INGENIX®

ingenix *e*solutions
Electronic coding, billing & reimbursement products

Electronic coding, billing and reimbursement products.

Ingenix provides a robust suite of eSolutions to solve a wide variety of coding, billing and reimbursement issues. As the industry moves to electronic products, you can rely on Ingenix to help support you through the transition.

← Web-based applications for all markets
← Dedicated support
← Environmentally responsible

Key Features and Benefits

Using eSolutions is a step in the right direction when it comes to streamlining your coding, billing and reimbursement practices. Ingenix eSolutions can help you save time and increase your efficiency with accurate and on-time content.

SAVE UP TO 20%
with source code FB10E

 Visit **www.shopingenix.com** and enter the source code to save 20%.

 Call toll-free **1-800-INGENIX** (464-3649), option 1 and save 15%.

- **Rely on a leader in health care.** Ingenix has been producing quality coding products for over 25 years. All of the expert content that goes into our books goes into our electronic resources.

- **Save time and money.** Ingenix eSolutions combine the content of over 37 code books and data files.

- **Go Green.** Eco-friendly electronic products are not only faster and easier to use than books, they require less storage space, less paper and leave a lighter carbon footprint.

- **Increase accuracy.** Electronic solutions are updated regularly so you know you're always working with the most current content available.

- **Get the training and support you need.** Convenient, online training and customized training programs are available to meet your specific needs.

- **Take baby steps.** Transition at your pace with code book and solution packages that let you keep your books while you learn how to become a whiz with your electronic products.

- **Get Started.** Visit **shopingenix.com/eSolutions** for product listing.

Ingenix | Information is the Lifeblood of Health Care | Call toll-free **1-800-INGENIX (464-3649), option 1.**

100% Money Back Guarantee If our merchandise ever fails to meet your expectations, please contact our Customer Service Department toll-free at 1-800-INGENIX (464-3649), option 1, for an immediate response. Software: Credit will be granted for unopened packages only.

Also available from your medical bookstore or distributor.

FB10E

www.shopingenix.com

INGENIX®
Learning and Development Services

Information is what keeps an expert an expert.

Ingenix Learning and Development Services provides comprehensive education and training programs that provide opportunities for health care professionals to increase their knowledge, enhance their skills and keep pace with industry trends. The result is a more capable workforce that enables health care organizations to continually improve their services.

← Convenient web-based eCourses

← Deep and diverse industry expertise

← Comprehensive coding curriculum

SAVE UP TO 20%
with source code FB10G

 Visit **www.shopingenix.com** and enter the source code to save 20%.

 Call toll-free **1-800-INGENIX** (464-3649), option 1 and save 15%.

Key Features and Benefits

Ingenix coding and reimbursement eCourses provide a robust curriculum with a variety of courses that focus on urgent coding and claims review training needs. Easy tracking and documentation of training results, timely content updates and higher information retention rates make our online courses a powerful resource.

- **Satisfy your coding needs by creating your own coder.** Customized curriculum to meet your individual practice needs.

- **Keep up-to-date with coding and regulatory changes.** Ingenix experts develop new classes based on current guidelines and rules so you and your staff are always up-to-date and prepared in case of an audit.

- **Streamline your revenue cycle with knowledgeable coding professionals.** Quickly reap the benefits of knowledgeable coding professionals: fewer denied claims, faster reimbursements and increased revenue.

- **Save time and money.** Reduce overall training costs by eliminating travel expenses and reducing costs associated with instructor time and salary.

- **Keep your staff's credentials current and relevant.** Earn CEU credentials provided by the American Academy of Professional Coders and the American Health Information Management Association.

For our full curriculum, visit Learning and Development Services on www.shopingenix.com.

Ingenix | Information is the Lifeblood of Health Care | Call toll-free 1-800-INGENIX (464-3649), option 1.

100% Money Back Guarantee If our merchandise ever fails to meet your expectations, please contact our Customer Service Department toll-free at 1-800-INGENIX (464-3649), option 1, for an immediate response. Software: Credit will be granted for unopened packages only.

Also available from your medical bookstore or distributor.

www.shopingenix.com

INGENIX
2010 Specialty References

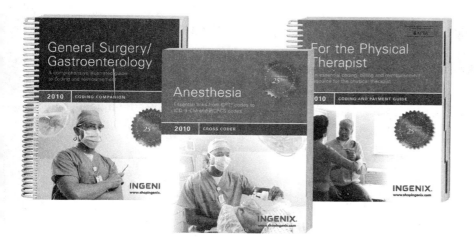

To view our full line of specialty resources, please visit www.shopingenix.com/specialty.

Simplify a coder's job with quick-find reference guides.

Increase cash flow in your specialty practice with the all-in-one solutions equipped with the specialty-specific information your practice needs for accurate and efficient coding and billing.

← Lay description for CPT® codes, customized to specialty

← Links from CPT® codes to appropriate ICD-9-CM and HCPCS codes

← Industry-leading content available in over 20 specialties

SAVE UP TO 20%
with source code FB10A

 Visit **www.shopingenix.com** and enter the source code to save 20%.

 Call toll-free **1-800-INGENIX** (464-3649), option 1 and save 15%.

Key Features and Benefits

Boost your coders' efficiency with these specialty-specific books that offer the most up-to-date coding information in a quick-search format.

2010 Coding Companions
- Essential procedures for each specialty is listed by CPT® code and crosswalks to ICD-9-CM diagnosis, procedure and anesthesia codes
- Includes Medicare RVUs, follow-up days and assistant-at-surgery indicators
- Organized by CPT® code, all the information you need is on one illustrated page
- Receive quarterly CCI edits via email

2010 Cross Coders
- Numerical organization by CPT® code allows for quick location of diagnosis and procedure code information
- Appendix offers a complete listing of add-on and unlisted codes, as well as CPT® and HCPCS modifiers

2010 Coding and Payment Guides
- Specialty-specific CPT® code sets with clear, concise definitions, coding tips, terminology and crosswalks to ICD-9-CM and HCPCS Level II codes, all in a one-page format
- Separate chapters on reimbursement, documentation and claims processing
- Medicare payment information with RVUs and Pub. 100 guidelines

---

Ingenix | Information is the Lifeblood of Health Care | Call toll-free 1-800-INGENIX (464-3649), option 1.

100% Money Back Guarantee If our merchandise ever fails to meet your expectations, please contact our Customer Service Department toll-free at 1-800-INGENIX (464-3649), option 1, for an immediate response. Software: Credit will be granted for unopened packages only.

Also available from your medical bookstore or distributor. CPT is a registered trademark of the American Medical Association.

FB10A

www.shopingenix.com

INGENIX
2010 Essential Coding Resources

ICD-9-CM Resources
Available: Sept. 2009

CPT® Resources
Available: Dec. 2009

HCPCS Resources
Available: Dec. 2009

SAVE UP TO 20%
with source code FB10D

 Visit www.shopingenix.com and enter the source code to save 20%.

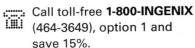 Call toll-free **1-800-INGENIX** (464-3649), option 1 and save 15%.

2010 Essential Coding Resources

Looks can be deceiving. Competitors attempt to imitate Ingenix code books because interpreting coding and reimbursement rules correctly and understanding the professional workflow is what we've helped coding professionals do successfully for 25 years. Count on Ingenix to deliver the accurate information, familiar features, industry-leading content and innovative additions that help you improve coding practices, comply with HIPAA code set regulations, and realize proper reimbursement.

← **A professional team's expertise**

← **Trusted and proven ICD-9-CM, CPT® and HCPCS resources**

← **Industry-leading content**

← **More value, competitive prices**

Key Features and Benefits

Rely on our team of highly experienced coding professionals to stay current with 2010 regulatory changes and promote accurate coding and proper reimbursement. Select from a range of formats for your ICD-9-CM, CPT,® and HCPCS resources to fit your individual preferences, skill level, business needs and budget—you can trust your resource to be accurate and complimentary to your daily work when it's under an Ingenix cover.

2010 ICD-9-CM: Physicians, Hospitals and Postacute editions available
- New! Official coding tips integrated with the codes
- New! Coding instructional note alerts
- New! ICD-10-CM Spotlight
- New! *ICD-9-CM Changes: An Insider's View* section
- Facility-specific resources in each *Expert* edition
- E-mail alerts for special reports

2010 Current Procedural Coding Expert
- Easy-to-navigate with CPT® codes arranged to facilitate coding, billing, and reimbursement for an office setting
- Comprehensive and up-to-date listings with an extensive, user-friendly index
- Reimbursement information and PQRI icons

2010 HCPCS Level II Expert
- Comprehensive code updates for accurate reporting of supplies and services
- User-friendly format and expanded index to ease code look-up
- Important coding indicators and icons, detailed illustrations, glossary of terms, and special MUEs

Ingenix | Information is the Lifeblood of Health Care | Call toll-free 1-800-INGENIX (464-3649), option 1.

100% Money Back Guarantee If our merchandise ever fails to meet your expectations, please contact our Customer Service Department toll-free at 1-800-INGENIX (464-3649), option 1, for an immediate response. Software: Credit will be granted for unopened packages only.

Also available from your medical bookstore or distributor. CPT is a registered trademark of the American Medical Association.

www.shopingenix.com

INGENIX

2010 Coders' Desk References for Specialties

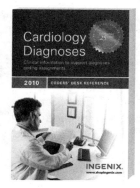

ISBN: 978-1-60151-333-5
Item Number: 1472
Available: Oct. 2009
Price: $129.95

ISBN: 978-1-60151-329-8
Item Number: 1423
Available: Jan. 2010
Price: $129.95

ISBN: 978-1-60151-332-8
Item Number: 1471
Available: Oct. 2009
Price: $129.95

Vital information about coding for specialty services—in one comprehensive resource

In order to accurately code for specialty services, it's beneficial to understand the clinical background of diseases, medical procedures and anatomy. But all too often, this important information is listed in multiple, disparate resources. To help boost coding accuracy and save time, we've compiled all this vital information into a single, specialty-specific resource.

← Reduce coding errors

← Understand coding and billing rules

← Distinguish between similar codes

SAVE UP TO 20%

with source code FB10B

 Visit **www.shopingenix.com** and enter the source code to save 20%.

 Call toll-free **1-800-INGENIX** (464-3649), option 1 and save 15%.

Key Features and Benefits

Get clear, concise information about diagnoses common to your specialty in one information-packed resource. This is the place to turn to when the code book and coding guidelines cannot give you answers.

- Know the key commonalities between codes in similar classifications

- Match up symptoms associated with diseases. Know what should and should not be coded

- Identify conditions that typically complicate diagnoses

- See diagnostic procedures linked to diseases

- Recognize conditions that may present in a similar manner but require separate reporting

- Know what associated conditions may also occur and be considered for separate reporting

---

Ingenix | Information is the Lifeblood of Health Care | Call toll-free 1-800-INGENIX (464-3649), option 1.

100% Money Back Guarantee If our merchandise ever fails to meet your expectations, please contact our Customer Service Department toll-free at 1-800-INGENIX (464-3649), option 1, for an immediate response. Software: Credit will be granted for unopened packages only.

Also available from your medical bookstore or distributor.

FB10B

| www.shopingenix.com |

INGENIX

Create Your Own Package

SAVE UP TO 30%
with source code FB10H

 Visit **www.shopingenix.com** and enter the source code to save up to 30%.

 Call toll-free **1-800-INGENIX (464-3649), option 1.**

Build your own coding library with the resources you need.

Ingenix resources are tailored to meet your specific needs. Now, you can combine the resources you want—nothing more, nothing less.

← Buy 2–3 items – save 20%

← Buy 4–5 items – save 25%

← Buy 6 or more – save 30%

Key Features and Benefits

Imagine how much time you could save if you could get to the code information you needed, faster. Our resources are designed to shave time off the coding process so you can work smarter, not harder. In addition, we have a dedicated team of experts who research changes in codes and regulations so our resources are updated with the most current information to help you stay compliant.

Buy more and save on the following product categories:

- 2010 Essential Code Books
- 2010 Specialty Reference
- 2010 Desk References
- Coding, Billing and Payment
- Training
- Electronic Resources

Visit **www.shopingenix.com/packages1** to determine what products apply.

Ingenix | Information is the Lifeblood of Health Care | Call toll-free **1-800-INGENIX (464-3649), option 1.**

100% Money Back Guarantee If our merchandise ever fails to meet your expectations, please contact our Customer Service Department toll-free at 1-800-INGENIX (464-3649), option 1, for an immediate response. Software: Credit will be granted for unopened packages only.

Also available from your medical bookstore or distributor.

FB10H

www.ingenix.com

INGENIX®
Physician Solutions

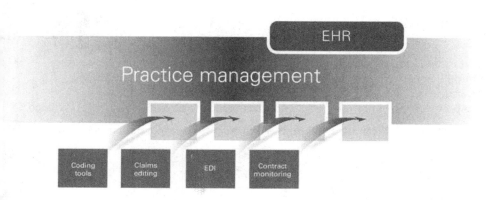

FOR PRICING DETAILS

 Visit **www.ingenix.com**

 Call toll-free **1-800-765-6704** and mention source code **FB10I**

Have a Fully Integrated Practice.

More companies rely on our medical coding expertise than anyone in the industry. That first-hand knowledge of all the stakeholders gives us unique insight, and we use it to create integrated information, technology and consulting solutions that address the range of financial and clinical challenges practices face.

← **Payers** – Connect with thousands of payer sources to verify eligibility and manage referral requirements, remittances and claims.

← **Clinical partners** – Work with real-time clinical data form labs, pharmacies, radiologists, hospitals and other key partners.

← **Patients** – Automate your appointment confirms, statements, letters and inbound patient calls.

Powerful solutions that work as one.

Start with your practice management platform or ours. Then plug in the powerful applications you need to enhance care or optimize your revenue cycle.

- **Electronic health records (EHR).** Low-cost, web-based EHR that puts your practice and your patients first. Ingenix CareTracker integrates with all the operational functions of the practice, improves quality and reduces costs.

- **Practice management.** Next-generation, web-based practice management with today's financial and administrative productivity. Our automated billing process electronically connects to more than 1,000 national insurance plans and submits your claims for you, overnight.

- **Coding tools.** The industry's broadest and most preferred coding tools. Our ever-evolving coding solutions are available in multiple formats to meet your needs.

- **Claims editing.** Powerful claims software that leverages our information and your rules. The industry's average resubmission cost is $25 per claims— our solutions help you get paid faster.

- **Electronic data interchange (EDI).** The way to navigate EDI your way, through clearinghouse connections, direct connections or both. Our connectivity solutions are HIPAA compliant, easy-to-use, efficient and affordable.

- **Contract monitoring.** Organizing and managing your payer agreements for automated reimbursement and compliance. If your total claims value is underpaid by 5%, you're losing about a day's worth of earnings every month.

Ingenix | Information is the Lifeblood of Health Care | Call toll-free 1-800-765-6704.

INGENIX®
Ingenix CareTracker EMR

Qualify for the stimulus incentive with CareTracker.

Ingenix CareTracker is a web-based, CCHIT-certified® EHR solution that is fully integrated with all operational functions of a practice, helping you cut administrative costs by automating tasks and improving communication. CareTracker offers attractive economics that facilitate meaningful, efficient improvements within your practice and enhance the physician-patient experience.

CareTracker EMR can help you capture the stimulus reimbursement through:

← Auto-prompting for Physician Quality Reporting Index (PQRI)

← A CCHIT-certified electronic medical record application

← Automatically generated prescriptions sent to appropriate pharmacies

← Safe and secure transmission of electronic health records through real-time connections with labs, pharmacies, hospitals and more

FOR PRICING DETAILS

 Visit **www.ingenix.com/caretracker**

 Call toll-free **1-866-427-6802** and mention source code **FB10F**

Key Features and Benefits

Ingenix CareTracker offers you the benefits of an EHR solution developed to meet physicians' specific needs:

- **Web-based**
- **CCHIT-certified**
- **Easy to implement**
- **Instant access to updates**
- **Affordable monthly subscription**
- **Minimal upfront investment**
- **Embedded analytics**
- **Point-of-care information delivery**
- **Built-in coding expertise**

Ingenix | Information is the Lifeblood of Health Care | Call toll-free 1-866-427-6802.

100% Money Back Guarantee If our merchandise ever fails to meet your expectations, please contact our Customer Service Department toll-free at 1-800-INGENIX (464-3649), option 1, for an immediate response. Software: Credit will be granted for unopened packages only.

Also available from your medical bookstore or distributor.

Current Procedural
Coding Expert

2010

Notice

The *2010 Current Procedural Coding Expert* is designed to be an accurate and authoritative source of information about the CPT® coding system. Every effort has been made to verify the accuracy of the listings, and all information is believed reliable at the time of publication. Absolute accuracy cannot be guaranteed, however. This publication is made available with the understanding that the publisher is not engaged in rendering legal or other services that require a professional license.

American Medical Association Notice

CPT only © 2009 American Medical Association. All rights reserved.

Fee schedules, relative value units, conversion factors and/or related components are not assigned by the AMA, are not part of CPT, and the AMA is not recommending their use. The AMA does not directly or indirectly practice medicine or dispense medical services. The AMA assumes no liability for data contained or not contained herein.

CPT is a registered trademark of the American Medical Association.

Copyright

Copyright © 2009

All rights reserved. No part of this publication may be reproduced or transmitted in any form or by any means electronic or mechanical, including photocopy, recording or storage in a database or retrieval system, without the prior written permission of the publisher.

Made in the USA

ISBN 978-1-934902-71-4

Acknowledgments

Steven Woodward, *Product Manager*
Karen Schmidt, BSN, *Technical Director*
Stacy Perry, *Manager, Desktop Publishing*
Lisa Singley, *Project Manager*
Wendy Gabbert, CPC, CPC-H, PCS, FCS *Clinical/Technical Editor*
LaJuana Green RHIA, CCS, *Clinical/Technical Editor*
Karen H. Kachur, RN, CPC, *Clinical/Technical Editor*
Anita D. Schmidt, RHIT, *Clinical/Technical Editor*
Tracy Betzler, *Desktop Publishing Specialist*
Hope M. Dunn, *Desktop Publishing Specialist*
Toni R. Stewart, *Desktop Publishing Specialist*
Kate Holden, *Editor*

About the Contributors

Wendy Gabbert, CPC, CPC-H, PCS, FCS

Ms. Gabbert has more than 25 years of experience in the health care field. She has extensive background in CPT/HCPCS and ICD-9-CM coding. She served several years as a coding consultant. Her areas of expertise include physician and hospital CPT coding assessments, chargemaster reviews, and the outpatient prospective payment system (OPPS). She is a member of the American Academy of Professional Coders and American College of Medical Coding Specialists.

Karen H. Kachur, RN, CPC

Ms. Kachur is a clinical/technical editor for Ingenix with expertise in CPT/HCPCS and ICD-9-CM coding, in addition to physician billing, compliance, and fraud and abuse. Prior to joining Ingenix, she worked for many years as a staff RN in a variety of clinical settings, including medicine, surgery, intensive care, and psychiatry. In addition to her clinical background, Ms. Kachur served as assistant director of a hospital utilization management and quality assurance department and has extensive experience as a nurse reviewer for Blue Cross/Blue Shield. She is an active member of the American Academy of Professional Coders and the American College of Medical Coding Specialists.

Contents

Introduction i
Anatomical Illustrations v
Interventional Radiology Illustrations xxviii
Index Index-1
00100–01999 1
10021–19499 13
20000–29999 37
30000–39599 95
40490–49999 143
50010–59899 179
60000–69990 214
70010–79999 257
80047–89398 297
90281–99607 347
Evaluation & Management 411
0001F–7025F 435
0016T–0222T 449
Appendix A—Modifiers 457
Appendix B—New, Changed, Deleted, and Modified Codes .. 464
Appendix C—Crosswalk of Deleted Codes 472
Appendix D—Resequenced Codes 473
Appendix E—Add-on, Modifier 51 Exempt, Modifier 63 Exempt, and Moderate Sedation Codes 474
Appendix F—Place of Service and Type of Service 475
Appendix G—Pub 100 References 479
Appendix H—Glossary 594
Appendix I— Listing of Sensory, Motor, and Mixed Nerves .. 603
Appendix J—Vascular Families 605
Appendix K—Physician Quality Reporting Program (PQRI) .. 608
Appendix L—Medically Unlikely Edits (MUEs) 615
    Professional 615
    OPPS 632

Introduction

Welcome to *Current Procedural Coding Expert*, an exciting Medicare coding and reimbursement tool and definitive procedure coding source that combines the work of the Centers for Medicare and Medicaid Services, American Medical Association, and other experts with the technical components you need for proper reimbursement and coding accuracy.

This new approach to CPT Medicare coding utilizes new, more intuitive ways of communicating the information you need to code claims accurately and efficiently. *Includes* and *Excludes* notes similar to those found in your ICD-9-CM manuals, help determine what services are related to the codes you are reporting. New and expanded icons help you crosswalk the code you are reporting to laboratory and radiology procedures necessary for proper reimbursement. CMS-mandated icons and relative value units (RVUs) help you determine which codes are most appropriate for the service you are reporting. In addition, icons denoting codes that apply to Physician Quality Reporting Initiative (PQRI) quality indicators are included along with their denominators. Add to that additional information identifying age and sex edits, ambulatory surgery center (ASC) and ambulatory payment classification (APC) indicators, and Medicare coverage and payment rule citations and *Current Procedural Coding Expert* provides the best in Medicare procedure reporting.

Current Procedural Coding Expert includes the information needed to submit claims to federal contractors and most commercial payers, and is correct at the time of printing. However, CMS, federal contractors, and commercial payers may change payment rules at any time throughout the year. *Current Procedural Coding Expert* includes effective codes that will not be published in the AMA's *Current Procedural Terminology* until the following year. Commercial payers will announce changes through monthly news or information posted on their websites. CMS will post changes in policy on its website at http://www.cms.hhs.gov/transmittals. National and local coverage determinations (NCDs and LCDs) provide universal and individual contractor guidelines for specific services. The existence of a procedure code does not imply coverage under any given insurance plan.

Current Procedural Coding Expert is based on the AMA's *Current Procedural Terminology* coding system, which is copyrighted and owned by the physician organization. CPT is the nation's official, Health Information Portability and Accountability Act (HIPAA) compliant code set for procedures and services provided by physicians, ASCs, and hospital outpatient services, as well as laboratories, imaging centers, physical therapy clinics, urgent care centers, and others.

GETTING STARTED WITH *CURRENT PROCEDURAL CODING EXPERT*

Current Procedural Coding Expert is an exciting tool combining the most current material at publication time from the AMA's *CPT 2010*, CMS's online manual system, the Correct Coding Initiative (CCI), CMS fee schedules, and official Medicare guidelines for reimbursement and coverage.

Note: The AMA releases code changes quarterly. *Current Procedural Coding Expert* contains the most current information from the AMA, including new, changed, and deleted codes that are released on its website for future inclusion in the CPT book. Some of these changes will not appear in the AMA's CPT book until the following year.

Another feature of *Current Procedural Coding Expert* that differs from the official CPT book is the addition to appendix H, "Glossary," of the devices used for cardiovascular monitoring defined by the AMA.

Material is presented in a logical fashion for those billing Medicare, Medicaid, and private payers. The new format, based on customer comments, better addresses what customers tell us they need in a comprehensive Medicare procedure coding guide.

Designed to be easy to use and full of information, this product is an excellent companion to your AMA CPT manual and to Medicare or other resources.

General Conventions
Sources of information in this book can be determined by color:

- Publisher-developed information derived by our experts is in blue ink.
- Medicare-derived information is in red ink.
- Codes, descriptions, and evaluation and management (E/M) guidelines from the American Medical Association are in black ink.

Icons derived from AMA guidelines or coding conventions are presented as circles. Icons derived from federal guidelines, data, or rules are square.

GUIDELINES

Coding guidelines have been incorporated into more specific section notes, code notes, icons, and the glossary. Section notes are listed under a range of codes. These guidelines apply to all the codes in that code range. Code notes are found under individual codes. These notes apply to a single code. Definitions of coding terms are listed in the glossary and can be found in appendix H.

RESEQUENCING OF CPT CODES

The American Medical Association (AMA) is introducing a new numbering methodology beginning in 2010. Resequencing is the practice of displaying codes outside of their numerical order according to the description relationship. According to the AMA, there are instances in which a new code is needed within an existing grouping of codes but an unused code number is not available. In these situations, the AMA will resequence the codes. In other words, it will assign a code that is not in numeric sequence with the related codes. However, the code and description will appear in the CPT manual with the other related codes.

An example of resequencing from *Current Procedural Coding Expert* follows:

▲   21555   **Excision, tumor, soft tissue of neck or anterior thorax, subcutaneous; less than 3 cm**

#●   21552   **3 cm or greater**

▲   21556   **Excision, tumor, soft tissue of neck or anterior thorax, subfascial (eg, intramuscular); less than 5 cm**

#●   21554   **5 cm or greater**

Note that codes 21552 and 21554 are out of numeric sequence. However, as they are indented codes, they are in the correct place.

In *Current Procedural Coding Expert* the resequenced codes are listed twice. They appear in their resequenced position as shown above as well as in their original numeric position with a note indicating that the code is out of numerical sequence and where it can be found. (See example below.)

#+▲   51797   *Resequenced code. See code following 51729.*

This differs from the AMA CPT book, in which the coder is directed to a code range that contains the resequenced code and description, rather than to a specific location.

CPT appendix D identifies all CPT codes that are resequenced.

This book displays the resequenced coding as assigned by the AMA in its CPT products so that the user may understand the code description relationships.

Each particular group of CPT codes in *Current Procedural Coding Expert* is organized in a more intuitive fashion for Medicare billing, being grouped by the Medicare rules and regulations that govern payment of these particular procedures and services, as in this example:

99241–99255 Consultations
CMS 100-3,70.1 Consultations with a Beneficiary's Family and Associates

CMS 100-2,15,30 Physician Services

CMS 100-1,5,70 Definition of Physician

CMS 100-4,12,30.6.10 Consultation Services

Introduction

Current Procedural Coding Expert

ICONS

● **New Codes**
Codes that have been added since the last edition of the book was printed.

▲ **Revised Codes**
Codes that have been revised since the last edition of the book was printed.

\# **Resequenced Codes**
Codes that are out of numeric order but apply to the appropriate category.

Red Color Bar—Not Covered by Medicare
Services and procedures identified by this color bar are never covered benefits under Medicare. Services and procedures that are not covered may be billed directly to the patient at the time of the service.

Yellow Color Bar—Unlisted Procedure
Unlisted CPT codes report procedures that have not been assigned a specific code number. An unlisted code delays payment due to the extra time necessary for review. When using an unlisted procedure code, include a cover letter, documentation of medical necessity, and operative reports as appropriate.

Blue Color Bar—Resequenced Codes
Resequenced codes are codes that are out of numeric sequence—they are indicated with a blue color bar. They are listed twice, in their resequenced position as well as in their original numeric position with a note that the code is out of numerical sequence and where the resequenced code and description can be found.

[INCLUDES] **Includes notes**
Includes notes identify procedures and services that would be bundled in the procedure code. These are derived from AMA, CMS, and CCI coding guidelines. This is not meant to be an all-inclusive list.

[EXCLUDES] **Excludes notes**
Excludes notes may lead the user to other codes. They may identify services that are not bundled and may be separately reported, or may lead the user to another more appropriate code. These are derived from AMA, CMS, and CCI coding guidelines.

Laboratory/Pathology Crosswalk
This icon denotes CPT codes in the laboratory and pathology section of CPT that may be reported separately with the primary CPT code.

Radiology Crosswalk
This icon denotes codes in the radiology section that may be used with the primary CPT code being reported.

[TC] **Technical Component Only**
Codes with this icon represent only the technical component (staff and equipment costs) of a procedure or service. Do not use either modifier 26 (physician component) or TC (technical component) with these codes.

[26] **Professional Component**
Only codes with this icon represent the physician's work or professional component of a procedure or service. Do not use either modifier 26 (physician component) or TC (technical component) with these codes.

[50] **Bilateral Procedure**
This icon identifies codes that can be reported bilaterally when the same surgeon provides the service for the same patient on the same date. Medicare allows payment for both procedures at 150 percent of the usual amount for one procedure. The modifier does not apply to bilateral procedures inclusive to one code.

[80] **Assist-at-Surgery Allowed**
Services noted by this icon are allowed an assist at surgery with a Medicare payment equal to 16 percent of the allowed amount for the global surgery for that procedure. No documentation is required.

[80] **Assist-at-Surgery Allowed with Documentation**
Services noted by this icon are allowed an assistant at surgery with a Medicare payment equal to 16 percent of the allowed amount for the global surgery for that procedure. Documentation is required.

+ **Add-on Codes**
This icon identifies procedures reported in addition to the primary procedure. The icon "+" denotes add-on codes. An add-on code is neither a stand-alone code nor subject to multiple procedure rules since it describes work in addition to the primary procedure.

⊘ **Modifier 51 Exempt**
Codes identified by this icon indicate that the procedure should not be reported with modifier 51 (Multiple procedures).

Correct Coding Initiative (CCI)
Current Procedural Coding Expert identifies those codes with corresponding CCI edits. The CCI edits define correct coding practices that serve as the basis of the national Medicare policy for paying claims. The code noted is the major service/procedure. The code may represent a column 1 code within the column 1/column 2 correct coding edits table or a code pair that is mutually exclusive of each other.

☒ **CLIA Waived Test**
This symbol is used to distinguish those laboratory tests that can be performed using test systems that are waived from regulatory oversight established by the Clinical Laboratory Improvement Amendments of 1988 (CLIA). The applicable CPT code for a CLIA waived test may be reported by providers who perform the testing but do not hold a CLIA license.

(63) **Modifier 63 Exempt**
This icon identifies procedures performed on infants that weigh less than 4 kg. Due to the complexity of performing procedures on infants less than 4 kg, modifier 63 may be added to the surgery codes to inform the payers of the special circumstances involved.

[A2]-[Z3] **ASC Payment Indicators**
These icons identify ASC payment status. They indicate how the ASC payment rate was derived and/or how the procedure, item, or service is treated under the revised ASC payment system.

[A2] Surgical procedure on ASC list in calendar year (CY) 2007; payment based on OPPS relative payment weight.

[F4] Corneal tissue acquisition; hepatitis B vaccine; paid at reasonable cost.

[G2] Non-office-based surgical procedure added in CY 2008 or later; payment based on outpatient prospective payment system (OPPS) relative payment weight.

[H7] Brachytherapy source paid separately when provided integral to a surgical procedure on ASC list; payment contractor-priced.

[H8] Device-intensive procedure on ASC list in CY 2007; paid at adjusted rate.

[J7] OPPS pass-through device paid separately when provided integral to a surgical procedure on ASC list; payment contractor-priced.

[J8] Device-intensive procedure added to ASC list in CY 2008 or later; paid at adjusted rate.

[K2] Drugs and biologicals paid separately when provided integral to a surgical procedure on ASC list; payment based on OPPS rate.

[K7] Unclassified drugs and biologicals; payment contractor-priced.

[L1] Influenza vaccine; pneumococcal vaccine. Packaged item/service; no separate payment made.

[L6] New technology intraocular lens (NTIOL); special payment.

[N1] Packaged service/item; no separate payment made.

Current Procedural Coding Expert

Introduction

P2 — Office-based surgical procedure added to ASC list in CY 2008 or later with Medicare physician fee schedule (MPFS) nonfacility practice expense (PE) RVUs; payment based on OPPS relative payment weight.

P3 — Office-based surgical procedure added to ASC list in CY 2008 or later with MPFS nonfacility PE RVUs; payment based on MPFS nonfacility PE RVUs.

R2 — Office-based surgical procedure added to ASC list in CY 2008 or later without MPFS nonfacility PE RVUs; payment based on OPPS relative payment weight.

Z2 — Radiology service paid separately when provided integral to a surgical procedure on ASC list; payment based on OPPS relative payment weight.

Z3 — Radiology service paid separately when provided integral to a surgical procedure on ASC list; payment based on MPFS nonfacility PE RVUs

⊙ **Moderate Sedation**
This icon identifies procedures that include moderate sedation. Moderate sedation codes should not be reported separately with these procedures.

A **Age Edit**
This icon denotes codes intended for use with a specific age group, such as neonate, newborn, pediatric, and adult. Carefully review the code description to ensure the code you report most appropriately reflects the patient's age.

M **Maternity**
This icon identifies procedures that by definition should be used only for maternity patients generally between 12 and 55 years of age.

♀ **Female Only**
This icon identifies procedures that some payers may consider for females only.

♂ **Male Only**
This icon identifies procedures that some payers may consider for males only.

🚑 **Facility RVU**
This icon precedes the facility RVU from CMS's 2010 physician fee schedule (PFS). It can be found under the code description.

🏃 **Nonfacility RVU**
This icon precedes the nonfacility RVU from CMS's 2010 PFS. It can be found under the code description.

Global Days The global period is the time following surgery during which routine care by the physician is considered postoperative and included in the surgical fee. Office visits or other routine care related to the original surgery cannot be separately reported if provided during the global period. Global days are sometimes referred to as "follow-up days," or FUDs. The statuses are:

000   No follow-up care included in this procedure

010   Normal postoperative care is included in this procedure for ten days

090   Normal postoperative care is included in the procedure for 90 days

MMM   Maternity codes; usual global period does not apply

XXX   The global concept does not apply to the code

YYY   The carrier is to determine whether the global concept applies and establishes postoperative period, if appropriate, at time of pricing

ZZZ   The code is related to another service and is always included in the global period of the other service

CMS: This notation indicates that there is a specific CMS guideline pertaining to this code in the CMS Online Manual System which includes the internet-only manual (IOM) *National Coverage Determinations Manual;* (NCD). These CMS sources present the rules for submitting these services to the federal government or its contractors and are included in the appendix G of this book.

AMA: This indicates discussion of the code in the American Medical Association's *CPT Assistant* newsletter. Use the citation to find the correct issue.

✗ **Drug Not Approved by FDA**
The AMA CPT Editorial Panel is publishing new vaccine product codes prior to Food and Drug Administration approval. This symbol indicates which of these codes are pending FDA approval at press time.

PQ **Physician Quality Reporting Initiative (PQRI)**
This icon denotes CPT codes that specifically address one or more of the CMS-determined quality measures. See appendix K for a list of denominators that apply to those codes.

A–**Y** **OPPS Status Indicators (OPSI)**
Status indicators identify how individual CPT codes are paid or not paid under the latest available hospital outpatient prospective payment system (OPPS). The same status indicator is assigned to all the codes within an ambulatory payment classification (APC). Consult your payer or other resource to learn which CPT codes fall within various APCs.

A   Services not paid under OPPS; paid under fee schedule or other payment system.

B   Non-allowed item or service for OPPS

C   Inpatient procedure

E   Non-allowed item or service

F   Corneal tissue acquisition; certain CRNA services and hepatitis B vaccines

G   Drug/biological pass-through

H   Pass-through device categories

K   Non-pass-through drugs and nonimplantable biologics, including therapeutic radiopharmaceuticals

L   Flu/PPV vaccines

M   Service not billable to the FI/MAC

N   Items and services packaged into APC rates

P   Partial hospitalization service

Q1   STVX-packaged codes

Q2   Packaged codes

Q3   Codes that may be paid through a composite APC

R   Blood and blood products

S   Significant procedure not subject to multiple procedure discounting

T   Significant procedure subject to multiple procedure discounting

U   Brachytherapy services

V   Clinic or emergency department visit

X   Ancillary service

Y   Non-implantable DME

APPENDIXES

Appendix A: Modifiers—This appendix identifies the modifiers. A modifier is a two-position alphabetic or numeric code that is appended to a CPT or HCPCS code to clarify the services being billed. Modifiers provide a means by which a service can be altered without changing the procedure code. They add more information, such as anatomical site, to the code. In addition, they help eliminate the appearance of duplicate billing and unbundling. Modifiers are used to increase the accuracy in reimbursement and coding consistency, ease editing, and capture payment data.

Appendix B: New, Changed, and Deleted Codes—This is a list of new, changed, and deleted CPT and HCPCS codes for the current year.

Appendix C: Crosswalk of Deleted Codes—This appendix is a cross-reference from a deleted CPT code to an active code when one is available. The deleted code cross-reference will also appear under the deleted code description in the tabular section of the book.

Appendix D: Resequenced Codes—This appendix contains a list of codes that are not in numeric order in the book. AMA resequenced some of the code numbers to relocate codes in the same category but not in numeric sequence.

Appendix E: Add-on, Modifier 51 Exempt, Modifier 63 Exempt, and Moderate Sedation Codes—This list includes add-on codes that cannot be reported alone, codes that are exempt from modifier 51, codes that should not be reported with modifier 63, and codes that include moderate sedation.

Appendix F: Place of Service and Type of Service—This appendix contains lists of place-of-service codes that should be used on professional claims and type-of-service codes used by the Medicare Common Working File.

Appendix G: Pub. 100 References—This appendix contains a verbatim printout of the Medicare Internet Only Manual references that pertain to specific codes. The reference, when available, is listed after the header in the CPT section. For example:

60600–60605 CAROTID BODY PROCEDURES

CMS 100-3, 20.18, Carotid Body Resection/Carotid Body Denervation

Since appendix G contains this reference from the *Medicare Claims Processing Manual*, Pub. 100-3 chapter 20, section 20.18, there is no need to search the Medicare website for the applicable reference.

Appendix H: Glossary—This appendix contains general terms and definitions as well as those that would apply to or be helpful for ASC billing and reimbursement and a definition of the devices used for cardiovascular monitoring as defined by the AMA. Appendix H contains term definitions.

Appendix I: Listing of Sensory, Motor, and Mixed Nerves—This appendix lists a summary of each sensory, motor, and mixed nerve with its appropriate nerve conduction study code.

Appendix J: Vascular Families—Appendix J contains a table of vascular families starting with the aorta. Additional information can be found in the interventional radiology illustrations located behind the index.

Appendix K: Physician Quality Reporting Initiative (PQRI)—Lists the numerators and denominators applicable to Medicare PQRI.

Appendix L: Medically Unlikely Edits—This appendix contains the published medically unlikely edits (MUEs). These edits establish maximum daily allowable units of service. The edits will be applied to the services provided to the same patient, for the same CPT or HCPCS code, on the same date of service when billed by the same provider. Included are the physician and facility edits.

For more information about ongoing development of the CPT coding system, consult the AMA website at URL http://www.ama-assn.org/.

Note: All data current as of November 10, 2009

Anatomical Illustrations

BODY PLANES AND MOVEMENTS

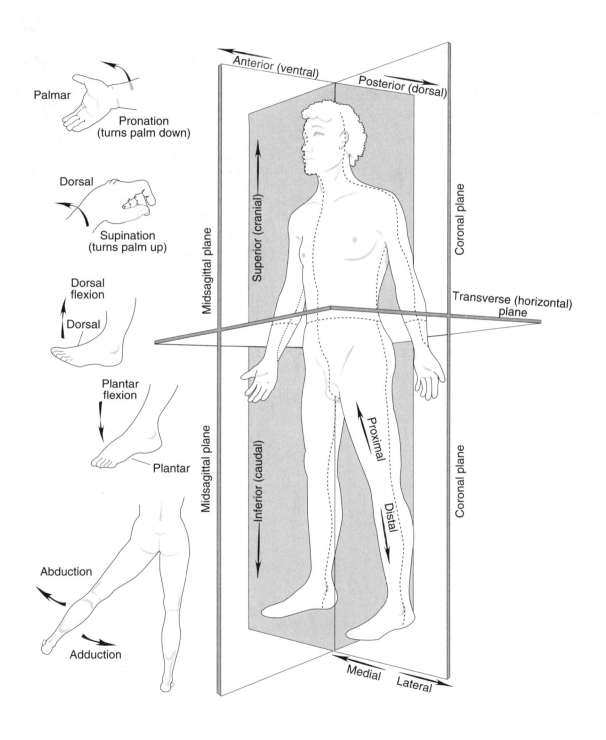

Anatomical Illustrations

MUSCULOSKELETAL SYSTEM

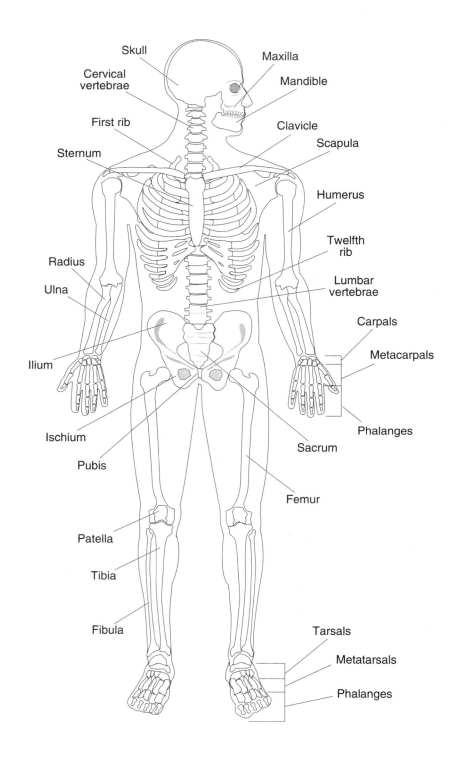

Current Procedural Coding Expert
Anatomical Illustrations
MUSCULOSKELETAL SYSTEM

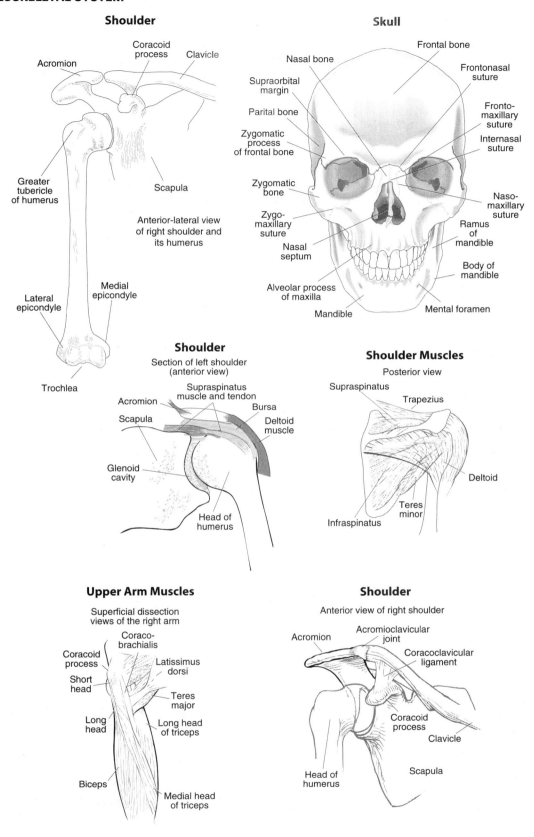

Anatomical Illustrations

MUSCULOSKELETAL SYSTEM

Elbow
Anterior view of right arm and elbow
- Humerus
- Radial fossa
- Lateral epicondyle
- Capitulum
- Radius
- Coronoid fossa
- Medial epicondyle
- Trochlea
- Ulna

Elbow
Anterior view of right elbow
- Humerus
- Joint capsule
- Lateral epicondyle
- Radial collateral ligament
- Radius
- Medial epicondyle
- Ulnar collateral ligament
- Ulna

Lateral view of right elbow joint
- Body of humerus
- Head of radius
- Joint capsule
- Radial collateral ligament
- Annular ligament of radius

Elbow
Posterior view of right elbow
- Triceps muscle
- Medial epicondyle of humerus
- Olecranon of ulna
- Flexor ulnaris
- Brachioradialis
- Extensor carpi radialis longus
- Extensor carpi radialis brevis
- Extensor digitorum
- Extensor carpi ulnaris

Lower Arm
- Radius
- Olecranon process
- Coronoid process
- Ulna
- Shafts
- Radial styloid process
- Ulnar styloid process
- Carpal bones

Finger
Medial schematic of finger joints
- Carpometacarpal joint
- Metacarpal
- Metacarpophalangeal (MP) joint
- Proximal phalange
- Proximal interphalangeal (PIP) joint
- Middle phalange
- Distal interphalangeal (DIP) joint
- Distal phalange

Hand
Palmar view
- Flexor carpi ulnaris
- Ulnar collateral ligament
- Ulna
- Radial collateral ligament
- Palmar radiocarpal ligament
- Radius

Dorsal view
- Radial collateral ligament
- Dorsal radiocarpal ligament
- Ulnar collateral ligament
- Ulnocarpal ligament

Hand
Dorsal view
- Trapezium
- Trapezoid
- Navicular
- Hamate
- Cuboid
- Triquetral
- Pisiform
- Lunate
- Carpals
- Radius
- Ulna

MUSCULOSKELETAL SYSTEM

Ankle

Lateral and posterior views of right ankle

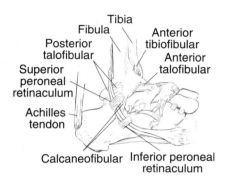

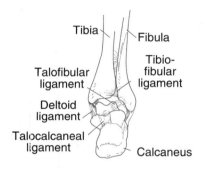

Achilles tendon not shown

Foot

Select extensors of the foot

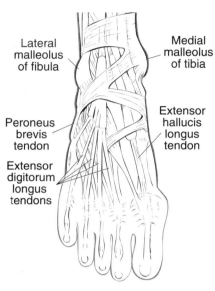

Foot

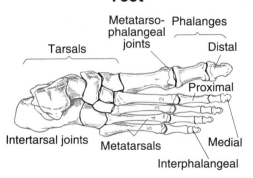

Foot

Tarsals, excluding talus and calcaneus (dark), superior view

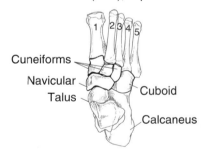

Anatomical Illustrations Current Procedural Coding Expert

MUSCULOSKELETAL SYSTEM

Leg

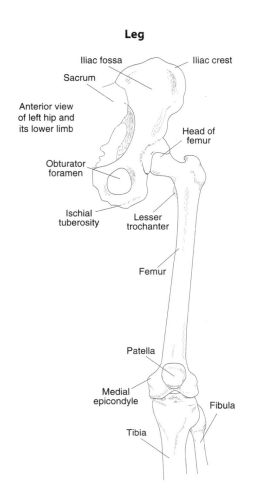

Hip

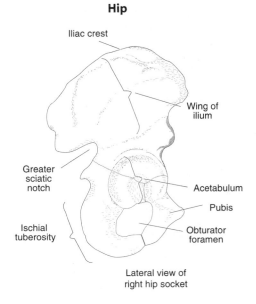

Lateral view of right hip socket

Lower Leg

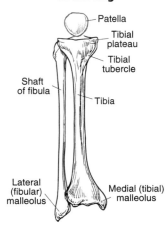

Knee

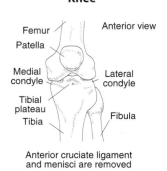

Anterior view of right knee

Knee

Anterior view

Anterior cruciate ligament and menisci are removed

RULE OF NINES FOR BURNS

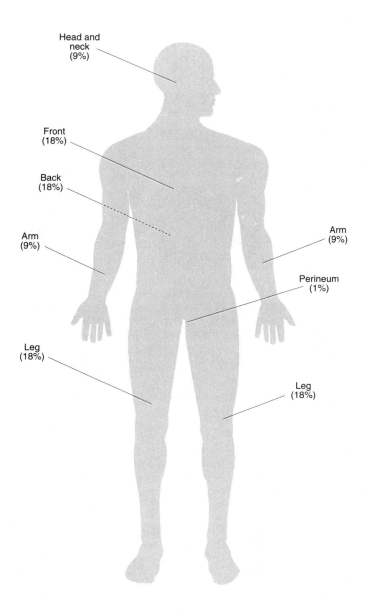

First-degree burns involve surface layers only and tissue destruction is minimal.

Second-degree burns damage deeper epidermal layers and upper layers of the dermis; damage to sweat glands, hair follicles, and sebaceous glands may occur.

Third-degree burns include destruction of both epidermis and dermis and tissue death extends below the hair follicles and sweat glands.

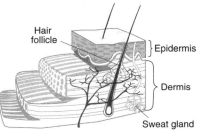

Anatomical Illustrations

DIGESTIVE SYSTEM

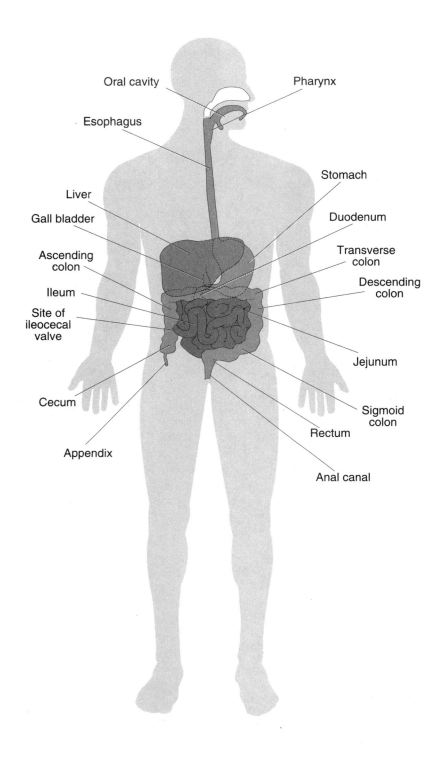

Current Procedural Coding Expert — Anatomical Illustrations

DIGESTIVE SYSTEM

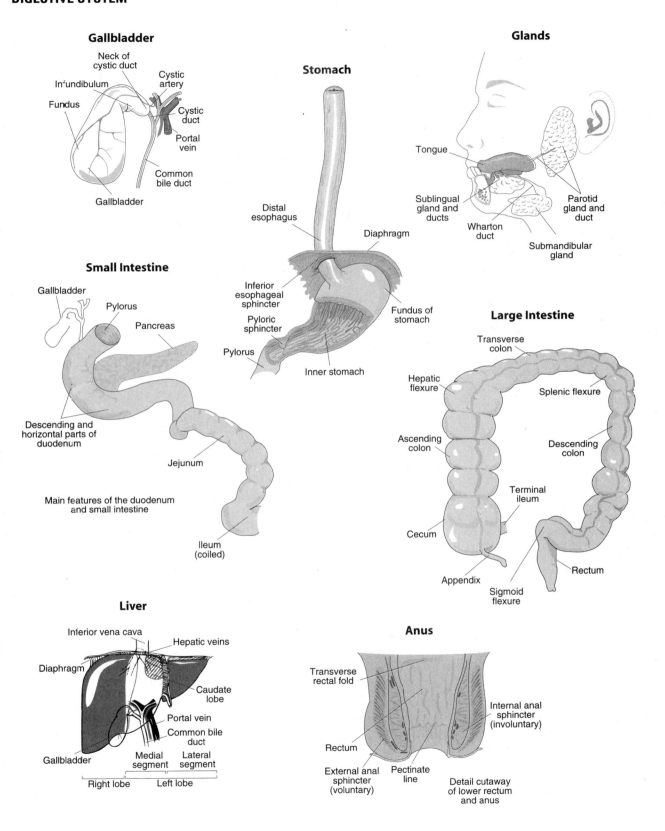

Anatomical Illustrations

ARTERIAL SYSTEM

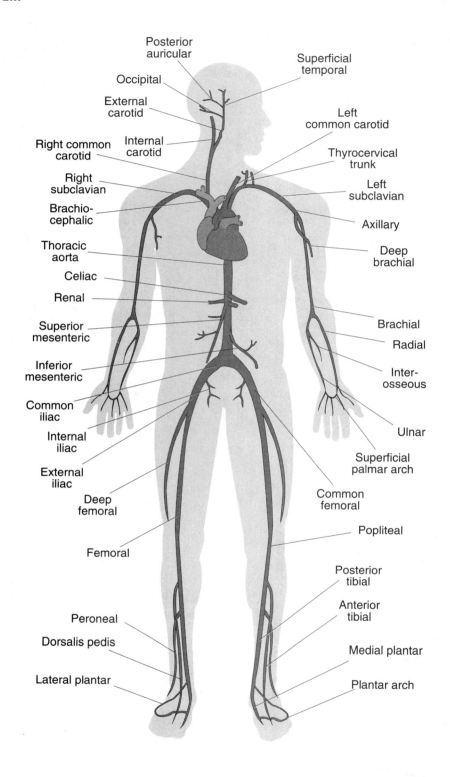

ARTERIAL SYSTEM

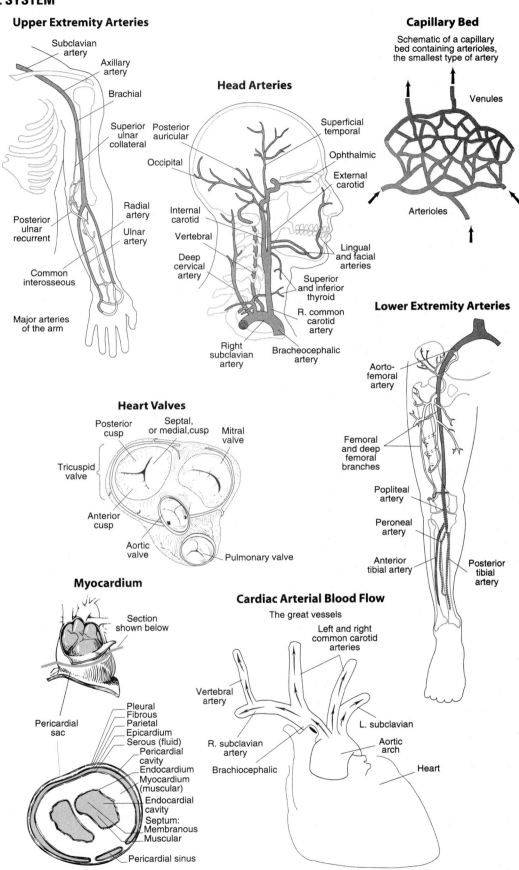

Anatomical Illustrations

VENOUS SYSTEM

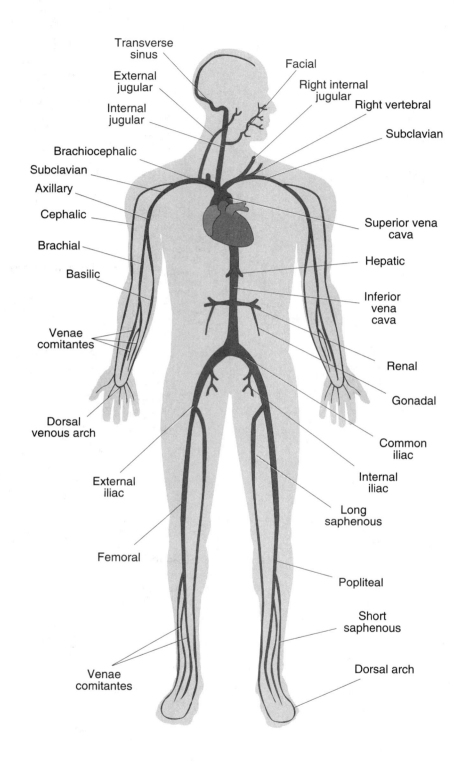

VENOUS SYSTEM

Upper Extremity Veins
Heart Veins
Venae Comitantes
Venous Blood Flow
Head Veins
Cardiac Venous Blood Flow
Abdominal Veins

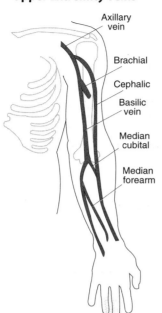
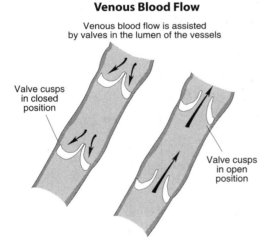
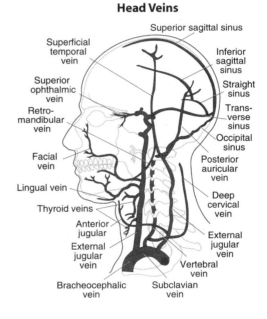
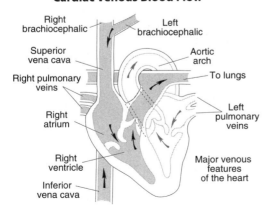
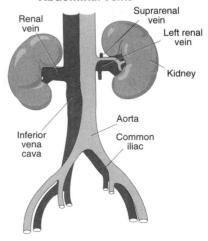

Anatomical Illustrations

NERVOUS SYSTEM

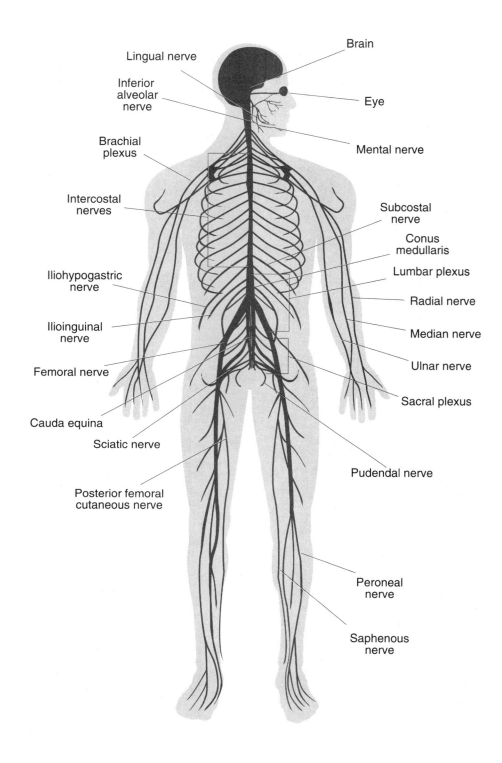

NERVOUS SYSTEM

Brain

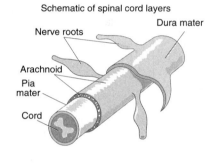

Cranial Nerves

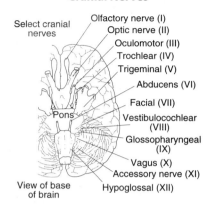

View of base of brain

Spinal Cord

Schematic of spinal cord layers

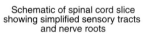

Spinal Column

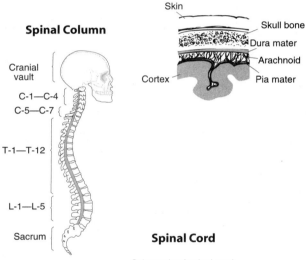

Cranial Layers

Spinal Cord

Schematic of spinal cord slice showing simplified sensory tracts and nerve roots

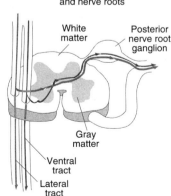

Spinal Cord

Schematic of spinal cord showing nerve roots

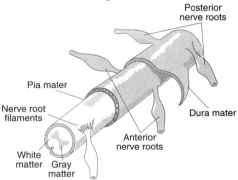

Anatomical Illustrations

LYMPHATIC SYSTEM

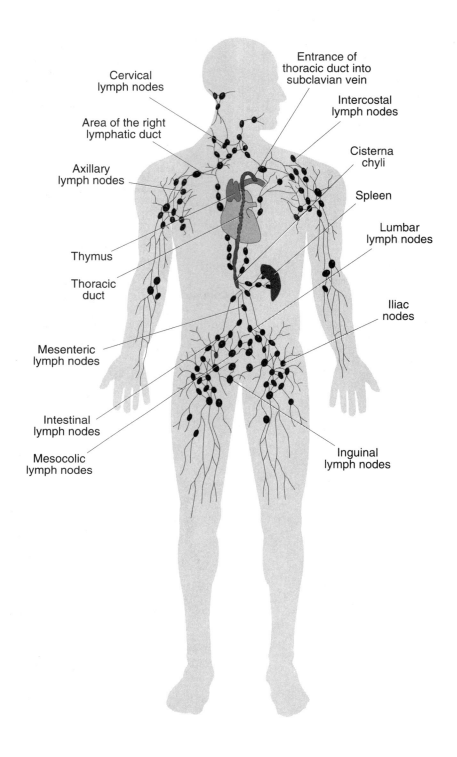

LYMPHATIC SYSTEM

Axillary Lymph Nodes

Lymphatic Capillaries

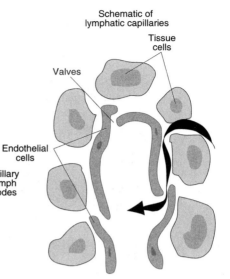

Lymphatic Drainage

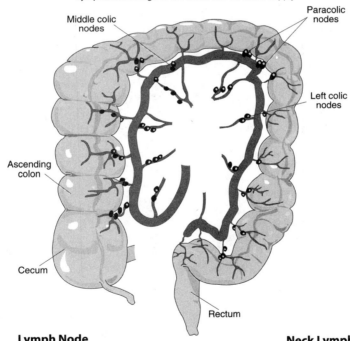

Lymph Node

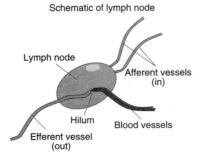

Neck Lymph Nodes

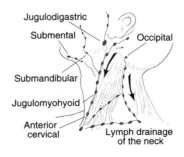

Anatomical Illustrations

ENDOCRINE SYSTEM

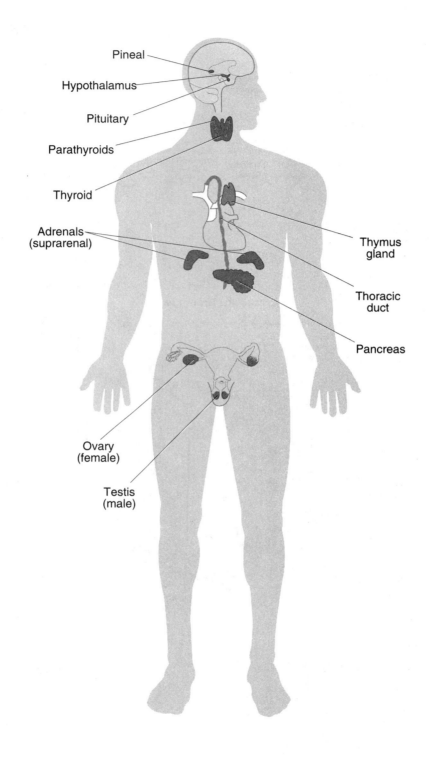

ENDOCRINE SYSTEM

Thyroid Glands

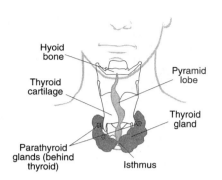

Pituitary Glands

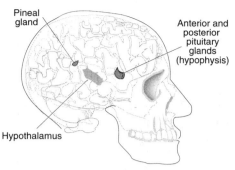

The pituitary gland and its controller, the hypothalamus, control body growth and stimulate and regulate other glands

Thyroid

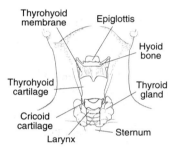

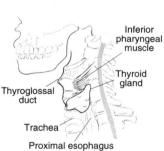

Thyroid

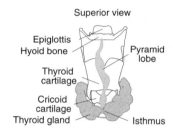

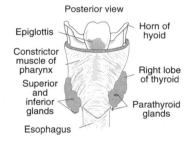

Placenta

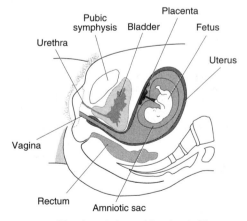

The placenta is considered part of the endocrine system, secreting chorionic gonadotropin, estrogen, progesterone, and somatomammotropin

Anatomical Illustrations

GENITOURINARY SYSTEM

Kidney

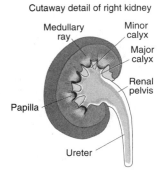

Cutaway detail of right kidney

Nephron

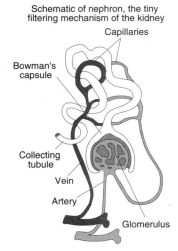

Schematic of nephron, the tiny filtering mechanism of the kidney

Urinary

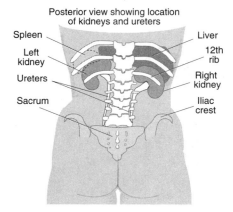

Posterior view showing location of kidneys and ureters

Male Urinary

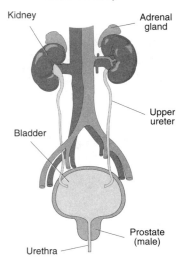

Male Genitourinary

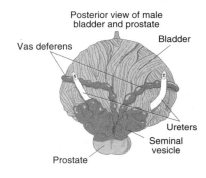

Posterior view of male bladder and prostate

Male Reproductive

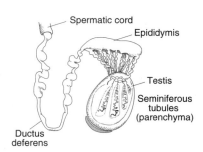

Current Procedural Coding Expert — Anatomical Illustrations

GENITOURINARY SYSTEM

Female Genitourinary
Sideview schematic of female urogenital system

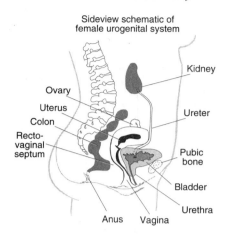

Female Rectoperineal
Lateral schematic showing the female rectoperineal area

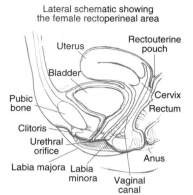

Female Bladder

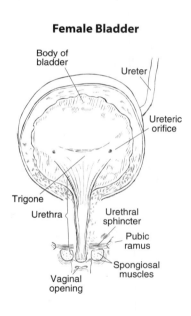

Female Reproductive

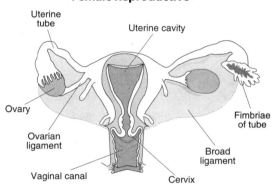

Female Reproductive
Sideview schematic of female breast

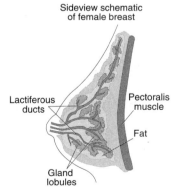

Anatomical Illustrations

RESPIRATORY SYSTEM

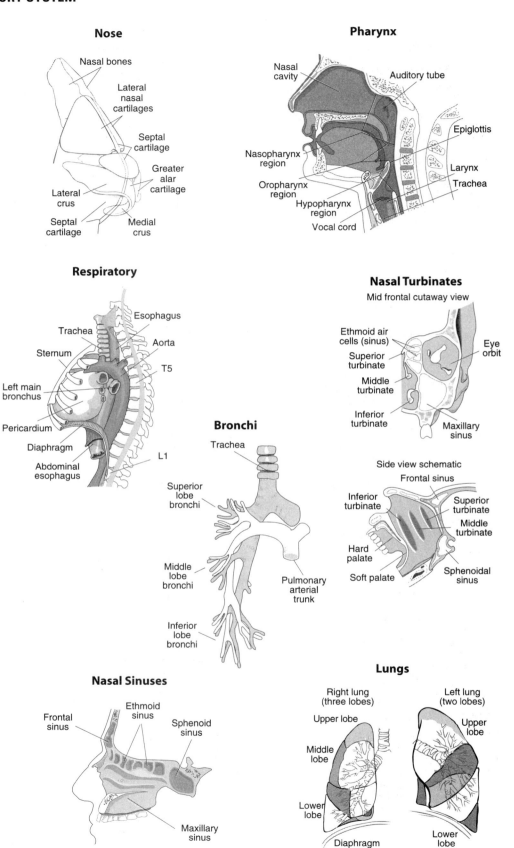

EYE

Eye
Muscles of the right eye

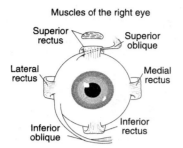

Lacrimal System

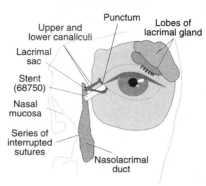

Eye
Anterior and posterior chambers of the eye

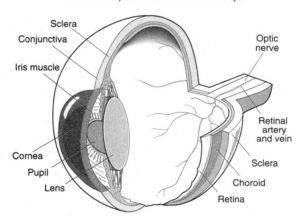

EAR

Ear

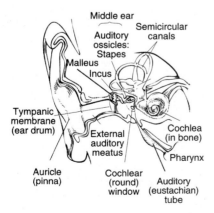

Middle Ear

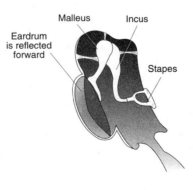

Normal Aortic Arch and Branch Anatomy – Transfemoral Approach

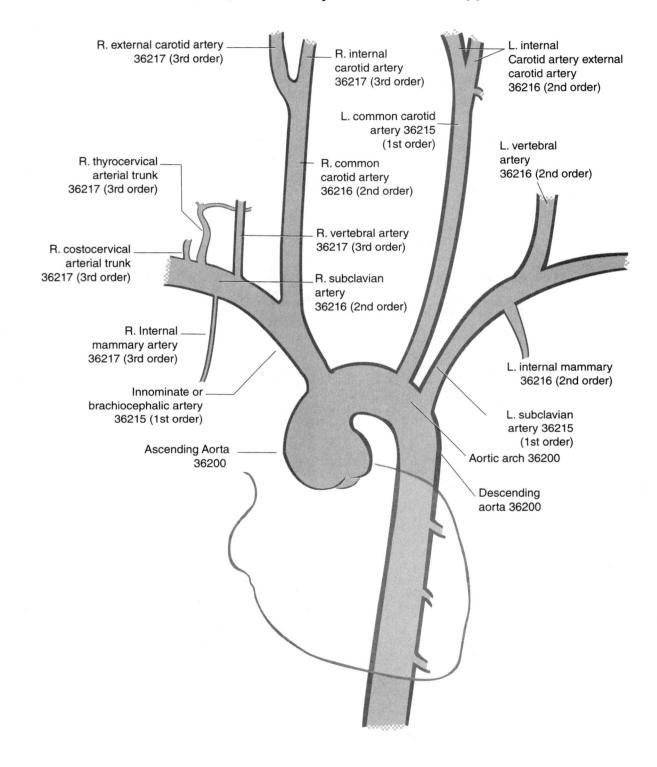

Superior and Inferior Mesenteric Arteries and Branches

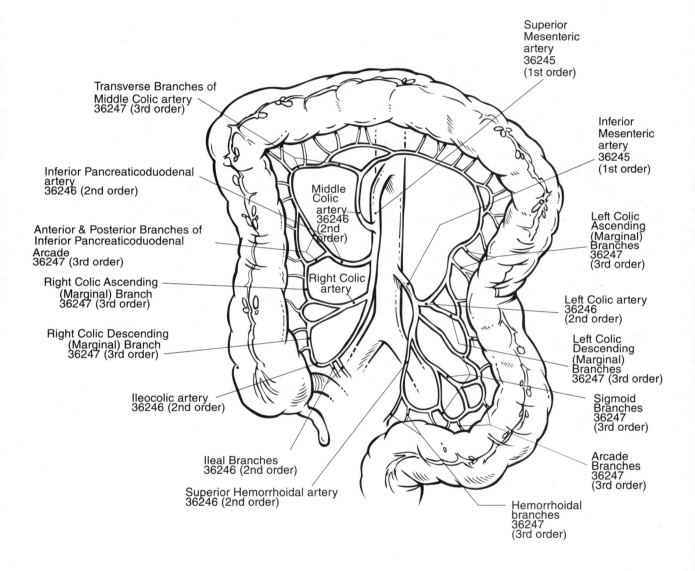

Portal System

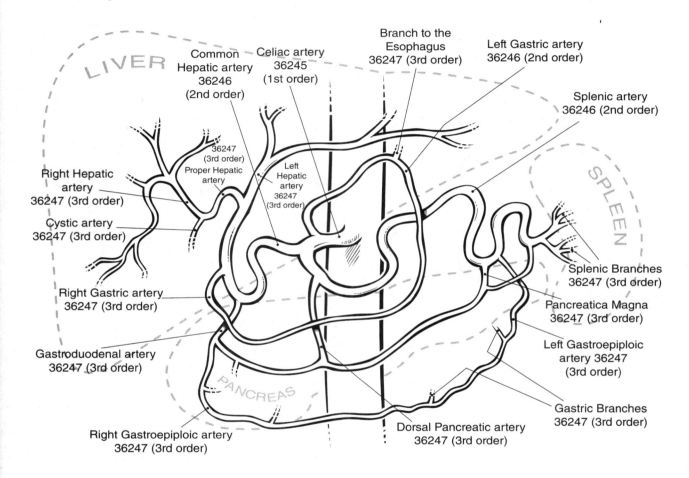

Renal Artery Anatomy–Femoral Approach

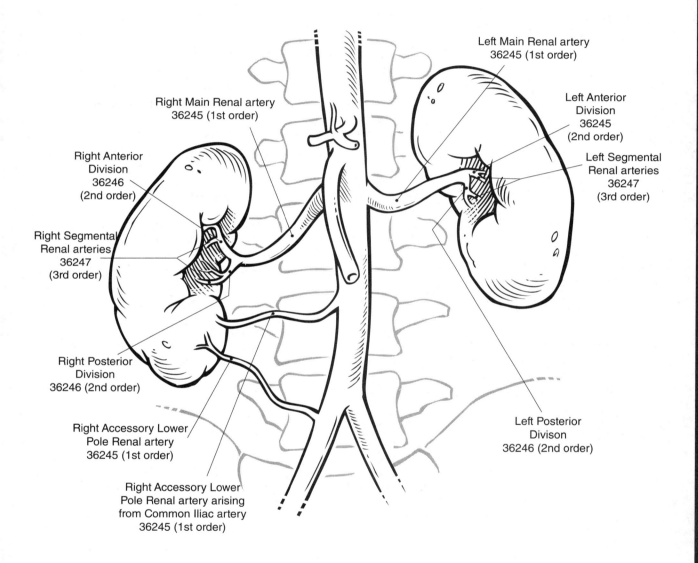

Upper Extremity Arterial Anatomy–Transfemoral or Contralateral Approach

- Subclavian artery R. 36216 (2nd order)
  L. 36215 (1st order)
- Axillary Artery (2nd order) R. 36216
  L. 36215 (1st order)
- Thoracoacromial artery
- Anterior humeral circumflex artery R. 36217
  L. 36216 (2nd order)
- Posterior circumflex humeral artery (3rd order) R. 36217
  (2nd order) L. 36216
- Deep brachial artery R. 36217 (3rd order or more)
  L. 36217 (3rd order or more)
- Brachial artery R. 36217, L. 36217 (3rd order or more)
- Superior ulnar collateral artery R. 36217 (3rd order or more)
  L. 36217 (3rd order or more)
- Radial collateral artery R. 36217, L. 36217 (3rd order or more)
- Inferior ulnar collateral artery R. 36217, L. 36217 (3rd order or more)
- Radial recurrent artery R. 36217, L. 36217 (3rd order or more)
- Recurrent interosseous artery R. 36217
  L. 36217 (3rd order or more)
- Common interosseous artery R. 36217, L. 36217 (3rd order or more)
- Anterior interosseous artery R. 36217, L. 36217 (3rd order or more)
- Radial artery R. 36217, L. 36217 (3rd order or more)
- Ulnar artery R. 36217
  L. 36217 (3rd order or more)
- Posterior interosseous artery R. 36217, L. 36217 (3rd order or more)
- Superficial palmar branch of radial artery R. 36217, L. 36217 (3rd order or more)
- Deep palmar arch R. 36217, L. 36217 (3rd order or more)
- Digital arteries

Lower Extremity Arterial Anatomy–Contralateral, Axillary or Brachial Approach

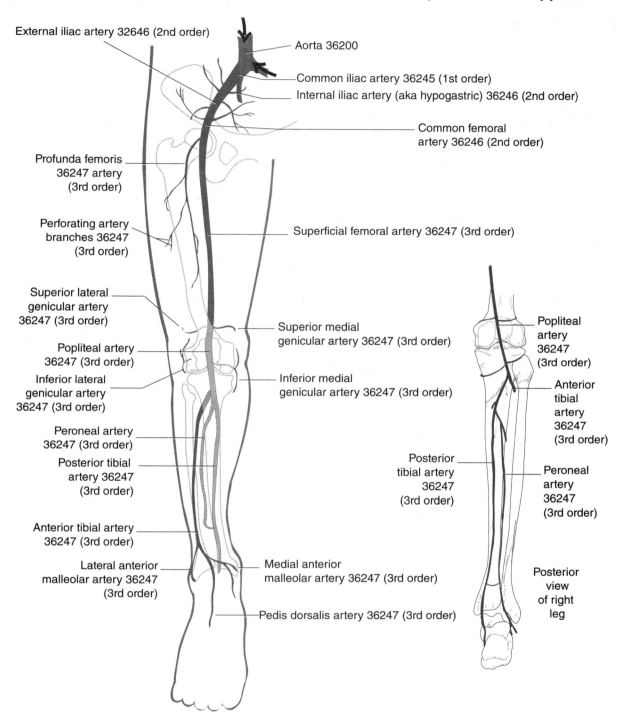

Portal System

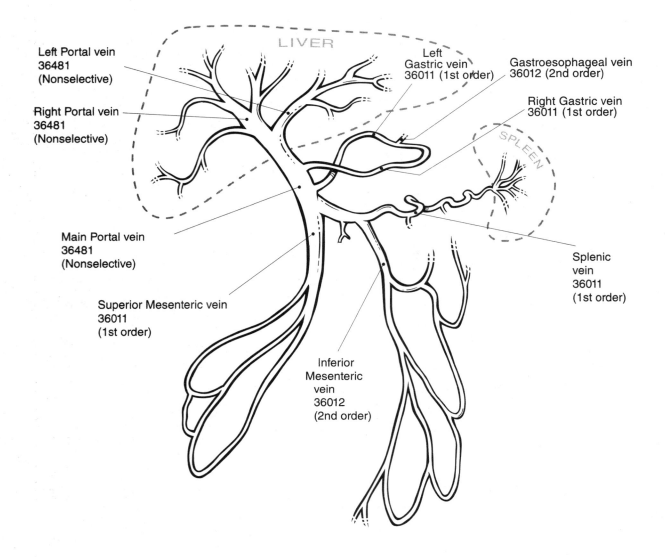

Coronary Arteries Anterior View

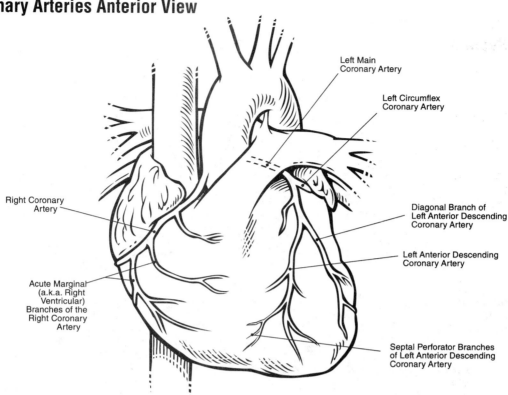

Left Heart Catheterization

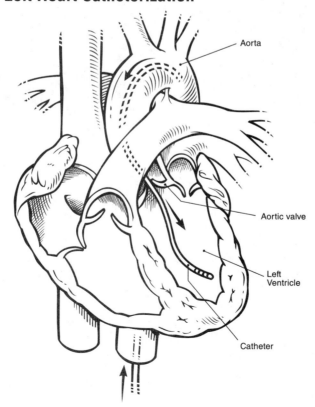

Heart Conduction System

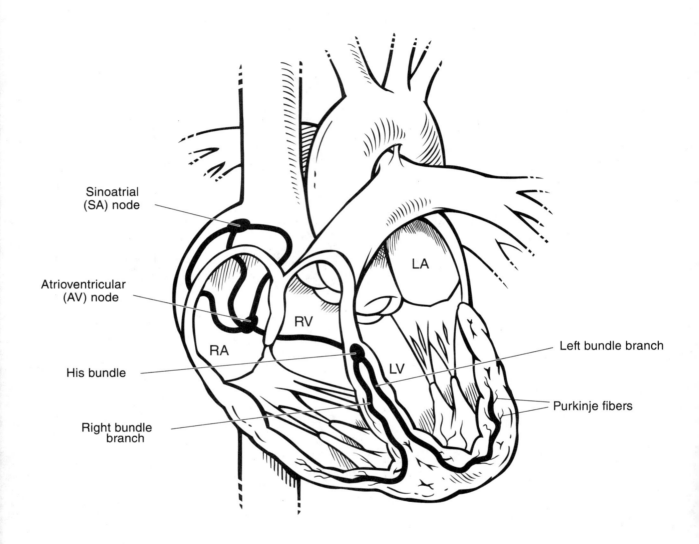

Index

A

Abbe–Estlander Procedure, 40527
ABBI Biopsy, 19103
Abdomen, Abdominal
  Abdominal Aorta
    Angiography, 75635
  Abdominal Wall
    Reconstruction, 49905
    Removal
      Mesh, 11008
      Prosthesis, 11008
    Repair
      Hernia, 49491-49557
        by Laparoscopy, 49650, 49651
    Tumor, 22900-22905
    Unlisted Services and Procedures, 22999
  Abscess
    Drainage, 49020, 49040
      Fluid, 49080, 49081
      Peritoneal
        Open, 49020
        Percutaneous, 49021
      Peritonitis, localized, 49020
      Retroperitoneal
        Open, 49060
        Percutaneous, 49061
      Skin and Subcutaneous Tissue
        Complicated, 10061
        Multiple, 10061
        Simple, 10060
        Single, 10060
      Subdiaphragmatic
        Open, 49040
        Percutaneous, 49041
      Subphrenic, 49040
    Incision and drainage, 49020, 49040
      Open, 49040
    Pancreatitis, 48000
    Percutaneous, 49021
    Peritoneal, 49020
    Peritonitis, Localized, 49020
    Retroperitoneal, 49060
    Skin and Subcutaneous Tissue
      Complicated, 10061
      Multiple, 10061
      Simple, 10060
      Single, 10060
    Subdiaphragmatic, 49040
    Subphrenic, 49040
  Angiography, 74175, 75635
  Anorectal Exam with Anesthesia, 45990
  Aorta
    Aneurysm, 0078T-0081T, 34800-34805, 34825-34832, 35081-35103, 75952, 75953
    Thromboendarterectomy, 35331
  Aortic Aneurysm, 0078T-0081T, 34800-34805, 34825-34832, 35081-35103, 75952, 75953
  Artery
    Ligation, 37617
  Biopsy
    Open, 49000
    Percutaneous, 49180
    Skin and Subcutaneous Tissue, 11100, 11101
  Bypass Graft, 35907
  Cannula/catheter
    Insertion, 49420, 49421
    Removal, 49422
  Celiotomy
    for Staging, 49220
  CT Scan, 74150-74175, 75635
  Cyst
    Destruction/Excision, 49203-49205
  Delivery
    with Hysterectomy, 59525

Abdomen, Abdominal — *continued*
  Delivery — *continued*
    After Attempted Vaginal Delivery
      Delivery Only, 59620
      Postpartum Care, 59622
      Routine Care, 59618
    Delivery Only, 59514
    Postpartum Care, 59515
    Routine Care, 59510
    Tubal Ligation at Time of, 58611
  Drainage
    Fluid, 49080, 49081
  Ectopic Pregnancy, 59130
  Endometrioma, 49203-49205
    Destruction/Excision, 49203-49205
  Excision
    Excess Skin, 15830
    Tumor, Abdominal Wall, 22900
  Exploration, 49000, 49002
    Blood Vessel, 35840
    Staging, 58960
  Hernia Repair, 49495-49525, 49560-49587
  Incision, 49000
    Staging, 58960
  Incision and Drainage
    Pancreatitis, 48000
  Infraumbilical Panniculectomy, 15830
  Injection
    Air, 49400
    Contrast Material, 49400
  Insertion
    Catheter, 49419-49421
    Venous Shunt, 49425
  Intraperitoneal
    Catheter Exit Site, 49436
    Catheter Insertion, 49324, 49435
    Catheter Removal, 49422
    Catheter Revision, 49325
    Shunt
      Ligation, 49428
      Removal, 49429
  Laparotomy
    with Biopsy, 49000
    Exploration, 47015, 49000-49002, 58960
    Hemorrhage Control, 49002
    Second Look, 58960
    Staging, 49220, 58960
  Magnetic Resonance Imaging (MRI), 74181-74183
  Needle Biopsy
    Mass, 49180
  Peritoneocentesis, 49080, 49081
  Radical Resection, 51597
  Repair
    Blood Vessel, 35221
    with
      Other Graft, 35281
      Vein Graft, 35251
    Hernia, 49491-49525, 49560-49587
    Suture, 49900
  Revision
    Venous Shunt, 49426
  Suture, 49900
  Tumor
    Destruction/Excision, 49203-49205
  Ultrasound, 76700, 76705
  Unlisted Services and Procedures, 49999
  Wound Exploration
    Penetrating, 20102
  X-ray, 74000-74022
Abdominal Lymphangiogram, 75805, 75807
Abdominal Paracentesis, 49080-49081
Abdominal Wall
  See Abdomen, X–Ray
  Debridement
    Infected, 11005-11006
  Reconstruction, 49905

Abdominal Wall — *continued*
  Removal
    Mesh, 11008
    Prosthesis, 11008
  Surgery, 22999
  Tumor
    Excision, 22900
Abdominohysterectomy
  Radical, 58210
  Resection of Ovarian Malignancy, 58951, 58953-58954, 58956
  Supracervical, 58180
  Total, 58150, 58200
    with Colpo-Urethrocystopexy, 58152
    with Omentectomy, 58956
    with Partial Vaginectomy, 58200
Abdominoplasty, 15830, 15847, 17999
ABG, 82803, 82805
Ablation
  Anal
    Polyp, 46615
    Tumor, 46615
  Atria, 33257-33259
  Bone Tumor, 20982
  Colon
    Tumor, 45339
  Cryosurgical
    Fibroadenoma, 19105
    Renal mass, 50250
    Renal Tumor
      Percutaneous, 50593
  CT Scan Guidance, 77013
  Endometrial, 58353, 58356, 58563
  Endometrium
    Ultrasound Guidance, 58356
  Heart
    Arrhythmogenic Focus, 93650-93652
    Atrioventricular Node Function, 93650
    Intracardiac Pacing and Mapping, 93631
      Follow-up Study, 93624
      Stimulation and Pacing, 93623
  Liver
    Tumor, 47380-47382
      Laparoscopic, 47370, 47371
      Open, 47380-47382
  Lung
    Tumor
      Radiofrequency, 32998
  Magnetic Resonance Guidance, 77022
  Parenchymal Tissue
    CT Scan Guidance, 77013
  Prostate, 55873
  Pulmonary Tumor, 32998
  Radiofrequency, 32998
  Renal
    Cyst, 50541
    Mass, 50542
      Radiofrequency, 50592
    Tumor, 50593
      Cryotherapy
        Percutaneous, 50593
  Supraventricular Arrhythmogenic Focus, 33250-33251
  Tongue Base, 41530
  Turbinate Mucosa, 30801, 30802
  Ultrasound
    Guidance, 76940
    Ultrasound Focused, 0071T-0072T
    Uterine Tumor, 0071T-0072T
  Uterine Leiomyomata, 0071T, 0072T
  Uterine Tumor
    Ultrasound, Focused, 0071T-0072T
  Vein
    Endovenous, 36475-36479
  Ventricular Arrhythmogenic Focus, 33261
ABLB Test, 92562
ABO, 86900

Abortion
  See Obstetrical Care
  Incomplete, 59812
  Induced by
    with Hysterotomy, 59100, 59852, 59857
    Amniocentesis Injection, 59850-59852
    Dilation and Curettage, 59840
    Dilation and Evacuation, 59841
    Saline, 59850, 59851
    Vaginal Suppositories, 59855, 59856
  Missed
    First Trimester, 59820
    Second Trimester, 59821
  Septic, 59830
  Spontaneous, 59812
  Therapeutic, 59840-59852
    by Saline, 59850
      with Dilatation and Curettage, 59851
    with Hysterotomy, 59852
ABR, 92585-92586
Abrasion, Skin
  Chemical Peel, 15788-15793
  Dermabrasion, 15780-15783
  Lesion, 15786, 15787
ABS, 86255, 86403, 86850
Abscess
  Abdomen, 49040, 49041
    Drainage, 49020, 49040
      Peritoneal
        Open, 49020
        Percutaneous, 49021
      Peritonitis, Localized, 49020
      Retroperitoneal
        Open, 49060
        Percutaneous, 49061
      Skin and Subcutaneous Tissue
        Complicated, 10061
        Multiple, 10061
        Simple, 10060
        Single, 10060
      Subdiaphragmatic, 49040
        Open, 49040
        Percutaneous, 49041
      Subphrenic, 49040
    Incision and Drainage
      Open, 49040
      Percutaneous, 49021
  Anal
    Incision and Drainage, 46045, 46050
  Ankle
    Incision and Drainage, 27603
  Appendix
    Incision and Drainage, 44900
      Open, 44900
      Percutaneous, 44901
  Arm, Lower, 25028
    Excision, 25145
    Incision and Drainage, 25035
  Arm, Upper
    Incision and Drainage, 23930-23935
  Auditory Canal, External, 69020
  Bartholin's Gland
    Incision and Drainage, 56420
  Bladder
    Incision and Drainage, 51080
  Brain
    Drainage by
      Burr Hole, 61150, 61151
      Craniotomy/Craniectomy, 61320, 61321
    Excision, 61514, 61522
    Incision and Drainage, 61320-61321
  Breast
    Incision and Drainage, 19020
  Carpals
    Incision, Deep, 25035
  Clavicle
    Sequestrectomy, 23170

Abscess

Abscess — *continued*
- Drainage
  - with X-ray, 75989, 76080
  - Contrast Injection, 49424
- Ear, External
  - Complicated, 69005
  - Simple, 69000
- Elbow
  - Incision and Drainage, 23930-23935
- Epididymis
  - Incision and Drainage, 54700
- Excision
  - Olecranon Process, 24138
  - Radius, 24136
  - Ulna, 24138
- Eyelid
  - Incision and Drainage, 67700
- Facial Bone(s)
  - Excision, 21026
- Finger, 26010-26011
  - Incision and Drainage, 26010, 26011, 26034
- Foot
  - Incision, 28005
- Gums
  - Incision and Drainage, 41800
- Hand
  - Incision and Drainage, 26034
- Hematoma
  - Incision and Drainage, 27603
- Hip
  - Incision and Drainage, 26990-26992
- Humeral Head, 23174
- Humerus
  - Excision, 24134
  - Incision and Drainage, 23935
- Kidney
  - Incision and Drainage
    - Open, 50020
    - Percutaneous, 50021
- Leg, Lower
  - Incision and Drainage, 27603
- Liver
  - Incision and Drainage
    - Open, 47010
    - Percutaneous, 47011
  - Injection, 47015
  - Repair, 47300
- Localization
  - Nuclear Medicine, 78806, 78807
- Lung
  - Percutaneous Drainage, 32200, 32201
- Lymph Node, 38300, 38305
  - Incision and Drainage, 38300-38305
- Lymphocele
  - Drainage, 49062
- Mandible
  - Excision, 21025
- Mouth
  - Incision and Drainage, 40800, 40801, 41005-41009, 41015-41018
- Nasal
  - Incision and Drainage, 30000, 30020
- Nasal Septum
  - Incision and Drainage, 30020
- Neck
  - Incision and Drainage, 21501, 21502
- Nose
  - Incision and Drainage, 30000, 30020
- Ovarian
  - Incision and Drainage, 58820-58822
    - Abdominal Approach, 58822
    - Vaginal Approach, 58820
- Ovary
  - Drainage
    - Percutaneous, 58823

Abscess — *continued*
- Ovary — *continued*
  - Incision and Drainage
    - Abdominal Approach, 58822
    - Vaginal Approach, 58820
- Palate
  - Incision and Drainage, 42000
- Paraurethral Gland
  - Incision and Drainage, 53060
- Parotid Gland
  - Drainage, 42300, 42305
- Pelvic
  - Drainage
    - Percutaneous, 58823
- Pelvis, 26990
  - Incision and Drainage, 26990-26992, 45000
  - Percutaneous, 58823
- Pericolic
  - Drainage
    - Percutaneous, 58823
- Perineum
  - Incision and Drainage, 56405
- Perirenal or Renal
  - Drainage, 50020-50021
  - Open, 50020
  - Percutaneous, 50021
- Peritoneum
  - Incision and Drainage
    - Open, 49020
    - Percutaneous, 49021
- Posterior Spine, 22010, 22015
- Prostate
  - Incision and Drainage, 55720-55725
    - Prostatotomy, 55720, 55725
    - Transurethral, 52700
- Radius
  - Incision, Deep, 25035
- Rectum
  - Incision and Drainage, 45005, 45020, 46040, 46060
- Retroperitoneal, 49060-49061
  - Drainage
    - Open, 49060
    - Percutaneous, 49061
- Salivary Gland
  - Drainage, 42300-42320
- Scapula
  - Sequestrectomy, 23172
- Scrotum
  - Incision and Drainage, 54700, 55100
- Shoulder
  - Incision and Drainage, 23030
- Skene's Gland
  - Incision and Drainage, 53060
- Skin
  - Incision and Drainage, 10060-10061
    - Complicated, 10061
    - Multiple, 10061
    - Simple, 10060
    - Single, 10060
  - Puncture Aspiration, 10160
- Soft Tissue
  - Incision, 20000, 20005
- Spine
  - Incision and Drainage, 22010-22015
- Subdiaphragmatic, 49040-49041
  - Incision and Drainage
    - Open, 49040
    - Percutaneous, 49041
- Sublingual Gland
  - Drainage, 42310, 42320
- Submaxillary Gland
  - Drainage, 42310, 42320
- Subphrenic, 49040, 49041
- Testis
  - Incision and Drainage, 54700
- Thoracostomy, 32551
- Thorax
  - Incision and Drainage, 21501, 21502

Abscess — *continued*
- Throat
  - Incision and Drainage, 42700-42725
- Tongue
  - Incision and Drainage, 41000-41006
- Tonsil
  - Incision and Drainage, 42700
- Ulna
  - Incision, Deep, 25035
- Urethra
  - Incision and Drainage, 53040
- Uvula
  - Incision and Drainage, 42000
- Vagina
  - Incision and Drainage, 57010
- Vulva
  - Incision and Drainage, 56405
- Wrist
  - Excision, 25145
  - Incision and Drainage, 25028, 25035
- X-ray, 76080

Absolute Neutrophil Count (ANC), 85048

Absorptiometry
- Dual Energy, 3095F-3096F
  - Bone
    - Appendicular, 77079
    - Axial Skeleton, 77078
    - Vertebral, 77080-77082
- Dual Photon
  - Bone, 78351
- Radiographic
  - Photodensity, 77083
- Single Photon
  - Bone, 78350

Absorption Spectrophotometry, 82190
- Atomic, 82190

ACB, 82045

ACBE, 74280

Accessory Nerve
- Incision, 63191
- Section, 63191
- Spinal — *See* Nerves, Spinal Accessory

Accessory, Toes, 28344

Accoustic Immittance Testing, 92570

ACD, 63075, 63076

ACE (Angiotensin Converting Enzyme), 82164

Acellular Immunization, 90700

Acetabuloplasty, 27120, 27122

Acetabulum
- Fracture
  - with Manipulation, 27222
  - without Manipulation, 27220
  - Closed Treatment, 27220, 27222
  - Open Treatment, 27226-27228
- Reconstruction, 27120
  - with Resection, Femoral Head, 27122
- Tumor
  - Excision, 27076

Acetaldehyde
- Blood, 82000

Acetaminophen
- Urine, 82003

Acetic Anhydrides, 84600

Acetone
- Blood or Urine, 82009, 82010

Acetone Body, 82009, 82010

Acetylcholinesterase
- Blood or Urine, 82013

AcG, 85220

Achilles Tendon
- Incision, 27605, 27606
- Lengthening, 27612
- Repair, 27650-27654

Achillotomy, 27605-27606

ACI, 27412, 29870

Acid
- Adenylic, 82030
- Amino
  - Blood or Urine, 82127-82139

Acid — *continued*
- Aminolevulinic
  - Urine or Blood, 82135
- Ascorbic
  - Blood, 82180
- Bile, 82239
  - Blood, 82240
- Deoxyribonucleic
  - Antibody, 86225-86226
- Diethylamide, Lysergic, 80102-80103, 80299
- Fast Bacilli (AFB)
  - Culture, 87116
- Fast Stain, 88312
- Fatty
  - Blood, 82725
  - Very Long Chain, 82726
- Folic, 82746
  - RBC, 82747
- Gastric, 82926, 82928
- Glycocholic, 82240
- Guanylic, 83008
- Lactic, 83605
- N-Acetylneuraminic, 84275
- Perfusion Test
  - Esophagus, 91012, 91030
- Phenylethylbarbituric, 82205
  - Assay, 80184
- Phosphatase, 84060-84066
- Probes, Nucleic
  - *See* Nucleic Acid Probe
- Reflux Test, 91034-91038
- Salic, 84275
- Uric
  - Blood, 84550
  - Other Source, 84560
  - Urine, 84560

Acid Diethylamide, Lysergic, 80102-80103, 80299

Acidity/Alkalinity
- Blood Gasses, 82800-82805
- Body Fluid, Not Otherwise Specified, 83986
- Exhaled Breath Condensate, 83987

ACL Repair
- Arthroscopy aided, 29888
- Open, 27407, 27409

Acne Surgery
- Incision and Drainage
  - Abscess, 10060, 10061
    - Puncture Aspiration, 10160
  - Bulla
    - Puncture Aspiration, 10160
  - Comedones, 10040
  - Cyst, 10040
    - Puncture Aspiration, 10160
  - Milia, Multiple, 10040
  - Pustules, 10040

Acne Treatment
- Abrasion, 15786, 15787
- Chemical Peel, 15788-15793
- Cryotherapy, 17340
- Dermabrasion, 15780-15783
- Exfoliation
  - Chemical, 17360

Acoustic Evoked Brain Stem Potential, 92585, 92586

Acoustic Neuroma
- Brainstem
  - Biopsy, 61575, 61576
  - Decompression, 61575, 61576
  - Evoked Potentials, 92585
  - Lesion Excision, 61575, 61576
- Brain Tumor Excision, 61510, 61518, 61520, 61521, 61526, 61530, 61545
- Mesencephalon
  - Tractotomy, 61480
- Skull Base Surgery
  - Anterior Cranial Fossa
    - Bicoronal Approach, 61586
    - Craniofacial Approach, 61580-61583
    - Extradural, 61600, 61601
    - LeFort I Osteotomy Approach, 61586

Index

Acoustic Neuroma — *continued*
  Skull Base Surgery — *continued*
    Anterior Cranial Fossa — *continued*
      Orbitocranial Approach, 61584, 61585
      Transzygomatic Approach, 61586
    Carotid Aneurysm, 61613
    Carotid Artery, 61610
      Transection
        Ligation, 61609-61612
    Craniotomy, 62121
    Dura
      Repair of Cerebrospinal Fluid Leak, 61618, 61619
    Middle Cranial Fossa
      Extradural, 61605-61607
      Infratemporal Approach, 61590, 61591
      Intradural, 61606-61608
      Orbitocranial Zygomatic Approach, 61592
    Posterior Cranial Fossa
      Extradural, 61615
      Intradural, 61616
      Transcondylar Approach, 61596, 61597
      Transpetrosal Approach, 61598
      Transtemporal Approach, 61595
Acoustic Recording
  Heart Sounds, 93799
Acoustic Reflex Testing, 92512
Acoustic Rhinometry, 92512
ACP, 84060-84066
Acromioclavicular Joint
  Arthrocentesis, 20605
  Arthrotomy, 23044
    with Biopsy, 23101
  Dislocation, 23540-23552
    Open Treatment, 23550, 23552
  X-ray, 73050
Acromion
  Excision
    Shoulder, 23130
Acromionectomy
  Partial, 23130
Acromioplasty, 23415, 23420
  Partial, 23130
ACTH (Adrenocorticotropic Hormone), 80400-80406, 80412, 80418, 82024
ActHIB, 90648
ACTH Releasing Factor, 80412
Actigraphy, 95803
Actinomyces
  Antibody, 86602
Actinomycosis, 86000
Actinomycotic Infection
  See Actinomycosis
Actinotherapy, 96900
Activated Factor X, 85260
Activated Partial Thromboplastin Time, 85730, 85732
Activation, Lymphocyte, 86353
Activities of Daily Living (ADL), 97535, 99509
  See Physical Medicine/Therapy/Occupational Therapy
  Training, 97535, 97537
Activity, Glomerular Procoagulant
  See Thromboplastin
Acupuncture
  One or More Needles
    with Electrical Stimulation, 97813-97814
    without Electrical Stimulation, 97810-97811
Acute Poliomyelitis
  See Polio
Acylcarnitines, 82016, 82017
Adacel, 90715
Adamantinoma, Pituitary
  See Craniopharyngioma

ADAMTS-13, 85397
Addam Operation, 26040-26045
Adductor Tenotomy of Hip
  See Tenotomy, Hip, Adductor
Adelson
  Crosby Immersion Method, 85999
Adenoidectomy
  with Tonsillectomy, 42820, 42821
  Primary
    Age 12 or Over, 42831
    Younger Than Age 12, 42830
  Secondary
    Age 12 or Over, 42836
    Younger Than Age 12, 42835
Adenoids
  Excision, 42830-42836
    with Tonsillectomy, 42820, 42821
  Unlisted Services and Procedures, 42999
Adenoma
  Pancreas
    Excision, 48120
  Thyroid Gland
    Excision, 60200
Adenosine 3', 5' Monophosphate, 82030
Adenosine Diphosphate
  Blood, 82030
Adenosine Monophosphate (AMP)
  Blood, 82030
Adenovirus
  Antibody, 86603
  Antigen Detection
    Enzyme Immunoassay, 87301-87451
    Immunofluorescence, 87260
Adenovirus Vaccine, 90476-90477
ADH (Antidiuretic Hormone), 84588
Adhesion, Adhesions
  Epidural, 62263, 62264
  Eye
    Corneovitreal, 65880
    Incision
      Anterior Segment, 65860-65870
      Posterior Segment, 65875
    Intermarginal
      Construction, 67880
        Transposition of Tarsal Plate, 67882
  Intestinal
    Enterolysis, 44005
    Laparoscopic, 44180
  Intracranial
    Lysis, 62161
  Intrauterine
    Lysis, 58559
  Labial
    Lysis, 56441
  Lungs
    Lysis, 32124
  Pelvic
    Lysis, 58660, 58662, 58740
  Penile
    Lysis
      Post-circumcision, 54162
  Preputial
    Lysis, 54450
  Urethral
    Lysis, 53500
Adipectomy, 15830-15839, 15876-15879
Adjustment
  External Fixation, 20693, 20696
ADL
  Activities of Daily Living, 97535, 97537
Administration
  Immunization
    Each Additional Vaccine/Toxoid, 90472, 90474
      with Counseling, 90466, 90468
    H1N1, 90470
    One (single) Vaccine/Toxoid, 90471, 90473

Administration — *continued*
  Immunization — *continued*
    One Vaccine/Toxoid — *continued*
      with Counseling, 90465, 90467
    Injection
      Intramuscular Antibiotic, 96372
      Therapeutic, Diagnostic, Prophylactic
        Intra-arterial, 96373
        Intramuscular, 96372
        Intravenous, 96374-96376
        Subcutaneous, 96372
ADP (Adenosine Diphosphate), 82030
Adrenal Cortex Hormone, 83491
Adrenalectomy, 60540
  with Excision Retroperitoneal Tumor, 60545
  Anesthesia, 00866
  Laparoscopic, 60650
Adrenal Gland
  Biopsy, 60540, 60545
  Excision
    Laparoscopy, 60650
    Retroperitoneal, 60545
  Exploration, 60540, 60545
  Nuclear Medicine
    Imaging, 78075
Adrenalin
  Blood, 82383, 82384
  Fractionated, 82384
  Urine, 82382, 82384
Adrenaline or Noradrenaline
  Testing, 82382-82384
Adrenal Medulla
  See Medulla
Adrenocorticotropic Hormone (ACTH), 80400-80406, 80412, 80418, 82024
  Blood or Urine, 82024
  Stimulation Panel, 80400-80406
Adrenogenital Syndrome, 56805, 57335
Adson Test, 95870
Adult T Cell Leukemia Lymphoma Virus I, 86687, 86689
Advanced Life Support
  Emergency Department Services, 99281-99288
  Physician Direction, 99288
Advancement
  Genioglossus, 21199
  Tendon
    Foot, 28238
    Genioglossus, 21199
Advancement Flap
  Skin, Adjacent Tissue Transfer, 14000-14350
AEP, 92585, 92586
Aerosol Inhalation
  Inhalation Treatment, 94640, 94664
  Pentamidine, 94642
AFB (Acid Fast Bacilli), 87116
AFBG, 35539, 35540, 35646
Afferent Nerve
  See Sensory Nerve
AFGE, 66020
AFI, 76815
AFP, 82105, 82106
After Hours Medical Services, 99050-99060
Afterloading Brachytherapy, 77785-77787
Agents, Anticoagulant
  See Clotting Inhibitors
Agglutinin
  Cold, 86156, 86157
  Febrile, 86000
Aggregation
  Platelet, 85576
AGTT, 82951, 82952
AHG (Antihemophilic Globulin), 85240
Ahmed Glaucoma Valve
  Insertion, 66180
  Removal, 67120

Ahmed Glaucoma Valve — *continued*
  Revision, 66185
AICD (Pacing Cardioverter–Defibrillator), 33223, 93282, 93289, 93292, 93295
  Heart
    Defibrillator, 33240-33249, 93282, 93288, 93292, 93295
    Pacemaker, 33212-33214, 33233-33237
Aid, Hearing
  Bone Conduction, 69710-69711
  Check, 92590-92595
AIDS
  Antibodies, 86687-86689, 86701-86703
  Virus, 86701, 86703
A–II (Angiotensin II), 82163
Air Contrast Barium Enema (ACBE), 74280
Akin Operation, 28298
ALA (Aminolevulinic Acid), 82135
Alanine 2 Oxoglutarate Aminotransferase
  See Transaminase, Glutamic Pyruvic
Alanine Amino (ALT), 84460
Alanine Transaminase
  See Transaminase, Glutamic Pyruvic
Albarran Test
  Water Load Test, 89235
Albumin
  Cobalt Binding (ACB), 82045
  Ischemia Modified, 82045
  Serum, 82040
  Urine, 82042-82044
Alcohol
  Abuse Screening and Intervention, 99408-99409
  Breath, 82075
  Ethyl
    Blood, 82055
    Urine, 82055
  Ethylene Glycol, 82693
Alcohol Dehydrogenase
  See Antidiuretic Hormone
Alcohol, Isopropyl
  See Isopropyl Alcohol
Alcohol, Methyl
  See Methanol
Aldolase
  Blood, 82085
Aldosterone
  Blood, 82088
  Suppression Evaluation, 80408
  Urine, 82088
Alexander's Operation, 58400-58410
ALIF (Anterior Lumbar Interbody Fusion), 22558-22585
Alimentary Canal
  See Gastrointestinal Tract
ALK (Automated Lamellar Keratoplasty), 65710
Alkaline Phosphatase, 84075-84080
  Leukocyte, 85540
  WBC, 85540
Alkaloids
  See Specific Drug
  Urine, 82101
Allergen Bronchial Provocation Tests
  See Allergy Tests; Bronchial Challenge Test
Allergen Challenge, Endobronchial
  See Bronchial Challenge Test
Allergen Immunotherapy
  Allergen
    with Extract Supply, 95144
    Injection, 95115-95117
    Prescription/Supply/Injection, 95120-95125
  Antigens, 95144
  IgE, 86003, 86005
  IgG, 86001

Allergen Immunotherapy

Allergen Immunotherapy — *continued*
  Injection
    with Extract Supply, 95120, 95125
    without Extract Supply, 95115, 95117
  Insect Venom
    Prescription
      Supply, 95145-95149
        Injection, 95130-95134
    Prescription
      Supply, 95165
        Insect, Whole Body, 95170
    Rapid Desensitization, 95180
Allergy Services/Procedures
  See Office and/or Other Outpatient Services, Allergen and Immunotherapy
  Education and Counseling, 99201-99215
  Unlisted Services and Procedures, 95199
Allergy Tests
  Challenge Test
    Bronchial, 95070, 95071
    Ingestion, 95075
  Eye Allergy, 95060
  Food Allergy, 95075
  Intradermal
    Allergen Extract, 95024, 95028
    Biologicals, 95015
    Drugs, 95015
    Incremental, 95027
    Venoms, 95015
  Nasal Mucous Membrane Test, 95065
  Nose Allergy, 95065
  Patch
    Application Tests, 95044
    Photo Patch, 95052
  Photosensitivity, 95056
  Skin Tests
    Allergen Extract, 95004, 95024, 95027
    Biologicals, 95010
    Drugs, 95010
    End Point Titration, 95027
    Venoms, 95010
Allogeneic Donor
  Backbench Preparation
    Intestine, 44715-44721
    Kidney, 50323-50329
    Liver, 47143-47147
    Pancreas, 48551-48552
  Lymphocyte Infusion, 38242
Allogeneic Transplantation
  See Homograft
  Backbench Preparation, 44715-44721
    Intestine, 44715-44721
    Kidney, 50323-50329
    Liver, 47143-47147
    Pancreas, 48551-48552
Allograft
  Acellular Dermal, 15330-15331, 15335-15336
  Aortic Valve, 33406, 33413
  Bone, Structural, 20931
  Cartilage
    Knee, 27415
  for Temporary Wound Closure, 15300-15301, 15320-15321
  Lung Transplant, 32850
  Skin, 15300-15336
  Spine Surgery
    Morselized, 20930
    Structural, 20931
Allograft Preparation
  Heart, 33933, 33944
  Intestines, 44715-44721
  Kidney, 50323-50329
  Liver, 47143-47147
  Lung, 32855-32856, 33933
  Pancreas, 48551-48552
  Renal, 50323-50329

Alloplastic Dressing
  Burns, 15002, 15004-15005
Allotransplantation
  Intestines, 44135, 44136
  Islets of Langerhans, 48999
  Renal, 50360, 50365
    Removal, 50370
Almen Test
  Blood, Feces, 82270
ALP, 84075-84080, 85540
Alpha-2 Antiplasmin, 85410
Alpha-Fetoprotein
  Amniotic Fluid, 82106
  Serum, 82105
Alpha-1-Antitrypsin, 82103, 82104
Alphatocopherol, 84446
ALS, 99288
ALT, 84460
Altemeier Procedure
  Rectum Prolapse, Excision, 45130, 45135
Alternate Binaural Loudness Balance Test (ABLB), 92562
Aluminum
  Blood, 82108
Alveola
  Fracture
    Closed Treatment, 21421
    Open Treatment, 21422-21423
Alveolar Cleft
  Ungrafted Bilateral, 21147
  Ungrafted Unilateral, 21146
Alveolar Nerve
  Avulsion, 64738
  Incision, 64738
  Transection, 64738
Alveolar Ridge
  Fracture
    Closed Treatment, 21440
    Open Treatment, 21445
Alveolectomy, 41830
Alveoli
  Fracture
    Closed Treatment, 21421
    Open Treatment, 21422, 21423
Alveoloplasty, 41874
Alveolus
  Excision, 41830
Amide, Procaine, 80190-80192
Amikacin
  Assay, 80150
Amine
  Vaginal Fluid, 82120
Amino Acids
  Blood or Urine, 82127-82139
Aminolevulinic Acid (ALA)
  Blood or Urine, 82135
Aminotransferase
  Alanine (SGPT), 84460
  Aspartate (SGOT), 84450
Amitriptyline
  Assay, 80152
Ammonia
  Blood, 82140
  Urine, 82140
Amniocentesis, 59000
  with Amniotic Fluid Reduction, 59001
  See Chromosome Analysis
  Induced Abortion, 59850
    with Dilation and Curettage, 59851
    with Dilation and Evacuation, 59851
    with Hysterotomy, 59852
  Urine
    with Amniotic Fluid Reduction, 59001
Amnioinfusion
  Transabdominal, 59070
Amnion
  Amniocentesis, 59000
    with Amniotic Fluid Reduction, 59001
  Amnioinfusion
    Transabdominal, 59070

Amniotic Fluid
  Alpha-Fetoprotein, 82106
  Index, 76815
  Scan, 82143
  Testing, 83661, 83663, 83664
Amniotic Membrane
  transplant (AMT), 65780
Amobarbital, 82205
AMP (Adenosine Monophosphate), 82030
AMP, Cyclic, 82030
Amphetamine
  Blood or Urine, 82145
Amputation
  Ankle, 27888
  Arm and Shoulder, 23900-23921
  Arm, Lower, 25900, 25905, 25915
    with Implant, 24931, 24935
    Cineplasty, 24940
    Revision, 25907, 25909
  Arm, Upper, 24900, 24920
    with Implant, 24931, 24935
    and Shoulder, 23900-23921
    Revision, 24925, 24930
  Boyd, 27880-27889
  Cervix
    Total, 57530
  Ear
    Partial, 69110
    Total, 69120
  Finger, 26910-26952
  Foot, 28800, 28805
  Hand
    at Metacarpals, 25927
    at Wrist, 25920
      Revision, 25922
    Revision, 25924, 25929, 25931
  Interpelviabdominal, 27290
  Interthoracoscapular, 23900
  Knee joint Disarticulation, 27598
  Leg, Lower, 27598, 27880-27882
    Revision, 27884, 27886
  Leg, Upper, 27590-27592
    at Hip, 27290, 27295
    Revision, 27594, 27596
  Metacarpal, 26910
  Metatarsal, 28810
  Penis
    Partial, 54120
    Radical, 54130, 54135
    Total, 54125
  Thumb, 26910-26952
  Toe, 28810-28825
  Tuft of Distal Phalanx, 11752
  Upper Extremity
    Cineplasty, 24940
Amputation, Nose
  See Resection, Nose
Amputation through Hand
  See Hand, Amputation
AMT, 65780
Amussat's Operation, 44025
Amygdalohippocampectomy, 61566
Amylase
  Blood, 82150
  Urine, 82150
ANA (Antinuclear Antibodies), 86038, 86039
Anabolic Steroid
  Androstenedione, 82160
Anal
  Abscess, 46045
  Bleeding, 46614
  Fissurectomy, 46200, 46261
  Fistula, 46262-46288, 46706-46707, 46715-46716
  Fistulectomy, 46270-46285
  Fistulotomy, 46270-46280
  Polyp, 46615
  Sphincter
    Dilation, 45905
    Incision, 46080
  Tumor, 46615
Analgesia, 99143-99150
  See also Anesthesia, Sedation

Analgesic Cutaneous Electrostimulation
  See Application, Neurostimulation
Analysis
  Algorithmic
    Electrocardiographic-derived Data, 0206T
  Cardio-Defibrillator, 93287, 93289, 93295-93296
  Cardiovascular Monitoring System, 93290, 93292, 93297, 93299
  Computer Data, 99090
  Electroencephalogram
    Digital, 95957
  Electronic
    Antitachycardia Pacemaker, 93724
    Drug Infusion Pump, 62367, 62368
    Pulse Generator, 95970-95971, 95980-95982
  Loop Recorder, 93291, 93298-93299
  Pacemaker, 93288, 93293-93294
  Patient Specific Findings, 0185T
  Physiologic Data, Remote, 99091
  Protein
    Tissue
      Western Blot, 88372
  Semen, 89320-89322
    Sperm Isolation, 89260, 89261
  Spectrum, 82190
Anaspadias
  See Epispadias
Anastomosis
  Arteriovenous Fistula
    with Bypass Graft, 35686
    with Graft, 36825, 36830, 36832
    with Thrombectomy, 36831
    Direct, 36821
    Revision, 36832, 36833
      with Thrombectomy, 36833
      without Thrombectomy, 36832
  Artery
    to Aorta, 33606
    to Artery
      Cranial, 61711
  Bile Duct
    to Bile Duct, 47800
    to Intestines, 47760, 47780
  Bile Duct to Gastrointestinal, 47785
  Broncho-Bronchial, 32486
  Caval to Mesenteric, 37160
  Cavopulmonary, 33768
  Colorectal, 44620
  Epididymis
    to Vas Deferens
      Bilateral, 54901
      Unilateral, 54900
  Excision
    Trachea, 31780, 31781
    Cervical, 31780
  Fallopian Tube, 58750
  Gallbladder to Intestine, 47720-47740
  Gallbladder to Pancreas, 47999
  Hepatic Duct to Intestine, 47765, 47802
  Ileo-Anal, 45113
  Intestines
    Colo-anal, 45119
    Cystectomy, 51590
    Enterocystoplasty, 51960
    Enterostomy, 44620-44626
    Ileoanal, 44157-44158
    Resection
      Laparoscopic, 44202-44205
    Intestine to Intestine, 44130
    Intrahepatic Portosystemic, 37182, 37183
  Jejunum, 43825
  Microvascular
    Free Transfer Jejunum, 43496
  Nerve
    Facial to Hypoglossal, 64868
    Facial to Phrenic, 64870

Index

Anesthesia

Anastomosis — *continued*
  Nerve — *continued*
    Facial to Spinal Accessory, 64864, 64865
  Oviduct, 58750
  Pancreas to Intestines, 48520, 48540, 48548
  Polya, 43632
  Portocaval, 37140
  Pulmonary, 33606
  Renoportal, 37145
  Splenorenal, 37180, 37181
  Stomach, 43825
    to Duodenum, 43810, 43855
      Revision, 43850
    to Jejunum, 43820, 43825, 43860, 43865
  Tubotubal, 58750
  Ureter
    to Bladder, 50780-50785
    to Colon, 50810, 50815
      Removal, 50830
    to Intestine, 50800, 50820, 50825
      Removal, 50830
    to Kidney, 50727-50750
    to Ureter, 50727, 50760, 50770
  Vein
    Saphenopopliteal, 34530
  Vein to Vein, 37140-37183

Anastomosis, Aorta–Pulmonary Artery
  See Aorta, Anastomosis, to Pulmonary Artery

Anastomosis, Bladder, to Intestine
  See Enterocystoplasty

Anastomosis, Hepatic Duct
  See Hepatic Duct, Anastomosis

Anastomosis of Lacrimal Sac to Conjunctival Sac
  See Conjunctivorhinostomy

Anastomosis of Pancreas
  See Pancreas, Anastomosis

ANC, 85048

Anderson Tibial Lengthening, 27715

Androstanediol Glucuronide, 82154

Androstanolone
  See Dihydrotestosterone

Androstenedione
  Blood or Urine, 82157

Androstenolone
  See Dehydroepiandrosterone

Androsterone
  Blood or Urine, 82160

Anesthesia
  See also Analgesia
  Abbe–Estlander Procedure, 00102
  Abdomen
    Abdominal Wall, 00700-00730, 00800, 00802, 00820-00836
      Halsted Repair, 00750-00756
    Blood Vessels, 00770, 00880-00882, 01930, 01931
      Inferior Vena Cava Ligation, 00882
      Transvenous Umbrella Insertion, 01930
    Endoscopy, 00740, 00810
    Extraperitoneal, 00860, 00862, 00866-00868, 00870
    Hernia Repair, 00830-00836
      Diaphragmatic, 00756
      Halsted Repair, 00750-00756
      Omphalocele, 00754
    Intraperitoneal, 00790-00797, 00840, 00842
    Laparoscopy, 00790
    Liver Transplant, 00796
    Pancreatectomy, 00794
    Renal Transplant, 00868
  Abdominoperineal Resection, 00844
  Abortion
    Incomplete, 01965
    Induced, 01966
  Achilles Tendon Repair, 01472
  Acromioclavicular Joint, 01620
  Adrenalectomy, 00866

Anesthesia — *continued*
  Amniocentesis, 00842
  Amputation
    Femur, 01232
    Forequarter, 01636
    Interthoracoscapular, 01636
    Penis
      Complete, 00932
      Radical with Bilateral Inguinal and Iliac Lymphadenectomy, 00936
      Radical with Bilateral Inguinal Lymphadenectomy, 00934
  Aneurysm
    Axillary–Brachial, 01652
    Knee, 01444
    Popliteal Artery, 01444
  Angiography, 01920
  Angioplasty, 01924-01926
  Ankle, 00400, 01462-01522
    Achilles Tendon, 01472
    Nerves, Muscles, Tendons, 01470
    Skin, 00400
  Anorectal Procedure, 00902
  Anus, 00902
  Arm
    Lower, 00400, 01810-01860
      Arteries, 01842
      Bones, Closed, 01820
      Bones, Open, 01830
      Cast Application, 01860
      Cast Removal, 01860
      Embolectomy, 01842
      Nerves, Muscle, Tendons, 01810
      Phleborrhaphy, 01852
      Shunt Revision, 01844
      Skin, 00400
      Total Wrist, 01832
      Veins, 01850
    Upper Arm, and Elbow, 00400, 01710-01782
      Nerves, Muscles, Tendons, 01710
      Tenodesis, 01716
      Tenoplasty, 01714
      Tenotomy, 01712
      Skin, 00400
  Arrhythmias, 00410
  Arteriograms, 01916
  Arteriography, 01916
  Arteriovenous (AV) Fistula, 01432
  Arthroplasty
    Hip, 01214, 01215
    Knee, 01402
  Arthroscopic Procedures
    Ankle, 01464
    Elbow, 01732-01740
    Foot, 01464
    Hip, 01202
    Knee, 01382, 01400, 01464
    Shoulder, 01622-01630
    Wrist, 01829-01830
  Auditory Canal, External
    Removal Foreign Body, 69205
  Axilla, 00400, 01610-01682
  Back Skin, 00300
  Batch–Spittler–McFaddin Operation, 01404
  Biopsy, 00100
    Anorectal, 00902
    Clavicle, 00450
    External ear, 00120
    Inner ear, 00120
    Intraoral, 00170
    Liver, 00702
    Middle ear, 00120
    Nose, 00164
    Parotid gland, 00100
    Salivary gland, 00100
    Sinuses, accessory, 00164
    Sublingual gland, 00100
    Submandibular gland, 00100
  Bladder, 00870, 00912
  Blepharoplasty, 00103

Anesthesia — *continued*
  Brain, 00210-00218, 00220-00222
  Breast, 00402-00406
    Augmentation Mammoplasty, 00402
    Breast Reduction, 00402
    Muscle Flaps, 00402
  Bronchi, 00542
    Intrathoracic Repair of Trauma, 00548
    Reconstruction, 00539
  Bronchoscopy, 00520
  Burns
    Debridement and/or Excision, 01951-01953
    Dressings and/or Debridement, 16020-16030
  Burr Hole, 00214
  Bypass Graft
    with pump oxygenator, younger than one year of age, 00561
    Coronary Artery without Pump Oxygenator, 00566
    Leg
      Lower, 01500
      Upper, 01270
    Shoulder, Axillary, 01654, 01656
  Cardiac Catheterization, 01920
  Cardioverter, 00534, 00560
  Cast
    Application
      Body Cast, 01130
      Forearm, 01860
      Hand, 01860
      Knee Joint, 01420
      Lower Leg, 01490
      Pelvis, 01130
      Shoulder, 01680-01682
      Shoulder Spica, 01682
      Wrist, 01860
    Removal
      Forearm, 01860
      Hand, 01860
      Knee Joint, 01420
      Lower Leg, 01490
      Shoulder, 01680
      Shoulder Spica, 01682
    Repair
      Forearm, 01860
      Hand, 01860
      Knee Joint, 01420
      Lower Leg, 01490
      Shoulder, 01680
      Shoulder Spica, 01682
  Central Venous Circulation, 00532
  Cervical Cerclage, 00948
  Cervix, 00948
  Cesarean Section, 01961, 01963, 01968, 01969
  Chemonucleolysis, 00634
  Chest, 00400-00410, 00470-00474, 00522, 00530-00539, 00542, 00546-00550
  Chest Skin, 00400
  Childbirth
    Cesarean Delivery, 01961, 01963, 01968, 01969
    External Cephalic Version, 01958
    Vaginal Delivery, 01960, 01967
  Clavicle, 00450-00454
  Cleft Lip Repair, 00102
  Cleft Palate Repair, 00172
  Colpectomy, 00942
  Colporrhaphy, 00942
  Colpotomy, 00942
  Conscious Sedation, 99143-99150
  Corneal Transplant, 00144
  Coronary Procedures, 00560-00580
  Cranioplasty, 00215
  Culdoscopy, 00950
  Cystectomy, 00864
  Cystolithotomy, 00870
  Cystourethroscopy
    Local, 52265
    Spinal, 52260
  Decortication, 00542

Anesthesia — *continued*
  Defibrillator, 00534, 00560
  Diaphragm, 00540
  Disarticulation
    Hip, 01212
    Knee, 01404
    Shoulder, 01634
  Discography, 01935-01936
  Donor
    Nephrectomy, 00862
  Dressing Change, 15852
  Drug Administration
    Epidural or Subarachnoid, 01996
  Ear, 00120-00126
  ECT, 00104
  Elbow, 00400, 01710-01782
  Electrocoagulation
    Intracranial Nerve, 00222
  Electroconvulsive Therapy (ECT), 00104
  Embolectomy
    Arm, Upper, 01772
    Femoral, 01274
    Femoral Artery, 01274
    Forearm, Wrist and Hand, 01842
    Leg, Lower, 01502
  Endoscopy
    Arm, Lower, 01830
    Gastrointestinal, 00740
    Intestines, 00810
    Uterus, 00952
    Vaginal, 00950
  Esophagoscopy, 00520
  Esophagus, 00320, 00500
  Excision
    Adrenal gland, 00866
    Bladder
      Total, 00864
    Gland
      Adrenal, 00866
    Iris, 00147
    Prostate, 00865
    Retropharyngeal tumor, 00174
    Testes
      Abdominal, 00928
      Inguinal, 00926
    Uterus
      Vaginal, 00944
    Vulva, 00906
  External Cephalic Version, 01958
  External Fixation System
    Adjustment/Revision, 20693
    Removal, 20694
  Eye, 00140-00148
    Corneal Transplant, 00144
    Iridectomy, 00147
    Iris, 00147
    Lens Surgery, 00142
    Ophthalmoscopy, 00148
    Vitrectomy, 00145
  Eyelid, 00103
  Facial Bones, 00190, 00192
    Mandibular, 00190
    Midface, 00190
    Zygomatic, 00190
  Fallopian Tube
    Ligation, 00851
  Femoral Artery
    Ligation, 01272
  Femur, 01220, 01234, 01340, 01360
  Fibula, 01390, 01392
  Foot, 00400, 01462-01522
  Forearm, 00400, 01810-01860
  Fowler–Stephens Orchiopexy, 00930
  Gastrocnemius Recession, 01474
  Gastrointestinal Endoscopy, 00740
  Genitalia
    Female, 00940-00952, 01958-01969
    Male, 00920-00938
  Great Vessels of Chest, 00560-00563
  Hand, 00400, 01810-01860
  Harrington Rod Technique, 00670
  Head, 00222, 00300
    Muscles, 00300
    Nerves, 00300

Anesthesia

Anesthesia — *continued*
Heart, 00560-00580
  Coronary Artery Bypass Grafting, 00566
  Electrophysiology/Ablation, 00537
  Transplant, 00580
Hepatectomy
  Partial, 00792
Hernia Repair
  Abdomen
    Lower, 00830-00836
    Upper, 00750, 00752, 00756
  Hip, 01200-01215
  Humerus, 01620, 01730, 01740-01744, 01758
Hysterectomy, 01962
  Cesarean, 01963, 01969
  Radial, 00846
  Vaginal, 00944
Hysterosalpingography, 00952
Hysteroscopy, 00952
Incomplete Abortion, 01965
Induced Abortion, 01966
Inferior Vena Cava Ligation, 00882
Injection procedures
  Discography
    Cervical, 01935-01936
    Lumbar, 01935-01936
  Myelography
    Cervical, 01935-01936
    Lumbar, 01935-01936
    Posterior Fossa, 01935-01936
  Nerve Blocks, 01991, 01992
  Pneumoencephalography, 01935-01936
Integumentary System
  Anterior Chest, 00400
  Anterior Pelvis, 00400
  Anterior Trunk, 00400
  Arm, Upper, 00400
  Axilla, 00400
  Elbow, 00400
  Extremity, 00400
  Forearm, 00400
  Hand, 00400
  Head, 00300
  Knee, 00400
  Leg, Lower, 00400
  Leg, Upper, 00400
  Neck, 00300
  Perineum, 00400
  Popliteal Area, 00400
  Posterior Chest, 00300
  Posterior Pelvis, 00300
  Posterior Trunk, 00300
  Shoulder, 00400
  Wrist, 00400
Intestines
  Endoscopy, 00810
Intracranial Procedures, 00210-00222
  Elevation of Depressed Skull Fracture, 00215
  Sitting Position, 00218
  Spinal Fluid Shunting, 00220
  Vascular Procedures, 00216
Intrahepatic or Portal Circulation Shunt(s), 01931
Intraoral Procedures, 00170-00176
  Radical Surgery, 00176
  Repair Cleft Palate, 00172
  Retropharyngeal Tumor Repair, 00174
Intrathoracic Procedures
  Bronchi, 00539, 00548
  Trachea, 00539, 00548
Intrathoracic System, 00500, 00520-00529, 00530-00548, 00550, 00560-00566, 00580
Iridectomy, 00147
Keen Operation, 00604
Kidney, 00862, 00868, 00872, 00873
Knee, 00400, 01320-01444
Knee Skin, 00400
Laminectomy, 00604

Anesthesia — *continued*
Laparoscopy, 00790-00792, 00840
Larynx, 00320, 00326
Leg
  Lower, 00400, 01462-01522
  Upper, 01200-01274
Lens, 00142
Leriche Operation, 00622
Life Support for Organ Donor, 01990
Ligation
  Fallopian Tube, 00851
Lips
  Repair of Cleft, 00102
Lithotripsy, 00872, 00873
Liver, 00702, 00792, 00796
  Hemorrhage, 00792
  Percutaneous Biopsy, 00702
  Transplant, 00796, 01990
Lumbar Puncture, 00635
Lungs, 00522, 00539-00548
  Transplant, 00580
Lymphadenectomy, 00934, 00936
  Bilateral, Inguinal and Iliac with Radical Amputation Penis, 00936
  Bilateral, Inguinal with Radical Amputation Penis, 00934
Lymphatic System, 00320, 00322
Malunion
  Humerus, 01744
Mammoplasty, 00402
Manipulation
  Spine, 22505
Manipulation of Temporomandibular Joint(s) (TMJ)
  Therapeutic, 21073
Marcellation Operation, 00944
Mediastinoscopy, 00528-00529
Mediastinum, 00528-00529, 00540-00541
Mouth, 00170, 00172
Myelography, 01935-01936
  Cervical, 01935-01936
  Injection Lumbar, 01935-01936
  Posterior Fossa, 01935-01936
Myringotomy, 69421
Neck, 00300-00352
Needle Biopsy
  Pleura, 00522
  Thyroid, 00322
Nephrectomy, 00862
Neuraxial
  Cesarean Delivery, 01968, 01969
  Labor, 01967-01969
  Vaginal Delivery, 01967
Neurectomy, 01180, 01190
Nose, 00160-00164
  Removal
    Foreign Body, 30310
Omphalocele, 00754
Ophthalmoscopy, 00148
Orchiectomy, 00926-00928
  Abdominal, 00928
  Inguinal, 00926
Orchiopexy, 00930
  Torek Procedure, 00930
Organ Harvesting
  Brain–Dead Patient, 01990
Osteoplasty
  Tibia/Fibula, 01484
Osteotomy
  Humerus, 01742
  Tibia/Fibula, 01484
Other Procedures, 01990-01999
Otoscopy, 00124
Pacemaker Insertion, 00530
Pacing Cardioverter/Defibrillator, 00534
Pancreas, 00794
Pancreatectomy, 00794
Panniculectomy, 00802
Parotid Gland, 00100
Patella, 01390, 01392
Pectus Excavatum, 00474
Pelvic Exenteration, 00848
Pelvis, 00400, 00865, 01112-01190

Anesthesia — *continued*
Pelvis — *continued*
  Amputation, 01140
  Bone, 01120
  Bone Marrow, 01112
  Examination, 57400
  Extraperitoneal, 00864
  Intraperitoneal, 00844-00851
  Repair, 01173
  Skin, 00300, 00400
Penis, 00932-00938
Percutaneous
  Liver Biopsy, 00702
  Spine and Spinal Cord, 01935-01936
Pericardial Sac, 00560-00563
Pericardium, 00560-00563
Perineum, 00904-00908
Pharynx, 00174, 00176
Phleborrhaphy
  Arm, Upper, 01782
  Forearm, Wrist and Hand, 01852
Pleura, 00540-00541
  Needle Biopsy, 00522
Pleurectomy, 32310-32320, 32656
Pneumocentesis, 00524
Popliteal Area, 00400, 01320, 01430-01444
Prognathism, 00192
Prostate, 00865, 00908, 00914
Prostatectomy
  Perineal, 00908
  Radical, 00865
    Retropubic, 00865
    Suprapubic, 00865
  Walsh Modified Radical, 00865
Ptosis Surgery, 00103
Radical Surgery, Procedures, Resections
  Ankle Resection, 01482
  Breast, Radical or Modified, 00402
  Breast with Internal Mammary Node Dissection, 00406
  Clavicle, 00452
  Elbow, 01756
  Facial Bones, 00192
  Femur, 01234
  Foot Resection, 01482
  Hip Joint Resection, 01234
  Humeral Head and Neck Resection, 01630
  Humerus, 01756
  Hysterectomy, 00846
  Intraoral Procedures, 00176
  Lower Leg Bone Resection, 01482
  Nose, 00162
  Orchiectomy, Abdominal, 00928
  Orchiectomy, Inguinal, 00926
  Pectus Excavatum, 00474
  Pelvis, 01150
  Penis Amputation with Bilateral Inguinal and Iliac Lymphadenectomy, 00936
  Penis Amputation with Bilateral Inguinal Lymphadenectomy, 00934
  Perineal, 00904
  Prognathism, 00192
  Prostatectomy, 00865
  Scapula, 00452
  Shoulder Joint Resection, 01630-01638
  Sinuses, Accessory, 00162
  Sternoclavicular Joint resection, 01630
  Testes
    Abdominal, 00928
    Inguinal, 00926
Radiologic Procedures, 00100-01922
  Arterial
    Therapeutic, 01924-01926
  Arteriograms
    Needle, Carotid, Vertebral, 01916

Anesthesia — *continued*
Radiologic Procedures — *continued*
  Arteriograms — *continued*
    Retrograde, Brachial, Femoral, 01916
  Cardiac Catheterization, 01920
  Discography Lumbar, 01935-01936
  Injection Hysterosalpingography, 00952
  Spine and Spinal Cord
    Percutaneous Image, Guided, 01935-01936
  Venous/Lymphatic, 01930-01933
    Therapeutic, 01930-01933
Reconstructive Procedures
  Blepharoplasty, 00103
  Breast, 00402
  Ptosis Surgery, 00103
Renal Procedures, 00862
Repair
  Achilles Tendon, Ruptured, with or without Graft, 01472
  Cast
    Forearm, 01860
    Hand, 01860
    Knee Joint, 01420
    Lower Leg, 01490
    Shoulder, 01680
    Shoulder Spica, 01682
    Wrist, 01860
  Cleft Lip, 00102
  Cleft Palate, 00172
  Humerus
    Malunion, 01744
    Nonunion, 01744
  Knee Joint, 01420
Repair of Skull, 00215
Repair, Plastic
  Cleft Lip, 00102
  Cleft Palate, 00172
Replacement
  Ankle, 01486
  Elbow, 01760
  Hip, 01212-01215
  Knee, 01402
  Shoulder, 01638
  Wrist, 01832
Restriction
  Gastric
    for Obesity, 00797
Retropharyngeal Tumor Excision, 00174
Rib Resection, 00470-00474
Sacroiliac Joint, 01160, 01170, 27096
Salivary Glands, 00100
Scheie Procedure, 00147
Second Degree Burn, 01953
Sedation
  Moderate, 99148-99150
    with Independent Observation, 99143-99145
Seminal Vesicles, 00922
Shoulder, 00400-00454, 01610-01682
  Dislocation
    Closed Treatment, 23655
Shunt
  Spinal Fluid, 00220
Sinuses
  Accessory, 00160-00164
    Biopsy, Soft Tissue, 00164
    Radical Surgery, 00162
Skin
  Anterior Chest, 00400
  Anterior Pelvis, 00400
  Arm, Upper, 00400
  Axilla, 00400
  Elbow, 00400
  Forearm, 00400
  Hand, 00400
  Head, 00300
  Knee, 00400
  Leg, Lower, 00400

Index

Anesthesia — *continued*
 Skin — *continued*
  Leg, Upper, 00400
  Neck, 00300
  Perineum, 00400
  Popliteal Area, 00400
  Posterior Chest, 00300
  Posterior Pelvis, 00300
  Shoulder, 00400
  Wrist, 00400
 Skull, 00190
 Skull Fracture
  Elevation, 00215
 Special Circumstances
  Emergency, 99140
  Extreme Age, 99100
  Hypotension, 99135
  Hypothermia, 99116
 Spinal Instrumentation, 00670
 Spinal Manipulation, 00640
 Spine and Spinal Cord, 00600-00670
  Cervical, 00600-00604, 00640, 00670
   Injection, 62310-62319
  Lumbar, 00630-00635, 00640, 00670
   Percutaneous Image Guided, 01935-01936
  Thoracic, 00620-00626, 00640, 00670
  Vascular, 00670
 Sternoclavicular Joint, 01620
 Sternum, 00550
 Stomach
  Restriction
   for Obesity, 00797
 Strayer Procedure, 01474
 Subcutaneous Tissue
  Anterior Chest, 00400
  Anterior Pelvis, 00400
  Arm, Upper, 00400
  Axilla, 00400
  Elbow, 00400
  Forearm, 00400
  Hand, 00400
  Head, 00100
  Knee, 00400
  Leg, Lower, 00400
  Leg, Upper, 00400
  Neck, 00300
  Perineum, 00400
  Popliteal Area, 00400
  Posterior Chest, 00300
  Posterior Pelvis, 00300
  Shoulder, 00400
  Wrist, 00400
 Subdural Taps, 00212
 Sublingual Gland, 00100
 Submandibular (Submaxillary) Gland, 00100
 Suture Removal, 15850-15851
 Sympathectomy
  Lumbar, 00632
  Thoracolumbar, 00622
 Symphysis Pubis, 01160, 01170
 Temporomandibular Joint, 21073
 Tenodesis, 01716
 Tenoplasty, 01714
 Tenotomy, 01712
 Testis, 00924-00930
 Third Degree Burn, 01951-01953
 Thoracoplasty, 00472
 Thoracoscopy, 00528-00529, 00540-00541
 Thoracotomy, 00540-00541
 Thorax, 00400-00474
 Thromboendarterectomy, 01442
 Thyroid, 00320-00322
 Tibia, 01390, 01392, 01484
 TIPS, 01931
 Trachea, 00320, 00326, 00542, 00548
  Reconstruction, 00539
 Transplant
  Cornea, 00144
  Heart, 00580

Anesthesia — *continued*
 Transplant — *continued*
  Kidney, 00868
  Liver, 00796, 01990
  Lungs, 00580
  Organ Harvesting, 01990
 Transurethral Procedures, 00910-00918
  Fragmentation
   Removal Ureteral Calculus, 00918
  Resection Bleeding, 00916
  Resection of Bladder Tumors, 00912
  Resection of Prostate, 00914
 Tubal Ligation, 00851
 Tuffier Vaginal Hysterectomy, 00944
 TURP, 00914
 Tympanostomy, 00120
 Tympanotomy, 00126
 Unlisted Services and Procedures, 01999
 Urethra, 00910, 00918, 00920, 00942
 Urethrocystoscopy, 00910
 Urinary Bladder, 00864, 00870, 00912
 Urinary Tract, 00860
 Uterus, 00952
 Vagina, 00940, 00942, 00950
  Dilation, 57400
  Removal
   Foreign Body, 57415
 Vaginal Delivery, 01960
 Vascular Access, 00532
 Vascular Shunt, 01844
 Vascular Surgery
  Abdomen, Lower, 00880, 00882
  Abdomen, Upper, 00770
  Arm, Lower, 01840-01852
  Arm, Upper, 01770-01782
  Brain, 00216
  Elbow, 01770-01782
  Hand, 01840-01852
  Knee, 01430-01444
  Leg, Lower, 01500-01522
  Leg, Upper, 01260-01274
  Neck, 00350, 00352
  Shoulder, 01650-01670
  Wrist, 01840-01852
 Vas Deferens
  Excision, 00921
 Vasectomy, 00921
 VATS, 00520
 Venography, 01916
 Ventriculography, 00214, 01920
 Vertebral Process
  Fracture/Dislocation
   Closed Treatment, 22315
 Vertebroplasty, 01935-01936
 Vitrectomy, 00145
 Vitreoretinal Surgery, 00145
 Vitreous Body, 00145
 Vulva, 00906
 Vulvectomy, 00906
 Wertheim Operation, 00846
 Wound
  Dehiscence
   Abdomen
    Upper, 00752
 Wrist, 00400, 01810-01860
Aneurysm, Aorta, Abdominal
 See Aorta, Abdominal, Aneurysm
Aneurysm, Artery, Femoral
 See Artery, Femoral, Aneurysm
Aneurysm, Artery, Radial
 See Artery, Radial, Aneurysm
Aneurysm, Artery, Renal
 See Artery, Renal, Aneurysm
Aneurysm, Basilar Artery
 See Artery, Basilar, Aneurysm

Aneurysm Repair
 Aorta
  Abdominal, 0078T-0081T, 34800-34805, 34825-34832, 35081-35103, 75952, 75953
  Thoracoabdominal, 33877
 Axillary Artery, 35011, 35013
 Basilar Artery, 61698, 61702
 Brachial Artery, 35011, 35013
 Carotid Artery, 35001, 35002, 61613, 61697, 61700, 61703
 Celiac Artery, 35121, 35122
 Femoral Artery, 35141, 35142
 Hepatic Artery, 35121, 35122
 Iliac Artery, 34900, 35131-35132, 75953-75954
 Innominate Artery, 35021, 35022
 Intracranial Artery, 61705, 61708
 Mesenteric Artery, 35121, 35122
 Popliteal Artery, 35151, 35152
 Radial Artery, 35045
 Renal Artery, 35121, 35122
 Splenic Artery, 35111, 35112
 Subclavian Artery, 35001, 35002, 35021, 35022
 Thoracic Aorta, 33880-33889, 75956-75959
 Thoracoabdominal Aorta, 33877
 Ulnar Artery, 35045
 Vascular Malformation or Carotid Cavernous Fistula, 61710
 Vertebral Artery, 61698, 61702
Angel Dust, 83992
Anginal Symptoms and Level of Activity Assessment, 1002F
Angiocardiographies
 See Heart, Angiography
Angiography
 Abdomen, 74175, 74185, 75635, 75726
 Abdominal Aorta, 0080T-0081T, 75635, 75952, 75953
 Adrenal Artery, 75731, 75733
 Aortography, 75600-75630
  Injection, 93544
 Arm Artery, 73206, 75710, 75716
 Arteriovenous Shunt, 75791
 Atrial, 93542-93543
 Brachial Artery, 75658
 Brain, 70496
 Carotid Artery, 75660, 75671
  Cervical
   Bilateral, 75680
   Unilateral, 75676
 Chest, 71275, 71555
 Coronary Artery
  Coronary Calcium Evaluation, 75571
  Flow Velocity Measurement During Angiography, 93571, 93572
 Coronary Bypass, 93508, 93556
 Endovascular Repair, 0080T-0081T, 75952, 75953
 Extremity, Lower, 73725
 Extremity, Upper, 73225
 Fluorescein, 92235
 Head, 70496, 70544-70546
  Artery, 75650
 Heart
  with Catheterization, 93543-93545
 Heart Vessels
  with Catheterization, 93510
  Aortocoronary Bypass, 93539, 93540
  Injection, 93545
 Indocyanine-Green, 92240
 Left Heart
  Injection, 93543
 Leg Artery, 73706, 75635, 75710, 75716
 Lung
  Injection, 93541

Angiography — *continued*
 Lung — *continued*
  Injection — *continued*
   See Cardiac Catheterization, Injection
  Mammary Artery, 75756
  Neck, 70498, 70547-70549
   Artery, 75650
  Nuclear Medicine, 78445
  Other Artery, 75774
  Pelvic Artery, 72198, 75736
  Pelvis, 72191
  Pulmonary Artery, 75741-75746
  Renal Artery, 75722, 75724
  Right Heart
   Injection, 93542
  Shunt, 75791
  Spinal Artery, 75705
  Spinal Canal, 72159
  Thorax, 71275
  Transcatheter Therapy
   Embolization, 75894, 75898
   Infusion, 75896, 75898
  Vertebral, 75685
Angioma
 See Lesion, Skin
Angioplasty
 Aorta
  Intraoperative, 35452
  Percutaneous, 35472
 Axillary Artery
  Intraoperative, 35458
 Brachiocephalic Artery
  Intraoperative, 35458
  Percutaneous, 35475
 Coronary Artery
  Percutaneous Transluminal, 92982, 92984
 Femoral Artery
  Intraoperative, 35456
  Percutaneous, 35474
 Iliac Artery
  Intraoperative, 35454
  Percutaneous, 35473
 Intracranial, 61630, 61635
  Percutaneous, 61630
 Percutaneous Transluminal Angioplasty, 92982, 92984, 92997, 92998
 Popliteal Artery
  Intraoperative, 35456
  Percutaneous, 35474
 Pulmonary Artery
  Percutaneous Transluminal, 92997, 92998
 Renal or Visceral Artery
  Intraoperative, 35450
  Percutaneous, 35471
 Subclavian Artery
  Intraoperative, 35458
 Tibioperoneal Artery
  Intraoperative, 35459
  Percutaneous, 35470
 Transluminal
  Arterial, 75962-75968
  Venous, 75978
 Venous
  Intraoperative, 35460
  Percutaneous, 35476
 Visceral Artery
  Intraoperative, 35450
  Percutaneous, 35471
Angioscopy
 Noncoronary vessels, 35400
Angiotensin Converting Enzyme (ACE), 82164
Angiotensin Forming Enzyme
 See Renin
Angiotensin I, 84244
 Riboflavin, 84252
Angiotensin II
 Blood or Urine, 82163
Angle Deformity
 Reconstruction
  Toe, 28313

Anhyrides, Acetic

Anhyrides, Acetic
 See Acetic Anhydrides
Animal Inoculation, 87001, 87003, 87250
Ankle
 See also Fibula, Leg, Lower; Tibia, Tibiofibular Joint
 Abscess
  Incision and Drainage, 27603
 Amputation, 27888
 Arthrocentesis, 20605
 Arthrodesis, 27870
 Arthrography, 73615
 Arthroplasty, 27700, 27702, 27703
 Arthroscopy
  Surgical, 29891-29899
 Arthrotomy, 27610, 27612, 27620-27626
 Biopsy, 27613, 27614, 27620
 Bursa
  Incision and Drainage, 27604
 Disarticulation, 27889
 Dislocation
  Closed Treatment, 27840, 27842
  Open Treatment, 27846, 27848
 Exploration, 27610, 27620
 Fracture
  Bimalleolar, 27808-27814
  Lateral, 27786-27814
  Medial, 27760-27766, 27808-27814
  Posterior, 27767-27769, 27808-27814
  Trimalleolar, 27816-27823
 Fusion, 27870
 Hematoma
  Incision and Drainage, 27603
 Incision, 27607
 Injection
  Radiologic, 27648
 Lesion
  Excision, 27630
 Magnetic Resonance Imaging (MRI), 73721-73723
 Manipulation, 27860
 Removal
  Foreign Body, 27610, 27620
  Implant, 27704
  Loose Body, 27620
 Repair
  Achilles Tendon, 27650-27654
  Ligament, 27695-27698
  Tendon, 27612, 27680-27687
 Strapping, 29540
 Synovium
  Excision, 27625, 27626
 Tenotomy, 27605, 27606
 Tumor, 26535, 27615-27638 [27632, 27634], 27645-27647
 Unlisted Services and Procedures, 27899
 X-ray, 73600, 73610
  with Contrast, 73615
Ankylosis (Surgical)
 See Arthrodesis
Annuloplasty
 Percutaneous, Intradiscal, 22526-22527, 22899
Anogenital Region
 See Perineum
Anoplasty
 Stricture, 46700, 46705
Anorectal Exam (Surgical), 45990
Anorectal Myomectomy, 45108
Anorectal Procedure
 Biofeedback, 90911
Anorectovaginoplasty, 46744, 46746
Anoscopy
 Ablation
  Polyp, 46615
  Tumor, 46615
 Biopsy, 46606
 Dilation, 46604
 Exploration, 46600
 Hemorrhage, 46614

Anoscopy — *continued*
 Removal
  Foreign Body, 46608
  Polyp, 46610-46612
  Tumor, 46610-46612
Antebrachium
 See Forearm
Antecedent, Plasma Thromboplastin, 85270
Antepartum Care
 Antepartum Care Only, 59425, 59426
 Cesarean Delivery, 59510
  Previous, 59610-59618
 Included with
  Cesarean Delivery, 59510
   Failed NSVD, Previous C-Section, 59618
  Vaginal Delivery, 59400
   Previous C-Section, 59610
 Vaginal Delivery, 59425-59426
Anterior Ramus of Thoracic Nerve
 See Intercostal Nerve
Antesternal Esophagostomy, 43499
Anthrax Vaccine, 90581
Anthrogon, 80418, 80426, 83001
Anti Australia Antigens
 See Antibody, Hepatitis B
Antibiotic Administration
 Injection, 96372
 Prescribed or Dispensed, 4120F-4124F
Antibiotic Sensitivity, 87181, 87184, 87188
 Enzyme Detection, 87185
 Minimum Bactericidal Concentration, 87187
 Minimum Inhibitory Concentration, 87186
Antibodies, Thyroid-Stimulating, 84445
 See Immunoglobulin, Thyroid Stimulating
Antibodies, Viral
 See Viral Antibodies
Antibody
 Actinomyces, 86602
 Adenovirus, 86603
 Antinuclear, 86038, 86039
 Anti-Phosphatidylserine (Phospholipid), 86148
 Antiprothrombin, 0030T
 Antistreptolysin O, 86060, 86063
 Aspergillus, 86606
 Bacterium, 86609
 Bartonella, 86611
 Beta 2 Glycoprotein I, 86146
 Blastomyces, 86612
 Blood Crossmatch, 86920-86923
 Bordetella, 86615
 Borrelia, 86618, 86619
 Brucella, 86622
 Campylobacter, 86625
 Candida, 86628
 Cardiolipin, 86147
 Chlamydia, 86631, 86632
 Coccidioides, 86635
 Coxiella Burnetii, 86638
 Cryptococcus, 86641
 Cyclic Citrullinated Peptide (CCP), 86200
 Cytomegalovirus, 86644, 86645
 Cytotoxic Screen, 86807, 86808
 Deoxyribonuclease, 86215
 Deoxyribonucleic Acid (DNA), 86225, 86226
 Diphtheria, 86648
 Ehrlichia, 86666
 Encephalitis, 86651-86654
 Enterovirus, 86658
 Epstein-Barr Virus, 86663-86665
 Fluorescent, 86255, 86256
 Francisella Tularensis, 86668
 Fungus, 86671
 Giardia Lamblia, 86674
 Growth Hormone, 86277

Antibody — *continued*
 Helicobacter Pylori, 86677
 Helminth, 86682
 Hemoglobin, Fecal, 82274
 Hemophilus Influenza, 86684
 Hepatitis A, 86708, 86709
 Hepatitis B
  Core, 86704
  IgM, 86705
  Surface, 86706
 Hepatitis Be, 86707
 Hepatitis C, 86803, 86804
 Hepatitis, Delta Agent, 86692
 Herpes Simplex, 86694-86696
 Heterophile, 86308-86310
 Histoplasma, 86698
 HIV, 86689, 86701-86703
 HIV-1, 86701, 86703
 HIV-2, 86702, 86703
 HTLV-I, 86687, 86689
 HTLV-II, 86688
 Influenza Virus, 86710
 Insulin, 86337
 Intrinsic Factor, 86340
 Islet Cell, 86341
 Legionella, 86713
 Leishmania, 86717
 Leptospira, 86720
 Listeria Monocytogenes, 86723
 Lyme Disease, 86617
 Lymphocytic Choriomeningitis, 86727
 Lymphogranuloma Venereum, 86729
 Microsomal, 86376
 Mucormycosis, 86732
 Mumps, 86735
 Mycoplasma, 86738
 Neisseria Meningitidis, 86741
 Nocardia, 86744
 Nuclear Antigen, 86235
 Other Virus, 86790
 Parvovirus, 86747
 Phospholipid, 86147
  Cofactor, 0030T
 Plasmodium, 86750
 Platelet, 86022, 86023
 Protozoa, 86753
 Red Blood Cell, 86850-86870
 Respiratory Syncytial Virus, 86756
 Rickettsia, 86757
 Rotavirus, 86759
 Rubella, 86762
 Rubeola, 86765
 Salmonella, 86768
 Shigella, 86771
 Sperm, 89325
 Streptokinase, 86590
 Tetanus, 86774
 Thyroglobulin, 86800
 Toxoplasma, 86777, 86778
 Treponema Pallidum, 86780
 Trichinella, 86784
 Varicella-Zoster, 86787
 West Nile Virus, 86788-86789
 White Blood Cell, 86021
 Yersinia, 86793
Antibody Identification
 Leukocyte Antibodies, 86021
 Platelet, 86022, 86023
 Red Blood Cell
  Pretreatment, 86970-86972
 Serum
  Pretreatment, 86975-86978
Antibody Neutralization Test, 86382
Antibody Receptor, 86243
Anticoagulant, 85300-85305, 85307
Anticoagulant Management, 99363-99364
Antidiabetic Hormone, 82943
Anti D Immunoglobulin, 90384-90386
Antidiuretic Hormone, 84588
Antidiuretic Hormone Measurement
 See Vasopressin
Anti-DNA Autoantibody, 86038-86039
Antigen
 Allergen Immunotherapy, 95144

Antigen — *continued*
 Carcinoembryonic, 82378
 Mononuclear Cell, 86356
 Prostate Specific
  Complexed, 84152
  Free, 84154
  Total, 84153
 Skin Test, 86486
Antigen, Australia
 See Hepatitis Antigen, B Surface
Antigen Bronchial Provocation Tests
 See Bronchial Challenge Test
Antigen, CD4, 86360
Antigen, CD8, 86360
Antigen Detection
 Direct Fluorescence, 87265-87272, 87276, 87278, 87280, 87285, 87290
  Bordetella, 87265
  Chlamydia Trachomatis, 87270
  Cryptosporidium, 87272
  Cytomegalovirus, 87271
  Enterovirus, 87267
  Giardia, 87269
  Influenza A, 87276
  Legionella Pneumophila, 87278
  Not Otherwise Specified, 87299
  Respiratory Syncytial Virus, 87280
  Treponema Pallidum, 87285
  Varicella Zoster, 87290
 Enzyme Immunoassay, 87301-87451
  Adenovirus, 87301
  Aspergillus, 87305
  Chlamydia Trachomatis, 87320
  Clostridium Difficile, 87324
  Cryptococcus Neoformans, 87327
  Cryptosporidium, 87328
  Cytomegalovirus, 87332
  Entamoeba Histolytica Dispar Group, 87336
  Entamoeba Histolytica Group, 87337
  Escherichia Coli 0157, 87335
  Giardia, 87329
  Helicobacter Pylori, 87338, 87339
  Hepatitis Be Antigen (HBeAg), 87350
  Hepatitis B Surface Antigen (HBsAg), 87340
  Hepatitis B Surface Antigen (HBsAg) Neutralization, 87341
  Hepatitis Delta Agent, 87380
  Histoplasma Capsulatum, 87385
  HIV-1, 87390
  HIV-2, 87391
  Influenza A, 87400
  Influenza B, 87400
  Multiple Step Method, 87301-87449
  Polyvalent, 87451
  Not Otherwise Specified, 87449, 87451
  Respiratory Syncytial Virus, 87420
  Rotavirus, 87425
  Shigella-like Toxin, 87427
  Single Step Method, 87450
  Streptococcus, Group A, 87430
 Immunoassay
  Direct Optical
   Clostridium Difficile Toxin A, 87803
   Influenza, 87804
   Respiratory Syncytial Virus, 87807
   Streptococcus, Group B, 87802
   Trichomonas Vaginalis, 87808
 Immunofluorescence, 87260, 87273-87275, 87277, 87279, 87281, 87283, 87299, 87300
  Adenovirus, 87260
  Herpes Simplex, 87273, 87274
  Influenza B, 87275
  Legionella Micdadei, 87277

Index

Antigen Detection — *continued*
  Immunofluorescence — *continued*
    Not otherwise specified, 87299
    Parainfluenza Virus, 87279
    Pneumocystis Carinii, 87281
    Polyvalent, 87300
    Rubeola, 87283
Antigens, CD142
  See Thromboplastin
Antigens, CD143, 82164
Antigens, E, 87350
Antigens, Hepatitis
  See Hepatitis Antigen
Antigens, Hepatitis B, 87515-87517
Antihemophilic Factor B, 85250
Antihemophilic Factor C, 85270
Antihemophilic Globulin (AHG), 85240
Antihuman Globulin, 86880-86886
Anti–Human Globulin Consumption Test
  See Coombs Test
Anti–inflammatory/Analgesic Agent Prescribed, 4016F
Antimony, 83015
Antinuclear Antibodies (ANA), 86038, 86039
  Fluorescent Technique, 86255, 86256
Anti–Phosphatidylserine (Phospholipid) Antibody, 86148
Anti–Phospholipid Antibody, 86147
Antiplasmin, Alpha–2, 85410
Antiprotease, Alpha 1
  See Alpha–1 Antitrypsin
Antiprothrombin Antibody, 0030T
Antistreptococcal Antibody, 86215
Antistreptokinase Titer, 86590
Antistreptolysin O, 86060, 86063
Antithrombin III, 85300, 85301
Antithrombin VI
  See Alpha Degradation Products
Antitoxin Assay, 87230
Antiviral Antibody
  See Viral Antibodies
Antrostomy
  Sinus/Maxillary, 31256-31267
Antrotomy
  Sinus
    Maxillary, 31020-31032
    Transmastoid, 69501
Antrum of Highmore
  See Sinus, Maxillary
Antrum Puncture
  Sinus
    Maxillary, 31000
    Sphenoid, 31002
Anus
  Ablation, 46615
  Abscess
    Incision and Drainage, 46045, 46050
  Biofeedback, 90911
  Biopsy
    Endoscopic, 46606
  Dilation
    Endoscopy, 46604
  Endoscopy
    Biopsy, 46606
    Dilation, 46604
    Exploration, 46600
    Hemorrhage, 46614
    Removal
      Foreign Body, 46608
      Polyp, 46610, 46612
      Tumor, 46610, 46612
  Excision
    Tag, 46230, [46220]
  Exploration
    Endoscopic, 46600
    Surgical, 45990
  Fissure
    Destruction, 46940, 46942
    Excision, 46200
  Fistula
    Excision, 46270-46285
    Repair, 46706-46707

Anus — *continued*
  Hemorrhage
    Endoscopic Control, 46614
  Hemorrhoids
    Clot Excision, [46320]
    Destruction, 46930
    Excision, 46250-46262
    Injection, 46500
    Ligation, 46221, [46945], [46946]
    Stapling, [46947]
    Suture, [46945], [46946]
  Imperforated
    Repair, 46715-46742
  Incision
    Septum, 46070
  Lesion
    Destruction, 46900-46917, 46924
    Excision, 45108, 46922
  Manometry, 91122
  Placement
    Seton, 46020
  Polyp, 46615
  Reconstruction, 46742
    with Graft, 46735
    with Implant, 46762
    Congenital Absence, 46730-46740
    Sphincter, 46750, 46751, 46760-46762
  Removal
    Foreign Body, 46608
    Seton, 46030
    Suture, 46754
    Wire, 46754
  Repair
    Anovaginal Fistula, 46715, 46716
    Cloacal Anomaly, 46748
    Fistula, 46706-46707
    Stricture, 46700, 46705
  Sphincter
    Chemodenervation, 46505
    Electromyography, 51784, 51785
    Needle, 51785
  Tumor, 46615
  Unlisted Procedure, 46999
Aorta
  Abdominal
    Aneurysm, 0078T-0081T, 34800-34805, 34825-34832, 35081-35103, 75952, 75953
    Thromboendarterectomy, 35331
  Anastomosis
    to Pulmonary Artery, 33606
  Angiogram
    Radiologic Injection, 93544
      Cardiac Catheterization, Injection, 93539-93545
  Angioplasty, 35452
  Aortography, 75600-75630
  Ascending
    Graft, 33864
    Balloon, 33967, 33970
    Catheterization
      Catheter, 36200
      Intracatheter, 36160
      Needle, 36160
    Circulation Assist, 33967, 33970
    Conduit to Heart, 33404
    Excision
      Coarctation, 33840-33851
      Graft, 33860-33864, 33875
    Insertion
      Balloon Device, 33967
      Graft, 33330-33335, 33864
      Intracatheter, 36160
      Needle, 36160
    Removal
      Balloon Assist Device, 33968, 33971
    Repair, 33320-33322, 33802, 33803
      Aortic Anomalies, 33800-33803
      Coarctation, 33840-33851
      Graft, 33860-33877
        Ascending, 33864

Aorta — *continued*
  Repair — *continued*
    Hypoplastic or Interrupted Aortic Arch
      with Cardiopulmonary Bypass, 33853
      without Cardiopulmonary Bypass, 33852
    Sinus of Valsalva, 33702-33720
    Thoracic Aneurysm with Graft, 33860-33877
      Endovascular, 33880-33891, 75956-75959
    Transposition of the Great Vessels, 33770-33781
  Suspension, 33800
  Suture, 33320-33322
  Thoracic
    Aneurysm, 33880-33889, 75956-75959
    Repair, 75956-75959
      Endovascular, 33880-33891
  Ultrasound, 76770, 76775
  Valve
    Incision, 33415
    Repair, 33400-33403
      Left Ventricle, 33414
      Supravalvular Stenosis, 33417
    Replacement, 33405-33413
  X-ray with Contrast, 75600-75630
Aorta–Pulmonary ART Transposition
  See Transposition, Great Arteries
Aortic Sinus
  See Sinus of Valsalva
Aortic Stenosis
  Repair, 33415
    Supravalvular, 33417
Aortic Valve
  See Heart, Aortic Valve
Aortic Valve Replacement
  See Replacement, Aortic Valve
Aortocoronary Bypass
  See Coronary Artery Bypass Graft (CABG)
Aortocoronary Bypass for Heart Revascularization
  See Artery, Coronary, Bypass
Aortography, 75600, 75605, 75630, 93544
  with Ileofemoral Artery, 75630
  See Angiography
  Serial, 75625
Aortoiliac
  Embolectomy, 34151, 34201
  Thrombectomy, 34151, 34201
Aortopexy, 33800
Aortoplasty
  Supravalvular Stenosis, 33417
AP, [51797]
APBI (Accelerated Partial Breast Irradiation), 19296-19298
Apendico-Vesicostomy, 50845
Apert–Gallais Syndrome
  See Adrenogenital Syndrome
Apexcardiogram, 93799
Aphasia Testing, 96105
Apheresis
  Therapeutic, 36511-36516
Apical–Aortic Conduit, 33404
Apicectomy
  with Mastoidectomy, 69530, 69605
  Petrous, 69530
Apicoectomy, 41899
Apoaminotransferase, Aspartate, 84550
Apolipoprotein
  Blood or Urine, 82172
Appendectomy, 44950-44960
  Laparoscopic, 44970
Appendiceal Abscess
  See Abscess, Appendix
Appendico–Stomy, 44799
Appendico–Vesicostomy
  Cutaneous, 50845

Appendix
  Abscess
    Incision and Drainage, 44900
      Open, 44900
      Percutaneous, 44901
  Excision, 44950-44960
Application
  Allergy Tests, 95044
  Bone Fixation Device
    Multiplane, 20692
    Uniplane, 20690
  Caliper, 20660
  Cranial Tongs, 20660
  Fixation Device
    Shoulder, 23700
  Halo
    Cranial, 20661
      Thin Skull Osteology, 20664
    Femoral, 20663
    Maxillofacial Fixation, 21100
    Pelvic, 20662
  Interdental Fixation Device, 21110
  Intervertebral Device, 22851
  Neurostimulation, 64550
  Radioelement, 77761-77778
    with Ultrasound, 76965
  Surface, 77789
  Stereotactic Frame, 20660, 61800
Application of External Fixation Device
  See Fixation (Device), Application, External
APPT
  See Thromboplastin, Partial, Time
APPY, 44950-44960
APTT
  See Thromboplastin, Partial, Time
Aquatic Therapy
  with Exercises, 97113
Aqueous Shunt
  to Extraocular Reservoir, 66180
  Revision, 66185
Arch, Zygomatic
  See Zygomatic Arch
Arm
  See Radius; Ulna; Wrist
  Excision
    Bone, 25145
    Excess Skin, 15836
    Lipectomy, Suction Assisted, 15878
  Removal
    Foreign Body
      Forearm or Wrist, 25248
  Repair
    Muscle, 24341
    Tendon, 24341
  Skin Graft
    Delay of Flap, 15610
    Full Thickness, 15220, 15221
    Muscle, Myocutaneous, or Fasciocutaneous Flaps, 15736
    Pedicle Flap, 15572
    Split, 15100-15111
  Tendon
    Excision, 25109
  Tissue Transfer, Adjacent, 14020, 14021
Arm, Lower
  Abscess, 25028
    Excision, 25145
    Incision and Drainage Bone, 25035
  Amputation, 24900, 24920, 25900, 25905, 25915
    Cineplasty, 24940
    Revision, 25907, 25909
  Angiography, 73206
  Artery
    Ligation, 37618
  Biopsy, 25065, 25066
  Bursa
    Incision and Drainage, 25031
  Bypass Graft, 35903
  Cast, 29075
  CT Scan, 73200-73206
  Decompression, 25020-25025

Arm, Lower — Index

Arm, Lower — *continued*
- Exploration
  - Blood Vessel, 35860
- Fasciotomy, 24495, 25020-25025
- Hematoma, 25028
- Incision and Drainage, 23930
- Lesion, Tendon Sheath
  - Excision, 25110
- Magnetic Resonance Imaging (MRI), 73218-73220, 73223
- Reconstruction
  - Ulna, 25337
- Removal
  - Foreign Body, 25248
- Repair
  - Blood Vessel with Other Graft, 35266
  - Blood Vessel with Vein Graft, 35236
  - Decompression, 24495
  - Muscle, 25260, 25263, 25270
    - Secondary, 25265
  - Secondary
    - Muscle or Tendon, 25272, 25274
  - Tendon, 25260-25274, 25280-25295, 25310-25316
    - Secondary, 25265
  - Tendon Sheath, 25275
- Replantation, 20805
- Splint, 29125, 29126
- Tenotomy, 25290
- Tumor, 25075-25078 [25071, 25073], 25120-25126
- Ultrasound, 76880
- Unlisted Services and Procedures, 25999
- X-ray, 73090
  - with Upper Arm, 73092

Arm, Upper
- Abscess
  - Incision and Drainage, 23930
    - *See* Elbow; Humerus
- Amputation, 23900-23921, 24900, 24920
  - with Implant, 24931, 24935
  - Cineplasty, 24940
  - Revision, 24925, 24930
- Anesthesia, 00400, 01710-01782
- Angiography, 73206
- Artery
  - Ligation, 37618
- Biopsy, 24065, 24066
- Bypass Graft, 35903
- Cast, 29065
- CT Scan, 73200-73206
- Exploration
  - Blood Vessel, 35860
- Hematoma
  - Incision and Drainage, 23930
- Magnetic Resonance Imaging (MRI), 73218-73220, 73223
- Muscle Revision, 24330, 24331
- Removal
  - Cast, 29705
  - Foreign Body, 24200, 24201
- Repair
  - Blood Vessel with Other Graft, 35266
  - Blood Vessel with Vein Graft, 35236
  - Muscle Revision, 24301, 24320
  - Muscle Transfer, 24301, 24320
  - Tendon, 24332
  - Tendon Lengthening, 24305
  - Tendon Revision, 24320
  - Tendon Transfer, 24301
  - Tenotomy, 24310
- Replantation, 20802
- Splint, 29105
- Tumor, 24075-24079 [24071, 24073]
- Ultrasound, 76880
- Unlisted Services and Procedures, 24999
- Wound Exploration, 20103
  - Penetrating, 20103

Arm, Upper — *continued*
- X-ray, 73060
- X-ray with Lower Arm
  - Infant, 73092

Arnold-Chiari Malformation Repair, 61343

AROM, 95851, 95852, 97110, 97530

Arrest, Epiphyseal
- Femur, 20150, 27185, 27475, 27479, 27485, 27742
- Fibula, 20150, 27477-27485, 27730-27742
- Radius, 20150, 25450, 25455
- Tibia, 20150, 27477-27485, 27730, 27734-27742
- Ulna, 20150, 25450, 25455

Arrhythmias
- Electrical Conversion Anesthesia, 00410
- Induction, 93618

Arrhythmogenic Focus
- Heart
  - Catheter Ablation, 93650-93652
  - Destruction, 33250-33251, 33261

Arsenic, 83015
- Blood or Urine, 82175
- Heavy Metal Screen, 83015

ART, 86592, 86593

Arterial Catheterization
- *See* Cannulation, Arterial

Arterial Dilatation, Transluminal
- *See* Angioplasty, Transluminal

Arterial Grafting for Coronary Artery Bypass
- *See* Bypass Graft, Coronary Artery, Arterial

Arterial Pressure
- *See* Blood Pressure

Arterial Puncture, 36600

Arteriography, Aorta
- *See* Aortography

Arteriosus, Ductus
- *See* Ductus Arteriosus

Arteriosus, Truncus
- *See* Truncus Arteriosus

Arteriotomy
- *See* Incision, Artery; Transection, Artery

Arteriovenous Anastomosis, 36818-36820

Arteriovenous Fistula
- Cannulization
  - Vein, 36815
- Hemodialysis via Fistula, 4052F
- Referral, 4051F
- Repair
  - Abdomen, 35182
    - Acquired or Traumatic, 35189
  - Head, 35180
    - Acquired or Traumatic, 35188
  - Lower Extremity, 35184
    - Acquired or Traumatic, 35190
  - Neck, 35180
    - Acquired or Traumatic, 35188
  - Thorax, 35182
    - Acquired or Traumatic, 35189
  - Upper Extremity, 35184
    - Acquired or Traumatic, 35190
- Revision
  - Hemodialysis Graft or Fistula
    - with Thrombectomy, 36833
    - without Thrombectomy, 36832
- Thrombectomy
  - Dialysis Graft
    - without Revision, 36831
  - Graft, 36870

Arteriovenous Malformation
- Cranial
  - Repair, 61680-61692, 61705, 61708
- Spinal
  - Excision, 63250-63252
  - Injection, 62294
  - Repair, 63250-63252

Arteriovenous Shunt
- Angiography, 75791

Arteriovenous Shunt — *continued*
- Catheterization, 36147-36148

Artery
- Abdomen
  - Angiography, 75726
  - Catheterization, 36245-36248
  - Ligation, 37617
- Adrenal
  - Angiography, 75731, 75733
- Anastomosis
  - Cranial, 61711
- Angiography, Visceral, 75726
- Angioplasty, 75962-75968
- Aorta
  - Angioplasty, 35452
  - Atherectomy, 35481, 35491
- Aortobifemoral
  - Bypass Graft, 35540
- Aortobi-iliac
  - Bypass Graft, 35538, 35638
- Aortofemoral
  - Bypass Graft, 35539
- Aortoiliac
  - Bypass Graft, 35537, 35637
  - Embolectomy, 34151, 34201
  - Thrombectomy, 34151, 34201
- Aortoiliofemoral, 35363
- Arm
  - Angiography, 75710, 75716
  - Harvest of Artery for Coronary Artery Bypass Graft, 35600
- Atherectomy
  - Open, 35480-35485
  - Percutaneous, 35490-35495, 92995, 92996
- Axillary
  - Aneurysm, 35011, 35013
  - Angioplasty, 35458
  - Bypass Graft, 35516-35522, 35533, 35616-35623, 35650, 35654
  - Embolectomy, 34101
  - Thrombectomy, 34101
  - Thromboendarterectomy, 35321
- Basilar
  - Aneurysm, 61698, 61702
- Biopsy
  - Transcatheter, 75970
- Brachial
  - Aneurysm, 35011, 35013
  - Angiography, 75658
  - Bypass Graft, 35510, 35512, 35522, 35525
  - Catheterization, 36120
  - Embolectomy, 34101
  - Exploration, 24495
  - Exposure, 34834
  - Thrombectomy, 34101
  - Thromboendarterectomy, 35321
- Brachiocephalic
  - Angioplasty, 35458
  - Atherectomy, 35484, 35494, 75992, 75993
  - Catheterization, 36215-36218
- Bypass Graft
  - with Composite Graft, 35681-35683
  - Autogenous
    - Three or More Segments
      - Two Locations, 35683
    - Two Segments
      - Two Locations, 35682
- Cannulization
  - for Extra Corporeal Circulation, 36823
  - to Vein, 36810-36821
- Carotid
  - Aneurysm, 35001-35005, 61697-61705
    - Vascular Malformation or Carotid Cavernous Fistula, 61710
  - Angiography, 75660-75680
  - Bypass Graft, 33891, 35500-35510, 35526, 35601-35606, 35626, 35642

Artery — *continued*
- Carotid — *continued*
  - Catheterization, 36100
  - Decompression, 61590, 61591, 61595, 61596
  - Embolectomy, 34001
  - Exploration, 35701
  - Ligation, 37600-37606, 61611, 61612
  - Stenosis
    - Imaging Study Measurement, 3100F
  - Thrombectomy, 34001
  - Thromboendarterectomy, 35301, 35390
  - Transection, 61611, 61612
  - Transposition, 33889
- Carotid, Common Intima-Media Thickness Study, 0126T
- Celiac
  - Aneurysm, 35121, 35122
  - Bypass Graft, 35531, 35631
  - Embolectomy, 34151
  - Thrombectomy, 34151
  - Thromboendarterectomy, 35341
- Chest
  - Ligation, 37616
- Coronary
  - Angiography, 93556
  - X-ray, Artery (Atherectomy), 75992-75996
  - Atherectomy, 92995, 92996
  - Bypass, 33517-33519
    - Arterial, 33533-33536
    - Bypass Venous Graft, 33510-33517, 35523
    - Internal Mammary Artery Graft, 4110F
  - Graft, 33503-33505
  - Ligation, 33502
  - Repair, 33500-33507
  - Thrombectomy
    - Percutaneous, 92973
- Digital
  - Sympathectomy, 64820
- Ethmoidal
  - Ligation, 30915
- Extra Corporeal Circulation
  - for Regional Chemotherapy of Extremity, 36823
- Extracranial
  - Vascular Studies
    - Non-invasive, Physiologic, 93875
- Extremities
  - Vascular Studies, 93922, 93923
- Extremity
  - Bypass Graft Revision, 35879-35884
  - Catheterization, 36140
  - Ligation, 37618
- Femoral
  - Aneurysm, 35141, 35142
  - Angioplasty, 35456
  - Atherectomy, 35483, 35493
  - Bypass Graft, 35521, 35533, 35539, 35540, 35551-35558, 35566, 35621, 35646, 35647, 35651-35661, 35666, 35700
  - Bypass Graft Revision, 35883-35884
  - Bypass In Situ, 35583-35585
  - Embolectomy, 34201
  - Exploration, 35721
  - Exposure, 34812, 34813
  - Thrombectomy, 34201
  - Thromboendarterectomy, 35302, 35371-35372
- Great Vessel Repair, 33770-33781
- Head
  - Angiography, 75650
- Hepatic
  - Aneurysm, 35121, 35122
- Iliac
  - Aneurysm, 35131-35132, 75954

Index

Artery — continued
Iliac — continued
Angioplasty, 35454
Atherectomy, 35482, 35492
Bypass Graft, 35537, 35538, 35563, 35637, 35638, 35663
Embolectomy, 34151, 34201
Exposure, 34820, 34833
Graft, 34900
Occlusion Device, 34808
Thrombectomy, 34151, 34201
Thromboendarterectomy, 35351, 35361, 35363
Iliofemoral
Bypass Graft, 35548, 35549, 35565, 35665
Thromboendarterectomy, 35355, 35363
X-ray with Contrast, 75630
Innominate
Aneurysm, 35021, 35022
Embolectomy, 34001, 34101
Thrombectomy, 34001, 34101
Thromboendarterectomy, 35311
Leg
Angiography, 75710, 75716
Catheterization, 36245-36248
Mammary
Angiography, 75756
Maxillary
Ligation, 30920
Mesenteric
Aneurysm, 35121, 35122
Bypass Graft, 35331, 35631
Embolectomy, 34151
Thrombectomy, 34151
Thromboendarterectomy, 35341
Middle Cerebral Artery, Fetal Vascular Studies, 76821
Neck
Angiography, 75650
Ligation, 37615
Nose
Incision, 30915, 30920
Other Angiography, 75774
Other Artery
Exploration, 35761
Pelvic
Angiography, 75736
Catheterization, 36245-36248
Peripheral Arterial Rehabilitation, 93668
Peroneal
Bypass Graft, 35566, 35571, 35666, 35671
Bypass In Situ, 35585, 35587
Embolectomy, 34203
Thrombectomy, 34203
Thromboendarterectomy, 35305-35306
Popliteal
Aneurysm, 35151, 35152
Angioplasty, 35456
Atherectomy, 35483, 35493
Bypass Graft, 35551, 35556, 35571, 35623, 35651, 35656, 35671, 35700
Bypass In Situ, 35583, 35587
Embolectomy, 34203
Exploration, 35741
Thrombectomy, 34203
Thromboendarterectomy, 35303
Pulmonary
Anastomosis, 33606
Angiography, 75741-75746
Repair, 33690, 33925-33926
Radial
Aneurysm, 35045
Embolectomy, 34111
Sympathectomy, 64821
Thrombectomy, 34111
Rehabilitation, 93668
Reimplantation
Carotid, 35691, 35694, 35695
Subclavian, 35693-35695

Artery — continued
Reimplantation — continued
Vertebral, 35691-35693
Visceral, 35697
Renal
Aneurysm, 35121, 35122
Angiography, 75722, 75724
Angioplasty, 35450
Atherectomy, 35480, 35490
Bypass Graft, 35536, 35560, 35631, 35636
Embolectomy, 34151
Thrombectomy, 34151
Thromboendarterectomy, 35341
Repair
with Other Graft, 35261-35286
with Vein Graft, 35231-35256
Aneurysm, 61697-61708
Angioplasty, 75962-75968
Direct, 35201-35226
Revision
Hemodialysis Graft or Fistula
with Thrombectomy, 36833
without Thrombectomy, 36832
Spinal
Angiography, 75705
Splenic
Aneurysm, 35111, 35112
Angioplasty, 35458
Bypass Graft, 35536, 35636
Subclavian
Aneurysm, 35001-35002, 35021-35022
Angioplasty, 35458
Bypass Graft, 35506, 35511-35516, 35526, 35606-35616, 35626, 35645
Embolectomy, 34001-34101
Thrombectomy, 34001-34101
Thromboendarterectomy, 35301, 35311
Transposition, 33889
Unlisted Services and Procedures, 37799
Superficial Femoral
Thromboendarterectomy, 35302
Superficial Palmar Arch
Sympathectomy, 64823
Temporal
Biopsy, 37609
Ligation, 37609
Thoracic
Catheterization, 36215-36218
Thrombectomy, 37184-37186
Hemodialysis Graft or Fistula, 36831
Other than Hemodialysis Graft or Fistula, 35875, 36870
Tibial
Bypass Graft, 35566, 35571, 35623, 35666, 35671
Bypass In Situ, 35585, 35587
Embolectomy, 34203
Thrombectomy, 34203
Thromboendarterectomy, 35305-35306
Tibioperoneal
Angioplasty, 35459, 35470
Atherectomy, 35485, 35495
Transcatheter Therapy, 75894, 75896
with Angiography, 75894
Transposition
Carotid, 33889, 35691, 35694, 35695
Subclavian, 33889, 35693-35695
Vertebral, 35691, 35693
Ulnar
Aneurysm, 35045
Embolectomy, 34111
Sympathectomy, 64822
Thrombectomy, 34111
Unlisted Services and Procedures, 37799
Vascular Study
Extremities, 93922, 93923

Artery — continued
Vertebral
Aneurysm, 35005, 61698, 61702
Angiography, 75685
Bypass Graft, 35508, 35515, 35642, 35645
Catheterization, 36100
Decompression, 61597
Thromboendarterectomy, 35301
Visceral
Angioplasty, 35450, 35471
Atherectomy, 35480, 35490
Reimplantation, 35697

Artery Catheterization, Pulmonary
See Catheterization, Pulmonary Artery

Artherectomies, Coronary
See Artery, Coronary, Atherectomy

Arthrectomy
Elbow, 24155

Arthrocentesis
Intermediate Joint, 20605
Large Joint, 20610
Small Joint, 20600

Arthrodesis
Ankle, 27870
Tibiotalar and Fibulotalar Joints, 29899
Arthroscopy
Subtalar Joint, 29907
Blair, 27870
Campbell, 27870
Carpometacarpal Joint
Hand, 26843, 26844
Thumb, 26841, 26842
Cervical Anterior
with Discectomy, 22554
Elbow, 24800, 24802
Finger Joint, 26850-26863
Interphalangeal, 26860-26863
Metacarpophalangeal, 26850
Foot Joint, 28705-28735, 28740
with Advancement, 28737
with Lengthening, 28737
Pantalar, 28705
Subtalar, 28725
Triple, 28715
Grice, 28725
Hand Joint, 26843, 26844
Hip Joint, 27284, 27286
Intercarpal Joint, 25820
with Autograft, 25825
Great Toe, 28755
with Tendon Transfer, 28760
Interphalangeal Joint, 26860-26863
Great Toe, 28755
with Tendon Transfer, 28760
Knee, 27580
Metacarpophalangeal Joint, 26850-26852
Great Toe, 28750
Metatarsophalangeal Joint
Great Toe, 28750
Pre-Sacral Interbody, 0195T-0196T
Pubic Symphysis, 27282
Radioulnar Joint, Distal, 25830
with Resection of Ulna, 25830
Sacroiliac Joint, 27280
Shoulder
See Shoulder, Arthrodesis
Shoulder Joint, 23800
with Autogenous Graft, 23802
Subtalar Joint, 29907
Talus
Pantalar, 28705
Subtalar, 28725
Triple, 28715
Tarsal Joint, 28730, 28735, 28740
with Advancement, 28737
with Lengthening, 28737
Tarsometatarsal Joint, 28730, 28735, 28740
Thumb Joint, 26841, 26842
Tibiofibular Joint, 27871

Arthrodesis — continued
Vertebra
Additional Interspace
Anterior/Anterolateral Approach, 22585
Lateral Extracavitary, 22534
Posterior/Posterolateral and/or Lateral Transverse Process, 22632
Cervical
Anterior/Anterolateral Approach, 22548
Posterior/Posterolateral and/or Lateral Transverse Process, 22590-22600
Lumbar
Anterior/Anterolateral Approach, 22558
Lateral Extracavitary, 22533
Posterior/Interbody, 22630
Posterior/Posterolateral and/or Lateral Transverse Process, 22612, 22630
Presacral Interbody Technique, 0195T-0196T
Spinal Deformity
Anterior Approach, 22808-22812
Posterior Approach, 22800, 22802, 22804
Spinal Fusion
Exploration, 22830
Thoracic
Anterior/Anterolateral Approach, 22556
Lateral Extracavitary, 22532
Posterior/Posterolateral and/or Lateral Traverse Process, 22610
Vertebrae
Posterior, 22614
Wrist, 25800
with Graft, 25810
with Sliding Graft, 25805
Radioulnar Joint, Distal, 25830

Arthrography
Ankle, 73615
Injection, 27648
Elbow, 73085
Injection, 24220
Hip, 73525
Injection, 27093, 27095
Knee, 73580
Injection, 27370
Sacroiliac Joint, 73542
Injection, 27096
Shoulder, 73040
Injection, 23350
Temporomandibular Joint (TMJ), 70328-70332
Injection, 21116
Wrist, 73115
Injection, 25246

Arthroplasty
Ankle, 27700-27703
Bower's, 25332
Cervical, 0092T, 22856
Elbow, 24360
with Implant, 24361, 24362
Total Replacement, 24363
Hip, 27132
Partial Replacement, 27125
Revision, 27134-27138
Total Replacement, 27130
Interphalangeal Joint, 26535, 26536
Knee, 27437-27443, 27446, 27447
with Prosthesis, 27438, 27445
Implantation, 27445
Revision, 27486, 27487
Lumbar, 0092T, 22857
Metacarpophalangeal Joint, 26530, 26531
Radius, 24365
with Implant, 24366

Arthroplasty

Arthroplasty — *continued*
  Reconstruction
    Prosthesis
      Hip, 27125
  Removal
    Cervical, 22864
    Each Additional Interspace, 0095T
    Lumbar, 22865
  Revision
    Cervical, 22861
    Each Additional Interspace, 0098T
    Lumbar, 22862
  Shoulder Joint
    with Implant, 23470, 23472
  Spine
    Cervical, 22856
    Each Additional Interspace, 0092T
    Lumbar, 22857
  Temporomandibular Joint, 21240-21243
  Vertebral, 0201T-0202T
  Wrist, 25332, 25441-25447
    with Implant, 25441-25445
    Carpal, 25443
    Lunate, 25444
    Navicular, 25443
    Pseudarthrosis Type, 25332
    Radius, 25441
    Revision, 25449
    Total Replacement, 25446
    Trapezium, 25445
    Ulna, 25442

Arthropods
  Examination, 87168

Arthroscopy
  Diagnostic
    Elbow, 29830
    Hip, 29860
    Knee, 29870, 29871
    Metacarpophalangeal Joint, 29900
    Shoulder, 29805
    Temporomandibular Joint, 29800
    Wrist, 29840
  Surgical
    Ankle, 29891-29899
    Elbow, 29834-29838
    Foot, 29999
    Hip, 29861-29863
    Knee, 29871-29889
      Cartilage Allograft, 29867
      Cartilage Autograft, 29866
      Meniscal Transplantation, 29868
      Osteochrondral Autograft, 29866
    Metacarpophalangeal Joint, 29901, 29902
    Shoulder, 29806-29828
      Biceps Tenodesis, 29828
    Subtalar Joint
      Arthrodesis, 29907
      Debridement, 29906
      Removal of Loose or Foreign Body, 29904
      Synovectomy, 29905
    Temporomandibular Joint, 29804
    Toe, 29999
    Wrist, 29843-29848
  Unlisted Services and Procedures, 29999

Arthroscopy of Ankle
  See Ankle, Arthroscopy

Arthrotomy
  with Biopsy
    Acromioclavicular Joint, 23101
    Glenohumeral Joint, 23100
    Hip Joint, 27052
    Knee Joint, 27330
    Sacroiliac Joint
      Hip Joint, 27050
    Sternoclavicular Joint, 23101

Arthrotomy — *continued*
  with Synovectomy
    Glenohumeral Joint, 23105
    Sternoclavicular Joint, 23106
  Acromioclavicular Joint, 23044, 23101
  Ankle, 27610, 27612, 27620
  Ankle Joint, 27625, 27626
  Carpometacarpal Joint, 26070, 26100
    with Synovial Biopsy, 26100
  Elbow, 24000
    with Joint Exploration, 24101
    with Synovectomy, 24102
    with Synovial Biopsy, 24100
    Capsular Release, 24006
  Finger Joint, 26075
    Interphalangeal with Synovial Biopsy, 26110
    Metacarpophalangeal with Biopsy, Synovium, 26105
  Glenohumeral Joint, 23040
  Hip, 27033
    with Synovectomy, 27054
    for Infection with Drainage, 27030
  Interphalangeal Joint, 26080, 26110
    Toe, 28024, 28054
  Intertarsal Joint, 28020, 28050
  Knee, 27310, 27330-27335, 27403, 29868
  Metacarpophalangeal Joint, 26075, 26105
  Metatarsophalangeal Joint, 28022, 28052
  Sacroiliac Joint, 27050
  Shoulder, 23044, 23105-23107
  Shoulder Joint, 23100, 23101
    Exploration and/or Removal of Loose Foreign Body, 23107
  Sternoclavicular Joint, 23044, 23101
  Tarsometatarsal Joint, 28020, 28050, 28052
  Temporomandibular Joint, 21010
  Wrist, 25040, 25100-25107

Arthrotomy for Removal of Prosthesis of Ankle
  See Ankle, Removal, Implant

Arthrotomy for Removal of Prosthesis of Hip
  See Hip, Removal, Prosthesis

Arthrotomy for Removal of Prosthesis of Wrist
  See Prosthesis, Wrist, Removal

Articular Ligament
  See Ligament

Artificial Abortion
  See Abortion

Artificial Cardiac Pacemaker
  See Heart, Pacemaker

Artificial Eye
  Prosthesis
    Cornea, 65770
    Ocular, 21077, 65770, 66983-66985, 92358

Artificial Genitourinary Sphincter
  See Prosthesis, Urethral Sphincter

Artificial Insemination, 58976
  See In Vitro Fertilization
  Intra-Cervical, 58321
  Intra-Uterine, 58322
  In Vitro Fertilization
    Culture Oocyte, 89250, 89272
    Fertilize Oocyte, 89280, 89281
    Retrieve Oocyte, 58970
    Transfer Embryo, 58974, 58976
    Transfer Gamete, 58976
  Sperm Washing, 58323

Artificial Knee Joints
  See Prosthesis, Knee

Artificial Penis
  See Penile Prosthesis

Artificial Pneumothorax
  See Pneumothorax, Therapeutic

Arytenoid
  Excision
    Endoscopic, 31560, 31561

Arytenoid Cartilage
  Excision, 31400
  Repair, 31400

Arytenoidectomy, 31400
  Endoscopic, 31560

Arytenoidopexy, 31400

ASAT, 84450

Ascorbic Acid
  Blood, 82180

ASO, 86060, 86063

Aspartate Aminotransferase, 84450

Aspergillus
  Antibody, 86606
  Antigen Detection
    Enzyme Immunoassay, 87305

Aspiration
  See Puncture Aspiration
  Amniotic Fluid
    Diagnostic, 59000
    Therapeutic, 59001
  Bladder, 51100-51102
  Bone Marrow, 38220
  Brain Lesion
    Stereotactic, 61750, 61751
  Bronchi
    Endoscopy, 31645, 31646
  Bronchus
    Nasotracheal, 31720
  Bursa, 20600-20610
  Catheter
    Nasotracheal, 31720
    Tracheobronchial, 31725
  Cyst
    Bone, 20615
    Kidney, 50390
    Pelvis, 50390
    Spinal Cord, 62268
    Thyroid, 60300
  Duodenal, 89100, 89105
  Fetal Fluid, 59074
  Ganglion Cyst, 20612
  Hydrocele
    Tunica Vaginalis, 55000
  Joint, 20600-20610
  Laryngoscopy
    Direct, 31515
  Lens Material, 66840
  Liver, 47015
  Lung, 32420
  Nucleus of Disc
    Diagnostic, 62267
  Orbital Contents, 67415
  Pelvis
    Endoscopy, 49322
  Pericardium, 33010, 33011
  Pleural Cavity, 32421-32422
  Puncture
    Cyst, Breast, 19000, 19001
  Spermatocele, 54699, 55899
  Spinal Cord
    Stereotaxis, 63615
  Syrinx
    Spinal Cord, 62268
  Thyroid, 60300
  Trachea, 31612
    Nasotracheal, 31720
    Puncture, 31612
  Tunica Vaginalis
    Hydrocele, 55000
  Vitreous, 67015

Aspiration, Chest
  See Thoracentesis

Aspiration Lipectomies
  See Liposuction

Aspiration, Lung Puncture
  See Pneumocentesis

Aspiration, Nail
  See Evacuation, Hematoma, Subungual

Aspiration of Bone Marrow from Donor for Transplant
  See Bone Marrow Harvesting

Atrial Electrogram

Aspiration, Spinal Puncture
  See Spinal Tap

Assay Tobramycin
  See Tobramycin

Assay, Very Long Chain Fatty Acids
  See Fatty Acid, Very Long Chain

Assessment
  Asthma, 1005F
  Heart Failure, 0001F
  Level of Activity, 1003F
  On-Line
    Nonphysician, 98969
    Physician, 99444
  Osteoarthritis, 0005F, 1006F
  Risk Factor
    Coronary Heart Disease, 0126T
    Gastrointestinal and Renal, 1008F
  Telephone
    Nonphysician, 98966-98968
    Physician, 99441-99443
  Use of Anti-inflammatory or analgesic (OTC) medications, 1007F
  Volume Overload, 1004F, 2002F

Assisted
  Circulation, 33960-33961, 33967, 33970-33971, 92970-92971
  Zonal Hatching (AZH), 89253

AST, 84450

Asthma, Long Term Control Medication, 4015F

Astragalectomy, 28130

Astragalus
  See Talus

Asymmetry, Face
  See Hemifacial Microsomia

Ataxia Telangiectasia
  Chromosome Analysis, 88248

Ataxy, Telangiectasia, 88248

Atherectomy
  See X-Ray, Artery
  Open
    Aorta, 35481
    Brachiocephalic, 35484
    Femoral, 35483
    Iliac, 35482
    Popliteal, 35483
    Renal, 35483
    Tibioperoneal, 35485
    Visceral, 35480
  Percutaneous
    Aorta, 35491
    Brachiocephalic, 35494
    Coronary, 92995, 92996
      See Artery, Coronary
    Femoral, 35493
    Iliac, 35492
    Popliteal, 35493
    Renal, 35490
    Tibioperoneal, 35495
    Visceral, 35490
  X-ray
    Peripheral Artery, 75992, 75993
    Renal Artery, 75994
    Visceral Artery, 75995, 75996

ATLV, 86687, 86689

ATLV Antibodies, 86687, 86689

Atomic Absorption Spectroscopy, 82190

ATP Creatine Phosphotransferase, 82550, 82552

Atresia, Choanal
  See Choanal Atresia

Atresia, Congenital
  Auditory Canal, External
    Reconstruction, 69320

Atria
  Ablation, 33254-33256, 33265-33266
  Reconstruction, 33254-33256, 33265-33266
  Surgical, 33265-33266

Atrial Electrogram
  See Cardiology, Diagnostic
  Esophageal Recording, 93615, 93616

Index

Atrial Fibrillation
See Fibrillation, Atrial
Atrioseptopexy
See Heart, Repair, Atrial Septum
Atrioseptoplasty
See Heart, Repair, Atrial Septum
Attachment
See Fixation
Attendance and Resuscitation Services
Newborn, 99464
ATTENUVAX, 90705
Atticotomy, 69631, 69635
Audiologic Function Tests
Acoustic Reflex, 92568
Acoustic Reflex Decay, 92570
Audiometry
Bekesy, 92560, 92561
Comprehensive, 92557
Conditioning Play, 92582
Groups, 92559
Pure Tone, 92552, 92553
Select Picture, 92583
Speech, 92555, 92556
Visual Reinforcement, 92579
Central Auditory Function, 92620, 92621
Diagnostic Analysis
Auditory Brainstem Implant, 92640
Electrocochleography, 92584
Evoked Otoacoustic Emissions, 92587, 92588
Filtered Speech, 92571
Lombard Test, 92700
Loudness Balance, 92562
Screening, 92551
Sensorineural Acuity, 92575
Short Increment Sensitivity Index, 92564
Staggered Spondaic Word Test, 92572
Stenger Test, 92565, 92577
Synthetic Sentence Test, 92576
Tinnitus Assessment, 92625
Tone Decay, 92563
Audiometry
Bekesy, 92560, 92561
Brainstem Evoked Response, 92585, 92586
Comprehensive, 92557
Conditioning Play, 92582
Evoked Otoacoustic Emissions, 92587, 92588
Groups, 92559
Pure Tone, 92552, 92553
Select Picture, 92583
Speech, 92555, 92556
Tympanometry, 92567
Visual Reinforcement, 92579
Auditory Brain Stem Evoked Response, 92585-92586
Auditory Canal
Decompression, 61591
External
Abscess
Incision and Drainage, 69020
Atresia, Congenital, 69320
Biopsy, 69105
Lesion
Excision, 69140-69155
Reconstruction, 69310, 69320
for Congenital Atresia, 69320
for Stenosis, 69310
Removal
Cerumen, 69210
Ear Wax, 69210
Foreign Body, 69200, 69205
Internal
Decompression, 69960
Auditory Canal Atresia, External
See Atresia, Congenital, Auditory Canal, External
Auditory Evoked Otoacoustic Emission, 92587, 92588

Auditory Evoked Potentials, 92585, 92586
Auditory Labyrinth
See Ear, Inner
Auditory Meatus
X-ray, 70134
Auditory Tube
See Eustachian Tube
Augmentation
Chin, 21120, 21123
Chin, 21120, 21123
Facial Bones, 21208
Malar, 21270
Malar, 21270
Mammoplasty, 19324-19325
Mandibular Body
with Bone Graft, 21127
with Prosthesis, 21125
Osteoplasty
Facial Bones, 21208
Percutaneous
Spine, 0200T-0201T, 22523-22525
Sacral, 0200T-0201T
Spine, 22523-22525
Vertebral, 22523-22525
Augmented Histamine Test, 91052
Gastric Analysis Test, 91052
Aural Rehabilitation Test, 92626-92633
Auricle (Heart)
See Atria
Auricular Fibrillation
See Fibrillation, Atrial
Auricular Prosthesis, 21086
Australia Antigen
Core, 86704
IgM, 86705
Surface, 86706
Autograft
Bone
Local, 20936
Morselized, 20937
Structural, 20938
Chondrocytes
Knee, 27412
Dermal, 15130-15136
Epidermal, 15110-15111, 15115-15116, 15150-15152, 15155-15157
Osteochondral
Knee, 27416
Talus, 28446
Skin
Dermal, 15130-15136
Epidermal, 15110-15116, 15150-15157
Harvesting
for Tissue Culture, 15040
Spine Surgery
Local, 20936
Morselized, 20937
Structural, 20938
Autologous Blood Transfusion
See Autotransfusion
Autologous Transplantation
See Autograft
Automated Lamellar Keratoplasty (ALK), 65710
Autonomic Nervous System Function
Heart Rate Response, 95921-95923
Pseudomotor Response, 95921-95923
Sympathetic Function, 95921-95923
AutoPap, 88152
Autoprothrombin C
See Thrombokinase
Autoprothrombin I
See Proconvertin
Autoprothrombin II
See Christmas Factor
Autoprothrombin III
See Stuart-Prower Factor
Autopsy
Coroner's Examination, 88045
Forensic Examination, 88040

Autopsy — continued
Gross and Microscopic
Examination, 88020-88029
Infant with Brain, 88028
Stillborn or Newborn with Brain, 88029
Gross Examination, 88000-88016
Organ, 88037
Regional, 88036
Unlisted Services and Procedures, 88099
Autotransfusion
Blood, 86890, 86891
Autotransplant
See Autograft
Autotransplantation
Renal, 50380
AVF, 35180-35190, 36815
AV Fistula (Arteriovenous Fistula)
Cannulization
Vein, 36815
Repair
Abdomen, 35182
Acquired or Traumatic, 35189
Head, 35180
Acquired or Traumatic, 35188
Lower Extremity, 35184
Acquired or Traumatic, 35190
Neck, 35180
Acquired or Traumatic, 35188
Thorax, 35182
Acquired or Traumatic, 35189
Upper Extremity, 35184
Acquired or Traumatic, 35190
Revision
Hemodialysis Graft or Fistula
with Thrombectomy, 36833
without Thrombectomy, 36832
Thrombectomy
Dialysis Graft
without Revision, 36831
A Vitamin, 84590
AV Shunt (Arteriovenous Shunt), 36147-36148, 75791
Avulsion
Nails, 11730, 11732
Nerves, 64732-64772
Axilla
Skin Graft
Delay of Flap, 15620
Full Thickness, 15240, 15241
Pedicle Flap, 15574
Tissue Transfer, Adjacent, 14040, 14041
Axillary Arteries
See Artery, Axillary
Axillary Nerve
Injection
Anesthetic, 64417
Axis, Dens
See Odontoid Process
AZH (Assisted Zonal Hatching), 89253

B

Bacillus Calmette Guerin Vaccine
See BCG Vaccine
Backbench Reconstruction Prior to Implant
Intestine, 44715-44721
Kidney, 50323-50329
Liver, 47143-47147
Pancreas, 48551-48552
Wound Exploration, Penetrating, 20102
Backbone
See Spine
Back/Flank
Biopsy, 21920, 21925
Repair
Hernia, 49540
Tumor, 21930-21936
Wound Exploration
Penetrating, 20102
Bacteria Culture
Additional Methods, 87077
Aerobic, 87040-87071

Bacteria Culture — continued
Anaerobic, 87073-87076
Blood, 87040
Feces, 87045, 87046
Nose, 87070
Other Source, 87070-87075
Screening, 87081
Stool, 87045-87046
Throat, 87070
Urine, 87086, 87088
Bacterial Endotoxins, 87176
Bacterial Overgrowth Breath Test, 91065
Homogenization, Tissue, for Culture, 87176
Bactericidal Titer, Serum, 87197
Bacterium
Antibody, 86609
BAEP (Brainstem Auditory Evoked Potential), 92585-92586
BAER, 92585-92586
Baker's Cyst, 27345
Baker Tube
Decompression of Bowel, 44021
Balanoplasty
See Penis, Repair
Baldy-Webster Operation, 58400
Balkan Grippe, 86000, 86638
Balloon Angioplasty
See Angioplasty
Balloon Assisted Device
Aorta, 33967-33974
Balloon, Cardiac Catheter, Insertion, 33967
Banding
Artery
Fistula, 37607
Pulmonary, 33690
Band, Pulmonary Artery
See Banding, Artery, Pulmonary
Bankart Procedure, 23455
Bank, Blood
See Blood Banking
B Antibodies, Hepatitis
See Antibody, Hepatitis B
B Antigens, Hepatitis
See Hepatitis Antigen, B
Barany Caloric Test, 92533
Barbiturates
Blood or Urine, 82205
Bardenheurer Operation, 37616
Bariatric Surgery, 43644-43645, 43770-43774, 43842-43848, 43886-43888
Barium, 83015
Barium Enema, 74270, 74280
Intussusception, 74283
Barker Operation, 28120
Barr Bodies, 88130
Barrel-Stave Procedure, 61559
Barr Procedure, 27690-27692
Barsky's Procedures, 26580
Bartholin's Gland
Abscess
Incision and Drainage, 56420
Cyst
Repair, 56440
Excision, 56740
Marsupialization, 56440
Bartonella
Antibody, 86611
Bartonella Detection, 87470-87472
Basic Life Services, 99450
Basic Proteins, Myelin
See Myelin Basic Protein
Basilar Arteries
See Artery, Basilar
Bassett's Operation, 56630-56640
Batch-Spittler-McFaddin Operation, 27598
Battle's Operation, 44950, 44960
Bayley Scales of Infant Development
Developmental Testing, 96110, 96111
B Cells
Total Count, 86355

BCG Vaccine

BCG Vaccine, 90585, 90586
B Complex Vitamins
    B-12 Absorption, 78270-78272
B–DNA
    See Deoxyribonucleic Acid
BE, 74270-74283
Be Antigens, Hepatitis
    See Hepatitis Antigen, Be
Bed Sores, 15920-15999
    Pressure Ulcer-Decubitus, Excision, 15999
Bekesy Audiometry
    See Audiometry, Bekesy
Belsey IV Procedure, 43324
Bender–Gestalt Test, 96101-96103
Benedict Test for Urea, 81005
Benign Cystic Mucinous Tumor
    See Ganglion
Benign Neoplasm of Cranial Nerves
    See Cranial Nerve
Bennett Fracture
    Other Than Thumb
        Closed Treatment, 26670, 26675
        Open Treatment, 26685, 26686
        Percutaneous Treatment, 26676
    Thumb Fracture
        with Dislocation, 26645, 26650
        Open Treatment, 26665
Bennett Procedure, 27430
Benzidine Test
    Blood, Feces, 82270, 82272
Benzodiazepines
    Assay, 80154
Benzoyl Cholinesterase
    See Cholinesterase
Bernstein Test, 91030
    Acid Perfusion Test, Esophagus, 91012, 91030
Beryllium, 83015
Beta 2 Glycoprotein I Antibody, 86146
Beta–2–Microglobulin
    Blood, 82232
    Urine, 82232
Beta Blocker Therapy, 4006F
Beta Glucosidase, 82963
Beta–Hydroxydehydrogenase, 80406
Beta Hypophamine
    See Antidiuretic Hormone
Beta Lipoproteins
    See Lipoprotein, LDL
Beta Test, 96101-96103
    Psychiatric Diagnosis, Psychological Testing, 96101-96103
Bethesda System, 88164-88167
Bevan's Operation, 54640
b-Hexosaminidase, 83080
Bicarbonate, 82374
Biceps Tendon
    Insertion, 24342
    Tenodesis, 23430, 29828
Bichloride, Methylene
    See Dichloromethane
Bicompartmental Knee Replacement, 27447
Bicuspid Valve
    Incision, 33420, 33422
    Repair, 33420-33427
    Replacement, 33430
Biesenberger Mammaplasty, 19318
Bifrontal Craniotomy, 61557
Bile Acids, 82239
    Blood, 82240
Bile Duct
    See Gallbladder
    Anastomosis
        with Intestines, 47760, 47780, 47785
    Biopsy
        Endoscopy, 47553
    Catheterization, 75982
    Change Catheter Tube, 75984
    Destruction
        Calculi (Stone), 43265
    Dilation
        Endoscopic, 43271, 47555, 47556

Bile Duct — *continued*
    Drainage
        Transhepatic, 75980
    Endoscopy
        Biopsy, 47553
        Destruction
            Calculi (Stone), 43265
            Tumor, 43272
        Dilation, 43271, 47555, 47556
        Exploration, 47552
        Intraoperative, 47550
        Removal
            Calculi, 43264, 47554
            Foreign Body, 43269
            Stent, 43269
        Specimen Collection, 43260
        Sphincterotomy, 43262
        Sphincter Pressure, 43263
        Tube Placement, 43267, 43268
    Exploration
        Atresia, 47700
        Endoscopy, 47552
    Incision
        Sphincter, 43262, 47460
    Incision and Drainage, 47420, 47425
    Insertion
        Catheter, 47510, 47525, 75982
            Revision, 47530
        Stent, 47511, 47801
    Nuclear Medicine
        Imaging, 78223
    Reconstruction
        Anastomosis, 47800
    Removal
        Calculi (Stone), 43264, 47420, 47425, 47554
        Percutaneous, 47630
        Foreign Body, 43269
        Stent, 43269
    Repair, 47701
        with Intestines, 47760, 47780
        Gastrointestinal Tract, 47785
    Tube Placement
        Nasobiliary, 43267
        Stent, 43268
    Tumor
        Destruction, 43271
        Excision, 47711, 47712
    Unlisted Services and Procedures, Biliary Tract, 47999
    X-ray
        with Contrast, 74300-74320
        Calculus Removal, 74327
        Guide Catheter, 74328, 74330
        Guide Dilation, 74360
Bile Duct, Common, Cystic Dilatation
    See Cyst, Choledochal
Bilirubin
    Blood, 82247, 82248
    Feces, 82252
    Total
        Direct, 82247, 82248
        Transcutaneous, 88720
    Total Blood, 82247, 82248
Billroth I or II, 43631-43634
Bilobectomy, 32482
Bimone
    See Testosterone
Binding Globulin, Testosterone Estradiol
    See Globulin, Sex Hormone Binding
Binet–Simon Test, 96101-96103
Binet Test, 96101-96103
Binocular Microscopy, 92504
Biofeedback
    Anorectal, 90911
    Blood–flow, 90901
    Blood Pressure, 90901
    Brainwaves, 90901
    EEG (Electroencephalogram), 90901
    Electromyogram, 90901
    Electro–Oculogram, 90901
    EMG (with Anorectal), 90911
    Eyelids, 90901
    Nerve Conduction, 90901
    Other (unlisted) biofeedback, 90901

Biofeedback — *continued*
    Perineal Muscles, 90911
    Psychiatric Treatment, 90875, 90876
    Urethral Sphincter, 90911
Bioimpedance
    Cardiovascular Analysis, 93701
Biological Skin Grafts
    See Allograft, Skin
Biometry
    Eye, 76516, 76519, 92136
Biopsies, Needle
    See Needle Biopsy
Biopsy
    with Arthrotomy
        Acromioclavicular Joint, 23101
        Glenohumeral Joint, 23100
        Sternoclavicular Joint, 23101
    with Cystourethroscopy, 52354
    See also Brush Biopsy; Needle Biopsy
    ABBI, 19103
    Abdomen, 49000
    Adenoids (and Tonsils), 42999
    Adrenal Gland, 60540-60545
        Laparoscopic, 60650
        Open, 60540, 60545, 60699
        Percutaneous, 49180
    Alveolus, 41899
    Anal
        Endoscopy, 46606
    Ankle, 27613, 27614, 27620
    Arm, Lower, 25065, 25066
    Arm, Upper, 24065, 24066
    Artery
        Temporal, 37609
    Auditory Canal, External, 69105
    Back/Flank, 21920, 21925
    Bile Duct
        Endoscopic, 47553
        Open, 47999
    Bladder, 52354
        Cystourethroscope, 52204
        Cystourethroscopy, 52224, 52250
            with Fulguration, 52224
            with Radioactive Substance, 52250
        Open, 53899
    Blood Vessel
        Transcatheter, 75970
    Bone, 20220-20245
    Bone Marrow, 38221
    Brain, 61140
        Stereotactic, 61750, 61751
    Brainstem, 61575-61576
    Breast, 19100-19103
        ABBI, 19103
        Stereotactic Localization, 77031
    Bronchi
        Catheterization, 31717
        Endoscopic, 31625-31629, 31632, 31633
        Open, 31899
    Brush
        with Cystourethroscopy, 52204
        Bronchi, 31717
        Renal Pelvis, 52007
        Ureter, 52007
    Carpometacarpal Joint
        Synovium, 26100
    Cervix, 57454, 57455, 57460, 57500, 57520
    Chorionic Villus, 59015
    Colon, 44025, 44100
        Endoscopic, 44137, 44389, 45380, 45391-45392
        Multiple
            with Colostomy, Cecostomy, 44322
    Colon–Sigmoid
        Endoscopic, 45305, 45331
    Conjunctiva, 68100
    Cornea, 65410
    Duodenum, 44010
    Ear
        External, 69100
        Inner, 69949
        Middle, 69799

Biopsy — *continued*
    Elbow, 24065, 24066, 24101
        Synovium, 24100
    Embryo Blastomere, 89290, 89291
    Endometrium, 58100, 58110, 58558
    Epididymis, 54800, 54865
    Esophagus
        Endoscopic, 43202
        Forceps, 3150F
        Open, 43499
    Eye
        Iris, Prolapsed, 66999
    Eyelid, 67810
    Eye Muscle, 67346
    Fallopian Tube, 58999
    Forearm, Soft Tissue, 25065, 25066
    Gallbladder
        Endoscopic, 43261
        Open, 47999
    Gastrointestinal, Upper
        Endoscopic, 43239
    Gum, 41899
    Hand Joint
        Synovium, 26100
    Heart, 93505
    Hip, 27040, 27041
        Joint, 27052
    Hypopharynx, 42802
    Ileum
        Endoscopic, 44382
    Interphalangeal Joint
        Finger, 26110
        Finger Synovium, 26110
        Toe, 28054
    Intertarsal Joint
        Synovial, 28050
        Toe, 28050
    Intestines, Small, 44020, 44100
        Endoscopic, 44361, 44377
    Kidney, 50200-50205
        Endoscopic, 50555-50557, 50574-50576, 52354
    Knee, 27323, 27324
        Synovium, 27330
    Knee Joint
        Synovium, 27330
    Lacrimal Gland, 68510
    Lacrimal Sac, 68525
    Larynx
        Endoscopy, 31510, 31535, 31536, 31576
    Leg
        Lower, 27613, 27614
        Upper, 27323, 27324
    Lip, 40490
    Liver, 47000, 47001, 47100
    Lung
        Needle, 32405
        Thoracotomy, 32095, 32100
    Lymph Nodes, 38500-38530, 38570
        Injection Procedure
            Identification of Sentinel Node, 38792
        Laparoscopic, 38570-38572
        Needle, 38505
        Open, 38500, 38510-38530
        Superficial, 38500
    Mediastinum, 39400
        Needle, 32405
    Metacarpophalangeal Joint, 26105
    Metatarsophalangeal Joint, 28052
    Mouth, 40808, 41108
    Muscle, 20200-20206
    Nail, 11755
    Nasopharynx, 42804, 42806
    Neck, 21550
    Needle
        Abdomen
            Mass, 49180
    Nerve, 64795
    Nose
        Endoscopic, 31237
        Intranasal, 30100
    Oocyte Polar Body, 89290, 89291
    Orbit, 61332
        Exploration, 67400, 67450

Index

Biopsy — *continued*
Orbit — *continued*
Fine Needle Aspiration, 67415
Oropharynx, 42800
Ovary, 58900
Palate, 42100
Pancreas, 48100
Parathyroid Gland, 60699
Pelvis, 27040, 27041
Penis, 54100
Cutaneous, 54100
Deep Structures, 54105
Percutaneous Needle
Spinal Cord, 62269
Perineum, 56605, 56606
Periprostatic Tissue, 54699, 55899
Perirenal Tissue, 53899
Peritoneum
Endoscopic, 47561, 49321
Periurethral Tissue, 53899
Perivesical Tissue, 53899
Pharynx, 42800-42806
Pineal Gland, 60699
Pituitary Gland, 60699
Pleura
Needle, 32400, 32402
Thoracotomy, 32095, 32100
Pleural
Open, 32402
Prostate, 55700, 55705, 55706
Rectum, 45100
Retroperitoneal Area, 49010
Sacroiliac Joint, 27050
Salivary Gland, 42405
Seminal Vesicles, 54699, 55899
Shoulder
Deep, 23066
Joint, 23100, 23101
Soft Tissue, 23065
Sinus
Sphenoid, 31050, 31051
Skin Lesion, 11100, 11101
Spinal Cord, 63275-63290
Percutaneous, 62269
Stereotactic, 63615
Spleen, 38999
Stomach, 43600, 43605
Tarsometatarsal Joint
Synovial, 28050
Testis, 54500, 54505
Thorax, 21550
Throat, 42800-42806
Thymus, 38999, 60699
Thyroid Gland, 60699
Tongue, 41100, 41105
Tonsils (and Adenoids), 42999
Transcatheter, 37200
Tunica Vaginalis, 54699, 55899
Ureter, 52354
Endoscopic, 50955-50957, 50974-50976
Open, 53899
Urethra, 52204, 52354, 53200
Uterus
Endometrial, 58100-58110
Endoscopic, 58558
Endocervical, 57454
Vagina, 57100, 57105, 57421
Vertebral Body, 20250, 20251
Vulva, 56605, 56606, 56821
Wrist, 25065, 25066, 25100, 25101
Biopsy, Skin
See Skin, Biopsy
Biopsy, Vein
See Vein, Biopsy
Biostatistics
See Biometry
Biosterol
See Vitamin, A
Biotinidase, 82261
BiPAP, 94660
Bird's Nest Filter Insertion, 37620
Birthing Room
Newborn Care, 99460, 99463-99465

Bischof Procedure
Laminectomy, Surgical, 63170, 63172
Bismuth, 83015
Bizzozero's Corpuscle/Cell
See Blood, Platelet
BKA, 27598, 27880-27882
Bladder
Abscess
Incision and Drainage, 51080
Anastomosis, 51960
with Intestine, 51960
Anesthesia, 00864, 00870, 00912
Aspiration, 51100-51102
Biopsy, 52204
by Cystourethroscopy, 52204
Catheterization, 51045, 51701-51703
Change Tube, 51705, 51710
Creation/Stoma, 51980
Cyst
Urachal
Excision, 51500
Destruction
Endoscopic, 52214-52240, 52354
Dilation
Ureter, 52260, 52265, 52341, 52342, 52344, 52345
Diverticulum
Excision, 51525
Incision, 52305
Resection, 52305
Endoscopy, 52000
with Urethrotomy, 52270-52276
Biopsy, 52204, 52354
Catheterization, 52005, 52010
Destruction, 52214, 52224, 52400
Dilation, 52260, 52265
Urethra, 52281
Diverticulum, 52305
Evacuation
Clot, 52001
Excision
Tumor, 52234-52240, 52355
Exploration, 52351
Injection, 52283
Insertion of Stent, 52332, 52334
Lithotripsy, 52353
Radiotracer, 52250
Removal
Calculus, 52310, 52315, 52352
Foreign Body, 52310, 52315
Sphincter Surgery, 52277
Tumor
Excision, 52355
Ureter Surgery, 52290, 52300
Urethral Syndrome, 52285
Excision
Partial, 51550-51565
Total, 51570, 51580, 51590-51597
with Nodes, 51575, 51585, 51595
Transurethral of Neck, 52640
Tumor, 52234-52240
Incision
with
Cryosurgery, 51030
Destruction, 51020, 51030
Fulguration, 51020
Insertion Radioactive, 51020
Radiotracer, 51020
Catheter or Stent, 51045
Incision and Drainage, 51040
Injection
Radiologic, 51600-51610
Insertion
Stent, 51045, 52282, 52334
Instillation
Drugs, 51720
Irrigation, 51700
Laparoscopy, 51999
Lesion
Destruction, 51030

Bladder — *continued*
Neck
Endoscopy
Injection of Implant Material, 51715
Excision, 51520
Nuclear Medicine
Residual Study, 78730
Radiotracer, 52250
Reconstruction
with Intestines, 51960
with Urethra, 51800, 51820
Removal
Calculus, 51050, 52310, 52315
Foreign Body, 52310, 52315
Urethral Stent, 52310, 52315
Repair
Diverticulum, 52305
Exstrophy, 51940
Fistula, 44660, 44661, 45800, 45805, 51880-51925
Neck, 51845
Wound, 51860, 51865
Resection, 52500
Residual Study, 78730
Sphincter Surgery, 52277
Suspension, 51990
Suture
Fistula, 44660, 44661, 45800, 45805, 51880-51925
Wound, 51860, 51865
Tumor
Excision, 51530
Unlisted Services and Procedures, 53899
Urethrocystography, 74450, 74455
Urethrotomy, 52270-52276
Urinary Incontinence Procedures
Laparoscopy, 51990, 51992
Plan of Care Documented, 0509F
Remodeling, 0193T
X-ray, 74430
with Contrast, 74450, 74455
Bladder Neck
Endoscopy
Injection of Implant Material, 51715
Bladder Voiding Pressure Studies, 51727-51729 [51797]
Blair Arthrodesis, 27870
Blalock-Hanlon Procedure, 33735-33737
Blalock-Taussig Procedure, 33750
Blastocyst Transfer
See Embryo Transfer
Blastogenesis, 86353
Blastomyces
Antibody, 86612
Blastomycosis, European
See Cryptococcus
Blast Transformation
See Blastogenesis
Blatt Capsulodesis, 25320
Bleeding
See Hemorrhage
Bleeding, Anal
See Anus, Hemorrhage
Bleeding Disorder
See Coagulopathy
Bleeding Time, 85002
Bleeding, Uterine
See Hemorrhage, Uterus
Bleeding, Vaginal
See Hemorrhage, Vagina
Blepharelosis Repair, 67921-67924
Blepharoplasty, 15820-15823
See Canthoplasty
Anesthesia, 00103
Ectropion
Excision Tarsal Wedge, 67916
Extensive, 67917
Entropion
Excision Tarsal Wedge, 67923
Extensive, 67924
Blepharoptosis
Repair, 67901-67909

Blepharoptosis — *continued*
Repair — *continued*
Frontalis Muscle Technique, 67901
with Fascial Sling, 67902
Superior Rectus Technique with Fascial Sling, 67906
Tarso Levator Resection Advancement
External Approach, 67904
Internal Approach, 67903
Blepharorrhaphy
See Tarsorrhaphy
Blepharospasm
Chemodenervation, 64612
Blepharotomy, 67700
Blister
See Bulla
Blom-Singer Prosthesis, 31611
Blood
Bleeding Time, 85002
Blood Clot
Assay, 85396
Clotting
Factor, 85250-85293
Factor Test, 85210
Inhibitors, 85300-85302, 85305, 85307
Coagulation Time, 85345-85348
Lysis Time, 85175
Retraction, 85170
Thrombolytic Agents
Tissue Plasminogen Activator (tPA), 4077F
Collection, for Autotransfusion
Intraoperative, 86891
Preoperative, 86890
Feces, 82270, 82272
by Hemoglobin Immunoassay, 82274
Gastric Contents, 82271
Harvesting of Stem Cells, 38205-38206
Hemoglobin A1c (HbA1c) Level, 3044F-3045F
Hemoglobin Concentration, 85046
Nuclear Medicine
Flow Imaging, 78445
Red Cell, 78140
Red Cell Survival, 78130, 78135
Occult, 82270
Osmolality, 83930
Other Sources, 82271
Patch, 62273
Plasma
Exchange, 36514-36516
Platelet
Aggregation, 85576
Automated Count, 85049
Count, 85008
Manual Count, 85032
Reticulocyte, 85046
Stem Cell
Count, 86367
Donor Search, 38204
Erythropoietin Therapy, 3160F, 4090F-4095F
Harvesting, 38205-38206
Transplantation, 38240-38242
Cell Concentration, 38215
Cryopreservation, 38207, 88240
Plasma Depletion, 38214
Platelet Depletion, 38213
Red Blood Cell Depletion, 38212
T-cell Depletion, 38210
Thawing, 38208-38209, 88241
Tumor Cell Depletion, 38211
Washing, 38209
Transfusion, 36430, 36440
Exchange, 36455
Newborn, 36450
Fetal, 36460
Push
Infant, 36440

Blood

Blood — *continued*
  Unlisted Services and Procedures, 85999
  Viscosity, 85810
Blood Banking
  Frozen Blood Preparation, 86930-86932
  Frozen Plasma Preparation, 86927
  Physician Services, 86077-86079
Blood Cell
  CD4 and CD8
    Including Ratio, 86360
  Enzyme Activity, 82657
  Exchange, 36511-36513
  Sedimentation Rate
    Automated, 85652
    Manual, 85651
Blood Cell Count
  Automated, 85049
  B-Cells, 86355
  Blood Smear, 85007, 85008
  Differential WBC Count, 85004-85007, 85009
  Hematocrit, 85014
  Hemoglobin, 85018
  Hemogram
    Added Indices, 85025-85027
    Automated, 85025-85027
    Manual, 85032
  Microhematocrit, 85013
  Natural Killer (NK) Cells, 86357
  Red
    See Red Blood Cell (RBC), Count
  Red Blood Cell, 85041
  Red Blood Cells, 85032-85041
  Reticulocyte, 85044-85046
  Stem Cells, 86367
  T Cell, 86359-86361
  White
    See White Blood Cell, Count
  White Blood Cell, 85032, 85048, 89055
Blood Clot
  Assay, 85396
  Clot Lysis Time, 85175
  Clot Retraction, 85170
  Clotting Factor, 85250-85293
  Clotting Factor Test, 85210-85244
  Clotting Inhibitors, 85300-85302, 85305, 85307
  Coagulation Time, 85345-85348
  Factor Inhibitor Test, 85335
Blood Coagulation
  Factor I, 85384, 85385
  Factor II, 85210
  Factor III, 85730, 85732
  Factor IV, 82310
  Factor IX, 85250
  Factor V, 85220
  Factor VII, 85230
  Factor VIII, 85244, 85247
  Factor X, 85260
  Factor XI, 85270
  Factor XIII, 85290, 85291
Blood Coagulation Defect
  See Coagulopathy
Blood Coagulation Disorders
  See Clot
Blood Coagulation Test
  See Coagulation
Blood Component Removal
  See Apheresis
Blood Count, Complete
  See Complete Blood Count (CBC)
Blood Flow Check, Graft, 15860, 90940
Blood Gases
  by Pulse Oximetry, 94760
  CO2, 82803
  HCO3, 82803
  Hemoglobin–Oxygen Affinity, 82820
  O2, 82803-82810
  O2 Saturation, 82805, 82810
  pCO2, 82803
  pH, 82800, 82803
  pO2, 82803

Blood Letting
  See Phlebotomy
Blood Lipoprotein
  See Lipoprotein
Blood, Occult
  See Occult Blood
Blood Patch, 62273
Blood Pool Imaging, 78472, 78473, 78481, 78483, 78494, 78496
Blood Pressure
  Monitoring, 24 hour, 93784-93790
  Systolic, 3074F-3075F
  Venous, 93770
Blood Products
  Irradiation, 86945
  Pooling, 86965
  Splitting, 86985
  Volume Reduction, 86960
Blood Sample
  Fetal, 59030
Blood Serum
  See Serum
Blood Smear, 85060
Blood Syndrome
  Chromosomal Analysis, 88245, 88248
Blood Test(s)
  Iron Stores, 3160F
  Kt/V, 3082F-3084F
  Nuclear Medicine
    Plasma Volume, 78110, 78111
    Platelet Survival, 78190, 78191
    Red Cell Volume, 78120, 78121
    Whole Blood Volume, 78122
  Panels
    Electrolyte, 80051
    General Health Panel, 80050
    Hepatic Function, 80076
    Hepatitis, Acute, 80074
    Lipid Panel, 80061
    Metabolic Panel, Basic
      Basic, 80048
      Comprehensive, 80053
      Ionized Calcium, 80047
      Total Calcium, 80048
    Obstetric Panel, 80055
    Renal Function, 80069
  Volume Determination, 78122
Blood Transfusion, Autologous
  See Autotransfusion
Blood Typing
  ABO Only, 86900
  Antigen Screen, 86903, 86904
  Crossmatch, 86920-86922
  Other RBC Antigens, 86905
  Paternity Testing, 86910, 86911
  Rh(D), 86901
  Rh Phenotype, 86906
Blood Urea Nitrogen, 84520, 84525
Blood Vessel(s)
  See Artery; Vein
  Angioscopy
    Noncoronary, 35400
  Endoscopy
    Surgical, 37500
  Excision
    Arteriovenous
      Malformation, 63250-63252
  Exploration
    Abdomen, 35840
    Chest, 35820
    Extremity, 35860
    Neck, 35800
  Great
    Suture, 33320-33322
  Harvest
    Endoscopic, 33508
    Lower Extremity Vein, 35572
    Upper Extremity Artery, 35600
    Upper Extremity Vein, 35500
  Kidney
    Repair, 50100
  Repair
    Abdomen, 35221, 35251, 35281
      with Composite Graft, 35681-35683

Blood Vessel(s) — *continued*
  Repair — *continued*
    Abdomen — *continued*
      with Other Graft, 35281
      with Vein Graft, 35251
      See Aneurysm Repair; Fistula, Repair
    Aneurysm, 61705-61710
    Arteriovenous Malformation, 61680-61692, 61705-61710, 63250-63252
    Chest, 35211, 35216
      with Composite Graft, 35681-35683
      with Other Graft, 35271, 35276
      with Vein Graft, 35241, 35246
    Direct, 35201-35226
    Finger, 35207
    Graft Defect, 35870
    Hand, 35207
    Kidney, 50100
    Lower Extremity, 35226
      with Composite Graft, 35681-35683
      with Other Graft, 35281
      with Vein Graft, 35251
    Neck, 35201
      with Composite Graft, 35681-35683
      with Other Graft, 35261
      with Vein Graft, 35231
    Upper Extremity, 35206
      with Composite Graft, 35681-35683
      with Other Graft, 35266
      with Vein Graft, 35236
  Shunt Creation
    with Bypass Graft, 35686
    with Graft, 36825, 36830
    Direct, 36821
    Thomas Shunt, 36835
  Shunt Revision
    with Graft, 36832
  Suture Repair, Great Vessels, 33320-33322
Bloom Syndrome
  Chromosome Analysis, 88245
Blot Test, Ink
  See Inkblot Test
Blotting, Western
  See Western Blot
Blount Osteotomy, 27455, 27475-27485
Blow-Out Fracture
  Orbital Floor, 21385-21395
Blue, Dome Cyst
  See Breast, Cyst
BMAC (Breath Methylated Alkane Contour), 0085T
BMT, 38240, 38241, 38242
Boarding Home Care, 99324-99337
Bodies, Acetone
  See Acetone Body
Bodies, Barr
  See Barr Bodies
Bodies, Carotid
  See Carotid Body
Bodies, Ciliary
  See Ciliary Body
Bodies, Heinz
  See Heinz Bodies
Bodies, Inclusion
  See Inclusion Bodies
Bodies, Ketone
  See Ketone Bodies
Body Cast
  Halo, 29000
  Removal, 29700, 29710, 29715
  Repair, 29720
  Risser Jacket, 29010, 29015
  Turnbuckle Jacket, 29020, 29025
  Upper Body and One Leg, 29044
  Upper Body Only, 29035
  Upper Body with Head, 29040
  Upper Body with Legs, 29046

Body Fluid
  Crystal Identification, 89060
Body of Vertebra
  See Vertebral Body
Body Section
  X-ray, 76100
  Motion, 76101, 76102
Body System, Neurologic
  See Nervous System
BOH, 93600
Bohler Procedure, 28405
Bohler Splinting, 29515
Boil
  See Furuncle
Boil, Vulva
  See Abscess, Vulva
Bone
  See Specific Bone
  Ablation
    Tumor, 20982
  Biopsy, 20220-20245
  CT Scan
    Density Study, 77078-77079
  Cyst
    Drainage, 20615
    Injection, 20615
  Dual Energy X-ray
    Absorptiometry, 77080-77081
  Excision
    Epiphyseal Bar, 20150
    Facial Bones, 21026
    Mandible, 21025
  Fixation
    Caliper, 20660
    Cranial Tong, 20660
    External, 20690
    Halo, 20661-20663, 21100
    Interdental, 21110
    Multiplane, 20692
    Pin
      Wire, 20650
    Skeletal
      Humeral Epicondyle
        Percutaneous, 24566
      Stereotactic Frame, 20660
      Uniplane, 20690
  Fracture
    Hyoid
      See Hyoid Bone
    Osteoporosis Screening, 5015F
  Insertion
    Needle, 36680
    Osseointegrated Implant
      for External Speech Processor/Cochlear Stimulator, 69714-69718
  Marrow
    Cytogenic Testing, 3155F
  Nuclear Medicine
    Density Study, 78350, 78351
    Imaging, 78300-78320
    SPECT, 78320
    Unlisted Services and Procedures, 78399
  Osteoporosis
    Pharmacologic Therapy, 4005F
  Protein, 83937
  Removal
    Fixation Device, 20670, 20680
  Replacement
    Osseointegrated Implant
      for External Speech Processor/Cochlear Stimulator, 69717-69718
  X-ray
    Age Study, 77072
    Dual Energy Absorptiometry, 77080-77081
    Length Study, 77073
    Osseous Survey, 77074-77077
Bone 4-Carboxyglutamic Protein
  See Osteocalcin
Bone, Carpal
  See Carpal Bone
Bone, Cheek
  See Cheekbone

Index

Bone Conduction Hearing Device, Electromagnetic
  Implantation
    Replacement, 69710
  Removal
    Repair, 69711
Bone Density Study
  Appendicular Skeleton, 77079, 77081
  Axial Skeleton, 77078, 77080
  Ultrasound, 76977
  Vertebral Fracture Assessment, 77082
Bone, Facial
  See Facial Bone
Bone Graft
  Allograft
    Morselized, 20930
    Structural, 20931
  Any Donor Area, 20900-20902
  Augmentation
    Mandibular Body, 21127
  Autograft, 20936
    Morselized, 20937
    Structural, 20938
  Femur, 27170
  Fracture
    Orbit, 21408
  Harvesting, 20900, 20902
  Malar Area, 21210
  Mandible, 21215
  Mandibular Ramus, 21194
  Maxilla, 21210
  Microvascular Anastomosis
    Fibula, 20955
    Iliac Crest, 20956
    Metatarsal Bone, 20957
    Other, 20962
    Rib, 20962
  Nasal Area, 21210
  Nasomaxillary Complex Fracture, 21348
  Open Treatment
    Craniofacial Separation, 21436
  Osteocutaneous Flap, 20969-20973
  Patella, 27599
  Reconstruction
    Mandibular Ramis, 21194
    Midface, 21145-21160
  Skull, 61316
    Excision, 62148
  Spine Surgery
    Allograft
      Morselized, 20930
      Structural, 20931
    Autograft
      Local, 20936
      Morselized, 20937
      Structural, 20938
  Vascular Pedicle, 25430
Bone Healing
  Electrical Stimulation
    Invasive, 20975
    Noninvasive, 20974
  Ultrasound Stimulation, 20979
Bone, Hyoid
  See Hyoid Bone
Bone Infection
  See Osteomyelitis
Bone Marrow
  Aspiration, 38220
  Harvesting, 38230
  Magnetic Resonance Imaging (MRI), 77084
  Needle Biopsy, 38221
  Nuclear Medicine
    Imaging, 78102-78104
  Smear, 85097
  T-Cell
    Transplantation, 38240, 38241, 38242
  Trocar Biopsy, 38221
Bone, Metatarsal
  See Metatarsal
Bone, Nasal
  See Nasal Bone

Bone, Navicular
  See Navicular
Bone Osseous Survey, 77074-77075
Bone Plate
  Mandible, 21244
Bone, Scan
  See Bone, Nuclear Medicine; Nuclear Medicine
Bone, Semilunar
  See Lunate
Bone, Sesamoid
  See Sesamoid Bone
Bone Spur, 28119
Bone, Tarsal
  See Ankle Bone
Bone, Temporal
  See Temporal, Bone
Bone Wedge Reversal
  Osteotomy, 21122
BOOSTRIX, 90715
Bordetella
  Antibody, 86615
  Antigen Detection
    Direct Fluorescent Antibody, 87265
Borrelia
  Antibody, 86618, 86619
  Antigen, 87475-87477
Borrelia burgdorferi ab, 86618-86619
Borreliosis, Lyme, 86617-86618
Borthen Operation, 66165
Bost Fusion
  Arthrodesis, Wrist, 25800-25810
Bosworth Operation, 23550, 23552
Bottle Type Procedure, 55060
Botulinum Toxin
  Chemodenervation
    Extraocular Muscle, 67345
    Facial Muscle, 64612
    Neck Muscle, 64613
Boutonniere Deformity, 26426, 26428
Bowel
  See Intestine(s)
Bower's Arthroplasty, 25332
Bowleg Repair, 27455, 27457
Boxer's Fracture Treatment, 26600-26615
Boyce Operation, 50040, 50045
Boyd Amputation, 27880-27889
Boyd Hip Disarticulation, 27590
Brace
  See Cast
  for Leg Cast, 29358
Brachial Arteries
  See Artery, Brachial
Brachial Plexus
  Decompression, 64713
  Injection
    Anesthetic, 64415, 64416
  Neuroplasty, 64713
  Release, 64713
  Repair
    Suture, 64861
Brachiocephalic Artery
  See Artery, Brachiocephalic
Brachycephaly, 21175
Brachytherapy, 0182T, 77761-77778, 77789
  Dose Plan, 77326-77328
    High Dose Electronic, 0182T
  Remote Afterloading
    1 Channel, 77785
    2-12 Channels, 77786
    Over 12 Channels, 77787
  Unlisted Services and Procedures, 77799
Bradykinin
  Blood or Urine, 82286
Brain
  Abscess
    Drainage, 61150, 61151
    Excision, 61514, 61522
    Incision and Drainage, 61320, 61321
  Adhesions
    Lysis, 62161

Brain — continued
  Anesthesia, 00210-00218, 00220-00222
  Angiography, 70496
  Biopsy, 61140
    Stereotactic, 61750, 61751
  Catheter
    Irrigation, 62194, 62225
    Replacement, 62160, 62194, 62225
  Catheter Placement
    for Chemotherapy, 0169T
  Cisternography, 70015
  Computer Assisted
    Surgery, 61795
  Cortex
    Magnetic Stimulation, 0160T-0161T
  Craniopharyngioma, 61545
    Excision, 61545
  CT Scan, 0042T, 70450-70470, 70496
  Cyst
    Drainage, 61150, 61151, 62161, 62162
    Excision, 61516, 61524, 62162
  Doppler Transcranial, 93886-93893
  Epileptogenic Focus
    Excision, 61534, 61536
  Excision
    Amygdala, 61566
    Choroid Plexus, 61544
    Hemisphere, 61542-61543
    Hemispherectomy, 61542, 61543
    Hippocampus, 61566
    Other Lobe, 61323, 61539, 61540
    Temporal Lobe, 61537, 61538
  Exploration
    Infratentorial, 61305
    Supratentorial, 61304
  Hematoma
    Drainage, 61154
    Incision and Drainage, 61312-61315
  Implantation
    Chemotherapeutic Agent, 61517
    Electrode, 61850-61875
    Pulse Generator, 61885, 61886
    Receiver, 61885, 61886
    Thermal Perfusion Probe, 61107, 61210
  Incision
    Corpus Callosum, 61541
    Frontal Lobe, 61490
    Mesencephalic Tract, 61480
    Subpial, 61567
  Infusion, 0169T
  Insertion
    Catheter, 61210
    Electrode, 61531, 61533, 61850-61875
    Pulse Generator, 61885, 61886
    Receiver, 61885, 61886
    Reservoir, 61210, 61215
  Lesion
    Aspiration, Stereotactic, 61750, 61751
    Excision, 61534, 61536, 61600-61608, 61615, 61616
  Magnetic Resonance Imaging (MRI), 70551-70555
    Intraoperative, 70557-70559
  Magnetic Stimulation
    Transcranial, 0160T-0161T
  Meningioma
    Excision, 61512, 61519
  Myelography, 70010
  Nuclear Medicine
    Blood Flow, 78610
    Cerebrospinal Fluid, 78630-78650
    Imaging, 78600-78607
      Vascular Flow, 78610
    Shunt Evaluation, 78645
  Positron Emission Tomography (PET), 78608, 78609

Brain — continued
  Removal
    Electrode, 61535, 61880
    Foreign Body, 61570, 62163
    Pulse Generator, 61888
    Receiver, 61888
    Shunt, 62256, 62258
  Repair
    Dura, 61618
    Wound, 61571
  Shunt
    Creation, 62180-62192, 62200-62223
    Removal, 62256, 62258
    Replacement, 62160, 62194, 62225-62258
    Reprogramming, 62252
  Skull
    Transcochlear Approach, 61596
    Transcondylar Approach, 61597
    Transpetrosal Approach, 61598
    Transtemporal Approach, 61595
  Skull Base
    Craniofacial Approach, 61580-61585
    Infratemporal Approach, 61590, 61591
    Orbitocranial Zygomatic Approach, 61592
  Stereotactic
    Aspiration, 61750, 61751
    Biopsy, 61750, 61751
    Catheter Placement, 0169T
    Create Lesion, 61720, 61735, 61790, 61791
    Localization for Placement Therapy Fields, 61770
    Radiation Treatment, 77432
    Radiosurgery, 61796-61800, 63620-63621, 77371-77373, 77435
    Surgery, 61795
    Trigeminal Tract, 61791
  Transection
    Subpial, 61567
  Tumor
    Excision, 61510, 61518, 61520, 61521, 61526, 61530, 61545, 62164
  X-ray with Contrast, 70010, 70015
Brain Coverings
  Tumor
    Excision, 61512, 61519
Brain Death
  Determination, 95824
Brainstem (Brain Stem)
  See Brain
  Biopsy, 61575, 61576
  Decompression, 61575, 61576
  Evoked Potentials, 92585, 92586
  Lesion
    Excision, 61575, 61576
Brain Stem Auditory Evoked Potential, 92585-92586
Brain Surface Electrode
  Stimulation, 95961-95962
Brain Tumor, Acoustic Neuroma
  See Brain, Tumor, Excision
Brain Tumor, Craniopharyngioma
  See Craniopharyngioma
Brain Tumor, Meningioma
  See Meningioma
Brain Ventriculography
  See Ventriculography
Branchial Cleft
  Cyst
    Excision, 42810, 42815
Branchioma
  See Branchial Cleft, Cyst
Braun Procedure, 23405-23406
Breast
  Ablation
    Cryosurgery, 19105
  Abscess
    Incision and Drainage, 19020
  Augmentation, 19324, 19325

Breast

Breast — *continued*
- Biopsy, 19100-19103
  - ABBI, 19103
- Catheter Placement
  - for Interstitial Radioelement Application, 19296-19298, 20555, 41019
- Cyst
  - Puncture Aspiration, 19000, 19001
- Excision
  - Biopsy, 19100-19103
  - Capsules, 19371
  - Chest Wall Tumor, 19260-19272
  - Cyst, 19120
  - Lactiferous Duct Fistula, 19112
  - Lesion, 19120-19126
    - by Needle Localization, 19125, 19126
  - Mastectomy, 19300-19307
  - Nipple Exploration, 19110
- Exploration, 19020
- Implants
  - Insertion, 19340, 19342
  - Preparation of Moulage, 19396
  - Removal, 19328, 19330
  - Supply, 19396
- Incision
  - Capsules, 19370
- Injection
  - Radiologic, 19030
- Magnetic Resonance Imaging (MRI), 77058-77059
  - with Computer-aided Detection, 0159T
- Mammoplasty
  - Augmentation, 19324, 19325
  - Reduction, 19318
- Mastopexy, 19316
- Metallic Localization Clip Placement, 19295
- Needle Biopsy, 19100
- Needle Wire Placement, 19290, 19291
- Periprosthetic Capsulectomy, 19371
- Periprosthetic Capsulotomy, 19370
- Reconstruction, 19357-19369
  - with Free Flap, 19364
  - with Latissimus Dorsi Flap, 19361
  - with Other Techniques, 19366
  - with Tissue Expander, 19357
  - with Transverse Rectus Abdominis Myocutaneous (TRAM) Flap, 19367-19369
  - Augmentation, 19324, 19325
  - Mammaplasty, 19318-19325
  - Nipple, 19350-19355
    - Areola, 19350
  - Nipple and Areola, 19350
    - Correction Inverted Nipples, 19355
  - Revision, 19380
- Reduction, 19318
- Removal
  - Capsules, 19371
  - Modified Radical, 19307
  - Partial, 19300-19302
  - Radical, 19305-19306
  - Simple, Complete, 19303
  - Subcutaneous, 19304
- Repair
  - Suspension, 19316
- Stereotactic Localization, 77031
- Ultrasound, 76645
- Unlisted Services and Procedures, 19499
- X-ray, 77055-77056, 77057
  - with Computer-aided Detection, 77051-77052
    - Mammography, 77051-77052
  - Localization Nodule, 77032

Breathing, Inspiratory Positive-Pressure
See Intermittent Positive Pressure Breathing (IPPB)

Breath Methylated Alkane Contour, 0085T

Breath Odor Alcohol
See Alcohol, Breath

Breath Test
- Alcohol, Ethyl, 82075
- Heart Transplant Rejection, 0085T
- Helicobacter Pylori, 78267, 78268, 83013, 83014
- Hydrogen, 91065

Bricker Operation
- Intestines Anastomosis, 50820

Brisement Injection, 20550-20551

Bristow Procedure, 23450-23462
- Capsulorrhaphy, Anterior, 23450-23462

Brock Operation, 33470-33475
- Valvotomy, Pulmonary Valve, 33470-33474

Broken, Nose
See Fracture, Nasal Bone

Bronchi
- Aspiration
  - Catheter, 31720-31725
  - Endoscopic, 31645-31646
- Biopsy
  - Endoscopic, 31625-31629, 31632, 31633
- Brushing
  - Protected Brushing, 31623
- Catheterization
  - with Bronchial Brush Biopsy, 31717
  - Insertion
    - with Intracavitary Radioelement, 31643
- Endoscopy
  - Aspiration, 31645, 31646
  - Biopsy, 31625, 31628, 31629, 31632, 31633
  - Destruction
    - Tumor, 31641
  - Dilation, 31630-31631, 31636-31638
  - Excision
    - Lesion, 31640
  - Exploration, 31622
  - Foreign Body Removal, 31635
  - Fracture, 31630
  - Injection, 31656
  - Lesion, 31640, 31641
  - Stenosis, 31641
  - Tumor, 31640, 31641
  - Ultrasound, 31620
- Exploration
  - Endoscopic, 31622
- Fracture
  - Endoscopy, 31630
- Injection
  - X-ray, 31656, 31715
- Needle Biopsy, 31629, 31633
- Reconstruction
  - Graft Repair, 31770
  - Stenosis, 31775
- Removal
  - Foreign Body, 31635
- Repair
  - Fistula, 32815
- Stenosis
  - Endoscopic Treatment, 31641
- Stent
  - Placement, 31636-31637
  - Revision, 31638
- Tumor
  - Excision, 31640
- Ultrasound, 31620
- Unlisted Services and Procedures, 31899
- X-ray
  - with Contrast, 71040, 71060

Bronchial Allergen Challenge
See Bronchial Challenge Test

Bronchial Alveolar Lavage, 31624

Bronchial Brush Biopsy
- with Catheterization, 31717

Bronchial Brushings
- Protected Brushing, 31623

Bronchial Challenge Test
- with Antigens or Gases, 95070
- with Chemicals, 95071
- See also Allergy Tests

Bronchial Provocation Test
See Allergy Tests, Challenge Test, Bronchial

Bronchoalveolar Lavage, 31624

Broncho–Bronchial Anastomosis, 32486

Bronchography, 71040, 71060
- Injection
  - Transtracheal, 31715
- Segmental
  - Injection, 31656

Bronchoplasty, 32501
- Excision Stenosis and Anastomosis, 31775
- Graft Repair, 31770
- Reconstruction, Bronchi, 32501
  - Graft Repair, 31770
- Stenosis, 31775

Bronchopneumonia, Hiberno–Vernal
See Q Fever

Bronchopulmonary Lavage, 31624

Bronchoscopy
- Alveolar Lavage, 31624
- Aspiration, 31645, 31646
- Biopsy, 31625-31629, 31632, 31633
- Brushing, Protected Brushing, 31623
- Catheter Placement
  - Intracavity Radioelement, 31643
- Diagnostic, 31622-31624, 31643
- Dilation, 31630-31631, 31636-31638
- Exploration, 31622
- Fracture, 31630
- Injection, 31656
- Needle Biopsy, 31629, 31633
- Removal
  - Foreign Body, 31635
  - Tumor, 31640, 31641
- Stenosis, 31641
- Stent Placement, 31631, 31636-31637
- Stent Revision, 31638
- Ultrasound, 31620
- X-ray Contrast, 31656

Bronchospasm Evaluation, 94060, 94070
- Pulmonology, Diagnostic, Spirometry, 94010-94070

Bronkodyl
See Theophylline

Browne's Operation, 54324

Brow Ptosis
- Repair, 67900

Brucella, 86000
- Antibody, 86622

Bruise
See Hematoma

Brunschwig Operation, 58240
- Pelvis, Exenteration, 58240

Brush Biopsy
- Bronchi, 31717

Brush Border ab
See Antibody, Heterophile

BSO, 58720

Bucca
See Cheek

Buccal Mucosa
See Mouth, Mucosa

Bulbourethral Gland
- Excision, 53250

Bulla
- Incision and Drainage
  - Puncture Aspiration, 10160
- Lung
  - Excision–Plication, 32141
  - Endoscopic, 32655

BUN, 84520-84545

Bunionectomy
- with Implant, 28293
- Chevron Procedure, 28296
- Concentric Procedure, 28296

Bunionectomy — *continued*
- Joplin Procedure, 28294
- Keller Procedure, 28292
- Lapidus Procedure, 28297
- Mayo Procedure, 28292
- McBride Procedure, 28292
- Mitchell, 28296
- Reverdin, 28296
- Silver Procedure, 28290

Bunion Repair, 28296-28299
- with Implant, 28293
- Bunionectomy, 28290-28299
- Chevron Procedure, 28296
- Concentric Procedure, 28296
- Joplin Procedure, 28294
- Keller Procedure, 28292
- Lapidus Procedure, 28297
- Mayo Procedure, 28292
- McBride Procedure, 28292
- Mitchell Procedure, 28296
- Reverdin, 28296
- Silver Procedure, 28290

Bunnell Procedure, 24301

Burch Operation, 51840-51841
- Laparoscopic, 58152

Burgess Amputation
- Disarticulation, Ankle, 27889

Burhenne Procedure, 43500
- Bile Duct, Removal of Calculus, 43264, 47420, 47425, 47554
- Percutaneous, 47630

Burkitt Herpevirus
See Epstein–Barr Virus

Burns
- Allograft, 15300-15321, 15330-15336
- Anesthesia, 01951-01953
- Debridement, 01951-01953, 15002-15003, 15004-15005, 16020-16030
- Dressing, 16020-16030
- Escharotomy, 16035, 16036
- Excision, 01951-01953, 15002, 15004-15005
- Initial Treatment, 16000
- Tissue Culture Skin Grafts, 15100-15157
- Xenograft, 15400-15431

Burr Hole
- Anesthesia, 00214
- Skull
  - with Injection, 61120
  - Biopsy, Brain, 61140
  - Catheterization, 61210
  - Drainage
    - Abscess, 61150, 61151
    - Cyst, 61150, 61151
    - Hematoma, 61154, 61156
  - Exploration
    - Infratentorial, 61253
    - Supratentorial, 61250
  - Implant
    - Cerebral Thermal Perfusion Probe, 61107, 61210
    - Neurostimulator Array, 61863-61868
  - Injection, Contrast Media, 61120
  - Insertion
    - Catheter, 61210
    - Reservoir, 61210

Burrow's Operation, 14000-14350

Bursa
- Ankle, 27604
- Arm, Lower, 25031
- Elbow
  - Excision, 24105
  - Incision and Drainage, 23931
- Femur
  - Excision, 27062
- Foot
  - Incision and Drainage, 28001
- Hip
  - Incision and Drainage, 26991
- Injection, 20600-20610
- Ischial
  - Excision, 27060

Bursa — *continued*
  Joint
    Aspiration, 20600-20610
    Drainage, 20600-20610
    Injection, 20600-20610
  Knee
    Excision, 27340
  Leg, Lower, 27604
  Palm
    Incision and Drainage, 26025, 26030
  Pelvis
    Incision and Drainage, 26991
  Shoulder
    Drainage, 23031
  Wrist, 25031
    Excision, 25115, 25116
    Incision and Drainage, 25020
    Infected Bursa, 25031
Bursectomy
  of Hand, 26989
Bursitis, Radiohumeral
  See Tennis Elbow
Bursocentesis
  See Aspiration, Bursa
Buttock
  Excision
    Excess Skin, 15835
Button
  Nasal Septal Prosthesis
    Insertion, 30220
Butyrylcholine Esterase
  See Cholinesterase
B Vitamins
  B-1 (Thiamine), 84425
  B-12 (Cyanocobalamin), 82607, 82608
    Absorption Study, 78270-78272
  B-2 (Riboflavin), 84252
  B-6 (Pyridoxal Phosphate), 84207
Bypass, Cardiopulmonary
  See Cardiopulmonary Bypass
Bypass Graft
  with Composite Graft, 35681-35683
    Autogenous
      Three or More Segments
        Two Locations, 35683
      Two Segments
        Two Locations, 35682
  Aortobifemoral, 35540
  Aortobi-iliac, 35538, 35638
  Aortofemoral, 35539
  Aortoiliac, 35537, 35637
  Axillary Artery, 35516-35522, 35533, 35616-35623, 35650, 35654
  Brachial Artery, 35510, 35512, 35522-35525
  Brachial-Ulnar or -Radial, 35523
  Carotid Artery, 33891, 35501-35510, 35526, 35601, 35606, 35626, 35642
  Celiac Artery, 35331, 35631
  Coronary Artery
    Angiography, 93556
    Arterial, 33533-33536
    Venous Graft, 33510-33516
  Excision
    Abdomen, 35907
    Extremity, 35903
    Neck, 35901
    Thorax, 35905
  Femoral Artery, 35521, 35533, 35539, 35540, 35551-35558, 35566, 35621, 35646, 35647, 35651-35661, 35666, 35700
  Harvest
    Endoscopic, 33508
    Upper Extremity Vein, 35500
  Hepatorenal, 35535
  Iliac Artery, 35537, 35538, 35563, 35637, 35638, 35663
  Ilio-Celiac, 35632
  Iliofemoral Artery, 35548, 35549, 35565, 35665
  Ilio-Mesenteric, 35633
  Iliorenal, 35634

Bypass Graft — *continued*
  Mesenteric Artery, 35531, 35631
  Peroneal Artery, 35566, 35571, 35666, 35671
  Placement
    Vein Patch, 35685
  Popliteal Artery, 35551-35558, 35571, 35623, 35651, 35656, 35671, 35700
  Renal Artery, 35536, 35560, 35631, 35636
  Reoperation, 35700
  Repair
    Abdomen, 35907
    Extremity, 35903
      Lower Extremity
        with Composite Graft, 35681-35683
    Neck, 35901
    Thorax, 35905
  Revascularization
    Extremity, 35903
    Neck, 35901
    Thorax, 35905
  Revision
    Lower Extremity
      with Angioplasty, 35879
      with Vein Interposition, 35881
    Femoral Artery, 35883-35884
  Secondary Repair, 35870
  Splenic Artery, 35536, 35636
  Subclavian Artery, 35506, 35511-35516, 35526, 35606-35616, 35626, 35645, 35693
  Thrombectomy, 35875, 35876, 37184-37186
    Other Than Hemodialysis Graft or Fistula, 35875-35876
  Tibial Artery, 35566, 35571, 35623, 35666, 35671
  Vertebral Artery, 35508, 35515, 35642, 35645
Bypass In Situ
  Femoral Artery, 35583-35585
  Peroneal Artery, 35585, 35587
  Popliteal Artery, 35583, 35587
  Tibial Artery, 35585, 35587

C

C-13
  Urea Breath Test, 83013, 83014
  Urease Activity, 83013, 83014
C-14
  Urea Breath Test, 78267, 78268
  Urease Activity, 83013, 83014
CA, 82310-82340
CABG, 33503-33505, 33510-33536
Cadmium
  Urine, 82300
Caffeine Halothane Contracture Test (CHCT), 89049
Calcaneus
  Craterization, 28120
  Cyst
    Excision, 28100-28103
  Diaphysectomy, 28120
  Excision, 28118-28120
  Fracture
    with Manipulation, 28405, 28406
    without Manipulation, 28400
    Open Treatment, 28415, 28420
    Percutaneous Fixation, 28406
  Repair
    Osteotomy, 28300
    Saucerization, 28120
  Spur, 28119
  Tumor
    Excision, 27647, 28100-28103
    X-ray, 73650
Calcareous Deposits
  Subdeltoid
    Removal, 23000
Calcifediol Assay
  See Calciferol
Calcification
  See Calcium, Deposits

Calciol
  See Calcifediol
Calcitonin
  Blood or Urine, 82308
  Stimulation Panel, 80410
Calcium
  Blood
    Infusion Test, 82331
  Deposits
    Removal, Calculi–Stone
      Bile Duct, 43264, 47420, 47425, 47554, 47630
      Bladder, 51050, 52310-52318
      Gallbladder, 47480
      Hepatic Duct, 47400
      Kidney, 50060-50081, 50130, 50561, 50580
      Pancreas, 48020
      Pancreatic Duct, 43264
      Salivary Gland, 42330-42340
      Ureter, 50610-50630, 50961, 50980, 51060, 51065, 52320-52330
      Urethra, 52310, 52315
  Ionized, 82330
    Panel, 80047
  Total, 82310
    Panel, 80048
  Urine, 82340
Calcium–Binding Protein, Vitamin K–Dependent
  See Osteocalcin
Calcium–Pentagastrin Stimulation, 80410
Calculus
  Analysis, 82355-82370
  Destruction
    Bile Duct, 43265
    Pancreatic Duct, 43265
  Removal
    Bile Duct, 43264, 47554, 74327
    Bladder, 51050, 52310-52318, 52352
    Kidney, 50060-50081, 50130, 50561, 50580, 52352
    Pancreatic Duct, 43264
    Ureter, 50610-50630, 50961, 50980, 51060, 51065, 52320, 52325, 52352
    Urethra, 52310, 52315, 52352
Calculus of Kidney
  See Calculus, Removal, Kidney
Caldwell–Luc Procedure(s), 21385, 31030, 31032
  Orbital Floor Blowout Fracture, 21385
  Sinusotomy, 31030, 31032
Caliper
  Application
    Removal, 20660
Callander Knee Disarticulation, 27598
Callosum, Corpus
  See Corpus Callosum
Calmette Guerin Bacillus Vaccine
  See BCG Vaccine
Caloric Vestibular Test, 92533, 92543
Calprotectin
  Fecal, 83993
Calycoplasty, 50405
Camey Enterocystoplasty, 50825
CAMP
  See Cyclic AMP
Campbell Arthrodesis, 27870
Campbell Procedure, 27422
Campylobacter
  Antibody, 86625
  Antigen, 86628
  Skin Test, 86485
Canal, Ear
  See Auditory Canal
Canalith Repositioning Procedure, 95992
Canaloplasty, 69631, 69635
Canal, Semicircular
  See Semicircular Canal

Candida
  Antibody, 86628
  Antigen, 87480-87482
  Skin Test, 86485
Cannulation
  Arterial, 36620, 36625
  Endoscopic
    Papilla, 43273
  Pancreatic Duct, 48999
  Sinus
    Maxillary, 31000
    Sphenoid, 31002
  Thoracic Duct, 38794
Cannulation, Renoportal
  See Anastomosis, Renoportal
Cannulization
  See Catheterization
  Arteriovenous (AV), 36147-36148, 36810, 36815
  Chemotherapy, 36823
  Declotting, 36593, 36860, 36861
  ECMO, 36822
    Isolated with Chemotherapy Perfusion, 36823
  Vas Deferens, 55200
  Vein to Vein, 36800
Canthocystostomy
  See Conjunctivorhinostomy
Canthopexy
  Lateral, 21282
  Medial, 21280
Canthoplasty, 67950
Canthorrhaphy, 67880, 67882
Canthotomy, 67715
Canthus
  Reconstruction, 67950
Cap, Cervical
  See Cervical Cap
CAPD, 90945, 90947
Capsule
  See Capsulodesis
  Elbow
    Arthrotomy, 24006
    Excision, 24006
  Foot, 28260-28264
  Interphalangeal Joint
    Excision, 26525
    Incision, 26525
  Knee, 27435
  Metacarpophalangeal Joint
    Excision, 26520
    Incision, 26520
  Metatarsophalangeal Joint Release, 28289
  Shoulder, Incision, 23020
  Wrist
    Excision, 25320
Capsulectomy
  Breast, Periprosthetic, 19371
Capsulodesis
  Blatt, 25320
  Metacarpophalangeal Joint, 26516-26518
Capsulorrhaphy
  Anterior, 23450-23462
  Multi–Directional Instability, 23466
  Posterior, 23465
  Wrist, 25320
Capsulotomy
  Breast
    Periprosthetic, 19370
  Foot, 28260-28262
  Hip with Release, Flexor Muscles, 27036
  Interphalangeal Joint, 28272
  Knee, 27435
  Metacarpophalangeal Joint, 26520
  Metatarsophalangeal Joint, 28270
  Toe, 28270, 28272
  Wrist, 25085
Captopril, 80416, 80417
Carbamazepine
  Assay, 80156, 80157
Carbazepin
  See Carbamazepine

Index

Carbinol
See Methanol
Carbohydrate Deficient Transferin, 82373
Carbon Dioxide
  Blood or Urine, 82374
Carbon Tetrachloride, 84600
Carboxycathepsin
  See Angiotensin Converting Enzyme (ACE)
Carboxyhemoglobin, 82375-82376, 88740
Carbuncle
  Incision and Drainage, 10060, 10061
Carcinoembryonal Antigen
  See Antigen, Carcinoembryonic
Carcinoembryonic Antigen, 82378
Cardiac Arrhythmia, Tachycardia
  See Tachycardia
Cardiac Atria
  See Atria
Cardiac Catheterization
  Combined Left and Right Heart, 93526-93529
  Flow Directed, 93503
  for Biopsy, 93505
  for Congenital Anomalies
    Right and Retrograde Left, 93531
    Transseptal and Retrograde Left, 93532, 93533
  for Dilution Studies, 93561, 93562
  Imaging, 93555, 93556
  Injection, 93539-93545
  Left Heart, 93510-93529
  Pacemaker, 33210
  Right Heart, 93501, 93503
    for Congenital Anomalies, 93530
Cardiac Electroversion
  See Cardioversion
Cardiac Event Recorder (wearable), 93224-93272
  Implantation, 33282
  Removal, 33284
Cardiac Magnetic Resonance Imaging (CMRI)
  With Contrast, 75561-75563
  Without Contrast, 75557-75559
  Morphology, 75557, 75561
  Velocity Flow Mapping, 75565
Cardiac Massage
  Thoracotomy, 32160
Cardiac Output Measurement
  by Indicator Dilution, 93561, 93562
  Inert Gas Rebreathing
    During Exercise, 0105T
    During Rest, 0104T
Cardiac Pacemaker
  See Heart, Pacemaker
Cardiac Rehabilitation, 93797, 93798
Cardiac Septal Defect
  See Septal Defect
Cardiac Transplantation
  See Heart, Transplantation
Cardiectomy
  Donor, 33930, 33940
Cardioassist, 92970, 92971
Cardiolipin Antibody, 86147
Cardiology
  Diagnostic
    Atrial Electrogram
      Esophageal Recording, 93615, 93616
    Cardioverter-Defibrillator
      Evaluation and Testing, 93282, 93289, 93292, 93295, 93640-93642
    Echocardiography
      Doppler, 93303-93321, 93662
      Intracardiac, 93662
      Transesophageal, 93318
      Transthoracic, 93303-93317, 93350
    Electrocardiogram
      Evaluation, 93000, 93010, 93014

Cardiology — continued
  Diagnostic — continued
    Electrocardiogram — continued
      Microvolt T-wave, Alternans, 93025
      Monitoring, 93224-93237
      Patient-Demand, Single Event, 93268-93272
      Rhythm, 93040-93042
      Tracing, 93005
      Transmission, 93012
    Electrophysiologic
      Follow-Up Study, 93624
      Ergonovine Provocation Test, 93024
    Evaluation
      Heart Device, 93640
    Heart
      Stimulation and Pacing, 93623
    Implantable Loop Recorder System, 93285, 93291, 93298
    Intracardiac Pacing and Mapping, 93631
      3-D Mapping, 93613
      Follow-up Study, 93624
      Stimulation and Pacing, 93623
    Intracardiac Pacing and Recording
      Arrhythmia Induction, 93618-93620
      Bundle of His, 93600
      Comprehensive, 93619-93622
      Intra-Atrial, 93602, 93610
      Right Ventricle, 93603
      Tachycardia Sites, 93609
      Ventricular, 93612
    Intravascular Ultrasound, 92978, 92979
    M Mode and Real Time, 93307-93321
    Pacemaker Testing, 93642
      Antitachycardia System, 93724
      Dual Chamber, 93280, 93288, 93293
      Leads, 93641
      Single Chamber, 93279, 93288, 93294
    Perfusion Imaging, 78451-78454, 78491-78492
    Stress Tests
      Cardiovascular, 93015-93018
      Drug Induced, 93024
      MUGA (Multiple Gated Acquisition), 78483
    Tilt Table Evaluation, 93660
    Vectorcardiogram
      Evaluation, 93799
      Tracing, 93799
  Therapeutic
    Angioplasty
      Percutaneous, Transluminal, 92982, 92984
    Cardioassist, 92970, 92971
    Cardio Defibrillator Initial Set-up and Programming, 93745
    Cardiopulmonary Resuscitation, 92950
    Cardioversion, 92960, 92961
    Intravascular Ultrasound, 92978, 92979
    Pacing
      Transcutaneous, Temporary, 92953
    Thrombolysis
      Coronary Vessel, 92975, 92977
    Thrombolysis, Coronary, 92977
    Valvuloplasty
      Percutaneous, 92986, 92990
Cardiomyotomy
  See Esophagomyotomy
Cardioplasty, 43320

Cardioplegia, 33999
Cardiopulmonary Bypass
  with Prosthetic Valve Repair, 33496
  Lung Transplant with
    Double, 32854
    Single, 32852
Cardiopulmonary Resuscitation, 92950
Cardiotomy, 33310, 33315
Cardiovascular Stress Test
  See Exercise Stress Tests
Cardioversion, 92960, 92961
Care, Custodial
  See Nursing Facility Services
Care, Intensive
  See Intensive Care
Care, Neonatal Intensive
  See Intensive Care, Neonatal
Care Plan Oversight Services
  Home Health Agency Care, 99374, 99375
  Hospice, 99377, 99378
  Nursing Facility, 99379, 99380
Care, Self
  See Self Care
Carneous Mole
  See Abortion
Carnitine Total and Free, 82379
Carotene, 82380
Carotid Artery
  Aneurysm Repair
    Vascular Malformation or Carotid Cavernous Fistula, 61710
  Excision, 60605
  Ligation, 37600-37606
  Stent, Transcatheter Placement, 0075T-0076T
  Transection
    with Skull Base Surgery, 61609
Carotid Body
  Lesion
    Carotid Artery, 60605
    Excision, 60600
Carotid, Common, 0126T
Carotid Pulse Tracing
  with ECG Lead, 93799
Carpal Bone
  See Wrist
  Arthroplasty
    with Implant, 25443
  Cyst
    Excision, 25130-25136
  Dislocation
    Closed Treatment, 25690
    Open Treatment, 25695
  Excision, 25210, 25215
    Partial, 25145
  Fracture, 25622-25628
    with Manipulation, 25624, 25635
    without Manipulation, 25630
    Closed Treatment, 25622, 25630
    Open Treatment, 25628, 25645
  Incision and Drainage, 26034
  Insertion
    Vascular Pedicle, 25430
  Osteoplasty, 25394
  Repair, 25431-25440
  Sequestrectomy, 25145
  Tumor
    Excision, 25130-25136
Carpals
  Incision and Drainage, 25035
Carpal Tunnel
  Injection
    Therapeutic, 20526
Carpal Tunnel Syndrome
  Decompression, 64721
  Arthroscopy, 29848
  Injection, 20526
Carpectomy, 25210, 25215
Carpometacarpal Joint
  Arthrodesis
    Hand, 26843, 26844
    Thumb, 26841, 26842
  Arthrotomy, 26070, 26100

Carpometacarpal Joint — continued
  Biopsy
    Synovium, 26100
  Dislocation
    Closed Treatment, 26670
      with Manipulation, 26675, 26676
    Open Treatment, 26685, 26686
  Exploration, 26070
  Fusion
    Hand, 26843, 26844
    Thumb, 26841, 26842
  Removal
    Foreign Body, 26070
  Repair, 25447
  Synovectomy, 26130
Carpue's Operation, 30400
Cartilage, Arytenoid
  See Arytenoid
Cartilage, Ear
  See Ear Cartilage
Cartilage Graft
  Ear to Face, 21235
  Harvesting, 20910, 20912
  Rib to Face, 21230
Cartilaginous Exostosis
  See Exostosis
Case Management Services
  Team Conferences, 99366-99368
  Telephone Calls
    Nonphysician, 98966-98968
    Physician, 99441-99443
Cast
  See Brace; Splint
  Body
    Halo, 29000
    Risser Jacket, 29010, 29015
    Turnbuckle Jacket, 29020, 29025
    Upper Body and Head, 29040
    Upper Body and Legs, 29046
    Upper Body and One Leg, 29044
    Upper Body Only, 29035
  Clubfoot, 29450
  Cylinder, 29365
  Finger, 29086
  Hand, 29085
  Hip, 29305, 29325
  Leg
    Rigid Total Contact, 29445
    Long Arm, 29065
    Long Leg, 29345, 29355, 29365, 29450
    Long Leg Brace, 29358
    Patellar Tendon Bearing (PTB), 29435
    Removal, 29700-29715
    Repair, 29720
    Short Arm, 29075
    Short Leg, 29405-29435, 29450
    Shoulder, 29049-29058
    Unlisted Services and Procedures, 29799
    Walking, 29355, 29425
    Revision, 29440
    Wedging, 29740, 29750
    Windowing, 29730
    Wrist, 29085
Casting
  Unlisted Services and Procedures, 29799
Castration
  See Orchiectomy
Castration, Female
  See Oophorectomy
Cataract
  Excision, 66830
  Incision, 66820, 66821
    Laser, 66821
    Stab Incision, 66820
  Removal
    Extraction
      Extracapsular, 66982, 66984
      Intracapsular, 66983
Catecholamines, 80424, 82382-82384
  Blood, 82383
  Urine, 82382
Cathepsin-D, 82387

Index

Catheter
See Cannulization; Venipuncture
Aspiration
  Nasotracheal, 31720
  Tracheobronchial, 31725
Bladder, 51701-51703
  Irrigation, 51700
Breast
  for Interstitial Radioelement Application, 19296-19298
Bronchus for Intracavitary Radioelement Application, 31643
Central Venous
  Repair, 36575
  Replacement, 36580, 36581, 36584
  Repositioning, 36597
Coronary Artery without Concomitant Left Heart Catheterization, 93508
Venous Coronary Bypass Graft without Concomitant Left Heart Catheterization, 93508
Declotting, 36593
Exchange
  Drainage, 49423
  Intravascular, 37209, 75900
Intracatheter
  Irrigation, 99507
  Obstruction Clearance, 36596
Pericatheter
  Obstruction Clearance, 36595
Placement
  Arterial Coronary Conduit without Concomitant Left Heart Catheterization, 93508
  Head and/or Neck, 41019
  Muscle and/or Soft Tissue, 20555
Removal
  Central Venous, 36589
  Peritoneum, 49422
  Pleural catheter, 32552
  Spinal Cord, 62355

Catheterization
Abdomen, 49420, 49421
Abdominal Artery, 36245-36248
Aorta, 36160-36215
Arterial
  Cutdown, 36625
  Intracatheter/Needle, 36100-36140
  Percutaneous, 36620
Arteriovenous Shunt, 36147-36148
Bile Duct, 47510, 47530
  Change, 47525
  Percutaneous, 47510
Bladder, 51045, 51102
Brachiocephalic Artery, 36215-36218
Brain, 61210
  Replacement, 62160, 62194, 62225
Bronchography
  with Bronchial Brush Biopsy, 31717
Cardiac
  Combined Left and Right Heart, 93526-93529
  Flow Directed, 93503
  for Biopsy, 93505
  for Congenital Anomalies
    Right and Retrograde Left, 93531
    Transseptal and Retrograde Left, 93532, 93533
  for Dilution Studies, 93561, 93562
  Imaging, 93555, 93556
  Injection, 93539-93545
  Left Heart, 93510-93529
  Pacemaker, 33210
  Right Heart, 36013, 93501, 93503
  for Congenital Cardiac Anomalies, 93530
Central, 36555-36566

Catheterization — continued
Cerebral Artery, 36215
Cystourethroscopy
  Ejaculatory Duct, 52010
  Urethral, 52005
Ear, Middle, 69405
Eustachian Tube, 69405
Fallopian Tube, 58345, 74742
Intracardiac
  Ablation, 93650-93652
Jejunum
  for Enteral Therapy, 44015
Kidney
  with Ureter, 50393
  Drainage, 50392
Legs, 36245-36248
Nasotracheal, 31720
Nasotracheobronchi, 31720
Newborn
  Umbilical Vein, 36510
Pelvic Artery, 36245-36248
Peripheral, 36568-36571
Placement
  Arterial Coronary Conduit without Concomitant Left Heart Catheterization, 93508
  Coronary Artery without Concomitant Left Heart Catheterization, 93508
  Venous Coronary Bypass Graft without Concomitant Left Heart Catheterization, 93508
Pleural Cavity, 32550
Portal Vein, 36481
Pulmonary Artery, 36013-36015
Radioelement Application, 55875
Removal
  Fractured Catheter, 75961
  Obstructive Material
    Intracatheter, 36596
    Pericatheter, 36595
Salivary Duct, 42660
Skull, 61107
Spinal Cord, 62350, 62351
Spinal Epidural or Intrathecal, 62350, 62351, 62360-62362
  Removal, 62355
Thoracic Artery, 36215-36218
Tracheobronchi, 31725
Umbilical Artery, 36660
Umbilical Vein, 36510
Ureter
  Endoscopic, 50553, 50572, 50953, 50972, 52005
  Injection, 50394, 50684
  Manometric Studies, 50396, 50686
Uterus, 58340
  Radiology, 58340
Vena Cava, 36010
Venous
  Central-Line, 36555, 36556, 36568, 36569, 36580, 36584
  First Order, 36011
  Intracatheter, 36000
  Needle, 36000
  Organ Blood, 36500
  Second Order, 36012
  Umbilical Vein, 36510
Ventricular, 61020, 61026, 61210, 61215

CAT Scan
See CT Scan

Cauda Equina
See Spinal Cord
Decompression, 63005, 63011, 63017, 63047-63048, 63055
Exploration, 63005, 63011, 63017

Cauterization
Anal Fissure, 46940, 46942
Cervix, 57522
  Cryocautery, 57511

Cauterization — continued
Cervix — continued
  Electro or Thermal, 57510
  Laser Ablation, 57513
Chemical
  Granulation Tissue, 17250
Everted Punctum, 68705
Lower Esophageal Sphincter
  Thermal via Endoscopy, 43257
Nasopharyngeal Hemorrhage, 42970
Nose
  Hemorrhage, 30901-30906
Skin Lesion
  Benign, 17000-17004
  Malignant, 17260-17286
  Pre-Malignant, 17000-17004
Skin Tags, 11200, 11201
Turbinate Mucosa, 30801, 30802

CAVB, 93650

Cavernitides, Fibrous
See Peyronie Disease

Cavernosography
Corpora, 54230

Cavernosometry, 54231

Cavities, Pleural
See Pleural Cavity

Cavus Foot Correction, 28309

CBC (Complete Blood Count), 85025-85027

CCL4, 84600

CCU (Critical Care Unit)
See Critical Care Services

CD142 Antigens, 85250

CD143 Antigens, 82164

CD4, 86360

CD8, 86360

CEA (Carcinoembryonic Antigen), 82378

Cecil Repair, 54318

Cecostomy Tube Placement, 44300

Celestin Procedure, 43510

Celiac Plexus
Destruction, 64680
Injection
  Anesthetic, 64530
  Neurolytic, 64680

Celiac Trunk Artery
See Artery, Celiac

Celioscopy
See Endoscopy, Peritoneum

Celiotomy, 49000
Abdomen
  for Staging, 49220

Cell, Blood
See Blood Cell

Cell Count
Body Fluid, 89050, 89051

Cell, Islet
Antibody, 86341

Cell, Mother
See Stem Cell

Cellobiase, 82963

Cell-Stimulating Hormone, Interstitial
See Luteinizing Hormone (LH)

Cellular Function Assay, 86352

Cellular Inclusion
See Inclusion Bodies

Central Shunt, 33764

Central Venous Catheter (CVC)
Insertion
  Central, 36555-36558
  Peripheral, 36568, 36569
Removal, 36589
Repair, 36575
Replacement, 36580-36585
Repositioning, 36597

Central Venous Catheter Removal, 36589

Cephalic Version
of Fetus
  External, 59412

Cephalocele
See Encephalocele

Cephalogram, Orthodontic
See Orthodontic Cephalogram

Cerclage
Cervix, 57700
  Abdominal Approach, 59325
  Removal under Anesthesia, 59871
  Vaginal Approach, 59320
McDonald, 57700

Cerebellopontine Angle Tumor
Excision, 61510, 61518, 61520, 61521, 61526, 61530, 61545

Cerebral Cortex Decortication
See Decortication

Cerebral Death, 95824

Cerebral Hernia
See Encephalocele

Cerebral Perfusion Analysis, 0042T

Cerebral Thermography
See Thermogram, Cephalic

Cerebral Ventriculographies
See Ventriculography

Cerebral Vessel(s)
Occlusion, 61623

Cerebrose
See Galactose

Cerebrospinal Fluid, 86325
Nuclear Imaging, 78630-78650

Cerebrospinal Fluid Leak, 63744
Brain
  Repair, 61618, 61619, 62100
Nasal
  Sinus Endoscopy Repair, 31290, 31291
Spinal Cord
  Repair, 63707, 63709

Cerebrospinal Fluid Shunt, 63740-63746
Creation, 62180-62192, 62200-62223
Irrigation, 62194
Removal, 62256, 62258
Replacement, 62160, 62194, 62225, 62230
Reprogramming, 62252

Ceruloplasmin, 82390

Cerumen
Removal, 69210

Cervical Canal
Instrumental Dilation of, 57800

Cervical Cap, 57170

Cervical Cerclage
Abdominal Approach, 59325
Removal under Anesthesia, 59871
Vaginal Approach, 59320

Cervical Lymphadenectomy, 38720, 38724

Cervical Mucus Penetration Test, 89330

Cervical Plexus
Injection
  Anesthetic, 64413

Cervical Pregnancy, 59140

Cervical Puncture, 61050, 61055

Cervical Smears, 88141, 88155, 88164-88167, 88174-88175
See Cytopathology

Cervical Spine
See Vertebra, Cervical

Cervical Stump
Dilation and Curettage of, 57558

Cervical Sympathectomy
See Sympathectomy, Cervical

Cervicectomy, 57530

Cervicoplasty, 15819

Cervicothoracic Ganglia
See Stellate Ganglion

Cervix
See Cytopathology
Amputation
  Total, 57530
Biopsy, 57500, 57520
Colposcopy, 57454, 57455, 57460
Cauterization, 57522
  Cryocautery, 57511
  Electro or Thermal, 57510
  Laser Ablation, 57513
Cerclage, 57700
  Abdominal, 59325

Cervix

Cervix — *continued*
  Cerclage — *continued*
    Removal under Anesthesia, 59871
    Vaginal, 59320
  Colposcopy, 57452-57461
  Conization, 57461, 57520, 57522
  Curettage
    Endocervical, 57454, 57456, 57505
  Dilation
    Canal, 57800
    Stump, 57558
  Dilation and Curettage, 57558
  Ectopic Pregnancy, 59140
  Excision
    Electrode, 57460
    Radical, 57531
    Stump
      Abdominal Approach, 57540, 57545
      Vaginal Approach, 57550-57556
    Total, 57530
  Exploration
    Endoscopy, 57452
  Insertion
    Dilation, 59200
    Laminaria, 59200
    Prostaglandin, 59200
  Repair
    Cerclage, 57700
      Abdominal, 59325
      Vaginal, 59320
    Suture, 57720
  Stump, 57558
  Suture, 57720
  Unlisted Services and Procedures, 58999

Cesarean Delivery
  with Hysterectomy, 59525
  Antepartum Care, 59610, 59618
  Delivery
    After Attempted Vaginal Delivery, 59618
      Delivery Only, 59620
      Postpartum Care, 59622
      Routine Care, 59618
    Routine Care, 59610
  Delivery Only, 59514
  Postpartum Care, 59515
  Routine Care, 59510
  Tubal Ligation at Time of, 58611

CGM (Continuous Glucose Monitoring System), 95250-95251

CGMP, 83008

Chalazion
  Excision, 67800-67808
  Multiple
    Different Lids, 67805
    Same Lids, 67801
  Single, 67800
  Under Anesthesia, 67808

Challenge Tests
  Bronchial Ingestion, 95070-95075

Chambers Procedure, 28300

Change
  Catheter
    With Contrast, 75984
  Fetal Position
    by Manipulation, 59412
  Tube or Stent (Endoscopic), Bile or Pancreatic Duct, 43269

Change, Gastrostomy Tube
  See Gastrostomy Tube, Change of

Change of, Dressing
  See Dressings, Change

CHCT (Caffeine Halothane Contracture Test), 89049

Cheek
  Bone
    Excision, 21030, 21034
    Fracture
      Closed Treatment with Manipulation, 21355
      Open Treatment, 21360-21366

Cheek — *continued*
  Bone — *continued*
    Fracture — *continued*
      Reconstruction, 21270
    Fascia Graft, 15840
    Muscle Graft, 15841-15845
    Muscle Transfer, 15845
    Rhytidectomy, 15828
    Skin Graft
      Delay of Flap, 15620
      Full Thickness, 15240, 15241
      Pedicle Flap, 15574
      Split, 15120-15121
    Tissue Transfer, Adjacent, 14040, 14041

Cheekbone
  Fracture
    Closed Treatment Manipulation, 21355
    Open Treatment, 21360-21366
    Reconstruction, 21270

Cheilectomy
  Metatarsophalangeal Joint Release, 28289

Cheiloplasty
  See Lip, Repair

Cheiloschisis
  See Cleft, Lip

Cheilotomy
  See Incision, Lip

Chemical
  Cauterization
    Granulation Tissue, 17250
  Exfoliation, 15788-15793, 17360
  Peel, 15788-15793, 17360

Chemiluminescent Assay, 82397

Chemistry Tests
  Organ or Disease Oriented Panel
    Electrolyte, 80051
    General Health Panel, 80050
    Hepatic Function Panel, 80076
    Hepatitis Panel, Acute, 80074
    Lipid Panel, 80061
    Metabolic
      Basic, 80047-80048
      Calcium
        Ionized, 80047
        Total, 80048
      Comprehensive, 80053
    Obstetric Panel, 80055
  Unlisted Services and Procedures, 84999

Chemocauterization
  Corneal Epithelium, 65435
    with Chelating Agent, 65436

Chemodenervation
  Eccrine Glands, 64650, 64653
  Electrical Stimulation for Guidance, 95873
  Extraocular Muscle, 67345
  Extremity Muscle, 64614
  Facial Muscle, 64612
  Internal Anal Sphincter, 46505
  Neck Muscle, 64613
  Trunk Muscle, 64614

Chemonucleolysis, 62292

Chemosurgery
  Mohs Technique, 17311-17315
  Skin Lesion, 17004, 17110, 17270, 17280

Chemotaxis Assay, 86155

Chemotherapy
  Arterial Catheterization, 36640
  Bladder Instillation, 51720
  Central Nervous System, 61517, 96450
  Extracorporeal Circulation Membrane Oxygenation, 36822
    Isolated with Chemotherapy Perfusion, 36823
  Home Infusion Procedures, 99601, 99602
  Intra–Arterial, 96420-96425
  Intralesional, 96405, 96406
  Intramuscular, 96401-96402
  Intravenous, 96409-96417

Chemotherapy — *continued*
  Kidney Instillation, 50391
  Peritoneal Cavity, 96445
  Pleural Cavity, 96440
  Pump Services
    Implantable, 96522
    Initiation, 96416
    Maintenance, 95990-95991, 96521-96522
    Portable, 96521
  Reservoir Filling, 96542
  Subcutaneous, 96401-96402
  Unlisted Services and Procedures, 96549
  Ureteral Instillation, 50391

Chest
  See Mediastinum; Thorax
  Angiography, 71275
  Artery
    Ligation, 37616
  CT Scan, 71250-71275
  Exploration
    Blood Vessel, 35820
  Magnetic Resonance Imaging (MRI), 71550-71552
  Repair
    Blood Vessel, 35211, 35216
      with Other Graft, 35271, 35276
      with Vein Graft, 35241, 35246
  Tube, 32551
  Ultrasound, 76604
  Wound Exploration
    Penetrating, 20101
  X-ray, 71010-71035
    Complete (four views) with Fluoroscopy, 71034
    Insertion Pacemaker, 71090
    Partial (two views) with Fluoroscopy, 71023
    Stereo, 71015

Chest Cavity
  Bypass Graft, 35905
  Endoscopy
    Exploration, 32601-32606
    Surgical, 32650-32665
    Therapeutic, 32654-32665

Chest, Funnel
  Anesthesia, 00474
  Reconstructive Repair, 21740-21742
    with Thoracoscopy, 21743

Chest Wall
  Manipulation, 94667, 94668
  Reconstruction, 49904
    Trauma, 32820
  Repair, 32905
    Closure, 32810
    Fistula, 32906
  Tumor
    Excision, 19260-19272
  Unlisted Services and Procedures, 32999

Chest Wall Fistula
  See Fistula, Chest Wall

Chevron Procedure, 28296

Chiari Osteotomy of the Pelvis
  See Osteotomy, Pelvis

Chicken Pox (Varicella)
  Immunization, 90716

Child Procedure, 48146
  See also Excision, Pancreas, Partial

Chin
  Repair
    Augmentation, 21120
    Osteotomy, 21121-21123
    Rhytidectomy, 15828
  Skin Graft
    Delay of Flap, 15620
    Full Thickness, 15240, 15241
    Pedicle Flap, 15574
    Split, 15120-15121
  Tissue Transfer, Adjacent, 14040, 14041

Chinidin, 80194

Chiropractic Manipulation
  See Manipulation, Chiropractic

Chiropractic Treatment
  Spinal
    Extraspinal, 98940-98943

Chlamydia
  Antibody, 86631, 86632
  Antigen Detection
    Direct
      Optical Observation, 87810
    Direct Fluorescent, 87270
    Enzyme Immunoassay, 87320
    Nucleic Acid, 87485-87492
  Culture, 87110

Chloramphenicol, 82415

Chlorhydrocarbon, 82441

Chloride
  Blood, 82435
  Other Source, 82438
  Spinal Fluid, 82438
  Urine, 82436

Chloride, Methylene
  See Dichloromethane

Chlorinated Hydrocarbons, 82441

Chlorohydrocarbon, 82441

Chlorpromazine, 84022

Choanal Atresia
  Repair, 30540, 30545

CHOL, 82465, 83718-83721

Cholangiogram
  Intravenous, 76499

Cholangiography
  with Cholecystectomy, 47563, 47605
  Injection, 47500, 47505
  Intraoperative, 74300, 74301
  Percutaneous, 74320
    with Laparoscopy, 47560, 47561
    with Peritoneoscopy, 47560, 47561
  Postoperative, 74305
  Repair
    with Bile Duct Exploration, 47700
    with Cholecystectomy, 47620

Cholangiopancreatography, 43260
  with Biopsy, 43261
  with Surgery, 43262-43267, 43269
  See Bile Duct, Pancreatic Duct

Cholangiostomy
  See Hepaticostomy

Cholangiotomy
  See Hepaticostomy

Cholecystectomy
  Laparoscopic, 47562-47570
    with Cholangiography, 47563
    with Exploration Common Duct, 47564
  Open Approach, 47600-47620
    with Cholangiography, 47605, 47620
    with Exploration Common Duct, 47610

Cholecystenterostomy, 47570, 47720-47741

Cholecystography, 74290, 74291

Cholecystostomy, 47480

Cholecystotomy, 47480, 48001
  Percutaneous, 47490

Choledochoplasty
  See Bile Duct, Repair

Choledochoscopy, 47550

Choledochostomy, 47420, 47425

Choledochotomy, 47420, 47425

Choledochus, Cyst
  See Cyst, Choledochal

Cholera Vaccine
  Injectable, 90725

Cholesterol
  Measurement, 83721
  Serum, 82465
  Testing, 83718, 83719

Choline Esterase I, 82013

Choline Esterase II, 82480, 82482

Cholinesterase
  Blood, 82480, 82482

Cholyglycine
  Blood, 82240

Chondroitin Sulfate, 82485

Index — Closure

Chondromalacia Patella
  Repair, 27418
Chondropathia Patellae
  See Chondromalacia Patella
Chondroplasty, 29877, 29879
Chondrosteoma
  See Exostosis
Chopart Procedure, 28800
  Amputation, Foot, 28800, 28805
Chordotomies
  See Cordotomy
Chorioangioma
  See Lesion, Skin
Choriogonadotropin, 80414, 84702-84703
  Stimulation, 80414-80415
Choriomeningitides, Lymphocytic, 86727
Chorionic Gonadotropin, 80414, 84702-84704
  Stimulation, 80414, 80415
Chorionic Growth Hormone, 83632
Chorionic Tumor
  See Hydatidiform Mole
Chorionic Villi, 59015
Chorionic Villus
  Biopsy, 59015
Choroid
  Destruction
    Lesion, 0016T, 67220-67225
Choroidopathy, 67208-67218
Choroid Plexus
  Excision, 61544
Christmas Factor, 85250
Chromaffinoma, Medullary
  See Pheochromocytoma
Chromatin, Sex
  See Barr Bodies
Chromatography
  Column
    Mass Spectrometry, 82541-82544
  Gas–Liquid or HPLC, 82486, 82491, 82492
  Paper, 82487, 82488
  Thin–Layer, 82489
Chromium, 82495
Chromogenic Substrate Assay, 85130
Chromosome Analysis
  Added Study, 88280-88289
  Amniotic Fluid, 88267, 88269
    Culture, 88235
  Biopsy Culture
    Tissue, 88233
  Bone Marrow Culture, 88237
  Chorionic Villus, 88267
    5 Cells, 88261
    15-20 Cells, 88262
    20-25 Cells, 88264
    45 Cells, 88263
    Culture, 88235
  for Breakage Syndromes, 88245-88249
  Fragile–X, 88248
  Lymphocyte Culture, 88230
  Pregnancy Associated Plasma Protein A, 84163
  Skin Culture
    Tissue, 88233
  Tissue Culture, 88239
  Unlisted Services and Procedures, 88299
Chromotubation
  Oviduct, 58350
Chronic Erection
  See Priapism
Chronic Interstitial Cystitides
  See Cystitis, Interstitial
Ciliary Body
  Cyst
    Destruction
      Cryotherapy, 66720
      Cyclodialysis, 66740
      Cyclophotocoagulation, 66710-66711
      Diathermy, 66700
      Nonexcisional, 66770

Ciliary Body — continued
  Destruction
    Cyclophotcoagulation, 66710, 66711
    Endoscopic, 66711
  Lesion
    Destruction, 66770
    Repair, 66680
Cimino Type Procedure, 36821
Cinefluorographies
  See Cineradiography
Cineplasty
  Arm, Lower, 24940
  Arm, Upper, 24940
Cineradiography
  Esophagus, 74230
  Pharynx, 70371, 74230
  Speech Evaluation, 70371
  Swallowing Evaluation, 74230
  Unlisted Services and Procedures, 76120, 76125
Cingulotomy, 61490
Circulation Assist
  Aortic, 33967, 33970
  Balloon Counterpulsation, 33967, 33970
    Removal, 33971
  Cardioassist Method
    External, 92971
    Internal, 92970
  External, 33960, 33961
Circulation, Extracorporeal
  See Extracorporeal Circulation
Circulatory Assist
  Aortic, 33967, 33970
  Balloon, 33967, 33970
  External, 33960-33961
Circumcision
  with Clamp or Other Device, 54150
  Repair, 54163
  Surgical Excision
    28 days or less, 54160
    Older than 28 days, 54161
Cisternal Puncture, 61050, 61055
Cisternography, 70015
  Nuclear, 78630
Citrate
  Blood or Urine, 82507
CK, 82550-82554
  Total, 82550
Cl, 82435-82438
Clagett Procedure
  Chest Wall, Repair, Closure, 32810
Clavicle
  Craterization, 23180
  Cyst
    Excision, 23140
      with Allograft, 23146
      with Autograft, 23145
  Diaphysectomy, 23180
  Dislocation
    without Manipulation, 23540
    Acromioclavicular Joint
      Closed Treatment, 23540, 23545
      Open Treatment, 23550, 23552
    Sternoclavicular Joint
      Closed Treatment, 23520, 23525
      Open Treatment, 23530, 23532
  Excision, 23170
    Partial, 23120, 23180
    Total, 23125
  Fracture
    Closed Treatment
      with Manipulation, 23505
      without Manipulation, 23500
    Open Treatment, 23515
  Osteotomy, 23480, 23485
  Pinning, Wiring, Etc., 23490
  Prophylactic Treatment, 23490
  Repair Osteotomy, 23480, 23485
  Saucerization, 23180
  Sequestrectomy, 23170

Clavicle — continued
  Tumor
    Excision, 23140, 23146, 23200
      with Allograft, 23146
      with Autograft, 23145
    Radical Resection, 23200
  X–ray, 73000
Clavicula
  See Clavicle
Claviculectomy
  Partial, 23120
  Total, 23125
Claw Finger Repair, 26499
Clayton Procedure, 28114
Cleft, Branchial
  See Branchial Cleft
Cleft Cyst, Branchial
  See Branchial Cleft, Cyst
Cleft Foot
  Reconstruction, 28360
Cleft Hand
  Repair, 26580
Cleft Lip
  Repair, 40700-40761
  Rhinoplasty, 30460, 30462
Cleft Palate
  Repair, 42200-42225
  Rhinoplasty, 30460, 30462
Clinical Act of Insertion
  See Insertion
Clinical Investigation
  FDA-approved Drugs
    Single Patient
      by Pharmacist, 0130T
Clitoroplasty
  for Intersex State, 56805
Closed [Transurethral] Biopsy of Bladder
  See Biopsy, Bladder, Cystourethroscopy
Clostridial Tetanus
  See Tetanus
Clostridium Botulinum Toxin
  See Chemodenervation
Clostridium Difficile Toxin
  Amplified Probe Technique, 87493
  Antigen Detection
    Enzyme Immunoassay, 87324
  by Immunoassay
    with Direct Optical Observation, 87803
Clostridium Tetani ab
  See Antibody, Tetanus
Closure, 12001-13160
  Anal Fistula, 46288
  Appendiceal Fistula, 44799
  Atrioventricular Valve, 33600
  Cardiac Valve, 33600, 33602
  Cystostomy, 51880
  Diaphragm
    Fistula, 39599
  Enterostomy, 44620-44626
  Lacrimal Fistula, 68770
  Lacrimal Punctum
    Plug, 68761
    Thermocauterization, Ligation, or Laser Surgery, 68760
  Rectovaginal Fistula, 57300-57308
  Semilunar Valve, 33602
  Septal Defect, 33615
  Skin
    Abdomen
      Complex, 13100-13102
      Intermediate, 12031-12037
      Layered, 12031-12037
      Simple, 12001-12007
      Superficial, 12001-12007
    Arm, Arms
      Complex, 13120-13122
      Intermediate, 12031-12037
      Layered, 12031-12037
      Simple, 12001-12007
      Superficial, 12001-12007
    Axilla, Axillae
      Complex, 13131-13133
      Intermediate, 12031-12037

Closure — continued
  Skin — continued
    Axilla, Axillae — continued
      Layered, 12031-12037
      Simple, 12001-12007
      Superficial, 12001-12007
    Back
      Complex, 13100-13102
      Intermediate, 12031-12037
      Layered, 12031-12037
      Simple, 12001-12007
      Superficial, 12001-12007
    Breast
      Complex, 13100-13102
      Intermediate, 12031-12037
      Layered, 12031-12037
      Simple, 12001-12007
      Superficial, 12001-12007
    Buttock
      Complex, 13100-13102
      Intermediate, 12031-12037
      Layered, 12031-12037
      Simple, 12001-12007
      Superficial, 12001-12007
    Cheek, Cheeks
      Complex, 13131-13133
      Intermediate, 12051-12057
      Layered, 12051-12057
      Simple, 12011-12018
      Superficial, 12011-12018
    Chest
      Complex, 13100-13102
      Intermediate, 12031-12037
      Layered, 12031-12037
      Simple, 12001-12007
      Superficial, 12001-12007
    Chin
      Complex, 13131-13133
      Intermediate, 12051-12057
      Layered, 12051-12057
      Simple, 12011-12018
      Superficial, 12011-12018
    Ear, Ears
      Complex, 13150-13153
      Intermediate, 12051-12057
      Layered, 12051-12057
      2.5 cm or less, 12051
      Simple, 12011-12018
      Superficial, 12011-12018
    External
      Genitalia
        Intermediate, 12041-12047
        Layered, 12041-12047
        Simple, 12001-12007
        Superficial, 12001-12007
    Extremity, Extremities
      Intermediate, 12031-12037
      Layered, 12031-12037
      Simple, 12001-12007
      Superficial, 12001-12007
    Eyelid, Eyelids
      Complex, 13150-13153
      Intermediate, 12051-12057
      Layered, 12051-12057
      Simple, 12011-12018
      Superficial, 12011-12018
    Face
      Complex, 13131-13133
      Intermediate, 12051-12057
      Layered, 12051-12057
      Simple, 12011-12018
      Superficial, 12011-12018
    Feet
      Complex, 13131-13133
      Intermediate, 12041-12047
      Layered, 12041-12047
      Simple, 12001-12007
      Superficial, 12001-12007
    Finger, Fingers
      Complex, 13131-13133
      Intermediate, 12041-12047
      Layered, 12041-12047
      Simple, 12001-12007
      Superficial, 12001-12007
    Foot
      Complex, 13131-13133

Closure

Closure — *continued*
Skin — *continued*
Foot — *continued*
Intermediate, 12041-12047
Layered, 12041-12047
Simple, 12001-12007
Superficial, 12001-12007
Forearm, Forearms
Complex, 13120-13122
Intermediate, 12031-12037
Layered, 12031-12037
Simple, 12001-12007
Superficial, 12001-12007
Forehead
Complex, 13131-13133
Intermediate, 12051-12057
Layered, 12051-12057
Simple, 12011-12018
Superficial, 12011-12018
Genitalia
Complex, 13131-13133
External
Intermediate, 12041-12047
Layered, 12041-12047
Simple, 12001-12007
Superficial, 12001-12007
Hand, Hands
Complex, 13131-13133
Intermediate, 12041-12047
Layered, 12041-12047
Simple, 12001-12007
Superficial, 12001-12007
Leg, Legs
Complex, 13120-13122
Intermediate, 12031-12037
Layered, 12031-12037
Simple, 12001-12007
Superficial, 12001-12007
Lip, Lips
Complex, 13150-13153
Intermediate, 12051-12057
Layered, 12051-12057
Simple, 12011-12018
Superficial, 12011-12018
Lower
Arm, Arms
Complex, 13120-13122
Intermediate, 12031-12037
Layered, 12031-12037
Simple, 12001-12007
Superficial, 12001-12007
Extremity, Extremities
Intermediate, 12031-12037
Layered, 12031-12037
Simple, 12001-12007
Superficial, 12001-12007
Leg, Legs
Complex, 13120-13122
Intermediate, 12031-12037
Layered, 12031-12037
Simple, 12001-12007
Superficial, 12001-12007
Mouth
Complex, 13131-13133
Mucous Membrane, Mucous Membranes
Intermediate, 12051-12057
Layered, 12051-12057
Simple, 12011-12018
Superficial, 12011-12018
Neck
Complex, 13131-13133
Intermediate, 12041-12047
Layered, 12041-12047
Simple, 12001-12007
Superficial, 12001-12007
Nose
Complex, 13150-13153
Intermediate, 12051-12057
Layered, 12051-12057
Simple, 12011-12018
Superficial, 12011-12018
Palm, Palms
Complex, 13131-13133
Intermediate, 12041-12047
Layered, 12041-12047

Closure — *continued*
Skin — *continued*
Palm, Palms — *continued*
Simple, 12001-12007
Superficial, 12001-12007
Scalp
Complex, 13120-13122
Intermediate, 12031-12037
Layered, 12031-12037
Simple, 12001-12007
Superficial, 12001-12007
Toe, Toes
Complex, 13131-13133
Intermediate, 12041-12047
Layered, 12041-12047
Simple, 12001-12007
Superficial, 12001-12007
Trunk
Complex, 13100-13102
Intermediate, 12031-12037
Layered, 12031-12037
Simple, 12001-12007
Superficial, 12001-12007
Upper
Arm, Arms
Complex, 13120-13122
Intermediate, 12031-12037
Layered, 12031-12037
Simple, 12001-12007
Superficial, 12001-12007
Extremity
Intermediate, 12031-12037
Layered, 12031-12037
Simple, 12001-12007
Superficial, 12001-12007
Leg, Legs
Complex, 13120-13122
Intermediate, 12031-12037
Layered, 12031-12037
Simple, 12001-12007
Superficial, 12001-12007
Sternotomy, 21750
Ventricular Tunnel, 33722
Closure, Atrial Septal Defect
See Heart, Repair, Atrial Septum
Closure, Cranial Sutures, Premature
See Craniosynostosis
Closure, Fistula, Vesicouterine
See Fistula, Vesicouterine, Closure
Closure, Meningocele, Spinal
See Meningocele Repair
Closure of Esophagostomy
See Esophagostomy, Closure
Closure of Gastrostomy
See Gastrostomy, Closure
Closure, Vagina
See Vagina, Closure
Clot, 34001-34490, 35875, 35876, 50230
Clot Lysis Time, 85175
Clot Retraction, 85170
Clotting Disorder
See Coagulopathy
Clotting Factor, 85210-85293
Clotting Inhibitors, 85300-85305, 85307
Clotting Operation
Excision, Nail Fold, 11765
Clotting Test
Protein C, 85303, 85307
Protein S, 85306
Clotting Time
See Coagulation
Cloverleaf Skull
Suture of, 61558
Clubfoot Cast, 29450
Wedging, 29750
CMG (Cystometrogram), 51725-51729
CMRI (Cardiac Magnetic Resonance Imaging)
With Contrast, 75561-75563
Without Contrast, 75557-75559
for Morphology and Function, 75557-75563
Velocity Flow Mapping, 75565

CMV (Cytomegalovirus)
Antibody, 86644, 86645
Antigen Detection
Enzyme Immunoassay, 87332
Nucleic Acid, 87495-87497
CNP, 94662
CNPB (Continuous Negative Pressure Breathing), 94662
CO₂
See Carbon Dioxide
Coagulation
Factor I, 85384, 85385
Factor II, 85210
Factor III, 85730, 85732
Factor IV, 82310
Factor IX, 85250
Factor V, 85220
Factor VII, 85230
Factor VIII, 85244, 85247
Factor X, 85260
Factor XI, 85270
Factor XII, 85280
Factor XIII, 85290, 85291
Fibrinolysis, 85396-85397
Time, 85345-85348
Unlisted Services and Procedures, 85999
Coagulation Defect, 85390
Assay, 85130
Coagulation Factor
Factor I, 85384-85385
Factor II, 85210
Factor III, 85347, 85705, 85730-85732
Factor IV, 82310, 82330-82331
Factor IX, 85250
Factor VII, 85230
Factor VIII, 85210-85293
Factor X, 85260
Factor Xa, 85260
Factor XI, 85270
Factor XII, 85280
Factor XIII, 85290-85291
Coagulation Time, 85345-85348
Coagulin
See Thromboplastin
Coagulopathy, 85390
Assay, 85130
Cocaine
Blood or Urine, 82520
Screen, 82486
Coccidioides
Antibody, 86635
Coccidioidin Test
Streptokinase, Antibody, 86590
Coccidioidomycosis
Skin Test, 86490
Coccygeal Spine Fracture
See Coccyx, Fracture
Coccygectomy, 15920, 15922, 27080
Coccyx
Excision, 27080
Fracture
Closed Treatment, 27200
Open Treatment, 27202
Pressure Ulcer, 15920, 15922
Tumor
Excision, 49215
X-ray, 72220
Cochlear Device
Insertion, 69930
Programming, 92601-92604
Codeine
Alkaloid Screening, 82101
Codeine Screen, 82486
Co–Factor I, Heparin
See Antithrombin III
Cofactor Protein S
See Protein S
Coffey Operation
Uterus, Repair, Suspension, 58400
with Presacral Sympathectomy, 58410
Cognitive Function Tests, 96116, 96125
See Neurology, Diagnostic

Cognitive Skills Development, 97532
See Physical Medicine/Therapy/Occupational Therapy
COHB, 82375-82376
Cold Agglutinin, 86156, 86157
Cold Pack Treatment, 97010
Cold Preservation
See Cryopreservation
Cold Therapies
See Cryotherapy
Colectomy
Miles', 44155
Partial, 44140
with
Anastomosis, 44140
Laparoscopic, 44204, 44207, 44208
Coloproctostomy, 44145, 44146
Colostomy, 44141-44144
Laparoscopic, 44206, 44208
Ileocolostomy
Laparoscopic, 44205
Ileostomy, 44144
Ileum Removal, 44160
Transcanal Approach, 44147
Total
Laparoscopic
with
Proctectomy and Ileostomy, 44211, 44212
without
Proctectomy, 44210
Open
with
Anastomosis, 44799
Ileal Reservoir, 44799
Ileostomy, 44150, 44151
Proctectomy, 44155, 44156, 45121
Collagen Cross Links, 82523
Collagen Injection, 11950-11954
Collar Bone
Craterization, 23180
Cyst
Excision, 23140
with
Allograft, 23146
Autograft, 23145
Diaphysectomy, 23180
Dislocation
with Manipulation, 23540
Acromioclavicular Joint
Closed Treatment, 23540, 23545
Open Treatment, 23550, 23552
Sternoclavicular Joint
Closed Treatment, 23520, 23525
Open Treatment, 23530, 23532
Excision
Partial, 23120, 23180
Total, 23125
Fracture
Closed Treatment
with Manipulation, 23505
without Manipulation, 23500
Open Treatment, 23515
Osteotomy, 23480, 23485
Pinning, Wiring, Etc., 23490
Prophylactic Treatment, 23490
Repair Osteotomy, 23480, 23485
Saucerization, 23180
Sequestrectomy, 23170
Tumor
Excision, 23140
with Allograft, 23146
with Autograft, 23145
Radical Resection, 23200
X-ray, 73000
Collateral Ligament
Ankle
Repair, 27695-27698

INDEX

Collateral Ligament — *continued*
  Interphalangeal Joint, 26545
  Knee Joint
    Repair, 27409
  Knee Repair, 27405
  Metacarpophalangeal Joint Repair, 26540-26542
  Repair
    Ankle, 27695-27698
Collection and Processing
  Allogenic Blood
    Harvesting of Stem Cells, 38205
  Autologous Blood
    Harvesting of Stem Cells, 38206
    Intraoperative, 86891
    Preoperative, 86890
  Specimen
    Capillary Blood, 36416
    Venous Blood, 36415, 36591-36592
  Washings
    Esophagus, 91000
    Stomach, 91055
Colles Fracture, 25600-25609
Colles Fracture Reversed
  See Smith Fracture
Collins Syndrome, Treacher
  See Treacher-Collins Syndrome
Collis Procedure, 43326
Colon
  See Colon-Sigmoid
  Biopsy, 44025, 44100, 44322
    by Colonoscopy, 45378
    Endoscopy, 44389, 45380, 45391-45392
  Colostomy, 44320, 44322
    Revision, 44340-44346
  Colotomy, 44322
    Colostomy, 44320
  CT Scan
    Colonography, 74261-74263
    Virtual Colonoscopy, 74261-74263
  Destruction
    Lesion, 44393, 45383
    Tumor, 44393, 45383
  Endoscopy
    Biopsy, 44389, 45380, 45391-45392
    Destruction
      Lesion, 44393
      Tumor, 44393, 45383
    Dilation, 45386
    Exploration, 44388, 45378, 45381, 45386
    Hemorrhage, 44391, 45382
    Injection
      Submucosal, 45381
    Placement
      Stent, 45387
    Removal
      Foreign Body, 44390, 45379
      Polyp, 44392, 45384, 45385
      Tumor, 45384, 45385
    Specimen Collection, 45380
  Excision
    Partial, 44140-44147, 44160
      Laparoscopic, 44204-44208
    Total, 44150-44156
      Laparoscopic, 44210-44212
  Exclusion, 44700
  Exploration, 44025
    Endoscopic, 44388, 45378, 45381, 45386
  Hemorrhage
    Endoscopic Control, 44391, 45382
  Hernia, 44050
  Incision
    Creation
      Stoma, 44320, 44322
      Exploration, 44025
    Revision
      Stoma, 44340-44346
  Lavage
    Intraoperative, 44701

Colon — *continued*
  Lesion
    Destruction, 45383
    Excision, 44110, 44111
  Lysis
    Adhesions, 44005
  Obstruction, 44025, 44050
  Reconstruction
    Bladder from, 50810
  Removal
    Foreign Body, 44025, 44390, 45379
    Polyp, 44392
  Repair
    Diverticula, 44605
    Fistula, 44650-44661
    Hernia, 44050
    Malrotation, 44055
    Obstruction, 44050
    Ulcer, 44605
    Volvulus, 44050
    Wound, 44605
  Stoma Closure, 44620, 44625
  Suture
    Diverticula, 44605
    Fistula, 44650-44661
    Plication, 44680
    Stoma, 44620, 44625
    Ulcer, 44605
    Wound, 44605
  Tumor
    Ablation, 45339
    Destruction, 45383
  Ultrasound
    Endoscopic, 45391-45392
    via Colotomy, 45355
    via Stoma, 44388-44397
  Unlisted Services and Procedures, 44799
  X-ray with Contrast
    Barium Enema, 74270, 74280
Colonna Procedure, 27120
  Acetabulum, Reconstruction, 27120
    with Resection, Femoral Head, 27122
Colonography
  CT Scan, 74261-74263
Colonoscopy
  Biopsy, 45380
    Collection of Specimen, 45380
    via Colotomy, 45355
  Destruction
    Lesion, 45383
    Tumor, 45383
  Dilation, 45386
  Hemorrhage Control, 45382
  Injection, Submucosal, 45381
  Placement
    Stent, 45387
  Removal
    Foreign Body, 45379
    Polyp, 45384, 45385
  Ultrasound, 45391-45392
    Tumor, 45384, 45385
  via Stoma, 44388-44390
    Biopsy, 44393
    Destruction
      of Lesion, 44393
      of Tumor, 44393
    Exploration, 44388
    Hemorrhage, 44391
    Placement
      Stent, 44397
    Removal
      Foreign Body, 44390
      Polyp, 44392, 44394
      Tumor, 44392, 44394
  Virtual, 74261-74263
Colon-Sigmoid
  See Colon
  Biopsy
    Endoscopy, 45331
  Endoscopy
    Ablation
      Polyp, 45339
      Tumor, 45339

Colon-Sigmoid — *continued*
  Endoscopy — *continued*
    Biopsy, 45331
    Dilation, 45340
    Exploration, 45330, 45335
    Hemorrhage, 45334
    Needle Biopsy, 45342
    Placement
      Stent, 45327, 45345
    Removal
      Foreign Body, 45332
      Polyp, 45333, 45338
      Tumor, 45333, 45338
    Ultrasound, 45341, 45342
    Volvulus, 45337
  Exploration
    Endoscopy, 45330, 45335
  Hemorrhage
    Endoscopy, 45334
  Needle Biopsy
    Endoscopy, 45342
  Removal
    Foreign Body, 45332
  Repair
    Volvulus
      Endoscopy, 45337
  Ultrasound
    Endoscopy, 45341, 45342
Colorrhaphy, 44604
Color Vision Examination, 92283
Colostomy, 44320, 45563
  Abdominal
    Establishment, 50810
  Delayed Opening, 44799
  Home Visit, 99505
  Intestine, Large
    with Suture, 44605
  Perineal
    Establishment, 50810
  Revision, 44340
    Paracolostomy Hernia, 44345, 44346
Colotomy, 44025
Colpectomy
  with Hysterectomy, 58275
    with Repair of Enterocele, 58280
  Partial, 57106
  Total, 57110
Colpoceliocentesis
  See Colpocentesis
Colpocentesis, 57020
Colpocleisis, 57120
Colpocleisis Complete
  See Vagina, Closure
Colpohysterectomies
  See Excision, Uterus, Vaginal
Colpoperineorrhaphy, 57210
Colpopexy, 57280
  Extra-peritoneal, 57282
  Intraperitoneal, 57283
  Laparoscopic, 57425
Colpoplasty
  See Repair, Vagina
Colporrhaphy
  Anterior, 57240, 57289
    with Insertion of Mesh, 57267
    with Insertion of Prosthesis, 57267
  Anteroposterior, 57260, 57265
    with Enterocele Repair, 57265
    with Insertion of Mesh, 57267
    with Insertion of Prosthesis, 57267
  Manchester, 58400
  Nonobstetrical, 57200
  Posterior, 57250
Colposcopy
  Biopsy, 56821, 57421, 57454-57455, 57460
    Endometrial, 58110
  Cervix, 57421, 57452-57461
  Exploration, 57452
  Loop Electrode Biopsy, 57460
  Loop Electrode Conization, 57461
  Perineum, 99170
  Vagina, 57420-57421

Colposcopy — *continued*
  Vulva, 56820
    Biopsy, 56821
Colpotomy
  Drainage
    Abscess, 57010
  Exploration, 57000
Colpo-Urethrocystopexy, 58152, 58267, 58293
  Marshall-Marchetti-Krantz procedure, 58152, 58267, 58293
  Pereyra Procedure, 58267, 58293
Colprosterone
  See Progesterone
Columna Vertebralis
  See Spine
Column Chromatography/Mass Spectrometry, 82541-82544
Combined Heart-Lung Transplantation
  See Transplantation, Heart-Lung
Combined Right and Left Heart Cardiac Catheterization
  See Cardiac Catheterization, Combined Left and Right Heart
Combined Vaccine, 90710
Comedones
  Opening or Removal of (Incision and Drainage)
    Acne Surgery, 10040
Commando-Type Procedure, 41155
Commissurotomy
  Right Ventricular, 33476, 33478
Common Sensory Nerve
  Repair, Suture, 64834
Common Truncus
  See Truncus, Arteriosus
Communication Device
  Non-speech-generating, 92605-92606
  Speech-generating, 92607-92609
Community/Work Reintegration
  See Physical Medicine/Therapy/Occupational Therapy
  Training, 97537
Compatibility Test
  Blood, 86920
  Electronic, 86923
Complement
  Antigen, 86160
  Fixation Test, 86171
  Functional Activity, 86161
  Hemolytic
    Total, 86162
  Total, 86162
Complete Blood Count, 85025-85027
Complete Colectomy
  See Colectomy, Total
Complete Pneumonectomy
  See Pneumonectomy, Completion
Complete Transposition of Great Vessels
  See Transposition, Great Arteries
Complex, Factor IX
  See Christmas Factor
Complex, Vitamin B
  See B Complex Vitamins
Component Removal, Blood
  See Apheresis
Composite Graft, 15760, 15770
  Vein, 35681-35683
    Autogenous
      Three or More Segments
        Two Locations, 35683
      Two Segments
        Two Locations, 35682
Compound B
  See Corticosterone
Compound F
  See Cortisol
Compression, Nerve, Median
  See Carpal Tunnel Syndrome
Computed Tomographic Scintigraphy
  See Emission Computerized Tomography

Computed Tomography (CT Scan)

Computed Tomography (CT Scan)
  with Contrast
    Abdomen, 74160, 74175
    Arm, 73201, 73206
    Brain, 70460
    Cardiac Structure and Morphology, 75572-75573
    Chest, 71275
    Ear, 70481
    Face, 70487
    Head, 70460, 70496
    Heart, 75572-75574
    Leg, 73701, 73706
    Maxilla, 70487
    Neck, 70491, 70498
    Orbit, 70481
    Pelvis, 72191, 72193
    Sella Turcica, 70481
    Spine
      Cervical, 72126
      Lumbar, 72132
      Thoracic, 72129
    Thorax, 71260
  without Contrast
    Abdomen, 74150
    Arm, 73200
    Brain, 70450
    Ear, 70480
    Face, 70486
    Head, 70450
    Heart, 75571
    Leg, 73700
    Maxilla, 70486
    Neck, 70490
    Orbit, 70480
    Pelvis, 72192
    Sella Turcica, 70480
    Spine, Cervical, 72125
    Spine, Lumbar, 72131
    Spine, Thoracic, 72128
    Thorax, 71250
  without Contrast, followed by Contrast
    Abdomen, 74170
    Arm, 73202
    Brain, 70470
    Ear, 70482
    Face, 70488
    Leg, 73702
    Maxilla, 70488
    Neck, 70492
    Orbit, 70482
    Pelvis, 72194
    Sella Turcica, 70482
    Spine
      Cervical, 72127
      Lumbar, 72133
      Thoracic, 72130
    Thorax, 71270
  Bone
    Density Study, 77078-77083
  Colon
    Colonography, 74261-74263
      Diagnostic, 74261-74262
      Screening, 74263
    Virtual Colonoscopy, 74261-74263
  Drainage, 75898
  Follow-up Study, 76380
  Guidance
    3D Rendering, 76376-76377
    Cyst Aspiration, 77012
    Localization, 77011
    Needle Biopsy, 77012
    Radiation Therapy, 77014
  Heart, 75571-75574
Computer-aided Detection
  Chest Radiograph, 0174T-0175T
  Mammography
    Diagnostic, 77051
    Screening, 77052
Computer Assisted Navigation
Computer-Assisted Navigation, 0054T-0055T, 20985
  Orthopedic Surgery, 20985
Computer-Assisted Surgical Navigation
  with Image Guidance
    Imageless, 20985
      Image Guidance
        Intraoperative, 20985
Computer-Assisted Testing
  Neuropsychological, 96120
  Psychological, 96103
Computer Data Analysis, 99090
Computerized Emission Tomography
  See Emission Computerized Tomography
COMVAX, 90748
Concentration, Hydrogen-Ion
  See pH
Concentration, Minimum Inhibitory
  See Minimum Inhibitory Concentration
Concentration of Specimen, 87015
Concentration Test for Renal Function
  Water Load Test, 89235
Concentric Procedure, 28296
Concha Bullosa Resection
  with Nasal/Sinus Endoscopy, 31240
Conchae Nasale
  See Nasal Turbinate
Conduction, Nerve
  See Nerve Conduction
Conduit, Ileal
  See Ileal Conduit
Condyle
  Humerus
    Fracture
      Closed Treatment, 24576, 24577
      Open Treatment, 24579
      Percutaneous, 24582
  Metatarsal
    Excision, 28288
  Phalanges
    Toe
      Excision, 28126
Condylectomy
  with Skull Base Surgery, 61596, 61597
  Temporomandibular Joint, 21050
Condyle, Mandibular
  See Mandibular Condyle
Condyloma
  Destruction
    Anal, 46900-46924
    Penis, 54050-54065
    Vagina, 57061, 57065
    Vulva, 56501, 56515
Conference
  Medical
    with Interdisciplinary Team, 99366-99368
Confirmation
  Drug, 80102
Congenital Arteriovenous Malformation
  See Arteriovenous Malformation
Congenital Elevation of Scapula
  See Sprengal's Deformity
Congenital Heart Septum Defect
  See Septal Defect
Congenital Kidney Abnormality
  Nephrolithotomy, 50070
  Pyeloplasty, 50405
  Pyelotomy, 50135
Congenital Laryngocele
  See Laryngocele
Congenital Vascular Anomaly
  See Vascular Malformation
Conisation
  See Cervix, Conization
Conization
  Cervix, 57461, 57520, 57522
Conjoint Psychotherapy, 90847
Conjunctiva
  Biopsy, 68100
  Cyst
    Incision and Drainage, 68020

Conjunctiva — *continued*
  Fistulize for Drainage
    with Tube, 68750
    without Tube, 68745
  Insertion Stent, 68750
  Lesion
    Destruction, 68135
    Excision, 68110-68130
      with Adjacent Sclera, 68130
      over 1 cm, 68115
    Reconstruction, 68320-68335
      with Flap
        Bridge or Partial, 68360
        Total, 68362
      Symblepharon
        with Graft, 68335
        without Graft, 68330
        Total, 68362
    Repair
      Symblepharon
        with Graft, 68335
        without Graft, 68330
        Division, 68340
      Wound
        Direct Closure, 65270
        Mobilization and Rearrangement, 65272, 65273
    Unlisted Services and Procedure, 68399
Conjunctivoccystorhinostomy
  See Conjunctivorhinostomy
Conjunctivodacryocystostomy
  See Conjunctivorhinostomy
Conjunctivoplasty, 68320-68330
  with Extensive Rearrangement, 68320
  with Graft, 68320
    Buccal Mucous Membrane, 68325
  Reconstruction Cul-de-Sac
    with Extensive Rearrangement, 68326
    with Graft, 68328
      Buccal Mucous Membrane, 68328
Conjunctivorhinostomy
  with Tube, 68750
  without Tube, 68745
Conjunctivo-Tarso-Levator
  Resection, 67908
Conjunctivo-Tarso-Muller Resection, 67908
Conscious Sedation
  See Sedation
Construction
  Finger
    Toe to Hand Transfer, 26551-26556
  IMRT Device, 77332-77334
  Multi-leaf Collimator (MLC) Device, 77338
  Neobladder, 51596
  Vagina
    with Graft, 57292
    without Graft, 57291
Consultation
  See Second Opinion; Third Opinion
  Clinical Pathology, 80500, 80502
  Initial Inpatient
    New or Established Patient, 99251-99255
  Office and/or Other Outpatient
    New or Established Patient, 99241-99245
  Pathology
    During Surgery, 88333-88334
  Psychiatric, with Family, 90887
  Radiation Therapy
    Radiation Physics, 77336, 77370
    Surgical Pathology, 88321-88325
      Intraoperation, 88329-88332
    X-ray, 76140
Consumption Test, Antiglobulin
  See Coombs Test
Contact Lens Services
  Fitting and Prescription, 92070, 92310-92313

Contact Lens Services — *continued*
  Modification, 92325
  Prescription, 92314-92317
  Replacement, 92326
Continuous Epidural Analgesia, 01967-01969
Continuous Glucose Monitoring System (CGMS), 95250-95251
Continuous Negative Pressure Breathing (CNPB), 94662
Continuous Positive Airway Pressure (CPAP), 94660
  Intermittent Positive Pressure Breathing, 94660
Contouring
  Silicone Injections, 11950-11954
  Tumor
    Facial Bone, 21029
Contraception
  Cervical Cap
    Fitting, 57170
  Diaphragm
    Fitting, 57170
  Intrauterine Device (IUD)
    Insertion, 58300
    Removal, 58301
Contraceptive Capsules, Implantable
  Insertion, 11975
  Removal, 11976
  with Reinsertion, 11977
Contraceptive Device, Intrauterine
  See Intrauterine Device (IUD)
Contracture
  Elbow
    Release with Radical Resection of Capsule, 24149
  Palm
    Release, 26121-26125
  Thumb
    Release, 26508
Contracture of Palmar Fascia
  See Dupuytren's Contracture
Contralateral Ligament
  Repair, Knee, 27405
Contrast Aortogram
  See Aortography
Contrast Bath Therapy, 97034
  See Physical Medicine/Therapy/Occupational Therapy
Contrast Material
  Injection
    Central Venous Access Device, 36598
    Gastrostomy, Duodenostomy, Jejunostomy, Gastro-jejunostomy, or Cecostomy Tube, Percutaneous, 49465
    via Peritoneal Catheter, 49424
  Instillation
    Bronchography, 31656, 31715
Contrast Phlebogram
  See Venography
Contusion
  See Hematoma
Converting Enzyme, Angiotensin
  See Angiotensin Converting Enzyme (ACE)
Coombs Test, 86880
Copper, 82525
Coprobilinogen
  Feces, 84577
Coproporphyrin, 84120
Coracoacromial Ligament Release, 23415
Coracoid Process Transfer, 23462
Cordectomy, 31300
Cordocentesis, 59012
Cordotomy, 63194-63199
Cord, Spermatic
  See Spermatic Cord
Cord, Spinal
  See Spinal Cord
Cord, Vocal
  See Vocal Cords
Corectomy, 66500, 66505
Coreoplasty, 66762

Index

Cornea
  Biopsy, 65410
  Curettage, 65435, 65436
    with Chelating Agent, 65436
  Epithelium
    Excision, 65435, 65436
      with Chelating Agent, 65436
  Lesion
    Destruction, 65450
    Excision, 65400
      with Graft, 65426
      without Graft, 65420
  Pachymetry, 76514
  Prosthesis, 65770
  Pterygium
    with Graft, 65426
    Excision, 65420
  Puncture, 65600
  Relaxing Incisions, 65772, 65775
  Repair
    with Glue, 65286
    Astigmatism, 65772, 65775
    Wedge Resection, 65775
    Wound
      Nonperforating, 65275
      Perforating, 65280, 65285
    Tissue Glue, 65286
  Reshape
    Epikeratoplasty, 65765
    Keratomileusis, 65760
    Keratoprosthesis, 65767
  Scraping
    Smear, 65430
  Tattoo, 65600
  Thickness Measurement, 76514
  Transplantation
    Autograft or Homograft
      Lamellar, 65710
      Penetrating, 65730-65755
    for Aphakia, 65750
Coronary
  Atherectomy, Percutaneous, 92995, 92996
  Thrombectomy
    Percutaneous, 92973
Coronary Angioplasty, Transluminal Balloon
  See Percutaneous Transluminal Angioplasty
Coronary Arteriography
  Anesthesia, 01920
Coronary Artery
  Insertion
    Stent, 92980, 92981
  Ligation, 33502
  Placement
    Radiation Delivery Device, 92974
  Repair, 33500-33507
Coronary Artery Bypass Graft (CABG), 33503-33505, 33510-33516
  Arterial, 33533-33536
  Arterial-Venous, 33517-33523
  Harvest
    Upper Extremity Artery, 35600
  Reoperation, 33530
  Venous, 33510-33516
Coronary Endarterectomy, 33572
Coroner's Exam, 88045
Coronoidectomy
  Temporomandibular Joint, 21070
Corpectomy, 63101-63103
Corpora Cavernosa
  Corpus Spongiosum Shunt, 54430
  Glans Penis Fistulization, 54435
  Injection, 54235
  Irrigation
    Priapism, 54220
  Saphenous Vein Shunt, 54420
  X-ray with Contrast, 74445
Corpora Cavernosa, Plastic Induraton
  See Peyronie Disease
Corpora Cavernosography, 74445
Corpus Callosum
  Transection, 61541
Corpus Uteri, 58100-58285

Corpus Vertebrae (Vertebrale)
  See Vertebral Body
Correction of Cleft Palate
  See Cleft Palate, Repair
Correction of Lid Retraction
  See Repair, Eyelid, Retraction
Correction of Malrotation of Duodenum
  See Ladd Procedure
Correction of Syndactyly, 26560-26562
Correction of Ureteropelvic Junction
  See Pyeloplasty
Cortex Decortication, Cerebral
  See Decortication
Cortical Mapping
  Transection by Electric Stimulation, 95961, 95962
Corticoids
  See Corticosteroids
Corticoliberin
  See Corticotropic Releasing Hormone (CRH)
Corticosteroid Binding Globulin, 84449
Corticosteroid Binding Protein, 84449
Corticosteroids
  Blood, 83491
  Urine, 83491
Corticosterone
  Blood or Urine, 82528
Corticotropic Releasing Hormone (CRH), 80412
Cortisol, 80400-80406, 80418, 80420, 80436, 82530
  Stimulation Panel, 80412
  Total, 82533
Cortisol Binding Globulin, 84449
Costectomy
  See Resection, Ribs
Costen Syndrome
  See Temporomandibular
Costotransversectomy, 21610
COTD (Cardiac Output Thermodilution), 93561-93562
Cothromboplastin
  See Proconvertin
Cotte Operation, 58400, 58410
  Repair, Uterus, Suspension, 58400, 58410
Cotting Operation
  Excision, Nail Fold, 11765
Cotton (Bohler) Procedure, 28405
Cotton Scoop Procedure, 28118
Counseling
  See Preventive Medicine
  Smoking and Tobacco Use Cessation, 99406-99407
Counseling and /or Risk Factor Reduction Intervention – Preventive Medicine, Individual Counseling
  Behavior Change Interventions, 99406-99409
  Preventive Medicine, 99411-99412, 99420
Counseling, Preventive
  Group, 99411, 99412
  Individual, 99401-99404
  Other, 99420, 99429
Count, Blood Cell
  See Blood Cell Count
Count, Blood Platelet
  See Blood, Platelet, Count
Count, Cell
  See Cell Count
Count,Complete Blood
  See Complete Blood Count (CBC)
Counterimmunoelectrophoresis, 86185
Counters, Cell
  See Cell Count
Countershock, Electric
  See Cardioversion
Count, Erythrocyte
  See Red Blood Cell (RBC), Count

Count, Leukocyte
  See White Blood Cell, Count
Count, Reticulocyte
  See Reticulocyte, Count
Coventry Tibial Wedge Osteotomy
  See Osteotomy, Tibia
Cowper's Gland
  Excision, 53250
Coxa
  See Hip
Coxiella Brunetii
  Antibody, 86638
Coxsackie
  Antibody, 86658
CPAP (Continuous Positive Airway Pressure), 94660
CPB, 32852, 32854, 33496, 33503-33505, 33510-33523, 33533-33536
C-Peptide, 80432, 84681
CPK
  Isoenzymes, 82252
  Isoforms, 82554
  MB Fraction Only, 82553
  Total, 82550
CPR (Cardiopulmonary Resuscitation), 92950
CR, 82565-82575
Cranial Bone
  Halo
    for Thin Skull Osteology, 20664
  Reconstruction
    Extracranial, 21181-21184
  Tumor
    Excision, 61563, 61564
Cranial Halo, 20661
Cranial Nerve
  Avulsion, 64732-64760, 64771
  Decompression, 61458, 64716
  Implantation
    Electrode, 64553, 64573
  Incision, 64732-64752, 64760, 65771
  Injection
    Anesthetic, 64400-64408, 64412
    Neurolytic, 64600-64610
  Insertion
    Electrode, 64553, 64573
  Neuroplasty, 64716
  Release, 64716
  Repair
    Suture, with or without Graft, 64864, 64865
  Section, 61460
  Transection, 64732-64760, 64771
  Transposition, 64716
Cranial Nerve II
  See Optic Nerve
Cranial Nerve V
  See Trigeminal Nerve
Cranial Nerve VII
  See Facial Nerve
Cranial Nerve X
  See Vagus Nerve
Cranial Nerve XI
  See Accessory Nerve
Cranial Nerve XII
  See Hypoglossal Nerve
Cranial Tongs
  Application
    Removal, 20660
  Removal, 20665
Craniectomy
  See Craniotomy
  Excision
    for Osteomyelitis, 61501
    of Lesion or Tumor, 61500
  Exploratory, 61304, 61305
  Extensive, for Craniosynostosis, 61558, 61559
  for
    Abscess, Drainage
      Infratentorial, 61321
      Supratentorial, 61320
    Decompression of
      Medulla, 61343

Craniotomy

Craniectomy — continued
  for — continued
    Decompression of — continued
      Orbit Only, 61330
      Spinal Column, 61343
    Electrode Placement, 61860-61875
    Foreign Body, 61570
    Hematoma Evacuation, 61312-61315
    Penetrating Wound, 61571
    Surgical, 61312-61315, 61320-61323, 61440-61480, 61500-61522
Craniofacial and Maxillofacial
  Unlisted Services and Procedures, 21299
Craniofacial Procedures
  Unlisted Services and Procedures, 21299
Craniofacial Separation
  Closed Treatment, 21431
  Open Treatment, 21432-21436
  Wire Fixation, 21431
Craniomegalic Skull
  Reduction, 62115-62117
Craniopharyngioma
  Excision, 61545
Cranioplasty, 62120
  with Autograft, 62146, 62147
  with Bone Graft, 61316, 62146, 62147
  Encephalocele Repair, 62120
  for Defect, 62140, 62141, 62145
Craniostenosis
  See Craniosynostosis
Craniosynostosis
  Bifrontal Craniotomy, 61557
  Extensive Craniectomy, 61558, 61559
Craniotomy
  with Bone Flap, 61510-61516, 61526, 61530, 61533-61545
  for Bone Lesion, 61500
  with Cingulotomy, 61490
  Barrel-Stave Procedure, 61559
  Bifrontal Bone Flap, 61557
  Cloverleaf Skull, 61558
  Decompression, 61322-61323
  Excision Brain Tumor
    Benign of Cranial Bone, 61563
      with Optic Nerve Decompression, 61564
    Cerebellopontine Angle Tumor, 61520
    Cyst, Supratentorial, 61516
    Infratentorial or posterior fossa, 61518
    Meningioma, 61519
    Midline at Skull Base, 61521
    Supratentorial, 61510
  Excision Epileptogenic Focus
    with Electrocorticography, 61536
    without Electrocorticography, 61534
  Foreign Body, 61570
  Pituitary Tumor, 61546, 61548
  Exploratory, 61304, 61305
  Orbit with Biopsy, 61332
  Removal
    Frontal Bone, 61334
    Lesion, 61333
  for Abscess Drainage
    Infratentorial, 61321
    Supratentorial, 61320
  for Craniosynostosis, 61556-61557
  for Decompression
    Orbit Only, 61330
    Other, Supratentorial, 61340
    Posterior Fossa, 61345
  Foreign Body, 61570
  for Encephalocele, 62121
  Frontal Bone Flap, 61556
  Hematoma, 61312-61315
  Implantation Electrodes, 61531, 61533

Craniotomy

Craniotomy — *continued*
  Implantation Electrodes — *continued*
    Stereotactic, 61760
  Lobectomy
    with Electrocorticography, 61538
  Medullary Tractotomy, 61470
  Meningioma, 61519
  Mesencephalic Tractotomy or Pedunculotomy, 61480
  Multiple Osteotomies and Bone Autografts, 61559
  Neurostimulators, 61850-61875
  Osteomyelitis, 61501
  Parietal Bone Flap, 61556
  Penetrating Wound, 61571
  Recontouring, 61559
  Removal of Electrode Array, 61535
  Suboccipital
    with Cervical Laminectomy, 61343
    for Cranial Nerves, 61458
    Subtemporal, 61450
  Surgery, 61312-61323, 61440, 61490, 61546, 61570-61571, 61582-61583, 61590, 61592, 61760, 62120
  Tentorium Cerebelli, 61440
  Transoral Approach, 61575
    requiring Splitting Tongue and/or Mandible, 61576

Cranium
  See Skull

Craterization
  Calcaneus, 28120
  Clavicle, 23180
  Femur, 27070, 27071, 27360
  Fibula, 27360, 27641
  Hip, 27070, 27071
  Humerus, 23184, 24140
  Ileum, 27070, 27071
  Metacarpal, 26230
  Metatarsal, 28122
  Olecranon Process, 24147
  Phalanges
    Finger, 26235, 26236
    Toe, 28124
  Pubis, 27070, 27071
  Radius, 24145, 25151
  Scapula, 23182
  Talus, 28120
  Tarsal, 28122
  Tibia, 27360, 27640
  Ulna, 24147, 25150

C-Reactive Protein, 86140, 86141

Creatine, 82553, 82554
  Blood or Urine, 82540

Creatine Kinase (Total), 82550

Creatine Phosphokinase
  Blood, 82552
  Total, 82550

Creatinine
  Blood, 82565
  Clearance, 82575
  Other Source, 82570
  Urine, 82570, 82575

Creation
  Arteriovenous
    Fistula/Autogenous Graft, 36825
  Colonic Reservoir, 45119
  Complete Heart Block, 93650
  Cutaneoperitoneal Fistula, 49999
  Defect, 40720
  Ileal Reservoir, 44799, 45113
  Lesion, 61790, 63600
    Gasserian Ganglion, 61790
    Spinal Cord, 63600
    Trigeminal Tract, 61791
  Mucofistula, 44144
  Pericardial Window, 32659
  Recipient Site, 15002-15003, 15004-15005
  Shunt
    Cerebrospinal Fluid, 62200
    Subarachnoid
      Lumbar-Peritoneal, 63740

Creation — *continued*
  Shunt — *continued*
    Subarachnoid-Subdural, 62190
    Ventriculo, 62220
  Sigmoid Bladder, 50810
  Speech Prosthesis, 31611
  Stoma
    Bladder, 51980
    Kidney, 50395
    Renal Pelvis, 50395
    Tympanic Membrane, 69433, 69436
    Ureter, 50860
  Ventral Hernia, 39503

CRF, 80412

CRH (Corticotropic Releasing Hormone), 80412

Cricoid Cartilage Split, 31587

Cricothyroid Membrane
  Incision, 31605

Cristobalite
  See Silica

CRIT, 85013

Critical Care Services, 99291
  Evaluation and Management, 99291-99292, 99468-99476
  Gastric Intubation, 91105
  Interfacility Transport, 99466-99467
  Ipecac Administration for Poison, 99175
  Neonatal
    Initial, 99468
    Subsequent, 99469
  Pediatric
    Initial, 99471, 99475
    Interfacility Transport, 99466-99467
    Subsequent, 99472, 99476
  Remote Interactive Videoconferenced, 0188T-0189T

Cross Finger Flap, 15574

Crossmatch, 86920-86922

Crossmatching, Tissue
  See Tissue Typing

CRP, 86140

Cruciate Ligament
  Arthroscopic Repair, 29888, 29889
  Repair, 27407, 27409
    Knee with Collateral Ligament, 27409

Cryoablation
  See Cryosurgery

Cryofibrinogen, 82585

Cryofixation
  Cells, 38207-38209, 88240-88241
  Embryo, 89258
  for Transplantation, 32850, 33930, 33940, 44132, 47133, 47140, 48550, 50300-50320, 50547
  Freezing and Storage, 38207, 88240
  Oocyte, 89240
  Ovarian Tissue, 89240
  Sperm, 89259
  Testes, 89335
  Thawing
    Embryo, 89352
    Oocytes, 89353
    Reproductive Tissue, 89354
    Sperm, 89356

Cryoglobulin, 82595

Cryopreservation
  Cells, 38207-38208, 88240-88241
  Embryo, 89258
  Freezing and Storage, 38207, 88240
  Oocyte, 89240
  Ovarian Tissue, 89240
  Sperm, 89259
  Testes, 89335
    Embryo, 89352
    Oocytes, 89353
    Reproductive Tissue, 89354
    Sperm, 89356

Cryosurgery, 17000-17286, 47371, 47381
  See Destruction
  Cervix, 57511

Cryosurgery — *continued*
  Labyrinthotomy, 69801
  Lesion
    Anus, 46916, 46924
    Mouth, 40820
    Penis, 54056, 54065
    Skin
      Benign, 17000-17004
      Malignant, 17260-17286
      Pre Malignant, 17000-17004
    Vagina, 57061-57065
    Vulva, 56501-56515
    Warts, flat, 17110, 17111

Cryotherapy
  Acne, 17340
  Destruction
    Ciliary body, 66720
  Lesion
    Cornea, 65450
    Retina, 67208, 67227
  Renal Tumor, 50593
  Retinal Detachment
    Prophylaxis, 67141
    Repair, 67101, 67113
  Retinopathy, 67229
  Trichiasis
    Correction, 67825

Cryptococcus
  Antibody, 86641
  Antigen Detection
    Enzyme Immunoassay, 87327

Cryptococcus Neoformans
  Antigen Detection
    Enzyme Immunoassay, 87327

Cryptorchism
  See Testis, Undescended

Cryptosporidium
  Antigen Detection
    Direct Fluorescent Antibody, 87272
    Enzyme Immunoassay, 87328

Crystal Identification
  Any Body Fluid, 89060

CS, 99143-99150

C-Section, 59510-59515, 59618-59622
  See also Cesarean Delivery

CSF, 86325, 89050, 89051

CST, 59020

CT Angiography
  Heart, 75571-75574

CTS, 29848, 64721

CT Scan
  with Contrast
    Abdomen, 74160, 74175
    Arm, 73201, 73206
    Brain, 70460, 70496
    Chest, 71275
    Ear, 70481
    Face, 70487
    Head, 70460, 70496
    Leg, 73701, 73706
    Maxilla, 70487
    Neck, 70491
    Orbit, 70481
    Pelvis, 72191, 72193
    Sella Turcica, 70481
    Spine
      Cervical, 72126
      Lumbar, 72132
      Thoracic, 72129
    Thorax, 71260
  without Contrast
    Abdomen, 74150
    Arm, 73200
    Brain, 70450
    Ear, 70480
    Face, 70486
    Head, 70450
    Leg, 73700
    Maxilla, 70486
    Neck, 70490
    Orbit, 70480
    Pelvis, 72192
    Sella Turcica, 70480
    Spine
      Cervical, 72125

CT Scan — *continued*
  without Contrast — *continued*
    Spine — *continued*
      Lumbar, 72131
      Thoracic, 72128
    Thorax, 71250
  without Contrast, followed by Contrast
    Abdomen, 74170
    Arm, 73202, 73220, 73223
    Brain, 70470
    Ear, 70482
    Face, 70488
    Head, 70470
    Leg, 73702
    Maxilla, 70488
    Neck, 70492
    Orbit, 70482
    Pelvis, 72194
    Sella Turcica, 70482
    Spine
      Cervical, 72127
      Lumbar, 72133
      Thoracic, 72130
    Thorax, 71270
  3D Rendering, 76376-76377
  Bone
    Density Study, 77078-77083
  Colon
    Diagnostic, 74261-74262
    Screening, 74263
  Drainage, 75989
  Follow-up Study, 76380
  Guidance
    Localization, 77011
    Needle Biopsy, 77012
    Radiation Therapy, 77014
    Tissue Ablation, 77013
    Vertebroplasty, 72292

CT Scan, Radionuclide
  See Emission Computerized Tomography

Cuff, Rotator
  See Rotator Cuff

Culdocentesis, 57020

Culdoplasty
  McCall, 57283

Culdoscopy, 57452

Culdotomy, 57000

Culture
  Acid Fast Bacilli, 87116
  Amniotic Fluid
    Chromosome Analysis, 88235
  Bacteria
    Additional Methods, 87077
    Aerobic, 87040-87070
    Anaerobic, 87073-87076
    Blood, 87040
    Feces, 87045, 87046
    Other, 87070-87073
    Screening, 87081
    Urine, 87086, 87088
  Bone Marrow
    Chromosome Analysis, 88237
  Chlamydia, 87110
  Chorionic Villus
    Chromosome Analysis, 88235
  Fertilized Oocyte
    for In Vitro Fertilization, 89250
    with Co-Culture of Embryo, 89251
    Assisted Microtechnique, 89280, 89281
  Fungus
    Blood, 87103
    Hair, 87101
    Identification, 87106
    Nail, 87101
    Other, 87102
    Skin, 87101
  Lymphocyte
    Chromosome Analysis, 88230
  Mold, 87107
  Mycobacteria, 87116-87118
  Mycoplasma, 87109

Culture — *continued*
- Oocyte/Embryo
  - Extended Culture, 89272
  - for In Vitro Fertilization, 89250
    - with Co–Culture of Embryo, 89251
- Pathogen
  - by Kit, 87084
- Skin
  - Chromosome Analysis, 88233
- Tissue
  - Toxin
    - Antitoxin, 87230
  - Toxin Virus, 87252, 87253
- Tubercle Bacilli, 87116
- Typing, 87140-87158
  - Culture, 87140-87158
- Unlisted Services and Procedures, 87999
- Yeast, 87106

Curettage
- *See* Dilation and Curettage
- Cervix
  - Endocervical, 57454, 57456, 57505
- Cornea, 65435, 65436
  - Chelating Agent, 65436
- Hydatidiform Mole, 59870
- Postpartum, 59160

Curettage and Dilatation
- *See* Dilation and Curettage

Curettage, Uterus
- *See* Uterus, Curettage

Curettement
- Skin Lesion, 11055-11057, 17004, 17110, 17270, 17280

Curietherapy
- *See* Brachytherapy

Custodial Care
- *See* Domiciliary Services; Nursing Facility Services

Cutaneolipectomy
- *See* Lipectomy

Cutaneous Electrostimulation, Analgesic
- *See* Application, Neurostimulation

Cutaneous Tag
- *See* Skin, Tags

Cutaneous Tissue
- *See* Integumentary System

Cutaneous–Vesicostomy
- *See* Vesicostomy, Cutaneous

CVAD (Central Venous Access Device)
- Insertion
  - Central, 36555-36558
  - Peripheral, 36568-36569
- Removal, 36589
- Repair, 36575
- Replacement, 36580-36585
- Repositioning, 36597

CVS, 59015

CXR, 71010-71035, 71090

Cyanide
- Blood, 82600
- Tissue, 82600

Cyanocobalamin, 82607, 82608

Cyclic AMP, 82030

Cyclic Citrullinated Peptide (CCP), Antibody, 86200

Cyclic GMP, 83008

Cyclic Somatostatin
- *See* Somatostatin

Cyclocryotherapy
- *See* Cryotherapy, Destruction, Ciliary Body

Cyclodialysis
- Destruction
  - Ciliary Body, 66740

Cyclophotocoagulation
- Destruction
  - Ciliary Body, 66710, 66711

Cyclosporine
- Assay, 80158

Cyst
- Abdomen
  - Destruction, 49203-49205

Cyst — *continued*
- Abdomen — *continued*
  - Excision, 49203-49205
- Ankle
  - Capsule, 27630
  - Tendon Sheath, 27630
- Bartholin's Gland
  - Excision, 56740
  - Repair, 56440
- Bile Duct
  - Excision, 47715
- Bladder
  - Excision, 51500
- Bone
  - Drainage, 20615
  - Injection, 20615
- Brain
  - Drainage, 61150, 61151, 61156, 62161, 62162
  - Excision, 61516, 61524, 62162
- Branchial Cleft
  - Excision, 42810, 42815
- Breast
  - Incision and Drainage, 19020
  - Puncture Aspiration, 19000, 19001
- Calcaneus, 28100-28103
- Carpal, 25130-25136
- Choledochal
  - Excision, 47715
- Ciliary Body
  - Destruction, 66770
- Clavicle
  - Excision, 23140-23146
- Conjunctiva, 68020
- Dermoid
  - Nose
    - Excision, 30124, 30125
- Drainage
  - Contrast Injection, 49424
    - with X-ray, 76080
- Excision
  - Cheekbone, 21030
  - Clavicle, 23140
    - with Allograft, 23146
    - with Autograft, 23145
  - Femur, 27355, 27357, 27358
  - Ganglion
    - *See* Ganglion
  - Humerus
    - with Allograft, 23156
    - with Autograft, 23155
  - Hydatid
    - *See* Echinococcosis
  - Lymphatic
    - *See* Lymphocele
  - Maxilla, 21030
  - Mediastinum, 32662
  - Olecranon Process
    - with Allograft, 24126
    - with Autograft, 24125
  - Pericardial, 32661
  - Pilonidal, 11770-11772
  - Radius
    - with Allograft, 24126
    - with Autograft, 24125
  - Scapula, 23140
    - with Allograft, 23146
    - with Autograft, 23145
  - Ulna
    - with Allograft, 24126
    - with Autograft, 24125
  - Zygoma, 21030
- Facial Bones
  - Excision, 21030
- Femur
  - Excision, 27065-27067, 27355-27358
- Fibula, 27635-27638
- Ganglion
  - Aspiration/Injection, 20612
- Gums
  - Incision and Drainage, 41800
- Hip, 27065-27067
- Humerus
  - Excision, 23150-23156, 24110

Cyst — *continued*
- Humerus — *continued*
  - Excision — *continued*
    - with Allograft, 24116
    - with Autograft, 24115
- Ileum, 27065-27067
- Incision and Drainage, 10060, 10061
  - Pilonidal, 10080, 10081
  - Puncture Aspiration, 10160
- Iris
  - Destruction, 66770
- Kidney
  - Ablation, 50541
  - Aspiration, 50390
  - Excision, 50280, 50290
  - Injection, 50390
  - X-ray, 74470
- Knee
  - Baker's, 27345
  - Excision, 27347
- Leg, Lower
  - Capsule, 27630
  - Tendon Sheath, 27630
- Liver
  - Incision and Drainage
    - Open, 47010
    - Percutaneous, 47011
  - Repair, 47300
- Lung
  - Incision and Drainage, 32200
  - Removal, 32140
- Lymph Node
  - Axillary
    - Cervical
      - Excision, 38550, 38555
- Mandible
  - Excision, 21040, 21046, 21047
- Mediastinal
  - Excision, 39200
- Metacarpal, 26200, 26205
- Metatarsal, 28104-28107
- Mouth, 41005-41009, 41015-41018
  - Incision and Drainage, 40800, 40801
- Mullerian Duct
  - Excision, 55680
- Nose
  - Excision, 30124, 30125
- Olecranon, 24120
- Opening or Removal of (Incision and Drainage)
  - Acne Surgery, 10040
- Ovarian
  - Excision, 58925
  - Incision and Drainage, 58800, 58805
- Pancreas, 48500
  - Anastomosis, 48520, 48540
  - Excision, 48120
- Pelvis
  - Aspiration, 50390
  - Injection, 50390
- Pericardial
  - Excision, 33050
- Phalanges
  - Finger, 26210, 26215
  - Toe, 28108
- Pilonidal
  - Excision, 11770-11772
  - Incision and Drainage, 10080, 10081
- Pubis, 27065-27067
- Radius
  - Excision, 24120, 25120-25126
- Rathke's Pouch
  - *See* Craniopharyngioma
- Removal
  - Skin, 10040
- Retroperitoneum
  - Destruction, 49203-49205
  - Excision, 49203-49205
- Salivary Gland
  - Drainage, 42409
  - Excision, 42408
- Scapula
  - Excision, 23140-23146

Cyst — *continued*
- Seminal Vesicles
  - Excision, 55680
- Skin
  - Puncture Aspiration, 10160
- Spinal Cord
  - Aspiration, 62268
  - Incision and Drainage, 63172, 63173
- Sublingual Gland
  - Drainage, 42409
  - Excision, 42408
- Talus, 28100-28103
- Tarsal, 28104-28107
- Thyroglossal Duct
  - Excision, 60280, 60281
  - Incision and Drainage, 60000
- Thyroid Gland
  - Aspiration, 60300
  - Excision, 60200
  - Injection, 60300
- Tibia
  - Excision, 27635-27638
- Tongue
  - Incision and Drainage, 41000-41006, 41015
- Ulna, 24120, 25120-25126
- Urachal
  - Bladder
    - Excision, 51500
- Vaginal
  - Excision, 57135
- Wrist, 25130-25136
  - Excision, 25111, 25112
- Zygoma
  - Excision, 21030

Cystatin C, 82610

Cystatins, Kininogen
- *See* Kininogen

Cystectomy
- Complete, 51570
  - with Bilateral Pelvic Lymphadenectomy, 51575, 51585, 51595
  - with Continent Diversion, 51596
  - with Ureteroileal Conduit, 51590
  - with Ureterosigmoidostomy, 51580
- Ovarian
  - Laparoscopic, 58661
  - Open, 58925
- Partial, 51550
  - Complicated, 51555
  - Reimplantation of Ureters, 51565
  - Simple, 51550

Cystic Hygroma
- *See* Hygroma

Cystine
- Urine, 82615

Cystitis
- Interstitial, 52260, 52265

Cystography, 74430
- Injection, 52281
- Radiologic, 51600

Cystolithotomy, 51050

Cystometrogram, 51725-51729

Cystoplasty, 51800

Cystorrhaphy, 51860, 51865

Cystoscopy, 52000

Cystoscopy, with Biopsy
- *See* Biopsy, Bladder, Cystourethroscopy

Cystostomy
- with Fulguration, 51020
- with Insertion
  - Radioactive Material, 51020
- with Urethrectomy
  - Female, 53210
  - Male, 53215
- Change Tube, 51705, 51710
- Closure, 51880
- Home Visit, 99505

Cystotomy
- with Calculus Basket Extraction, 51065
- with Destruction Intravesical Lesion, 51030

Cystotomy · Index

Cystotomy — *continued*
  with Drainage, 51040
  with Fulguration, 51020
  with Insertion
    Radioactive Material, 51020
    Urethral Catheter, 51045
  with Removal Calculus, 51050, 51065
  Excision
    Bladder Diverticulum, 51525
    Bladder Tumor, 51530
    Diverticulum, 51525
    Repair of Ureterocele, 51535
    Vesical Neck, 51520
  Repair Ureterocele, 51535
Cystourethrogram, Retrograde, 51610
Cystourethropexy, 51840-51841
Cystourethroplasty, 51800, 51820
Cystourethroscopy, 52000, 52351, 52601, 52647, 52648, 53500
  with Direct Vision Internal Urethrotomy, 52276
  with Ejaculatory Duct Catheterization, 52010
  with Fulguration, 52214, 52354
    Lesion, 52224
    Tumor, 52234-52240
  with Internal Urethrotomy
    Female, 52270
    Male, 52275
  with Steroid Injection, 52283
  with Urethral Catheterization, 52005
  with Urethral Meatotomy, 52290, 52300, 52305
  Biopsy, 52204, 52354
    Brush, 52007
  Calibration and/or Dilation Urethral Stricture or Stenosis, 52281
  Catheterization
    Ejaculatory Duct, 52010
    Ureteral, 52005
  Destruction
    Lesion, 52400
  Dilation
    Bladder, 52260, 52265
    Intra–Renal Stricture, 52343, 52346
    Ureter, 52341, 52342, 52344, 52345
    Urethra, 52281
  Evacuation
    Clot, 52001
  Female Urethral Syndrome, 52285
  Incision
    Ejaculatory Duct, 52402
  Injection of Implant Material, 52327
  Insertion
    Indwelling Urethral Stent, 50947, 52332
    Radioactive Substance, 52250
    Ureteral Guide Wire, 52334
    Urethral Stent, 52282
  Lithotripsy, 52353
  Manipulation of Ureteral Calculus, 52330
  Meatotomy
    Urethral, 52290-52305
  Removal
    Calculus, 52310, 52315, 52320, 52325, 52352
    Foreign Body, 52310, 52315
    Urethral Stent, 52310, 52315
  Resection
    Ejaculatory Duct, 52402
    External Sphincter, 52277
    Tumor, 52355
  Urethral Syndrome, 52285
  Vasectomy
    Transurethral, 52402
  Vasotomy
    Transurethral, 52402
Cyst, Ovary
  See Ovary, Cyst
Cytochrome, Reductase, Lactic
  See Lactic Dehydrogenase

Cytogenetic Study
  Molecular DNA Probe, 88271-88275, 88291, 88365
  Unlisted Services and Procedures, 88299
Cytomegalovirus
  Antibody, 86644, 86645
  Antigen Detection
    Direct Fluorescence, 87271
    Enzyme Immunoassay, 87332
    Nucleic Acid, 87495-87497
Cytometries, Flow
  See Flow Cytometry
Cytopathology
  Cervical or Vaginal
    Requiring Interpretation by Physician, 88141
    Thin Layer Prep, 88142-88143, 88174-88175
  Concentration Technique, 88108
  Evaluation, 88172
  Fluids, Washings, Brushings, 88104-88108
  Forensic, 88125
  Other Source, 88160-88162
  Smears
    Cervical or Vaginal, 88141-88155, 88164-88167, 88174-88175
    Other Source, 88160-88162
  Unlisted Services and Procedures, 88199
Cytoscopy
  See Bladder, Endoscopy
Cytosol Aminopeptidase, 83670
Cytotoxic Screen
  Lymphocyte, 86805, 86806
  Percent Reactive Antibody (PRA), 86807, 86808
  Serum Antibodies, 86807, 86808

D

D2, Vitamin
  See Calciferol
Dacrocystogram
  See Dacrocystography
Dacryoadenectomy
  Partial, 68505
  Total, 68500
Dacryocystectomy, 68520
Dacryocystography, 68850, 70170
  with Nuclear Imaging, 78660
Dacryocystorhinostomy, 68720
  Total
    with Nasal
      Sinus Endoscopy, 31239
Dacryocystostomy, 68420
Daily Living Activities
  See Activities of Daily Living
D&C Yellow No. 7
  See Fluorescein
Damus–Kaye–Stansel Procedure, 33606
Dana Operation, 63185, 63190
  Rhizotomy, 63185, 63190
D and C (Dilation and Curettage), 59840
D and E (Dilation and Evacuation), 59841-59851
Dandy Operation, 62200
DAPTACEL, 90700
Dark Adaptation Examination, 92284
Dark Field Examination, 87164, 87166
Darkroom Test, 92140
Darrach Procedure, 25240
  See Excision, Ulna, Partial
David Procedure, 33864
Day Test, 82270
DCP, 83951
DCR, 31239, 68720
DDST, 96101-96103
Death, Brain
  See Brain Death
Debridement
  Brain, 62010
  Burns, 16020-16030

Debridement — *continued*
  Burns — *continued*
    Anesthesia, 01951-01953
  Mastoid Cavity
    Complex, 69222
    Simple, 69220
  Metatarsophalangeal Joint, 28289
  Muscle
    Infected, 11004-11006
  Nails, 11720, 11721
  Necrotizing Soft Tissue, 11004-11008
  Nose
    Endoscopic, 31237
  Pancreatic Tissue, 48105
  Skin, 11040-11041
    with Open Fracture and/or Dislocation, 11010-11012
    Eczematous, 11000, 11001
    Full Thickness, 11041
    Infected, 11000, 11001
    Partial Thickness, 11040
    Subcutaneous Tissue, 11042-11044
    Infected, 11004-11006
  Sternum, 21627
  Wound
    Non–Selective, 97602
    Selective, 97597-97598
Debulking Procedure
  Ovary
    Pelvis, 58952-58954
Decapsulation
  of Kidney, 53899
DECAVAC, 90714
Declotting
  Vascular Access Device, 36593
Decompression
  with Nasal
    Sinus Endoscopy
      Optic Nerve, 31294
      Orbit Wall, 31292, 31293
  Arm, Lower, 24495, 25020-25025
  Auditory Canal, Internal, 69960
  Brainstem, 61575, 61576
  Buttocks, 27057
  Carpal Tunnel, 64721
  Cauda Equina, 63011, 63017, 63047, 63048, 63056, 63057, 63087-63091
  Cranial Nerves, 61458
  Esophagogastric Varices, 37181
  Facial Nerve, 61590
    Intratemporal
      Lateral to Geniculate Ganglion, 69720, 69740
      Medial to Geniculate Ganglion, 69725, 69745
    Total, 69955
  Finger, 26035
  Gasserian Ganglion
    Sensory Root, 61450
  Gill Type procedure, 63012
  Hand, 26035, 26037
  Intestines
    Small, 44021
  Jejunostomy
    Laparoscopic, 44186
  Leg
    Fasciotomy, 27600-27602
    Nerve, 64702-64727
    Root, 63020-63048, 63055-63103
  Nucleus of Disc
    Lumbar, 62287
  Optic Nerve, 67570
  Orbit, 61330
    Removal of Bone, 67414, 67445
  Pelvis, 27057
  Posterior Tibial Nerve, 28035
  Skull, 61322-61323, 61340-61345
  Spinal Cord, 63001-63017, 63045-63103
    Anterolateral Approach, 63075-63091
    Posterior Approach, 63001-63048
      Cauda Equina, 63001-63017

Decompression — *continued*
  Spinal Cord — *continued*
    Posterior Approach — *continued*
      Cervical, 63001, 63015, 63020, 63035, 63045, 63048
      Gill Type Procedure, 63012
      Lumbar, 63005, 63017, 63030, 63042, 63047, 63048
      Sacral, 63011
      Thoracic, 63003, 63016, 63046, 63048
    Transpedicular or Costovertebral Approach, 63055-63066
  Tarsal Tunnel Release, 28035
  Volvulus, 45321, 45337
  Wrist, 25020-25025
Decortication
  Lung, 32220, 32225, 32320, 32651-32652
    with Parietal Pleurectomy, 32320
    Endoscopic, 32651, 32652
    Partial, 32225
    Total, 32220
Decubiti
  See Pressure Ulcer (Decubitus)
Decubitus Ulcers
  See Debridement; Pressure Ulcer (Decubitus); Skin Graft and Flap
Deetjeen's Body
  See Blood, Platelet
Defect, Coagulation
  See Coagulopathy
Defect, Heart Septal
  See Septal Defect
Defect, Septal Closure, Atrial
  See Heart, Repair, Atrial Septum
Deferens, Ductus
  See Vas Deferens
Defibrillation
  See Cardioversion
Defibrillator, Heart
  See Pacemaker, Heart
  Evaluation, 93283, 93287, 93289, 93292, 93295-93296, 93640-93642
  Insertion, 33240
  Interrogation, 93289, 93295-93296
  Pacemaker or Cardioverter Defibrillator
    Electrodes, 33216, 33217, 33224-33225
    Pulse Generator, 33240
    Removal, 33243, 33244
      Pulse Generator Only, 33241
    Programming, 93282-93284, 93287
    Repair
      Leads, Dual Chamber, 33220
      Leads, Single Chamber, 33218
    Repositioning
      Electrodes, 33215, 33226
    Revise Pocket Chest, 33223
    Wearable Device, 93292, 93745
Deformity, Boutonniere
  See Boutonniere Deformity
Deformity, Sprengel's
  See Sprengel's Deformity
Degenerative, Articular Cartilage, Patella
  See Chondromalacia Patella
Degradation Products, Fibrin
  See Fibrin Degradation Products
Dehiscence
  Suture
    Abdominal Wall, 49900
    Skin and Subcutaneous Tissue
      Complex, 13160
      Complicated, 13160
      Extensive, 13160
    Skin and Subcutaneous Tissue
      Simple, 12020
      with Packing, 12021

Index

Dehiscence — continued
Suture — continued
Skin and Subcutaneous Tissue — continued
Superficial, 12020
with Packing, 12021
Wound
Abdominal Wall, 49900
Skin and Subcutaneous Tissue
Complex, 13160
Complicated, 13160
Extensive, 13160
Skin and Subcutaneous Tissue
Simple, 12020
with Packing, 12021
Superficial, 12020
with Packing, 12021

Dehydroepiandrosterone, 82626
Dehydroepiandrosterone–Sulfate, 82627
Dehydrogenase, 6–Phosphogluconate
See Phosphogluconate-6, Dehydrogenase
Dehydrogenase, Alcohol
See Antidiuretic Hormone
Dehydrogenase, Glucose–6–Phosphate
See Glucose-6-Phosphate, Dehydrogenase
Dehydrogenase, Glutamate
See Glutamate Dehydrogenase
Dehydrogenase, Isocitrate
See Isocitric Dehydrogenase
Dehydrogenase, Lactate
See Lactic Dehydrogenase
Dehydrogenase, Malate
See Malate Dehydrogenase
Dehydroisoandrosterone Sulfate
See Dehydroepiandrosterone Sulfate
Delay of Flap, 15600-15630
Deligation
Ureter, 50940
Deliveries, Abdominal
See Cesarean Delivery
Delivery
See Cesarean Delivery, Vaginal Delivery
Pharmacologic Agent
Suprachoroidal, 0186T
Delorme Operation, 33030
Denervation
Hip
Femoral Nerve, 27035
Obturator Nerve, 27035
Sciatic Nerve, 27035
Denervation, Sympathetic
See Excision, Nerve, Sympathetic
Denis–Browne Splint, 29590
Dens Axis
See Odontoid Process
Denver Developmental Screening Test, 96101-96103
Denver Krupin Procedure, 66180
Denver Shunt
Patency Test, 78291
Deoxycorticosterone, 82633
Deoxycortisol, 80436, 82634
Deoxyephedrine
See Methamphetamine
Deoxyribonuclease
Antibody, 86215
Deoxyribonuclease I
See DNAse
Deoxyribonucleic Acid
Antibody, 86225, 86226
Depilation
See Removal, Hair
Depletion
Plasma, 38214
Platelet, 38213
T–Cell, 38210
Tumor Cell, 38211
Deposit Calcium
See Calcium, Deposits
Depth Electrode
Insertion, 61760

DeQuervain's Disease Treatment, 25000
Dermabrasion, 15780-15783
Derma–Fat–Fascia Graft, 15770
Dermatology
Actinotherapy, 96900
Examination of Hair
Microscopic, 96902
Ultraviolet A Treatment, 96912
Ultraviolet B Treatment, 96910-96913
Ultraviolet Light Treatment, 96900-96913
Unlisted Services and Procedures, 96999
Dermatoplasty
Septal, 30620
Dermoid
See Cyst, Dermoid
Derrick–Burnet Disease
See Q Fever
Descending Abdominal Aorta
See Aorta, Abdominal
Design
Collimator, 77338
IMRT Devices, 77332-77334
Desipramine
Assay, 80160
Desmotomy
See Ligament, Release
Desoxycorticosterone, 82633
Desoxycortone
See Desoxycorticosterone
Desoxyephedrine
See Methamphetamine
Desoxynorephedrin
See Amphetamine
Desoxyphenobarbital
See Primidone
Desquamation
See Exfoliation
Destruction
with Cystourethroscopy, 52354
Acne, 17340, 17360
Cryotherapy, 17340
Arrhythmogenic Focus
Heart, 33250, 33251, 33261
Bladder, 51020, 52214, 52224, 52354
Endoscopic, 52214
Large Tumors, 52240
Medium Tumors, 52235
Minor Lesions, 52224
Small Tumors, 52234
Calculus
Bile Duct, 43265
Kidney, 50590
Pancreatic Duct, 43265
Chemical Cauterization
Granulation Tissue, 17250
Ciliary Body
Cryotherapy, 66720
Cyclodialysis, 66740
Cyclophotocoagulation, 66710, 66711
Diathermy, 66700
Endoscopic, 66711
Condyloma
Anal, 46900-46924
Penis, 54050-54065
Vagina, 57061-57065
Vulva, 56501-56515
Cyst
Abdomen, 49203-49205
Ciliary Body, 66770
Iris, 66770
Retroperitoneal, 49203-49205
Endometrial Ablation, 58356
Endometriomas
Abdomen, 49203-49205
Retroperitoneal, 49203-49205
Fissure
Anal, 46940, 46942
Hemorrhoids, 46930
Kidney, 52354
Endoscopic, 50557, 50576

Destruction — continued
Lesion
Anus, 46900-46917, 46924
Bladder, 51030
Choroid, 0016T, 67220-67225
Ciliary Body, 66770
Colon, 45383
Conjunctiva, 68135
Cornea, 65450
Eyelid, 67850
Facial, 17000-17108, 17280-17286
Gastrointestinal, Upper, 43258
Gums, 41850
Intestines
Large, 44393
Small, 44369
Iris, 66770
Mouth, 40820
Nose
Intranasal, 30117, 30118
Palate, 42160
Penis
Cryosurgery, 54056
Electrodesiccation, 54055
Extensive, 54065
Laser Surgery, 54057
Simple, 54050-54060
Surgical Excision, 54060
Pharynx, 42808
Prostate, 55320
Thermotherapy, 53850-53852
Microwave, 53850
Radio Frequency, 53852
Rectum, 45320
Retina
Cryotherapy, Diathermy, 67208, 67227
Photocoagulation, 0017T, 67210, 67228
Radiation by Implantation of Source, 67218
Skin
Benign, 17000-17250
Malignant, 17260-17286, 96567
Premalignant, 96567
Spinal Cord, 62280-62282
Tumor or Polyp
Rectum, 45320
Ureter, 52341, 52342, 52344, 52345
Urethra, 52400, 53265
Uvula, 42160
Vagina
Extensive, 57065
Simple, 57061
Vascular, Cutaneous, 17106-17108
Vulva
Extensive, 56515
Simple, 56501
Molluscum Contagiosum, 17110, 17111
Muscle Endplate
Extraocular, 67345
Extremity, 64614
Facial, 64612
Neck Muscle, 64613
Trunk, 64614
Nerve, 64600-64681
Laryngeal, Recurrent, 31595
Plantar Common Digital Nerve, 64632
Polyp
Aural, 69540
Nasal, 30110, 30115
Urethra, 53260
Prostate, 55873
Prostate Tissue
Transurethral
Thermotherapy, 53850-53852
Sinus
Frontal, 31080-31085
Skene's Gland, 53270

Destruction — continued
Skin Lesion
Benign, 17000-17004
Fifteen or More Lesions, 17004
Two to Fourteen Lesions, 17003
Malignant, 17260-17286
by Photodynamic Therapy, 96567
Premalignant, 17000-17004
by Photodynamic Therapy, 96567
Fifteen or More Lesions, 17004
Two to Fourteen Lesions, 17003
Skin Tags, 11200, 11201
Tonsil
Lingual, 42870
Tumor
Abdomen, 49203-49205
Bile Duct, 43272
Chemosurgery, 17311-17315
Colon, 45383
Intestines
Large, 44393
Small, 44369
Pancreatic Duct, 43272
Rectum, 45190, 45320
Retroperitoneal, 49203-49205
Urethra, 53220
Tumor or Polyp
Rectum, 45320
Turbinate Mucosa, 30801, 30802
Unlisted Services and Procedures, 17999
Ureter
Endoscopic, 50957, 50976
Urethra, 52214, 52224, 52354
Prolapse, 53275
Warts
Flat, 17110, 17111

Determination, Blood Pressure
See Blood Pressure
Developmental Testing
Evaluation
Extended, 96111
Limited, 96110
Device
Adjustable Gastric Restrictive Device, 43770-43774
Contraceptive, Intrauterine
Insertion, 58300
Removal, 58301
Iliac Artery Occlusion Device
Insertion, 34808
Muti-leaf Collimator Design and Construction, 77338
Venous Access
Collection of Blood Specimen, 36591
Fluoroscopic Guidance, 77001
Insertion
Catheter, 36578
Central, 36560-36566
Imaging, 75901, 75902
Obstruction Clearance, 36595, 36596
Peripheral, 36570, 36571
Removal, 36590
Repair, 36576
Replacement, 36582, 36583, 36585
Ventricular Assist
Extracorporeal Removal, 0050T
Device Handling, 99002
Device, Orthotic
See Orthotics
Dexamethasone
Suppression Test, 80420
D Galactose
See Galactose
D Glucose
See Glucose

Index

DHA Sulfate
See Dehydroepiandrosterone Sulfate
DHEA (Dehydroepiandrosterone), 82626
DHEAS, 82627
DHT (Dihydrotestosterone), 82651
Diagnosis, Psychiatric
See Psychiatric Diagnosis
Diagnostic Amniocentesis
See Amniocentesis
Diagnostic Aspiration of Anterior Chamber of Eye
See Eye, Paracentesis, Anterior Chamber, with Diagnostic Aspiration of Aqueous
Dialysis
Arteriovenous Fistula
Revision
without Thrombectomy, 36832
Arteriovenous Shunt, 36147-36148, 75791
Revision
with Thrombectomy, 36833
End Stage Renal Disease, 90951-90953, 90963, 90967
Hemodialysis, 90935, 90937
Blood Flow Study, 90940
Hemoperfusion, 90997
Patient Training
Completed Course, 90989
Per Session, 90993
Peritoneal, 90945, 90947
Unlisted Procedures, 90999
Dialysis, Extracorporeal
See Hemodialysis
DI–Amphetamine
See Amphetamine
Diaphragm
Anesthesia, 00540
Hernia Repair, 00756
Repair
for Eventration, 39545
Hernia, 39502-39541
Laceration, 39501
Resection, 39560, 39561
Unlisted Procedures, 39599
Vagina
Fitting, 57170
Diaphragm Contraception, 57170
Diaphysectomy
Calcaneus, 28120
Clavicle, 23180
Femur, 27360
Fibula, 27360, 27641
Humerus, 23184, 24140
Metacarpal, 26230
Metatarsal, 28122
Olecranon Process, 24147
Phalanges
Finger, 26235, 26236
Toe, 28124
Radius, 24145, 25151
Scapula, 23182
Talus, 28120
Tarsal, 28122
Tibia, 27360, 27640
Ulna, 24147, 25150
Diastase
See Amylase
Diastasis
See Separation
Diathermy, 97024
See Physical Medicine/ Therapy/Occupational
Destruction
Ciliary Body, 66700
Lesion
Retina, 67208, 67227
Retinal Detachment
Prophylaxis, 67141
Repair, 67101
Diathermy, Surgical
See Electrocautery
Dibucaine Number, 82638
Dichloride, Methylene
See Dichloromethane

Dichlorides, Ethylene
See Dichloroethane
Dichloroethane, 84600
Dichloromethane, 84600
Diethylamide, Lysergic Acid
See Lysergic Acid Diethylamide
Diethylether, 84600
Differential Count
White Blood Cell Count, 85007, 85009, 85540
Differentiation Reversal Factor
See Prothrombin
Diffusion Test, Gel
See Immunodiffusion
Digestive Tract
See Gastrointestinal Tract
Digit(s)
See also Finger, Toe
Pinch Graft, 15050
Replantation, 20816, 20822
Skin Graft
Split, 15120, 15121
Digital Artery Sympathectomy, 64820
Digital Slit–Beam Radiograph
See Scanogram
Digoxin
Assay, 80162
Blood or Urine, 80162
Dihydrocodeinone, 82646
Dihydrocodeinone Screen, 82486
Dihydrohydroxycodeinone
See Oxycodinone
Dihydromorphinone, 82486, 82649
Dihydrotestosterone, 82651
Dihydroxyethanes
See Ethylene Glycol
Dilatation, Transluminal Arterial
See Angioplasty, Transluminal
Dilation
See Dilation and Curettage
Anal
Endoscopic, 46604
Sphincter, 45905
Bile Duct
Endoscopic, 43271, 47555, 47556
Bladder
Cystourethroscopy, 52260, 52265
Bronchi
Endoscopy, 31630, 31636-31638
Cervix
Canal, 57800
Stump, 57558
Colon
Endoscopy, 45386
Colon–Sigmoid
Endoscopy, 45340
Curettage, 57558
Enterostomy Stoma, 44799
Esophagus, 43450-43458
Endoscopic Balloon, 43249
Endoscopy, 43220-43226, 43249
Surgical, 43510
Frontonasal Duct, 30999
Intestines, Small
Endoscopy, 44370
Intracranial Vasospasm, 61640-61642
Kidney, 50395
Intra–Renal Stricture, 52343, 52346
Lacrimal Punctum, 68801
Larynx
Endoscopy, 31528, 31529
Pancreatic Duct
Endoscopy, 43271
Rectum
Endoscopy, 45303
Sphincter, 45910
Salivary Duct, 42650, 42660
Schlemm's Canal, 0176T-0177T
Trachea
Endoscopic, 31630, 31631, 31636-31638
Ureter, 50395, 52341, 52342, 52344, 52345

Dilation — continued
Ureter — continued
Endoscopic, 50553, 50572, 50953, 50972
Urethra, 52260, 52265
General, 53665
Suppository and/or Instillation, 53660, 53661
Urethral
Stenosis, 52281
Stricture, 52281, 53600-53621
Vagina, 57400
Dilation and Curettage
See Curettage; Dilation
Cervical Stump, 57558
Cervix, 57558, 57800
Corpus Uteri, 58120
Hysteroscopy, 58558
Induced Abortion, 59840
with Amniotic Injections, 59851
with Vaginal Suppositories, 59856
Postpartum, 59160
Dilation and Evacuation, 59841
with Amniotic Injections, 59851
Dimethadione, 82654
Dioxide, Carbon
See Carbon Dioxide
Dioxide Silicon
See Silica
Dipeptidyl Peptidase A
See Angiotensin Converting Enzyme (ACE)
Diphenylhydantoin
See Phenytoin
Diphosphate, Adenosine
See Adenosine Diphosphate
Diphtheria
Antibody, 86648
Immunization, 90698, 90700-90702, 90714-90715, 90718-90723
Dipropylacetic Acid
Assay, 80164
Direct Pedicle Flap
Formation, 15570-15576
Disability Evaluation Services
Basic Life and/or Disability Evaluation, 99450
Work–Related or Medical Disability Evaluation, 99455, 99456
Disarticulation
Ankle, 27889
Elbow, 20999
Hip, 27295
Knee, 27598
Shoulder, 23920, 23921
Wrist, 25920, 25924
Revision, 25922
Disarticulation of Shoulder
See Shoulder, Disarticulation
Disc Chemolyses, Intervertebral
See Chemonucleolysis
Discectomies
See Discectomy
Discectomies, Percutaneous
See Discectomy, Percutaneous
Discectomy
Anterior with Decompression
Cervical Interspace, 63075
Each Additional, 63076
Thoracic Interspace, 63077
Each Additional, 63078
Arthrodesis
Additional Interspace, 22534, 22585
Lumbar, 22533, 22558, 22630
Thoracic, 22532, 22556
Vertebra
Cervical, 22554
Cervical, 22220
Lumbar, 22224, 22630
Thoracic, 22222
Additional Segment, 22226
Discharge, Body Substance
See Drainage

Discharge Instructions
Heart Failure, 4014F
Discharge Services
See Hospital Services
Hospital, 99238, 99239
Nursing Facility, 99315, 99316
Observation Care, 99234-99236
Disc, Intervertebral
See Intervertebral Disc
Discission
Cataract
Laser Surgery, 66821
Stab Incision, 66820
Vitreous Strands, 67030
Discography
Cervical Disc, 72285
Injection, 62290, 62291
Lumbar Disc, 72295
Thoracic, 72285
Discolysis
See Chemonucleolysis
Disease
Durand–Nicolas–Favre
See Lymphogranuloma Venereum
Erb–Goldflam
See Myasthenia Gravis
Heine–Medin
See Polio
Hydatid
See Echinococcosis
Lyme
See Lyme Disease
Ormond
See Retroperitoneal Fibrosis
Peyronie
See Peyronie Disease
Posada–Wernicke
See Coccidioidomycosis
Disease/Organ Panel
See Organ/Disease Panel
Diskectomy
See Discectomy
Dislocated Elbow
See Dislocation, Elbow
Dislocated Hip
See Dislocation, Hip Joint
Dislocated Jaw
See Dislocation, Temporomandibular Joint
Dislocated Joint
See Dislocation
Dislocated Shoulder
See Dislocation, Shoulder
Dislocation
Acromioclavicular Joint
Open Treatment, 23550, 23552
Ankle Joint
Closed Treatment, 27840, 27842
Open Treatment, 27846, 27848
Carpal, 25690
Closed Treatment, 25690
Open Treatment, 25695
Carpometacarpal Joint
Closed Treatment, 26641, 26645, 26670
with Anesthesia, 26675
Open Treatment, 26665, 26685, 26686
Percutaneous Fixation, 26676
Clavicle
with Manipulation, 23545
without Manipulation, 23540
Closed Treatment, 23540, 23545
Open Treatment, 23550, 23552
Elbow
with Manipulation, 24620, 24640
Closed Treatment, 24600, 24605, 24640
Open Treatment, 24586, 24615
Hip Joint
without Trauma, 27265, 27266
Closed Treatment, 27250, 27252, 27265, 27266
Congenital, 27256-27259
Open Treatment, 27253, 27254, 27258, 27259

Index

Dislocation — continued
Interphalangeal Joint
  Finger(s)/Hand
    Closed Treatment, 26770, 26775
    Open Treatment, 26785
    Percutaneous Fixation, 26776
  Toe(s)/Foot, 28660-28675
    Closed Treatment, 28660, 28665
    Open Treatment, 28675
    Percutaneous Fixation, 28666
Knee
  Closed Treatment, 27550, 27552
  Open Treatment, 27556-27558, 27566, 27730
  Recurrent, 27420-27424
Lunate, 25690-25695
  with Manipulation, 25690, 26670-26676, 26700-26706
  Closed Treatment, 25690
  Open Treatment, 25695
Metacarpophalangeal Joint
  Closed Treatment, 26700-26706
  Open Treatment, 26715
Metatarsophalangeal Joint
  Closed Treatment, 28630, 28635
  Open Treatment, 28645
  Percutaneous Fixation, 28636
Patella
  Closed Treatment, 27560, 27562
  Open Treatment, 27566
  Recurrent, 27420-27424
Pelvic Ring
  Closed Treatment, 27193, 27194
  Open Treatment, 27217, 27218
  Percutaneous Fixation, 27216
Percutaneous Fixation
  Metacarpophalangeal, 26705
Peroneal Tendons, 27675, 27676
Radiocarpal Joint, 25660
Radioulnar Joint
  Closed Treatment, 25675
    with Radial Fracture, 25520
  Open Treatment, 25676
    with Radial Fracture, 25525, 25526
Radius
  with Fracture, 24620, 24635
    Closed Treatment, 24620
    Open Treatment, 24635
  Closed Treatment, 24640
Shoulder
  Closed Treatment
    with Manipulation, 23650, 23655
    with Fracture of Greater Humeral Tuberosity, 23665
  Open Treatment, 23670
    with Surgical or Anatomical Neck Fracture, 23675
  Open Treatment, 25680
  Open Treatment, 23660
  Recurrent, 23450-23466
Sternoclavicular Joint
  Closed Treatment
    with Manipulation, 23525
    without Manipulation, 23520
  Open Treatment, 23530, 23532
Talotarsal Joint
  Closed Treatment, 28570, 28575
  Open Treatment, 28546
  Percutaneous Fixation, 28576
Tarsal
  Closed Treatment, 28540, 28545
  Open Treatment, 28555
  Percutaneous Fixation, 28545, 28546
Tarsometatarsal Joint
  Closed Treatment, 28600, 28605
  Open Treatment, 28615
  Percutaneous Fixation, 28606

Dislocation — continued
Temporomandibular Joint
  Closed Treatment, 21480, 21485
  Open Treatment, 21490
Thumb
  with Fracture, 26645
    Open Treatment, 26665
    Percutaneous Fixation, 26650, 26665
  with Manipulation, 26641-26650
    Closed Treatment, 26641, 26645
    Open Treatment, 26665
    Percutaneous Fixation, 26650
Tibiofibular Joint
  Closed Treatment, 27830, 27831
  Open Treatment, 27832
Vertebrae
  Additional Segment, Any Level
    Open Treatment, 22328
  Cervical
    Open Treatment, 22326
  Closed Treatment
    with Manipulation, Casting and/or Bracing, 22315
    without Manipulation, 22310
  Lumbar
    Open Treatment, 22325
  Thoracic
    Open Treatment, 22327
Wrist
  with Fracture
    Closed Treatment, 25680
    Open Treatment, 25685
  Intercarpal
    Closed Treatment, 25660
    Open Treatment, 25670
  Percutaneous, 25671
  Radiocarpal
    Closed Treatment, 25660
    Open Treatment, 25670
  Radioulnar
    Closed Treatment, 25675
    Open Treatment, 25676
    Percutaneous Fixation, 25671
Dislocation, Radiocarpal Joint
  See Radiocarpal Joint, Dislocation
Disorder
  Blood Coagulation
    See Coagulopathy
  Penis
    See Penis
  Retinal
    See Retina
Displacement Therapy
  Nose, 30210
Dissection
  Hygroma, Cystic
    Axillary, 38550, 38555
    Cervical, 38550, 38555
  Lymph Nodes, 38542
Dissection, Neck, Radical
  See Radical Neck Dissection
Distention
  See Dilation
Diverticulectomy, 44800
  Esophagus, 43130, 43135
Diverticulectomy, Meckel's
  See Meckel's Diverticulum, Excision
Diverticulopexy
  Esophagus, 43499
  Pharynx, 43499
Diverticulum
  Bladder
    See Bladder, Diverticulum
  Meckel's
    Excision, 44800
  Repair
    Urethra, 53400, 53405
Division
  Muscle
    Foot, 28250
  Plantar Fascia
    Foot, 28250
Division, Isthmus, Horseshoe Kidney
  See Symphysiotomy, Horseshoe Kidney

Division, Scalenus Anticus Muscle
See Muscle Division, Scalenus Anticus
DMO
  See Dimethadione
DNA Antibody, 86225, 86226
DNA Endonuclease
  See DNAse
DNA Probe
  See Cytogenetics Studies; Nucleic Acid Probe
DNAse, 86215
DNAse Antibody, 86215
Domiciliary Services
  See Nursing Facility Services
  Assisted Living, 99339-99340
  Care Plan Oversight, 99339-99340
  Discharge Services, 99315, 99316
  Established Patient, 99334-99337
  New Patient, 99324-99328
Donor Procedures
  Backbench Preparation Prior to Transplantation
    Intestine, 44715-44721
    Kidney, 50323-50329
    Liver, 47143-47147
    Pancreas, 48551-48552
  Conjunctival Graft, 68371
  Heart Excision, 33940
  Heart-Lung Excision, 33930
  Liver Segment, 47140-47142
  Stem Cells
    Donor Search, 38204
Dopamine
  See Catecholamines
  Blood, 82383, 82384
  Urine, 82382, 82384
Doppler Echocardiography, 76827, 76828, 93320-93350
  Extracranial, 93875
  Hemodialysis Access, 93990
  Intracardiac, 93662
Doppler Scan
  Arterial Studies, Extremities, 93922-93924
  Fetal
    Middle Cerebral Artery, 76821
    Umbilical Artery, 76820
  Extremities, 93965
  Intracranial Arteries, 93886, 93888
Dor Procedure, 33548
Dorsal Vertebra
  See Vertebra, Thoracic
Dose Plan
  Radiation Therapy, 77300, 77331, 77399
  Brachytherapy, 77326-77328
  Teletherapy, 77305-77321
Dosimetry
  Radiation Therapy, 77300, 77331, 77399
  Brachytherapy, 77326-77328
  Intensity Modulation, 77301
  Teletherapy, 77305-77321
Double-J Stent, 52332
  Cystourethroscopy, 52000, 52601, 52647, 52648
Double-Stranded DNA
  See Deoxyribonucleic Acid
Douglas-Type Procedure, 41510
Doxepin
  Assay, 80166
DPH
  See Phenytoin
DPT, 90701
Drainage
  See Excision; Incision; Incision and Drainage
  Abdomen
    Abdominal Fluid, 49080, 49081
    Paracentesis, 49080, 49081
    Peritoneal, 49020
    Peritoneal Lavage, 49080, 49081
    Peritonitis, Localized, 49020
    Retroperitoneal, 49060
    Subdiaphragmatic, 49040

Drainage — continued
Abdomen — continued
  Subphrenic, 49040
Wall
  Skin and Subcutaneous Tissue, 10060, 10061
    Complicated, 10061
    Multiple, 10061
    Simple, 10060
    Single, 10060
Abscess
  Abdomen, 49040, 49041
    Fluid, 49080, 49081
  Peritoneal
    Open, 49020
    Percutaneous, 49021
  Peritonitis, localized, 49020
  Retroperitoneal
    Open, 49060
    Percutaneous, 49061
  Skin and Subcutaneous Tissue
    Complicated, 10061
    Multiple, 10061
    Simple, 10060
    Single, 10060
  Subdiaphragmatic, 49040
    Open, 49040
    Percutaneous, 49041
  Subphrenic, 49040
Anal
  Incision and Drainage, 46045, 46050
Ankle
  Incision and Drainage, 27603
Appendix
  Incision and Drainage, 44900
    Open, 44900
    Percutaneous, 44901
Arm, Lower, 25028
  Incision and Drainage, 25035
Arm, Upper
  Incision and Drainage, 23930-23935
Auditory Canal, External, 69020
Bartholin's Gland
  Incision and Drainage, 56420
Bladder
  Incision and Drainage, 51080
Brain
  by
    Burrhole, 61150, 61151
    Craniotomy/Craniectomy, 61320, 61321
Breast
  Incision and Drainage, 19020
Carpals
  Incision, Deep, 25035
Clavicle
  Sequestrectomy, 23170
Contrast Injection, 49424
  with X-ray, 75989, 76080
Ear, External
  Complicated, 69005
  Simple, 69000
Elbow
  Incision and Drainage, 23930-23935
Epididymis
  Incision and Drainage, 54700
Eyelid
  Incision and Drainage, 67700
Facial Bone(s)
  Excision, 21026
Finger
  Incision and Drainage, 26010, 26011, 26034
Foot
  Incision, 28005
Ganglion Cyst, 20600-20605
Gums
  Incision and Drainage, 41800
Hand
  Incision and Drainage, 26034
Hematoma
  Brain, 61154-61156

Drainage

Drainage — continued
  Abscess — continued
    Hematoma — continued
      Incision and Drainage, 27603
      Vagina, 57022, 57023
    Hip
      Incision and Drainage, 26990-26992
    Humeral Head, 23174
    Humerus
      Incision and Drainage, 23935
    Kidney
      Incision and Drainage, 50020
      Open, 50020
      Percutaneous, 50021
    Leg, Lower, 27603
      Incision and Drainage, 27603
    Liver
      Incision and Drainage
      Open, 47010
      Percutaneous, 47011
      Injection, 47015
      Repair, 47300
    Localization
      Nuclear Medicine, 78806, 78807
    Lung
      Percutaneous Drainage, 32200, 32201
    Lymph Node, 38300, 38305
    Lymphocele, 49062
    Mandible
      Excision, 21025
    Mouth
      Incision and Drainage, 40800, 40801, 41005-41009, 41015-41018
    Nasal Septum
      Incision and Drainage, 30020
    Neck
      Incision and Drainage, 21501, 21502
    Nose
      Incision and Drainage, 30000, 30020
    Ovary
      Incision and Drainage
        Abdominal Approach, 58822
        Percutaneous, 58823
        Vaginal Approach, 58820
    Palate
      Incision and Drainage, 42000
    Paraurethral Gland
      Incision and Drainage, 53060
    Parotid Gland, 42300, 42305
    Pelvic
      Percutaneous, 58823
    Pelvis, 26990
      Incision and Drainage, 26990-26992, 45000
      Percutaneous, 58823
    Pericolic
      Percutaneous, 58823
    Perineum
      Incision and Drainage, 56405
    Perirenal or Renal
      Open, 50020
      Percutaneous, 50021
    Peritoneum, 49020
      Open, 49020
      Percutaneous, 49021
    Prostate
      Incision and Drainage
        Prostatotomy, 55720, 55725
        Transurethral, 52700
    Radius
      Incision, Deep, 25035
    Rectum
      Incision and Drainage, 45005, 45020, 46040, 46060
    Retroperitoneal
      Open, 49060
      Percutaneous, 49061
    Salivary Gland, 42300-42320

Drainage — continued
  Abscess — continued
    Scapula
      Sequestrectomy, 23172
    Scrotum
      Incision and Drainage, 54700, 55100
    Shoulder
      Incision and Drainage, 23030
    Skene's Gland
      Incision and Drainage, 53060
    Skin
      Incision and Drainage
        Complicated, 10061
        Multiple, 10061
        Simple, 10060
        Single, 10060
      Puncture Aspiration, 10160
    Soft Tissue
      Incision, 20000, 20005
    Subdiaphragmatic
      Incision and Drainage
        Open, 49040
        Percutaneous, 49041
    Sublingual Gland, 42310, 42320
    Submaxillary Gland, 42310, 42320
    Subphrenic, 49040, 49041
    Testis
      Incision and Drainage, 54700
    Thoracostomy, 32551
    Thorax
      Incision and Drainage, 21501, 21502
    Throat
      Incision and Drainage, 42700-42725
    Tongue
      Incision and Drainage, 41000-41006, 41015-41018
    Tonsil
      Incision and Drainage, 42700
    Ulna
      Incision, Deep, 25035
    Urethra
      Incision and Drainage, 53040
    Uvula
      Incision and Drainage, 42000
    Vagina
      Incision and Drainage, 57010
    Vulva
      Incision and Drainage, 56405
    Wrist
      Incision and Drainage, 25028, 25035
    X-ray, 76080
  Amniotic Fluid
    Diagnostic Aspiration, 59000
    Therapeutic Aspiration, 59001
  Aqueous, 0191T-0192T
  Bile Duct
    Transhepatic, 47510
  Brain Fluid, 61070
  Bursa, 20600-20610
  Cerebrospinal Fluid, 61000-61020, 61050, 61070, 62272
  Cervical Fluid, 61050
  Cisternal Fluid, 61050
  Cyst
    Bone, 20615
    Brain, 61150, 61151, 62161, 62162
    Breast, 19000, 19001
    Ganglion, 20612
    Liver, 47010, 47011
      Percutaneous, 47011
    Salivary Gland, 42409
    Sublingual Gland, 42409
  Extraperitoneal Lymphocele
    Laparoscopic, 49323
    Open, 49062
  Eye
    Anterior Chamber
      Paracentesis
        with Diagnostic Aspiration of Aqueous, 65800

Drainage — continued
  Eye — continued
    Anterior Chamber — continued
      Paracentesis — continued
        with Therapeutic Release of Aqueous, 65805
        Removal Blood, 65815
        Removal Vitreous and/or Discission Anterior Hyaloid Membrane, 65810
  Fetal Fluid, 59074
  Ganglion Cyst, 20612
  Hematoma
    Brain, 61154, 61156
    Subungual, 11740
    Vagina, 57022, 57023
  Joint, 20600-20610
  Liver
    Abscess or Cyst, 47010, 47011
    Percutaneous, 47011
  Lymphocele
    Endoscopic, 49323
  Onychia, 10060, 10061
  Orbit, 67405, 67440
  Pancreas
    See Anastomosis, Pancreas to Intestines
    Pseudocyst, 48510, 48511
    Percutaneous, 48511
  Paronychia, 10060, 10061
  Pericardial Sac, 32659
  Pericardium
    See Aspiration, Pericardium
  Pseudocyst
    Gastrointestinal, Upper
      Transmural Endoscopic, 43240
    Pancreas, 48510
      Open, 48510
      Percutaneous, 48511
  Puncture
    Chest, 32421-32422
    Skin, 10040-10180
  Spinal Cord
    Cerebrospinal Fluid, 62272
    Subdural Fluid, 61000, 61001
  Urethra
    Extravasation, 53080, 53085
  Ventricular Fluid, 61020
Drainage Implant, Glaucoma
  See Aqueous Shunt
Dressings
  Burns, 16020-16030
  Change under Anesthesia, 15852
DREZ Procedure, 63170
Drill Hole
  Skull
    Catheter, 61107
    Drain Hematoma, 61108
    Exploration, 61105
    Implant Electrode, 61850
      Twist Drill Hole, 61105
    Surgery, 61105-61108
Drinking Test for Glaucoma
  Glaucoma Provocative Test, 92140
Drug
  See also Drug Assay
  Confirmation, 80102
  Implant Infusion Device, 62360-62362
  Screening, 80100, 80101
  Tissue Preparation, 80103
Drug Assay
  Amikacin, 80150
  Amitriptyline, 80152
  Benzodiazepine, 80154
  Carbamazepine, 80156, 80157
  Cyclosporine, 80158
  Desipramine, 80160
  Digoxin, 80162
  Dipropylacetic Acid, 80164
  Doxepin, 80166
  Ethosuximide, 80168
  Gentamicin, 80170
  Gold, 80172

Drug Assay — continued
  Haloperidol, 80173
  Imipramine, 80174
  Lidocaine, 80176
  Lithium, 80178
  Nortriptyline, 80182
  Phenobarbital, 80184
  Phenytoin, 80185, 80186
  Primidone, 80188
  Procainamide, 80190, 80192
  Quantitative
    Other, 80299
  Quinidine, 80194
  Salicylate, 80196
  Tacrolimus, 80197
  Theophylline, 80198
  Tobramycin, 80200
  Topiramate, 80201
  Vancomycin, 80202
Drug Confirmation, 80102
Drug Delivery Implant
  Insertion, 11981
  Maintenance
    Brain, 95990, 95991
    Epidural, 95990, 95991
    Intra-arterial, 96522
    Intrathecal, 95990, 95991
    Intravenous, 96522
    Intraventricular, 95990, 95991
  Removal, 11982, 11983
    with Reinsertion, 11983
Drug Instillation
  See Instillation, Drugs
Drug Management
  Psychiatric, 90862
Drugs, Anticoagulant
  See Clotting Inhibitors
Drug Screen, 80100, 80101, 82486
DST, 80420
DT, 90702
DTaP, 90700
DTaP–HepB–IPV Immunization, 90723
DTaP with Hib, 90721
DTP, 90701
DTP with Hib, 90720
DT Shots, 90702
Dual X-ray Absorptiometry (DXA)
  See Absorptiometry, Dual Photon
  Appendicular, 77081
  Axial Skeleton, 77080
  Vertebral Fracture, 77082
Duct, Bile
  See Bile Duct
Duct, Hepatic
  See Hepatic Duct
Duct, Nasolacrimal
  See Nasolacrimal Duct
Ductogram, Mammary
  See Galactogram
Duct, Omphalomesenteric
  See Omphalomesenteric Duct
Duct, Pancreatic
  See Pancreatic Duct
Duct, Salivary
  See Salivary Duct
Duct, Stensen's
  See Parotid Duct
Duct, Thoracic
  See Thoracic Duct
Ductus Arteriosus
  Repair, 33820-33824
Ductus Deferens
  See Vas Deferens
Duhamel Procedure, 45120
Dunn Operation, 28725
Duodenectomy
  Near Total, 48153, 48154
  Total, 48150, 48152
Duodenography, 74260
Duodenotomy, 44010
Duodenum
  Biopsy, 44010
  Exclusion, 48547
  Exploration, 44010
  Incision, 44010
  Removal/Foreign Body, 44010

Index — Elbow

Duodenum — *continued*
X-ray, 74260
Duplex Scan
See Vascular Studies
Arterial Studies
Aorta, 93978, 93979
Extracranial, 93880, 93882
Lower Extremity, 93925, 93926
Penile, 93980, 93981
Upper Extremity, 93930, 93931
Visceral, 93975-93979
Hemodialysis Access, 93990
Venous Studies
Extremity, 93970, 93971
Penile, 93980, 93981
Dupuy–Dutemp Operation, 67971
Dupuytren's Contracture, 26040, 26045
Durand–Nicolas–Favre Disease
See Lymphogranuloma Venereum
Dust, Angel
See Phencyclidine
Duvries Operation
See Tenoplasty
D Vitamin
See Vitamin, D
Multileaf Collimator Device (MLC), 77338
Dwyer Procedure, 28300
DXA (Dual Energy X-ray Absorptiometry), 77080-77082
D-Xylose Absorption Test, 84620
Dynamometry
See Osteotomy, Calcaneus
Venous Studies
with Ophthalmoscopy, 92260

E

E1, 82679
E2, 82677
E3, 82677
E Antigens
See Hepatitis Antigen, Be
Ear
Collection of Blood from, 36415, 36416
Drum, 69420, 69421, 69433, 69436, 69450, 69610, 69620
See Tympanic Membrane
External
Abscess
Incision and Drainage
Complicated, 69005
Simple, 69000
Biopsy, 69100
Excision
Partial, 69110
Total, 69120
Hematoma
Incision and Drainage, 69000, 69005
Reconstruction, 69300
Unlisted Services and Procedures, 69399
Inner
CT Scan, 70480-70482
Excision
Labyrinth, 69905, 69910
Exploration
Endolymphatic Sac, 69805, 69806
Incision
Labyrinth, 69801, 69802
Semicircular Canal, 69840
Insertion
Cochlear Device, 69930
Semicircular Canal, 69820
Unlisted Services and Procedures, 69949
Middle
Catheterization, 69405
CT Scan, 70480-70482
Exploration, 69440
Inflation
with Catheterization, 69400

Ear — *continued*
Middle — *continued*
Inflation — *continued*
without Catheterization, 69401
Insertion
Catheter, 69405
Lesion
Excision, 69540
Reconstruction
Tympanoplasty with Antrotomy or Mastoidectomy, 69635-69637
Tympanoplasty with Mastoidectomy, 69641-69646
Tympanoplasty without Mastoidectomy, 69631-69633
Removal
Ventilating Tube, 69424
Repair
Oval Window, 69666
Round Window, 69667
Revision
Stapes, 69662
Tumor
Excision, 69550-69554
Unlisted Services and Procedures, 69799
Outer
CT Scan, 70480-70482
Skin Graft
Delay of Flap, 15630
Full Thickness, 15260, 15261
Pedicle Flap, 15576
Split, 15120, 15121
Tissue Transfer, Adjacent, 14060-14061
Ear Canal
See Auditory Canal
Ear Cartilage
Graft
to Face, 21235
Ear Lobes
Pierce, 69090
Ear, Nose, and Throat
Audiologic Function Tests
Acoustic Reflex, 92568
Acoustic Reflex Decay, 92570
Audiometry
Bekesy, 92560, 92561
Comprehensive, 92557
Conditioning Play, 92582
Evoked Response, 92585, 92586
Groups, 92559
Pure Tone, 92552, 92553
Select Picture, 92583
Speech, 92555, 92556
Brainstem Evoked Response, 92585, 92586
Central Auditory Function, 92620-92621
Ear Protector Evaluation, 92596
Electrocochleography, 92584
Filtered Speech, 92571
Hearing Aid Evaluation, 92590-92595
Lombard Test, 92700
Loudness Balance, 92562
Screening Test, 92551
Sensorineural Acuity, 92575
Short Increment Sensitivity Index (SISI), 92564
Staggered Spondaic Word Test, 92572
Stenger Test, 92565, 92577
Synthetic Sentence Test, 92576
Tone Decay, 92563
Tympanometry, 92567
Ear Protector Attenuation, 92596
See Hearing Aid Services
Ear Wax
See Cerumen
Ebstein Anomaly Repair, 33468
EBV, 86663-86665

E B Virus
See Epstein–Barr Virus
ECCE, 66840-66852, 66940
ECG, 3120F, 93000-93024, 93040-93278
Signal-Averaged, 93278
Transmission, 93012-93014
Wearable, 93224-93278
Echinococcosis, 86171, 93278
ECHO, 76825, 93303-93312, 93314, 93315, 93317-93321, 93350
Echocardiography
Cardiac, 93320-93350
Intracardiac, 93662
Transesophageal, 93318
Transthoracic, 93303-93317
Doppler, 93303-93321, 93350, 93662
Fetal Heart, 76825-76828
Doppler
Complete, 76827
Follow-up or Repeat Study, 76828
for Congenital Anomalies
Transesophageal, 93315-93317
Transthoracic, 93303, 93304
Intracardiac, 93662
M Mode and Real Time, 99306
Stress Test, 93350-93351
with Contrast, 93352
Transesophageal, 93312-93317
for Congenital Anomalies, 93315-93317
Transthoracic, 93303-93317, 93350
for Congenital Anomalies, 93303, 93304
Echoencephalography, 76506
Echography
Abdomen, 76700, 76705
Arm, 76880
Breast, 76645
Cardiac, 93303-93317, 93320, 93321, 93350, 93662
Guidance, 76932
Chest, 76604
Extracranial Arteries, 93880, 93882
Eyes, 76510-76529
Follow-Up, 76970
Head, 76536
Heart
Radiologic Guidance, 76932
Hip
Infant, 76885, 76886
Intracranial Arteries, 93886-93893
Intraoperative, 76998
Kidney
Transplant, 76776
Leg, 76880
Neck, 76536
Pelvis, 76856, 76857
Placement Therapy Fields, 76950
Pregnant Uterus, 76801-76817
Prostate, 76872-76873
Retroperitoneal, 76770, 76775
Scrotum, 76870
Spine, 76880
Transrectal, 76872, 76873
Transvaginal, 76817, 76830
Unlisted Services and Procedures, 76999
Vagina, 76817, 76830
Echotomography
See Echography
ECMO (Extracorporeal Circulation Membrane Oxygenation), 36822
Isolated with Chemotherapy Perfusion, 36823
ECS
See Emission Computerized Tomography
ECSF (Erythrocyte Colony Stimulating Factor)
See Erythropoietin
ECT (Emission Computerized Tomography), 78607

ECT (Electroconvulsive Therapy), 90870
Ectasia
See Dilation
Ectopic Pregnancy
See Obstetrical Care
Abdominal, 59130
Cervix, 59140
Interstitial
Partial Resection Uterus, 59136
Total Hysterectomy, 59135
Laparoscopy, 59150
with Salpingectomy and/or Oophorectomy, 59151
Tubal, 59121
with Salpingectomy and/or Oophorectomy, 59120
Ectropion
Repair
Blepharoplasty
Excision Tarsal Wedge, 67916
Extensive, 67917
Suture, 67914
Thermocauterization, 67915
ED, 99281-99288
Education, 99078
Patient
for Heart Failure, 4003F
Self-management by nonphysician, 98960-98962
Services (Group), 99078
Supplies, 99071
EEG, 95812-95827, 95830, 95950-95953, 95956-95958
See also Electroencephalography
EGD, 43235, 43239, 43241, 43243-43255, 43258, 43259
Egg
See Ova
Eggers Procedure, 27100
Ehrlichia, 86666
EKG, 93000-93010
Signal Averaged, 93278
Transmission, 93012-93014
Wearable, 93224-93272
Elastase, 82656
Elbow
See Humerus; Radius; Ulna
Abscess
Incision and Drainage, 23930, 23935
Arthrectomy, 24155
Arthrocentesis, 20605
Arthrodesis, 24800, 24802
Arthroplasty, 24360
with Implant, 24361, 24362
Total Replacement, 24363
Arthroscopy
Diagnostic, 29830
Surgical, 29834-29838
Arthrotomy, 24000
with Joint Exploration, 24101
with Synovectomy, 24102
with Synovial Biopsy, 24101
Capsular Release, 24006
Biopsy, 24065, 24066, 24101
Bursa
Incision and Drainage, 23931
Dislocation
Closed Treatment, 24600, 24605, 24640
Open Treatment, 24615
Partial, 24640
Subluxate, 24640
Excision, 24155
Bursa, 24105
Synovium, 24102
Tumor, 24075-24079 [24071, 24073], 24120-24126, 24152
Exploration, 24000-24101 [24071, 24073]
Fracture
Monteggia, 24620, 24635
Open Treatment, 24586, 24587

Elbow

Elbow — *continued*
  Hematoma
    Incision and Drainage, 23930
  Implant
    Removal, 24164
  Incision and Drainage, 24000
  Injection
    Arthrography (Radiologic), 24220
    Magnetic Resonance Imaging (MRI), 73221
  Manipulation, 24300
  Radical Resection
    Capsule, Soft Tissue and Bone with Contracture Release, 24149
  Removal
    Foreign Body, 24000, 24101, 24200, 24201
    Implant, 24160
    Loose Body, 24101
  Repair
    Epicondylitis, 24357-24359
    Fasciotomy, 24357-24359
    Flexorplasty, 24330
    Hemiephyseal Arrest, 24470
    Ligament, 24343-24346
    Muscle, 24341
    Muscle Transfer, 24301
    Tendon, 24340-24342
      Lengthening, 24305
      Transfer, 24301
    Tennis Elbow, 24357-24359
  Steindler Advancement, 24330
  Strapping, 29260
  Tenotomy, 24357-24359
  Unlisted Services and Procedures, 24999
  X-ray, 73070, 73080
    with Contrast, 73085
Elbow, Golfer, 24357-24359
Elbow, Tennis, 24357-24359
Electrical Stimulation
  Bone Healing
    Invasive, 20975
    Noninvasive, 20974
  Brain Surface, 95961, 95962
  Cardiac, 93623
  Physical Therapy
    Attended, Manual, 97032
    Unattended, 97014
Electric Countershock
  See Cardioversion
Electric Stimulation
  See Electrical Stimulation
Electric Stimulation, Transcutaneous
  See Application, Neurostimulator
Electrocardiogram, 93000-93010
  Signal-Averaged, 93278
  Transmission, 93012-93014
  Wearable, 93224-93272
Electrocardiography
  24-hour Monitoring, 93224-93272
  Doppler
    Color Flow Velocity, 93325
    Pulsed
      Continuous Wave, 93320, 93321
  Evaluation, 93000, 93010, 93014
  Monitoring, 93224-93237
  Patient-Demand Recording
    Transmission and Evaluation, 93270
  Rhythm, 93040
    Evaluation, 93042
    Interpretation and Report, 93042
    Microvolt T-wave Alternans, 93025
    Tracing and Evaluation, 93040
  Signal Averaged, 93278
  Tracing, 93005
  Transmission, 93012
Electrocautery, 17000-17286
  See Destruction
Electrochemistry
  See Electolysis
Electroconvulsive Therapy, 90870

Electrocorticogram
  Intraoperative, 95829
Electrode, Depth
  See Depth Electrode
Electrodesiccation, 17000-17286
  Lesion
    Penis, 54055
Electroejaculation, 55870
Electroencephalography (EEG)
  Brain Death, 95824
  Coma, 95822
  Digital Analysis, 95957
  Electrode Placement, 95830
  Intraoperative, 95955
  Monitoring, 95812, 95813, 95950-95953, 95956
    with Drug Activation, 95954
    with Physical Activation, 95954
    with WADA Activation, 95958
  Sleep, 95819, 95822, 95827
  Standard, 95816, 95819
Electrogastrography, 91132, 91133
Electrogram, Atrial
  Esophageal Recording, 93615, 93616
Electro-Hydraulic Procedure, 52325
Electrolysis, 17380
Electromyographs
  See Electromyography, Needle
Electromyography
  Anus
    Biofeedback, 90911
  Fine Wire
    Dynamic, 96004
  for Guidance with Chemodenervation, 95874
  Hemidiaphragm, 95866
  Larynx, 95865
  Needle
    Extremities, 95861-95864
    Extremity, 95860
    Face and Neck Muscles, 95867, 95868
    Ocular, 92265
    Other than Paraspinal, 95870
    Single Fiber Electrode, 95872
    Thoracic Paraspinal Muscles, 95869
  Rectum
    Biofeedback, 90911
  Sphincter Muscles
    Anus, 51784
      Needle, 51785
    Urethra, 51784, 51785
      Needle, 51785
  Surface
    Dynamic, 96002-96004
Electronic Analysis
  Cardioverter-Defibrillator
    with Reprogramming, 93282, 93289, 93292, 93295
    without Reprogramming, 93283, 93289, 93295
  Defibrillator, 93282, 93289, 93292, 93295
  Drug Infusion Pump, 62367, 62368
  Implantable Loop Recorder System, 93285, 93291, 93298
  Neurostimulator Pulse Generator, 95970-95979
  Pulse Generator, 95970, 95971
Electron Microscopy, 88348, 88349
Electro-oculography, 92270
Electrophoresis
  Counterimmuno-, 86185
  Immuno-, 86320-86327
  Immunofixation, 86334-86335
  Protein, 84165-84166
  Unlisted Services and Procedures, 82664
Electrophysiology Procedure, 93600-93660
Electroretinography, 92275
Electrostimulation, Analgesic Cutaneous
  See Application, Neurostimulation

Electrosurgery
  Skin Lesion, 17000-17111, 17260-17286
  Skin Tags, 11200, 11201
  Trichiasis
    Correction, 67825
Electroversion, Cardiac
  See Cardioversion
Elevation, Scapula, Congenital
  See Sprengel's Deformity
Elliot Operation, 66130
  Excision, Lesion, Sclera, 66130
Eloesser Procedure, 32035, 32036
Eloesser Thoracoplasty, 32905
Embolectomy
  Aortoiliac Artery, 34151, 34201
  Axillary Artery, 34101
  Brachial Artery, 34101
  Carotid Artery, 34001
  Celiac Artery, 34151
  Femoral, 34201
  Iliac, 34151, 34201
  Innominate Artery, 34001-34101
  Mesentery Artery, 34151
  Peroneal Artery, 34203
  Popliteal Artery, 34203
  Pulmonary Artery, 33910-33916
  Radial Artery, 34111
  Renal Artery, 34151
  Subclavian Artery, 34001-34101
  Tibial Artery, 34203
  Ulnar Artery, 34111
Embryo
  Biopsy, 89290, 89291
  Cryopreservation, 89258
  Cryopreserved
    Preparation/Thawing, 89352
  Culture, 89250
    with Co-Culture Oocyte, 89251
  Hatching
    Assisted Microtechnique, 89253
  Preparation for Transfer, 89255
  Storage, 89342
Embryo/Fetus Monitoring
  See Monitoring, Fetal
Embryo Implantation
  See Implantation
Embryonated Eggs
  Inoculation, 87250
Embryo Transfer
  In Vitro Fertilization, 58974, 58976
    Intrafallopian Transfer, 58976
    Intrauterine Transfer, 58974
Emergency Department Services, 99281-99288
  See Critical Care; Emergency Department
  Anesthesia, 99140
    in Office, 99058
  Physician Direction of Advanced Life Support, 99288
Emesis Induction, 99175
EMG (Electromyography, Needle), 51784, 51785, 92265, 95860-95872
EMI Scan
  See CT Scan
Emission Computerized Tomography, 78607, 78647
Emission Computerized Tomography, Single-Photon
  See SPECT
Emmet Operation, 57720
Empyema
  Closure
    Chest Wall, 32810
  Thoracostomy, 32035, 32036, 32551
Empyema, Lung
  See Abscess, Thorax
Empyemectomy, 32540
EMS, 99288
Encephalitis
  Antibody, 86651-86654
Encephalitis Virus Vaccine, 90735
Encephalocele
  Repair, 62120

Encephalocele — *continued*
  Repair — *continued*
    Craniotomy, 62121
Encephalography, A-Mode, 76506
Encephalon
  See Brain
Endarterectomy
  Coronary Artery, 33572
  Pulmonary, 33916
Endemic Flea-Borne Typhus
  See Murine Typhus
End-Expiratory Pressure, Positive
  See Pressure Breathing, Positive
Endobronchial Challenge Tests
  See Bronchial Challenge Test
Endocavitary Fulguration
  See Electrocautery
Endocrine System
  Unlisted Services and Procedures, 60699, 78099
Endolymphatic Sac
  Exploration
    with Shunt, 69806
    without Shunt, 69805
Endometrial Ablation, 58353, 58356, 58563
  Curettage, 58356
  Exploration via Hysteroscopy, 58563
Endometrioma
  Abdomen
    Destruction, 49203-49205
    Excision, 49203-49205
  Retroperitoneal
    Destruction, 49203-49205
    Excision, 49203-49205
Endometriosis, Adhesive
  See Adhesions, Intrauterine
Endometrium
  Ablation, 58356
  Biopsy, 58100, 58558
Endonuclease, DNA
  See DNAse
Endopyelotomy, 50575
Endorectal Pull-Through
  Proctectomy, Total, 45110, 45112, 45120, 45121
Endoscopic Retrograde Cannulation of Pancreatic Duct (ERCP)
  See Cholangiopancreatography
Endoscopies, Pleural
  See Thoracoscopy
Endoscopy
  See Arthroscopy; Thoracoscopy
  Adrenal Gland
    Biopsy, 60650
    Excision, 60650
  Anal
    Biopsy, 46606
    Dilation, 46604
    Exploration, 46600
    Hemorrhage, 46614
    Removal
      Foreign Body, 46608
      Polyp, 46610, 46612
      Tumor, 46610, 46612
  Bile Duct
    Biopsy, 47553
    Destruction
      Calculi (Stone), 43265
      Tumor, 43272
    Dilation, 43271, 47555, 47556
    Exploration, 47552
    Intraoperative, 47550
    Percutaneous, 47552-47555
    Removal
      Calculi (Stone), 43264, 47554
      Foreign Body, 43269
      Stent, 43269
    Specimen Collection, 43260
    Sphincterotomy, 43262
    Sphincter Pressure, 43263
    Tube Placement, 43267, 43268
  Bladder
    Biopsy, 52007, 52204, 52354
    Catheterization, 52005, 52010
    Destruction, 52354

Index — End Stage Renal Disease Services

Endoscopy — *continued*
  Bladder — *continued*
    Destruction — *continued*
      Lesion, 52400
    Diagnostic, 52000
    Evacuation
      Clot, 52001
    Excision
      Tumor, 52355
    Exploration, 52351
    Lithotripsy, 52353
    Removal
      Calculus, 52352
      Urethral Stent Insertion, 52282, 53855
  Bladder Neck
    Injection of Implant Material, 51715
  Brain
    Shunt Creation, 62201
  Bronchi
    Aspiration, 31645, 31646
    Biopsy, 31625-31629, 31632, 31633
    Destruction
      Lesion, 31641
    Dilation, 31630, 31631, 31636-31638
    Exploration, 31622
    Injection, 31656
    Lesion, 31641
      Destruction, 31641
    Needle Biopsy, 31629, 31633
    Placement
      Stent, 31631, 31636-31637
    Revision
      Stent, 31638
    Stenosis, 31641
    Tumor, 31641
    Ultrasound, 31620
      Destruction, 31641
      Excision, 31640
  Cannulization
    Papilla, 43273
  Cervix
    Biopsy, 57454, 57455, 57460
    Curettage, 57454, 57456
    Exploration, 57452
    Loop Electrode Biopsy, 57460
    Loop Electrode Conization, 57461
  Chest Cavity
    Exploration, 32601-32606
    Surgical, 32650-32665
  Colon
    Biopsy, 44389, 45380
    Destruction
      Lesion, 44393, 45383
      Tumor, 44393, 45383
    Exploration, 44388, 45378
    Hemorrhage, 44391, 45382
    Injection, 45381
    Placement
      Stent, 45387
    Removal
      Foreign Body, 44390, 45379
      Polyp, 44392, 45384, 45385
      Tumor, 44392, 45384, 45385
    Specimen Collection, 45380
    Ultrasound, 45391-45392
    via Colotomy, 45355
    via Stoma (Colostomy), 44388-44393, 44397
    Virtual, 74261-74263
  Colon–Sigmoid
    Ablation
      Polyp, 45339
      Tumor, 45339
    Biopsy, 45331
    Dilation, 45340
    Exploration, 45330
      Specimen Collection, 45331
    Hemorrhage, 45334
    Injection, 45335
    Needle Biopsy, 45342
    Placement
      Stent, 45327, 45345

Endoscopy — *continued*
  Colon–Sigmoid — *continued*
    Removal
      Foreign Body, 45332
      Polyp, 45333, 45338
      Tumor, 45333, 45338
    Specimen Collection, 45331
    Ultrasound, 45341, 45342
    Volvulus, 45337
  Esophagus
    Biopsy, 43202
    Dilation, 43220, 43226
    Exploration, 43200
    Hemorrhage, 43227
    Injection, 43201, 43204
    Insertion Stent, 43219
    Needle Biopsy, 43232
    Removal
      Foreign Body, 43215
      Polyp, 43216, 43217, 43228
      Tumor, 43216, 43228
    Ultrasound, 43231-43232
    Vein Ligation, 43205
  Eye, 66990
  Foot
    Plantar Fasciotomy, 29893
  Gastrointestinal
    Upper
      Biopsy, 43239
      Catheterization, 43241
      Destruction of Lesion, 43258
      Dilation, 43245, 43248, 43249
      Drainage of Pseudocyst, 43240
      Exploration, 43234, 43235
      Foreign Body, 43247
      Gastric Bypass, 43644-43645
      Gastroenterostomy, 43644-43645
      Hemorrhage, 43255
      Injection, 43236
      Inject Varices, 43243
      Needle Biopsy, 43232, 43238
      Removal, 43247, 43250, 43251
      Roux-En-Y, 43644
      Stent Placement, 43256
      Thermal Radiation, 43257
      Tube Placement, 43246
      Ultrasound, 43237-43242, 43259, 76975
      Vein Ligation, 43244
  Ileum
    via Stoma, 44383
  Intestines, Small
    Biopsy, 44361, 44377
    Destruction
      Lesion, 44369
      Tumor, 44369
    Diagnostic, 44376
    Exploration, 44360
    Hemorrhage, 44366, 44378
    Insertion
      Stent, 44370, 44379
      Tube, 44379
    Pelvic Pouch, 44385, 44386
    Removal
      Foreign Body, 44363
      Lesion, 44365
      Polyp, 44364, 44365
      Tumor, 44364, 44365
    Tube Placement, 44372
    Tube Revision, 44373
    via Stoma, 44380, 44382
    Tumor, 44364, 44365
  Intracranial, 62160-62165
  Kidney
    Biopsy, 50555, 50574-50576, 52354
    Catheterization, 50553, 50572
    Destruction, 50557, 50576, 52354
    Dilation of Ureter, 50553
    Excision
      Tumor, 52355
    Exploration, 52351

Endoscopy — *continued*
  Kidney — *continued*
    Lithotripsy, 52353
    Removal
      Calculus, 50561, 50580, 52352
      Foreign Body, 50561, 50580
      via Incision, 50562-50576, 50580
      via Stoma, 50551-50557, 50561
  Larynx
    with Injection, 31570
    Biopsy, 31510, 31535, 31536
    Direct, 31515-31571
    Exploration, 31505, 31520-31526, 31575
    Fiberoptic, 31575-31579
    Indirect, 31505-31513
    Operative, 31530-31561
    Removal
      Foreign Body, 31530, 31531
      Lesion, 31511, 31545-31546
  Mediastinoscopy
    Biopsy, 39400
    Exploration, 39400
  Nose
    Diagnostic, 31231-31235
    Surgical, 31237-31294
    Unlisted Procedure, Accessory Sinuses, 31299
  Pancreatic Duct
    Destruction
      Stone, 43265
      Tumor, 43272
    Dilation, 43271
    Removal
      Calculi (Stone), 43264
      Foreign Body, 43269
      Stent, 43269
    Specimen Collection, 43260
    Sphincterotomy, 43262
    Sphincter Pressure, 43263
    Tube Placement, 43267, 43268
  Pelvis
    Aspiration, 49322
    Destruction of Lesions, 58662
    Lysis of Adhesions, 58660
    Oviduct Surgery, 58670, 58671
    Removal of Adnexal Structures, 58661
  Peritoneum
    Biopsy, 47561
    Drainage Lymphocele, 49323, 54690
    Radiologic, 47560
  Rectum
    Biopsy, 45305
    Destruction
      Tumor, 45320
    Dilation, 45303
    Exploration, 45300
    Hemorrhage, 45317
    Removal
      Foreign Body, 45307
      Polyp, 45308-45315
      Tumor, 45308-45315
    Volvulus, 45321
  Spleen
    Removal, 38120
  Testis
    Removal, 54690
  Trachea
    Dilation, 31630-31631, 31636-31638
    via Tracheostomy, 31615
  Ureter
    Biopsy, 50955-50957, 50974-50976, 52354
    Catheterization, 50953, 50972
    Destruction, 50957, 50976, 52354
    Excision
      Tumor, 52355
    Exploration, 52351
    Injection of Implant Material, 52327
    Lithotripsy, 52353

Endoscopy — *continued*
  Ureter — *continued*
    Manipulation of Ureteral Calculus, 52330
    Placement
      Stent, 50947
    Removal
      Calculus, 50961, 50980, 52352
      Foreign Body, 50961, 50980
    Resection, 52355
      via Incision, 50970-50976, 50980
      via Stoma, 50951-50957, 50961
      via Ureterotomy, 50970-50980
  Ureteral
    Biopsy, 52007
    Catheterization, 52005
  Urethra, 52000, 52010
    Biopsy, 52007, 52204, 52354
    Catheterization, 52005, 52010
    Destruction, 52354
      Lesion, 52400
    Evacuation
      Clot, 52001
    Excision
      Tumor, 52355
    Exploration, 52351
    Incision
      Ejaculatory Duct, 52402
    Injection of Implant Material, 51715
    Lithotripsy, 52353
    Removal
      Calculus, 52352
    Resection
      Ejaculatory Duct, 52402
    Vasectomy, 52402
    Vasotomy, 52402
  Uterus
    Anesthesia, 00952
    Hysteroscopy
      with Division
        Resection Intrauterine Septum, 58560
      with Lysis of Intrauterine Adhesions, 58559
      Diagnostic, 58555
      Placement
        Fallopian Tube, 58565
      Removal
        Endometrial, 58563
        Impacted Foreign Body, 58562
        Leiomyomata, 58561
      Surgical with Biopsy, 58558
  Vagina
    Biopsy, 57454
    Exploration, 57452
  Vascular
    Surgical, 33508, 37500, 37501
  Virtual
    Colon, 74261-74263
Endosteal Implant
  Reconstruction
    Mandible, 21248, 21249
    Maxilla, 21248, 21249
Endothelioma, Dural
  See Meningioma
Endotoxin
  Bacteria, 87176
Endotracheal Tube
  Intubation, 31500
Endovascular Repair, 0078T-0081T, 33880-33891, 34800-34805, 34812-34826, 34833-34900, 75952-75959
  Angiography, 75952-75954
  Imaging Neck, 75956-75959
Endovascular Therapy
  Ablation
    Vein, 36475-36479
  Occlusion, 61623
Endrocrine, Pancreas
  See Islet Cell
End Stage Renal Disease Services, 90951-90962, 90967-90970
  Home, 90963-90966

Enema

Enema
  Air Contrast, 74280
  Diagnostic, 74000, 74280
  Home Visit for Fecal Impaction, 99511
  Therapeutic
    for Intussusception, 74283
Energies, Electromagnetic
  See Irradiation
ENERGIX-B, 90744, 90746-90747
ENG, 92541, 92542, 92544
ENT
  See Ear, Nose, and Throat; Otorhinolaryngology, Diagnostic
  Therapeutic
    See Otorhinolaryngology
Entamoeba Histolytica
  Antigen Detection
    Enzyme Immunoassay, 87336, 87337
Enterectomy, 44126-44128, 44137, 44202
  with Enterostomy, 44125
  Donor, 44132, 44133
  Resection, 44120, 44121
Enterocele
  Repair, 57556
    Hysterectomy
      with Colpectomy, 58280
      with Colpo-Urethrocystopexy, 58270
Enterocystoplasty, 51960
  Camey, 50825
Enteroenterostomy, 44130
Enterolysis, 44005
  Laparoscopic, 44180
Enteropancreatostomy
  See Anastomosis, Pancreas to Intestines
Enterorrhaphy, 44602, 44603, 44615
Enteroscopy
  Intestines, Small
    Biopsy, 44361, 44377
    Control of Bleeding, 44378
    Destruction
      Lesion, 44369
      Tumor, 44369
    Diagnostic, 44376
    Exploration, 44360
    Hemorrhage, 44366
    Pelvic Pouch, 44385, 44386
    Removal
      Foreign Body, 44363
      Lesion, 44364, 44365
      Polyp, 44364, 44365
      Tumor, 44364, 44365
    Tube Placement, 44372
    Tube Revision, 44373
    via Stoma, 44380, 44382
    Tumor, 44364, 44365
Enterostomy Tube Placement, 44300
  with Enterectomy
    Intestine, Small, 44125
  Closure, 44625, 44626
Enterotomy, 44615
Enterovirus
  Antibody, 86658
  Antigen Detection
    Direct Fluorescence, 87265-87272, 87276, 87278, 87280, 87285-87290
Entropion
  Repair, 67921-67924
    Blepharoplasty
      Excision Tarsal Wedge, 67923
      Extensive, 67923
      Suture, 67921
      Thermocauterization, 67922
Enucleation
  Eye
    with Implant, 65103
      Muscles Attached, 65105
    without Implant, 65101
  Pleural, 32540
  Prostate, 52649

Enucleation, Cyst, Ovarian
  See Cystectomy, Ovarian
Environmental Intervention
  for Psychiatric Patients, 90882
Enzyme Activity, 82657
  Radioactive Substrate, 82658
Enzyme, Angiotensin Converting
  See Angiotensin Converting Enzyme (ACE)
Enzyme, Angiotensin-Forming
  See Renin
EOG (Electro-Oculography), 92270
Eosinocyte
  See Eosinophils
Eosinophils
  Nasal Smear, 89190
Epiandrosterone, 82666
Epicondylitis, 24357-24359
Epidemic Parotitis
  See Mumps
Epididymectomy
  Bilateral, 54861
  Unilateral, 54860
Epididymis
  Abscess
    Incision and Drainage, 54700
  Anastomosis
    to Vas Deferens
      Bilateral, 54901
      Unilateral, 54900
  Biopsy, 54800, 54865
  Epididymography, 74440
  Excision
    Bilateral, 54861
    Unilateral, 54860
  Exploration
    Biopsy, 54865
  Hematoma
    Incision and Drainage, 54700
  Lesion
    Excision
      Local, 54830
      Spermatocele, 54840
    Needle Biopsy, 54800
    Repair, 54900, 54901
    Spermatocele
      Excision, 54840
    Unlisted Procedures, Male Genital, 54699, 55899
    X-ray with Contrast, 74440
Epididymograms, 55300
Epididymography, 74440
Epididymoplasty
  See Repair, Epididymis
Epididymovasostomy
  Bilateral, 54901
  Unilateral, 54900
Epidural
  Analgesia
    Continuous, 01967-01969
    Drug Administration, 01996
  Electrode
    Insertion, 61531
    Removal, 61535
  Injection, 62281, 62282, 62310-62319, 64479-64484
  Lysis, 62263, 62264
Epidurography, 72275
Epigastric
  Hernia Repair, 49572
Epiglottidectomy, 31420
Epiglottis
  Excision, 31420
Epikeratoplasty, 65767
Epilation, 17380
Epinephrine
  See Catecholamines
  Blood, 82383, 82384
  Urine, 82384
Epiphyseal Arrest
  Femur, 20150, 27185, 27475, 27479, 27485, 27742
  Fibula, 20150, 27477-27485, 27730-27742
  Radius, 20150, 25450, 25455

Epiphyseal Arrest — continued
  Tibia, 20150, 27477-27485, 27730, 27734-27742
  Ulna, 20150, 25450, 25455
Epiphyseal Separation
  Radius
    Closed Treatment, 25600
    Open Treatment, 25607, 25608-25609
Epiphysiodesis
  See Epiphyseal Arrest
Epiphysis
  See Bone; Specific Bone
Epiploectomy, 49255
EPIS, 59300, 92585, 95925-95930
Episiotomy, 59300
Epispadias
  Penis
    Reconstruction, 54385
    Repair, 54380-54390
      with Exstrophy of Bladder, 54390
      with Incontinence, 54380, 54385
Epistaxis
  with Nasal
    Sinus Endoscopy, 31238
    Control, 30901-30906
Epley Maneuver, 95992
EPO, 82668
EPS, 93600-93660
Epstein-Barr Virus
  Antibody, 86663-86665
Equina, Cauda
  Decompression, 63005, 63011, 63017, 63047-63048, 63055
  Exploration, 63005, 63011, 63017
ER, 99281-99288
ERCP (Cholangiopancreatography), 43260-43272
ERG (Electroretinography), 92275
Ergocalciferol
  See Calciferol
Ergocalciferols
  See Calciferol
Ergonovine Provocation Test, 93024
Erythrocyte
  See Red Blood Bell (RBC)
Erythrocyte ab
  See Antibody, Red Blood Cell
Erythrocyte Count
  See Red Blood Cell (RBC), Count
Erythropoietin, 82668
Escharotomy
  Burns, 16035, 16036
Escherichia Coli 0157
  Antigen Detection
    Enzyme Immunoassay, 87335
ESD
  See Endoscopy, Gastrointestinal, Upper
Esophageal Acid Infusion Test, 91012, 91030
Esophageal Polyp
  See Polyp, Esophagus
Esophageal Tumor
  See Tumor, Esophagus
Esophageal Varices
  Injection Sclerosis, 43204, 43243
  Ligation, 43205, 43244, 43400
  Repair/Transection, 43401
Esophagectomy
  Partial, 43116-43124
  Total, 43107-43113, 43124
Esophagoenterostomy
  with Total Gastrectomy, 43260
Esophagogastroduodenoscopies
  See Endoscopy, Gastrointestinal, Upper
Esophagogastrostomy, 43320
Esophagojejunostomy, 43340, 43341
Esophagomyotomy, 32665, 43330, 43331
  Laparoscopic, 43279
Esophagoplasty, 43300-43312
Esophagorrphaphy
  See Esophagus, Suture

Esophagoscopies
  See Endoscopy, Esophagus
Esophagoscopy
  Operative By Incision, 43499
  Through Artificial Stoma, 43499
Esophagostomy, 43350-43352
  Closure, 43420, 43425
Esophagotomy, 43020, 43045
Esophagotracheal Fistula
  See Fistula, Tracheoesophageal
Esophagus
  Acid Perfusion Test, 91012, 91030
  Acid Reflux Tests, 91034-91035, 91037-91038
  Balloon Distension
    Provocation Study, 91040
  Biopsy
    Endoscopy, 43202
  Cineradiography, 74230
  Dilation, 43450-43458
    Endoscopic, 43220, 43226, 43248, 43249
    Surgical, 43510
  Endoscopy
    Biopsy, 43202
    Dilation, 43220, 43226
    Exploration, 43200
    Hemorrhage, 43227
    Injection, 43201, 43204
    Insertion Stent, 43219
    Needle Biopsy, 43232
    Removal
      Foreign Body, 43215
      Polyp, 43216, 43217, 43228
      Tumor, 43216, 43228
    Ultrasound, 43231, 43232
    Vein Ligation, 43205
  Excision
    Diverticula, 43130, 43135
    Partial, 43116-43124
    Total, 43107-43113, 43124
  Exploration
    Endoscopy, 43200
    Hemorrhage, 43227
    Incision, 43020, 43045
    Muscle, 43030
  Injection
    Sclerosis Agent, 43204
    Submucosal, 43201
  Insertion
    Stent, 43219
    Tamponade, 43460
    Tube, 43510
    Intubation with Specimen Collection, 91000
  Lesion
    Excision, 43100, 43101
    Ligation, 43405
    Motility Study, 78258, 91010-91012
  Needle Biopsy
    Endoscopy, 43232
  Nuclear Medicine
    Imaging (Motility), 78258
    Reflux Study, 78262
  Reconstruction, 43300, 43310, 43313
    Creation
      Stoma, 43350-43352
      Esophagostomy, 43350
      Fistula, 43305, 43312, 43314
      Gastrointestinal, 43360, 43361
  Removal
    Foreign Bodies, 43020, 43045, 43215, 74235
    Lesion, 43216
    Polyp, 43216, 43217, 43228
  Repair, 43300, 43310, 43313
    Esophagogastric Fundoplasty, 43324, 43325
      Laparoscopic, 43280
    Esophagogastrostomy, 43320
    Esophagojejunostomy, 43340, 43341
    Fistula, 43305, 43312, 43314, 43420, 43425
    Muscle, 43330, 43331

Index

Esophagus — continued
Repair — continued
- Pre-existing Perforation, 43405
- Varices, 43401
- Wound, 43410, 43415
- Stapling Gastroesophageal Junction, 43405
- Suture
  - Gastroesophageal Junction, 43405
  - Wound, 43410, 43415
- Ultrasound, 43231, 43232
- Unlisted Services and Procedures, 43289, 43499
- Vein
  - Ligation, 43205, 43400
- Video, 74230
- X-ray, 74220

Esophagus Neoplasm
See Tumor, Esophagus

Esophagus, Varix
See Esophageal Varices

ESR, 85651, 85652
ESRD, 90951-90961, 90967-90970
- Home, 90963-90966

EST, 90870

Established Patient
- Domiciliary or Rest Home Visit, 99334-99337
- Emergency Department Services, 99281-99285
- Home Services, 99347-99350
- Hospital Inpatient Services, 99221-99239
- Hospital Observation Services, 99217-99220
- Initial Inpatient Consultation, 99251-99255
- Office and/or Other Outpatient Consultations, 99241-99245
- Office Visit, 99211-99215
- Online Evaluation and Management Services
  - Nonphysician, 98969
  - Physician, 99444
- Outpatient Visit, 99211-99215

Establishment
- Colostomy
  - Abdominal, 50810
  - Perineal, 50810

Estes Operation
See Ovary, Transposition

Estlander Procedure, 40525, 40527
Estradiol, 82670
- Response, 80415

Estriol
- Blood or Urine, 82677

Estrogen
- Blood or Urine, 82671, 82672
- Receptor, 84233

Estrone
- Blood or Urine, 82679

ESWL, 50590

Ethanediols
See Ethylene Glycol

Ethanol
- Blood, 82055
- Breath, 82075
- Urine, 82055

Ethchlorvynol
- Blood, 82690
- Urine, 82690

Ethmoid
- Fracture
  - with Fixation, 21340

Ethmoidectomy, 31200-31205
- with Nasal
  - Sinus Endoscopy, 31254, 31255
- Endoscopic, 31254, 31255
- Skull Base Surgery, 61580, 61581

Ethmoid, Sinus
See Sinus, Ethmoid

Ethosuccimid
See Ethosuximide

Ethosuximide, 80168
- Assay, 80168

Ethyl Alcohol (Ethanol)
- Blood, 82055
- Breath, 82075
- Urine, 82055

Ethylene Dichlorides
See Dichloroethane

Ethylene Glycol, 82693

Ethylmethylsuccimide
See Ethosuximide

Etiocholanolone, 82696

Etiocholanolone Measurement
See Etiocholanolone

ETOH, 82055, 82075
EUA, 57410, 92018, 92019, 92502
Euglobulin Lysis, 85360

European Blastomycosis
See Cryptococcus

Eustachian Tube
- Catheterization, 69405
- Inflation
  - with Catheterization, 69400
  - without Catheterization, 69401
- Myringotomy, 69420
- Anesthesia, 69421
- Insertion
  - Catheter, 69405

Eutelegenesis
See Artificial Insemination

Evacuation
- Cervical Pregnancy, 59140
- Hematoma
  - Brain, 61312-61315
  - Subungual, 11740
- Hydatidiform Mole, 59870
- Meibomian Glands, 0207T

Evaluation
- Asthma Symptoms, 1005F
- Multiple Molecular Probes, 88384-88386
- Occupation Therapy
  - Re-evaluation, 97004
- Physical Therapy
  - Re-evaluation, 97002
- Vestibular, basic, 92540

Evaluation and Management
- Alcohold and/or Substance Abuse, 99408-99409
- Anticoagulant Management, 99363-99364
- Assistive Technology Assessment, 97755
- Athletic Training
  - Evaluation, 97005
  - Re-evaluation, 97006
- Basic Life and/or Disability Evaluation Services, 99450
- Birthing Center, 99460, 99462-99465
- Care Plan Oversight Services, 99374-99380
  - Home Health Agency Care, 99374
  - Hospice, 99377
  - Nursing Facility, 99379, 99380
- Case Management Services, 99366-99368
- Consultation, 99241-99255
- Critical Care, 99291, 99292
  - Interfacility Pediatric Transport, 99466-99467
- Domiciliary or Rest Home, 99324-99337
- Emergency Department, 99281-99288
- Health Behavior
  - Assessment, 96150
  - Family Intervention, 96154, 96155
  - Group Intervention, 96153
  - Individual Intervention, 96152
  - Re-assessment, 96151
- Home Services, 99341-99350
- Hospital, 99221-99233
- Hospital Discharge, 99238, 99239
- Hospital Services
  - Initial, 99221-99233, 99460-99463, 99477

Evaluation and Management — continued
- Hospital Services — continued
  - Intensive Care
    - Low Birth Weight, 99478-99480
    - Neonate, 99477
  - Observation Care, 99217-99220
  - Subsequent, 99231, 99462-99463
- Insurance Examination, 99455-99456
- Internet Communication
  - Nonphysician, 98969
  - Physician, 99444
- Low Birth Weight Infant, 99468-99469, 99478-99480
- Medical
  - with Individual Psychotherapy
    - Hospital or Residential Care, 90817, 90819, 90822, 90824, 90827, 90829
    - Office or Outpatient, 90805, 90807, 90809
  - with Individual Psychotherapy, Interactive
    - Office or Outpatient, 90811, 90813, 90815
- Neonatal
  - Critical Care, 99468-99469
  - Intensive Observation, 99477-99480
- Newborn Care, 99460-99465
- Nursing Facility, 99304-99318
- Observation Care, 99217-99220
- Occupation Therapy Evaluation, 97003
  - Re-evaluation, 97004
- Office and Other Outpatient, 99201-99215
- On-line Assessment
  - Nonphysician, 98969
  - Physician, 99444
- Online Evaluation
  - Nonphysician, 98969
  - Physician, 99444
- Pediatric
  - Critical Care, 99471-99472
  - Interfacility Transport, 99466-99467
- Physical Therapy Evaluation, 97001
  - Re-evaluation, 97002
- Physician Standby Services, 99360
- Preventive Services, 4000F-4001F, 99381-99429
- Prolonged Services, 99356, 99357
- Psychiatric/Records or Reports, 90885
- Smoking and Tobacco Cessation Counseling, 99406-99407
- Telephone Assessment
  - Nonphysician, 98966-98968
  - Physician, 99441-99443
- Unlisted Service and Procedures, 99499
- Work-Related and/or Medical Disability Evaluation, 99450

Evaluation Studies, Drug, Preclinical
See Drug Screen

EVAR (Endovascular Aortic Repair), 34800-34826

Evisceration
- Ocular Contents
  - with Implant, 65093
  - without Implant, 65091
- Repair
  - Abdominal Wall, 49900
- Suture
  - Abdominal Wall, 49900

Evisceration, Pelvic
See Exenteration, Pelvis

E Vitamin
See Tocopherol

Evocative/Suppression Test, 80400-80440

Evocative/Suppression Test — continued
- Stimulation Panel, 80410

Evoked Potential
See Audiologic Function Tests
- Auditory Brainstem, 92585, 92586
- Central Motor
  - Transcranial Motor Stimulation, 95928-95929
- Somatosensory Testing, 95925-95927
- Visual, CNS, 95930

Ewart Procedure
- Palate, Reconstruction, Lengthening, 42226, 42227

Examination
- Anorectal, 45990
- Involved Joint, 2004F

Excavatum, Pectus
See Pectus Excavatum

Exchange
- Arterial Catheter, 37209, 75900
- Drainage Catheter
  - under Radiologic Guidance, 49423
- External Fixation, 20697
- Intraocular Lens, 66986

Exchange Transfusion
See Blood, Transfusion, Exchange

Excision
See Also Debridement; Destruction
- Abscess
  - Brain, 61514, 61522
  - Olecranon Process, 24138
  - Radius, 24136
  - Ulna, 24138
- Acromion, 23130
- Shoulder, 23130
- Adenoids
  - with Tonsils, 42820, 42821
  - Primary
    - 12 or over, 42831
    - Younger Than Age 12, 42830
  - Secondary
    - 12 or over, 42836
    - Younger Than Age 12, 42835
- Adenoma
  - Thyroid Gland, 60200
- Adrenal Gland, 60540
  - with Excision Retroperitoneal Tumor, 60545
  - Laparoscopic, 60650
- Alveolus, 41830
- Anal Fissure, 46200
- Anal Tag, 46230 [46220]
- Aorta
  - Coarctation, 33840-33851
- Appendix, 44950-44960
- Arteriovenous Malformation
  - Spinal, 63250-63252
- Arytenoid Cartilage, 31400
  - Endoscopic, 31560, 31561
- Atrial Septum, 33735-33737
- Bartholin's Gland, 56740
- Bladder
  - Diverticulum, 51525
  - Neck, 51520
  - Partial, 51550-51565
  - Total, 51570, 51580, 51590-51597
    - with Nodes, 51575, 51585, 51595
  - Transurethral, 52640
  - Tumor, 51530
- Bladder Neck Contracture, Postoperative, 52640
- Bone
  - Femur, 20150
  - Fibula, 20150
  - Radius, 20150
  - Tibia, 20150
  - Ulna, 20150
- Bone Abscess
  - Facial, 21026
  - Mandible, 21025

Excision

Excision — *continued*
- Brain
  - Amygdala, 61566
  - Epileptogenic Focus, 61536
  - Hemisphere, 61542, 61543
  - Hippocampus, 61566
  - Other Lobe, 61323, 61539-61540
  - Temporal Lobe, 61537, 61538
- Brain Lobe
  - *See* Lobectomy, Brain
- Breast
  - Biopsy, 19100-19103
  - Chest Wall Tumor, 19260-19272
  - Cyst, 19120-19126
  - Lactiferous Duct Fistula, 19112
  - Lesion, 19120-19126
    - by Needle Localization, 19125, 19126
  - Mastectomy, 19300-19307
  - Nipple Exploration, 19110
- Bulbourethral Gland, 53250
- Bullae
  - Lung, 32141
    - Endoscopic, 32655
- Burns, 15002-15003, 15004-15005
- Bursa
  - Elbow, 24105
  - Excision, 27060
  - Femur, 27062
  - Ischial, 27060
  - Knee, 27340
  - Wrist, 25115, 25116
- Bypass Graft, 35901-35907
- Calcaneus, 28118-28120
- Calculi (Stone)
  - Biliary Duct, 47630
  - Parotid Gland, 42330, 42340
  - Salivary Gland, 42330-42340
  - Sublingual Gland, 42330, 42335
  - Submandibular Gland, 42330, 42335
- Carotid Artery, 60605
- Carpal, 25145, 25210, 25215
- Cartilage
  - Knee Joint, 27332, 27333
  - Shoulder Joint, 23101
  - Temporomandibular Joint, 21060
  - Wrist, 25107
- Caruncle, Urethra, 53265
- Cataract
  - Secondary, 66830
- Cervix
  - Electrode, 57460
  - Radical, 57531
  - Stump
    - Abdominal Approach, 57540, 57545
    - Vaginal Approach, 57550-57556
  - Total, 57530
- Chalazion
  - with Anesthesia, 67808
  - Multiple
    - Different Lids, 67805
    - Same Lid, 67801
  - Single, 67800
- Chest Wall Tumor, 19260-19272
- Choroid Plexus, 61544
- Clavicle
  - Partial, 23120, 23180
  - Sequestrectomy, 23170
  - Total, 23125
  - Tumor
    - Radical Resection, 23200
- Coccyx, 27080
- Colon
  - Excision
    - Partial, 44140-44147, 44160
      - with Anastomosis, 44140
    - Total, 44150-44156
  - Laparoscopic
    - with Anastomosis, 44204, 44207-44208
    - with Colostomy, 44206, 44208
    - with Ileocolostomy, 44205

Excision — *continued*
- Condyle
  - Temporomandibular Joint, 21050
- Condylectomy, 21050
- Constricting Ring
  - Finger, 26596
- Cornea
  - Epithelium, 65435
    - with Chelating Agent, 65436
  - Scraping, 65430
- Coronoidectomy, 21070
- Cowper's Gland, 53250
- Cranial Bone
  - Tumor, 61563, 61564
- Cyst
  - *See* Ganglion Cyst
  - Bile Duct, 47715
  - Bladder, 51500
  - Brain, 61516, 61524, 62162
  - Branchial, 42810, 42815
  - Breast, 19120
  - Calcaneus, 28100-28103
  - Carpal, 25130-25136
  - Cheekbone, 21030
  - Clavicle, 23140
    - with Allograft, 23146
    - with Autograft, 23145
  - Facial Bone, 21030
  - Femur, 27065-27067, 27355-27358
  - Fibula, 27635-27638
  - Finger, 26034, 26160
  - Foot, 28090
  - Hand, 26160
  - Hip, 27065-27067
  - Humerus, 23150, 24110
    - with Allograft, 23156, 24116
    - with Autograft, 23155, 24115
  - Ileum, 27065-27067
  - Intra-abdominal, 49203-49205
  - Kidney, 50280, 50290
  - Knee, 27345, 27347
  - Lung, 32140
  - Mandible, 21040, 21046-21047
  - Maxilla, 21030, 21048-21049
  - Mediastinal, 39200
  - Mediastinum, 32662
  - Metacarpal, 26200, 26205
  - Metatarsal, 28104-28107
  - Mullerian Duct, 55680
  - Nose, 30124-30125
  - Olecranon (Process), 24120
    - with Allograft, 24126
    - with Autograft, 24125
  - Ovarian, 58925
    - *See* Cystectomy, Ovarian
  - Pericardial, 33050
    - Endoscopic, 32661
  - Phalanges
    - Finger, 26210, 26215
    - Toe, 28108
  - Pilonidal, 11770-11772
  - Pubis, 27066, 27067
  - Radius, 24120, 25120-25126
    - with Allograft, 24126
    - with Autograft, 24125
  - Salivary Gland, 42408
  - Scapula, 23140
    - with Allograft, 23146
    - with Autograft, 23145
  - Seminal Vesicle, 55680
  - Sublingual Gland, 42408
  - Talus, 28100-28103
  - Tarsal, 28104-28107
  - Thyroglossal Duct, 60280, 60281
  - Thyroid Gland, 60200
  - Tibia, 27635-27638
  - Toe, 28092
  - Ulna, 24120, 25120-25126
    - with Allograft, 24126
    - with Autograft, 24125
- Urachal
  - Bladder, 51500
- Vaginal, 57135

Excision — *continued*
- Destruction of the Vestibule of the Mouth
  - *See* Mouth, Vestibule of, Excision, Destruction
- Diverticulum, Meckel's
  - *See* Meckel's Diverticulum, Excision
- Ear, External
  - Partial, 69110
  - Total, 69120
- Elbow Joint, 24155
- Electrode, 57522
- Embolectomy/Thrombectomy
  - Aortoiliac Artery, 34151, 34201
  - Axillary Artery, 34101
  - Brachial Artery, 34101
  - Carotid Artery, 34001
  - Celiac Artery, 34151
  - Femoral Artery, 34201
  - Iliac Artery, 34151, 34201
  - Innominate Artery, 34001-34101
  - Mesentery Artery, 34151
  - Peroneal Artery, 34203
  - Popliteal Artery, 34203
  - Radial Artery, 34111
  - Renal Artery, 34151
  - Subclavian Artery, 34001-34101
  - Tibial Artery, 34203
  - Ulnar Artery, 34111
- Embolism
  - Pulmonary Artery, 33910-33916
- Empyema
  - Lung, 32540
  - Pleural, 32540
- Endometriomas
  - Intra-abdominal, 49203-49205
- Epididymis
  - Bilateral, 54861
  - Unilateral, 54860
- Epiglottis, 31420
- Epikeratoplasty, 65767
- Epiphyseal Bar, 20150
- Esophagus
  - Diverticulum, 43130, 43135
  - Partial, 43116-43124
  - Total, 43107-43113, 43124
- Excess Skin
  - Abdomen, 15830
- Eye
  - *See* Enucleation, Eye
- Fallopian Tubes
  - Salpingectomy, 58700
  - Salpingo-Oophorectomy, 58720
- Fascia
  - *See* Fasciectomy
- Femur, 27360
  - Partial, 27070, 27071
- Fibula, 27360, 27455, 27457, 27641
- Fistula
  - Anal, 46270-46285
- Foot
  - Fasciectomy, 28060
    - Radical, 28060, 28062
- Gallbladder
  - Open, 47600-47620
  - via Laparoscopy
    - Cholecystectomy, 47562, 47563
      - with Cholangiography, 47563
      - with Exploration Common Duct, 47564
- Ganglion Cyst
  - Knee, 27347
  - Wrist, 25111, 25112
- Gingiva, 41820
- Gums, 41820
  - Alveolus, 41830
  - Operculum, 41821
- Heart
  - Donor, 33940
  - Lung
    - Donor, 33930
- Hemangioma, 11400-11446
- Hemorrhoids, 46221, 46250

Excision — *continued*
- Hemorrhoids — *continued*
  - with Fissurectomy, 46257, 46258
  - Clot, [46320]
  - Complex, 46260-46262
  - Simple, 46255
- Hip
  - Partial, 27070, 27071
- Hippocampus, 61566
- Humeral Head
  - Resection, 23195
  - Sequestrectomy, 23174
- Humerus, 23184, 23220, 24134, 24140, 24150
- Hydrocele
  - Spermatic Cord, 55500
  - Tunica Vaginalis, 55040, 55041
    - Bilateral, 55041
    - Unilateral, 55040
- Hygroma, Cystic
  - Axillary
    - Cervical, 38550, 38555
- Hymenotomy, 56700
  - *See* Hymen, Excision
- Ileum
  - Ileoanal Reservoir, 45136
  - Partial, 27070, 27071
- Inner Ear
  - *See* Ear, Inner, Excision
- Interphalangeal Joint
  - Toe, 28160
- Intervertebral Disc
  - Decompression, 63075-63078
  - Hemilaminectomy, 63040, 63043, 63044
  - Herniated, 63020-63044, 63055-63066
- Intestine
  - Laparoscopic
    - with Anastomosis, 44202, 44203
- Intestines
  - Donor, 44132, 44133
- Intestines, Small, 44120-44128
  - Transplantation, 44137
- Iris
  - Iridectomy
    - with Corneoscleral or Corneal Section, 66600
    - with Cyclectomy, 66605
    - Optical, 66635
    - Peripheral, 66625
    - Sector, 66630
- Kidney
  - with Ureters, 50220-50236
  - Donor, 50300, 50320, 50547
  - Partial, 50240
  - Recipient, 50340
  - Transplantation, 50370
- Kneecap, 27350
- Labyrinth
  - with Mastoidectomy, 69910
  - Transcanal, 69905
- Lacrimal Gland
  - Partial, 68505
  - Total, 68500
- Lacrimal Sac, 68520
- Laparoscopy
  - Adrenalectomy, 60650
- Larynx
  - with Pharynx, 31390, 31395
  - Endoscopic, 31545-31546
- Leg, Lower, 27630
- Lesion
  - Anal, 45108, 46922
  - Ankle, 27630
    - Arthroscopic, 29891
  - Arm, Lower, 25110
  - Auditory Canal, External
    - Exostosis, 69140
    - Radical with Neck Dissection, 69155
    - Radical without Neck Dissection, 69150
    - Soft Tissue, 69145
  - Bladder, 52224

Index

Excision

Excision — *continued*
  Lesion — *continued*
    Brain, 61534, 61536-61540
    Brainstem, 61575, 61576
    Carotid Body, 60600, 60605
    Colon, 44110, 44111
    Conjunctiva, 68110-68130
      with Adjacent Sclera, 68130
      over One Centimeter, 68115
    Cornea, 65400
      without Graft, 65420
    Ear, Middle, 69540
    Epididymis
      Local, 54830
      Spermatocele, 54840
    Esophagus, 43100, 43101
    Eye, 65900
    Eyelid
      without Closure, 67840
      Multiple, Different Lids, 67805
      Multiple, Same Lid, 67801
      Single, 67800
      under Anesthesia, 67808
    Femur, 27062
    Finger, 26160
    Foot, 28080, 28090
    Gums, 41822-41828
    Hand, 26160
    Intestines, 44110
      Small, 43250, 44111
    Intraspinal, 63265-63273
    Knee, 27347
  Lesion, Arthroscopic
    Ankle, 29891
    Talus, 29891
    Tibia, 29891
  Lesion, Tendon Sheath
    Arm, Lower, 25110
    Foot, 28090
    Hand/Finger, 26160
    Leg/Ankle, 27630
  Lip, 40500-40530
    Frenum, 40819
  Liver
    Allotransplantation, 47135
      Heterotopic, 47136
    Biopsy, wedge, 47100
    Donor, 47133-47142
    Extensive, 47122
      Lobectomy, total
        Left, 47125
        Right, 47130
    Resection
      Partial, 47120, 47125, 47140-47142
      Total, 47133
    Trisegmentectomy, 47122
  Lung, 32440-32445, 32488
    Bronchus Resection, 32486
    Bullae
      Endoscopic, 32655
    Completion, 32488
    Emphysematous, 32491
    Heart
      Donor, 33930
    Lobe, 32480, 32482
    Segment, 32484
    Total, 32440-32445
    Wedge Resection, 32500
    Endoscopic, 32657
  Lymph Nodes, 38500, 38510-38530
    Abdominal, 38747
    Axillary, 38740
      Complete, 38745
    Cervical, 38720, 38724
    Cloquet's node, 38760
    Deep
      Axillary, 38525
      Cervical, 38510, 38520
      Mammary, 38530
    Inguinofemoral, 38760, 38765
    Limited, for Staging
      Para–Aortic, 38562
      Pelvic, 38562
      Retroperitoneal, 38564
    Mediastinal, 38746

Excision — *continued*
  Lymph Nodes — *continued*
    Pelvic, 38770
    Peritracheal, 38746
    Radical
      Axillary, 38740, 38745
      Cervical, 38720, 38724
      Suprahyoid, 38700
      Retroperitoneal Transabdominal, 38780
    Superficial
      Needle, 38505
      Open, 38500
    Suprahyoid, 38700
    Thoracic, 38746
  Mandibular, Exostosis, 21031
  Mastoid
    Complete, 69502
    Radical, 69511
      Modified, 69505
    Petrous Apicectomy, 69530
    Simple, 69501
  Maxilla
    Exostosis, 21032
  Maxillary Torus Palatinus, 21032
  Meningioma
    Brain, 61512, 61519
  Meniscectomy
    Temporomandibular Joint, 21060
  Meniscus, 27347
  Mesentery, 44820
  Metacarpal, 26230
  Metatarsal, 28110-28114, 28122, 28140
    Condyle, 28288
  Mouth, 40810-40816, 41115, 41116
  Mucosa
    Gums, 41828
    Mouth, 40818
  Mucous Membrane
    Sphenoid Sinus, 31288
  Nail Fold, 11765
  Nails, 11750, 11752
  Nasopharynx, 61586, 61600
  Nerve
    Foot, 28055
    Hamstring, 27325
    Leg, Upper, 27325
    Popliteal, 27326
    Sympathetic, 64802-64818
  Neurofibroma, 64788, 64790
  Neurolemmoma, 64788-64792
  Neuroma, 64774-64786
  Nose, 30117-30118
    Dermoid Cyst
      Complex, 30125
      Simple, 30124
    Polyp, 30110, 30115
    Rhinectomy, 30150, 30160
    Skin, 30120
    Submucous Resection
      Nasal Septum, 30520
      Turbinate, 30140
    Turbinate, 30130, 30140
  Odontoid Process, 22548
  Olecranon, 24147
  Omentum, 49255
  Orbit, 61333
    Lateral Approach, 67420
    Removal, 67412
  Ovary
    Partial
      Oophorectomy, 58940
      Ovarian Malignancy, 58943
      Peritoneal Malignancy, 58943
      Tubal Malignancy, 58943
      Wedge Resection, 58920
    Total, 58940, 58943
  Oviduct, 58720
  Palate, 42104-42120, 42145
  Pancreas, 48120
    Ampulla of Vater, 48148
    Duct, 48148
    Lesion, 48120
    Partial, 48140-48154, 48160
    Peripancreatic Tissue, 48105

Excision — *continued*
  Pancreas — *continued*
    Total, 48155, 48160
  Papilla
    Anus, 46230 [46220]
  Parathyroid Gland, 60500, 60502
  Parotid Gland, 42340
    Partial, 42410, 42415
    Total, 42420-42426
  Partial, 31367-31382
  Patella, 27350
    See Patellectomy
  Penile Adhesions
    Post–circumcision, 54162
  Penis, 54110-54112
    Frenulum, 54164
    Partial, 54120
    Penile Plaque, 54110-54112
    Prepuce, 54150-54161, 54163
    Radical, 54130, 54135
    Total, 54125, 54135
  Pericardium, 33030, 33031
    Endoscopic, 32659-32660
  Petrous Temporal
    Apex, 69530
  Phalanges
    Finger, 26235, 26236
    Toe, 28124, 28126, 28150-28160
  Pharynx, 42145
    with Larynx, 31390, 31395
    Lesion, 42808
    Partial, 42890
    Resection, 42892, 42894
  Pituitary Gland, 61546, 61548
  Pleura, 32310, 32320
    Endoscopic, 32656
  Polyp
    Intestines, 43250
    Nose
      Extensive, 30115
      Simple, 30110
    Sinus, 31032
    Urethra, 53260
  Pressure Ulcers, 15920-15999
    See Skin Graft and Flap
    Coccygeal, 15920, 15922
    Ischial, 15940-15946
    Sacral, 15931-15936
    Trochanteric, 15950-15958
    Unlisted Procedure, Excision, 15999
  Prostate
    Abdominoperineal, 45119
    Partial, 55801, 55821, 55831
    Perineal, 55801-55815
    Radical, 55810-55815, 55840-55845
    Regrowth, 52630
    Residual Obstructive Tissue, 52630
    Retropubic, 55831-55845
    Suprapubic, 55821
    Transurethral, 52601
  Pterygium
    with Graft, 65426
  Pubis
    Partial, 27070, 27071
  Radical Synovium
    Wrist, 25115, 25116
  Radius, 24130, 24136, 24145, 24152, 25145
    Styloid Process, 25230
  Rectum
    with Colon, 45121
    Partial, 45111, 45113-45116, 45123
    Prolapse, 45130, 45135
    Stricture, 45150
    Total, 45119, 45120
    Tumor, 0184T
  Redundant Skin of Eyelid
    See Blepharoplasty
  Ribs, 21600-21616, 32900
  Scapula
    Ostectomy, 23190
    Partial, 23182

Excision — *continued*
  Scapula — *continued*
    Sequestrectomy, 23172
    Tumor
      Radical Resection, 23210
  Sclera, 66130, 66160
  Scrotum, 55150
  Semilunar Cartilage of Knee
    See Knee, Meniscectomy
  Seminal Vesicle, 55650
  Sesamoid Bone
    Foot, 28315
  Sinus
    Ethmoid, 31200-31205
      Endoscopic, 31254, 31255
    Frontal
      Endoscopic, 31276
    Maxillary, 31225, 31230
    Maxillectomy, 31230, 31255
      Endoscopic, 31267
    Unlisted Procedure, Accessory Sinuses, 31299
  Skene's Gland, 53270
  Skin, 11400-11471, 11600-11646
    Excess, 15830-15839
    Lesion
      Benign, 11400-11471
      Malignant, 11600-11646
    Nose, 30120
  Skin Graft
    Preparation of Site, 15002-15003, 15004-15005
  Skull, 61500-61501, 61615, 61616
  Spermatic Cord, 55520
  Spermatic Veins, 55530-55540
    with Hernia Repair, 55540
    Abdominal Approach, 55535
  Spinal Cord, 63300-63308
  Spleen, 38100-38102
    Laparoscopic, 38120
  Stapes
    with Footplate Drill Out, 69661
    without Foreign Material, 69660
  Sternum, 21620, 21630, 21632
  Stomach
    Partial, 43631-43635, 43845
    Total, 43620-43622, 43634
    Tumor or ulcer, 43610-43611
  Sublingual Gland, 42450
  Submandibular Gland, 42440, 42508
  Sweat Glands
    Axillary, 11450, 11451
    Inguinal, 11462, 11463
    Perianal, 11470, 11471
    Perineal, 11470, 11471
    Umbilical, 11470, 11471
  Synovium
    Ankle, 27625, 27626
    Carpometacarpal Joint, 26130
    Elbow, 24102
    Hip Joint, 27054
    Interphalangeal Joint, Finger, 26140
    Intertarsal Joint, 28070
    Knee Joint, 27334, 27335
    Metacarpophalangeal Joint, 26135
    Metatarsophalangeal Joint, 28072
    Shoulder, 23105, 23106
    Tarsometatarsal Joint, 28070
    Wrist, 25105, 25115-25119
  Tag
    Anus, 46230 [46220]
    Skin, 11200-11201
  Talus, 28120, 28130
    Arthroscopic, 29891
  Tarsal, 28116, 28122
  Temporal Bone, 69535
  Temporal, Petrous
    Apex, 69530
  Tendon
    Finger, 26180, 26390, 26415
    Hand, 26390, 26415
    Palm, 26170
  Tendon Sheath
    Finger, 26145

Excision

Excision — *continued*
Tendon Sheath — *continued*
  Foot, 28086, 28088
  Forearm, 25110
  Palm, 26145
  Wrist, 25115, 25116
Testis
  Extraparenchymal lesion, 54512
  Laparoscopic, 54690
  Partial, 54522
  Radical, 54530, 54535
  Simple, 54520
  Tumor, 54530, 54535
Thrombectomy
  Axillary Vein, 34490
  Bypass Graft, 35875, 35876
  Femoropopliteal Vein, 34401-34451
  Iliac Vein, 34401-34451
  Subclavian Vein, 34471, 34490
  Vena Cava, 34401-34451
Thromboendarterectomy
  Aorta, Abdominal, 35331
  Aortoiliac, 35361
  Aortoiliofemoral, 35363
  Axillary Artery, 35321
  Brachial Artery, 35321
  Carotid Artery, 35301, 35390
  Celiac Artery, 35341
  Femoral Artery, 35302, 35371, 35372
  Iliac, 35361, 35363
  Iliac Artery, 35351
  Iliofemoral Artery, 35355, 35363
  Innominate Artery, 35311
  Mesenteric Artery, 35341
  Peroneal Artery, 35305-35306
  Popliteal Artery, 35303
  Renal Artery, 35341
  Subclavian Artery, 35301, 35311, 35331, 35390
  Tibial Artery, 35305-35306
  Vertebral Artery, 35301, 35390
Thymus Gland, 60521
Thyroid Gland
  for Malignancy, 60252, 60254
    Limited Neck Dissection, 60252
    Radical Neck Dissection, 60254
  Partial, 60210-60225
  Removal All Thyroid Tissue, 60260
  Secondary, 60260
  Total, 60240
    Cervical Approach, 60271
    Sternal Split Transthoracic, 60270
Tibia, 27360, 27640
  Arthroscopic, 29891
Toe, 28092
Tongue
  with Mouth Resection, 41150, 41153
  with Radical Neck Dissection, 41135, 41145-41155
  Complete, 41140-41155
  Frenum, 41115
  Partial, 41120-41135
Tonsils
  Lingual, 42870
  Radical, 42842-42845
    Closure Local Flap, 42844, 42845
  Tag, 42860
    Anus, 46230 [46220]
    Skin, 11200-11201
  Tonsillectomy and Adenoidectomy
    Age 12 or Over, 42821
    Younger Than Age 12, 42820
  Tonsillectomy, Primary or Secondary
    Age 12 or Over, 42826
    Younger Than Age 12, 42825
Torus Mandibularis, 21031
Total, 31360, 31365

Excision — *continued*
Trachea
  Stenosis, 31780, 31781
Transcervical Approach, 60520
Tricuspid Valve, 33460-33465
Tumor
  Abdomen, 49203-49205
  Abdominal Wall, 22900-22905
  Acetabulum, 27076
  Ankle, 27615-27619 [27632, 27634], 27647
  Arm, Lower, 25075-25078 [25071, 25073], 25120-25126, 25170
  Arm, Upper, 23220, 24075-24079 [24071, 24073], 24110-24126, 24150-24152
  Back
    Flank, 21930, 21935
  Bile Duct, 47711, 47712
  Bladder, 51530, 52234-52240, 52355
  Brain, 61510, 61518, 61520, 61521, 61526, 61530, 61545, 62164
  Bronchi, 31640, 31641
  Calcaneus, 27647, 28100-28103
    with Allograft, 28103
    with Autograft, 28102
  Carpal, 25075-25078 [25071, 25073], 25130-25136
  Cheekbone, 21030, 21034, 21048-21049
  Clavicle, 23075-23078 [23071, 23073], 23140-23146, 23200
  Ear, Middle
    Extended, 69554
    Transcanal, 69550
    Transmastoid, 69552
  Elbow, 24075-24079 [24071, 24073], 24120-24126, 24152
  Esophagus
    Endoscopic Ablation, 43228
  Face or Scalp, 21011-21016
  Facial Bones, 21029, 21030, 21034, 21040, 21046-21049
  Femur, 27327-27328 [27337, 27339], 27355-27358, 27364-27365 [27329]
  Fibula, 27615-27619 [27632, 27634], 27635-27638, 27646
  Finger, 26115-26118 [26111, 26113], 26210-26215, 26260-26262
  Foot, 27647, 28043-28047 [28039, 28041], 28100-28107, 28171-28175
  Gums, 41825-41827
  Hand, 26115-26118 [26111, 26113], 26200-26205, 26250
  Heart, 33120, 33130
  Hip, 27047-27049 [27043, 27045, 27059], 27065-27067, 27076-27078
  Humerus, 23150-23156, 23220, 24075-24079 [24071, 24073], 24110-24116, 24150
  Ilium, 27047-27049 [27043, 27045, 27059], 27065-27067
  Innominate, 27047-27049 [27043, 27045, 27059], 27077
  Intestines
    Small, 43250
  Ischial, 27047-27049 [27043, 27045, 27059], 27078
  Kidney, 52355

Excision — *continued*
Tumor — *continued*
  Knee, 27327-27328 [27337, 27339], 27364-27365 [27329]
  Lacrimal Gland
    Frontal Approach, 68540
    Involving Osteotomy, 68550
  Larynx, 31300, 31320
    Endoscopic, 31540, 31541, 31578
  Leg, Lower, 27615-27619 [27632, 27634], 27635-27638, 27645-27647
  Leg, Upper, 27327-27328 [27337, 27339], 27355-27358, 27364-27365 [27329]
  Mandible, 21040-21047
  Maxilla, 21030, 21034, 21048, 21049
  Mediastinal, 39220
  Mediastinum, 32662
  Metacarpal, 26115-26118 [26111, 26113], 26200-26205
  Metatarsal, 28043-28047 [28039, 28041], 28100-28107, 28173
  Neck, 21555-21558 [21552, 21554]
  Olecranon Process, 24075-24079 [24071, 24073], 24120-24126
  Parotid Gland, 42410-42426
  Pelvis, 27047-27049 [27043, 27045, 27059], 27065-27067
  Pericardial, 33050
  Pericardium, 32661
  Phalanges
    Finger, 26115-26118 [26111, 26113], 26210, 26215, 26260-26262
    Toe, 28043-28047 [28039, 28041], 28108, 28175
  Pituitary Gland, 61546, 61548, 62165
  Presacral, 49215
  Pubis, 27065-27067
  Radius, 24152
  Rectum, 0184T, 45160, 45171-45172
  Retropharyngeal
    Anesthesia, 00174
  Sacrococcygeal, 49215
  Scalp or Face, 21011-21014
  Scapula, 23140
    with Allograft, 23146
    with Autograft, 23145
  Shoulder, 23075-23078 [23071, 23073]
  Skull, 61500
  Spermatocele
    See Spermatocele, Excision
  Spinal Cord, 63275-63290
  Spleen, Total
    See Splenectomy, Total
  Sternum, 21630
  Stomach, 43610
  Talus, 27647
  Tarsal
    Benign, 28104
      with Allograft, 28107
      with Autograft, 28106
    Radical, 28171
  Thigh, 27327-27328 [27337, 27339], 27355-27358, 27364-27365 [27329]
  Thorax, 21555-21558 [21552, 21554]
  Thyroid, 60200
  Tibia, 27615-27619 [27632, 27634], 27635-27638, 27645
  Toe, 28043-28047 [28039, 28041], 28108, 28175

Excision — *continued*
Tumor — *continued*
  Trachea
    Cervical, 31785
    Thoracic, 31786
  Ulna, 25075-25078 [25071, 25073], 25120-25126, 25170
  Ureter, 52355
  Urethra, 52234, 52235, 52240, 52355, 53220
  Uterus
    Abdominal Approach, 58140, 58146
    Vaginal Approach, 58145
  Vagina, 57135
  Vertebra
    Lumbar, 22102
    Thoracic, 22101
  Wrist, 25075-25078 [25071, 25073], 25120-25126
  Zygoma, 21030, 21034
Turbinate, 30130, 30140
Tympanic Nerve, 69676
Ulcer
  Stomach, 43610
Ulna, 24147, 25145
  Complete, 25240
  Partial, 24147, 25150, 25240
  Radical, 25170
Umbilicus, 49250
Ureter
  See Ureterectomy
Ureterocele, 51535
Urethra
  Diverticulum, 53230, 53235
  Prolapse, 53275
  Total
    Female, 53210
    Male, 53215
Uterus
  with Colo-urethrocystopexy, 58267, 58293
  with Colpectomy, 58275-58280
  with Repair of Enterocele, 58270, 58292, 58294
  Laparoscopic, 58550
  Partial, 58180
  Radical, 58210, 58285
  Removal Tubes and/or Ovaries, 58262-58263, 58291, 58552, 58554
  Total, 58150, 58152, 58200
  Vaginal, 58260, 58290-58294, 58550, 58553
    with Colpectomy, 58275-58280
    with Colpo-Urethrocystopexy, 58267, 58293
    with Repair of Enterocele, 58270, 58292, 58294
  Removal Tubes and or Ovaries, 58262, 58263, 58291, 58552, 58554
Uvula, 42104-42107, 42140, 42145
Vagina
  with Hysterectomy, 58275, 58280
  with Colpectomy, 58275
  Repair of Enterocele, 58280
  Closure, 57120
  Complete
    with Removal of Paravaginal Tissue with Lymphadenectomy, 57112
    with Removal of Paravaginal Tissue, 57111
    with Removal of Vaginal Wall, 57110
  Partial
    with Removal of Paravaginal Tissue with Lymphadenectomy, 57109
    with Removal of Paravaginal Tissue, 57107

Index — Eye

Excision — *continued*
  Vagina — *continued*
    Partial — *continued*
      with Removal of Vaginal Wall, 57106
    Septum, 57130
    Total, 57110
  Varicocele
    Spermatic Cord, 55530-55540
      with Hernia Repair, 55540
        Abdominal Approach, 55535
  Vascular Malformation
    Finger, 26115
    Hand, 26115
  Vas Deferens, 55250
  Vein
    Varicose, 37765, 37766
  Vertebra
    Additional Segment, 22103, 22116
    Cervical, 22110
      for Tumor, 22100, 22110
    Lumbar, 22102
      for Tumor, 22114
    Thoracic, 22112
      for Tumor, 22101
  Vertebral Body
    Decompression, 63081-63091
    Lesion, 63300-63308
  Vitreous
    with Retinal Surgery, 67108, 67113
    Mechanical, Pars Plana Approach, 67036-67043
  Vulva
    Radical
      Complete, 56633-56640
      Partial, 56630-56632
    Simple
      Complete, 56625
      Partial, 56620
  Wrist Tendon, 25110
Exclusion
  Duodenum, 48547
  Small Bowel, 44700
Exenteration
  Eye
    with Muscle or Myocutaneous Flap, 65114
    Removal Orbital Contents, 65110
    Therapeutic Removal of Bone, 65112
  Pelvis, 45126, 58240
    for Colorectal Malignancy, 45126
Exercise Stress Tests, 93015-93018
Exercise Test
  See Electromyography, Needle
  Ischemic Limb, 95875
Exercise Therapy, 97110-97113
  See Physical Medicine/Therapy/Occupational
Exfoliation
  Chemical, 17360
Exhaled Breath Condensate pH, 83987
Exocrine, Pancreas
  See Pancreas
Exomphalos
  See Omphalocele
Exostectomy, 28288, 28290
Exostoses, Cartilaginous
  See Exostosis
Exostosis
  Excision, 69140
Expander, Tissue, Inflatable
  Breast reconstruction with insertion, 19357
  Skin
    Insertion, 11960
    Removal, 11971
    Replacement, 11970
Expired Gas Analysis, 94680-94690, 94770
Exploration
  Abdomen, 49000, 49002
    Blood Vessel, 35840
    Penetrating Wound, 20102

Exploration — *continued*
  Abdomen — *continued*
    Staging, 58960
    Adrenal Gland, 60540, 60545
  Anal
    Endoscopy, 46600
  Ankle, 27610, 27620
  Arm, Lower, 25248
  Artery
    Brachial, 24495
    Carotid, 35701
    Femoral, 35721
    Other, 35761
    Popliteal, 35741
    Unlisted Services and Procedures, 35761
  Back, Penetrating Wound, 20102
  Bile Duct
    Atresia, 47700
    Endoscopy, 47552, 47553
  Blood Vessel
    Abdomen, 35840
    Chest, 35820
    Extremity, 35860
    Neck, 35800
  Brain
    Infratentorial, 61305
    Supratentorial, 61304
    via Burr Hole
      Infratentorial, 61253
      Supratentorial, 61250
  Breast, 19020
  Bronchi
    Endoscopy, 31622
  Bronchoscopy, 31622
  Cauda Equina, 63005, 63011, 63017
  Chest, Penetrating Wound, 20101
  Colon
    Endoscopic, 44388, 45378
  Colon, Sigmoid
    Endoscopy, 45330, 45335
  Common Bile Duct
    with Cholecystectomy, 47610
  Duodenum, 44010
  Ear, Inner
    Endolymphatic Sac
      with Shunt, 69806
      without Shunt, 69805
  Ear, Middle, 69440
  Elbow, 24000-24101 [24071, 24073]
  Epididymis, 54865
    Exploration, 54865
  Esophagus
    Endoscopy, 43200
  Extremity
    Penetrating Wound, 20103
  Finger Joint, 26075, 26080
  Flank
    Penetrating Wound, 20102
  Gallbladder, 47480
  Gastrointestinal Tract, Upper
    Endoscopy, 43234, 43235
  Hand Joint, 26070
  Heart, 33310, 33315
  Hepatic Duct, 47400
  Hip, 27033
  Interphalangeal Joint
    Toe, 28024
  Intertarsal Joint, 28020
  Intestines, Small
    Endoscopy, 43360
    Enterotomy, 44020
  Kidney, 50010, 50045, 50120, 50135
  Knee, 27310, 27331
  Lacrimal Duct, 68810
    with Anesthesia, 68811
    with Insertion Tube or Stent, 68815
    Canaliculi, 68840
  Laryngoscopy, 31575
  Larynx, 31320, 31505, 31520-31526, 31575
  Liver
    Wound, 47361, 47362
  Mediastinum, 39000, 39010
  Metatarsophalangeal Joint, 28022

Exploration — *continued*
  Nasolacrimal Duct, 68810
    with Anesthesia, 68811
    with Insertion Tube or Stent, 68815
  Neck
    Lymph Nodes, 38542
    Penetrating Wound, 20100
  Nipple, 19110
  Nose
    Endoscopy, 31231-31235
  Orbit, 61332-61334
    without Bone Flap, 67400
    with/without Biopsy, 67450
  Parathyroid Gland, 60500-60505
  Pelvis, 49320
  Peritoneum
    Endoscopic, 49320
  Prostate, 55860
    with Nodes, 55862, 55865
  Pterygomaxillary Fossa, 31040
  Rectum
    Endoscopic, 45300
    Injury, 45562, 45563
  Retroperitoneal Area, 49010
  Scrotum, 55110
  Shoulder Joint, 23040, 23044, 23107
  Sinus
    Frontal, 31070, 31075
      Endoscopic, 31276
      Transorbital, 31075
    Maxillary, 31020, 31030
    Sphenoid, 31050
  Skull, Drill Hole, 61105
  Spinal Cord, 63001-63011, 63015-63017, 63040-63044
    Facetectomy, Foraminotomy
      Partial Cervical, 63045
        Additional Segments, 63048
      Partial Lumbar, 63047
        Additional Segments, 63048
      Partial Thoracic, 63046
        Additional Segments, 63048
    Fusion, 22830
    Hemilaminectomy (including partial Facetectomy, Foraminotomy)
      Cervical, 63045
        Additional Segments, 63048
      Lumbar, 63047
        Additional Segments, 63048
      Thoracic, 63046
        Additional Segments, 63048
    Laminectomy
      Cervical, 63001, 63015
      Lumbar, 63005, 63017
      Thoracic, 63003, 63016
    Laminotomy
      Initial
        Cervical, 63020
          Each Additional Space, 63035
        Lumbar, 63030
      Reexploration
        Cervical, 63040
          Each Additional Space, 63043
        Lumbar, 63042
          Each Additional Interspace, 63044
  Stomach, 43500
  Tarsometatarsal Joint, 28020
  Testis
    Undescended, 54550, 54560
  Toe Joint, 28024
  Ureter, 50600, 50650, 50660
  Vagina, 57000
    Endoscopic Endocervical, 57452
  Wrist, 25101, 25248

Exploration — *continued*
  Wrist — *continued*
    Joint, 25040
Exploration, Larynx by Incision
  See Laryngotomy, Diagnostic
Exploratory Laparotomy
  See Abdomen, Exploration
Expression
  Lesion
    Conjunctiva, 68040
Exteriorization, Small Intestine
  See Enterostomy
External Auditory Canal
  See Auditory Canal
External Cephalic Version, 59412
External Ear
  See Ear, External
External Extoses
  See Exostosis
External Fixation (System)
  Adjustment/Revision, 20693
  Application, 20690, 20692
  Mandibular Fracture
    Open Treatment, 21454
    Percutaneous Treatment, 21452
  Removal, 20694
Extirpation, Lacrimal Sac
  See Dacryocystectomy
Extracorporeal Circulation, 33960, 33961
  Regional Chemotherapy
    Extremity, 36823
Extracorporeal Dialysis
  See Hemodialysis
Extracorporeal Membrane Oxygenation
  Cannulization, 36822
  Initial 24 Hours, 33960
Extracorporeal Photochemotherapies
  See Photopheresis
Extracorporeal Shock Wave Therapy
  See Lithotripsy
  Lateral Humeral Epicondyle, 0102T
  Musculoskeletal, 0019T, 0101T
  Plantar Fascia, 28890
Extraction
  Lens
    Extracapsular, 66940
    Intracapsular, 66920
    Dislocated Lens, 66930
Extraction, Cataract
  See Cataract, Excision
Extradural Anesthesia
  See Anesthesia, Epidural
Extradural Injection
  See Epidural, Injection
Extraocular Muscle
  See Eye Muscles
Extrauterine Pregnancy
  See Ectopic Pregnancy
Extravasation Blood
  See Hemorrhage
Extremity
  Lower
    Harvest of Vein for Bypass Graft, 35500
    Harvest of Vein for Vascular Reconstruction, 35572
    Repair of Blood Vessel, 35286
    Revision, 35879, 35881
  Penetrating Wound, 20103
  Upper
    Harvest of Artery for Coronary Artery Bypass Graft, 35600
    Harvest of Vein for Bypass Graft, 35500
    Repair of Blood Vessel, 35206
Extremity Testing
  Physical Therapy, 97750
  Vascular Diagnostics, 93924
Eye
  with Muscle or Myocutaneous Flap, 65114
    Muscles Attached, 65105
    Ocular Contents
      with Implant, 65093

Eye

Eye — *continued*
  with Muscle or Myocutaneous Flap — *continued*
    Ocular Contents — *continued*
      without Implant, 65091
      Orbital Contents, 65110
        without Implant, 65101
    See Ciliary Body; Cornea; Iris; Lens; Retina; Sclera; Vitreous
  Biometry, 76516, 76519, 92136
  Drainage
    with Removal of Vitreous and/or Discission of Anterior Hyaloid Membrane, 65810
    with Therapeutic Release of Aqueous, 65805
    Anterior Chamber, 65800-65815
      with Diagnostic Aspiration of Aqueous, 65800
      with Removal of Blood, 65815
  Endoscopy, 66990
  Goniotomy, 65820
  Incision
    Adhesions
      Anterior Synechiae, 65860, 65870
      Corneovitreal Adhesions, 65880
      Goniosynechiae, 65865
      Posterior Synechiae, 65875
    Anterior Chamber, 65820
    Trabecula, 65850
  Injection
    Air, 66020
    Medication, 66030
  Insertion
    Implantation
      Drug Delivery System, 67027
      Foreign Material for Reinforcement, 65155
      Muscles Attached, 65140
      Muscles Not Attached, 65135
      Reinsertion, 65150
      Scleral Shell, 65130
  Interferometry
    Biometry, 92136
  Lesion
    Excision, 65900
  Nerve
    Destruction, 67345
  Paracentesis
    Anterior Chamber
      with Diagnostic Aspiration of Aqueous, 65800
      with Removal of Blood, 65815
    Removal of Vitreous and/or Discission Anterior Hyaloid Membrane, 65810
    with Therapeutic Release of Aqueous, 65805
  Radial Keratotomy, 65771
  Reconstruction
    Amniotic Membrane, 65780
    Conjunctiva, 65782
  Removal
    Blood Clot, 65930
    Bone, 65112
    Foreign Body
      Conjunctival Embedded, 65210
      Conjunctival Superficial, 65205
      Corneal without Slit Lamp, 65220
      Corneal with Slit Lamp, 65222
      Intraocular, 65235-65265
    Implant, 65175
      Anterior Segment, 65920
      Muscles not Attached, 65103
      Posterior Segment, 67120, 67121
  Repair
    Conjunctiva
      by Mobilization and Rearrangement with Hospitalization, 65273

Eye — *continued*
  Repair — *continued*
    Conjunctiva — *continued*
      by Mobilization and Rearrangement without Hospitalization, 65272
      Direct Closure, 65270
    Cornea
      Nonperforating, 65275
      Perforating, 65280, 65285
    Muscles, 65290
    Sclera
      with Graft, 66225
      with Tissue Glue, 65286
      without Graft, 66220
    Anterior Segment, 66250
    Trabeculae, 65855
    Wound
      by Mobilization and Rearrangement, 65272, 65273
      Direct Closure, 65270
  Shunt, Aqueous
    to Extraocular Reservoir, 66180
  Ultrasound, 76510-76514
    Biometry, 76516, 76519
    Foreign Body, 76529
  Unlisted Services and Procedures
    Anterior Segment, 66999
    Posterior Segment, 67299
  X-ray, 70030
Eye Allergy Test, 95060
  See Allergy Tests
Eyebrow
  Repair
    Ptosis, 67900
Eye Evisceration
  See Evisceration, Ocular Contents
Eye Exam
  with Anesthesia, 92018, 92019
  Established Patient, 92012, 92014
  New Patient, 92002, 92004
  Radiologic, 70030
Eye Exercises
  Training, 92065
Eyeglasses
  See Spectacle Services
Eyelashes
  Repair Trichiasis
    Epilation
      by Forceps Only, 67820
      by Other than Forceps, 67825
    Incision of Lid Margin, 67830
      with Free Mucous Membrane Graft, 67835
Eyelid
  Abscess
    Incision and Drainage, 67700
  Biopsy, 67810
  Blepharoplasty, 15820-15823
  Chalazion
    Excision
      with Anesthesia, 67808
      Multiple, 67801, 67805
      Single, 67800
    Closure by Suture, 67875
  Incision
    Canthus, 67715
  Injection
    Subconjunctival, 68200
    Sutures, 67710
  Lesion
    Destruction, 67850
    Excision
      with Anesthesia, 67808
      without Closure, 67840
      Multiple, 67801, 67805
      Single, 67800
  Reconstruction
    Canthus, 67950
    Total Eyelid
      Conjunctivo–Tarso–Muller's Muscle–Levator Resection, 67908
      Lower, 67973
      Second Stage, 67975

Eyelid — *continued*
  Reconstruction — *continued*
    Canthus — *continued*
    Total Eyelid — *continued*
      Upper, 67974
      Second Stage, 67975
      Transfer of Tarsoconjunctival Flap from Opposing Eyelid, 67971
  Removal
    Foreign Body, 67938
  Repair, 21280, 21282
    Blepharoptosis
      Reduction Overcorrection of Ptosis, 67909
      Superior Rectus Technique with Fascial Sling, 67906
    Ectropion
      Excision Tarsal Wedge, 67916
      Extensive, 67917
      Suture, 67914
      Thermocauterization, 67915
    Entropion
      Excision Tarsal Wedge, 67923
      Extensive, 67924
      Frontalis Muscle Technique, 67901-67904
      Suture, 67921
      Thermocauterization, 67922
    Excisional, 67961
      over One-Fourth of Lid Margin, 67966
    Lagophthalmos, 67912
    Lashes
      Epilation, by Forceps Only, 67820
      Epilation by Other than Forceps, 67825
      Lid Margin, 67830, 67835
    Wound
      Full Thickness, 67935
      Partial Thickness, 67930
  Repair with Graft
    Retraction, 67911
  Skin Graft
    Delay of Flap, 15630
    Full Thickness, 15260, 15261, 67961
    Pedicle Flap, 15576
    Split, 15120, 15121, 67961
  Suture, 67880
    with Transposition of Tarsal Plate, 67882
  Tissue Transfer, Adjacent, 14060, 14061, 67961
  Unlisted Services and Procedures, 67999
Eyelid Ptoses
  See Blepharoptosis
Eye Muscles
  Biopsy, 67346
    Extraocular muscle, 67346
  Repair
    Strabismus
      with Scarring Extraocular Muscles, 67332
      with Superior Oblique Muscle, 67318
      Adjustable Sutures, 67335
      Exploration and/or Repair Detached Extraocular Muscle, 67340
      One Vertical Muscle, 67314
      on Patient with Previous Surgery, 67331
      Posterior Fixation Suture, 67334
      Recession or Resection, 67311, 67312
      Release of Scar Tissue without Detaching Extraocular Muscle, 67343
      Two or More Vertical Muscles, 67316
    Transposition, 67320

Eye Muscles — *continued*
  Unlisted Procedure, Ocular Muscle, 67399
Eye Prosthesis
  See Prosthesis
Eye Socket
  See Orbit; Orbital Contents; Orbital Floor; Periorbital Region

F

Face
  CT Scan, 70486-70488
  Lesion
    Destruction, 17000-17108, 17280-17286
    Magnetic Resonance Imaging (MRI), 70540-70543
  Skin Graft
    Split, 15120, 15121
  Tumor Resection, 21011-21016
Face Lift, 15824-15828
Facial Asymmetries
  See Hemifacial Microsomia
Facial Bone
  See Mandible; Maxilla
  Tumor
    Excision, 21034
Facial Bones
  Abscess
    Excision, 21026
  Anesthesia, 00190, 00192
  Reconstruction
    Secondary, 21275
  Repair, 21208, 21209
  Tumor
    Excision, 21029, 21030, 21034
    Resection
      Radical, 21015
  X-ray
    Complete, Minimum Three Views, 70150
    Less than Three Views, 70140
    Nasal Bones, 70160
Facial Nerve
  Anastomosis
    to Hypoglossal Nerve, 64868
    to Phrenic Nerve, 64870
    to Spinal Accessory Nerve, 64866
  Avulsion, 64742
  Decompression, 61590, 61596
    Intratemporal
      Lateral to Geniculate Ganglion, 69720, 69740
      Medial to Geniculate Ganglion, 69725, 69745
    Total, 69955
  Function Study, 92516
  Incision, 64742
  Injection
    Anesthetic, 64402
  Mobilization, 61590
  Paralysis Repair, 15840-15845
  Repair
    Lateral to Geniculate Ganglion, 69740
    Medial to Geniculate Ganglion, 69745
    Suture with or without Graft, 64864, 64865
  Suture
    Lateral to Geniculate Ganglion, 69740
    Medial to Geniculate Ganglion, 69745
  Transection, 64742
Facial Nerve Function Study, 92516
Facial Nerve Paralysis
  Graft, 15840-15845
  Repair, 15840-15845
Facial Prosthesis, 21088
Facial Rhytidectomy
  See Face Lift
Factor
  I, 85384, 85385
  II, 85210
  III, 85730, 85732

Index

Factor — continued
- IV, 82310
- IX, 85250
- V, 85220
- VII, 85230
- VIII, 85244, 85247
- X, 85260
- XI, 85270
- XIII, 85290, 85291

Factor, ACTH–Releasing
See Corticotropic Releasing Hormone (CRH)

Factor, Antinuclear
See Antinuclear Antibodies (ANA)

Factor, Fitzgerald
See Fitzgerald Factor

Factor, Fletcher
See Fletcher Factor

Factor, Hyperglycemic–Glycogenolytic
See Glucagon

Factor Inhibitor Test, 85335

Factor, Intrinsic
See Intrinsic Factor

Factor, Sulfation
See Somatomedin

Fallopian Tube
- Anastomosis, 58750
- Catheterization, 58345, 74742
- Destruction
  - Endoscopy, 58670
- Ectopic Pregnancy, 59121
  - with Salpingectomy and/or Oophorectomy, 59120
- Excision, 58700, 58720
- Ligation, 58600-58611
- Lysis
  - Adhesions, 58740
- Occlusion, 58615
  - Endoscopy, 58671
- Placement
  - Implant for Occlusion, 58565
- Repair, 58752
  - Anastomosis, 58750
  - Creation of Stoma, 58770
- Tumor
  - Resection, 58950, 58952-58956
- Unlisted Procedure, Female Genital System, 58999
- X-ray, 74742

Fallopian Tube Pregnancy
See Ectopic Pregnancy, Tubal

Fallot, Tetralogy of
See Tetralogy of Fallot

Family Psychotherapy
See Psychotherapy, Family

Fanconi Anemia, 88248
- Chromosome Analysis, 88248

Fan Type Procedure, 40525

Farnsworth-Musell Color Test, 92283

Farr Test, 82784, 82785

Fasanella–Servat Procedure, 67908

Fascia Graft, 15840
- Free Microvascular Anastomosis, 15758
- Harvesting, 20920, 20922
- Open Treatment, Sternoclavicular Dislocation, 23532

Fascia Lata Graft
- Harvesting, 20920, 20922

Fascial Defect
- Repair, 50728

Fascial Graft
- Free
  - Microvascular Anastomosis, 15758
- Open Treatment
  - Sternoclavicular Dislocation, 23532

Fasciectomy
- Foot, 28060
- Radical, 28060, 28062
- Palm, 26121-26125

Fasciocutaneous Flap, 15732-15738
- Head and Neck, 15732
- Lower Extremity, 15738
- Trunk, 15734

Fasciocutaneous Flap — continued
- Upper Extremity, 15736

Fasciotomy
- Arm, Lower, 24495, 25020-25025
- Buttocks, 27057
- Elbow, 24357-24359
- Foot, 28008
- Hand, Decompression, 26037
- Hip, 27025
- Knee, 27305, 27496-27499
- Leg, Lower, 27600-27602, 27892-27894
- Leg, Upper, 27305, 27496-27499, 27892-27894
- Palm, 26040, 26045
- Pelvis, 27057
- Plantar
  - Endoscopic, 29893
- Thigh, 27025
- Toe, 28008
- Wrist, 25020-25025

FAST
See Allergen Immunotherapy

Fat
- Feces, 82705-82715
- Removal
  - Lipectomy, 15876-15879
- Respiratory Secretions, 89125

Fat Stain
- Feces, 89125
- Respiratory Secretions, 89125
- Sputum, 89125
- Urine, 89125

Fatty Acid
- Blood, 82725
- Very Long Chain, 82726

Favre–Durand Disease
See Lymphogranuloma Venereum

FC Receptor, 86243

FDP (Fibrin Degradation Products), 85362-85379

Fe, 83540

Feedback, Psychophysiologic
See Biofeedback; Training, Biofeedback

Female Castration
See Oophorectomy

Female Gonad
See Ovary

Femoral Artery
See Artery, Femoral
- Embolectomy
  - Anesthesia, 01274
- Ligation
  - Anesthesia, 01272

Femoral Nerve
- Injection
  - Anesthetic, 64447-64448

Femoral Stem Prosthesis
- Arthroplasty, Hip, 27132
  - Partial Replacement, 27125
  - Revision, 27134-27138
  - Total Replacement, 27130
  - Incision, 27303

Femoral Vein
See Vein, Femoral

Femur
See Hip; Knee; Leg, Upper
- Bursa
  - Excision, 27062
- Craterization, 27070, 27071, 27360
- Cyst
  - Excision, 27065-27067, 27355-27358
- Diaphysectomy, 27360
- Drainage, 27303
- Excision, 27070, 27071, 27360
- Epiphyseal Bar, 20150
- Fracture
  - Closed Treatment, 27501-27503
  - Distal, 27508, 27510, 27514
  - Distal, Medial or Lateral Condyle, 27509
  - Epiphysis, 27516-27519
  - Intertrochanteric, 27238-27245
    - with Implant, 27245

Femur — continued
- Fracture — continued
  - Intertrochanteric — continued
    - with Manipulation, 27240
    - Closed Treatment, 27238
    - Open Treatment, 27244
  - Neck, 27230-27236
    - Closed Treatment, 27230, 27232
    - Open Treatment, 27236
    - Percutaneous Fixation, 27235
    - Open Treatment, 27244, 27245, 27506, 27507, 27511, 27513
  - Percutaneous Fixation, 27509
  - Peritrochanteric, 27238-27245
    - with Implant, 27245
    - with Manipulation, 27240
    - Closed Treatment, 27238
    - Open Treatment, 27244
  - Shaft, 27500, 27502, 27506, 27507
  - Subtrochanteric, 27238-27245
    - with Implant, 27245
    - with Manipulation, 27240
    - Closed Treatment, 27238
    - Open Treatment, 27244
  - Supracondylar, 27501-27503, 27509, 27511, 27513
  - Transcondylar, 27501-27503, 27509, 27511, 27513
  - Trochanteric, 27246, 27248
    - with Manipulation, 27503
    - without Manipulation, 27501
    - Closed Treatment, 27246
    - Open Treatment, 27248
- Halo, 20663
- Lesion
  - Excision, 27062
- Osteoplasty
  - Lengthening, 27466, 27468
  - Shortening, 27465, 27468
- Osteotomy
  - without Fixation, 27448
- Prophylactic Treatment, 27187, 27495
- Realignment on Intramedullary Rod, 27454
- Reconstruction, 27468
  - at Knee, 27442, 27443, 27446
  - Lengthening, 27466, 27468
  - Shortening, 27465, 27468
- Repair, 27470, 27472
  - with Graft, 27170
  - Epiphysis, 27181, 27742
    - Arrest, 27185, 27475, 27479
  - Muscle Transfer, 27110
  - Osteotomy, 27448, 27450
    - with Open Reduction, Hip, 27156
    - and Transfer of Greater Trochanter, 27140
    - as part of other, 27151
  - Femoral Neck, 27161
  - Intertrochanteric or Subtrochanteric, 27165
  - Multiple, Shaft, 27454
  - Shaft or Supracondylar, 27448
- Saucerization, 27070, 27071, 27360
- Tumor
  - Excision, 27065-27067, 27355-27358, 27365
- X-ray, 73550

Fenestration, Pericardium
See Pericardiostomy

Fenestration Procedure
- Lempert's, 69820
- Semicircular Canal, 69820
- Revision, 69840
- Tracheostomy, 31610

Fern Test
- Smear and Stain, Wet Mount, 87210

Ferric Chloride
- Urine, 81005

Fibrinolysis

Ferrihemoglobin
See Methemoglobin

Ferritin
- Blood or Urine, 82728

Ferroxidase
See Ceruloplasmin

Fertility Control
See Contraception

Fertility Test
- Semen Analysis, 89300-89322
- Sperm Evaluation
  - Cervical Mucus Penetration Test, 89330
  - Hamster Penetration, 89329

Fertilization
- Oocytes (Eggs)
  - In Vitro, 89250-89251
    - with Co–Culture of Embryo, 89251
    - Assisted (Microtechnique), 89280, 89281

Fertilization in Vitro
See In Vitro Fertilization

Fetal Biophysical Profile, 76818, 76819

Fetal Contraction Stress Test, 59020

Fetal Hemoglobin, 83030, 83033, 85460, 85461

Fetal Lung Maturity Assessment, Lecithin Sphingomyelin Ratio, 83661

Fetal Monitoring
See Monitoring, Fetal

Fetal Non-Stress Test, 59025
- Ultrasound, 76818

Fetal Procedure
- Amnioinfusion, 59070
- Cord Occlusion, 59072
- Fluid Drainage, 59074
- Shunt Placement, 59076
- Unlisted Procedure, 59897

Fetal Testing
- Biophysical Profile, 76818-76819
- Lung Maturity, 83661, 83663, 83664
- Heart, 76825, 76826
  - Doppler
    - Complete, 76827
    - Follow–up or Repeat Study, 76828
- Hemoglobin, 83030, 83033, 85460, 85461
- Scalp Blood Sampling, 59020
- Ultrasound, 76801-76828
  - Heart, 76825
  - Middle Cerebral Artery, 76821
  - Umbilical Artery, 76820

Fetuin
See Alpha–Fetoprotein

Fever, Australian Q
See Q Fever

Fever, Japanese River
See Scrub Typhus

FFL (Flexible Fiberoptic Laryngoscopy), 31575-31579

Fibrillation
- Atrial, 33254, 33255-33256

Fibrillation, Heart
See Heart, Fibrillation

Fibrinase
See Plasmin

Fibrin Degradation Products, 85362-85380

Fibrin Deposit
- Removal, 32150

Fibrinogen, 85384, 85385

Fibrinolysin
See Plasmin

Fibrinolysins, 85390

Fibrinolysis
- Alpha–2 Antiplasmin, 85410
- Assay, 85396
- Functional Activity, 85397
- Plasmin, 85400
- Plasminogen, 85420, 85421
- Plasminogen Activator, 85415

Fibrin Stabilizing Factor, 85290, 85291
Fibroadenoma
  Excision, 19120-19126
Fibroblastoma, Arachnoidal
  See Meningioma
Fibrocutaneous Tags
  Destruction, 11200, 11201
Fibroids Tumor of Uterus
  Excision
    Abdominal Approach, 58140
    Vaginal Approach, 58145
Fibromatosis, Dupuytrens's
  See Dupuytren's Contracture
Fibromatosis, Penile
  See Peyronie Disease
Fibromyoma
  See Leiomyomata
Fibronectin, Fetal, 82731
Fibrosis, Penile
  See Peyronie Disease
Fibrosis, Retroperitoneal
  See Retroperitoneal Fibrosis
Fibrous Cavernitides
  See Peyronie Disease
Fibrous Dysplasia, 21029, 21181-21184
  Reconstruction
    Cranial, 21181
    Facial, 21029
    Orbital Walls, 21182
      40 cm to 80 cm, 21183
      80 cm or More, 21184
Fibula
  See Ankle; Knee; Tibia
  Bone Graft with Microvascular Anastomosis, 20955
  Craterization, 27360, 27641
  Cyst
    Excision, 27635-27638
  Diaphysectomy, 27360, 27641
  Excision, 27360, 27641
  Epiphyseal Bar, 20150
  Fracture
    Malleolus
      Bimalleolar
        Closed Treatment, 27808
          with Manipulation, 27810
        Open Treatment, 27814
      Lateral
        Closed Treatment, 27786
          with Manipulation, 27788
        Open Treatment, 27792
      Medial
        Closed Treatment, 27760
          with Manipulation, 27762
        Open Treatment, 27766
      Trimalleolar
        Closed Treatment, 27816
          with Manipulation, 27818
        Open Treatment, 27822
          with Fixation, 27823
    Shaft
      Closed Treatment, 27780
        with Manipulation, 27781
      Open Treatment, 27784
  Incision, 27607
  Osteoplasty
    Lengthening, 27715
  Repair
    Epiphysis, 27477-27485, 27730-27742
    Osteotomy, 27707-27712
  Saucerization, 27360, 27641
  Tumor
    Excision, 27635-27638, 27646
  X-ray, 73590
Figure of Eight Cast, 29049
Filariasis, 86280
Filtering Operation
  Incision, Sclera, Fistulization
    with Iridectomy, 66160

Filtering Operation — *continued*
  Incision, Sclera, Fistulization — *continued*
    Iridencleisis or Iridotasis, 66165
    Sclerectomy with Punch or Scissors with Iridectomy, 66160
    Thermocauterization with Iridectomy, 66155
    Trabeculectomy ab Externo in Absence Previous Surgery, 66170
    Trephination with Iridectomy, 66150
Filtration
  Transciliary, 0123T
Filtration Implant, Glaucoma
  See Aqueous Shunt
Fimbrioplasty, 58760
  Laparoscopic, 58672
Fine Needle Aspiration, 10021, 10022
  Evaluation, 88172, 88173
Finger
  See Phalanx, Finger
  Abscess
    Bone
      Incision and Drainage, 26034
    Incision and Drainage, 26010, 26011
  Amputation, 26951
    with Exploration or Removal, 26910
  Arthrocentesis, 20600
  Arthrodesis
    Interphalangeal Joint, 26860-26863
    Metacarpophalangeal Joint, 26850, 26852
  Bone
    Incision and Drainage, 26034
  Cast, 29086
  Collection of Blood, 36415, 36416
  Decompression, 26035
  Excision, 26235-26236
    Constricting Ring, 26596
    Tendon, 26180, 26390, 26415
  Insertion
    Tendon Graft, 26392
  Magnetic Resonance Imaging (MRI), 73221
  Reconstruction
    Extra Digit, 26587
    Toe to Hand Transfer, 26551-26554, 26556
  Removal
    Implantation, 26320
    Tube, 26392, 26416
  Repair
    Blood Vessel, 35207
    Claw Finger, 26499
    Extra Digit, 26587
    Macrodactylia, 26590
    Tendon
      Dorsum, 26418, 26420
      Extensor, 26415-26434, 26445, 26449, 26460
        Central Slip, 26426, 26428
        Distal Insertion, 26432, 26433
        Excision with Implantation, 26415
        Hand, 26410
          with Graft, 26412
        Realignment, Hand, 26437
      Flexor, 26356-26358, 26440, 26442, 26455
      Flexor Excision with Implantation, 26390
      Lengthening, 26476, 26478
      Opponensplasty, 26490-26496
      Profundus, 26370-26373
      Removal Tube or Rod
        Extensor, 26416
        Flexor, 26392
      Shortening, 26477, 26479
      Tenodesis, 26471, 26474

Finger — *continued*
  Repair — *continued*
    Tendon — *continued*
      Tenolysis, 26440-26449
      Tenotomy, 26450-26460
      Transfer or Transplant, 26485, 26489, 26497, 26498
    Volar Plate, 26548
    Web Finger, 26560-26562
  Replantation, 20816, 20822
  Reposition, 26555
  Sesamoidectomy, 26185
  Splint, 29130, 29131
  Strapping, 29280
  Tendon Sheath
    Excision, 26145
    Incision, 26055
    Incision and Drainage, 26020
  Tenotomy, 26060, 26460
    Flexor, 26455
  Tumor, 25120, 26115-26118 [26111, 26113], 26260-28260 [27043, 27045, 27059, 27329, 27337, 27339, 27632, 27634, 28039, 28041]
  Unlisted Services and Procedures/Hands or Fingers, 26989
  X-ray, 73140
Finger Flap
  Tissue Transfer, 14350
Finger Joint
  See Intercarpal Joint
Finney Operation, 43850
FISH, 88365
Fishberg Concentration Test
  Water Load Test, 89235
Fissurectomy, 46200, 46261-46262
Fissure in Ano
  See Anus, Fissure
Fistula
  Anal
    Repair, 46262-46288, 46706-46707
  Arteriovenous, 36831-36833
    Injection, 36147-36148
    Revision
      with Thrombectomy, 36831
      without Thrombectomy, 36832
    Thrombectomy without revision, 36831
    Autogenous Graft, 36825
  Bronchi
    Repair, 32815
  Carotid–Cavernous Repair, 61710
  Chest Wall
    Repair, 32906
  Conjunctiva
    with Tube or Stent, 68750
    without Tube, 68745
  Enterovesical
    Closure, 44660, 44661
  Kidney, 50520-50526
  Lacrimal Gland
    Closure, 68770
    Dacryocystorhinostomy, 68720
  Nose
    Repair, 30580, 30600
    Window, 69666
  Oval Window, 69666
  Postauricular, 69700
  Rectovaginal
    with Concomitant Colostomy, 57307
    Abdominal Approach, 57305
    Transperineal Approach, 57308
  Round Window, 69667
  Sclera
    Iridencleisis or Iridotasis, 66165
    Sclerectomy with Punch or Scissors with Iridectomy, 66160
    Thermocauterization with Iridectomy, 66155

Fistula — *continued*
  Sclera — *continued*
    Trabeculectomy ab Externo in Absence Previous Surgery, 66170
    Trabeculectomy ab Externo with Scarring, 66172
    Trephination with Iridectomy, 66150
  Suture
    Kidney, 50520-50526
    Ureter, 50920, 50930
  Trachea, 31755
  Tracheoesophageal
    Repair, 43305, 43312, 43314
    Speech Prosthesis, 31611
  Transperineal Approach, 57308
  Ureter, 50920, 50930
  Urethra, 53400, 53405
  Urethrovaginal, 57310
    with Bulbocavernosus Transplant, 57311
  Vesicouterine
    Closure, 51920, 51925
  Vesicovaginal
    Closure, 51900
    Transvesical and Vaginal Approach, 57330
    Vaginal Approach, 57320
  X-ray, 76080
Fistula Arteriovenous
  See Arteriovenous Fistula
Fistulectomy
  Anal, 46060, 46262-46285
Fistulization
  Conjunction to Nasal Cavity, 68745
  Esophagus, 43350-43352
  Intestines, 44300-44346
  Lacrimal Sac to Nasal Cavity, 68720
  Penis, 54435
  Pharynx, 42955
  Sclera, 0123T
  Tracheopharyngeal, 31755
Fistulization, Interatrial
  See Septostomy, Atrial
Fistulotomy
  Anal, 46270-46280
Fitting
  Cervical Cap, 57170
  Contact Lens, 92070, 92310-92313
    See Contact Lens Services
  Diaphragm, 57170
  Low Vision Aid, 92354, 92355
    See Spectacle Services
  Spectacle Prosthesis, 92352, 92353
  Spectacles, 92340-92342
Fitzgerald Factor, 85293
Fixation (Device)
  See Application; Bone; Fixation; Spinal Instrumentation
  Application, External, 20690-20697
  Insertion, 20690-20697, 22841-22844
    Prosthetic, 22851
    Reinsertion, 22849
  Interdental without Fracture, 21497
  Pelvic
    Insertion, 22848
  Removal
    External, 20694
    Internal, 20670, 20680
  Sacrospinous Ligament
    Vaginal Prolapse, 57282
  Shoulder, 23700
  Skeletal
    Humeral Epicondyle
      Percutaneous, 24566
  Spinal
    Insertion, 22841-22847
    Prosthetic, 22851
    Reinsertion, 22849
Fixation, External
  See External Fixation
Fixation, Kidney
  See Nephropexy

Index — Foreign Body

Fixation, Rectum
　See Proctopexy
Fixation Test Complement
　See Complement, Fixation Test
Fixation, Tongue
　See Tongue, Fixation
Flank
　See Back/Flank
Flap
　See Skin Graft and Flap
　Delay of Flap at Trunk, 15600
　　at Eyelids, Nose Ears, or Lips, 15630
　　at Forehead, Cheeks, Chin, Neck, Axillae, Genitalia, Hands, Feet, 15620
　　at Scalp, Arms, or Legs, 15610
　　Section Pedicle of Cross Finger, 15620
　Free
　　Breast Reconstruction, 19364
　　Microvascular Transfer, 15756-15758
　Grafts, 15574-15650, 15842
　　Composite, 15760
　　　Derma–Fat–Fascia, 15770
　　Cross Finger Flap, 15574
　　Punch for Hair Transplant
　　　Less than 15, 15775
　　　More than 15, 15776
　Island Pedicle, 15740
　　Neurovascular Pedicle, 15750
　Latissimus Dorsi
　　Breast Reconstruction, 19361
　Omentum
　　Free
　　　with Microvascular Anastomosis, 49906
　Transfer
　　Intermediate of Any Pedicle, 15650
　Transverse Rectus Abdominis Myocutaneous
　　Breast Reconstruction, 19367-19369
Flatfoot Correction, 28735
Flea Typhus
　See Murine Typhus
Fletcher Factor, 85292
Flick Method Testing, 93561-93562
Flow Cytometry, 86356, 88182-88189
Flow Volume Loop/Pulmonary, 94375
　See Pulmonology, Diagnostic
FLUARIX, 90656
Fluid, Amniotic
　See Amniotic Fluid
Fluid, Body
　See Body Fluid
Fluid, Cerebrospinal
　See Cerebrospinal Fluid
Fluid Collection
　Incision and Drainage
　　Skin, 10140
Fluid Drainage
　Abdomen, 49080, 49081
FluMist, 90660
Fluorescein
　Angiography, Ocular, 92287
　Intravenous Injection
　　Vascular Flow Check, Graft, 15860
Fluorescein, Angiography
　See Angiography, Fluorescein
Fluorescent Antibody, 86255, 86256
Fluorescent In Situ Hybridization, 88365
Fluoride
　Blood, 82735
　Urine, 82735
Fluoroscopy
　Bile Duct
　　Calculus Removal, 74327
　　Guide for Catheter, 74328, 74330
　Chest
　　Bronchoscopy, 31622-31646
　　Complete (four views), 71034

Fluoroscopy — continued
　Chest — continued
　　Partial (two views), 71023
　　Drain Abscess, 75989
　GI Tract
　　Guidance Intubation, 74340
　Hourly, 76000, 76001
　Introduction
　　GI Tube, 74340
　Larynx, 70370
　Nasogastric, 43752
　Needle Biopsy, 77002
　Pancreatic Duct
　　Catheter, 74329, 74330
　Pharynx, 70370
　Renal
　　Guide Catheter, 74475
　Spine/Paraspinous
　　Guide Catheter
　　　Needle, 77003
　Unlisted Procedure, 76496
　Ureter
　　Guidance Catheter, 74480
　Vertebra
　　Osteoplasty, 72291-72292
　X-ray with Contrast
　　Guidance Catheter, 74475
Flurazepam
　Blood or Urine, 82742
Flush Aortogram, 75722, 75724
Flu Vaccines, 90645-90660
Fluvirin, 90656, 90658
Fluzone, 90655-90658
fMRI (Functional MRI), 70554-70555
FNA (Fine Needle Aspiration), 10021-10022
Foam Stability Test, 83662
FOBT (Fecal Occult Blood Test), 82270, 82272, 82274
Fold, Vocal
　See Vocal Cords
Foley Operation Pyeloplasty
　See Pyeloplasty
Foley Y–Pyeloplasty, 50400, 50405
Folic Acid, 82746
　RBC, 82747
Follicle Stimulating Hormone (FSH), 80418, 80426, 83001
Folliculin
　See Estrone
Follitropin
　See Follicle Stimulating Hormone (FSH)
Follow–Up Services
　See Hospital Services; Office and/or Other Outpatient Services
　Post-Op, 99024
Fontan Procedure, 33615, 33617
Food Allergy Test, 95075
　See Allergy Tests
Foot
　See Metatarsal; Tarsal
　Amputation, 28800, 28805
　Bursa
　　Incision and Drainage, 28001
　Capsulotomy, 28260-28264
　Cast, 29450
　Cock Up Fifth Toe, 28286
　Fasciectomy, 28060
　　Radical, 28060, 28062
　Fasciotomy, 28008
　　Endoscopic, 29893
　Hammertoe Operation, 28285
　Incision, 28002-28005
　Joint
　　See Talotarsal Joint; Tarsometatarsal Joint
　　Magnetic Resonance Imaging (MRI), 73721-73723
　Lesion
　　Excision, 28080, 28090
　Magnetic Resonance Imaging (MRI), 73718-73720
　Nerve
　　Excision, 28055
　　Incision, 28035

Foot — continued
　Neuroma
　　Excision, 28080
　Ostectomy, Metatarsal Head, 28288
　Reconstruction
　　Cleft Foot, 28360
　Removal
　　Foreign Body, 28190-28193
　Repair
　　Muscle, 28250
　　Tendon
　　　Advancement Posterior Tibial, 28238
　　　Capsulotomy; Metatarsophalangeal, 28270
　　　　Interphalangeal, 28272
　　　Capsulotomy, Midfoot; Medial Release, 26820
　　　Capsulotomy, Midtarsal (Heyman Type), 28264
　　　Extensor, Single, 28208
　　　　Secondary with Free Graft, 28210
　　　Flexor, Single, with Free Graft, 28200
　　　　Secondary with Free Graft, 28202
　　　Tenolysis, Extensor
　　　　Multiple through Same Incision, 28226
　　　Tenolysis, Flexor
　　　　Multiple through Same Incision, 28222
　　　　Single, 28220
　　　Tenotomy, Open, Extensor
　　　　Foot or Toe, 28234
　　　Tenotomy, Open, Flexor, 28230
　　　　Toe, Single Procedure, 28232
　Replantation, 20838
　Sesamoid
　　Excision, 28315
　Skin Graft
　　Delay of Flap, 15620
　　Full Thickness, 15240, 15241
　　Pedicle Flap, 15574
　　Split, 15100, 15101
　Splint, 29590
　Strapping, 29540, 29590
　Suture
　　Tendon, 28200-28210
　Tendon Sheath
　　Excision, 28086, 28088
　　Tenolysis, 28220-28226
　　Tenotomy, 28230-28234
　Tissue Transfer, Adjacent, 14040, 14041
　Tumor, 28043-28047 [28039, 28041], 28100-28107, 28171-28173
　Unlisted Services and Procedures, 28899
　X–ray, 73620, 73630
Foot Abscess
　See Abscess, Foot
Foot Navicular Bone
　See Navicular
Forced Expiratory Fllows, 94011-94012
Forearm
　See Arm, Lower
Forehead
　Reconstruction, 21179-21180, 21182-21184
　　Midface, 21159, 21160
　Reduction, 21137-21139
　Rhytidectomy, 15824, 15826
　Skin Graft
　　Delay of Flap, 15620
　　Full Thickness, 15240, 15241
　　Pedicle Flap, 15574
　Tissue Transfer, Adjacent, 14040, 14041
Forehead and Orbital Rim
　Reconstruction, 21172-21180

Foreign Body
　Removal
　　Adenoid, 42999
　　Anal, 46608
　　Ankle Joint, 27610, 27620
　　Arm
　　　Lower, 25248
　　　Upper, 24200, 24201
　　Auditory Canal, External, 69200
　　　with Anesthesia, 69205
　　Bile Duct, 43269
　　Bladder, 52310, 52315
　　Brain, 61570
　　Bronchi, 31635
　　Colon, 44025, 44390, 45379
　　Colon–Sigmoid, 45332
　　Conjunctival Embedded, 65210
　　Cornea
　　　with Slip Lamp, 65222
　　　without Slit Lamp, 65220
　　Duodenum, 44010
　　Elbow, 24000, 24101, 24200, 24201
　　Esophagus, 43020, 43045, 43215, 74235
　　External Eye, 65205
　　Eyelid, 67938
　　Finger, 26075, 26080
　　Foot, 28190-28193
　　Gastrointestinal, Upper, 43247
　　Gum, 41805
　　Hand, 26070
　　Hip, 27033, 27086, 27087
　　Hysteroscopy, 58562
　　Interphalangeal Joint
　　　Toe, 28024
　　Intertarsal Joint, 28020
　　Intestines, Small, 44020, 44363
　　Intraocular, 65235
　　Kidney, 50561, 50580
　　Knee Joint, 27310, 27331, 27372
　　Lacrimal Duct, 68530
　　Lacrimal Gland, 68530
　　Larynx, 31511, 31530, 31531, 31577
　　Leg, Upper, 27372
　　Lung, 32151
　　Mandible, 41806
　　Maxillary Sinus, 31299
　　Mediastinum, 39000, 39010
　　Metatarsophalangeal Joint, 28022
　　Mouth, 40804, 40805
　　Muscle, 20520, 20525
　　　Stimulator
　　　　Skeletal, 20999
　　Nose, 30300
　　　Anesthesia, under, 30310
　　　Lateral Rhinotomy, 30320
　　Orbit, 61334, 67413, 67430
　　　with Bone Flap, 67430
　　　without Bone Flap, 67413
　　Pancreatic Duct, 43269
　　Pelvis, 27086, 27087
　　Penile Tissue, 54115
　　Penis, 54115
　　Pericardium, 33020
　　　Endoscopic, 32658
　　Peritoneum, 49402
　　Pharynx, 42809
　　Pleura, 32150, 32151
　　　Endoscopic, 32653
　　Posterior Segment
　　　Magnetic Extraction, 65260
　　　Nonmagnetic Extraction, 65265
　　Rectum, 45307, 45915
　　Scrotum, 55120
　　Shoulder, 23040, 23044
　　　Complicated, 23332
　　　Deep, 23331
　　　Subcutaneous, 23330
　　Skin
　　　with Debridement, 11010-11012
　　Stomach, 43500
　　Subcutaneous, 10120, 10121

Foreign Body

Foreign Body — *continued*
  Removal — *continued*
    Subcutaneous — *continued*
      with Debridement, 11010-11012
    Tarsometatarsal Joint, 28020
    Tendon Sheath, 20520, 20525
    Toe, 28022
    Ureter, 50961, 50980
    Urethra, 52310, 52315
    Uterus, 58562
    Vagina, 57415
    Wrist, 25040, 25101, 25248
Forensic Exam, 88040
  Cytopathology, 88125
  Phosphatase, Acid, 84061
Foreskin of Penis
  See Penis, Prepuce
Formycin Diphosphate
  See Fibrin Degradation Products
Fournier's Gangrene
  See Debridement, Skin, Subcutaneous Tissue, Infected
Fowler Procedure
  Osteotomy, 28305
Fowler-Stephens Orchiopexy, 54650
Fox Operation, 67923
Fraction, Factor IX
  See Christmas Factor
Fracture, Treatment
  Acetabulum
    with Manipulation, 27222
    without Manipulation, 27220
    Closed Treatment, 27220, 27222
    Open Treatment, 27226-27228
  Alveola
    Closed Treatment, 21421
    Open Treatment, 21422, 21423
  Alveolar Ridge
    Closed Treatment, 21440
    Open Treatment, 21445
  Ankle
    with Manipulation, 27818
    without Manipulation, 27816
    Closed Treatment, 27816, 27818
    Lateral, 27786, 27792, 27822
      Closed Treatment, 27786
        with Manipulation, 27788
      Open Treatment, 27792
    Malleolus
      Bimalleolar
        Closed Treatment, 27808
          with Manipulation, 27810
        Open Treatment, 27814
      Posterior, 27767-27769
      Medial, 27760-27766, 27808-27814
        Closed Treatment, 27760
          with Manipulation, 27762
        Open Treatment, 27766
      Open Treatment, 27822, 27823
      Trimalleolar, 27816-27823
        Closed Treatment, 27816
          with Manipulation, 27818
        Open Treatment, 27822
          with Fixation, 27823
  Ankle Bone
    Medial, 27760, 27762
    Posterior, 27767-27769
  Bennett's
    See Thumb, Fracture
  Boxer's, 26600-26615
  Bronchi
    Endoscopy, 31630
  Calcaneus
    with Manipulation, 28405, 28406
    without Manipulation, 28400
    Closed Treatment, 28400, 28405
    Open Treatment, 28415, 28420
    Percutaneous Fixation, 28436
  Carpal, 25622-25628
    Closed Treatment
      with Manipulation, 25624, 25635

Fracture, Treatment — *continued*
  Carpal — *continued*
    Closed Treatment — *continued*
      without Manipulation, 25622, 25630
    Open Treatment, 25628, 25645
  Carpal Scaphoid
    Closed Treatment, 25622
  Carpometacarpal
    Closed Treatment, 26645
    Open Treatment, 26665
    Percutaneous Fixation, 26650
  Cheekbone
    with Manipulation, 21355
    Open Treatment, 21360-21366
  Clavicle
    Closed Treatment, 23500, 23505
      with Manipulation, 23505
      without Manipulation, 23500
    Open Treatment, 23515
  Coccyx
    Closed Treatment, 27200
    Open Treatment, 27202
  Colles-Reversed
    See Smith Fracture
  Craniofacial
    Closed Treatment, 21431
    Open Treatment, 21432-21435
  Debridement
    with Open Fracture, 11040-11044
  Elbow
    Closed Treatment, 24620, 24640
    Open Treatment, 24586, 24587, 24635
  Femur
    with Manipulation, 27232, 27502, 27503, 27510
    without Manipulation, 27230, 27238, 27246, 27500, 27501, 27503, 27516, 27517, 27520
    Closed Treatment, 27230, 27238, 27240, 27246, 27500-27503, 27510, 27516, 27517
    Distal, 27508, 27510, 27514
    Epiphysis, 27516-27519
    Intertrochanteric
      Closed Treatment, 27238
        with Manipulation, 27240
      Intramedullary Implant, Shaft, 27245
      Open Treatment, 27244
        with Implant, 27245
    Neck
      Closed Treatment, 27230
        with Manipulation, 27232
      Open Treatment, 27236
      Percutaneous Fixation, 27235
    Open Treatment, 27244, 27245, 27248, 27506, 27507, 27511-27514, 27519
    Percutaneous Fixation, 27235, 27509
    Peritrochanteric
      Closed Treatment, 27238
        with Manipulation, 27240
      Intermedullary Implant Shaft, 27245, 27500, 27502, 27506-27507
      Open Treatment, 27244, 27245
    Proximal, 27267-27269
    Shaft, 27500, 27502, 27506, 27507
    Subtrochanteric
      Closed Treatment, 27238
        with Manipulation, 27240
      Intramedullary Implant, 27245
      Open Treatment, 27244, 27245
    Supracondylar, 27501-27503, 27509, 27511, 27513
    Transcondylar, 27501-27503, 27509, 27511, 27513

Fracture, Treatment — *continued*
  Femur — *continued*
    Trochanteric
      Closed Treatment, 27246
      Open Treatment, 27248
  Fibula
    with Manipulation, 27781, 27788, 27810
    without Manipulation, 27780, 27786, 27808
    Closed Treatment, 27780, 27781, 27786, 27788, 27808, 27810
    Malleolus, 27786-27814
    Open Treatment, 27784, 27792, 27814
    Shaft, 27780-27786, 27808
  Frontal Sinus
    Open Treatment, 21343, 21344
  Great Toe
    Closed Treatment, 28490
      with Manipulation, 28490
  Heel
    Closed Treatment
      with Manipulation, 28405, 28406
      without Manipulation, 28400
    Open Treatment, 28415, 28420
  Humerus
    with Dislocation
      Closed Treatment, 23665
      Open Treatment, 23670
    with Shoulder Dislocation
      Closed Treatment, 23675
      Open Treatment, 23680
    Closed Treatment, 24500, 24505
      with Manipulation, 23605
      without Manipulation, 23600
    Condyle, 24582
      Closed Treatment, 24576, 24577
      Open Treatment, 24579
      Percutaneous, 24582
    Epicondyle
      Closed Treatment, 24560, 24565
      Open Treatment, 24575
      Percutaneous Fixation, 24566
    Greater Tuberosity Fracture
      Closed Treatment with Manipulation, 23625
      Closed Treatment without Manipulation, 23620
      Open Treatment, 23630
    Open Treatment, 23615, 23616
    Shaft, 24500
      Open Treatment, 24515, 24516
    Supracondylar
      Closed Treatment, 24530, 24535
      Open Treatment, 24545, 24546
      Percutaneous Fixation, 24538
    Transcondylar
      Closed Treatment, 24530, 24535
      Open Treatment, 24545, 24546
      Percutaneous Fixation, 24538
  Hyoid Bone
    Open Treatment, 21495
  Ilium
    Open Treatment, 27215, 27218
    Percutaneous Fixation, 27216
  Knee, 27520
    Arthroscopic Treatment, 29850, 29851
    Open Treatment, 27524
  Larynx
    Open Treatment, 31584

Fracture, Treatment — *continued*
  Leg
    Femur
      Closed Treatment
        With manipulation, 27502, 27503, 27510, 27516
        Without manipulation, 27500, 27501, 27508, 27517
      Open Treatment, 27506, 27507, 27511-27514, 27519
      Percutaneous fixation, 27509
    Fibula
      Closed Treatment
        With manipulation, 27752, 27781, 27788
        Without manipulation, 27750, 27780, 27786
      Open Treatment, 27758, 27759, 27784, 27792, 27826-27832
    Tibia
      Closed Treatment
        With manipulation, 27752, 27825
        Without manipulation, 27750, 27824, 27830, 27831
      Open Treatment, 27758, 27759, 27826-27829, 27832
      Percutaneous fixation, 27756
  Malar Area
    with Bone Graft, 21366
    with Manipulation, 21355
    Open Treatment, 21360-21366
  Mandible
    Closed Treatment
      with Manipulation, 21451
      without Manipulation, 21450
      Interdental Fixation, 21453
    Open Treatment, 21454-21470
      with Interdental Fixation, 21462
      without Interdental Fixation, 21461
    External Fixation, 21454
    Percutaneous Treatment, 21452
  Maxilla
    Closed Treatment, 21421
    Open Treatment, 21422, 21423
  Metacarpal
    with Manipulation, 26605, 26607
    without Manipulation, 26600
    Closed Treatment, 26600, 26605
      with Fixation, 26607
    Open Treatment, 26615
    Percutaneous Fixation, 26608
  Metatarsal
    with Manipulation, 28475, 28476
    without Manipulation, 28450, 28470
    Closed Treatment, 28470, 28475
    Open Treatment, 28485
    Percutaneous Fixation, 28476
  Monteggia
    See Fracture, Ulna; Monteggia Fracture
  Nasal Bone
    with Manipulation, 21315, 21320
    without Manipulation, 21310
    Closed Treatment, 21310-21320
    Open Treatment, 21325-21335
  Nasal Septum
    Closed Treatment, 21337
    Open Treatment, 21336
  Nasal Turbinate
    Therapeutic, 30930
  Nasoethmoid
    with Fixation, 21340
    Open Treatment, 21338, 21339
    Percutaneous Treatment, 21340

Index — Frontal Sinusotomy

Fracture, Treatment — *continued*
- Nasomaxillary
  - with Bone Grafting, 21348
  - with Fixation, 21345-21347
  - Closed Treatment, 21345
  - Open Treatment, 21346-21348
- Navicular
  - with Manipulation, 25624
  - Closed Treatment, 25622
  - Open Treatment, 25628
- Odontoid
  - Open Treatment
    - with Graft, 22319
    - without Graft, 22318
- Orbit
  - Closed Treatment, 21400
    - with Manipulation, 21401
    - without Manipulation, 21400
  - Open Treatment, 21406-21408
    - Blowout Fracture, 21385-21395
- Orbital Floor
  - Blow Out, 21385-21395
- Palate
  - Closed Treatment, 21421
  - Open Treatment, 21422, 21423
- Patella
  - Closed Treatment
    - without Manipulation, 27520
  - Open Treatment, 27524
- Pelvic Ring
  - Closed Treatment, 27193, 27194
    - without Manipulation, 27193, 27194
  - Open Treatment
    - Anterior, 27217
    - Posterior, 27218
  - Percutaneous Fixation, 27216
- Phalanges
  - Finger(s)
    - Articular
      - with Manipulation, 26742
      - Closed Treatment, 26740
      - Open Treatment, 26746
    - Closed Treatment
      - with Manipulation, 26725, 26742, 26755
      - without Manipulation, 26720, 26740, 26750
    - Distal, 26755, 26756
      - Closed Treatment, 26750
      - Open Treatment, 26765
      - Percutaneous Fixation, 26756
  - Finger/Thumb
    - with Manipulation, 26725, 26727
    - Bennett Fracture, 26650, 26665
    - Closed Treatment, 26720, 26725
    - Percutaneous Fixation, 26650, 26727, 26756
    - Shaft, 26720-26727
  - Great Toe, 28490
    - Closed Treatment, 28490, 28495
    - Open Treatment, 28505
    - Percutaneous Fixation, 28496
      - without Manipulation, 28496
    - Open Treatment, 26735, 26746
      - Distal, 26765
    - Shaft
      - Closed Treatment, 26725
      - Open Treatment, 26735
      - Percutaneous Fixation, 26727
    - Toe
      - with Manipulation, 28515
      - without Manipulation, 28510
      - Closed Treatment, 28515
      - Open Treatment, 28525
- Radius
  - with Manipulation, 25565, 25605
  - with Ulna, 25560, 25565

Fracture, Treatment — *continued*
- Radius — *continued*
  - with Ulna — *continued*
    - Open Treatment, 25575
    - without Manipulation, 25560, 25600
    - Closed Treatment, 24650, 24655, 25500, 25505, 25520, 25560, 25565, 25600, 25605
    - Colles, 25600, 25605
    - Distal, 25600-25609
      - Open Treatment, 25607, 25608-25609
      - Smith, 25600-25605, 25606, 25607, 25609
    - Head/Neck
      - Closed Treatment, 24650, 24655
      - Open Treatment, 24665, 24666
    - Open Treatment, 25515, 25607, 25608-25609
    - Percutaneous Fixation, 25606
    - Shaft, 25500, 25525, 25526
      - Closed Treatment, 25500, 25505, 25520
      - Open Treatment, 25515, 25525, 25526, 25574
- Rib
  - Closed Treatment, 21800
  - External Fixation, 21810
  - Open Treatment, 21805
- Scaphoid
  - with Dislocation
    - Closed Treatment, 25680
    - Open Treatment, 25685
  - with Manipulation, 25624
  - Closed Treatment, 25622
  - Open Treatment, 25628
- Scapula
  - Closed Treatment
    - with Manipulation, 23575
    - without Manipulation, 23570
  - Open Treatment, 23585
- Sesamoid
  - Closed Treatment, 28530
  - Foot, 28530, 28531
  - Open Treatment, 28531
- Shoulder
  - Closed Treatment
    - with Greater Tuberosity Fracture, 23620, 23655
    - with Surgical or Anatomical Neck Fracture, 23600, 23675
  - Open Treatment, 23630, 23680
- Skull, 62000-62010
- Sternum
  - Closed Treatment, 21820
  - Open Treatment, 21825
- Talus
  - with Manipulation, 28435, 28436
  - without Manipulation, 28430
  - Closed Treatment, 28430, 28435
  - Open Treatment, 28445
- Tarsal
  - with Manipulation, 28455, 28456
  - without Manipulation, 28450
  - Open Treatment, 28465
  - Percutaneous Fixation, 28456
- Thigh
  - Femur
    - Closed Treatment
      - with manipulation, 27502, 27503, 27510, 27517
      - Without manipulation, 27500, 27501, 27508, 27516, 27520
    - Open Treatment, 27506, 27507, 27511, 27513, 27514, 27519, 27524
    - Percutaneous fixation, 27509

Fracture, Treatment — *continued*
- Thumb
  - with Dislocation, 26645, 26650
    - Open Treatment, 26665
    - Closed Treatment, 26645, 26650
    - Percutaneous Fixation, 26650
- Tibia
  - with Manipulation, 27752, 27762, 27810
  - without Manipulation, 27530, 27750, 27760, 27808, 27825
  - Arthroscopic Treatment, 29855, 29856
  - Closed Treatment, 27530, 27532, 27538, 27750, 27752, 27760, 27762, 27808, 27810, 27824, 27825
    - with Traction, 27532, 27825
  - Distal, 27824-27828
  - Intercondylar Spines, 27538, 27540
  - Malformation, 27810
  - Malleolus, 27760-27766, 27808-27814
  - Open Treatment, 27535, 27536, 27540, 27758, 27759, 27766, 27814, 27826-27828
  - Percutaneous Fixation, 27756
  - Bimalleolar
    - Closed Treatment, 27808
    - with Manipulation, 27810
    - Open Treatment, 27814
  - Lateral
    - Closed Treatment, 27786
    - with Manipulation, 27788
    - Open Treatment, 27792
  - Medial
    - Closed Treatment, 27760
    - with Manipulation, 27762
    - Open Treatment, 27766
  - Trimalleolar
    - Closed Treatment, 27816
    - with Manipulation, 27818
    - Open Treatment, 27822
    - with Fixation, 27823
  - Plateau, 27530-27536, 29855, 29856
  - Shaft, 27750-27759
    - with Manipulation, 27752, 27762, 27825
    - without Manipulation, 27530, 27750, 27760, 27824
- Tibia and Fibula
  - Malleolar, 27808-27814
- Trachea
  - Endoscopy Repair, 31630
- Turbinate
  - Therapeutic, 30930
- Ulna
  - with Dislocation, 24620, 24635
    - Closed Treatment, 24620
    - Monteggia, 24620, 24635
    - Open Treatment, 24635
  - with Manipulation, 25535, 25565
  - with Radius, 25560, 25565
    - Open Treatment, 25575
  - without Manipulation, 25530, 25560
  - *See* Elbow; Humerus; Radius
  - Closed Treatment, 25560, 25565
    - Monteggia type, 24620
    - of Shaft, 25530, 25535
      - with Manipulation, 25535
      - and Radial, 25560
        - with Manipulation, 25565
  - Proximal end, 24670
    - with Manipulation, 24675
  - Ulnar Styloid, 25650

Fracture, Treatment — *continued*
- Ulna — *continued*
  - Olecranon
    - Closed Treatment, 24670, 24675
      - with Manipulation, 24675
    - Open Treatment, 24685
  - Open Treatment, 25574, 25575
    - Proximal End, 24685
    - Radial AND Ulnar Shaft, 25574, 25575
    - Shaft, 25545
  - Shaft
    - Closed Treatment, 25530, 25535
    - Open Treatment, 25545, 25574
  - Styloid Process
    - Closed Treatment, 25650
    - Open Treatment, 25652
    - Percutaneous Fixation, 25651
- Vertebra
  - Additional Segment
    - Open Treatment, 22328
  - Cervical
    - Open Treatment, 22326
  - Closed Treatment
    - with Manipulation, Casting and/or Bracing, 22315
    - without Manipulation, 22310
  - Lumbar
    - Open Treatment, 22325
  - Posterior
    - Open Treatment, 22325-22327
  - Thoracic
    - Open Treatment, 22327
- Vertebral Process
  - Closed Treatment, 22305
- Wrist
  - with Dislocation, 25680, 25685
    - Closed Treatment, 25680
    - Open Treatment, 25685
- Zygomatic Arch
  - Open Treatment, 21356, 21360-21366
  - with Manipulation, 21355

Fragile–X
- Chromosome Analysis, 88248

Fragility
- Red Blood Cell
  - Mechanical, 85547
  - Osmotic, 85555, 85557

Frames, Stereotactic
- *See* Stereotactic Frame

Francisella, 86000
- Antibody, 86668

Frazier-Spiller Procedure, 61450

Fredet–Ramstedt Procedure, 43520

Free E3
- *See* Estriol

Free Skin Graft
- *See* Skin, Grafts, Free

Free T4
- *See* Thyroxine, Free

Frei Disease
- *See* Lymphogranuloma Venereum

Frenectomy, 40819, 41115

Frenectomy, Lingual
- *See* Excision, Tongue, Frenum

Frenoplasty, 41520

Frenotomy, 40806, 41010

Frenulectomy, 40819

Frenuloplasty, 41520

Frenum
- *See* Lip
- Lip
  - Incision, 40806

Frenumectomy, 40819

Frickman Operation, 45550

Frontal Craniotomy, 61556

Frontal Sinus
- *See* Sinus, Frontal

Frontal Sinusotomy
- *See* Exploration, Sinus, Frontal

Frost Suture
Eyelid
Closure by Suture, 67875
Frozen Blood Preparation, 86930-86932
Fructose, 84375
Semen, 82757
Fructose Intolerance Breath Test, 91065
Fruit Sugar
See Fructose
FSF, 85290, 85291
FSH, 83001
with Additional Tests, 80418, 80426
FSP, 85362-85380
FT-4, 84439
FTG, 15200-15261
FTI, 84439
FTSG, 15200-15261
Fulguration
See Destruction
Bladder, 51020
Cystourethroscopy with, 52214
Lesion, 52224
Tumor, 52234-52240
Ureter, 50957, 50976
Ureterocele
Ectopic, 52301
Orthotopic, 52300
Fulguration, Endocavitary
See Electrocautery
Full Thickness Graft, 15200-15261
Functional Ability
See Activities of Daily Living
Functional MRI, 70554-70555
Function, Study, Nasal
See Nasal Function Study
Function Test, Lung
See Pulmonology, Diagnostic
Function Test, Vestibular
See Vestibular Function Tests
Fundoplasty
Esophagogastric, 43324, 43325
with Gastroplasty, 43326
Laparoscopic, 43280
Fundoplication
See Fundoplasty, Esophagogastric
Fungal Wet Prep, 87220
Fungus
Antibody, 86671
Culture
Blood, 87103
Hair, 87101
Identification, 87106
Nail, 87101
Other, 87102
Skin, 87101
Tissue Exam, 87220
Funnel Chest
See Pectus Excavatum
Furuncle
Incision and Drainage, 10060, 10061
Furuncle, Vulva
See Abscess, Vulva
Fusion
See Arthrodesis
Pleural Cavity, 32560
Thumb
in Opposition, 26820
Fusion, Epiphyseal–Diaphyseal
See Epiphyseal Arrest
Fusion, Joint
See Arthrodesis
Fusion, Joint, Ankle
See Ankle, Arthrodesis
Fusion, Joint, Interphalangeal, Finger
See Arthrodesis, Finger Joint, Interphalangeal

G

GA, 91052
Gago Procedure
Repair, Tricuspid Valve, 33463-33465
Gait Training, 97116
Galactogram, 77053, 77054
Galactogram — *continued*
Injection, 19030
Galactokinase
Blood, 82759
Galactose
Blood, 82760
Urine, 82760
Galactose–1–Phosphate
Uridyl Transferase, 82775-82776
Galeazzi Dislocation
Fracture
Closed Treatment, 25520
Open Treatment, 25525, 25526
Gallbladder
See Bile Duct
Anastomosis
with Intestines, 47720-47741
Cholecystectomy
Laparoscopic, 47562
with Cholangiogram, 47564
Open, 47600
with Cholangiogram, 47605
with Choledochoenterostomy, 47612
with Exploration Common Duct, 47610
with Transduodenal Sphincterotomy or Sphincteroplasty, 47620
Cholecystostomy
for Drainage, 47480
for Exploration, 47480
for Removal of Stone, 47480
Percutaneous, 47490
Excision, 47562-47564, 47600-47620
Exploration, 47480
Incision, 47490
Incision and Drainage, 47480
Nuclear Medicine
Imaging, 78223
Removal Calculi, 47480
Repair
with Gastroenterostomy, 47741
with Intestines, 47720-47740
Unlisted Services and Procedures, 47999
X-ray with Contrast, 74290, 74291
Galvanocautery
See Electrocautery
Galvanoionization
See Iontophoresis
Gamete Intrafallopian Transfer (GIFT), 58976
Gamete Transfer
In Vitro Fertilization, 58976
Gamma Camera Imaging
See Nuclear Medicine
Gammacorten
See Dexamethasone
Gammaglobulin
Blood, 82784-82787
Gamma Glutamyl Transferase, 82977
Gamma Seminoprotein
See Antigen, Prostate Specific
Gamulin Rh
See Imune Globulins, Rho (D)
Ganglia, Trigeminal
See Gasserian Ganglion
Ganglion
See Gasserian Ganglion
Cyst
Aspiration/Injection, 20612
Drainage, 20612
Wrist
Excision, 25111, 25112
Injection
Anesthetic, 64505, 64510
Ganglion Cervicothoracicum
See Stellate Ganglion
Ganglion, Gasser's
See Gasserian Ganglion
Ganglion Pterygopalatinum
See Sphenopalatine Ganglion
GARDASIL, 90649
Gardasil, 90650
Gardnerella Vaginalis Detection, 87510-87512
Gardner Operation, 63700, 63702
Gasser Ganglion
See Gasserian Ganglion
Gasserian Ganglion
Sensory Root
Decompression, 61450
Section, 61450
Stereotactic, 61790
Gastrectomy
Partial, 43631
with Gastroduodenostomy, 43631
with Roux–en–Y Reconstruction, 43633
with Gastrojejunostomy, 43632
with Intestinal Pouch, 43634
Distal with Vagotomy, 43635
Total, 43621, 43622
with Esophagoenterostomy, 43620
with Intestinal Pouch, 43622
Gastric Acid, 82926, 82928
Gastric Analysis Test, 91052
Gastric Intubation, 89130-89141, 91105
Gastric Lavage
Therapeutic, 91105
Gastric Restrictive Procedure
Laparoscopy, 43770-43774
Open, 43886-43888
Gastric Tests
Manometry, 91020
Gastric Ulcer Disease
See Stomach, Ulcer
Gastrin, 82938, 82941
Gastrocnemius Recession
Leg, Lower, 27687
Gastroduodenostomy, 43810
with Gastrectomy, 43631, 43632
Revision of Anastomosis with Reconstruction, 43850
with Vagotomy, 43855
Gastroenterology, Diagnostic
Breath Hydrogen Test, 91065
Esophagus Tests
Acid Perfusion, 91030
Acid Reflux Test, 91034-91038
Balloon Distension Provocation Study, 91040
Intubation with Specimen Collection, 91100
Manometry, 91020
Motility Study, 91010-91012
Gastric Tests
Manometry, 91020
Gastroesophageal Reflux Test
See Acid Reflux, 91034-91038
Manometry, 91020
Rectum
Manometry, 91122
Sensation, Tone, and Compliance Test, 91120
Stomach
Intubation with Specimen Prep, 91055
Manometry, 91020
Stimulation of Secretion, 91052
Unlisted Services and Procedures, 91299
Gastroenterostomy
for Obesity, 43644-43645, 43842-43848
Gastroesophageal Reflux Test, 91034-91038
Gastrointestinal Endoscopies
See Endoscopy, Gastrointestinal
Gastrointestinal Exam
Nuclear Medicine
Blood Loss Study, 78278
Protein Loss Study, 78282
Shunt Testing, 78291
Unlisted Services and Procedures, 78299
Gastrointestinal Prophylaxis for NSAID Use Prescribed, 4017F
Gastrointestinal Tract
Imaging Intraluminal, 91110
Reconstruction, 43360, 43361
Upper
Dilation, 43249
X-ray, 74240-74245
with Contrast, 74246-74249
Guide Dilator, 74360
Guide Intubation, 49440, 74340
Gastrointestinal, Upper
Biopsy
Endoscopy, 43239
Dilation
Endoscopy, 43245
Esophagus, 43248
Endoscopy
Catheterization, 43241
Destruction
Lesion, 43258
Dilation, 43245
Drainage
Pseudocyst, 43240
Exploration, 43234, 43235
Hemorrhage, 43255
Inject Varices, 43243
Needle Biopsy, 43238, 43242
Removal
Foreign Body, 43247
Lesion, 43251
Polyp, 43251
Tumor, 43251
Stent Placement, 43256
Thermal Radiation, 43257
Tube Placement, 43246
Ultrasound, 43237, 43238, 43242, 76975
Exploration
Endoscopy, 43234, 43235
Hemorrhage
Endoscopic Control, 43255
Injection
Submucosal, 43236
Varices, 43243
Lesion
Destruction, 43258
Ligation of Vein, 43244
Needle Biopsy
Endoscopy, 43238, 43242
Removal
Foreign body, 43247
Lesion, 43250
Polyp, 43250, 43251
Tumor, 43250
Stent Placement, 43256
Tube Placement
Endoscopy, 43237, 43238, 43246
Ultrasound
Endoscopy, 43237, 43238, 43242, 43259, 76975
Gastrojejunostomy, 43860, 43865
with Duodenal Exclusion, 48547
with Partial Gastrectomy, 43632
with Vagotomy, 43825
without Vagotomy, 43820
Revision, 43860
with Vagotomy, 43865
Gastroplasty
with Esophagogastric Fundoplasty, 43326
for Obesity, 43644-43645, 43842-43848
Restrictive for Obesity, 43842
Other than Vertical Banded, 43843
Gastrorrhaphy, 43840
Gastroschisis, 49605
Gastrostomy
with Pancreatic Drain, 48001
with Pyloroplasty, 43640
with Vagotomy, 43640
Closure, 43870
Laparoscopic
Permanent, 43832
Temporary, 43653
Temporary, 43830
Laparoscopic, 43653

Index

Gastrostomy — *continued*
  Temporary — *continued*
    Neonatal, 43831
Gastrostomy Tube
  Change of, 43760
  Conversion to Gastro-jejunostomy Tube, 49446
  Directed Placement
    Endoscopic, 43246
  Insertion
    Percutaneous, 43246, 49440
  Percutaneous, 49440
  Replacement, 49450
  Repositioning, 43761
Gastrotomy, 43500, 43501, 43510
GDH, 82965
GE
  Reflux, 78262
Gel Diffusion, 86331
Gene Product
  See Protein
Genioplasty, 21120-21123
  Augmentation, 21120, 21123
  Osteotomy, 21121-21123
Genitalia
  Female
    Anesthesia, 00940-00952
  Male
    Anesthesia, 00920-00938
  Skin Graft
    Delay of Flap, 15620
    Full Thickness, 15240, 15241
    Pedicle Flap, 15574
    Split, 15120, 15121
    Tissue Transfer, Adjacent, 14040, 14041
Genitourinary Sphincter, Artificial
  See Prosthesis, Urethral Sphincter
Genotype Analysis
  by Nucleic Acid
    Infectious Agent
      Hepatitis C Virus, 87902
      HIV-1 Protease/Reverse Transcriptase, 87901
Gentamicin, 80170
  Assay, 80170
Gentiobiase, 82963
Genus: Human Cytomegalovirus Group
  See Cytomegalovirus
GERD
  See Gastroesophageal Reflux Test
German Measles
  See Rubella
Gestational Trophoblastic Tumor
  See Hydatidiform Mole
GGT, 82977
GH, 83003
GHb, 83036
Giardia
  Antigen Detection
    Enzyme Immunoassay, 87329
    Immunofluorescence, 87269
Giardia Lamblia
  Antibody, 86674
Gibbons Stent, 52332
GIF, 84307
GIFT, 58976
Gillies Approach
  Fracture
    Zygomatic Arch, 21356
Gill Operation, 63012
Gingiva
  See Gums
Gingiva, Abscess
  See Abscess
  Fracture
    See Abscess, Gums; Gums
    Zygomatic Arch
      See Abscess, Gums; Gums, Abscess
Gingivectomy, 41820
Gingivoplasty, 41872
Girdlestone Laminectomy
  See Laminectomy

Girdlestone Procedure
  Acetabulum, Reconstruction, 27120, 27122
GI Tract
  See Gastrointestinal Tract
  X-Rays, 74240-74249, 74340, 74360
Glabellar Frown Lines
  Rhytidectomy, 15826
Gland
  See Specific Gland
Gland, Adrenal
  See Adrenal Gland
Gland, Bartholin's
  See Bartholin's Gland
Gland, Bulbourethral
  See Bulbourethral Gland
Gland, Lacrimal
  See Lacrimal Gland
Gland, Mammary
  See Breast
Gland, Parathyroid
  See Parathyroid Gland
Gland, Parotid
  See Parotid Gland
Gland, Pituitary
  See Pituitary Gland
Gland, Salivary
  See Salivary Glands
Gland, Sublingual
  See Sublingual Gland
Gland, Sweat
  See Sweat Glands
Gland, Thymus
  See Thymus Gland
Gland, Thyroid
  See Thyroid Gland
Gla Protein (Bone)
  See Osteocalcin
Glasses
  See Spectacle Services
Glaucoma
  Cryotherapy, 66720
  Cyclophotocoagulation, 66710, 66711
  Diathermy, 66700
  Fistulization of Sclera, 66150
  Provocative Test, 92140
Glaucoma Drainage Implant
  See Aqueous Shunt
GLC, 82486
Glenn Procedure, 33766, 33767
Glenohumeral Joint
  Arthrotomy, 23040
    with Biopsy, 23100
    with Synovectomy, 23105
  Exploration, 23107
  Removal
    Foreign or Loose Body, 23107
Glenoid Fossa
  Reconstruction, 21255
GLN, 82975
Globulin
  Antihuman, 86880-86886
  Immune, 90281-90399
  Sex Hormone Binding, 84270
Globulin, Corticosteroid-Binding, 84449
Globulin, Rh Immune, 90384-90386
Globulin, Thyroxine-Binding, 84442
Glomerular Procoagulant Activity
  See Thromboplastin
Glomus Caroticum
  See Carotid Body
Glossectomies, 41120-41155
Glossectomy, 41120-41155
Glossopexy, 41500
Glossorrhaphy
  See Suture, Tongue
Glucagon, 82943
  Tolerance Panel, 80422, 80424
  Tolerance Test, 82946
Glucose, 80422, 80424, 80430-80435, 95250
  Blood Test, 82947-82950, 82962
  Body Fluid, 82945
  Hormone Panel, 80430

Glucose — *continued*
  Interstitial Fluid
    Continuous Monitoring, 95250
  Tolerance Test, 82951, 82952
    with Tolbutamide, 82953
Glucose-6-Phosphate
  Dehydrogenase, 82955, 82960
Glucose Phosphate Isomerase, 84087
Glucose Phosphate Isomerase Measurement, 84087
Glucosidase, 82963
Glucuronide Androstanediol, 82154
Glue
  Cornea Wound, 65286
  Sclera Wound, 65286
Glukagon
  See Glucagon
Glutamate Dehydrogenase, 82965
Glutamate Pyruvate Transaminase, 84460
Glutamic Alanine Transaminase, 84460
Glutamic Aspartic Transaminase, 84450
Glutamic Dehydrogenase, 82965
Glutamine, 82975
Glutamyltransferase, Gamma, 82977
Glutathione, 82978
  Glutathione Reductase, 82979
Glutethimide, 82980
Glycanhydrolase, N-Acetylmuramide
  See Lysozyme
Glycated Hemoglobins
  See Glycohemoglobin
Glycated Protein, 82985
Glycerol, Phosphatidyl
  See Phosphatidylglycerol
Glycerol Phosphoglycerides
  See Phosphatidylglycerol
Glycerophosphatase
  See Alkaline Phophatase
Glycinate, Theophylline Sodium
  See Theophylline
Glycocholic Acid
  See Cholylglycine
Glycohemoglobin, 83036-83037
Glycol, Ethylene
  See Ethylene Glycol
Glycols, Ethylene
  See Ethylene Glycol
Glycosaminoglycan
  See Mucopolysaccharides
GMP (Guanosine Monophosphate), 83008
GMP, Cyclic
  See Guanosine Monophosphate
Goeckerman Treatment
  Photochemotherapy, 96910-96913
Gold
  Assay, 80172
  Blood, 80172
Goldwaite Procedure
  Reconstruction, Patella, for Instability, 27422
Golfer's Elbow, 24357-24359
Gol-Vernet Operation, 50120
Gonadectomy, Female
  See Oophorectomy
Gonadectomy, Male
  See Excision, Testis
Gonadotropin
  Chorionic, 84702, 84703
  FSH, 83001
  ICSH, 83002
  LH, 83002
Gonadotropin Panel, 80426
Goniophotography, 92285
Gonioscopy, 92020
Goniotomy, 65820
Gonococcus
  See Neisseria Gonorrhoeae
Goodenough Harris Drawing Test, 96101-96103
GOTT
  See Transaminase, Glutamic Oxaloacetic

GPUT
  See Galactose-1-Phosphate, uridyl Transferase
Graefe's Operation, 66830
Graft
  See Bone Graft; Bypass Graft
  Anal, 46753
  Aorta, 33840, 33845, 33852, 33860-33877
  Artery
    Coronary, 33503-33505
  Bone
    See Bone Marrow, Transplantation
    Anastomosis, 20969-20973
    Harvesting, 20900, 20902
    Microvascular Anastomosis, 20955-20962
    Osteocutaneous Flap with Microvascular Anastomosis, 20969-20973
    Vascular Pedicle, 25430
  Bone and Skin, 20969-20973
  Cartilage
    Ear to Face, 21235
    Harvesting, 20910, 20912
    See Cartilage Graft
    Rib to Face, 21230
    Three or More Segments
    Two Locations, 35682, 35683
  Composite, 35681-35683
  Conjunctiva, 65782
  Eye
    Amniotic Membrane, 65780
    Conjunctiva, 65782
    Stem Cell, 65781
  Cornea
    with Lesion Excision, 65426
  Corneal Transplant
    in Aphakia, 65750
    in Pseudophakia, 65755
    Lamellar, 65710
    Penetrating, 65730
  Dura
    Spinal Cord, 63710
  Endovascular, 34900
  Facial Nerve Paralysis, 15840-15845
  Fascia Graft
    Cheek, 15840
  Fascia Lata
    Harvesting, 20920, 20922
  Gum Mucosa, 41870
  Heart
    See Heart, Transplantation
  Heart Lung
    See Transplantation, Heart-Lung
  Hepatorenal, 35535
  Kidney
    See Kidney, Transplantation
  Liver
    See Liver, Transplantation
  Lung
    See Lung, Transplantation
  Muscle
    Cheek, 15841-15845
  Nail Bed Reconstruction, 11762
  Nerve, 64885-64907
  Oral Mucosa, 40818
  Organ
    See Transplantation
  Osteochondral
    Knee, 27415-27416
    Talus, 28446
  Pancreas
    See Pancreas, Transplantation
  Peroneal-Tibial, 35570
  Skin
    Allograft, 15300-15336
    Tissue Cultured
      Dermal Substitute, 15360-15361, 15365-15366
      Skin Substitute, 15340-15341

Graft

Graft — *continued*
- Skin — *continued*
  - Bilaminate Skin Substitute, 15170-15176, 15340-15341, 15360-15366
  - Blood Flow Check, Graft, 15860
    - *See* Skin Graft and Flap
  - Composite, 15760, 15770
  - Delayed Flap, 15600-15630
  - Free Flap, 15757
  - Full Thickness, Free
    - Axillae, 15240, 15241
    - Cheeks, Chin, 15240, 15241
    - Ears, Eyelids, 15260, 15261
    - Extremities (Excluding Hands/Feet), 15240, 15241
    - Feet, Hands, 15240, 15241
    - Forehead, 15240, 15241
    - Genitalia, 15240, 15241
    - Lips, Nose, 15260, 15261
    - Mouth, Neck, 15240, 15241
    - Scalp, 15220, 15221
    - Trunk, 15200, 15201
  - Pedicle
    - Direct, 15570, 15576
    - Transfer, 15650
  - Pinch Graft, 15050
  - Preparation Recipient Site, 15002, 15004-15005
  - Split Graft, 15100, 15101, 15120, 15121
  - Vascular Flow Check, Graft, 15860
  - Xenograft, 15400, 15401, 15420-15421, 15430-15431
- Tendon
  - Finger, 26392
  - Hand, 26392
  - Harvesting, 20924
  - Tibial/peroneal Trunk-Tibial, 35570
  - Tibial-Tibial, 35570
- Tissue
  - Harvesting, 20926
- Vein
  - Cross-Over, 34520

Grain Alcohol
- *See* Alcohol, Ethyl

Granulation Tissue
- Cauterization, Chemical, 17250

Gravi, Myasthenia
- *See* Myasthenia Gravis

Gravities, Specific
- *See* Specific Gravity

Greater Tuberosity Fracture
- with Shoulder Dislocation
  - Closed Treatment, 23665
  - Open Treatment, 23670

Greater Vestibular Gland
- *See* Bartholin's Gland

Great Toe
- Free Osteocutaneous Flap with Microvascular Anastomosis, 20973

Great Vessel(s)
- Shunt
  - Aorta to Pulmonary Artery
    - Ascending, 33755
    - Descending, 33762
  - Central, 33764
  - Subclavian to Pulmonary Artery, 33750
  - Vena Cava to Pulmonary Artery, 33766, 33767
- Unlisted Services and Procedures, 33999

Great Vessels Transposition
- *See* Transposition, Great Arteries

Greenfield Filter Insertion, 37620

Green Operation
- *See* Scapulopexy

Grice Arthrodesis, 28725

Gridley Stain, 88312

Grippe, Balkan
- *See* Q Fever

Gritti Operation, 27590-27592

Gritti Operation — *continued*
- *See* Amputation, Leg, Upper; Radical Resection; Replantation

Groin Area
- Repair
  - Hernia, 49550-49557

Gross Type Procedure, 49610, 49611

Group Health Education, 99078

Grouping, Blood
- *See* Blood Typing

Growth Factors, Insulin-Like
- *See* Somatomedin

Growth Hormone, 83003
- with Arginine Tolerance Test, 80428
- Human, 80418, 80428, 80430, 86277

Growth Hormone Release Inhibiting Factor
- *See* Somatostatin

GTT, 82951, 82952

Guaiac Test
- Blood in Feces, 82270

Guanosine Monophosphate, 83008

Guanosine Monophosphate, Cyclic
- *See* Cyclic GMP

Guanylic Acids
- *See* Guanosine Monophosphate

Guard Stain, 88313

Gullet
- *See* Esophagus

Gums
- Abscess
  - Incision and Drainage, 41800
- Alveolus
  - Excision, 41830
- Cyst
  - Incision and Drainage, 41800
- Excision
  - Gingiva, 41820
  - Operculum, 41821
- Graft
  - Mucosa, 41870
- Hematoma
  - Incision and Drainage, 41800
- Lesion
  - Destruction, 41850
  - Excision, 41822-41828
- Mucosa
  - Excision, 41828
- Reconstruction
  - Alveolus, 41874
  - Gingiva, 41872
- Removal
  - Foreign Body, 41805
- Tumor
  - Excision, 41825-41827
- Unlisted Services and Procedures, 41899

Gunning-Lieben Test, 82009, 82010

Gunther Tulip Filter Insertion, 37620

Guthrie Test, 84030

H

H1N1 Vaccine, 90663
- Administration, 90470

HAA (Hepatitis Associated Antigen), 87340-87380, 87515-87527
- *See* Hepatitis Antigen, B Surface

HAAb (Antibody, Hepatitis), 86708, 86709

Haemoglobin F
- *See* Fetal Hemoglobin

Haemorrhage
- *See* Hemorrhage

Haemorrhage Rectum
- *See* Hemorrhage, Rectum

Hageman Factor, 85280
- Clotting Factor, 85210-85293

Haglund's Deformity Repair, 28119

HAI (Hemagglutination Inhibition Test), 86280

Hair
- Electrolysis, 17380
- KOH Examination, 87220
- Microscopic Evaluation, 96902

Hair — *continued*
- Transplant
  - Punch Graft, 15775, 15776
  - Strip Graft, 15220, 15221

Hair Removal
- *See* Removal, Hair

Hallux
- *See* Great Toe

Hallux Rigidus
- Correction with Cheilectomy, 28289

Halo
- Body Cast, 29000
- Cranial, 20661
  - for Thin Skull Osteology, 20664
- Femur, 20663
- Maxillofacial, 21100
- Pelvic, 20662
- Removal, 20665

Haloperidol
- Assay, 80173

Halsted Mastectomy, 19305

Halsted Repair
- Hernia, 49495

Hammertoe Repair, 28285, 28286

Hamster Penetration Test, 89329

Ham Test
- Hemolysins, 85475
- with Agglutinins, 86940, 86941

Hand
- *See* Carpometacarpal Joint; Intercarpal Joint
- Amputation
  - at Metacarpal, 25927
  - at Wrist, 25920
    - Revision, 25922
  - Revision, 25924, 25929, 25931
- Arthrodesis
  - Carpometacarpal Joint, 26843, 26844
  - Intercarpal Joint, 25820, 25825
- Bone
  - Incision and Drainage, 26034
- Cast, 29085
- Decompression, 26035, 26037
- Excision
  - Excess Skin, 15837
- Fracture
  - Metacarpal, 26600
- Implantation
  - Removal, 26320
  - Tube/Rod, 26392, 26416
  - Tube/Rod, 26390
- Insertion
  - Tendon Graft, 26392
- Magnetic Resonance Imaging (MRI), 73218-73223
- Reconstruction
  - Tendon Pulley, 26500-26502
- Repair
  - Blood Vessel, 35207
  - Cleft Hand, 26580
  - Muscle, 26591, 26593
  - Release, 26593
- Tendon
  - Extensor, 26410-26416, 26426, 26428, 26433-26437
  - Flexor, 26350-26358, 26440
  - Profundus, 26370-26373
- Replantation, 20808
- Skin Graft
  - Delay of Flap, 15620
  - Full Thickness, 15240, 15241
  - Pedicle Flap, 15574
  - Split, 15100, 15101
- Strapping, 29280
- Tendon
  - Excision, 26390
  - Extensor, 26415
- Tenotomy, 26450, 26460
- Tissue Transfer, Adjacent, 14040, 14041
- Tumor, 26115-26118 [26111, 26113], 26200-26205
- Unlisted Services and Procedures, 26989

Hand — *continued*
- X-ray, 73120, 73130

Hand Abscess
- *See* Abscess, Hand

Hand(s) Dupuytren's Contracture(s)
- *See* Dupuytren's Contracture

Handling
- Device, 99002
- Radioelement, 77790
- Specimen, 99000, 99001

Hand Phalange
- *See* Finger, Bone

Hanganutziu Deicher Antibodies
- *See* Antibody, Heterophile

Haptoglobin, 83010, 83012

Hard Palate
- *See* Palate

Harelip Operation
- *See* Cleft Lip, Repair

Harii Procedure (Carpal Bone), 25430

Harrington Rod
- Insertion, 22840
- Removal, 22850

Hartley-Krause, 61450

Hartmann Procedure, 44143
- Laparoscopy
  - Partial Colectomy with Colostomy, 44206
- Open, 44143

Harvesting
- Bone Graft, 20900, 20902
- Bone Marrow, 38230
- Cartilage, 20910, 20912
- Conjunctival Graft, 68371
- Eggs for In Vitro Fertilization, 58970
- Endoscopic
  - Vein for Bypass Graft, 33508
- Fascia Lata Graft, 20920, 20922
- Intestines, 44132, 44133
- Kidney, 50300, 50320, 50547
- Liver, 47133, 47140-47142
- Lower Extremity Vein for Vascular Reconstruction, 35572
- Skin, 15040
- Stem Cell, 38205, 38206
- Tendon Graft, 20924
- Tissue Grafts, 20926
- Upper Extremity Artery
  - for Coronary Artery Bypass Graft, 35600
- Upper Extremity Vein
  - for Bypass Graft, 35500

Hauser Procedure
- Reconstruction, Patella, for Instability, 27420

HAVRIX, 90632-90634

Hayem's Elementary Corpuscle
- *See* Blood, Platelet

Haygroves Procedure, 27120, 27122

HBcAb, 86704, 86705

HBeAb, 86707

HBeAg, 87350

HBsAb, 86706

HBsAg (Hepatitis B Surface Antigen), 87340

HCG, 84702-84704

HCO3
- *See* Bicarbonate

Hct, 85013, 85014

HCV Antibodies
- *See* Antibody, Hepatitis C

HD, 27295

HDL (High Density Lipoprotein), 83718

Head
- Angiography, 70496, 70544-70546
- CT Scan, 70450-70470, 70496
- Excision, 21015-21070
- Fracture and/or Dislocation, 21310-21497
- Incision, 21010, 61316, 62148
- Introduction, 21076-21116
- Lipectomy, Suction Assisted, 15876
- Magnetic Resonance Angiography (MRA), 70544-70546
- Nerve
  - Graft, 64885, 64886

Index

Head — *continued*
Other Procedures, 21299, 21499
Repair
Revision and/or Reconstruction, 21120-21296
Ultrasound Examination, 76506, 76536
Unlisted Services and Procedures, 21499
X-ray, 70350
Headbrace
Application, 21100
Removal, 20661
Head Rings, Stereotactic
See Stereotactic Frame
Heaf Test
TB Test, 86580
Health Behavior
Alcohol and/or Substance Abuse, 99408-99409
Assessment, 96150
Family Intervention, 96154-96155
Group Intervention, 96153
Individual Intervention, 96152
Re-assessment, 96151
Smoking and Tobacco Cessation, 99406-99407
Health Risk Assessment Instrument, 99420
Hearing Aid
Bone Conduction
Implant, 69710
Removal, 69711
Repair, 69711
Replace, 69710
Check, 92592, 92593
Hearing Aid Services
Electroacoustic Test, 92594, 92595
Examination, 92590, 92591
Hearing Evaluation, 92506
Hearing Tests
See Audiologic Function Tests; Hearing Evaluation
Hearing Therapy, 92507, 92601-92604
Heart
Ablation
Ventricular Septum
Non-surgical, 93799
Allograft Preparation, 33933, 33944
Angiocardiography, 93555
Angiography
Injection, 93542, 93543
See Cardiac Catheterization; Injection
Aortic Arch
with Cardiopulmonary Bypass, 33853
without Cardiopulmonary Bypass, 33852
Aortic Valve
Repair, Left Ventricle, 33414
Replacement, 33405-33413
Arrhythmogenic Focus
Catheter Ablation, 93650-93652
Destruction, 33250, 33251, 33261
Atria
See Atria
Biopsy, 93505
Radiologic Guidance, 76932
Blood Vessel
Repair, 33320-33322
Cardiac Output Measurements
by Indicator Dilution, 93561-93562
Inert Gas Rebreathing
During Exercise, 0105T
During Rest, 0104T
Cardiac Rehabilitation, 93797, 93798
Cardioassist, 92970, 92971
Cardiopulmonary Bypass
with Lung Transplant, 32852, 32854
Cardioverter-Defibrillator
Evaluation and Testing, 93640, 93641, 93642

Heart — *continued*
Catheterization, 93501, 93510-93533
Combined Right and Retrograde Left for Congenital Cardiac Anomalies, 93531
Combined Right and Transseptal Left for Congenital Cardiac Anomalies, 93532, 93533
Flow-Directed, 93503
Right for Congenital Cardiac Anomalies, 93530
See Catheterization, Cardiac
Closure
Septal Defect, 33615
Valve
Atrioventricular, 33600
Semilunar, 33602
Commissurotomy, Right Ventricle, 33476, 33478
Defibrillator
Removal, 33243, 33244
Pulse Generator Only, 33241
Repair, 33218, 33220
Replacement, Leads, 33216, 33217, 33249
Destruction
Arrhythmogenic Focus, 33250, 33261
Electrical Recording
3-D Mapping, 93613
Atria, 93602
Atrial Electrogram, Esophageal (or Trans-esophageal), 93615, 93616
Bundle of His, 93600
Comprehensive, 93619, 93620
Right Ventricle, 93603
Tachycardia Sites, 93609
Electroconversion, 92960, 92961
Electrophysiologic Follow-Up Study, 93624
Evaluation of Device, 93640
Excision
Donor, 33930, 33940
Tricuspid Valve, 33460, 33465
Exploration, 33310, 33315
Fibrillation
Atrial, 33254, 33255-33256
Great Vessels
See Great Vessels
Heart-Lung Bypass
See Cardiopulmonary Bypass
Heart-Lung Transplantation
See Transplantation, Heart-Lung
Implantation
Artificial Heart, Intracorporeal, 0051T
Total Replacement Heart System, Intracorporeal, 0051T
Ventricular Assist Device, 33976
Extracorporeal, 0048T
Incision
Atrial, 33254, 33255-33256
Exploration, 33310, 33315
Injection
Radiologic, 93542, 93543
See Cardiac Catheterization, Injection
Insertion
Balloon Device, 33973
Defibrillator, 33212-33213
Electrode, 33210, 33211, 33214-33217, 33224-33225
Pacemaker, 33206-33208, 33212, 33213
Catheter, 33210
Pulse Generator, 33212-33214
Ventricular Assist Device, 33975
Intraoperative Pacing and Mapping, 93631
Ligation
Fistula, 37607
Magnetic Resonance Imaging (MRI)/with Contrast Material, 75561-75563
with contrast, 75561-75563

Heart — *continued*
Magnetic Resonance Imaging/with Contrast Material — *continued*
without Contrast Material, 75557-75559
Mitral Valve
See Mitral Valve
Muscle
See Myocardium
Myocardium
Imaging, Nuclear, 78466-78469
Perfusion Study, 78451-78454
Nuclear Medicine
Blood Flow Study, 78414
Blood Pool Imaging, 78472, 78473, 78481, 78483, 78494, 78496
Myocardial Imaging, 78466-78469
Myocardial Perfusion, 78451-78454
Shunt Detection (Test), 78428
Unlisted Services and Procedures, 78499
Open Chest Massage, 32160
Pacemaker
Conversion, 93214
Insertion, 33206-33208
Pulse Generator, 33212, 33213
Removal, 33233-33237
Replacement, 33206-33208
Catheter, 33210
Upgrade, 33214
Pacing
Arrhythmia Induction, 93618
Atria, 93610
Transcutaneous
Temporary, 92953
Ventricular, 93612
Pacing Cardioverter-Defibrillator
Evaluation and Testing, 93282-93283, 93289, 93292, 93295, 93640-93642
Insertion Electrodes, 33216, 33217, 33224-33225, 33249
Pulse Generator, 33240
Reposition Electrodes, 33215, 33226
Positron Emission Tomography (PET), 78459
Perfusion Study, 78491, 78492
Pulmonary Valve
See Pulmonary Valve
Rate Increase
See Tachycardia
Reconstruction
Atrial Septum, 33735-33737
Vena Cava, 34502
Recording
Left Ventricle, 93622
Right Ventricle, 93603
Tachycardia Sites, 93609
Reduction
Ventricular Septum
Non-surgical, 93799
Removal
Balloon Device, 33974
Electrode, 33238
Ventricular Assist Device, 33977, 33978
Extracorporeal, 0050T
Intracorporeal, 33980
Removal Single/Dual Chamber
Electrodes, 33243, 33244
Pulse Generator, 33241
Repair, 33218, 33220
Repair
Anomaly, 33615, 33617
Aortic Sinus, 33702-33722
Artificial Heart, Intracorporeal, 0052T, 0053T
Atrial Septum, 33254, 33255-33256, 33641, 33647

Heart — *continued*
Repair — *continued*
Atrioventricular Canal, 33660, 33665
Complete, 33670
Atrioventricular Valve, 33660, 33665
Cor Triatriatum, 33732
Electrode, 33218
Fenestration, 93580
Prosthetic Valve, 33670
Infundibular, 33476, 33478
Mitral Valve, 33420-33430
Myocardium, 33542
Outflow Tract, 33476, 33478
Postinfarction, 33542, 33545
Prosthetic Valve Dysfunction, 33496
Septal Defect, 33608, 33610, 33660, 33813, 33814, 93581
Sinus of Valsalva, 33702-33722
Sinus Venosus, 33645
Tetralogy of Fallot, 33692-33697, 33924
Total Replacement Heart System, Intracorporeal, 0052T, 0053T
Tricuspid Valve, 33460-33468
Ventricle, 33611, 33612
Obstruction, 33619
Ventricular Septum, 33545, 33647, 33681-33688, 33692-33697, 93581
Ventricular Tunnel, 33722
Wound, 33300, 33305
Replacement
Artificial Heart, Intracorporeal, 0052T, 0053T
Electrode, 33210, 33211, 33217
Mitral Valve, 33430
Total Replacement Heart System, Intracorporeal, 0052T, 0053T
Repositioning
Electrode, 33215, 33217, 33226
Tricuspid Valve, 33468
Resuscitation, 92950
Stimulation and Pacing, 93623
Thrombectomy, 33310-33315
Ventricular Assist Device, 33976
Intracorporeal, 33979
Transplantation, 33935, 33945
Anesthesia, 00580
Tricuspid Valve
See Tricuspid Valve
Tumor
Excision, 33120, 33130
Ultrasound
Radiologic Guidance, 76932
Unlisted Services and Procedures, 33999
Ventriculography
See Ventriculography
Ventriculomyectomy, 33416
Ventriculomyotomy, 33416
Wound
Repair, 33300, 33305
Heart Biopsy
Ultrasound, Radiologic Guidance, 76932
Heartsbreath Test, 0085T
Heart Vessels
Angiography
Injection, 93545
Angioplasty
Percutaneous, 92982, 92984
See Angioplasty; Percutaneous Transluminal Angioplasty
Injection
Radiologic, 93545
Insertion
Graft, 33330-33335
Thrombolysis, 92975, 92977

Heart Vessels — Hernia

Heart Vessels — *continued*
  Valvuloplasty
    See Valvuloplasty
    Percutaneous, 92986-92990
Heat Unstable Haemoglobin
  See Hemoglobin, Thermolabile
Heavy Lipoproteins
  See Lipoprotein
Heavy Metal, 83015, 83018
Heel
  See Calcaneus
  Collection of Blood, 36415, 36416
  X-ray, 73650
Heel Bone
  See Calcaneus
Heel Fracture
  See Calcaneus, Fracture
Heel Spur
  Excision, 28119
Heine–Medin Disease
  See Polio
Heine Operation
  See Cyclodialysis
Heinz Bodies, 85441, 85445
Helicobacter Pylori
  Antibody, 86677
  Antigen Detection
    Enzyme Immunoassay, 87338, 87339
    Breath Test, 78267, 78268, 83013
    Stool, 87338
    Urease Activity, 83009, 83013, 83014
Heller Procedure, 32665, 43279, 43330-43331
Helminth
  Antibody, 86682
Hemagglutination Inhibition Test, 86280
Hemangioma, 17106-17108
Hemapheresis, 36511-36516
Hematochezia, 82270, 82274
Hematologic Test
  See Blood Tests
Hematology
  Unlisted Services and Procedures, 85999
Hematoma
  Ankle, 27603
  Arm, Lower, 25028
  Arm, Upper
    Incision and Drainage, 23930
  Brain
    Drainage, 61154, 61156
    Evacuation, 61312-61315
    Incision and Drainage, 61312-61315
    Drain, 61108
  Ear, External
    Complicated, 69005
    Simple, 69000
  Elbow
    Incision and Drainage, 23930
  Epididymis
    Incision and Drainage, 54700
  Gums
    Incision and Drainage, 41800
  Hip, 26990
  Incision and Drainage
    Neck, 21501, 21502
    Skin, 10140
    Thorax, 21501, 21502
  Knee, 27301
  Leg, Lower, 27603
  Leg, Upper, 27301
  Mouth, 41005-41009, 41015-41018
    Incision and Drainage, 40800, 40801
  Nasal Septum
    Incision and Drainage, 30020
  Nose
    Incision and Drainage, 30000, 30020
  Pelvis, 26990
  Puncture Aspiration, 10160

Hematoma — *continued*
  Scrotum
    Incision and Drainage, 54700
  Shoulder
    Drainage, 23030
  Skin
    Incision and Drainage, 10140
    Puncture Aspiration, 10160
  Subdural, 61108
  Subungual
    Evacuation, 11740
  Testis
    Incision and Drainage, 54700
  Tongue, 41000-41006, 41015
  Vagina
    Incision and Drainage, 57022, 57023
  Wrist, 25028
Hematopoietic Stem Cell Transplantation
  See Stem Cell, Transplantation
Hematopoietin
  See Erythropoietin
Hematuria
  See Blood, Urine
Hemic System
  Unlisted Procedure, 38999
Hemiephyseal Arrest
  Elbow, 24470
Hemifacial Microsomia
  Reconstruction Mandibular Condyle, 21247
Hemilaminectomy, 63020-63044
Hemilaryngectomy, 31370-31382
Hemipelvectomies
  See Amputation, Interperviabdominal
Hemiphalangectomy
  Toe, 28160
Hemispherectomy
  Partial, 61543
  Total, 61542
Hemocytoblast
  See Stem Cell
Hemodialysis, 90935, 90937, 99512
  Blood Flow Study, 90940
  Duplex Scan of Access, 93990
Hemofiltration, 90945, 90947
  Hemodialysis, 90935, 90937
  Peritoneal Dialysis, 90945, 90947
Hemoglobin
  A1C, 83036
  Analysis
    O2 Affinity, 82820
  Antibody
    Fecal, 82274
  Carboxyhemoglobin, 82375-82376
  Chromatography, 83021
  Electrophoresis, 83020
  Fetal, 83030, 83033, 85460, 85461
  Fractionation and Quantitation, 83020
  Glycated, 83036
  Methemoglobin, 83045, 83050
  Non–Automated, 83026
  Plasma, 83051
  Sulfhemoglobin, 83055, 83060
  Thermolabile, 83065, 83068
  Transcutaneous
    Carboxyhemoglobin, 88740
    Methemoglobin, 88741
  Urine, 83069
Hemoglobin F
  Fetal
    Chemical, 83030
    Qualitative, 83033
Hemoglobin, Glycosylated, 83036-83037
Hemoglobin (Hgb) quantitative
  transcutaneous, 88738-88741
Hemogram
  Added Indices, 85025-85027
  Automated, 85025-85027
  Manual, 85014, 85018, 85032
Hemolysins, 85475
  with Agglutinins, 86940, 86941

Hemolytic Complement
  See Complement, Hemolytic
Hemolytic Complement, Total
  See Complement, Hemolytic, Total
Hemoperfusion, 90997
Hemophil
  See Clotting Factor
Hemophilus Influenza
  Antibody, 86684
  B Vaccine, 90645-90648, 90720-90721, 90748
Hemorrhage
  Abdomen, 49002
  Anal
    Endoscopic Control, 46614
  Bladder
    Postoperative, 52214
  Chest Cavity
    Endoscopic Control, 32654
  Colon
    Endoscopic Control, 44391, 45382
  Colon–Sigmoid
    Endoscopic Control, 45334
  Esophagus
    Endoscopic Control, 43227
  Gastrointestinal, Upper
    Endoscopic Control, 43255
  Intestines, Small
    Endoscopic Control, 44366, 44378
  Liver
    Control, 47350
  Lung, 32110
  Nasal
    Cauterization, 30901-30906
    Endoscopic Control, 31238
  Nasopharynx, 42970-42972
  Nose
    Cauterization, 30901-30906
  Oropharynx, 42960-42962
  Rectum
    Endoscopic Control, 45317
  Throat, 42960-42962
  Uterus
    Postpartum, 59160
  Vagina, 57180
Hemorrhoidectomy
  External, 46250, [46320]
  Internal and External, 46255-46262
  Ligation, 46221 [46945, 46946]
  Whitehead, 46260
Hemorrhoidopexy, [46947]
Hemorrhoids
  Destruction, 46930
  Excision, 46250-46262, [46320]
  Incision, 46083
  Injection
    Sclerosing Solution, 46500
  Ligation, 46221 [46945, 46946]
  Stapling, [46947]
Hemosiderin, 83070, 83071
Hemothorax
  Thoracostomy, 32551
Heparin, 85520
  Clotting Inhibitors, 85300-85305
  Neutralization, 85525
  Protamine Tolerance Test, 85530
Heparin Cofactor I
  See Antithrombin III
Hepatectomy
  Extensive, 47122
  Left Lobe, 47125
  Partial
    Donor, 47140-47142
    Lobe, 47120
  Right Lobe, 47130
  Total
    Donor, 47133
Hepatic Abscess
  See Abscess, Liver
Hepatic Arteries
  See Artery, Hepatic
Hepatic Artery Aneurysm
  See Artery, Hepatic, Aneurysm

Hepatic Duct
  Anastomosis
    with Intestines, 47765, 47802
  Exploration, 47400
  Incision and Drainage, 47400
  Nuclear Medicine
    Imaging, 78223
  Removal
    Calculi (Stone), 47400
  Repair
    with Intestines, 47765, 47802
  Unlisted Services and Procedures, 47999
Hepatic Haemorrhage
  See Hemorrhage, Liver
Hepaticodochotomy
  See Hepaticostomy
Hepaticoenterostomy, 47802
Hepaticostomy, 47400
Hepaticotomy, 47400
Hepatic Portal Vein
  See Vein, Hepatic Portal
Hepatic Portoenterostomies
  See Hepaticoenterostomy
Hepatic Transplantation
  See Liver, Transplantation
Hepatitis A and Hepatitis B, 90636
Hepatitis Antibody
  A, 86708, 86709
  B core, 86704, 86705
  Be, 86707
  B Surface, 86706
  C, 86803, 86804
  Delta Agent, 86692
  IgG, 86704, 86708
  IgM, 86704, 86705, 86708, 86709
Hepatitis Antigen
  B, 87515-87517
  Be, 87350
  B Surface, 87340, 87341
  C, 87520-87522
  Delta Agent, 87380
  G, 87525-87527
Hepatitis A Vaccine
  Adolescent
  Pediatric
    Three Dose Schedule, 90634
    Two Dose Schedule, 90633
  Adult Dosage, 90632
Hepatitis B and Hib, 90748
Hepatitis B Immunization, 90740-90747
Hepatitis B Vaccine
  Dosage
    Adolescent, 90743
    Adult, 90746
    Immunosuppressed, 90740, 90747
    Pediatric, 90744
    Adolescent, 90743-90744
Hepatitis B Virus E Antibody
  See Antibody, Hepatitis
Hepatitis B Virus Surface ab
  See Antibody, Hepatitis B, Surface
Hepatorrhaphy
  See Liver, Repair
Hepatotomy
  Abscess, 47010, 47011
    Percutaneous, 47011
  Cyst, 47010, 47011
    Percutaneous, 47011
Hernia
  Repair
    with Spermatic Cord, 55540
    Abdominal, 49560, 49565, 49590
      Incisional, 49560
      Recurrent, 49565
    Diaphragmatic, 39502-39541
      Chronic, 39541
      Esophageal Hiatal, 39520
      Neonatal, 39503
    Epigastric, 49570
      Incarcerated, 49572
    Femoral, 49550
      Incarcerated, 49553
      Recurrent, 49555

Index

Hernia — continued
Repair — continued
  Femoral — continued
    Recurrent Incarcerated, 49557
    Reducible, 49550
  Incisional, 49561, 49566
    Incarcerated, 49561
  Inguinal, 49491, 49495-49500, 49505
    Incarcerated, 49492, 49496, 49501, 49507, 49521
    Infant, Incarcerated Strangulated, 49496, 49501
    Infant, Reducible, 49495, 49500
    Laparoscopic, 49650, 49651
    Pediatric, Reducible, 49500, 49505
    Recurrent, Incarcerated Strangulated, 49521
    Recurrent, Reducible, 49520
    Sliding, 49525
    Strangulated, 49492
  Lumbar, 49540
  Lung, 32800
  Mayo, 49585
  Orchiopexy, 54640
  Recurrent Incisional Incarcerated, 49566
  Umbilicus, 49580, 49585
    Incarcerated, 49582, 49587
  Spigelian, 49590

Hernia, Cerebral
See Encephalocele

Hernia, Rectovaginal
See Rectocele

Hernia, Umbilical
See Omphalocele

Heroin, Alkaloid Screening, 82101
Heroin Screen, 82486

Herpes Simplex Virus
Antibody, 86696
Antigen Detection
  Immunofluorescence, 87273, 87274
  Nucleic Acid, 87528-87530
Identification
  Smear and Stain, 87207

Herpes Smear, 87207

Herpesvirus 4 (Gamma), Human
See Epstein–Barr Virus

Herpes Virus–6 Detection, 87531-87533

Herpetic Vesicle
Destruction, 54050, 54065

Heteroantibodies
See Antibody, Heterophile

Heterograft
Skin, 15400-15431

Heterologous Tranplantations
See Heterograft

Heterologous Transplant
See Xenograft

Heterophile Antibody, 86308-86310

Heterotropia
See Strabismus

Hexadecadrol
See Dexamethasone

Hex B
See b–Hexosaminidase

Hexosephosphate Isomerase
See Phosphohexose Isomerase

Heyman Procedure, 27179, 28264

H Flu
See Hemophilus Influenza

Hgb, 85018
HGB, 83036, 83051, 83065, 83068

Hg Factor
See Glucagon

HGH (Human Growth Hormone), 80418, 80428, 80430, 83003, 86277

HHV–4
See Epstein–Barr Virus

HIAA (Hydroxyindolacetic Acid, Urine), 83497
Hibb Operation, 22841
HibTITER, 90645

Hib Vaccine
Four Dose Schedule
  HbOC, 90645
  PRP-T, 90648
  PRP-D/Booster, 90646
  PRP-OMP
Three Dose Schedule, 90647

Hickmann Catheterization
See Cannulization; Catheterization, Venous, Central Line; Venipuncture

Hicks–Pitney Test
Thromboplastin, Partial Time, 85730, 85732

Hidradenitis
See Sweat Gland
Excision, 11450-11471
Suppurative
  Incision and Drainage, 10060, 10061

High Altitude Simulation Test, 94452-94453
High Density Lipoprotein, 83718
Highly Selective Vagotomy
See Vagotomy, Highly Selective
High Molecular Weight Kininogen
See Fitzgerald Factor

Highmore Antrum
See Sinus, Maxillary

Hill Procedure, 43324
Laparoscopic, 43280

Hinton Positive
See RPR

Hip
See Femur; Pelvis
Abscess
  Incision and Drainage, 26990
Arthrocentesis, 20610
Arthrodesis, 27284, 27286
Arthrography, 73525
Arthroplasty, 27130, 27132
Arthroscopy, 29860-29863
Arthrotomy, 27030, 27033
Biopsy, 27040, 27041
Bone
  Drainage, 26992
Bursa
  Incision and Drainage, 26991
Capsulectomy
  with Release, Flexor Muscles, 27036
Cast, 29305, 29325
Craterization, 27070, 27071
Cyst
  Excision, 27065-27067
Denervation, 27035
Echography
  Infant, 76885, 76886
Endoprosthesis
  See Prosthesis, Hip
Excision, 27070
  Excess Skin, 15834
Exploration, 27033
Fasciotomy, 27025
Fusion, 27284, 27286
Hematoma
  Incision and Drainage, 26990
Injection
  Radiologic, 27093, 27095, 27096
Manipulation, 27275
Reconstruction
  Total Replacement, 27130
Removal
  Cast, 29710
  Foreign Body, 27033, 27086, 27087
    Arthroscopic, 29861
  Loose Body
    Arthroscopic, 29861
  Prosthesis, 27090, 27091

Hip — continued
Repair
  Muscle Transfer, 27100-27105, 27111
  Osteotomy, 27146-27156
  Tendon, 27097
Saucerization, 27070
Stem Prostheses
  See Arthroplasty, Hip
Strapping, 29520
Tenotomy
  Abductor Tendon, 27006
  Adductor Tendon, 27000-27003
  Iliopsoas Tendon, 27005
Total Replacement, 27130, 27132
Tumor
  Excision, 27047-27049 [27043, 27045, 27059], 27065-27067, 27075-27078
Ultrasound
  Infant, 76885, 76886
X-ray, 73500-73520, 73540
  with Contrast, 73525
  Intraoperative, 73530

Hip Joint
Arthroplasty, 27132
  Revision, 27134-27138
Arthrotomy, 27502
Biopsy, 27502
Capsulotomy
  with Release, Flexor Muscles, 27036
Dislocation, 27250, 27252
  without Trauma, 27265, 27266
  Congenital, 27256-27259
  Open Treatment, 27253, 27254
  Manipulation, 27275
Reconstruction
  Revision, 27134-27138
Synovium
  Excision, 27054
  Arthroscopic, 29863
Total Replacement, 27132

Hippocampus
Excision, 61566

Hip Stem Prosthesis
See Arthroplasty, Hip

Histalog Test
Gastric Analysis Test, 91052

Histamine, 83088
Histamine Release Test, 86343
Histochemistry, 88318, 88319

Histocompatibility Testing
See Tissue Typing

Histoplasma
Antibody, 86698
Antigen, 87385

Histoplasma Capsulatum
Antigen Detection
  Enzyme Immunoassay, 87385

Histoplasmin Test
See Histoplasmosis, Skin Test

Histoplasmoses
See Histoplasmosis

Histoplasmosis
Skin Test, 86510

History and Physical
See Evaluation and Management, Office and/or Other Outpatient Services
Pelvic Exam under Anesthesia, 57410
Preventive
  Established Patient, 99391-99397
  New Patient, 99381-99387

HIV, 86689, 86701-86703, 87390, 87391, 87534-87539
Antibody
  Confirmation Test, 86689

HIV-1
Antigen Detection
  Enzyme Immunoassay, 87390

HIV-2
Antigen Detection
  Enzyme Immunoassay, 87391

HIV Antibody, 86701-86703

HIV Detection
Antibody, 86701-86703
Antigen, 87390, 87391, 87534-87539
Confirmation Test, 86689

HK3 Kallikrein
See Antigen, Prostate Specific

HLA, 86812-86817
HLA Typing, 86812-86817

HMRK
See Fitzgerald Factor

Hoffman Apparatus, 20690
Hofmeister Operation, 43632

Holotranscobalamin
Quantitative, 0103T

Holten Test, 82575
Holter Monitor, 93235

Home Services
Activities of Daily Living, 99509
Catheter Care, 99507
Enema Administration, 99511
Established Patient, 99347-99350
Hemodialysis, 99512
Home Infusion Procedures, 99601, 99602
Individual or Family Counseling, 99510
Intramuscular Injections, 99506
Mechanical Ventilation, 99504
Newborn Care, 99502
New Patient, 99341-99345
Postnatal Assessment, 99501
Prenatal Monitoring, 99500
Respiratory Therapy., 99503
Sleep Studies, 95805-95811
Stoma Care, 99505
Unlisted Services and Procedures, 99600

Homocystine, 83090
Urine, 82615
Homogenization, Tissue, 87176

Homograft
Skin, 15300-15336

Homologous Grafts
See Graft

Homologous Transplantation
See Homograft

Homovanillic Acid
Urine, 83150

Hormone Adrenocorticotrophic
See Adrenocorticotropic Hormone (ACTH)

Hormone Assay
ACTH, 82024
Aldosterone
  Blood or Urine, 82088
Androstenedione
  Blood or Urine, 82157
Androsterone
  Blood or Urine, 82160
Angiotensin II, 82163
Corticosterone, 82528
Cortisol
  Total, 82533
Dehydroepiandrosterone, 82626-82627
Dihydroelestosterone, 82651
Dihydrotestosterone, 82651
Epiandrosterone, 82666
Estradiol, 82670
Estriol, 82677
Estrogen, 82671, 82672
Estrone, 82679
Follicle Stimulating Hormone, 83001
Growth Hormone, 83003
  Suppression Panel, 80430
Hydroxyprogesterone, 83498, 83499
Luteinizing Hormone, 83002
Somatotropin, 80430, 83003
Testosterone, 84403
Vasopressin, 84588

Hormone–Binding Globulin, Sex
See Globulin, Sex Hormone Binding

Hormone, Corticotropin–Releasing
See Corticotropic Releasing Hormone (CRH)

Hormone, Growth

Hormone, Growth
  See Growth Hormone
Hormone, Human Growth
  See Gowth Hormone, Human
Hormone, Interstitial Cell–Stimulation
  See Luteinizing Hormone (LH)
Hormone, Parathyroid
  See Parathormone
Hormone Pellet Implantation, 11980
Hormone, Pituitary Lactogenic
  See Prolactin
Hormone, Placental Lactogen
  See Lactogen, Human Placental
Hormones, Adrenal Cortex
  See Corticosteroids
Hormones, Antidiuretic
  See Antidiuretic Hormone
Hormone, Somatotropin Release–Inhibiting
  See Somatostatin
Hormone, Thyroid–Stimulating
  See Thyroid Stimulating Hormone (TSH)
Hospital Discharge Services
  See Discharge Services, Hospital
Hospital Services
  Inpatient Services
    Discharge Services, 99238, 99239
    Initial Care New or Established Patient, 99221-99223
    Initial Hospital Care, 99221-99223
    Neonate, 99477
    Newborn, 99460-99465, 99466-99480
    Prolonged Services, 99356, 99357
    Subsequent Hospital Care, 99231-99233
  Normal Newborn, 99460-99463
  Observation
    Discharge Services, 99234-99236
    Initial Care, 99218-99220
    New or Established Patient, 99218-99220
    Intensive Neonatal, 99477
  Same Day Admission
    Discharge Services, 99234-99236
    Subsequent Newborn Care, 99462
Hot Pack Treatment, 97010
  See Physical Medicine and Rehabilitation
House Calls, 99341-99350
Howard Test
  Cystourethroscopy, Catheterization, Ureter, 52005
HP, 83010, 83012
HPL, 83632
H–Reflex Study, 95934, 95936
HSG, 58340, 74740
HTLV I
  Antibody
    Confirmatory Test, 86689
    Detection, 86687
HTLV–II
  Antibody, 86688
HTLV III
  See HIV
HTLV III Antibodies
  See Antibody, HIV
HTLV–IV
  See HIV-2
Hubbard Tank Therapy, 97036
  with Exercises, 97036, 97113
  See Physical Medicine/ Therapy/Occupational Therapy
Hue Test, 92283
Huggin Operation, 54520
Huhner Test, 89300-89320
Human
  Epididymis Protein 4 (HE4), 86305
  Growth Hormone, 80418, 80428, 80430
  Leukocyte Antigen, 86812-86826
  Papillomavirus Detection, 87620-87622

Human — *continued*
  Papillomavirus (HPV) Vaccine, 90649-90650
Human Chorionic Gonadotropin
  See Chorionic Gonadotropin
Human Chorionic Somatomammotropin
  See Lactogen, HumanPlacental
Human Cytomegalovirus Group
  See Cytomegalovirus
Human Herpes Virus 4
  See Epstein–Barr Virus
Human Immunodeficiency Virus
  See HIV
Human Immunodeficiency Virus 1
  See HIV-1
Human Immunodeficiency Virus 2
  See HIV-2
Human Placental Lactogen, 83632
Human T Cell Leukemia Virus I
  See HTLV I
Human T Cell Leukemia Virus I Antibodies
  See Antibody, HTLV–I
Human T Cell Leukemia Virus II
  See HTLV II
Human T Cell Leukemia Virus II Antibodies
  See Antibody, HTLV–II
Humeral Epicondylitides, Lateral
  See Tennis Elbow
Humeral Fracture
  See Fracture, Humerus
Humerus
  See Arm, Upper; Shoulder
  Abscess
    Incision and Drainage, 23935
  Craterization, 23184, 24140
  Cyst
    Excision, 23150, 24110
      with Allograft, 23156, 24116
      with Autograft, 23155, 24115
  Diaphysectomy, 23184, 24140
  Excision, 23174, 23184, 23195, 23220, 24077-24079, 24110-24116, 24134, 24140, 24150
  Fracture
    with Dislocation, 23665, 23670
    Closed Treatment, 24500, 24505
      with Manipulation, 23605
      without Manipulation, 23600
    Condyle
      Closed Treatment, 24576, 24577
      Open Treatment, 24579
      Percutaneous Fixation, 24582
    Epicondyle
      Closed Treatment, 24560, 24565
      Open Treatment, 24575
      Percutaneous Fixation, 24566
    Greater Tuberosity Fracture
      Closed Treatment with Manipulation, 23625
      Closed Treatment without Manipulation, 23620
      Open Treatment, 23630
    Open Treatment, 23615, 23616
    Shaft
      Closed Treatment, 24500, 24505, 24516
      Open Treatment, 24515
    Supracondylar
      Closed Treatment, 24530, 24535
      Open Treatment, 24545, 24546
      Percutaneous Fixation, 24538
    Transcondylar
      Closed Treatment, 24530, 24535
      Open Treatment, 24545, 24546
      Percutaneous Fixation, 24538
  Osteomyelitis, 24134
  Pinning, Wiring, 23491, 24498

Humerus — *continued*
  Prophylactic Treatment, 23491, 24498
  Radical Resection, 23220, 24077-24079
  Repair, 24430
    with Graft, 24435
    Nonunion, Malunion, 24430, 24435
    Osteoplasty, 24420
    Osteotomy, 24400, 24410
  Resection Head, 23195
  Saucerization, 23184, 24140
  Sequestrectomy, 23174, 24134
  Tumor
    Excision, 23150-23156, 23220, 24075-24079 [24071, 24073], 24110-24116
  X-ray, 73060
Hummelshein Operation, 67340
  Strabismus Repair
    Adjustable Sutures, 67335
    Extraocular Muscles, 67340
    One Horizontal Muscle, 67311
    One Vertical Muscle, 67314
    Posterior Fixation Suture Technique, 67335
    Previous Surgery not Involving Extraocular Muscles, 67331
    Release Extensive Scar Tissue, 67343
    Superior Oblique Muscle, 67318
    Transposition, 67320
    Two Horizontal Muscles, 67312
    Two or More Vertical Muscles, 67316
Humor Shunt, Aqueous
  See Aqueous Shunt
HVA (Homovanillic Acid), 83150
Hybridization Probes, DNA
  See Nucleic Acid Probe
Hydatid Disease
  See Echinococcosis
Hydatidiform Mole
  Evacuation and Curettage, 59870
  Excision, 59100
Hydatid Mole
  See Hydatidiform Mole
Hydration, 96360-96361
Hydrocarbons, Chlorinated
  See Chlorinated Hydrocarbons
Hydrocele
  Aspiration, 55000
  Excision
    Bilateral, Tunica Vaginalis, 55041
    Unilateral
      Spermatic Cord, 55500
      Tunica Vaginalis, 55040
  Repair, 55060
Hydrocelectomy, 49495-49501
Hydrocele, Tunica Vaginalis
  See Tunica Vaginalis, Hydrocele
Hydrochloric Acid, Gastric
  See Acid, Gastric
Hydrochloride, Vancomycin
  See Vancomycin
Hydrocodon
  See Dihydrocodeinone
Hydrogen Ion Concentration
  See pH
Hydrolase, Acetylcholine
  See Acetylcholinesterase
Hydrolases, Phosphoric Monoester
  See Phosphatase
Hydrolase, Triacylglycerol
  See Lipase
Hydrotherapy (Hubbard Tank), 97036
  with Exercises, 97036, 97113
  See Physical Medicine/Therapy/ Occupational Therapy
Hydrotubation, 58350
Hydroxyacetanilide
  See Acetaminophen
Hydroxycorticosteroid, 83491
Hydroxyindolacetic Acid, 83497
  Urine, 83497

Hydroxypregnenolone, 80406, 84143
Hydroxyprogesterone, 80402, 80406, 83498, 83500
Hydroxyproline, 83500, 83505
Hydroxytyramine
  See Dopamine
Hygroma, Cystic
  Axillary or Cervical Excision, 38550, 38555
Hymen
  Excision, 56700
  Incision, 56442
Hymenal Ring
  Revision, 56700
Hymenectomy, 56700
Hymenotomy, 56442
Hyoid Bone
  Fracture
    Open Treatment, 21495
Hyperbaric Oxygen Pressurization, 99183
Hypercycloidal X–ray, 76101, 76102
Hyperdactylies
  See Supernumerary Digit
Hyperglycemic Glycogenolytic Factor
  See Glucagon
HyperRAB, 90375-90376
HyperTED, 90389
Hypertelorism of Orbit
  See Orbital Hypertelorism
Hyperthermia Therapy
  See Thermotherapy
Hyperthermia Treatment, 77600-77620
Hypnotherapy, 90880
Hypodermis
  See Subcutaneous Tissue
Hypogastric Plexus
  Destruction, 64681
  Injection
    Anesthetic, 64517
    Neurolytic, 64681
Hypoglossal–Facial Anastomosis
  See Anastomosis, Nerve, Facial to Hypoglossal
Hypoglossal Nerve
  Anastomosis
    to Facial Nerve, 64868
Hypopharynges
  See Hypopharynx
Hypopharynx
  Biopsy, 42802
Hypophysectomy, 61546, 61548, 62165
Hypophysis
  See Pituitary Gland
Hypopyrexia
  See Hypothermia
Hypospadias
  Repair, 54300, 54352
  Complications, 54340-54348
  First Stage, 54304
    Meatal Advancement, 54322
    Perineal, 54336
    Proximal Penile or Penoscrotal, 54332
  One Stage
    Meatal Advancement, 54322
    Perineal, 54336
  Urethroplasty by
    Local Skin Flaps, 54324
    Local Skin Flaps and Mobilization of Urethra, 54326
    Local Skin Flaps, Skin Graft Patch and/or Island Flap, 54328
  Urethroplasty for Second Stage, 54308-54316
    Free Skin Graft, 54316
  Urethroplasty for Third Stage, 54318
Hypotensive Anesthesia, 99135
Hypothermia, 99116
Hypothermic Anesthesia, 99116
Hypoxia
  Breathing Response, 94450

Index

Hypoxia — *continued*
  High Altitude Simulation Test, 94452-94453
Hysterectomy
  Abdominal
    Radical, 58210
      Resection of Ovarian Malignancy, 58951, 58953-58954, 58956
    Supracervical, 58180
    Total, 58150, 58200
      with Colpo–Urethrocystopexy, 58152
      with Omentectomy, 58956
      with Partial Vaginectomy, 58200
  Cesarean
    with Closure of Vesicouterine Fistula, 51925
    After Cesarean Section, 59525
  Removal
    Lesion, 59100
  Vaginal, 58260-58270, 58290-58294, 58550-58554
    with Colpectomy, 58275, 58280
    with Colpo–Urethrocystopexy, 58267, 58293
    See Lysis, Adhesions, Uterus
    Laparoscopic, 58550
    Radical, 58285
    Removal Tubes
      Ovaries, 52402, 58262, 58263, 58291-58292, 58552-58554
      Repair of Enterocele, 58263, 58292, 58294
  Wertheim, 58210
Hysterolysis, 58559
Hysteroplasty, 58540
Hysterorrhaphy, 58520, 59350
Hysterosalpingography, 74740
  Catheterization, 58345
  Introduction of Contrast, 58340
Hysterosalpingostomy
  See Implantation, Tubouterine
Hysteroscopy
  with Endometrial Ablation, 58563
  with Lysis of Adhesions, 58559
  Ablation
    Endometrial, 58563
  Diagnostic, 58555
  Lysis
    Adhesions, 58559
  Placement
    Fallopian Tube Implants, 58565
  Removal
    Impacted Foreign Body, 58562
    Leiomyomata, 58561
  Resection
    of Intrauterine Septum, 58560
  Surgical with Biopsy, 58558
  Unlisted Services and Procedures, 58579
Hysterosonography, 76831
  See Ultrasound
Hysterotomy, 59100
  See Ligation, Uterus
  Induced Abortion
    with Amniotic Injections, 59852
    with Vaginal Suppositories, 59857
Hysterotrachelectomy, 57530

I

IA, 36100-36140, 36260
IAB, 33970-33974
IABP, 33970-33974
IAC, 33970-33974
I Angiotensin, 84244
I Antibodies, HTLV, 86687, 86689
IBC, 83550
ICCE, 66920, 66930
Ichthyosis, Sex-Linked, 86592-86593
I Coagulation Factor, 85384-85385
ICSH, 80418, 80426, 83002

Identification
  Oocyte from Follicular Fluid, 89254
  Sentinel Node from Injection, 38792
  Sperm
    from Aspiration, 89257
    from Tissue, 89264
IDH (Isocitric Dehydrogenase, Blood), 83570
IG, 82787, 84445, 86023
IgA, Gammaglobulin, 82784
IgD, Gammaglobulin, 82784
IgE
  Allergen Specific, 86003, 86005
  Gammaglobulin, 82785
IgG
  Allergen Specific, 86001
  Gammaglobulin, 82784
IgM, Gammaglobulin, 82784
I Heparin Co-Factor, 85300-85301
II, Coagulation Factor, 85610-85611
II, CranialNerve
  See Optic Nerve
Ileal Conduit
  Visualization, 50690
Ileocolostomy, 44160
Ileoproctostomy, 44150
Ileoscopy, 44380, 44382
  via Stoma, 44383
Ileostomy, 44310, 45136
  Continent (Kock Pouch), 44316
  Laparoscopic, 44186-44187
  Nontube, 44187
  Revision, 44312, 44314
Iliac Arteries
  See Artery, Iliac
Iliac Crest
  Free Osteocutaneous flap with Microvascular Anastomosis, 20970
Iliohypogastric Nerve
  Injection
    Anesthetic, 64425
Ilioinguinal Nerve
  Injection
    Anesthetic, 64425
Ilium
  Craterization, 27070, 27071
  Cyst, 27065-27067
  Excision, 27070-27071
  Fracture
    Open Treatment, 27215, 27218
    Saucerization, 27070, 27071
  Tumor, 27065-27067
Ilizarov Procedure
  Application, Bone Fixation Device, 20690, 20692
  Monticelli Type, 20692
Imaging
  See Vascular Studies
Imaging, Gamma Camera
  See Nuclear Medicine
Imaging, Magnetic Resonance
  See Magnetic Resonance Imaging (MRI)
Imaging, Ultrasonic
  See Echography
Imbrication
  Diaphragm, 39545
Imidobenzyle
  See Imipramine
IM Injection
  Chemotherapy/Complex Biological, 96401-96402
  Diagnostic, Prophylactic, Therapeutic, 96372
  Antineoplastic
    Hormonal, 96402
    Non-hormonal, 96401
Imipramine
  Assay, 80174
Immune Complex Assay, 86332
Immune Globulin Administration, 96365-96368, 96372, 96374-96375
Immune Globulin E, 82785

Immune Globulins
  Antitoxin
    Botulinum, 90287
    Diptheria, 90296
  Botulism, 90288
  Cytomegalovirus, 90291
  Hepatitis B, 90371
  Human, 90281, 90283-90284
  Rabies, 90375, 90376
  Rho (D), 90384-90386
  Tetanus, 90389
  Unlisted Immune Globulin, 90399
  Vaccinia, 90393
  Varicella–Zoster, 90396
Immune Serum Globulin
  Immunization, 90281, 90283
Immunization
  Active
    Acellular Pertussis, 90700, 90721-90723
    BCG, 90585, 90586
    Cholera, 90725
    Diphtheria, 90700-90702, 90718-90723
    Diphtheria, Tetanus, Pertussis (DTP), 90701, 90720
    Diphtheria, Tetanus Toxoids, Acellular Pertussis, 90700, 90720-90723
    Diptheria, Tetanus Acellular Influenza B and Poliovirus Inactivated, Vaccine, 90698
    Hemophilus Influenza B, 90645-90648, 90720-90721, 90748
    Hepatitis A, 90632-90636
    Hepatitis B, 90740-90747, 90748
    Hepatitis B, Hemophilus Influenza B (HIB), 90748
    Influenza, 90655-90660
    Influenza B, 90645-90648
    Japanese Encephalitis, 90735
    Lyme Disease, 90665
    Measles, 90705
    Measles, Mumps, Rubella, 90707
    Measles, Mumps, Rubella, Varicella Vaccine, 90710
    Measles, Rubella, 90708
    Meningococcal Conjugate, 90734
    Meningococcal Polysaccharide, 90733
    Mumps, 90704
    Plague, 90727
    Pneumococcal, 90732
    Poliomyelitis, 90713
    Poliovirus, 90712
    Rabies, 90675, 90676
    Rotavirus Vaccine, 90680
    Rubella, 90706
    Tetanus and Diphtheria, 90700-90702, 90718, 90720-90723
    Tetanus Diphtheria and Acellular Pertussis, 90715
    Tetanus Toxoid, 90703
    Typhoid, 90690-90693
    Varicella (Chicken Pox), 90716
    Yellow Fever, 90717
  Administration
    Each Additional Vaccine/Toxoid, 90472, 90474
      with Counseling, 90466, 90468
    One Vaccine/Toxoid, 90471, 90473
      with Counseling, 90465, 90467
  Inactive
    Japanese Encephalitis Virus, 90738
  Passive
    Hyperimmune Serum Globulin, 90287-90399
    Immune Serum Globulin, 90281, 90283

Immunization — *continued*
  Unlisted Services and Procedures, 90749
Immunization Administration
  Each Additional Vaccine/Toxoid, 90472, 90474
    with Counseling, 90466, 90468
  One Vaccine/Toxoid, 90471, 90473
    with Counseling, 90465, 90467
  Single Vaccine
    Toxoid, 90471, 90473
  Two or More Vaccines, Each Additional
    Toxoids, 90472, 90474
Immunoassay
  Analyte, 83518-83520
  Calprotectin, Fecal, 83993
  Infectious Agent, 86317, 86318, 87449-87451, 87809
  Nonantibody, 83516-83519
  Tumor Antigen, 86294, 86316
  CA 125, 86304
  CA 15-3, 86300
  CA 19-9, 86301
Immunoblotting, Western
  HIV, 86689
  Protein, 84181-84182
  Tissue Analysis, 88371-88372
Immunochemical, Lysozyme (Muramidase), 85549
Immunocytochemistry, 88342
Immunodeficiency Virus, Human
  See HIV
Immunodeficiency Virus Type 1, Human, 87390
Immunodeficiency Virus Type 2, Human, 87391
Immunodiffusion, 86329, 86331
Immunoelectrophoresis, 86320-86327, 86334-86335
Immunofixation Electrophoresis, 86334-86335
Immunofluorescent Study, 88346, 88347
Immunogen
  See Antigen
Immunoglobulin, 82787
  Platelet Associated, 86023
  Thyroid Stimulating, 84445
Immunoglobulin E, 86003-86005
Immunoglobulin Receptor Assay, 86243
Immunologic Skin Test
  See Skin, Tests
Immunology
  Unlisted Services and Procedures, 86849
Immunotherapies, Allergen
  See Allergen Immunotherapy
IMOVAX RABIES, 90675
Impedance Testing, 92567
  See Audiologic Function Tests
Imperfectly Descended Testis, 54550-54560
Implantation
  Artificial Heart, Intracorporeal, 0051T
  Bone
    for External Speech Processor/Cochlear Stimulator, 69714-69718
  Brain
    Chemotherapy, 61517
    Thermal Perfusion Probe, 61107, 61210
  Cardiac Event Recorder, 33282
  Cerebral Thermal Perfusion Probe, 61107, 61210
  Contraceptive Capsules, 11975, 11977
  Corneal Ring Segment
    Intrastomal, 0099T
  Drug Delivery Device, 11981, 11983, 61517
  Electrode
    Brain, 61850-61875

Implantation

Implantation — *continued*
  Electrode — *continued*
    Gastric Implantation
      Laparoscopic
        Neurostimulator, 43647
        Stimulation, 0155T
    Nerve, 64553-64581
    Spinal Cord, 63650, 63655
    Stomach, 0155T, 0157T
  Eye
    Anterior Segment, 65920
    Aqueous Shunt to Extraocular Reservoir, 66180
      Revision, 66185
    Corneal Ring Segments, 0099T
    Placement or Replacement of Pegs, 65125
    Posterior Segment
      Extraocular, 67120
      Intraocular, 67121
    Replacement of Pegs, 65125
    Reservoir, 66180
    Vitreous
      Drug Delivery System, 67027
  Fallopian Tube, 58565
  Hearing Aid
    Bone Conduction, 69710
  Hip Prosthesis
    See Arthroplasty, Hip
  Hormone Pellet, 11980
  Intraocular Lens
    See Insertion, Intraocular Lens
  Intraocular Retinal Electrode Array, 0100T
  Intrastomal Corneal Ring Segments, 0099T
  Joint
    See Arthroplasty
  Mesh
    Closure of Necrotizing Soft Tissue Infection, 49568
    Hernia Repair, 49568, 49652-49657
    Vaginal Repair, 57267
  Nerve
    into Bone, 64787
    into Muscle, 64787
  Neurostimulators
    Gastric, 95980-95982
    Implantation
      Laparoscopic
        Neurostimulator, 43647
        Stimulation, 0157T
      Open
        Neurostimulator, 43881
        Stimulation, 0157T
    Pulse Generator, 61885
    Receiver, 61886
  Ovum, 58976
  Pulsatile Heart Assist System, 33999
  Pulse Generator
    Brain, 61885, 61886
    Spinal Cord, 63685
  Receiver
    Brain, 61885, 61886
    Nerve, 64590
    Spinal Cord, 63685
  Removal, 20670, 20680
    Anesthesia, External Fixation, 20694
    Elbow, 24164
    Radius, 24164
    Wire, Pin, Rod, 20670
    Wire, Pin, Rod/Deep, 20680
  Reservoir Vascular Access Device
    Declotting, 36593
  Retinal Electrode Array, 0100T
  Total Replacement Heart System, Intracorporeal, 0051T
  Tubouterine, 58752
  Ventricular Assist Device, 33976
    Extracorporeal, 0048T
    Intracorporeal, 33979
Implant, Breast
  See Breast,Implants

Implant, Glaucoma Drainage, 66180-66185
Implant, Orbital
  Insertion, 67550
  Removal, 67560
Implant, Penile
  See Penile Prosthesis
Implant,Penile Prosthesis, Inflatable
  See Penile Prosthesis, Insertion, Inflatable
Implant Removal
  See Specific Anatomical Site
Implant, Subperiosteal
  See Subperiosteal Implant
Implant, Ureters into, Bladder
  See Anastomosis, Ureter, to Bladder
Impression, Maxillofacial, 21076-21089
  Auricular Prosthesis, 21086
  Definitive Obturator Prosthesis, 21080
  Facial Prosthesis, 21088
  Interim Obturator, 21079
  Mandibular Resection Prosthesis, 21081
  Nasal Prosthesis, 21087
  Oral Surgical Splint, 21085
  Orbital Prosthesis, 21077
  Palatal Augmentation Prosthesis, 21082
  Palatal Lift Prosthesis, 21083
  Speech Aid Prosthesis, 21084
  Surgical Obturator, 21076
IMRT (Intensity Modulated Radiation Therapy)
  Plan, 77301
  Treatment, 77418
IMT Testing, 0126T
Incision
  See Incision and Drainage
  Abdomen, 49000
    Exploration, 58960
  Abscess
    Soft Tissue, 20000, 20005
  Accessory Nerve, 63191
  Anal
    Fistula, 46270, 46280
    Septum, 46070
    Sphincter, 46080
  Ankle, 27607
    Tendon, 27605, 27606
  Anus
    See Anus, Incision
  Aortic Valve, 33401, 33403
    for Stenosis, 33415
  Artery
    Nose, 30915, 30920
  Atrial Septum, 33735-33737
  Bile Duct
    Sphincter, 43262, 47460
  Bladder
    with Destruction, 51020, 51030
    with Radiotracer, 51020
    Catheterization, 51045
  Bladder Diverticulum, 52305
  Brachial Artery
    Exposure, 34834
  Brain
    Amygdalohippocampectomy, 61566
    Subpial, 61567
  Breast
    Capsules, 19370
  Bronchus, 31899
  Burn Scab, 16035, 16036
  Cataract
    Secondary
      Laser Surgery, 66821
      Stab Incision Technique, 66820
  Chest
    Biopsy, 32095, 32100
  Colon
    Exploration, 44025
    Stoma
      Creation, 44320, 44322

Incision — *continued*
  Colon — *continued*
    Stoma — *continued*
      Revision, 44340-44346
  Cornea
    for Astigmatism, 65772
  Corpus Callosum, 61541
  Cricothyroid Membrane, 31605
  Dentate Ligament, 63180, 63182
  Duodenum, 44010
  Ear, Inner
    Labyrinth
      with Mastoidectomy, 69802
      with or without Cryosurgery, 69801
  Elbow, 24000
  Esophagus, 43020, 43045
    Esophageal Web, 43499
    Muscle, 43030
  Exploration
    Heart, 33310-33315
    Kidney, 50010
  Eye
    Adhesions, 65880
      Anterior Segment, 65860, 65865
      Anterior Synechiae, 65870
      Corneovitreal, 65880
      Posterior, 65875
    Anterior Chamber, 65820
    Conjunctiva, 0124T
    Trabecular, 65850
  Eyelid
    Canthus, 67715
    Sutures, 67710
  Femoral Artery
    Exposure, 34812, 34813
  Fibula, 27607
  Finger
    Decompression, 26035
    Tendon, 26060, 26455, 26460
    Tendon Sheath, 26055, 26060, 26455, 26460
  Foot
    Bone Cortex, 28005
    Capsule, 28260-28264
    Fascia, 28008
    for Infection, 28002, 28003
    Tendon, 28230, 28234
  Frontal Lobe, 61490
  Gallbladder, 47490
  Hand Decompression, 26035, 26037
    Tendon, 26450, 26460
  Heart
    Exploration, 33310, 33315
    Incision, Not Specified, 33999
  Hemorrhoid
    External, 46083
  Hepatic Ducts
    See Hepaticostomy
  Hip
    Denervation, 27035
    Exploration, 27033
    Fasciotomy, 27025
    Joint Capsule for Flexor Release, 27036
    Tendon
      Abductor, 27006
      Adductor, 27000-27003
      Iliopsoas, 27005
  Hymen
    See Hymen, Incision
  Hymenotomy, 56442
  Hyoid, Muscle, 21685
  Iliac Artery
    Exposure, 34820, 34833
  Intercarpal Joint
    Dislocation, 25670
  Interphalangeal Joint
    Capsule, 26525
  Intestines (Except Rectum)
    See Enterotomy
  Intestines, Small, 44010
    Biopsy, 44020
    Creation
      Pouch, 44316

Incision — *continued*
  Intestines, Small — *continued*
    Creation — *continued*
      Stoma, 44300-44314
    Decompression, 44021
    Exploration, 44020
    Incision, 44020
    Removal
      Foreign Body, 44020
    Revision
      Stoma, 44312
  Intracranial Vessels, 37799
  Iris, 66500, 66505
  Kidney, 50010, 50045
    Calculus Removal, 50130
      Complicated, 50135
    Exploration, 50010
    Nephrotomy, with Exploration, 50045
    Pyelotomy, with exploration, 50120
  Knee
    Capsule, 27435
    Exploration, 27310
    Fasciotomy, 27305
    Removal of Foreign Body, 27310
  Lacrimal Punctum, 68440
  Lacrimal Sac
    See Dacryocystotomy
  Larynx, 31300, 31320
  Leg, Lower
    Fasciotomy, 27600-27602
  Leg, Upper
    Fasciotomy, 27025, 27305
    Tenotomy, 27306, 27307, 27390-27392
  Lip
    Frenum, 40806
  Liver
    See Hepatotomy
  Lung
    Biopsy, 32095, 32100
    Decortication
      Partial, 32225
      Total, 32220
  Lymphatic Channels, 38308
  Mastoid
    See Mastoidotomy
  Medullary Tract, 61470
  Mesencephalic Tract, 61480
  Metacarpophalangeal Joint
    Capsule, 26520
  Mitral Valve, 33420, 33422
  Muscle
    See Myotomy
  Nerve, 64573-64580, 64585, 64595, 64702-64772
    Foot, 28035
    Root, 63185, 63190
    Sacral, 64581
    Vagus, 43640, 43641
  Nose
    See Rhinotomy
  Orbit
    See Orbitotomy
  Palm
    Fasciotomy, 26040, 26045
  Pancreas
    Sphincter, 43262
  Penis
    Prepuce, 54000, 54001
      Newborn, 54000
  Pericardium, 33030, 33031
    with Clot Removal, 33020
    with Foreign Body Removal, 33020
    with Tube Insertion, 33015
  Pharynx
    Stoma, 42955
  Pleura, 32320
    Biopsy, 32095, 32100
  Pleural Cavity
    Empyema, 32035, 32036
    Pneumothorax, 32551

Index

Incision — continued
Prostate
  Exposure
    Bilateral Pelvic Lymphadenectomy, 55865
    Insertion Radioactive Substance, 55860
    Lymph Node Biopsy, 55862
    Transurethral, 52450
Pterygomaxillary Fossa, 31040
Pulmonary Valve, 33470-33474
Pyloric Sphincter, 43520
Retina
  Encircling Material, 67115
Sclera
  Fistulization
    with Iridectomy, 66160
    Iridencleisis or Iridotasis, 66165
    Sclerectomy with Punch or Scissors with Iridectomy, 66160
    Thermocauterization with Iridectomy, 66155
    Trabeculectomy ab Externo in Absence Previous Surgery, 66170
    Trephination with Iridectomy, 66150
Semicircular Canal Revision, 69840
  Fenestration, 69820
Seminal Vesicle, 55600-55605
  Complicated, 55605
Shoulder
  Bone, 23035
  Capsule Contracture Release, 23020
  Removal
    Calcareous Deposits, 23000
  Tenomyotomy, 23405-23406
Shoulder Joint, 23040, 23044
Sinus
  Frontal, 31070-31087
  Maxillary, 31020-31032
    Endoscopic, 31256, 31267
    Multiple, 31090
  Sphenoid
    Sinusotomy, 31050, 31051
Skin, 10040-10180
Skull, 61316, 62148
  Suture, 61550, 61552
Spinal Cord, 63200
  Tract, 63170, 63194-63199
Stomach
  Creation
    Stoma, 43830-43832
  Exploration, 43500
  Pyloric Sphincter, 43520
Synovectomy, 26140
Temporomandibular Joint, 21010-21070
Tendon
  Arm, Upper, 24310
Thigh
  Fasciotomy, 27025
Thorax
  Empyema, 32035, 32036
  Pneumothorax, 32551
Thyroid Gland
  See Thyrotomy
Tibia, 27607
Toe
  Capsule, 28270, 28272
  Fasciotomy, 28008
  Tendon, 28232, 28234
  Tenotomy, 28010, 28011
Tongue
  Frenum, 41010
Trachea
  with Flaps, 31610
  Emergency, 31603, 31605
  Planned, 31600
    Younger Than Two Years, 31601
Tympanic Membrane, 69420
  with Anesthesia, 69421

Incision — continued
Ureter, 50600
Ureterocele, 51535
Urethra, 53000, 53010
  Meatus, 53020, 53025
Uterus
  Remove Lesion, 59100
Vagina
  Exploration, 57000
Vas Deferens, 55200
  for X-ray, 55300
Vestibule of Mouth
  See Mouth, Vestibule of, Incision
Vitreous Strands
  Laser Surgery, 67031
  Pars Plana Approach, 67030
Wrist, 25100-25105
  Capsule, 25085
  Decompression, 25020-25025
  Tendon Sheath, 25000, 25001

Incisional Hernia Repair
  See Hernia, Repair, Incisional

Incision and Drainage
  See Drainage; Incision
Abdomen
  Fluid, 49080-49081
  Pancreatitis, 48000
Abscess
  Abdomen, Abdominal
    Open, 49040
    Pancreatitis, 48000
    Percutaneous, 49021
    Peritoneal, 49020
    Peritonitis, Localized, 49020
    Retroperitoneal, 49060
    Skin and Subcutaneous Tissue
      Complicated, 10061
      Multiple, 10061
      Simple, 10060
      Single, 10060
    Subdiaphragmatic, 49040
    Subphrenic, 49040
  Acne Surgery
    Comedones, 10040
    Cysts, 10040
    Marsupialization, 10040
    Milia, Multiple, 10040
    Pustules, 10040
  Anal, 46045, 46050
  Ankle, 27603
  Appendix
    Open, 44900
    Percutaneous, 44901
  Arm, Lower, 25028, 25035
  Arm, Upper, 23930, 23931
  Auditory Canal, External, 69020
  Bartholin's Gland, 56420
  Bladder, 51080
  Brain, 61320, 61321
  Breast, 19020
  Ear, External
    Complicated, 69005
    Simple, 69000
  Elbow, 23930
  Epididymis, 54700
  Eyelid, 67700
  Finger, 26010, 26011
  Gums, 41800
  Hip, 26990
  Kidney
    Open, 50020
    Percutaneous, 50021
  Knee, 27301
  Leg, Lower, 27603
  Leg, Upper, 27301
  Liver
    Open, 47010
    Percutaneous, 47011
  Lung, 32200
    Percutaneous, 32201
  Lymph Node, 38300, 38305
  Mouth, 40800, 40801, 41005-41009, 41015-41018
  Nasal Septum, 30020
  Neck, 21501, 21502

Incision and Drainage — continued
Abscess — continued
  Nose, 30000, 30020
  Ovary, 58820, 58822
    Abdominal Approach, 58822
    Vaginal Approach, 58820
  Palate, 42000
  Paraurethral Gland, 53060
  Parotid Gland, 42300, 42305
  Pelvis, 26990, 45000
  Perineum, 56405
  Peritoneum
    Open, 49020
    Percutaneous, 49021
  Prostate, 55720, 55725
  Rectum, 45005, 45020, 46040, 46050, 46060
  Retroperitoneal, 49061
    Open, 49060
  Salivary Gland, 42300-42320
  Scrotum, 54700, 55100
  Shoulder, 23035
  Skene's Gland, 53060
  Skin, 10060, 10061
  Spine, 22010-22015
  Subdiaphragmatic
    Open, 49040
    Percutaneous, 49041
  Sublingual Gland, 42310, 42320
  Submaxillary Gland, 42310, 42320
  Subphrenic
    Open, 49040
    Percutaneous, 49041
  Testis, 54700
  Thorax, 21501, 21502
  Throat, 42700-42725
  Tongue, 41000-41006, 41015
  Tonsil, 42700
  Urethra, 53040
  Uvula, 42000
  Vagina, 57010, 57020
  Vulva, 56405
  Wrist, 25028, 25040
Ankle, 27610
Bile Duct, 47420, 47425
Bladder, 51040
Bulla
  Skin
    Puncture Aspiration, 10160
Bursa
  Ankle, 27604
  Arm, Lower, 25031
  Elbow, 23931
  Foot, 28001
  Hip, 26991
  Knee, 27301
  Leg, Lower, 27604
  Leg, Upper, 27301
  Palm, 26025, 26030
  Pelvis, 26991
  Wrist, 25031
Carbuncle
  Skin, 10060, 10061
Carpals, 25035, 26034
Comedones
  Skin, 10040
Cyst
  Conjunctiva, 68020
  Gums, 41800
  Liver
    Open, 47010
    Percutaneous, 47011
  Lung, 32200
    Percutaneous, 32201
  Mouth, 40800, 40801, 41005-41009, 41015-41018
  Ovarian, 58800, 58805
  Skin, 10040-10061
    Pilonidal, 10080, 10081
    Puncture Aspiration, 10160
  Spinal Cord, 63172, 63173
  Thyroid Gland, 60000
  Tongue, 41000-41006, 41015, 60000

Incision and Drainage — continued
Elbow
  Abscess, 23935
  Arthrotomy, 24000
Femur, 27303
Fluid Collection
  Skin, 10140
Foreign Body
  Skin, 10120, 10121
Furuncle, 10060, 10061
Gallbladder, 47480
Hematoma
  Ankle, 27603
  Arm, Lower, 25028
  Arm, Upper, 23930
  Brain, 61312-61315
  Ear, External
    Complicated, 69005
    Simple, 69000
  Elbow, 23930
  Epididymis, 54700
  Gums, 41800
  Hip, 26990
  Knee, 27301
  Leg, Lower, 27603
  Leg, Upper, 27301
  Mouth, 40800, 40801, 41005-41009, 41015-41018
  Nasal Septum, 30020
  Neck, 21501, 21502
  Nose, 30000, 30020
  Pelvis, 26990
  Scrotum, 54700
  Shoulder, 23030
  Skin, 10140
    Puncture Aspiration, 10160
  Skull, 61312-61315
  Testis, 54700
  Thorax, 21501, 21502
  Tongue, 41000-41006, 41015
  Vagina, 57022, 57023
  Wrist, 25028
Hepatic Duct, 47400
Hip
  Bone, 26992, 27030
Humerus
  Abscess, 23935
Interphalangeal Joint
  Toe, 28024
Intertarsal Joint, 28020
Kidney, 50040, 50125
Knee, 27303, 27310
Lacrimal Gland, 68400
Lacrimal Sac, 68420
Liver
  Abscess or Cyst, 47010, 47011
    Percutaneous, 47011
Mediastinum, 39000, 39010
Metatarsophalangeal Joint, 28022
Milia, Multiple, 10040
Onychia, 10060, 10061
Orbit, 67405, 67440
Paronychia, 10060, 10061
Pelvic/Bone, 26992
Penis, 54015
Pericardium, 33025
Phalanges
  Finger, 26034
Pilonidal Cyst, 10080, 10081
Pustules
  Skin, 10040
Radius, 25035
Seroma
  Skin, 10140
Shoulder
  Abscess, 23030
  Arthrotomy
    Acromioclavicular Joint, 23044
    Glenohumeral Joint, 23040
    Sternoclavicular Joint, 23044
  Bursa, 23031
  Hematoma, 23030
Shoulder Joint
  Arthrotomy, Glenohumeral Joint, 23040

Incision and Drainage

Incision and Drainage — *continued*
  Tarsometatarsal Joint, 28020
  Tendon Sheath
    Finger, 26020
    Palm, 26020
  Thorax
    Deep, 21510
  Toe, 28024
  Ulna, 25035
  Ureter, 50600
  Vagina, 57020
  Wound Infection
    Skin, 10180
  Wrist, 25028, 25040
Inclusion Bodies
  Fluid, 88106
  Smear, 87207, 87210
Incomplete
  Abortion, 59812
Incomplete Abortion, 59812
Indicator Dilution Studies, 93561, 93562
Induced
  Abortion
    with Hysterotomy, 59100, 59852, 59857
    by Dilation and Curettage, 59840
    by Dilation and Evacuation, 59841
    by Saline, 59850, 59851
    by Vaginal Suppositories, 59855, 59856
Induced Hyperthermia, 53850-53852
Induced Hypothermia, 99116
Induratio Penis Plastica
  with Graft, 54110-54112
  Injection, 54200
  Surgical Exposure, 54205
Infantile Paralysis
  See Polio
Infant, Newborn, Intensive Care
  See Intensive Care, Neonatal
INFARIX, 90700
Infection
  Actinomyces, 86602
  Diagnosis
    Group A Strep Test, 3210F
  Drainage
    Postoperative Wound, 10180
  Filarioidea, 86280
  Immunoassay, 86317, 86318
  Rapid Test, 86403, 86406
  Treatment
    Antibiotics Prescribed, 4045F
Infection, Bone
  See Osteomyelitis
Infection, Wound
  See Wound, Infection
Infectious Agent Detection
  Antigen Detection
    Direct Fluorescence
      Bordetella, 87265
      Chlamydia Trachomatis, 87270
      Cryptosporidium, 87272
      Cytomegalovirus, 87271
      Enterovirus, 87267
      Giardia, 87269
      Influenza A, 87276
      Legionella Pneumophila, 87278
      Pertussis, 87265
      Respiratory Syncytial Virus, 87280
      Treponema Pallidum, 87285
      Varicella Zoster, 87290
    Direct Probe
      Vancomycin Resistance, 87500
    Enzyme Immunoassay
      Adenovirus, 87301
      Aspergillus, 87305
      Chlamydia Trachomatis, 87320
      Clostridium Difficile Toxin A, 87324

Infectious Agent Detection — *continued*
  Antigen Detection — *continued*
    Enzyme Immunoassay — *continued*
      Cryptococcus Neoformans, 87327
      Cryptosporidium, 87328
      Cytomegalovirus, 87332
      Entamoeba Histolytica Dispar Group, 87336
      Entamoeba Histolytica Group, 87337
      Escherichia coli 0157, 87335
      Giardia, 87329
      Helicobacter Pylori, 87338, 87339
      Hepatitis Be Antigen (HBeAg), 87350
      Hepatitis B Surface Antigen (HBsAg), 87340
      Hepatitis B Surface Antigen (HBsAg) Neutralization, 87341
      Hepatitis, Delta Agent, 87380
      Histoplasma Capsulatum, 87385
      HIV-1, 87390
      HIV-2, 87391
      Influenza A, 87400
      Influenza B, 87400
      Multiple Step Method, 87301-87449, 87451
      See specific agent
      Not Otherwise Specified, 87449-87451
      Respiratory Syncytial Virus, 87420
      Rotavirus, 87425
      Shiga-like Toxin, 87427
      Single Step Method, 87450
      Streptococcus, Group A, 87430
    Immunoassay
      Adenovirus, 87809
    Immunofluorescence, 87260, 87273-87275, 87277, 87279, 87281-87283, 87299-87300
      Adenovirus, 87260
      Herpes Simplex, 87273, 87274
      Influenza B, 87275
      Legionella Micdadei, 87277
      Not otherwise Specified, 87299
      Parainfluenza Virus, 87279
      Pneumocystis Carinii, 87281
      Polyvalent, 87300
      Rubeola, 87283
    Nucleic Acid
      Vancomycin Resistance, 87500
  Concentration, 87015
  Detection
    by Immunoassay
      with Direct Optical Observation, 87802-87899
      Chlamydia Trachomatis, 87810
      Clostridium difficile, 87803
      Influenza, 87804
      Neisseria Gonorrhoeae, 87850
      Not Otherwise Specified, 87899
      Respiratory Syncytial Virus, 87807
      Streptococcus, Group A, 87880
      Streptococcus, Group B, 87802
      Trichomonas Vaginalis, 87808
    by Nucleic Acid
      Bartonella Henselae, 87470-87472
      Bartonella Quintana, 87470-87472

Infectious Agent Detection — *continued*
  Detection — *continued*
    by Nucleic Acid — *continued*
      Borrelia Burgdorferi, 87475-87477
      Candida Species, 87480-87482
      Chlamydia Pneumoniae, 87485-87487
      Chlamydia Trachomatis, 87490-87492
      Cytomegalovirus, 87495-87497
      Gardnerella Vaginalis, 87510-87512
      Hepatitis B Virus, 87515-87517
      Hepatitis C, 87520-87522
      Hepatitis G, 87525-87527
      Herpes Simplex Virus, 87528-87530
      Herpes Virus-6, 87531-87533
      HIV-1, 87534-87536
      HIV-2, 87537-87539
      Intracellulare, 87560-87562
      Legionella Pneumophila, 87540-87542
      Multiple Organisms, 87800, 87801
      Mycobacteria Avium-Intracellularae, 87560-87562
      Mycobacteria Species, 87550-87552
      Mycobacteria Tuberculosis, 87555-87557
      Mycoplasma Pneumoniae, 87580-87582
      Neisseria Gonorrhoeae, 87590-87592
      Not Otherwise Specified, 87797-87799
      Papillomavirus, Human, 87620-87622
      Staphylococcus Aureus, 87640-87641
      Streptococcus
        Group A, 87650-87652
        Group B, 87653
      Trichomonas Vaginalis, 87660
  Genotype Analysis
    by Nucleic Acid
      Hepatitis C Virus, 87902
      HIV-1 Protease/Reverse Transcriptase, 87901
  Phenotype Analysis
    by Nucleic Acid
      HIV-1 Drug Resistance, 87903, 87904
      HIV-1 Drug Resistance, 87900
  Phenotype Prediction
    by Genetic Database, 87900
  Vancomycin Resistance, 87500
Infectious Agent Enzymatic Activity, 87905
Infectious Mononucleosis Virus
  See Epstein-Barr Virus
Inflammatory Process
  Localization
    Nuclear Medicine, 78805-78807
Inflation
  Ear, Middle
    Eustachian Tube
      with Catheterization, 69400
      without Catheterization, 69401
  Eustachian Tube
    Myringotomy, 69420
    Anesthesia, 69424
Influenza A
  Antigen Detection
    Direct Fluorescent, 87276
    Enzyme Immunoassay, 87400

Influenza B
  Antigen Detection
    Enzyme Immunoassay, 87400
    Immunofluorescence, 87275
Influenza B Vaccine, 90645-90648, 90720-90721, 90748
Influenza Vaccine
  See Vaccines
Influenza Virus
  Antibody, 86710
  Vaccine, 90657-90660
  by Immunoassay
    with Direct Optical Observation, 87804
Infraorbital Nerve
  Avulsion, 64734
  Incision, 64734
  Transection, 64734
Infrared Light Treatment, 97026
  See Physical Medicine/Therapy/Occupational Therapy
Infratentorial Craniotomy, 61520, 61521
Infusion
  Amnion, Transabdominal, 59072
  Cerebral
    Intravenous for Thrombolysis, 37195
  Chemotherapy, 96413-96417, 96423, 96425
  Hydration, 96360-96361
  Intra-Arterial
    Chemotherapy or Complex Biological Agent, 96422-96425
    Diagnostic, Prophylactic, Diagnostic, 96373
    Unlisted, Intra-arterial, 96379
  Intraosseous, 36680
  IV
    Chemotherapy, Complex Biological Agent, 96413-96417
    Diagnostic, Prophylactic, Therapeutic, 96365-96368
    Hydration, 96360-96361
    Unlisted Intravenous Infusion, 96379
  Radioelement, 77750
  Subcutaneous, 96369-96371
  Transcatheter Therapy, 37201, 37202
Infusion Pump
  Electronic Analysis
    Spinal Cord, 62367, 62368
  Insertion
    Intraarterial, 36260
    Intraarterial
      Removal, 36262
      Revision, 36261
    Intravenous
      Insertion, 36563
      Removal, 36590
      Revision, 36576, 36578
  Maintenance, 95990-95991, 96521-96522
  Chemotherapy, Pump Services, 96521-96522
  Spinal Cord, 62361, 62362
  Ventricular Catheter, 61215
Infusion Therapy, 62350, 62351, 62360-62362
  See Injection, Chemotherapy
  Arterial Catheterization, 36640
  Chemotherapy, 96401-96542, 96549
  Home Infusion Procedures, 99601-99602
  Intravenous, 96360-96361, 96365-96368
  Pain, 62360-62362, 62367-62368
  Transcatheter Therapy, 75896
Ingestion Challenge Test, 95075
Inguinal Hernia Repair
  See Hernia, Repair, Inguinal
INH
  See Drug Assay
Inhalation
  Pentamidine, 94642

Index

Inhalation Provocation Tests
  See Bronchial Challenge Test
Inhalation Treatment, 94640-94645, 94664, 99503
  See Pulmonology, Therapeutic
Inhibin A, 86336
Inhibition, Fertilization
  See Contraception
Inhibition Test, Hemagglutination, 86280
Inhibitor, Alpha 1–Protease, 82103-82104
Inhibitor, Alpha 2–Plasmin, 85410
Inhibitory Concentration, Minimum
  See Minimum Inhibitory Concentration
Initial Inpatient Consultations
  See Consultation, Initial Inpatient
Injection
  Abdomen
    Air, 49400
    Contrast Material, 49400
  Allergen, 95115-95134
  Anesthetic
    Morton's Neuroma, 64455
    Paravertebral Facet, 64490-64495
    Plantar Common Digit, 64455
    Sympathetic Nerves, 64505-64530
    Transforaminal, 64479-64484
  Angiography
    Coronary, 93556
    Pulmonary, 75746
  Ankle
    Radial, 27648
  Antigen (Allergen), 95115-95125, 95145-95170
  Aorta (Aortography)
    Radiologic, 93544
  Aponeurosis, 20550
  Bladder
    Radiologic, 51600-51610
  Bone Marrow, into, 38999
  Brain Canal, 61070
  Breast
    Radiologic, 19030
  Brisement, 20550-20551
  Bronchography
    Segmental, 31656
  Bursa, 20600-20610
  Cardiac Catheterization, 93539-93545
  Carpal Tunnel
    Therapeutic, 20526
  Chemotherapy, 96401-96549
  Cistern
    Medication or Other, 61055
  Contrast
    Central Venous Access Device, 36598
    Gastrostomy, Duodenostomy, Jejunostomy, Gastro-jejunostomy, or Cecostomy Tube, Percutaneous, 49465
    via Peritoneal Catheter, 49424
  Corpora Cavernosa, 54235
  Cyst
    Bone, 20615
    Kidney, 50390
    Pelvis, 50390
    Thyroid, 60300
  Elbow
    Arthrography, Radiologic, 24220
  Epidural
    See Epidural, Injection
  Esophageal Varices
    Endoscopy, 43243
  Esophagus
    Sclerosing Agent, 43204
    Submucosal, 43201
  Extremity
    Pseudoaneurysm, 36002
  Eye
    Air, 66020
    Medication, 66030

Injection — continued
  Eyelid
    Subconjunctival, 68200
  Ganglion
    Anesthetic, 64505, 64510
  Ganglion Cyst, 20612
  Gastric Secretion Stimulant, 91052
  Gastric Varices
    Endoscopy, 43243
  Heart
    Therapeutic Substance into Pericardium, 33999
  Heart Vessels
    Cardiac Catheterization, 93539-93545
      See Catheterization, Cardiac
    Radiologic, 93545
  Hemorrhoids
    Sclerosing Solution, 46500
  Hip
    Radiologic, 27093, 27095
  Hydration, 96360-96361
  Insect Venom, 95130-95134
  Intervertebral Disc
    Chemonucleolysis Agent, 62292
    Radiological, 62290, 62291
  Intra-amniotic, 59850-59852
  Intra-arterial, 96373
    Chemotherapy, 96420-96425
  Intradermal, Tattooing, 11920-11922
  Intralesional, Skin, 11900, 11901
    Chemotherapy, 96405-96406
  Intramuscular, 96372, 99506
    Chemotherapy, 96401-96402
  Intravenous, 96365-96368
    Chemotherapy, 96409-96417
    Diagnostic, 96365-96368
    Thrombolytic, 37187-37188
    Vascular Flow Check, Graft, 15860
  Intravitreal
    Pharmacologic Agent, 67028
  Joint, 20600-20610
  Kidney
    Drugs, 50391
    Radiologic, 50394
  Knee
    Radiologic, 27370
  Lacrimal Gland
    Radiologic, 68850
  Left Heart
    Radiologic, 93543
  Lesion, Skin, 11900, 11901
    Chemotherapy, 96405-96411
  Ligament, 20550
  Liver, 47015
    Radiologic, 47500, 47505
  Lungs
    Radiologic, 93541
  Lymphangiography, 38790
  Mammary Ductogram
    Galactogram, 19030
  Muscle Endplate
    Cervical Spinal, 64613
    Extremity, 64614
    Facial, 64612
    Trunk, 64614
  Nerve
    Anesthetic, 01991-01992, 64400-64530
    Neurolytic Agent, 64600-64681
  Orbit
    Retrobulbar
      Alcohol, 67505
      Medication, 67500
    Tenon's Capsule, 67515
  Pancreatography, 48400
  Paravertebral Facet Joint, 0213T-0218T, 64490-64495
  Penis
    for Erection, 54235
    Peyronie Disease, 54200
      with Surgical Exposure of Plaque, 54205
    Radiology, 54230
    Vasoactive Drugs, 54231

Injection — continued
  Pericardium
    Injection of Therapeutic Substance, 33999
  Peritoneal Cavity Air
    See Pneumoperitoneum
  Radiologic
    Breast, 19030
  Radiopharmaceutical, 78808
  Rectum
    Sclerosing Solution, 45520
  Right Heart
    Injection of Radiologic Substance, 93542
  Sacroiliac Joint
    for Arthrography, 27096
  Salivary Duct, 42660
  Salivary Gland
    Radiologic, 42550
  Sclerosing Agent
    Esophagus, 43204
    Intravenous, 36470, 36471
  Sentinel Node Identification, 38792
  Shoulder
    Arthrography, Radiologic, 23350
  Shunt
    Peritoneal
      Venous, 49427
  Sinus Tract, 20500
    Diagnostic, 20501
  Spider Veins
    Telangiectasia, 36468, 36469
  Spinal Artery, 62294
  Spinal Cord
    Anesthetic, 62310-62319
    Blood, 62273
    Neurolytic Agent, 62280-62282
    Other, 62310, 62311
    Radiologic, 62284
  Spleen
    Radiologic, 38200
  Steroids, 52283
    Morton's Neuroma, 64455
    Paravertebral Facet Joint, 64490-64495
    Plantar Common Digital Nerve, 64455
    Stricture, 52283
    Sympathetic Nerves, 64505-64530
    Transforaminal, 64479-64484
  Subcutaneous, 96369-96371
    Chemotherapy, 96401-96402
  Temporomandibular Joint
    Arthrography, 21116
  Tendon Origin, Insertion, 20551
  Tendon Sheath, 20550
  Therapeutic
    Extremity Pseudoaneurysm, 36002
    Lung, 32960
    Thyroid, 60300
    Turbinate, 30200
  Thoracic Cavity
    See Pleurodesis, Chemical
  Thrombolytic, 37184-37186
  Trachea
    Puncture, 31612
  Transtracheal
    Bronchography, 31715
  Trigger Point(s)
    One or Two Muscle Groups, 20552
    Three or More Muscle Groups, 20553
  Turbinate, 30200
  Unlisted, 96379
  Ureter
    Drugs, 50391
    Radiologic, 50684
  Ureteropyelography, 50690
  Venography, 36005
  Ventricular
    Dye, 61120
    Medication or Other, 61026
  Vitreous, 67028

Injection — continued
  Vitreous — continued
    Fluid Substitute, 67025
  Vocal Cords
    Therapeutic, 31513, 31570, 31571
  Wrist
    Carpal Tunnel
      Therapeutic, 20526
    Radiologic, 25246
  Zygapophyseal, 0213T-0218T, 64490-64495
Inkblot Test, 96101-96103
Inner Ear
  See Ear, Inner
Innominate
  Tumor
    Excision, 27077
Innominate Arteries
  See Artery, Brachiocephalic
Inorganic Sulfates
  See Sulfate
Inpatient Consultations, 99251-99255
INR Test Review, 99363-99364
Insemination
  Artificial, 58321, 58322, 89268
Insertion
  See Implantation; Intubation; Transplantation Baffle
  Aqueous Drainage Device, 0191T-0192T
  Balloon
    Intra–Aortic, 33967, 33973
  Breast
    Implants, 19340, 19342
  Cannula
    Arteriovenous, 36810, 36815
    ECMO, 36822
    Extra Corporeal Circulation for Regional Chemotherapy of Extremity, 36823
    Thoracic Duct, 38794
    Vein to Vein, 36800
  Cardio-Defibrillator
    Leads, 33216-33220, 33224-33225
    Pulse Generator Only, 33240, 33241
  Catheter
    Abdomen, 49324, 49419-49421, 49435
    Abdominal Artery, 36245-36248
    Aorta, 36200
    Bile Duct, 47525, 47530, 75982
      Percutaneous, 47510
    Bladder, 51045, 51701-51703
    Brachiocephalic Artery, 36215-36218
    Brain, 0169T, 61210, 61770
    Breast
      for Interstitial Radioelement Application, 19296-19298, 20555
    Bronchi, 31717
    Bronchus
      for Intracavity Radioelement Application, 31643
    Cardiac
      See Catheterization, Cardiac
      Flow Directed, 93503
    Ear, Middle, 69405
    Eustachian Tube, 69405
    Flow Directed, 93503
    Gastrointestinal, Upper, 43241
    Head and/or Neck, 41019
    Jejunum, 44015
    Kidney, 50392
    Lower Extremity Artery, 36245-36248
    Nasotracheal, 31720
    Pelvic Artery, 36245-36248
    Pelvic Organs and/or Genitalia, 55920
    Pleural Cavity, 32550
    Portal Vein, 36481
    Prostate, 55875

Insertion

Insertion — *continued*
  Catheter — *continued*
    Pulmonary Artery, 36013-36015
    Right Heart, 36013
    Skull, 61107
    Spinal Cord, 62350, 62351
    Suprapubic, 51102
    Thoracic Artery, 36215-36218
    Tracheobronchial, 31725
    Ureter via Kidney, 50393
    Urethra, 51701-51703
    Vena Cava, 36010
    Venous, 36011, 36012, 36400-36425, 36500, 36510, 36555-36558, 36568-36569
  Cecostomy Tube, 49442
  Cervical Dilator, 59200
  Cochlear Device, 69930
  Colonic Tube, 49442
  Contraceptive Capsules, 11975, 11977
  Defibrillator
    Heart, 33212, 33213
      Leads, 33216, 33217
      Pulse Generator Only, 33240
  Drug Delivery Implant, 11981, 11983
  Electrode
    Brain, 61531, 61533, 61760, 61850-61875
    Heart, 33202-33203, 33210-33217, 33224-33225, 93620-93622
    Nerve, 64553-64581
    Retina, 0100T
    Sphenoidal, 95830
    Spinal Cord, 63650, 63655
    Stomach
      Laparoscopic
        Neurostimulator, 43647
        Stimulation, 0155T
      Open
        Neurostimulator, 43881
        Stimulation, 0157T
  Endotracheal Tube
    Emergency Intubation, 31500
  Filiform
    Urethra, 53620
  Filter
    Bird's Nest, 37620
  Gastrostomy Tube
    Laparoscopic, 43653
    Percutaneous, 43246, 49440
  Graft
    Aorta, 33330-33335
    Heart Vessel, 33330-33335
  Guide
    Kidney, Pelvis, 50395
  Guide Wire
    Endoscopy, 43248
    Esophagoscopy, 43248
      with Dilation, 43226
  Heyman Capsule
    Uterus
      for Brachytherapy, 58346
  Iliac Artery
    Occlusion Device, 34808
  Implant
    Bone
      for External Speech Processor/Cochlear Stimulator, 69714-69718
  Infusion Pump
    Intraarterial, 36260
    Intravenous, 36563
    Spinal Cord, 62361, 62362
  Intracatheter/Needle
    Aorta, 36160
    Arteriovenous Shunt, 36147-36148
    Intraarterial, 36100-36140
    Intravenous, 36000
    Kidney, 50392
    Venous, 36000
  Intraocular Lens, 66983

Insertion — *continued*
  Intraocular Lens — *continued*
    Manual or Mechanical Technique, 66982, 66984
    not Associated with Concurrent Cataract Removal, 66985
  Intrauterine Device (IUD), 58300
  IVC Filter, 37620
  Jejunostomy Tube
    Endoscopy, 44372
    Percutaneous, 49441
  Keel
    Laryngoplasty, 31580
  Laminaria, 59200
  Mesh
    Pelvic Floor, 57267
  Nasobiliary Tube
    Endoscopy, 43267
  Nasopancreatic Tube
    Endoscopy, 43267
  Needle
    Bone, 36680
    Head and/or Neck, 41019
    Intraosseous, 36680
    Pelvic Organs and/or Genitalia, 55920
    Prostate, 55875
  Needle Wire Dilator
    Stent
      Trachea, 31730
      Transtracheal for Oxygen, 31720
  Neurostimulator
    Pulse Generator, 64590
    Receiver, 64590
  Nose
    Septal Prosthesis, 30220
  Obturator/Larynx, 31527
  Ocular Implant
    with Foreign Material, 65155
    with or without Conjunctival Graft, 65150
    in Scleral Shell, 65130, 67550
    Muscles Attached, 65140
    Muscles not Attached, 65135
  Orbital Transplant, 67550
  Oviduct
    Chromotubation, 58350
    Hydrotubation, 58350
  Ovoid
    Vagina
      for Brachytherapy, 57155
  Pacemaker
    Fluoroscopy
      Radiography, 71090
    Heart, 33206-33208, 33212, 33213
  Packing
    Vagina, 57180
  Penile Prosthesis Inflatable
    See Penile Prosthesis, Insertion, Inflatable
  Pessary
    Vagina, 57160
  PICC Line, 36568-36569
  Pin
    Skeletal Traction, 20650
  Posterior Spinous Process Distraction Devices, 0171T-0172T
  Probe
    Brain, 61770
  Prostaglandin, 59200
  Prostate
    Radioactive Substance, 55860
  Prosthesis
    Knee, 27438, 27445
    Nasal Septal, 30220
    Palate, 42281
    Pelvic Floor, 57267
    Penis
      Inflatable, 54401-54405
      Non-inflatable, 54400
    Speech, 31611
    Testis, 54660
    Urethral Sphincter, 53444-53445

Insertion — *continued*
  Pulse Generator
    Brain, 61885, 61886
    Heart, 33212, 33213
    Spinal Cord, 63685
  Radioactive Material
    Bladder, 51020
    Cystourethroscopy, 52250
    Interstitial Brachytherapy, 77776-77778
    Intracavitary Brachytherapy, 77761, 77762
    Intraocular, 0190T
    Prostate, 55860, 55875
    Remote Afterloading Brachytherapy, 77785-77787
  Receiver
    Brain, 61885, 61886
    Spinal Cord, 63685
  Reservoir
    Brain, 61210, 61215
    Spinal Cord, 62360
    Subcutaneous, 49419
  Shunt, 36835
    Abdomen
      Vein, 49425
      Venous, 49426
    Intrahepatic Portosystemic, 37182
  Spinal Instrument, 22849
    Spinous Process, 0171T-0172T, 22841
  Spinal Instrumentation
    Anterior, 22845-22847
    Internal Spinal Fixation, 22841
    Pelvic Fixation, 22848
    Posterior Non-segmental Harrington Rod Technique, 22840
    Posterior Segmental, 22842-22844
    Prosthetic Device, 22851
  Stent
    Bile Duct, 43268, 47801
      Percutaneous, 47511
    Bladder, 51045
    Conjunctiva, 68750
    Coronary, 92980, 92981
    Esophagus, 43219
    Gastrointestinal, Upper, 43256
    Ileum, 44383
    Indwelling, 50605
    Intracoronary, 92980, 92981
    Lacrimal Duct, 68810-68815
    Pancreatic Duct, 43268
    Small Intestines, 44370, 44379
    Ureteral, 50688, 50947, 52332
    Ureter via Kidney, 50393
    Urethral, 52282, 53855
  Tamponade
    Esophagus, 43460
  Tandem
    Uterus
      for Brachytherapy, 57155
  Tendon Graft
    Finger, 26392
    Hand, 26392
  Testicular Prosthesis
    See Prosthesis, Testicular, Insertion
  Tissue Expanders, Skin, 11960-11971
  Tube
    Bile Duct, 43268
    Cecostomy, 49442
    Chest, 32422
    Duodenostomy or Jejunostomy, 49441
    Esophagus, 43510
    Gastrointestinal, Upper, 43241
    Gastrostomy, 49440
    Ileum, 44383
    Kidney, 50398
    Pancreatic Duct, 43268
    Small Intestines, 44379
    Trachea, 31730

Insertion — *continued*
  Tube — *continued*
    Ureter, 50688
  Urethral
    Catheter, 51701-51703
    Guide Wire, 52344
    Implant Material, 51715
    Suppository, 53660-53661
  Vascular Pedicle
    Carpal Bone, 25430
  Venous Access Device
    Central, 36560-36566
    Peripheral, 36570, 36571
  Venous Shunt
    Abdomen, 49425
  Ventilating Tube, 69433
  Ventricular Assist Device, 33975
  Wire
    Skeletal Traction, 20650

In Situ Hybridization
  See Nucleic Acid Probe, Cytogenic Studies, Morphometric Analysis

Inspiratory Positive Pressure Breathing
  See Intermittent Positive Pressure Breathing (IPPB)

Instillation
  Agent for Pleurodesis, 32560-32562
  Drugs
    Bladder, 51720
    Kidney, 50391
    Ureter, 50391

Instillation, Bladder
  See Bladder, Instillation

Instrumentation
  See Application; Bone; Fixation; Spinal Instrumentation
  Spinal
    Insertion, 22840-22848, 22851
    Reinsertion, 22849
    Removal, 22850, 22852, 22855

Insufflation, Eustachian Tube
  See Eustachian Tube, Inflation

Insulin, 80422, 80432-80435
  Antibody, 86337
  Blood, 83525
  Free, 83527

Insulin C-Peptide Measurement
  See C-Peptide

Insulin Like Growth Factors
  See Somatomedin

Insurance
  Basic Life and/or Disability Evaluation Services, 99450
  Examination, 99450-99456

Integumentary System
  Ablation
    Breast, 19105
  Biopsy, 11100, 11101
  Breast
    Ablation, 19105
    Excision, 19100-19272
    Incision, 19000-19030
    Metallic Localization Clip Placement, 19295
    Preoperative Placement of Needle Localization, 19290-19291
    Reconstruction, 19316-19396
    Repair, 19316-19396
    Unlisted Services and Procedures, 19499
  Burns, 15002-15003, 15005, 15100-15121, 15400-15431, 16000-16036
  Debridement, 11000-11006, 11010-11044
  Destruction
    See Dermatology
    Actinotherapy, 96900
    Benign Lesion, 17000-17004
      by Photodynamic Therapy, 96567
    Chemical Exfoliation, 17360
    Cryotherapy, 17340
    Electrolysis Epilation, 17380

Index

Integumentary System — continued
Destruction — continued
- Malignant Lesion, 17260-17286
  - by Photodynamic Therapy, 96567
- Mohs Micrographic Surgery, 17311-17315
- Photodynamic Therapy, 96567, 96570, 96571
- Premalignant Lesion, 17000-17004
- Unlisted Services and Procedures, 17999

Drainage, 10040-10180
Excision
- Benign Lesion, 11400-11471
- Debridement, 11000-11006, 11010-11044
- Malignant Lesion, 11600-11646

Graft
- Acellular Dermal Replacement, 15170-15176
- Allograft, 15300-15366
- Autograft, 15040-15157
- Surgical Preparation, 15002-15005
- Xenograft, 15400-15431

Incision, 10040-10180
Introduction, 11900-11977
- Drug Delivery Implant, 11981, 11983

Nails, 11719-11765
Paring, 11055-11057
Photography, 96904
Pressure Ulcers, 15920-15999
Removal
- Drug Delivery Implant, 11982, 11983

Repair
- Adjacent Tissue Transfer Rearrangement, 14000-14350
- Complex, 13100-13160
- Flaps
  - Other, 15740-15776
- Free Skin Grafts, 15002-15005, 15050-15136, 15200-15321, 15420-15431
- Intermediate, 12031-12057
- Other Procedures, 15780-15879
- Simple, 12001-12021
- Skin and/or Deep Tissue, 15570-15738

Shaving of Epidermal or Dermal Lesion, 11300-11313
Skin Tags
- Removal, 11200, 11201

Integumentum Commune
See Integumentary System

Intelligence Test
- Computer-Assisted, 96103
- Psychiatric Diagnosis, Psychological Testing, 96101-96103

Intensity Modulated Radiation Therapy (IMRT)
- Plan, 77301
- Treatment, 77418

Intensive Care
- Low Birth Weight Infant, 99478-99479
- Neonatal
  - Initial Care, 99479
  - Subsequent Care, 99478

Intercarpal Joint
- Arthrodesis, 25820, 25825
- Dislocation
  - Closed Treatment, 25660
- Repair, 25447

Intercostal Nerve
- Destruction, 64620
- Injection
  - Anesthetic, 64420, 64421
  - Neurolytic Agent, 64620

Intercranial Arterial Perfusion
- Thrombolysis, 61624

Interdental Fixation
- without Fracture, 21497

Interdental Fixation — continued
Device
- Application, 21110
Mandibular Fracture
- Closed Treatment, 21453
- Open Treatment, 21462

Interdental Papilla
See Gums

Interdental Wire Fixation
Closed Treatment
- Craniofacial Separation, 21431

Interferometry
Eye
- Biometry, 92136

Intermediate Care Facility (ICF) Visits, 99304-99318

Intermittent Positive Pressure Breathing (IPPB)
See Continuous Negative Pressure Breathing (CNPB); Continuous Positive Airway Pressure (CPAP)

Internal Breast Prostheses
See Breast, Implants

Internal Ear
See Ear, Inner

Internal Rigid Fixation
Reconstruction
- Mandibular Rami, 21196

International Normalized Ratio
Test Review, 99363-99364

Internet E/M Service
- Nonphysician, 98969
- Physician, 99444

Interphalangeal Joint
- Arthrodesis, 26860-26863
- Arthroplasty, 26535, 26536
- Arthrotomy, 26080, 28054
- Biopsy
  - Synovium, 26110
- Capsule
  - Excision, 26525
  - Incision, 26525
- Dislocation
  - with Manipulation, 26340
  - Closed Treatment, 26770
  - Fingers/Hand
    - with Manipulation, 26340
    - Closed Treatment, 26770, 26775
    - Open Treatment, 26785
    - Percutaneous Fixation, 26776
  - Open Treatment, 26785
  - Percutaneous Fixation, 26776
  - Toes/Foot
    - Closed Treatment, 28660, 28665
    - Open Treatment, 28675
    - Percutaneous Fixation, 28666
- Excision, 28160
- Exploration, 26080, 28024
- Fracture
  - with Manipulation, 26742
  - Closed Treatment, 26740
  - Open Treatment, 26746
- Fusion, 26860-26863
- Great Toe
  - Arthrodesis, 28755
    - with Tendon Transfer, 28760
  - Fusion, 28755
    - with Tendon Transfer, 28760
- Removal
  - Foreign Body, 26080
  - Loose Body, 28024
- Repair
  - Collateral Ligament, 26545
  - Volar Plate, 26548
- Synovectomy, 26140
- Synovial
  - Biopsy, 28054
- Toe, 28272
  - Arthrotomy, 28024
  - Biopsy
    - Synovial, 28054
  - Dislocation, 28660-28665, 28675
    - Percutaneous Fixation, 28666

Interphalangeal Joint — continued
Toe — continued
- Excision, 28160
- Exploration, 28024
- Removal
  - Foreign Body, 28024
  - Loose Body, 28024
- Synovial
  - Biopsy, 28054

Interrogation
- Cardio-Defibrillator, 93289, 93292, 93295
- Cardiovascular Monitoring System, 93290, 93297, 93299
- Loop Recorder, 93291, 93298-93299
- Pacemaker, 93288, 93294, 93296

Interruption
Vein
- Femoral, 37650
- Iliac, 37660
- Vena Cava, 37620

Intersex State
- Clitoroplasty, 56805
- Vaginoplasty, 57335

Intersex Surgery
- Female to Male, 55980
- Male to Female, 55970

Interstitial Cell Stimulating Hormone
See Luteinizing Hormone (LH)
- Cystitides, Chronic
  See Cystitis, Interstitial
- Cystitis
  See Cystitis, Interstitial
- Fluid Pressure
  - Monitoring, 20950

Interstitual Cell Stimulating Hormone
See Luteinizing Hormone (LH)

Intertarsal Joint
- Arthrotomy, 28020, 28050
- Biopsy
  - Synovial, 28050
- Exploration, 28020
- Removal
  - Foreign Body, 28020
  - Loose Body, 28020
- Synovial
  - Biopsy, 28050
  - Excision, 28070

Interthoracoscapular Amputation
See Amputation, Interthoracoscapular

Intertrochanteric Femur Fracture
See Femur, Fracture, Intertrochanteric

Intervertebral Chemonucleolysis
See Chemonucleolysis

Intervertebral Disc
- Annuloplasty, 22526-22527
- Arthroplasty
  - Cervical Interspace, 22856
  - Each Additional Interspace, 0092T
  - Lumbar Interspace, 0163T, 22857-22865
  - Removal, 0095T, 0164T
  - Removal, 0095T
  - Revision, 0098T, 0165T
- Discography
  - Cervical, 72285
  - Lumbar, 72295
  - Thoracic, 72285
- Excision
  - Decompression, 63075-63078
  - Herniated, 63020-63044, 63055-63066
- Injection
  - Chemonucleolysis Agent, 62292
  - X-ray, 62290, 62291
- X-ray with Contrast
  - Cervical, 72285
  - Lumbar, 72295

Intestinal Anastomosis
See Anastomosis, Intestines

Intestinal Invagination
See Intussusception

Intestines, Small

Intestinal Peptide, Vasoconstrictive
See Vasoactive Intestinal Peptide

Intestine(s)
- Allotransplantation, 44135, 44136
  - Removal, 44137
- Anastomosis, 44625, 44626
  - Laparoscopic, 44227
- Biopsy, 44100
- Closure
  - Enterostomy
    - Large or Small, 44625, 44626
  - Stoma, 44620, 44625
- Excision
  - Donor, 44132, 44133
- Exclusion, 44700
- Laparoscopic Resection with Anastomosis, 44202, 44203, 44207, 44208
- Lesion
  - Excision, 44110, 44111
- Lysis of Adhesions
  - Laparoscopic, 44180
- Nuclear Medicine
  - Imaging, 78290
- Reconstruction
  - Bladder, 50820
  - Colonic Reservoir, 45119
- Repair
  - Diverticula, 44605
  - Obstruction, 44615
  - Ulcer, 44605
  - Wound, 44605
- Resection, 44227
- Suture
  - Diverticula, 44605
  - Stoma, 44620, 44625
  - Ulcer, 44605
  - Wound, 44605
- Transplantation
  - Allograft Preparation, 44715-44721
  - Donor Enterectomy, 44132, 44133
  - Removal of Allograft, 44137
- Unlisted Laparoscopic Procedure, 44238

Intestines, Large
See Anus; Cecum; Colon; Rectum

Intestines, Small
- Anastomosis, 43845, 44130
- Biopsy, 44020, 44100
- Endoscopy, 44361
- Catheterization
  - Jejunum, 44015
- Closure
  - Stoma, 44620, 44625
- Decompression, 44021
- Destruction
  - Lesion, 44369
  - Tumor, 44369
- Endoscopy, 44360
  - Biopsy, 44361, 44377
  - Control of Bleeding, 44366, 44378
  - via Stoma, 44382
  - Destruction
    - Lesion, 44369
    - Tumor, 44369
  - Diagnostic, 44376
  - Exploration, 44360
  - Hemorrhage, 44366
  - Insertion
    - Stent, 44370, 44379
    - Tube, 44379
  - Pelvic Pouch, 44385, 44386
  - Place Tube, 44372
  - Removal
    - Foreign Body, 44363
    - Lesion, 44365
    - Polyp, 44364, 44365
    - Tumor, 44364, 44365
  - Tube Placement, 44372
  - Tube Revision, 44373
  - via Stoma, 44380, 44382
- Enterostomy, 44620-44626
  - Tube Placement, 44300

Intestines, Small — Index

Intestines, Small — *continued*
  Excision, 44120-44128
    Partial with Anastomosis, 44140
  Exclusion, 44700
  Exploration, 44020
  Gastrostomy Tube, 44373
  Hemorrhage, 44378
  Hemorrhage Control, 44366
  Ileostomy, 44310-44314, 44316, 45136
    Continent, 44316
  Incision, 44010, 44020
    Creation
      Pouch, 44316
      Stoma, 44300-44310
    Decompression, 44021
    Exploration, 44020
    Revision
      Stoma, 44312
      Stoma Closure, 44620-44626
  Insertion
    Catheter, 44015
    Duodenostomy Tube, 49441
    Jejunostomy Tube, 44015, 44372
  Jejunostomy, 44310
    Laparoscopic, 44186
  Lesion
    Excision, 44110, 44111
  Lysis
    Adhesions, 44005
  Removal
    Foreign Body, 44020, 44363
  Repair
    Diverticula, 44602-44603
    Enterocele
      Abdominal Approach, 57270
      Vaginal Approach, 57268
    Fistula, 44640-44661
    Hernia, 44050
    Malrotation, 44055
    Obstruction, 44050, 44615
    Ulcer, 44602, 44603, 44605
    Volvulus, 44050
    Wound, 44602, 44603, 44605
  Revision
    Jejunostomy Tube, 44373, 49451-49452
  Specimen Collection, 89100, 89105
  Suture
    Diverticula, 44602, 44603, 44605
    Fistula, 44640-44661
    Plication, 44680
    Stoma, 44620, 44625
    Ulcer, 44602, 44603, 44605
    Wound, 44602, 44603, 44605
  Unlisted Services and Procedures, 44799
  X–ray, 74245, 74249-74251
    Guide Intubation, 74355
Intestinovesical Fistula
  See Fistula, Enterovesical
Intima-Media Thickness Testing
  Artery
    Carotid, Common, 0126T
Intimectomy
  See Endarterectomy
Intra–Abdominal Manipulation
  Intestines, 44799
Intra–Abdominal Voiding Pressure Studies, [51797]
Intra-Aortic Balloon Pump Insertion, 33967-33974
Intra-Arterial Infusion Pump, 36260-36262
Intracapsular Extraction of Lens
  See Extraction, Lens, Intracapsular
Intracardiac Echocardiography, 93662
Intracranial
  Biopsy, 61140
  Microdissection, 69990
    with Surgical Microscope, 69990
Intracranial Arterial Perfusion
  Thrombolysis, 61624
Intracranial Neoplasm, Acoustic Neuroma
  See Brain, Tumor, Excision

Intracranial Neoplasm, Craniopharyngioma
  See Craniopharyngioma
Intracranial Neoplasm, Meningioma
  See Meningioma
Intracranial Nerve
  Electrocoagulation
    Anesthesia, 00222
Intracranial Procedures
  Anesthesia, 00190, 00210-00222
Intradiscal Electrothermal Therapy (IDET), 22526-22527
Intrafallopian Transfer, Gamete
  See GIFT
Intra-Fraction Localization and Tracking
  Patient Motion During Radiation Therapy, 0197T
Intraluminal Angioplasty
  See Angioplasty
Intraocular Lens
  Exchange, 66986
  Insertion, 66983
    Manual or Mechanical Technique, 66982, 66984
    not Associated with Concurrent Cataract Removal, 66985
Intraoperative Manipulation of Stomach, 43659, 43999
Intraoral
  Skin Graft
    Pedicle Flap, 15576
Intra–Osseous Infusion
  See Infusion, Intrasosseous
Intrathoracic Esophagoesophagostomy, 43499
Intrathoracic System
  Anesthesia, 00500-00580
Intratracheal Intubation
  See Insertion, Endotracheal Tube
Intrauterine
  Contraceptive Device (IUD)
    Insertion, 58300
    Removal, 58301
  Insemination, 58322
Intrauterine Synechiae
  Lysis, 58559
Intravascular Sensor
  Pressure
    Complete Study, 93982
Intravascular Stent
  See Transcatheter, Placement, Intravascular Stents
  X-ray, 75960
Intravascular Ultrasound
  Intraoperative, 37250, 37251
Intravenous Pyelogram
  See Urography, Intravenous
Intravenous Therapy, 96360-96361, 96365-96368, 96374-96379
  See Injection, Chemotherapy
Intravesical Instillation
  See Bladder, Instillation
Intrinsic Factor, 83528
  Antibodies, 86340
Introduction
  Breast
    Metallic Localization Clip Placement, 19295
    Preoperative Placement, Needle, 19290-19291
  Contraceptive Capsules
    Implantable, 11975-11977
  Drug Delivery Implant, 11981, 11983
  Gastrointestinal Tube, 44500
    with Fluoroscopic Guidance, 74340
  Injections
    Intradermal, 11920-11922
    Intralesional, 11900, 11901
    Subcutaneous, 11950-11954
  Needle or Catheter
    Aorta, 36100, 36200
    Arterial System
      Brachiocephalic Branch, 36215-36218

Introduction — *continued*
  Needle or Catheter — *continued*
    Arterial System — *continued*
      Lower Extremity, 36245-36248
      Pelvic Branch, 36245-36248
      AV Shunt, 36147-36148
      Brachial Artery, 36120
      Carotid, 36100
      Extremity Artery, 36140
      Vertebral Artery, 31600
  Tissue Expanders, Skin, 11960-11971
Intubation
  See Insertion
  Endotracheal Tube, 31500
  Eustachian Tube
    See Catheterization, Eustachian Tube
  for Specimen Collection
    Esophagus, 91000
    Stomach, 91055
    Gastric, 89130-89141, 91105
Intubation Tube
  See Endotracheal Tube
Intussusception
  Barium Enema, 74283
  Reduction
    Laparotomy, 44050
Invagination, Intestinal
  See Intussesception
Inversion, Nipple, 19355
Investigation
  FDA Approved Chronic Care Drugs, 0130T
In Vitro Fertilization
  Biopsy Oocyte, 89290, 89291
  Culture Oocyte, 89250, 89251
    Extended, 89272
  Embryo Hatching, 89253
  Fertilze Oocyte, 89250
    Microtechnique, 89280, 89281
  Identify Oocyte, 89254
  Insemination of Oocyte, 89268
  Prepare Embryo, 89255, 89352
  Retrieve Oocyte, 58970
  Transfer Embryo, 58974, 58976
  Transfer Gamete, 58976
In Vivo NMR Spectroscopy
  See Magnetic Resonance Spectroscopy
Iodide Test
  Nuclear Medicine, Thyroid Uptake, 78000-78003
Iodine Test, 89225
IOL, 66825, 66983-66986
Ionization, Medical
  See Iontophoresis
Iontophoresis, 97033
  Sweat Collection, 89230
IP
  See Allergen Immunotherapy
Ipecac Administration, 99175
IPOL, 90713
IPV, 90713
Iridectomy
  with Corneoscleral or Corneal Section, 66600
  with Sclerectomy with Punch or Scissors, 66160
  with Thermocauterizaton, 66155
  with Transfixion as for Iris Bombe, 66605
  with Trephination, 66150
  by Laser Surgery, 66761
  Peripheral for Glaucoma, 66625
Iridencleisis, 66165
Iridocapsulectomy, 66830
Iridocapsulotomy, 66830
Iridodialysis, 66680
Iridoplasty, 66762
Iridotasis, 66165
Iridotomy
  by Laser Surgery, 66761
  by Stab Incision, 66500

Iridotomy — *continued*
  Excision
    with Corneoscleral or Corneal Section, 66600
    with Cyclectomy, 66605
    Optical, 66635
    Peripheral, 66625
  Incision
    with Transfixion as for Iris Bombe, 66505
    Stab, 66500
    Optical, 66635
    Peripheral, 66625
    Sector, 66630
Iris
  Cyst
    Destruction, 66770
  Excision
    Iridectomy
      with Corneoscleral or Corneal Section, 66600
      with Cyclectomy, 66605
      Optical, 66635
      Peripheral, 66625
      Sector, 66630
  Incision
    Iridotomy
      with Transfixion as for Iris Bombe, 66505
      Stab, 66500
  Lesion
    Destruction, 66770
  Repair, 66680
    Suture, 66682
  Revision
    Laser Surgery, 66761
    Photocoagulation, 66762
  Suture
    with Ciliary Body, 66682
Iron, 83540
Iron Binding Capacity, 83550
Iron Hematoxylin Stain, 88312
Iron Stain, 85536, 88313
Irradiation
  Blood Products, 86945
Irrigation
  Bladder, 51700
  Caloric Vestibular Test, 92533, 92543
  Catheter, 96523
    Brain, 62194, 62225
  Corpora Cavernosa
    Priapism, 54220
  Penis
    Priapism, 54220
  Peritoneal
    See Peritoneal Lavage
  Rectum
    for Fecal Impaction, 91123
  Shunt
    Spinal Cord, 63744
  Sinus
    Maxillary, 31000
    Sphenoid, 31002
  Vagina, 57150
Irving Sterilization
  Ligation, Fallopian Tube, Oviduct, 58600-58611, 58670
Ischemic Stroke
  Onset, 1065F-1066F
  Tissue Plasminogen Activator (tPA)
    Documentation That Administration Was Considered, 4077F
Ischial
  Excision
    Bursa, 27060
    Tumor, 27078
Ischiectomy, 15941
Ischium
  Pressure Ulcer, 15940-15946
ISG Immunization, 90281, 90283
Ishihara Test, 92283
Island Pedicle Flaps, 15740
Islands of Langerhans
  See Islet Cell

Index

Islet Cell
  Antibody, 86341
Isocitrate Dehydrogenase
  See Isocitric Dehydrogenase
Isocitric Dehydrogenase
  Blood, 83570
Isolation
  Sperm, 89260, 89261
Isomerase, Glucose 6 Phophate
  See Phosphohexose Isomerase
Isopropanol
  See Isopropyl Alcohol
Isopropyl Alcohol, 84600
Isthmusectomy
  Thyroid Gland, 60210-60225
IUD, 58300, 58301
  Insertion, 58300
  Removal, 58301
IUI (Intrauterine Insemination), 58322
IV, 96365-96368, 96374-96376
  Chemotherapy, 96413-96417
  Hydration, 96360-96361
IVC Filter
  Insertion, 37620
IV, Coagulation Factor
  See Calcium
IVF (In Vitro Fertilization), 58970-58976, 89250-89255
IV Infusion Therapy, 96365-96368
  Chemotherapy, 96409, 96411, 96413-96417, 96542
  Hydration, 96360-96361
IV Injection, 96374-96376
  Chemotherapy, 96409-96417
Ivor Lewis, 43117
IVP, 50394, 74400
Ivy Bleeding Time, 85002
IX Complex, Factor
  See Christmas Factor

J

Jaboulay Operation
  Gastroduodenostomy, 43810, 43850, 43855
Jannetta Procedure
  Decompression, Cranial Nerves, 61458
Japanese Encephalitis Virus Vaccine, 90735, 90738
Japanese, River Fever
  See Scrub Typhus
Jatene Procedure
  Repair, Great Arteries, 33770-33781
Jaw Joint
  See Facial Bones; Mandible; Maxilla
Jaws
  Muscle Reduction, 21295, 21296
  X-ray
    for Orthodontics, 70355
Jejunostomy
  with Pancreatic Drain, 48001
  Catheterization, 44015
  Insertion
    Catheter, 44015
  Laparoscopic, 44186
  Non-Tube, 44310
Jejunum
  Transfer with Microvascular Anastomosis, Free, 43496
JE-VAX, 90735
Johannsen Procedure, 53400
Johanson Operation
  See Reconstruction, Urethra
Joint
  See Specific Joint
  Acromioclavicular
    See Acromioclavicular Joint
  Arthrocentesis, 20600-20610
  Aspiration, 20600-20610
  Dislocation
    See Dislocation
  Drainage, 20600-20610
  Finger
    See Intercarpal Joint
  Fixation (Surgical)
    See Arthrodesis

Joint — continued
  Foot
    See Foot, Joint
  Hip
    See Hip, Joint
  Injection, 20600-20610
  Intertarsal
    See Intertarsal Joint
  Knee
    See Knee Joint
  Ligament
    See Ligament
  Metacarpophalangeal
    See Metacarpophalangeal Joint
  Metatarsophalangeal
    See Metatarsophalangeal Joint
  Mobilization, 97140
  Nuclear Medicine
    Imaging, 78300-78315
  Radiology
    Stress Views, 77071
  Sacroiliac
    See Sacroiliac Joint
  Shoulder
    See Glenohumeral Joint
  Sternoclavicular
    See Sternoclavicular Joint
  Survey, 77077
  Temporomandibular
    See Temporomandibular Joint (TMJ)
  Dislocation Temporomandibular
    See Dislocation, Temporomandibular Joint
  Implant
    See Prosthesis, Temporomandibular Joint
  Wrist
    See Radiocarpal Joint
Joint Syndrome, Temporomandibular
  See Temporomandibular Joint (TMJ)
Jones and Cantarow Test
  Clearance, Urea Nitrogen, 84545
Jones Procedure
  Arthrodesis, Interphalangeal Joint, Great Toe, 28760
Joplin Procedure, 28294
Jugal Bone
  See Cheekbone
Jugular Vein
  See Vein, Jugular

K

K+, 84132
Kader Operation
  Incision, Stomach, Creation of Stoma, 43830-43832
Kala Azar Smear, 87207
Kallidin I / Kallidin 9
  See Bradykinin
Kallidrein HK3
  See Antigen, Prostate Specific
Kallikreinogen
  See Fletcher Factor
Kasai Procedure, 47701
Kedani Fever, 86000
Keel
  Insertion
    Removal
      Laryngoplasty, 31580
Keen Operation, 63198
  Laminectomy, 63600
Keitzer Test, 51727, 51729
Kelikian Procedure, 28280
Keller Procedure, 28292
Kelly Urethral Plication, 57220
Keratectomy
  Partial
    for Lesion, 65400
Keratomileusis, 65760
Keratophakia, 65765
Keratoplasty
  Lamellar, 65710
    in Aphakia, 65750
    in Pseudophakia, 65755
    Penetrating, 65730

Keratoprosthesis, 65770
Keratotomy
  Radial, 65771
Ketogenic Steroids, 83582
Ketone Body
  Acetone, 82009, 82010
Ketosteroids, 83586, 83593
Kidner Procedure, 28238
Kidney
  Abscess
    Incision and Drainage
      Open, 50020
      Percutaneous, 50021
  Allograft Preparation, 50323-50329
    Donor Nephrectomy, 50300, 50320, 50547
    Implantation of Graft, 50360
    Recipient Nephrectomy, 50340, 50365
    Reimplantation Kidney, 50380
    Removal Transplant Renal Autograft, 50370
  Anesthesia
    Donor, 00862
    Recipient, 00868
  Biopsy, 50200, 50205
    Endoscopic, 50555-50557, 52354
  Catheterization
    Endoscopic, 50572
  Cyst
    Ablation, 50541
    Aspiration, 50390
    Excision, 50280, 50290
    Injection, 50390
    X-ray, 74470
  Destruction
    Calculus, 50590
    Endoscopic, 50557, 50576, 52354
  Dilation, 50395
  Endoscopy
    with Endopyelotomy, 50575
    Biopsy, 50555, 50574-50576, 52354
    Catheterization, 50553, 50572
    Destruction, 50557, 50576, 52354
    Dilation
      Intra-Renal Stricture, 52343, 52346
      Ureter, 50553
    Excision
      Tumor, 52355
    Exploration, 52351
    Lithotripsy, 52353
    Removal
      Calculus, 50561, 50580, 52352
      Foreign Body, 50561, 50580
      via Incision, 50570-50580
      via Stoma, 50551-50561
  Excision
    with Ureters, 50220-50236
    Donor, 50300, 50320, 50547
    Partial, 50240
    Recipient, 50340
    Transplantation, 50370
  Exploration, 50010, 50045, 50120
  Incision, 50010, 50045, 50120, 50130, 50135
  Incision and Drainage, 50040, 50125
  Injection
    Drugs, 50391
    Radiologic, 50394
  Insertion
    Catheter, 50392, 50393
    Guide, 50395
    Intracatheter, 50392
    Stent, 50393
    Tube, 50398
  Instillation
    Drugs, 50391
  Lithotripsy, 50590
  Manometry
    Pressure, 50396

Kidney — continued
  Mass
    Ablation, 50542
      Cryosurgical, 50250
      Radiofrequency, 50592
  Mass Ablation, 50542
  Needle Biopsy, 50200
  Nuclear Medicine
    Blood Flow, 78701-78709
    Function Study, 78725
    Imaging, 78700-78707, 78710
    Unlisted Services and Procedures, 78799
  Removal
    Calculus, 50060-50081, 50130, 50561
    Foreign Body, 50561, 50580
    Tube
      Nephrostomy, 50389
  Renal Pelvis, 50405
  Repair
    Blood Vessels, 50100
    Fistula, 50520-50526
    Horseshoe Kidney, 50540
    Renal Pelvis, 50400, 50405
    Wound, 50500
  Solitary, 50405
  Suture
    Fistula, 50520-50526
    Horseshoe Kidney, 50540
  Transplantation
    Allograft Preparation, 50323-50329
    Anesthesia
      Donor, 00862
      Recipient, 00868
    Donor Nephrectomy, 50300-50320, 50547
    Graft Implantation, 50360-50365
    Implantation of Graft, 50360
    Recipient Nephrectomy, 50340, 50365
    Reimplantation Kidney, 50380
    Removal Transplant Allograft, 50370
  Tumor
    Ablation
      Cryotherapy, 50250, 50593
  Ultrasound, 76770-76775, 76776
  X-ray with Contrast
    Guide Catheter, 74475
Kidney Stone
  Removal, Calculi, 50060-50081, 50130, 50561, 50580
Killian Operation, 31020
  Sinusotomy, Frontal, 31070-31087
Kinase Creatine
  Blood, 82550-82552
Kineplasty
  Arm, Lower or Upper, 24940
Kinetic Therapy, 97530
Kininase A, 82164
Kininogen, 85293
Kininogen, High Molecular Weight, 85293
Kleihauer-Betke Test, 85460
Kloramfenikol, 82415
Knee
  See Femur; Fibula; Patella; Tibia
  Abscess, 27301
  Arthrocentesis, 20610
  Arthrodesis, 27580
  Arthroplasty, 27440-27445, 27447
    Revision, 27486, 27487
  Arthroscopy
    Diagnostic, 29870
    Surgical, 29866-29868, 29871-29889
  Arthrotomy, 27310, 27330-27335, 27403
  Autograft, Osteochondral, Open, 27416
  Biopsy, 27323, 27324, 27330, 27331
    Synovium, 27330
  Bone
    Drainage, 27303

Knee — Index

Knee — *continued*
  Bursa, 27301
    Excision, 27340
  Cyst
    Excision, 27345, 27347
  Disarticulation, 27598
  Dislocation
    Closed Treatment, 27550, 27552, 27560, 27562
    Open Treatment, 27556-27558, 27566
  Drainage, 27310
  Excision
    Cartilage, 27332, 27333
    Ganglion, 27347
    Lesion, 27347
    Synovial Lining, 27334, 27335
  Exploration, 27310, 27331
  Fasciotomy, 27305, 27496-27499
  Fracture, 27520, 27524
    Arthroscopic Treatment, 29850, 29851
  Fusion, 27580
  Hematoma, 27301
  Incision
    Capsule, 27435
  Injection
    X-ray, 27370
  Magnetic Resonance Imaging (MRI), 73721-73723
  Manipulation, 27570
  Meniscectomy, 27332, 27333
  Osteochondral Graft, 27415-27416
  Reconstruction, 27437, 27438
    with Implantation, 27445
    with Prosthesis, 27445
    Ligament, 27427-27429
  Removal
    Foreign Body, 27310, 27331, 27372
    Loose Body, 27331
    Prosthesis, 27488
  Repair
    Ligament, 27405-27409
      Collateral, 27405
      Collateral and Cruciate, 27409
      Cruciate, 27407, 27409
    Meniscus, 27403
    Tendon, 27380, 27381
  Replacement, 27447
  Retinacular
    Release, 27425
  Strapping, 29530
  Suture
    Tendon, 27380, 27381
  Transplantation
    Chondrocytes, 27412
    Meniscus, 29868
    Osteochondral
      Allograft, 27415, 29867
      Autograft, 27412, 29866
  Tumor, 27327-27328 [27337, 27339], 27335-27358, 27364-27365 [27329]
  Unlisted Services and Procedures, 27599
  X-ray, 73560-73564
    Arthrography, 73580
    Bilateral, 73565
  X-ray with Contrast
    Angiography, 73706
    Arthrography, 73580

Kneecap
  Excision, 27350
  Repair
    Instability, 27420-27424

Knee Joint
  Arthroplasty, 27446

Knee Prosthesis
  See Prosthesis, Knee

Knock-Knee Repair, 27455, 27457

Kocher Operation, 23650-23680
  See Clavicle; Scapula; Shoulder, Dislocation, Closed Treatment

Kocher Pylorectomy
  Gastrectomy, Partial, 43631

Kock Pouch, 44316
  Formation, 50825

Kock Procedure, 44316

KOH
  Hair, Nails, Tissue, Examination for Fungi, 87220

Konno Procedure, 33412

Koop Inguinal Orchiopexy, 54640

Kraske Procedure, 45116

Krause Operation
  Gasserian Ganglion, Sensory Root, Decompression, 61450

Kroenlein Procedure, 67420

Krukenberg Procedure, 25915

Krupin-Denver Valve
  Implant, 66180
  Removal, 67120
  Revision, 66185

KS, 83586, 83593

KUB, 74241, 74247, 74270, 74420

Kuhlmann Test, 96101-96103

Kuhnt–Szymanowski Procedure, 67917

K-Wire Fixation
  Tongue, 41500

Kyphectomy
  More than Two Segments, 22819
  Up to Two Segments, 22818

Kyphoplasty, 22523-22525

L

Labial Adhesions
  Lysis, 56441

Labyrinth
  See Ear, Inner

Labyrinthectomy
  with Mastoidectomy, 69910
  with Skull Base Surgery, 61596
  Transcanal, 69905

Labyrinthotomy
  with Mastoidectomy, 69802
  with Skull Base Surgery, 61596
  Inner Ear, 69949
  Transcanal
    with/without Cryosurgery, 69801

Laceration Repair
  See Repair, Laceration, Skin

Lacrimal Duct
  Balloon, 68816
  Canaliculi
    Incision, 68899
    Repair, 68700
  Dilation, 68816
  Exploration, 68810
    with Anesthesia, 68811
    Canaliculi, 68840
    Stent, 68815
  Insertion
    Stent, 68815
  Nasolacrimal Duct Probing, 68816
  Removal
    Dacryolith, 68530
    Foreign Body, 68530
  X-ray with Contrast, 70170

Lacrimal Gland
  Biopsy, 68510
  Close Fistula, 68770
  Excision
    Partial, 68505
    Total, 68500
  Fistulization, 68720
  Incision and Drainage, 68400
  Injection
    X-ray, 68850
  Nuclear Medicine
    Tear Flow, 78660
  Removal
    Dacryolith, 68530
    Foreign Body, 68530
  Repair
    Fistula, 68770
  Tumor
    Excision
      with Osteotomy, 68550
      without Closure, 68540
  X-Ray, 70170

Lacrimal Punctum
  Closure
    by Plug, 68761
    by Thermocauterization, Ligation or Laser Surgery, 68760
  Dilation, 68801
  Incision, 68440
  Repair, 68705

Lacrimal Sac
  Biopsy, 68525
  Excision, 68520
  Incision and Drainage, 68420

Lacrimal System
  Unlisted Services and Procedures, 68899

Lacryoaptography
  Nuclear, 78660

Lactase Deficiency Breath Test, 91065

Lactate, 83605

Lactic Acid, 83605

Lactic Acid Measurement
  See Lactate

Lactic Cytochrome Reductase
  See Lactic Dehydrogenase

Lactic Dehydrogenase, 83615, 83625

Lactiferous Duct
  Excision, 19112
  Exploration, 19110

Lactoferrin
  Fecal, 83630-83631

Lactogen, Human Placental, 83632

Lactogenic Hormone
  See Prolactin

Lactose
  Urine, 83633, 83634

Ladd Procedure, 44055

Lagophthalmos
  Repair, 67912

Laki Lorand Factor
  See Fibrin Stabilizing Factor

L-Alanine
  See Aminolevulinic Acid (ALA)

Lamblia Intestinalis
  See Giardia Lamblia

Lambrinudi Operation
  Arthrodesis, Foot Joints, 28730, 28735, 28740

Lamellar Keratoplasties
  See Keratoplasty, Lamellar

Laminaria
  Insertion, 59200

Laminectomy, 62351, 63001, 63005-63011, 63015-63044, 63180-63200, 63265-63290, 63600-63655
  with Facetectomy, 63045-63048
  Decompression
    Cervical, 63001, 63015
      with Facetectomy and Foraminotomy, 63045, 63048
    Laminotomy
      Initial
        Cervical, 63020
        Each Additional Space, 63035
        Lumbar, 63030
      Reexploration
        Cervical, 63040
        Each Additional Interspace, 63043
        Lumbar, 63042
        Each Additional Interspace, 63044
    Lumbar, 63005, 63017
      with Facetectomy and Foraminotomy, 63046, 63048
    Sacral, 63011
    Thoracic, 63003, 63016
      with Facetectomy and Foraminotomy, 63047, 63048
  Excision
    Lesion, 63250-63273
    Neoplasm, 63275-63290

Laminectomy — *continued*
  Lumbar, 22630, 63012
  Surgical, 63170-63200

Laminoplasty
  Cervical, 63050-63051

Laminotomy
  Cervical, One Interspace, 63020
  Lumbar, 63042
    One Interspace, 63030
    Each Additional, 63035
  Re-exploration, Cervical, 63040

Landboldt's Operation, 67971, 67973, 67975

Lane's Operation, 44150

Langerhans Islands
  See Islet Cell

Language Evaluation, 92506

Language Therapy, 92507, 92508

LAP, 83670

Laparoscopy
  with X-ray, 47560
  Abdominal, 49320-49329
  Adrenalectomy, 60650
  Adrenal Gland
    Biopsy, 60650
    Excision, 60650
  Appendectomy, 44970
  Aspiration, 49322
  Biopsy, 47561, 49321
    Lymph Nodes, 38570
    Ovary, 49321
  Bladder
    Repair
      Sling Procedure, 51992
      Urethral Suspension, 51990
    Unlisted, 51999
  Cecostomy, 44188
  Cholangiography, 47560, 47561
  Cholecystectomy, 47562-47564
  Cholecystoenterostomy, 47570
  Closure
    Enterostomy, 44227
  Colectomy
    Partial, 44204-44208, 44213
    Total, 44210-44212
  Colostomy, 44188
  Destruction
    Lesion, 58662
  Diagnostic, 49320
  Drainage
    Extraperitoneal Lymphocele, 49323
  Ectopic Pregnancy, 59150
    with Salpingectomy and/or Oophorectomy, 59151
  Electrode
    Implantation
      Gastric, 0156T, 43647-43648
    Removal
      Gastric, 0156T, 43648
    Replacement
      Gastric, 0156T, 43647
    Revision
      Gastric, 0156T, 43648
  Enterectomy, 44202
  Enterolysis, 44180
  Enterostomy
    Closure, 44227
  Esophagogastric Fundoplasty, 43280
  Esophagomyotomy, 43279
  Fimbrioplasty, 58672
  Gastric Restrictive Procedures, 43644-43645, 43770-43774
  Gastrostomy
    Temporary, 43653
  Graft Revision
    Vaginal, 57426
  Hernia Repair
    Epigastric, 49652
      Incarcerated or Strangulated, 49653
    Incisional, 49654
      Incarcerated or Strangulated, 49655
      Recurrent, 49656

Index

Laparoscopy — *continued*
  Hernia Repair — *continued*
    Incisional — *continued*
      Recurrent — *continued*
        Incarcerated or Strangulated, 49657
      Initial, 49650
      Recurrent, 49651
    Spigelian, 49652
      Incarcerated or Strangulated, 49653
    Umbilical, 49652
      Incarcerated or Strangulated, 49653
    Ventral, 49652
      Incarcerated or Strangulated, 49653
  Hysterectomy, 58541-58554, 58570-58573
    Radical, 58548
    Total, 58570-58573
  Ileostomy, 44187
  Incontinence Repair, 51990, 51992
  In Vitro Fertilization, 58976
    Retrieve Oocyte, 58970
    Transfer Embryo, 58974
    Transfer Gamete, 58976
  Jejunostomy, 44186-44187
  Kidney
    Ablation, 50541-50542
  Ligation
    Veins, Spermatic, 55500
  Liver
    Ablation
      Tumor, 47370, 47371
  Lymphadenectomy, 38571-38572
  Lymphatic, 38570-38589
  Lysis of Adhesions, 58660
  Lysis of Intestinal Adhesions, 44180
  Mobilization
    Splenic Flexure, 44213
  Nephrectomy, 50545-50548
    Partial, 50543
  Omentopexy, 49326
  Orchiectomy, 54690
  Orchiopexy, 54692
  Ovary
    Biopsy, 49321
    Reimplantation, 59898
    Suture, 59898
  Oviduct Surgery, 58670, 58671, 58679
  Pancreatic Islet Cell Transplantation, 0143T
  Pelvis, 49320
  Proctectomy, 45395, 45397
    with Creation of Colonic Reservoir, 45397
    Complete, 45395
  Proctopexy, 45400, 45402
  Prostatectomy, 55866
  Pyloplasty, 50544
  Rectum
    Resection, 45395-45397
    Unlisted, 45499
  Removal
    Fallopian Tubes, 58661
    Leiomyomata, 58545-58546
    Ovaries, 58661
    Spleen, 38120
    Testis, 54690
  Resection
    Intestines
      with Anastomosis, 44202, 44203
    Rectum, 45395-45397
  Salpingostomy, 58673
  Splenectomy, 38120, 38129
  Splenic Flexure
    Mobilization, 44213
  Stomach, 43651-43659
    Gastric Bypass, 43644-43645
    Gastric Restrictive Procedures, 43770-43774, 43848, 43886-43888
    Gastroenterostomy, 43644-43645

Laparoscopy — *continued*
  Stomach — *continued*
    Roux–en–Y, 43644
    Surgical, 38570-38572, 43651-43653, 44180-44188, 44212, 44213, 44227, 44970, 45395-45402, 45400-45402, 47370, 47371, 49321-49323, 49650, 49651, 50541, 50543, 50545, 50945-50948, 51992, 54690, 54692, 55550, 55866, 57425, 58545, 58546, 58552, 58554
    with Guided Transhepatic Cholangiography, 47560-47561
  Transplantation
    Islet Cell, 0143T
  Unlisted Services and Procedures, 38129, 38589, 43289, 43659, 44238, 44979, 45499, 47379, 47579, 49329, 49659, 50549, 50949, 51999, 54699, 55559, 58578, 58579, 58679, 59898
  Ureterolithotomy, 50945
  Ureteroneocystostomy, 50947-50948
  Urethral Suspension, 51990
  Vaginal Hysterectomy, 58550-58554
  Vaginal Suspension, 57425
  Vagus Nerves Transection, 43651, 43652

Laparotomy
  with Biopsy, 49000
  Electrode
    Gastric
      Implantation, 0157T, 43881
      Removal, 0158T, 43882
      Replacement, 0157T, 43881
      Revision, 0158T, 43882
  Exploration, 47015, 49000, 49002, 58960
  for Staging, 49220
  Hemorrhage Control, 49002
  Second Look, 58960
  Staging, 58960
  Surgical, 44050

Laparotomy, Exploratory
  See Abdomen, Exploration

Lapidus Procedure, 28297

Large Bowel
  See Anus; Cecum; Rectum

Laroyenne Operation
  Vagina, Abscess, Incision and Drainage, 57010

Laryngeal Function Study, 92520
Laryngeal Sensory Testing, 92614-92617
Laryngectomy, 31360-31382
  Partial, 31367-31382
  Subtotal, 31367, 31368
  Total, 31360, 31365

Laryngocele
  Removal, 31300
Laryngofissure, 31300
Laryngography, 70373
Laryngopharyngectomy
  Excision, Larynx, with Pharynx, 31390, 31395
Laryngopharynx
  See Hypopharynx
Laryngoplasty
  Burns, 31588
  Cricoid Split, 31587
  Laryngeal Stenosis, 31582
  Laryngeal Web, 31580
  Open Reduction of Fracture, 31584
Laryngoscopy
  Diagnostic, 31505
  Direct, 31515-31571
  Exploration, 31505, 31520-31526, 31575
  Fiberoptic, 31575-31579
    with Stroboscopy, 31579
  Indirect, 31505-31513
  Newborn, 31520
  Operative, 31530-31561

Laryngotomy
  Diagnostic, 31320
  Partial, 31370-31382
  Removal
    Tumor, 31300
  Total, 31360-31368
Larynx
  Aspiration
    Endoscopy, 31515
  Biopsy
    Endoscopy, 31510, 31535, 31536, 31576
  Dilation
    Endoscopic, 31528, 31529
  Electromyography
    Needle, 95865
  Endoscopy
    Direct, 31515-31571
    Excision, 31545-31546
    Exploration, 31505, 31520-31526, 31575
    Fiberoptic, 31575-31579
      with Stroboscopy, 31579
    Indirect, 31505-31513
    Operative, 31530-31561
  Excision
    with Pharynx, 31390, 31395
    Lesion, 31512, 31578
      Endoscopic, 31545-31546
    Partial, 31367-31382
    Total, 31360, 31365
  Exploration
    Endoscopic, 31505, 31520-31526, 31575
  Fracture
    Open Treatment, 31584
  Insertion
    Obturator, 31527
  Nerve
    Destruction, 31595
  Pharynx
    with Pharynx, 31390
  Reconstruction
    with Pharynx, 31395
    Burns, 31588
    Cricoid Split, 31587
    Other, 31588
    Stenosis, 31582
    Web, 31580
  Removal
    Foreign Body
      Endoscopic, 31511, 31530, 31531, 31577
    Lesion
      Endoscopic, 31512, 31545-31546, 31578
  Repair
    Reinnervation Neuromuscular Pedicle, 31590
  Stroboscopy, 31579
  Tumor
    Excision, 31300
    Endoscopic, 31540, 31541
  Unlisted Services and Procedures, 31599
  Vocal Cord
    Injection, 31513, 31570, 31571
  X–ray, 70370
    with Contrast, 70373

L Ascorbic Acid
  See Ascorbic Acid
LASEK, 65760
Laser Surgery
  Anal, 46917
  Cautery
    Esophagus, 43227
  Lacrimal Punctum, 68760
  Lens
    Posterior, 66821
  Lesion
    Mouth, 40820
    Nose, 30117, 30118
    Penis, 54057
    Skin, 17000-17111, 17260-17286
    Prostate, 52647-52649

Laser Surgery — *continued*
  Spine
    Diskectomy, 62287
  Tumor
    Urethra and Bladder, 52234-52240
  Urethra and Bladder, 52214
Laser Treatment, 17000-17286, 96920-96922
  See Destruction
Lash Procedure
  Tracheoplasty, 31750-31760
LASIK, 65760
L Aspartate 2 Oxoglutarate Aminotransferase
  See Transaminase, Glutamic Oxaloacetic
Lateral Epicondylitis
  See Tennis Elbow
Latex Fixation, 86403, 86406
LATS, 80438, 80439
Latzko Procedure
  Colpocleisis, 57120
LAV
  See HIV
LAV–2, 86702-86703
Lavage
  Colon, 44701
  Lung
    Bronchial, 31624
    Total, 32997
  Peritoneal, 49080
LAV Antibodies, 86689, 86701-86703
LCM
  Antibody, 86727
LD (Lactic Dehydrogenase), 83615
LDH, 83615, 83625
LDL, 83721
Lead, 83655
Leadbetter Procedure, 53431
Lecithin C
  See Tissue Typing
Lecithin–Sphingomyelin Ratio, 83661
Lee and White Test, 85345
LEEP Procedure, 57460
LeFort III Procedure
  Craniofacial Separation, 21431-21436
  Midface Reconstruction, 21154-21159
LeFort II Procedure
  Midface Reconstruction, 21150, 21151
  Nasomaxillary Complex Fracture, 21345-21348
LeFort I Procedure
  Midface Reconstruction, 21141-21147, 21155, 21160
  Palatal or Maxillary Fracture, 21421-21423
LeFort Procedure
  Vagina, 57120
Left Atrioventricular Valve
  See Mitral Valve
Left Heart Cardiac Catheterization
  See Cardiac Catheterization, Left Heart
Leg
  Cast
    Rigid Total Contact, 29445
  Excision
    Excess Skin, 15833
  Lipectomy, Suction Assisted, 15879
  Lower
    See Ankle; Fibula; Knee; Tibia
    Abscess
      Incision and Drainage, 27603
    Amputation, 27598, 27880-27882
      Revision, 27884, 27886
    Angiography, 73706
    Artery
      Ligation, 37618
    Biopsy, 27613, 27614
    Bursa
      Incision and Drainage, 27604
    Bypass Graft, 35903

Leg | Index

Leg — continued
  Lower — continued
    Cast, 29405-29435, 29450
    CT Scan, 73700-73706
    Decompression, 27600-27602
    Exploration
      Blood Vessel, 35860
    Fasciotomy, 27600-27602, 27892-27894
    Hematoma
      Incision and Drainage, 27603
    Lesion
      Excision, 27630
    Magnetic Resonance Imaging, 73718-73720
    Repair
      Blood Vessel, 35226
        with Other Graft, 35286
        with Vein Graft, 35256
      Fascia, 27656
      Tendon, 27658-27692
    Skin Graft
      Delay of Flap, 15610
      Full Thickness, 15220, 15221
      Pedicle Flap, 15572
      Split, 15100, 15101
    Splint, 29515
    Strapping, 29580
    Tendon, 27658-27665
    Tissue Transfer, Adjacent, 14020, 14021
    Tumor, 27615-27619 [27632, 27634], 27635-27638, 27645-27647
    Ultrasound, 76880
    Unlisted Services and Procedures, 27899
    Unna Boot, 29580
    X-ray, 73592
  Upper
    See Femur
    Abscess, 27301
    Amputation, 27590-27592
      at Hip, 27290, 27295
      Revision, 27594, 27596
    Angiography, 73706, 75635
    Artery
      Ligation, 37618
    Biopsy, 27323, 27324
    Bursa, 27301
    Bypass Graft, 35903
    Cast, 29345-29365, 29450
    Cast Brace, 29358
    CT Scan, 73700-73706, 75635
    Exploration
      Blood Vessel, 35860
    Fasciotomy, 27305, 27496-27499, 27892-27894
    Halo Application, 20663
    Hematoma, 27301
    Magnetic Resonance Imaging, 73718-73720
    Neurectomy, 27325, 27326
    Pressure Ulcer, 15950-15958
    Removal
      Cast, 29705
      Foreign Body, 27372
    Repair
      Blood Vessel
        with Other Graft, 35286
        with Vein Graft, 35256
      Muscle, 27385, 27386, 27400, 27430
      Tendon, 27393-27400
    Splint, 29505
    Strapping, 29580
    Suture
      Muscle, 27385, 27386
      Tendon, 27658-27665
    Tenotomy, 27306, 27307, 27390-27392
    Tumor
      Excision, 27327-27360 [27329, 27337, 27339]
    Ultrasound, 76880

Leg — continued
  Upper — continued
    Unlisted Services and Procedures, 27599
    Unna Boot, 29580
    X-ray, 73592
  Wound Exploration
    Penetrating, 20103
Legionella
  Antibody, 86713
  Antigen, 87277, 87278, 87540-87542
Legionella Micdadei
  Immunofluorescence, 87277
Legionella Pneumophilia
  Antigen Detection
    Direct Fluorescence, 87278
Leg Length Measurement X-Ray
  See Scanogram
Leiomyomata
  Embolization, 37210
  Removal, 58140, 58545-58546, 58561
Leishmania
  Antibody, 86717
Lempert's Fenestration, 69820
Lengthening, Tendon
  See Tendon, Lengthening
Lens
  Extracapsular, 66940
  Intracapsular, 66920
    Dislocated, 66930
  Intraocular
    Exchange, 66986
    Reposition, 66825
  Prosthesis
    Insertion, 66983
      Manual or Mechanical Technique, 66982, 66984
      not associated with Concurrent Cataract Removal, 66985
  Removal
    Lens Material
      Aspiration Technique, 66840
      Extracapsular, 66940
      Intracapsular, 66920, 66930
      Pars Plana Approach, 66852
      Phacofragmentation Technique, 66850
Lens Material
  Aspiration Technique, 66840
  Pars Plana Approach, 66852
  Phacofragmentation Technique, 66850
Leptomeningioma
  See Meningioma
Leptospira
  Antibody, 86720
Leriche Operation
  Sympathectomy, Thoracolumbar, 64809
Lesion
  See Tumor
  Anal
    Destruction, 46900-46917, 46924
    Excision, 45108, 46922
  Ankle
    Tendon Sheath, 27630
  Arm, Lower
    Tendon Sheath Excision, 25110
  Auditory Canal, External
    Excision
      Exostosis, 69140
      Radical with Neck Dissection, 69155
      Radical without Neck Dissection, 69150
      Soft Tissue, 69145
  Bladder
    Destruction, 51030
  Brain
    Excision, 61534, 61536, 61600-61608, 61615, 61616
    Radiation Treatment, 77432
  Brainstem
    Excision, 61575, 61576

Lesion — continued
  Breast
    Excision, 19120-19126
  Carotid Body
    Excision, 60600, 60605
  Chemotherapy, 96405, 96406
    Destruction, 67220-67225
  Choroid
    Destruction, 0016T
  Ciliary Body
    Destruction, 66770
  Colon
    Destruction, 44393, 45383
    Excision, 44110, 44111
  Conjunctiva
    Destruction, 68135
    Excision, 68110-68130
      with Adjacent Sclera, 68130
      over 1 cm, 68115
    Expression, 68040
  Cornea
    Destruction, 65450
    Excision, 65400
      of Pterygium, 65420, 65426
  Cranium, 77432
  Destruction
    Ureter, 52341, 52342, 52344, 52345, 52354
  Ear, Middle
    Excision, 69540
  Epididymis
    Excision, 54830
  Esophagus
    Ablation, 43228
    Excision, 43100, 43101
    Removal, 43216
  Excision, 59100
    Bladder, 52224
    Urethra, 52224, 53265
  Eye
    Excision, 65900
  Eyelid
    Destruction, 67850
    Excision
      without Closure, 67840
      Multiple, Different Lids, 67805
      Multiple, Same Lid, 67801
      Single, 67800
      under Anesthesia, 67808
  Facial
    Destruction, 17000-17108, 17280-17286
  Femur
    Excision, 27062
  Finger
    Tendon Sheath, 26160
  Foot
    Excision, 28080, 28090
  Gums
    Destruction, 41850
    Excision, 41822-41828
  Hand
    Tendon Sheath, 26160
  Intestines
    Excision, 44110
  Intestines, Small
    Destruction, 44369
    Excision, 44111
  Iris
    Destruction, 66770
  Larynx
    Excision, 31545-31546
  Leg, Lower
    Tendon Sheath, 27630
  Lymph Node
    Incision and Drainage, 38300, 38305
  Mesentery
    Excision, 44820
  Mouth
    Destruction, 40820
    Excision, 40810-40816, 41116
    Vestibule
      Destruction, 40820
      Repair, 40830

Lesion — continued
  Nasopharynx
    Excision, 61586, 61600
  Nerve
    Excision, 64774-64792
  Nose
    Intranasal
      External Approach, 30118
      Internal Approach, 30117
  Orbit
    Excision, 61333, 67412
  Palate
    Destruction, 42160
    Excision, 42104-42120
  Pancreas
    Excision, 48120
  Pelvis
    Destruction, 58662
  Penis
    Destruction
      Any Method, 54065
      Cryosurgery, 54056
      Electrodesiccation, 54055
      Extensive, 54065
      Laser Surgery, 54057
      Simple, 54050-54060
      Surgical Excision, 54060
    Excision, 54060
      Penile Plaque, 54110-54112
  Pharynx
    Destruction, 42808
    Excision, 42808
  Rectum
    Excision, 45108
  Removal
    Larynx, 31512, 31578
  Resection, 52354
  Retina
    Destruction
      Extensive, 67227, 67228
      Localized, 0017T, 67208, 67210
    Radiation by Implantation of Source, 67218
  Sciatic Nerve
    Excision, 64786
  Sclera
    Excision, 66130
  Skin
    Abrasion, 15786, 15787
    Biopsy, 11100, 11101
    Destruction
      Benign, 17000-17250
      Malignant, 17260-17286
        by Photodynamic Therapy, 96567
      Premalignant, 17000-17004
    Excision
      Benign, 11400-11471
      Malignant, 11600-11646
    Injection, 11900, 11901
    Paring or Curettement, 11055-11057
      Benign Hyperkeratotic, 11055-11057
    Shaving, 11300-11313
  Skin Tags
    Removal, 11200, 11201
  Skull
    Excision, 61500, 61600-61608, 61615, 61616
  Spermatic Cord
    Excision, 55520
  Spinal Cord
    Destruction, 62280-62282
    Excision, 63265-63273
  Stomach
    Excision, 43611
  Testis
    Excision, 54512
  Toe
    Excision, 28092
  Tongue
    Excision, 41110-41114
  Uvula
    Destruction, 42145

Index

Lesion — *continued*
  Uvula — *continued*
    Excision, 42104-42107
  Vagina
    Destruction, 57061, 57065
  Vulva
    Destruction
      Extensive, 56515
      Simple, 56501
  Wrist Tendon
    Excision, 25110
Lesion of Sciatic Nerve
  See Sciatic Nerve, Lesion
Leu 2 Antigens
  See CD8
Leucine Aminopeptidase, 83670
Leukapheresis, 36511
Leukemia Lymphoma Virus I, Adult T Cell
  See HTLV-I
Leukemia Lymphoma Virus I Antibodies, Human T Cell
  See Antibody, HTLV-I
Leukemia Lymphoma Virus II Antibodies, Human T Cell
  See Antibody, HTLV-II
Leukemia Virus II, Hairy Cell Associated, Human T Cell
  See HTLV-II
Leukoagglutinins, 86021
Leukocyte
  See White Blood Cell
  Alkaline Phosphatase, 85540
  Antibody, 86021
  Histamine Release Test, 86343
  Phagocytosis, 86344
  Transfusion, 86950
Leukocyte Count, 85032, 85048, 89055
Leukocyte Histamine Release Test, 86343
Levarterenol
  See Noradrenalin
Levator Muscle Rep
  Blepharoptosis, Repair, 67901-67909
LeVeen Shunt
  Insertion, 49425
  Patency Test, 78291
  Revision, 49426
Levulose
  See Fructose
L Glutamine
  See Glutamine
LGV
  Antibody, 86729
LH (Luteinizing Hormone), 80418, 80426, 83002
LHR (Leukocyte Histamine Release Test), 86343
Liberatory Maneuver, 69710
Lidocaine
  Assay, 80176
Lid Suture
  Blepharoptosis, Repair, 67901-67909
Life Support
  Organ Donor, 01990
Lift, Face
  See Face Lift
Ligament
  See Specific Site
  Collateral
    Repair, Knee with Cruciate Ligament, 27409
  Dentate
    Incision, 63180, 63182
    Section, 63180, 63182
    Injection, 20550
  Release
    Coracoacromial, 23415
    Transverse Carpal, 29848
  Repair
    Elbow, 24343-24346
    Knee Joint, 27405-27409
Ligation
  Appendage
    Dermal, 11200

Ligation — *continued*
  Artery
    Abdomen, 37617
    Carotid, 37600-37606
    Chest, 37616
    Coronary, 33502
    Coronary Artery, 33502
    Ethmoidal, 30915
    Extremity, 37618
    Fistula, 37607
    Maxillary, 30920
    Neck, 37615
    Temporal, 37609
  Bronchus, 31899
  Esophageal Varices, 43204, 43400
  Fallopian Tube
    Oviduct, 58600-58611, 58670
  Gastroesophageal, 43405
  Hemorrhoids, 46221 *[46945, 46946]*
  Oviducts, 59100
  Salivary Duct, 42665
  Shunt
    Aorta
      Pulmonary, 33924
    Peritoneal
      Venous, 49428
  Thoracic Duct, 38380
    Abdominal Approach, 38382
    Thoracic Approach, 38381
  Thyroid Vessels, 37615
  Ureter, 53899
  Vas Deferens, 55450
  Vein
    Clusters, 37785
    Esophagus, 43205, 43244, 43400
    Femoral, 37650
    Gastric, 43244
    Iliac, 37660
    Jugular, Internal, 37565
    Perforator, 37760-37761
    Saphenous, 37700-37735, 37780
    Vena Cava, 37620
Ligature Strangulation
  Skin Tags, 11200, 11201
Light Coagulation
  See Photocoagulation
Light Scattering Measurement
  See Nephelometry
Light Therapy, UV
  See Actinotherapy
Limb
  See Extremity
Limited Lymphadenectomy for Staging
  See Lymphadenectomy, Limited, for Staging
Limited Neck Dissection
  with Thyroidectomy, 60252
Limited Resection Mastectomies
  See Breast, Excision, Lesion
Lindholm Operation
  See Tenoplasty
Lingual Bone
  See Hyoid Bone
Lingual Frenectomy
  See Excision, Tongue, Frenum
Lingual Nerve
  Avulsion, 64740
  Incision, 64740
  Transection, 64740
Lingual Tonsil
  See Tonsils, Lingual
Linton Procedure, 37760
Lip
  Biopsy, 40490
  Excision, 40500-40530
    Frenum, 40819
  Incision
    Frenum, 40806
  Reconstruction, 40525, 40527
  Repair, 40650-40654
    Cleft Lip, 40700-40761
    Fistula, 42260
  Unlisted Services and Procedures, 40799
Lipase, 83690

Lip, Cleft
  See Cleft Lip
Lipectomies, Aspiration
  See Liposuction
Lipectomy
  Excision, 15830-15839
  Suction Assisted, 15876-15879
Lipids
  Feces, 82705, 82710
Lipo–Lutin
  See Progesterone
Lipolysis, Aspiration
  See Liposuction
Lipophosphodiesterase I
  See Tissue Typing
Lipoprotein
  (a), 83695
  Blood, 83695, 83700-83721
  LDL, 83700-83701, 83721
  Phospholipase A2, 83698
Lipoprotein, Alpha
  See Lipoprotein
Lipoprotein, Pre–Beta
  See Lipoprotein, Blood
Liposuction, 15876-15879
Lips
  Skin Graft
    Delay of Flap, 15630
    Full Thickness, 15260, 15261
    Pedicle Flap, 15576
    Tissue Transfer, Adjacent, 14060, 14061
Lisfranc Operation
  Amputation, Foot, 28800, 28805
Listeria Monocytogenes
  Antibody, 86723
Lithium
  Assay, 80178
Litholapaxy, 52317, 52318
Lithotripsy
  with Cystourethroscopy, 52353
  See Extracorporeal Shock Wave Therapy
  Bile Duct Calculi (Stone)
    Endoscopy, 43265
  Bladder, 52353
  Kidney, 50590, 52353
  Pancreatic Duct Calculi (Stone)
    Endoscopy, 43265
  Ureter, 52353
  Urethra, 52353
Lithotrity
  See Litholapaxy
Liver
  See Hepatic Duct
  Ablation
    Tumor, 47380-47382
      Laparoscopic, 47370, 47371
  Abscess
    Aspiration, 47015
    Incision and Drainage
      Closed, 47011
      Open, 47010
      Percutaneous, 47011
    Injection, 47015
  Aspiration, 47015
  Biopsy, 47100
    Anesthesia, 00702
  Cyst
    Aspiration, 47015
    Incision and Drainage
      Open, 47010
      Percutaneous, 47011
    Excision
      Extensive, 47122
      Partial, 47120, 47125, 47130, 47140-47142
      Total, 47133
    Injection, 47015
    Radiologic, 47505
    X-ray, 47500
  Lobectomy, 47125, 47130
    Partial, 47120
  Needle Biopsy, 47000, 47001
  Nuclear Medicine
    Function Study, 78220

Liver — *continued*
  Nuclear Medicine — *continued*
    Imaging, 78201-78216
    Vascular Flow, 78206
  Repair
    Abscess, 47300
    Cyst, 47300
    Wound, 47350-47362
  Suture
    Wound, 47350-47362
  Transplantation, 47135, 47136
    Allograft preparation, 47143-47147
    Anesthesia, 00796, 01990
  Trisegmentectomy, 47122
  Ultrasound Scan (LUSS), 76705
  Unlisted Services and Procedures, 47379, 47399
Living Activities, Daily, 97535, 97537
LKP, 65710
L–Leucylnaphthylamidase, 83670
Lobectomy
  Brain, 61323, 61537-61540
  Contralateral Subtotal
    Thyroid Gland, 60212, 60225
  Liver, 47120-47130
  Lung, 32480-32482
    Sleeve, 32486
  Parotid Gland, 42410, 42415
  Segmental, 32663
  Sleeve, 32486
  Temporal Lobe, 61537, 61538
  Thyroid Gland
    Partial, 60210, 60212
    Total, 60220, 60225
  Total, 32663
Lobotomy
  Frontal, 61490
Local Excision Mastectomies
  See Breast, Excision, Lesion
Local Excision of Lesion or Tissue of Femur
  See Excision, Lesion, Femur
Localization
  Nodule Radiographic, Breast, 77032
  Patient Motion, 0197T
Log Hydrogen Ion Concentration
  See pH
Lombard Test, 92700
Long Acting Thyroid Stimulator
  See Thyrotropin Releasing Hormone (TRH)
Long Chain (C20–C22) Omega-3 Fatty Acids in RBC Membranes, 0111T
Longmire Operation, 47765
Long Term Care Facility Visits
  Annual Assessment, 99318
  Care Plan Oversight Services, 99379-99380
  Discharge Services, 99315-99316
  Inital, 99304-99306
  Subsequent, 99307-99310
Loopogram
  See Urography, Antegrade
Loopscopy, 53899
Loose Body
  Removal
    Ankle, 27620
    Carpometacarpal, 26070
    Elbow, 24101
    Interphalangeal Joint, 28020
      Toe, 28024
    Knee Joint, 27331
    Metatarsophalangeal Joint, 28022
    Tarsometatarsal Joint, 28020
    Toe, 28022
    Wrist, 25101
Lord Procedure
  Anal Sphincter, Dilation, 45905
Lorenz's Operation, 27258
Louis Bar Syndrome, 88248
Low Birth Weight Intensive Care Services, 99478-99480
Low Density Lipoprotein
  See Lipoprotein, LDL

Lower Extremities

Lower Extremities
  See Extremity, Lower
Lower GI Series
  See Barium Enema
Low Frequency Ultrasound, 0183T
Lowsley's Operation, 54380
Low Vision Aids
  Fitting, 92354, 92355
LP, 62270
LRH (Luteinizing Releasing Hormone), 83727
L/S, 83661
LSD (Lysergic Acid Diethylamide), 80100-80103, 80299
L/S Ratio
  Amniotic Fluid, 83661
LTH
  See Prolactin
Lucentis Injection, 67028
Lumbar
  See Spine
Lumbar Plexus
  Decompression, 64714
  Injection, Anesthetic, 64449
  Neuroplasty, 64714
  Release, 64714
  Repair
    Suture, 64862
Lumbar Puncture
  See Spinal Tap
Lumbar Spine Fracture
  See Fracture, Vertebra, Lumbar
Lumbar Sympathectomy
  See Sympathectomy, Lumbar
Lumbar Vertebra
  See Vertebra, Lumbar
Lumen Dilation, 74360
Lumpectomy, 19301-19302
Lunate
  Arthroplasty
    with Implant, 25444
  Dislocation
    Closed Treatment, 25690
    Open Treatment, 25695
Lung
  Ablation, 32998
  Abscess
    Incision and Drainage
      Open, 32200
      Percutaneous Drainage, 32200, 32201
  Angiography
    Injection, 93541
  Aspiration, 32420
  Biopsy, 32095, 32100
  Bullae
    Excision, 32141
      Endoscopic, 32655
  Cyst
    Incision and Drainage
      Open, 32200
      Percutaneous, 32201
    Removal, 32140
  Decortication
    with Parietal Pleurectomy, 32320
    Endoscopic, 32651, 32652
    Partial, 32225
    Total, 32220
  Empyema
    Excision, 32540
  Excision
    Bronchus Resection, 32486
    Completion, 32488
    Donor, 33930
      Heart Lung, 33930
      Lung, 32850
    Emphysematous, 32491
    Empyema, 32540
    Lobe, 32480, 32482
    Segment, 32484
    Total, 32440-32445
    Tumor, 32503-32504
    Wedge Resection, 32500
      Endoscopic, 32657
  Foreign Body
    Removal, 32151

Lung — continued
  Hemorrhage, 32110
  Injection
    Radiologic, 93541
  Lavage
    Bronchial, 31624
    Total, 32997
  Lysis
    Adhesions, 32124
  Needle Biopsy, 32405
  Nuclear Medicine
    Imaging, Perfusion, 78580-78585
    Imaging, Ventilation, 78586-78594
    Unlisted Services and Procedures, 78599
  Pneumocentesis, 32420
  Pneumolysis, 32940
  Pneumothorax, 32960
  Puncture, 32420
  Removal
    Bronchoplasty, 32501
    Completion Pneumonectomy, 32488
    Extrapleural, 32445
    Single Lobe, 32480
    Single Segment, 32484
    Sleeve Lobectomy, 32486
    Sleeve Pneumonectomy, 32442
    Total Pneumonectomy, 32440-32445
    Two Lobes, 32482
    Volume Reduction, 32491
    Wedge Resection, 32500
  Repair
    Hernia, 32800
  Segmentectomy, 32484
  Tear
    Repair, 32110
  Thoracotomy, 32110-32160
    with Excision–Plication of Bullae, 32141
    with Open Intrapleural Pneumonolysis, 32124
    Biopsy, 32095, 32100
    Cardiac Massage, 32160
    for Post–Operative Complications, 32120
    Removal
      Bullae, 32141
      Cyst, 32140
      Intrapleural Foreign Body, 32150
      Intrapulmonary Foreign Body, 32151
    Repair, 32110
  Transplantation, 32851-32854, 33935
    Allograft Preparation, 32855-32856, 33933
    Donor Pneumonectomy
      Heart–Lung, 33930
      Lung, 32850
  Tumor
    Removal, 32503-32504
  Unlisted Services and Procedures, 32999
  Volume Reduction
    Emphysematous, 32491
Lung Function Tests
  See Pulmonology, Diagnostic
Lupus Anticoagulant Assay, 85705
Lupus Band Test
  Immunofluorescent Study, 88346, 88347
Luschke Procedure, 45120
LUSCS, 59514-59515, 59618, 59620, 59622
LUSS (Liver Ultrasound Scan), 76705
Luteinizing Hormone (LH), 80418, 80426, 83002
Luteinizing Release Factor, 83727
Luteotropic Hormone, 80418, 80440, 84146
Luteotropin, 80418, 80440, 84146
Luteotropin Placental, 83632

Lutrepulse Injection, 11980
LVRS, 32491
Lyme Disease, 86617, 86618
Lyme Disease ab, 86617
Lyme Disease Vaccine, 90665
Lymphadenectomy
  Abdominal, 38747
  Bilateral Inguinofemoral, 54130, 56632, 56637
  Bilateral Pelvic, 51575, 51585, 51595, 54135, 55845, 55865
  Total, 38571, 38572, 57531, 58210
  Diaphragmatic Assessment, 58960
  Gastric, 38747
  Inguinofemoral, 38760, 38765
  Inguinofemoral, Iliac and Pelvic, 56640
  Injection
    Sentinel Node, 38792
  Limited, for Staging
    Para–Aortic, 38562
    Pelvic, 38562
    Retroperitoneal, 38564
  Limited Para–Aortic, Resection of Ovarian Malignancy, 58951
  Limited Pelvic, 55852, 55862, 58954
  Malignancy, 58951, 58954
  Mediastinal, 21632
  Para-Aortic, 58958
  Pelvic, 58958
  Peripancreatic, 38747
  Portal, 38747
  Radical
    Axillary, 38740, 38745
    Cervical, 38720, 38724
    Groin Area, 38760, 38765
    Pelvic, 54135, 55845, 58548
    Suprahyoid, 38700
  Regional, 50230
  Retroperitoneal Transabdominal, 38780
  Thoracic, 38746
  Unilateral Inguinofemoral, 56631, 56634
Lymphadenitis
  Incision and Drainage, 38300, 38305
Lymphadenopathy Associated Antibodies
  See Antibody, HIV
Lymphadenopathy Associated Virus
  See HIV
Lymphangiogram, Abdominal
  See Lymphangiography, Abdomen
Lymphangiography
  Abdomen, 75805, 75807
  Arm, 75801, 75803
  Injection, 38790
  Leg, 75801, 75803
  Pelvis, 75805, 75807
Lymphangioma, Cystic
  See Hygroma
Lymphangiotomy, 38308
Lymphatic Channels
  Incision, 38308
Lymphatic Cyst
  Drainage
    Laparoscopic, 49323
    Open, 49062
Lymphatic System
  Anesthesia, 00320
  Unlisted Procedure, 38999
Lymph Duct
  Injection, 38790
Lymph Node(s)
  Abscess
    Incision and Drainage, 38300, 38305
  Biopsy, 38500, 38510-38530, 38570
    Needle, 38505
  Dissection, 38542
  Excision, 38500, 38510-38530
    Abdominal, 38747
    Inguinofemoral, 38760, 38765
    Laparoscopic, 38571, 38572

Lymph Node(s) — continued
  Excision — continued
    Limited, for Staging
      Para–Aortic, 38562
      Pelvic, 38562
      Retroperitoneal, 38564
    Pelvic, 38770
    Radical
      Axillary, 38740, 38745
      Cervical, 38720, 38724
      Suprahyoid, 38720, 38724
      Retroperitoneal Transabdominal, 38780
    Thoracic, 38746
  Exploration, 38542
  Hygroma, Cystic
    Axillary
    Cervical
      Excision, 38550, 38555
  Nuclear Medicine
    Imaging, 78195
  Removal
    Abdominal, 38747
    Inguinofemoral, 38760, 38765
    Pelvic, 38747, 38770
    Retroperitoneal Transabdominal, 38780
    Thoracic, 38746
Lymphoblast Transformation
  See Blastogenesis
Lymphocele
  Drainage
    Laparoscopic, 49323
  Extraperitoneal
    Open Drainage, 49062
Lymphocyte
  Culture, 86821, 86822
  Toxicity Assay, 86805, 86806
  Transformation, 86353
Lymphocytes, CD4
  See CD4
Lymphocytes, CD8
  See CD8
Lymphocyte, Thymus–Dependent
  See T-Cells
Lymphocytic Choriomeningitis
  Antibody, 86727
Lymphocytotoxicity, 86805, 86806
Lymphogranuloma Venereum
  Antibody, 86729
Lymphoma Virus, Burkitt
  See Epstein–Barr Virus
Lymph Vessels
  Imaging
    Lymphangiography
      Abdomen, 75805-75807
      Arm, 75801-75803
      Leg, 75801-75803
      Pelvis, 75805-75807
    Nuclear Medicine, 78195
  Incision, 38308
Lynch Procedure, 31075
Lysergic Acid Diethylamide, 80102, 80103, 80299
Lysergide, 80102-80103, 80299
Lysis
  Adhesions
    Bladder
      Intraluminal, 53899
    Corneovitreal, 65880
    Epidural, 62263, 62264
    Fallopian Tube, 58740
    Foreskin, 54450
    Intestinal, 44005
    Labial, 56441
    Lung, 32124
    Nose, 30560
    Ovary, 58740
    Oviduct, 58740
    Penile
      Post–circumcision, 54162
    Spermatic Cord, 54699, 55899
    Tongue, 41599
    Ureter, 50715-50725
      Intraluminal, 53899
    Urethra, 53500

Lysis — *continued*
  Adhesions — *continued*
    Uterus, 58559
    Euglobulin, 85360
    Eye
      Goniosynechiae, 65865
      Synechiae
        Anterior, 65870
        Posterior, 65875
    Labial
      Adhesions, 56441
    Nose
      Intranasal Synechia, 30560
    Transurethral
      Adhesions, 53899
Lysozyme, 85549

M

MacEwen Operation
  Hernia Repair, Inguinal, 49495-49500, 49505
    Incarcerated, 49496, 49501, 49507, 49521
    Laparoscopic, 49650, 49651
    Recurrent, 49520
    Sliding, 49525
Machado Test
  Complement, Fixation Test, 86171
MacLean–De Wesselow Test
  Clearance, Urea Nitrogen, 84540, 84545
Macrodactylia
  Repair, 26590
Macrosopic examination and tissue preparation, 88387
  intraoperative, 88388
Maculopathy, 67208-67218
Madlener Operation, 58600
Magnesium, 83735
Magnetic Resonance Angiography (MRA)
  Abdomen, 74185
  Arm, 73225
  Chest, 71555
  Head, 70544-70546
  Leg, 73725
  Neck, 70547-70549
  Pelvis, 72198
  Spine, 72159
Magnetic Resonance Spectroscopy, 76390
Magnetic Stimulation
  Transcranial, 0160T-0161T
Magnetoencephalography (MEG), 95965-95967
Magnet Operation
  Eye, Removal of Foreign Body
    Conjunctival Embedded, 65210
    Conjunctival Superficial, 65205
    Corneal without Slit Lamp, 65220
    Corneal with Slit Lamp, 65222
    Intraocular, 65235-65265
Magnuson Procedure, 23450
MAGPI Operation, 54322
Magpi Procedure, 54322
Major Vestibular Gland
  See Bartholin's Gland
Malar Area
  Augmentation, 21270
  Bone Graft, 21210
  Fracture
    with Bone Grafting, 21366
    with Manipulation, 21355
    Open Treatment, 21360-21366
  Reconstruction, 21270
Malar Bone
  See Cheekbone
Malaria Antibody, 86750
Malaria Smear, 87207
Malate Dehydrogenase, 83775
Maldescent, Testis
  See Testis, Undescended
Male Circumcision
  See Circumcision
Malformation, Arteriovenous
  See Arteriovenous Malformation

Malic Dehydrogenase
  See Malate Dehydrogenase
Malignant Hyperthermia Susceptibility
  Caffeine Halothane Contracture Test (CHCT), 89049
Malleolus
  See Ankle; Fibula; Leg, Lower; Tibia; Tibiofibular Joint
  Metatarsophalangeal Joint, 27889
Mallet Finger Repair, 26432
Mallory–Weiss Procedure, 43502
Maltose
  Tolerance Test, 82951, 82952
Malunion Repair
  Femur
    with Graft, 27472
    without Graft, 27470
  Metatarsal, 28322
  Tarsal Joint, 28320
Mammalian Oviduct
  See Fallopian Tube
Mammaplasties
  See Breast, Reconstruction
Mammaplasty, 19318-19325
Mammary Abscess, 19020
Mammary Arteries
  See Artery, Mammary
Mammary Duct
  X-ray with Contrast, 77053, 77054
Mammary Ductogram
  Injection, 19030
  Radiologic Supervision and Interpretation, 77053-77054
Mammary Node
  Dissection
    Anesthesia, 00406
Mammary Stimulating Hormone, 80418, 80440, 84146
Mammilliplasty, 19350
Mammogram
  with Computer-Aided Detection, 77051-77052
  Breast
    Localization Nodule, 77032
  Magnetic Resonance Imaging (MRI)
    with Computer-aided Detection, 0159T
  Screening, 77057
Mammography
  with Computer-Aided Detection, 77051-77052
  Assessment, 3340F-3350F
  Diagnostic, 77055, 77056
    with Computer-aided Detection, 77051
  Magnetic Resonance Imaging (MRI)
    with Computer-Aided Detection, 0159T
  Screening, 77057
    with Computer-aided Detection, 77052
Mammoplasty
  Anesthesia, 00402
  Augmentation, 19324, 19325
  Reduction, 19318
Mammotomy
  See Mastotomy
Mammotropic Hormone, Pituitary, 80418, 80440, 84146
Mammotropic Hormone, Placental, 83632
Mammotropin, 80418, 80440, 84146
Manchester Colporrhaphy, 58400
Mandated Services
  Hospital, on call, 99026, 99027
Mandible
  See Facial Bones; Maxilla; Temporomandibular Joint (TMJ)
  Abscess
    Excision, 21025
  Bone Graft, 21215
  Cyst
    Excision, 21040, 21046, 21047
  Dysostosis Repair, 21150-21151

Mandible — *continued*
  Fracture
    Closed Treatment
      with Interdental Fixation, 21453
      with Manipulation, 21451
      without Manipulation, 21450
    Open Treatment, 21454-21470
      with Interdental Fixation, 21462
      without Interdental Fixation, 21461
      External Fixation, 21454
    Percutaneous Treatment, 21452
  Osteotomy, 21198, 21199
  Reconstruction
    with Implant, 21244-21246, 21248, 21249
  Removal
    Foreign Body, 41806
  Torus Mandibularis
    Excision, 21031
  Tumor
    Excision, 21040-21047
  X-ray, 70100, 70110
Mandibular Body
  Augmentation
    with Bone Graft, 21127
    with Prosthesis, 21125
Mandibular Condyle
  Fracture
    Open Treatment, 21465, 21470
  Reconstruction, 21247
Mandibular Condylectomy
  See Condylectomy
Mandibular Fracture
  See Fracture, Mandible
Mandibular Rami
  Reconstruction
    with Bone Graft, 21194
    with Internal Rigid Fixation, 21196
    without Bone Graft, 21193
    without Internal Rigid Fixation, 21195
Mandibular Resection Prosthesis, 21081
Mandibular Staple Bone Plate
  Reconstruction
    Mandible, 21244
Manganese, 83785
Manipulation
  Chest Wall, 94667, 94668
  Chiropractic, 98940-98943
  Dislocation and/or Fracture
    Acetabulum, 27222
    Acromioclavicular, 23545
    Ankle, 27810, 27818, 27860
    Carpometacarpal, 26670-26676
    Chest Wall, 94667, 94668
    Clavicle, 23505
    Elbow, 24300, 24640
    Epicondyle, 24565
    Femoral, 27232, 27502, 27510, 27517
      Petrochanteric, 27240
    Fibula, 27781, 27788
    Finger, 26725, 26727, 26742, 26755
    Greater Tuberosity
      Humeral, 23625
    Hand, 26670-26676
    Heel, 28405, 28406
    Hip, 27257
    Hip Socket, 27222
    Humeral, 23605, 24505, 24535, 24577
      Epicondyle, 24565
    Intercarpal, 25660
    Interphalangeal Joint, 26340, 26770-26776
    Lunate, 25690
    Malar Area, 21355
    Mandibular, 21451
    Metacarpal, 26605, 26607

Manipulation — *continued*
  Dislocation and/or Fracture — *continued*
    Metacarpophalangeal, 26700-26706, 26742
    Metacarpophalangeal Joint, 26340
    Metatarsal Fracture, 28475, 28476
    Nasal Bone, 21315, 21320
    Orbit, 21401
    Phalangeal Shaft, 26727
      Distal, Finger or Thumb, 26755
    Phalanges, Finger/Thumb, 26725
    Phalanges
      Finger, 26742, 26755, 26770-26776
      Finger/Thumb, 26727
      Great Toe, 28495, 28496
      Toes, 28515
    Radial, 24655, 25565
    Radial Shaft, 25505
    Radiocarpal, 25660
    Radioulnar, 25675
    Scapula, 23575
    Shoulder, 23650, 23655
      with Greater Tuberosity, 23665
      with Surgical or Anatomical Neck, 23675
    Sternoclavicular, 23525
      with Surgical or Anatomical Neck, 23675
    Talus, 28435, 28436
    Tarsal, 28455, 28456
    Thumb, 26641-26650
    Tibial, 27532, 27752
    Trans–Scaphoperilunar, 25680
    Ulnar, 24675, 25535, 25565
    Vertebral, 22315
    Wrist, 25259, 25624, 25635, 25660, 25675, 25680, 25690
  Foreskin, 54450
  Globe, 92018, 92019
  Hip, 27275
  Interphalangeal Joint, Proximal, 26742
  Knee, 27570
  Osteopathic, 98925-98929
  Physical Therapy, 97140
  Shoulder
    Application of Fixation Apparatus, 23700
  Spine
    Anesthesia, 22505
  Stoma, 44799
  Temporomandibular Joint (TMJ), 21073
  Tibial, Distal, 27762
Manometric Studies
  Kidney
    Pressure, 50396
  Rectum
    Anus, 91122
  Ureter
    Pressure, 50686
  Ureterostomy, 50686
Manometry
  Esophageal, 43499
  Esophagogastric, 91020
  Rectum
    Anus, 90911
Mantoux Test
  Skin Test, 86580
Manual Therapy, 97140
Maquet Procedure, 27418
Marcellation Operation
  Hysterectomy, Vaginal, 58260-58270, 58550
Marrow, Bone
  Aspiration, 38220
  Harvesting, 38230

Marrow, Bone

Marrow, Bone — *continued*
  Magnetic Resonance Imaging (MRI), 77084
  Needle Biopsy, 38221
  Nuclear Medicine Imaging, 78102-78104
  Smear, 85097
  T-Cell Transplantation, 38240-38242
Marshall–Marchetti–Krantz Procedure, 51840, 51841, 58152, 58267, 58293
Marsupialization
  Bartholin's Gland Cyst, 56440
  Cyst
    Acne, 10040
    Bartholin's Gland, 56440
    Laryngeal, 31599
    Splenic, 38999
    Sublingual Salivary, 42409
  Lesion
    Kidney, 53899
  Liver
    Cyst or Abscess, 47300
  Pancreatic Cyst, 48500
  Skin, 10040
  Urethral Diverticulum, 53240
Mass
  Kidney
    Ablation, 50542
    Cryosurgery, 50250
Massage
  Cardiac, 32160
  Therapy, 97124
  See Physical Medicine/Therapy/Occupational Therapy
Masseter Muscle/Bone
  Reduction, 21295, 21296
Mass Spectrometry and Tandem Mass Spectrometry
  Analyte
    Qualitative, 83788
    Quantitative, 83789
Mastectomy
  Gynecomastia, 19300
  Modified Radical, 19307
  Partial, 19301-19302
  Radical, 19305-19306
  Simple, Complete, 19303
  Subcutaneous, 19304
Mastectomy, Halsted
  See Mastectomy, Radical
Masters' 2–Step Stress Test, 93799
Mastoid
  Excision
    Complete, 69502
    Radical, 69511
      Modified, 69505
      Petrous Apicectomy, 69530
      Simple, 69501
      Total, 69502
  Obliteration, 69670
  Repair
    with Apicectomy, 69605
    with Tympanoplasty, 69604
    by Excision, 69601-69603
    Fistula, 69700
Mastoid Cavity
  Debridement, 69220, 69222
Mastoidectomy
  with Apicectomy, 69605
  with Labyrinthectomy, 69910
  with Labyrinthotomy, 69802
  with Petrous Apicectomy, 69530
  with Skull Base Surgery, 61590, 61597
    Decompression, 61595
    Facial Nerve, 61595
  with Tympanoplasty, 69604, 69641-69646
    Ossicular Chain Reconstruction, 69636
    and Synthetic Prosthesis, 69636
  Cochlear Device Implantation, 69930
  Complete, 69502
  Revision, 69601-69605

Mastoidectomy — *continued*
  Osseointegrated Implant
    for External Speech Processor/Cochlear Stimulator, 69715, 69718
  Ossicular Chain Reconstruction, 69605
  Radical, 69511
    Modified, 69505
    Revision, 69602, 69603
  Revision, 69601
  Simple, 69501
Mastoidotomy, 69635-69637
  with Tympanoplasty, 69635
    Ossicular Chain Reconstruction, 69636
    and Synthetic Prosthesis, 69637
Mastoids
  Polytomography, 76101, 76102
  X-ray, 70120, 70130
Mastopexy, 19316
Mastotomy, 19020
Maternity Care and Delivery, 0500F-0502F, 0503F, 59400-59898
  See also Abortion, Cesarean Delivery, Ectopic Pregnancy, Vaginal Delivery
Maxilla
  See Facial Bones; Mandible
  Bone Graft, 21210
  CT Scan, 70486-70488
  Cyst, Excision, 21048, 21049
  Excision, 21030, 21032-21034
  Fracture
    with Fixation, 21345-21347
    Closed Treatment, 21345, 21421
    Open Treatment, 21346-21348, 21422, 21423
  Osteotomy, 21206
  Reconstruction
    with Implant, 21245, 21246, 21248, 21249
  Tumor
    Excision, 21048-21049
Maxillary Arteries
  See Artery, Maxillary
Maxillary Sinus
  See Sinus, Maxillary
Maxillary Torus Palatinus
  Tumor Excision, 21032
Maxillectomy, 31225, 31230
Maxillofacial Fixation
  Application
    Halo Type Appliance, 21100
Maxillofacial Impressions
  Auricular Prosthesis, 21086
  Definitive Obturator Prosthesis, 21080
  Facial Prosthesis, 21088
  Interim Obturator Prosthesis, 21079
  Mandibular Resection Prosthesis, 21081
  Nasal Prosthesis, 21087
  Oral Surgical Splint, 21085
  Orbital Prosthesis, 21077
  Palatal Augmentation Prosthesis, 21082
  Palatal Lift Prosthesis, 21083
  Speech Aid Prosthesis, 21084
  Surgical Obturator Prosthesis, 21076
Maxillofacial Procedures
  Unlisted Services and Procedures, 21299
Maxillofacial Prosthetics, 21076-21088
  Unlisted Services and Procedures, 21089
Maydl Operation, 45563, 50810
Mayo Hernia Repair, 49580-49587
Mayo Operation
  Varicose Vein Removal, 37700-37735, 37780, 37785
Mayo Procedure, 28292
Maze Procedure, 33254-33259, 33265-33266
MBC, 87181-87190

McBride Procedure, 28292
McBurney Operation
  Hernia Repair, Inguinal, 49495-49500, 49505
    Incarcerated, 49496, 49501, 49507, 49521
    Recurrent, 49520
    Sliding, 49525
McCall Culdoplasty, 57283
McCannel Procedure, 66682
McCauley Procedure, 28240
McDonald Operation, 57700
McKissock Surgery, 19318
McIndoe Procedure, 57291
McVay Operation
  Hernia Repair, Inguinal, 49495-49500, 49505
    Incarcerated, 49496, 49501, 49507, 49521
    Laparoscopic, 49650, 49651
    Recurrent, 49520
    Sliding, 49525
MEA (Microwave Endometrial Ablation, 58563
Measles, German
  Antibody, 86756
  Vaccine, 90706-90710
Measles Immunization, 90705, 90707-90708, 90710
Measles, Mumps, Rubella Vaccine, 90707
Measles Uncomplicated
  Antibody, 86765
  Antigen Detection, 87283
Measles Vaccine, 90702, 90705, 90708, 90710
Measurement
  Ocular Blood Flow, 0198T
  Spirometric Forced Expiratory Flow, 94011-94012
Meat Fibers
  Feces, 89160
Meatoplasty, 69310
Meatotomy, 53020-53025
  Contact Laser Vaporization with/without Transurethral Resection of Prostate, 52648
    with Cystourethroscopy, 52281
  Infant, 53025
  Non–Contact Laser Coagulation Prostate, 52647
  Prostate
    Laser Coagulation, 52647
    Laser Vaporization, 52648
    Transurethral Electrosurgical Resection Prostate, 52601
  Ureter, 52290
  Urethral
    Cystourethroscopy, 52290-52305
Meckel's Diverticulum
  Excision, 44800
  Unlisted Services and Procedures, 44899
Median Nerve
  Decompression, 64721
  Neuroplasty, 64721
  Release, 64721
  Repair
    Suture
      Motor, 64835
    Transposition, 64721
Median Nerve Compression
  Decompression, 64721
  Endoscopy, 29848
  Injection, 20526
Mediastinal Cyst, 32662, 39200
Mediastinoscopy, 39400
Mediastinotomy
  Cervical Approach, 39000
  Transthoracic Approach, 39010
Mediastinum
  See Chest; Thorax
  Cyst
    Excision, 32662, 39200

Mediastinum — *continued*
  Endoscopy
    Biopsy, 39400
    Exploration, 39400
  Exploration, 39000, 39010
  Incision and Drainage, 39000, 39010
  Needle Biopsy, 32405
  Removal
    Foreign Body, 39000, 39010
  Tumor
    Excision, 32662, 39220
  Unlisted Procedures, 39499
Medical Disability Evaluation Services, 99455, 99456
Medical Genetics
  Counseling, 96040
Medical Nutrition Therapy, 97802-97804
Medical Team Conference, 99366-99368
Medical Testimony, 99075
Medication Therapy Management
  By a Pharmacist
    Initial Encounter, 99605-99606
    Subsequent Encounter, 99607
    Each Additional 15 Minutes, 99607
Medicine, Preventive
  See Preventive Medicine
Medicine, Pulmonary
  See Pulmonology
Medulla
  Tractotomy, 61470
Medullary Tract
  Incision, 61470
  Section, 61470
MEG (Magnetoencephalography), 95965-95967
Meibomian Cyst
  Excision, 67805
  Multiple
    Different Lids, 67805
    Same Lid, 67801
  Single, 67800
  Under Anesthesia, 67808
Membrane, Mucous
  See Mucosa
Membrane Oxygenation, Extracorporeal
  Cannulization, 36822
Membrane, Tympanic
  See Ear, Drum
Menactra, 90734
Meninges
  Tumor
    Excision, 61512, 61519
Meningioma
  Excision, 61512, 61519
  Tumor
    Excision, 61512, 61519
Meningitis, Lymphocytic Benign
  Antibody, 86727
Meningocele Repair, 63700, 63702
Meningococcal Vaccine
  Conjugate, serogroups A, C, Y, W-135, 90734
  Polysaccharide, any groups, 90733
Meningococcus, 86741
Meningomyelocele
  Repair, 63704-63706
Meniscal Temporal Lobectomy, 61566
Meniscectomy
  Knee Joint, 27332, 27333
  Temporomandibular Joint, 21060
Meniscus
  Knee
    Excision, 27332, 27333
    Repair, 27403
    Transplantation, 29868
Menomune, 90733
Mental Nerve
  Avulsion, 64736
  Incision, 64736
  Transection, 64736
Meprobamate, 83805
Mercury, 83015, 83825

Index

Merskey Test
  Fibrin Degradation Products, 85362-85379
MERUVAX, 90706
Mesencephalic Tract
  Incision, 61480
  Section, 61480
Mesencephalon
  Tractotomy, 61480
Mesenteric Arteries
  See Artery, Mesenteric
Mesentery
  Lesion
    Excision, 44820
  Repair, 44850
  Suture, 44850
  Unlisted Services and Procedures, 44899
Mesh
  Implantation
    Hernia, 49568
  Insertion
    Pelvic Floor, 57267
  Removal
    Abdominal Infected, 11008
Mesh Implantation
  Closure of Necrotizing Soft Tissue Infection, 49568
  Incisional or Ventral Hernia, 49568
  Vagina, 57267
Metabisulfite Test
  Red Blood Cell, Sickling, 85660
Metabolic Panel
  Calcium Ionized, 80047
  Calcium Total, 80048
  Comprehensive, 80053
Metabolite, 82520
  Thromboxane, 84431
Metacarpal
  Amputation, 26910
  Craterization, 26230
  Cyst
    Excision, 26200, 26205
  Diaphysectomy, 26230
  Excision, 26230
    Radical for Tumor, 26250
  Fracture
    with Manipulation, 26605, 26607
    without Manipulation, 26600
    Closed Treatment, 26605
      with Fixation, 26607
    Open Treatment, 26615
    Percutaneous Fixation, 26608
  Ostectomy
    Radical
      for Tumor, 26250
  Repair
    Lengthening, 26568
    Nonunion, 26546
    Osteotomy, 26565
    Saucerization, 26230
  Tumor
    Excision, 26200, 26205
Metacarpophalangeal Joint
  Arthrodesis, 26850, 26852
  Arthroplasty, 26530, 26531
  Arthroscopy
    Diagnostic, 29900
    Surgical, 29901, 29902
  Arthrotomy, 26075
  Biopsy
    Synovium, 26105
  Capsule
    Excision, 26520
    Incision, 26520
  Capsulodesis, 26516-26518
  Dislocation
    with Manipulation, 26340
    Closed Treatment, 26700
    Open Treatment, 26715
    Percutaneous Fixation, 26705, 26706
  Exploration, 26075
  Fracture
    with Manipulation, 26742
    Closed Treatment, 26740

Metacarpophalangeal Joint — *continued*
  Fracture — *continued*
    Open Treatment, 26746
  Fusion, 26516-26518, 26850, 26852
  Removal of Foreign Body, 26075
  Repair
    Collateral Ligament, 26540-26542
  Synovectomy, 26135
Metadrenaline, 83835
Metals, Heavy, 83015, 83018
Metamfetamine, 82145
Metanephrine, 83835
Metatarsal
  See Foot
  Amputation, 28810
  Condyle
    Excision, 28288
  Craterization, 28122
  Cyst
    Excision, 28104-28107
  Diaphysectomy, 28122
  Excision, 28110-28114, 28122, 28140
  Fracture
    Closed Treatment
      with Manipulation, 28475, 28476
      without Manipulation, 28470
    Open Treatment, 28485
    Percutaneous Fixation, 28476
  Free Osteocutaneous Flap with Microvascular Anastomosis, 20972
  Repair, 28322
    Lengthening, 28306, 28307
    Osteotomy, 28306-28309
    Saucerization, 28122
  Tumor
    Excision, 28104-28107, 28173
Metatarsectomy, 28140
Metatarsophalangeal Joint
  Arthrotomy, 28022, 28052
  Cheilectomy, 28289
  Dislocation, 28630, 28635, 28645
    Open Treatment, 28645
    Percutaneous Fixation, 28636
  Exploration, 28022
  Great Toe
    Arthrodesis, 28750
    Fusion, 28750
  Release, 28289
  Removal
    of Foreign Body, 28022
    of Loose Body, 28022
  Repair
    Hallux Rigidus, 28289
  Synovial
    Biopsy, 28052
    Excision, 28072
  Toe, 28270
Methadone, 83840
Methaemoglobin, 83045-83050
Methamphetamine
  Blood or Urine, 82145
Methanol, 84600
Methbipyranone, 80436
Methemalbumin, 83857
Methemoglobin, 83045, 83050, 88741
Methenamine Silver Stain, 88312
Methopyrapone, 80436
Methoxyhydroxymandelic Acid, 84585
Methsuximide, 83858
Methyl Alcohol, 84600
Methylamphetamine, 82145
Methylene Bichloride, 84600
Methylfluorprednisolone, 80420
Methylmorphine
  See Codeine
Metroplasty, 58540
Metyrapone, 80436
Mg, 83735
MIC (Minimum Inhibitory Concentration), 87186
Microalbumin
  Urine, 82043, 82044

Microbiology, 87001-87999
Microdissection, 88380-88381
Microfluorometries, Flow, 88182-88189
  Diagnostic/Pretreatment, 3170F
Microglobulin, Beta 2
  Blood, 82232
  Urine, 82232
Micrographic Surgery
  Mohs Technique, 17311-17315
Micro-Ophthalmia
  Orbit Reconstruction, 21256
Micropigmentation
  Correction, 11920-11922
Micro-Remodeling Female Bladder, 0193T
Microscope, Surgical
  See Operating Microscope
Microscopic Evaluation
  Hair, 96902
Microscopies, Electron
  See Electron Microscopy
Microscopy
  Ear Exam, 92504
Microsomal Antibody, 86376
Microsomia, Hemifacial
  See Hemifacial Microsomia
Microsurgery
  Operating Microscope, 69990
Microvascular Anastomosis
  Bone Graft
    Fibula, 20955
    Other, 20962
  Facial Flap, Free, 15758
  Muscle Flap, Free, 15756
  Osteocutaneous Flap with, 20969-20973
  Skin Flap, Free, 15757
Microvite A, 84590
Microvolt T-Wave Altemans, 93025
Microwave Therapy, 97024
  See Physical Medicine/Therapy/Occupational Therapy
Midbrain
  See Brain; Brainstem; Mesencephalon; Skull Base Surgery
Midcarpal Mediooccipital Joint
  Arthrotomy, 25040
Middle Cerebral artery Velocimetry, 76821
Middle Ear
  See Ear, Middle
Midface
  Reconstruction
    with Bone Graft, 21145-21159, 21188
    without Bone Graft, 21141-21143
    Forehead Advancement, 21159, 21160
MIF (Migration Inhibitory Factor), 86378
Migration Inhibitory Factor (MIF), 86378
Mile Operation, 44155, 44156
Milia, Multiple
  Removal, 10040
Miller–Abbott Intubation, 44500, 44340
Miller Procedure, 28737
Millin-Read Operation, 57288
Minerva Cast, 29040
  Removal, 29710
Minimum Inhibitory Concentration, 87186
Minimum Lethal Concentration, 87187
Minnesota Multiple Personality Inventory, 96101-96103
Miscarriage
  Incomplete Abortion, 59812
  Missed Abortion
    First Trimester, 59820
    Second Trimester, 59821
  Septic Abortion, 59830
Missed Abortion
  First Trimester, 59820

Missed Abortion — *continued*
  Second Trimester, 59821
Mitchell Procedure, 28296
Mitochondrial Antibody, 86255, 86256
Mitogen Blastogenesis, 86353
Mitral Valve
  Incision, 33420, 33422
  Repair, 33420-33427
    Incision, 33420, 33422
  Replacement, 33430
Mitrofanoff Operation, 50845
Miyagawanella
  See Chlamydia
  Antibody, 86631-86632
  Antigen Detection
    Direct Fluorescence, 87270
    Enzyme Immunoassay, 87320
  Culture, 87110
MLB Test, 92562
MLC, 86821
MMK, 51841
MMPI, 96101-96103
  Computer Assisted, 96103
MMRV, 90710
MMR Vaccine, 90707
Mobilization
  Splenic Flexure, 44139
    Laparoscopic, 44213
  Stapes, 69650
Moderate Sedation, 99143-99150
Modified Radical Mastectomy, 19307
Mohs Micrographic Surgery, 17311-17315
Molar Pregnancy
  Evacuation and Curettage, 59870
  Excision, 59100
Mold
  Culture, 87107
Mole, Carneous
  See Abortion
Molecular Cytogenetics, 88271-88275
  Interpretation and Report, 88291
Molecular Diagnostics, 83890-83914
  Amplification, 83898-83901, 83908
  Cell Lysis, 83907
  Dot/Slot Procedure, 83893
  Enzymatic Digestion, 83892
  Extraction, 83890, 83891
  Interpretation, 83912
  Lysis of Cells, 83907
  Molecular Isolation (Extraction), 83890
  Mutation Identification, 83904-83906
    Enzymatic Ligation, 83914
  Mutation Scanning, 83903
  Nucleic Acid Amplification, 83900-83901, 83908
  Nucleic Acid Extraction, 83907
  Nucleic Acid Probe, 83896
  Nucleic Acid Transfer, 83897
  Polymerase Reaction Chain, 83898
  Reverse Transcription, 83902
  RNA Stabilization, 83913
  Separation, 83894, 83909
  Signal Amplification, 83908
Molecular Oxygen Saturation, 82805-82810
Mole, Hydatid
  Evacuation and Curettage, 59870
  Excision, 59100
Molluscum Contagiosum Destruction
  Penis, 54050-54060
  Skin, 17110-17111
  Vulva, 56501-56515
Molteno Procedure, 66180
Molteno Valve
  Insertion, 66180
  Removal, 67120
  Revision, 66185
Monilia
  Antibody, 86628
  Skin Test, 86485
Monitoring
  Blood Pressure, 24 hour, 93784-93790

Monitoring — continued

Monitoring — continued
  Electrocardiogram
    Transmission, 93012-93014
    Wearable, 93224-93272
  Electroencephalogram, 95812,
      95813, 95950-95953, 95956
    with Drug Activation, 95954
    with Physical Activation, 95954
    with WADA Activation, 95958
  Fetal
    During Labor, 59050, 59051,
      99500
    Interpretation Only, 59051
  Glucose
    Interstitial Fluid, 95250-95251
  Interstitial Fluid Pressure, 20950
  Intraocular Pressure, 0173T
  Pediatric Apnea, 94774-94777
  Prolonged, with Physician Attendance, 99354-99360
  Seizure, 61531, 61760
Monitoring, Sleep, 95808-95811
Monoethylene Glycol, 82693
Mononuclear Cell Antigen
  Quantitative, 86356
Mononucleosis Virus, Infectious, 86663-86665
Monophosphate, Adenosine, 82030
Monophosphate, Adenosine Cyclic, 82030
Monophosphate, Guanosine, 83008
Monophosphate, Guanosine Cyclic, 83008
Monospot Test, 86308
Monteggia Fracture, 24620, 24635
Monticelli Procedure, 20690, 20692
Morbilli
  See Rubeola
Morphine Methyl Ether
  See Codeine
Morphometric Analysis
  Nerve, 88356
  Skeletal Muscle, 88355
  Tumor, 88358-88361
Morton's Neuroma
  Excision, 28080
Mosaicplasty, 27416, 29866-29867
Moschcowitz Operation
  Repair, Hernia, Femoral, 49550-49557
Mosenthal Test, 81002
Mother Cell
  See Stem Cell
Motility Study
  Duodenal, 91022
  Esophagus, 91010-91012
    Imaging, 78258
  Sperm, 89300
Motion Analysis
  by Video and 3-D Kinematics, 96000, 96004
  Computer-based, 96000, 96004
Motor and/or Sensory Nerve Conduction, 95900-95905
Mousseaux-Barbin Procedure, 43510
Mouth
  Abscess
    Incision and Drainage, 40800, 40801, 41005-41009, 41015-41018
  Biopsy, 40808, 41108
  Cyst
    Incision and Drainage, 40800, 40801, 41005-41009, 41015-41018
  Excision
    Frenum, 40819
  Hematoma
    Incision and Drainage, 40800, 40801, 41005-41009, 41015-41018
  Lesion
    Destruction, 40820
    Excision, 40810-40816, 41116
    Vestibule of
      Destruction, 40820

Mouth — continued
  Lesion — continued
    Vestibule of — continued
      Repair, 40830
  Mucosa
    Excision, 40818
    Reconstruction, 40840-40845
    Removal
      Foreign Body, 40804, 40805
    Repair
      Laceration, 40830, 40831
    Skin Graft
      Full Thickness, 15240, 15241
      Pedicle Flap, 15574
      Split, 15120, 15121
    Tissue Transfer, Adjacent, 14040, 14041
    Unlisted Services and Procedures, 40899, 41599
  Vestibule
    Excision
      Destruction, 40808-40820
    Incision, 40800-40806
    Other Procedures, 40899
    Removal
      Foreign Body, 40804
    Repair, 40830-40845
Move
  See Transfer
  Finger, 26555
  Toe Joint, 26556
  Toe to Hand, 26551-26554
Moynihan Test
  Gastrointestinal Tract, X-ray, with Contrast, 74246-74249
MPR (Multifetal Pregnancy Reduction), 59866
MRA (Magnetic Resonance Angiography), 71555, 72159, 72198, 73225, 73725, 74185
MRCP (Magnetic Resonance Cholangiopancreatography), 74181
MRI (Magnetic Resonance Imaging)
  3D Rendering, 76376-76377
  Abdomen, 74181-74183
  Ankle, 73721-73723
  Arm, 73218-73220, 73223
  Bone Marrow Study, 77084
  Brain, 70551-70553
    Functional, 70554-70555
    Intraoperative, 70557-70559
  Breast, 77058-77059
    with Computer-Aided Detection, 0159T
  Chest, 71550-71552
  Elbow, 73221
  Face, 70540-70543
  Finger Joint, 73221
  Foot, 73718, 73719
  Foot Joints, 73721-73723
  Guidance
    Needle Placement, 77021
    Parenchymal Tissue Ablation, 77022
    Tissue Ablation, 77022
  Hand, 73218-73220, 73223
  Heart, 75557-75563
    Complete Study, 75557-75563, 75565
    Flow Mapping, 75565
    Morphology, 75557-75563
  Joint
    Lower Extremity, 73721-73723
    Upper Extremity, 73221-73223
  Knee, 73721-73723
  Leg, 73718-73720
  Neck, 70540-70543
  Orbit, 70540-70543
  Pelvis, 72195-72197
  Radiology
    Unlisted Diagnostic Procedure, 76499
  Spectroscopy, 76390
  Spine
    Cervical, 72141, 72142, 72156-72158

MRI (Magnetic Resonance Imaging) — continued
  Spine — continued
    Lumbar, 72148-72158
    Thoracic, 72146, 72147, 72156-72158
  Temporomandibular Joint (TMJ), 70336
  Toe, 73721-73723
  Unlisted, 76498
  Wrist, 73221
MRS (Magnetic Resonance Spectroscopy), 76390
MR Spectroscopy
  See Magnetic Resonance Spectroscopy
MSLT, 95805
MTWA (Microvolt T-Wave Alternans), 93025
Mucin
  Synovial Fluid, 83872
Mucocele
  Sinusotomy
    Frontal, 31075
Mucopolysaccharides, 83864, 83866
Mucormycoses
  See Mucormycosis
Mucormycosis
  Antibody, 86732
Mucosa
  Cautery, 30801-30802
  Destruction
    Cautery, 30801-30802
    Photodynamic Therapy, 96567
  Ectopic Gastric Imaging, 78290
  Excision of Lesion
    Alveolar, Hyperplastic, 41828
    Vestibule of Mouth, 40810-40818
    via Esophagoscopy, 43228
    via Small Intestinal Endoscopy, 44369
    via Upper GI Endoscopy, 43258
  Periodontal Grafting, 41870
  Urethra, Mucosal Advancement, 53450
  Vaginal Biopsy, 57100, 57105
Mucosa, Buccal
  See Mouth, Mucosa
Mucosectomy
  Rectal, 44799, 45113
Mucous Cyst
  Antibody
  Hand or Finger, 26160
Mucous Membrane
  See Mouth, Mucosa
  Cutaneous
    Biopsy, 11100, 11101
    Excision
      Benign Lesion, 11440-11446
      Malignant, 11640-11646
    Layer Closure, Wounds, 12051-12057
    Simple Repair, Wounds, 12011-12018
  Excision
    Sphenoid Sinus, 31288
  Lid Margin
    Correction of Trichiasis, 67835
  Nasal Test, 95065
  Ophthalmic Test, 95060
  Rectum
    Proctoplasty for Prolapse, 45505
Mucus Cyst
  See Mucous Cyst
MUGA (Multiple Gated Acquisition), 78453, 78454, 78472-78473, 78483
Muller Procedure
  Attended, 95806
  Unattended, 95807
Multifetal Pregnancy Reduction, 59866

Multiple Sleep Latency Testing (MSLT), 95805
Multiple Valve Procedures
  See Valvuloplasty
Mumford Operation, 29824
Mumford Procedure, 23120, 29824
Mumps
  Antibody, 86735
  Immunization, 90704, 90707, 90710
  Vaccine, 90704
    MMR, 90707
    MMRV, 90710
MUMPSVAX, 90704
Muramidase, 85549
Murine Typhus, 86000
Muscle
  See Specific Muscle
  Abdomen
    See Abdominal Wall
  Biofeedback Training, 90911
  Biopsy, 20200-20206
  Debridement
    Infected, 11004-11006
  Heart
    See Myocardium
  Neck
    See Neck Muscle
  Removal
    Foreign Body, 20520, 20525
  Repair
    Extraocular, 65290
    Forearm, 25260-25274
    Wrist, 25260-25274
  Revision
    Arm, Upper, 24330, 24331
    Elbow, 24301
  Transfer
    Arm, Upper, 24301, 24320
    Elbow, 24301
    Femur, 27110
    Hip, 27100-27105, 27111
    Shoulder, 23395, 23397, 24301, 24320
Muscle Compartment Syndrome
  Detection, 20950
Muscle Denervation
  See Denervation
Muscle Division
  Scalenus Anticus, 21700, 21705
  Sternocleidomastoid, 21720, 21725
Muscle Flaps, 15731-15738
  Free, 15756
Muscle Grafts, 15841-15845
Muscle, Oculomotor
  See Eye Muscles
Muscles
  Repair
    Extraocular, 65290
Muscle Testing
  Dynamometry, Eye, 92260
  Extraocular Multiple Muscles, 92265
  Manual, 95831-95834
Musculoplasty
  See Muscle, Repair
Musculoskeletal System
  Computer Assisted Surgical Navigational Procedure, 0054T-0055T, 20985
  Unlisted Services and Procedures, 20999, 21499, 24999, 25999, 26989, 27299, 27599, 27899
  Unlisted Services and Procedures, Head, 21499
Musculotendinous (Rotator) Cuff
  Repair, 23410, 23412
Mustard Procedure, 33774-33777
  See Repair, Great Arteries, Revision
Mutation Identification, 83914
MVD (Microvascular Decompression), 61450
MVR, 33430
Myasthenia Gravis
  Tensilon Test, 95857
Myasthenic, Gravis
  See Myasthenia Gravis

Index

Mycobacteria
  Culture, 87116
  Identification, 87118
  Detection, 87550-87562
  Sensitivity Studies, 87190
Mycoplasma
  Antibody, 86738
  Culture, 87109
  Detection, 87580-87582
Mycota
  See Fungus
Myectomy, Anorectal
  See Myomectomy, Anorectal
Myelencephalon
  See Medulla
Myelin Basic Protein
  Cerebrospinal Fluid, 83873
Myelography
  Brain, 70010
  Spine
    Cervical, 72240
    Lumbosacral, 72265
    Thoracic, 72255
    Total, 72270
Myelomeningocele
  Repair, 63704, 63706
  Stereotaxis
    Creation Lesion, 63600
Myelotomy, 63170
Myocardial
  Imaging, 78466, 78468, 78469
  Perfusion Imaging, 78451-78454
    See Nuclear Medicine
  Positron Emission Tomography (PET), 78459, 78491, 78492
  Repair
    Postinfarction, 33542
Myocardium, 33140-33141
Myocutaneous Flaps, 15732-15738, 15756
Myofascial Pain Dysfunction Syndrome
  See Temporomandibular Joint (TMJ)
Myofascial Release, 97140
Myofibroma
  Embolization, 37210
  Removal, 58140, 58545-58546, 58561
Myoglobin, 83874
Myomectomy
  Anorectal, 45108
  Uterus, 58140-58146, 58545, 58546
Myoplasty
  Extraocular, 65290, 67346
Myotomy
  Esophagus, 43030
  Hyoid, 21685
  Sigmoid Colon
    Intestine, 44799
    Rectum, 45999
Myringoplasty, 69620
Myringostomy, 69420-69421
Myringotomy, 69420, 69421
Myxoid Cyst
  Aspiration/Injection, 20612
  Drainage, 20610
  Wrist
    Excision, 25111-25112

N

Na, 84295
Nabi-HIB, 90371
Naffziger Operation, 61330
Nagel Test, 92283
Nail Bed
  Reconstruction, 11762
  Repair, 11760
Nail Fold
  Excision
    Wedge, 11765
Nail Plate Separation
  See Onychia
Nails
  Avulsion, 11730, 11732
  Biopsy, 11755
  Debridement, 11720, 11721

Nails — *continued*
  Drainage, 10060-10061
  Evacuation
    Hematoma, Subungual, 11740
  Excision, 11750, 11752
    Cyst
      Pilonidal, 11770-11772
    KOH Examination, 87220
    Removal, 11730, 11732, 11750, 11752
    Trimming, 11719
Narcoanalysis, 90865
Narcosynthesis
  Diagnostic and Therapeutic, 90865
Nasal Abscess, 30000-30020
Nasal Area
  Bone Graft, 21210
Nasal Bleeding
  See Epistaxis
Nasal Bone
  Fracture
    with Manipulation, 21315, 21320
    without Manipulation, 21310
    Closed Treatment, 21310-21320
    Open Treatment, 21325-21335
  X-ray, 70160
Nasal Deformity
  Repair, 40700-40761
Nasal Function Study, 92512
Nasal Polyp
  Excision
    Extensive, 30115
    Simple, 30110
Nasal Prosthesis
  Impression, 21087
Nasal Septum
  Abscess
    Incision and Drainage, 30020
  Fracture
    Closed Treatment, 21337
    Open Treatment, 21336
  Hematoma
    Incision and Drainage, 30020
    Repair, 30630
  Submucous Resection, 30520
Nasal Sinuses
  See Sinus; Sinuses
Nasal Smear
  Eosinophils, 89190
Nasal Turbinate
  Fracture
    Therapeutic, 30930
Nasoethmoid Complex
  Fracture
    Open Treatment, 21338, 21339
    Percutaneous Treatment, 21340
  Reconstruction, 21182-21184
Nasogastric Tube
  Placement, 43752
Nasolacrimal Duct
  Exploration, 68810
    with Anesthesia, 68811
  Insertion
    Stent, 68815
  Probing, 68816
  X-ray
    with Contrast, 70170
Nasomaxillary
  Fracture
    with Bone Grafting, 21348
    Closed Treatment, 21345
    Open Treatment, 21346-21348
Nasopharynges
  See Nasopharynx
Nasopharyngoscopy, 92511
Nasopharynx
  See Pharynx
  Biopsy, 42804, 42806
  Hemorrhage, 42970-42972
  Unlisted Services and Procedures, 42999
Natriuretic Peptide, 83880
Natural Killer Cells (NK)
  Total Count, 86357

Natural Ostium
  Sinus
    Maxillary, 31000
    Sphenoid, 31002
Navicular
  Arthroplasty
    with Implant, 25443
  Fracture
    with Manipulation, 25624
    Closed Treatment, 25622
    Open Treatment, 25628
  Repair, 25440
Navigation
  Computer Assisted, 20985
NCS (Nerve Conduction Study), 95900-95904
Neck
  Angiography, 70498, 70547-70549
  Artery
    Ligation, 37615
  Biopsy, 21550
  Bypass Graft, 35901
  CT Scan, 70490-70492, 70498
  Dissection, Radical
    See Radical Neck Dissection
  Exploration
    Blood Vessels, 35800
    Lymph Nodes, 38542
  Incision and Drainage
    Abscess, 21501, 21502
    Hematoma, 21501, 21502
  Lipectomy, Suction Assisted, 15876
  Magnetic Resonance Angiography (MRA), 70547-70549
  Magnetic Resonance Imaging (MRI), 70540-70543
  Nerve
    Graft, 64885, 64886
  Repair
    with Other Graft, 35261
    with Vein Graft, 35231
    Blood Vessel, 35201
  Rhytidectomy, 15825, 15828
  Skin
    Revision, 15819
  Skin Graft
    Delay of Flap, 15620
    Full Thickness, 15240, 15241
    Pedicle Flap, 15574
    Split, 15120, 15121
  Surgery, Unlisted, 21899
  Tissue Transfer, Adjacent, 14040, 14041
  Tumor, 21555-21558 [21552, 21554]
  Ultrasound Exam, 76536
  Unlisted Services and Procedures, 21899
  Urinary Bladder
    See Bladder, Neck
  Wound Exploration
    Penetrating, 20100
  X-ray, 70360
Neck, Humerus
  Fracture
    with Shoulder Dislocation
      Closed Treatment, 23680
      Open Treatment, 23675
Neck Muscle
  Division, Scalenus Anticus, 21700, 21705
  Sternocleidomastoid, 21720-21725
Necropsy
  Coroner Examination, 88045
  Forensic Examination, 88040
  Gross and Microscopic Examination, 88020-88029
  Gross Examination, 88000-88016
  Organ, 88037
  Regional, 88036
  Unlisted Services and Procedures, 88099
Needle Biopsy
  See Biopsy
  Abdomen Mass, 49180
  Bone, 20220, 20225

Needle Biopsy — *continued*
  Bone Marrow, 38221
  Breast, 19100
  Colon
    Endoscopy, 45392
  Colon Sigmoid
    Endoscopy, 45342
  CT Scan Guidance, 77012
  Epididymis, 54800
  Esophagus
    Endoscopy, 43232, 43238
  Fluoroscopic Guidance, 77002
  Gastrointestinal, Upper
    Endoscopy, 43238, 43242
  Kidney, 50200
  Liver, 47000, 47001
  Lung, 32405
  Lymph Node, 38505
  Mediastinum, 32405
  Muscle, 20206
  Pancreas, 48102
  Pleura, 32400
  Prostate, 55700
  Retroperitoneal Mass, 49180
  Salivary Gland, 42400
  Spinal Cord, 62269
  Testis, 54500
  Thyroid Gland, 60100
  Transbronchial, 31629, 31633
Needle Localization
  Breast
    with Lesion Excision, 19125, 19126
    Placement, 19290, 19291
  Magnetic Resonance Guidance, 77021
Needle Manometer Technique, 20950
Needle Wire
  Introduction
    Trachea, 31730
  Placement
    Breast, 19290, 19291
Neer Procedure, 23470
Negative Pressure Wound Therapy (NPWT), 97605-97606
Neisseria Gonorrhoeae, 87590-87592, 87850
Neisseria Meningitidis
  Antibody, 86741
Neobladder
  Construction, 51596
Neonatal Critical Care, 99468-99469
Neonatal Intensive Care
  See Newborn Care
  Initial, 99477-99480
  Subsequent, 99478-99480
Neoplasm
  See Tumor
Neoplastic Growth
  See Tumor
Nephelometry, 83883
Nephrectomy
  with Ureters, 50220-50236, 50546, 50548
  Donor, 50300, 50320, 50547
  Laparoscopic, 50545-50548
  Partial, 50240
    Laparoscopic, 50543
  Recipient, 50340
Nephrolith
  See Calculus, Removal, Kidney
Nephrolithotomy, 50060-50075
Nephropexy, 50400, 50405
Nephroplasty
  See Kidney, Repair
Nephropyeloplasty, 50400-50405, 50544
Nephrorrhaphy, 50500
Nephroscopy
  See Endoscopy, Kidney
Nephrostogram, 50394
Nephrostolithotomy
  Percutaneous, 50080, 50081
Nephrostomy
  Change Tube, 50398
  with Drainage, 50400

Nephrostomy

Nephrostomy — continued
  Closure, 53899
  Endoscopic, 50562-50570
    with Exploration, 50045
  Percutaneous, 52334
  X-ray with Contrast
    to Guide Dilation, 74485
Nephrostomy Tract
  Establishment, 50395
Nephrotomogram
  See Nephrotomography
Nephrotomography, 74415
Nephrotomy, 50040, 50045
  with Exploration, 50045
Nerve
  Cranial
    See Cranial Nerve
  Facial
    See Facial Nerve
  Foot
    Incision, 28035
  Intercostal
    See Intercostal Nerve
  Median
    See Median Nerve
  Obturator
    See Obturator Nerve
  Peripheral
    See Peripheral Nerve
  Phrenic
    See Phrenic Nerve
  Sciatic
    See Sciatic Nerve
  Spinal
    See Spinal Nerve
  Tibial
    See Tibial Nerve
  Ulnar
    See Ulnar Nerve
  Vestibular
    See Vestibular Nerve
Nerve Conduction
  Motor and/or Sensory, 95905
  Motor Nerve, 95900, 95903
  Sensory Nerve, 95904
Nerve II, Cranial
  See Optic Nerve
Nerve Root
  See Cauda Equina; Spinal Cord
  Decompression, 63020-63048, 63055-63103
  Incision, 63185, 63190
  Section, 63185, 63190
Nerves
  Anastomosis
    Facial to Hypoglossal, 64868
    Facial to Phrenic, 64870
    Facial to Spinal Accessory, 64866
  Avulsion, 64732-64772
  Biopsy, 64795
  Decompression, 64702-64727
  Destruction, 64600-64681
    Laryngeal, Recurrent, 31595
  Foot
    Excision, 28055
    Incision, 28035
  Graft, 64885-64907
  Implantation
    Electrode, 64553-64581
      to Bone, 64787
      to Muscle, 64787
  Incision, 43640, 43641, 64732-64772
  Injection
    Anesthetic, 01991-01992, 64400-64530
    Neurolytic Agent, 64600-64681
  Insertion
    Electrode, 64553-64581
  Lesion
    Excision, 64774-64792
  Neurofibroma
    Excision, 64788-64792
  Neurolemmoma
    Excision, 64788-64792

Nerves — continued
  Neurolytic
    Internal, 64727
  Neuroma
    Excision, 64774-64786
  Neuroplasty, 64702-64721
  Nuclear Medicine
    Unlisted Services and Procedures, 78699
  Removal
    Electrode, 64585
  Repair
    Graft, 64885-64911
    Microdissection
      with Surgical Microscope, 69990
    Suture, 64831-64876
  Spinal Accessory
    Incision, 63191
    Section, 63191
  Suture, 64831-64876
  Sympathectomy
    Excision, 64802-64818
    Transection, 43640, 43641, 64732-64772
    Transposition, 64718-64721
  Unlisted Services and Procedures, 64999
Nerve Stimulation, Transcutaneous
  See Application, Neurostimulation
Nerve Teasing, 88362
Nerve V, Cranial
  See Trigeminal Nerve
Nerve VII, Cranial
  See Facial Nerve
Nerve X, Cranial
  See Vagus Nerve
Nerve XI, Cranial
  See Accessory Nerve
Nerve XII, Cranial
  See Hypoglossal Nerve
Nervous System
  Nuclear Medicine
    Unlisted Services and Procedures, 78699
Nesidioblast
  See Islet Cell
Neurectasis, 64999
Neurectomy
  Foot, 28055
  Gastrocnemius, 27326
  Hamstring Muscle, 27325
  Leg, Lower, 27326
  Leg, Upper, 27325
  Popliteal, 27326
  Tympanic, 69676
Neuroendoscopy
  Intracranial, 62160-62165
Neurofibroma
  Cutaneous Nerve
    Excision, 64788
  Extensive
    Excision, 64792
  Peripheral Nerve
    Excision, 64790
Neurolemmoma
  Cutaneous Nerve
    Excision, 64788
  Extensive
    Excision, 64792
  Peripheral Nerve
    Excision, 64790
Neurologic System
  See Nervous System
Neurology
  Brain
    Cortex Magnetic Stimulation, 0160T-0161T
    Mapping, 96020
    Surface Electrode Stimulation, 95961-95962
  Central Motor
    Electrocorticogram
      Intraoperative, 95829
    Electroencephalogram (EEG)
      Brain Death, 95824

Neurology — continued
  Central Motor — continued
    Electroencephalogram — continued
      Electrode Placement, 95830
      Intraoperative, 95955
      Monitoring, 95812, 95813, 95950-95953, 95956
      Physical or Drug Activation, 95954
      Sleep, 95808, 95810, 95822, 95827
      Attended, 95806, 95807
      Standard, 95819
      WADA activation, 95958
    Electroencephalography (EEG)
      Digital Analysis, 95957
    Electromyography
      See Electromyography
      Fine Wire
        Dynamic, 96004
      Ischemic Limb Exercise Test, 95875
      Needle, 51785, 95860-95872
      Surface
        Dynamic, 96002-96004
    Higher Cerebral Function
      Aphasia Test, 96105
      Cognitive Function Tests, 96116
      Developmental Tests, 96110, 96111
      Magnetoencephalography (MEG), 95965-95967
    Motion Analysis
      by Video and 3-D Kinematics, 96000, 96004
      Computer-based, 96000, 96004
    Muscle Testing
      Manual, 95831-95834
    Nerve Conduction
      Motor Nerve, 95900, 95903
      Sensory Nerve, 95904
    Neuromuscular Junction Tests, 95937
    Neurophysiological Testing
      Intraoperative, 95920
    Neuropsychological Testing, 96118-96120
    Plantar Pressure Measurements
      Dynamic, 96001, 96004
    Polysomnography, 95808-95811
    Range of Motion Test, 95851, 95852
    Reflex
      H-Reflex, 95933, 95934
    Reflex Test
      Blink Reflex, 95933
    Sleep Study, 95808, 95810
      Attended, 95806
      Unattended, 95807
    Somatosensory Testing, 95925-95927
    Tension Test, 95857
    Transcranial Motor Stimulation, 95928-95929
    Unlisted Services and Procedures, 95999
    Urethral Sphincter, 51785
    Visual Evoked Potential, CNS, 95930
  Cognitive Performance, 96125
  Diagnostic
    Anal Sphincter, 51785
    Autonomic Nervous Function
      Heart Rate Response, 95921-95923
      Pseudomotor Response, 95921-95923
      Sympathetic Function, 95921-95923
    Brain Cortex Magnetic Stimulation, 0160T-0161T
    Brain Surface Electrode Stimulation, 95961, 95962

Neurolysis
  Nerve, 64704, 64708
  Internal, 64727
Neuroma
  Acoustic
    See Brain, Tumor, Excision
  Cutaneous Nerve
    Excision, 64774
  Digital Nerve
    Excision, 64776, 64778
  Excision, 64774
  Foot Nerve
    Excision, 28080, 64782, 64783
  Hand Nerve
    Excision, 64782, 64783
  Interdigital, 28080
  Peripheral Nerve
    Excision, 64784
  Sciatic Nerve
    Excision, 64786
Neuromuscular Junction Tests, 95937
Neuromuscular Pedicle
  Reinnervation
    Larynx, 31590
Neuromuscular Reeducation, 97112
  See Physical Medicine/Therapy/Occupational Therapy
  Intraoperative, Per Hour, 95920
Neurophysiological Testing, 96118-96120
Neurophysiologic Testing
  Autonomic Nervous Function
    Heart Rate Response, 95921-95923
    Pseudomotor Response, 95921-95923
    Sympathetic Function, 95921-95923
  Intraoperative, Per Hour, 95920
Neuroplasty, 64712
  Cranial Nerve, 64716
  Digital Nerve, 64702, 64704
  Peripheral Nerve, 64708-64714, 64718-64721
Neuropsychological Testing, 96118-96120
  Computer Assisted, 96120
Neurorrhaphy, 64831-64876
  Peripheral Nerve
    with Graft, 64885-64907
    Conduit, 64910-64911
Neurostimulation
  Application, 64550
Neurostimulator
  Analysis, 95970-95982
  Implantation, 64553-64565
    Electrodes, 43647, 43881
  Insertion
    Pulse Generator, 61885-61886, 64590
    Receiver, 61885-61886, 64590
  Removal
    Electrodes, 43648, 43882, 61880, 63661-63662
    Pulse Generator, 61888, 64595
    Receiver, 61888, 64595
  Replacement, 61885
    Electrodes, 43647, 43881, 63663-63664
    Pulse Generator, 63685
    Receiver, 63685
  Revision
    Electrode, 63663-63664
    Pulse Generator, 63688
    Receiver, 63688
Neurotomy, Sympathetic
  See Gasserian Ganglion, Sensory Root, Decompression
Neurovascular Pedicle Flaps, 15750
Neutralization Test
  Virus, 86382
Newborn Care, 99460-99465, 99502
  Attendance at Delivery, 99464
  Birthing Room, 99460-99463
  Blood Transfusion, 36450
  See Neonatal Intensive Care

Index — Nuclear Medicine

Newborn Care — *continued*
- Circumcision
  - Clamp or Other Device, 54150
  - Surgical Excision, 54160
- Laryngoscopy, 31520
- Normal, 99460-99463
- Prepuce Slitting, 54000
- Preventive
  - Office, 99461
- Resuscitation, 99465
- Standby for C–Section, 99360
- Subsequent Hospital Care, 99462
- Umbilical Artery Catheterization, 36660

New Patient
- Domiciliary or Rest Home Visit, 99324-99328
- Emergency Department Services, 99281-99288
- Home Services, 99341-99345
- Hospital Inpatient Services, 99221-99239
- Hospital Observation Services, 99217-99220
- Initial Inpatient Consultations, 99251-99255
- Initial Office Visit, 99201-99205
  - See Evaluation and Management, Office and Other Outpatient
- Office and/or Other Outpatient Consultations, 99241-99245
- Outpatient Visit, 99211-99215

Nickel, 83885

Nicolas–Durand–Favre Disease
- See Lymphogranuloma Venerum

Nicotine, 83887

Nidation
- See Implantation

Nikaidoh Procedure, 33782-33783

Nipples
- See Breast
- Inverted, 19355
- Reconstruction, 19350

Nissen Operation
- See Fundoplasty, Esophagogastric

Nissen Procedure, 43324
- Laparoscopic, 43280

Nitrate Reduction Test
- Urinalysis, 81000-81099

Nitric Oxide, 95012

Nitroblue Tetrazolium Dye Test, 86384

Nitrogen, Blood Urea
- See Blood Urea Nitrogen

N. Meningitidis, 86741

NMR Imaging
- See Magnetic Resonance Spectroscopy

NMR Spectroscopies
- See Magnetic Resonance Spectroscopy

Noble Procedure, 44680

Nocardia
- Antibody, 86744

Nocturnal Penile Rigidity Test, 54250

Nocturnal Penile Tumescence Test, 54250

Node Dissection, Lymph, 38542

Node, Lymph
- See Lymph Nodes

Nodes
- See Lymph Nodes

No Man's Land
- Tendon Repair, 26356-26358

Non–Invasive Vascular Imaging
- See Vascular Studies

Non–Office Medical Services, 99056
- Emergency Care, 99060

Non–Stress Test, Fetal, 59025

Nonunion Repair
- Femur
  - with Graft, 27472
  - without Graft, 27470
- Fibula, 27726
- Metatarsal, 28322
- Tarsal Joint, 28320

Noradrenalin
- Blood, 82383, 82384
- Urine, 82382

Norchlorimipramine
- See Imipramine

Norepinephrine
- See Catecholamines
- Blood, 82383, 82384
- Urine, 82382

Nortriptyline
- Assay, 80182

Norwood Procedure, 33611, 33612, 33619
- See Repair, Heart, Ventricle; Revision

Nose
- Abscess
  - Incision and Drainage, 30000, 30020
- Actinotherapy, Intranasal, 0168T
- Artery
  - Incision, 30915, 30920
- Biopsy
  - Intranasal, 30100
- Dermoid Cyst
  - Excision
    - Complex, 30125
    - Simple, 30124
- Displacement Therapy, 30210
- Endoscopy
  - Diagnostic, 31231-31235
  - Surgical, 31237-31294
- Excision
  - Rhinectomy, 30150, 30160
- Fracture
  - with Fixation, 21330, 21340, 21345-21347
  - Closed Treatment, 21345
  - Open Treatment, 21325-21336, 21338, 21339, 21346, 21347
  - Percutaneous Treatment, 21340
- Hematoma
  - Hemorrhage
    - Cauterization, 30901-30906
  - Incision and Drainage, 30000, 30020
- Insertion
  - Septal Prosthesis, 30220
- Intranasal
  - Actinotherapy, 0168T
  - Lesion
    - External Approach, 30118
    - Internal Approach, 30117
  - Phototherapy, 0168T
- Lysis of Adhesions, 30560
- Polyp
  - Excision
    - Extensive, 30115
    - Simple, 30110
- Reconstruction
  - Cleft Lip
    - Cleft Palate, 30460, 30462
  - Dermatoplasty, 30620
  - Primary, 30400-30420
  - Secondary, 30430-30450
  - Septum, 30520
- Removal
  - Foreign Body, 30300
    - with Anesthesia, 30310
    - by Lateral Rhinotomy, 30320
- Repair
  - Adhesions, 30560
  - Cleft Lip, 40700-40761
  - Fistula, 30580, 30600, 42260
  - Rhinophyma, 30120
  - Septum, 30540, 30545, 30630
  - Synechia, 30560
  - Vestibular Stenosis, 30465
- Skin
  - Excision, 30120
  - Surgical Planing, 30120
- Skin Graft
  - Delay of Flap, 15630
  - Full Thickness, 15260, 15261
  - Pedicle Flap, 15576

Nose — *continued*
- Submucous Resection Turbinate
  - Excision, 30140
- Tissue Transfer, Adjacent, 14060, 14061
- Turbinate
  - Excision, 30130, 30140
  - Fracture, 30930
  - Injection, 30200
- Turbinate Mucosa
  - Cauterization, 30801, 30802
- Unlisted Services and Procedures, 30999

Nose Bleed, 30901-30906
- See Hemorrhage, Nasal

NPWT (Negative Pressure Wound Therapy), 97605-97606

NST, 59025

NSVD, 59400-59410, 59610-59614

NTD (Nitroblue Tetrazolium Dye Test), 86384

Nuclear Antigen
- Antibody, 86235

Nuclear Imaging
- See Nuclear Medicine

Nuclear Magnetic Resonance Imaging
- See Magnetic Resonance Imaging (MRI)

Nuclear Magnetic Resonance Spectroscopy
- See Magnetic Resonance Spectroscopy

Nuclear Medicine
- Abscess Localization, 78805, 78806, 78807
- Adrenal Gland Imaging, 78075
- Bile Duct Imaging, 78223
- Bladder
  - Residual Study, 78730
- Blood
  - Flow Imaging, 78445
  - Iron
    - Plasma Volume, 78110, 78111
    - Platelet Survival, 78190, 78191
    - Red Cells, 78120, 78121, 78130-78140
    - Red Cell Survival, 78130, 78135
  - Unlisted Services and Procedures, 78199
  - Whole Blood Volume, 78122
- Bone
  - Density Study, 78350, 78351
  - Imaging, 78300-78320
  - SPECT, 78320
  - Ultrasound, 76977
  - Unlisted Services and Procedures, 78399
- Bone Marrow
  - Imaging, 78102-78104
- Brain
  - Blood Flow, 78610
  - Cerebrospinal Fluid, 78630-78650
  - Imaging, 78600-78609
  - Vascular Flow, 78610
- Endocrine Glands
  - Unlisted Services and Procedures, 78099
- Esophagus
  - Imaging (Motility), 78258
  - Reflux Study, 78262
- Gallbladder
  - Imaging, 78223
- Gastric Mucosa
  - Imaging, 78261
- Gastrointestinal
  - Blood Loss Study, 78278
  - Protein Loss Study, 78282
  - Shunt Testing, 78291
  - Unlisted Services and Procedures, 78299
- Genitourinary System
  - Unlisted Services and Procedures, 78799

Nuclear Medicine — *continued*
- Heart
  - Blood Flow, 78414
  - Blood Pool Imaging, 78472, 78473, 78481, 78483, 78494, 78496
  - Myocardial Imaging, 78459, 78466-78469
  - Myocardial Perfusion, 78451-78454, 78491, 78492
  - Shunt Detection, 78428
  - Unlisted Services and Procedures, 78499
- Hepatic Duct
  - Imaging, 78223
- Inflammatory Process, 78805-78807
- Intestines
  - Imaging, 78290
- Kidney
  - Blood Flow, 78701-78709
  - Function Study, 78725
  - Imaging, 78700-78710
- Lacrimal Gland
  - Tear Flow, 78660
- Liver
  - Function Study, 78220
  - Imaging, 78201-78216
  - Vascular Flow, 78206
- Lung
  - Imaging Perfusion, 78580-78585
  - Imaging Ventilation, 78586-78594
  - Unlisted Services and Procedures, 78599
- Lymphatics, 78195
  - Unlisted Services and Procedures, 78199
- Lymph Nodes, 78195
- Musculoskeletal System
  - Unlisted Services and Procedures, 78399
- Nervous System
  - Unlisted Services and Procedures, 78699
- Parathyroid Glands
  - Imaging, 78070
- Pulmonary Perfusion Imaging, 78588
- Salivary Gland
  - Function Study, 78232
  - Imaging, 78230, 78231
- Spleen
  - Imaging, 78185, 78215, 78216
  - Unlisted Services and Procedures, 78199
- Stomach
  - Blood Loss Study, 78278
  - Emptying Study, 78264
  - Protein Loss Study, 78282
  - Reflux Study, 78262
  - Vitamin B–12 Absorption, 78270-78272
- Testes
  - Imaging, 78761
- Therapeutic
  - Heart, 79440
  - Interstitial, 79300
  - Intra–arterial, 79445
  - Intra–articular, 79440
  - Intracavitary, 79200
  - Intravascular, 79101
  - Intravenous, 79101
  - Intravenous Infusion, 79101, 79403
  - Oral Administration, 79005
  - Radioactive Colloid Therapy, 79200, 79300
  - Thyroid, 79200, 79300
  - Unlisted Services and Procedures, 79999
- Thyroid
  - Imaging, 78010
    - with Flow, 78011
    - with Uptake, 78006
    - for Metastases, 78015-78018
  - Metastases Uptake, 78020
  - Uptake, 78000-78003

Nuclear Medicine — Index

Nuclear Medicine — *continued*
  Tumor Imaging
    Positron Emission Tomography, 78811-78816
      with Computed Tomography, 78814-78816
    Tumor Localization, 78800-78804
  Unlisted Services and Procedures, 78999
  Urea Breath Test, 78267, 78268
  Ureter
    Reflux Study, 78740
  Vein
    Thrombosis Imaging, 78456-78458
Nucleases, DNA
  Antibody, 86215
Nucleic Acid Probe, 83896
  Amplified Probe Detection
    Infectious Agent
      Bartonella henselae, 87471
      Bartonella quintana, 87471
      Borrelia burgdorferi, 87476
      Candida species, 87481
      Chlamydia pneumoniae, 87486
      Chlamydia trachomatis, 87491
      Cytomegalovirus, 87496
      Enterovirus, 87498, 87500
      Gardnerella vaginalis, 87511
      Hepatitis B virus, 87516
      Hepatitis C, 87521
      Hepatitis G, 87526
      Herpes simplex virus, 87529
      Herpes virus-6, 87532
      HIV-1, 87535
      HIV-2, 87538
      Legionella pneumophila, 87541
      Multiple Organisms, 87801
      Mycobacteria avium–intracellulare, 87561
      Mycobacteria species, 87551
      Mycobacteria tuberculosis, 87556
      Mycoplasma pneumoniae, 87581
      Neisseria gonorrhoeae, 87591
      Not Otherwise Specified, 87798, 87801
      Papillomavirus, human, 87621
      Staphylococcus aureus, 87640-87641
      Streptococcus, group A, 87651
      Streptococcus, group B, 87653
  Direct Probe Detection
    Infectious Agent
      Bartonella henselae, 87470
      Bartonella quintana, 87470
      Borrelia burgdorferi, 87475
      Candida species, 87480
      Chlamydia pneumoniae, 87485
      Chlamydia trachomatis, 87490
      Cytomegalovirus, 87495
      Gardnerella vaginalis, 87510
      Hepatitis B virus, 87515
      Hepatitis C, 87520
      Hepatitis G, 87525
      Herpes simplex virus, 87528
      Herpes virus-6, 87531
      HIV-1, 87534
      HIV-2, 87537
      Legionella pneumophila, 87540
      Multiple Organisms, 87800
      Mycobacteria avium–intracellulare, 87560
      Mycobacteria species, 87550
      Mycobacteria tuberculosis, 87555

Nucleic Acid Probe — *continued*
  Direct Probe Detection — *continued*
    Infectious Agent — *continued*
      Mycoplasma pneumoniae, 87580
      Neisseria gonorrhoeae, 87590
      Not Otherwise Specified, 87797
      Papillomavirus, human, 87620
      Streptococcus, group A, 87650
      Trichomonas Vaginalis, 87660
  Genotype Analysis
    Infectious Agent
      Hepatitis C Virus, 87902
      HIV-1, 87901
  In Situ Hybridization, 88365-88368
  Molecular Diagnostics, 83896
  Nucleic Acid Microbial Identification, 87797-87799
  Phenotype Analysis
    Infectious Agent
      HIV-1 Drug Resistance, 87903, 87904
  Quantification
    Infectious Agent
      Bartonella henselae, 87472
      Bartonella quintana, 87472
      Borrelia burgdorferi, 87477
      Candida species, 87482
      Chlamydia pneumoniae, 87487
      Chlamydia trachomatis, 87492
      Cytomegalovirus, 87497
      Gardnerella vaginalis, 87512
      Hepatitis B virus, 87517
      Hepatitis C, 87522
      Hepatitis G, 87527
      Herpes simplex virus, 87530
      Herpes virus-6, 87533
      HIV-1, 87536
      HIV-2, 87539
      Legionella pneumophila, 87542
      Mycobacteria avium–intracellulare, 87562
      Mycobacteria species, 87552
      Mycobacteria tuberculosis, 87557
      Mycoplasma pneumoniae, 87582
      Neisseria gonorrhoeae, 87592
      Not Otherwise Specified, 87799
      Papillomavirus, human, 87622
      Streptococcus, group A, 87652
Nuclear Medicine
  Vein
    Thrombosis Imaging, 78456-78458
Nucleolysis, Intervertebral Disc
  See Chemonucleolysis
Nucleotidase, 83915
Nursemaid Elbow, 24640
Nursing Facility Services
  Annual Assessment, 99318
  Care Plan Oversight Services, 99379, 99380
  Discharge Services, 1110F-1111F, 99315-99316
  Initial, 99304-99306
  Subsequent Nursing Facility Care, 99307-99310
    New or Established Patient, 99307-99310
  See also Domiciliary Services
Nuss Procedure
  with Thoracoscopy, 21743
  without Thoracoscopy, 21742
Nutrition Therapy
  Group, 97804
  Home Infusion, 99601, 99602
  Initial Assessment, 97802

Nutrition Therapy — *continued*
  Reassessment, 97803
Nystagmus Tests
  See Vestibular Function Tests
  Optokinetic, 92534, 92544
  Positional, 92532, 92542
  Spontaneous, 92531, 92541

O

O2 Saturation, 82805-82810, 94760-94762
OAE Test, 92587-92588
Ober–Yount Procedure, 27025
Obliteration
  Mastoid, 69670
  Vaginal
    Total, 57110-57112
    Vault, 57120
Obliteration, Total Excision of Vagina, 57110-57112
Obliteration, Vaginal Vault, 57120
Oblongata, Medulla
  Tractotomy, 61470
Observation
  Discharge, 99217
  Initial, 99218-99220
  Same Date Admit/Discharge, 99234-99236
Obstetrical Care
  See Also Abortion; Cesarean Delivery; Ectopic Pregnancy
  Abortion
    Induced
      by Amniocentesis Injection, 59850-59852
      by Dilation and Curettage, 59840
      by Dilation and Evaluation, 59841
    Missed
      First Trimester, 59820
      Second Trimester, 59821
    Spontaneous, 59812
    Therapeutic, 59840-59852
  Antepartum Care, 59425-59426
  Cesarean Section
    with Hysterectomy, 59525
    with Postpartum Care, 59515
    for Failed VBAC
      with Postpartum Care, 59622
      Only, 59620
      Routine (Global), 59618
    Only, 59514
    Routine (Global), 59510
  Curettage
    Hydatidiform Mole, 59870
  Evacuation
    Hydatidiform Mole, 59870
  External Cephalic Version, 59412
  Miscarriage
    Surgical Completion, 59812-59821
  Placenta Delivery, 59414
  Postpartum Care
    Cesarean Delivery, 59510
    Following Vaginal Delivery After Prior Cesarean Section, 59610, 59614, 59618, 59622
    Postpartum care only, 59430
    Vaginal, 59400, 59410
  Septic Abortion, 59830
  Total (Global), 59400, 59510, 59610, 59618
  Unlisted Services and Procedures, 59898-59899
  Vaginal Delivery
    with Postpartum Care, 59410
    After C/S-VBAC (Global), 59610
      with Postpartum Care, 59614
      Delivery Only, 59612
    Only, 59409
    Routine (Global), 59400
Obstetric Tamponade
  Uterus, 59899
  Vagina, 59899

Obstruction
  Extracranial, 61623
  Fallopian Tube, 58565, 58615
  Head/Neck, 61623
  Intracranial, 61623
  Penis (Vein), 37790
  Umbilical Cord, 59072
Obstruction Clearance
  Venous Access Device, 36595-36596
Obstruction Colon, 44025-44050
Obstructive Material Removal
  Gastrostomy, Duodenostomy, Jejunostomy, Gastro-jejunostomy, or Cecostomy Tube, 49460
Obturator Nerve
  Avulsion, 64763-64766
  Incision, 64763-64766
  Transection, 64763-64766
Obturator Prosthesis
  Impression/Custom Preparation
    Definitive, 21080
    Interim, 21079
    Surgical, 21076
  Insertion
    Larynx, 31527
Occipital Nerve, Greater
  Avulsion, 64744
  Incision, 64744
  Injection
    Anesthetic, 64405
  Transection, 64744
Occlusion
  Extracranial/Intracranial, 61623
  Fallopian Tubes
    Oviduct, 58565, 58615
  Penis
    Vein, 37790
  Umbilical Cord, 59072
Occlusive Disease of Artery, 35001, 35005-35021, 35045-35081, 35091, 35102, 35111, 35121, 35131, 35141, 35151
  See Also Repair, Artery; Revision
Occult Blood, 82270-82272
  by Hemoglobin Immunoassay, 82274
Occupational Therapy
  Evaluation, 97003-97004
OCT (Oxytocin Challenge), 59020
Ocular Implant
  See Also Orbital Implant
  Insertion
    in Scleral Shell, 65130
    Muscles Attached, 65140
    Muscles not Attached, 65135
  Modification, 65125
  Reinsertion, 65150
    with Foreign Material, 65155
  Removal, 65175
Ocular Muscle, 67311-67399
Ocular Orbit
  See Orbit
Ocular Photoscreening, 99174
Ocular Prostheses, 21077, 65770, 66982-66985, 92358
Oculomotor Muscle, 67311-67399
Oddi Sphincter
  Pressure Measurement, 43263
ODM, 92260
Odontoid Dislocation
  Open Treatment
    Reduction, 22318
      with Grafting, 22319
Odontoid Fracture
  Open Treatment
    Reduction, 22318
      With Grafting, 22319
Odontoid Process
  Excisions, 22548
Oesophageal Neoplasm
  Endoscopic Removal
    Ablation, 43228
    Bipolar Cautery, 43216
    Hot Biopsy Forceps, 43216
    Snare, 43217
  Excision, Open, 43100-43101

Index

Oesophageal Varices
  Injection Sclerosis, 43204, 43243
  Ligation, 43205, 43244, 43400
  Repair/Transection, 43401
Oesophagus
  See Esophagus
Oestradiol, 82670
  Response, 80415
Office and/or Other Outpatient Visits
  Consultation, 99241-99245
  Established Patient, 99211-99215
  New Patient, 99201-99205
  Normal Newborn, 99461
  Office Visit
    Established Patient, 99211-99215
    New Patient, 99201-99205
    Prolonged Service, 99354-99355
  Outpatient Visit
    Established Patient, 99211-99215
    New Patient, 99201-99205
    Prolonged Service, 99354-99355
Office Medical Services
  After Hours, 99050
  Emergency Care, 99058
  Extended Hours, 99051
Office or Other Outpatient Consultations, 99241-99245, 99354-99355
Olecranon
  See Also Elbow; Humerus; Radius; Ulna
  Bone Cyst
    Excision, 24120-24126
  Bursa
    Arthrocentesis, 20605
    Excision, 24105
  Tumor, Benign, 25120-25126
    Cyst, 24120
    Excision, 24125, 24126
Olecranon Process
  Craterization, 24147
  Diaphysectomy, 24147
  Excision
    Cyst/Tumor, 24120-24126
    Partial, 24147
  Fracture
    Closed Treatment, 24670-24675
    Open Treatment, 24685
  Osteomyelitis, 24138, 24147
  Saucerization, 24147
  Sequestrectomy, 24138
Oligoclonal Immunoglobulin
  Cerebrospinal Fluid, 83916
Omentectomy, 49255, 58950-58958
  Laparotomy, 58960
  Oophorectomy, 58943
  Resection Ovarian Malignancy, 58950-58958
  Resection Peritoneal Malignancy, 58950-58958
  Resection Tubal Malignancy, 58950-58958
Omentum
  Excision, 49255, 58950-58958
  Flap, 49904-49905
    Free
      with Microvascular Anastomosis, 49906
  Unlisted Services and Procedures, 49999
Omphalectomy, 49250
Omphalocele
  Repair, 49600-49611
Omphalomesenteric Duct
  Excision, 44800
Omphalomesenteric Duct, Persistent
  Excision, 44800
OMT, 98925-98929
Oncoprotein
  des-gamma-carboxy-prothrombin (DCP), 83951
  HER-2/neu, 83950
One Stage Prothrombin Time, 85610-85611
On-Line Internet Assessment/Management
  Nonphysician, 98969

On-Line Internet Assessment/Management — continued
  Physician, 99444
On-Line Medical Evaluation
  Non-Physician, 98969
  Physician, 99444
ONSD, 67570
Onychectomy, 11750-11752
Onychia
  Drainage, 10060-10061
Onychoplasty, 11760-11762
Oocyte
  Assisted Fertilization, Microtechnique, 89280-89281
  Biopsy, 89290-89291
  Cryopreservation, 88240
  Culture
    with Co-Culture, 89251
    Extended, 89272
    Less than 4 days, 89250
  Identification, Follicular Fluid, 89254
  Insemination, 89268
  Retrieval
    for In Vitro Fertilization, 58970
  Storage, 89346
  Thawing, 89356
Oophorectomy, 58262-58263, 58291-58292, 58552, 58554, 58661, 58940-58943
  Ectopic Pregnancy
    Laparoscopic Treatment, 59151
    Surgical Treatment, 59120
Oophorectomy, Partial, 58920, 58940-58943
Oophorocystectomy, 58925
  Laparoscopic, 58661
Open Biopsy, Adrenal Gland, 60540-60545
Opening (Incision and Drainage)
  Acne
    Comedones, 10040
    Cysts, 10040
    Milia, Multiple, 10040
    Pustules, 10040
Operating Microscope, 69990
Operation Microscopes, 69990
Operation/Procedure
  Belsey IV, 43324
  Blalock-Hanlon, 33735
  Blalock-Taussig Subclavian-Pulmonary Anastomosis, 33750
  Borthen, 66165
  Collis, 43326
  Damus-Kaye-Stansel, 33606
  Dana, 63185
  Dor, 33548
  Dunn, 28715
  Duvries, 27675-27676
  Estes, 58825
  Flip-flap, 54324
  Foley Pyeloplasty, 50400-50405
  Fontan, 33615-33617
  Fowler-Stephens, 54650
  Fox, 67923
  Fredet-Ramstedt, 43520
  Gardner, 63700-63702
  Green, 23400
  Harelip, 40700, 40761
  Heine, 66740
  Heller, 32665, 43330-43331
  Iris, Inclusion, 66165
  Jaboulay Gastroduodenostomy, 43810, 43850-43855
  Johannsen, 53400
  Keller, 28292
  Krause, 61450
  Kuhnt-Szymanowski, 67917
  Leadbetter Urethroplasty, 53431
  Maquet, 27418
  Mumford, 23120, 29824
  Nissen, 43280, 43324-43326
  Norwood, 33619
  Peet, 64802-64818
  Ramstedt, 43520

Operation/Procedure — continued
  Richardson Hysterectomy
    See Hysterectomy, Abdominal, Total
  Richardson Urethromeatoplasty, 53460
  Schanz, 27448
  Schlatter Total Gastrectomy, 43620-43622
  Smithwick, 64802-64818
  Stamm, 43830
    Laparoscopic, 43653
  SVR, SAVER, 33548
  Tenago, 53431
  Toupet, 43280
  Winiwarter Cholecystoenterostomy, 47720-47740
  Winter, 54435
Operculectomy, 41821
Operculum
  See Gums
Ophthalmic Biometry, 76516-76519, 92136
Ophthalmic Mucous Membrane Test, 95060
Ophthalmology
  Unlisted Services and Procedures, 92499
    See Also Opthalmology, Diagnostic
Ophthalmology, Diagnostic
  Color Vision Exam, 92283
  Computerized Scanning, 0187T, 92135
  Computerized Screening, 99172, 99174
  Dark Adaptation, 92284
  Electromyography, Needle, 92265
  Electro-oculography, 92270
  Electroretinography, 92275
  Endoscopy, 66990
  Eye Exam
    with Anesthesia, 92018-92019
    Established Patient, 92012-92014
    New Patient, 92002-92004
  Glaucoma Provocative Test, 92140
  Gonioscopy, 92020
  Ocular Photography
    External, 92285
    Internal, 92286-92287
  Ophthalmoscopy, 92225-92226
    with Angiography, 92235
    with Angioscopy, 92230
    with Dynamometry, 92260
    with Fluorescein Angiography, 92235
    with Fluorescein Angioscopy, 92230
    with Fundus Photography, 92250
    with Indocyanine-Green Angiography, 92240
  Photoscreening, 99174
  Refractive Determination, 92015
  Rotation Tests, 92499
  Sensorimotor Exam, 92060
  Tonography, 92120
    with Provocation, 92130
  Tonometry
    Serial, 92100
  Ultrasound, 76510-76529
  Visual Acuity Screen, 99172-99173
  Visual Field Exam, 92081-92083
  Visual Function Screen, 99172, 99174
Ophthalmoscopy, 92225-92226
  See Also Ophthalmology, Diagnostic
Opiates, 83925
Opinion, Second
  See Confirmatory Consultations
Optic Nerve
  Decompression, 67570
    with Nasal/Sinus Endoscopy, 31294
  Head Evaluation, 2027F
Optokinectic Nystagmus Test, 92534, 92544

OPV, 90712
Oral Lactose Tolerance Test, 82951-82953
Oral Mucosa
  Excision, 40818
Oral Surgical Splint, 21085
Orbit
  See Also Orbital Contents; Orbital Floor; Periorbital Region
  Biopsy, 61332
  Exploration, 67450
  Fine Needle Aspiration or Orbital Contents, 67415
  Orbitotomy without Bone Flap, 67400
  CT Scan, 70480-70482
  Decompression, 61330
    Bone Removal, 67414, 67445
  Exploration, 61332, 67400, 67450
  Lesion
    Excision, 61333
  Fracture
    Closed Treatment
      with Manipulation, 21401
      without Manipulation, 21400
    Open Treatment, 21406-21408
      Blowout Fracture, 21385-21395
  Incision and Drainage, 67405, 67440
  Injection
    Retrobulbar, 67500-67505
    Tenon's Capsule, 67515
  Insertion
    Implant, 67550
  Lesion
    Excision, 67412, 67420
  Magnetic Resonance Imaging (MRI), 70540-70543
  Removal
    Decompression, 67445
    Exploration, 61334
    Foreign Body, 61334, 67413, 67430
    Implant, 67560
    Sella Turcica, 70482
  Unlisted Services and Procedures, 67599
  X-ray, 70190-70200
Orbital Contents
  Aspiration, 67415
Orbital Floor
  See Also Orbit; Periorbital Region
  Fracture
    Blow-Out, 21385-21395
Orbital Hypertelorism
  Osteotomy
    Periorbital, 21260-21263
Orbital Implant
  See Also Ocular Implant
  Insertion, 67550
  Removal, 67560
Orbital Prosthesis, 21077
Orbital Rim and Forehead
  Reconstruction, 21172-21180
Orbital Rims
  Reconstruction, 21182-21184
Orbital Transplant, 67560
Orbital Walls
  Reconstruction, 21182-21184
Orbit Area
  Reconstruction
    Secondary, 21275
Orbitocraniofacial Reconstruction
  Secondary, 21275
Orbitotomy
  with Bone Flap
    with Biopsy, 67450
    with Bone Removal for Decompression, 67445
    with Drainage, 67440
    with Foreign Body Removal, 67430
    with Lesion Removal, 67420
    for Exploration, 67450
  without Bone Flap
    with Biopsy, 67400

Orbitotomy

Orbitotomy — *continued*
  without Bone Flap — *continued*
    with Bone Removal for Decompression, 67414
    with Drainage, 67405
    with Foreign Body Removal, 67413
    with Lesion Removal, 67412
    for Exploration, 67400
  Frontal Approach, 67400-67414
  Lateral Approach, 67420-67450
  Transconjunctival Approach, 67400-67414

Orbits
  Skin Graft
    Split, 15120-15121

Orbit Wall(s)
  Decompression
    with Nasal
      Sinus Endoscopy, 31292, 31293
  Reconstruction, 21182-21184

Orchidectomies
  Laparoscopic, 54690
  Partial, 54522
  Radical, 54530-54535
  Simple, 54520
  Tumor, 54530-54535

Orchidopexy, 54640-54650, 54692

Orchidoplasty
  Injury, 54670
  Suspension, 54620-54640
  Torsion, 54600

Orchiectomy
  Laparoscopic, 54690
  Partial, 54522
  Radical
    Abdominal Exploration, 54535
    Inguinal Approach, 54530
  Simple, 54520

Orchiopexy
  Abdominal Approach, 54650
  Inguinal Approach, 54640
  Intra–Abdominal Testis, 54692
  Koop Inguinal, 54640

Orchioplasty
  Injury, 54670
  Suspension, 54620-54640
  Torsion, 54600

Organ Donor
  Life Support, 01990

Organ Grafting
  See Transplantation

Organic Acids, 83918-83921

Organ or Disease Oriented Panel
  Electrolyte, 80051
  General Health Panel, 80050
  Hepatic Function Panel, 80076
  Hepatitis Panel, 80074
  Lipid Panel, 80061
  Metabolic
    Basic
      Calcium Ionized, 80047
      Calcium Total, 80048
    Comprehensive, 80053
  Obstetric Panel, 80055
  Renal Function, 80069

Organ System, Neurologic
  See Nervous System

ORIF
  Dislocation
    Ankle, 27848
    Bennett, 26685-26686
    Bennett Thumb, 26665
    Carpometacarpal, 26685-26686
      Thumb, 26665
    Elbow, 24635
      Monteggia, 24635
    Galeazzi, 25525-25526
      with
        Repair
          Triangular Cartilage, 25526
    Hip
      Spontaneous, 27258

ORIF — *continued*
  Dislocation — *continued*
    Hip — *continued*
      Spontaneous — *continued*
        with
          Femoral Shaft Shortening, 27259
      Traumatic, 27254
        with
          Fracture
            Acetabular Wall, 27254
            Femoral Head, 27254
    Interphalangeal
      Foot, 28675
      Hand, 26785
    Knee, 27556
      with
        Ligament, Ligamentous
          Augmentation, 27558
          Reconstruction, 27558
          Repair, 27557-27558
    Lunate, 25695
    Metacarpophalangeal, 26715
    Metatarsophalangeal Joint, 28645
    Monteggia, 24635
    Odontoid, 22318-22319
    Pelvic, Pelvis
      Ring
        Anterior
          Open, 27217
          Pubis Symphysis, 27217
          Rami, 27217
        Posterior
          Open, 27218
      Sacroiliac joint
        Open, 27218
    Radioulnar
      Distal, 25676
    Sacroiliac Joint, 27218
    Sacrum, 27218
    Shoulder
      with
        Fracture
          Humeral, Humerus
            Anatomical Neck, 23680
            Surgical Neck, 23680
            Tuberosity, 23670
    Talotarsal Joint, 28585
    Tarsal, 28555
    Tarsometatarsal Joint, 28615
    Temporomandibular, 21490
    Tibiofibular Joint, 27832
      with
        Excision
          Proximal
            Fibula, 27832
    TMJ, 21490
    Trans–Scaphoperilunar, 25685
  Fracture
    Acetabulum, Acetabular
      Column
        Anterior, 27227-27228
        Posterior, 27227-27228
      T-fracture, 27228
      Wall
        Anterior, 27226, 27228
        Posterior, 27226, 27228
      Traumatic, 27254
        with
          Dislocation of Hip, 27254
    Alveolar Ridge, 21445
    Ankle
      Bimalleolar, 27814
      Trimalleolar, 27822
        with
          Fixation
            Posterior Lip, 27823
          Malleolus Fracture
            Lateral, 27822-27823

ORIF — *continued*
  Fracture — *continued*
    Ankle — *continued*
      Trimalleolar — *continued*
        with — *continued*
          Malleolus Fracture — *continued*
            Medial, 27822-27823
    Calcaneal, Calcaneus, 28415
      with
        Bone Graft, 28420
    Capitate, 25645
    Carpal (Other), 25645
      Navicular, 25628
      Scaphoid, 25628
    Clavicle, 23515
    Clavicular, 23515
    Coccyx, Coccygeal, 27202
    Colles, 25607-25609
    Craniofacial, 21432-21436
    Cuboid, 28465
    Cuneiforms, 28465
    Elbow
      Monteggia, 24635
      Periarticular, 24586-24587
    Epiphysis, Epiphyseal, 27519
    Femur, Femoral
      Condyle
        Lateral, 27514
        Medial, 27514
      Distal, 27514
        Lateral Condyle, 27514
        Medial Condyle, 27514
      Epiphysis, Epiphyseal, 27519
      Head, 27254
        Traumatic, 27254
          with
            Dislocation Hip, 27254
      Intertrochanteric, Intertrochanter, 27244-27245
        with/Intermedullary Implant, 27245
      Lateral condyle, 27514
      Medial condyle, 27514
      Peritrochanteric, Peritrochanter, 27244-27245
        with
          Intermedullary Implant, 27245
      Proximal End, 27236
        with
          Prosthetic Replacement, 27236
      Proximal Neck, 27236
        with
          Prosthetic Replacement, 27236
      Shaft, 27506-27507
        with
          Intermedullary Implant, 27245
      Subtrochanteric, Subtrochanter, 27244-27245
      Supracondylar, 27511-27513
        with
          Intercondylar Extension, 27513
      Transcondylar, 27511-27513
        with
          Intercondylar Extension, 27513
      Trochanteric, Trochanter
        Greater, 27248
        Intertrochanteric, Intertrochanter, 27244-27245
          with
            Intermedullary Implant, 27245

ORIF — *continued*
  Fracture — *continued*
    Femur, Femoral — *continued*
      Trochanteric, Trochanter — *continued*
        Peritrochanteric, Peritrochanter, 27244-27245
          with
            Intermedullary implant, 27245
        Subtrochanteric, Subtrochanter, 27244-27245
          with
            Intermedullary Implant, 27245
    Fibula and Tibia, 27828
      Distal
        with
          Tibia Fracture, 27826
    Fibula, Fibular
      Distal, 27792
      Malleolus
        Lateral, 27792
      Proximal, 27784
      Shaft, 27784
    Foot
      Sesamoid, 28531
    Frontal Sinus, 21343-21344
    Galeazzi, 25525-25526
      with
        Fracture
          Radial Shaft, 25525-25526
        Repair
          Triangular Cartilage, 25526
    Great Toe, 28505
    Hamate, 25645
    Heel, 28415
      with
        Bone Graft, 28420
    Humeral, Humerus
      Anatomical Neck, 23615-23616
      Condylar
        Lateral, 24579
        Medial, 24579
      Epicondylar
        Lateral, 24575
        Medial, 24575
      Proximal, 23615-23616
      Shaft, 24515-24516
      Supracondylar, 24545-24546
        with
          Intercondylar Extension, 24546
      Surgical Neck, 23615-23616
      Transcondylar, 24545-24546
        with
          Intercondylar Extension, 24546
      Tuberosity, 23630
    Hyoid, 21495
    Interphalangeal, 26746
    Knee
      Intercondylar Spine, 27540
      Tuberosity, 27540
    Larynx, Laryngeal, 31584
    LeFort I, 21422-21423
    LeFort II, 21346-21348
    LeFort III, 21432-21436
    Lunate, 25645
    Malar (Area), 21365-21366
      with Malar Tripod, 21365-21366
      with Zygomatic Arch, 21365-21366
    Malleolus
      Lateral, 27792
        with
          Ankle Fracture
            Trimalleolar, 27822-27823
      Medial, 27766

ORIF — *continued*
  Fracture — *continued*
    Malleolus — *continued*
      Medial — *continued*
        with
          Ankle Fracture
            Trimalleolar, 27822-27823
    Mandibular, Mandible, 21462, 21470
      Alveolar Ridge, 21445
      Condylar, Condyle, 21465
    Maxillary, Maxilla, 21422-21423
      Alveolar Ridge, 21445
    Metacarpal, 26615
    Metacarpophalangeal, 26715
    Metatarsal, 28485
    Monteggia, 24635
    Nasal Bone, 21330-21335
      with Nasal Septum, 21335
    Nasal Septum, 21335
    Nasoethmoid, 21339
    Nasomaxillary, 21346-21348
    Navicular
      Foot, 28465
      Hand, 25628
    Odontoid, 22318-22319
    Olecranon process, 24685
    Orbit, 21406-21408
    Palate, Palatal, 21422-21423
    Patella, Patellar, 27524
      with
        Patellectomy
          Complete, 27524
          Partial, 27524
        Repair
          Soft Tissue, 27524
    Phalange, Phalangeal
      Foot, 28525
        Great Toe, 28505
      Hand, 26735
        Distal, 26765
    Pisiform, 25645
    Radial, Radius
      and
        Ulnar, Ulna, 25575
      Distal, 25606-25609
        with Fracture
          Ulnar Styloid
      Head, 24665-24666
      Neck, 24665-24666
      or
        Ulnar, Ulna, 25574
      Shaft, 25515, 25525-25526
        with Dislocation
          Distal
            Radio–Ulnar Joint, 25525-25526
          with Repair
            Triangular Cartilage, 25526
    Rib, 21810
    Scaphoid, 25628
    Scapula, Scapular, 23585
    Sesamoid, 28531
    Smith, 25607, 25608-25609
    Sternum, 21825
    Talar, Talus, 28445
    Tarsal
      Calcaneal, 28415
        with Bone Graft, 28420
      Cuboid, 28465
      Cuneiforms, 28465
      Navicular, 28465
      Talus, 28445
    T–Fracture, 27228
    Thigh
      Femur, Femoral
        Condyle
          Lateral, 27514
          Medial, 27514
        Distal, 27514
          Lateral Condyle, 27514
          Medial Condyle, 27514
        Epiphysis, Epiphyseal, 27519

ORIF — *continued*
  Fracture — *continued*
    Thigh — *continued*
      Femur, Femoral — *continued*
        Head, 27254
          Traumatic, 27254
            with Dislocation
              Hip, 27254
        Intertrochanteric, Intertrochanter, 27244-27245
          with Intermedullary Implant, 27245
        Lateral Condyle, 27514
        Medial Condyle, 27514
        Peritrochanteric, Peritrochanter, 27244-27245
          with Intermedullary Implant, 27245
        Proximal End, 27236
          with Prosthetic Replacement, 27236
        Proximal Neck, 27236
          with Prosthetic Replacement, 27236
        Shaft, 27506-27507
          with Intermedullary Implant, 27245
        Subtrochanteric, Subtrochanter, 27244-27245
        Supracondylar, 27511-27513
          with Intercondylar Extension, 27513
        Transcondylar, 27511-27513
          with Intercondylar Extension, 27513
        Trochanteric, Trochanter
          Greater, 27248
          Intertrochanteric, Intertrochanter, 27244-27245
            with Intermedullary Implant, 27245
          Peritrochanteric, Peritrochanter, 27244-27245
            with Intermedullary Implant, 27245
          Subtrochanteric, Subtrochanter, 27244-27245
            with Intermedullary Implant, 27245
    Thumb, 26665
    Tibia and Fibula, 27828
    Tibia, Tibial
      Articular Surface, 27827
        with Fibula, Fibular Fracture, 27828
      Bicondylar, 27536
      Condylar
        Bicondylar, 27536
        Unicondylar, 27535
      Distal, 27826
      Pilon, 27827
        with Fibula, Fibular Fracture, 27828
      Plafond, 27827
        with Fibula, Fibular Fracture, 27828
      Plateau, 27535-27536
        Proximal, 27535-27536
      Shaft, 27758-27759
        with Fibula, Fibular Fracture, 27758-27759
        with Intermedullary Implant, 27759
      Unicondylar, 27535

ORIF — *continued*
  Fracture — *continued*
    Toe, 28525
      Great, 28505
    Trapezium, 25645
    Trapezoid, 25645
    Triquetral, 25645
    Ulna, Ulnar
      and Radial, Radius, 25575
      Monteggia, 24635
      Proximal, 24635, 24685
      Shaft, 25545
        or Radial, Radius, 25574
    Vertebral, 22325-22328
    Zygomatic Arch, 21365-21366
Ormond Disease
  Ureterolysis, 50715
Orogastric Tube
  Placement, 43752
Oropharynx
  Biopsy, 42800
Orthodontic Cephalogram, 70350
Orthomyxoviridae
  Antibody, 86710
    by Immunoassay with Direct Optical Observation, 87804
Orthomyxovirus, 86710, 87804
Orthopantogram, 70355
Orthopedic Cast
  See Cast
Orthopedic Surgery
  Computer Assisted Navigation, 20985
  Stereotaxis
    Computer Assisted, 20985
Orthoptic Training, 92065
Orthoroentgenogram, 77073
Orthosis/Orthotics
  Check–Out, 97762
  Management/Training, 97760
Os Calcis Fracture
  with Manipulation, 28405-28406
  without Manipulation, 28400
  Open Treatment, 28415-28420
  Percutaneous Fixation, 28406
Osmolality
  Blood, 83930
  Urine, 83935
Osseous Survey, 77074-77076
Osseous Tissue
  See Bone
Ossicles
  Excision
    Stapes
      with Footplate Drill Out, 69661
      without Foreign Material, 69660-69661
  Reconstruction
    Ossicular Chain
      Tympanoplasty with Antrotomy or Mastoidotomy, 69636-69637
      Tympanoplasty with Mastoidectomy, 69642, 69644, 69646
      Tympanoplasty without Mastoidectomy, 69632-69633
  Release
    Stapes, 69650
  Replacement
    with Prosthesis, 69633, 69637
OST, 59020
Ostectomy
  Carpal, 25215
  Femur, 27365
  Humerus, 24999
  Metacarpal, 26250
  Metatarsal, 28288
  Phalanges
    Fingers, 26260-26262
  Pressure Ulcer
    Ischial, 15941, 15945
    Sacral, 15933, 15935, 15937

Ostectomy — *continued*
  Pressure Ulcer — *continued*
    Trochanteric, 15951, 15953, 15958
  Radius, 25999
  Scapula, 23190
  Sternum, 21620
  Ulna, 25999
Osteocalcin, 83937
Osteocartilaginous Exostoses
  Auditory Canal
    Excision, 69140
Osteochondroma
  Auditory Canal
    Excision, 69140
Osteoclasis
  Carpal, 26989
  Clavicle, 23929
  Femur, 27599
  Humerus, 24999
  Metacarpal, 26989
  Metatarsal, 28899
  Patella, 27599
  Radius, 26989
  Scapula, 23929
  Tarsal, 28899
  Thorax, 23929
  Ulna, 26989
Osteocutaneous Flap
  with Microvascular Anastomosis, 20969-20973
Osteoma
  Sinusotomy
    Frontal, 31075
Osteomyelitis
  Excision
    Clavicle, 23180
    Facial, 21026
    Femur, 27360
    Fibula
      Distal, 27641
      Proximal, 27360
    Humerus, 24140
      Proximal, 23184
    Mandible, 21025
    Metacarpal, 26230
    Olecranon Process, 24147
    Pelvis/Hip Joint
      Deep, 27071
      Superficial, 27070
    Phalanx (Toe), 28124
    Phalanx (Finger)
      Distal, 26236
      Proximal or Middle, 26235
    Radial Head/Neck, 24145
    Scapula, 23182
    Talus/Calcaneous, 28120
    Tarsal/Metatarsal, 28122
    Tibia
      Distal, 27640
      Proximal, 27360
    Ulna, 25150
  Incision
    Elbow, 23935
    Femur, 27303
    Foot, 28005
    Forearm, 25035
    Hand/Finger, 26034
    Hip Joint, 26992
    Humerus, 23935
    Knee, 27303
    Leg/Ankle, 27607
    Pelvis, 26992
    Shoulder, 23035
    Soft Tissue, 20000-20005
    Thorax, 21510
    Wrist, 25035
  Sequestrectomy
    Clavicle, 23170
    Forearm, 25145
    Humeral Head, 23174
    Humerus, Shaft or Distal, 24134
    Olecranon Process, 24138
    Radial Head/Neck, 24136
    Scapula, 23172
    Skull, 61501

Index

Osteomyelitis — continued
- Sequestrectomy — continued
  - Wrist, 25145
- **Osteopathic Manipulation**, 98925-98929
- **Osteophytectomy**, 63075-63078
- **Osteoplasty**
  - Carpal Bone, 25394
  - Facial Bones
    - Augmentation, 21208
    - Reduction, 21209
  - Femoral Neck, 27179
  - Femur, 27179
    - Lengthening, 27466-27468
    - Shortening, 27465, 27468
  - Fibula
    - Lengthening, 27715
  - Humerus, 24420
  - Metacarpal, 26568
  - Phalanges
    - Finger, 26568
    - Toe, 28299, 28310-28312
  - Radius, 25390-25393
  - Tibia
    - Lengthening, 27715
  - Ulna, 25390-25393
  - Vertebra, 72291-72292
    - Lumbar, 22521-22522
    - Thoracic, 22520, 22522
- **Osteotomy**
  - with Graft
    - Reconstruction
      - Periorbital Region, 21267-21268
  - Blount, 27455, 27475-27485
  - Calcaneus, 28300
  - Chin, 21121-21123
  - Clavicle, 23480-23485
  - Femur
    - with Fixation, 27165
    - with Open Reduction of Hip, 27156
    - with Realignment, 27454
    - without Fixation, 27448-27450
    - Femoral Neck, 27161
    - for Slipped Epiphysis, 27181
    - Greater Trochanter, 27140
  - Fibula, 27707-27712
  - Hip, 27146-27156
    - Femoral
      - with Open Reduction, 27156
    - Femur, 27151
  - Humerus, 24400-24410
  - Mandible, 21198-21199
    - Extra-oral, 21047
    - Intra-oral, 21046
  - Maxilla, 21206
    - Extra-oral, 21049
    - Intra-oral, 21048
  - Metacarpal, 26565
  - Metatarsal, 28306-28309
  - Orbit Reconstruction, 21256
  - Patella
    - Wedge, 27448
  - Pelvis, 27158
  - Pemberton, 27147
  - Periorbital
    - Orbital Hypertelorism, 21260-21263
    - Osteotomy with Graft, 21267-21268
  - Phalanges
    - Finger, 26567
    - Toe, 28299, 28310-28312
  - Radius
    - and Ulna, 25365, 25375
    - Distal Third, 25350
    - Middle or Proximal Third, 25355
    - Multiple, 25370
  - Salter, 27146
  - Skull Base, 61582-61585, 61592
  - Spine
    - Anterior, 22220-22226
    - Posterior/Posterolateral, 22210-22214
      - Cervical, 22210

Osteotomy — continued
- Spine — continued
  - Posterior/Posterolateral — continued
    - Each Additional Vertebral Segment, 22208, 22216
    - Lumbar, 22207, 22214
    - Thoracic, 22206, 22212
    - Three-Column, 22206-22208
  - Talus, 28302
  - Tarsal, 28304-28305
  - Tibia, 27455-27457, 27705, 27709-27712
  - Ulna, 25360
    - and Radius, 25365, 25375
    - Multiple, 25370
  - Vertebra
    - Additional Segment
      - Anterior Approach, 22226
      - Posterior/Posterolateral Approach, 22208, 22216
    - Cervical
      - Anterior Approach, 22220
      - Posterior/Posterolateral Approach, 22210
    - Lumbar
      - Anterior Approach, 22224
      - Posterior/Posterolateral Approach, 22214
    - Thoracic
      - Anterior Approach, 22222
      - Posterior/Posterolateral Approach, 22212
- **Other Nonoperative Measurements and Examinations**
  - Acid Perfusion
    - Esophagus, 91030
  - Acid Reflux
    - Esophagus, 91034-91035, 91037-91038
  - Attenuation Measurements
    - Ear Protector, 92596
  - Bernstein Test, 91030
  - Breath Hydrogen, 91065
  - Bronchial Challenge Testing, 95070-95071
  - Esophageal Intubation, 91000
  - Gastric Analysis, 91052
  - Gastric Motility (Manometric) Studies, 91020
  - Information
    - Analysis of Data, 99090
  - Ingestion Challenge Test, 95075
  - Iontophoresis, 90733
  - Laryngeal Function Studies, 92520
  - Manometry
    - Anorectal, 91122
  - Photography
    - Anterior Segment, 92286
    - External Ocular, 92285
  - Provocative Testing
    - for Glaucoma, 92140
- **Otoacoustic Emission Test**, 92587-92588
- **Otolaryngology**
  - Diagnostic
    - Exam under Anesthesia, 92502
- **Otomy**
  - See Incision
- **Otoplasty**, 69300
- **Otorhinolaryngology**
  - Diagnostic
    - Otolaryngology Exam, 92502
  - Unlisted Services and Procedures, 92700
- **Ouchterlony Immunodiffusion**, 86331
- **Outer Ear**
  - CT Scan, 70480-70482
- **Outpatient Visit**, 99201-99215
- **Output, Cardiac**
  - by Indicator Dilution, 93561-93562
  - Inert Gas Rebreathing
    - During Exercise, 0105T
    - During Rest, 0104T
- **Ova**
  - Smear, 87177

Oval Window
- Repair Fistula, 69666
Oval Window Fistula
- Repair, 69666
Ovarian Cyst
- Excision, 58925
- Incision and Drainage, 58800-58805
Ovarian Vein Syndrome
- Uterolysis, 50722
Ovariectomies, 58940-58943
- with Hysterectomy, 58262-58263, 58291-58292, 58542, 58544, 58552, 58554, 58571, 58573
- for Ectopic Pregnancy, 59120, 59151
Ovariolysis, 58740
Ovary
- Abscess
  - Incision and Drainage, 58820-58822
    - Abdominal Approach, 58822
    - Vaginal Approach, 58820
- Biopsy, 58900
- Cryopreservation, 88240
- Cyst
  - Incision and Drainage, 58800-58805
  - Ovarian, 58805
- Excision, 58662, 58720
  - Cyst, 58925
  - Partial
    - Oophorectomy, 58661, 58940
    - Ovarian Malignancy, 58943
    - Peritoneal Malignancy, 58943
    - Tubal Malignancy, 58943
    - Wedge Resection, 58920
  - Total, 58940-58943
- Laparoscopy, 58660-58662, 58679
- Lysis
  - Adhesions, 58660, 58740
- Radical Resection, 58950-58952
- Transposition, 58825
- Tumor
  - Resection, 58950-58958
- Unlisted Services and Procedures, 58679, 58999
- Wedge Resection, 58920
Oviduct
- Anastomosis, 58750
- Chromotubation, 58350
- Ectopic Pregnancy, 59120-59121
- Excision, 58700-58720
- Fulguration
  - Laparoscopic, 58670
- Hysterosalpingography, 74740
- Laparoscopy, 58679
- Ligation, 58600-58611
- Lysis
  - Adhesions, 58740
- Occlusion, 58615
  - Laparoscopic, 58671
- Repair, 58752
  - Anastomosis, 58750
  - Create Stoma, 58770
- Unlisted Services and Procedures, 58679, 58999
- X-ray with Contrast, 74740
Ovocyte
- See Oocyte
Ovulation Tests, 84830
Ovum Implantation, 58976
Ovum Transfer Surgery, 58976
Oxalate, 83945
Oxidase, Ceruloplasmin, 82390
Oxidoreductase, Alcohol-Nad+, 84588
Oximetry (Noninvasive)
- See Also Pulmonology, Diagnostic
- Blood O2 Saturation
  - Ear or Pulse, 94760-94762
Oxoisomerase, 84087
Oxosteroids, 83586-83593
Oxycodinone, 80102-80103, 83925
Oxygenation, Extracorporeal Membrane
- Cannulization, 36822
Oxygen Saturation, 82805-82810
- Ear Oximetry, 94760-94762

Oxygen Saturation — continued
- Pulse Oximetry, 94760-94762
Oxyproline, 83500-83505
Oxytocin Stress Test, Fetal, 59020

P

Pacemaker, Heart
- See Also Cardiology, Defibrillator, Heart
- Conversion, 33214
- Electronic Analysis
  - Antitachycardia System, 93724
- Electrophysiologic Evaluation, 93640-93642
- Evaluation, 93286, 93288, 93293-93294, 93296
- Insertion, 33206-33208
  - Electrode(s), 33202-33203, 33210-33211, 33216-33217, 33224-33225
  - Pulse Generator, 33212-33213, 33240
- Interrogation, 93288, 93294, 93296
- Programming, 93279-93281
- Removal, 33236-33237
  - Electrodes, 33234-33235, 33238, 33243-33244
  - Pulse Generator
    - Cardioverter-Defibrillator, 33241
    - Pacemaker, 33233
- Repair
  - Electrode(s), 33218-33220
  - Leads, 33218-33220
- Replacement, 33206-33208
  - Catheter, 33210
  - Electrode(s), 33210-33211
  - Leads, 33210-33211
  - Pulse Generator, 33212-33213
- Repositioning
  - Electrodes, 33215, 33226, 33249
- Revision
  - Skin Pocket, 33222-33223
- Telephonic Analysis, 93293-93294, 93296
- Upgrade, 33214
P-Acetamidophenol
- Urine, 82003
Pachymetry
- Eye, 76514
Packing
- Nasal Hemorrhage, 30901-30906
Pain Management
- Epidural, 62350-62351, 62360-62362, 99601-99602
- Intrathecal, 62350-62351, 62360-62362, 99601-99602
- Intravenous Therapy, 96360-96368, 96374-96376
Pain Therapy, 62350-62365
Palatal Augmentation Prosthesis, 21082
Palatal Lift Prosthesis, 21083
Palate
- Abscess
  - Incision and Drainage, 42000
- Biopsy, 42100
- Excision, 42120, 42145
- Fracture
  - Closed Treatment, 21421
  - Open Treatment, 21422-21423
- Lesion
  - Destruction, 42160
  - Excision, 42104-42120
- Prosthesis
  - Augmentation, 21082
  - Impression, 42280
  - Insertion, 42281
  - Lift, 21089
- Reconstruction
  - Lengthening, 42226-42227
- Repair
  - Cleft Palate, 42200-42225
  - Laceration, 42180-42182
  - Vomer Flap, 42235

Index

Palate — *continued*
Unlisted Services and Procedures, 42299
Palate, Cleft
Repair, 42200-42225
Rhinoplasty, 30460-30462
Palatopharyngoplasty, 42145
Palatoplasty, 42200-42225
Palatoschisis, 42200-42225
Palm
Bursa
Incision and Drainage, 26025-26030
Fasciectomy, 26121-26125
Fasciotomy, 26040-26045
Tendon
Excision, 26170
Tendon Sheath
Excision, 26145
Incision and Drainage, 26020
Palsy, Seventh Nerve
Graft/Repair, 15840-15845
P&P, 85230
Pancoast Tumor Resection, 32503-32504
Pancreas
Anastomosis
with Intestines, 48520-48540, 48548
Anesthesia, 00794
Biopsy, 48100
Needle Biopsy, 48102
Cyst
Anastomosis, 48520-48540
Repair, 48500
Debridement
Peripancreatic Tissue, 48105
Excision
Ampulla of Vater, 48148
Duct, 48148
Partial, 48140-48146, 48150-48154, 48160
Peripancreatic Tissue, 48105
Total, 48155-48160
Lesion
Excision, 48120
Needle Biopsy, 48102
Placement
Drains, 48000-48001
Pseudocyst
Drainage
Open, 48510
Percutaneous, 48511
Removal
Calculi (Stone), 48020
Removal Transplanted Allograft, 48556
Repair
Cyst, 48500
Resection, 48105
Suture, 48545
Transplantation, 48160, 48550, 48554-48556
Allograft Preparation, 48550-48552
Islet Cell, 0141T-0143T
Unlisted Services and Procedures, 48999
X-ray with Contrast, 74300-74305
Injection Procedure, 48400
Pancreas, Endocrine Only
Islet Cell
Antibody, 86341
Transplantation, 0141T-0143T
Pancreatectomy
with Transplantation, 48160
Donor, 48550
Partial, 48140-48146, 48150-48154, 48160
Total, 48155-48160
Pancreatic DNAse
See DNAse
Pancreatic Duct
Destruction
Calculi (Stone), 43265

Pancreatic Duct — *continued*
Dilation
Endoscopy, 43271
Drainage
of Cyst, 48999
Endoscopy
Collection
Specimen, 43260
Destruction
Calculi (Stone), 43265
Tumor, 43272
Dilation, 43271
Removal (Endoscopic)
Calculi (Stone), 43264
Foreign Body, 43269
Stent, 43269
Sphincterotomy, 43262
Sphincter Pressure, 43263
Tube Placement, 43267-43268
Incision
Sphincter, 43262
Removal
Calculi (Stone), 43264
Foreign Body, 43269
Stent, 43269
Tube Placement
Nasopancreatic, 43267
Stent, 43268
Tumor
Destruction, 43272
X-ray with Contrast
Guide Catheter, 74329-74330
Pancreatic Elastase 1 (PE1), 82656
Pancreatic Islet Cell AB, 86341
Pancreaticojejunostomy, 48548
Pancreatitis
Incision and Drainage, 48000
Pancreatography
Injection Procedure, 48400
Intraoperative, 74300-74301
Postoperative, 74305
Pancreatojejunostomies
See Pancreaticojejunostomy
Pancreatorrhaphy, 48545
Pancreatotomy
Sphincter, 43262
Pancreozymin-Secretin Test, 82938
Panel
See Blood Tests; Organ or Disease Oriented panel
Panniculectomy, 15830
PAP, 88141-88167, 88174-88175
Paper, Chromatography, 82487-82488
Papilla Excision, 46230 [46220]
Papilla, Interdental
See Gums
Papilloma
Destruction
Anus, 46900-46924
Penis, 54050-54065
Papillotomy, 43262
Destruction
Anus, 46900-46924
Penis, 54050-54065
PAPP D, 83632
Pap Smears, 88141-88155, 88164-88167, 88174-88175
Paracentesis
Abdomen, 49080-49081
Eye
Anterior Chamber
with Diagnostic Aspiration of Aqueous, 65800
with Removal of Blood, 65815
with Removal Vitreous and or Discission of Anterior Hyaloid Membrane, 65810
with Therapeutic Release of Aqueous, 65805
Thorax, 32421-32422
Paracervical Nerve
Injection
Anesthetic, 64435
Paraffin Bath Therapy, 97018
Paraganglioma, Medullary, 80424

Parainfluenza Virus
Antigen Detection
Immunofluorescence, 87279
Paralysis, Facial Nerve
Graft, 15840-15845
Repair, 15840-15845
Paralysis, Infantile
Polio
Antibody, 86658
Vaccine, 90712-90713
Paranasal Sinuses
See Sinus
Parasites
Blood, 87206-87209
Concentration, 87015
Examination, 87169
Smear, 87177
Tissue, 87220
Parasitic Worms, 86682
Parathormone, 83970
Parathyrin, 83970
Parathyroid Autotransplantation, 60512
Parathyroidectomy, 60500-60505
Parathyroid Gland
Autotransplant, 60512
Biopsy, 60699
Excision, 60500-60502
Exploration, 60500-60505
Nuclear Medicine
Imaging, 78070
Parathyroid Hormone, 83970
Parathyroid Hormone Measurement, 83970
Parathyroid Transplantation, 60512
Para-Tyrosine, 84510
Paraurethral Gland
Abscess
Incision and Drainage, 53060
Paravertebral Nerve
Destruction, 64622-64627
Injection
Anesthetic, 64490-64495
Neurolytic, 64622-64627
Parietal Cell Vagotomies, 43641
Parietal Craniotomy, 61556
Paring
Skin Lesion
Benign Hyperkeratotic
More than Four Lesions, 11057
Single Lesion, 11055
Two to Four Lesions, 11056
Park Posterior Anal Repair, 46761
Paronychia
Incision and Drainage, 10060-10061
Parotid Duct
Diversion, 42507-42510
Reconstruction, 42507-42510
Parotidectomy, 61590
Parotid Gland
Abscess
Incision and Drainage, 42300-42305
Calculi (Stone)
Excision, 42330, 42340
Excision
Partial, 42410-42415
Total, 42420-42426
Tumor
Excision, 42410-42426
Parotitides, Epidemic
See Mumps
Pars Abdominalis Aortae
See Aorta, Abdominal
Partial Claviculectomy, 23120, 23180
Partial Colectomy, 44140-44147, 44160, 44204-44208, 44213
Partial Cystectomy, 51550-51565
Partial Esophagectomy, 43116-43124
Partial Gastrectomy, 43631-43635, 43845
Partial Glossectomy, 41120-41135
Partial Hepatectomy, 47120, 47125-47130, 47140-47142
Partial Mastectomies, 19301-19302

Partial Mastectomies — *continued*
See Also Breast, Excision, Lesion
Partial Nephrectomy, 50240, 50543
Partial Pancreatectomy, 48140-48146, 48150, 48153-48154, 48160
Partial Splenectomy, 38101, 38120
Partial Thromboplastin Time, 85730-85732
Partial Ureterectomy, 50220, 50546
Particle Agglutination, 86403-86406
Parvovirus
Antibody, 86747
Patch
Allergy Tests, 95044
Patella
See Also Knee
Dislocation, 27560-27566
Excision, 27350
with Reconstruction, 27424
Fracture, 27520-27524
Reconstruction, 27437-27438
Repair
Chondromalacia, 27418
Instability, 27420-27424
Patellar Tendon Bearing (PTB) Cast, 29435
Patellectomy, 27350, 27524, 27566
with Reconstruction, 27424
Paternity Testing, 86910-86911
Patey's Operation
Mastectomy, Modified Radical, 19307
Pathologic Dilatation
See Dilation
Pathology
Clinical
Consultation, 80500-80502
Surgical
Consultation, 88321-88325
Intraoperative, 88329-88332
Decalcification Procedure, 88311
Electron Microscopy, 88348-88349
Gross and Micro Exam
Level II, 88302
Level III, 88304
Level IV, 88305
Level V, 88307
Level VI, 88309
Gross Exam
Level I, 88300
Histochemistry, 88318-88319
Immunocytochemistry, 88342
Immunofluorescent Study, 88346-88347
Morphometry
Nerve, 88356
Skeletal Muscle, 88355
Tumor, 88358, 88361
Nerve Teasing, 88362
Special Stain, 88312-88314
Staining, 88312-88314
Tissue Hybridization, 88365
Unlisted Services and Procedures, 88399, 89240
Patient
Dialysis Training
Completed Course, 90989
Education
Heart Failure, 4003F
Patterson's Test
Blood Urea Nitrogen, 84520, 84525
Paul-Bunnell Test
See Antibody; Antibody Identification; Microsomal Antibody
P B Antibodies, 86308-86310
PBG
Urine, 84106-84110
PBSCT (Peripheral Blood Stem Cell Transplant), 38240-38242
PCL, 27407, 29889
PCP, 83992
PCR (Polymerase Chain Reaction), 83898-83902, 83904-83912
Peak Flow Rate, 94150

Pean's Operation

Pean's Operation
  Amputation, Leg, Upper, at Hip, 27290
Pectoral Cavity
  See Chest Cavity
Pectus Carinatum
  Reconstructive Repair, 21740-21742
    with Thoracoscopy, 21743
Pectus Excavatum Repair
  Anesthesia, 00474
  Reconstructive Repair, 21740-21742
    with Thoracoscopy, 21743
PEDIARIX, 90723
Pediatric Critical Care
  Initial, 99471
  Subsequent, 99472
Pedicle Fixation, 22842-22844
Pedicle Flap
  Formation, 15570-15576
  Island, 15740
  Neurovascular, 15750
  Transfer, 15650
PedvaxHIB, 90647
PEEP, 94660
Peet Operation
  See Nerves, Sympathectomy, Excision
PEG, 43246
Pelvic Adhesions, 58660, 58662, 58740
Pelvic Bone
  Drainage, 26990
Pelvic Exam, 57410
Pelvic Exenteration, 51597
  for Colorectal Malignancy, 45126
Pelvic Fixation
  Insertion, 22848
Pelvic Lymphadenectomy, 38562, 38765
  with Hysterectomy, 58210, 58548, 58951, 58954
  with Prostatectomy, 55812-55815, 55842-55845
  with Prostate Exposure, 55862-55865
  with Trachelectomy, 57531
  with Vaginectomy, 57112
  with Vulvectomy, 56640
  for Malignancy, 58951, 58958-58960
  Laparoscopic, 38571-38572, 58548
Pelvimetry, 74710
Pelviolithotomy, 50130
Pelvis
  See Also Hip
  Abscess
    Incision and Drainage, 26990, 45000
  Angiography, 72191
  Biopsy, 27040-27041
  Bone
    Drainage, 26992
  Brace Application, 20662
  Bursa
    Incision and Drainage, 26991
  CT Scan, 72191-72194
  Cyst
    Aspiration, 50390
    Injection, 50390
  Destruction
    Lesion, 58662
  Endoscopy
    Destruction of Lesions, 58662
    Lysis of Adhesions, 58660
    Oviduct Surgery, 58670-58671
  Exclusion
    Small Intestine, 44700
  Exenteration
    for Colorectal Malignancy, 45126
    for Gynecologic Malignancy, 58240
    for Prostatic Malignancy, 51597
    for Urethral Malignancy, 51597
    for Vesical Malignancy, 51597
  Halo, 20662
  Hematoma
    Incision and Drainage, 26990

Pelvis — continued
  Lysis
    Adhesions, 58660
  Magnetic Resonance Angiography, 72198
  Magnetic Resonance Imaging (MRI), 72195-72197
  Removal
    Foreign Body, 27086-27087
  Repair
    Osteotomy, 27158
    Tendon, 27098
  Ring
    Dislocation, 27193-27194, 27216-27218
    Fracture, 27216-27218
      Closed Treatment, 27193-27194
  Tumor, 27047-27049 [27043, 27045], 27065, 27075-27078
  Ultrasound, 76856-76857
  Unlisted Services and Procedures, 27299
  X-ray, 72170-72190, 73540
  Manometry, 74710
Pelvi-Ureteroplasty, 50400-50405
Pemberton Osteotomy of Pelvis, 27158
Penectomy, 54120-54135
Penetrating Keratoplasties, 65730-65755
Penile Induration
  Injection, 54200
    with Surgical Exposure, 54205
  Plaque Excision, 54110
    with Graft, 54111-54112
Penile Prosthesis
  Insertion
    Inflatable, 54401-54405
    Semi-Rigid, 54400
  Removal Only
    Inflatable, 54406, 54415
    Semi-Rigid, 54415
  Repair
    Inflatable, 54408
  Replacement
    Inflatable, 54410-54411, 54416-54417
    Semi-Rigid, 54416-54417
Penile Rigidity Test, 54250
Penile Tumescence Test, 54250
Penis
  Amputation
    Partial, 54120
    Radical, 54130-54135
    Total, 54125-54135
  Biopsy, 54100-54105
  Circumcision
    with Clamp or Other Device, 54150
    Newborn, 54150
    Repair, 54163
    Surgical Excision, 54161
    Newborn, 54160
  Excision
    Partial, 54120
    Prepuce, 54150-54161, 54163
    Total, 54125-54135
  Frenulum
    Excision, 54164
  Incision
    and Drainage, 54015
    Prepuce, 54000-54001
  Injection
    for Erection, 54235
    Peyronie Disease, 54200
      Surgical Exposure Plaque, 54205
    Vasoactive Drugs, 54231
    X-ray, 54230
  Insertion
    Prosthesis
      Inflatable, 54401-54405
      Noninflatable, 54400
  Irrigation
    Priapism, 54220

Penis — continued
  Lesion
    Destruction
      Any Method
        Extensive, 54065
        Cryosurgery, 54056
        Electrodesiccation, 54055
        Laser Surgery, 54057
        Simple, 54050-54060
        Surgical Excision, 54060
    Excision, 54060
      Penile Plaque, 54110-54112
    Nocturnal Tumescence Test, 54250
  Occlusion
    Vein, 37790
  Plaque
    Excision, 54110-54112
    Plethysmography, 54240
  Prepuce
    Stretch, 54450
  Reconstruction
    Angulation, 54360
    Chordee, 54300-54304, 54328
    Complications, 54340-54348
    Epispadias, 54380-54390
    Hypospadias, 54328-54352
    Injury, 54440
  Removal
    Foreign Body, 54115
    Prosthesis
      Inflatable, 54406, 54415
      Semi-Rigid, 54415
  Repair
    Fistulization, 54435
    Priapism with Shunt, 54420-54430
    Prosthesis
      Inflatable, 54408
  Replacement
    Prosthesis
      Inflatable, 54410-54411, 54416-54417
      Semi-Rigid, 54416-54417
  Revascularization, 37788
  Rigidity Test, 54250
  Test Erection, 54250
  Unlisted Services and Procedures, 54699, 55899
  Venous Studies, 93980-93981
Penis Adhesions
  Lysis
    Post-circumcision, 54162
Penis Prostheses
  See Penile Prosthesis
Pentagastrin Test
  Gastric Analysis Test, 91052
Pentamidine
  Inhalation Treatment, 94640-94644
Peptidase P
  Angiotensin Converting Enzyme (ACE), 82164
Peptidase S
  Leucine Aminopeptidase, 83670
Peptide, Connecting, 80432, 84681
Peptide, Vasoactive Intestinal, 84586
Peptidyl Dipeptidase A
  Angiotensin Converting Enzyme (ACE), 82164
Percutaneous Abdominal Paracentesis, 49080-49081
Percutaneous Aspiration
  Bartholin's Gland, 58999
  Gallbladder, 47999
  Seminal Vesicle, 54699, 55899
Percutaneous Atherectomies, 35490-35495
Percutaneous Biopsy, Gallbladder/Bile Ducts, 47553
Percutaneous Cardiopulmonary Bypass, 33999
Percutaneous Cystostomy, 53899
Percutaneous Discectomies, 62287
  Diagnostic, 62267
Percutaneous Electric Nerve Stimulation
  Electrode Insertion, 64553-64565

Percutaneous Lumbar Discectomy, 62287
Percutaneous Lysis, 62263-62264
Percutaneous Nephrostomies, 50395, 52334
Percutaneous Transluminal Angioplasty
  Artery
    Aortic, 35472
    Brachiocephalic, 35475
    Coronary, 92982, 92984
    Femoral-Popliteal, 35474
    Iliac, 35473
    Pulmonary, 92997, 92998
    Renal, 35471
    Tibioperoneal, 35470
    Visceral, 35471
  Venous, 35476
Percutaneous Transluminal Coronary Angioplasty
  See Percutaneous Transluminal Angioplasty
Percutaneous Vertebroplasty, 22520-22522
Pereyra Procedure, 51845, 57289, 58267, 58293
Performance Measures
  See Also Physician Quality Reporting Indicators (PQRI)
  ACE Inhibitor Therapy, 4009F
  Acute Otitis
    Examination
      Membrane Mobility, 2035F
    History
      Auricular Pain, 1116F
    Intervention
      Antimicrobial Therapy, 4131F-4132F
      Effusion Antihistamines, 4133F-4134F
      Systemic Antimicrobials, 4131F-4132F
      Systemic Steroids, 4135F-4136F
      Topical Therapy, 4130F
  Anginal Symptom Assessment, 1002F
  Antiplatelet Therapy, 4011F
  Beta-Blocker Therapy, 4006F
  Blood Pressure, 2000F
    Postpartum Care Visit, 0503F
    Prenatal Care Visit Initial, 0500F
    Prenatal Care Visit Subsequent, 0502F
    Prenatal Flow Sheet, 0501F
  Statin Therapy, 4002F
  Tobacco Use
    Assessment, 1000F, 1034F-1036F
    Counseling, 4000F
    Pharmacologic Therapy, 4001F
Performance Test
  See Also Physical Medicine/Therapy/Occupational Therapy
  Cognitive, 96125
  Performance Test Physical Therapy, 97750
  Psychological Test, 96101-96103
    Computer-Assisted, 96103
Perfusion
  Brain
    Imaging, 0042T
  Myocardial, 78451-78454
    Imaging, 78466-78469
    Positron Emission Tomography (PET)
      Myocardial Imaging, 78491-78492
Perfusion, Intracranial Arterial
  Thrombolysis, 61624
Perfusion Pump
  See Infusion Pump
Pericardectomies, 33030-33031
  See Excision, Pericardium
  Endoscopic, 32659, 32660
Pericardial Cyst
  See Cyst, Pericardial

Index

Pericardial Cyst — *continued*
  Excision, 33050
    Thoracoscopic, 32661
Pericardial Sac
  Drainage, 32659
Pericardial Window
  for Drainage, 33025
    Thoracoscopic, 32659
Pericardiectomy
  Complete, 33030-33031
  Subtotal, 33030-33031
  via Thoracoscopy, 32659-32660
Pericardiocentesis, 33010-33011
  Ultrasound Guidance, 76930
Pericardiostomy
  Tube, 33015
Pericardiotomy
  Removal
    Clot/Foreign Body, 33020
      via Thoracoscopy, 32658
Pericardium
  Cyst
    Excision, 32661, 33050
  Excision, 32659, 33030-33031
  Incision, 33030-33031
    with Tube, 33015
    Removal
      Clot, 33020
      Foreign Body, 33020
  Incision and Drainage, 33025
  Lung
    Pneumonocentesis, 32420
  Puncture Aspiration, 33010-33011
  Removal
    Clot
      Endoscopic, 32658
    Foreign Body
      Endoscopic, 32658
  Tumor
    Excision, 32661, 33050
Peridural Anesthesia
  See Anesthesia, Epidural
Peridural Injection, 62281-62282, 62310-62319, 64479-64484
Perineal Prostatectomy
  Partial, 55801
  Radical, 55810-55815
Perineoplasty, 56810
Perineorrhaphy
  Repair
    Rectocele, 57250
Perineum
  Abscess
    Incision and Drainage, 56405
  Biopsy, 56605-56606
  Colposcopy, 99170
  Debridement
    Infected, 11004, 11006
  Removal
    Prosthesis, 53442
  Repair, 56810
  X-ray with Contrast, 74775
Perionychia, 10060-10061
Periorbital Region
  Reconstruction–Osteotomy
    with Graft, 21267-21268
  Repair–Osteotomy, 21260-21263
Peripheral Artery Disease (PAD) Rehabilitation, 93668
Peripheral Blood Stem Cell Transplant, 38240-38242
Peripheral Nerve
  Repair/Suture
    Major, 64856, 64859
Periprosthetic Capsulotomy
  Breast, 19371
Peristaltic Pumps
  See Infusion Pump
Peritoneal Dialysis, 4055F, 90945-90947
  Kt/V Level, 3082F-3084F
  Training
    Counseling, 90989, 90993
Peritoneal Free Air, 49400
Peritoneal Lavage, 49080-49081
Peritoneocentesis, 49080-49081

Peritoneoscopy
  Biopsy, 47561, 49321
  Exploration, 49320
  Radiologic, 47560
Peritoneum
  Abscess
    Incision and Drainage, 49020
      Percutaneous, 49021
  Chemotherapy Administration, 96445
    See Chemotherapy
  Endoscopy
    Biopsy, 47561
    Drainage
      Lymphocele, 49323
    X-ray, 47560
  Exchange
    Drainage Catheter, 49423
  Injection
    Contrast
      Via Catheter, 49424
  Ligation
    Shunt, 49428
  Removal
    Cannula
      Catheter, 49422
    Foreign Body, 49402
    Shunt, 49429
  Tumor
    Resection, 58950-58954
  Unlisted Services and Procedures, 49999
  Venous Shunt, 49427
  X-ray, 74190
Persistent, Omphalomesenteric Duct
  Excision, 44800
Persistent Truncus Arteriosus
  See Truncus Arteriosus
  Repair, 33786
Personal Care
  See Self Care
Personality Test, 96101-96103
  Computer-Assisted, 96103
Pertussis Immunization, 90698-90701, 90715, 90720-90723
Pessary
  Insertion, 57160
Pesticides
  Chlorinated Hydrocarbons, 82441
PET
  With Computed Tomography (CT)
    Limited Area, 78814
    Skull Base to Mid-thigh, 78815
    Whole Body, 78816
  Brain, 78608-78609
  Heart, 78459
  Limited Area, 78811
  Myocardial Imaging Perfusion Study, 78491-78492
  Skull Base to Mid-thigh, 78812
  Whole Body, 78813
Petrous Temporal
  Excision
    Apex, 69530
Peyreva Procedure, 51845
Peyronie Disease
  with Graft, 54110-54112
  Injection, 54200
  Surgical Exposure, 54205
PFG (Percutaneous Fluoroscopic Gastrostomy), 49440
PFT (Pulmonary Function Test), 94010-94799
PG, 84081, 84150
pH
  Blood Gases, 82800-82805
  Body Fluid, Not Otherwise Specified, 83986
  Exhaled Breath Condensate, 83987
Phacoemulsification
  Removal
    Extracapsular Cataract, 66982, 66984
    Secondary Membranous Cataract, 66850

Phagocytosis
  White Blood Cells, 86344
Phalangectomy
  Toe, 28150
    Partial, 28160
Phalanges (Hand)
  See Also Finger, Bone
  Incision, Bone Cortex, 26034
Phalanx, Finger
  Craterization, 26235, 26236
  Cyst
    Excision, 26210, 26215
  Diaphysectomy, 26235, 26236
  Excision, 26235, 26236
    Radical
      for Tumor, 26260-26262
  Fracture
    Articular
      with Manipulation, 26742
      Closed Treatment, 26740
      Open Treatment, 26746
    Distal, 26755, 26756
      Closed Treatment, 26750
      Open Treatment, 26765
      Percutaneous, 26756
    Open Treatment, 26735
      Distal, 26765
    Percutaneous Fixation, 26756
    Shaft, 26720-26727
      Open Treatment, 26735
  Incision and Drainage, 26034
  Ostectomy
    Radical
      for Tumor, 26260-26262
  Repair
    Lengthening, 26568
    Nonunion, 26546
    Osteotomy, 26567
  Saucerization, 26235, 26236
  Thumb
    Fracture
      Shaft, 26720-26727
  Tumor, 26115-26118 [26111, 26113], 26210-26215, 26260-26262
Phalanx, Great Toe
  See Also Phalanx, Toe
  Fracture
    Closed Treatment, 28490
      with Manipulation, 28495
    Open Treatment, 28505
    Percutaneous Skeletal Fixation, 28496
Phalanx, Toe
  Condyle
    Excision, 28126
  Craterization, 28124
  Cyst
    Excision, 28108
  Diaphysectomy, 28124
  Excision, 28124, 28150-28160
  Fracture
    with Manipulation, 28515
    without Manipulation, 28510
    Open Treatment, 28525
  Repair
    Osteotomy, 28310, 28312
  Saucerization, 28124
  Tumor
    Excision, 28108, 28175
Pharmaceutic Preparations
  See Drug
Pharmacotherapies
  See Chemotherapy
Pharyngeal Tonsil
  Excision, 42830-42836
    with Tonsils, 42820-42821
  Unlisted Services/Procedures, 42999
Pharyngectomy
  Partial, 42890
Pharyngolaryngectomy, 31390, 31395
Pharyngoplasty, 42950
Pharyngorrhaphy, 42900
Pharyngostomy, 42955
Pharyngotomy
  See Incision, Pharynx

Pharyngotympanic Tube
  Catheterization, 69405
  Inflation, 69400-69401
    with Myringotomy, 69420-69421
Pharynx
  See Also Nasopharynx; Throat
  Biopsy, 42800-42806
  Cineradiography, 70371, 74230
  Creation
    Stoma, 42955
  Excision, 42145
    with Larynx, 31390, 31395
    Partial, 42890
    Resection, 42892, 42894
  Hemorrhage, 42960-42962
  Lesion
    Destruction, 42808
    Excision, 42808
  Reconstruction, 42950
  Removal, Foreign Body, 42809
  Repair
    with Esophagus, 42953
  Unlisted Services and Procedures, 42999
  Video, 70371, 74230
  X-ray, 70370, 74210
Phencyclidine, 83992
Phenobarbital, 82205
  Assay, 80184
Phenothiazine, 84022
Phenotype Analysis
  by Nucleic Acid
    Infectious Agent
      HIV-1 Drug Resistance, 87903, 87904
Phenotype Prediction
  by Generic Database
    HIV-1
      Drug Susceptibility, 87900
    Using Regularly Updated Genotypic
      Bioinformatics, 87900
Phenylalanine, 84030
Phenylalanine–Tyrosine Ratio, 84030
Phenylketones, 84035
Phenylketonuria, 84030
Phenytoin
  Assay, 80185, 80186
Pheochromocytoma, 80424
Pheresis, 36511-36516
Phlebectasia
  with Tissue Excision, 37735-37760
  Ablation, 36475-36479
  Removal, 37718-37735, 37765-37785
Phlebectomy
  Stab, 37765-37766
Phlebographies, 75820-75880, 75885, 75893, 78445, 78457-78458
  Injection, 36005
Phleborheography, 93965
Phleborrhaphy
  Femoral, 37650
  Iliac, 37660
  Vena Cava, 37620
Phlebotomy
  Therapeutic, 99195
Phonocardiogram
  Evaluation, 93799
  Intracardiac, 93799
  Tracing, 93799
Phoria
  See Strabismus
Phosphatase
  Alkaline, 84075, 84080
    Blood, 84078
    Forensic Examination, 84061
Phosphatase, Acid, 84060
  Blood, 84066
Phosphate, Pyridoxal, 84207
Phosphatidylcholine Cholinephosphohydrolase
  See Tissue Typing
Phosphatidyl Glycerol, 84081
Phosphatidylglycerol, 84081
Phosphocreatine Phosphotransferase, ADP, 82550-82552

Phosphogluconate–6
Dehydrogenase, 84085
Phosphoglycerides, Glycerol, 84081
Phosphohexose Isomerase, 84087
Phosphohydrolases
Alkaline, 84075-84080
Forensic Examination, 84061
Phosphokinase, Creatine, 82550-82552
Phospholipase C
See Tissue Typing
Phospholipid Antibody, 86147, 86148
Phospholipid Cofactor Antibody, 0030T
Phosphomonoesterase, 84061, 84075-84080
Phosphoric Monoester Hydrolases, 84061, 84075-84080
Phosphorous, 84100
Urine, 84105
Phosphotransferase, ADP Phosphocreatine, 82550-82552
Photochemotherapies, Extracorporeal, 36522
Photochemotherapy, 96910-96913
See Also Dermatology
Endoscopic Light, 96570-96571
Photocoagulation
Endolaser Panretinal
Vitrectomy, 67040
Focal Endolaser
Vitrectomy, 67040
Iridoplasty, 66762
Lesion
Cornea, 65450
Retina, 0017T, 67210, 67227, 67228
Retinal Detachment
Prophylaxis, 67145
Repair, 67105, 67113
Retinopathy, 67229
Photodensity
Radiographic Absorptiometry, 77083
Photodynamic Therapy
External, 96567
Photography
Ocular
Anterior Segment, 92286, 92287
External, 92285
Fundus, 92250
Skin, Diagnostic, 96904
Photo Patch
Allergy Test, 95052
See Also Allergy Tests
Photopheresis
Extracorporeal, 36522
Photophoresis
See Actinotherapy; Photochemotherapy
Photoradiation Therapies
See Actinotherapy
Photoscreen
Ocular, 99174
Photosensitivity Testing, 95056
See Also Allergy Tests
Phototherapies
See Actinotherapy
Phototherapy, Ultraviolet, 0168T, 96900
Phrenic Nerve
Anastomosis
to Facial Nerve, 64870
Avulsion, 64746
Incision, 64746
Injection
Anesthetic, 64410
Transection, 64746
Physical Examination
Office and/or Other Outpatient Services, 99201-99205
Physical Medicine/Therapy/Occupational Therapy
See Also Neurology, Diagnostic
Activities of Daily Living, 97535, 99509

Physical Medicine/Therapy/Occupational Therapy — continued
Aquatic Therapy
with Exercises, 97113
Athletic Training
Evaluation, 97005
Re-evaluation, 97006
Check-Out
Orthotics/Prosthetics
ADL, 97762
Cognitive Skills Development, 97532
Community/Work Reintegration, 97537
Evaluation, 97001, 97002
Hydrotherapy
Hubbard Tank, 97036
Pool with Exercises, 97036, 97113
Joint Mobilization, 97140
Kinetic Therapy, 97530
Manipulation, 97140
Manual Therapy, 97140
Modalities
Contrast Baths, 97034
Diathermy Treatment, 97024
Electric Stimulation
Attended, Manual, 97032
Unattended, 97014
Hot or Cold Pack, 97010
Hydrotherapy (Hubbard Tank), 97036
Infrared Light Treatment, 97026
Iontophoresis, 97033
Microwave Therapy, 97024
Paraffin Bath, 97018
Traction, 97012
Ultrasound, 97035
Ultraviolet Light, 97028
Unlisted Services and Procedures, 97039
Vasopneumatic Device, 97016
Whirlpool Therapy, 97022
Orthotics Training, 97760
Osteopathic Manipulation, 98925-98929
Procedures
Aquatic Therapy, 97113
Direct, 97032
Gait Training, 97116
Group Therapeutic, 97150
Massage Therapy, 97124
Neuromuscular Reeducation, 97112
Physical Performance Test, 97750
Supervised, 97010-97028
Therapeutic Exercises, 4018F, 97110
Traction Therapy, 97140
Work Hardening, 97545, 97546
Prosthetic Training, 97761
Sensory Integration, 97533
Therapeutic Activities, 97530
Unlisted Services and Procedures, 97139, 97799
Wheelchair Management, 97542
Work Reintegration, 97537
Physical Therapy
See Physical Medicine/Therapy/Occupational Therapy
Physician Quality Reporting Indicators (PQRI)
A1c, 3044F-3046F
ABO and RH Blood Typing, 3293F
Advance Care Plan
Discussion, 1123F-1124F, 1158F
Document, 1157F
Age-Related Eye Disease Study (AREDS), 4177F
Alarm Symptoms, 1070F-1071F
Alcohol Use, 4320F
American Joint Committee on Cancer (AJCC) Staging, 3300F, 3321F, 3370F-3390F
Anesthesia
Duration, 4255F-4256F

Physician Quality Reporting Indicators (PQRI) — continued
Antibiotic Therapy, 4120F, 4124F
Antidepressant Therapy, 4063F-4064F
Antihistamines or Decongestant, 4133F-4134F
Antimicrobial Therapy, 4131F-4132F
Antiretroviral Therapy, 4270F-4271F, 4276F
Arterio-venous (AV) Fistula, 4051F
Aspirin Therapy, 4084F
Assessment
Alarm Symptoms, 1070F-1071F
Angina, 1002F
Anti-Inflamatory/Analgesic Medications, 1007F
Asthma, 1005F, 1038F-1039F
Auricular or Periauricular Pain, 1116F
Back Pain and Function, 1130F
Cataract Surgery, 0014F
Chest X-ray, 3006F
Colonoscopy, 3018F
Colorectal Cancer Screening, 3017F
Community Acquired Bacterial Pneumonia, 0012F
Comorbid Conditions, 1026F
COPD, 1015F, 1018F-1019F
Depression, 1040F
DXA Results, 3095F-3096F
Dysphagia, 6010F, 6015F
Dyspnea, 1018F-1019F
Fall Risk, 1100F-1101F, 3288F
Functional Expiratory Volume, 3040F, 3042F
Functional Status, 1170F
Gastrointestinal and Renal Risk Factors, 1008F
GERD, 1118F
Heart Failure, 0001F
Hemoglobin A1c, 3044F-3046F
Hydration Status, 2018F, 2030F-2031F
Influenza Immunization, 1030F
LDL, 3048F-3050F
Left Ventricle, 3020F-3022F
Level of Activity, 1002F
Lipid Panel, 3011F
Mammogram, 3014F, 3340F-3350F
Mental Status, 2014F, 2044F
Microalbuminuria, 3060F-3062F
Mobility
Tympanic Membrane, 2035F
Moles, 1050F
Optic Nerve Head, 2027F
Osteoarthritis, 0005F, 1006F-1008F, 2004F
Oxygen Saturation, 3028F, 3035F, 3037F
Pneumococcus Immunization, 1022F
Pneumonia, 0012F
Preoperative, 3325F
Rehabilitation, 4079F
Retinopathy, 3072F
Rh, 3290F-3291F
Rheumatoid Arthritis Prognosis, 3475F-3476F
Risk Factors
Thromboembolism, 1180F
Screen
Depression, 1220F, 3351F-3354F
Suicide Risk, 3085F
Spirometry, 3023F, 3025F, 3027F
Tissue Plasminogen Activator (t-PA), 4077F
Tobacco Use, 1000F, 1034F-1036F
Tympanic Membrane, 2035F
Urinary Incontinence, 1090F-1091F

Physician Quality Reporting Indicators (PQRI) — continued
Assessment — continued
Visual Function, 1055F
Volume Overload, 1004F, 2002F
Asthma, 1038F-1039F
Barium Swallow, 3142F, 3200F
Barrett's Esophagus, 3140F
Beta Blocker, 4115F
Biopsy
Site Other Than Primary Tumor, 3250F
Biphosphonate Therapy, 4100F
Blood Pressure, 0513F, 2000F, 3074F-3080F
Body Mass Index (BMI), 3008F
Bone Scan, 3269F-3270F
Breast Imaging-Reporting and Data System (BI-RADS), 3340F-3345F
Information Entered into Internal Database, 7020F
Cancer
American Joint Committee on Cancer (AJCC), 3300F, 3321F-3322F, 3370F-3390F
Breast, 3315F-3316F
Metastatic, 3301F
Pathology Report, 3317F-3318F
Stage, 3301F
Carotid, 3100F
Imaging Report, 3100F
Cataract
Preoperative Assessment, 0014F
Presurgical Axial Length, 3073F
Visual Acuity, 4175F
CD4+, 3500F
Chemotherapy
Colon Cancer, 4180F
Planned Chemotherapy Regimen, 0519F
Chest X-ray, 3006F
Colonoscopy
Follow-up (10 years), 0528F
Interval 3+ Years, 0529F
Communication
Diagnostic Mammogram, 5060F, 5062F
Risk
Fracture, 5100F
Treatment Plan, 5050F
Treatment Summary, 5020F
Compression Therapy, 4267F-4269F
Coronary Artery Bypass Graft (CABG), 4110F
Corticosteroids, 4135F-4136F
Counseling
Against Bed Rest, 4248F
Age-Related Eye Disease Study (AREDS), 4177F
Alcohol, 4320F
Risk with Hep-C, 4158F
Contraceptive, 4159F
Epilepsy, 4330F, 4340F, 6070F
Exercise, 4242F
Exercise and Calcium/Vitamin D, 4019F
Glaucoma, 4174F
Prostate Cancer, 4163F
Resume Normal Activities, 4245F
Self Examination for Moles, 5005F
Tobacco, 4004F
Treatment Options
Alcohol, 4320F
Opioid, 4306F
UV Protection, 4176F
CT or MRI
Brain, 3111F-3112F
Epilepsy, Ordered, Reviewed, or Requested, 3324F
Hemorrhage, Mass Lesion, and Acute Infarction, 3110F

Index — Physician Services

Physician Quality Reporting Indicators (PQRI) — *continued*
Culture
  Wound, 4260F-4261F
Cytogenic Testing
  Bone Marrow, 3155F
Deep Vein Thrombosis (DVT) Prophylaxis, 4070F
Depression, 0545F, 1040F, 2060F, 3092F-3093F, 3351F-3354F
Diagnostic Imaging Studies
  Not Ordered, 3331F
  Ordered, 3319F-3320F, 3330F
Discharge
  Inpatient Facility, 1110F
Instructions
  Heart Failure, 4014F
  Medications Reconciled, 1111F
  Within Last 60 Days, 1110F
Disease Activity
  Rheumatoid Arthritis (RA), 3470F-3472F
Dressing, 4265F-4266F
Dual-energy X-ray Absorptiometry (DXA), 3095F-3096F
ECG, 3120F
Education
  Alcohol Risk, 4158F
  Foot Care, 4305F
  Gastroenteritis, 4058F
  Heart Failure, 4003F
EEG, 3650F
Electroconvulsive Therapy (ECT), 4066F-4067F
Elevation
  Head of Bed, 4167F
Endoscopy
  Upper, 3140F-3141F
Epilepsy, 1205F, 5200F, 6070F
Erythropoietin Therapy, 4090F, 4095F, 4171F-4172F
Evaluation Hepatitis C
  Initial, 1119F
  Subsequent, 1121F
Exam
  Back, 2040F
  Foot, 2028F
  Fundus, 2020F-2021F, 5010F
  Joints, 2004F
  Macular, 2019F, 2021F
  Retina, 2022F
  Skin, 2029F
Exercise
  Counseling, 4019F, 4242F
  Instruction, 4240F
  Therapeutic, 4018F
Fibrillation, 1060F-1061F
Follow-Up
  Colonoscopy, 0528F-0529F
  Melanoma, 0015F
Functional Expiratory Volume, 3040F-3042F
GERD, 1118F, 3130F-3142F, 3150F
Glucocorticoid Therapy, 0540F, 4192F-4194F
Goals of care, 1152F-1153F
Hearing Test, 3230F
Hemodialysis, 0505F, 4052F-4054F
Hemoglobin Level, 3279F-3281F
Hepatitis, 1119F, 1121F, 3215F-3216F, 3218F, 3220F, 3265F-3266F, 3514F-3515F, 4148F-4159F, 4275F
History
  AIDS-Defining Condition, 3490F
  Moles, 1050F
  HIV Status, 3292F, 3491F-3503F
Hypertension, 4050F
ICU, 4168F-4169F
Influenza Immunization, 4035F, 4037F, 4274F
International Normalization Ratio, 3555F
Intraocular Pressure (IOP), 3284F-3285F
Iron Stores, 3160F

Physician Quality Reporting Indicators (PQRI) — *continued*
Ischemic Stroke Symptoms, 1065F-1066F
Kt/V, 3082F-3084F
LDL-C, 3048F-3050F
Lipid Panel, 3011F
Medications Documented and Reviewed, 1159F-1160F
Medication Therapy
  Angiotensin Converting Enzyme (ACE) or Angiotensin Receptor Blockers (ARB), 4210F
  Anticonvulsant Medication, 4230F
  Digoxin, 4220F
  Diuretic Medication, 4221F
Melanoma
  Follow-Up, 0015F
  Greater than AJCC Stage 0 or 1A, 3321F-3322F
Microalbuminuria, 3060F-3062F
Nephropathy Treatment, 3066F
Normothermia Maintained Intraoperatively, 4250F
Not Prescribed
  Antibiotic, 4124F
  Corticosteroids, 4192F
NPO Ordered, 6020F
Oral Rehydration, 4056F
Ordered
  Calcium, Phosphorus, Parathyroid Hormone, Lipid Profile, 3278F
  Imaging Studies, 3319F, 3330F
Osteoporosis
  Fracture, 5015F
  Pharmacologic Therapy, 4005F
Otitis Externa, 4130F
Oxygen Saturation, 3028F, 3035F, 3037F
Pain
  Auricular or Periauricular, 1116F
  Back, 1130F, 1134F-1137F, 2044F
  Severity, 1125F-1126F
Pathology, 3260F
Patient Information
  Entered into Internal Database, 7010F
  Entered into Reminder System, 7025F
Peginterferon and Ribavirin, 4153F
Performance Status Before Surgery, 3328F
Peritoneal Dialysis, 0507F, 4055F
Plan of Care
  Advance, 1123F-1124F
  Anemia, 0516F
  Blood Pressure, 0513F
  Chemotherapy, 0519F
  Depression, 0545F
  Dyspnea Management, 0535F
  Falls, 0518F
  Glaucoma, 0517F
  Glucorticoid Management, 0540F
  Hemodialysis, 0505F
  Hemoglobin Level, 0514F
  HIV RNA Control, 0575F
  Hypertension, 4050F
  Pain, 0521F
  Severity, 1125F-1126F
  Peritoneal dialysis, 0507F
  Urinary Incontinence, 0509F
Pneumatic Otoscopy, 2035F
Pneumococcal Vaccine Administration, 4040F
Postpartum Care, 0503F
Prenatal
  Rh, 3290F-3291F
Prenatal Care, 0500F-0502F
  Anti-D Immune Globulin, 4178F
Prescribed
  ACE Inhibitor or ARB Therapy, 4009F

Physician Quality Reporting Indicators (PQRI) — *continued*
Prescribed — *continued*
  Adjuvant chemotherapy perscribed, 4180F
  Age Related Eye Disease Study (AREDS), 4177F
  Antibiotic, 4120F, 4124F
  Anticoagulant, 4075F
  Antidepressant, 4064F
  Antihistamines or Decongestants, 4133F
  Anti-inflammatory Agent, 4016F
  Anti-inflammatory/Analgesic, 4016F
  Antimicrobial, 4131F-4132F
  Antiplatelet Therapy, 4011F, 4073F
  Antipsychotic, 4065F
  Antiviral, 4150F
  Asthma Treatment, 4015F
  Beta Blocker Therapy, 4006F
  Corticosteroids, 4135F
  Disease Modifying Anti-Rheumatic Drug Therapy Prescribed or Dispensed., 4187F
  Empiric Antibiotic, 4045F
  GI Prophylaxis for NSAIDS, 4017F
  Inhaled Bronchodilator, 4025F
  Osteoporosis Therapy, 4005F
  Otitis Externa Medication, 4130F
  Oxygen Therapy, 4030F
  Statin Therapy, 4002F
  Tamoxifen, 4179F
  Therapeutic Exercise, 4018F
  Warfarin Therapy, 4012F
Prophylaxis
  Antibiotic, 4041F-4043F, 4046F-4049F
  Cefazolin or Cefuroxime, 4041F
  for Deep Vein Thrombosis (DVT), 4070F
  for NSAID, 4017F
  Pneumocystis jiroveci pneumonia, 4279F-4280F
Prostate, 3268F-3274F
Prostate Specific Antigen (PSA), 3268F
Proton Pump Inhibitor (PPI) or Histamine H2 Receptor Antagonist (H2RA), 4185F-4186F
Psychotherapy, 4060F, 4062F
Pulmonary
  Function Test, 3038F
  Rehabilitation, 4033F
Radiation Therapy
  Conformal Radiation Therapy Not Received, 4182F
  Conformal Radiation Therapy Received, 4181F
  Dose Limits Established, 0520F
  Dose Reduction Device, 6040F
  Exposure Time, 6045F
  External Beam Radiotherapy, 4200F-4201F
  Prostate Cancer, 4164F-4165F
  Rationale for Level of Care, 6005F
Recall System in Place, 7010F
Referral
  Arterio Venous (AV) Fistula, 4051F
  Electroconvulsive Therapy (ECT), 4066F
  Psychotherapy, 4062F
Results Reviewed
  Colorectal Cancer Screening, 3017F
  Malignancy, 3317F-3318F
  Mammography, 3014F
  Microalbuminuria Test Results, 3060F-3062F
  MRI or CT, 3324F
Retinopathy, 3072F
Rheumatoid Arthritis, 4192F-4196F

Physician Quality Reporting Indicators (PQRI) — *continued*
Risk
  Death within 1 year, 1150F-1151F
  Fracture, 3572F-3573F
  Prostate Cancer, 3272F-3274F
  Thromboembolism, 3550F-3552F
Scintigraphy Study, 3570F
Screening
  Alcohol Use, 3016F
  Cervical Cancer, 3015F
  Colorectal Cancer, 3017F
  Depression, 1220F
  Drug Use, 4290F
  Dyspnea, 3450F-3452F
  Future Fall Risk, 1100F-1101F
  Group B Strep, 3294F
  Hepatitis B, 3513F
  Hepatitis C, 3514F
  High-Risk Behavior, 4290F, 4293F
  Mammography, 3014F
  STD, 3511F-3512F
  Suicide, 3085F
  TB, 3455F, 3510F
  Tobacco Use, 4004F
Seizure
  Type, 1200F
Spirometry, 3023F, 3025F-3027F
Stereoscopic Photos, 2024F, 2026F
Sterile Barrier, 6030F
Strep Test
  Group A, 3210F
Stroke, 1066F, 3110F-3112F
TB Screening, 3455F, 3510F
Therapeutic Monitoring
  Angiotensin Converting Enzyme (ACE)/Angiotensin Receptor Blockers (ARB), 4188F
  Anticonvulsant, 4191F
  Digoxin, 4189F
  Diuretic, 4190F
Thromboembolism, 3550F
Tobacco
  Cessation, 4000F-4001F
  Use, 1035F-1036F
Treatment Plan, 5050F
Tympanometry, 2035F
Urinary Incontinence, 0509F, 1090F-1091F
Vaccine
  Hepatitis
    A, 4155F
    B, 4157F, 4275F
  Influenza, 4037F
  Pneumococcal, 4040F
Vital Signs Documented and Reviewed, 2010F
Volume Overload, 2002F
Warfarin Therapy, 4300F-4301F
Warming
  Intraoperative, 4250F
Weight Recorded, 2001F
Wound, 2050F
  Culture, 4260F-4261F
  Dressings, 4265F-4266F
Physician Services
Care Plan Oversight Services, 99339-99340, 99374-99380
  Domiciliary Facility, 99339-99340
  Home Health Agency Care, 99374
  Home/Rest Home Care, 99339-99340
  Hospice, 99377, 99378
  Nursing Facility, 99379, 99380
Case Management Services, 99366-99368
Direction, Advanced Life Support, 99288
Online, 99444
Prolonged
  with Direct Patient Contact, 99354-99357
  Outpatient Office, 99354, 99355

Physician Services — Index

Physician Services — *continued*
  Prolonged — *continued*
    with Direct Patient Services
      Inpatient, 99356, 99357
    without Direct Patient Contact, 99358, 99359
    Standby, 99360
  Supervision, Care Plan Oversight Services, 99339-99340, 99374-99380
  Team Conference, 99367
  Telephone, 99441-99443
Physiologic recording of tremor, 0199T
PICC Line Insertion, 36568-36569
Pierce Ears, 69090
Piercing of Ear Lobe, 69090
Piles
  See Hemorrhoids
Pilon Fracture Treatment, 27824
Pilonidal Cyst
  Excision, 11770-11772
  Incision and Drainage, 10080, 10081
Pin
  See Also Wire
  Insertion
    Removal
      Skeletal Traction, 20650
  Prophylactic Treatment
    Femur, 27187
    Humerus, 24498
    Shoulder, 23490, 23491
Pinch Graft, 15050
Pineal Gland
  Excision
    Partial, 60699
    Total, 60699
  Incision, 60699
Pinna
  See Ear, External
Pinworms
  Examination, 87172
Pirogoff Procedure, 27888
Pituitary Epidermoid Tumor
  See Craniopharyngioma
Pituitary Fossa
  Exploration, 60699
Pituitary Gland
  Excision, 61546, 61548
  Incision, 60699
  Tumor
    Excision, 61546, 61548, 62165
Pituitary Growth Hormone
  See Growth Hormone
Pituitary Lactogenic Hormone
  See Prolactin
Pituitectomy
  See Excision, Pituitary Gland
PKP, 65730-65755
PKU, 84030
PL, 80418, 80440, 84146
Placement
  Adjustable Gastric Restrictive Device, 43770
  Aqueous Drainage Device, 0191T-0192T
  Bronchial Stent, 31636-31637
  Catheter
    Aneurysm Sac Pressure Sensor, 34806
    Complete Study, 93982
    Bile Duct, 75982
    Brain for Chemotherapy, 0169T
    Bronchus
      for Intracavitary Radioelement Application, 31643
      See Catheterization
    for Interstitial Radioelement Application
      Breast, 19296-19298
      Genitalia, 55920
      Head/Neck, 41019
      Muscle, 20555
      Pelvic Organs, 55920
      Prostate, 55875
      Soft Tissue, 20555

Placement — *continued*
  Catheter — *continued*
    Pleural, 32550
  Catheter, Cardiac, 93503
    See Also Catheterization, Cardiac
  Cecostomy Tube, 44300, 49442
  Colonic Stent, 44397, 45327, 45345, 45387
  Dosimeter
    Prostate, 55876
  Drainage
    Pancreas, 48001
  Duodenostomy Tube, 49441
  Endovascular Prosthesis, Aorta, 33883-33886
  Enterostomy Tube, 44300
  Fiducial Markers
    intra-abdominal, 49411
    intra-pelvic, 49411
    intrathoracic, 32553
    Prostate, 55876
    retroperitoneum, 49411
  Gastrostomy Tube, 43246, 49440
  Guidance Catheter
    Abscess, 75989
    Bile, 75982
    Specimen, 75989
  Interstitial Device
    Intra-abdominal, 49411
    Intra-pelvic, 49411
    Intra-thoracic, 32553
    Prostate, 55876
    Retroperitoneum, 49411
  Intrafacet Implant(s), 0219T-0222T
  Intravascular Stent
    Coronary, 92980-92981
    Intracranial, 61635
  IVC Filter, 75940
  Jejunostomy Tube
    Endoscopic, 44372
    Percutaneous, 49441
  Metallic Localization Clip
    Breast, 19295
  Nasogastric Tube, 43752
  Needle
    Bone, 36680
    for Interstitial Radioelement Application
      Genitalia, 55920
      Head, 41019
      Muscle, 20555
      Neck, 41019
      Pelvic Organs, 55920
      Prostate, 55875
      Soft Tissue, 20555
    Head and/or Neck, 41019
    Muscle or Soft Tissue
      for Radioelement Application, 20555
    Pelvic Organs and/or Genitalia, 55920
    Prostate, 55875-55876
  Needle Wire
    Breast, 19290, 19291
  Orogastric Tube, 43752
  Pharmacological Agent
    Posterior Juxtascleral, 0124T
  Pressure Sensor, 34806
  Prosthesis, Thoracic Aorta, 75958-75959
  Radiation Delivery Device
    Intracoronary Artery, 92974
    Intraocular, 0190T
  Sensor, Wireless
    Endovascular Repair, 34806
  Seton
    Anal, 46020
  Stereotactic Frame, 20660
    Head Frame, 61800
  Subconjunctival Retinal Prosthesis Receiver, 0100T
  Tracheal Stent, 31631
  Transcatheter
    Extracranial, 0075T-0076T
    Physiologic Sensor, 34806
  Ureteral Stent, 50947

Placenta
  Delivery, 59414
Placental Lactogen, 83632
Placental Villi
  See Chorionic Villus
Plafond Fracture Treatment
  Tibial, 27824
Plagiocephaly, 21175
Plague Vaccine, 90727
Planing
  Nose
    Skin, 30120
Plantar Digital Nerve
  Decompression, 64726
Plantar Pressure Measurements
  Dynamic, 96001, 96004
Plasma
  Frozen Preparation, 86927
  Volume Determination, 78110, 78111
Plasma Prokallikrein
  See Fletcher Factor
Plasma Protein–A, Pregnancy Associated (PAPP–A), 84163
Plasma Test
  Volume Determination, 78110-78111
Plasma Thromboplastin
  Antecedent, 85270
  Component, 85250
  Frozen Preparation, 86927
Plasmin, 85400
Plasmin Antiactivator
  See Alpha–2 Antiplasmin
Plasminogen, 85420, 85421
Plasmodium
  Antibody, 86750
Plastic Repair of Mouth
  See Mouth, Repair
Plate, Bone
  See Bone Plate
Platelet
  See Also Blood Cell Count; Complete Blood Count
  Aggregation, 85576
  Antibody, 86022, 86023
  Assay, 85055
  Blood, 85025
  Count, 85032, 85049
  Neutralization, 85597
Platelet Cofactor I
  See Clotting Factor
Platelet Test
  Survival Test, 78190, 78191
Platelet Thromboplastin Antecedent, 85270
Platysmal Flap, 15825
PLC, 86822
Pleoptic Training, 92065
Plethysmography
  See Vascular Studies
  Extremities, 93922, 93923
  Veins, 93965
  Penis, 54240
  Total Body, 93720-93722
Pleura
  Biopsy, 32095, 32100, 32400, 32402
  Decortication, 32320
  Empyema
    Excision, 32540
  Excision, 32310, 32320
    Endoscopic, 32656
  Foreign Body
    Removal, 32150, 32151
  Incision, 32320
  Needle Biopsy, 32400
  Removal
    Foreign Body, 32150, 32653
  Repair, 32215
  Thoracotomy, 32095, 32100
  Unlisted Services and Procedures, 32999
Pleural Cavity
  Aspiration, 32421-32422
  Catheterization, 32550
  Chemotherapy Administration, 96440

Pleural Cavity — *continued*
  Chemotherapy Administration — *continued*
    See Chemotherapy
  Fusion, 32560
  Incision
    Empyema, 32035, 32036
    Pneumothorax, 32551
  Puncture and Drainage, 32421-32422
  Thoracostomy, 32035, 32036
Pleural Endoscopies
  See Thoracoscopy
Pleural Scarification
  for Repeat Pneumothorax, 32215
Pleural Tap
  See Thoracentesis
Pleurectomy
  Anesthesia, 00542
  Parietal, 32310, 32320
  Endoscopic, 32656
Pleuritis, Purulent, 21501-21502
Pleurocentesis, 32422
Pleurodesis
  Agent for Pleurodesis, 32560
  Endoscopic, 32650
Pleurosclerosis
  See Pleurodesis
Pleurosclerosis, Chemical
  See Pleurodesis, Chemical
Plexectomy, Choroid
  See Choroid Plexus, Excision
Plexus Brachialis
  See Brachial Plexus
Plexus Cervicalis
  See Cervical Plexus
Plexus, Choroid
  See Choroid Plexus
Plexus Coeliacus
  See Celiac Plexus
Plexus Lumbalis
  See Lumbar Plexus
PLGN
  See Plasminogen
Plication
  Diaphragm, 39599
Plication, Sphincter, Urinary Bladder
  See Bladder, Repair, Neck
PLIF (Posterior Lumbar Interbody Fusion), 22630
Pneumocentesis
  Lung, 32420
Pneumocisternogram
  See Cisternography
Pneumococcal Vaccine, 90669-90670, 90732
Pneumocystis Carinii
  Antigen Detection, 87281
Pneumoencephalogram, 78635
Pneumoencephalography
  Anesthesia, 01935-01936
Pneumogastric Nerve
  See Vagus Nerve
Pneumogram
  Pediatric, 94772
Pneumolysis, 32940
Pneumonectomy, 32440-32500
  Completion, 32488
  Donor, 32850, 33930
  Sleeve, 32442
  Total, 32440-32445
Pneumonology
  See Pulmonology
Pneumonolysis, 32940
  Intrapleural, 32652
  Open Intrapleural, 32124
Pneumonostomy, 32200-32201
Pneumonotomy
  See Incision, Lung
Pneumoperitoneum, 49400
Pneumoplethysmography
  Ocular, 93875
Pneumothorax
  Agent for Pleurodesis, 32560
  Pleural Scarification for Repeat, 32215

Index

Pneumothorax — *continued*
  Therapeutic
    Injection Intrapleural Air, 32960
    Thoracentesis with Tube Insertion, 32422
PNEUMOVAX 23, 90732
Polio
  Antibody, 86658
  Vaccine, 90698, 90712, 90713
Poliovirus Vaccine, Inactivated
  See Vaccines
Pollicization
  Digit, 26550
Polya Anastomosis, 43632
Polya Gastrectomy, 43632
Polydactylism, 26587, 28344
Polydactylous Digit
  Excision, Soft Tissue Only, 11200
  Reconstruction, 26587
  Repair, 26587
Polydactyly, Toes, 28344
Polymerase Chain Reaction, 83898
Polyp
  Antrochoanal
    Removal, 31032
  Esophagus
    Ablation, 43228
  Nose
    Excision
      Endoscopic, 31237-31240
      Extensive, 30115
      Simple, 30110
    Removal
      Sphenoid Sinus, 31051
  Urethra
    Excision, 53260
Polypectomy
  Nose
    Endoscopic, 31237
  Uterus, 58558
Polypeptide, Vasoactive Intestinal
  See Vasoactive Intestinal Peptide
Polysomnography, 95808-95811
Polyuria Test
  Water Load Test, 89235
Pomeroy's Operation
  Tubal Ligation, 58600
Pooling
  Blood Products, 86965
Pool Therapy with Exercises, 97036, 97113
Popliteal Arteries
  See Artery, Popliteal
Popliteal Synovial Cyst
  See Baker's Cyst
Poradenitistras
  See Lymphogranuloma Venereum
PORP (Partial Ossicular Replacement Prosthesis), 69633, 69637
Porphobilinogen
  Urine, 84106, 84110
Porphyrin Precursors, 82135
Porphyrins
  Feces, 84126, 84127
  Urine, 84119, 84120
Port
  Peripheral
    Insertion, 36569-36571
    Removal, 36590
    Replacement, 36578, 36585
  Venous Access
    Insertion, 36560-36561, 36566
    Removal, 36590
    Repair, 36576
    Replacement, 36578, 36582-36583
Port-A-Cath
  Insertion, 36560-36571
  Removal, 36589-36590
  Replacement, 36575-36585
Portal Vein
  See Vein, Hepatic Portal
Porter–Silber Test
  Corticosteroid, Blood, 82528
Port Film, 77417
Portoenterostomy, 47701

Portoenterostomy, Hepatic, 47802
Posadas–Wernicke Disease, 86490
Positional Nystagmus Test
  See Nystagmus Test, Positional
Positive End Expiratory Pressure
  See Pressure Breathing, Positive
Positive–Pressure Breathing, Inspiratory
  See Intermittent Positive Pressure Breathing (IPPB)
Positron Emission Tomography (PET)
  With Computed Tomography (CT)
    Limited, 78814
    Skull Base to Mid-thigh, 78815
    Whole Body, 78816
  Brain, 78608, 78609
  Heart, 78459
  Limited, 78811
  Myocardial Imaging Perfusion Study, 78491-78492
  Perfusion Study, 78491, 78492
  Skull Base to Mid-thigh, 78812
  Whole Body, 78813
Postauricular Fistula
  See Fistula, Postauricular
Postcaval Ureter
  See Retrocaval Ureter
Postmortem
  See Autopsy
Postoperative Wound Infection
  Incision and Drainage, 10180
Postop Vas Reconstruction
  See Vasovasorrhaphy
Post–Op Visit, 99024
Postpartum Care
  Cesarean Section, 59515
    After Attempted Vaginal Delivery, 59622
    Previous, 59610, 59614-59618, 59622
  Postpartum Care Only, 59430
  Vaginal Delivery, 59410, 59430
    After Previous Cesarean Delivery, 59614
Potassium
  Hydroxide Examination, 87220
  Serum, 84132
  Urine, 84133
Potential, Auditory Evoked
  See Auditory Evoked Potentials
Potential, Evoked
  See Evoked Potential
Potts-Smith Procedure, 33762
Pouch, Kock
  See Kock Pouch
PPD, 86580
PPH, 59160
PPP, 85362-85379
PRA, 86805-86808
Prealbumin, 84134
Prebeta Lipoproteins
  See Lipoprotein, Blood
Pregl's Test
  Cystourethroscopy, Catheterization, Urethral, 52005
Pregnancy
  Abortion
    Induced, 59855-59857
      by Amniocentesis Injection, 59850-59852
      by Dilation and Curettage, 59840
      by Dilation and Evacuation, 59841
    Septic, 59830
    Therapeutic
      by Dilation and Curettage, 59851
      by Hysterotomy, 59852
      by Saline, 59850
  Antepartum Care, 0500F-0502F, 59425, 59426
  Cesarean Section, 59618-59622
    with Hysterectomy, 59525
    Only, 59514

Pregnancy — *continued*
  Cesarean Section — *continued*
    Postpartum Care, 0503F, 59514, 59515
    Routine Care, 59510
    Vaginal Birth After, 59610-59614
  Ectopic
    Abdominal, 59130
    Cervix, 59140
    Interstitial
      Partial Resection Uterus, 59136
      Total Hysterectomy, 59135
    Laparoscopy
      with Salpingectomy and/or Oophorectomy, 59151
      without Salpingectomy and/or Oophorectomy, 59150
    Miscarriage
      Surgical completion
        Any Trimester, 59812
        First Trimester, 59820
        Second Trimester, 59821
    Molar
      See Hydatidiform Mole
    Multifetal Reduction, 59866
    Placenta Delivery, 59414
    Tubal, 59121
      with Salpingectomy and/or Oophorectomy, 59120
    Vaginal Delivery, 59409, 59410
      After Cesarean Section, 59610-59614
      Antepartum Care, 59425-59426
      Postpartum Care, 59430
      Total Obstetrical Care, 59400, 59610, 59618
Pregnancy Test
  Blood, 84702-84703
  Urine, 81025
Pregnanediol, 84135
Pregnanetriol, 84138
Pregnenolone, 84140
Prekallikrein
  See Fletcher Factor
Prekallikrein Factor, 85292
Premature, Closure, Cranial Suture
  See Craniosynostosis
Prenatal Procedure
  Amnioinfusion
    Transabdominal, 59070
  Drainage
    Fluid, 59074
  Occlusion
    Umbilical Cord, 59072
  Shunt, 59076
  Unlisted Procedure, 59897
Prenatal Testing
  Amniocentesis, 59000
    with Amniotic Fluid Reduction, 59001
  Chorionic Villus Sampling, 59015
  Cordocentesis, 59012
  Fetal Blood Sample, 59030
  Fetal Monitoring, 59050
    Interpretation Only, 59051
  Non–Stress Test, Fetal, 59025, 99500
  Oxytocin Stress Test, 59020
  Stress Test
    Oxytocin, 59020
  Ultrasound, 76801-76817
    Fetal Biophysical Profile, 76818, 76819
    Fetal Heart, 76825
Prentiss Operation
  Orchiopexy, Inguinal Approach, 54640
Preparation
  for Transfer
    Embryo, 89255
  for Transplantation
    Heart, 33933, 33944
    Heart/Lung, 33933
    Intestines, 44715-44721
    Kidney, 50323-50329
    Liver, 47143-47147

Preparation — *continued*
  for Transplantation — *continued*
    Lung, 32855-32856, 33933
    Pancreas, 48551-48552
    Renal, 50323-50329
  Thawing
    Embryo
      Cryopreserved, 89352
    Oocytes
      Cryopreserved, 89356
    Reproductive Tissue
      Cryopreserved, 89354
    Sperm
      Cryopreserved, 89353
Presacral Sympathectomy
  See Sympathectomy, Presacral
Prescription
  Contact Lens, 92310-92317
  See Contact Lens Services
Pressure, Blood, 2000F, 2010F
  24-Hour Monitoring, 93784-93790
  Diastolic, 3078F-3080F
  Systolic, 3074F-3075F
  Venous, 93770
Pressure Breathing
  See Pulmonology, Therapeutic
  Negative
    Continuous (CNP), 94662
  Positive
    Continuous (CPAP), 94660
Pressure Measurement of Sphincter of Oddi, 43263
Pressure Sensor, Aneurysm, 34806
Pressure Trousers
  Application, 99199
Pressure Ulcer (Decubitus)
  See Also Debridement; Skin Graft and Flap
  Excision, 15920-15999
    Coccygeal, 15920, 15922
    Ischial, 15940-15946
    Sacral, 15931-15937
    Trochanter, 15950-15958
    Unlisted Procedures and Services, 15999
Pressure, Venous, 93770
Pretreatment
  Red Blood Cell
    Antibody Identification, 86970-86972
  Serum
    Antibody Identification, 86975-86978
Prevention and Control
  See Prophylaxis/Prophylactic Treatment
Preventive Medicine, 99381-99387
  See Also Immunization; Newborn Care, Normal; Office and/or Other Outpatient Services; Prophylactic Treatment
  Administration and Interpretation of Health Risk Assessment, 99420
  Counseling and/or Risk Factor Reduction Intervention, 99401-99429
  Established Patient, 99382-99397
  Established Patient Exam, 99391-99397
  Intervention, 99401-99429
    Behavior Change, 99406-99408
    Calcium/Vitamin D Use, 4019F
    Exercise, 4019F
    Group Counseling, 99411-99412
    Individual Counseling, 99401-99404
      Self-Examination for Moles, 5005F
  Newborn Care, 99461
  New Patient Exam, 99381-99387
  Respiratory Pattern Recording, 94772
  Unlisted Services and Procedures, 99429
Prevnar, 90669

Priapism

Priapism
  Repair
    with Shunt, 54420, 54430
    Fistulization, 54435
Primidone
  Assay, 80188
PRITS (Partial Resection Inferior Turbinates), 30140
PRL
  See Prolactin
Proalbumin
  See Prealbumin
Probes, DNA
  See Nucleic Acid Probe
Probes, Nucleic Acid
  See Nucleic Acid Probe
Probing
  Nasolacrimal Duct, 68816
Procainamide
  Assay, 80190, 80192
Procalcitonin (PCT), 84145
Procedure, Fontan
  See Repair, Heart, Anomaly
Procedure, Maxillofacial
  See Maxillofacial Procedures
Process
  See anatomic Term (e.g., coracoid, odontoid)
Process, Odontoid
  See Odontoid Process
Procidentia
  Rectal
    Excision, 45130, 45135
    Repair, 45900
Procoagulant Activity, Glomerular
  See Thromboplastin
Proconvertin, 85230
Proctectasis
  See Dilation, Rectum
Proctectomy
  Laparoscopic, 45395-45397
    with Colectomy/Ileostomy, 44211-44212
  Open Approach, 45110-45123
    with Colectomy, 45121
    with Colectomy/Ileostomy, 44155-44158
Proctocele
  See Rectocele
Proctopexy, 45400-45402, 45540-45550
  with Sigmoid Excision, 45550
Proctoplasty, 45500, 45505
Proctorrhaphy
  Fistula, 45800-45825
  Prolapse, 45540-45541
Proctoscopies
  See Anoscopy
Proctosigmoidoscopy
  Ablation
    Polyp or Lesion, 45320
  Biopsy, 45305
  Destruction
    Tumor, 45320
  Dilation, 45303
  Exploration, 45300
  Hemorrhage Control, 45317
  Placement
    Stent, 45327
  Removal
    Foreign Body, 45307
    Polyp, 45308-45315
    Tumor, 45315
  Stoma
    through Artificial, 45999
  Volvulus Repair, 45321
Proctostomy
  Closure, 45999
Proctotomy, 45160
Products, Gene
  See Protein
Proetz Therapy, 30210
Profibrinolysin, 85420-85421
Progenitor Cell
  See Stemm Cell
Progesterone, 84144

Progesterone Receptors, 84234
Progestin Receptors, 84234
Programming
  Cardioverter-Defibrillator, 93282-93284, 93287
  Loop Recorder, 93285
  Pacemaker, 93279-93281, 93286
Proinsulin, 84206
Pro–Insulin C Peptide
  See C–Peptide
Projective Test, 96101-96103
Prokallikrein, 85292
Prokallikrein, Plasma, 85292
Prokinogenase, 85292
Prolactin, 80418, 80440, 84146
Prolapse
  See procidentia
Prolapse, Rectal
  See Procidentia, Rectum
Prolastin
  See Alpha–1 Antitrypsin
Prolonged Services
  with Direct Patient Contact, 99354-99357
  without Direct Patient Contact, 99358, 99359
  Physician Standby Services, 99360
PROM, 95851, 95852, 97110, 97530
Pronuclear Stage Tube Transfer (PROST), 58976
Prophylactic Treatment
  See Also Preventive Medicine
  Antibiotic Documentation, 4042F-4043F, 4045F-4049F
  Antimicrobial Documentation, 4041F
  Clavicle, 23490
  Femoral Neck and Proximal Femur
    Nailing, 27187
    Pinning, 27187
    Wiring, 27187
  Femur, 27495
    Nailing, 27495
    Pinning, 27495
    Wiring, 27495
  Humerus, 23491
    Pinning, Wiring, 24498
  Radius, 25490, 25492
    Nailing, 25490, 25492
    Pinning, 25490, 25492
    Plating, 25490, 25492
    Wiring, 25490, 25492
  Shoulder
    Clavicle, 23490
    Humerus, 23491
  Tibia, 27745
  Ulna, 25491, 25492
    Nailing, 25491, 25492
    Pinning, 25491, 25492
    Plating, 25491, 25492
    Wiring, 25491, 25492
  Venous Thromboembolism (VTE), 4044F
Prophylaxis
  Anticoagulant Therapy, 4075F
  Deep Vein Thrombosis (DVT), 4070F
  Retinal Detachment
    Cryotherapy, 67141
      Cryotherapy, Diathermy, 67141
      Photocoagulation, 67145
    Diathermy, 67141
    Photocoagulation, 67145
ProQuad, 90710
PROST (Pronuclear Stage Tube Transfer), 58976
Prostaglandin, 84150
  Insertion, 59200
Prostanoids
  See Prostaglandin
Prostate
  Ablation
    Cryosurgery, 55873
  Abscess
    Drainage, 52700
    Incision and Drainage, 55720, 55725

Prostate — continued
  Biopsy, 55700, 55705, 55706
  Brachytherapy
    Needle Insertion, 55875
  Coagulation
    Laser, 52647
  Destruction
    Cryosurgery, 55873
    Thermotherapy, 53850
      Microwave, 53850
      Radio Frequency, 53852
  Enucleation, Laser, 52649
  Excision
    Partial, 55801, 55821, 55831
    Perineal, 55801-55815
    Radical, 55810-55815, 55840-55845
    Retropubic, 55831-55845
    Suprapubic, 55821
    Transurethral, 52402, 52601
  Exploration
    with Nodes, 55862, 55865
    Exposure, 55860
  Incision
    Exposure, 55860-55865
    Transurethral, 52450
  Insertion
    Catheter, 55875
    Needle, 55875
    Radioactive Substance, 55860
  Needle Biopsy, 55700, 55706
  Placement
    Catheter, 55875
    Dosimeter, 55876
    Fiducial Marker, 55876
    Interstitial Device, 55876
    Needle, 55875
  Thermotherapy
    Transurethral, 53850
  Ultrasound, 76872, 76873
  Unlisted Services and Procedures, 54699, 55899
    Urinary System, 53899
  Urethra
    Stent Insertion, 53855
  Vaporization
    Laser, 52648
Prostatectomy, 52601
  Laparoscopic, 55866
  Perineal
    Partial, 55801
    Radical, 55810, 55815
  Retropubic
    Partial, 55831
    Radical, 55840-55845, 55866
  Suprapubic
    Partial, 55821
  Transurethral, 52601
  Walsh Modified Radical, 55810
Prostate Specific Antigen
  Complexed, 84152
  Free, 84154
  Total, 84153
Prostatic Abscess
  Incision and Drainage, 55720, 55725
    Prostatotomy, 55720, 55725
    Transurethral, 52700
Prostatotomy, 55720, 55725
Prosthesis
  Augmentation
    Mandibular Body, 21125
  Auricular, 21086
  Breast
    Insertion, 19340, 19342
    Removal, 19328, 19330
    Supply, 19396
  Check–Out, 97762
    See Physical Medicine/Therapy/Occupational Therapy
  Cornea, 65770
  Endovascular
    Thoracic Aorta, 33883-33886
  Facial, 21088
  Hernia
    Mesh, 49568

Prosthesis — continued
  Hip
    Removal, 27090, 27091
    Impression and Custom Preparation (by Physician)
      Auricular, 21086
      Facial, 21088
      Mandibular Resection, 21081
      Nasal, 21087
      Obturator
        Definitive, 21080
        Interim, 21079
        Surgical, 21076
      Oral Surgical Splint, 21085
      Orbital, 21077
      Palatal
        Augmentation, 21082
        Lift, 21083
      Speech Aid, 21084
  Intestines, 44700
  Knee
    Insertion, 27438, 27445
  Lens
    Insertion, 66982-66985
    Manual or Mechanical Technique, 66982-66984
    not Associated with Concurrent Cataract Removal, 66985
  Mandibular Resection, 21081
  Nasal, 21087
  Nasal Septum
    Insertion, 30220
  Obturator, 21076
    Definitive, 21080
    Interim, 21079
  Ocular, 21077, 65770, 66982-66985, 92358
    Fitting and Prescription, 92002-92014
    Loan, 92358
    Prescription, 92002-92014
  Orbital, 21077
  Orthotic
    Check-Out, 97762
    Training, 97761
  Ossicular Chain
    Partial or Total, 69633, 69637
  Palatal Augmentation, 21082
  Palatal Lift, 21083
  Palate, 42280, 42281
  Penile
    Fitting, 54699, 55899
    Insertion, 54400-54405
    Removal, 54406, 54410-54417
    Repair, 54408
    Replacement, 54410, 54411, 54416, 54417
  Perineum
    Removal, 53442
  Skull Plate
    Removal, 62142
    Replacement, 62143
  Spectacle
    Fitting, 92352, 92353
    Repair, 92371
  Speech Aid, 21084
  Spinal
    Insertion, 22851
  Synthetic, 69633, 69637
  Temporomandibular Joint
    Arthroplasty, 21243
  Testicular
    Insertion, 54660
  Training, 97761
  Urethral Sphincter
    Insertion, 53444, 53445
    Removal, 53446, 53447
    Repair, 53449
    Replacement, 53448
  Vagina
    Insertion, 57267
  Wrist
    Removal, 25250, 25251
Protease F, 85400
Protein
  A, Plasma (PAPP-A), 84163

Index

Protein — *continued*
C–Reactive, 86140-86141
Electrophoresis, 84165-84166
Glycated, 82985
Myelin Basic, 83873
Osteocalcin, 83937
Other Fluids, 84166
Other Source, 84157
Prealbumin, 84134
Serum, 84155, 84165
Total, 84155-84160
Urine, 84156
by Dipstick, 81000-81003
Western Blot, 84181, 84182, 88372
Protein Analysis, Tissue
Western Blot, 88371-88372
Protein Blotting, 84181-84182
Protein C Activator, 85337
Protein C Antigen, 85302
Protein C Assay, 85303
Protein C Resistance Assay, 85307
Protein S
Assay, 85306
Total, 85305
Prothrombase, 85260
Prothrombin, 85210
Prothrombinase
Inhibition, 85705
Inhibition Test, 85347
Partial Time, 85730, 85732
Prothrombin Time, 85610, 85611
Prothrombokinase, 85230
Protime, 85610-85611
Proton Treatment Delivery
Complex, 77525
Intermediate, 77523
Simple, 77520, 77522
Protoporphyrin, 84202, 84203
Protozoa
Antibody, 86753
Provitamin A, 84590
Provocation Test
for Glaucoma, 92140
Provocation Tonography, 92130
Prower Factor, 85260
PRP, 67040
PSA, 84152
Free, 84154
Total, 84153
Pseudocyst, Pancreas
Drainage
Open, 48510
Percutaneous, 48511
PSG, 95808-95811
Psoriasis Treatment, 96910-96922
Psychiatric Diagnosis
Evaluation of Records, Reports, and Tests, 90885
Interventional Evaluation
Interactive, 90802
Interview and Evaluation, 90801-90802
Interactive, 90802
Major Depressive Disorder (MDD), 3088F-3093F
Diagnostic and Statistical Manual (DSM) Criteria Documented, 1040F
Narcosynthesis, 90865
Psychological Testing, 96101-96103
Cognitive Performance, 96125
Computer-Assisted, 96103
Suicide Risk Assessment, 3085F
Unlisted Services and Procedures, 90899
Psychiatric Treatment
Biofeedback Training, 90875-90876
Consultation with Family, 90887
Drug Management, 90862
Electroconvulsive Therapy, 4066F, 90870
Referral Documented, 4067F
Environmental Intervention, 90882
Family, 90846-90849, 99510
Group, 90853-90857
Hypnotherapy, 90880

Psychiatric Treatment — *continued*
Individual
Insight–Oriented
Home Visit, 99510
Hospital or Residential Care, 90816-90822
Office or Outpatient, 90804-90809
Interactive
Home Visit, 99510
Hospital or Residential Care, 90823-90829
Office or Outpatient, 90810-90815
Narcosynthesis
Analysis, 90865
Pharmacotherapy
Antidepressant, 4064F
Antipsychotic, 4065F
Psychoanalysis, 90845
Psychotherapy
Family, 90846-90849
Group, 90853-90857
Individual
Insight–Oriented
Hospital or Residential Care, 90816-90822
Office or Outpatient, 90804-90809
Interactive
Hospital or Residential Care, 90823-90829
Office or Outpatient, 90810-90815
Report Preparation, 90889
Residential
Facility Care, 90816-90829
Suicide Risk Assessment, 3085F
Unlisted Services/Procedures, 90899
Psychoanalysis, 90845
Psychodrama, 90899
Psychophysiologic Feedback, 90875-90876
Psychotherapy, 4060F-4062F
Family, 90846-90849, 99510
Group, 90853-90857
Individual
Insight–Oriented
Hospital or Residential Care, 90816-90822
Office or Outpatient, 90804-90809
Interactive
Hospital or Residential Care, 90823-90829
Office or Outpatient, 90810-90815
Referral Documented, 4062F
PT, 85610-85611, 97001-97755
PTA (Factor XI), 85210-85293
PTA, 35470-35476, 85270, 92997-92998
PTB, 29435
PTC, 85250
PTCA, 92982, 92984
Artery Aortic, 35472
Brachiocephalic, 35475
Coronary, 92982, 92984
Femoral–Popliteal, 35474
Iliac, 35473
Pulmonary, 92997, 92998
Renal, 35471
Tibioperoneal, 35470
Venous, 35476
Visceral, 35471
PTC Factor, 85250
PTE (Prolonged Tissue Expansion), 11960, 19357
Pteroylglutamic Acid, 82746, 82747
Pterygium
Excision, 65420
with Graft, 65426
Pterygomaxillary Fossa
Incision, 31040

Pterygopalatine Ganglion
Injection
anesthetic, 64505
PTH, 83970
PTHC (Percutaneous Transhepatic Cholangiography), 74320
PTK, 65400
Ptosis
See Blepharoptosis; Procidentia
PTT, 85730, 85732
Ptyalectasis, 42650-42660
Pubic Symphysis, 27282
Pubiotomy, 59899
Pubis
Craterization, 27070, 27071
Cyst
Excision, 27065-27067
Excision, 27070
Saucerization, 27070, 27071
Tumor
Excision, 27065-27067
PUBS (Percutaneous Umbilical Blood Sampling), 59012
Pudendal Nerve
Avulsion, 64761
Destruction, 64630
Incision, 64761
Injection
Anesthetic, 64430
Neurolytic, 64630
Transection, 64761
Puestow Procedure, 48548
Pulled Elbow, 24640
Pulmonary Artery, 33690
Angioplasty, 92997, 92998
Banding, 33690
Catheterization, 36013-36015
Embolism, 33910-33916
Excision, 33910-33916
Percutaneous Transluminal Angioplasty, 92997, 92998
Reimplantation, 33788
Repair, 33690, 33917-33920
Reimplantation, 33788
Shunt
from Aorta, 33755, 33762, 33924
from Vena Cava, 33766, 33767
Subclavian, 33750
Transection, 33922
Pulmonary Decortication, 32220, 32225, 32320, 32651-32652
Pulmonary Function Study, 78596
Pulmonary Haemorrhage, 32110
Pulmonary Perfusion Imaging
Nuclear Medicine, 78588
Pulmonary Valve
Incision, 33470-33474
Repair, 33470-33474
Replacement, 33475
Pulmonary Vein
Repair
Complete, 33730
Partial, 33724
Stenosis, 33726
Stenosis
Repair, 33726
Pulmonology
Diagnostic
Airway Closing Volume, 94370
Apnea Monitoring, Pediatric, 94774-94777
Bronchodilation, 94664
Bronchospasm Evaluation, 94060, 94070
Carbon Dioxide Response Curve, 94400
Carbon Monoxide Diffusion Capacity, 94720
Expired Gas Analysis
Carbon Dioxide, 94770
CO2, 94770
NO, 95012
O2 and CO2, 94681
O2 Uptake, Direct, 94680
O2 Uptake, Indirect, 94690

Pulmonology — *continued*
Diagnostic — *continued*
Expired Gas Analysis — *continued*
Oxygen and Carbon Dioxide, 94681
Oxygen Uptake, 94680
Oxygen Uptake, Indirect, 94690
Quantitative, 94250
Flow–Volume Loop, 94375
Functional Residual Capacity, 94240
Function Study, 78596
Hemoglobin Oxygen Affinity, 82820
High Altitude Simulation Test (HAST), 94452-94453
Hypoxia Response Curve, 94450
Inhalation Treatment, 94640
Maldistribution of Inspired Air, 94350
Maximum Breathing Capacity, 94200
Maximum Voluntary Ventilation, 94200
Membrane Compliance, 94750
Membrane Diffusion Capacity, 94725
Nitrogen Washout Curve, 94350
Oximetry
Ear or Pulse, 94760-94762
Resistance to Airflow, 94360
Spirometry, 94010-94070
with Bronchospasm Evaluation, 94070
Patient Initiated, 94014-94016
Sputum Mobilization with Inhalants, 94664
Stress Test, 94621
Stress Test, Pulmonary, 94620
Thoracic Gas Volume, 94260
Unlisted Services and Procedures, 94799
Vital Capacity, 94150
Therapeutic
Expired Gas Analysis, 94250
Inhalation
Pentamidine, 94642
Inhalation Treatment, 94640, 94644-94645, 94664, 99503
Intrapulmonary Surfactant Administration, 94610
Manipulation of Chest Wall, 94667, 94668
Pressure Ventilation
Negative CNPB, 94662
Positive CPAP, 94660
Ventilation Assist, 94002-94005, 99504
Unlisted Services and Procedures, 94799
Pulse Generator
Electronic Analysis, 95970-95971, 95980-95982
Heart
Insertion/Replacement, 33212, 33213
Pulse Rate Increased
Heart
Recording, 93609
Pump
See Chemotherapy, Pump Services; Infusion Pump
Pump, Infusion
See Infusion Pump
Pump Services
Oxygenator/Heat Exchange, 99190-99192
Pump Stomach for Poison, 91105
Punch Graft, 15775, 15776
Puncture
Artery, 36600
Chest
Drainage, 32421-32422

Puncture — *continued*
  Cisternal, 61050-61055
  Lumbar, 62270-62272
  Lung, 32420
  Pericardium, 33010, 33011
  Pleural Cavity
    Drainage, 32421-32422
  Skull
    Drain Fluid, 61000-61020
      Cistern, 61050
    Inject Cistern, 61055
    Inject Ventricle, 61026
    Shunt
      Drainage of Fluid, 61070
      Injection, 61070
  Spinal Cord
    Diagnostic, 62270
    Drainage Fluid, 62272
    Lumbar, 62270
  Spleen, 38999
  Tracheal
    Aspiration and/or Injection, 31612
Puncture Aspiration
  Abscess
    Skin, 10160
  Bulla, 10160
  Cyst
    Breast, 19000, 19001
    Skin, 10160
  Hematoma, 10160
Puncturing
  See Puncture
Pure–Tone Audiometry, 0208T-0209T, 92552, 92553
Pustules
  Removal, 10040
Putti–Platt Procedure, 23450
PUVA, 96912, 96913
PV, 90712, 90713
PVA (Percutaneous Vertebral Augmentation), 22523-22525
Pyelogram
  See Urography, Intravenous; Urography, Retrograde
Pyelography, 74400, 74425
  Injection, 50394
Pyelolithotomy, 50130
  Anatrophic, 50075
  Coagulum, 50130
Pyeloplasty, 50400, 50405, 50544
  Change Tube, 50398
  Repair
    Horseshoe Kidney, 50540
    Secondary, 50405
Pyeloscopy
  with Cystourethroscopy, 52351
    Biopsy, 52354
    Destruction, 52354
    Lithotripsy, 52353
    Removal
      Calculus, 52352
    Tumor Excision, 52355
Pyelostogram, 50394
Pyelostolithotomy
  Percutaneous, 50080, 50081
Pyelostomy, 50125, 50400, 50405
  Change Tube, 50398
  Closure, 53899
Pyelotomy
  with Drainage, 50125
  with Removal Calculus, 50130
  Complicated, 50135
  Endoscopic, 50570
  Exploration, 50120
Pyeloureterogram
  Antegrade, 50394
Pyeloureteroplasty, 50400, 50405, 50544
Pyloric Sphincter
  Incision, 43520
  Reconstruction, 43800
Pyloromyotomy, 43520
Pyloroplasty, 43800
  with Vagotomy, 43640

Pyothorax
  Incision and Drainage, 21501, 21502
Pyridoxal Phosphate, 84207
Pyrophosphate, Adenosine, 82030
Pyrophosphorylase, Udp Galactose, 82775-82776
Pyruvate, 84210, 84220

Q

Q Fever, 86000, 86638
Q Fever ab, 86638
QSART, 95923
QST (Quantitative Sensory Testing), 0106T-0110T
Quadrentectomy, 19301-19302
Quadriceps Repair, 27430
Qualifying Circumstances
  Anesthesia, 99100, 99116, 99135, 99140
Quantitative Sensory Testing (QST)
  Using Cooling Stimuli, 0108T
  Using Heat–Pain Stimuli, 0109T
  Using Other Stimuli, 0110T
  Using Touch Pressure Stimuli, 0106T
  Using Vibration Stimuli, 0107T
Quick Test
  Prothrombin Time, 85610, 85611
Quinidine
  Assay, 80194
Quinine, 84228

R

RabAvert, 90675
Rabies
  Immune Globulin, 90375-90376
  Vaccine, 90675-90676
Race Thin
  Special, 77470
Rachicentesis, 62270-62272
Radial Arteries
  Aneurysm, 35045
  Embolectomy, 34111
  Sympathectomy, 64821
  Thrombectomy, 34111
Radial Head, Subluxation, 24640
Radial Keratotomy, 65771
Radiation
  Blood Products, 86945
Radiation Physics
  Consultation, 77336-77370
  Unlisted Services and Procedures, 77399
Radiation Therapy
  Consultation
    Radiation Physics, 77336-77370
  CT Scan Guidance, 77014
  Dose Plan, 77300, 77305-77331
    Brachytherapy, 77326-77328
    Intensity Modulation, 77301
    Teletherapy, 77305-77321
  Field Set–Up, 77280-77295
  Localization of Patient Movement, 0197T
  Multi-leaf Collimator Device Design and Construction, 77338
  Planning, 77261-77263, 77299
  Special, 77470
  Stereotactic, 77371-77373, 77432
    Body, 77373
    Cranial Lesion, 77371-77372, 77432
  Sterioscopic X-ray Guidance, 77421
  Treatment Delivery
    Beam Modulation, 0073T
    High Energy Neutron, 77422-77423
    Intensity Modulation, 77418
    Proton Beam, 77520-77525
    Single, 77402-77406
    Stereotactic
      Body, 77373
      Cranial Lesion(s), 77371-77372
    Superficial, 77401

Radiation Therapy — *continued*
  Treatment Delivery — *continued*
    Three or More Areas, 77412-77416
    Two Areas, 77407-77411
    Weekly, 77427
  Treatment Device, 77332-77334
  Treatment Management
    One or Two Fractions Only, 77431
    Stereotactic
      Body, 77435
      Cerebral, 77432
    Unlisted Services and Procedures, 77499
    Weekly, 77427
Radiation X
  See X-Ray
Radical Excision of Lymph Nodes
  Axillary, 38740-38745
  Cervical, 38720-38724
  Suprahyoid, 38700
Radical Mastectomies, Modified, 19307
Radical Neck Dissection
  with Auditory Canal Surgery, 69155
  with Thyroidectomy, 60254
  with Tongue Excision, 41135, 41145, 41153, 41155
  Laryngectomy, 31365-31368
  Pharyngolaryngectomy, 31390, 31395
Radical Vaginal Hysterectomy, 58285
Radical Vulvectomy, 56630-56640
Radioactive Colloid Therapy, 79300
Radioactive Substance
  Insertion
    Prostate, 55860
Radiocarpal Joint
  Arthrotomy, 25040
  Dislocation
    Closed Treatment, 25660
Radiocinematographies
  Esophagus, 74230
  Pharynx, 70371, 74230
  Speech Evaluation, 70371
  Swallowing Evaluation, 74230
  Unlisted Services and Procedures, 76120-76125
Radio–Cobalt B12 Schilling Test
  Vitamin B12 Absorption Study, 78270-78272
Radioelement
  Application, 77761-77778
    with Ultrasound, 76965
  Surface, 77789
  Handling, 77790
  Infusion, 77750
Radioelement Substance
  Catheterization, 55875
  Catheter Placement
    Breast, 19296-19298
    Bronchus, 31643
    Head and/or Neck, 41019
    Muscle and/or Soft Tissue, 20555
    Pelvic Organs or Genitalia, 55920
    Prostate, 55875
  Needle Placement
    Head and/or Neck, 41019
    Muscle and/or Soft Tissue, 20555
    Pelvic Organs and Genitalia, 55920
    Prostate, 55875
Radiography
  See Radiology, Diagnostic; X-Ray
Radioimmunosorbent Test
  Gammaglobulin, Blood, 82784-82785
Radioisotope Brachytherapy
  See Brachytherapy
Radioisotope Scan
  See Nuclear Medicine
Radiological Marker
  Preoperative Placement
    Excision of Breast Lesion, 19125, 19126

Radiology
  See Also Nuclear Medicine, Radiation Therapy, X–Ray, Ultrasound
  Diagnostic
    Unlisted Services and Procedures, 76499
  Examination, 70030
    Stress Views, 77071
  Joint Survey, 77077
  Therapeutic
    Field Set-Up, 77280-77290
    Planning, 77261-77263, 77299
    Port Film, 77417
Radionuclide Therapy
  Heart, 79440
  Interstitial, 79300
  Intra–arterial, 79445
  Intra–articular, 79440
  Intracavitary, 79200
  Intravascular, 79101
  Intravenous, 79101, 79403
  Intravenous Infusion, 79101, 79403
  Oral, 79005
  Remote Afterloading, 77785-77787
  Unlisted Services and Procedures, 79999
Radionuclide Tomography, Single–Photon Emission–Computed
  Abscess Localization, 78807
  Bone, 78320
  Brain, 78607
  Cerebrospinal Fluid, 78647
  Heart, 78451-78454
  Joint, 78320
  Kidney, 78710
  Liver, 78205
  Tumor Localization, 78803
Radiopharmaceutical Therapy
  Heart, 79440
  Interstitial, 79300
    Colloid Administration, 79300
  Intra–arterial particulate, 79445
  Intra–articular, 79440
  Intracavitary, 79200
  Intravascular, 79101
  Intravenous, 78808, 79101, 79403
  Oral, 79005
  Unlisted Services and Procedures, 79999
Radiosurgery
  Cranial Lesion, 61796-61799
  Spinal Lesion, 63620-63621
Radiotherapeutic
  See Radiation Therapy
Radiotherapies
  See Irradiation
Radiotherapy
  Afterloading, 77785-77787
    Catheter Insertion, 19296-19298
  Planning, 77326-77328
Radiotherapy, Surface, 77789
Radioulnar Joint
  Arthrodesis
    with Ulnar Resection, 25830
  Dislocation
    Closed Treatment, 25525, 25675
    Open Treatment, 25676
    Percutaneous Fixation, 25671
Radius
  See Also Arm, Lower; Elbow; Ulna
  Arthroplasty, 24365
    with Implant, 24366, 25441
  Craterization, 24145, 25151
  Cyst
    Excision, 24125, 24126, 25120-25126
  Diaphysectomy, 24145, 25151
  Dislocation
    with Fracture
      Closed Treatment, 24620
      Open Treatment, 24635
    Partial, 24640
    Subluxate, 24640
  Excision, 24130, 24136, 24145, 24152
    Epiphyseal Bar, 20150

Index

Radius — continued
Excision — continued
- Partial, 25145
- Styloid Process, 25230

Fracture, 25605
- with Ulna, 25560, 25565
  - Open Treatment, 25575
- Closed Treatment, 25500, 25505, 25520, 25600, 25605
  - with Manipulation, 25605
  - without Manipulation, 25600
- Colles, 25600, 25605
- Distal, 25600-25609
  - Closed Treatment, 25600-25605
  - Open Treatment, 25607-25609
- Head/Neck
  - Closed Treatment, 24650, 24655
  - Open Treatment, 24665, 24666
- Open Treatment, 25515, 25525, 25526, 25574
- Percutaneous Fixation, 25606
- Shaft, 25500-25526
  - Open Treatment, 25515, 25574-25575

Implant
- Removal, 24164

Incision and Drainage, 25035
Osteomyelitis, 24136, 24145
Osteoplasty, 25390-25393
Prophylactic Treatment, 25490, 25492

Repair
- with Graft, 25405, 25420-25426
- Epiphyseal Arrest, 25450, 25455
- Epiphyseal Separation
  - Closed, 25600
  - Closed with Manipulation, 25605
  - Open Treatment, 25607, 25608-25609
  - Percutaneous Fixation, 25606
- Malunion or Nonunion, 25400, 25415
- Osteotomy, 25350, 25355, 25370, 25375
- and Ulna, 25365

Saucerization, 24145, 25151
Sequestrectomy, 24136, 25145
Subluxation, 24640
Tumor
- Cyst, 24120
- Excision, 24125, 24126, 25120-25126, 25170

RA Factor
- Qualitative, 86430
- Quantitative, 86431

Ramstedt Operation
- Pyloromyotomy, 43520

Ramus Anterior, Nervus Thoracicus
- Destruction, 64620
- Injection
  - Anesthetic, 64420-64421
  - Neurolytic, 64620

Range of Motion Test
- Extremities, 95851
- Eye, 92018, 92019
- Hand, 95852
- Rectum
  - Biofeedback, 90911
- Trunk, 97530

Ranula
- Treatment of, 42408

Rapid Heart Rate
- Heart
  - Recording, 93609
  - Recording, 93609

Rapid Plasma Reagin Test, 86592, 86593

Rapid Test for Infection, 86308, 86403, 86406
- Monospot Test, 86308

Rapoport Test, 52005

Raskind Procedure, 33735-33737
Rastelli Procedure, 33786
Rathke Pouch Tumor
- Excision, 61545

Rat Typhus, 86000
Rays, Roentgen
- See X-Ray

Raz Procedure, 51845
RBC, 78120, 78121, 78130-78140, 85007, 85014, 85041, 85547, 85555, 85557, 85651-85660, 86850-86870, 86970-86978

RBC ab, 86850-86870
RBL (Rubber Band Ligation)
- Hemorrhoids, [46945, 46946]
- Skin Tags, 11200-11201

Reaction
- Lip
  - without Reconstruction, 40530

Reaction, Polymerase Chain, 83898
Realignment
- Femur, with Osteotomy, 27454
- Knee, Extensor, 27422
- Muscle, 20999
  - Hand, 26989
- Tendon, Extensor, 26437

Reattachment
- Muscle, 20999
- Thigh, 27599

Receptor
- Antibody, 86243
- CD4, 86360
- Estrogen, 84233
- FC, 86243
- Progesterone, 84234
- Progestin, 84234

Receptor Assay
- Hormone, 84233
- Immunoglobulin, 86243
- Non-Hormone, 84238

Recession
- Gastrocnemius
  - Leg, Lower, 27687
- Tendon
  - Hand, 26989

RECOMBIVAX HB, 90740, 90743-90744, 90746

Reconstruction
See Also Revision
- Abdominal Wall
  - Ometal Flap, 49905
- Acetabulum, 27120, 27122
- Anal
  - with Implant, 46762
  - Congenital Absence, 46730-46740
  - Fistula, 46742
  - Graft, 46753
  - Sphincter, 46750, 46751, 46760-46762
- Ankle, 27700-27703
- Apical-Aortic Conduit, 33404
- Atrial, 33254-33259
  - Endoscopic, 33265-33266
  - Open, 33254-33259
- Auditory Canal, External, 69310, 69320
- Bile Duct
  - Anastomosis, 47800
- Bladder
  - with Urethra, 51800, 51820
  - from Colon, 50810
  - from Intestines, 50820, 51960
- Breast
  - with Free Flap, 19364
  - with Latissimus Dorsi Flap, 19361
  - with Other Techniques, 19366
  - with Tissue Expander, 19357
  - Augmentation, 19324, 19325
  - Mammoplasty, 19318-19325
    - Biesenberger, 19318
  - Nipple, 19350, 19355
  - Revision, 19380

Reconstruction — continued
- Breast — continued
  - Transverse Rectus Abdominis Myocutaneous Flap, 19367-19369
- Bronchi
  - with Lobectomy, 32501
  - with Segmentectomy, 32501
  - Graft Repair, 31770
  - Stenosis, 31775
- Canthus, 67950
- Carpal, 25443
- Carpal Bone, 25394, 25430
- Cheekbone, 21270
- Chest Wall
  - Omental Flap, 49905
  - Trauma, 32820
- Cleft Palate, 42200-42225
- Conduit
  - Apical-Aortic, 33404
- Conjunctiva, 68320-68335
  - with Flap
    - Bridge or Partial, 68360
    - Total, 68362
- Cranial Bone
  - Extracranial, 21181-21184
- Ear, Middle
  - Tympanoplasty with Antrotomy or Mastoidectomy
    - with Ossicular Chain Reconstruction, 69636, 69637
  - Tympanoplasty with Mastoidectomy, 69641
    - with Intact or Reconstructed Wall, 69643, 69644
    - with Ossicular Chain Reconstruction, 69642
    - Radical or Complete, 69644, 69645
  - Tympanoplasty without Mastoidectomy, 69631
    - with Ossicular Chain Reconstruction, 69632, 69633
- Elbow, 24360
  - with Implant, 24361, 24362
  - Total Replacement, 24363
- Esophagus, 43300, 43310, 43313
  - Creation
    - Stoma, 43350-43352
  - Esophagostomy, 43350
  - Fistula, 43305, 43312, 43314
  - Gastrointestinal, 43360, 43361
- Eye
  - Graft
    - Conjunctiva, 65782
    - Stem Cell, 65781
  - Transplantation
    - Amniotic Membrane, 65780
- Eyelid
  - Canthus, 67950
  - Second Stage, 67975
  - Total, 67973-67975
  - Total Eyelid
    - Lower, One Stage, 67973
    - Upper, One Stage, 67974
  - Transfer Tarsoconjunctival Flap from Opposing Eyelid, 67971
- Facial Bones
  - Secondary, 21275
- Fallopian Tube, 58673, 58750-58752, 58770
- Femur
  - Knee, 27442, 27443
  - Lengthening, 27466, 27468
  - Shortening, 27465, 27468
- Fibula
  - Lengthening, 27715
- Finger
  - Polydactylous, 26587
- Foot
  - Cleft, 28360
- Forehead, 21172-21180, 21182-21184
- Glenoid Fossa, 21255

Reconstruction — continued
- Gums
  - Alveolus, 41874
  - Gingiva, 41872
- Hand
  - Tendon Pulley, 26500-26502
  - Toe to Finger Transfer, 26551-26556
- Heart
  - Atrial, 33254-33259
    - Endoscopic, 33265-33266
    - Open, 33254-33259
  - Atrial Septum, 33735-33737
  - Pulmonary Artery Shunt, 33924
  - Vena Cava, 34502
- Hip
  - Replacement, 27130, 27132
  - Secondary, 27134-27138
- Hip Joint
  - with Prosthesis, 27125
- Interphalangeal Joint, 26535, 26536
  - Collateral Ligament, 26545
- Intestines, Small
  - Anastomosis, 44130
- Knee, 27437, 27438
  - with Implantation, 27445
  - with Prosthesis, 27438, 27445
  - Femur, 27442, 27443, 27446
  - Instability, 27420, 27424
  - Ligament, 27427-27429
  - Replacement, 27447
  - Revision, 27486, 27487
  - Tibia
    - Plateau, 27440-27443, 27446
- Kneecap
  - Instability, 27420-27424
- Larynx
  - Burns, 31588
  - Cricoid Split, 31587
  - Other, 31545-31546, 31588
  - Stenosis, 31582
  - Web, 31580
- Lip, 40525, 40527, 40761
- Lunate, 25444
- Malar Augmentation
  - with Bone Graft, 21210
  - Prosthetic Material, 21270
- Mandible
  - with Implant, 21244-21246, 21248, 21249
- Mandibular Condyle, 21247
- Mandibular Rami
  - with Bone Graft, 21194
  - with Internal Rigid Fixation, 21196
  - without Bone Graft, 21193
  - without Internal Rigid Fixation, 21195
- Maxilla
  - with Implant, 21245, 21246, 21248, 21249
- Metacarpophalangeal Joint, 26530, 26531
- Midface, 21188
  - with Bone Graft, 21145-21160, 21188
  - with Internal Rigid Fixation, 21196
  - without Bone Graft, 21141-21143
  - without Internal Rigid Fixation, 21195
  - Forehead Advancement, 21159, 21160
- Mouth, 40840-40845
- Nail Bed, 11762
- Nasoethmoid Complex, 21182-21184
- Navicular, 25443
- Nose
  - Cleft Lip
    - Cleft Palate, 30460, 30462
  - Dermatoplasty, 30620
  - Primary, 30400-30420
  - Secondary, 30430-30462
  - Septum, 30520
- Orbit, 21256
- Orbital Rim, 21172-21180

Reconstruction — Reduction

Reconstruction — continued
Orbital Walls, 21182-21184
Orbit Area
  Secondary, 21275
Orbitocraniofacial
  Secondary Revision, 21275
Orbit, with Bone Grafting, 21182-21184
Oviduct
  Fimbrioplasty, 58760
Palate
  Cleft Palate, 42200-42225
  Lengthening, 42226, 42227
Parotid Duct
  Diversion, 42507-42510
Patella, 27437, 27438
  Instability, 27420-27424
Penis
  Angulation, 54360
  Chordee, 54300, 54304
  Complications, 54340-54348
  Epispadias, 54380-54390
  Hypospadias, 54332, 54352
    One Stage Distal with Urethroplasty, 54324-54328
    One Stage Perineal, 54336
Periorbital Region
  Osteotomy with Graft, 21267, 21268
Pharynx, 42950
Pyloric Sphincter, 43800
Radius, 24365, 25390-25393, 25441
  Arthroplasty
    with Implant, 24366
Shoulder Joint
  with Implant, 23470, 23472
Skull, 21172-21180
  Defect, 62140, 62141, 62145
Sternum, 21740-21742
  with Thoracoscopy, 21743
Stomach
  with Duodenum, 43810, 43850, 43855, 43865
  with Jejunum, 43820, 43825, 43860
  for Obesity, 43644-43645, 43845-43848
    Gastric Bypass, 43644-43846
    Roux–en–Y, 43644, 43846
Superior–Lateral Orbital Rim and Forehead, 21172, 21175
Supraorbital Rim and Forehead, 21179, 21180
Symblepharon, 68335
Temporomandibular Joint
  Arthroplasty, 21240-21243
Throat, 42950
Thumb
  from Finger, 26550
  Opponensplasty, 26490-26496
Tibia
  Lengthening, 27715
  Tubercle, 27418
Toe
  Angle Deformity, 28313
  Extra, 28344
  Hammertoe, 28285, 28286
  Macrodactyly, 28340, 28341
  Polydactylous, 26587
  Syndactyly, 28345
  Webbed Toe, 28345
Tongue
  Frenum, 41520
Trachea
  Carina, 31766
  Cervical, 31750
  Fistula, 31755
  Graft Repair, 31770
  Intrathoracic, 31760
Trapezium, 25445
Tympanic Membrane, 69620
Ulna, 25390-25393, 25442
  Radioulnar, 25337
Ureter, 50700
  with Intestines, 50840
Urethra, 53410-53440, 53445

Reconstruction — continued
Urethra — continued
  Complications, 54340-54348
  Hypospadias
    Meatus, 53450, 53460
    One Stage Distal with Meatal Advancement, 54322
    One Stage Distal with Urethroplasty, 54324-54328
    Suture to Bladder, 51840, 51841
    Urethroplasty for Second Stage, 54308-54316
    Urethroplasty for Third Stage, 54318
Uterus, 58540
Vas Deferens, 55400
Vena Cava, 34502
  with Resection, 37799
Wound Repair, 13100-13160
Wrist, 25332
  Capsulectomy, 25320
  Capsulorrhaphy, 25320
  Realign, 25335
Zygomatic Arch, 21255
Recording
  tremor, 0199T
Rectal Bleeding
  Endoscopic Control, 45317
Rectal Packing, 45999
Rectal Prolapse
  Excision, 45130-45135
  Repair, 45900
Rectal Sphincter
  Dilation, 45910
Rectocele
  Repair, 45560
Rectopexy
  Laparoscopic, 45400-45402
  Open, 45540-45550
Rectoplasty, 45500-45505
Rectorrhaphy, 45540-45541, 45800-45825
Rectovaginal Fistula
  See Fistula, Rectovaginal
Rectovaginal Hernia
  See Rectocele
Rectum
  See Also Anus
  Abscess
    Incision and Drainage, 45005, 45020, 46040, 46060
  Biopsy, 45100
  Dilation
    Endoscopy, 45303
  Endoscopy
    Destruction
      Tumor, 45320
    Dilation, 45303
    Exploration, 45300
    Hemorrhage, 45317
    Removal
      Foreign Body, 45307
      Polyp, 45308-45315
      Tumor, 45308-45315
    Volvulus, 45321
  Excision
    with Colon, 45121
    Partial, 45111, 45113-45116, 45123
    Total, 45110, 45112, 45119, 45120
  Exploration
    Endoscopic, 45300
    Surgical, 45990
  Hemorrhage
    Endoscopic, 45317
  Injection
    Sclerosing Solution, 45520
  Laparoscopy, 45499
  Lesion
    Excision, 45108
  Manometry, 91122
  Prolapse
    Excision, 45130, 45135

Rectum — continued
Pulsed Irrigation
  Fecal Impaction, 91123
Removal
  Fecal Impaction, 45915
    by Pulsed Irrigation, 91123
  Foreign Body, 45307, 45915
Repair
  with Sigmoid Excision, 45550
  Fistula, 45800-45825, 46706-46707
  Injury, 45562, 45563
  Prolapse, 45505-45541, 45900
  Rectocele, 45560
  Stenosis, 45500
Sensation, Tone, and Compliance Test, 91120
Stricture
  Excision, 45150
Suture
  Fistula, 45800-45825
  Prolapse, 45540, 45541
Tumor
  Destruction, 45190, 45320
  Excision, 45160, 45171-45172
Unlisted Services and Procedures, 45999
Red Blood Cell (RBC)
  Antibody, 86850-86870
    Pretreatment, 86970-86972
  Count, 85032-85041
  Fragility
    Mechanical, 85547
    Osmotic, 85555, 85557
  Hematocrit, 85014
  Morphology, 85007
  Platelet Estimation, 85007
  Sedimentation Rate
    Automated, 85652
    Manual, 85651
  Sequestration, 78140
  Sickling, 85660
  Survival Test, 78130, 78135
  Volume Determination, 78120, 78121
Red Blood Cell ab, 86850-86870
Reductase, Glutathione, 82978
Reductase, Lactic Cytochrome, 83615, 83625
Reduction
  Blood Volume, 86960
  Dislocation
    Acromioclavicular
      Closed Treatment, 23545
      Open Treatment, 23550, 23552
    Ankle
      Closed Treatment, 27840, 27842
      Open Treatment, 27846, 27848
    Bennet's
      Closed Treatment, 26670, 26675
      Open Treatment, 26665, 26685, 26686
      Percutaneous Fixation, 26650, 26676
    Carpometacarpal
      Closed Treatment, 26641, 26645, 26670, 26675
      Open Treatment, 26665, 26685, 26686
      Percutaneous Fixation, 26650, 26676
    Clavicle
      Closed Treatment, 23540, 23545
      Open Treatment, 23550, 23552
    Elbow
      Closed Treatment, 24600, 24605, 24620, 24640
      Monteggia, 24620
      Open Treatment
        Acute, 24615

Reduction — continued
Dislocation — continued
  Elbow — continued
    Open Treatment — continued
      Chronic, 24615
      Monteggia, 24635
      Periarticular, 24586, 24587
  Galeazzi
    Closed Treatment, 25520
    Open Treatment, 25525, 25526
    with Fracture
      Radial Shaft, 25525, 25526
    with Repair
      Triangular Cartilage, 25526
  Hip
    Post Arthroplasty
      Closed Treatment, 27265, 27266
    Spontaneous/Pathologic
      Closed Treatment, 27257
    Developmental/Congenital
      Closed Treatment, 27257
      Open Treatment, 27258
      with Femoral Shaft Shortening, 27259
      Open Treatment, 27258
      with Femoral Shaft shortening, 27259
    Traumatic
      Closed Treatment, 27250, 27252
      Open Treatment, 27253, 27254
      with Fracture
        Acetabular Wall, 27254
        Femoral Head, 27254
  Intercarpal
    Closed Treatment, 25660
    Open Treatment, 25670
  Interphalangeal Joint
    Foot/Toe
      Closed Treatment, 28660, 28665
      Open Treatment, 28675
      Percutaneous Fixation, 28666
    Hand/Finger
      Closed Treatment, 26770, 26775
      Open Treatment, 26785
      Percutaneous Fixation, 26776
  Knee
    Closed Treatment, 27550, 27552
    Open Treatment, 27556-27558
  Lunate
    Closed Treatment, 25690
    Open Treatment, 25695
  Metacarpophalangeal Joint
    Closed Treatment, 26700-26706
    Open Treatment, 26715
  Metatarsophalangeal joint
    Closed Treatment, 28630, 28635
    Open Treatment, 28645
    Percutaneous Fixation, 28636
  Monteggia, 24635
  Odontoid
    Open Treatment, 22318, 22319
  Patella, Patellar
    Acute
      Closed Treatment, 27560, 27562

Index

Reduction — *continued*
  Dislocation — *continued*
    Patella, Patellar — *continued*
      Acute — *continued*
        Open Treatment, 27566
        Partial, 27566
        Total, 27566
      Recurrent, 27420-27424
        with Patellectomy, 27424
    Pelvic, Ring
      Closed Treatment, 27193, 27194
      Open Treatment, 27217, 27218
      Percutaneous Fixation, 27216
    Radiocarpal
      Closed Treatment, 25660
      Open Treatment, 25670
    Radio–ulnar Joint
      Closed Treatment, 25675
        with Radial Fracture, 25520
      Open Treatment, 25676
        with Radial Fracture, 25525, 25526
    Radius
      with Fracture
        Closed Treatment, 24620
        Open Treatment, 24635
      Closed Treatment, 24640
    Sacrum, 27218
    Shoulder
      Closed Treatment with Manipulation, 23650, 23655
        with Fracture of Greater Humeral Tuberosity, 23665
        with Surgical or Anatomical Neck Fracture, 23675
      Open Treatment, 23660
      Recurrent, 23450-23466
    Sternoclavicular
      Closed Treatment, 23525
      Open Treatment, 23530, 23532
    Talotarsal joint
      Closed Treatment, 28570, 28575
      Open Treatment, 28585
      Percutaneous Fixation, 28576
    Tarsal
      Closed Treatment, 28540, 28545
      Open Treatment, 28555
      Percutaneous Fixation, 28546
    Tarsometatarsal joint
      Closed Treatment, 28600
      Open Treatment, 28615
      Percutaneous Fixation, 28606
    Temporomandibular
      Closed Treatment, 21480, 21485
      Open Treatment, 21490
    Tibiofibular Joint
      Closed Treatment, 27830, 27831
      Open Treatment, 27832
    TMJ
      Closed Treatment, 21480, 21485
      Open Treatment, 21490
    Vertebral
      Closed Treatment, 22315
      Open Treatment, 22325, 22326-22328
  Forehead, 21137-21139
  Fracture
    Acetabulum, Acetabular
      Closed Treatment, 27222
      Open Treatment, 27227, 27228
        with Dislocation hip, 27254
    Alveolar Ridge
      Closed Treatment, 21440

Reduction — *continued*
  Fracture — *continued*
    Alveolar Ridge — *continued*
      Open Treatment, 21445
    Ankle
      Bimalleolar
        Closed Treatment, 27810
        Open Treatment, 27814
      Trimalleolar
        Closed Treatment, 27818
        Open Treatment, 27822
          with Fixation
            Posterior Lip, 27823
          with Malleolus Fracture
            Lateral, 27822, 27823
            Medial, 27822, 27823
    Bennett
      Closed Treatment, 26670, 26675
      Open Treatment, 26665, 26685, 26686
      Percutaneous Fixation, 26650, 26676
    Blowout
      Open Treatment, 21385-21395
    Bronchi, Bronchus
      Closed
        Endoscopic Treatment, 31630
    Calcaneal, Calcaneus
      Closed Treatment, 28405
      Open Treatment, 28415
        with
          Bone graft, 28420
      Percutaneous Fixation, 28406
    Carpal Bone(s)
      Closed Treatment, 25624, 25635
        Capitate, 25635
        Hamate, 25635
        Lunate, 25635
        Navicular, 25624
        Pisiform, 25635
        Scaphoid, 25624
        Trapezium, 25635
        Trapezoid, 25635
        Triquetral, 25635
      Open Treatment, 25628, 25645
        Capitate, 25645
        Hamate, 25645
        Lunate, 25645
        Navicular, 25628
        Pisiform, 25645
        Scaphoid, 25628
        Trapezium, 25645
        Trapezoid, 25645
        Triquetral, 25645
    Carpometacarpal
      Closed Treatment, 26645
      Open Treatment, 26665
      Percutaneous Fixation, 26650
    Cheek
      Percutaneous, 21355
    Clavicle
      Closed Treatment, 23505
      Open Treatment, 23515
    Coccyx, Coccygeal
      Open Treatment, 27202
    Colles
      Closed Treatment, 25605
      Open Treatment, 25607, 25608-25609
      Percutaneous Fixation, 25606
    Craniofacial
      Open Treatment, 21432-21436
    Cuboid
      Closed Treatment, 28455
      Open Treatment, 28465
    Cuneiforms
      Closed Treatment, 28455
      Open Treatment, 28465

Reduction — *continued*
  Fracture — *continued*
    Elbow
      Closed Treatment, 24620
      Open Treatment, 24586, 24587
    Epiphysis, Epiphyseal
      Closed Treatment, 27517
      Open Treatment, 27519
    Femur, Femoral
      Condyle
        Lateral
          Closed Treatment, 27510
          Open Treatment, 27514
        Medial
          Closed Treatment, 27510
          Open Treatment, 27514
      Distal
        Closed Treatment, 27510
          Lateral condyle, 27510
          Medial condyle, 27510
        Open Treatment, 27514
          Lateral condyle, 27514
          Medial condyle, 27514
      Epiphysis, Epiphyseal
        Closed Treatment, 27517
        Open Treatment, 27519
      Greater Trochanteric
        Open Treatment, 27248
      Head
        Traumatic, 27254
          with Dislocation Hip, 27254
        with Greater
          Trochanteric
          Open Treatment, 27248
      Intertrochanteric, Intertrochanter
        Closed Treatment, 27238, 27240
        Open Treatment, 27244, 27245
          with Intermedullary Implant, 27245
      Peritrochanteric, Peritrochanter
        Closed Treatment, 27240
        Open Treatment, 27244, 27245
          with Intermedullary Implant, 27245
      Proximal End
        Closed Treatment, 27232
        Open Treatment, 27236
          with Prosthetic Replacement, 27236
      Proximal Neck
        Closed, 27232
        Open Treatment, 27236
          with Prosthetic Replacement, 27236
      Shaft
        Closed Treatment, 27502
        Open Treatment, 27506, 27507
          with Intermedullary Implant, 27245
      Subtrochanteric, Subtrochanter
        Closed Treatment, 27240
        Open Treatment, 27244, 27245
      Supracondylar
        Closed Treatment, 27503
          with Intercondylar Extension, 27503
        Open Treatment, 27511, 27513
          with Intercondylar Extension, 27513
      Transcondylar
        Closed Treatment, 27503

Reduction — *continued*
  Fracture — *continued*
    Femur, Femoral — *continued*
      Transcondylar — *continued*
        Open Treatment, 27511, 27513
          with Intercondylar Extension, 27513
    Fibula and Tibia, 27828
    Fibula, Fibular
      Distal
        Closed Treatment, 27788
        Open Treatment, 27792
          with Fracture
            Tibia, 27828
      Malleolus
        Lateral
          Closed Treatment, 27788
          Open Treatment, 27792
      Proximal
        Closed Treatment, 27781
        Open Treatment, 27784
      Shaft
        Closed Treatment, 27781
        Open Treatment, 27784
    Foot
      Sesamoid
        Open Treatment, 28531
    Frontal Sinus
      Open Treatment, 21343, 21344
    Great Toe
      Closed Treatment, 28495
      Open Treatment, 28505
      Percutaneous Fixation, 28496
    Heel
      Closed Treatment, 28405
      Open Treatment, 28415
        with Bone graft, 28420
    Humeral, Humerus
      Anatomical neck
        Closed Treatment, 23605
        Open Treatment, 23615, 23616
      Condylar
        Lateral
          Closed Treatment, 24577
          Open Treatment, 24579
          Percutaneous Fixation, 24582
        Medial
          Closed Treatment, 24577
          Open Treatment, 24579
          Percutaneous Fixation, 24566
      Epicondylar
        Lateral
          Closed Treatment, 24565
          Open Treatment, 24575
          Percutaneous Fixation, 24566
        Medial
          Closed Treatment, 24565
          Open, 24575
          Percutaneous Fixation, 24566
      Proximal
        Closed Treatment, 23605
        Open Treatment, 23615, 23616
      Shaft
        Closed Treatment, 24505
        Open Treatment, 24515, 24516
      Supracondylar
        Closed Treatment, 24535
        Open Treatment, 24545, 24546
          with Intercondylar Extension, 24546

Reduction

Reduction — *continued*
  Fracture — *continued*
    Humeral, Humerus — *continued*
      Surgical Neck
        Closed Treatment, 23605
        Open Treatment, 23615, 23616
      Transcondylar
        Closed Treatment, 24535
        Open Treatment, 24545, 24546
        with Intercondylar Extension, 24546
      Tuberosity
        Closed Treatment, 23625
        Open Treatment, 23630
    Hyoid
      Open Treatment, 21495
    Iliac, Ilium
      Open Treatment
        Spine, 27215
        Tuberosity, 27215
        Wing, 27215
    Interphalangeal
      Closed Treatment
        Articular, 26742
      Open Treatment
        Articular, 26746
    Knee
      Intercondylar
        Spine
          Closed Treatment, 27538
          Open Treatment, 27540
        Tuberosity
          Open Treatment, 27540
    Larynx, Laryngeal
      Open Treatment, 31584
    LeFort I
      Open Treatment, 21422, 21423
    LeFort II
      Open Treatment, 21346-21348
    LeFort III
      Open Treatment, 21432-21436
    Lunate
      Closed Treatment, 25635
      Open Treatment, 25645
    Malar Area
      Open Treatment, 21360-21366
      Percutaneous Fixation, 21355
    Malar Tripod
      Open Treatment, 21360-21366
      Percutaneous Treatment, 21355
    Malleolus
      Lateral
        Closed Treatment, 27788
        Open Treatment, 27792
          with Fracture
            Ankle, Trimalleolar, 27822
      Medial
        Closed Treatment, 27762
        Open Treatment, 27766
          with Fracture
            Ankle, Trimalleolar, 27822
    Mandibular, Mandible
      Alveolar Ridge
        Closed Treatment, 21440
        Open Treatment, 21445
      Closed Treatment, 21451
      Condylar, Condyle
        Open Treatment, 21465
      Open Treatment, 21454-21462, 21470
    Metacarpal
      Closed Treatment, 26605, 26607
      Open Treatment, 26615

Reduction — *continued*
  Fracture — *continued*
    Metacarpal — *continued*
      Percutaneous Fixation, 26608
    Metacarpophalangeal
      Closed
        Articular, 26742
      Open
        Articular, 26746
    Metatarsal
      Closed Treatment, 28475
      Open Treatment, 28485
      Percutaneous Fixation, 28476
    Monteggia, 24635
    Nasal Bone
      Closed Treatment
        with Stabilization, 21320
        without Stabilization, 21315
      Open Treatment
        with External Fixation, 21330, 21335
        with Fractured Septum, 21335
    Nasal, Nose
      Closed Treatment
        with Stabilization, 21320
        without Stabilization, 21315
      Open Treatment
        with External Fixation, 21330, 21335
        with Fractured Septum, 21335
        with Internal Fixation, 21330, 21335
    Nasal Septum
      Closed Treatment, 21337
        with Stabilization, 21337
        without Stabilization, 21337
      Open Treatment
        with Nasal Bone, 21335
        with Stabilization, 21336
        without Stabilization, 21336
    Nasoethmoid
      Open Treatment
        with External Fixation, 21339
        without External Fixation, 21338
    Nasomaxillary
      Closed Treatment
        LeFort II, 21345
      Open Treatment
        LeFort II, 21346-21348
    Navicular
      Foot
        Closed Treatment, 28455
        Open Treatment, 28465
        Percutaneous Fixation, 28456
      Hand
        Closed Treatment, 25624
        Open Treatment, 25628
    Odontoid
      Open Treatment, 22318, 22319
    Olecranon process
      Closed Treatment, 24675
      Open Treatment, 24685
    Orbit
      Closed Treatment, 21401
      Open Treatment, 21406-21408
    Orbital Floor
      Blowout, 21385-21395
      Open Treatment, 21385-21395
    Palate, Palatal
      Open Treatment, 21422, 21423
    Patella, Patellar
      Open Treatment, 27524

Reduction — *continued*
  Fracture — *continued*
    Pelvic, Pelvis
      Iliac, Ilium
        Open Treatment
          Spine, 27215
          Tuberosity, 27215
          Wing, 27215
      Pelvic Ring
        Closed Treatment, 27194
        Open Treatment, 27217, 27218
        Percutaneous Fixation, 27216
    Phalange, Phalanges, Phalangeal
      Foot
        Closed Treatment, 28515
          Great Toe, 28495, 28505
        Open Treatment, 28525
          Great Toe, 28505
        Percutaneous Fixation, 28496
          Great Toe, 28496
      Hand
        Closed Treatment, 26725
          Distal, 26755
        Open Treatment, 26735
          Distal, 26765
        Percutaneous Fixation, 26727, 26756
    Pisiform
      Closed Treatment, 25635
      Open Treatment, 25645
    Radial, Radius
      Colles
        Closed Treatment, 25605
        Open Treatment, 25607, 25608-25609
        Percutaneous Fixation, 25606
      Distal
        Closed Treatment, 25605
          with Fracture
            Ulnar Styloid, 25600, 25605
        Open Treatment, 25607, 25608-25609
      Head
        Closed Treatment, 24655
        Open Treatment, 24665, 24666
      Neck
        Closed Treatment, 24655
        Open Treatment, 24665, 24666
      Shaft
        Closed Treatment, 25505
          with Dislocation
            Radio–Ulnar Joint, Distal, 25520
        Open Treatment, 25515
          with Dislocation
            Radio–Ulnar Joint, Distal, 25525, 25526
          Repair, Triangular Cartilage, 25526
      Smith
        Closed Treatment, 25605
        Open Treatment, 25607, 25608-25609
        Percutaneous Fixation, 25606
    Rib
      Open Treatment, 21805, 21810
    Sacroiliac Joint, 27218
    Sacrum, 27218
    Scaphoid
      Closed Treatment, 25624
      Open Treatment, 25628
    Scapula, Scapular
      Closed Treatment, 23575
      Open Treatment, 23585

Reduction — *continued*
  Fracture — *continued*
    Sesamoid
      Open Treatment, 28531
    Sternum
      Open Treatment, 21825
    Talar, Talus
      Closed Treatment, 28435
      Open Treatment, 28445
      Percutaneous Fixation, 28436
    Tarsal
      Calcaneal
        Closed Treatment, 28405
        Open Treatment, 28415
          With Bone Graft, 28420
        Percutaneous Fixation, 28456
      Cuboid
        Closed Treatment, 28455
        Open Treatment, 28465
        Percutaneous Fixation, 28456
      Cuneiforms
        Closed Treatment, 28455
        Open Treatment, 28465
        Percutaneous Fixation, 28456
      Navicular
        Closed Treatment, 28465
        Open Treatment, 28465
        Percutaneous Fixation, 28456
      Navicular Talus
        Closed Treatment, 28435
        Open Treatment, 28445
        Percutaneous Fixation, 28436
    T–Fracture, 27228
    Thigh
      Femur, Femoral
        Condyle
          Lateral
            Closed Treatment, 27510
            Open Treatment, 27514
          Medial
            Closed Treatment, 27510
            Open Treatment, 27514
        Distal
          Closed Treatment, 27510
          Lateral condyle, 27510
          Medial condyle, 27510
          Open, 27514
          Lateral condyle, 27514
          Medial condyle, 27514
        Epiphysis, Epiphyseal
          Closed, 27517
          Open, 27519
        Greater Trochanteric
          Open Treatment, 27248
        Head
          Traumatic, 27254
            with Dislocation
              Hip, 27254
        Intertrochanter
          Closed Treatment, 27240
          Open Treatment, 27244, 27245
            with Intermedullary Implant, 27245
        Peritrochanteric, Peritrochanter
          Closed Treatment, 27240
          Open Treatment, 27244, 27245

Index

Reduction — *continued*
  Fracture — *continued*
    Thigh — *continued*
      Femur, Femoral — *continued*
        Peritrochanteric, Peritrochanter — *continued*
          Open Treatment — *continued*
            with Intermedullary Implant, 27245
        Proximal End
          Closed Treatment, 27232
          Open Treatment, 27236
            with Prosthetic Replacement, 27236
        Proximal Neck
          Closed Treatment, 27232
          Open Treatment, 27236
            with Prosthetic Replacement, 27236
        Shaft
          Closed Treatment, 27502
          Open Treatment, 27506, 27507
            with Intermedullary Implant, 27245
        Subtrochanteric, Subtrochanter
          Closed Treatment, 27240
          Open Treatment, 27244, 27245
        Supracondylar
          Closed Treatment, 27503
            with Intercondylar Extension, 27503
        Transcondylar
          Closed Treatment, 27503
            with Intercondylar Extension, 27503
          Open Treatment, 27511
            with Intercondylar Extension, 27513
    Thumb
      Bennett, 26645
      Closed Treatment, 26645
      Open Treatment, 26665
      Percutaneous Fixation, 26650
    Tibia and Fibula, 27828
    Tibia, Tibial
      Articular Surface
        Closed Treatment, 27825
        Open Treatment, 27827
          with Fibula, Fibular Fracture, 27828
      Condylar
        Bicondylar, 27536
        Unicondylar, 27535
      Distal
        Closed Treatment, 27825
        Open Treatment, 27826
      Pilon
        Closed Treatment, 27825
        Open Treatment, 27827
          with Fibula, Fibular Fracture, 27828
      Plafond
        Closed Treatment, 27825
        Open Treatment, 27827
          with Fibula, Fibular Fracture, 27828

Reduction — *continued*
  Fracture — *continued*
    Tibia, Tibial — *continued*
      Plateau
        Closed Treatment, 27532
        Open Treatment, 27535, 27536
      Proximal Plateau
        Closed Treatment, 27532
        Open Treatment, 27535, 27536
      Shaft
        Closed Treatment, 27752
          with Fibula, Fibular Fracture, 27752
        Open Treatment, 27758, 27759
          with Fibula, Fibular Fracture, 27758, 27759
          with Intermedullary Implant, 27759
        Percutaneous Fixation, 27756
    Toe
      Closed Treatment, 28515
        Great, 28495
      Open Treatment, 28525
        Great, 28505
      Percutaneous Fixation, 28496
        Great, 28496
    Trachea, Tracheal
      Closed
        Endoscopic Treatment, 31630
    Trans–Scaphoperilunar
      Closed Treatment, 25680
      Open Treatment, 25685
    Trapezium
      Closed Treatment, 25635
      Open Treatment, 25645
    Trapezoid
      Closed Treatment, 25635
      Open Treatment, 25645
    Triquetral
      Closed Treatment, 25635
      Open Treatment, 25645
    Ulna, Ulnar
      Proximal
        Closed Treatment, 24675
        Open Treatment, 24685
          with Dislocation
            Radial Head, 24635
            Monteggia, 24635
      Shaft
        Closed Treatment, 25535
        And
          Radial, Radius, 25565
        Open Treatment, 25545
        and
          Radial, Radius, 25574, 25575
      Styloid, 25650
    Vertebral
      Closed Treatment, 22315
      Open Treatment, 22325-22328, 63081-63091
    Zygomatic Arch, 21356-21366
      Open Treatment, 21356-21366
        with Malar Area, 21360
        with Malar Tripod, 21360
      Percutaneous, 21355
  Lung Volume, 32491
  Mammoplasty, 19318
  Masseter Muscle/Bone, 21295, 21296
  Osteoplasty
    Facial Bones, 21209
  Pregnancy
    Multifetal, 59866
  Renal Pedicle
    Torsion, 53899

Reduction — *continued*
  Separation
    Craniofacial
      Open, 21432-21436
  Skull
    Craniomegalic, 62115-62117
  Subluxation
    Pelvic ring
      Closed, 27194
    Radial, 24640
      Head, 24640
      Neck, 24640
  Tongue Base
    Radiofrequency, 41530
  Ventricular Septum
    Non–surgical, 93799
Reflex Test
  Blink, Reflex, 95933
  H Reflex, 95934, 95936
Reflux Study, 78262
  Gastroesophageal, 91034-91038
Refraction, 92015
Regnolli's Excision, 41140
Rehabilitation
  Artery
    Occlusive Disease, 93668
  Auditory
    Postlingual Hearing Loss, 92633
    Prelingual Hearing Loss, 92630
    Status Evaluation, 92626-92627
  Cardiac, 93797, 93798
  Services Considered Documentation, 4079F
Rehabilitation Facility
  Discharge Services, 1110F-1111F
Rehabilitative
  See Rehabilitation
Rehfuss Test, 91055
Rehydration, 96360-96361
Reichstein's Substance S, 80436, 82634
Reimplantation
  Arteries
    Aorta Prosthesis, 35697
    Carotid, 35691, 35694, 35695
    Subclavian, 35693-35695
    Vertebral, 35691, 35693
    Visceral, 35697
  Coronary Ostia, 33783
  Kidney, 50380
  Ovary, 58825
  Pulmonary Artery, 33788
  Ureter
    to Bladder, 50780-50785
  Ureters, 51565
Reinnervation
  Larynx
    Neuromuscular Pedicle, 31590
Reinsch Test, 83015
Reinsertion
  Drug Delivery Implant, 11983
  Implantable Contraceptive Capsules, 11977
  Spinal Fixation Device, 22849
Relative Density
  Body Fluid, 84315
Release
  Carpal Tunnel, 64721
  Elbow Contracture
    with Radical Release of Capsule, 24149
  Flexor Muscles
    Hip, 27036
  Muscle
    Knee, 27422
    Thumb Contracture, 26508
  Nerve, 64702-64726
    Carpal Tunnel, 64721
    Neurolytic, 64727
  Retina
    Encircling Material, 67115
  Spinal Cord, 63200
  Stapes, 69650
  Tarsal Tunnel, 28035
  Tendon, 24332, 25295
  Thumb Contracture, 26508

Release–Inhibiting Hormone, Somatotropin, 84307
Remodeling
  Bladder/Urethra, 0193T
Remote Afterloading
  Brachytherapy, 77785-77787
Removal
  Adjustable Gastric Restrictive Device, 43772-43774
  Adrenal Gland, 60650
  Allograft
    Intestinal, 44137
  Artificial Disc, 0095T, 0164T, 22864-22865
  Artificial Intervertebral Disc
    Cervical Interspace, 0095T, 22864
    Lumbar Interspace, 0164T, 22865
  Balloon
    Gastric, 43659, 43999
    Intra–Aortic, 33974
  Balloon Assist Device
    Intra–Aortic, 33968, 33971
  Bladder, 51597
    Electronic Stimulator, 53899
  Blood Clot
    Eye, 65930
  Blood Component
    Apheresis, 36511-36516
  Breast
    Capsules, 19371
    Implants, 19328, 19330
    Modified Radical, 19307
    Partial, 19301-19302
    Radical, 19305, 19306
    Simple, Complete, 19303
    Subcutaneous, 19304
  Calcaneous Deposits
    Subdeltoid, 23000
  Calculi (Stone)
    Bile Duct, 43264, 47420, 47425
      Percutaneous, 47554, 47630
    Bladder, 51050, 52310-52318, 52352
    Gallbladder, 47480
    Hepatic Duct, 47400
    Kidney, 50060-50081, 50130, 50561, 50580, 52352
    Pancreas, 48020
    Pancreatic Duct, 43264
    Salivary Gland, 42330-42340
    Ureter, 50610-50630, 50961, 50980, 51060, 51065, 52320-52330, 52352
    Urethra, 52310, 52315, 52352
  Cardiac Event Recorder, 33284
  Cast, 29700-29715
  Cataract
    with Replacement
      Extracapsular, 66982, 66984
      Intracapsular, 66983
      Not Associated with Concurrent, 66983
    Dilated Fundus Evaluation, 2021F
  Catheter
    Central Venous, 36589
    Fractured, 75961
    Peritoneum, 49422
    Pleural, 32552
    Spinal Cord, 62355
  Cerclage
    Cervix, 59871
  Cerumen
    Auditory Canal, External, 69210
  Clot
    Pericardium, 33020
    Endoscopic, 32658
  Comedones, 10040
  Contraceptive Capsules, 11976, 11977
  Cranial Tongs, 20665
  Cyst, 10040
  Dacryolith
    Lacrimal Duct, 68530
    Lacrimal Gland, 68530

Removal

Removal — *continued*
- Defibrillator
  - Heart, 33244
    - Pulse Generator Only, 33241
    - via Thoracotomy, 33243
- Disc, 22864-22865
- Drug Delivery Implant, 11982, 11983
- Ear Wax
  - Auditory Canal, External, 69210
- Electrode
  - Brain, 61535, 61880
  - Heart, 33238
  - Nerve, 64585
  - Spinal Cord, 63661-63664
  - Stomach, 0156T, 0158T, 43648, 43882
- Embolus, Artery
  - Aortoiliac, 34151-34201
  - Axillary, 34101
  - Brachial, 34101
  - Carotid, 34001
  - Celiac, 34151
  - Femoropopliteal, 34201
  - Iliac, 34151, 34201
  - Innominate, 34001-34101
  - Mesentery, 34151
  - Peroneal, 34203
  - Popliteal, 34203
  - Pulmonary, 33910-33916
  - Radial, 34111
  - Renal, 34151
  - Subclavian, 34001-34101
  - Tibial, 34203
  - Ulnar, 34111
- External Fixation System, 20694, 20697
- Eye
  - with Bone, 65112
  - with Implant
    - Muscles Attached, 65105
    - Muscles not Attached, 65103
    - with Muscle or Myocutaneous Flap, 65114
  - without Implant, 65101
  - Bone, 67414, 67445
  - Ocular Contents
    - with Implant, 65093
    - without Implant, 65091
  - Orbital Contents Only, 65110
- Fallopian Tube
  - Laparoscopy, 58661
    - with Hysterectomy, 58542, 58544, 58548
- Fat
  - Lipectomy, 15876-15879
- Fecal Impaction
  - Rectum, 45915
- Fibrin Deposit, 32150
- Fixation Device, 20670, 20680
- Foreign Bodies
  - Adenoid, 42999
  - Anal, 46608
  - Ankle Joint, 27610, 27620
  - Arm
    - Lower, 25248
    - Upper, 24200, 24201
  - Auditory Canal, External, 69200
    - with Anesthesia, 69205
  - Bile Duct, 43269
  - Bladder, 52310, 52315
  - Brain, 61570, 62163
  - Bronchi, 31635
  - Colon, 44025, 44390, 45379
  - Colon–Sigmoid, 45332
  - Conjunctival Embedded, 65210
  - Cornea
    - with Slip Lamp, 65222
    - without Slit Lamp, 65220
  - Duodenum, 44010
  - Elbow, 24000, 24101, 24200, 24201
  - Esophagus, 43020, 43045, 43215, 74235
  - External Eye, 65205
  - Eyelid, 67938
  - Finger, 26075, 26080

Removal — *continued*
- Foreign Bodies — *continued*
  - Foot, 28190-28193
  - Gastrointestinal, Upper, 43247
  - Gum, 41805
  - Hand, 26070
  - Hip, 27033, 27086, 27087
  - Hysteroscopy, 58562
  - Interphalangeal Joint
    - Toe, 28024
  - Intertarsal Joint, 28020
  - Intestines, Small, 44020, 44363
  - Intraocular, 65235
  - Kidney, 50561, 50580
  - Knee Joint, 27310, 27331, 27372
  - Lacrimal Duct, 68530
  - Lacrimal Gland, 68530
  - Larynx, 31511, 31530, 31531, 31577
  - Leg, Upper, 27372
  - Lung, 32151
  - Mandible, 41806
  - Maxillary Sinus, 31299
  - Mediastinum, 39000, 39010
  - Metatarsophalangeal Joint, 28022
  - Mouth, 40804, 40805
  - Muscle, 20520, 20525
    - Stimulator
      - Skeletal, 20999
  - Nose, 30300
    - Anesthesia, under, 30310
    - Lateral Rhinotomy, 30320
  - Orbit, 61334, 67413, 67430
    - with Bone Flap, 67430
    - without Bone Flap, 67413
  - Pancreatic Duct, 43269
  - Patella
    - *See* Patellectomy
  - Pelvis, 27086, 27087
  - Penile Tissue, 54115
  - Penis, 54115
  - Pericardium, 33020
    - Endoscopic, 32658
  - Peritoneum, 49402
  - Pharynx, 42809
  - Pleura, 32150, 32151
    - Endoscopic, 32653
  - Posterior Segment
    - Magnetic Extraction, 65260
    - Nonmagnetic Extraction, 65265
  - Rectum, 45307, 45915
  - Scrotum, 55120
  - Shoulder, 23040, 23044
    - Complicated, 23332
    - Deep, 23331
    - Subcutaneous, 23330
  - Skin
    - with Debridement, 11010-11012
  - Stomach, 43500
  - Subcutaneous, 10120, 10121
    - with Debridement, 11010-11012
  - Tarsometatarsal Joint, 28020
  - Tendon Sheath, 20520, 20525
  - Toe, 28022
  - Ureter, 50961, 50980
  - Urethra, 52310, 52315
  - Uterus, 58562
  - Vagina, 57415
  - Wrist, 25040, 25101, 25248
- Hair
  - by Electrolysis, 17380
- Halo, 20665
- Harrington Rod, 22850
- Hearing Aid
  - Bone Conduction, 69711
- Hematoma
  - Brain, 61312-61315
- Implant, 20670, 20680
  - Ankle, 27704
  - Contraceptive Capsules, 11976, 11977
  - Disc, 0164T, 22865
  - Elbow, 24160

Removal — *continued*
- Implant — *continued*
  - Eye, 67120, 67121
  - Finger, 26320
  - Hand, 26320
  - Pin, 20670, 20680
  - Radius, 24164
  - Rod, 20670, 20680
  - Screw, 20670, 20680
  - Wrist, 25449
- Infusion Pump
  - Intra-Arterial, 36262
  - Intravenous, 36590
  - Spinal Cord, 62365
- Intra-Aortic Balloon, 33974
  - Assist Device, 33968, 33971
- Intrauterine Device (IUD), 58301
- Keel
  - Laryngoplasty, 31580
- Kidney
  - Mechanical, 53899
- Lacrimal Gland
  - Partial, 68505
  - Total, 68500
- Lacrimal Sac
  - Excision, 68520
- Laryngocele, 31300
- Leiomyomata, 58545, 58546, 58561
- Lens, 66920-66940
- Lens Material, 66840-66852
- Lesion
  - Conjunctiva, 68040
  - Larynx, 31512, 31578
    - Endoscopic, 31545-31546
- Loose Body
  - Ankle, 27620
  - Carpometacarpal Joint, 26070
  - Elbow, 24101
  - Foot, 28020
  - Interphalangeal Joint, Toe, 28024
  - Intertarsal Joint, 28020
  - Knee Joint, 27331
  - Metatarsophalangeal Joint, 28022
  - Tarsometatarsal Joint, 28020
  - Toe, 28022
  - Wrist, 25101
- Lung
  - Apical Tumor, 32503-32504
  - Bronchoplasty, 32501
  - Completion Pneumonectomy, 32488
  - Cyst, 32140
  - Extrapleural, 32445
  - Single Lobe, 32480
  - Single Segment, 32484
  - Sleeve Lobectomy, 32486
  - Sleeve Pneumonectomy, 32442
  - Total Pneumonectomy, 32440-32445
  - Two Lobes, 32482
  - Volume Reduction, 32491
  - Wedge Resection, 32500
- Lymph Nodes
  - Abdominal, 38747
  - Inguinofemoral, 38760, 38765
  - Pelvic, 38770
  - Retroperitoneal Transabdominal, 38780
  - Thoracic, 38746
- Mammary Implant, 19328, 19330
- Mastoid
  - Air Cells, 69670
- Mesh
  - Abdominal Wall, 11008
- Milia, Multiple, 10040
- Nail, 11730, 11732, 11750, 11752
- Nephrostomy Tube, 50389
- Neurostimulator
  - Electrode, 63661-63662
  - Pulse Generator, 64595
  - Receiver, 64595
- Obstructive Material
  - Gastrostomy, Duodenostomy, Jejunostomy, Gastro-jejunostomy, or Cecostomy Tube, 49460

Removal — *continued*
- Ocular Implant, 65175, 65920
- Orbital Implant, 67560
- Ovaries
  - Laparoscopy, 58661
    - with Hysterectomy, 58542, 58544, 58548
- Pacemaker
  - Heart, 33233-33237
- Patella, Complete, 27424
- Plate
  - Skull, 62142
- Polyp
  - Anal, 46610, 46612
  - Antrochoanal, 31032
  - Colon, 44392, 45385
  - Colon–Sigmoid, 45333
  - Endoscopy, 44364, 44365, 44394
  - Esophagus, 43217, 43250
  - Gastrointestinal, Upper, 43250, 43251
  - Rectum, 45315
  - Sphenoid Sinus, 31051
- Prosthesis
  - Abdomen, 49606
  - Abdominal Wall, 11008
  - Hip, 27090, 27091
  - Knee, 27488
  - Penis, 54406, 54410-54417
  - Perineum, 53442
  - Skull, 62142
  - Urethral Sphincter, 53446, 53447
  - Wrist, 25250, 25251
- Pulse Generator
  - Brain, 61888
  - Spinal Cord, 63688
- Pustules, 10040
- Receiver
  - Brain, 61888
  - Spinal Cord, 63688
  - Reservoir, 62365
- Seton
  - Anal, 46030
- Shoulder Joint
  - Foreign or Loose Body, 23107
- Shunt
  - Brain, 62256, 62258
  - Heart, 33924
  - Peritoneum, 49429
  - Spinal Cord, 63746
- Skin Tags, 11200, 11201
- Sling
  - Urethra, 53442
  - Vagina, 57287
- Spinal Instrumentation
  - Anterior, 22855
  - Posterior Nonsegmental
    - Harrington Rod, 22850
  - Posterior Segmental, 22852
- Stent
  - Bile Duct, 43269
  - Pancreatic Duct, 43269
  - Ureteral, 50382-50387
- Stone (Calculi)
  - Bile Duct, 43264, 47420, 47425
    - Percutaneous, 47554, 47630
  - Bladder, 51050, 52310-52318, 52352
  - Gallbladder, 47480
  - Hepatic Duct, 47400
  - Kidney, 50060-50081, 50130, 50561, 50580, 52352
  - Pancreas, 48020
  - Pancreatic Duct, 43264
  - Salivary Gland, 42330-42340
  - Ureter, 50610-50630, 50961, 50980, 51060, 51065, 52320-52330, 52352
  - Urethra, 52310, 52315, 52352
- Subcutaneous Port for Gastric Restrictive Procedure, 43887-43888
- Suture
  - Anal, 46754
  - Anesthesia, 15850, 15851

Index

Removal — *continued*
  Thrombus
    See Thrombectomy
  Tissue
    Vaginal, Partial, 57107
  Tissue Expanders, 11971
  Transplant Intestines, 44137
  Transplant Kidney, 50370
  Tube
    Ear, Middle, 69424
    Finger, 26392, 26416
    Hand, 26392, 26416
    Nephrostomy, 50389
  Tumor
    Temporal Bone, 69970
  Ureter
    Ligature, 50940
    Stent, 50382-50387
  Urethral Stent
    Bladder, 52310, 52315
    Urethra, 52310, 52315
  Vagina
    Partial
      with Nodes, 57109
      Tissue, 57106
      Wall, 57107, 57110, 57111
  Vein
    Clusters, 37785
    Perforation, 37760
    Saphenous, 37718-37735, 37780
    Secondary, 37785
    Varicose, 37765, 37766
  Venous Access Device
    Obstruction, 75901-75902
  Ventilating Tube
    Ear, Middle, 69424
  Ventricular Assist Device, 33977, 33978
    Extracorporeal, 0050T
    Intracorporeal, 33980
  Vitreous
    Partial, 67005, 67010
  Wire
    Anal, 46754

Renal Abscess
  Incision and Drainage, 50020-50021

Renal Arteries
  Aneurysm, 35121-35122
  Angiography, 75722-75724
  Angioplasty, 35450
  Atherectomy, 35480, 35490
  Bypass Graft, 35536, 35560, 35631-35636
  Embolectomy, 34151
  Thrombectomy, 34151
  Thromboendarterectomy, 35341

Renal Autotransplantation, 50380

Renal Calculus
  Removal, 50060-50081, 50130, 50561, 50580, 52352

Renal Cyst
  Ablation, 50541
  Aspiration, 50390
  Excision, 50280, 50290
  Injection, 50390
  Xray, 74470

Renal Dialysis
  Blood Flow Study, 90940
  Documented Plan of Care, 0505F
  Duplex Scan of Access, 93990
  Kt/V Level, 3082F-3084F
  via Catheter, 4054F
  via Functioning Arteriovenous Fistula, 4052F
  via Functioning Arteriovenous Graft, 4053F

Renal Disease Services
  Arteriovenous Fistula
    Revision, 36832, 36833
    Thrombectomy, 36831
  Arteriovenous Shunt
    Revision, 36832, 36833
    Thrombectomy, 36831
  End Stage Renal Disease, 90951-90956, 90964, 90968
  Hemodialysis, 90935, 90937

Renal Disease Services — *continued*
  Hemodialysis — *continued*
    Blood Flow Study, 90940
  Hemoperfusion, 90997
  Patient Training, 90989, 90993
  Peritoneal Dialysis, 90945-90947

Renal Transplantation
  Allograft Preparation, 50323-50329
  Anesthesia
    Donor, 00862
    Recipient, 00868
  Donor Nephrectomy, 50300-50320, 50547
  Graft Implantation, 50360-50365
  Recipient Nephrectomy, 50340, 50365
  Reimplantation Kidney, 50380
  Removal Transplanted Allograft, 50370

Renin, 80408, 80416, 84244
  Peripheral Vein, 80417

Renin–Converting Enzyme, 82164

Reoperation
  Carotid
    Thromboendarterectomy, 35390
  Coronary Artery Bypass
    Valve Procedure, 33530
  Distal Vessel Bypass, 35700

Repair
  See Also Revision
  Abdomen, 49900
    Hernia, 49491-49525, 49565, 49570, 49582-49590
    Omphalocele, 49600-49611
    Suture, 49900
  Abdominal Wall, 15830, 15847, 17999
  Anal
    Anomaly, 46744-46748
    Fistula, 46288, 46706-46716
    High Imperforate, 46730, 46735, 46740, 46742
    Low Imperforate, 46715-46716
    Park Posterior, 46761
    Stricture, 46700, 46705
  Aneurysm
    Aorta
      Abdominal, 0078T-0081T, 34800-34805, 34825-34826, 35081-35103
      Iliac Vessels, 35102-35103
      Visceral Vessels, 35091-35092
      Infrarenal, 34800-34805, 34825-34832
      Imaging, 75952-75953
      Thoracic, 33877-33886
    Arteriovenous, 36832
    Axillary-Brachial Artery, 35011, 35013
    Carotid Artery, 35001-35002
    Femoral, 35141-35142
    Hepatic, Celiac, Renal, or Mesenteric Artery, 35121-35122
    Iliac Artery, 34825-34826, 34900, 35131-35132
      Imaging, 75954
    Innominate, Subclavian Artery, 35021-35022
    Intracranial Artery, 61697-61708
    Popliteal Artery, 35151-35152
    Radial or Ulnar Artery, 35045
    Sinus of Valsalva, 33720
    Subclavian Artery, 35001-35002, 35021-35022
    Vertebral Artery, 35005
  Ankle
    Ligament, 27695-27698
    Tendon, 27612, 27650-27654, 27680-27687
  Anomaly
    Artery Arborization, 33925-33926
    Cardiac, 33608, 33610, 33615, 33617
    Coronary Artery, 33502-33507
    Pulmonary Venous Return, 33730

Repair — *continued*
  Aorta, 33320-33322, 33802, 33803
    Coarctation, 33840-33851
    Graft, 33860-33877
    Sinus of Valsalva, 33702-33720
    Thoracic
      Endovascular, 33880-33891
      Prosthesis Placement, 33886
      Radiological Supervision and Interpretation, 75956-75959
  Aortic Arch
    with Cardiopulmonary Bypass, 33853
    without Cardiopulmonary Bypass, 33852
  Aortic Valve, 33400-33403
    Obstruction
      Outflow Tract, 33414
      Septal Hypertrophy, 33416
    Stenosis, 33415
    Valvuloplasty, 33400-33403
  Arm
    Lower, 25260, 25263, 25270
      Fasciotomy, 24495
      Secondary, 25265, 25272, 25274
      Tendon, 25290
      Tendon Sheath, 25275
      Muscle, 24341
      Tendon, 24332, 24341, 25280, 25295, 25310-25316
    Upper
      Muscle Revision, 24330, 24331
      Muscle Transfer, 24301, 24320
      Tendon Lengthening, 24305
      Tendon Revision, 24320
      Tendon Transfer, 24301
      Tenotomy, 24310
  Arteriovenous Aneurysm, 36832
  Arteriovenous Fistula
    Abdomen, 35182
      Acquired or Traumatic, 35189
    Extremities, 35184
      Acquired or Traumatic, 35190
    Head, 35180
      Acquired or Traumatic, 35188
    Neck, 35180
      Acquired or Traumatic, 35188
    Thorax, 35182
      Acquired or Traumatic, 35189
  Arteriovenous Malformation
    Intracranial, 61680-61692
    Intracranial Artery, 61705, 61708
    Spinal Artery, 62294
    Spinal Cord, 63250-63252
  Arterioventricular Canal, 33665, 33670
  Artery
    Angioplasty, 75962-75968
    Aorta, 35452, 35472
    Axillary, 35458
    Brachiocephalic, 35458, 35475
    Bypass Graft, 35501-35571, 35601-35683, 35691-35700
    Bypass In-Situ, 35583-35587
    Bypass Venous Graft, 33510-33516, 35510-35525
    Coronary
      Anomalous, 33502-33507
    Femoral, 35456, 35474
    Iliac, 34900, 35454, 35473
    Occlusive Disease, 35001, 35005-35021, 35045, 35081, 35091, 35102, 35111, 35121, 35131, 35141, 35151
    Popliteal, 35456, 35474
    Pulmonary, 33690, 33925-33926
    Renal, 35450
    Renal or Visceral, 35471
    Subclavian, 35458

Repair — *continued*
  Artery — *continued*
    Thromboendarterectomy, 35301-35321, 35341-35390
    Tibioperoneal, 35459, 35470
    Venous Graft, 33510-33516, 35510-35525
    Viscera, 35450, 35471
  Arytenoid Cartilage, 31400
  Atria
    Laparoscopic, 33265-33266
    Open, 33254-33256
  Atrial Fibrillation, 33254, 33255-33256
  Bile Duct, 47701
    with Intestines, 47760, 47780, 47785
    Wound, 47900
  Bladder
    Exstrophy, 51940
    Fistula, 44660, 44661, 45800, 45805, 51880-51925
    Neck, 51845
    Resection, 52500
    Wound, 51860, 51865
  Blepharoptosis
    Conjunctivo-Tarso-Muller's Muscle Resection, 67908
    Frontalis Muscle Technique with Fascial Sling, 67902
    Superior Rectus Technique with Fascial Sling, 67906
    Tarso Levator Resection or Advancement, 67903-67904
  Blood Vessel(s)
    Abdomen, 35221, 35251, 35281
      with Other Graft, 35281
      with Vein Graft, 35251
    Chest, 35211, 35216
      with Other Graft, 35271, 35276
      with Vein Graft, 35241, 35246
    Finger, 35207
    Graft Defect, 35870
    Hand, 35207
    Intrathoracic, 35211, 35216, 35241, 35246, 35271, 35276
    Kidney, 50100
    Lower Extremity, 35226, 35256, 35286
      with Other Graft, 35286
      with Vein Graft, 35256
    Neck, 35201, 35231, 35261
      with Other Graft, 35261
      with Vein Graft, 35231
    Upper Extremity, 35206, 35236, 35266
      with Other Graft, 35266
      with Vein Graft, 35236
  Body Cast, 29720
  Brain
    Wound, 61571
  Breast
    Suspension, 19316
  Bronchi, 31770, 32501
    Fistula, 32815
  Brow Ptosis, 67900
  Bunion, 28290-28299
  Bypass Graft, 35901-35907
    Fistula, 35870
  Calcaneus
    Osteotomy, 28300
  Canaliculi, 68700
  Cannula, 36860, 36861
  Carpal, 25440
  Carpal Bone, 25431
  Cast
    Spica, body, or jacket, 29720
  Central Venous Catheter, 36575-36576
  Cervix
    Cerclage, 57700
      Abdominal, 59320, 59325
    Suture, 57720
    Vaginal Approach, 57720

Repair

Repair — *continued*
Chest Wall, 32905
  Closure, 32810
  Fistula, 32906
  Pectus Excavatum, 21740
Chin
  Augmentation, 21120, 21123
  Osteotomy, 21121-21123
Choanal Atresia, 30540, 30545
Chordee, 54304
Ciliary Body, 66680
Circumcision, 54163
Clavicle
  Osteotomy, 23480, 23485
Cleft
  Hand, 26580
  Lip, 40525, 40527, 40700
  Nasal Deformity, 40700, 40701, 40720, 40761
Cleft Palate, 42200-42225
  See Cleft Palate Repair
Cloacal anomaly, 46744, 46746, 46748
Colon
  Fistula, 44650-44661
  Hernia, 44050
  Malrotation, 44055
  Obstruction, 44050
Conjunctiva, 65270, 65272
Cornea, 65275, 65280, 65285
Coronary Chamber Fistula, 33500, 33501
Cor Triatriatum or Supravalvular Mitral Ring, 33732
Cyst
  Bartholin's Gland, 56440
  Liver, 47300
Cystocele, 57240
Defect
  Atrial Septal, 33647
  Radius, 25425-25426
  Septal, 33813-33814
  Ulna, 25425-25426
  Ventricular Septal, 33545
Defibrillator, Heart, 33218, 33220
Diaphragm
  for Eventration, 39545
  Hernia, 39502-39541
  Lacerations, 39501
Dislocation
  Ankle, 27846, 27848
  Knee, 27556-27558
Ductus Arteriosus, 33820-33824
Dura, 61618-61619, 62010
Dura/Cerebrospinal Fluid Leak, 63707, 63709
Dysfunction
  Prosthetic Valve, 33406
Ear, Middle
  Oval Window Fistula, 69666
  Round Window Fistula, 69667
Ectropion
  Excision Tarsal Wedge, 67916, 67923
  Extensive, 67917
  Suture, 67914, 67921
  Thermocauterization, 67915, 67922
Elbow
  Fasciotomy, 24357-24359
  Hemiepiphyseal Arrest, 24470
  Ligament, 24343-24346
  Muscle, 24341
  Muscle Transfer, 24301
  Tendon, 24340-24342
    Each, 24341
  Tendon Lengthening, 24305
  Tendon Transfer, 24301
  Tennis Elbow, 24357-24359
Electrode, 33218-33220
Electromagnetic Bone Conduction Hearing Device, 69711
Encephalocele, 62121
Enterocele
  with Colporrhaphy, 57265

Repair — *continued*
Enterocele — *continued*
  Hysterectomy, 58263, 58270, 58292, 58294
  Vaginal Approach, 57268
Entropion, 67924
Epididymis, 54900, 54901
Episiotomy, 59300
Epispadias, 54380-54390
Esophagus, 43300, 43310, 43312-43314
  Esophagogastrostomy, 43320
  Esophagojejunostomy, 43340, 43341
  Fistula, 43305, 43312, 43314, 43420, 43425
  Fundoplasty, 43324, 43325
  Muscle, 43330, 43331
  Preexisting Perforation, 43405
  Varices, 43401
  Wound, 43410, 43415
Esophogeal Varices, 43401
Extraocular muscle, 67340
Eye
  Ciliary Body, 66680
  Suture, 66682
  Conjunctiva, 65270-65273
    Wound, 65270-65273
  Cornea, 65275
    with Glue, 65286
    Astigmatism, 65772, 65775
    Wound, 65275-65285
      Dehiscence, 66250
  Fistula
    Lacrimal Gland, 68770
  Iris
    with Ciliary Body, 66680
    Suture, 66682
  Lacrimal Duct
    Canaliculi, 68700
  Lacrimal Punctum, 68705
  Retina
    Detachment, 67101-67112
  Sclera
    with Glue, 65286
    with Graft, 66225
    Reinforcement, 67250, 67255
    Staphyloma, 66220, 66225
    Wound, 65286, 66250
  Strabismus
    Chemodenervation, 67345
  Symblepharon
    with Graft, 68335
    without Graft, 68330
    Division, 68340
  Trabeculae, 65855
Eyebrow
  Ptosis, 67900
Eyelashes
  Epilation
    by Forceps, 67820
    by Other than Forceps, 67825
  Incision of Lid Margin, 67830
    with Free Mucous Membrane Graft, 67835
Eyelid, 21280, 21282, 67961, 67966
  Ectropion
    Excision Tarsal Wedge, 67916
    Suture, 67914
    Tarsal Strip Operation, 67917
    Thermocauterization, 67915
  Entropion
    Capsulopalpebral Fascia Repair, 67924
    Excision Tarsal Wedge, 67923
    Suture, 67921-67924
    Tarsal Strip, 67924
    Thermocauterization, 67922
  Excisional, 67961, 67966
  Lagophthalmos, 67912
  Ptosis
    Conjunctivo–Tarso–Muller's Muscle–Levator Resection, 67908
    Frontalis Muscle Technique, 67901, 67902

Repair — *continued*
Eyelid — *continued*
  Ptosis — *continued*
    Levator Resection, 67903, 67904
    Reduction of Overcorrection, 67909
    Superior Rectus Technique, 67906
  Retraction, 67911
  Wound
    Extraocular Muscle, 65290
    Suture, 67930, 67935
Eye Muscles
  Strabismus
    Adjustable Sutures, 67335
    One Horizontal Muscle, 67311
    One Vertical Muscle, 67314
    Posterior Fixation Suture Technique, 67334, 67335
    Previous Surgery not Involving Extraocular Muscles, 67331
    Release Extensive Scar Tissue, 67343
    Superior Oblique Muscle, 67318
    Two Horizontal Muscles, 67312
    Two or More Vertical Muscles, 67316
  Wound
    Extraocular Muscle, 65290
Facial Bones, 21208, 21209
Facial Nerve
  Paralysis, 15840-15845
  Suture
    Intratemporal, Lateral to Geniculate Ganglion, 69740
    Intratemporal, Medial to Geniculate Ganglion, 69745
Fallopian Tube, 58752
  Anastomosis, 58750
  Create Stoma, 58770
Fascial Defect, 50728
  Leg, 27656
Femur, 27470, 27472
  with Graft, 27170
  Epiphysis, 27475-27485, 27742
  Arrest, 27185
  by Pinning, 27176
  by Traction, 27175
  Open Treatment, 27177, 27178
  Osteoplasty, 27179
  Osteotomy, 27181
  Muscle Transfer, 27110
  Osteotomy, 27140, 27151, 27450, 27454
    with Fixation, 27165
    with Open Reduction, 27156
  Femoral Neck, 27161
Fibula
  Epiphysis, 27477-27485, 27730-27742
  Nonunion or Malunion, 27726
  Osteotomy, 27707-27712
Finger
  Claw Finger, 26499
  Macrodactyly, 26590
  Polydactylous, 26587
  Syndactyly, 26560-26562
  Tendon
    Extensor, 26415-26434, 26445, 26449, 26455
    Flexor, 26356-26358, 26440, 26442
  Joint Stabilization, 26474
  PIP Joint, 26471
  Toe Transfer, 26551-26556
  Trigger, 26055
  Volar Plate, 26548
  Web Finger, 26560

Repair — *continued*
Fistula
  Anal, 46706
  Anoperineal, 46715-46716
  Anorectal, 46707
  Carotid–Cavernous, 61710
  Coronary, 33500-33501
  Graft-Enteric Fistula, 35870
  Ileoanal Pouch, 46710-46712
  Mastoid, 69700
  Nasolabial, 42260
  Neurovisceral, 50525-50526
  Oromaxillary, 30580
  Oronasal, 30600
  Rectourethral, 46740-46742
  Rectovaginal, 46740-46742, 57308
  Sinus of Valsalva, 33702, 33710
  Ureterovisceral, 50930
Foot
  Fascia, 28250
  Muscles, 28250
  Tendon, 28200-28226, 28238
Fracture
  Nasoethmoid, 21340
  Patella, 27524
  Radius, 25526
  Talar Dome, 29892
  Tibial Plafond, 29892
Gallbladder
  with Gastroenterostomy, 47741
  with Intestines, 47720-47740
  Laceration, 47999
Great Arteries, 33770-33781
Great Vessel, 33320-33322
Hallux Valgus, 28290-28299
Hammertoe, 28285-28286
Hamstring, 27097
Hand
  Cleft Hand, 26580
  Muscles, 26591, 26593
  Tendon
    Extensor, 26410-26416, 26426, 26428, 26433-26437
    Flexor, 26350-26358, 26440
    Profundus, 26370-26373
Hearing Aid
  Bone Conduction, 69711
Heart
  Anomaly, 33600-33617
  Aortic Sinus, 33702-33722
  Artificial Heart
    Intracorporeal, 0052T, 0053T
  Atria
    Laparoscopic, 33265-33266
    Open, 33254-33256
  Atrioventricular Canal, 33660, 33665
  Complete, 33670
  Atrioventricular Valve, 33660, 33665
  Blood Vessel, 33320-33322
  Cor Triatriatum, 33732
  Fibrillation, 33254, 33255-33256
  Infundibular, 33476, 33478
  Mitral Valve, 33420-33427
  Myocardium, 33542
  Outflow Tract, 33476, 33478
  Post–Infarction, 33542, 33545
  Prosthetic Valve, 33670, 33852, 33853
  Prosthetic Valve Dysfunction, 33496
  Pulmonary Artery Shunt, 33924
  Pulmonary Valve, 33470-33474
  Septal Defect, 33545, 33608, 33610, 33681-33688, 33692-33697
    Atrial and Ventricular, 33647
    Atrium, 33641
  Sinus of Valsalva, 33702-33722
  Sinus Venosus, 33645
  Tetralogy of Fallot, 33692
  Total Replacement Heart System
    Intracorporeal, 0052T, 0053T

Index — Repair

Repair — *continued*
- Heart — *continued*
  - Tricuspid Valve, 33465
  - Ventricle, 33611, 33612
    - Obstruction, 33619
  - Ventricular Tunnel, 33722
  - Wound, 33300, 33305
- Hepatic Duct
  - with Intestines, 47765, 47802
- Hernia
  - with Mesh, 49568
  - with Spermatic Cord, 54640
  - Abdomen, 49565, 49590
    - Incisional or Ventral, 49560
  - Diaphragmatic, 39520, 39530-39531, 39540-39541, 39560, 39561
  - Epigastric
    - Incarcerated, 49572
    - Reducible, 49570
  - Femoral, 49550
    - Incarcerated, 49553
    - Initial
      - Incarcerated, 49553
      - Reducible, 49550
    - Recurrent, 49555
      - Recurrent Incarcerated, 49557
      - Reducible Recurrent, 49555
  - Hiatus, 39502
  - Incisional
    - Initial
      - Incarcerated, 49566
      - Reducible, 49560
    - Recurrent
      - Reducible, 49565
  - Inguinal, 49420
    - Initial
      - by Laparoscopy, 49650
      - Incarcerated, 49496, 49501, 49507
      - Reducible, 49491, 49495, 49500, 49505
      - Strangulated, 49492, 49496, 49501, 49507
    - Laparoscopy, 49650-49651
    - Older Than 50 Weeks, Younger than 6 Months, 49496
    - Preterm Older than 50 weeks and younger than 6 months, full term infant younger than 6 months, 49495-49496
    - Preterm up to 50 Weeks, 49491-49492
    - Recurrent
      - by Laparoscopy, 49651
      - Incarcerated, 49521
      - Reducible, 49520
      - Strangulated, 49521
    - Sliding, 49525
  - Intestinal, 44025, 44050
  - Lumbar, 49540
  - Lung, 32800
  - Orchiopexy, 54640
  - Paracolostomy, 44346
  - Parasternal, 49999
  - Pretern Infant
    - Birth up to 50 Weeks, 49491-49492
    - Older than 50 weeks, 49495-49496
  - Reducible
    - Initial
      - Epigastric, 49570
      - Femoral, 49550
      - Incisional, 49560
      - Inguinal, 49495, 49500, 49505
      - Umbilical, 49580, 49585
      - Ventral, 49560
    - Recurrent
      - Femoral, 49555
      - Incisional, 49565
      - Inguinal, 49520

Repair — *continued*
- Hernia — *continued*
  - Reducible — *continued*
    - Recurrent — *continued*
      - Ventral, 49560
    - Sliding, 49525
    - Spigelian, 49590
    - Umbilical, 49580, 49585
      - Incarcerated, 49582, 49587
      - Reducible, 49580, 49585
    - Ventral
      - Initial
        - Incarcerated, 49561
        - Reducible, 49565
- Hip
  - Muscle Transfer, 27100-27105, 27111
  - Osteotomy, 27146-27156
  - Tendon, 27097
- Humerus, 24420, 24430
  - with Graft, 24435
  - Osteotomy, 24400, 24410
- Hypoplasia
  - Aortic Arch, 33619
- Hypospadias, 54308, 54312, 54316, 54318, 54322, 54326, 54328, 54332, 54336, 54340, 54344, 54348, 54352
- Ileoanal Pouch, 46710-46712
- Ileostomy, 44310, 45136
  - Continent (Kock Pouch), 44316
- Interphalangeal Joint
  - Volar Plate, 26548
- Intestine
  - Large
    - Ulcer, 44605
    - Wound, 44605
- Intestines
  - Enterocele
    - Abdominal Approach, 57270
    - Vaginal Approach, 57268
  - Large
    - Closure Enterostomy, 44620-44626
    - Diverticula, 44605
    - Obstruction, 44615
- Intestines, Small
  - Closure Enterostomy, 44620-44626
  - Diverticula, 44602, 44603
  - Fistula, 44640-44661
  - Hernia, 44050
  - Malrotation, 44055
  - Obstruction, 44025, 44050
  - Ulcer, 44602, 44603
  - Wound, 44602, 44603
- Introitus, Vagina, 56800
- Iris, Ciliary Body, 66680
- Jejunum
  - Free Transfer with Microvascular Anastomosis, 43496
- Kidney
  - Fistula, 50520-50526
  - Horseshoe, 50540
  - Renal Pelvis, 50400, 50405
  - Wound, 50500
- Knee
  - Cartilage, 27403
  - Instability, 27420
  - Ligament, 27405-27409
    - Collateral, 27405
    - Collateral and Cruciate, 27409
    - Cruciate, 27407, 27409
  - Meniscus, 27403
  - Tendons, 27380, 27381
- Laceration, Skin
  - Abdomen
    - Complex, 13100-13102
    - Intermediate, 12031-12037
    - Layered, 12031-12037
    - Simple, 12001-12007
    - Superficial, 12001-12007
  - Arm, Arms
    - Complex, 13120-13122
    - Intermediate, 12031-12037
    - Layered, 12031-12037

Repair — *continued*
- Laceration, Skin — *continued*
  - Arm, Arms — *continued*
    - Simple, 12001-12007
    - Superficial, 12001-12007
  - Axilla, Axillae
    - Complex, 13131-13133
    - Intermediate, 12031-12037
    - Layered, 12031-12037
    - Simple, 12001-12007
    - Superficial, 12001-12007
  - Back
    - Complex, 13100-13102
    - Intermediate, 12031-12037
    - Layered, 12031-12037
    - Simple, 12001-12007
    - Superficial, 12001-12007
  - Breast
    - Complex, 13100-13102
    - Intermediate, 12031-12037
    - Layered, 12031-12037
    - Simple, 12001-12007
    - Superficial, 12001-12007
  - Buttock
    - Complex, 13100-13102
    - Intermediate, 12031-12037
    - Layered, 12031-12037
    - Simple, 12001-12007
    - Superficial, 12001-12007
  - Cheek, Cheeks
    - Complex, 13131-13133
    - Intermediate, 12051-12057
    - Layered, 12051-12057
    - Simple, 12011-12018
    - Superficial, 12011-12018
  - Chest
    - Complex, 13100-13102
    - Intermediate, 12031-12037
    - Layered, 12031-12037
    - Simple, 12001-12007
    - Superficial, 12001-12007
  - Chin
    - Complex, 13131-13133
    - Intermediate, 12051-12057
    - Layered, 12051-12057
    - Simple, 12011-12018
    - Superficial, 12011-12018
  - Ear, Ears
    - Complex, 13150-13153
    - Intermediate, 12051-12057
    - Layered, 12051-12057
    - 2.5 cm or less, 12051
    - Simple, 12011-12018
    - Superficial, 12011-12018
  - External
    - Genitalia
      - Complex/Intermediate, 12041-12047
      - Layered, 12041-12047
      - Simple, 12001-12007
      - Superficial, 12041-12047
  - Extremity, Extremities
    - Complex, 13150-13153
    - Complex/Intermediate, 12031-12037
    - Intermediate, 12051-12057
    - Layered, 12031-12037
    - Simple, 12001-12007
    - Superficial, 12001-12007
  - Face
    - Complex/Intermediate, 12051-12057
    - Layered, 12051-12057
    - Simple, 12011-12018
    - Superficial, 12011-12018
  - Feet
    - Complex, 13131-13133
    - Intermediate, 12041-12047
    - Layered, 12041-12047
    - Simple, 12001-12007
    - Superficial, 12001-12007
  - Finger, Fingers
    - Complex, 13131-13133
    - Intermediate, 12041-12047
    - Layered, 12041-12047
    - Simple, 12001-12007

Repair — *continued*
- Laceration, Skin — *continued*
  - Finger, Fingers — *continued*
    - Superficial, 12001-12007
  - Foot
    - Complex, 13131-13133
    - Intermediate, 12041-12047
    - Layered, 12041-12047
    - Simple, 12001-12007
    - Superficial, 12001-12007
  - Forearm, Forearms
    - Complex, 13120-13122
    - Intermediate, 12031-12037
    - Layered, 12031-12037
    - Simple, 12001-12007
    - Superficial, 12001-12007
  - Forehead
    - Complex, 13131-13133
    - Intermediate, 12051-12057
    - Layered, 12051-12057
    - Simple, 12011-12018
    - Superficial, 12011-12018
  - Genitalia
    - Complex, 13131-13133
    - External
      - Complex/Intermediate, 12041-12047
      - Layered, 12041-12047
      - Simple, 12001-12007
      - Superficial, 12001-12007
  - Hand, Hands
    - Complex, 13131-13133
    - Intermediate, 12041-12047
    - Layered, 12041-12047
    - Simple, 12001-12007
    - Superficial, 12001-12007
  - Leg, Legs
    - Complex, 13120-13122
    - Intermediate, 12031-12037
    - Layered, 12031-12037
    - Simple, 12001-12007
    - Superficial, 12001-12007
  - Lip, Lips
    - Complex, 13150-13153
    - Intermediate, 12051-12057
    - Layered, 12051-12057
    - Simple, 12011-12018
    - Superficial, 12011-12018
  - Lower
    - Arm, Arms
      - Complex, 13120-13122
      - Intermediate, 12031-12037
      - Layered, 12031-12037
      - Simple, 12001-12007
      - Superficial, 12001-12007
    - Extremity, Extremities
      - Complex, 13120-13122
      - Intermediate, 12031-12037
      - Layered, 12031-12037
      - Simple, 12001-12007
      - Superficial, 12001-12007
    - Leg, Legs
      - Complex, 13120-13122
      - Intermediate, 12031-12037
      - Layered, 12031-12037
      - Simple, 12001-12007
      - Superficial, 12001-12007
  - Mouth
    - Complex, 13131-13133
  - Mucous Membrane
    - Complex/Intermediate, 12051-12057
    - Layered, 12051-12057
    - Simple, 12011-12018
    - Superficial, 12011-12018
  - Neck
    - Complex, 13131-13133
    - Intermediate, 12041-12047
    - Layered, 12041-12047
    - Simple, 12001-12007
    - Superficial, 12001-12007
  - Nose
    - Complex, 13150-13153
    - Complex/Intermediate, 12051-12057
    - Layered, 12051-12057

Repair

Repair — *continued*
  Laceration, Skin — *continued*
    Nose — *continued*
      Simple, 12011-12018
      Superficial, 12011-12018
    Palm, Palms
      Complex, 13131-13133
      Intermediate, 12041-12047
      Layered, 12041-12047
      Layered Simple, 12001-12007
      Superficial, 12001-12007
    Scalp
      Complex, 13120-13122
      Intermediate, 12031-12037
      Layered, 12031-12037
      Simple, 12001-12007
      Superficial, 12001-12007
    Toe, Toes
      Complex, 13131-13133
      Intermediate, 12041-12047
      Layered, 12041-12047
      Simple, 12001-12007
      Superficial, 12001-12007
    Trunk
      Complex, 13100-13102
      Intermediate, 12031-12037
      Layered, 12031-12037
      Simple, 12001-12007
      Superficial, 12001-12007
    Upper
      Arm, Arms
        Complex, 13120-13122
        Intermediate, 12031-12037
        Layered, 12031-12037
        Simple, 12001-12007
        Superficial, 12001-12007
      Extremity
        Complex, 13120-13122
        Intermediate, 12031-12037
        Layered, 12031-12037
        Simple, 12001-12007
        Superficial, 12001-12007
    Leg, Legs
      Complex, 13120-13122
      Intermediate, 12031-12037
      Layered, 12031-12037
      Simple, 12001-12007
      Superficial, 12001-12007
  Larynx
    Fracture, 31584
    Reinnervation
      Neuromuscular Pedicle, 31590
  Leak
    Cerebrospinal Fluid, 31290-31291
  Leg
    Lower
      Fascia, 27656
      Tendon, 27658-27692
    Upper
      Muscles, 27385, 27386, 27400, 27430
      Tendon, 27393-27400
  Ligament
    Ankle, 27695-27696, 27698
    Anterior Cruciate, 29888
    Collateral
      Elbow, 24343, 24345
      Metacarpophalangeal or interphalangeal joint, 26540
    Knee, 27405, 27407, 27409
    Posterior Cruciate Ligament, 29889
  Lip, 40650-40654
    Cleft Lip, 40700-40761
    Fistula, 42260
  Liver
    Abscess, 47300
    Cyst, 47300
    Wound, 47350-47361
  Lung
    Hernia, 32800
    Pneumolysis, 32940
    Tear, 32110
  Macrodactylia, 26590

Repair — *continued*
  Malunion
    Femur, 27470, 27472
    Fibula, 27726
    Humerus, 24430
    Metatarsal, 28322
    Radius, 25400, 25405, 25415, 25420
    Tarsal Bones, 28320
    Tibia, 27720, 27722, 27724-27725
    Ulna, 25400, 25405, 25415, 25420
  Mastoidectomy
    with Apicectomy, 69605
    with Tympanoplasty, 69604
    Complete, 69601
    Modified Radical, 69602
    Radical, 69603
  Maxilla
    Osteotomy, 21206
  Meningocele, 63700, 63702
  Meniscus
    Knee, 27403, 29882-29883
  Mesentery, 44850
  Metacarpal
    Lengthen, 26568
    Nonunion, 26546
    Osteotomy, 26565
  Metacarpophalangeal Joint
    Capsulodesis, 26516-26518
    Collateral Ligament, 26540-26542
    Fusion, 26516-26518
  Metatarsal, 28322
    Osteotomy, 28306-28309
  Microsurgery, 69990
  Mitral Valve, 33420-33427
  Mouth
    Floor, 41250
    Laceration, 40830, 40831
    Vestibule of, 40830-40845
  Muscle
    Hand, 26591
    Upper Arm or Elbow, 24341
  Musculotendinous Cuff, 23410, 23412
  Myelomeningocele, 63704, 63706
  Nail Bed, 11760
  Nasal Deformity
    Cleft Lip, 40700-40761
  Nasal Septum, 30630
  Navicular, 25440
  Neck Muscles
    Scalenus Anticus, 21700, 21705
    Sternocleidomastoid, 21720, 21725
  Nerve, 64876
    Facial, 69955
    Graft, 64885-64907
    Microrepair
      with Surgical Microscope, 69990
    Suture, 64831-64876
  Nonunion
    Carpal Bone, 25431
    Femur, 27470, 27472
    Fibula, 27726
    Humerus, 24430
    Metacarpal, 26546
    Metatarsal, 28322
    Navicular, 25440
    Phalanx, 26546
    Radius, 25400, 25405, 25415, 25420
    Scaphoid, 25440
    Tarsal Bones, 28320
    Tibia, 27720, 27722, 27724-27725
    Ulna, 25400, 25405, 25415, 25420
  Nose
    Adhesions, 30560
    Fistula, 30580, 30600, 42260
    Rhinophyma, 30120
    Septum, 30540, 30545, 30630
    Synechia, 30560

Repair — *continued*
  Nose — *continued*
    Vestibular Stenosis, 30465
  Obstruction
    Ventricular Outflow, 33414, 33619
  Omentum, 49999
  Omphalocele, 49600-49611
  Osteochondritis Dissecans Lesion, 29892
  Osteotomy
    Femoral Neck, 27161
    Radius and Ulna, 25365
    Ulna and Radius, 25365
    Vertebra
      Additional Segment, 22216, 22226
      Cervical, 22210, 22220
      Lumbar, 22214, 22224
      Thoracic, 22212, 22222
  Oval Window
    Fistula, 69666-69667
  Oviduct, 58752
    Create Stoma, 58770
  Pacemaker
    Heart
      Electrode(s), 33218, 33220
  Palate
    Laceration, 42180, 42182
    Vomer Flap, 42235
  Pancreas
    Cyst, 48500
    Pseudocyst, 48510, 48511
      Percutaneous, 48511
  Paravaginal Defect, 57284-57285, 57423
  Pectus Carinatum, 21740-21742
    with Thoracoscopy, 21743
  Pectus Excavatum, 21740-21742
    with Thoracoscopy, 21743
  Pectus Excavatum or Carinatum, 21740, 21742-21743
  Pelvic Floor
    with Prosthesis, 57267
  Pelvis
    Osteotomy, 27158
    Tendon, 27098
  Penis
    Fistulization, 54435
    Injury, 54440
    Priapism, 54420-54435
    Prosthesis, 54408
    Shunt, 54420, 54430
  Perforation
    Septal, 30630
  Perineum, 56810
  Periorbital Region
    Osteotomy, 21260-21263
  Peritoneum, 49999
  Phalanges
    Finger
      Lengthening, 26568
      Osteotomy, 26567
      Nonunion, 26546
    Toe
      Osteotomy, 28310, 28312
  Pharynx
    with Esophagus, 42953
  Pleura, 32215
  Prosthesis
    Penis, 54408
  Pseudarthrosis
    Tibia, 27727
  Pulmonary Artery, 33917, 33920, 33925-33926
    Reimplantation, 33788
  Pulmonary Valve, 33470-33474
  Pulmonary Venous
    Anomaly, 33724
    Stenosis, 33726
  Quadriceps, 27430
  Radius
    with Graft, 25405, 25420-25426
    Epiphyseal, 25450, 25455
    Malunion or Nonunion, 25400-25420

Repair — *continued*
  Radius — *continued*
    Osteotomy, 25350, 25355, 25370, 25375
  Rectocele, 45560, 57250
  Rectovaginal Fistula, 57308
  Rectum
    with Sigmoid Excision, 45550
    Fistula, 45800-45825, 46706-46707, 46715-46716, 46740, 46742
    Injury, 45562-45563
    Prolapse, 45505-45541, 45900
    Rectocele, 45560, 57250
    Stenosis, 45500
  Retinal Detachment, 67101-67113
    Diathermy, 67101
  Rotator Cuff, 23410-23412, 23420, 29827
  Salivary Duct, 42500, 42505
    Fistula, 42600
  Scalenus Anticus, 21700, 21705
  Scapula
    Fixation, 23400
    Scapulopexy, 23400
  Sclera
    with Glue, 65286
    Reinforcement
      with Graft, 67255
      without Graft, 67250
    Staphyloma
      with Graft, 66225
      without Graft, 66220
    Wound
      Operative, 66250
      Tissue Glue, 65286
  Scrotum, 55175, 55180
  Septal Defect, 33813-33814
  Septum, Nasal, 30420
  Shoulder
    Capsule, 23450-23466
    Cuff, 23410, 23412
    Ligament Release, 23415
    Muscle Transfer, 23395, 23397
    Musculotendinous (Rotator) Cuff, 23410, 23412
    Rotator Cuff, 23415, 23420
    Tendon, 23410, 23412, 23430, 23434
    Tenomyotomy, 23405, 23406
  Simple, Integumentary System, 12001-12021
  Sinus
    Ethmoid
      Cerebrospinal Fluid Leak, 31290
    Meningocele, 63700, 63702
    Myelomeningocele, 63704, 63706
    Sphenoid
      Cerebrospinal Fluid Leak, 31291
  Sinus of Valsalva, 33702-33722
  Skin
    See also Repair, Laceration
    Wound
      Complex, 13100-13160
      Intermediate, 12031-12057
      Simple, 12020, 12021
  Skull
    Cerebrospinal Fluid Leak, 62100
    Encephalocele, 62120
  SLAP Lesion, 29807
  Spectacles, 92370, 92371
    Prosthesis, 92371
  Sphincter, 53449
  Spica Cast, 29720
  Spinal Cord, 63700
    Cerebrospinal Fluid Leak, 63707, 63709
    Meningocele, 63700, 63702
    Myelomeningocele, 63704, 63706
  Spinal Meningocele, 63700-63702
  Spine
    Lumbar Vertebra, 22521-22522, 22524-22525
    Osteotomy, 22210-22226

Index

Repair — *continued*
Spine — *continued*
Thoracic Vertebra, 22520, 22522, 22523, 22525
Spleen, 38115
Stenosis
Nasal Vestibular, 30465
Pulmonary, 33782-33783
Sternocleidomastoid, 21720, 21725
Stomach
Esophagogastrostomy, 43320
Fistula, 43880
Fundoplasty, 43324, 43325
Laceration, 43501, 43502
Stoma, 43870
Ulcer, 43501
Symblepharon, 68330, 68335, 68340
Syndactyly, 26560-26562
Talus
Osteotomy, 28302
Tarsal, 28320
Osteotomy, 28304, 28305
Tear
Lung, 32110
Tendon
Achilles, 27650, 27652, 27654
Extensor, 26410, 26412, 26418, 26420, 26426, 26428, 26433-26434, 27664-27665
Foot, 28208, 28210
Flexor, 26350, 26352, 26356-26358, 27658-27659
Leg, 28200, 28202
Foot, 28200, 28202, 28208, 28210
Leg, 27658-27659, 27664-27665
Peroneal, 27675-27676
Profundus, 26370, 26372-26373
Upper Arm or Elbow, 24341
Testis
Injury, 54670
Suspension, 54620, 54640
Torsion, 54600
Tetralogy of Fallot, 33692, 33694, 33697
Throat
Pharyngoesophageal, 42953
Wound, 42900
Thumb
Muscle, 26508
Tendon, 26510
Tibia, 27720-27725
Epiphysis, 27477-27485, 27730-27742
Osteotomy, 27455, 27457, 27705, 27709, 27712
Pseudoarthrosis, 27727
Toe(s)
Bunion, 28290-28299
Macrodactyly, 26590
Muscle, 28240
Polydactylous, 26587
Ruiz–Mora Procedure, 28286
Tendon, 28240
Webbed Toe, 28280, 28345
Tongue, 41250-41252
Fixation, 41500
Laceration, 41250-41252
Mechanical, 41500
Suture, 41510
Trachea
Fistula, 31755
with Plastic Repair, 31825
without Plastic Repair, 31820
Stenosis, 31780, 31781
Stoma, 31613, 31614
with Plastic Repair, 31825
without Plastic Repair, 31820
Scar, 31830
Wound
Cervical, 31800
Intrathoracic, 31805
Transposition
Great Arteries, 33770-33771, 33774-33781

Repair — *continued*
Triangular Fibrocartilage, 29846
Tricuspid Valve, 33463-33465
Trigger Finger, 26055
Truncus Arteriosus
Rastelli Type, 33786
Tunica Vaginalis
Hydrocele, 55060
Tympanic Membrane, 69450, 69610, 69635-69637, 69641-69646
Ulcer, 43501
Ulna
with Graft, 25405, 25420
Epiphyseal, 25450, 25455
Malunion or Nonunion, 25400-25415
Osteotomy, 25360, 25370, 25375, 25425, 25426
Umbilicus
Omphalocele, 49600-49611
Ureter
Anastomosis, 50740-50825
Continent Diversion, 50825
Deligation, 50940
Fistula, 50920, 50930
Lysis Adhesions, 50715-50725
Suture, 50900
Urinary Undiversion, 50830
Ureterocele, 51535
Urethra
Artificial Sphincter, 53449
Diverticulum, 53240, 53400, 53405
Fistula, 45820, 45825, 53400, 53405, 53520
Prostatic or Membranous Urethra, 53415, 53420, 53425
Stoma, 53520
Stricture, 53400, 53405
Urethrocele, 57230
Wound, 53502-53515
Urethral Sphincter, 57220
Urinary Incontinence, 53431, 53440, 53445
Uterus
Anomaly, 58540
Fistula, 51920, 51925
Rupture, 58520, 59350
Suspension, 58400, 58410
Presacral Sympathectomy, 58410
Vagina
Anterior, 57240, 57289
with Insertion of Mesh, 57267
with Insertion of Prosthesis, 57267
Cystocele, 57240, 57260
Enterocele, 57265
Episiotomy, 59300
Fistula, 46715, 46716, 51900
Rectovaginal, 57300-57307
Transvesical and Vaginal Approach, 57330
Urethrovaginal, 57310, 57311
Vaginoenteric, 58999
Vesicovaginal, 57320, 57330
Hysterectomy, 58267, 58293
Incontinence, 57288
Pereyra Procedure, 57289
Postpartum, 59300
Prolapse, 57282, 57284
Rectocele, 57250, 57260
Suspension, 57280-57284
Laparoscopic, 57425
Wound, 57200, 57210
Vaginal Wall Prolapse
Anterior, 57240, 57267, 57289
Anteroposterior, 57260-57267
Nonobstetrical, 57200
Posterior, 57250, 57267
Vas Deferens
Suture, 55400
Vein
Angioplasty, 35460, 35476, 75978
Femoral, 34501

Repair — *continued*
Vein — *continued*
Graft, 34520
Pulmonary, 33730
Transposition, 34510
Ventricle, 33545, 33611-33612, 33782-33783
Vulva
Postpartum, 59300
Wound
Cardiac, 33300, 33305
Complex, 13100-13160
Extraocular Muscle, 65290
Intermediate, 12031-12057
Operative Wound Anterior Segment, 66250
Simple, 12001-12021
Wound Dehiscence
Abdominal Wall, 49900
Skin and Subcutaneous Tissue
Complex, 13160
Simple, 12020, 12021
Wrist, 25260, 25263, 25270, 25447
Bones, 25440
Carpal Bone, 25431
Cartilage, 25107
Muscles, 25260-25274
Removal
Implant, 25449
Secondary, 25265, 25272, 25274
Tendon, 25280-25316
Sheath, 25275
Total Replacement, 25446
Repeat Surgeries
Carotid
Thromboendarterectomy, 35390
Coronary Artery Bypass
Valve Procedure, 33530
Distal Vessel Bypass, 35700
Replacement
Acellular Dermal, 15170-15176
Adjustable Gastric Restrictive Device, 43773
Aortic Valve, 33405-33413
Arthroplasty
Hip, 27125-27138
Spine, 22856-22857, 22861-22862
Artificial Heart
Intracorporeal, 0052T-0053T
Cecostomy Tube, 49450
Cerebrospinal Fluid Shunt, 62160, 62194, 62225, 62230
Colonic Tube, 49450
Contact Lens, 92326
See Also Contact Lens Services
Duodenostomy Tube, 49451
Elbow
Total, 24363
Electrode
Heart, 33210, 33211, 33216, 33217
Stomach, 0155T, 0157T, 43647
External Fixation, 20697
Eye
Drug Delivery System, 67121
Gastro-jejunostomy Tube, 49452
Gastrostomy Tube, 43760, 49450
Hearing Aid
Bone Conduction, 69710
Heart
Defibrillator
Leads, 33249
Hip, 27130, 27132
Revision, 27134-27138
Implant
Bone
for External Speech Processor/Cochlear Stimulator, 69717, 69718
Intervertebral Disc
Cervical Interspace, 0092T, 22856
Lumbar Interspace, 0163T, 22862
Jejunostomy Tube, 49451

Replacement — *continued*
Knee
Total, 27447
Mitral Valve, 33430
Nephrostomy Tube, 50398
Nerve, 64726
Neurostimulator
Electrode, 63663-63664
Pulse Generator/Receiver
Intracranial, 61885
Peripheral Nerve, 64590
Spinal, 63685
Ossicles
with Prosthesis, 69633, 69637
Ossicular Replacement, 69633, 69637
Pacemaker, 33206-33208
Catheter, 33210
Electrode, 33210, 33211, 33216, 33217
Pacing Cardioverter–Defibrillator
Leads, 33243, 33244
Pulse Generator Only, 33241
Penile
Prosthesis, 54410, 54411, 54416, 54417
Prosthesis
Skull, 62143
Urethral Sphincter, 53448
Pulmonary Valve, 33475
Pulse Generator
Brain, 61885
Peripheral Nerve, 64590
Spinal Cord, 63685
Pyelostomy Tube, 50398
Receiver
Brain, 61885
Peripheral Nerve, 64590
Spinal Cord, 63685
Skin
Acellular Dermal Matrix, 15170-15176
Skull Plate, 62143
Spinal Cord
Reservoir, 62360
Stent
Ureteral, 50382, 50385, 50387
Strut, 20697
Subcutaneous Port for Gastric Restrictive Procedure, 43888
Tissue Expanders
Skin, 11970
Total Replacement Heart System
Intracorporeal, 0052T-0053T
Total Replacement Hip, 27130-27132
Tricuspid Valve, 33465
Ureter
with Intestines, 50840
Electronic Stimulator, 53899
Uterus
Inverted, 59899
Venous Access Device, 36582, 36583, 36585
Catheter, 36578
Venous Catheter
Central, 36580, 36581, 36584
Ventricular Assist Device, 33981-33983
Replantation, Reimplantation
Adrenal Tissue, 60699
Arm, Upper, 20802
Digit, 20816, 20822
Foot, 20838
Forearm, 20805
Hand, 20808
Scalp, 17999
Thumb, 20824, 20827
Report Preparation
Extended, Medical, 99080
Psychiatric, 90889
Reposition
Toe to Hand, 26551-26556
Repositioning
Canalith, 95992
Central Venous Catheter, Previously Placed, 36597

Repositioning — *continued*
  Electrode
    Heart, 33215, 33216, 33217, 33226
  Gastrostomy Tube, 43761
  Heart
    Defibrillator
      Leads, 33215, 33216, 33226, 33249
  Intraocular Lens, 66825
  Tricuspid Valve, 33468

Reproductive Tissue
  Preparation
    Thawing, 89354
  Storage, 89344

Reprogramming
  Shunt
    Brain, 62252

Reptilase
  Test, 85635
  Time, 85670-85675

Resection
  Abdomen, 51597
  Aortic Valve Stenosis, 33415
  Bladder Diverticulum, 52305
  Bladder Neck
    Transurethral, 52500
  Brain Lobe, 61323, 61537-61540
  Chest Wall, 19260-19272
  Diaphragm, 39560-39561
  Endaural, 69905-69910
  Humeral Head, 23195
  Intestines, Small
    Laparoscopic, 44202-44203
  Lung, 32503-32504
  Mouth
    with Tongue Excision, 41153
  Myocardium
    Aneurysm, 33542
    Septal Defect, 33545
  Nasal Septum, Submucous, 30520
  Nose
    Septum, 30520
  Ovary, Wedge, 58920
  Palate, 42120
  Pancoast Tumor, 32503-32504
  Phalangeal Head
    Toe, 28153
  Prostate, Transurethral, 52601
  Radical
    Abdomen, 22904-22905, 51597
    Acetabulum, 27049 [27059], 27076
    Ankle, 27615-27616, 27645-27647
    Arm, Lower, 24152, 25077-25078, 25170
    Arm, Upper, 23220, 24077-24079, 24150
    Back, 21935-21936
    Calcaneus, 27615-27616, 27647
    Elbow, 24077-24079, 24152
      Capsule Soft Tissue, 24149
    Face, 21015-21016
    Femur, 27364-27365 [27329]
    Fibula, 27615-27616, 27646
    Finger, 26117-26118, 26260-26262
    Flank, 21935-21936
    Foot, 28046-28047, 28171-28173
    Forearm, 25077-25078, 25170
    Hand, 26117-26118, 26250
    Hip, 27049 [27059], 27075-27078
    Humerus, 23220, 24077-24079
    Innominate, 27049 [27059], 27077
    Ischial, 27049 [27059], 27078
    Knee, 27364-27365 [27329]
    Lymph Node(s)
      Abdomen, 38747
      Axillary, 38740, 38745
      Cervical, 38720, 38724
      Groin Area, 38760, 38765
      Pelvic, 38770
      Retroperitoneal, 38780
      Suprahyoid, 38700

Resection — *continued*
  Radical — *continued*
    Lymph Node(s) — *continued*
      Thoracic, 38746
    Metacarpal, 26117-26118, 26250
    Metatarsal, 28046-28047, 28173
    Mouth
      with Tongue Excision, 41150, 41155
    Neck, 21557-21558
    Ovarian Tumor
      with Radical Dissection for Debulking, 58952-58954
      with Total Abdominal Hysterectomy, 58951, 58953-58956
      Bilateral Salpingo-Oophorectomy-Omentectomy, 58950-58954
      Omentectomy, 58950-58956
    Pelvis, 27049 [27059], 27075-27078
    Peritoneal Tumor
      with Radical Dissection for Debulking, 58952-58954
      Bilateral Salpingo-Oophorectomy-Omentectomy, 58952-58954
    Phalanges
      Fingers, 26117-26118, 26260-26262
      Toes, 28046-28047, 28175
    Radius, 24152, 25077-25078, 25170
    Scalp, 21015-21016
    Scapula, 23077-23078, 23210
    Shoulder, 23077-23078, 23220
    Sternum, 21557-21558, 21630-21632
    Talus, 27615-27616, 27647
    Tarsal, 28046-28047, 28171
    Thigh, 27364-27365 [27329]
    Thorax, 21557-21558
    Tibia, 27615-27616, 27645
    Tonsil, 42842-42845
    Ulna, 25077-25078, 25170
    Wrist, 25077-25078, 25115-25116, 25170
  Rhinectomy
    Partial, 30150
    Total, 30160
  Ribs, 19260-19272, 32900
  Synovial Membrane
    See Synovectomy
  Temporal Bone, 69535
  Tumor
    Fallopian Tube, 58957-58958
    Lung, 32503-32504
    Ovary, 58957-58958
    Peritoneum, 58957-58958
  Ulna
    Arthrodesis
      Radioulnar Joint, 25830
  Ureterocele
    Ectopic, 52301
    Orthotopic, 52300
  Vena Cava
    with Reconstruction, 37799

Residual Urine Collection, 51701
Resonance Spectroscopy, Magnetic, 76390
Respiration, Positive-Pressure, 94660
Respiratory Pattern Recording
  Preventive
    Infant, 94772
Respiratory Syncytial Virus
  Antibody, 86756
  Antigen Detection
    Direct Fluorescent Antibody, 87280
    Direct Optical Observation, 87807
    Enzyme Immunoassay, 87420
  Recombinant, 90378

Response, Auditory Evoked, 92585-92586
  See Also Audiologic Function Tests
Rest Home Visit
  Care Plan Oversight Services, 99339-99340
  Established Patient, 99334-99337
  New Patient, 99324-99328
Restoration
  Ventricular, 33548
Resuscitation
  Cardiac Massage via Thoracotomy, 32160
  Cardiopulmonary (CPR), 92950
  Newborn, 99460-99465
Reticulocyte
  Count, 85044-85045
Retina
  Examination, Macula/Fundus, Dilated, 2019F-2021F
    Communication of Findings for Diabetes Management, 5010F
  Incision
    Encircling Material, 67115
  Lesion
    Extensive
      Destruction, 67227-67228
    Localized
      Destruction, 0017T, 67208-67218
  Repair
    Detachment
      with Vitrectomy, 67108, 67112-67113
      by Scleral Buckling, 67112
      Cryotherapy or Diathermy, 67101
      Injection of Air, 67110
      Photocoagulation, 67105
      Scleral Dissection, 67107
    Prophylaxis
      Detachment, 67141, 67145
  Retinopathy
    Destruction
      Cryotherapy, Diathermy, 67227, 67229
      Photocoagulation, 67228-67229
      Preterm Infant, 67229
Retinacular
  Knee
    Release, 27425
Retinopathy
  Destruction/Treatment
    Cryotherapy, Diathermy, 67227, 67229
    Photocoagulation, 67228-67229
Retinopexy, Pneumatic, 67110
Retraction, Clot
  See Clot Retraction
Retrieval
  Transcatheter Foreign Body, 37203
Retrocaval Ureter
  Ureterolysis, 50725
Retrograde Cholangiopancreatographies, Endoscopic
  See Cholangiopancreatography
Retrograde Cystourethrogram
  See Urethrocystography, Retrograde
Retrograde Pyelogram
  See Urography, Retrograde
Retroperitoneal Area
  Abscess
    Incision and Drainage
      Open, 49060
      Percutaneous, 49061
  Biopsy, 49010
  Cyst
    Destruction/Excision, 49203-49205
  Endometriomas
    Destruction/Excision, 49203-49205
  Exploration, 49010

Retroperitoneal Area — *continued*
  Needle Biopsy
    Mass, 49180
  Tumor
    Destruction
      Excision, 49203-49205
Retroperitoneal Fibrosis
  Ureterolysis, 50715
Retropubic Prostatectomies
  See Prostatectomy, Retropubic
Revascularization
  Distal Upper Extremity
    with Interval Ligation, 36838
  Heart
    Arterial Implant, 33999
    Myocardial Resection, 33542
    Other Tissue Grafts, 20926
  Interval Ligation
    Distal Upper Extremity, 36838
  Penis, 37788
  Transmyocardial, 33140-33141
Reverdin Bunionectomy, 28296
Reversal, Vasectomy
  See Vasovasorrhaphy
Reverse T3, 84482
Reverse Triiodothyronine, 84482
Revision
  See Also Reconstruction
  Abdomen
    Intraperitoneal Catheter, 49325
    Peritoneal-Venous Shunt, 49426
  Adjustable Gastric Restrictive Device, 43771
  Aorta, 33404
  Arthroplasty
    Hip, 27125-27138
    Spine, 22861-22862
    Atrial, 33254-33256
    Blepharoplasty, 15820-15823
  Breast
    Implant, 19380
  Bronchial Stent, 31638
  Bronchus, 32501
  Bypass Graft
    Vein Patch, 35685
  Cervicoplasty, 15819
  Colostomy, 44340
    Paracolostomy Hernia, 44345-44346
  Cornea
    Prosthesis, 65770
    Reshaping
      Epikeratoplasty, 65767
      Keratomileusis, 65760
      Keratophakia, 65765
  Defibrillator Site
    Chest, 33223
  Ear, Middle, 69662
  Electrode, Stomach, 0156T, 0158T, 43648, 43882
  External Fixation System, 20693
  Eye
    Aqueous Shunt, 66185
  Gastric Restrictive Device, Adjustable, 43771
  Gastric Restrictive Procedure, 43848
    Adjustable Gastric Restrictive Device Component, 43771
    Subcutaneous Port Component, 43886
  Gastrostomy Tube, 44373
  Graft
    Vaginal, 57295-57296, 57426
  Hip Replacement
    See Replacement, Hip, Revision
  Hymenal Ring, 56700
  Ileostomy, 44312-44314
  Infusion Pump
    Intra-Arterial, 36261
    Intravenous, 36576-36578, 36582-36583
  Iris
    Iridoplasty, 66762
    Iridotomy, 66761
  Jejunostomy Tube, 44373

Index

Revision — *continued*
  Lower Extremity Arterial Bypass, 35879-35881
  Neurostimulator
    Electrode, 63663-63664
    Pulse Generator, 63688
    Receiver, 63688
  Pacemaker Site
    Chest, 33222
  Rhytidectomy, 15824-15829
  Semicircular Canal
    Fenestration, 69840
  Shunt
    Intrahepatic Portosystemic, 37183
  Skin Pocket, Chest
    for Implantable Cardioverter–Defibrillator, 33223
    for Pacemaker, 33222
  Sling, 53442
  Stapedectomy, 69662
  Stomach
    for Obesity, 43848
  Subcutaneous Port for Gastric Restrictive Procedure, 43886
  Tracheostomy
    Scar, 31830
  Urinary–Cutaneous Anastomosis, 50727-50728
  Vagina
    Graft, 57295-57296, 57426
    Sling
      Stress Incontinence, 57287
  Venous Access Device, 36576-36578, 36582-36583, 36585
  Ventricle
    Ventriculomyectomy, 33416
    Ventriculomyotomy, 33416
  Vesicostomy, 51880
Rh (D), 86901
Rheumatoid Factor, 86430-86431
Rh Immune Globulin, 90384-90386
Rhinectomy
  Partial, 30150
  Total, 30160
Rhinomanometry, 92512
Rhinopharynx
  Biopsy, 42804-42806
  Hemorrhage, 42970-42972
  Unlisted Services/Procedures, 42999
Rhinophototherapy, 0168T
Rhinophyma
  Repair, 30120
Rhinoplasty
  Cleft Lip
    Cleft Palate, 30460-30462
  Primary, 30400-30420
  Secondary, 30430-30450
Rhinoscopy
  Diagnostic, 31231-31235
  Surgical, 31237-31294
  Unlisted Services/Procedures, 31299
Rhinotomy
  Lateral, 30118, 30320
Rhizotomy, 63185, 63190
Rho(D) Vaccine, 90384-90386
Rho Variant Du, 86905
Rh Type, 86901
Rhytidectomy, 15824-15829
  Cheek, 15828
  Chin, 15828
  Forehead, 15824
  Glabellar Frown Lines, 15826
  Neck, 15825, 15828
  Superficial Musculoaponeurotic System, 15829
Rhytidoplasties, 15824-15829
Rib
  Antibody, 86756
  Antigen Detection by Immunoassay with Direct Optical Observation
    Direct Fluorescence, 87280
    Enzyme Immunoassay, 87420
  Bone Graft
    with Microvascular Anastomosis, 20962

Rib — *continued*
  Excision, 21600-21616, 32900
  Fracture
    Closed Treatment, 21800
    External Fixation, 21810
    Open Treatment, 21805
  Free Osteocutaneous Flap with Microvascular Anastomosis, 20969
  Graft
    to Face, 21230
  Resection, 19260-19272, 32900
  X-ray, 71100-71111
Riboflavin, 84252
Richardson Operation Hysterectomy, 58150
  See Also Hysterectomy, Abdominal, Total
Richardson Procedure, 53460
Rickettsia
  Antibody, 86757
Ridell Operation
  Sinusotomy, Frontal, 31075-31087
Ridge, Alveolar
  Fracture Treatment
    Closed, 21440
    Open, 21445
RIG (Rabies Immune Globulin), 90375-90376
Right Atrioventricular Valve, 33460-33468
Right Heart Cardiac Catheterization, 93501-93503
  Congenital Cardiac Anomalies, 93530
Ripstein Operation
  Laparoscopic, 45400
    with Sigmoid Resection, 45402
  Open, 45540-45541
    with Sigmoid Excision, 45550
Risk Factor Reduction Intervention
  Behavior Change Interventions, 99406-99409
  Group Counseling, 99411-99412
  Individual Counseling, 99401-99404
Risser Jacket, 29010-29015
  Removal, 29710
RK, 65771
Rocky Mountain Spotted Fever, 86000
Roentgenographic
  See X-Ray
Roentgenography
  See Radiology, Diagnostic
Roentgen Rays
  See X-Ray
ROM, 95851-95852, 97110, 97530
Ropes Test, 83872
Rorschach Test, 96101-96103
Ross Information Processing Assessment, 96125
Ross Procedure, 33413
Rotarix, 90681
RotaTeq, 90680
Rotation Flap, 14000-14350
Rotator Cuff
  Repair, 23410-23420
Rotavirus
  Antibody, 86759
  Antigen Detection
    Enzyme Immunoassay, 87425
Rotavirus Vaccine, 90680-90681
Round Window
  Repair Fistula, 69667
Round Window Fistula, 69667
Roux-en-Y Procedures
  Biliary Tract, 47740-47741, 47780-47785
  Pancreas, 48540
  Stomach, 43621, 43633, 43644, 43846
    Laparoscopic, 43644
RPP (Radical Perineal Prostatectomy), 55810-55815
RPR, 86592-86593
RRP (Radical Retropubic Prostatectomy), 55840-55845

RSV
  Antibody, 86756
  Antigen Detection
    Direct Fluorescent Antibody, 87280
    Enzyme Immunoassay, 87420
    Recombinant, 90378
RT3, 84482
Rubber Band Ligation
  Hemorrhoids, [46945, 46946]
  Skin Tags, 11200-11201
Rubella
  Antibody, 86762
  Vaccine, 90706-90710
Rubella HI Test
  Hemagglutination Inhibition Test, 86280
Rubella Immunization, 90706
  with Measles, 90708
  MMR, 90707
  MMRV, 90710
Rubeola
  Antibody, 86765
  Antigen Detection
    Immunofluorescence, 87283
Ruiz–Mora Procedure, 28286
Russel Viper Venom Time, 85612-85613

S

Saccomanno Technique, 88108
Sac, Endolymphatic
  Exploration, 69805-69806
Sacral Nerve
  Implantation
    Electrode, 64561, 64581
  Insertion
    Electrode, 64561, 64581
Sacroiliac Joint
  Arthrodesis, 27280
  Arthrotomy, 27050
  Biopsy, 27050
  Dislocation
    Open Treatment, 27218
  Fusion, 27280
  Injection for Arthrography, 27096
  X-ray, 72200-72202, 73542
Sacroplasty, 0200T-0201T
Sacrum
  augmentation, 0200T-0201T
  Pressure Ulcer, 15931-15937
  Tumor
    Excision, 49215
  X-ray, 72220
SAECG, 93278
SAH, 61566
Sahli Test
  Stomach, Intubation with Specimen Prep., 91055
Salabrasion, 15780-15787
Salicylate
  Assay, 80196
Saline–Solution Abortion, 59850-59851
Salivary Duct
  Catheterization, 42660
  Dilation, 42650-42660
  Ligation, 42665
  Repair, 42500-42505
  Fistula, 42600
Salivary Glands
  Abscess
    Incision and Drainage, 42310-42320
  Biopsy, 42405
  Calculi (Stone)
    Excision, 42330-42340
  Cyst
    Drainage, 42409
    Excision, 42408
  Injection
    X-ray, 42550
  Needle Biopsy, 42400
  Nuclear Medicine
    Function Study, 78232
    Imaging, 78230-78231

Salivary Glands — *continued*
  Parotid
    Abscess, 42300-42305
  Unlisted Services and Procedures, 42699
  X-ray, 70380-70390
    with Contrast, 70390
Salivary Gland Virus
  Antibody, 86644-86645
  Antigen Detection
    Direct Fluorescence, 87271
    Enzyme Immunoassay, 87332
    Nucleic Acid, 87495-87497
Salmonella
  Antibody, 86768
Salpingectomy, 58262-58263, 58291-58292, 58552, 58554, 58661, 58700
  Ectopic Pregnancy
    Laparoscopic Treatment, 59151
    Surgical Treatment, 59120
  Oophorectomy, 58943
Salpingohysterostomy, 58752
Salpingolysis, 58740
Salpingoneostomy, 58673, 58770
Salpingo–Oophorectomy, 58720
  Resection Ovarian Malignancy, 58950-58956
  Resection Peritoneal Malignancy, 58950-58956
  Resection Tubal Malignancy, 58950-58956
Salpingostomy, 58673, 58770
  Laparoscopic, 58673
SALT, 84460
Salter Osteotomy of the Pelvis, 27146
Sampling
  See Biopsy; Brush Biopsy; Needle Biopsy
Sang–Park Procedure
  Septectomy, Atrial, 33735-33737
    Balloon (Rashkind Type), 92992
    Blade Method (Park), 92993
Sao Paulo Typhus, 86000
SAST, 84450
Saucerization
  Calcaneus, 28120
  Clavicle, 23180
  Femur, 27070, 27360
  Fibula, 27360, 27641
  Hip, 27070
  Humerus, 23184, 24140
  Ileum, 27070
  Metacarpal, 26230
  Metatarsal, 28122
  Olecranon Process, 24147
  Phalanges
    Finger, 26235-26236
    Toe, 28124
  Pubis, 27070
  Radius, 24145, 25151
  Scapula, 23182
  Talus, 28120
  Tarsal, 28122
  Tibia, 27360, 27640
  Ulna, 24147, 25150
Saundby Test, 82270, 82272
Sauve–Kapandji Procedure
  Arthrodesis, Distal Radioulnar Joint, 25830
SAVER (Surgical Anterior Ventricular Endocardial Restoration), 33548
SBFT, 74249
SBRT (Stereotactic Body Radiation Therapy), 77373
Scabies, 87220
Scalenotomy, 21700-21705
Scalenus Anticus
  Division, 21700-21705
Scaling
  Chemical for Acne, 17360
Scalp
  Skin Graft
    Delay of Flap, 15610
    Full Thickness, 15220-15221
    Pedicle Flap, 15572

Scalp

Scalp — *continued*
  Skin Graft — *continued*
    Split, 15100-15101
    Tissue Transfer, Adjacent, 14020-14021
  Tumor Excision, 21011-21016
Scalp Blood Sampling, 59030
Scan
  See Also Specific Site; Nuclear Medicine
  Abdomen
    Computed Tomography, 74150-74175, 75635
  Computerized
    Ophthalmic, 0187T
  CT
    See CT Scan
  MRI
    See Magnetic Resonance Imaging
  PET
    With Computed Tomography (CT)
      Limted, 78814
      Skull Base to Mid-thigh, 78815
      Whole Body, 78816
    Brain, 78608-78609
    Heart, 78459
    Limited Area, 78811
    Myocardial Imaging Perfusion Study, 78491-78492
    Skull Base to Mid-Thigh, 78812
    Whole Body, 78813
  Radionuclide, Brain, 78607
Scanning Radioiosotope
  See Nuclear Medicine
Scanogram, 77073
Scaphoid
  Fracture
    with Manipulation, 25624
    Closed Treatment, 25622
    Open Treatment, 25628
Scapula
  Craterization, 23182
  Cyst
    Excision, 23140
      with Allograft, 23146
      with Autograft, 23145
  Diaphysectomy, 23182
  Excision, 23172, 23190
    Partial, 23182
  Fracture
    Closed Treatment
      with Manipulation, 23575
      without Manipulation, 23570
    Open Treatment, 23585
  Ostectomy, 23190
  Repair
    Fixation, 23400
    Scapulopexy, 23400
  Saucerization, 23182
  Sequestrectomy, 23172
  Tumor
    Excision, 23140, 23210
      with Allograft, 23146
      with Autograft, 23145
    Radical Resection, 23210
  X–ray, 73010
Scapulopexy, 23400
Scarification
  Pleural, 32215
Scarification of Pleura
  Agent for Pleurodesis, 32560
  Endoscopic, 32650
SCBE (Single Contrast Barium Enema), 74270
Schanz Operation, 27448
Schauta Operation, 58285
Schede Procedure, 32905-32906
Scheie Procedure, 66155
Schilling Test, 78270-78272
Schlatter Operation, 43620
Schlemm's Canal Dilation, 0176T-0177T
Schlicter Test, 87197
Schocket Procedure, 66180

Schuchard Procedure
  Osteotomy
    Maxilla, 21206
Schwannoma, Acoustic
  See Brain, Tumor, Excision
Sciatic Nerve
  Decompression, 64712
  Injection
    Anesthetic, 64445-64446
  Lesion
    Excision, 64786
  Neuroma
    Excision, 64786
  Neuroplasty, 64712
  Release, 64712
  Repair
    Suture, 64858
Scintigraphy
  See Emission Computerized Tomography
  See Nuclear Medicine
Scissoring
  Skin Tags, 11200-11201
Sclera
  Excision, 66130
    Sclerectomy with Punch or Scissors, 66160
  Fistulization
    for Glaucoma, 0123T
    Iridencleisis or Iridotasis, 66165
    Sclerectomy with Punch or Scissors with Iridectomy, 66160
    Thermocauterization with Iridectomy, 66155
    Trabeculectomy ab Externo in Absence of Previous Surgery, 66170
    Trephination with Iridectomy, 66150
  Incision (Fistulization)
    Iridencleisis or Iridotasis, 66165
    Sclerectomy with Punch or Scissors with Iridectomy, 66160
    Thermocauterization with Iridectomy, 66155
    Trabeculectomy ab Externo in Absence of Previous Surgery, 66170
    Trephination with Iridectomy, 66150
  Lesion
    Excision, 66130
  Repair
    with Glue, 65286
    Reinforcement
      with Graft, 67255
      without Graft, 67250
    Staphyloma
      with Graft, 66225
      without Graft, 66220
    Wound (Operative), 66250
    Tissue Glue, 65286
Scleral Buckling Operation
  Retina, Repair, Detachment, 67107-67112
Scleral Ectasia
  Repair, 66220
    with Graft, 66225
Sclerectomy, 66160
Sclerotherapy
  Venous, 36468-36471
Sclerotomy, 66150-66170
Screening, Drug
  Alcohol and/or Substance Abuse, 99408-99409
  Qualitative, 80100-80101
Scribner Cannulization, 36810
Scrotal Varices
  Excision, 55530-55540
Scrotoplasty, 55175-55180
Scrotum
  Abscess
    Incision and Drainage, 54700, 55100
  Excision, 55150
  Exploration, 55110

Scrotum — *continued*
  Hematoma
    Incision and Drainage, 54700
  Removal
    Foreign Body, 55120
  Repair, 55175-55180
  Ultrasound, 76870
  Unlisted Services and Procedures, 55899
Scrub Typhus, 86000
Second Look Surgery
  Carotid Thromboendarterectomy, 35390
  Coronary Artery Bypass, 33530
  Distal Vessel Bypass, 35700
  Valve Procedure, 33530
Section
  See Also Decompression
  Cesarean
    See Cesarean Delivery
  Cranial Nerve, 61460
    Spinal Access, 63191
  Dentate Ligament, 63180-63182
  Gasserian Ganglion
    Sensory Root, 61450
  Medullary Tract, 61470
  Mesencephalic Tract, 61480
  Nerve Root, 63185-63190
  Spinal Accessory Nerve, 63191
  Spinal Cord Tract, 63194-63199
  Tentorium Cerebelli, 61440
  Vestibular Nerve
    Transcranial Approach, 69950
    Translabyrinthine Approach, 69915
Sedation
  Conscious (Moderate), 99143-99150
    with Independent Observation, 99143-99145
Seddon–Brookes Procedure, 24320
Sedimentation Rate
  Blood Cell
    Automated, 85652
    Manual, 85651
Segmentectomy
  Breast, 19301-19302
  Lung, 32484
Selective Cellular Enhancement Technique, 88112
Selenium, 84255
Self Care
  See Also Physical Medicine/Therapy/Occupational Therapy
  Training, 97535, 98960-98962, 99509
Sella Turcica
  CT Scan, 70480-70482
  X-ray, 70240
Semen
  Cryopreservation
    Storage (per year), 89343
    Thawing, each aliquot, 89353
Semen Analysis, 89300-89322
  with Sperm Isolation, 89260-89261
  Sperm Analysis, 89331
  Antibodies, 89325
Semenogelase, 84152-84154
Semicircular Canal
  Incision
    Fenestration, 69820
    Revised, 69840
Semilunar
  Bone
    See Lunate
  Ganglion
    See Gasserian Ganglion
Seminal Vesicle
  Cyst
    Excision, 55680
  Excision, 55650
  Incision, 55600, 55605
  Mullerian Duct
    Excision, 55680
  Unlisted Services and Procedures, 55899

Seminal Vesicles
  Vesiculography, 74440
  X-ray with Contrast, 74440
Seminin, 84152-84154
Semiquantitative, 81005
Semont Maneuver, 95992
Sengstaaken Tamponade
  Esophagus, 43460
Senning Procedure
  Repair, Great Arteries, 33774-33777
Senning Type, 33774-33777
Sensitivity Study
  Antibiotic
    Agar, 87181
    Disc, 87184
    Enzyme Detection, 87185
    Macrobroth, 87188
    MIC, 87186
    Microtiter, 87186
    MLC, 87187
    Mycobacteria, 87190
  Antiviral Drugs
    HIV–1
      Tissue Culture, 87904
Sensorimotor Exam, 92060
Sensor, Transcatheter Placement, 34806
Sensory Nerve
  Common
    Repair/Suture, 64834
Sensory Testing
  Quantitative (QST), Per Extremity
    Cooling Stimuli, 0108T
    Heat–Pain Stimuli, 0109T
    Touch Pressure Stimuli, 0106T
    Using Other Stimuli, 0110T
    Vibration Stimuli, 0107T
Sentinel Node
  Injection Procedure, 38792
SEP (Somatosensory Evoked Potentials), 95925-95927
Separation
  Craniofacial
    Closed Treatment, 21431
    Open Treatment, 21432-21436
Septal Defect
  Repair, 33813-33814
  Ventricular
    Closure
      Open, 33675-33688
      Percutaneous, 93581
      Transmyocardial, 0166T-0167T
Septectomy
  Atrial, 33735-33737
    Balloon Type, 92992
    Blade Method, 92993
  Closed, 33735
  Submucous Nasal, 30520
Septic Abortion, 59830
Septoplasty, 30520
Septostomy
  Atrial, 33735-33737
    Balloon Type, 92992
    Blade Method, 92993
Septum, Nasal
  See Nasal Septum
Sequestrectomy
  with Alveolectomy, 41830
  Calcaneus, 28120
  Carpal, 25145
  Clavicle, 23170
  Forearm, 25145
  Humeral Head, 23174
  Humerus, 24134
  Olecranon Process, 24138
  Radius, 24136, 25145
  Scapula, 23172
  Skull, 61501
  Talus, 28120
  Ulna, 24138, 25145
  Wrist, 25145
Serialography
  Aorta, 75625
Serodiagnosis, Syphilis, 86592-86593

Index

Serologic Test for Syphilis, 86592-86593
Seroma, 10140
  Incision and Drainage
    Skin, 10140
Serotonin, 84260
Serum
  Albumin, 82040
  Antibody Identification
    Pretreatment, 86975-86978
  CPK, 82550
  Serum Immune Globulin, 90281-90284
Serum Globulin Immunization, 90281-90284
Sesamoid Bone
  Excision, 28315
  Finger
    Excision, 26185
  Foot
    Fracture, 28530-28531
  Thumb
    Excision, 26185
Sesamoidectomy
  Toe, 28315
Severing of Blepharorrhaphy, 67710
Sever Procedure, 23020
Sex Change Operation
  Female to Male, 55980
  Male to Female, 55970
Sex Chromatin, 88130
Sex Chromatin Identification, 88130-88140
Sex Hormone Binding Globulin, 84270
Sex–Linked Ichthyoses, 86592-86593
SG, 84315, 93503
SGOT, 84450
SGPT, 84460
Shaving
  Skin Lesion, 11300-11313
SHBG, 84270
Shelf Procedure
  Osteotomy, Hip, 27146-27151
    Femoral with Open Reduction, 27156
Shiga–Like Toxin
  Antigen Detection
    Enzyme Immunoassay, 87427
Shigella
  Antibody, 86771
Shirodkar Operation, 57700
Shock Wave Lithotripsy, 50590
Shock Wave (Extracorporeal) Therapy, 0019T, 0101T-0102T, 28890
Shock Wave, Ultrasonic
  See Ultrasound
Shop Typhus of Malaya, 86000
Shoulder
  See Also Clavicle; Scapula
  Abscess
    Drainage, 23030
  Amputation, 23900-23921
  Arthrocentesis, 20610
  Arthrodesis, 23800
    with Autogenous Graft, 23802
  Arthrography
    Injection
      Radiologic, 23350
  Arthroplasty
    with Implant, 23470-23472
  Arthroscopy
    Diagnostic, 29805
    Surgical, 29806-29828
  Arthrotomy
    with Removal Loose or Foreign Body, 23107
  Biopsy
    Deep, 23066
    Soft Tissue, 23065
  Blade
    See Scapula
  Bone
    Excision
      Acromion, 23130
      Clavicle, 23120-23125
      Clavicle Tumor, 23140-23146

Shoulder — continued
  Bone — continued
    Incision, 23035
    Tumor
      Excision, 23140-23146
  Bursa
    Drainage, 23031
  Capsular Contracture Release, 23020
  Cast
    Figure Eight, 29049
    Removal, 29710
    Spica, 29055
    Velpeau, 29058
  Disarticulation, 23920-23921
  Dislocation
    with Greater Tuberosity Fracture
      Closed Treatment, 23665
      Open Treatment, 23670
    with Surgical or Anatomical Neck Fracture
      Closed Treatment with Manipulation, 23675
      Open Treatment, 23680
    Closed Treatment
      with Manipulation, 23650, 23655
    Open Treatment, 23660
  Excision
    Acromion, 23130
    Torn Cartilage, 23101
  Exploration, 23107
  Hematoma
    Drainage, 23030
  Incision and Drainage, 23040-23044
    Superficial, 10060-10061
  Joint
    X-ray, 73050
  Manipulation
    Application of Fixation Apparatus, 23700
  Prophylactic Treatment, 23490-23491
  Radical Resection, 23077
  Removal
    Calcareous Deposits, 23000
    Cast, 29710
    Foreign Body, 23040-23044
      Complicated, 23332
      Deep, 23331
      Subcutaneous, 23330
    Foreign or Loose Body, 23107
  Repair
    Capsule, 23450-23466
    Ligament Release, 23415
    Muscle Transfer, 23395-23397
    Rotator Cuff, 23410-23420
    Tendon, 23410-23412, 23430-23440
    Tenomyotomy, 23405-23406
  Strapping, 29240
  Surgery
    Unlisted Services and Procedures, 23929
  Tumor, 23075-23078 [23071, 23073]
  Unlisted Services and Procedures, 23929
  X-ray, 73020-73030
    with Contrast, 73040
Shoulder Bone
  Excision
    Acromion, 23130
    Clavicle, 23120-23125
  Tumor
    Excision, 23140-23146
Shoulder Joint
  See Also Clavicle; Scapula
  Arthroplasty
    with Implant, 23470-23472
  Arthrotomy
    with Biopsy, 23100-23101
    with Synovectomy, 23105-23106
  Dislocation
    with Greater Tuberosity Fracture
      Closed Treatment, 23665
      Open Treatment, 23670

Shoulder Joint — continued
  Dislocation — continued
    with Surgical or Anatomical Neck Fracture
      Closed Treatment with Manipulation, 23675
      Open Treatment, 23680
    Open Treatment, 23660
  Excision
    Torn Cartilage, 23101
  Exploration, 23040-23044, 23107
  Foreign Body Removal, 23040-23044
  Incision and Drainage, 23040-23044
  X-ray, 73050
Shunt(s)
  Aqueous
    Revision, 66185
    to Extraocular Reservoir, 66180
  Arteriovenous Shunt
    Angiography, 75791
    Catheterization, 36147-36148
  Brain
    Creation, 62180-62223
    Removal, 62256-62258
    Replacement, 62160, 62194, 62225-62230, 62258
    Reprogramming, 62252
  Cerebrospinal Fluid, 62180-62258, 63740-63746
  Creation
    Arteriovenous
      with Bypass Graft, 35686
      with Graft, 36825-36830
      Direct, 36821
      ECMO, 36822
        Isolated with Chemotherapy Perfusion, 36823
    Thomas Shunt, 36835
    Transposition, 36818
  Fetal, 59076
  Great Vessel
    Aorta
      Pulmonary, 33924
    Aortic Pulmonary Artery
      Ascending, 33755
      Descending, 33762
    Central, 33764
    Subclavian–Pulmonary Artery, 33750
    Vena Cava to Pulmonary Artery, 33766-33768
  Intra-atrial, 33735-33737
  LeVeen
    Insertion, 49425
    Ligation, 49428
    Patency Test, 78291
    Removal, 49429
    Revision, 49426
  Nonvascular
    X-ray, 75809
  Peritoneal
  Venous
    Injection, 49427
    Ligation, 49428
    Removal, 49429
    X-ray, 75809
  Pulmonary Artery
    from Aorta, 33755-33762, 33924
    from Vena Cava, 33766-33767
    Subclavian, 33750
  Revision
    Arteriovenous, 36832
  Spinal Cord
    Creation, 63740-63741
    Irrigation, 63744
    Removal, 63746
    Replacement, 63744
  Superior Mesenteric–Cavel
    See Anastomosis, Caval to Mesenteric
  Transvenous Intrahepatic Portosystemic, 37182-37183
  Ureter to Colon, 50815
  Ventriculocisternal with Valve, 62180, 62200-62201
Shuntogram, 75809

Sialic Acid, 84275
Sialodochoplasty, 42500-42505
Sialogram, 70390
Sialography, 70390
Sialolithotomy, 42330-42340
Sickling
  Electrophoresis, 83020
Siderocytes, 85536
Siderophilin, 84466
Sigmoid
  See Colon–Sigmoid
Sigmoid Bladder
  Cystectomy, 51590
Sigmoidoscopy
  Ablation
    Polyp, 45339
    Tumor, 45339
  Biopsy, 45331
  Collection
    Specimen, 45331
  Exploration, 45330
  Hemorrhage Control, 45334
  Injection
    Submucosal, 45335
  Needle Biopsy, 45342
  Placement
    Stent, 45345
  Removal
    Foreign Body, 45332
    Polyp, 45333, 45338
    Tumor, 45333, 45338
  Repair
    Volvulus, 45337
  Ultrasound, 45341-45342
Signal–Averaged Electrocardiography, 93278
Silica, 84285
Silicon Dioxide, 84285
Silicone
  Contouring Injections, 11950-11954
Silver Procedure, 28290
Simon Nitinol Filter Insertion, 37620
Simple Mastectomies
  See Mastectomy
Single Photon Absorptiometry
  Bone Density, 78350
Single Photon Emission Computed Tomography
  See SPECT
Sinogram, 76080
Sinus
  Ethmoidectomy
    Excision, 31254
  Pilonidal
    Excision, 11770-11772
    Incision and Drainage, 10080-10081
Sinusectomy, Ethmoid
  Endoscopic, 31254-31255
  Extranasal, 31205
  Intranasal, 31200-31201
Sinuses
  Ethmoid
    with Nasal
      Sinus Endoscopy, 31254-31255
    Excision, 31200-31205
    Repair of Cerebrospinal Leak, 31290
  Frontal
    Destruction, 31080-31085
    Exploration, 31070-31075
      with Nasal
        Sinus Endoscopy, 31276
    Fracture
      Open Treatment, 21343-21344
    Incision, 31070-31087
    Injection, 20500
    Diagnostic, 20501
  Maxillary
    Antrostomy, 31256-31267
    Excision, 31225-31230
    Exploration, 31020-31032
      with Nasal/Sinus Endoscopy, 31233

Index

Sinuses — *continued*
  Maxillary — *continued*
    Incision, 31020-31032, 31256-31267
    Irrigation, 31000
    Skull Base Surgery, 61581
    Surgery, 61581
  Multiple
    Incision, 31090
    Paranasal Incision, 31090
  Repair of Cerebrospinal Leak, 31290
  Sphenoid
    Biopsy, 31050-31051
    Exploration, 31050-31051
      with Nasal
        Sinus Endoscopy, 31235
    Incision, 31050-31051
      with Nasal Sinus Endoscopy, 31287-31288
    Irrigation, 31002
    Repair of Cerebrospinal Leak, 31291
    Sinusotomy, 31050-31051
    Skull Base Surgery, 61580-61581
  Unlisted Services and Procedures, 31299
  X-ray, 70210-70220
Sinus of Valsalva
  Repair, 33702-33722
Sinusoidal Rotational Testing, 92546
Sinusoscopy
  Sinus
    Maxillary, 31233
    Sphenoid, 31235
Sinusotomy
  Combined, 31090
  Frontal Sinus
    Exploratory, 31070-31075
    Non–Obliterative, 31086-31087
    Obliterative, 31080-31085
  Maxillary, 31020-31032
  Multiple
    Paranasal, 31090
  Ridell, 31080
  Sphenoid Sinus, 31050-31051
Sinu, Sphenoid
  See Sinuses, Sphenoid
Sinus Venosus
  Repair, 33645
Sirolimus Drug Assay, 80195
SISI Test, 92564
Sistrunk Operation
  Cyst, Thyroid Gland, Excision, 60200
Six-Minute Walk Test, 94620
Size Reduction, Breast, 19318
Skeletal Fixation
  Humeral Epicondyle
    Percutaneous, 24566
Skeletal Traction
  Insertion/Removal, 20650
  Pin/Wire, 20650
Skene's Gland
  Abscess
    Incision and Drainage, 53060
  Destruction, 53270
  Excision, 53270
Skilled Nursing Facilities (SNFs)
  Annual Assessment, 99318
  Care Plan Oversight, 99379-99380
  Discharge Services, 1110F-1111F, 99315-99316
  Initial Care, 99304-99306
  Subsequent Care, 99307-99310
Skin
  Abrasion, 15786-15787
    Chemical Peel, 15788-15793
    Dermabrasion, 15780-15783
  Abscess
    Incision and Drainage, 10060-10061
    Puncture Aspiration, 10160
  Adjacent Tissue Transfer, 14000-14350
  Allogenic Substitute, 15340-15341
    Dermal, 15360-15366
  Allografts, 15300-15336

Skin — *continued*
  Biopsy, 11100-11101
  Chemical Exfoliation, 17360
  Cyst
    Puncture Aspiration, 10160
  Debridement, 11000-11006, 11010-11044
    with Open Fracture and/or Dislocation, 11010-11012
    Eczematous, 11000-11001
    Full Thickness, 11041
    Infected, 11000-11006
    Partial Thickness, 11040
    Subcutaneous Tissue, 11042-11044
    Infected, 11004-11006
  Decubitus Ulcer(s)
    Excision, 15920-15999
  Desquamation, 17360
  Destruction
    Benign Lesion
      Fifteen or More Lesions, 17111
      One to Fourteen Lesions, 17110
    Flat Warts, 17110-17111
    Lesion(s), 17106-17108
    Malignant Lesion, 17260-17286
      by Photodynamic Therapy, 96567
    Premalignant Lesions
      by Photodynamic Therapy, 96567
      Fifteen or More Lesions, 17004
      First Lesion, 17000
      Two to Fourteen Lesions, 17003
  Excision
    Debridement, 11000-11006, 11010-11044
    Excess Skin, 15830-15839, 15847
    Hemangioma, 11400-11446
    Lesion
      Benign, 11400-11446
      Malignant, 11600-11646
  Fasciocutaneous Flaps, 15732-15738
  Grafts
    Free, 15200-15261
    Harvesting for Tissue Culture, 15040
  Homografts, 15300-15336
  Incision and Drainage, 10040-10180
    See Also Incision, Skin
  Lesion
    See Lesion; Tumor
    Verrucous
      Destruction, 17110-17111
  Mole
    History, 1050F
    Patient Self-Examination Counseling, 5005F
  Muscle Flaps, 15732-15738
  Myocutaneous Flap, 15732-15738
  Nevi
    History, 1050F
    Patient Self-Examination Counseling, 5005F
  Nose
    Surgical Planing, 30120
  Paring, 11055-11057
  Photography
    Diagnostic, 96904
  Removal
    Skin Tag, 11200-11201
  Revision
    Blepharoplasty, 15820-15823
    Cervicoplasty, 15819
    Rhytidectomy, 15824-15829
  Shaving, 11300-11313
  Tags
    Removal, 11200, 11201
  Tests
    See Also Allergy Tests
    Candida, 86485

Skin — *continued*
  Tests — *continued*
    Coccidioidomycosis, 86490
    Histoplasmosis, 86510
    Other Antigen, 86356, 86486
    Tuberculosis, 86580
    Unlisted Antigen, 86486
  Unlisted Services and Procedures, 17999
  Wound Repair
    Abdomen
      Complex, 13100-13102
      Intermediate, 12031-12037
      Layered, 12031-12037
      Simple, 12001-12007
      Superficial, 12001-12007
    Arm, Arms
      Complex, 13120-13122
      Intermediate, 12031-12037
      Layered, 12031-12037
      Simple, 12001-12007
      Superficial, 12001-12007
    Axilla, Axillae
      Complex, 13131-13133
      Intermediate, 12031-12037
      Layered, 12031-12037
      Simple, 12001-12007
      Superficial, 12001-12007
    Back
      Complex, 13100-13102
      Intermediate, 12031-12037
      Layered, 12031-12037
      Simple, 12001-12007
      Superficial, 12001-12007
    Breast
      Complex, 13100-13102
      Intermediate, 12031-12037
      Layered, 12031-12037
      Simple, 12001-12007
      Superficial, 12001-12007
    Buttock
      Complex, 13100-13102
      Intermediate, 12031-12037
      Layered, 12031-12037
      Simple, 12001-12007
      Superficial, 12001-12007
    Cheek, Cheeks
      Complex, 13131-13133
      Intermediate, 12051-12057
      Layered, 12051-12057
      Simple, 12011-12018
      Superficial, 12011-12018
    Chest
      Complex, 13100-13102
      Intermediate, 12031-12037
      Layered, 12031-12037
      Simple, 12001-12007
      Superficial, 12001-12007
    Chin
      Complex, 13131-13133
      Intermediate, 12051-12057
      Layered, 12051-12057
      Simple, 12011-12018
      Superficial, 12011-12018
    Ear, Ears
      Complex, 13150-13153
      Intermediate, 12051-12057
      Layered, 12051-12057
      2.5 cm or less, 12051
      Simple, 12011-12018
      Superficial, 12011-12018
    External
      Genitalia
        Complex/Intermediate, 12041-12047
        Layered, 12041-12047
        Simple, 12001-12007
        Superficial, 12041-12047
    Extremity, Extremities
      Complex/Intermediate, 12031-12037
      Layered, 12031-12037
      Simple, 12001-12007
      Superficial, 12001-12007
    Eyelid, Eyelids
      Complex, 13150-13153

Skin — *continued*
  Wound Repair — *continued*
    Eyelid, Eyelids — *continued*
      Intermediate, 12051-12057
      Layered, 12051-12057
      Simple, 12011-12018
      Superficial, 12011-12018
    Face
      Complex/Intermediate, 12051-12057
      Layered, 12051-12057
      Simple, 12011-12018
      Superficial, 12011-12018
    Feet
      Complex, 13131-13133
      Intermediate, 12041-12047
      Layered, 12041-12047
      Simple, 12001-12007
      Superficial, 12001-12007
    Finger, Fingers
      Complex, 13131-13133
      Intermediate, 12041-12047
      Layered, 12041-12047
      Simple, 12001-12007
      Superficial, 12001-12007
    Foot
      Complex, 13131-13133
      Intermediate, 12041-12047
      Layered, 12041-12047
      Simple, 12001-12007
      Superficial, 12001-12007
    Forearm, Forearms
      Complex, 13120-13122
      Intermediate, 12031-12037
      Layered, 12031-12037
      Simple, 12001-12007
      Superficial, 12001-12007
    Forehead
      Complex, 13131-13133
      Intermediate, 12051-12057
      Layered, 12051-12057
      Simple, 12011-12018
      Superficial, 12011-12018
    Genitalia
      Complex, 13131-13133
      External
        Complex/Intermediate, 12041-12047
        Layered, 12041-12047
        Simple, 12001-12007
        Superficial, 12001-12007
    Hand, Hands
      Complex, 13131-13133
      Intermediate, 12041-12047
      Layered, 12041-12047
      Simple, 12001-12007
      Superficial, 12001-12007
    Leg, Legs
      Complex, 13120-13122
      Intermediate, 12031-12037
      Layered, 12031-12037
      Simple, 12001-12007
      Superficial, 12001-12007
    Lip, Lips
      Complex, 13150-13153
      Intermediate, 12051-12057
      Layered, 12051-12057
      Simple, 12011-12018
      Superficial, 12011-12018
    Lower
      Arm, Arms
        Complex, 13120-13122
        Intermediate, 12031-12037
        Layered, 12031-12037
        Simple, 12001-12007
        Superficial, 12001-12007
      Extremity, Extremities
        Complex, 13120-13122
        Intermediate, 12031-12037
        Layered, 12031-12037
        Simple, 12001-12007
        Superficial, 12001-12007
      Leg, Legs
        Complex, 13120-13122
        Intermediate, 12031-12037
        Layered, 12031-12037

Index

Skin — continued
  Wound Repair — continued
    Lower — continued
      Leg, Legs — continued
        Simple, 12001-12007
        Superficial, 12001-12007
    Mouth
      Complex, 13131-13133
    Mucous Membrane
      Complex/Intermediate, 12051-12057
      Layered, 12051-12057
      Simple, 12011-12018
      Superficial, 12011-12018
    Neck
      Complex, 13131-13133
      Intermediate, 12041-12047
      Layered, 12041-12047
      Simple, 12001-12007
      Superficial, 12001-12007
    Nose
      Complex, 13150-13153
      Intermediate, 12051-12057
      Layered, 12051-12057
      Simple, 12011-12018
      Superficial, 12011-12018
    Palm, Palms
      Complex, 13131-13133
      Intermediate, 12041-12047
      Layered, 12041-12047
      Simple, 12001-12007
      Superficial, 12001-12007
    Scalp
      Complex, 13120-13122
      Intermediate, 12031-12057
      Layered, 12031-12037
      Simple, 12001-12007
      Superficial, 12001-12007
    Toe, Toes
      Complex, 13131-13133
      Intermediate, 12041-12047
      Layered, 12041-12047
      Simple, 12001-12007
      Superficial, 12001-12007
    Trunk
      Complex, 13100-13102
      Intermediate, 12031-12037
      Layered, 12031-12037
      Simple, 12001-12007
      Superficial, 12001-12007
    Upper
      Arm, Arms
        Complex, 13120-13122
        Intermediate, 12031-12037
        Layered, 12031-12037
        Simple, 12001-12007
        Superficial, 12001-12007
      Extremity
        Complex, 13120-13122
        Intermediate, 12031-12037
        Layered, 12031-12037
        Simple, 12001-12007
        Superficial, 12001-12007
      Leg, Legs
        Complex, 13120-13122
        Intermediate, 12031-12037
        Layered, 12031-12037
        Simple, 12001-12007
        Superficial, 12001-12007

Skin Graft and Flap
  Acellular Dermal Replacement, 15170-15176
  Allogenic Skin Substitute, 15340-15341
    Dermal, 15360-15366
  Allograft, 15300-15336
  Autograft
    Dermal, 15130-15136
    Epidermal, 15110-15116, 15150-15157
    Split-Thickness, 15100-15101, 15120-15121
  Composite Graft, 15760-15770
  Cross Finger Flap, 15574
  Delay of Flap, 15600-15630
  Derma-Fat-Fascia Graft, 15770

Skin Graft and Flap — continued
  Fascial
    Free, 15758
  Fasciocutaneous Flap, 15732-15738
  Formation, 15570-15576
  Free
    Microvascular Anastomosis, 15756-15758
  Free Skin Graft
    Full Thickness, 15200-15261
  Island Pedicle Flap, 15740
  Muscle, 15732-15738, 15842
    Free, 15756
  Myocutaneous, 15732-15738, 15756
  Pedicle Flap
    Formation, 15570-15576
    Island, 15740
    Neurovascular, 15750
    Transfer, 15650
  Pinch Graft, 15050
  Platysmal, 15825
  Punch Graft, 15775-15776
    for Hair Transplant, 15775-15776
  Recipient Site Preparation, 15002-15005
  Skin
    Free, 15757
  Split Graft, 15100-15101, 15120-15121
  Superficial Musculoaponeurotic System, 15829
  Tissue-Cultured, 15150-15157, 15340-15366
  Tissue Transfer, 14000-14350
  Transfer, 15650
  Vascular Flow Check, 15860
  Xenograft, 15400-15421
    Acellular Implant, 15430-15431

Skull
  Burr Hole
    with Injection, 61120
    Biopsy Brain, 61140
    Drainage
      Abscess, 61150-61151
      Cyst, 61150-61151
      Hematoma, 61154-61156
    Exploration
      Infratentorial, 61253
      Supratentorial, 61250
    Insertion
      Catheter, 61210
      EEG Electrode, 61210
      Reservoir, 61210
    Intracranial Biopsy, 61140
  Decompression, 61322-61323, 61340-61345
  Orbit, 61330
  Drill Hole
    Catheter, 61107
    Drainage Hematoma, 61108
    Exploration, 61105
  Excision, 61501
  Exploration Drill Hole, 61105
  Fracture, 62000-62010
  Hematoma Drainage, 61108
  Incision
    Suture, 61550-61552
  Insertion
    Catheter, 61107
  Lesion
    Excision, 61500, 61600-61608, 61615-61616
  Orbit
    Biopsy, 61332
    Excision
      Lesion, 61333
    Exploration, 61332-61334
    Removal of Foreign Body, 61334
  Puncture
    Cervical, 61050
    Cisternal, 61050
    Drain Fluid, 61070
    Injection, 61070
    Subdural, 61000-61001
    Ventricular Fluid, 61020
  Reconstruction, 21172-21180

Skull — continued
  Reconstruction — continued
    Defect, 62140-62141, 62145
  Reduction
    Craniomegalic, 62115-62117
  Removal
    Plate, 62142
    Prosthesis, 62142
  Repair
    Cerebrospinal Fluid Leak, 62100
    Encephalocele, 62120
  Replacement
    Plate, 62143
    Prosthesis, 62143
  Tumor
    Excision, 61500
  X-ray, 70250, 70260

Skull Base Surgery
  Anterior Cranial Fossa
    Bicoronal Approach, 61586
    Craniofacial Approach, 61580-61583
    Extradural, 61600, 61601
    LeFort I Osteotomy Approach, 61586
    Orbitocranial Approach, 61584, 61585
    Transzygomatic Approach, 61586
  Carotid Aneurysm, 61613
  Carotid Artery, 61610
    Transection
      Ligation, 61609-61612
  Craniotomy, 62121
  Dura
    Repair of Cerebrospinal Fluid Leak, 61618, 61619
  Middle Cranial Fossa
    Extradural, 61605, 61607
    Infratemporal Approach, 61590, 61591
    Intradural, 61606, 61608
    Orbitocranial Zygomatic Approach, 61592
  Posterior Cranial Fossa
    Extradural, 61615
    Intradural, 61616
    Transcondylar Approach, 61596, 61597
    Transpetrosal Approach, 61598
    Transtemporal Approach, 61595

Sleep Study, 95803-95807
  Polysomnography, 95808-95811
  Unattended, 0203T-0204T

Sliding Inlay Graft, Tibia
  Tibia, Repair, 27720-27725

Sling Operation
  Incontinence, 53440
    Removal, 53442
  Stress Incontinence, 51992, 57287
  Vagina, 57287, 57288

Small Bowel
  See Also Intestines, Small
  Endoscopy, 44360-44386
    with Tumor Removal
      Ablation, 44369
      Bipolar Cautery, 44365
      Hot Biopsy Forceps, 44365
      Snare Technique, 44364
  Enterectomy, 44120-44128
    Laparoscopic, 44202-44203
  Enterotomy, 44020-44021
    for Lesion Removal, 44110-44111

SMAS Flap, 15829

Smear
  Cervical, 88141-88143, 88155, 88164-88167, 88174-88175
  Papanicolaou, 88141-88155, 88164-88167, 88174-88175

Smear and Stain
  Cervical/Vaginal, 88141-88167, 88174-88175
  Cornea, 65430
  Fluorescent, 87206
  Gram or Giesma, 87205
  Intracellular Parasites, 87207

Special Services

Smear and Stain — continued
  Ova
    Parasite, 87177, 87209
  Parasites, 87206-87209
  Wet Mount, 87210
Smith Fracture, 25600-25605, 25607, 25608-25609
Smith-Robinson Operation
  Arthrodesis, Vertebra, 22614
Smoking and Tobacco Cessation, 99406-99407
Smooth Muscle Antibody, 86255
SO4
  Chondroitin Sulfate, 82485
  Dehydroepiandrosterone Sulfate, 82627
  Urine, 84392
Soave Procedure, 45120
Sodium, 84295, 84302
  Urine, 84300
Sodium Glycinate, Theophylline, 80198
Sofield Procedure, 24410
Soft Tissue
  Abscess, 20000-20005
Solar Plexus
  Destruction, 64680
  Injection
    Anesthetic, 64530
    Neurolytic, 64680
Solitary Cyst, Bone
  Drainage, 20615
  Injection, 20615
Somatomammotropin, Chorionic, 83632
Somatomedin, 84305
Somatosensory Testing
  Lower Limbs, 95926
  Trunk or Head, 95927
  Upper Limbs, 95925
Somatostatin, 84307
Somatotropin, 83003
  Release Inhibiting Hormone, 84307
Somatropin, 80418, 80428-80430, 86277
Somnography, 95808-95811
Somophyllin T, 80198
Sonography
  See Echography
Sonohysterography, 76831
  Saline Infusion
    Injection Procedure, 58340
Sore, Bed
  Excision, 15920-15999
Spasm, Eyelid
  Chemodenervation, 64612
Special Services
  After Hours Medical Services, 99050
  Analysis
    Remote Physiologic Data, 99091
    Computer Data Analysis, 99090
  Device Handling, 99002
  Emergency Care in Office, 99058
    Out of Office, 99060
  Extended Hours, 99051-99053
  Group Education, 99078
    Self-Management, 98961-98962
  Hyperbaric Oxygen, 99183
  Hypothermia, 99116
  Individual Education
    Self-Management, 98960
  Medical Testimony, 99075
  Non-Office Medical Services, 99056
  On Call, Hospital Mandated, 99026, 99027
  Phlebotomy, 99199
  Postoperative Visit, 99024
  Prolonged Attendance, 99354-99360
  Psychiatric, 90889
  Pump Services, 99190-99192
  Reports and Forms
    Medical, 99080
    Psychiaric, 90889
  Specimen Handling, 99000, 99001
  Supply of Materials, 99070
    Educational, 99071

Special Services

Special Services — *continued*
  Unlisted Services and Procedures, 99199
  Unusual Travel, 99082
Specific Gravity
  with Urinalysis, 81000-81003
  Body Fluid, 84315
Specimen Collection
  Intestines, 89100, 89105
  Stomach, 89130-89141
  Venous Catheter, 36591-36592
Specimen Concentration, 87015
Specimen Handling, 99000, 99001
Specimen X-ray Examination, 76098
SPECT
  See Also Emission Computerized Tomography
  Abscess Localization, 78807
  Bone, 78320
  Brain, 78607
  Cerebrospinal Fluid, 78647
  Heart, 78451-78452
  Kidney, 78710
  Liver, 78205-78206
  Localization
    Inflammatory Process, 78807
    Tumor, 78803
Spectacle Services
  Fitting
    Low Vision Aid, 92354, 92355
    Spectacle Prosthesis, 92352, 92353
    Spectacles, 92340-92342
  Repair, 92370, 92371
Spectometry
  Mass
    Analyte
      Qualitative, 83788
      Quantitative, 83789
Spectrophotometry, 84311
  Atomic Absorption, 82190
Spectroscopy
  Atomic Absorption, 82190
  Coronary Vessel or Graft, 0205T
  Magnetic Resonance, 76390
Spectrum Analyses, 84311
Speech
  Audiometry Threshold, 0210T-0211T
  Evaluation, 92506
    Cine, 70371
    for Prosthesis, 92597, 92607, 92608
    Video, 70371
  Prosthesis
    Creation, 31611
    Evaluation for Speech, 92567, 92607, 92608
    Insertion, 31611
    Preparation of, 21084
  Therapy, 92507, 92508
Speech Evaluation, 92506
Sperm
  Antibodies, 89325
  Cryopreservation, 89259
  Evaluation, 89329-89331
  Identification
    from Aspiration, 89257
    from Testis Tissue, 89264
    Medicolegal, 88125
  Isolation, 89260-89261
  Storage (per year), 89343
  Thawing, 89353
Sperm Analysis
  Antibodies, 89325
  Cervical Mucus Penetration Test, 89330
  Cryopreservation, 89259
  Hamster Penetration Test, 89329
  Identification
    from Aspiration, 89257
    from Testis Tissue, 89264
  Isolation and Preparation, 89260-89261
Spermatic Cord
  Hydrocele
    Excision, 55500

Spermatic Cord — *continued*
  Laparoscopy, 55559
  Lesion
    Excision, 55520
  Repair
    Veins, 55530
      with Hernia Repair, 55540
      Abdominal Approach, 55535
  Varicocele
    Excision, 55530-55540
Spermatic Veins
  Excision, 55530-55540
  Ligation, 55500
Spermatocele
  Excision, 54840
Spermatocystectomy, 54840
Sperm Evaluation, Cervical Mucus Penetration Test, 89330
Sperm Washing, 58323
Sphenoidotomy
  with Nasal
    Sinus Endoscopy, 31287, 31288
Sphenoid Sinus
  See Sinuses, Sphenoid
Sphenopalatine Ganglion
  Injection
    Anesthetic, 64505
Sphenopalatine Ganglionectomy, 64999
Sphincter
  See Also Specific Sphincter
  Anal
    Dilation, 45905
    Incision, 46080
  Artificial Genitourinary, 53444-53449
  Pyloric
    Incision, 43520
    Reconstruction, 43800
Sphincter of Oddi
  Pressure Measurement
    Endoscopy, 43263
Sphincteroplasty
  Anal, 46750-46751, 46760-46761
    with Implant, 46762
  Bile Duct, 47460
  Bladder Neck, 51800, 51845
  Pancreatic, 48999
Sphincterotomy
  Anal, 46080
  Bile Duct, 47460
  Bladder, 52277
Spica Cast
  Hip, 29305, 29325
  Repair, 29720
  Shoulder, 29055
Spinal Accessory Nerve
  Anastomosis
    to Facial Nerve, 64866
  Incision, 63191
  Injection
    Anesthetic, 64412
  Section, 63191
Spinal Column
  See Spine
Spinal Cord
  Biopsy, 63275-63290
  Cyst
    Aspiration, 62268
    Incision and Drainage, 63172, 63173
  Decompression, 63001-63103
    with Cervical Laminoplasty, 63050-63051
  Drain Fluid, 62272
  Exploration, 63001-63044
  Graft
    Dura, 63710
  Implantation
    Electrode, 63650, 63655
    Pulse Generator, 63685
    Receiver, 63685
  Incision, 63200
    Dentate Ligament, 63180-63182
    Nerve Root, 63185-63190
    Tract, 63170, 63194-63199

Spinal Cord — *continued*
  Injection
    Anesthesia, 62310, 62311, 62319
    Blood, 62273
    CT Scan, 62284
    Neurolytic Agent, 62280-62282
    Other, 62310-62311
    X-ray, 62284
  Insertion
    Electrode, 63650, 63655
    Pulse Generator, 63685
    Receiver, 63685
  Lesion
    Destruction, 62280-62282
    Excision, 63265-63273, 63300-63308
  Needle Biopsy, 62269
  Neoplasm
    Excision, 63275-63290
  Puncture (Tap)
    Diagnostic, 62270
    Drainage of Fluid, 62272
    Lumbar, 62270
  Reconstruction
    Dorsal Spine Elements, 63295
  Release, 63200
  Removal
    Catheter, 62355
    Electrode, 63661-63662
    Pulse Generator, 63688
    Pump, 62365
    Receiver, 63688
    Reservoir, 62365
  Repair
    Cerebrospinal Fluid Leak, 63707-63709
    Meningocele, 63700-63702
    Myelomenigocele, 63704-63706
  Revision
    Electrode, 63663-63664
    Neurostimulator, 63688
  Section
    Dentate Ligament, 63180, 63182
    Nerve Root, 63185-63190
    Tract, 63194-63199
  Shunt
    Create, 63740, 63741
    Irrigation, 63744
    Removal, 63746
    Replacement, 63744
  Stereotaxis
    Aspiration, 63615
    Biopsy, 63615
    Creation Lesion, 63600
    Excision Lesion, 63615
    Stimulation, 63610
  Syrinx
    Aspiration, 62268
  Tumor
    Excision, 63275-63290
Spinal Cord Neoplasms
  Excision, 63275-63290
Spinal Fluid
  Immunoelectrophoresis, 86325
  Nuclear Imagine, 78630-78650
Spinal Fracture
  See Fracture, Vertebra
Spinal Instrumentation
  Anterior, 22845-22847
  Removal, 22855
  Internal Fixation, 22841
  Pelvic Fixation, 22848
  Posterior Nonsegmental
    Harrington Rod Technique, 22840
    Harrington Rod Technique Removal, 22850
  Posterior Segmental, 22842-22844
  Posterior Segmental Removal, 22852
  Prosthetic Device, 22851
  Reinsertion of Spinal Fixation Device, 22849
Spinal Manipulation, 98940-98942
Spinal Nerve
  Avulsion, 64772
  Transection, 64772

Spinal Tap
  Cervical Puncture, 61050-61055
  Cisternal Puncture, 61050-61055
  Drainage of Fluid, 62272
  Lumbar, 62270
  Subdural Tap, 61000-61001
  Ventricular Puncture, 61020-61026, 61105-61120
Spine
  See Also Intervertebral Disc; Spinal Cord; Vertebra; Vertebral Body; Vertebral Process
  Allograft
    Morselized, 20930
    Structural, 20931
  Arthroplasty
    Cervical, 0098T, 22861
    Lumbar, 0163T-0165T, 22857-22865
  Augmentation
    Lumbar Vertebra, 22524-22525
    Thoracic Vertebra, 22523, 22525
  Autograft
    Local, 20936
    Morselized, 20937
    Structural, 20938
  Biopsy, 20250, 20251
  CT Scan
    Cervical, 72125-72127
    Lumbar, 72131-72133
    Thoracic, 72128-72130
  Fixation, 22842
  Fusion
    Anterior, 22808-22812
    Anterior Approach, 22548-22585, 22812
    Exploration, 22830
    Lateral Extracavitary, 22532-22534
    Posterior Approach, 22590-22802
  Incision and Drainage
    Abscess, 22010-22015
  Insertion
    Instrumentation, 22840-22848, 22851
  Kyphectomy, 22818, 22819
  Magnetic Resonance Angiography, 72159
  Magnetic Resonance Imaging
    Cervical, 72141, 72142, 72156-72158
    Lumbar, 72148-72158
    Thoracic, 72146, 72147, 72156-72158
  Manipulation
    Anesthesia, 22505
  Myelography
    Cervical, 72240
    Lumbosacral, 72265
    Thoracic, 72255
    Total, 72270
  Reconstruction
    Dorsal Spine Elements, 63295
  Reinsertion Instrumentation, 22849
  Removal Instrumentation, 22850, 22852-22855
  Repair, Osteotomy
    Anterior, 22220-22226
    Posterior, 22210-22214
      Cervical Laminoplasty, 63050-63051
      Posterolateral, 22216
  Standing X-ray, 72069
  Surgery, NOS, 22899
  Ultrasound, 76800
  Unlisted Services and Procedures, 22899
  X-Ray, 72020, 72090
    with Contrast
      Cervical, 72240
      Lumbosacral, 72265
      Thoracic, 72255
      Total, 72270
    Absorptiometry, 77080, 77082
    Cervical, 72040-72052
    Lumbosacral, 72100-72120

Index

Spine — *continued*
  X–Ray — *continued*
    Standing, 72069
    Thoracic, 72070-72074
    Thoracolumbar, 72080
    Total, 72010
Spine Chemotherapy
  Administration, 96450
  See Also Chemotherapy
Spirometry, 94010-94070
  Patient Initiated, 94014-94016
Splanchnicectomy, 64802-64818
Spleen
  Excision, 38100-38102
    Laparoscopic, 38120
  Injection
    Radiologic, 38200
  Nuclear Medicine
    Imaging, 78185, 78215, 78216
  Repair, 38115
Splenectomy
  Laparoscopic, 38120
  Partial, 38101
  Partial with Repair, Ruptured Spleen, 38115
  Total, 38100
    En Bloc, 38102
Splenoplasty, 38115
Splenoportography, 75810
  Injection Procedures, 38200
Splenorrhaphy, 38115
Splenotomy, 38999
Splint
  See Also Casting; Strapping
  Arm
    Long, 29105
    Short, 29125-29126
  Finger, 29130-29131
  Foot, 29590
  Leg
    Long, 29505
    Short, 29515
  Oral Surgical, 21085
  Ureteral, 50400-50405
Split Grafts, 15100-15101, 15120-15121
Split Renal Function Test, 52005
Splitting
  Blood Products, 86985
SPR (Selective Posterior Rhizotomy), 63185, 63190
Sprengel's Deformity, 23400
Spring Water Cyst, 33050
  Excision, 33050
    via Thoracoscopy, 32661
Spur, Bone
  See Also Exostosis
  Calcaneal, 28119
  External Auditory Canal, 69140
Sputum Analysis, 89220
SQ, 96369-96372
SRIH, 84307
SRS (Stereotactic Radiosurgery), 61796-61800, 63620-63621
SRT (Speech Reception Threshold), 92555
Ssabanejew-Frank Operation
  Incision, Stomach, Creation of Stoma, 43830-43832
Stabilizing Factor, Fibrin, 85290-85291
Stable Factor, 85230
Stallard Procedure
  with Tube, 68750
  without Tube, 68745
Stamey Procedure, 51845
Standby Services, Physician, 99360
Standing X-ray, 72069, 73564, 73565
Stanford-Binet Test, 96101-96103
Stanftan, 96101-96103
Stapedectomy
  with Footplate Drill Out, 69661
  without Foreign Material, 69660
  Revision, 69662
Stapedotomy
  with Footplate Drill Out, 69661

Stapedotomy — *continued*
  without Foreign Material, 69660
  Revision, 69662
Stapes
  Excision
    with Footplate Drill Out, 69661
    without Foreign Material, 69660
  Mobilization
    See Mobilization, Stapes
  Release, 69650
  Revision, 69662
Staphyloma
  Sclera
    Repair
      with Graft, 66225
      without Graft, 66220
Starch Granules
  Feces, 89225
State Operation
  Proctectomy
    Partial, 45111, 45113-45116, 45123
    Total, 45110, 45112, 45120
    with Colon, 45121
Statin Therapy, 4002F
Statistics/Biometry, 76516-76519, 92136
Steindler Stripping, 28250
Steindler Type Advancement, 24330
Stellate Ganglion
  Injection
    Anesthetic, 64510
Stem, Brain
  Biopsy, 61575-61576
  Decompression, 61575-61576
  Evoked Potentials, 92585-92586
  Lesion Excision, 61575-61576
Stem Cell
  Cell Concentration, 38215
  Count, 86367
    Total Count, 86367
  Cryopreservation, 38207, 88240
  Donor Search, 38204
  Harvesting, 38205-38206
  Limbal
    Allograft, 65781
  Plasma Depletion, 38214
  Platelet Depletion, 38213
  Red Blood Cell Depletion, 38212
  T-cell Depletion, 38210
  Thawing, 38208, 38209, 88241
  Transplantation, 38240-38242
  Tumor Cell Depletion, 38211
  Washing, 38209
Stenger Test
  Pure Tone, 92565
  Speech, 92577
Stenosis
  Aortic
    Repair, 33415
      Supravalvular, 33417
  Bronchi, 31641
    Reconstruction, 31775
  Excision
    Trachea, 31780, 31781
  Laryngoplasty, 31582
  Reconstruction
    Auditory Canal, External, 69310
  Repair
    Trachea, 31780, 31781
    Tracheal, 31780-31781
  Urethral Stenosis, 52281
Stenson Duct, 42507-42510
Stent
  Indwelling
    Insertion
      Ureter, 50605
    Intravascular, 0075T-0076T, 37205-37208, 37215-37216
  Placement
    Bronchoscopy, 31631, 31636-31637
    Colonoscopy, 45387
    via Stoma, 44397

Stent — *continued*
  Placement — *continued*
    Endoscopy
      Gastrointestinal, Upper, 43256
    Enteroscopy, 44370
    Proctosigmoidoscopy, 45327
    Sigmoidoscopy, 45345
    Transcatheter
      Intravascular, 37205-37208, 37215, 37216
      Extracranial, 0075T-0076T
    Ureteroneocystomy, 50947, 50948
    Urethral, 52282, 53855
  Revision
    Bronchoscopy, 31638
    Spanner, 53855
  Tracheal
    via Bronchoscopy, 31631
    Revision, 31638
  Ureteral
    Insertion, 50605, 52332
    Removal, 50384, 50386
    and Replacement, 50382, 50385, 50387
  Urethra, 52282
    Insertion, 52282, 53855
    Prostatic, 53855
Stereotactic Frame
  Application
  Removal, 20660
Stereotactic Radiosurgery
  Cranial Lesion, 61797-61799
  Spinal Lesion, 63620-63621
Stereotaxis
  Aspiration
    Brain Lesion, 61750
      with CT Scan and/or MRI, 61751
    Spinal Cord, 63615
  Biopsy
    Aspiration
      Brain Lesion, 61750
    Brain, 61750
    Brain with CT Scan and/or MRI, 61751
    Breast, 77031
    Spinal Cord, 63615
  Catheter Placement
    Brain
      Infusion, 0169T
      Radiation Source, 61770
  Computer-Assisted
    Brain Surgery, 61795
    Orthopedic Surgery, 20985
  Creation Lesion
    Brain
      Deep, 61720-61735
      Percutaneous, 61790
    Gasserian Ganglion, 61790
    Spinal Cord, 63600
    Trigeminal Tract, 61791
  CT Scan
    Aspiration, 61751
    Biopsy, 61751
  Excision Lesion
    Brain, 61750
    Spinal Cord, 63615
  Focus Beam
    Radiosurgery, 61796-61800, 63620-63621
  Localization
    Brain, 61770
  Radiation Therapy, 77371-77373, 77432
  Stimulation
    Spinal Cord, 63610
  Target Volume Guidance, 77421
Sterile Coverings
  Burns, 16020-16030
  Change
    under Anesthesia, 15852
Sternal Fracture
  Closed Treatment, 21820
  Open Treatment, 21825

Stomach

Sternoclavicular Joint
  Arthrotomy, 23044
    with Biopsy, 23101
    with Synovectomy, 23106
  Dislocation
    Closed Treatment
      with Manipulation, 23525
      without Manipulation, 23520
    Open Treatment, 23530-23532
      with Fascial Graft, 23532
Sternocleidomastoid
  Division, 21720-21725
Sternotomy
  Closure, 21750
Sternum
  Debridement, 21627
  Excision, 21620, 21630-21632
  Fracture
    Closed Treatment, 21820
    Open Treatment, 21825
  Ostectomy, 21620
  Radical Resection, 21630-21632
  Reconstruction, 21740-21742, 21750
    with Thoracoscopy, 21743
  X–Ray, 71120-71130
Steroid–Binding Protein, Sex, 84270
Steroids
  Anabolic
    See Androstenedione
  Injection
    Morton's Neuroma, 64455
    Paravertebral Facet Joint, 64490-64495
    Plantar Common Digital Nerve, 64455
    Sympathetic Nerves, 64505-64530
    Transforaminal Epidural, 64479-64484
    Urethral Stricture, 52283
  Ketogenic
    Urine, 83582
STG, 15100-15121
STH, 83003
Stimson's Method Reduction, 23650, 23655
Stimulating Antibody, Thyroid, 84445
Stimulation
  Electric
    See Also Electrical Stimulation
    Brain Surface, 95961-95962
  Lymphocyte, 86353
  Spinal Cord
    Stereotaxis, 63610
  Transcutaneous Electric, 64550
Stimulator, Long–Acting Thyroid, 80438-80439
Stimulators, Cardiac, 33202-33213
  See Also Heart, Pacemaker
Stimulus Evoked Response, 51792
Stoffel Operation
  Rhizotomy, 63185, 63190
Stoma
  Closure
    Intestines, 44620
  Creation
    Bladder, 51980
    Kidney, 50551-50561
    Stomach
      Neonatal, 43831
      Permanent, 43832
      Temporary, 43830, 43831
    Ureter, 50860
  Revision
    Colostomy, 44345
    Ileostomy
      Complicated, 44314
      Simple, 44312
  Ureter
    Endoscopy via, 50951-50961
Stomach
  Anastomosis
    with Duodenum, 43810, 43850-43855
    with Jejunum, 43820-43825, 43860-43865

Stomach — Index

Stomach — *continued*
- Biopsy, 43600-43605
- Creation
  - Stoma
    - Permanent, 43832
    - Temporary, 43830-43831
      - Laparoscopic, 43653
- Electrode
  - Implantation, 0155T, 0157T, 43647, 43881
  - Removal/Revision, 0156T, 0158T, 43882
- Electrogastrography, 91132-91133
- Excision
  - Partial, 43631-43635, 43845
  - Total, 43620-43622
- Exploration, 43500
- Gastric Bypass, 43644-43645, 43846-43847
- Revision, 43848
- Gastric Restrictive Procedures, 43644-43645, 43770-43774, 43842-43848, 43886-43888
- Gastropexy, 43659, 43999
- Implantation
  - Electrodes, 0155T, 0157T, 43647, 43881
- Incision, 43830-43832
  - Exploration, 43500
  - Pyloric Sphincter, 43520
- Removal
  - Foreign Body, 43500
- Intubation with Specimen Prep, 91055
- Laparoscopy, 0155T-0156T, 43647-43648
- Nuclear Medicine
  - Blood Loss Study, 78278
  - Emptying Study, 78264
  - Imaging, 78261
  - Protein Loss Study, 78282
  - Reflux Study, 78262
  - Vitamin B-12
    - Absorption, 78270-78272
- Reconstruction
  - for Obesity, 43644-43645, 43842-43847
  - Roux-en-Y, 43644, 43846
- Removal
  - Foreign Body, 43500
- Repair, 48547
  - Fistula, 43880
  - Fundoplasty, 43324, 43325
    - Laparoscopic, 43280
  - Laceration, 43501, 43502
  - Stoma, 43870
  - Ulcer, 43501
- Specimen Collection, 89130-89141
- Stimulation of Secretion, 91052
- Suture
  - Fistula, 43880
  - for Obesity, 43842, 43843
  - Stoma, 43870
  - Ulcer, 43840
  - Wound, 43840
- Tumor
  - Excision, 43610, 43611
- Ulcer
  - Excision, 43610
- Unlisted Services and Procedures, 43659, 43999

Stomatoplasty
- Vestibule, 40840-40845

Stone
- Calculi
  - Bile Duct, 43264, 47420, 47425
    - Percutaneous, 47554, 47630
  - Bladder, 51050, 52310-52318, 52352
  - Gallbladder, 47480
  - Hepatic Duct, 47400
  - Kidney, 50060-50081, 50130, 50561, 50580, 52352
  - Pancreas, 48020
  - Pancreatic Duct, 43264
  - Salivary Gland, 42330-42340

Stone — *continued*
- Calculi — *continued*
  - Ureter, 50610-50630, 50961, 50980, 51060, 51065, 52320-52330, 52352
  - Urethra, 52310, 52315, 52352

Stone, Kidney
- Removal, 50060-50081, 50130, 50561, 50580, 52352

Stookey-Scarff Procedure
- Ventriculocisternostomy, 62200

Stool Blood, 82270, 82272-82274

Storage
- Embryo, 89342
- Oocyte, 89346
- Reproductive Tissue, 89344
- Sperm, 89343

Strabismus
- Chemodenervation, 67345
- Repair
  - Adjustable Sutures, 67335
  - Extraocular Muscles, 67340
  - One Horizontal Muscle, 67311
  - One Vertical Muscle, 67314
  - Posterior Fixation Suture Technique, 67334, 67335
  - Previous Surgery not Involving Extraocular Muscles, 67331
  - Release Extensive Scar Tissue, 67343
  - Superior Oblique Muscle, 67318
  - Transposition, 67320
  - Two Horizontal Muscles, 67312
  - Two or More Vertical Muscles, 67316

Strapping
- *See Also* Cast; Splint
- Ankle, 29540
- Chest, 29200
- Elbow, 29260
- Finger, 29280
- Foot, 29540, 29590
- Hand, 29280
- Hip, 29520
- Knee, 29530
- Shoulder, 29240
- Thorax, 29200
- Toes, 29550
- Unlisted Services and Procedures, 29799
- Unna Boot, 29580
- Wrist, 29260

Strassman Procedure, 58540
Strayer Procedure, 27687
Strep Quick Test, 86403
Streptococcus, Group A
- Antigen Detection
  - Enzyme Immunoassay, 87430
  - Nucleic Acid, 87650-87652
  - Direct Optical Observation, 87880

Streptococcus, Group B
- by Immunoassay
  - with Direct Optical Observation, 87802

Streptococcus pneumoniae Vaccine
- *See* Vaccines

Streptokinase, Antibody, 86590
Stress Tests
- Cardiovascular, 93015-93024
  - Echocardiography, 93350-93351
    - with Contrast, 93352
  - Multiple Gated Acquisition (MUGA), 78472, 78473
  - Myocardial Perfusion Imaging, 78451-78454
- Pulmonary, 94620, 94621
  - *See* Pulmonology, Diagnostic

Stricture
- Urethra
  - Dilation, 52281
  - Repair, 53400

Stricturoplasty
- Intestines, 44615

Stroboscopy
- Larynx, 31579

STS, 86592-86593

STSG, 15100-15121
Stuart-Prower Factor, 85260
Study
- Color Vision, 92283
- Common Carotid Intima-media Thickness (IMT), 0126T
- Implanted Wireless Pressure Sensor, 93982

Sturmdorf Procedure, 57520
Styloidectomy
- Radial, 25230

Styloid Process
- Fracture, 25645, 25650
- Radial
  - Excision, 25230

Stypven Time, 85612-85613
Subacromial Bursa
- Arthrocentesis, 20610

Subarachnoid Drug Administration, 0186T, 01996

Subclavian Arteries
- Aneurysm, 35001-35002, 35021-35022
- Angioplasty, 35458, 35475
- Bypass Graft, 35506, 35511-35516, 35526, 35606-35616, 35626, 35645
- Embolectomy, 34001-34101
- Thrombectomy, 34001-34101
- Thromboendarterectomy, 35301, 35311
- Transposition, 33889
- Unlisted Services/Procedures, 37799

Subcutaneous
- Chemotherapy, 96401-96402
- Infusion, 96369-96371
- Injecton, 96372

Subcutaneous Mastectomies, 19304
Subcutaneous Tissue
- Excision, 15830-15839, 15847
- Repair
  - Complex, 13100-13160
  - Intermediate, 12031-12057
  - Simple, 12020, 12021

Subdiaphragmatic Abscess, 49040-49041
Subdural Electrode
- Insertion, 61531-61533
- Removal, 61535

Subdural Hematoma, 61108, 61154
Subdural Puncture, 61105-61108
Subdural Tap, 61000, 61001
Sublingual Gland
- Abscess
  - Incision and Drainage, 42310, 42320
- Calculi (Stone)
  - Excision, 42330
- Cyst
  - Drainage, 42409
  - Excision, 42408
- Excision, 42450

Subluxation
- Elbow, 24640

Submandibular Gland
- Calculi (Stone)
  - Excision, 42330, 42335
- Excision, 42440

Submaxillary Gland
- Abscess
  - Incision and Drainage, 42310-42320

Submental Fat Pad
- Excision
  - Excess Skin, 15838

Submucous Resection of Nasal Septum, 30520
Subperiosteal Implant
- Reconstruction
  - Mandible, 21245, 21246
  - Maxilla, 21245, 21246

Subphrenic Abscess, 49040-49041
Substance and/or Alcohol Abuse Screening and Intervention, 99408-99409

Substance S, Reichstein's, 80436, 82634
Subtrochanteric Fracture
- with Implant, 27244-27245
- Closed Treatment, 27238
- with Manipulation, 27240

Sucrose Hemolysis Test, 85555-85557
Suction Lipectomies, 15876-15879
Sudiferous Gland
- Excision
  - Axillary, 11450-11451
  - Inguinal, 11462-11463
  - Perianal, 11470-11471
  - Perineal, 11470-11471
  - Umbilical, 11470-11471

Sugars, 84375-84379
Sugar Water Test, 85555-85557
Sugiura Procedure
- Esophagus, Repair, Varices, 43401

Sulfate
- Chondroitin, 82485
- DHA, 82627
- Urine, 84392

Sulfation Factor, 84305
Sulphates
- Chondroitin, 82485
- DHA, 82627
- Urine, 84392

Sumatran Mite Fever, 86000
Sunrise View X-Ray, 73560-73564
Superficial Musculoaponeurotic Systems (SMAS) Flap
- Rhytidectomy, 15829

Supernumerary Digit
- Reconstruction, 26587
- Repair, 26587

Supply
- Chemotherapeutic Agent
  - *See* Chemotherapy
- Educational Materials, 99071
- Low Vision Aids
  - Fitting, 92354-92355
  - Repair, 92370
- Materials, 99070
- Prosthesis
  - Breast, 19396

Suppositories, Vaginal, 57160
- for Induced Abortion, 59855-59857

Suppression, 80400-80408
Suppression/Testing, 80400-80440
Suppressor T Lymphocyte Marker, 86360

Suppurative Hidradenitides
- Incision and Drainage, 10060-10061

Suprahyoid
- Lymphadenectomy, 38700

Supraorbital Nerve
- Avulsion, 64732
- Incision, 64732
- Transection, 64732

Supraorbital Rim and Forehead
- Reconstruction, 21179-21180

Suprapubic Prostatectomies, 55821
Suprarenal
- Gland
  - Biopsy, 60540-60545, 60650
  - Excision, 60540-60545, 60650
  - Exploration, 60540-60545, 60650
  - Nuclear Medicine Imaging, 78075
- Vein
  - Venography, 75840-75842

Suprascapular Nerve
- Injection
  - Anesthetic, 64418

Suprasellar Cyst, 61545
Surface CD4 Receptor, 86360
Surface Radiotherapy, 77789
Surgeries
- Breast-Conserving, 19120-19126, 19301
- Laser
  - Anus, 46614, 46917
  - Bladder/Urethra, 52214-52240
  - Esophagus, 43227
  - Lacrimal Punctum, 68760
  - Lens, Posterior, 66821

Index

Surgeries — *continued*
  Laser — *continued*
    Lesion
      Mouth, 40820
      Nose, 30117-30118
      Penis, 54057
      Skin, 17000-17111, 17260-17286
    Myocardium, 33140-33141
    Prostate, 52647-52648
    Spine, 62287
  Mohs, 17311-17315
  Repeat
    Cardiac Valve Procedure, 33530
    Carotid Thromboendarterectomy, 35390
    Coronary Artery Bypass, 33530
    Distal Vessel Bypass, 35700
  Surgical
    Avulsion
      Nails, 11730-11732
      Nerve, 64732-64772
    Cartilage
      Excision, 21060
    Cataract Removal, 3073F, 66830, 66982-66984
    Collapse Therapy, Thoracoplasty, 32905-32906
    Diathermy
      Ciliary Body, 66700
      Lesions
        Benign, 17000-17111
        Malignant, 17260-17286
        Premalignant, 17000-17111
    Galvanism, 17380
    Incision
      See Incision
    Meniscectomy, 21060
    Microscopes, 69990
    Pathology
      See Pathology, Surgical
    Planing
      Nose
        Skin, 30120
    Pneumoperitoneum, 49400
    Removal, Eye
      with Implant, 65103-65105
      without Implant, 65101
    Revision
      Cardiac Valve Procedure, 33530
      Carotid Thromboendarterectomy, 35390
      Coronary Artery Bypass, 33530
      Distal Vessel Bypass, 35700
    Services
      Postoperative Visit, 99024
    Ventricular Restoration, 33548
Surgical Correction
  Uterus
    Inverted, 59899
Surgical Services
  Post–Operative Visit, 99024
Surveillance
  See Monitoring
Suspension
  Aorta, 33800
  Hyoid, 21685
  Kidney, 50400-50405
  Tongue Base, 41512
  Urethra, 51990, 57289
  Uterine, 58400-58410
  Vagina, 57280-57283, 57425
  Vesical Neck, 51845
Suture
  See Also Repair
  Abdomen, 49900
  Anus, 46999
  Aorta, 33320, 33321
  Bile Duct
    Wound, 47900
  Bladder
    Fistulization, 44660-44661, 45800-45805, 51880-51925
      Vesicouterine, 51920-51925
      Vesicovaginal, 51900

Suture — *continued*
  Bladder — *continued*
    Wound, 51860-51865
  Cervix, 57720
  Colon
    Diverticula, 44604-44605
    Fistula, 44650-44661
    Plication, 44680
    Stoma, 44620-44625
    Ulcer, 44604-44605
    Wound, 44604-44605
  Esophagus
    Wound, 43410, 43415
  Eyelid, 67880
    with Transposition of Tarsal Plate, 67882
    Closure of, 67875
    Wound
      Full Thickness, 67935
      Partial Thickness, 67930
  Facial Nerve
    Intratemporal
      Lateral to Geniculate Ganglion, 69740
      Medial to Geniculate Ganglion, 69745
  Fallopian Tube
    Simple, 58999
  Foot
    Tendon, 28200-28210
  Gastroesophageal, 43405
  Great Vessel, 33320-33322
  Hemorrhoids, [46945], [46946]
  Hepatic Duct, 47765, 47802
  Intestines
    Large, 44604-44605
    Small, 44602-44603
      Fistula, 44640-44661
      Plication, 44680
      Stoma, 44620-44625
  Iris
    with Ciliary Body, 66682
  Kidney
    Fistula, 50520-50526
    Horseshoe, 50540
    Wound, 50500
  Leg, Lower
    Tendon, 27658-27665
  Leg, Upper
    Muscles, 27385, 27386
  Liver
    Wound, 47350-47361
  Mesentery, 44850
  Nerve, 64831-64876
  Pancreas, 48545
  Pharynx
    Wound, 42900
  Rectum
    Fistula, 45800-45825
    Prolapse, 45540, 45541
    Removal
      Anesthesia, 15850, 15851
  Spleen, 38115
  Stomach
    Fistula, 43880
    Laceration, 43501, 43502
    Stoma, 43870
    Ulcer, 43501, 43840
    Wound, 43840
  Tendon
    Foot, 28200-28210
    Knee, 27380, 27381
  Testis
    Injury, 54670
    Suspension, 54620, 54640
  Thoracic Duct
    Abdominal Approach, 38382
    Cervical Approach, 38380
    Thoracic Approach, 38381
  Throat
    Wound, 42900
  Tongue
    to Lip, 41510
  Trachea
    Fistula, 31825
      with Plastic Repair, 31825

Suture — *continued*
  Trachea — *continued*
    Fistula — *continued*
      without Plastic Repair, 31820
    Stoma, 31825
      with Plastic Repair, 31825
      without Plastic Repair, 31820
    Wound
      Cervical, 31800
      Intrathoracic, 31805
  Ulcer, 44604-44605
  Ureter, 50900, 50940
    Deligation, 50940
    Fistula, 50920-50930
  Urethra
    Fistula, 45820-45825, 53520
    Stoma, 53520
    to Bladder, 51840-51841
    Wound, 53502-53515
  Uterus
    Fistula, 51920-51925
    Rupture, 58520, 59350
    Suspension, 58400-58410
  Vagina
    Cystocele, 57240, 57260
    Enterocele, 57265
    Fistula
      Rectovaginal, 57300-57307
      Transvesical and Vaginal Approach, 57330
      Urethrovaginal, 57310-57311
      Vesicovaginal, 51900, 57320-57330
    Rectocele, 57250-57260
    Suspension, 57280-57283
    Wound, 57200-57210
  Vas Deferens, 55400
  Vein
    Femoral, 37650
    Iliac, 37660
    Vena Cava, 37620
  Wound, 44604-44605
    Skin
      Complex, 13100-13160
      Intermediate, 12031-12057
      Simple, 12020-12021
SUZI (Sub-Zonal Insemination), 89280
SVR (Surgical Ventricular Restoration), 33548
Swallowing
  Cine, 74230
  Evaluation, 92610-92613, 92616-92617
  Therapy, 92526
  Video, 74230
Swan-Gans Catheter Insertion, 93503
Swanson Procedure
  Repair, Metatarsal, 28322
  Osteotomy, 28306-28309
Sweat Collection
  Iontophoresis, 89230
Sweat Glands
  Excision
    Axillary, 11450, 11451
    Inguinal, 11462, 11463
    Perianal, 11470, 11471
    Perineal, 11470, 11471
    Umbilical, 11470, 11471
Sweat Test
  Chloride, Blood, 82435
Swenson Procedure, 45120
Swine Flu Vaccine, 90663
  Administration, 90470
Syme Procedure, 27888
Sympathectomy
  with Rib Excision, 21616
  Artery
    Digital, 64820
    Radial, 64821
    Superficial Palmar Arch, 64823
    Ulnar, 64822
  Cervical, 64802
  Cervicothoracic, 64804
  Digital Artery with Magnification, 64820
  Lumbar, 64818

Sympathectomy — *continued*
  Presacral, 58410
  Thoracic, 32664
  Thoracolumbar, 64809
Sympathetic Nerve
  Excision, 64802-64818
  Injection
    Anesthetic, 64508, 64520-64530
Sympathins, 80424, 82382-82384
Symphysiotomy
  Horseshoe Kidney, 50540
Symphysis, Pubic, 27282
Syncytial Virus, Respiratory
  Antibody, 86756
  Antigen Detection
    Direct Fluorescence, 87280
    Direct Optical Observation, 87807
    Enzyme Immunoassay, 87420
Syndactylism, Toes, 28280
Syndactyly
  Repair, 26560-26562
Syndesmotomy
  Coracoacromial
    Arthroscopic, 29826
    Open, 23130, 23415
  Lateral Retinacular
    Endoscopic, 29873
    Open, 27425
  Transverse Carpal, 29848
Syndrome
  Adrenogenital, 56805, 57335
  Ataxia–Telangiectasia
    Chromosome Analysis, 88248
  Bloom
    Chromosome Analysis, 88245
  Carpal Tunnel
    Decompression, 64721
  Costen's
    See Temporomandibular Joint (TMJ)
  Erb–Goldflam
    Tensilon Test, 95857
  Ovarian Vein
    Ureterolysis, 50722
  Synechiae, Intrauterine
    Lysis, 58559
  Treacher Collins
    Midface Reconstruction, 21150-21151
  Urethral
    Cystourethroscopy, 52285
Syngesterone, 84144
Synostosis (Cranial)
  Bifrontal Craniotomy, 61557
  Extensive Craniectomy, 61558-61559
  Frontal Craniotomy, 61556
  Parietal Craniotomy, 61556
Synovectomy
  Arthrotomy with
    Glenohumeral Joint, 23105
    Sternoclavicular Joint, 23106
  Elbow, 24102
  Excision
    Carpometacarpal Joint, 26130
    Finger Joint, 26135-26140
    Hip Joint, 27054
    Interphalangeal Joint, 26140
    Knee Joint, 27334-27335
    Metacarpophalangeal Joint, 26135
    Palm, 26145
  Wrist, 25105, 25115-25119
    Radical, 25115-25116
Synovial
  Bursa
    See Also Bursa
    Joint Aspiration, 20600-20610
  Cyst
    See Also Ganglion
    Aspiration, 20612
  Membrane
    See Synovium
  Popliteal Space, 27345
Synovium
  Biopsy
    Carpometacarpal Joint, 26100

Synovium

Synovium — *continued*
- Biopsy — *continued*
  - Interphalangeal Joint, 26110
  - Knee Joint, 27330
  - Metacarpophalangeal Joint
    - with Synovial Biopsy, 26105
- Excision
  - Carpometacarpal Joint, 26130
  - Finger Joint, 26135-26140
  - Hip Joint, 27054
  - Interphalangeal Joint, 26140
  - Knee Joint, 27334-27335

Syphilis Nontreponemal Antibody, 86592-86593

Syphilis Test, 86592, 86593

Syrinx
- Spinal Cord
  - Aspiration, 62268

System
- Auditory, 69000-69979
- Cardiovascular, 33010-37799
- Digestive, 40490-49999 *[46220, 46320, 46945, 46946, 46947]*
- Endocrine, 60000-60699
- Eye/Ocular Adnexa, 65091-68899
- Genital
  - Female, 56405-58999
  - Male, 54000-55899
- Hemic/Lymphatic, 38100-38999
- Integumentary, 10040-19499
- Mediastinum/Diaphragm, 39000-39599
- Musculoskeletal, 20000-29999 *[21552, 21554, 23071, 23073, 24071, 24073, 25071, 25073, 26111, 26113, 27043, 27045, 27059, 27329, 27337, 27339, 27632, 27634, 28039, 28041]*
- Nervous, 61000-64999
- Respiratory, 30000-32999
- Urinary, 50010-53899 *[51797]*

T

T-3, 84480
T3 Free, 84481
T-4
- T Cells, 86360-86361
- Thyroxine, 84436-84439

T4 Molecule, 86360
T4 Total, 84436
T-7 Index
- Thyroxine, Total, 84436
- Triiodothyronine, 84480-84482

T-8, 86360
Taarnhoj Procedure
- Decompression, Gasserian Ganglion, Sensory Root, 61450

Tachycardia
- Heart
  - Recording, 93609

Tacrolimus
- Drug Assay, 80197

Tag
- Anus, 46230 *[46220]*
- Skin Removal, 11200-11201

TAH, 51925, 58150, 58152, 58200-58240, 58951, 59525
TAHBSO, 58150, 58152, 58200-58240, 58951
Tail Bone
- Excision, 27080
- Fracture, 27200, 27202

Takeuchi Procedure, 33505
Talectomy, 28130
Talotarsal Joint
- Dislocation, 28570, 28575, 28585
- Percutaneous Fixation, 28576

Talus
- Arthrodesis
  - Pantalar, 28705
  - Subtalar, 28725
  - Triple, 28715
- Arthroscopy
  - Surgical, 29891, 29892
- Craterization, 28120

Talus — *continued*
- Cyst
  - Excision, 28100-28103
- Diaphysectomy, 28120
- Excision, 28120, 28130
- Fracture
  - with Manipulation, 28435, 28436
  - without Manipulation, 28430
  - Open Treatment, 28445
  - Percutaneous Fixation, 28436
- Osteochondral Graft, 28446
- Repair
  - Osteochondritis Dissecans, 29892
  - Osteotomy, 28302
- Saucerization, 28120
- Tumor
  - Excision, 27647, 28100-28103

T&A, 42820-42821
Tap
- Cisternal, 61050-61055
- Lumbar Diagnostic, 62270

Tarsal
- Fracture
  - Percutaneous Fixation, 28456

Tarsal Bone
- *See* Ankle Bone

Tarsal Joint
- *See Also* Foot
- Arthrodesis, 28730, 28735, 28740
  - with Advancement, 28737
  - with Lengthening, 28737
- Craterization, 28122
- Cyst
  - Excision, 28104-28107
- Diaphysectomy, 28122
- Dislocation, 28540, 28545, 28555
  - Percutaneous Fixation, 28545, 28546
- Excision, 28116, 28122
- Fracture
  - with Manipulation, 28455, 28456
  - without Manipulation, 28450
  - Open Treatment, 28465
- Fusion, 28730, 28735, 28740
  - with Advancement, 28737
  - with Lengthening, 28737
- Repair, 28320
  - Osteotomy, 28304, 28305
- Saucerization, 28122
- Tumor
  - Excision, 28104-28107, 28171

Tarsal Strip Procedure, 67917, 67924
Tarsal Tunnel Release, 28035
Tarsal Wedge Procedure, 67916, 67923
Tarsometatarsal Joint
- Arthrodesis, 28730, 28735, 28740
- Arthrotomy, 28020, 28050
- Biopsy
  - Synovial, 28050, 28052
- Dislocation, 28600, 28605, 28615
  - Percutaneous Fixation, 28606
- Exploration, 28020
- Fusion, 28730, 28735, 28740
- Removal
  - Foreign Body, 28020
  - Loose Body, 28020
- Synovial
  - Biopsy, 28050
  - Excision, 28070

Tarsorrhaphy, 67875
- Median, 67880
- Severing, 67710
  - with Transposition of Tarsal Plate, 67882

Tattoo
- Cornea, 65600
- Skin, 11920-11922

TB, 87015, 87116, 87190
TBG, 84442
TBNA (Transbronchial Needle Aspiration), 31629, 31633
TBS, 88164, 88166
TB Test
- Antigen Response, 86480
- Cell Mediated Immunity Measurement, 86480

TB Test — *continued*
- Skin Test, 86580

TCD (Transcranial Doppler), 93886-93893
T Cell Leukemia Virus I Antibodies, Adult, 86687, 86689
T Cell Leukemia Virus I, Human, 86687, 86689
T Cell Leukemia Virus II Antibodies, Human, 86688
T Cell Leukemia Virus II, Human, 86688
T-Cell T8 Antigens, 86360
TCF (Transciliary Filtration), 0123T
TCT, 85670
Td, 90718
Tear Duct
- *See* Lacrimal Gland

Tear Gland
- *See* Lacrimal Gland

Technique
- Pericardial Window, 33015

TEE, 93312-93318
Teeth
- X-ray, 70300-70320

Telangiectasia
- Chromosome Analysis, 88248
- Injection, 36468

Telangiectasia, Cerebello-Oculocutaneous
- Chromosome Analysis, 88248

Telephone
- Non-Face-to-Face
  - Nonphysician, 98966-98968
  - Physician, 99441-99443
- Pacemaker Analysis, 93293
- Transmission of ECG, 93012

Teletherapy
- Dose Plan, 77305-77321

Temperature Gradient Studies, 93740
Temporal Arteries
- Biopsy, 37609
- Ligation, 37609

Temporal, Bone
- Electromagnetic Bone Conduction Hearing Device
  - Implantation/Replacement, 69710
  - Removal/Repair, 69711
- Excision, 69535
- Resection, 69535
- Tumor
  - Removal, 69970
- Unlisted Services and Procedures, 69979

Temporal, Petrous
- Excision
  - Apex, 69530

Temporomandibular Joint (TMJ)
- Arthrocentesis, 20605
- Arthrography, 70328-70332
  - Injection, 21116
- Arthroplasty, 21240-21243
- Arthroscopy
  - Diagnostic, 29800
  - Surgical, 29804
- Arthrotomy, 21010
- Cartilage
  - Excision, 21060
- Condylectomy, 21050
- Coronoidectomy, 21070
- Dislocation
  - Closed Treatment, 21480, 21485
  - Open Treatment, 21490
- Injection
  - Radiologic, 21116
- Magnetic Resonance Imaging, 70336
- Manipulation, 21073
- Meniscectomy, 21060
- Prostheses, 21243
- Reconstruction, 21240-21243
- X-ray with Contrast, 70328-70332

Tenago Procedure, 53431
Tendinosuture
- Foot, 28200-28210
- Knee, 27380-27381

Tendon
- Achilles
  - Incision, 27605-27606
  - Lengthening, 27612
  - Repair, 27650-27654
- Arm, Upper
  - Revision, 24320
- Finger
  - Excision, 26180
- Forearm
  - Repair, 25260-25274
- Graft
  - Harvesting, 20924
- Insertion
  - Biceps Tendon, 24342
- Lengthening
  - Ankle, 27685, 27686
  - Arm, Lower, 25280
  - Arm, Upper, 24305
  - Elbow, 24305
  - Finger, 26476, 26478
  - Forearm, 25280
  - Hand, 26476, 26478
  - Leg, Lower, 27685, 27686
  - Leg, Upper, 27393-27395
  - Toe, 28240
  - Wrist, 25280
- Palm
  - Excision, 26170
- Release
  - Arm, Lower, 25295
  - Arm, Upper, 24332
  - Wrist, 25295
- Shortening
  - Ankle, 27685, 27686
  - Finger, 26477, 26479
  - Hand, 26477, 26479
  - Leg, Lower, 27685, 27686
- Transfer
  - Arm, Lower, 25310, 25312, 25316
  - Arm, Upper, 24301
  - Elbow, 24301
  - Finger, 26497, 26498
  - Hand, 26480-26483
  - Leg, Lower, 27690-27692
  - Leg, Upper, 27400
  - Pelvis, 27098
  - Thumb, 26490, 26492, 26510
  - Wrist, 25310, 25312, 25316, 25320
- Transplant
  - Leg, Upper, 27396, 27397
- Wrist
  - Repair, 25260-25274

Tendon Origin
- Insertion
  - Injection, 20551

Tendon Pulley Reconstruction of Hand, 26500-26502
Tendon Sheath
- Arm
  - Lower
    - Repair, 25275
- Finger
  - Incision, 26055
  - Incision and Drainage, 26020
  - Lesion, 26160
- Foot
  - Excision, 28086, 28088
- Hand
  - Lesion, 26160
- Injection, 20550
- Palm
  - Incision and Drainage, 26020
- Removal
  - Foreign Body, 20520, 20525
- Wrist
  - Excision, 25115, 25116
  - Incision, 25000, 25001
  - Repair, 25275

Tendon Shortening
- Ankle, 27685, 27686
- Leg, Lower, 27685, 27686

Tenectomy, Tendon Sheath
- Foot, 28090

Index

Tenectomy, Tendon Sheath — *continued*
  Forearm/Wrist, 25110
  Hand/Finger, 26160
  Leg/Ankle, 27630
Tennis Elbow
  Repair, 24357-24359
Tenodesis
  Biceps Tendon
    at Elbow, 24340
    at Shoulder, 23430, 29828
  Finger, 26471, 26474
  Wrist, 25300, 25301
Tenolysis
  Ankle, 27680, 27681
  Arm, Lower, 25295
  Arm, Upper, 24332
  Finger
    Extensor, 26445, 26449
    Flexor, 26440, 26442
  Foot, 28220-28226
  Hand
    Extensor, 26445, 26449
    Flexor, 26440, 26442
  Leg, Lower, 27680, 27681
  Wrist, 25295
Tenomyotomy, 23405, 23406
Tenon's Capsule
  Injection, 67515
Tenoplasty
  Anesthesia, 01714
Tenorrhaphy
  Foot, 28200-28210, 28270
  Knee, 27380-27381
Tenosuspension
  at Wrist, 25300-25301
  Biceps, 29828
    at Elbow, 24340
    Long Tendon, 23430
  Interphalangeal Joint, 26471-26474
Tenosuture
  Foot, 28200-28210
  Knee, 27380-27381
Tenosynovectomy, 26145, 27626
Tenotomy
  Achilles Tendon, 27605, 27606
  Anesthesia, 01712
  Ankle, 27605, 27606
  Arm, Lower, 25290
  Arm, Upper, 24310
  Elbow, 24357
  Finger, 26060, 26455, 26460
  Foot, 28230, 28234
  Hand, 26450, 26460
  Hip
    Abductor, 27006
    Adductor, 27000-27003
    Iliopsoas Tendon, 27005
  Leg, Upper, 27306, 27307, 27390-27392
  Toe, 28010, 28011, 28232, 28234, 28240
  Wrist, 25290
TENS, 64550, 97014, 97032
Tensilon Test, 95857
Tentorium Cerebelli
  Section, 61440
TEP (Tracheoesophageal Puncture), 31611
Terman–Merrill Test, 96101-96103
Termination, Pregnancy
  See Abortion
TEST (Tubal Embyo Stage Transfer), 58974
Tester, Color Vision, 92283
Testes
  Cryopreservation, 89335
  Nuclear Medicine
    Imaging, 78761
  Undescended
    Exploration, 54550-54560
Testicular Vein
  Excision, 55530-55540
  Ligation, 55530-55540, 55550
Testimony, Medical, 99075

Testing
  Accousti Immittance, 92570
  Actigraphy, 95803
  Cognitive Performance, 96125
  Neurobehavioral, 96116
  Neuropsychological, 96118-96120
    Intraoperative, 95920
  Psychological, 96101-96103
  Range of Motion
    Extremities, 95851
    Eye, 92018-92019
    Hand, 95852
    Rectum
      Biofeedback, 90911
    Trunk, 97530
Testing, Histocompatibility, 86812-86817, 86821-86822
Testis
  Abscess
    Incision and Drainage, 54700
  Biopsy, 54500, 54505
  Cryopreservation, 89335
  Excision
    Laparoscopic, 54690
    Partial, 54522
    Radical, 54530, 54535
    Simple, 54520
  Hematoma
    Incision and Drainage, 54700
  Insertion
    Prosthesis, 54660
  Lesion
    Excision, 54512
    Needle Biopsy, 54500
  Nuclear Medicine
    Imaging, 78761
  Repair
    Injury, 54670
    Suspension, 54620, 54640
    Torsion, 54600
  Suture
    Injury, 54670
    Suspension, 54620, 54640
  Transplantation
    to Thigh, 54680
  Tumor
    Excision, 54530, 54535
  Undescended
    Exploration, 54550, 54560
  Unlisted Services and Procedures, 54699, 55899
Testosterone, 84402
  Response, 80414
    Stimulation, 80414, 80415
  Total, 84403
Testosterone Estradiol Binding Globulin, 84270
Test Tube Fertilization, 58321-58322
Tetanus, 86280
  Antibody, 86774
  Immunoglobulin, 90389
  Vaccine, 90703
Tetanus Immunization, 90698-90703, 90715, 90718, 90720-90723
Tetrachloride, Carbon, 84600
Tetralogy of Fallot, 33692-33697, 33924
THA, 27130-27134
Thal–Nissen Procedure, 43325
Thawing
  Cryopreserved
    Embryo, 89352
    Oocytes, 89356
    Reproductive Tissue, 89354
    Sperm, 89353
  Previously Frozen Cells, 38208, 38209
Thawing and Expansion
  of Frozen Cell, 88241
THBR, 84479
Theleplasty, 19350
Theophylline
  Assay, 80198
TheraCys, 90586
Therapeutic
  Abortion, 59850-59852

Therapeutic — *continued*
  Apheresis, 36511-36516
  Drug Assay
    See Drug Assay
  Mobilization
    See Mobilization
  Photopheresis
    See Photopheresis
  Radiology
    See Radiation Therapy
Therapeutic Activities
  Music
    Per 15 Minutes, 97530
Therapies
  Cold
    See Cryotherapy
  Exercise, 97110-97113
  Family, 99510
    Psychotherapy, 90846-90849
  Language, 92507-92508
  Milieu, 90882
  Occupational
    Evaluation, 97003-97004
  Photodynamic, 67221, 96567-96571
    See Photochemotherapy
  Photoradiation, 0168T, 96900
  Physical
    See Physical Medicine/ Therapy/Occupational Therapy
  Speech, 92507-92508
  Tocolytic, 59412
  Ultraviolet, 0168T, 96900
Therapy
  ACE Inhibitor Therapy, 4009F
  Beta Blocker Therapy, 4006F
  Desensitization, 95180
  Hemodialysis
    See Hemodialysis
  Hot Pack, 97010
  Pharmacologic, for Cessation of Tobacco Use, 4001F
  Radiation
    Blood Products, 86945
  Speech, 92507-92508
  Statin Therapy, Prescribed, 4002F
  Warfarin, 4012F
Thermocauterization
  Ectropion
    Repair, 67922
  Lesion
    Cornea, 65450
Thermocoagulation, 17000-17286
Thermotherapy
  Prostate, 53850-53852
    Microwave, 53850
    Radiofrequency, 53852
Thiamine, 84425
Thiersch Operation
  Pinch Graft, 15050
Thiersch Procedure, 46753
Thigh
  Excision
    Excess Skin, 15832
    Tumor, 27327-27328 [27337, 27339], 27365, [27329]
  Fasciotomy, 27025
Thin Layer Chromatographies, 82489
ThinPrep, 88142
Thiocyanate, 84430
Thompson Procedure, 27430
Thompson Test
  Smear and Stain, Routine, 87205
  Urinalysis, Glass Test, 81020
Thoracectomy, 32905-32906
Thoracentesis, 32421-32422
Thoracic
  Anterior Ramus
    Anesthetic Injection, 64420-64421
    Destruction, 64620
    Neurolytic Injection, 64620
  Arteries
    Catheterization, 36215-36218
  Cavity
    Bypass Graft Excision, 35905

Thoracic — *continued*
  Cavity — *continued*
    Endoscopy
      Exploration, 32601-32606
      Surgical, 32650-32665
  Duct
    Cannulation, 38794
    Ligation, 38380
      Abdominal Approach, 38382
      Thoracic Approach, 38381
    Suture, 38380
      Abdominal Approach, 38382
      Cervical Approach, 38380
      Thoracic Approach, 38381
  Empyema
    Incision and Drainage, 21501-21502
  Surgery
    Video–Assisted
      See Thoracoscopy
  Vertebra
    See Also Vertebra, Thoracic
    Corpectomy, 63085-63101, 63103
      Intraspinal Lesion, 63301-63302, 63305-63306, 63308
    Decompression, 63055, 63057, 63064-63066
    Discectomy, 63077-63078
    Excision for Lesion, 22101, 22112
    Injection Procedure
      Diagnostic/Therapeutic, 62310, 62318
      for Discography, 62291
      for Neurolysis, 62281
      Paravertebral, 64490-64495
    Laminectomy, 63003, 63016, 63046, 63048
  Wall
    See Chest Wall
Thoracocentesis, 32421-32422
Thoracoplasty, 32905
  with Closure Bronchopleural Fistula, 32906
Thoracoscopy
  Diagnostic, 32601, 32606
    with Biopsy, 32602, 32604, 32606
    without Biopsy, 32601, 32603, 32605
  Surgical, 32650-32665
    with Control Traumatic Hemorrhage, 32654
    with Creation Pericardial Window, 32659
    with Esophagomyotomy, 32665
    with Excision Mediastinal Cyst, Tumor and/or Mass, 32662
    with Excision Pericardial Cyst, Tumor and/or Mass, 32661
    with Excision–Plication of Bullae, 32655
    with Lobectomy, 32663
    with Parietal Pleurectomy, 32656
    with Partial Pulmonary Decortication, 32651
    with Pleurodesis, 32650
    with Removal Clot
      Foreign Body, 32658
    with Removal Intrapleural Foreign Body, 32653
    with Sternum Reconstruction, 21743
    with Thoracic Sympathectomy, 32664
    with Total Pericardiectomy, 32660
    with Total Pulmonary Decortication, 32652
    with Wedge Resection of Lung, 32657
Thoracostomy
  Empyema, 32035, 32036
  Tube, 32551
Thoracotomy
  with Biopsy, 32095, 32100

Thoracotomy | Index

Thoracotomy — *continued*
  with Excision–Plication of Bullae, 32141
  with Lung Repair, 32110
  with Open Intrapleural Pneumolysis, 32124
  Cardiac Massage, 32160
  for Postoperative Complications, 32120
  Hemorrhage, 32110
  Removal
    Bullae, 32141
    Cyst, 32140
    Defibrillator, 33243
    Electrodes, 33238
    Foreign Body
      Intrapleural, 32150
      Intrapulmonary, 32151
    Pacemaker, 33236, 33237
  Transmyocardial Laser Revascularization, 33140, 33141
Thorax
  See Also Chest; Chest Cavity; Mediastinum
  Angiography, 71275
  Biopsy, 21550
  CT Scan, 71250-71275
  Incision
    Empyema, 32035, 32036
    Pneumothorax, 32551
  Incision and Drainage
    Abscess, 21501, 21502
    Deep, 21510
    Hematoma, 21501, 21502
  Strapping, 29200
  Tumor, 21555-21558 *[21552, 21554]*
  Unlisted Services and Procedures, 21899
Three–Day Measles
  Antibody, 86762
  Vaccine, 90706-90710
Three Glass Test
  Urinalysis, Glass Test, 81020
Throat
  See Also Pharynx
  Abscess
    Incision and Drainage, 42700-42725
  Biopsy, 42800-42806
  Hemorrhage, 42960-42962
  Reconstruction, 42950
  Removal
    Foreign Body, 42809
  Repair
    Pharyngoesophageal, 42953
    Wound, 42900
  Suture
    Wound, 42900
  Unlisted Services and Procedures, 42999
Thrombectomy
  Aortoiliac Artery, 34151, 34201
  Arterial, Mechanical, 37184-37185
  Arteriovenous Fistula
    Graft, 36870
  Axillary Artery, 34101
  Axillary Vein, 34490
  Brachial Artery, 34101
  Bypass Graft, 35875, 35876
    Noncoronary, 37184-37186
  Carotid Artery, 34001
  Celiac Artery, 34151
  Dialysis Graft
    without Revision, 36831
  Femoral, 34201
  Femoropopliteal Vein, 34421, 34451
  Iliac Artery, 34151, 34201
  Iliac Vein, 34401-34451
  Innominate Artery, 34001-34101
  Mesenteric Artery, 34151
  Percutaneous
    Coronary Artery, 92973
    Noncoronary, 37184-37186
    Vein, 37187-37188
  Peroneal Artery, 34203
  Popliteal Artery, 34203

Thrombectomy — *continued*
  Radial Artery, 34111
  Renal Artery, 34151
  Subclavian Artery, 34001-34101
  Subclavian Vein, 34471, 34490
  Tibial Artery, 34203
  Ulnar Artery, 34111
  Vena Cava, 34401-34451
  Vena Caval, 50230
  Venous, Mechanical, 37187-37188
Thrombin Inhibitor I, 85300-85301
Thrombin Time, 85670, 85675
Thrombocyte (Platelet)
  Aggregation, 85576
  Automated Count, 85049
  Count, 85008
  Manual Count, 85032
Thrombocyte ab, 86022-86023
Thromboendarterectomy
  See Also Thrombectomy
  Aorta, Abdominal, 35331
  Aortoiliofemoral Artery, 35363
  Axillary Artery, 35321
  Brachial Artery, 35321
  Carotid Artery, 35301, 35390
  Celiac Artery, 35341
  Femoral Artery, 35302, 35371-35372
  Iliac Artery, 35351, 35361, 35363
  Iliofemoral Artery, 35355, 35363
  Innominate Artery, 35311
  Mesenteric Artery, 35341
  Peroneal Artery, 35305-35306
  Popliteal Artery, 35303
  Renal Artery, 35341
  Subclavian Artery, 35301, 35311
  Tibial Artery, 35305-35306
  Vertebral Artery, 35301
Thrombokinase, 85260
Thrombolysin, 85400
Thrombolysis
  Catheter Exchange
    Arterial, 37209, 75900
  Cerebral
    Intravenous Infusion, 37195
  Coronary Vessels, 92975, 92977
  Cranial Vessels, 37195
Thrombolysis Biopsy Intracranial
  Arterial Perfusion, 61624
Thrombolysis Intracranial, 65205
  See Also Ciliary Body; Cornea; Eye, Removal, Foreign Body; Iris; Lens; Retina; Sclera; Vitreous
Thrombomodulin, 85337
Thromboplastin
  Inhibition, 85705
  Inhibition Test, 85347
  Partial Time, 85730, 85732
Thromboplastin Antecedent, Plasma, 85270
Thromboplastinogen, 85210-85293
Thromboplastinogen B, 85250
Thromboxane Metabolite(s), 84431
Thumb
  Amputation, 26910-26952
  Arthrodesis
    Carpometacarpal Joint, 26841, 26842
  Dislocation
    with Fracture, 26645, 26650
      Open Treatment, 26665
    with Manipulation, 26641
  Fracture
    with Dislocation, 26645, 26650
    Open Treatment, 26665
  Fusion
    in Opposition, 26820
  Reconstruction
    from Finger, 26550
    Opponensplasty, 26490-26496
  Repair
    Muscle, 26508
    Muscle Transfer, 26494
    Tendon Transfer, 26510
  Replantation, 20824, 20827
  Sesamoidectomy, 26185

Thumb — *continued*
  Unlisted Services and Procedures, 26989
Thymectomy, 60520, 60521
  Sternal Split
    Transthoracic Approach, 60521, 60522
  Transcervical Approach, 60520
Thymotaxin, 82232
Thymus Gland, 60520
  Excision, 60520, 60521
  Exploration
    Thymus Field, 60699
  Incision, 60699
  Other Operations, 60699
  Repair, 60699
  Transplantation, 60699
Thyramine, 82145
Thyrocalcitonin, 80410, 82308
Thyroglobulin, 84432
  Antibody, 86800
Thyroglossal Duct
  Cyst
    Excision, 60280, 60281
Thyroidectomy
  Partial, 60210-60225
  Secondary, 60260
  Total, 60240, 60271
    Cervical Approach, 60271
      for Malignancy
        Limited Neck Dissection, 60252
        Radical Neck Dissection, 60254
      Removal All Thyroid Tissue, 60260
    Sternal Split
      Transthoracic Approach, 60270
Thyroid Gland
  Biopsy
    Open, 60699
  Cyst
    Aspiration, 60300
    Excision, 60200
    Incision and Drainage, 60000
    Injection, 60300
  Excision
    for Malignancy
      Limited Neck Dissection, 60252
      Radical Neck Dissection, 60254
    Partial, 60210-60225
    Secondary, 60260
    Total, 60240, 60271
      Cervical Approach, 60271
      Removal All Thyroid Tissue, 60260
      Sternal Split
        Transthoracic Approach, 60270
      Transcervical Approach, 60520
  Metastatic Cancer
    Nuclear Imaging, 78015-78018
  Needle Biopsy, 60100
  Nuclear Medicine
    Imaging, 78010
    Imaging for Metastases, 78015-78018
    Imaging with Flow, 78011
    Imaging with Uptake, 78006, 78007
    Metastases Uptake, 78020
    Uptake, 78000-78003
  Suture, 60699
  Tissue
    Reimplantation, 60699
  Tumor
    Excision, 60200
Thyroid Hormone Binding Ratio, 84479
Thyroid Hormone Uptake, 84479
Thyroid Isthmus
  Transection, 60200

Thyroid Simulator, Long Acting, 80438-80439
Thyroid Stimulating Hormone (TSH), 80418, 80438-80440, 84443
Thyroid Stimulating Hormone Receptor ab, 80438-80439
Thyroid Stimulating Immune Globulins (TSI), 84445
Thyroid Suppression Test
  Nuclear Medicine, Thyroid Uptake, 78000-78003
Thyrolingual Cyst
  Incision and Drainage, 60000
Thyrotomy, 31300
Thyrotropin Receptor ab, 80438-80439
Thyrotropin Releasing Hormone (TRH), 80438, 80439
Thyrotropin Stimulating Immunoglobulins, 84445
Thyroxine
  Free, 84439
  Neonatal, 84437
  Total, 84436
  True, 84436
Thyroxine Binding Globulin, 84442
TIBC, 83550
Tibia
  See Also Ankle
  Arthroscopy Surgical, 29891, 29892
  Craterization, 27360, 27640
  Cyst
    Excision, 27635-27638
  Diaphysectomy, 27360, 27640
  Excision, 27360, 27640
    Epiphyseal Bar, 20150
  Fracture
    with Manipulation, 27825
    without Manipulation, 27824
      Incision, 27607
    Arthroscopic Treatment, 29855, 29856
    Plafond, 29892
    Closed Treatment, 27824, 27825
      with Manipulation, 27825
      without Manipulation, 27824
    Distal, 27824-27828
    Intercondylar, 27538, 27540
    Malleolus, 27760-27766, 27808-27814
    Open Treatment, 27535, 27536, 27758, 27759, 27826-27828
    Plateau, 29855, 29856
      Closed Treatment, 27530, 27532
    Shaft, 27752-27759
  Osteoplasty
    Lengthening, 27715
  Prophylactic Treatment, 27745
  Reconstruction, 27418
    at Knee, 27440-27443, 27446
  Repair, 27720-27725
    Epiphysis, 27477-27485, 27730-27742
    Osteochondritis Dissecans
      Arthroscopy, 29892
    Osteotomy, 27455, 27457, 27705, 27709, 27712
    Pseudoarthrosis, 27727
  Saucerization, 27360, 27640
  Tumor
    Excision, 27635-27638, 27645
  X–ray, 73590
Tibial
  Arteries
    Bypass Graft, 35566-35571, 35666-35671
    Bypass In-Situ, 35585-35587
    Embolectomy, 34203
    Thrombectomy, 34203
    Thromboendarterectomy, 35305-35306
  Nerve
    Repair/Suture
      Posterior, 64840

Index

Tibiofibular Joint
  Arthrodesis, 27871
  Dislocation, 27830-27832
  Disruption
    Open Treatment, 27829
  Fusion, 27871
TIG, 90389
TIG (Tetanus Immune Globulin) Vaccine, 90389
Time
  Bleeding, 85002
  Prothrombin, 85610-85611
  Reptilase, 85670-85675
Tinnitus
  Assessment, 92625
TIPS (Transvenous Intrahepatic Portosystemic Shunt) Procedure, 37182-37183
  Anesthesia, 01931
Tissue
  Closure
    Abdomen
      Complex, 13100-13102
      Intermediate, 12031-12037
      Intermediate Layered, 12031-12037
      Simple, 12001-12007
      Superficial, 12001-12007
    Arm, Arms
      Complex, 13120-13122
      Intermediate, 12031-12037
      Layered, 12031-12037
      Simple, 12001-12007
      Superficial, 12001-12007
    Axilla, Axillae
      Complex, 13131-13133
      Intermediate, 12031-12037
      Layered, 12031-12037
      Simple, 12001-12007
      Superficial, 12001-12007
    Back
      Complex, 13100-13102
      Intermediate, 12031-12037
      Layered, 12031-12037
      Simple, 12001-12007
      Superficial, 12001-12007
    Breast
      Complex, 13100-13102
      Intermediate, 12031-12037
      Layered, 12031-12037
      Simple, 12001-12007
      Superficial, 12001-12007
    Buttock
      Complex, 13100-13102
      Intermediate, 12031-12037
      Layered, 12031-12037
      Simple, 12001-12007
      Superficial, 12001-12007
    Cheek, Cheeks
      Complex, 13131-13133
      Intermediate, 12051-12057
      Layered, 12051-12057
      Simple, 12011-12018
      Superficial, 12011-12018
    Chest
      Complex, 13100-13102
      Intermediate, 12031-12037
      Layered, 12031-12037
      Simple, 12001-12007
      Superficial, 12001-12007
    Chin
      Complex, 13131-13133
      Intermediate, 12051-12057
      Layered, 12051-12057
      Simple, 12011-12018
      Superficial, 12011-12018
    Ear, Ears
      Complex, 13150-13153
      Intermediate, 12051-12057
      Layered, 12051-12057
        2.5 cm or less, 12051
      Simple, 12011-12018
      Superficial, 12011-12018

Tissue — *continued*
  Closure — *continued*
    External
      Genitalia
        Complex/Intermediate, 12041-12047
        Layered, 12041-12047
        Simple, 12001-12007
        Superficial, 12041-12047
    Extremity, Extremities
      Complex/Intermediate, 12031-12037
      Layered, 12031-12037
      Simple, 12001-12007
      Superficial, 12001-12007
    Face
      Complex/Intermediate, 12051-12057
      Layered, 12051-12057
      Simple, 12011-12018
      Superficial, 12011-12018
    Feet
      Complex, 13131-13133
      Intermediate, 12041-12047
      Layered, 12041-12047
      Simple, 12001-12007
      Superficial, 12001-12007
    Finger, Fingers
      Complex, 13131-13133
      Intermediate, 12041-12047
      Layered, 12041-12047
      Simple, 12001-12007
      Superficial, 12001-12007
    Foot
      Complex, 13131-13133
      Intermediate, 12041-12047
      Layered, 12041-12047
      Simple, 12001-12007
      Superficial, 12001-12007
    Forearm, Forearms
      Complex, 13120-13122
      Intermediate, 12031-12037
      Layered, 12031-12037
      Simple, 12001-12007
      Superficial, 12001-12007
    Forehead
      Complex, 13131-13133
      Intermediate, 12051-12057
      Layered, 12051-12057
      Simple, 12011-12018
      Superficial, 12011-12018
    Genitalia
      Complex, 13131-13133
      External
        Complex/Intermediate, 12041-12047
        Layered, 12041-12047
        Simple, 12001-12007
        Superficial, 12001-12007
    Hand, Hands
      Complex, 13131-13133
      Intermediate, 12041-12047
      Layered, 12041-12047
      Simple, 12001-12007
      Superficial, 12001-12007
    Leg, Legs
      Complex, 13120-13122
      Intermediate, 12031-12037
      Layered, 12031-12037
      Simple, 12001-12007
      Superficial, 12001-12007
    Lip, Lips
      Complex, 13150-13153
      Intermediate, 12051-12057
      Layered, 12051-12057
      Simple, 12011-12018
      Superficial, 12011-12018
    Lower
      Arm, Arms
        Complex, 13120-13122
        Intermediate, 12031-12037
        Layered, 12031-12037
        Simple, 12001-12007
        Superficial, 12001-12007
      Extremity, Extremities
        Complex, 13120-13122

Tissue — *continued*
  Closure — *continued*
    Lower — *continued*
      Extremity, Extremities — *continued*
        Intermediate, 12031-12037
        Layered, 12031-12037
        Simple, 12001-12007
        Superficial, 12001-12007
      Leg, Legs
        Complex, 13120-13122
        Intermediate, 12031-12037
        Layered, 12031-12037
        Simple, 12001-12007
        Superficial, 12001-12007
    Mouth
      Complex, 13131-13133
    Mucous Membrane
      Complex/Intermediate, 12051-12057
      Layered, 12051-12057
      Simple, 12011-12018
      Superficial, 12011-12018
    Neck
      Complex, 13131-13133
      Intermediate, 12041-12047
      Layered, 12041-12047
      Simple, 12001-12007
      Superficial, 12001-12007
    Nose
      Complex, 13150-13153
      Intermediate, 12051-12057
      Layered, 12051-12057
      Simple, 12011-12018
      Superficial, 12011-12018
    Palm, Palms
      Complex, 13131-13133
      Intermediate, 12041-12047
      Layered, 12041-12047
      Simple, 12001-12007
      Superficial, 12001-12007
    Scalp
      Complex, 13120-13122
      Intermediate, 12031-13133
      Layered, 12031-12037
      Simple, 12001-12007
      Superficial, 12001-12007
    Skin/Eyelid, Eyelids
      Complex, 13150-13153
      Intermediate, 12051-12057
      Layered, 12051-12057
      Simple, 12011-12018
      Superficial, 12011-12018
    Toe, Toes
      Complex, 13131-13133
      Intermediate, 12041-12047
      Layered, 12041-12047
      Simple, 12001-12007
      Superficial, 12001-12007
    Trunk
      Complex, 13100-13102
      Intermediate, 12031-12037
      Layered, 12031-12037
      Simple, 12001-12007
      Superficial, 12001-12007
    Upper
      Arm, Arms
        Complex, 13120-13122
        Intermediate, 12031-12037
        Layered, 12031-12037
        Simple, 12001-12007
        Superficial, 12001-12007
      Extremity
        Complex, 13120-13122
        Intermediate, 12031-12037
        Layered, 12031-12037
        Simple, 12001-12007
        Superficial, 12001-12007
      Leg, Legs
        Complex, 13120-13122
        Intermediate, 12031-12037
        Layered, 12031-12037
        Simple, 12001-12007
        Superficial, 12001-12007

Tissue — *continued*
  Culture
    Chromosome Analysis, 88230-88239
    Homogenization, 87176
    Non–neoplastic Disorder, 88230, 88237
    Skin Grafts, 15040-15157
    Solid tumor, 88239
    Toxin/Antitoxin, 87230
    Virus, 87252, 87253
  Enzyme Activity, 82657
  Examination for Ectoparasites, 87220
  Examination for Fungi, 87220
  Expander
    Breast Reconstruction with, 19357
    Insertion
      Skin, 11960
    Removal
      Skin, 11971
    Replacement
      Skin, 11970
  Grafts
    Harvesting, 20926
  Granulation
    Cauterization, 17250
  Homogenization, 87176
  Hybridization In Situ, 88365-88368
  Mucosal
    See Mucosa
  Preparation
    Drug Analysis, 80103
  Soft
    Abscess, 20000, 20005
  Subcutaneous Tissue
    Abdomen
      Complex, 13100-13102
      Intermediate, 12031-12037
      Layered, 12031-12037
      Simple, 12001-12007
      Superficial, 12001-12007
    Arm, Arms
      Complex, 13120-13122
      Intermediate, 12031-12037
      Layered, 12031-12037
      Simple, 12001-12007
      Superficial, 12001-12007
    Axilla, Axillae
      Complex, 13131-13133
      Intermediate, 12031-12037
      Layered, 12031-12037
      Simple, 12001-12007
      Superficial, 12001-12007
    Back
      Complex, 13100-13102
      Intermediate, 12031-12037
      Layered, 12031-12037
      Simple, 12001-12007
      Superficial, 12001-12007
    Breast
      Complex, 13100-13102
      Intermediate, 12031-12037
      Layered, 12031-12037
      Simple, 12001-12007
      Superficial, 12001-12007
    Buttock
      Complex, 13100-13102
      Intermediate, 12031-12037
      Layered, 12031-12037
      Simple, 12001-12007
      Superficial, 12001-12007
    Cheek, Cheeks
      Complex, 13131-13133
      Intermediate, 12051-12057
      Layered, 12051-12057
      Simple, 12011-12018
      Superficial, 12011-12018
    Chest
      Complex, 13100-13102
      Intermediate, 12031-12037
      Layered, 12031-12037
      Simple, 12001-12007
      Superficial, 12001-12007

Tissue

Tissue — *continued*
  Subcutaneous Tissue — *continued*
    Chin
      Complex, 13131-13133
      Intermediate, 12051-12057
      Layered, 12051-12057
      Simple, 12011-12018
      Superficial, 12011-12018
    Ear, Ears
      Complex, 13150-13153
      Intermediate, 12051-12057
      Layered, 12051-12057
      2.5 cm or less, 12051
      Simple, 12011-12018
      Superficial, 12011-12018
    External
      Genitalia
        Complex/Intermediate, 12041-12047
        Layered, 12041-12047
        Simple, 12001-12007
        Superficial, 12041-12047
    Extremity, Extremities
      Complex/Intermediate, 12031-12037
      Layered, 12031-12037
      Simple, 12001-12007
      Superficial, 12001-12007
    Eyelid, Eyelids
      Complex, 13150-13153
      Intermediate, 12051-12057
      Layered, 12051-12057
      Simple, 12011-12018
      Superficial, 12011-12018
    Face
      Complex/Intermediate, 12051-12057
      Layered, 12051-12057
      Simple, 12011-12018
      Superficial, 12011-12018
    Feet
      Complex, 13131-13133
      Intermediate, 12041-12047
      Layered, 12041-12047
      Simple, 12001-12007
      Superficial, 12001-12007
    Finger, Fingers
      Complex, 13131-13133
      Intermediate, 12041-12047
      Layered, 12041-12047
      Simple, 12001-12007
      Superficial, 12001-12007
    Foot
      Complex, 13131-13133
      Intermediate, 12041-12047
      Layered, 12041-12047
      Simple, 12001-12007
      Superficial, 12001-12007
    Forearm, Forearms
      Complex, 13120-13122
      Intermediate, 12031-12037
      Layered, 12031-12037
      Simple, 12001-12007
      Superficial, 12001-12007
    Forehead
      Complex, 13131-13133
      Intermediate, 12051-12057
      Layered, 12051-12057
      Simple, 12011-12018
      Superficial, 12011-12018
    Genitalia
      Complex, 13131-13133
      External
        Complex/Intermediate, 12041-12047
        Complex Layered, 12041-12047
        Simple, 12001-12007
        Superficial, 12001-12007
    Hand, Hands
      Complex, 13131-13133
      Intermediate, 12041-12047
      Layered, 12041-12047
      Simple, 12001-12007
      Superficial, 12001-12007

Tissue — *continued*
  Subcutaneous Tissue — *continued*
    Leg, Legs
      Complex, 13120-13122
      Intermediate, 12031-12037
      Layered, 12031-12037
      Simple, 12001-12007
      Superficial, 12001-12007
    Lip, Lips
      Complex, 13150-13153
      Intermediate, 12051-12057
      Layered, 12051-12057
      Simple, 12011-12018
      Superficial, 12011-12018
    Lower
      Arm, Arms
        Complex, 13120-13122
        Intermediate, 12031-12037
        Layered, 12031-12037
        Simple, 12001-12007
        Superficial, 12001-12007
      Extremity, Extremities
        Complex, 13120-13122
        Intermediate, 12031-12037
        Layered, 12031-12037
        Simple, 12001-12007
        Superficial, 12001-12007
      Leg, Legs
        Complex, 13120-13122
        Intermediate, 12031-12037
        Layered, 12031-12037
        Simple, 12001-12007
        Superficial, 12001-12007
    Mouth
      Complex, 13131-13133
    Mucous Membrane
      Complex/Intermediate, 12051-12057
      Layered, 12051-12057
      Simple, 12011-12018
    Neck
      Complex, 13131-13133
      Intermediate, 12041-12047
      Layered, 12041-12047
      Simple, 12001-12007
      Superficial, 12001-12007
    Nose
      Complex, 13150-13153
      Intermediate, 12051-12057
      Layered, 12051-12057
      Simple, 12011-12018
      Superficial, 12011-12018
    Palm, Palms
      Complex, 13131-13133
      Intermediate, 12041-12047
      Layered, 12041-12047
      Simple, 12001-12007
      Superficial, 12001-12007
    Scalp
      Complex, 13120-13122
      Intermediate, 12031-12037
      Layered, 12031-12037
      Simple, 12001-12007
      Superficial, 12001-12007
    Toe, Toes
      Complex, 13131-13133
      Intermediate, 12041-12047
      Layered, 12041-12047
      Simple, 12001-12007
      Superficial, 12001-12007
    Trunk
      Complex, 13100-13102
      Intermediate, 12031-12037
      Layered, 12031-12037
      Simple, 12001-12007
      Superficial, 12001-12007
    Upper
      Arm, Arms
        Complex, 13120-13122
        Intermediate, 12031-12037
        Layered, 12031-12037
        Simple, 12001-12007
        Superficial, 12001-12007
      Extremity
        Complex, 13120-13122

Tissue — *continued*
  Subcutaneous Tissue — *continued*
    Upper — *continued*
      Extremity — *continued*
        Intermediate, 12031-12037
        Layered, 12031-12037
        Simple, 12001-12007
        Superficial, 12001-12007
      Leg, Legs
        Complex, 13120-13122
        Intermediate, 12031-12037
        Layered, 12031-12037
        Simple, 12001-12007
        Superficial, 12001-12007
    Transfer
      Adjacent
        Eyelids, 67961
        Skin, 14000-14350
        Facial Muscles, 15845
        Finger Flap, 14350
        Toe Flap, 14350
      Typing
        HLA Antibodies, 86812-86817
        Lymphocyte Culture, 86821, 86822
  Tissue Factor
    Inhibition, 85705
    Inhibition Test, 85347
    Partial Time, 85730-85732
  Tissue Glue
    See Tissue, Adhesive
  Tissue Transfer
    Adjacent
      Arms, 14020, 14021
      Axillae, 14040, 14041
      Cheeks, 14040, 14041
      Chin, 14040, 14041
      Ears, 14060, 14061
      Eyelids, 67961
      Face, 14040-14061
      Feet, 14040, 14041
      Finger, 14350
      Forehead, 14040, 14041
      Genitalia, 14040, 14041
      Hand, 14040, 14041
      Legs, 14020, 14021
      Limbs, 14020, 14021
      Lips, 14060, 14061
      Mouth, 14040, 14041
      Neck, 14040, 14041
      Nose, 14060, 14061
      Scalp, 14020, 14021
      Skin, 14000-14350
      Trunk, 14000, 14001
      Facial Muscles, 15845
      Finger Flap, 14350
      Toe Flap, 14350
  Tissue Typing
    HLA Antibodies, 86812-86817
    Lymphocyte Culture, 86821, 86822
  TLC Screen, 82489, 84375
  TMJ
    Arthrocentesis, 20605
    Arthrography, 70328-70332
      Injection, 21116
    Arthroplasty, 21240-21243
    Arthroscopy
      Diagnostic, 29800
  TMR (Transmyocardial Revascularization), 33140-33141
  TNA (Total Nail Avulsion), 11730, 11732
  TNS, 64550
  Tobacco Use
    Assessment, 1000F, 1034F-1036F
    Counseling, 4000F
    Pharmacologic Therapy, 4001F
  Tobramycin, 80200
    Assay, 80200
  Tocolysis, 59412
  Tocopherol, 84446
  Toe
    See Also Interphalangeal Joint, Toe; Metatarsophalangeal Joint; Phalanx

Index

Toe — *continued*
  Amputation, 28810-28825
  Arthrocentesis, 20600
  Bunionectomy, 28290-28299
  Capsulotomy, 28270, 28272
  Dislocation
    See Specific Joint
  Fasciotomy, 28008
  Flap
    Tissue Transfer, 14350
  Lesion
    Excision, 28092
  Magnetic Resonance Imaging (MRI), 73721
  Reconstruction
    Angle Deformity, 28313
    Extra Digit, 26587
    Extra Toes, 28344
    Hammer Toe, 28285, 28286
    Macrodactyly, 28340, 28341
    Syndactyly, 28345
    Webbed Toe, 28345
  Repair, 26590
    Bunion, 28290-28299
    Extra Digit, 26587
    Macrodactylia, 26590
    Muscle, 28240
    Tendon, 28232, 28234, 28240
    Webbed, 28280, 28345
    Webbed Toe, 28345
  Reposition, 20973, 26551-26554
  Reposition to Hand, 26551-26554, 26556
  Strapping, 29550
  Tenotomy, 28010, 28011, 28232, 28234
  Tumor, 28043-28047 *[28039, 28041]*, 28108, 28175
  Unlisted Services and Procedures, 28899
  X–Ray, 73660
  X-ray, 73660
Tolbutamide Tolerance Test, 82953
Tolerance Test(s)
  Glucagon, 82946
  Glucose, 82951, 82952
    with Tolbutamide, 82953
  Heparin–Protamine, 85530
  Insulin, 80434, 80435
  Maltose, 82951, 82952
  Tolbutamide, 82953
Tomodensitometries
  See CT Scan
Tomographic Scintigraphy, Computed, 78607, 78647
Tomographic SPECT
  Myocardial Imaging, 78469
Tomographies, Computed X–Ray
  See CT Scan
Tomography, Computed
  Abdomen, 74150-74175, 75635
  Head, 70450-70470, 70496
  Heart, 75572-75574
Tomography, Emission Computed
  Single Photon
    See SPECT
Tompkins Metroplasty
  Uterus Reconstruction, 58540
Tongue
  Ablation, 41530
  Abscess
    Incision and Drainage, 41000-41006, 41015
  Biopsy, 41100, 41105
  Cyst
    Incision and Drainage, 41000-41006, 41015, 60000
  Excision
    with Mouth Resection, 41150, 41153
    with Radical Neck, 41135, 41145, 41153, 41155
  Base
    Radiofrequency, 41530
    Complete, 41140-41155
    Frenum, 41115

Index

Tongue — *continued*
 Excision — *continued*
  Partial, 41120-41135
 Fixation, 41500
 Hematoma
  Incision and Drainage, 41000-41006, 41015
 Incision
  Frenum, 41010
 Lesion
  Excision, 41110-41114
 Reconstruction
  Frenum, 41520
 Reduction for Sleep Apnea, 41530
 Repair
  Laceration, 41250-41252
  Suture, 41510
 Suspension, 41512
 Unlisted Services and Procedures, 41599
Tonography, 92120
 with Provocation, 92130
Tonometry, Serial, 92100
Tonsillectomy, 42820-42826
 with Adenoidectomy
  Age 12 or Over, 42821
  Younger Than Age 12, 42820
 Primary
  Age 12 or Over, 42826
  Younger Than Age 12, 42825
 Secondary
  Age 12 or Over, 42826
  Younger Than Age 12, 42825
Tonsil, Pharyngeal
 Excision, 42830-42836
  with Tonsillectomy, 42820-42821
 Unlisted Services/Procedures, 42999
Tonsils
 Abscess
  Incision and Drainage, 42700
 Excision, 42825, 42826
 Excision with Adenoids, 42820, 42821
  Lingual, 42870
  Radical, 42842-42845
  Tag, 42860
 Lingual
  Destruction, 42870
 Removal
  Foreign Body, 42999
 Unlisted Services and Procedures, 42999
Topiramate
 Assay, 80201
Torek Procedure
 Orchiopexy, 54650
Torkildsen Procedure, 62180
TORP (Total Ossicular Replacement Prosthesis), 69633, 69637
Torsion Swing Test, 92546
Torula, 86641, 87327
Torus Mandibularis
 Tumor Excision, 21031
Total
 Abdominal Hysterectomy, 58150
  with Colpo-Urethrocystopexy, 58152
  with Omentectomy, 58956
  with Partial Vaginectomy, 58200
 Bilirubin Level, 82247-82248, 88720
 Catecholamines, 82382
 Cystectomy, 51570-51597
 Dacryoadenectomy, 68500
 Elbow Replacement, 24363
 Esophagectomy, 43107-43113, 43124
 Gastrectomy, 43620-43622
 Hemolytic Complement, 86162
 Hip Arthroplasty, 27130-27132
 Knee Arthroplasty, 27447
 Mastectomies
  See Mastectomy
 Ostectomy of Patella, 27424
 Splenectomy, 38100, 38102
Toupet Procedure, 43280

Touroff Operation/Ligation, Artery, Neck, 37615
Toxicology Screen, 80100-80103
Toxin Assay, 87230
 Tissue Culture, 87230
Toxin, Botulinum
 Chemodenervation
  Eccrine Glands, 64650-64653
  Extraocular Muscle, 67345
  Extremity Muscle, 64614
   for Blepharospasm, 64612
   for Hemifacial Spasm, 64612
  Internal Anal Sphincter, 46505
  Neck Muscle, 64613
  Trunk Muscle, 64614
Toxoplasma
 Antibody, 86777, 86778
T-Phyl, 80198
TR3SVR, 33548
Trabeculectomies, 65855
Trabeculectomy Ab Externo
 with Scarring Previous Surgery, 66172
 in Absence of Previous Surgery, 66170
Trabeculoplasty
 by Laser Surgery, 65855
Trabeculotomy Ab Externo
 Eye, 65850
Trachea
 Aspiration, 31720
  Catheter, 31720, 31725
 Dilation, 31630-31631, 31636-31638
 Endoscopy
  via Tracheostomy, 31615
 Excision
  Stenosis, 31780, 31781
 Fistula
  with Plastic Repair, 31825
  without Plastic Repair, 31820
  Repair, 31825
 Fracture
  Endoscopy, 31630
 Incision
  with Flaps, 31610
  Emergency, 31603, 31605
  Planned, 31600, 31601
 Introduction
  Needle Wire, 31730
 Puncture
  Aspiration and or Injection, 31612
 Reconstruction
  Carina, 31766
  Cervical, 31750
  Fistula, 31755
  Graft Repair, 31770
  Intrathoracic, 31760
 Repair
  Cervical, 31750
  Fistula, 31755
  Intrathoracic, 31760
  Stoma, 31613, 31614
 Revision/Stoma/Scars, 31830
 Scar
  Revision, 31830
 Stenosis
  Excision, 31780, 31781
  Repair, 31780, 31781
 Stoma
  Repair, 31825
   with Plastic Repair, 31825
   without Plastic Repair, 31820
  Revision
   Scars, 31830
 Tumor
  Excision
   Cervical, 31785
   Thoracic, 31786
 Unlisted Services and Procedures, 31899
 Bronchi, 31899
 Wound
  Suture
   Cervical, 31800
   Intrathoracic, 31805

Tracheal
 Stent
  Placement, 31631
 Tube, 31500
Trachelectomy, 57530
 Radical, 57531
Trachelorrhaphy, 57720
Tracheobronchoscopy
 via Tracheostomy, 31615
Tracheo-Esophageal Fistula
 Repair, 43305, 43312, 43314
 Speech Prosthesis, 31611
Tracheoplasty
 Cervical, 31750
 Intrathoracic, 31760
 Tracheopharyngeal Fistulization, 31755
Tracheoscopy, 31515-31529
Tracheostoma
 Revision, 31613, 31614
Tracheostomy
 with Flaps, 31610
 Emergency, 31603, 31605
 Planned, 31600, 31601
 Revision
  Scar, 31830
 Surgical Closure
  with Plastic Repair, 31825
  without Plastic Repair, 31820
 Tracheobronchoscopy through, 31615
Tracheotomy
 Tube Change, 31502
Tracking Tests (Ocular), 92545
Traction Therapy
 Manual, 97140
 Mechanical, 97012
 Skeletal, 20999
Tractotomy
 Medulla, 61470
 Mesencephalon, 61480
Tract, Urinary
 X-Ray with Contrast, 74400-74425
Training
 Activities of Daily Living, 97535, 99509
 Biofeedback, 90901, 90911
 Cognitive Skills, 97532
 Community
  Work Reintegration, 97537
 Home Management, 97535, 99509
 Management
  Propulsion, 97542
 Orthoptic
  Pleoptic, 92065
 Orthotics, 97760
 Prosthetics, 97761
 Seeing Impaired, 97799
  Braille, or Moon, 97799
  Lead Dog, Use of, 97799
 Self Care, 97535, 99509
 Sensory Integration, 97533
 Walking (Physical Therapy), 97116
 Wheelchair Management
  Propulsion, 97542
TRAM Flap
 Breast Reconstruction, 19367-19369
Transabdominal Endoscopy
 Intestine, Large, 45355
Transaminase
 Glutamic Oxaloacetic, 84450
 Glutamic Pyruvic, 84460
Transbronchial Needle Aspiration (TBNA), 31629, 31633
Transcatheter
 Biopsy, 37200
 Closure
  Percutaneous, Heart, 93580, 93581
 Embolization
  Percutaneous, 37204
  Cranial, 61624, 61626
 Occlusion
  Percutaneous, 37204
  Cranial, 61624, 61626

Transcatheter — *continued*
 Placement
  Intravascular Stent(s), 0075T-0076T, 37205-37208, 37215-37216
  Wireless Physiologic Sensor, 34806
 Therapy
  Embolization, 75894
  Infusion, 37201, 37202, 75896, 75898
 Perfusion
  Cranial, 61624, 61626
 Retrieval, 75961
Transcatheter Foreign Body
 Retrieval, 37203
Transcortin, 84449
Transcranial
 Doppler Study (TCP), 93886-93893
 Stimulation, Motor, 95928-95929
Transcutaneous Electric Nerve Stimulation, 64550
Transdermal Electrostimulation, 64550
Transection
 Artery
  Carotid, 61610, 61612
 Blood Vessel
  Kidney, 50100
 Brain
  Subpial, 61597
 Carotid
  with Skull Base Surgery, 61609
 Nerve, 64732-64772
  Vagus, 43640, 43641
 Pulmonary Artery, 33922
Transesophageal
 Echocardiography, 93312-93318
Transfer
 Adjacent Tissue, 14000-14350
 Blastocyst, 58974-58976
 Cryopreserved, 89352
 Finger Position, 26555
 Gamete Intrafalopian, 58976
 Jejunum
  with Microvascular Anastomosis Preparation/Embryo, 89255
 Free, 43496
 Toe Joint, 26556
 Toe to Hand, 26551-26554, 26556
 Tubal Embyo Stage, 58974
Transferase
 Aspartate Amino, 84450
 Glutamic Oxaloacetic, 84450
Transferrin, 84466
Transformation
 Lymphocyte, 86353
Transfusion
 Blood, 36430
  Exchange, 36450, 36455
  Fetal, 36460
  Push
   Infant, 36440
  Unlisted Services and Procedures, 86999
 White Blood Cells, 86950
Transfusion, Blood, Autologous, 86890-86891
Transillumination
 Skull
  Newborn, 95999
Translocation
 Aortic Root, 33782-33783
Transluminal
 Angioplasty
  Arterial, 75962-75968
 Atherectomies, 35490-35495, 92995-92996
 Coronary Balloon Dilatation, 92982-92984
Transmyocardial Laser Revascularization, 33140, 33141
Transosteal Bone Plate
 Reconstruction
  Mandible, 21244

Index

Transpeptidase, Gamma-Glutamyl, 82977
Transplant
　See Also Graft
　Bone
　　See Also Bone Graft
　　Allograft, Spine, 20930-20931
　　Autograft, Spine, 20936-20938
　Hair, 15775-15776
　　See Hair, Transplant
Transplantation
　See Also Graft
　Allogenic, 15300-15336
　Amniotic Membrane, 65780
　Autologous
　　See Autograft
　Backbench Preparation Prior to Transplantation
　　Intestine, 44715-44721
　　Kidney, 50323-50329
　　Liver, 47143-47147
　　Pancreas, 48551-48552
　Bone Marrow, 38240, 38241
　　Harvesting, 38230
　Cartilage
　　Knee, 27415, 29867
　　　Allograft, 27415, 29867
　　　Autograft, 27412, 29866
　Chondrocytes
　　Knee, 27412
　Conjunctiva, 65782
　Cornea
　　Autograft/Homograft
　　　Lamellar, 65710
　　　Penetrating, 65730-65755
　　for Aphakia, 65750
　Eye
　　Amniotic Membrane, 65780
　　Conjunctiva, 65782
　　Stem Cell, 65781
　Hair
　　Punch Graft, 15775, 15776
　　Strip, 15220, 15221
　Heart, 33945
　　Allograft Preparation, 33933, 33944
　Heart-Lung, 33935
　Heterologous
　　Skin, 15400-15431
　Intestines
　　Allograft Preparation, 44715-44721
　　Allotransplantation, 44135, 44136
　　Donor Enterectomy, 44132, 44133
　　Removal of Allograft, 44137
　Liver, 47135
　　Allograft Preparation, 47143-47147
　　Heterotopic, 47136
　Lung
　　Allograft Preparation, 32855-32856, 33933
　　Donor Pneumonectomy, 32850
　　Double with Cardiopulmonary Bypass, 32854
　　Double, without Cardiopulmonary Bypass, 32853
　　Single, with Cardiopulmonary Bypass, 32852
　　Single, without Cardiopulmonary Bypass, 32851
　Meniscus
　　Knee, 29868
　Muscle, 15731-15738, 15756
　Ovary, 58999
　Pancreas, 48550, 48554-48556
　　Allograft Preparation, 48551-48552
　Pancreatic Islet Cell
　　Laparoscopy, 0143T
　　Open, 0142T
　　Percutaneous, 0141T
　Parathyroid, 60512

Transplantation — *continued*
　Renal
　　Allograft Preparation, 50323-50329
　　Allotransplantation, 50360
　　　with Recipient Nephrectomy, 50365
　　Autotransplantation, 50380
　　Donor Nephrectomy, 50300, 50320, 50547
　　Recipient Nephrectomy, 50340
　　Removal Transplanted Renal Allograft, 50370
　Spleen, 38999
　Stem Cells, 38240, 38241, 38242
　　Cell Concentration, 38215
　　Cryopreservation, 38207, 88240
　　Donor Search, 38204
　　Harvesting, 38205-38206
　　Plasma Depletion, 38214
　　Platelet Depletion, 38213
　　Red Blood Cell Depletion, 38212
　　T-cell Depletion, 38210
　　Thawing, 38208, 38241
　　Tumor Cell Depletion, 38211
　　Washing, 38209
　Testis
　　to Thigh, 54680
　Tissue, Harvesting, 20926
Transpleural Thoracoscopy
　See Thoracoscopy
Transposition
　Arteries
　　Carotid, 33889, 35691, 35694, 35695
　　Subclavian, 33889, 35693-35695
　　Vertebral, 35691, 35693
　Cranial Nerve, 64716
　Eye Muscles, 67320
　Great Arteries
　　Repair, 33770-33781
　Nerve, 64718-64721
　Nipple, 19499
　Ovary, 58825
　Peripheral Nerve
　　Major, 64856
　Vein Valve, 34510
Trans-Scaphoperilunar
　Fracture
　　Dislocation, 25680, 25685
　　　Closed Treatment, 25680
　　　Open Treatment, 25685
Transthoracic Echocardiography, 93303-93350
Transthyretin, 84134
Transureteroureterostomy, 50770
Transurethral
　See Also Specific Procedure
　Fulguration
　　Postoperative Bleeding, 52214
　Prostate
　　Incision, 52450
　　Resection, 52601
　　Thermotherapy, 53850-53852
　　　Microwave, 53850
　　　Radiofrequency, 53852
　Radiofrequency Micro-Remodeling Female Bladder, 0193T
Trapezium
　Arthroplasty
　　with Implant, 25445
Travel, Unusual, 99082
Treacher-Collins Syndrome
　Midface Reconstruction, 21150, 21151
Treatment, Tocolytic, 59412
Trendelenburg Operation, 37785
Trephine Procedure
　Sinusotomy
　　Frontal, 31070
Treponema Pallidum
　Antibody, 86780
　Antigen Detection
　　Direct Fluorescent Antibody, 87285

TRF (Thyrotropin Releasing Factor), 80439
TRH, 80438, 80439
Triacylglycerol, 84478
Triacylglycerol Hydrolase, 83690
Triangular Cartilage
　Repair with Fracture
　　Radial shaft, 25526
Triangular Fibrocartilage
　Excision, 29846
Tributyrinase, 83690
Trichiasis
　Repair, 67825
　　Epilation, by Forceps, 67820
　　Epilation, by Other than Forceps, 67825
　　Incision of Lid Margin, 67830
　　　with Free Mucous Membrane Graft, 67835
Trichina, 86784, 96902
Trichinella
　Antibody, 86784
Trichogram, 96902
Trichomonas Vaginalis
　Antigen Detection
　　Nucleic Acid, 87660
Trichrome Stain, 88313
Tricuspid Valve
　Excision, 33460
　Repair, 33463-33465
　Replace, 33465
　Repositioning, 33468
Tridymite, 84285
Trigeminal Ganglia, 61450, 61790
Trigeminal Nerve
　Destruction, 64600-64610
　Injection
　　Anesthetic, 64400
　　Neurolytic, 64600, 64605
Trigeminal Tract
　Stereotactic
　　Create Lesion, 61791
Trigger Finger Repair, 26055
Trigger Point
　Injection
　　One or Two Muscle Groups, 20552
　　Two or More Muscle Groups, 20553
Triglyceridase, 83690
Triglyceride Lipase, 83690
Triglycerides, 84478
Trigonocephaly, 21175
TriHIBt, 90721
Triiodothyronine
　Free, 84481
　Resin Uptake, 84479
　Reverse, 84482
　Total, 84480
　True, 84480
Triolean Hydrolase, 83690
Trioxopurine, 84550, 84560
Tripcellim
　Duodenum, 84485
　Feces, 84488-84490
Tripedia, 90700
Trisegmentectomy, 47122
Trocar Biopsy
　Bone Marrow, 38221
Trochanter
　Pressure Ulcer, 15950-15958
Trochanteric Femur Fracture, 27246-27248
Trophoblastic Tumor GTT, 59100, 59870
Troponin
　Qualitative, 84512
　Quantitative, 84484
Truncal Vagotomies, 43640
Truncus Arteriosus
　Repair, 33786
Truncus Brachiocephalicus
　Angiography, 35458
　Atherectomy, 35484, 35494, 75992-75993
　Catheterization, 36215-36218

Trunk
　Lipectomy, Suction Assisted, 15877
　Skin Graft
　　Delay of Flap, 15600
　　Full Thickness, 15200
　　Muscle, Myocutaneous, or Fasciocutaneous Flaps, 15734
　　Split, 15100, 15101
　　Tissue Transfer, Adjacent, 14000
TRUSP (Transrectal Ultrasound of Prostate), 76873
Trypanosomiases, 86171, 86280
Trypanosomiasis, 86171, 86280
Trypsin
　Duodenum, 84485
　Feces, 84488-84490
Trypsin Inhibitor, Alpha 1-Antitrypsin, 82103-82104
Trypure
　Duodenum, 84485
　Feces, 84488-84490
TSA, 86316
Tsalicylate Intoxication, 80196
TSH, 80418, 80438-80440, 84443
TSI, 84445
Tsutsugamushi Disease, 86000
TT, 85670-85675
TT-3, 84480
TT-4, 84436
Tuba, Auditoria (Auditiva)
　Eustachian Tube Procedures, 69400-69421
Tubal Embryo Stage Transfer, 58976
Tubal Ligation, 58600
　with Cesarean Section, 58611
　Laparoscopic, 58670
　Postpartum, 58605
Tubal Occlusion
　with Cesarean Delivery
　　See Fallopian Tube, Occlusion; Occlusion
　Create Lesion
　　See Fallopian Tube, Occlusion; Occlusion, Fallopian Tube
　See Fallopian Tube
Tubal Pregnancy, 59121
　with Salpingectomy and/or Oophorectomy, 59120
Tube Change
　Tracheotomy, 31502
Tubectomy, 58700, 58720
Tubed Pedicle Flap
　Formation, 15570-15576
　Walking Tube, 15650
Tube, Fallopian
　See Fallopian Tube
Tube Placement
　Chest, 32551
　Endoscopic
　　Bile Duct, Pancreatic Duct, 43268
　　Nasobiliary, Nasopancreatic for Drainage, 43267
　　Gastrostomy Tube, 43246
　　Nasogastric Tube, 43752
　　Orogastric Tube, 43752
Tubercle Bacilli
　Culture, 87116
Tubercleplasty, Anterior Tibial, 27418
Tuberculin Test, 86580
Tuberculosis
　Antigen Response Test, 86480
　Culture, 87116
　Skin Test, 86580
Tuberculosis Vaccine (BCG), 90585, 90586
Tubes
　Endotracheal, 31500
　Gastrostomy, 43246, 49440
　See Also Gastrostomy Tube
Tudor "Rabbit Ear"
　Urethra, Repair
　　Diverticulum, 53240, 53400, 53405
　　Fistula, 45820, 45825, 53400, 53405, 53520

Index

Tudor "Rabbit Ear" — continued
Urethra, Repair — continued
- Sphincter, 57220
- Stricture, 53400, 53405
- Urethrocele, 57230
- Wound, 53502-53515

Tuffier Vaginal Hysterectomy
See Hysterectomy, Vaginal

TULIP, 52647-52648

Tumor
- Abdomen
  - Destruction
    - Excision, 49203-49205
- Abdominal Wall, 22900-22905
- Acetabulum
  - Excision, 27076
- Ankle, 27615-27619 [27632]
- Arm, Lower, 24152, 25075-25078 [25071, 25073]
- Arm, Upper, 23220, 24075-24079 [24071, 24073], 24110-24126, 24150
- Back, 21930-21936
- Bile Duct
  - Destruction, 43272
  - Extrahepatic, 47711
  - Intrahepatic, 47712
- Bladder, 52234-52240
  - Excision, 51530, 52355
- Brain, 61510
  - Excision, 61518, 61520, 61521, 61526, 61530, 61545, 62164
- Breast
  - Excision, 19120-19126
- Bronchi
  - Excision, 31640
- Calcaneus, 28100-28103
  - Excision, 27647
- Carpal, 25130-25136
- Chest Wall
  - Excision, 19260-19272
- Clavicle
  - Excision, 23140, 23200
  - with Allograft, 23146
  - with Autograft, 23145
- Coccyx, 49215
- Colon
  - Destruction, 44393, 45383
- Cranial Bone
  - Reconstruction, 21181, 21182
- Destruction
  - Abdomen, 49203-49205
  - Chemosurgery, 17311-17315
  - Urethra, 53220
- Ear, Middle
  - Extended, 69554
  - Transcanal, 69550
  - Transmastoid, 69552
- Elbow, 24075-24079 [24071, 24073], 24120-24126, 24152
- Esophagus
  - Ablation, 43228
- Excision
  - Femur, 27355-27358
- Face, 21011-21016
- Facial Bones, 21029, 21030, 21034
- Fallopian Tube
  - Resection, 58950, 58952-58956
- Femoral, 27355-27358
  - Excision, 27365
- Femur, 27065-27067
  - Excision, 27365
- Fibula, 27635-27638
  - Excision, 27646
- Finger
  - Excision, 26115-26117 [26111, 26113]
  - Foot, 28043, 28045, 28046
- Flank, 21930-21936
- Forearm
  - Radical Resection, 25077
- Gums
  - Excision, 41825-41827
- Hand, 26115-26117 [26111, 26113]

Tumor — continued
- Heart
  - Excision, 33120, 33130
- Hip, 27047-27049 [27043, 27045], 27065-27067
  - Excision, 27075, 27076
- Humerus, 23155-23156, 23220, 24115-24116, 24150
- Ileum, 27065-27067
- Immunoassay for Antigen, 86294, 86316
  - CA 125, 86304
  - CA 15-3, 86300
  - CA 19-9, 86301
- Innominate
  - Excision, 27077
- Intestines, Small
  - Destruction, 44369
- Ischial Tuberosity, 27078
- Kidney
  - Excision, 52355
- Knee
  - Excision, 27327-27360 [27329, 27337, 27339], 27365
- Lacrimal Gland
  - Excision
    - with Osteotomy, 68550
    - Frontal Approach, 68540
- Larynx, 31540, 31541
  - Excision, 31300
    - Endoscopic, 31540, 31541, 31578
  - Incision, 31300
- Leg, Lower, 27615-27619 [27632]
- Leg, Upper
  - Excision, 27327-27360 [27329, 27337, 27339]
- Localization
  - with Nuclear Medicine, 78800-78803
- Mandible, 21040-21045
- Maxillary Torus Palatinus, 21032
- Mediastinal
  - Excision, 39220
- Mediastinum, 32662
- Meningioma
  - Excision, 61519
- Metacarpal, 26200, 26205, 26250
- Metatarsal, 28104-28107
  - Excision, 28173
- Neck, 21555-21558 [21552, 21554]
- Olecranon Process, 24075-24077 [24071, 24073], 24120-24126
- Ovary
  - Resection, 58950, 58952-58954
- Pancreatic Duct
  - Destruction, 43272
- Parotid Gland
  - Excision, 42410-42426
- Pelvis, 27047-27049 [27043, 27045]
- Pericardial
  - Endoscopic, 32661
  - Excision, 33050
- Peritoneum
  - Resection, 58950-58956
- Phalanges
  - Finger, 26210, 26215, 26260-26262
  - Toe, 28108
    - Excision, 28175
- Pituitary Gland
  - Excision, 61546, 61548
- Pubis, 27065-27067
- Radiation Therapy, 77295
- Radius, 25120-25126, 25170
  - with Allograft, 24126
  - with Autograft, 24125
  - Excision, 24120
- Rectum, 0184T, 45160, 45171-45172, 45190
- Resection
  - with Cystourethroscopy, 52355
- Face, 21015
- Scalp, 21015

Tumor — continued
- Retroperitoneal
  - Destruction
    - Excision, 49203-49205
- Sacrum, 49215
- Scalp, 21011-21016
- Scapula, 23140
  - Excision, 23140, 23210
    - with Allograft, 23146
    - with Autograft, 23145
- Shoulder, 23075-23078 [23071, 23073]
- Skull
  - Excision, 61500
- Soft Tissue
  - Elbow
    - Excision, 24075
  - Finger
    - Excision, 26115
  - Forearm
    - Radical Resection, 25077
  - Hand
    - Excision, 26115
- Spinal Cord
  - Excision, 63275-63290
- Stomach
  - Excision, 43610, 43611
- Talus, 28100-28103
  - Excision, 27647
- Tarsal, 28104-28107
  - Excision, 28171
- Temporal Bone
  - Removal, 69970
- Testis
  - Excision, 54530, 54535
- Thorax, 21555-21558 [21552, 21554]
- Thyroid
  - Excision, 60200
- Tibia, 27365, 27635-27638
  - Excision, 27645
- Torus Mandibularis, 21031
- Trachea
  - Excision
    - Cervical, 31785
    - Thoracic, 31786
- Ulna, 25120-25126, 25170
  - with Allograft
    - Excision, 24126
  - with Autograft
    - Excision, 24125
  - Excision, 24120
- Ureter
  - Excision, 52355
- Urethra, 52234-52240, 53220
  - Excision, 52355
- Uterus
  - Excision, 58140, 58145
- Vagina
  - Excision, 57135
- Vertebra
  - Additional Segment
    - Excision, 22103, 22116
  - Cervical
    - Excision, 22100
  - Lumbar, 22102
  - Thoracic
    - Excision, 22101
- Wrist, 25075-25078 [25071, 25073]

TUMT (Transurethral Microwave Thermotherapy), 53850

TUNA, 53852

Tunica Vaginalis
- Hydrocele
  - Aspiration, 55000
  - Excision, 55040, 55041
  - Repair, 55060

Turbinate
- Excision, 30130, 30140
- Fracture
  - Therapeutic, 30930
- Injection, 30200
- Submucous Resection
  - Nose
    - Excision, 30140

Turbinate Mucosa
- Ablation, 30801, 30802

Ulcer

Turcica, Sella, 70240, 70480-70482

Turnbuckle Jacket, 29020, 29025
- Removal, 29715

TURP, 52601, 52630

TVCB (Transvaginal Chorionic Villus Biopsy), 59015

TVH (Total Vaginal Hysterectomy), 58262-58263, 58285, 58291-58292

TVS (Transvaginal Sonography), 76817, 76830

TWINRIX, 90636

Tylectomy, 19120-19126

Tylenol
- Urine, 82003

Tympanic Membrane
- Create Stoma, 69433, 69436
- Incision, 69420, 69421
- Reconstruction, 69620
- Repair, 69450, 69610

Tympanic Nerve
- Excision, 69676

Tympanolysis, 69450

Tympanometry, 92550, 92567

Tympanoplasty
- with Antrotomy or Mastoidectomy, 69635
  - with Ossicular Chain Reconstruction, 69636
    - and Synthetic Prosthesis, 69637
- with Mastoidectomy, 69641
  - with Intact or Reconstructed Wall without Ossicular Chain Reconstruction, 69643
    - and Ossicular Chain Reconstruction, 69644
    - and Ossicular Chain Reconstruction, 69644
- without Mastoidectomy, 69631
  - with Ossicular Chain Reconstruction, 69632
    - and Synthetic Prosthesis, 69633
- Myringoplasty, 69620
- Radical or Complete, 69645
  - with Ossicular Chain Reconstruction, 69646

Tympanostomy, 69433, 69436

Tympanotomy, 69420-69421

Typhin Vi, 90691

Typhoid Vaccine, 90690-90693
- AKD, 90693
- H-P, 90692
- Oral, 90690
- Polysaccharide, 90691

Typhus
- Endemic, 86000
- Mite-Bone, 86000
- Sao Paulo, 86000
- Tropical, 86000

Typing, Blood
See Blood Typing

Typing, HLA, 86812-86817

Typing, Tissue, 86812-86817, 86821-86822

Tyrosine, 84510

Tzanck Smear, 88160-88161

U

UAC, 36660

Uchida Procedure
- Tubal Ligation, 58600

UCX (Urine Culture), 87086-87088

UDP Galactose Pyrophysphorylase, 82775-82776

UFE, 37210

UFR, 51736, 51741

Ulcer
- Anal
  - Destruction, 46940-46942
  - Excision, 46200
- Decubitus
  - See Debridement; Pressure Ulcer (Decubitus); Skin Graft and Flap

ULCER

Ulcer — *continued*
  Pinch Graft, 15050
  Pressure, 15920-15999
  Stomach
    Excision, 43610
Ulcerative, Cystitis, 52260-52265
Ulna
  See Also Arm, Lower; Elbow; Humerus; Radius
  Arthrodesis
    Radioulnar Joint
      with Resection, 25830
  Arthroplasty
    with Implant, 25442
  Centralization of Wrist, 25335
  Craterization, 24147, 25150
  Cyst
    Excision, 24125, 24126, 25120-25126
  Diaphysectomy, 24147, 25150, 25151
  Excision, 24147
    Abscess, 24138
    Complete, 25240
    Epiphyseal Bar, 20150
    Partial, 25145-25151, 25240
  Fracture, 25605
    with Dislocation
      Closed Treatment, 24620
      Open Treatment, 24635
    with Manipulation, 25535
    with Radius, 25560, 25565
      Open Treatment, 25575
    without Manipulation, 25530
    Closed Treatment, 25530, 25535
    Olecranon, 24670, 24675
      Open Treatment, 24685
    Open Treatment, 25545
    Shaft, 25530-25545
      Open Treatment, 25574
    Styloid Process
      Closed Treatment, 25650
      Open Treatment, 25652
      Percutaneous Fixation, 25651
  Incision and Drainage, 25035
  Osteoplasty, 25390-25393
  Prophylactic Treatment, 25491, 25492
  Reconstruction
    Radioulnar, 25337
  Repair, 25400, 25415
    with Graft, 25405, 25420-25426
      Malunion or Nonunion, 25400, 25415
    Epiphyseal Arrest, 25450, 25455
    Osteotomy, 25360, 25370, 25375
      and Radius, 25365
  Saucerization, 24147, 24150, 25151
  Sequestrectomy, 24138, 25145
  Tumor
    Cyst, 24120
    Excision, 24125, 24126, 25120-25126, 25170
Ulnar Arteries
  Aneurysm Repair, 35045
  Embolectomy, 34111
  Sympathectomy, 64822
  Thrombectomy, 34111
Ulnar Nerve
  Decompression, 64718
  Neuroplasty, 64718, 64719
  Reconstruction, 64718, 64719
  Release, 64718, 64719
  Repair
    Suture
      Motor, 64836
  Transposition, 64718, 64719
Ultrasonic Cardiography
  See Echocardiography
Ultrasonic Procedure, 52325
Ultrasonography
  See Echography
Ultrasound
  3D Rendering, 76376-76377
  See Also Echocardiography; Echography

Ultrasound — *continued*
  Abdomen, 76700, 76705
  Ablation
    Uterine Leiomyomata, 0071T, 0072T
  Arm, 76880
  Artery
    Intracranial, 93886-93893
    Middle Cerebral, 76821
    Umbilical, 76820
  Bladder, 51798
  Bone Density Study, 76977
  Breast, 76645
  Bronchi
    Endoscopy, 31620
  Chest, 76604
  Colon
    Endoscopic, 45391-45392
  Colon–Sigmoid
    Endoscopic, 45341, 45342
  Computer Aided Surgical Navigation
    Intraoperative, 0054T-0055T
  Drainage
    Abscess, 75989
  Echoencephalography, 76506
  Esophagus
    Endoscopy, 43231, 43232
  Eye, 76511-76513
    Arteries, 93875
    Biometry, 76514-76519
    Foreign Body, 76529
    Pachymetry, 76514
  Fetus, 76818, 76819
  Follow-Up, 76970
  for Physical Therapy, 97035
  Gastrointestinal, 76975
  Gastrointestinal, Upper
    Endoscopic, 43242, 43259
  Guidance
    Amniocentesis, 59001, 76946
    Amnioinfusion, 59070
    Arteriovenous Fistulae, 76936
    Chorionic Villus Sampling, 76945
    Cryosurgery, 55873
    Drainage
      Fetal Fluid, 59074
    Endometrial Ablation, 58356
    Fetal Cordocentesis, 76941
    Fetal Transfusion, 76941
    Heart Biopsy, 76932
    Injection Facet Joint, 0213T-0218T
    Needle Biopsy, 43232, 43242, 45342, 76942
    Occlusion
      Umbilical Cord, 59072
    Ova Retrieval, 76948
    Pericardiocentesis, 76930
    Pseudoaneurysm, 76936
    Radiation Therapy, 76950
    Radioelement, 76965
    Radiofrequency Ablation, 76940, 77013, 77022
    Shunt Placement
      Fetal, 59076
    Thoracentesis, 76942
    Vascular Access, 76937
  Head, 76506, 76536
  Heart
    Fetal, 76825
  Hips
    Infant, 76885, 76886
  Hysterosonography, 76831
  Intraoperative, 76998
  Intravascular
    Intraoperative, 37250, 37251
  Kidney, 76770-76776
  Leg, 76880
  Neck, 76536
  Needle or Catheter Insertion, 20555
  Noncoronary
    Intravascular, 75945, 75946
  Pelvis, 76856, 76857
  Physical Therapy, 97035
  Pregnant Uterus, 76801-76817
  Prostate, 76872, 76873

Ultrasound — *continued*
  Rectal, 76872, 76873
  Retroperitoneal, 76770, 76775
  Scrotum, 76870
  Sonohysterography, 76831
  Spine, 76880
  Stimulation to Aid Bone Healing, 20979
  Umbilical Artery, 76820
  Unlisted Services and Procedures, 76999
  Uterus
    Tumor Ablation, 0071T-0072T
  Vagina, 76830
Ultraviolet A Therapy, 96912
Ultraviolet B Therapy, 96910
Ultraviolet Light Therapy
  Dermatology, 96900
    Ultraviolet A, 96912
    Ultraviolet B, 96910
  for Physical Medicine, 97028
Umbilectomy, 49250
Umbilical
  Artery Ultrasound, 76820
  Hernia
    Repair, 49580-49587
      Omphalocele, 49600-49611
  Vein Catheterization, 36510
Umbilical Cord
  Occlusion, 59072
Umbilicus
  Excision, 49250
  Repair
    Hernia, 49580-49587
    Omphalocele, 49600-49611
Undescended Testicle
  Exploration, 54550-54560
Unguis
  See Nails
Unilateral Simple Mastectomy, 19303
Unlisted Services or Procedures, 99499
  Abdomen, 22999, 49329, 49999
  Allergy
    Immunology, 95199
  Anal, 46999
  Anesthesia, 01999
  Arm, Upper, 24999
  Arthroscopy, 29999
  Autopsy, 88099
  Bile Duct, 47999
  Bladder, 53899
  Brachytherapy, 77799
  Breast, 19499
  Bronchi, 31899
  Cardiac, 33999
  Cardiovascular Studies, 93799
  Casting, 29799
  Cervix, 58999
  Chemistry Procedure, 84999
  Chemotherapy, 96549
  Chest, 32999
  Coagulation, 85999
  Colon, 44799
  Conjunctiva Surgery, 68399
  Craniofacial, 21299
  CT Scan, 76497
  Cytogenetic Study, 88299
  Cytopathology, 88199
  Dermatology, 96999
  Dialysis, 90999
  Diaphragm, 39599
  Ear
    External, 69399
    Inner, 69949
    Middle, 69799
  Endocrine System, 60699
  Epididymis, 55899
  Esophagus, 43289, 43499
  Evaluation and Management Services, 99499
  Eyelid, 67999
  Eye Muscle, 67399
  Eye Surgery
    Anterior Segment, 66999
    Posterior Segment, 67299

Unlisted Services or Procedures — *continued*
  Fluoroscopy, 76496
  Forearm, 25999
  Gallbladder Surgery, 47999
  Gastroenterology Test, 91299
  Gum Surgery, 41899
  Hand, 26989
  Hemic System, 38999
  Hepatic Duct, 47999
  Hip Joint, 27299
  Hysteroscopy, 58579
  Immunization, 90749
  Immunology, 86849
  Infusion, 96379
  Injection, 96379
  Injection of Medication, 96379
  Intestine, 44799
  Kidney, 49659
  Lacrimal System, 68899
  Laparoscopy, 38129, 38589, 43289, 43659, 44799, 47379, 47579, 49329, 49659, 50549, 50949, 54699, 55559, 58578, 58679, 59898, 60659
  Larynx, 31599
  Lip, 40799
  Liver, 47379, 47399
  Lungs, 32999
  Lymphatic System, 38999
  Magnetic Resonance, 76498
  Maxillofacial, 21299
  Maxillofacial Prosthetics, 21089
  Meckel's Diverticulum, 44899
  Mediastinum, 39499
  Mesentery Surgery, 44899
  Microbiology, 87999
  Mouth, 40899, 41599
  Musculoskeletal, 25999, 26989
  Musculoskeletal Surgery
    Abdominal Wall, 22999
    Neck, 21899
    Spine, 22899
    Thorax, 21899
  Musculoskeletal System, 20999
    Ankle, 27899
    Arm, Upper, 24999
    Elbow, 24999
    Head, 21499
    Knee, 27599
    Leg, Lower, 27899
    Leg, Upper, 27599
  Necropsy, 88099
  Nervous System Surgery, 64999
  Neurology
    Neuromuscular Testing, 95999
  Nose, 30999
  Nuclear Medicine, 78999
    Blood, 78199
    Bone, 78399
    Endocrine Procedure, 78099
    Genitourinary System, 78799
    Heart, 78499
    Hematopoietic System, 78199
    Lymphatic System, 78199
    Musculoskeletal System, 78399
    Nervous System, 78699
    Therapeutic, 79999
  Obstetric Care, 59898, 59899
  Omentum, 49329, 49999
  Ophthalmology, 92499
  Orbit, 67599
  Otorhinolaryngology, 92700
  Ovary, 58679, 58999
  Oviduct, 58679, 58999
  Palate, 42299
  Pancreas Surgery, 48999
  Pathology, 89240
  Pelvis, 27299
  Penis, 55899
  Peritoneum, 49329, 49999
  Pharynx, 42999
  Physical Therapy, 97039, 97139, 97799
  Pleura, 32999
  Pressure Ulcer, 15999

Index

Unlisted Services or Procedures — *continued*
  Preventive Medicine, 99429
  Prostate, 55899
  Psychiatric, 90899
  Pulmonology, 94799
  Radiation Physics, 77399
  Radiation Therapy, 77499
    Planning, 77299
  Radiology, Diagnostic, 76499
  Radionuclide Therapy, 79999
  Radiopharmaceutical Therapy, 79999
  Rectum, 45999
  Reproductive Medicine Lab, 89398
  Salivary Gland, 42699
  Scrotum, 55899
  Seminal Vesicle, 54699, 55899
  Shoulder, 23929
  Sinuses, 31299
  Skin, 17999
  Special Services and Reports, 99199
  Spine, 22899
  Stomach, 43659, 43999
  Strapping, 29799
  Surgical Pathology, 88399
  Temporal Bone, 69979
  Testis, 54699, 55899
  Throat, 42999
  Toe, 28899
  Tongue, 41599
  Tonsil
    Adenoid, 42999
  Toxoid, 90749
  Trachea, 31899
  Transfusion, 86999
  Ultrasound, 76999
  Ureter, 50949
  Urinary System, 53899
  Uterus, 58578, 58579, 58999
  Uvula, 42299
  Vaccine, 90749
  Vagina, 58999
  Vascular, 37799
  Vascular Endoscopy, 37501
  Vascular Injection, 36299
  Vascular Studies, 93799
  Vas Deferens, 55899
  Wrist, 25999
Unna Paste Boot, 29580
  Removal, 29700
UPP (Urethral Pressure Profile), 51727, 51729
Upper
  Digestive System Endoscopy
    See Endoscopy, Gastrointestinal, Upper
  Extremity
    See Arm, Upper; Elbow; Humerus
  Gastrointestinal Bleeding
    Endoscopic Control, 43255
  Gastrointestinal Endoscopy, Biopsy, 43239
  GI Tract
    See Gastrointestinal Tract, Upper
UPPP (Uvulopalatopharyngoplasty), 42145
Urachal Cyst
  Bladder
    Excision, 51500
Urea Breath Test, 78267, 78268, 83014
Urea Nitrogen, 84525
  Blood, 84520, 84525
  Clearance, 84545
  Quantitative, 84520
  Semiquantitative, 84525
  Urine, 84540
Urecholine Supersensitivity Test
  Cystometrogram, 51725, 51726
Ureter
  Anastomosis
    to Bladder, 50780-50785
    to Colon, 50810, 50815
    to Intestine, 50800, 50820, 50825
    to Kidney, 50740, 50750
    to Ureter, 50760, 50770

Ureter — *continued*
  Biopsy, 50955-50957, 50974-50976, 52007
  Catheterization, 52005
  Continent Diversion, 50825
  Creation
    Stoma, 50860
  Destruction
    Endoscopic, 50957, 50976
  Dilation, 52341, 52342, 52344, 52345
    Endoscopic, 50553, 50572, 50953, 50972
  Endoscopy
    Biopsy, 50955-50957, 50974-50976, 52007, 52354
    Catheterization, 50953, 50972, 52005
    Destruction, 50957, 50976, 52354
    Endoscopic, 50957, 50976
    Dilation, 52341, 52342, 52344, 52345
    Excision
      Tumor, 52355
    Exploration, 52351
    Injection of Implant Material, 52327
    Insertion
      Stent, 50947, 52332, 52334
    Lithotripsy, 52353
    Manipulation of Ureteral Calculus, 52330
    Removal
      Calculus, 50961, 50980, 52320, 52325, 52352
      Foreign Body, 50961, 50980
    Resection, 50970-50980, 52355
      via Incision, 50970-50980
      via Stoma, 50951-50961
  Exploration, 50600
  Incision and Drainage, 50600
  Injection
    Drugs, 50391
    Radiologic, 50684, 50690
  Insertion
    Catheter, 50393
    Stent, 50393, 50947, 52332, 52334
    Tube, 50688
  Instillation
    Drugs, 50391
  Lesion
    Destruction, 52354
  Lithotripsy, 52353
  Lysis
    Adhesions, 50715-50725
  Manometric Studies
    Pressure, 50686
  Meatotomy, 52290
  Nuclear Medicine
    Reflux Study, 78740
  Postcaval
    Ureterolysis, 50725
  Reconstruction, 50700
    with Intestines, 50840
  Reflux Study, 78740
  Reimplantation, 51565
  Removal
    Anastomosis, 50830
    Calculus, 50610-50630, 50961, 51060, 51065, 52320, 52325
    Foreign Body, 50961
    Stent, 50382-50387
  Repair, 50900
    Anastomosis, 50740-50825
    Continent Diversion, 50825
    Deligation, 50940
    Fistula, 50920, 50930
    Lysis of Adhesions, 50715-50725
    Ureterocele, 51535
      Ectopic, 52301
      Orthotopic, 52300
    Urinary Undiversion, 50830

Ureter — *continued*
  Replacement
    with Intestines, 50840
    Stent, 50382, 50387
  Resection, 52355
  Revision
    Anastomosis, 50727, 50728
  Stent
    Change, 50382, 50387, 50688
    Insertion, 50688
    Removal, 50382-50387
    Replacement, 50382, 50387, 50688
  Suture, 50900
    Deligation, 50940
    Fistula, 50920, 50930
  Tube
    Change, 50688
    Insertion, 50688
  Tumor Resection, 50949
  Unlisted Services and Procedures, 53899
  Ureterocele
    Excision, 51535
    Incision, 51535
    Repair, 51535
  X-ray with Contrast
    Guidance Catheter, 74480
    Guide Dilation, 74485
Ureteral
  Biopsy, 52007
  Catheterization
    Endoscopic, 50553, 50572, 50953, 50972, 52005
    Injection, 50394, 50684
    Manometric Studies, 50396, 50686
  Endoscopy
    Biopsy, 52007
    Catheterization, 52005
    Guide Wire Insertion, 52334
    Meatotomy, 52290
      Splinting, 50400-50405
      Stent Insertion, 52332
Ureteral Splinting, 50400, 50405
Ureteral Stent
  Insertion, 52332
  Removal, 50384-50387
  Replacement, 50382, 50385, 50387
Ureteral Wire
  Insertion, 52334
Ureterectomy, 50650, 50660
  Partial, 50220
  Total, 50548
Ureterocalycostomy, 50750
  Excision, 51535
  Fulguration, 52300
    Ectopic, 52301
    Orthotopic, 52300
  Incision, 51535
  Repair, 51535
  Resection, 52300
    Ectopic, 52301
    Orthotopic, 52300
Ureterocolon Conduit, 50815
Ureteroenterostomy, 50800
  Revision, 50830
Ureterography
  Injection Procedure, 50684
Ureteroileal Conduit, 50820
  Cystectomy, 51590
  Removal, 50830
Ureterolithotomy, 50610-50630
  Laparoscopy, 50945
  Transvesical, 51060
Ureterolysis
  for Ovarian Vein Syndrome, 50722
  for Retrocaval Ureter, 50725
  for Retroperitoneal Fibrosis, 50715
Ureteroneocystostomy, 50780-50785, 50830, 51565
  Laparoscopic, 50947, 50948
Ureteropexy, 53899
Ureteroplasty, 50700
Ureteropyelography, 50951, 52005
  Injection Procedure, 50684, 50690

Ureteropyelostomy, 50740
Ureterorrhaphy, 50900
Ureteroscopy
  Dilation
    Intra-Renal Stricture, 52346
    Ureter, 52344, 52345
  Third Stage with Cystourethroscopy, 52351
  Biopsy, 52354
  Destruction, 52354
  Lithotripsy, 52354
  Removal
    Calculus, 52352
  Tumor Excision, 52355
Ureterosigmoidostomy, 50810
  Revision, 50830
Ureterostomy, 50860, 50951
  Injection Procedure, 50684
  Manometric Studies, 50686
  Stent
    Change, 50688
Ureterostomy Tube
  Change, 50688
Ureterotomy, 50600
  Insertion Indwelling Stent, 50605
Ureteroureterostomy, 50760, 50770, 50830
Urethra
  Abscess
    Incision and Drainage, 53040
  Adhesions
    Lysis, 53500
  Artificial Sphincter
    Repair, 53449
  Biopsy, 52204, 52354, 53200
  Destruction, 52214, 52224
  Dilation, 52260, 52265, 53600, 53621
    General, 53665
    Suppository and/or Instillation, 53660, 53661
  Diverticulum
    Biopsy, 52204
    Catheterization, 52010
    Destruction, 52214, 52224
    Endoscopy, 52000
    Excision, 53230, 53235
    Extravasation, 53080, 53085
    Injection of Implant Material, 51715
    Marsupialization, 53240
    Repair, 53240
  Drainage
    Extravasation, 53080, 53085
  Endoscopy, 52000
    Biopsy, 52204, 52354
    Catheterization, 52010
    Destruction, 52354, 52400
    Evacuation
      Clot, 52001
    Excision
      Tumor, 52355
    Exploration, 52351
    Incision
      Ejaculatory Duct, 52402
      Injection of Implant Material, 51715
    Lithotripsy, 52353
    Removal
      Calculus, 52352
    Resection
      Ejaculatory Duct, 52402
      Vasectomy, 52402
      Vasotomy, 52402
  Excision
    Diverticulum, 53230, 53235
    Total
      Female, 53210
      Male, 53215
  Incision, 53000, 53010
    Meatus, 53020, 53025
  Incision and Drainage, 53060
  Insertion
    Catheter, 51701-51703
    Filiform, 53620, 53621
    Stent, 52282, 53855

Urethra — Index

Urethra — *continued*
  Lesion
    Destruction, 53265
    Excision, 53260
  Lysis
    Adhesions, 53500
  Paraurethral Gland
    Incision and Drainage, 53060
  Polyp
    Destruction, 53260
    Excision, 53260
  Prolapse
    Destruction, 53275
    Excision, 53275
    Repair, 53275
  Radiotracer, 52250
  Reconstruction, 53410-53440, 53445
  Reconstruction and Bladder, 51800, 51820
    Complications, 54340-54348
    Hypospadias
      First Stage, 54322-54328
      Second Stage, 54308-54316
      Third Stage, 54318
    Meatus, 53450, 53460
  Removal
    Calculus, 52310, 52315
    Foreign Body, 52310, 52315
    Sling, 53442
    Urethral Stent, 52315
  Repair
    Diverticulum, 53240, 53400, 53405
    Fistula, 45820, 45825, 53400, 53405, 53520
    Sphincter, 57220
    Stricture, 53400, 53405
    Urethrocele, 57230
    Wound, 53502-53515
  Skene's Gland
    Incision and Drainage, 53060
  Sphincter, 52277
    Electromyography, 51784, 51785
      Needle, 51785
    Insertion
      Prosthesis, 53444
    Reconstruction, 53445
    Removal
      Prosthesis, 53446, 53447
    Repair
      Prosthesis, 53449
    Replacement
      Prosthesis, 53448
  Suture
    Fistula, 45820, 45825, 53520
    to Bladder, 51840, 51841
    Wound, 53502-53515
  Thermotherapy, 53850-53852
  Tumor
    Destruction, 53220
    Excision, 53220
  Unlisted Services and Procedures, 53899
  Urethrocystography, 74450, 74455
  Urethrotomy, 52270-52276
  X-ray with Contrast, 74450, 74455

Urethral
  Diverticulum Marsupialization, 53240
  Meatus, Dorsal
    Reconstruction, 54385
    Repair, 54380-54390
  Pressure Profile, 51727, 51729
  Sphincter
    Biofeedback Training, 90911
    Insertion
      Prosthesis, 53444
    Removal
      Prosthesis, 53447
    Replacement
      Prosthesis, 53448
  Stenosis
    Dilation, 52281
  Stent
    Insertion, 52282, 53855

Urethral — *continued*
  Stent — *continued*
    Removal
      Bladder, 52310, 52315
      Urethra, 52310, 52315
  Stricture
    Dilation, 52281, 53600-53621
    Injection
      Steroids, 52283
  Syndrome
    Cystourethroscopy, 52285
Urethral Calculus
  Anesthesia, 00918
Urethral Diverticulum
  Marsupialization, 53240
Urethral Guide Wire
  Insertion, 52334
Urethral Pressure Profile, 51727, 51729
Urethral Sphincter
  Biofeedback Training, 90911
  Removal
    Prosthesis, 53447
Urethral Stenosis
  Dilation, 52281
Urethral Stent
  Insertion, 52332
  Removal
    Bladder, 52310, 52315
    Urethra, 52310, 52315
Urethral Stricture
  Dilation, 52281, 53600, 53621
  Injection
    Steroids, 52283
Urethral Syndrome
  Cystourethroscopy, 52285
Urethrectomy, 50650, 50660
  Partial, 50220
  Total
    Female, 53210
    Male, 53215
Urethrocele
  Repair, 57230-57240
Urethrocystography, 74450, 74455
  Contrast and/or Chain, 51605
  Retrograde, 51610
  Voiding, 51600
Urethrocystopexy, 51840-51841
Urethromeatoplasty, 53450, 53460
Urethropexy, 51840, 51841
Urethroplasty, 46744, 46746
  First Stage, 53410
    Hypospadias, 54322-54328
  Reconstruction
    Female Urethra, 53430
    Male Anterior Urethra, 53410
    Prostatic
      Membranous Urethra
        First Stage, 53420
        One Stage, 53415
        Second Stage, 53425
  Second Stage, 53405
    Hypospadias, 54308-54316
  Third Stage
    Hypospadias, 54318
Urethrorrhaphy, 53502-53515
Urethroscopy, 52000-52315, 52320-52402
  Perineal, 53899
Urethrostomy, 53000, 53010
Urethrotomy, 53000, 53010
  with Cystourethroscopy
    Female, 52270
    Male, 52275
  Direct Vision
    with Cystourethroscopy, 52276
  Internal, 52601, 52647, 52648
Uric Acid
  Blood, 84550
  Other Source, 84560
  Urine, 84560
Uridyltransferase, Galactose–1–Phosphate, 82775-82776
Uridylyltransferase, Galactosephophate, 82775-82776
Urinalysis, 81000-81099

Urinalysis — *continued*
  without Microscopy, 81002
  Automated, 81001, 81003
  Glass Test, 81020
  Microalbumin, 82043, 82044
  Microscopic, 81015
  Pregnancy Test, 81025
  Qualitative, 81005
  Routine, 81002
  Screen, 81007
  Semiquantitative, 81005
  Unlisted Services and Procedures, 81099
  Volume Measurement, 81050
  Water Load Test, 89235
Urinary Bladder
  See Bladder
Urinary Catheter Irrigation, 51700
Urinary Concentration Test, 89235
Urinary Sphincter, Artificial
  Insertion, 53445
  Removal, 53446
    with Replacement, 53447-53448
  Repair, 53449
Urinary Tract
  X-ray with Contrast, 74400-74425
Urine
  Albumin, 82042-82044
  Blood, 81000-81005
  Colony Count, 87086
  Pregnancy Test, 81025
  Tests, 81000-81099
Urine Sensitivity Test, 87181-87190
Urobilinogen
  Feces, 84577
  Urine, 84578-84583
Urodynamic Tests
  Bladder Capacity
    Ultrasound, 51798
  Cystometrogram, 51725-51729
  Electromyography Studies
    Needle, 51785
  Rectal, [51797]
  Residual Urine
    Ultrasound, 51798
  Stimulus Evoked Response, 51792
  Urethra Pressure Profile, [51797]
  Uroflowmetry, 51736, 51741
  Voiding Pressure Studies
    Bladder, 51728-51729
    Intra–Abdominal, [51797]
Uroflowmetry, 51736, 51741
Urography
  Antegrade, 74425
  Infusion, 74410, 74415
  Intravenous, 74400-74415
  Retrograde, 74420
Uroporphyrin, 84120
Urostomy, 50727, 50728
Urothromboplastin
  Inhibition, 85705
  Inhibition Test, 85347
  Partial Time, 85730-85732
Uterine
  Adhesion
    Lysis, 58559
  Cervix
    See Cervix
  Endoscopies
    See Endoscopy, Uterus
  Hemorrhage
    Postpartum, 59160
Uterus
  Ablation
    Endometrium, 58353-58356
    Tumor
      Ultrasound Focused, 0071T-0072T
  Biopsy
    Endometrium, 58100
    Endoscopy, 58558
  Catheterization
    X-ray, 58340
  Chromotubation, 58350
  Curettage, 58356
    Postpartum, 59160

Uterus — *continued*
  Dilation and Curettage, 58120
    Postpartum, 59160
  Ectopic Pregnancy
    Interstitial
      Partial Resection Uterus, 59136
      Total Hysterectomy, 59135
  Embolization
    Fibroid, 37210
  Endoscopy
    Endometrial Ablation, 58563
    Exploration, 58555
    Surgery, 58558-58565
    Treatment, 58558-58565
  Excision
    Laparoscopic, 58550
      with Removal of Ovaries, 58552, 58554
    Total, 58570-58573
    Partial, 58180
    Radical
      Laparoscopic, 58548
      Open, 58210, 58285
    Removal of Tubes and/or Ovaries, 58262, 58263, 58291-58293, 58552, 58554
    Sonohysterography, 76831
    Total, 58150-58152, 58200, 58953-58956
    Vaginal, 58260-58270, 58290-58294, 58550-58554
      with Colpectomy, 58275, 58280
      with Colpo–Urethrocystopexy, 58267
      with Repair of Enterocele, 58270, 58294
  Hemorrhage
    Postpartum, 59160
  Hydatidiform Mole
    Excision, 59100
  Hydrotubation, 58350
  Hysterosalpingography, 74740
  Hysterosonography, 76831
  Incision
    Removal of Lesion, 59100
  Insertion
    Heyman Capsule
      for Brachytherapy, 58346
    Intrauterine Device, 58300
    Tandem
      for Brachytherapy, 57155
  Laparoscopy, 58578
  Lesion
    Excision, 58545, 58546, 59100
  Reconstruction, 58540
  Removal
    Intrauterine Device (IUD), 58301
  Repair
    Fistula, 51920, 51925
    Rupture, 58520, 59350
    Suspension, 58400
      with Presacral Sympathectomy, 58410
  Sonohysterography, 76831
  Suture
    Rupture, 59350
  Tumor
    Ablation
      Ultrasound Focused, 0071T-0072T
    Embolization, 37210
    Excision
      Abdominal Approach, 58140, 58146
      Vaginal Approach, 58145
  Unlisted Services and Procedures, 58578, 58999
  X-ray with Contrast, 74740
UTP Hexose 1 Phosphate Uridylyltransferase, 82775-82776
UVC, 36510
UV Light Therapy, 96900

Index

Uvula
  Abscess
    Incision and Drainage, 42000
  Biopsy, 42100
  Excision, 42140, 42145
  Lesion
    Destruction, 42145
    Excision, 42104-42107
  Unlisted Services and Procedures, 42299
Uvulectomy, 42140
Uvulopalatopharyngoplasty, 42145
Uvulopharyngoplasty, 42145

V

Vaccines
  Adenovirus, 90476, 90477
  Anthrax, 90581
  Chicken Pox, 90716
  Cholera Injectable, 90725
  Diphtheria, Tetanus (DT), 90702
  Diphtheria, Tetanus, Acellular Pertussis (DTaP), 90700
  Diphtheria, Tetanus, Acellular Pertussis and Hemophilus Influenza B (Hib) (DtaP–Hib), 90721
  Diphtheria, Tetanus, Acellular Pertussis, Hemophilus Influenza B, and Poliovirus Inactivated (DTaP–Hib–IPV), 90696, 90698
  Diphtheria, Tetanus, Acellular Pertussis, Hepatitis B, and Inactivated Poliovirus (DTaP–HepB–IPV), 90723
  Diphtheria, Tetanus, and Acellular Pertussis, (Tdap), 90715
  Diphtheria, Tetanus, Whole Cell Pertussis (DTP), 90701
  Diphtheria, Tetanus, Whole Cell Pertussis and Hemophilus Influenza B (DTP–Hib), 90720
  Diphtheria Toxoid, 90719
  Encephalitis, Japanese, 90735, 90738
  H1N1, 90663
  Hemophilus Influenza b, 90645-90648
  Hepatitis A, 90632-90634
  Hepatitis A and Hepatitis B, 90636
  Hepatitis B, 90740-90747
  Hepatitis B and Hemophilus Influenza B (HepB–Hib), 90748
  Human Papilloma Virus (HPV), 90649-90650
  Influenza, 90655-90660
  Japanese Encephalitis, 90738
  Lyme Disease, 90665
  Measles, 90705
  Measles and Rubella, 90708
  Measles, Mumps and Rubella (MMR), 90707
  Measles, Mumps, Rubella and Varicella (MMRV), 90710
  Meningococcal, 90733, 90734
  Mumps, 90704
  Plague, 90727
  Pneumococcal, 90669-90670, 90732
  Poliovirus, Inactivated
    Intramuscular, 90713
    Subcutaneous, 90713
  Poliovirus, Live
    Oral, 90712
  Rabies, 90675, 90676
  Rotavirus, 90680-90681
  Rubella, 90706
  Swine Flu, 90663
  Tetanus and Diphtheria, 90714, 90718
  Tetanus, Diphtheria and Acellular Pertussis (Tdap), 90715
  Tetanus, Diphtheria, and Acellular Pertussis (TdaP), 90715
  Tetanus Toxoid, 90703
  Tuberculosis (BCG), 90585
  Typhoid, 90690-90693

Vaccines — *continued*
  Unlisted Vaccine
    Toxoid, 90749
  Varicella (Chicken Pox), 90716
  Yellow Fever, 90717
  Zoster, 90736
VAD, 0048T, 33975-33980
Vagina
  Abscess
    Incision and Drainage, 57010
  Amines Test, 82120
  Biopsy
    Colposcopy, 57421
    Endocervical, 57454
    Extensive, 57105
    Simple, 57100
  Closure, 57120
  Colposcopy, 57420-57421, 57455-57456, 57461
  Construction
    with Graft, 57292
    without Graft, 57291
  Cyst
    Excision, 57135
  Dilation, 57400
  Endocervical
    Biopsy, 57454
    Exploration, 57452
  Excision
    Closure, 57120
    Complete
      with Removal of Paravaginal Tissue with Lymphadenectomy, 57112
      with Removal of Paravaginal Tissue, 57111
      with Removal of Vaginal Wall, 57110
    Partial
      with Removal of Paravaginal Tissue with Lymphadenectomy, 57109
      with Removal of Paravaginal Tissue, 57107
      with Removal of Vaginal Wall, 57106
    Total, 57110
      with Hysterectomy, 58275, 58280
      with Repair of Enterocele, 58280
  Exploration
    Endocervical, 57452
    Incision, 57000
  Hematoma
    Incision and Drainage, 57022, 57023
  Hemorrhage, 57180
  Hysterectomy, 58290, 58550, 58552-58554
  Incision and Drainage, 57020
  Insertion
    Ovoid
      for Brachytherapy, 57155
    Packing for Bleeding, 57180
    Pessary, 57160
  Irrigation, 57150
  Lesion
    Destruction, 57061, 57065
      Extensive, 57065
      Simple, 57061
  Prolapse
    Sacrospinous Ligament Fixation, 57282
  Removal
    Foreign Body, 57415
    Prosthetic Graft, 57295-57296
    Sling
      Stress Incontinence, 57287
    Tissue, Partial, 57106
    Wall, Partial, 57107
  Repair, 56800
    Cystocele, 57240, 57260
      Combined Anteroposterior, 57260, 57265
      Posterior, 57240

Vagina — *continued*
  Repair — *continued*
    Enterocele, 57265
    Fistula, 51900
      Rectovaginal, 57300-57308
      Transvesical and Vaginal Approach, 57330
      Urethrovaginal, 57310, 57311
      Vesicovaginal, 51900, 57320, 57330
    Hysterectomy, 58267, 58293
    Incontinence, 57288
    Obstetric, 59300
    Paravaginal Defect, 57284
    Pereyra Procedure, 57289
    Prolapse, 57282, 57284
    Prosthesis Insertion, 57267
    Rectocele
      Combined Anteroposterior, 57260, 57265
      Posterior, 57250
    Suspension, 57280-57283
      Laparoscopic, 57425
    Urethra Sphincter, 57220
    Wound, 57200, 57210
      Colpoperineorrhaphy, 57210
      Colporrhaphy, 57200
  Revision
    Prosthetic Graft, 57295-57296, 57426
  Sling
    Stress Incontinence, 57287
  Septum
    Excision, 57130
  Suspension, 57280-57283
    Laparoscopic, 57425
  Suture
    Cystocele, 57240, 57260
    Enterocele, 57265
    Fistula, 51900, 57300-57330
    Rectocele, 57250, 57260
    Wound, 57200, 57210
  Tumor
    Excision, 57135
  Ultrasound, 76830
  Unlisted Services and Procedures, 58999
  X-ray with Contrast, 74775
Vaginal Delivery, 59400, 59610-59614
  After Previous Cesarean Section, 59610, 59612
  Attempted, 59618-59622
  Antepartum Care Only, 59425, 59426
  Attempted, 59618-59622
  Cesarean Delivery After Attempted with Postpartum Care, 59622
  Delivery Only, 59620
  Delivery After Previous Vaginal Delivery Only
    with Postpartum Care, 59614
  Delivery Only, 59409
  External Cephalic Version, 59412
  Placenta, 59414
  Postpartum Care only, 59410
  Routine Care, 59400
Vaginal Smear, 88141-88155, 88164-88167, 88174-88175
Vaginal Suppositories
  Induced Abortion, 59855
    with Dilation and Curettage, 59856
    with Hysterotomy, 59857
Vaginal Tissue
  Removal, Partial, 57106
Vaginal Wall
  Removal, Partial, 57107
Vaginectomy
  Partial, 57109
    with Nodes, 57109
Vaginoplasty
  Intersex State, 57335
Vaginorrhaphy, 57200
  See Also Colporrhaphy
Vaginoscopy
  Biopsy, 57454

Vaginoscopy — *continued*
  Exploration, 57452
Vaginotomy, 57000-57010
Vagotomy
  With Gastroduodenostomy Revision/Reconstruction, 43855
  With Gastrojejunostomy Revision/Reconstruction, 43865
  With Partial Distal Gastrectomy, 43635
  Abdominal, 64760
  Highly Selective, 43641
  Parietal Cell, 43641, 64755
  Reconstruction, 43855
    with Gastroduodenostomy Revision, 43855
    with Gastrojejunostomy Revision, Reconstruction, 43865
  Selective, 43640
  Transthoracic, 64752
  Truncal, 43640
Vagus Nerve
  Avulsion
    Abdominal, 64760
    Selective, 64755
    Thoracic, 64752
  Incision, 43640, 43641
    Abdominal, 64760
    Selective, 64755
    Thoracic, 64752
  Injection
    Anesthetic, 64408
  Transection, 43640, 43641
    Abdominal, 64760
    Selective, 43652, 64755
    Thoracic, 64752
    Truncal, 43651
Valentine's Test
  Urinalysis, Glass Test, 81020
Valproic Acid, 80164
Valproic Acid Measurement, 80164
Valsalva Sinus
  Repair, 33702-33720
Valva Atrioventricularis Sinistra (Valva Mitralis)
  Incision, 33420, 33422
  Repair, 33420-33427
  Replacement, 33430
Valve
  Aortic
    Repair, Left Ventricle, 33414
    Replacement, 33405-33413
  Bicuspid
    Incision, 33420, 33422
    Repair, 33420-33427
    Replacement, 33430
  Mitral
    Incision, 33420, 33422
    Repair, 33420-33427
    Replacement, 33430
  Pulmonary
    Incision, 33470-33474
    Repair, 33470-33474
    Replacement, 33475
  Tricuspid
    Excision, 33460
    Repair, 33463-33465
    Replace, 33465
    Reposition, 33468
Valvectomy
  Tricuspid Valve, 33460
Valve Stenoses, Aortic
  Repair, 33415
    Supravalvular, 33417
Valvotomy
  Mitral Valve, 33420, 33422
  Pulmonary Valve, 33470-33474
  Reoperation, 33530
Valvuloplasty
  Aortic Valve, 33400-33403
  Femoral Vein, 34501
  Mitral Valve, 33425-33427
  Percutaneous Balloon
    Aortic Valve, 92986
    Mitral Valve, 92987
    Pulmonary Valve, 92990

Valvuloplasty — continued
- Prosthetic Valve, 33496
- Reoperation, 33530
- Tricuspid Valve, 33460-33465

Vancomycin
- Assay, 80202
- Resistance, 87500

Van Den Bergh Test, 82247, 82248

Vanillymandelic Acid
- Urine, 84585

Vanilmandelic Acid
- Urine, 84585

VAQTA, 90632-90633

Varicella (Chicken Pox)
- Immunization, 90710, 90716

Varicella-Zoster
- Antibody, 86787
- Antigen Detection
  - Direct Fluorescent Antibody, 87290

Varices, Esophageal
- Ligation, 43205, 43400
- Transection and Repair, 43401

Varicocele
- Spermatic Cord
  - Excision, 55530-55540

Varicose Vein
- with Tissue Excision, 37735, 37760
- Ablation, 36475-36479
- Removal, 37718, 37722, 37735, 37765-37785
- Secondary Varicosity, 37785

VARIVAX, 90716

Vascular Flow Check, Graft, 15860

Vascular Injection
- Unlisted Services and Procedures, 36299

Vascular Lesion
- Cranial
  - Excision, 61600-61608, 61615, 61616
- Cutaneous
  - Destruction, 17106-17108

Vascular Malformation
- Cerebral
  - Repair, 61710
- Finger
  - Excision, 26115
- Hand
  - Excision, 26115

Vascular Procedure
- Angioscopy
  - Noncoronary Vessels, 35400
- Brachytherapy
  - Intracoronary Artery, 92974
- Endoscopy
  - Surgical, 37500
- Harvest
  - Lower Extremity Vein, 35572
- Intravascular Ultrasound
  - Coronary Vessels, 92978, 92979
  - Noncoronary Vessels, 75945-75946
- Stent
  - Intracoronary, 92980, 92981
- Thrombolysis
  - Coronary Vessels, 92975-92977
  - Cranial Vessels, 37195

Vascular Procedures
- Angioscopy
  - Noncoronary Vessels, 35400
- Endoscopy
  - Surgical, 37500
- Harvest
  - Lower Extremity Vein, 35572
- Intravascular Ultrasound
  - Non-Coronary Vessels, 75945, 75946
- Stent
  - Intracoronary, 92980-92981
- Thrombolysis
  - Coronary Vessels, 92975, 92977
  - Cranial Vessels, 37195

Vascular Rehabilitation, 93668

Vascular Studies
- See Also Doppler Scan, Duplex, Plethysmography
- Angioscopy
  - Aorta, 93978, 93979
  - Noncoronary Vessels, 35400
- Artery Studies
  - Extracranial, 93875-93882
  - Extremities, 93922-93924
  - Intracranial, 93886, 93888
  - Lower Extremity, 93922-93926
  - Middle Cerebral Artery, Fetal, 76821
  - Umbilical Artery, Fetal, 76820
  - Upper Extremity, 93930, 93931
- Blood Pressure Monitoring, 24 Hour, 93784-93790
- Cardiac Catheterization
  - Imaging, 93555, 93556
- Hemodialysis Access, 93990
- Kidney
  - Multiple Study with Pharmacological Intervention, 78709
  - Single Study with Pharmacological Intervention, 78708
- Penile Vessels, 93980, 93981
- Plethysmography
  - Total Body, 93720-93722
  - Temperature Gradient, 93740
- Unlisted Services and Procedures, 93799
- Venous Studies
  - Extremities, 93965-93971
  - Venous Pressure, 93770
- Visceral Studies, 93975-93979

Vascular Surgery
- Arm, Upper
  - Anesthesia, 01770-01782
- Elbow
  - Anesthesia, 01770-01782
- Endoscopy, 37500
- Unlisted Services and Procedures, 37799

Vas Deferens
- Anastomosis
  - to Epididymis, 54900, 54901
- Excision, 55250
- Incision, 55200
  - for X-Ray, 55300
- Ligation, 55450
- Repair
  - Suture, 55400
- Unlisted Services and Procedures, 55899
- Vasography, 74440
- X-Ray with Contrast, 74440

Vasectomy, 55250
- Laser Coagulation of Prostate, 52647
- Laser Vaporization of Prostate, 52648
- Reversal, 55400
- Transurethral
  - Cystourethroscopic, 52402
  - Transurethral Electrosurgical Resection of Prostate, 52601
  - Transurethral Resection of Prostate, 52648

Vasoactive Drugs
- Injection
  - Penis, 54231

Vasoactive Intestinal Peptide, 84586

Vasogram, 74440

Vasography, 74440

Vasointestinal Peptide, 84586

Vasopneumatic Device Therapy, 97016
- See Also Physical Medicine/Therapy/Occupational Therapy

Vasopressin, 84588

Vasotomy, 55200, 55300
- Transurethral
  - Cystourethroscopic, 52402

Vasovasorrhaphy, 55400

Vasovasostomy, 55400

VATS
- See Thoracoscopy

VBAC, 59610-59614

VBG (Vertical Banding Gastroplasty), 43842

V, Cranial Nerve
- Destruction, 64600-64610
- Injection
  - Anesthetic, 64400
  - Neurolytic, 64600-64610

VCU (Voiding Cystourethrogram), 51600

VCUG (Voiding Cystourethrogram), 51600

VDRL, 86592-86593

Vectorcardiogram
- Evaluation, 93799
- Tracing, 93799

Vein
- Ablation
  - Endovenous, 36475-36479
- Adrenal
  - Venography, 75840, 75842
- Anastomosis
  - Caval to Mesenteric, 37160
  - Intrahepatic Portosystemic, 37182-37183
  - Portocaval, 37140
  - Reniportal, 37145
  - Saphenopopliteal, 34530
  - Splenorenal, 37180, 37181
  - Vein, 34530, 37180, 37181
    - to Vein, 37140-37160, 37182-37183
- Angioplasty
  - Transluminal, 35460
- Arm
  - Harvest of Vein for Bypass Graft, 35500
  - Venography, 75820, 75822
- Axillary
  - Thrombectomy, 34490
- Biopsy
  - Transcatheter, 75970
- Cannulization
  - to Artery, 36810, 36815
  - to Vein, 36800
- Catheterization
  - Central Insertion, 36555-36558
  - Organ Blood, 36500
  - Peripheral Insertion, 36568, 36569
  - Removal, 36589
  - Repair, 36575
  - Replacement, 36578-36581, 36584
  - Umbilical, 36510
- Endoscopic Harvest
  - for Bypass Graft, 33508
- External Cannula Declotting, 36860, 36861
- Extremity
  - Non-Invasive Studies, 93965-93971
- Femoral
  - Repair, 34501
- Femoropopliteal
  - Thrombectomy, 34421, 34451
- Guidance
  - Fluoroscopic, 77001
  - Ultrasound, 76937
- Hepatic Portal
  - Splenoportography, 75810
  - Venography, 75885, 75887
- Iliac
  - Thrombectomy, 34401, 34421, 34451
- Injection
  - Sclerosing Agent, 36468-36471
- Insertion
  - IVC Filter, 75940
- Interrupt
  - Femoral Vein, 37650
  - Iliac, 37660
  - Vena Cava, 37620
- Jugular
  - Venography, 75860

Vein — continued
- Leg
  - Harvest for Vascular Reconstruction, 35572
  - Venography, 75820, 75822
- Ligation
  - Clusters, 37785
  - Esophagus, 43205
  - Jugular, 37565
  - Perforation, 37760
  - Saphenous, 37700-37735, 37780
  - Secondary, 37785
- Liver
  - Venography, 75860, 75889, 75891
- Neck
  - Venography, 75860
- Nuclear Medicine
  - Thrombosis Imaging, 78456-78458
- Orbit
  - Venography, 75880
- Portal
  - Catheterization, 36481
- Pulmonary
  - Repair, 33730
- Removal
  - Clusters, 37785
  - Saphenous, 37700-37735, 37780
  - Varicose, 37765, 37766
- Renal
  - Venography, 75831, 75833
- Repair
  - Aneurysm, 36832
  - Angioplasty, 75978
  - Graft, 34520
- Sampling
  - Venography, 75893
- Sinus
  - Venography, 75870
- Skull
  - Venography, 75870, 75872
- Spermatic
  - Excision, 55530-55540
  - Ligation, 55500
- Splenic
  - Splenoportography, 75810
- Stripping
  - Saphenous, 37700-37735, 37780
- Subclavian
  - Thrombectomy, 34471, 34490
- Thrombectomy
  - Other than Hemodialysis Graft or Fistula, 35875, 35876
- Unlisted Services and Procedures, 37799
- Valve Transposition, 34510
- Varicose
  - with Tissue Excision, 37735, 37760
  - Ablation, 36475-36479
  - Removal, 37718-37735, 37765-37785
  - Secondary Varicosity, 37785
- Vena Cava
  - Thrombectomy, 34401-34451
  - Venography, 75825, 75827

Velpeau Cast, 29058

Vena Cava
- Catheterization, 36010
- Interruption, 37620
- Reconstruction, 34502
- Resection with Reconstruction, 37799

Vena Caval
- Thrombectomy, 50230

Venereal Disease Research Laboratory (VDRL), 86592-86593

Venesection
- Therapeutic, 99195

Venipuncture
- See Also Cannulation; Catheterization
- Child/Adult
  - Cutdown, 36425
  - Percutaneous, 36410

Index

Venipuncture — *continued*
  Infant
    Cutdown, 36420
    Percutaneous, 36400-36406
  Routine, 36415
Venography
  Adrenal, 75840, 75842
  Arm, 75820, 75822
  Epidural, 75872
  Hepatic Portal, 75885, 75887
  Injection, 36005
  Jugular, 75860
  Leg, 75820, 75822
  Liver, 75889, 75891
  Neck, 75860
  Nuclear Medicine, 78445, 78457, 78458
  Orbit, 75880
  Renal, 75831, 75833
  Sagittal Sinus, 75870
  Thoracic, 22520-22522
  Vena Cava, 75825, 75827
  Venous Sampling, 75893
Venorrhaphy
  Femoral, 37650
  Iliac, 37660
  Vena Cava, 37620
Venotomy
  Therapeutic, 99195
Venous Access Device
  Blood Collection, 36591-36592
  Declotting, 36593
  Fluoroscopic Guidance, 77001
  Insertion
    Central, 36560-36566
    Peripheral, 36570, 36571
  Obstruction Clearance, 36595, 36596
  Guidance, 75901, 75902
  Removal, 36590
  Repair, 36576
  Replacement, 36582, 36583, 36585
  Catheter Only, 36578
Venous Blood Pressure, 93770
Venovenostomy
  Saphenopopliteal, 34530
Ventilating Tube
  Insertion, 69433
  Removal, 69424
Ventilation Assist, 94002-94005, 99504
Ventricular
  Aneurysmectomy, 33542
  Assist Device, 0048T, 33975-33980
  Puncture, 61020, 61026, 61105-61120
Ventriculocisternostomy, 62180, 62200, 62201
Ventriculography
  Anesthesia
    Brain, 00214
    Cardia, 01920
    Burr Holes, 01920
  Cerebrospinal Fluid Flow, 78635
  Nuclear Imaging, 78635
Ventriculomyectomy, 33416
Ventriculomyotomy, 33416
VEP, 95930
Vermiform Appendix
  Abscess
    Incision and Drainage, 44900-44901
  Excision, 44950-44960
Vermilionectomy, 40500
Verruca(e)
  Destruction, 17110-17111
Verruca Plana
  Destruction, 17110-17111
Version, Cephalic
  External, of Fetus, 59412
Vertebra
  See Also Spinal Cord; Spine; Vertebral Body; Vertebral Process
  Additional Segment
    Excision, 22103, 22116

Vertebra — *continued*
  Arthrodesis
    Anterior, 22548-22585
    Exploration, 22830
    Lateral Extracavitary, 22532-22534
    Posterior, 22590-22802
    Spinal Deformity
      Anterior Approach, 22808-22812
      Posterior Approach, 22800-22804
  Arthroplasty, 0202T
  Cervical
    Artificial Disc, 22864
    Excision for Tumor, 22100, 22110
    Fracture, 23675, 23680
  Fracture
    Dislocation
      Additional Segment
        Open Treatment, 22328
      Cervical
        Open Treatment, 22326
      Lumbar
        Open Treatment, 22325
      Thoracic
        Open Treatment, 22327
  Kyphectomy, 22818, 22819
  Lumbar
    Artificial Disc, 22865
    Distraction Device, 0171T-0172T
    Excision for Tumor, 22102, 22114
  Osteoplasty
    CT Scan, 72292
    Fluoroscopy, 72291
    Lumbar, 22521, 22522
    Thoracic, 22520-22522
  Osteotomy
    Additional Segment
      Anterior Approach, 22226
      Posterior/Posterolateral Approach, 22216
    Cervical
      Anterior Approach, 22220
      Posterior/Posterolateral Approach, 22210
    Lumbar
      Anterior Approach, 22224
      Posterior/Posterolateral Approach, 22214
    Thoracic
      Anterior Approach, 22222
      Posterior/Posterolateral Approach, 22212
  Thoracic
    Excision for Tumor, 22101, 22112
Vertebrae
  See Also Vertebra
  Arthrodesis
    Anterior, 22548-22585
    Lateral Extracavitary, 22532-22534
    Spinal Deformity, 22818, 22819
Vertebral
  Arteries
    Aneurysm, 35005, 61698, 61702
    Angiography, 75685
    Bypass Graft, 35508, 35515, 35542-35645
    Catheterization, 36100
    Decompression, 61597
    Thromboendarterectomy, 35301
Vertebral Body
  Biopsy, 20250, 20251
  Excision
    with Skull Base Surgery, 61597
    Decompression, 63081-63091
    Lesion, 63300-63308
  Fracture
    Dislocation
      Closed Treatment, 22305
      without Manipulation, 22310

Vertebral Body — *continued*
  Kyphectomy, 22818, 22819
Vertebral Column
  See Spine
Vertebral Corpectomy, 63081-63308
Vertebral Fracture
  Closed Treatment
    with Manipulation, Casting, and/or Bracing, 22315
    without Manipulation, 22310
  Open Treatment
    Additional Segment, 22328
    Cervical, 22326
    Lumbar, 22325
    Posterior, 22325-22327
    Thoracic, 22327
Vertebral Process
  Fracture
    Closed Treatment, 22305
Vertical Banding Gastroplasty (VBG), 43842
Very Low Density Lipoprotein, 83719
Vesication
  Puncture Aspiration, 10160
Vesicle, Seminal
  Excision, 55650
  Cyst, 55680
    Mullerian Duct, 55680
  Incision, 55600, 55605
  Unlisted Services/Procedures, 55899
  Vesiculography, 74440
  X-Ray with Contrast, 74440
Vesico-Psoas Hitch, 50785
Vesicostomy
  Cutaneous, 51980
Vesicourethropexy, 51840-51841
Vesicovaginal Fistula
  Closure
    Abdominal Approach, 51900
    Transvesical/Vaginal Approach, 57330
    Vaginal Approach, 57320
Vesiculectomy, 55650
Vesiculogram, Seminal, 55300, 74440
Vesiculography, 55300, 74440
Vesiculotomy, 55600, 55605
  Complicated, 55605
Vessel, Blood
  See Blood Vessels
Vessels Transposition, Great
  Repair, 33770-33781
Vestibular Function Tests
  Additional Electrodes, 92547
  Caloric Tests, 92533, 92543
  Nystagmus
    Optokinetic, 92534, 92544
    Positional, 92532, 92542
    Spontaneous, 92531, 92541
  Posturography, 92548
  Sinusoidal Rotational Testing, 92546
  Torsion Swing Test, 92546
  Tracking Test, 92545
Vestibular Nerve
  Section
    Transcranial Approach, 69950
    Translabyrinthine Approach, 69915
Vestibule of Mouth
  Biopsy, 40808
  Excision
    Lesion, 40810-40816
    Destruction, 40820
    Mucosa for Graft, 40818
Vestibuloplasty, 40840-40845
VF, 92081-92083
V-Flap Procedure
  One Stage Distal Hypospadias Repair, 54322
Vibration Perception Threshold (VPT), 0107T
ViCPs, 90691
Vicq D'Azyr Operation, 31600-31605
Vidal Procedure
  Varicocele, Spermatic Cord, Excision, 55530-55540

Video
  Esophagus, 74230
  Pharynx, 70371-74230
  Speech Evaluation, 70371
  Swallowing Evaluation, 74230
Video-Assisted Thoracoscopic Surgery
  See Thoracoscopy
Videoradiography
  Unlisted Services and Procedures, 76120-76125
VII, Coagulation Factor, 85230
  See Proconvertin
VII, Cranial Nerve
  See Facial Nerve
VIII, Coagulation Factor, 85240-85247
Villus, Chorionic
  Biopsy, 59015
Villusectomy
  See Synovectomy
VIP, 84586
Viral
  AIDS, 87390
  Burkitt Lymphoma
    Antibody, 86663-86665
  Human Immunodeficiency
    Antibody, 86701-86703
    Antigen, 87390-87391, 87534-87539
    Confirmation Test, 86689
  Influenza
    Antibody, 86710
    Antigen Detection, 87804
    Vaccine, 90657-90660
  Respiratory Syncytial
    Antibody, 86756
    Antigen Detection, 87280, 87420, 87807
    Recombinant, 90378
  Salivary Gland
    Cytomegalovirus
      Antibody, 86644-86645
      Antigen Detection, 87271, 87332, 87495-87497
Viral Antibodies, 86280
Viral Warts
  Destruction, 17110-17111
Virtual Colonoscopy
  Diagnostic, 74261-74262
  Screening, 74263
Virus Identification
  Immunofluorescence, 87254
Virus Isolation, 87250-87255
Visceral Larval Migrans, 86280
Viscosities, Blood, 85810
Visit, Home, 99341-99350
Vistibular Evaluation, 92540
Visual Acuity Screen, 99172, 99173
Visual Field Exam, 92081-92083
Visual Function Screen, 1055F, 99172
Visualization
  Ideal Conduit, 50690
Visual Reinforcement Audiometry, 92579
Vital Capacity Measurement, 94150
Vitamin
  A, 84590
  B-1, 84425
  B-12, 82607-82608
    Absorption Study, 78270-78272
  B-2, 84252
  B-6, 84207
  B-6 Measurement, 84207
  BC, 82746-82747
  B Complex, 78270-78272
  C, 82180
  D, 82306 *[82652]*
  E, 84446
  K, 84597
    Dependent Bone Protein, 83937
    Dependent Protein S, 85305-85306
Vitelline Duct
  Excision, 44800
Vitrectomy
  with Endolaser Panretinal Photocoagulation, 67040

Vitrectomy

Vitrectomy — *continued*
  with Epiretinal Membrane Stripping, 67041-67043
  with Focal Endolaser Photocoagulation, 67039
  with Implantation of Intra-ocular Retinal Electrode Array, 0100T
  with Implantation or Replacement Drug Delivery System, 67027
  with Placement of Subconjunctival Retinal Prosthesis Receiver, 0100T
  Anterior Approach
    Partial, 67005
  for Retinal Detachment, 67112-67113
  Monitoring of Intraocular Pressure, 0173T
  Pars Plana Approach, 67036, 67041-67043
  Partial, 67005, 67010
  Subtotal, 67010
Vitreous
  Aspiration, 67015
  Excision
    with Epiretinal Membrane Stripping, 67041-67043
    with Focal Endolaser Photocoagulation, 67039
    Pars Plana Approach, 67036
  Implantation
    Drug Delivery System, 67027
  Incision
    Strands, 67030, 67031
  Injection
    Fluid Substitute, 67025
    Pharmacologic Agent, 67028
  Removal
    Anterior Approach, 67005
    Subtotal, 67010
  Replacement
    Drug Delivery System, 67027
  Strands
    Discission, 67030
    Severing, 67031
  Subtotal, 67010
Vitreous Humor
  Anesthesia, 00145
Vivotif Berna, 90690
VLDL, 83719
VMA, 84585
Vocal Cords
  Injection
    Endoscopy, 31513
    Therapeutic, 31570, 31571
Voice Button
  Speech Prosthesis, Creation, 31611
Voiding
  EMG, 51784-51785
  Pressure Studies
    Abdominal, [51797]
    Bladder, 51728-51729 [51797]
    Rectum, [51797]
Volatiles, 84600
Volhard's Test
  Water Load Test, 89235
Volkman Contracture, 25315, 25316
Volume Reduction
  Blood Products, 86960
Volume Reduction, Lung, 32491
Von Kraske Proctectomy
  Proctectomy, Partial, 45111-45123
VP, 51728-51729, [51797]
VPT (Vibration Perception Threshold), 0107T
VRA, 92579
Vulva
  Abscess
    Incision and Drainage, 56405
  Colposcopy., 56820
    Biopsy, 56821
  Excision
    Complete, 56625, 56633-56640
    Partial, 56620, 56630-56632
    Radical, 56630, 56631, 56633-56640

Vulva — *continued*
  Excision — *continued*
    Radical — *continued*
      Complete, 56633-56640
      Partial, 56630-56632
    Simple
      Complete, 56625
      Partial, 56620
  Lesion
    Destruction, 56501, 56515
  Perineum
    Biopsy, 56605, 56606
    Incision and Drainage, 56405
  Repair
    Obstetric, 59300
Vulvectomy
  Complete, 56625, 56633-56640
  Partial, 56620, 56630-56632
  Radical, 56630-56640
    Complete
      with Bilateral Inguinofemoral Lymphadenectomy, 56637
      with Inguinofemoral, Iliac, and Pelvic Lymphadenectomy, 56640
      with Unilateral Inguinofemoral Lymphadenectomy, 56634
    Partial, 56630-56632
  Simple
    Complete, 56625
    Partial, 56620
  Tricuspid Valve, 33460-33465
V-Y Operation, Bladder, Neck, 51845
V-Y Plasty
  Skin, Adjacent Tissue Transfer, 14000-14350
VZIG, 90396
YF-VAX, 90717

W

WADA Activation Test, 95958
WAIS, 96101-96103
  Psychiatric Diagnosis, Psychological Testing, 96101-96103
Waldius Procedure, 27445
Wall, Abdominal
  See Abdominal Wall
Walsh Modified Radical Prostatectomy, 55810
Warfarin Therapy, 4012F
Warts
  Flat
    Destruction, 17110, 17111
Washing
  Sperm, 58323
Wasserman Test
  Syphilis Test, 86592-86593
Wassmund Procedure
  Osteotomy
    Maxilla, 21206
Water Load Test, 89235
Waterston Procedure, 33755
Water Wart
  Destruction
    Penis, 54050-54060
    Skin, 17110-17111
    Vulva, 56501-56515
Watson-Jones Procedure
  Repair, Ankle, Ligament, 27695-27698
Wave, Ultrasonic Shock
  See Ultrasound
WBC, 85007, 85009, 85025, 85048, 85540
Webbed
  Toe
    Repair, 28280
Wechsler Memory Scales, 96118-96119
Wedge Excision
  Osteotomy, 21122
Wedge Resection
  Ovary, 58920
Weight Recorded, 2001F

Well Child Care, 99381-99384, 99391-99394, 99460-99463
Wellness Behavior
  Alcohol and/or Substance Abuse, 99408-99409
  Assessment, 96150
  Family Intervention, 96154-96155
  Group Intervention, 96153
  Re-assessment, 96151
  Smoking and Tobacco Cessation Counseling, 99406-99407
Wernicke-Posadas Disease, 86490
Wertheim Hysterectomy, 58210
Wertheim Operation, 58210
Westergren Test
  Sedimentation Rate, Blood Cell, 85651, 85652
Western Blot
  HIV, 86689
  Protein, 84181, 84182
  Tissue Analysis, 88371, 88372
West Nile Virus
  Antibody, 86788-86789
Wharton Ducts
  Ligation of, 42510
Wheelchair Management
  Propulsion
    Training, 97542
Wheeler Knife Procedure, 66820
Wheeler Procedure
  Blepharoplasty, 67924
  Discission Secondary Membranous Cataract, 66820
Whipple Procedure, 48150
  without Pancreatojejunostomy, 48152
Whirlpool Therapy, 97022
White Blood Cell
  Alkaline Phosphatase, 85540
  Antibody, 86021
  Count, 85032, 85048, 89055
  Differential, 85004-85007, 85009
  Histamine Release Test, 86343
  Phagocytosis, 86344
  Transfusion, 86950
Whitehead Hemorrhoidectomy, 46260
Whitemead Operation, 46260
Whitman Astragalectomy, 28120, 28130
Whitman Procedure (Hip), 27120
Wick Catheter Technique, 20950
Widal Serum Test
  Agglutinin, Febrile, 86000
Wilke Type Procedure, 42507
Window
  Oval
    Fistula Repair, 69666
  Round
    Fistula Repair, 69667
Window Technic, Pericardial, 33015
Windpipe
  See Trachea
Winiwarter Operation, 47720-47740
Winter Procedure, 54435
Wintrobe Test
  Sedimentation Rate, Blood Cell, 85651, 85652
Wire
  Insertion
    Removal
      Skeletal Traction, 20650
    Intradental
      without Fracture, 21497
Wiring
  Prophylactic Treatment
    Humerus, 24498
Wirsung Duct
  See Pancreatic Duct
Wisconsin Card Sorting Test, 96118-96120
Witzel Operation, 43500, 43520, 43830-43832
Wolff-Parkinson-White Procedure, 33250
Womb
  See Uterus

Wood Alcohol, 84600
Work Hardening, 97545-97546
Work Reintegration, 97545, 97546
Work Related Evaluation Services, 99455, 99456
Worm
  Helminth Antibody, 86682
Wound
  Abdominal wall, 49900
  Closure
    Temporary
      Skin Allograft, 15300-15321
      Skin Xenograft, 15420-15421
  Debridement
    Non-Selective, 97602
    Selective, 97597-97598
  Dehiscence
    Repair
      Abdominal wall, 49900
      Secondary
        Abdominal wall, 49900
        Skin and subcutaneous tissue
          Complex, 13160
          Complicated, 13160
          Extensive, 13160
        Skin and subcutaneous tissue
          Simple, 12020
            with packing, 12021
          Superficial, 12020
            with packing, 12021
    Suture
      Secondary
        Abdominal wall, 49900
        Skin and subcutaneous tissue
          Complex, 13160
          Complicated, 13160
          Extensive, 13160
        Skin and subcutaneous tissue
          Simple, 12020
            with packing, 12021
          Superficial, 12020
            with packing, 12021
  Exploration
    Parathyroidectomy, 60502
    Penetrating
      Abdomen/Flank/Back, 20102
      Chest, 20101
      Extremity, 20103
      Neck, 20100
      Penetrating Trauma, 20100-20103
  Infection
    Incision and Drainage
      Postoperative, 10180
    Negative Pressure Therapy, 97605-97606
  Repair
    Skin
      Complex, 13100-13160
      Intermediate, 12031-12057
      Simple, 12001-12021
      Urethra, 53502-53515
    Secondary
      Abdominal wall, 49900
      Skin and subcutaneous tissue
        Complex, 13160
        Complicated, 13160
        Extensive, 13160
        Simple, 12020
        Simple with packing, 12021
        Superficial, 12020
          with packing, 12021
    Suture
      Bladder, 51860, 51865
      Kidney, 50500
      Trachea
        Cervical, 31800
        Intrathoracic, 31805
      Urethra, 53502-53515
    Vagina
      Repair, 57200, 57210
W-Plasty
  Skin Surgery, Adjacent Tissue Transfer, 14000-14350

Index

Wrist
See Also Arm, Lower; Carpal Bone
Abscess, 25028
Arthrocentesis, 20605
Arthrodesis, 25800
  with Graft, 25810
  with Sliding Graft, 25805
Arthrography, 73115
Arthroplasty, 25332, 25443, 25447
  with Implant, 25441, 25442, 25444, 25445
  Revision, 25449
  Total Replacement, 25446
Arthroscopy
  Diagnostic, 29840
  Surgical, 29843-29848
Arthrotomy, 25040, 25100-25105
  for Repair, 25107
Biopsy, 25065, 25066, 25100, 25101
Bursa
  Excision, 25115, 25116
    Incision and Drainage, 25031
Capsule
  Incision, 25085
Cast, 29085
Cyst, 25130-25136
Decompression, 25020, 25023
Disarticulation, 25920
  Reamputation, 25924
  Revision, 25922
Dislocation
  with Fracture
    Closed Treatment, 25680
    Open Treatment, 25685
  with Manipulation, 25259, 25660, 25675
  Closed Treatment, 25660
  Intercarpal, 25660
    Open Treatment, 25670
  Open Treatment, 25660, 25670, 25676
  Percutaneous Fixation, 25671
  Radiocarpal, 25660
    Open Treatment, 25670
  Radioulnar
    Closed Treatment, 25675
    Percutaneous Fixation, 25671
Excision
  Carpal, 25210, 25215
  Cartilage, 25107
  Tendon Sheath, 25115, 25116
  Tumor, 25075-25078 *[25071, 25073]*
Exploration, 25040, 25101
Fasciotomy, 25020-25025
Fracture, 25645
  with Dislocation, 25680, 25685
  with Manipulation, 25259, 25624, 25635
  Closed Treatment, 25622, 25630
  Open Treatment, 25628
Ganglion Cyst
  Excision, 25111, 25112
Hematoma, 25028
Incision, 25040, 25100-25105
  Tendon Sheath, 25000, 25001
Injection
  Carpal Tunnel
    Therapeutic, 20526
  X-ray, 25246
Joint
  See Radiocarpal Joint
Lesion
  Excision, 25110
  Tendon Sheath, 25000
Magnetic Resonance Imaging, 73221
Reconstruction
  Capsulectomy, 25320
  Capsulorrhaphy, 25320
  Carpal Bone, 25394, 25430
  Realign, 25335
Removal
  Foreign Body, 25040, 25101, 25248
  Implant, 25449
  Loose Body, 25101

Wrist — continued
Removal — continued
  Prosthesis, 25250, 25251
Repair, 25447
  Bone, 25440
  Carpal Bone, 25431
  Muscle, 25260, 25270
    Secondary, 25263, 25265, 25272, 25274
  Tendon, 25260, 25270, 25280-25316
    Secondary, 25263, 25265, 25272, 25274
  Tendon Sheath, 25275
Strapping, 29260
Synovium
  Excision, 25105, 25115-25119
Tendon
  Excision, 25109
Tendon Sheath
  Excision, 25115, 25116
Tenodesis, 25300, 25301
Tenotomy, 25290
Unlisted Services and Procedures, 25999
X-ray, 73100, 73110
  with Contrast, 73115

X

Xa, Coagulation Factor, 85260
X, Coagulation Factor, 85260
X, Cranial Nerve
  See Vagus Nerve
Xenoantibodies, 86308-86310
Xenograft, 15400-15401, 15420-15421, 15430-15431
Xenotransplantation
  Skin, 15400-15431
Xerography, 76150
Xeroradiography, 76150
XI, Coagulation Factor, 85270
XI, Cranial Nerve
  See Accessory Nerve
XII, Coagulation Factor, 85280
XII, Cranial Nerve
  Hypoglossal Nerve
    Anastomosis to Facial Nerve, 64868
XIII, Coagulation Factor, 85290-85291
X-Linked Ichthyoses, 86592-86593
X-ray
  with Contrast
    Ankle, 73615
    Aorta, 0080T-0081T, 75600-75630, 75952, 75953
    Artery
      with Additional Vessels, 75774
      Abdominal, 75726
      Adrenal, 75731, 75733
      Arm, 75710, 75716
      Arteriovenous Shunt, 75791
      Brachial, 75658
      Carotid, 75660-75680
      Coronary, 93556
      Coronary Bypass, 93556
      Head and Neck, 75650
      Leg, 75710, 75716
      Mammary, 75756
      Pelvic, 75736
      Pulmonary, 75741-75746
      Renal, 75722, 75724
      Spine, 75705
      Transcatheter Therapy, 75894-75898
        Angiogram, 75898
        Embolization, 75894
        Infusion, 75896
      Vertebral, 75685
    Bile Duct, 74300-74320
      Calculus Removal, 74327
      Catheterization, 75982
      Drainage, 75980, 75982
      Guide Catheter, 74328, 74330
    Bladder, 74430, 74450, 74455
    Brain, 70010, 70015
    Bronchi, 71040, 71060

X-ray — continued
with Contrast — continued
  Central Venous Access Device, 36598
  Colon
    Barium Enema, 74270, 74280
  Corpora Cavernosa, 74445
  Elbow, 73085
  Epididymis, 74440
  Gallbladder, 74290, 74291
  Gastrointestinal Tract, 74246-74249
  Hip, 73525
  Iliac, 75953
  Iliofemoral Artery, 75630
  Intervertebral Disc
    Cervical, 72285
    Lumbar, 72295
    Thoracic, 72285
  Joint
    Stress Views, 77071
  Kidney
    Cyst, 74470
    Guide Catheter, 74475
  Knee, 73560-73564, 73580
  Lacrimal Duct, 70170
  Larynx, 70373
  Lymph Vessel, 75805, 75807
    Abdomen, 75805, 75807
    Arm, 75801, 75803
    Leg, 75801, 75803
  Mammary Duct, 77053-77054
  Nasolacrimal Duct, 70170
    Guide Dilation, 74485
  Oviduct, 74740
  Pancreas, 74300, 74301, 74305
  Pancreatic Duct
    Guide Catheter, 74329, 74330
  Perineum, 74775
  Peritoneum, 74190
  Salivary Gland, 70390
  Seminal Vesicles, 74440
  Shoulder, 73040
  Spine
    Cervical, 72240
    Lumbosacral, 72265
    Thoracic, 72255
    Total, 72270
  Subtraction Method, 76350
  Temporomandibular Joint (TMJ), 70328-70332
  Ureter
    Guide Catheter, 74480
    Guide Dilation, 74485
  Urethra, 74450, 74455
  Urinary Tract, 74400-74425
  Uterus, 74740
  Vas Deferens, 74440
  Vein
    Adrenal, 75840, 75842
    Arm, 75820, 75822
      Hepatic Portal, 75810, 75885, 75887
    Jugular, 75860
    Leg, 75820, 75822
    Liver, 75889, 75891
    Neck, 75860
    Orbit, 75880
    Renal, 75831, 75833
    Sampling, 75893
    Sinus, 75870
    Skull, 75870, 75872
    Splenic, 75810
    Vena Cava, 75825, 75827
  Wrist, 73115
Abdomen, 74000-74022
Abscess, 76080
Acromioclavicular Joint, 73050
Ankle, 73600, 73610
Arm, Lower, 73090
Arm, Upper, 73092
Artery
  Atherectomy, 75992-75996
    Transluminal, 75992
      Additional, 75993
      Renal, 75994

X-ray — continued
Artery — continued
  Atherectomy — continued
    Transluminal — continued
      Visceral, 75995
Auditory Meatus, 70134
Barium Swallow Test, 3142F, 3200F
Bile Duct
  Guide Dilation, 74360
Body Section, 76100
  Motion, 76101, 76102
Bone
  Age Study, 77072
  Dual Energy Absorptiometry, 77080-77082
  Length Study, 77073
  Osseous Survey, 77074-77076
    Complete, 77075
    Infant, 77076
    Limited, 77074
  Ultrasound, 76977
Breast, 77055-77057
  with Computer-aided Detection, 77051-77052
  Localization Nodule, 77032
Calcaneus, 73650
Chest, 71010-71035
  with Computer-Aided Detection, 0174T-0175T
  with Fluoroscopy, 71090
  Complete (four views)
    with Fluoroscopy, 71034
  Insert Pacemaker, 71090
  Localization, Transbronchial Biopsy
    Insertion Pacemaker, 71090
  Partial (two views)
    with Fluoroscopy, 71023
  Stereo, 71015
Clavicle, 73000
Coccyx, 72220
Consultation, 76140
Duodenum, 74260
Elbow, 73070, 73080
Esophagus, 74220
Eye, 70030
Facial Bones, 70140, 70150
Fallopian Tube, 74742
Femur, 73550
Fibula, 73590
Fingers, 73140
Fistula, 76080
Foot, 73620, 73630
Gastrointestinal Tract, 74240-74245
  Guide Dilation, 74360
  Guide Intubation, 49440, 74340
  Upper, 3142F, 3200F
Hand, 73120, 73130
Head, 70350
Heel, 73650
  Intraoperative, 73530
Hip, 73500-73520, 73540
  Intraoperative, 73530
Humerus, 73060
Intestines, Small, 74245, 74249-74251
  Guide Intubation, 74355
Intravascular Stent, 75960
Jaws, 70355
Joint
  Stress Views, 77071
Knee, 73560-73564, 73580
  Bilateral, 73565
Larynx, 70370
Leg, 73592
Lumen Dilator, 74360
Mandible, 70100, 70110
Mastoids, 70120, 70130
Nasal Bones, 70160
Neck, 70360
Nose to Rectum
  Foreign Body
    Child, 76010
Orbit, 70190, 70200
Pelvis, 72170, 72190, 73540
  Manometry, 74710

X-ray

X-ray — *continued*
  Peritoneum, 74190
  Pharynx, 70370, 74210
  Ribs, 71100-71111
  Sacroiliac Joint, 72200, 72202, 73542
  Sacrum, 72220
  Salivary Gland, 70380
  Scapula, 73010
  Sella Turcica, 70240
  Shoulder, 73020, 73030, 73050
  Sinuses, 70210, 70220
  Sinus Tract, 76080
  Skull, 70250, 70260
  Specimen
    Surgical, 76098
  Spine, 72020, 72090
    Cervical, 72040-72052
    Lumbosacral, 72100-72120

X-ray — *continued*
  Spine — *continued*
    Thoracic, 72070-72074
    Thoracolumbar, 72080
    Total, 72010
  Standing
    Spine, 72069
  Sternum, 71120, 71130
  Teeth, 70300-70320
  Tibia, 73590
  Toe, 73660
  Total Body
    Foreign Body, 76010
  Unlisted Services and Procedures, 76120, 76125
  Upper Gastrointestinal Series (Upper GI Series), 3142F, 3200F
  Wrist, 73100, 73110

X-Ray Tomography, Computed
  See CT Scan
Xylose Absorption Test
  Blood, 84620
  Urine, 84620

Y

Yacoub Procedure, 33864
YAG, 66821
Yeast
  Culture, 87106
Yellow Fever Vaccine, 90717
Yersinia
  Antibody, 86793
Y-Plasty, 51800

Z

Ziegler Procedure
  Discission Secondary Membranous Cataract, 66820
ZIFT, 58976
Zinc, 84630
Zinc Manganese Leucine Aminopeptidase, 83670
ZOSTAVAX, 90736
Z-Plasty, 26121-26125, 41520
Zygoma
  Fracture Treatment, 21355-21366
  Reconstruction, 21270
Zygomatic Arch
  Fracture
    with Manipulation, 21355
    Open Treatment, 21356-21366
  Reconstruction, 21255

Current Procedural Coding Expert – Anesthesia

00100-00126 Anesthesia for Gland, Cleft Lip, Eyelid, ECT, and Ear Procedures

CMS 100-4,4,10.4 — Packaging Rules Under OPPS
CMS 100-4,4,20.6 — Modifier Use Under OPPS
CMS 100-4,4,20.6.4 — Modifiers for Discontinued Services
CMS 100-4,12,50 — Anesthesia Services
CMS 100-4,12,140 — Certified Registered Nurse Anesthetist Services
CMS 100-4,12,140.2 — Payment for CRNA Services
CMS 100-4,12,140.3.2 — Calculation of Anesthesia Time

00100 Anesthesia for procedures on salivary glands, including biopsy
0.00   0.00   Global Days XXX
AMA: 2009, Jan, 11-31; 2008, Jan, 10-25; 2008, Apr, 3-4; 2007, January, 13-27; 2006, March, 15; 2006, December, 10-12; 2006, February, 10-15

00102 Anesthesia for procedures involving plastic repair of cleft lip
0.00   0.00   Global Days XXX
AMA: 2009, Jan, 11-31; 2008, Apr, 3-4

00103 Anesthesia for reconstructive procedures of eyelid (eg, blepharoplasty, ptosis surgery)
0.00   0.00   Global Days XXX
AMA: 2009, Jan, 11-31; 2008, Apr, 3-4; 2006, February, 10-15

00104 Anesthesia for electroconvulsive therapy
0.00   0.00   Global Days XXX
AMA: 2009, Jan, 11-31; 2008, Apr, 3-4; 2006, December, 10-12; 2006, February, 10-15; 2006, March, 15

00120 Anesthesia for procedures on external, middle, and inner ear including biopsy; not otherwise specified
0.00   0.00   Global Days XXX
AMA: 2009, Jan, 11-31; 2008, Apr, 3-4; 2006, December, 10-12; 2006, March, 15; 2006, February, 10-15

00124 otoscopy
0.00   0.00   Global Days XXX
AMA: 2009, Jan, 11-31; 2008, Apr, 3-4; 2006, March, 15; 2006, December, 10-12; 2006, February, 10-15

00126 tympanotomy
0.00   0.00   Global Days XXX
AMA: 2009, Jan, 11-31; 2008, Apr, 3-4; 2006, December, 10-12; 2006, February, 10-15; 2006, March, 15

00140-00148 Anesthesia for Eye Procedures

CMS 100-3,230.1 — Visual Tests Prior to and General Anesthesia During Cataract Surgery
CMS 100-4,4,10.4 — Packaging Rules Under OPPS
CMS 100-4,4,20.6 — Modifier Use Under OPPS
CMS 100-4,4,20.6.4 — Modifiers for Discontinued Services
CMS 100-4,12,50 — Anesthesia Services
CMS 100-4,12,140 — Certified Registered Nurse Anesthetist Services
CMS 100-4,12,140.3.2 — Calculation of Anesthesia Time

00140 Anesthesia for procedures on eye; not otherwise specified
0.00   0.00   Global Days XXX
AMA: 2009, Jan, 11-31; 2008, Apr, 3-4; 2006, March, 15; 2006, December, 10-12; 2006, February, 10-15

00142 lens surgery
0.00   0.00   Global Days XXX
AMA: 2009, Jan, 11-31; 2008, Apr, 3-4; 2006, December, 10-12; 2006, March, 15; 2006, February, 10-15

00144 corneal transplant
0.00   0.00   Global Days XXX
AMA: 2009, Jan, 11-31; 2008, Apr, 3-4; 2006, December, 10-12; 2006, February, 10-15; 2006, March, 15

00145 vitreoretinal surgery
0.00   0.00   Global Days XXX
AMA: 2009, Jan, 11-31; 2008, Apr, 3-4; 2006, December, 10-12; 2006, March, 15; 2006, February, 10-15

00147 iridectomy
0.00   0.00   Global Days XXX
AMA: 2009, Jan, 11-31; 2008, Apr, 3-4; 2006, December, 10-12; 2006, March, 15; 2006, February, 10-15

00148 ophthalmoscopy
0.00   0.00   Global Days XXX
AMA: 2009, Jan, 11-31; 2008, Apr, 3-4; 2006, December, 10-12; 2006, March, 15; 2006, February, 10-15

00160-00326 Anesthesia for Face and Head Procedures

CMS 100-4,4,10.4 — Packaging Rules Under OPPS
CMS 100-4,4,20.6 — Modifier Use Under OPPS
CMS 100-4,12,50 — Anesthesia Services
CMS 100-4,12,140 — Certified Registered Nurse Anesthetist Services
CMS 100-4,12,140.2 — Payment for CRNA Services
CMS 100-4,12,140.3.2 — Calculation of Anesthesia Time

00160 Anesthesia for procedures on nose and accessory sinuses; not otherwise specified
0.00   0.00   Global Days XXX
AMA: 2009, Jan, 11-31; 2008, Apr, 3-4; 2006, December, 10-12; 2006, March, 15; 2006, February, 10-15

00162 radical surgery
0.00   0.00   Global Days XXX
AMA: 2009, Jan, 11-31; 2008, Apr, 3-4; 2006, December, 10-12; 2006, February, 10-15; 2006, March, 15

00164 biopsy, soft tissue
0.00   0.00   Global Days XXX
AMA: 2009, Jan, 11-31; 2008, Apr, 3-4; 2006, March, 15; 2006, December, 10-12; 2006, February, 10-15

00170 Anesthesia for intraoral procedures, including biopsy; not otherwise specified
0.00   0.00   Global Days XXX
AMA: 2009, Jan, 11-31; 2008, Apr, 3-4; 2006, December, 10-12; 2006, March, 15; 2006, February, 10-15

00172 repair of cleft palate
0.00   0.00   Global Days XXX
AMA: 2009, Jan, 11-31; 2008, Apr, 3-4; 2006, December, 10-12; 2006, February, 10-15; 2006, March, 15

00174 excision of retropharyngeal tumor
0.00   0.00   Global Days XXX
AMA: 2009, Jan, 11-31; 2008, Apr, 3-4; 2006, March, 15; 2006, December, 10-12; 2006, February, 10-15

00176 radical surgery
0.00   0.00   Global Days XXX
AMA: 2009, Jan, 11-31; 2008, Apr, 3-4; 2006, December, 10-12; 2006, March, 15; 2006, February, 10-15

00190 Anesthesia for procedures on facial bones or skull; not otherwise specified
0.00   0.00   Global Days XXX
AMA: 2009, Jan, 11-31; 2008, Apr, 3-4; 2006, December, 10-12; 2006, February, 10-15; 2006, March, 15

00192 radical surgery (including prognathism)
0.00   0.00   Global Days XXX
AMA: 2009, Jan, 11-31; 2008, Apr, 3-4; 2006, December, 10-12; 2006, March, 15; 2006, February, 10-15

00210 Anesthesia for intracranial procedures; not otherwise specified
0.00   0.00   Global Days XXX
AMA: 2009, Jan, 11-31; 2008, Apr, 3-4; 2006, March, 15; 2006, December, 10-12; 2006, February, 10-15

● New Code   ▲ Revised Code   M Maternity   A Age   Unlisted   Not Covered   # Resequenced
CCI   + Add-on   ⊘ Mod 51 Exempt   Mod 63 Exempt   ⊙ Mod Sedation   PQRI

© 2009 Publisher (Blue Ink)   CPT only © 2009 American Medical Association. All Rights Reserved. (Black Ink)   Medicare (Red Ink)

00211

00211 craniotomy or craniectomy for evacuation of hematoma
0.00 0.00 Global Days XXX
AMA: 2009, Jan, 11-31

00212 subdural taps
0.00 0.00 Global Days XXX
AMA: 2009, Jan, 11-31; 2008, Apr, 3-4; 2006, December, 10-12; 2006, February, 10-15; 2006, March, 15

00214 burr holes, including ventriculography
0.00 0.00 Global Days XXX
AMA: 2009, Jan, 11-31; 2008, Apr, 3-4; 2006, December, 10-12; 2006, March, 15; 2006, February, 10-15

00215 cranioplasty or elevation of depressed skull fracture, extradural (simple or compound)
0.00 0.00 Global Days XXX
AMA: 2009, Jan, 11-31; 2008, Apr, 3-4; 2006, March, 15; 2006, December, 10-12; 2006, February, 10-15

00216 vascular procedures
0.00 0.00 Global Days XXX
AMA: 2009, Jan, 11-31; 2008, Apr, 3-4; 2006, March, 15; 2006, December, 10-12; 2006, February, 10-15

00218 procedures in sitting position
0.00 0.00 Global Days XXX
AMA: 2009, Jan, 11-31; 2008, Apr, 3-4; 2006, December, 10-12; 2006, March, 15; 2006, February, 10-15

00220 cerebrospinal fluid shunting procedures
0.00 0.00 Global Days XXX
AMA: 2009, Jan, 11-31; 2008, Apr, 3-4; 2006, December, 10-12; 2006, February, 10-15; 2006, March, 15

00222 electrocoagulation of intracranial nerve
0.00 0.00 Global Days XXX
AMA: 2009, Jan, 11-31; 2008, Apr, 3-4; 2006, December, 10-12; 2006, March, 15; 2006, February, 10-15

00300 Anesthesia for all procedures on the integumentary system, muscles and nerves of head, neck, and posterior trunk, not otherwise specified
0.00 0.00 Global Days XXX
AMA: 2009, Jan, 11-31; 2008, Apr, 3-4; 2006, March, 15; 2006, December, 10-12; 2006, February, 10-15

00320 Anesthesia for all procedures on esophagus, thyroid, larynx, trachea and lymphatic system of neck; not otherwise specified, age 1 year or older
0.00 0.00 Global Days XXX
AMA: 2009, Jan, 11-31; 2008, Apr, 3-4; 2006, December, 10-12; 2006, February, 10-15; 2006, March, 15

00322 needle biopsy of thyroid
EXCLUDES Cervical spine and spinal cord procedures (00600, 00604, 00670)
0.00 0.00 Global Days XXX
AMA: 2009, Jan, 11-31; 2008, Apr, 3-4; 2006, December, 10-12; 2006, March, 15; 2006, February, 10-15

00326 Anesthesia for all procedures on the larynx and trachea in children younger than 1 year of age
Do not report with (99100)
0.00 0.00 Global Days XXX
AMA: 2009, Jan, 11-31; 2008, Apr, 3-4; 2006, December, 10-12; 2006, February, 10-15; 2006, March, 15

00350-00352 Anesthesia for Neck Vessel Procedures

CMS 100-4,4,10.4 — Packaging Rules Under OPPS
CMS 100-4,4,20.6 — Modifier Use Under OPPS
CMS 100-4,4,20.6.4 — Modifiers for Discontinued Services
CMS 100-4,12,50 — Anesthesia Services
CMS 100-4,12,140 — Certified Registered Nurse Anesthetist Services
CMS 100-4,12,140.2 — Payment for CRNA Services
CMS 100-4,12,140.3.2 — Calculation of Anesthesia Time
EXCLUDES Arteriography (01916)

00350 Anesthesia for procedures on major vessels of neck; not otherwise specified
0.00 0.00 Global Days XXX
AMA: 2009, Jan, 11-31; 2008, Apr, 3-4; 2006, December, 10-12; 2006, March, 15; 2006, February, 10-15

00352 simple ligation
0.00 0.00 Global Days XXX
AMA: 2009, Jan, 11-31; 2008, Apr, 3-4; 2006, March, 15; 2006, February, 10-15

00400-00529 Anesthesia for Chest Procedures

CMS 100-4,4,10.4 — Packaging Rules Under OPPS
CMS 100-4,4,20.6 — Modifier Use Under OPPS
CMS 100-4,4,20.6.4 — Modifiers for Discontinued Services
CMS 100-4,12,50 — Anesthesia Services
CMS 100-4,12,140 — Certified Registered Nurse Anesthetist Services
CMS 100-4,12,140.2 — Payment for CRNA Services
CMS 100-4,12,140.3.2 — Calculation of Anesthesia Time

00400 Anesthesia for procedures on the integumentary system on the extremities, anterior trunk and perineum; not otherwise specified
0.00 0.00 Global Days XXX
AMA: 2009, Jan, 11-31; 2008, Apr, 3-4; 2006, December, 10-12; 2006, March, 15; 2006, February, 10-15

00402 reconstructive procedures on breast (eg, reduction or augmentation mammoplasty, muscle flaps)
0.00 0.00 Global Days XXX
AMA: 2009, Jan, 11-31; 2008, Apr, 3-4; 2006, December, 10-12; 2006, February, 10-15; 2006, March, 15

00404 radical or modified radical procedures on breast
0.00 0.00 Global Days XXX
AMA: 2009, Jan, 11-31; 2008, Apr, 3-4; 2006, December, 10-12; 2006, March, 15; 2006, February, 10-15

00406 radical or modified radical procedures on breast with internal mammary node dissection
0.00 0.00 Global Days XXX
AMA: 2009, Jan, 11-31; 2008, Apr, 3-4; 2006, December, 10-12; 2006, March, 15; 2006, February, 10-15

00410 electrical conversion of arrhythmias
0.00 0.00 Global Days XXX
AMA: 2009, Jan, 11-31; 2008, Apr, 3-4; 2006, December, 10-12; 2006, February, 10-15; 2006, March, 15

00450 Anesthesia for procedures on clavicle and scapula; not otherwise specified
0.00 0.00 Global Days XXX
AMA: 2009, Jan, 11-31; 2008, Apr, 3-4; 2006, December, 10-12; 2006, March, 15; 2006, February, 10-15

00452 radical surgery
0.00 0.00 Global Days XXX
AMA: 2009, Jan, 11-31; 2008, Apr, 3-4; 2006, December, 10-12; 2006, March, 15; 2006, February, 10-15

Current Procedural Coding Expert – Anesthesia

00454 biopsy of clavicle
0.00 0.00 Global Days XXX
AMA: 2009, Jan, 11-31; 2008, Apr, 3-4; 2006, December, 10-12; 2006, February, 10-15; 2006, March, 15

00470 Anesthesia for partial rib resection; not otherwise specified
0.00 0.00 Global Days XXX
AMA: 2009, Jan, 11-31; 2008, Apr, 3-4; 2006, December, 10-12; 2006, March, 15; 2006, February, 10-15

00472 thoracoplasty (any type)
0.00 0.00 Global Days XXX
AMA: 2009, Jan, 11-31; 2008, Apr, 3-4; 2006, March, 15; 2006, December, 10-12; 2006, February, 10-15

00474 radical procedures (eg, pectus excavatum)
0.00 0.00 Global Days XXX
AMA: 2009, Jan, 11-31; 2008, Apr, 3-4; 2006, February, 10-15; 2006, December, 10-12; 2006, March, 15

00500 Anesthesia for all procedures on esophagus
0.00 0.00 Global Days XXX
AMA: 2009, Jan, 11-31; 2008, Apr, 3-4; 2006, February, 10-15; 2006, December, 10-12; 2006, March, 15

00520 Anesthesia for closed chest procedures; (including bronchoscopy) not otherwise specified
0.00 0.00 Global Days XXX
AMA: 2009, Jan, 11-31; 2008, Apr, 3-4; 2006, February, 10-15; 2006, December, 10-12; 2006, March, 15

00522 needle biopsy of pleura
0.00 0.00 Global Days XXX
AMA: 2009, Jan, 11-31; 2008, Apr, 3-4; 2006, December, 10-12; 2006, March, 15; 2006, February, 10-15

00524 pneumocentesis
0.00 0.00 Global Days XXX
AMA: 2009, Jan, 11-31; 2008, Apr, 3-4; 2006, December, 10-12; 2006, March, 15; 2006, February, 10-15

00528 mediastinoscopy and diagnostic thoracoscopy not utilizing 1 lung ventilation
EXCLUDES Transbronchial reconstruction (00539)
0.00 0.00 Global Days XXX
AMA: 2009, Jan, 11-31; 2008, Apr, 3-4; 2006, February, 10-15; 2006, December, 10-12; 2006, March, 15

00529 mediastinoscopy and diagnostic thoracoscopy utilizing 1 lung ventilation
0.00 0.00 Global Days XXX
AMA: 2009, Jan, 11-31; 2008, Apr, 3-4; 2006, December, 10-12; 2006, February, 10-15; 2006, March, 15

00530 Anesthesia for Cardiac Pacemaker Procedure

CMS Certified Registered Nurse Anesthetist Services
CMS 100-4,4,10.4 Packaging Rules Under OPPS
CMS 100-4,4,20.6 Modifier Use Under OPPS
CMS 100-4,4,20.6.4 Modifiers for Discontinued Services
CMS 100-4,12,50 Anesthesia Services
CMS 100-4,12,140.2 Payment for CRNA Services
CMS 100-4,12,140.3.2 Calculation of Anesthesia Time

00530 Anesthesia for permanent transvenous pacemaker insertion
0.00 0.00 Global Days XXX
AMA: 2009, Jan, 11-31; 2008, Apr, 3-4; 2006, December, 10-12; 2006, March, 15; 2006, February, 10-15

00532-00550 Anesthesia for Heart and Lung Procedures

CMS 100-4,4,10.4 Packaging Rules Under OPPS
CMS 100-4,4,20.6 Modifier Use Under OPPS
CMS 100-4,12,50 Anesthesia Services
CMS 100-4,12,140 Certified Registered Nurse Anesthetist Services
CMS 100-4,12,140.2 Payment for CRNA Services
CMS 100-4,12,140.3.2 Calculation of Anesthesia Time

00532 Anesthesia for access to central venous circulation
0.00 0.00 Global Days XXX
AMA: 2009, Jan, 11-31; 2008, Apr, 3-4; 2006, February, 10-15; 2006, December, 10-12; 2006, March, 15

00534 Anesthesia for transvenous insertion or replacement of pacing cardioverter-defibrillator
EXCLUDES Transthoracic approach (00560)
0.00 0.00 Global Days XXX
AMA: 2009, Jan, 11-31; 2008, Apr, 3-4; 2006, February, 10-15; 2006, December, 10-12; 2006, March, 15

00537 Anesthesia for cardiac electrophysiologic procedures including radiofrequency ablation
0.00 0.00 Global Days XXX
AMA: 2009, Jan, 11-31; 2008, Apr, 3-4; 2006, February, 10-15; 2006, December, 10-12; 2006, March, 15

00539 Anesthesia for tracheobronchial reconstruction
0.00 0.00 Global Days XXX
AMA: 2009, Jan, 11-31; 2008, Apr, 3-4; 2006, December, 10-12; 2006, February, 10-15; 2006, March, 15

00540 Anesthesia for thoracotomy procedures involving lungs, pleura, diaphragm, and mediastinum (including surgical thoracoscopy); not otherwise specified
EXCLUDES Thoracic spine and spinal cord procedures via anterior transthoracic approach (00625-00626)
0.00 0.00 Global Days XXX
AMA: 2009, Jan, 11-31; 2008, Apr, 3-4; 2006, February, 10-15; 2006, December, 10-12; 2006, March, 15

00541 utilizing 1 lung ventilation
EXCLUDES Thoracic spine and spinal cord procedures via anterior transthoracic approach (00625-00626)
0.00 0.00 Global Days XXX
AMA: 2009, Jan, 11-31; 2008, Apr, 3-4; 2006, February, 10-15; 2006, December, 10-12; 2006, March, 15

00542 decortication
0.00 0.00 Global Days XXX
AMA: 2009, Jan, 11-31; 2008, Apr, 3-4; 2006, December, 10-12; 2006, March, 15; 2006, February, 10-15

00546 pulmonary resection with thoracoplasty
0.00 0.00 Global Days XXX
AMA: 2009, Jan, 11-31; 2008, Apr, 3-4; 2006, February, 10-15; 2006, December, 10-12; 2006, March, 15

00548 intrathoracic procedures on the trachea and bronchi
0.00 0.00 Global Days XXX
AMA: 2009, Jan, 11-31; 2008, Apr, 3-4; 2006, February, 10-15; 2006, December, 10-12; 2006, March, 15

00550 Anesthesia for sternal debridement
0.00 0.00 Global Days XXX
AMA: 2009, Jan, 11-31; 2008, Apr, 3-4; 2006, February, 10-15; 2006, December, 10-12; 2006, March, 15

● New Code   ▲ Revised Code   M Maternity   A Age   Unlisted   Not Covered   # Resequenced
CCI   + Add-on   ⊘ Mod 51 Exempt   Mod 63 Exempt   ⊙ Mod Sedation   PQRI

© 2009 Publisher (Blue Ink)   CPT only © 2009 American Medical Association. All Rights Reserved. (Black Ink)   Medicare (Red Ink)

00560–00580 Anesthesia for Open Heart Procedures

CMS 100-3,160.9 — Electroencephalographic (EEG) Monitoring During Open-Heart Surgery
CMS 100-4,12,50 — Anesthesia Services
CMS 100-4,12,140 — Certified Registered Nurse Anesthetist Services
CMS 100-4,12,140.2 — Payment for CRNA Services
CMS 100-4,12,140.3.2 — Calculation of Anesthesia Time

00560 Anesthesia for procedures on heart, pericardial sac, and great vessels of chest; without pump oxygenator
 0.00 0.00 Global Days XXX
 AMA: 2009, Jan, 11-31; 2008, Apr, 3-4; 2006, February, 10-15; 2006, December, 10-12; 2006, March, 15

00561 with pump oxygenator, younger than 1 year of age
 Do not report with (99100, 99116, 99135)
 0.00 0.00 Global Days XXX
 AMA: 2009, Jan, 11-31; 2008, Apr, 3-4; 2006, December, 10-12; 2006, February, 10-15; 2006, March, 15

00562 with pump oxygenator, age 1 year or older, for all non-coronary bypass procedures (eg, valve procedures) or for re-operation for coronary bypass more than 1 month after original operation
 0.00 0.00 Global Days XXX
 AMA: 2009, Jan, 11-31; 2008, Apr, 3-4; 2006, February, 10-15; 2006, December, 10-12; 2006, March, 15

00563 with pump oxygenator with hypothermic circulatory arrest
 0.00 0.00 Global Days XXX
 AMA: 2009, Jan, 11-31; 2008, Apr, 3-4; 2006, February, 10-15; 2006, December, 10-12; 2006, March, 15

00566 Anesthesia for direct coronary artery bypass grafting; without pump oxygenator
 0.00 0.00 Global Days XXX
 AMA: 2009, Jan, 11-31; 2008, Apr, 3-4; 2006, December, 10-12; 2006, February, 10-15; 2006, March, 15

00567 with pump oxygenator
 0.00 0.00 Global Days XXX
 AMA: 2009, Jan, 11-31

00580 Anesthesia for heart transplant or heart/lung transplant
 0.00 0.00 Global Days XXX
 AMA: 2009, Jan, 11-31; 2008, Apr, 3-4; 2006, December, 10-12; 2006, February, 10-15; 2006, March, 15

00600–00670 Anesthesia for Spinal Procedures

CMS 100-4,4,10.4 — Packaging Rules Under OPPS
CMS 100-4,4,20.6 — Modifier Use Under OPPS
CMS 100-4,4,20.6.4 — Modifiers for Discontinued Services
CMS 100-4,12,50 — Anesthesia Services
CMS 100-4,12,140 — Certified Registered Nurse Anesthetist Services
CMS 100-4,12,140.2 — Payment for CRNA Services
CMS 100-4,12,140.3.2 — Calculation of Anesthesia Time

00600 Anesthesia for procedures on cervical spine and cord; not otherwise specified
 EXCLUDES Percutaneous image-guided spinal cord anesthesia services (01935-01936)
 0.00 0.00 Global Days XXX
 AMA: 2009, Jan, 11-31; 2008, Jan, 10-25; 2008, Apr, 3-4; 2006, March, 15; 2006, December, 10-12; 2006, February, 10-15

00604 procedures with patient in the sitting position
 0.00 0.00 Global Days XXX
 AMA: 2009, Jan, 11-31; 2008, Apr, 3-4; 2006, December, 10-12; 2006, February, 10-15; 2006, March, 15

00620 Anesthesia for procedures on thoracic spine and cord; not otherwise specified
 0.00 0.00 Global Days XXX
 AMA: 2009, Jan, 11-31; 2008, Jan, 10-25; 2008, Apr, 3-4; 2007, March, 9-11; 2006, December, 10-12; 2006, February, 10-15; 2006, March, 15

00622 thoracolumbar sympathectomy
 0.00 0.00 Global Days XXX
 AMA: 2009, Jan, 11-31; 2008, Jan, 10-25; 2008, Apr, 3-4; 2007, March, 9-11; 2006, February, 10-15; 2006, March, 15; 2006, December, 10-12

00625 Anesthesia for procedures on the thoracic spine and cord, via an anterior transthoracic approach; not utilizing 1 lung ventilation
 EXCLUDES Anesthesia services for thoracotomy procedures other than spine (00540-00541)
 0.00 0.00 Global Days XXX
 AMA: 2009, Jan, 11-31; 2008, Jan, 10-25; 2008, Apr, 3-4; 2007, March, 9-11; 2006, December, 10-12

00626 utilizing 1 lung ventilation
 EXCLUDES Anesthesia services for thoracotomy procedures other than spine (00540-00541)
 0.00 0.00 Global Days XXX
 AMA: 2009, Jan, 11-31; 2008, Jan, 10-25; 2008, Apr, 3-4; 2007, March, 9-11; 2006, December, 10-12

00630 Anesthesia for procedures in lumbar region; not otherwise specified
 0.00 0.00 Global Days XXX
 AMA: 2009, Jan, 11-31; 2008, Apr, 3-4; 2006, February, 10-15; 2006, December, 10-12; 2006, March, 15

00632 lumbar sympathectomy
 0.00 0.00 Global Days XXX
 AMA: 2009, Jan, 11-31; 2008, Apr, 3-4; 2006, December, 10-12; 2006, March, 15; 2006, February, 10-15

00634 chemonucleolysis
 0.00 0.00 Global Days XXX
 AMA: 2009, Jan, 11-31; 2008, Apr, 3-4; 2006, December, 10-12; 2006, February, 10-15; 2006, March, 15

00635 diagnostic or therapeutic lumbar puncture
 0.00 0.00 Global Days XXX
 AMA: 2009, Jan, 11-31; 2008, Apr, 3-4; 2006, February, 10-15; 2006, December, 10-12; 2006, March, 15

00640 Anesthesia for manipulation of the spine or for closed procedures on the cervical, thoracic or lumbar spine
 0.00 0.00 Global Days XXX
 AMA: 2009, Jan, 11-31; 2008, Apr, 3-4; 2006, February, 10-15; 2006, December, 10-12; 2006, March, 15

00670 Anesthesia for extensive spine and spinal cord procedures (eg, spinal instrumentation or vascular procedures)
 0.00 0.00 Global Days XXX
 AMA: 2009, Jan, 11-31; 2008, Apr, 3-4; 2006, February, 10-15; 2006, December, 10-12; 2006, March, 15

Current Procedural Coding Expert – Anesthesia 00836

00700-00882 Anesthesia for Abdominal Procedures

CMS 100-4,4,10.4	Packaging Rules Under OPPS
CMS 100-4,4,20.6	Modifier Use Under OPPS
CMS 100-4,4,20.6.4	Modifiers for Discontinued Services
CMS 100-4,12,50	Anesthesia Services
CMS 100-4,12,140	Certified Registered Nurse Anesthetist Services
CMS 100-4,12,140.2	Payment for CRNA Services
CMS 100-4,12,140.3.2	Calculation of Anesthesia Time

00700 Anesthesia for procedures on upper anterior abdominal wall; not otherwise specified
0.00 0.00 Global Days XXX
AMA: 2009, Jan, 11-31; 2008, Apr, 3-4; 2006, December, 10-12; 2006, March, 15; 2006, February, 10-15

00702 percutaneous liver biopsy
0.00 0.00 Global Days XXX
AMA: 2009, Jan, 11-31; 2008, Apr, 3-4; 2006, February, 10-15; 2006, December, 10-12; 2006, March, 15

00730 Anesthesia for procedures on upper posterior abdominal wall
0.00 0.00 Global Days XXX
AMA: 2009, Jan, 11-31; 2008, Apr, 3-4; 2006, February, 10-15; 2006, March, 15; 2006, December, 10-12

00740 Anesthesia for upper gastrointestinal endoscopic procedures, endoscope introduced proximal to duodenum
0.00 0.00 Global Days XXX
AMA: 2009, Jan, 11-31; 2008, Apr, 3-4; 2006, December, 10-12; 2006, March, 15; 2006, February, 10-15

00750 Anesthesia for hernia repairs in upper abdomen; not otherwise specified
0.00 0.00 Global Days XXX
AMA: 2009, Jan, 11-31; 2008, Apr, 3-4; 2006, February, 10-15; 2006, December, 10-12; 2006, March, 15

00752 lumbar and ventral (incisional) hernias and/or wound dehiscence
0.00 0.00 Global Days XXX
AMA: 2009, Jan, 11-31; 2008, Apr, 3-4; 2006, February, 10-15; 2006, December, 10-12; 2006, March, 15

00754 omphalocele
0.00 0.00 Global Days XXX
AMA: 2009, Jan, 11-31; 2008, Apr, 3-4; 2006, December, 10-12; 2006, February, 10-15; 2006, March, 15

00756 transabdominal repair of diaphragmatic hernia
0.00 0.00 Global Days XXX
AMA: 2009, Jan, 11-31; 2008, Apr, 3-4; 2006, December, 10-12; 2006, March, 15; 2006, February, 10-15

00770 Anesthesia for all procedures on major abdominal blood vessels
0.00 0.00 Global Days XXX
AMA: 2009, Jan, 11-31; 2008, Apr, 3-4; 2006, February, 10-15; 2006, December, 10-12; 2006, March, 15

00790 Anesthesia for intraperitoneal procedures in upper abdomen including laparoscopy; not otherwise specified
0.00 0.00 Global Days XXX
AMA: 2009, Jan, 11-31; 2008, Apr, 3-4; 2006, December, 10-12; 2006, February, 10-15; 2006, March, 15

00792 partial hepatectomy or management of liver hemorrhage (excluding liver biopsy)
0.00 0.00 Global Days XXX
AMA: 2009, Jan, 11-31; 2008, Apr, 3-4; 2006, December, 10-12; 2006, March, 15; 2006, February, 10-15

00794 pancreatectomy, partial or total (eg, Whipple procedure)
0.00 0.00 Global Days XXX
AMA: 2009, Jan, 11-31; 2008, Apr, 3-4; 2006, December, 10-12; 2006, February, 10-15; 2006, March, 15

00796 liver transplant (recipient)
EXCLUDES Physiological support during liver harvest (01990)
0.00 0.00 Global Days XXX
AMA: 2009, Jan, 11-31; 2008, Apr, 3-4; 2006, December, 10-12; 2006, March, 15; 2006, February, 10-15

00797 gastric restrictive procedure for morbid obesity
0.00 0.00 Global Days XXX
AMA: 2009, Jan, 11-31; 2008, Apr, 3-4; 2006, February, 10-15; 2006, December, 10-12; 2006, March, 15

00800 Anesthesia for procedures on lower anterior abdominal wall; not otherwise specified
0.00 0.00 Global Days XXX
AMA: 2009, Jan, 11-31; 2008, Apr, 3-4; 2006, December, 10-12; 2006, February, 10-15; 2006, March, 15

00802 panniculectomy
0.00 0.00 Global Days XXX
AMA: 2009, Jan, 11-31; 2008, Apr, 3-4; 2006, December, 10-12; 2006, March, 15; 2006, February, 10-15

00810 Anesthesia for lower intestinal endoscopic procedures, endoscope introduced distal to duodenum
0.00 0.00 Global Days XXX
AMA: 2009, Jan, 11-31; 2008, Apr, 3-4; 2006, February, 10-15; 2006, December, 10-12; 2006, March, 15

00820 Anesthesia for procedures on lower posterior abdominal wall
0.00 0.00 Global Days XXX
AMA: 2009, Jan, 11-31; 2008, Apr, 3-4; 2006, December, 10-12; 2006, February, 10-15; 2006, March, 15

00830 Anesthesia for hernia repairs in lower abdomen; not otherwise specified
EXCLUDES Anesthesia for hernia repairs on infants one year old or younger (00834, 00836)
0.00 0.00 Global Days XXX
AMA: 2009, Jan, 11-31; 2008, Apr, 3-4; 2006, December, 10-12; 2006, March, 15; 2006, February, 10-15

00832 ventral and incisional hernias
EXCLUDES Anesthesia for hernia repairs on infants one year old or younger (00834, 00836)
0.00 0.00 Global Days XXX
AMA: 2009, Jan, 11-31; 2008, Apr, 3-4; 2006, December, 10-12; 2006, February, 10-15; 2006, March, 15

00834 Anesthesia for hernia repairs in the lower abdomen not otherwise specified, younger than 1 year of age
Do not report with (99100)
0.00 0.00 Global Days XXX
AMA: 2009, Jan, 11-31; 2008, Apr, 3-4; 2006, December, 10-12; 2006, February, 10-15; 2006, March, 15

00836 Anesthesia for hernia repairs in the lower abdomen not otherwise specified, infants younger than 37 weeks gestational age at birth and younger than 50 weeks gestational age at time of surgery
Do not report with (99100)
0.00 0.00 Global Days XXX
AMA: 2009, Jan, 11-31; 2008, Apr, 3-4; 2006, December, 10-12; 2006, February, 10-15; 2006, March, 15

● New Code ▲ Revised Code M Maternity A Age Unlisted Not Covered # Resequenced
CCI + Add-on Mod 51 Exempt Mod 63 Exempt Mod Sedation PQRI

© 2009 Publisher (Blue Ink) CPT only © 2009 American Medical Association. All Rights Reserved. (Black Ink) Medicare (Red Ink)

00840

00840	Anesthesia for intraperitoneal procedures in lower abdomen including laparoscopy; not otherwise specified N P0 🚗 0.00 ✂ 0.00 **Global Days XXX** **AMA:** 2009, Jan, 11-31; 2008, Apr, 3-4; 2006, December, 10-12; 2006, March, 15; 2006, February, 10-15
00842	amniocentesis M ♀ N P0 🚗 0.00 ✂ 0.00 **Global Days XXX** **AMA:** 2009, Jan, 11-31; 2008, Apr, 3-4; 2006, February, 10-15; 2006, December, 10-12; 2006, March, 15
00844	abdominoperineal resection C P0 🚗 0.00 ✂ 0.00 **Global Days XXX** **AMA:** 2009, Jan, 11-31; 2008, Apr, 3-4; 2006, December, 10-12; 2006, March, 15; 2006, February, 10-15
00846	radical hysterectomy ♀ C P0 🚗 0.00 ✂ 0.00 **Global Days XXX** **AMA:** 2009, Jan, 11-31; 2008, Apr, 3-4; 2006, December, 10-12; 2006, March, 15; 2006, February, 10-15
00848	pelvic exenteration C P0 🚗 0.00 ✂ 0.00 **Global Days XXX** **AMA:** 2009, Jan, 11-31; 2008, Apr, 3-4; 2006, December, 10-12; 2006, February, 10-15; 2006, March, 15
00851	tubal ligation/transection ♀ N P0 🚗 0.00 ✂ 0.00 **Global Days XXX** **AMA:** 2009, Jan, 11-31; 2008, Apr, 3-4; 2006, February, 10-15; 2006, December, 10-12; 2006, March, 15
00860	Anesthesia for extraperitoneal procedures in lower abdomen, including urinary tract; not otherwise specified N P0 🚗 0.00 ✂ 0.00 **Global Days XXX** **AMA:** 2009, Jan, 11-31; 2008, Apr, 3-4; 2006, December, 10-12; 2006, February, 10-15; 2006, March, 15
00862	renal procedures, including upper one-third of ureter, or donor nephrectomy N P0 🚗 0.00 ✂ 0.00 **Global Days XXX** **AMA:** 2009, Jan, 11-31; 2008, Apr, 3-4; 2006, December, 10-12; 2006, March, 15; 2006, February, 10-15
00864	total cystectomy C P0 🚗 0.00 ✂ 0.00 **Global Days XXX** **AMA:** 2009, Jan, 11-31; 2008, Apr, 3-4; 2006, February, 10-15; 2006, December, 10-12; 2006, March, 15
00865	radical prostatectomy (suprapubic, retropubic) ♂ C P0 🚗 0.00 ✂ 0.00 **Global Days XXX** **AMA:** 2009, Jan, 11-31; 2008, Apr, 3-4; 2006, February, 10-15; 2006, March, 15; 2006, December, 10-12
00866	adrenalectomy C P0 🚗 0.00 ✂ 0.00 **Global Days XXX** **AMA:** 2009, Jan, 11-31; 2008, Apr, 3-4; 2006, December, 10-12; 2006, March, 15; 2006, February, 10-15
00868	renal transplant (recipient) C P0 **EXCLUDES** Anesthesia for donor nephrectomy (00862) Harvesting kidney from brain dead patient (01990) 🚗 0.00 ✂ 0.00 **Global Days XXX** **AMA:** 2009, Jan, 11-31; 2008, Apr, 3-4; 2006, December, 10-12; 2006, February, 10-15
00870	cystolithotomy N P0 🚗 0.00 ✂ 0.00 **Global Days XXX** **AMA:** 2009, Jan, 11-31; 2008, Apr, 3-4; 2006, December, 10-12; 2006, February, 10-15; 2006, March, 15
00872	Anesthesia for lithotripsy, extracorporeal shock wave; with water bath N P0 🚗 0.00 ✂ 0.00 **Global Days XXX** **AMA:** 2009, Jan, 11-31; 2008, Apr, 3-4; 2006, December, 10-12; 2006, February, 10-15; 2006, March, 15
00873	without water bath N P0 🚗 0.00 ✂ 0.00 **Global Days XXX** **AMA:** 2009, Jan, 11-31; 2008, Apr, 3-4; 2006, February, 10-15; 2006, December, 10-12; 2006, March, 15
00880	Anesthesia for procedures on major lower abdominal vessels; not otherwise specified N P0 🚗 0.00 ✂ 0.00 **Global Days XXX** **AMA:** 2009, Jan, 11-31; 2008, Apr, 3-4; 2006, December, 10-12; 2006, March, 15; 2006, February, 10-15
00882	inferior vena cava ligation C P0 🚗 0.00 ✂ 0.00 **Global Days XXX** **AMA:** 2009, Jan, 11-31; 2008, Apr, 3-4; 2006, February, 10-15; 2006, December, 10-12; 2006, March, 15

00902-00952 Anesthesia for Genitourinary Procedures

CMS 100-4,4,10.4 — Packaging Rules Under OPPS
CMS 100-4,4,20.6 — Modifier Use Under OPPS
CMS 100-4,4,20.6.4 — Modifiers for Discontinued Services
CMS 100-4,12,50 — Anesthesia Services
CMS 100-4,12,140 — Certified Registered Nurse Anesthetist Services
CMS 100-4,12,140.2 — Payment for CRNA Services
CMS 100-4,12,140.3.2 — Calculation of Anesthesia Time

EXCLUDES Perineal procedures on skin, muscles, and nerves (00300, 00400)

00902	Anesthesia for; anorectal procedure N P0 🚗 0.00 ✂ 0.00 **Global Days XXX** **AMA:** 2009, Jan, 11-31; 2008, Apr, 3-4; 2006, December, 10-12; 2006, February, 10-15; 2006, March, 15
00904	radical perineal procedure C P0 🚗 0.00 ✂ 0.00 **Global Days XXX** **AMA:** 2009, Jan, 11-31; 2008, Apr, 3-4; 2006, December, 10-12; 2006, March, 15; 2006, February, 10-15
00906	vulvectomy ♀ N P0 🚗 0.00 ✂ 0.00 **Global Days XXX** **AMA:** 2009, Jan, 11-31; 2008, Apr, 3-4; 2006, December, 10-12; 2006, February, 10-15; 2006, March, 15
00908	perineal prostatectomy ♂ C P0 🚗 0.00 ✂ 0.00 **Global Days XXX** **AMA:** 2009, Jan, 11-31; 2008, Apr, 3-4; 2006, December, 10-12; 2006, February, 10-15; 2006, March, 15
00910	Anesthesia for transurethral procedures (including urethrocystoscopy); not otherwise specified N P0 🚗 0.00 ✂ 0.00 **Global Days XXX** **AMA:** 2009, Jan, 11-31; 2008, Apr, 3-4; 2006, February, 10-15; 2006, December, 10-12; 2006, March, 15
00912	transurethral resection of bladder tumor(s) N P0 🚗 0.00 ✂ 0.00 **Global Days XXX** **AMA:** 2009, Jan, 11-31; 2008, Apr, 3-4; 2006, March, 15; 2006, December, 10-12; 2006, February, 10-15
00914	transurethral resection of prostate ♂ N P0 🚗 0.00 ✂ 0.00 **Global Days XXX** **AMA:** 2009, Jan, 11-31; 2008, Apr, 3-4; 2006, February, 10-15; 2006, December, 10-12; 2006, March, 15
00916	post-transurethral resection bleeding N P0 🚗 0.00 ✂ 0.00 **Global Days XXX** **AMA:** 2009, Jan, 11-31; 2008, Apr, 3-4; 2006, February, 10-15; 2006, December, 10-12; 2006, March, 15
00918	with fragmentation, manipulation and/or removal of ureteral calculus N P0 🚗 0.00 ✂ 0.00 **Global Days XXX** **AMA:** 2009, Jan, 11-31; 2008, Apr, 3-4; 2006, December, 10-12; 2006, March, 15; 2006, February, 10-15

Current Procedural Coding Expert – Anesthesia   01180

00920 Anesthesia for procedures on male genitalia (including open urethral procedures); not otherwise specified ♂ N 🖥 P0
 0.00   0.00 Global Days XXX
AMA: 2009, Jan, 11-31; 2008, Apr, 3-4; 2006, February, 10-15; 2006, March, 15; 2006, December, 10-12

00921 vasectomy, unilateral or bilateral ♂ N 🖥 P0
 0.00   0.00 Global Days XXX
AMA: 2009, Jan, 11-31; 2008, Apr, 3-4; 2006, December, 10-12; 2006, February, 10-15; 2006, March, 15

00922 seminal vesicles ♂ N 🖥 P0
 0.00   0.00 Global Days XXX
AMA: 2009, Jan, 11-31; 2008, Apr, 3-4; 2006, February, 10-15; 2006, March, 15; 2006, December, 10-12

00924 undescended testis, unilateral or bilateral ♂ N 🖥 P0
 0.00   0.00 Global Days XXX
AMA: 2009, Jan, 11-31; 2008, Apr, 3-4; 2006, February, 10-15; 2006, December, 10-12; 2006, March, 15

00926 radical orchiectomy, inguinal ♂ N 🖥 P0
 0.00   0.00 Global Days XXX
AMA: 2009, Jan, 11-31; 2008, Apr, 3-4; 2006, March, 15; 2006, December, 10-12; 2006, February, 10-15

00928 radical orchiectomy, abdominal ♂ N 🖥 P0
 0.00   0.00 Global Days XXX
AMA: 2009, Jan, 11-31; 2008, Apr, 3-4; 2006, February, 10-15; 2006, March, 15; 2006, December, 10-12

00930 orchiopexy, unilateral or bilateral ♂ N 🖥 P0
 0.00   0.00 Global Days XXX
AMA: 2009, Jan, 11-31; 2008, Apr, 3-4; 2006, February, 10-15; 2006, December, 10-12; 2006, March, 15

00932 complete amputation of penis ♂ C 🖥 P0
 0.00   0.00 Global Days XXX
AMA: 2009, Jan, 11-31; 2008, Apr, 3-4; 2006, March, 15; 2006, December, 10-12; 2006, February, 10-15

00934 radical amputation of penis with bilateral inguinal lymphadenectomy ♂ C 🖥 P0
 0.00   0.00 Global Days XXX
AMA: 2009, Jan, 11-31; 2008, Apr, 3-4; 2006, December, 10-12; 2006, February, 10-15; 2006, March, 15

00936 radical amputation of penis with bilateral inguinal and iliac lymphadenectomy ♂ C 🖥 P0
 0.00   0.00 Global Days XXX
AMA: 2009, Jan, 11-31; 2008, Apr, 3-4; 2006, February, 10-15; 2006, December, 10-12; 2006, March, 15

00938 insertion of penile prosthesis (perineal approach) ♂ N 🖥 P0
 0.00   0.00 Global Days XXX
AMA: 2009, Jan, 11-31; 2008, Apr, 3-4; 2006, February, 10-15; 2006, March, 15; 2006, December, 10-12

00940 Anesthesia for vaginal procedures (including biopsy of labia, vagina, cervix or endometrium); not otherwise specified ♀ N 🖥 P0
 0.00   0.00 Global Days XXX
AMA: 2009, Jan, 11-31; 2008, Apr, 3-4; 2006, March, 15; 2006, December, 10-12; 2006, February, 10-15

00942 colpotomy, vaginectomy, colporrhaphy, and open urethral procedures ♀ N 🖥 P0
 0.00   0.00 Global Days XXX
AMA: 2009, Jan, 11-31; 2008, Apr, 3-4; 2006, February, 10-15; 2006, March, 15; 2006, December, 10-12

00944 vaginal hysterectomy ♀ C 🖥 P0
 0.00   0.00 Global Days XXX
AMA: 2009, Jan, 11-31; 2008, Apr, 3-4; 2006, March, 15; 2006, December, 10-12; 2006, February, 10-15

00948 cervical cerclage ♀ N 🖥 P0
 0.00   0.00 Global Days XXX
AMA: 2009, Jan, 11-31; 2008, Apr, 3-4; 2006, February, 10-15; 2006, December, 10-12; 2006, March, 15

00950 culdoscopy ♀ N 🖥 P0
 0.00   0.00 Global Days XXX
AMA: 2009, Jan, 11-31; 2008, Apr, 3-4; 2006, March, 15; 2006, December, 10-12; 2006, February, 10-15

00952 hysteroscopy and/or hysterosalpingography ♀ N 🖥 P0
 0.00   0.00 Global Days XXX
AMA: 2009, Jan, 11-31; 2008, Apr, 3-4; 2006, December, 10-12; 2006, March, 15; 2006, February, 10-15

01112-01522 Anesthesia for Lower Extremity Procedures

CMS 100-4,4,10.4 Packaging Rules Under OPPS
CMS 100-4,4,20.6 Modifier Use Under OPPS
CMS 100-4,4,20.6.4 Modifiers for Discontinued Services
CMS 100-4,12,50 Anesthesia Services
CMS 100-4,12,140 Certified Registered Nurse Anesthetist Services
CMS 100-4,12,140.2 Payment for CRNA Services
CMS 100-4,12,140.3.2 Calculation of Anesthesia Time

01112 Anesthesia for bone marrow aspiration and/or biopsy, anterior or posterior iliac crest N 🖥 P0
 0.00   0.00 Global Days XXX
AMA: 2009, Jan, 11-31; 2008, Apr, 3-4; 2006, December, 10-12; 2006, February, 10-15; 2006, March, 15

01120 Anesthesia for procedures on bony pelvis N 🖥 P0
 0.00   0.00 Global Days XXX
AMA: 2009, Jan, 11-31; 2008, Apr, 3-4; 2006, December, 10-12; 2006, February, 10-15; 2006, March, 15

01130 Anesthesia for body cast application or revision N 🖥 P0
 0.00   0.00 Global Days XXX
AMA: 2009, Jan, 11-31; 2008, Apr, 3-4; 2006, March, 15; 2006, February, 10-15; 2006, December, 10-12

01140 Anesthesia for interpelviabdominal (hindquarter) amputation C 🖥 P0
 0.00   0.00 Global Days XXX
AMA: 2009, Jan, 11-31; 2008, Apr, 3-4; 2006, December, 10-12; 2006, March, 15; 2006, February, 10-15

01150 Anesthesia for radical procedures for tumor of pelvis, except hindquarter amputation C 🖥 P0
 0.00   0.00 Global Days XXX
AMA: 2009, Jan, 11-31; 2008, Apr, 3-4; 2006, March, 15; 2006, February, 10-15; 2006, December, 10-12

01160 Anesthesia for closed procedures involving symphysis pubis or sacroiliac joint N 🖥 P0
 0.00   0.00 Global Days XXX
AMA: 2009, Jan, 11-31; 2008, Apr, 3-4; 2006, March, 15; 2006, February, 10-15; 2006, December, 10-12

01170 Anesthesia for open procedures involving symphysis pubis or sacroiliac joint N 🖥 P0
 0.00   0.00 Global Days XXX
AMA: 2009, Jan, 11-31; 2008, Apr, 3-4; 2006, March, 15; 2006, February, 10-15; 2006, December, 10-12

01173 Anesthesia for open repair of fracture disruption of pelvis or column fracture involving acetabulum N 🖥 P0
 0.00   0.00 Global Days XXX
AMA: 2009, Jan, 11-31; 2008, Apr, 3-4; 2006, December, 10-12; 2006, March, 15; 2006, February, 10-15

01180 Anesthesia for obturator neurectomy; extrapelvic N 🖥 P0
 0.00   0.00 Global Days XXX
AMA: 2009, Jan, 11-31; 2008, Apr, 3-4; 2006, March, 15; 2006, February, 10-15; 2006, December, 10-12

● New Code   ▲ Revised Code   M Maternity   A Age   Unlisted   Not Covered   # Resequenced
CCI   + Add-on   ⊘ Mod 51 Exempt   Mod 63 Exempt   ⊙ Mod Sedation   P0 PQRI

© 2009 Publisher *(Blue Ink)*   CPT only © 2009 American Medical Association. All Rights Reserved. (Black Ink)   Medicare (Red Ink)

Current Procedural Coding Expert – Anesthesia

01190	intrapelvic
	0.00 0.00 Global Days XXX
	AMA: 2009, Jan, 11-31; 2008, Apr, 3-4; 2006, March, 15; 2006, February, 10-15; 2006, December, 10-12

01200	Anesthesia for all closed procedures involving hip joint
	0.00 0.00 Global Days XXX
	AMA: 2009, Jan, 11-31; 2008, Apr, 3-4; 2006, March, 15; 2006, February, 10-15; 2006, December, 10-12

01202	Anesthesia for arthroscopic procedures of hip joint
	0.00 0.00 Global Days XXX
	AMA: 2009, Jan, 11-31; 2008, Apr, 3-4; 2006, December, 10-12; 2006, March, 15; 2006, February, 10-15

01210	Anesthesia for open procedures involving hip joint; not otherwise specified
	0.00 0.00 Global Days XXX
	AMA: 2009, Jan, 11-31; 2008, Apr, 3-4; 2006, March, 15; 2006, December, 10-12; 2006, February, 10-15

01212	hip disarticulation
	0.00 0.00 Global Days XXX
	AMA: 2009, Jan, 11-31; 2008, Apr, 3-4; 2006, March, 15; 2006, February, 10-15; 2006, December, 10-12

01214	total hip arthroplasty
	0.00 0.00 Global Days XXX
	AMA: 2009, Jan, 11-31; 2008, Apr, 3-4; 2006, December, 10-12; 2006, March, 15; 2006, February, 10-15

01215	revision of total hip arthroplasty
	0.00 0.00 Global Days XXX
	AMA: 2009, Jan, 11-31; 2008, Apr, 3-4; 2006, March, 15; 2006, December, 10-12; 2006, February, 10-15

01220	Anesthesia for all closed procedures involving upper 2/3 of femur
	0.00 0.00 Global Days XXX
	AMA: 2009, Jan, 11-31; 2008, Apr, 3-4; 2006, February, 10-15; 2006, March, 15; 2006, December, 10-12

01230	Anesthesia for open procedures involving upper 2/3 of femur; not otherwise specified
	0.00 0.00 Global Days XXX
	AMA: 2009, Jan, 11-31; 2008, Apr, 3-4; 2006, December, 10-12; 2006, February, 10-15; 2006, March, 15

01232	amputation
	0.00 0.00 Global Days XXX
	AMA: 2009, Jan, 11-31; 2008, Apr, 3-4; 2006, March, 15; 2006, February, 10-15; 2006, December, 10-12

01234	radical resection
	0.00 0.00 Global Days XXX
	AMA: 2009, Jan, 11-31; 2008, Apr, 3-4; 2006, December, 10-12; 2006, March, 15; 2006, February, 10-15

01250	Anesthesia for all procedures on nerves, muscles, tendons, fascia, and bursae of upper leg
	0.00 0.00 Global Days XXX
	AMA: 2009, Jan, 11-31; 2008, Apr, 3-4; 2006, March, 15; 2006, December, 10-12; 2006, February, 10-15

01260	Anesthesia for all procedures involving veins of upper leg, including exploration
	0.00 0.00 Global Days XXX
	AMA: 2009, Jan, 11-31; 2008, Apr, 3-4; 2006, March, 15; 2006, February, 10-15; 2006, December, 10-12

01270	Anesthesia for procedures involving arteries of upper leg, including bypass graft; not otherwise specified
	0.00 0.00 Global Days XXX
	AMA: 2009, Jan, 11-31; 2008, Apr, 3-4; 2006, December, 10-12; 2006, March, 15; 2006, February, 10-15

01272	femoral artery ligation
	0.00 0.00 Global Days XXX
	AMA: 2009, Jan, 11-31; 2008, Apr, 3-4; 2006, March, 15; 2006, December, 10-12; 2006, February, 10-15

01274	femoral artery embolectomy
	0.00 0.00 Global Days XXX
	AMA: 2009, Jan, 11-31; 2008, Apr, 3-4; 2006, March, 15; 2006, December, 10-12; 2006, February, 10-15

01320	Anesthesia for all procedures on nerves, muscles, tendons, fascia, and bursae of knee and/or popliteal area
	0.00 0.00 Global Days XXX
	AMA: 2009, Jan, 11-31; 2008, Apr, 3-4; 2006, December, 10-12; 2006, February, 10-15; 2006, March, 15

01340	Anesthesia for all closed procedures on lower 1/3 of femur
	0.00 0.00 Global Days XXX
	AMA: 2009, Jan, 11-31; 2008, Apr, 3-4; 2006, December, 10-12; 2006, March, 15; 2006, February, 10-15

01360	Anesthesia for all open procedures on lower 1/3 of femur
	0.00 0.00 Global Days XXX
	AMA: 2009, Jan, 11-31; 2008, Apr, 3-4; 2006, March, 15; 2006, February, 10-15; 2006, December, 10-12

01380	Anesthesia for all closed procedures on knee joint
	0.00 0.00 Global Days XXX
	AMA: 2009, Jan, 11-31; 2008, Apr, 3-4; 2006, December, 10-12; 2006, February, 10-15; 2006, March, 15

01382	Anesthesia for diagnostic arthroscopic procedures of knee joint
	0.00 0.00 Global Days XXX
	AMA: 2009, Jan, 11-31; 2008, Apr, 3-4; 2006, December, 10-12; 2006, March, 15; 2006, February, 10-15

01390	Anesthesia for all closed procedures on upper ends of tibia, fibula, and/or patella
	0.00 0.00 Global Days XXX
	AMA: 2009, Jan, 11-31; 2008, Apr, 3-4; 2006, March, 15; 2006, December, 10-12; 2006, February, 10-15

01392	Anesthesia for all open procedures on upper ends of tibia, fibula, and/or patella
	0.00 0.00 Global Days XXX
	AMA: 2009, Jan, 11-31; 2008, Apr, 3-4; 2006, March, 15; 2006, December, 10-12; 2006, February, 10-15

01400	Anesthesia for open or surgical arthroscopic procedures on knee joint; not otherwise specified
	0.00 0.00 Global Days XXX
	AMA: 2009, Jan, 11-31; 2008, Apr, 3-4; 2006, December, 10-12; 2006, February, 10-15; 2006, March, 15

01402	total knee arthroplasty
	0.00 0.00 Global Days XXX
	AMA: 2009, Jan, 11-31; 2008, Apr, 3-4; 2006, March, 15; 2006, December, 10-12; 2006, February, 10-15

01404	disarticulation at knee
	0.00 0.00 Global Days XXX
	AMA: 2009, Jan, 11-31; 2008, Apr, 3-4; 2006, March, 15; 2006, December, 10-12; 2006, February, 10-15

01420	Anesthesia for all cast applications, removal, or repair involving knee joint
	0.00 0.00 Global Days XXX
	AMA: 2009, Jan, 11-31; 2008, Apr, 3-4; 2006, March, 15; 2006, December, 10-12; 2006, February, 10-15

26/TC PC/TC Comp Only   A2- ASC Pmt   50 Bilateral   ♂ Male Only   ♀ Female Only   Facility RVU   Non-Facility RVU
AMA: CPT Asst   **MED:** Pub 100   A- Y OPPSI   80/80 Surg Assist Allowed / w/Doc   Lab Crosswalk   Radiology Crosswalk
Medicare (Red Ink)   © 2009 Publisher (Blue Ink)

CPT only © 2009 American Medical Association. All Rights Reserved. (Black Ink)

Current Procedural Coding Expert – Anesthesia

01430 Anesthesia for procedures on veins of knee and popliteal area; not otherwise specified
 0.00 0.00 Global Days XXX
AMA: 2009, Jan, 11-31; 2008, Apr, 3-4; 2006, December, 10-12; 2006, February, 10-15; 2006, March, 15

01432 arteriovenous fistula
 0.00 0.00 Global Days XXX
AMA: 2009, Jan, 11-31; 2008, Apr, 3-4; 2006, March, 15; 2006, December, 10-12; 2006, February, 10-15

01440 Anesthesia for procedures on arteries of knee and popliteal area; not otherwise specified
 0.00 0.00 Global Days XXX
AMA: 2009, Jan, 11-31; 2008, Apr, 3-4; 2006, March, 15; 2006, December, 10-12; 2006, February, 10-15

01442 popliteal thromboendarterectomy, with or without patch graft
 0.00 0.00 Global Days XXX
AMA: 2009, Jan, 11-31; 2008, Apr, 3-4; 2006, December, 10-12; 2006, February, 10-15; 2006, March, 15

01444 popliteal excision and graft or repair for occlusion or aneurysm
 0.00 0.00 Global Days XXX
AMA: 2009, Jan, 11-31; 2008, Apr, 3-4; 2006, March, 15; 2006, December, 10-12; 2006, February, 10-15

01462 Anesthesia for all closed procedures on lower leg, ankle, and foot
 0.00 0.00 Global Days XXX
AMA: 2009, Jan, 11-31; 2008, Apr, 3-4; 2006, March, 15; 2006, December, 10-12; 2006, February, 10-15

01464 Anesthesia for arthroscopic procedures of ankle and/or foot
 0.00 0.00 Global Days XXX
AMA: 2009, Jan, 11-31; 2008, Apr, 3-4; 2006, December, 10-12; 2006, February, 10-15; 2006, March, 15

01470 Anesthesia for procedures on nerves, muscles, tendons, and fascia of lower leg, ankle, and foot; not otherwise specified
 0.00 0.00 Global Days XXX
AMA: 2009, Jan, 11-31; 2008, Apr, 3-4; 2006, March, 15; 2006, December, 10-12; 2006, February, 10-15

01472 repair of ruptured Achilles tendon, with or without graft
 0.00 0.00 Global Days XXX
AMA: 2009, Jan, 11-31; 2008, Apr, 3-4; 2006, March, 15; 2006, March, 15; 2006, February, 10-15

01474 gastrocnemius recession (eg, Strayer procedure)
 0.00 0.00 Global Days XXX
AMA: 2009, Jan, 11-31; 2008, Apr, 3-4; 2006, March, 15; 2006, December, 10-12; 2006, February, 10-15

01480 Anesthesia for open procedures on bones of lower leg, ankle, and foot; not otherwise specified
 0.00 0.00 Global Days XXX
AMA: 2009, Jan, 11-31; 2008, Apr, 3-4; 2006, March, 15; 2006, December, 10-12; 2006, February, 10-15

01482 radical resection (including below knee amputation)
 0.00 0.00 Global Days XXX
AMA: 2009, Jan, 11-31; 2008, Apr, 3-4; 2006, December, 10-12; 2006, February, 10-15; 2006, March, 15

01484 osteotomy or osteoplasty of tibia and/or fibula
 0.00 0.00 Global Days XXX
AMA: 2009, Jan, 11-31; 2008, Apr, 3-4; 2006, March, 15; 2006, December, 10-12; 2006, February, 10-15

01486 total ankle replacement
 0.00 0.00 Global Days XXX
AMA: 2009, Jan, 11-31; 2008, Apr, 3-4; 2006, March, 15; 2006, December, 10-12; 2006, February, 10-15

01490 Anesthesia for lower leg cast application, removal, or repair
 0.00 0.00 Global Days XXX
AMA: 2009, Jan, 11-31; 2008, Apr, 3-4; 2006, December, 10-12; 2006, February, 10-15; 2006, March, 15

01500 Anesthesia for procedures on arteries of lower leg, including bypass graft; not otherwise specified
 0.00 0.00 Global Days XXX
AMA: 2009, Jan, 11-31; 2008, Apr, 3-4; 2006, March, 15; 2006, December, 10-12; 2006, February, 10-15

01502 embolectomy, direct or with catheter
 0.00 0.00 Global Days XXX
AMA: 2009, Jan, 11-31; 2008, Apr, 3-4; 2006, December, 10-12; 2006, March, 15; 2006, February, 10-15

01520 Anesthesia for procedures on veins of lower leg; not otherwise specified
 0.00 0.00 Global Days XXX
AMA: 2009, Jan, 11-31; 2008, Apr, 3-4; 2006, December, 10-12; 2006, February, 10-15; 2006, March, 15

01522 venous thrombectomy, direct or with catheter
 0.00 0.00 Global Days XXX
AMA: 2009, Jan, 11-31; 2008, Apr, 3-4; 2006, March, 15; 2006, December, 10-12; 2006, February, 10-15

01610-01682 Anesthesia for Shoulder Procedures

CMS 100-4,12,50 Anesthesia Services
CMS 100-4,12,140 Certified Registered Nurse Anesthetist Services
CMS 100-4,12,140.2 Payment for CRNA Services
CMS 100-4,12,140.3.2 Calculation of Anesthesia Time
INCLUDES
Acromioclavicular joint
Humeral head and neck
Shoulder joint
Sternoclavicular joint

01610 Anesthesia for all procedures on nerves, muscles, tendons, fascia, and bursae of shoulder and axilla
 0.00 0.00 Global Days XXX
AMA: 2009, Jan, 11-31; 2008, Apr, 3-4; 2006, March, 15; 2006, December, 10-12; 2006, February, 10-15

01620 Anesthesia for all closed procedures on humeral head and neck, sternoclavicular joint, acromioclavicular joint, and shoulder joint
 0.00 0.00 Global Days XXX
AMA: 2009, Jan, 11-31; 2008, Apr, 3-4; 2006, December, 10-12; 2006, February, 10-15; 2006, March, 15

01622 Anesthesia for diagnostic arthroscopic procedures of shoulder joint
 0.00 0.00 Global Days XXX
AMA: 2009, Jan, 11-31; 2008, Apr, 3-4; 2006, December, 10-12; 2006, March, 15; 2006, February, 10-15

01630 Anesthesia for open or surgical arthroscopic procedures on humeral head and neck, sternoclavicular joint, acromioclavicular joint, and shoulder joint; not otherwise specified
 0.00 0.00 Global Days XXX
AMA: 2009, Jan, 11-31; 2008, Apr, 3-4; 2006, December, 10-12; 2006, March, 15; 2006, February, 10-15

~~**01632**~~ ~~radical resection~~
To report, see code 01630, 01638

● New Code ▲ Revised Code Ⓜ Maternity Ⓐ Age Unlisted Not Covered # Resequenced
 CCI + Add-on ⊘ Mod 51 Exempt ⊚ Mod 63 Exempt ⊙ Mod Sedation PQRI
© 2009 Publisher *(Blue Ink)* CPT only © 2009 American Medical Association. All Rights Reserved. (Black Ink) Medicare (Red Ink)

01634 — Current Procedural Coding Expert – Anesthesia

01634	shoulder disarticulation
	0.00 0.00 Global Days XXX
	AMA: 2009, Jan, 11-31; 2008, Apr, 3-4; 2006, March, 15; 2006, February, 10-15; 2006, December, 10-12

01636	interthoracoscapular (forequarter) amputation
	0.00 0.00 Global Days XXX
	AMA: 2009, Jan, 11-31; 2008, Apr, 3-4; 2006, March, 15; 2006, December, 10-12; 2006, February, 10-15

01638	total shoulder replacement
	0.00 0.00 Global Days XXX
	AMA: 2009, Jan, 11-31; 2008, Apr, 3-4; 2006, December, 10-12; 2006, February, 10-15; 2006, March, 15

01650	Anesthesia for procedures on arteries of shoulder and axilla; not otherwise specified
	0.00 0.00 Global Days XXX
	AMA: 2009, Jan, 11-31; 2008, Apr, 3-4; 2006, March, 15; 2006, December, 10-12; 2006, February, 10-15

01652	axillary-brachial aneurysm
	0.00 0.00 Global Days XXX
	AMA: 2009, Jan, 11-31; 2008, Apr, 3-4; 2006, March, 15; 2006, December, 10-12; 2006, February, 10-15

01654	bypass graft
	0.00 0.00 Global Days XXX
	AMA: 2009, Jan, 11-31; 2008, Apr, 3-4; 2006, December, 10-12; 2006, February, 10-15; 2006, March, 15

01656	axillary-femoral bypass graft
	0.00 0.00 Global Days XXX
	AMA: 2009, Jan, 11-31; 2008, Apr, 3-4; 2006, March, 15; 2006, December, 10-12; 2006, February, 10-15

01670	Anesthesia for all procedures on veins of shoulder and axilla
	0.00 0.00 Global Days XXX
	AMA: 2009, Jan, 11-31; 2008, Apr, 3-4; 2006, December, 10-12; 2006, March, 15; 2006, February, 10-15

01680	Anesthesia for shoulder cast application, removal or repair; not otherwise specified
	0.00 0.00 Global Days XXX
	AMA: 2009, Jan, 11-31; 2008, Apr, 3-4; 2006, December, 10-12; 2006, February, 10-15; 2006, March, 15

01682	shoulder spica
	0.00 0.00 Global Days XXX
	AMA: 2009, Jan, 11-31; 2008, Apr, 3-4; 2006, March, 15; 2006, December, 10-12; 2006, February, 10-15

01710-01860 Anesthesia for Upper Extremity Procedures

CMS 100-4,12,50   Anesthesia Services
CMS 100-4,12,140   Certified Registered Nurse Anesthetist Services
CMS 100-4,12,140.2   Payment for CRNA Services
CMS 100-4,12,140.3.2   Calculation of Anesthesia Time

01710	Anesthesia for procedures on nerves, muscles, tendons, fascia, and bursae of upper arm and elbow; not otherwise specified
	0.00 0.00 Global Days XXX
	AMA: 2009, Jan, 11-31; 2008, Apr, 3-4; 2006, March, 15; 2006, December, 10-12; 2006, February, 10-15

01712	tenotomy, elbow to shoulder, open
	0.00 0.00 Global Days XXX
	AMA: 2009, Jan, 11-31; 2008, Apr, 3-4; 2006, March, 15; 2006, December, 10-12; 2006, February, 10-15

01714	tenoplasty, elbow to shoulder
	0.00 0.00 Global Days XXX
	AMA: 2009, Jan, 11-31; 2008, Apr, 3-4; 2006, December, 10-12; 2006, February, 10-15; 2006, March, 15

01716	tenodesis, rupture of long tendon of biceps
	0.00 0.00 Global Days XXX
	AMA: 2009, Jan, 11-31; 2008, Apr, 3-4; 2006, March, 15; 2006, February, 10-15; 2006, December, 10-12

01730	Anesthesia for all closed procedures on humerus and elbow
	0.00 0.00 Global Days XXX
	AMA: 2009, Jan, 11-31; 2008, Apr, 3-4; 2006, December, 10-12; 2006, March, 15; 2006, February, 10-15

01732	Anesthesia for diagnostic arthroscopic procedures of elbow joint
	0.00 0.00 Global Days XXX
	AMA: 2009, Jan, 11-31; 2008, Apr, 3-4; 2006, December, 10-12; 2006, March, 15; 2006, February, 10-15

01740	Anesthesia for open or surgical arthroscopic procedures of the elbow; not otherwise specified
	0.00 0.00 Global Days XXX
	AMA: 2009, Jan, 11-31; 2008, Apr, 3-4; 2006, December, 10-12; 2006, February, 10-15; 2006, March, 15

01742	osteotomy of humerus
	0.00 0.00 Global Days XXX
	AMA: 2009, Jan, 11-31; 2008, Apr, 3-4; 2006, March, 15; 2006, December, 10-12; 2006, February, 10-15

01744	repair of nonunion or malunion of humerus
	0.00 0.00 Global Days XXX
	AMA: 2009, Jan, 11-31; 2008, Apr, 3-4; 2006, March, 15; 2006, December, 10-12; 2006, February, 10-15

01756	radical procedures
	0.00 0.00 Global Days XXX
	AMA: 2009, Jan, 11-31; 2008, Apr, 3-4; 2006, December, 10-12; 2006, February, 10-15; 2006, March, 15

01758	excision of cyst or tumor of humerus
	0.00 0.00 Global Days XXX
	AMA: 2009, Jan, 11-31; 2008, Apr, 3-4; 2006, March, 15; 2006, December, 10-12; 2006, February, 10-15

01760	total elbow replacement
	0.00 0.00 Global Days XXX
	AMA: 2009, Jan, 11-31; 2008, Apr, 3-4; 2006, March, 15; 2006, December, 10-12; 2006, February, 10-15

01770	Anesthesia for procedures on arteries of upper arm and elbow; not otherwise specified
	0.00 0.00 Global Days XXX
	AMA: 2009, Jan, 11-31; 2008, Apr, 3-4; 2006, March, 15; 2006, December, 10-12; 2006, February, 10-15

01772	embolectomy
	0.00 0.00 Global Days XXX
	AMA: 2009, Jan, 11-31; 2008, Apr, 3-4; 2006, February, 10-15; 2006, December, 10-12; 2006, March, 15

01780	Anesthesia for procedures on veins of upper arm and elbow; not otherwise specified
	0.00 0.00 Global Days XXX
	AMA: 2009, Jan, 11-31; 2008, Apr, 3-4; 2006, March, 15; 2006, December, 10-12; 2006, February, 10-15

01782	phleborrhaphy
	0.00 0.00 Global Days XXX
	AMA: 2009, Jan, 11-31; 2008, Apr, 3-4; 2006, March, 15; 2006, December, 10-12; 2006, February, 10-15

01810	Anesthesia for all procedures on nerves, muscles, tendons, fascia, and bursae of forearm, wrist, and hand
	0.00 0.00 Global Days XXX
	AMA: 2009, Jan, 11-31; 2008, Apr, 3-4; 2006, December, 10-12; 2006, February, 10-15; 2006, March, 15

Current Procedural Coding Expert – Anesthesia

01820   Anesthesia for all closed procedures on radius, ulna, wrist, or hand bones
0.00   0.00   **Global Days XXX**
AMA: 2009, Jan, 11-31; 2008, Apr, 3-4; 2006, March, 15; 2006, December, 10-12; 2006, February, 10-15

01829   Anesthesia for diagnostic arthroscopic procedures on the wrist
0.00   0.00   **Global Days XXX**
AMA: 2009, Jan, 11-31; 2008, Apr, 3-4; 2006, December, 10-12; 2006, February, 10-15; 2006, March, 15

01830   Anesthesia for open or surgical arthroscopic/endoscopic procedures on distal radius, distal ulna, wrist, or hand joints; not otherwise specified
0.00   0.00   **Global Days XXX**
AMA: 2009, Jan, 11-31; 2008, Apr, 3-4; 2006, March, 15; 2006, December, 10-12; 2006, February, 10-15

01832   total wrist replacement
0.00   0.00   **Global Days XXX**
AMA: 2009, Jan, 11-31; 2008, Apr, 3-4; 2006, December, 10-12; 2006, March, 15; 2006, February, 10-15

01840   Anesthesia for procedures on arteries of forearm, wrist, and hand; not otherwise specified
0.00   0.00   **Global Days XXX**
AMA: 2009, Jan, 11-31; 2008, Apr, 3-4; 2006, December, 10-12; 2006, February, 10-15; 2006, March, 15

01842   embolectomy
0.00   0.00   **Global Days XXX**
AMA: 2009, Jan, 11-31; 2008, Apr, 3-4; 2006, March, 15; 2006, December, 10-12; 2006, February, 10-15

01844   Anesthesia for vascular shunt, or shunt revision, any type (eg, dialysis)
0.00   0.00   **Global Days XXX**
AMA: 2009, Jan, 11-31; 2008, Apr, 3-4; 2006, March, 15; 2006, February, 10-15; 2006, December, 10-12

01850   Anesthesia for procedures on veins of forearm, wrist, and hand; not otherwise specified
0.00   0.00   **Global Days XXX**
AMA: 2009, Jan, 11-31; 2008, Apr, 3-4; 2006, March, 15; 2006, December, 10-12; 2006, February, 10-15

01852   phleborrhaphy
0.00   0.00   **Global Days XXX**
AMA: 2009, Jan, 11-31; 2008, Apr, 3-4; 2006, December, 10-12; 2006, February, 10-15; 2006, March, 15

01860   Anesthesia for forearm, wrist, or hand cast application, removal, or repair
0.00   0.00   **Global Days XXX**
AMA: 2009, Jan, 11-31; 2008, Apr, 3-4; 2006, February, 10-15; 2006, December, 10-12

01916-01936 Anesthesia for Interventional Radiology Procedures

CMS 100-4,12,50   Anesthesia Services
CMS 100-4,12,140   Certified Registered Nurse Anesthetist Services
CMS 100-4,12,140.2   Payment for CRNA Services
CMS 100-4,12,140.3.2   Calculation of Anesthesia Time

01916   Anesthesia for diagnostic arteriography/venography
Do not report with (01924-01926, 01930-01933)
0.00   0.00   **Global Days XXX**
AMA: 2009, Jan, 11-31; 2008, Apr, 3-4; 2006, March, 15; 2006, December, 10-12; 2006, February, 10-15

01920   Anesthesia for cardiac catheterization including coronary angiography and ventriculography (not to include Swan-Ganz catheter)
0.00   0.00   **Global Days XXX**
AMA: 2009, Jan, 11-31; 2008, Apr, 3-4; 2006, February, 10-15; 2006, December, 10-12; 2006, March, 15

01922   Anesthesia for non-invasive imaging or radiation therapy
0.00   0.00   **Global Days XXX**
AMA: 2009, Jan, 11-31; 2008, Apr, 3-4; 2006, March, 15; 2006, December, 10-12; 2006, February, 10-15

01924   Anesthesia for therapeutic interventional radiological procedures involving the arterial system; not otherwise specified
0.00   0.00   **Global Days XXX**
AMA: 2009, Jan, 11-31; 2008, Apr, 3-4; 2006, March, 15; 2006, December, 10-12; 2006, February, 10-15

01925   carotid or coronary
0.00   0.00   **Global Days XXX**
AMA: 2009, Jan, 11-31; 2008, Apr, 3-4; 2006, December, 10-12; 2006, February, 10-15; 2006, March, 15

01926   intracranial, intracardiac, or aortic
0.00   0.00   **Global Days XXX**
AMA: 2009, Jan, 11-31; 2008, Apr, 3-4; 2006, March, 15; 2006, December, 10-12; 2006, February, 10-15

01930   Anesthesia for therapeutic interventional radiological procedures involving the venous/lymphatic system (not to include access to the central circulation); not otherwise specified
0.00   0.00   **Global Days XXX**
AMA: 2009, Jan, 11-31; 2008, Apr, 3-4; 2006, March, 15; 2006, December, 10-12; 2006, February, 10-15

01931   intrahepatic or portal circulation (eg, transvenous intrahepatic portosystemic shunt[s] [TIPS])
0.00   0.00   **Global Days XXX**
AMA: 2009, Jan, 11-31; 2008, Apr, 3-4; 2006, December, 10-12; 2006, February, 10-15; 2006, March, 15

01932   intrathoracic or jugular
0.00   0.00   **Global Days XXX**
AMA: 2009, Jan, 11-31; 2008, Apr, 3-4; 2006, March, 15; 2006, December, 10-12; 2006, February, 10-15

01933   intracranial
0.00   0.00   **Global Days XXX**
AMA: 2009, Jan, 11-31; 2008, Apr, 3-4; 2006, March, 15; 2006, December, 10-12; 2006, February, 10-15

01935   Anesthesia for percutaneous image guided procedures on the spine and spinal cord; diagnostic
0.00   0.00   **Global Days XXX**
AMA: 2009, Jan, 11-31; 2008, Apr, 3-4

01936   therapeutic
0.00   0.00   **Global Days XXX**
AMA: 2009, Jan, 11-31; 2008, Apr, 3-4

01951-01953 Anesthesia for Burn Procedures

CMS 100-4,3,20.1.2.8   Special Payments for Burn Cases
CMS 100-4,12,50   Anesthesia Services
CMS 100-4,12,140   Certified Registered Nurse Anesthetist Services
CMS 100-4,12,140.2   Payment for CRNA Services
CMS 100-4,12,140.3.2   Calculation of Anesthesia Time

01951   Anesthesia for second- and third-degree burn excision or debridement with or without skin grafting, any site, for total body surface area (TBSA) treated during anesthesia and surgery; less than 4% total body surface area
0.00   0.00   **Global Days XXX**
AMA: 2009, Jan, 11-31; 2008, Apr, 3-4; 2006, March, 15; 2006, December, 10-12; 2006, February, 10-15

01952   between 4% and 9% of total body surface area
0.00   0.00   **Global Days XXX**
AMA: 2009, Jan, 11-31; 2008, Apr, 3-4; 2006, December, 10-12; 2006, February, 10-15; 2006, March, 15

● New Code   ▲ Revised Code   M Maternity   A Age   Unlisted   Not Covered   # Resequenced
CCI   + Add-on   Mod 51 Exempt   Mod 63 Exempt   Mod Sedation   PQRI
© 2009 Publisher (*Blue Ink*)   CPT only © 2009 American Medical Association. All Rights Reserved. (Black Ink)   Medicare (Red Ink)

+ 01953 each additional 9% total body surface area or part thereof (List separately in addition to code for primary procedure)
Code first 01952
0.00 0.00 Global Days XXX
AMA: 2009, Jan, 11-31; 2008, Apr, 3-4; 2006, March, 15; 2006, December, 10-12; 2006, February, 10-15

01958-01969 Anesthesia for Obstetric Procedures

CMS 100-4,12,50 — Anesthesia Services
CMS 100-4,12,140 — Certified Registered Nurse Anesthetist Services
CMS 100-4,12,140.2 — Payment for CRNA Services
CMS 100-4,12,140.3.2 — Calculation of Anesthesia Time

01958 Anesthesia for external cephalic version procedure
0.00 0.00 Global Days XXX
AMA: 2009, Jan, 11-31; 2008, Apr, 3-4; 2006, March, 15; 2006, December, 10-12; 2006, February, 10-15

01960 Anesthesia for vaginal delivery only
0.00 0.00 Global Days XXX
AMA: 2009, Jan, 11-31; 2008, Apr, 3-4; 2006, March, 15; 2006, December, 10-12; 2006, February, 10-15

01961 Anesthesia for cesarean delivery only
0.00 0.00 Global Days XXX
AMA: 2009, Jan, 11-31; 2008, Apr, 3-4; 2006, December, 10-12; 2006, February, 10-15; 2006, March, 15

01962 Anesthesia for urgent hysterectomy following delivery
0.00 0.00 Global Days XXX
AMA: 2009, Jan, 11-31; 2008, Apr, 3-4; 2006, December, 10-12; 2006, March, 15; 2006, February, 10-15

01963 Anesthesia for cesarean hysterectomy without any labor analgesia/anesthesia care
0.00 0.00 Global Days XXX
AMA: 2009, Jan, 11-31; 2008, Apr, 3-4; 2006, March, 15; 2006, December, 10-12; 2006, February, 10-15

01965 Anesthesia for incomplete or missed abortion procedures
0.00 0.00 Global Days XXX
AMA: 2009, Jan, 11-31; 2008, Apr, 3-4; 2006, December, 10-12; 2006, February, 10-15; 2006, March, 15

01966 Anesthesia for induced abortion procedures
0.00 0.00 Global Days XXX
AMA: 2009, Jan, 11-31; 2008, Apr, 3-4; 2006, December, 10-12; 2006, March, 15; 2006, February, 10-15

01967 Neuraxial labor analgesia/anesthesia for planned vaginal delivery (this includes any repeat subarachnoid needle placement and drug injection and/or any necessary replacement of an epidural catheter during labor)
0.00 0.00 Global Days XXX
AMA: 2009, Jan, 11-31; 2008, Apr, 3-4; 2006, March, 15; 2006, December, 10-12; 2006, February, 10-15

+ 01968 Anesthesia for cesarean delivery following neuraxial labor analgesia/anesthesia (List separately in addition to code for primary procedure performed)
Code first (01967)
0.00 0.00 Global Days XXX
AMA: 2009, Jan, 11-31; 2008, Apr, 3-4; 2006, March, 15; 2006, December, 10-12; 2006, February, 10-15

+ 01969 Anesthesia for cesarean hysterectomy following neuraxial labor analgesia/anesthesia (List separately in addition to code for primary procedure performed)
Code first (01967)
0.00 0.00 Global Days XXX
AMA: 2009, Jan, 11-31; 2008, Apr, 3-4; 2006, December, 10-12; 2006, February, 10-15; 2006, March, 15

01990-01999 Anesthesia Miscellaneous

CMS 100-4,12,50 — Anesthesia Services
CMS 100-4,12,140 — Certified Registered Nurse Anesthetist Services
CMS 100-4,12,140.2 — Payment for CRNA Services
CMS 100-4,12,140.3.2 — Calculation of Anesthesia Time

01990 Physiological support for harvesting of organ(s) from brain-dead patient
0.00 0.00 Global Days XXX
AMA: 2009, Jan, 11-31; 2008, Apr, 3-4; 2006, March, 15; 2006, December, 10-12; 2006, February, 10-15

01991 Anesthesia for diagnostic or therapeutic nerve blocks and injections (when block or injection is performed by a different provider); other than the prone position
Do not report with (99143-99150)
EXCLUDES Bier block for pain management (64999)
IV or intra-arterial injections (96373-96374)
Regional or local anesthesia of arms or legs for surgical procedure
0.00 0.00 Global Days XXX
AMA: 2009, Jan, 11-31; 2008, Apr, 3-4; 2006, March, 15; 2006, December, 10-12; 2006, February, 10-15

01992 prone position
Do not report with (99143-99150)
EXCLUDES Bier block for pain management (64999)
Pain management via intra-arterial or intravenous therapy (96373-96374)
Regional or local anesthesia of arms or legs for surgical procedure
0.00 0.00 Global Days XXX
AMA: 2009, Jan, 11-31; 2008, Apr, 3-4; 2006, March, 15; 2006, December, 10-12; 2006, February, 10-15

01996 Daily hospital management of epidural or subarachnoid continuous drug administration
INCLUDES Continuous epidural or subarachnoid drug services performed after insertion of an epidural or subarachnoid catheter
0.00 0.00 Global Days XXX
AMA: 2009, Jan, 11-31; 2008, Apr, 3-4; 2006, March, 15; 2006, December, 10-12; 2006, February, 10-15

01999 Unlisted anesthesia procedure(s)
0.00 0.00 Global Days XXX
AMA: 2009, Jan, 11-31; 2008, Jan, 10-25; 2008, Apr, 3-4; 2007, January, 13-27; 2006, March, 15; 2006, February, 10-15; 2006, December, 10-12

CURRENT PROCEDURAL CODING EXPERT – Integumentary System   11004

10021-10022 Fine Needle Aspiration

CMS 100-4,13,80.1   Supervision and Interpretation Codes
CMS 100-4,13,80.2   S&I Multiple Procedure Reduction
EXCLUDES Percutaneous localization clip placement during breast biopsy (19295)
Percutaneous needle biopsy of:
 Abdominal or retroperitoneal mass (49180)
 Bone (20220, 20225)
 Bone marrow (38221)
 Breast (19100)
 Epididymis (54800)
 Kidney (50200)
 Liver (47000-47001)
 Lung or mediastinum (32405)
 Lymph node (38505)
 Muscle (20206)
 Nucleus pulposus, paravertebral tissue or intervertebral disc (62267)
 Pancreas (48102)
 Pleura (32400)
 Prostate (55700)
 Salivary gland (42400)
 Spinal cord (62269)
 Testis (54500)
 Thyroid (60100)

10021 Fine needle aspiration; without imaging guidance   [P2] [T] [80]
   88172-88173
   1.94   3.73   Global Days XXX
   AMA: 2009, Jan, 11-31; 2008, Jan, 10-25; 2007, January, 13-27; 2005, March, 11-15

10022 with imaging guidance   [G2] [T] [80]
   88172-88173
   76942, 77002, 77012, 77021
   1.80   3.43   Global Days XXX
   AMA: 2009, Jan, 11-31; 2008, Jan, 10-25; 2007, June, 10-11

10040-10180 Treatment of Fluid-filled Lesions: Skin and Subcutaneous Tissues

CMS 100-4,12,30   Correct Coding Policy
CMS 100-4,13,80.1   Physician Presence
CMS 100-4,13,80.2   S&I Multiple Procedure Reduction

10040 Acne surgery (eg, marsupialization, opening or removal of multiple milia, comedones, cysts, pustules)   [P2] [T]
   2.38   2.69   Global Days 010
   AMA: 2009, Jan, 11-31

10060 Incision and drainage of abscess (eg, carbuncle, suppurative hidradenitis, cutaneous or subcutaneous abscess, cyst, furuncle, or paronychia); simple or single   [P3] [T]
   2.53   2.98   Global Days 010
   AMA: 2009, Jan, 11-31; 2008, Jan, 10-25; 2007, January, 13-27; 2006, December, 14-15

10061 complicated or multiple   [P2] [T]
   4.36   4.97   Global Days 010
   AMA: 2006, December, 14-15

10080 Incision and drainage of pilonidal cyst; simple   [P2] [T]
   2.68   4.40   Global Days 010
   AMA: 2007, May, 5-8; 2006, December, 14-15

10081 complicated   [P3] [T]
   EXCLUDES Excision of pilonidal cyst (11770-11772)
   4.66   6.96   Global Days 010
   AMA: 2007, May, 5-8; 2006, December, 14-15

10120 Incision and removal of foreign body, subcutaneous tissues; simple   [P3] [T]
   2.50   3.62   Global Days 010
   AMA: 2006, December, 14-15

10121 complicated   [A2] [T]
   EXCLUDES Debridement associated with a fracture or dislocation (11010-11012)
   Exploration penetrating wound (20100-20103)
   4.97   7.02   Global Days 010
   AMA: 2006, December, 14-15

Hematoma may be decompressed with a hemostat
Drain may be placed to allow further drainage

10140 Incision and drainage of hematoma, seroma or fluid collection   [P3] [T]
   76942, 77012, 77021
   3.13   4.18   Global Days 010
   AMA: 2009, Jan, 11-31; 2008, Jan, 10-25; 2007, January, 13-27

10160 Puncture aspiration of abscess, hematoma, bulla, or cyst   [P3] [T]
   76942, 77012, 77021
   2.56   3.38   Global Days 010

10180 Incision and drainage, complex, postoperative wound infection   [A2] [T]
   EXCLUDES Wound dehiscence (12020-12021, 13160)
   4.75   6.33   Global Days 010
   AMA: 2009, Jan, 11-31; 2008, Jan, 10-25

11000-11012 Removal of Foreign Substances and Infected/Devitalized Tissue

CMS 100-4,12,40.1   Global Surgery Package
CMS 100-4,12,40.2   Billing Requirements for Global Surgeries
EXCLUDES Burn debridement or treatment (16000-16035)
Dermabrasions (15780-15783)
Nail debridement (11720-11721)

11000 Debridement of extensive eczematous or infected skin; up to 10% of body surface   [P3] [T]
   EXCLUDES Necrotizing soft tissue infection of:
    Abdominal wall (11005-11006)
    External genitalia and perineum (11004, 11006)
   0.81   1.41   Global Days 000

+ 11001 each additional 10% of the body surface, or part thereof (List separately in addition to code for primary procedure)   [P3] [T]
   Code first 11000
   0.41   0.57   Global Days ZZZ

11004 Debridement of skin, subcutaneous tissue, muscle and fascia for necrotizing soft tissue infection; external genitalia and perineum   [C]
   EXCLUDES Skin grafts or flaps (14000-14350, 15040-15770)
   16.06   16.06   Global Days 000

● New Code   ▲ Revised Code   [M] Maternity   [A] Age   Unlisted   Not Covered   # Resequenced
[CCI] CCI   + Add-on   ⊘ Mod 51 Exempt   ⊘ Mod 63 Exempt   ☉ Mod Sedation   [PQ] PQRI

© 2009 Publisher (Blue Ink)   CPT only © 2009 American Medical Association. All Rights Reserved. (Black Ink)   Medicare (Red Ink)   13

11005

Current Procedural Coding Expert – Integumentary System

11005	abdominal wall, with or without fascial closure
	21.70 21.70 Global Days 000
11006	external genitalia, perineum and abdominal wall, with or without fascial closure
	19.62 19.62 Global Days 000
+ 11008	Removal of prosthetic material or mesh, abdominal wall for infection (eg, for chronic or recurrent mesh infection or necrotizing soft tissue infection) (List separately in addition to code for primary procedure)

INCLUDES Debridement:
  Associated with an open fracture
  Bone
  Extensive eczematous or infected skin
  Muscle
  Skin
  Subcutaneous tissue

EXCLUDES Insertion of mesh (49568)
  Orchiectomy (54520)
  Skin grafts or flaps (14000-14350, 15040-15770)
  Testicular transplantation (54680)

Code first (10180, 11004-11006)
Do not report with (11000-11001, 11010-11044)
 7.62 7.62 Global Days ZZZ

11010	Debridement including removal of foreign material associated with open fracture(s) and/or dislocation(s); skin and subcutaneous tissues
	7.63 12.64 Global Days 010
	AMA: 2009, Jan, 11-31; 2008, Jan, 10-25; 2007, January, 13-27
11011	skin, subcutaneous tissue, muscle fascia, and muscle
	8.25 13.72 Global Days 000
11012	skin, subcutaneous tissue, muscle fascia, muscle, and bone
	11.69 18.31 Global Days 000
	AMA: 2009, Jan, 11-31; 2008, Jan, 10-25; 2007, January, 13-27

11040-11044 Removal of Infected/Devitalized Tissue

CMS 100-2,15,260   Covered ASC Procedures
CMS 100-4,12,40.1   Global Surgery Definition
CMS 100-4,12,40.2   Billing Requirements for Global Surgeries
CMS 100-4,14,10   ASC Procedures

INCLUDES Active wound care management
  Removal of devitalized tissue

EXCLUDES Burn debridement or treatment (16000-16035)
  Dermabrasions (15780-15783)
  Nail debridement (11720-11721)

Do not report with (97597-97602)

11040	Debridement; skin, partial thickness
	0.69 1.25 Global Days 000
	AMA: 2009, Jan, 11-31; 2008, Jan, 10-25; 2007, January, 13-27; 2005, June, 9-11; 2005, June, 1-4
11041	skin, full thickness
	0.84 1.41 Global Days 000
	AMA: 2005, June, 1-4
11042	skin, and subcutaneous tissue
	1.17 1.95 Global Days 000
	AMA: 2005, June, 1-4; 2005, June, 9-11
11043	skin, subcutaneous tissue, and muscle
	6.57 7.57 Global Days 010
	AMA: 2009, Jan, 11-31; 2008, Jan, 10-25; 2007, January, 13-27; 2005, June, 1-4; 2005, June, 9-11
11044	skin, subcutaneous tissue, muscle, and bone
	9.05 10.46 Global Days 010
	AMA: 2009, Jan, 11-31; 2008, Jan, 10-25; 2007, January, 13-27; 2005, June, 9-11; 2005, June, 1-4

11055-11057 Excision Benign Hypertrophic Skin Lesions

CMS 100-2,15,290   Routine Foot Care
EXCLUDES Destruction (17000-17004)

11055	Paring or cutting of benign hyperkeratotic lesion (eg, corn or callus); single lesion
	0.55 1.29 Global Days 000
	AMA: 2009, Jan, 11-31; 2008, Jan, 10-25; 2007, January, 13-27
11056	2 to 4 lesions
	0.79 1.56 Global Days 000
11057	more than 4 lesions
	1.02 1.85 Global Days 000

11100-11101 Surgical Biopsy Skin and Mucous Membranes

CMS 100-4,12,30   Correct Coding Policy

INCLUDES Attaining tissue for pathologic exam

EXCLUDES Biopsy of:
  Conjunctiva (68100)
  Eyelid (67810)

11100	Biopsy of skin, subcutaneous tissue and/or mucous membrane (including simple closure), unless otherwise listed; single lesion
	1.36 2.63 Global Days 000
	AMA: 2008, Feb, 1; 2006, December, 1-3
+ 11101	each separate/additional lesion (List separately in addition to code for primary procedure)
	Code first 11100
	0.69 0.87 Global Days ZZZ
	AMA: 2008, Feb, 1; 2006, December, 1-3

Unrelated and separately distinct biopsies

11200-11201 Skin Tag Removal - All Techniques

CMS 100-4,12,30   Correct Coding Policy
CMS 100-4,12,40.1   Global Surgery Package Definition
CMS 100-4,12,40.2   Billing Requirements for Global Surgeries

INCLUDES Chemical destruction
  Electrocauterization
  Electrosurgical destruction
  Ligature strangulation
  Removal with or without local anesthesia
  Sharp excision or scissoring

EXCLUDES Extensive or complicated secondary wound closure (13160)

11200	Removal of skin tags, multiple fibrocutaneous tags, any area; up to and including 15 lesions
	1.91 2.24 Global Days 010
	AMA: 2009, Jan, 11-31; 2008, Jan, 10-25; 2007, January, 13-27
+ 11201	each additional 10 lesions, or part thereof (List separately in addition to code for primary procedure)
	Code first 11200
	0.47 0.52 Global Days ZZZ

26/ TC PC/TC Comp Only	A2- 23 ASC Pmt	50 Bilateral	♂ Male Only	♀ Female Only	Facility RVU	Non-Facility RVU
AMA: CPT Asst	**MED:** Pub 100	A- Y OPPSI	80/ 80 Surg Assist Allowed / w/Doc		Lab Crosswalk	Radiology Crosswalk

CPT only © 2009 American Medical Association. All Rights Reserved. (Black Ink)   Medicare (Red Ink)   © 2009 Publisher (Blue Ink)

Current Procedural Coding Expert – Integumentary System

11300-11313 Skin Lesion Removal: Shaving

CMS 100-4,12,40.1 Global Surgery Package Definition
CMS 100-4,12,40.2 Global Surgery Billing Requirements
CMS 100-4,12,50 Local anesthesia

INCLUDES
Local anesthesia
Partial thickness excision by horizontal slicing
Wound cauterization

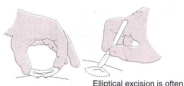

Shave excision of an elevated lesion; technique also used to biopsy

Elliptical excision is often used when tissue removal is larger than 4 mm or when deep pathology is suspected

A punch biopsy cuts a core of tissue as the tool is twisted downward

The skin is the largest organ of the human body and accounts for about 20 percent of total body weight. It serves mainly as a protective barrier, a temperature regulator, and as a sensory device. The epidermis is outermost and is the thinnest of the skin layers; the major part of the dermis is high in collagen and is notable for its great elasticity and strength; the major blood and nerve network is found in the middermis. Adnexal structures are the hair follicles, sebaceous glands, sweat glands, and the follicles that produce fingernails and toenails. Lesions are small areas of skin disease and may be solitary or multiple

11300 Shaving of epidermal or dermal lesion, single lesion, trunk, arms or legs; lesion diameter 0.5 cm or less
0.83 1.77 Global Days 000
AMA: 2009, Jan, 11-31; 2008, Jan, 10-25; 2008, Feb, 1; 2007, January, 13-27

11301 lesion diameter 0.6 to 1.0 cm
1.42 2.41 Global Days 000
AMA: 2009, Jan, 11-31; 2008, Jan, 10-25; 2008, Feb, 1; 2007, January, 13-27

11302 lesion diameter 1.1 to 2.0 cm
1.76 2.88 Global Days 000
AMA: 2009, Jan, 11-31; 2008, Jan, 10-25; 2008, Feb, 1; 2007, January, 13-27

11303 lesion diameter over 2.0 cm
2.06 3.38 Global Days 000
AMA: 2009, Jan, 11-31; 2008, Jan, 10-25; 2008, Feb, 1; 2007, January, 13-27

11305 Shaving of epidermal or dermal lesion, single lesion, scalp, neck, hands, feet, genitalia; lesion diameter 0.5 cm or less
0.94 1.84 Global Days 000
AMA: 2009, Jan, 11-31; 2008, Jan, 10-25; 2008, Feb, 1; 2007, January, 13-27

11306 lesion diameter 0.6 to 1.0 cm
1.50 2.50 Global Days 000
AMA: 2009, Jan, 11-31; 2008, Jan, 10-25; 2008, Feb, 1; 2007, January, 13-27

11307 lesion diameter 1.1 to 2.0 cm
1.82 2.95 Global Days 000
AMA: 2009, Jan, 11-31; 2008, Jan, 10-25; 2008, Feb, 1; 2007, January, 13-27

11308 lesion diameter over 2.0 cm
2.07 3.28 Global Days 000
AMA: 2009, Jan, 11-31; 2008, Jan, 10-25; 2008, Feb, 1; 2007, January, 13-27

11310 Shaving of epidermal or dermal lesion, single lesion, face, ears, eyelids, nose, lips, mucous membrane; lesion diameter 0.5 cm or less
1.21 2.19 Global Days 000
AMA: 2009, Jan, 11-31; 2008, Jan, 10-25; 2008, Feb, 1; 2007, January, 13-27

11311 lesion diameter 0.6 to 1.0 cm
1.76 2.77 Global Days 000
AMA: 2009, Jan, 11-31; 2008, Jan, 10-25; 2008, Feb, 1; 2007, January, 13-27

11312 lesion diameter 1.1 to 2.0 cm
2.02 3.20 Global Days 000
AMA: 2009, Jan, 11-31; 2008, Jan, 10-25; 2008, Feb, 1; 2007, January, 13-27

11313 lesion diameter over 2.0 cm
2.70 3.99 Global Days 000
AMA: 2009, Jan, 11-31; 2008, Jan, 10-25; 2008, Feb, 1; 2007, January, 13-27

11400-11446 Skin Lesion Removal: Benign

CMS 100-2,16,120 Cosmetic Procedures
CMS 100-4,12,40.1 Global Surgery Package Definition
CMS 100-4,12,40.2 Billing Requirements for Global Surgeries
CMS 100-4,12,50 Local anesthesia

INCLUDES
Biopsy on same lesion
Full thickness removal including margins
Local anesthesia
Lesion measurement before excision at largest diameter plus margin
Simple, nonlayered closure

EXCLUDES
Biopsy of eyelid (67810)
Destruction of eyelid lesion (67850)
Excision and reconstruction of eyelid (67961-67975)
Excision of chalazion (67800-67808)
Eyelid procedures involving more than skin (67800 and subsequent codes)
Shave removal (11300-11313)

Code also intermediate closure (12031-12057)
Code also reconstruction (15002-15261, 15570-15770)
Code also complex closure (13100-13153)
Code also modifier 22 if excision is complicated or unusual
Code also each separate lesion
Do not report with adjacent tissue transfer. Report only adjacent tissue transfer code. (14000-14302)

11400 Excision, benign lesion including margins, except skin tag (unless listed elsewhere), trunk, arms or legs; excised diameter 0.5 cm or less
2.10 3.09 Global Days 010
AMA: 2009, Jan, 11-31; 2008, Jan, 10-25; 2008, Jul, 5-6&15; 2007, January, 13-27; 2006, August, 12-14

11401 excised diameter 0.6 to 1.0 cm
2.74 3.77 Global Days 010
AMA: 2008, Jul, 5-6&15; 2006, August, 12-14

11402 excised diameter 1.1 to 2.0 cm
3.02 4.20 Global Days 010
AMA: 2008, Jul, 5-6&15; 2006, August, 12-14

11403 excised diameter 2.1 to 3.0 cm
3.89 4.89 Global Days 010
AMA: 2008, Jul, 5-6&15; 2006, August, 12-14

11404 excised diameter 3.1 to 4.0 cm
4.31 5.58 Global Days 010
AMA: 2008, Jul, 5-6&15; 2006, August, 12-14

11406 excised diameter over 4.0 cm
6.59 8.12 Global Days 010
AMA: 2008, Jul, 5-6&15; 2006, August, 12-14

● New Code ▲ Revised Code Ⓜ Maternity Ⓐ Age Unlisted Not Covered # Resequenced
CCI + Add-on ⊘ Mod 51 Exempt Mod 63 Exempt ⊙ Mod Sedation PQRI
© 2009 Publisher *(Blue Ink)* CPT only © 2009 American Medical Association. All Rights Reserved. *(Black Ink)* Medicare *(Red Ink)*

11420 — **Current Procedural Coding Expert – Integumentary System**

11420	Excision, benign lesion including margins, except skin tag (unless listed elsewhere), scalp, neck, hands, feet, genitalia; excised diameter 0.5 cm or less
	2.17 3.12 Global Days 010
	AMA: 2008, Jul, 5-6&15; 2006, August, 12-14
11421	excised diameter 0.6 to 1.0 cm
	2.94 4.01 Global Days 010
	AMA: 2008, Jul, 5-6&15; 2006, August, 12-14
11422	excised diameter 1.1 to 2.0 cm
	3.58 4.48 Global Days 010
	AMA: 2008, Jul, 5-6&15; 2006, August, 12-14
11423	excised diameter 2.1 to 3.0 cm
	4.20 5.22 Global Days 010
	AMA: 2008, Jul, 5-6&15; 2006, August, 12-14
11424	excised diameter 3.1 to 4.0 cm
	4.83 6.06 Global Days 010
	AMA: 2008, Jul, 5-6&15; 2006, August, 12-14
11426	excised diameter over 4.0 cm
	7.39 8.72 Global Days 010
	AMA: 2008, Jul, 5-6&15; 2006, August, 12-14

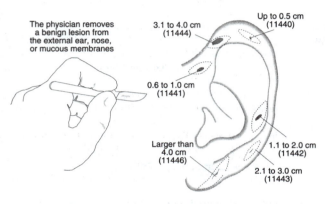

The physician removes a benign lesion from the external ear, nose, or mucous membranes

Up to 0.5 cm (11440)
3.1 to 4.0 cm (11444)
0.6 to 1.0 cm (11441)
Larger than 4.0 cm (11446)
1.1 to 2.0 cm (11442)
2.1 to 3.0 cm (11443)

11440	Excision, other benign lesion including margins, except skin tag (unless listed elsewhere), face, ears, eyelids, nose, lips, mucous membrane; excised diameter 0.5 cm or less
	2.67 3.38 Global Days 010
	AMA: 2008, Jul, 5-6&15; 2006, August, 12-14
11441	excised diameter 0.6 to 1.0 cm
	3.47 4.29 Global Days 010
	AMA: 2008, Jul, 5-6&15; 2006, August, 12-14
11442	excised diameter 1.1 to 2.0 cm
	3.86 4.82 Global Days 010
	AMA: 2009, Jan, 11-31; 2008, Jun, 14-15; 2008, Jul, 5-6&15; 2006, August, 12-14
11443	excised diameter 2.1 to 3.0 cm
	4.76 5.80 Global Days 010
	AMA: 2008, Jul, 5-6&15; 2006, August, 12-14
11444	excised diameter 3.1 to 4.0 cm
	6.16 7.38 Global Days 010
	AMA: 2008, Jul, 5-6&15; 2006, August, 12-14
11446	excised diameter over 4.0 cm
	8.81 10.27 Global Days 010
	AMA: 2009, Jan, 11-31; 2008, Jan, 10-25; 2008, Jul, 5-6&15; 2007, January, 13-27; 2006, August, 12-14

11450-11471 Treatment of Hidradenitis: Excision and Repair

CMS 100-2,15,260   Covered ASC Procedures
CMS 100-4,4,20.5   HCPCS Under OPPS
CMS 100-4,12,90.3   MD Services in ASCs
CMS 100-4,14,10   General ASC Services

Code also closure by skin graft or flap (14000-14350, 15040-15770)

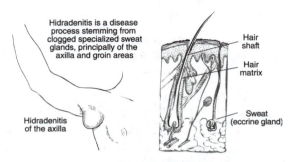

Hidradenitis is a disease process stemming from clogged specialized sweat glands, principally of the axilla and groin areas

Hidradenitis of the axilla

Hair shaft
Hair matrix
Sweat (eccrine gland)

11450	Excision of skin and subcutaneous tissue for hidradenitis, axillary; with simple or intermediate repair
	6.66 9.64 Global Days 090
11451	with complex repair
	8.61 12.29 Global Days 090
11462	Excision of skin and subcutaneous tissue for hidradenitis, inguinal; with simple or intermediate repair
	6.42 9.50 Global Days 090
11463	with complex repair
	8.71 12.55 Global Days 090
11470	Excision of skin and subcutaneous tissue for hidradenitis, perianal, perineal, or umbilical; with simple or intermediate repair
	7.51 10.57 Global Days 090
11471	with complex repair
	9.32 13.03 Global Days 090

11600-11646 Skin Lesion Removal: Malignant

CMS 100-2,15,260   Covered ASC Procedures
CMS 100-4,4,20.5   HCPCS Under OPPS
CMS 100-4,12,90.3   MD Services in ASCs
CMS 100-4,14,10   General ASC Services

INCLUDES
Biopsy on same lesion
Excision of additional margin at same operative session
Full thickness removal including margins
Lesion measurement before excision at largest diameter plus margin
Local anesthesia
Simple, nonlayered closure

EXCLUDES
Destruction (17260-17286)
Excision of additional margin at subsequent operative session (11600-11646)

Code also complex closure (13100-13153)
Code also each separate lesion
Code also intermediate closure (12031-12057)
Code also modifier 58 if re-excision is performed during postoperative period
Code also reconstruction (15002-15261, 15570-15770)
Do not report with adjacent tissue transfer. Report only adjacent tissue transfer code. (14000-14302)

11600	Excision, malignant lesion including margins, trunk, arms, or legs; excised diameter 0.5 cm or less
	3.19 4.85 Global Days 010
	AMA: 2009, Jan, 11-31; 2008, Jan, 10-25; 2008, Feb, 8-9; 2008, Jul, 5-6&15; 2007, January, 13-27

26/TC PC/TC Comp Only   A2-Z3 ASC Pmt   50 Bilateral   ♂ Male Only   ♀ Female Only   Facility RVU   Non-Facility RVU
AMA: CPT Asst   **MED:** Pub 100   A-Y OPPSI   80/B0 Surg Assist Allowed / w/Doc   Lab Crosswalk   Radiology Crosswalk

16   CPT only © 2009 American Medical Association. All Rights Reserved. (Black Ink)   Medicare (Red Ink)   © 2009 Publisher (Blue Ink)

Current Procedural Coding Expert – Integumentary System

11601	excised diameter 0.6 to 1.0 cm
	4.02 5.84 Global Days 010
	AMA: 2008, Feb, 8-9; 2008, Jul, 5-6&15
11602	excised diameter 1.1 to 2.0 cm
	4.42 6.35 Global Days 010
	AMA: 2008, Feb, 8-9; 2008, Jul, 5-6&15
11603	excised diameter 2.1 to 3.0 cm
	5.31 7.31 Global Days 010
	AMA: 2008, Feb, 8-9; 2008, Jul, 5-6&15
11604	excised diameter 3.1 to 4.0 cm
	5.84 8.12 Global Days 010
	AMA: 2008, Feb, 8-9; 2008, Jul, 5-6&15
11606	excised diameter over 4.0 cm
	8.75 11.75 Global Days 010
	AMA: 2008, Feb, 8-9; 2008, Jul, 5-6&15
11620	Excision, malignant lesion including margins, scalp, neck, hands, feet, genitalia; excised diameter 0.5 cm or less
	3.25 4.93 Global Days 010
	AMA: 2008, Feb, 8-9; 2008, Jul, 5-6&15
11621	excised diameter 0.6 to 1.0 cm
	4.06 5.89 Global Days 010
	AMA: 2008, Feb, 8-9; 2008, Jul, 5-6&15
11622	excised diameter 1.1 to 2.0 cm
	4.66 6.60 Global Days 010
	AMA: 2008, Feb, 8-9; 2008, Jul, 5-6&15
11623	excised diameter 2.1 to 3.0 cm
	5.79 7.81 Global Days 010
	AMA: 2008, Feb, 8-9; 2008, Jul, 5-6&15
11624	excised diameter 3.1 to 4.0 cm
	6.58 8.83 Global Days 010
	AMA: 2008, Feb, 8-9; 2008, Jul, 5-6&15
11626	excised diameter over 4.0 cm
	8.10 10.72 Global Days 010
	AMA: 2008, Feb, 8-9; 2008, Jul, 5-6&15
11640	Excision, malignant lesion including margins, face, ears, eyelids, nose, lips; excised diameter 0.5 cm or less
	EXCLUDES Eyelid excision involving more than skin (67800 and subsequent codes)
	3.36 5.08 Global Days 010
	AMA: 2008, Feb, 8-9; 2008, Jul, 5-6&15
11641	excised diameter 0.6 to 1.0 cm
	EXCLUDES Eyelid excision involving more than skin (67800 and subsequent codes)
	4.24 6.10 Global Days 010
	AMA: 2008, Feb, 8-9; 2008, Jul, 5-6&15
11642	excised diameter 1.1 to 2.0 cm
	EXCLUDES Eyelid excision involving more than skin (67800 and subsequent codes)
	5.02 7.02 Global Days 010
	AMA: 2008, Feb, 8-9; 2008, Jul, 5-6&15
11643	excised diameter 2.1 to 3.0 cm
	EXCLUDES Eyelid excision involving more than skin (67800 and subsequent codes)
	6.32 8.36 Global Days 010
	AMA: 2008, Feb, 8-9; 2008, Jul, 5-6&15
11644	excised diameter 3.1 to 4.0 cm
	EXCLUDES Eyelid excision involving more than skin (67800 and subsequent codes)
	7.84 10.34 Global Days 010
	AMA: 2008, Feb, 8-9; 2008, Jul, 5-6&15
11646	excised diameter over 4.0 cm
	EXCLUDES Eyelid excision involving more than skin (67800 and subsequent codes)
	10.96 13.68 Global Days 010
	AMA: 2009, Jan, 11-31; 2008, Jan, 10-25; 2008, Feb, 8-9; 2008, Jul, 5-6&15; 2007, January, 13-27

11719-11765 Nails and Supporting Structures

CMS 100-2,15,290 Foot Care
CMS 100-4,4,20.5 HCPCS Under OPPS
EXCLUDES Drainage of paronychia or onychia (10060-10061)

11719	Trimming of nondystrophic nails, any number
	0.22 0.57 Global Days 000
11720	Debridement of nail(s) by any method(s); 1 to 5
	0.42 0.82 Global Days 000
11721	6 or more
	0.70 1.13 Global Days 000
11730	Avulsion of nail plate, partial or complete, simple; single
	1.43 2.55 Global Days 000
	AMA: 2009, Jan, 11-31; 2008, Jan, 10-25; 2007, January, 13-27
+11732	each additional nail plate (List separately in addition to code for primary procedure)
	Code first 11730
	0.74 1.17 Global Days ZZZ
11740	Evacuation of subungual hematoma
	0.84 1.23 Global Days 000
11750	Excision of nail and nail matrix, partial or complete (eg, ingrown or deformed nail), for permanent removal;
	EXCLUDES Skin graft (15050)
	4.63 5.78 Global Days 010
11752	with amputation of tuft of distal phalanx
	EXCLUDES Skin graft (15050)
	6.96 8.36 Global Days 010
11755	Biopsy of nail unit (eg, plate, bed, matrix, hyponychium, proximal and lateral nail folds) (separate procedure)
	2.19 3.51 Global Days 000
	AMA: 2009, Jan, 11-31; 2008, Jan, 10-25; 2007, January, 13-27
11760	Repair of nail bed
	3.52 5.81 Global Days 010
11762	Reconstruction of nail bed with graft
	5.04 7.30 Global Days 010
11765	Wedge excision of skin of nail fold (eg, for ingrown toenail)
	INCLUDES Cotting's operation
	1.85 3.62 Global Days 010

11770-11772 Treatment Pilonidal Cyst: Excision

CMS 100-2,15,260 Covered ASC Procedures
CMS 100-4,4,20.5 HCPCS Under OPPS
CMS 100-4,12,90.3 MD Services in ASCs
EXCLUDES Incision of pilonidal cyst (10080-10081)

11770	Excision of pilonidal cyst or sinus; simple
	4.93 7.08 Global Days 010
11771	extensive
	11.63 14.90 Global Days 090
11772	complicated
	15.19 17.91 Global Days 090

● New Code   ▲ Revised Code   Maternity   Age   Unlisted   Not Covered   # Resequenced
CCI   + Add-on   ⊘ Mod 51 Exempt   Mod 63 Exempt   ⊙ Mod Sedation   P0 PQRI
© 2009 Publisher *(Blue Ink)*   CPT only © 2009 American Medical Association. All Rights Reserved. (Black Ink)   Medicare (Red Ink)

11900 — 12004 Integumentary System

11900-11901 Treatment of Lesions: Injection

CMS 100-4,17,20.5.7   Injection Services
EXCLUDES   Injection of veins (36470-36471)
     Intralesional chemotherapy (96405-96406)

Do not report for local anesthetic injection performed preoperatively

- **11900**   Injection, intralesional; up to and including 7 lesions   [P3][T]
  - 0.87   1.44   Global Days 000
  - **AMA:** 2009, Jan, 11-31; 2008, Jan, 10-25; 2007, January, 13-27; 2006, December, 10-12

- **11901**   more than 7 lesions   [P3][T]
  - 1.36   1.87   Global Days 000
  - **AMA:** 2009, Jan, 11-31; 2008, Jan, 10-25; 2007, January, 13-27; 2006, December, 10-12

11920-11971 Tattoos, Tissue Expanders, and Dermal Fillers

CMS 100-2,16,10   Exclusions from Coverage
CMS 100-2,16,120   Cosmetic Procedures
CMS 100-2,16,180   Services Related to Noncovered Procedures
CMS 100-4,4,20.5   HCPCS Under OPPS

- **11920**   Tattooing, intradermal introduction of insoluble opaque pigments to correct color defects of skin, including micropigmentation; 6.0 sq cm or less   [P3][T][80]
  - 3.15   4.45   Global Days 000

- **11921**   6.1 to 20.0 sq cm   [P3][T][80]
  - 3.72   5.19   Global Days 000

- **+ 11922**   each additional 20.0 sq cm, or part thereof (List separately in addition to code for primary procedure)   [P3][T][80]
  - Code first 11921
  - 0.84   1.59   Global Days ZZZ

- **11950**   Subcutaneous injection of filling material (eg, collagen); 1 cc or less   [P3][T][80]
  - 1.46   1.97   Global Days 000

- **11951**   1.1 to 5.0 cc   [P3][T][80]
  - 2.10   2.81   Global Days 000

- **11952**   5.1 to 10.0 cc   [P3][T][80]
  - 2.53   3.29   Global Days 000

- **11954**   over 10.0 cc   [P2][T][80]
  - 3.24   4.29   Global Days 000

- **11960**   Insertion of tissue expander(s) for other than breast, including subsequent expansion   [A2][T]
  - **EXCLUDES**   Breast reconstruction with tissue expander(s) (19357)
  - 24.41   24.41   Global Days 090

- **11970**   Replacement of tissue expander with permanent prosthesis   [A2][T]
  - 16.54   16.54   Global Days 090
  - **AMA:** 2005, August, 1-3

- **11971**   Removal of tissue expander(s) without insertion of prosthesis   [A2][T][80]
  - 8.48   12.01   Global Days 090
  - **AMA:** 2009, Jan, 11-31; 2008, Jan, 10-25; 2007, January, 13-27; 2005, June, 9-11

11975-11983 Drug Implantation

CMS 100-2,15,50   Drugs and Biologicals
CMS 100-2,16,20   General Exclusions

- **11975**   Insertion, implantable contraceptive capsules   ♀ [E]
  - 2.09   3.36   Global Days XXX

- **11976**   Removal, implantable contraceptive capsules   ♀ [P3][T][80]
  - 2.68   3.80   Global Days 000

- **11977**   Removal with reinsertion, implantable contraceptive capsules   ♀ [E]
  - 4.67   5.97   Global Days XXX

- **11980**   Subcutaneous hormone pellet implantation (implantation of estradiol and/or testosterone pellets beneath the skin)   [P2][X]
  - 2.26   2.80   Global Days 000

- **11981**   Insertion, non-biodegradable drug delivery implant   [P2][X][80]
  - 2.23   3.43   Global Days XXX
  - **AMA:** 2009, Jan, 11-31; 2007, Dec, 10-179

- **11982**   Removal, non-biodegradable drug delivery implant   [P2][X][80]
  - 2.64   3.76   Global Days XXX

- **11983**   Removal with reinsertion, non-biodegradable drug delivery implant   [P2][X][80]
  - 4.68   5.68   Global Days XXX

12001-12021 Suturing of Superficial Wounds

CMS 100-2,15,260   Covered ASC Procedures
CMS 100-4,4,20.5   HCPCS Under OPPS
CMS 100-4,14,10   ASC Procedures

INCLUDES
- Administration of local anesthesia
- Cauterization without closure
- Simple:
  - Exploration nerves, blood vessels, tendons
  - Vessel ligation, in wound
- Simple repair that involves:
  - Routine debridement and decontamination
  - Simple one layer closure
  - Superficial tissues
  - Sutures, staples, tissue adhesives
  - Total length of several repairs in same code category

EXCLUDES
- Adhesive strips only (99201-99499)
- Debridement:
  - Performed separately, no closure (11040-11044)
  - That requires:
    - Comprehensive cleaning
    - Removal of significant tissue
    - Removal soft tissue and/or bone, no fracture/dislocation (11040-11044)
    - Removal soft tissue and/or bone with open fracture/dislocation (11010-11012)
- Deep tissue repair (12031-13153)
- Major exploration (20100-20103)
- Repair nerves, blood vessels, tendons (see appropriate anatomical section)
- Secondary closure/dehiscense (13160)

- **12001**   Simple repair of superficial wounds of scalp, neck, axillae, external genitalia, trunk and/or extremities (including hands and feet); 2.5 cm or less   [P2][T]
  - 2.92   4.11   Global Days 010
  - **AMA:** 2009, Jan, 11-31; 2008, Jan, 10-25; 2008, Feb, 8-9; 2007, January, 13-27; 2007, February, 10-11

- **12002**   2.6 cm to 7.5 cm   [P2][T]
  - 3.23   4.36   Global Days 010
  - **AMA:** 2009, Jan, 11-31; 2008, Jan, 10-25; 2008, Feb, 8-9; February, 10-11; 2007, January, 13-27

- **12004**   7.6 cm to 12.5 cm   [P2][T]
  - 3.76   5.11   Global Days 010
  - **AMA:** 2009, Jan, 11-31; 2008, Jan, 10-25; 2008, Feb, 8-9; February, 10-11; 2007, January, 13-27

[26/TC] PC/TC Comp Only   [A2-Z3] ASC Pmt   [50] Bilateral   ♂ Male Only   ♀ Female Only   Facility RVU   Non-Facility RVU
AMA: CPT Asst   **MED:** Pub 100   [A-Y] OPPSI   [80/80] Surg Assist Allowed / w/Doc   Lab Crosswalk   Radiology Crosswalk

CPT only © 2009 American Medical Association. All Rights Reserved. (Black Ink)   Medicare (Red Ink)   © 2009 Publisher (Blue Ink)

Current Procedural Coding Expert – Integumentary System

12005	12.6 cm to 20.0 cm
	4.63 6.34 Global Days 010
	AMA: 2009, Jan, 11-31; 2008, Jan, 10-25; 2008, Feb, 8-9; 2007, January, 13-27; 2007, February, 10-11
12006	20.1 cm to 30.0 cm
	5.82 7.83 Global Days 010
	AMA: 2009, Jan, 11-31; 2008, Jan, 10-25; 2008, Feb, 8-9; 2007, February, 10-11; 2007, January, 13-27
12007	over 30.0 cm
	6.52 8.67 Global Days 010
	AMA: 2009, Jan, 11-31; 2008, Jan, 10-25; 2008, Feb, 8-9; 2007, February, 10-11; 2007, January, 13-27
12011	Simple repair of superficial wounds of face, ears, eyelids, nose, lips and/or mucous membranes; 2.5 cm or less
	2.99 4.34 Global Days 010
	AMA: 2009, Jan, 11-31; 2008, Jan, 10-25; 2008, Feb, 8-9; 2007, January, 13-27; 2007, February, 10-11
12013	2.6 cm to 5.0 cm
	3.40 4.78 Global Days 010
	AMA: 2009, Jan, 11-31; 2008, Jan, 10-25; 2008, Feb, 8-9; 2007, February, 10-11; 2007, January, 13-27
12014	5.1 cm to 7.5 cm
	4.03 5.58 Global Days 010
	AMA: 2009, Jan, 11-31; 2008, Feb, 8-9; 2008, Jan, 10-25; 2007, February, 10-11; 2007, January, 13-27
12015	7.6 cm to 12.5 cm
	5.04 6.98 Global Days 010
	AMA: 2009, Jan, 11-31; 2008, Feb, 8-9; 2008, Jan, 10-25; 2007, February, 10-11; 2007, January, 13-27
12016	12.6 cm to 20.0 cm
	6.07 8.29 Global Days 010
	AMA: 2009, Jan, 11-31; 2008, Jan, 10-25; 2008, Feb, 8-9; 2007, January, 13-27; 2007, February, 10-11
12017	20.1 cm to 30.0 cm
	6.86 6.86 Global Days 010
	AMA: 2009, Jan, 11-31; 2008, Jan, 10-25; 2008, Feb, 8-9; 2007, February, 10-11; 2007, January, 13-27
12018	over 30.0 cm
	7.91 7.91 Global Days 010
	AMA: 2009, Jan, 11-31; 2008, Jan, 10-25; 2008, Feb, 8-9; 2007, February, 10-11; 2007, January, 13-27
12020	Treatment of superficial wound dehiscence; simple closure
	EXCLUDES Secondary closure major/complex wound (13160)
	5.05 7.13 Global Days 010
	AMA: 2009, Jan, 11-31; 2008, Jan, 10-25; 2008, Feb, 8-9; 2007, January, 13-27
12021	with packing
	EXCLUDES Secondary closure major/complex wound (13160)
	3.67 4.22 Global Days 010
	AMA: 2009, Jan, 11-31; 2008, Jan, 10-25; 2008, Feb, 8-9; 2007, January, 13-27

12031-12057 Suturing of Intermediate Wounds

CMS 100-4,4,20.5   HCPCS Under OPPS
CMS 100-4,12,90.3   MD Services in ASCs
CMS 100-4,14,10   General ASC Services

INCLUDES
Administration of local anesthesia
Intermediate repair that involves:
  Closure of contaminated single layer wound
  Layer closure (e.g., subcutaneous tissue, superficial fascia)
  Removal foreign material (e.g. gravel, glass)
  Routine debridement and decontamination
Simple:
  Exploration nerves, blood vessels, tendons in wound
Total length of several repairs in same code category

EXCLUDES
Debridement
  Performed separately, no closure (11040-11044)
  That requires:
    Removal soft tissue and/or bone, no fracture/dislocation (11040-11044)
    Removal soft tissue/bone due to open fracture/dislocation (11010-11012)
Major exploration (20100-20103)
Repair nerves, blood vessels, tendons (see appropriate anatomical section)
Secondary closure major/complex wound or dehiscense (13160)
Wound repair involving more than layer closure

12031	Repair, intermediate, wounds of scalp, axillae, trunk and/or extremities (excluding hands and feet); 2.5 cm or less
	4.44 6.42 Global Days 010
	AMA: 2009, Jan, 11-31; 2008, Jan, 10-25; 2007, January, 13-27; 2007, February, 10-11
12032	2.6 cm to 7.5 cm
	5.24 7.83 Global Days 010
	AMA: 2009, Jan, 11-31; 2008, Jan, 10-25; 2007, January, 13-27; 2007, February, 10-11
12034	7.6 cm to 12.5 cm
	5.57 8.06 Global Days 010
	AMA: 2009, Jan, 11-31; 2008, Jan, 10-25; 2007, February, 10-11; 2007, January, 13-27
12035	12.6 cm to 20.0 cm
	6.43 9.77 Global Days 010
	AMA: 2009, Jan, 11-31; 2008, Jan, 10-25; 2007, February, 10-11; 2007, January, 13-27
12036	20.1 cm to 30.0 cm
	7.36 10.75 Global Days 010
	AMA: 2009, Jan, 11-31; 2008, Jan, 10-25; 2007, February, 10-11; 2007, January, 13-27
12037	over 30.0 cm
	8.51 12.02 Global Days 010
	AMA: 2009, Jan, 11-31; 2008, Jan, 10-25; 2007, February, 10-11; 2007, January, 13-27
12041	Repair, intermediate, wounds of neck, hands, feet and/or external genitalia; 2.5 cm or less
	4.72 6.73 Global Days 010
	AMA: 2009, Jan, 11-31; 2008, Jan, 10-25; 2007, February, 10-11; 2007, January, 13-27
12042	2.6 cm to 7.5 cm
	5.42 7.54 Global Days 010
	AMA: 2009, Jan, 11-31; 2008, Jan, 10-25; 2007, February, 10-11; 2007, January, 13-27

● New Code   ▲ Revised Code   Maternity    Age   Unlisted   Not Covered   # Resequenced
CCI   + Add-on   Mod 51 Exempt   Mod 63 Exempt   Mod Sedation   PQRI

© 2009 Publisher *(Blue Ink)*   CPT only © 2009 American Medical Association. All Rights Reserved. *(Black Ink)*   Medicare *(Red Ink)*

12044	7.6 cm to 12.5 cm	A2 T
	🚑 5.79 ✂ 9.21 Global Days 010	
	AMA: 2009, Jan, 11-31; 2008, Jan, 10-25; 2007, January, 13-27; 2007, February, 10-11	
12045	12.6 cm to 20.0 cm	A2 T
	🚑 6.63 ✂ 9.79 Global Days 010	
	AMA: 2009, Jan, 11-31; 2008, Jan, 10-25; 2007, February, 10-11; 2007, January, 13-27	
12046	20.1 cm to 30.0 cm	A2 T 80
	🚑 8.41 ✂ 12.93 Global Days 010	
	AMA: 2009, Jan, 11-31; 2008, Jan, 10-25; 2007, February, 10-11; 2007, January, 13-27	
12047	over 30.0 cm	A2 T 80
	🚑 9.33 ✂ 13.59 Global Days 010	
	AMA: 2009, Jan, 11-31; 2008, Jan, 10-25; 2007, February, 10-11; 2007, January, 13-27	
12051	Repair, intermediate, wounds of face, ears, eyelids, nose, lips and/or mucous membranes; 2.5 cm or less	P2 T
	🚑 4.95 ✂ 6.98 Global Days 010	
	AMA: 2009, Jan, 11-31; 2008, Jan, 10-25; 2007, January, 13-27; 2007, February, 10-11	
12052	2.6 cm to 5.0 cm	P2 T
	🚑 5.93 ✂ 7.97 Global Days 010	
	AMA: 2009, Jan, 11-31; 2008, Jan, 10-25; 2008, Jul, 5-6&15; 2007, February, 10-11; 2007, January, 13-27	
12053	5.1 cm to 7.5 cm	P2 T
	🚑 5.89 ✂ 8.91 Global Days 010	
	AMA: 2009, Jan, 11-31; 2008, Jan, 10-25; 2007, February, 10-11; 2007, January, 13-27	
12054	7.6 cm to 12.5 cm	A2 T
	🚑 6.22 ✂ 9.54 Global Days 010	
	AMA: 2009, Jan, 11-31; 2008, Jan, 10-25; 2007, January, 13-27; 2007, February, 10-11	
12055	12.6 cm to 20.0 cm	A2 T
	🚑 7.59 ✂ 11.48 Global Days 010	
	AMA: 2009, Jan, 11-31; 2008, Jan, 10-25; 2007, February, 10-11; 2007, January, 13-27	
12056	20.1 cm to 30.0 cm	A2 T 80
	🚑 7.81 ✂ 13.58 Global Days 010	
	AMA: 2009, Jan, 11-31; 2008, Jan, 10-25; 2007, February, 10-11; 2007, January, 13-27	
12057	over 30.0 cm	A2 T 80
	🚑 9.96 ✂ 14.49 Global Days 010	
	AMA: 2009, Jan, 11-31; 2008, Jan, 10-25; 2007, February, 10-11; 2007, January, 13-27	

13100-13160 Suturing of Complicated Wounds

CMS 100-4,4,20.5 — HCPCS Under OPPS
CMS 100-4,12,90.3 — MD Services in ASCs
CMS 100-4,14,10 — General ASC Services

INCLUDES
Creation of defect for repair, such as scar removal
Debridement complicated wounds/avulsions
More complicated than layered closure
Simple:
   Exploration nerves, vessels, tendons in wound
   Vessel ligation in wound
Total length of several repairs in same code category
Undermining, stents, retention sutures

EXCLUDES
Complex/secondary wound closure or dehiscence
Debridement:
   Performed separately, no closure (11040-11044)
   Soft tissue and/or bone due to open fracture/dislocation (11010-11012)
   Soft tissue and/or bone, no fracture/dislocation (11040-11044)
Excision:
   Benign lesions (11400-11446)
   Malignant lesions (11600-11646)
Extensive exploration (20100-20103)
Repair nerves, blood vessels, tendons (see appropriate anatomical section)

13100	Repair, complex, trunk; 1.1 cm to 2.5 cm	A2 T
	EXCLUDES Complex repair 1.0 cm or less (12001, 12031)	
	🚑 6.30 ✂ 8.10 Global Days 010	
	AMA: 2009, Jan, 11-31; 2008, Jan, 10-25; 2007, January, 13-27	
13101	2.6 cm to 7.5 cm	A2 T
	🚑 7.69 ✂ 10.27 Global Days 010	
	AMA: 2009, Jan, 11-31; 2008, Jan, 10-25; 2007, January, 13-27	
+ 13102	each additional 5 cm or less (List separately in addition to code for primary procedure)	A2 T
	Code first 13101	
	🚑 2.07 ✂ 2.85 Global Days ZZZ	
	AMA: 2009, Jan, 11-31; 2008, Jan, 10-25; 2007, January, 13-27	
13120	Repair, complex, scalp, arms, and/or legs; 1.1 cm to 2.5 cm	A2 T
	EXCLUDES Complex repair 1.0 cm or less (12001, 12031)	
	🚑 6.60 ✂ 8.41 Global Days 010	
	AMA: 2009, Jan, 11-31; 2008, Jan, 10-25; 2007, January, 13-27	
13121	2.6 cm to 7.5 cm	A2 T
	🚑 8.83 ✂ 11.48 Global Days 010	
	AMA: 2009, Jan, 11-31; 2008, Jan, 10-25; 2007, January, 13-27	
+ 13122	each additional 5 cm or less (List separately in addition to code for primary procedure)	A2 T
	Code first 13121	
	🚑 2.37 ✂ 3.13 Global Days ZZZ	
	AMA: 2009, Jan, 11-31; 2008, Jan, 10-25; 2007, January, 13-27	
13131	Repair, complex, forehead, cheeks, chin, mouth, neck, axillae, genitalia, hands and/or feet; 1.1 cm to 2.5 cm	A2 T
	EXCLUDES Complex repair 1.0 cm or less (12001, 12011, 12031, 12041, 12051)	
	🚑 7.43 ✂ 9.31 Global Days 010	
	AMA: 2009, Jan, 11-31; 2008, Jan, 10-25; 2007, January, 13-27	
13132	2.6 cm to 7.5 cm	A2 T
	🚑 12.71 ✂ 15.21 Global Days 010	
	AMA: 2009, Jan, 11-31; 2008, Jan, 10-25; 2007, January, 13-27	
+ 13133	each additional 5 cm or less (List separately in addition to code for primary procedure)	A2 T
	Code first 13132	
	🚑 3.67 ✂ 4.48 Global Days ZZZ	
	AMA: 2009, Jan, 11-31; 2008, Jan, 10-25; 2007, January, 13-27	

Current Procedural Coding Expert – Integumentary System

13150 Repair, complex, eyelids, nose, ears and/or lips; 1.0 cm or less
  7.44 9.32 Global Days 010
  AMA: 2009, Jan, 11-31; 2008, Jan, 10-25; 2007, January, 13-27

13151 1.1 cm to 2.5 cm
  8.58 10.59 Global Days 010
  AMA: 2009, Jan, 11-31; 2008, Jan, 10-25; 2007, January, 13-27

13152 2.6 cm to 7.5 cm
  11.56 14.71 Global Days 010
  AMA: 2009, Jan, 11-31; 2008, Jan, 10-25; 2007, January, 13-27

+ **13153** each additional 5 cm or less (List separately in addition to code for primary procedure)
  Code first 13152
  3.97 4.94 Global Days ZZZ
  AMA: 2009, Jan, 11-31; 2008, Jan, 10-25; 2007, January, 13-27

13160 Secondary closure of surgical wound or dehiscence, extensive or complicated
  EXCLUDES Packing or simple secondary wound closure (12020-12021)
  21.94 21.94 Global Days 090
  AMA: 2009, Jan, 11-31; 2008, Jan, 10-25; 2007, January, 13-27

14000-14350 Reposition Contiguous Tissue

CMS 100-2,16,120   Cosmetic Procedures
CMS 100-4,4,20.5   HCPCS Under OPPS
CMS 100-4,12,90.3 MD Services in ASCs
CMS 100-4,14,10   Part B ASC Payment

INCLUDES Excision of lesion with repair by adjacent tissue transfer or tissue rearrangement
Z-plasty, W-plasty, VY-plasty, rotation flap, advancement flap, double pedicle flap

EXCLUDES Full thickness closure of:
Eyelid (67930-67935, 67961-67975)
Lip (40650-40654)
Skin graft necessary to repair secondary defect (flap defect)

Do not report with (11400-11446, 11600-11646)

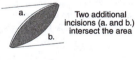
Example of common Z-plasty. Lesion is removed with oval-shaped incision
Two additional incisions (a. and b.) intersect the area

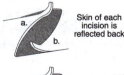
Skin of each incision is reflected back

The flaps are then transposed and the repair is closed

An adjacent flap, or other rearrangement flap, is performed to repair a defect of 10 sq cm or less (14000); a larger defect (up to 30 sq cm) is coded 14001

14000 Adjacent tissue transfer or rearrangement, trunk; defect 10 sq cm or less
  INCLUDES Burrow's operation
  13.56 16.29 Global Days 090
  AMA: 2009, Jan, 11-31; 2008, Jan, 10-25; 2008, Jul, 5-6&15; 2007, January, 13-27; 2006, January, 46-47; 2006, December, 14-15

14001 defect 10.1 sq cm to 30.0 sq cm
  17.78 21.06 Global Days 090
  AMA: 2009, Jan, 11-31; 2008, Jan, 10-25; 2008, Jul, 5-6&15; 2007, January, 13-27; 2006, December, 14-15; 2006, January, 46-47

14020 Adjacent tissue transfer or rearrangement, scalp, arms and/or legs; defect 10 sq cm or less
  15.34 18.24 Global Days 090
  AMA: 2009, Jan, 11-31; 2008, Jan, 10-25; 2008, Jul, 5-6&15; 2007, January, 13-27; 2006, January, 46-47; 2006, December, 14-15

14021 defect 10.1 sq cm to 30.0 sq cm
  19.56 22.97 Global Days 090
  AMA: 2009, Jan, 11-31; 2008, Jan, 10-25; 2008, Jul, 5-6&15; 2007, January, 13-27; 2006, January, 46-47; 2006, December, 14-15

14040 Adjacent tissue transfer or rearrangement, forehead, cheeks, chin, mouth, neck, axillae, genitalia, hands and/or feet; defect 10 sq cm or less
  INCLUDES Krimer's palatoplasty
  17.30 20.20 Global Days 090
  AMA: 2009, Jan, 11-31; 2008, Jan, 10-25; 2008, Jul, 5-6&15; 2007, January, 13-27; 2006, January, 46-47; 2006, December, 14-15

14041 defect 10.1 sq cm to 30.0 sq cm
  21.29 24.98 Global Days 090
  AMA: 2009, Jan, 11-31; 2008, Jan, 10-25; 2008, Jul, 5-6&15; 2007, January, 13-27; 2006, December, 14-15; 2006, January, 46-47

14060 Adjacent tissue transfer or rearrangement, eyelids, nose, ears and/or lips; defect 10 sq cm or less
  INCLUDES Denonvillier's operation
  EXCLUDES Eyelid, full thickness (67961 and subsequent codes)
  18.38 20.66 Global Days 090
  AMA: 2009, Jan, 11-31; 2008, Jan, 10-25; 2008, Jul, 5-6&15; 2007, January, 13-27; 2006, January, 46-47; 2006, December, 14-15

14061 defect 10.1 sq cm to 30.0 sq cm
  EXCLUDES Eyelid, full thickness (67961 and subsequent codes)
  22.73 26.81 Global Days 090
  AMA: 2009, Jan, 11-31; 2008, Jan, 10-25; 2008, Jul, 5-6&15; 2007, January, 13-27; 2006, January, 46-47; 2006, December, 14-15

~~**14300** Adjacent tissue transfer or rearrangement, more than 30 sq cm, unusual or complicated, any area~~
  To report, see code 14301-14302

● **14301** Adjacent tissue transfer or rearrangement, any area; defect 30.1 sq cm to 60.0 sq cm
  24.14 28.52 Global Days 090

+ ● **14302** each additional 30.0 sq cm, or part thereof (List separately in addition to code for primary procedure)
  Code first 14301
  6.26 6.26 Global Days ZZZ

● New Code   ▲ Revised Code   Maternity   Age   Unlisted   Not Covered   # Resequenced
CCI   + Add-on   Mod 51 Exempt   Mod 63 Exempt   Mod Sedation   PQRI

14350

14350 Filleted finger or toe flap, including preparation of recipient site
🔗 19.87 🔗 19.87 Global Days 090
AMA: 2009, Jan, 11-31; 2008, Jan, 10-25; 2008, Jul, 5-6&15; 2007, January, 13-27; 2006, January, 46-47

15002-15005 Development of Base for Tissue Grafting

CMS 100-4,3,20.1.2.8   Special Payments for Burn Cases
CMS 100-4,12,90.3   MD Services in ASCs
CMS 100-4,14,10   Part B ASC Payment

INCLUDES
Excision of scar or burn eschar or release of scar contracture without graft with application of dressing or other material only
Fixation and anchoring skin graft
Initial wound preparation such as scar or burn eschar removal or release of scar contracture
Routine dressing
Simple tissue debridement
Wound size by percentage of body area for children younger than age 10
Wound size in centimeters for adults age 10 or older

EXCLUDES
Acellular dermal graft (15170-15176)
Autologous skin graft (15100-15261)
Autologous tissue cultured skin graft (15150-15157)
Excision of:
  Benign lesion (11400-11471)
  Malignant lesion (11600-11646)
Grafting with skin or skin replacements (15100-15431)
Harvesting of tissue for autologous skin grafts (15040)
Microvascular repair (15756-15758)
Primary procedure such as radical mastectomy, extensive tumor removal, orbitectomy (see appropriate anatomical site)
Repair of donor site with skin grafts or flaps (14000-14350, 15050-15770)
Simple graft application alone
Simple placement of stabilization dressings only

Code also any immediate:
  Allograft skin applications (15300-15336, 15360-15366)
  Skin grafting (15050-15261)
  Xenogenic dermis application (15400-15421)
Code also modifier 58 for staged procedures

15002 Surgical preparation or creation of recipient site by excision of open wounds, burn eschar, or scar (including subcutaneous tissues), or incisional release of scar contracture, trunk, arms, legs; first 100 sq cm or 1% of body area of infants and children
🔗 6.27 🔗 9.01 Global Days 000
AMA: 2009, Jan, 11-31; 2008, Mar, 14-15; 2008, Jan, 10-25; 2007, January, 13-27

+ **15003** each additional 100 sq cm, or part thereof, or each additional 1% of body area of infants and children (List separately in addition to code for primary procedure)
Code first 15002
🔗 1.27 🔗 1.96 Global Days ZZZ
AMA: 2009, Jan, 11-31; 2008, Jan, 10-25; 2007, January, 13-27

15004 Surgical preparation or creation of recipient site by excision of open wounds, burn eschar, or scar (including subcutaneous tissues), or incisional release of scar contracture, face, scalp, eyelids, mouth, neck, ears, orbits, genitalia, hands, feet and/or multiple digits; first 100 sq cm or 1% of body area of infants and children
🔗 7.55 🔗 10.53 Global Days 000
AMA: 2009, Jan, 11-31; 2008, Jan, 10-25; 2007, January, 13-27

+ **15005** each additional 100 sq cm, or part thereof, or each additional 1% of body area of infants and children (List separately in addition to code for primary procedure)
Code first 15004
🔗 2.56 🔗 3.32 Global Days ZZZ
AMA: 2009, Jan, 11-31; 2008, Jan, 10-25; 2007, January, 13-27

15040 Obtain Autograft

CMS 100-4,3,20.1.2.8   Special Payments for Burn Cases
CMS 100-4,12,90.3   MD Services in ASCs

15040 Harvest of skin for tissue cultured skin autograft, 100 sq cm or less
🔗 3.57 🔗 6.62 Global Days 000
AMA: 2009, Jan, 11-31; 2008, Jan, 10-25; 2008, Feb, 3-4; 2007, January, 13-27; 2006, August, 12-14

15050-15261 Skin Grafts and Replacements

CMS 100-4,3,20.1.2.8   Special Payments for Burn Cases
CMS 100-4,12,90.3   MD Services in ASCs
CMS 100-4,14,10   Part B ASC Payment

INCLUDES
Fixation and anchoring skin graft
Routine dressing
Simple tissue debridement
Wound size by percentage of body area for children younger than age 10
Wound size in centimeters for adults age 10 or older (15100-15101)

EXCLUDES
Excision of:
  Benign lesion (11400-11471)
  Burn eschar or scar (15002-15005)
  Malignant lesion (11600-11646)
Harvesting of tissue for autologous skin graft (15040)
Microvascular repair (15756-15758)
Primary procedures such as radical mastectomy, extensive tumor removal, orbitectomy (see appropriate anatomical site)
Reconstruction of eyelid (67961-67975)
Repair of donor site with skin grafts or flaps (14000-14350, 15050-15431)

15050 Pinch graft, single or multiple, to cover small ulcer, tip of digit, or other minimal open area (except on face), up to defect size 2 cm diameter
🔗 12.01 🔗 14.81 Global Days 090
AMA: 2009, Jan, 11-31; 2008, Jan, 10-25; 2007, January, 13-27; 2006, August, 12-14; 2005, February, 10-12

15100 Split-thickness autograft, trunk, arms, legs; first 100 sq cm or less, or 1% of body area of infants and children (except 15050)
🔗 19.42 🔗 22.69 Global Days 090
AMA: 2009, Jan, 11-31; 2008, Jan, 10-25; 2008, Feb, 3-4; 2007, January, 13-27; 2006, August, 12-14

+ **15101** each additional 100 sq cm, or each additional 1% of body area of infants and children, or part thereof (List separately in addition to code for primary procedure)
Code first 15100
🔗 3.04 🔗 4.78 Global Days ZZZ
AMA: 2009, Jan, 11-31; 2008, Jan, 10-25; 2008, Feb, 3-4; 2007, January, 13-27; 2006, August, 12-14

15110 Epidermal autograft, trunk, arms, legs; first 100 sq cm or less, or 1% of body area of infants and children
🔗 20.28 🔗 22.84 Global Days 090
AMA: 2009, Jan, 11-31; 2008, Jan, 10-25; 2008, Feb, 3-4; 2007, January, 13-27; 2006, August, 12-14

Current Procedural Coding Expert – Integumentary System   15175

+	15111	each additional 100 sq cm, or each additional 1% of body area of infants and children, or part thereof (List separately in addition to code for primary procedure) A2 T Code first 15110 2.91 3.18 Global Days ZZZ **AMA:** 2009, Jan, 11-31; 2008, Jan, 10-25; 2008, Feb, 3-4; 2007, January, 13-27; 2006, August, 12-14
	15115	Epidermal autograft, face, scalp, eyelids, mouth, neck, ears, orbits, genitalia, hands, feet, and/or multiple digits; first 100 sq cm or less, or 1% of body area of infants and children A2 T 20.55 23.06 Global Days 090 **AMA:** 2009, Jan, 11-31; 2008, Jan, 10-25; 2008, Feb, 3-4; 2007, January, 13-27; 2006, August, 12-14
+	15116	each additional 100 sq cm, or each additional 1% of body area of infants and children, or part thereof (List separately in addition to code for primary procedure) A2 T Code first 15115 4.31 4.67 Global Days ZZZ **AMA:** 2009, Jan, 11-31; 2008, Feb, 3-4; 2008, Jan, 10-25; 2007, January, 13-27; 2006, August, 12-14
	15120	Split-thickness autograft, face, scalp, eyelids, mouth, neck, ears, orbits, genitalia, hands, feet, and/or multiple digits; first 100 sq cm or less, or 1% of body area of infants and children (except 15050) A2 T 21.53 25.47 Global Days 090 **AMA:** 2009, Jan, 11-31; 2008, Jan, 10-25; 2008, Feb, 3-4; 2008, Jul, 5-6&15; 2007, January, 13-27; 2006, August, 12-14
+	15121	each additional 100 sq cm, or each additional 1% of body area of infants and children, or part thereof (List separately in addition to code for primary procedure) A2 T Code first 15120 4.69 6.95 Global Days ZZZ **AMA:** 2009, Jan, 11-31; 2008, Jan, 10-25; 2008, Feb, 3-4; 2007, January, 13-27; 2006, August, 12-14
	15130	Dermal autograft, trunk, arms, legs; first 100 sq cm or less, or 1% of body area of infants and children A2 T 15.15 17.68 Global Days 090 **AMA:** 2009, Jan, 11-31; 2008, Jan, 10-25; 2008, Feb, 3-4; 2007, January, 13-27; 2006, August, 12-14
+	15131	each additional 100 sq cm, or each additional 1% of body area of infants and children, or part thereof (List separately in addition to code for primary procedure) A2 T Code first 15130 2.28 2.48 Global Days ZZZ **AMA:** 2009, Jan, 11-31; 2008, Jan, 10-25; 2008, Feb, 3-4; 2007, January, 13-27; 2006, August, 12-14
	15135	Dermal autograft, face, scalp, eyelids, mouth, neck, ears, orbits, genitalia, hands, feet, and/or multiple digits; first 100 sq cm or less, or 1% of body area of infants and children A2 T 20.82 23.31 Global Days 090 **AMA:** 2009, Jan, 11-31; 2008, Jan, 10-25; 2008, Feb, 3-4; 2007, January, 13-27; 2006, August, 12-14
+	15136	each additional 100 sq cm, or each additional 1% of body area of infants and children, or part thereof (List separately in addition to code for primary procedure) A2 T Code first (15135) 2.17 2.30 Global Days ZZZ **AMA:** 2009, Jan, 11-31; 2008, Feb, 3-4; 2008, Jan, 10-25; 2007, January, 13-27; 2006, August, 12-14

	15150	Tissue cultured epidermal autograft, trunk, arms, legs; first 25 sq cm or less A2 T 17.07 18.49 Global Days 090 **AMA:** 2009, Jan, 11-31; 2008, Jan, 10-25; 2008, Feb, 3-4; 2007, January, 13-27; 2006, August, 12-14
+	15151	additional 1 sq cm to 75 sq cm (List separately in addition to code for primary procedure) A2 T Code first 15150 **EXCLUDES** Grafts over 75 sq cm (15152) 3.05 3.27 Global Days ZZZ **AMA:** 2009, Jan, 11-31; 2008, Jan, 10-25; 2008, Feb, 3-4; 2007, January, 13-27; 2006, August, 12-14
+	15152	each additional 100 sq cm, or each additional 1% of body area of infants and children, or part thereof (List separately in addition to code for primary procedure) A2 T Code first 15151 3.79 4.02 Global Days ZZZ **AMA:** 2009, Jan, 11-31; 2008, Jan, 10-25; 2008, Feb, 3-4; 2007, January, 13-27; 2006, August, 12-14
	15155	Tissue cultured epidermal autograft, face, scalp, eyelids, mouth, neck, ears, orbits, genitalia, hands, feet, and/or multiple digits; first 25 sq cm or less A2 T 15.29 16.43 Global Days 090 **AMA:** 2009, Jan, 11-31; 2008, Jan, 10-25; 2008, Feb, 3-4; 2007, January, 13-27; 2006, August, 12-14
+	15156	additional 1 sq cm to 75 sq cm (List separately in addition to code for primary procedure) A2 T Code first 15155 **EXCLUDES** Grafts over 75 sq cm (15157) 4.43 4.63 Global Days ZZZ **AMA:** 2009, Jan, 11-31; 2008, Feb, 3-4; 2008, Jan, 10-25; 2007, January, 13-27; 2006, August, 12-14
+	15157	each additional 100 sq cm, or each additional 1% of body area of infants and children, or part thereof (List separately in addition to code for primary procedure) A2 T Code first 15156 4.25 4.50 Global Days ZZZ **AMA:** 2009, Jan, 11-31; 2008, Jan, 10-25; 2008, Feb, 3-4; 2007, January, 13-27; 2006, August, 12-14
	15170	Acellular dermal replacement, trunk, arms, legs; first 100 sq cm or less, or 1% of body area of infants and children G2 T 10.25 11.80 Global Days 090 **AMA:** 2009, Jan, 11-31; 2008, Jan, 10-25; 2008, Feb, 3-4; 2007, January, 13-27; 2006, August, 12-14
+	15171	each additional 100 sq cm, or each additional 1% of body area of infants and children, or part thereof (List separately in addition to code for primary procedure) G2 T Code first 15170 2.43 2.58 Global Days ZZZ **AMA:** 2009, Jan, 11-31; 2008, Jan, 10-25; 2008, Feb, 3-4; 2007, January, 13-27; 2006, August, 12-14
	15175	Acellular dermal replacement, face, scalp, eyelids, mouth, neck, ears, orbits, genitalia, hands, feet, and/or multiple digits; first 100 sq cm or less, or 1% of body area of infants and children G2 T 12.52 13.96 Global Days 090 **AMA:** 2009, Jan, 11-31; 2008, Feb, 3-4; 2008, Jan, 10-25; 2007, January, 13-27; 2006, August, 12-14

● New Code   ▲ Revised Code   M Maternity   A Age   Unlisted   Not Covered   # Resequenced
CCI   + Add-on   Mod 51 Exempt   Mod 63 Exempt   Mod Sedation   PQRI
© 2009 Publisher *(Blue Ink)*   CPT only © 2009 American Medical Association. All Rights Reserved. (Black Ink)   Medicare (Red Ink)

+	15176	each additional 100 sq cm, or each additional 1% of body area of infants and children, or part thereof (List separately in addition to code for primary procedure)

Code first 15175
3.74 4.01 Global Days ZZZ
AMA: 2009, Jan, 11-31; 2008, Feb, 3-4; 2008, Jan, 10-25; 2007, January, 13-27; 2006, August, 12-14

	15200	Full thickness graft, free, including direct closure of donor site, trunk; 20 sq cm or less

18.19 21.82 Global Days 090
AMA: 2009, Jan, 11-31; 2008, Jan, 10-25; 2008, Mar, 14-15; 2008, Feb, 3-4; 2007, January, 13-27; 2006, August, 12-14

+	15201	each additional 20 sq cm, or part thereof (List separately in addition to code for primary procedure)

Code first 15200
2.13 3.80 Global Days ZZZ
AMA: 2009, Jan, 11-31; 2008, Jan, 10-25; 2008, Mar, 14-15; 2008, Feb, 3-4; 2007, January, 13-27; 2006, August, 12-14

	15220	Full thickness graft, free, including direct closure of donor site, scalp, arms, and/or legs; 20 sq cm or less

16.66 20.21 Global Days 090
AMA: 2009, Jan, 11-31; 2008, Jan, 10-25; 2008, Mar, 14-15; 2008, Feb, 3-4; 2007, January, 13-27; 2006, August, 12-14

+	15221	each additional 20 sq cm, or part thereof (List separately in addition to code for primary procedure)

Code first 15220
2.01 3.54 Global Days ZZZ
AMA: 2009, Jan, 11-31; 2008, Jan, 10-25; 2008, Feb, 3-4; 2008, Mar, 14-15; 2007, January, 13-27; 2006, August, 12-14

	15240	Full thickness graft, free, including direct closure of donor site, forehead, cheeks, chin, mouth, neck, axillae, genitalia, hands, and/or feet; 20 sq cm or less

EXCLUDES Finger tip graft (15050)
            Syndactyly repair fingers (26560-26562)

21.69 24.64 Global Days 090
AMA: 2009, Jan, 11-31; 2008, Mar, 14-15; 2008, Jan, 10-25; 2008, Feb, 3-4; 2007, January, 13-27; 2006, August, 12-14

+	15241	each additional 20 sq cm, or part thereof (List separately in addition to code for primary procedure)

Code first 15240
3.14 4.86 Global Days ZZZ
AMA: 2009, Jan, 11-31; 2008, Jan, 10-25; 2008, Feb, 3-4; 2008, Mar, 14-15; 2007, January, 13-27; 2006, August, 12-14

	15260	Full thickness graft, free, including direct closure of donor site, nose, ears, eyelids, and/or lips; 20 sq cm or less

23.39 26.69 Global Days 090
AMA: 2009, Jan, 11-31; 2008, Mar, 14-15; 2008, Feb, 3-4; 2008, Jan, 10-25; 2007, January, 13-27; 2006, August, 12-14

+	15261	each additional 20 sq cm, or part thereof (List separately in addition to code for primary procedure)

Code first 15260
EXCLUDES Eyelid reconstruction (67961-67975)

3.94 5.68 Global Days ZZZ
AMA: 2009, Jan, 11-31; 2008, Mar, 14-15; 2008, Jan, 10-25; 2008, Feb, 3-4; 2007, January, 13-27; 2006, August, 12-14

15300-15366 Homografts

CMS 100-4,3,20.1.2.8 Special Payments for Burn Cases
CMS 100-4,4,20.5 HCPCS Under OPPS

INCLUDES Fixation and anchoring skin graft
Non-autologous human skin graft to repair wound caused by:
   Burns
   Infection of skin and subcutaneous tissues
   Necrosis
   Surgical wounds
   Traumatic injury
Routine dressing
Simple tissue debridement

EXCLUDES *Autologous tissue cultured skin graft (15150-15157)*
Excision of:
   Benign lesion (11400-11471)
   Burn eschar or scar (15002-15005)
   Malignant lesion (11600-11646)
Harvesting tissue for autologous skin graft (15040)
Microvascular repair (15756-15758)
Primary procedures such as a radical mastectomy, extensive tumor removal, orbitectomy (see appropriate anatomical site)
Repair of donor site with skin grafts or flaps (14000-14350, 15050-15431)

	15300	Allograft skin for temporary wound closure, trunk, arms, legs; first 100 sq cm or less, or 1% of body area of infants and children

8.05 9.49 Global Days 090
AMA: 2009, Jan, 11-31; 2008, Jan, 10-25; 2007, January, 13-27; 2006, August, 12-14

+	15301	each additional 100 sq cm, or each additional 1% of body area of infants and children, or part thereof (List separately in addition to code for primary procedure)

Code first 15300
1.59 1.74 Global Days ZZZ
AMA: 2009, Jan, 11-31; 2008, Jan, 10-25; 2007, January, 13-27; 2006, August, 12-14

	15320	Allograft skin for temporary wound closure, face, scalp, eyelids, mouth, neck, ears, orbits, genitalia, hands, feet, and/or multiple digits; first 100 sq cm or less, or 1% of body area of infants and children

8.59 10.14 Global Days 090
AMA: 2009, Jan, 11-31; 2008, Jan, 10-25; 2007, January, 13-27; 2006, August, 12-14

+	15321	each additional 100 sq cm, or each additional 1% of body area of infants and children, or part thereof (List separately in addition to code for primary procedure)

Code first 15320
2.39 2.58 Global Days ZZZ
AMA: 2009, Jan, 11-31; 2008, Jan, 10-25; 2007, January, 13-27; 2006, August, 12-14

	15330	Acellular dermal allograft, trunk, arms, legs; first 100 sq cm or less, or 1% of body area of infants and children

7.27 8.74 Global Days 090
AMA: 2009, Jan, 11-31; 2008, Jan, 10-25; 2007, January, 13-27; 2006, August, 12-14

Current Procedural Coding Expert – Integumentary System

+ 15331 each additional 100 sq cm, or each additional 1% of body area of infants and children, or part thereof (List separately in addition to code for primary procedure) [A2] [T]
Code first 15330
 1.60 1.74 Global Days ZZZ
AMA: 2009, Jan, 11-31; 2008, Jan, 10-25; 2007, January, 13-27; 2006, August, 12-14

15335 Acellular dermal allograft, face, scalp, eyelids, mouth, neck, ears, orbits, genitalia, hands, feet, and/or multiple digits; first 100 sq cm or less, or 1% of body area of infants and children [A2] [T]
 7.12 8.50 Global Days 090
AMA: 2009, Jan, 11-31; 2008, Jan, 10-25; 2007, January, 13-27; 2006, August, 12-14

+ 15336 each additional 100 sq cm, or each additional 1% of body area of infants and children, or part thereof (List separately in addition to code for primary procedure) [A2] [T]
Code first 15335
 1.86 2.06 Global Days ZZZ
AMA: 2009, Jan, 11-31; 2008, Jan, 10-25; 2007, January, 13-27; 2006, August, 12-14

15340 Tissue cultured allogeneic skin substitute; first 25 sq cm or less [G2] [T]
INCLUDES Debridement
Surgical creation or preparation of recipient site

Do not report with (11040-11042, 15002-15005)
 7.22 8.38 Global Days 010
AMA: 2009, Jan, 11-31; 2008, Jan, 10-25; 2007, January, 13-27; 2006, August, 12-14

+ 15341 each additional 25 sq cm, or part thereof (List separately in addition to code for primary procedure) [G2] [T]
Code first 15340
Do not report with (11040-11042, 15002-15005)
 0.71 1.26 Global Days ZZZ
AMA: 2009, Jan, 11-31; 2008, Jan, 10-25; 2007, January, 13-27; 2006, August, 12-14

15360 Tissue cultured allogeneic dermal substitute, trunk, arms, legs; first 100 sq cm or less, or 1% of body area of infants and children [G2] [T]
 8.11 9.44 Global Days 090
AMA: 2009, Jan, 11-31; 2008, Jan, 10-25; 2008, Feb, 3-4; 2007, January, 13-27; 2006, August, 12-14

+ 15361 each additional 100 sq cm, or each additional 1% of body area of infants and children, or part thereof (List separately in addition to code for primary procedure) [G2] [T]
Code first 15360
 1.73 1.92 Global Days ZZZ
AMA: 2009, Jan, 11-31; 2008, Jan, 10-25; 2008, Feb, 3-4; 2007, January, 13-27; 2006, August, 12-14

15365 Tissue cultured allogeneic dermal substitute, face, scalp, eyelids, mouth, neck, ears, orbits, genitalia, hands, feet, and/or multiple digits; first 100 sq cm or less, or 1% of body area of infants and children [G2] [T]
 7.82 9.01 Global Days 090
AMA: 2009, Jan, 11-31; 2008, Jan, 10-25; 2008, Feb, 3-4; 2007, January, 13-27; 2006, August, 12-14

+ 15366 each additional 100 sq cm, or each additional 1% of body area of infants and children, or part thereof (List separately in addition to code for primary procedure) [G2] [T]
Code first 15365
 1.99 2.18 Global Days ZZZ
AMA: 2009, Jan, 11-31; 2008, Jan, 10-25; 2007, January, 13-27; 2006, August, 12-14

15400-15431 Heterografts

CMS 100-4,3,20.1.2.8   Special Payments for Burn Cases
INCLUDES Fixation and anchoring skin graft
Porcine tissue, pig skin, or nonhuman skin replacement
Routine dressing
Simple tissue debridement
Xenograft to repair wound caused by:
  Burns
  Infection of skin and subcutaneous tissues
  Necrosis
  Surgical wounds
  Traumatic injury

EXCLUDES Autologous tissue cultured skin graft (15150-15157)
Excision of:
  Benign lesion (11400-11471)
  Burn eschar or scar (15002-15005)
  Malignant lesion (11600-11646)
Primary procedures such as a radical mastectomy, extensive tumor removal, orbitectomy (see appropriate anatomical site)

15400 Xenograft, skin (dermal), for temporary wound closure, trunk, arms, legs; first 100 sq cm or less, or 1% of body area of infants and children [A2] [T]
 9.56 10.90 Global Days 090
AMA: 2009, Jan, 11-31; 2008, Jan, 10-25; 2007, January, 13-27; 2006, August, 12-14; 2006, January, 2-4,48

+ 15401 each additional 100 sq cm, or each additional 1% of body area of infants and children, or part thereof (List separately in addition to code for primary procedure) [A2] [T]
Code first 15400
 1.57 2.29 Global Days ZZZ
AMA: 2009, Jan, 11-31; 2008, Jan, 10-25; 2007, January, 13-27; 2006, January, 2-4,48; 2006, August, 12-14

15420 Xenograft skin (dermal), for temporary wound closure, face, scalp, eyelids, mouth, neck, ears, orbits, genitalia, hands, feet, and/or multiple digits; first 100 sq cm or less, or 1% of body area of infants and children [A2] [T]
 10.34 11.61 Global Days 090
AMA: 2009, Jan, 11-31; 2008, Jan, 10-25; 2007, January, 13-27; 2006, August, 12-14

+ 15421 each additional 100 sq cm, or each additional 1% of body area of infants and children, or part thereof (List separately in addition to code for primary procedure) [A2] [T]
Code first 15420
 2.39 3.11 Global Days ZZZ
AMA: 2009, Jan, 11-31; 2008, Jan, 10-25; 2007, January, 13-27; 2006, August, 12-14

● New Code   ▲ Revised Code   M Maternity   A Age   Unlisted   Not Covered   # Resequenced
CCI   + Add-on   Mod 51 Exempt   Mod 63 Exempt   Mod Sedation   PQRI
© 2009 Publisher (Blue Ink)   CPT only © 2009 American Medical Association. All Rights Reserved. (Black Ink)   Medicare (Red Ink)

15430   Acellular xenograft implant; first 100 sq cm or less, or 1% of body area of infants and children
    INCLUDES   Debridement
                   Surgical creation or preparation of recipient site
     Do not report with (11040-11042, 15002-15005, 46707)
     13.93   14.54   **Global Days 090**
     AMA: 2009, Jan, 11-31; 2008, Jan, 10-25; 2008, Jun, 3-6; 2007, January, 13-27; 2006, August, 12-14

+ 15431   each additional 100 sq cm, or each additional 1% of body area of infants and children, or part thereof (List separately in addition to code for primary procedure)
     Code first 15430
     Do not report with (11040-11042, 15002-15005, 46707)
     0.00   0.00   **Global Days ZZZ**
     AMA: 2009, Jan, 11-31; 2008, Jan, 10-25; 2008, Jun, 3-6; 2007, January, 13-27; 2006, August, 12-14

15570-15750 Wound Reconstruction: Skin Flaps

CMS 100-4,3,20.1.2.8   Special Payments for Burn Cases
CMS 100-4,4,20.5   HCPCS Under OPPS

INCLUDES
- Fixation and anchoring skin graft
- Routine dressing
- Simple tissue debridement
- Tube formation for later transfer
- Xenogenic dermis application

EXCLUDES
- Acellular dermal graft (15170-15176)
- Adjacent tissue transfer (14000-14302)
- Application of extensive immobilization apparatus
- Autologous skin graft (15100-15261)
- Autologous tissue cultured skin graft (15040)
- Excision of:
  - Benign lesion (11400-11471)
  - Burn eschar or scar (15002-15005)
  - Malignant lesion (11600-11646)
- Microvascular repair (15756-15758)
- Primary procedure such as radical mastectomy, extensive tumor removal, orbitectomy (see appropriate anatomical site)
- Repair of donor site with skin grafts or flaps (14000-14350, 15050-15431)

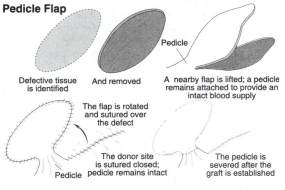

Pedicle Flap

Defective tissue is identified. And removed. A nearby flap is lifted; a pedicle remains attached to provide an intact blood supply. The flap is rotated and sutured over the defect. The donor site is sutured closed; pedicle remains intact. The pedicle is severed after the graft is established.

15570   Formation of direct or tubed pedicle, with or without transfer; trunk
     19.65   23.67   **Global Days 090**

15572   scalp, arms, or legs
     20.03   23.16   **Global Days 090**

15574   forehead, cheeks, chin, mouth, neck, axillae, genitalia, hands or feet
     20.94   24.29   **Global Days 090**

15576   eyelids, nose, ears, lips, or intraoral
     18.40   21.46   **Global Days 090**

15600   Delay of flap or sectioning of flap (division and inset); at trunk
     5.41   8.10   **Global Days 090**

15610   at scalp, arms, or legs
     6.36   8.98   **Global Days 090**

15620   at forehead, cheeks, chin, neck, axillae, genitalia, hands, or feet
     8.66   11.26   **Global Days 090**

15630   at eyelids, nose, ears, or lips
     9.29   11.89   **Global Days 090**

15650   Transfer, intermediate, of any pedicle flap (eg, abdomen to wrist, Walking tube), any location
     EXCLUDES   Defatting, revision, or rearranging of transferred pedicle flap or skin graft (13100-14302)
     10.26   13.05   **Global Days 090**

15731   Forehead flap with preservation of vascular pedicle (eg, axial pattern flap, paramedian forehead flap)
     EXCLUDES   Muscle, myocutaneous, or fasciocutaneous flap of the head or neck (15732)
     27.95   30.63   **Global Days 090**

15732   Muscle, myocutaneous, or fasciocutaneous flap; head and neck (eg, temporalis, masseter muscle, sternocleidomastoid, levator scapulae)
     EXCLUDES   Forehead flap with preservation of vascular pedicle (15731)
     36.98   40.66   **Global Days 090**

15734   trunk
     36.95   41.04   **Global Days 090**

15736   upper extremity
     31.61   35.62   **Global Days 090**

15738   lower extremity
     34.35   38.12   **Global Days 090**
     AMA: 2009, Jan, 11-31; 2008, Jan, 10-25; 2007, January, 13-27

15740   Flap; island pedicle
     EXCLUDES   V-Y subcutaneous flaps, random island flaps, and other flaps from adjacent areas (14000-14302)
     23.44   27.04   **Global Days 090**
     AMA: 2009, Jan, 11-31; 2008, Jan, 10-25; 2007, January, 13-27

15750   neurovascular pedicle
     EXCLUDES   V-Y subcutaneous flaps, random island flaps, and other flaps from adjacent areas (14000-14302)
     25.05   25.05   **Global Days 090**

CURRENT PROCEDURAL CODING EXPERT – INTEGUMENTARY SYSTEM 15822

15756-15758 Wound Reconstruction: Free Flaps

CMS 100-4,3,20.1.2.8 — Special Payments for Burn Cases
CMS 104-4,12,30 — Correct Coding Policy

INCLUDES
Fixation and anchoring skin graft
Operating microscope (69990)
Routine dressing
Simple tissue debridement

EXCLUDES
Acellular dermal graft (15170-15176)
Adjacent tissue transfer (14000-14302)
Autologous skin graft (15100-15261)
Autologous tissue cultured graft (15040)
Excision of:
   Benign lesion (11400-11471)
   Burn eschar or scar (15002-15005)
   Malignant lesion (11600-11646)
Flaps without addition of a vascular pedicle (15570-15576)
Primary procedure such as radical mastectomy, extensive tumor removal, orbitectomy (see appropriate anatomical section)
Repair of donor site with skin grafts or flaps (14000-14350, 15050-15431)

15756 Free muscle or myocutaneous flap with microvascular anastomosis   C 80
     65.31   65.31   Global Days 090

15757 Free skin flap with microvascular anastomosis   C 80
     64.70   64.70   Global Days 090

15758 Free fascial flap with microvascular anastomosis   C 80
     64.17   64.17   Global Days 090

15760-15770 Grafts Comprising Multiple Tissue Types

CMS 100-4,3,20.1.2.8 — Special Payments for Burn Cases
CMS 100-4,4,20.5 — HCPCS Under OPPS

INCLUDES
Fixation and anchoring skin graft
Routine dressing
Simple tissue debridement

EXCLUDES
Acellular dermal graft (15170-15176)
Adjacent tissue transfer (14000-14302)
Autologous skin graft (15100-15261)
Excision of:
   Benign lesion (11400-11471)
   Burn eschar or scar (15002-15005)
   Malignant lesion (11600-11646)
Flaps without addition of a vascular pedicle (15570-15576)
Microvascular repair (15756-15758)
Primary procedure such as extensive tumor removal (see appropriate anatomical site)
Repair of donor site with skin grafts or flaps (14000-14350, 15050-15431)

15760 Graft; composite (eg, full thickness of external ear or nasal ala), including primary closure, donor area   A2 T
     19.40   22.70   Global Days 090

15770 derma-fat-fascia   A2 T 80
     18.23   18.23   Global Days 090

15775-15839 Plastic, Reconstructive, and Aesthetic Surgery

CMS 100-2,16,10 — Exclusions from Coverage
CMS 100-2,16,120 — Cosmetic Procedures
CMS 100-2,16,180 — Services Related to Noncovered Procedures

EXCLUDES *Strip transplant (15220)*

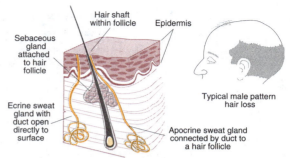

Alopecia means hair loss and the condition is separated into two major categories: that which occurs with associated, visible scalp disease, and that which occurs in the absence of visible disease. Male and female pattern hair loss is of the latter category. Hirsutism is excess hair growth, particularly in women, and is often a sign of a systemic medical syndrome

15775 Punch graft for hair transplant; 1 to 15 punch grafts   A2 T 80
     5.93   7.68   Global Days 000

15776 more than 15 punch grafts   A2 T 80
     8.17   10.65   Global Days 000

15780 Dermabrasion; total face (eg, for acne scarring, fine wrinkling, rhytids, general keratosis)   P3 T 80
     16.69   21.36   Global Days 090
     AMA: 2009, Jan, 11-31; 2008, Jan, 10-25; 2007, January, 13-27

15781 segmental, face   P2 T
     11.40   14.11   Global Days 090

15782 regional, other than face   P2 T 80
     11.34   15.29   Global Days 090

15783 superficial, any site (eg, tattoo removal)   P2 T 80
     9.99   12.50   Global Days 090

15786 Abrasion; single lesion (eg, keratosis, scar)   P2 T
     3.84   6.44   Global Days 010

+ 15787 each additional 4 lesions or less (List separately in addition to code for primary procedure)   P3 T
     Code first 15786
     0.52   1.28   Global Days ZZZ

15788 Chemical peel, facial; epidermal   P2 T
     6.53   11.60   Global Days 090

15789 dermal   P2 T
     11.03   14.03   Global Days 090

15792 Chemical peel, nonfacial; epidermal   P2 T 80
     6.74   10.89   Global Days 090

15793 dermal   P2 T 80
     9.57   12.45   Global Days 090

15819 Cervicoplasty   G2 T 80
     20.24   20.24   Global Days 090

15820 Blepharoplasty, lower eyelid;   A2 T 80 50
     13.90   15.15   Global Days 090
     AMA: 2009, Jan, 11-31; 2008, Jan, 10-25; 2007, January, 13-27; 2005, January, 46-47; 2005, February, 13-16

15821 with extensive herniated fat pad   A2 T 80 50
     14.91   16.32   Global Days 090
     AMA: 2005, February, 13-16

15822 Blepharoplasty, upper eyelid;   A2 T 50
     10.50   11.73   Global Days 090
     AMA: 2005, February, 13-16

● New Code   ▲ Revised Code   M Maternity   A Age   Unlisted   Not Covered   # Resequenced

CCI   + Add-on   ⊘ Mod 51 Exempt   ⊚ Mod 63 Exempt   ⊙ Mod Sedation   PQ PQRI

15823

15823	with excessive skin weighting down lid	A2 T 50
	17.71 19.09 Global Days 090	
	AMA: 2005, February, 13-16	

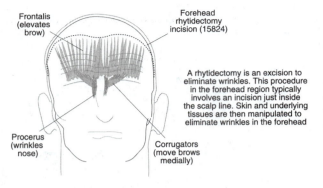

A rhytidectomy is an excision to eliminate wrinkles. This procedure in the forehead region typically involves an incision just inside the scalp line. Skin and underlying tissues are then manipulated to eliminate wrinkles in the forehead

15824	Rhytidectomy; forehead	A2 T 80 50
	EXCLUDES Repair of brow ptosis (67900)	
	0.00 0.00 Global Days 000	
15825	neck with platysmal tightening (platysmal flap, P-flap)	A2 T 80 50
	0.00 0.00 Global Days 000	
15826	glabellar frown lines	A2 T 80 50
	0.00 0.00 Global Days 000	
15828	cheek, chin, and neck	A2 T 80 50
	0.00 0.00 Global Days 000	
15829	superficial musculoaponeurotic system (SMAS) flap	A2 T 80 50
	0.00 0.00 Global Days 000	
15830	Excision, excessive skin and subcutaneous tissue (includes lipectomy); abdomen, infraumbilical panniculectomy	A2 T 80
	EXCLUDES Other abdominoplasty (17999)	
	Code also 15847 for abdominoplasty with panniculectomy	
	Do not report with (12031-12032, 12034-12037, 13100-13102, 14000-14001, 14302)	
	32.03 32.03 Global Days 090	
15832	thigh	A2 T 80
	24.54 24.54 Global Days 090	
15833	leg	A2 T 80
	23.92 23.92 Global Days 090	
15834	hip	A2 T 80
	24.39 24.39 Global Days 090	
15835	buttock	A2 T 80
	25.79 25.79 Global Days 090	
15836	arm	A2 T 80
	19.38 19.38 Global Days 090	
15837	forearm or hand	G2 T 80
	17.81 21.20 Global Days 090	
15838	submental fat pad	G2 T 80
	15.79 15.79 Global Days 090	
15839	other area	A2 T 80
	19.96 23.34 Global Days 090	

15840-15845 Reanimation of the Paralyzed Face

CMS 100-2,15,260   Covered ASC Procedures
CMS 100-4,4,20.5   HCPCS Under OPPS
CMS 100-4,12,40.7   Bilateral Procedures
CMS 100-4,12,90.3   MD Services in ASCs

EXCLUDES Intravenous fluorescein evaluation of blood flow in graft or flap (15860)
Nerve:
  Decompression (69720, 69725, 69955)
  Pedicle transfer (64905, 64907)
  Suture (64831-64876, 69740, 69745)

15840	Graft for facial nerve paralysis; free fascia graft (including obtaining fascia)	A2 T
	28.26 28.26 Global Days 090	
15841	free muscle graft (including obtaining graft)	A2 T 80
	44.99 44.99 Global Days 090	
15842	free muscle flap by microsurgical technique	G2 T 80
	INCLUDES Operating microscope (69990)	
	64.91 64.91 Global Days 090	
15845	regional muscle transfer	A2 T 80
	27.55 27.55 Global Days 090	

15847 Removal of Excess Abdominal Tissue Add-on

+ 15847	Excision, excessive skin and subcutaneous tissue (includes lipectomy), abdomen (eg, abdominoplasty) (includes umbilical transposition and fascial plication) (List separately in addition to code for primary procedure)	A2 T 80
	Code first (15830)	
	EXCLUDES Abdominal wall hernia repair (49491-49587)	
	Other abdominoplasty (17999)	
	0.00 0.00 Global Days YYY	

15850-15852 Suture Removal/Dressing Change: Anesthesia Required

CMS 100-4,12,40.1   Global Surgery Package Definition
CMS 100-4,12,50   Anesthesia Services

15850	Removal of sutures under anesthesia (other than local), same surgeon	G2 T
	1.10 2.19 Global Days XXX	
15851	Removal of sutures under anesthesia (other than local), other surgeon	P3 T
	1.29 2.49 Global Days 000	
15852	Dressing change (for other than burns) under anesthesia (other than local)	R2 X
	EXCLUDES Dressing change for burns (16020-16030)	
	1.30 1.30 Global Days 000	

15860 Injection for Vascular Flow Determination

15860	Intravenous injection of agent (eg, fluorescein) to test vascular flow in flap or graft	G2 X 80
	3.38 3.38 Global Days 000	

Current Procedural Coding Expert – Integumentary System

15876-15879 Liposuction

CMS 100-2,16,10 — Exclusions from Coverage
CMS 100-2,16,120 — Cosmetic Procedures
CMS 100-2,16,180 — Services Related to Noncovered Procedures
CMS 100-4,12,20.4.3 — Payment for Assistant at Surgery

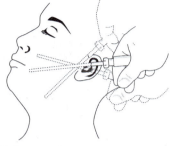

Cannula typically inserted through incision in front of ear

In 15876, a liposuction cannula is inserted through fat deposits creating tunnels and removing excess deposits

- **15876** Suction assisted lipectomy; head and neck
  0.00 0.00 Global Days 000
- **15877** trunk
  0.00 0.00 Global Days 000
  AMA: 2009, Jan, 11-31; 2008, Jan, 10-25; 2007, January, 13-27; 2005, February, 13-16
- **15878** upper extremity
  0.00 0.00 Global Days 000
- **15879** lower extremity
  0.00 0.00 Global Days 000

15920-15999 Treatment of Decubitus Ulcers

CMS 100-3,270.4 — Treatment of Decubitus
CMS 100-4,12,20.4.3 — Payment for Assistant at Surgery
CMS 100-4,12,40.6 — Multiple procedures
CMS 100-4,12,40.8 — Co-surgery and team surgery
Code also free skin graft to repair ulcer or donor site

- **15920** Excision, coccygeal pressure ulcer, with coccygectomy; with primary suture
  16.30 16.30 Global Days 090
- **15922** with flap closure
  19.17 19.17 Global Days 090
- **15931** Excision, sacral pressure ulcer, with primary suture;
  18.44 18.44 Global Days 090
- **15933** with ostectomy
  22.86 22.86 Global Days 090
- **15934** Excision, sacral pressure ulcer, with skin flap closure;
  25.30 25.30 Global Days 090
- **15935** with ostectomy
  30.12 30.12 Global Days 090
- **15936** Excision, sacral pressure ulcer, in preparation for muscle or myocutaneous flap or skin graft closure;
  Code also any defect repair with:
    Muscle or myocutaneous flap (15734, 15738)
    Split skin graft (15100-15101)
  24.32 24.32 Global Days 090
- **15937** with ostectomy
  Code also any defect repair with:
    Muscle or myocutaneous flap (15734, 15738)
    Split skin graft (15100-15101)
  28.31 28.31 Global Days 090
- **15940** Excision, ischial pressure ulcer, with primary suture;
  18.86 18.86 Global Days 090
- **15941** with ostectomy (ischiectomy)
  24.61 24.61 Global Days 090
- **15944** Excision, ischial pressure ulcer, with skin flap closure;
  24.22 24.22 Global Days 090
- **15945** with ostectomy
  26.92 26.92 Global Days 090
- **15946** Excision, ischial pressure ulcer, with ostectomy, in preparation for muscle or myocutaneous flap or skin graft closure
  Code also any defect repair with:
    Muscle or myocutaneous flap (15734, 15738)
    Split skin graft (15100-15101)
  44.86 44.86 Global Days 090
  AMA: 2009, Jan, 11-31; 2008, Jan, 10-25; 2007, January, 13-27
- **15950** Excision, trochanteric pressure ulcer, with primary suture;
  15.51 15.51 Global Days 090
- **15951** with ostectomy
  21.56 21.56 Global Days 090
- **15952** Excision, trochanteric pressure ulcer, with skin flap closure;
  22.34 22.34 Global Days 090
- **15953** with ostectomy
  27.29 27.29 Global Days 090
- **15956** Excision, trochanteric pressure ulcer, in preparation for muscle or myocutaneous flap or skin graft closure;
  Code also any defect repair with:
    muscle or myocutaneous flap (15734, 15738)
    split skin graft (15100-15101)
  31.24 31.24 Global Days 090
- **15958** with ostectomy
  Code also any defect repair with:
    Muscle or myocutaneous flap (15734-15738)
    Split skin graft (15100-15101)
  31.87 31.87 Global Days 090
- **15999** Unlisted procedure, excision pressure ulcer
  0.00 0.00 Global Days YYY

● New Code   ▲ Revised Code   Ⓜ Maternity   Ⓐ Age   Unlisted   Not Covered   # Resequenced
CCI   + Add-on   ⊘ Mod 51 Exempt   Mod 63 Exempt   ⊙ Mod Sedation   PQRI
© 2009 Publisher *(Blue Ink)*   CPT only © 2009 American Medical Association. All Rights Reserved. *(Black Ink)*   Medicare *(Red Ink)*   29

16000-16036 Burn Care

CMS 100-4,3,20.1.2.8   Special Payments for Burn Cases
INCLUDES   Local care of burn only
EXCLUDES   Application of skin grafts (15100-15650)
Evaluation and management services

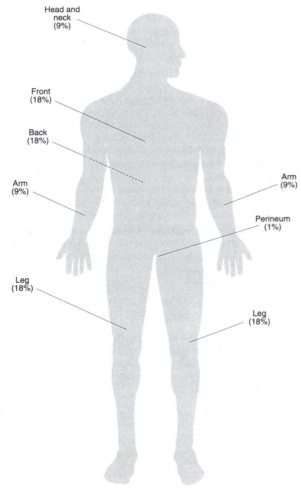

Rule of Nines for Burns
- Head and neck (9%)
- Front (18%)
- Back (18%)
- Arm (9%)
- Arm (9%)
- Perineum (1%)
- Leg (18%)
- Leg (18%)

16000   Initial treatment, first degree burn, when no more than local treatment is required
1.32   1.88   Global Days 000

16020   Dressings and/or debridement of partial-thickness burns, initial or subsequent; small (less than 5% total body surface area)
INCLUDES   Wound coverage other than skin graft
1.59   2.22   Global Days 000

16025   medium (eg, whole face or whole extremity, or 5% to 10% total body surface area)
INCLUDES   Wound coverage other than skin graft
3.22   4.04   Global Days 000
AMA: 2009, Jan, 11-31; 2008, Jun, 14-15

16030   large (eg, more than 1 extremity, or greater than 10% total body surface area)
INCLUDES   Wound coverage other than skin graft
3.67   4.83   Global Days 000
AMA: 2009, Jan, 11-31; 2008, Jun, 14-15

16035   Escharotomy; initial incision
EXCLUDES   Debridement or scraping of burn wound (16020-16030)
5.54   5.54   Global Days 000

+ **16036**   each additional incision (List separately in addition to code for primary procedure)
EXCLUDES   Debridement or scraping of burn wound (16020-16030)
Code first 16035
2.32   2.32   Global Days ZZZ

17000-17004 Destruction Any Method: Premalignant Lesion

CMS 100-2,16,10   Exclusions from Coverage
CMS 100-2,16,120   Cosmetic Procedures
CMS 100-2,16,180   Services Related to Noncovered Procedures
CMS 100-3,140.5   Laser Procedures
CMS 100-4,4,20.5   HCPCS Under OPPS
CMS 100-4,12,40.6   Multiple procedures
EXCLUDES   Cryotherapy acne (17340)
Destruction of lesion of:
   Anus (46900-46917, 46924)
   Conjunctiva (68135)
   Eyelid (67850)
   Penis (54050-54057, 54065)
   Vagina (57061, 57065)
   Vestibule of mouth (40820)
   Vulva (56501, 56515)
Destruction of plantar warts (17110-17111)
Destruction or excision of skin tags (11200-11201)
Localized chemotherapy treatment (99201-99499)
Paring or excision of benign hyperkeratotic lesion (11055-11057)
Shaving skin lesions (11300-11313)
Treatment of inflammatory skin disease via laser (96920-96922)

17000   Destruction (eg, laser surgery, electrosurgery, cryosurgery, chemosurgery, surgical curettement), premalignant lesions (eg, actinic keratoses); first lesion
1.48   2.07   Global Days 010
AMA: 2009, Jan, 11-31; 2008, Jan, 10-25; 2007, February, 10-11; 2007, January, 13-27; 2006, April, 11-18; 2006, May, 16-20; 2005, March, 11-15

+ **17003**   second through 14 lesions, each (List separately in addition to code for first lesion)
Code first 17000
0.12   0.18   Global Days ZZZ
AMA: 2009, Jan, 11-31; 2008, Jan, 10-25; 2007, February, 10-11; 2007, January, 13-27; 2006, May, 16-20

17004   Destruction (eg, laser surgery, electrosurgery, cryosurgery, chemosurgery, surgical curettement), premalignant lesions (eg, actinic keratoses), 15 or more lesions
Do not report with (17000-17003)
3.55   4.45   Global Days 010
AMA: 2009, Jan, 11-31; 2008, Jan, 10-25; 2007, January, 13-27; 2007, February, 10-11

Current Procedural Coding Expert – Integumentary System

17106-17250 Destruction, Any Method: Vascular Proliferative Lesion

CMS 100-2,16,10   Exclusions from Coverage
CMS 100-2,16,120   Cosmetic Procedures
CMS 100-2,16,180   Services Related to Noncovered Procedures

EXCLUDES *Destruction of lesion of:*
    Anus (46900-46917, 46924)
    Conjunctiva (68135)
    Eyelid (67850)
    Penis (54050-54057, 54065)
    Vagina (57061, 57065)
    Vestibule of mouth (40820)
    Vulva (56501, 56515)
Treatment of inflammatory skin disease via laser (96920-96922)

17106   Destruction of cutaneous vascular proliferative lesions (eg, laser technique); less than 10 sq cm
     7.35   8.89   Global Days 090
     AMA: 2009, Jan, 11-31; 2008, Jan, 10-25; 2008, Jun, 14-15; 2007, April, 11-12

17107   10.0 to 50.0 sq cm
     9.30   11.32   Global Days 090
     AMA: 2009, Jan, 11-31; 2008, Jan, 10-25; 2008, Jun, 14-15; 2007, April, 11-12

17108   over 50.0 sq cm
     13.79   16.47   Global Days 090
     AMA: 2009, Jan, 11-31; 2008, Jan, 10-25; 2008, Jun, 14-15; 2007, April, 11-12

17110   Destruction (eg, laser surgery, electrosurgery, cryosurgery, chemosurgery, surgical curettement), of benign lesions other than skin tags or cutaneous vascular proliferative lesions; up to 14 lesions
     1.82   2.77   Global Days 010
     AMA: 2009, Jan, 11-31; 2008, Jan, 10-25; 2008, Nov, 10-11; 2007, February, 10-11; 2007, April, 11-12

17111   15 or more lesions
     2.27   3.33   Global Days 010
     AMA: 2009, Jan, 11-31; 2008, Jan, 10-25; 2008, Nov, 10-11; 2007, February, 10-11; 2007, April, 11-12

17250   Chemical cauterization of granulation tissue (proud flesh, sinus or fistula)
     Do not report with excision/removal codes for the same lesion
     0.98   1.98   Global Days 000

17260-17286 Destruction, Any Method: Malignant Lesion

CMS 100-3,140.5   Laser Procedures
CMS 100-4,12,30   Correct Coding Policy

EXCLUDES *Destruction of lesion of:*
    Anus (46900-46917, 46924)
    Conjunctiva (68135)
    Eyelid (67850)
    Localized chemotherapy treatment (99201-99499)
    Penis (54050-54057, 54065)
    Shaving skin lesion (11300-11313)
    Vestibule of mouth (40820)
    Vulva (56501-56515)
Treatment of inflammatory skin disease via laser (96920-96922)

17260   Destruction, malignant lesion (eg, laser surgery, electrosurgery, cryosurgery, chemosurgery, surgical curettement), trunk, arms or legs; lesion diameter 0.5 cm or less
     1.85   2.45   Global Days 010
     AMA: 2006, April, 11-18

17261   lesion diameter 0.6 to 1.0 cm
     2.47   3.65   Global Days 010

17262   lesion diameter 1.1 to 2.0 cm
     3.17   4.46   Global Days 010

17263   lesion diameter 2.1 to 3.0 cm
     3.52   4.92   Global Days 010

17264   lesion diameter 3.1 to 4.0 cm
     3.76   5.29   Global Days 010

17266   lesion diameter over 4.0 cm
     4.43   6.04   Global Days 010

17270   Destruction, malignant lesion (eg, laser surgery, electrosurgery, cryosurgery, chemosurgery, surgical curettement), scalp, neck, hands, feet, genitalia; lesion diameter 0.5 cm or less
     2.70   3.85   Global Days 010

17271   lesion diameter 0.6 to 1.0 cm
     3.01   4.21   Global Days 010

17272   lesion diameter 1.1 to 2.0 cm
     3.49   4.82   Global Days 010

17273   lesion diameter 2.1 to 3.0 cm
     3.96   5.38   Global Days 010

17274   lesion diameter 3.1 to 4.0 cm
     4.86   6.41   Global Days 010

17276   lesion diameter over 4.0 cm
     5.87   7.49   Global Days 010

17280   Destruction, malignant lesion (eg, laser surgery, electrosurgery, cryosurgery, chemosurgery, surgical curettement), face, ears, eyelids, nose, lips, mucous membrane; lesion diameter 0.5 cm or less
     2.45   3.58   Global Days 010

17281   lesion diameter 0.6 to 1.0 cm
     3.40   4.57   Global Days 010

17282   lesion diameter 1.1 to 2.0 cm
     3.94   5.31   Global Days 010

17283   lesion diameter 2.1 to 3.0 cm
     4.95   6.44   Global Days 010

17284   lesion diameter 3.1 to 4.0 cm
     5.90   7.52   Global Days 010

17286   lesion diameter over 4.0 cm
     7.92   9.63   Global Days 010

● New Code   ▲ Revised Code   M Maternity   A Age   Unlisted   Not Covered   # Resequenced
CCI   + Add-on   Mod 51 Exempt   Mod 63 Exempt   Mod Sedation   PQRI
© 2009 Publisher (Blue Ink)   CPT only © 2009 American Medical Association. All Rights Reserved. (Black Ink)   Medicare (Red Ink)

Current Procedural Coding Expert – Integumentary System

17311-17315 Mohs Surgery

CMS 100-4,12,40.1   Global Surgery Package Definition

INCLUDES   The following surgical/pathological services performed by the same physician:
Evaluation of skin margins by surgeon
Pathology exam on Mohs surgery specimen (88302-88309)
Routine frozen section stain (88314)
Tumor removal, mapping, preparation, and examination of lesion

EXCLUDES   *Complex repair (13100-13160)*
Flaps or grafts (14000-14350, 15050-15770)
Frozen section if no prior diagnosis determination has been performed (88331)
Intermediate repair (12031-12057)
Simple repair (12001-12021)

Code also any histochemical stain on a frozen section, nonroutine (with modifier 59) (88314)

Code also biopsy if no prior diagnosis determination has been performed (11100-11101)

17311   Mohs micrographic technique, including removal of all gross tumor, surgical excision of tissue specimens, mapping, color coding of specimens, microscopic examination of specimens by the surgeon, and histopathologic preparation including routine stain(s) (eg, hematoxylin and eosin, toluidine blue), head, neck, hands, feet, genitalia, or any location with surgery directly involving muscle, cartilage, bone, tendon, major nerves, or vessels; first stage, up to 5 tissue blocks   [P2] [T]
   10.55   16.83   Global Days 000
   AMA: 2006, December, 1-3; 2006, December, 10-12

+ **17312**   each additional stage after the first stage, up to 5 tissue blocks (List separately in addition to code for primary procedure)   [P3] [T]
   Code first 17311
   5.62   9.94   Global Days ZZZ
   AMA: 2006, December, 1-3

17313   Mohs micrographic technique, including removal of all gross tumor, surgical excision of tissue specimens, mapping, color coding of specimens, microscopic examination of specimens by the surgeon, and histopathologic preparation including routine stain(s) (eg, hematoxylin and eosin, toluidine blue), of the trunk, arms, or legs; first stage, up to 5 tissue blocks   [P2] [T]
   9.47   15.33   Global Days 000
   AMA: 2006, December, 1-3; 2006, December, 10-12

+ **17314**   each additional stage after the first stage, up to 5 tissue blocks (List separately in addition to code for primary procedure)   [P3] [T]
   Code first 17313
   5.20   9.21   Global Days ZZZ
   AMA: 2006, December, 1-3

+ **17315**   Mohs micrographic technique, including removal of all gross tumor, surgical excision of tissue specimens, mapping, color coding of specimens, microscopic examination of specimens by the surgeon, and histopathologic preparation including routine stain(s) (eg, hematoxylin and eosin, toluidine blue), each additional block after the first 5 tissue blocks, any stage (List separately in addition to code for primary procedure)   [P3] [T]
   Code first 17311-17314
   1.48   2.07   Global Days ZZZ
   AMA: 2006, December, 1-3

17340-17999 Treatment for Active Acne and Permanent Hair Removal

17340   Cryotherapy (CO2 slush, liquid N2) for acne   [P3] [T]
   1.33   1.39   Global Days 010

17360   Chemical exfoliation for acne (eg, acne paste, acid)   [P2] [T]
   2.73   3.42   Global Days 010

17380   Electrolysis epilation, each 30 minutes   [R2] [T] [80]
   EXCLUDES   *Actinotherapy (96900)*
   0.00   0.00   Global Days 000

17999   Unlisted procedure, skin, mucous membrane and subcutaneous tissue   [T] [80]
   0.00   0.00   Global Days YYY
   AMA: 2009, Jan, 11-31; 2008, Jan, 10-25; 2008, Nov, 10-11; 2007, January, 13-27; 2005, June, 9-11

19000-19030 Treatment of Breast Abscess and Cyst with Injection, Aspiration, Incision

19000   Puncture aspiration of cyst of breast;   [P3] [T]
   76942, 77021, 77031, 77032
   1.19   2.74   Global Days 000
   AMA: 2008, Nov, 10-11; 2005, April, 6-9

+ **19001**   each additional cyst (List separately in addition to code for primary procedure)   [P3] [T]
   Code first 19000
   76942, 77021, 77031, 77032
   0.59   0.71   Global Days ZZZ
   AMA: 2005, April, 6-9

19020   Mastotomy with exploration or drainage of abscess, deep   [A2] [T] [50]
   8.03   11.92   Global Days 090
   AMA: 2005, April, 6-9

19030   Injection procedure only for mammary ductogram or galactogram   [N1] [N] [50]
   77053-77054
   2.10   4.00   Global Days 000
   AMA: 2005, April, 6-9

Current Procedural Coding Expert – Integumentary System

19100-19103 Breast Biopsy
CMS 100-2,15,260 — Covered ASC Procedures
CMS 100-3,220.13 — Percutaneous Image-guided Breast Biopsy
CMS 100-4,13,80.1 — Supervision and Interpretation Codes
CMS 100-4,13,80.2 — Physician Presence
INCLUDES Open removal of breast mass without concentration on surgical margins
EXCLUDES Lesion removal without concentration on surgical margins (19110-19126)
Partial mastectomy (19301-19302)
Total mastectomy (19303-19307)

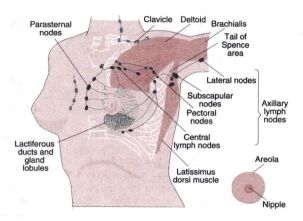

19100 Biopsy of breast; percutaneous, needle core, not using imaging guidance (separate procedure)
EXCLUDES Fine needle aspiration (10021)
Radiology guided breast biopsy (10022, 19102-19103)
1.93   3.82   Global Days 000
AMA: 2009, Jan, 11-31; 2008, Jan, 10-25; 2008, Nov, 10-11; 2007, January, 13-27; 2006, December, 10-12; 2005, April, 6-9

19101 open, incisional
5.93   8.75   Global Days 010
AMA: 2009, Jan, 11-31; 2008, Jan, 10-25; 2007, January, 13-27; 2005, April, 6-9

19102 percutaneous, needle core, using imaging guidance
EXCLUDES Insertion of percutaneous localization clip if appropriate (19295)
76942, 77002, 77012, 77021, 77031-77032
2.77   5.28   Global Days 000
AMA: 2009, Jan, 11-31; 2008, Jan, 10-25; 2008, Nov, 10-11; 2007, January, 13-27; 2005, April, 6-9

19103 percutaneous, automated vacuum assisted or rotating biopsy device, using imaging guidance
INCLUDES ABBI biopsy
EXCLUDES Insertion of percutaneous localization clip if appropriate (19295)
76942, 77012, 77021, 77031-77032
5.21   13.46   Global Days 000
AMA: 2009, Jan, 11-31; 2008, Jan, 10-25; 2008, Nov, 10-11; 2007, January, 13-27; 2005, April, 6-9

19105 Treatment of Fibroadenoma: Cryoablation
CMS 100-4,13,80.1 — Supervision and Interpretation Codes
CMS 100-4,13,80.2 — Physician Presence
INCLUDES Adjacent lesions treated with one cryoprobe
Ultrasound guidance

19105 Ablation, cryosurgical, of fibroadenoma, including ultrasound guidance, each fibroadenoma
Do not report with (76940, 76942)
5.28   47.37   Global Days 000
AMA: 2007, March, 7-8

19110-19126 Excisional Procedures: Breast
CMS 100-4,12,40.7 — Bilateral Procedures

19110 Nipple exploration, with or without excision of a solitary lactiferous duct or a papilloma lactiferous duct
9.10   12.57   Global Days 090
AMA: 2005, April, 6-9

19112 Excision of lactiferous duct fistula
8.25   11.79   Global Days 090
AMA: 2005, April, 6-9

19120 Excision of cyst, fibroadenoma, or other benign or malignant tumor, aberrant breast tissue, duct lesion, nipple or areolar lesion (except 19300), open, male or female, 1 or more lesions
11.05   12.93   Global Days 090
AMA: 2009, Jan, 11-31; 2008, Jan, 10-25; 2007, January, 13-27; 2005, April, 13-14; 2005, April, 6-9

19125 Excision of breast lesion identified by preoperative placement of radiological marker, open; single lesion
12.32   14.41   Global Days 090
AMA: 2009, Jan, 11-31; 2008, Jan, 10-25; 2007, January, 13-27; 2005, April, 6-9

+ **19126** each additional lesion separately identified by a preoperative radiological marker (List separately in addition to code for primary procedure)
Code first 19125
4.46   4.46   Global Days ZZZ
AMA: 2009, Jan, 11-31; 2008, Jan, 10-25; 2007, January, 13-27; 2005, April, 6-9

19260-19272 Excisional Procedures: Chest Wall
CMS 100-4,12,20.4.3 — Payment for Assistant at Surgery
Do not report with (32100, 32422, 32503-32504, 32551)

19260 Excision of chest wall tumor including ribs
32.70   32.70   Global Days 090
AMA: 2007, February, 4-5; 2005, April, 6-9

19271 Excision of chest wall tumor involving ribs, with plastic reconstruction; without mediastinal lymphadenectomy
44.11   44.11   Global Days 090
AMA: 2007, February, 4-5; 2005, April, 6-9

19272 with mediastinal lymphadenectomy
48.54   48.54   Global Days 090
AMA: 2007, February, 4-5; 2005, April, 6-9

● New Code   ▲ Revised Code   Maternity   Age   Unlisted   Not Covered   # Resequenced
CCI   + Add-on   Mod 51 Exempt   Mod 63 Exempt   Mod Sedation   PQRI
© 2009 Publisher (Blue Ink)   CPT only © 2009 American Medical Association. All Rights Reserved. (Black Ink)   Medicare (Red Ink)

19290-19298 Placement of Localization Markers and Brachytherapy Catheters

CMS 100-4,12,40.7 — Bilateral Procedures
CMS 100-4,13,80.1 — Supervision and Interpretation Codes
CMS 100-4,13,80.2 — Physician Presence

19290 Preoperative placement of needle localization wire, breast; [N1] [N] [50]
  76942, 77031-77032
  1.74   3.93   Global Days 000
  AMA: 2005, April, 6-9

+ **19291** each additional lesion (List separately in addition to code for primary procedure) [N1] [N] [80]
  Code first 19290
  76942, 77031-77032
  0.87   1.70   Global Days ZZZ
  AMA: 2005, April, 6-9

+ ▲ **19295** Image guided placement, metallic localization clip, percutaneous, during breast biopsy/aspiration (List separately in addition to code for primary procedure) [N1] [N] [80]
  Code first (10022, 19102-19103)
  76942, 77031-77032
  2.09   2.09   Global Days ZZZ
  AMA: 2009, Jan, 11-31; 2008, Nov, 10-11; 2005, April, 6-9

19296 Placement of radiotherapy afterloading expandable catheter (single or multichannel) into the breast for interstitial radioelement application following partial mastectomy, includes imaging guidance; on date separate from partial mastectomy [A2] [T] [80] [50]
  Code also (C1728)
  5.78   97.30   Global Days 000
  AMA: 2007, February, 4-5; 2005, April, 6-9; 2005, November, 14-15

+ **19297** concurrent with partial mastectomy (List separately in addition to code for primary procedure) [A2] [T] [80]
  Code also (C1728)
  Code first (19301-19302)
  2.62   2.62   Global Days ZZZ
  AMA: 2007, February, 4-5; 2005, November, 14-15; 2005, April, 6-9

⊙ **19298** Placement of radiotherapy afterloading brachytherapy catheters (multiple tube and button type) into the breast for interstitial radioelement application following (at the time of or subsequent to) partial mastectomy, includes imaging guidance [A2] [T] [80] [50]
  Code also (C1728)
  9.15   28.92   Global Days 000
  AMA: 2007, February, 4-5; 2005, November, 14-15; 2005, April, 6-9

19300-19307 Mastectomies: Partial, Simple, Radical

CMS 100-4,12,20.4.3 — Payment for Assistant at Surgery
CMS 100-4,12,40.7 — Bilateral Procedures
EXCLUDES Instantaneous or postponed insertion of prosthesis (19340, 19342)

19300 Mastectomy for gynecomastia ♂ [A2] [T] [50]
  10.84   13.45   Global Days 090
  AMA: 2007, February, 4-5

19301 Mastectomy, partial (eg, lumpectomy, tylectomy, quadrantectomy, segmentectomy); [A2] [T] [80] [50] [P0]
  EXCLUDES Insertion of radiotherapy afterloading balloon or brachytherapy catheters (19296-19298)
  17.67   17.67   Global Days 090
  AMA: 2009, Jan, 11-31; 2008, Sep, 5-6; 2007, Dec, 7-8; 2007, February, 4-5

19302 with axillary lymphadenectomy [A2] [T] [80] [50] [P0]
  EXCLUDES Insertion of radiotherapy afterloading balloon or brachytherapy catheters (19296-19298)
  24.18   24.18   Global Days 090
  AMA: 2009, Jan, 11-31; 2008, Jan, 10-25; 2008, Sep, 5-6; 2007, Dec, 7-8; 2007, February, 4-5

19303 Mastectomy, simple, complete [A2] [T] [80] [50] [P0]
  EXCLUDES Gynecomastia (19300)
  27.42   27.42   Global Days 090
  AMA: 2007, February, 4-5

19304 Mastectomy, subcutaneous [A2] [T] [80] [50] [P0]
  15.28   15.28   Global Days 090
  AMA: 2009, Jan, 11-31; 2008, Jan, 10-25; 2007, Dec, 7-8; 2007, February, 4-5

19305 Mastectomy, radical, including pectoral muscles, axillary lymph nodes [C] [80] [50] [P0]
  30.62   30.62   Global Days 090
  AMA: 2008, Sep, 5-6; 2007, February, 4-5

19306 Mastectomy, radical, including pectoral muscles, axillary and internal mammary lymph nodes (Urban type operation) [C] [80] [50] [P0]
  32.36   32.36   Global Days 090
  AMA: 2008, Sep, 5-6; 2007, February, 4-5

19307 Mastectomy, modified radical, including axillary lymph nodes, with or without pectoralis minor muscle, but excluding pectoralis major muscle [T] [80] [50] [P0]
  32.33   32.33   Global Days 090
  AMA: 2008, Sep, 5-6; 2007, February, 4-5

19316-19499 Plastic, Reconstructive, and Aesthetic Breast Procedures

CMS 100-2,16,120 — Cosmetic Procedures
CMS 100-2,16,180 — Services Related to Noncovered Procedures
CMS 100-3,140.2 — Breast Reconstruction Following Mastectomy
CMS 100-4,12,40.7 — Bilateral Procedures

19316 Mastopexy [A2] [T] [80] [50] [P0]
  21.06   21.06   Global Days 090
  AMA: 2005, April, 6-9

19318 Reduction mammaplasty ♀ [A2] [T] [80] [50] [P0]
  INCLUDES Aries-Pitanguy mammaplasty
  Biesenberger mammaplasty
  30.49   30.49   Global Days 090
  AMA: 2009, Jan, 11-31; 2008, Jan, 10-25; 2007, January, 13-27; 2005, April, 6-9

19324 Mammaplasty, augmentation; without prosthetic implant [A2] [T] [80] [50] [P0]
  13.08   13.08   Global Days 090
  AMA: 2005, April, 6-9

19325 with prosthetic implant [A2] [T] [80] [50] [P0]
  Code also (C1789, L8600)
  EXCLUDES Flap or graft (15100-15650)
  17.57   17.57   Global Days 090
  AMA: 2005, April, 6-9

Current Procedural Coding Expert – Integumentary System

19328 Removal of intact mammary implant
- 13.41 13.41 Global Days 090
- AMA: 2005, April, 6-9

19330 Removal of mammary implant material
- 17.19 17.19 Global Days 090
- AMA: 2009, Jan, 11-31; 2008, Jan, 10-25; 2007, January, 13-27; 2005, April, 6-9

19340 Immediate insertion of breast prosthesis following mastopexy, mastectomy or in reconstruction
- EXCLUDES Supply of prosthetic implant (99070, L8030, L8039, L8600)
- 26.12 26.12 Global Days 090
- AMA: 2007, February, 4-5; 2005, August, 1-3; 2005, April, 6-9

19342 Delayed insertion of breast prosthesis following mastopexy, mastectomy or in reconstruction
- EXCLUDES Preparation of moulage for custom breast implant (19396)
  Supply of prosthetic implant (99070, L8030, L8039, L8600)
- Code also (C1789, L8600)
- 25.30 25.30 Global Days 090
- AMA: 2007, February, 4-5; 2005, August, 1-3; 2005, April, 6-9

19350 Nipple/areola reconstruction
- 18.35 21.82 Global Days 090
- AMA: 2009, Jan, 11-31; 2008, Jan, 10-25; 2007, January, 13-27; 2005, April, 6-9

19355 Correction of inverted nipples
- 15.36 18.47 Global Days 090
- AMA: 2005, April, 6-9

19357 Breast reconstruction, immediate or delayed, with tissue expander, including subsequent expansion
- 42.74 42.74 Global Days 090
- AMA: 2005, August, 1-3; 2005, April, 6-9

19361 Breast reconstruction with latissimus dorsi flap, without prosthetic implant
- EXCLUDES Implant of prosthesis (19340)
- 46.91 46.91 Global Days 090
- AMA: 2005, August, 1-3; 2005, April, 6-9

19364 Breast reconstruction with free flap
- INCLUDES Closure of donor site
  Harvesting of skin graft
  Inset shaping of flap into breast
  Microvascular repair
  Operating microscope (69990)
- 76.70 76.70 Global Days 090
- AMA: 2005, August, 1-3; 2005, April, 6-9

19366 Breast reconstruction with other technique
- EXCLUDES Implant of prosthesis if appropriate (19340, 19342)
  Operating microscope (69990)
- 38.04 38.04 Global Days 090
- AMA: 2005, April, 6-9

19367 Breast reconstruction with transverse rectus abdominis myocutaneous flap (TRAM), single pedicle, including closure of donor site;
- 49.50 49.50 Global Days 090
- AMA: 2005, April, 6-9; 2005, August, 1-3

19368 with microvascular anastomosis (supercharging)
- INCLUDES Operating microscope (69990)
- 61.65 61.65 Global Days 090
- AMA: 2005, August, 1-3; 2005, April, 6-9

19369 Breast reconstruction with transverse rectus abdominis myocutaneous flap (TRAM), double pedicle, including closure of donor site
- 57.17 57.17 Global Days 090
- AMA: 2005, August, 1-3; 2005, April, 6-9

19370 Open periprosthetic capsulotomy, breast
- 18.67 18.67 Global Days 090
- AMA: 2005, April, 6-9

19371 Periprosthetic capsulectomy, breast
- 21.42 21.42 Global Days 090
- AMA: 2009, Jan, 11-31; 2008, Jan, 10-25; 2007, January, 13-27; 2005, April, 6-9

19380 Revision of reconstructed breast
- 21.06 21.06 Global Days 090
- AMA: 2005, April, 6-9

19396 Preparation of moulage for custom breast implant
- 3.62 7.13 Global Days 000
- AMA: 2005, April, 6-9

19499 Unlisted procedure, breast
- 0.00 0.00 Global Days YYY
- AMA: 2005, April, 6-9

● New Code   ▲ Revised Code   Maternity   Age   Unlisted   Not Covered   # Resequenced

CCI   + Add-on   Mod 51 Exempt   Mod 63 Exempt   Mod Sedation   PQRI

© 2009 Publisher *(Blue Ink)*   CPT only © 2009 American Medical Association. All Rights Reserved. (Black Ink)   Medicare (Red Ink)   35

Current Procedural Coding Expert – Musculoskeletal System

20000-20005 Incisional Treatment Soft Tissue Abscess

20000 Incision of soft tissue abscess (eg, secondary to osteomyelitis); superficial
 4.04   5.36   Global Days 010

20005 deep or complicated
 6.36   8.16   Global Days 010

20100-20103 Exploratory Surgery of Traumatic Wound

EXCLUDES
Laparotomy (49000-49010)
Thoracotomy (32100-32160)
Repair of major vessels of:
 Neck (35201, 35231, 35261)
 Chest (35211, 35216, 35241, 35246, 35271, 35276)
 Abdomen (35221, 35251, 35281)
 Extremity (35206-35207, 35226, 35236, 35256, 35266, 35286)

INCLUDES
Debridement
Extraction of foreign material
Open examination
Tying or coagulation of small vessels

20100 Exploration of penetrating wound (separate procedure); neck
 16.65   16.65   Global Days 010
AMA: 2009, Jan, 11-31; 2008, Jan, 10-25; 2007, January, 13-27; 2006, September, 14-16

20101 chest
 5.42   10.18   Global Days 010
AMA: 2009, Jan, 11-31; 2008, Jan, 10-25; 2007, January, 13-27; 2006, September, 14-16

20102 abdomen/flank/back
 6.92   12.46   Global Days 010
AMA: 2009, Jan, 11-31; 2008, Jan, 10-25; 2007, January, 13-27; 2006, September, 14-16

20103 extremity
 9.51   15.05   Global Days 010
AMA: 2009, Jan, 11-31; 2008, Jan, 10-25; 2007, January, 13-27; 2006, September, 14-16

20150 Epiphyseal Bar Resection

EXCLUDES Bone marrow aspiration (38220)

20150 Excision of epiphyseal bar, with or without autogenous soft tissue graft obtained through same fascial incision
 25.13   25.13   Global Days 090

20200-20206 Muscle Biopsy

EXCLUDES Removal of muscle tumor (see appropriate anatomic section)

20200 Biopsy, muscle; superficial
 2.54   5.11   Global Days 000

20205 deep
 4.17   7.24   Global Days 000

20206 Biopsy, muscle, percutaneous needle
INCLUDES Fluoroscopic guidance (77002)
EXCLUDES Fine needle aspiration (10021-10022)
 88172-88173
 76942, 77012, 77021
 1.59   5.86   Global Days 000

20220-20225 Percutaneous Bone Biopsy

CMS 100-3,150.3   Bone (Mineral) Density Studies
EXCLUDES Bone marrow biopsy (38221)

20220 Biopsy, bone, trocar, or needle; superficial (eg, ilium, sternum, spinous process, ribs)
 77002, 77012, 77021
 1.98   3.83   Global Days 000

20225 deep (eg, vertebral body, femur)
 77002, 77012, 77021
 2.99   13.34   Global Days 000

20240-20251 Open Bone Biopsy

CMS 100-3,150.3   Bone (Mineral) Density Studies
EXCLUDES Sequestrectomy or incision and drainage of bone abscess of:
 Skull (61501)
 Humeral head (23174)
 Radius (24136, 25145)
 Olecranon process (24138)
 Calcaneus (28120)
 Carpal bone (25145)
 Scapula (23172)
 Clavicle (23170)
 Humerus (24134)
 Talus (28120)
 Ulna (24138, 24145)

20240 Biopsy, bone, open; superficial (eg, ilium, sternum, spinous process, ribs, trochanter of femur)
 6.06   6.06   Global Days 010
AMA: 2009, Jan, 11-31; 2008, Jan, 10-25; 2007, January, 13-27; 2005, August, 13-15

20245 deep (eg, humerus, ischium, femur)
 16.98   16.98   Global Days 010

20250 Biopsy, vertebral body, open; thoracic
 10.18   10.18   Global Days 010

20251 lumbar or cervical
 11.11   11.11   Global Days 010

20500-20501 Injection Fistula/Sinus Tract

CMS 100-4,13,80.1   Supervision and Interpretation Codes
CMS 100-4,13,80.2   Physician Presence
EXCLUDES Arthrography injection of:
 Ankle (27648)
 Elbow (24220)
 Hip (27093, 27095)
 Sacroiliac joint (27096)
 Knee (27370)
 Temporomandibular joint (TMJ) (21116)
 Shoulder (23350)
 Wrist (25246)

20500 Injection of sinus tract; therapeutic (separate procedure)
 76080
 2.26   2.72   Global Days 010

20501 diagnostic (sinogram)
EXCLUDES Contrast injection or injections for radiological evaluation of existing gastrostomy, duodenostomy, jejunostomy, gastro-jejunostomy, or cecostomy (or other colonic) tube from percutaneous approach (49465)
 76080
 1.04   2.93   Global Days 000

20520-20525 Foreign Body Removal

CMS 100-4,12,30   Correct Coding Policy

- **20520** Removal of foreign body in muscle or tendon sheath; simple
  - 3.88   5.19   Global Days 010
- **20525** deep or complicated
  - 6.70   12.16   Global Days 010

20526 Injection for Carpal Tunnel

CMS 100-4,17,20.5.7   Injection Services

- **20526** Injection, therapeutic (eg, local anesthetic, corticosteroid), carpal tunnel
  - 1.56   1.99   Global Days 000
  - AMA: 2009, Jan, 11-31; 2008, Jan, 10-25; 2007, January, 13-27

20550-20553 Therapeutic Injections: Tendons, Trigger Points

CMS 100-3,150.7   Prolotherapy, Joint Sclerotherapy, and Ligamentous Injections with Sclerosing Agents
CMS 100-4,12,30   Correct Coding Policy
CMS 100-4,13,80.1   Supervision and Interpretation Codes
CMS 100-4,13,80.2   Physician Presence

- **20550** Injection(s); single tendon sheath, or ligament, aponeurosis (eg, plantar "fascia")
  - EXCLUDES   Morton's neuroma injection (64455, 64632)
  - 76942, 77002, 77021
  - 1.14   1.52   Global Days 000
  - AMA: 2009, Jan, 11-31; 2009, Jan, 6&9; 2008, Jan, 10-25; 2007, January, 13-27
- **20551** single tendon origin/insertion
  - 76942, 77002, 77021
  - 1.19   1.59   Global Days 000
  - AMA: 2009, Jan, 11-31; 2008, Jan, 10-25; 2007, January, 13-27
- **20552** single or multiple trigger point(s), 1 or 2 muscle(s)
  - 76942, 77002, 77021
  - 1.04   1.42   Global Days 000
  - AMA: 2009, Jan, 11-31; 2008, Jan, 10-25; 2007, January, 13-27
- **20553** single or multiple trigger point(s), 3 or more muscle(s)
  - 76942, 77002, 77021
  - 1.18   1.64   Global Days 000
  - AMA: 2009, Jan, 11-31; 2008, Jan, 10-25; 2008, Jun, 8-11; 2007, January, 13-27

20555 Placement of Catheters/Needles for Brachytherapy

- **20555** Placement of needles or catheters into muscle and/or soft tissue for subsequent interstitial radioelement application (at the time of or subsequent to the procedure)
  - EXCLUDES   Interstitial radioelement:
    - Devices placed into the breast (19296-19298)
    - Placement of needle, catheters, or devices into muscle or soft tissue of the head and neck (41019)
    - Placement of needles or catheters into pelvic organs or genitalia (55920)
    - Placement of needles or catheters into prostate (55875)
    - Radioelement application (77776-77778, 77785-77787)
  - 76942, 77002, 77012, 77021
  - 9.22   9.22   Global Days 000
  - AMA: 2009, Jan, 11-31; 2008, Feb, 8-9; 2008, Jun, 8-11; 2007, Dec, 1-2

20600-20610 Aspiration and/or Injection of Joint

CMS 100-3,150.6   Vitamin B12 Injections to Strenghen Tendons, Ligaments of Foot
CMS 100-3,150.7   Prolotherapy, Joint Sclerotherapy, and Ligamentous Injections with Sclerosing Agents
CMS 100-4,12,30   Correct Coding Policy
CMS 100-4,13,80.1   Supervision and Interpretation Codes
CMS 100-4,13,80.2   Physician Presence

- **20600** Arthrocentesis, aspiration and/or injection; small joint or bursa (eg, fingers, toes)
  - 76942, 77002, 77012, 77021
  - 1.06   1.43   Global Days 000
  - AMA: 2007, Dec, 10-179
- **20605** intermediate joint or bursa (eg, temporomandibular, acromioclavicular, wrist, elbow or ankle, olecranon bursa)
  - 76942, 77002, 77012, 77021
  - 1.12   1.56   Global Days 000
  - AMA: 2007, Dec, 10-179
- **20610** major joint or bursa (eg, shoulder, hip, knee joint, subacromial bursa)
  - 76942, 77002, 77012, 77021
  - 1.37   2.08   Global Days 000
  - AMA: 2009, Jan, 11-31; 2008, Jan, 10-25; 2008, Jun, 8-11; 2008, Jul, 9; 2007, Dec, 10-179; 2007, January, 13-27; 2006, April, 19-20; 2005, March, 11-15

20612-20615 Aspiration and/or Injection of Cyst

CMS 100-4,12,30   Correct Coding Policy

- **20612** Aspiration and/or injection of ganglion cyst(s) any location
  - 1.15   1.58   Global Days 000
- **20615** Aspiration and injection for treatment of bone cyst
  - 4.19   5.57   Global Days 010

Current Procedural Coding Expert – Musculoskeletal System

20650-20697 Devices Related to External Fixation
CMS 100-4,12,30   Correct Coding Policy

20650 Insertion of wire or pin with application of skeletal traction, including removal (separate procedure)
4.09   5.22   Global Days 010

20660 Application of cranial tongs, caliper, or stereotactic frame, including removal (separate procedure)
6.63   6.63   Global Days 000
AMA: 2009, Jan, 11-31; 2008, Jan, 10-25; 2008, Feb, 8-9; 2008, Jul, 10&13; 2007, Dec, 1-2; 2007, January, 13-27; 2006, December, 10-12; 2006, January, 46-47

20661 Application of halo, including removal; cranial
13.01   13.01   Global Days 090

20662 pelvic
10.82   10.82   Global Days 090

20663 femoral
12.35   12.35   Global Days 090

20664 Application of halo, including removal, cranial, 6 or more pins placed, for thin skull osteology (eg, pediatric patients, hydrocephalus, osteogenesis imperfecta), requiring general anesthesia
22.70   22.70   Global Days 090

20665 Removal of tongs or halo applied by another physician
2.52   2.87   Global Days 010
AMA: 2006, December, 10-12

20670 Removal of implant; superficial (eg, buried wire, pin or rod) (separate procedure)
3.93   9.48   Global Days 010
AMA: 2009, Jan, 11-31; 2009, Jun, 7-8; 2008, Jan, 10-25; 2007, Dec, 7-8

20680 deep (eg, buried wire, pin, screw, metal band, nail, rod or plate)
11.49   16.08   Global Days 090
AMA: 2009, Jun, 7-8

20690 Application of a uniplane (pins or wires in 1 plane), unilateral, external fixation system
15.94   15.94   Global Days 090
AMA: 2009, Jan, 11-31; 2009, Jun, 7-8; 2008, Feb, 8-9; 2008, Jan, 4-5; 2008, Jan, 10-25; 2007, January, 13-27; 2005, June, 9-11

20692 Application of a multiplane (pins or wires in more than 1 plane), unilateral, external fixation system (eg, Ilizarov, Monticelli type)
30.21   30.21   Global Days 090
AMA: 2009, Jan, 11-31; 2009, Jun, 7-8; 2008, Jan, 10-25; 2008, Jan, 4-5; 2008, Feb, 8-9; 2007, January, 13-27

20693 Adjustment or revision of external fixation system requiring anesthesia (eg, new pin[s] or wire[s] and/or new ring[s] or bar[s])
12.17   12.17   Global Days 090
AMA: 2009, Jun, 7-8; 2009, Jan, 11-31; 2008, Jan, 10-25; 2007, January, 13-27

20694 Removal, under anesthesia, of external fixation system
9.01   11.04   Global Days 090
AMA: 2009, Jan, 11-31; 2009, Jun, 7-8; 2008, Jan, 10-25; 2007, January, 13-27

20696 Application of multiplane (pins or wires in more than 1 plane), unilateral, external fixation with stereotactic computer-assisted adjustment (eg, spatial frame), including imaging; initial and subsequent alignment(s), assessment(s), and computation(s) of adjustment schedule(s)
Do not report with (20692, 20697)
28.39   28.39   Global Days 090
AMA: 2009, Jun, 7-8

20697 exchange (ie, removal and replacement) of strut, each
Do not report with (20692, 20696)
38.73   38.73   Global Days 000
AMA: 2009, Jun, 7-8

20802-20838 Reimplantation Procedures
CMS 100-4,12,30   Correct Coding Policy
CMS 100-4,12,40.1   Global Surgery Package Definition
EXCLUDES Repair of incomplete amputation (see individual repair codes for bone(s), ligament(s), tendon(s), nerve(s), or blood vessel(s))

20802 Replantation, arm (includes surgical neck of humerus through elbow joint), complete amputation
64.03   64.03   Global Days 090

20805 Replantation, forearm (includes radius and ulna to radial carpal joint), complete amputation
89.65   89.65   Global Days 090

20808 Replantation, hand (includes hand through metacarpophalangeal joints), complete amputation
114.06   114.06   Global Days 090

20816 Replantation, digit, excluding thumb (includes metacarpophalangeal joint to insertion of flexor sublimis tendon), complete amputation
54.63   54.63   Global Days 090
AMA: 2009, Jan, 11-31; 2008, Jan, 10-25; 2007, January, 13-27

20822 Replantation, digit, excluding thumb (includes distal tip to sublimis tendon insertion), complete amputation
48.13   48.13   Global Days 090

20824 Replantation, thumb (includes carpometacarpal joint to MP joint), complete amputation
56.39   56.39   Global Days 090

20827 Replantation, thumb (includes distal tip to MP joint), complete amputation
49.48   49.48   Global Days 090

20838 Replantation, foot, complete amputation
66.18   66.18   Global Days 090

20900-20926 Bone and Tissue Autografts
CMS 100-4,12,30   Correct Coding Policy
EXCLUDES Acquisition of autogenous bone graft, cartilage, tendon, fascia lata through distinct incision unless included in the code description
Bone graft procedures on the spine (20930-20938)

20900 Bone graft, any donor area; minor or small (eg, dowel or button)
5.90   10.64   Global Days 000
AMA: 2009, Jan, 11-31; 2008, Jan, 10-25; 2007, January, 13-27

20902 major or large
8.36   8.36   Global Days 000
AMA: 2009, Jan, 11-31; 2008, Jan, 10-25; 2007, January, 13-27

20910 Cartilage graft; costochondral
EXCLUDES Graft with ear cartilage (21235)
11.26   11.26   Global Days 090

● New Code   ▲ Revised Code   M Maternity   A Age   Unlisted   Not Covered   # Resequenced
CCI   + Add-on   ⊘ Mod 51 Exempt   @ Mod 63 Exempt   ⊙ Mod Sedation   PQRI

© 2009 Publisher *(Blue Ink)*   CPT only © 2009 American Medical Association. All Rights Reserved. *(Black Ink)*   Medicare *(Red Ink)*

20912	nasal septum
	EXCLUDES Graft with ear cartilage (21235)
	13.18 13.18 Global Days 090
20920	Fascia lata graft; by stripper
	10.89 10.89 Global Days 090
	AMA: 2005, January, 7-13
20922	by incision and area exposure, complex or sheet
	13.28 15.74 Global Days 090
	AMA: 2005, January, 7-13
20924	Tendon graft, from a distance (eg, palmaris, toe extensor, plantaris)
	13.49 13.49 Global Days 090
	AMA: 2005, January, 7-13
20926	Tissue grafts, other (eg, paratenon, fat, dermis)
	11.82 11.82 Global Days 090
	AMA: 2009, Jan, 11-31; 2008, Jan, 10-25; 2007, March, 9-11; 2007, January, 13-27; 2006, May, 16-20

20930-20938 Bone Allograft and Autograft of Spine

CMS 100-4,12,40.1 Global Surgery Package Definition
EXCLUDES Bone marrow aspiration for grafting (38220)

+ 20930	Allograft for spine surgery only; morselized (List separately in addition to code for primary procedure)
	Code first (0195T-0196T, 22319, 22532-22533, 22548-22558, 22590-22612, 22630, 22800-22812)
	0.00 0.00 Global Days XXX
	AMA: 2009, Jan, 11-31; 2008, Feb, 8-9; 2008, Jan, 10-25; 2007, Dec, 1-2; 2007, January, 13-27
+ 20931	structural (List separately in addition to code for primary procedure)
	Code first (22319, 22532-22533, 22548-22558, 22590-22612, 22630, 22800-22812)
	3.06 3.06 Global Days ZZZ
	AMA: 2009, Jan, 11-31; 2008, Feb, 8-9; 2007, Dec, 1-2; 2005, February, 13-16
+ 20936	Autograft for spine surgery only (includes harvesting the graft); local (eg, ribs, spinous process, or laminar fragments) obtained from same incision (List separately in addition to code for primary procedure)
	Code first (0195T-0196T, 22319, 22532-22533, 22548-22558, 22590-22612, 22630, 22800-22812)
	0.00 0.00 Global Days XXX
	AMA: 2009, Jan, 11-31; 2008, Feb, 8-9; 2007, Dec, 1-2
+ 20937	morselized (through separate skin or fascial incision) (List separately in addition to code for primary procedure)
	Code first (0195T-0196T, 22319, 22532-22533, 22548-22558, 22590-22612, 22630, 22800-22812)
	4.63 4.63 Global Days ZZZ
	AMA: 2009, Jan, 11-31; 2008, Feb, 8-9; 2007, Dec, 1-2
+ 20938	structural, bicortical or tricortical (through separate skin or fascial incision) (List separately in addition to code for primary procedure)
	Code first (22319, 22532-22533, 22548-22558, 22590-22612, 22630)
	5.06 5.06 Global Days ZZZ
	AMA: 2009, Jan, 11-31; 2008, Feb, 8-9; 2007, Dec, 1-2

20950 Measurement of Intracompartmental Pressure

CMS 100-4,12,20.4.3 Payment for Assistant at Surgery
CMS 100-4,12,30 Correct Coding Policy

20950	Monitoring of interstitial fluid pressure (includes insertion of device, eg, wick catheter technique, needle manometer technique) in detection of muscle compartment syndrome
	2.43 6.06 Global Days 000
	AMA: 2009, Jan, 11-31; 2008, Jan, 10-25

20955-20973 Bone and Osteocutaneous Grafts

CMS 100-4,12,20.4.3 Payment for Assistant at Surgery
CMS 100-4,12,30 Correct Coding Policy
INCLUDES Operating microscope (69990)

20955	Bone graft with microvascular anastomosis; fibula
	69.94 69.94 Global Days 090
20956	iliac crest
	72.29 72.29 Global Days 090
20957	metatarsal
	75.12 75.12 Global Days 090
20962	other than fibula, iliac crest, or metatarsal
	72.25 72.25 Global Days 090
20969	Free osteocutaneous flap with microvascular anastomosis; other than iliac crest, metatarsal, or great toe
	77.80 77.80 Global Days 090
20970	iliac crest
	78.21 78.21 Global Days 090
20972	metatarsal
	61.52 61.52 Global Days 090
20973	great toe with web space
	EXCLUDES Wrap-around repair (26551)
	70.46 70.46 Global Days 090

20974-20979 Osteogenic Stimulation

CMS 100-3,150.2 Osteogenic Stimulation
CMS 100-4,12,20.4.3 Payment for Assistant at Surgery
CMS 100-4,12,30 Correct Coding Policy

20974	Electrical stimulation to aid bone healing; noninvasive (nonoperative)
	1.32 1.92 Global Days 000
	AMA: 2009, Jan, 11-31; 2008, Jan, 10-25; 2007, January, 13-27
20975	invasive (operative)
	4.76 4.76 Global Days 000
20979	Low intensity ultrasound stimulation to aid bone healing, noninvasive (nonoperative)
	0.91 1.38 Global Days 000
	AMA: 2009, Jan, 11-31; 2008, Jan, 10-25; 2007, January, 13-27

20982-20999 General Musculoskeletal Procedures

CMS 100-4,12,20.4.3 Payment for Assistant at Surgery
CMS 100-4,12,30 Correct Coding Policy
CMS 100-4,12,40.7 Bilateral Procedures

20982	Ablation, bone tumor(s) (eg, osteoid osteoma, metastasis) radiofrequency, percutaneous, including computed tomographic guidance
	Do not report with (77013)
	10.34 83.50 Global Days 000

Current Procedural Coding Expert – Musculoskeletal System

+ **20985** Computer-assisted surgical navigational procedure for musculoskeletal procedures, image-less (List separately in addition to code for primary procedure)
  - **EXCLUDES** *Image guidance derived from intraoperative and preoperative obtained images (0054T-0055T)*
  - Do not report with (61795)
  - 4.07 4.07 Global Days ZZZ
  - **AMA:** 2007, Dec, 1-2

20999 Unlisted procedure, musculoskeletal system, general
  - 0.00 0.00 Global Days YYY

21010 Temporomandibular Joint Arthrotomy

21010 Arthrotomy, temporomandibular joint
  - **EXCLUDES** *Excision of foreign body from dentoalveolar site (41805-41806)*
  - *Simple abscess and hematoma drainage (20000)*
  - 21.03 21.03 Global Days 090

21011-21016 Excision Soft Tissue Tumors Face and Scalp

- **CMS** 100-4,4,20.5 HCPCS Under OPPS
- **CMS** 100-4,12,30   Correct Coding Policy
- **CMS** 100-4,12,90.3 MD Services in ASCs
- **CMS** 100-4,14,10   General ASC Services

INCLUDES Any necessary elevation of tissue planes or dissection
Measurement of tumor and necessary margin at greatest diameter prior to excision
Simple and intermediate repairs
Types of excisions:
  Fascial or subfascial soft tissue tumors: simple and marginal resection of most often benign and intramuscular tumors found either in or below the deep fascia, not involving bone
  Radical resection soft tissue tumor: wide resection of tumor, mostly malignant or aggressive benign, involving large margins of normal tissue and may involve tissue removal from one or more layers
  Subcutaneous: simple and marginal resection of most often benign tumors found in the subcutaneous tissue above the deep fascia

EXCLUDES *Complex repair*
Radical resection of cutaneous tumors (e.g., melanoma) (11600-11646)
Significant exploration of vessels or neuroplasty

● **21011** Excision, tumor, soft tissue of face or scalp, subcutaneous; less than 2 cm
  - 6.64 8.49 Global Days 090

● **21012** 2 cm or greater
  - 9.09 9.09 Global Days 090

● **21013** Excision, tumor, soft tissue of face and scalp, subfascial (eg, subgaleal, intramuscular); less than 2 cm
  - 10.70 13.19 Global Days 090

● **21014** 2 cm or greater
  - 14.04 14.04 Global Days 090

▲ **21015** Radical resection of tumor (eg, malignant neoplasm), soft tissue of face or scalp; less than 2 cm
  - **EXCLUDES** *Removal of cranial tumor for osteomyelitis (61501)*
  - 18.60 18.60 Global Days 090

● **21016** 2 cm or greater
  - 28.23 28.23 Global Days 090

21025-21070 Procedures of Cranial and Facial Bones

21025 Excision of bone (eg, for osteomyelitis or bone abscess); mandible
  - 20.42 23.70 Global Days 090

21026 facial bone(s)
  - 13.31 16.15 Global Days 090

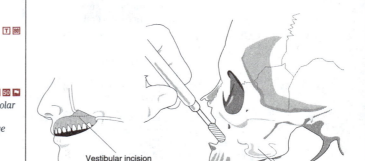

Vestibular incision
Burs, files, and osteotomes used to remove bone
Area of benign bone growth

21029 Removal by contouring of benign tumor of facial bone (eg, fibrous dysplasia)
  - 17.51 20.59 Global Days 090

21030 Excision of benign tumor or cyst of maxilla or zygoma by enucleation and curettage
  - 11.15 13.53 Global Days 090

21031 Excision of torus mandibularis
  - 7.81 10.14 Global Days 090

21032 Excision of maxillary torus palatinus
  - 7.76 10.29 Global Days 090

21034 Excision of malignant tumor of maxilla or zygoma
  - 32.13 35.93 Global Days 090

21040 Excision of benign tumor or cyst of mandible, by enucleation and/or curettage
  - **INCLUDES** Removal of benign tumor or cyst without osteotomy
  - **EXCLUDES** *Removal of benign tumor or cyst with osteotomy (21046-21047)*
  - 11.21 13.65 Global Days 090

21044 Excision of malignant tumor of mandible;
  - 24.31 24.31 Global Days 090

21045	**radical resection**
	INCLUDES: Any necessary elevation of tissue planes or dissection; Measurement of tumor and necessary margin prior to excision; Radical resection of bone tumor involves resection of the tumor (may include entire bone) and wide margins of normal tissue primarily for malignant or aggressive benign tumors; Simple and intermediate repairs
	EXCLUDES: Bone graft procedure (21215); Complex repair; Radical resection of cutaneous tumors (e.g., melanoma) (11600-11646); Significant exploration of vessels, neuroplasty, reconstruction, or complex bone repair
	Do not report excision of soft tissue codes when adjacent soft tissue is removed during the bone tumor resection (21011-21016)
	33.99 33.99 Global Days 090
21046	**Excision of benign tumor or cyst of mandible; requiring intra-oral osteotomy (eg, locally aggressive or destructive lesion(s))**
	30.01 30.01 Global Days 090
21047	**requiring extra-oral osteotomy and partial mandibulectomy (eg, locally aggressive or destructive lesion(s))**
	36.08 36.08 Global Days 090
21048	**Excision of benign tumor or cyst of maxilla; requiring intra-oral osteotomy (eg, locally aggressive or destructive lesion(s))**
	30.81 30.81 Global Days 090
21049	**requiring extra-oral osteotomy and partial maxillectomy (eg, locally aggressive or destructive lesion(s))**
	34.16 34.16 Global Days 090
21050	**Condylectomy, temporomandibular joint (separate procedure)**
	23.74 23.74 Global Days 090
21060	**Meniscectomy, partial or complete, temporomandibular joint (separate procedure)**
	22.81 22.81 Global Days 090
21070	**Coronoidectomy (separate procedure)**
	17.50 17.50 Global Days 090

21073 Temporomandibular Joint Manipulation with Anesthesia

CMS 100-3,150.1 Manipulation

21073	**Manipulation of temporomandibular joint(s) (TMJ), therapeutic, requiring an anesthesia service (ie, general or monitored anesthesia care)**
	EXCLUDES: Closed treatment of TMJ dislocation (21480, 21485); Manipulation of TMJ without an anesthesia service (97140, 98925-98929, 98943)
	7.09 9.91 Global Days 090
	AMA: 2009, Jan, 11-31; 2008, Feb, 8-9; 2007, Dec, 1-2

21076-21089 Medical Impressions for Fabrication Maxillofacial Prosthesis

CMS 100-4,12,30 Correct Coding Policy
INCLUDES: Professional services by a physician and not an outside lab
EXCLUDES: Application or removal of caliper or tongs (20660, 20665)

21076	**Impression and custom preparation; surgical obturator prosthesis**
	23.20 26.30 Global Days 010
	AMA: 2009, Jan, 11-31; 2008, Jan, 10-25; 2007, January, 13-27; 2006, December, 10-12; 2006, September, 14-16
21077	**orbital prosthesis**
	58.50 64.59 Global Days 090
	AMA: 2006, December, 10-12; 2006, September, 14-16
21079	**interim obturator prosthesis**
	38.88 44.35 Global Days 090
	AMA: 2006, September, 14-16; 2006, December, 10-12
21080	**definitive obturator prosthesis**
	43.40 50.05 Global Days 090
	AMA: 2006, December, 10-12; 2006, September, 14-16
21081	**mandibular resection prosthesis**
	39.69 45.86 Global Days 090
	AMA: 2006, December, 10-12; 2006, September, 14-16
21082	**palatal augmentation prosthesis**
	37.17 43.23 Global Days 090
	AMA: 2006, December, 10-12; 2006, September, 14-16
21083	**palatal lift prosthesis**
	33.66 40.17 Global Days 090
	AMA: 2006, December, 10-12; 2006, September, 14-16
21084	**speech aid prosthesis**
	39.95 47.09 Global Days 090
	AMA: 2006, December, 10-12; 2006, September, 14-16
21085	**oral surgical splint**
	17.34 20.55 Global Days 010
	AMA: 2006, December, 10-12; 2006, September, 14-16
21086	**auricular prosthesis**
	43.05 47.18 Global Days 090
	AMA: 2006, December, 10-12; 2006, September, 14-16
21087	**nasal prosthesis**
	42.81 46.98 Global Days 090
	AMA: 2006, December, 10-12; 2006, September, 14-16
21088	**facial prosthesis**
	0.00 0.00 Global Days 090
	AMA: 2006, December, 10-12; 2006, September, 14-16
21089	**Unlisted maxillofacial prosthetic procedure**
	0.00 0.00 Global Days YYY
	AMA: 2009, Jan, 11-31; 2008, Jan, 10-25; 2007, January, 13-27; 2006, December, 10-12; 2006, September, 14-16

21100-21110 Application Fixation Device

CMS 100-4,12,40.1 Global Surgery Package Definition

21100	**Application of halo type appliance for maxillofacial fixation, includes removal (separate procedure)**
	10.21 18.19 Global Days 090
21110	**Application of interdental fixation device for conditions other than fracture or dislocation, includes removal**
	EXCLUDES: Removal of interdental fixation by another doctor (20670-20680)
	17.48 20.56 Global Days 090
	AMA: 2009, Jan, 11-31; 2008, Jan, 10-25; 2007, January, 13-27

Current Procedural Coding Expert – Musculoskeletal System

21116 Injection for TMJ Arthrogram

CMS 100-4,13,80.1 Supervision and Interpretation Codes
CMS 100-4,13,80.2 Physician Presence

21116 Injection procedure for temporomandibular joint arthrography
 70332
 1.25 4.01 Global Days 000

21120-21299 Repair/Reconstruction Craniofacial Bones

CMS 100-2,16,10 Exclusions from Coverage
CMS 100-2,16,120 Cosmetic Procedures
CMS 100-2,16,180 Services Related to Noncovered Procedures
CMS 100-4,12,40.1 Global Surgery Package Definition
EXCLUDES Cranioplasty (62116, 62120, 62140-62147)

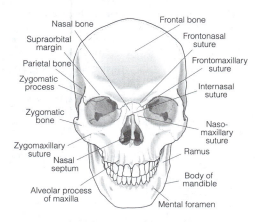

21120 Genioplasty; augmentation (autograft, allograft, prosthetic material)
 13.83 17.04 Global Days 090

21121 sliding osteotomy, single piece
 16.92 19.98 Global Days 090

21122 sliding osteotomies, 2 or more osteotomies (eg, wedge excision or bone wedge reversal for asymmetrical chin)
 17.03 17.03 Global Days 090

21123 sliding, augmentation with interpositional bone grafts (includes obtaining autografts)
 23.75 23.75 Global Days 090

21125 Augmentation, mandibular body or angle; prosthetic material
 22.27 88.33 Global Days 090

21127 with bone graft, onlay or interpositional (includes obtaining autograft)
 22.65 97.75 Global Days 090

21137 Reduction forehead; contouring only
 20.69 20.69 Global Days 090

21138 contouring and application of prosthetic material or bone graft (includes obtaining autograft)
 24.56 24.56 Global Days 090

21139 contouring and setback of anterior frontal sinus wall
 25.03 25.03 Global Days 090

21141 Reconstruction midface, LeFort I; single piece, segment movement in any direction (eg, for Long Face Syndrome), without bone graft
 37.45 37.45 Global Days 090

21142 2 pieces, segment movement in any direction, without bone graft
 39.51 39.51 Global Days 090

21143 3 or more pieces, segment movement in any direction, without bone graft
 37.82 37.82 Global Days 090

21145 single piece, segment movement in any direction, requiring bone grafts (includes obtaining autografts)
 43.36 43.36 Global Days 090

21146 2 pieces, segment movement in any direction, requiring bone grafts (includes obtaining autografts) (eg, ungrafted unilateral alveolar cleft)
 47.89 47.89 Global Days 090

21147 3 or more pieces, segment movement in any direction, requiring bone grafts (includes obtaining autografts) (eg, ungrafted bilateral alveolar cleft or multiple osteotomies)
 46.40 46.40 Global Days 090

21150 Reconstruction midface, LeFort II; anterior intrusion (eg, Treacher-Collins Syndrome)
 42.01 42.01 Global Days 090

21151 any direction, requiring bone grafts (includes obtaining autografts)
 51.96 51.96 Global Days 090

21154 Reconstruction midface, LeFort III (extracranial), any type, requiring bone grafts (includes obtaining autografts); without LeFort I
 55.89 55.89 Global Days 090

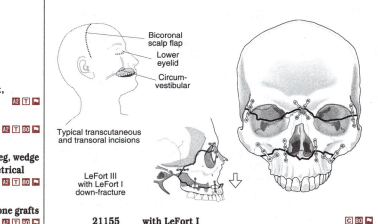

21155 with LeFort I
 62.38 62.38 Global Days 090

21159 Reconstruction midface, LeFort III (extra and intracranial) with forehead advancement (eg, mono bloc), requiring bone grafts (includes obtaining autografts); without LeFort I
 74.55 74.55 Global Days 090

21160 with LeFort I
 72.36 72.36 Global Days 090

21172 Reconstruction superior-lateral orbital rim and lower forehead, advancement or alteration, with or without grafts (includes obtaining autografts)
EXCLUDES Frontal or parietal craniotomy for craniosynostosis (61556)
 50.94 50.94 Global Days 090

● New Code ▲ Revised Code M Maternity A Age Unlisted Not Covered # Resequenced
CCI + Add-on Mod 51 Exempt Mod 63 Exempt Mod Sedation PQRI
© 2009 Publisher (Blue Ink) CPT only © 2009 American Medical Association. All Rights Reserved. (Black Ink) Medicare (Red Ink) 43

Code	Description	Facility RVU	Non-Facility RVU	Global Days
21175	Reconstruction, bifrontal, superior-lateral orbital rims and lower forehead, advancement or alteration (eg, plagiocephaly, trigonocephaly, brachycephaly), with or without grafts (includes obtaining autografts) [T][80]	63.96	63.96	090
	EXCLUDES: Bifrontal craniotomy for craniosynostosis (61557)			
21179	Reconstruction, entire or majority of forehead and/or supraorbital rims; with grafts (allograft or prosthetic material) [C][80]	39.68	39.68	090
	EXCLUDES: Extensive craniotomy for numerous suture craniosynostosis (61558-61559)			
21180	with autograft (includes obtaining grafts) [C][80]	43.26	43.26	090
	EXCLUDES: Extensive craniotomy for numerous suture craniosynostosis (61558-61559)			
21181	Reconstruction by contouring of benign tumor of cranial bones (eg, fibrous dysplasia), extracranial [A2][T][80]	18.58	18.58	090
21182	Reconstruction of orbital walls, rims, forehead, nasoethmoid complex following intra- and extracranial excision of benign tumor of cranial bone (eg, fibrous dysplasia), with multiple autografts (includes obtaining grafts); total area of bone grafting less than 40 sq cm [C][80]	54.24	54.24	090
	EXCLUDES: Removal of benign tumor of the skull (61563-61564)			
21183	total area of bone grafting greater than 40 sq cm but less than 80 sq cm [C][80]	64.73	64.73	090
	EXCLUDES: Removal of benign tumor of the skull (61563-61564)			
21184	total area of bone grafting greater than 80 sq cm [C][80]	67.24	67.24	090
	EXCLUDES: Removal of benign tumor of the skull (61563-61564)			
21188	Reconstruction midface, osteotomies (other than LeFort type) and bone grafts (includes obtaining autografts) [C][80]	46.87	46.87	090
21193	Reconstruction of mandibular rami, horizontal, vertical, C, or L osteotomy; without bone graft [C][80]	31.95	31.95	090
	AMA: 2009, Jan, 11-31; 2008, Jan, 10-25; 2007, January, 13-27			
21194	with bone graft (includes obtaining graft) [C][80]	38.32	38.32	090
21195	Reconstruction of mandibular rami and/or body, sagittal split; without internal rigid fixation [T][80]	37.01	37.01	090
	AMA: 2009, Jan, 11-31; 2008, Jan, 10-25; 2007, January, 13-27			
21196	with internal rigid fixation [C][80]	40.42	40.42	090
	AMA: 2009, Jan, 11-31; 2008, Jan, 10-25; 2007, January, 13-27			
21198	Osteotomy, mandible, segmental; [G2][T][80]	31.46	31.46	090
	EXCLUDES: Total maxillary osteotomy (21141-21160)			
21199	with genioglossus advancement [G2][T][80]	28.42	28.42	090
	EXCLUDES: Total maxillary osteotomy (21141-21160)			
21206	Osteotomy, maxilla, segmental (eg, Wassmund or Schuchard) [A2][T][80]	33.87	33.87	090
21208	Osteoplasty, facial bones; augmentation (autograft, allograft, or prosthetic implant) [A2][T][80]	23.20	49.48	090
21209	reduction [A2][T][80]	18.61	23.89	090
21210	Graft, bone; nasal, maxillary or malar areas (includes obtaining graft) [A2][T]	23.37	57.14	090
	EXCLUDES: Cleft palate treatment (42200-42225)			
21215	mandible (includes obtaining graft) [A2][T]	24.95	99.82	090
21230	Graft; rib cartilage, autogenous, to face, chin, nose or ear (includes obtaining graft) [A2][T][80]	21.90	21.90	090
	EXCLUDES: Augmentation graft of the facial bones (21208)			
21235	ear cartilage, autogenous, to nose or ear (includes obtaining graft) [A2][T]	15.49	19.29	090
	EXCLUDES: Augmentation graft of the facial bones (21208)			
	AMA: 2009, Jan, 11-31; 2008, Jan, 10-25; 2007, March, 9-11			
21240	Arthroplasty, temporomandibular joint, with or without autograft (includes obtaining graft) [A2][T][80][50]	30.37	30.37	090
21242	Arthroplasty, temporomandibular joint, with allograft [A2][T][80][50]	27.76	27.76	090
21243	Arthroplasty, temporomandibular joint, with prosthetic joint replacement [A2][T][80][50]	47.13	47.13	090
21244	Reconstruction of mandible, extraoral, with transosteal bone plate (eg, mandibular staple bone plate) [A2][T][80]	28.96	28.96	090
21245	Reconstruction of mandible or maxilla, subperiosteal implant; partial [A2][T][80]	24.62	30.12	090
21246	complete [A2][T][80]	23.01	23.01	090
21247	Reconstruction of mandibular condyle with bone and cartilage autografts (includes obtaining grafts) (eg, for hemifacial microsomia) [C][80]	44.09	44.09	090

TMJ syndrome is often related to stress and tooth-grinding; in other cases, arthritis, injury, poorly aligned teeth, or ill-fitting dentures may be the cause

Cutaway view of temporomandibular joint (TMJ) — Upper joint space, Lower joint space, Articular disc (meniscus), Condyle, Mandible, Cutaway detail

Symptoms include facial pain and chewing problems; TMJ syndrome occurs more frequently in women

Current Procedural Coding Expert – Musculoskeletal System 21348

21248	Reconstruction of mandible or maxilla, endosteal implant (eg, blade, cylinder); partial
	EXCLUDES: Midface reconstruction (21141-21160)
	24.63 29.47 Global Days 090
21249	complete
	EXCLUDES: Midface reconstruction (21141-21160)
	35.22 40.69 Global Days 090
21255	Reconstruction of zygomatic arch and glenoid fossa with bone and cartilage (includes obtaining autografts)
	36.58 36.58 Global Days 090
21256	Reconstruction of orbit with osteotomies (extracranial) and with bone grafts (includes obtaining autografts) (eg, micro-ophthalmia)
	33.21 33.21 Global Days 090
21260	Periorbital osteotomies for orbital hypertelorism, with bone grafts; extracranial approach
	31.00 31.00 Global Days 090
21261	combined intra- and extracranial approach
	62.40 62.40 Global Days 090

In 21263, a frontal craniotomy is performed, the brain retracted, and the orbit approached from inside the skull; frontal bone is advanced and secured

Osteotomies are cut 360 degrees around the orbit; portions of nasal and ethmoid bones are removed

Grafts are placed and the bony orbits realigned

21263	with forehead advancement
	51.27 51.27 Global Days 090
21267	Orbital repositioning, periorbital osteotomies, unilateral, with bone grafts; extracranial approach
	43.97 43.97 Global Days 090
21268	combined intra- and extracranial approach
	58.86 58.86 Global Days 090
21270	Malar augmentation, prosthetic material
	EXCLUDES: Bone graft (21210)
	20.34 25.88 Global Days 090
21275	Secondary revision of orbitocraniofacial reconstruction
	23.13 23.13 Global Days 090
21280	Medial canthopexy (separate procedure)
	EXCLUDES: Reconstruction of canthus (67950)
	15.57 15.57 Global Days 090
21282	Lateral canthopexy
	10.18 10.18 Global Days 090
21295	Reduction of masseter muscle and bone (eg, for treatment of benign masseteric hypertrophy); extraoral approach
	4.76 4.76 Global Days 090
21296	intraoral approach
	11.79 11.79 Global Days 090
21299	**Unlisted craniofacial and maxillofacial procedure**
	0.00 0.00 Global Days YYY

21310-21499 Care of Fractures/Dislocations of the Cranial and Facial Bones

- CMS 100-4,4,20.5   HCPCS Under OPPS
- CMS 100-4,12,40.1   Global Surgery Package Definition
- CMS 100-4,12,90.3   MD Services in ASCs
- CMS 100-4,14,10   General ASC Services

EXCLUDES:
Closed treatment of skull fracture (99201-99499)
Open treatment of skull fracture (62000-62010)

21310	Closed treatment of nasal bone fracture without manipulation
	0.79 3.00 Global Days 000
21315	Closed treatment of nasal bone fracture; without stabilization
	4.01 7.05 Global Days 010
21320	with stabilization
	3.72 6.67 Global Days 010
21325	Open treatment of nasal fracture; uncomplicated
	12.34 12.34 Global Days 090
21330	complicated, with internal and/or external skeletal fixation
	14.97 14.97 Global Days 090
21335	with concomitant open treatment of fractured septum
	19.80 19.80 Global Days 090
21336	Open treatment of nasal septal fracture, with or without stabilization
	17.21 17.21 Global Days 090
21337	Closed treatment of nasal septal fracture, with or without stabilization
	7.90 10.52 Global Days 090
21338	Open treatment of nasoethmoid fracture; without external fixation
	19.68 19.68 Global Days 090
21339	with external fixation
	22.50 22.50 Global Days 090
21340	Percutaneous treatment of nasoethmoid complex fracture, with splint, wire or headcap fixation, including repair of canthal ligaments and/or the nasolacrimal apparatus
	20.92 20.92 Global Days 090
21343	Open treatment of depressed frontal sinus fracture
	32.82 32.82 Global Days 090
21344	Open treatment of complicated (eg, comminuted or involving posterior wall) frontal sinus fracture, via coronal or multiple approaches
	45.26 45.26 Global Days 090
21345	Closed treatment of nasomaxillary complex fracture (LeFort II type), with interdental wire fixation or fixation of denture or splint
	17.44 21.23 Global Days 090
21346	Open treatment of nasomaxillary complex fracture (LeFort II type); with wiring and/or local fixation
	24.82 24.82 Global Days 090
21347	requiring multiple open approaches
	27.91 27.91 Global Days 090
21348	with bone grafting (includes obtaining graft)
	30.56 30.56 Global Days 090

● New Code   ▲ Revised Code   M Maternity   Age   Unlisted   Not Covered   # Resequenced
CCI   + Add-on   ⊘ Mod 51 Exempt   Mod 63 Exempt   ⊙ Mod Sedation   PQRI
© 2009 Publisher (Blue Ink)   CPT only © 2009 American Medical Association. All Rights Reserved. (Black Ink)   Medicare (Red Ink)

Code	Description	Facility RVU	Non-Facility RVU	Global Days
21355	Percutaneous treatment of fracture of malar area, including zygomatic arch and malar tripod, with manipulation	8.87	11.55	010
21356	Open treatment of depressed zygomatic arch fracture (eg, Gillies approach)	10.17	13.05	010
21360	Open treatment of depressed malar fracture, including zygomatic arch and malar tripod	14.49	14.49	090
21365	Open treatment of complicated (eg, comminuted or involving cranial nerve foramina) fracture(s) of malar area, including zygomatic arch and malar tripod; with internal fixation and multiple surgical approaches	30.84	30.84	090
21366	with bone grafting (includes obtaining graft)	35.45	35.45	090
21385	Open treatment of orbital floor blowout fracture; transantral approach (Caldwell-Luc type operation)	18.90	18.90	090
21386	periorbital approach	17.92	17.92	090
21387	combined approach	20.24	20.24	090
21390	periorbital approach, with alloplastic or other implant	21.87	21.87	090
21395	periorbital approach with bone graft (includes obtaining graft)	25.50	25.50	090
21400	Closed treatment of fracture of orbit, except blowout; without manipulation	4.00	4.84	090
21401	with manipulation	8.03	12.21	090
21406	Open treatment of fracture of orbit, except blowout; without implant	14.24	14.24	090
21407	with implant	17.82	17.82	090
21408	with bone grafting (includes obtaining graft)	24.93	24.93	090
21421	Closed treatment of palatal or maxillary fracture (LeFort I type), with interdental wire fixation or fixation of denture or splint	17.50	20.81	090
21422	Open treatment of palatal or maxillary fracture (LeFort I type);	18.08	18.08	090
21423	complicated (comminuted or involving cranial nerve foramina), multiple approaches	21.78	21.78	090
21431	Closed treatment of craniofacial separation (LeFort III type) using interdental wire fixation of denture or splint	20.96	20.96	090
21432	Open treatment of craniofacial separation (LeFort III type); with wiring and/or internal fixation	18.09	18.09	090
21433	complicated (eg, comminuted or involving cranial nerve foramina), multiple surgical approaches	45.60	45.60	090
21435	complicated, utilizing internal and/or external fixation techniques (eg, head cap, halo device, and/or intermaxillary fixation)	35.50	35.50	090
	EXCLUDES Removal of internal or external fixation (20670)			
21436	complicated, multiple surgical approaches, internal fixation, with bone grafting (includes obtaining graft)	56.97	56.97	090
21440	Closed treatment of mandibular or maxillary alveolar ridge fracture (separate procedure)	12.06	14.61	090
21445	Open treatment of mandibular or maxillary alveolar ridge fracture (separate procedure)	16.42	19.82	090
21450	Closed treatment of mandibular fracture; without manipulation	12.46	15.25	090
21451	with manipulation	16.61	19.52	090
21452	Percutaneous treatment of mandibular fracture, with external fixation	8.74	13.96	090
21453	Closed treatment of mandibular fracture with interdental fixation	20.21	23.27	090
	AMA: 2009, Jan, 11-31; 2008, Jan, 10-25; 2007, Dec, 7-8			
21454	Open treatment of mandibular fracture with external fixation	15.39	15.39	090
21461	Open treatment of mandibular fracture; without interdental fixation	24.85	53.49	090
21462	with interdental fixation	27.54	56.73	090
21465	Open treatment of mandibular condylar fracture	25.82	25.82	090
21470	Open treatment of complicated mandibular fracture by multiple surgical approaches including internal fixation, interdental fixation, and/or wiring of dentures or splints	33.29	33.29	090
	AMA: 2009, Jan, 11-31; 2008, Jan, 10-25; 2007, January, 13-27			
21480	Closed treatment of temporomandibular dislocation; initial or subsequent	0.91	2.35	000

In 21452, external fixation is necessary

Comminuted fractures
Metal or acrylic bar
Rods and pins placed in drilled holes

Current Procedural Coding Expert – Musculoskeletal System 21632

21485	complicated (eg, recurrent requiring intermaxillary fixation or splinting), initial or subsequent [A2][T][80][50]
	🚑 15.15 ⚕ 17.91 Global Days 090
21490	Open treatment of temporomandibular dislocation [A2][T][80][50]
	EXCLUDES Interdental wiring (21497)
	🚑 25.48 ⚕ 25.48 Global Days 090
21495	Open treatment of hyoid fracture [C2][T][80]
	EXCLUDES Closed treatment of larynx fracture (99201-99499) Laryngoplasty with fracture repair (31584)
	🚑 18.97 ⚕ 18.97 Global Days 090
21497	Interdental wiring, for condition other than fracture [A2][T][80]
	🚑 15.05 ⚕ 17.59 Global Days 090
	AMA: 2009, Jan, 11-31; 2008, Jan, 10-25; 2007, January, 13-27
21499	Unlisted musculoskeletal procedure, head [T][80]
	EXCLUDES Unlisted procedures of craniofacial or maxillofacial areas
	🚑 0.00 ⚕ 0.00 Global Days YYY

21501-21510 Surgical Incision for Drainage: Chest and Soft Tissues of Neck

EXCLUDES Biopsy of the flank or back (21920-21925)
Simple incision and drainage of abscess or hematoma (10060, 10140)
Tumor removal of flank or back (21930-21935)

21501	Incision and drainage, deep abscess or hematoma, soft tissues of neck or thorax; [A2][T]
	EXCLUDES Deep incision and drainage of posterior spine (22010-22015)
	🚑 8.63 ⚕ 11.83 Global Days 090
21502	with partial rib ostectomy [A2][T][80]
	🚑 14.37 ⚕ 14.37 Global Days 090
21510	Incision, deep, with opening of bone cortex (eg, for osteomyelitis or bone abscess), thorax [C][80]
	🚑 11.97 ⚕ 11.97 Global Days 090

21550 Soft Tissue Biopsy of Chest or Neck

EXCLUDES Biopsy of bone (20220-20251)
Soft tissue needle biopsy (20206)

21550	Biopsy, soft tissue of neck or thorax [C2][T]
	🚑 4.21 ⚕ 6.63 Global Days 010

21552-21558 [21552, 21554] Resection Soft Tissues of Chest and Neck

INCLUDES Any necessary elevation of tissue planes or dissection
Measurement of tumor and necessary margin at greatest diameter prior to excision
Resection without removal of significant normal tissue
Simple and intermediate repairs
Types of Excisions:
  Fascial or subfascial soft tissue tumors: simple and marginal resection of most often benign and intramuscular tumors found either in or below the deep fascia, not involving bone
  Radical resection soft tissue tumor: wide resection of tumor, mostly malignant or aggressive benign, involving large margins of normal tissue and may involve tissue removal from one or more layers
  Subcutaneous: simple and marginal resection of most often benign tumors found in the subcutaneous tissue above the deep fascia

EXCLUDES Complex repair
Radical resection of cutaneous tumors (e.g., melanoma) (11600-11646)
Significant exploration of the vessels or neuroplasty

21552	*Resequenced code. See code following 21555.*
21554	*Resequenced code. See code following 21556.*
▲ 21555	Excision, tumor, soft tissue of neck or anterior thorax, subcutaneous; less than 3 cm [P3][T]
	🚑 8.36 ⚕ 10.89 Global Days 090
	AMA: 2009, Jan, 11-31; 2008, Jan, 10-25; 2007, January, 13-27
#● 21552	3 cm or greater [C2][T][80]
	🚑 12.14 ⚕ 12.14 Global Days 090
▲ 21556	Excision, tumor, soft tissue of neck or anterior thorax, subfascial (eg, intramuscular); less than 5 cm [C2][T]
	🚑 14.20 ⚕ 14.20 Global Days 090
#● 21554	5 cm or greater [C2][T][80]
	🚑 19.94 ⚕ 19.94 Global Days 090
▲ 21557	Radical resection of tumor (eg, malignant neoplasm), soft tissue of neck or anterior thorax; less than 5 cm [C2][T][80]
	🚑 25.63 ⚕ 25.63 Global Days 090
● 21558	5 cm or greater [C2][T][80]
	🚑 37.43 ⚕ 37.43 Global Days 090

21600-21632 Bony Resection Chest and Neck

21600	Excision of rib, partial [A2][T][80]
	EXCLUDES Extensive debridement (11040-11044) Extensive tumor removal (19260)
	🚑 15.23 ⚕ 15.23 Global Days 090
21610	Costotransversectomy (separate procedure) [A2][T][80]
	🚑 31.83 ⚕ 31.83 Global Days 090
21615	Excision first and/or cervical rib; [C][80][50]
	🚑 18.20 ⚕ 18.20 Global Days 090
21616	with sympathectomy [C][80][50]
	🚑 21.06 ⚕ 21.06 Global Days 090
21620	Ostectomy of sternum, partial [C][80]
	🚑 14.01 ⚕ 14.01 Global Days 090
21627	Sternal debridement [C][80][PQ]
	EXCLUDES Sternotomy closure (21750)
	🚑 14.82 ⚕ 14.82 Global Days 090
21630	Radical resection of sternum; [C][80]
	🚑 34.31 ⚕ 34.31 Global Days 090
21632	with mediastinal lymphadenectomy [C][80][PQ]
	🚑 34.25 ⚕ 34.25 Global Days 090

● New Code   ▲ Revised Code   M Maternity   A Age   **Unlisted**   **Not Covered**   # Resequenced
□ CCI   + Add-on   ⊘ Mod 51 Exempt   ⊛ Mod 63 Exempt   ⊙ Mod Sedation   PQ PQRI

© 2009 Publisher *(Blue Ink)*   CPT only © 2009 American Medical Association. All Rights Reserved. *(Black Ink)*   Medicare *(Red Ink)*   47

21685-21750 Repair/Reconstruction Chest and Soft Tissues Neck

EXCLUDES
Biopsy of flank or back (21920-21925)
Repair of simple wounds (12001-12007)
Tumor removal of flank or back (21930, 21935)

21685 Hyoid myotomy and suspension
27.70 27.70 Global Days 090
AMA: 2009, Jan, 11-31; 2008, Jan, 10-25; 2007, January, 13-27

21700 Division of scalenus anticus; without resection of cervical rib
10.56 10.56 Global Days 090

21705 with resection of cervical rib
15.85 15.85 Global Days 090

21720 Division of sternocleidomastoid for torticollis, open operation; without cast application
EXCLUDES Transection of spinal accessory and cervical nerves (63191, 64722)
12.15 12.15 Global Days 090

21725 with cast application
EXCLUDES Transection of spinal accessory and cervical nerves (63191, 64722)
14.39 14.39 Global Days 090

21740 Reconstructive repair of pectus excavatum or carinatum; open
28.18 28.18 Global Days 090

21742 minimally invasive approach (Nuss procedure), without thoracoscopy
0.00 0.00 Global Days 090

21743 minimally invasive approach (Nuss procedure), with thoracoscopy
0.00 0.00 Global Days 090

21750 Closure of median sternotomy separation with or without debridement (separate procedure)
19.21 19.21 Global Days 090

21800-21899 Fracture Care: Ribs and Sternum

21800 Closed treatment of rib fracture, uncomplicated, each
2.84 2.77 Global Days 090

21805 Open treatment of rib fracture without fixation, each
7.00 7.00 Global Days 090

21810 Treatment of rib fracture requiring external fixation (flail chest)
13.63 13.63 Global Days 090

21820 Closed treatment of sternum fracture
3.69 3.62 Global Days 090

21825 Open treatment of sternum fracture with or without skeletal fixation
EXCLUDES Treatment of sternoclavicular dislocation (23520-23532)
15.38 15.38 Global Days 090

21899 Unlisted procedure, neck or thorax
0.00 0.00 Global Days YYY

21920-21925 Biopsy Soft Tissue of Back and Flank

EXCLUDES Soft tissue needle biopsy (20206)

21920 Biopsy, soft tissue of back or flank; superficial
EXCLUDES Needle biopsy (20206)
4.36 6.66 Global Days 010

21925 deep
EXCLUDES Needle biopsy (20206)
9.32 11.44 Global Days 090

21930-21936 Excision Soft Tissue Tumor Back or Flank

INCLUDES
Any necessary elevation of tissue planes or dissection
Measurement of tumor and necessary margin at greatest diameter prior to excision
Resection without removal of significant normal tissue
Simple and intermediate repairs
Types of Excision:
  Fascial or subfascial soft tissue tumors: simple and marginal resection of most often benign and intramuscular tumors found either in or below the deep fascia, not involving bone
  Radical resection soft tissue tumor: wide resection of tumor, mostly malignant or aggressive benign, involving large margins of normal tissue and may involve tissue removal from one or more layers
  Subcutaneous: simple and marginal resection of most often benign tumors found in the subcutaneous tissue above the deep fascia

EXCLUDES
Complex repair
Radical resection of cutaneous tumors (e.g., melanoma) (11600-11646)
Significant exploration of the vessels or neuroplasty

▲ **21930** Excision, tumor, soft tissue of back or flank, subcutaneous; less than 3 cm
9.82 12.30 Global Days 090
AMA: 2009, Jan, 11-31; 2008, Jan, 10-25; 2007, January, 13-27; 2006, August, 12-14

● **21931** 3 cm or greater
12.71 12.71 Global Days 090

● **21932** Excision, tumor, soft tissue of back or flank, subfascial (eg, intramuscular); less than 5 cm
18.27 18.27 Global Days 090

● **21933** 5 cm or greater
20.15 20.15 Global Days 090

▲ **21935** Radical resection of tumor (eg, malignant neoplasm), soft tissue of back or flank; less than 5 cm
28.39 28.39 Global Days 090

● **21936** 5 cm or greater
38.99 38.99 Global Days 090

22010-22015 Incision for Drainage of Deep Spinal Abscess

EXCLUDES
Incision and drainage of hematoma (10060, 10140)
Injection:
  Chemonucleolysis (62292)
  Discography (62290-62291)
  Facet joint (64490-64495, 64622-64627)
  Myelography (62284)
Needle/trocar biopsy (20220-20225)

22010 Incision and drainage, open, of deep abscess (subfascial), posterior spine; cervical, thoracic, or cervicothoracic
25.09 25.09 Global Days 090

22015 lumbar, sacral, or lumbosacral
Do not report with (10180, 22010, 22850, 22852)
24.84 24.84 Global Days 090

Current Procedural Coding Expert – Musculoskeletal System

22100-22103 Partial Resection Vertebral Component

EXCLUDES
Back or flank biopsy (21920-21925)
Bone biopsy (20220-20251)
Bone grafting procedures (20930-20938)
Injection
  Chemonucleolysis (62292)
  Discography (62290-62291)
  Facet joint (64490-64495, 64622-64627)
  Myelography (62284)
Removal of tumor flank or back (21930)
Soft tissue needle biopsy (20206)

22100 Partial excision of posterior vertebral component (eg, spinous process, lamina or facet) for intrinsic bony lesion, single vertebral segment; cervical
  23.39 23.39 Global Days 090

22101 thoracic
  24.34 24.34 Global Days 090

22102 lumbar
  EXCLUDES Insertion of posterior spinous process distraction devices (0171T-0172T)
  21.97 21.97 Global Days 090

+ **22103** each additional segment (List separately in addition to code for primary procedure)
  Code first 22100-22102
  3.95 3.95 Global Days ZZZ

22110-22116 Partial Resection Vertebral Component without Decompression

EXCLUDES
Back or flank biopsy (21920-21925)
Bone biopsy (20220-20251)
Bone grafting procedures (20930-20938)
Harvest bone graft (20931, 20938)
Injection:
  Chemonucleolysis (62292)
  Discography (62290-62291)
  Facet joint (64490-64495, 64622-64627)
  Myelography (62284)
Osteotomy (22210-22226)
Removal of tumor flank or back (21930)
Restoration after vertebral body resection (22585, 63082, or 63086, or 63088, or 63091)
Spinal restoration with graft:
  Cervical (20931, or 20938, 22554, 63081)
  Lumbar (20931, or 20938, 22558, 63087, or 63090)
  Thoracic (20931, or 20938, 22556, 63085, or 63087)
Spinal restoration with prosthesis:
  Cervical (20931, or 20938, 22554, 22851, 63081)
  Lumbar (20931, or 20938, 22558, 22851, 63087, or 63090)
  Thoracic (20931, or 20938, 22556, 22851, 63085, or 63087)
Vertebral corpectomy (63081-63091)

22110 Partial excision of vertebral body, for intrinsic bony lesion, without decompression of spinal cord or nerve root(s), single vertebral segment; cervical
  28.39 28.39 Global Days 090

22112 thoracic
  29.51 29.51 Global Days 090

22114 lumbar
  26.95 26.95 Global Days 090

+ **22116** each additional vertebral segment (List separately in addition to code for primary procedure)
  Code first 22110-22114
  3.86 3.86 Global Days ZZZ

22206-22216 Spinal Osteotomy: Posterior/Posterolateral Approach

CMS 100-4,12,40.8 Co-surgery and team surgery
EXCLUDES Decompression of the spinal cord and/or nerve roots (63001-63308)
Injection:
  Chemonucleolysis (62292)
  Discography (62290-62292)
  Facet joint (64490-64495, 64622-64627)
  Myelography (62284)
Repair of vertebral fracture by the anterior approach, see appropriate arthrodesis, bone graft, instrumentation codes, and (63081-63091)

Code also arthrodesis (22590-22632)
Code also bone grafting procedures (20930-20938)
Code also spinal instrumentation (22840-22855)

22206 Osteotomy of spine, posterior or posterolateral approach, 3 columns, 1 vertebral segment (eg, pedicle/vertebral body subtraction); thoracic
  Do not report with (22207)
  Do not report with the following codes if performed at same level (22210-22226, 22830, 63001-63048, 63055-63066, 63075-63091, 63101-63103)
  64.40 64.40 Global Days 090
  AMA: 2009, Jan, 11-31; 2008, Feb, 8-9; 2007, Dec, 1-2

22207 lumbar
  Do not report with (22206)
  Do not report with the following codes if performed at the same level (22210-22226, 22830, 63001-63048, 63055-63066, 63075-63091, 63101-63103)
  65.18 65.18 Global Days 090
  AMA: 2009, Jan, 11-31; 2008, Feb, 8-9; 2007, Dec, 1-2

+ **22208** each additional vertebral segment (List separately in addition to code for primary procedure)
  Code first (22206, or 22207)
  Do not report with the following codes if performed at the same level (22210-22226, 22830, 63001-63048, 63055-63066, 63075-63091, 63101-63103)
  16.24 16.24 Global Days ZZZ
  AMA: 2009, Jan, 11-31; 2008, Feb, 8-9; 2007, Dec, 1-2

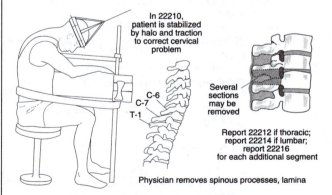

In 22210, patient is stabilized by halo and traction to correct cervical problem
C-6
C-7
T-1
Several sections may be removed
Report 22212 if thoracic; report 22214 if lumbar; report 22216 for each additional segment
Physician removes spinous processes, lamina

22210 Osteotomy of spine, posterior or posterolateral approach, 1 vertebral segment; cervical
  47.52 47.52 Global Days 090
  AMA: 2007, Dec, 1-2

22212 thoracic
  39.69 39.69 Global Days 090
  AMA: 2007, Dec, 1-2

● New Code ▲ Revised Code M Maternity A Age Unlisted Not Covered # Resequenced
CCI + Add-on ⊘ Mod 51 Exempt @ Mod 63 Exempt ⊙ Mod Sedation PQRI

© 2009 Publisher (Blue Ink) CPT only © 2009 American Medical Association. All Rights Reserved. (Black Ink) Medicare (Red Ink) 49

	22214	lumbar
		39.90 39.90 Global Days 090
		AMA: 2007, Dec, 1-2
+	22216	each additional vertebral segment (List separately in addition to primary procedure)
		Code first 22210-22214
		10.04 10.04 Global Days ZZZ
		AMA: 2007, Dec, 1-2

22220-22226 Spinal Osteotomy: Anterior Approach

CMS 100-4,12,40.8 Co-surgery and team surgery

EXCLUDES Corpectomy (63081-63091)
Decompression of the spinal cord and/or nerve roots (63001-63308)
Injection:
    Chemonucleolysis (62292)
    Discography (62290-62291)
    Facet joint (64490-64495, 64622-64627)
    Myelography (62284)
    Needle/trocar biopsy (20220-20225)
Repair of vertebral fracture by the anterior approach, see appropriate arthrodesis, bone graft, instrumentation codes, and (63081-63091)

Code also arthrodesis (22590-22632)
Code also spinal instrumentation (22840-22855)
Code also bone grafting procedures (20930-20938)

	22220	Osteotomy of spine, including discectomy, anterior approach, single vertebral segment; cervical
		43.64 43.64 Global Days 090
	22222	thoracic
		42.33 42.33 Global Days 090
	22224	lumbar
		42.60 42.60 Global Days 090
+	22226	each additional vertebral segment (List separately in addition to code for primary procedure)
		Code first 22220-22224
		10.03 10.03 Global Days ZZZ

22305-22315 Closed Treatment Vertebral Fractures

EXCLUDES Injection:
    Chemonucleolysis (62292)
    Discography (62290-62291)
    Facet joint (64490-64495, 64622-64627)
    Myelography (62284)

	22305	Closed treatment of vertebral process fracture(s)
		4.61 5.01 Global Days 090
	22310	Closed treatment of vertebral body fracture(s), without manipulation, requiring and including casting or bracing
		7.53 8.09 Global Days 090
		AMA: 2009, Jan, 11-31; 2008, Jan, 10-25; 2007, January, 13-27; 2006, June, 16-17
	22315	Closed treatment of vertebral fracture(s) and/or dislocation(s) requiring casting or bracing, with and including casting and/or bracing, with or without anesthesia, by manipulation or traction
		EXCLUDES Spinal manipulation (97140)
		20.68 23.31 Global Days 090

22318-22319 Open Treatment Odontoid Fracture: Anterior Approach

EXCLUDES Injection:
    Chemonucleolysis (62292)
    Discography (62290-62291)
    Facet joint (64490-64495, 64622-64627)
    Myelography (62284)
    Needle/trocar biopsy (20220-20225)

Code also arthrodesis (22590-22632)
Code also bone grafting procedures (20930-20938)
Code also spinal instrumentation (22840-22855)

	22318	Open treatment and/or reduction of odontoid fracture(s) and or dislocation(s) (including os odontoideum), anterior approach, including placement of internal fixation; without grafting
		43.67 43.67 Global Days 090
	22319	with grafting
		48.73 48.73 Global Days 090

22325-22328 Open Treatment Vertebral Fractures: Posterior Approach

EXCLUDES Corpectomy (63081-63091)
Injection:
    Chemonucleolysis (62292)
    Discography (62290-62291)
    Facet joint (64490-64495, 64622-64627)
    Myelography (62284)
    Needle/trocar biopsy (20220-20225)
Spine decompression (63001-63091)
Vertebral fracture care frontal approach (63081-63091)

Code also arthrodesis (22548-22632)
Code also bone grafting procedure (20930-20938)
Code also spinal instrumentation (22840-22855)

	22325	Open treatment and/or reduction of vertebral fracture(s) and/or dislocation(s), posterior approach, 1 fractured vertebra or dislocated segment; lumbar
		38.50 38.50 Global Days 090
	22326	cervical
		39.83 39.83 Global Days 090
	22327	thoracic
		39.71 39.71 Global Days 090
+	22328	each additional fractured vertebra or dislocated segment (List separately in addition to code for primary procedure)
		Code first 22325-22327
		7.78 7.78 Global Days ZZZ

22505 Spinal Manipulation with Anesthesia

EXCLUDES Manipulation not requiring anesthesia (97140)

	22505	Manipulation of spine requiring anesthesia, any region
		3.23 3.23 Global Days 010
		AMA: 2009, Jan, 11-31; 2008, Jan, 10-25; 2007, January, 13-27

22520-22525 Percutaneous Vertebroplasty/Kyphoplasty

EXCLUDES Injection:
    Chemonucleolysis (62292)
    Discography (62290-62291)
    Facet joint (64490-64495, 64622-64627)
    Myelography (62284)
    Needle/trocar biopsy (20220-20225)

72291-72292

- ⊙ **22520** Percutaneous vertebroplasty, 1 vertebral body, unilateral or bilateral injection; thoracic
    13.86 54.17 Global Days 010

- ⊙ **22521** lumbar
    13.10 53.49 Global Days 010

- + **22522** each additional thoracic or lumbar vertebral body (List separately in addition to code for primary procedure)
Code first 22520-22521
    6.23 6.23 Global Days ZZZ

- **22523** Percutaneous vertebral augmentation, including cavity creation (fracture reduction and bone biopsy included when performed) using mechanical device, 1 vertebral body, unilateral or bilateral cannulation (eg, kyphoplasty); thoracic
    15.67 15.67 Global Days 010

- **22524** lumbar
    15.05 15.05 Global Days 010

- + **22525** each additional thoracic or lumbar vertebral body (List separately in addition to code for primary procedure)
Code first 22523-22524
Do not report with augmentation at the same level (22523-22525)
    7.09 7.09 Global Days ZZZ

22526-22527 Percutaneous Annuloplasty

EXCLUDES Needle/trocar biopsy (20220-20225)
Injection:
    Chemonucleolysis (62292)
    Discography (62290-62291)
    Facet joint (64490-64495, 64622-64627)
    Myelography (62284)
    Procedure performed by other methods (22899)

Do not report with (77002, 77003)

- ⊙ **22526** Percutaneous intradiscal electrothermal annuloplasty, unilateral or bilateral including fluoroscopic guidance; single level
    INCLUDES Contrast injection during fluoroscopic guidance/localization (77003)
    EXCLUDES Percutaneous intradiscal annuloplasty other than electrothermal (22899)
    9.40 56.71 Global Days 010
    AMA: 2009, Jan, 11-31; 2008, Jan, 10-25; 2007, March, 7-8

- + ⊙ ▲ **22527** Percutaneous intradiscal electrothermal annuloplasty, unilateral or bilateral, including fluoroscopic guidance; 1 or more additional levels (List separately in addition to code for primary procedure)
    INCLUDES Contrast injection during fluoroscopic guidance/localization (77003)
    EXCLUDES Percutaneous intradiscal annuloplasty other than electrothermal (22899)
Code first (22526)
    4.31 46.34 Global Days ZZZ
    AMA: 2007, March, 7-8

22532-22534 Spinal Fusion: Lateral Extracavitary Approach

CMS 100-3,150.2 Osteogenic Stimulation
EXCLUDES Corpectomy (63101-63103)
Exploration of spinal fusion (22830)
Fracture care (22305-22328)
Injection:
    Chemonucleolysis (62292)
    Discography (62290-62291)
    Facet joint (64490-64495, 64622-64627)
    Myelography (62284)
Laminectomy (63001-63017)
Needle/trocar biopsy (20220-20225)
Osteotomy (22206)

Code also bone grafting procedures (20930-20938)
Code also spinal instrumentation (22840-22855)

- **22532** Arthrodesis, lateral extracavitary technique, including minimal discectomy to prepare interspace (other than for decompression); thoracic
    48.28 48.28 Global Days 090

- **22533** lumbar
    45.78 45.78 Global Days 090

- + **22534** thoracic or lumbar, each additional vertebral segment (List separately in addition to code for primary procedure)
Code first 22532-22533
    10.01 10.01 Global Days ZZZ

22548-22632 Spinal Fusion: Anterior and Posterior Approach

CMS 100-3,150.2 Osteogenic Stimulation
EXCLUDES Corpectomy (63081-63091)
Exploration of spinal fusion (22830)
Fracture care (22305-22328)
Injection:
    Chemonucleolysis (62292)
    Discography (62290-62291)
    Facet joint (64490-64495, 64622-64627)
    Myelography (62284)
Laminectomy (63001-63017)
Needle/trocar biopsy (20220-20225)
Osteotomy (22206)

Code also bone grafting procedures (20930-20938)
Code also spinal instrumentation (22840-22855)

- **22548** Arthrodesis, anterior transoral or extraoral technique, clivus-C1-C2 (atlas-axis), with or without excision of odontoid process
    EXCLUDES Laminectomy or laminotomy with disc removal (63020-63042)
    51.95 51.95 Global Days 090
    AMA: 2009, Jan, 11-31; 2008, Jan, 10-25; 2007, January, 13-27

● New Code ▲ Revised Code M Maternity A Age Unlisted Not Covered # Resequenced
CCI + Add-on ⊘ Mod 51 Exempt ⊚ Mod 63 Exempt ⊙ Mod Sedation PQRI

© 2009 Publisher *(Blue Ink)* CPT only © 2009 American Medical Association. All Rights Reserved. *(Black Ink)* Medicare *(Red Ink)*

22554	Arthrodesis, anterior interbody technique, including minimal discectomy to prepare interspace (other than for decompression); cervical below C2	C 80 P0
	34.17 34.17 Global Days 090	
	AMA: 2009, Jan, 11-31; 2008, Jan, 10-25; 2007, January, 13-27	
22556	thoracic	C 80 P0
	45.05 45.05 Global Days 090	
	AMA: 2009, Jan, 11-31; 2008, Jan, 10-25; 2007, January, 13-27	

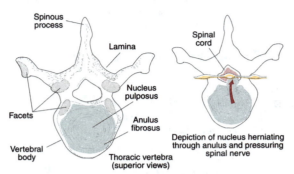

Intervertebral disc displacement and prolapse are major causes of disability among working people. When a disc prolapses, nuclear material bursts through the anulus fibrosus damaging ligaments, nerve roots, and other structures. The herniated matter usually fibroses and shrinks over time

22558	lumbar	C 80 P0
	41.94 41.94 Global Days 090	
	AMA: 2009, Jan, 11-31; 2008, Jan, 10-25; 2008, Apr, -11; 2007, June, 1-3; 2007, January, 13-27	
+ 22585	each additional interspace (List separately in addition to code for primary procedure)	C 80 P0
	Code first 22554-22558	
	9.27 9.27 Global Days ZZZ	
	AMA: 2009, Jan, 11-31; 2008, Jan, 10-25; 2008, Apr, -11; 2007, June, 1-3; 2007, January, 13-27	

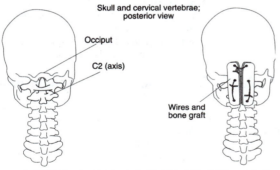

In 22590, the physician fuses skull to C2 (axis) to stabilize cervical vertebrae; anchor holes are drilled in the occiput of the skull

22590	Arthrodesis, posterior technique, craniocervical (occiput-C2)	C 80 P0
	42.23 42.23 Global Days 090	
22595	Arthrodesis, posterior technique, atlas-axis (C1-C2)	C 80 P0
	40.18 40.18 Global Days 090	
22600	Arthrodesis, posterior or posterolateral technique, single level; cervical below C2 segment	C 80 P0
	34.36 34.36 Global Days 090	
22610	thoracic (with or without lateral transverse technique)	C 80
	33.68 33.68 Global Days 090	
22612	lumbar (with or without lateral transverse technique)	T 80 P0
	43.22 43.22 Global Days 090	
	AMA: 2009, Jan, 11-31; 2008, Jan, 10-25; 2008, Apr, -11; 2008, Jul, 7-8&15; 2007, January, 13-27	
+ 22614	each additional vertebral segment (List separately in addition to code for primary procedure)	T 80 P0
	Code first 22600-22612	
	10.78 10.78 Global Days ZZZ	
22630	Arthrodesis, posterior interbody technique, including laminectomy and/or discectomy to prepare interspace (other than for decompression), single interspace; lumbar	C 80 P0
	41.67 41.67 Global Days 090	
	AMA: 2009, Jan, 11-31; 2008, Jan, 10-25; 2007, January, 13-27	
+ 22632	each additional interspace (List separately in addition to code for primary procedure)	C 80 P0
	Code first 22630	
	8.80 8.80 Global Days ZZZ	

22800-22819 Procedures to Correct Anomalous Spinal Vertebrae

Code also bone grafting procedures (20930-20938)
Code also spinal instrumentation (22840-22855)

22800	Arthrodesis, posterior, for spinal deformity, with or without cast; up to 6 vertebral segments	C 80 P0
	36.62 36.62 Global Days 090	
22802	7 to 12 vertebral segments	C 80 P0
	57.20 57.20 Global Days 090	
	AMA: 2009, Jan, 11-31; 2008, Jan, 10-25; 2007, January, 13-27	
22804	13 or more vertebral segments	C 80 P0
	65.85 65.85 Global Days 090	
22808	Arthrodesis, anterior, for spinal deformity, with or without cast; 2 to 3 vertebral segments	C 80
	INCLUDES Smith-Robinson arthrodesis	
	49.54 49.54 Global Days 090	
22810	4 to 7 vertebral segments	C 80
	55.61 55.61 Global Days 090	
22812	8 or more vertebral segments	C 80
	60.41 60.41 Global Days 090	
22818	Kyphectomy, circumferential exposure of spine and resection of vertebral segment(s) (including body and posterior elements); single or 2 segments	C 80 P0
	EXCLUDES Arthrodesis (22800-22804)	
	59.52 59.52 Global Days 090	

Scoliosis is the lateral curvature of the spine; most commonly diagnosed during adolescence; occurrence is higher among females

Excessively kyphotic thoracic spine may be caused by Scheuermann's disease or juvenile kyphosis

Excessive convexity in the thoracic region is known as kyphosis

Excessive concavity in the lumbar region is known as lordosis

Current Procedural Coding Expert – Musculoskeletal System

22819   3 or more segments
     EXCLUDES   Arthrodesis (22800-22804)
     73.61   73.61   **Global Days 090**

22830 Surgical Exploration Previous Spinal Fusion

CMS 100-3,150.2   Osteogenic Stimulation
EXCLUDES   Arthrodesis (22532-22819)
     Bone grafting procedures (20930-20938)
     Spinal decompression (63001-63103)

Code also spinal instrumentation (22840-22855)

22830   **Exploration of spinal fusion**
     Do not report with (22850, 22852, 22855)
     21.77   21.77   **Global Days 090**
     AMA: 2009, Jan, 11-31; 2008, Jan, 10-25; 2007, January, 13-27

22840-22855 Spinal Instrumentation: Segmental/Non-segmental

EXCLUDES   Arthrodesis (22532-22534, 22548-22812)
     Bone grafting procedures (20930-20938)
     Exploration of spinal fusion (22830)
     Fracture treatment (22325-22328)

+ 22840   **Posterior non-segmental instrumentation (eg, Harrington rod technique, pedicle fixation across 1 interspace, atlantoaxial transarticular screw fixation, sublaminar wiring at C1, facet screw fixation) (List separately in addition to code for primary procedure)**
     EXCLUDES   Insertion of posterior spinous process distraction devices (0171T-0172T)
     Code first (22100-22102, 22110-22114, 22206-22207, 22210-22214, 22220-22224, 22305-22327, 22532-22533, 22548-22558, 22590-22612, 22630, 22800-22812, 63001-63030, 63040-63042, 63045-63047, 63050-63056, 63064, 63075, 63077, 63081, 63085, 63087, 63090, 63101-63102, 63170-63290, 63300-63307)
     21.06   21.06   **Global Days ZZZ**
     AMA: 2009, Jan, 11-31; 2008, Jan, 10-25; 2007, January, 13-27

+ 22841   **Internal spinal fixation by wiring of spinous processes (List separately in addition to code for primary procedure)**
     INCLUDES   Hibb's fusion
     Code first (22100-22102, 22110-22114, 22206-22207, 22210-22214, 22220-22224, 22305-22327, 22532-22533, 22548-22558, 22590-22612, 22630, 22800-22812, 63001-63030, 63040-63042, 63045-63047, 63050-63056, 63064, 63075, 63077, 63081, 63085, 63087, 63090, 63101-63102, 63170-63290, 63300-63307)
     0.00   0.00   **Global Days XXX**

+ 22842   **Posterior segmental instrumentation (eg, pedicle fixation, dual rods with multiple hooks and sublaminar wires); 3 to 6 vertebral segments (List separately in addition to code for primary procedure)**
     Code first (22100-22102, 22110-22114, 22206-22207, 22210-22214, 22220-22224, 22305-22327, 22532-22533, 22548-22558, 22590-22612, 22630, 22800-22812, 63001-63030, 63040-63042, 63045-63047, 63050-63056, 63064, 63075, 63077, 63081, 63085, 63087, 63090, 63101-63102, 63170-63290, 63300-63307)
     21.08   21.08   **Global Days ZZZ**

+ 22843   **7 to 12 vertebral segments (List separately in addition to code for primary procedure)**
     Code first (22100-22102, 22110-22114, 22206-22207, 22210-22214, 22220-22224, 22305-22327, 22532-22533, 22548-22558, 22590-22612, 22630, 22800-22812, 63001-63102, 63170-63290, 63300-63307)
     22.43   22.43   **Global Days ZZZ**

+ 22844   **13 or more vertebral segments (List separately in addition to code for primary procedure)**
     Code first (22100-22102, 22206-22207, 22210-22214, 22210-22214, 22220-22224, 22305-22327, 22532-22533, 22548-22558, 22590-22612, 22630, 22800-22812, 63001-63030, 63040-63042, 63045-63047, 63050-63056, 63064, 63075, 63077, 63081, 63085, 63087, 63090, 63101-63102, 63170-63290, 63300-63307)
     27.10   27.10   **Global Days ZZZ**

+ 22845   **Anterior instrumentation; 2 to 3 vertebral segments (List separately in addition to code for primary procedure)**
     INCLUDES   Dwyer instrumentation technique
     Code first (22100-22102, 22110-22114, 22206-22207, 22210-22214, 22220-22224, 22305-22327, 22532-22533, 22548-22558, 22590-22612, 22630, 22800-22812, 63001-63030, 63040-63042, 63045-63047, 63050-63056, 63064, 63075, 63077, 63081, 63085, 63087, 63090, 63101-63102, 63170-63290, 63300-63307)
     20.25   20.25   **Global Days ZZZ**
     AMA: 2009, Jan, 11-31; 2008, Jan, 10-25; 2007, June, 1-3; 2007, January, 13-27

+ 22846   **4 to 7 vertebral segments (List separately in addition to code for primary procedure)**
     INCLUDES   Dwyer instrumentation technique
     Code first (22100-22102, 22110-22114, 22206-22207, 22210-22214, 22220-22224, 22305-22327, 22532-22533, 22548-22558, 22590-22612, 22630, 22800-22812, 63001-63030, 63040-63042, 63045-63047, 63050-63056, 63064, 63075, 63077, 63081, 63085, 63087, 63090, 63101-63102, 63170-63290, 63300-63307)
     21.02   21.02   **Global Days ZZZ**
     AMA: 2009, Jan, 11-31; 2008, Jan, 10-25

+ 22847   **8 or more vertebral segments (List separately in addition to code for primary procedure)**
     INCLUDES   Dwyer instrumentation technique
     Code first (22100-22102, 22110-22114, 22206-22207, 22210-22214, 22220-22224, 22305-22327, 22532-22533, 22548-22558, 22590-22612, 22630, 22800-22812, 63001-63030, 63040-63042, 63045-63047, 63050-63056, 63064, 63075, 63077, 63081, 63085, 63087, 63090, 63101-63102, 63170-63290, 63300-63307)
     23.78   23.78   **Global Days ZZZ**
     AMA: 2009, Jan, 11-31; 2008, Jan, 10-25

+ 22848   **Pelvic fixation (attachment of caudal end of instrumentation to pelvic bony structures) other than sacrum (List separately in addition to code for primary procedure)**
     Code first (22100-22102, 22110-22114, 22206-22207, 22210-22214, 22220-22224, 22305-22327, 22532-22533, 22548-22558, 22590-22612, 22630, 22800-22812, 63001-63030, 63040-63042, 63045-63047, 63050-63056, 63064, 63075, 63077, 63081, 63085, 63087, 63090, 63101-63102, 63170-63290, 63300-63307)
     9.92   9.92   **Global Days ZZZ**

22849   **Reinsertion of spinal fixation device**
     Do not report with removal of instrumentation at the same level (22850, 22852, 22855)
     35.29   35.29   **Global Days 090**

22850-22855

22850 Removal of posterior nonsegmental instrumentation (eg, Harrington rod) [C][80]
 19.35 19.35 Global Days 090

+ 22851 Application of intervertebral biomechanical device(s) (eg, synthetic cage(s), threaded bone dowel(s), methylmethacrylate) to vertebral defect or interspace (List separately in addition to code for primary procedure) [T][80]
 EXCLUDES Insertion of posterior spinous process distraction devices (0171T-0172T)
 Code first (22100-22102, 22110-22114, 22206-22207, 22210-22214, 22220-22224, 22305-22327, 22532-22533, 22548-22558, 22590-22612, 22630, 22800-22812, 63001-63030, 63040-63042, 63045-63047, 63050-63056, 63064, 63075, 63077, 63081, 63085, 63087, 63090, 63101-63102, 63170-63290, 63300-63307)
 11.27 11.27 Global Days ZZZ
 AMA: 2009, Jan, 11-31; 2008, Jan, 10-25; 2007, January, 13-27; 2007, June, 1-3; 2005, June, 6-8; 2005, February, 13-16

22852 Removal of posterior segmental instrumentation [C][80]
 18.51 18.51 Global Days 090
 AMA: 2009, Jan, 11-31; 2008, Jan, 10-25; 2007, January, 13-27; 2006, May, 16-20

22855 Removal of anterior instrumentation [C][80]
 30.16 30.16 Global Days 090

22856-22899 Artificial Disc Replacement

CMS 100-3,150.10 Lumbar Artificial Disc Replacement (LADR)
 INCLUDES Fluoroscopy (76000-76001)
 EXCLUDES Spinal decompression (63001-63048)

22856 Total disc arthroplasty (artificial disc), anterior approach, including discectomy with end plate preparation (includes osteophytectomy for nerve root or spinal cord decompression and microdissection), single interspace, cervical [C][80]
 INCLUDES Operating microscope (69990)
  Same level:
   Arthrodesis (22554)
   Discectomy (63075)
   Instrumentation (22845, 22851)
 EXCLUDES Cervical total disc arthroplasty with additional interspace revision (0092T)
 44.62 44.62 Global Days 090

22857 Total disc arthroplasty (artificial disc), anterior approach, including discectomy to prepare interspace (other than for decompression), single interspace, lumbar [C][80]
 INCLUDES Operating microscope (69990)
  Same level:
   Arthrodesis (22558)
   Instrumentation (22845, 22851)
   Retroperitoneal exploration (49010)
 EXCLUDES Arthroplasty more than one interspace (0163T)
 45.04 45.04 Global Days 090
 AMA: 2007, June, 1-3

22861 Revision including replacement of total disc arthroplasty (artificial disc), anterior approach, single interspace; cervical [C][80]
 INCLUDES Operating microscope (69990)
 EXCLUDES Revision of additional cervical arthroplasty (0098T)
  Same level:
   Discectomy (63075)
   Instrumentation (22845, 22851)
   Removal of artificial disc (22864)
 49.56 49.56 Global Days 090

22862 lumbar [C][80]
 INCLUDES Same level:
   Arthrodesis (22558)
   Instrumentation (22845, 22851)
   Removal artificial disc (22865)
   Retroperitoneal exploration (49010)
 EXCLUDES Arthroplasty revision more than one interspace (0165T)
 53.04 53.04 Global Days 090
 AMA: 2007, June, 1-3

22864 Removal of total disc arthroplasty (artificial disc), anterior approach, single interspace; cervical [C][80]
 INCLUDES Operating microscope (69990)
 EXCLUDES Cervical total disc arthroplasty with additional interspace removal (0095T)
 Do not report with (22861)
 43.96 43.96 Global Days 090

22865 lumbar [C][80]
 EXCLUDES Arthroplasty more than one level (0164T)
 Do not report with (49010)
 55.98 55.98 Global Days 090
 AMA: 2007, June, 1-3

22899 Unlisted procedure, spine [T][80]
 0.00 0.00 Global Days YYY
 AMA: 2009, Jan, 11-31; 2008, Jan, 10-25; 2007, January, 13-27; 2006, May, 16-20

22900-22999 Musculoskeletal Procedures of Abdomen

INCLUDES Any necessary elevation of tissue planes or dissection
 Measurement of tumor and necessary margin at greatest diameter prior to excision
 Resection without removal of significant normal tissue
 Simple and intermediate repairs
 Types of Excision:
  Fascial or subfascial soft tissue tumors: simple and marginal resection of most often benign and intramuscular tumors found either in or below the deep fascia, not involving bone
  Radical resection soft tissue tumor: wide resection of tumor, mostly malignant or aggressive benign, involving large margins of normal tissue and may involve tissue removal from one or more layers
  Subcutaneous: simple and marginal resection of most often benign tumors found in the subcutaneous tissue above the deep fascia

EXCLUDES Complex repair
 Radical resection of cutaneous tumors (e.g., melanoma) (11600-11646)
 Significant exploration of the vessels or neuroplasty

▲ **22900** Excision, tumor, soft tissue of abdominal wall, subfascial (eg, intramuscular); less than 5 cm [62][T][80]
 14.92 14.92 Global Days 090

● **22901** 5 cm or greater [62][T][80]
 17.98 17.98 Global Days 090

Current Procedural Coding Expert – Musculoskeletal System   23106

- **22902** Excision, tumor, soft tissue of abdominal wall, subcutaneous; less than 3 cm G2 T 80
  - 9.07 11.34 Global Days 090
- **22903** 3 cm or greater G2 T 80
  - 11.88 11.88 Global Days 090
- **22904** Radical resection of tumor (eg, malignant neoplasm), soft tissue of abdominal wall; less than 5 cm G2 T 80
  - 28.16 28.16 Global Days 090
- **22905** 5 cm or greater G2 T 80
  - 36.50 36.50 Global Days 090
- **22999** Unlisted procedure, abdomen, musculoskeletal system T 80
  - 0.00 0.00 Global Days YYY

23000-23044 Surgical Incision Shoulder: Drainage, Removal Foreign Body, Release Contracture

- **23000** Removal of subdeltoid calcareous deposits, open A2 T 80
  - EXCLUDES Arthroscopic calcium deposit removal (29999)
  - 9.71 14.57 Global Days 090
- **23020** Capsular contracture release (eg, Sever type procedure) A2 T 80 50
  - EXCLUDES Simple incision and drainage (10040-10160)
  - 18.48 18.48 Global Days 090
- **23030** Incision and drainage, shoulder area; deep abscess or hematoma A2 T
  - 6.80 11.09 Global Days 010

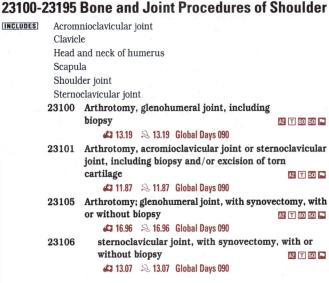

- **23031** infected bursa A2 T 50
  - 5.66 10.12 Global Days 010
- **23035** Incision, bone cortex (eg, osteomyelitis or bone abscess), shoulder area A2 T 80 50
  - 18.18 18.18 Global Days 090
- **23040** Arthrotomy, glenohumeral joint, including exploration, drainage, or removal of foreign body A2 T 80 50
  - 19.24 19.24 Global Days 090
- **23044** Arthrotomy, acromioclavicular, sternoclavicular joint, including exploration, drainage, or removal of foreign body A2 T 50
  - 15.34 15.34 Global Days 090

23065-23066 Shoulder Biopsy

EXCLUDES Soft tissue needle biopsy (20206)

- **23065** Biopsy, soft tissue of shoulder area; superficial P3 T 50
  - 4.52 5.69 Global Days 010
- **23066** deep A2 T 50
  - 9.26 13.84 Global Days 090

23071-23078 [23071, 23073] Resection Soft Tissues of Shoulder

INCLUDES
- Any necessary elevation of tissue planes or dissection
- Measurement of tumor and necessary margin at greatest diameter prior to excision
- Resection without removal of significant normal tissue
- Simple and intermediate repairs
- Types of Excision:
  - Fascial or subfascial soft tissue tumors: simple and marginal resection of most often benign and intramuscular tumors found either in or below the deep fascia, not involving bone
  - Radical resection soft tissue tumor: wide resection of tumor, mostly malignant or aggressive benign, involving large margins of normal tissue and may involve tissue removal from one or more layers
  - Subcutaneous: simple and marginal resection of most often benign tumors found in the subcutaneous tissue above the deep fascia

EXCLUDES
- Complex repair
- Significant exploration of the vessels or neuroplasty

| 23071 | Resequenced code. See code following 23075. |
| 23073 | Resequenced code. See code following 23076. |

- ▲ **23075** Excision, tumor, soft tissue of shoulder area, subcutaneous; less than 3 cm P3 T 50
  - 8.49 11.63 Global Days 090
- #● **23071** 3 cm or greater G2 T 80 50
  - 11.29 11.29 Global Days 090
- ▲ **23076** Excision, tumor, soft tissue of shoulder area, subfascial (eg, intramuscular); less than 5 cm G2 T 50
  - 14.43 14.43 Global Days 090
- #● **23073** 5 cm or greater G2 T 80 50
  - 18.72 18.72 Global Days 090
- ▲ **23077** Radical resection of tumor (eg, malignant neoplasm), soft tissue of shoulder area; less than 5 cm G2 T 80 50
  - 31.51 31.51 Global Days 090
- ● **23078** 5 cm or greater G2 T 80 50
  - 37.98 37.98 Global Days 090

23100-23195 Bone and Joint Procedures of Shoulder

INCLUDES
- Acromnioclavicular joint
- Clavicle
- Head and neck of humerus
- Scapula
- Shoulder joint
- Sternoclavicular joint

- **23100** Arthrotomy, glenohumeral joint, including biopsy A2 T 80 50
  - 13.19 13.19 Global Days 090
- **23101** Arthrotomy, acromioclavicular joint or sternoclavicular joint, including biopsy and/or excision of torn cartilage A2 T 50
  - 11.87 11.87 Global Days 090
- **23105** Arthrotomy; glenohumeral joint, with synovectomy, with or without biopsy A2 T 80 50
  - 16.96 16.96 Global Days 090
- **23106** sternoclavicular joint, with synovectomy, with or without biopsy A2 T 50
  - 13.07 13.07 Global Days 090

● New Code   ▲ Revised Code   M Maternity   A Age   Unlisted   Not Covered   # Resequenced
CCI   + Add-on   ⊘ Mod 51 Exempt   Mod 63 Exempt   ⊙ Mod Sedation   PQRI

© 2009 Publisher *(Blue Ink)*   CPT only © 2009 American Medical Association. All Rights Reserved. (Black Ink)   Medicare (Red Ink)   55

Code	Description	RVU (Facility)	RVU (Non-Facility)	Global Days
23107	Arthrotomy, glenohumeral joint, with joint exploration, with or without removal of loose or foreign body	17.64	17.64	090
23120	Claviculectomy; partial	15.53	15.53	090
	INCLUDES: Mumford operation			
	EXCLUDES: Arthroscopic claviculectomy (29824)			
23125	total	18.93	18.93	090
23130	Acromioplasty or acromionectomy, partial, with or without coracoacromial ligament release	16.12	16.12	090
	AMA: 2009, Jan, 11-31; 2008, Jan, 10-25; 2007, January, 13-27			
23140	Excision or curettage of bone cyst or benign tumor of clavicle or scapula;	13.94	13.94	090
23145	with autograft (includes obtaining graft)	18.54	18.54	090
23146	with allograft	16.47	16.47	090
23150	Excision or curettage of bone cyst or benign tumor of proximal humerus;	17.66	17.66	090
23155	with autograft (includes obtaining graft)	21.20	21.20	090
23156	with allograft	18.07	18.07	090
23170	Sequestrectomy (eg, for osteomyelitis or bone abscess), clavicle	14.84	14.84	090
23172	Sequestrectomy (eg, for osteomyelitis or bone abscess), scapula	15.00	15.00	090
23174	Sequestrectomy (eg, for osteomyelitis or bone abscess), humeral head to surgical neck	20.19	20.19	090
23180	Partial excision (craterization, saucerization, or diaphysectomy) bone (eg, osteomyelitis), clavicle	17.84	17.84	090
23182	Partial excision (craterization, saucerization, or diaphysectomy) bone (eg, osteomyelitis), scapula	17.61	17.61	090
23184	Partial excision (craterization, saucerization, or diaphysectomy) bone (eg, osteomyelitis), proximal humerus	19.64	19.64	090
23190	Ostectomy of scapula, partial (eg, superior medial angle)	15.18	15.18	090
23195	Resection, humeral head	20.20	20.20	090
	EXCLUDES: Arthroplasty with replacement with implant (23470)			

23200-23220 Radical Resection of Bone Tumors of Shoulder

INCLUDES:
- Any necessary elevation of tissue planes or dissection
- Measurement of tumor and necessary margin at greatest diameter prior to excision
- Simple and intermediate repairs

EXCLUDES:
- Complex repair
- Significant exploration of vessels, neuroplasty, reconstruction, or complex bone repair

Do not report excision of soft tissue codes when adjacent soft tissue is removed during the bone tumor resection (23076-23078 [23071, 23073])

Code	Description	RVU (Facility)	RVU (Non-Facility)	Global Days
▲ 23200	Radical resection of tumor; clavicle	39.74	39.74	090
▲ 23210	scapula	46.51	46.51	090
▲ 23220	Radical resection of tumor, proximal humerus	51.05	51.05	090

23330-23332 Foreign Body Removal: Shoulder

EXCLUDES:
- Bursal arthrocentesis or needling (20610)
- K-wire or pin insertion (20650)
- K-wire or pin removal (20670, 20680)

Code	Description	RVU (Facility)	RVU (Non-Facility)	Global Days
23330	Removal of foreign body, shoulder; subcutaneous	4.08	6.16	010
23331	deep (eg, Neer hemiarthroplasty removal)	15.70	15.70	090
23332	complicated (eg, total shoulder)	23.74	23.74	090

AMA: 2009, Jan, 11-31; 2008, Jan, 10-25; 2007, January, 13-27

23350 Injection for Shoulder Arthrogram

Code	Description	RVU (Facility)	RVU (Non-Facility)	Global Days
23350	Injection procedure for shoulder arthrography or enhanced CT/MRI shoulder arthrography	1.39	3.58	000

EXCLUDES: Shoulder biopsy (29805-29826)

73040, 73201-73202, 73222-73223, 77002

23395-23491 Repair/Reconstruction of Shoulder

Code	Description	RVU (Facility)	RVU (Non-Facility)	Global Days
23395	Muscle transfer, any type, shoulder or upper arm; single	34.77	34.77	090
23397	multiple	30.83	30.83	090
23400	Scapulopexy (eg, Sprengels deformity or for paralysis)	26.13	26.13	090
23405	Tenotomy, shoulder area; single tendon	16.87	16.87	090
23406	multiple tendons through same incision	20.93	20.93	090
23410	Repair of ruptured musculotendinous cuff (eg, rotator cuff) open; acute	22.07	22.07	090

EXCLUDES: Arthroscopic repair (29827)

AMA: 2009, Jan, 11-31; 2008, Jan, 10-25; 2007, January, 13-27

Current Procedural Coding Expert – Musculoskeletal System   23616

23412	chronic A2 T 80 50	
	EXCLUDES Arthroscopic repair (29827)	
	🔨 22.98 ⚕ 22.98 Global Days 090	
	AMA: 2009, Jan, 11-31; 2008, Jan, 10-25; 2007, January, 13-27	
23415	Coracoacromial ligament release, with or without acromioplasty A2 T 50	
	EXCLUDES Arthroscopic repair (29826)	
	🔨 18.49 ⚕ 18.49 Global Days 090	
23420	Reconstruction of complete shoulder (rotator) cuff avulsion, chronic (includes acromioplasty) A2 T 80 50	
	🔨 26.08 ⚕ 26.08 Global Days 090	
	AMA: 2009, Jan, 11-31; 2008, Jan, 10-25; 2007, January, 13-27; 2005, October, 23-24	
23430	Tenodesis of long tendon of biceps A2 T 80 50	
	EXCLUDES Arthroscopic biceps tenodesis (29828)	
	🔨 19.79 ⚕ 19.79 Global Days 090	
23440	Resection or transplantation of long tendon of biceps A2 T 80 50	
	🔨 20.36 ⚕ 20.36 Global Days 090	
23450	Capsulorrhaphy, anterior; Putti-Platt procedure or Magnuson type operation A2 T 80 50	
	EXCLUDES Arthroscopic thermal capsulorrhaphy (29999)	
	🔨 25.58 ⚕ 25.58 Global Days 090	
23455	with labral repair (eg, Bankart procedure) A2 T 80 50	
	EXCLUDES Arthroscopic repair (29806)	
	🔨 27.14 ⚕ 27.14 Global Days 090	
23460	Capsulorrhaphy, anterior, any type; with bone block A2 T 80 50	
	INCLUDES Bristow procedure	
	🔨 29.41 ⚕ 29.41 Global Days 090	
23462	with coracoid process transfer A2 T 80 50	
	EXCLUDES Open thermal capsulorrhaphy (23929)	
	🔨 28.97 ⚕ 28.97 Global Days 090	
23465	Capsulorrhaphy, glenohumeral joint, posterior, with or without bone block A2 T 80 50	
	EXCLUDES Sternoclavicular and acromioclavicular joint repair (23530, 23550)	
	🔨 30.13 ⚕ 30.13 Global Days 090	
23466	Capsulorrhaphy, glenohumeral joint, any type multi-directional instability A2 T 80 50	
	🔨 30.29 ⚕ 30.29 Global Days 090	
23470	Arthroplasty, glenohumeral joint; hemiarthroplasty T 80 50	
	🔨 32.79 ⚕ 32.79 Global Days 090	
23472	total shoulder (glenoid and proximal humeral replacement (eg, total shoulder)) C 80 50	
	EXCLUDES Proximal humerus osteotomy (24400) Removal of total shoulder components (23331-23332)	
	🔨 40.72 ⚕ 40.72 Global Days 090	
	AMA: 2009, Jan, 11-31; 2008, Jan, 10-25; 2007, January, 13-27	
23480	Osteotomy, clavicle, with or without internal fixation; A2 T 50	
	🔨 22.04 ⚕ 22.04 Global Days 090	
23485	with bone graft for nonunion or malunion (includes obtaining graft and/or necessary fixation) A2 T 80 50	
	🔨 25.90 ⚕ 25.90 Global Days 090	
23490	Prophylactic treatment (nailing, pinning, plating or wiring) with or without methylmethacrylate; clavicle A2 T 80 50	
	🔨 23.16 ⚕ 23.16 Global Days 090	
23491	proximal humerus A2 T 80 50	
	🔨 27.36 ⚕ 27.36 Global Days 090	

23500-23680 Treatment of Shoulder Fracture/Dislocation

23500	Closed treatment of clavicular fracture; without manipulation A2 T 50	
	🔨 5.70 ⚕ 5.62 Global Days 090	
23505	with manipulation A2 T 50	
	🔨 8.68 ⚕ 9.13 Global Days 090	
23515	Open treatment of clavicular fracture, includes internal fixation, when performed A2 T 80 50	
	🔨 19.49 ⚕ 19.49 Global Days 090	
	AMA: 2008, Jan, 4-5	
23520	Closed treatment of sternoclavicular dislocation; without manipulation A2 T 80 50	
	🔨 6.01 ⚕ 5.93 Global Days 090	
23525	with manipulation A2 T 80 50	
	🔨 9.20 ⚕ 9.87 Global Days 090	
23530	Open treatment of sternoclavicular dislocation, acute or chronic; A2 T 80 50	
	🔨 15.19 ⚕ 15.19 Global Days 090	
23532	with fascial graft (includes obtaining graft) A2 T 80 50	
	🔨 16.58 ⚕ 16.58 Global Days 090	
23540	Closed treatment of acromioclavicular dislocation; without manipulation A2 T 50	
	🔨 5.83 ⚕ 5.75 Global Days 090	
23545	with manipulation A2 T 80 50	
	🔨 7.68 ⚕ 8.37 Global Days 090	
23550	Open treatment of acromioclavicular dislocation, acute or chronic; A2 T 80 50	
	🔨 15.22 ⚕ 15.22 Global Days 090	
23552	with fascial graft (includes obtaining graft) A2 T 80 50	
	🔨 17.60 ⚕ 17.60 Global Days 090	
23570	Closed treatment of scapular fracture; without manipulation A2 T 50	
	🔨 6.14 ⚕ 5.98 Global Days 090	
23575	with manipulation, with or without skeletal traction (with or without shoulder joint involvement) A2 T 80 50	
	🔨 9.78 ⚕ 10.36 Global Days 090	
23585	Open treatment of scapular fracture (body, glenoid or acromion) includes internal fixation, when performed A2 T 80 50	
	🔨 26.63 ⚕ 26.63 Global Days 090	
	AMA: 2009, Jan, 11-31; 2008, Jan, 10-25; 2007, January, 13-27	
23600	Closed treatment of proximal humeral (surgical or anatomical neck) fracture; without manipulation P2 T 50	
	🔨 7.85 ⚕ 8.32 Global Days 090	
23605	with manipulation, with or without skeletal traction A2 T 50	
	🔨 11.19 ⚕ 12.08 Global Days 090	
23615	Open treatment of proximal humeral (surgical or anatomical neck) fracture, includes internal fixation, when performed, includes repair of tuberosity(s), when performed; A2 T 80 50	
	🔨 23.82 ⚕ 23.82 Global Days 090	
	AMA: 2008, Jan, 4-5	
23616	with proximal humeral prosthetic replacement A2 T 80 50	
	🔨 33.75 ⚕ 33.75 Global Days 090	

● New Code   ▲ Revised Code   M Maternity   A Age   Unlisted   Not Covered   # Resequenced

 CCI   + Add-on   ⊘ Mod 51 Exempt   ⊚ Mod 63 Exempt   ⊙ Mod Sedation   PQRI

© 2009 Publisher (Blue Ink)   CPT only © 2009 American Medical Association. All Rights Reserved. (Black Ink)   Medicare (Red Ink)   57

23620 — Current Procedural Coding Expert – Musculoskeletal System

23620 Closed treatment of greater humeral tuberosity fracture; without manipulation P2 T 50
 6.61 6.91 Global Days 090

23625 with manipulation A2 T 50
 9.29 9.88 Global Days 090

23630 Open treatment of greater humeral tuberosity fracture, includes internal fixation, when performed A2 T 80 50
 20.97 20.97 Global Days 090

23650 Closed treatment of shoulder dislocation, with manipulation; without anesthesia A2 T 50
 7.29 7.84 Global Days 090

23655 requiring anesthesia A2 T 50
 10.37 10.37 Global Days 090

23660 Open treatment of acute shoulder dislocation A2 T 80 50
 EXCLUDES Chronic dislocation repair (23450-23466)
 15.57 15.57 Global Days 090

23665 Closed treatment of shoulder dislocation, with fracture of greater humeral tuberosity, with manipulation A2 T 50
 10.39 11.06 Global Days 090

23670 Open treatment of shoulder dislocation, with fracture of greater humeral tuberosity, includes internal fixation, when performed A2 T 80 50
 23.65 23.65 Global Days 090

23675 Closed treatment of shoulder dislocation, with surgical or anatomical neck fracture, with manipulation A2 T 50
 13.11 14.24 Global Days 090

23680 Open treatment of shoulder dislocation, with surgical or anatomical neck fracture, includes internal fixation, when performed A2 T 80 50
 25.03 25.03 Global Days 090

23700-23929 Other/Unlisted Shoulder Procedures

23700 Manipulation under anesthesia, shoulder joint, including application of fixation apparatus (dislocation excluded) A2 T 50
 5.19 5.19 Global Days 010
 AMA: 2009, Jan, 11-31; 2009, May, 8-9&11; 2008, Jan, 10-25; 2007, January, 13-27; 2005, April, 13-14

23800 Arthrodesis, glenohumeral joint; A2 T 80 50
 27.62 27.62 Global Days 090

23802 with autogenous graft (includes obtaining graft) A2 T 80
 34.59 34.59 Global Days 090

23900 Interthoracoscapular amputation (forequarter) C 80
 37.61 37.61 Global Days 090

23920 Disarticulation of shoulder; C 80
 30.38 30.38 Global Days 090

23921 secondary closure or scar revision A2 T
 11.48 11.48 Global Days 090

23929 Unlisted procedure, shoulder T 80
 0.00 0.00 Global Days YYY

23930-24006 Surgical Incision Elbow/Upper Arm

EXCLUDES Simple incision and drainage procedures (10040-10160)

23930 Incision and drainage, upper arm or elbow area; deep abscess or hematoma A2 T 50
 5.81 9.12 Global Days 010

23931 bursa A2 T 50
 4.18 7.09 Global Days 010

23935 Incision, deep, with opening of bone cortex (eg, for osteomyelitis or bone abscess), humerus or elbow A2 T 80 50
 13.24 13.24 Global Days 090

24000 Arthrotomy, elbow, including exploration, drainage, or removal of foreign body A2 T 80 50
 12.64 12.64 Global Days 090

24006 Arthrotomy of the elbow, with capsular excision for capsular release (separate procedure) A2 T 80 50
 19.02 19.02 Global Days 090

24065-24066 Biopsy of Elbow/Upper Arm

24065 Biopsy, soft tissue of upper arm or elbow area; superficial P3 T 50
 EXCLUDES Soft tissue needle biopsy (20206)
 4.48 6.57 Global Days 010

24066 deep (subfascial or intramuscular) A2 T 50
 EXCLUDES Soft tissue needle biopsy (20206)
 10.91 15.73 Global Days 090

24071-24079 [24071, 24073] Excision Soft Tissue Tumor Elbow/Upper Arm

INCLUDES
Any necessary elevation of tissue planes or dissection
Measurement of tumor and necessary margin at greatest diameter prior to excision
Resection without removal of significant normal tissue
Types of Excision:
 Fascial or subfascial soft tissue tumors: simple and marginal resection of most often benign and intramuscular tumors found either in or below the deep fascia, not involving bone
 Radical resection of tumor: wide resection of soft tissue tumor, mostly malignant or aggressive benign, involving large margins of normal tissue and may involve tissue removal from one or more layers
 Subcutaneous: simple and marginal resection of most often benign tumors found in the subcutaneous tissue above the deep fascia

EXCLUDES
Complex repair
Radical resection of cutaneous tumors (e.g., melanoma) (11600-11646)
Significant exploration of vessels or neuroplasty

24071 *Resequenced code. See code following 24075.*

24073 *Resequenced code. See code following 24076.*

▲ **24075** Excision, tumor, soft tissue of upper arm or elbow area, subcutaneous; less than 3 cm P3 T 50
 8.80 12.36 Global Days 090

#● **24071** 3 cm or greater G2 T 80 50
 10.96 10.96 Global Days 090

▲ **24076** Excision, tumor, soft tissue of upper arm or elbow area, subfascial (eg, intramuscular); less than 5 cm G2 T 50
 14.36 14.36 Global Days 090

#● **24073** 5 cm or greater G2 T 80 50
 18.81 18.81 Global Days 090

▲ **24077** Radical resection of tumor (eg, malignant neoplasm), soft tissue of upper arm or elbow area; less than 5 cm G2 T 50
 27.75 27.75 Global Days 090

● **24079** 5 cm or greater G2 T 80 50
 35.02 35.02 Global Days 090

---

26 PC PC/TC Comp Only   A2 Z3 ASC Pmt   50 Bilateral   ♂ Male Only   ♀ Female Only   Facility RVU   Non-Facility RVU
AMA: CPT Asst   **MED:** Pub 100   A Y OPPSI   80/80 Surg Assist Allowed / w/Doc   Lab Crosswalk   Radiology Crosswalk
58 CPT only © 2009 American Medical Association. All Rights Reserved. (Black Ink) Medicare (Red Ink) © 2009 Publisher (Blue Ink)

24100-24149 Bone and Joint Procedures of Upper Arm and Elbow

24100 Arthrotomy, elbow; with synovial biopsy only
 10.98 10.98 Global Days 090

24101 with joint exploration, with or without biopsy, with or without removal of loose or foreign body
 13.20 13.20 Global Days 090

24102 with synovectomy
 16.42 16.42 Global Days 090

24105 Excision, olecranon bursa
 9.08 9.08 Global Days 090

24110 Excision or curettage of bone cyst or benign tumor, humerus;
 15.57 15.57 Global Days 090

24115 with autograft (includes obtaining graft)
 18.46 18.46 Global Days 090

24116 with allograft
 23.18 23.18 Global Days 090

24120 Excision or curettage of bone cyst or benign tumor of head or neck of radius or olecranon process;
 13.98 13.98 Global Days 090

24125 with autograft (includes obtaining graft)
 16.48 16.48 Global Days 090

24126 with allograft
 17.27 17.27 Global Days 090

24130 Excision, radial head
 EXCLUDES That with replacement with implant (24366)
 13.45 13.45 Global Days 090

24134 Sequestrectomy (eg, for osteomyelitis or bone abscess), shaft or distal humerus
 19.97 19.97 Global Days 090

24136 Sequestrectomy (eg, for osteomyelitis or bone abscess), radial head or neck
 16.79 16.79 Global Days 090

24138 Sequestrectomy (eg, for osteomyelitis or bone abscess), olecranon process
 17.83 17.83 Global Days 090

24140 Partial excision (craterization, saucerization, or diaphysectomy) bone (eg, osteomyelitis), humerus
 18.80 18.80 Global Days 090

24145 Partial excision (craterization, saucerization, or diaphysectomy) bone (eg, osteomyelitis), radial head or neck
 15.72 15.72 Global Days 090

24147 Partial excision (craterization, saucerization, or diaphysectomy) bone (eg, osteomyelitis), olecranon process
 16.43 16.43 Global Days 090

24149 Radical resection of capsule, soft tissue, and heterotopic bone, elbow, with contracture release (separate procedure)
 EXCLUDES Capsular and soft tissue release (24006)
 31.50 31.50 Global Days 090

24150-24152 Radical Resection of Bone Tumor Upper Arm

INCLUDES
Any necessary elevation of tissue planes or dissection
Measurement of tumor and necessary margin at greatest diameter prior to excision
Radical resection of bone tumor: resection of the tumor (may include entire bone) and wide margins of normal tissue primarily for malignant or aggressive benign tumors
Simple and intermediate repairs

EXCLUDES
Complex repair
Significant exploration of vessels, neuroplasty, reconstruction, or complex bone repair

Do not report excision of soft tissue codes when adjacent soft tissue is removed during the bone tumor resection (24076-24079 [24071, 24073])

▲ **24150** Radical resection of tumor, shaft, or distal humerus
 40.91 40.91 Global Days 090

~~24151~~ ~~Radical resection for tumor, shaft or distal humerus; with autograft (includes obtaining graft)~~
To report, see code 24150

▲ **24152** Radical resection of tumor, radial head or neck
 35.23 35.23 Global Days 090

24155 Elbow Arthrectomy

24155 Resection of elbow joint (arthrectomy)
 22.94 22.94 Global Days 090

24160-24201 Removal Implant/Foreign Body from Elbow/Upper Arm

EXCLUDES
Bursal or joint arthrocentesis or needling (20605)
K-wire or pin insertion (20650)
K-wire or pin removal (20670, 20680)

24160 Implant removal; elbow joint
 16.12 16.12 Global Days 090

24164 radial head
 13.19 13.19 Global Days 090

24200 Removal of foreign body, upper arm or elbow area; subcutaneous
 3.72 5.25 Global Days 010

24201 deep (subfascial or intramuscular)
 9.73 14.27 Global Days 090

24220 Injection for Elbow Arthrogram

24220 Injection procedure for elbow arthrography
 EXCLUDES Injection tennis elbow (20550)
 73085
 1.86 4.00 Global Days 000

24300-24498 Repair/Reconstruction of Elbow/Upper Arm

24300 Manipulation, elbow, under anesthesia
 EXCLUDES Application of external fixation (20690, 20692)
 10.50 10.50 Global Days 090

24301 Muscle or tendon transfer, any type, upper arm or elbow, single (excluding 24320-24331)
 20.13 20.13 Global Days 090

Code	Description	Facility RVU	Non-Facility RVU	Global Days
24305	Tendon lengthening, upper arm or elbow, each tendon	15.42	15.42	090
24310	Tenotomy, open, elbow to shoulder, each tendon	12.69	12.69	090
24320	Tenoplasty, with muscle transfer, with or without free graft, elbow to shoulder, single (Seddon-Brookes type procedure)	20.93	20.93	090
24330	Flexor-plasty, elbow (eg, Steindler type advancement);	19.16	19.16	090
24331	with extensor advancement	21.07	21.07	090
24332	Tenolysis, triceps	16.23	16.23	090
24340	Tenodesis of biceps tendon at elbow (separate procedure)	16.34	16.34	090
24341	Repair, tendon or muscle, upper arm or elbow, each tendon or muscle, primary or secondary (excludes rotator cuff)	19.84	19.84	090
24342	Reinsertion of ruptured biceps or triceps tendon, distal, with or without tendon graft	20.92	20.92	090
24343	Repair lateral collateral ligament, elbow, with local tissue	18.85	18.85	090
24344	Reconstruction lateral collateral ligament, elbow, with tendon graft (includes harvesting of graft)	29.43	29.43	090
24345	Repair medial collateral ligament, elbow, with local tissue	18.73	18.73	090
24346	Reconstruction medial collateral ligament, elbow, with tendon graft (includes harvesting of graft)	29.43	29.43	090
24357	Tenotomy, elbow, lateral or medial (eg, epicondylitis, tennis elbow, golfer's elbow); percutaneous Do not report with (29837-29838) AMA: 2008, Jan, 4-5	11.79	11.79	090
24358	debridement, soft tissue and/or bone, open Do not report with (29837-29838) AMA: 2008, Jan, 4-5	13.87	13.87	090
24359	debridement, soft tissue and/or bone, open with tendon repair or reattachment Do not report with (29837-29838) AMA: 2008, Jan, 4-5	17.66	17.66	090
24360	Arthroplasty, elbow; with membrane (eg, fascial)	24.15	24.15	090
24361	with distal humeral prosthetic replacement Code also (C1776)	27.09	27.09	090
24362	with implant and fascia lata ligament reconstruction	28.57	28.57	090
24363	with distal humerus and proximal ulnar prosthetic replacement (eg, total elbow) Code also (C1776)	40.76	40.76	090
24365	Arthroplasty, radial head;	17.04	17.04	090
24366	with implant Code also implant supply (C1776)	18.23	18.23	090
24400	Osteotomy, humerus, with or without internal fixation	22.01	22.01	090
24410	Multiple osteotomies with realignment on intramedullary rod, humeral shaft (Sofield type procedure)	28.45	28.45	090
24420	Osteoplasty, humerus (eg, shortening or lengthening) (excluding 64876)	26.56	26.56	090
24430	Repair of nonunion or malunion, humerus; without graft (eg, compression technique)	28.62	28.62	090
24435	with iliac or other autograft (includes obtaining graft)	29.00	29.00	090
24470	Hemiepiphyseal arrest (eg, cubitus varus or valgus, distal humerus)	17.85	17.85	090
24495	Decompression fasciotomy, forearm, with brachial artery exploration	17.16	17.16	090
24498	Prophylactic treatment (nailing, pinning, plating or wiring), with or without methylmethacrylate, humeral shaft	23.31	23.31	090

24500-24685 Treatment of Fracture/Dislocation of Elbow/Upper Arm

Code	Description	Facility RVU	Non-Facility RVU	Global Days
24500	Closed treatment of humeral shaft fracture; without manipulation	8.39	9.12	090
24505	with manipulation, with or without skeletal traction	11.88	12.98	090
24515	Open treatment of humeral shaft fracture with plate/screws, with or without cerclage	23.54	23.54	090
24516	Treatment of humeral shaft fracture, with insertion of intramedullary implant, with or without cerclage and/or locking screws AMA: 2009, Jun, 7-8	23.20	23.20	090
24530	Closed treatment of supracondylar or transcondylar humeral fracture, with or without intercondylar extension; without manipulation	8.93	9.76	090
24535	with manipulation, with or without skin or skeletal traction	15.07	16.16	090
24538	Percutaneous skeletal fixation of supracondylar or transcondylar humeral fracture, with or without intercondylar extension	19.72	19.72	090

Current Procedural Coding Expert – Musculoskeletal System

24545	Open treatment of humeral supracondylar or transcondylar fracture, includes internal fixation, when performed; without intercondylar extension A2 T 80 50
25.05 25.05 Global Days 090
24546	with intercondylar extension A2 T 80 50
28.05 28.05 Global Days 090
24560	Closed treatment of humeral epicondylar fracture, medial or lateral; without manipulation A2 T 50
7.43 8.20 Global Days 090
24565	with manipulation A2 T 50
12.80 13.82 Global Days 090
24566	Percutaneous skeletal fixation of humeral epicondylar fracture, medial or lateral, with manipulation A2 T 50
18.96 18.96 Global Days 090
24575	Open treatment of humeral epicondylar fracture, medial or lateral, includes internal fixation, when performed A2 T 80 50
19.54 19.54 Global Days 090
24576	Closed treatment of humeral condylar fracture, medial or lateral; without manipulation A2 T 50
7.89 8.69 Global Days 090
24577	with manipulation A2 T 50
13.17 14.25 Global Days 090
24579	Open treatment of humeral condylar fracture, medial or lateral, includes internal fixation, when performed A2 T 80 50
EXCLUDES Closed treatment without manipulation (24530, 24560, 24576, 24650, 24670)
Repair with manipulation (24535, 24565, 24577, 24675)
22.40 22.40 Global Days 090
24582	Percutaneous skeletal fixation of humeral condylar fracture, medial or lateral, with manipulation A2 T 50
21.36 21.36 Global Days 090
24586	Open treatment of periarticular fracture and/or dislocation of the elbow (fracture distal humerus and proximal ulna and/or proximal radius); A2 T 80 50
29.30 29.30 Global Days 090
24587	with implant arthroplasty A2 T 80 50
EXCLUDES Distal humerus arthroplasty (24361)
29.41 29.41 Global Days 090
24600	Treatment of closed elbow dislocation; without anesthesia A2 T 50
8.74 9.41 Global Days 090
24605	requiring anesthesia A2 T 50
12.28 12.28 Global Days 090
24615	Open treatment of acute or chronic elbow dislocation A2 T 80 50
19.07 19.07 Global Days 090
24620	Closed treatment of Monteggia type of fracture dislocation at elbow (fracture proximal end of ulna with dislocation of radial head), with manipulation A2 T 80 50
14.52 14.52 Global Days 090
24635	Open treatment of Monteggia type of fracture dislocation at elbow (fracture proximal end of ulna with dislocation of radial head), includes internal fixation, when performed A2 T 80 50
17.92 17.92 Global Days 090
24640	Closed treatment of radial head subluxation in child, nursemaid elbow, with manipulation A P3 T 80 50
2.38 3.37 Global Days 010
24650	Closed treatment of radial head or neck fracture; without manipulation P2 T 50
6.16 6.65 Global Days 090
24655	with manipulation A2 T 50
10.44 11.34 Global Days 090
24665	Open treatment of radial head or neck fracture, includes internal fixation or radial head excision, when performed; A2 T 80 50
17.31 17.31 Global Days 090
24666	with radial head prosthetic replacement A2 T 80 50
19.60 19.60 Global Days 090
24670	Closed treatment of ulnar fracture, proximal end (eg, olecranon or coronoid process[es]); without manipulation A2 T 50
6.76 7.41 Global Days 090
24675	with manipulation A2 T 50
10.88 11.80 Global Days 090
24685	Open treatment of ulnar fracture, proximal end (eg, olecranon or coronoid process[es]), includes internal fixation, when performed A2 T 80 50
Do not report with (24100-24102)
17.37 17.37 Global Days 090

24800-24999 Other/Unlisted Elbow/Upper Arm Procedures

24800	Arthrodesis, elbow joint; local A2 T 80 50
22.19 22.19 Global Days 090
24802	with autogenous graft (includes obtaining graft) A2 T 80 50
26.95 26.95 Global Days 090
24900	Amputation, arm through humerus; with primary closure C 80 50
19.58 19.58 Global Days 090
24920	open, circular (guillotine) C 80 50
19.61 19.61 Global Days 090
24925	secondary closure or scar revision A2 T 80 50
14.98 14.98 Global Days 090
24930	re-amputation C 80 50
20.75 20.75 Global Days 090
24931	with implant C 80 50
21.15 21.15 Global Days 090
24935	Stump elongation, upper extremity T 80 50
31.00 31.00 Global Days 090
24940	Cineplasty, upper extremity, complete procedure C 80 50
0.00 0.00 Global Days 090
24999	**Unlisted procedure, humerus or elbow** T 80 50
0.00 0.00 Global Days YYY

25000-25001 Incision Tendon Sheath of Wrist

25000	Incision, extensor tendon sheath, wrist (eg, deQuervains disease) A2 T 50
EXCLUDES Carpal tunnel release (64721)
8.72 8.72 Global Days 090
25001	Incision, flexor tendon sheath, wrist (eg, flexor carpi radialis) G2 T 50
8.94 8.94 Global Days 090

● New Code   ▲ Revised Code   M Maternity   A Age   Unlisted   Not Covered   # Resequenced
CCI   + Add-on   Mod 51 Exempt   Mod 63 Exempt   Mod Sedation   PQRI
© 2009 Publisher (Blue Ink)   CPT only © 2009 American Medical Association. All Rights Reserved. (Black Ink)   Medicare (Red Ink)

25020-25025 Decompression Fasciotomy Forearm/Wrist

25020 Decompression fasciotomy, forearm and/or wrist, flexor OR extensor compartment; without debridement of nonviable muscle and/or nerve
  EXCLUDES Brachial artery exploration (24495)
  Superficial incision and drainage (10060-10160)
  14.95 14.95 Global Days 090

25023 with debridement of nonviable muscle and/or nerve
  EXCLUDES Brachial artery exploration (24495)
  Debridement (11000-11044)
  Superficial incision and drainage (10060-10160)
  29.81 29.81 Global Days 090

25024 Decompression fasciotomy, forearm and/or wrist, flexor AND extensor compartment; without debridement of nonviable muscle and/or nerve
  20.76 20.76 Global Days 090

25025 with debridement of nonviable muscle and/or nerve
  33.11 33.11 Global Days 090

25028-25040 Incision for Drainage/Foreign Body Removal

25028 Incision and drainage, forearm and/or wrist; deep abscess or hematoma
  13.50 13.50 Global Days 090

25031 bursa
  9.53 9.53 Global Days 090

25035 Incision, deep, bone cortex, forearm and/or wrist (eg, osteomyelitis or bone abscess)
  15.21 15.21 Global Days 090

25040 Arthrotomy, radiocarpal or midcarpal joint, with exploration, drainage, or removal of foreign body
  14.97 14.97 Global Days 090

25065-25066 Biopsy Forearm/Wrist

EXCLUDES Soft tissue needle biopsy (20206)

25065 Biopsy, soft tissue of forearm and/or wrist; superficial
  4.39 6.53 Global Days 010

25066 deep (subfascial or intramuscular)
  9.36 9.36 Global Days 090

25071-25078 [25071, 25073] Excision Soft Tissue Tumor Forearm/Wrist

INCLUDES Any necessary elevation of tissue planes or dissection
Measurement of tumor and necessary margin at greatest diameter prior to excision
Resection without removal of significant normal tissue
Simple and intermediate repairs
Types of Excision:
  Fascial or subfascial soft tissue tumors: simple and marginal resection of most often benign and intramuscular tumors found either in or below the deep fascia, not involving bone
  Radical resection of tumor: wide resection of tumor, mostly malignant or aggressive benign, involving large margins of normal tissue and may involve tissue removal from one or more layers
  Subcutaneous: simple and marginal resection of most often benign tumors found in the subcutaneous tissue above the deep fascia

EXCLUDES Complex repair
Radical resection of cutaneous tumors (e.g., melanoma) (11600-11646)
Significant exploration of vessels or neuroplasty

25071 Resequenced code. See code following 25075.
25073 Resequenced code. See code following 25076.

▲ **25075** Excision, tumor, soft tissue of forearm and/or wrist area, subcutaneous; less than 3 cm
  8.46 12.06 Global Days 090

#● **25071** 3 cm or greater
  11.48 11.48 Global Days 090

▲ **25076** Excision, tumor, soft tissue of forearm and/or wrist area, subfascial (eg, intramuscular); less than 3 cm
  13.44 13.44 Global Days 090

#● **25073** 3 cm or greater
  14.29 14.29 Global Days 090

▲ **25077** Radical resection of tumor (eg, malignant neoplasm), soft tissue of forearm and/or wrist area; less than 3 cm
  23.50 23.50 Global Days 090

● **25078** 3 cm or greater
  30.58 30.58 Global Days 090

25085-25240 Procedures of Bones and Joints Lower Arm and Wrist

25085 Capsulotomy, wrist (eg, contracture)
  11.91 11.91 Global Days 090

25100 Arthrotomy, wrist joint; with biopsy
  9.05 9.05 Global Days 090

25101 with joint exploration, with or without biopsy, with or without removal of loose or foreign body
  10.64 10.64 Global Days 090

25105 with synovectomy
  12.80 12.80 Global Days 090

25107 Arthrotomy, distal radioulnar joint including repair of triangular cartilage, complex
  16.32 16.32 Global Days 090

25109 Excision of tendon, forearm and/or wrist, flexor or extensor, each
  14.29 14.29 Global Days 090

25110 Excision, lesion of tendon sheath, forearm and/or wrist
  8.93 8.93 Global Days 090

Current Procedural Coding Expert – Musculoskeletal System

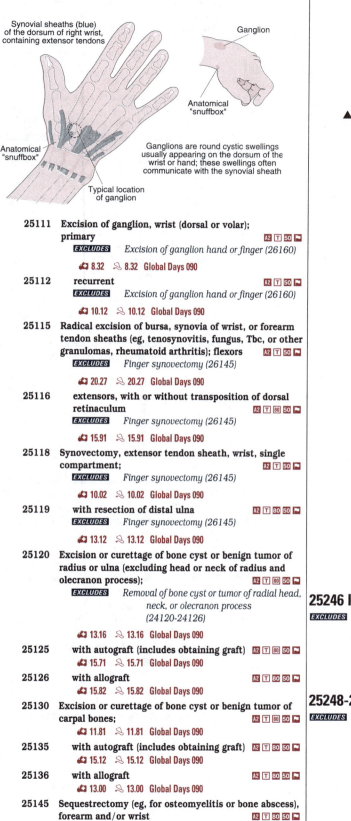

25111	**Excision of ganglion, wrist (dorsal or volar); primary** [A2][T][50]
	EXCLUDES: Excision of ganglion hand or finger (26160)
	8.32 8.32 Global Days 090
25112	**recurrent** [A2][T][50]
	EXCLUDES: Excision of ganglion hand or finger (26160)
	10.12 10.12 Global Days 090
25115	**Radical excision of bursa, synovia of wrist, or forearm tendon sheaths (eg, tenosynovitis, fungus, Tbc, or other granulomas, rheumatoid arthritis); flexors** [A2][T][50]
	EXCLUDES: Finger synovectomy (26145)
	20.27 20.27 Global Days 090
25116	**extensors, with or without transposition of dorsal retinaculum** [A2][T][80][50]
	EXCLUDES: Finger synovectomy (26145)
	15.91 15.91 Global Days 090
25118	**Synovectomy, extensor tendon sheath, wrist, single compartment;** [A2][T][50]
	EXCLUDES: Finger synovectomy (26145)
	10.02 10.02 Global Days 090
25119	**with resection of distal ulna** [A2][T][80][50]
	EXCLUDES: Finger synovectomy (26145)
	13.12 13.12 Global Days 090
25120	**Excision or curettage of bone cyst or benign tumor of radius or ulna (excluding head or neck of radius and olecranon process);** [A2][T][80][50]
	EXCLUDES: Removal of bone cyst or tumor of radial head, neck, or olecranon process (24120-24126)
	13.16 13.16 Global Days 090
25125	**with autograft (includes obtaining graft)** [A2][T][80][50]
	15.71 15.71 Global Days 090
25126	**with allograft** [A2][T][80][50]
	15.82 15.82 Global Days 090
25130	**Excision or curettage of bone cyst or benign tumor of carpal bones;** [A2][T][80][50]
	11.81 11.81 Global Days 090
25135	**with autograft (includes obtaining graft)** [A2][T][80][50]
	15.12 15.12 Global Days 090
25136	**with allograft** [A2][T][80][50]
	13.00 13.00 Global Days 090
25145	**Sequestrectomy (eg, for osteomyelitis or bone abscess), forearm and/or wrist** [A2][T][80][50]
	13.65 13.65 Global Days 090
25150	**Partial excision (craterization, saucerization, or diaphysectomy) of bone (eg, for osteomyelitis); ulna** [A2][T][50]
	14.98 14.98 Global Days 090
25151	**radius** [A2][T][80][50]
	EXCLUDES: Partial removal of radial head, neck, or olecranon process (24145, 24147)
	15.66 15.66 Global Days 090
▲ 25170	**Radical resection of tumor, radius or ulna** [T][80][50]
	INCLUDES: Any necessary elevation of tissue planes or dissection
	Measurement of tumor and necessary margin at greatest diameter prior to excision
	Radical resection of tumor: wide resection of soft tissue tumor, mostly malignant or aggressive benign, involving large margins of normal tissue and may involve tissue removal from one or more layers
	Resection without removal of significant normal tissue
	Simple and intermediate repairs
	EXCLUDES: Complex repair
	Significant exploration of vessels, neuroplasty, reconstruction, or complex bone repair
	Do not report radical excision of soft tissue codes when adjacent soft tissue is removed during the bone tumor resection (25076-25078 [25071, 25073])
	38.60 38.60 Global Days 090
25210	**Carpectomy; 1 bone** [A2][T][80]
	EXCLUDES: Carpectomy with insertion of implant (25441-25445)
	12.94 12.94 Global Days 090
25215	**all bones of proximal row** [A2][T][80]
	16.45 16.45 Global Days 090
25230	**Radial styloidectomy (separate procedure)** [A2][T][50]
	11.40 11.40 Global Days 090
25240	**Excision distal ulna partial or complete (eg, Darrach type or matched resection)** [A2][T][80][50]
	EXCLUDES: Acquisition of fascia for interposition (20920, 20922)
	Implant replacement (25442)
	11.34 11.34 Global Days 090

25246 Injection for Wrist Arthrogram

EXCLUDES: Excision of foreign body (20520)
K-wire, pin, or rod placement or removal (20650, 20670, 20680)

25246	**Injection procedure for wrist arthrography** [M][N][50]
	73115
	2.05 4.08 Global Days 000

25248-25251 Removal Foreign Body of Wrist

EXCLUDES: Excision of superficial foreign body (20520)
K-wire, pin, or rod placement or removal (20650, 20670, 20680)

25248	**Exploration with removal of deep foreign body, forearm or wrist** [A2][T][50]
	10.96 10.96 Global Days 090
25250	**Removal of wrist prosthesis; (separate procedure)** [A2][T][80][50]
	14.02 14.02 Global Days 090
25251	**complicated, including total wrist** [A2][T][80]
	19.22 19.22 Global Days 090

● New Code ▲ Revised Code [M] Maternity [A] Age Unlisted Not Covered # Resequenced
□ CCI + Add-on ⊘ Mod 51 Exempt @ Mod 63 Exempt ⊙ Mod Sedation PQ PQRI

© 2009 Publisher *(Blue Ink)*   CPT only © 2009 American Medical Association. All Rights Reserved. (Black Ink)   Medicare (Red Ink)   63

25259 Manipulation of Wrist with Anesthesia

25259 Manipulation, wrist, under anesthesia [62] [T] [50]
EXCLUDES Application of external fixation (20690, 20692)
🦴 10.56   ✂ 10.56   Global Days 090
AMA: 2009, Jan, 11-31; 2008, Jan, 10-25; 2007, January, 13-27; 2005, June, 9-11

25260-25492 Repair/Reconstruction of Forearm/Wrist

25260 Repair, tendon or muscle, flexor, forearm and/or wrist; primary, single, each tendon or muscle [A2] [T]
🦴 16.72   ✂ 16.72   Global Days 090

25263 secondary, single, each tendon or muscle [A2] [T] [80]
🦴 16.59   ✂ 16.59   Global Days 090

25265 secondary, with free graft (includes obtaining graft), each tendon or muscle [A2] [T] [80]
🦴 19.96   ✂ 19.96   Global Days 090

25270 Repair, tendon or muscle, extensor, forearm and/or wrist; primary, single, each tendon or muscle [A2] [T] [80]
🦴 13.04   ✂ 13.04   Global Days 090

25272 secondary, single, each tendon or muscle [A2] [T] [80]
🦴 14.70   ✂ 14.70   Global Days 090

25274 secondary, with free graft (includes obtaining graft), each tendon or muscle [A2] [T] [80]
🦴 17.78   ✂ 17.78   Global Days 090

25275 Repair, tendon sheath, extensor, forearm and/or wrist, with free graft (includes obtaining graft) (eg, for extensor carpi ulnaris subluxation) [A2] [T] [80] [50]
🦴 17.94   ✂ 17.94   Global Days 090

25280 Lengthening or shortening of flexor or extensor tendon, forearm and/or wrist, single, each tendon [A2] [T] [80]
🦴 15.06   ✂ 15.06   Global Days 090

25290 Tenotomy, open, flexor or extensor tendon, forearm and/or wrist, single, each tendon [A2] [T]
🦴 11.51   ✂ 11.51   Global Days 090

25295 Tenolysis, flexor or extensor tendon, forearm and/or wrist, single, each tendon [A2] [T]
🦴 13.87   ✂ 13.87   Global Days 090
AMA: 2009, Jan, 11-31; 2008, Jan, 10-25; 2007, January, 13-27

25300 Tenodesis at wrist; flexors of fingers [A2] [T] [80] [50]
🦴 18.18   ✂ 18.18   Global Days 090

25301 extensors of fingers [A2] [T] [80] [50]
🦴 17.21   ✂ 17.21   Global Days 090

25310 Tendon transplantation or transfer, flexor or extensor, forearm and/or wrist, single; each tendon [A2] [T] [80]
🦴 16.49   ✂ 16.49   Global Days 090
AMA: 2009, Jan, 11-31; 2008, Jan, 10-25; 2007, January, 13-27; 2005, January, 7-13

25312 with tendon graft(s) (includes obtaining graft), each tendon [A2] [T] [80]
🦴 19.27   ✂ 19.27   Global Days 090

25315 Flexor origin slide (eg, for cerebral palsy, Volkmann contracture), forearm and/or wrist; [A2] [T] [80] [50]
🦴 20.63   ✂ 20.63   Global Days 090

25316 with tendon(s) transfer [A2] [T] [80] [50]
🦴 24.65   ✂ 24.65   Global Days 090

25320 Capsulorrhaphy or reconstruction, wrist, open (eg, capsulodesis, ligament repair, tendon transfer or graft) (includes synovectomy, capsulotomy and open reduction) for carpal instability [A2] [T] [80] [50]
🦴 26.33   ✂ 26.33   Global Days 090

25332 Arthroplasty, wrist, with or without interposition, with or without external or internal fixation [A2] [T] [80] [50]
EXCLUDES Acquiring fascia for interposition (20920, 20922)
Arthroplasty with prosthesis (25441-25446)
🦴 22.56   ✂ 22.56   Global Days 090
AMA: 2005, January, 7-13

25335 Centralization of wrist on ulna (eg, radial club hand) [A2] [T] [80] [50]
🦴 21.26   ✂ 21.26   Global Days 090

25337 Reconstruction for stabilization of unstable distal ulna or distal radioulnar joint, secondary by soft tissue stabilization (eg, tendon transfer, tendon graft or weave, or tenodesis) with or without open reduction of distal radioulnar joint [A2] [T] [80]
EXCLUDES Acquiring fascia lata graft (20920, 20922)
🦴 23.72   ✂ 23.72   Global Days 090

25350 Osteotomy, radius; distal third [A2] [T] [80] [50]
🦴 17.99   ✂ 17.99   Global Days 090

25355 middle or proximal third [A2] [T] [80] [50]
🦴 20.49   ✂ 20.49   Global Days 090

25360 Osteotomy; ulna [A2] [T] [80] [50]
🦴 17.45   ✂ 17.45   Global Days 090

25365 radius AND ulna [A2] [T] [80] [50]
🦴 24.56   ✂ 24.56   Global Days 090

25370 Multiple osteotomies, with realignment on intramedullary rod (Sofield type procedure); radius OR ulna [A2] [T] [80] [50]
🦴 26.99   ✂ 26.99   Global Days 090

25375 radius AND ulna [A2] [T] [80] [50]
🦴 21.49   ✂ 21.49   Global Days 090

25390 Osteoplasty, radius OR ulna; shortening [A2] [T] [80] [50]
🦴 20.69   ✂ 20.69   Global Days 090

25391 lengthening with autograft [A2] [T] [80] [50]
🦴 26.80   ✂ 26.80   Global Days 090

25392 Osteoplasty, radius AND ulna; shortening (excluding 64876) [A2] [T] [80] [50]
🦴 27.29   ✂ 27.29   Global Days 090

25393 lengthening with autograft [A2] [T] [80] [50]
🦴 30.52   ✂ 30.52   Global Days 090

25394 Osteoplasty, carpal bone, shortening [62] [T] [80] [50]
🦴 20.97   ✂ 20.97   Global Days 090

25400 Repair of nonunion or malunion, radius OR ulna; without graft (eg, compression technique) [A2] [T] [80] [50]
🦴 21.65   ✂ 21.65   Global Days 090

25405 with autograft (includes obtaining graft) [A2] [T] [80] [50]
🦴 28.00   ✂ 28.00   Global Days 090

25415 Repair of nonunion or malunion, radius AND ulna; without graft (eg, compression technique) [A2] [T] [80] [50]
🦴 26.44   ✂ 26.44   Global Days 090

25420 with autograft (includes obtaining graft) [A2] [T] [80] [50]
🦴 31.52   ✂ 31.52   Global Days 090

25425 Repair of defect with autograft; radius OR ulna [A2] [T] [80] [50]
🦴 25.88   ✂ 25.88   Global Days 090

25426 radius AND ulna [A2] [T] [80] [50]
🦴 30.34   ✂ 30.34   Global Days 090

25430 Insertion of vascular pedicle into carpal bone (eg, Hori procedure) [62] [T] [50]
INCLUDES Harii procedure
🦴 19.50   ✂ 19.50   Global Days 090

---

[26]/[TC] PC/TC Comp Only   [A2]-[Z3] ASC Pmt   [50] Bilateral   ♂ Male Only   ♀ Female Only   🦴 Facility RVU   ✂ Non-Facility RVU
AMA: CPT Asst   MED: Pub 100   [A]-[Y] OPPSI   [80]/[80] Surg Assist Allowed / w/Doc   🔬 Lab Crosswalk   📊 Radiology Crosswalk

Current Procedural Coding Expert – Musculoskeletal System

25431 Repair of nonunion of carpal bone (excluding carpal scaphoid (navicular)) (includes obtaining graft and necessary fixation), each bone
21.11 21.11 Global Days 090

25440 Repair of nonunion, scaphoid carpal (navicular) bone, with or without radial styloidectomy (includes obtaining graft and necessary fixation)
20.47 20.47 Global Days 090

25441 Arthroplasty with prosthetic replacement; distal radius
Code also (C1776)
25.28 25.28 Global Days 090
AMA: 2005, January, 7-13

25442 distal ulna
Code also (C1776)
21.32 21.32 Global Days 090
AMA: 2005, January, 7-13

25443 scaphoid carpal (navicular)
20.86 20.86 Global Days 090
AMA: 2005, January, 7-13

25444 lunate
18.47 18.47 Global Days 090
AMA: 2005, January, 7-13

25445 trapezium
19.27 19.27 Global Days 090
AMA: 2005, January, 7-13

25446 distal radius and partial or entire carpus (total wrist)
Code also (C1776)
31.71 31.71 Global Days 090
AMA: 2005, January, 7-13

25447 Arthroplasty, interposition, intercarpal or carpometacarpal joints
EXCLUDES Wrist arthroplasty (25332)
22.14 22.14 Global Days 090
AMA: 2005, January, 7-13

25449 Revision of arthroplasty, including removal of implant, wrist joint
27.86 27.86 Global Days 090

25450 Epiphyseal arrest by epiphysiodesis or stapling; distal radius OR ulna
15.61 15.61 Global Days 090

25455 distal radius AND ulna
16.06 16.06 Global Days 090

25490 Prophylactic treatment (nailing, pinning, plating or wiring) with or without methylmethacrylate; radius
17.93 17.93 Global Days 090

25491 ulna
19.77 19.77 Global Days 090

25492 radius AND ulna
24.25 24.25 Global Days 090

25500-25695 Treatment of Fracture/Dislocation of Forearm/Wrist

EXCLUDES External fixation application (20690)

25500 Closed treatment of radial shaft fracture; without manipulation
6.40 6.91 Global Days 090

25505 with manipulation
12.13 13.09 Global Days 090

25515 Open treatment of radial shaft fracture, includes internal fixation, when performed
17.82 17.82 Global Days 090

25520 Closed treatment of radial shaft fracture and closed treatment of dislocation of distal radioulnar joint (Galeazzi fracture/dislocation)
14.12 14.80 Global Days 090

25525 Open treatment of radial shaft fracture, includes internal fixation, when performed, and closed treatment of distal radioulnar joint dislocation (Galeazzi fracture/dislocation), includes percutaneous skeletal fixation, when performed
20.89 20.89 Global Days 090

25526 Open treatment of radial shaft fracture, includes internal fixation, when performed, and open treatment of distal radioulnar joint dislocation (Galeazzi fracture/dislocation), includes internal fixation, when performed, includes repair of triangular fibrocartilage complex
25.43 25.43 Global Days 090

25530 Closed treatment of ulnar shaft fracture; without manipulation
6.05 6.63 Global Days 090

25535 with manipulation
11.91 12.74 Global Days 090

25545 Open treatment of ulnar shaft fracture, includes internal fixation, when performed
16.52 16.52 Global Days 090

25560 Closed treatment of radial and ulnar shaft fractures; without manipulation
6.41 7.02 Global Days 090

25565 with manipulation
12.48 13.60 Global Days 090

25574 Open treatment of radial AND ulnar shaft fractures, with internal fixation, when performed; of radius OR ulna
17.95 17.95 Global Days 090

25575 of radius AND ulna
24.10 24.10 Global Days 090

25600 Closed treatment of distal radial fracture (eg, Colles or Smith type) or epiphyseal separation, includes closed treatment of fracture of ulnar styloid, when performed; without manipulation
Do not report with (25650)
6.91 7.49 Global Days 090

25605 with manipulation
Do not report with (25650)
15.53 16.36 Global Days 090

25606 Percutaneous skeletal fixation of distal radial fracture or epiphyseal separation
EXCLUDES Open repair of ulnar styloid fracture (25652)
Percutaneous repair of ulnar styloid fracture (25651)
Do not report with (25650)
17.49 17.49 Global Days 090

25607 Open treatment of distal radial extra-articular fracture or epiphyseal separation, with internal fixation
EXCLUDES Open repair of ulnar styloid fracture (25652)
Percutaneous repair of ulnar styloid fracture (25651)
Do not report with (25650)
19.55 19.55 Global Days 090

● New Code   ▲ Revised Code   M Maternity   A Age   Unlisted   Not Covered   # Resequenced
CCI   + Add-on   ⊘ Mod 51 Exempt   ⓔ Mod 63 Exempt   ⊙ Mod Sedation   PQ PQRI

Current Procedural Coding Expert – Musculoskeletal System

Code	Description	Facility RVU	Non-Facility RVU	Global Days
25608	Open treatment of distal radial intra-articular fracture or epiphyseal separation; with internal fixation of 2 fragments	22.04	22.04	090
	EXCLUDES Open repair of ulnar styloid fracture (25652); Percutaneous repair of ulnar styloid fracture (25651)			
	Do not report with (25609, 25650)			
25609	with internal fixation of 3 or more fragments	28.09	28.09	090
	EXCLUDES Open repair of ulnar styloid fracture (25652); Percutaneous repair of ulnar styloid fracture (25651)			
	Do not report with (25650)			
25622	Closed treatment of carpal scaphoid (navicular) fracture; without manipulation	7.15	7.78	090
25624	with manipulation	11.04	12.01	090
25628	Open treatment of carpal scaphoid (navicular) fracture, includes internal fixation, when performed	19.22	19.22	090
25630	Closed treatment of carpal bone fracture (excluding carpal scaphoid [navicular]); without manipulation, each bone	7.31	7.89	090
25635	with manipulation, each bone	10.79	11.71	090
25645	Open treatment of carpal bone fracture (other than carpal scaphoid [navicular]), each bone	15.09	15.09	090
25650	Closed treatment of ulnar styloid fracture	7.75	8.21	090
	Do not report with (25600, 25605, 25607-25609)			
25651	Percutaneous skeletal fixation of ulnar styloid fracture	12.78	12.78	090
25652	Open treatment of ulnar styloid fracture	16.54	16.54	090
25660	Closed treatment of radiocarpal or intercarpal dislocation, 1 or more bones, with manipulation	10.81	10.81	090
25670	Open treatment of radiocarpal or intercarpal dislocation, 1 or more bones	16.17	16.17	090
25671	Percutaneous skeletal fixation of distal radioulnar dislocation	13.96	13.96	090
25675	Closed treatment of distal radioulnar dislocation with manipulation	10.42	11.26	090
25676	Open treatment of distal radioulnar dislocation, acute or chronic	16.70	16.70	090
25680	Closed treatment of trans-scaphoperilunar type of fracture dislocation, with manipulation	12.44	12.44	090
25685	Open treatment of trans-scaphoperilunar type of fracture dislocation	19.67	19.67	090
25690	Closed treatment of lunate dislocation, with manipulation	12.59	12.59	090
25695	Open treatment of lunate dislocation	16.86	16.86	090

25800-25830 Wrist Fusion

Code	Description	Facility RVU	Non-Facility RVU	Global Days
25800	Arthrodesis, wrist; complete, without bone graft (includes radiocarpal and/or intercarpal and/or carpometacarpal joints)	19.66	19.66	090
25805	with sliding graft	22.62	22.62	090
25810	with iliac or other autograft (includes obtaining graft)	23.26	23.26	090
25820	limited, without bone graft (eg, intercarpal or radiocarpal)	16.30	16.30	090
25825	with autograft (includes obtaining graft)	20.11	20.11	090
25830	Arthrodesis, distal radioulnar joint with segmental resection of ulna, with or without bone graft (eg, Sauve-Kapandji procedure)	25.01	25.01	090

25900-25999 Amputation Through Forearm/Wrist

Code	Description	Facility RVU	Non-Facility RVU	Global Days
25900	Amputation, forearm, through radius and ulna;	18.91	18.91	090
25905	open, circular (guillotine)	18.73	18.73	090
25907	secondary closure or scar revision	16.27	16.27	090
25909	re-amputation	18.27	18.27	090
25915	Krukenberg procedure	26.27	26.27	090
25920	Disarticulation through wrist;	18.47	18.47	090
25922	secondary closure or scar revision	13.26	13.26	090
25924	re-amputation	18.02	18.02	090
25927	Transmetacarpal amputation;	21.13	21.13	090
25929	secondary closure or scar revision	15.84	15.84	090
25931	re-amputation	17.82	17.82	090
25999	Unlisted procedure, forearm or wrist	0.00	0.00	YYY

Current Procedural Coding Expert – Musculoskeletal System

26010-26037 Incision Hand/Fingers

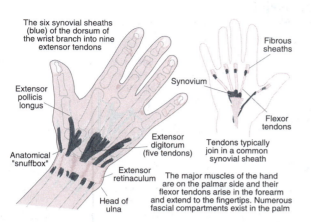

26010	Drainage of finger abscess; simple
	3.61 6.49 Global Days 010
26011	complicated (eg, felon)
	4.90 9.66 Global Days 010
26020	Drainage of tendon sheath, digit and/or palm, each
	11.41 11.41 Global Days 090
26025	Drainage of palmar bursa; single, bursa
	11.17 11.17 Global Days 090
26030	multiple bursa
	13.09 13.09 Global Days 090
26034	Incision, bone cortex, hand or finger (eg, osteomyelitis or bone abscess)
	14.19 14.19 Global Days 090
26035	Decompression fingers and/or hand, injection injury (eg, grease gun)
	22.81 22.81 Global Days 090
26037	Decompressive fasciotomy, hand (excludes 26035)
	EXCLUDES Injection injury (26035)
	15.24 15.24 Global Days 090

26040-26045 Incision Palmar Fascia

EXCLUDES Fasciectomy (26121, 26123, 26125)

26040	Fasciotomy, palmar (eg, Dupuytren's contracture); percutaneous
	8.14 8.14 Global Days 090
26045	open, partial
	12.34 12.34 Global Days 090

26055-26080 Incision Tendon/Joint of Fingers/Hand

26055	Tendon sheath incision (eg, for trigger finger)
	8.01 13.82 Global Days 090
26060	Tenotomy, percutaneous, single, each digit
	EXCLUDES Arthrocentesis (20610)
	6.96 6.96 Global Days 090
26070	Arthrotomy, with exploration, drainage, or removal of loose or foreign body; carpometacarpal joint
	8.10 8.10 Global Days 090
26075	metacarpophalangeal joint, each
	8.53 8.53 Global Days 090
26080	interphalangeal joint, each
	10.18 10.18 Global Days 090

26100-26110 Arthrotomy with Biopsy of Joint Hand/Fingers

26100	Arthrotomy with biopsy; carpometacarpal joint, each
	8.73 8.73 Global Days 090
26105	metacarpophalangeal joint, each
	8.79 8.79 Global Days 090
26110	interphalangeal joint, each
	8.41 8.41 Global Days 090

26111-26118 [26111, 26113] Excision Soft Tissue Tumor Fingers and Hand

INCLUDES
- Any necessary elevation of tissue planes or dissection
- Measurement of tumor and necessary margin prior to excision
- Resection without removal of significant normal tissue
- Simple and intermediate repairs
- Type of Excisions:
  - Fascial or subfascial soft tissue tumors: simple and marginal resection of most often benign and intramuscular tumors found either in or below the deep fascia, not involving bone
  - Radical resection soft tissue tumor: wide resection of tumor, mostly malignant or aggressive benign, involving large margins of normal tissue and may involve tissue removal from one or more layers
  - Subcutaneous: simple and marginal resection of most often benign tumors found in the subcutaneous tissue above the deep fascia

EXCLUDES
- Complex repair
- Radical resection of cutaneous tumors (e.g., melanoma) (11600-11646)
- Significant exploration of the vessels or neuroplasty

26111	Resequenced code. See code following 26115.
26113	Resequenced code. See code following 26116.
▲ 26115	Excision, tumor or vascular malformation, soft tissue of hand or finger, subcutaneous; less than 1.5 cm
	8.83 12.54 Global Days 090
#● 26111	1.5 cm or greater
	11.12 11.12 Global Days 090
▲ 26116	Excision, tumor, soft tissue, or vascular malformation, of hand or finger, subfascial (eg, intramuscular); less than 1.5 cm
	13.86 13.86 Global Days 090
#● 26113	1.5 cm or greater
	14.63 14.63 Global Days 090
▲ 26117	Radical resection of tumor (eg, malignant neoplasm), soft tissue of hand or finger; less than 3 cm
	19.86 19.86 Global Days 090
● 26118	3 cm or greater
	28.73 28.73 Global Days 090

26121-26236 Procedures of Bones, Fascia, Joints and Tendons Hands and Fingers

26121	Fasciectomy, palm only, with or without Z-plasty, other local tissue rearrangement, or skin grafting (includes obtaining graft)
	EXCLUDES Fasciotomy (26040, 26045)
	15.88 15.88 Global Days 090

● New Code   ▲ Revised Code   M Maternity   Age   Unlisted   Not Covered   # Resequenced
CCI   + Add-on   Mod 51 Exempt   Mod 63 Exempt   Mod Sedation   PQRI

© 2009 Publisher (Blue Ink)   CPT only © 2009 American Medical Association. All Rights Reserved. (Black Ink)   Medicare (Red Ink)

26123	Fasciectomy, partial palmar with release of single digit including proximal interphalangeal joint, with or without Z-plasty, other local tissue rearrangement, or skin grafting (includes obtaining graft);
	EXCLUDES Fasciotomy (26040, 26045)
	22.21 22.21 Global Days 090
+ 26125	each additional digit (List separately in addition to code for primary procedure)
	Code first 26123 (26123)
	EXCLUDES Fasciotomy (26040, 26045)
	7.60 7.60 Global Days ZZZ
26130	Synovectomy, carpometacarpal joint
	12.13 12.13 Global Days 090
26135	Synovectomy, metacarpophalangeal joint including intrinsic release and extensor hood reconstruction, each digit
	14.59 14.59 Global Days 090
26140	Synovectomy, proximal interphalangeal joint, including extensor reconstruction, each interphalangeal joint
	13.34 13.34 Global Days 090
26145	Synovectomy, tendon sheath, radical (tenosynovectomy), flexor tendon, palm and/or finger, each tendon
	EXCLUDES Wrist synovectomy (25115-25116)
	13.56 13.56 Global Days 090
26160	Excision of lesion of tendon sheath or joint capsule (eg, cyst, mucous cyst, or ganglion), hand or finger
	EXCLUDES Trigger finger (26055)
	Wrist ganglion removal (25111-25112)
	8.69 14.30 Global Days 090
26170	Excision of tendon, palm, flexor or extensor, single, each tendon
	Do not report with (26390, 26415)
	10.73 10.73 Global Days 090
26180	Excision of tendon, finger, flexor or extensor, each tendon
	Do not report with (26390, 26415)
	11.72 11.72 Global Days 090
26185	Sesamoidectomy, thumb or finger (separate procedure)
	14.42 14.42 Global Days 090
26200	Excision or curettage of bone cyst or benign tumor of metacarpal;
	11.90 11.90 Global Days 090
26205	with autograft (includes obtaining graft)
	15.98 15.98 Global Days 090
26210	Excision or curettage of bone cyst or benign tumor of proximal, middle, or distal phalanx of finger;
	11.63 11.63 Global Days 090
26215	with autograft (includes obtaining graft)
	14.91 14.91 Global Days 090
26230	Partial excision (craterization, saucerization, or diaphysectomy) bone (eg, osteomyelitis); metacarpal
	13.22 13.22 Global Days 090
26235	proximal or middle phalanx of finger
	13.11 13.11 Global Days 090
26236	distal phalanx of finger
	11.68 11.68 Global Days 090

26250-26262 Radical Resection Bone Tumor of Hand/Finger

INCLUDES
- Any necessary elevation of tissue planes or dissection
- Measurement of tumor and necessary margin at greatest diameter prior to excision
- Radical resection of bone tumor: resection of the tumor (may include entire bone) and wide margins of normal tissue primarily for malignant or aggressive benign tumors
- Simple and intermediate repairs

EXCLUDES
- Complex repair
- Significant exploration of vessels, neuroplasty, reconstruction, or complex bone repair

Do not report radical excision of soft tissue codes when adjacent soft tissue is removed during the bone tumor resection (26116-26118 [26111, 26113])

▲ 26250	Radical resection of tumor, metacarpal
	27.72 27.72 Global Days 090
26255	Radical resection, metacarpal (eg, tumor); with autograft (includes obtaining graft)
	To report, see code 26250
▲ 26260	Radical resection of tumor, proximal or middle phalanx of finger
	20.97 20.97 Global Days 090
26261	Radical resection, proximal or middle phalanx of finger (eg, tumor); with autograft (includes obtaining graft)
	To report, see code 26260
▲ 26262	Radical resection of tumor, distal phalanx of finger
	16.49 16.49 Global Days 090

26320 Implant Removal Hand/Finger

26320	Removal of implant from finger or hand
	EXCLUDES Excision of foreign body (20520, 20525)
	9.11 9.11 Global Days 090

26340-26548 Repair/Reconstruction of Fingers and Hand

26340	Manipulation, finger joint, under anesthesia, each joint
	EXCLUDES Application of external fixation (20690, 20692)
	8.51 8.51 Global Days 090
	AMA: 2009, Jan, 11-31; 2008, Jan, 10-25; 2007, January, 13-27
26350	Repair or advancement, flexor tendon, not in zone 2 digital flexor tendon sheath (eg, no man's land); primary or secondary without free graft, each tendon
	17.93 17.93 Global Days 090
26352	secondary with free graft (includes obtaining graft), each tendon
	20.73 20.73 Global Days 090
26356	Repair or advancement, flexor tendon, in zone 2 digital flexor tendon sheath (eg, no man's land); primary, without free graft, each tendon
	27.95 27.95 Global Days 090
	AMA: 2009, Jan, 11-31; 2008, Jan, 10-25; 2007, January, 13-27
26357	secondary, without free graft, each tendon
	22.21 22.21 Global Days 090
26358	secondary, with free graft (includes obtaining graft), each tendon
	23.44 23.44 Global Days 090

Current Procedural Coding Expert – Musculoskeletal System

26370	Repair or advancement of profundus tendon, with intact superficialis tendon; primary, each tendon
	19.36 19.36 Global Days 090
26372	secondary with free graft (includes obtaining graft), each tendon
	22.59 22.59 Global Days 090
26373	secondary without free graft, each tendon
	21.62 21.62 Global Days 090
26390	Excision flexor tendon, with implantation of synthetic rod for delayed tendon graft, hand or finger, each rod
	21.59 21.59 Global Days 090
26392	Removal of synthetic rod and insertion of flexor tendon graft, hand or finger (includes obtaining graft), each rod
	25.03 25.03 Global Days 090
26410	Repair, extensor tendon, hand, primary or secondary; without free graft, each tendon
	14.21 14.21 Global Days 090
26412	with free graft (includes obtaining graft), each tendon
	17.33 17.33 Global Days 090
26415	Excision of extensor tendon, with implantation of synthetic rod for delayed tendon graft, hand or finger, each rod
	18.22 18.22 Global Days 090
26416	Removal of synthetic rod and insertion of extensor tendon graft (includes obtaining graft), hand or finger, each rod
	22.76 22.76 Global Days 090
26418	Repair, extensor tendon, finger, primary or secondary; without free graft, each tendon
	14.41 14.41 Global Days 090
	AMA: 2009, Jan, 11-31; 2008, Jan, 10-25; 2007, January, 13-27
26420	with free graft (includes obtaining graft) each tendon
	18.27 18.27 Global Days 090
26426	Repair of extensor tendon, central slip, secondary (eg, boutonniere deformity); using local tissue(s), including lateral band(s), each finger
	13.29 13.29 Global Days 090
26428	with free graft (includes obtaining graft), each finger
	19.23 19.23 Global Days 090
26432	Closed treatment of distal extensor tendon insertion, with or without percutaneous pinning (eg, mallet finger)
	12.55 12.55 Global Days 090
26433	Repair of extensor tendon, distal insertion, primary or secondary; without graft (eg, mallet finger)
	EXCLUDES Trigger finger (26055)
	13.39 13.39 Global Days 090
26434	with free graft (includes obtaining graft)
	EXCLUDES Trigger finger (26055)
	16.42 16.42 Global Days 090
26437	Realignment of extensor tendon, hand, each tendon
	15.80 15.80 Global Days 090
26440	Tenolysis, flexor tendon; palm OR finger, each tendon
	15.58 15.58 Global Days 090
	AMA: 2009, Jan, 11-31; 2008, Jan, 10-25; 2007, January, 13-27
26442	palm AND finger, each tendon
	24.76 24.76 Global Days 090
26445	Tenolysis, extensor tendon, hand OR finger, each tendon
	14.44 14.44 Global Days 090
	AMA: 2009, Jan, 11-31; 2008, Jan, 10-25; 2007, January, 13-27
26449	Tenolysis, complex, extensor tendon, finger, including forearm, each tendon
	18.44 18.44 Global Days 090
26450	Tenotomy, flexor, palm, open, each tendon
	10.35 10.35 Global Days 090
26455	Tenotomy, flexor, finger, open, each tendon
	10.25 10.25 Global Days 090
26460	Tenotomy, extensor, hand or finger, open, each tendon
	9.94 9.94 Global Days 090
26471	Tenodesis; of proximal interphalangeal joint, each joint
	15.66 15.66 Global Days 090
26474	of distal joint, each joint
	15.16 15.16 Global Days 090
26476	Lengthening of tendon, extensor, hand or finger, each tendon
	14.93 14.93 Global Days 090
26477	Shortening of tendon, extensor, hand or finger, each tendon
	14.78 14.78 Global Days 090
26478	Lengthening of tendon, flexor, hand or finger, each tendon
	15.84 15.84 Global Days 090
26479	Shortening of tendon, flexor, hand or finger, each tendon
	15.84 15.84 Global Days 090
26480	Transfer or transplant of tendon, carpometacarpal area or dorsum of hand; without free graft, each tendon
	19.11 19.11 Global Days 090
	AMA: 2005, January, 7-13
26483	with free tendon graft (includes obtaining graft), each tendon
	21.42 21.42 Global Days 090
26485	Transfer or transplant of tendon, palmar; without free tendon graft, each tendon
	20.56 20.56 Global Days 090
26489	with free tendon graft (includes obtaining graft), each tendon
	23.99 23.99 Global Days 090
26490	Opponensplasty; superficialis tendon transfer type, each tendon
	EXCLUDES Thumb fusion (26820)
	20.19 20.19 Global Days 090
26492	tendon transfer with graft (includes obtaining graft), each tendon
	EXCLUDES Thumb fusion (26820)
	22.76 22.76 Global Days 090
26494	hypothenar muscle transfer
	EXCLUDES Thumb fusion (26820)
	20.55 20.55 Global Days 090
26496	other methods
	EXCLUDES Thumb fusion (26820)
	22.30 22.30 Global Days 090
26497	Transfer of tendon to restore intrinsic function; ring and small finger
	22.35 22.35 Global Days 090

● New Code   ▲ Revised Code   M Maternity   A Age   Unlisted   Not Covered   # Resequenced
CCI   + Add-on   Mod 51 Exempt   Mod 63 Exempt   Mod Sedation   PQRI
© 2009 Publisher (Blue Ink)   CPT only © 2009 American Medical Association. All Rights Reserved. (Black Ink)   Medicare (Red Ink)

Code	Description	RVU Fac	RVU Non-Fac	Global Days
26498	all 4 fingers	29.91	29.91	090
26499	Correction claw finger, other methods	21.39	21.39	090
26500	Reconstruction of tendon pulley, each tendon; with local tissues (separate procedure)	15.98	15.98	090
26502	with tendon or fascial graft (includes obtaining graft) (separate procedure)	18.13	18.13	090
26508	Release of thenar muscle(s) (eg, thumb contracture)	15.90	15.90	090
26510	Cross intrinsic transfer, each tendon	15.14	15.14	090
26516	Capsulodesis, metacarpophalangeal joint; single digit	18.00	18.00	090
26517	2 digits	21.23	21.23	090
26518	3 or 4 digits	21.55	21.55	090
26520	Capsulectomy or capsulotomy; metacarpophalangeal joint, each joint	16.38	16.38	090
	EXCLUDES Carpometacarpal joint arthroplasty (25447)			
26525	interphalangeal joint, each joint	16.40	16.40	090
	EXCLUDES Carpometacarpal joint arthroplasty (25447)			
	AMA: 2009, Jan, 11-31; 2008, Jan, 10-25; 2007, January, 13-27			
26530	Arthroplasty, metacarpophalangeal joint; each joint	14.25	14.25	090
	EXCLUDES Carpometacarpal joint arthroplasty (25447)			
26531	with prosthetic implant, each joint	16.60	16.60	090
	EXCLUDES Carpometacarpal joint arthroplasty (25447)			
26535	Arthroplasty, interphalangeal joint; each joint	11.03	11.03	090
	EXCLUDES Carpometacarpal joint arthroplasty (25447)			
26536	with prosthetic implant, each joint	18.10	18.10	090
	EXCLUDES Carpometacarpal joint arthroplasty (25447)			
26540	Repair of collateral ligament, metacarpophalangeal or interphalangeal joint	16.82	16.82	090
26541	Reconstruction, collateral ligament, metacarpophalangeal joint, single; with tendon or fascial graft (includes obtaining graft)	20.72	20.72	090
26542	with local tissue (eg, adductor advancement)	17.19	17.19	090
26545	Reconstruction, collateral ligament, interphalangeal joint, single, including graft, each joint	17.85	17.85	090
26546	Repair non-union, metacarpal or phalanx (includes obtaining bone graft with or without external or internal fixation)	25.36	25.36	090
26548	Repair and reconstruction, finger, volar plate, interphalangeal joint	19.58	19.58	090

26550-26556 Reconstruction Procedures with Finger and Toe Transplants

Code	Description	RVU Fac	RVU Non-Fac	Global Days
26550	Pollicization of a digit	43.44	43.44	090
26551	Transfer, toe-to-hand with microvascular anastomosis; great toe wrap-around with bone graft	88.80	88.80	090
	INCLUDES Operating microscope (69990)			
	EXCLUDES Big toe with web space (20973)			
26553	other than great toe, single	74.55	74.55	090
	INCLUDES Operating microscope (69990)			
26554	other than great toe, double	87.39	87.39	090
	INCLUDES Operating microscope (69990)			
26555	Transfer, finger to another position without microvascular anastomosis	36.81	36.81	090
26556	Transfer, free toe joint, with microvascular anastomosis	66.27	66.27	090
	INCLUDES Operating microscope (69990)			
	EXCLUDES Big toe to hand transfer (20973)			

26560-26596 Repair of Other Deformities of the Fingers/Hand

Code	Description	RVU Fac	RVU Non-Fac	Global Days
26560	Repair of syndactyly (web finger) each web space; with skin flaps	14.72	14.72	090
26561	with skin flaps and grafts	22.69	22.69	090
26562	complex (eg, involving bone, nails)	28.89	28.89	090
26565	Osteotomy; metacarpal, each	17.44	17.44	090
26567	phalanx of finger, each	17.47	17.47	090
26568	Osteoplasty, lengthening, metacarpal or phalanx	23.02	23.02	090
26580	Repair cleft hand	39.89	39.89	090
	INCLUDES Barsky's procedure			
26587	Reconstruction of polydactylous digit, soft tissue and bone	25.83	25.83	090
	EXCLUDES Soft tissue removal only (11200)			
	AMA: 2009, Jan, 11-31; 2008, Jan, 10-25; 2007, January, 13-27			
26590	Repair macrodactylia, each digit	37.20	37.20	090
	AMA: 2009, Jan, 11-31; 2008, Jan, 10-25; 2007, January, 13-27			
26591	Repair, intrinsic muscles of hand, each muscle	10.76	10.76	090
	AMA: 2009, Jan, 11-31; 2008, Jan, 10-25; 2007, January, 13-27			
26593	Release, intrinsic muscles of hand, each muscle	15.25	15.25	090

Current Procedural Coding Expert – Musculoskeletal System

26596 Excision of constricting ring of finger, with multiple Z-plasties
EXCLUDES *Release of scar contracture or treatment with graft (11041-11042, 14040-14041, 15120, 15240)*
19.86   19.86   Global Days 090

26600-26785 Treatment of Fracture/Dislocation of Fingers and Hand

26600 Closed treatment of metacarpal fracture, single; without manipulation, each bone
7.08   7.48   Global Days 090

26605   with manipulation, each bone
7.58   8.24   Global Days 090

26607 Closed treatment of metacarpal fracture, with manipulation, with external fixation, each bone
11.96   11.96   Global Days 090

26608 Percutaneous skeletal fixation of metacarpal fracture, each bone
12.51   12.51   Global Days 090

26615 Open treatment of metacarpal fracture, single, includes internal fixation, when performed, each bone
15.20   15.20   Global Days 090

26641 Closed treatment of carpometacarpal dislocation, thumb, with manipulation
8.81   9.54   Global Days 090

26645 Closed treatment of carpometacarpal fracture dislocation, thumb (Bennett fracture), with manipulation
10.25   11.06   Global Days 090

26650 Percutaneous skeletal fixation of carpometacarpal fracture dislocation, thumb (Bennett fracture), with manipulation
12.49   12.49   Global Days 090

26665 Open treatment of carpometacarpal fracture dislocation, thumb (Bennett fracture), includes internal fixation, when performed
16.65   16.65   Global Days 090

26670 Closed treatment of carpometacarpal dislocation, other than thumb, with manipulation, each joint; without anesthesia
7.95   8.65   Global Days 090

26675   requiring anesthesia
10.90   11.75   Global Days 090

26676 Percutaneous skeletal fixation of carpometacarpal dislocation, other than thumb, with manipulation, each joint
13.10   13.10   Global Days 090

26685 Open treatment of carpometacarpal dislocation, other than thumb; includes internal fixation, when performed, each joint
15.25   15.25   Global Days 090

26686   complex, multiple, or delayed reduction
16.54   16.54   Global Days 090

26700 Closed treatment of metacarpophalangeal dislocation, single, with manipulation; without anesthesia
7.87   8.31   Global Days 090

26705   requiring anesthesia
9.90   10.74   Global Days 090

26706 Percutaneous skeletal fixation of metacarpophalangeal dislocation, single, with manipulation
11.60   11.60   Global Days 090

26715 Open treatment of metacarpophalangeal dislocation, single, includes internal fixation, when performed
15.07   15.07   Global Days 090

26720 Closed treatment of phalangeal shaft fracture, proximal or middle phalanx, finger or thumb; without manipulation, each
4.71   5.03   Global Days 090

26725   with manipulation, with or without skin or skeletal traction, each
7.99   8.75   Global Days 090

26727 Percutaneous skeletal fixation of unstable phalangeal shaft fracture, proximal or middle phalanx, finger or thumb, with manipulation, each
12.30   12.30   Global Days 090

26735 Open treatment of phalangeal shaft fracture, proximal or middle phalanx, finger or thumb, includes internal fixation, when performed, each
15.78   15.78   Global Days 090

26740 Closed treatment of articular fracture, involving metacarpophalangeal or interphalangeal joint; without manipulation, each
5.52   5.84   Global Days 090

26742   with manipulation, each
8.77   9.55   Global Days 090

26746 Open treatment of articular fracture, involving metacarpophalangeal or interphalangeal joint, includes internal fixation, when performed, each
19.79   19.79   Global Days 090

26750 Closed treatment of distal phalangeal fracture, finger or thumb; without manipulation, each
4.73   4.72   Global Days 090

26755   with manipulation, each
7.16   8.07   Global Days 090

26756 Percutaneous skeletal fixation of distal phalangeal fracture, finger or thumb, each
10.89   10.89   Global Days 090

26765 Open treatment of distal phalangeal fracture, finger or thumb, includes internal fixation, when performed, each
13.17   13.17   Global Days 090

26770 Closed treatment of interphalangeal joint dislocation, single, with manipulation; without anesthesia
6.63   7.08   Global Days 090

26775   requiring anesthesia
9.02   9.87   Global Days 090

26776 Percutaneous skeletal fixation of interphalangeal joint dislocation, single, with manipulation
11.54   11.54   Global Days 090

26785 Open treatment of interphalangeal joint dislocation, includes internal fixation, when performed, single
14.39   14.39   Global Days 090

26820-26863 Fusion of Joint(s) of Fingers or Hand

26820 Fusion in opposition, thumb, with autogenous graft (includes obtaining graft)
20.20   20.20   Global Days 090

26841 Arthrodesis, carpometacarpal joint, thumb, with or without internal fixation;
18.63   18.63   Global Days 090

26842   with autograft (includes obtaining graft)
20.27   20.27   Global Days 090

● New Code   ▲ Revised Code   M Maternity   A Age   Unlisted   Not Covered   # Resequenced
CCI   + Add-on   ⊘ Mod 51 Exempt   ⊛ Mod 63 Exempt   ⊙ Mod Sedation   PQRI
© 2009 Publisher *(Blue Ink)*   CPT only © 2009 American Medical Association. All Rights Reserved. (Black Ink)   Medicare (Red Ink)

26843 — Current Procedural Coding Expert – Musculoskeletal System

26843	Arthrodesis, carpometacarpal joint, digit, other than thumb, each; A2 T 80
	18.90 18.90 Global Days 090
	AMA: 2009, Jan, 11-31; 2008, Jan, 10-25; 2007, January, 13-27
26844	with autograft (includes obtaining graft) A2 T 80
	21.07 21.07 Global Days 090
26850	Arthrodesis, metacarpophalangeal joint, with or without internal fixation; A2 T 80
	17.74 17.74 Global Days 090
26852	with autograft (includes obtaining graft) A2 T 80
	20.50 20.50 Global Days 090
26860	Arthrodesis, interphalangeal joint, with or without internal fixation; A2 T
	14.20 14.20 Global Days 090
	AMA: 2009, Jul, 10
+ 26861	each additional interphalangeal joint (List separately in addition to code for primary procedure) A2 T
	Code first 26860
	2.86 2.86 Global Days ZZZ
	AMA: 2009, Jul, 10
26862	with autograft (includes obtaining graft) A2 T 80
	18.67 18.67 Global Days 090
+ 26863	with autograft (includes obtaining graft), each additional joint (List separately in addition to code for primary procedure) A2 T 80
	Code first 26862
	6.35 6.35 Global Days ZZZ

26910-26989 Amputation Finger/Hand

26910	Amputation, metacarpal, with finger or thumb (ray amputation), single, with or without interosseous transfer A2 T
	EXCLUDES Repositioning (26550, 26555)
	Transmetacarpal amputation of hand (25927)
	18.50 18.50 Global Days 090
26951	Amputation, finger or thumb, primary or secondary, any joint or phalanx, single, including neurectomies; with direct closure A2 T
	EXCLUDES Repair necessitating flaps or grafts (15050-15758)
	Transmetacarpal amputation of hand (25927)
	16.58 16.58 Global Days 090
26952	with local advancement flaps (V-Y, hood) A2 T
	EXCLUDES Repair necessitating flaps or grafts (15050-15758)
	Transmetacarpal amputation of hand (25927)
	16.49 16.49 Global Days 090
26989	Unlisted procedure, hands or fingers T
	0.00 0.00 Global Days YYY

26990-26992 Incision for Drainage of Pelvis or Hip

EXCLUDES Simple incision and drainage procedures (10040-10160)

26990	Incision and drainage, pelvis or hip joint area; deep abscess or hematoma A2 T
	16.50 16.50 Global Days 090
26991	infected bursa A2 T 80
	14.01 18.25 Global Days 090
26992	Incision, bone cortex, pelvis and/or hip joint (eg, osteomyelitis or bone abscess) C 80
	25.82 25.82 Global Days 090
	AMA: 2009, Jan, 11-31; 2008, Jan, 10-25; 2007, January, 13-27

27000-27006 Tenotomy Procedures of Hip

27000	Tenotomy, adductor of hip, percutaneous (separate procedure) A2 T 50
	11.54 11.54 Global Days 090
27001	Tenotomy, adductor of hip, open A2 T 80 50
	14.41 14.41 Global Days 090
27003	Tenotomy, adductor, subcutaneous, open, with obturator neurectomy A2 T 80 50
	15.82 15.82 Global Days 090
27005	Tenotomy, hip flexor(s), open (separate procedure) C 80 50
	19.51 19.51 Global Days 090
27006	Tenotomy, abductors and/or extensor(s) of hip, open (separate procedure) T 80 50
	19.71 19.71 Global Days 090

27025-27036 Surgical Incision of Hip

CMS 100-3,160.1 Induced Lesions of Nerve Tracts

27025	Fasciotomy, hip or thigh, any type C 80 50
	24.57 24.57 Global Days 090
27027	Decompression fasciotomy(ies), pelvic (buttock) compartment(s) (eg, gluteus medius-minimus, gluteus maximus, iliopsoas, and/or tensor fascia lata muscle), unilateral T 80 50
	22.78 22.78 Global Days 090
27030	Arthrotomy, hip, with drainage (eg, infection) C 80 50
	25.36 25.36 Global Days 090
27033	Arthrotomy, hip, including exploration or removal of loose or foreign body A2 T 80 50
	26.28 26.28 Global Days 090
27035	Denervation, hip joint, intrapelvic or extrapelvic intra-articular branches of sciatic, femoral, or obturator nerves A2 T 80 50
	EXCLUDES Transection of obturator nerve (64763, 64766)
	31.84 31.84 Global Days 090
27036	Capsulectomy or capsulotomy, hip, with or without excision of heterotopic bone, with release of hip flexor muscles (ie, gluteus medius, gluteus minimus, tensor fascia latae, rectus femoris, sartorius, iliopsoas) C 80 50
	27.09 27.09 Global Days 090

27040-27041 Biopsy of Hip/Pelvis

EXCLUDES Soft tissue needle biopsy (20206)

27040	Biopsy, soft tissue of pelvis and hip area; superficial A2 T 50
	5.34 8.70 Global Days 010
27041	deep, subfascial or intramuscular A2 T 50
	18.08 18.08 Global Days 090

26/TC PC/TC Comp Only   A2-Z3 ASC Pmt   50 Bilateral   ♂ Male Only   ♀ Female Only   Facility RVU   Non-Facility RVU
AMA: CPT Asst   MED: Pub 100   A-Y OPPSI   80/80 Surg Assist Allowed / w/Doc   Lab Crosswalk   Radiology Crosswalk

Current Procedural Coding Expert – Musculoskeletal System

27043-27059 [27043, 27045, 27059] Excision Soft Tissue Tumor Hip/Pelvis

INCLUDES
- Any necessary elevation of tissue planes or dissection
- Measurement of tumor and necessary margin at greatest diameter prior to excision
- Simple and intermediate repairs
- Types of Exision:
  - Fascial or subfascial soft tissue tumors: simple and marginal resection of most often benign and intramuscular tumors found either in or below the deep fascia, not involving bone
  - Radical resection of tumor: wide resection of tumor, mostly malignant or aggressive benign, involving large margins of normal tissue and may involve tissue removal from one or more layers
  - Subcutaneous: simple and marginal resection of most often benign tumors found in the subcutaneous tissue above the deep fascia

EXCLUDES
- Complex repair
- Radical resection of cutaneous tumors (e.g., melanoma) (11600-11646)
- Significant exploration of vessels, neuroplasty, reconstruction, or complex bone repair

27043	Resequenced code. See code following 27047.
27045	Resequenced code. See code following 27048.
▲ 27047	Excision, tumor, soft tissue of pelvis and hip area, subcutaneous; less than 3 cm 10.18 12.63 Global Days 090
#● 27043	3 cm or greater 12.69 12.69 Global Days 090
▲ 27048	Excision, tumor, soft tissue of pelvis and hip area, subfascial (eg, intramuscular); less than 5 cm 16.14 16.14 Global Days 090
#● 27045	5 cm or greater 20.18 20.18 Global Days 090
▲ 27049	Radical resection of tumor (eg, malignant neoplasm), soft tissue of pelvis and hip area; less than 5 cm 36.17 36.17 Global Days 090
#● 27059	5 cm or greater 49.47 49.47 Global Days 090

27050-27071 Procedures of Bones and Joints of Hip and Pelvis

27050	Arthrotomy, with biopsy; sacroiliac joint 10.53 10.53 Global Days 090
27052	hip joint 15.30 15.30 Global Days 090
27054	Arthrotomy with synovectomy, hip joint 18.32 18.32 Global Days 090
27057	Decompression fasciotomy(ies), pelvic (buttock) compartment(s) (eg, gluteus medius-minimus, gluteus maximus, iliopsoas, and/or tensor fascia lata muscle) with debridement of nonviable muscle, unilateral 26.04 26.04 Global Days 090
27059	Resequenced code. See code following 27049.
27060	Excision; ischial bursa 11.30 11.30 Global Days 090
27062	trochanteric bursa or calcification **EXCLUDES** Arthrocentesis (20610) 12.06 12.06 Global Days 090
27065	Excision of bone cyst or benign tumor; superficial (wing of ilium, symphysis pubis, or greater trochanter of femur) with or without autograft 13.49 13.49 Global Days 090
27066	deep, with or without autograft 21.79 21.79 Global Days 090
27067	with autograft requiring separate incision 27.82 27.82 Global Days 090
27070	Partial excision (craterization, saucerization) (eg, osteomyelitis or bone abscess); superficial (eg, wing of ilium, symphysis pubis, or greater trochanter of femur) 22.88 22.88 Global Days 090
27071	deep (subfascial or intramuscular) 24.40 24.40 Global Days 090

27075-27078 Radical Resection Bone Tumor of Hip/Pelvis

INCLUDES
- Any necessary elevation of tissue planes or dissection
- Measurement of tumor and necessary margin at greatest diameter prior to excision
- Radical resection of bone tumor: resection of the tumor (may include entire bone) and wide margins of normal tissue primarily for malignant or aggressive benign tumors
- Simple and intermediate repairs

EXCLUDES
- Complex repair
- Significant exploration of vessels, neuroplasty, reconstruction, or complex bone repair

Do not report radical excision of soft tissue codes when adjacent soft tissue is removed during the bone tumor resection (27048-27049 [27043, 27045, 27059])

▲ 27075	Radical resection of tumor; wing of ilium, 1 pubic or ischial ramus or symphysis pubis 57.13 57.13 Global Days 090
▲ 27076	ilium, including acetabulum, both pubic rami, or ischium and acetabulum 66.53 66.53 Global Days 090
▲ 27077	innominate bone, total 77.44 77.44 Global Days 090
▲ 27078	ischial tuberosity and greater trochanter of femur 54.07 54.07 Global Days 090

27080 Excision of Coccyx

EXCLUDES Surgical excision of decubitus ulcers (15920, 15922, 15931-15958)

27080	Coccygectomy, primary 13.66 13.66 Global Days 090

27086-27091 Removal Foreign Body or Hip Prosthesis

27086	Removal of foreign body, pelvis or hip; subcutaneous tissue 3.89 6.22 Global Days 010
27087	deep (subfascial or intramuscular) 17.01 17.01 Global Days 090
27090	Removal of hip prosthesis; (separate procedure) 22.33 22.33 Global Days 090
27091	complicated, including total hip prosthesis, methylmethacrylate with or without insertion of spacer 43.65 43.65 Global Days 090

● New Code   ▲ Revised Code   M Maternity   A Age   Unlisted   Not Covered   # Resequenced
CCI   + Add-on   ⊘ Mod 51 Exempt   ⊚ Mod 63 Exempt   ⊙ Mod Sedation   PQRI

© 2009 Publisher (Blue Ink)   CPT only © 2009 American Medical Association. All Rights Reserved. (Black Ink)   Medicare (Red Ink)

27093-27096 Injection for Arthrogram Hip/Sacroiliac Joint

- **27093** Injection procedure for hip arthrography; without anesthesia [N1][N][50]
  - 73525
  - 1.95 4.80 Global Days 000
- **27095** with anesthesia [N1][N][50]
  - 73525
  - 2.26 5.86 Global Days 000
- **27096** Injection procedure for sacroiliac joint, arthrography and/or anesthetic/steroid [B][50]
  - INCLUDES: Verification of position
  - 73542, 77003
  - 2.04 4.92 Global Days 000
  - AMA: 2009, Jan, 11-31; 2008, Jan, 10-25; 2008, Jul, 9; 2007, January, 13-27

27097-27187 Revision/Reconstruction Hip and Pelvis

- **27097** Release or recession, hamstring, proximal [A2][T][80][50]
  - 18.20 18.20 Global Days 090
- **27098** Transfer, adductor to ischium [A2][T][80][50]
  - 16.51 16.51 Global Days 090
- **27100** Transfer external oblique muscle to greater trochanter including fascial or tendon extension (graft) [A2][T][80][50]
  - INCLUDES: Eggers procedure
  - 22.09 22.09 Global Days 090
- **27105** Transfer paraspinal muscle to hip (includes fascial or tendon extension graft) [A2][T][80][50]
  - 23.23 23.23 Global Days 090
- **27110** Transfer iliopsoas; to greater trochanter of femur [A2][T][80][50]
  - 26.06 26.06 Global Days 090
- **27111** to femoral neck [A2][T][80][50]
  - 24.14 24.14 Global Days 090
- **27120** Acetabuloplasty; (eg, Whitman, Colonna, Haygroves, or cup type) [C][80][50]
  - 35.19 35.19 Global Days 090
- **27122** resection, femoral head (eg, Girdlestone procedure) [C][80][50]
  - 29.80 29.80 Global Days 090
- **27125** Hemiarthroplasty, hip, partial (eg, femoral stem prosthesis, bipolar arthroplasty) [C][80][50][P0]
  - EXCLUDES: Total joint following hip fracture (27236)
  - 30.71 30.71 Global Days 090
  - AMA: 2009, Jan, 11-31; 2008, Jan, 10-25; 2007, January, 13-27
- **27130** Arthroplasty, acetabular and proximal femoral prosthetic replacement (total hip arthroplasty), with or without autograft or allograft [C][80][50][P0]
  - 39.32 39.32 Global Days 090
  - AMA: 2007, January, 1-5
- **27132** Conversion of previous hip surgery to total hip arthroplasty, with or without autograft or allograft [C][80][50][P0]
  - 45.83 45.83 Global Days 090
- **27134** Revision of total hip arthroplasty; both components, with or without autograft or allograft [C][80][50][P0]
  - 52.71 52.71 Global Days 090
- **27137** acetabular component only, with or without autograft or allograft [C][80][50][P0]
  - 40.34 40.34 Global Days 090
- **27138** femoral component only, with or without allograft [C][80][50][P0]
  - 41.97 41.97 Global Days 090
- **27140** Osteotomy and transfer of greater trochanter of femur (separate procedure) [C][80][50]
  - 24.17 24.17 Global Days 090
- **27146** Osteotomy, iliac, acetabular or innominate bone; [C][80][50]
  - INCLUDES: Salter osteotomy
  - 34.77 34.77 Global Days 090
  - AMA: 2009, Jan, 11-31; 2008, Jan, 10-25; 2007, January, 13-27
- **27147** with open reduction of hip [C][80][50]
  - INCLUDES: Pemberton osteotomy
  - 39.91 39.91 Global Days 090
- **27151** with femoral osteotomy [C][80][50]
  - 43.26 43.26 Global Days 090
- **27156** with femoral osteotomy and with open reduction of hip [C][80][50]
  - INCLUDES: Chiari osteotomy
  - 46.70 46.70 Global Days 090
- **27158** Osteotomy, pelvis, bilateral (eg, congenital malformation) [C][80]
  - 38.04 38.04 Global Days 090
- **27161** Osteotomy, femoral neck (separate procedure) [C][80][50]
  - 32.90 32.90 Global Days 090
- **27165** Osteotomy, intertrochanteric or subtrochanteric including internal or external fixation and/or cast [C][80][50]
  - 37.30 37.30 Global Days 090
- **27170** Bone graft, femoral head, neck, intertrochanteric or subtrochanteric area (includes obtaining bone graft) [C][80][50]
  - 32.02 32.02 Global Days 090
- **27175** Treatment of slipped femoral epiphysis; by traction, without reduction [C][80][50]
  - 17.90 17.90 Global Days 090
- **27176** by single or multiple pinning, in situ [C][80][50]
  - 24.67 24.67 Global Days 090
- **27177** Open treatment of slipped femoral epiphysis; single or multiple pinning or bone graft (includes obtaining graft) [C][80][50]
  - 30.05 30.05 Global Days 090
- **27178** closed manipulation with single or multiple pinning [C][80][50]
  - 24.67 24.67 Global Days 090
- **27179** osteoplasty of femoral neck (Heyman type procedure) [T][80][50]
  - 26.28 26.28 Global Days 090
- **27181** osteotomy and internal fixation [C][80][50]
  - 30.29 30.29 Global Days 090
- **27185** Epiphyseal arrest by epiphysiodesis or stapling, greater trochanter of femur [C][50]
  - 15.98 15.98 Global Days 090
- **27187** Prophylactic treatment (nailing, pinning, plating or wiring) with or without methylmethacrylate, femoral neck and proximal femur [C][80][50]
  - 26.78 26.78 Global Days 090

Current Procedural Coding Expert – Musculoskeletal System

27193-27269 Treatment of Fracture/Dislocation Hip/Pelvis

27193 Closed treatment of pelvic ring fracture, dislocation, diastasis or subluxation; without manipulation A2 T
12.65   12.50   Global Days 090

27194 with manipulation, requiring more than local anesthesia A2 T 80
18.52   18.52   Global Days 090

27200 Closed treatment of coccygeal fracture P3 T
4.85   4.68   Global Days 090

27202 Open treatment of coccygeal fracture A2 T 80
14.24   14.24   Global Days 090

27215 Open treatment of iliac spine(s), tuberosity avulsion, or iliac wing fracture(s), unilateral, for pelvic bone fracture patterns that do not disrupt the pelvic ring, includes internal fixation, when performed E
17.45   17.45   Global Days 090

27216 Percutaneous skeletal fixation of posterior pelvic bone fracture and/or dislocation, for fracture patterns that disrupt the pelvic ring, unilateral (includes ipsilateral ilium, sacroiliac joint and/or sacrum) E
25.91   25.91   Global Days 090

27217 Open treatment of anterior pelvic bone fracture and/or dislocation for fracture patterns that disrupt the pelvic ring, unilateral, includes internal fixation, when performed (includes pubic symphysis and/or ipsilateral superior/inferior rami) E
24.30   24.30   Global Days 090

27218 Open treatment of posterior pelvic bone fracture and/or dislocation, for fracture patterns that disrupt the pelvic ring, unilateral, includes internal fixation, when performed (includes ipsilateral ilium, sacroiliac joint and/or sacrum) E
33.85   33.85   Global Days 090

27220 Closed treatment of acetabulum (hip socket) fracture(s); without manipulation G2 T 50
13.99   14.10   Global Days 090

27222 with manipulation, with or without skeletal traction C 50
26.31   26.31   Global Days 090

27226 Open treatment of posterior or anterior acetabular wall fracture, with internal fixation C 80 50
28.70   28.70   Global Days 090

27227 Open treatment of acetabular fracture(s) involving anterior or posterior (1) column, or a fracture running transversely across the acetabulum, with internal fixation C 80 50
45.32   45.32   Global Days 090

27228 Open treatment of acetabular fracture(s) involving anterior and posterior (2) columns, includes T-fracture and both column fracture with complete articular detachment, or single column or transverse fracture with associated acetabular wall fracture, with internal fixation C 80 50
51.75   51.75   Global Days 090

27230 Closed treatment of femoral fracture, proximal end, neck; without manipulation A2 T 50 P0
12.48   12.56   Global Days 090

27232 with manipulation, with or without skeletal traction C 50 P0
20.69   20.69   Global Days 090

27235 Percutaneous skeletal fixation of femoral fracture, proximal end, neck T 50 P0
24.49   24.49   Global Days 090

27236 Open treatment of femoral fracture, proximal end, neck, internal fixation or prosthetic replacement C 80 50 P0
32.47   32.47   Global Days 090
AMA: 2009, Jan, 11-31; 2008, Jan, 10-25; 2007, January, 1-5; 2007, January, 13-27

27238 Closed treatment of intertrochanteric, peritrochanteric, or subtrochanteric femoral fracture; without manipulation A2 T 50 P0
12.18   12.18   Global Days 090

27240 with manipulation, with or without skin or skeletal traction C 50
25.85   25.85   Global Days 090

27244 Treatment of intertrochanteric, peritrochanteric, or subtrochanteric femoral fracture; with plate/screw type implant, with or without cerclage C 80 50 P0
33.39   33.39   Global Days 090

27245 with intramedullary implant, with or without interlocking screws and/or cerclage C 80 50 P0
33.42   33.42   Global Days 090

27246 Closed treatment of greater trochanteric fracture, without manipulation A2 T 50 P0
10.22   10.18   Global Days 090

27248 Open treatment of greater trochanteric fracture, includes internal fixation, when performed C 80 50 P0
20.11   20.11   Global Days 090

27250 Closed treatment of hip dislocation, traumatic; without anesthesia A2 T 50
5.11   5.11   Global Days 000

27252 requiring anesthesia A2 T 50
20.45   20.45   Global Days 090

27253 Open treatment of hip dislocation, traumatic, without internal fixation C 80 50
25.44   25.44   Global Days 090

27254 Open treatment of hip dislocation, traumatic, with acetabular wall and femoral head fracture, with or without internal or external fixation C 80 50
EXCLUDES Acetabular fracture treatment (27226-27227)
34.34   34.34   Global Days 090

27256 Treatment of spontaneous hip dislocation (developmental, including congenital or pathological), by abduction, splint or traction; without anesthesia, without manipulation G2 T 80 50
6.56   7.75   Global Days 010

27257 with manipulation, requiring anesthesia A2 T 80 50
9.00   9.00   Global Days 010

27258 Open treatment of spontaneous hip dislocation (developmental, including congenital or pathological), replacement of femoral head in acetabulum (including tenotomy, etc); C 80 50
INCLUDES Lorenz's operation
29.99   29.99   Global Days 090

27259 with femoral shaft shortening C 80 50
42.12   42.12   Global Days 090

27265 Closed treatment of post hip arthroplasty dislocation; without anesthesia A2 T 50
10.41   10.41   Global Days 090

27266 requiring regional or general anesthesia A2 T 50
15.48   15.48   Global Days 090

27267 Closed treatment of femoral fracture, proximal end, head; without manipulation G2 T 80 50
11.66   11.66   Global Days 090
AMA: 2008, Jan, 4-5

● New Code   ▲ Revised Code   M Maternity   A Age   Unlisted   Not Covered   # Resequenced
CCI   + Add-on   ⊘ Mod 51 Exempt   Mod 63 Exempt   ⊙ Mod Sedation   P0 PQRI

© 2009 Publisher *(Blue Ink)*   CPT only © 2009 American Medical Association. All Rights Reserved. *(Black Ink)*   Medicare *(Red Ink)*   75

27268	with manipulation	C 80 50
	🩸 14.31 🔪 14.31 Global Days 090	
	AMA: 2008, Jan, 4-5	
27269	Open treatment of femoral fracture, proximal end, head, includes internal fixation, when performed	C 80 50 P0
	Do not report with (27033, 27253)	
	🩸 33.85 🔪 33.85 Global Days 090	
	AMA: 2008, Jan, 4-5	

27275 Hip Manipulation with Anesthesia

27275	Manipulation, hip joint, requiring general anesthesia	A2 T
	🩸 4.66 🔪 4.66 Global Days 010	

27280-27286 Arthrodesis of Hip and Pelvis

27280	Arthrodesis, sacroiliac joint (including obtaining graft)	C 80 50
	🩸 27.81 🔪 27.81 Global Days 090	
27282	Arthrodesis, symphysis pubis (including obtaining graft)	C 80
	🩸 22.91 🔪 22.91 Global Days 090	
27284	Arthrodesis, hip joint (including obtaining graft);	C 80 50
	🩸 44.16 🔪 44.16 Global Days 090	
27286	with subtrochanteric osteotomy	C 80 50
	🩸 44.97 🔪 44.97 Global Days 090	

27290-27299 Amputations and Unlisted Procedures of Hip and Pelvis

27290	Interpelviabdominal amputation (hindquarter amputation)	C 80
	INCLUDES Pean's amputation	
	🩸 44.13 🔪 44.13 Global Days 090	
27295	Disarticulation of hip	C 80
	🩸 34.42 🔪 34.42 Global Days 090	
27299	Unlisted procedure, pelvis or hip joint	T 80 50
	🩸 0.00 🔪 0.00 Global Days YYY	
	AMA: 2009, Jan, 11-31; 2008, Jan, 10-25; 2007, January, 13-27; 2005, December, 9-11	

27301-27303 Incision for Drainage Femur or Knee

INCLUDES Superficial incision and drainage (10040-10160)

27301	Incision and drainage, deep abscess, bursa, or hematoma, thigh or knee region	A2 T 50
	🩸 13.38 🔪 17.36 Global Days 090	
27303	Incision, deep, with opening of bone cortex, femur or knee (eg, osteomyelitis or bone abscess)	C 80 50
	🩸 17.11 🔪 17.11 Global Days 090	

27305-27310 Other Incisional Procedures Femur and Knee

EXCLUDES Superficial incision and drainage (10040-10160)

27305	Fasciotomy, iliotibial (tenotomy), open	A2 T 80 50
	EXCLUDES Ober-Yount (gluteal-iliotibial) fasciotomy (27025)	
	🩸 12.70 🔪 12.70 Global Days 090	
27306	Tenotomy, percutaneous, adductor or hamstring; single tendon (separate procedure)	A2 T 80 50
	🩸 10.31 🔪 10.31 Global Days 090	

27307	multiple tendons	A2 T 80 50
	🩸 12.68 🔪 12.68 Global Days 090	
27310	Arthrotomy, knee, with exploration, drainage, or removal of foreign body (eg, infection)	A2 T 80 50
	🩸 19.60 🔪 19.60 Global Days 090	

27323-27324 Biopsy Femur or Knee

EXCLUDES Soft tissue needle biopsy (20206)

27323	Biopsy, soft tissue of thigh or knee area; superficial	A2 T 50
	🩸 4.78 🔪 7.01 Global Days 010	
27324	deep (subfascial or intramuscular)	A2 T 50
	🩸 10.36 🔪 10.36 Global Days 090	
	AMA: 2006, March, 6-9	

27325-27326 Neurectomy

27325	Neurectomy, hamstring muscle	A2 T 80 50
	🩸 14.77 🔪 14.77 Global Days 090	
27326	Neurectomy, popliteal (gastrocnemius)	A2 T 80 50
	🩸 13.57 🔪 13.57 Global Days 090	

27327-27329 [27337, 27339] Excision Soft Tissue Tumors Femur/Knee

INCLUDES Any necessary elevation of tissue planes or dissection
Measurement of tumor and necessary margin prior to excision
Resection without removal of significant normal tissue
Simple and intermediate repairs
Types of Excision:
  Fascial or subfascial soft tissue tumors: simple and marginal resection of most often benign and intramuscular tumors found either in or below the deep fascia, not involving bone
  Radical resection of tumor: wide resection of tumor, mostly malignant or aggressive benign, involving large margins of normal tissue and may involve tissue removal from one or more layers
  Subcutaneous: simple and marginal resection of most often benign tumors found in the subcutaneous tissue above the deep fascia

EXCLUDES Complex repair
Radical resection of cutaneous tumors (e.g., melanoma) (11600-11646)
Significant exploration of vessels or neuroplasty

▲ 27327	Excision, tumor, soft tissue of thigh or knee area, subcutaneous; less than 3 cm	P3 T 50
	🩸 8.46 🔪 11.82 Global Days 090	
#● 27337	3 cm or greater	
	🩸 11.32 🔪 11.32 Global Days 090	
▲ 27328	Excision, tumor, soft tissue of thigh or knee area, subfascial (eg, intramuscular); less than 5 cm	G2 T 50
	🩸 16.20 🔪 16.20 Global Days 090	
#● 27339	5 cm or greater	
	🩸 20.39 🔪 20.39 Global Days 090	
27329	Resequenced code. See code following 27360.	

27330-27360 Resection Procedures Thigh/Knee

27330	Arthrotomy, knee; with synovial biopsy only	A2 T 50
	🩸 10.58 🔪 10.58 Global Days 090	
27331	including joint exploration, biopsy, or removal of loose or foreign bodies	A2 T 80 50
	🩸 12.60 🔪 12.60 Global Days 090	

Current Procedural Coding Expert – Musculoskeletal System

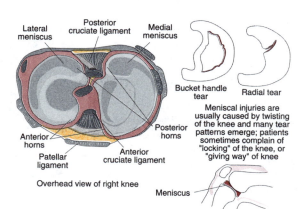

Overhead view of right knee. Meniscal injuries are usually caused by twisting of the knee and many tear patterns emerge; patients sometimes complain of "locking" of the knee, or "giving way" of knee

27332	Arthrotomy, with excision of semilunar cartilage (meniscectomy) knee; medial OR lateral 17.08 17.08 Global Days 090
27333	medial AND lateral 15.52 15.52 Global Days 090
27334	Arthrotomy, with synovectomy, knee; anterior OR posterior 18.27 18.27 Global Days 090
27335	anterior AND posterior including popliteal area 20.53 20.53 Global Days 090
27337	Resequenced code. See code following 27327.
27339	Resequenced code. See code following 27328.
27340	Excision, prepatellar bursa 9.73 9.73 Global Days 090
27345	Excision of synovial cyst of popliteal space (eg, Baker's cyst) 12.82 12.82 Global Days 090
27347	Excision of lesion of meniscus or capsule (eg, cyst, ganglion), knee 13.99 13.99 Global Days 090
27350	Patellectomy or hemipatellectomy 17.41 17.41 Global Days 090
27355	Excision or curettage of bone cyst or benign tumor of femur; 16.08 16.08 Global Days 090
27356	with allograft 19.77 19.77 Global Days 090
27357	with autograft (includes obtaining graft) 21.77 21.77 Global Days 090 AMA: 2009, Jan, 11-31; 2008, Jan, 10-25; 2007, January, 13-27
+27358	with internal fixation (List in addition to code for primary procedure) Code first 27355-27357 7.72 7.72 Global Days ZZZ
27360	Partial excision (craterization, saucerization, or diaphysectomy) bone, femur, proximal tibia and/or fibula (eg, osteomyelitis or bone abscess) 22.77 22.77 Global Days 090

27329-27365 [27329] Radical Resection Bone Tumor Knee/Thigh

INCLUDES
- Any necessary elevation of tissue planes or dissection
- Measurement of tumor and necessary margin at greatest diameter prior to excision
- Radical resection soft tissue tumor: wide resection of tumor, mostly malignant or aggressive benign, involving large margins of normal tissue and may involve tissue removal from one or more layers
- Simple and intermediate repairs

EXCLUDES
- Complex repair
- Significant exploration of vessels, neuroplasty, reconstruction, or complex bone repair

Do not report radical excision of soft tissue codes when adjacent soft tissue is removed during the bone tumor resection (27327-27360 [27329, 27337, 27339])

#▲ 27329	Radical resection of tumor (eg, malignant neoplasm), soft tissue of thigh or knee area; less than 5 cm 28.39 28.39 Global Days 090
● 27364	5 cm or greater 42.59 42.59 Global Days 090
▲ 27365	Radical resection of tumor, femur or knee EXCLUDES Soft tissue tumor excision thigh or knee area ([27329], 27364) 54.56 54.56 Global Days 090

27370 Injection for Arthrogram of Knee

27370	Injection procedure for knee arthrography 73580 1.48 4.31 Global Days 000

27372 Foreign Body Removal Femur or Knee

27372	Removal of foreign body, deep, thigh region or knee area EXCLUDES Arthroscopic procedures (29870-29887) Knee prosthesis (27488) 10.80 15.57 Global Days 090

27380-27499 Repair/Reconstruction of Femur or Knee

27380	Suture of infrapatellar tendon; primary 15.73 15.73 Global Days 090
27381	secondary reconstruction, including fascial or tendon graft 21.39 21.39 Global Days 090
27385	Suture of quadriceps or hamstring muscle rupture; primary 16.81 16.81 Global Days 090
27386	secondary reconstruction, including fascial or tendon graft 22.23 22.23 Global Days 090
27390	Tenotomy, open, hamstring, knee to hip; single tendon 11.81 11.81 Global Days 090
27391	multiple tendons, 1 leg 15.29 15.29 Global Days 090
27392	multiple tendons, bilateral 19.00 19.00 Global Days 090
27393	Lengthening of hamstring tendon; single tendon 13.52 13.52 Global Days 090

● New Code   ▲ Revised Code   M Maternity   A Age   Unlisted   Not Covered   # Resequenced
CCI   + Add-on   Mod 51 Exempt   Mod 63 Exempt   Mod Sedation   PQRI

© 2009 Publisher (Blue Ink)   CPT only © 2009 American Medical Association. All Rights Reserved. (Black Ink)   Medicare (Red Ink)

27394	multiple tendons, 1 leg
	17.46 17.46 Global Days 090
27395	multiple tendons, bilateral
	23.56 23.56 Global Days 090
27396	Transplant or transfer (with muscle redirection or rerouting), thigh (eg, extensor to flexor); single tendon
	16.37 16.37 Global Days 090
27397	multiple tendons
	24.55 24.55 Global Days 090
27400	Transfer, tendon or muscle, hamstrings to femur (eg, Egger's type procedure)
	18.51 18.51 Global Days 090
27403	Arthrotomy with meniscus repair, knee
	EXCLUDES Arthroscopic treatment (29882)
	17.13 17.13 Global Days 090
27405	Repair, primary, torn ligament and/or capsule, knee; collateral
	18.08 18.08 Global Days 090
27407	cruciate
	EXCLUDES Reconstruction (27427)
	21.18 21.18 Global Days 090
27409	collateral and cruciate ligaments
	EXCLUDES Reconstruction (27427-27429)
	25.96 25.96 Global Days 090
27412	Autologous chondrocyte implantation, knee
	INCLUDES Knee arthrotomy (27331) Manipulation of knee joint (27570) Tissue graft (20926)
	EXCLUDES Obtaining chondrocytes (29870)
	44.89 44.89 Global Days 090
27415	Osteochondral allograft, knee, open
	EXCLUDES Arthroscopic procedure (29867)
	Do not report with (27416)
	37.13 37.13 Global Days 090
	AMA: 2009, Jan, 11-31
27416	Osteochondral autograft(s), knee, open (eg, mosaicplasty) (includes harvesting of autograft[s])
	EXCLUDES Surgical arthroscopy of the knee with osteochondral autograft(s) (29866)
	Do not report with the following procedures in the same compartment (29874, 29877, 29879, 29885-29887)
	Do not report with the following procedures performed at the same surgical session (27415, 29870-29871, 29875, 29884)
	26.44 26.44 Global Days 090
	AMA: 2008, Jan, 4-5
27418	Anterior tibial tubercleplasty (eg, Maquet type procedure)
	22.34 22.34 Global Days 090

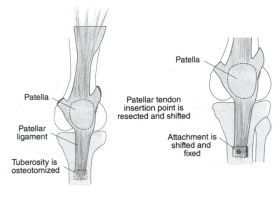

27420	Reconstruction of dislocating patella; (eg, Hauser type procedure)
	20.01 20.01 Global Days 090
27422	with extensor realignment and/or muscle advancement or release (eg, Campbell, Goldwaite type procedure)
	19.97 19.97 Global Days 090
27424	with patellectomy
	20.01 20.01 Global Days 090

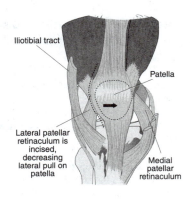

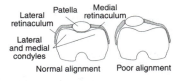

27425	Lateral retinacular release, open
	EXCLUDES Arthroscopic release (29873)
	11.76 11.76 Global Days 090
	AMA: 2009, Jan, 11-31; 2008, Jan, 10-25; 2007, January, 13-27
27427	Ligamentous reconstruction (augmentation), knee; extra-articular
	EXCLUDES Primary repair of ligament(s) (27405, 27407, 27409)
	19.28 19.28 Global Days 090
27428	intra-articular (open)
	EXCLUDES Primary repair of ligament(s) (27405, 27407, 27409)
	29.93 29.93 Global Days 090

Current Procedural Coding Expert – Musculoskeletal System 27502

27429	intra-articular (open) and extra-articular [A2][T][80][50]
	EXCLUDES Primary repair of ligament(s) (27405, 27407, 27409)
	33.71 33.71 Global Days 090
27430	Quadricepsplasty (eg, Bennett or Thompson type) [A2][T][80][50]
	19.87 19.87 Global Days 090
27435	Capsulotomy, posterior capsular release, knee [A2][T][80][50]
	21.68 21.68 Global Days 090
27437	Arthroplasty, patella; without prosthesis [A2][T][50]
	17.63 17.63 Global Days 090
27438	with prosthesis [A2][T][80][50]
	22.70 22.70 Global Days 090
27440	Arthroplasty, knee, tibial plateau; [G2][T][80][50][PQ]
	21.38 21.38 Global Days 090
27441	with debridement and partial synovectomy [A2][T][80][50][PQ]
	22.11 22.11 Global Days 090
27442	Arthroplasty, femoral condyles or tibial plateau(s), knee; [A2][T][80][50][PQ]
	23.52 23.52 Global Days 090
27443	with debridement and partial synovectomy [A2][T][80][50][PQ]
	21.90 21.90 Global Days 090
27445	Arthroplasty, knee, hinge prosthesis (eg, Walldius type) [C][80][50][PQ]
	EXCLUDES Removal knee prosthesis (27488)
	Revision knee arthroplasty (27487)
	34.10 34.10 Global Days 090
27446	Arthroplasty, knee, condyle and plateau; medial OR lateral compartment [J8][T][80][50][PQ]
	EXCLUDES Removal knee prosthesis (27488)
	Revision knee arthroplasty (27487)
	Code also (C1776)
	30.05 30.05 Global Days 090
27447	medial AND lateral compartments with or without patella resurfacing (total knee arthroplasty) [C][80][50][PQ]
	EXCLUDES Removal knee prosthesis (27488)
	Revision knee arthroplasty (27487)
	41.99 41.99 Global Days 090
	AMA: 2007, January, 1-5; 2005, March, 11-15
27448	Osteotomy, femur, shaft or supracondylar; without fixation [C][80][50]
	22.01 22.01 Global Days 090
27450	with fixation [C][80][50]
	27.47 27.47 Global Days 090
27454	Osteotomy, multiple, with realignment on intramedullary rod, femoral shaft (eg, Sofield type procedure) [C][80][50]
	35.17 35.17 Global Days 090
27455	Osteotomy, proximal tibia, including fibular excision or osteotomy (includes correction of genu varus [bowleg] or genu valgus [knock-knee]); before epiphyseal closure [C][80][50]
	25.34 25.34 Global Days 090
27457	after epiphyseal closure [C][80][50]
	26.01 26.01 Global Days 090
27465	Osteoplasty, femur; shortening (excluding 64876) [C][80][50]
	33.95 33.95 Global Days 090
27466	lengthening [C][80][50]
	32.12 32.12 Global Days 090
27468	combined, lengthening and shortening with femoral segment transfer [C][80][50]
	36.38 36.38 Global Days 090
27470	Repair, nonunion or malunion, femur, distal to head and neck; without graft (eg, compression technique) [C][80][50]
	31.92 31.92 Global Days 090
27472	with iliac or other autogenous bone graft (includes obtaining graft) [C][80][50]
	34.36 34.36 Global Days 090
27475	Arrest, epiphyseal, any method (eg, epiphysiodesis); distal femur [G2][T][50]
	17.64 17.64 Global Days 090
27477	tibia and fibula, proximal [C][50]
	19.62 19.62 Global Days 090
27479	combined distal femur, proximal tibia and fibula [G2][T][80][50]
	20.81 20.81 Global Days 090
27485	Arrest, hemiepiphyseal, distal femur or proximal tibia or fibula (eg, genu varus or valgus) [C][50]
	17.90 17.90 Global Days 090
27486	Revision of total knee arthroplasty, with or without allograft; 1 component [C][80][50]
	38.37 38.37 Global Days 090
27487	femoral and entire tibial component [C][80][50]
	48.17 48.17 Global Days 090
27488	Removal of prosthesis, including total knee prosthesis, methylmethacrylate with or without insertion of spacer, knee [C][80][50]
	32.61 32.61 Global Days 090
27495	Prophylactic treatment (nailing, pinning, plating, or wiring) with or without methylmethacrylate, femur [C][80][50]
	30.59 30.59 Global Days 090
27496	Decompression fasciotomy, thigh and/or knee, 1 compartment (flexor or extensor or adductor); [A2][T][50]
	14.35 14.35 Global Days 090
27497	with debridement of nonviable muscle and/or nerve [A2][T][80][50]
	15.50 15.50 Global Days 090
27498	Decompression fasciotomy, thigh and/or knee, multiple compartments; [A2][T][80][50]
	17.41 17.41 Global Days 090
27499	with debridement of nonviable muscle and/or nerve [A2][T][80][50]
	18.67 18.67 Global Days 090

27500-27566 Treatment of Fracture/Dislocation of Femur/Knee

27500	Closed treatment of femoral shaft fracture, without manipulation [A2][T][50]
	12.78 13.68 Global Days 090
27501	Closed treatment of supracondylar or transcondylar femoral fracture with or without intercondylar extension, without manipulation [A2][T][80][50]
	13.26 13.36 Global Days 090
27502	Closed treatment of femoral shaft fracture, with manipulation, with or without skin or skeletal traction [A2][T][50]
	21.12 21.12 Global Days 090

● New Code   ▲ Revised Code   Ⓜ Maternity   Ⓐ Age   Unlisted   Not Covered   # Resequenced

CCI   + Add-on   ⊘ Mod 51 Exempt   @ Mod 63 Exempt   ⊙ Mod Sedation   PQRI

© 2009 Publisher (*Blue Ink*)   CPT only © 2009 American Medical Association. All Rights Reserved. (Black Ink)   Medicare (Red Ink)   79

Code	Description	Facility RVU	Non-Facility RVU	Global Days
27503	Closed treatment of supracondylar or transcondylar femoral fracture with or without intercondylar extension, with manipulation, with or without skin or skeletal traction	21.57	21.57	090
27506	Open treatment of femoral shaft fracture, with or without external fixation, with insertion of intramedullary implant, with or without cerclage and/or locking screws	36.29	36.29	090
	AMA: 2009, Jun, 7-8			
27507	Open treatment of femoral shaft fracture with plate/screws, with or without cerclage	26.46	26.46	090
27508	Closed treatment of femoral fracture, distal end, medial or lateral condyle, without manipulation	13.11	13.83	090
27509	Percutaneous skeletal fixation of femoral fracture, distal end, medial or lateral condyle, or supracondylar or transcondylar, with or without intercondylar extension, or distal femoral epiphyseal separation	17.11	17.11	090
27510	Closed treatment of femoral fracture, distal end, medial or lateral condyle, with manipulation	18.63	18.63	090
27511	Open treatment of femoral supracondylar or transcondylar fracture without intercondylar extension, includes internal fixation, when performed	27.17	27.17	090
27513	Open treatment of femoral supracondylar or transcondylar fracture with intercondylar extension, includes internal fixation, when performed	33.93	33.93	090
27514	Open treatment of femoral fracture, distal end, medial or lateral condyle, includes internal fixation, when performed	26.33	26.33	090
27516	Closed treatment of distal femoral epiphyseal separation; without manipulation	12.49	13.21	090
27517	with manipulation, with or without skin or skeletal traction	18.26	18.26	090
27519	Open treatment of distal femoral epiphyseal separation, includes internal fixation, when performed	24.14	24.14	090
27520	Closed treatment of patellar fracture, without manipulation	7.63	8.29	090
27524	Open treatment of patellar fracture, with internal fixation and/or partial or complete patellectomy and soft tissue repair	20.21	20.21	090
27530	Closed treatment of tibial fracture, proximal (plateau); without manipulation	9.71	10.34	090
	EXCLUDES Arthroscopic repair (29855-29856)			
27532	with or without manipulation, with skeletal traction	15.37	16.25	090
	EXCLUDES Arthroscopic repair (29855-29856)			
27535	Open treatment of tibial fracture, proximal (plateau); unicondylar, includes internal fixation, when performed	24.40	24.40	090
	EXCLUDES Arthroscopic repair (29855-29856)			
27536	bicondylar, with or without internal fixation	32.27	32.27	090
	EXCLUDES Arthroscopic repair (29855-29856)			
27538	Closed treatment of intercondylar spine(s) and/or tuberosity fracture(s) of knee, with or without manipulation	11.56	12.25	090
	EXCLUDES Arthroscopic repair (29850-29851)			
27540	Open treatment of intercondylar spine(s) and/or tuberosity fracture(s) of the knee, includes internal fixation, when performed	21.85	21.85	090
27550	Closed treatment of knee dislocation; without anesthesia	12.14	12.97	090
27552	requiring anesthesia	16.65	16.65	090
27556	Open treatment of knee dislocation, includes internal fixation, when performed; without primary ligamentous repair or augmentation/reconstruction	23.74	23.74	090
27557	with primary ligamentous repair	28.47	28.47	090
27558	with primary ligamentous repair, with augmentation/reconstruction	32.53	32.53	090
27560	Closed treatment of patellar dislocation; without anesthesia	9.23	9.85	090
	EXCLUDES Recurrent dislocation (27420-27424)			
27562	requiring anesthesia	12.74	12.74	090
	EXCLUDES Recurrent dislocation (27420-27424)			
27566	Open treatment of patellar dislocation, with or without partial or total patellectomy	24.05	24.05	090
	EXCLUDES Recurrent dislocation (27420-27424)			

27570 Knee Manipulation with Anesthesia

Code	Description	Facility RVU	Non-Facility RVU	Global Days
27570	Manipulation of knee joint under general anesthesia (includes application of traction or other fixation devices)	3.96	3.96	010

27580 Knee Arthrodesis

Code	Description	Facility RVU	Non-Facility RVU	Global Days
27580	Arthrodesis, knee, any technique	39.05	39.05	090
	INCLUDES Albert's operation			

27590-27599 Amputations at Femur or Knee

Code	Description	Facility RVU	Non-Facility RVU	Global Days
27590	Amputation, thigh, through femur, any level;	22.92	22.92	090
27591	immediate fitting technique including first cast	24.76	24.76	090

Current Procedural Coding Expert – Musculoskeletal System

27592 open, circular (guillotine) C 80 50
    19.24   19.24 Global Days 090

27594 secondary closure or scar revision A2 T 50
    14.03   14.03 Global Days 090

27596 re-amputation C 50
    20.21   20.21 Global Days 090

27598 Disarticulation at knee C 80 50
    INCLUDES Batch-Spittler-McFaddin operation
                Callandar knee disarticulation
                Gritti amputation
    20.51   20.51 Global Days 090

27599 Unlisted procedure, femur or knee T 80 50
    0.00   0.00 Global Days YYY
    AMA: 2009, Jan, 11-31; 2008, Jan, 4-5; 2008, Mar, 14-15

27600-27602 Decompression Fasciotomy of Leg

EXCLUDES Fasciotomy with debridement (27892-27894)
    Simple incision and drainage (10140-10160)

27600 Decompression fasciotomy, leg; anterior and/or lateral compartments only A2 T 50
    11.37   11.37 Global Days 090

27601 posterior compartment(s) only A2 T 50
    12.00   12.00 Global Days 090

27602 anterior and/or lateral, and posterior compartment(s) A2 T 80 50
    14.05   14.05 Global Days 090

27603-27612 Incisional Procedures Lower Leg and Ankle

27603 Incision and drainage, leg or ankle; deep abscess or hematoma A2 T 50
    10.59   14.07 Global Days 090

27604 infected bursa A2 T 80 50
    9.10   12.47 Global Days 090

27605 Tenotomy, percutaneous, Achilles tendon (separate procedure); local anesthesia A2 T 80 50
    5.07   8.86 Global Days 010

27606 general anesthesia A2 T 50
    7.77   7.77 Global Days 010

27607 Incision (eg, osteomyelitis or bone abscess), leg or ankle A2 T 50
    16.53   16.53 Global Days 090

27610 Arthrotomy, ankle, including exploration, drainage, or removal of foreign body A2 T 50
    17.58   17.58 Global Days 090

27612 Arthrotomy, posterior capsular release, ankle, with or without Achilles tendon lengthening A2 T 80 50
    EXCLUDES Lengthening or shortening tendon (27685)
    15.01   15.01 Global Days 090

27613-27614 Biopsy Lower Leg and Ankle

EXCLUDES Needle biopsy (20206)

27613 Biopsy, soft tissue of leg or ankle area; superficial P3 T 50
    4.40   6.53 Global Days 010

27614 deep (subfascial or intramuscular) A2 T 50
    11.05   15.21 Global Days 090

27615-27634 [27632, 27634] Excision Soft Tissue Tumor Lower Leg/Ankle

INCLUDES
Any necessary elevation of tissue planes or dissection
Measurement of tumor and necessary margin prior to excision
Resection without removal of significant normal tissue
Simple and intermediate repairs
Types of Excision:
    Fascial or subfascial soft tissue tumors: simple and marginal resection of most often benign and intramuscular tumors found either in or below the deep fascia, not involving bone
    Radical resection soft tissue tumor: wide resection of tumor, mostly malignant or aggressive benign, involving large margins of normal tissue and may involve tissue removal from one or more layers
    Subcutaneous: simple and marginal resection of most often benign tumors found in the subcutaneous tissue above the deep fascia

EXCLUDES Complex repair
Radical resection of cutaneous tumors (e.g., melanoma) (11600-11646)
Significant exploration of vessels or neuroplasty

▲ 27615 Radical resection of tumor (eg, malignant neoplasm), soft tissue of leg or ankle area; less than 5 cm 62 T 80 50
    27.91   27.91 Global Days 090

● 27616 5 cm or greater 62 T 80 50
    34.76   34.76 Global Days 090

▲ 27618 Excision, tumor, soft tissue of leg or ankle area, subcutaneous; less than 3 cm P3 T 50
    8.42   11.70 Global Days 090

#● 27632 3 cm or greater 62 T 80 50
    11.18   11.18 Global Days 090

▲ 27619 Excision, tumor, soft tissue of leg or ankle area, subfascial (eg, intramuscular); less than 5 cm 62 T 50
    13.28   13.28 Global Days 090

#● 27634 5 cm or greater 62 T 80 50
    18.22   18.22 Global Days 090

27620-27641 Bone and Joint Procedures Ankle/Leg

27620 Arthrotomy, ankle, with joint exploration, with or without biopsy, with or without removal of loose or foreign body A2 T 80 50
    12.31   12.31 Global Days 090

27625 Arthrotomy, with synovectomy, ankle; A2 T 80 50
    15.53   15.53 Global Days 090

27626 including tenosynovectomy A2 T 80 50
    17.06   17.06 Global Days 090

27630 Excision of lesion of tendon sheath or capsule (eg, cyst or ganglion), leg and/or ankle A2 T 50
    9.81   14.42 Global Days 090

27632 *Resequenced code. See code following 27618.*

27634 *Resequenced code. See code following 27619.*

27635 Excision or curettage of bone cyst or benign tumor, tibia or fibula; A2 T 50
    15.85   15.85 Global Days 090

27637 with autograft (includes obtaining graft) A2 T 80 50
    20.40   20.40 Global Days 090

27638 with allograft A2 T 80 50
    20.99   20.99 Global Days 090

● New Code   ▲ Revised Code   M Maternity   A Age   Unlisted   Not Covered   # Resequenced
CCI   + Add-on   Mod 51 Exempt   Mod 63 Exempt   Mod Sedation   PQ PQRI
© 2009 Publisher *(Blue Ink)*   CPT only © 2009 American Medical Association. All Rights Reserved. *(Black Ink)*   Medicare *(Red Ink)*

27640

Code	Description	RVU (Facility)	RVU (Non-Facility)	Global Days
▲ 27640	Partial excision (craterization, saucerization, or diaphysectomy), bone (eg, osteomyelitis); tibia	22.68	22.68	090
	EXCLUDES Excision of exostosis (27635)			
▲ 27641	fibula	18.22	18.22	090
	EXCLUDES Excision of exostosis (27635)			

27645-27647 Radical Resection Bone Tumor Ankle/Leg

INCLUDES
- Any necessary elevation of tissue planes or dissection
- Measurement of tumor and necessary margin at greatest diameter prior to excision
- Radical resection of bone tumor: resection of the tumor (may include entire bone) and wide margins of normal tissue primarily for malignant or aggressive benign tumors
- Simple and intermediate repairs

EXCLUDES
- Complex repair
- Significant exploration of vessels, neuroplasty, reconstruction, or complex bone repair

Do not report radical excision of soft tissue codes when adjacent soft tissue is removed during the bone tumor resection (27615-27619 [27632, 27634])

Code	Description	Facility RVU	Non-Facility RVU	Global Days
▲ 27645	Radical resection of tumor; tibia	46.74	46.74	090
▲ 27646	fibula	40.56	40.56	090
▲ 27647	talus or calcaneus	29.59	29.59	090

27648 Injection for Ankle Arthrogram

EXCLUDES Arthroscopy (29894-29898)

27648	Injection procedure for ankle arthrography	1.46	4.20	000
	73615			

27650-27745 Repair/Reconstruction Lower Leg/Ankle

Code	Description	Facility RVU	Non-Facility RVU	Global Days
27650	Repair, primary, open or percutaneous, ruptured Achilles tendon;	17.97	17.97	090
27652	with graft (includes obtaining graft)	18.84	18.84	090
27654	Repair, secondary, Achilles tendon, with or without graft	19.14	19.14	090
27656	Repair, fascial defect of leg	10.42	16.00	090
27658	Repair, flexor tendon, leg; primary, without graft, each tendon	10.18	10.18	090
27659	secondary, with or without graft, each tendon	12.93	12.93	090
27664	Repair, extensor tendon, leg; primary, without graft, each tendon	9.69	9.69	090
27665	secondary, with or without graft, each tendon	11.19	11.19	090
27675	Repair, dislocating peroneal tendons; without fibular osteotomy	13.27	13.27	090
27676	with fibular osteotomy	16.59	16.59	090
27680	Tenolysis, flexor or extensor tendon, leg and/or ankle; single, each tendon	11.49	11.49	090
27681	multiple tendons (through separate incision(s))	14.49	14.49	090
27685	Lengthening or shortening of tendon, leg or ankle; single tendon (separate procedure)	12.52	17.25	090
27686	multiple tendons (through same incision), each	14.80	14.80	090
27687	Gastrocnemius recession (eg, Strayer procedure)	12.32	12.32	090
27690	Transfer or transplant of single tendon (with muscle redirection or rerouting); superficial (eg, anterior tibial extensors into midfoot)	17.18	17.18	090
	INCLUDES Toe extensors considered a single tendon with transplant into midfoot			
27691	deep (eg, anterior tibial or posterior tibial through interosseous space, flexor digitorum longus, flexor hallucis longus, or peroneal tendon to midfoot or hindfoot)	20.36	20.36	090
	INCLUDES Barr procedure; Toe extensors considered a single tendon with transplant into midfoot			
+ 27692	each additional tendon (List separately in addition to code for primary procedure)	2.97	2.97	ZZZ
	INCLUDES Toe extensors considered a single tendon with transplant into midfoot			
	Code first 27690-27691			

Lateral view of right ankle showing components of the collateral ligament

The components of the collateral ligament are often affected in sprained ankle type of injuries. Code 27695 reports first time repair of a disrupted collateral ligament. Report 27696 for repair to more than one collateral ligament

(Tibia, Fibula, Anterior talofibular, Posterior talofibular, Calcaneus, Calcaneofibular)

Code	Description	Facility RVU	Non-Facility RVU	Global Days
27695	Repair, primary, disrupted ligament, ankle; collateral	13.07	13.07	090
	AMA: 2009, Mar, 10-11			
27696	both collateral ligaments	15.04	15.04	090
27698	Repair, secondary, disrupted ligament, ankle, collateral (eg, Watson-Jones procedure)	17.45	17.45	090
27700	Arthroplasty, ankle;	16.37	16.37	090
27702	with implant (total ankle)	26.51	26.51	090

Current Procedural Coding Expert – Musculoskeletal System

27703	revision, total ankle [C][80][50][P0]
	30.98 30.98 Global Days 090
27704	Removal of ankle implant [A2][T][50][P0]
	15.42 15.42 Global Days 090
27705	Osteotomy; tibia [A2][T][80][50]
	EXCLUDES Genu varus or genu valgus repair (27455-27457)
	20.61 20.61 Global Days 090
27707	fibula [A2][T][50]
	EXCLUDES Genu varus or genu valgus repair (27455-27457)
	10.69 10.69 Global Days 090
27709	tibia and fibula [A2][T][80][50]
	EXCLUDES Genu varus or genu valgus repair (27455-27457)
	31.81 31.81 Global Days 090
27712	multiple, with realignment on intramedullary rod (eg, Sofield type procedure) [C][80][50]
	EXCLUDES Genu varus or genu valgus repair (27455-27457)
	29.80 29.80 Global Days 090
27715	Osteoplasty, tibia and fibula, lengthening or shortening [C][80][50]
	INCLUDES Anderson tibial lengthening
	28.88 28.88 Global Days 090
27720	Repair of nonunion or malunion, tibia; without graft, (eg, compression technique) [G2][T][80][50]
	23.67 23.67 Global Days 090
27722	with sliding graft [T][80][50]
	23.90 23.90 Global Days 090
27724	with iliac or other autograft (includes obtaining graft) [C][80][50]
	34.60 34.60 Global Days 090
27725	by synostosis, with fibula, any method [C][80][50]
	32.86 32.86 Global Days 090
27726	Repair of fibula nonunion and/or malunion with internal fixation [G2][T][50]
	Do not report with (27707)
	26.43 26.43 Global Days 090
	AMA: 2008, Jan, 4-5
27727	Repair of congenital pseudarthrosis, tibia [C][80][50]
	27.93 27.93 Global Days 090
27730	Arrest, epiphyseal (epiphysiodesis), open; distal tibia [A2][T][50]
	15.58 15.58 Global Days 090
27732	distal fibula [A2][T][50]
	11.78 11.78 Global Days 090
27734	distal tibia and fibula [A2][T][50]
	14.55 14.55 Global Days 090
27740	Arrest, epiphyseal (epiphysiodesis), any method, combined, proximal and distal tibia and fibula; [A2][T][80][50]
	EXCLUDES Epiphyseal arrest of proximal tibia and fibula (27477)
	18.91 18.91 Global Days 090
27742	and distal femur [A2][T][80][50]
	EXCLUDES Epiphyseal arrest of proximal tibia and fibula (27477)
	20.82 20.82 Global Days 090
27745	Prophylactic treatment (nailing, pinning, plating or wiring) with or without methylmethacrylate, tibia [T][80][50]
	20.37 20.37 Global Days 090

27750-27848 Treatment of Fracture/Dislocation Lower Leg/Ankle

27750	Closed treatment of tibial shaft fracture (with or without fibular fracture); without manipulation [A2][T][50]
	8.26 8.92 Global Days 090
	AMA: 2009, Jan, 11-31; 2008, Jan, 10-25; 2007, January, 13-27
27752	with manipulation, with or without skeletal traction [A2][T][50]
	13.18 14.14 Global Days 090
27756	Percutaneous skeletal fixation of tibial shaft fracture (with or without fibular fracture) (eg, pins or screws) [A2][T][80][50][P0]
	15.32 15.32 Global Days 090
27758	Open treatment of tibial shaft fracture (with or without fibular fracture), with plate/screws, with or without cerclage [A2][T][80][50][P0]
	24.02 24.02 Global Days 090
	AMA: 2009, Jan, 11-31; 2008, Jan, 10-25; 2007, January, 13-27
27759	Treatment of tibial shaft fracture (with or without fibular fracture) by intramedullary implant, with or without interlocking screws and/or cerclage [A2][T][80][50][P0]
	27.02 27.02 Global Days 090
27760	Closed treatment of medial malleolus fracture; without manipulation [A2][T][50]
	7.93 8.62 Global Days 090
27762	with manipulation, with or without skin or skeletal traction [A2][T][50]
	11.63 12.57 Global Days 090
27766	Open treatment of medial malleolus fracture, includes internal fixation, when performed [A2][T][50][P0]
	16.25 16.25 Global Days 090
27767	Closed treatment of posterior malleolus fracture; without manipulation [G2][T][50]
	Do not report with (27808-27823)
	7.32 7.28 Global Days 090
27768	with manipulation [G2][T][50]
	Do not report with (27808-27823)
	11.52 11.52 Global Days 090
27769	Open treatment of posterior malleolus fracture, includes internal fixation, when performed [G2][T][50][P0]
	Do not report with (27808-27823)
	19.74 19.74 Global Days 090
27780	Closed treatment of proximal fibula or shaft fracture; without manipulation [A2][T][50]
	7.18 7.82 Global Days 090
27781	with manipulation [A2][T][50]
	10.40 11.11 Global Days 090
27784	Open treatment of proximal fibula or shaft fracture, includes internal fixation, when performed [A2][T][50]
	19.22 19.22 Global Days 090
	AMA: 2009, Jan, 11-31; 2008, Jan, 10-25; 2007, January, 13-27
27786	Closed treatment of distal fibular fracture (lateral malleolus); without manipulation [A2][T][50]
	7.47 8.18 Global Days 090
27788	with manipulation [A2][T][50]
	10.19 11.03 Global Days 090

● New Code ▲ Revised Code M Maternity A Age Unlisted Not Covered # Resequenced
CCI + Add-on ⊘ Mod 51 Exempt ⊚ Mod 63 Exempt ⊙ Mod Sedation PQ PQRI

Code	Description	RVU (Facility)	RVU (Non-Facility)	Global Days
27792	Open treatment of distal fibular fracture (lateral malleolus), includes internal fixation, when performed	19.14	19.14	090
	EXCLUDES: Repair of tibia and fibula shaft fracture (27750-27759)			
	AMA: 2009, Mar, 10-11			
27808	Closed treatment of bimalleolar ankle fracture (eg, lateral and medial malleoli, or lateral and posterior malleoli or medial and posterior malleoli); without manipulation	7.77	8.56	090
27810	with manipulation	11.35	12.32	090
27814	Open treatment of bimalleolar ankle fracture (eg, lateral and medial malleoli, or lateral and posterior malleoli, or medial and posterior malleoli), includes internal fixation, when performed	20.81	20.81	090
27816	Closed treatment of trimalleolar ankle fracture; without manipulation	7.43	8.19	090
27818	with manipulation	11.55	12.67	090
27822	Open treatment of trimalleolar ankle fracture, includes internal fixation, when performed, medial and/or lateral malleolus; without fixation of posterior lip	22.58	22.58	090
27823	with fixation of posterior lip	25.75	25.75	090
27824	Closed treatment of fracture of weight bearing articular portion of distal tibia (eg, pilon or tibial plafond), with or without anesthesia; without manipulation	7.91	8.12	090
27825	with skeletal traction and/or requiring manipulation	13.31	14.48	090
27826	Open treatment of fracture of weight bearing articular surface/portion of distal tibia (eg, pilon or tibial plafond), with internal fixation, when performed; of fibula only	22.38	22.38	090
27827	of tibia only	29.08	29.08	090
27828	of both tibia and fibula	35.07	35.07	090
27829	Open treatment of distal tibiofibular joint (syndesmosis) disruption, includes internal fixation, when performed	18.34	18.34	090
	AMA: 2009, Mar, 10-11			
27830	Closed treatment of proximal tibiofibular joint dislocation; without anesthesia	9.24	9.85	090
27831	requiring anesthesia	10.49	10.49	090
27832	Open treatment of proximal tibiofibular joint dislocation, includes internal fixation, when performed, or with excision of proximal fibula	20.18	20.18	090
27840	Closed treatment of ankle dislocation; without anesthesia	9.56	9.56	090
27842	requiring anesthesia, with or without percutaneous skeletal fixation	13.08	13.08	090
27846	Open treatment of ankle dislocation, with or without percutaneous skeletal fixation; without repair or internal fixation	19.81	19.81	090
	EXCLUDES: Arthroscopy (29894-29898)			
27848	with repair or internal or external fixation	22.20	22.20	090
	EXCLUDES: Arthroscopy (29894-29898)			

27860 Ankle Manipulation with Anesthesia

Code	Description	RVU (Facility)	RVU (Non-Facility)	Global Days
27860	Manipulation of ankle under general anesthesia (includes application of traction or other fixation apparatus)	4.66	4.66	010

27870-27871 Arthrodesis Lower Leg/Ankle

Code	Description	RVU (Facility)	RVU (Non-Facility)	Global Days
27870	Arthrodesis, ankle, open	28.30	28.30	090
	EXCLUDES: Arthroscopic arthrodesis of ankle (29899)			
27871	Arthrodesis, tibiofibular joint, proximal or distal	18.70	18.70	090

27880-27889 Amputations of Lower Leg/Ankle

Code	Description	RVU (Facility)	RVU (Non-Facility)	Global Days
27880	Amputation, leg, through tibia and fibula;	25.96	25.96	090
	INCLUDES: Burgess amputation			
27881	with immediate fitting technique including application of first cast	24.33	24.33	090
27882	open, circular (guillotine)	17.14	17.14	090
27884	secondary closure or scar revision	16.10	16.10	090
27886	re-amputation	18.41	18.41	090
27888	Amputation, ankle, through malleoli of tibia and fibula (eg, Syme, Pirogoff type procedures), with plastic closure and resection of nerves	18.91	18.91	090
27889	Ankle disarticulation	18.55	18.55	090

27892-27899 Decompression Fasciotomy Lower Leg

EXCLUDES: Decompression fasciotomy without debridement (27600-27602)

Code	Description	RVU (Facility)	RVU (Non-Facility)	Global Days
27892	Decompression fasciotomy, leg; anterior and/or lateral compartments only, with debridement of nonviable muscle and/or nerve	15.12	15.12	090
27893	posterior compartment(s) only, with debridement of nonviable muscle and/or nerve	14.98	14.98	090
27894	anterior and/or lateral, and posterior compartment(s), with debridement of nonviable muscle and/or nerve	23.41	23.41	090

Current Procedural Coding Expert – Musculoskeletal System   28070

27899 Unlisted procedure, leg or ankle
   0.00   0.00 Global Days YYY
   AMA: 2009, Jan, 11-31; 2008, Jan, 10-25; 2007, January, 13-27

28001-28008 Surgical Incision Foot/Toe
EXCLUDES Simple incision and drainage (10140-10160)

28001 Incision and drainage, bursa, foot
   4.59   7.14 Global Days 010

28002 Incision and drainage below fascia, with or without tendon sheath involvement, foot; single bursal space
   10.29   13.67 Global Days 010

28003 multiple areas
   14.72   18.19 Global Days 090

28005 Incision, bone cortex (eg, osteomyelitis or bone abscess), foot
   16.11   16.11 Global Days 090

28008 Fasciotomy, foot and/or toe
   EXCLUDES Plantar fascia division (28250)
   Plantar fasciectomy (28060, 28062)
   7.94   11.29 Global Days 090

28010-28011 Tenotomy/Toe
EXCLUDES Open tenotomy (28230-28234)
Simple incision and drainage (10140-10160)

28010 Tenotomy, percutaneous, toe; single tendon
   5.63   6.18 Global Days 090

28011 multiple tendons
   7.97   8.82 Global Days 090

28020-28024 Arthrotomy Foot/Toe
EXCLUDES Simple incision and drainage (10140-10160)

28020 Arthrotomy, including exploration, drainage, or removal of loose or foreign body; intertarsal or tarsometatarsal joint
   9.61   13.80 Global Days 090

28022 metatarsophalangeal joint
   8.65   12.51 Global Days 090

28024 interphalangeal joint
   8.11   11.80 Global Days 090

28035 Tarsal Tunnel Release
EXCLUDES Other nerve decompression (64722)
Other neuroplasty (64704)

28035 Release, tarsal tunnel (posterior tibial nerve decompression)
   9.68   13.84 Global Days 090

28039-28047 [28039, 28041] Excision Soft Tissue Tumor Foot/Toe
INCLUDES Any necessary elevation of tissue planes or dissection
Measurement of tumor and necessary margin at greatest diameter prior to excision
Resection without removal of significant normal tissue
Simple and intermediate repairs
Types of Excision:
   Fascial or subfascial soft tissue tumors: simple and marginal resection of most often benign and intramuscular tumors found either in or below the deep fascia, not involving bone
   Radical resection soft tissue tumor: wide resection of tumor, mostly malignant or aggressive benign, involving large margins of normal tissue and may involve tissue removal from one or more layers
   Subcutaneous: simple and marginal resection of most often benign tumors found in the subcutaneous tissue above the deep fascia

EXCLUDES Complex repair
Radical resection of cutaneous tumors (e.g., melanoma) (11600-11646)
Significant exploration of vessels, neuroplasty or reconstruction

28039 Resequenced code. See code following 28043.

28041 Resequenced code. See code following 28045.

▲ **28043** Excision, tumor, soft tissue of foot or toe, subcutaneous; less than 1.5 cm
   7.18   10.56 Global Days 090

#● **28039**   1.5 cm or greater
   9.20   12.85 Global Days 090

▲ **28045** Excision, tumor, soft tissue of foot or toe, subfascial (eg, intramuscular); less than 1.5 cm
   9.62   13.31 Global Days 090

#● **28041**   1.5 cm or greater
   12.09   12.09 Global Days 090

▲ **28046** Radical resection of tumor (eg, malignant neoplasm), soft tissue of foot or toe; less than 3 cm
   20.35   20.35 Global Days 090

● **28047**   3 cm or greater
   25.46   25.46 Global Days 090

28050-28160 Resection Procedures Foot/Toes

28050 Arthrotomy with biopsy; intertarsal or tarsometatarsal joint
   7.85   11.52 Global Days 090

28052 metatarsophalangeal joint
   7.75   11.74 Global Days 090

28054 interphalangeal joint
   6.36   9.74 Global Days 090

28055 Neurectomy, intrinsic musculature of foot
   10.29   10.29 Global Days 090

28060 Fasciectomy, plantar fascia; partial (separate procedure)
   EXCLUDES Plantar fasciotomy (28008, 28250)
   9.60   13.47 Global Days 090
   AMA: 2009, Jan, 11-31; 2008, Mar, 14-15

28062 radical (separate procedure)
   EXCLUDES Plantar fasciotomy (28008, 28250)
   11.08   15.38 Global Days 090

28070 Synovectomy; intertarsal or tarsometatarsal joint, each
   9.26   13.31 Global Days 090

● New Code ▲ Revised Code M Maternity A Age Unlisted Not Covered # Resequenced
CCI + Add-on ⊘ Mod 51 Exempt ⊘ Mod 63 Exempt ⊙ Mod Sedation PQRI
© 2009 Publisher (Blue Ink)   CPT only © 2009 American Medical Association. All Rights Reserved. (Black Ink)   Medicare (Red Ink)   85

Code	Description	RVU (F)	RVU (NF)	Global
28072	metatarsophalangeal joint, each	9.19	13.60	090

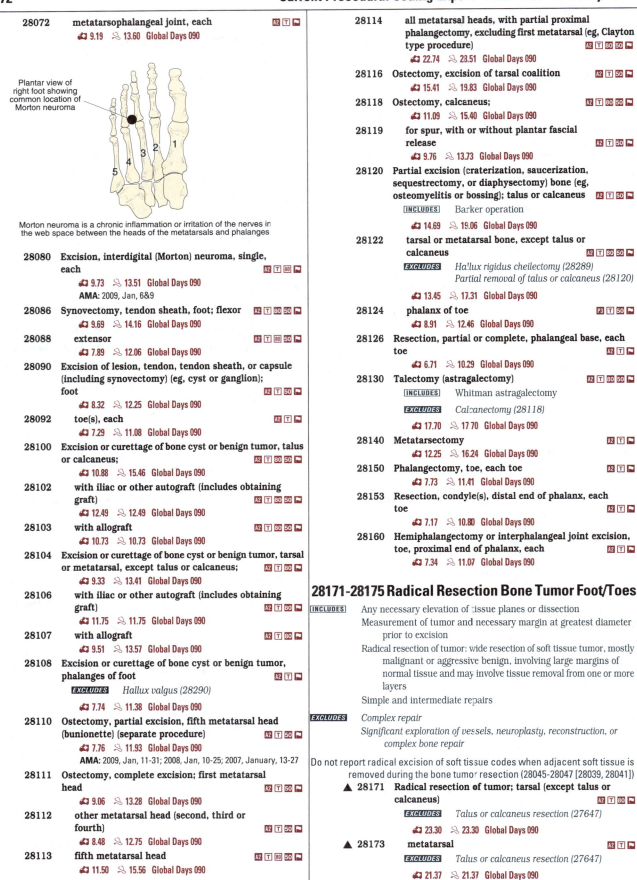

Morton neuroma is a chronic inflammation or irritation of the nerves in the web space between the heads of the metatarsals and phalanges

Plantar view of right foot showing common location of Morton neuroma

Code	Description	RVU (F)	RVU (NF)	Global
28080	Excision, interdigital (Morton) neuroma, single, each	9.73	13.51	090

AMA: 2009, Jan, 6&9

Code	Description	RVU (F)	RVU (NF)	Global
28086	Synovectomy, tendon sheath, foot; flexor	9.69	14.16	090
28088	extensor	7.89	12.06	090
28090	Excision of lesion, tendon, tendon sheath, or capsule (including synovectomy) (eg, cyst or ganglion); foot	8.32	12.25	090
28092	toe(s), each	7.29	11.08	090
28100	Excision or curettage of bone cyst or benign tumor, talus or calcaneus;	10.88	15.46	090
28102	with iliac or other autograft (includes obtaining graft)	12.49	12.49	090
28103	with allograft	10.73	10.73	090
28104	Excision or curettage of bone cyst or benign tumor, tarsal or metatarsal, except talus or calcaneus;	9.33	13.41	090
28106	with iliac or other autograft (includes obtaining graft)	11.75	11.75	090
28107	with allograft	9.51	13.57	090
28108	Excision or curettage of bone cyst or benign tumor, phalanges of foot	7.74	11.38	090

EXCLUDES Hallux valgus (28290)

Code	Description	RVU (F)	RVU (NF)	Global
28110	Ostectomy, partial excision, fifth metatarsal head (bunionette) (separate procedure)	7.76	11.93	090

AMA: 2009, Jan, 11-31; 2008, Jan, 10-25; 2007, January, 13-27

Code	Description	RVU (F)	RVU (NF)	Global
28111	Ostectomy, complete excision; first metatarsal head	9.06	13.28	090
28112	other metatarsal head (second, third or fourth)	8.48	12.75	090
28113	fifth metatarsal head	11.50	15.56	090
28114	all metatarsal heads, with partial proximal phalangectomy, excluding first metatarsal (eg, Clayton type procedure)	22.74	23.51	090
28116	Ostectomy, excision of tarsal coalition	15.41	19.83	090
28118	Ostectomy, calcaneus;	11.09	15.40	090
28119	for spur, with or without plantar fascial release	9.76	13.73	090
28120	Partial excision (craterization, saucerization, sequestrectomy, or diaphysectomy) bone (eg, osteomyelitis or bossing); talus or calcaneus	14.69	19.06	090

INCLUDES Barker operation

Code	Description	RVU (F)	RVU (NF)	Global
28122	tarsal or metatarsal bone, except talus or calcaneus	13.45	17.31	090

EXCLUDES Hallux rigidus cheilectomy (28289)
Partial removal of talus or calcaneus (28120)

Code	Description	RVU (F)	RVU (NF)	Global
28124	phalanx of toe	8.91	12.46	090
28126	Resection, partial or complete, phalangeal base, each toe	6.71	10.29	090
28130	Talectomy (astragalectomy)	17.70	17.70	090

INCLUDES Whitman astragalectomy
EXCLUDES Calcanectomy (28118)

Code	Description	RVU (F)	RVU (NF)	Global
28140	Metatarsectomy	12.25	16.24	090
28150	Phalangectomy, toe, each toe	7.73	11.41	090
28153	Resection, condyle(s), distal end of phalanx, each toe	7.17	10.80	090
28160	Hemiphalangectomy or interphalangeal joint excision, toe, proximal end of phalanx, each	7.34	11.07	090

28171-28175 Radical Resection Bone Tumor Foot/Toes

INCLUDES
Any necessary elevation of tissue planes or dissection
Measurement of tumor and necessary margin at greatest diameter prior to excision
Radical resection of tumor: wide resection of soft tissue tumor, mostly malignant or aggressive benign, involving large margins of normal tissue and may involve tissue removal from one or more layers
Simple and intermediate repairs

EXCLUDES
Complex repair
Significant exploration of vessels, neuroplasty, reconstruction, or complex bone repair

Do not report radical excision of soft tissue codes when adjacent soft tissue is removed during the bone tumor resection (28045-28047 [28039, 28041])

Code	Description	RVU (F)	RVU (NF)	Global
▲ 28171	Radical resection of tumor; tarsal (except talus or calcaneus)	23.30	23.30	090

EXCLUDES Talus or calcaneus resection (27647)

Code	Description	RVU (F)	RVU (NF)	Global
▲ 28173	metatarsal	21.37	21.37	090

EXCLUDES Talus or calcaneus resection (27647)

Current Procedural Coding Expert – Musculoskeletal System

▲ 28175	phalanx of toe	A2 T
	EXCLUDES Talus or calcaneus resection (27647)	
	13.55 13.55 Global Days 090	

28190-28193 Foreign Body Removal: Foot

28190	Removal of foreign body, foot; subcutaneous	P3 T 50
	3.62 6.55 Global Days 010	
28192	deep	A2 T 50 PQ
	8.52 12.32 Global Days 090	
28193	complicated	A2 T 50 PQ
	10.11 14.08 Global Days 090	

28200-28360 Repair/Reconstruction of Foot/Toe

28200	Repair, tendon, flexor, foot; primary or secondary, without free graft, each tendon	A2 T
	8.43 12.33 Global Days 090	
28202	secondary with free graft, each tendon (includes obtaining graft)	A2 T 80
	11.64 15.77 Global Days 090	
28208	Repair, tendon, extensor, foot; primary or secondary, each tendon	A2 T
	8.35 12.25 Global Days 090	
28210	secondary with free graft, each tendon (includes obtaining graft)	A2 T 80
	11.08 15.05 Global Days 090	
28220	Tenolysis, flexor, foot; single tendon	P3 T
	8.19 11.79 Global Days 090	
28222	multiple tendons	A2 T
	9.56 13.39 Global Days 090	
28225	Tenolysis, extensor, foot; single tendon	A2 T
	6.86 10.39 Global Days 090	
28226	multiple tendons	A2 T
	7.95 11.54 Global Days 090	
28230	Tenotomy, open, tendon flexor; foot, single or multiple tendon(s) (separate procedure)	P3 T
	7.63 11.26 Global Days 090	
28232	toe, single tendon (separate procedure)	P3 T
	6.59 10.12 Global Days 090	
28234	Tenotomy, open, extensor, foot or toe, each tendon	A2 T
	EXCLUDES Tendon transfer (27690-27691)	
	7.11 10.66 Global Days 090	
28238	Reconstruction (advancement), posterior tibial tendon with excision of accessory tarsal navicular bone (eg, Kidner type procedure)	A2 T 80 50
	EXCLUDES Extensor hallucis longus transfer with big toe fusion (28760)	
	Jones procedure (28760)	
	Subcutaneous tenotomy (28010-28011)	
	Transfer or transplant of tendon with muscle redirection or rerouting (27690-27692)	
	13.38 17.87 Global Days 090	
28240	Tenotomy, lengthening, or release, abductor hallucis muscle	A2 T 50
	7.93 11.63 Global Days 090	
28250	Division of plantar fascia and muscle (eg, Steindler stripping) (separate procedure)	A2 T 80 50
	10.89 15.08 Global Days 090	
28260	Capsulotomy, midfoot; medial release only (separate procedure)	A2 T 80 50
	14.17 18.54 Global Days 090	
28261	with tendon lengthening	A2 T 80 50
	20.60 25.29 Global Days 090	
28262	extensive, including posterior talotibial capsulotomy and tendon(s) lengthening (eg, resistant clubfoot deformity)	A2 T 80 50
	30.84 37.36 Global Days 090	
28264	Capsulotomy, midtarsal (eg, Heyman type procedure)	A2 T 80 50
	16.06 20.03 Global Days 090	
28270	Capsulotomy; metatarsophalangeal joint, with or without tenorrhaphy, each joint (separate procedure)	A2 T 50
	9.00 12.82 Global Days 090	
28272	interphalangeal joint, each joint (separate procedure)	P3 T 50
	6.87 10.26 Global Days 090	
	AMA: 2009, Jan, 11-31; 2008, Jan, 10-25; 2007, January, 13-27	
28280	Syndactylization, toes (eg, webbing or Kelikian type procedure)	A2 T 80 50
	9.54 13.64 Global Days 090	
28285	Correction, hammertoe (eg, interphalangeal fusion, partial or total phalangectomy)	A2 T 50
	8.66 12.33 Global Days 090	
	AMA: 2009, Jan, 11-31; 2008, Jan, 10-25; 2007, January, 13-27; 2006, May, 16-20	
28286	Correction, cock-up fifth toe, with plastic skin closure (eg, Ruiz-Mora type procedure)	A2 T
	8.15 11.86 Global Days 090	
28288	Ostectomy, partial, exostectomy or condylectomy, metatarsal head, each metatarsal head	A2 T
	11.62 15.92 Global Days 090	
28289	Hallux rigidus correction with cheilectomy, debridement and capsular release of the first metatarsophalangeal joint	A2 T 80 50
	14.89 19.41 Global Days 090	

Cuneiform bones, Metatarsals, Phalanges, Cuboid, Metatarsophalangeal joint, Metatarsophalangeal joint, Tenorrhaphy, Interphalangeal joints

Tarsals, metatarsals, and phalanges

The metatarsophalangeal joint capsule is incised (capsulotomy)

Hallux valgus bunion, Base of proximal phalanx is resected, Kirshner wires stabilize the osteotomy, Keller type approach, Medial emminence of metatarsal bone, A portion of the metatarsal head is resected, Prosthetic implant placed in the joint, Right foot, Correction of hallux valgus bunion by resection of joint

● New Code   ▲ Revised Code   M Maternity   A Age   Unlisted   Not Covered   # Resequenced
CCI   + Add-on   ⊘ Mod 51 Exempt   @ Mod 63 Exempt   ⊙ Mod Sedation   PQ PQRI

Code	Description	Indicators	Facility RVU	Non-Facility RVU	Global Days
28290	Correction, hallux valgus (bunion), with or without sesamoidectomy; simple exostectomy (eg, Silver type procedure)	A2 T 50	10.66	15.31	090
	AMA: 2009, Jan, 11-31; 2008, Jan, 10-25; 2007, January, 28-31				
28292	Keller, McBride, or Mayo type procedure	A2 T 80 50	16.29	20.86	090
	AMA: 2007, January, 28-31				
28293	resection of joint with implant	A2 T 80 50 P0	19.31	27.38	090
	AMA: 2007, January, 28-31				
28294	with tendon transplants (eg, Joplin type procedure)	A2 T 80 50	14.60	19.79	090
	AMA: 2007, January, 28-31				
28296	with metatarsal osteotomy (eg, Mitchell, Chevron, or concentric type procedures)	A2 T 80 50 P0	14.19	18.86	090
	AMA: 2009, Jan, 11-31; 2008, Jan, 10-25; 2007, January, 28-31; 2007, January, 13-27				
28297	Lapidus-type procedure	A2 T 80 50	16.14	21.83	090
	AMA: 2007, January, 28-31				
28298	by phalanx osteotomy	A2 T 80 50			
	INCLUDES Akin Procedure		13.76	18.98	090
	AMA: 2007, January, 28-31				
28299	by double osteotomy	A2 T 80 50 P0	18.48	23.78	090
	AMA: 2009, Jan, 11-31; 2008, Jan, 10-25; 2007, January, 28-31				
28300	Osteotomy; calcaneus (eg, Dwyer or Chambers type procedure), with or without internal fixation	A2 T 80 50 P0	17.90	17.90	090
28302	talus	A2 T 80 50	19.12	19.12	090
28304	Osteotomy, tarsal bones, other than calcaneus or talus;	A2 T 80 50	16.08	21.15	090
28305	with autograft (includes obtaining graft) (eg, Fowler type)	A2 T 80 50	18.00	18.00	090
28306	Osteotomy, with or without lengthening, shortening or angular correction, metatarsal; first metatarsal	A2 T 80 50 P0	11.08	16.25	090
28307	first metatarsal with autograft (other than first toe)	A2 T 80 50 P0	13.59	20.15	090
28308	other than first metatarsal, each	A2 T 80 50 P0	10.13	14.70	090
28309	multiple (eg, Swanson type cavus foot procedure)	A2 T 80 50 P0	24.50	24.50	090
28310	Osteotomy, shortening, angular or rotational correction; proximal phalanx, first toe (separate procedure)	A2 T P0	9.58	14.06	090
28312	other phalanges, any toe	A2 T	8.56	13.13	090
28313	Reconstruction, angular deformity of toe, soft tissue procedures only (eg, overlapping second toe, fifth toe, curly toes)	A2 T	9.82	14.03	090
28315	Sesamoidectomy, first toe (separate procedure)	A2 T 50	8.77	12.53	090
28320	Repair, nonunion or malunion; tarsal bones	A2 T 80 P0	16.77	16.77	090
28322	metatarsal, with or without bone graft (includes obtaining graft)	A2 T 80 P0	15.78	20.91	090
28340	Reconstruction, toe, macrodactyly; soft tissue resection	A2 T	11.35	15.38	090
28341	requiring bone resection	A2 T	13.55	17.92	090
28344	Reconstruction, toe(s); polydactyly	A2 T	7.61	11.18	090
28345	syndactyly, with or without skin graft(s), each web	A2 T 80	9.98	13.81	090
28360	Reconstruction, cleft foot	T 80	26.94	26.94	090

28400-28675 Treatment of Fracture/Dislocation of Foot/Toe

Code	Description	Indicators	Facility RVU	Non-Facility RVU	Global Days
28400	Closed treatment of calcaneal fracture; without manipulation	A2 T 50	5.95	6.45	090
28405	with manipulation	A2 T 80 50			
	INCLUDES Bohler reduction		9.29	10.12	090
28406	Percutaneous skeletal fixation of calcaneal fracture, with manipulation	A2 T 80 50 P0	13.84	13.84	090
28415	Open treatment of calcaneal fracture, includes internal fixation, when performed;	A2 T 80 50 P0	30.24	30.24	090
28420	with primary iliac or other autogenous bone graft (includes obtaining graft)	A2 T 80 50 P0	33.69	33.69	090
28430	Closed treatment of talus fracture; without manipulation	P2 T 50	5.46	6.09	090
28435	with manipulation	A2 T 80 50	8.39	9.29	090
28436	Percutaneous skeletal fixation of talus fracture, with manipulation	A2 T 50 P0	11.70	11.70	090
28445	Open treatment of talus fracture, includes internal fixation, when performed	A2 T 80 50 P0	28.98	28.98	090
28446	Open osteochondral autograft, talus (includes obtaining graft[s])	G2 T 80 50			
	EXCLUDES Arthroscopically aided osteochondral talus graft (29892)				
	Open osteochondral allograft or repairs with industrial grafts (28899)				
	Do not report with (27705-27707)		33.05	33.05	090
	AMA: 2008, Jan, 4-5				
28450	Treatment of tarsal bone fracture (except talus and calcaneus); without manipulation, each	P2 T	5.03	5.59	090
	AMA: 2009, Jan, 11-31; 2008, Jan, 10-25; 2007, January, 13-27				

Current Procedural Coding Expert – Musculoskeletal System

28455	with manipulation, each 7.18 7.92 Global Days 090
28456	Percutaneous skeletal fixation of tarsal bone fracture (except talus and calcaneus), with manipulation, each 8.36 8.36 Global Days 090
28465	Open treatment of tarsal bone fracture (except talus and calcaneus), includes internal fixation, when performed, each 16.47 16.47 Global Days 090
28470	Closed treatment of metatarsal fracture; without manipulation, each 5.00 5.50 Global Days 090
28475	with manipulation, each 6.07 6.76 Global Days 090
28476	Percutaneous skeletal fixation of metatarsal fracture, with manipulation, each 8.87 8.87 Global Days 090
28485	Open treatment of metatarsal fracture, includes internal fixation, when performed, each 14.33 14.33 Global Days 090
28490	Closed treatment of fracture great toe, phalanx or phalanges; without manipulation 3.24 3.72 Global Days 090
28495	with manipulation 3.89 4.56 Global Days 090
28496	Percutaneous skeletal fixation of fracture great toe, phalanx or phalanges, with manipulation 6.03 10.88 Global Days 090
28505	Open treatment of fracture, great toe, phalanx or phalanges, includes internal fixation, when performed 13.51 17.58 Global Days 090
28510	Closed treatment of fracture, phalanx or phalanges, other than great toe; without manipulation, each 3.11 3.19 Global Days 090
28515	with manipulation, each 3.71 4.15 Global Days 090
28525	Open treatment of fracture, phalanx or phalanges, other than great toe, includes internal fixation, when performed, each 10.79 14.90 Global Days 090
28530	Closed treatment of sesamoid fracture 2.69 3.01 Global Days 090
28531	Open treatment of sesamoid fracture, with or without internal fixation 6.43 12.03 Global Days 090
28540	Closed treatment of tarsal bone dislocation, other than talotarsal; without anesthesia 4.78 5.25 Global Days 090
28545	requiring anesthesia 6.77 7.56 Global Days 090
28546	Percutaneous skeletal fixation of tarsal bone dislocation, other than talotarsal, with manipulation 8.78 14.44 Global Days 090
28555	Open treatment of tarsal bone dislocation, includes internal fixation, when performed 18.13 23.25 Global Days 090
28570	Closed treatment of talotarsal joint dislocation; without anesthesia 3.69 4.24 Global Days 090
28575	requiring anesthesia 8.56 9.39 Global Days 090
28576	Percutaneous skeletal fixation of talotarsal joint dislocation, with manipulation 10.38 10.38 Global Days 090
28585	Open treatment of talotarsal joint dislocation, includes internal fixation, when performed 20.23 25.37 Global Days 090
28600	Closed treatment of tarsometatarsal joint dislocation; without anesthesia 4.92 5.65 Global Days 090
28605	requiring anesthesia 7.58 8.35 Global Days 090
28606	Percutaneous skeletal fixation of tarsometatarsal joint dislocation, with manipulation 10.49 10.49 Global Days 090
28615	Open treatment of tarsometatarsal joint dislocation, includes internal fixation, when performed 21.04 21.04 Global Days 090
28630	Closed treatment of metatarsophalangeal joint dislocation; without anesthesia 2.97 4.04 Global Days 010
28635	requiring anesthesia 3.51 4.52 Global Days 010
28636	Percutaneous skeletal fixation of metatarsophalangeal joint dislocation, with manipulation 5.32 7.90 Global Days 010
28645	Open treatment of metatarsophalangeal joint dislocation, includes internal fixation, when performed 12.97 17.03 Global Days 090
28660	Closed treatment of interphalangeal joint dislocation; without anesthesia 2.37 2.99 Global Days 010
28665	requiring anesthesia 3.61 4.16 Global Days 010
28666	Percutaneous skeletal fixation of interphalangeal joint dislocation, with manipulation 5.61 5.61 Global Days 010
28675	Open treatment of interphalangeal joint dislocation, includes internal fixation, when performed 11.15 15.39 Global Days 090

28705-28760 Arthrodesis of Foot/Toe

28705	Arthrodesis; pantalar 35.44 35.44 Global Days 090
28715	triple 26.42 26.42 Global Days 090
28725	subtalar **INCLUDES** Dunn arthrodesis Grice arthrosis 21.39 21.39 Global Days 090
28730	Arthrodesis, midtarsal or tarsometatarsal, multiple or transverse; **INCLUDES** Lambrinudi arthrodesis 22.78 22.78 Global Days 090
28735	with osteotomy (eg, flatfoot correction) 21.53 21.53 Global Days 090
28737	Arthrodesis, with tendon lengthening and advancement, midtarsal, tarsal navicular-cuneiform (eg, Miller type procedure) 18.51 18.51 Global Days 090
28740	Arthrodesis, midtarsal or tarsometatarsal, single joint 17.14 22.67 Global Days 090

● New Code   ▲ Revised Code   M Maternity   Age   Unlisted   Not Covered   # Resequenced
CCI   + Add-on   Mod 51 Exempt   @ Mod 63 Exempt   Mod Sedation   PQRI

Code	Description	Facility RVU	Non-Facility RVU	Global Days
28750	Arthrodesis, great toe; metatarsophalangeal joint [A2][T][80][50][P0]	16.30	21.84	090
28755	interphalangeal joint [A2][T][50][P0]	8.85	13.13	090
28760	Arthrodesis, with extensor hallucis longus transfer to first metatarsal neck, great toe, interphalangeal joint (eg, Jones type procedure) [A2][T][80][50][P0] **EXCLUDES** Hammer toe repair or interphalangeal fusion (28285)	15.81	21.00	090

28800-28825 Amputation Foot/Toe

Code	Description	Facility RVU	Non-Facility RVU	Global Days
28800	Amputation, foot; midtarsal (eg, Chopart type procedure) [C][80][50]	15.31	15.31	090
28805	transmetatarsal [T][80][50]	20.90	20.90	090
28810	Amputation, metatarsal, with toe, single [A2][T][80] **EXCLUDES** Removal of tuft of distal phalanx (11752)	12.10	12.10	090
28820	Amputation, toe; metatarsophalangeal joint [A2][T] **EXCLUDES** Removal of tuft of distal phalanx (11752)	9.44	13.84	090
28825	interphalangeal joint [A2][T] **EXCLUDES** Removal of tuft of distal phalanx (11752)	11.15	15.41	090

28890-28899 Other/Unlisted Procedures Foot/Toe

Code	Description	Facility RVU	Non-Facility RVU	Global Days
28890	Extracorporeal shock wave, high energy, performed by a physician, requiring anesthesia other than local, including ultrasound guidance, involving the plantar fascia [P3][T][50] **EXCLUDES** Extracorporeal shock wave therapy of musculoskeletal system not otherwise specified (0019T, 0101T, 0102T)	6.21	8.90	090
	AMA: 2009, Jan, 11-31; 2008, Jan, 10-25; 2007, January, 13-27; 2006, March, 1-5; 2005, December, 9-11			
28899	Unlisted procedure, foot or toes [T][80]	0.00	0.00	YYY
	AMA: 2009, Jan, 6&9; 2008, Jan, 4-5			

29000-29086 Casting: Arm/Shoulder/Torso

CMS 100-2,15,100 Surgical Dressings, Splints, Casts, and Devices for Reductions of Fractures/Dislocations
CMS 100-4,4,240 Inpatient Part B Hospital Services Paid Under OPPS
EXCLUDES Cast or splint material (99070, Q4001-Q4051)
Orthotic supervision and training (97760-97762)

Code	Description	Facility RVU	Non-Facility RVU	Global Days
29000	Application of halo type body cast (see 20661-20663 for insertion) [G2][S][80]	4.14	5.97	000
	AMA: 2009, May, 8-9&11			
29010	Application of Risser jacket, localizer, body; only [P2][S][80]	3.20	4.66	000
29015	including head [P2][S][80]	4.06	6.39	000
29020	Application of turnbuckle jacket, body; only [G2][S][80]	3.46	5.47	000
29025	including head [P2][S][80]	4.84	7.44	000
29035	Application of body cast, shoulder to hips; [P2][S][80]	3.66	5.99	000
29040	including head, Minerva type [G2][S][80]	4.20	6.29	000
29044	including 1 thigh [P2][S][80]	4.24	6.63	000
29046	including both thighs [G2][S][80]	4.66	7.02	000
29049	Application, cast; figure-of-eight [P3][S][80]	1.86	2.54	000
	AMA: 2007, February, 8-9			
29055	shoulder spica [P3][S][80]	3.69	5.64	000
29058	plaster Velpeau [P3][S][80]	2.17	2.96	000
29065	shoulder to hand (long arm) [P3][S][50]	1.83	2.48	000
29075	elbow to finger (short arm) [P3][S][50]	1.66	2.30	000
29085	hand and lower forearm (gauntlet) [P3][S][50]	1.81	2.46	000
	AMA: 2009, Jan, 11-31; 2008, Jan, 10-25; 2007, January, 13-27			
29086	finger (eg, contracture) [P3][S][50]	1.37	1.99	000

29105-29280 Splinting and Strapping: Torso/Upper Extremities

CMS 100-2,15,100 Surgical Dressings, Splints, Casts, and Devices for Reductions of Fractures/Dislocations
CMS 100-4,4,240 Inpatient Part B Hospital Services Paid Under OPPS
EXCLUDES Orthotic supervision and training (97760-97762)

Code	Description	Facility RVU	Non-Facility RVU	Global Days
29105	Application of long arm splint (shoulder to hand) [P3][S][50]	1.63	2.27	000
	AMA: 2009, May, 8-9&11			
29125	Application of short arm splint (forearm to hand); static [P3][S][50]	1.18	1.81	000
29126	dynamic [P3][S][50]	1.45	2.06	000
29130	Application of finger splint; static [P3][S][50]	0.80	1.08	000
29131	dynamic [P3][S][50]	0.92	1.34	000
29200	Strapping; thorax [P3][S] **EXCLUDES** Strapping of low back (29799)	1.12	1.44	000
~~29220~~	~~low back~~ To report, see code 29799			
29240	shoulder (eg, Velpeau) [P3][S]	1.19	1.50	000
29260	elbow or wrist [P3][S][50]	1.03	1.36	000
29280	hand or finger [P3][S][50]	0.98	1.31	000

Current Procedural Coding Expert – Musculoskeletal System

29305-29450 Casting: Legs

CMS 100-2,15,100 — Surgical Dressings, Splints, Casts, and Devices for Reductions of Fractures/Dislocations
CMS 100-4,4,240 — Inpatient Part B Hospital Services Paid Under OPPS
EXCLUDES Cast or splint supplies (99070, Q4001-Q4051)
Orthotic supervision and training (97760-97762)

- **29305** Application of hip spica cast; 1 leg
  - **EXCLUDES** Hip spica cast thighs only (29046)
  - 4.24 / 6.28 Global Days 000
- **29325** 1 and 1/2 spica or both legs
  - **EXCLUDES** Hip spica cast thighs only (29046)
  - 4.77 / 6.97 Global Days 000
- **29345** Application of long leg cast (thigh to toes);
  - 2.72 / 3.54 Global Days 000
- **29355** walker or ambulatory type
  - 2.87 / 3.66 Global Days 000
- **29358** Application of long leg cast brace
  - 2.79 / 4.10 Global Days 000
- **29365** Application of cylinder cast (thigh to ankle)
  - 2.35 / 3.17 Global Days 000
- **29405** Application of short leg cast (below knee to toes);
  - 1.72 / 2.33 Global Days 000
- **29425** walking or ambulatory type
  - 1.85 / 2.49 Global Days 000
- **29435** Application of patellar tendon bearing (PTB) cast
  - 2.29 / 3.09 Global Days 000
- **29440** Adding walker to previously applied cast
  - 0.94 / 1.38 Global Days 000
- **29445** Application of rigid total contact leg cast
  - 2.97 / 3.73 Global Days 000
- **29450** Application of clubfoot cast with molding or manipulation, long or short leg
  - 3.14 / 3.88 Global Days 000

29505-29590 Splinting and Strapping Ankle/Foot/Leg/Toes

CMS 100-2,15,100 — Surgical Dressings, Splints, Casts, and Devices for Reductions of Fractures/Dislocations
CMS 100-4,4,240 — Inpatient Part B Hospital Services Paid Under OPPS
EXCLUDES Orthotic supervision and training (97760-97762)

- **29505** Application of long leg splint (thigh to ankle or toes)
  - 1.34 / 2.06 Global Days 000
  - **AMA:** 2009, May, 8-9&11
- **29515** Application of short leg splint (calf to foot)
  - 1.35 / 1.92 Global Days 000
- **29520** Strapping; hip
  - 0.97 / 1.28 Global Days 000
- **29530** knee
  - 1.03 / 1.36 Global Days 000
- **29540** ankle and/or foot
  - Do not report with (29581)
  - 0.85 / 1.11 Global Days 000
- **29550** toes
  - 0.81 / 1.09 Global Days 000
- **29580** Unna boot
  - Do not report with (29581)
  - 0.98 / 1.39 Global Days 000
  - **AMA:** 2009, Jan, 11-31; 2008, Jan, 10-25; 2007, January, 13-27
- **●29581** Application of multi-layer venous wound compression system, below knee
  - Do not report with (29540, 29580)
  - 0.89 / 2.40 Global Days 000
- **29590** Denis-Browne splint strapping
  - 1.06 / 1.43 Global Days 000

29700-29799 Casting Services Other Than Application

INCLUDES Casts applied by treating physician

- **29700** Removal or bivalving; gauntlet, boot or body cast
  - 0.93 / 1.67 Global Days 000
- **29705** full arm or full leg cast
  - 1.31 / 1.77 Global Days 000
- **29710** shoulder or hip spica, Minerva, or Risser jacket, etc.
  - 2.29 / 3.22 Global Days 000
- **29715** turnbuckle jacket
  - 1.46 / 2.11 Global Days 000
- **29720** Repair of spica, body cast or jacket
  - 1.19 / 2.12 Global Days 000
- **29730** Windowing of cast
  - 1.25 / 1.72 Global Days 000
- **29740** Wedging of cast (except clubfoot casts)
  - 1.76 / 2.37 Global Days 000
- **29750** Wedging of clubfoot cast
  - 2.15 / 2.82 Global Days 000
- **29799** Unlisted procedure, casting or strapping
  - 0.00 / 0.00 Global Days YYY

29800-29999 Arthroscopic Musculoskeletal Procedures

INCLUDES Diagnostic arthroscopy with surgical arthroscopy

- **29800** Arthroscopy, temporomandibular joint, diagnostic, with or without synovial biopsy (separate procedure)
  - 14.01 / 14.01 Global Days 090
- **29804** Arthroscopy, temporomandibular joint, surgical
  - **EXCLUDES** Open surgery (21010)
  - 17.75 / 17.75 Global Days 090
- **29805** Arthroscopy, shoulder, diagnostic, with or without synovial biopsy (separate procedure)
  - **EXCLUDES** Open surgery (23065-23066, 23100-23101)
  - 12.51 / 12.51 Global Days 090
- **29806** Arthroscopy, shoulder, surgical; capsulorrhaphy
  - **EXCLUDES** Capsulorrhaphy (29999)
  - Open surgery (23450-23466)
  - 28.62 / 28.62 Global Days 090
- **29807** repair of SLAP lesion
  - 27.88 / 27.88 Global Days 090
- **29819** with removal of loose body or foreign body
  - **EXCLUDES** Open surgery (23040-23044, 23107)
  - 15.64 / 15.64 Global Days 090
- **29820** synovectomy, partial
  - **EXCLUDES** Open surgery (23105)
  - 14.42 / 14.42 Global Days 090

● New Code ▲ Revised Code M Maternity A Age Unlisted Not Covered # Resequenced
CCI + Add-on Mod 51 Exempt @ Mod 63 Exempt ⊙ Mod Sedation PQRI
© 2009 Publisher (Blue Ink) CPT only © 2009 American Medical Association. All Rights Reserved. (Black Ink) Medicare (Red Ink)

Code	Description	Indicators	Facility RVU	Non-Facility RVU	Global Days
29821	synovectomy, complete	A2 T 80 50	15.82	15.82	090
	EXCLUDES: Open surgery (23105)				
29822	debridement, limited	A2 T 80 50	15.38	15.38	090
	EXCLUDES: Open surgery (see specific shoulder section)				
29823	debridement, extensive	A2 T 80 50	16.82	16.82	090
	EXCLUDES: Open surgery (see specific shoulder section)				
29824	distal claviculectomy including distal articular surface (Mumford procedure)	A2 T 80 50	18.12	18.12	090
	INCLUDES: Mumford procedure				
	EXCLUDES: Open surgery (23120)				
29825	with lysis and resection of adhesions, with or without manipulation	A2 T 80 50	15.67	15.67	090
	EXCLUDES: Open surgery (see specific shoulder section)				
29826	decompression of subacromial space with partial acromioplasty, with or without coracoacromial release	A2 T 80 50	17.92	17.92	090
	EXCLUDES: Open surgery (23130, 23415)				
29827	with rotator cuff repair	A2 T 80 50	29.13	29.13	090
	EXCLUDES: Distal clavicle excision (29824); Open surgery (23412); Subacromial decompression (29826)				
	AMA: 2009, Jan, 11-31; 2008, Mar, 14-15				
29828	biceps tenodesis	62 T 80 50	24.99	24.99	090
	EXCLUDES: Tenodesis of long tendon of biceps (23430)				
	Do not report with (29805, 29820, 29822)				
	AMA: 2009, Jan, 11-31; 2008, Feb, 8-9				
29830	Arthroscopy, elbow, diagnostic, with or without synovial biopsy (separate procedure)	A2 T 50	12.08	12.08	090
29834	Arthroscopy, elbow, surgical; with removal of loose body or foreign body	A2 T 80 50	13.14	13.14	090
29835	synovectomy, partial	A2 T 80 50	13.50	13.50	090
29836	synovectomy, complete	A2 T 80 50	15.57	15.57	090
29837	debridement, limited	A2 T 80 50	14.12	14.12	090
29838	debridement, extensive	A2 T 80 50	15.78	15.78	090
29840	Arthroscopy, wrist, diagnostic, with or without synovial biopsy (separate procedure)	A2 T 80 50	11.96	11.96	090
29843	Arthroscopy, wrist, surgical; for infection, lavage and drainage	A2 T 80 50	12.82	12.82	090
29844	synovectomy, partial	A2 T 80 50	13.32	13.32	090
29845	synovectomy, complete	A2 T 80 50	15.28	15.28	090
	AMA: 2009, Jan, 11-31; 2008, Jan, 10-25; 2007, January, 13-27				
29846	excision and/or repair of triangular fibrocartilage and/or joint debridement	A2 T 80 50	13.93	13.93	090
	AMA: 2009, Jan, 11-31; 2008, Jan, 10-25; 2007, January, 13-27				
29847	internal fixation for fracture or instability	A2 T 80 50	14.47	14.47	090
29848	Endoscopy, wrist, surgical, with release of transverse carpal ligament	A2 T 50	13.56	13.56	090
	EXCLUDES: Open surgery (64721)				
29850	Arthroscopically aided treatment of intercondylar spine(s) and/or tuberosity fracture(s) of the knee, with or without manipulation; without internal or external fixation (includes arthroscopy)	A2 T 80 50	16.63	16.63	090
29851	with internal or external fixation (includes arthroscopy)	A2 T 80 50	25.10	25.10	090
	EXCLUDES: Bone graft (20900, 20902)				
29855	Arthroscopically aided treatment of tibial fracture, proximal (plateau); unicondylar, includes internal fixation, when performed (includes arthroscopy)	A2 T 80 50	21.12	21.12	090
29856	bicondylar, includes internal fixation, when performed (includes arthroscopy)	A2 T 80 50	26.87	26.87	090
	EXCLUDES: Bone graft (20900, 20902)				
29860	Arthroscopy, hip, diagnostic with or without synovial biopsy (separate procedure)	A2 T 80 50	17.82	17.82	090
29861	Arthroscopy, hip, surgical; with removal of loose body or foreign body	A2 T 80 50	19.62	19.62	090
29862	with debridement/shaving of articular cartilage (chondroplasty), abrasion arthroplasty, and/or resection of labrum	A2 T 80 50	21.94	21.94	090
29863	with synovectomy	A2 T 80 50	21.99	21.99	090

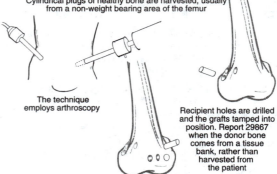

Cylindrical plugs of healthy bone are harvested, usually from a non-weight bearing area of the femur

The technique employs arthroscopy

Recipient holes are drilled and the grafts tamped into position. Report 29867 when the donor bone comes from a tissue bank, rather than harvested from the patient

---

Legend:
- 26/TC PC/TC Comp Only
- A2-Z3 ASC Pmt
- 50 Bilateral
- ♂ Male Only
- ♀ Female Only
- Facility RVU
- Non-Facility RVU
- AMA: CPT Asst
- MED: Pub 100
- A-Y OPPSI
- 80/80 Surg Assist Allowed / w/Doc
- Lab Crosswalk
- Radiology Crosswalk

CPT only © 2009 American Medical Association. All Rights Reserved. (Black Ink) Medicare (Red Ink) © 2009 Publisher (Blue Ink)

Current Procedural Coding Expert – Musculoskeletal System 29893

29866 Arthroscopy, knee, surgical; osteochondral autograft(s) (eg, mosaicplasty) (includes harvesting of the autograft[s])
  EXCLUDES Open osteochondral autograft of the knee (27416)
  Do not report with procedure performed in the same compartment (29874, 29877, 29879, 29885-29887)
  Do not report with procedure performed at the same surgical session (29870, 29871, 29875, 29884)
  28.20 28.20 Global Days 090

29867 osteochondral allograft (eg, mosaicplasty)
  Do not report with procedures performed in the same compartment (29874, 29877, 29879, 29885-29887)
  Do not report with procedures performed at the same surgical session (27415, 27570, 29870-29871, 29875, 29884)
  34.50 34.50 Global Days 090

29868 meniscal transplantation (includes arthrotomy for meniscal insertion), medial or lateral
  Do not report with procedure performed in same compartment (29874, 29877, 29881-29882)
  Do not report with procedures performed at same surgical session (29870-29871, 29875, 29880, 29883-29884)
  45.45 45.45 Global Days 090

29870 Arthroscopy, knee, diagnostic, with or without synovial biopsy (separate procedure)
  EXCLUDES Open procedure (27412)
  10.93 14.96 Global Days 090
  AMA: 2009, Jan, 11-31; 2007, Dec, 10-179

29871 Arthroscopy, knee, surgical; for infection, lavage and drainage
  EXCLUDES Osteochondral graft (27412, 27415, 29866-29867)
  13.68 13.68 Global Days 090
  AMA: 2007, Dec, 10-179

29873 with lateral release
  EXCLUDES Open procedure (27425)
  13.80 13.80 Global Days 090
  AMA: 2007, Dec, 10-179

29874 for removal of loose body or foreign body (eg, osteochondritis dissecans fragmentation, chondral fragmentation)
  14.36 14.36 Global Days 090
  AMA: 2007, Dec, 10-179

29875 synovectomy, limited (eg, plica or shelf resection) (separate procedure)
  13.20 13.20 Global Days 090
  AMA: 2007, Dec, 10-179

29876 synovectomy, major, 2 or more compartments (eg, medial or lateral)
  17.56 17.56 Global Days 090
  AMA: 2007, Dec, 10-179

29877 debridement/shaving of articular cartilage (chondroplasty)
  16.65 16.65 Global Days 090
  AMA: 2009, Jan, 11-31; 2008, Jan, 10-25; 2007, Dec, 10-179; 2007, January, 13-27; 2005, April, 13-14

29879 abrasion arthroplasty (includes chondroplasty where necessary) or multiple drilling or microfracture
  17.76 17.76 Global Days 090
  AMA: 2007, Dec, 10-179

29880 with meniscectomy (medial AND lateral, including any meniscal shaving)
  18.52 18.52 Global Days 090
  AMA: 2007, Dec, 10-179

29881 with meniscectomy (medial OR lateral, including any meniscal shaving)
  17.31 17.31 Global Days 090
  AMA: 2009, Jan, 11-31; 2008, Jan, 10-25; 2007, Dec, 10-179; 2007, January, 13-27; 2005, April, 13-14

29882 with meniscus repair (medial OR lateral)
  EXCLUDES Meniscus transplant (29868)
  18.73 18.73 Global Days 090
  AMA: 2009, Jan, 11-31; 2008, Jan, 10-25; 2007, Dec, 10-179; 2007, January, 13-27

29883 with meniscus repair (medial AND lateral)
  EXCLUDES Meniscus transplant (29868)
  22.61 22.61 Global Days 090
  AMA: 2009, Jan, 11-31; 2008, Jan, 10-25; 2007, Dec, 10-179; 2007, January, 13-27

29884 with lysis of adhesions, with or without manipulation (separate procedure)
  16.62 16.62 Global Days 090
  AMA: 2007, Dec, 10-179

29885 drilling for osteochondritis dissecans with bone grafting, with or without internal fixation (including debridement of base of lesion)
  20.13 20.13 Global Days 090
  AMA: 2007, Dec, 10-179

29886 drilling for intact osteochondritis dissecans lesion
  16.98 16.98 Global Days 090
  AMA: 2007, Dec, 10-179

29887 drilling for intact osteochondritis dissecans lesion with internal fixation
  20.02 20.02 Global Days 090
  AMA: 2007, Dec, 10-179

29888 Arthroscopically aided anterior cruciate ligament repair/augmentation or reconstruction
  Do not report with ligamentous reconstruction (27427-27429)
  26.80 26.80 Global Days 090
  AMA: 2009, Jan, 11-31; 2008, Jan, 10-25; 2007, Dec, 10-179; 2007, January, 13-27

29889 Arthroscopically aided posterior cruciate ligament repair/augmentation or reconstruction
  Do not report with ligamentous reconstruction (27427-27429)
  32.85 32.85 Global Days 090
  AMA: 2009, Jan, 11-31; 2008, Jan, 10-25; 2007, Dec, 10-179; 2007, January, 13-27

29891 Arthroscopy, ankle, surgical, excision of osteochondral defect of talus and/or tibia, including drilling of the defect
  18.63 18.63 Global Days 090

29892 Arthroscopically aided repair of large osteochondritis dissecans lesion, talar dome fracture, or tibial plafond fracture, with or without internal fixation (includes arthroscopy)
  20.53 20.53 Global Days 090

29893 Endoscopic plantar fasciotomy
  11.52 15.96 Global Days 090

● New Code   ▲ Revised Code   Maternity   Age   Unlisted   Not Covered   # Resequenced
CCI   + Add-on   Mod 51 Exempt   Mod 63 Exempt   Mod Sedation   PQRI
© 2009 Publisher (Blue Ink)   CPT only © 2009 American Medical Association. All Rights Reserved. (Black Ink)   Medicare (Red Ink)   93

Code	Description	Indicators
29894	Arthroscopy, ankle (tibiotalar and fibulotalar joints), surgical; with removal of loose body or foreign body	A2 T 80 50
	13.86 13.86 Global Days 090	
29895	synovectomy, partial	A2 T 80 50
	13.21 13.21 Global Days 090	
29897	debridement, limited	A2 T 80 50
	13.91 13.91 Global Days 090	
29898	debridement, extensive	A2 T 80 50
	15.48 15.48 Global Days 090	
29899	with ankle arthrodesis	A2 T 80 50
	EXCLUDES Open procedure (27870)	
	28.37 28.37 Global Days 090	
29900	Arthroscopy, metacarpophalangeal joint, diagnostic, includes synovial biopsy	A2 T 80 50
	Do not report with (29901-29902)	
	10.61 10.61 Global Days 090	
29901	Arthroscopy, metacarpophalangeal joint, surgical; with debridement	A2 T 80 50
	14.08 14.08 Global Days 090	
29902	with reduction of displaced ulnar collateral ligament (eg, Stenar lesion)	A2 T 80 50
	16.96 16.96 Global Days 090	
29904	Arthroscopy, subtalar joint, surgical; with removal of loose body or foreign body	G2 T 80 50
	17.06 17.06 Global Days 090	
29905	with synovectomy	G2 T 80 50
	18.41 18.41 Global Days 090	
29906	with debridement	G2 T 80 50
	19.38 19.38 Global Days 090	
29907	with subtalar arthrodesis	G2 T 80 50
	23.53 23.53 Global Days 090	
29999	Unlisted procedure, arthroscopy	T 80 50
	0.00 0.00 Global Days YYY	
	AMA: 2009, Jan, 11-31; 2009, Mar, 10-11; 2008, Jan, 10-25; 2008, Nov, 10-11; 2007, January, 13-27	

Current Procedural Coding Expert – Respiratory System

30000-30115 I&D, Biopsy, Excision Procedures of the Nose

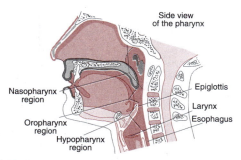

The nasopharynx is the membranous passage above the level of the soft palate; the oropharynx is the region between the soft palate and the upper edge of the epiglottis; the hypopharynx is the region of the epiglottis to the juncture of the larynx and esophagus; the three regions are collectively known as the pharynx

30000 Drainage abscess or hematoma, nasal, internal approach
 EXCLUDES Incision and drainage (10060, 10140)
 3.21 5.99 Global Days 010
 AMA: 2005, May, 13-14

30020 Drainage abscess or hematoma, nasal septum
 EXCLUDES Lateral rhinotomy incision (30118, 30320)
 3.24 6.03 Global Days 010

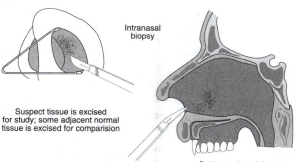

Suspect tissue is excised for study; some adjacent normal tissue is excised for comparison

Only a wedge of tissue is removed for larger lesions

30100 Biopsy, intranasal
 EXCLUDES Superficial biopsy of nose (11100-11101)
 1.88 3.69 Global Days 000

30110 Excision, nasal polyp(s), simple
 3.55 6.01 Global Days 010

30115 Excision, nasal polyp(s), extensive
 11.52 11.52 Global Days 090

30117-30118 Destruction Procedures Nose

CMS 100-3,140.5   Laser Procedures

30117 Excision or destruction (eg, laser), intranasal lesion; internal approach
 8.98 22.22 Global Days 090

30118 external approach (lateral rhinotomy)
 20.82 20.82 Global Days 090

30120-30140 Excision Procedures Nose, Turbinate

30120 Excision or surgical planing of skin of nose for rhinophyma
 11.78 13.71 Global Days 090
 AMA: 2009, Jan, 11-31; 2008, Jan, 10-25; 2007, May, 9-11

30124 Excision dermoid cyst, nose; simple, skin, subcutaneous
 7.35 7.35 Global Days 090

30125 complex, under bone or cartilage
 16.48 16.48 Global Days 090

30130 Excision inferior turbinate, partial or complete, any method
 EXCLUDES Excision middle/superior turbinate(s) (30999)
 Do not report with (30801, 30802, 30930)
 10.07 10.07 Global Days 090
 AMA: 2009, Jan, 11-31; 2008, Jan, 10-25; 2007, January, 13-27

30140 Submucous resection inferior turbinate, partial or complete, any method
 EXCLUDES Endoscopic resection of concha bullosa of middle turbinate (31240)
 Reduction of turbinates, report 30140-52 (30140)
 Submucous resection:
 Nasal septum (30520)
 Superior or middle turbinate (30999)

 Do not report with (30801, 30802, 30930)
 11.57 11.57 Global Days 090
 AMA: 2009, Jan, 11-31; 2008, Jan, 10-25; 2008, Mar, 14-15; 2007, January, 13-27

30150-30160 Surgical Removal: Nose

EXCLUDES Reconstruction and/or closure (primary or delayed primary intention) (13150-13160, 14060-14302, 15120-15121, 15260-15261, 15261, 15760, 20900-20912)

30150 Rhinectomy; partial
 20.90 20.90 Global Days 090

30160 total
 21.10 21.10 Global Days 090

30200-30320 Turbinate Injection, Removal Foreign Substance in the Nose

30200 Injection into turbinate(s), therapeutic
 1.64 2.98 Global Days 000
 AMA: 2009, Jan, 11-31; 2008, Jan, 10-25; 2007, January, 13-27

30210 Displacement therapy (Proetz type)
 2.69 3.93 Global Days 010

30220 Insertion, nasal septal prosthesis (button)
 3.42 7.83 Global Days 010

30300 Removal foreign body, intranasal; office type procedure
 3.32 5.87 Global Days 010

30310 requiring general anesthesia
 5.47 5.47 Global Days 010

30320 by lateral rhinotomy
 12.07 12.07 Global Days 090

● New Code ▲ Revised Code M Maternity A Age Unlisted Not Covered # Resequenced
CCI + Add-on ⊘ Mod 51 Exempt Mod 63 Exempt ⊙ Mod Sedation PQ PQRI

30400-30630 Reconstruction or Repair of Nose

EXCLUDES *Bone/tissue grafts (20900-20926, 21210)*

- **30400** Rhinoplasty, primary; lateral and alar cartilages and/or elevation of nasal tip
  - **INCLUDES** Carpue's operation
  - **EXCLUDES** *Reconstruction of columella (13150-13153)*
  - 27.04   27.04   Global Days 090
- **30410** complete, external parts including bony pyramid, lateral and alar cartilages, and/or elevation of nasal tip
  - 31.99   31.99   Global Days 090
- **30420** including major septal repair
  - 37.16   37.16   Global Days 090
- **30430** Rhinoplasty, secondary; minor revision (small amount of nasal tip work)
  - 23.31   23.31   Global Days 090
- **30435** intermediate revision (bony work with osteotomies)
  - 29.99   29.99   Global Days 090
- **30450** major revision (nasal tip work and osteotomies)
  - 40.91   40.91   Global Days 090

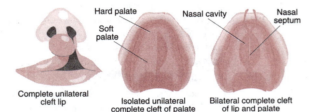

- **30460** Rhinoplasty for nasal deformity secondary to congenital cleft lip and/or palate, including columellar lengthening; tip only
  - 22.08   22.08   Global Days 090
- **30462** tip, septum, osteotomies
  - 39.67   39.67   Global Days 090
- **30465** Repair of nasal vestibular stenosis (eg, spreader grafting, lateral nasal wall reconstruction)
  - 26.65   26.65   Global Days 090
- **30520** Septoplasty or submucous resection, with or without cartilage scoring, contouring or replacement with graft
  - **EXCLUDES** *Turbinate resection (30140)*
  - 16.81   16.81   Global Days 090
  - **AMA:** 2009, Jan, 11-31; 2008, Jan, 10-25; 2007, January, 13-27
- **30540** Repair choanal atresia; intranasal
  - 18.55   18.55   Global Days 090
- **30545** transpalatine
  - 22.56   22.56   Global Days 090
- **30560** Lysis intranasal synechia
  - 3.67   6.94   Global Days 010
- **30580** Repair fistula; oromaxillary (combine with 31030 if antrotomy is included)
  - 13.76   17.07   Global Days 090
- **30600** oronasal
  - 11.84   15.36   Global Days 090
- **30620** Septal or other intranasal dermatoplasty (does not include obtaining graft)
  - 16.54   16.54   Global Days 090
- **30630** Repair nasal septal perforations
  - 16.82   16.82   Global Days 090

30801-30802 Turbinate Destruction

EXCLUDES *Cautery to stop nasal bleeding (30901-30906)*

Do not report with (30130, 30140)

- ▲ **30801** Ablation, soft tissue of inferior turbinates, unilateral or bilateral, any method (eg, electrocautery, radiofrequency ablation, or tissue volume reduction); superficial
  - **EXCLUDES** *Ablation middle/superior turbinates (30999)*
  - Do not report with (30802)
  - 3.59   5.83   Global Days 010
- ▲ **30802** intramural (ie, submucosal)
  - 5.11   7.58   Global Days 010
  - **AMA:** 2009, Jan, 11-31; 2008, Mar, 14-15

30901-30999 Control Nose Bleed

- **30901** Control nasal hemorrhage, anterior, simple (limited cautery and/or packing) any method
  - 1.76   2.80   Global Days 000
- **30903** Control nasal hemorrhage, anterior, complex (extensive cautery and/or packing) any method
  - 2.29   5.26   Global Days 000
- **30905** Control nasal hemorrhage, posterior, with posterior nasal packs and/or cautery, any method; initial
  - 2.88   6.51   Global Days 000
- **30906** subsequent
  - 3.78   7.38   Global Days 000
- **30915** Ligation arteries; ethmoidal
  - **EXCLUDES** *External carotid artery (37600)*
  - 15.79   15.79   Global Days 090
- **30920** internal maxillary artery, transantral
  - **EXCLUDES** *External carotid artery (37600)*
  - 22.85   22.85   Global Days 090

Current Procedural Coding Expert – Respiratory System

30930	Fracture nasal inferior turbinate(s), therapeutic	A2 T 50
	EXCLUDES *Fracture of superior or middle turbinate(s) (30999)*	
	Do not report with (30130, 30140)	
	3.31　3.31　Global Days 010	
	AMA: 2009, Jan, 11-31; 2008, Jan, 10-25; 2007, January, 13-27	
30999	Unlisted procedure, nose	T 80
	0.00　0.00　Global Days YYY	

31000-31230 Opening Sinuses

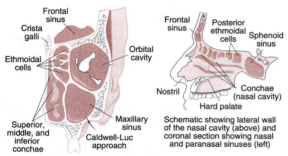

Schematic showing lateral wall of the nasal cavity (above) and coronal section showing nasal and paranasal sinuses (left)

The nasal sinuses are air filled cavities in the cranial bones that bear their names; all are lined with mucous membrane continuous with the nasal cavity and all drain fluids into the nasal cavity. The ethmoid cells vary in size and number and feature very thin septa, or walls. The maxillary sinuses are the largest and are the most frequently infected.

31000	Lavage by cannulation; maxillary sinus (antrum puncture or natural ostium)	P3 T 50
	2.80　4.66　Global Days 010	
31002	sphenoid sinus	R2 T 80 50
	5.30　5.30　Global Days 010	
31020	Sinusotomy, maxillary (antrotomy); intranasal	A2 T 50
	9.32　12.34　Global Days 090	
31030	radical (Caldwell-Luc) without removal of antrochoanal polyps	A2 T 50
	13.99　17.95　Global Days 090	
31032	radical (Caldwell-Luc) with removal of antrochoanal polyps	A2 T 50
	15.41　15.41　Global Days 090	
31040	Pterygomaxillary fossa surgery, any approach	R2 T
	EXCLUDES *Transantral ligation internal maxillary artery (30920)*	
	20.45　20.45　Global Days 090	
31050	Sinusotomy, sphenoid, with or without biopsy;	A2 T 50
	13.20　13.20　Global Days 090	
31051	with mucosal stripping or removal of polyp(s)	A2 T 50
	17.37　17.37　Global Days 090	
31070	Sinusotomy frontal; external, simple (trephine operation)	A2 T 50
	INCLUDES Killian operation	
	EXCLUDES *Intranasal frontal sinusotomy (31276)*	
	11.70　11.70　Global Days 090	
31075	transorbital, unilateral (for mucocele or osteoma, Lynch type)	A2 T 80 50
	21.18　21.18　Global Days 090	

31080	obliterative without osteoplastic flap, brow incision (includes ablation)	A2 T 80 50
	INCLUDES Ridell sinusotomy	
	27.97　27.97　Global Days 090	
31081	obliterative, without osteoplastic flap, coronal incision (includes ablation)	A2 T 80 50
	38.29　38.29　Global Days 090	
31084	obliterative, with osteoplastic flap, brow incision	A2 T 80 50
	31.44　31.44　Global Days 090	
31085	obliterative, with osteoplastic flap, coronal incision	A2 T 80 50
	40.78　40.78　Global Days 090	
31086	nonobliterative, with osteoplastic flap, brow incision	A2 T 80 50
	30.52　30.52　Global Days 090	
31087	nonobliterative, with osteoplastic flap, coronal incision	A2 T 80 50
	29.60　29.60　Global Days 090	
31090	Sinusotomy, unilateral, 3 or more paranasal sinuses (frontal, maxillary, ethmoid, sphenoid)	A2 T 50
	27.50　27.50　Global Days 090	
31200	Ethmoidectomy; intranasal, anterior	A2 T 50
	14.61　14.61　Global Days 090	
31201	intranasal, total	A2 T 50
	19.90　19.90　Global Days 090	
31205	extranasal, total	A2 T 80 50
	23.87　23.87　Global Days 090	
31225	Maxillectomy; without orbital exenteration	C 80 50
	51.47　51.47　Global Days 090	
31230	with orbital exenteration (en bloc)	C 80 50
	EXCLUDES *Orbital exenteration without maxillectomy (65110-65114)*	
	Skin grafts (15120-15121)	
	57.53　57.53　Global Days 090	

31231-31235 Nasal Endoscopy, Diagnostic

CMS 100-3, 100.2　Endoscopy
CMS 100-4, 12, 40.6　Multiple procedures

INCLUDES Complete sinus exam (e.g., nasal cavity, turbinates, sphenoethmoidal recess)

31231	Nasal endoscopy, diagnostic, unilateral or bilateral (separate procedure)	P2 T
	2.13　4.97　Global Days 000	
31233	Nasal/sinus endoscopy, diagnostic with maxillary sinusoscopy (via inferior meatus or canine fossa puncture)	A2 T 50
	3.83　6.98　Global Days 000	
31235	Nasal/sinus endoscopy, diagnostic with sphenoid sinusoscopy (via puncture of sphenoidal face or cannulation of ostium)	A2 T 50
	4.54　7.93　Global Days 000	

31237-31240 Nasal Endoscopy, Surgical

CMS 100-3,100.2 — Endoscopy

INCLUDES
Diagnostic nasal/sinus endoscopy
Sinusotomy, when applicable

EXCLUDES
Endoscopic frontal sinus exploration, osteomeatal complex (OMC) resection and/or anterior ethmoidectomy:
  With antrostomy, with/without polyp removal, report all: (31254, 31256, 31276)
  With/without polyp removal, report both: (31254, 31276)
Endoscopic frontal sinus exploration, osteomeatal complex (OMC) resection, antrostomy, removal of antral mucosal disease and/or anterior ethmoidectomy, with/without polyp removal, report all: (31254, 31267, 31276)
Endoscopic osteomeatal complex (OMC) resection with antrostomy:
  And/or anterior ethmoidectomy, with/without polyp removal, report both: (31254, 31256)
  Removal of antral mucosal disease, and/or anterior ethmoidectomy, with/without polyp removal, report both: (31254, 31267)

31237 Nasal/sinus endoscopy, surgical; with biopsy, polypectomy or debridement (separate procedure) [A2][T][50]
  5.10 8.62 Global Days 000
  AMA: 2009, Jan, 11-31; 2008, Jan, 10-25; 2007, January, 13-27

31238 with control of nasal hemorrhage [A2][T][80][50]
  5.54 8.89 Global Days 000

31239 with dacryocystorhinostomy [A2][T][80][50]
  18.69 18.69 Global Days 010

31240 with concha bullosa resection [A2][T][80][50]
  4.51 4.51 Global Days 000

31254-31255 Nasal Endoscopy with Ethmoid Removal

CMS 100-3,100.2 — Endoscopy
CMS 100-4,12,40.6 — Multiple procedures

INCLUDES
Diagnostic nasal/sinus endoscopy
Sinusotomy, when applicable

31254 Nasal/sinus endoscopy, surgical; with ethmoidectomy, partial (anterior) [A2][T][50]

  EXCLUDES
  Endoscopic exploration frontal sinus, resection osteomeatal complex (OMC), antrostomy:
    And/or anterior ethmoidectomy, with/without polyp removal, report all (31254, 31256, 31276)
    Removal of antral mucosal disease and/or anterior ethmoidectomy, with/without polyp removal, report all: (31254, 31267, 31276)
  Endoscopic frontal sinus exploration, osteomeatal complex (OMC) resection and/or anterior ethmoidectomy, with/without polyp removal, report both: (31254, 31276)
  Endoscopic resection osteomeatal complex (OMC):
    And antrostomy, removal antral mucosal disease, and/or anterior ethmoidectomy, with/without polyp removal, report both: (31254, 31276)
    Antrostomy, and/or anterior ethmoidectomy, with/without polyp removal, report both: (31254, 31256, 31267, 31276)

  7.72 7.72 Global Days 000
  AMA: 2009, Jan, 11-31; 2008, Jan, 10-25; 2007, January, 13-27

31255 with ethmoidectomy, total (anterior and posterior) [A2][T][50]

  EXCLUDES
  Endoscopic anterior and posterior ethmoidectomy (APE), antrostomy:
    With removal disease of antral mucosa, with/without polyp removal, report both: (31255, 31267)
    With/without polyp removal, report both: (31255, 31256)
  Endoscopic anterior and posterior ethmoidectomy and sphenoidotomy (APS), antrostomy:
    And removal of diseased antral mucosa, with/without polyp removal, report 31255 and 31267 with 31287, or 31288: (31255, 31267, 31287 or 31288)
    With/without polyp removal, report 31255 and 31256 with: (31287 or 31288)
  Endoscopic anterior and posterior ethmoidectomy and sphenoidotomy (APS), with/without polyp removal, report 31255 with: (31287, or 31288)
  Endoscopic frontal sinus exploration, anterior and posterior ethmoidectomy and sphenoidotomy (APS):
    Antrostomy, removal diseased antral mucosa, with/without polyp removal, report 31255, 31267, and 31276 with: (31287 or 31288)
    Antrostomy, with/without polyp removal, report 31255, 31256, and 31276 with: (31287 or 31288)
    With/without polyp removal, report 31255 and 31276 with: (31287 or 31288)
  Endoscopic frontal sinus exploration, anterior and posterior ethmoidectomy (APE):
    Antrostomy, removal diseased antral mucosa, with/without polyp removal, report all: (31255, 31267, 31276)
    Antrostomy, with/without polyp removal, report all: (31255, 31256, 31276)
    With/without polyp removal, report both: (31255, 31276)

  11.33 11.33 Global Days 000
  AMA: 2009, Jan, 11-31; 2008, Jan, 10-25; 2007, January, 13-27

Current Procedural Coding Expert – Respiratory System

31256-31267 Nasal Endoscopy with Maxillary Procedures

CMS 100-3,100.2 — Endoscopy
CMS 100-4,12,40.6 — Multiple procedures
INCLUDES Diagnostic nasal/sinus endoscopy
Sinusotomy, when applicable

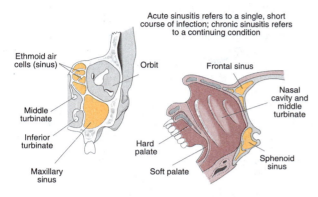

Acute sinusitis refers to a single, short course of infection; chronic sinusitis refers to a continuing condition

- 31256   Nasal/sinus endoscopy, surgical, with maxillary antrostomy;

  EXCLUDES *Endoscopic anterior and posterior ethmoidectomy and sphenoidotomy (APS):*
  Antrostomy, with/without polyp removal, report 31255 and 31256 with: (31287 or 31288)
  Frontal sinus exploration, and antrostomy, with/without polyp removal, report 31255, 31256 and 31276 with: (31287 or 31288)
  Endoscopic anterior and posterior ethmoidectomy (APE):
  Antrostomy, with/without polyp removal, report both: (31255, 31256)
  Frontal sinus exploration, antrostomy, with/without polyp removal, report all: (31255, 31256, 31276)

  5.59   5.59   Global Days 000

- 31267   with removal of tissue from maxillary sinus

  EXCLUDES *Endoscopic anterior and posterior ethmoidectomy and sphenoidotomy (APS):*
  Antrostomy, and removal of diseased antral mucosal, with/without polyp removal, report 31255, 31267 with: (31287 or 31288)
  Frontal sinus exploration, antrostomy, and removal of diseased antral mucosa, with/without polyp removal, report 31255, 31267 and 31276 with: (31287 or 31288)
  Endoscopic anterior and posterior ethmoidectomy (APE)
  Antrostomy, removal of antral mucosal disease, with/without polyp removal, report both: (31255, 31267)
  Frontal sinus exploration, antrostomy and removal of antral mucosal disease, with/without polyp removal, report all: (31255, 31267, 31276)

  8.99   8.99   Global Days 000

  AMA: 2009, Jan, 11-31; 2008, Jan, 10-25; 2007, January, 13-27

31276 Nasal Endoscopy with Frontal Sinus Examination

CMS 100-3,100.2 — Endoscopy
CMS 100-4,12,40.6 — Multiple procedures
INCLUDES Diagnostic nasal/sinus endoscopy
Sinusotomy, when applicable

EXCLUDES *Endoscopic anterior and posterior ethmoidectomy and sphenoidotomy (APS):*
Frontal sinus exploration, with/without polyp removal, report: 31255 and 31276 and (31287 or 31288)
With frontal sinus exploration, antrostomy and removal of antral mucosal disease, with/without polyp removal, report: 31255 and 31267 and 31276 and (31287 or 31288)
With/without polyp removal, with frontal sinus exploration and antrostomy report: 31255 and 31256 and 31276 and (31287 or 31288)
Endoscopic anterior and posterior ethmoidectomy (APE), frontal sinus exploration, with/without polyp removal, report both: (31255, 31276)
Unilateral endoscopy two or more sinuses (31231-31235)

- 31276   Nasal/sinus endoscopy, surgical with frontal sinus exploration, with or without removal of tissue from frontal sinus

  14.32   14.32   Global Days 000

31287-31288 Nasal Endoscopy with Sphenoid Procedures

CMS 100-3,100.2 — Endoscopy
CMS 100-4,12,40.6 — Multiple procedures

- 31287   Nasal/sinus endoscopy, surgical, with sphenoidotomy;

  6.56   6.56   Global Days 000

- 31288   with removal of tissue from the sphenoid sinus

  7.61   7.61   Global Days 000

31290

31290-31299 Nasal Endoscopy with Repair and Decompression

CMS 100-3,100.2   Endoscopy
CMS 100-4,12,40.6 Multiple procedures
INCLUDES Diagnostic nasal/sinus endoscopy
          Sinusotomy, when applicable

- **31290** Nasal/sinus endoscopy, surgical, with repair of cerebrospinal fluid leak; ethmoid region
  32.44 32.44 Global Days 010
- **31291** sphenoid region
  34.22 34.22 Global Days 010
- **31292** Nasal/sinus endoscopy, surgical; with medial or inferior orbital wall decompression
  28.00 28.00 Global Days 010
- **31293** with medial orbital wall and inferior orbital wall decompression
  30.46 30.46 Global Days 010
- **31294** with optic nerve decompression
  34.94 34.94 Global Days 010
- **31299** Unlisted procedure, accessory sinuses
  EXCLUDES Hypophysectomy (61546, 61548)
  0.00 0.00 Global Days YYY

31300-31502 Procedures of the Larynx

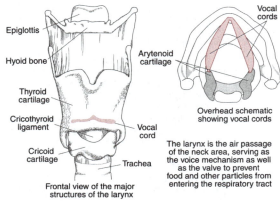

Frontal view of the major structures of the larynx
Overhead schematic showing vocal cords
The larynx is the air passage of the neck area, serving as the voice mechanism as well as the valve to prevent food and other particles from entering the respiratory tract

- **31300** Laryngotomy (thyrotomy, laryngofissure); with removal of tumor or laryngocele, cordectomy
  34.62 34.62 Global Days 090
- **31320** diagnostic
  17.36 17.36 Global Days 090
- **31360** Laryngectomy; total, without radical neck dissection
  57.41 57.41 Global Days 090
- **31365** total, with radical neck dissection
  71.46 71.46 Global Days 090
  AMA: 2009, Jan, 11-31; 2008, Jan, 10-25; 2007, January, 13-27
- **31367** subtotal supraglottic, without radical neck dissection
  60.66 60.66 Global Days 090
- **31368** subtotal supraglottic, with radical neck dissection
  67.33 67.33 Global Days 090
- **31370** Partial laryngectomy (hemilaryngectomy); horizontal
  56.77 56.77 Global Days 090
- **31375** laterovertical
  53.86 53.86 Global Days 090
- **31380** anterovertical
  53.07 53.07 Global Days 090
- **31382** antero-latero-vertical
  58.34 58.34 Global Days 090
- **31390** Pharyngolaryngectomy, with radical neck dissection; without reconstruction
  78.68 78.68 Global Days 090
- **31395** with reconstruction
  83.21 83.21 Global Days 090
- **31400** Arytenoidectomy or arytenoidopexy, external approach
  EXCLUDES Endoscopic arytenoidectomy (31560)
  26.98 26.98 Global Days 090

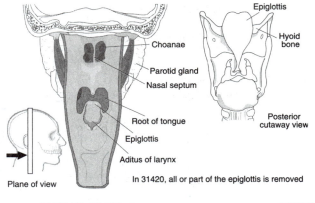

In 31420, all or part of the epiglottis is removed

- **31420** Epiglottidectomy
  22.96 22.96 Global Days 090
- **31500** Intubation, endotracheal, emergency procedure
  EXCLUDES Injection of contrast for segmental bronchography (31656)
  3.06 3.06 Global Days 000
  AMA: 2007, April, 3-6; 2007, Jul, 1-4; 2006, May, 1-9
- **31502** Tracheotomy tube change prior to establishment of fistula tract
  0.99 0.99 Global Days 000

31505-31541 Endoscopy of the Larynx

CMS 100-3,100.2   Endoscopy
CMS 100-4,12,40.6 Multiple procedures

- **31505** Laryngoscopy, indirect; diagnostic (separate procedure)
  1.35 2.18 Global Days 000
- **31510** with biopsy
  3.38 5.58 Global Days 000
- **31511** with removal of foreign body
  3.62 5.62 Global Days 000
- **31512** with removal of lesion
  3.66 5.56 Global Days 000
- **31513** with vocal cord injection
  3.72 3.72 Global Days 000
- **31515** Laryngoscopy direct, with or without tracheoscopy; for aspiration
  3.09 5.49 Global Days 000
- **31520** diagnostic, newborn
  4.44 4.44 Global Days 000
- **31525** diagnostic, except newborn
  4.48 6.71 Global Days 000

Current Procedural Coding Expert – Respiratory System

31526	diagnostic, with operating microscope or telescope
	INCLUDES Operating microscope (69990)
	4.45 4.45 Global Days 000
31527	with insertion of obturator
	5.55 5.55 Global Days 000
31528	with dilation, initial
	4.09 4.09 Global Days 000
31529	with dilation, subsequent
	4.56 4.56 Global Days 000
31530	Laryngoscopy, direct, operative, with foreign body removal;
	5.60 5.60 Global Days 000
31531	with operating microscope or telescope
	INCLUDES Operating microscope (69990)
	6.03 6.03 Global Days 000
31535	Laryngoscopy, direct, operative, with biopsy;
	5.38 5.38 Global Days 000
31536	with operating microscope or telescope
	INCLUDES Operating microscope (69990)
	5.99 5.99 Global Days 000
31540	Laryngoscopy, direct, operative, with excision of tumor and/or stripping of vocal cords or epiglottis;
	6.89 6.89 Global Days 000
31541	with operating microscope or telescope
	INCLUDES Operating microscope (69990)
	7.52 7.52 Global Days 000

31545-31546 Endoscopy of Larynx with Reconstruction

INCLUDES   Operating microscope (69990)
EXCLUDES   Vocal cord reconstruction with allograft (31599)
Do not report with (31540, 31541, 69990)

31545	Laryngoscopy, direct, operative, with operating microscope or telescope, with submucosal removal of non-neoplastic lesion(s) of vocal cord; reconstruction with local tissue flap(s)
	10.35 10.35 Global Days 000
31546	reconstruction with graft(s) (includes obtaining autograft)
	Do not report with (20926)
	15.76 15.76 Global Days 000
	AMA: 2009, Jan, 11-31; 2008, Jan, 10-25; 2007, January, 13-27; 2006, May, 16-20

31560-31571 Endoscopy of Larynx with Arytenoid Removal, Vocal Cord Injection

CMS 100-3,100.2   Endoscopy
CMS 100-4,12,40.6   Multiple procedures

31560	Laryngoscopy, direct, operative, with arytenoidectomy;
	8.95 8.95 Global Days 000
31561	with operating microscope or telescope
	INCLUDES Operating microscope (69990)
	9.78 9.78 Global Days 000
31570	Laryngoscopy, direct, with injection into vocal cord(s), therapeutic;
	6.45 9.06 Global Days 000
31571	with operating microscope or telescope
	INCLUDES Operating microscope (69990)
	7.12 7.12 Global Days 000

31575-31579 Endoscopy of Larynx, Flexible Fiberoptic

EXCLUDES   Evaluation by flexible fiberoptic endoscope:
    Sensory assessment (92614-92615)
    Swallowing (92612-92613)
    Swallowing and sensory assessment (92616-92617)
    Flexible fiberoptic endoscopic examination/testing by cine or video recording (92612-92617)

31575	Laryngoscopy, flexible fiberoptic; diagnostic
	2.13 3.06 Global Days 000
31576	with biopsy
	3.46 5.92 Global Days 000
31577	with removal of foreign body
	4.20 6.46 Global Days 000
31578	with removal of lesion
	4.87 7.51 Global Days 000
31579	Laryngoscopy, flexible or rigid fiberoptic, with stroboscopy
	3.96 5.68 Global Days 000

31580-31599 Larynx Reconstruction

31580	Laryngoplasty; for laryngeal web, 2-stage, with keel insertion and removal
	33.17 33.17 Global Days 090
31582	for laryngeal stenosis, with graft or core mold, including tracheotomy
	51.55 51.55 Global Days 090
31584	with open reduction of fracture
	41.47 41.47 Global Days 090
31587	Laryngoplasty, cricoid split
	27.92 27.92 Global Days 090
31588	Laryngoplasty, not otherwise specified (eg, for burns, reconstruction after partial laryngectomy)
	31.25 31.25 Global Days 090
	AMA: 2009, Jan, 11-31; 2008, Jan, 10-25; 2007, January, 13-27
31590	Laryngeal reinnervation by neuromuscular pedicle
	23.57 23.57 Global Days 090

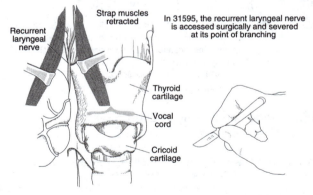

In 31595, the recurrent laryngeal nerve is accessed surgically and severed at its point of branching

31595	Section recurrent laryngeal nerve, therapeutic (separate procedure), unilateral
	20.67 20.67 Global Days 090
31599	Unlisted procedure, larynx
	0.00 0.00 Global Days YYY

● New Code   ▲ Revised Code   M Maternity   A Age   Unlisted   Not Covered   # Resequenced
CCI   + Add-on   ⊘ Mod 51 Exempt   Ⓜ Mod 63 Exempt   ⊙ Mod Sedation   PQRI
© 2009 Publisher (Blue Ink)   CPT only © 2009 American Medical Association. All Rights Reserved. (Black Ink)   Medicare (Red Ink)   101

31600-31610 Stoma Creation: Trachea

EXCLUDES Aspiration of trachea, direct vision (31515)
Endotracheal intubation (31500)

- **31600** Tracheostomy, planned (separate procedure); [A] [T] [■]
  11.13 11.13 Global Days 000

- **31601** younger than 2 years [A] [T] [80] [■]
  7.36 7.36 Global Days 000

- **31603** Tracheostomy, emergency procedure; transtracheal [A2] [T] [■]
  6.29 6.29 Global Days 000

- **31605** cricothyroid membrane [G2] [T] [■]
  5.12 5.12 Global Days 000

- **31610** Tracheostomy, fenestration procedure with skin flaps [T] [■]
  19.49 19.49 Global Days 090

31611-31614 Procedures of the Trachea

- **31611** Construction of tracheoesophageal fistula and subsequent insertion of an alaryngeal speech prosthesis (eg, voice button, Blom-Singer prosthesis) [A2] [T] [80] [■]
  14.56 14.56 Global Days 090

- **31612** Tracheal puncture, percutaneous with transtracheal aspiration and/or injection [A2] [T] [80] [■]
  EXCLUDES Tracheal aspiration under direct vision (31515)
  1.35 2.17 Global Days 000

- **31613** Tracheostoma revision; simple, without flap rotation [A2] [T] [■]
  12.14 12.14 Global Days 090

- **31614** complex, with flap rotation [A2] [T] [■]
  20.38 20.38 Global Days 090

31615 Endoscopy Through Tracheostomy

INCLUDES Diagnostic bronchoscopy

- ⊙ **31615** Tracheobronchoscopy through established tracheostomy incision [A2] [T] [■]
  3.58 4.86 Global Days 000

31620 Endobronchial Ultrasound (EBUS)

- +⊙ **31620** Endobronchial ultrasound (EBUS) during bronchoscopic diagnostic or therapeutic intervention(s) (List separately in addition to code for primary procedure[s]) [N1] [N]
  Code first (31622-31646)
  1.90 6.72 Global Days ZZZ
  AMA: 2005, August, 4-6

31622-31656 Endoscopy of Lung

INCLUDES Diagnostic bronchoscopy with surgical bronchoscopy procedures
Fluoroscopic guidance for codes 31622-31646

- ⊙ ▲ **31622** Bronchoscopy, rigid or flexible, including fluoroscopic guidance, when performed; diagnostic, with cell washing, when performed (separate procedure) [A2] [T] [■]
  4.06 7.91 Global Days 000
  AMA: 2009, Jan, 11-31; 2008, Jan, 10-25; 2007, January, 13-27; 2005, August, 4-6

- ⊙ ▲ **31623** with brushing or protected brushings [A2] [T] [■]
  4.08 8.33 Global Days 000
  AMA: 2009, Jan, 11-31; 2008, Jan, 10-25; 2008, May, 9-11; 2007, January, 13-27; 2005, August, 4-6

- ⊙ ▲ **31624** with bronchial alveolar lavage [A2] [T] [■]
  4.09 7.87 Global Days 000
  AMA: 2009, Jan, 11-31; 2008, Jan, 10-25; 2008, May, 9-11; 2007, January, 13-27; 2005, August, 4-6

- ⊙ ▲ **31625** with bronchial or endobronchial biopsy(s), single or multiple sites [A2] [T] [■]
  4.76 8.55 Global Days 000
  AMA: 2009, Jan, 11-31; 2008, Jan, 10-25; 2007, January, 13-27; 2005, August, 4-6

- ⊙ ● **31626** with placement of fiducial markers, single or multiple [G2] [T] [80]
  device
  5.85 11.72 Global Days 000

- +⊙ ● **31627** with computer-assisted, image-guided navigation (List separately in addition to code for primary procedure[s]) [N1] [N] [80]
  INCLUDES 3D reconstruction
  Code first (31615, 31622-31631, 31635-31636, 31638-31643)
  Do not report with (76376-76377)
  2.84 32.29 Global Days ZZZ

- ⊙ **31628** with transbronchial lung biopsy(s), single lobe [A2] [T] [■]
  INCLUDES All biopsies taken from lobe
  EXCLUDES Transbronchial biopsies by needle aspiration (31629, 31633)
  Transbronchial biopsies of additional lobe(s) (31632)
  5.29 9.70 Global Days 000
  AMA: 2009, Jan, 11-31; 2008, Jan, 10-25; 2008, May, 9-11; 2007, January, 13-27; 2005, August, 4-6

- ⊙ **31629** with transbronchial needle aspiration biopsy(s), trachea, main stem and/or lobar bronchus(i) [A2] [T] [■]
  INCLUDES All biopsies from same lobe
  EXCLUDES Transbronchial biopsies of lung (31628, 31632)
  Transbronchial needle biopsies of another lobe(s) (31633)
  5.70 14.70 Global Days 000
  AMA: 2009, Jan, 11-31; 2008, Jan, 10-25; 2007, January, 13-27; 2005, August, 4-6

- **31630** with tracheal/bronchial dilation or closed reduction of fracture [A2] [T] [■]
  5.63 5.63 Global Days 000
  AMA: 2005, August, 4-6

- **31631** with placement of tracheal stent(s) (includes tracheal/bronchial dilation as required) [A2] [T] [■]
  EXCLUDES Bronchial stent placement (31636-31637)
  Revision bronchial or tracheal stent (31638)
  6.43 6.43 Global Days 000
  AMA: 2005, August, 4-6

- + ▲ **31632** with transbronchial lung biopsy(s), each additional lobe (List separately in addition to code for primary procedure) [G2] [T] [■]
  INCLUDES All biopsies of additional lobe of lung
  Code first (31628)
  1.39 1.90 Global Days ZZZ
  AMA: 2005, August, 4-6

Current Procedural Coding Expert – Respiratory System 31825

+ ▲ 31633	with transbronchial needle aspiration biopsy(s), each additional lobe (List separately in addition to code for primary procedure)

INCLUDES All needle biopsies from another lobe or from trachea

Code first 31629
1.78 2.34 Global Days ZZZ
AMA: 2009, Jan, 11-31; 2008, Jan, 10-25; 2007, January, 13-27; 2005, August, 4-6

⊙ 31635 with removal of foreign body
5.26 8.81 Global Days 000
AMA: 2009, Jan, 11-31; 2008, Jan, 10-25; 2007, January, 13-27; 2005, August, 4-6

31636 with placement of bronchial stent(s) (includes tracheal/bronchial dilation as required), initial bronchus
6.21 6.21 Global Days 000
AMA: 2005, August, 4-6

+ 31637 each additional major bronchus stented (List separately in addition to code for primary procedure)
Code first 31636
2.09 2.09 Global Days ZZZ
AMA: 2005, August, 4-6

31638 with revision of tracheal or bronchial stent inserted at previous session (includes tracheal/bronchial dilation as required)
7.12 7.12 Global Days 000
AMA: 2005, August, 4-6

31640 with excision of tumor
7.18 7.18 Global Days 000
AMA: 2005, August, 4-6

▲ 31641 with destruction of tumor or relief of stenosis by any method other than excision (eg, laser therapy, cryotherapy)
Code also any photodynamic therapy via bronchoscopy (96570-96571)
7.21 7.21 Global Days 000
AMA: 2005, August, 4-6

▲ 31643 with placement of catheter(s) for intracavitary radioelement application
Code also if appropriate (77761-77763, 77785-77787)
4.85 4.85 Global Days 000
AMA: 2005, August, 4-6

⊙ ▲ 31645 with therapeutic aspiration of tracheobronchial tree, initial (eg, drainage of lung abscess)
EXCLUDES Bedside aspiration of trachea, bronchi (31725)
4.47 7.69 Global Days 000
AMA: 2005, August, 4-6

⊙ ▲ 31646 with therapeutic aspiration of tracheobronchial tree, subsequent
EXCLUDES Bedside aspiration of trachea, bronchi (31725)
3.87 6.94 Global Days 000
AMA: 2005, August, 4-6

⊙ ▲ 31656 with injection of contrast material for segmental bronchography (fiberscope only)
71040, 71060
3.05 7.38 Global Days 000

31715-31899 Respiratory Procedures

EXCLUDES Endotracheal intubation (31500)
Tracheal aspiration under direct vision (31515)

31715 Transtracheal injection for bronchography
EXCLUDES Prolonged services (99354-99360)
71040, 71060
1.46 1.46 Global Days 000

31717 Catheterization with bronchial brush biopsy
2.98 6.39 Global Days 000
AMA: 2009, Jan, 11-31; 2008, Jan, 10-25; 2007, January, 13-27

31720 Catheter aspiration (separate procedure); nasotracheal
1.43 1.43 Global Days 000

⊙ 31725 tracheobronchial with fiberscope, bedside
2.65 2.65 Global Days 000

31730 Transtracheal (percutaneous) introduction of needle wire dilator/stent or indwelling tube for oxygen therapy
4.17 29.09 Global Days 000

31750 Tracheoplasty; cervical
36.70 36.70 Global Days 090

31755 tracheopharyngeal fistulization, each stage
46.21 46.21 Global Days 090

31760 intrathoracic
38.06 38.06 Global Days 090

31766 Carinal reconstruction
52.00 52.00 Global Days 090

31770 Bronchoplasty; graft repair
EXCLUDES Bronchoplasty done with lobectomy (32501)
37.12 37.12 Global Days 090

31775 excision stenosis and anastomosis
EXCLUDES Bronchoplasty done with lobectomy (32501)
38.95 38.95 Global Days 090

31780 Excision tracheal stenosis and anastomosis; cervical
33.31 33.31 Global Days 090

31781 cervicothoracic
43.05 43.05 Global Days 090

31785 Excision of tracheal tumor or carcinoma; cervical
30.42 30.42 Global Days 090

31786 thoracic
40.17 40.17 Global Days 090

31800 Suture of tracheal wound or injury; cervical
19.30 19.30 Global Days 090

31805 intrathoracic
23.67 23.67 Global Days 090

31820 Surgical closure tracheostomy or fistula; without plastic repair
EXCLUDES Tracheoesophageal fistula repair (43305, 43312)
9.06 11.70 Global Days 090

31825 with plastic repair
EXCLUDES Tracheoesophageal fistula repair (43305, 43312)
13.32 16.32 Global Days 090

● New Code   ▲ Revised Code   M Maternity   A Age   Unlisted   Not Covered   # Resequenced
CCI   + Add-on   ⊘ Mod 51 Exempt   63 Mod 63 Exempt   ⊙ Mod Sedation   PQ PQRI
© 2009 Publisher (Blue Ink)   CPT only © 2009 American Medical Association. All Rights Reserved. (Black Ink)   Medicare (Red Ink)   103

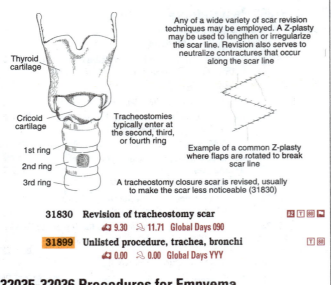

31830	Revision of tracheostomy scar	A2 T 80	
	9.30 11.71 Global Days 090		
31899	Unlisted procedure, trachea, bronchi	T 80	
	0.00 0.00 Global Days YYY		

32035-32036 Procedures for Empyema

32035	Thoracostomy; with rib resection for empyema	C 80
	19.91 19.91 Global Days 090	
32036	with open flap drainage for empyema	C 80
	21.53 21.53 Global Days 090	

32095-32160 Open Procedures: Chest

INCLUDES Exploration of penetrating wound of chest
EXCLUDES Lung resection (32480-32504)

32095	Thoracotomy, limited, for biopsy of lung or pleura	C 80 P0
	EXCLUDES Exploration without thoracotomy of wound due to penetrating trauma (20102)	
	17.61 17.61 Global Days 090	
32100	Thoracotomy, major; with exploration and biopsy	C 80 P0
	Do not report with (19260, 19271-19272, 32503-32504)	
	26.72 26.72 Global Days 090	
	AMA: 2007, March, 1-3	
32110	with control of traumatic hemorrhage and/or repair of lung tear	C 80 P0
	40.79 40.79 Global Days 090	
32120	for postoperative complications	C 80 P0
	24.35 24.35 Global Days 090	
32124	with open intrapleural pneumonolysis	C 80 P0
	26.00 26.00 Global Days 090	
32140	with cyst(s) removal, with or without a pleural procedure	C 80 P0
	27.90 27.90 Global Days 090	
32141	with excision-plication of bullae, with or without any pleural procedure	C 80 P0
	EXCLUDES Lung volume reduction (32491)	
	43.24 43.24 Global Days 090	
32150	with removal of intrapleural foreign body or fibrin deposit	C 80 P0
	28.06 28.06 Global Days 090	
32151	with removal of intrapulmonary foreign body	C 80
	27.90 27.90 Global Days 090	
32160	with cardiac massage	C 80
	21.86 21.86 Global Days 090	

32200-32320 Open Procedures: Lung

32200	Pneumonostomy; with open drainage of abscess or cyst	C 80
	75989	
	31.65 31.65 Global Days 090	
32201	with percutaneous drainage of abscess or cyst	T
	75989	
	5.46 22.07 Global Days 000	
32215	Pleural scarification for repeat pneumothorax	C 80 P0
	22.34 22.34 Global Days 090	
32220	Decortication, pulmonary (separate procedure); total	C 80 P0
	44.50 44.50 Global Days 090	
32225	partial	C 80 P0
	27.88 27.88 Global Days 090	
32310	Pleurectomy, parietal (separate procedure)	C 80 P0
	25.73 25.73 Global Days 090	
32320	Decortication and parietal pleurectomy	C 80 P0
	44.83 44.83 Global Days 090	

32400-32405 Lung Biopsy

EXCLUDES Fine needle aspiration biopsy (10021, 10022)

32400	Biopsy, pleura; percutaneous needle	A2 T
	76942, 77002, 77012, 77021	
	88172-88173	
	2.40 3.81 Global Days 000	
32402	open	C 80 P0
	15.75 15.75 Global Days 090	
32405	Biopsy, lung or mediastinum, percutaneous needle	A2 T
	76942, 77002, 77012, 77021	
	88172-88173	
	2.63 2.63 Global Days 000	
	AMA: 2009, Jan, 11-31; 2008, Jan, 10-25; 2007, January, 13-27	

32420-32422 Needle Insertion: Chest

32420	Pneumocentesis, puncture of lung for aspiration	A2 T
	3.00 3.00 Global Days 000	
32421	Thoracentesis, puncture of pleural cavity for aspiration, initial or subsequent	A2 T 50
	EXCLUDES Total lung lavage (32997)	
	76942, 77002, 77012	
	2.13 3.87 Global Days 000	
32422	Thoracentesis with insertion of tube, includes water seal (eg, for pneumothorax), when performed (separate procedure)	G2 T 50
	Do not report with (19260, 19271-19272, 32503-32504)	
	76942, 77002, 77012	
	3.34 4.99 Global Days 000	

Current Procedural Coding Expert – Respiratory System

32440-32501 Lung Resection
Code also resection of chest wall tumor, as appropriate, (19260-19272)

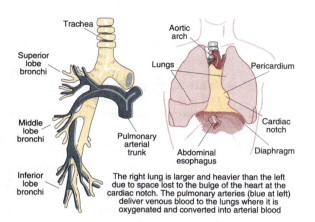

The right lung is larger and heavier than the left due to space lost to the bulge of the heart at the cardiac notch. The pulmonary arteries (blue at left) deliver venous blood to the lungs where it is oxygenated and converted into arterial blood.

32440 Removal of lung, total pneumonectomy;
44.09 44.09 Global Days 090

32442 with resection of segment of trachea followed by broncho-tracheal anastomosis (sleeve pneumonectomy)
76.54 76.54 Global Days 090

32445 extrapleural
EXCLUDES Empyemectomy with extrapleural pneumonectomy (32540)
98.82 98.82 Global Days 090

32480 Removal of lung, other than total pneumonectomy; single lobe (lobectomy)
EXCLUDES Lung removal with bronchoplasty (32501)
Code also (32320)
41.71 41.71 Global Days 090

32482 2 lobes (bilobectomy)
EXCLUDES Lung removal with bronchoplasty (32501)
Code also (32320)
44.60 44.60 Global Days 090
AMA: 2009, Jan, 11-31; 2008, Jan, 10-25; 2007, January, 28-31

32484 single segment (segmentectomy)
EXCLUDES Lung removal with bronchoplasty (32501)
Code also (32320)
40.48 40.48 Global Days 090

32486 with circumferential resection of segment of bronchus followed by broncho-bronchial anastomosis (sleeve lobectomy)
Code also (32320)
66.48 66.48 Global Days 090

32488 all remaining lung following previous removal of a portion of lung (completion pneumonectomy)
Code also (32320)
67.49 67.49 Global Days 090

32491 excision-plication of emphysematous lung(s) (bullous or non-bullous) for lung volume reduction, sternal split or transthoracic approach, with or without any pleural procedure
41.04 41.04 Global Days 090

32500 wedge resection, single or multiple
40.36 40.36 Global Days 090

+ 32501 Resection and repair of portion of bronchus (bronchoplasty) when performed at time of lobectomy or segmentectomy (List separately in addition to code for primary procedure)
Code first 32480-32484
6.95 6.95 Global Days ZZZ

32503-32504 Excision of Lung Neoplasm
EXCLUDES Lung resection performed in conjunction with chest wall resection
Do not report with (19260, 19271-19272, 32100, 32422, 32551)

32503 Resection of apical lung tumor (eg, Pancoast tumor), including chest wall resection, rib(s) resection(s), neurovascular dissection, when performed; without chest wall reconstruction(s)
50.54 50.54 Global Days 090

32504 with chest wall reconstruction
57.73 57.73 Global Days 090

32540 Removal of Empyema

32540 Extrapleural enucleation of empyema (empyemectomy)
EXCLUDES Lung removal code when empyemectomy is performed with lobectomy (see appropriate lung removal code)
Code also appropriate removal of lung code when done with lobectomy (32480-32488)
48.68 48.68 Global Days 090

32550-32552 Chest Tube/Catheter

32550 Insertion of indwelling tunneled pleural catheter with cuff
Code also drainage catheter (C1729)
Do not report with (32421-32422)
75989
6.25 19.68 Global Days 000

32551 Tube thoracostomy, includes water seal (eg, for abscess, hemothorax, empyema), when performed (separate procedure)
Do not report with (19260, 19271-19272, 32503-32504)
75989
4.75 4.75 Global Days 000

● 32552 Removal of indwelling tunneled pleural catheter with cuff
4.44 5.01 Global Days 010

32553 Intrathoracic Placement Radiation Therapy Devices

● 32553 Placement of interstitial device(s) for radiation therapy guidance (eg, fiducial markers, dosimeter), percutaneous, intra-thoracic, single or multiple
EXCLUDES Percutaneous placement of interstitial device(s) for radiation therapy guidance: intra-abdominal, intrapelvic, and/or retroperitoneal (49411) device
76942, 77002, 77012, 77021
5.73 16.11 Global Days 000

32560-32562 Instillation Drug/Chemical by Chest Tube

EXCLUDES Insertion of chest tube (32551)

▲ **32560** Instillation, via chest tube/catheter, agent for pleurodesis (eg, talc for recurrent or persistent pneumothorax) T
 2.30 6.30 Global Days 000

● **32561** Instillation(s), via chest tube/catheter, agent for fibrinolysis (eg, fibrinolytic agent for break-up of multiloculated effusion); initial day T 80
 Do not report more than one time on the date of initial treatment
 2.00 2.61 Global Days 000

● **32562** subsequent day T 80
 Do not report more than one time on each day of subsequent treatment
 1.79 2.32 Global Days 000

32601-32820 Endoscopy of Chest, Repair, Reconstruction

CMS 100-3,100.2 Endoscopy
CMS 100-4,12,40.6 Multiple procedures
INCLUDES Diagnostic thoracoscopy in surgical thoracoscopy

32601 Thoracoscopy, diagnostic (separate procedure); lungs and pleural space, without biopsy T 80
 8.64 8.64 Global Days 000

32602 lungs and pleural space, with biopsy T 80
 9.38 9.38 Global Days 000

32603 pericardial sac, without biopsy T 80
 12.22 12.22 Global Days 000

32604 pericardial sac, with biopsy T 80
 13.49 13.49 Global Days 000

32605 mediastinal space, without biopsy T 80
 10.76 10.76 Global Days 000

32606 mediastinal space, with biopsy T 80
 13.05 13.05 Global Days 000

32650 Thoracoscopy, surgical; with pleurodesis (eg, mechanical or chemical) C 80
 18.59 18.59 Global Days 090

32651 with partial pulmonary decortication C 80
 30.67 30.67 Global Days 090

32652 with total pulmonary decortication, including intrapleural pneumonolysis C 80
 46.56 46.56 Global Days 090

32653 with removal of intrapleural foreign body or fibrin deposit C 80
 29.48 29.48 Global Days 090

32654 with control of traumatic hemorrhage C 80
 33.09 33.09 Global Days 090

32655 with excision-plication of bullae, including any pleural procedure C 80
 26.82 26.82 Global Days 090
 AMA: 2009, Jan, 11-31; 2008, Jan, 10-25; 2007, January, 13-27; 2005, August, 13-15

32656 with parietal pleurectomy C 80
 22.23 22.23 Global Days 090

32657 with wedge resection of lung, single or multiple C 80 P0
 21.89 21.89 Global Days 090

32658 with removal of clot or foreign body from pericardial sac C 80
 19.73 19.73 Global Days 090

32659 with creation of pericardial window or partial resection of pericardial sac for drainage C 80
 20.32 20.32 Global Days 090

32660 with total pericardiectomy C 80
 29.00 29.00 Global Days 090

32661 with excision of pericardial cyst, tumor, or mass C 80
 22.11 22.11 Global Days 090

32662 with excision of mediastinal cyst, tumor, or mass C 80
 25.01 25.01 Global Days 090
 AMA: 2009, Jan, 11-31; 2007, Dec, 10-179

32663 with lobectomy, total or segmental C 80
 39.24 39.24 Global Days 090

32664 with thoracic sympathectomy C 80 50
 23.51 23.51 Global Days 090
 AMA: 2009, Jan, 11-31; 2008, Jan, 10-25; 2007, January, 13-27

32665 with esophagomyotomy (Heller type) C 80
 35.69 35.69 Global Days 090

32800 Repair lung hernia through chest wall C 80 P0
 24.65 24.65 Global Days 090

32810 Closure of chest wall following open flap drainage for empyema (Clagett type procedure) C 80 P0
 24.93 24.93 Global Days 090

32815 Open closure of major bronchial fistula C 80 P0
 79.12 79.12 Global Days 090

32820 Major reconstruction, chest wall (posttraumatic) C 80
 36.89 36.89 Global Days 090

32850-32856 Lung Transplant Procedures

INCLUDES Harvesting donor lung(s), cold preservation, preparation of donor lung(s), transplantation into recipient
EXCLUDES Repairs or resection of donor lung(s) (32491, 32500, 35216, 35276)

32850 Donor pneumonectomy(s) (including cold preservation), from cadaver donor C
 0.00 0.00 Global Days XXX

32851 Lung transplant, single; without cardiopulmonary bypass C 80
 71.24 71.24 Global Days 090

32852 with cardiopulmonary bypass C 80
 78.52 78.52 Global Days 090

32853 Lung transplant, double (bilateral sequential or en bloc); without cardiopulmonary bypass C 80
 84.90 84.90 Global Days 090

32854 with cardiopulmonary bypass C 80
 92.86 92.86 Global Days 090

32855 Backbench standard preparation of cadaver donor lung allograft prior to transplantation, including dissection of allograft from surrounding soft tissues to prepare pulmonary venous/atrial cuff, pulmonary artery, and bronchus; unilateral C 80
 0.00 0.00 Global Days XXX

32856 bilateral C 80
 0.00 0.00 Global Days XXX

32900-32997 Chest and Respiratory Procedures

CMS 100-4,12,40.6 Multiple procedures

32900 Resection of ribs, extrapleural, all stages C 80 P0
 38.65 38.65 Global Days 090

32905 Thoracoplasty, Schede type or extrapleural (all stages); C 80 P0
 37.20 37.20 Global Days 090

Current Procedural Coding Expert – Respiratory System

32906 with closure of bronchopleural fistula [C] [80] [P0]
EXCLUDES Open closure of bronchial fistula (32815)
Resection first rib for thoracic compression (21615, 21616)

    46.05   46.05 Global Days 090

32940 Pneumonolysis, extraperiosteal, including filling or packing procedures [C] [80] [P0]

    34.33   34.33 Global Days 090

32960 Pneumothorax, therapeutic, intrapleural injection of air [G2] [T]

    2.88   4.01 Global Days 000

32997 Total lung lavage (unilateral) [C]
EXCLUDES Broncho-alveolar lavage by bronchoscopy (31624)

    10.08   10.08 Global Days 000

32998-32999 Destruction of Lung Neoplasm

32998 Ablation therapy for reduction or eradication of 1 or more pulmonary tumor(s) including pleura or chest wall when involved by tumor extension, percutaneous, radiofrequency, unilateral [G2] [T] [80]

    76940, 77013, 77022

    7.92   68.88 Global Days 000

32999 Unlisted procedure, lungs and pleura [T]

    0.00   0.00 Global Days YYY

AMA: 2009, Jan, 11-31; 2008, Jan, 10-25; 2008, Jul, 10&13; 2007, January, 13-27

● New Code   ▲ Revised Code   M Maternity   A Age   Unlisted   Not Covered   # Resequenced
CCI   + Add-on   ⊘ Mod 51 Exempt   Mod 63 Exempt   ⊙ Mod Sedation   P0 PQRI
© 2009 Publisher (*Blue Ink*)   CPT only © 2009 American Medical Association. All Rights Reserved. (Black Ink)   Medicare (*Red Ink*)

33010-33050 Procedures of the Pericardial Sac

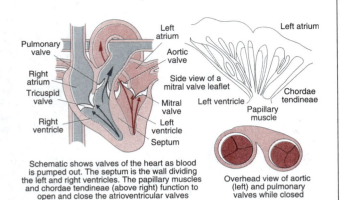

Schematic shows valves of the heart as blood is pumped out. The septum is the wall dividing the left and right ventricles. The papillary muscles and chordae tendineae (above right) function to open and close the atrioventricular valves

Overhead view of aortic (left) and pulmonary valves while closed

⊙ **33010** Pericardiocentesis; initial A2 T ▣
 76930
 3.29 3.29 Global Days 000

⊙ **33011** subsequent A2 T 80 ▣
 76930
 3.34 3.34 Global Days 000

33015 Tube pericardiostomy C ▣
 13.84 13.84 Global Days 090

33020 Pericardiotomy for removal of clot or foreign body (primary procedure) C 80 ▣ P0
 24.60 24.60 Global Days 090

33025 Creation of pericardial window or partial resection for drainage C 80 ▣ P0
 22.53 22.53 Global Days 090

33030 Pericardiectomy, subtotal or complete; without cardiopulmonary bypass C 80 ▣ P0
 INCLUDES Delorme pericardiectomy
 36.28 36.28 Global Days 090

33031 with cardiopulmonary bypass C 80 ▣ P0
 40.42 40.42 Global Days 090

33050 Excision of pericardial cyst or tumor C 80 ▣ P0
 28.07 28.07 Global Days 090

33120-33130 Neoplasms of Heart

33120 Excision of intracardiac tumor, resection with cardiopulmonary bypass C 80 ▣ P0
 43.97 43.97 Global Days 090
 AMA: 2007, March, 1-3

33130 Resection of external cardiac tumor C 80 ▣ P0
 46.06 46.06 Global Days 090
 AMA: 2007, March, 1-3

33140-33141 Transmyocardial Revascularization

CMS 100-3,20.6 Transmyocardial Revascularization (TMR) for Severe Angina

33140 Transmyocardial laser revascularization, by thoracotomy; (separate procedure) C 80 ▣ P0
 44.68 44.68 Global Days 090
 AMA: 2009, Jan, 11-31; 2008, Jan, 10-25; 2007, January, 13-27

+ **33141** performed at the time of other open cardiac procedure(s) (List separately in addition to code for primary procedure) C 80 P0
 Code first 33400-33496, 33510-33536, 33542
 3.80 3.80 Global Days ZZZ

33202-33249 Pacemakers/Implantable Defibrillators

CMS 100-3,20.4 Implantable Automatic Defibrillators
CMS 100-3,20.8 Cardiac Pacemakers
CMS 100-3,20.8.1 Cardiac Pacemaker Evaluation Services
CMS 100-3,20.8.1.1 Transtelephonic Monitoring of Cardiac Pacemakers
CMS 100-3,20.8.2 Self-contained Pacemaker Monitors
EXCLUDES Electronic analysis of internal pacemaker (93279-93280, 93288, 93293-93294)

33202 Insertion of epicardial electrode(s); open incision (eg, thoracotomy, median sternotomy, subxiphoid approach) C P0
 Code also insertion of pulse generator by same physician/same surgical session (33212-33213)
 71090
 21.65 21.65 Global Days 090

33203 endoscopic approach (eg, thoracoscopy, pericardioscopy) C P0
 Code also insertion of pulse generator by same physician/same surgical session (33212-33213)
 71090
 22.41 22.41 Global Days 090

⊙ **33206** Insertion or replacement of permanent pacemaker with transvenous electrode(s); atrial J8 T ▣ P0
 INCLUDES Pulse generator insertion/electrode placement
 Code also (C1779, C1785, C1786, C1898, C2619, C2620, C2621)
 71090
 12.31 12.31 Global Days 090
 AMA: 2009, Jan, 11-31; 2008, Jun, 14-15

⊙ **33207** ventricular J8 T ▣ P0
 INCLUDES Pulse generator insertion/electrode placement
 Code also (C1779, C1785, C1786, C1898, C2619, C2620, C2621)
 71090
 13.10 13.10 Global Days 090
 AMA: 2009, Jan, 11-31; 2008, Jun, 14-15

⊙ **33208** atrial and ventricular J8 T ▣ P0
 INCLUDES Pulse generator insertion/electrode placement
 Code also (C1779, C1785, C1898, C2619, C2621)
 71090
 14.17 14.17 Global Days 090
 AMA: 2009, Jan, 11-31; 2008, Jan, 10-25; 2008, Jun, 14-15; 2007, January, 13-27

⊙ **33210** Insertion or replacement of temporary transvenous single chamber cardiac electrode or pacemaker catheter (separate procedure) 62 T ▣
 71090
 4.90 4.90 Global Days 000
 AMA: 2007, March, 1-3

⊙ **33211** Insertion or replacement of temporary transvenous dual chamber pacing electrodes (separate procedure) 62 T ▣
 Code also (C1779, C1898)
 71090
 5.03 5.03 Global Days 000
 AMA: 2007, March, 1-3

Current Procedural Coding Expert – Cardiovascular System

33212 — Insertion or replacement of pacemaker pulse generator only; single chamber, atrial or ventricular [H8][T][CCI][PQ]
  Code also placement of epicardial leads by same physician/same surgical session (33202-33203)
  Code also (C1786, C2620, C2621)
  71090
  9.11   9.11 Global Days 090
  AMA: 2009, Jan, 11-31; 2008, Jan, 10-25; 2008, Jun, 14-15; 2007, January, 13-27

33213 — dual chamber [H8][T][CCI][PQ]
  Code also placement of epicardial leads by same physician/same surgical session (33202-33203)
  Code also (C1785, C2619, C2621)
  71090
  10.37   10.37 Global Days 090
  AMA: 2009, Jan, 11-31; 2008, Jan, 10-25; 2008, Jun, 14-15; 2007, January, 13-27

33214 — Upgrade of implanted pacemaker system, conversion of single chamber system to dual chamber system (includes removal of previously placed pulse generator, testing of existing lead, insertion of new lead, insertion of new pulse generator) [J8][T][80][CCI][PQ]
  Code also placement of epicardial leads by same physician/same surgical session when appropriate (33202-33203)
  Code also (C1779, C1785, C1898, C2619, C2621)
  Do not report with (33216-33217)
  71090
  13.01   13.01 Global Days 090
  AMA: 2008, Jun, 14-15

33215 — Repositioning of previously implanted transvenous pacemaker or pacing cardioverter-defibrillator (right atrial or right ventricular) electrode [G2][T][CCI][PQ]
  71090
  8.17   8.17 Global Days 090

▲ **33216** — Insertion of a single transvenous electrode, permanent pacemaker or cardioverter-defibrillator [G2][T][CCI][PQ]
  EXCLUDES *Insertion or replacement of a lead for a cardiac venous system (33224-33225)*
  Code also (C1777, C1779, C1895, C1896, C1898, C1899)
  Do not report with (33214)
  71090
  10.02   10.02 Global Days 090
  AMA: 2009, Jan, 11-31; 2008, Jan, 10-25; 2007, January, 13-27

▲ **33217** — Insertion of 2 transvenous electrodes, permanent pacemaker or cardioverter-defibrillator [G2][T][CCI][PQ]
  EXCLUDES *Insertion or replacement of a lead for a cardiac venous system (33224-33225)*
  Code also (C1777, C1779, C1895, C1896, C1898, C1899)
  Do not report with (33214)
  71090
  9.99   9.99 Global Days 090
  AMA: 2009, Jan, 11-31; 2008, Jan, 10-25; 2007, January, 13-27

33218 — Repair of single transvenous electrode for a single chamber, permanent pacemaker or single chamber pacing cardioverter-defibrillator [G2][T][CCI][PQ]
  Code also insertion of pulse generator replacement when appropriate (33212, or 33213)
  71090
  10.45   10.45 Global Days 090
  AMA: 2009, Jan, 11-31; 2008, Jan, 10-25; 2007, January, 13-27; 2005, January, 46-47

33220 — Repair of 2 transvenous electrodes for a dual chamber permanent pacemaker or dual chamber pacing cardioverter-defibrillator [G2][T][CCI][PQ]
  Code also pulse generator replacement when appropriate (33212, or 33213)
  71090
  10.60   10.60 Global Days 090
  AMA: 2009, Jan, 11-31; 2008, Jun, 14-15

33222 — Revision or relocation of skin pocket for pacemaker [A2][T][CCI][PQ]
  71090
  9.23   9.23 Global Days 090
  AMA: 2008, Jun, 14-15

▲ **33223** — Revision of skin pocket for cardioverter-defibrillator [A2][T][80][CCI][PQ]
  71090
  11.04   11.04 Global Days 090
  AMA: 2008, Jun, 14-15

33224 — Insertion of pacing electrode, cardiac venous system, for left ventricular pacing, with attachment to previously placed pacemaker or pacing cardioverter-defibrillator pulse generator (including revision of pocket, removal, insertion, and/or replacement of generator) [J8][T][CCI][PQ]
  Code also placement of epicardial electrode when appropriate (33202-33203)
  Code also (C1900)
  71090
  13.81   13.81 Global Days 000
  AMA: 2009, Jan, 11-31; 2007, Dec, 10-179

+ **33225** — Insertion of pacing electrode, cardiac venous system, for left ventricular pacing, at time of insertion of pacing cardioverter-defibrillator or pacemaker pulse generator (including upgrade to dual chamber system) (List separately in addition to code for primary procedure) [J8][T][CCI][PQ]
  Code also (33206-33208, 33212-33214, 33216-33217, 33222, 33233-33235, 33240, 33249, C1900)
  71090
  12.42   12.42 Global Days ZZZ
  AMA: 2009, Jan, 11-31; 2007, Dec, 10-179

33226 — Repositioning of previously implanted cardiac venous system (left ventricular) electrode (including removal, insertion and/or replacement of generator) [G2][T][CCI][PQ]
  71090
  13.27   13.27 Global Days 000

33233 — Removal of permanent pacemaker pulse generator [A2][T][CCI][PQ]
  71090
  6.26   6.26 Global Days 090
  AMA: 2009, Jan, 11-31; 2008, Jan, 10-25; 2007, January, 13-27

33234 — Removal of transvenous pacemaker electrode(s); single lead system, atrial or ventricular [G2][T][CCI][PQ]
  71090
  13.07   13.07 Global Days 090

33235 — dual lead system [G2][T][CCI][PQ]
  71090
  17.04   17.04 Global Days 090

33236 — Removal of permanent epicardial pacemaker and electrodes by thoracotomy; single lead system, atrial or ventricular [C][80][CCI][PQ]
  EXCLUDES *Removal of pacing cardioverter-defibrillator electrode(s) by thoracotomy (33243)*
  Removal of transvenous pacemaker electrodes, single or dual lead system (33234, 33235)
  71090
  22.00   22.00 Global Days 090

● New Code   ▲ Revised Code   Ⓜ Maternity   Ⓐ Age   Unlisted   Not Covered   # Resequenced
CCI   + Add-on   Mod 51 Exempt   Mod 63 Exempt   Mod Sedation   PQRI

© 2009 Publisher *(Blue Ink)*   CPT only © 2009 American Medical Association. All Rights Reserved. *(Black Ink)*   Medicare *(Red Ink)*

33237

	33237	dual lead system	C 80 P0
		EXCLUDES Removal of pacing cardioverter-defibrillator electrode(s) by thoracotomy (33243) Removal of transvenous pacemaker electrodes, single or dual lead system (33234, 33235)	
		71090	
		22.70 22.70 Global Days 090	
	33238	Removal of permanent transvenous electrode(s) by thoracotomy	C 80 P0
		EXCLUDES Removal of pacing cardioverter-defibrillator electrode(s) by thoracotomy (33243) Removal of transvenous pacemaker electrodes, single or dual lead system (33234, 33235)	
		71090	
		26.19 26.19 Global Days 090	
⊙	33240	Insertion of single or dual chamber pacing cardioverter-defibrillator pulse generator	J8 T 80 P0
		Code also cardioverter-defibrillator (C1721-C1722, C1882) Code also placement of epicardial leads by same physican/same surgical session (33202-33203)	
		71090	
		12.37 12.37 Global Days 090	
		AMA: 2009, Jan, 11-31; 2008, Jan, 10-25; 2008, Jun, 14-15; 2007, January, 13-27	
⊙	33241	Subcutaneous removal of single or dual chamber pacing cardioverter-defibrillator pulse generator	62 T 80 P0
		EXCLUDES Repair cardioverter-defibrillator generator and/or leads (33218, 33220)	
		Code also electrode removal if applicable (33243-33244) Code also removal with reinsertion of pacing cardioverter-defibrillator system; report with (33243, or 33244, 33249)	
		71090	
		5.89 5.89 Global Days 090	
	33243	Removal of single or dual chamber pacing cardioverter-defibrillator electrode(s); by thoracotomy	C 80 P0
		Code also subcutaneous removal pulse generator (33241)	
		71090	
		38.31 38.31 Global Days 090	
⊙	33244	by transvenous extraction	T 80 P0
		Code also subcutaneous removal pulse generator (33241)	
		71090	
		22.91 22.91 Global Days 090	
⊙	33249	Insertion or repositioning of electrode lead(s) for single or dual chamber pacing cardioverter-defibrillator and insertion of pulse generator	J8 T 80 P0
		EXCLUDES ICD lead insertion without thoracotomy (33216)	
		Code also cardio-defibrillator (C1721-C1722, C1882) Code also removal/reinsertion pacing cardioverter-defibrillator system; report (33241, 33243, or 33244, 33249)	
		71090	
		24.34 24.34 Global Days 090	
		AMA: 2008, May, 9-11; 2008, Jun, 14-15	

33250-33251 Surgical Ablation Arrhythmogenic Foci, Supraventricular

INCLUDES Procedures using cryotherapy, laser, microwave, radiofrequency, and ultrasound

33250	Operative ablation of supraventricular arrhythmogenic focus or pathway (eg, Wolff-Parkinson-White, atrioventricular node re-entry), tract(s) and/or focus (foci); without cardiopulmonary bypass	C 80 P0
	EXCLUDES Pacing and mapping during surgery by other provider (93631)	
	41.55 41.55 Global Days 090	
33251	with cardiopulmonary bypass	C 80 P0
	46.70 46.70 Global Days 090	

33254-33256 Surgical Ablation Arrhythmogenic Foci, Atrial (e.g., Maze)

INCLUDES Excision or isolation of the left atrial appendage
Procedures using cryotherapy, laser, microwave, radiofrequency, and ultrasound

Do not report with (32100, 32551, 33120, 33130, 33210-33211, 33400-33507, 33510-33523, 33533-33548, 33600-33853, 33860-33864, 33910-33920)

33254	Operative tissue ablation and reconstruction of atria, limited (eg, modified maze procedure)	C 80 P0
	38.76 38.76 Global Days 090	
	AMA: 2007, March, 1-3	
33255	Operative tissue ablation and reconstruction of atria, extensive (eg, maze procedure); without cardiopulmonary bypass	C 80 P0
	46.68 46.68 Global Days 090	
	AMA: 2007, March, 1-3	
33256	with cardiopulmonary bypass	C 80 P0
	55.46 55.46 Global Days 090	
	AMA: 2007, March, 1-3	

33257-33259 Surgical Ablation Arrhythmogenic Foci, Atrial, with Other Heart Procedure(s)

Do not report with (32551, 33210-33211, 33254-33256, 33265-33266)

+ 33257	Operative tissue ablation and reconstruction of atria, performed at the time of other cardiac procedure(s), limited (eg, modified maze procedure) (List separately in addition to code for primary procedure)	C 80
	Code first (33120-33130, 33250-33251, 33261, 33300-33335, 33400-33496, 33500-33507, 33510-33516, 33533-33548, 33600-33619, 33641-33697, 33702-33732, 33735-33767, 33770-33814, 33840-33877, 33910-33922, 33925-33926, 33935, 33945, 33975-33980)	
	16.50 16.50 Global Days ZZZ	
+ 33258	Operative tissue ablation and reconstruction of atria, performed at the time of other cardiac procedure(s), extensive (eg, maze procedure), without cardiopulmonary bypass (List separately in addition to code for primary procedure)	C 80
	Code first (33130, 33250, 33300, 33310, 33320-33321, 33330, 33332, 33401, 33414-33417, 33420, 33470-33472, 33501-33503, 33510-33516, 33533-33536, 33690, 33735, 33737, 33800-33813, 33840-33852, 33915, 33925)	
	18.57 18.57 Global Days ZZZ	

Current Procedural Coding Expert – Cardiovascular System

+ 33259 Operative tissue ablation and reconstruction of atria, performed at the time of other cardiac procedure(s), extensive (eg, maze procedure), with cardiopulmonary bypass (List separately in addition to code for primary procedure) [C][80]
Code first (33120, 33251, 33261, 33305, 33315, 33322, 33335, 33400, 33403-33413, 33422-33468, 33474-33478, 33496, 33500, 33504-33507, 33510-33516, 33533-33548, 33600-33688, 33692-33722, 33730, 33732, 33736, 33750-33767, 33770-33781, 33786-33788, 33814, 33853, 33860-33877, 33910, 33916-33922, 33926, 33935, 33945, 33975-33980)
23.95   23.95   Global Days ZZZ

33261 Surgical Ablation Arrhythmogenic Foci, Ventricular

33261 Operative ablation of ventricular arrhythmogenic focus with cardiopulmonary bypass [C][80][P0]
46.06   46.06   Global Days 090

33265-33266 Surgical Ablation Arrhythmogenic Foci, Endoscopic

Do not report with (32551, 33210-33211)

33265 Endoscopy, surgical; operative tissue ablation and reconstruction of atria, limited (eg, modified maze procedure), without cardiopulmonary bypass [C][80]
38.44   38.44   Global Days 090
AMA: 2007, March, 1-3

33266 operative tissue ablation and reconstruction of atria, extensive (eg, maze procedure), without cardiopulmonary bypass [C][80]
52.45   52.45   Global Days 090
AMA: 2007, March, 1-3

33282-33284 Implantable Loop Recorder

CMS 100-3,20.15   Electrocardiographic Services

33282 Implantation of patient-activated cardiac event recorder [J8][S]
INCLUDES Initial programming of device
EXCLUDES Subsequent electronic analysis and/or reprogramming of device (93285, 93291, 93298)
Code also (C1764)
8.49   8.49   Global Days 090
AMA: 2009, Jan, 11-31; 2009, Mar, 5-7; 2009, Feb, 3-12; 2008, Jun, 14-15

33284 Removal of an implantable, patient-activated cardiac event recorder [62][T]
6.03   6.03   Global Days 090

33300-33315 Procedures for Injury of the Heart

33300 Repair of cardiac wound; without bypass [C][80][P0]
69.54   69.54   Global Days 090

33305 with cardiopulmonary bypass [C][80][P0]
117.07   117.07   Global Days 090

33310 Cardiotomy, exploratory (includes removal of foreign body, atrial or ventricular thrombus); without bypass [C][80][P0]
Do not report with other cardiac procedures unless separate incision into heart is necessary in order to remove thrombus
32.91   32.91   Global Days 090

33315 with cardiopulmonary bypass [C][80][P0]
Code also excision of thrombus with cardiopulmonary bypass as appropriate if separate incision is required (33120, 33130, 33420-33430, 33460-33468, 33496, 33542, 33545, 33641-33647, 33670, 33681, 33975-33980)
Do not report with other cardiac procedures unless separate incision into heart is necessary in order to remove thrombus; in this case, append modifier 59
41.99   41.99   Global Days 090

33320-33335 Procedures for Injury of the Aorta/Great Vessels

33320 Suture repair of aorta or great vessels; without shunt or cardiopulmonary bypass [C][80][P0]
29.84   29.84   Global Days 090

33321 with shunt bypass [C][80][P0]
33.41   33.41   Global Days 090

33322 with cardiopulmonary bypass [C][80][P0]
39.53   39.53   Global Days 090

33330 Insertion of graft, aorta or great vessels; without shunt, or cardiopulmonary bypass [C][80]
42.39   42.39   Global Days 090

33332 with shunt bypass [C][80][P0]
39.42   39.42   Global Days 090

33335 with cardiopulmonary bypass [C][80][P0]
53.93   53.93   Global Days 090

33400-33415 Aortic Valve Procedures

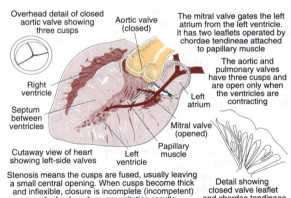

33400 Valvuloplasty, aortic valve; open, with cardiopulmonary bypass [C][80][P0]
64.92   64.92   Global Days 090
AMA: 2007, March, 1-3; 2005, February, 13-16

33401 open, with inflow occlusion [C][80][63][P0]
39.09   39.09   Global Days 090
AMA: 2007, March, 1-3; 2005, February, 13-16

33403 using transventricular dilation, with cardiopulmonary bypass [C][80][63][P0]
41.95   41.95   Global Days 090
AMA: 2007, March, 1-3; 2005, February, 13-16

33404 Construction of apical-aortic conduit [C][80][P0]
49.79   49.79   Global Days 090
AMA: 2009, Jan, 11-31; 2008, Jan, 10-25; 2007, January, 13-27; 2007, March, 1-3; 2005, February, 13-16

● New Code   ▲ Revised Code   M Maternity   A Age   Unlisted   Not Covered   # Resequenced
□ CCI   + Add-on   ⊘ Mod 51 Exempt   ⊘ Mod 63 Exempt   ⊙ Mod Sedation   P0 PQRI
© 2009 Publisher (Blue Ink)   CPT only © 2009 American Medical Association. All Rights Reserved. (Black Ink)   Medicare (Red Ink)

33405

Current Procedural Coding Expert – Cardiovascular System

33405	Replacement, aortic valve, with cardiopulmonary bypass; with prosthetic valve other than homograft or stentless valve			C 80 P0
	EXCLUDES	Valvotomy of aortic valve:
		With cardiopulmonary bypass (33403)
		With inflow occlusion (33401)
	65.24 65.24 Global Days 090
	AMA: 2007, March, 1-3; 2005, February, 13-16
33406	with allograft valve (freehand)		C 80 P0
	EXCLUDES	Valvotomy of aortic valve:
		With cardiopulmonary bypass (33403)
		With inflow occlusion (33401)
	82.22 82.22 Global Days 090
	AMA: 2007, March, 1-3; 2005, February, 13-16
33410	with stentless tissue valve		C 80 P0
	72.86 72.86 Global Days 090
	AMA: 2007, March, 1-3; 2005, February, 13-16
33411	Replacement, aortic valve; with aortic annulus enlargement, noncoronary cusp		C 80 P0
	96.30 96.30 Global Days 090
	AMA: 2007, March, 1-3; 2005, February, 13-16
33412	with transventricular aortic annulus enlargement (Konno procedure)		C 80
	69.72 69.72 Global Days 090
	AMA: 2007, March, 1-3; 2005, February, 13-16
33413	by translocation of autologous pulmonary valve with allograft replacement of pulmonary valve (Ross procedure)		C 80 P0
	91.49 91.49 Global Days 090
	AMA: 2007, March, 1-3; 2005, February, 13-16
33414	Repair of left ventricular outflow tract obstruction by patch enlargement of the outflow tract		C 80
	61.51 61.51 Global Days 090
	AMA: 2007, March, 1-3; 2005, February, 13-16
33415	Resection or incision of subvalvular tissue for discrete subvalvular aortic stenosis		C 80
	58.03 58.03 Global Days 090
	AMA: 2007, March, 1-3; 2005, February, 13-16

33416 Ventriculectomy

CMS 100-3,20.26   Partial Ventriculectomy

33416	Ventriculomyotomy (-myectomy) for idiopathic hypertrophic subaortic stenosis (eg, asymmetric septal hypertrophy)	C 80 P0
	58.13 58.13 Global Days 090
	AMA: 2007, March, 1-3; 2005, February, 13-16

33417 Repair of Supravalvular Stenosis by Aortoplasty

33417	Aortoplasty (gusset) for supravalvular stenosis	C 80
	47.39 47.39 Global Days 090
	AMA: 2007, March, 1-3; 2005, February, 13-16

33420-33468 Mitral and Tricuspid Valve Procedures

INCLUDES   Procedures on mitral and tricuspid valves

Code also removal of thrombus through a separate heart incision if applicable (33310, 33315)

33420	Valvotomy, mitral valve; closed heart	C
	40.22 40.22 Global Days 090
	AMA: 2007, March, 1-3; 2005, February, 13-16
33422	open heart, with cardiopulmonary bypass	C 80 P0
	47.54 47.54 Global Days 090
	AMA: 2007, March, 1-3; 2005, February, 13-16
33425	Valvuloplasty, mitral valve, with cardiopulmonary bypass;	C 80 P0
	77.90 77.90 Global Days 090
	AMA: 2009, Jan, 11-31; 2008, Jan, 10-25; 2007, March, 1-3; 2007, January, 13-27; 2005, February, 13-16
33426	with prosthetic ring	C 80 P0
	68.25 68.25 Global Days 090
	AMA: 2007, March, 1-3; 2005, February, 13-16
33427	radical reconstruction, with or without ring	C 80 P0
	69.94 69.94 Global Days 090
	AMA: 2007, March, 1-3; 2005, February, 13-16
33430	Replacement, mitral valve, with cardiopulmonary bypass	C 80 P0
	80.29 80.29 Global Days 090
	AMA: 2007, March, 1-3; 2005, February, 13-16
33460	Valvectomy, tricuspid valve, with cardiopulmonary bypass	C 80 P0
	81.80 81.80 Global Days 090
	AMA: 2007, March, 1-3; 2005, February, 13-16
33463	Valvuloplasty, tricuspid valve; without ring insertion	C 80 P0
	88.54 88.54 Global Days 090
	AMA: 2007, March, 1-3; 2005, February, 13-16
33464	with ring insertion	C 80 P0
	70.30 70.30 Global Days 090
	AMA: 2007, March, 1-3; 2005, February, 13-16
33465	Replacement, tricuspid valve, with cardiopulmonary bypass	C 80 P0
	79.00 79.00 Global Days 090
	AMA: 2007, March, 1-3; 2005, February, 13-16
33468	Tricuspid valve repositioning and plication for Ebstein anomaly	C 80
	52.08 52.08 Global Days 090
	AMA: 2007, March, 1-3; 2005, February, 13-16

33470-33474 Pulmonary Valvotomy

INCLUDES   Brock's operation

Code also the concurrent ligation/takedown of a systemic-to-pulmonary artery shunt (33924)

33470	Valvotomy, pulmonary valve, closed heart; transventricular	C 80 50
	34.51 34.51 Global Days 090
	AMA: 2007, March, 1-3; 2005, February, 13-16
33471	via pulmonary artery	C 80
	EXCLUDES	Percutaneous valvuloplasty of pulmonary valve (92990)
	35.03 35.03 Global Days 090
	AMA: 2007, March, 1-3; 2005, February, 13-16
33472	Valvotomy, pulmonary valve, open heart; with inflow occlusion	C 80 50
	34.69 34.69 Global Days 090
	AMA: 2007, March, 1-3; 2005, February, 13-16
33474	with cardiopulmonary bypass	C 80
	61.06 61.06 Global Days 090
	AMA: 2007, March, 1-3; 2005, February, 13-16

33475-33478 Other Procedures Pulmonary Valve

33475	Replacement, pulmonary valve	C 80 P0
	EXCLUDES	Concurrent ligation/takedown of a systemic-to-pulmonary artery shunt (33924)
	66.56 66.56 Global Days 090
	AMA: 2007, March, 1-3; 2005, February, 13-16

26/TC PC/TC Comp Only	A2-Z3 ASC Pmt	50 Bilateral	♂ Male Only	♀ Female Only	Facility RVU	Non-Facility RVU
AMA: CPT Asst	**MED:** Pub 100	A-Y OPPSI	80/80 Surg Assist Allowed / w/Doc	Lab Crosswalk	Radiology Crosswalk

112   CPT only © 2009 American Medical Association. All Rights Reserved. (Black Ink)    Medicare (Red Ink)   © 2009 Publisher (Blue Ink)

Current Procedural Coding Expert – Cardiovascular System

33476 Right ventricular resection for infundibular stenosis, with or without commissurotomy
INCLUDES Brock's operation
43.01 43.01 Global Days 090
AMA: 2007, March, 1-3; 2005, February, 13-16

33478 Outflow tract augmentation (gusset), with or without commissurotomy or infundibular resection
Code also 33768 for cavopulmonary anastomosis to a second superior vena cava
44.45 44.45 Global Days 090
AMA: 2007, March, 1-3; 2005, February, 13-16

33496 Prosthetic Valve Repair

Code also reoperation if performed (33530)
Code also separate incision into heart to remove thrombus if applicable; append modifier 59 to (33315)

33496 Repair of non-structural prosthetic valve dysfunction with cardiopulmonary bypass (separate procedure)
47.62 47.62 Global Days 090
AMA: 2007, March, 1-3; 2005, February, 13-16

33500-33507 Repair Aberrant Coronary Artery Anatomy

INCLUDES Angioplasty and/or endarterectomy

33500 Repair of coronary arteriovenous or arteriocardiac chamber fistula; with cardiopulmonary bypass
44.59 44.59 Global Days 090
AMA: 2007, March, 1-3

33501 without cardiopulmonary bypass
31.78 31.78 Global Days 090
AMA: 2007, March, 1-3

33502 Repair of anomalous coronary artery from pulmonary artery origin; by ligation
35.97 35.97 Global Days 090
AMA: 2007, March, 1-3

33503 by graft, without cardiopulmonary bypass
35.93 35.93 Global Days 090
AMA: 2007, March, 1-3

33504 by graft, with cardiopulmonary bypass
41.40 41.40 Global Days 090
AMA: 2007, March, 1-3

33505 with construction of intrapulmonary artery tunnel (Takeuchi procedure)
58.52 58.52 Global Days 090
AMA: 2007, March, 1-3

33506 by translocation from pulmonary artery to aorta
57.76 57.76 Global Days 090
AMA: 2007, March, 1-3

33507 Repair of anomalous (eg, intramural) aortic origin of coronary artery by unroofing or translocation
48.40 48.40 Global Days 090
AMA: 2007, March, 1-3

33508 Endoscopic Harvesting of Venous Graft

+ **33508** Endoscopy, surgical, including video-assisted harvest of vein(s) for coronary artery bypass procedure (List separately in addition to code for primary procedure)
EXCLUDES Harvesting of vein of upper extremity (35500)
Code first 33510-33523
0.46 0.46 Global Days ZZZ

33510-33516 Coronary Artery Bypass: Venous Grafts

INCLUDES Harvesting of saphenous vein grafts
Venous grafting only
EXCLUDES Arterial grafting only (33533-33536)
Combined arterial-venous grafts; 33517-33523 and (33533-33535)
Harvesting of vein graft:
  Of femoropopliteal vein (35572)
  Of upper extremity vein (35500)
  Performed by surgical assistant

33510 Coronary artery bypass, vein only; single coronary venous graft
55.58 55.58 Global Days 090
AMA: 2009, Jan, 11-31; 2008, Jan, 10-25; 2007, January, 13-27; 2007, January, 7-10; 2007, March, 1-3; 2005, February, 13-16

33511 2 coronary venous grafts
60.94 60.94 Global Days 090
AMA: 2007, March, 1-3; 2007, January, 7-10; 2005, February, 13-16

33512 3 coronary venous grafts
69.13 69.13 Global Days 090
AMA: 2007, March, 1-3; 2007, January, 7-10; 2005, February, 13-16

33513 4 coronary venous grafts
71.17 71.17 Global Days 090
AMA: 2007, January, 7-10; 2007, March, 1-3; 2005, February, 13-16

33514 5 coronary venous grafts
75.22 75.22 Global Days 090
AMA: 2007, January, 7-10; 2007, March, 1-3; 2005, February, 13-16

33516 6 or more coronary venous grafts
77.59 77.59 Global Days 090
AMA: 2007, January, 7-10; 2007, March, 1-3; 2005, February, 13-16

33517-33523 Coronary Artery Bypass: Venous AND Arterial Grafts

INCLUDES Harvesting of saphenous vein grafts
EXCLUDES Harvesting of artery: from upper extremity (35600)
Femoropopliteal vein graft (35572)
Vein of upper extremity (35500)
Venous or arterial graft by surgical assistant
Code also appropriate code from (33533-33536)

+ **33517** Coronary artery bypass, using venous graft(s) and arterial graft(s); single vein graft (List separately in addition to code for primary procedure)
5.40 5.40 Global Days ZZZ
AMA: 2007, January, 7-10; 2007, March, 1-3; 2005, February, 13-16

+ **33518** 2 venous grafts (List separately in addition to code for primary procedure)
11.87 11.87 Global Days ZZZ
AMA: 2007, March, 1-3; 2007, January, 7-10; 2005, February, 13-16

+ **33519** 3 venous grafts (List separately in addition to code for primary procedure)
15.74 15.74 Global Days ZZZ
AMA: 2007, January, 7-10; 2007, March, 1-3; 2005, February, 13-16

Current Procedural Coding Expert – Cardiovascular System

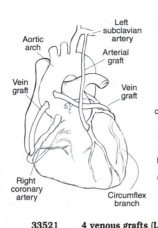

33521: four vein grafts
33522: five vein grafts
33523: six or more

The left internal thoracic (or mammary) artery is the most commonly used arterial graft. Arising from the subclavian artery, each side descends just behind the rib cartilage. The artery is left intact at the subclavian end and anastomosed to the coronary just beyond the occlusion. These codes are not reported alone; code the arterial preparation separately

+ **33521** 4 venous grafts (List separately in addition to code for primary procedure) C 80 P0
  18.89 18.89 Global Days ZZZ
  AMA: 2007, January, 7-10; 2007, March, 1-3; 2005, February, 13-16

+ **33522** 5 venous grafts (List separately in addition to code for primary procedure) C 80 P0
  21.24 21.24 Global Days ZZZ
  AMA: 2007, January, 7-10; 2007, March, 1-3; 2005, February, 13-16

+ **33523** 6 or more venous grafts (List separately in addition to code for primary procedure) C 80 P0
  24.08 24.08 Global Days ZZZ
  AMA: 2007, January, 7-10; 2007, March, 1-3; 2005, February, 13-16

33530 Reoperative Coronary Artery Bypass Graft or Valve Procedure

+ **33530** Reoperation, coronary artery bypass procedure or valve procedure, more than 1 month after original operation (List separately in addition to code for primary procedure) C 80 P0
  Code first (33400-33496, 33510-33536, 33863)
  15.17 15.17 Global Days ZZZ
  AMA: 2009, Jan, 11-31; 2008, Jan, 10-25; 2007, January, 7-10; 2007, January, 13-27; 2005, February, 13-16

33533-33536 Coronary Artery Bypass: Arterial Grafts

INCLUDES Harvesting of arterial graft excluding upper extremity (e.g., epigastric, internal mammary, gastroepiploic and others)
EXCLUDES Harvesting of arterial/venous grafts:
  Of femoropopliteal vein (35572)
  Of upper extremity vein or artery (35500, 35600)
  Performed by surgical assistant
  Venous grafts only (33510-33516)
Code also appropriate code from 33517-33523 to report combined arterial-venous grafts

33533 Coronary artery bypass, using arterial graft(s); single arterial graft C 80 P0
  53.54 53.54 Global Days 090
  AMA: 2007, January, 7-10; 2007, March, 1-3; 2005, March, 11-15; 2005, February, 13-16

33534 2 coronary arterial grafts C 80 P0
  63.05 63.05 Global Days 090
  AMA: 2007, January, 7-10; 2007, March, 1-3; 2005, February, 13-16

33535 3 coronary arterial grafts C 80 P0
  70.35 70.35 Global Days 090
  AMA: 2007, January, 7-10; 2007, March, 1-3; 2005, February, 13-16

33536 4 or more coronary arterial grafts C 80 P0
  76.10 76.10 Global Days 090
  AMA: 2007, March, 1-3; 2007, January, 7-10; 2005, February, 13-16

33542-33548 Ventricular Reconstruction

CMS 100-3,20.26   Partial Ventriculectomy

33542 Myocardial resection (eg, ventricular aneurysmectomy) C 80 P0
  Code also separate incision in heart to remove thrombus
  75.24 75.24 Global Days 090
  AMA: 2007, March, 1-3

33545 Repair of postinfarction ventricular septal defect, with or without myocardial resection C 80 P0
  Code also separate incision in heart to remove thrombus
  88.03 88.03 Global Days 090
  AMA: 2007, March, 1-3

33548 Surgical ventricular restoration procedure, includes prosthetic patch, when performed (eg, ventricular remodeling, SVR, SAVER, Dor procedures) C 80 P0
  EXCLUDES Batista procedure or pachopexy (33999)
  Do not report with (33210-33211, 33251, 33310, 33315)
  84.95 84.95 Global Days 090
  AMA: 2009, Jan, 11-31; 2008, Jan, 10-25; 2007, March, 1-3; 2007, January, 13-27; 2006, December, 10-12

33572 Endarterectomy with CABG (LAD, RCA, Cx)

+ **33572** Coronary endarterectomy, open, any method, of left anterior descending, circumflex, or right coronary artery performed in conjunction with coronary artery bypass graft procedure, each vessel (List separately in addition to primary procedure) C 80 P0
  Code first (33510-33516, 33533-33536)
  6.64 6.64 Global Days ZZZ

33600-33619 Repair Aberrant Heart Anatomy

Code also the concurrent ligation/takedown of a systemic-to-pulmonary artery shunt (33924)

33600 Closure of atrioventricular valve (mitral or tricuspid) by suture or patch C 80
  48.04 48.04 Global Days 090
  AMA: 2007, March, 1-3

33602 Closure of semilunar valve (aortic or pulmonary) by suture or patch C 80
  48.43 48.43 Global Days 090
  AMA: 2007, March, 1-3

33606 Anastomosis of pulmonary artery to aorta (Damus-Kaye-Stansel procedure) C 80
  51.65 51.65 Global Days 090
  AMA: 2007, March, 1-3

33608 Repair of complex cardiac anomaly other than pulmonary atresia with ventricular septal defect by construction or replacement of conduit from right or left ventricle to pulmonary artery C 80
  EXCLUDES Unifocalization of arborization anomalies of pulmonary artery (33925, 33926)
  50.35 50.35 Global Days 090
  AMA: 2007, March, 1-3

26/TC PC/TC Comp Only   A2/Z3 ASC Pmt   50 Bilateral   ♂ Male Only   ♀ Female Only   Facility RVU   Non-Facility RVU
AMA: CPT Asst   **MED:** Pub 100   A-/Y OPPSI   80/80 Surg Assist Allowed / w/Doc   Lab Crosswalk   Radiology Crosswalk
114   CPT only © 2009 American Medical Association. All Rights Reserved. (Black Ink)   Medicare (Red Ink)   © 2009 Publisher (Blue Ink)

Current Procedural Coding Expert – Cardiovascular System

33610 Repair of complex cardiac anomalies (eg, single ventricle with subaortic obstruction) by surgical enlargement of ventricular septal defect
49.64 49.64 Global Days 090
AMA: 2007, March, 1-3

33611 Repair of double outlet right ventricle with intraventricular tunnel repair;
55.47 55.47 Global Days 090
AMA: 2007, March, 1-3

33612 with repair of right ventricular outflow tract obstruction
56.04 56.04 Global Days 090
AMA: 2007, March, 1-3

33615 Repair of complex cardiac anomalies (eg, tricuspid atresia) by closure of atrial septal defect and anastomosis of atria or vena cava to pulmonary artery (simple Fontan procedure)
55.94 55.94 Global Days 090
AMA: 2007, March, 1-3

33617 Repair of complex cardiac anomalies (eg, single ventricle) by modified Fontan procedure
Code also 33768 for cavopulmonary anastomosis to a second superior vena cava
60.65 60.65 Global Days 090
AMA: 2007, March, 1-3

33619 Repair of single ventricle with aortic outflow obstruction and aortic arch hypoplasia (hypoplastic left heart syndrome) (eg, Norwood procedure)
76.34 76.34 Global Days 090
AMA: 2007, March, 1-3

33641-33645 Closure of Defect: Atrium

33641 Repair atrial septal defect, secundum, with cardiopulmonary bypass, with or without patch
47.01 47.01 Global Days 090
AMA: 2007, March, 1-3

33645 Direct or patch closure, sinus venosus, with or without anomalous pulmonary venous drainage
Do not report with (33724, 33726)
44.65 44.65 Global Days 090
AMA: 2007, March, 1-3

33647 Closure of Septal Defect: Atrial AND Ventricular

33647 Repair of atrial septal defect and ventricular septal defect, with direct or patch closure
EXCLUDES Tricuspid atresia repair procedures (33615)
56.10 56.10 Global Days 090
AMA: 2007, March, 1-3

33660-33670 Closure of Defect: Atrioventricular Canal

33660 Repair of incomplete or partial atrioventricular canal (ostium primum atrial septal defect), with or without atrioventricular valve repair
49.91 49.91 Global Days 090
AMA: 2007, March, 1-3

33665 Repair of intermediate or transitional atrioventricular canal, with or without atrioventricular valve repair
64.41 64.41 Global Days 090
AMA: 2007, March, 1-3

33670 Repair of complete atrioventricular canal, with or without prosthetic valve
56.22 56.22 Global Days 090
AMA: 2007, March, 1-3

33675-33677 Closure of Multiple Septal Defects: Ventricle

EXCLUDES Percutaneous closure (93581)
Transmyocardial closure ventricular septal defect (0166T, 0167T)

Do not report with (32100, 32422, 32551, 33210, 33681, 33684, 33688)

33675 Closure of multiple ventricular septal defects;
55.81 55.81 Global Days 090
AMA: 2007, March, 1-3

33676 with pulmonary valvotomy or infundibular resection (acyanotic)
54.33 54.33 Global Days 090
AMA: 2007, March, 1-3

33677 with removal of pulmonary artery band, with or without gusset
56.45 56.45 Global Days 090
AMA: 2007, March, 1-3

33681-33688 Closure of Septal Defect: Ventricle

EXCLUDES Repair of pulmonary vein that requires creating an atrial septal defect (33724)

33681 Closure of single ventricular septal defect, with or without patch;
52.34 52.34 Global Days 090
AMA: 2007, March, 1-3

33684 with pulmonary valvotomy or infundibular resection (acyanotic)
Code also concurrent ligation/takedown of a systemic-to-pulmonary artery shunt if performed (33924)
63.19 63.19 Global Days 090
AMA: 2007, March, 1-3

33688 with removal of pulmonary artery band, with or without gusset
Code also the concurrent ligation/takedown of a systemic-to-pulmonary artery shunt if performed (33924)
53.65 53.65 Global Days 090
AMA: 2007, March, 1-3

33690 Reduce Pulmonary Overcirculation in Septal Defects

33690 Banding of pulmonary artery
33.39 33.39 Global Days 090
AMA: 2007, March, 1-3

33692-33697 Repair of Defects of Tetralogy of Fallot

Code also the concurrent ligation/takedown of a systemic-to-pulmonary artery shunt (33924)

33692 Complete repair tetralogy of Fallot without pulmonary atresia;
46.73 46.73 Global Days 090
AMA: 2007, March, 1-3

33694 with transannular patch
55.21 55.21 Global Days 090
AMA: 2007, March, 1-3

● New Code   ▲ Revised Code   M Maternity   A Age   Unlisted   Not Covered   # Resequenced
CCI   + Add-on   Mod 51 Exempt   Mod 63 Exempt   Mod Sedation   PQRI
© 2009 Publisher (Blue Ink)   CPT only © 2009 American Medical Association. All Rights Reserved. (Black Ink)   Medicare (Red Ink)

33697 — Current Procedural Coding Expert – Cardiovascular System

33697   Complete repair tetralogy of Fallot with pulmonary atresia including construction of conduit from right ventricle to pulmonary artery and closure of ventricular septal defect   [C][80]
    57.53   57.53   Global Days 090
    AMA: 2007, March, 1-3

33702-33722 Repair Anomalies Sinus of Valsalva

33702   Repair sinus of Valsalva fistula, with cardiopulmonary bypass;   [C][80]
    43.74   43.74   Global Days 090
    AMA: 2007, March, 1-3

33710   with repair of ventricular septal defect   [C][80]
    47.89   47.89   Global Days 090
    AMA: 2007, March, 1-3

33720   Repair sinus of Valsalva aneurysm, with cardiopulmonary bypass   [C][80]
    43.25   43.25   Global Days 090
    AMA: 2007, March, 1-3

33722   Closure of aortico-left ventricular tunnel   [C][80]
    45.89   45.89   Global Days 090
    AMA: 2007, March, 1-3

33724-33732 Repair Aberrant Pulmonary Venous Connection

33724   Repair of isolated partial anomalous pulmonary venous return (eg, Scimitar Syndrome)   [C][80]
    Do not report with (32551, 33210-33211)
    43.16   43.16   Global Days 090
    AMA: 2007, March, 1-3

33726   Repair of pulmonary venous stenosis   [C][80]
    Do not report with (32551, 33210-33211)
    57.82   57.82   Global Days 090
    AMA: 2007, March, 1-3

33730   Complete repair of anomalous pulmonary venous return (supracardiac, intracardiac, or infracardiac types)   [C][80]
    EXCLUDES   Partial anomalous pulmonary venous return (33724)
              Repair of pulmonary venous stenosis (33726)
    56.90   56.90   Global Days 090
    AMA: 2007, March, 1-3

33732   Repair of cor triatriatum or supravalvular mitral ring by resection of left atrial membrane   [C][80]
    46.62   46.62   Global Days 090
    AMA: 2007, March, 1-3

33735-33737 Creation of Atrial Septal Defect

Code also the concurrent ligation/takedown of a systemic-to-pulmonary artery shunt (33924)

33735   Atrial septectomy or septostomy; closed heart (Blalock-Hanlon type operation)   [C][80]
    36.34   36.34   Global Days 090
    AMA: 2007, March, 1-3

33736   open heart with cardiopulmonary bypass   [C][80]
    39.70   39.70   Global Days 090
    AMA: 2007, March, 1-3

33737   open heart, with inflow occlusion   [C][80]
    EXCLUDES   Atrial septectomy/septostomy:
              Blade method (92993)
              Transvenous balloon method (92992)
    36.19   36.19   Global Days 090
    AMA: 2007, March, 1-3

33750-33767 Systemic Vessel to Pulmonary Artery Shunts

Code also the concurrent ligation/takedown of a systemic-to-pulmonary artery shunt (33924)

33750   Shunt; subclavian to pulmonary artery (Blalock-Taussig type operation)   [C][80]
    42.65   42.65   Global Days 090
    AMA: 2007, March, 1-3

33755   ascending aorta to pulmonary artery (Waterston type operation)   [C][80]
    35.85   35.85   Global Days 090
    AMA: 2007, March, 1-3

33762   descending aorta to pulmonary artery (Potts-Smith type operation)   [C][80]
    34.06   34.06   Global Days 090
    AMA: 2007, March, 1-3

33764   central, with prosthetic graft   [C][80]
    38.17   38.17   Global Days 090
    AMA: 2007, March, 1-3

33766   superior vena cava to pulmonary artery for flow to 1 lung (classical Glenn procedure)   [C][80]
    36.74   36.74   Global Days 090
    AMA: 2007, March, 1-3

33767   superior vena cava to pulmonary artery for flow to both lungs (bidirectional Glenn procedure)   [C][80]
    40.09   40.09   Global Days 090
    AMA: 2007, March, 1-3

33768 Cavopulmonary Anastomosis to Decrease Volume Load

Do not report with (32551, 33210-33211)

+ 33768   Anastomosis, cavopulmonary, second superior vena cava (List separately in addition to primary procedure)   [C][80]
    Code first (33478, 33617, 33767)
    11.32   11.32   Global Days ZZZ
    AMA: 2007, March, 1-3

33770-33783 Repair Aberrant Anatomy: Transposition Great Vessels

Code also the concurrent ligation/takedown of a systemic-to-pulmonary artery shunt (33924)

33770   Repair of transposition of the great arteries with ventricular septal defect and subpulmonary stenosis; without surgical enlargement of ventricular septal defect   [C][80]
    62.24   62.24   Global Days 090
    AMA: 2007, March, 1-3

33771   with surgical enlargement of ventricular septal defect   [C][80]
    58.78   58.78   Global Days 090
    AMA: 2007, March, 1-3

33774   Repair of transposition of the great arteries, atrial baffle procedure (eg, Mustard or Senning type) with cardiopulmonary bypass;   [C][80]
    50.91   50.91   Global Days 090
    AMA: 2007, March, 1-3

33775   with removal of pulmonary band   [C][80]
    49.40   49.40   Global Days 090
    AMA: 2007, March, 1-3

33776   with closure of ventricular septal defect   [C][80]
    52.18   52.18   Global Days 090
    AMA: 2007, March, 1-3

[26/TC] PC/TC Comp Only	[A2-Z3] ASC Pmt	[50] Bilateral	♂ Male Only	♀ Female Only	Facility RVU Non-Facility RVU
AMA: CPT Asst	**MED:** Pub 100	[A-Y] OPPSI	[80/80] Surg Assist Allowed w/Doc		Lab Crosswalk Radiology Crosswalk

116   CPT only © 2009 American Medical Association. All Rights Reserved. (Black Ink)   Medicare (Red Ink)   © 2009 Publisher (Blue Ink)

Current Procedural Coding Expert – Cardiovascular System

33777	with repair of subpulmonic obstruction	
	50.60 50.60 Global Days 090	
	AMA: 2007, March, 1-3	
33778	Repair of transposition of the great arteries, aortic pulmonary artery reconstruction (eg, Jatene type);	
	62.98 62.98 Global Days 090	
	AMA: 2007, March, 1-3	
33779	with removal of pulmonary band	
	62.70 62.70 Global Days 090	
	AMA: 2007, March, 1-3	
33780	with closure of ventricular septal defect	
	74.24 74.24 Global Days 090	
	AMA: 2007, March, 1-3	
33781	with repair of subpulmonic obstruction	
	62.43 62.43 Global Days 090	
	AMA: 2007, March, 1-3	
● 33782	Aortic root translocation with ventricular septal defect and pulmonary stenosis repair (ie, Nikaidoh procedure); without coronary ostium reimplantation	
	Do not report with (33412-33413, 33608, 33681, 33770-33771, 33778, 33780, 33920)	
	90.92 90.92 Global Days 090	
● 33783	with reimplantation of 1 or both coronary ostia	
	98.28 98.28 Global Days 090	

33786-33788 Repair Aberrant Anatomy: Truncus Arteriosus

33786	Total repair, truncus arteriosus (Rastelli type operation)	
	Code also the concurrent ligation/takedown of a systemic-to-pulmonary artery shunt (33924)	
	61.18 61.18 Global Days 090	
	AMA: 2007, March, 1-3	
33788	Reimplantation of an anomalous pulmonary artery	
	EXCLUDES Pulmonary artery banding (33690)	
	40.89 40.89 Global Days 090	
	AMA: 2007, March, 1-3	

33800-33853 Repair Aberrant Anatomy: Aorta

33800	Aortic suspension (aortopexy) for tracheal decompression (eg, for tracheomalacia) (separate procedure)	
	27.92 27.92 Global Days 090	
	AMA: 2007, March, 1-3	
33802	Division of aberrant vessel (vascular ring);	
	30.37 30.37 Global Days 090	
	AMA: 2007, March, 1-3	
33803	with reanastomosis	
	32.39 32.39 Global Days 090	
	AMA: 2007, March, 1-3	
33813	Obliteration of aortopulmonary septal defect; without cardiopulmonary bypass	
	34.56 34.56 Global Days 090	
	AMA: 2007, March, 1-3	
33814	with cardiopulmonary bypass	
	43.05 43.05 Global Days 090	
	AMA: 2007, March, 1-3	
33820	Repair of patent ductus arteriosus; by ligation	
	27.35 27.35 Global Days 090	
	AMA: 2007, March, 1-3	
33822	by division, younger than 18 years	
	27.05 27.05 Global Days 090	
	AMA: 2007, March, 1-3	
33824	by division, 18 years and older	
	33.98 33.98 Global Days 090	
	AMA: 2007, March, 1-3	
33840	Excision of coarctation of aorta, with or without associated patent ductus arteriosus; with direct anastomosis	
	34.27 34.27 Global Days 090	
	AMA: 2007, March, 1-3	
33845	with graft	
	37.62 37.62 Global Days 090	
	AMA: 2007, March, 1-3	
33851	repair using either left subclavian artery or prosthetic material as gusset for enlargement	
	35.72 35.72 Global Days 090	
	AMA: 2007, March, 1-3	
33852	Repair of hypoplastic or interrupted aortic arch using autogenous or prosthetic material; without cardiopulmonary bypass	
	EXCLUDES Hypoplastic left heart syndrome repair by excision of coarctation of aorta (33619)	
	46.70 46.70 Global Days 090	
	AMA: 2007, March, 1-3	

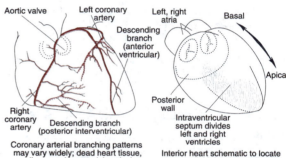

Aortic valve — Left coronary artery — Descending branch (anterior ventricular) — Left, right atria — Basal — Apical — Right coronary artery — Descending branch (posterior interventricular) — Posterior wall — Intraventricular septum divides left and right ventricles

Coronary arterial branching patterns may vary widely; dead heart tissue, usually caused by arterial occlusion, is called a myocardial infarct and about 1.5 million cases are reported annually. Inadequate blood supply can lead to "angina pectoris," or chest pain

Interior heart schematic to locate a myocardial infarction; walls of the left ventrical are much thicker and more than half of MI occurrences will see some degree of transient impairment to the left ventricle

33853	with cardiopulmonary bypass	
	EXCLUDES Hypoplastic left heart syndrome repair by excision of coarctation of aorta (33619)	
	61.37 61.37 Global Days 090	
	AMA: 2007, March, 1-3	

33860-33877 Aortic Graft Procedures

33860	Ascending aorta graft, with cardiopulmonary bypass, with or without valve suspension;	
	Code also concurrent aortic valve replacement (33405, or 33406)	
	91.84 91.84 Global Days 090	
	AMA: 2007, March, 1-3	
33861	with coronary reconstruction	
	Code also concurrent aortic valve replacement (33405, or 33406)	
	69.03 69.03 Global Days 090	
	AMA: 2007, March, 1-3	
33863	with aortic root replacement using composite prosthesis and coronary reconstruction	
	90.10 90.10 Global Days 090	
	AMA: 2007, March, 1-3; 2005, February, 13-16	

● New Code   ▲ Revised Code   M Maternity   A Age   Unlisted   Not Covered   # Resequenced
CCI   + Add-on   ⊘ Mod 51 Exempt   Mod 63 Exempt   ⊙ Mod Sedation   PQRI
© 2009 Publisher (Blue Ink)   CPT only © 2009 American Medical Association. All Rights Reserved. (Black Ink)   Medicare (Red Ink)

33864 Ascending aorta graft, with cardiopulmonary bypass with valve suspension, with coronary reconstruction and valve-sparing aortic annulus remodeling (eg, David Procedure, Yacoub Procedure) C 80

Do not report with (32551, 33210-33211, 33400, 33860-33863)

92.23   92.23   Global Days 090

33870 Transverse arch graft, with cardiopulmonary bypass   C 80

71.74   71.74   Global Days 090

33875 Descending thoracic aorta graft, with or without bypass   C 80

55.84   55.84   Global Days 090

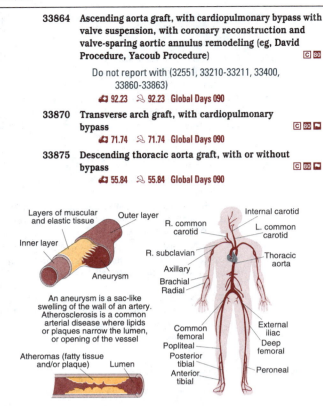

33877 Repair of thoracoabdominal aortic aneurysm with graft, with or without cardiopulmonary bypass   C 80 P0

104.18   104.18   Global Days 090

33880-33891 Endovascular Repair Aortic Aneurysm: Thoracic

INCLUDES   Balloon angioplasty
Introduction, manipulation, placement, and deployment of the device

EXCLUDES   Additional interventional procedures provided during the endovascular repair
Carotid-carotid bypass (33891)
Guidewire and catheter insertion (36140, 36200-36218)
Open exposure of artery/subsequent closure (34812, 34820, 34833, 34834)
Study, interpretation, and report of implanted wireless pressure sensor in an aneurysmal sac (93982)
Subclavian to carotid artery transposition (33889)
Substantial artery repair/replacement (35226, 35286)
Transcatheter insertion of wireless physiologic sensor in an aneurysmal sac (34806)

33880 Endovascular repair of descending thoracic aorta (eg, aneurysm, pseudoaneurysm, dissection, penetrating ulcer, intramural hematoma, or traumatic disruption); involving coverage of left subclavian artery origin, initial endoprosthesis plus descending thoracic aortic extension(s), if required, to level of celiac artery origin   C 80 P0

INCLUDES   Placement of distal extensions
EXCLUDES   Proximal extensions
75956
52.22   52.22   Global Days 090
AMA: 2006, May, 10-11

33881 not involving coverage of left subclavian artery origin, initial endoprosthesis plus descending thoracic aortic extension(s), if required, to level of celiac artery origin   C 80 P0

INCLUDES   Placement of distal extensions in distal thoracic aorta
EXCLUDES   Proximal extensions
75957
44.82   44.82   Global Days 090
AMA: 2006, May, 10-11

33883 Placement of proximal extension prosthesis for endovascular repair of descending thoracic aorta (eg, aneurysm, pseudoaneurysm, dissection, penetrating ulcer, intramural hematoma, or traumatic disruption); initial extension   C 80 P0

75958
32.43   32.43   Global Days 090
AMA: 2006, May, 10-11

+ **33884** each additional proximal extension (List separately in addition to code for primary procedure)   C 80

Code first 33883
75958
11.93   11.93   Global Days ZZZ
AMA: 2006, May, 10-11

33886 Placement of distal extension prosthesis(s) delayed after endovascular repair of descending thoracic aorta   C 80 P0

INCLUDES   All modules deployed
Do not report with (33880, 33881)
75959
27.57   27.57   Global Days 090
AMA: 2006, May, 10-11

33889 Open subclavian to carotid artery transposition performed in conjunction with endovascular repair of descending thoracic aorta, by neck incision, unilateral   C 80 50

Do not report with (35694)
22.94   22.94   Global Days 000
AMA: 2006, May, 10-11

33891 Bypass graft, with other than vein, transcervical retropharyngeal carotid-carotid, performed in conjunction with endovascular repair of descending thoracic aorta, by neck incision   C 80 50 P0

Do not report with (35509, 35601)
28.81   28.81   Global Days 000
AMA: 2006, May, 10-11

33910-33926 Surgical Procedures of Pulmonary Artery

CMS 100-3,240.6   Transvenous (Catheter) Pulmonary Embolectomy

33910 Pulmonary artery embolectomy; with cardiopulmonary bypass   C 80

47.64   47.64   Global Days 090
AMA: 2007, March, 1-3

33915 without cardiopulmonary bypass   C 80

38.56   38.56   Global Days 090
AMA: 2007, March, 1-3

33916 Pulmonary endarterectomy, with or without embolectomy, with cardiopulmonary bypass   C 80

45.09   45.09   Global Days 090
AMA: 2007, March, 1-3

33917 Repair of pulmonary artery stenosis by reconstruction with patch or graft   C 80

40.66   40.66   Global Days 090
AMA: 2007, March, 1-3

26/TC PC/TC Comp Only   A2-A3 ASC Pmt   50 Bilateral   ♂ Male Only   ♀ Female Only   Facility RVU   Non-Facility RVU
AMA: CPT Asst   MED: Pub 100   A-Y OPPSI   80/80 Surg Assist Allowed / w/Doc   Lab Crosswalk   Radiology Crosswalk

Current Procedural Coding Expert – Cardiovascular System 33976

33920 Repair of pulmonary atresia with ventricular septal defect, by construction or replacement of conduit from right or left ventricle to pulmonary artery C 80
- EXCLUDES: Repair of complicated cardiac anomalies by creating/replacing conduit from ventricle to pulmonary artery (33608)
- Code also the concurrent ligation/takedown of a systemic-to-pulmonary artery shunt (33924)
- 51.12 51.12 Global Days 090
- AMA: 2007, March, 1-3

33922 Transection of pulmonary artery with cardiopulmonary bypass C 80 63
- Code also the concurrent ligation/takedown of a systemic-to-pulmonary artery shunt (33924)
- 39.25 39.25 Global Days 090

+ 33924 Ligation and takedown of a systemic-to-pulmonary artery shunt, performed in conjunction with a congenital heart procedure (List separately in addition to code for primary procedure) C 80
- Code first (33470-33475, 33600-33619, 33684-33688, 33692-33697, 33735-33767, 33770-33781, 33786, 33920-33922)
- 8.08 8.08 Global Days ZZZ

33925 Repair of pulmonary artery arborization anomalies by unifocalization; without cardiopulmonary bypass C 80
- Do not report with (33697)
- 48.25 48.25 Global Days 090

33926 with cardiopulmonary bypass C 80
- Do not report with (33697)
- 71.71 71.71 Global Days 090

33930-33945 Heart and Heart-Lung Transplants

CMS 100-4,3,90.2 Heart Transplants
CMS 100-4,3,90.2.1 Artificial Hearts and Related Devices

- INCLUDES: Backbench work to prepare the donor heart and/or lungs for transplantation (33933, 33944)
  - Harvesting of donor organs with cold preservation (33930, 33940)
  - Transplantation of heart and/or lungs into recipient (33935, 33945)
- EXCLUDES: Implantation/repair/replacement of artificial heart or components (0051T-0053T)
  - Procedures performed on donor heart (33300, 33310, 33320, 33400, 33463, 33464, 33510, 33641, 35216, 35276, 35685)

33930 Donor cardiectomy-pneumonectomy (including cold preservation) C
- 0.00 0.00 Global Days XXX

33933 Backbench standard preparation of cadaver donor heart/lung allograft prior to transplantation, including dissection of allograft from surrounding soft tissues to prepare aorta, superior vena cava, inferior vena cava, and trachea for implantation C 80
- 0.00 0.00 Global Days XXX

33935 Heart-lung transplant with recipient cardiectomy-pneumonectomy C 80
- 97.92 97.92 Global Days 090

33940 Donor cardiectomy (including cold preservation) C
- 0.00 0.00 Global Days XXX
- AMA: 2005, April, 10-12

33944 Backbench standard preparation of cadaver donor heart allograft prior to transplantation, including dissection of allograft from surrounding soft tissues to prepare aorta, superior vena cava, inferior vena cava, pulmonary artery, and left atrium for implantation C 80
- 0.00 0.00 Global Days XXX

33945 Heart transplant, with or without recipient cardiectomy C 80
- 137.73 137.73 Global Days 090

33960-33999 Mechanical Circulatory Support

CMS 100-4,3,90.2.1 Artificial Hearts and Related Devices
- EXCLUDES: Implantation or removal of extracorporeal ventricular assist device via percutaneous transseptal access approach, extracorporeal (0048T, 0050T)
  - Replacement of a ventricular assist device, percutaneous transseptal access, extracorporeal (33999)

33960 Prolonged extracorporeal circulation for cardiopulmonary insufficiency; initial 24 hours C 80 63
- EXCLUDES: Cannula insertion for prolonged extracorporeal circulation (36822)
- 28.17 28.17 Global Days 000

+ 33961 each additional 24 hours (List separately in addition to code for primary procedure) C 63
- EXCLUDES: Cannula insertion for prolonged extracorporeal circulation (36822)
- Code first 33960
- 15.40 15.40 Global Days ZZZ

33967 Insertion of intra-aortic balloon assist device, percutaneous C 80
- 7.21 7.21 Global Days 000

33968 Removal of intra-aortic balloon assist device, percutaneous C
- 0.96 0.96 Global Days 000
- AMA: 2009, Jan, 11-31; 2008, Jan, 10-25; 2007, January, 13-27

33970 Insertion of intra-aortic balloon assist device through the femoral artery, open approach C 80
- EXCLUDES: Percutaneous insertion of intra-aortic balloon assist device (33967)
- 10.05 10.05 Global Days 000

33971 Removal of intra-aortic balloon assist device including repair of femoral artery, with or without graft C
- 19.91 19.91 Global Days 090

33973 Insertion of intra-aortic balloon assist device through the ascending aorta C 80
- 14.52 14.52 Global Days 000

33974 Removal of intra-aortic balloon assist device from the ascending aorta, including repair of the ascending aorta, with or without graft C
- 25.09 25.09 Global Days 090

33975 Insertion of ventricular assist device; extracorporeal, single ventricle C 80
- INCLUDES: Replacement of the entire ventricular assist device system, including pump(s) and cannulas
- Code also removal atrial/ventricular thrombi through a separate incision
- 31.30 31.30 Global Days XXX
- AMA: 2009, Jan, 11-31; 2008, Jan, 10-25; 2007, January, 13-27

33976 extracorporeal, biventricular C 80
- INCLUDES: Replacement of the entire ventricular assist device system, including pump(s) and cannulas
- Code also removal atrial/ventricular thrombi through a separate incision
- 34.23 34.23 Global Days XXX

● New Code   ▲ Revised Code   # Resequenced

□ CCI   + Add-on   ⊘ Mod 51 Exempt   Mod 63 Exempt   Mod Sedation   PQRI

© 2009 Publisher (Blue Ink)   CPT only © 2009 American Medical Association. All Rights Reserved. (Black Ink)   Medicare (Red Ink)

33977

33977 Removal of ventricular assist device; extracorporeal, single ventricle
   INCLUDES Removal of the entire device and the cannulas

   Code also removal atrial/ventricular thrombi through a separate incision

   Do not report replacement of the ventricular assist device when performed at the time of of insertion of a new device

   34.03 34.03 Global Days 090

33978 extracorporeal, biventricular
   INCLUDES Removal of the entire device and the cannulas

   Code also removal atrial/ventricular thrombi through a separate incision

   Do not report replacement of the ventricular assist device when performed at the time of of insertion of a new device

   37.82 37.82 Global Days 090

33979 Insertion of ventricular assist device, implantable intracorporeal, single ventricle
   INCLUDES Replacement of the entire ventricular assist device system, including pump(s) and cannulas

   Code also removal atrial/ventricular thrombi through a separate incision

   68.20 68.20 Global Days XXX

33980 Removal of ventricular assist device, implantable intracorporeal, single ventricle
   INCLUDES Removal of the entire device and the cannulas

   Code also removal atrial/ventricular thrombi through a separate incision

   Do not report replacement of the ventricular assist device when performed at the time of insertion of a new device

   102.72 102.72 Global Days 090

● **33981** Replacement of extracorporeal ventricular assist device, single or biventricular, pump(s), single or each pump
   INCLUDES Insertion of the new pump with de-airing, connection, and initiation
             Removal of the old pump

   0.00 0.00 Global Days XXX

● **33982** Replacement of ventricular assist device pump(s); implantable intracorporeal, single ventricle, without cardiopulmonary bypass
   INCLUDES New pump insertion with connection, de-airing, and initiation
             Removal of the old pump

   0.00 0.00 Global Days XXX

● **33983** implantable intracorporeal, single ventricle, with cardiopulmonary bypass
   INCLUDES Insertion of the new pump with de-airing, connection, and initiation
             Removal of the old pump

   0.00 0.00 Global Days XXX

33999 Unlisted procedure, cardiac surgery
   0.00 0.00 Global Days YYY
   AMA: 2009, Jan, 11-31; 2008, Jan, 10-25; 2007, January, 13-27; 2007, March, 1-3

34001-34530 Surgical Revascularization: Veins and Arteries

INCLUDES Repair of blood vessel
          Surgeon's component of operative arteriogram

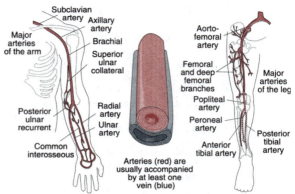

34001 Embolectomy or thrombectomy, with or without catheter; carotid, subclavian or innominate artery, by neck incision
   28.44 28.44 Global Days 090

34051 innominate, subclavian artery, by thoracic incision
   28.11 28.11 Global Days 090

34101 axillary, brachial, innominate, subclavian artery, by arm incision
   17.74 17.74 Global Days 090

34111 radial or ulnar artery, by arm incision
   17.78 17.78 Global Days 090

34151 renal, celiac, mesentery, aortoiliac artery, by abdominal incision
   41.22 41.22 Global Days 090

34201 femoropopliteal, aortoiliac artery, by leg incision
   30.49 30.49 Global Days 090

34203 popliteal-tibio-peroneal artery, by leg incision
   28.28 28.28 Global Days 090

34401 Thrombectomy, direct or with catheter; vena cava, iliac vein, by abdominal incision
   41.52 41.52 Global Days 090

34421 vena cava, iliac, femoropopliteal vein, by leg incision
   21.48 21.48 Global Days 090

34451 vena cava, iliac, femoropopliteal vein, by abdominal and leg incision
   42.71 42.71 Global Days 090

34471 subclavian vein, by neck incision
   34.74 34.74 Global Days 090

34490 axillary and subclavian vein, by arm incision
   17.85 17.85 Global Days 090

34501 Valvuloplasty, femoral vein
   26.45 26.45 Global Days 090

34502 Reconstruction of vena cava, any method
   43.82 43.82 Global Days 090

34510 Venous valve transposition, any vein donor
   32.93 32.93 Global Days 090

34520	Cross-over vein graft to venous system
	29.35 29.35 Global Days 090
34530	Saphenopopliteal vein anastomosis
	30.47 30.47 Global Days 090

34800-34834 Endovascular Stent Grafting for Abdominal Aneurysms

CMS 100-3,20.23   *Fabric Wrapping of Abdominal Aneurysms*

INCLUDES
Balloon angioplasty
Introduction, manipulation, placement, and deployment
Open exposure of artery/subsequent closure
Thromboendarterectomy at site of aneurysm

EXCLUDES
Additional interventional procedures
Guidewire and catheter insertion (36140, 36200, 36245-36248)
Substantial artery repair/replacement (35226, 35286)

75952, 75953

34800	Endovascular repair of infrarenal abdominal aortic aneurysm or dissection; using aorto-aortic tube prosthesis
	Code also open arterial exposure as appropriate (34812, 34820, 34833, 34834)
	75952
	32.82 32.82 Global Days 090
	AMA: 2009, Jan, 11-31; 2008, Jan, 10-25; 2007, January, 13-27; 2006, April, 11-18; 2005, June, 6-8
34802	using modular bifurcated prosthesis (1 docking limb)
	Code also open arterial exposure as appropriate (34812, 34820, 34833, 34834)
	75952
	36.37 36.37 Global Days 090
	AMA: 2009, Jan, 11-31; 2008, Jan, 10-25; 2007, January, 13-27; 2006, April, 11-18; 2005, June, 6-8
34803	using modular bifurcated prosthesis (2 docking limbs)
	EXCLUDES Use of prosthesis for associated visceral vessels (0078T, 0079T)
	Code also open arterial exposure as appropriate (34812, 34820, 34833, 34834)
	75952
	37.65 37.65 Global Days 090
	AMA: 2006, April, 11-18; 2005, June, 6-8
34804	using unibody bifurcated prosthesis
	Code also open arterial exposure as appropriate (34812, 34820, 34833, 34834)
	75952
	36.43 36.43 Global Days 090
	AMA: 2006, April, 11-18; 2005, June, 6-8
34805	using aorto-uniiliac or aorto-unifemoral prosthesis
	Code also open arterial exposure as appropriate (34812, 34820, 34833, 34834)
	75952
	34.59 34.59 Global Days 090
	AMA: 2009, Jan, 11-31; 2008, Jan, 10-25; 2007, January, 13-27; 2006, April, 11-18; 2005, June, 6-8

+ 34806	Transcatheter placement of wireless physiologic sensor in aneurysmal sac during endovascular repair, including radiological supervision and interpretation, instrument calibration, and collection of pressure data (List separately in addition to code for primary procedure)
	Code first (33880-33881, 33886, 34800-34805, 34825, 34900)
	Code also open arterial exposure as appropriate (34812, 34820, 34833-34834)
	Do not report with (93982)
	3.00 3.00 Global Days ZZZ
+ 34808	Endovascular placement of iliac artery occlusion device (List separately in addition to code for primary procedure)
	Code first 34800, 34805, 34813, 34825, 34826
	Code also open arterial exposure as appropriate (34812, 34820, 34833-34834)
	75952
	5.99 5.99 Global Days ZZZ
	AMA: 2005, June, 6-8
34812	Open femoral artery exposure for delivery of endovascular prosthesis, by groin incision, unilateral
	Code also as appropriate (34800-34808)
	9.93 9.93 Global Days 000
	AMA: 2009, Jan, 11-31; 2008, Jan, 10-25; 2007, January, 13-27; 2006, May, 10-11; 2005, June, 6-8
+ 34813	Placement of femoral-femoral prosthetic graft during endovascular aortic aneurysm repair (List separately in addition to code for primary procedure)
	EXCLUDES Grafting of femoral artery (35521, 35533, 35539, 35540, 35551-35558, 35566, 35621, 35646, 35651-35661, 35666, 35700)
	Code first 34812
	7.01 7.01 Global Days ZZZ
	AMA: 2005, June, 6-8
34820	Open iliac artery exposure for delivery of endovascular prosthesis or iliac occlusion during endovascular therapy, by abdominal or retroperitoneal incision, unilateral
	Code also endovascular repair of abdominal aorta aneurysm as appropriate (34800-34808)
	14.22 14.22 Global Days 000
	AMA: 2009, Jan, 11-31; 2008, Jan, 10-25; 2007, January, 13-27; 2006, May, 10-11; 2005, June, 6-8
34825	Placement of proximal or distal extension prosthesis for endovascular repair of infrarenal abdominal aortic or iliac aneurysm, false aneurysm, or dissection; initial vessel
	Code also endovascular repair of abdominal aorta or iliac aneurysm as appropriate (34800-34808, 34900)
	75953
	20.31 20.31 Global Days 090
	AMA: 2005, June, 6-8
+ 34826	each additional vessel (List separately in addition to code for primary procedure)
	Code first 34825
	Code also endovascular repair of abdominal aorta or iliac aneurysm as appropriate (34800-34808, 34900)
	75953
	6.02 6.02 Global Days ZZZ
	AMA: 2005, June, 6-8
34830	Open repair of infrarenal aortic aneurysm or dissection, plus repair of associated arterial trauma, following unsuccessful endovascular repair; tube prosthesis
	52.46 52.46 Global Days 090
	AMA: 2009, Jan, 11-31; 2008, Oct, 10-11

34831

34831	aorto-bi-iliac prosthesis
	56.42 56.42 Global Days 090
	AMA: 2009, Jan, 11-31; 2008, Oct, 10-11

34832	aorto-bifemoral prosthesis
	56.42 56.42 Global Days 090
	AMA: 2009, Jan, 11-31; 2008, Oct, 10-11

34833	Open iliac artery exposure with creation of conduit for delivery of aortic or iliac endovascular prosthesis, by abdominal or retroperitoneal incision, unilateral
	Do not report with (34820)
	17.86 17.86 Global Days 000
	AMA: 2009, Jan, 11-31; 2008, Jan, 10-25; 2007, January, 13-27; 2006, May, 10-11

34834	Open brachial artery exposure to assist in the deployment of aortic or iliac endovascular prosthesis by arm incision, unilateral
	8.04 8.04 Global Days 000
	AMA: 2006, May, 10-11

34900 Endovascular Stent Grafting Iliac Artery

INCLUDES
Balloon angioplasty
Introduction, manipulation, placement, and deployment

EXCLUDES
Insertion guidewires, catheters (36200, 36215-36218)
Open exposure femoral or iliac artery (34812, 34820)
Other concurrent interventional procedures
Placement extension prosthesis (34825)
Substantial artery repair/replacemt (35206-35286)

34900	Endovascular graft placement for repair of iliac artery (eg, aneurysm, pseudoaneurysm, arteriovenous malformation, trauma)
	75954
	26.14 26.14 Global Days 090
	AMA: 2006, April, 11-18

35001-35152 Repair Aneurysm, False Aneurysm, Related Arterial Disease

INCLUDES Endarterectomy procedures

EXCLUDES Endovascular repairs of:
Abdominal aortic aneurysm (34800-34826)
Aneurysm of iliac artery (34900)
Thoracic aortic aneurysm (33880)
Intracranial aneurysms (61697-61710)
Open repairs thoracic aortic aneurysm (33860-33875)
Repairs related to occlusive disease only (35201-35286)

35001	Direct repair of aneurysm, pseudoaneurysm, or excision (partial or total) and graft insertion, with or without patch graft; for aneurysm and associated occlusive disease, carotid, subclavian artery, by neck incision
	33.09 33.09 Global Days 090

35002	for ruptured aneurysm, carotid, subclavian artery, by neck incision
	36.55 36.55 Global Days 090

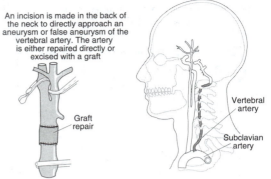

An incision is made in the back of the neck to directly approach an aneurysm or false aneurysm of the vertebral artery. The artery is either repaired directly or excised with a graft

Graft repair

Vertebral artery

Subclavian artery

35005	for aneurysm, pseudoaneurysm, and associated occlusive disease, vertebral artery
	29.49 29.49 Global Days 090

35011	for aneurysm and associated occlusive disease, axillary-brachial artery, by arm incision
	29.25 29.25 Global Days 090

35013	for ruptured aneurysm, axillary-brachial artery, by arm incision
	36.43 36.43 Global Days 090

35021	for aneurysm, pseudoaneurysm, and associated occlusive disease, innominate, subclavian artery, by thoracic incision
	35.39 35.39 Global Days 090

35022	for ruptured aneurysm, innominate, subclavian artery, by thoracic incision
	40.58 40.58 Global Days 090

35045	for aneurysm, pseudoaneurysm, and associated occlusive disease, radial or ulnar artery
	28.79 28.79 Global Days 090

35081	for aneurysm, pseudoaneurysm, and associated occlusive disease, abdominal aorta
	51.85 51.85 Global Days 090
	AMA: 2009, Jan, 11-31; 2008, Jan, 10-25; 2007, January, 13-27; 2005, June, 6-8

35082	for ruptured aneurysm, abdominal aorta
	64.60 64.60 Global Days 090

35091	for aneurysm, pseudoaneurysm, and associated occlusive disease, abdominal aorta involving visceral vessels (mesenteric, celiac, renal)
	53.38 53.38 Global Days 090

35092	for ruptured aneurysm, abdominal aorta involving visceral vessels (mesenteric, celiac, renal)
	77.31 77.31 Global Days 090

35102	for aneurysm, pseudoaneurysm, and associated occlusive disease, abdominal aorta involving iliac vessels (common, hypogastric, external)
	56.13 56.13 Global Days 090
	AMA: 2005, June, 6-8

35103	for ruptured aneurysm, abdominal aorta involving iliac vessels (common, hypogastric, external)
	66.37 66.37 Global Days 090

35111	for aneurysm, pseudoaneurysm, and associated occlusive disease, splenic artery
	42.61 42.61 Global Days 090

35112	for ruptured aneurysm, splenic artery
	52.33 52.33 Global Days 090

Current Procedural Coding Expert – Cardiovascular System

35121	for aneurysm, pseudoaneurysm, and associated occlusive disease, hepatic, celiac, renal, or mesenteric artery	C 80 50
	48.54 48.54 Global Days 090	
35122	for ruptured aneurysm, hepatic, celiac, renal, or mesenteric artery	C 80 50
	60.43 60.43 Global Days 090	
35131	for aneurysm, pseudoaneurysm, and associated occlusive disease, iliac artery (common, hypogastric, external)	C 80 50 PQ
	41.15 41.15 Global Days 090	
35132	for ruptured aneurysm, iliac artery (common, hypogastric, external)	C 80 50
	50.04 50.04 Global Days 090	
35141	for aneurysm, pseudoaneurysm, and associated occlusive disease, common femoral artery (profunda femoris, superficial femoral)	C 80 50 PQ
	32.64 32.64 Global Days 090	
35142	for ruptured aneurysm, common femoral artery (profunda femoris, superficial femoral)	C 80 50
	39.10 39.10 Global Days 090	
35151	for aneurysm, pseudoaneurysm, and associated occlusive disease, popliteal artery	C 80 50 PQ
	36.86 36.86 Global Days 090	
35152	for ruptured aneurysm, popliteal artery	C 80 50
	41.55 41.55 Global Days 090	

35180-35190 Repair Arteriovenous Malformations

35180	Repair, congenital arteriovenous fistula; head and neck	T 80
	24.43 24.43 Global Days 090	
35182	thorax and abdomen	C 80
	51.91 51.91 Global Days 090	
35184	extremities	T 80
	31.07 31.07 Global Days 090	
35188	Repair, acquired or traumatic arteriovenous fistula; head and neck	A2 T 80
	25.79 25.79 Global Days 090	
35189	thorax and abdomen	C 80
	47.18 47.18 Global Days 090	
35190	extremities	T 80
	21.90 21.90 Global Days 090	

35201-35286 Surgical Repair Artery or Vein

EXCLUDES Arteriovenous fistula repair (35180-35190)

Do not report with a primary open vascular procedure.

35201	Repair blood vessel, direct; neck	T 80 50
	27.42 27.42 Global Days 090	
35206	upper extremity	T 80 50
	22.42 22.42 Global Days 090	
35207	hand, finger	A2 T 50
	20.48 20.48 Global Days 090	
35211	intrathoracic, with bypass	C 80 50 PQ
	39.71 39.71 Global Days 090	
35216	intrathoracic, without bypass	C 80 50 PQ
	58.17 58.17 Global Days 090	
	AMA: 2005, April, 10-12	
35221	intra-abdominal	C 80 50
	41.50 41.50 Global Days 090	
35226	lower extremity	T 80 50
	24.31 24.31 Global Days 090	
	AMA: 2006, May, 10-11	
35231	Repair blood vessel with vein graft; neck	T 80 50
	34.69 34.69 Global Days 090	
35236	upper extremity	T 80 50
	28.62 28.62 Global Days 090	
35241	intrathoracic, with bypass	C 80 50 PQ
	41.32 41.32 Global Days 090	
35246	intrathoracic, without bypass	C 80 50 PQ
	42.49 42.49 Global Days 090	
35251	intra-abdominal	C 80 50
	49.25 49.25 Global Days 090	
35256	lower extremity	T 80 50
	29.91 29.91 Global Days 090	
35261	Repair blood vessel with graft other than vein; neck	T 80 50
	Code also (C1768, L8670)	
	30.82 30.82 Global Days 090	
35266	upper extremity	T 80 50
	Code also (C1768, L8670)	
	25.25 25.25 Global Days 090	
35271	intrathoracic, with bypass	C 80 50 PQ
	39.67 39.67 Global Days 090	
35276	intrathoracic, without bypass	C 80 50 PQ
	41.01 41.01 Global Days 090	
35281	intra-abdominal	C 80 50
	46.65 46.65 Global Days 090	
35286	lower extremity	T 80 50
	Code also (C1768, L8670)	
	27.48 27.48 Global Days 090	
	AMA: 2006, May, 10-11	

35301-35390 Surgical Thromboendarterectomy Peripheral and Visceral Arteries

CMS 100-3,20.1 — Vertebral Artery Surgery
CMS 100-3,160.8 — Electroencephalographic Monitoring During Cerebral Vasculature Surgery

INCLUDES Obtaining saphenous or arm vein for graft
Thrombectomy/embolectomy

EXCLUDES Coronary artery bypass procedures (33510-33536, 33572)
Thromboendarterectomy for vascular occlusion on a different vessel during the same session

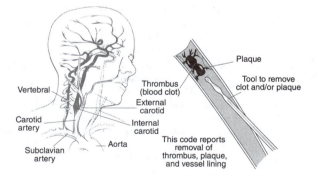

35301	Thromboendarterectomy, including patch graft, if performed; carotid, vertebral, subclavian, by neck incision	C 80 50 PQ
	30.92 30.92 Global Days 090	
	AMA: 2007, January, 7-10	

35302

	35302	**superficial femoral artery** [C] [80] [50]
		Do not report with (35483, 35500)
		33.24 33.24 Global Days 090
		AMA: 2007, January, 7-10; 2007, May, 9-11
	35303	**popliteal artery** [C] [80] [50]
		Do not report with (35483, 35500)
		36.59 36.59 Global Days 090
		AMA: 2007, May, 9-11; 2007, January, 7-10
	35304	**tibioperoneal trunk artery** [C] [80] [50]
		Do not report with (35485, 35500)
		38.00 38.00 Global Days 090
		AMA: 2007, May, 9-11; 2007, January, 7-10
	35305	**tibial or peroneal artery, initial vessel** [C] [80] [50]
		Do not report with (35485, 35500)
		36.56 36.56 Global Days 090
		AMA: 2009, Jan, 11-31; 2008, Jan, 10-25; 2007, January, 7-10; 2007, May, 9-11
+	35306	**each additional tibial or peroneal artery** (List separately in addition to code for primary procedure) [C] [80]
		Code first (35305)
		Do not report with (35485, 35500)
		13.33 13.33 Global Days ZZZ
		AMA: 2007, January, 7-10; 2007, May, 9-11
	35311	**subclavian, innominate, by thoracic incision** [C] [80] [50] [P0]
		44.06 44.06 Global Days 090
	35321	**axillary-brachial** [T] [80] [50]
		26.36 26.36 Global Days 090
	35331	**abdominal aorta** [C] [80] [50]
		43.07 43.07 Global Days 090
	35341	**mesenteric, celiac, or renal** [C] [80] [50]
		40.36 40.36 Global Days 090
	35351	**iliac** [C] [80] [50]
		38.05 38.05 Global Days 090
	35355	**iliofemoral** [C] [80] [50]
		30.87 30.87 Global Days 090
	35361	**combined aortoiliac** [C] [80] [50]
		45.28 45.28 Global Days 090
	35363	**combined aortoiliofemoral** [C] [80] [50]
		50.12 50.12 Global Days 090
	35371	**common femoral** [C] [80] [50]
		24.25 24.25 Global Days 090
		AMA: 2007, January, 7-10
	35372	**deep (profunda) femoral** [C] [80] [50]
		29.05 29.05 Global Days 090
		AMA: 2007, January, 7-10
+	35390	**Reoperation, carotid, thromboendarterectomy, more than 1 month after original operation** (List separately in addition to code for primary procedure) [C] [80]
		Code first 35301
		4.72 4.72 Global Days ZZZ

35400 Endoscopic Visualization of Vessels

+ 35400 **Angioscopy (non-coronary vessels or grafts) during therapeutic intervention** (List separately in addition to code for primary procedure) [C] [80]
  Code first the therapeutic intervention
  4.40 4.40 Global Days ZZZ

35450-35460 Transluminal Angioplasty: Open

35450	**Transluminal balloon angioplasty, open; renal or other visceral artery** [C] [80] [50]
	75962-75968, 75978
	14.97 14.97 Global Days 000
35452	**aortic** [C] [80] [50]
	75962-75968, 75978
	10.46 10.46 Global Days 000
	AMA: 2005, June, 6-8
35454	**iliac** [C] [80] [50]
	75962-75968, 75978
	9.10 9.10 Global Days 000
	AMA: 2005, June, 6-8
35456	**femoral-popliteal** [C] [80] [50]
	75962-75968, 75978
	11.09 11.09 Global Days 000
35458	**brachiocephalic trunk or branches, each vessel** [T] [80] [50]
	Code also (C1725, C1874, C1876, C1885, C2625)
	75962-75968, 75978
	14.35 14.35 Global Days 000
	AMA: 2009, Jan, 11-31; 2008, Jan, 10-25; 2007, January, 13-27
35459	**tibioperoneal trunk and branches** [T] [80] [50]
	Code also (C1725, C1874, C1876, C1885, C2625)
	75962-75968, 75978
	13.00 13.00 Global Days 000
35460	**venous** [62] [T] [50]
	Code also (C1725, C1874, C1876, C1885, C2625)
	75962-75968, 75978
	9.22 9.22 Global Days 000

35470-35476 Transluminal Angioplasty: Percutaneous

CMS 100-3,20.7 Percutaneous Transluminal Angioplasty (PTA)
EXCLUDES Catheter placement

○ 35470 **Transluminal balloon angioplasty, percutaneous; tibioperoneal trunk or branches, each vessel** [T] [50]
  75966, 75968
  Code also (C1725, C1874, C1876, C1885, C2625)
  12.78 62.60 Global Days 000

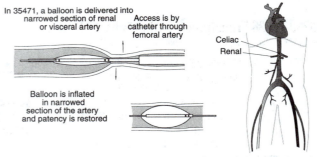

○ 35471 **renal or visceral artery** [T] [50]
  Code also (C1725, C1874, C1876, C1885, C2625)
  75966, 75968
  14.93 64.15 Global Days 000

○ 35472 **aortic** [T] [80] [50]
  Code also (C1725, C1874, C1876, C1885, C2625)
  75966, 75968
  10.33 49.36 Global Days 000
  AMA: 2005, June, 6-8

Current Procedural Coding Expert – Cardiovascular System

35473	iliac
	Code also (C1725, C1874, C1876, C1885, C2625)
	75962, 75964
	9.03 47.01 Global Days 000
	AMA: 2009, Jan, 11-31; 2007, Dec, 10-179

35474	femoral-popliteal
	Code also (C1725, C1874, C1876, C1885, C2625)
	75962, 75964
	10.94 60.56 Global Days 000
	AMA: 2009, Jan, 11-31; 2008, Jan, 10-25; 2007, Dec, 10-179; 2007, January, 13-27; 2006, August, 12-14

35475	brachiocephalic trunk or branches, each vessel
	Code also (C1725, C1874, C1876, C1885, C2625)
	75966, 75968
	13.78 57.39 Global Days 000
	AMA: 2009, Jan, 11-31; 2008, Sep, 10-11

35476	venous
	Code also (C1725, C1874, C1876, C1885, C2625)
	75978
	8.75 42.77 Global Days 000

35480-35485 Transluminal Atherectomy via Cutdown

35480	Transluminal peripheral atherectomy, open; renal or other visceral artery
	75992-75996
	16.15 16.15 Global Days 000

35481	aortic
	75992-75996
	11.58 11.58 Global Days 000

35482	iliac
	75992-75996
	9.77 9.77 Global Days 000

35483	femoral-popliteal
	75992-75996
	12.36 12.36 Global Days 000

35484	brachiocephalic trunk or branches, each vessel
	75992-75996
	15.22 15.22 Global Days 000

35485	tibioperoneal trunk and branches
	75992-75996
	14.46 14.46 Global Days 000

35490-35495 Transluminal Atherectomy, Percutaneous

EXCLUDES Catheter placement

35490	Transluminal peripheral atherectomy, percutaneous; renal or other visceral artery
	75992-75996
	16.97 16.97 Global Days 000

35491	aortic
	75992-75996
	11.93 11.93 Global Days 000

35492	iliac
	75992-75996
	10.33 10.33 Global Days 000

35493	femoral-popliteal
	75992-75996
	12.47 12.47 Global Days 000

35494	brachiocephalic trunk or branches, each vessel
	75992-75996
	15.94 15.94 Global Days 000

35495	tibioperoneal trunk and branches
	75992-75996
	14.55 14.55 Global Days 000
	AMA: 2009, Jan, 11-31; 2008, Jan, 10-25; 2007, Jul, 12-13

35500 Obtain Arm Vein for Graft

EXCLUDES Endoscopic harvest (33508)
Harvesting of multiple vein segments (35682, 35683)

+ 35500	Harvest of upper extremity vein, 1 segment, for lower extremity or coronary artery bypass procedure (List separately in addition to code for primary procedure)
	Code first (33510-33536, 35556, 35566, 35571, 35583-35587)
	9.56 9.56 Global Days ZZZ
	AMA: 2007, January, 7-10

35501-35571 Arterial Bypass Using Vein Grafts

CMS 100-3,20.1 Vertebral Artery Surgery
CMS 100-3,20.2 Extracranial-intracranial (EC-IC) Arterial Bypass Surgery
CMS 100-3,160.8 Electroencephalographic Monitoring During Cerebral Vasculature Surgery
INCLUDES Harvesting of saphenous vein grafts
EXCLUDES Harvesting of multiple vein segments (35682, 35683)
Harvesting of vein graft, upper extremity or femoropopliteal (35500, 35572)
Treatment of different sites with different bypass procedures during the same operative session

35501	Bypass graft, with vein; common carotid-ipsilateral internal carotid
	46.36 46.36 Global Days 090
	AMA: 2007, January, 7-10

35506	carotid-subclavian or subclavian-carotid
	39.30 39.30 Global Days 090
	AMA: 2007, January, 7-10

35508	carotid-vertebral
	INCLUDES Endoscopic procedure
	41.69 41.69 Global Days 090

35509	carotid-contralateral carotid
	43.69 43.69 Global Days 090
	AMA: 2009, Jan, 11-31; 2008, Jan, 10-25; 2007, May, 9-11; 2007, January, 7-10; 2006, May, 10-11

35510	carotid-brachial
	36.62 36.62 Global Days 090
	AMA: 2009, Jan, 11-31; 2008, Jan, 10-25

35511	subclavian-subclavian
	36.35 36.35 Global Days 090

35512	subclavian-brachial
	35.89 35.89 Global Days 090

35515	subclavian-vertebral
	41.25 41.25 Global Days 090

35516	subclavian-axillary
	36.31 36.31 Global Days 090

35518	axillary-axillary
	33.99 33.99 Global Days 090

35521	axillary-femoral
	EXCLUDES Synthetic graft (35621)
	36.47 36.47 Global Days 090

35522	axillary-brachial
	36.26 36.26 Global Days 090

● New Code   ▲ Revised Code   M Maternity   A Age   Unlisted   Not Covered   # Resequenced
CCI   + Add-on   ⊘ Mod 51 Exempt   ⊛ Mod 63 Exempt   ⊙ Mod Sedation   PQ PQRI

35523	brachial-ulnar or -radial	C 80 50
	EXCLUDES Bypass graft performed with synthetic conduit (37799)	
	Do not report with (35206, 35500, 35525, 36838)	
	🚗 37.95 🐍 37.95 **Global Days 090**	
35525	brachial-brachial	C 80 50
	🚗 33.75 🐍 33.75 **Global Days 090**	
35526	aortosubclavian or carotid	C 80 50 P0
	EXCLUDES Synthetic graft (35626)	
	🚗 49.56 🐍 49.56 **Global Days 090**	
35531	aortoceliac or aortomesenteric	C 80 50
	🚗 59.85 🐍 59.85 **Global Days 090**	
35533	axillary-femoral-femoral	C 80 50
	EXCLUDES Synthetic graft (35654)	
	🚗 48.82 🐍 48.82 **Global Days 090**	
35535	hepatorenal	C 80 50
	Do not report with (35221, 35251, 35281, 35500, 35536, 35560, 35631, 35636)	
	🚗 54.36 🐍 54.36 **Global Days 090**	
35536	splenorenal	C 80 50
	🚗 50.31 🐍 50.31 **Global Days 090**	
	AMA: 2009, Jan, 11-31; 2008, Jan, 10-25; 2007, January, 13-27	
35537	aortoiliac	C 80
	EXCLUDES Synthetic graft (35637)	
	Do not report with (35538)	
	🚗 62.12 🐍 62.12 **Global Days 090**	
	AMA: 2007, January, 7-10	
35538	aortobi-iliac	C 80
	EXCLUDES Synthetic graft (35638)	
	Do not report with (35537)	
	🚗 69.55 🐍 69.55 **Global Days 090**	
	AMA: 2007, January, 7-10	
35539	aortofemoral	C 80 50
	EXCLUDES Synthetic graft (35647)	
	Do not report with (35540)	
	🚗 65.33 🐍 65.33 **Global Days 090**	
	AMA: 2007, January, 7-10	
35540	aortobifemoral	C 50
	EXCLUDES Synthetic graft (35646)	
	Do not report with (35539)	
	🚗 75.25 🐍 75.25 **Global Days 090**	
	AMA: 2007, January, 7-10	
35548	aortoiliofemoral, unilateral	C 80
	EXCLUDES Synthetic graft (37799)	
	🚗 34.37 🐍 34.37 **Global Days 090**	
35549	aortoiliofemoral, bilateral	C 80
	EXCLUDES Synthetic graft (37799)	
	🚗 36.50 🐍 36.50 **Global Days 090**	
35551	aortofemoral-popliteal	C 80 50
	🚗 45.09 🐍 45.09 **Global Days 090**	
35556	femoral-popliteal	C 80 50
	🚗 41.64 🐍 41.64 **Global Days 090**	
	AMA: 2007, January, 7-10	
35558	femoral-femoral	C 80 50
	🚗 36.34 🐍 36.34 **Global Days 090**	
35560	aortorenal	C 80 50
	🚗 52.49 🐍 52.49 **Global Days 090**	
	AMA: 2009, Jan, 11-31; 2008, Jan, 10-25; 2007, January, 13-27	
35563	ilioiliac	C 80 50
	🚗 42.96 🐍 42.96 **Global Days 090**	
35565	iliofemoral	C 80 50
	🚗 38.98 🐍 38.98 **Global Days 090**	
35566	femoral-anterior tibial, posterior tibial, peroneal artery or other distal vessels	C 80 50
	🚗 49.70 🐍 49.70 **Global Days 090**	
	AMA: 2007, January, 7-10	
35570	tibial-tibial, peroneal-tibial, or tibial/peroneal trunk-tibial	C 80 50
	Do not report with (35256, 35286)	
	🚗 42.15 🐍 42.15 **Global Days 090**	
35571	popliteal-tibial, -peroneal artery or other distal vessels	C 80 50
	🚗 39.47 🐍 39.47 **Global Days 090**	
	AMA: 2007, January, 7-10	

35572 Obtain Femoropopliteal Vein for Graft

+ 35572 Harvest of femoropopliteal vein, 1 segment, for vascular reconstruction procedure (eg, aortic, vena caval, coronary, peripheral artery) (List separately in addition to code for primary procedure)   N1 N 80

Code first (33510-33523, 33533-33536, 34502, 34520, 35001, 35002, 35011-35022, 35102-35103, 35121-35152, 35231-35256, 35501-35587, 35879-35907)

🚗 10.13   🐍 10.13   **Global Days ZZZ**

AMA: 2009, Jan, 11-31; 2008, Jan, 10-25; 2007, January, 28-31

35583-35587 Lower Extremity Revascularization: In-situ Vein Bypass

INCLUDES Harvesting of saphenous vein grafts

EXCLUDES Harvesting of multiple vein segments (35682, 35683)

Harvesting of vein graft, upper extremity or femoropopliteal (35500, 35572)

35583	In-situ vein bypass; femoral-popliteal	C 80 50
	Code also concurrent aortobifemoral bypass (synthetic) (35646)	
	Code also concurrent aortofemoral bypass (synthetic) (35647)	
	Code also concurrent aortobifemoral bypass (vein) (35539)	
	🚗 42.99 🐍 42.99 **Global Days 090**	
	AMA: 2007, January, 7-10	
35585	femoral-anterior tibial, posterior tibial, or peroneal artery	C 80 50
	🚗 49.96 🐍 49.96 **Global Days 090**	
	AMA: 2007, January, 7-10	
35587	popliteal-tibial, peroneal	C 80 50
	🚗 40.60 🐍 40.60 **Global Days 090**	
	AMA: 2007, January, 7-10	

35600 Obtain Arm Artery for Coronary Bypass

EXCLUDES Arterial reimplantation (35691-35695)

Transposition of arteries (35691-35695)

+ 35600 Harvest of upper extremity artery, 1 segment, for coronary artery bypass procedure (List separately in addition to code for primary procedure)   C 80

Code first (33533-33536)

🚗 7.47   🐍 7.47   **Global Days ZZZ**

AMA: 2009, Jan, 11-31; 2008, Jan, 10-25

Current Procedural Coding Expert – Cardiovascular System

35601-35671 Arterial Bypass with Synthetic Grafts

CMS 100-3,20.1   Vertebral Artery Surgery
CMS 100-3,20.2   Extracranial-intracranial (EC-IC) Arterial Bypass Surgery
CMS 100-3,160.8   Electroencephalographic Monitoring During Cerebral Vasculature Surgery
EXCLUDES Transposition and/or reimplantation of arteries (35691-35695)

35601   Bypass graft, with other than vein; common carotid-ipsilateral internal carotid
    EXCLUDES Open transcervical common carotid-common carotid bypass with endovascular repair of descending thoracic aorta (33891)
    43.77   43.77   Global Days 090
    AMA: 2007, January, 7-10; 2006, May, 10-11

35606   carotid-subclavian
    EXCLUDES Open subclavian to carotid artery transposition performed with endovascular thoracic aneurysm repair via neck incision (33889)
    34.78   34.78   Global Days 090

35612   subclavian-subclavian
    25.93   25.93   Global Days 090

35616   subclavian-axillary
    35.39   35.39   Global Days 090

35621   axillary-femoral
    32.68   32.68   Global Days 090
    AMA: 2007, January, 7-10

35623   axillary-popliteal or -tibial
    39.05   39.05   Global Days 090

35626   aortosubclavian or carotid
    45.60   45.60   Global Days 090

In 35631, a bypass graft of material other than vein is surgically installed from the aorta to the celiac, mesenteric, or renal arteries. The graft is typically placed in an end-to-side fashion on both the aorta and the recipient vessel downstream from the blockage.

35631   aortoceliac, aortomesenteric, aortorenal
    54.56   54.56   Global Days 090

35632   ilio-celiac
    Do not report with (35221, 35251, 35281, 35531, 35631)
    51.62   51.62   Global Days 090

35633   ilio-mesenteric
    Do not report with (35221, 35251, 35281, 35531, 35631)
    55.70   55.70   Global Days 090

35634   iliorenal
    Do not report with (35221, 35251, 35281, 35536, 35560, 35631)
    50.52   50.52   Global Days 090

35636   splenorenal (splenic to renal arterial anastomosis)
    47.46   47.46   Global Days 090

35637   aortoiliac
    Do not report with (35638, 35646)
    51.14   51.14   Global Days 090
    AMA: 2009, Jan, 11-31; 2008, Jan, 10-25; 2007, January, 7-10

35638   aortobi-iliac
    EXCLUDES Open placement of aorto-bi-iliac prosthesis after a failed endovascular repair (34831)
    Do not report with (35637, 35646)
    51.91   51.91   Global Days 090
    AMA: 2009, Jan, 11-31; 2008, Jan, 10-25; 2007, January, 7-10

35642   carotid-vertebral
    29.27   29.27   Global Days 090

35645   subclavian-vertebral
    29.58   29.58   Global Days 090

35646   aortobifemoral
    EXCLUDES Bypass graft using vein graft (35540)
    Open placement of aortobifemoral prostheses after a failed endovascular repair (34832)
    50.90   50.90   Global Days 090
    AMA: 2007, January, 7-10

35647   aortofemoral
    EXCLUDES Bypass graft using vein graft (35539)
    45.87   45.87   Global Days 090
    AMA: 2007, January, 7-10

35650   axillary-axillary
    31.55   31.55   Global Days 090

35651   aortofemoral-popliteal
    42.42   42.42   Global Days 090

35654   axillary-femoral-femoral
    40.69   40.69   Global Days 090
    AMA: 2007, January, 7-10

35656   femoral-popliteal
    32.07   32.07   Global Days 090

35661   femoral-femoral
    32.18   32.18   Global Days 090
    AMA: 2007, January, 7-10

35663   ilioiliac
    37.17   37.17   Global Days 090

35665   iliofemoral
    34.80   34.80   Global Days 090
    AMA: 2007, January, 7-10

35666   femoral-anterior tibial, posterior tibial, or peroneal artery
    37.60   37.60   Global Days 090

35671   popliteal-tibial or -peroneal artery
    33.16   33.16   Global Days 090

35681-35686 Arterial Bypass Using Combination Synthetic and Donor Graft

+ 35681   Bypass graft; composite, prosthetic and vein (List separately in addition to code for primary procedure)
    Do not report with (35682, 35683)
    2.37   2.37   Global Days ZZZ
    AMA: 2009, Jan, 11-31; 2008, Jan, 10-25; 2007, January, 13-27

Current Procedural Coding Expert – Cardiovascular System

+ 35682 autogenous composite, 2 segments of veins from 2 locations (List separately in addition to code for primary procedure) C 80
Code first (35556, 35566, 35571, 35583-35587)
Do not report with (35681, 35683)
🚗 10.51 ✂ 10.51 Global Days ZZZ
AMA: 2009, Jan, 11-31; 2008, Jan, 10-25; 2007, January, 13-27

+ 35683 autogenous composite, 3 or more segments of vein from 2 or more locations (List separately in addition to code for primary procedure) C 80
Code first (35556, 35566, 35571, 35583-35587)
Do not report with (35681, 35682)
🚗 12.23 ✂ 12.23 Global Days ZZZ
AMA: 2009, Jan, 11-31; 2008, Jan, 10-25; 2007, January, 13-27

+ 35685 Placement of vein patch or cuff at distal anastomosis of bypass graft, synthetic conduit (List separately in addition to code for primary procedure) T 80
EXCLUDES Composite grafts (35681-35683)
Code first (35656, 35666, or 35671)
🚗 5.93 ✂ 5.93 Global Days ZZZ

+ 35686 Creation of distal arteriovenous fistula during lower extremity bypass surgery (non-hemodialysis) (List separately in addition to code for primary procedure) T 80
EXCLUDES Composite grafts (35681-35683)
Code first (35556, 35566, 35571, 35583-35587, 35623, 35656, 35666, 35671)
🚗 4.90 ✂ 4.90 Global Days ZZZ

35691-35697 Arterial Translocation

CMS 100-3,20.1 Vertebral Artery Surgery
CMS 100-3,20.2 Extracranial-intracranial (EC-IC) Arterial Bypass Surgery
CMS 100-3,160.8 Electroencephalographic Monitoring During Cerebral Vasculature Surgery

35691 Transposition and/or reimplantation; vertebral to carotid artery C 80 50
🚗 28.07 ✂ 28.07 Global Days 090

35693 vertebral to subclavian artery C 80 50
🚗 24.73 ✂ 24.73 Global Days 090

35694 subclavian to carotid artery C 80 50
EXCLUDES Subclavian to carotid artery transposition procedure (open) with concurrent repair of descending thoracic aorta (endovascular) (33889)
🚗 29.32 ✂ 29.32 Global Days 090

35695 carotid to subclavian artery C 80 50
🚗 30.45 ✂ 30.45 Global Days 090

+ 35697 Reimplantation, visceral artery to infrarenal aortic prosthesis, each artery (List separately in addition to code for primary procedure) C 80
Do not report with (33877)
🚗 4.40 ✂ 4.40 Global Days ZZZ

35700 Reoperative Bypass Lower Extremities

+ 35700 Reoperation, femoral-popliteal or femoral (popliteal)-anterior tibial, posterior tibial, peroneal artery, or other distal vessels, more than 1 month after original operation (List separately in addition to code for primary procedure) C 80
Code first (35556, 35566, 35571, 35583, 35585, 35587, 35656, 35666, 35671)
🚗 4.53 ✂ 4.53 Global Days ZZZ

35701-35761 Arterial Exploration without Repair

35701 Exploration (not followed by surgical repair), with or without lysis of artery; carotid artery C 80 50
🚗 15.89 ✂ 15.89 Global Days 090

35721 femoral artery C 80 50
🚗 13.12 ✂ 13.12 Global Days 090

35741 popliteal artery C 80 50
🚗 14.75 ✂ 14.75 Global Days 090

35761 other vessels G2 T 80 50
🚗 10.96 ✂ 10.96 Global Days 090

35800-35860 Arterial Exploration for Postoperative Complication

INCLUDES Return to the operating room for postoperative hemorrhage

35800 Exploration for postoperative hemorrhage, thrombosis or infection; neck C 80
🚗 14.03 ✂ 14.03 Global Days 090

35820 chest C 80
🚗 57.31 ✂ 57.31 Global Days 090

35840 abdomen C 80
🚗 18.54 ✂ 18.54 Global Days 090

35860 extremity T 80
🚗 11.84 ✂ 11.84 Global Days 090

35870 Repair Secondary Aortoenteric Fistula

35870 Repair of graft-enteric fistula C 80
🚗 37.00 ✂ 37.00 Global Days 090

35875-35876 Removal of Thrombus from Graft

EXCLUDES Thrombectomy dialysis fistula or graft (36831, 36833)
Thrombectomy with blood vessel repair, lower extremity, vein graft (35256)
Thrombectomy with blood vessel repair, lower extremity, with/without patch angioplasty (35226)

35875 Thrombectomy of arterial or venous graft (other than hemodialysis graft or fistula); A2 T
🚗 17.49 ✂ 17.49 Global Days 090
AMA: 2009, Jan, 11-31; 2008, Jan, 10-25; 2007, January, 13-27

35876 with revision of arterial or venous graft A2 T 80
🚗 28.00 ✂ 28.00 Global Days 090

35879-35884 Revision Lower Extremity Bypass Graft

EXCLUDES Removal of infected graft (35901-35907)
Revascularization following removal of infected graft(s)

35879 Revision, lower extremity arterial bypass, without thrombectomy, open; with vein patch angioplasty T 80 50
🚗 27.52 ✂ 27.52 Global Days 090
AMA: 2007, January, 7-10

35881 with segmental vein interposition T 80 50
EXCLUDES Revision of femoral anastomosis of synthetic arterial bypass graft (35883-35884)
🚗 30.22 ✂ 30.22 Global Days 090
AMA: 2007, January, 7-10

35883 Revision, femoral anastomosis of synthetic arterial bypass graft in groin, open; with nonautogenous patch graft (eg, Dacron, ePTFE, bovine pericardium) T 80 50
Do not report with (35700, 35875-35876, 35884)
🚗 35.76 ✂ 35.76 Global Days 090
AMA: 2009, Jan, 11-31; 2008, Jan, 10-25; 2007, January, 7-10

26/16 PC/TC Comp Only   A2- ASC Pmt   50 Bilateral   ♂ Male Only   ♀ Female Only   🚗 Facility RVU   ✂ Non-Facility RVU
AMA: CPT Asst   MED: Pub 100   A-Y OPPSI   80/89 Surg Assist Allowed / w/Doc   Lab Crosswalk   Radiology Crosswalk
128   CPT only © 2009 American Medical Association. All Rights Reserved. (Black Ink)   Medicare (Red Ink)   © 2009 Publisher (Blue Ink)

Current Procedural Coding Expert – Cardiovascular System

35884 with autogenous vein patch graft ⊺ 80 50
Do not report with (35700, 35875-35876, 35883)
💰 36.93 ⚕ 36.93 Global Days 090
AMA: 2009, Jan, 11-31; 2008, Jan, 10-25; 2007, January, 7-10

35901-35907 Removal of Infected Graft

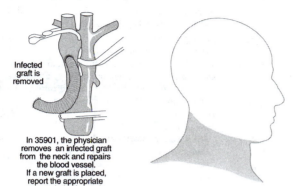

In 35901, the physician removes an infected graft from the neck and repairs the blood vessel. If a new graft is placed, report the appropriate revascularization code.

35901 Excision of infected graft; neck C 80
💰 14.64 ⚕ 14.64 Global Days 090

35903 extremity ⊺ 80
💰 16.47 ⚕ 16.47 Global Days 090

35905 thorax C 80
💰 50.00 ⚕ 50.00 Global Days 090

35907 abdomen C 80
💰 56.59 ⚕ 56.59 Global Days 090

36000 Intravenous Access Established

INCLUDES Venous access for phlebotomy, prophylactic intravenous access, infusion therapy, chemotherapy, hydration, transfusion, drug administration, etc. which is included in the work value of the primary procedure

36000 Introduction of needle or intracatheter, vein M N 50
💰 0.27 ⚕ 0.61 Global Days XXX
AMA: 2009, Jan, 11-31; 2008, Jan, 10-25; 2007, January, 13-27; 2007, February, 10-11; 2007, Jul, 1-4; 2006, May, 1-9

36002 Injection Treatment of Pseudoaneurysm

INCLUDES Insertion of needle or catheter, local anesthesia, injection of contrast, power injections

EXCLUDES Compression repair pseudoaneurysm, ultrasound guided (76936)
Medications, contrast material, catheters

36002 Injection procedures (eg, thrombin) for percutaneous treatment of extremity pseudoaneurysm 62 S 50
76942, 77002, 77012, 77021
💰 2.97 ⚕ 4.25 Global Days 000

36005-36015 Insertion Needle or Intracatheter: Venous

INCLUDES Insertion of needle/catheter, local anesthesia, injection of contrast, power injections

EXCLUDES Medications, contrast materials, catheters

Code also catheterization of second order vessels (or higher) supplied by the same first order branch, same vascular family

Code also each vascular family (e.g., bilateral procedures are separate vascular families)

36005 Injection procedure for extremity venography (including introduction of needle or intracatheter) M N 80 50
75820, 75822
💰 1.36 ⚕ 8.32 Global Days 000

36010 Introduction of catheter, superior or inferior vena cava M N 50
💰 3.43 ⚕ 12.98 Global Days XXX
AMA: 2009, Jan, 7-8; 2009, Jan, 11-31; 2008, Jan, 10-25; 2008, Oct, 10-11; 2007, January, 13-27

36011 Selective catheter placement, venous system; first order branch (eg, renal vein, jugular vein) M N 50
💰 4.46 ⚕ 22.04 Global Days XXX

36012 second order, or more selective, branch (eg, left adrenal vein, petrosal sinus) M N 50
💰 4.97 ⚕ 22.12 Global Days XXX

36013 Introduction of catheter, right heart or main pulmonary artery M N
💰 3.65 ⚕ 19.27 Global Days XXX
AMA: 2009, Jan, 7-8; 2009, Jan, 11-31; 2008, Oct, 10-11

36014 Selective catheter placement, left or right pulmonary artery M N 50
💰 4.20 ⚕ 20.59 Global Days XXX

36015 Selective catheter placement, segmental or subsegmental pulmonary artery M N 50
EXCLUDES Placement of Swan Ganz/other flow directed catheter for monitoring (93503)
Selective blood sampling, specific organs (36500)
💰 4.85 ⚕ 22.15 Global Days XXX

36100-36248 Insertion Needle or Intracatheter: Arterial

INCLUDES Introduction of the catheter and catheterization of all lesser order vessels used for the approach
Local anesthesia, placement of catheter/needle, injection of contrast, power injections

EXCLUDES Angiography (36147, 75600-75774, 75791)
Angioplasty (35470-35475)
Injection procedures for cardiac catheterizations (93541-93545)
Medications, contrast, catheters
Transcatheter procedures (37200-37208, 61624, 61626)

Code also catheterization of second and third order vessels supplied by the same first order branch, same vascular family (36218, 36248)

75600-75791

36100 Introduction of needle or intracatheter, carotid or vertebral artery M N 50
💰 4.47 ⚕ 12.61 Global Days XXX

36120 Introduction of needle or intracatheter; retrograde brachial artery M N
💰 2.82 ⚕ 11.20 Global Days XXX
AMA: 2009, Jun, 10-11

● New Code ▲ Revised Code M Maternity A Age Unlisted Not Covered # Resequenced
CCI + Add-on ⊘ Mod 51 Exempt Mod 63 Exempt ⊙ Mod Sedation PQRI

© 2009 Publisher (Blue Ink) CPT only © 2009 American Medical Association. All Rights Reserved. (Black Ink) Medicare (Red Ink)

36140 — 36415 Cardiovascular System

36140	**extremity artery** [N1][N][□] 2.93 11.48 Global Days XXX AMA: 2009, Jan, 11-31; 2009, Jun, 10-11; 2007, Dec, 10-179; 2007, Jul, 1-4; 2006, May, 10-11; 2006, May, 1-9
~~36145~~	~~arteriovenous shunt created for dialysis (cannula, fistula, or graft)~~ To report, see code 36147-36148
⊙● 36147	**Introduction of needle and/or catheter, arteriovenous shunt created for dialysis (graft/fistula); initial access with complete radiological evaluation of dialysis access, including fluoroscopy, image documentation and report (includes access of shunt, injection[s] of contrast, and all necessary imaging from the arterial anastomosis and adjacent artery through entire venous outflow, including the inferior or superior vena cava)** [P2][T][80] Code also the second shunt catheterization when 36147 indicates the need for a therapeutic interventional procedure (36148) Do not report with (75791) 5.38 21.28 Global Days XXX
+⊙● 36148	**additional access for therapeutic intervention (List separately in addition to code for primary procedure)** [N1][N][□] Code first (36147) 1.41 6.70 Global Days ZZZ
36160	**Introduction of needle or intracatheter, aortic, translumbar** [N1][N][□] 3.54 12.33 Global Days XXX AMA: 2007, Dec, 10-179
36200	**Introduction of catheter, aorta** [N1][N][50][□] 4.37 15.84 Global Days XXX AMA: 2009, Jan, 11-31; 2008, Apr, -11; 2007, Dec, 10-179; 2006, May, 10-11
36215	**Selective catheter placement, arterial system; each first order thoracic or brachiocephalic branch, within a vascular family** [N1][N][□] EXCLUDES Placement of catheter for coronary angiography (93508) 6.80 27.91 Global Days XXX AMA: 2009, Jan, 11-31; 2008, Jan, 10-25; 2007, Dec, 10-179; 2007, January, 13-27; 2006, May, 10-11
36216	**initial second order thoracic or brachiocephalic branch, within a vascular family** [N1][N][□] 7.67 30.65 Global Days XXX AMA: 2007, Dec, 10-179; 2006, May, 10-11
36217	**initial third order or more selective thoracic or brachiocephalic branch, within a vascular family** [N1][N][□] 9.13 49.34 Global Days XXX AMA: 2007, Dec, 10-179; 2006, May, 10-11
+ 36218	**additional second order, third order, and beyond, thoracic or brachiocephalic branch, within a vascular family (List in addition to code for initial second or third order vessel as appropriate)** [N1][N][□] Code first (36216, 36217) 1.46 4.60 Global Days ZZZ AMA: 2007, Dec, 10-179; 2006, May, 10-11
36245	**each first order abdominal, pelvic, or lower extremity artery branch, within a vascular family** [N1][N][50][□] 6.83 28.06 Global Days XXX AMA: 2009, Jan, 11-31; 2008, Jan, 10-25; 2007, Dec, 10-179; 2007, January, 7-10; 2007, January, 13-27
36246	**initial second order abdominal, pelvic, or lower extremity artery branch, within a vascular family** [N1][N][50][□] 7.62 29.59 Global Days XXX AMA: 2009, Jan, 11-31; 2008, Jan, 10-25; 2007, Dec, 10-179; 2007, January, 13-27; 2007, January, 7-10
36247	**initial third order or more selective abdominal, pelvic, or lower extremity artery branch, within a vascular family** [N1][N][50][□] 9.10 46.29 Global Days XXX AMA: 2009, Jan, 11-31; 2008, Jan, 10-25; 2007, January, 7-10; 2007, January, 13-27; 2007, Dec, 10-179
+ 36248	**additional second order, third order, and beyond, abdominal, pelvic, or lower extremity artery branch, within a vascular family (List in addition to code for initial second or third order vessel as appropriate)** [N1][N][□] Code first (36246, 36247) 1.44 3.88 Global Days ZZZ AMA: 2009, Jan, 11-31; 2008, Jan, 10-25; 2007, January, 7-10; 2007, January, 13-27

36260-36299 Implanted Infusion Pumps: Intra-arterial

CMS 100-3,280.14 Infusion Pumps

36260	**Insertion of implantable intra-arterial infusion pump (eg, for chemotherapy of liver)** [A2][T][□] Code also (C1772, C1891, C2626) 17.56 17.56 Global Days 090
36261	**Revision of implanted intra-arterial infusion pump** [A2][T][80][□] 10.09 10.09 Global Days 090
36262	**Removal of implanted intra-arterial infusion pump** [A2][T][□] 8.06 8.06 Global Days 090
36299	**Unlisted procedure, vascular injection** [N][80] 0.00 0.00 Global Days YYY

36400-36425 Specimen Collection: Phlebotomy

EXCLUDES Collection of specimen from:
A completely implantable device (36591)
An established catheter (36592)

36400	**Venipuncture, younger than age 3 years, necessitating physician's skill, not to be used for routine venipuncture; femoral or jugular vein** [A][N1][N][□] 0.57 0.80 Global Days XXX AMA: 2007, Jul, 1-4; 2006, May, 1-9
36405	**scalp vein** [A][N1][N][□] 0.47 0.73 Global Days XXX AMA: 2007, Jul, 1-4; 2006, May, 1-9
36406	**other vein** [A][N1][N][□] 0.27 0.50 Global Days XXX AMA: 2007, Jul, 1-4; 2006, May, 1-9
36410	**Venipuncture, age 3 years or older, necessitating physician's skill (separate procedure), for diagnostic or therapeutic purposes (not to be used for routine venipuncture)** [N1][N][□] 0.27 0.55 Global Days XXX AMA: 2009, Jan, 11-31; 2008, Jan, 10-25; 2007, January, 13-27; 2007, February, 10-11; 2007, Jul, 1-4
36415	**Collection of venous blood by venipuncture** [A][⊙] 0.00 0.00 Global Days XXX AMA: 2009, Jan, 11-31; 2008, Jan, 10-25; 2008, Apr, -9; 2007, January, 13-27; 2007, February, 10-11; 2007, Jul, 1-4

[26/TC] PC/TC Comp Only [A2-Z3] ASC Pmt [50] Bilateral ♂ Male Only ♀ Female Only   Facility RVU   Non-Facility RVU
AMA: CPT Asst MED: Pub 100 [A-Y] OPPSI [80/80] Surg Assist Allowed / w/Doc   Lab Crosswalk   Radiology Crosswalk
130 CPT only © 2009 American Medical Association. All Rights Reserved. (Black Ink) Medicare (Red Ink) © 2009 Publisher (Blue Ink)

Current Procedural Coding Expert – Cardiovascular System

36416 Collection of capillary blood specimen (eg, finger, heel, ear stick)
    0.00 0.00 **Global Days** XXX
    AMA: 2008, Apr, -9

36420 Venipuncture, cutdown; younger than age 1 year
    1.49 1.49 **Global Days** XXX
    AMA: 2007, Jul, 1-4; 2006, May, 1-9

36425 age 1 or over
    1.12 1.12 **Global Days** XXX

36430-36460 Transfusions

CMS 100-1,3,20.5   Blood Deductibles
CMS 100-1,3,20.5.2   Part B Blood Deductible
CMS 100-2,1,10   Inpatient Hospital Services Covered Under Part A
CMS 100-3,110.5   Granulocyte Transfulsions
CMS 100-3,110.7   Blood Transfusions
CMS 100-3,110.8   Blood Platelet Transfusions
CMS 100-3,110.16   Nonselective (Random) Transfusions and Living-Related Donor Specific Transfusions (DST) in Kidney Transplantation
CMS 100-4,3,40.2.2   Beneficiary Charges for Part A Services

36430 Transfusion, blood or blood components
    0.76 0.76 **Global Days** XXX
    AMA: 2009, Jan, 11-31; 2008, Jan, 10-25; 2007, January, 13-27; 2007, Jul, 1-4; 2006, May, 1-9

36440 Push transfusion, blood, 2 years or younger
    1.60 1.60 **Global Days** XXX
    AMA: 2007, Jul, 1-4; 2006, May, 1-9

36450 Exchange transfusion, blood; newborn
    3.18 3.18 **Global Days** XXX

36455 other than newborn
    3.50 3.50 **Global Days** XXX

36460 Transfusion, intrauterine, fetal
    76941
    10.02 10.02 **Global Days** XXX

36468-36479 Destruction of Veins

CMS 100-2,16,10   Exclusions from Coverage
CMS 100-2,16,120   Cosmetic Procedures
CMS 100-2,16,180   Services Related to Noncovered Procedures

36468 Single or multiple injections of sclerosing solutions, spider veins (telangiectasia); limb or trunk
    0.00 0.00 **Global Days** 000

36469 face
    0.00 0.00 **Global Days** 000

36470 Injection of sclerosing solution; single vein
    2.02 3.88 **Global Days** 010

36471 multiple veins, same leg
    2.83 4.67 **Global Days** 010

36475 Endovenous ablation therapy of incompetent vein, extremity, inclusive of all imaging guidance and monitoring, percutaneous, radiofrequency; first vein treated
    Do not report with (36000-36005, 36410, 36425, 36478-36479, 37204, 75894, 76000-76001, 76937, 76942, 76998, 77022, 93970-93971)
    10.11 46.05 **Global Days** 000

+ 36476 second and subsequent veins treated in a single extremity, each through separate access sites (List separately in addition to code for primary procedure)
    Code first (36475)
    Do not report with (36000-36005, 36410, 36425, 36478-36479, 37204, 75894, 76000-76001, 76937, 76942, 76998, 77022, 93970-93971)
    4.98 10.48 **Global Days** ZZZ

36478 Endovenous ablation therapy of incompetent vein, extremity, inclusive of all imaging guidance and monitoring, percutaneous, laser; first vein treated
    Do not report with (36000-36005, 36410, 36425, 36475-36476, 37204, 75894, 76000-76001, 76937, 76942, 76998, 77022, 93970-93971)
    10.03 36.62 **Global Days** 000

+ 36479 second and subsequent veins treated in a single extremity, each through separate access sites (List separately in addition to code for primary procedure)
    Code first (36478)
    Do not report with (36000-36005, 36410, 36425, 36475-36476, 37204, 75894, 76000-76001, 76937, 76942, 76998, 77022, 93970-93971)
    4.96 10.48 **Global Days** ZZZ

36481-36510 Other Venous Catheterization Procedures

EXCLUDES Collection of a specimen from:
    A completely implantable device (36591)
    An established catheter (36592)

36481 Percutaneous portal vein catheterization by any method
    75885, 75887
    10.04 53.01 **Global Days** 000
    AMA: 2009, Jan, 11-31; 2008, Jan, 10-25; 2007, January, 13-27; 2006, April, 11-18

36500 Venous catheterization for selective organ blood sampling
    EXCLUDES Inferior or superior vena cava catheterization (36010)
    75893
    5.03 5.03 **Global Days** 000

36510 Catheterization of umbilical vein for diagnosis or therapy, newborn
    EXCLUDES Collection of a specimen from:
        Capillary blood (36416)
        Venipuncture (36415)
    1.69 2.52 **Global Days** 000
    AMA: 2007, Jul, 1-4; 2006, May, 1-9

36511-36516 Apheresis

CMS 100-1,3,20.5.2   Part B Blood Deductible
CMS 100-3,110.14   Apheresis (Therapeutic Pheresis)
EXCLUDES Collection of a specimen from:
    A completely implantable device (36591)
    An established catheter (36592)

36511 Therapeutic apheresis; for white blood cells
    2.66 2.66 **Global Days** 000
    AMA: 2009, Jun, 3-6&11

36512 for red blood cells
    2.57 2.57 **Global Days** 000
    AMA: 2009, Jun, 3-6&11

36513-36571

36513	for platelets		
	2.72 2.72 Global Days 000		
	AMA: 2009, Mar, 10-11; 2009, Jun, 3-6&11		
36514	for plasma pheresis		
	2.58 12.25 Global Days 000		
	AMA: 2009, Jun, 3-6&11		
36515	with extracorporeal immunoadsorption and plasma reinfusion		
	2.57 46.46 Global Days 000		
	AMA: 2009, Jun, 3-6&11		
36516	with extracorporeal selective adsorption or selective filtration and plasma reinfusion		
	1.93 47.88 Global Days 000		
	AMA: 2009, Jun, 3-6&11		

36522 Extracorporeal Photopheresis

CMS 100-3,110.4   Extracorporeal Photopheresis

36522	Photopheresis, extracorporeal
	2.79 31.76 Global Days 000
	AMA: 2009, Jun, 3-6&11

36555-36571 Placement of Implantable Venous Access Device

INCLUDES Devices that are inserted via cutdown or percutaneous access, either centrally (e.g., femoral, jugular, subclavian veins, or vena cava) or peripherally (e.g., basilic or cephalic)
Devices that terminate in the brachiocephalic (innominate), iliac, or subclavian veins, vena cava, or right atrium

EXCLUDES Maintenance/refilling of implantable pump/reservoir (96522)

76937, 77001

- **36555** Insertion of non-tunneled centrally inserted central venous catheter; younger than 5 years of age
  EXCLUDES That by peripheral insertion (36568)
  3.28 6.40 Global Days 000
  AMA: 2008, Jun, 8-11; 2007, Jul, 1-4; 2006, May, 1-9

- **36556** age 5 years or older
  EXCLUDES That by peripheral insertion (36569)
  3.41 5.99 Global Days 000
  AMA: 2008, Jun, 8-11

A tunneled centrally inserted CVC is inserted. Report 36557 for a patient under age 5 and 36558 for patients older than age 5

- **36557** Insertion of tunneled centrally inserted central venous catheter, without subcutaneous port or pump; younger than 5 years of age
  Code also (C1750, C1751, C1752)
  9.00 25.54 Global Days 010
  AMA: 2008, Jun, 8-11

- **36558** age 5 years or older
  EXCLUDES That by peripheral insertion (36571)
  Code also (C1750, C1751, C1752)
  7.76 19.91 Global Days 010
  AMA: 2008, Jun, 8-11

- **36560** Insertion of tunneled centrally inserted central venous access device, with subcutaneous port; younger than 5 years of age
  EXCLUDES That by peripheral insertion (36570)
  Code also (C1751, C1788)
  9.35 24.54 Global Days 010
  AMA: 2008, Jun, 8-11

- **36561** age 5 years or older
  EXCLUDES That by peripheral insertion (36571)
  Code also (C1751, C1788)
  9.91 30.11 Global Days 010
  AMA: 2008, Jun, 8-11

- **36563** Insertion of tunneled centrally inserted central venous access device with subcutaneous pump
  Code also (C1772, C1891, C2626)
  10.47 32.79 Global Days 010
  AMA: 2008, Jun, 8-11

- **36565** Insertion of tunneled centrally inserted central venous access device, requiring 2 catheters via 2 separate venous access sites; without subcutaneous port or pump (eg, Tesio type catheter)
  Code also (C1750, C1751, C1752)
  9.87 25.82 Global Days 010
  AMA: 2008, Jun, 8-11

- **36566** with subcutaneous port(s)
  Code also (C1881)
  10.65 129.86 Global Days 010
  AMA: 2008, Jun, 8-11

- **36568** Insertion of peripherally inserted central venous catheter (PICC), without subcutaneous port or pump; younger than 5 years of age
  EXCLUDES Centrally inserted placement (36555)
  2.65 6.95 Global Days 000
  AMA: 2009, Jan, 11-31; 2008, Jan, 10-25; 2008, Jun, 8-11; 2007, January, 13-27; 2005, May, 13-14

- **36569** age 5 years or older
  EXCLUDES Centrally inserted placement (36556)
  2.56 6.16 Global Days 000
  AMA: 2009, Jan, 11-31; 2008, Jan, 10-25; 2008, Jun, 8-11; 2007, January, 13-27; 2005, May, 13-14

- **36570** Insertion of peripherally inserted central venous access device, with subcutaneous port; younger than 5 years of age
  EXCLUDES Centrally inserted placement (36560)
  Code also (C1751, C1788)
  8.22 26.46 Global Days 010
  AMA: 2008, Jun, 8-11

- **36571** age 5 years or older
  EXCLUDES Centrally inserted placement (36561)
  Code also (C1751, C1788)
  8.92 32.32 Global Days 010
  AMA: 2008, Jun, 8-11

26/TC PC/TC Comp Only   A2-Z3 ASC Pmt   50 Bilateral   ♂ Male Only   ♀ Female Only   Facility RVU   Non-Facility RVU
AMA: CPT Asst   MED: Pub 100   A-Y OPPSI   80/8P Surg Assist Allowed / w/Doc   Lab Crosswalk   Radiology Crosswalk
CPT only © 2009 American Medical Association. All Rights Reserved. (Black Ink)   Medicare (Red Ink)   © 2009 Publisher (Blue Ink)

Current Procedural Coding Expert – Cardiovascular System

36575-36590 Repair, Removal, and Replacement Implantable Venous Access Device

INCLUDES
Complete removal/all components (36589-36590)
Complete replacement (replace all components/same access site) (36580-36585)
Partial replacement (catheter only) (36578)
Repair of the device without replacing any parts (36575-36576)

EXCLUDES
Mechanical removal obstructive material, pericatheter/intraluminal (36595, 36596)

36575 Repair of tunneled or non-tunneled central venous access catheter, without subcutaneous port or pump, central or peripheral insertion site
0.99   4.03   Global Days 000
AMA: 2008, Jun, 8-11

36576 Repair of central venous access device, with subcutaneous port or pump, central or peripheral insertion site
5.43   9.89   Global Days 010
AMA: 2008, Jun, 8-11

36578 Replacement, catheter only, of central venous access device, with subcutaneous port or pump, central or peripheral insertion site
Code also hemodialysis catheter (C1752)
Code also implantable dialysis access system (C1881)
Code also infusion catheter (C1751)
5.94   13.02   Global Days 010
AMA: 2008, Jun, 8-11

36580 Replacement, complete, of a non-tunneled centrally inserted central venous catheter, without subcutaneous port or pump, through same venous access
1.88   5.35   Global Days 000
AMA: 2008, Jun, 8-11

36581 Replacement, complete, of a tunneled centrally inserted central venous catheter, without subcutaneous port or pump, through same venous access
Code also (C1750, C1751, C1752)
5.46   18.81   Global Days 010
AMA: 2008, Jun, 8-11

36582 Replacement, complete, of a tunneled centrally inserted central venous access device, with subcutaneous port, through same venous access
Code also (C1751, C1788, C1881)
8.53   27.87   Global Days 010
AMA: 2008, Jun, 8-11

36583 Replacement, complete, of a tunneled centrally inserted central venous access device, with subcutaneous pump, through same venous access
Code also (C1772, C1891, C2626)
9.22   33.87   Global Days 010
AMA: 2008, Jun, 8-11

36584 Replacement, complete, of a peripherally inserted central venous catheter (PICC), without subcutaneous port or pump, through same venous access
1.83   5.00   Global Days 000
AMA: 2008, Jun, 8-11

36585 Replacement, complete, of a peripherally inserted central venous access device, with subcutaneous port, through same venous access
Code also (C1751, C1788)
7.72   27.00   Global Days 010
AMA: 2008, Jun, 8-11

36589 Removal of tunneled central venous catheter, without subcutaneous port or pump
EXCLUDES *Non-tunneled central venous catheter removal; report appropriate E/M code*
3.88   4.52   Global Days 010
AMA: 2008, Jun, 8-11

36590 Removal of tunneled central venous access device, with subcutaneous port or pump, central or peripheral insertion
Do not report with non-tunneled central venous catheter removal; report appropriate E/M code
5.70   7.82   Global Days 010
AMA: 2008, Jun, 8-11

36591-36592 Obtain Blood Specimen from Implanted Device or Catheter

36591 Collection of blood specimen from a completely implantable venous access device
EXCLUDES *Collection of:*
Capillary blood specimen (36416)
Venous blood specimen by venipuncture (36415)
Do not report with any other service
0.52   0.52   Global Days XXX
AMA: 2008, Apr, -9

36592 Collection of blood specimen using established central or peripheral catheter, venous, not otherwise specified
EXCLUDES *Collection of blood from an established arterial catheter (37799)*
Do not report with any other service
0.59   0.59   Global Days XXX
AMA: 2008, Apr, -9

36593-36596 Restore Patency of Occluded Catheter or Device

EXCLUDES *Venous catheterization (36010-36012)*

36593 Declotting by thrombolytic agent of implanted vascular access device or catheter
0.70   0.70   Global Days XXX
AMA: 2008, Apr, -9

36595 Mechanical removal of pericatheter obstructive material (eg, fibrin sheath) from central venous device via separate venous access
EXCLUDES *Venous catheterization (36010-36012)*
Do not report with (36593)
75901
5.16   13.89   Global Days 000

36596 Mechanical removal of intraluminal (intracatheter) obstructive material from central venous device through device lumen
EXCLUDES *Venous catheterization (36010-36012)*
Do not report with (36593)
75902
1.23   3.25   Global Days 000

● New Code   ▲ Revised Code   Ⓜ Maternity   Ⓐ Age   Unlisted   Not Covered   # Resequenced
CCI   + Add-on   ⊘ Mod 51 Exempt   Mod 63 Exempt   ⊙ Mod Sedation   PQRI
© 2009 Publisher (*Blue Ink*)   CPT only © 2009 American Medical Association. All Rights Reserved. (Black Ink)   Medicare (Red Ink)

36597-36598 Repositioning or Assessment of In Situ Venous Access Device

36597 Repositioning of previously placed central venous catheter under fluoroscopic guidance
  76000
  1.70 3.16 Global Days 000

36598 Contrast injection(s) for radiologic evaluation of existing central venous access device, including fluoroscopy, image documentation and report
  EXCLUDES Complete venography studies (75820, 75825, 75827)
  Do not report with (36595-36596, 76000)
  1.01 2.75 Global Days 000

36600-36660 Insertion Needle or Catheter: Artery

36600 Arterial puncture, withdrawal of blood for diagnosis
  Do not report with critical care services
  0.43 0.79 Global Days XXX
  AMA: 2007, Jul, 1-4; 2007, February, 10-11; 2006, May, 1-9; 2005, July, 11-12

36620 Arterial catheterization or cannulation for sampling, monitoring or transfusion (separate procedure); percutaneous
  1.43 1.43 Global Days 000
  AMA: 2007, Jul, 1-4; 2006, May, 1-9

36625 cutdown
  3.03 3.03 Global Days 000

36640 Arterial catheterization for prolonged infusion therapy (chemotherapy), cutdown
  EXCLUDES Intraarterial chemotherapy (96420-96425)
  Transcatheter embolization (75894)
  Code also (C1751)
  3.44 3.44 Global Days 000

36660 Catheterization, umbilical artery, newborn, for diagnosis or therapy
  1.87 1.87 Global Days 000
  AMA: 2007, Jul, 1-4; 2006, May, 1-9

36680 Percutaneous Placement of Catheter/Needle into Bone Marrow Cavity

36680 Placement of needle for intraosseous infusion
  1.63 1.63 Global Days 000

36800-36821 Vascular Access for Hemodialysis

36800 Insertion of cannula for hemodialysis, other purpose (separate procedure); vein to vein
  Code also (C1750, C1752)
  4.48 4.48 Global Days 000

36810 arteriovenous, external (Scribner type)
  Code also (C1750, C1752)
  6.09 6.09 Global Days 000

36815 arteriovenous, external revision, or closure
  4.31 4.31 Global Days 000

36818 Arteriovenous anastomosis, open; by upper arm cephalic vein transposition
  19.36 19.36 Global Days 090
  AMA: 2005, July, 9-10

36819 by upper arm basilic vein transposition
  23.10 23.10 Global Days 090
  AMA: 2005, July, 9-10

36820 by forearm vein transposition
  23.32 23.32 Global Days 090
  AMA: 2005, July, 9-10

36821 direct, any site (eg, Cimino type) (separate procedure)
  20.00 20.00 Global Days 090
  AMA: 2005, July, 9-10

36822-36823 Vascular Access for Extracorporeal Circulation

EXCLUDES Maintenance for prolonged extracorporeal circulation (33960, 33961)

36822 Insertion of cannula(s) for prolonged extracorporeal circulation for cardiopulmonary insufficiency (ECMO) (separate procedure)
  EXCLUDES Maintenance for prolonged circulation (33960, 33961)
  10.63 10.63 Global Days 090
  AMA: 2009, Jan, 11-31; 2008, Jan, 10-25; 2007, January, 13-27

36823 Insertion of arterial and venous cannula(s) for isolated extracorporeal circulation including regional chemotherapy perfusion to an extremity, with or without hyperthermia, with removal of cannula(s) and repair of arteriotomy and venotomy sites
  INCLUDES Chemotherapy perfusion
  Do not report with (96409-96425)
  37.54 37.54 Global Days 090

36825-36835 Permanent Vascular Access Procedures

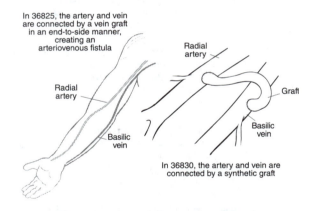

In 36825, the artery and vein are connected by a vein graft in an end-to-side manner, creating an arteriovenous fistula

In 36830, the artery and vein are connected by a synthetic graft

36825 Creation of arteriovenous fistula by other than direct arteriovenous anastomosis (separate procedure); autogenous graft
  EXCLUDES Direct arteriovenous (AV) anastomosis (36821)
  23.54 23.54 Global Days 090
  AMA: 2005, July, 9-10

36830 nonautogenous graft (eg, biological collagen, thermoplastic graft)
  EXCLUDES Direct arteriovenous (AV) anastomosis (36821)
  19.08 19.08 Global Days 090
  AMA: 2005, July, 9-10

36831 Thrombectomy, open, arteriovenous fistula without revision, autogenous or nonautogenous dialysis graft (separate procedure)
  13.22 13.22 Global Days 090
  AMA: 2009, Jan, 11-31; 2008, Jan, 10-25; 2007, January, 13-27

Current Procedural Coding Expert – Cardiovascular System

36832 Revision, open, arteriovenous fistula; without thrombectomy, autogenous or nonautogenous dialysis graft (separate procedure) [A2] [T] [80]
INCLUDES Revision of an arteriovenous access fistula or graft
🔹 16.86 🔹 16.86 Global Days 090
AMA: 2009, Jan, 11-31; 2008, Jan, 10-25; 2007, January, 13-27

36833 with thrombectomy, autogenous or nonautogenous dialysis graft (separate procedure) [A2] [T] [80]
🔹 19.04 🔹 19.04 Global Days 090
AMA: 2009, Jan, 11-31; 2008, Jan, 10-25; 2007, January, 13-27

~~**36834** Plastic repair of arteriovenous aneurysm (separate procedure)~~
To report, see code 36832

36835 Insertion of Thomas shunt (separate procedure) [A2] [T]
Code also (C1750, C1752)
🔹 13.84 🔹 13.84 Global Days 090

36838 DRIL Procedure for Ischemic Steal Syndrome

INCLUDES Banding/ligation angioaccess arteriovenous (AV) fistula
Ligation artery of extremity
Open revision arteriovenous (AV) fistula
Subclavian-brachial or axillary-brachial bypass grafts

Do not report with (35512, 35522-35523, 36832, 37607, 37618)

36838 Distal revascularization and interval ligation (DRIL), upper extremity hemodialysis access (steal syndrome) [T] [80] [50]
🔹 33.86 🔹 33.86 Global Days 090

36860-36870 Restore Patency of Occluded Cannula or Arteriovenous Fistula

36860 External cannula declotting (separate procedure); without balloon catheter [A2] [T]
76000
🔹 3.01 🔹 5.46 Global Days 000

36861 with balloon catheter [A2] [T]
Code also (C1757)
76000
🔹 4.33 🔹 4.33 Global Days 000

⊙ **36870** Thrombectomy, percutaneous, arteriovenous fistula, autogenous or nonautogenous graft (includes mechanical thrombus extraction and intra-graft thrombolysis) [A2] [T] [50]
INCLUDES Declotting using thrombolytics
EXCLUDES Catheterization (36147-36148)
Catheterization for arteriovenous (AV) shunt (36145)
Do not report with (36593)
36147, 75791
🔹 8.32 🔹 45.18 Global Days 090

37140-37181 Open Decompression of Portal Circulation

EXCLUDES Peritoneal-venous shunt (49425)

37140 Venous anastomosis, open; portocaval [C]
🔹 41.13 🔹 41.13 Global Days 090

37145 renoportal [C] [80]
🔹 42.67 🔹 42.67 Global Days 090

37160 caval-mesenteric [C] [80]
🔹 38.09 🔹 38.09 Global Days 090

37180 splenorenal, proximal [C] [80]
🔹 42.66 🔹 42.66 Global Days 090

37181 splenorenal, distal (selective decompression of esophagogastric varices, any technique) [C] [80]
EXCLUDES Percutaneous procedure (37182)
🔹 45.91 🔹 45.91 Global Days 090

37182-37183 Transvenous Decompression of Portal Circulation

Do not report with (75885, 75887)

37182 Insertion of transvenous intrahepatic portosystemic shunt(s) (TIPS) (includes venous access, hepatic and portal vein catheterization, portography with hemodynamic evaluation, intrahepatic tract formation/dilatation, stent placement and all associated imaging guidance and documentation) [C] [80] [PQ]
EXCLUDES Open procedure (37140)
🔹 23.29 🔹 23.29 Global Days 000
AMA: 2009, Jan, 11-31; 2008, Jan, 10-25; 2007, January, 13-27

⊙ **37183** Revision of transvenous intrahepatic portosystemic shunt(s) (TIPS) (includes venous access, hepatic and portal vein catheterization, portography with hemodynamic evaluation, intrahepatic tract recanulization/dilatation, stent placement and all associated imaging guidance and documentation) [T] [80] [PQ]
EXCLUDES Arteriovenous (AV) aneurysm repair (36832)
🔹 10.98 🔹 136.49 Global Days 000
AMA: 2009, Jan, 11-31; 2008, Jan, 10-25; 2007, January, 13-27

37184-37188 Removal of Thrombus from Vessel: Percutaneous

INCLUDES Fluoroscopic guidance
Injection(s) of thrombolytics during the procedure
Postprocedure evaluation
Pretreatment planning

EXCLUDES Continuous infusion of thrombolytics prior to and after the procedure (37201, 75896, 75898)
Diagnostic studies
Mechanical thrombectomy, coronary (92973)
Other interventions performed percutaneously (e.g., balloon angioplasty)
Percutaneous thrombectomy of an arteriovenous fistula (36870)
Placement of catheters
Radiological supervision/interpretation

⊙ **37184** Primary percutaneous transluminal mechanical thrombectomy, noncoronary, arterial or arterial bypass graft, including fluoroscopic guidance and intraprocedural pharmacological thrombolytic injection(s); initial vessel [G2] [T] [50] [PQ]
EXCLUDES Mechanical thrombectomy of another vascular family, separate access site, append modifier 51 to code, as appropriate
Seconday mechanical thrombectomy for treating of embolus/thrombus complicating another percutaneous intervention (37186)
Code also (C1757)
Do not report with (76000-76001, 96374, 99143-99150)
🔹 12.72 🔹 56.02 Global Days 000

● New Code ▲ Revised Code Ⓜ Maternity Ⓐ Age Unlisted Not Covered # Resequenced
CCI + Add-on ⊘ Mod 51 Exempt ⊘ Mod 63 Exempt ⊙ Mod Sedation PQ PQRI
© 2009 Publisher (Blue Ink) CPT only © 2009 American Medical Association. All Rights Reserved. (Black Ink) Medicare (Red Ink)

Current Procedural Coding Expert – Cardiovascular System

+ ⊙ 37185 second and all subsequent vessel(s) within the same vascular family (List separately in addition to code for primary mechanical thrombectomy procedure) [G2] [T]

  INCLUDES Treatment of second and all succeeding vessel(s) in same vascular family

  EXCLUDES Intravenous drug injections administered subsequent to an initial service
  Mechanical thrombectomy for embolus/thrombus complicating another percutaneous interventional procedure (37186)
  Mechanical thrombectomy of another vascular family/separate access site, append modifier 51 to code as appropriate

  Code first (37184)
  Do not report with (76000-76001, 96375)
  🔴 4.74   ⚕ 18.60 Global Days ZZZ

+ ⊙ 37186 Secondary percutaneous transluminal thrombectomy (eg, nonprimary mechanical, snare basket, suction technique), noncoronary, arterial or arterial bypass graft, including fluoroscopic guidance and intraprocedural pharmacological thrombolytic injections, provided in conjunction with another percutaneous intervention other than primary mechanical thrombectomy (List separately in addition to code for primary procedure) [G2] [T]

  INCLUDES Removal of small emboli/thrombi prior to or after another percutaneous procedure

  Code first primary procedure
  Do not report with (76000-76001, 96375)
  🔴 7.14   ⚕ 35.38 Global Days ZZZ
  AMA: 2009, Jan, 11-31; 2008, May, 9-11

⊙ 37187 Percutaneous transluminal mechanical thrombectomy, vein(s), including intraprocedural pharmacological thrombolytic injections and fluoroscopic guidance [G2] [T] [50] [P0]

  INCLUDES Secondary or subsequent intravenous injection after another initial service

  Code also (C1757)
  Do not report with (76000-76001, 96375)
  🔴 11.52   ⚕ 53.58 Global Days 000

⊙ 37188 Percutaneous transluminal mechanical thrombectomy, vein(s), including intraprocedural pharmacological thrombolytic injections and fluoroscopic guidance, repeat treatment on subsequent day during course of thrombolytic therapy [G2] [T] [50] [P0]

  Code also (C1757)
  Do not report with (76000-76001, 96375)
  🔴 8.30   ⚕ 44.08 Global Days 000

37195-37203 Miscellaneous Transcatheter Procedures: Infusions, Biopsy, Foreign Body Removal

37195 Thrombolysis, cerebral, by intravenous infusion [T] [80]
  🔴 0.00   ⚕ 0.00 Global Days XXX

37200 Transcatheter biopsy [G2] [T]
  📷 75970
  🔴 6.19   ⚕ 6.19 Global Days 000

37201 Transcatheter therapy, infusion for thrombolysis other than coronary [T]
  EXCLUDES Thrombolysis of coronary vessels (92975-92977)
  📷 75896
  🔴 7.64   ⚕ 7.64 Global Days 000
  AMA: 2009, Jan, 11-31; 2008, Jan, 10-25; 2007, January, 13-27

37202 Transcatheter therapy, infusion other than for thrombolysis, any type (eg, spasmolytic, vasoconstrictive) [T]
  EXCLUDES Thrombolysis of coronary vessels (92975-92977)
  📷 75896
  🔴 9.25   ⚕ 9.25 Global Days 000
  AMA: 2009, Jan, 11-31; 2008, Jan, 10-25; 2007, January, 13-27

⊙ 37203 Transcatheter retrieval, percutaneous, of intravascular foreign body (eg, fractured venous or arterial catheter) [G2] [T]
  📷 75961
  🔴 7.27   ⚕ 32.66 Global Days 000
  AMA: 2009, Jan, 11-31; 2009, Jan, 7-8; 2008, Oct, 10-11

37204 Therapeutic Embolization (Except UFE)

CMS 100-3,20.28   Therapeutic Embolization
INCLUDES Ob/Gyn procedures except uterine fibroid embolization
EXCLUDES Embolization/uterine fibroids (37210)
Transcatheter occlusion or embolization for treatment of a tumor, vascular malformation, or hemorrhage (61624, 61626)

37204 Transcatheter occlusion or embolization (eg, for tumor destruction, to achieve hemostasis, to occlude a vascular malformation), percutaneous, any method, non-central nervous system, non-head or neck [T]
  📷 75894
  🔴 25.11   ⚕ 25.11 Global Days 000
  AMA: 2009, Jan, 11-31; 2008, Feb, 5-6; 2008, Jan, 10-25; 2007, January, 7-10; 2007, January, 13-27

37205-37208 Insertion Intravascular Stent

EXCLUDES Placement stent(s):
  Extracranial vertebral or intrathoracic carotid artery (0075T, 0076T)
  Intracoronary (92980, 92981)
  Intracranial (61635)
  Intravascular cervical carotid artery (37215-37216)
  Selective catheter placement (36215-36248)

37205 Transcatheter placement of an intravascular stent(s) (except coronary, carotid, and vertebral vessel), percutaneous; initial vessel [T] [80]
  📷 75960
  Code also (C1874, C1875, C1876, C1877, C2617, C2625)
  🔴 12.00   ⚕ 102.34 Global Days 000
  AMA: 2005, June, 6-8

+ 37206 each additional vessel (List separately in addition to code for primary procedure) [T] [80]
  📷 75960
  Code first (37205)
  Code also (C1874, C1875, C1876, C1877, C2617, C2625)
  🔴 5.99   ⚕ 61.53 Global Days ZZZ
  AMA: 2005, June, 6-8

37207 Transcatheter placement of an intravascular stent(s) (non-coronary vessel), open; initial vessel [T] [80] [50]
  📷 75960
  Code also (C1874, C1875, C1876, C1877, C2617, C2625)
  🔴 12.48   ⚕ 12.48 Global Days 000
  AMA: 2005, June, 6-8

+ 37208 each additional vessel (List separately in addition to code for primary procedure) [T] [80]
  📷 75960
  Code first (37207)
  Code also (C1874, C1875, C1876, C1877, C2617, C2625)
  🔴 6.03   ⚕ 6.03 Global Days ZZZ
  AMA: 2005, June, 6-8

Current Procedural Coding Expert – Cardiovascular System

37209 Replace Intravascular Catheter

- **37209** Exchange of a previously placed intravascular catheter during thrombolytic therapy
  - Code also hemodialysis catheter (C1750, C1752)
  - Code also infusion catheter (C1751)
  - 75900
  - 3.18   3.18   Global Days 000

37210 Therapeutic Embolization, Uterine Fibroid

CMS 100-3,20.28   Therapeutic Embolization

INCLUDES
- Access and imaging
- Angiography follow-up evaluation
- Transcatheter therapy, radiological supervision and interpretation
- Vascular access procedures

EXCLUDES
- Ob/Gyn procedures other than UFE
- Transcatheter embolization for conditions other than CNS/head or neck (37204)

Do not report with (36200, 36245-36248, 37204, 75894, 75898)

- **37210** Uterine fibroid embolization (UFE, embolization of the uterine arteries to treat uterine fibroids, leiomyomata), percutaneous approach inclusive of vascular access, vessel selection, embolization, and all radiological supervision and interpretation, intraprocedural roadmapping, and imaging guidance necessary to complete the procedure
  - 14.49   86.94   Global Days 000
  - **AMA:** 2009, Jan, 11-31; 2008, Jan, 10-25; 2008, Feb, 5-6; 2007, January, 7-10

37215-37216 Stenting of Carotid Artery with/without Insertion Distal Embolic Protection Device

INCLUDES
- Carotid stenting, if required
- Iplilateral diagnostic imaging/supervision and interpretation
- Ipsilateral selective carotid catheterization

EXCLUDES
- Carotid catheterization and imaging, if carotid stenting not required
- Percutaneous placement intravascular stents besides coronary, carotid, vertebral (37205, 37206)
- Transcatheter placement extracranial vertebral or intrathoracic carotid artery stents (0075T, 0076T)

Do not report with (75671, 75680)

- **37215** Transcatheter placement of intravascular stent(s), cervical carotid artery, percutaneous; with distal embolic protection
  - 30.33   30.33   Global Days 090
  - **AMA:** 2005, May, 7-12

- **37216** without distal embolic protection
  - 28.31   28.31   Global Days 090
  - **AMA:** 2005, May, 7-12

37250-37251 Intravascular Ultrasound: Noncoronary

CMS 100-3,220.5   Ultrasound Diagnostic Procedures

INCLUDES Manipulation and repositioning of the transducer prior to and after therapeutic interventional procedures

EXCLUDES
- Selective catheter placement for access (36215-36248)
- Transcatheter procedures (37200-37208, 61624, 61626)

- + **37250** Intravascular ultrasound (non-coronary vessel) during diagnostic evaluation and/or therapeutic intervention; initial vessel (List separately in addition to code for primary procedure)
  - 75945-75946
  - 3.08   3.08   Global Days ZZZ

- + **37251** each additional vessel (List separately in addition to code for primary procedure)
  - 75945-75946
  - Code first (37250)
  - 2.33   2.33   Global Days ZZZ

37500-37501 Vascular Endoscopic Procedures

INCLUDES Diagnostic endoscopy

EXCLUDES Open procedure (37760)

- **37500** Vascular endoscopy, surgical, with ligation of perforator veins, subfascial (SEPS)
  - 20.02   20.02   Global Days 090

- **37501** Unlisted vascular endoscopy procedure
  - 0.00   0.00   Global Days YYY

37565-37606 Ligation Procedures: Jugular Vein, Carotid Arteries

CMS 100-3,160.8   Electroencephalographic Monitoring During Cerebral Vasculature Surgery

EXCLUDES
- Arterial balloon occlusion, endovascular, temporary (61623)
- For treatment intracranial aneurysm (61703)
- Suture of arteries and veins (35201-35286)
- Transcatheter arterial embolization/occlusion, permanent (61624, 61626)

- **37565** Ligation, internal jugular vein
  - 20.52   20.52   Global Days 090

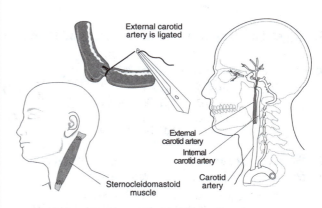

- **37600** Ligation; external carotid artery
  - 20.52   20.52   Global Days 090
- **37605** internal or common carotid artery
  - 23.33   23.33   Global Days 090
- **37606** internal or common carotid artery, with gradual occlusion, as with Selverstone or Crutchfield clamp
  - 15.78   15.78   Global Days 090

37607-37609 Ligation Hemodialysis Angioaccess or Temporal Artery

EXCLUDES Suture of arteries and veins (35201-35286)

- **37607** Ligation or banding of angioaccess arteriovenous fistula
  - 10.82   10.82   Global Days 090
- **37609** Ligation or biopsy, temporal artery
  - 5.79   8.33   Global Days 010

● New Code   ▲ Revised Code   M Maternity   A Age   Unlisted   Not Covered   # Resequenced
□ CCI   + Add-on   ⊘ Mod 51 Exempt   ⊚ Mod 63 Exempt   ⊙ Mod Sedation   PQRI

© 2009 Publisher (Blue Ink)   CPT only © 2009 American Medical Association. All Rights Reserved. (Black Ink)   Medicare (Red Ink)

Current Procedural Coding Expert – Hemic/Lymphatic

37615-37618 Arterial Ligation, Major Vessel, for Injury/Rupture

EXCLUDES *Suture of arteries and veins (35201-35286)*

37615 Ligation, major artery (eg, post-traumatic, rupture); neck
   INCLUDES Touroff ligation
   14.15   14.15   Global Days 090

37616 chest
   INCLUDES Bardenheuer operation
   31.04   31.04   Global Days 090

37617 abdomen
   37.56   37.56   Global Days 090

37618 extremity
   10.87   10.87   Global Days 090

37620 Ligation, Any Method, Inferior Vena Cava

EXCLUDES *Suture of arteries and veins (35201-35286)*

37620 Interruption, partial or complete, of inferior vena cava by suture, ligation, plication, clip, extravascular, intravascular (umbrella device)
   75940
   17.86   17.86   Global Days 090
   AMA: 2009, Jan, 11-31; 2008, Jan, 10-25; 2008, Oct, 10-11; 2007, January, 13-27

37650-37660 Venous Ligation, Femoral and Common Iliac

EXCLUDES *Suture of arteries and veins (35201-35286)*

37650 Ligation of femoral vein
   14.19   14.19   Global Days 090

37660 Ligation of common iliac vein
   36.10   36.10   Global Days 090

37700-37785 Treatment of Varicose Veins of Legs

EXCLUDES *Suture of arteries and veins (35201-35286)*

37700 Ligation and division of long saphenous vein at saphenofemoral junction, or distal interruptions
   INCLUDES Babcock operation
   Do not report with (37718, 37722)
   7.16   7.16   Global Days 090
   AMA: 2009, Jan, 11-31; 2008, Jan, 10-25; 2007, January, 13-27

37718 Ligation, division, and stripping, short saphenous vein
   Do not report with (37735, 37780)
   12.47   12.47   Global Days 090

37722 Ligation, division, and stripping, long (greater) saphenous veins from saphenofemoral junction to knee or below
   EXCLUDES *Ligation/division/stripping short saphenous vein (37718)*
   Do not report with (37700, 37735)
   13.91   13.91   Global Days 090

37735 Ligation and division and complete stripping of long or short saphenous veins with radical excision of ulcer and skin graft and/or interruption of communicating veins of lower leg, with excision of deep fascia
   Do not report with (37700, 37718, 37722, 37780)
   17.93   17.93   Global Days 090

▲ **37760** Ligation of perforator veins, subfascial, radical (Linton type), including skin graft, when performed, open, 1 leg
   Do not report with (76937, 76942, 76998, 93971)
   EXCLUDES *Ligation of subfascial perforator veins, endoscopic (37500)*
   18.79   18.79   Global Days 090

● **37761** Ligation of perforator vein(s), subfascial, open, including ultrasound guidance, when performed, 1 leg
   EXCLUDES *Ligation of subfascial perforator veins, endoscopic (37500)*
   Do not report with (76937, 76942, 76998, 93971)
   15.91   15.91   Global Days 090

37765 Stab phlebectomy of varicose veins, 1 extremity; 10-20 stab incisions
   EXCLUDES *Fewer than 10 incisions (37799)*
   12.93   12.93   Global Days 090

37766 more than 20 incisions
   EXCLUDES *Fewer than 10 incisions (37799)*
   15.89   15.89   Global Days 090

37780 Ligation and division of short saphenous vein at saphenopopliteal junction (separate procedure)
   7.39   7.39   Global Days 090
   AMA: 2009, Jan, 11-31; 2008, Jan, 10-25; 2007, January, 13-27

37785 Ligation, division, and/or excision of varicose vein cluster(s), 1 leg
   7.43   9.83   Global Days 090

37788-37799 Treatment of Vascular Disease of the Penis

37788 Penile revascularization, artery, with or without vein graft
   38.00   38.00   Global Days 090

37790 Penile venous occlusive procedure
   13.24   13.24   Global Days 090

37799 Unlisted procedure, vascular surgery
   0.00   0.00   Global Days YYY
   AMA: 2009, Jan, 11-31; 2008, Jan, 10-25; 2007, January, 13-27

38100-38200 Splenic Procedures

38100 Splenectomy; total (separate procedure)
   31.67   31.67   Global Days 090

38101 partial (separate procedure)
   31.95   31.95   Global Days 090

+ **38102** total, en bloc for extensive disease, in conjunction with other procedure (List in addition to code for primary procedure)
   Code first primary procedure
   7.26   7.26   Global Days ZZZ

38115 Repair of ruptured spleen (splenorrhaphy) with or without partial splenectomy
   35.01   35.01   Global Days 090

Current Procedural Coding Expert – Hemic/Lymphatic

38120	Laparoscopy, surgical, splenectomy
	INCLUDES: Diagnostic laparoscopy
	28.83 28.83 Global Days 090

38129	Unlisted laparoscopy procedure, spleen
	0.00 0.00 Global Days YYY

38200	Injection procedure for splenoportography
	75810
	4.13 4.13 Global Days 000

38204-38215 Hematopoietic Stem Cell Procedures

CMS 100-3,110.8.1   Stem Cell Transplantation

INCLUDES:
- Preservation, preparation, purification before transplant or reinfusion
- Bone marrow
- Stem cells
- Reporting each code no more than once per day

Do not report with flow cytometry (88182, 88184-88189)

38204 Management of recipient hematopoietic progenitor cell donor search and cell acquisition
2.83   2.83   Global Days XXX
AMA: 2009, Jun, 3-6&11

38205 Blood-derived hematopoietic progenitor cell harvesting for transplantation, per collection; allogenic
2.23   2.23   Global Days 000
AMA: 2009, Jun, 3-6&11

38206 autologous
2.23   2.23   Global Days 000
AMA: 2009, Jun, 3-6&11

38207 Transplant preparation of hematopoietic progenitor cells; cryopreservation and storage
88240
1.37   1.37   Global Days XXX
AMA: 2009, Jun, 3-6&11

38208 thawing of previously frozen harvest, without washing
88241
0.87   0.87   Global Days XXX
AMA: 2009, Jun, 3-6&11

38209 thawing of previously frozen harvest, with washing
0.37   0.37   Global Days XXX
AMA: 2009, Jun, 3-6&11

38210 specific cell depletion within harvest, T-cell depletion
2.43   2.43   Global Days XXX
AMA: 2009, Jun, 3-6&11

38211 tumor cell depletion
2.19   2.19   Global Days XXX
AMA: 2009, Jun, 3-6&11

38212 red blood cell removal
1.45   1.45   Global Days XXX
AMA: 2009, Jun, 3-6&11

38213 platelet depletion
0.37   0.37   Global Days XXX
AMA: 2009, Jun, 3-6&11

38214 plasma (volume) depletion
1.25   1.25   Global Days XXX
AMA: 2009, Jun, 3-6&11

38215 cell concentration in plasma, mononuclear, or buffy coat layer
1.45   1.45   Global Days XXX
AMA: 2009, Jun, 3-6&11

38220-38242 Bone Marrow Procedures

CMS 100-1,5,90.2   Laboratory Defined
CMS 100-2,15,80   Physician Supervision Requirements for Diagnostic Tests
CMS 100-2,15,80.1   Payment for Clinical Laboratory Services
CMS 100-3,110.8.1   Stem Cell Transplantation
CMS 100-4,3,90.3   Stem Cell Transplantation
CMS 100-4,3,90.3.1   Allogeneic Stem Cell Transplantation
CMS 100-4,3,90.3.3   Billing for Stem Cell Transplantation
CMS 100-4,32,90   Billing for Stem Cell Transplantation

EXCLUDES:
- Expansion and thawing of blood-derived stem cell specimens for transplantation (38208-38209)
- Modification, treatment, processing of bone marrow/blood-derived stem cell specimens for transplantation (38210-38213)
- Storage, freezing, and cryopreservation of blood-derived stem cell specimens for transplantation (38207)

38220 Bone marrow; aspiration only
1.68   3.58   Global Days XXX
AMA: 2009, Jan, 11-31; 2009, Jun, 3-6&11; 2008, Jan, 10-25; 2007, June, 10-11; 2007, January, 13-27

38221 biopsy, needle or trocar
88305
2.07   3.89   Global Days XXX
AMA: 2009, Jun, 3-6&11

38230 Bone marrow harvesting for transplantation
EXCLUDES: Allogenic blood-derived hematopoietic progenitor cell harvesting for transplant (38205)
Autologous blood-derived hematopoietic progenitor cell harvesting for transplant (38206)
86812-86822, 88240-88241
9.22   9.22   Global Days 010
AMA: 2009, Jun, 3-6&11

38240 Bone marrow or blood-derived peripheral stem cell transplantation; allogenic
86812-86822, 88240-88241
3.43   3.43   Global Days XXX
AMA: 2009, Jun, 3-6&11

38241 autologous
86812-86822, 88240-88241
3.43   3.43   Global Days XXX
AMA: 2009, Jun, 3-6&11

38242 allogeneic donor lymphocyte infusions
86812-86822, 88240-88241
2.63   2.63   Global Days 000
AMA: 2009, Jun, 3-6&11

38300-38382 Incision Lymphatic Vessels

38300 Drainage of lymph node abscess or lymphadenitis; simple
4.87   6.97   Global Days 010

38305 extensive
12.53   12.53   Global Days 090

● New Code   ▲ Revised Code   M Maternity   A Age   Unlisted   Not Covered   # Resequenced
CCI   + Add-on   ⊘ Mod 51 Exempt   ⊘ Mod 63 Exempt   ⊙ Mod Sedation   PQRI

© 2009 Publisher (Blue Ink)   CPT only © 2009 American Medical Association. All Rights Reserved. (Black Ink)   Medicare (Red Ink)

38308

Current Procedural Coding Expert – Hemic/Lymphatic

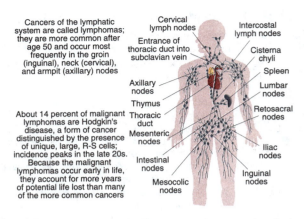

Cancers of the lymphatic system are called lymphomas; they are more common after age 50 and occur most frequently in the groin (inguinal), neck (cervical), and armpit (axillary) nodes

About 14 percent of malignant lymphomas are Hodgkin's disease, a form of cancer distinguished by the presence of unique, large, R-S cells; incidence peaks in the late 20s. Because the malignant lymphomas occur early in life, they account for more years of potential life lost than many of the more common cancers

38308 Lymphangiotomy or other operations on lymphatic channels
 12.29 12.29 Global Days 090

38380 Suture and/or ligation of thoracic duct; cervical approach
 15.92 15.92 Global Days 090

38381 thoracic approach
 22.33 22.33 Global Days 090

38382 abdominal approach
 19.33 19.33 Global Days 090

38500-38555 Biopsy/Excision Lymphatic Vessels

CMS 100-4,12,30 Correct Coding Policy

EXCLUDES Injection for sentinel node identification (38792)
Percutaneous needle biopsy retroperitoneal mass (49180)

38500 Biopsy or excision of lymph node(s); open, superficial
 Do not report with (38700-38780)
 6.89 8.75 Global Days 010
 AMA: 2009, Jan, 7-8; 2009, Jan, 11-31; 2008, Jan, 10-25; 2008, Sep, 5-6; 2007, Dec, 7-8; 2007, January, 13-27; 2005, October, 23-24

38505 by needle, superficial (eg, cervical, inguinal, axillary)
 EXCLUDES Fine needle aspiration (10021-10022)
  76942, 77012, 77021
  88172, 88173
 1.94 3.21 Global Days 000
 AMA: 2009, Jan, 7-8

38510 open, deep cervical node(s)
 11.62 14.03 Global Days 010
 AMA: 2009, Jan, 11-31; 2008, Jan, 10-25; 2007, January, 13-27

38520 open, deep cervical node(s) with excision scalene fat pad
 12.69 12.69 Global Days 090
 AMA: 2009, Jan, 11-31; 2008, Jan, 10-25; 2007, January, 13-27

38525 open, deep axillary node(s)
 11.78 11.78 Global Days 090
 AMA: 2009, Jan, 11-31; 2008, Jan, 10-25; 2008, Sep, 5-6; 2007, Dec, 7-8; 2007, January, 13-27; 2005, October, 23-24

38530 open, internal mammary node(s)
 EXCLUDES Fine needle aspiration (10022)
 Do not report with (38720-38746)
 14.93 14.93 Global Days 090
 AMA: 2008, Sep, 5-6

38542 Dissection, deep jugular node(s)
 EXCLUDES Complete cervical lymphadenectomy (38720)
 14.35 14.35 Global Days 090

38550 Excision of cystic hygroma, axillary or cervical; without deep neurovascular dissection
 13.63 13.63 Global Days 090

38555 with deep neurovascular dissection
 27.04 27.04 Global Days 090

38562-38564 Limited Lymphadenectomy: Staging

38562 Limited lymphadenectomy for staging (separate procedure); pelvic and para-aortic
 EXCLUDES With prostatectomy (55812, 55842)
 With radioactive substance inserted into prostate (55862)
 18.98 18.98 Global Days 090
 AMA: 2009, Jan, 11-31; 2008, Jan, 10-25; 2007, January, 13-27

38564 retroperitoneal (aortic and/or splenic)
 19.32 19.32 Global Days 090

38570-38589 Laparoscopic Lymph Node Procedures

INCLUDES Diagnostic laparoscopy
EXCLUDES Laparoscopy with draining of lymphocele to peritoneal cavity (49323)

38570 Laparoscopy, surgical; with retroperitoneal lymph node sampling (biopsy), single or multiple
 14.75 14.75 Global Days 010

38571 with bilateral total pelvic lymphadenectomy
 21.75 21.75 Global Days 010

38572 with bilateral total pelvic lymphadenectomy and peri-aortic lymph node sampling (biopsy), single or multiple
 26.12 26.12 Global Days 010

38589 Unlisted laparoscopy procedure, lymphatic system
 0.00 0.00 Global Days YYY

38700-38780 Lymphadenectomy Procedures

INCLUDES Lymph node biopsy/excision
EXCLUDES Excision of lymphedematous skin and subcutaneous tissue (15004-15005)
Limited lymphadenectomy
  Pelvic (38562)
  Retroperitoneal (38564)
Repair of lymphedematous skin and subcutaneous tissue (15570-15650)
Do not report with (38500)

38700 Suprahyoid lymphadenectomy
 22.61 22.61 Global Days 090

38720 Cervical lymphadenectomy (complete)
 37.64 37.64 Global Days 090
 AMA: 2009, Jan, 11-31; 2008, Jan, 10-25; 2007, January, 13-27

38724 Cervical lymphadenectomy (modified radical neck dissection)
 40.94 40.94 Global Days 090
 AMA: 2009, Jan, 11-31; 2008, Jan, 10-25; 2007, January, 13-27

38740 Axillary lymphadenectomy; superficial
 18.78 18.78 Global Days 090

38745 complete
 23.88 23.88 Global Days 090

 PC/TC Comp Only   ASC Pmt   Bilateral ♂ Male Only ♀ Female Only   Facility RVU   Non-Facility RVU
AMA: CPT Asst MED: Pub 100   OPPSI   Surg Assist Allowed / w/Doc   Lab Crosswalk   Radiology Crosswalk
140 CPT only © 2009 American Medical Association. All Rights Reserved. (Black Ink) Medicare (Red Ink) © 2009 Publisher (Blue Ink)

Current Procedural Coding Expert – Mediastinum

+ **38746** Thoracic lymphadenectomy, regional, including mediastinal and peritracheal nodes (List separately in addition to code for primary procedure)
Code first primary procedure
7.26 7.26 Global Days ZZZ

+ **38747** Abdominal lymphadenectomy, regional, including celiac, gastric, portal, peripancreatic, with or without para-aortic and vena caval nodes (List separately in addition to code for primary procedure)
Code first primary procedure
7.41 7.41 Global Days ZZZ

38760 Inguinofemoral lymphadenectomy, superficial, including Cloquets node (separate procedure)
23.02 23.02 Global Days 090
AMA: 2009, Jan, 7-8

38765 Inguinofemoral lymphadenectomy, superficial, in continuity with pelvic lymphadenectomy, including external iliac, hypogastric, and obturator nodes (separate procedure)
INCLUDES Lymph node biopsy/excision
EXCLUDES Limited lymphadenectomy
  Pelvic (38562)
  Retroperitoneal (38564)
35.48 35.48 Global Days 090
AMA: 2009, Jan, 7-8

38770 Pelvic lymphadenectomy, including external iliac, hypogastric, and obturator nodes (separate procedure)
INCLUDES Lymph node biopsy/excision
EXCLUDES Limited lymphadenectomy
  Pelvic (38562)
  Retroperitoneal (38564)
21.96 21.96 Global Days 090

38780 Retroperitoneal transabdominal lymphadenectomy, extensive, including pelvic, aortic, and renal nodes (separate procedure)
INCLUDES Lymph node biopsy/excision
EXCLUDES Limited lymphadenectomy
  Pelvic (38562)
  Retroperitoneal (38564)
28.21 28.21 Global Days 090

38790-38999 Cannulation/Injection/Other Procedures

38790 Injection procedure; lymphangiography
75801-75807
2.27 2.27 Global Days 000

38792 for identification of sentinel node
EXCLUDES Sentinel node excision (38500-38542)
78195
1.09 1.09 Global Days 000
AMA: 2008, Jan, 10-25; 2008, Sep, 5-6; 2007, Dec, 7-8

38794 Cannulation, thoracic duct
7.73 7.73 Global Days 090

38999 Unlisted procedure, hemic or lymphatic system
0.00 0.00 Global Days YYY
AMA: 2009, Jan, 11-31; 2008, Jan, 10-25; 2007, January, 13-27

39000-39499 Surgical Procedures: Mediastinum

39000 Mediastinotomy with exploration, drainage, removal of foreign body, or biopsy; cervical approach
13.69 13.69 Global Days 090

39010 transthoracic approach, including either transthoracic or median sternotomy
22.14 22.14 Global Days 090

39200 Excision of mediastinal cyst
24.64 24.64 Global Days 090

39220 Excision of mediastinal tumor
EXCLUDES Thymectomy (60520)
  Thyroidectomy, substernal (60270)
31.94 31.94 Global Days 090

39400 Mediastinoscopy, with or without biopsy
14.01 14.01 Global Days 010

39499 Unlisted procedure, mediastinum
0.00 0.00 Global Days YYY

39501-39599 Surgical Procedures: Diaphragm
EXCLUDES Transabdominal repair of diaphragmatic hernia (43324-43325)

39501 Repair, laceration of diaphragm, any approach
23.38 23.38 Global Days 090

39502 Repair, paraesophageal hiatus hernia, transabdominal, with or without fundoplasty, vagotomy, and/or pyloroplasty, except neonatal
EXCLUDES Paraesophageal hernia repair, laparoscopic (43281-43282)
28.48 28.48 Global Days 090
AMA: 2008, Jun, 3-6

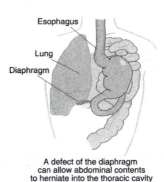

A defect of the diaphragm can allow abdominal contents to herniate into the thoracic cavity

Code 39503 reports the repair of a diaphragmatic hernia in a neonate. The nature of the repair may necessitate the creation of a ventral hernia (an opening in the anterior abdomen to accommodate the viscera). A chest tube may or may not be required

The code is reserved for procedures on neonates

39503 Repair, neonatal diaphragmatic hernia, with or without chest tube insertion and with or without creation of ventral hernia
169.86 169.86 Global Days 090
AMA: 2008, Jun, 3-6

39520 Repair, diaphragmatic hernia (esophageal hiatal); transthoracic
EXCLUDES Paraesophageal hernia repair, laparoscopic (43281-43282)
27.68 27.68 Global Days 090
AMA: 2008, Jun, 3-6

39530 combined, thoracoabdominal
26.78 26.78 Global Days 090
AMA: 2008, Jun, 3-6

39531 combined, thoracoabdominal, with dilation of stricture (with or without gastroplasty)
28.69 28.69 Global Days 090
AMA: 2008, Jun, 3-6

39540 Repair, diaphragmatic hernia (other than neonatal), traumatic; acute
24.02 24.02 Global Days 090
AMA: 2008, Jun, 3-6

● New Code   ▲ Revised Code   M Maternity   A Age   Unlisted   Not Covered   # Resequenced
CCI   + Add-on   ⊘ Mod 51 Exempt   ⊚ Mod 63 Exempt   ⊙ Mod Sedation   PQRI

39541	chronic	C 80 ▪ P0
	26.09 26.09 Global Days 090
	AMA: 2008, Jun, 3-6
39545	Imbrication of diaphragm for eventration, transthoracic or transabdominal, paralytic or nonparalytic	C 80 ▪ P0
	24.84 24.84 Global Days 090
39560	Resection, diaphragm; with simple repair (eg, primary suture)	C 80 ▪ P0
	21.83 21.83 Global Days 090
39561	with complex repair (eg, prosthetic material, local muscle flap)	C 80 ▪ P0
	34.61 34.61 Global Days 090
39599	Unlisted procedure, diaphragm	C 80
	0.00 0.00 Global Days YYY

Current Procedural Coding Expert – Digestive

40490-40799 Resection and Repair Procedures of the Lips

EXCLUDES Procedures on the skin of lips (10040-17999)

- **40490** Biopsy of lip
  - 2.06 3.33 Global Days 000
- **40500** Vermilionectomy (lip shave), with mucosal advancement
  - 9.90 13.29 Global Days 090
- **40510** Excision of lip; transverse wedge excision with primary closure
  - EXCLUDES Excision of mucous lesions (40810-40816)
  - 9.78 12.83 Global Days 090
- **40520** V-excision with primary direct linear closure
  - EXCLUDES Excision of mucous lesions (40810-40816)
  - 9.86 12.99 Global Days 090
- **40525** full thickness, reconstruction with local flap (eg, Estlander or fan)
  - 15.25 15.25 Global Days 090
- **40527** full thickness, reconstruction with cross lip flap (Abbe-Estlander)
  - EXCLUDES Cleft lip repair with cross lip pedicle flap (40761)
  - 17.33 17.33 Global Days 090
- **40530** Resection of lip, more than 1/4, without reconstruction
  - EXCLUDES Reconstruction (13131-13153)
  - 11.19 14.45 Global Days 090
- **40650** Repair lip, full thickness; vermilion only
  - 7.89 10.95 Global Days 090
  - AMA: 2009, Jan, 11-31; 2008, Jan, 10-25; 2007, January, 13-27
- **40652** up to half vertical height
  - 9.58 12.84 Global Days 090
  - AMA: 2009, Jan, 11-31; 2008, Jan, 10-25; 2007, January, 13-27
- **40654** over 1/2 vertical height, or complex
  - 11.57 14.98 Global Days 090
- **40700** Plastic repair of cleft lip/nasal deformity; primary, partial or complete, unilateral
  - EXCLUDES Cleft lip repair with cross lip pedicle flap (Abbe-Estlander type) (40761)
  Rhinoplasty for nasal deformity secondary to congenital cleft lip (30460, 30462)
  - 25.44 25.44 Global Days 090
- **40701** primary bilateral, 1-stage procedure
  - EXCLUDES Cleft lip repair with cross lip pedicle flap (Abbe-Estlander type) (40761)
  Rhinoplasty for nasal deformity secondary to congenital cleft lip (30460, 30462)
  - 30.28 30.28 Global Days 090
- **40702** primary bilateral, 1 of 2 stages
  - EXCLUDES Cleft lip repair with cross lip pedicle flap (Abbe-Estlander type) (40761)
  Rhinoplasty for nasal deformity secondary to congenital cleft lip (30460, 30462)
  - 22.63 22.63 Global Days 090
- **40720** secondary, by recreation of defect and reclosure
  - EXCLUDES Cleft lip repair with cross lip pedicle flap (Abbe-Estlander type) (40761)
  Rhinoplasty for nasal deformity secondary to congenital cleft lip (30460, 30462)
  - 28.64 28.64 Global Days 090
- **40761** with cross lip pedicle flap (Abbe-Estlander type), including sectioning and inserting of pedicle
  - EXCLUDES Cleft palate repair (42200-42225)
  Other reconstructive procedures (14060, 14061, 15120-15261, 15574, 15576, 15630)
  - 30.31 30.31 Global Days 090
- **40799** Unlisted procedure, lips
  - 0.00 0.00 Global Days YYY

40800-40819 Incision and Resection of Buccal Cavity

INCLUDES Mucosal/submucosal tissue of lips/cheeks
Oral cavity outside the dentoalveolar structures

- **40800** Drainage of abscess, cyst, hematoma, vestibule of mouth; simple
  - 3.48 5.40 Global Days 010
- **40801** complicated
  - 6.03 8.30 Global Days 010
- **40804** Removal of embedded foreign body, vestibule of mouth; simple
  - 3.59 5.64 Global Days 010
- **40805** complicated
  - 6.29 8.40 Global Days 010
- **40806** Incision of labial frenum (frenotomy)
  - 0.89 2.54 Global Days 000
- **40808** Biopsy, vestibule of mouth
  - 2.89 4.80 Global Days 010
- **40810** Excision of lesion of mucosa and submucosa, vestibule of mouth; without repair
  - 3.45 5.36 Global Days 010
- **40812** with simple repair
  - 5.38 7.55 Global Days 010
- **40814** with complex repair
  - 8.28 10.19 Global Days 090
- **40816** complex, with excision of underlying muscle
  - 8.67 10.74 Global Days 090
- **40818** Excision of mucosa of vestibule of mouth as donor graft
  - 7.26 9.30 Global Days 090
- **40819** Excision of frenum, labial or buccal (frenumectomy, frenulectomy, frenectomy)
  - 6.35 8.10 Global Days 090

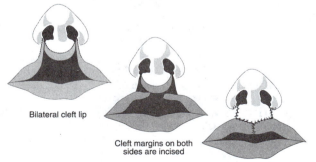

Bilateral cleft lip

Cleft margins on both sides are incised

Margins are closed, correcting cleft

● New Code   ▲ Revised Code   M Maternity   A Age   Unlisted   Not Covered   # Resequenced
□ CCI   + Add-on   ⊘ Mod 51 Exempt   ⊕ Mod 63 Exempt   ⊙ Mod Sedation   PQRI

© 2009 Publisher (Blue Ink)   CPT only © 2009 American Medical Association. All Rights Reserved. (Black Ink)   Medicare (Red Ink)   143

40820 Destruction of Lesion of Buccal Cavity

CMS 100-3,140.5 — Laser Procedures

INCLUDES
Mucosal/submucosal tissue of lips/cheeks
Oral cavity outside the dentoalveolar structures

- **40820** Destruction of lesion or scar of vestibule of mouth by physical methods (eg, laser, thermal, cryo, chemical)
  4.53 6.77 Global Days 010

40830-40899 Repair Procedures of the Buccal Cavity

INCLUDES
Mucosal/submucosal tissue of lips/cheeks
Oral cavity outside the dentoalveolar structures

EXCLUDES Skin grafts (15002-15630)

- **40830** Closure of laceration, vestibule of mouth; 2.5 cm or less
  4.40 6.68 Global Days 010
- **40831** over 2.5 cm or complex
  6.02 8.72 Global Days 010
- **40840** Vestibuloplasty; anterior
  16.91 21.36 Global Days 090
- **40842** posterior, unilateral
  18.13 23.04 Global Days 090
- **40843** posterior, bilateral
  22.27 28.01 Global Days 090
- **40844** entire arch
  30.64 36.68 Global Days 090
- **40845** complex (including ridge extension, muscle repositioning)
  34.38 40.05 Global Days 090
- **40899** Unlisted procedure, vestibule of mouth
  0.00 0.00 Global Days YYY

41000-41018 Surgical Incision of Floor of Mouth or Tongue

EXCLUDES Frenoplasty (41520)

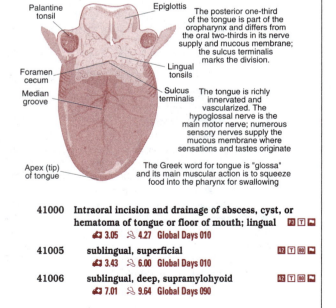

The posterior one-third of the tongue is part of the oropharynx and differs from the oral two-thirds in its nerve supply and mucous membrane; the sulcus terminalis marks the division.

The tongue is richly innervated and vascularized. The hypoglossal nerve is the main motor nerve; numerous sensory nerves supply the mucous membrane where sensations and tastes originate

The Greek word for tongue is "glossa" and its main muscular action is to squeeze food into the pharynx for swallowing

- **41000** Intraoral incision and drainage of abscess, cyst, or hematoma of tongue or floor of mouth; lingual
  3.05 4.27 Global Days 010
- **41005** sublingual, superficial
  3.43 6.00 Global Days 010
- **41006** sublingual, deep, supramylohyoid
  7.01 9.64 Global Days 090
- **41007** submental space
  6.79 9.46 Global Days 090
- **41008** submandibular space
  7.32 9.96 Global Days 090
- **41009** masticator space
  7.99 10.57 Global Days 090
- **41010** Incision of lingual frenum (frenotomy)
  2.96 5.33 Global Days 010
- **41015** Extraoral incision and drainage of abscess, cyst, or hematoma of floor of mouth; sublingual
  9.30 11.35 Global Days 090
- **41016** submental
  9.56 11.48 Global Days 090
- **41017** submandibular
  9.56 11.73 Global Days 090
- **41018** masticator space
  11.31 13.32 Global Days 090

41019 Placement of Devices for Brachytherapy

- **41019** Placement of needles, catheters, or other device(s) into the head and/or neck region (percutaneous, transoral, or transnasal) for subsequent interstitial radioelement application

  EXCLUDES Application of interstitial radioelements (77776-77787)
  Intracranial brachytherapy radiation sources with stereotactic insertion (61770)

  76942, 77002, 77012, 77021
  13.45 13.45 Global Days 000

41100-41599 Resection and Repair of the Tongue

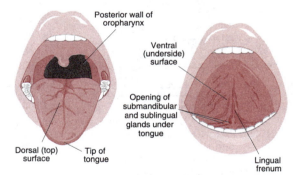

Anterior (front) two-thirds of tongue comprises most of easily visible portions; the base, or root, comprises the remainder of tongue

- **41100** Biopsy of tongue; anterior 2/3
  2.97 4.45 Global Days 010
- **41105** posterior 1/3
  3.08 4.53 Global Days 010
- **41108** Biopsy of floor of mouth
  2.48 3.89 Global Days 010
- **41110** Excision of lesion of tongue without closure
  3.61 5.60 Global Days 010
- **41112** Excision of lesion of tongue with closure; anterior 2/3
  6.86 8.83 Global Days 090
- **41113** posterior 1/3
  7.62 9.67 Global Days 090

Current Procedural Coding Expert – Digestive 41870

Code	Description	Symbols
41114	with local tongue flap	A2 T 80
	Code also excision lesion of tongue with closure anterior/posterior two-thirds (41112, 41113)	
	17.65 17.65 Global Days 090	
41115	Excision of lingual frenum (frenectomy)	P3 T 80
	4.11 6.37 Global Days 010	
41116	Excision, lesion of floor of mouth	A2 T
	6.01 8.72 Global Days 090	
41120	Glossectomy; less than 1/2 tongue	A2 T 80
	28.32 28.32 Global Days 090	
41130	hemiglossectomy	C 80 P0
	35.63 35.63 Global Days 090	
41135	partial, with unilateral radical neck dissection	C 80 P0
	59.70 59.70 Global Days 090	
41140	complete or total, with or without tracheostomy, without radical neck dissection	C 80 P0
	INCLUDES Regnolli's excision	
	60.21 60.21 Global Days 090	
41145	complete or total, with or without tracheostomy, with unilateral radical neck dissection	C 80 P0
	76.37 76.37 Global Days 090	
41150	composite procedure with resection floor of mouth and mandibular resection, without radical neck dissection	C 80 P0
	60.56 60.56 Global Days 090	
41153	composite procedure with resection floor of mouth, with suprahyoid neck dissection	C 80 P0
	66.05 66.05 Global Days 090	
41155	composite procedure with resection floor of mouth, mandibular resection, and radical neck dissection (Commando type)	C 80 P0
	83.42 83.42 Global Days 090	
	AMA: 2009, Jan, 11-31; 2008, Jan, 10-25; 2007, January, 13-27	
41250	Repair of laceration 2.5 cm or less; floor of mouth and/or anterior 2/3 of tongue	A2 T 80
	4.11 6.63 Global Days 010	
41251	posterior 1/3 of tongue	A2 T 80
	4.64 7.08 Global Days 010	
41252	Repair of laceration of tongue, floor of mouth, over 2.6 cm or complex	A2 T 80
	5.91 8.45 Global Days 010	
41500	Fixation of tongue, mechanical, other than suture (eg, K-wire)	A2 T 80
	12.24 12.24 Global Days 090	
41510	Suture of tongue to lip for micrognathia (Douglas type procedure)	A2 T 80
	11.78 11.78 Global Days 090	
41512	Tongue base suspension, permanent suture technique	G2 T 80
	EXCLUDES Mechanical fixation of tongue, other than suture (41500)	
	Suture tongue to lip for micrognathia (41510)	
	17.01 17.01 Global Days 090	
41520	Frenoplasty (surgical revision of frenum, eg, with Z-plasty)	A2 T 80
	EXCLUDES Frenotomy (40806, 41010)	
	6.90 9.17 Global Days 090	
41530	Submucosal ablation of the tongue base, radiofrequency, 1 or more sites, per session	G2 T 80
	10.92 79.57 Global Days 010	
41599	**Unlisted procedure, tongue, floor of mouth**	T 80
	0.00 0.00 Global Days YYY	
	AMA: 2009, Jan, 11-31; 2008, Jan, 10-25; 2007, January, 13-27	

41800-41899 Procedures of the Teeth and Supporting Structures

CMS 100-2,15,150   Dental Services

Code	Description	Symbols
41800	Drainage of abscess, cyst, hematoma from dentoalveolar structures	A2 T
	3.81 6.67 Global Days 010	
41805	Removal of embedded foreign body from dentoalveolar structures; soft tissues	P3 T 80
	4.75 6.91 Global Days 010	
41806	bone	P3 T 80
	7.09 9.33 Global Days 010	

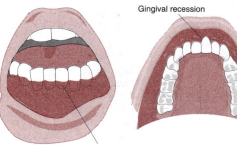

Gingivitis is an inflammatory response to bacteria on the teeth; it is characterized by tender, red, swollen gums and can lead to gingival recession

Code	Description	Symbols
41820	Gingivectomy, excision gingiva, each quadrant	R2 T 80
	0.00 0.00 Global Days 000	
41821	Operculectomy, excision pericoronal tissues	G2 T 80
	0.00 0.00 Global Days 000	
41822	Excision of fibrous tuberosities, dentoalveolar structures	P3 T 80
	5.01 7.58 Global Days 010	
41823	Excision of osseous tuberosities, dentoalveolar structures	P3 T 80
	8.75 11.21 Global Days 090	
41825	Excision of lesion or tumor (except listed above), dentoalveolar structures; without repair	P3 T
	EXCLUDES Lesion destruction nonexcisional (41850)	
	3.30 5.44 Global Days 010	
41826	with simple repair	P3 T
	EXCLUDES Lesion destruction nonexcisional (41850)	
	5.73 8.15 Global Days 010	
41827	with complex repair	A2 T
	EXCLUDES Lesion destruction nonexcisional (41850)	
	8.42 11.60 Global Days 090	
41828	Excision of hyperplastic alveolar mucosa, each quadrant (specify)	P3 T 80
	5.93 8.14 Global Days 010	
41830	Alveolectomy, including curettage of osteitis or sequestrectomy	P3 T 80
	7.70 10.28 Global Days 010	
41850	Destruction of lesion (except excision), dentoalveolar structures	R2 T 80
	0.00 0.00 Global Days 000	
41870	Periodontal mucosal grafting	G2 T 80
	0.00 0.00 Global Days 000	

● New Code   ▲ Revised Code   M Maternity   A Age   Unlisted   Not Covered   # Resequenced

CCI   + Add-on   ⊘ Mod 51 Exempt   ⊚ Mod 63 Exempt   ⊙ Mod Sedation   P0 PQRI

41872	Gingivoplasty, each quadrant (specify)	A2 T 80
	🚗 7.23 👤 9.66 Global Days 090	
41874	Alveoloplasty, each quadrant (specify)	A2 T 80
	EXCLUDES Fracture reduction (21421-21490)	
	Laceration closure (40830, 40831)	
	Maxilla osteotomy, segmental (21206)	
	🚗 6.95 👤 9.74 Global Days 090	
41899	Unlisted procedure, dentoalveolar structures	T 80
	🚗 0.00 👤 0.00 Global Days YYY	

42000-42299 Procedures of the Palate and Uvula

42000	Drainage of abscess of palate, uvula	A2 T 80
	🚗 2.86 👤 4.13 Global Days 010	
42100	Biopsy of palate, uvula	P3 T
	🚗 3.01 👤 3.99 Global Days 010	
42104	Excision, lesion of palate, uvula; without closure	P3 T
	🚗 3.82 👤 5.69 Global Days 010	
42106	with simple primary closure	P3 T
	🚗 4.86 👤 7.14 Global Days 010	
42107	with local flap closure	A2 T
	EXCLUDES Mucosal graft (40818)	
	Skin graft (14040-14302)	
	🚗 9.55 👤 12.31 Global Days 090	
42120	Resection of palate or extensive resection of lesion	A2 T 80
	EXCLUDES Reconstruction of palate with extraoral tissue (14040-14302, 15050, 15120, 15240, 15576)	
	🚗 27.18 👤 27.18 Global Days 090	
42140	Uvulectomy, excision of uvula	A2 T
	🚗 4.23 👤 6.69 Global Days 090	
42145	Palatopharyngoplasty (eg, uvulopalatopharyngoplasty, uvulopharyngoplasty)	A2 T
	EXCLUDES Removal of exostosis of the bony palate (21031, 21032)	
	🚗 30.98 👤 30.98 Global Days 090	
	AMA: 2009, Jan, 11-31; 2008, Jan, 10-25; 2007, January, 13-27; 2005, January, 46-47	
42160	Destruction of lesion, palate or uvula (thermal, cryo or chemical)	P3 T 80
	🚗 4.04 👤 6.14 Global Days 010	
42180	Repair, laceration of palate; up to 2 cm	A2 T 80
	🚗 5.13 👤 6.64 Global Days 010	
42182	over 2 cm or complex	A2 T 80
	🚗 7.22 👤 8.82 Global Days 010	
42200	Palatoplasty for cleft palate, soft and/or hard palate only	A2 T 80
	🚗 23.84 👤 23.84 Global Days 090	
42205	Palatoplasty for cleft palate, with closure of alveolar ridge; soft tissue only	A2 T 80
	🚗 25.00 👤 25.00 Global Days 090	
42210	with bone graft to alveolar ridge (includes obtaining graft)	A2 T 80
	🚗 29.96 👤 29.96 Global Days 090	
42215	Palatoplasty for cleft palate; major revision	A2 T 80
	🚗 18.41 👤 18.41 Global Days 090	
42220	secondary lengthening procedure	A2 T 80
	🚗 14.93 👤 14.93 Global Days 090	
42225	attachment pharyngeal flap	G2 T 80
	🚗 23.97 👤 23.97 Global Days 090	
	AMA: 2009, Jan, 11-31; 2008, Jan, 10-25; 2007, January, 13-27	
42226	Lengthening of palate, and pharyngeal flap	A2 T 80
	🚗 24.47 👤 24.47 Global Days 090	
42227	Lengthening of palate, with island flap	G2 T 80
	🚗 22.99 👤 22.99 Global Days 090	
42235	Repair of anterior palate, including vomer flap	A2 T 80
	EXCLUDES Oronasal fistula repair (30600)	
	🚗 20.01 👤 20.01 Global Days 090	
42260	Repair of nasolabial fistula	A2 T 80
	EXCLUDES Cleft lip repair (40700-40761)	
	🚗 18.59 👤 22.38 Global Days 090	
42280	Maxillary impression for palatal prosthesis	P3 T 80
	🚗 3.13 👤 4.41 Global Days 010	
42281	Insertion of pin-retained palatal prosthesis	G2 T 80
	🚗 4.20 👤 5.55 Global Days 010	
42299	Unlisted procedure, palate, uvula	T 80
	🚗 0.00 👤 0.00 Global Days YYY	
	AMA: 2009, Jan, 11-31; 2008, Jan, 10-25; 2007, January, 13-27; 2005, January, 46-47	

42300-42699 Procedures of the Salivary Ducts and Glands

42300	Drainage of abscess; parotid, simple	A2 T
	🚗 4.20 👤 5.60 Global Days 010	
42305	parotid, complicated	A2 T
	🚗 12.02 👤 12.02 Global Days 090	
42310	submaxillary or sublingual, intraoral	A2 T
	🚗 3.45 👤 4.34 Global Days 010	
42320	submaxillary, external	A2 T 80
	🚗 4.90 👤 6.76 Global Days 010	
42330	Sialolithotomy; submandibular (submaxillary), sublingual or parotid, uncomplicated, intraoral	P3 T
	🚗 4.59 👤 6.25 Global Days 010	
42335	submandibular (submaxillary), complicated, intraoral	P3 T
	🚗 7.15 👤 10.03 Global Days 090	
42340	parotid, extraoral or complicated intraoral	A2 T 80
	🚗 9.38 👤 12.60 Global Days 090	
42400	Biopsy of salivary gland; needle	P3 T
	EXCLUDES Fine needle aspiration (10021, 10022)	
	🔬 88172, 88173	
	📡 76942, 77002, 77012, 77021	
	🚗 1.55 👤 2.85 Global Days 000	
42405	incisional	A2 T
	📡 76942, 77002, 77012, 77021	
	🚗 6.27 👤 8.02 Global Days 010	
42408	Excision of sublingual salivary cyst (ranula)	A2 T 80
	🚗 9.12 👤 12.28 Global Days 090	
42409	Marsupialization of sublingual salivary cyst (ranula)	A2 T 80
	🚗 6.17 👤 8.95 Global Days 090	

Current Procedural Coding Expert – Digestive

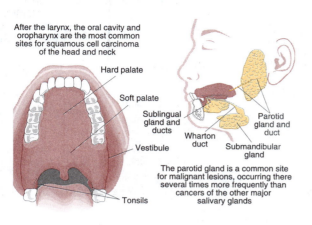

After the larynx, the oral cavity and oropharynx are the most common sites for squamous cell carcinoma of the head and neck

Hard palate
Soft palate
Sublingual gland and ducts
Wharton duct
Vestibule
Parotid gland and duct
Submandibular gland
Tonsils

The parotid gland is a common site for malignant lesions, occurring there several times more frequently than cancers of the other major salivary glands

42410 Excision of parotid tumor or parotid gland; lateral lobe, without nerve dissection A2 T 80
   EXCLUDES Facial nerve suture or graft (64864, 64865, 69740, 69745)
   17.38 17.38 Global Days 090

42415 lateral lobe, with dissection and preservation of facial nerve A2 T 80
   EXCLUDES Facial nerve suture or graft (64864, 64865, 69740, 69745)
   31.30 31.30 Global Days 090

42420 total, with dissection and preservation of facial nerve A2 T 80
   EXCLUDES Facial nerve suture or graft (64864, 64865, 69740, 69745)
   35.84 35.84 Global Days 090

42425 total, en bloc removal with sacrifice of facial nerve A2 T 80
   EXCLUDES Facial nerve suture or graft (64864, 64865, 69740, 69745)
   23.54 23.54 Global Days 090

42426 total, with unilateral radical neck dissection C 80
   EXCLUDES Facial nerve suture or graft (64864, 64865, 69740, 69745)
   38.22 38.22 Global Days 090

42440 Excision of submandibular (submaxillary) gland A2 T 80
   13.08 13.08 Global Days 090

42450 Excision of sublingual gland A2 T 80
   9.96 12.28 Global Days 090

42500 Plastic repair of salivary duct, sialodochoplasty; primary or simple A2 T 80
   9.46 11.73 Global Days 090

42505 secondary or complicated A2 T
   12.66 15.17 Global Days 090

42507 Parotid duct diversion, bilateral (Wilke type procedure); A2 T 80
   14.13 14.13 Global Days 090

42508 with excision of 1 submandibular gland A2 T 80
   19.74 19.74 Global Days 090

42509 with excision of both submandibular glands A2 T 80
   24.15 24.15 Global Days 090

42510 with ligation of both submandibular (Wharton's) ducts A2 T 80
   17.43 17.43 Global Days 090

42550 Injection procedure for sialography N1 N
   70390
   1.70 3.33 Global Days 000

42600 Closure salivary fistula A2 T 80
   9.73 13.01 Global Days 090

42650 Dilation salivary duct P3 T
   1.62 2.24 Global Days 000

42660 Dilation and catheterization of salivary duct, with or without injection P3 T 80
   2.19 2.90 Global Days 000

42665 Ligation salivary duct, intraoral A2 T 80
   5.73 8.41 Global Days 090

42699 Unlisted procedure, salivary glands or ducts T 80
   0.00 0.00 Global Days YYY

42700-42999 Procedures of the Adenoids/Throat/Tonsils

42700 Incision and drainage abscess; peritonsillar A2 T
   3.73 5.07 Global Days 010

42720 retropharyngeal or parapharyngeal, intraoral approach A2 T 80
   11.07 12.60 Global Days 010

42725 retropharyngeal or parapharyngeal, external approach A2 T 80
   22.63 22.63 Global Days 090

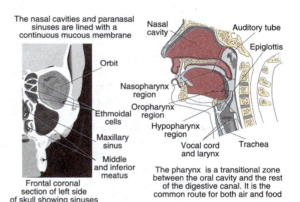

The nasal cavities and paranasal sinuses are lined with a continuous mucous membrane

Nasal cavity
Auditory tube
Epiglottis
Orbit
Nasopharynx region
Ethmoidal cells
Oropharynx region
Maxillary sinus
Hypopharynx region
Middle and inferior meatus
Vocal cord and larynx
Trachea
Frontal coronal section of left side of skull showing sinuses

The pharynx is a transitional zone between the oral cavity and the rest of the digestive canal. It is the common route for both air and food

42800 Biopsy; oropharynx P3 T
   EXCLUDES Laryngoscopy with biopsy (31510, 31535, 31536)
   3.10 4.26 Global Days 010

42802 hypopharynx A2 T
   EXCLUDES Laryngoscopy with biopsy (31510, 31535, 31536)
   3.67 6.14 Global Days 010

42804 nasopharynx, visible lesion, simple A2 T
   EXCLUDES Laryngoscopy with biopsy (31510, 31535, 31536)
   3.11 5.20 Global Days 010

42806 nasopharynx, survey for unknown primary lesion A2 T
   EXCLUDES Laryngoscopy with biopsy (31510, 31535, 31536)
   3.65 5.87 Global Days 010

42808 Excision or destruction of lesion of pharynx, any method A2 T
   4.55 6.17 Global Days 010

● New Code ▲ Revised Code M Maternity A Age Unlisted Not Covered # Resequenced
CCI + Add-on ⊘ Mod 51 Exempt @ Mod 63 Exempt ⊙ Mod Sedation PQRI

Code	Description	Facility RVU	Non-Facility RVU	Global Days
42809	Removal of foreign body from pharynx	3.64	4.61	010
42810	Excision branchial cleft cyst or vestige, confined to skin and subcutaneous tissues	7.96	10.44	090
42815	Excision branchial cleft cyst, vestige, or fistula, extending beneath subcutaneous tissues and/or into pharynx	15.44	15.44	090
42820	Tonsillectomy and adenoidectomy; younger than age 12	8.13	8.13	090

AMA: 2009, Jan, 11-31; 2008, Mar, 14-15; 2008, Jan, 10-25; 2008, May, 9-11; 2007, January, 13-27

Code	Description	Facility RVU	Non-Facility RVU	Global Days
42821	age 12 or over	8.42	8.42	090

AMA: 2009, Jan, 11-31; 2008, May, 9-11; 2008, Mar, 14-15

Code	Description	Facility RVU	Non-Facility RVU	Global Days
42825	Tonsillectomy, primary or secondary; younger than age 12	7.28	7.28	090

AMA: 2009, Jan, 11-31; 2008, Mar, 14-15

Code	Description	Facility RVU	Non-Facility RVU	Global Days
42826	age 12 or over	6.99	6.99	090

AMA: 2009, Jan, 11-31; 2008, Mar, 14-15

Code	Description	Facility RVU	Non-Facility RVU	Global Days
42830	Adenoidectomy, primary; younger than age 12	5.74	5.74	090
42831	age 12 or over	6.17	6.17	090
42835	Adenoidectomy, secondary; younger than age 12	5.32	5.32	090
42836	age 12 or over	6.70	6.70	090
42842	Radical resection of tonsil, tonsillar pillars, and/or retromolar trigone; without closure	27.36	27.36	090
42844	closure with local flap (eg, tongue, buccal)	37.77	37.77	090
42845	closure with other flap	61.99	61.99	090

Code also closure with other flap(s)
Code also radical neck dissection when combined (38720)

Code	Description	Facility RVU	Non-Facility RVU	Global Days
42860	Excision of tonsil tags	5.19	5.19	090
42870	Excision or destruction lingual tonsil, any method (separate procedure)	15.58	15.58	090

EXCLUDES: Nasopharynx resection (juvenile angiofibroma) by transzygomatic/bicoronal approach (61586, 61600)

Side view of the pharynx
- Nasopharynx region
- Oropharynx region
- Hypopharynx region
- Epiglottis
- Larynx
- Esophagus

The nasopharynx is the membranous passage above the level of the soft palate; the oropharynx is the region between the soft palate and the upper edge of the epiglottis; the hypopharynx is the region of the epiglottis to the juncture of the larynx and esophagus; the three regions are collectively known as the pharynx

Code	Description	Facility RVU	Non-Facility RVU	Global Days
42890	Limited pharyngectomy	39.15	39.15	090
42892	Resection of lateral pharyngeal wall or pyriform sinus, direct closure by advancement of lateral and posterior pharyngeal walls	51.92	51.92	090

Code also radical neck dissection when combined (38720)

▲ 42894 Resection of pharyngeal wall requiring closure with myocutaneous or fasciocutaneous flap or free muscle, skin, or fascial flap with microvascular anastomosis — 65.94 / 65.94 Global Days 090

EXCLUDES: Flap used for reconstruction (15732, 15734, 15756-15758)
Limited pharyngectomy with radical neck dissection (38720 and 42890)

Code also radical neck dissection when combined (38720)

AMA: 2009, Jan, 11-31; 2008, Jan, 10-25

Code	Description	Facility RVU	Non-Facility RVU	Global Days
42900	Suture pharynx for wound or injury	9.56	9.56	010
42950	Pharyngoplasty (plastic or reconstructive operation on pharynx)	21.43	21.43	090

EXCLUDES: Pharyngeal flap (42225)

Code	Description	Facility RVU	Non-Facility RVU	Global Days
42953	Pharyngoesophageal repair	25.75	25.75	090

Code also closure using myocutaneous or other flap

Code	Description	Facility RVU	Non-Facility RVU	Global Days
42955	Pharyngostomy (fistulization of pharynx, external for feeding)	20.45	20.45	090
42960	Control oropharyngeal hemorrhage, primary or secondary (eg, post-tonsillectomy); simple	4.73	4.73	010
42961	complicated, requiring hospitalization	11.70	11.70	090
42962	with secondary surgical intervention	14.47	14.47	090

Current Procedural Coding Expert – Digestive

42970 Control of nasopharyngeal hemorrhage, primary or secondary (eg, postadenoidectomy); simple, with posterior nasal packs, with or without anterior packs and/or cautery
10.97 10.97 Global Days 090

42971 complicated, requiring hospitalization
12.81 12.81 Global Days 090

42972 with secondary surgical intervention
14.36 14.36 Global Days 090

42999 Unlisted procedure, pharynx, adenoids, or tonsils
0.00 0.00 Global Days YYY

43020-43135 Incision/Resection of Esophagus

EXCLUDES Gastrointestinal reconstruction for previous esophagectomy (43360, 43361)
Gastrotomy with intraluminal tube insertion (43510)

43020 Esophagotomy, cervical approach, with removal of foreign body
EXCLUDES Laparotomy with esophageal intubation (43510)
15.17 15.17 Global Days 090

43030 Cricopharyngeal myotomy
EXCLUDES Laparotomy with esophageal intubation (43510)
14.52 14.52 Global Days 090

43045 Esophagotomy, thoracic approach, with removal of foreign body
EXCLUDES Laparotomy with esophageal intubation (43510)
36.07 36.07 Global Days 090

43100 Excision of lesion, esophagus, with primary repair; cervical approach
EXCLUDES Wide excision of malignant lesion of cervical esophagus with total laryngectomy: (31365, 43107, 43116, 43124)
With radical neck dissection (31365, 43107, 43116, 43124)
Without radical neck dissection (31360, 43107, 43116, 43124)
17.64 17.64 Global Days 090

43101 thoracic or abdominal approach
EXCLUDES Wide excision of malignant lesion of cervical esophagus with total laryngectomy: (31365, 43107, 43116, 43124)
With radical neck dissection
Without radical neck dissection (31360, 43107, 43116, 43124)
27.94 27.94 Global Days 090

43107 Total or near total esophagectomy, without thoracotomy; with pharyngogastrostomy or cervical esophagogastrostomy, with or without pyloroplasty (transhiatal)
70.88 70.88 Global Days 090

43108 with colon interposition or small intestine reconstruction, including intestine mobilization, preparation and anastomosis(es)
129.80 129.80 Global Days 090

43112 Total or near total esophagectomy, with thoracotomy; with pharyngogastrostomy or cervical esophagogastrostomy, with or without pyloroplasty
75.14 75.14 Global Days 090

43113 with colon interposition or small intestine reconstruction, including intestine mobilization, preparation, and anastomosis(es)
126.70 126.70 Global Days 090

43116 Partial esophagectomy, cervical, with free intestinal graft, including microvascular anastomosis, obtaining the graft and intestinal reconstruction
INCLUDES Operating microscope (69990)
EXCLUDES Free jejunal graft with microvascular anastomosis done by a different physician (43496)
Code also modifier 52 if intestinal or free jejunal graft with microvascular anastomosis is done by another physician
149.60 149.60 Global Days 090

43117 Partial esophagectomy, distal 2/3, with thoracotomy and separate abdominal incision, with or without proximal gastrectomy; with thoracic esophagogastrostomy, with or without pyloroplasty (Ivor Lewis)
EXCLUDES Esophagogastrectomy (lower third) and vagotomy (43122)
Total esophagectomy with gastropharyngostomy (43107, 43124)
68.97 68.97 Global Days 090

43118 with colon interposition or small intestine reconstruction, including intestine mobilization, preparation, and anastomosis(es)
EXCLUDES Esophagogastrectomy (lower third) and vagotomy (43122)
Total esophagectomy with gastropharyngostomy (43107, 43124)
105.73 105.73 Global Days 090

43121 Partial esophagectomy, distal 2/3, with thoracotomy only, with or without proximal gastrectomy, with thoracic esophagogastrostomy, with or without pyloroplasty
80.00 80.00 Global Days 090

43122 Partial esophagectomy, thoracoabdominal or abdominal approach, with or without proximal gastrectomy; with esophagogastrostomy, with or without pyloroplasty
71.12 71.12 Global Days 090

43123 with colon interposition or small intestine reconstruction, including intestine mobilization, preparation, and anastomosis(es)
131.37 131.37 Global Days 090

43124 Total or partial esophagectomy, without reconstruction (any approach), with cervical esophagostomy
106.69 106.69 Global Days 090

43130 Diverticulectomy of hypopharynx or esophagus, with or without myotomy; cervical approach
22.06 22.06 Global Days 090

43135 thoracic approach
41.74 41.74 Global Days 090

43200-43259 Endoscopic Procedures: Upper GI

CMS 100-3,100.2 Endoscopy
INCLUDES Diagnostic endoscopy with surgical endoscopy
Code also appropriate endoscopy of each anatomic site examined

43200 Esophagoscopy, rigid or flexible; diagnostic, with or without collection of specimen(s) by brushing or washing (separate procedure)
2.89 5.55 Global Days 000
AMA: 2009, Jan, 11-31; 2008, Jan, 10-25; 2008, Oct, 6-7; 2007, January, 13-27

● New Code ▲ Revised Code M Maternity A Age Unlisted Not Covered # Resequenced
CCI + Add-on Mod 51 Exempt Mod 63 Exempt Mod Sedation PQRI
© 2009 Publisher (Blue Ink) CPT only © 2009 American Medical Association. All Rights Reserved. (Black Ink) Medicare (Red Ink) 149

43201

Code	Description	Facility RVU	Non-Facility RVU	Global Days
43201	with directed submucosal injection(s), any substance	3.51	7.44	000

EXCLUDES Injection sclerosis of esophageal varices (43204)

AMA: 2008, Oct, 6-7

| 43202 | with biopsy, single or multiple | 3.18 | 7.16 | 000 |

AMA: 2008, Oct, 6-7

| 43204 | with injection sclerosis of esophageal varices | 6.08 | 6.08 | 000 |

AMA: 2008, Oct, 6-7

| 43205 | with band ligation of esophageal varices | 6.09 | 6.09 | 000 |

AMA: 2008, Oct, 6-7

| 43215 | with removal of foreign body | 4.27 | 4.27 | 000 |

74235

AMA: 2008, Oct, 6-7

| 43216 | with removal of tumor(s), polyp(s), or other lesion(s) by hot biopsy forceps or bipolar cautery | 3.94 | 5.66 | 000 |

AMA: 2008, Oct, 6-7

| 43217 | with removal of tumor(s), polyp(s), or other lesion(s) by snare technique | 4.72 | 9.57 | 000 |

AMA: 2008, Oct, 6-7

| 43219 | with insertion of plastic tube or stent | 4.67 | 4.67 | 000 |

AMA: 2008, Oct, 6-7

| 43220 | with balloon dilation (less than 30 mm diameter) | 3.51 | 3.51 | 000 |

EXCLUDES Dilation of esophagus: (43458)
With balloon 30 mm diameter or larger
Without visualization (43450-43453)
Fiberoptic esophagogastroscopy:
Diagnostic (43200, 43235)
With biopsy or collection of specimen (43200, 43202, 43235, 43239)
With removal of foreign body (43215, 43247)
With removal of polyps(s) (43217, 43251)

74360

AMA: 2009, Jan, 11-31; 2008, Jan, 10-25; 2008, Oct, 6-7; 2007, January, 13-27; 2005, May, 3-6

| 43226 | with insertion of guide wire followed by dilation over guide wire | 3.88 | 3.88 | 000 |

74360

AMA: 2008, Oct, 6-7

| 43227 | with control of bleeding (eg, injection, bipolar cautery, unipolar cautery, laser, heater probe, stapler, plasma coagulator) | 5.78 | 5.78 | 000 |

AMA: 2008, Oct, 6-7

| 43228 | with ablation of tumor(s), polyp(s), or other lesion(s), not amenable to removal by hot biopsy forceps, bipolar cautery or snare technique | 6.07 | 6.07 | 000 |

Code also esophagoscopic photodynamic therapy if performed (96570, 96571)

AMA: 2008, Oct, 6-7

| 43231 | with endoscopic ultrasound examination | 5.18 | 5.18 | 000 |

Do not report with (76975)

AMA: 2009, Mar, 8-9; 2008, Oct, 6-7

| 43232 | with transendoscopic ultrasound-guided intramural or transmural fine needle aspiration/biopsy(s) | 7.14 | 7.14 | 000 |

Do not report with (76942, 76975)

88172-88173

AMA: 2009, Jan, 11-31; 2009, Mar, 8-9; 2008, Jan, 10-25; 2008, Oct, 6-7; 2007, January, 13-27

| 43234 | Upper gastrointestinal endoscopy, simple primary examination (eg, with small diameter flexible endoscope) (separate procedure) | 3.34 | 7.09 | 000 |

AMA: 2009, Jan, 11-31; 2008, Jan, 10-25; 2007, May, 9-11

| 43235 | Upper gastrointestinal endoscopy including esophagus, stomach, and either the duodenum and/or jejunum as appropriate; diagnostic, with or without collection of specimen(s) by brushing or washing (separate procedure) | 3.95 | 7.38 | 000 |

AMA: 2009, May, 8-9&11; 2009, Jan, 11-31; 2008, Jan, 10-25; 2008, Oct, 6-7; 2007, January, 13-27

| 43236 | with directed submucosal injection(s), any substance | 4.78 | 9.10 | 000 |

EXCLUDES Injection sclerosis of varices, esophageal/gastric (43243)

AMA: 2008, Oct, 6-7

| 43237 | with endoscopic ultrasound examination limited to the esophagus | 6.41 | 6.41 | 000 |

Do not report with (76942, 76975)

AMA: 2009, Mar, 8-9; 2008, Oct, 6-7

| 43238 | with transendoscopic ultrasound-guided intramural or transmural fine needle aspiration/biopsy(s), esophagus (includes endoscopic ultrasound examination limited to the esophagus) | 7.99 | 7.99 | 000 |

Do not report with (76942, 76975)

AMA: 2009, Mar, 8-9; 2008, Oct, 6-7

| 43239 | with biopsy, single or multiple | 4.69 | 8.62 | 000 |

AMA: 2009, Jan, 11-31; 2008, Jan, 10-25; 2008, Oct, 6-7; 2007, January, 13-27; 2005, March, 11-15

| 43240 | with transmural drainage of pseudocyst | 10.83 | 10.83 | 000 |

AMA: 2008, Oct, 6-7

| 43241 | with transendoscopic intraluminal tube or catheter placement | 4.25 | 4.25 | 000 |

AMA: 2008, Oct, 6-7

Current Procedural Coding Expert – Digestive 43268

| | 43242 | with transendoscopic ultrasound-guided intramural or transmural fine needle aspiration/biopsy(s) (includes endoscopic ultrasound examination of the esophagus, stomach, and either the duodenum and/or jejunum as appropriate) [A2][T][80] |

EXCLUDES: Fine needle biopsy/aspiration, transendoscopic, of only the esophagus (43238)

Do not report with (76942, 76975)
88172-88173
11.54   11.54   Global Days 000
AMA: 2009, Mar, 8-9; 2008, Oct, 6-7

| | 43243 | with injection sclerosis of esophageal and/or gastric varices [A2][T] |
7.29   7.29   Global Days 000
AMA: 2008, Oct, 6-7

| | 43244 | with band ligation of esophageal and/or gastric varices [A2][T][80] |
8.04   8.04   Global Days 000
AMA: 2008, Oct, 6-7

| | 43245 | with dilation of gastric outlet for obstruction (eg, balloon, guide wire, bougie) [A2][T] |

Do not report with (43256)
5.16   5.16   Global Days 000
AMA: 2009, Jan, 11-31; 2008, Jan, 10-25; 2008, Oct, 6-7; 2007, January, 13-27

| | 43246 | with directed placement of percutaneous gastrostomy tube [A2][T][80] |

EXCLUDES: Percutaneous insertion of gastrostomy tube, nonendoscopic (49440)
6.91   6.91   Global Days 000
AMA: 2009, Jan, 11-31; 2008, Jan, 10-25; 2008, Oct, 6-7; 2007, January, 13-27

| | 43247 | with removal of foreign body [A2][T] |
74235
5.48   5.48   Global Days 000
AMA: 2009, Jan, 11-31; 2008, Jan, 10-25; 2008, Oct, 6-7; 2007, Dec, 7-8

| | 43248 | with insertion of guide wire followed by dilation of esophagus over guide wire [A2][T] |
5.13   5.13   Global Days 000
AMA: 2009, Jan, 11-31; 2008, Jan, 10-25; 2008, Oct, 6-7; 2007, January, 13-27

| | 43249 | with balloon dilation of esophagus (less than 30 mm diameter) [A2][T] |
4.74   4.74   Global Days 000
AMA: 2008, Oct, 6-7; 2005, May, 3-6

| | 43250 | with removal of tumor(s), polyp(s), or other lesion(s) by hot biopsy forceps or bipolar cautery [A2][T] |
5.19   5.19   Global Days 000
AMA: 2009, Jan, 11-31; 2008, Jan, 10-25; 2008, Oct, 6-7; 2007, January, 13-27

| | 43251 | with removal of tumor(s), polyp(s), or other lesion(s) by snare technique [A2][T] |
5.96   5.96   Global Days 000
AMA: 2008, Oct, 6-7

| | 43255 | with control of bleeding, any method [A2][T] |
7.69   7.69   Global Days 000
AMA: 2008, Oct, 6-7

| | 43256 | with transendoscopic stent placement (includes predilation) [A2][T] |
Code also (C1874, C1875, C1876, C1877, C2617, C2625)
6.94   6.94   Global Days 000
AMA: 2008, Oct, 6-7

| | 43257 | with delivery of thermal energy to the muscle of lower esophageal sphincter and/or gastric cardia, for treatment of gastroesophageal reflux disease [A2][T] |
8.82   8.82   Global Days 000
AMA: 2008, Oct, 6-7; 2005, May, 3-6

| | 43258 | with ablation of tumor(s), polyp(s), or other lesion(s) not amenable to removal by hot biopsy forceps, bipolar cautery or snare technique |

EXCLUDES: Esophagoscopy with injection sclerosis of esophageal varices (43204)
Upper gastrointestinal endoscopy with injection sclerosis of esophageal varices (43243)
7.27   7.27   Global Days 000
AMA: 2008, Oct, 6-7

| | 43259 | with endoscopic ultrasound examination, including the esophagus, stomach, and either the duodenum and/or jejunum as appropriate [A2][T][80] |

Do not report with (76975)
8.27   8.27   Global Days 000
AMA: 2009, Mar, 8-9; 2008, Oct, 6-7

43260-43273 Endoscopic Procedures: ERCP

INCLUDES: Diagnostic endoscopy with surgical endoscopy

Code also appropriate endoscopy of each anatomic site examined.

| | 43260 | Endoscopic retrograde cholangiopancreatography (ERCP); diagnostic, with or without collection of specimen(s) by brushing or washing (separate procedure) [A2][T][P0] |
74328-74330
9.44   9.44   Global Days 000
AMA: 2009, Jan, 11-31; 2008, May, 9-11

| | 43261 | with biopsy, single or multiple [A2][T][P0] |
74328-74330
9.94   9.94   Global Days 000

| | 43262 | with sphincterotomy/papillotomy [A2][T][P0] |
74328-74330
11.66   11.66   Global Days 000
AMA: 2009, Jul, 10

| | 43263 | with pressure measurement of sphincter of Oddi (pancreatic duct or common bile duct) [A2][T][P0] |
74328-74330
11.47   11.47   Global Days 000

| | 43264 | with endoscopic retrograde removal of calculus/calculi from biliary and/or pancreatic ducts [A2][T][P0] |
Code also sphincterotomy, when performed (43262)
74328-74330
13.99   13.99   Global Days 000
AMA: 2009, Jan, 11-31; 2007, Dec, 10-179

| | 43265 | with endoscopic retrograde destruction, lithotripsy of calculus/calculi, any method [A2][T][P0] |
Code also sphincterotomy, when performed (43262)
74328-74330
15.71   15.71   Global Days 000

| | 43267 | with endoscopic retrograde insertion of nasobiliary or nasopancreatic drainage tube [A2][T][P0] |
Code also sphincterotomy, when performed (43262)
74328-74330
11.64   11.64   Global Days 000

| | 43268 | with endoscopic retrograde insertion of tube or stent into bile or pancreatic duct [A2][T][P0] |
Code also sphincterotomy, when performed (43262)
74328-74330
11.79   11.79   Global Days 000
AMA: 2009, Jan, 11-31; 2008, Jan, 10-25; 2007, January, 13-27

● New Code   ▲ Revised Code   M Maternity   Age   Unlisted   Not Covered   # Resequenced
□ CCI   + Add-on   ⊘ Mod 51 Exempt   Ⓡ Mod 63 Exempt   ⊙ Mod Sedation   P0 PQRI

© 2009 Publisher *(Blue Ink)*   CPT only © 2009 American Medical Association. All Rights Reserved. (Black Ink)   Medicare *(Red Ink)*   151

	43269	with endoscopic retrograde removal of foreign body and/or change of tube or stent [A2][T][▢][P0]
		Code also sphincterotomy, when performed (43262)
		⊞ 74328-74330
		🗞 12.94 🔍 12.94 Global Days 000
⊙	43271	with endoscopic retrograde balloon dilation of ampulla, biliary and/or pancreatic duct(s) [A2][T][▢][P0]
		Code also sphincterotomy, when performed (43262)
		⊞ 74328-74330
		🗞 11.66 🔍 11.66 Global Days 000
⊙	43272	with ablation of tumor(s), polyp(s), or other lesion(s) not amenable to removal by hot biopsy forceps, bipolar cautery or snare technique [A2][T][80][▢][P0]
		⊞ 74328-74330
		🗞 11.66 🔍 11.66 Global Days 000
+⊙	43273	Endoscopic cannulation of papilla with direct visualization of common bile duct(s) and/or pancreatic duct(s) (List separately in addition to code(s) for primary procedure) [G2][T][80]
		Code first (43260-43261, 43263-43265, 43267-43272)
		🗞 3.33 🔍 3.33 Global Days ZZZ
		AMA: 2009, Jul, 10

43279-43289 Laparoscopic Procedures of Esophagus

	43279	Laparoscopy, surgical, esophagomyotomy (Heller type), with fundoplasty, when performed [C][80][P0]
		INCLUDES Diagnostic laparoscopy with surgical laparoscopy
		EXCLUDES Esophagomyotomy, open method (43330-43331)
		Do not report with (43280)
		🗞 33.59 🔍 33.59 Global Days 090
	43280	Laparoscopy, surgical, esophagogastric fundoplasty (eg, Nissen, Toupet procedures) [T][80][▢][P0]
		INCLUDES Diagnostic laparoscopy with surgical laparoscopy
		EXCLUDES Esophagogastric fundoplasty, open method (43324)
		Do not report with (43279)
		🗞 29.77 🔍 29.77 Global Days 090
●	43281	Laparoscopy, surgical, repair of paraesophageal hernia, includes fundoplasty, when performed; without implantation of mesh [C][80]
		EXCLUDES Transabdominal paraesophageal hernia repair (39502)
		Transthoracic paraesophageal hernia repair (39520)
		Do not report with (43280, 43450, 43453, 43456, 43458, 49568)
		🗞 42.71 🔍 42.71 Global Days 090
●	43282	with implantation of mesh [C][80]
		Transthoracic paraesophageal hernia repair (39520)
		Do not report with (43280, 43450, 43453, 43456, 43458, 49568)
		EXCLUDES Transabdominal paraesophageal hernia repair (39502)
		🗞 48.04 🔍 48.04 Global Days 090
	43289	Unlisted laparoscopy procedure, esophagus [T][80][50]
		🗞 0.00 🔍 0.00 Global Days YYY

43300-43425 Open Esophageal Repair Procedures

43300	Esophagoplasty (plastic repair or reconstruction), cervical approach; without repair of tracheoesophageal fistula [C][80][▢][P0]
	🗞 17.29 🔍 17.29 Global Days 090
43305	with repair of tracheoesophageal fistula [C][80][▢][P0]
	🗞 30.98 🔍 30.98 Global Days 090
43310	Esophagoplasty (plastic repair or reconstruction), thoracic approach; without repair of tracheoesophageal fistula [C][80][▢][P0]
	🗞 42.30 🔍 42.30 Global Days 090
43312	with repair of tracheoesophageal fistula [C][80][▢][P0]
	🗞 44.78 🔍 44.78 Global Days 090
43313	Esophagoplasty for congenital defect (plastic repair or reconstruction), thoracic approach; without repair of congenital tracheoesophageal fistula [C][80][♀][▢][P0]
	🗞 76.30 🔍 76.30 Global Days 090
43314	with repair of congenital tracheoesophageal fistula [C][80][♀][▢][P0]
	🗞 87.75 🔍 87.75 Global Days 090
43320	Esophagogastrostomy (cardioplasty), with or without vagotomy and pyloroplasty, transabdominal or transthoracic approach [C][80][▢][P0]
	🗞 38.11 🔍 38.11 Global Days 090
43324	Esophagogastric fundoplasty (eg, Nissen, Belsey IV, Hill procedures) [C][80][▢][P0]
	EXCLUDES Laparoscopic approach (43280)
	🗞 37.47 🔍 37.47 Global Days 090
	AMA: 2009, Jan, 11-31; 2008, Jan, 10-25; 2007, January, 13-27; 2005, May, 3-6
43325	Esophagogastric fundoplasty; with fundic patch (Thal-Nissen procedure) [C][80][▢][P0]
	EXCLUDES Myotomy, cricopharyngeal (43030)
	🗞 37.19 🔍 37.19 Global Days 090
43326	with gastroplasty (eg, Collis) [C][80][▢][P0]
	🗞 36.78 🔍 36.78 Global Days 090
43330	Esophagomyotomy (Heller type); abdominal approach [C][80][▢][P0]
	EXCLUDES Esophagomyotomy, laparoscopic method (43279)
	🗞 36.25 🔍 36.25 Global Days 090
43331	thoracic approach [C][80][▢][P0]
	EXCLUDES Thoracoscopy with esophagomyotomy (32665)
	🗞 37.29 🔍 37.29 Global Days 090

| 26/TC PC/TC Comp Only | A2-73 ASC Pmt | 50 Bilateral | ♂ Male Only | ♀ Female Only | 🗞 Facility RVU | 🔍 Non-Facility RVU |
| AMA: CPT Asst | MED: Pub 100 | A-Y OPPSI | 80/80 Surg Assist Allowed / w/Doc | ▢ Lab Crosswalk | ⊞ Radiology Crosswalk |

Current Procedural Coding Expert – Digestive

43340 Esophagojejunostomy (without total gastrectomy); abdominal approach C 80 P0
  37.78 37.78 Global Days 090

43341 thoracic approach C 80 P0
  40.94 40.94 Global Days 090

43350 Esophagostomy, fistulization of esophagus, external; abdominal approach C 80 P0
  33.01 33.01 Global Days 090

43351 thoracic approach C 80 P0
  36.48 36.48 Global Days 090

43352 cervical approach C 80 P0
  29.57 29.57 Global Days 090

43360 Gastrointestinal reconstruction for previous esophagectomy, for obstructing esophageal lesion or fistula, or for previous esophageal exclusion; with stomach, with or without pyloroplasty C 80 P0
  62.98 62.98 Global Days 090

43361 with colon interposition or small intestine reconstruction, including intestine mobilization, preparation, and anastomosis(es) C 80 P0
  74.00 74.00 Global Days 090

43400 Ligation, direct, esophageal varices C 80 P0
  42.07 42.07 Global Days 090

43401 Transection of esophagus with repair, for esophageal varices C 80 P0
  43.11 43.11 Global Days 090

43405 Ligation or stapling at gastroesophageal junction for pre-existing esophageal perforation C 80 P0
  42.08 42.08 Global Days 090

43410 Suture of esophageal wound or injury; cervical approach C 80 P0
  27.52 27.52 Global Days 090

43415 transthoracic or transabdominal approach C 80 P0
  47.78 47.78 Global Days 090

43420 Closure of esophagostomy or fistula; cervical approach T 80 P0
  28.87 28.87 Global Days 090

43425 transthoracic or transabdominal approach C 80 P0
  EXCLUDES Esophageal hiatal hernia repair (39520-39531)
  41.81 41.81 Global Days 090

43450-43458 Esophageal Dilation

43450 Dilation of esophagus, by unguided sound or bougie, single or multiple passes A2 T
  74220, 74360
  2.39 3.90 Global Days 000
  AMA: 2009, Jan, 11-31; 2008, Jan, 10-25; 2007, January, 13-27

⊙ **43453** Dilation of esophagus, over guide wire A2 T
  EXCLUDES Dilation performed with direct visualization (43220)
  Esophagus dilation performed by dilator or balloon (43220, 43458, 74360)
  74220, 74360
  2.59 7.10 Global Days 000
  AMA: 2009, Jan, 11-31; 2008, Jan, 10-25; 2007, January, 13-27

⊙ **43456** Dilation of esophagus, by balloon or dilator, retrograde A2 T
  74220, 74360
  4.23 14.29 Global Days 000
  AMA: 2005, May, 3-6

⊙ **43458** Dilation of esophagus with balloon (30 mm diameter or larger) for achalasia A2 T
  EXCLUDES Balloon dilation less than 30 mm diameter (43220)
  74220, 74360
  4.99 9.72 Global Days 000
  AMA: 2009, Jan, 11-31; 2008, Jan, 10-25; 2008, Oct, 6-7; 2007, January, 13-27; 2005, May, 3-6

43460-43499 Other and Unlisted Esophageal Procedures

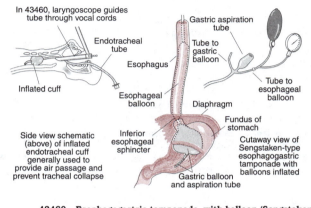

43460 Esophagogastric tamponade, with balloon (Sengstaken type) C
  EXCLUDES Removal of foreign body of the esophagus with balloon catheter (43215, 43247, 74235)
  6.12 6.12 Global Days 000

43496 Free jejunum transfer with microvascular anastomosis C 80 P0
  INCLUDES Operating microscope (69990)
  0.00 0.00 Global Days 090

43499 Unlisted procedure, esophagus T
  0.00 0.00 Global Days YYY
  AMA: 2009, Jan, 11-31; 2008, Jan, 10-25; 2007, May, 9-11

43500-43641 Open Gastric Incisional and Resection Procedures

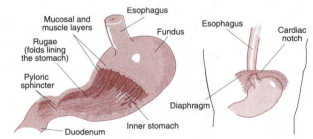

The stomach is a highly distensible organ that serves as a reservoir to mix food and break it down with digestive juices. The esophagus pierces the diaphragm at the cardiac notch, where the stomach begins. The pyloric sphincter marks the inferior border of the stomach. The vagal nerve trunks run down the front and back of the esophagus and serve the stomach by controlling secretion of digestive acids

43500 Gastrotomy; with exploration or foreign body removal C 80 P0
  21.51 21.51 Global Days 090

● New Code ▲ Revised Code M Maternity A Age Unlisted Not Covered # Resequenced
CCI + Add-on ⊘ Mod 51 Exempt ⊚ Mod 63 Exempt ⊙ Mod Sedation P0 PQRI
© 2009 Publisher (Blue Ink) CPT only © 2009 American Medical Association. All Rights Reserved. (Black Ink) Medicare (Red Ink) 153

43501	with suture repair of bleeding ulcer		C 80 P0
	36.93 36.93 Global Days 090		
43502	with suture repair of pre-existing esophagogastric laceration (eg, Mallory-Weiss)		C 80 P0
	41.85 41.85 Global Days 090		
43510	with esophageal dilation and insertion of permanent intraluminal tube (eg, Celestin or Mousseaux-Barbin)		T 80 P0
	25.82 25.82 Global Days 090		
43520	Pyloromyotomy, cutting of pyloric muscle (Fredet-Ramstedt type operation)		C 80 ♂ P0
	18.97 18.97 Global Days 090		
43600	Biopsy of stomach; by capsule, tube, peroral (1 or more specimens)		A2 T
	2.91 2.91 Global Days 000		
43605	by laparotomy		C 80 P0
	22.88 22.88 Global Days 090		
43610	Excision, local; ulcer or benign tumor of stomach		C 80 P0
	26.93 26.93 Global Days 090		
43611	malignant tumor of stomach		C 80 P0
	33.58 33.58 Global Days 090		
43620	Gastrectomy, total; with esophagoenterostomy		C 80 P0
	54.31 54.31 Global Days 090		
43621	with Roux-en-Y reconstruction		C 80 P0
	62.70 62.70 Global Days 090		
43622	with formation of intestinal pouch, any type		C 80 P0
	63.51 63.51 Global Days 090		
43631	Gastrectomy, partial, distal; with gastroduodenostomy		C 80 P0
	INCLUDES Billroth operation		
	39.90 39.90 Global Days 090		
43632	with gastrojejunostomy		C 80 P0
	INCLUDES Polya anastomosis		
	56.08 56.08 Global Days 090		
43633	with Roux-en-Y reconstruction		C 80 P0
	52.95 52.95 Global Days 090		
43634	with formation of intestinal pouch		C 80 P0
	58.54 58.54 Global Days 090		
+ 43635	Vagotomy when performed with partial distal gastrectomy (List separately in addition to code[s] for primary procedure)		C 80
	Code first as appropriate (43631-43634)		
	3.14 3.14 Global Days ZZZ		
43640	Vagotomy including pyloroplasty, with or without gastrostomy; truncal or selective		C 80 P0
	EXCLUDES Pyloroplasty (43800) Vagotomy (64752-64760)		
	32.40 32.40 Global Days 090		
43641	parietal cell (highly selective)		C 80 P0
	EXCLUDES Upper gastrointestinal endoscopy (43234-43259)		
	32.89 32.89 Global Days 090		

43644-43645 Laparoscopic Gastric Bypass with Small Bowel Resection

CMS 100-3,40.5 — Treatment of Obesity
CMS 100-3,100.1 — Bariatric Surgery for Treatment of Morbid Obesity
CMS 100-3,100.8 — Intestinal Bypass Surgery

INCLUDES Diagnostic laparoscopy

EXCLUDES *Endoscopy, upper gastrointestinal, (esophagus/stomach/duodenum/jejunum) (43235-43259)*

43644 Laparoscopy, surgical, gastric restrictive procedure; with gastric bypass and Roux-en-Y gastroenterostomy (roux limb 150 cm or less) C 80 P0

EXCLUDES *Open method (43846)*
Roux limb greater than 150 cm (43645)

Do not report with (43846, 49320)
 47.76 47.76 Global Days 090
AMA: 2005, May, 3-6

43645 with gastric bypass and small intestine reconstruction to limit absorption C 80 P0

Do not report with (43847, 49320)
 51.13 51.13 Global Days 090
AMA: 2005, May, 3-6

43647-43659 Other and Unlisted Laparoscopic Gastric Procedures

INCLUDES Diagnostic laparoscopy

EXCLUDES *Endoscopy, upper gastrointestinal, (esophagus/stomach/duodenum/jejunum) (43235-43259)*

43647 Laparoscopy, surgical; implantation or replacement of gastric neurostimulator electrodes, antrum S 80

EXCLUDES *Electronic analysis/programming gastric neurostimulator pulse generator (95980-95982)*
Electronic analysis / programming / reprogramming gastric neurostimulator pulse generator, lesser curvature (morbid obesity) (95980-95982)
Implantation or replacement of gastric stimulation electrodes, lesser curvature, performed laparoscopically (0155T)
Insertion/replacement gastric neurostimulator pulse generator (64590)
Open method (43881)

Code also neurostimulator lead (C1778, C1897)
 0.00 0.00 Global Days YYY
AMA: 2009, Jan, 11-31; 2008, Jan, 8-9; 2007, March, 4-5

43648 revision or removal of gastric neurostimulator electrodes, antrum T 80

EXCLUDES *Electronic analysis/programming gastric neurostimulator (95980-95982)*
Open method (43882)
Revision or removal of gastric stimulation electrodes, lesser curvature, performed laparoscopically (0156T)
Revision/removal gastric neurostimulator pulse generator (64595)

 0.00 0.00 Global Days YYY
AMA: 2007, March, 4-5

43651 transection of vagus nerves, truncal T 80 P0
 17.80 17.80 Global Days 090

Current Procedural Coding Expert – Digestive

43652 transection of vagus nerves, selective or highly selective
 20.85 20.85 Global Days 090

43653 gastrostomy, without construction of gastric tube (eg, Stamm procedure) (separate procedure)
 15.47 15.47 Global Days 090

43659 Unlisted laparoscopy procedure, stomach
 0.00 0.00 Global Days YYY
AMA: 2009, Jan, 11-31; 2008, Jan, 10-25; 2007, Dec, 10-179; 2007, January, 13-27; 2006, June, 16-17; 2006, April, 19-20

43752-43761 Nonsurgical Gastric Tube Procedures

CMS 100-4,20,50.3 Payment for Replacement of Parenteral and Enteral Pumps
CMS 100-4,20,100.2.2 Medical Necessity for Parenteral and Enteral Nutrition Therapy

43752 Naso- or oro-gastric tube placement, requiring physician's skill and fluoroscopic guidance (includes fluoroscopy, image documentation and report)
EXCLUDES Percutaneous insertion of gastrostomy tube (43246, 49440)
Placement of enteric tube (44500, 74340)
Do not report with (99291-99292, 99468-99469, 99471-99472, 99478-99479)
 1.13 1.13 Global Days 000
AMA: 2009, Jan, 11-31; 2008, Jan, 10-25; 2007, January, 13-27; 2007, February, 10-11; 2007, Jul, 1-4; 2006, May, 1-9

43760 Change of gastrostomy tube, percutaneous, without imaging or endoscopic guidance
EXCLUDES Fluoroscopically guided gastrostomy replacement (49450)
Gastrostomy tube, placed endoscopically (43246)
 1.35 11.24 Global Days 000
AMA: 2009, Jan, 11-31; 2008, Apr, -11

▲ **43761** Repositioning of a naso- or oro-gastric feeding tube, through the duodenum for enteric nutrition
EXCLUDES Gastrostomy tube converted endoscopically to jejunostomy tube (44373)
Introduction of long gastrointestinal tube into the duodenum (44500)
Do not report with (44500, 49446)
 76000
 2.86 3.18 Global Days 000
AMA: 2008, Jun, 8-11

43770-43775 Laparoscopic Bariatric Procedures

CMS 100-3,100.1 Bariatric Surgery for Treatment of Morbid Obesity
INCLUDES Diagnostic laparoscopy
Stomach/duodenum/jejunum/ileum
Subsequent band adjustments (change of the gastric band component diameter by injection/aspriation of fluid through the subcutaneous port component) during the postoperative period

43770 Laparoscopy, surgical, gastric restrictive procedure; placement of adjustable gastric restrictive device (eg, gastric band and subcutaneous port components)
Code also modifier 52 for placement of individual component
 30.60 30.60 Global Days 090
AMA: 2009, Jan, 11-31; 2008, Jan, 10-25; 2007, January, 13-27; 2006, April, 1-7; 2006, April, 19-20

43771 revision of adjustable gastric restrictive device component only
 34.92 34.92 Global Days 090
AMA: 2006, April, 1-7

43772 removal of adjustable gastric restrictive device component only
 26.17 26.17 Global Days 090
AMA: 2006, April, 1-7

43773 removal and replacement of adjustable gastric restrictive device component only
Do not report with (43772)
 34.92 34.92 Global Days 090
AMA: 2006, April, 1-7

43774 removal of adjustable gastric restrictive device and subcutaneous port components
EXCLUDES Removal/replacement of subcutaneous port components and gastric band (43659)
 26.33 26.33 Global Days 090
AMA: 2009, Jan, 11-31; 2008, Jan, 10-25; 2007, January, 13-27; 2006, June, 16-17; 2006, April, 19-20; 2006, April, 1-7

● **43775** longitudinal gastrectomy (ie, sleeve gastrectomy)
EXCLUDES Open gastric restrictive procedure for morbid obesity, without gastric bypass, other than vertical-banded gastroplasty (43843)
 35.86 35.86 Global Days 090

43800-43840 Open Gastric Incisional/Repair/Resection Procedures

43800 Pyloroplasty
EXCLUDES Vagotomy with pyloroplasty (43640)
 25.57 25.57 Global Days 090

43810 Gastroduodenostomy
 27.88 27.88 Global Days 090

43820 Gastrojejunostomy; without vagotomy
 36.87 36.87 Global Days 090

43825 with vagotomy, any type
 35.75 35.75 Global Days 090

43830 Gastrostomy, open; without construction of gastric tube (eg, Stamm procedure) (separate procedure)
 19.02 19.02 Global Days 090

43831 neonatal, for feeding
EXCLUDES Change of gastrostomy tube (43760)
 16.02 16.02 Global Days 090

43832 with construction of gastric tube (eg, Janeway procedure)
EXCLUDES Endoscopic placement of percutaneous gastrostomy tube (43246)
 28.82 28.82 Global Days 090

43840 Gastrorrhaphy, suture of perforated duodenal or gastric ulcer, wound, or injury
 37.30 37.30 Global Days 090

43842-43848 Open Bariatric Procedures for Morbid Obesity

CMS 100-3,40.5 Treatment of Obesity
CMS 100-3,100.1 Bariatric Surgery for Treatment of Morbid Obesity
CMS 100-3,100.8 Intestinal Bypass Surgery

43842 Gastric restrictive procedure, without gastric bypass, for morbid obesity; vertical-banded gastroplasty
 31.82 31.82 Global Days 090

● New Code   ▲ Revised Code   Maternity   Age   Unlisted   Not Covered   # Resequenced
CCI   + Add-on   Mod 51 Exempt   Mod 63 Exempt   Mod Sedation   PQRI

© 2009 Publisher (Blue Ink)   CPT only © 2009 American Medical Association. All Rights Reserved. (Black Ink)   Medicare (Red Ink)

43843

43843	other than vertical-banded gastroplasty	C 80 P0
	INCLUDES Laparoscopic longitudinal gastrectomy {ie, sleeve gastrectomy} (43775)	
	🚗 34.68 ⚕ 34.68 **Global Days 090**	
43845	Gastric restrictive procedure with partial gastrectomy, pylorus-preserving duodenoileostomy and ileoileostomy (50 to 100 cm common channel) to limit absorption (biliopancreatic diversion with duodenal switch)	C 80 P0
	Do not report with (43633, 43847, 44130, 49000)	
	🚗 54.18 ⚕ 54.18 **Global Days 090**	
	AMA: 2005, May, 3-6	
43846	Gastric restrictive procedure, with gastric bypass for morbid obesity; with short limb (150 cm or less) Roux-en-Y gastroenterostomy	C 80 P0
	EXCLUDES Gastric bypass with Roux-en-Y gastroenterostomy performed laparoscopically (43644) More than 150 cm (43847)	
	🚗 45.04 ⚕ 45.04 **Global Days 090**	
	AMA: 2005, May, 3-6	
43847	with small intestine reconstruction to limit absorption	C 80 P0
	🚗 49.45 ⚕ 49.45 **Global Days 090**	
43848	Revision, open, of gastric restrictive procedure for morbid obesity, other than adjustable gastric restrictive device (separate procedure)	C 80 P0
	EXCLUDES Procedures for adjustable gastric restrictive devices (43770-43774, 43886-43888)	
	🚗 53.12 ⚕ 53.12 **Global Days 090**	
	AMA: 2006, April, 1-7	

43850-43882 Open Gastric Procedures: Closure/Implantation/Replacement/Revision

43850	Revision of gastroduodenal anastomosis (gastroduodenostomy) with reconstruction; without vagotomy	C 80 P0
	🚗 44.74 ⚕ 44.74 **Global Days 090**	
43855	with vagotomy	C 80 P0
	🚗 45.61 ⚕ 45.61 **Global Days 090**	
43860	Revision of gastrojejunal anastomosis (gastrojejunostomy) with reconstruction, with or without partial gastrectomy or intestine resection; without vagotomy	C 80 P0
	🚗 45.16 ⚕ 45.16 **Global Days 090**	
43865	with vagotomy	C 80 P0
	🚗 46.97 ⚕ 46.97 **Global Days 090**	
43870	Closure of gastrostomy, surgical	A2 T 80 P0
	🚗 19.47 ⚕ 19.47 **Global Days 090**	
43880	Closure of gastrocolic fistula	C 80 P0
	🚗 43.97 ⚕ 43.97 **Global Days 090**	

43881	Implantation or replacement of gastric neurostimulator electrodes, antrum, open	C 80
	EXCLUDES Electronic analysis / programming / reprogramming gastric neurostimulator pulse generator, lesser curvature (morbid obesity) (95980-95982) Gastric neurostimulator pulse generator programming / electronic analysis (95999) Implantation / replacement performed laparoscopically (43647) Insertion / replacement gastric neurostimulator pulse generator (64590) Laparotomy with implantation, replacement, revision, or removal of gastric stimulation electrodes, lesser curvature (0157T, 0158T)	
	🚗 0.00 ⚕ 0.00 **Global Days YYY**	
	AMA: 2007, March, 4-5	
43882	Revision or removal of gastric neurostimulator electrodes, antrum, open	C 80
	EXCLUDES Electronic analysis and programming (95980-95982) Insertion of gastric neurostimulator pulse generator (64590) Laparotomy with implantation, replacement, revision, or removal of gastric stimulation electrodes, lesser curvature (0157T, 0158T) Revision / removal gastric neurostimulator pulse generator (64595) Revision / removal performed laparoscopically (43648)	
	🚗 0.00 ⚕ 0.00 **Global Days YYY**	
	AMA: 2007, March, 4-5	

43886-43999 Bariatric Procedures: Removal/Replacement/Revision Port Components

CMS 100-3,40.5   Treatment of Obesity
CMS 100-3,100.1   Bariatric Surgery for Treatment of Morbid Obesity

43886	Gastric restrictive procedure, open; revision of subcutaneous port component only	62 T 80 P0
	🚗 9.66 ⚕ 9.66 **Global Days 090**	
	AMA: 2006, April, 1-7	
43887	removal of subcutaneous port component only	62 T 80 P0
	EXCLUDES Gastric band and subcutaneous port components: Removal and replacement (43659) Removal performed laparascopically (43774)	
	🚗 8.74 ⚕ 8.74 **Global Days 090**	
	AMA: 2006, April, 1-7	
43888	removal and replacement of subcutaneous port component only	62 T 80 P0
	EXCLUDES Gastric band and subcutaneous port components: Removal and replacement (43659) Removal performed laparoscopically (43774)	
	Do not report with (43774, 43887)	
	🚗 12.39 ⚕ 12.39 **Global Days 090**	
	AMA: 2006, April, 1-7	
43999	Unlisted procedure, stomach	T 80
	🚗 0.00 ⚕ 0.00 **Global Days YYY**	

26/TC PC/TC Comp Only   A2-Z3 ASC Pmt   50 Bilateral   ♂ Male Only   ♀ Female Only   🚗 Facility RVU   ⚕ Non-Facility RVU
AMA: CPT Asst   **MED:** Pub 100   A-Y OPPSI   80/66 Surg Assist Allowed / w/Doc   🔬 Lab Crosswalk   ☢ Radiology Crosswalk

44005-44130 Incisional and Resection Procedures of Bowel

44005 Enterolysis (freeing of intestinal adhesion) (separate procedure) [C][80][CCI][PQ]
  EXCLUDES Enterolysis performed laparoscopically (44180)
  Do not report with (45136)
  30.08 30.08 Global Days 090
  AMA: 2009, Jan, 11-31; 2008, Jan, 10-25; 2007, January, 13-27

44010 Duodenotomy, for exploration, biopsy(s), or foreign body removal [C][80][CCI][PQ]
  23.69 23.69 Global Days 090

+ **44015** Tube or needle catheter jejunostomy for enteral alimentation, intraoperative, any method (List separately in addition to primary procedure) [C][80][CCI]
  Code first the primary procedure
  3.96 3.96 Global Days ZZZ
  AMA: 2009, Jan, 11-31; 2008, Jan, 10-25; 2007, January, 13-27

44020 Enterotomy, small intestine, other than duodenum; for exploration, biopsy(s), or foreign body removal [C][80][CCI][PQ]
  26.65 26.65 Global Days 090

Anterior abdominal skin — Baker-type tube — Peritoneum — Bowel lumen
Depicted at left is a tube threaded through intestine for decompression
Note that the bowel is sutured to the abdominal wall

In 44021, a select portion of intestine is surgically approached and incised. A tube is inserted into the bowel lumen and threaded distally, often to a point of obstruction. The tube is used to decompress the bowel segment it passes through, often during or immediately following surgery for bowel obstruction.

44021 for decompression (eg, Baker tube) [C][80][CCI][PQ]
  26.84 26.84 Global Days 090

44025 Colotomy, for exploration, biopsy(s), or foreign body removal [C][80][CCI][PQ]
  INCLUDES Amussat's operation
  EXCLUDES Intestine exteriorization (Mikulicz resection with crushing of spur) (44602-44605)
  27.15 27.15 Global Days 090

44050 Reduction of volvulus, intussusception, internal hernia, by laparotomy [C][80][CCI][PQ]
  25.68 25.68 Global Days 090

44055 Correction of malrotation by lysis of duodenal bands and/or reduction of midgut volvulus (eg, Ladd procedure) [C][80][63][CCI][PQ]
  41.15 41.15 Global Days 090

44100 Biopsy of intestine by capsule, tube, peroral (1 or more specimens) [A2][T][CCI][PQ]
  3.10 3.10 Global Days 000

44110 Excision of 1 or more lesions of small or large intestine not requiring anastomosis, exteriorization, or fistulization; single enterotomy [C][80][CCI][PQ]
  23.33 23.33 Global Days 090

44111 multiple enterotomies [C][80][CCI][PQ]
  27.15 27.15 Global Days 090

44120 Enterectomy, resection of small intestine; single resection and anastomosis [C][80][CCI][PQ]
  Do not report with (45136)
  33.68 33.68 Global Days 090

+ **44121** each additional resection and anastomosis (List separately in addition to code for primary procedure) [C][80][CCI]
  Code first single resection of small intestine (44120)
  6.73 6.73 Global Days ZZZ

44125 with enterostomy [C][80][CCI][PQ]
  32.54 32.54 Global Days 090

44126 Enterectomy, resection of small intestine for congenital atresia, single resection and anastomosis of proximal segment of intestine; without tapering [C][80][63][CCI][PQ]
  67.85 67.85 Global Days 090

44127 with tapering [C][80][63][CCI][PQ]
  78.53 78.53 Global Days 090

+ **44128** each additional resection and anastomosis (List separately in addition to code for primary procedure) [C][80][63][CCI]
  Code first single resection of small intestine (44126, 44127)
  6.76 6.76 Global Days ZZZ

44130 Enteroenterostomy, anastomosis of intestine, with or without cutaneous enterostomy (separate procedure) [C][80][CCI][PQ]
  36.11 36.11 Global Days 090

44132-44137 Intestine Transplant Procedures

CMS 100-3,260.5 Intestinal and Multi-Visceral Transplantation
CMS 100-4,3,90.6 Intestinal and Multi-Visceral Transplants

44132 Donor enterectomy (including cold preservation), open; from cadaver donor [C][80][CCI][PQ]
  INCLUDES Graft:
    Cold preservation
    Harvest
  0.00 0.00 Global Days XXX

44133 partial, from living donor [C][80][CCI][PQ]
  INCLUDES Donor care
    Graft:
    Cold preservation
    Harvest
  EXCLUDES Preparation/reconstruction of backbench intestinal graft (44715, 44720, 44721)
  0.00 0.00 Global Days XXX

44135 Intestinal allotransplantation; from cadaver donor [C][80][CCI][PQ]
  INCLUDES Allograft transplantation
    Recipient care
  0.00 0.00 Global Days XXX

44136 from living donor [C][80][CCI][PQ]
  INCLUDES Allograft transplantation
    Recipient care
  0.00 0.00 Global Days XXX

44137 Removal of transplanted intestinal allograft, complete [C][80][CCI]
  EXCLUDES Partial removal of transplant allograft (44120, 44121, 44140)
  0.00 0.00 Global Days XXX

44139-44160 Colon Resection Procedures

+ **44139** Mobilization (take-down) of splenic flexure performed in conjunction with partial colectomy (List separately in addition to primary procedure) [C] [80] [■]
Code first partial colectomy (44140-44147)
🚑 3.38 ✂ 3.38 **Global Days ZZZ**
AMA: 2006, April, 1-7

44140 Colectomy, partial; with anastomosis [C] [80] [■] [P0]
EXCLUDES Partial colectomy with anastomosis performed laparoscopically (44204)
🚑 36.91 ✂ 36.91 **Global Days 090**
AMA: 2008, Nov, 7-9

44141 with skin level cecostomy or colostomy [C] [80] [■] [P0]
🚑 50.08 ✂ 50.08 **Global Days 090**
AMA: 2008, Nov, 7-9

44143 with end colostomy and closure of distal segment (Hartmann type procedure) [C] [80] [■] [P0]
EXCLUDES Laparoscopic method (44206)
🚑 45.77 ✂ 45.77 **Global Days 090**
AMA: 2008, Nov, 7-9

44144 with resection, with colostomy or ileostomy and creation of mucofistula [C] [80] [■] [P0]
🚑 48.76 ✂ 48.76 **Global Days 090**
AMA: 2008, Nov, 7-9

44145 with coloproctostomy (low pelvic anastomosis) [C] [80] [■] [P0]
EXCLUDES Laparoscopic method (44207)
🚑 45.84 ✂ 45.84 **Global Days 090**
AMA: 2008, Nov, 7-9

44146 with coloproctostomy (low pelvic anastomosis), with colostomy [C] [80] [■] [P0]
EXCLUDES Laparoscopic method (44208)
🚑 58.31 ✂ 58.31 **Global Days 090**
AMA: 2008, Nov, 7-9

44147 abdominal and transanal approach [C] [80] [■] [P0]
🚑 53.59 ✂ 53.59 **Global Days 090**
AMA: 2008, Nov, 7-9

44150 Colectomy, total, abdominal, without proctectomy; with ileostomy or ileoproctostomy [C] [80] [■] [P0]
INCLUDES Lane's operation
EXCLUDES Laparoscopic method (44210)
🚑 51.33 ✂ 51.33 **Global Days 090**
AMA: 2008, Nov, 7-9

44151 with continent ileostomy [C] [80] [■] [P0]
🚑 58.63 ✂ 58.63 **Global Days 090**
AMA: 2008, Nov, 7-9

44155 Colectomy, total, abdominal, with proctectomy; with ileostomy [C] [80] [■] [P0]
INCLUDES Miles' colectomy
EXCLUDES Laparoscopic method (44212)
🚑 57.28 ✂ 57.28 **Global Days 090**
AMA: 2008, Nov, 7-9

44156 with continent ileostomy [C] [80] [■] [P0]
🚑 63.26 ✂ 63.26 **Global Days 090**
AMA: 2008, Nov, 7-9

44157 with ileoanal anastomosis, includes loop ileostomy, and rectal mucosectomy, when performed [C] [80] [■] [P0]
🚑 60.02 ✂ 60.02 **Global Days 090**
AMA: 2008, Nov, 7-9

44158 with ileoanal anastomosis, creation of ileal reservoir (S or J), includes loop ileostomy, and rectal mucosectomy, when performed [C] [80] [■] [P0]
EXCLUDES Laparoscopic method (44211)
🚑 61.32 ✂ 61.32 **Global Days 090**
AMA: 2008, Nov, 7-9

44160 Colectomy, partial, with removal of terminal ileum with ileocolostomy [C] [80] [■] [P0]
EXCLUDES Laparoscopic method (44205)
🚑 34.20 ✂ 34.20 **Global Days 090**
AMA: 2008, Nov, 7-9

44180 Laparoscopic Enterolysis

INCLUDES Diagnostic laparoscopy when performed with a surgical laparoscopy

44180 Laparoscopy, surgical, enterolysis (freeing of intestinal adhesion) (separate procedure) [T] [80] [P0]
EXCLUDES Laparoscopic salpingolysis/ovariolysis (58660)
🚑 25.24 ✂ 25.24 **Global Days 090**
AMA: 2006, April, 1-7

44186-44238 Laparoscopic Enterostomy Procedures

INCLUDES Diagnostic laparoscopy when performed with a surgical laparoscopy

44186 Laparoscopy, surgical; jejunostomy (eg, for decompression or feeding) [T] [80] [P0]
🚑 17.82 ✂ 17.82 **Global Days 090**
AMA: 2006, April, 1-7

44187 ileostomy or jejunostomy, non-tube [C] [80] [P0]
EXCLUDES Open method (44310)
🚑 30.32 ✂ 30.32 **Global Days 090**
AMA: 2006, April, 1-7

44188 Laparoscopy, surgical, colostomy or skin level cecostomy [C] [80] [P0]
EXCLUDES Open method (44320)
Do not report with (44970)
🚑 33.55 ✂ 33.55 **Global Days 090**
AMA: 2009, Jan, 11-31; 2008, Jan, 10-25; 2007, January, 13-27; 2006, April, 1-7; 2006, April, 19-20

44202 Laparoscopy, surgical; enterectomy, resection of small intestine, single resection and anastomosis [C] [80] [■] [P0]
EXCLUDES Open method (44120)
🚑 38.22 ✂ 38.22 **Global Days 090**
AMA: 2006, April, 1-7; 2005, December, 9-11

+ **44203** each additional small intestine resection and anastomosis (List separately in addition to code for primary procedure) [C] [80] [■]
EXCLUDES Open method (44121)
Code first single resection of small intestine (44202)
🚑 6.76 ✂ 6.76 **Global Days ZZZ**

44204 colectomy, partial, with anastomosis [C] [80] [■] [P0]
EXCLUDES Open method (44140)
🚑 42.57 ✂ 42.57 **Global Days 090**
AMA: 2009, Jan, 11-31; 2008, Jan, 10-25; 2007, January, 13-27; 2006, April, 1-7; 2006, April, 19-20

44205 colectomy, partial, with removal of terminal ileum with ileocolostomy [C] [80] [■] [P0]
EXCLUDES Open method (44160)
🚑 37.07 ✂ 37.07 **Global Days 090**
AMA: 2006, April, 1-7

Current Procedural Coding Expert – Digestive

44206 colectomy, partial, with end colostomy and closure of distal segment (Hartmann type procedure) [T][80][P0]
EXCLUDES Open method (44143)
48.46 48.46 Global Days 090
AMA: 2006, April, 1-7

44207 colectomy, partial, with anastomosis, with coloproctostomy (low pelvic anastomosis) [T][80][P0]
EXCLUDES Open method (44145)
50.71 50.71 Global Days 090
AMA: 2006, April, 1-7

44208 colectomy, partial, with anastomosis, with coloproctostomy (low pelvic anastomosis) with colostomy [T][80][P0]
EXCLUDES Open method (44146)
55.17 55.17 Global Days 090
AMA: 2006, April, 1-7

44210 colectomy, total, abdominal, without proctectomy, with ileostomy or ileoproctostomy [C][80][P0]
EXCLUDES Open method (44150)
49.59 49.59 Global Days 090

44211 colectomy, total, abdominal, with proctectomy, with ileoanal anastomosis, creation of ileal reservoir (S or J), with loop ileostomy, includes rectal mucosectomy, when performed [C][80][P0]
EXCLUDES Open method (44157, 44158)
61.85 61.85 Global Days 090

44212 colectomy, total, abdominal, with proctectomy, with ileostomy [C][80][P0]
EXCLUDES Open method (44155)
56.99 56.99 Global Days 090

+ 44213 Laparoscopy, surgical, mobilization (take-down) of splenic flexure performed in conjunction with partial colectomy (List separately in addition to primary procedure) [T][80]
EXCLUDES Open method (44139)
Code first partial colectomy (44204-44208)
5.28 5.28 Global Days ZZZ
AMA: 2009, Jan, 11-31; 2008, Jan, 10-25; 2007, January, 13-27; 2006, April, 19-20; 2006, April, 1-7

44227 Laparoscopy, surgical, closure of enterostomy, large or small intestine, with resection and anastomosis [C][80][P0]
EXCLUDES Open method (44625, 44626)
46.20 46.20 Global Days 090
AMA: 2006, April, 1-7

44238 Unlisted laparoscopy procedure, intestine (except rectum) [T][80][50]
0.00 0.00 Global Days YYY

44300-44346 Open Enterostomy Procedures

44300 Placement, enterostomy or cecostomy, tube open (eg, for feeding or decompression) (separate procedure) [C][80]
EXCLUDES Other colonic tube(s) placed percutaneously with fluoroscopic imaging guidance (49441-49442)
23.11 23.11 Global Days 090
AMA: 2009, Jan, 11-31; 2008, Jan, 10-25; 2007, January, 13-27

44310 Ileostomy or jejunostomy, non-tube [C][80][P0]
EXCLUDES Laparoscopic method (44187)
Do not report with (44144, 44150-44151, 44155-44156, 45113, 45119, 45136)
28.76 28.76 Global Days 090
AMA: 2009, Jan, 11-31; 2008, Jan, 10-25; 2007, January, 13-27; 2006, April, 1-7

44312 Revision of ileostomy; simple (release of superficial scar) (separate procedure) [A2][T][80][P0]
16.15 16.15 Global Days 090

44314 complicated (reconstruction in-depth) (separate procedure) [C][80][P0]
27.70 27.70 Global Days 090

44316 Continent ileostomy (Kock procedure) (separate procedure) [C][80][P0]
EXCLUDES Fiberoptic evaluation (44385)
38.76 38.76 Global Days 090

44320 Colostomy or skin level cecostomy; [C][80][P0]
EXCLUDES Laparoscopic method (44188)
Do not report with (44141, 44144, 44146, 44605, 45110, 45119, 45126, 45563, 45805, 45825, 50810, 51597, 57307, 58240)
33.00 33.00 Global Days 090
AMA: 2006, April, 1-7

44322 with multiple biopsies (eg, for congenital megacolon) (separate procedure) [C][80][P0]
26.83 26.83 Global Days 090

44340 Revision of colostomy; simple (release of superficial scar) (separate procedure) [A2][T][80][P0]
16.92 16.92 Global Days 090

44345 complicated (reconstruction in-depth) (separate procedure) [C][80][P0]
28.88 28.88 Global Days 090

In 44346, the site of the colostomy may be moved. The bowel is mobilized and trimmed of any herniations. The former site is closed.

44346 with repair of paracolostomy hernia (separate procedure) [C][80][P0]
32.58 32.58 Global Days 090

44360-44386 Endoscopy of Small Intestine

CMS 100-3,100.2 Endoscopy
INCLUDES Diagnostic endoscopy performed with a surgical endoscopy
EXCLUDES Endoscopy, upper gastrointestinal (43234-43258)

⊙ **44360** Small intestinal endoscopy, enteroscopy beyond second portion of duodenum, not including ileum; diagnostic, with or without collection of specimen(s) by brushing or washing (separate procedure) [A2][T]
4.27 4.27 Global Days 000

⊙ **44361** with biopsy, single or multiple [A2][T]
4.70 4.70 Global Days 000

● New Code ▲ Revised Code M Maternity A Age Unlisted Not Covered # Resequenced
CCI + Add-on ⊘ Mod 51 Exempt ⊚ Mod 63 Exempt ⊙ Mod Sedation PQRI

© 2009 Publisher (Blue Ink) CPT only © 2009 American Medical Association. All Rights Reserved. (Black Ink) Medicare (Red Ink) 159

	44363	with removal of foreign body [A2] [T] [80]
⊙		5.62 5.62 Global Days 000
⊙	44364	with removal of tumor(s), polyp(s), or other lesion(s) by snare technique [A2] [T] [80]
		6.02 6.02 Global Days 000
⊙	44365	with removal of tumor(s), polyp(s), or other lesion(s) by hot biopsy forceps or bipolar cautery [A2] [T] [80]
		5.38 5.38 Global Days 000
⊙	44366	with control of bleeding (eg, injection, bipolar cautery, unipolar cautery, laser, heater probe, stapler, plasma coagulator) [A2] [T]
		7.07 7.07 Global Days 000
⊙	44369	with ablation of tumor(s), polyp(s), or other lesion(s) not amenable to removal by hot biopsy forceps, bipolar cautery or snare technique [A2] [T] [80]
		7.24 7.24 Global Days 000
⊙	44370	with transendoscopic stent placement (includes predilation) [A2] [T] [80]
		Code also (C1874, C1875, C1876, C1877, C2617, C2625)
		7.82 7.82 Global Days 000
⊙	44372	with placement of percutaneous jejunostomy tube [A2] [T]
		7.02 7.02 Global Days 000
⊙	44373	with conversion of percutaneous gastrostomy tube to percutaneous jejunostomy tube [A2] [T]
		EXCLUDES Jejunostomy, fiberoptic, through stoma (43235)
		5.62 5.62 Global Days 000
⊙	44376	Small intestinal endoscopy, enteroscopy beyond second portion of duodenum, including ileum; diagnostic, with or without collection of specimen(s) by brushing or washing (separate procedure) [A2] [T] [80]
		8.33 8.33 Global Days 000
⊙	44377	with biopsy, single or multiple [A2] [T] [80]
		8.78 8.78 Global Days 000
⊙	44378	with control of bleeding (eg, injection, bipolar cautery, unipolar cautery, laser, heater probe, stapler, plasma coagulator) [A2] [T] [80]
		11.25 11.25 Global Days 000
⊙	44379	with transendoscopic stent placement (includes predilation) [A2] [T] [80]
		Code also (C1874, C1875, C1876, C1877, C2617, C2625)
		11.96 11.96 Global Days 000
⊙	44380	Ileoscopy, through stoma; diagnostic, with or without collection of specimen(s) by brushing or washing (separate procedure) [A2] [T]
		1.85 1.85 Global Days 000
⊙	44382	with biopsy, single or multiple [A2] [T]
		2.22 2.22 Global Days 000
⊙	44383	with transendoscopic stent placement (includes predilation) [A2] [T]
		Code also (C1874, C1875, C1876, C1877, C2617, C2625)
		4.52 4.52 Global Days 000
⊙	44385	Endoscopic evaluation of small intestinal (abdominal or pelvic) pouch; diagnostic, with or without collection of specimen(s) by brushing or washing (separate procedure) [A2] [T]
		2.94 6.56 Global Days 000
⊙	44386	with biopsy, single or multiple [A2] [T] [80]
		3.49 8.76 Global Days 000

44388-44397 Colonoscopy Via Stoma

CMS 100-3,100.2   Endoscopy
INCLUDES   Diagnostic endoscopy when performed with a surgical endoscopy
EXCLUDES   Endoscopy, upper gastrointestinal (43234-43258)

	44388	Colonoscopy through stoma; diagnostic, with or without collection of specimen(s) by brushing or washing (separate procedure) [A2] [T] [P0]
⊙		4.59 8.99 Global Days 000
		AMA: 2009, Jan, 11-31; 2008, Jan, 10-25
⊙	44389	with biopsy, single or multiple [A2] [T] [P0]
		5.07 10.04 Global Days 000
⊙	44390	with removal of foreign body [A2] [T] [80]
		6.18 11.81 Global Days 000
⊙	44391	with control of bleeding (eg, injection, bipolar cautery, unipolar cautery, laser, heater probe, stapler, plasma coagulator) [A2] [T] [80]
		6.87 12.65 Global Days 000
⊙	44392	with removal of tumor(s), polyp(s), or other lesion(s) by hot biopsy forceps or bipolar cautery [A2] [T] [P0]
		6.08 11.30 Global Days 000

Anatomical distribution of large bowel cancers

Cancer of the colon and rectum is a major cause of mortality in the U.S. with about 140,000 new cases identified annually; peak incidence is about 70 years of age; rectal cancer is more common among men, colon cancer among women

⊙	44393	with ablation of tumor(s), polyp(s), or other lesion(s) not amenable to removal by hot biopsy forceps, bipolar cautery or snare technique [A2] [T] [P0]
		7.66 13.00 Global Days 000
⊙	44394	with removal of tumor(s), polyp(s), or other lesion(s) by snare technique [A2] [T]
		EXCLUDES Colonoscopy / rectum (45330-45385)
		7.05 12.80 Global Days 000
⊙	44397	with transendoscopic stent placement (includes predilation) [A2] [T]
		Code also (C1874, C1875-C1877, C2617, C2625)
		7.53 7.53 Global Days 000

44500 Gastrointestinal Intubation

⊘ ⊙	44500	Introduction of long gastrointestinal tube (eg, Miller-Abbott) (separate procedure) [G2] [T] [80] [P0]
		EXCLUDES Placement of oro- or naso-gastric tube (43752)
		74340
		0.68 0.68 Global Days 000

CURRENT PROCEDURAL CODING EXPERT – Digestive

44602-44680 Open Repair Procedures of Intestines

44602 Suture of small intestine (enterorrhaphy) for perforated ulcer, diverticulum, wound, injury or rupture; single perforation
38.99 38.99 Global Days 090

44603 multiple perforations
44.72 44.72 Global Days 090

44604 Suture of large intestine (colorrhaphy) for perforated ulcer, diverticulum, wound, injury or rupture (single or multiple perforations); without colostomy
29.12 29.12 Global Days 090

44605 with colostomy
36.06 36.06 Global Days 090

44615 Intestinal stricturoplasty (enterotomy and enterorrhaphy) with or without dilation, for intestinal obstruction
29.63 29.63 Global Days 090

44620 Closure of enterostomy, large or small intestine;
23.88 23.88 Global Days 090

44625 with resection and anastomosis other than colorectal
EXCLUDES Laparoscopic method (44227)
28.17 28.17 Global Days 090

44626 with resection and colorectal anastomosis (eg, closure of Hartmann type procedure)
EXCLUDES Laparoscopic method (44227)
44.42 44.42 Global Days 090

44640 Closure of intestinal cutaneous fistula
38.70 38.70 Global Days 090

44650 Closure of enteroenteric or enterocolic fistula
40.05 40.05 Global Days 090

44660 Closure of enterovesical fistula; without intestinal or bladder resection
EXCLUDES Closure of fistula:
Gastrocolic (43880)
Rectovesical (45800, 45805)
Renocolic (50525, 50526)
36.95 36.95 Global Days 090

44661 with intestine and/or bladder resection
EXCLUDES Closure of fistula:
Gastrocolic (43880)
Rectovesical (45800, 45805)
Renocolic (50525, 50526)
42.99 42.99 Global Days 090

44680 Intestinal plication (separate procedure)
INCLUDES Noble intestinal plication
29.56 29.56 Global Days 090

44700-44701 Other Intestinal Procedures

44700 Exclusion of small intestine from pelvis by mesh or other prosthesis, or native tissue (eg, bladder or omentum)
EXCLUDES Therapeutic radiation clinical treatment (77261-77799)
28.13 28.13 Global Days 090

+ 44701 Intraoperative colonic lavage (List separately in addition to code for primary procedure)
Code first as appropriate (44140, 44145, 44150, 44604)
Do not report with (44300, 44950-44960)
4.66 4.66 Global Days ZZZ

44715-44799 Backbench Transplant Procedures

CMS 100-3,260.5 Intestinal and Multi-Visceral Transplantation
CMS 100-4,3,90.6 Intestinal and Multi-Visceral Transplants

44715 Backbench standard preparation of cadaver or living donor intestine allograft prior to transplantation, including mobilization and fashioning of the superior mesenteric artery and vein
INCLUDES Mobilization/fashioning of superior mesenteric vein/artery
0.00 0.00 Global Days XXX

44720 Backbench reconstruction of cadaver or living donor intestine allograft prior to transplantation; venous anastomosis, each
7.08 7.08 Global Days XXX

44721 arterial anastomosis, each
10.66 10.66 Global Days XXX
AMA: 2005, April, 10-12

44799 Unlisted procedure, intestine
0.00 0.00 Global Days YYY
AMA: 2009, Jan, 11-31; 2008, Jan, 10-25; 2008, May, 9-11; 2008, Nov, 10-11; 2007, January, 13-27

44800-44899 Meckel's Diverticulum and Mesentery Procedures

44800 Excision of Meckel's diverticulum (diverticulectomy) or omphalomesenteric duct
20.82 20.82 Global Days 090

44820 Excision of lesion of mesentery (separate procedure)
EXCLUDES Resection of intestine (44120-44128, 44140-44160)
23.00 23.00 Global Days 090

44850 Suture of mesentery (separate procedure)
EXCLUDES Internal hernia repair/reduction (44050)
20.35 20.35 Global Days 090

44899 Unlisted procedure, Meckel's diverticulum and the mesentery
0.00 0.00 Global Days YYY

44900-44979 Open and Endoscopic Appendix Procedures

44900 Incision and drainage of appendiceal abscess; open
21.18 21.18 Global Days 090

⊙ **44901** percutaneous
75989
4.65 21.84 Global Days 000

44950 — Current Procedural Coding Expert – Digestive

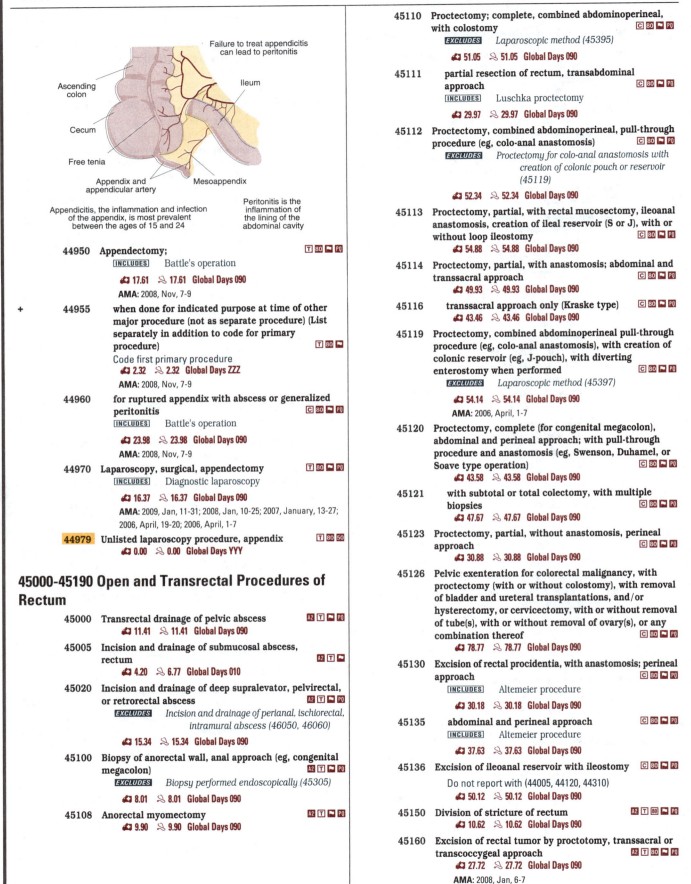

44950	**Appendectomy;** [T][80]
	INCLUDES: Battle's operation
	17.61 / 17.61 Global Days 090
	AMA: 2008, Nov, 7-9
+**44955**	when done for indicated purpose at time of other major procedure (not as separate procedure) (List separately in addition to code for primary procedure) [T][80]
	Code first primary procedure
	2.32 / 2.32 Global Days ZZZ
	AMA: 2008, Nov, 7-9
44960	for ruptured appendix with abscess or generalized peritonitis [C][80][P0]
	INCLUDES: Battle's operation
	23.98 / 23.98 Global Days 090
	AMA: 2008, Nov, 7-9
44970	**Laparoscopy, surgical, appendectomy** [T][80][P0]
	INCLUDES: Diagnostic laparoscopy
	16.37 / 16.37 Global Days 090
	AMA: 2009, Jan, 11-31; 2008, Jan, 10-25; 2007, January, 13-27; 2006, April, 19-20; 2006, April, 1-7
44979	Unlisted laparoscopy procedure, appendix [T][80][50]
	0.00 / 0.00 Global Days YYY

45000-45190 Open and Transrectal Procedures of Rectum

45000	**Transrectal drainage of pelvic abscess** [A2][T][P0]
	11.41 / 11.41 Global Days 090
45005	**Incision and drainage of submucosal abscess, rectum** [A2][T]
	4.20 / 6.77 Global Days 010
45020	**Incision and drainage of deep supralevator, pelvirectal, or retrorectal abscess** [A2][T][P0]
	EXCLUDES: Incision and drainage of perianal, ischiorectal, intramural abscess (46050, 46060)
	15.34 / 15.34 Global Days 090
45100	**Biopsy of anorectal wall, anal approach (eg, congenital megacolon)** [A2][T][P0]
	EXCLUDES: Biopsy performed endoscopically (45305)
	8.01 / 8.01 Global Days 090
45108	**Anorectal myomectomy** [A2][T][P0]
	9.90 / 9.90 Global Days 090
45110	**Proctectomy; complete, combined abdominoperineal, with colostomy** [C][80][P0]
	EXCLUDES: Laparoscopic method (45395)
	51.05 / 51.05 Global Days 090
45111	partial resection of rectum, transabdominal approach [C][80][P0]
	INCLUDES: Luschka proctectomy
	29.97 / 29.97 Global Days 090
45112	**Proctectomy, combined abdominoperineal, pull-through procedure (eg, colo-anal anastomosis)** [C][80][P0]
	EXCLUDES: Proctectomy for colo-anal anastomosis with creation of colonic pouch or reservoir (45119)
	52.34 / 52.34 Global Days 090
45113	**Proctectomy, partial, with rectal mucosectomy, ileoanal anastomosis, creation of ileal reservoir (S or J), with or without loop ileostomy** [C][80][P0]
	54.88 / 54.88 Global Days 090
45114	**Proctectomy, partial, with anastomosis; abdominal and transsacral approach** [C][80][P0]
	49.93 / 49.93 Global Days 090
45116	transsacral approach only (Kraske type) [C][80][P0]
	43.46 / 43.46 Global Days 090
45119	**Proctectomy, combined abdominoperineal pull-through procedure (eg, colo-anal anastomosis), with creation of colonic reservoir (eg, J-pouch), with diverting enterostomy when performed** [C][80][P0]
	EXCLUDES: Laparoscopic method (45397)
	54.14 / 54.14 Global Days 090
	AMA: 2006, April, 1-7
45120	**Proctectomy, complete (for congenital megacolon), abdominal and perineal approach; with pull-through procedure and anastomosis (eg, Swenson, Duhamel, or Soave type operation)** [C][80][P0]
	43.58 / 43.58 Global Days 090
45121	with subtotal or total colectomy, with multiple biopsies [C][80][P0]
	47.67 / 47.67 Global Days 090
45123	**Proctectomy, partial, without anastomosis, perineal approach** [C][80][P0]
	30.88 / 30.88 Global Days 090
45126	**Pelvic exenteration for colorectal malignancy, with proctectomy (with or without colostomy), with removal of bladder and ureteral transplantations, and/or hysterectomy, or cervicectomy, with or without removal of tube(s), with or without removal of ovary(s), or any combination thereof** [C][80][P0]
	78.77 / 78.77 Global Days 090
45130	**Excision of rectal procidentia, with anastomosis; perineal approach** [C][80][P0]
	INCLUDES: Altemeier procedure
	30.18 / 30.18 Global Days 090
45135	abdominal and perineal approach [C][80][P0]
	INCLUDES: Altemeier procedure
	37.63 / 37.63 Global Days 090
45136	**Excision of ileoanal reservoir with ileostomy** [C][80][P0]
	Do not report with (44005, 44120, 44310)
	50.12 / 50.12 Global Days 090
45150	**Division of stricture of rectum** [A2][T][80][P0]
	10.62 / 10.62 Global Days 090
45160	**Excision of rectal tumor by proctotomy, transsacral or transcoccygeal approach** [A2][T][80][P0]
	27.72 / 27.72 Global Days 090
	AMA: 2008, Jan, 6-7

Current Procedural Coding Expert – Digestive

	~~45170~~	~~Excision of rectal tumor, transanal approach~~ To report, see code 45171-45172
●	45171	Excision of rectal tumor, transanal approach; not including muscularis propria (ie, partial thickness) [G2] [T] [80] EXCLUDES Transanal destruction of rectal tumor (45190) 🕭 16.09 ✄ 16.09 Global Days 090
●	45172	including muscularis propria (ie, full thickness) [G2] [T] [80] EXCLUDES Transanal destruction of rectal tumor (45190) 🕭 22.11 ✄ 22.11 Global Days 090
	45190	Destruction of rectal tumor (eg, electrodesiccation, electrosurgery, laser ablation, laser resection, cryosurgery) transanal approach [A2] [T] [□] [PQ] EXCLUDES Transanal excision of rectal tumor (45171-45172) 🕭 18.84 ✄ 18.84 Global Days 090 AMA: 2006, December, 10-12

45300-45327 Rigid Proctosigmoidoscopy Procedures

CMS 100-3,100.2   Endoscopy
INCLUDES Exam of:
  Rectum
  Sigmoid colon
EXCLUDES Computed tomographic colonography (74261-74263)

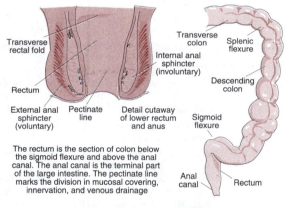

The rectum is the section of colon below the sigmoid flexure and above the anal canal. The anal canal is the terminal part of the large intestine. The pectinate line marks the division in mucosal covering, innervation, and venous drainage

	45300	Proctosigmoidoscopy, rigid; diagnostic, with or without collection of specimen(s) by brushing or washing (separate procedure) [P3] [T] [□] 🕭 1.47 ✄ 3.10 Global Days 000 AMA: 2008, Jan, 6-7; 2006, April, 1-7
⊙	45303	with dilation (eg, balloon, guide wire, bougie) [P2] [T] [□] 74360 🕭 2.52 ✄ 22.82 Global Days 000 AMA: 2008, Jan, 6-7; 2006, April, 1-7
⊙	45305	with biopsy, single or multiple [A2] [T] [□] 🕭 2.16 ✄ 4.88 Global Days 000 AMA: 2008, Jan, 6-7; 2006, April, 1-7
⊙	45307	with removal of foreign body [A2] [T] [80] [□] 🕭 2.84 ✄ 5.64 Global Days 000 AMA: 2008, Jan, 6-7; 2006, April, 1-7
⊙	45308	with removal of single tumor, polyp, or other lesion by hot biopsy forceps or bipolar cautery [A2] [T] [□] 🕭 2.39 ✄ 5.33 Global Days 000 AMA: 2008, Jan, 6-7; 2006, April, 1-7
⊙	45309	with removal of single tumor, polyp, or other lesion by snare technique [A2] [T] [□] 🕭 2.54 ✄ 5.51 Global Days 000 AMA: 2008, Jan, 6-7; 2006, April, 1-7
⊙	45315	with removal of multiple tumors, polyps, or other lesions by hot biopsy forceps, bipolar cautery or snare technique [A2] [T] [□] 🕭 3.00 ✄ 5.91 Global Days 000 AMA: 2008, Jan, 6-7; 2006, April, 1-7
⊙	45317	with control of bleeding (eg, injection, bipolar cautery, unipolar cautery, laser, heater probe, stapler, plasma coagulator) [A2] [T] [□] 🕭 3.27 ✄ 6.01 Global Days 000 AMA: 2008, Jan, 6-7; 2006, April, 1-7
⊙	45320	with ablation of tumor(s), polyp(s), or other lesion(s) not amenable to removal by hot biopsy forceps, bipolar cautery or snare technique (eg, laser) [A2] [T] [□] 🕭 2.97 ✄ 5.63 Global Days 000 AMA: 2008, Jan, 6-7; 2006, April, 1-7
⊙	45321	with decompression of volvulus [A2] [T] [□] 🕭 2.95 ✄ 2.95 Global Days 000 AMA: 2008, Jan, 6-7; 2006, April, 1-7
⊙	45327	with transendoscopic stent placement (includes predilation) [A2] [T] [□] Code also (C1874, C1875, C1876, C1877, C2617, C2625) 🕭 3.46 ✄ 3.46 Global Days 000 AMA: 2008, Jan, 6-7; 2006, April, 1-7

45330-45345 Flexible Sigmoidoscopy Procedures

CMS 100-3,100.2   Endoscopy
INCLUDES Exam of:
  Entire rectum
  Entire sigmoid colon
  Portion of descending colon (may include)
EXCLUDES Computed tomographic colonography (74261-74263)

	45330	Sigmoidoscopy, flexible; diagnostic, with or without collection of specimen(s) by brushing or washing (separate procedure) [P3] [T] [□] 🕭 1.72 ✄ 3.51 Global Days 000 AMA: 2009, Jan, 11-31; 2008, Jan, 10-25; 2007, May, 9-11; 2005, May, 3-6
	45331	with biopsy, single or multiple [A2] [T] [□] 🕭 2.04 ✄ 4.22 Global Days 000 AMA: 2009, Jan, 11-31; 2008, Jan, 10-25; 2007, January, 28-31
⊙	45332	with removal of foreign body [A2] [T] [□] 🕭 3.01 ✄ 7.17 Global Days 000
⊙	45333	with removal of tumor(s), polyp(s), or other lesion(s) by hot biopsy forceps or bipolar cautery [A2] [T] [□] 🕭 3.01 ✄ 7.30 Global Days 000
⊙	45334	with control of bleeding (eg, injection, bipolar cautery, unipolar cautery, laser, heater probe, stapler, plasma coagulator) [A2] [T] [□] 🕭 4.46 ✄ 4.46 Global Days 000 AMA: 2009, Jan, 11-31; 2008, Jan, 10-25; 2007, January, 28-31
⊙	45335	with directed submucosal injection(s), any substance [A2] [T] [□] 🕭 2.50 ✄ 6.46 Global Days 000 AMA: 2009, Jan, 11-31; 2008, Jan, 10-25; 2007, January, 13-27
⊙	45337	with decompression of volvulus, any method [A2] [T] [□] 🕭 3.90 ✄ 3.90 Global Days 000
⊙	45338	with removal of tumor(s), polyp(s), or other lesion(s) by snare technique [A2] [T] [□] 🕭 3.86 ✄ 7.95 Global Days 000

● New Code   ▲ Revised Code   Ⓜ Maternity   Ⓐ Age   Unlisted   Not Covered   # Resequenced
□ CCI   + Add-on   ⊘ Mod 51 Exempt   ⊕ Mod 63 Exempt   ⊙ Mod Sedation   PQ PQRI

© 2009 Publisher (Blue Ink)   CPT only © 2009 American Medical Association. All Rights Reserved. (Black Ink)   Medicare (Red Ink)

Current Procedural Coding Expert – Digestive

45339	with ablation of tumor(s), polyp(s), or other lesion(s) not amenable to removal by hot biopsy forceps, bipolar cautery or snare technique [A2][T][▢] 💰 5.10 ⚕ 8.66 Global Days 000
45340	with dilation by balloon, 1 or more strictures [A2][T][▢] Do not report with (45345) 💰 3.16 ⚕ 11.58 Global Days 000
45341	with endoscopic ultrasound examination [A2][T][▢] Do not report with (76942, 76975) 💰 4.27 ⚕ 4.27 Global Days 000 **AMA:** 2009, Mar, 8-9; 2005, May, 3-6
45342	with transendoscopic ultrasound guided intramural or transmural fine needle aspiration/biopsy(s) [A2][T][▢] **EXCLUDES** Transrectal ultrasound with rigid probe device (76872) Do not report with (76942, 76975) ■ 88172-88173 💰 6.51 ⚕ 6.51 Global Days 000 **AMA:** 2009, Mar, 8-9; 2005, May, 3-6
45345	with transendoscopic stent placement (includes predilation) [A2][T][▢] Code also (C1874, C1875, C1876, C1877, C2617, C2625) 💰 4.75 ⚕ 4.75 Global Days 000

45355-45392 Flexible and Rigid Colonoscopy Procedures

CMS 100-3,100.2   Endoscopy

INCLUDES   Exam of:
Entire colon (rectum to cecum)
Terminal ileum (may include)

EXCLUDES   Computed tomographic colonography (74261-74263)

45355	Colonoscopy, rigid or flexible, transabdominal via colotomy, single or multiple [A2][T][▢][PQ] **EXCLUDES** Colonoscopy, fiberoptic, past 25cm to splenic flexure (45330-45345) 💰 5.63 ⚕ 5.63 Global Days 000
45378	Colonoscopy, flexible, proximal to splenic flexure; diagnostic, with or without collection of specimen(s) by brushing or washing, with or without colon decompression (separate procedure) [A2][T][▢][PQ] 💰 5.94 ⚕ 10.01 Global Days 000 **AMA:** 2005, May, 3-6; 2005, March, 11-15
45379	with removal of foreign body [A2][T][▢] 💰 7.46 ⚕ 12.82 Global Days 000
45380	with biopsy, single or multiple [A2][T][▢][PQ] 💰 7.09 ⚕ 11.91 Global Days 000 **AMA:** 2009, Jan, 11-31; 2008, Jan, 10-25; 2007, January, 13-27
45381	with directed submucosal injection(s), any substance [A2][T][▢][PQ] 💰 6.71 ⚕ 11.53 Global Days 000 **AMA:** 2009, Jan, 11-31; 2008, Jan, 10-25; 2007, January, 13-27
45382	with control of bleeding (eg, injection, bipolar cautery, unipolar cautery, laser, heater probe, stapler, plasma coagulator) [A2][T][▢] 💰 9.02 ⚕ 15.43 Global Days 000
45383	with ablation of tumor(s), polyp(s), or other lesion(s) not amenable to removal by hot biopsy forceps, bipolar cautery or snare technique [A2][T][▢][PQ] 💰 9.24 ⚕ 14.61 Global Days 000
45384	with removal of tumor(s), polyp(s), or other lesion(s) by hot biopsy forceps or bipolar cautery [A2][T][▢][PQ] 💰 7.46 ⚕ 11.99 Global Days 000 **AMA:** 2009, Jan, 11-31; 2008, Jan, 10-25; 2007, January, 13-27
45385	with removal of tumor(s), polyp(s), or other lesion(s) by snare technique [A2][T][▢][PQ] **EXCLUDES** Endoscopy, small intestine/stomal (44360-44393) 💰 8.42 ⚕ 13.48 Global Days 000 **AMA:** 2009, Jan, 11-31; 2008, Jan, 10-25; 2007, January, 13-27; 2005, March, 11-15
45386	with dilation by balloon, 1 or more strictures [A2][T][▢] Do not report with (45387) 💰 7.28 ⚕ 16.35 Global Days 000
45387	with transendoscopic stent placement (includes predilation) [A2][T][▢] Code also (C1874, C1875, C1876, C1877, C2617, C2625) 💰 9.46 ⚕ 9.46 Global Days 000
45391	with endoscopic ultrasound examination [A2][T][▢] Do not report with (45330, 45341-45342, 45378, 76872) 💰 8.09 ⚕ 8.09 Global Days 000 **AMA:** 2005, May, 3-6
45392	with transendoscopic ultrasound guided intramural or transmural fine needle aspiration/biopsy(s) [A2][T][▢] Do not report with (45330, 45341-45342, 45378, 76872) 💰 10.35 ⚕ 10.35 Global Days 000 **AMA:** 2005, May, 3-6

45395-45499 Laparoscopic Procedures of Rectum

INCLUDES   Diagnostic laparoscopy

45395	Laparoscopy, surgical; proctectomy, complete, combined abdominoperineal, with colostomy [C][80][PQ] **EXCLUDES** Open method (45110) 💰 55.00 ⚕ 55.00 Global Days 090 **AMA:** 2006, April, 1-7
45397	proctectomy, combined abdominoperineal pull-through procedure (eg, colo-anal anastomosis), with creation of colonic reservoir (eg, J-pouch), with diverting enterostomy, when performed [C][80][PQ] **EXCLUDES** Open method (45119) 💰 59.57 ⚕ 59.57 Global Days 090 **AMA:** 2009, Jan, 11-31; 2008, Jan, 10-25; 2007, January, 13-27; 2006, April, 19-20; 2006, April, 1-7
45400	proctopexy (for prolapse) [C][80][PQ] **EXCLUDES** Open method (45540, 45541) 💰 31.85 ⚕ 31.85 Global Days 090 **AMA:** 2006, April, 1-7
45402	proctopexy (for prolapse), with sigmoid resection [C][80][PQ] **EXCLUDES** Open method (45550) 💰 42.47 ⚕ 42.47 Global Days 090 **AMA:** 2006, April, 1-7
45499	Unlisted laparoscopy procedure, rectum [T][80] 💰 0.00 ⚕ 0.00 Global Days YYY

45500-45825 Open Repairs of Rectum

45500	Proctoplasty; for stenosis [A2][T][80][▢][PQ] 💰 14.19 ⚕ 14.19 Global Days 090
45505	for prolapse of mucous membrane [A2][T][▢][PQ] 💰 15.90 ⚕ 15.90 Global Days 090

---

[26]/[TC] PC/TC Comp Only   [A2]-[Z3] ASC Pmt   [50] Bilateral   ♂ Male Only   ♀ Female Only   💰 Facility RVU   ⚕ Non-Facility RVU
AMA: CPT Asst   **MED:** Pub 100   [A]-[Y] OPPSI   [80]/[80] Surg Assist Allowed / w/Doc   ■ Lab Crosswalk   ▢ Radiology Crosswalk

Current Procedural Coding Expert – Digestive

45520	Perirectal injection of sclerosing solution for prolapse
	1.09 3.82 Global Days 000
	AMA: 2009, Jan, 11-31; 2008, Jan, 10-25; 2007, January, 13-27
45540	Proctopexy (eg, for prolapse); abdominal approach
	EXCLUDES Laparoscopic method (45400)
	29.24 29.24 Global Days 090
45541	perineal approach
	25.45 25.45 Global Days 090
45550	with sigmoid resection, abdominal approach
	INCLUDES Frickman proctopexy
	EXCLUDES Laparoscopic method (45402)
	40.53 40.53 Global Days 090
45560	Repair of rectocele (separate procedure)
	EXCLUDES Posterior colporrhaphy with rectocele repair (57250)
	19.11 19.11 Global Days 090
45562	Exploration, repair, and presacral drainage for rectal injury;
	30.44 30.44 Global Days 090
45563	with colostomy
	INCLUDES Maydl colostomy
	44.92 44.92 Global Days 090

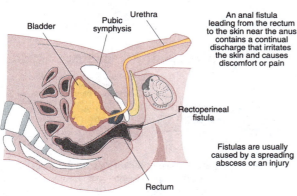

An anal fistula leading from the rectum to the skin near the anus contains a continual discharge that irritates the skin and causes discomfort or pain

Fistulas are usually caused by a spreading abscess or an injury

45800	Closure of rectovesical fistula;
	32.72 32.72 Global Days 090
45805	with colostomy
	39.84 39.84 Global Days 090
45820	Closure of rectourethral fistula;
	EXCLUDES Closure of fistula, rectovaginal (57300-57308)
	30.85 30.85 Global Days 090
45825	with colostomy
	EXCLUDES Closure of fistula, rectovaginal (57300-57308)
	40.34 40.34 Global Days 090

45900-45999 Closed Procedures of Rectum With Anesthesia

45900	Reduction of procidentia (separate procedure) under anesthesia
	5.47 5.47 Global Days 010
45905	Dilation of anal sphincter (separate procedure) under anesthesia other than local
	4.54 4.54 Global Days 010
45910	Dilation of rectal stricture (separate procedure) under anesthesia other than local
	5.24 5.24 Global Days 010
45915	Removal of fecal impaction or foreign body (separate procedure) under anesthesia
	6.00 8.33 Global Days 010
	AMA: 2009, Jan, 11-31; 2008, Jan, 10-25; 2007, January, 13-27; 2006, June, 16-17
45990	Anorectal exam, surgical, requiring anesthesia (general, spinal, or epidural), diagnostic
	INCLUDES Diagnostic: Anoscopy Proctoscopy, rigid Exam: Pelvic (when performed) Perineal, external Rectal, digital
	Do not report with (45300-45327, 46600, 57410, 99170)
	2.97 2.97 Global Days 000
	AMA: 2009, Jan, 11-31; 2008, Jan, 10-25; 2007, January, 13-27; 2006, April, 1-7; 2006, May, 16-20
45999	Unlisted procedure, rectum
	0.00 0.00 Global Days YYY
	AMA: 2006, April, 1-7

46020-46083 Surgical Incision of Anus

EXCLUDES Cryosurgical destruction of hemorrhoid(s) (46999)
Fistulotomy, subcutaneous (46270)
Hemorrhoidopexy ([46947])
Injection of hemorrhoid(s) (46500)
Thermal energy destruction of internal hemorrhoid(s) (46930)

46020	Placement of seton
	Do not report with (46060, 46280, 46600)
	6.26 7.23 Global Days 010
46030	Removal of anal seton, other marker
	2.43 3.59 Global Days 010
46040	Incision and drainage of ischiorectal and/or perirectal abscess (separate procedure)
	10.99 13.79 Global Days 090
46045	Incision and drainage of intramural, intramuscular, or submucosal abscess, transanal, under anesthesia
	11.59 11.59 Global Days 090
46050	Incision and drainage, perianal abscess, superficial
	EXCLUDES Incision and drainage abscess Ischiorectal/intramural (46060) Supralevator/pelvirectal/retrorectal (45020)
	2.60 5.06 Global Days 010
46060	Incision and drainage of ischiorectal or intramural abscess, with fistulectomy or fistulotomy, submuscular, with or without placement of seton
	EXCLUDES Incision and drainage abscess Supralevator/pelvirectal/retrorectal (45020)
	Do not report with (46020)
	12.70 12.70 Global Days 090
46070	Incision, anal septum (infant)
	EXCLUDES Anoplasty (46700-46705)
	5.77 5.77 Global Days 090
46080	Sphincterotomy, anal, division of sphincter (separate procedure)
	4.35 6.47 Global Days 010

● New Code ▲ Revised Code M Maternity A Age Unlisted Not Covered # Resequenced
CCI + Add-on ⊘ Mod 51 Exempt ⊘ Mod 63 Exempt ⊙ Mod Sedation PQRI
© 2009 Publisher (Blue Ink) CPT only © 2009 American Medical Association. All Rights Reserved. (Black Ink) Medicare (Red Ink)

46083   **Current Procedural Coding Expert – Digestive**

46083   Incision of thrombosed hemorrhoid, external
     2.86   4.43   Global Days 010
     AMA: 2009, Jan, 11-31; 2008, Jan, 10-25; 2007, January, 13-27

46200-46262 [46220, 46320, 46945, 46946] Anal Resection and Hemorrhoidectomies

EXCLUDES *Cryosurgical destruction of hemorrhoid(s) (46999)*
Hemorrhoidopexy ([46947])
Injection of hemorrhoid(s) (46500)
Thermal energy destruction of internal hemorrhoid(s) (46930)

▲ 46200   Fissurectomy, including sphincterotomy, when performed
    8.51   11.30   Global Days 090

~~46210~~   ~~Cryptectomy; single~~
    To report, see code 46999

~~46211~~   ~~multiple (separate procedure)~~
    To report, see code 46999

46220   Resequenced code. See code above 46230.

▲ 46221   Hemorrhoidectomy, internal, by rubber band ligation(s)
    5.05   6.91   Global Days 010

#▲ 46945   Hemorrhoidectomy, internal, by ligation other than rubber band; single hemorrhoid column/group
    EXCLUDES *Other hemorrhoid procedures:*
       Destruction (46930)
       Excision (46250-46262)
       Injection sclerosing solution (46500)
    5.83   7.74   Global Days 090

#▲ 46946   2 or more hemorrhoid columns/groups
    5.87   7.88   Global Days 090

#▲ 46220   Excision of single external papilla or tag, anus
    3.19   5.26   Global Days 010

▲ 46230   Excision of multiple external papillae or tags, anus
    4.69   7.09   Global Days 010

#▲ 46320   Excision of thrombosed hemorrhoid, external
    3.00   4.71   Global Days 010

▲ 46250   Hemorrhoidectomy, external, 2 or more columns/groups
    EXCLUDES *Hemorrhoidectomy, external, single column/group (46999)*
    8.38   11.85   Global Days 090

▲ 46255   Hemorrhoidectomy, internal and external, single column/group;
    9.49   13.07   Global Days 090

▲ 46257   with fissurectomy
    11.33   11.33   Global Days 090

▲ 46258   with fistulectomy, including fissurectomy, when performed
    12.57   12.57   Global Days 090

▲ 46260   Hemorrhoidectomy, internal and external, 2 or more columns/groups;
    INCLUDES Whitehead hemorrhoidectomy
    12.76   12.76   Global Days 090

▲ 46261   with fissurectomy
    14.29   14.29   Global Days 090

▲ 46262   with fistulectomy, including fissurectomy, when performed
    14.89   14.89   Global Days 090
    AMA: 2005, May, 3-6

46270-46320 Resection of Anal Fistula

46270   Surgical treatment of anal fistula (fistulectomy/fistulotomy); subcutaneous
    10.39   13.10   Global Days 090

▲ 46275   intersphincteric
    11.03   13.93   Global Days 090

▲ 46280   transsphincteric, suprasphincteric, extrasphincteric or multiple, including placement of seton, when performed
    Do not report with (46020)
    12.54   12.54   Global Days 090

46285   second stage
    11.01   13.83   Global Days 090

46288   Closure of anal fistula with rectal advancement flap
    14.75   14.75   Global Days 090

46320   Resequenced code. See code following 46230.

46500 Other Hemorrhoid Procedures

Varicose veins commonly develop in the lower legs, particularly in the elderly, when impaired valves cause the vessels to swell and become inflamed; the risk of clot formation increases with inflamed veins; thrombophlebitis is the inflammation which may result in blood clots in veins

Rectum
Valve cusps become incompetent in the varicose vein causing blood to pool
Anal sphincter
Internal hemorrhoid
External hemorrhoid
Thrombus (blood clot)

Varicose veins and hemorrhoids (varicose rectal veins) are often associated; internal hemorrhoids (also called piles) are varicosities of the tributaries of the superior rectal veins and are covered by mucous membranes; external hemorrhoids are of the inferior rectal veins and are covered by skin

46500   Injection of sclerosing solution, hemorrhoids
    3.45   6.01   Global Days 010
    AMA: 2005, May, 3-6

46505 Chemodenervation Anal Sphincter

46505   Chemodenervation of internal anal sphincter
    EXCLUDES *Chemodenervation of:*
       Extremity/trunk muscles (64614)
       Muscles/facial nerve (64612)
       Neck muscles (64613)
       Other peripheral nerve/branch (64640)
    Code also drug(s)/substance(s) given
    6.42   7.52   Global Days 010
    AMA: 2006, April, 1-7

46600-46615 Anoscopic Procedures

CMS 100-3,100.2   Endoscopy

46600   Anoscopy; diagnostic, with or without collection of specimen(s) by brushing or washing (separate procedure)
    Do not report with (46020)
    1.09   2.19   Global Days 000
    AMA: 2006, April, 1-7

PC/TC Comp Only   ASC Pmt   Bilateral   ♂ Male Only   ♀ Female Only   Facility RVU   Non-Facility RVU
AMA: CPT Asst   **MED:** Pub 100   OPPSI   Surg Assist Allowed / w/Doc   Lab Crosswalk   Radiology Crosswalk

Current Procedural Coding Expert – Digestive

46604	with dilation (eg, balloon, guide wire, bougie) P3 T
	INCLUDES Diagnostic anosocpy (46600)
	1.81 14.76 Global Days 000
46606	with biopsy, single or multiple P3 T
	INCLUDES Diagnostic anoscopy (46600)
	2.09 5.60 Global Days 000
46608	with removal of foreign body A2 T 80
	INCLUDES Diagnostic anoscopy (46600)
	2.17 5.81 Global Days 000
46610	with removal of single tumor, polyp, or other lesion by hot biopsy forceps or bipolar cautery A2 T
	INCLUDES Diagnostic anoscopy (46600)
	2.23 5.68 Global Days 000
46611	with removal of single tumor, polyp, or other lesion by snare technique A2 T 80
	INCLUDES Diagnostic anoscopy (46600)
	2.22 4.39 Global Days 000
46612	with removal of multiple tumors, polyps, or other lesions by hot biopsy forceps, bipolar cautery or snare technique A2 T 80
	INCLUDES Diagnostic anoscopy (46600)
	2.59 6.65 Global Days 000
46614	with control of bleeding (eg, injection, bipolar cautery, unipolar cautery, laser, heater probe, stapler, plasma coagulator) P3 T
	INCLUDES Diagnostic anoscopy (46600)
	1.76 3.25 Global Days 000
46615	with ablation of tumor(s), polyp(s), or other lesion(s) not amenable to removal by hot biopsy forceps, bipolar cautery or snare technique A2 T 80
	INCLUDES Diagnostic anoscopy (46600)
	2.55 3.71 Global Days 000

46700-46947 [46947] Anal Repairs and Stapled Hemorrhoidpexy

46700	Anoplasty, plastic operation for stricture; adult A2 T
	17.72 17.72 Global Days 090
46705	infant C 80 63
	EXCLUDES Anal septum incision (46070)
	13.03 13.03 Global Days 090
46706	Repair of anal fistula with fibrin glue A2 T
	4.54 4.54 Global Days 010
● 46707	Repair of anorectal fistula with plug (eg, porcine small intestine submucosa [SIS]) G2 T 80
	12.31 12.31 Global Days 090
46710	Repair of ileoanal pouch fistula/sinus (eg, perineal or vaginal), pouch advancement; transperineal approach C 80
	30.00 30.00 Global Days 090
	AMA: 2006, April, 1-7
46712	combined transperineal and transabdominal approach C 80
	55.61 55.61 Global Days 090
	AMA: 2006, April, 1-7
46715	Repair of low imperforate anus; with anoperineal fistula (cut-back procedure) ♀ C 80 P0
	12.92 12.92 Global Days 090
46716	with transposition of anoperineal or anovestibular fistula ♀ C 80 63 P0
	29.12 29.12 Global Days 090
46730	Repair of high imperforate anus without fistula; perineal or sacroperineal approach C 80 63 P0
	57.02 57.02 Global Days 090
46735	combined transabdominal and sacroperineal approaches C 80 63 P0
	56.06 56.06 Global Days 090
46740	Repair of high imperforate anus with rectourethral or rectovaginal fistula; perineal or sacroperineal approach C 80 63 P0
	58.28 58.28 Global Days 090
46742	combined transabdominal and sacroperineal approaches C 80 63 P0
	67.70 67.70 Global Days 090
46744	Repair of cloacal anomaly by anorectovaginoplasty and urethroplasty, sacroperineal approach ♀ C 80 63 P0
	92.63 92.63 Global Days 090
46746	Repair of cloacal anomaly by anorectovaginoplasty and urethroplasty, combined abdominal and sacroperineal approach; ♀ C 80 P0
	97.63 97.63 Global Days 090
46748	with vaginal lengthening by intestinal graft or pedicle flaps ♀ C 80 P0
	106.09 106.09 Global Days 090
46750	Sphincteroplasty, anal, for incontinence or prolapse; adult A2 T 80 P0
	20.86 20.86 Global Days 090
46751	child A C 80
	16.14 16.14 Global Days 090
46753	Graft (Thiersch operation) for rectal incontinence and/or prolapse A2 T P0
	15.86 15.86 Global Days 090
46754	Removal of Thiersch wire or suture, anal canal A2 T 80
	6.12 7.64 Global Days 010
46760	Sphincteroplasty, anal, for incontinence, adult; muscle transplant A2 T 80 P0
	29.88 29.88 Global Days 090
46761	levator muscle imbrication (Park posterior anal repair) A2 T 80 P0
	25.68 25.68 Global Days 090
46762	implantation artificial sphincter A2 T 80 P0
	25.23 25.23 Global Days 090
# 46947	**Hemorrhoidopexy (eg, for prolapsing internal hemorrhoids) by stapling** A2 T
	10.32 10.32 Global Days 090
	AMA: 2009, Jan, 11-31; 2008, Jan, 10-25; 2007, January, 13-27; 2005, May, 13-14; 2005, May, 3-6

46900-46999 Destruction Procedures: Anus

46900	Destruction of lesion(s), anus (eg, condyloma, papilloma, molluscum contagiosum, herpetic vesicle), simple; chemical P3 T
	3.73 6.17 Global Days 010
46910	electrodesiccation P3 T
	3.64 6.49 Global Days 010
46916	cryosurgery P2 T
	3.87 5.89 Global Days 010
46917	laser surgery A2 T
	3.58 11.28 Global Days 010
46922	surgical excision A2 T
	3.65 6.78 Global Days 010

46924 — Current Procedural Coding Expert – Digestive

46924 Destruction of lesion(s), anus (eg, condyloma, papilloma, molluscum contagiosum, herpetic vesicle), extensive (eg, laser surgery, electrosurgery, cryosurgery, chemosurgery) [A2] [T]
  5.04 13.41 Global Days 010

46930 Destruction of internal hemorrhoid(s) by thermal energy (eg, infrared coagulation, cautery, radiofrequency) [P3] [T] [80]
  EXCLUDES Other hemorrhoid procedures:
    Cryosurgery destruction (46999)
    Destruction with heat (46930)
    Excision ([46320], 46250-46262)
    Hemorrhoidopexy ([46947])
    Incision (46083)
    Injection sclerosing solution (46500)
    Ligation (46221, [46945, 46946])
  3.69 4.99 Global Days 090

~~46937~~ ~~Cryosurgery of rectal tumor; benign~~
  To report, see code 45190

~~46938~~ ~~malignant~~
  To report, see code 45190

46940 Curettage or cautery of anal fissure, including dilation of anal sphincter (separate procedure); initial [P3] [T]
  4.02 5.96 Global Days 010

46942 subsequent [P3] [T] [80]
  3.60 5.61 Global Days 010

46945 Resequenced code. See code range 46221-46230.
46946 Resequenced code. See code range 46221-46230.
46947 Resequenced code. See code following 46762.

46999 Unlisted procedure, anus [T] [80]
  0.00 0.00 Global Days YYY

47000-47001 Needle Biopsy of Liver
EXCLUDES Fine needle aspiration (10021, 10022)

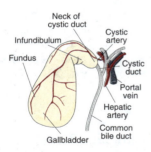

The liver is divided into four lobes for descriptive purposes, although the left and right halves are functionally separate, each receiving its own arterial supply and venous drainage. The liver is the largest gland in the body and serves many metabolic purposes including secretion of bile. The gallbladder is located on the visceral side of the quadrate lobe and stores bile between active phases of digestion; positions of the sac and its structures vary

47000 Biopsy of liver, needle; percutaneous [A2] [T]
   88172-88173
   76942, 77002, 77012, 77021
  2.64 8.94 Global Days 000
  AMA: 2009, Jan, 11-31; 2008, Jan, 10-25; 2007, June, 10-11

+ **47001** when done for indicated purpose at time of other major procedure (List separately in addition to code for primary procedure) [M] [N]
  Code first primary procedure
   88172-88173
   76942, 77002
  2.87 2.87 Global Days ZZZ
  AMA: 2009, Jan, 11-31; 2008, Jan, 10-25; 2007, June, 10-11

47010-47130 Open Incisional and Resection Procedures of Liver

47010 Hepatotomy; for open drainage of abscess or cyst, 1 or 2 stages [C] [80] [P0]
  32.66 32.66 Global Days 090

⊙ **47011** for percutaneous drainage of abscess or cyst, 1 or 2 stages [T]
   75989
  5.06 5.06 Global Days 000

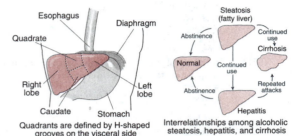

Quadrants are defined by H-shaped grooves on the visceral side

Interrelationships among alcoholic steatosis, hepatitis, and cirrhosis

The liver is the largest gland in the body and serves many metabolic purposes including secretion of bile. Chronic alcohol use leads to three similar forms of alcoholic liver disease: steatosis (fatty liver), hepatitis, and cirrhosis. The conditions have many overlapping features and each may occur without involvement of alcohol. Alcoholic cirrhosis accounts for about 60 percent of all cirrhosis cases and the risk appears to rise with the amount of alcohol consumed daily. The liver tends to shrink and become fibrotic

47015 Laparotomy, with aspiration and/or injection of hepatic parasitic (eg, amoebic or echinococcal) cyst(s) or abscess(es) [C] [80]
  31.69 31.69 Global Days 090

47100 Biopsy of liver, wedge [C] [80] [P0]
  22.93 22.93 Global Days 090

47120 Hepatectomy, resection of liver; partial lobectomy [C] [80] [P0]
  63.91 63.91 Global Days 090
  AMA: 2009, Jan, 11-31; 2008, Jan, 10-25; 2007, January, 13-27

47122 trisegmentectomy [C] [80] [P0]
  94.59 94.59 Global Days 090

47125 total left lobectomy [C] [80] [P0]
  84.70 84.70 Global Days 090

47130 total right lobectomy [C] [80] [P0]
  90.83 90.83 Global Days 090

CURRENT PROCEDURAL CODING EXPERT – Digestive

47399

47133-47147 Liver Transplant Procedures

CMS 100-3,260.1   Adult Liver Transplantation
CMS 100-3,260.2   Pediatric Liver Transplantation
CMS 100-4,3,90.4   Liver Transplants
CMS 100-4,3,90.4.1   Standard Liver Acquisition Charge
CMS 100-4,3,90.4.2   Billing for Liver Transplant and Acquisition Services
CMS 100-4,3,90.6   Intestinal and Multi-Visceral Transplants

47133   Donor hepatectomy (including cold preservation), from cadaver donor
    INCLUDES   Graft:
                  Cold preservation
                  Harvest
    0.00   0.00   Global Days XXX

47135   Liver allotransplantation; orthotopic, partial or whole, from cadaver or living donor, any age
    INCLUDES   Partial/whole recipient hepatectomy
                  Partial/whole transplant of allograft
                  Recipient care
    134.48   134.48   Global Days 090

47136   heterotopic, partial or whole, from cadaver or living donor, any age
    INCLUDES   Partial/whole recipient hepatectomy
                  Partial/whole transplant of allograft
                  Recipient care
    115.14   115.14   Global Days 090

47140   Donor hepatectomy (including cold preservation), from living donor; left lateral segment only (segments II and III)
    INCLUDES   Donor care
                  Graft:
                  Cold preservation
                  Harvest
    97.79   97.79   Global Days 090

47141   total left lobectomy (segments II, III and IV)
    INCLUDES   Donor care
                  Graft:
                  Cold preservation
                  Harvest
    107.18   107.18   Global Days 090

47142   total right lobectomy (segments V, VI, VII and VIII)
    INCLUDES   Donor care
                  Graft:
                  Cold preservation
                  Harvest
    129.06   129.06   Global Days 090

47143   Backbench standard preparation of cadaver donor whole liver graft prior to allotransplantation, including cholecystectomy, if necessary, and dissection and removal of surrounding soft tissues to prepare the vena cava, portal vein, hepatic artery, and common bile duct for implantation; without trisegment or lobe split
    Do not report with (47120-47125, 47600, 47610)
    0.00   0.00   Global Days XXX
    AMA: 2005, April, 10-12

47144   with trisegment split of whole liver graft into 2 partial liver grafts (ie, left lateral segment [segments II and III] and right trisegment [segments I and IV through VIII])
    Do not report with (47120-47125, 47600, 47610)
    0.00   0.00   Global Days 090

47145   with lobe split of whole liver graft into 2 partial liver grafts (ie, left lobe [segments II, III, and IV] and right lobe [segments I and V through VIII])
    Do not report with (47120-47125, 47600, 47610)
    0.00   0.00   Global Days XXX

47146   Backbench reconstruction of cadaver or living donor liver graft prior to allotransplantation; venous anastomosis, each
    Do not report with (47120-47125, 47600, 47610)
    9.13   9.13   Global Days XXX

47147   arterial anastomosis, each
    Do not report with (47120-47125, 47600, 47610)
    10.64   10.64   Global Days XXX

47300-47362 Open Repair of Liver

47300   Marsupialization of cyst or abscess of liver
    31.02   31.02   Global Days 090

47350   Management of liver hemorrhage; simple suture of liver wound or injury
    37.52   37.52   Global Days 090

47360   complex suture of liver wound or injury, with or without hepatic artery ligation
    50.98   50.98   Global Days 090

47361   exploration of hepatic wound, extensive debridement, coagulation and/or suture, with or without packing of liver
    83.01   83.01   Global Days 090

47362   re-exploration of hepatic wound for removal of packing
    39.39   39.39   Global Days 090

47370-47379 Laparoscopic Ablation Liver Tumors

47370   Laparoscopy, surgical, ablation of 1 or more liver tumor(s); radiofrequency
    INCLUDES   Diagnostic laparoscopy
    76940
    33.95   33.95   Global Days 090

47371   cryosurgical
    INCLUDES   Diagnostic laparoscopy
    76940
    34.40   34.40   Global Days 090

47379   Unlisted laparoscopic procedure, liver
    0.00   0.00   Global Days YYY
    AMA: 2009, Jan, 11-31; 2008, Jan, 10-25; 2007, Dec, 10-179; 2007, January, 13-27; 2006, August, 12-14

47380-47399 Open and Percutaneous Ablation of Liver Tumors

47380   Ablation, open, of 1 or more liver tumor(s); radiofrequency
    76940
    39.48   39.48   Global Days 090

47381   cryosurgical
    76940
    40.60   40.60   Global Days 090

47382   Ablation, 1 or more liver tumor(s), percutaneous, radiofrequency
    76940, 77013, 77022
    21.33   118.39   Global Days 010

47399   Unlisted procedure, liver
    0.00   0.00   Global Days YYY

● New Code   ▲ Revised Code   M Maternity   △ Age   Unlisted   Not Covered   # Resequenced
CCI   + Add-on   ⊘ Mod 51 Exempt   63 Mod 63 Exempt   ⊙ Mod Sedation   PQ PQRI

© 2009 Publisher (Blue Ink)   CPT only © 2009 American Medical Association. All Rights Reserved. (Black Ink)   Medicare (Red Ink)

47400-47490 Surgical Incision Biliary Tract

47400 Hepaticotomy or hepaticostomy with exploration, drainage, or removal of calculus [C][80][P0]
59.15　59.15　Global Days 090

47420 Choledochotomy or choledochostomy with exploration, drainage, or removal of calculus, with or without cholecystotomy; without transduodenal sphincterotomy or sphincteroplasty [C][80][P0]
36.74　36.74　Global Days 090

47425 with transduodenal sphincterotomy or sphincteroplasty [C][80][P0]
37.36　37.36　Global Days 090

47460 Transduodenal sphincterotomy or sphincteroplasty, with or without transduodenal extraction of calculus (separate procedure) [C][80][P0]
34.79　34.79　Global Days 090

The gallbladder is incised, explored, and possibly drained of infection or other fluids. Calculi, if present, are removed

Access is usually by a subcostal or upper midline incision. A drainage tube, if used, will be brought through the skin surface via a separate stab incision

47480 Cholecystotomy or cholecystostomy with exploration, drainage, or removal of calculus (separate procedure) [C][80][P0]
23.61　23.61　Global Days 090

47490 Percutaneous cholecystostomy [T]
75989
13.26　13.26　Global Days 090

47500-47530 Injection/Insertion Procedures of Biliary Tract

47500 Injection procedure for percutaneous transhepatic cholangiography [M1][N][P0]
74320
2.68　2.68　Global Days 000

47505 Injection procedure for cholangiography through an existing catheter (eg, percutaneous transhepatic or T-tube) [M1][N][80][P0]
74305
1.04　1.04　Global Days 000

47510 Introduction of percutaneous transhepatic catheter for biliary drainage [A2][T]
75980
12.61　12.61　Global Days 090

47511 Introduction of percutaneous transhepatic stent for internal and external biliary drainage [A2][T][50]
75982
15.73　15.73　Global Days 090

⊙ **47525** Change of percutaneous biliary drainage catheter [A2][T][50]
Code also (C1729)
75984
2.31　12.11　Global Days 000

47530 Revision and/or reinsertion of transhepatic tube [A2][T]
75984
9.47　34.54　Global Days 090

47550-47556 Endoscopic Procedures of the Biliary Tract

CMS 100-3,100.2　　Endoscopy

+ **47550** Biliary endoscopy, intraoperative (choledochoscopy) (List separately in addition to code for primary procedure) [C][80]
Code first primary procedure
4.59　4.59　Global Days ZZZ

47552 Biliary endoscopy, percutaneous via T-tube or other tract; diagnostic, with or without collection of specimen(s) by brushing and/or washing (separate procedure) [A2][T]
8.64　8.64　Global Days 000
AMA: 2009, Jan, 11-31

47553 with biopsy, single or multiple [A2][T]
INCLUDES　Diagnostic endoscopy
8.70　8.70　Global Days 000
AMA: 2009, Jan, 11-31

47554 with removal of calculus/calculi [A2][T]
INCLUDES　Diagnostic endoscopy
13.54　13.54　Global Days 000
AMA: 2009, Jan, 11-31

47555 with dilation of biliary duct stricture(s) without stent [A2][T]
INCLUDES　Diagnostic endoscopy
10.26　10.26　Global Days 000
AMA: 2009, Jan, 11-31

47556 with dilation of biliary duct stricture(s) with stent [A2][T]
INCLUDES　Diagnostic endoscopy
EXCLUDES　Endoscopic retrograde cholangiopancreatography (ERCP) (43260-43272, 74363)
74363, 75982
11.65　11.65　Global Days 000
AMA: 2009, Jan, 11-31

47560-47579 Laparoscopic Gallbladder Procedures

CMS 100-3,100.13　　Laparoscopic Cholecystectomy
INCLUDES　Diagnostic laparoscopy

47560 Laparoscopy, surgical; with guided transhepatic cholangiography, without biopsy [A2][T][80][P0]
7.43　7.43　Global Days 000

47561 with guided transhepatic cholangiography with biopsy [A2][T][80][P0]
8.12　8.12　Global Days 000

47562 cholecystectomy [G2][T][80][P0]
20.44　20.44　Global Days 090
AMA: 2009, Jan, 11-31; 2007, Dec, 10-179

47563 cholecystectomy with cholangiography [G2][T][80][P0]
20.68　20.68　Global Days 090
AMA: 2009, Jan, 11-31; 2008, Jan, 10-25; 2007, Dec, 10-179; 2007, January, 13-27

47564 cholecystectomy with exploration of common duct [G2][T][80][P0]
23.67　23.67　Global Days 090
AMA: 2009, Jan, 11-31; 2007, Dec, 10-179

Current Procedural Coding Expert – Digestive

47570	cholecystoenterostomy
	21.19 21.19 Global Days 090
47579	Unlisted laparoscopy procedure, biliary tract
	0.00 0.00 Global Days YYY

47600-47620 Open Gallbladder Procedures

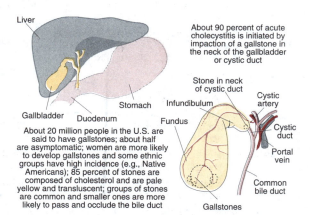

About 90 percent of acute cholecystitis is initiated by impaction of a gallstone in the neck of the gallbladder or cystic duct

About 20 million people in the U.S. are said to have gallstones; about half are asymptomatic; women are more likely to develop gallstones and some ethnic groups have high incidence (e.g., Native Americans); 85 percent of stones are composed of cholesterol and are pale yellow and translucent; groups of stones are common and smaller ones are more likely to pass and occlude the bile duct

47600	Cholecystectomy;
	EXCLUDES Laparoscopic method (47562)
	29.66 29.66 Global Days 090
47605	with cholangiography
	EXCLUDES Laparoscopic method (47564)
	26.88 26.88 Global Days 090
	AMA: 2009, Jan, 11-31; 2008, Jan, 10-25; 2007, January, 13-27
47610	Cholecystectomy with exploration of common duct;
	Code also biliary endoscopy when performed in conjunction with cholecystectomy with exploration of common duct (47550)
	34.45 34.45 Global Days 090
	AMA: 2009, Jan, 11-31; 2008, Jan, 10-25; 2007, January, 13-27
47612	with choledochoenterostomy
	34.79 34.79 Global Days 090
47620	with transduodenal sphincterotomy or sphincteroplasty, with or without cholangiography
	37.66 37.66 Global Days 090

47630-47999 Open Resection and Repair of Biliary Tract

47630	Biliary duct stone extraction, percutaneous via T-tube tract, basket, or snare (eg, Burhenne technique)
	74327
	14.88 14.88 Global Days 090
	AMA: 2009, Jan, 11-31; 2008, Jan, 10-25; 2007, January, 13-27
47700	Exploration for congenital atresia of bile ducts, without repair, with or without liver biopsy, with or without cholangiography
	28.64 28.64 Global Days 090
47701	Portoenterostomy (eg, Kasai procedure)
	47.51 47.51 Global Days 090
47711	Excision of bile duct tumor, with or without primary repair of bile duct; extrahepatic
	42.67 42.67 Global Days 090

47712	intrahepatic
	EXCLUDES Anastomosis (47760-47800)
	54.88 54.88 Global Days 090
47715	Excision of choledochal cyst
	36.33 36.33 Global Days 090
47720	Cholecystoenterostomy; direct
	EXCLUDES Laparoscopic method (47570)
	31.44 31.44 Global Days 090
47721	with gastroenterostomy
	37.00 37.00 Global Days 090
47740	Roux-en-Y
	35.84 35.84 Global Days 090
47741	Roux-en-Y with gastroenterostomy
	40.38 40.38 Global Days 090
47760	Anastomosis, of extrahepatic biliary ducts and gastrointestinal tract
	61.98 61.98 Global Days 090
47765	Anastomosis, of intrahepatic ducts and gastrointestinal tract
	INCLUDES Longmire anastomosis
	83.62 83.62 Global Days 090
47780	Anastomosis, Roux-en-Y, of extrahepatic biliary ducts and gastrointestinal tract
	68.11 68.11 Global Days 090
47785	Anastomosis, Roux-en-Y, of intrahepatic biliary ducts and gastrointestinal tract
	89.57 89.57 Global Days 090
47800	Reconstruction, plastic, of extrahepatic biliary ducts with end-to-end anastomosis
	43.26 43.26 Global Days 090
47801	Placement of choledochal stent
	27.52 27.52 Global Days 090
47802	U-tube hepaticoenterostomy
	41.73 41.73 Global Days 090
47900	Suture of extrahepatic biliary duct for pre-existing injury (separate procedure)
	37.49 37.49 Global Days 090
47999	Unlisted procedure, biliary tract
	0.00 0.00 Global Days YYY

48000-48548 Open Procedures of the Pancreas

EXCLUDES   Peroral pancreatic procedures performed endoscopically (43260-43272)

48000	Placement of drains, peripancreatic, for acute pancreatitis;
	50.68 50.68 Global Days 090
48001	with cholecystostomy, gastrostomy, and jejunostomy
	63.54 63.54 Global Days 090

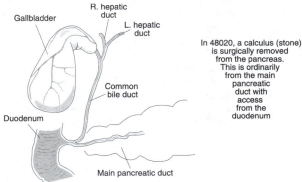

In 48020, a calculus (stone) is surgically removed from the pancreas. This is ordinarily from the main pancreatic duct with access from the duodenum

● New Code   ▲ Revised Code   Maternity   Age   Unlisted   Not Covered   # Resequenced
CCI   + Add-on   ⊘ Mod 51 Exempt   Mod 63 Exempt   ⊙ Mod Sedation   PQRI

© 2009 Publisher (Blue Ink)   CPT only © 2009 American Medical Association. All Rights Reserved. (Black Ink)   Medicare (Red Ink)

Current Procedural Coding Expert – Digestive

48020	Removal of pancreatic calculus 32.16 32.16 Global Days 090
48100	Biopsy of pancreas, open (eg, fine needle aspiration, needle core biopsy, wedge biopsy) 24.21 24.21 Global Days 090
48102	Biopsy of pancreas, percutaneous needle EXCLUDES Aspiration, fine needle (10022) 88172, 88173 76942, 77002, 77012, 77021 6.62 13.57 Global Days 010
48105	Resection or debridement of pancreas and peripancreatic tissue for acute necrotizing pancreatitis 78.56 78.56 Global Days 090
48120	Excision of lesion of pancreas (eg, cyst, adenoma) 30.38 30.38 Global Days 090
48140	Pancreatectomy, distal subtotal, with or without splenectomy; without pancreaticojejunostomy 42.92 42.92 Global Days 090
48145	with pancreaticojejunostomy 44.81 44.81 Global Days 090

48146	Pancreatectomy, distal, near-total with preservation of duodenum (Child-type procedure) 51.00 51.00 Global Days 090
48148	Excision of ampulla of Vater 34.13 34.13 Global Days 090
48150	Pancreatectomy, proximal subtotal with total duodenectomy, partial gastrectomy, choledochoenterostomy and gastrojejunostomy (Whipple-type procedure); with pancreatojejunostomy 85.41 85.41 Global Days 090
48152	without pancreatojejunostomy 79.24 79.24 Global Days 090
48153	Pancreatectomy, proximal subtotal with near-total duodenectomy, choledochoenterostomy and duodenojejunostomy (pylorus-sparing, Whipple-type procedure); with pancreatojejunostomy 85.27 85.27 Global Days 090
48154	without pancreatojejunostomy 79.59 79.59 Global Days 090
48155	Pancreatectomy, total 49.55 49.55 Global Days 090
48160	Pancreatectomy, total or subtotal, with autologous transplantation of pancreas or pancreatic islet cells 0.00 0.00 Global Days XXX

+**48400**	Injection procedure for intraoperative pancreatography (List separately in addition to code for primary procedure) Code first primary procedure 74300-74305 3.03 3.03 Global Days ZZZ AMA: 2009, Jan, 11-31; 2007, Dec, 10-179
48500	Marsupialization of pancreatic cyst 31.35 31.35 Global Days 090
48510	External drainage, pseudocyst of pancreas; open 29.57 29.57 Global Days 090
⊙ **48511**	percutaneous 75989 5.46 22.59 Global Days 000
48520	Internal anastomosis of pancreatic cyst to gastrointestinal tract; direct 30.00 30.00 Global Days 090
48540	Roux-en-Y 35.95 35.95 Global Days 090
48545	Pancreatorrhaphy for injury 36.84 36.84 Global Days 090
48547	Duodenal exclusion with gastrojejunostomy for pancreatic injury 49.25 49.25 Global Days 090
48548	Pancreaticojejunostomy, side-to-side anastomosis (Puestow-type operation) 45.59 45.59 Global Days 090

48550-48999 Pancreas Transplant Procedures

CMS 100-3,260.3 Pancreas Transplants
CMS 100-4,3,90.5 Pancreas Transplants with Kidney Transplants

48550	Donor pancreatectomy (including cold preservation), with or without duodenal segment for transplantation INCLUDES Graft: Cold preservation Harvest (with or without duodenal segment) 0.00 0.00 Global Days XXX AMA: 2005, April, 10-12
48551	Backbench standard preparation of cadaver donor pancreas allograft prior to transplantation, including dissection of allograft from surrounding soft tissues, splenectomy, duodenotomy, ligation of bile duct, ligation of mesenteric vessels, and Y-graft arterial anastomoses from iliac artery to superior mesenteric artery and to splenic artery Do not report with (35531, 35563, 35685, 38100-38102, 44010, 44820, 44850, 47460, 47505-47525, 47550-47556, 48100-48120, 48545) 0.00 0.00 Global Days XXX
48552	Backbench reconstruction of cadaver donor pancreas allograft prior to transplantation, venous anastomosis, each Do not report with (35531, 35563, 35685, 38100-38102, 44010, 44820, 44850, 47460, 47505-47525, 47550-47556, 48100-48120, 48545) 6.55 6.55 Global Days XXX
48554	Transplantation of pancreatic allograft INCLUDES Allograft transplant Recipient care 69.16 69.16 Global Days 090

PC/TC Comp Only ASC Pmt Bilateral ♂ Male Only ♀ Female Only   Facility RVU   Non-Facility RVU
AMA: CPT Asst **MED:** Pub 100 OPPSI Surg Assist Allowed / w/Doc   Lab Crosswalk   Radiology Crosswalk
CPT only © 2009 American Medical Association. All Rights Reserved. (Black Ink) Medicare (Red Ink) © 2009 Publisher (Blue Ink)

Current Procedural Coding Expert – Digestive

48556 Removal of transplanted pancreatic allograft
 34.58 34.58 Global Days 090

48999 Unlisted procedure, pancreas
 0.00 0.00 Global Days YYY
AMA: 2009, Jan, 11-31; 2007, Dec, 10-179

49000-49081 Exploratory and Drainage Procedures: Abdomen/Peritoneum

49000 Exploratory laparotomy, exploratory celiotomy with or without biopsy(s) (separate procedure)
EXCLUDES Exploration of penetrating wound without laparotomy (20102)
 21.09 21.09 Global Days 090
AMA: 2009, Jan, 11-31; 2008, Jan, 10-25; 2008, Nov, 7-9; 2007, January, 13-27; 2006, April, 11-18

49002 Reopening of recent laparotomy
EXCLUDES Hepatic wound re-exploration for packing removal (47362)
 28.75 28.75 Global Days 090
AMA: 2008, Nov, 7-9; 2006, April, 11-18

49010 Exploration, retroperitoneal area with or without biopsy(s) (separate procedure)
EXCLUDES Exploration of penetrating wound without laparotomy (20102)
 25.85 25.85 Global Days 090
AMA: 2007, June, 1-3; 2005, June, 6-8

49020 Drainage of peritoneal abscess or localized peritonitis, exclusive of appendiceal abscess; open
EXCLUDES Appendiceal abscess (44900)
 43.61 43.61 Global Days 090

49021 percutaneous
75989
 4.61 21.40 Global Days 000

49040 Drainage of subdiaphragmatic or subphrenic abscess; open
 27.42 27.42 Global Days 090

49041 percutaneous
75989
 5.45 22.20 Global Days 000

49060 Drainage of retroperitoneal abscess; open
EXCLUDES Drainage performed laparoscopically (49323)
 30.11 30.11 Global Days 090
AMA: 2009, Jan, 11-31; 2008, Jan, 10-25; 2007, January, 13-27

49061 percutaneous
EXCLUDES Drainage performed laparoscopically (49323)
75989
 5.04 21.79 Global Days 000
AMA: 2009, Jan, 11-31; 2008, Jan, 10-25; 2007, January, 13-27

49062 Drainage of extraperitoneal lymphocele to peritoneal cavity, open
 20.15 20.15 Global Days 090
AMA: 2009, Jan, 11-31; 2008, Jan, 10-25; 2007, January, 13-27

49080 Peritoneocentesis, abdominal paracentesis, or peritoneal lavage (diagnostic or therapeutic); initial
76942, 77012
 1.89 3.96 Global Days 000

49081 subsequent
76942, 77012
 1.84 4.17 Global Days 000

49180 Biopsy of Mass: Abdomen/Retroperitoneum

49180 Biopsy, abdominal or retroperitoneal mass, percutaneous needle
EXCLUDES Aspiration, fine needle (10021, 10022)
Lysis of intestinal adhesions (44005)
76942, 77002, 77012, 77021
88172, 88173
 2.37 4.06 Global Days 000

49203-49205 Open Destruction or Excision: Abdominal Tumors

EXCLUDES Cryoablation of renal tumor (50250, 50593)
Lysis of intestinal adhesions (44005)
Primary, recurrent ovarian, uterine, or tubal resection (58957-58958)

Code also colectomy (44140)
Code also small bowel resection (44120)
Code also total nephrectomy (50220, or 50240)
Code also vena caval resection with reconstruction (37799)
Do not report with (38770, 38780, 49000, 49010, 49215, 50010, 50205, 50225, 50236, 50250, 50290, 58900-58960)

49203 Excision or destruction, open, intra-abdominal tumors, cysts or endometriomas, 1 or more peritoneal, mesenteric, or retroperitoneal primary or secondary tumors; largest tumor 5 cm diameter or less
 32.78 32.78 Global Days 090

49204 largest tumor 5.1-10.0 cm diameter
 41.81 41.81 Global Days 090

49205 largest tumor greater than 10.0 cm diameter
 48.05 48.05 Global Days 090

49215 Resection Presacral/Sacrococcygeal Tumor

49215 Excision of presacral or sacrococcygeal tumor
 60.25 60.25 Global Days 090

49220-49255 Other Open Abdominal Procedures

EXCLUDES Lysis of intestinal adhesions (44005)

49220 Staging laparotomy for Hodgkins disease or lymphoma (includes splenectomy, needle or open biopsies of both liver lobes, possibly also removal of abdominal nodes, abdominal node and/or bone marrow biopsies, ovarian repositioning)
 26.52 26.52 Global Days 090

49250 Umbilectomy, omphalectomy, excision of umbilicus (separate procedure)
 15.76 15.76 Global Days 090

49255 Omentectomy, epiploectomy, resection of omentum (separate procedure)
 21.51 21.51 Global Days 090

49320-49329 Laparoscopic Procedures of the Abdomen/Peritoneum/Omentum

INCLUDES Diagnostic laparoscopy

EXCLUDES Fulguration/excision of lesions of ovary/pelvic viscera/peritoneal surface, performed laparoscopically (58662)

49320 Laparoscopy, abdomen, peritoneum, and omentum, diagnostic, with or without collection of specimen(s) by brushing or washing (separate procedure)
 8.90 8.90 Global Days 010
 AMA: 2009, Jan, 11-31; 2008, Jan, 10-25; 2007, March, 4-5; 2007, January, 13-27; 2006, April, 11-18; 2006, April, 19-20

49321 Laparoscopy, surgical; with biopsy (single or multiple)
 9.44 9.44 Global Days 010

49322 with aspiration of cavity or cyst (eg, ovarian cyst) (single or multiple)
 10.11 10.11 Global Days 010

49323 with drainage of lymphocele to peritoneal cavity
 EXCLUDES Retroperitoneal abscess drainage:
  Open (49060)
  Percutaneous (49061)
 17.37 17.37 Global Days 090
 AMA: 2009, Jan, 11-31; 2008, Jan, 10-25; 2007, January, 13-27

49324 with insertion of intraperitoneal cannula or catheter, permanent
 EXCLUDES Open approach (49421)
 Code also insertion of subcutaneous extension to intraperitoneal cannula with remote chest exit site, when appropriate (49435)
 10.82 10.82 Global Days 010

49325 with revision of previously placed intraperitoneal cannula or catheter, with removal of intraluminal obstructive material if performed
 11.57 11.57 Global Days 010

+ 49326 with omentopexy (omental tacking procedure) (List separately in addition to code for primary procedure)
 Code first laparoscopy with permanent intraperitoneal cannula or catheter insertion or revision of previously placed catheter/cannula (49324, 49325)
 5.30 5.30 Global Days ZZZ

49329 Unlisted laparoscopy procedure, abdomen, peritoneum and omentum
 0.00 0.00 Global Days YYY
 AMA: 2009, Jan, 11-31; 2008, Jan, 10-25; 2007, January, 13-27

49400-49436 Peritoneal Procedures: Insertion/Modifications/Removal

49400 Injection of air or contrast into peritoneal cavity (separate procedure)
 Code also (49446)
 2.64 4.41 Global Days 000

49402 Removal of peritoneal foreign body from peritoneal cavity
 EXCLUDES Enterolysis (44005)
 23.39 23.39 Global Days 090

49411 Placement of interstitial device(s) for radiation therapy guidance (eg, fiducial markers, dosimeter), percutaneous, intra-abdominal, intra-pelvic (except prostate), and/or retroperitoneum, single or multiple
 EXCLUDES Placement (percutaneous) of interstitial device(s) for intrathoracic radiation therapy guidance (32553)
 Code also supply of device
  76942, 77002, 77012, 77021
 5.50 13.99 Global Days 000

49419 Insertion of intraperitoneal cannula or catheter, with subcutaneous reservoir, permanent (ie, totally implantable)
 EXCLUDES Removal of catheter/cannula (49422)
 Code also (C1788)
 11.96 11.96 Global Days 090

49420 Insertion of intraperitoneal cannula or catheter for drainage or dialysis; temporary
 3.65 3.65 Global Days 000

49421 permanent
 EXCLUDES Laparoscopic approach (49324)
 Code also insertion of subcutaneous extension to intraperitoneal cannula with remote chest exit site, when appropriate (49435)
 10.41 10.41 Global Days 090
 AMA: 2009, Jan, 11-31; 2008, Jan, 10-25; 2007, January, 13-27; 2006, May, 16-20

49422 Removal of permanent intraperitoneal cannula or catheter
 EXCLUDES Removal temporary catheter or cannula (99201-99499)
 10.51 10.51 Global Days 010

49423 Exchange of previously placed abscess or cyst drainage catheter under radiological guidance (separate procedure)
 Code also drainage catheter (C1729)
  75984
 2.02 13.53 Global Days 000

49424 Contrast injection for assessment of abscess or cyst via previously placed drainage catheter or tube (separate procedure)
  76080
 1.06 3.62 Global Days 000
 AMA: 2009, Jan, 11-31; 2008, Jan, 10-25; 2007, January, 13-27

49425 Insertion of peritoneal-venous shunt
 20.59 20.59 Global Days 090

49426 Revision of peritoneal-venous shunt
 EXCLUDES Shunt patency test (78291)
 17.32 17.32 Global Days 090

49427 Injection procedure (eg, contrast media) for evaluation of previously placed peritoneal-venous shunt
  75809, 78291
 1.25 1.25 Global Days 000

49428 Ligation of peritoneal-venous shunt
 11.76 11.76 Global Days 010

49429 Removal of peritoneal-venous shunt
 12.19 12.19 Global Days 010

+ 49435 Insertion of subcutaneous extension to intraperitoneal cannula or catheter with remote chest exit site (List separately in addition to code for primary procedure)
 Code first permanent insertion of intraperitoneal catheter/cannula (49324, 49421)
 3.35 3.35 Global Days ZZZ

Current Procedural Coding Expert – Digestive

49436	Delayed creation of exit site from embedded subcutaneous segment of intraperitoneal cannula or catheter G2 T 80
	5.06 5.06 Global Days 010

49440-49442 Insertion of Percutaneous Gastrointestinal Tube

Do not report with (43752)

⊙ 49440	Insertion of gastrostomy tube, percutaneous, under fluoroscopic guidance including contrast injection(s), image documentation and report G2 T 80 P0
	EXCLUDES Gastrostomy tube to gastrojejunostomy tube when gastrostomy first placed, report 49440 and (49446)
	6.18 25.85 Global Days 010
	AMA: 2009, Jan, 11-31; 2008, Jan, 8-9; 2008, Jun, 8-11; 2007, Dec, 10-179

⊙ 49441	Insertion of duodenostomy or jejunostomy tube, percutaneous, under fluoroscopic guidance including contrast injection(s), image documentation and report G2 T 80 P0
	EXCLUDES Gastrostrostomy tube to gastrojejunostomy tube conversion (49446)
	7.01 28.08 Global Days 010
	AMA: 2009, Jan, 11-31; 2008, Jan, 8-9; 2008, Jun, 8-11; 2007, Dec, 10-179

⊙ 49442	Insertion of cecostomy or other colonic tube, percutaneous, under fluoroscopic guidance including contrast injection(s), image documentation and report G2 T 80 P0
	5.91 22.55 Global Days 010
	AMA: 2009, Jan, 11-31; 2008, Jan, 8-9; 2008, Jun, 8-11; 2007, Dec, 10-179

49446 Percutaneous Conversion: Gastrostomy to Gastro-jejunostomy Tube

⊙ 49446	Conversion of gastrostomy tube to gastro-jejunostomy tube, percutaneous, under fluoroscopic guidance including contrast injection(s), image documentation and report G2 T 80 P0
	EXCLUDES Gastrostomy tube to gastrojejunostomy tube conversion when gastrostomy tube first placed, report 49446 and (49440)
	4.53 24.01 Global Days 000
	AMA: 2009, Jan, 11-31; 2008, Jun, 8-11; 2007, Dec, 10-179

49450-49452 Replacement Gastrointestinal Tube

EXCLUDES Placement of new tube whether gastrostomy, jejunostomy, duodenostomy, gastro-jejunostomy, or cecostomy at different percutaneous site (49440-49442)

49450	Replacement of gastrostomy or cecostomy (or other colonic) tube, percutaneous, under fluoroscopic guidance including contrast injection(s), image documentation and report G2 T 80 P0
	EXCLUDES Change of gastrostomy tube, percutaneous, without imaging or endoscopic guidance (43760)
	1.88 16.02 Global Days 000
	AMA: 2008, Jun, 8-11

49451	Replacement of duodenostomy or jejunostomy tube, percutaneous, under fluoroscopic guidance including contrast injection(s), image documentation and report G2 T 80 P0
	2.55 17.44 Global Days 000
	AMA: 2009, Jan, 11-31; 2008, Jan, 8-9; 2008, Jun, 8-11; 2007, Dec, 10-179

49452	Replacement of gastro-jejunostomy tube, percutaneous, under fluoroscopic guidance including contrast injection(s), image documentation and report G2 T 80 P0
	3.92 21.57 Global Days 000
	AMA: 2008, Jun, 8-11

49460-49465 Removal of Obstruction/Injection for Contrast Through Gastrointestinal Tube

49460	Mechanical removal of obstructive material from gastrostomy, duodenostomy, jejunostomy, gastro-jejunostomy, or cecostomy (or other colonic) tube, any method, under fluoroscopic guidance including contrast injection(s), if performed, image documentation and report G2 T 80 P0
	Do not report with (49450-49452, 49465)
	1.34 17.44 Global Days 000
	AMA: 2008, Jun, 8-11

49465	Contrast injection(s) for radiological evaluation of existing gastrostomy, duodenostomy, jejunostomy, gastro-jejunostomy, or cecostomy (or other colonic) tube, from a percutaneous approach including image documentation and report N1 01 80 P0
	Do not report with (49450-49460)
	0.85 4.15 Global Days 000
	AMA: 2008, Jun, 8-11

49491-49492 Inguinal Hernia Repair on Premature Infant

INCLUDES Hernia repairs done on preterm infants younger than or equal to 50 weeks postconception age but younger than 6 months of age since birth
Initial repair: no previous repair required
Mesh or other prosthesis

EXCLUDES Abdominal wall debridement (11042, 11043)
Intra-abdominal hernia repair/reduction (44050)

Code also repair or excision of testicle(s), intestine, ovaries if performed (44120, 54520, 58940)

49491	Repair, initial inguinal hernia, preterm infant (younger than 37 weeks gestation at birth), performed from birth up to 50 weeks postconception age, with or without hydrocelectomy; reducible A T 80 50 ⊛
	21.59 21.59 Global Days 090
	AMA: 2009, Jan, 11-31; 2008, Jan, 10-25; 2008, Jun, 3-6

49492	incarcerated or strangulated A T 80 50 ⊛
	24.40 24.40 Global Days 090
	AMA: 2008, Jun, 3-6

CURRENT PROCEDURAL CODING EXPERT – Digestive

49495-49557 Hernia Repair: Femoral/Inguinal/Lumbar

INCLUDES
- Initial repair: no previous repair required
- Mesh or other prosthesis
- Recurrent repair: required previous repair(s)

EXCLUDES
- Abdominal wall debridement (11042, 11043)
- Intra-abdominal hernia repair/reduction (44050)

Code also repair or excision of testicle(s), intestine, ovaries if performed (44120, 54520, 58940)

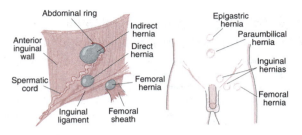

A hernia is a protrusion, usually through an abdominal wall containment. Often, hernias are congenital. Groin hernias are common among both sexes and all age groups. In males, indirect hernias are often associated with incomplete closure of the path the testicle takes as it descends just prior to birth (the processus vaginalis). Direct hernias simply protrude through the wall. Femoral hernias occur below the inguinal ligament. Strangulation and necrosis of the protruding bowel section can occur. Umbilical hernias are often linked to incomplete closure of the umbilicus.

49495 Repair, initial inguinal hernia, full term infant younger than age 6 months, or preterm infant older than 50 weeks postconception age and younger than age 6 months at the time of surgery, with or without hydrocelectomy; reducible
    INCLUDES Hernia repairs done on preterm infants older than 50 weeks postconception age and younger than 6 months
    11.09 11.09 Global Days 090
    AMA: 2009, Jan, 11-31; 2008, Jan, 10-25; 2008, Jun, 3-6; 2007, January, 13-27

49496 incarcerated or strangulated
    INCLUDES Hernia repairs done on preterm infants older than 50 weeks postconception age and younger than 6 months
    16.78 16.78 Global Days 090
    AMA: 2009, Jan, 11-31; 2008, Jan, 10-25; 2008, Jun, 3-6; 2007, January, 13-27

49500 Repair initial inguinal hernia, age 6 months to younger than 5 years, with or without hydrocelectomy; reducible
    INCLUDES Repairs performed on patients 6 months to younger than 5 years old
    11.05 11.05 Global Days 090
    AMA: 2009, Jan, 11-31; 2008, Jan, 10-25; 2008, Jun, 3-6; 2007, January, 13-27

49501 incarcerated or strangulated
    INCLUDES Repairs performed on patients 6 months to younger than 5 years old
    16.43 16.43 Global Days 090
    AMA: 2009, Jan, 11-31; 2008, Jan, 10-25; 2008, Jun, 3-6; 2007, January, 13-27

49505 Repair initial inguinal hernia, age 5 years or older; reducible
    INCLUDES MacEwen hernia repair
    Code also when performed:
      Excision of hydrocele (55040)
      Excision of spermatocele (54840)
      Simple orchiectomy (54520)
    14.12 14.12 Global Days 090
    AMA: 2009, Jan, 11-31; 2008, Jan, 10-25; 2008, Jun, 3-6; 2007, January, 13-27

49507 incarcerated or strangulated
    Code also when performed:
      Excision of hydrocele (55040)
      Excision of spermatocele (54840)
      Simple orchiectomy (54520)
    17.36 17.36 Global Days 090
    AMA: 2009, Jan, 11-31; 2008, Jan, 10-25; 2008, Jun, 3-6; 2007, January, 13-27

49520 Repair recurrent inguinal hernia, any age; reducible
    17.21 17.21 Global Days 090
    AMA: 2009, Jan, 11-31; 2008, Jan, 10-25; 2008, Jun, 3-6; 2007, January, 13-27

49521 incarcerated or strangulated
    20.90 20.90 Global Days 090
    AMA: 2009, Jan, 11-31; 2008, Jan, 10-25; 2008, Jun, 3-6; 2007, January, 13-27

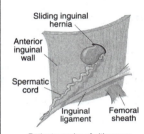
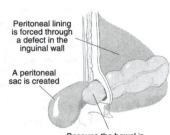

In 49525, a sliding inguinal hernia (depicted above, right) is repaired in a patient of any age

49525 Repair inguinal hernia, sliding, any age
    EXCLUDES Inguinal hernia repair, incarcerated/strangulated (49496, 49501, 49507, 49521)
    15.58 15.58 Global Days 090
    AMA: 2009, Jan, 11-31; 2008, Jan, 10-25; 2008, Jun, 3-6; 2007, January, 13-27

49540 Repair lumbar hernia
    18.43 18.43 Global Days 090
    AMA: 2008, Jun, 3-6

49550 Repair initial femoral hernia, any age; reducible
    15.67 15.67 Global Days 090
    AMA: 2008, Jun, 3-6

49553 incarcerated or strangulated
    17.19 17.19 Global Days 090
    AMA: 2008, Jun, 3-6

49555 Repair recurrent femoral hernia; reducible
    16.34 16.34 Global Days 090
    AMA: 2008, Jun, 3-6

49557 incarcerated or strangulated
    19.79 19.79 Global Days 090
    AMA: 2008, Jun, 3-6

26/TC PC/TC Comp Only	A2-Z3 ASC Pmt	50 Bilateral	♂ Male Only	♀ Female Only	Facility RVU	Non-Facility RVU
AMA: CPT Asst	MED: Pub 100	A-Y OPPSI	80/80 Surg Assist Allowed / w/Doc		Lab Crosswalk	Radiology Crosswalk

CPT only © 2009 American Medical Association. All Rights Reserved. (Black Ink) Medicare (Red Ink) © 2009 Publisher (Blue Ink)

Current Procedural Coding Expert – Digestive

49560-49568 Hernia Repair: Incisional/Ventral

INCLUDES Initial repair: no previous repair required
Recurrent repair: required previous repair(s)

EXCLUDES Abdominal wall debridement (11042, 11043)
Intra-abdominal hernia repair/reduction (44050)

Code also repair or excision of testicle(s), intestine, ovaries if performed (44120, 54520, 58940)

49560 Repair initial incisional or ventral hernia; reducible
Code also implantation of mesh or other prosthesis if performed (49568)
20.16 20.16 Global Days 090
AMA: 2008, Jun, 3-6

49561 incarcerated or strangulated
Code also implantation of mesh or other prosthesis if performed (49568)
25.48 25.48 Global Days 090
AMA: 2008, Jun, 3-6

49565 Repair recurrent incisional or ventral hernia; reducible
Code also implantation of mesh or other prosthesis if performed (49568)
20.98 20.98 Global Days 090
AMA: 2008, Jun, 3-6

49566 incarcerated or strangulated
Code also implantation of mesh or other prosthesis if performed (49568)
25.74 25.74 Global Days 090
AMA: 2008, Jun, 3-6

+ **49568** Implantation of mesh or other prosthesis for open incisional or ventral hernia repair or mesh for closure of debridement for necrotizing soft tissue infection (List separately in addition to code for the incisional or ventral hernia repair)
Code first (11004-11006, 49560-49566)
7.42 7.42 Global Days ZZZ
AMA: 2009, Jan, 11-31; 2008, Jan, 10-25; 2008, Jun, 3-6; 2007, January, 13-27; 2005, November, 14-15

49570-49590 Hernia Repair: Epigastric/Lateral Ventral/Umbilical

INCLUDES Mesh or other prosthesis

EXCLUDES Abdominal wall debridement (11042, 11043)
Intra-abdominal hernia repair/reduction (44050)

Code also repair or excision of testicle(s), intestine, ovaries if performed (44120, 54520, 58940)

49570 Repair epigastric hernia (eg, preperitoneal fat); reducible (separate procedure)
11.22 11.22 Global Days 090
AMA: 2008, Jun, 3-6

49572 incarcerated or strangulated
13.97 13.97 Global Days 090
AMA: 2008, Jun, 3-6

49580 Repair umbilical hernia, younger than age 5 years; reducible
9.93 9.93 Global Days 090
AMA: 2008, Jun, 3-6

49582 incarcerated or strangulated
13.02 13.02 Global Days 090
AMA: 2008, Jun, 3-6

49585 Repair umbilical hernia, age 5 years or older; reducible
INCLUDES Mayo hernia repair
12.01 12.01 Global Days 090
AMA: 2008, Jun, 3-6

49587 incarcerated or strangulated
14.23 14.23 Global Days 090
AMA: 2008, Jun, 3-6

49590 Repair spigelian hernia
15.54 15.54 Global Days 090
AMA: 2008, Jun, 3-6

49600-49611 Repair Birth Defect Abdominal Wall: Omphalocele/Gastroschisis

INCLUDES Mesh or other prosthesis

EXCLUDES Abdominal wall debridement (11042, 11043)
Intra-abdominal hernia repair/reduction (44050)
Repair of:
  Diaphragmatic or hiatal hernia (39502-39541)
  Omentum (49999)

49600 Repair of small omphalocele, with primary closure
19.88 19.88 Global Days 090
AMA: 2008, Jun, 3-6

49605 Repair of large omphalocele or gastroschisis; with or without prosthesis
136.23 136.23 Global Days 090
AMA: 2008, Jun, 3-6

49606 with removal of prosthesis, final reduction and closure, in operating room
31.05 31.05 Global Days 090
AMA: 2008, Jun, 3-6

49610 Repair of omphalocele (Gross type operation); first stage
18.72 18.72 Global Days 090
AMA: 2008, Jun, 3-6

49611 second stage
14.85 14.85 Global Days 090
AMA: 2009, Jan, 11-31; 2008, Jan, 10-25; 2008, Jun, 3-6

49650-49659 Laparoscopic Hernia Repair

INCLUDES Diagnostic laparoscopy

49650 Laparoscopy, surgical; repair initial inguinal hernia
11.59 11.59 Global Days 090
AMA: 2008, Jun, 3-6

49651 repair recurrent inguinal hernia
15.09 15.09 Global Days 090
AMA: 2008, Jun, 3-6

49652 Laparoscopy, surgical, repair, ventral, umbilical, spigelian or epigastric hernia (includes mesh insertion, when performed); reducible
Do not report with (44180, 49568)
20.48 20.48 Global Days 090

49653 incarcerated or strangulated
Do not report with (44180, 49568)
25.64 25.64 Global Days 090

49654 Laparoscopy, surgical, repair, incisional hernia (includes mesh insertion, when performed); reducible
Do not report with (44180, 49568)
23.53 23.53 Global Days 090

● New Code ▲ Revised Code M Maternity A Age Unlisted Not Covered # Resequenced
 CCI + Add-on ⊘ Mod 51 Exempt ⊚ Mod 63 Exempt ⊙ Mod Sedation PQRI

© 2009 Publisher (Blue Ink) CPT only © 2009 American Medical Association. All Rights Reserved. (Black Ink) Medicare (Red Ink)

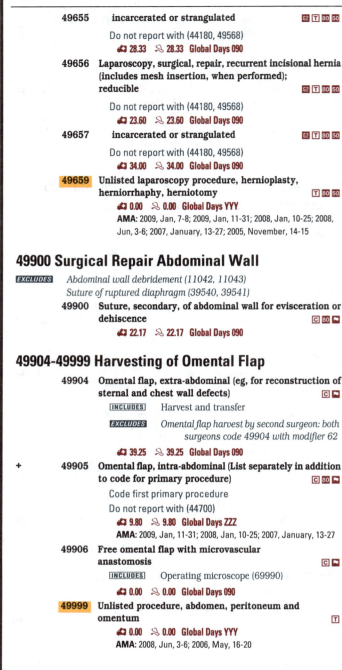

49655 incarcerated or strangulated
Do not report with (44180, 49568)
28.33 28.33 Global Days 090

49656 Laparoscopy, surgical, repair, recurrent incisional hernia (includes mesh insertion, when performed); reducible
Do not report with (44180, 49568)
23.60 23.60 Global Days 090

49657 incarcerated or strangulated
Do not report with (44180, 49568)
34.00 34.00 Global Days 090

49659 Unlisted laparoscopy procedure, hernioplasty, herniorrhaphy, herniotomy
0.00 0.00 Global Days YYY
AMA: 2009, Jan, 7-8; 2009, Jan, 11-31; 2008, Jan, 10-25; 2008, Jun, 3-6; 2007, January, 13-27; 2005, November, 14-15

49900 Surgical Repair Abdominal Wall

EXCLUDES Abdominal wall debridement (11042, 11043)
Suture of ruptured diaphragm (39540, 39541)

49900 Suture, secondary, of abdominal wall for evisceration or dehiscence
22.17 22.17 Global Days 090

49904-49999 Harvesting of Omental Flap

49904 Omental flap, extra-abdominal (eg, for reconstruction of sternal and chest wall defects)
INCLUDES Harvest and transfer
EXCLUDES Omental flap harvest by second surgeon: both surgeons code 49904 with modifier 62
39.25 39.25 Global Days 090

+ 49905 Omental flap, intra-abdominal (List separately in addition to code for primary procedure)
Code first primary procedure
Do not report with (44700)
9.80 9.80 Global Days ZZZ
AMA: 2009, Jan, 11-31; 2008, Jan, 10-25; 2007, January, 13-27

49906 Free omental flap with microvascular anastomosis
INCLUDES Operating microscope (69990)
0.00 0.00 Global Days 090

49999 Unlisted procedure, abdomen, peritoneum and omentum
0.00 0.00 Global Days YYY
AMA: 2008, Jun, 3-6; 2006, May, 16-20

Current Procedural Coding Expert – Urinary System

50010-50045 Kidney Procedures for Exploration or Drainage

EXCLUDES Retroperitoneal
 Abscess drainage (49060)
 Exploration (49010)
 Tumor/cyst excision (49203-49205)

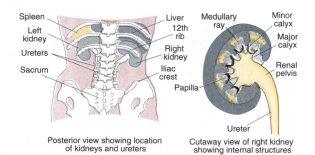

Posterior view showing location of kidneys and ureters
Cutaway view of right kidney showing internal structures

The kidneys remove waste products of protein metabolism and other excess materials and fluids from the blood. Variations in kidney anatomy are fairly common, though abnormalities can complicate procedures. "Pyelo" refers to the renal pelvis, an important access site to the inner kidney. Each kidney is imbedded in a mass of peritoneal fat that helps to enclose and position it

50010 Renal exploration, not necessitating other specific procedures
 EXCLUDES Laparoscopic ablation of mass lesions of kidney (50542)
 19.93 19.93 Global Days 090

50020 Drainage of perirenal or renal abscess; open
 28.76 28.76 Global Days 090

50021 percutaneous
 75989
 4.60 22.62 Global Days 000

50040 Nephrostomy, nephrotomy with drainage
 25.27 25.27 Global Days 090

50045 Nephrotomy, with exploration
 EXCLUDES Renal endoscopy through nephrotomy (50570-50580)
 25.48 25.48 Global Days 090

50060-50081 Treatment of Kidney Stones

CMS 100-3,230.1 Treatment of Kidney Stones
EXCLUDES Retroperitoneal
 Abscess drainage (49060)
 Exploration (49010)
 Tumor/cyst excision (49203-49205)

50060 Nephrolithotomy; removal of calculus
 31.27 31.27 Global Days 090

50065 secondary surgical operation for calculus
 33.18 33.18 Global Days 090

50070 complicated by congenital kidney abnormality
 32.53 32.53 Global Days 090

50075 removal of large staghorn calculus filling renal pelvis and calyces (including anatrophic pyelolithotomy)
 40.05 40.05 Global Days 090

50080 Percutaneous nephrostolithotomy or pyelostolithotomy, with or without dilation, endoscopy, lithotripsy, stenting, or basket extraction; up to 2 cm
 EXCLUDES Nephrostomy without nephrostolithotomy (50040, 50395, 52334)
 23.80 23.80 Global Days 090
 AMA: 2009, Jun, 10-11

50081 over 2 cm
 EXCLUDES Nephrostomy without nephrostolithotomy (50040, 50395, 52334)
 76000, 76001
 35.08 35.08 Global Days 090
 AMA: 2009, Jun, 10-11

50100 Repair of Anomalous Vessels of the Kidney

EXCLUDES Retroperitoneal:
 Abscess drainage (49060)
 Exploration (49010)
 Tumor/cyst excision (49203-49205)

50100 Transection or repositioning of aberrant renal vessels (separate procedure)
 29.43 29.43 Global Days 090

50120-50135 Procedures of Renal Pelvis

EXCLUDES Retroperitoneal:
 Abscess drainage (49060)
 Exploration (49010)
 Tumor/cyst excision (49203-49205)

50120 Pyelotomy; with exploration
 INCLUDES Gol-Vernet pyelotomy
 EXCLUDES Renal endoscopy through pyelotomy (50570-50580)
 25.97 25.97 Global Days 090

50125 with drainage, pyelostomy
 28.50 28.50 Global Days 090

50130 with removal of calculus (pyelolithotomy, pelviolithotomy, including coagulum pyelolithotomy)
 28.28 28.28 Global Days 090

50135 complicated (eg, secondary operation, congenital kidney abnormality)
 30.76 30.76 Global Days 090

50200-50205 Biopsy of Kidney

CMS 100-3,190.4 Electron Microscope
EXCLUDES Laparoscopic renal mass lesion ablation (50542)
 Retroperitoneal tumor/cyst excision (49203-49205)

50200 Renal biopsy; percutaneous, by trocar or needle
 EXCLUDES Evaluation of fine needle aspirate (88172, 88173)
 Fine needle aspiration (10022)
 76942, 77002, 77012, 77021
 3.93 14.96 Global Days 000

50205 by surgical exposure of kidney
 20.51 20.51 Global Days 090

50220-50240 Nephrectomy Procedures

EXCLUDES Retroperitoneal tumor/cyst excision (49203-49205)

50220 Nephrectomy, including partial ureterectomy, any open approach including rib resection;
 28.62 28.62 Global Days 090

● New Code ▲ Revised Code M Maternity A Age Unlisted Not Covered # Resequenced
CCI + Add-on ⊘ Mod 51 Exempt ⊚ Mod 63 Exempt ⊙ Mod Sedation PQRI

© 2009 Publisher (Blue Ink) CPT only © 2009 American Medical Association. All Rights Reserved. (Black Ink) Medicare (Red Ink)

50225 complicated because of previous surgery on same kidney [C][80][50][▪][P0]
    🔁 32.97   ✂ 32.97 **Global Days 090**

50230 radical, with regional lymphadenectomy and/or vena caval thrombectomy [C][80][50][▪][P0]
   EXCLUDES   Vena caval resection with reconstruction (37799)
    🔁 35.28   ✂ 35.28 **Global Days 090**

50234 Nephrectomy with total ureterectomy and bladder cuff; through same incision [C][80][▪][P0]
    🔁 35.79   ✂ 35.79 **Global Days 090**

50236 through separate incision [C][80][▪][P0]
    🔁 40.25   ✂ 40.25 **Global Days 090**

50240 Nephrectomy, partial [C][80][▪][P0]
   EXCLUDES   Laparoscopic partial nephrectomy (50543)
    🔁 36.35   ✂ 36.35 **Global Days 090**
   AMA: 2005, April, 10-12

50250-50290 Open Removal Kidney Lesions

50250 Ablation, open, 1 or more renal mass lesion(s), cryosurgical, including intraoperative ultrasound, if performed [C][80]
   EXCLUDES   Cryoablation of renal tumors (50593)
                 Laparoscopic renal mass lesion ablation (50542)
                 Open destruction or excision intra-abdominal tumors (49203-49205)
    🔁 33.49   ✂ 33.49 **Global Days 090**
   AMA: 2009, Jan, 11-31; 2008, Jan, 10-25; 2007, January, 13-27; 2006, May, 16-20

50280 Excision or unroofing of cyst(s) of kidney [C][80][▪]
   EXCLUDES   Renal cyst laparoscopic ablation (50541)
    🔁 26.13   ✂ 26.13 **Global Days 090**

50290 Excision of perinephric cyst [C][80][▪]
   EXCLUDES   Open destruction or excision intra-abdominal tumors (49203-49205)
    🔁 24.54   ✂ 24.54 **Global Days 090**

50300-50380 Kidney Transplant Procedures

CMS 100-3,20.3   Thoracic Duct Drainage (TDD) in Renal Transplants
CMS 100-3,110.16   Nonselective (Random) Transfusions and Living-Related Donor Specific Transfusions (DST) in Kidney Transplantation
CMS 100-3,190.1   Histocompatibility Testing
CMS 100-3,260.7   Lymphocyte Immune Globulin, Anti-Thymocyte Globulin (Equine)
CMS 100-4,3,90.1   Kidney Transplant - General
CMS 100-4,3,90.1.1   Standard Kidney Acquisition Charge
CMS 100-4,3,90.1.2   Billing for Kidney Transplant and Acquisition Services
EXCLUDES   Lymphocele drainage to peritoneal cavity performed laparoscopically (49323)

50300 Donor nephrectomy (including cold preservation); from cadaver donor, unilateral or bilateral [C][▪][P0]
   INCLUDES   Graft:
                 Cold preservation
                 Harvesting
    🔁 0.00   ✂ 0.00 **Global Days XXX**
   AMA: 2005, April, 10-12

50320 open, from living donor [C][80][50][▪][P0]
   INCLUDES   Donor care
                 Graft:
                     Cold preservation
                     Harvesting
   EXCLUDES   Donor nephrectomy performed laparoscopically (50547)
    🔁 38.64   ✂ 38.64 **Global Days 090**

50323 Backbench standard preparation of cadaver donor renal allograft prior to transplantation, including dissection and removal of perinephric fat, diaphragmatic and retroperitoneal attachments, excision of adrenal gland, and preparation of ureter(s), renal vein(s), and renal artery(s), ligating branches, as necessary [C][80][▪]
   Do not report with (60540, 60545)
    🔁 0.00   ✂ 0.00 **Global Days XXX**
   AMA: 2005, April, 10-12

50325 Backbench standard preparation of living donor renal allograft (open or laparoscopic) prior to transplantation, including dissection and removal of perinephric fat and preparation of ureter(s), renal vein(s), and renal artery(s), ligating branches, as necessary [C][80][▪]
    🔁 0.00   ✂ 0.00 **Global Days XXX**

50327 Backbench reconstruction of cadaver or living donor renal allograft prior to transplantation; venous anastomosis, each [C][80][▪]
    🔁 6.01   ✂ 6.01 **Global Days XXX**

50328 arterial anastomosis, each [C][80][▪]
    🔁 5.23   ✂ 5.23 **Global Days XXX**

50329 ureteral anastomosis, each [C][80][▪]
    🔁 4.83   ✂ 4.83 **Global Days XXX**

50340 Recipient nephrectomy (separate procedure) [C][80][50][▪][P0]
    🔁 25.61   ✂ 25.61 **Global Days 090**

50360 Renal allotransplantation, implantation of graft; without recipient nephrectomy [C][80][▪][P0]
   INCLUDES   Allograft transplantation
                 Recipient care
    🔁 69.97   ✂ 69.97 **Global Days 090**

50365 with recipient nephrectomy [C][80][50][▪][P0]
   INCLUDES   Allograft transplantation
                 Recipient care
    🔁 77.99   ✂ 77.99 **Global Days 090**
   AMA: 2005, April, 10-12

50370 Removal of transplanted renal allograft [C][80][▪][P0]
    🔁 32.52   ✂ 32.52 **Global Days 090**

50380 Renal autotransplantation, reimplantation of kidney [C][80][▪][P0]
   INCLUDES   Reimplantation of autograft
   Code also nephrolithotomy (50060-50075)
   Code also partial nephrectomy (50240, 50543)
    🔁 54.16   ✂ 54.16 **Global Days 090**
   AMA: 2005, April, 10-12

[26/TC] PC/TC Comp Only   [A2-Z3] ASC Pmt   [50] Bilateral   ♂ Male Only   ♀ Female Only   🔁 Facility RVU   ✂ Non-Facility RVU
AMA: CPT Asst   **MED:** Pub 100   [A-Y] OPPSI   [80/80] Surg Assist Allowed / w/Doc   📘 Lab Crosswalk   📕 Radiology Crosswalk
CPT only © 2009 American Medical Association. All Rights Reserved. (Black Ink)   Medicare (Red Ink)   © 2009 Publisher (Blue Ink)

Current Procedural Coding Expert – Urinary System

50382-50386 Removal With/Without Replacement Internal Ureteral Stent

INCLUDES   Radiological supervision and interpretation

⊙ **50382** Removal (via snare/capture) and replacement of internally dwelling ureteral stent via percutaneous approach, including radiological supervision and interpretation
EXCLUDES   *Removal and replacement of an internally dwelling ureteral stent using a transurethral approach (50385)*
Do not report with (50395)
7.58 29.50 Global Days 000
AMA: 2008, Oct, 8-9; 2006, September, 1-4

⊙ **50384** Removal (via snare/capture) of internally dwelling ureteral stent via percutaneous approach, including radiological supervision and interpretation
EXCLUDES   *Removal of an internally dwelling ureteral stent using a transurethral approach (50386)*
Do not report with (50395)
6.89 24.02 Global Days 000
AMA: 2008, Oct, 8-9; 2006, September, 1-4

⊙ **50385** Removal (via snare/capture) and replacement of internally dwelling ureteral stent via transurethral approach, without use of cystoscopy, including radiological supervision and interpretation
6.36 28.80 Global Days 000
AMA: 2008, Oct, 8-9

⊙ **50386** Removal (via snare/capture) of internally dwelling ureteral stent via transurethral approach, without use of cystoscopy, including radiological supervision and interpretation
4.82 19.00 Global Days 000
AMA: 2008, Oct, 8-9

50387 Remove/Replace Accessible Ureteral Stent

CMS 100-4,4,61.2 Requirements for Specific Procedures to be Reported With Device Codes
EXCLUDES   *Removal and replacement of ureterostomy tube or externally accessible ureteral stent via ileal conduit (50688)*
Removal without replacement of externally accessible ureteral stent without fluoroscopic guidance (99201-99499)

⊙ **50387** Removal and replacement of externally accessible transnephric ureteral stent (eg, external/internal stent) requiring fluoroscopic guidance, including radiological supervision and interpretation
Code also (C1875, C1877, C2617, C2625)
2.73 13.53 Global Days 000
AMA: 2006, September, 1-4

50389-50398 Percutaneous and Injection Procedures With/Without Indwelling Tube/Catheter Access

50389 Removal of nephrostomy tube, requiring fluoroscopic guidance (eg, with concurrent indwelling ureteral stent)
EXCLUDES   *Nephrostomy tube removal without fluoroscopic guidance (99201-99499)*
1.50 7.16 Global Days 000
AMA: 2006, September, 1-4

50390 Aspiration and/or injection of renal cyst or pelvis by needle, percutaneous
88172-88173
74425, 74470, 76942, 77002, 77012, 77021
2.67 2.67 Global Days 000
AMA: 2008, Oct, 8-9; 2005, October, 18-22

50391 Instillation(s) of therapeutic agent into renal pelvis and/or ureter through established nephrostomy, pyelostomy or ureterostomy tube (eg, anticarcinogenic or antifungal agent)
2.80 3.36 Global Days 000
AMA: 2005, October, 18-22

50392 Introduction of intracatheter or catheter into renal pelvis for drainage and/or injection, percutaneous
74475, 76942, 77012
4.87 4.87 Global Days 000
AMA: 2008, Oct, 8-9; 2005, October, 18-22

50393 Introduction of ureteral catheter or stent into ureter through renal pelvis for drainage and/or injection, percutaneous
74480, 76942, 77002, 77012
5.93 5.93 Global Days 000
AMA: 2005, October, 18-22

50394 Injection procedure for pyelography (as nephrostogram, pyelostogram, antegrade pyeloureterograms) through nephrostomy or pyelostomy tube, or indwelling ureteral catheter
74425
1.31 2.48 Global Days 000
AMA: 2005, October, 18-22

50395 Introduction of guide into renal pelvis and/or ureter with dilation to establish nephrostomy tract, percutaneous
EXCLUDES   *Percutaneous nephrostolithotomy (50080, 50081)*
Renal endoscopy (50551-50561)
Retrograde percutaneous nephrostomy (52334)
74475, 74480, 74485
4.90 4.90 Global Days 000
AMA: 2009, Jan, 7-8; 2006, September, 1-4; 2005, October, 18-22

50396 Manometric studies through nephrostomy or pyelostomy tube, or indwelling ureteral catheter
74425, 74475, 74480
3.11 3.11 Global Days 000

50398 Change of nephrostomy or pyelostomy tube
Code also (C1729)
75984
2.03 12.32 Global Days 000
AMA: 2005, October, 18-22

50400-50540 Open Surgical Procedures of Kidney

50400 Pyeloplasty (Foley Y-pyeloplasty), plastic operation on renal pelvis, with or without plastic operation on ureter, nephropexy, nephrostomy, pyelostomy, or ureteral splinting; simple
EXCLUDES   *Laparoscopic pyeloplasty (50544)*
31.77 31.77 Global Days 090

50405 complicated (congenital kidney abnormality, secondary pyeloplasty, solitary kidney, calycoplasty)
EXCLUDES   *Laparoscopic pyeloplasty (50544)*
38.34 38.34 Global Days 090

● New Code   ▲ Revised Code   M Maternity   A Age   Unlisted   Not Covered   # Resequenced
CCI   + Add-on   ⊘ Mod 51 Exempt   Mod 63 Exempt   ⊙ Mod Sedation   PQRI
© 2009 Publisher *(Blue Ink)*   CPT only © 2009 American Medical Association. All Rights Reserved. *(Black Ink)*   Medicare *(Red Ink)*

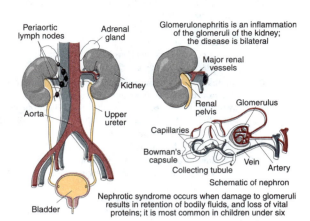

50500 Nephrorrhaphy, suture of kidney wound or injury
 34.74 34.74 Global Days 090

50520 Closure of nephrocutaneous or pyelocutaneous fistula
 28.36 28.36 Global Days 090

50525 Closure of nephrovisceral fistula (eg, renocolic), including visceral repair; abdominal approach
 40.18 40.18 Global Days 090

50526 thoracic approach
 39.50 39.50 Global Days 090

50540 Symphysiotomy for horseshoe kidney with or without pyeloplasty and/or other plastic procedure, unilateral or bilateral (1 operation)
 31.48 31.48 Global Days 090

50541-50549 Laparoscopic Surgical Procedures of the Kidney

INCLUDES Diagnostic laparoscopy
EXCLUDES Laparoscopic drainage of lymphocele to peritoneal cavity (49323)

50541 Laparoscopy, surgical; ablation of renal cysts
 25.30 25.30 Global Days 090

50542 ablation of renal mass lesion(s)
EXCLUDES Cryosurgical open ablation of renal mass lesion(s) (50250)
Nephrectomy, open approach (50220-50240)
 32.06 32.06 Global Days 090
AMA: 2009, Jan, 11-31; 2008, Jan, 10-25; 2007, January, 13-27

50543 partial nephrectomy
EXCLUDES Partial nephrectomy, open approach (50240)
 40.96 40.96 Global Days 090

50544 pyeloplasty
 34.39 34.39 Global Days 090

50545 radical nephrectomy (includes removal of Gerota's fascia and surrounding fatty tissue, removal of regional lymph nodes, and adrenalectomy)
EXCLUDES Radical nephrectomy, open approach (50230)
 36.99 36.99 Global Days 090

50546 nephrectomy, including partial ureterectomy
 33.00 33.00 Global Days 090

50547 donor nephrectomy (including cold preservation), from living donor
INCLUDES Donor care
Graft:
Cold preservation
Harvesting
EXCLUDES Backbench reconstruction renal allograft prior to transplantation (50327-50329)
Backbench standard preparation of living donor renal allograft prior to transplantation (50325)
Donor nephrectomy, open approach (50320)
 43.74 43.74 Global Days 090

50548 nephrectomy with total ureterectomy
EXCLUDES Nephrectomy, open approach (50234, 50236)
 37.18 37.18 Global Days 090

50549 Unlisted laparoscopy procedure, renal
 0.00 0.00 Global Days YYY
AMA: 2009, Jan, 11-31; 2008, Jan, 10-25; 2007, January, 13-27

50551-50562 Endoscopic Procedures of Kidney via Established Nephrostomy/Pyelostomy Access

EXCLUDES Materials and supplies (99070)

50551 Renal endoscopy through established nephrostomy or pyelostomy, with or without irrigation, instillation, or ureteropyelography, exclusive of radiologic service;
 8.15 9.61 Global Days 000

50553 with ureteral catheterization, with or without dilation of ureter
 8.67 10.28 Global Days 000

50555 with biopsy
 9.44 11.01 Global Days 000

50557 with fulguration and/or incision, with or without biopsy
 9.56 11.20 Global Days 000

50561 with removal of foreign body or calculus
 10.93 12.74 Global Days 000

50562 with resection of tumor
 16.00 16.00 Global Days 090

50570-50580 Endoscopic Procedures of Kidney via Nephrotomy/Pyelotomy Access

EXCLUDES Materials and supplies (99070)
Nephrotomy (50045)
Pyelotomy (50120)

50570 Renal endoscopy through nephrotomy or pyelotomy, with or without irrigation, instillation, or ureteropyelography, exclusive of radiologic service;
 13.62 13.62 Global Days 000

50572 with ureteral catheterization, with or without dilation of ureter
 14.73 14.73 Global Days 000

50574 with biopsy
 15.67 15.67 Global Days 000

50575 with endopyelotomy (includes cystoscopy, ureteroscopy, dilation of ureter and ureteral pelvic junction, incision of ureteral pelvic junction and insertion of endopyelotomy stent)
 19.82 19.82 Global Days 000
AMA: 2009, Jan, 11-31; 2008, Jan, 10-25; 2007, January, 13-27

Current Procedural Coding Expert – Urinary System

50576 with fulguration and/or incision, with or without biopsy
 15.63   15.63   Global Days 000

50580 with removal of foreign body or calculus
 16.85   16.85   Global Days 000

50590-50593 Noninvasive and Minimally Invasive Procedures of the Kidney

CMS 100-3,230.1   Treatment of Kidney Stones

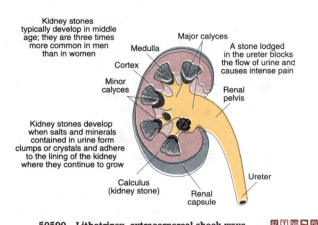

50590 Lithotripsy, extracorporeal shock wave
 15.36   23.54   Global Days 090
AMA: 2009, Jan, 11-31; 2008, Jan, 10-25; 2007, January, 13-27

● **50592** Ablation, 1 or more renal tumor(s), percutaneous, unilateral, radiofrequency
76940, 77013, 77022
 9.85   71.97   Global Days 010

● **50593** Ablation, renal tumor(s), unilateral, percutaneous, cryotherapy
76940, 77013, 77022
 13.24   108.02   Global Days 010

50600-50940 Open and Injection Procedures of Ureter

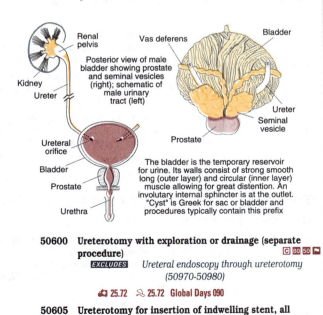

50600 Ureterotomy with exploration or drainage (separate procedure)
EXCLUDES   Ureteral endoscopy through ureterotomy (50970-50980)
 25.72   25.72   Global Days 090

50605 Ureterotomy for insertion of indwelling stent, all types
 26.55   26.55   Global Days 090

50610 Ureterolithotomy; upper 1/3 of ureter
EXCLUDES   Cystotomy with calculus basket extraction of ureteral calculus (51065)
Transvesical ureterolithotomy (51060)
Ureteral calculus manipulation/extraction performed endoscopically (50080, 50081, 50561, 50961, 50980, 52320-52330, 52352, 52353)
Ureterolithotomy performed laparoscopically (50945)
 25.89   25.89   Global Days 090

50620 middle 1/3 of ureter
EXCLUDES   Cystotomy with calculus basket extraction of ureteral calculus (51065)
Transvesical ureterolithotomy (51060)
Ureteral calculus manipulation/extraction performed endoscopically (50080, 50081, 50561, 50961, 50980, 52320-52330, 52352, 52353)
Ureterolithotomy performed laparoscopically (50945)
 24.74   24.74   Global Days 090

50630 lower 1/3 of ureter
EXCLUDES   Cystotomy with calculus basket extraction of ureteral calculus (51065)
Transvesical ureterolithotomy (51060)
Ureteral calculus manipulation/extraction performed endoscopically (50080, 50081, 50561, 50961, 50980, 52320-52330, 52352, 52353)
Ureterolithotomy performed laparoscopically (50945)
 24.44   24.44   Global Days 090

50650 Ureterectomy, with bladder cuff (separate procedure)
EXCLUDES   Ureterocele (51535, 52300)
 28.38   28.38   Global Days 090

50660 Ureterectomy, total, ectopic ureter, combination abdominal, vaginal and/or perineal approach
EXCLUDES   Ureterocele (51535, 52300)
 31.36   31.36   Global Days 090

50684 Injection procedure for ureterography or ureteropyelography through ureterostomy or indwelling ureteral catheter
74425
 1.33   4.13   Global Days 000

50686 Manometric studies through ureterostomy or indwelling ureteral catheter
 2.54   3.95   Global Days 000

50688 Change of ureterostomy tube or externally accessible ureteral stent via ileal conduit
Code also (C1729, C1758, C2617, C2625)
75984
 2.11   2.11   Global Days 010

50690 Injection procedure for visualization of ileal conduit and/or ureteropyelography, exclusive of radiologic service
74425
 1.87   2.48   Global Days 000

50700 Ureteroplasty, plastic operation on ureter (eg, stricture)
 25.52   25.52   Global Days 090

50715 Ureterolysis, with or without repositioning of ureter for retroperitoneal fibrosis
 32.49   32.49   Global Days 090

● New Code   ▲ Revised Code   M Maternity   A Age   Unlisted   Not Covered   # Resequenced
CCI   + Add-on   ⊘ Mod 51 Exempt   63 Mod 63 Exempt   ⊙ Mod Sedation   PQRI
© 2009 Publisher (Blue Ink)   CPT only © 2009 American Medical Association. All Rights Reserved. (Black Ink)   Medicare (Red Ink)   183

Current Procedural Coding Expert – Urinary System

Code	Description	RVU (Facility)	RVU (Non-Facility)	Global Days
50722	Ureterolysis for ovarian vein syndrome ♀	28.90	28.90	090
50725	Ureterolysis for retrocaval ureter, with reanastomosis of upper urinary tract or vena cava	30.21	30.21	090
50727	Revision of urinary-cutaneous anastomosis (any type urostomy);	13.61	13.61	090
50728	with repair of fascial defect and hernia	18.99	18.99	090
50740	Ureteropyelostomy, anastomosis of ureter and renal pelvis	33.42	33.42	090
50750	Ureterocalycostomy, anastomosis of ureter to renal calyx	31.65	31.65	090
50760	Ureteroureterostomy	30.96	30.96	090
50770	Transureteroureterostomy, anastomosis of ureter to contralateral ureter	31.65	31.65	090
50780	Ureteroneocystostomy; anastomosis of single ureter to bladder **INCLUDES** Minor procedures to prevent vesicoureteral reflux **EXCLUDES** Cystourethroplasty with ureteroneocystostomy (51820)	30.41	30.41	090
50782	anastomosis of duplicated ureter to bladder **INCLUDES** Minor procedures to prevent vesicoureteral reflux	31.11	31.11	090
50783	with extensive ureteral tailoring **INCLUDES** Minor procedures to prevent vesicoureteral reflux	32.65	32.65	090
50785	with vesico-psoas hitch or bladder flap **INCLUDES** Minor procedures to prevent vesicoureteral reflux	33.26	33.26	090
50800	Ureteroenterostomy, direct anastomosis of ureter to intestine **EXCLUDES** Cystectomy with ureterosigmoidostomy/ureteroileal conduit (51580-51595)	25.25	25.25	090
50810	Ureterosigmoidostomy, with creation of sigmoid bladder and establishment of abdominal or perineal colostomy, including intestine anastomosis **EXCLUDES** Cystectomy with ureterosigmoidostomy/ureteroileal conduit (51580-51595)	38.11	38.11	090
50815	Ureterocolon conduit, including intestine anastomosis **EXCLUDES** Cystectomy with ureterosigmoidostomy/ureteroileal conduit (51580-51595)	33.48	33.48	090
50820	Ureteroileal conduit (ileal bladder), including intestine anastomosis (Bricker operation) **EXCLUDES** Cystectomy with ureterosigmoidostomy/ureteroileal conduit (51580-51595)	36.29	36.29	090
50825	Continent diversion, including intestine anastomosis using any segment of small and/or large intestine (Kock pouch or Camey enterocystoplasty)	45.52	45.52	090
50830	Urinary undiversion (eg, taking down of ureteroileal conduit, ureterosigmoidostomy or ureteroenterostomy with ureteroureterostomy or ureteroneocystostomy)	49.59	49.59	090
50840	Replacement of all or part of ureter by intestine segment, including intestine anastomosis	33.66	33.66	090
50845	Cutaneous appendico-vesicostomy **INCLUDES** Mitrofanoff operation	34.14	34.14	090
50860	Ureterostomy, transplantation of ureter to skin	25.85	25.85	090
50900	Ureterorrhaphy, suture of ureter (separate procedure)	23.29	23.29	090
50920	Closure of ureterocutaneous fistula	24.07	24.07	090
50930	Closure of ureterovisceral fistula (including visceral repair)	31.89	31.89	090
50940	Deligation of ureter **EXCLUDES** Ureteroplasty/ureterolysis (50700-50860)	24.24	24.24	090

50945-50949 Laparoscopic Procedures of Ureter

INCLUDES Diagnostic laparoscopy
EXCLUDES Ureteroneocystostomy, open approach (50780-50785)

Code	Description	RVU (Facility)	RVU (Non-Facility)	Global Days
50945	Laparoscopy, surgical; ureterolithotomy	26.71	26.71	090

AMA: 2009, Jan, 11-31; 2008, Jan, 10-25; 2007, January, 13-27; 2006, September, 14-16

50947	ureteroneocystostomy with cystoscopy and ureteral stent placement	38.04	38.04	090
50948	ureteroneocystostomy without cystoscopy and ureteral stent placement	35.08	35.08	090
50949	Unlisted laparoscopy procedure, ureter	0.00	0.00	YYY

50951-50961 Endoscopic Procedures of Ureter via Established Ureterostomy Access

| 50951 | Ureteral endoscopy through established ureterostomy, with or without irrigation, instillation, or ureteropyelography, exclusive of radiologic service; | 8.49 | 10.03 | 000 |

AMA: 2009, Jan, 11-31; 2008, Jan, 10-25; 2007, March, 9-11

Current Procedural Coding Expert – Urinary System

50953 with ureteral catheterization, with or without dilation of ureter [A2] [T] [80] [50]
9.32 10.63 Global Days 000
AMA: 2007, March, 9-11

50955 with biopsy [A2] [T] [80] [50]
10.04 11.37 Global Days 000
AMA: 2007, March, 9-11

50957 with fulguration and/or incision, with or without biopsy [A2] [T] [80] [50]
9.81 11.48 Global Days 000
AMA: 2007, March, 9-11

50961 with removal of foreign body or calculus [A2] [T] [80] [50]
8.76 10.31 Global Days 000
AMA: 2009, Jan, 11-31; 2008, Jan, 10-25; 2007, April, 11-12; 2007, March, 9-11

50970-50980 Endoscopic Procedures of Ureter via Ureterotomy

EXCLUDES *Ureterotomy (50600)*

50970 Ureteral endoscopy through ureterotomy, with or without irrigation, instillation, or ureteropyelography, exclusive of radiologic service; [A2] [T] [80] [50]
10.26 10.26 Global Days 000

50972 with ureteral catheterization, with or without dilation of ureter [A2] [T] [80] [50]
9.91 9.91 Global Days 000

50974 with biopsy [A2] [T] [80] [50]
13.10 13.10 Global Days 000

50976 with fulguration and/or incision, with or without biopsy [A2] [T] [80] [50]
12.91 12.91 Global Days 000

50980 with removal of foreign body or calculus [A2] [T] [80] [50]
9.86 9.86 Global Days 000

51020-51080 Open Incisional Procedures of Bladder

51020 Cystotomy or cystostomy; with fulguration and/or insertion of radioactive material [A2] [T] [80]
12.67 12.67 Global Days 090

51030 with cryosurgical destruction of intravesical lesion [A2] [T] [80]
12.39 12.39 Global Days 090

51040 Cystostomy, cystotomy with drainage [A2] [T] [80]
7.76 7.76 Global Days 090

51045 Cystotomy, with insertion of ureteral catheter or stent (separate procedure) [A2] [T] [80]
13.22 13.22 Global Days 090

51050 Cystolithotomy, cystotomy with removal of calculus, without vesical neck resection [A2] [T] [80]
12.80 12.80 Global Days 090

51060 Transvesical ureterolithotomy [T] [80]
15.76 15.76 Global Days 090

51065 Cystotomy, with calculus basket extraction and/or ultrasonic or electrohydraulic fragmentation of ureteral calculus [A2] [T] [80]
15.70 15.70 Global Days 090

51080 Drainage of perivesical or prevesical space abscess [A2] [T] [80]
11.01 11.01 Global Days 090

51100-51102 Bladder Aspiration Procedures

76942, 77002, 77012

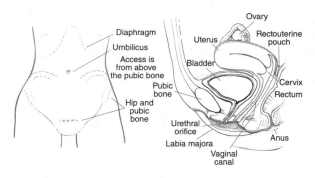

51100 Aspiration of bladder; by needle [P3] [T]
1.09 1.64 Global Days 000
AMA: 2008, Jun, 8-11

51101 by trocar or intracatheter [P2] [T]
1.48 3.22 Global Days 000
AMA: 2008, Jun, 8-11

51102 with insertion of suprapubic catheter [A2] [T]
4.01 5.89 Global Days 000
AMA: 2008, Jun, 8-11; 2007, Dec, 10-179

51500-51597 Open Excisional Procedures of Bladder

51500 Excision of urachal cyst or sinus, with or without umbilical hernia repair [A2] [T] [80]
17.29 17.29 Global Days 090

51520 Cystotomy; for simple excision of vesical neck (separate procedure) [A2] [T] [80]
16.13 16.13 Global Days 090

51525 for excision of bladder diverticulum, single or multiple (separate procedure) [C] [80]
EXCLUDES *Transurethral resection (52305)*
23.54 23.54 Global Days 090

51530 for excision of bladder tumor [C] [80]
EXCLUDES *Transurethral resection (52234-52240)*
21.48 21.48 Global Days 090

51535 Cystotomy for excision, incision, or repair of ureterocele [G2] [T] [80] [50]
EXCLUDES *Transurethral excision (52300)*
21.26 21.26 Global Days 090

51550 Cystectomy, partial; simple [C] [80] [PQ]
26.57 26.57 Global Days 090

51555 complicated (eg, postradiation, previous surgery, difficult location) [C] [80] [PQ]
34.94 34.94 Global Days 090

51565 Cystectomy, partial, with reimplantation of ureter(s) into bladder (ureteroneocystostomy) [C] [80] [PQ]
35.57 35.57 Global Days 090

51570 Cystectomy, complete; (separate procedure) [C] [80] [PQ]
40.73 40.73 Global Days 090

51575 with bilateral pelvic lymphadenectomy, including external iliac, hypogastric, and obturator nodes [C] [80] [PQ]
50.20 50.20 Global Days 090

51580 Cystectomy, complete, with ureterosigmoidostomy or ureterocutaneous transplantations; [C] [80] [PQ]
52.12 52.12 Global Days 090

CURRENT PROCEDURAL CODING EXPERT – Urinary System

51585	with bilateral pelvic lymphadenectomy, including external iliac, hypogastric, and obturator nodes
	58.09 58.09 Global Days 090
51590	Cystectomy, complete, with ureteroileal conduit or sigmoid bladder, including intestine anastomosis;
	53.27 53.27 Global Days 090
51595	with bilateral pelvic lymphadenectomy, including external iliac, hypogastric, and obturator nodes
	60.40 60.40 Global Days 090
51596	Cystectomy, complete, with continent diversion, any open technique, using any segment of small and/or large intestine to construct neobladder
	64.82 64.82 Global Days 090
51597	Pelvic exenteration, complete, for vesical, prostatic or urethral malignancy, with removal of bladder and ureteral transplantations, with or without hysterectomy and/or abdominoperineal resection of rectum and colon and colostomy, or any combination thereof
	EXCLUDES Pelvic exenteration for gynecologic malignancy (58240)
	63.30 63.30 Global Days 090

51600-51720 Injection/Insertion/Instillation Procedures of Bladder

51600	Injection procedure for cystography or voiding urethrocystography
	74430, 74455
	1.22 4.51 Global Days 000
51605	Injection procedure and placement of chain for contrast and/or chain urethrocystography
	74430
	1.03 1.03 Global Days 000
51610	Injection procedure for retrograde urethrocystography
	74450
	1.71 2.72 Global Days 000
51700	Bladder irrigation, simple, lavage and/or instillation
	1.25 2.14 Global Days 000
51701	Insertion of non-indwelling bladder catheter (eg, straight catheterization for residual urine)
	EXCLUDES Catheterization for specimen collection (P9612)
	Do not report with insertion of catheter as an inclusive component of another procedure
	0.76 1.39 Global Days 000
	AMA: 2009, Jan, 11-31; 2008, Jan, 10-25; 2007, Jul, 1-4; 2007, January, 28-31; 2006, May, 1-9
51702	Insertion of temporary indwelling bladder catheter; simple (eg, Foley)
	Do not report with insertion of catheter as an inclusive component of another procedure
	0.82 1.77 Global Days 000
	AMA: 2009, Jan, 11-31; 2008, Jan, 10-25; 2007, Jul, 1-4; 2007, January, 28-31; 2007, January, 13-27; 2006, May, 1-9
51703	complicated (eg, altered anatomy, fractured catheter/balloon)
	2.24 3.36 Global Days 000
	AMA: 2007, January, 28-31
51705	Change of cystostomy tube; simple
	1.81 2.70 Global Days 010
	AMA: 2009, Jan, 11-31; 2008, Jan, 10-25; 2007, Dec, 10-179; 2007, January, 28-31
51710	complicated
	Code also (C2627)
	75984
	2.57 3.74 Global Days 010
	AMA: 2007, Dec, 10-179
51715	Endoscopic injection of implant material into the submucosal tissues of the urethra and/or bladder neck
	Code also (L8603, L8604, L8606)
	5.53 7.57 Global Days 000
51720	Bladder instillation of anticarcinogenic agent (including retention time)
	2.22 2.88 Global Days 000
	AMA: 2009, Jan, 11-31; 2008, Jan, 10-25; 2007, January, 13-27

51725-51798 [51797] Uroflowmetric Evaluations

CMS 100-3,230.2   Uroflowmetric Evaluations

51725	Simple cystometrogram (CMG) (eg, spinal manometer)
	4.96 4.96 Global Days 000
▲ 51726	Complex cystometrogram (ie, calibrated electronic equipment);
	7.42 7.42 Global Days 000
● 51727	with urethral pressure profile studies (ie, urethral closure pressure profile), any technique
	8.07 8.07 Global Days 000
● 51728	with voiding pressure studies (ie, bladder voiding pressure), any technique
	8.06 8.06 Global Days 000
● 51729	with voiding pressure studies (ie, bladder voiding pressure) and urethral pressure profile studies (ie, urethral closure pressure profile), any technique
	8.14 8.14 Global Days 000
+ #▲ 51797	**Voiding pressure studies, intra-abdominal (ie, rectal, gastric, intraperitoneal) (List separately in addition to code for primary procedure)**
	Code first (51728-51729)
	2.79 2.79 Global Days ZZZ
	AMA: 2009, Jan, 11-31; 2008, Jan, 10-25; 2007, January, 13-27
51736	Simple uroflowmetry (UFR) (eg, stop-watch flow rate, mechanical uroflowmeter)
	1.38 1.38 Global Days 000
51741	Complex uroflowmetry (eg, calibrated electronic equipment)
	2.19 2.19 Global Days 000
~~51772~~	~~Urethral pressure profile studies (UPP) (urethral closure pressure profile), any technique~~
	To report, see code 51727, 51729
51784	Electromyography studies (EMG) of anal or urethral sphincter, other than needle, any technique
	4.94 4.94 Global Days 000
51785	Needle electromyography studies (EMG) of anal or urethral sphincter, any technique
	5.41 5.41 Global Days 000
	AMA: 2009, Jan, 11-31; 2008, Jan, 10-25; 2007, January, 13-27
51792	Stimulus evoked response (eg, measurement of bulbocavernosus reflex latency time)
	5.21 5.21 Global Days 000
~~51795~~	~~Voiding pressure studies (VP); bladder voiding pressure, any technique~~
	To report, see code 51728-51729
51797	*Resequenced code. See code following 51729.*

Current Procedural Coding Expert – Urinary System

51798 Measurement of post-voiding residual urine and/or bladder capacity by ultrasound, non-imaging
 0.45   0.45 Global Days XXX
AMA: 2005, December, 3-6

51800-51980 Open Repairs Urinary System

51800 Cystoplasty or cystourethroplasty, plastic operation on bladder and/or vesical neck (anterior Y-plasty, vesical fundus resection), any procedure, with or without wedge resection of posterior vesical neck
 28.64   28.64 Global Days 090

51820 Cystourethroplasty with unilateral or bilateral ureteroneocystostomy
 29.63   29.63 Global Days 090

51840 Anterior vesicourethropexy, or urethropexy (eg, Marshall-Marchetti-Krantz, Burch); simple
EXCLUDES Pereyra type urethropexy (57289)
 18.18   18.18 Global Days 090
AMA: 2009, Jan, 11-31; 2008, Jan, 10-25; 2007, January, 13-27; 2006, May, 16-20

51841 complicated (eg, secondary repair)
EXCLUDES Pereyra type urethropexy (57289)
 21.61   21.61 Global Days 090

51845 Abdomino-vaginal vesical neck suspension, with or without endoscopic control (eg, Stamey, Raz, modified Pereyra)
 16.11   16.11 Global Days 090

51860 Cystorrhaphy, suture of bladder wound, injury or rupture; simple
 20.42   20.42 Global Days 090

51865 complicated
 24.58   24.58 Global Days 090

51880 Closure of cystostomy (separate procedure)
 12.79   12.79 Global Days 090

51900 Closure of vesicovaginal fistula, abdominal approach
EXCLUDES Vesicovaginal fistula closure, vaginal approach (57320-57330)
 22.75   22.75 Global Days 090

51920 Closure of vesicouterine fistula;
EXCLUDES Enterovesical fistula closure (44660, 44661)
Rectovesical fistula closure (45800-45805)
 20.78   20.78 Global Days 090

51925 with hysterectomy
EXCLUDES Enterovesical fistula closure (44660, 44661)
Rectovesical fistula closure (45800-45805)
 28.66   28.66 Global Days 090

51940 Closure, exstrophy of bladder
EXCLUDES Epispadias reconstruction with exstropy of bladder (54390)
 45.14   45.14 Global Days 090

51960 Enterocystoplasty, including intestinal anastomosis
 38.17   38.17 Global Days 090

51980 Cutaneous vesicostomy
 19.42   19.42 Global Days 090

51990-51999 Laparoscopic Procedures of Urinary System
INCLUDES Diagnostic laparoscopy

51990 Laparoscopy, surgical; urethral suspension for stress incontinence
 21.04   21.04 Global Days 090

51992 sling operation for stress incontinence (eg, fascia or synthetic)
EXCLUDES Removal/revision of sling for stress incontinence (57287)
Sling operation for stress incontinence, open approach (57288)
 23.54   23.54 Global Days 090

51999 Unlisted laparoscopy procedure, bladder
 0.00   0.00 Global Days YYY

52000-52318 Endoscopic Procedures via Urethra: Bladder and Urethra

52000 Cystourethroscopy (separate procedure)
 3.44   5.20 Global Days 000
AMA: 2009, Jan, 11-31; 2008, Jan, 10-25; 2007, January, 13-27; 2005, March, 11-15; 2005, October, 23-24

52001 Cystourethroscopy with irrigation and evacuation of multiple obstructing clots
Do not report with (52000)
 7.94   9.81 Global Days 000

52005 Cystourethroscopy, with ureteral catheterization, with or without irrigation, instillation, or ureteropyelography, exclusive of radiologic service;
INCLUDES Howard test
 3.64   6.89 Global Days 000
AMA: 2009, Jan, 11-31; 2008, Jan, 10-25; 2007, January, 13-27

52007 with brush biopsy of ureter and/or renal pelvis
 4.54   11.38 Global Days 000

52010 Cystourethroscopy, with ejaculatory duct catheterization, with or without irrigation, instillation, or duct radiography, exclusive of radiologic service
74440
 4.54   9.38 Global Days 000

52204 Cystourethroscopy, with biopsy(s)
 3.88   9.06 Global Days 000
AMA: 2009, Jan, 11-31; 2008, Jan, 10-25; 2007, January, 13-27

52214 Cystourethroscopy, with fulguration (including cryosurgery or laser surgery) of trigone, bladder neck, prostatic fossa, urethra, or periurethral glands
 5.44   15.82 Global Days 000

52224 Cystourethroscopy, with fulguration (including cryosurgery or laser surgery) or treatment of MINOR (less than 0.5 cm) lesion(s) with or without biopsy
 4.65   14.62 Global Days 000
AMA: 2009, Jan, 11-31; 2009, Jun, 10-11; 2008, Jan, 10-25; 2007, Dec, 7-8

52234 Cystourethroscopy, with fulguration (including cryosurgery or laser surgery) and/or resection of; SMALL bladder tumor(s) (0.5 up to 2.0 cm)
EXCLUDES Bladder tumor excision through cystotomy (51530)
 6.79   6.79 Global Days 000
AMA: 2009, Jan, 11-31; 2009, Jun, 10-11; 2008, Jan, 10-25; 2007, Dec, 7-8; 2007, January, 13-27

● New Code ▲ Revised Code   Maternity   Age   Unlisted   Not Covered   # Resequenced
 CCI + Add-on   Mod 51 Exempt   Mod 63 Exempt   Mod Sedation   PQRI
© 2009 Publisher *(Blue Ink)*   CPT only © 2009 American Medical Association. All Rights Reserved. *(Black Ink)*   Medicare *(Red Ink)*

Code	Description	Facility RVU	Non-Facility RVU	Global Days
52235	MEDIUM bladder tumor(s) (2.0 to 5.0 cm) [A2][T]	7.95	7.95	000
	EXCLUDES Bladder tumor excision through cystotomy (51530)			
	AMA: 2009, Jun, 10-11			
52240	LARGE bladder tumor(s) [A2][T]	13.94	13.94	000
	EXCLUDES Bladder tumor excision through cystotomy (51530)			
	AMA: 2009, Jun, 10-11			
52250	Cystourethroscopy with insertion of radioactive substance, with or without biopsy or fulguration [A2][T]	6.70	6.70	000
52260	Cystourethroscopy, with dilation of bladder for interstitial cystitis; general or conduction (spinal) anesthesia [A2][T]	5.80	5.80	000
	AMA: 2009, Jan, 11-31; 2008, Jan, 10-25; 2007, January, 13-27; 2005, October, 23-24			
52265	local anesthesia [P3][T]	4.52	9.19	000
52270	Cystourethroscopy, with internal urethrotomy; female ♀ [A2][T]	5.00	8.94	000
52275	male ♂ [A2][T]	6.86	12.10	000
52276	Cystourethroscopy with direct vision internal urethrotomy [A2][T]	7.32	7.32	000
	AMA: 2009, May, 8-9&11			
52277	Cystourethroscopy, with resection of external sphincter (sphincterotomy) [A2][T][80]	9.27	9.27	000
52281	Cystourethroscopy, with calibration and/or dilation of urethral stricture or stenosis, with or without meatotomy, with or without injection procedure for cystography, male or female [A2][T]	4.24	7.03	000
	AMA: 2009, Jan, 11-31; 2008, Jan, 10-25; 2007, June, 10-11			
▲ 52282	Cystourethroscopy, with insertion of permanent urethral stent [A2][T]	9.33	9.33	000
	EXCLUDES Placement of temporary prostatic urethral stent (53855)			
52283	Cystourethroscopy, with steroid injection into stricture [A2][T]	5.56	7.24	000
52285	Cystourethroscopy for treatment of the female urethral syndrome with any or all of the following: urethral meatotomy, urethral dilation, internal urethrotomy, lysis of urethrovaginal septal fibrosis, lateral incisions of the bladder neck, and fulguration of polyp(s) of urethra, bladder neck, and/or trigone ♀ [A2][T]	5.39	7.26	000
52290	Cystourethroscopy; with ureteral meatotomy, unilateral or bilateral [A2][T]	6.74	6.74	000
52300	with resection or fulguration of orthotopic ureterocele(s), unilateral or bilateral [A2][T][80]	7.86	7.86	000
52301	with resection or fulguration of ectopic ureterocele(s), unilateral or bilateral [A2][T][80]	8.07	8.07	000
52305	with incision or resection of orifice of bladder diverticulum, single or multiple [A2][T]	7.70	7.70	000
52310	Cystourethroscopy, with removal of foreign body, calculus, or ureteral stent from urethra or bladder (separate procedure); simple [A2][T]	4.17	6.10	000
52315	complicated [A2][T]	7.57	10.68	000
52317	Litholapaxy: crushing or fragmentation of calculus by any means in bladder and removal of fragments; simple or small (less than 2.5 cm) [A2][T]	9.62	20.11	000
52318	complicated or large (over 2.5 cm) [A2][T]	13.12	13.12	000

52320-52355 Endoscopic Procedures via Urethra: Renal Pelvis and Ureter

INCLUDES Diagnostic cystourethroscopy with therapeutic cystourethroscopy
Insertion/removal of temporary ureteral catheter

EXCLUDES Diagnostic cystourethroscopy only (52000)
Self-retaining/indwelling ureteral stent removal by cystourethroscope (52310, 52315)

Code also the insertion of an indwelling stent performed in addition to other procedures within this section (52332)

Do not report with (52005)

Code	Description	Facility RVU	Non-Facility RVU	Global Days
52320	Cystourethroscopy (including ureteral catheterization); with removal of ureteral calculus [A2][T][50]	6.82	6.82	000
	Do not report with (52000)			
	AMA: 2009, Jan, 11-31; 2008, Jan, 10-25; 2007, January, 13-27			
52325	with fragmentation of ureteral calculus (eg, ultrasonic or electro-hydraulic technique) [A2][T][50]	8.86	8.86	000
	Do not report with (52000)			
	AMA: 2009, Jan, 11-31; 2007, Dec, 10-179			
52327	with suburetic injection of implant material [A2][T][50]	7.28	7.28	000
	Do not report with (52000)			
52330	with manipulation, without removal of ureteral calculus [A2][T][50]	7.30	12.51	000
	Do not report with (52000)			
	AMA: 2009, Jan, 11-31; 2008, Jan, 10-25; 2007, January, 13-27			

Diverticulum of bladder — Diverticula are pouches that push out through the wall of an organ; bladder diverticula may be acquired or congenital and may cause urinary incontinence or increased urgency to urinate. This condition is most common in older men.

Current Procedural Coding Expert – Urinary System 52500

52332 Cystourethroscopy, with insertion of indwelling ureteral stent (eg, Gibbons or double-J type) [A2] [T] [50]
- Do not report with (52000)
- 4.28   12.39   Global Days 000
- **AMA:** 2009, Jan, 11-31; 2008, Jan, 10-25; 2007, January, 13-27; 2005, October, 18-22

52334 Cystourethroscopy with insertion of ureteral guide wire through kidney to establish a percutaneous nephrostomy, retrograde [A2] [T] [50]
- EXCLUDES Cystourethroscopy with incision/fulguration/resection of congenital posterior urethral valves/obstructive hypertrophic mucosal folds (52400)
  Cystourethroscopy with pyeloscopy and/or ureteroscopy (52351-52355)
  Nephrostomy tract establishment only (50395)
  Percutaneous nephrolithotomy (50080, 50081)
- Do not report with (52000)
- 7.06   7.06   Global Days 000

52341 Cystourethroscopy; with treatment of ureteral stricture (eg, balloon dilation, laser, electrocautery, and incision) [A2] [T] [50]
- INCLUDES Diagnostic cystourethroscopy with ureteroscopy/pyeloscopy
- Do not report with (52000, 52341)
- 7.95   7.95   Global Days 000

52342 with treatment of ureteropelvic junction stricture (eg, balloon dilation, laser, electrocautery, and incision) [A2] [T] [50]
- INCLUDES Diagnostic cystourethroscopy with ureteroscopy/pyeloscopy
- Do not report with (52000, 52351)
- 8.64   8.64   Global Days 000
- **AMA:** 2009, Jan, 11-31; 2008, Jan, 10-25; 2007, January, 13-27

52343 with treatment of intra-renal stricture (eg, balloon dilation, laser, electrocautery, and incision) [A2] [T] [50]
- INCLUDES Diagnostic cystourethroscopy with ureteroscopy/pyeloscopy
- Do not report with (52000, 52351)
- 9.62   9.62   Global Days 000

52344 Cystourethroscopy with ureteroscopy; with treatment of ureteral stricture (eg, balloon dilation, laser, electrocautery, and incision) [A2] [T] [50]
- INCLUDES Diagnostic cystourethroscopy with ureteroscopy/pyeloscopy
- Do not report with (52351)
- 10.45   10.45   Global Days 000

52345 with treatment of ureteropelvic junction stricture (eg, balloon dilation, laser, electrocautery, and incision) [A2] [T] [80]
- INCLUDES Diagnostic cystourethroscopy with ureteroscopy/pyeloscopy
- Do not report with (52351)
- 11.15   11.15   Global Days 000

52346 with treatment of intra-renal stricture (eg, balloon dilation, laser, electrocautery, and incision) [A2] [T] [80]
- INCLUDES Diagnostic cystourethroscopy with ureteroscopy/pyeloscopy
- EXCLUDES Cystourethroscopy with transurethral resection or incision of ejaculatory ducts (52402)
- Do not report with (52351)
- 12.58   12.58   Global Days 000

52351 Cystourethroscopy, with ureteroscopy and/or pyeloscopy; diagnostic [A2] [T]
- Do not report with (52341-52346, 52352-52355)
- 74485
- 8.64   8.64   Global Days 000

52352 with removal or manipulation of calculus (ureteral catheterization is included) [A2] [T] [50]
- INCLUDES Diagnostic cystourethroscopy with ureteroscopy/pyeloscopy
- Do not report with (52351)
- 10.15   10.15   Global Days 000
- **AMA:** 2009, Jan, 11-31; 2008, Jan, 10-25; 2007, June, 10-11

52353 with lithotripsy (ureteral catheterization is included) [A2] [T] [50]
- INCLUDES Diagnostic cystourethroscopy with ureteroscopy/pyeloscopy
- Do not report with (52351)
- 11.67   11.67   Global Days 000
- **AMA:** 2009, Jan, 11-31; 2007, Dec, 10-179

52354 with biopsy and/or fulguration of ureteral or renal pelvic lesion [A2] [T] [50]
- INCLUDES Diagnostic cystourethroscopy with ureteroscopy/pyeloscopy
- Do not report with (52351)
- 10.80   10.80   Global Days 000

52355 with resection of ureteral or renal pelvic tumor [A2] [T] [50]
- INCLUDES Diagnostic cystourethroscopy with ureteroscopy/pyeloscopy
- Do not report with (52351)
- 12.86   12.86   Global Days 000

52400-52700 Endoscopic Procedures via Urethra: Prostate and Vesical Neck

52400 Cystourethroscopy with incision, fulguration, or resection of congenital posterior urethral valves, or congenital obstructive hypertrophic mucosal folds [A2] [T]
- 12.11   12.11   Global Days 090

52402 Cystourethroscopy with transurethral resection or incision of ejaculatory ducts ♂ [A2] [T] [80]
- 7.41   7.41   Global Days 000

52450 Transurethral incision of prostate ♂ [A2] [T] [P0]
- 12.69   12.69   Global Days 090
- **AMA:** 2009, Jan, 11-31; 2008, Jan, 10-25; 2007, January, 13-27; 2005, July, 13-16

52500 Transurethral resection of bladder neck (separate procedure) [A2] [T]
- 13.19   13.19   Global Days 090
- **AMA:** 2009, Jan, 11-31; 2009, May, 8-9&11; 2008, Jan, 10-25; 2007, January, 13-27; 2005, July, 13-16

● New Code   ▲ Revised Code   Ⓜ Maternity   Age   Unlisted   Not Covered   # Resequenced
CCI   + Add-on   ⊘ Mod 51 Exempt   Mod 63 Exempt   ⊙ Mod Sedation   PQRI

52601

52601 Transurethral electrosurgical resection of prostate, including control of postoperative bleeding, complete (vasectomy, meatotomy, cystourethroscopy, urethral calibration and/or dilation, and internal urethrotomy are included) ♂ A2 T P0
  EXCLUDES Excision of prostate (55801-55845)
  🚗 23.13 ⚕ 23.13 **Global Days 090**

52630 Transurethral resection; residual or regrowth of obstructive prostate tissue including control of postoperative bleeding, complete (vasectomy, meatotomy, cystourethroscopy, urethral calibration and/or dilation, and internal urethrotomy are included) ♂ A2 T P0
  EXCLUDES Excision of prostate (55801-55845)
  🚗 12.11 ⚕ 12.11 **Global Days 090**

52640 of postoperative bladder neck contracture ♂ A2 T
  EXCLUDES Excision of prostate (55801-55845)
  🚗 7.93 ⚕ 7.93 **Global Days 090**

52647 Laser coagulation of prostate, including control of postoperative bleeding, complete (vasectomy, meatotomy, cystourethroscopy, urethral calibration and/or dilation, and internal urethrotomy are included if performed) ♂ A2 T P0
  🚗 17.61 ⚕ 43.71 **Global Days 090**
  AMA: 2009, Jan, 11-31; 2008, Jan, 10-25; 2007, January, 13-27; 2006, December, 10-12

52648 Laser vaporization of prostate, including control of postoperative bleeding, complete (vasectomy, meatotomy, cystourethroscopy, urethral calibration and/or dilation, internal urethrotomy and transurethral resection of prostate are included if performed) ♂ A2 T P0
  🚗 18.81 ⚕ 45.13 **Global Days 090**
  AMA: 2009, Jan, 11-31; 2008, Jan, 10-25; 2007, January, 13-27; 2006, December, 10-12; 2005, July, 13-16

52649 Laser enucleation of the prostate with morcellation, including control of postoperative bleeding, complete (vasectomy, meatotomy, cystourethroscopy, urethral calibration and/or dilation, internal urethrotomy and transurethral resection of prostate are included if performed) ♂ T 80 P0
  Do not report with (52000, 52276, 52281, 52601, 52647-52648, 53020, 55250)
  🚗 26.01 ⚕ 26.01 **Global Days 090**

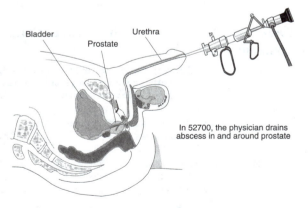

In 52700, the physician drains abscess in and around prostate

52700 Transurethral drainage of prostatic abscess ♂ A2 T 80
  EXCLUDES Litholapaxy (52317, 52318)
  🚗 11.95 ⚕ 11.95 **Global Days 090**

53000-53520 Open Surgical Procedures of Urethra

53000 Urethrotomy or urethrostomy, external (separate procedure); pendulous urethra A2 T
  EXCLUDES Endoscopic procedures; cystoscopy, urethroscopy, cystourethroscopy (52000-52700)
  Urethrocystography injection procedure (51600-51610)
  🚗 4.00 ⚕ 4.00 **Global Days 010**

53010 perineal urethra, external A2 T
  EXCLUDES Endoscopic procedures; cystoscopy, urethroscopy, cystourethroscopy (52000-52700)
  Urethrocystography injection procedure (51600-51610)
  🚗 7.86 ⚕ 7.86 **Global Days 090**

53020 Meatotomy, cutting of meatus (separate procedure); except infant A2 T
  🚗 2.67 ⚕ 2.67 **Global Days 000**

53025 infant A R2 T 80
  🚗 1.89 ⚕ 1.89 **Global Days 000**

53040 Drainage of deep periurethral abscess A2 T 80
  EXCLUDES Incision and drainage of subcutaneous abscess (10060, 10061)
  🚗 10.61 ⚕ 10.61 **Global Days 090**

53060 Drainage of Skene's gland abscess or cyst ♀ P3 T
  🚗 4.58 ⚕ 5.01 **Global Days 010**

53080 Drainage of perineal urinary extravasation; uncomplicated (separate procedure) A2 T
  🚗 11.34 ⚕ 11.34 **Global Days 090**

53085 complicated 62 T 80
  🚗 17.63 ⚕ 17.63 **Global Days 090**

53200 Biopsy of urethra A2 T
  🚗 3.89 ⚕ 4.20 **Global Days 000**

53210 Urethrectomy, total, including cystostomy; female ♀ T 80
  🚗 21.10 ⚕ 21.10 **Global Days 090**

53215 male ♂ T 80
  🚗 25.42 ⚕ 25.42 **Global Days 090**

53220 Excision or fulguration of carcinoma of urethra A2 T 80
  🚗 12.31 ⚕ 12.31 **Global Days 090**

53230 Excision of urethral diverticulum (separate procedure); female ♀ T 80
  🚗 16.58 ⚕ 16.58 **Global Days 090**

53235 male ♂ T 80
  🚗 17.19 ⚕ 17.19 **Global Days 090**

53240 Marsupialization of urethral diverticulum, male or female A2 T
  🚗 11.47 ⚕ 11.47 **Global Days 090**

53250 Excision of bulbourethral gland (Cowper's gland) ♂ A2 T
  🚗 11.03 ⚕ 11.03 **Global Days 090**

53260 Excision or fulguration; urethral polyp(s), distal urethra A2 T
  EXCLUDES Endoscopic method (52214, 52224)
  🚗 4.93 ⚕ 5.41 **Global Days 010**

53265 urethral caruncle A2 T
  EXCLUDES Endoscopic method (52214, 52224)
  🚗 5.07 ⚕ 5.79 **Global Days 010**

26/TC PC/TC Comp Only | A2/Z3 ASC Pmt | 50 Bilateral | ♂ Male Only | ♀ Female Only | 🚗 Facility RVU | ⚕ Non-Facility RVU
AMA: CPT Asst | **MED:** Pub 100 | A/Y OPPSI | 80/ Surg Assist Allowed / w/Doc | Lab Crosswalk | Radiology Crosswalk

Current Procedural Coding Expert – Urinary System

53270	Skene's glands ♀ A2 T
	EXCLUDES Endoscopic method (52214, 52224)
	5.28 5.75 Global Days 010
53275	urethral prolapse ♀ A2 T
	EXCLUDES Endoscopic method (52214, 52224)
	7.14 7.14 Global Days 010
53400	Urethroplasty; first stage, for fistula, diverticulum, or stricture (eg, Johannsen type) A2 T 80
	EXCLUDES Hypospadias repair (54300-54352)
	21.89 21.89 Global Days 090
53405	second stage (formation of urethra), including urinary diversion A2 T 80
	EXCLUDES Hypospadias repair (54300-54352)
	23.86 23.86 Global Days 090
53410	Urethroplasty, 1-stage reconstruction of male anterior urethra ♂ A2 T 80
	EXCLUDES Hypospadias repair (54300-54352)
	26.80 26.80 Global Days 090
53415	Urethroplasty, transpubic or perineal, 1-stage, for reconstruction or repair of prostatic or membranous urethra ♂ C 80
	31.08 31.08 Global Days 090
53420	Urethroplasty, 2-stage reconstruction or repair of prostatic or membranous urethra; first stage ♂ A2 T
	22.99 22.99 Global Days 090
53425	second stage ♂ A2 T 80
	25.65 25.65 Global Days 090
53430	Urethroplasty, reconstruction of female urethra ♀ A2 T 80
	26.64 26.64 Global Days 090
53431	Urethroplasty with tubularization of posterior urethra and/or lower bladder for incontinence (eg, Tenago, Leadbetter procedure) A2 T 80
	31.65 31.65 Global Days 090
53440	Sling operation for correction of male urinary incontinence (eg, fascia or synthetic) ♂ H8 S 80
	Code also (C1762, C1763, C1771, C1781, C2631)
	24.11 24.11 Global Days 090
53442	Removal or revision of sling for male urinary incontinence (eg, fascia or synthetic) ♂ A2 T 80
	21.27 21.27 Global Days 090
53444	Insertion of tandem cuff (dual cuff) H8 S 80
	Code also (C1815)
	21.68 21.68 Global Days 090
53445	Insertion of inflatable urethral/bladder neck sphincter, including placement of pump, reservoir, and cuff H8 S 80
	Code also (C1815)
	23.89 23.89 Global Days 090
53446	Removal of inflatable urethral/bladder neck sphincter, including pump, reservoir, and cuff A2 T 80
	17.46 17.46 Global Days 090
53447	Removal and replacement of inflatable urethral/bladder neck sphincter including pump, reservoir, and cuff at the same operative session H8 S 80
	Code also (C1815)
	22.08 22.08 Global Days 090
53448	Removal and replacement of inflatable urethral/bladder neck sphincter including pump, reservoir, and cuff through an infected field at the same operative session including irrigation and debridement of infected tissue C 80
	Do not report with (11040-11043)
	35.09 35.09 Global Days 090
53449	Repair of inflatable urethral/bladder neck sphincter, including pump, reservoir, and cuff A2 T 80
	16.63 16.63 Global Days 090
53450	Urethromeatoplasty, with mucosal advancement A2 T
	EXCLUDES Meatotomy (53020, 53025)
	11.05 11.05 Global Days 090
53460	Urethromeatoplasty, with partial excision of distal urethral segment (Richardson type procedure) A2 T 80
	12.40 12.40 Global Days 090
53500	Urethrolysis, transvaginal, secondary, open, including cystourethroscopy (eg, postsurgical obstruction, scarring) ♀ T 80
	EXCLUDES Retropubic approach (53899)
	Do not report with (52000)
	20.50 20.50 Global Days 090
53502	Urethrorrhaphy, suture of urethral wound or injury, female ♀ A2 T
	13.18 13.18 Global Days 090
53505	Urethrorrhaphy, suture of urethral wound or injury; penile ♂ A2 T 80
	13.17 13.17 Global Days 090
53510	perineal A2 T 80
	17.16 17.16 Global Days 090
53515	prostatomembranous ♂ A2 T 80
	21.72 21.72 Global Days 090
53520	Closure of urethrostomy or urethrocutaneous fistula, male (separate procedure) ♂ A2 T
	EXCLUDES Closure of fistula: Urethrorectal (45820, 45825) Urethrovaginal (57310)
	15.08 15.08 Global Days 090

53600-53665 Urethral Dilation

EXCLUDES Endoscopic procedures; cystoscopy, urethroscopy, cystourethroscopy (52000-52700)
Urethral catheterization (51701-51703)
Urethrocystography injection procedure (51600-51610)

74485

53600	Dilation of urethral stricture by passage of sound or urethral dilator, male; initial ♂ P3 T
	1.77 2.21 Global Days 000
53601	subsequent ♂ P3 T
	1.47 2.10 Global Days 000
53605	Dilation of urethral stricture or vesical neck by passage of sound or urethral dilator, male, general or conduction (spinal) anesthesia ♂ A2 T
	EXCLUDES Procedure performed under local anesthesia (53600-53601, 53620-53621)
	1.79 1.79 Global Days 000
53620	Dilation of urethral stricture by passage of filiform and follower, male; initial ♂ P3 T
	2.40 3.05 Global Days 000
53621	subsequent ♂ P3 T
	1.98 2.83 Global Days 000
53660	Dilation of female urethra including suppository and/or instillation; initial ♀ P3 T
	1.13 1.79 Global Days 000
53661	subsequent ♀ P3 T
	1.11 1.77 Global Days 000

53665 Dilation of female urethra, general or conduction (spinal) anesthesia
  EXCLUDES Procedure performed under local anesthesia (53660-53661)
  74485
  1.09 1.09 Global Days 000

53850-53899 Endoscopic Procedures via Urethra: Prostate

EXCLUDES Endoscopic procedures; cystoscopy, urethroscopy, cystourethroscopy (52000-52700)
Urethrocystography injection procedure (51600-51610)

53850 Transurethral destruction of prostate tissue; by microwave thermotherapy
  81020
  15.50 47.86 Global Days 090

53852 by radiofrequency thermotherapy
  81020
  16.92 46.53 Global Days 090

● **53855** Insertion of a temporary prostatic urethral stent, including urethral measurement
  EXCLUDES Permanent urethral stent insertion (52282)
  2.29 18.06 Global Days 000

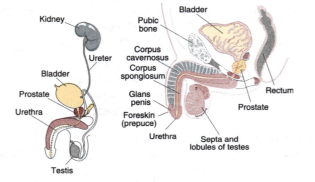

53899 Unlisted procedure, urinary system
  81020
  0.00 0.00 Global Days YYY
  AMA: 2009, Jan, 11-31; 2008, Jan, 10-25; 2007, January, 13-27; 2006, February, 16-18; 2005, October, 23-24; 2005, October, 18-22

Current Procedural Coding Expert – Male Genital System

54000-54015 Procedures of Penis: Incisional

EXCLUDES Debridement of abdominal perineal gangrene (11004-11006)

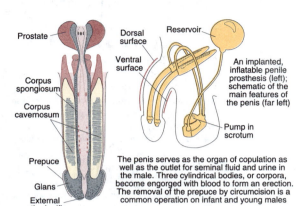

54000	Slitting of prepuce, dorsal or lateral (separate procedure); newborn
	2.87 3.78 Global Days 010
54001	except newborn
	3.74 4.79 Global Days 010
54015	Incision and drainage of penis, deep
	EXCLUDES Abscess, skin/subcutaneous (10060-10160)
	8.45 8.45 Global Days 010

54050-54065 Destruction of Penis Lesions: Multiple Methods

CMS 100-3,140.5   Laser Procedures

EXCLUDES Excision/destruction other lesions (11420-11426, 11620-11626, 17000-17250, 17270-17276)

54050	Destruction of lesion(s), penis (eg, condyloma, papilloma, molluscum contagiosum, herpetic vesicle), simple; chemical
	2.80 3.42 Global Days 010
54055	electrodesiccation
	2.46 3.06 Global Days 010
54056	cryosurgery
	2.96 3.67 Global Days 010
54057	laser surgery
	2.52 3.50 Global Days 010
54060	surgical excision
	3.51 4.64 Global Days 010
54065	Destruction of lesion(s), penis (eg, condyloma, papilloma, molluscum contagiosum, herpetic vesicle), extensive (eg, laser surgery, electrosurgery, cryosurgery, chemosurgery)
	4.67 5.75 Global Days 010

54100-54115 Procedures of Penis: Excisional

54100	Biopsy of penis; (separate procedure)
	3.44 5.06 Global Days 000
54105	deep structures
	5.76 6.93 Global Days 010
54110	Excision of penile plaque (Peyronie disease);
	16.99 16.99 Global Days 090
54111	with graft to 5 cm in length
	21.88 21.88 Global Days 090
	AMA: 2009, Jan, 11-31; 2008, Jan, 10-25; 2007, January, 13-27
54112	with graft greater than 5 cm in length
	25.65 25.65 Global Days 090
54115	Removal foreign body from deep penile tissue (eg, plastic implant)
	11.43 12.05 Global Days 090

54120-54135 Amputation of Penis

EXCLUDES Lymphadenectomy (separate procedure) (38760-38770)

54120	Amputation of penis; partial
	17.21 17.21 Global Days 090
54125	complete
	22.26 22.26 Global Days 090
54130	Amputation of penis, radical; with bilateral inguinofemoral lymphadenectomy
	32.71 32.71 Global Days 090
54135	in continuity with bilateral pelvic lymphadenectomy, including external iliac, hypogastric and obturator nodes
	41.56 41.56 Global Days 090

54150-54164 Circumcision Procedures

54150	Circumcision, using clamp or other device with regional dorsal penile or ring block
	Code also modifier 52 when performed without dorsal penile or ring block
	2.74 4.08 Global Days 000
	AMA: 2009, Mar, 3,4&7; 2009, Jan, 11-31; 2008, Jan, 10-25; 2007, May, 9-11; 2007, January, 13-27; 2007, Jul, 5
54160	Circumcision, surgical excision other than clamp, device, or dorsal slit; neonate (28 days of age or less)
	3.93 5.67 Global Days 010
	AMA: 2009, Jan, 11-31; 2008, Jan, 10-25; 2007, May, 9-11; 2007, January, 13-27; 2007, Jul, 5
54161	older than 28 days of age
	5.34 5.34 Global Days 010
	AMA: 2009, Jan, 11-31; 2008, Jan, 10-25; 2007, May, 9-11; 2007, January, 13-27; 2007, Jul, 5
54162	Lysis or excision of penile post-circumcision adhesions
	5.40 6.72 Global Days 010
54163	Repair incomplete circumcision
	5.83 5.83 Global Days 010
54164	Frenulotomy of penis
	Do not report with (54150, 54160-54163)
	5.14 5.14 Global Days 010

54200-54250 Evaluation and Treatment of Erectile Abnormalities

54200	Injection procedure for Peyronie disease;
	2.22 2.76 Global Days 010
54205	with surgical exposure of plaque
	14.41 14.41 Global Days 090
54220	Irrigation of corpora cavernosa for priapism
	3.70 5.20 Global Days 000
54230	Injection procedure for corpora cavernosography
	74445
	2.16 2.54 Global Days 000

● New Code ▲ Revised Code M Maternity A Age Unlisted Not Covered # Resequenced

CCI + Add-on ○ Mod 51 Exempt @ Mod 63 Exempt ☉ Mod Sedation PQ PQRI

© 2009 Publisher (Blue Ink) CPT only © 2009 American Medical Association. All Rights Reserved. (Black Ink) Medicare (Red Ink)

54231	Dynamic cavernosometry, including intracavernosal injection of vasoactive drugs (eg, papaverine, phentolamine) ♂ P3 T 3.17 3.71 Global Days 000
54235	Injection of corpora cavernosa with pharmacologic agent(s) (eg, papaverine, phentolamine) ♂ P3 T 1.99 2.38 Global Days 000 AMA: 2009, Jan, 11-31; 2008, Jan, 10-25; 2007, January, 13-27
54240	Penile plethysmography ♂ P3 T 80 2.60 2.60 Global Days 000
54250	Nocturnal penile tumescence and/or rigidity test ♂ P3 T 80 3.35 3.35 Global Days 000

54300-54390 Hypospadias Repair and Related Procedures

EXCLUDES Other urethroplasties (53400-53430)
Revascularization of penis (37788)

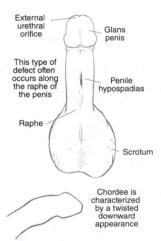

Plastic repair is performed on the penis. Report 54300 to straighten chordee and 54304 to otherwise address chordee and or hypospadias repair

54300	Plastic operation of penis for straightening of chordee (eg, hypospadias), with or without mobilization of urethra ♂ A2 T 80 17.48 17.48 Global Days 090
54304	Plastic operation on penis for correction of chordee or for first stage hypospadias repair with or without transplantation of prepuce and/or skin flaps ♂ A2 T 80 20.45 20.45 Global Days 090
54308	Urethroplasty for second stage hypospadias repair (including urinary diversion); less than 3 cm ♂ A2 T 80 19.48 19.48 Global Days 090
54312	greater than 3 cm ♂ A2 T 80 22.32 22.32 Global Days 090
54316	Urethroplasty for second stage hypospadias repair (including urinary diversion) with free skin graft obtained from site other than genitalia ♂ A2 T 80 27.29 27.29 Global Days 090
54318	Urethroplasty for third stage hypospadias repair to release penis from scrotum (eg, third stage Cecil repair) ♂ A2 T 80 19.72 19.72 Global Days 090
54322	1-stage distal hypospadias repair (with or without chordee or circumcision); with simple meatal advancement (eg, Magpi, V-flap) ♂ A2 T 80 21.32 21.32 Global Days 090
54324	with urethroplasty by local skin flaps (eg, flip-flap, prepucial flap) ♂ A2 T 80 **INCLUDES** Browne's operation 26.51 26.51 Global Days 090
54326	with urethroplasty by local skin flaps and mobilization of urethra ♂ A2 T 80 25.85 25.85 Global Days 090
54328	with extensive dissection to correct chordee and urethroplasty with local skin flaps, skin graft patch, and/or island flap ♂ A2 T 80 **EXCLUDES** Urethroplasty/straightening of chordee (54308) 25.67 25.67 Global Days 090 AMA: 2009, Jan, 11-31; 2008, Jan, 10-25; 2007, January, 13-27
54332	1-stage proximal penile or penoscrotal hypospadias repair requiring extensive dissection to correct chordee and urethroplasty by use of skin graft tube and/or island flap ♂ T 80 27.75 27.75 Global Days 090 AMA: 2009, Jan, 11-31; 2008, Jan, 10-25; 2007, January, 13-27
54336	1-stage perineal hypospadias repair requiring extensive dissection to correct chordee and urethroplasty by use of skin graft tube and/or island flap ♂ T 80 32.57 32.57 Global Days 090 AMA: 2009, Jan, 11-31; 2008, Jan, 10-25; 2007, January, 13-27
54340	Repair of hypospadias complications (ie, fistula, stricture, diverticula); by closure, incision, or excision, simple ♂ A2 T 80 15.45 15.45 Global Days 090
54344	requiring mobilization of skin flaps and urethroplasty with flap or patch graft ♂ A2 T 80 25.90 25.90 Global Days 090
54348	requiring extensive dissection and urethroplasty with flap, patch or tubed graft (includes urinary diversion) ♂ A2 T 80 28.21 28.21 Global Days 090
54352	Repair of hypospadias cripple requiring extensive dissection and excision of previously constructed structures including re-release of chordee and reconstruction of urethra and penis by use of local skin as grafts and island flaps and skin brought in as flaps or grafts ♂ A2 T 80 38.89 38.89 Global Days 090
54360	Plastic operation on penis to correct angulation ♂ A2 T 80 19.67 19.67 Global Days 090
54380	Plastic operation on penis for epispadias distal to external sphincter; ♂ A2 T 80 **INCLUDES** Lowsley's operation 21.79 21.79 Global Days 090
54385	with incontinence ♂ A2 T 80 28.40 28.40 Global Days 090
54390	with exstrophy of bladder ♂ C 80 34.02 34.02 Global Days 090

Current Procedural Coding Expert – Male Genital System

54400-54417 Procedures to Treat Impotence

CMS 100-3,230.4 Diagnosis and Treatment of Impotence
EXCLUDES Other urethroplasties (53400-53430)
Revascularization of penis (37788)

54400 Insertion of penile prosthesis; non-inflatable (semi-rigid)
EXCLUDES Replacement/removal penile prosthesis (54415, 54416)
Code also (C2622)
14.40 14.40 Global Days 090

54401 inflatable (self-contained)
EXCLUDES Replacement/removal penile prosthesis (54415, 54416)
Code also (C1813)
17.61 17.61 Global Days 090

54405 Insertion of multi-component, inflatable penile prosthesis, including placement of pump, cylinders, and reservoir
Code also modifier 52 for reduced services
Code also (C1813)
22.12 22.12 Global Days 090

54406 Removal of all components of a multi-component, inflatable penile prosthesis without replacement of prosthesis
Code also modifier 52 for reduced services
19.91 19.91 Global Days 090

54408 Repair of component(s) of a multi-component, inflatable penile prosthesis
21.57 21.57 Global Days 090

54410 Removal and replacement of all component(s) of a multi-component, inflatable penile prosthesis at the same operative session
Code also (C1813)
23.46 23.46 Global Days 090

54411 Removal and replacement of all components of a multi-component inflatable penile prosthesis through an infected field at the same operative session, including irrigation and debridement of infected tissue
Code also modifier 52 for reduced services
Do not report with (11040-11043)
28.08 28.08 Global Days 090

54415 Removal of non-inflatable (semi-rigid) or inflatable (self-contained) penile prosthesis, without replacement of prosthesis
14.31 14.31 Global Days 090

54416 Removal and replacement of non-inflatable (semi-rigid) or inflatable (self-contained) penile prosthesis at the same operative session
Code also (C1813, C2622)
19.25 19.25 Global Days 090

54417 Removal and replacement of non-inflatable (semi-rigid) or inflatable (self-contained) penile prosthesis through an infected field at the same operative session, including irrigation and debridement of infected tissue
Do not report with (11040-11043)
24.55 24.55 Global Days 090

54420-54450 Other Procedures of the Penis

EXCLUDES Other urethroplasties (53400-53430)
Revascularization of penis (37788)

54420 Corpora cavernosa-saphenous vein shunt (priapism operation), unilateral or bilateral
19.19 19.19 Global Days 090

54430 Corpora cavernosa-corpus spongiosum shunt (priapism operation), unilateral or bilateral
17.39 17.39 Global Days 090

54435 Corpora cavernosa-glans penis fistulization (eg, biopsy needle, Winter procedure, rongeur, or punch) for priapism
11.23 11.23 Global Days 090

54440 Plastic operation of penis for injury
0.00 0.00 Global Days 090

54450 Foreskin manipulation including lysis of preputial adhesions and stretching
1.60 1.88 Global Days 000

54500-54560 Testicular Procedures: Incisional

EXCLUDES Debridement of abdominal perineal gangrene (11004-11006)

54500 Biopsy of testis, needle (separate procedure)
EXCLUDES Fine needle aspiration (10021, 10022)
88172, 88173
2.03 2.03 Global Days 000

54505 Biopsy of testis, incisional (separate procedure)
Code also vasotomy for vasogram, seminal vesiculogram, epididymogram when combined (55300)
5.67 5.67 Global Days 010

54512 Excision of extraparenchymal lesion of testis
14.66 14.66 Global Days 090
AMA: 2009, Jan, 11-31; 2008, Jan, 10-25; 2007, January, 13-27; 2005, August, 13-15

54520 Orchiectomy, simple (including subcapsular), with or without testicular prosthesis, scrotal or inguinal approach
INCLUDES Huggins' orchiectomy
EXCLUDES Lymphadenectomy, radical retroperitoneal (38780)
Code also hernia repair if performed (49505, 49507)
8.84 8.84 Global Days 090

54522 Orchiectomy, partial
EXCLUDES Lymphadenectomy, radical retroperitoneal (38780)
16.04 16.04 Global Days 090

54530 Orchiectomy, radical, for tumor; inguinal approach
EXCLUDES Lymphadenectomy, radical retroperitoneal (38780)
13.71 13.71 Global Days 090

54535 with abdominal exploration
EXCLUDES Lymphadenectomy, radical retroperitoneal (38780)
20.28 20.28 Global Days 090

● New Code ▲ Revised Code Maternity Age Unlisted Not Covered # Resequenced
CCI + Add-on ⊘ Mod 51 Exempt Mod 63 Exempt ⊙ Mod Sedation PQRI

© 2009 Publisher (Blue Ink)   Medicare (Red Ink)

54550

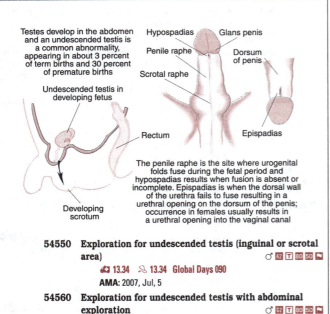

Testes develop in the abdomen and an undescended testis is a common abnormality, appearing in about 3 percent of term births and 30 percent of premature births

The penile raphe is the site where urogenital folds fuse during the fetal period and hypospadias results when fusion is absent or incomplete. Epispadias is when the dorsal wall of the urethra fails to fuse resulting in a urethral opening on the dorsum of the penis; occurrence in females usually results in a urethral opening into the vaginal canal

54550 Exploration for undescended testis (inguinal or scrotal area) ♂ A2 T 80 50
 13.34 13.34 Global Days 090
AMA: 2007, Jul, 5

54560 Exploration for undescended testis with abdominal exploration ♂ 62 T 80 50
 18.71 18.71 Global Days 090
AMA: 2007, Jul, 5

54600-54699 Open and Laparoscopic Testicular Procedures

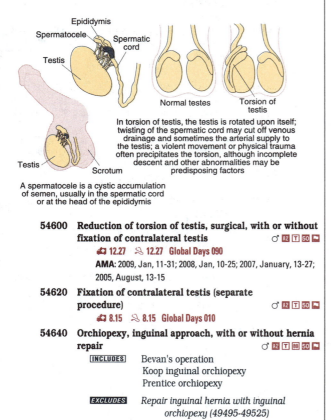

In torsion of testis, the testis is rotated upon itself; twisting of the spermatic cord may cut off venous drainage and sometimes the arterial supply to the testis; a violent movement or physical trauma often precipitates the torsion, although incomplete descent and other abnormalities may be predisposing factors

A spermatocele is a cystic accumulation of semen, usually in the spermatic cord or at the head of the epididymis

54600 Reduction of torsion of testis, surgical, with or without fixation of contralateral testis ♂ A2 T 50
 12.27 12.27 Global Days 090
AMA: 2009, Jan, 11-31; 2008, Jan, 10-25; 2007, January, 13-27; 2005, August, 13-15

54620 Fixation of contralateral testis (separate procedure) ♂ A2 T 50
 8.15 8.15 Global Days 010

54640 Orchiopexy, inguinal approach, with or without hernia repair ♂ A2 T 80 50
INCLUDES Bevan's operation
  Koop inguinal orchiopexy
  Prentice orchiopexy
EXCLUDES Repair inguinal hernia with inguinal orchiopexy (49495-49525)
 12.92 12.92 Global Days 090
AMA: 2009, Jan, 11-31; 2008, Jan, 10-25; 2008, Jun, 3-6; 2007, January, 13-27

54650 Orchiopexy, abdominal approach, for intra-abdominal testis (eg, Fowler-Stephens) ♂ C 80 50
EXCLUDES Laparoscopic orchiopexy (54692)
 19.35 19.35 Global Days 090

54660 Insertion of testicular prosthesis (separate procedure) ♂ A2 T 80 50
 9.61 9.61 Global Days 090

54670 Suture or repair of testicular injury ♂ A2 T 80 50
 10.93 10.93 Global Days 090

54680 Transplantation of testis(es) to thigh (because of scrotal destruction) ♂ A2 T 80 50
 21.48 21.48 Global Days 090

54690 Laparoscopy, surgical; orchiectomy ♂ A2 T 80 50
INCLUDES Diagnostic laparoscopy
 20.12 20.12 Global Days 090

54692 orchiopexy for intra-abdominal testis ♂ 62 T 50
INCLUDES Diagnostic laparoscopy
 20.77 20.77 Global Days 090

54699 Unlisted laparoscopy procedure, testis ♂ T 80 50
 0.00 0.00 Global Days YYY

54700-54901 Open Procedures of the Epididymis

54700 Incision and drainage of epididymis, testis and/or scrotal space (eg, abscess or hematoma) ♂ A2 T
EXCLUDES Debridement of genitalia for necrotizing soft tissue infection (11004-11006)
 5.81 5.81 Global Days 010

54800 Biopsy of epididymis, needle ♂ A2 T 80
EXCLUDES Fine needle aspiration (10021, 10022)
 88172, 88173
 4.23 4.23 Global Days 000
AMA: 2007, Jul, 5

54830 Excision of local lesion of epididymis ♂ A2 T 80
 10.08 10.08 Global Days 090

54840 Excision of spermatocele, with or without epididymectomy ♂ A2 T
 8.66 8.66 Global Days 090

54860 Epididymectomy; unilateral ♂ A2 T
 11.32 11.32 Global Days 090

54861 bilateral ♂ A2 T 80
 15.35 15.35 Global Days 090

54865 Exploration of epididymis, with or without biopsy ♂ A2 T 80
 9.65 9.65 Global Days 090
AMA: 2007, Jul, 5

54900 Epididymovasostomy, anastomosis of epididymis to vas deferens; unilateral ♂ A2 T 80
EXCLUDES Operating microscope (69990)
 22.22 22.22 Global Days 090
AMA: 2009, Jan, 11-31; 2008, Jan, 10-25; 2007, January, 13-27

54901 bilateral ♂ A2 T 80
EXCLUDES Operating microscope (69990)
 29.38 29.38 Global Days 090
AMA: 2009, Jan, 11-31; 2008, Jan, 10-25; 2007, January, 13-27

Current Procedural Coding Expert – Male Genital System

55000-55180 Procedures of the Tunica Vaginalis and Scrotum

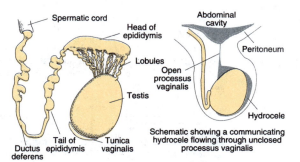

The tunica vaginalis is a closed sac within the scrotum and is the lower remnant of the path taken by the testis as it descends from the abdomen just prior to birth. The presence of fluid in this pathway is called a hydrocele. The testes, or testicles, are the male reproductive organs. Each produces sperm and male sex hormones

55000 Puncture aspiration of hydrocele, tunica vaginalis, with or without injection of medication
  2.32 3.06 Global Days 000

55040 Excision of hydrocele; unilateral
  EXCLUDES Repair of hernia with hydrocelectomy (49495-49501)
  9.16 9.16 Global Days 090
  AMA: 2008, Jun, 3-6

55041 bilateral
  EXCLUDES Repair of hernia with hydrocelectomy (49495-49501)
  13.84 13.84 Global Days 090

55060 Repair of tunica vaginalis hydrocele (Bottle type)
  10.30 10.30 Global Days 090

55100 Drainage of scrotal wall abscess
  EXCLUDES Debridement of genitalia for necrotizing soft tissue infection (11004-11006)
  Incision and drainage of scrotal space (54700)
  4.46 5.58 Global Days 010

55110 Scrotal exploration
  10.48 10.48 Global Days 090

55120 Removal of foreign body in scrotum
  9.65 9.65 Global Days 090

55150 Resection of scrotum
  EXCLUDES Lesion excision of skin of scrotum (11420-11426, 11620-11626)
  13.29 13.29 Global Days 090

55175 Scrotoplasty; simple
  9.79 9.79 Global Days 090

55180 complicated
  18.77 18.77 Global Days 090

55200-55680 Procedures of Other Male Genital Ducts and Glands

55200 Vasotomy, cannulization with or without incision of vas, unilateral or bilateral (separate procedure)
  7.51 11.11 Global Days 090

55250 Vasectomy, unilateral or bilateral (separate procedure), including postoperative semen examination(s)
  6.04 9.64 Global Days 090
  AMA: 2009, Jan, 11-31; 2008, Jan, 10-25; 2007, January, 13-27

55300 Vasotomy for vasograms, seminal vesiculograms, or epididymograms, unilateral or bilateral
  Code also biopsy of testis when combined (54505)
  74440
  5.16 5.16 Global Days 000

55400 Vasovasostomy, vasovasorrhaphy
  EXCLUDES Operating microscope (69990)
  13.54 13.54 Global Days 090
  AMA: 2009, Jan, 11-31; 2008, Jan, 10-25; 2007, January, 13-27

55450 Ligation (percutaneous) of vas deferens, unilateral or bilateral (separate procedure)
  6.99 9.31 Global Days 010

55500 Excision of hydrocele of spermatic cord, unilateral (separate procedure)
  10.75 10.75 Global Days 090

55520 Excision of lesion of spermatic cord (separate procedure)
  12.22 12.22 Global Days 090
  AMA: 2009, Jan, 11-31; 2008, Jan, 10-25; 2007, January, 13-27

55530 Excision of varicocele or ligation of spermatic veins for varicocele; (separate procedure)
  9.54 9.54 Global Days 090

55535 abdominal approach
  11.64 11.64 Global Days 090

55540 with hernia repair
  14.60 14.60 Global Days 090

55550 Laparoscopy, surgical, with ligation of spermatic veins for varicocele
  INCLUDES Diagnostic laparoscopy
  11.60 11.60 Global Days 090

55559 Unlisted laparoscopy procedure, spermatic cord
  0.00 0.00 Global Days YYY

55600 Vesiculotomy;
  11.38 11.38 Global Days 090

55605 complicated
  14.09 14.09 Global Days 090

55650 Vesiculectomy, any approach
  19.60 19.60 Global Days 090

55680 Excision of Mullerian duct cyst
  EXCLUDES Injection procedure (52010, 55300)
  9.33 9.33 Global Days 090

● New Code ▲ Revised Code Ⓜ Maternity Age Unlisted Not Covered # Resequenced
CCI + Add-on Mod 51 Exempt Mod 63 Exempt Mod Sedation PQRI

© 2009 Publisher (Blue Ink) CPT only © 2009 American Medical Association. All Rights Reserved. (Black Ink) Medicare (Red Ink) 197

55700-55725 Procedures of Prostate: Incisional

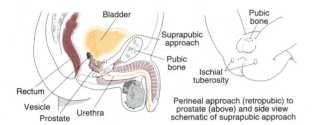

Perineal approach (retropubic) to prostate (above) and side view schematic of suprapubic approach

The walnut-sized prostate gland secretes a thin, milky fluid that mixes with spermatic fluids during ejaculation; its secretion constitutes about one-third of the volume of seminal fluid. The prostate is palpable via the rectum. Some procedures are via the urethra, which can be dilated to accommodate instruments. The seminal vesicles may also be palpated via the rectum. Each is a long, coiled tube which secretes a thick fluid that mixes with sperm as it passes along the ejaculatory ducts. The ejaculatory ducts are the union of the seminal vesicles and the sperm-carrying ductus deferens

55700 Biopsy, prostate; needle or punch, single or multiple, any approach
  EXCLUDES: Fine needle aspiration (10021, 10022)
  Needle biopsy of prostate, saturation sampling for prostate mapping (55706)
  88172, 88173
  76942
  3.83 5.62 Global Days 000
  AMA: 2006, April, 11-18

55705 incisional, any approach
  7.24 7.24 Global Days 010

55706 Biopsies, prostate, needle, transperineal, stereotactic template guided saturation sampling, including imaging guidance
  Do not report with (55700)
  10.01 10.01 Global Days 010

55720 Prostatotomy, external drainage of prostatic abscess, any approach; simple
  EXCLUDES: Drainage of prostatic abscess, transurethral (52700)
  12.27 12.27 Global Days 090

55725 complicated
  EXCLUDES: Drainage of prostatic abscess, transurethral (52700)
  16.07 16.07 Global Days 090

55801-55845 Open Prostatectomy

EXCLUDES: Node dissection, independent (38770-38780)
Pelvic limited lymphadenectomy for staging (separate procedure) (38562)
Transurethral prostate
  Destruction (53850-53852)
  Resection (52601-52640)

55801 Prostatectomy, perineal, subtotal (including control of postoperative bleeding, vasectomy, meatotomy, urethral calibration and/or dilation, and internal urethrotomy)
  29.91 29.91 Global Days 090

55810 Prostatectomy, perineal radical;
  INCLUDES: Walsh modified radical prostatectomy
  36.28 36.28 Global Days 090

55812 with lymph node biopsy(s) (limited pelvic lymphadenectomy)
  44.22 44.22 Global Days 090

55815 with bilateral pelvic lymphadenectomy, including external iliac, hypogastric and obturator nodes
  EXCLUDES: Perineal radical prostatectomy when performed on a separate day from bilateral pelvic lymphadenectomy (38770, 55810)
  48.50 48.50 Global Days 090

55821 Prostatectomy (including control of postoperative bleeding, vasectomy, meatotomy, urethral calibration and/or dilation, and internal urethrotomy); suprapubic, subtotal, 1 or 2 stages
  23.93 23.93 Global Days 090

55831 retropubic, subtotal
  25.93 25.93 Global Days 090

55840 Prostatectomy, retropubic radical, with or without nerve sparing;
  EXCLUDES: Prostatectomy, radical retropubic, performed laparoscopically (55866)
  36.76 36.76 Global Days 090

55842 with lymph node biopsy(s) (limited pelvic lymphadenectomy)
  39.35 39.35 Global Days 090

55845 with bilateral pelvic lymphadenectomy, including external iliac, hypogastric, and obturator nodes
  EXCLUDES: Radical retropubic prostatectomy when performed on a separate day from bilateral pelvic lymphadenectomy (38770, 55840)
  45.09 45.09 Global Days 090

55860-55865 Prostate Exposure for Radiation Source Application

55860 Exposure of prostate, any approach, for insertion of radioactive substance;
  77776-77778
  23.90 23.90 Global Days 090

55862 with lymph node biopsy(s) (limited pelvic lymphadenectomy)
  30.06 30.06 Global Days 090

55865 with bilateral pelvic lymphadenectomy, including external iliac, hypogastric and obturator nodes
  36.62 36.62 Global Days 090

55866 Laparoscopic Prostatectomy

55866 Laparoscopy, surgical prostatectomy, retropubic radical, including nerve sparing
  INCLUDES: Diagnostic laparoscopy
  EXCLUDES: Open method (55840)
  47.95 47.95 Global Days 090

55870-55899 Miscellaneous Prostate Procedures

55870 Electroejaculation
  EXCLUDES: Artificial insemination (58321-58322)
  3.90 4.65 Global Days 000

▲ **55873** Cryosurgical ablation of the prostate (includes ultrasonic guidance and monitoring)
  Code also (C2618)
  21.36 162.12 Global Days 090
  AMA: 2006, April, 11-18

Current Procedural Coding Expert – Female Genital System

55875 Transperineal placement of needles or catheters into prostate for interstitial radioelement application, with or without cystoscopy
EXCLUDES: The placement of needles or catheters into the pelvic organs and/or genitalia (except for the prostate) for interstitial radioelement application (55920)
76965, 77776-77787
20.85 20.85 Global Days 090
AMA: 2008, Jun, 8-11; 2007, May, 1-2; 2007, March, 7-8

▲ **55876** Placement of interstitial device(s) for radiation therapy guidance (eg, fiducial markers, dosimeter), percutaneous, prostate, single or multiple
Code also supply of device
76942, 77002, 77012, 77021
2.75 3.56 Global Days 000
AMA: 2007, May, 1-2

55899 Unlisted procedure, male genital system
0.00 0.00 Global Days YYY
AMA: 2007, May, 1-2

55920 Insertion Brachytherapy Catheters/Needles Pelvis/Genitalia, Male/Female

55920 Placement of needles or catheters into pelvic organs and/or genitalia (except prostate) for subsequent interstitial radioelement application
EXCLUDES: Insertion of Heyman capsules for purposes of brachytherapy (58346)
Insertion of vaginal ovoids and/or uterine tandems for purposes of brachytherapy (57155)
Placement of catheters or needles, prostate (55875)
12.59 12.59 Global Days 000

55970-55980 Transsexual Surgery

CMS 100-2,16,180 Services Related to Noncovered Procedures
CMS 100-3,140.3 Transexual Surgery

55970 Intersex surgery; male to female
0.00 0.00 Global Days XXX

55980 female to male
0.00 0.00 Global Days XXX

56405-56420 Incision and Drainage of Abscess

EXCLUDES: Incision and drainage Skene's gland cyst/abscess (53060)
Incision and drainage subcutaneous abscess/cyst/furuncle (10040, 10060, 10061)

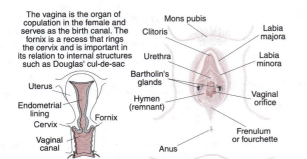

The vagina is the organ of copulation in the female and serves as the birth canal. The fornix is a recess that rings the cervix and is important in its relation to internal structures such as Douglas' cul-de-sac

Labels: Mons pubis, Clitoris, Urethra, Bartholin's glands, Hymen (remnant), Labia majora, Labia minora, Vaginal orifice, Frenulum or fourchette, Anus, Uterus, Endometrial lining, Cervix, Fornix, Vaginal canal

The external female genital region is collectively known as the vulva, or sometimes, the pudendum. A Bartholin's gland is located on either side of the orifice. The perineum is the space between the anus and the vagina, but is often generally defined as the entire pelvic floor and its related structures. Introitus is a general term for the vaginal entrance

56405 Incision and drainage of vulva or perineal abscess
2.92 2.94 Global Days 010

56420 Incision and drainage of Bartholin's gland abscess
2.51 3.21 Global Days 010

56440-56442 Other Female Genital Incisional Procedures

EXCLUDES: Incision and drainage subcutaneous abscess/cyst/furuncle (10040, 10060, 10061)

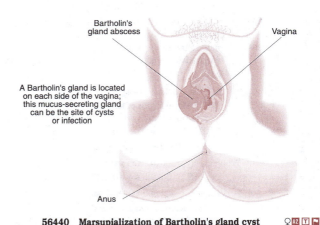

A Bartholin's gland is located on each side of the vagina; this mucus-secreting gland can be the site of cysts or infection

Labels: Bartholin's gland abscess, Vagina, Anus

56440 Marsupialization of Bartholin's gland cyst
5.03 5.03 Global Days 010

56441 Lysis of labial adhesions
3.71 3.83 Global Days 010

56442 Hymenotomy, simple incision
1.29 1.29 Global Days 000

56501-56515 Destruction of Vulvar Lesions, Any Method

CMS 100-3,140.5 Laser Procedures
EXCLUDES: Excision/fulguration/destruction Skene's glands (53270)
Urethral caruncle (53265)

56501 Destruction of lesion(s), vulva; simple (eg, laser surgery, electrosurgery, cryosurgery, chemosurgery)
3.08 3.45 Global Days 010
AMA: 2006, April, 11-18

56515 extensive (eg, laser surgery, electrosurgery, cryosurgery, chemosurgery)
5.43 6.00 Global Days 010

56605-56606 Vulvar and Perineal Biopsies

EXCLUDES: Excision local lesion (11420-11426, 11620-11626)

56605 Biopsy of vulva or perineum (separate procedure); 1 lesion
1.69 2.20 Global Days 000
AMA: 2008, Jun, 3-6

+ **56606** each separate additional lesion (List separately in addition to code for primary procedure)
Code first (56605)
0.83 1.02 Global Days ZZZ

● New Code   ▲ Revised Code   M Maternity   Age   Unlisted   Not Covered   # Resequenced
CCI   + Add-on   Mod 51 Exempt   Mod 63 Exempt   Mod Sedation   PQRI
© 2009 Publisher (Blue Ink)   CPT only © 2009 American Medical Association. All Rights Reserved. (Black Ink)   Medicare (Red Ink)

56620-56640 Vulvectomy Procedures

INCLUDES Removal of:
Greater than 80% of the vulvar area - complete procedure
Less than 80% of the vulvar area - partial procedure
Skin and deep subcutaneous tissue - radical procedure
Skin and superficial subcutaneous tissues - simple procedure

EXCLUDES Skin graft (15004-15005, 15120, 15121, 15240, 15241)

56620	Vulvectomy simple; partial	
	13.65 13.65 Global Days 090	
56625	complete	
	16.57 16.57 Global Days 090	
56630	Vulvectomy, radical, partial;	
	24.48 24.48 Global Days 090	
56631	with unilateral inguinofemoral lymphadenectomy	
	INCLUDES Bassett's operation	
	31.14 31.14 Global Days 090	
56632	with bilateral inguinofemoral lymphadenectomy	
	INCLUDES Bassett's operation	
	36.20 36.20 Global Days 090	
56633	Vulvectomy, radical, complete;	
	INCLUDES Bassett's operation	
	31.99 31.99 Global Days 090	
56634	with unilateral inguinofemoral lymphadenectomy	
	INCLUDES Bassett's operation	
	33.75 33.75 Global Days 090	
56637	with bilateral inguinofemoral lymphadenectomy	
	INCLUDES Bassett's operation	
	39.65 39.65 Global Days 090	
56640	Vulvectomy, radical, complete, with inguinofemoral, iliac, and pelvic lymphadenectomy	
	INCLUDES Bassett's operation	
	EXCLUDES Lymphadenectomy (38760-38780)	
	39.63 39.63 Global Days 090	

56700-56740 Other Excisional Procedures: External Female Genitalia

56700 Partial hymenectomy or revision of hymenal ring
  5.10 5.10 Global Days 010

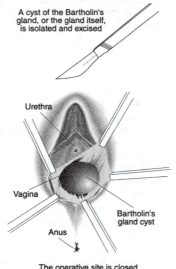

56740 Excision of Bartholin's gland or cyst
EXCLUDES Excision/fulguration/marsupialization:
Skene's glands (53270)
Urethral carcinoma (53220)
Urethral caruncle (53265)
Urethral diverticulum (53230, 53240)
  8.21 8.21 Global Days 010

56800-56810 Repair/Reconstruction External Female Genitalia

EXCLUDES Repair of urethra for mucosal prolapse (53275)

56800 Plastic repair of introitus
INCLUDES Emmet's operation
  6.61 6.61 Global Days 010

56805 Clitoroplasty for intersex state
  31.87 31.87 Global Days 090

56810 Perineoplasty, repair of perineum, nonobstetrical (separate procedure)
INCLUDES Emmet's operation
EXCLUDES Genitalia wound repair (12001-12007, 12041-12047, 13131-13133)
Introitus plastic repair (56800)
Sphincteroplasty, anal (46750, 46751)
Vaginal/perineum recent injury repair, nonobstetrical (57210)
Vulva/perineum episiorrhaphy/episioperineorrhaphy for recent injury, nonobstetrical (57210)
  7.15 7.15 Global Days 010

56820-56821 Vulvar Colposcopy with/without Biopsy

EXCLUDES Colposcopic procedures and/or examinations:
Cervix (57452-57461)
Vagina (57420, 57421)

56820 Colposcopy of the vulva;
  2.36 2.95 Global Days 000

56821 with biopsy(s)
  3.20 3.93 Global Days 000

Current Procedural Coding Expert – Female Genital System   57267

57000-57023 Incisional Procedures: Vagina

57000 Colpotomy; with exploration
  5.19   5.19   Global Days 010

57010 with drainage of pelvic abscess
  INCLUDES Laroyenne operation
  11.89   11.89   Global Days 090

57020 Colpocentesis (separate procedure)
  2.28   2.56   Global Days 000

57022 Incision and drainage of vaginal hematoma; obstetrical/postpartum
  4.63   4.63   Global Days 010

57023 non-obstetrical (eg, post-trauma, spontaneous bleeding)
  8.58   8.58   Global Days 010

57061-57065 Destruction of Vaginal Lesions, Any Method

CMS 100-3,140.5   Laser Procedures

57061 Destruction of vaginal lesion(s); simple (eg, laser surgery, electrosurgery, cryosurgery, chemosurgery)
  2.62   2.98   Global Days 010
  AMA: 2009, Jan, 11-31; 2008, Jan, 10-25; 2007, January, 13-27

57065 extensive (eg, laser surgery, electrosurgery, cryosurgery, chemosurgery)
  4.67   5.14   Global Days 010
  AMA: 2009, Jan, 11-31; 2008, Jan, 10-25; 2007, January, 13-27

57100-57135 Excisional Procedures: Vagina

57100 Biopsy of vaginal mucosa; simple (separate procedure)
  1.84   2.35   Global Days 000

57105 extensive, requiring suture (including cysts)
  3.34   3.57   Global Days 010

57106 Vaginectomy, partial removal of vaginal wall;
  13.17   13.17   Global Days 090

57107 with removal of paravaginal tissue (radical vaginectomy)
  39.10   39.10   Global Days 090

57109 with removal of paravaginal tissue (radical vaginectomy) with bilateral total pelvic lymphadenectomy and para-aortic lymph node sampling (biopsy)
  45.34   45.34   Global Days 090

57110 Vaginectomy, complete removal of vaginal wall;
  24.91   24.91   Global Days 090

57111 with removal of paravaginal tissue (radical vaginectomy)
  45.34   45.34   Global Days 090

57112 with removal of paravaginal tissue (radical vaginectomy) with bilateral total pelvic lymphadenectomy and para-aortic lymph node sampling (biopsy)
  46.61   46.61   Global Days 090

57120 Colpocleisis (Le Fort type)
  14.02   14.02   Global Days 090

57130 Excision of vaginal septum
  4.35   4.77   Global Days 010

57135 Excision of vaginal cyst or tumor
  4.71   5.14   Global Days 010

57150-57180 Irrigation/Insertion/Introduction Vaginal Medication or Supply

57150 Irrigation of vagina and/or application of medicament for treatment of bacterial, parasitic, or fungoid disease
  0.83   1.20   Global Days 000

57155 Insertion of uterine tandems and/or vaginal ovoids for clinical brachytherapy
  EXCLUDES The placement of needles or catheters into the pelvic organs and/or genitalia (except for the prostate) for interstitial radioelement application (55920)
  77761-77763, 77785-77787
  11.38   11.38   Global Days 090

57160 Fitting and insertion of pessary or other intravaginal support device
  1.33   2.01   Global Days 000
  AMA: 2009, Jan, 11-31; 2008, Jan, 10-25; 2007, January, 13-27

57170 Diaphragm or cervical cap fitting with instructions
  1.37   1.65   Global Days 000

57180 Introduction of any hemostatic agent or pack for spontaneous or traumatic nonobstetrical vaginal hemorrhage (separate procedure)
  2.88   3.69   Global Days 010

57200-57335 Vaginal Repair and Reconstruction

CMS 100-3,230.10   Incontinence Control Devices
EXCLUDES Marshall-Marchetti-Kranz type urethral suspension, abdominal approach (51840, 51841)
Urethral suspension performed laparoscopically (51990)

57200 Colporrhaphy, suture of injury of vagina (nonobstetrical)
  8.07   8.07   Global Days 090

57210 Colpoperineorrhaphy, suture of injury of vagina and/or perineum (nonobstetrical)
  9.99   9.99   Global Days 090

57220 Plastic operation on urethral sphincter, vaginal approach (eg, Kelly urethral plication)
  8.71   8.71   Global Days 090

57230 Plastic repair of urethrocele
  10.85   10.85   Global Days 090

57240 Anterior colporrhaphy, repair of cystocele with or without repair of urethrocele
  18.45   18.45   Global Days 090

57250 Posterior colporrhaphy, repair of rectocele with or without perineorrhaphy
  EXCLUDES Rectocele repair (separate procedure) without posterior colporrhaphy (45560)
  18.74   18.74   Global Days 090

57260 Combined anteroposterior colporrhaphy;
  23.18   23.18   Global Days 090

57265 with enterocele repair
  25.37   25.37   Global Days 090

+ **57267** Insertion of mesh or other prosthesis for repair of pelvic floor defect, each site (anterior, posterior compartment), vaginal approach (List separately in addition to code for primary procedure)
  Code first (45560, 57240-57265, 57285)
  7.21   7.21   Global Days ZZZ
  AMA: 2009, Jan, 11-31; 2008, Jan, 10-25; 2007, January, 13-27; 2005, July, 13-16

● New Code   ▲ Revised Code   M Maternity   △ Age   Unlisted   Not Covered   # Resequenced
□ CCI   + Add-on   ⊘ Mod 51 Exempt   ⊗ Mod 63 Exempt   ⊙ Mod Sedation   PQRI

© 2009 Publisher (Blue Ink)   CPT only © 2009 American Medical Association. All Rights Reserved. (Black Ink)   Medicare (Red Ink)   201

Code	Description	RVU (Facility)	RVU (Non-Facility)	Global Days
57268	Repair of enterocele, vaginal approach (separate procedure) ♀ A2 T 80	13.18	13.18	090
57270	Repair of enterocele, abdominal approach (separate procedure) ♀ C 80	22.18	22.18	090
57280	Colpopexy, abdominal approach ♀ C 80	26.47	26.47	090
57282	Colpopexy, vaginal; extra-peritoneal approach (sacrospinous, iliococcygeus) ♀ T 80	13.71	13.71	090
57283	intra-peritoneal approach (uterosacral, levator myorrhaphy) ♀ T 80	19.11	19.11	090
57284	Paravaginal defect repair (including repair of cystocele, if performed); open abdominal approach ♀ T 80	22.61	22.61	090

Do not report with (51840-51841, 51990, 57240, 57260-57265, 58152, 58267)

AMA: 2009, Jan, 11-31; 2008, Jan, 10-25; 2007, January, 13-27; 2005, July, 13-16

Code	Description	RVU (Facility)	RVU (Non-Facility)	Global Days
57285	vaginal approach ♀ T			

Do not report with (51990, 57240, 57260-57265, 58267)

18.64 / 18.64 Global Days 090

| 57287 | Removal or revision of sling for stress incontinence (eg, fascia or synthetic) ♀ 62 T 80 | 18.52 | 18.52 | 090 |

AMA: 2009, Jan, 11-31; 2008, Jan, 10-25

| 57288 | Sling operation for stress incontinence (eg, fascia or synthetic) ♀ A2 T 80 |

INCLUDES Millin-Read operation

EXCLUDES Sling operation for stress incontinence performed laparoscopically (51992)

Code also (C1762, C1763, C1771, C1781, C2631)

19.28 / 19.28 Global Days 090

AMA: 2009, Jan, 11-31; 2008, Jan, 10-25; 2007, January, 13-27

| 57289 | Pereyra procedure, including anterior colporrhaphy ♀ A2 T 80 | 19.84 | 19.84 | 090 |
| 57291 | Construction of artificial vagina; without graft ♀ A2 T 80 | | | |

INCLUDES McIndoe vaginal construction

14.60 / 14.60 Global Days 090

| 57292 | with graft ♀ T 80 | 22.98 | 22.98 | 090 |
| 57295 | Revision (including removal) of prosthetic vaginal graft; vaginal approach ♀ 62 T 80 | | | |

EXCLUDES Laparoscopic approach (57426)

13.12 / 13.12 Global Days 090

| 57296 | open abdominal approach ♀ C 80 | | | |

EXCLUDES Laparoscopic approach (57426)

26.49 / 26.49 Global Days 090

57300	Closure of rectovaginal fistula; vaginal or transanal approach ♀ A2 T 80	15.29	15.29	090
57305	abdominal approach ♀ C 80	25.63	25.63	090
57307	abdominal approach, with concomitant colostomy ♀ C 80	29.18	29.18	090
57308	transperineal approach, with perineal body reconstruction, with or without levator plication ♀ C 80	17.66	17.66	090
57310	Closure of urethrovaginal fistula; ♀ T 80	12.44	12.44	090
57311	with bulbocavernosus transplant ♀ C 80	14.20	14.20	090
57320	Closure of vesicovaginal fistula; vaginal approach ♀ 62 T 80			

EXCLUDES Cystostomy, concomitant (51020-51040, 51101-51102)

14.46 / 14.46 Global Days 090

| 57330 | transvesical and vaginal approach ♀ T 80 | | | |

EXCLUDES Vesicovaginal fistula closure, abdominal approach (51900)

20.18 / 20.18 Global Days 090

| 57335 | Vaginoplasty for intersex state ♀ T 80 | 32.18 | 32.18 | 090 |

57400-57415 Treatment of Vaginal Disorders Under Anesthesia

| 57400 | Dilation of vagina under anesthesia (other than local) ♀ A2 T 80 | 3.69 | 3.69 | 000 |
| 57410 | Pelvic examination under anesthesia (other than local) ♀ A2 T | 2.95 | 2.95 | 000 |

AMA: 2006, April, 1-7

| 57415 | Removal of impacted vaginal foreign body (separate procedure) under anesthesia (other than local) ♀ A2 T 80 | | | |

EXCLUDES Removal of impacted vaginal foreign body without anesthesia (99201-99499)

4.34 / 4.34 Global Days 010

57420-57426 Endoscopic Vaginal Procedures

| 57420 | Colposcopy of the entire vagina, with cervix if present; ♀ P3 T | | | |

EXCLUDES Colposcopic procedures and/or examinations:
Cervix (57452-57461)
Vulva (56820-56821)
Colposcopy of cervix and upper adjacent vagina (57452)
Endometrial sampling (biopsy) performed at the same time as colposcopy (58110)

2.51 / 3.10 Global Days 000

| 57421 | with biopsy(s) of vagina/cervix ♀ P3 T | | | |

EXCLUDES Colposcopic procedures and/or examinations:
Cervix (57452-57461)
Vulva (56820-56821)
Colposcopy of cervix and upper adjacent vagina (57452)
Endometrial sampling (biopsy) performed at the same time as colposcopy (58110)

3.43 / 4.18 Global Days 000

AMA: 2009, Jan, 11-31; 2008, Jan, 10-25; 2007, January, 13-27; 2006, June, 16-17

Current Procedural Coding Expert – Female Genital System 57800

57423	Paravaginal defect repair (including repair of cystocele, if performed), laparoscopic approach ♀ T 80	
	Do not report with (49320, 51840-51841, 51990, 57240, 57260, 58152, 58267)	
	25.50 25.50 Global Days 090	
57425	Laparoscopy, surgical, colpopexy (suspension of vaginal apex) ♀ T 80	
	27.02 27.02 Global Days 090	
● 57426	Revision (including removal) of prosthetic vaginal graft, laparoscopic approach ♀ 62 T 80	
	EXCLUDES Open abdominal approach (57296) Vaginal approach (57295)	
	23.65 23.65 Global Days 090	

57452-57461 Endoscopic Cervical Procedures

Code also endometrial sampling (biopsy) performed at the same time as colposcopy (58110)

EXCLUDES Cervicography
Colposcopic procedures and/or examinations:
Vagina (57420-57421)
Vulva (56820-56821)

57452	Colposcopy of the cervix including upper/adjacent vagina; ♀ P3 T	
	Do not report with (57454-57461)	
	2.52 2.90 Global Days 000	
57454	with biopsy(s) of the cervix and endocervical curettage ♀ P3 T	
	3.78 4.17 Global Days 000	
57455	with biopsy(s) of the cervix ♀ P3 T	
	3.10 3.83 Global Days 000	
57456	with endocervical curettage ♀ P3 T	
	Do not report with (57461)	
	2.88 3.61 Global Days 000	
	AMA: 2009, Jan, 11-31; 2008, Jan, 10-25; 2007, January, 13-27	
57460	with loop electrode biopsy(s) of the cervix ♀ P3 T	
	4.53 7.32 Global Days 000	
	AMA: 2009, Jan, 11-31; 2008, Jan, 10-25; 2007, January, 13-27; 2005, July, 13-16	
57461	with loop electrode conization of the cervix ♀ P3 T	
	Do not report with (57456)	
	5.27 8.32 Global Days 000	
	AMA: 2009, Jan, 11-31; 2008, Jan, 10-25; 2007, January, 13-27; 2006, December, 14-15	

57500-57556 Cervical Procedures: Multiple Techniques

EXCLUDES Destruction/excision of endometriomas, open method (49203-49205, 58957-58958)
Radical surgical procedures (58200-58240)

57500	Biopsy of cervix, single or multiple, or local excision of lesion, with or without fulguration (separate procedure) ♀ P3 T	
	2.08 3.28 Global Days 000	
57505	Endocervical curettage (not done as part of a dilation and curettage) ♀ P3 T	
	2.44 2.67 Global Days 010	
	AMA: 2009, Jan, 11-31; 2008, Jan, 10-25; 2007, January, 13-27; 2005, July, 13-16	
57510	Cautery of cervix; electro or thermal ♀ P3 T	
	3.19 3.54 Global Days 010	
57511	cryocautery, initial or repeat ♀ P3 T	
	3.59 3.88 Global Days 010	
57513	laser ablation ♀ A2 T	
	3.58 3.84 Global Days 010	
57520	Conization of cervix, with or without fulguration, with or without dilation and curettage, with or without repair; cold knife or laser ♀ A2 T	
	EXCLUDES Dilation and curettage, diagnostic/therapeutic, nonobstetrical (58120)	
	7.40 8.15 Global Days 090	
57522	loop electrode excision ♀ A2 T	
	6.60 7.05 Global Days 090	
	AMA: 2009, Jan, 11-31; 2008, Jan, 10-25; 2007, January, 13-27	
57530	Trachelectomy (cervicectomy), amputation of cervix (separate procedure) ♀ A2 T 80	
	9.38 9.38 Global Days 090	
57531	Radical trachelectomy, with bilateral total pelvic lymphadenectomy and para-aortic lymph node sampling biopsy, with or without removal of tube(s), with or without removal of ovary(s) ♀ C 80	
	47.86 47.86 Global Days 090	
57540	Excision of cervical stump, abdominal approach; ♀ C 80	
	21.61 21.61 Global Days 090	
57545	with pelvic floor repair ♀ C 80	
	22.85 22.85 Global Days 090	
57550	Excision of cervical stump, vaginal approach; ♀ A2 T 80	
	11.14 11.14 Global Days 090	
57555	with anterior and/or posterior repair ♀ T 80	
	16.59 16.59 Global Days 090	
57556	with repair of enterocele ♀ A2 T 80	
	EXCLUDES Insertion of hemostatic agent/pack for spontaneous/traumatic nonobstetrical vaginal hemorrhage (57180) Intrauterine device insertion (58300)	
	15.57 15.57 Global Days 090	

57558-57800 Cervical Procedures: Dilation, Suturing, or Instrumentation

EXCLUDES Destruction/excision of endometriomas, open method (49203-49205, 58957-58958)

57558	Dilation and curettage of cervical stump ♀ A2 T	
	EXCLUDES Radical surgical procedures (58200-58240)	
	3.10 3.35 Global Days 010	
57700	Cerclage of uterine cervix, nonobstetrical ♀ A2 T 80	
	INCLUDES McDonald cerclage Shirodker operation	
	8.37 8.37 Global Days 090	
57720	Trachelorrhaphy, plastic repair of uterine cervix, vaginal approach ♀ A2 T 80	
	INCLUDES Emmet operation	
	8.36 8.36 Global Days 090	
57800	Dilation of cervical canal, instrumental (separate procedure) ♀ P3 T	
	1.33 1.60 Global Days 000	

● New Code   ▲ Revised Code   M Maternity   A Age   Unlisted   Not Covered   # Resequenced
CCI   + Add-on   ⊘ Mod 51 Exempt   @ Mod 63 Exempt   ⊙ Mod Sedation   PQRI

© 2009 Publisher (Blue Ink)   CPT only © 2009 American Medical Association. All Rights Reserved. (Black Ink)   Medicare (Red Ink)   203

Current Procedural Coding Expert – Female Genital System

58100-58120 Procedures Involving the Endometrium

CMS 100-3,230.6   Vabra Aspirator

58100 Endometrial sampling (biopsy) with or without endocervical sampling (biopsy), without cervical dilation, any method (separate procedure)
- **EXCLUDES** Endocervical curettage only (57505)
  Endometrial sampling (biopsy) performed in conjunction with colposcopy (58110)
- 2.44   2.93   Global Days 000

+ 58110 Endometrial sampling (biopsy) performed in conjunction with colposcopy (List separately in addition to code for primary procedure)
- Code first colposcopy (57420-57421, 57452-57461)
- 1.16   1.32   Global Days ZZZ
- **AMA:** 2006, June, 16-17

58120 Dilation and curettage, diagnostic and/or therapeutic (nonobstetrical)
- **EXCLUDES** Postpartum hemorrhage (59160)
- 6.00   6.90   Global Days 010
- **AMA:** 2009, Jan, 11-31; 2008, Jan, 10-25; 2007, January, 13-27

58140-58146 Myomectomy Procedures

58140 Myomectomy, excision of fibroid tumor(s) of uterus, 1 to 4 intramural myoma(s) with total weight of 250 g or less and/or removal of surface myomas; abdominal approach
- 25.55   25.55   Global Days 090
- **AMA:** 2009, Jan, 11-31; 2008, Jan, 10-25; 2007, January, 13-27

58145   vaginal approach
- 14.97   14.97   Global Days 090

58146 Myomectomy, excision of fibroid tumor(s) of uterus, 5 or more intramural myomas and/or intramural myomas with total weight greater than 250 g, abdominal approach
- Do not report with (58140-58145, 58150-58240)
- 32.18   32.18   Global Days 090
- **AMA:** 2009, Jan, 11-31; 2008, Jan, 10-25; 2007, January, 13-27

58150-58294 Abdominal and Vaginal Hysterectomies

CMS 100-3,230.3   Sterilization

EXCLUDES Destruction/excision of endometriomas, open method (49203-49205, 58957-58958)

58150 Total abdominal hysterectomy (corpus and cervix), with or without removal of tube(s), with or without removal of ovary(s);
- 27.71   27.71   Global Days 090
- **AMA:** 2009, Jan, 11-31; 2008, Jan, 10-25; 2007, January, 13-27

58152   with colpo-urethrocystopexy (eg, Marshall-Marchetti-Krantz, Burch)
- **EXCLUDES** Urethrocystopexy without hysterectomy (51840, 51841)
- 34.73   34.73   Global Days 090

58180 Supracervical abdominal hysterectomy (subtotal hysterectomy), with or without removal of tube(s), with or without removal of ovary(s)
- 26.62   26.62   Global Days 090

58200 Total abdominal hysterectomy, including partial vaginectomy, with para-aortic and pelvic lymph node sampling, with or without removal of tube(s), with or without removal of ovary(s)
- 36.61   36.61   Global Days 090

58210 Radical abdominal hysterectomy, with bilateral total pelvic lymphadenectomy and para-aortic lymph node sampling (biopsy), with or without removal of tube(s), with or without removal of ovary(s)
- **INCLUDES** Wertheim hysterectomy
- **EXCLUDES** Hysterectomy, radical, with transposition of ovary(s) (58825)
- 48.97   48.97   Global Days 090

58240 Pelvic exenteration for gynecologic malignancy, with total abdominal hysterectomy or cervicectomy, with or without removal of tube(s), with or without removal of ovary(s), with removal of bladder and ureteral transplantations, and/or abdominoperineal resection of rectum and colon and colostomy, or any combination thereof
- **EXCLUDES** Pelvic exenteration for male genital malignancy or lower urinary tract (51597)
- 77.66   77.66   Global Days 090

58260 Vaginal hysterectomy, for uterus 250 g or less;
- 22.96   22.96   Global Days 090

58262   with removal of tube(s), and/or ovary(s)
- 25.64   25.64   Global Days 090

58263   with removal of tube(s), and/or ovary(s), with repair of enterocele
- Do not report with (57283)
- 27.61   27.61   Global Days 090

58267   with colpo-urethrocystopexy (Marshall-Marchetti-Krantz type, Pereyra type) with or without endoscopic control
- 29.38   29.38   Global Days 090

58270   with repair of enterocele
- **EXCLUDES** Vaginal hysterectomy with repair of enterocele and removal of tubes and/or ovaries (58263)
- 24.52   24.52   Global Days 090

58275 Vaginal hysterectomy, with total or partial vaginectomy;
- 27.37   27.37   Global Days 090

58280   with repair of enterocele
- 29.34   29.34   Global Days 090

58285 Vaginal hysterectomy, radical (Schauta type operation)
- 36.64   36.64   Global Days 090

58290 Vaginal hysterectomy, for uterus greater than 250 g;
- 32.07   32.07   Global Days 090

58291   with removal of tube(s) and/or ovary(s)
- 34.77   34.77   Global Days 090

58292   with removal of tube(s) and/or ovary(s), with repair of enterocele
- 36.72   36.72   Global Days 090

58293   with colpo-urethrocystopexy (Marshall-Marchetti-Krantz type, Pereyra type) with or without endoscopic control
- 38.19   38.19   Global Days 090

58294   with repair of enterocele
- 34.00   34.00   Global Days 090

26/TC PC/TC Comp Only	A2-73 ASC Pmt	50 Bilateral	♂ Male Only	♀ Female Only	Facility RVU	Non-Facility RVU
AMA: CPT Asst	**MED:** Pub 100	A-Y OPPSI	80/80 Surg Assist Allowed / w/Doc	Lab Crosswalk	Radiology Crosswalk

CPT only © 2009 American Medical Association. All Rights Reserved. (Black Ink)   Medicare (Red Ink)   © 2009 Publisher (Blue Ink)

Current Procedural Coding Expert – Female Genital System 58544

58300-58323 Contraception and Reproduction Procedures

58300 Insertion of intrauterine device (IUD) ♀ E
  EXCLUDES Insertion and/or removal of implantable contraceptive capsules (11975-11977)
  🩸 1.43 🔬 1.85 Global Days XXX
  AMA: 2009, Jan, 11-31; 2008, Jan, 10-25; 2007, January, 13-27

58301 Removal of intrauterine device (IUD) ♀ P3 T 80
  EXCLUDES Insertion and/or removal of implantable contraceptive capsules (11975-11977)
  🩸 1.91 🔬 2.54 Global Days 000
  AMA: 2009, Jan, 11-31; 2008, Jan, 10-25; 2007, January, 13-27

58321 Artificial insemination; intra-cervical ♀ P3 T 80
  🩸 1.31 🔬 2.03 Global Days 000

58322 intra-uterine ♀ P3 T 80
  🩸 1.65 🔬 2.28 Global Days 000

58323 Sperm washing for artificial insemination ♀ P3 T 80
  🩸 0.35 🔬 0.42 Global Days 000

58340-58350 Fallopian Tube Patency and Brachytherapy Procedures

58340 Catheterization and introduction of saline or contrast material for saline infusion sonohysterography (SIS) or hysterosalpingography ♀ N1 N
  📷 74740, 76831
  🩸 1.58 🔬 2.96 Global Days 000
  AMA: 2009, Mar, 10-11

58345 Transcervical introduction of fallopian tube catheter for diagnosis and/or re-establishing patency (any method), with or without hysterosalpingography ♀ R2 T 80 50
  📷 74742
  🩸 7.73 🔬 7.73 Global Days 010
  AMA: 2009, Mar, 10-11

58346 Insertion of Heyman capsules for clinical brachytherapy ♀ A2 T
  EXCLUDES The placement of needles or catheters into the pelvic organs and/or genitalia (except for the prostate) for interstitial radioelement application (55920)
  📷 77761-77763, 77785-77787
  🩸 12.49 🔬 12.49 Global Days 090

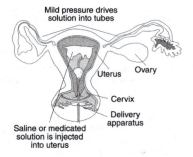

58350 Chromotubation of oviduct, including materials ♀ A2 T
  EXCLUDES Materials and supplies provided by the physician (99070)
  🩸 2.11 🔬 2.52 Global Days 010
  AMA: 2009, Jan, 11-31; 2008, Jan, 10-25; 2007, January, 13-27

58353-58356 Ablation of Endometrium

58353 Endometrial ablation, thermal, without hysteroscopic guidance ♀ A2 T
  EXCLUDES Endometrial ablation performed hysteroscopically (58563)
  🩸 6.04 🔬 24.28 Global Days 010
  AMA: 2009, Jan, 11-31; 2008, Jan, 10-25; 2007, January, 13-27

58356 Endometrial cryoablation with ultrasonic guidance, including endometrial curettage, when performed ♀ P3 T 80
  Code also (C2618)
  Do not report with (58100, 58120, 58340, 76700, 76856)
  🩸 9.72 🔬 45.56 Global Days 010

58400-58540 Uterine Repairs: Vaginal and Abdominal

58400 Uterine suspension, with or without shortening of round ligaments, with or without shortening of sacrouterine ligaments; (separate procedure) ♀ C 80
  INCLUDES Alexander's operation
             Baldy-Webster operation
             Manchester colporrhaphy
  EXCLUDES Anastomosis of tubes to uterus (58752)
  🩸 12.07 🔬 12.07 Global Days 090

58410 with presacral sympathectomy ♀ C 80
  INCLUDES Alexander's operation
  EXCLUDES Anastomosis of tubes to uterus (58752)
  🩸 22.35 🔬 22.35 Global Days 090
  AMA: 2009, Jan, 11-31; 2008, Jan, 10-25; 2007, March, 9-11

58520 Hysterorrhaphy, repair of ruptured uterus (nonobstetrical) ♀ C 80
  🩸 22.93 🔬 22.93 Global Days 090

58540 Hysteroplasty, repair of uterine anomaly (Strassman type) ♀ C 80
  INCLUDES Strassman type
  EXCLUDES Vesicouterine fistula closure (51920)
  🩸 25.28 🔬 25.28 Global Days 090

58541-58579 Endoscopic Procedures of the Uterus

INCLUDES Diagnostic laparoscopy
EXCLUDES Diagnostic hysteroscopy (58555)

58541 Laparoscopy, surgical, supracervical hysterectomy, for uterus 250 g or less; ♀ T 80
  Do not report with (49320, 57000, 57180, 57410, 58140-58146, 58545-58546, 58561, 58661, 58670-58671)
  🩸 23.98 🔬 23.98 Global Days 090

58542 with removal of tube(s) and/or ovary(s) ♀ T 80
  Do not report with (49320, 57000, 57180, 57410, 58140-58146, 58545-58546, 58561, 58661, 58670-58671)
  🩸 26.79 🔬 26.79 Global Days 090

58543 Laparoscopy, surgical, supracervical hysterectomy, for uterus greater than 250 g; ♀ T 80
  Do not report with (49320, 57000, 57180, 57410, 58140-58146, 58545-58546, 58561, 58661, 58670-58671)
  🩸 27.30 🔬 27.30 Global Days 090

58544 with removal of tube(s) and/or ovary(s) ♀ T 80
  Do not report with (49320, 57000, 57180, 57410, 58140-58146, 58545-58546, 58561, 58661, 58670-58671)
  🩸 29.52 🔬 29.52 Global Days 090

● New Code   ▲ Revised Code   M Maternity   A Age   Unlisted   Not Covered   # Resequenced
□ CCI   + Add-on   ⊘ Mod 51 Exempt   ⊙ Mod 63 Exempt   ⊙ Mod Sedation   PQ PQRI

© 2009 Publisher (Blue Ink)   CPT only © 2009 American Medical Association. All Rights Reserved. (Black Ink)   Medicare (Red Ink)   205

58545 — 58605

58545	Laparoscopy, surgical, myomectomy, excision; 1 to 4 intramural myomas with total weight of 250 g or less and/or removal of surface myomas ♀ A2 T 80
	24.90 24.90 Global Days 090
58546	5 or more intramural myomas and/or intramural myomas with total weight greater than 250 g ♀ A2 T 80
	31.42 31.42 Global Days 090
	AMA: 2009, Jan, 11-31; 2008, Jan, 10-25; 2007, January, 13-27
58548	Laparoscopy, surgical, with radical hysterectomy, with bilateral total pelvic lymphadenectomy and para-aortic lymph node sampling (biopsy), with removal of tube(s) and ovary(s), if performed ♀ C 80
	Do not report with (38570-38572, 58210, 58285, 58550-58554)
	50.28 50.28 Global Days 090
58550	Laparoscopy, surgical, with vaginal hysterectomy, for uterus 250 g or less; ♀ A2 T 80
	Do not report with (49320, 57000, 57180, 57410, 58140-58146, 58545-58546, 58561, 58661, 58670-58671)
	24.49 24.49 Global Days 090
58552	with removal of tube(s) and/or ovary(s) ♀ G2 T 80
	Do not report with (49320, 57000, 57180, 57410, 58140-58146, 58545-58546, 58561, 58661, 58670-58671)
	27.22 27.22 Global Days 090
58553	Laparoscopy, surgical, with vaginal hysterectomy, for uterus greater than 250 g; ♀ T 80
	Do not report with (49320, 57000, 57180, 57410, 58140-58146, 58545-58546, 58561, 58661, 58670-58671)
	31.63 31.63 Global Days 090
58554	with removal of tube(s) and/or ovary(s) ♀ T 80
	Do not report with (49320, 57000, 57180, 57410, 58140-58146, 58545-58546, 58561, 58661, 58670-58671)
	36.60 36.60 Global Days 090

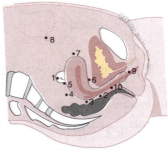

Some common sites of endometriosis, in descending order of frequency:
(1) ovary,
(2) cul de sac,
(3) uterosacral ligaments,
(4) broad ligaments,
(5) fallopian tube,
(6) uterovesical fold,
(7) round ligament,
(8) vermiform appendix,
(9) vagina,
(10) rectovaginal septum

Endometriosis is a benign condition in which endometrial matter is present outside of the endometrial cavity; it is estimated that 15 percent of women have some degree of the disease; occurrence is most common in the ovaries and about 60 percent of patients will have ovarian involvement, many with cyst development

58555	Hysteroscopy, diagnostic (separate procedure) ♀ A2 T 80
	5.28 7.91 Global Days 000
58558	Hysteroscopy, surgical; with sampling (biopsy) of endometrium and/or polypectomy, with or without D & C ♀ A2 T
	7.44 10.44 Global Days 000
	AMA: 2009, Jan, 11-31; 2008, Jan, 10-25; 2007, January, 13-27
58559	with lysis of intrauterine adhesions (any method) ♀ A2 T
	9.58 9.58 Global Days 000
58560	with division or resection of intrauterine septum (any method) ♀ A2 T 80
	10.83 10.83 Global Days 000
58561	with removal of leiomyomata ♀ A2 T 80
	15.34 15.34 Global Days 000
58562	with removal of impacted foreign body ♀ A2 T
	8.10 10.89 Global Days 000
	AMA: 2009, Jan, 11-31; 2008, Jan, 10-25
58563	with endometrial ablation (eg, endometrial resection, electrosurgical ablation, thermoablation) ♀ A2 T 80
	9.57 40.22 Global Days 000
	AMA: 2009, Jan, 11-31; 2008, Jan, 10-25; 2007, January, 13-27
58565	with bilateral fallopian tube cannulation to induce occlusion by placement of permanent implants ♀ A2 T
	Do not report with (57800, 58555)
	11.95 45.23 Global Days 090
58570	Laparoscopy, surgical, with total hysterectomy, for uterus 250 g or less; ♀ T 80
	Do not report with (49320, 57000, 57180, 57410, 58140-58146, 58150, 58545, 58546, 58561, 58661, 58670, 58671)
	25.81 25.81 Global Days 090
58571	with removal of tube(s) and/or ovary(s) ♀ T 80
	Do not report with (49320, 57100, 57180, 57410, 58140-58146, 58150, 58545, 58546, 58561, 58661, 58670, 58671)
	28.69 28.69 Global Days 090
58572	Laparoscopy, surgical, with total hysterectomy, for uterus greater than 250 g; ♀ T 80
	Do not report with (49320, 57000, 57180, 57410, 58140-58146, 58150, 58545, 58546, 58561, 58661, 58670, 58671)
	32.09 32.09 Global Days 090
58573	with removal of tube(s) and/or ovary(s) ♀ T 80
	Do not report with (49320, 57000, 57180, 57410, 58140-58146, 58150, 58545, 58546, 58561, 58661, 58670, 58671)
	36.87 36.87 Global Days 090
58578	Unlisted laparoscopy procedure, uterus ♀ T 80 50
	0.00 0.00 Global Days YYY
	AMA: 2009, Jan, 11-31; 2008, Jan, 10-25; 2007, March, 9-11
58579	Unlisted hysteroscopy procedure, uterus ♀ T 80 50
	0.00 0.00 Global Days YYY

58600-58615 Sterilization by Tubal Interruption

CMS 100-3,230.3   Sterilization
EXCLUDES (49203-49205, 58957-58958)

58600	Ligation or transection of fallopian tube(s), abdominal or vaginal approach, unilateral or bilateral ♀ G2 T 80
	INCLUDES Madlener operation
	10.02 10.02 Global Days 090
58605	Ligation or transection of fallopian tube(s), abdominal or vaginal approach, postpartum, unilateral or bilateral, during same hospitalization (separate procedure) ♀ C 80
	EXCLUDES Laparoscopic methods (58670, 58671)
	9.05 9.05 Global Days 090

Current Procedural Coding Expert – Female Genital System

+ 58611 Ligation or transection of fallopian tube(s) when done at the time of cesarean delivery or intra-abdominal surgery (not a separate procedure) (List separately in addition to code for primary procedure) ♀ C 80
Code first primary procedure
2.19   2.19   Global Days ZZZ

58615 Occlusion of fallopian tube(s) by device (eg, band, clip, Falope ring) vaginal or suprapubic approach ♀ 62 T 80
EXCLUDES   Laparoscopic method (58671)
Lysis of adnexal adhesions (58740)
6.71   6.71   Global Days 010

58660-58679 Endoscopic Procedures Fallopian Tubes and/or Ovaries

CMS 100-3,230.3   Sterilization
INCLUDES   Diagnostic laparoscopy
EXCLUDES   Laparoscopy with biopsy of fallopian tube or ovary (49321)
Laparoscopy with ovarian cyst aspiration (49322)

58660 Laparoscopy, surgical; with lysis of adhesions (salpingolysis, ovariolysis) (separate procedure) ♀ A2 T 80
18.71   18.71   Global Days 090
AMA: 2009, Jan, 11-31; 2008, Jan, 10-25; 2007, January, 13-27

58661 with removal of adnexal structures (partial or total oophorectomy and/or salpingectomy) ♀ A2 T 80 50
17.92   17.92   Global Days 010
AMA: 2009, Jan, 11-31; 2008, Jan, 10-25; 2007, January, 13-27

58662 with fulguration or excision of lesions of the ovary, pelvic viscera, or peritoneal surface by any method ♀ A2 T 80
19.58   19.58   Global Days 090

58670 with fulguration of oviducts (with or without transection) ♀ A2 T
10.06   10.06   Global Days 090

58671 with occlusion of oviducts by device (eg, band, clip, or Falope ring) ♀ A2 T
10.05   10.05   Global Days 090

58672 with fimbrioplasty ♀ A2 T 80 50
20.51   20.51   Global Days 090

58673 with salpingostomy (salpingoneostomy) ♀ A2 T 80 50
22.30   22.30   Global Days 090
AMA: 2009, Jan, 11-31; 2008, Jan, 10-25; 2007, January, 13-27

58679 Unlisted laparoscopy procedure, oviduct, ovary ♀ T 80 50
0.00   0.00   Global Days YYY

58700-58770 Open Procedures Fallopian Tubes, with/without Ovaries

EXCLUDES   Destruction/excision of endometriomas, open method (49203-49205, 58957-58958)

58700 Salpingectomy, complete or partial, unilateral or bilateral (separate procedure) ♀ C 80
21.54   21.54   Global Days 090

58720 Salpingo-oophorectomy, complete or partial, unilateral or bilateral (separate procedure) ♀ C 80
20.00   20.00   Global Days 090
AMA: 2009, Jan, 11-31; 2008, Jan, 10-25; 2007, January, 13-27; 2006, May, 16-20

58740 Lysis of adhesions (salpingolysis, ovariolysis) ♀ C 80
EXCLUDES   Excision/fulguration of lesions performed laparoscopically (58662)
Laparoscopic method (58660)
24.31   24.31   Global Days 090

Occluded section of tube is excised
Tube ends are sutured
Ovary

58750 Tubotubal anastomosis ♀ C 80
25.08   25.08   Global Days 090

58752 Tubouterine implantation ♀ C 80
23.81   23.81   Global Days 090

58760 Fimbrioplasty ♀ C 80 50
EXCLUDES   Laparoscopic method (58672)
22.50   22.50   Global Days 090

58770 Salpingostomy (salpingoneostomy) ♀ T 80 50
EXCLUDES   Laparoscopic method (58673)
23.72   23.72   Global Days 090

58800-58925 Open Procedures: Ovary

CMS 100-3,230.3   Sterilization
EXCLUDES   Destruction/excision of endometriomas, open method (49203-49205, 58957-58958)

58800 Drainage of ovarian cyst(s), unilateral or bilateral (separate procedure); vaginal approach ♀ A2 T
8.15   8.60   Global Days 090

58805 abdominal approach ♀ 62 T 80
11.09   11.09   Global Days 090

58820 Drainage of ovarian abscess; vaginal approach, open ♀ A2 T 80
8.50   8.50   Global Days 090

58822 abdominal approach ♀ C 80
20.47   20.47   Global Days 090

⊙ **58823** Drainage of pelvic abscess, transvaginal or transrectal approach, percutaneous (eg, ovarian, pericolic) ♀ T
75989
4.68   22.04   Global Days 000

58825 Transposition, ovary(s) ♀ C 80
19.26   19.26   Global Days 090

58900 Biopsy of ovary, unilateral or bilateral (separate procedure) ♀ A2 T
EXCLUDES   Laparoscopy with biopsy of fallopian tube or ovary (49321)
12.23   12.23   Global Days 090

58920 Wedge resection or bisection of ovary, unilateral or bilateral ♀ T 80
19.43   19.43   Global Days 090

58925 Ovarian cystectomy, unilateral or bilateral ♀ T 80
20.51   20.51   Global Days 090

● New Code   ▲ Revised Code   M Maternity   A Age   Unlisted   Not Covered   # Resequenced
CCI   + Add-on   ⊘ Mod 51 Exempt   @ Mod 63 Exempt   ⊙ Mod Sedation   PQRI
© 2009 Publisher (Blue Ink)   CPT only © 2009 American Medical Association. All Rights Reserved. (Black Ink)   Medicare (Red Ink)

58940-58960 Removal Ovary(s) with/without Multiple Procedures for Malignancy

EXCLUDES *Destruction/excision of endometriomas, open method (49203-49205, 58957-58958)*

58940 Oophorectomy, partial or total, unilateral or bilateral; ♀ C 80

    EXCLUDES *Oophorectomy with concomitant debulking for ovarian malignancy (58952)*

    14.17   14.17   Global Days 090

58943 for ovarian, tubal or primary peritoneal malignancy, with para-aortic and pelvic lymph node biopsies, peritoneal washings, peritoneal biopsies, diaphragmatic assessments, with or without salpingectomy(s), with or without omentectomy ♀ C 80

    31.39   31.39   Global Days 090

58950 Resection (initial) of ovarian, tubal or primary peritoneal malignancy with bilateral salpingo-oophorectomy and omentectomy; ♀ C 80

    29.95   29.95   Global Days 090

58951 with total abdominal hysterectomy, pelvic and limited para-aortic lymphadenectomy ♀ C 80 P0

    EXCLUDES *Resection/tumor debulking of recurrent ovarian/tubal/primary peritoneal/uterine malignancy (58957, 58958)*

    38.59   38.59   Global Days 090

    AMA: 2009, Jan, 11-31; 2008, Jan, 10-25; 2007, January, 13-27

58952 with radical dissection for debulking (ie, radical excision or destruction, intra-abdominal or retroperitoneal tumors) ♀ C 80

    EXCLUDES *Resection/tumor debulking of recurrent ovarian/tubal/primary peritoneal/uterine malignancy (58957, 58958)*

    43.57   43.57   Global Days 090

    AMA: 2009, Jan, 11-31; 2008, Jan, 10-25; 2007, January, 13-27

58953 Bilateral salpingo-oophorectomy with omentectomy, total abdominal hysterectomy and radical dissection for debulking; ♀ C 80 P0

    54.02   54.02   Global Days 090

58954 with pelvic lymphadenectomy and limited para-aortic lymphadenectomy ♀ C 80 P0

    58.56   58.56   Global Days 090

58956 Bilateral salpingo-oophorectomy with total omentectomy, total abdominal hysterectomy for malignancy ♀ C 80 P0

    Do not report with (49255, 58150, 58180, 58262-58263, 58550, 58661, 58700, 58720, 58900, 58925, 58940, 58957-58958)

    36.75   36.75   Global Days 090

58957 Resection (tumor debulking) of recurrent ovarian, tubal, primary peritoneal, uterine malignancy (intra-abdominal, retroperitoneal tumors), with omentectomy, if performed; ♀ C 80

    Do not report with (38770, 38780, 44005, 49000, 49203-49215, 49255, 58900-58960)

    42.18   42.18   Global Days 090

58958 with pelvic lymphadenectomy and limited para-aortic lymphadenectomy ♀ C 80

    Do not report with (38770, 38780, 44005, 49000, 49203-49215, 49255, 58900-58960)

    46.54   46.54   Global Days 090

58960 Laparotomy, for staging or restaging of ovarian, tubal, or primary peritoneal malignancy (second look), with or without omentectomy, peritoneal washing, biopsy of abdominal and pelvic peritoneum, diaphragmatic assessment with pelvic and limited para-aortic lymphadenectomy ♀ C 80

    Do not report with (58957, 58958)

    25.76   25.76   Global Days 090

58970-58999 Procedural Components: In Vitro Fertilization

58970 Follicle puncture for oocyte retrieval, any method ♀ A2 T 80

    76948

    5.33   5.90   Global Days 000

58974 Embryo transfer, intrauterine M ♀ A2 T 80

    0.00   0.00   Global Days 000

58976 Gamete, zygote, or embryo intrafallopian transfer, any method M ♀ A2 T 80

    EXCLUDES *Adnexal procedures performed laparoscopically (58660-58673)*

    5.75   6.53   Global Days 000

58999 Unlisted procedure, female genital system (nonobstetrical) ♀ T

    0.00   0.00   Global Days YYY

59000-59001 Aspiration of Amniotic Fluid

CMS 100-3,220.5   Ultrasound Diagnostic Procedures

EXCLUDES *Intrauterine fetal transfusion (36460)*
Unlisted fetal invasive procedure (59897)

59000 Amniocentesis; diagnostic M ♀ P3 T

    76946

    2.23   3.27   Global Days 000

59001 therapeutic amniotic fluid reduction (includes ultrasound guidance) M ♀ R2 T

    4.98   4.98   Global Days 000

59012-59076 Fetal Testing and Treatment

EXCLUDES *Newborn circumcision (54150, 54160)*
Intrauterine fetal transfusion (36460)
Unlisted fetal invasive procedures (59897)

59012 Cordocentesis (intrauterine), any method M ♀ B2 T 80

    76941

    5.64   5.64   Global Days 000

59015 Chorionic villus sampling, any method M ♀ P3 T 80

    76945

    3.67   4.21   Global Days 000

59020 Fetal contraction stress test M ♀ P3 T 80

    1.82   1.82   Global Days 000

59025 Fetal non-stress test M ♀ P3 T 80

    1.25   1.25   Global Days 000

    AMA: 2009, Jan, 11-31; 2008, Jan, 10-25; 2007, January, 13-27

59030 Fetal scalp blood sampling M ♀ T 80

    2.82   2.82   Global Days 000

26/TC PC/TC Comp Only	A2-Z3 ASC Pmt	50 Bilateral	♂ Male Only	♀ Female Only	Facility RVU	Non-Facility RVU
AMA: CPT Asst	**MED:** Pub 100	A-Y OPPSI	80/80 Surg Assist Allowed / w/Doc		Lab Crosswalk	Radiology Crosswalk

CPT only © 2009 American Medical Association. All Rights Reserved. (Black Ink)   Medicare (Red Ink)   © 2009 Publisher (Blue Ink)

Current Procedural Coding Expert – Maternity Care/Delivery

59050 Fetal monitoring during labor by consulting physician (ie, non-attending physician) with written report; supervision and interpretation
1.41 1.41 Global Days XXX

59051 interpretation only
1.17 1.17 Global Days XXX

59070 Transabdominal amnioinfusion, including ultrasound guidance
8.62 10.97 Global Days 000
AMA: 2009, Jan, 11-31; 2008, Jan, 10-25; 2007, January, 13-27

59072 Fetal umbilical cord occlusion, including ultrasound guidance
14.63 14.63 Global Days 000
AMA: 2009, Jan, 11-31; 2008, Jan, 10-25; 2007, January, 13-27

59074 Fetal fluid drainage (eg, vesicocentesis, thoracocentesis, paracentesis), including ultrasound guidance
8.78 11.21 Global Days 000
AMA: 2009, Jan, 11-31; 2008, Jan, 10-25; 2007, January, 13-27

59076 Fetal shunt placement, including ultrasound guidance
14.63 14.63 Global Days 000
AMA: 2009, Jan, 11-31; 2008, Jan, 10-25; 2007, January, 13-27

59100-59151 Tubal Pregnancy/Hysterotomy Procedures

CMS 100-3,230.3   Sterilization

59100 Hysterotomy, abdominal (eg, for hydatidiform mole, abortion)
Code also ligation of fallopian tubes when performed at the same time as hysterotomy (58611)
22.96 22.96 Global Days 090

59120 Surgical treatment of ectopic pregnancy; tubal or ovarian, requiring salpingectomy and/or oophorectomy, abdominal or vaginal approach
21.84 21.84 Global Days 090

59121 tubal or ovarian, without salpingectomy and/or oophorectomy
21.88 21.88 Global Days 090

59130 abdominal pregnancy
23.18 23.18 Global Days 090

59135 interstitial, uterine pregnancy requiring total hysterectomy
22.89 22.89 Global Days 090

59136 interstitial, uterine pregnancy with partial resection of uterus
24.23 24.23 Global Days 090

59140 cervical, with evacuation
10.07 10.07 Global Days 090

59150 Laparoscopic treatment of ectopic pregnancy; without salpingectomy and/or oophorectomy
21.17 21.17 Global Days 090

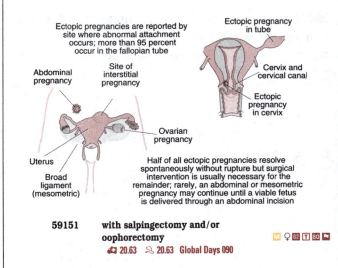

Ectopic pregnancies are reported by site where abnormal attachment occurs; more than 95 percent occur in the fallopian tube

Half of all ectopic pregnancies resolve spontaneously without rupture but surgical intervention is usually necessary for the remainder; rarely, an abdominal or mesometric pregnancy may continue until a viable fetus is delivered through an abdominal incision

59151 with salpingectomy and/or oophorectomy
20.63 20.63 Global Days 090

59160-59200 Procedures of Uterus Prior To/After Delivery

59160 Curettage, postpartum
4.75 5.46 Global Days 010
AMA: 2009, Jan, 11-31; 2008, Jan, 10-25; 2007, January, 13-27

59200 Insertion of cervical dilator (eg, laminaria, prostaglandin) (separate procedure)
EXCLUDES Fetal transfusion, intrauterine (36460)
Hypertonic solution/prostaglandin introduction for labor initiation (59850-59857)
1.25 1.88 Global Days 000
AMA: 2005, July, 13-16

59300-59350 Postpartum Vaginal/Cervical/Uterine Repairs

EXCLUDES Nonpregnancy-related cerclage (57700)

59300 Episiotomy or vaginal repair, by other than attending physician
EXCLUDES Tracheloplasty (57700)
4.11 5.14 Global Days 000

59320 Cerclage of cervix, during pregnancy; vaginal
4.21 4.21 Global Days 000
AMA: 2009, Jan, 11-31; 2008, Jan, 10-25; 2007, February, 10-11; 2007, January, 13-27; 2006, December, 10-12

59325 abdominal
6.05 6.05 Global Days 000
AMA: 2009, Jan, 11-31; 2008, Jan, 10-25; 2007, January, 13-27; 2007, February, 10-11; 2006, December, 10-12

59350 Hysterorrhaphy of ruptured uterus
7.83 7.83 Global Days 000

59400-59410 Vaginal Delivery: Comprehensive and Component Services

CMS 100-2,15,20.1 Physician Expense for Surgery, Childbirth, and Treatment for Infertility
CMS 100-2,15,180 Nurse-Midwife (CNM) Services

INCLUDES
Admission history
Admission to hospital
Management of uncomplicated labor
Physical exam
Vaginal delivery with or without episiotomy or forceps

EXCLUDES
Medical complications of pregnancy:
  Cardiac problems
  Diabetes
  Hyperemesis
  Hypertension
  Neurological problems
  Premature rupture of membranes
  Pre-term labor
  Toxemia
Medical problems complicating labor and delivery
Newborn circumcision (54150, 54160)
Surgical complications of pregnancy:
  Appendectomy
  Bartholin cyst
  Hernia
  Ovarian cyst

Breech presentation (left) and Simpson forceps delivery of aftercoming head (right)

Vacuum extractor attached to posterior fontanelle to flex head downward (below left)

Obstetric forceps provide traction, rotation, or both to the birthing head and designs vary to accomplish specific tasks (e.g., Kielland forceps to rotate the head). Low forceps is application when skull is at station plus 2 or lower; mid forceps is application above station plus 2; high forceps is application at point of engagement. Vacuum extraction holds certain advantages, especially when forced rotation is not wanted, but it is not used for breech presentations

59400 Routine obstetric care including antepartum care, vaginal delivery (with or without episiotomy, and/or forceps) and postpartum care

INCLUDES
Biweekly visits to 36 weeks gestation
Fetal heart tones
Hospital/office visits following cesarean section or vaginal delivery
Initial/subsequent history
Monthly visits up to 28 weeks gestation
Physical exams
Recording of weight/blood pressures
Routine chemical urinalysis
Weekly visits until delivery

49.43 49.43 Global Days MMM
AMA: 2009, Jan, 11-31; 2008, Jan, 10-25; 2007, January, 13-27

59409 Vaginal delivery only (with or without episiotomy and/or forceps);
21.39 21.39 Global Days MMM
AMA: 2009, Jun, 10-11; 2009, Jan, 11-31; 2008, Jan, 10-25; 2007, Dec, 10-179; 2007, January, 13-27

59410 including postpartum care
INCLUDES Hospital/office visits following cesarean section or vaginal delivery
25.01 25.01 Global Days MMM
AMA: 2006, December, 1-3

59412-59414 Other Maternity Services

Complete breech presentation at term

"Footling"

Malposition and malpresentation occur when the fetus is in any presentation other than vertex; breech is most common at about 3 percent of deliveries; prematurity is a major predisposing factor

Shoulder presentation

Brow presentation

59412 External cephalic version, with or without tocolysis
Code also delivery code(s)
2.86 2.86 Global Days MMM

59414 Delivery of placenta (separate procedure)
2.56 2.56 Global Days MMM
AMA: 2009, Jan, 11-31; 2008, Jan, 10-25; 2007, January, 13-27

Current Procedural Coding Expert – Maternity Care/Delivery   59510

59425-59430 Prenatal and Postpartum Visits

CMS 100-2,15,20.1 Physician Expense for Surgery, Childbirth, and Treatment for Infertility
CMS 100-2,15,180 Nurse-Midwife (CNM) Services

INCLUDES Physician providing all or a portion of antepartum/postpartum care, but no delivery due to
  Referral to another physician for delivery
  Termination of pregnancy by abortion

EXCLUDES Antepartum care, 1-3 visits (99201-99499)
  Medical complications of pregnancy:
    Cardiac problems
    Diabetes
    Hyperemesis
    Hypertension
    Neurological problems
    Premature rupture of membranes
    Pre-term labor
    Toxemia
  Newborn circumcision (54150, 54160)
  Surgical complications of pregnancy:
    Appendectomy
    Bartholin cyst
    Hernia
    Ovarian cyst

59425 Antepartum care only; 4-6 visits
  INCLUDES Biweekly visits to 36 weeks gestation
    Fetal heart tones
    Initial/subsequent history
    Monthly visits up to 28 weeks gestation
    Physical exams
    Recording of weight/blood pressures
    Routine chemical urinalysis
    Weekly visits until delivery

  10.22 12.51 Global Days MMM
  AMA: 2009, Jan, 11-31; 2008, Jan, 10-25; 2007, January, 13-27

59426 7 or more visits
  INCLUDES Biweekly visits to 36 weeks gestation
    Fetal heart tones
    Initial/subsequent history
    Monthly visits up to 28 weeks gestation
    Physical exams
    Recording of weight/blood pressures
    Routine chemical urinalysis
    Weekly visits until delivery

  18.16 22.49 Global Days MMM
  AMA: 2009, Jan, 11-31; 2008, Jan, 10-25; 2007, January, 13-27

59430 Postpartum care only (separate procedure)
  INCLUDES Hospital/office visits following cesarean section or vaginal delivery

  3.48 3.81 Global Days MMM
  AMA: 2009, Jan, 11-31; 2008, Jan, 10-25; 2007, January, 13-27

59510-59525 Cesarean Section Delivery: Comprehensive and Components of Care

INCLUDES Classic cesarean section
  Low cervical cesarean section

EXCLUDES Infant standby attendance (99360)
  Medical complications of pregnancy:
    Cardiac problems
    Diabetes
    Hyperemesis
    Hypertension
    Neurological problems
    Premature rupture of membranes
    Pre-term labor
    Toxemia
  Newborn circumcision (54150, 54160)
  Surgical complications of pregnancy:
    Appendectomy
    Bartholin cyst
    Hernia
    Ovarian cyst

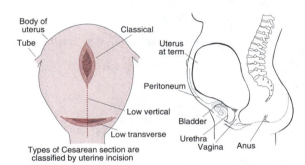

Types of Cesarean section are classified by uterine incision

Cesarean section is delivery through incisions in the anterior abdominal and uterine walls and is indicated for numerous conditions in both the fetus and the mother. Although other approaches may be warranted, low transverse is preferred to decrease chance of uterine rupture during future pregnancies

59510 Routine obstetric care including antepartum care, cesarean delivery, and postpartum care
  INCLUDES Admission history
    Admission to hospital
    Biweekly visits to 36 weeks gestation
    Cesarean delivery
    Fetal heart tones
    Hospital/office visits following cesarean section
    Initial/subsequent history
    Management of uncomplicated labor
    Monthly visits up to 28 weeks gestation
    Physical exam
    Recording of weight/blood pressures
    Routine chemical urinalysis
    Weekly visits until delivery
  EXCLUDES Medical problems complicating labor and delivery

  55.90 55.90 Global Days MMM
  AMA: 2009, Jan, 11-31; 2008, Jan, 10-25; 2007, January, 13-27

Current Procedural Coding Expert – Maternity Care/Delivery

59514 Cesarean delivery only;
  INCLUDES
   Admission history
   Admission to hospital
   Cesarean delivery
   Management of uncomplicated labor
   Physical exam
  EXCLUDES
   Medical problems complicating labor and delivery
  25.44 25.44 Global Days MMM
  AMA: 2009, Jan, 11-31; 2008, Jan, 10-25; 2007, January, 13-27

59515 including postpartum care
  INCLUDES
   Admission history
   Admission to hospital
   Cesarean delivery
   Hospital/office visits following cesarean section or vaginal delivery
   Management of uncomplicated labor
   Physical exam
  EXCLUDES
   Medical problems complicating labor and delivery
  30.19 30.19 Global Days MMM

+ **59525** Subtotal or total hysterectomy after cesarean delivery (List separately in addition to code for primary procedure)
   Code first cesarean delivery (59510, 59514, 59515, 59618, 59620, 59622)
   13.60 13.60 Global Days ZZZ

59610-59614 Vaginal Delivery After Prior Cesarean Section: Comprehensive and Components of Care

CMS 100-2,15,20.1 Physician Expense for Surgery, Childbirth, and Treatment for Infertility
CMS 100-2,15,180   Nurse-Midwife (CNM) Services

INCLUDES
 Admission history
 Admission to hospital
 Management of uncomplicated labor
 Patients with previous cesarean delivery who present with the expectation of a vaginal delivery
 Physical exam
 Successful vaginal delivery after previous cesarean delivery (VBAC)
 Vaginal delivery with or without episiotomy or forceps

EXCLUDES
 Elective cesarean delivery (59510, 59514, 59515)
 Medical complications of pregnancy:
  Cardiac problems
  Diabetes
  Hyperemesis
  Hypertension
  Neurological problems
  Premature rupture of membranes
  Pre-term labor
  Toxemia
 Medical problems complicating labor and delivery
 Newborn circumcision (54150, 54160)
 Surgical complications of pregnancy:
  Appendectomy
  Bartholin cyst
  Hernia
  Ovarian cyst

59610 Routine obstetric care including antepartum care, vaginal delivery (with or without episiotomy, and/or forceps) and postpartum care, after previous cesarean delivery
  INCLUDES
   Biweekly visits to 36 weeks gestation
   Fetal heart tones
   Hospital/office visits following cesarean section or vaginal delivery
   Initial/subsequent history
   Monthly visits up to 28 weeks gestation
   Physical exams
   Recording of weight/blood pressures
   Routine chemical urinalysis
   Weekly visits until delivery
  52.06 52.06 Global Days MMM

59612 Vaginal delivery only, after previous cesarean delivery (with or without episiotomy and/or forceps);
  24.01 24.01 Global Days MMM

59614 including postpartum care
  INCLUDES
   Hospital/office visits following cesarean section or vaginal delivery
  26.96 26.96 Global Days MMM

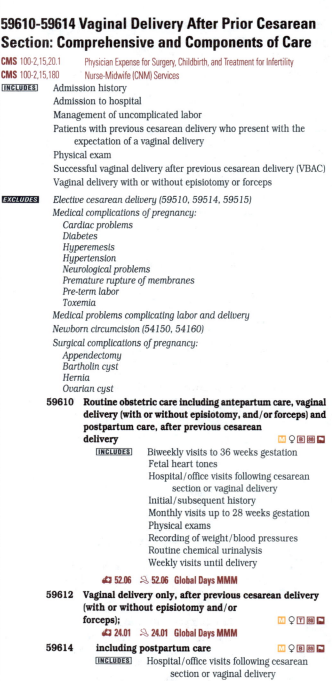

26/TC PC/TC Comp Only   A2-Z3 ASC Pmt   50 Bilateral   ♂ Male Only   ♀ Female Only   Facility RVU   Non-Facility RVU
AMA: CPT Asst   **MED:** Pub 100   A-Y OPPSI   80/80 Surg Assist Allowed / w/Doc   Lab Crosswalk   Radiology Crosswalk
212   CPT only © 2009 American Medical Association. All Rights Reserved. (Black Ink)   Medicare (Red Ink)   © 2009 Publisher (Blue Ink)

Current Procedural Coding Expert – Maternity Care/Delivery

59618-59622 Cesarean Section After Attempted Vaginal Birth/Prior C-Section

INCLUDES
Admission history
Admission to hospital
Cesarean delivery
Cesarean delivery following an unsuccessful vaginal delivery attempt after previous cesarean delivery
Management of uncomplicated labor
Patients with previous cesarean delivery who present with the expectation of a vaginal delivery
Physical exam

EXCLUDES
Elective cesarean delivery (59510, 59514, 59515)
Medical complications of pregnancy:
  Cardiac problems
  Diabetes
  Hyperemesis
  Hypertension
  Neurological problems
  Premature rupture of membranes
  Pre-term labor
  Toxemia
Medical problems complicating labor and delivery
Newborn circumcision (54150, 54160)
Surgical complications of pregnancy:
  Appendectomy
  Bartholin cyst
  Hernia
  Ovarian cyst

59618 Routine obstetric care including antepartum care, cesarean delivery, and postpartum care, following attempted vaginal delivery after previous cesarean delivery
  INCLUDES
  Biweekly visits to 36 weeks gestation
  Fetal heart tones
  Hospital/office visits following cesarean section or vaginal delivery
  Initial/subsequent history
  Monthly visits up to 28 weeks gestation
  Physical exams
  Recording of weight/blood pressures
  Routine chemical urinalysis
  Weekly visits until delivery
  58.33   58.33   Global Days MMM

59620 Cesarean delivery only, following attempted vaginal delivery after previous cesarean delivery;
  27.93   27.93   Global Days MMM

59622 including postpartum care
  INCLUDES Hospital/office visits following cesarean section or vaginal delivery
  32.68   32.68   Global Days MMM

59812-59830 Treatment of Miscarriage

EXCLUDES Medical treatment of spontaneous complete abortion, any trimester (99201-99233)

59812 Treatment of incomplete abortion, any trimester, completed surgically
  INCLUDES Surgical treatment of spontaneous abortion
  8.04   8.68   Global Days 090

59820 Treatment of missed abortion, completed surgically; first trimester
  9.55   10.08   Global Days 090

59821 second trimester
  9.64   10.21   Global Days 090

59830 Treatment of septic abortion, completed surgically
  11.89   11.89   Global Days 090

59840-59866 Elective Abortions

CMS 100-3,140.1   Abortion
CMS 100-4,3,100.1   Billing for Abortion Services

59840 Induced abortion, by dilation and curettage
  5.62   5.83   Global Days 010
  AMA: 2009, Jan, 11-31; 2008, Jan, 10-25; 2007, January, 13-27

59841 Induced abortion, by dilation and evacuation
  9.87   10.37   Global Days 010

59850 Induced abortion, by 1 or more intra-amniotic injections (amniocentesis injections), including hospital admission and visits, delivery of fetus and secundines;
  EXCLUDES Cervical dilator insertion (59200)
  9.52   9.52   Global Days 090

59851 with dilation and curettage and/or evacuation
  EXCLUDES Cervical dilator insertion (59200)
  10.85   10.85   Global Days 090

59852 with hysterotomy (failed intra-amniotic injection)
  EXCLUDES Cervical dilator insertion (59200)
  13.69   13.69   Global Days 090

59855 Induced abortion, by 1 or more vaginal suppositories (eg, prostaglandin) with or without cervical dilation (eg, laminaria), including hospital admission and visits, delivery of fetus and secundines;
  11.35   11.35   Global Days 090

59856 with dilation and curettage and/or evacuation
  13.41   13.41   Global Days 090

59857 with hysterotomy (failed medical evacuation)
  14.27   14.27   Global Days 090

59866 Multifetal pregnancy reduction(s) (MPR)
  5.99   5.99   Global Days 000

59870-59899 Miscellaneous Obstetrical Procedures

59870 Uterine evacuation and curettage for hydatidiform mole
  12.70   12.70   Global Days 090
  AMA: 2009, Jan, 11-31; 2008, Jan, 10-25; 2007, January, 13-27

59871 Removal of cerclage suture under anesthesia (other than local)
  3.69   3.69   Global Days 000
  AMA: 2007, February, 10-11; 2006, December, 10-12

▲ **59897** Unlisted fetal invasive procedure, including ultrasound guidance, when performed
  0.00   0.00   Global Days YYY
  AMA: 2005, July, 13-16

59898 Unlisted laparoscopy procedure, maternity care and delivery
  0.00   0.00   Global Days YYY

59899 Unlisted procedure, maternity care and delivery
  0.00   0.00   Global Days YYY
  AMA: 2009, Jan, 11-31; 2008, Jan, 10-25; 2007, January, 13-27

● New Code ▲ Revised Code M Maternity A Age Unlisted Not Covered # Resequenced
CCI + Add-on ⊘ Mod 51 Exempt ⊚ Mod 63 Exempt ⊙ Mod Sedation PQRI

© 2009 Publisher (Blue Ink)   CPT only © 2009 American Medical Association. All Rights Reserved. (Black Ink)   Medicare (Red Ink)   213

60000 I&D of Infected Thyroglossal Cyst

60000 Incision and drainage of thyroglossal duct cyst, infected A2 T 80
3.93 4.34 Global Days 010

60100 Core Needle Biopsy: Thyroid
EXCLUDES Fine needle aspiration (10021-10022)

60100 Biopsy thyroid, percutaneous core needle P3 T
88172-88173
76942, 77002, 77012, 77021
2.17 2.91 Global Days 000
AMA: 2009, Jan, 11-31; 2008, Jan, 10-25; 2008, Jun, 8-11; 2007, June, 10-11

60200 Surgical Removal Thyroid Cyst or Mass; Division of Isthmus

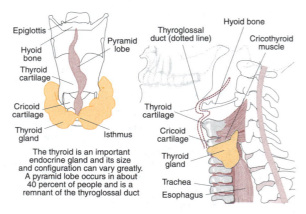

The thyroid is an important endocrine gland and its size and configuration can vary greatly. A pyramid lobe occurs in about 40 percent of people and is a remnant of the thyroglossal duct

60200 Excision of cyst or adenoma of thyroid, or transection of isthmus A2 T 80 PQ
18.15 18.15 Global Days 090

60210-60225 Subtotal Thyroidectomy
CMS 100-4, 12, 40.7   Bilateral Procedures

60210 Partial thyroid lobectomy, unilateral; with or without isthmusectomy G2 T 80 PQ
19.51 19.51 Global Days 090

60212 with contralateral subtotal lobectomy, including isthmusectomy G2 T 80 PQ
27.96 27.96 Global Days 090

60220 Total thyroid lobectomy, unilateral; with or without isthmusectomy G2 T 80 PQ
21.36 21.36 Global Days 090

60225 with contralateral subtotal lobectomy, including isthmusectomy G2 T 80 PQ
25.68 25.68 Global Days 090

60240-60271 Complete Thyroidectomy Procedures

60240 Thyroidectomy, total or complete T 80 PQ
EXCLUDES Subtotal or partial thyroidectomy (60271)
27.00 27.00 Global Days 090

60252 Thyroidectomy, total or subtotal for malignancy; with limited neck dissection T 80 PQ
36.70 36.70 Global Days 090
AMA: 2009, Jan, 11-31; 2008, Jan, 10-25; 2007, January, 13-27

60254 with radical neck dissection C 80 PQ
46.89 46.89 Global Days 090
AMA: 2009, Jan, 11-31; 2008, Jan, 10-25; 2007, January, 13-27

60260 Thyroidectomy, removal of all remaining thyroid tissue following previous removal of a portion of thyroid T 80 50 PQ
30.49 30.49 Global Days 090

60270 Thyroidectomy, including substernal thyroid; sternal split or transthoracic approach C 80 PQ
38.24 38.24 Global Days 090

60271 cervical approach T 80 PQ
29.45 29.45 Global Days 090

60280-60300 Treatment of Cyst/Sinus of Thyroid

60280 Excision of thyroglossal duct cyst or sinus; A2 T 80 PQ
EXCLUDES Thyroid ultrasound (76536)
12.22 12.22 Global Days 090

60281 recurrent A2 T 80 PQ
EXCLUDES Thyroid ultrasound (76536)
16.42 16.42 Global Days 090

60300 Aspiration and/or injection, thyroid cyst P3 T
EXCLUDES Fine needle aspiration (10021-10022)
76942, 77012
1.36 2.86 Global Days 000

60500-60512 Parathyroid Procedures

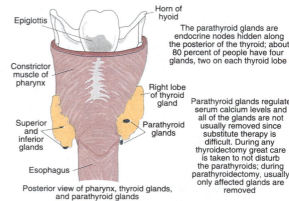

Posterior view of pharynx, thyroid glands, and parathyroid glands

The parathyroid glands are endocrine nodes hidden along the posterior of the thyroid; about 80 percent of people have four glands, two on each thyroid lobe

Parathyroid glands regulate serum calcium levels and all of the glands are not usually removed since substitute therapy is difficult. During any thyroidectomy great care is taken to not disturb the parathyroids; during parathyroidectomy, usually only affected glands are removed

60500 Parathyroidectomy or exploration of parathyroid(s); T 80 PQ
28.27 28.27 Global Days 090

60502 re-exploration T 80 PQ
35.45 35.45 Global Days 090

60505 with mediastinal exploration, sternal split or transthoracic approach C 80 PQ
38.70 38.70 Global Days 090

+ **60512** Parathyroid autotransplantation (List separately in addition to code for primary procedure) T 80
Code first 60212, 60225, 60240, 60252, 60254, 60260, 60270-60271, 60500, 60502, 60505
6.80 6.80 Global Days ZZZ

60520-60522 Thymus Procedures

60520 Thymectomy, partial or total; transcervical approach (separate procedure) T 80 PQ
28.51 28.51 Global Days 090

Current Procedural Coding Expert – Endocrine System

	60521	sternal split or transthoracic approach, without radical mediastinal dissection (separate procedure) [C] [80] [PQ]
		🚚 31.62 ✂ 31.62 Global Days 090
		AMA: 2009, Jan, 11-31; 2007, Dec, 10-179
	60522	sternal split or transthoracic approach, with radical mediastinal dissection (separate procedure) [C] [80] [PQ]
		🚚 38.37 ✂ 38.37 Global Days 090

60540-60545 Adrenal Gland Procedures

EXCLUDES Laparoscopic approach (60650)
Removal of remote or disseminated pheochromocytoma (49203-49205)

Do not report with (50323)

	60540	Adrenalectomy, partial or complete, or exploration of adrenal gland with or without biopsy, transabdominal, lumbar or dorsal (separate procedure); [C] [80] [50] [PQ]
		🚚 28.91 ✂ 28.91 Global Days 090
	60545	with excision of adjacent retroperitoneal tumor [C] [80] [PQ]
		🚚 33.48 ✂ 33.48 Global Days 090

60600-60605 Carotid Body Procedures

CMS 100-3,20.18   Carotid Body Resection/Carotid Body Denervation

	60600	Excision of carotid body tumor; without excision of carotid artery [C] [80] [PQ]
		🚚 39.74 ✂ 39.74 Global Days 090
	60605	with excision of carotid artery [C] [80] [PQ]
		🚚 54.00 ✂ 54.00 Global Days 090

60650-60699 Laparoscopic and Unlisted Procedures

INCLUDES Diagnostic laparoscopy

	60650	Laparoscopy, surgical, with adrenalectomy, partial or complete, or exploration of adrenal gland with or without biopsy, transabdominal, lumbar or dorsal [C] [80] [50] [PQ]
		🚚 32.91 ✂ 32.91 Global Days 090
	60659	Unlisted laparoscopy procedure, endocrine system [T] [80] [50]
		🚚 0.00 ✂ 0.00 Global Days YYY
	60699	Unlisted procedure, endocrine system [T] [80]
		🚚 0.00 ✂ 0.00 Global Days YYY
		AMA: 2009, Jan, 11-31; 2008, Jan, 10-25; 2007, Dec, 10-179; 2007, January, 13-27

● New Code   ▲ Revised Code   [M] Maternity   [A] Age   Unlisted   Not Covered   # Resequenced
[CCI]   + Add-on   ⊘ Mod 51 Exempt   ⊛ Mod 63 Exempt   ⊙ Mod Sedation   [PQ] PQRI

Current Procedural Coding Expert – Nervous System

61000-61253 Transcranial Access via Puncture, Burr Hole, Twist Hole, or Trephine

EXCLUDES Injection for:
Cerebral angiography (36100-36218)

61000 Subdural tap through fontanelle, or suture, infant, unilateral or bilateral; initial
  EXCLUDES Injection for:
  Cerebral angiography (36100-36218)
  Pneumoencephalography (61055)
  Ventriculography (61026, 61120)
  3.00 3.00 Global Days 000

61001 subsequent taps
  3.87 3.87 Global Days 000

61020 Ventricular puncture through previous burr hole, fontanelle, suture, or implanted ventricular catheter/reservoir; without injection
  3.56 3.56 Global Days 000

61026 with injection of medication or other substance for diagnosis or treatment
  3.40 3.40 Global Days 000

61050 Cisternal or lateral cervical (C1-C2) puncture; without injection (separate procedure)
  2.77 2.77 Global Days 000

61055 with injection of medication or other substance for diagnosis or treatment (eg, C1-C2)
  INCLUDES Injection for pneumoencephalography
  EXCLUDES Radiology procedures
  3.62 3.62 Global Days 000

61070 Puncture of shunt tubing or reservoir for aspiration or injection procedure
  75809
  2.22 2.22 Global Days 000
  AMA: 2009, Jan, 11-31; 2008, Jul, 10&13; 2008, Sep, 10-11

61105 Twist drill hole for subdural or ventricular puncture
  11.97 11.97 Global Days 090

61107 Twist drill hole(s) for subdural, intracerebral, or ventricular puncture; for implanting ventricular catheter, pressure recording device, or other intracerebral monitoring device
  EXCLUDES Intracranial neuroendoscopic ventricular catheter insertion or reinsertion (62160)
  8.57 8.57 Global Days 000
  AMA: 2007, June, 10-11; 2005, May, 7-12

61108 for evacuation and/or drainage of subdural hematoma
  23.99 23.99 Global Days 090

61120 Burr hole(s) for ventricular puncture (including injection of gas, contrast media, dye, or radioactive material)
  19.82 19.82 Global Days 090

61140 Burr hole(s) or trephine; with biopsy of brain or intracranial lesion
  33.55 33.55 Global Days 090

61150 with drainage of brain abscess or cyst
  36.26 36.26 Global Days 090

61151 with subsequent tapping (aspiration) of intracranial abscess or cyst
  26.53 26.53 Global Days 090

61154 Burr hole(s) with evacuation and/or drainage of hematoma, extradural or subdural
  33.82 33.82 Global Days 090

61156 Burr hole(s); with aspiration of hematoma or cyst, intracerebral
  33.27 33.27 Global Days 090

61210 for implanting ventricular catheter, reservoir, EEG electrode(s), pressure recording device, or other cerebral monitoring device (separate procedure)
  EXCLUDES Intracranial neuroendoscopic ventricular insertion (62160)
  10.03 10.03 Global Days 000
  AMA: 2009, Jan, 11-31; 2008, May, 9-11; 2008, Jul, 4; 2007, June, 10-11

61215 Insertion of subcutaneous reservoir, pump or continuous infusion system for connection to ventricular catheter
  EXCLUDES Chemotherapy (96450)
  Refilling and maintenance of implantable infusion pump (95990)
  13.24 13.24 Global Days 090

61250 Burr hole(s) or trephine, supratentorial, exploratory, not followed by other surgery
  23.08 23.08 Global Days 090

61253 Burr hole(s) or trephine, infratentorial, unilateral or bilateral
  EXCLUDES Burr hole or trephine followed by craniotomy at same operative session (61304-61321)
  23.10 23.10 Global Days 090
  AMA: 2009, Jan, 11-31; 2008, Jan, 10-25; 2007, January, 13-27

61304-61323 Craniectomy/Craniotomy: By Indication/Specific Area of Brain

EXCLUDES Injection for:
Cerebral angiography (36100-36218)
Pneumoencephalography (61055)
Ventriculography (61026, 61120)

61304 Craniectomy or craniotomy, exploratory; supratentorial
  44.06 44.06 Global Days 090

61305 infratentorial (posterior fossa)
  53.93 53.93 Global Days 090

61312 Craniectomy or craniotomy for evacuation of hematoma, supratentorial; extradural or subdural
  55.96 55.96 Global Days 090

61313 intracerebral
  53.18 53.18 Global Days 090

61314 Craniectomy or craniotomy for evacuation of hematoma, infratentorial; extradural or subdural
  49.07 49.07 Global Days 090

61315 intracerebellar
  55.58 55.58 Global Days 090

61316 Incision and subcutaneous placement of cranial bone graft (List separately in addition to code for primary procedure)
  Code first (61304, 61312-61313, 61322-61323, 61340, 61570-61571, 61680-61705)
  2.39 2.39 Global Days ZZZ

61320 Craniectomy or craniotomy, drainage of intracranial abscess; supratentorial
  51.11 51.11 Global Days 090

61321 infratentorial
  57.19 57.19 Global Days 090

● New Code   ▲ Revised Code   M Maternity   A Age   Unlisted   Not Covered   # Resequenced
CCI   + Add-on   ⊘ Mod 51 Exempt   Mod 63 Exempt   Mod Sedation   PQRI
© 2009 Publisher (Blue Ink)   CPT only © 2009 American Medical Association. All Rights Reserved. (Black Ink)   Medicare (Red Ink)

61322

61322	Craniectomy or craniotomy, decompressive, with or without duraplasty, for treatment of intracranial hypertension, without evacuation of associated intraparenchymal hematoma; without lobectomy	C 80
	EXCLUDES: Subtemporal decompression (61340)	
	Do not report with (61313)	
	63.79 63.79 Global Days 090	
61323	with lobectomy	C
	EXCLUDES: Subtemporal decompression (61340)	
	Do not report with (61313)	
	64.23 64.23 Global Days 090	

61330-61530 Craniectomy/Craniotomy/Decompression Brain By Surgical Approach/Specific Area of Brain

EXCLUDES: Injection for:
  Cerebral angiography (36100-36218)
  Pneumoencephalography (61055)
  Ventriculography (61026, 61120)

61330	Decompression of orbit only, transcranial approach	62 T 80 50
	INCLUDES: Naffziger operation	
	46.61 46.61 Global Days 090	
61332	Exploration of orbit (transcranial approach); with biopsy	C 80
	53.34 53.34 Global Days 090	
61333	with removal of lesion	C 80
	56.37 56.37 Global Days 090	
61334	with removal of foreign body	62 T 80
	37.81 37.81 Global Days 090	
61340	Subtemporal cranial decompression (pseudotumor cerebri, slit ventricle syndrome)	C 80 50
	EXCLUDES: Decompression craniotomy or craniectomy for intracranial hypertension, without hematoma removal (61322-61323)	
	38.69 38.69 Global Days 090	
61343	Craniectomy, suboccipital with cervical laminectomy for decompression of medulla and spinal cord, with or without dural graft (eg, Arnold-Chiari malformation)	C 80
	59.14 59.14 Global Days 090	
61345	Other cranial decompression, posterior fossa	C 80
	EXCLUDES: Kroenlein procedure (67445) Orbital decompression using a lateral wall approach (67445)	
	54.78 54.78 Global Days 090	
61440	Craniotomy for section of tentorium cerebelli (separate procedure)	C 80
	53.79 53.79 Global Days 090	
61450	Craniectomy, subtemporal, for section, compression, or decompression of sensory root of gasserian ganglion	C 80
	INCLUDES: Frazier-Spiller procedure / Hartley-Krause / Krause decompression / Taarnhoj procedure	
	51.67 51.67 Global Days 090	
61458	Craniectomy, suboccipital; for exploration or decompression of cranial nerves	C 80
	INCLUDES: Jannetta decompression	
	53.86 53.86 Global Days 090	
61460	for section of 1 or more cranial nerves	C 80
	56.52 56.52 Global Days 090	
61470	for medullary tractotomy	C 80
	51.55 51.55 Global Days 090	
61480	for mesencephalic tractotomy or pedunculotomy	C 80
	41.52 41.52 Global Days 090	
61490	Craniotomy for lobotomy, including cingulotomy	C 80 50
	50.86 50.86 Global Days 090	
61500	Craniectomy; with excision of tumor or other bone lesion of skull	C 80
	36.16 36.16 Global Days 090	
61501	for osteomyelitis	C 80
	31.22 31.22 Global Days 090	
61510	Craniectomy, trephination, bone flap craniotomy; for excision of brain tumor, supratentorial, except meningioma	C 80 P0
	58.52 58.52 Global Days 090	
61512	for excision of meningioma, supratentorial	C 80 P0
	68.64 68.64 Global Days 090	
61514	for excision of brain abscess, supratentorial	C 80
	51.13 51.13 Global Days 090	
61516	for excision or fenestration of cyst, supratentorial	C 80
	EXCLUDES: Craniopharyngioma (61545) Pituitary tumor removal (61546, 61548)	
	49.51 49.51 Global Days 090	
+**61517**	Implantation of brain intracavitary chemotherapy agent (List separately in addition to code for primary procedure)	C
	EXCLUDES: Intracavity radioelement source or ribbon implantation (77785-77787)	
	Code first (61510, 61518)	
	2.37 2.37 Global Days ZZZ	
61518	Craniectomy for excision of brain tumor, infratentorial or posterior fossa; except meningioma, cerebellopontine angle tumor, or midline tumor at base of skull	C 80 P0
	74.25 74.25 Global Days 090	
61519	meningioma	C 80
	79.40 79.40 Global Days 090	
61520	cerebellopontine angle tumor	C 80 P0
	101.48 101.48 Global Days 090	
61521	midline tumor at base of skull	C 80
	85.81 85.81 Global Days 090	

Cancers of the central nervous system are grouped according to locations in the brain and spinal cord; many CNS tumors are grouped broadly as gliomas and rarely metastasize; secondary tumors are ones that have metastasized to the CNS and are often encountered with melanomas and lung cancers

Current Procedural Coding Expert – Nervous System

61564

61522	Craniectomy, infratentorial or posterior fossa; for excision of brain abscess
	58.76 58.76 Global Days 090
61524	for excision or fenestration of cyst
	55.92 55.92 Global Days 090
61526	Craniectomy, bone flap craniotomy, transtemporal (mastoid) for excision of cerebellopontine angle tumor;
	97.10 97.10 Global Days 090
61530	combined with middle/posterior fossa craniotomy/craniectomy
	82.96 82.96 Global Days 090

61531-61545 Procedures for Seizures/Implanted Electrodes/Choroid Plexus/Craniopharyngioma

CMS 100-3,160.5 Stereotaxic Depth Electrode Implantation

EXCLUDES Craniotomy for:
  Multiple subpial transections during procedure (61567)
  Selective amygdalohippocampectomy (61566)
Injection for:
  Cerebral angiography (36100-36218)
  Pneumoencephalography (61055)
  Ventriculography (61026, 61120)

61531	Subdural implantation of strip electrodes through 1 or more burr or trephine hole(s) for long-term seizure monitoring
	EXCLUDES Craniotomy for intracranial arteriovenous malformation removal (61680-61692) Stereotactic insertion of electrodes (61760)
	32.56 32.56 Global Days 090
61533	Craniotomy with elevation of bone flap; for subdural implantation of an electrode array, for long-term seizure monitoring
	EXCLUDES Continuous EEG observation (95950-95954)
	40.78 40.78 Global Days 090
61534	for excision of epileptogenic focus without electrocorticography during surgery
	44.04 44.04 Global Days 090
61535	for removal of epidural or subdural electrode array, without excision of cerebral tissue (separate procedure)
	26.57 26.57 Global Days 090
61536	for excision of cerebral epileptogenic focus, with electrocorticography during surgery (includes removal of electrode array)
	69.43 69.43 Global Days 090
61537	for lobectomy, temporal lobe, without electrocorticography during surgery
	66.26 66.26 Global Days 090
61538	for lobectomy, temporal lobe, with electrocorticography during surgery
	71.25 71.25 Global Days 090
61539	for lobectomy, other than temporal lobe, partial or total, with electrocorticography during surgery
	63.49 63.49 Global Days 090
61540	for lobectomy, other than temporal lobe, partial or total, without electrocorticography during surgery
	58.65 58.65 Global Days 090
61541	for transection of corpus callosum
	57.73 57.73 Global Days 090
61542	for total hemispherectomy
	61.43 61.43 Global Days 090

61543	for partial or subtotal (functional) hemispherectomy
	58.36 58.36 Global Days 090
61544	for excision or coagulation of choroid plexus
	51.10 51.10 Global Days 090
61545	for excision of craniopharyngioma
	85.69 85.69 Global Days 090

61546-61548 Removal Pituitary Gland/Tumor

EXCLUDES Injection for:
  Cerebral angiography (36100-36218)
  Pneumoencephalography (61055)
  Ventriculography (61026, 61120)

61546	Craniotomy for hypophysectomy or excision of pituitary tumor, intracranial approach
	62.04 62.04 Global Days 090
61548	Hypophysectomy or excision of pituitary tumor, transnasal or transseptal approach, nonstereotactic
	INCLUDES Operating microscope (69990)
	42.29 42.29 Global Days 090

61550-61559 Craniosynostosis Procedures

EXCLUDES Injection for:
  Cerebral angiography (36100-36218)
  Pneumoencephalography (61055)
  Ventriculography (61026, 61120)
Orbital hypertelorism reconstruction (21260-21263)
Reconstruction (21172-21180)

61550	Craniectomy for craniosynostosis; single cranial suture
	24.28 24.28 Global Days 090
61552	multiple cranial sutures
	30.97 30.97 Global Days 090
61556	Craniotomy for craniosynostosis; frontal or parietal bone flap
	45.68 45.68 Global Days 090
61557	bifrontal bone flap
	44.95 44.95 Global Days 090
61558	Extensive craniectomy for multiple cranial suture craniosynostosis (eg, cloverleaf skull); not requiring bone grafts
	50.31 50.31 Global Days 090
61559	recontouring with multiple osteotomies and bone autografts (eg, barrel-stave procedure) (includes obtaining grafts)
	50.78 50.78 Global Days 090

61563-61564 Removal Cranial Bone Tumor With/Without Optic Nerve Decompression

EXCLUDES Injection for:
  Cerebral angiography (36100-36218)
  Pneumoencephalography (61055)
  Ventriculography (61026, 61120)
Reconstruction (21181-21183)

61563	Excision, intra and extracranial, benign tumor of cranial bone (eg, fibrous dysplasia); without optic nerve decompression
	53.18 53.18 Global Days 090
61564	with optic nerve decompression
	64.68 64.68 Global Days 090

 New Code   Revised Code   Maternity   Age   Unlisted   Not Covered   Resequenced

CCI   + Add-on   Mod 51 Exempt   Mod 63 Exempt   Mod Sedation   PQRI

© 2009 Publisher (Blue Ink)   CPT only © 2009 American Medical Association. All Rights Reserved. (Black Ink)   Medicare (Red Ink)   219

61566-61567 Craniotomy for Seizures

EXCLUDES Injection for:
Cerebral angiography (36100-36218)
Pneumoencephalography (61055)
Ventriculography (61026, 61120)

61566 Craniotomy with elevation of bone flap; for selective amygdalohippocampectomy C 80
60.42   60.42   Global Days 090

61567 for multiple subpial transections, with electrocorticography during surgery C 80
68.88   68.88   Global Days 090

61570-61571 Removal of Foreign Body from Brain

EXCLUDES Injection for:
Cerebral angiography (36100-36218)
Pneumoencephalography (61055)
Ventriculography (61026, 61120)
Sequestrectomy for osteomyelitis (61501)

61570 Craniectomy or craniotomy; with excision of foreign body from brain C 80
50.07   50.07   Global Days 090

61571 with treatment of penetrating wound of brain C 80
53.38   53.38   Global Days 090

61575-61576 Transoral Approach Posterior Cranial Fossa/Upper Cervical Cord

EXCLUDES Arthrodesis (22548)
Injection for:
Cerebral angiography (36100-36218)
Pneumoencephalography (61055)
Ventriculography (61026, 61120)

61575 Transoral approach to skull base, brain stem or upper spinal cord for biopsy, decompression or excision of lesion; C 80
67.42   67.42   Global Days 090

61576 requiring splitting of tongue and/or mandible (including tracheostomy) C 80
96.45   96.45   Global Days 090

61580-61598 Surgical Approach: Cranial Fossae

EXCLUDES Definitive surgery (61600-61616)
Injection for:
Cerebral angiography (36100-36218)
Pneumoencephalography (61055)
Ventriculography (61026, 61120)
Primary closure (15732, 15756-15758)
Repair and/or reconstruction (61618-61619)

61580 Craniofacial approach to anterior cranial fossa; extradural, including lateral rhinotomy, ethmoidectomy, sphenoidectomy, without maxillectomy or orbital exenteration C 50
66.66   66.66   Global Days 090

61581 extradural, including lateral rhinotomy, orbital exenteration, ethmoidectomy, sphenoidectomy and/or maxillectomy C 50
74.68   74.68   Global Days 090

61582 extradural, including unilateral or bifrontal craniotomy, elevation of frontal lobe(s), osteotomy of base of anterior cranial fossa C 80
80.15   80.15   Global Days 090

61583 intradural, including unilateral or bifrontal craniotomy, elevation or resection of frontal lobe, osteotomy of base of anterior cranial fossa C 80
76.98   76.98   Global Days 090

61584 Orbitocranial approach to anterior cranial fossa, extradural, including supraorbital ridge osteotomy and elevation of frontal and/or temporal lobe(s); without orbital exenteration C 80 50
75.38   75.38   Global Days 090

61585 with orbital exenteration C 80 50
86.23   86.23   Global Days 090

61586 Bicoronal, transzygomatic and/or LeFort I osteotomy approach to anterior cranial fossa with or without internal fixation, without bone graft C 80
64.20   64.20   Global Days 090

61590 Infratemporal pre-auricular approach to middle cranial fossa (parapharyngeal space, infratemporal and midline skull base, nasopharynx), with or without disarticulation of the mandible, including parotidectomy, craniotomy, decompression and/or mobilization of the facial nerve and/or petrous carotid artery C 80 50
84.72   84.72   Global Days 090

61591 Infratemporal post-auricular approach to middle cranial fossa (internal auditory meatus, petrous apex, tentorium, cavernous sinus, parasellar area, infratemporal fossa) including mastoidectomy, resection of sigmoid sinus, with or without decompression and/or mobilization of contents of auditory canal or petrous carotid artery C 80 50 P0
85.39   85.39   Global Days 090

61592 Orbitocranial zygomatic approach to middle cranial fossa (cavernous sinus and carotid artery, clivus, basilar artery or petrous apex) including osteotomy of zygoma, craniotomy, extra- or intradural elevation of temporal lobe C 80 50
84.44   84.44   Global Days 090

61595 Transtemporal approach to posterior cranial fossa, jugular foramen or midline skull base, including mastoidectomy, decompression of sigmoid sinus and/or facial nerve, with or without mobilization C 50 P0
64.53   64.53   Global Days 090

61596 Transcochlear approach to posterior cranial fossa, jugular foramen or midline skull base, including labyrinthectomy, decompression, with or without mobilization of facial nerve and/or petrous carotid artery C 80 50 P0
69.11   69.11   Global Days 090

61597 Transcondylar (far lateral) approach to posterior cranial fossa, jugular foramen or midline skull base, including occipital condylectomy, mastoidectomy, resection of C1-C3 vertebral body(s), decompression of vertebral artery, with or without mobilization C 80 50
79.44   79.44   Global Days 090

61598 Transpetrosal approach to posterior cranial fossa, clivus or foramen magnum, including ligation of superior petrosal sinus and/or sigmoid sinus C 80 P0
75.29   75.29   Global Days 090

Current Procedural Coding Expert – Nervous System   61626

61600-61616 Definitive Procedures: Cranial Fossae

EXCLUDES
Injection for:
  Cerebral angiography (36100-36218)
  Pneumoencephalography (61055)
  Ventriculography (61026, 61120)
Primary closure (15732, 15756-15758)
Repair and/or reconstruction (61618-61619)
Surgical approach (61580-61598)

61600 Resection or excision of neoplastic, vascular or infectious lesion of base of anterior cranial fossa; extradural
58.66   58.66   Global Days 090

61601 intradural, including dural repair, with or without graft
63.41   63.41   Global Days 090

61605 Resection or excision of neoplastic, vascular or infectious lesion of infratemporal fossa, parapharyngeal space, petrous apex; extradural
60.63   60.63   Global Days 090

61606 intradural, including dural repair, with or without graft
80.70   80.70   Global Days 090

61607 Resection or excision of neoplastic, vascular or infectious lesion of parasellar area, cavernous sinus, clivus or midline skull base; extradural
78.55   78.55   Global Days 090

61608 intradural, including dural repair, with or without graft
86.67   86.67   Global Days 090

+ 61609 Transection or ligation, carotid artery in cavernous sinus; without repair (List separately in addition to code for primary procedure)
Code first (61605-61608)
17.22   17.22   Global Days ZZZ

+ 61610 with repair by anastomosis or graft (List separately in addition to code for primary procedure)
Code first (61605-61608)
51.13   51.13   Global Days ZZZ

+ 61611 Transection or ligation, carotid artery in petrous canal; without repair (List separately in addition to code for primary procedure)
Code first (61605-61608)
10.49   10.49   Global Days ZZZ

+ 61612 with repair by anastomosis or graft (List separately in addition to code for primary procedure)
Code first (61605-61608)
39.41   39.41   Global Days ZZZ

61613 Obliteration of carotid aneurysm, arteriovenous malformation, or carotid-cavernous fistula by dissection within cavernous sinus
87.75   87.75   Global Days 090

61615 Resection or excision of neoplastic, vascular or infectious lesion of base of posterior cranial fossa, jugular foramen, foramen magnum, or C1-C3 vertebral bodies; extradural
63.48   63.48   Global Days 090

61616 intradural, including dural repair, with or without graft
89.18   89.18   Global Days 090

61618-61619 Reconstruction Post-Surgical Cranial Fossae Defects

EXCLUDES
Definitive surgery (61600-61616)
Injection for:
  Cerebral angiography (36100-36218)
  Pneumoencephalography (61055)
  Ventriculography (61026, 61120)
Primary closure (15732, 15756-15758)
Surgical approach (61580-61598)

61618 Secondary repair of dura for cerebrospinal fluid leak, anterior, middle or posterior cranial fossa following surgery of the skull base; by free tissue graft (eg, pericranium, fascia, tensor fascia lata, adipose tissue, homologous or synthetic grafts)
35.16   35.16   Global Days 090
AMA: 2009, Jan, 11-31; 2008, Jan, 10-25; 2007, January, 13-27

61619 by local or regionalized vascularized pedicle flap or myocutaneous flap (including galea, temporalis, frontalis or occipitalis muscle)
40.40   40.40   Global Days 090
AMA: 2009, Jan, 11-31; 2008, Jan, 10-25; 2007, January, 13-27

61623-61642 Neurovascular Interventional Procedures

CMS 100-2,16,10   Exclusions from Coverage
CMS 100-2,16,180   Services Related to Noncovered Procedures
CMS 100-3,20.28   Therapeutic Embolization
CMS 100-4,4,61.1   Hospital Requirement for Device Codes on OPPS Claims
CMS 100-4,4,61.2   Requirements for Specific Procedures to be Reported With Device Codes

61623 Endovascular temporary balloon arterial occlusion, head or neck (extracranial/intracranial) including selective catheterization of vessel to be occluded, positioning and inflation of occlusion balloon, concomitant neurological monitoring, and radiologic supervision and interpretation of all angiography required for balloon occlusion and to exclude vascular injury post occlusion
Code also (C2628)
15.00   15.00   Global Days 000
AMA: 2006, December, 4-7

61624 Transcatheter permanent occlusion or embolization (eg, for tumor destruction, to achieve hemostasis, to occlude a vascular malformation), percutaneous, any method; central nervous system (intracranial, spinal cord)
EXCLUDES Transcatheter occlusion or embolization other than head or neck (37204)
75894
29.92   29.92   Global Days 000
AMA: 2009, Jan, 11-31; 2008, Jan, 10-25; 2007, January, 13-27; 2006, December, 4-7

61626 non-central nervous system, head or neck (extracranial, brachiocephalic branch)
EXCLUDES Transcatheter occlusion or embolization other than head or neck (37204)
Code also (C1769, C1887, C2628)
75894
23.35   23.35   Global Days 000
AMA: 2006, December, 4-7

● New Code   ▲ Revised Code   Ⓜ Maternity   Ⓐ Age   Unlisted   Not Covered   # Resequenced
CCI   + Add-on   ⊘ Mod 51 Exempt   Mod 63 Exempt   ⊙ Mod Sedation   PQRI

© 2009 Publisher *(Blue Ink)*   CPT only © 2009 American Medical Association. All Rights Reserved. *(Black Ink)*   Medicare *(Red Ink)*

61630   **Current Procedural Coding Expert – Nervous System**

61630   Balloon angioplasty, intracranial (eg, atherosclerotic stenosis), percutaneous   C 80
     INCLUDES   Diagnostic arteriogram if stent or angioplasty is necessary
                 Radiology services for arteriography of target vascular family
                 Selective catheterization of the target vascular family
     EXCLUDES   Diagnostic arteriogram if stent or angioplasty is not necessary (use applicable code for selective catheterization and radiology services)
     🔧 34.17   ✂ 34.17   Global Days XXX
     AMA: 2006, December, 4-7

61635   Transcatheter placement of intravascular stent(s), intracranial (eg, atherosclerotic stenosis), including balloon angioplasty, if performed   C 80
     INCLUDES   Diagnostic arteriogram if stent or angioplasty is necessary
                 Radiology services for arteriography of target vascular family
                 Selective catheterization of the target vascular family
     EXCLUDES   Diagnostic arteriogram if stent or angioplasty is not necessary (use applicable code for selective catheterization and radiology services)
     🔧 36.89   ✂ 36.89   Global Days XXX
     AMA: 2006, December, 4-7

61640   Balloon dilatation of intracranial vasospasm, percutaneous; initial vessel   E
     INCLUDES   Angiography after dilation of vessel
                 Fluoroscopic guidance
                 Injection of contrast material
                 Roadmapping
                 Selective catheterization of target vessel
                 Vessel analysis
     🔧 17.44   ✂ 17.44   Global Days 000
     AMA: 2006, December, 4-7

+ **61641**   each additional vessel in same vascular family (List separately in addition to code for primary procedure)   E
     INCLUDES   Angiography after dilation of vessel
                 Fluoroscopic guidance
                 Injection of contrast material
                 Roadmapping
                 Selective catheterization of target vessel
                 Vessel analysis
     Code first (61640)
     🔧 6.13   ✂ 6.13   Global Days ZZZ
     AMA: 2006, December, 4-7

+ **61642**   each additional vessel in different vascular family (List separately in addition to code for primary procedure)   E
     INCLUDES   Angiography after dilation of vessel
                 Fluoroscopic guidance
                 Injection of contrast material
                 Roadmapping
                 Selective catheterization of target vessel
                 Vessel analysis
     Code first (61640)
     🔧 12.25   ✂ 12.25   Global Days ZZZ
     AMA: 2006, December, 4-7

61680-61692 Surgical Treatment of Arteriovenous Malformation of the Brain

CMS 100-4,12,30   Correct Coding Policy
INCLUDES   Craniotomy

61680   Surgery of intracranial arteriovenous malformation; supratentorial, simple   C 80
     🔧 60.77   ✂ 60.77   Global Days 090

61682   supratentorial, complex   C 80
     🔧 113.00   ✂ 113.00   Global Days 090

61684   infratentorial, simple   C 80
     🔧 76.58   ✂ 76.58   Global Days 090

61686   infratentorial, complex   C 80
     🔧 121.57   ✂ 121.57   Global Days 090

61690   dural, simple   C 80
     🔧 58.68   ✂ 58.68   Global Days 090

61692   dural, complex   C 80
     🔧 98.82   ✂ 98.82   Global Days 090

61697-61703 Surgical Treatment Brain Aneurysm

INCLUDES   Craniotomy

61697   Surgery of complex intracranial aneurysm, intracranial approach; carotid circulation   C 80 P0
     INCLUDES   Aneurysms bigger than 15 mm
                 Calcification of the aneurysm neck
                 Inclusion of normal vessels in aneurysm neck
                 Surgery needing temporary vessel occlusion, trapping, or cardiopulmonary bypass to treat aneurysm
     🔧 113.88   ✂ 113.88   Global Days 090

61698   vertebrobasilar circulation   C 80
     INCLUDES   Aneurysm bigger than 15 mm
                 Calcification of aneurysm neck
                 Inclusion of normal vessels into aneurysm neck
                 Surgery needing temporary vessel occlusion, trapping, or cardiopulmonary bypass to treat aneurysm
     🔧 125.25   ✂ 125.25   Global Days 090

61700   Surgery of simple intracranial aneurysm, intracranial approach; carotid circulation   C 80 P0
     🔧 92.18   ✂ 92.18   Global Days 090
     AMA: 2009, Jan, 11-31; 2008, Jan, 10-25; 2007, January, 13-27

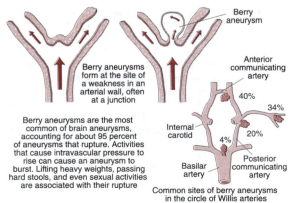

Berry aneurysms form at the site of a weakness in an arterial wall, often at a junction

Berry aneurysms are the most common of brain aneurysms, accounting for about 95 percent of aneurysms that rupture. Activities that cause intravascular pressure to rise can cause an aneurysm to burst. Lifting heavy weights, passing hard stools, and even sexual activities are associated with their rupture

Common sites of berry aneurysms in the circle of Willis arteries

61702   vertebrobasilar circulation   C 80
     🔧 108.71   ✂ 108.71   Global Days 090

Current Procedural Coding Expert – Nervous System

61703   Surgery of intracranial aneurysm, cervical approach by application of occluding clamp to cervical carotid artery (Selverstone-Crutchfield type)   C 80
     EXCLUDES   Cervical approach for direct ligation of carotid artery (37600-37606)
     36.33   36.33   Global Days 090

61705-61710 Other Procedures for Aneurysm, Arteriovenous Malformation, and Carotid-Cavernous Fistula

INCLUDES   Craniotomy
EXCLUDES   Ligation or gradual occlusion of internal common carotid artery (37605-37606)

61705   Surgery of aneurysm, vascular malformation or carotid-cavernous fistula; by intracranial and cervical occlusion of carotid artery   C 80
     70.09   70.09   Global Days 090

61708   by intracranial electrothrombosis   C 80
     EXCLUDES   Ligation or gradual occlusion of internal or common carotid artery (37605-37606)
     57.12   57.12   Global Days 090

61710   by intra-arterial embolization, injection procedure, or balloon catheter   C 80
     49.48   49.48   Global Days 090

61711 Extracranial-Intracranial Bypass

INCLUDES   Craniotomy

61711   Anastomosis, arterial, extracranial-intracranial (eg, middle cerebral/cortical) arteries   C 80
     EXCLUDES   Carotid or vertebral thromboendarterectomy (35301)
              Operating microscope (69990)
     69.82   69.82   Global Days 090

61720-61791 Stereotactic Procedures of the Brain

CMS 100-3,160.4   Stereotactic Cingulotomy as a Means of Psychosurgery--Not Covered
CMS 100-3,160.5   Stereotaxic Depth Electrode Implantation

Frontal section of the brain (left) and lateral view schematic showing the ventricular system in blue (right)

Cerebral spinal fluid (CSF) is secreted in the ventricles and flows generally from the laterals into the third ventricle via the interventricular foramina, and into the fourth ventricle via the cerebral aqueduct. Many brain disorders upset ventricular fluid pressures and shunts are employed to restore balance

61720   Creation of lesion by stereotactic method, including burr hole(s) and localizing and recording techniques, single or multiple stages; globus pallidus or thalamus   T
     33.96   33.96   Global Days 090

61735   subcortical structure(s) other than globus pallidus or thalamus   C
     42.58   42.58   Global Days 090

61750   Stereotactic biopsy, aspiration, or excision, including burr hole(s), for intracranial lesion;   C PQ
     37.64   37.64   Global Days 090

61751   with computed tomography and/or magnetic resonance guidance   C PQ
     70450, 70460, 70470, 70551-70553
     36.61   36.61   Global Days 090
     AMA: 2009, Jan, 11-31; 2008, Jan, 10-25; 2007, January, 13-27

61760   Stereotactic implantation of depth electrodes into the cerebrum for long-term seizure monitoring   C
     42.36   42.36   Global Days 090

61770   Stereotactic localization, including burr hole(s), with insertion of catheter(s) or probe(s) for placement of radiation source   G2 T
     42.99   42.99   Global Days 090

61790   Creation of lesion by stereotactic method, percutaneous, by neurolytic agent (eg, alcohol, thermal, electrical, radiofrequency); gasserian ganglion   A2 T
     23.22   23.22   Global Days 090

61791   trigeminal medullary tract   A2 T 80
     29.17   29.17   Global Days 090

61795-61800 Stereotactic Radiosurgery (SRS): Brain

INCLUDES   Planning, dosimetry, targeting, positioning or blocking performed by the neurosurgen
EXCLUDES   Intensity modulated beam delivery plan and treatment (77301, 77418)
         Stereotactic body radiation therapy (77435, 77373)
         Treatment planning, physics and dosimetry, and treatment delivery performed by the oncologist

Do not report more than once per lesion for a course of treatment
Do not report radiation treatment management and radiosurgery by the same physician (77427-77435)
Do not report with (20660)

+ 61795   Stereotactic computer-assisted volumetric (navigational) procedure, intracranial, extracranial, or spinal (List separately in addition to code for primary procedure)   N N
     Code first primary procedure
     Do not report with (61796-61799)
     6.68   6.68   Global Days ZZZ
     AMA: 2009, Jan, 11-31; 2008, May, 9-11; 2008, Jan, 10-25; 2008, Jul, 10&13; 2008, Oct, 10-11; 2007, Dec, 1-2; 2007, January, 13-27; 2006, January, 46-47

61796   Stereotactic radiosurgery (particle beam, gamma ray, or linear accelerator); 1 simple cranial lesion   B 80
     INCLUDES   Lesions less than 3.5 cm
     EXCLUDES   Brainstem lesions or lesions located <= 5 mm from the optic nerve, chasm, or tract (61798-61799)

Do not report more than once per treatment
Do not report with (61795, 61798)
     23.46   23.46   Global Days 090

+ 61797   each additional cranial lesion, simple (List separately in addition to code for primary procedure)   B 80
     INCLUDES   Lesions < 3.5 cm
     EXCLUDES   Brainstem lesions or lesions located <= 5 mm from the optic nerve, chasm, or tract (61798-61799)

Code first (61796, or 61798)
Do not report 61797 and 61799 more than four times in total per treatment course
Do not report with (61795)
     5.20   5.20   Global Days ZZZ

● New Code   ▲ Revised Code   M Maternity   A Age   Unlisted   Not Covered   # Resequenced
CCI   + Add-on   ⊘ Mod 51 Exempt   Ⓢ Mod 63 Exempt   ⊙ Mod Sedation   PQ PQRI

© 2009 Publisher (Blue Ink)   CPT only © 2009 American Medical Association. All Rights Reserved. (Black Ink)   Medicare (Red Ink)   223

61798

	61798	1 complex cranial lesion [B][80]
		INCLUDES: All lesions involved in therapeutic lesion creation procedures
		Arteriovenous malformations, cavernous sinus, parasellar, glomus, pineal region, pituary tumors, and Schwannomas
		Brainstem lesions or lesions located <= 5 mm from the optic nerve, chasm, or tract
		Lesions >= 3.5 cm
		Do not report more than once per lesion per treatment course
		Do not report with (61795-61796)
		32.01 32.01 Global Days 090
+	61799	each additional cranial lesion, complex (List separately in addition to code for primary procedure) [B][80]
		INCLUDES: All lesions created in therapeutic lesion creation procedures
		Brainstem lesions or lesions located <= 5 mm from the optic nerve, chasm, or tract
		Lesions >= 3.5 cm
		Code first (61798)
		Do not report more than once per lesion per treatment course
		Do not report 61797 and 61799 more than four times in total per treatment course
		Do not report with (61795)
		7.19 7.19 Global Days ZZZ
+	61800	Application of stereotactic headframe for stereotactic radiosurgery (List separately in addition to code for primary procedure) [B][80]
		Code first (61796, 61798)
		3.61 3.61 Global Days ZZZ

61850-61888 Intracranial Neurostimulation

CMS 100-3,160.2 Treatment of Motor Function Disorders with Electric Nerve Stimulation
CMS 100-3,160.7 Electrical Nerve Stimulators
CMS 100-4,32,50 Deep Brain Stimulation for Essential Tremor and Parkinson's Disease

INCLUDES: Microelectrode recording by same physician, if provided

EXCLUDES: Electronic analysis and reprogramming of neurostimulator pulse generator (95970-95975)
Neurophysiological mapping by another physician (95961-95962)

	61850	Twist drill or burr hole(s) for implantation of neurostimulator electrodes, cortical [C][80]
		26.19 26.19 Global Days 090
	61860	Craniectomy or craniotomy for implantation of neurostimulator electrodes, cerebral, cortical [C][80]
		41.97 41.97 Global Days 090
	61863	Twist drill, burr hole, craniotomy, or craniectomy with stereotactic implantation of neurostimulator electrode array in subcortical site (eg, thalamus, globus pallidus, subthalamic nucleus, periventricular, periaqueductal gray), without use of intraoperative microelectrode recording; first array [C][80][50]
		40.13 40.13 Global Days 090
+	61864	each additional array (List separately in addition to primary procedure) [C][80]
		Code first (61863)
		7.74 7.74 Global Days ZZZ

Current Procedural Coding Expert – Nervous System

	61867	Twist drill, burr hole, craniotomy, or craniectomy with stereotactic implantation of neurostimulator electrode array in subcortical site (eg, thalamus, globus pallidus, subthalamic nucleus, periventricular, periaqueductal gray), with use of intraoperative microelectrode recording; first array [C][80][50][P0]
		61.38 61.38 Global Days 090
+	61868	each additional array (List separately in addition to primary procedure) [C][80]
		Code first (61867)
		13.66 13.66 Global Days ZZZ
	61870	Craniectomy for implantation of neurostimulator electrodes, cerebellar; cortical [C][80]
		31.63 31.63 Global Days 090
	61875	subcortical [C][80]
		24.95 24.95 Global Days 090
	61880	Revision or removal of intracranial neurostimulator electrodes [G2][T][80][50]
		15.03 15.03 Global Days 090
	61885	Insertion or replacement of cranial neurostimulator pulse generator or receiver, direct or inductive coupling; with connection to a single electrode array [H8][S][80][50]
		EXCLUDES: Open surgery to place cranial nerve neurostimulator electrode(s) (64573)
		Percutaneous procedure to place cranial nerve neurostimulator electrode(s) (64553)
		Revision or removal of cranial nerve neurostimulator electrode(s) (64585)
		Code also (C1820, L8685-L8686)
		17.63 17.63 Global Days 090
	61886	with connection to 2 or more electrode arrays [H8][S][80]
		EXCLUDES: Open surgery to place cranial nerve neurostimulator electrode(s) (64573)
		Percutaneous procedure to place cranial nerve neurostimulator electrode(s) (64553)
		Revision or removal of cranial nerve neurostimulator electrode(s) (64585)
		Code also (C1767, C1820, L8688)
		22.15 22.15 Global Days 090
	61888	Revision or removal of cranial neurostimulator pulse generator or receiver [A2][T][50]
		Do not report with (61885-61886)
		10.36 10.36 Global Days 010

62000-62148 Repair of Skull and/or Cerebrospinal Fluid Leaks

	62000	Elevation of depressed skull fracture; simple, extradural [T]
		27.47 27.47 Global Days 090
	62005	compound or comminuted, extradural [C][80]
		33.98 33.98 Global Days 090
	62010	with repair of dura and/or debridement of brain [C][80]
		40.61 40.61 Global Days 090
	62100	Craniotomy for repair of dural/cerebrospinal fluid leak, including surgery for rhinorrhea/otorrhea [C][80]
		EXCLUDES: Repair of spinal fluid leak (63707, 63709)
		43.44 43.44 Global Days 090
	62115	Reduction of craniomegalic skull (eg, treated hydrocephalus); not requiring bone grafts or cranioplasty [C][80]
		34.89 34.89 Global Days 090

---

[26]/[TC] PC/TC Comp Only   [A2]-[Z3] ASC Pmt   [50] Bilateral   ♂ Male Only   ♀ Female Only   Facility RVU   Non-Facility RVU
AMA: CPT Asst   **MED:** Pub 100   [A]-[Y] OPPSI   [80]/[82] Surg Assist Allowed / w/Doc   Lab Crosswalk   Radiology Crosswalk

Current Procedural Coding Expert – Nervous System

62116	with simple cranioplasty
	47.52　47.52　Global Days 090
62117	requiring craniotomy and reconstruction with or without bone graft (includes obtaining grafts)
	46.84　46.84　Global Days 090
62120	Repair of encephalocele, skull vault, including cranioplasty
	46.50　46.50　Global Days 090
62121	Craniotomy for repair of encephalocele, skull base
	48.58　48.58　Global Days 090
62140	Cranioplasty for skull defect; up to 5 cm diameter
	27.91　27.91　Global Days 090
62141	larger than 5 cm diameter
	30.70　30.70　Global Days 090
62142	Removal of bone flap or prosthetic plate of skull
	23.65　23.65　Global Days 090
62143	Replacement of bone flap or prosthetic plate of skull
	27.75　27.75　Global Days 090
62145	Cranioplasty for skull defect with reparative brain surgery
	37.82　37.82　Global Days 090
62146	Cranioplasty with autograft (includes obtaining bone grafts); up to 5 cm diameter
	33.38　33.38　Global Days 090
62147	larger than 5 cm diameter
	39.23　39.23　Global Days 090
+ 62148	Incision and retrieval of subcutaneous cranial bone graft for cranioplasty (List separately in addition to code for primary procedure)
	Code first (62140-62147)
	3.45　3.45　Global Days ZZZ

62160-62165 Neuroendoscopic Procedures of the Brain

INCLUDES Diagnostic endoscopy

+ 62160	Neuroendoscopy, intracranial, for placement or replacement of ventricular catheter and attachment to shunt system or external drainage (List separately in addition to code for primary procedure)
	Code first (61107, 61210, 62220-62230, 62258)
	5.16　5.16　Global Days ZZZ
	AMA: 2009, Jan, 11-31; 2008, Jan, 10-25; 2008, May, 9-11; 2007, June, 10-11
62161	Neuroendoscopy, intracranial; with dissection of adhesions, fenestration of septum pellucidum or intraventricular cysts (including placement, replacement, or removal of ventricular catheter)
	40.75　40.75　Global Days 090
62162	with fenestration or excision of colloid cyst, including placement of external ventricular catheter for drainage
	50.69　50.69　Global Days 090
62163	with retrieval of foreign body
	32.63　32.63　Global Days 090
62164	with excision of brain tumor, including placement of external ventricular catheter for drainage
	55.98　55.98　Global Days 090
62165	with excision of pituitary tumor, transnasal or trans-sphenoidal approach
	42.30　42.30　Global Days 090

62180-62258 Cerebrospinal Fluid Diversion Procedures

62180	Ventriculocisternostomy (Torkildsen type operation)
	42.89　42.89　Global Days 090
62190	Creation of shunt; subarachnoid/subdural-atrial, -jugular, -auricular
	24.56　24.56　Global Days 090
62192	subarachnoid/subdural-peritoneal, -pleural, other terminus
	26.20　26.20　Global Days 090
62194	Replacement or irrigation, subarachnoid/subdural catheter
	11.30　11.30　Global Days 010
62200	Ventriculocisternostomy, third ventricle;
	INCLUDES Dandy ventriculocisternostomy
	36.84　36.84　Global Days 090
62201	stereotactic, neuroendoscopic method
	EXCLUDES Intracranial neuroendoscopic surgery (62161-62165)
	32.02　32.02　Global Days 090
	AMA: 2009, Jan, 11-31; 2008, Jan, 10-25; 2007, Aug, 15
62220	Creation of shunt; ventriculo-atrial, -jugular, -auricular
	EXCLUDES Intracranial neuroendoscopic ventricular catheter placement (62160)
	27.22　27.22　Global Days 090
	AMA: 2007, June, 10-11
62223	ventriculo-peritoneal, -pleural, other terminus
	EXCLUDES Intracranial neuroendoscopic ventricular catheter placement (62160)
	28.12　28.12　Global Days 090
	AMA: 2007, June, 10-11
62225	Replacement or irrigation, ventricular catheter
	EXCLUDES Intracranial neuroendoscopic ventricular catheter placement (62160)
	13.70　13.70　Global Days 090
	AMA: 2007, June, 10-11
62230	Replacement or revision of cerebrospinal fluid shunt, obstructed valve, or distal catheter in shunt system
	EXCLUDES Intracranial neuroendoscopic ventricular catheter placement (62160)
	22.50　22.50　Global Days 090
	AMA: 2007, June, 10-11
62252	Reprogramming of programmable cerebrospinal shunt
	EXCLUDES Intracranial neuroendoscopic ventricular catheter insertion (62160)
	Percutaneous irrigation or aspiraton of shunt reservoir (61070)
	2.70　2.70　Global Days XXX

● New Code　▲ Revised Code　M Maternity　A Age　Unlisted　Not Covered　# Resequenced
CCI　+ Add-on　⊘ Mod 51 Exempt　⊘ Mod 63 Exempt　⊙ Mod Sedation　PQ PQRI
© 2009 Publisher (Blue Ink)　CPT only © 2009 American Medical Association. All Rights Reserved. (Black Ink)　Medicare (Red Ink)

62256	Removal of complete cerebrospinal fluid shunt system; without replacement
	EXCLUDES *Intracranial neuroendoscopic ventricular catheter insertion (62160)*
	Percutaneous irrigation or aspiration of shunt reservoir (61070)
	Reprogramming cerebrospinal fluid (SCF) shunt (62252)
	15.77 15.77 Global Days 090
62258	with replacement by similar or other shunt at same operation
	EXCLUDES *Intracranial neuroendoscopic ventricular catheter placement (62160)*
	Percutaneous irrigation or aspiration of shunt reservoir (61070)
	Reprogramming of a cerebrospinal fluid (CSF) shunt (62252)
	30.14 30.14 Global Days 090
	AMA: 2007, June, 10-11

62263-62264 Lysis of Epidural Lesions with Injection of Solution/Mechanical Methods

INCLUDES Fluoroscopic guidance and epidurography (72275, 77003)

62263	Percutaneous lysis of epidural adhesions using solution injection (eg, hypertonic saline, enzyme) or mechanical means (eg, catheter) including radiologic localization (includes contrast when administered), multiple adhesiolysis sessions; 2 or more days
	INCLUDES All adhesiolysis treatments, injections, and infusions during course of treatment
	Contrast injection during fluoroscopic guidance/localization
	Fluoroscopic guidance and epidurography (72275, 77003)
	Percutaneous epidural catheter insertion and removal for neurolytic agent injections during serialized treatment sessions
	Do not report more than once for the complete series spanning two or more treatment days
	11.38 19.39 Global Days 010
	AMA: 2009, Jan, 11-31; 2008, Jan, 10-25; 2008, Jun, 8-11; 2008, Jul, 9; 2007, January, 13-27; 2005, November, 14-15
62264	1 day
	INCLUDES Contrast injection during fluoroscopic guidance/localization
	Multiple treatment sessions performed on the same day
	Do not report with (62263)
	6.76 11.37 Global Days 010
	AMA: 2009, Jan, 11-31; 2008, Jan, 10-25; 2008, Jul, 9; 2008, Jun, 8-11; 2007, January, 13-27; 2005, November, 14-15

62267-62269 Percutaneous Procedures of Spinal Cord

EXCLUDES *Fluoroscopic guidance and localization unless a formal contrast study is performed (77003)*

62267	Percutaneous aspiration within the nucleus pulposus, intervertebral disc, or paravertebral tissue for diagnostic purposes
	INCLUDES Contrast injection during fluoroscopic guidance/localization
	Do not report with (10022, 20225, 62287, 62290-62291)
	77003
	4.64 7.33 Global Days 000
62268	Percutaneous aspiration, spinal cord cyst or syrinx
	76942, 77002, 77012
	6.96 10.75 Global Days 000
62269	Biopsy of spinal cord, percutaneous needle
	EXCLUDES *Fine needle aspiration (10021-10022)*
	76942, 77002, 77012
	7.08 10.87 Global Days 000

62270-62272 Spinal Puncture, Subarachnoid Space, Diagnostic/Therapeutic

INCLUDES Contrast injection during fluoroscopic guidance/localization

EXCLUDES *Fluoroscopic guidance and localization unless a formal contrast study is performed (77003)*

Most common agent in neonates is E. coli; Haemophilus influenzae b and streptococcus pneumoniae are common agents in adult cases

The brain and spinal cord are encased in a tough fibrous membrane known as the meninges and meningitis is an inflammation of that tissue and commonly affects the underlying central nervous system tissues and fluids; causes are numerous and classification is based on type of infection; purulent refers to forms usually caused by bacteria; chronic meningitis is usually caused by mycobacteria and fungi; aseptic or abacterial meningitis is commonly associated with a viral infection and is reported with the underlying disease. Encephalitis is inflammation of the brain and is also usually associated with a viral infection and also is reported with the underlying disease

62270	Spinal puncture, lumbar, diagnostic
	INCLUDES Contrast injection during fluoroscopic guidance/localization
	2.12 3.94 Global Days 000
	AMA: 2007, Jul, 1-4; 2006, May, 1-9
62272	Spinal puncture, therapeutic, for drainage of cerebrospinal fluid (by needle or catheter)
	INCLUDES Contrast injection during fluoroscopic guidance/localization
	2.28 5.05 Global Days 000

Current Procedural Coding Expert – Nervous System

62273 Epidural Blood Patch

EXCLUDES *Fluoroscopic guidance and localization unless a formal contrast study is performed (77003)*
Injection of diagnostic or therapeutic material (62310-62311, 62318-62319)

62273 Injection, epidural, of blood or clot patch
INCLUDES Contrast injection during fluoroscopic guidance/localization
3.12 4.50 Global Days 000

62280-62282 Neurolysis

INCLUDES Contrast injection during fluoroscopic guidance/localization
EXCLUDES *Fluoroscopic guidance and localization unless a formal contrast study is performed (77003)*
Injection of diagnostic or therapeutic material only (62310-62311, 62318-62319)

62280 Injection/infusion of neurolytic substance (eg, alcohol, phenol, iced saline solutions), with or without other therapeutic substance; subarachnoid
4.43 8.24 Global Days 010
AMA: 2008, Jul, 9

62281 epidural, cervical or thoracic
4.33 7.96 Global Days 010
AMA: 2008, Jul, 9

62282 epidural, lumbar, sacral (caudal)
EXCLUDES *Fluoroscopic guidance and localization unless a formal contrast study is performed (77003)*
3.98 7.46 Global Days 010
AMA: 2009, Jan, 11-31; 2008, Jan, 10-25; 2008, Jul, 9; 2007, January, 13-27

62284-62294 Injection/Aspiration of Spine, Diagnostic/Therapeutic

62284 Injection procedure for myelography and/or computed tomography, spinal (other than C1-C2 and posterior fossa)
EXCLUDES *Injection at C1-C2 (61055)*
72126, 72129, 72132, 72240, 72255, 72265, 72270
2.33 5.19 Global Days 000
AMA: 2009, Jan, 11-31; 2008, Jan, 10-25; 2007, January, 13-27

62287 Decompression procedure, percutaneous, of nucleus pulposus of intervertebral disc, any method, single or multiple levels, lumbar (eg, manual or automated percutaneous discectomy, percutaneous laser discectomy)
EXCLUDES *Nonneurolytic injection (62310, 62311)*
Do not report with (62267)
77003
14.91 14.91 Global Days 090
AMA: 2009, Jan, 11-31; 2008, Jan, 10-25; 2008, Jun, 8-11; 2007, January, 13-27

62290 Injection procedure for discography, each level; lumbar
72295
4.76 8.72 Global Days 000
AMA: 2009, Jan, 11-31; 2008, Jan, 10-25; 2007, January, 13-27

62291 cervical or thoracic
72285
4.62 8.35 Global Days 000

62292 Injection procedure for chemonucleolysis, including discography, intervertebral disc, single or multiple levels, lumbar
14.04 14.04 Global Days 090
AMA: 2009, Jan, 11-31; 2008, Jan, 10-25; 2007, January, 13-27

62294 Injection procedure, arterial, for occlusion of arteriovenous malformation, spinal
16.90 16.90 Global Days 090

62310-62319 Injection/Infusion Diagnostic/Therapeutic Material

EXCLUDES *Daily management of continuous epidural or subarachnoid drug administration (01996)*
Fluoroscopic guidance and localization unless a formal contrast study is performed (77003)
Transforaminal epidural injection (64479-64484)

62310 Injection, single (not via indwelling catheter), not including neurolytic substances, with or without contrast (for either localization or epidurography), of diagnostic or therapeutic substance(s) (including anesthetic, antispasmodic, opioid, steroid, other solution), epidural or subarachnoid; cervical or thoracic
INCLUDES Contrast injection during fluoroscopic guidance/localization
EXCLUDES *Fluoroscopic guidance and localization unless a formal contrast study is performed (77003)*
2.98 6.24 Global Days 000
AMA: 2009, Jan, 11-31; 2008, Jan, 10-25; 2008, Jul, 9; 2008, Nov, 10-11; 2007, January, 13-27

62311 lumbar, sacral (caudal)
INCLUDES Contrast injection during fluoroscopic guidance/localization
EXCLUDES *Fluoroscopic guidance and localization unless a formal contrast study is performed (77003)*
2.43 5.21 Global Days 000
AMA: 2009, Jan, 11-31; 2008, Jan, 10-25; 2008, Jul, 9; 2008, Nov, 10-11; 2007, January, 13-27

62318 Injection, including catheter placement, continuous infusion or intermittent bolus, not including neurolytic substances, with or without contrast (for either localization or epidurography), of diagnostic or therapeutic substance(s) (including anesthetic, antispasmodic, opioid, steroid, other solution), epidural or subarachnoid; cervical or thoracic
INCLUDES Contrast injection during fluoroscopic guidance/localization
EXCLUDES *Daily hospital management of epidural or subarachnoid infusion (01996)*
Fluoroscopic guidance and localization unless a formal contrast study is performed (77003)
2.78 6.07 Global Days 000
AMA: 2009, Jan, 11-31; 2008, Jan, 10-25; 2008, Jul, 9; 2008, Nov, 10-11; 2007, January, 13-27

● New Code   ▲ Revised Code   M Maternity   A Age   Unlisted   Not Covered   # Resequenced
CCI   + Add-on   ⊘ Mod 51 Exempt   Mod 63 Exempt   ⊙ Mod Sedation   PQRI

© 2009 Publisher (Blue Ink)   CPT only © 2009 American Medical Association. All Rights Reserved. (Black Ink)   Medicare (Red Ink)

62319 lumbar, sacral (caudal)
  INCLUDES Contrast injection during fluoroscopic guidance/localization
  EXCLUDES Daily hospital management of epidural or subarachnoid infusion (01996)
  Fluoroscopic guidance and localization unless a formal contrast study is performed (77003)
  2.66   5.69   Global Days 000
  AMA: 2009, Jan, 11-31; 2008, Jan, 10-25; 2008, Jul, 9; 2008, Nov, 10-11; 2007, January, 13-27

62350-62368 Procedures Related to Epidural and Intrathecal Catheters

CMS 100-3,280.14   Infusion Pumps
EXCLUDES Infusion pump refilling and maintenance (95990-95991)
Percutaneous insertion of intrathecal or epidural catheter (62270-62273, 62280-62284, 62310-62319)

62350 Implantation, revision or repositioning of tunneled intrathecal or epidural catheter, for long-term medication administration via an external pump or implantable reservoir/infusion pump; without laminectomy
  10.87   10.87   Global Days 010

62351 with laminectomy
  23.44   23.44   Global Days 090

62355 Removal of previously implanted intrathecal or epidural catheter
  8.23   8.23   Global Days 010

62360 Implantation or replacement of device for intrathecal or epidural drug infusion; subcutaneous reservoir
  8.40   8.40   Global Days 010

62361 nonprogrammable pump
  Code also (C1891, C2626)
  10.67   10.67   Global Days 010

62362 programmable pump, including preparation of pump, with or without programming
  Code also (C1772)
  11.24   11.24   Global Days 010
  AMA: 2009, Jan, 11-31; 2008, Jan, 10-25; 2007, January, 13-27

62365 Removal of subcutaneous reservoir or pump, previously implanted for intrathecal or epidural infusion
  8.93   8.93   Global Days 010

62367 Electronic analysis of programmable, implanted pump for intrathecal or epidural drug infusion (includes evaluation of reservoir status, alarm status, drug prescription status); without reprogramming
  0.71   1.13   Global Days XXX
  AMA: 2006, April, 19-20

62368 with reprogramming
  1.12   1.65   Global Days XXX
  AMA: 2009, Jan, 11-31; 2008, Jan, 10-25; 2007, January, 13-27; 2006, April, 19-20

63001-63048 Posterior Midline Approach: Laminectomy/Laminotomy/Decompression

EXCLUDES Arthrodesis (22590-22614)

63001 Laminectomy with exploration and/or decompression of spinal cord and/or cauda equina, without facetectomy, foraminotomy or discectomy (eg, spinal stenosis), 1 or 2 vertebral segments; cervical
  33.20   33.20   Global Days 090
  AMA: 2009, Jan, 11-31; 2008, Jan, 10-25; 2007, June, 1-3; 2007, January, 13-27; 2005, June, 6-8

63003 thoracic
  33.34   33.34   Global Days 090
  AMA: 2009, Jan, 11-31; 2008, Jan, 10-25; 2007, January, 13-27; 2007, June, 1-3; 2005, June, 6-8

63005 lumbar, except for spondylolisthesis
  31.77   31.77   Global Days 090
  AMA: 2009, Jan, 11-31; 2008, Jan, 10-25; 2007, June, 1-3; 2007, January, 13-27; 2005, June, 6-8

63011 sacral
  29.64   29.64   Global Days 090
  AMA: 2009, Jan, 11-31; 2008, Jan, 10-25; 2007, June, 1-3; 2007, January, 13-27; 2005, June, 6-8

63012 Laminectomy with removal of abnormal facets and/or pars inter-articularis with decompression of cauda equina and nerve roots for spondylolisthesis, lumbar (Gill type procedure)
  32.01   32.01   Global Days 090
  AMA: 2009, Jan, 11-31; 2008, Jan, 10-25; 2007, January, 13-27; 2007, June, 1-3; 2005, June, 6-8

63015 Laminectomy with exploration and/or decompression of spinal cord and/or cauda equina, without facetectomy, foraminotomy or discectomy (eg, spinal stenosis), more than 2 vertebral segments; cervical
  39.82   39.82   Global Days 090
  AMA: 2009, Jan, 11-31; 2008, Jan, 10-25; 2007, June, 1-3; 2007, January, 13-27; 2005, June, 6-8

63016 thoracic
  40.82   40.82   Global Days 090
  AMA: 2009, Jan, 11-31; 2008, Jan, 10-25; 2007, June, 1-3; 2007, January, 13-27; 2005, June, 6-8

Quadraplegia is paralysis of both arms and both legs; quadraparesis is incomplete paralysis of both arms and both legs; paraplegia is paralysis of both legs; diplegia is paralysis of both arms.

Nerve root problems in C_5 through C_7 cause paralysis of the upper limb

Atlas (C_1)
Axis (C_2)
C_1 to C_4
C_5 to C_7

The specialized atlas allows for rotary motion, which turns the head

63017 lumbar
  33.49   33.49   Global Days 090
  AMA: 2009, Jan, 11-31; 2008, Jan, 10-25; 2007, January, 13-27; 2007, June, 1-3; 2005, June, 6-8

63020 Laminotomy (hemilaminectomy), with decompression of nerve root(s), including partial facetectomy, foraminotomy and/or excision of herniated intervertebral disc, including open and endoscopically-assisted approaches; 1 interspace, cervical
  31.42   31.42   Global Days 090
  AMA: 2009, Jan, 11-31; 2008, Jan, 10-25; 2007, June, 1-3; January, 13-27; 2005, June, 6-8

63030 1 interspace, lumbar
  26.03   26.03   Global Days 090
  AMA: 2009, Jan, 11-31; 2008, Jan, 10-25; 2008, Oct, 10-11; 2007, June, 1-3; 2007, January, 13-27; 2005, June, 6-8

+ **63035** each additional interspace, cervical or lumbar (List separately in addition to code for primary procedure)
  Code first (63020-63030)
  5.30   5.30   Global Days ZZZ
  AMA: 2009, Jan, 11-31; 2008, Jan, 10-25; 2007, January, 13-27; 2007, June, 1-3; 2005, June, 6-8

Current Procedural Coding Expert – Nervous System 63081

63040 Laminotomy (hemilaminectomy), with decompression of nerve root(s), including partial facetectomy, foraminotomy and/or excision of herniated intervertebral disc, reexploration, single interspace; cervical [T] [80] [50] [CCI] [PQ]
 37.99   37.99   Global Days 090
AMA: 2009, Jan, 11-31; 2008, Jan, 10-25; 2007, June, 1-3; 2007, January, 13-27; 2005, June, 6-8

63042 lumbar [T] [80] [50] [CCI] [PQ]
 35.17   35.17   Global Days 090
AMA: 2009, Jan, 11-31; 2008, Jan, 10-25; 2008, Oct, 10-11; 2007, January, 13-27; 2007, June, 1-3; 2005, June, 6-8

+ ▲ 63043 Laminotomy (hemilaminectomy), with decompression of nerve root(s), including partial facetectomy, foraminotomy and/or excision of herniated intervertebral disc, re-exploration, single interspace; each additional cervical interspace (List separately in addition to code for primary procedure) [C] [80] [50] [CCI] [PQ]
Code first (63040)
 0.00   0.00   Global Days ZZZ
AMA: 2009, Jan, 11-31; 2008, Jan, 10-25; 2007, June, 1-3; 2007, January, 13-27; 2005, June, 6-8

+ ▲ 63044 each additional lumbar interspace (List separately in addition to code for primary procedure) [C] [80] [50] [CCI] [PQ]
Code first (63042)
 0.00   0.00   Global Days ZZZ
AMA: 2009, Jan, 11-31; 2008, Jan, 10-25; 2007, June, 1-3; 2007, January, 13-27; 2005, June, 6-8

63045 Laminectomy, facetectomy and foraminotomy (unilateral or bilateral with decompression of spinal cord, cauda equina and/or nerve root[s], [eg, spinal or lateral recess stenosis]), single vertebral segment; cervical [T] [80] [CCI] [PQ]
 34.19   34.19   Global Days 090
AMA: 2009, Jan, 11-31; 2008, Jan, 10-25; 2007, January, 13-27; 2007, June, 1-3; 2005, June, 6-8

63046 thoracic [T] [80] [CCI] [PQ]
 32.65   32.65   Global Days 090
AMA: 2009, Jan, 11-31; 2008, Jan, 10-25; 2007, June, 1-3; 2007, January, 13-27; 2005, June, 6-8

63047 lumbar [T] [80] [CCI] [PQ]
 29.62   29.62   Global Days 090
AMA: 2009, Jan, 11-31; 2008, Jan, 10-25; 2008, Oct, 10-11; 2008, Jul, 7-8&15; 2008, Apr, -11; 2007, June, 1-3; 2007, January, 13-27; 2005, June, 6-8

+ 63048 each additional segment, cervical, thoracic, or lumbar (List separately in addition to code for primary procedure) [T] [80] [CCI] [PQ]
Code first (63045-63047)
 5.85   5.85   Global Days ZZZ
AMA: 2009, Jan, 11-31; 2008, Jan, 10-25; 2007, January, 13-27; 2007, June, 1-3; 2005, June, 6-8

63050-63051 Cervical Laminoplasty: Posterior Midline Approach

Do not report with procedure performed on the same vertebral segment(s) (22600, 22614, 22840-22842, 63001, 63015, 63045, 63048, 63295)

63050 Laminoplasty, cervical, with decompression of the spinal cord, 2 or more vertebral segments; [C] [80] [CCI]
 41.74   41.74   Global Days 090

63051 with reconstruction of the posterior bony elements (including the application of bridging bone graft and non-segmental fixation devices (eg, wire, suture, mini-plates), when performed) [C] [80] [CCI]
 46.48   46.48   Global Days 090

63055-63066 Spinal Cord/Nerve Root Decompression: Costovertebral or Transpedicular Approach

63055 Transpedicular approach with decompression of spinal cord, equina and/or nerve root(s) (eg, herniated intervertebral disc), single segment; thoracic [T] [80] [CCI] [PQ]
 43.85   43.85   Global Days 090

63056 lumbar (including transfacet, or lateral extraforaminal approach) (eg, far lateral herniated intervertebral disc) [T] [80] [CCI] [PQ]
 40.09   40.09   Global Days 090

+ 63057 each additional segment, thoracic or lumbar (List separately in addition to code for primary procedure) [T] [80] [CCI] [PQ]
Code first (63055-63056)
 8.85   8.85   Global Days ZZZ

63064 Costovertebral approach with decompression of spinal cord or nerve root(s) (eg, herniated intervertebral disc), thoracic; single segment [T] [80] [CCI] [PQ]
 47.91   47.91   Global Days 090

+ 63066 each additional segment (List separately in addition to code for primary procedure) [T] [80] [CCI] [PQ]
EXCLUDES Laminectomy with intraspinal thoracic lesion removal (63266, 63271, 63276, 63281, 63286)
Code first (63064)
 5.62   5.62   Global Days ZZZ

63075-63078 Discectomy: Anterior or Anterolateral Approach

INCLUDES Operating microscope (69990)

63075 Discectomy, anterior, with decompression of spinal cord and/or nerve root(s), including osteophytectomy; cervical, single interspace [T] [80] [CCI] [PQ]
 37.04   37.04   Global Days 090
AMA: 2009, Jan, 11-31; 2008, Jan, 10-25; 2007, January, 13-27

+ 63076 cervical, each additional interspace (List separately in addition to code for primary procedure) [T] [80] [CCI] [PQ]
Code first (63075)
 6.86   6.86   Global Days ZZZ
AMA: 2009, Jan, 11-31; 2008, Jan, 10-25; 2007, January, 13-27

63077 thoracic, single interspace [C] [80] [CCI] [PQ]
 40.70   40.70   Global Days 090
AMA: 2009, Jan, 11-31; 2008, Jan, 10-25; 2007, January, 13-27

+ 63078 thoracic, each additional interspace (List separately in addition to code for primary procedure) [C] [80] [CCI] [PQ]
Code first (63077)
 5.39   5.39   Global Days ZZZ
AMA: 2009, Jan, 11-31; 2008, Jan, 10-25; 2007, January, 13-27

63081-63091 Vertebral Corpectomy, All Levels, Anterior Approach

INCLUDES Disc removal at the level below and/or above vertebral segment
EXCLUDES Arthrodesis (22548-22812)
Code also reconstruction (20930-20938, 22548-22812, 22840-22855)

63081 Vertebral corpectomy (vertebral body resection), partial or complete, anterior approach with decompression of spinal cord and/or nerve root(s); cervical, single segment [C] [80] [CCI] [PQ]
EXCLUDES Transoral approach (61575-61576)
 47.95   47.95   Global Days 090

● New Code   ▲ Revised Code   M Maternity   A Age   Unlisted   Not Covered   # Resequenced
□ CCI   + Add-on   Ø Mod 51 Exempt   Ø Mod 63 Exempt   ⊙ Mod Sedation   PQ PQRI

© 2009 Publisher (Blue Ink)   CPT only © 2009 American Medical Association. All Rights Reserved. (Black Ink)   Medicare (Red Ink)   229

Current Procedural Coding Expert – Nervous System

+ 63082	cervical, each additional segment (List separately in addition to code for primary procedure) C 80 P0
	EXCLUDES Transoral approach (61575-61576)
	Code first (63081)
	7.39 7.39 Global Days ZZZ
63085	Vertebral corpectomy (vertebral body resection), partial or complete, transthoracic approach with decompression of spinal cord and/or nerve root(s); thoracic, single segment C 80 P0
	51.81 51.81 Global Days 090
+ 63086	thoracic, each additional segment (List separately in addition to code for primary procedure) C 80 P0
	Code first (63085)
	5.30 5.30 Global Days ZZZ
63087	Vertebral corpectomy (vertebral body resection), partial or complete, combined thoracolumbar approach with decompression of spinal cord, cauda equina or nerve root(s), lower thoracic or lumbar; single segment C 80 P0
	65.27 65.27 Global Days 090
+ 63088	each additional segment (List separately in addition to code for primary procedure) C 80 P0
	Code first (63087)
	7.13 7.13 Global Days ZZZ
63090	Vertebral corpectomy (vertebral body resection), partial or complete, transperitoneal or retroperitoneal approach with decompression of spinal cord, cauda equina or nerve root(s), lower thoracic, lumbar, or sacral; single segment C 80 P0
	53.80 53.80 Global Days 090
+ 63091	each additional segment (List separately in addition to code for primary procedure) C 80 P0
	Code first (63090)
	4.94 4.94 Global Days ZZZ

63101-63103 Corpectomy Lateral Extracavitary Approach

63101	Vertebral corpectomy (vertebral body resection), partial or complete, lateral extracavitary approach with decompression of spinal cord and/or nerve root(s) (eg, for tumor or retropulsed bone fragments); thoracic, single segment C 80 P0
	62.65 62.65 Global Days 090
63102	lumbar, single segment C 80 P0
	61.01 61.01 Global Days 090
+ 63103	thoracic or lumbar, each additional segment (List separately in addition to code for primary procedure) C 80 P0
	Code first (63101-63102)
	8.04 8.04 Global Days ZZZ

63170-63295 Laminectomies

63170	Laminectomy with myelotomy (eg, Bischof or DREZ type), cervical, thoracic, or thoracolumbar C 80 P0
	42.62 42.62 Global Days 090
63172	Laminectomy with drainage of intramedullary cyst/syrinx; to subarachnoid space C 80 P0
	37.54 37.54 Global Days 090
63173	to peritoneal or pleural space C 80 P0
	46.24 46.24 Global Days 090
63180	Laminectomy and section of dentate ligaments, with or without dural graft, cervical; 1 or 2 segments C 80 P0
	36.22 36.22 Global Days 090
63182	more than 2 segments C 80 P0
	43.67 43.67 Global Days 090
63185	Laminectomy with rhizotomy; 1 or 2 segments C 80 P0
	INCLUDES Dana rhizotomy
	Stoffel rhizotomy
	32.62 32.62 Global Days 090
63190	more than 2 segments C 80 P0
	34.57 34.57 Global Days 090
63191	Laminectomy with section of spinal accessory nerve C 80 50 P0
	EXCLUDES Division of sternocleidomastoid muscle for torticollis (21720)
	35.54 35.54 Global Days 090
63194	Laminectomy with cordotomy, with section of 1 spinothalamic tract, 1 stage; cervical C 80 P0
	37.43 37.43 Global Days 090
63195	thoracic C 80 P0
	41.19 41.19 Global Days 090
63196	Laminectomy with cordotomy, with section of both spinothalamic tracts, 1 stage; cervical C 80 P0
	37.77 37.77 Global Days 090
63197	thoracic C 80 P0
	45.84 45.84 Global Days 090
63198	Laminectomy with cordotomy with section of both spinothalamic tracts, 2 stages within 14 days; cervical C 80 P0
	INCLUDES Keen laminectomy
	44.52 44.52 Global Days 090
63199	thoracic C 80 P0
	46.74 46.74 Global Days 090
63200	Laminectomy, with release of tethered spinal cord, lumbar C 80 P0
	40.97 40.97 Global Days 090

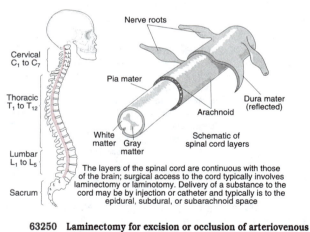

63250	Laminectomy for excision or occlusion of arteriovenous malformation of spinal cord; cervical C 80
	80.02 80.02 Global Days 090
63251	thoracic C 80
	81.76 81.76 Global Days 090
63252	thoracolumbar C 80
	81.73 81.73 Global Days 090
63265	Laminectomy for excision or evacuation of intraspinal lesion other than neoplasm, extradural; cervical C 80
	44.89 44.89 Global Days 090
63266	thoracic C 80
	46.36 46.36 Global Days 090

26/TC PC/TC Comp Only A2-Z3 ASC Pmt 50 Bilateral ♂ Male Only ♀ Female Only Facility RVU Non-Facility RVU
AMA: CPT Asst MED: Pub 100 A-Y OPPSI 80/80 Surg Assist Allowed / w/Doc Lab Crosswalk Radiology Crosswalk
CPT only © 2009 American Medical Association. All Rights Reserved. (Black Ink) Medicare (Red Ink) © 2009 Publisher (Blue Ink)

Current Procedural Coding Expert – Nervous System   63621

63267	lumbar C 80
	37.04 37.04 Global Days 090
63268	sacral C 80
	38.88 38.88 Global Days 090
63270	Laminectomy for excision of intraspinal lesion other than neoplasm, intradural; cervical C 80
	55.76 55.76 Global Days 090
63271	thoracic C 80
	55.72 55.72 Global Days 090
63272	lumbar C 80
	51.31 51.31 Global Days 090
63273	sacral C 80
	50.01 50.01 Global Days 090
63275	Laminectomy for biopsy/excision of intraspinal neoplasm; extradural, cervical C 80
	48.37 48.37 Global Days 090
63276	extradural, thoracic C 80 P0
	47.99 47.99 Global Days 090
63277	extradural, lumbar C 80
	41.85 41.85 Global Days 090
63278	extradural, sacral C 80
	42.51 42.51 Global Days 090
63280	intradural, extramedullary, cervical C 80
	56.85 56.85 Global Days 090
63281	intradural, extramedullary, thoracic C 80
	56.17 56.17 Global Days 090
63282	intradural, extramedullary, lumbar C 80
	53.03 53.03 Global Days 090
63283	intradural, sacral C 80
	50.90 50.90 Global Days 090
63285	intradural, intramedullary, cervical C 80
	70.31 70.31 Global Days 090
63286	intradural, intramedullary, thoracic C 80
	69.30 69.30 Global Days 090
63287	intradural, intramedullary, thoracolumbar C 80
	73.89 73.89 Global Days 090
63290	combined extradural-intradural lesion, any level C 80
	EXCLUDES Drainage intermedullary cyst or syrinx (63172-63173)
	75.17 75.17 Global Days 090
+ 63295	Osteoplastic reconstruction of dorsal spinal elements, following primary intraspinal procedure (List separately in addition to code for primary procedure) C 80
	Code first (63172-63173, 63185, 63190, 63200-63290)
	Do not report with procedure performed at the same vertebral segment(s) (22590-22614, 22840-22844, 63050-63051)
	9.05 9.05 Global Days ZZZ

63300-63308 Vertebral Corpectomy for Intraspinal Lesion: Anterior/Anterolateral Approach

EXCLUDES Arthrodesis (22548-22585)
Spinal reconstruction (20930-20938)

63300	Vertebral corpectomy (vertebral body resection), partial or complete, for excision of intraspinal lesion, single segment; extradural, cervical C 80
	49.47 49.47 Global Days 090
63301	extradural, thoracic by transthoracic approach C 80
	59.20 59.20 Global Days 090
63302	extradural, thoracic by thoracolumbar approach C 80
	58.48 58.48 Global Days 090
63303	extradural, lumbar or sacral by transperitoneal or retroperitoneal approach C 80
	60.46 60.46 Global Days 090
63304	intradural, cervical C 80
	63.13 63.13 Global Days 090
63305	intradural, thoracic by transthoracic approach C 80
	67.26 67.26 Global Days 090
63306	intradural, thoracic by thoracolumbar approach C 80
	66.06 66.06 Global Days 090
63307	intradural, lumbar or sacral by transperitoneal or retroperitoneal approach C 80
	59.79 59.79 Global Days 090
+ 63308	each additional segment (List separately in addition to codes for single segment) C 80
	Code first (63300-63307)
	8.77 8.77 Global Days ZZZ

63600-63615 Stereotactic Procedures of the Spinal Cord

63600	Creation of lesion of spinal cord by stereotactic method, percutaneous, any modality (including stimulation and/or recording) A2 T 80
	22.95 22.95 Global Days 090
63610	Stereotactic stimulation of spinal cord, percutaneous, separate procedure not followed by other surgery A2 T 80 P0
	10.88 23.00 Global Days 000
63615	Stereotactic biopsy, aspiration, or excision of lesion, spinal cord R2 T
	30.30 30.30 Global Days 090

63620-63621 Stereotactic Radiosurgery (SRS): Spine

INCLUDES Planning dosimetry, targeting, positioning, or blocking by neurosurgeon

EXCLUDES Arteriovenous malformations (see Radiation Oncology Section)
Intensity modulated beam delivery plan and treatment (77301, 77418)
Stereotactic body radiation therapy (77373, 77435)
Treatment planning, physics, dosimetry, treatment delivery and management provided by the oncologist (77261-77790)

Do not report more than once per lesion per treatment course
Do not report stereotactic radiosurgery services with radiation treatment management by the same physician (77427-77432)

63620	Stereotactic radiosurgery (particle beam, gamma ray, or linear accelerator); 1 spinal lesion B 80
	INCLUDES Computer-assisted planning
	Do not report more than once per treatment course
	Do not report with (61795)
	25.87 25.87 Global Days 090
+ 63621	each additional spinal lesion (List separately in addition to code for primary procedure) B 80
	Code first (63620)
	Do not report computer-assisted planning
	Do not report more than once per lesion
	Do not report more than twice per treatment course
	Do not report with (61795)
	5.98 5.98 Global Days ZZZ

● New Code   ▲ Revised Code   M Maternity   Age   Unlisted   Not Covered   # Resequenced
□ CCI   + Add-on   ⊘ Mod 51 Exempt   ⊛ Mod 63 Exempt   ⊙ Mod Sedation   P0 PQRI

© 2009 Publisher (Blue Ink)   CPT only © 2009 American Medical Association. All Rights Reserved. (Black Ink)   Medicare (Red Ink)

63650-63688 Spinal Neurostimulation

CMS 100-3,160.2 — Treatment of Motor Function Disorders with Electric Nerve Stimulation
CMS 100-3,160.7 — Electrical Nerve Stimulators
EXCLUDES Analysis and programming of neurostimulator pulse generator (95970-95975)

63650 Percutaneous implantation of neurostimulator electrode array, epidural
   INCLUDES The following are components of a neurostimulator system:
      Collection of contacts of which four or more provide the electrical stimulation in the epidural space
      Contacts on a catheter-type lead (array)
      Extension
      External controller
      Implanted neurostimulator
   Code also (C1778, C1897)
   11.95   11.95 Global Days 010
   AMA: 2009, Jan, 11-31; 2008, Jan, 10-25; 2007, January, 13-27

63655 Laminectomy for implantation of neurostimulator electrodes, plate/paddle, epidural
   INCLUDES The following are components of a neurostimulator system:
      Collection of contacts of which four or more provide the electrical stimulation in the epidural space
      Contacts on a plate or paddle-shaped surface for systems placed by open exposure
      Extension
      External controller
      Implanted neurostimulator
   Code also (C1778, C1897)
   23.25   23.25 Global Days 090

~~63660~~ ~~Revision or removal of spinal neurostimulator electrode percutaneous array(s) or plate/paddle(s)~~
   To report, see code 63661

● **63661** Removal of spinal neurostimulator electrode percutaneous array(s), including fluoroscopy, when performed
   INCLUDES The following are components of a neurostimulator system:
      Collection of contacts of which four or more provide the electrical stimulation in the epidural space
      Contacts on a catheter-type lead (array)
      Extension
      External controller
      Implanted neurostimulator
   Do not report when removing or replacing a temporary array placed percutaneously for an external generator
   8.28   14.82 Global Days 010

● **63662** Removal of spinal neurostimulator electrode plate/paddle(s) placed via laminotomy or laminectomy, including fluoroscopy, when performed
   INCLUDES The following are components of a neurostimulator system:
      Collection of contacts of which four or more provide the electrical stimulation in the epidural space
      Contacts on a catheter-type lead (array)
      Extension
      External controller
      Implanted neurostimulator
   19.04   19.04 Global Days 090

● **63663** Revision including replacement, when performed, of spinal neurostimulator electrode percutaneous array(s), including fluoroscopy, when performed
   INCLUDES The following are components of a neurostimulator system:
      Collection of contacts of which four or more provide the electrical stimulation in the epidural space
      Contacts on a catheter-type lead (array)
      Extension
      External controller
      Implanted neurostimulator
   Do not report when removing or replacing a temporary array placed percutaneously for an external generator
   Do not report with (63661-63662)
   12.80   21.96 Global Days 010

● **63664** Revision including replacement, when performed, of spinal neurostimulator electrode plate/paddle(s) placed via laminotomy or laminectomy, including fluoroscopy, when performed
   INCLUDES The following are components of a neurostimulator system:
      Collection of contacts of which four or more provide the electrical stimulation in the epidural space
      Contacts on a catheter-type lead (array)
      Extension
      External controller
      Implanted neurostimulator
   Do not report with (63661-63662)
   19.82   19.82 Global Days 090

63685 Insertion or replacement of spinal neurostimulator pulse generator or receiver, direct or inductive coupling
   Code also (C1767, C1820, L8685-L8688)
   Do not report with 63688 for the same pulse generator or receiver
   10.97   10.97 Global Days 010

63688 Revision or removal of implanted spinal neurostimulator pulse generator or receiver
   Do not report with 63685 for the same pulse generator or receiver
   9.95   9.95 Global Days 010

Current Procedural Coding Expert – Nervous System

63700-63706 Repair Congenital Neural Tube Defects

EXCLUDES Complex skin repair (see appropriate integumentary closure code)

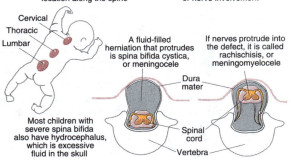

63700	Repair of meningocele; less than 5 cm diameter	C 80 63	
	34.59 34.59 Global Days 090		
63702	larger than 5 cm diameter	C 80 63	
	37.94 37.94 Global Days 090		
63704	Repair of myelomeningocele; less than 5 cm diameter	C 80 63	
	43.99 43.99 Global Days 090		
63706	larger than 5 cm diameter	C 80 63	
	49.01 49.01 Global Days 090		

63707-63710 Repair Dural Cerebrospinal Fluid Leak

63707	Repair of dural/cerebrospinal fluid leak, not requiring laminectomy	C 80
	24.48 24.48 Global Days 090	
63709	Repair of dural/cerebrospinal fluid leak or pseudomeningocele, with laminectomy	C 80
	29.71 29.71 Global Days 090	
63710	Dural graft, spinal	C 80
	EXCLUDES Laminectomy and section of dentate ligament (63180, 63182)	
	29.74 29.74 Global Days 090	

63740-63746 Cerebrospinal Fluid (CSF) Shunt: Lumbar

EXCLUDES Placement of subarachnoid catheter with reservoir and/or pump:
Not requiring laminectomy (62350, 62360-62362)
With laminectomy (62351, 62360-62362)

63740	Creation of shunt, lumbar, subarachnoid-peritoneal, -pleural, or other; including laminectomy	C 80
	25.22 25.22 Global Days 090	
63741	percutaneous, not requiring laminectomy	T 80
	16.37 16.37 Global Days 090	
63744	Replacement, irrigation or revision of lumbosubarachnoid shunt	A2 T 80
	17.98 17.98 Global Days 090	
63746	Removal of entire lumbosubarachnoid shunt system without replacement	A2 T 80
	15.82 15.82 Global Days 090	

64400-64455 Nerve Blocks

EXCLUDES Epidural or subarachnoid injection (62310-62319)
Nerve destruction (62280-62282, 64600-64681)

64400	Injection, anesthetic agent; trigeminal nerve, any division or branch	P3 T 50
	1.88 3.05 Global Days 000	
	AMA: 2009, Jan, 11-31; 2008, Jan, 10-25; 2008, Jun, 8-11; 2007, January, 13-27; 2005, April, 13-14	
64402	facial nerve	P3 T 50
	2.10 3.14 Global Days 000	
	AMA: 2009, Jan, 11-31; 2008, Jan, 10-25; 2008, Jun, 8-11; 2007, January, 13-27; 2005, April, 13-14	
64405	greater occipital nerve	P3 T 50
	2.23 3.11 Global Days 000	
	AMA: 2009, Jan, 11-31; 2008, Jan, 10-25; 2008, Jun, 8-11; 2007, January, 13-27; 2005, April, 13-14	
64408	vagus nerve	P3 T 80 50
	2.50 3.31 Global Days 000	
	AMA: 2009, Jan, 11-31; 2008, Jan, 10-25; 2008, Jun, 8-11; 2007, January, 13-27; 2005, April, 13-14	
64410	phrenic nerve	A2 T 80 50
	2.32 4.04 Global Days 000	
	AMA: 2009, Jan, 11-31; 2008, Jan, 10-25; 2008, Jun, 8-11; 2007, January, 13-27; 2005, April, 13-14	
64412	spinal accessory nerve	P3 T 50
	2.09 4.14 Global Days 000	
	AMA: 2009, Jan, 11-31; 2008, Jan, 10-25; 2008, Jun, 8-11; 2007, Aug, 15; 2007, January, 13-27; 2005, April, 13-14	
64413	cervical plexus	P3 T 50
	2.19 3.15 Global Days 000	
	AMA: 2009, Jan, 11-31; 2008, Jan, 10-25; 2008, Jun, 8-11; 2007, Aug, 15; 2007, January, 13-27; 2005, April, 13-14	
64415	brachial plexus, single	A2 T 50
	1.98 3.30 Global Days 000	
	AMA: 2009, Jan, 11-31; 2008, Jan, 10-25; 2008, Jun, 8-11; 2007, January, 13-27; 2006, December, 10-12; 2005, April, 13-14	
64416	brachial plexus, continuous infusion by catheter (including catheter placement)	G2 T 50
	Do not report with (01996)	
	2.22 2.22 Global Days 000	
	AMA: 2009, Jan, 11-31; 2008, Jan, 10-25; 2008, Jun, 8-11; 2007, January, 13-27; 2005, April, 13-14	
64417	axillary nerve	A2 T 50
	1.94 3.27 Global Days 000	
	AMA: 2009, Jan, 11-31; 2008, Jan, 10-25; 2008, Jun, 8-11; 2007, January, 13-27; 2005, April, 13-14	
64418	suprascapular nerve	P3 T 50
	2.10 3.66 Global Days 000	
	AMA: 2009, Jan, 11-31; 2008, Jan, 10-25; 2008, Jun, 8-11; 2007, Aug, 15; 2007, January, 13-27; 2005, April, 13-14	
64420	intercostal nerve, single	A2 T
	1.90 4.29 Global Days 000	
	AMA: 2009, Jan, 11-31; 2008, Jan, 10-25; 2008, Jun, 8-11; 2007, January, 13-27; 2005, April, 13-14	
64421	intercostal nerves, multiple, regional block	A2 T 50
	2.60 6.32 Global Days 000	
	AMA: 2009, Jan, 11-31; 2008, Jan, 10-25; 2008, Jun, 8-11; 2007, January, 13-27; 2005, April, 13-14	
64425	ilioinguinal, iliohypogastric nerves	P3 T 50
	2.67 3.61 Global Days 000	
	AMA: 2009, Jan, 11-31; 2008, Jan, 10-25; 2008, Jun, 8-11; 2007, January, 13-27; 2005, April, 13-14	

● New Code ▲ Revised Code M Maternity A Age Unlisted Not Covered # Resequenced
CCI + Add-on ○ Mod 51 Exempt ⊚ Mod 63 Exempt ⊙ Mod Sedation PQRI PQRI

64430

64430	**pudendal nerve** A2 T 50
	2.23 3.49 Global Days 000
	AMA: 2009, Jan, 11-31; 2008, Jan, 10-25; 2008, Jun, 8-11; 2007, January, 13-27; 2005, April, 13-14
64435	**paracervical (uterine) nerve** ♀ P3 50
	2.33 3.54 Global Days 000
	AMA: 2009, Jan, 11-31; 2008, Jan, 10-25; 2008, Jun, 8-11; 2007, January, 13-27; 2005, April, 13-14
64445	**sciatic nerve, single** P3 T 50
	2.23 3.52 Global Days 000
	AMA: 2008, Jun, 8-11; 2005, April, 13-14
64446	**sciatic nerve, continuous infusion by catheter (including catheter placement)** G2 T 50
	Do not report with (01996)
	2.24 2.24 Global Days 000
	AMA: 2008, Jun, 8-11; 2005, April, 13-14
64447	**femoral nerve, single** R2 T 50
	Do not report with (01996)
	1.84 1.84 Global Days 000
	AMA: 2008, Jun, 8-11; 2005, April, 13-14
64448	**femoral nerve, continuous infusion by catheter (including catheter placement)** G2 T 50
	Do not report with (01996)
	2.00 2.00 Global Days 000
	AMA: 2008, Jun, 8-11; 2005, April, 13-14
64449	**lumbar plexus, posterior approach, continuous infusion by catheter (including catheter placement)** G2 T 50
	Do not report with (01996)
	2.29 2.29 Global Days 000
	AMA: 2008, Jun, 8-11; 2005, April, 13-14
64450	**other peripheral nerve or branch** P3 T 50
	EXCLUDES Morton's neuroma (64455, 64632)
	1.90 2.77 Global Days 000
	AMA: 2009, Jan, 6&9; 2009, Jan, 11-31; 2008, Jan, 10-25; 2008, Jun, 8-11; 2007, January, 13-27; 2005, April, 13-14
64455	**Injection(s), anesthetic agent and/or steroid, plantar common digital nerve(s) (eg, Morton's neuroma)** P3 T 80 50
	Do not report with (64632)
	1.06 1.38 Global Days 000
	AMA: 2009, Jan, 6&9

64479-64484 Transforaminal Injection

EXCLUDES Epidural or subarachnoid injection (62310-62319)
Nerve destruction (62280-62282, 64600-64681)

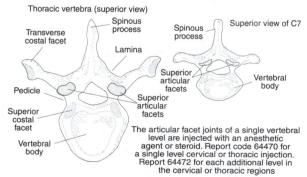

The articular facet joints of a single vertebral level are injected with an anesthetic agent or steroid. Report code 64470 for a single level cervical or thoracic injection. Report 64472 for each additional level in the cervical or thoracic regions

---

Current Procedural Coding Expert – Nervous System

~~64470~~	~~Injection, anesthetic agent and/or steroid, paravertebral facet joint or facet joint nerve; cervical or thoracic, single level~~
	To report, see code 64490
~~64472~~	~~cervical or thoracic, each additional level (List separately in addition to code for primary procedure)~~
	To report, see code 64491-64492
~~64475~~	~~lumbar or sacral, single level~~
	To report, see code 64493
~~64476~~	~~lumbar or sacral, each additional level (List separately in addition to code for primary procedure)~~
	To report, see code 64494-64495
64479	**Injection, anesthetic agent and/or steroid, transforaminal epidural; cervical or thoracic, single level** A2 T 50
	77003
	3.60 7.38 Global Days 000
	AMA: 2008, Jul, 9; 2008, Jun, 8-11; 2008, Nov, 10-11
+ 64480	**cervical or thoracic, each additional level (List separately in addition to code for primary procedure)** A2 T 50
	Code first (64479)
	77003
	2.36 3.86 Global Days ZZZ
	AMA: 2009, Jan, 11-31; 2008, Jan, 10-25; 2008, Jul, 9; 2008, Jun, 8-11; 2008, Nov, 10-11; 2007, January, 13-27; 2005, February, 13-16
64483	**lumbar or sacral, single level** A2 T 50
	77003
	3.12 7.05 Global Days 000
	AMA: 2008, Jun, 8-11; 2008, Jul, 9; 2008, Nov, 10-11
+ 64484	**lumbar or sacral, each additional level (List separately in addition to code for primary procedure)** A2 T 50
	Code first (64483)
	77003
	1.98 3.69 Global Days ZZZ
	AMA: 2009, Jan, 11-31; 2008, Jan, 10-25; 2008, Jul, 9; 2008, Jun, 8-11; 2008, Nov, 10-11; 2007, January, 13-27; 2005, February, 13-16

64490-64495 Paraspinal Nerve Injections

INCLUDES Image guidance (CT or fluoroscopy) and any contrast injection
EXCLUDES Ultrasonic guidance (0213T-0218T)

Do not report when imaging is not provided, instead report (20550-20553)

● 64490	**Injection(s), diagnostic or therapeutic agent, paravertebral facet (zygapophyseal) joint (or nerves innervating that joint) with image guidance (fluoroscopy or CT), cervical or thoracic; single level** G2 T 80 50
	2.98 4.53 Global Days 000
+ ● 64491	**second level (List separately in addition to code for primary procedure)** G2 T 80 50
	Code first (64490)
	1.71 2.23 Global Days ZZZ
+ ● 64492	**third and any additional level(s) (List separately in addition to code for primary procedure)** G2 T 80 50
	Code first (64490)
	Do not report more than one time per day
	1.74 2.26 Global Days ZZZ

| 26/TC PC/TC Comp Only | A2/23 ASC Pmt | 50 Bilateral | ♂ Male Only | ♀ Female Only | Facility RVU | Non-Facility RVU |
| AMA: CPT Asst | MED: Pub 100 | A-Y OPPSI | 80/80 Surg Assist Allowed / w/Doc | Lab Crosswalk | Radiology Crosswalk |

234 CPT only © 2009 American Medical Association. All Rights Reserved. (Black Ink) Medicare (Red Ink) © 2009 Publisher (Blue Ink)

Current Procedural Coding Expert – Nervous System

64590

● **64493** Injection(s), diagnostic or therapeutic agent, paravertebral facet (zygapophyseal) joint (or nerves innervating that joint) with image guidance (fluoroscopy or CT), lumbar or sacral; single level [62] [T] [80] [50]
INCLUDES Injection of T1-L1 joint and nerves that innervate that joint
🚗 2.53 ✂ 4.10 Global Days 000

+ ● **64494** second level (List separately in addition to code for primary procedure) [62] [T] [80] [50]
Code first (64493)
🚗 1.46 ✂ 2.00 Global Days ZZZ

+ ● **64495** third and any additional level(s) (List separately in addition to code for primary procedure) [62] [T] [80] [50]
Code first (64493)
Do not report more than one time per day
🚗 1.49 ✂ 2.03 Global Days ZZZ

64505-64530 Sympathetic Nerve Blocks

64505 Injection, anesthetic agent; sphenopalatine ganglion [P3] [T] 🗔
🚗 2.23 ✂ 2.58 Global Days 000
AMA: 2009, Jan, 11-31; 2008, Jan, 10-25; 2008, Jun, 8-11; 2007, January, 13-27; 2005, April, 13-14

64508 carotid sinus (separate procedure) [P3] [T] [80] 🗔
🚗 2.14 ✂ 4.39 Global Days 000
AMA: 2008, Jun, 8-11; 2005, April, 13-14

64510 stellate ganglion (cervical sympathetic) [A2] [T] 🗔 [P0]
🚗 2.00 ✂ 3.30 Global Days 000
AMA: 2008, Jun, 8-11; 2005, April, 13-14

64517 superior hypogastric plexus [A2] [T] 🗔
🚗 3.49 ✂ 4.88 Global Days 000
AMA: 2009, Jan, 11-31; 2008, Jan, 10-25; 2008, Jun, 8-11; 2007, January, 13-27; 2005, April, 13-14

64520 lumbar or thoracic (paravertebral sympathetic) [A2] [T] 🗔 [P0]
🚗 2.23 ✂ 4.98 Global Days 000
AMA: 2008, Jun, 8-11; 2005, April, 13-14

64530 celiac plexus, with or without radiologic monitoring [A2] [T] 🗔 [P0]
🚗 2.58 ✂ 5.10 Global Days 000
AMA: 2009, Jan, 11-31; 2008, Jan, 10-25; 2008, Jun, 8-11; 2007, January, 13-27; 2005, April, 13-14

64550 Transcutaneous Electrical Nerve Stimulation

CMS 100-3,160.2 Treatment of Motor Function Disorders with Electric Nerve Stimulation
CMS 100-3,160.7.1 Assessing Patients Suitability for Electrical Nerve Stimulation Therapy
CMS 100-3,160.13 Supplies Used for Transcutaneous Electrical Nerve Stimulation and Neuromuscular Electrical Stimulation (NMES)
CMS 100-3,280.13 Transcutaneous Electrical Nerve Stimulators (TENS)
CMS 100-4,4,20.5 HCPCS Under OPPS
EXCLUDES Analysis and programming neurostimulator pulse generator (95970-95975)

64550 Application of surface (transcutaneous) neurostimulator [A] 🗔
🚗 0.25 ✂ 0.43 Global Days 000
AMA: 2009, Jan, 11-31; 2008, Jan, 10-25; 2007, January, 13-27

64553-64565 Electrical Nerve Stimulation: Insertion/Replacement/Removal/Revision

CMS 100-3,160.2 Treatment of Motor Function Disorders with Electric Nerve Stimulation
CMS 100-3,160.7 Electrical Nerve Stimulators
CMS 100-3,160.7.1 Assessing Patients Suitability for Electrical Nerve Stimulation Therapy
CMS 100-3,160.12 Neuromuscular Electrical Stimulation (NMES)
CMS 100-3,160.13 Supplies Used for Transcutaneous Electrical Nerve Stimulation and Neuromuscular Electrical Stimulation (NMES)
CMS 100-4,32,40 Sacral Nerve Stimulation
EXCLUDES Analysis and programming of neurostimulator pulse generator (95970-95975)

64553 Percutaneous implantation of neurostimulator electrodes; cranial nerve [H8] [S] [80] 🗔
EXCLUDES Open procedure (61885-61886)
Code also (C1778, C1897)
🚗 4.42 ✂ 5.69 Global Days 010

64555 peripheral nerve (excludes sacral nerve) [J8] [S] 🗔
Code also (C1778, C1897)
🚗 3.93 ✂ 5.04 Global Days 010

64560 autonomic nerve [J8] [S] [80] 🗔
Code also (C1778, C1897)
🚗 4.04 ✂ 5.14 Global Days 010

64561 sacral nerve (transforaminal placement) [H8] [S] 🗔 [P0]
Code also (C1778, C1897)
🚗 10.97 ✂ 23.02 Global Days 010

64565 neuromuscular [J8] [S] 🗔
Code also (C1778, C1897)
🚗 3.50 ✂ 4.82 Global Days 010
AMA: 2009, Jan, 11-31; 2008, Jan, 10-25; 2007, January, 13-27

64573-64595 Implantation/Revision/Removal Neurostimulators: Incisional

64573 Incision for implantation of neurostimulator electrodes; cranial nerve [H8] [S] [80] 🗔
EXCLUDES Open procedure (61885-61886)
Removal or revision of cranial nerve neurostimulator pulse generator (61888)
Code also (C1778, C1897)
🚗 16.32 ✂ 16.32 Global Days 090

64575 peripheral nerve (excludes sacral nerve) [H8] [S] 🗔
Code also (C1778, C1897)
🚗 7.94 ✂ 7.94 Global Days 090

64577 autonomic nerve [H8] [S] 🗔
Code also (C1778, C1897)
🚗 10.98 ✂ 10.98 Global Days 090

64580 neuromuscular [H8] [S] [80] 🗔
Code also (C1778, C1897)
🚗 8.18 ✂ 8.18 Global Days 090

64581 sacral nerve (transforaminal placement) [H8] [S] 🗔
Code also (C1778, C1897)
🚗 21.15 ✂ 21.15 Global Days 090

64585 Revision or removal of peripheral neurostimulator electrodes [A2] [T] 🗔
🚗 3.90 ✂ 6.33 Global Days 010

64590 Insertion or replacement of peripheral or gastric neurostimulator pulse generator or receiver, direct or inductive coupling [H8] [S] 🗔
Code also (C1767, C1820, L8685-L8688)
Do not report with (64595)
🚗 4.31 ✂ 6.68 Global Days 010
AMA: 2007, March, 4-5; 2007, April, 7-10; 2006, May, 12-15

● New Code   ▲ Revised Code   M Maternity   A Age   Unlisted   Not Covered   # Resequenced
🗔 CCI   + Add-on   ⊘ Mod 51 Exempt   ⊗ Mod 63 Exempt   ⊙ Mod Sedation   [P0] PQRI

© 2009 Publisher (Blue Ink)   CPT only © 2009 American Medical Association. All Rights Reserved. (Black Ink)   Medicare (Red Ink)   235

64595

64595   Revision or removal of peripheral or gastric neurostimulator pulse generator or receiver   A2 T
Do not report with (64590)
◎ 3.37   ⚕ 6.15   Global Days 010
AMA: 2009, Jan, 11-31; 2008, Jan, 8-9; 2007, April, 7-10; 2007, March, 4-5; 2006, May, 12-15

64600-64610 Neurolysis Trigeminal Nerve

CMS 100-3,160.1   Induced Lesions of Nerve Tracts
INCLUDES   Injection of therapeutic medication
EXCLUDES   Treatments that do not destroy the target nerve (64999)

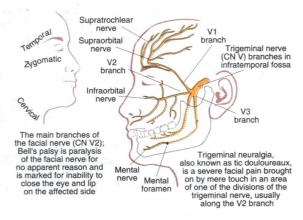

The main branches of the facial nerve (CN V2); Bell's palsy is paralysis of the facial nerve for no apparent reason and is marked for inability to close the eye and lip on the affected side

Trigeminal neuralgia, also known as tic douloureaux, is a severe facial pain brought on by mere touch in an area of one of the divisions of the trigeminal nerve, usually along the V2 branch

64600   Destruction by neurolytic agent, trigeminal nerve; supraorbital, infraorbital, mental, or inferior alveolar branch   A2 T
◎ 6.16   ⚕ 10.60   Global Days 010
AMA: 2008, Jun, 8-11; 2005, August, 13-15

64605   second and third division branches at foramen ovale   A2 T 80 P0
◎ 10.03   ⚕ 19.50   Global Days 010
AMA: 2008, Jun, 8-11; 2005, August, 13-15

64610   second and third division branches at foramen ovale under radiologic monitoring   A2 T P0
◎ 13.11   ⚕ 19.59   Global Days 010
AMA: 2008, Jun, 8-11; 2005, August, 13-15

64612-64614 Chemical Denervation of Muscles

CMS 100-3,160.1   Induced Lesions of Nerve Tracts
INCLUDES   Injection of therapeutic medication
EXCLUDES   Electromyography or muscle electric stimulation guidance (95873-95874)
Nerve destruction of:
  Anal sphincter (46505)
  Extraocular muscles to treat strabismus (67345)
Treatments that do not destroy the target nerve (64999)

64612   Chemodenervation of muscle(s); muscle(s) innervated by facial nerve (eg, for blepharospasm, hemifacial spasm)   P3 T 50
◎ 4.31   ⚕ 4.59   Global Days 010
AMA: 2009, Jan, 11-31; 2009, Jan, 7-8; 2008, Jan, 10-25; 2008, Jun, 8-11; 2007, January, 13-27; 2006, September, 5-8; 2005, August, 13-15

64613   neck muscle(s) (eg, for spasmodic torticollis, spasmodic dysphonia)   P3 T 50
◎ 4.01   ⚕ 4.32   Global Days 010
AMA: 2009, Jan, 7-8; 2009, Jan, 11-31; 2008, Jan, 10-25; 2008, Jun, 8-11; 2007, January, 13-27; 2006, September, 5-8; 2005, August, 13-15

64614   extremity(s) and/or trunk muscle(s) (eg, for dystonia, cerebral palsy, multiple sclerosis)   P3 T 50
◎ 4.22   ⚕ 4.64   Global Days 010
AMA: 2009, Jan, 11-31; 2008, Jan, 10-25; 2008, Jun, 8-11; 2007, January, 13-27; 2006, September, 5-8; 2005, February, 13-16; 2005, August, 13-15

64620-64640 Neurolysis: Intercostal, Facet Joint, and Pudendal Nerve

CMS 100-3,160.1   Induced Lesions of Nerve Tracts
INCLUDES   Injection of therapeutic medication
EXCLUDES   Treatments that do not destroy the target nerve (64999)

64620   Destruction by neurolytic agent, intercostal nerve   A2 T P0
◎ 4.87   ⚕ 7.77   Global Days 010
AMA: 2008, Jun, 8-11; 2005, August, 13-15

64622   Destruction by neurolytic agent, paravertebral facet joint nerve; lumbar or sacral, single level   A2 T 50 P0
  77003
◎ 5.29   ⚕ 9.03   Global Days 010
AMA: 2008, Jun, 8-11; 2005, August, 13-15

+ 64623   lumbar or sacral, each additional level (List separately in addition to code for primary procedure)   A2 T 50
Code first (64622)
  77003
◎ 1.46   ⚕ 3.36   Global Days ZZZ
AMA: 2008, Jun, 8-11; 2005, August, 13-15

64626   cervical or thoracic, single level   A2 T 50 P0
  77003
◎ 7.16   ⚕ 10.93   Global Days 010
AMA: 2008, Jun, 8-11; 2005, August, 13-15

+ 64627   cervical or thoracic, each additional level (List separately in addition to code for primary procedure)   A2 T 50
Code first (64626)
  77003
◎ 1.71   ⚕ 4.53   Global Days ZZZ
AMA: 2008, Jun, 8-11; 2005, August, 13-15

64630   Destruction by neurolytic agent; pudendal nerve   A2 T 80
◎ 5.02   ⚕ 5.84   Global Days 010
AMA: 2008, Jun, 8-11; 2005, August, 13-15

64632   plantar common digital nerve   P3 T 80 50
Do not report with (64455)
◎ 2.00   ⚕ 2.37   Global Days 010
AMA: 2009, Jan, 6&9

64640   other peripheral nerve or branch   P3 T 50
◎ 4.56   ⚕ 5.67   Global Days 010
AMA: 2008, Jun, 8-11; 2005, August, 13-15

64650-64653 Chemical Denervation Eccrine Glands

INCLUDES   Injection of therapeutic medication

64650   Chemodenervation of eccrine glands; both axillae   P3 T 80
◎ 1.14   ⚕ 1.91   Global Days 000
AMA: 2008, Jun, 8-11; 2005, August, 13-15

64653   other area(s) (eg, scalp, face, neck), per day   P3 T 80
EXCLUDES   Hands or feet (64999)
◎ 1.45   ⚕ 2.36   Global Days 000
AMA: 2008, Jun, 8-11; 2005, August, 13-15

Current Procedural Coding Expert – Nervous System

64680-64681 Neurolysis: Celiac Plexus, Superior Hypogastric Plexus

INCLUDES
- Injection of therapeutic medication
- Only for lesions that abut the dura matter or that affect the spinal neural tissue
- Planning, dosimetry, targeting, positioning, or blocking performed by the surgeon
- Radiation treatment management by the same physician (77427-77432)

Do not report more than once per lesion per course of treatment
Do not report with (61795)

64680 Destruction by neurolytic agent, with or without radiologic monitoring; celiac plexus
4.51   8.19   Global Days 010
AMA: 2009, Jan, 11-31; 2008, Jan, 10-25; 2008, Jun, 8-11; 2007, January, 13-27; 2005, August, 13-15

64681 superior hypogastric plexus
5.18   8.85   Global Days 010
AMA: 2009, Jan, 11-31; 2007, Dec, 10-179; 2005, August, 13-15

64702-64727 Decompression and/or Transposition of Nerve

INCLUDES Neuroplasty with nerve wrapping
EXCLUDES Facial nerve decompression (69720)
Neuroplasty with operating microscope (64727)

64702 Neuroplasty; digital, 1 or both, same digit
13.30   13.30   Global Days 090
AMA: 2009, Jan, 11-31; 2008, Jan, 10-25; 2007, January, 13-27

64704 nerve of hand or foot
8.74   8.74   Global Days 090
AMA: 2009, Jan, 11-31; 2008, Jan, 10-25; 2007, January, 13-27

64708 Neuroplasty, major peripheral nerve, arm or leg; other than specified
13.15   13.15   Global Days 090
AMA: 2009, Jan, 11-31; 2008, Jan, 10-25; 2007, January, 13-27

64712 sciatic nerve
14.78   14.78   Global Days 090
AMA: 2009, Jan, 11-31; 2008, Jan, 10-25; 2007, January, 13-27

64713 brachial plexus
20.88   20.88   Global Days 090
AMA: 2009, Jan, 11-31; 2008, Jan, 10-25; 2007, January, 13-27

64714 lumbar plexus
18.97   18.97   Global Days 090
AMA: 2009, Jan, 11-31; 2008, Jan, 10-25; 2007, January, 13-27

64716 Neuroplasty and/or transposition; cranial nerve (specify)
14.46   14.46   Global Days 090
AMA: 2009, Jan, 11-31; 2008, Jan, 10-25; 2007, January, 13-27

64718 ulnar nerve at elbow
15.69   15.69   Global Days 090
AMA: 2009, Jan, 11-31; 2009, Mar, 10-11; 2008, Jan, 10-25; 2007, January, 13-27

64719 ulnar nerve at wrist
10.59   10.59   Global Days 090
AMA: 2009, Jan, 11-31; 2009, Mar, 10-11; 2008, Jan, 10-25; 2007, January, 13-27

64721 median nerve at carpal tunnel
EXCLUDES Arthroscopic procedure (29848)
11.19   11.25   Global Days 090
AMA: 2009, Jan, 11-31; 2008, Jan, 10-25; 2007, January, 13-27; 2006, December, 10-12

64722 Decompression; unspecified nerve(s) (specify)
9.40   9.40   Global Days 090
AMA: 2009, Jan, 11-31; 2008, Jan, 10-25; 2007, January, 13-27

64726 plantar digital nerve
7.50   7.50   Global Days 090
AMA: 2009, Jan, 11-31; 2008, Jan, 10-25; 2007, January, 13-27

+ **64727** Internal neurolysis, requiring use of operating microscope (List separately in addition to code for neuroplasty) (Neuroplasty includes external neurolysis)
INCLUDES Neuroplasty with nerve wrapping
Operating microscope (69990)
5.06   5.06   Global Days ZZZ
AMA: 2009, Jan, 11-31; 2008, Jan, 10-25; 2007, January, 13-27

64732-64772 Surgical Avulsion/Transection of Nerve

CMS 100-3,160.1   Induced Lesions of Nerve Tracts
EXCLUDES Stereotactic lesion of gasserian ganglion (61790)

64732 Transection or avulsion of; supraorbital nerve
11.47   11.47   Global Days 090

64734 infraorbital nerve
12.09   12.09   Global Days 090

64736 mental nerve
12.45   12.45   Global Days 090

64738 inferior alveolar nerve by osteotomy
14.40   14.40   Global Days 090

64740 lingual nerve
12.61   12.61   Global Days 090

64742 facial nerve, differential or complete
13.45   13.45   Global Days 090

64744 greater occipital nerve
12.91   12.91   Global Days 090

64746 phrenic nerve
EXCLUDES Section of recurrent unilateral laryngeal nerve (31595)
12.86   12.86   Global Days 090

64752 vagus nerve (vagotomy), transthoracic
13.42   13.42   Global Days 090

64755 vagus nerves limited to proximal stomach (selective proximal vagotomy, proximal gastric vagotomy, parietal cell vagotomy, supra- or highly selective vagotomy)
EXCLUDES Laparoscopic procedure (43652)
25.12   25.12   Global Days 090

64760 vagus nerve (vagotomy), abdominal
EXCLUDES Laparoscopic procedure (43651)
13.86   13.86   Global Days 090

64761 pudendal nerve
12.37   12.37   Global Days 090

64763 Transection or avulsion of obturator nerve, extrapelvic, with or without adductor tenotomy
13.74   13.74   Global Days 090

64766 Transection or avulsion of obturator nerve, intrapelvic, with or without adductor tenotomy
16.15   16.15   Global Days 090

64771 Transection or avulsion of other cranial nerve, extradural
15.13   15.13   Global Days 090

● New Code   ▲ Revised Code   M Maternity   A Age   Unlisted   Not Covered   # Resequenced
CCI   + Add-on   ⊘ Mod 51 Exempt   ⊘ Mod 63 Exempt   ⊙ Mod Sedation   PQRI

© 2009 Publisher (Blue Ink)   CPT only © 2009 American Medical Association. All Rights Reserved. (Black Ink)   Medicare (Red Ink)   237

Current Procedural Coding Expert – Nervous System

64772	Transection or avulsion of other spinal nerve, extradural
	EXCLUDES: Removal of tender scar and soft tissue including neuroma if necessary (11400-11446, 13100-13153)
	15.51 15.51 Global Days 090

64774-64823 Excisional Nerve Procedures

EXCLUDES: Morton neuroma excision (28080)

64774	Excision of neuroma; cutaneous nerve, surgically identifiable
	11.24 11.24 Global Days 090
64776	digital nerve, 1 or both, same digit
	10.57 10.57 Global Days 090
+64778	digital nerve, each additional digit (List separately in addition to code for primary procedure)
	Code first (64776)
	5.08 5.08 Global Days ZZZ
64782	hand or foot, except digital nerve
	12.42 12.42 Global Days 090
+64783	hand or foot, each additional nerve, except same digit (List separately in addition to code for primary procedure)
	Code first (64782)
	6.13 6.13 Global Days ZZZ
64784	major peripheral nerve, except sciatic
	19.93 19.93 Global Days 090
64786	sciatic nerve
	29.35 29.35 Global Days 090
+64787	Implantation of nerve end into bone or muscle (List separately in addition to neuroma excision)
	Code first (64774-64786)
	6.72 6.72 Global Days ZZZ
64788	Excision of neurofibroma or neurolemmoma; cutaneous nerve
	10.64 10.64 Global Days 090
64790	major peripheral nerve
	22.53 22.53 Global Days 090
64792	extensive (including malignant type)
	31.62 31.62 Global Days 090
64795	Biopsy of nerve
	5.39 5.39 Global Days 000
64802	Sympathectomy, cervical
	18.27 18.27 Global Days 090
64804	Sympathectomy, cervicothoracic
	20.96 20.96 Global Days 090
64809	Sympathectomy, thoracolumbar
	INCLUDES: Leriche sympathectomy
	19.32 19.32 Global Days 090
64818	Sympathectomy, lumbar
	18.27 18.27 Global Days 090
64820	Sympathectomy; digital arteries, each digit
	INCLUDES: Operating microscope (69990)
	20.50 20.50 Global Days 090
	AMA: 2009, Jan, 11-31; 2008, Jan, 10-25; 2007, January, 13-27
64821	radial artery
	INCLUDES: Operating microscope (69990)
	18.48 18.48 Global Days 090
64822	ulnar artery
	INCLUDES: Operating microscope (69990)
	18.48 18.48 Global Days 090
64823	superficial palmar arch
	INCLUDES: Operating microscope (69990)
	21.11 21.11 Global Days 090

64831-64907 Nerve Repair: Suture and Nerve Grafts

64831	Suture of digital nerve, hand or foot; 1 nerve
	18.37 18.37 Global Days 090
+64832	each additional digital nerve (List separately in addition to code for primary procedure)
	Code first (64831)
	9.38 9.38 Global Days ZZZ
64834	Suture of 1 nerve; hand or foot, common sensory nerve
	20.10 20.10 Global Days 090
64835	median motor thenar
	21.96 21.96 Global Days 090
64836	ulnar motor
	21.96 21.96 Global Days 090
+64837	Suture of each additional nerve, hand or foot (List separately in addition to code for primary procedure)
	Code first (64834-64836)
	10.34 10.34 Global Days ZZZ
64840	Suture of posterior tibial nerve
	20.34 20.34 Global Days 090
64856	Suture of major peripheral nerve, arm or leg, except sciatic; including transposition
	27.70 27.70 Global Days 090
64857	without transposition
	28.96 28.96 Global Days 090
64858	Suture of sciatic nerve
	32.00 32.00 Global Days 090
+64859	Suture of each additional major peripheral nerve (List separately in addition to code for primary procedure)
	Code first (64856-64857)
	6.93 6.93 Global Days ZZZ
64861	Suture of; brachial plexus
	37.30 37.30 Global Days 090
64862	lumbar plexus
	40.67 40.67 Global Days 090
64864	Suture of facial nerve; extracranial
	23.83 23.83 Global Days 090
64865	infratemporal, with or without grafting
	30.92 30.92 Global Days 090
64866	Anastomosis; facial-spinal accessory
	32.09 32.09 Global Days 090
64868	facial-hypoglossal
	INCLUDES: Korte-Ballance anastomosis
	28.34 28.34 Global Days 090
64870	facial-phrenic
	30.43 30.43 Global Days 090
+64872	Suture of nerve; requiring secondary or delayed suture (List separately in addition to code for primary neurorrhaphy)
	Code first (64831-64865)
	3.29 3.29 Global Days ZZZ
+64874	requiring extensive mobilization, or transposition of nerve (List separately in addition to code for nerve suture)
	Code first (64831-64865)
	4.64 4.64 Global Days ZZZ

Current Procedural Coding Expert – Nervous System 64999

+ 64876 requiring shortening of bone of extremity (List separately in addition to code for nerve suture) [A2] [T] [80]
  Code first (64831-64865)
  5.83 5.83 Global Days ZZZ

64885 Nerve graft (includes obtaining graft), head or neck; up to 4 cm in length [A2] [T] [80]
  30.68 30.68 Global Days 090
  AMA: 2009, Jan, 11-31; 2008, Jan, 10-25; 2007, January, 13-27

64886 more than 4 cm length [A2] [T] [80]
  36.65 36.65 Global Days 090
  AMA: 2009, Jan, 11-31; 2008, Jan, 10-25; 2007, January, 13-27

64890 Nerve graft (includes obtaining graft), single strand, hand or foot; up to 4 cm length [A2] [T] [80]
  29.33 29.33 Global Days 090

64891 more than 4 cm length [A2] [T] [80]
  31.24 31.24 Global Days 090

64892 Nerve graft (includes obtaining graft), single strand, arm or leg; up to 4 cm length [A2] [T] [80]
  28.52 28.52 Global Days 090

64893 more than 4 cm length [A2] [T] [80]
  30.46 30.46 Global Days 090

64895 Nerve graft (includes obtaining graft), multiple strands (cable), hand or foot; up to 4 cm length [A2] [T] [80]
  36.20 36.20 Global Days 090

64896 more than 4 cm length [A2] [T] [80]
  43.08 43.08 Global Days 090

64897 Nerve graft (includes obtaining graft), multiple strands (cable), arm or leg; up to 4 cm length [A2] [T] [80]
  34.55 34.55 Global Days 090

64898 more than 4 cm length [A2] [T] [80]
  37.43 37.43 Global Days 090

+ 64901 Nerve graft, each additional nerve; single strand (List separately in addition to code for primary procedure) [A2] [T] [80]
  Code first (64885-64893)
  17.65 17.65 Global Days ZZZ

+ 64902 multiple strands (cable) (List separately in addition to code for primary procedure) [A2] [T] [80]
  Code first (64885-64886, 64895-64898)
  20.45 20.45 Global Days ZZZ

64905 Nerve pedicle transfer; first stage [A2] [T] [80]
  28.60 28.60 Global Days 090

64907 second stage [A2] [T] [80]
  30.22 30.22 Global Days 090

64910-64999 Nerve Repair: Synthetic and Vein Grafts

INCLUDES Operating microscope (69990)

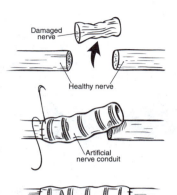

A synthetic "bridge" is affixed to each end of a severed nerve with sutures. This procedure is performed using an operating microscope

64910 Nerve repair; with synthetic conduit or vein allograft (eg, nerve tube), each nerve [62] [T] [80]
  22.43 22.43 Global Days 090

64911 with autogenous vein graft (includes harvest of vein graft), each nerve [T] [80]
  Do not report with (64910-64911)
  28.16 28.16 Global Days 090

64999 Unlisted procedure, nervous system [T] [80]
  0.00 0.00 Global Days YYY
  AMA: 2009, Jan, 11-31; 2008, Jan, 10-25; 2008, Jul, 9; 2008, Sep, 10-11; 2007, Dec, 7-8; 2007, January, 13-27; 2005, April, 13-14; 2005, September, 9-11; 2005, August, 13-15

65091-65093 Surgical Removal of Eyeball Contents

CMS 100-2,15,120   Prosthetic Devices
CMS 100-4,12,30   Correct Coding Policy
INCLUDES Operating microscope (69990)

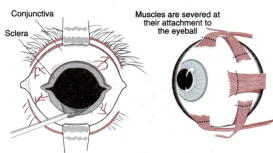

Conjunctiva / Sclera

Muscles are severed at their attachment to the eyeball

Evisceration involves removal of the contents of the eyeball: the vitreous; retina; choroid; lens; iris; and ciliary muscle. Only the scleral shell remains. A temporary or permanent implant is usually inserted

Enucleation involves severing the extraorbital muscles and optic nerve with removal of the eyeball. An implant is usually inserted and, if permanent, may involve attachment to the severed extraorbital muscles

65091   Evisceration of ocular contents; without implant   A2 T 80 50
     17.10   17.10   Global Days 090

65093   with implant   A2 T 50
     16.85   16.85   Global Days 090

65101-65105 Surgical Removal of Eyeball

CMS 100-2,15,120   Prosthetic Devices
CMS 100-4,12,30   Correct Coding Policy
INCLUDES Operating microscope (69990)
EXCLUDES Conjunctivoplasty following enucleation (68320-68340)

65101   Enucleation of eye; without implant   A2 T 50
     19.83   19.83   Global Days 090

65103   with implant, muscles not attached to implant   A2 T 50
     20.73   20.73   Global Days 090

65105   with implant, muscles attached to implant   A2 T 80 50
     22.97   22.97   Global Days 090

65110-65114 Surgical Removal of Orbital Contents

CMS 100-2,15,120   Prosthetic Devices
CMS 100-4,12,30   Correct Coding Policy
INCLUDES Operating microscope (69990)
EXCLUDES Free full thickness graft (15260-15261)
Repair more extensive than skin (67930-67975)
Skin graft (15120-15121)

65110   Exenteration of orbit (does not include skin graft), removal of orbital contents; only   A2 T 80 50
     32.52   32.52   Global Days 090

65112   with therapeutic removal of bone   A2 T 80 50
     38.14   38.14   Global Days 090

65114   with muscle or myocutaneous flap   A2 T 80 50
     40.06   40.06   Global Days 090

65125-65175 Implant Procedures: Insertion, Removal, and Revision

CMS 100-2,15,120   Prosthetic Devices
CMS 100-4,12,30   Correct Coding Policy
INCLUDES Operating microscope (69990)
EXCLUDES Orbit implant insertion outside muscle cone (67550)
Orbital implant removal or revision outside muscle cone (67560)

65125   Modification of ocular implant with placement or replacement of pegs (eg, drilling receptacle for prosthesis appendage) (separate procedure)   62 T 50
     7.86   11.60   Global Days 090

65130   Insertion of ocular implant secondary; after evisceration, in scleral shell   A2 T 50
     19.73   19.73   Global Days 090

65135   after enucleation, muscles not attached to implant   A2 T 50
     20.04   20.04   Global Days 090

65140   after enucleation, muscles attached to implant   A2 T 50
     21.38   21.38   Global Days 090

65150   Reinsertion of ocular implant; with or without conjunctival graft   A2 T 80 50
     14.92   14.92   Global Days 090

65155   with use of foreign material for reinforcement and/or attachment of muscles to implant   A2 T 50
     22.95   22.95   Global Days 090

65175   Removal of ocular implant   A2 T 50
     17.28   17.28   Global Days 090

65205-65265 Foreign Body Removal By Area of Eye

CMS 100-4,12,30   Correct Coding Policy
INCLUDES Operating microscope (69990)
EXCLUDES Removal:
     Anterior segment implant (65920)
     Orbital implant outside muscle cone (67560)
     Posterior segment implant (67120)
Removal of foreign body:
     Eyelid (67938)
     Frontal approach (67413)
     Lacrimal system (68530)
     Lateral approach (67430)
     Transcranial approach (61334)

65205   Removal of foreign body, external eye; conjunctival superficial   P3 S 50
     70030, 76529
     1.23   1.50   Global Days 000
     AMA: 2009, Jan, 11-31; 2008, Jan, 10-25; 2007, January, 13-27; 2005, March, 16-17

65210   conjunctival embedded (includes concretions), subconjunctival, or scleral nonperforating   P3 S 50
     70030, 76529
     1.50   1.85   Global Days 000

65220   corneal, without slit lamp   62 S 50
     EXCLUDES Repair of corneal wound with foreign body (65275)
     70030, 76529
     1.18   1.54   Global Days 000

65222   corneal, with slit lamp   P3 S 50
     EXCLUDES Repair of corneal wound with foreign body (65275)
     70030, 76529
     1.64   2.04   Global Days 000

26/TC PC/TC Comp Only   A2-Z3 ASC Pmt   50 Bilateral   ♂ Male Only   ♀ Female Only   Facility RVU   Non-Facility RVU
AMA: CPT Asst   **MED:** Pub 100   A-Y OPPSI   80/80 Surg Assist Allowed / w/Doc   Lab Crosswalk   Radiology Crosswalk

Current Procedural Coding Expert – Eye and Ocular Adnexa 65730

65235	Removal of foreign body, intraocular; from anterior chamber of eye or lens
	70030, 76529
	19.10 19.10 Global Days 090
65260	from posterior segment, magnetic extraction, anterior or posterior route
	70030, 76529
	25.29 25.29 Global Days 090
65265	from posterior segment, nonmagnetic extraction
	70030, 76529
	30.01 30.01 Global Days 090

65270-65290 Laceration Repair External Eye

CMS 100-4,12,30 — Correct Coding Policy

INCLUDES
Conjunctival flap
Operating microscope (69990)
Restoration of anterior chamber with air or saline injection

EXCLUDES
Repair:
  Ciliary body or iris (66680)
  Eyelid laceration (12011-12018, 12051-12057, 13150-13160, 67930, 67935)
  Lacrimal system injury (68700)
  Surgical wound (66250)
Treatment of orbit fracture (21385-21408)

65270	Repair of laceration; conjunctiva, with or without nonperforating laceration sclera, direct closure
	3.84 6.69 Global Days 010
65272	conjunctiva, by mobilization and rearrangement, without hospitalization
	9.28 12.71 Global Days 090
65273	conjunctiva, by mobilization and rearrangement, with hospitalization
	10.11 10.11 Global Days 090
65275	cornea, nonperforating, with or without removal foreign body
	12.58 15.22 Global Days 090
65280	cornea and/or sclera, perforating, not involving uveal tissue
	18.62 18.62 Global Days 090
65285	cornea and/or sclera, perforating, with reposition or resection of uveal tissue
	28.74 28.74 Global Days 090
65286	application of tissue glue, wounds of cornea and/or sclera
	13.45 18.18 Global Days 090
65290	Repair of wound, extraocular muscle, tendon and/or Tenon's capsule
	13.57 13.57 Global Days 090

65400-65600 Removal Corneal Lesions

CMS 100-4,12,30 — Correct Coding Policy
INCLUDES Operating microscope (69990)

65400	Excision of lesion, cornea (keratectomy, lamellar, partial), except pterygium
	16.18 17.92 Global Days 090
65410	Biopsy of cornea
	2.93 3.80 Global Days 000

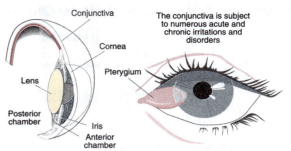

Keratitis is an often painful inflammation of the cornea, the clear membrane covering the anterior segment of the eye

The conjunctiva is subject to numerous acute and chronic irritations and disorders

A pterygium is a wedge of excess tissue extending from the medial canthus toward the cornea

65420	Excision or transposition of pterygium; without graft
	10.00 13.16 Global Days 090
	AMA: 2009, Jan, 11-31; 2007, Dec, 10-179
65426	with graft
	12.87 16.81 Global Days 090
	AMA: 2009, Jun, 9&11
65430	Scraping of cornea, diagnostic, for smear and/or culture
	2.83 3.08 Global Days 000
65435	Removal of corneal epithelium; with or without chemocauterization (abrasion, curettage)
	1.91 2.14 Global Days 000
65436	with application of chelating agent (eg, EDTA)
	10.16 10.52 Global Days 090
65450	Destruction of lesion of cornea by cryotherapy, photocoagulation or thermocauterization
	8.46 8.54 Global Days 090
65600	Multiple punctures of anterior cornea (eg, for corneal erosion, tattoo)
	9.20 10.34 Global Days 090

65710-65757 Corneal Transplants

CMS 100-3,80.7 — Refractive Keratoplasty
CMS 100-4,12,30 — Correct Coding Policy
INCLUDES Operating microscope (69990)
EXCLUDES Processing, preserving, and transporting corneal tissue (V2785)

Do not report with (92025)

65710	Keratoplasty (corneal transplant); anterior lamellar
	INCLUDES Use and preparation of fresh or preserved graft
	EXCLUDES Refractive keratoplasty surgery (65760, 65765, 65767)
	29.94 29.94 Global Days 090
65730	penetrating (except in aphakia or pseudophakia)
	INCLUDES Use and preparation of fresh or preserved graft
	EXCLUDES Refractive keratoplasty surgery (65760, 65765, 65767)
	33.30 33.30 Global Days 090
	AMA: 2006, February, 1-6

● New Code   ▲ Revised Code   Ⓜ Maternity   Ⓐ Age   Unlisted   Not Covered   # Resequenced
CCI   + Add-on   ⊘ Mod 51 Exempt   ⊚ Mod 63 Exempt   ⊙ Mod Sedation   PQRI

© 2009 Publisher *(Blue Ink)*   CPT only © 2009 American Medical Association. All Rights Reserved. *(Black Ink)*   Medicare *(Red Ink)*

65750

Code	Description	RVU Facility	RVU Non-Facility	Global Days
65750	penetrating (in aphakia)	33.51	33.51	090
	INCLUDES: Use and preparation of fresh or preserved graft			
	EXCLUDES: Refractive keratoplasty surgery (65760, 65765, 65767)			
65755	penetrating (in pseudophakia)	33.43	33.43	090
	INCLUDES: Use and preparation of fresh or preserved graft			
	EXCLUDES: Refractive keratoplasty surgery (65760, 65765, 65767)			
65756	endothelial	31.60	31.60	090
	Code also if appropriate (65757)			
+65757	Backbench preparation of corneal endothelial allograft prior to transplantation (List separately in addition to code for primary procedure)	0.00	0.00	ZZZ
	Code first (65756)			

65760-65775 Corneal Refractive Procedures

CMS 100-3,80.7 — Refractive Keratoplasty
INCLUDES: Operating microscope (69990)

Code	Description	RVU Facility	RVU Non-Facility	Global Days
65760	Keratomileusis	0.00	0.00	XXX
	Do not report with (92025)			
65765	Keratophakia	0.00	0.00	XXX
	Do not report with (92025)			
65767	Epikeratoplasty	0.00	0.00	XXX
	Do not report with (92025)			
65770	Keratoprosthesis	41.53	41.53	090
	Code also (C1818, L8609)			
	Do not report with (92025)			
65771	Radial keratotomy	0.00	0.00	XXX
	Do not report with (92025)			
65772	Corneal relaxing incision for correction of surgically induced astigmatism	10.88	11.90	090
65775	Corneal wedge resection for correction of surgically induced astigmatism	14.48	14.48	090
	EXCLUDES: Fitting of contact lens to treat disease (92070)			

65780-65782 Corneal Surface Reconstruction

CMS 100-4,4,200.4 — Billing for Amniotic Membrane
CMS 100-4,12,30 — Correct Coding Policy
INCLUDES: Operating microscope (69990)
EXCLUDES: Obtaining conjunctival allograft from a live donor (68371)

Code	Description	RVU Facility	RVU Non-Facility	Global Days
65780	Ocular surface reconstruction; amniotic membrane transplantation	23.64	23.64	090
	AMA: 2009, Jan, 11-31; 2009, Jun, 9&11; 2008, Jan, 10-25; 2007, January, 13-27			
65781	limbal stem cell allograft (eg, cadaveric or living donor)	35.41	35.41	090
65782	limbal conjunctival autograft (includes obtaining graft)	31.91	31.91	090
	AMA: 2009, Jan, 11-31; 2008, Jan, 10-25; 2007, January, 13-27; 2005, February, 13-16			

65800-66030 Anterior Chamber Procedures

INCLUDES: Operating microscope (69990)

Code	Description	RVU Facility	RVU Non-Facility	Global Days
65800	Paracentesis of anterior chamber of eye (separate procedure); with diagnostic aspiration of aqueous	3.59	4.00	000
65805	with therapeutic release of aqueous	3.65	4.38	000
65810	with removal of vitreous and/or discission of anterior hyaloid membrane, with or without air injection	12.71	12.71	090
65815	with removal of blood, with or without irrigation and/or air injection	12.99	16.63	090
	EXCLUDES: Injection only (66020-66030); Removal of blood clot only (65930)			
65820	Goniotomy	19.54	19.54	090
	INCLUDES: Barkan's operation			
	Code also ophthalmic endoscope if used (66990)			
	AMA: 2005, September, 5			
65850	Trabeculotomy ab externo	23.13	23.13	090
65855	Trabeculoplasty by laser surgery, 1 or more sessions (defined treatment series)	8.12	9.06	010
	EXCLUDES: Re-treatment after several months for more extensive disease; Trabeculectomy ab externo (66170)			
	AMA: 2009, Jan, 11-31; 2008, Jan, 10-25; 2007, January, 13-27			
65860	Severing adhesions of anterior segment, laser technique (separate procedure)	7.53	8.82	090
65865	Severing adhesions of anterior segment of eye, incisional technique (with or without injection of air or liquid) (separate procedure); goniosynechiae	12.36	12.36	090
	EXCLUDES: Laser trabeculectomy (65855)			
65870	anterior synechiae, except goniosynechiae	16.06	16.06	090
65875	posterior synechiae	16.89	16.89	090
	Code also ophthalmic endoscope if used (66990)			
	AMA: 2005, September, 5			
65880	corneovitreal adhesions	17.40	17.40	090
65900	Removal of epithelial downgrowth, anterior chamber of eye	25.42	25.42	090
65920	Removal of implanted material, anterior segment of eye	21.13	21.13	090
	Code also ophthalmic endoscope if used (66990)			
	AMA: 2005, September, 5			

Current Procedural Coding Expert – Eye and Ocular Adnexa

65930	Removal of blood clot, anterior segment of eye
	17.45 17.45 Global Days 090
66020	Injection, anterior chamber of eye (separate procedure); air or liquid
	3.45 4.70 Global Days 010
66030	medication
	2.95 4.20 Global Days 010

66130-66250 Scleral Procedures

CMS 100-4,12,30   Correct Coding Policy
INCLUDES Operating microscope (69990)
EXCLUDES Intraocular foreign body removal (65235)
Scleral procedures with retinal procedures (67101-67228)
Surgery on posterior sclera (67250, 67255)

66130	Excision of lesion, sclera
	15.93 18.82 Global Days 090
66150	Fistulization of sclera for glaucoma; trephination with iridectomy
	22.90 22.90 Global Days 090
66155	thermocauterization with iridectomy
	22.88 22.88 Global Days 090
66160	sclerectomy with punch or scissors, with iridectomy
	INCLUDES Knapp's operation
	25.95 25.95 Global Days 090

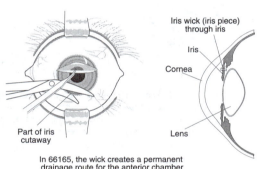

In 66165, the wick creates a permanent drainage route for the anterior chamber

66165	iridencleisis or iridotasis
	22.43 22.43 Global Days 090
66170	trabeculectomy ab externo in absence of previous surgery
	EXCLUDES Dilation of Schlemm's canal (0176T-0177T)
	Repair of surgical wound (66250)
	Trabeculectomy ab externo (65850)
	32.13 32.13 Global Days 090
66172	trabeculectomy ab externo with scarring from previous ocular surgery or trauma (includes injection of antifibrotic agents)
	EXCLUDES Fistulation of transciliary body sclera (0123T)
	40.53 40.53 Global Days 090
66180	Aqueous shunt to extraocular reservoir (eg, Molteno, Schocket, Denver-Krupin)
	INCLUDES Schocket implant
	31.72 31.72 Global Days 090
66185	Revision of aqueous shunt to extraocular reservoir
	EXCLUDES Implanted shunt removal (67120)
	20.45 20.45 Global Days 090

66220	Repair of scleral staphyloma; without graft
	19.95 19.95 Global Days 090
66225	with graft
	EXCLUDES Scleral reinforcement (67250, 67255)
	25.89 25.89 Global Days 090
66250	Revision or repair of operative wound of anterior segment, any type, early or late, major or minor procedure
	15.29 19.64 Global Days 090

66500-66505 Iridotomy With/Without Transfixion

CMS 100-4,12,30   Correct Coding Policy
INCLUDES Operating microscope (69990)
EXCLUDES Photocoagulation iridotomy (66761)

66500	Iridotomy by stab incision (separate procedure); except transfixion
	9.13 9.13 Global Days 090
66505	with transfixion as for iris bombe
	10.01 10.01 Global Days 090

66600-66635 Iridectomy Procedures

CMS 100-4,12,30   Correct Coding Policy
INCLUDES Operating microscope (69990)
EXCLUDES Photocoagulation coreoplasty (66762)

66600	Iridectomy, with corneoscleral or corneal section; for removal of lesion
	21.82 21.82 Global Days 090
66605	with cyclectomy
	28.02 28.02 Global Days 090
66625	peripheral for glaucoma (separate procedure)
	11.50 11.50 Global Days 090
66630	sector for glaucoma (separate procedure)
	15.50 15.50 Global Days 090
66635	optical (separate procedure)
	15.14 15.14 Global Days 090

66680-66770 Other Procedures of the Uveal Tract

CMS 100-4,12,30   Correct Coding Policy
INCLUDES Operating microscope (69990)

66680	Repair of iris, ciliary body (as for iridodialysis)
	14.19 14.19 Global Days 090
66682	Suture of iris, ciliary body (separate procedure) with retrieval of suture through small incision (eg, McCannel suture)
	17.20 17.20 Global Days 090
66700	Ciliary body destruction; diathermy
	INCLUDES Heine's operation
	10.48 11.79 Global Days 090
66710	cyclophotocoagulation, transscleral
	10.84 11.93 Global Days 090
	AMA: 2009, Jan, 11-31; 2008, Jan, 10-25; 2007, January, 13-27; 2005, March, 16-17; 2005, September, 5
66711	cyclophotocoagulation, endoscopic
	INCLUDES Operating microscope (66990)
	16.87 16.87 Global Days 090
	AMA: 2009, Jan, 11-31; 2008, Jan, 10-25; 2007, January, 13-27; 2005, March, 16-17; 2005, September, 5

● New Code   ▲ Revised Code   Ⓜ Maternity   Ⓐ Age   Unlisted   Not Covered   # Resequenced
□ CCI   + Add-on   ⊘ Mod 51 Exempt   ⊘ Mod 63 Exempt   ⊙ Mod Sedation   PQ PQRI

© 2009 Publisher *(Blue Ink)*   CPT only © 2009 American Medical Association. All Rights Reserved. (Black Ink)   Medicare (Red Ink)

66720

CURRENT PROCEDURAL CODING EXPERT – Eye and Ocular Adnexa

66720	cryotherapy	A2 T 50
	11.20 12.37 Global Days 090	
	AMA: 2006, April, 11-18	
66740	cyclodialysis	A2 T 50
	10.38 11.39 Global Days 090	
66761	Iridotomy/iridectomy by laser surgery (eg, for glaucoma) (1 or more sessions)	P3 T 50
	11.19 12.09 Global Days 090	
66762	Iridoplasty by photocoagulation (1 or more sessions) (eg, for improvement of vision, for widening of anterior chamber angle)	P3 T 50
	11.43 12.56 Global Days 090	
66770	Destruction of cyst or lesion iris or ciliary body (nonexcisional procedure)	P3 T 50
	EXCLUDES Excision:	
	Epithelial downgrowth (65900)	
	Iris, ciliary body lesion (66600-66605)	
	12.73 13.75 Global Days 090	

66820-66825 Post-Cataract Surgery Procedures

INCLUDES Operating microscope (69990)

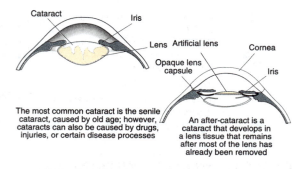

A cataract is a milky opacity on the normally clear lens of the eye; it obscures vision

The most common cataract is the senile cataract, caused by old age; however, cataracts can also be caused by drugs, injuries, or certain disease processes

An after-cataract is a cataract that develops in a lens tissue that remains after most of the lens has already been removed

66820	Discission of secondary membranous cataract (opacified posterior lens capsule and/or anterior hyaloid); stab incision technique (Ziegler or Wheeler knife)	G2 T 50
	10.37 10.37 Global Days 090	
66821	laser surgery (eg, YAG laser) (1 or more stages)	A2 T 50
	8.24 8.68 Global Days 090	
66825	Repositioning of intraocular lens prosthesis, requiring an incision (separate procedure)	A2 T 80 50
	20.17 20.17 Global Days 090	

66830-66940 Cataract Extraction; Without Insertion Intraocular Lens

CMS 100-3,80.10	Phacoemulsification Procedure--Cataract Extraction
CMS 100-3,80.11	Vitrectomy
CMS 100-4,12,30	Correct Coding Policy

INCLUDES
Anterior and/or posterior capsulotomy
Enzymatic zonulysis
Iridectomy/iridotomy
Lateral canthotomy
Medications
Operating microscope (69990)
Subconjunctival injection
Subtenon injection
Use of viscoelastic material

EXCLUDES *Removal of intralenticular foreign body without lens excision (65235)*
Repair of surgical laceration (66250)

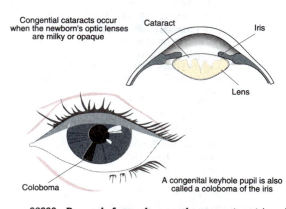

Congenital cataracts occur when the newborn's optic lenses are milky or opaque

A congenital keyhole pupil is also called a coloboma of the iris

66830	Removal of secondary membranous cataract (opacified posterior lens capsule and/or anterior hyaloid) with corneo-scleral section, with or without iridectomy (iridocapsulotomy, iridocapsulectomy)	A2 T 50
	INCLUDES Graefe's operation	
	18.87 18.87 Global Days 090	
66840	Removal of lens material; aspiration technique, 1 or more stages	A2 T 50
	INCLUDES Fukala's operation	
	19.24 19.24 Global Days 090	
	AMA: 2009, Jan, 7-8	
66850	phacofragmentation technique (mechanical or ultrasonic) (eg, phacoemulsification), with aspiration	A2 T 50
	21.48 21.48 Global Days 090	
	AMA: 2009, Jan, 7-8	
66852	pars plana approach, with or without vitrectomy	A2 T 80 50
	23.25 23.25 Global Days 090	
	AMA: 2009, Jan, 7-8	
66920	intracapsular	A2 T 80 50
	19.99 19.99 Global Days 090	
66930	intracapsular, for dislocated lens	A2 T 80 50
	22.71 22.71 Global Days 090	
66940	extracapsular (other than 66840, 66850, 66852)	A2 T 80 50
	21.41 21.41 Global Days 090	
	AMA: 2009, Jan, 7-8	

26/TC PC/TC Comp Only   A-Z ASC Pmt   50 Bilateral   ♂ Male Only   ♀ Female Only   Facility RVU   Non-Facility RVU
AMA: CPT Asst   **MED:** Pub 100   A-Y OPPSI   80/89 Surg Assist Allowed / w/Doc   Lab Crosswalk   Radiology Crosswalk

CPT only © 2009 American Medical Association. All Rights Reserved. (Black Ink)   Medicare (Red Ink)   © 2009 Publisher (Blue Ink)

Current Procedural Coding Expert – Eye and Ocular Adnexa 67030

66982-66986 Cataract Extraction: With Insertion Intraocular Lens

CMS 100-3,80.10 Phacoemulsification Procedure--Cataract Extraction
CMS 100-3,80.12 Intraocular Lenses (IOLs)
CMS 100-4,12,30 Correct Coding Policy

INCLUDES
Anterior or posterior capsulotomy
Enzymatic zonulysis
Iridectomy/iridotomy
Lateral canthotomy
Medications
Operating microscope (69990)
Subconjunctival injection
Subtenon injection
Use of viscoelastic material

EXCLUDES Intraocular lens (99070, C1780, Q1003-Q1005, V2630-V2632, V2788)

66982 Extracapsular cataract removal with insertion of intraocular lens prosthesis (1-stage procedure), manual or mechanical technique (eg, irrigation and aspiration or phacoemulsification), complex, requiring devices or techniques not generally used in routine cataract surgery (eg, iris expansion device, suture support for intraocular lens, or primary posterior capsulorrhexis) or performed on patients in the amblyogenic developmental stage
76519
29.09   29.09   Global Days 090
AMA: 2009, Jan, 11-31; 2008, Jan, 10-25; 2007, January, 13-27

66983 Intracapsular cataract extraction with insertion of intraocular lens prosthesis (1 stage procedure)
76519
19.74   19.74   Global Days 090

66984 Extracapsular cataract removal with insertion of intraocular lens prosthesis (1 stage procedure), manual or mechanical technique (eg, irrigation and aspiration or phacoemulsification)
EXCLUDES Complex extracapsular cataract removal (66982)
76519
20.85   20.85   Global Days 090
AMA: 2005, March, 11-15

66985 Insertion of intraocular lens prosthesis (secondary implant), not associated with concurrent cataract removal
EXCLUDES Insertion of lens at the time of cataract procedure (66982-66984)
Secondary suture (66682)
Code also ophthalmic endoscope if used (66990)
76519
20.74   20.74   Global Days 090
AMA: 2005, September, 5

66986 Exchange of intraocular lens
Code also ophthalmic endoscope if used (66990)
76519
24.61   24.61   Global Days 090
AMA: 2005, September, 5

66990-66999 Ophthalmic Endoscopy

CMS 100-3,80.10 Phacoemulsification Procedure--Cataract Extraction
CMS 100-3,80.11 Vitrectomy
CMS 100-4,12,30 Correct Coding Policy

+ 66990 Use of ophthalmic endoscope (List separately in addition to code for primary procedure)
Code first (65820, 65875, 65920, 66985-66986, 67036-67043, 67112-67113)
2.48   2.48   Global Days ZZZ
AMA: 2009, Jan, 11-31; 2008, Jan, 10-25; 2008, Oct, 1-5; 2007, January, 13-27; 2005, September, 5

66999 Unlisted procedure, anterior segment of eye
0.00   0.00   Global Days YYY

67005-67015 Vitrectomy: Partial and Subtotal

CMS 100-3,80.11 Vitrectomy
CMS 100-4,12,30 Correct Coding Policy
INCLUDES Operating microscope (69990)

67005 Removal of vitreous, anterior approach (open sky technique or limbal incision); partial removal
EXCLUDES Anterior chamber vitrectomy by paracentesis (65810)
Severing of corneovitreal adhesions (65880)
12.99   12.99   Global Days 090

67010 subtotal removal with mechanical vitrectomy
EXCLUDES Anterior chamber vitrectomy by paracentesis (65810)
Severing of corneovitreal adhesions (65880)
14.64   14.64   Global Days 090

67015 Aspiration or release of vitreous, subretinal or choroidal fluid, pars plana approach (posterior sclerotomy)
15.52   15.52   Global Days 090

67025-67028 Intravitreal Injection/Implantation

CMS 100-3,80.11 Vitrectomy
CMS 100-4,12,30 Correct Coding Policy
INCLUDES Operating microscope (69990)

67025 Injection of vitreous substitute, pars plana or limbal approach (fluid-gas exchange), with or without aspiration (separate procedure)
17.24   19.36   Global Days 090

67027 Implantation of intravitreal drug delivery system (eg, ganciclovir implant), includes concomitant removal of vitreous
EXCLUDES Removal of drug delivery system (67121)
23.49   23.49   Global Days 090
AMA: 2009, Jan, 11-31; 2007, Dec, 10-179

67028 Intravitreal injection of a pharmacologic agent (separate procedure)
4.65   5.64   Global Days 000

67030-67031 Incision of Vitreous Strands/Membranes

CMS 100-4,12,30 Correct Coding Policy
INCLUDES Operating microscope (69990)

67030 Discission of vitreous strands (without removal), pars plana approach
13.83   13.83   Global Days 090

● New Code   ▲ Revised Code   M Maternity   A Age   Unlisted   Not Covered   # Resequenced
CCI   + Add-on   ⊘ Mod 51 Exempt   @ Mod 63 Exempt   ⊙ Mod Sedation   PQRI

© 2009 Publisher (*Blue Ink*)   CPT only © 2009 American Medical Association. All Rights Reserved. (Black Ink)   Medicare (Red Ink)   245

67031 Severing of vitreous strands, vitreous face adhesions, sheets, membranes or opacities, laser surgery (1 or more stages) A2 T 50
🚑 9.56 🏥 10.28 Global Days 090

67036-67043 Pars Plana Mechanical Vitrectomy

CMS Vitrectomy
CMS 100-4,12,30 Correct Coding Policy
INCLUDES Operating microscope (69990)
EXCLUDES Foreign body removal (65260, 65265)
Lens removal (66850)
Vitrectomy in retinal detachment (67108, 67113)

Code also ophthalmic endoscope if used (66990)

67036 Vitrectomy, mechanical, pars plana approach; A2 T 80 50
Code also placement of intraocular radiation source applicator (0190T)
🚑 26.14 🏥 26.14 Global Days 090
AMA: 2008, Jan, 6-7; 2008, Oct, 1-5

67039 with focal endolaser photocoagulation A2 T 80 50
🚑 34.01 🏥 34.01 Global Days 090
AMA: 2009, Jan, 11-31; 2008, Jan, 10-25; 2008, Oct, 1-5; 2007, January, 13-27; 2005, September, 5

67040 with endolaser panretinal photocoagulation A2 T 80 50
🚑 38.68 🏥 38.68 Global Days 090
AMA: 2009, Jan, 11-31; 2008, Jan, 10-25; 2008, Oct, 1-5; 2007, Jul, 12-13; 2005, September, 5

67041 with removal of preretinal cellular membrane (eg, macular pucker) G2 T 80 50
🚑 36.40 🏥 36.40 Global Days 090
AMA: 2008, Oct, 1-5

67042 with removal of internal limiting membrane of retina (eg, for repair of macular hole, diabetic macular edema), includes, if performed, intraocular tamponade (ie, air, gas or silicone oil) G2 T 80 50
🚑 41.69 🏥 41.69 Global Days 090
AMA: 2008, Oct, 1-5

67043 with removal of subretinal membrane (eg, choroidal neovascularization), includes, if performed, intraocular tamponade (ie, air, gas or silicone oil) and laser photocoagulation G2 T 80 50
🚑 44.43 🏥 44.43 Global Days 090
AMA: 2008, Oct, 1-5

67101-67115 Detached Retina Repair

CMS 100-4,12,30 Correct Coding Policy
INCLUDES Operating microscope (69990)

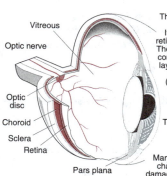

67101 Repair of retinal detachment, 1 or more sessions; cryotherapy or diathermy, with or without drainage of subretinal fluid P3 T 50
🚑 18.45 🏥 20.97 Global Days 090

67105 photocoagulation, with or without drainage of subretinal fluid P2 T 50
🚑 17.44 🏥 19.21 Global Days 090

67107 Repair of retinal detachment; scleral buckling (such as lamellar scleral dissection, imbrication or encircling procedure), with or without implant, with or without cryotherapy, photocoagulation, and drainage of subretinal fluid A2 T 80 50
INCLUDES Gonin's operation
🚑 33.57 🏥 33.57 Global Days 090

67108 with vitrectomy, any method, with or without air or gas tamponade, focal endolaser photocoagulation, cryotherapy, drainage of subretinal fluid, scleral buckling, and/or removal of lens by same technique A2 T 80 50
🚑 43.98 🏥 43.98 Global Days 090
AMA: 2009, Jan, 11-31; 2008, Jan, 10-25; 2008, Oct, 1-5; 2007, Jul, 12-13

67110 by injection of air or other gas (eg, pneumatic retinopexy) P3 T 50
🚑 20.90 🏥 23.04 Global Days 090

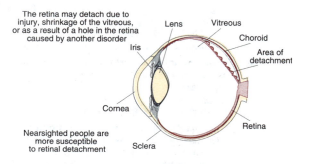

67112 by scleral buckling or vitrectomy, on patient having previous ipsilateral retinal detachment repair(s) using scleral buckling or vitrectomy techniques A2 T 80 50
EXCLUDES Aspiration or drainage of subretinal or subchoroidal fluid (67015)
Code also ophthalmic endoscope if used (66990)
🚑 36.27 🏥 36.27 Global Days 090
AMA: 2009, Jan, 7-8; 2008, Oct, 1-5

67113 Repair of complex retinal detachment (eg, proliferative vitreoretinopathy, stage C-1 or greater, diabetic traction retinal detachment, retinopathy of prematurity, retinal tear of greater than 90 degrees), with vitrectomy and membrane peeling, may include air, gas, or silicone oil tamponade, cryotherapy, endolaser photocoagulation, drainage of subretinal fluid, scleral buckling, and/or removal of lens G2 T 80 50
EXCLUDES Ophthalmic endoscope (66990)
Vitrectomy for other than retinal detachment, pars plana approach (67036-67043)
🚑 47.93 🏥 47.93 Global Days 090
AMA: 2008, Oct, 1-5

67115 Release of encircling material (posterior segment) A2 T 50
🚑 13.33 🏥 13.33 Global Days 090

Current Procedural Coding Expert – Eye and Ocular Adnexa

67120-67121 Removal of Previously Implanted Prosthetic Device

CMS 100-4,12,30   Correct Coding Policy
INCLUDES   Operating microscope (69990)
EXCLUDES   Foreign body removal (65260, 65265)
     Removal of implanted material anterior segment (65920)

- **67120** Removal of implanted material, posterior segment; extraocular
     15.30   17.56   Global Days 090
- **67121** intraocular
    EXCLUDES   Removal from anterior segment (65920)
       Removal of foreign body (65260, 65265)
     25.01   25.01   Global Days 090

67141-67145 Retinal Detachment: Preventative Procedures

CMS 100-4,12,30   Correct Coding Policy
INCLUDES   Operating microscope (69990)
     Treatment at one or more sessions that may occur at different encounters

Do not report more than one time during a defined period of treatment

- **67141** Prophylaxis of retinal detachment (eg, retinal break, lattice degeneration) without drainage, 1 or more sessions; cryotherapy, diathermy
     13.27   14.10   Global Days 090
  AMA: 2008, Oct, 1-5
- **67145** photocoagulation (laser or xenon arc)
     13.39   14.07   Global Days 090
  AMA: 2008, Oct, 1-5

67208-67218 Destruction of Retinal Lesions

CMS 100-3,140.5   Laser Procedures
CMS 100-4,12,30   Correct Coding Policy
INCLUDES   Operating microscope (69990)
     Treatment at one or more sessions that may occur at different encounters

Do not report more than one time during a defined period of treatment

- **67208** Destruction of localized lesion of retina (eg, macular edema, tumors), 1 or more sessions; cryotherapy, diathermy
     15.29   15.77   Global Days 090
  AMA: 2008, Oct, 1-5
- **67210** photocoagulation
     18.31   18.83   Global Days 090
  AMA: 2008, Oct, 1-5
- **67218** radiation by implantation of source (includes removal of source)
     37.10   37.10   Global Days 090
  AMA: 2008, Oct, 1-5

67220-67225 Destruction of Choroidal Lesions

CMS 100-3,80.2   Photodynamic Therapy
CMS 100-3,80.3   Photosensitive Drugs
CMS 100-3,140.5   Laser Procedures
CMS 100-4,12,30   Correct Coding Policy
INCLUDES   Operating microscope (69990)

- **67220** Destruction of localized lesion of choroid (eg, choroidal neovascularization); photocoagulation (eg, laser), 1 or more sessions
  INCLUDES   Treatment at one or more sessions that may occur at different encounters

  Do not report more than one time during a defined period of treatment
  EXCLUDES   Photocoagulation destruction of macular drusen (0017T)
       Transpupillary thermotherapy choroid lesion destruction (0016T)

     28.06   29.22   Global Days 090
  AMA: 2009, Jan, 11-31; 2008, Jan, 10-25; 2008, Oct, 1-5; 2007, January, 13-27
- **67221** photodynamic therapy (includes intravenous infusion)
     5.98   7.66   Global Days 000
  AMA: 2009, Jan, 11-31; 2008, Jan, 10-25; 2007, January, 13-27
- **+ 67225** photodynamic therapy, second eye, at single session (List separately in addition to code for primary eye treatment)
  Code first (67221)
     0.77   0.80   Global Days ZZZ
  AMA: 2009, Jan, 11-31; 2008, Jan, 10-25; 2007, January, 13-27

67227-67229 Destruction Retinopathy

CMS 100-4,12,30   Correct Coding Policy
INCLUDES   Operating microscope (69990)
     Treatment at one or more sessions that may occur at different encounters

Do not report more than one time during a defined period of treatment

- **67227** Destruction of extensive or progressive retinopathy (eg, diabetic retinopathy), 1 or more sessions, cryotherapy, diathermy
     15.09   16.00   Global Days 090
  AMA: 2009, Jan, 11-31; 2008, Jan, 10-25; 2008, Oct, 1-5; 2007, January, 13-27; 2006, April, 11-18
- **67228** Treatment of extensive or progressive retinopathy, 1 or more sessions; (eg, diabetic retinopathy), photocoagulation
     29.26   32.97   Global Days 090
  AMA: 2008, Oct, 1-5
- **67229** preterm infant (less than 37 weeks gestation at birth), performed from birth up to 1 year of age (eg, retinopathy of prematurity), photocoagulation or cryotherapy
     30.61   30.61   Global Days 090
  AMA: 2008, Oct, 1-5

67250-67255 Reinforcement of Posterior Sclera

CMS 100-4,12,30   Correct Coding Policy
INCLUDES Operating microscope (69990)
EXCLUDES Removal of lesion of sclera (66130)
Repair scleral staphyloma (66220, 66225)

- **67250** Scleral reinforcement (separate procedure); without graft
  - 21.11   21.11   Global Days 090
- **67255** with graft
  - 22.89   22.89   Global Days 090

67299 Unlisted Posterior Segment Procedure

- **67299** Unlisted procedure, posterior segment
  - 0.00   0.00   Global Days YYY
  - AMA: 2009, Jan, 11-31; 2007, Dec, 10-179

67311-67334 Strabismus Procedures on Extraocular Muscles

CMS 100-4,12,30   Correct Coding Policy
INCLUDES Operating microscope (69990)
Code also adjustable sutures (67335)

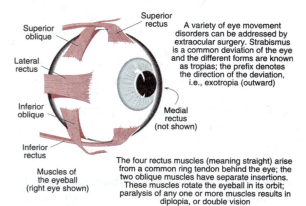

A variety of eye movement disorders can be addressed by extraocular surgery. Strabismus is a common deviation of the eye and the different forms are known as tropias; the prefix denotes the direction of the deviation, i.e., exotropia (outward)

The four rectus muscles (meaning straight) arise from a common ring tendon behind the eye; the two oblique muscles have separate insertions. These muscles rotate the eyeball in its orbit; paralysis of any one or more muscles results in diplopia, or double vision

Muscles of the eyeball (right eye shown)

- **67311** Strabismus surgery, recession or resection procedure; 1 horizontal muscle
  - 16.31   16.31   Global Days 090
  - AMA: 2009, Jan, 11-31; 2008, Jan, 10-25; 2007, January, 13-27
- **67312** 2 horizontal muscles
  - 19.75   19.75   Global Days 090
  - AMA: 2009, Jan, 11-31; 2008, Jan, 10-25; 2007, January, 13-27
- **67314** 1 vertical muscle (excluding superior oblique)
  - 18.36   18.36   Global Days 090
- **67316** 2 or more vertical muscles (excluding superior oblique)
  - 22.17   22.17   Global Days 090
- **67318** Strabismus surgery, any procedure, superior oblique muscle
  - 18.61   18.61   Global Days 090
- + **67320** Transposition procedure (eg, for paretic extraocular muscle), any extraocular muscle (specify) (List separately in addition to code for primary procedure)
  - Code first (67311-67318)
  - 8.84   8.84   Global Days ZZZ
- + **67331** Strabismus surgery on patient with previous eye surgery or injury that did not involve the extraocular muscles (List separately in addition to code for primary procedure)
  - Code first (67311-67318)
  - 8.74   8.74   Global Days ZZZ
- + **67332** Strabismus surgery on patient with scarring of extraocular muscles (eg, prior ocular injury, strabismus or retinal detachment surgery) or restrictive myopathy (eg, dysthyroid ophthalmopathy) (List separately in addition to code for primary procedure)
  - Code first (67311-67318)
  - 9.50   9.50   Global Days ZZZ
- + **67334** Strabismus surgery by posterior fixation suture technique, with or without muscle recession (List separately in addition to code for primary procedure)
  - Code first (67311-67318)
  - 8.28   8.28   Global Days ZZZ

67335-67399 Other Procedures of Extraocular Muscles

CMS 100-4,12,30   Correct Coding Policy
INCLUDES Operating microscope (69990)

- + **67335** Placement of adjustable suture(s) during strabismus surgery, including postoperative adjustment(s) of suture(s) (List separately in addition to code for specific strabismus surgery)
  - Code first (67311-67334)
  - 4.24   4.24   Global Days ZZZ
- + **67340** Strabismus surgery involving exploration and/or repair of detached extraocular muscle(s) (List separately in addition to code for primary procedure)
  - **INCLUDES** Hummelsheim operation
  - Code first (67311-67334)
  - 9.84   9.84   Global Days ZZZ
- **67343** Release of extensive scar tissue without detaching extraocular muscle (separate procedure)
  - Code also 67311-67340 if these procedures are performed on other than the affected muscle
  - 17.94   17.94   Global Days 090
- **67345** Chemodenervation of extraocular muscle
  - **EXCLUDES** Nerve destruction for blepharospasm and other neurological disorders (64612-64613)
  - 5.98   6.50   Global Days 010
- **67346** Biopsy of extraocular muscle
  - **EXCLUDES** Repair laceration extraocular muscle, tendon, or Tenon's capsule (65290)
  - 5.66   5.66   Global Days 000
- **67399** Unlisted procedure, ocular muscle
  - 0.00   0.00   Global Days YYY

67400-67415 Frontal Orbitotomy

CMS 100-4,12,30   Correct Coding Policy
INCLUDES Operating microscope (69990)

- **67400** Orbitotomy without bone flap (frontal or transconjunctival approach); for exploration, with or without biopsy
  - 25.19   25.19   Global Days 090
- **67405** with drainage only
  - 20.95   20.95   Global Days 090
  - AMA: 2009, Jun, 10-11
- **67412** with removal of lesion
  - 23.00   23.00   Global Days 090

Current Procedural Coding Expert – Eye and Ocular Adnexa

67413	with removal of foreign body
	23.24 23.24 Global Days 090
67414	with removal of bone for decompression
	35.87 35.87 Global Days 090
	AMA: 2009, Jan, 11-31; 2008, Jan, 10-25; 2007, January, 13-27
67415	Fine needle aspiration of orbital contents
	EXCLUDES *Decompression optic nerve (67570)*
	Exenteration, enucleation, and repair (65101-65114)
	2.97 2.97 Global Days 000

67420-67450 Lateral Orbitotomy

CMS 100-4,12,30 Correct Coding Policy
INCLUDES Operating microscope (69990)
EXCLUDES *Eyeball removal or repair after removal (65091-65175)*
Orbital implant (67550, 67560)
Transcranial approach orbitotomy (61330-61334)

67420	Orbitotomy with bone flap or window, lateral approach (eg, Kroenlein); with removal of lesion
	44.72 44.72 Global Days 090
67430	with removal of foreign body
	32.61 32.61 Global Days 090
67440	with drainage
	32.17 32.17 Global Days 090
67445	with removal of bone for decompression
	EXCLUDES *Decompression optic nerve sheath (67570)*
	38.85 38.85 Global Days 090
67450	for exploration, with or without biopsy
	33.46 33.46 Global Days 090

67500-67515 Eye Injections

CMS 100-4,12,30 Correct Coding Policy
INCLUDES Operating microscope (69990)

67500	Retrobulbar injection; medication (separate procedure, does not include supply of medication)
	2.20 2.36 Global Days 000
67505	alcohol
	2.32 2.50 Global Days 000
67515	Injection of medication or other substance into Tenon's capsule
	EXCLUDES *Subconjunctival injection (68200)*
	2.53 2.70 Global Days 000

67550-67560 Orbital Implant

CMS 100-4,12,30 Correct Coding Policy
INCLUDES Operating microscope (69990)
EXCLUDES *Fracture repair malar area, orbit (21355-21408)*
Ocular implant inside muscle cone (65093-65105, 65130-65175)

67550	Orbital implant (implant outside muscle cone); insertion
	26.29 26.29 Global Days 090
67560	removal or revision
	26.31 26.31 Global Days 090

67570-67599 Other and Unlisted Orbital Procedures

CMS 100-4,12,30 Correct Coding Policy
INCLUDES Operating microscope (69990)

67570	Optic nerve decompression (eg, incision or fenestration of optic nerve sheath)
	32.84 32.84 Global Days 090

67599	Unlisted procedure, orbit
	0.00 0.00 Global Days YYY

67700-67715 Incisional Procedures of Eyelids

CMS 100-4,12,30 Correct Coding Policy
INCLUDES Operating microscope (69990)

67700	Blepharotomy, drainage of abscess, eyelid
	3.10 6.53 Global Days 010
67710	Severing of tarsorrhaphy
	2.61 5.47 Global Days 010
67715	Canthotomy (separate procedure)
	EXCLUDES *Canthoplasty (67950)*
	Symblepharon division (68340)
	2.95 5.84 Global Days 010

67800-67808 Excision of Chalazion (Meibomian Cyst)

CMS 100-4,12,30 Correct Coding Policy
INCLUDES Lesion removal deeper than skin
Operating microscope (69990)
EXCLUDES *Blepharoplasty, graft, or reconstructive procedures (67930-67975)*
Lesion excision of skin (11310-11313, 11440-11446, 11640-11646, 17000-17004)

67800	Excision of chalazion; single
	2.85 3.38 Global Days 010
	AMA: 2009, Jan, 11-31; 2008, Jan, 10-25; 2007, January, 13-27
67801	multiple, same lid
	3.75 4.40 Global Days 010
67805	multiple, different lids
	4.59 5.44 Global Days 010
	AMA: 2009, Jan, 11-31; 2008, Jan, 10-25; 2007, January, 13-27
67808	under general anesthesia and/or requiring hospitalization, single or multiple
	10.07 10.07 Global Days 090

67810-67875 Other Eyelid Procedures

CMS 100-4,12,30 Correct Coding Policy
INCLUDES Operating microscope (69990)

67810	Biopsy of eyelid
	2.51 5.40 Global Days 000
	AMA: 2009, Jan, 11-31; 2008, Jan, 10-25; 2007, January, 13-27
67820	Correction of trichiasis; epilation, by forceps only
	1.46 1.38 Global Days 000
	AMA: 2009, Jan, 11-31; 2008, Jan, 10-25; 2007, January, 13-27
67825	epilation by other than forceps (eg, by electrosurgery, cryotherapy, laser surgery)
	3.28 3.43 Global Days 010
	AMA: 2009, Jan, 11-31; 2008, Jan, 10-25; 2007, January, 13-27
67830	incision of lid margin
	3.78 6.68 Global Days 010
67835	incision of lid margin, with free mucous membrane graft
	12.10 12.10 Global Days 090
67840	Excision of lesion of eyelid (except chalazion) without closure or with simple direct closure
	EXCLUDES *Eyelid removal and reconstruction (67961, 67966)*
	4.32 6.97 Global Days 010

67850	Destruction of lesion of lid margin (up to 1 cm) P3 T 50
	EXCLUDES Mohs micro procedures (17311-17315)
	Topical chemotherapy (99201-99215)
	3.65 5.47 Global Days 010
67875	Temporary closure of eyelids by suture (eg, Frost suture) G2 T 50
	2.70 4.38 Global Days 000

67880-67882 Suturing of the Eyelids

CMS 100-4,12,30 — Correct Coding Policy
INCLUDES Operating microscope (69990)
EXCLUDES Canthoplasty (67950)
Canthotomy (67715)
Severing of tarsorrhaphy (67710)

67880	Construction of intermarginal adhesions, median tarsorrhaphy, or canthorrhaphy; A2 T 50
	10.01 12.04 Global Days 090
67882	with transposition of tarsal plate A2 T 50
	12.96 15.03 Global Days 090

67900-67912 Repair of Ptosis/Retraction Eyelids, Eyebrows

CMS 100-2,16,120 — Cosmetic Procedures
CMS 100-4,12,30 — Correct Coding Policy
INCLUDES Operating microscope (69990)

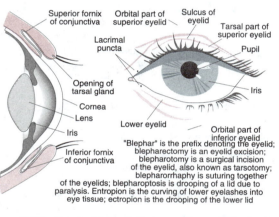

67900	Repair of brow ptosis (supraciliary, mid-forehead or coronal approach) A2 T 50
	EXCLUDES Forehead rhytidectomy (15824)
	14.00 16.98 Global Days 090
	AMA: 2009, Jan, 11-31; 2008, Jan, 10-25; 2007, January, 13-27; 2005, January, 46-47
67901	Repair of blepharoptosis; frontalis muscle technique with suture or other material (eg, banked fascia) A2 T 50
	15.89 19.91 Global Days 090
67902	frontalis muscle technique with autologous fascial sling (includes obtaining fascia) A2 T 50
	20.02 20.02 Global Days 090
67903	(tarso) levator resection or advancement, internal approach A2 T 50
	13.39 15.87 Global Days 090
67904	(tarso) levator resection or advancement, external approach A2 T 50
	INCLUDES Everbusch's operation
	16.48 19.53 Global Days 090
67906	superior rectus technique with fascial sling (includes obtaining fascia) A2 50
	13.50 13.50 Global Days 090
67908	conjunctivo-tarso-Muller's muscle-levator resection (eg, Fasanella-Servat type) A2 T 50
	11.62 13.18 Global Days 090
67909	Reduction of overcorrection of ptosis A2 T 50
	12.01 14.21 Global Days 090
67911	Correction of lid retraction A2 T 50
	EXCLUDES Graft harvest (20920, 20922, 20926)
	Mucous membrane graft repair of trichiasis (67835)
	15.50 15.50 Global Days 090
67912	Correction of lagophthalmos, with implantation of upper eyelid lid load (eg, gold weight) A2 T 50
	13.30 22.29 Global Days 090
	AMA: 2009, Jan, 11-31; 2008, Jan, 10-25; 2007, January, 13-27

67914-67924 Repair Ectropion/Entropion

CMS 100-4,12,30 — Correct Coding Policy
INCLUDES Operating microscope (69990)
EXCLUDES Cicatricial ectropion or entropion with scar excision or graft (67961-67966)

67914	Repair of ectropion; suture A2 T 50
	7.89 10.14 Global Days 090
67915	thermocauterization P3 50
	6.83 8.90 Global Days 090
67916	excision tarsal wedge A2 T 50
	11.76 14.17 Global Days 090
	AMA: 2009, Jan, 11-31; 2008, Jan, 10-25; 2007, January, 13-27; 2005, February, 13-16
67917	extensive (eg, tarsal strip operations) A2 T 50
	EXCLUDES Repair of everted punctum (68705)
	13.04 15.55 Global Days 090
	AMA: 2009, Jan, 11-31; 2008, Jan, 10-25; 2007, January, 13-27; 2005, January, 46-47
67921	Repair of entropion; suture A2 T 50
	7.45 9.69 Global Days 090
67922	thermocauterization P3 50
	6.59 8.62 Global Days 090
67923	excision tarsal wedge A2 T 50
	12.80 15.10 Global Days 090
67924	extensive (eg, tarsal strip or capsulopalpebral fascia repairs operation) A2 T 50
	12.35 15.45 Global Days 090

Current Procedural Coding Expert – Eye and Ocular Adnexa   68330

67930-67935 Repair Eyelid Wound
CMS 100-4,12,30   Correct Coding Policy
INCLUDES Operating microscope (69990)
EXCLUDES
Blepharoplasty for entropion or ectropion (67916-67917, 67923-67924)
Correction of lid retraction and blepharoptosis (67901-67911)
Free graft (15120-15121, 15260-15261)
Graft preparation (15004)
Plastic repair of lacrimal canaliculi (68700)
Procedures more extensive than skin repair (12011-12018, 12051-12057, 13150-13153)
Removal of eyelid lesion (67800-67810, 67840-67850)
Repair involving skin and subcutaneous tissue (12011, 12051-12057, 13150-13153)
Repair of blepharochalasis (15820-15823)
Skin adjacent tissue transfer (14060-14061)
Tarsorrhaphy, canthorrhaphy (67880, 67882)

67930 Suture of recent wound, eyelid, involving lid margin, tarsus, and/or palpebral conjunctiva direct closure; partial thickness
6.81   9.63 Global Days 010

67935 full thickness
12.37   15.81 Global Days 090

67938-67999 Eyelid Reconstruction/Repair/Removal Deep Foreign Body
CMS 100-4,12,30   Correct Coding Policy
INCLUDES Operating microscope (69990)
EXCLUDES
Blepharoplasty for entropion or ectropion (67916-67917, 67923-67924)
Correction of lid retraction and blepharoptosis (67901-67911)
Free graft (15120-15121, 15260-15261)
Graft preparation (15004)
Plastic repair of lacrimal canaliculi (68700)
Procedures more extensive than skin repair (12011-12018, 12051-12053, 13150-13153)
Removal of eyelid lesion (67800-67810, 67840-67850)
Repair of blepharochalasis (15820-15823)
Skin adjacent tissue transfer (14060-14061)
Tarsorrhaphy, canthoplasty (67880, 67882)

67938 Removal of embedded foreign body, eyelid
3.10   5.99 Global Days 010

67950 Canthoplasty (reconstruction of canthus)
12.69   15.16 Global Days 090

67961 Excision and repair of eyelid, involving lid margin, tarsus, conjunctiva, canthus, or full thickness, may include preparation for skin graft or pedicle flap with adjacent tissue transfer or rearrangement; up to 1/4 of lid margin
12.48   15.20 Global Days 090

67966 over 1/4 of lid margin
EXCLUDES
Canthoplasty (67950)
Delay flap (15630)
Flap attachment (15650)
Free skin grafts (15120-15121, 15260-15261)
Tubed pedicle flap preparation (15576)
18.21   20.72 Global Days 090

67971 Reconstruction of eyelid, full thickness by transfer of tarsoconjunctival flap from opposing eyelid; up to 2/3 of eyelid, 1 stage or first stage
INCLUDES Dupuy-Dutemp reconstruction
Landboldt's operation
20.15   20.15 Global Days 090

67973 total eyelid, lower, 1 stage or first stage
INCLUDES Landboldt's operation
26.05   26.05 Global Days 090

67974 total eyelid, upper, 1 stage or first stage
INCLUDES Landboldt's operation
26.00   26.00 Global Days 090

67975 second stage
INCLUDES Landboldt's operation
19.03   19.03 Global Days 090

67999 Unlisted procedure, eyelids
0.00   0.00 Global Days YYY
AMA: 2009, Jan, 11-31; 2008, Jan, 10-25; 2007, January, 13-27; 2005, January, 46-47

68020-68200 Conjunctival Biopsy/Injection/Treatment of Lesions
CMS 100-4,12,30   Correct Coding Policy
INCLUDES Operating microscope (69990)

68020 Incision of conjunctiva, drainage of cyst
2.97   3.17 Global Days 010

68040 Expression of conjunctival follicles (eg, for trachoma)
1.51   1.78 Global Days 000

68100 Biopsy of conjunctiva
2.68   4.29 Global Days 000

68110 Excision of lesion, conjunctiva; up to 1 cm
4.05   5.79 Global Days 010

68115 over 1 cm
4.96   7.84 Global Days 010

68130 with adjacent sclera
10.81   13.67 Global Days 090

68135 Destruction of lesion, conjunctiva
4.05   4.18 Global Days 010

68200 Subconjunctival injection
EXCLUDES Retrobulbar or Tenon's capsule injection (67500-67515)
0.97   1.15 Global Days 000
AMA: 2009, Jan, 11-31; 2008, Jan, 10-25; 2007, January, 13-27

68320-68340 Conjunctivoplasty Procedures
CMS 100-4,12,30   Correct Coding Policy
EXCLUDES Laceration repair (65270-65273)

68320 Conjunctivoplasty; with conjunctival graft or extensive rearrangement
14.72   18.93 Global Days 090
AMA: 2009, Jan, 11-31; 2008, Jan, 10-25; 2007, Dec, 10-179; 2007, January, 13-27

68325 with buccal mucous membrane graft (includes obtaining graft)
18.15   18.15 Global Days 090

68326 Conjunctivoplasty, reconstruction cul-de-sac; with conjunctival graft or extensive rearrangement
17.79   17.79 Global Days 090

68328 with buccal mucous membrane graft (includes obtaining graft)
19.62   19.62 Global Days 090

68330 Repair of symblepharon; conjunctivoplasty, without graft
12.64   15.88 Global Days 090

● New Code   ▲ Revised Code   M Maternity   A Age   Unlisted   Not Covered   # Resequenced

 CCI   + Add-on   Mod 51 Exempt   Mod 63 Exempt    Mod Sedation   PQRI

© 2009 Publisher (Blue Ink)   CPT only © 2009 American Medical Association. All Rights Reserved. (Black Ink)   Medicare (Red Ink)   251

Code	Description	Facility RVU	Non-Facility RVU	Global Days
68335	with free graft conjunctiva or buccal mucous membrane (includes obtaining graft) [A2][T][50]	17.87	17.87	090
68340	division of symblepharon, with or without insertion of conformer or contact lens [A2][T][80][50]	10.93	14.22	090

68360-68399 Conjunctival Transplant and Unlisted Procedures

CMS 100-4,12,30   Correct Coding Policy
INCLUDES Operating microscope (69990)

Code	Description	Facility RVU	Non-Facility RVU	Global Days
68360	Conjunctival flap; bridge or partial (separate procedure) [A2][T][50]			
	EXCLUDES Conjunctival flap for injury (65280, 65285)			
	Conjunctival foreign body removal (65205, 65210)			
	Surgical wound (66250)	11.27	13.97	090
68362	total (such as Gunderson thin flap or purse string flap) [A2][T][50]			
	EXCLUDES Conjunctival flap for injury (65280, 65285)			
	Conjunctival foreign body removal (65205, 65210)			
	Surgical wound (66250)	18.08	18.08	090
68371	Harvesting conjunctival allograft, living donor [A2][T][50]	10.83	10.83	010
68399	Unlisted procedure, conjunctiva [T][80][50]	0.00	0.00	YYY

68400-68899 Nasolacrimal System Procedures

CMS 100-4,12,30   Correct Coding Policy
INCLUDES Operating microscope (69990)

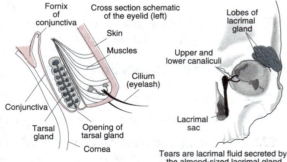

Fornix of conjunctiva; Cross section schematic of the eyelid (left); Lobes of lacrimal gland; Skin; Muscles; Upper and lower canaliculi; Cilium (eyelash); Conjunctiva; Lacrimal sac; Tarsal gland; Opening of tarsal gland; Cornea

The eyelid is a moveable fold covered by skin externally and highly vascularized conjunctiva internally. The tarsal glands secrete lubricant to the edges of the eyelid

Tears are lacrimal fluid secreted by the almond-sized lacrimal gland through ducts into the fornix of the conjunctiva; fluid is drained through the puncta and into the lacrimal sac and into the nose

Code	Description	Facility RVU	Non-Facility RVU	Global Days
68400	Incision, drainage of lacrimal gland [P2][T][50]	3.64	7.07	010
68420	Incision, drainage of lacrimal sac (dacryocystotomy or dacryocystostomy) [P3][T][50]	4.57	8.02	010
68440	Snip incision of lacrimal punctum [P3][T][50]	2.62	2.69	010
68500	Excision of lacrimal gland (dacryoadenectomy), except for tumor; total [A2][T][50]	27.27	27.27	090
68505	partial [A2][T][50]	26.79	26.79	090
68510	Biopsy of lacrimal gland [A2][T][80][50]	8.34	11.80	000
68520	Excision of lacrimal sac (dacryocystectomy) [A2][T][80][50]	18.44	18.44	090
68525	Biopsy of lacrimal sac [A2][T][50]	7.65	7.65	000
68530	Removal of foreign body or dacryolith, lacrimal passages [P2][T][50]			
	INCLUDES Meller's excision	7.21	11.05	010
68540	Excision of lacrimal gland tumor; frontal approach [A2][T][50]	25.05	25.05	090
68550	involving osteotomy [A2][T][50]	29.22	29.22	090
68700	Plastic repair of canaliculi [A2][T][50]	16.65	16.65	090
68705	Correction of everted punctum, cautery [P3][T][50]	4.57	6.15	010
68720	Dacryocystorhinostomy (fistulization of lacrimal sac to nasal cavity) [A2][T][80][50]	20.64	20.64	090
	AMA: 2009, Jan, 11-31; 2008, Jan, 10-25; 2007, January, 13-27			
68745	Conjunctivorhinostomy (fistulization of conjunctiva to nasal cavity); without tube [A2][T][80][50]	20.96	20.96	090
68750	with insertion of tube or stent [A2][T][80][50]	21.64	21.64	090
68760	Closure of the lacrimal punctum; by thermocauterization, ligation, or laser surgery [P3][T][50]	3.98	5.21	010
68761	by plug, each [P3][T][80][50]	3.18	3.82	010
	AMA: 2009, Jan, 11-31; 2008, Jan, 10-25; 2007, January, 28-31; 2007, January, 13-27			
68770	Closure of lacrimal fistula (separate procedure) [A2][T][80][50]	17.38	17.38	090
68801	Dilation of lacrimal punctum, with or without irrigation [P2][S][50]	2.84	3.23	010
68810	Probing of nasolacrimal duct, with or without irrigation; [A2][T][50]			
	EXCLUDES Ophthalmological exam under anesthesia (92018)	5.04	6.28	010
	AMA: 2008, Oct, 1-5			
68811	requiring general anesthesia [A2][T][50]			
	EXCLUDES Ophthalmological exam under anesthesia (92018)	5.61	5.61	010
	AMA: 2009, Jan, 11-31; 2008, Jan, 10-25; 2008, Oct, 1-5; 2007, January, 13-27			
68815	with insertion of tube or stent [A2][T][50]			
	EXCLUDES Ophthalmological exam under anesthesia (92018)	7.02	11.35	010
	AMA: 2009, Jan, 11-31; 2008, Jan, 10-25; 2008, Oct, 1-5; 2007, January, 13-27			

Current Procedural Coding Expert – Auditory System

68816	with transluminal balloon catheter dilation
	EXCLUDES Ophthalmological exam under anesthesia (92018)
	Do not report with (68810-68811, 68815)
	6.85 18.02 Global Days 010
	AMA: 2008, Oct, 1-5
68840	Probing of lacrimal canaliculi, with or without irrigation
	3.13 3.38 Global Days 010
68850	Injection of contrast medium for dacryocystography
	70170, 78660
	1.50 1.62 Global Days 000
	AMA: 2009, Jan, 11-31; 2008, Jan, 10-25; 2007, January, 13-27
68899	Unlisted procedure, lacrimal system
	0.00 0.00 Global Days YYY

69000-69020 Treatment Abscess/Hematoma External

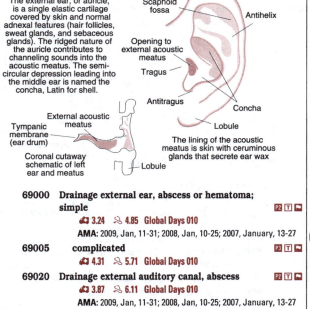

The external ear, or auricle, is a single elastic cartilage covered by skin and normal adnexal features (hair follicles, sweat glands, and sebaceous glands). The ridged nature of the auricle contributes to channeling sounds into the acoustic meatus. The semi-circular depression leading into the middle ear is named the concha, Latin for shell.

The lining of the acoustic meatus is skin with ceruminous glands that secrete ear wax.

Coronal cutaway schematic of left ear and meatus

69000	Drainage external ear, abscess or hematoma; simple
	3.24 4.85 Global Days 010
	AMA: 2009, Jan, 11-31; 2008, Jan, 10-25; 2007, January, 13-27
69005	complicated
	4.31 5.71 Global Days 010
69020	Drainage external auditory canal, abscess
	3.87 6.11 Global Days 010
	AMA: 2009, Jan, 11-31; 2008, Jan, 10-25; 2007, January, 13-27

69090 Cosmetic Ear Piercing

CMS 100-2,16,10   Exclusions from Coverage
CMS 100-2,16,120 Cosmetic Procedures

69090	Ear piercing
	0.00 0.00 Global Days XXX

69100-69222 Excisional Procedures External Ear/Auditory Canal

CMS 100-4,12,30   Correct Coding Policy
EXCLUDES Reconstruction of ear (see integumentary section codes)

69100	Biopsy external ear
	1.37 2.57 Global Days 000
69105	Biopsy external auditory canal
	1.76 3.66 Global Days 000

69110	Excision external ear; partial, simple repair
	EXCLUDES Reconstruction of ear (see integumentary section codes)
	8.69 11.89 Global Days 090
69120	complete amputation
	EXCLUDES Reconstruction of ear (see integumentary section codes)
	10.83 10.83 Global Days 090
69140	Excision exostosis(es), external auditory canal
	23.41 23.41 Global Days 090
69145	Excision soft tissue lesion, external auditory canal
	6.76 10.40 Global Days 090
69150	Radical excision external auditory canal lesion; without neck dissection
	EXCLUDES Skin graft (15004-15261) Temporal bone resection (69535)
	28.63 28.63 Global Days 090
69155	with neck dissection
	46.21 46.21 Global Days 090
69200	Removal foreign body from external auditory canal; without general anesthesia
	1.59 3.21 Global Days 000
69205	with general anesthesia
	2.75 2.75 Global Days 010
69210	Removal impacted cerumen (separate procedure), 1 or both ears
	0.93 1.38 Global Days 000
	AMA: 2009, Jan, 11-31; 2008, Jan, 10-25; 2007, January, 13-27; 2005, July, 13-16
69220	Debridement, mastoidectomy cavity, simple (eg, routine cleaning)
	1.72 3.61 Global Days 000
69222	Debridement, mastoidectomy cavity, complex (eg, with anesthesia or more than routine cleaning)
	3.71 5.77 Global Days 010

69300 Plastic Surgery for Prominent Ears

CMS 100-2,16,120 Cosmetic Procedures
CMS 100-2,16,180 Services Related to Noncovered Procedures
EXCLUDES Suture of laceration of external ear (12011-14302)

⊙ 69300	Otoplasty, protruding ear, with or without size reduction
	13.19 18.56 Global Days YYY

69310-69399 Reconstruction Auditory Canal: Postaural Approach

CMS 100-4,12,30   Correct Coding Policy
EXCLUDES Suture of laceration of external ear (12011-14302)

69310	Reconstruction of external auditory canal (meatoplasty) (eg, for stenosis due to injury, infection) (separate procedure)
	29.11 29.11 Global Days 090
69320	Reconstruction external auditory canal for congenital atresia, single stage
	EXCLUDES Other reconstruction surgery with graft (13150-15760, 21230-21235) Tympanoplasty (69631, 69641)
	41.47 41.47 Global Days 090
69399	Unlisted procedure, external ear
	0.00 0.00 Global Days YYY

● New Code   ▲ Revised Code   Ⓜ Maternity   Ⓐ Age   Unlisted   Not Covered   # Resequenced
CCI   + Add-on   ⊘ Mod 51 Exempt   Mod 63 Exempt   ⊙ Mod Sedation   PQRI
© 2009 Publisher (Blue Ink)   CPT only © 2009 American Medical Association. All Rights Reserved. (Black Ink)   Medicare (Red Ink)   253

69400-69405 Treatment of Eustachian Tube Obstruction

CMS 100-4,12,30   Correct Coding Policy

69400 Eustachian tube inflation, transnasal; with catheterization
   1.72   3.85   Global Days 000

69401 without catheterization
   1.35   2.28   Global Days 000

69405 Eustachian tube catheterization, transtympanic
   5.33   7.04   Global Days 010

69420-69450 Ear Drum Procedures

CMS 100-4,12,30   Correct Coding Policy

69420 Myringotomy including aspiration and/or eustachian tube inflation
   3.29   5.05   Global Days 010

69421 Myringotomy including aspiration and/or eustachian tube inflation requiring general anesthesia
   4.07   4.07   Global Days 010

69424 Ventilating tube removal requiring general anesthesia
   Do not report with (69205, 69210, 69420-69421, 69433-69676, 69710-69745, 69801-69930)
   1.72   3.37   Global Days 000
   AMA: 2009, Jan, 11-31; 2008, Jan, 10-25; 2007, January, 13-27; 2005, March, 16-17

69433 Tympanostomy (requiring insertion of ventilating tube), local or topical anesthesia
   3.55   5.28   Global Days 010

69436 Tympanostomy (requiring insertion of ventilating tube), general anesthesia
   4.41   4.41   Global Days 010
   AMA: 2009, Mar, 10-11; 2008, Sep, 10-11

69440 Middle ear exploration through postauricular or ear canal incision
   EXCLUDES Atticotomy (69601-69605)
   18.73   18.73   Global Days 090
   AMA: 2008, Sep, 10-11

69450 Tympanolysis, transcanal
   14.72   14.72   Global Days 090
   AMA: 2008, Sep, 10-11

69501-69535 Transmastoid Excision

CMS 100-4,12,30   Correct Coding Policy
EXCLUDES Mastoidectomy cavity debridement (69220, 69222)
Skin graft (15004-15770)

69501 Transmastoid antrotomy (simple mastoidectomy)
   20.10   20.10   Global Days 090

69502 Mastoidectomy; complete
   26.64   26.64   Global Days 090

69505 modified radical
   32.57   32.57   Global Days 090

69511 radical
   EXCLUDES Debridement of mastoid cavity (69220, 69222)
   Skin graft (15004-15431)
   33.42   33.42   Global Days 090

69530 Petrous apicectomy including radical mastoidectomy
   45.24   45.24   Global Days 090

69535 Resection temporal bone, external approach
   EXCLUDES Middle fossa approach (69950-69970)
   73.82   73.82   Global Days 090

69540-69554 Polyp and Glomus Tumor Removal

CMS 100-4,12,30   Correct Coding Policy

69540 Excision aural polyp
   3.42   5.45   Global Days 010

69550 Excision aural glomus tumor; transcanal
   28.14   28.14   Global Days 090

69552 transmastoid
   43.06   43.06   Global Days 090

69554 extended (extratemporal)
   67.77   67.77   Global Days 090

69601-69605 Revised Mastoidectomy

CMS 100-4,12,30   Correct Coding Policy
EXCLUDES Skin graft (15120-15121, 15260-15261)

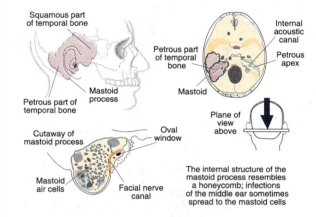

69601 Revision mastoidectomy; resulting in complete mastoidectomy
   28.80   28.80   Global Days 090

69602 resulting in modified radical mastoidectomy
   29.91   29.91   Global Days 090

69603 resulting in radical mastoidectomy
   34.21   34.21   Global Days 090

69604 resulting in tympanoplasty
   EXCLUDES Secondary tympanoplasty following mastoidectomy (69631-69632)
   30.60   30.60   Global Days 090

69605 with apicectomy
   EXCLUDES Skin graft (15120-15121, 15260-15261)
   42.59   42.59   Global Days 090

69610-69646 Eardrum Repair with/without Other Procedures

CMS 100-4,12,30   Correct Coding Policy

69610 Tympanic membrane repair, with or without site preparation of perforation for closure, with or without patch
   8.15   10.47   Global Days 010
   AMA: 2009, Jan, 11-31; 2008, Jan, 10-25; 2007, January, 13-27

Current Procedural Coding Expert – Auditory System

69620 Myringoplasty (surgery confined to drumhead and donor area) [A2] [T] [50]
13.34 18.41 Global Days 090
AMA: 2009, Jan, 11-31; 2008, Jan, 10-25; 2007, January, 13-27

69631 Tympanoplasty without mastoidectomy (including canalplasty, atticotomy and/or middle ear surgery), initial or revision; without ossicular chain reconstruction [A2] [T] [50]
24.06 24.06 Global Days 090
AMA: 2009, Jan, 11-31; 2008, Jan, 10-25; 2007, March, 9-11; 2007, January, 13-27

69632 with ossicular chain reconstruction (eg, postfenestration) [A2] [T] [50]
29.47 29.47 Global Days 090

69633 with ossicular chain reconstruction and synthetic prosthesis (eg, partial ossicular replacement prosthesis [PORP], total ossicular replacement prosthesis [TORP]) [A2] [T] [50]
28.46 28.46 Global Days 090

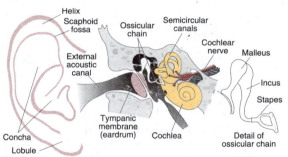

The tympanic membrane is a thin, sensitive tissue and is the gateway to the middle ear; the membrane vibrates in response to sound waves and the movement is transmitted via the ossicular chain to the internal ear. Many surgeries to the middle ear involve repair to the tympanic membrane and reconstruction to the various components of the ossicular chain.

69635 Tympanoplasty with antrotomy or mastoidotomy (including canalplasty, atticotomy, middle ear surgery, and/or tympanic membrane repair); without ossicular chain reconstruction [A2] [T] [50]
32.90 32.90 Global Days 090

69636 with ossicular chain reconstruction [A2] [T] [80] [50]
37.44 37.44 Global Days 090

69637 with ossicular chain reconstruction and synthetic prosthesis (eg, partial ossicular replacement prosthesis [PORP], total ossicular replacement prosthesis [TORP]) [A2] [T] [80] [50]
37.31 37.31 Global Days 090

69641 Tympanoplasty with mastoidectomy (including canalplasty, middle ear surgery, tympanic membrane repair); without ossicular chain reconstruction [A2] [T] [50]
28.54 28.54 Global Days 090

69642 with ossicular chain reconstruction [A2] [T] [50]
36.77 36.77 Global Days 090

69643 with intact or reconstructed wall, without ossicular chain reconstruction [A2] [T] [50]
33.61 33.61 Global Days 090

69644 with intact or reconstructed canal wall, with ossicular chain reconstruction [A2] [T] [50]
40.24 40.24 Global Days 090

69645 radical or complete, without ossicular chain reconstruction [A2] [T] [50]
39.43 39.43 Global Days 090

69646 radical or complete, with ossicular chain reconstruction [A2] [T] [80] [50]
42.06 42.06 Global Days 090

69650-69662 Stapes Procedures

CMS 100-4,12,30 Correct Coding Policy

69650 Stapes mobilization [A2] [T] [50]
22.02 22.02 Global Days 090

69660 Stapedectomy or stapedotomy with reestablishment of ossicular continuity, with or without use of foreign material; [A2] [T] [50]
25.50 25.50 Global Days 090

69661 with footplate drill out [A2] [T] [80] [50]
33.23 33.23 Global Days 090

69662 Revision of stapedectomy or stapedotomy [A2] [T] [50]
31.94 31.94 Global Days 090

69666-69700 Other Inner Ear Procedures

CMS 100-4,12,30 Correct Coding Policy

69666 Repair oval window fistula [A2] [T] [80] [50]
22.10 22.10 Global Days 090

69667 Repair round window fistula [A2] [T] [80] [50]
22.11 22.11 Global Days 090

69670 Mastoid obliteration (separate procedure) [A2] [T] [80] [50]
25.90 25.90 Global Days 090

69676 Tympanic neurectomy [A2] [T] [50]
22.69 22.69 Global Days 090

69700 Closure postauricular fistula, mastoid (separate procedure) [A2] [T] [50]
18.78 18.78 Global Days 090

69710-69718 Procedures Related to Hearing Aids/Auditory Implants

CMS 100-2,16,100 Hearing Devices
CMS 100-2,16,180 Services Related to Noncovered Procedures

69710 Implantation or replacement of electromagnetic bone conduction hearing device in temporal bone [E]
INCLUDES Removal of existing device when performing replacement procedure
0.00 0.00 Global Days XXX

69711 Removal or repair of electromagnetic bone conduction hearing device in temporal bone [A2] [T] [80] [50]
23.64 23.64 Global Days 090

69714 Implantation, osseointegrated implant, temporal bone, with percutaneous attachment to external speech processor/cochlear stimulator; without mastoidectomy [H8] [T] [50]
Code also (L8690)
29.70 29.70 Global Days 090

69715 with mastoidectomy [H8] [T] [50]
Code also (L8690)
36.98 36.98 Global Days 090

69717 Replacement (including removal of existing device), osseointegrated implant, temporal bone, with percutaneous attachment to external speech processor/cochlear stimulator; without mastoidectomy [H8] [T] [50]
Code also (L8690)
31.28 31.28 Global Days 090

69718 with mastoidectomy [H8] [T] [50]
Code also (L8690)
37.37 37.37 Global Days 090

● New Code   ▲ Revised Code   M Maternity   A Age   Unlisted   Not Covered   # Resequenced
CCI   + Add-on   ⊘ Mod 51 Exempt   Mod 63 Exempt   Mod Sedation   PQRI

69720 Current Procedural Coding Expert – Operating Microscope

69720-69799 Procedures of the Facial Nerve

CMS 100-4,12,30 Correct Coding Policy
EXCLUDES *Extracranial suture of facial nerve (64864)*

   69720 Decompression facial nerve, intratemporal; lateral to geniculate ganglion
      32.24 32.24 Global Days 090

   69725 including medial to geniculate ganglion
      52.49 52.49 Global Days 090

   69740 Suture facial nerve, intratemporal, with or without graft or decompression; lateral to geniculate ganglion
      32.41 32.41 Global Days 090

   69745 including medial to geniculate ganglion
      EXCLUDES *Extracranial suture of facial nerve (64864)*
      34.41 34.41 Global Days 090

   69799 Unlisted procedure, middle ear
      0.00 0.00 Global Days YYY

69801-69915 Procedures of the Labyrinth

CMS 100-4,12,30 Correct Coding Policy

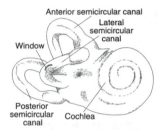

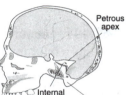

The mastoid process is a bony protrusion of the petrous part of the temporal bone. It houses a honeycomb-like sinus that resonates sounds. The petrous apex lies deep in the inner ear and is drilled and drained during an apicectomy.

   69801 Labyrinthotomy, with or without cryosurgery including other nonexcisional destructive procedures or perfusion of vestibuloactive drugs (single or multiple perfusions); transcanal
      INCLUDES Initial and subsequent infusions
      20.47 20.47 Global Days 090
      AMA: 2009, Jan, 11-31; 2008, Jan, 10-25; 2007, Dec, 7-8

   69802 with mastoidectomy
      28.68 28.68 Global Days 090

   69805 Endolymphatic sac operation; without shunt
      29.26 29.26 Global Days 090

   69806 with shunt
      26.11 26.11 Global Days 090

   69820 Fenestration semicircular canal
      INCLUDES Lempert's fenestration
      23.49 23.49 Global Days 090

   69840 Revision fenestration operation
      25.25 25.25 Global Days 090

   69905 Labyrinthectomy; transcanal
      25.15 25.15 Global Days 090

   69910 with mastoidectomy
      28.27 28.27 Global Days 090

   69915 Vestibular nerve section, translabyrinthine approach
      EXCLUDES *Transcranial approach (69950)*
      39.21 39.21 Global Days 090

69930-69949 Cochlear Implantation

CMS 100-2,16,100 Hearing Devices
CMS 100-3,50.3 Cochlear Implantation
CMS 100-4,32,100 Billing Requirements for Cochlear Implantation

   69930 Cochlear device implantation, with or without mastoidectomy
      Code also (L8614)
      34.05 34.05 Global Days 090

   69949 Unlisted procedure, inner ear
      0.00 0.00 Global Days YYY

69950-69979 Inner Ear Procedures via Craniotomy

CMS 100-4,12,30 Correct Coding Policy
EXCLUDES *External approach (69535)*

   69950 Vestibular nerve section, transcranial approach
      50.04 50.04 Global Days 090

   69955 Total facial nerve decompression and/or repair (may include graft)
      55.30 55.30 Global Days 090

   69960 Decompression internal auditory canal
      53.96 53.96 Global Days 090

   69970 Removal of tumor, temporal bone
      60.00 60.00 Global Days 090

   69979 Unlisted procedure, temporal bone, middle fossa approach
      0.00 0.00 Global Days YYY

69990 Operating Microscope

CMS 100-4,12,30 Correct Coding Policy
EXCLUDES *Magnifying loupes*

Code first primary procedure
+ 69990 Microsurgical techniques, requiring use of operating microscope (List separately in addition to code for primary procedure)

      Do not report with (0184T, 15756-15758, 15842, 19364, 19368, 20955-20962, 20969-20973, 22856-22861, 26551-26554, 26556, 31526, 31531, 31536, 31541, 31545-31546, 31561, 31571, 43116, 43496, 49906, 61548, 63075-63078, 64727, 64820-64823, 65091-68850)
      5.90 5.90 Global Days ZZZ
      AMA: 2009, Mar, 10-11; 2009, Jan, 11-31; 2008, Jan, 6-7; 2008, Jan, 10-25; 2008, Sep, 10-11; 2007, January, 13-27; 2005, August, 1-3; 2005, March, 11-15; 2005, July, 13-16

Current Procedural Coding Expert – Radiology

70010-70015 Radiography: Neurodiagnostic

CMS 100-2,6,10   Medical and Other Services Furnished to Inpatients
CMS 100-2,15,80   Physician Supervision Requirements for Diagnostic Tests
CMS 100-4,3,10.4   Payment of Nonphysician Services for Inpatients
CMS 100-4,13,100   Interpretation of Diagnostic Tests

EXCLUDES Intrathecal injection procedures (61055, 62284)

70010 Myelography, posterior fossa, radiological supervision and interpretation
3.77   3.77   Global Days XXX
AMA: 2005, March, 11-15

70015 Cisternography, positive contrast, radiological supervision and interpretation
3.84   3.84   Global Days XXX

70030-70390 Radiography: Head, Neck, Orofacial Structures

CMS 100-2,6,10   Medical and Other Services Furnished to Inpatients
CMS 100-2,15,80   Physician Supervision Requirements for Diagnostic Tests
CMS 100-4,3,10.4   Payment of Nonphysician Services for Inpatients
CMS 100-4,13,10   ICD-9-CM Coding for Diagnostic Tests
CMS 100-4,13,100   Interpretation of Diagnostic Tests

INCLUDES Minimum number of views or more views when needed to adequately complete the study
Radiographs that have to be repeated during the encounter due to substandard quality; only one unit of service is reported

EXCLUDES Obtaining more films after review of initial films, based on the discretion of the radiologist, an order for the test, and a change in the patient's condition

Do not report with a second interpretation by the requesting physician (included in E/M service)

70030 Radiologic examination, eye, for detection of foreign body
0.72   0.72   Global Days XXX

70100 Radiologic examination, mandible; partial, less than 4 views
0.81   0.81   Global Days XXX

70110 complete, minimum of 4 views
0.99   0.99   Global Days XXX

70120 Radiologic examination, mastoids; less than 3 views per side
0.95   0.95   Global Days XXX

70130 complete, minimum of 3 views per side
1.43   1.43   Global Days XXX

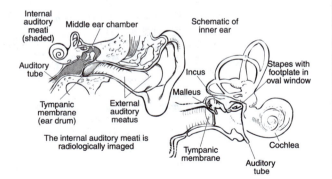

70134 Radiologic examination, internal auditory meati, complete
1.15   1.15   Global Days XXX

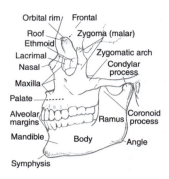

An x-ray of the facial bones is performed

70140 Radiologic examination, facial bones; less than 3 views
0.75   0.75   Global Days XXX

70150 complete, minimum of 3 views
1.07   1.07   Global Days XXX

70160 Radiologic examination, nasal bones, complete, minimum of 3 views
0.82   0.82   Global Days XXX

70170 Dacryocystography, nasolacrimal duct, radiological supervision and interpretation
EXCLUDES Procedure (68850)
0.00   0.00   Global Days XXX

70190 Radiologic examination; optic foramina
0.89   0.89   Global Days XXX

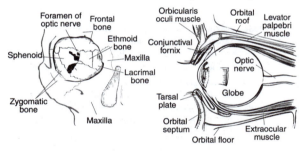

An x-ray of the orbits is performed

70200 orbits, complete, minimum of 4 views
1.09   1.09   Global Days XXX

70210 Radiologic examination, sinuses, paranasal, less than 3 views
0.78   0.78   Global Days XXX

70220 Radiologic examination, sinuses, paranasal, complete, minimum of 3 views
0.98   0.98   Global Days XXX

70240 Radiologic examination, sella turcica
0.73   0.73   Global Days XXX

70250 Radiologic examination, skull; less than 4 views
0.94   0.94   Global Days XXX

70260 complete, minimum of 4 views
1.19   1.19   Global Days XXX

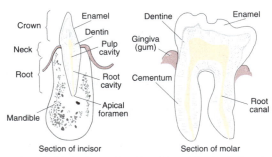

Normal adult dentition numbers 16 teeth in each jaw: four incisors, two canines, four premolars, and six molars. A common tooth eruption problem occurs with the third molars (wisdom teeth) which may be malposed and become impacted. Caries means "rotten" and is a decalcification of tooth enamel and sometimes penetration into the dentin and pulp. Disease processes may cause resorption of the dentin and cementum

70300 Radiologic examination, teeth; single view
 0.37 0.37 Global Days XXX

70310 partial examination, less than full mouth
 1.01 1.01 Global Days XXX

70320 complete, full mouth
 1.31 1.31 Global Days XXX

70328 Radiologic examination, temporomandibular joint, open and closed mouth; unilateral
 0.79 0.79 Global Days XXX

70330 bilateral
 1.21 1.21 Global Days XXX

70332 Temporomandibular joint arthrography, radiological supervision and interpretation
Do not report with fluoroscopic guidance (77002)
 2.14 2.14 Global Days XXX
AMA: 2009, Jan, 11-31; 2008, Jan, 10-25; 2008, Jun, 8-11; 2007, February, 10-11

70336 Magnetic resonance (eg, proton) imaging, temporomandibular joint(s)
 7.87 7.87 Global Days XXX
AMA: 2009, Jan, 11-31; 2008, Jan, 10-25; 2007, January, 13-27

70350 Cephalogram, orthodontic
 0.56 0.56 Global Days XXX

70355 Orthopantogram
 0.54 0.54 Global Days XXX

70360 Radiologic examination; neck, soft tissue
 0.69 0.69 Global Days XXX

70370 pharynx or larynx, including fluoroscopy and/or magnification technique
 2.10 2.10 Global Days XXX

70371 Complex dynamic pharyngeal and speech evaluation by cine or video recording
 2.34 2.34 Global Days XXX

70373 Laryngography, contrast, radiological supervision and interpretation
 2.11 2.11 Global Days XXX

70380 Radiologic examination, salivary gland for calculus
 1.02 1.02 Global Days XXX

70390 Sialography, radiological supervision and interpretation
 2.47 2.47 Global Days XXX

70450-70492 Computerized Tomography: Head, Neck, Face

CMS 100-2,6,10 — Medical and Other Services Furnished to Inpatients
CMS 100-2,15,80 — Physician Supervision Requirements for Diagnostic Tests
CMS 100-3,220.1 — Computerized Tomography
CMS 100-4,3,10.4 — Payment of Nonphysician Services for Inpatients
CMS 100-4,13,10 — ICD-9-CM Coding for Diagnostic Tests
CMS 100-4,13,100 — Interpretation of Diagnostic Tests

INCLUDES Imaging using tomographic technique enhanced by computer imaging to create a cross-sectional plane of the body

EXCLUDES 3D rendering (76376, 76377)

70450 Computed tomography, head or brain; without contrast material
 3.63 3.63 Global Days XXX
AMA: 2009, Jan, 11-31; 2008, Jan, 10-25; 2007, January, 13-27; 2005, March, 11-15

70460 with contrast material(s)
 4.82 4.82 Global Days XXX
AMA: 2009, Jan, 11-31; 2008, Jan, 10-25; 2007, January, 13-27

70470 without contrast material, followed by contrast material(s) and further sections
 5.75 5.75 Global Days XXX
AMA: 2009, Jan, 11-31; 2008, Jan, 10-25; 2007, January, 13-27

70480 Computed tomography, orbit, sella, or posterior fossa or outer, middle, or inner ear; without contrast material
 6.10 6.10 Global Days XXX
AMA: 2009, Jan, 11-31

70481 with contrast material(s)
 7.02 7.02 Global Days XXX
AMA: 2009, Jan, 11-31; 2008, Apr, -11

70482 without contrast material, followed by contrast material(s) and further sections
 7.81 7.81 Global Days XXX

70486 Computed tomography, maxillofacial area; without contrast material
 5.04 5.04 Global Days XXX
AMA: 2009, Jan, 11-31; 2008, Jan, 10-25; 2007, January, 13-27

70487 with contrast material(s)
 6.02 6.02 Global Days XXX

70488 without contrast material, followed by contrast material(s) and further sections
 7.22 7.22 Global Days XXX

70490 Computed tomography, soft tissue neck; without contrast material
EXCLUDES CT of the cervical spine (72125)
 4.97 4.97 Global Days XXX

70491 with contrast material(s)
EXCLUDES CT of the cervical spine (72126)
 5.94 5.94 Global Days XXX

70492 without contrast material followed by contrast material(s) and further sections
EXCLUDES CT of the cervical spine (72127)
 7.04 7.04 Global Days XXX

Current Procedural Coding Expert – Radiology

70496-70498 Computerized Tomographic Angiography: Head and Neck

CMS 100-2,6,10 — Medical and Other Services Furnished to Inpatients
CMS 100-2,15,80 — Physician Supervision Requirements for Diagnostic Tests
CMS 100-3,220.1 — Computerized Tomography
CMS 100-4,3,10.4 — Payment of Nonphysician Services for Inpatients
CMS 100-4,13,10 — ICD-9-CM Coding for Diagnostic Tests
CMS 100-4,13,30 — Computerized Axial Tomography (CT) Procedures
CMS 100-4,13,100 — Interpretation of Diagnostic Tests
INCLUDES Multiple rapid thin section CT scans to create cross-sectional images of bones, organs and tissues

70496 Computed tomographic angiography, head, with contrast material(s), including noncontrast images, if performed, and image postprocessing
 16.84 16.84 Global Days XXX
AMA: 2007, January, 28-31; 2005, December, 7

70498 Computed tomographic angiography, neck, with contrast material(s), including noncontrast images, if performed, and image postprocessing
 16.74 16.74 Global Days XXX
AMA: 2007, January, 28-31; 2005, December, 7

70540-70543 Magnetic Resonance Imaging: Face, Neck, Orbits

CMS 100-2,6,10 — Medical and Other Services Furnished to Inpatients
CMS 100-2,15,80 — Physician Supervision Requirements for Diagnostic Tests
CMS 100-3,220.2 — Magnetic Resonance Imaging
CMS 100-4,3,10.4 — Payment of Nonphysician Services for Inpatients
CMS 100-4,13,40 — Magnetic Resonance Imaging (MRI) Procedures
CMS 100-4,13,100 — Interpretation of Diagnostic Tests
INCLUDES Application of an external magnetic field that forces alignment of hydrogen atom nuclei in soft tissues which converts to sets of tomographic images that can be displayed as three-dimensional images
Maximum frequency with which codes may be reported for each imaging session (once)
EXCLUDES Magnetic resonance angiography head/neck (70544-70549)

70540 Magnetic resonance (eg, proton) imaging, orbit, face, and/or neck; without contrast material(s)
 8.70 8.70 Global Days XXX
AMA: 2007, March, 7-8

70542 with contrast material(s)
 9.79 9.79 Global Days XXX

70543 without contrast material(s), followed by contrast material(s) and further sequences
 12.13 12.13 Global Days XXX

70544-70549 Magnetic Resonance Angiography: Head and Neck

CMS 100-2,6,10 — Medical and Other Services Furnished to Inpatients
CMS 100-2,15,80 — Physician Supervision Requirements for Diagnostic Tests
CMS 100-3,220.3 — Magnetic Resonance Angiography
CMS 100-4,3,10.4 — Payment of Nonphysician Services for Inpatients
CMS 100-4,13,10 — ICD-9-CM Coding for Diagnostic Tests
CMS 100-4,13,40.1 — Magnetic Resonance Angiography
CMS 100-4,13,40.1.1 — Magnetic Resonance Angiography Coverage Summary
CMS 100-4,13,100 — Interpretation of Diagnostic Tests
INCLUDES Use of magnetic fields and radio waves to produce detailed cross-sectional images of internal body structures

70544 Magnetic resonance angiography, head; without contrast material(s)
 15.24 15.24 Global Days XXX
AMA: 2007, January, 28-31; 2005, December, 7

70545 with contrast material(s)
 15.09 15.09 Global Days XXX
AMA: 2007, January, 28-31; 2005, December, 7

70546 without contrast material(s), followed by contrast material(s) and further sequences
 23.13 23.13 Global Days XXX
AMA: 2007, January, 28-31; 2005, December, 7

70547 Magnetic resonance angiography, neck; without contrast material(s)
 15.20 15.20 Global Days XXX
AMA: 2007, January, 28-31; 2005, December, 7

70548 with contrast material(s)
 16.06 16.06 Global Days XXX
AMA: 2007, January, 28-31; 2005, December, 7

70549 without contrast material(s), followed by contrast material(s) and further sequences
 23.06 23.06 Global Days XXX
AMA: 2007, January, 28-31; 2005, December, 7

70551-70553 Magnetic Resonance Imaging: Brain and Brain Stem

CMS 100-2,6,10 — Medical and Other Services Furnished to Inpatients
CMS 100-2,15,80 — Physician Supervision Requirements for Diagnostic Tests
CMS 100-3,220.2 — Magnetic Resonance Imaging
CMS 100-4,3,10.4 — Payment of Nonphysician Services for Inpatients
CMS 100-4,13,10 — ICD-9-CM Coding for Diagnostic Tests
CMS 100-4,13,20.1 — Professional Component (PC)
CMS 100-4,13,40 — Magnetic Resonance Imaging (MRI) Procedures
CMS 100-4,13,100 — Interpretation of Diagnostic Tests
INCLUDES Application of an external magnetic field that forces alignment of hydrogen atom nuclei in soft tissues which converts to sets of tomographic images that can be displayed as three-dimensional images
EXCLUDES Magnetic spectroscopy (76390)

70551 Magnetic resonance (eg, proton) imaging, brain (including brain stem); without contrast material
 9.14 9.14 Global Days XXX
AMA: 2009, Jan, 11-31; 2008, Jan, 10-25; 2007, February, 6-7; 2007, January, 13-27; 2005, March, 16-17

70552 with contrast material(s)
 10.30 10.30 Global Days XXX
AMA: 2009, Jan, 11-31; 2008, Jan, 10-25; 2007, February, 6-7; 2007, January, 13-27; 2005, March, 16-17

70553 without contrast material, followed by contrast material(s) and further sequences
 12.19 12.19 Global Days XXX
AMA: 2009, Jan, 11-31; 2008, Jan, 10-25; 2007, February, 6-7; 2007, January, 13-27; 2005, March, 16-17; 2005, March, 11-15

70554-70555 Magnetic Resonance Imaging: Brain Mapping

INCLUDES Neuroimaging technique using MRI to identify and map signals related to brain activity
Do not report with the following codes unless a separate diagnostic MRI is performed (70551-70553)

70554 Magnetic resonance imaging, brain, functional MRI; including test selection and administration of repetitive body part movement and/or visual stimulation, not requiring physician or psychologist administration
INCLUDES Testing performed by a technologist, nonphysician, or nonpsychologist
Do not report with functional brain mapping (96020)
 11.22 11.22 Global Days XXX
AMA: 2009, Jan, 11-31; 2007, February, 6-7; 2007, March, 7-8

● New Code ▲ Revised Code Maternity Age Unlisted Not Covered # Resequenced
CCI + Add-on Mod 51 Exempt Mod 63 Exempt Mod Sedation PQRI
© 2009 Publisher (Blue Ink) CPT only © 2009 American Medical Association. All Rights Reserved. (Black Ink) Medicare (Red Ink) 259

70555 — CURRENT PROCEDURAL CODING EXPERT – Radiology

70555 requiring physician or psychologist administration of entire neurofunctional testing
INCLUDES Services provided by a physician or psychologist
Code also (96020)
0.00   0.00   Global Days XXX
AMA: 2007, March, 7-8; 2007, February, 6-7

70557-70559 Magnetic Resonance Imaging: Intraoperative
EXCLUDES Frequency greater than one for each code per operative session
Intracranial lesion stereotaxic biopsy with magnetic resonance guidance (61751)
Code also only if a separate report is generated (70557-70559)
Do not report with (61751, 77021, 77022)

70557 Magnetic resonance (eg, proton) imaging, brain (including brain stem and skull base), during open intracranial procedure (eg, to assess for residual tumor or residual vascular malformation); without contrast material
0.00   0.00   Global Days XXX

70558 with contrast material(s)
0.00   0.00   Global Days XXX

70559 without contrast material(s), followed by contrast material(s) and further sequences
0.00   0.00   Global Days XXX

71010-71130 Radiography: Thorax
CMS 100-2,6,10 Medical and Other Services Furnished to Inpatients
CMS 100-2,15,80 Physician Supervision Requirements for Diagnostic Tests
CMS 100-4,3,10.4 Payment of Nonphysician Services for Inpatients
CMS 100-4,13,10 ICD-9-CM Coding for Diagnostic Tests
CMS 100-4,13,100 Interpretation of Diagnostic Tests
EXCLUDES Needle placement guidance (76942, 77002)

71010 Radiologic examination, chest; single view, frontal
EXCLUDES Concurrent computer-aided detection (0174T)
Do not report with (99291-99292)
Do not report with remotely performed CAD (0175T)
0.59   0.59   Global Days XXX
AMA: 2009, Jan, 11-31; 2008, Jan, 10-25; 2007, February, 10-11; 2007, Jul, 6-10; 2007, Jul, 1-4; 2005, March, 11-15

71015 stereo, frontal
Do not report with (99291-99292)
0.77   0.77   Global Days XXX
AMA: 2007, Jul, 1-4; 2007, February, 10-11

71020 Radiologic examination, chest, 2 views, frontal and lateral;
Do not report with (99291-99292)
0.76   0.76   Global Days XXX
AMA: 2007, February, 10-11; 2007, Jul, 1-4; 2007, Jul, 6-10; 2005, March, 11-15

71021 with apical lordotic procedure
0.95   0.95   Global Days XXX

71022 with oblique projections
1.17   1.17   Global Days XXX
AMA: 2007, Jul, 6-10

71023 with fluoroscopy
1.77   1.77   Global Days XXX
AMA: 2009, Jan, 11-31; 2008, Jan, 10-25; 2008, Jun, 8-11; 2007, January, 13-27

71030 Radiologic examination, chest, complete, minimum of 4 views;
1.14   1.14   Global Days XXX
AMA: 2007, Jul, 6-10

71034 with fluoroscopy
EXCLUDES Separate fluoroscopy of chest (76000)
2.11   2.11   Global Days XXX
AMA: 2009, Jan, 11-31; 2008, Jan, 10-25; 2008, Jun, 8-11; 2007, January, 13-27

71035 Radiologic examination, chest, special views (eg, lateral decubitus, Bucky studies)
0.87   0.87   Global Days XXX

71040 Bronchography, unilateral, radiological supervision and interpretation
EXCLUDES Procedure (31656, 31715)
2.41   2.41   Global Days XXX

71060 Bronchography, bilateral, radiological supervision and interpretation
EXCLUDES Procedure (31656, 31715)
3.59   3.59   Global Days XXX

71090 Insertion pacemaker, fluoroscopy and radiography, radiological supervision and interpretation
EXCLUDES Pacemaker insertion procedure
0.00   0.00   Global Days XXX
AMA: 2009, Jan, 11-31; 2008, May, 9-11; 2008, Jan, 10-25; 2007, January, 13-27

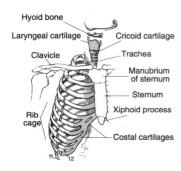

An x-ray of the ribs is performed unilaterally (71100-71101) or bilaterally (71110-71111)

71100 Radiologic examination, ribs, unilateral; 2 views
0.81   0.81   Global Days XXX

71101 including posteroanterior chest, minimum of 3 views
0.99   0.99   Global Days XXX

71110 Radiologic examination, ribs, bilateral; 3 views
1.02   1.02   Global Days XXX

71111 including posteroanterior chest, minimum of 4 views
1.33   1.33   Global Days XXX

71120 Radiologic examination; sternum, minimum of 2 views
0.78   0.78   Global Days XXX

71130 sternoclavicular joint or joints, minimum of 3 views
0.93   0.93   Global Days XXX

26/TC PC/TC Comp Only   A2-Z3 ASC Pmt   50 Bilateral   ♂ Male Only   ♀ Female Only   Facility RVU   Non-Facility RVU
AMA: CPT Asst   MED: Pub 100   A-Y OPPSI   80/80 Surg Assist Allowed / w/Doc   Lab Crosswalk   Radiology Crosswalk
260   CPT only © 2009 American Medical Association. All Rights Reserved. (Black Ink)   Medicare (Red Ink)   © 2009 Publisher (Blue Ink)

Current Procedural Coding Expert – Radiology

71250-71270 Computerized Tomography: Thorax

CMS 100-2,6,10 — Medical and Other Services Furnished to Inpatients
CMS 100-2,15,80 — Physician Supervision Requirements for Diagnostic Tests
CMS 100-3,220.1 — Computerized Tomography
CMS 100-4,3,10.4 — Payment of Nonphysician Services for Inpatients
CMS 100-4,13,10 — ICD-9-CM Coding for Diagnostic Tests
CMS 100-4,13,30 — Computerized Axial Tomography (CT) Procedures
CMS 100-4,13,100 — Interpretation of Diagnostic Tests

INCLUDES Imaging using tomographic technique enhanced by computer imaging to create a cross-sectional plane of the body

EXCLUDES 3D rendering (76376, 76377)
Cardiac computed tomography of the heart (75571-75574)

71250 Computed tomography, thorax; without contrast material
4.81   4.81 Global Days XXX
AMA: 2009, Jan, 11-31; 2008, Jan, 10-25; 2007, Jul, 12-13

71260 with contrast material(s)
5.76   5.76 Global Days XXX
AMA: 2009, Jan, 11-31; 2009, Jun, 9&11; 2008, Jan, 10-25; 2007, Jul, 12-13; 2005, March, 11-15

71270 without contrast material, followed by contrast material(s) and further sections
6.98   6.98 Global Days XXX
AMA: 2009, Jan, 11-31; 2008, Jan, 10-25; 2007, Jul, 12-13; 2007, January, 13-27

71275 Computerized Tomographic Angiography: Thorax

CMS 100-2,6,10 — Medical and Other Services Furnished to Inpatients
CMS 100-2,15,80 — Physician Supervision Requirements for Diagnostic Tests
CMS 100-3,220.1 — Computerized Tomography
CMS 100-4,3,10.4 — Payment of Nonphysician Services for Inpatients
CMS 100-4,13,10 — ICD-9-CM Coding for Diagnostic Tests
CMS 100-4,13,30 — Computerized Axial Tomography (CT) Procedures
CMS 100-4,13,100 — Interpretation of Diagnostic Tests

INCLUDES Multiple rapid thin section CT scans to create cross-sectional images of bones, organs and tissues

EXCLUDES Computed tomographic angiography of coronary arteries that includes calcification score and/or cardiac morphology (75574)

71275 Computed tomographic angiography, chest (noncoronary), with contrast material(s), including noncontrast images, if performed, and image postprocessing
12.28   12.28 Global Days XXX
AMA: 2009, Jan, 11-31; 2009, Jun, 9&11; 2008, Jan, 10-25; 2007, March, 7-8; 2007, January, 28-31; 2007, January, 13-27; 2005, June, 9-11; 2005, December, 7

71550-71552 Magnetic Resonance Imaging: Thorax

CMS 100-2,6,10 — Medical and Other Services Furnished to Inpatients
CMS 100-2,15,80 — Physician Supervision Requirements for Diagnostic Tests
CMS 100-3,220.2 — Magnetic Resonance Imaging
CMS 100-4,3,10.4 — Payment of Nonphysician Services for Inpatients
CMS 100-4,13,10 — ICD-9-CM Coding for Diagnostic Tests
CMS 100-4,13,40 — Magnetic Resonance Imaging (MRI) Procedures
CMS 100-4,13,100 — Interpretation of Diagnostic Tests

INCLUDES Application of an external magnetic field that forces alignment of hydrogen atom nuclei in soft tissues which converts to sets of tomographic images that can be displayed as three-dimensional images

EXCLUDES MRI of the breast (77058, 77059)

71550 Magnetic resonance (eg, proton) imaging, chest (eg, for evaluation of hilar and mediastinal lymphadenopathy); without contrast material(s)
9.94   9.94 Global Days XXX

71551 with contrast material(s)
11.31   11.31 Global Days XXX

71552 without contrast material(s), followed by contrast material(s) and further sequences
14.08   14.08 Global Days XXX

71555 Magnetic Resonance Angiography: Thorax

CMS 100-2,6,10 — Medical and Other Services Furnished to Inpatients
CMS 100-2,15,80 — Physician Supervision Requirements for Diagnostic Tests
CMS 100-3,220.3 — Magnetic Resonance Angiography
CMS 100-4,3,10.4 — Payment of Nonphysician Services for Inpatients
CMS 100-4,13,10 — ICD-9-CM Coding for Diagnostic Tests
CMS 100-4,13,40.1 — Magnetic Resonance Angiography
CMS 100-4,13,40.1.1 — Magnetic Resonance Angiography Coverage Summary
CMS 100-4,13,100 — Interpretation of Diagnostic Tests

71555 Magnetic resonance angiography, chest (excluding myocardium), with or without contrast material(s)
15.03   15.03 Global Days XXX
AMA: 2008, Jul, 3&14; 2007, January, 28-31; 2005, December, 7

72010-72120 Radiography: Spine

CMS 100-2,6,10 — Medical and Other Services Furnished to Inpatients
CMS 100-2,15,80 — Physician Supervision Requirements for Diagnostic Tests
CMS 100-4,3,10.4 — Payment of Nonphysician Services for Inpatients
CMS 100-4,13,10 — ICD-9-CM Coding for Diagnostic Tests
CMS 100-4,13,100 — Interpretation of Diagnostic Tests

INCLUDES Minimum number of views or more views when needed to adequately complete the study
Radiographs that have to be repeated during the encounter due to substandard quality; only one unit of service is reported

EXCLUDES Obtaining more films after review of initial films, based on the discretion of the radiologist, an order for the test, and a change in the patient's condition

Do not report with a second interpretation by the requesting physician (included in E/M service)

72010 Radiologic examination, spine, entire, survey study, anteroposterior and lateral
1.96   1.96 Global Days XXX
AMA: 2009, Jan, 11-31; 2008, Jan, 10-25; 2007, January, 28-31; 2007, January, 13-27

72020 Radiologic examination, spine, single view, specify level
0.59   0.59 Global Days XXX

72040

CURRENT PROCEDURAL CODING EXPERT – Radiology

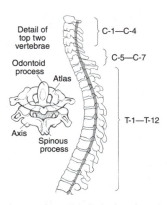

An x-ray of the cervical spine is performed

72040	Radiologic examination, spine, cervical; 2 or 3 views
	0.99 0.99 Global Days XXX
72050	minimum of 4 views
	1.31 1.31 Global Days XXX
72052	complete, including oblique and flexion and/or extension studies
	1.68 1.68 Global Days XXX
72069	Radiologic examination, spine, thoracolumbar, standing (scoliosis)
	0.96 0.96 Global Days XXX
72070	Radiologic examination, spine; thoracic, 2 views
	0.85 0.85 Global Days XXX
72072	thoracic, 3 views
	0.92 0.92 Global Days XXX
72074	thoracic, minimum of 4 views
	1.09 1.09 Global Days XXX
72080	thoracolumbar, 2 views
	0.93 0.93 Global Days XXX
72090	scoliosis study, including supine and erect studies
	1.28 1.28 Global Days XXX

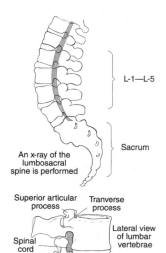

An x-ray of the lumbosacral spine is performed

72100	Radiologic examination, spine, lumbosacral; 2 or 3 views
	1.04 1.04 Global Days XXX
72110	minimum of 4 views
	1.38 1.38 Global Days XXX
72114	complete, including bending views
	1.91 1.91 Global Days XXX
72120	Radiologic examination, spine, lumbosacral, bending views only, minimum of 4 views
	1.33 1.33 Global Days XXX

72125-72133 Computerized Tomography: Spine

CMS 100-2,6,10 — Medical and Other Services Furnished to Inpatients
CMS 100-2,15,80 — Physician Supervision Requirements for Diagnostic Tests
CMS 100-3,220.1 — Computerized Tomography
CMS 100-4,13,10 — ICD-9-CM Coding for Diagnostic Tests
CMS 100-4,13,30 — Computerized Axial Tomography (CT) Procedures
CMS 100-4,13,100 — Interpretation of Diagnostic Tests

INCLUDES Imaging using tomographic technique enhanced by computer imaging to create a cross-sectional plane of the body

EXCLUDES 3D rendering (76376, 76377)

Code also intrathecal injection procedure when performed (61055, 62284)

72125	Computed tomography, cervical spine; without contrast material
	4.84 4.84 Global Days XXX
72126	with contrast material
	5.75 5.75 Global Days XXX
72127	without contrast material, followed by contrast material(s) and further sections
	6.85 6.85 Global Days XXX
72128	Computed tomography, thoracic spine; without contrast material
	4.83 4.83 Global Days XXX
72129	with contrast material
	5.76 5.76 Global Days XXX
72130	without contrast material, followed by contrast material(s) and further sections
	6.90 6.90 Global Days XXX
72131	Computed tomography, lumbar spine; without contrast material
	4.82 4.82 Global Days XXX
72132	with contrast material
	5.74 5.74 Global Days XXX
72133	without contrast material, followed by contrast material(s) and further sections
	6.86 6.86 Global Days XXX

26/TC PC/TC Comp Only   A2-Z3 ASC Pmt   50 Bilateral   ♂ Male Only   ♀ Female Only   Facility RVU   Non-Facility RVU
AMA: CPT Asst   **MED:** Pub 100   A-Y OPPSI   80/80 Surg Assist Allowed / w/Doc   Lab Crosswalk   Radiology Crosswalk

72141-72158 Magnetic Resonance Imaging: Spine

CMS 100-2,6,10 — Medical and Other Services Furnished to Inpatients
CMS 100-2,15,80 — Physician Supervision Requirements for Diagnostic Tests
CMS 100-3,220.2 — Magnetic Resonance Imaging
CMS 100-4,3,10.4 — Payment of Nonphysician Services for Inpatients
CMS 100-4,13,10 — ICD-9-CM Coding for Diagnostic Tests
CMS 100-4,13,40 — Magnetic Resonance Imaging (MRI) Procedures
CMS 100-4,13,100 — Interpretation of Diagnostic Tests

INCLUDES Application of an external magnetic field that forces alignment of hydrogen atom nuclei in soft tissues which converts to sets of tomographic images that can be displayed as three-dimensional images

Code also intrathecal injection procedure when performed (61055, 62284)

72141 Magnetic resonance (eg, proton) imaging, spinal canal and contents, cervical; without contrast material
8.27 8.27 Global Days XXX

72142 with contrast material(s)
EXCLUDES MRI of cervical spinal canal performed without contrast followed by repeating the study with contrast (72156)
10.55 10.55 Global Days XXX

72146 Magnetic resonance (eg, proton) imaging, spinal canal and contents, thoracic; without contrast material
8.28 8.28 Global Days XXX

72147 with contrast material(s)
EXCLUDES MRI of thoracic spinal canal performed without contrast followed by repeating the study with contrast (72157)
9.43 9.43 Global Days XXX
AMA: 2009, Jan, 11-31; 2008, Jan, 10-25; 2007, January, 13-27

72148 Magnetic resonance (eg, proton) imaging, spinal canal and contents, lumbar; without contrast material
8.12 8.12 Global Days XXX
AMA: 2009, Jan, 11-31; 2008, Jan, 10-25; 2007, January, 13-27; 2005, November, 14-15; 2005, March, 11-15

72149 with contrast material(s)
EXCLUDES MRI of lumbar spinal canal performed without contrast followed by repeating the study with contrast (72158)
10.25 10.25 Global Days XXX

72156 Magnetic resonance (eg, proton) imaging, spinal canal and contents, without contrast material, followed by contrast material(s) and further sequences; cervical
12.29 12.29 Global Days XXX

72157 thoracic
11.47 11.47 Global Days XXX

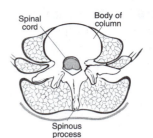

Superior view of thoracic spine and surrounding paraspinal muscles

An MRI of the lumbar spinal canal and its contents is performed without contrast material, and then with contrast. Report 72158 for the lumbar spine

72158 lumbar
11.97 11.97 Global Days XXX

72159 Magnetic Resonance Angiography: Spine

CMS 100-2,6,10 — Medical and Other Services Furnished to Inpatients
CMS 100-2,15,80 — Physician Supervision Requirements for Diagnostic Tests
CMS 100-3,220.3 — Magnetic Resonance Angiography
CMS 100-4,3,10.4 — Payment of Nonphysician Services for Inpatients
CMS 100-4,13,10 — ICD-9-CM Coding for Diagnostic Tests
CMS 100-4,13,40 — Magnetic Resonance Imaging (MRI) Procedures
CMS 100-4,13,100 — Interpretation of Diagnostic Tests

Code also intrathecal injection procedure when performed (61055, 62284)

72159 Magnetic resonance angiography, spinal canal and contents, with or without contrast material(s)
17.62 17.62 Global Days XXX
AMA: 2007, January, 28-31; 2005, December, 7

72170-72190 Radiography: Pelvis

CMS 100-2,6,10 — Medical and Other Services Furnished to Inpatients
CMS 100-2,15,80 — Physician Supervision Requirements for Diagnostic Tests
CMS 100-4,3,10.4 — Payment of Nonphysician Services for Inpatients
CMS 100-4,13,10 — ICD-9-CM Coding for Diagnostic Tests
CMS 100-4,13,100 — Interpretation of Diagnostic Tests

INCLUDES Minimum number of views or more views when needed to adequately complete the study
Radiographs that have to be repeated during the encounter due to substandard quality; only one unit of service is reported

EXCLUDES Obtaining more films after review of initial films, based on the discretion of the radiologist, an order for the test, and a change in the patient's condition
Pelvimetry (74710)

Do not report with a second interpretation by the requesting physician (included in E/M service)

72170 Radiologic examination, pelvis; 1 or 2 views
0.67 0.67 Global Days XXX
AMA: 2009, Jan, 11-31; 2008, Jan, 10-25; 2007, January, 13-27

72190 complete, minimum of 3 views
1.06 1.06 Global Days XXX

72191

72191 Computerized Tomographic Angiography: Pelvis

CMS 100-2,6,10	Medical and Other Services Furnished to Inpatients
CMS 100-2,15,80	Physician Supervision Requirements for Diagnostic Tests
CMS 100-3,220.1	Computerized Tomography
CMS 100-4,3,10.4	Payment of Nonphysician Services for Inpatients
CMS 100-4,13,10	ICD-9-CM Coding for Diagnostic Tests
CMS 100-4,13,30	Computerized Axial Tomography (CT) Procedures
CMS 100-4,13,100	Interpretation of Diagnostic Tests

INCLUDES Multiple rapid thin section CT scans to create cross-sectional images of bones, organs and tissues

EXCLUDES CTA aorto-iliofemoral runoff (75635)

72191 Computed tomographic angiography, pelvis, with contrast material(s), including noncontrast images, if performed, and image postprocessing
11.80   11.80   Global Days XXX
AMA: 2007, January, 28-31; 2005, December, 7

72192-72194 Computerized Tomography: Pelvis

CMS 100-2,6,10	Medical and Other Services Furnished to Inpatients
CMS 100-2,15,80	Physician Supervision Requirements for Diagnostic Tests
CMS 100-3,220.1	Computerized Tomography
CMS 100-4,3,10.4	Payment of Nonphysician Services for Inpatients
CMS 100-4,13,10	ICD-9-CM Coding for Diagnostic Tests
CMS 100-4,13,30	Computerized Axial Tomography (CT) Procedures
CMS 100-4,13,100	Interpretation of Diagnostic Tests

EXCLUDES 3D rendering (76376, 76377)
Computed tomographic colonography, diagnostic (74261-74262)
Computed tomographic colonography, screening (74263)

Do not report with (74261-74263)

72192 Computed tomography, pelvis; without contrast material
4.48   4.48   Global Days XXX
AMA: 2009, Jan, 11-31; 2008, Jan, 10-25; 2007, March, 9-11; 2005, March, 1-6

72193 with contrast material(s)
5.41   5.41   Global Days XXX
AMA: 2007, March, 9-11; 2005, March, 11-15; 2005, March, 1-6

72194 without contrast material, followed by contrast material(s) and further sections
6.84   6.84   Global Days XXX
AMA: 2009, Jan, 11-31; 2008, Jan, 10-25; 2007, March, 9-11; 2005, March, 1-6

72195-72197 Magnetic Resonance Imaging: Pelvis

CMS 100-2,6,10	Medical and Other Services Furnished to Inpatients
CMS 100-2,15,80	Physician Supervision Requirements for Diagnostic Tests
CMS 100-3,220.2	Magnetic Resonance Imaging
CMS 100-4,3,10.4	Payment of Nonphysician Services for Inpatients
CMS 100-4,13,10	ICD-9-CM Coding for Diagnostic Tests
CMS 100-4,13,40	Magnetic Resonance Imaging (MRI) Procedures
CMS 100-4,13,100	Interpretation of Diagnostic Tests

INCLUDES Application of an external magnetic field that forces alignment of hydrogen atom nuclei in soft tissues which converts to sets of tomographic images that can be displayed as three-dimensional images

72195 Magnetic resonance (eg, proton) imaging, pelvis; without contrast material(s)
9.08   9.08   Global Days XXX
AMA: 2009, Jan, 11-31; 2008, Jan, 10-25; 2007, January, 13-27; 2006, June, 16-17

72196 with contrast material(s)
10.15   10.15   Global Days XXX
AMA: 2009, Jan, 11-31; 2008, Jan, 10-25; 2007, January, 13-27; 2006, June, 16-17

72197 without contrast material(s), followed by contrast material(s) and further sequences
12.38   12.38   Global Days XXX

72198 Magnetic Resonance Angiography: Pelvis

CMS 100-2,6,10	Medical and Other Services Furnished to Inpatients
CMS 100-2,15,80	Physician Supervision Requirements for Diagnostic Tests
CMS 100-3,220.3	Magnetic Resonance Angiography
CMS 100-4,3,10.4	Payment of Nonphysician Services for Inpatients
CMS 100-4,13,10	ICD-9-CM Coding for Diagnostic Tests
CMS 100-4,13,40.1	Magnetic Resonance Angiography
CMS 100-4,13,40.1.1	Magnetic Resonance Angiography Coverage Summary
CMS 100-4,13,100	Interpretation of Diagnostic Tests

INCLUDES Use of magnetic fields and radio waves to produce detailed cross-sectional images of internal body structures

72198 Magnetic resonance angiography, pelvis, with or without contrast material(s)
15.04   15.04   Global Days XXX
AMA: 2007, January, 28-31; 2005, December, 7

72200-72220 Radiography: Pelvisacral

CMS 100-2,6,10	Medical and Other Services Furnished to Inpatients
CMS 100-2,15,80	Physician Supervision Requirements for Diagnostic Tests
CMS 100-4,3,10.4	Payment of Nonphysician Services for Inpatients
CMS 100-4,13,10	ICD-9-CM Coding for Diagnostic Tests
CMS 100-4,13,100	Interpretation of Diagnostic Tests

INCLUDES Minimum number of views or more views when needed to adequately complete the study
Radiographs that have to be repeated during the encounter due to substandard quality; only one unit of service is reported

EXCLUDES Obtaining more films after review of initial films, based on the discretion of the radiologist, an order for the test, and a change in the patient's condition

Do not report with second interpretation by the requesting physician (included in E/M service)

72200 Radiologic examination, sacroiliac joints; less than 3 views
0.74   0.74   Global Days XXX

72202 3 or more views
0.86   0.86   Global Days XXX

72220 Radiologic examination, sacrum and coccyx, minimum of 2 views
0.73   0.73   Global Days XXX

72240-72270 Radiography with Contrast: Spinal Cord

CMS 100-2,6,10	Medical and Other Services Furnished to Inpatients
CMS 100-2,15,80	Physician Supervision Requirements for Diagnostic Tests
CMS 100-4,3,10.4	Payment of Nonphysician Services for Inpatients
CMS 100-4,13,10	ICD-9-CM Coding for Diagnostic Tests
CMS 100-4,13,100	Interpretation of Diagnostic Tests

INCLUDES Fluoroscopic guidance for subarachnoid puncture for diagnostic radiographic myelography

Code also injection procedure (61055, 62284)
Do not report with (77003)

72240 Myelography, cervical, radiological supervision and interpretation
3.26   3.26   Global Days XXX

Current Procedural Coding Expert – Radiology

72255 Myelography, thoracic, radiological supervision and interpretation
  INCLUDES Fluoroscopic guidance for subarachnoid puncture for diagnostic radiographic myelography (77003)
  3.20 3.20 Global Days XXX

72265 Myelography, lumbosacral, radiological supervision and interpretation
  INCLUDES Fluoroscopic guidance for subarachnoid puncture for diagnostic radiographic myelography (77003)
  3.18 3.18 Global Days XXX

72270 Myelography, 2 or more regions (eg, lumbar/thoracic, cervical/thoracic, lumbar/cervical, lumbar/thoracic/cervical), radiological supervision and interpretation
  INCLUDES Fluoroscopic guidance for subarachnoid puncture for diagnostic radiographic myelography (77003)
  4.95 4.95 Global Days XXX

72275 Radiography: Epidural Space

CMS 100-2,15,80 Physician Supervision Requirements for Diagnostic Tests
CMS 100-4,3,10.4 Payment of Nonphysician Services for Inpatients
CMS 100-4,13,10 ICD-9-CM Coding for Diagnostic Tests
CMS 100-4,13,100 Interpretation of Diagnostic Tests
INCLUDES Epidurogram, documentation of images, formal written report
  Fluoroscopic guidance (77003)
Code also injection procedure as appropriate (62280-62282, 62310-62319, 64479-64484)

72275 Epidurography, radiological supervision and interpretation
  INCLUDES Fluoroscopic guidance (77003)
  3.00 3.00 Global Days XXX
  AMA: 2008, Jun, 8-11; 2008, Jul, 9

72285 Radiography: Intervertebral Disc (Cervical/Thoracic)

CMS 100-2,6,10 Medical and Other Services Furnished to Inpatients
CMS 100-2,15,80 Physician Supervision Requirements for Diagnostic Tests
CMS 100-4,3,10.4 Payment of Nonphysician Services for Inpatients
CMS 100-4,13,10 ICD-9-CM Coding for Diagnostic Tests
CMS 100-4,13,100 Interpretation of Diagnostic Tests
Code also discography injection procedure

72285 Discography, cervical or thoracic, radiological supervision and interpretation
  3.10 3.10 Global Days XXX

72291-72292 Radiography: Percutaneous Vertebral Augmentation

Code also percutaneous vertebroplasty/vertebral augmentation procedure(s) as appropriate (0200T-0201T, 22520-22525)

▲ **72291** Radiological supervision and interpretation, percutaneous vertebroplasty, vertebral augmentation, or sacral augmentation (sacroplasty), including cavity creation, per vertebral body or sacrum; under fluoroscopic guidance
  Code also procedure (0200T-0201T, 22520-22525)
  0.00 0.00 Global Days XXX
  AMA: 2007, March, 7-8

▲ **72292** under CT guidance
  Code also procedure (0200T-0201T, 22520-22525)
  0.00 0.00 Global Days XXX
  AMA: 2007, March, 7-8

72295 Radiography: Intervertebral Disc (Lumbar)

CMS 100-2,6,10 Medical and Other Services Furnished to Inpatients
CMS 100-2,15,80 Physician Supervision Requirements for Diagnostic Tests
CMS 100-4,3,10.4 Payment of Nonphysician Services for Inpatients
CMS 100-4,13,10 ICD-9-CM Coding for Diagnostic Tests
CMS 100-4,13,100 Interpretation of Diagnostic Tests
Code also discography injection procedure (62291)

72295 Discography, lumbar, radiological supervision and interpretation
  2.63 2.63 Global Days XXX
  AMA: 2009, Jan, 11-31; 2008, Jan, 10-25; 2007, January, 13-27

73000-73085 Radiography: Shoulder and Upper Arm

CMS 100-2,15,80 Physician Supervision Requirements for Diagnostic Tests
CMS 100-4,3,10.4 Payment of Nonphysician Services for Inpatients
CMS 100-4,13,10 ICD-9-CM Coding for Diagnostic Tests
CMS 100-4,13,100 Interpretation of Diagnostic Tests
INCLUDES Minimum number of views or more views when needed to adequately complete the study
  Radiographs that have to be repeated during the encounter due to substandard quality; only one unit of service is reported
EXCLUDES *Obtaining more films after review of initial films, based on the discretion of the radiologist, an order for the test, and a change in the patient's condition*
  Stress views of upper body joint(s), when performed (77071)
Do not report with a second interpretation by the requesting physician (included in E/M service)

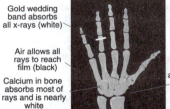
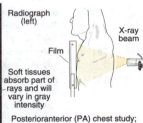

Traditional diagnostic radiography is defined by the x-ray. Radiographs, or x-rays, are "shadowgrams" of body structures and tissues and show radiopaque matter, such as bone, to be whiter and radiolucent substances, such as air, to be blacker. Each study is oriented by the direction path of the x-ray beam: e.g., PA, the most common, means the beam travels from posterior to anterior. Contrast agents are commonly used to highlight particular areas or structures

73000 Radiologic examination; clavicle, complete
  0.73 0.73 Global Days XXX

73010 scapula, complete
  0.80 0.80 Global Days XXX

73020 Radiologic examination, shoulder; 1 view
  0.61 0.61 Global Days XXX

73030 complete, minimum of 2 views
  0.78 0.78 Global Days XXX

73040 Radiologic examination, shoulder, arthrography, radiological supervision and interpretation
  Code also arthrography injection procedure (23350)
  Do not report with (77002)
  2.66 2.66 Global Days XXX
  AMA: 2009, Jan, 11-31; 2008, Jan, 10-25; 2008, Jun, 8-11; 2007, February, 10-11

73050 Radiologic examination; acromioclavicular joints, bilateral, with or without weighted distraction
  0.99 0.99 Global Days XXX

● New Code   ▲ Revised Code   Maternity   Age   Unlisted   Not Covered   # Resequenced
 CCI   + Add-on   ⊘ Mod 51 Exempt   @ Mod 63 Exempt   ⊙ Mod Sedation   PQRI

© 2009 Publisher *(Blue Ink)*   CPT only © 2009 American Medical Association. All Rights Reserved. (Black Ink)   Medicare (Red Ink)

73060 humerus, minimum of 2 views
 0.74   0.74 Global Days XXX

73070 Radiologic examination, elbow; 2 views
 0.72   0.72 Global Days XXX

73080 complete, minimum of 3 views
 0.90   0.90 Global Days XXX

73085 Radiologic examination, elbow, arthrography, radiological supervision and interpretation
Do not report with (77002)
Code also arthrography injection procedure (24220)
 2.41   2.41 Global Days XXX
AMA: 2008, Jun, 8-11; 2007, February, 10-11

73090-73140 Radiography: Forearm and Hand

CMS 100-2,15,80   Physician Supervision Requirements for Diagnostic Tests
CMS 100-4,3,10.4   Payment of Nonphysician Services for Inpatients
CMS 100-4,13,10   ICD-9-CM Coding for Diagnostic Tests
CMS 100-4,13,100   Interpretation of Diagnostic Tests

INCLUDES   Minimum number of views or more views when needed to adequately complete the study
Radiographs that have to be repeated during the encounter due to substandard quality; only one unit of service is reported

EXCLUDES   Obtaining more films after review of initial films, based on the discretion of the radiologist, an order for the test, and a change in the patient's condition

Code also stress views of upper body joint(s), when performed (77071)
Do not report with a second interpretation by the requesting physician (included in E/M service)

73090 Radiologic examination; forearm, 2 views
 0.70   0.70 Global Days XXX

73092 upper extremity, infant, minimum of 2 views
 0.76   0.76 Global Days XXX

73100 Radiologic examination, wrist; 2 views
 0.81   0.81 Global Days XXX

73110 complete, minimum of 3 views
 0.94   0.94 Global Days XXX
AMA: 2009, Jan, 11-31; 2008, Jan, 10-25; 2007, January, 13-27; 2006, December, 10-12

73115 Radiologic examination, wrist, arthrography, radiological supervision and interpretation
Code also arthrography injection procedure (25246)
Do not report with (77002)
 2.79   2.79 Global Days XXX
AMA: 2008, Jun, 8-11; 2007, February, 10-11

73120 Radiologic examination, hand; 2 views
 0.70   0.70 Global Days XXX

73130 minimum of 3 views
 0.81   0.81 Global Days XXX

73140 Radiologic examination, finger(s), minimum of 2 views
 0.83   0.83 Global Days XXX
AMA: 2007, January, 28-31

73200-73202 Computerized Tomography: Shoulder, Arm, Hand

CMS 100-2,6,10   Medical and Other Services Furnished to Inpatients
CMS 100-2,15,80   Physician Supervision Requirements for Diagnostic Tests
CMS 100-3,220.1   Computerized Tomography
CMS 100-4,3,10.4   Payment of Nonphysician Services for Inpatients
CMS 100-4,13,10   ICD-9-CM Coding for Diagnostic Tests
CMS 100-4,13,30   Computerized Axial Tomography (CT) Procedures
CMS 100-4,13,100   Interpretation of Diagnostic Tests

INCLUDES   Imaging using tomographic technique enhanced by computer imaging to create a cross-sectional plane of the body
Intravascular injection of contrast material
Intravascular, intrathecal, or intra-articular contrast materials when noted in code descriptor

EXCLUDES   3D rendering (76376-76377)

73200 Computed tomography, upper extremity; without contrast material
 4.71   4.71 Global Days XXX

73201 with contrast material(s)
 5.63   5.63 Global Days XXX

73202 without contrast material, followed by contrast material(s) and further sections
 7.10   7.10 Global Days XXX

73206 Computerized Tomographic Angiography: Shoulder, Arm, and Hand

CMS 100-2,6,10   Medical and Other Services Furnished to Inpatients
CMS 100-2,15,80   Physician Supervision Requirements for Diagnostic Tests
CMS 100-3,220.1   Computerized Tomography
CMS 100-4,3,10.4   Payment of Nonphysician Services for Inpatients
CMS 100-4,13,10   ICD-9-CM Coding for Diagnostic Tests
CMS 100-4,13,30   Computerized Axial Tomography (CT) Procedures
CMS 100-4,13,100   Interpretation of Diagnostic Tests

INCLUDES   Intravascular injection of contrast material
Intravascular, intrathecal, or intra-articular contrast materials when noted in code descriptor
Multiple rapid thin section CT scans to create cross-sectional images of bones, organs and tissues

73206 Computed tomographic angiography, upper extremity, with contrast material(s), including noncontrast images, if performed, and image postprocessing
 11.25   11.25 Global Days XXX
AMA: 2007, January, 28-31; 2005, December, 7

73218-73223 Magnetic Resonance Imaging: Shoulder, Arm, Hand

CMS 100-2,6,10   Medical and Other Services Furnished to Inpatients
CMS 100-2,15,80   Physician Supervision Requirements for Diagnostic Tests
CMS 100-3,220.2   Magnetic Resonance Imaging
CMS 100-4,3,10.4   Payment of Nonphysician Services for Inpatients
CMS 100-4,13,10   ICD-9-CM Coding for Diagnostic Tests
CMS 100-4,13,30   Computerized Axial Tomography (CT) Procedures
CMS 100-4,13,100   Interpretation of Diagnostic Tests

INCLUDES   Application of an external magnetic field that forces alignment of hydrogen atom nuclei in soft tissues which converts to sets of tomographic images that can be displayed as three-dimensional images
Intravascular injection of contrast material
Intravascular, intrathecal, or intra-articular contrast materials when noted in code descriptor

73218 Magnetic resonance (eg, proton) imaging, upper extremity, other than joint; without contrast material(s)
 8.95   8.95 Global Days XXX

 PC/TC Comp Only   ASC Pmt   50 Bilateral   ♂ Male Only   ♀ Female Only   Facility RVU   Non-Facility RVU
AMA: CPT Asst   **MED:** Pub 100   OPPSI   Surg Assist Allowed / w/Doc   Lab Crosswalk   Radiology Crosswalk

Current Procedural Coding Expert – Radiology

73219	with contrast material(s)
	10.00 10.00 Global Days XXX
73220	without contrast material(s), followed by contrast material(s) and further sequences
	12.36 12.36 Global Days XXX
73221	Magnetic resonance (eg, proton) imaging, any joint of upper extremity; without contrast material(s)
	8.57 8.57 Global Days XXX
73222	with contrast material(s)
	9.39 9.39 Global Days XXX
73223	without contrast material(s), followed by contrast material(s) and further sequences
	11.69 11.69 Global Days XXX

73225 Magnetic Resonance Angiography: Shoulder, Arm, Hand

- CMS 100-2,6,10 — Medical and Other Services Furnished to Inpatients
- CMS 100-2,15,80 — Physician Supervision Requirements for Diagnostic Tests
- CMS 100-3,220.3 — Magnetic Resonance Angiography
- CMS 100-4,3,10.4 — Payment of Nonphysician Services for Inpatients
- CMS 100-4,13,10 — ICD-9-CM Coding for Diagnostic Tests
- CMS 100-4,13,40.1 — Magnetic Resonance Angiography
- CMS 100-4,13,40.1.1 — Magnetic Resonance Angiography Coverage Summary
- CMS 100-4,13,100 — Interpretation of Diagnostic Tests

INCLUDES Intravascular injection of contrast material
Intravascular, intrathecal, or intra-articular contrast materials when noted in code descriptor
Use of magnetic fields and radio waves to produce detailed cross-sectional images of internal body structures

73225	Magnetic resonance angiography, upper extremity, with or without contrast material(s)
	17.52 17.52 Global Days XXX
	AMA: 2007, January, 28-31; 2005, December, 7

73500-73550 Radiography: Pelvic Region and Thigh

- CMS 100-2,6,10 — Medical and Other Services Furnished to Inpatients
- CMS 100-2,15,80 — Physician Supervision Requirements for Diagnostic Tests
- CMS 100-4,3,10.4 — Payment of Nonphysician Services for Inpatients
- CMS 100-4,13,10 — ICD-9-CM Coding for Diagnostic Tests
- CMS 100-4,13,100 — Interpretation of Diagnostic Tests

EXCLUDES Stress views any joint (77071)

73500	Radiologic examination, hip, unilateral; 1 view
	0.69 0.69 Global Days XXX
73510	complete, minimum of 2 views
	0.99 0.99 Global Days XXX
	AMA: 2009, Jan, 11-31; 2008, Jan, 10-25; 2007, January, 13-27
73520	Radiologic examination, hips, bilateral, minimum of 2 views of each hip, including anteroposterior view of pelvis
	1.04 1.04 Global Days XXX
	AMA: 2009, Jan, 11-31; 2008, Jan, 10-25; 2007, January, 13-27
73525	Radiologic examination, hip, arthrography, radiological supervision and interpretation
	Do not report with (77002)
	2.55 2.55 Global Days XXX
	AMA: 2008, Jun, 8-11; 2007, February, 10-11
73530	Radiologic examination, hip, during operative procedure
	0.00 0.00 Global Days XXX
73540	Radiologic examination, pelvis and hips, infant or child, minimum of 2 views
	1.12 1.12 Global Days XXX

73542	Radiological examination, sacroiliac joint arthrography, radiological supervision and interpretation
	EXCLUDES Fluoroscopic guidance for sacroiliac joint injection (77003)
	Injection procedure (27096)
	Do not report with (77002)
	2.19 2.19 Global Days XXX
	AMA: 2008, Jul, 9
73550	Radiologic examination, femur, 2 views
	0.71 0.71 Global Days XXX

73560-73660 Radiography: Lower Leg, Ankle, and Foot

- CMS 100-2,15,80 — Physician Supervision Requirements for Diagnostic Tests
- CMS 100-4,3,10.4 — Payment of Nonphysician Services for Inpatients
- CMS 100-4,13,10 — ICD-9-CM Coding for Diagnostic Tests
- CMS 100-4,13,100 — Interpretation of Diagnostic Tests

EXCLUDES Stress views, any joint (77071)

73560	Radiologic examination, knee; 1 or 2 views
	0.79 0.79 Global Days XXX
73562	3 views
	0.94 0.94 Global Days XXX
73564	complete, 4 or more views
	1.10 1.10 Global Days XXX
	AMA: 2009, Jan, 11-31; 2008, Jan, 10-25; 2007, January, 13-27
73565	both knees, standing, anteroposterior
	0.90 0.90 Global Days XXX
73580	Radiologic examination, knee, arthrography, radiological supervision and interpretation
	Do not report with (77002)
	3.47 3.47 Global Days XXX
	AMA: 2008, Jun, 8-11; 2007, February, 10-11
73590	Radiologic examination; tibia and fibula, 2 views
	0.70 0.70 Global Days XXX
73592	lower extremity, infant, minimum of 2 views
	0.80 0.80 Global Days XXX
73600	Radiologic examination, ankle; 2 views
	0.74 0.74 Global Days XXX
73610	complete, minimum of 3 views
	0.84 0.84 Global Days XXX
73615	Radiologic examination, ankle, arthrography, radiological supervision and interpretation
	Do not report with (77002)
	2.71 2.71 Global Days XXX
	AMA: 2008, Jun, 8-11; 2007, February, 10-11
73620	Radiologic examination, foot; 2 views
	0.71 0.71 Global Days XXX
73630	complete, minimum of 3 views
	0.82 0.82 Global Days XXX
73650	Radiologic examination; calcaneus, minimum of 2 views
	0.73 0.73 Global Days XXX
73660	toe(s), minimum of 2 views
	0.77 0.77 Global Days XXX

● New Code   ▲ Revised Code   Maternity   Age   Unlisted   Not Covered   # Resequenced
CCI   + Add-on   Mod 51 Exempt   Mod 63 Exempt   Mod Sedation   PQRI

© 2009 Publisher (Blue Ink)   CPT only © 2009 American Medical Association. All Rights Reserved. (Black Ink)   Medicare (Red Ink)

73700-73702 Computerized Tomography: Leg, Ankle, and Foot

CMS 100-2,6,10 — Medical and Other Services Furnished to Inpatients
CMS 100-2,15,80 — Physician Supervision Requirements for Diagnostic Tests
CMS 100-3,220.1 — Computerized Tomography
CMS 100-4,3,10.4 — Payment of Nonphysician Services for Inpatients
CMS 100-4,13,10 — ICD-9-CM Coding for Diagnostic Tests
CMS 100-4,13,100 — Interpretation of Diagnostic Tests
EXCLUDES Stress views, any joint (77071)

- **73700** Computed tomography, lower extremity; without contrast material
  4.71 4.71 Global Days XXX
  AMA: 2007, March, 9-11

- **73701** with contrast material(s)
  5.68 5.68 Global Days XXX
  AMA: 2007, March, 9-11

- **73702** without contrast material, followed by contrast material(s) and further sections
  EXCLUDES 3D rendering (76376, 76377)
  7.14 7.14 Global Days XXX
  AMA: 2007, March, 9-11

73706 Computerized Tomographic Angiography: Leg, Ankle, and Foot

CMS 100-2,6,10 — Medical and Other Services Furnished to Inpatients
CMS 100-2,15,80 — Physician Supervision Requirements for Diagnostic Tests
CMS 100-4,3,10.4 — Payment of Nonphysician Services for Inpatients
CMS 100-4,13,10 — ICD-9-CM Coding for Diagnostic Tests
CMS 100-4,13,100 — Interpretation of Diagnostic Tests
EXCLUDES Stress views, any joint (77071)

- **73706** Computed tomographic angiography, lower extremity, with contrast material(s), including noncontrast images, if performed, and image postprocessing
  EXCLUDES Computed tomographic angiography aorto-iliofemoral runoff (75635)
  12.51 12.51 Global Days XXX
  AMA: 2009, Jan, 11-31; 2007, January, 28-31; 2005, December, 7

73718-73723 Magnetic Resonance Imaging: Leg, Ankle, and Foot

CMS 100-2,6,10 — Medical and Other Services Furnished to Inpatients
CMS 100-2,15,80 — Physician Supervision Requirements for Diagnostic Tests
CMS 100-3,220.2 — Magnetic Resonance Imaging
CMS 100-4,3,10.4 — Payment of Nonphysician Services for Inpatients
CMS 100-4,13,10 — ICD-9-CM Coding for Diagnostic Tests
CMS 100-4,13,40 — Magnetic Resonance Imaging (MRI) Procedures
CMS 100-4,13,100 — Interpretation of Diagnostic Tests
EXCLUDES Stress views, any joint (77071)

- **73718** Magnetic resonance (eg, proton) imaging, lower extremity other than joint; without contrast material(s)
  8.85 8.85 Global Days XXX

- **73719** with contrast material(s)
  9.91 9.91 Global Days XXX

- **73720** without contrast material(s), followed by contrast material(s) and further sequences
  12.37 12.37 Global Days XXX

- **73721** Magnetic resonance (eg, proton) imaging, any joint of lower extremity; without contrast material
  8.76 8.76 Global Days XXX
  AMA: 2009, Jan, 11-31; 2008, Jan, 10-25; 2007, January, 13-27; 2006, June, 16-17

- **73722** with contrast material(s)
  9.57 9.57 Global Days XXX
  AMA: 2006, June, 16-17

- **73723** without contrast material(s), followed by contrast material(s) and further sequences
  11.67 11.67 Global Days XXX

73725 Magnetic Resonace Angiography: Leg, Ankle, and Foot

CMS 100-2,6,10 — Medical and Other Services Furnished to Inpatients
CMS 100-2,15,80 — Physician Supervision Requirements for Diagnostic Tests
CMS 100-3,220.3 — Magnetic Resonance Angiography
CMS 100-4,3,10.4 — Payment of Nonphysician Services for Inpatients
CMS 100-4,13,10 — ICD-9-CM Coding for Diagnostic Tests
CMS 100-4,13,40.1 — Magnetic Resonance Angiography
CMS 100-4,13,40.1.1 — Magnetic Resonance Angiography Coverage Summary
CMS 100-4,13,100 — Interpretation of Diagnostic Tests

- **73725** Magnetic resonance angiography, lower extremity, with or without contrast material(s)
  15.09 15.09 Global Days XXX
  AMA: 2007, January, 28-31; 2005, December, 7

74000-74022 Radiography: Abdomen--General

CMS 100-2,15,80 — Physician Supervision Requirements for Diagnostic Tests
CMS 100-4,3,10.4 — Payment of Nonphysician Services for Inpatients
CMS 100-4,13,10 — ICD-9-CM Coding for Diagnostic Tests
CMS 100-4,13,100 — Interpretation of Diagnostic Tests

- **74000** Radiologic examination, abdomen; single anteroposterior view
  0.61 0.61 Global Days XXX

- **74010** anteroposterior and additional oblique and cone views
  0.95 0.95 Global Days XXX
  AMA: 2007, January, 28-31

- **74020** complete, including decubitus and/or erect views
  1.00 1.00 Global Days XXX

- **74022** complete acute abdomen series, including supine, erect, and/or decubitus views, single view chest
  1.20 1.20 Global Days XXX

74150-74170 Computerized Tomography: Abdomen–General

CMS 100-2,6,10 — Medical and Other Services Furnished to Inpatients
CMS 100-2,15,80 — Physician Supervision Requirements for Diagnostic Tests
CMS 100-3,220.1 — Computerized Tomography
CMS 100-4,3,10.4 — Payment of Nonphysician Services for Inpatients
CMS 100-4,13,10 — ICD-9-CM Coding for Diagnostic Tests
CMS 100-4,13,30 — Computerized Axial Tomography (CT) Procedures
CMS 100-4,13,100 — Interpretation of Diagnostic Tests
EXCLUDES 3D rendering (76376-76377)
Computed tomographic colonography, diagnostic (74261-74262)
Computed tomographic colonography, screening (74263)

Do not report with computed tomographic colonography (74261-74263)

- **74150** Computed tomography, abdomen; without contrast material
  4.63 4.63 Global Days XXX
  AMA: 2009, Jan, 11-31; 2008, Jan, 10-25; 2007, January, 13-27; 2005, March, 1-6

- **74160** with contrast material(s)
  6.22 6.22 Global Days XXX
  AMA: 2005, March, 11-15; 2005, March, 1-6

Current Procedural Coding Expert – Radiology

74170 without contrast material, followed by contrast material(s) and further sections
8.18   8.18   Global Days XXX
AMA: 2005, March, 1-6

74175 Computerized Tomographic Angiography: Abdomen–General

CMS 100-2,6,10	Medical and Other Services Furnished to Inpatients
CMS 100-2,15,80	Physician Supervision Requirements for Diagnostic Tests
CMS 100-3,220.1	Computerized Tomography
CMS 100-4,3,10.4	Payment of Nonphysician Services for Inpatients
CMS 100-4,13,10	ICD-9-CM Coding for Diagnostic Tests
CMS 100-4,13,30	Computerized Axial Tomography (CT) Procedures
CMS 100-4,13,100	Interpretation of Diagnostic Tests

74175 Computed tomographic angiography, abdomen, with contrast material(s), including noncontrast images, if performed, and image postprocessing
EXCLUDES Computed tomographic angiography aorto-iliofemoral runoff (75635)
12.69   12.69   Global Days XXX
AMA: 2007, January, 28-31; 2005, December, 7

74181-74183 Magnetic Resonance Imaging: Abdomen–General

CMS 100-2,6,10	Medical and Other Services Furnished to Inpatients
CMS 100-2,15,80	Physician Supervision Requirements for Diagnostic Tests
CMS 100-3,220.2	Magnetic Resonance Imaging
CMS 100-4,3,10.4	Payment of Nonphysician Services for Inpatients
CMS 100-4,13,10	ICD-9-CM Coding for Diagnostic Tests
CMS 100-4,13,40	Magnetic Resonance Imaging (MRI) Procedures
CMS 100-4,13,100	Interpretation of Diagnostic Tests

74181 Magnetic resonance (eg, proton) imaging, abdomen; without contrast material(s)
8.07   8.07   Global Days XXX
AMA: 2009, May, 8-9&11; 2009, Jul, 10; 2009, Jan, 11-31; 2008, Jan, 10-25

74182 with contrast material(s)
11.06   11.06   Global Days XXX
AMA: 2009, May, 8-9&11; 2009, Jul, 10

74183 without contrast material(s), followed by with contrast material(s) and further sequences
12.42   12.42   Global Days XXX
AMA: 2009, May, 8-9&11; 2009, Jul, 10

74185 Magnetic Resonance Angiography: Abdomen–General

CMS 100-2,6,10	Medical and Other Services Furnished to Inpatients
CMS 100-2,15,80	Physician Supervision Requirements for Diagnostic Tests
CMS 100-3,220.3	Magnetic Resonance Angiography
CMS 100-4,3,10.4	Payment of Nonphysician Services for Inpatients
CMS 100-4,13,10	ICD-9-CM Coding for Diagnostic Tests
CMS 100-4,13,40.1	Magnetic Resonance Angiography
CMS 100-4,13,100	Interpretation of Diagnostic Tests

74185 Magnetic resonance angiography, abdomen, with or without contrast material(s)
14.97   14.97   Global Days XXX
AMA: 2007, January, 28-31; 2005, December, 7

74190 Peritoneography

CMS 100-2,15,80	Physician Supervision Requirements for Diagnostic Tests
CMS 100-4,3,10.4	Payment of Nonphysician Services for Inpatients
CMS 100-4,13,10	ICD-9-CM Coding for Diagnostic Tests
CMS 100-4,13,100	Interpretation of Diagnostic Tests

74190 Peritoneogram (eg, after injection of air or contrast), radiological supervision and interpretation
EXCLUDES Computed tomography, pelvis or abdomen (72192, 74150)
Code also injection procedure (49400)
0.00   0.00   Global Days XXX

74210-74235 Radiography: Throat and Esophagus

CMS 100-2,15,80	Physician Supervision Requirements for Diagnostic Tests
CMS 100-4,3,10.4	Payment of Nonphysician Services for Inpatients
CMS 100-4,13,10	ICD-9-CM Coding for Diagnostic Tests
CMS 100-4,13,100	Interpretation of Diagnostic Tests

EXCLUDES Percutaneous placement of gastrostomy tube, endoscopic (43246)
Percutaneous placement of gastrostomy tube, fluoroscopic guidance (49440)

74210 Radiologic examination; pharynx and/or cervical esophagus
1.93   1.93   Global Days XXX

74220 esophagus
2.27   2.27   Global Days XXX

74230 Swallowing function, with cineradiography/videoradiography
2.27   2.27   Global Days XXX

74235 Removal of foreign body(s), esophageal, with use of balloon catheter, radiological supervision and interpretation
Code also esophagoscopy/upper GI endoscopy (43215, 43247)
0.00   0.00   Global Days XXX

74240-74283 Radiography: Intestines

CMS 100-2,6,10	Medical and Other Services Furnished to Inpatients
CMS 100-2,15,80	Physician Supervision Requirements for Diagnostic Tests
CMS 100-4,3,10.4	Payment of Nonphysician Services for Inpatients
CMS 100-4,13,10	ICD-9-CM Coding for Diagnostic Tests
CMS 100-4,13,100	Interpretation of Diagnostic Tests

EXCLUDES Percutaneous placement of gastrostomy tube, endoscopic (43246)
Percutaneous placement of gastrostomy tube, fluoroscopic guidance (49440)

74240 Radiologic examination, gastrointestinal tract, upper; with or without delayed films, without KUB
2.77   2.77   Global Days XXX

74241 with or without delayed films, with KUB
2.99   2.99   Global Days XXX

74245 with small intestine, includes multiple serial films
4.41   4.41   Global Days XXX

74246 Radiological examination, gastrointestinal tract, upper, air contrast, with specific high density barium, effervescent agent, with or without glucagon; with or without delayed films, without KUB
INCLUDES Moynihan test
3.17   3.17   Global Days XXX

74247 with or without delayed films, with KUB
3.55   3.55   Global Days XXX

74249 with small intestine follow-through
4.77   4.77   Global Days XXX

● New Code   ▲ Revised Code   M Maternity   A Age   Unlisted   Not Covered   # Resequenced
CCI   + Add-on   ⊘ Mod 51 Exempt   ⊚ Mod 63 Exempt   ⊙ Mod Sedation   PQRI

© 2009 Publisher *(Blue Ink)*   CPT only © 2009 American Medical Association. All Rights Reserved. *(Black Ink)*   Medicare *(Red Ink)*

74250	Radiologic examination, small intestine, includes multiple serial films;	Z2 S 80 P0
	2.67 2.67 Global Days XXX	
74251	via enteroclysis tube	Z2 S 80 P0
	9.57 9.57 Global Days XXX	
74260	Duodenography, hypotonic	Z2 S 80 P0
	7.91 7.91 Global Days XXX	
● 74261	Computed tomographic (CT) colonography, diagnostic, including image postprocessing; without contrast material	Z2 Q3 80
	Do not report with (72192-72194, 74150-74170, 74263, 76376-76377)	
	16.82 16.82 Global Days XXX	
● 74262	with contrast material(s) including non-contrast images, if performed	Z2 Q3 80
	Do not report with (72192-72194, 74150-74170, 74263, 76376-76377)	
	18.83 18.83 Global Days XXX	
● 74263	Computed tomographic (CT) colonography, screening, including image postprocessing	E
	Do not report with (72192-72194, 74150-74170, 74261-74262, 76376-76377)	
	19.55 19.55 Global Days XXX	
74270	Radiologic examination, colon; contrast (eg, barium) enema, with or without KUB	Z2 S 80 P0
	3.87 3.87 Global Days XXX	
	AMA: 2009, Jan, 11-31; 2008, Jan, 10-25; 2007, January, 13-27	
74280	air contrast with specific high density barium, with or without glucagon	Z2 S 80 P0
	5.38 5.38 Global Days XXX	
74283	Therapeutic enema, contrast or air, for reduction of intussusception or other intraluminal obstruction (eg, meconium ileus)	Z2 S 80 P0
	5.21 5.21 Global Days XXX	

74290-74330 Radiography: Biliary Tract

CMS 100-2,15,80 Physician Supervision Requirements for Diagnostic Tests
CMS 100-4,3,10.4 Payment of Nonphysician Services for Inpatients
CMS 100-4,13,10 ICD-9-CM Coding for Diagnostic Tests
CMS 100-4,13,100 Interpretation of Diagnostic Tests

EXCLUDES Percutaneous placement of gastrostomy tube, endoscopic (43246)
Percutaneous placement of gastrostomy tube, fluoroscopic guidance (49440)

74290	Cholecystography, oral contrast;	Z3 S 80 P0
	1.76 1.76 Global Days XXX	
74291	additional or repeat examination or multiple day examination	Z3 S 80 P0
	1.70 1.70 Global Days XXX	
74300	Cholangiography and/or pancreatography; intraoperative, radiological supervision and interpretation	N1 N 80 P0
	0.00 0.00 Global Days XXX	
	AMA: 2009, Jan, 11-31; 2008, Jan, 10-25; 2007, January, 13-27	
+ 74301	additional set intraoperative, radiological supervision and interpretation (List separately in addition to code for primary procedure)	N1 N 80
	Code first primary procedure (74300)	
	0.00 0.00 Global Days ZZZ	
74305	through existing catheter, radiological supervision and interpretation	N1 Q2 80 P0
	EXCLUDES Percutaneous biliary duct stone extraction (47630, 74327)	
	Code also (47505, 47560-47561, 47563, 48400)	
	0.00 0.00 Global Days XXX	
74320	Cholangiography, percutaneous, transhepatic, radiological supervision and interpretation	N1 Q2 80 P0
	INCLUDES Needle placement with fluoroscopic guidance (77002)	
	2.47 2.47 Global Days XXX	
	AMA: 2008, Jun, 8-11; 2007, February, 10-11	
74327	Postoperative biliary duct calculus removal, percutaneous via T-tube tract, basket, or snare (eg, Burhenne technique), radiological supervision and interpretation	N1 N 80 P0
	Code also percutaneous biliary duct stone extraction (47630)	
	3.43 3.43 Global Days XXX	
74328	Endoscopic catheterization of the biliary ductal system, radiological supervision and interpretation	N1 N 80 P0
	Code also ERCP (43260-43272)	
	0.00 0.00 Global Days XXX	
	AMA: 2009, Jan, 11-31; 2008, May, 9-11	
74329	Endoscopic catheterization of the pancreatic ductal system, radiological supervision and interpretation	N1 N 80 P0
	Code also ERCP (43260-43272)	
	0.00 0.00 Global Days XXX	
74330	Combined endoscopic catheterization of the biliary and pancreatic ductal systems, radiological supervision and interpretation	N1 N 80 P0
	Code also ERCP (43260-43272)	
	0.00 0.00 Global Days XXX	

74340-74363 Radiography: Bilidigestive Intubation

CMS 100-2,15,80 Physician Supervision Requirements for Diagnostic Tests
CMS 100-4,3,10.4 Payment of Nonphysician Services for Inpatients
CMS 100-4,13,10 ICD-9-CM Coding for Diagnostic Tests
CMS 100-4,13,100 Interpretation of Diagnostic Tests

EXCLUDES Percutaneous insertion of gastrostomy tube, endoscopic (43246)
Percutaneous placement of gastrostomy tube, fluoroscopic guidance (49440)

74340	Introduction of long gastrointestinal tube (eg, Miller-Abbott), including multiple fluoroscopies and films, radiological supervision and interpretation	N1 N 80 P0
	Code also placement of tube (44500)	
	0.00 0.00 Global Days XXX	
74355	Percutaneous placement of enteroclysis tube, radiological supervision and interpretation	N1 N 80 P0
	INCLUDES Needle placement with fluoroscopic guidance (77002)	
	0.00 0.00 Global Days XXX	
	AMA: 2008, Jun, 8-11; 2007, February, 10-11	
74360	Intraluminal dilation of strictures and/or obstructions (eg, esophagus), radiological supervision and interpretation	N1 N 80 P0
	0.00 0.00 Global Days XXX	
	AMA: 2008, Oct, 6-7	
74363	Percutaneous transhepatic dilation of biliary duct stricture with or without placement of stent, radiological supervision and interpretation	N1 N 80 P0
	EXCLUDES Surgical procedure (47510, 47511, 47555, 47556)	
	0.00 0.00 Global Days XXX	

CURRENT PROCEDURAL CODING EXPERT – Radiology   74775

74400-74775 Radiography: Urogenital

CMS 100-2,15,80   Physician Supervision Requirements for Diagnostic Tests
CMS 100-4,3,10.4   Payment of Nonphysician Services for Inpatients
CMS 100-4,13,10   ICD-9-CM Coding for Diagnostic Tests
CMS 100-4,13,100   Interpretation of Diagnostic Tests

74400 Urography (pyelography), intravenous, with or without KUB, with or without tomography
 2.75 2.75 Global Days XXX

74410 Urography, infusion, drip technique and/or bolus technique;
 2.77 2.77 Global Days XXX

74415 with nephrotomography
 3.34 3.34 Global Days XXX

74420 Urography, retrograde, with or without KUB
 0.00 0.00 Global Days XXX
 AMA: 2009, Jan, 11-31; 2008, Jan, 10-25; 2007, January, 13-27

74425 Urography, antegrade (pyelostogram, nephrostogram, loopogram), radiological supervision and interpretation
 0.00 0.00 Global Days XXX
 AMA: 2005, October, 18-22

74430 Cystography, minimum of 3 views, radiological supervision and interpretation
 2.01 2.01 Global Days XXX

74440 Vasography, vesiculography, or epididymography, radiological supervision and interpretation
 2.14 2.14 Global Days XXX

74445 Corpora cavernosography, radiological supervision and interpretation
 INCLUDES Needle placement with fluoroscopic guidance (77002)
 0.00 0.00 Global Days XXX
 AMA: 2008, Jun, 8-11; 2007, February, 10-11

74450 Urethrocystography, retrograde, radiological supervision and interpretation
 0.00 0.00 Global Days XXX

74455 Urethrocystography, voiding, radiological supervision and interpretation
 2.13 2.13 Global Days XXX

74470 Radiologic examination, renal cyst study, translumbar, contrast visualization, radiological supervision and interpretation
 INCLUDES Needle placement with fluoroscopic guidance (77002)
 0.00 0.00 Global Days XXX
 AMA: 2008, Jun, 8-11; 2007, February, 10-11; 2005, October, 18-22

74475 Introduction of intracatheter or catheter into renal pelvis for drainage and/or injection, percutaneous, radiological supervision and interpretation
 INCLUDES Needle placement with fluoroscopic guidance (77002)
 2.45 2.45 Global Days XXX
 AMA: 2008, Jun, 8-11; 2007, February, 10-11; 2005, October, 18-22

74480 Introduction of ureteral catheter or stent into ureter through renal pelvis for drainage and/or injection, percutaneous, radiological supervision and interpretation
 EXCLUDES Code also ureter/pelvis transurethral surgery (52320-52355)
 2.45 2.45 Global Days XXX
 AMA: 2005, October, 18-22

74485 Dilation of nephrostomy, ureters, or urethra, radiological supervision and interpretation
 EXCLUDES Change of pyelostomy/nephrostomy tube (50398)
 Ureter dilation without radiologic guidance (52341, 52344)
 2.50 2.50 Global Days XXX
 AMA: 2009, Jan, 7-8; 2005, October, 18-22

74710 Pelvimetry, with or without placental localization
 EXCLUDES Imaging procedures on abdomen and pelvis (72170-72190, 74000-74170)
 0.92 0.92 Global Days XXX

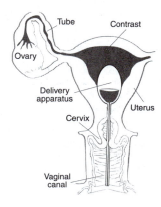

Hysterosalpingography (imaging of the uterus and tubes) is performed. Report for radiological supervision and interpretation

74740 Hysterosalpingography, radiological supervision and interpretation
 EXCLUDES Imaging procedures on abdomen and pelvis (72170-72190, 74000-74170)
 Code also injection of saline/contrast (58340)
 1.96 1.96 Global Days XXX
 AMA: 2009, Mar, 10-11

74742 Transcervical catheterization of fallopian tube, radiological supervision and interpretation
 EXCLUDES Imaging procedures on abdomen and pelvis (72170-72190, 74000-74170)
 Code also (58345)
 0.00 0.00 Global Days XXX
 AMA: 2009, Mar, 10-11

74775 Perineogram (eg, vaginogram, for sex determination or extent of anomalies)
 EXCLUDES Imaging procedures on abdomen and pelvis (72170-72190, 74000-74170)
 0.00 0.00 Global Days XXX

75557-75565 Magnetic Resonance Imaging: Heart Structure and Physiology

CMS 100-2,15,80	Physician Supervision Requirements for Diagnostic Tests
CMS 100-3,220.2	Magnetic Resonance Imaging
CMS 100-4,3,10.4	Payment of Nonphysician Services for Inpatients
CMS 100-4,13,10	ICD-9-CM Coding for Diagnostic Tests
CMS 100-4,13,40	Magnetic Resonance Imaging (MRI) Procedures

INCLUDES Physiologic evaluation of cardiac function
EXCLUDES Cardiac catherization procedures (93501-93556)
Code also separate vascular injection (36000-36299)
Do not report with (76376-76377)
Do not report with more than one code in this group per session

75557 Cardiac magnetic resonance imaging for morphology and function without contrast material;
8.27 8.27 Global Days XXX
AMA: 2008, Jul, 3&14

~~75558~~ ~~with flow/velocity quantification~~
To report, see code 75565

75559 with stress imaging
Code also for stress testing when performed (93015-93018)
INCLUDES Pharmacologic wall motion stress evaluation without contrast
Code also stress test (93015-93018)
11.80 11.80 Global Days XXX
AMA: 2008, Jul, 3&14

~~75560~~ ~~with flow/velocity quantification and stress~~
To report, see code 75565

75561 Cardiac magnetic resonance imaging for morphology and function without contrast material(s), followed by contrast material(s) and further sequences;
10.92 10.92 Global Days XXX
AMA: 2008, Jul, 3&14

~~75562~~ ~~with flow/velocity quantification~~
To report, see code 75565

75563 with stress imaging
Code also stress testing codes as appropriate (93015-93018)
INCLUDES Pharmacologic perfusion stress evaluation with contrast
Code also stress test (93015-93018)
13.04 13.04 Global Days XXX
AMA: 2008, Jul, 3&14

~~75564~~ ~~with flow/velocity quantification and stress~~
To report, see code 75565

+ ● **75565** Cardiac magnetic resonance imaging for velocity flow mapping (List separately in addition to code for primary procedure)
Code first (75557, 75559, 75561, 75563)
Code also to report flow with pharmacologic perfusion stress with (75563)
Code also for flow with pharmacologic wall motion stress evaluation without contrast with (75559)
2.54 2.54 Global Days XXX

75571-75574 Computed Tomographic Imaging: Heart

● **75571** Computed tomography, heart, without contrast material, with quantitative evaluation of coronary calcium
3.33 3.33 Global Days XXX

● **75572** Computed tomography, heart, with contrast material, for evaluation of cardiac structure and morphology (including 3D image postprocessing, assessment of cardiac function, and evaluation of venous structures, if performed)
3.80 3.80 Global Days XXX

● **75573** Computed tomography, heart, with contrast material, for evaluation of cardiac structure and morphology in the setting of congenital heart disease (including 3D image postprocessing, assessment of LV cardiac function, RV structure and function and evaluation of venous structures, if performed)
5.10 5.10 Global Days XXX

● **75574** Computed tomographic angiography, heart, coronary arteries and bypass grafts (when present), with contrast material, including 3D image postprocessing (including evaluation of cardiac structure and morphology, assessment of cardiac function, and evaluation of venous structures, if performed)
16.08 16.08 Global Days XXX

75600-75791 Radiography: Arterial

CMS 100-2,15,80	Physician Supervision Requirements for Diagnostic Tests
CMS 100-4,3,10.4	Payment of Nonphysician Services for Inpatients
CMS 100-4,13,10	ICD-9-CM Coding for Diagnostic Tests
CMS 100-4,13,100	Interpretation of Diagnostic Tests

INCLUDES Diagnostic angiography specifically included in the interventional code description
The following diagnostic procedures with interventional supervision and interpretation:
Angiography
Contrast injection
Fluoroscopic guidance for intervention
Post-angioplasty/stent angiography
Roadmapping
Vessel measurement

EXCLUDES Diagnostic angiogram during a separate encounter from the interventional procedure
Diagnostic angiography with interventional procedure if:
1. No previous catheter-based angiogram is accessible and a complete diagnostic procedure is performed and the decision to proceed with an interventional procedure is based on the diagnostic service, OR
2. The previous diagnostic angiogram is accessible but the documentation in the medical record specifies that:
    A. the patient's condition has changed
    B. there is insufficient imaging of the patient's anatomy and/or disease, OR
    C. there is a clinical change during the procedure that necessitates a new examination away from the site of the intervention
Intra-arterial procedures (36100-36248)
Intravenous procedures (36000-36013, 36400-36425)

75600 Aortography, thoracic, without serialography, radiological supervision and interpretation
Code also injection procedure (93544)
5.31 5.31 Global Days XXX

75605 Aortography, thoracic, by serialography, radiological supervision and interpretation
Code also injection procedure (93544)
3.95 3.95 Global Days XXX
AMA: 2009, Jan, 11-31; 2008, Jan, 10-25; 2007, January, 13-27

75625 Aortography, abdominal, by serialography, radiological supervision and interpretation
Code also injection procedure (93544)
4.05 4.05 Global Days XXX
AMA: 2009, Jan, 11-31; 2008, Jan, 10-25; 2008, Apr, -11; 2007, Dec, 10-179; 2007, January, 13-27

75630 Aortography, abdominal plus bilateral iliofemoral lower extremity, catheter, by serialography, radiological supervision and interpretation
4.91 4.91 Global Days XXX
AMA: 2009, Jan, 11-31; 2008, Jan, 10-25; 2008, Apr, -11; 2007, January, 13-27

75635 Computed tomographic angiography, abdominal aorta and bilateral iliofemoral lower extremity runoff, with contrast material(s), including noncontrast images, if performed, and image postprocessing
13.44 13.44 Global Days XXX
AMA: 2007, January, 28-31; 2005, December, 7

75650 Angiography, cervicocerebral, catheter, including vessel origin, radiological supervision and interpretation
4.51 4.51 Global Days XXX

75658 Angiography, brachial, retrograde, radiological supervision and interpretation
4.89 4.89 Global Days XXX

75660 Angiography, external carotid, unilateral, selective, radiological supervision and interpretation
4.81 4.81 Global Days XXX

75662 Angiography, external carotid, bilateral, selective, radiological supervision and interpretation
5.83 5.83 Global Days XXX

75665 Angiography, carotid, cerebral, unilateral, radiological supervision and interpretation
5.08 5.08 Global Days XXX

75671 Angiography, carotid, cerebral, bilateral, radiological supervision and interpretation
6.13 6.13 Global Days XXX

75676 Angiography, carotid, cervical, unilateral, radiological supervision and interpretation
4.79 4.79 Global Days XXX

75680 Angiography, carotid, cervical, bilateral, radiological supervision and interpretation
5.60 5.60 Global Days XXX

75685 Angiography, vertebral, cervical, and/or intracranial, radiological supervision and interpretation
4.81 4.81 Global Days XXX

An angiography of a specific area of the spine is performed

75705 Angiography, spinal, selective, radiological supervision and interpretation
6.01 6.01 Global Days XXX

75710 Angiography, extremity, unilateral, radiological supervision and interpretation
4.57 4.57 Global Days XXX
AMA: 2009, Jan, 11-31; 2008, Jan, 10-25; 2007, January, 13-27

75716 Angiography, extremity, bilateral, radiological supervision and interpretation
5.48 5.48 Global Days XXX
AMA: 2009, Jan, 11-31; 2008, Jan, 10-25; 2008, Apr, -11; 2007, Dec, 10-179; 2007, January, 13-27

75722 Angiography, renal, unilateral, selective (including flush aortogram), radiological supervision and interpretation
4.25 4.25 Global Days XXX

75724 Angiography, renal, bilateral, selective (including flush aortogram), radiological supervision and interpretation
5.18 5.18 Global Days XXX

75726 Angiography, visceral, selective or supraselective (with or without flush aortogram), radiological supervision and interpretation
EXCLUDES Selective angiography, each additional visceral vessel studied after basic examination (75774)
4.46 4.46 Global Days XXX

75731 Angiography, adrenal, unilateral, selective, radiological supervision and interpretation
4.23 4.23 Global Days XXX

75733 Angiography, adrenal, bilateral, selective, radiological supervision and interpretation
5.21 5.21 Global Days XXX

75736 Angiography, pelvic, selective or supraselective, radiological supervision and interpretation
4.41 4.41 Global Days XXX

75741 Angiography, pulmonary, unilateral, selective, radiological supervision and interpretation
Code also injection procedure (93541)
4.12 4.12 Global Days XXX

75743 Angiography, pulmonary, bilateral, selective, radiological supervision and interpretation
Code also injection procedure (93541)
4.86 4.86 Global Days XXX

75746 Angiography, pulmonary, by nonselective catheter or venous injection, radiological supervision and interpretation
Code also injection procedure (93541)
EXCLUDES Injection procedure, catheter introduction (93501-93533, 93539, 93540, 93545, 93556)
4.26 4.26 Global Days XXX

75756 Angiography, internal mammary, radiological supervision and interpretation
EXCLUDES Injection procedure, catheter introduction (93501-93533, 93545, 93556)
4.53 4.53 Global Days XXX

+ **75774** Angiography, selective, each additional vessel studied after basic examination, radiological supervision and interpretation (List separately in addition to code for primary procedure)
EXCLUDES Angiography (36147, 75600-75774, 75791)
Catheterizations (36215-36248)
Injection procedure, catheter introduction (93501-93533, 93545, 93555, 93556)
Code first initial vessel
2.53 2.53 Global Days ZZZ
AMA: 2009, Jan, 11-31; 2007, Dec, 10-179

75790 ~~Angiography, arteriovenous shunt (eg, dialysis patient), radiological supervision and interpretation~~
To report, see code 75791

- **75791** Angiography, arteriovenous shunt (eg, dialysis patient fistula/graft), complete evaluation of dialysis access, including fluoroscopy, image documentation and report (includes injections of contrast and all necessary imaging from the arterial anastomosis and adjacent artery through entire venous outflow, including the inferior or superior vena cava), radiological supervision and interpretation

  INCLUDES Radiological evaluation performed via existing access into the shunt or from an access that is not a direct puncture of the shunt

  EXCLUDES Catheter introduction, when performed (36140, 36215-36217, 36245-36247)
  Radiological evaluation with introduction of needle/catheter, AV dialysis shunt, complete procedure (36147)

  8.48   8.48 Global Days XXX

75801-75893 Radiography: Lymphatic and Venous

CMS 100-2,15,80 Physician Supervision Requirements for Diagnostic Tests
CMS 100-4,3,10.4 Payment of Nonphysician Services for Inpatients
CMS 100-4,13,10 ICD-9-CM Coding for Diagnostic Tests
CMS 100-4,13,100 Interpretation of Diagnostic Tests

INCLUDES Diagnostic venography specifically included in the interventional code description
The following diagnostic procedures with interventional supervision and interpretation:
  Contrast injection
  Fluoroscopic guidance for intervention
  Post-angioplasty/venography
  Roadmapping
  Venography
  Vessel measurement

EXCLUDES Diagnostic venogram during a separate encounter from the interventional procedure
Diagnostic venography with interventional procedure if:
  1. No previous catheter-based venogram is accessible and a complete diagnostic procedure is performed and the decision to proceed with an interventional procedure is based on the diagnostic service, OR
  2. The previous diagnostic venogram is accessible but the documentation in the medical record specifies that:
     A. the patient's condition has changed
     B. there is insufficient imaging of the patient's anatomy and/or disease, OR
     C. there is a clinical change during the procedure that necessitates a new examination away from the site of the intervention
Intravenous procedures (36000-36015, 36400-36510)
Lymphatic injection procedures (38790)

- **75801** Lymphangiography, extremity only, unilateral, radiological supervision and interpretation
  0.00   0.00 Global Days XXX

- **75803** Lymphangiography, extremity only, bilateral, radiological supervision and interpretation
  0.00   0.00 Global Days XXX

- **75805** Lymphangiography, pelvic/abdominal, unilateral, radiological supervision and interpretation
  0.00   0.00 Global Days XXX

- **75807** Lymphangiography, pelvic/abdominal, bilateral, radiological supervision and interpretation
  0.00   0.00 Global Days XXX

- **75809** Shuntogram for investigation of previously placed indwelling nonvascular shunt (eg, LeVeen shunt, ventriculoperitoneal shunt, indwelling infusion pump), radiological supervision and interpretation

  INCLUDES Needle placement with fluoroscopic guidance (77002)

  Code also surgical procedure (49427, 61070)
  2.53   2.53 Global Days XXX
  AMA: 2009, Jan, 11-31; 2008, Jul, 10&13; 2008, Sep, 10-11; 2008, Jun, 8-11; 2007, February, 10-11

- **75810** Splenoportography, radiological supervision and interpretation
  INCLUDES Needle placement with fluoroscopic guidance (77002)
  0.00   0.00 Global Days XXX
  AMA: 2008, Jun, 8-11; 2007, February, 10-11

- **75820** Venography, extremity, unilateral, radiological supervision and interpretation
  3.22   3.22 Global Days XXX
  AMA: 2009, Jan, 11-31; 2008, May, 9-11; 2008, Jan, 10-25; 2007, January, 13-27

- **75822** Venography, extremity, bilateral, radiological supervision and interpretation
  3.97   3.97 Global Days XXX

- **75825** Venography, caval, inferior, with serialography, radiological supervision and interpretation
  3.86   3.86 Global Days XXX
  AMA: 2009, Jan, 11-31; 2009, Jan, 7-8; 2008, Oct, 10-11

- **75827** Venography, caval, superior, with serialography, radiological supervision and interpretation
  4.00   4.00 Global Days XXX

- **75831** Venography, renal, unilateral, selective, radiological supervision and interpretation
  4.08   4.08 Global Days XXX

- **75833** Venography, renal, bilateral, selective, radiological supervision and interpretation
  4.86   4.86 Global Days XXX

- **75840** Venography, adrenal, unilateral, selective, radiological supervision and interpretation
  3.92   3.92 Global Days XXX

- **75842** Venography, adrenal, bilateral, selective, radiological supervision and interpretation
  4.79   4.79 Global Days XXX

- **75860** Venography, venous sinus (eg, petrosal and inferior sagittal) or jugular, catheter, radiological supervision and interpretation
  3.93   3.93 Global Days XXX

- **75870** Venography, superior sagittal sinus, radiological supervision and interpretation
  4.10   4.10 Global Days XXX

- **75872** Venography, epidural, radiological supervision and interpretation
  7.07   7.07 Global Days XXX

- **75880** Venography, orbital, radiological supervision and interpretation
  3.31   3.31 Global Days XXX

Current Procedural Coding Expert – Radiology 75900

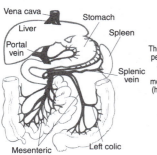

Schematic showing the portal vein

The portal vein is accessed by needle, percutaneously and through the liver, and contrast is delivered into the lumen. Measurement of blood movement through the vein are made (hemodynamic studies). Images are taken. Code 75885 reports the radiological supervision and interpretation of the studies

75885 Percutaneous transhepatic portography with hemodynamic evaluation, radiological supervision and interpretation
INCLUDES Needle placement with fluoroscopic guidance (77002)
4.30 4.30 Global Days XXX
AMA: 2009, Jan, 11-31; 2008, Jan, 10-25; 2008, Jun, 8-11; 2007, January, 13-27; 2007, February, 10-11

75887 Percutaneous transhepatic portography without hemodynamic evaluation, radiological supervision and interpretation
INCLUDES Needle placement with fluoroscopic guidance (77002)
4.43 4.43 Global Days XXX
AMA: 2009, Jan, 11-31; 2008, Jan, 10-25; 2008, Jun, 8-11; 2007, January, 13-27; 2007, February, 10-11; 2006, April, 11-18

75889 Hepatic venography, wedged or free, with hemodynamic evaluation, radiological supervision and interpretation
3.92 3.92 Global Days XXX

75891 Hepatic venography, wedged or free, without hemodynamic evaluation, radiological supervision and interpretation
3.91 3.91 Global Days XXX

75893 Venous sampling through catheter, with or without angiography (eg, for parathyroid hormone, renin), radiological supervision and interpretation
Code also surgical procedure (36500)
3.04 3.04 Global Days XXX

75894-75946 Transcatheter Procedures

CMS 100-2,15,80 Physician Supervision Requirements for Diagnostic Tests
CMS 100-3,20.28 Therapeutic Embolization
CMS 100-4,3,10.4 Payment of Nonphysician Services for Inpatients
CMS 100-4,13,10 ICD-9-CM Coding for Diagnostic Tests
CMS 100-4,13,100 Interpretation of Diagnostic Tests

INCLUDES The following diagnostic procedures with interventional supervision and interpretation:
Angiography/venography
Completion angiography/venography except for those services allowed by 75898
Contrast injection
Fluoroscopic guidance for intervention
Roadmapping
Vessel measurement
Transurethral approach to the removal or replacement of an internally dwelling ureteral stent (50385-50386)

EXCLUDES *Diagnostic angiography/venography performed at the same session as transcatheter therapy unless it is specifically included in the code descriptor or is excluded in the venography/angiography notes (75600-75893)*
Replacement of gastrostomy, duodenostomy, jejunostomy, gastrojejunostomy, or cecostomy tube, percutaneously, including guidance via fluoroscopy (49450-49452)

75894 Transcatheter therapy, embolization, any method, radiological supervision and interpretation
Code also obstetrical or postpartum hemorrhage embolization (37204)
Code also uterine fibroid embolization (37210)
0.00 0.00 Global Days XXX
AMA: 2008, Feb, 5-6; 2007, January, 7-10

75896 Transcatheter therapy, infusion, any method (eg, thrombolysis other than coronary), radiological supervision and interpretation
EXCLUDES Coronary disease infusion (92975, 92977)
0.00 0.00 Global Days XXX

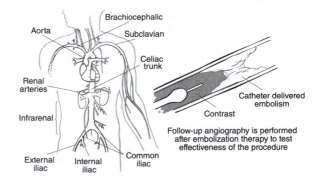

Follow-up angiography is performed after embolization therapy to test effectiveness of the procedure

75898 Angiography through existing catheter for follow-up study for transcatheter therapy, embolization or infusion
0.00 0.00 Global Days XXX
AMA: 2009, Jan, 11-31; 2007, Dec, 10-179; 2007, January, 7-10

75900 Exchange of a previously placed intravascular catheter during thrombolytic therapy with contrast monitoring, radiological supervision and interpretation
Code also surgical procedure (37209)
0.00 0.00 Global Days XXX

● New Code ▲ Revised Code M Maternity A Age Unlisted Not Covered # Resequenced
CCI + Add-on ⊘ Mod 51 Exempt ⊛ Mod 63 Exempt ⊙ Mod Sedation PQRI

© 2009 Publisher (Blue Ink) CPT only © 2009 American Medical Association. All Rights Reserved. (Black Ink) Medicare (Red Ink)

75901 Mechanical removal of pericatheter obstructive material (eg, fibrin sheath) from central venous device via separate venous access, radiologic supervision and interpretation
Code also surgical procedure (36595)
EXCLUDES Venous catheterization (36010-36012)
4.33 4.33 Global Days XXX

75902 Mechanical removal of intraluminal (intracatheter) obstructive material from central venous device through device lumen, radiologic supervision and interpretation
Code also surgical procedure (36596)
EXCLUDES Venous catheterization (36010-36012)
1.95 1.95 Global Days XXX

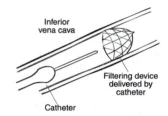

A filtering device is placed by catheter into the inferior vena cava (IVC). Code 75940 reports radiological supervision and interpretation of procedure

75940 Percutaneous placement of IVC filter, radiological supervision and interpretation
0.00 0.00 Global Days XXX
AMA: 2009, Jan, 11-31; 2008, Jan, 10-25; 2008, Oct, 10-11; 2007, January, 13-27

75945 Intravascular ultrasound (non-coronary vessel), radiological supervision and interpretation; initial vessel
0.00 0.00 Global Days XXX

+ **75946** each additional non-coronary vessel (List separately in addition to code for primary procedure)
Code first initial vessel (75945)
0.00 0.00 Global Days ZZZ

75952-75959 Endovascular Aneurysm Repair

CMS 100-4,3,10.4 Payment of Nonphysician Services for Inpatients
INCLUDES The following diagnostic procedures with interventional supervision and interpretation:
Angiography/venography
Completion angiography/venography except for those services allowed by 75898
Contrast injection
Fluoroscopic guidance for intervention
Roadmapping
Vessel measurement

EXCLUDES Diagnostic angiography/venography performed at the same session as transcatheter therapy unless it is specifically included in the code descriptor or is excluded in the venography/angiography notes (75600-75893)

75952 Endovascular repair of infrarenal abdominal aortic aneurysm or dissection, radiological supervision and interpretation
EXCLUDES Endovascular repair of abdominal aortic aneurysm, radiologic supervision and interpretation (0078T-0081T)
Implantation endovascular grafts (34800-34808)
0.00 0.00 Global Days XXX

75953 Placement of proximal or distal extension prosthesis for endovascular repair of infrarenal aortic or iliac artery aneurysm, pseudoaneurysm, or dissection, radiological supervision and interpretation
EXCLUDES Placement of endovascular extension prostheses (34825, 34826)
0.00 0.00 Global Days XXX

75954 Endovascular repair of iliac artery aneurysm, pseudoaneurysm, arteriovenous malformation, or trauma, radiological supervision and interpretation
EXCLUDES Placement of endovascular graft (34900)
0.00 0.00 Global Days XXX

75956 Endovascular repair of descending thoracic aorta (eg, aneurysm, pseudoaneurysm, dissection, penetrating ulcer, intramural hematoma, or traumatic disruption); involving coverage of left subclavian artery origin, initial endoprosthesis plus descending thoracic aortic extension(s), if required, to level of celiac artery origin, radiological supervision and interpretation
Code also endovascular graft implantation (33880)
0.00 0.00 Global Days XXX
AMA: 2006, May, 10-11

75957 not involving coverage of left subclavian artery origin, initial endoprosthesis plus descending thoracic aortic extension(s), if required, to level of celiac artery origin, radiological supervision and interpretation
Code also endovascular graft implantation (33881)
0.00 0.00 Global Days XXX
AMA: 2006, May, 10-11

75958 Placement of proximal extension prosthesis for endovascular repair of descending thoracic aorta (eg, aneurysm, pseudoaneurysm, dissection, penetrating ulcer, intramural hematoma, or traumatic disruption), radiological supervision and interpretation
INCLUDES Corresponding services for placement of each proximal thoracic endovascular extension
Code also placement of proximal endovascular extension (33883, 33884)
0.00 0.00 Global Days XXX
AMA: 2006, May, 10-11

Current Procedural Coding Expert – Radiology

75959 Placement of distal extension prosthesis(s) (delayed) after endovascular repair of descending thoracic aorta, as needed, to level of celiac origin, radiological supervision and interpretation
- **INCLUDES** Corresponding services for placement of distal thoracic endovascular extension(s) placed during procedure following the principal procedure
- Code also placement of distal endovascular extension (33886)
- Do not report with endovascular repair (75956, 75957)
- 0.00 0.00 Global Days XXX
- **AMA:** 2006, May, 10-11

75960-75961 Transcatheter Insertion and Removal

CMS 100-2,15,80 Physician Supervision Requirements for Diagnostic Tests
CMS 100-4,3,10.4 Payment of Nonphysician Services for Inpatients
CMS 100-4,13,10 ICD-9-CM Coding for Diagnostic Tests
CMS 100-4,13,100 Interpretation of Diagnostic Tests

INCLUDES The following diagnostic procedures with interventional supervision and interpretation:
- Angiography/venography
- Completion angiography/venography except for those services allowed by 75898
- Contrast injection
- Fluoroscopic guidance for intervention
- Roadmapping
- Vessel measurement

EXCLUDES Diagnostic angiography/venography performed at the same session as transcatheter therapy unless it is specifically included in the code descriptor or is excluded in the venography/angiography notes (75600-75893)

75960 Transcatheter introduction of intravascular stent(s) (except coronary, carotid, and vertebral vessel), percutaneous and/or open, radiological supervision and interpretation, each vessel
- **EXCLUDES** Transcatheter placement of extracranial vertebral/intrathoracic carotid artery stent(s) radiologic supervision and interpretation (0075T, 0076T)
- Code also surgical procedure (37205-37208)
- 3.14 3.14 Global Days XXX

75961 Transcatheter retrieval, percutaneous, of intravascular foreign body (eg, fractured venous or arterial catheter), radiological supervision and interpretation
- Code also surgical procedure (37203)
- 8.48 8.48 Global Days XXX
- **AMA:** 2009, Jan, 11-31; 2009, Jan, 7-8; 2008, Oct, 10-11

75962-75978 Percutaneous Transluminal Angioplasty

CMS 100-3,20.7 Percutaneous Transluminal Angioplasty (PTA)
CMS 100-4,3,10.4 Payment of Nonphysician Services for Inpatients

INCLUDES The following diagnostic procedures with interventional supervision and interpretation:
- Angiography/venography
- Completion angiography/venography except for those services allowed by 75898
- Contrast injection
- Fluoroscopic guidance for intervention
- Roadmapping
- Vessel measurement

EXCLUDES Diagnostic angiography/venography performed at the same session as transcatheter therapy unless it is specifically included in the code descriptor or is excluded in the venography/angiography notes (75600-75893)

75962 Transluminal balloon angioplasty, peripheral artery, radiological supervision and interpretation
- Code also angioplasty catheter (C1725, C1885)
- 3.56 3.56 Global Days XXX
- **AMA:** 2009, Jan, 11-31; 2007, Dec, 10-179

+ 75964 Transluminal balloon angioplasty, each additional peripheral artery, radiological supervision and interpretation (List separately in addition to code for primary procedure)
- Code first primary procedure (75962)
- 2.44 2.44 Global Days ZZZ
- **AMA:** 2009, Jan, 11-31; 2007, Dec, 10-179

75966 Transluminal balloon angioplasty, renal or other visceral artery, radiological supervision and interpretation
- Code also angioplasty catheter (C1725, C1885)
- 4.57 4.57 Global Days XXX

+ 75968 Transluminal balloon angioplasty, each additional visceral artery, radiological supervision and interpretation (List separately in addition to code for primary procedure)
- **EXCLUDES** Percutaneous transluminal coronary angioplasty (92982-92984)
- Code first primary procedure (75966)
- 2.27 2.27 Global Days ZZZ

75970 Transcatheter biopsy, radiological supervision and interpretation
- **EXCLUDES** Injection procedure only for transcatheter therapy or biopsy (36100-36299)
- Percutaneous needle biopsy
  - Pancreas (48102)
  - Retroperitoneal lymph node/mass (49180)
  - Transcatheter renal/ureteral biopsy (52007)
- 0.00 0.00 Global Days XXX

75978 Transluminal balloon angioplasty, venous (eg, subclavian stenosis), radiological supervision and interpretation
- Code also angioplasty catheter (C1725, C1885)
- 3.68 3.68 Global Days XXX

75980-75989 Percutaneous Drainage

CMS 100-3,220.1   Computerized Tomography
CMS 100-3,220.5   Ultrasound Diagnostic Procedures
CMS 100-4,3,10.4   Payment of Nonphysician Services for Inpatients

INCLUDES The following diagnostic procedures with interventional supervision and interpretation:
- Angiography/venography
- Completion angiography/venography except for those services allowed by 75898
- Contrast injection
- Fluoroscopic guidance for intervention
- Roadmapping
- Vessel measurement

EXCLUDES Diagnostic angiography/venography performed at the same session as transcatheter therapy unless it is specifically included in the code descriptor or is excluded in the venography/angiography notes (75600-75893)

75980 Percutaneous transhepatic biliary drainage with contrast monitoring, radiological supervision and interpretation   N1 N 80 P0
    INCLUDES Needle placement with fluoroscopic guidance (77002)
    0.00   0.00   **Global Days XXX**
    AMA: 2008, Jun, 8-11; 2007, February, 10-11

75982 Percutaneous placement of drainage catheter for combined internal and external biliary drainage or of a drainage stent for internal biliary drainage in patients with an inoperable mechanical biliary obstruction, radiological supervision and interpretation   N1 N 80 P0
    INCLUDES Needle placement with fluoroscopic guidance (77002)
    0.00   0.00   **Global Days XXX**
    AMA: 2008, Jun, 8-11; 2007, February, 10-11

75984 Change of percutaneous tube or drainage catheter with contrast monitoring (eg, genitourinary system, abscess), radiological supervision and interpretation   N1 N 80 P0
    EXCLUDES
- Change only of nephrostomy/pyelostomy tube (50398)
- Change only of percutaneous biliary drainage catheter (47525)
- Cholecystostomy, percutaneous (47490)
- Introduction procedure only for percutaneous biliary drainage (47510, 47511)
- Nephrostolithotomy/pyelostolithotomy, percutaneous (50080, 50081)
- Percutaneous replacement of gastrointestinal tube using fluoroscopic guidance (49450-49452)

    2.83   2.83   **Global Days XXX**
    AMA: 2005, October, 18-22

75989 Radiological guidance (ie, fluoroscopy, ultrasound, or computed tomography), for percutaneous drainage (eg, abscess, specimen collection), with placement of catheter, radiological supervision and interpretation   N N 80
    INCLUDES Needle placement with fluoroscopic guidance (77002)
    3.24   3.24   **Global Days XXX**
    AMA: 2008, Jun, 8-11; 2007, February, 10-11

75992-75996 Noncoronary Transluminal Atherectomy

CMS 100-4,3,10.4   Payment of Nonphysician Services for Inpatients

75992 Transluminal atherectomy, peripheral artery, radiological supervision and interpretation   N1 N 80 P0
    Code also surgical procedure (35481-35485, 35491-35495)
    0.00   0.00   **Global Days XXX**

+ 75993 Transluminal atherectomy, each additional peripheral artery, radiological supervision and interpretation (List separately in addition to code for primary procedure)   N1 N 80 P0
    Code also surgical procedure (35481-35485, 35491-35495)
    Code first primary procedure (75992)
    0.00   0.00   **Global Days ZZZ**

75994 Transluminal atherectomy, renal, radiological supervision and interpretation   N1 N 80 P0
    Code also surgical procedure (35480, 35490)
    0.00   0.00   **Global Days XXX**

75995 Transluminal atherectomy, visceral, radiological supervision and interpretation   N1 N 80 P0
    Code also surgical procedure (35480, 35490)
    0.00   0.00   **Global Days XXX**

+ 75996 Transluminal atherectomy, each additional visceral artery, radiological supervision and interpretation (List separately in addition to code for primary procedure)   N1 N 80 P0
    Code also surgical procedure (35480, 35490)
    Code first primary procedure (75995)
    0.00   0.00   **Global Days ZZZ**

76000-76150 Miscellaneous Techniques

CMS 100-4,3,10.4   Payment of Nonphysician Services for Inpatients

EXCLUDES Arthrography:
- Ankle (73615)
- Elbow (73085)
- Hip (73525)
- Knee (73580)
- Shoulder (73040)
- Wrist (73115)

CT cerebral perfusion test (0042T)

76000 Fluoroscopy (separate procedure), up to 1 hour physician time, other than 71023 or 71034 (eg, cardiac fluoroscopy)   N1 Q1 80 P0
    2.85   2.85   **Global Days XXX**
    AMA: 2009, Jan, 11-31; 2008, Jan, 10-25; 2008, Jul, 9; 2008, Jun, 8-11; 2007, January, 13-27

76001 Fluoroscopy, physician time more than 1 hour, assisting a nonradiologic physician (eg, nephrostolithotomy, ERCP, bronchoscopy, transbronchial biopsy)   N1 N 80 P0
    0.00   0.00   **Global Days XXX**
    AMA: 2009, Jan, 11-31; 2008, Jun, 8-11; 2008, Jul, 9

76010 Radiologic examination from nose to rectum for foreign body, single view, child   A Z3 X 80
    0.66   0.66   **Global Days XXX**

76080 Radiologic examination, abscess, fistula or sinus tract study, radiological supervision and interpretation   N1 Q2 80 P0
    EXCLUDES Contrast injections, radiology evaluation, and guidance via fluoroscopy of gastrostomy, duodenostomy, jejunostomy, gastro-jejunostomy, or cecostomy tube (49465)
    1.53   1.53   **Global Days XXX**
    AMA: 2009, Jan, 11-31; 2009, Jan, 7-8; 2008, Jan, 10-25; 2007, January, 13-27; 2006, December, 10-12

Current Procedural Coding Expert – Radiology

76098 Radiological examination, surgical specimen
🚚 0.46 ⚖ 0.46 Global Days XXX

76100 Radiologic examination, single plane body section (eg, tomography), other than with urography
🚚 2.62 ⚖ 2.62 Global Days XXX

76101 Radiologic examination, complex motion (ie, hypercycloidal) body section (eg, mastoid polytomography), other than with urography; unilateral
🚚 3.76 ⚖ 3.76 Global Days XXX

76102 bilateral
EXCLUDES Nephrotomography (74415)
🚚 5.02 ⚖ 5.02 Global Days XXX

76120 Cineradiography/videoradiography, except where specifically included
🚚 1.91 ⚖ 1.91 Global Days XXX

+ **76125** Cineradiography/videoradiography to complement routine examination (List separately in addition to code for primary procedure)
Code first primary procedure
🚚 0.00 ⚖ 0.00 Global Days ZZZ

76140 Consultation on X-ray examination made elsewhere, written report
🚚 0.00 ⚖ 0.00 Global Days XXX
AMA: 2009, Jan, 11-31; 2008, Jan, 10-25; 2007, Jul, 12-13

76150 Xeroradiography
INCLUDES Non-mammographic studies only
🚚 0.56 ⚖ 0.56 Global Days XXX

76350 Digital Subtraction Angiography

CMS 100-3,220.9 Digital Subtraction Angiography
EXCLUDES Arthrography:
Ankle (73615)
Elbow (73085)
Hip (73525)
Knee (73580)
Shoulder (73040)
Wrist (73115)
CT cerebral perfusion test (0042T)

76350 Subtraction in conjunction with contrast studies
EXCLUDES 3D rendering (76376, 76377)
🚚 0.00 ⚖ 0.00 Global Days XXX

76376-76377 Three-dimensional Manipulation

CMS 100-4,3,10.4 Payment of Nonphysician Services for Inpatients
EXCLUDES Arthrography:
Ankle (73615)
Elbow (73085)
Hip (73525)
Knee (73580)
Shoulder (73040)
Wrist (73115)
Computer-aided detection of MRI data for lesion, breast MRI (0159T)
CT cerebral perfusion test (0042T)

76376 3D rendering with interpretation and reporting of computed tomography, magnetic resonance imaging, ultrasound, or other tomographic modality; not requiring image postprocessing on an independent workstation
INCLUDES Concurrent physician supervision of image postprocessing 3D manipulation of volumetric data set/image rendering
Code also base imaging procedures
Do not report with (0159T, 31627, 70496, 70498, 70544-70549, 71275, 71555, 72159, 72191, 72198, 73206, 73225, 73706, 73725, 74175, 74185, 74261-74263, 75557-75565, 75571-75574, 75635, 76377, 78000-78999)
🚚 1.45 ⚖ 1.45 Global Days XXX
AMA: 2009, May, 8-9&11; 2009, Jun, 9&11; 2009, Jul, 10; 2009, Jan, 11-31; 2008, Jan, 10-25; 2008, Jul, 3&14; 2007, January, 28-31; 2007, January, 13-27; 2005, December, 3-6; 2005, December, 7; 2005, December, 1-2

76377 requiring image postprocessing on an independent workstation
Do not report with (0159T, 70496, 70498, 70544-70549, 71275, 71555, 72159, 72191, 72198, 73206, 73225, 73706, 73725, 74175, 74185, 74261-74263, 75557, 75559, 75561, 75563, 75565, 75571-75574, 75635, 76376, 78000-78999)
Code also base imaging procedures
🚚 2.03 ⚖ 2.03 Global Days XXX
AMA: 2009, May, 8-9&11; 2009, Jun, 9&11; 2009, Jul, 10; 2009, Jan, 11-31; 2008, Jan, 10-25; 2008, Jul, 3&14; 2007, January, 13-27; 2007, January, 28-31; 2005, December, 3-6; 2005, December, 7; 2005, December, 1-2

76380 Computerized Tomography: Delimited

CMS 100-3,220.1 Computerized Tomography
EXCLUDES Arthrography:
Ankle (73615)
Elbow (73085)
Hip (73525)
Knee (73580)
Shoulder (73040)
Wrist (73115)
CT cerebral perfusion test (0042T)

76380 Computed tomography, limited or localized follow-up study
🚚 5.22 ⚖ 5.22 Global Days XXX
AMA: 2007, Jul, 12-13

76390-76499 Magnetic Resonance Spectroscopy

CMS 100-3,220.2.1   Magnetic Resonance Spectroscopy

EXCLUDES   Arthrography:
    Ankle (73615)
    Elbow (73085)
    Hip (73525)
    Knee (73580)
    Shoulder (73040)
    Wrist (73115)
CT cerebral perfusion test (0042T)

76390   Magnetic resonance spectroscopy   [E]
    EXCLUDES   MRI
    11.61   11.61   Global Days XXX

76496   Unlisted fluoroscopic procedure (eg, diagnostic, interventional)
    0.00   0.00   Global Days XXX

76497   Unlisted computed tomography procedure (eg, diagnostic, interventional)
    0.00   0.00   Global Days XXX
    AMA: 2009, Jan, 11-31; 2008, Jan, 10-25; 2007, January, 13-27; 2005, June, 9-11

76498   Unlisted magnetic resonance procedure (eg, diagnostic, interventional)
    0.00   0.00   Global Days XXX
    AMA: 2009, May, 8-9&11; 2008, Jul, 3&14

76499   Unlisted diagnostic radiographic procedure
    0.00   0.00   Global Days XXX
    AMA: 2009, Jan, 11-31; 2008, Jan, 10-25; 2008, Mar, 14-15; 2007, January, 13-27; 2006, December, 10-12

76506 Ultrasound: Brain

CMS 100-3,220.5   Ultrasound Diagnostic Procedures

INCLUDES   Required permanent documentation of ultrasound images except when diagnostic purpose is biometric measurement
Written documentation

EXCLUDES   Doppler study of vessels, other than color flow (93875-93990)
Focused ultrasound ablation of uterine leiomyomata (0071T-0072T)
Noninvasive vascular studies, diagnostic (93875-93990)
Ultrasound exam that does not include thorough assessment of organ or site, recorded image, and written report

76506   Echoencephalography, real time with image documentation (gray scale) (for determination of ventricular size, delineation of cerebral contents, and detection of fluid masses or other intracranial abnormalities), including A-mode encephalography as secondary component where indicated
    3.16   3.16   Global Days XXX
    AMA: 2007, March, 7-8; 2006, December, 10-12

76510-76529 Ultrasound: Eyes

CMS 100-3,220.5   Ultrasound Diagnostic Procedures
CMS 100-3,230.1   Visual Tests Prior to and General Anesthesia During Cataract Surgery

INCLUDES   Required permanent documentation of ultrasound images except when diagnostic purpose is biometric measurement
Written documentation

EXCLUDES   Doppler study of vessels, other than color flow (93875-93990)
Focused ultrasound ablation of uterine leiomyomata (0071T-0072T)
Ultrasound exam that does not include thorough assessment of organ or site, recorded image, and written report

76510   Ophthalmic ultrasound, diagnostic; B-scan and quantitative A-scan performed during the same patient encounter
    4.51   4.51   Global Days XXX
    AMA: 2005, December, 3-6

76511   quantitative A-scan only
    2.59   2.59   Global Days XXX
    AMA: 2005, December, 3-6

76512   B-scan (with or without superimposed non-quantitative A-scan)
    2.42   2.42   Global Days XXX
    AMA: 2005, December, 3-6

76513   anterior segment ultrasound, immersion (water bath) B-scan or high resolution biomicroscopy
    EXCLUDES   Computerized ophthalmic testing other than by ultrasound (0187T, 92135)
    2.35   2.35   Global Days XXX

76514   corneal pachymetry, unilateral or bilateral (determination of corneal thickness)
    0.40   0.40   Global Days XXX
    AMA: 2009, Jan, 11-31; 2008, Jan, 10-25; 2007, January, 13-27; 2005, February, 13-16; 2005, December, 3-6; 2005, June, 9-11

76516   Ophthalmic biometry by ultrasound echography, A-scan;
    1.93   1.93   Global Days XXX
    AMA: 2009, Jan, 11-31; 2008, Jan, 10-25; 2007, January, 13-27; 2005, December, 3-6

76519   with intraocular lens power calculation
    EXCLUDES   Partial coherence interferometry (92136)
    2.07   2.07   Global Days XXX
    AMA: 2009, Jan, 11-31; 2008, Jan, 10-25; 2007, January, 13-27; 2005, December, 3-6

76529   Ophthalmic ultrasonic foreign body localization
    2.00   2.00   Global Days XXX

76536-76800 Ultrasound: Neck, Thorax, Abdomen, and Spine

CMS 100-2,15,80   Physician Supervision Requirements for Diagnostic Tests
CMS 100-3,220.5   Ultrasound Diagnostic Procedures
CMS 100-4,3,10.4   Payment of Nonphysician Services for Inpatients

INCLUDES   Required permanent documentation of ultrasound images except when diagnostic purpose is biometric measurement
Written documentation

EXCLUDES   Focused ultrasound ablation of uterine leiomyomata (0071T-0072T)
Ultrasound exam that does not include thorough assessment of organ or site, recorded image, and written report

76536   Ultrasound, soft tissues of head and neck (eg, thyroid, parathyroid, parotid), real time with image documentation
    3.02   3.02   Global Days XXX
    AMA: 2009, May, 7&10; 2007, March, 7-8

76604   Ultrasound, chest (includes mediastinum), real time with image documentation
    2.18   2.18   Global Days XXX
    AMA: 2009, May, 7&10; 2007, March, 7-8

76645   Ultrasound, breast(s) (unilateral or bilateral), real time with image documentation
    2.43   2.43   Global Days XXX
    AMA: 2007, March, 7-8

Current Procedural Coding Expert – Radiology 76810

76700 Ultrasound, abdominal, real time with image documentation; complete
INCLUDES Real time scans of:
Common bile duct
Gall bladder
Inferior vena cava
Kidneys
Liver
Pancreas
Spleen
Upper abdominal aorta
 3.52   3.52 Global Days XXX
AMA: 2009, May, 7&10; 2007, March, 7-8; 2005, December, 3-6

76705 limited (eg, single organ, quadrant, follow-up)
 2.67   2.67 Global Days XXX
AMA: 2009, Jan, 11-31; 2009, May, 7&10; 2009, Feb, 22; 2008, Jan, 10-25; 2007, January, 13-27; 2005, December, 3-6

76770 Ultrasound, retroperitoneal (eg, renal, aorta, nodes), real time with image documentation; complete
INCLUDES Complete assessment of kidneys and bladder if history indicates urinary pathology
Real time scans of:
Abdominal aorta
Common iliac artery origins
Inferior vena cava
Kidneys
 3.32   3.32 Global Days XXX
AMA: 2007, March, 7-8; 2005, December, 3-6

76775 limited
 2.68   2.68 Global Days XXX
AMA: 2009, Jan, 11-31; 2009, Feb, 22; 2008, Jan, 10-25; 2007, January, 13-27; 2005, December, 3-6

76776 Ultrasound, transplanted kidney, real time and duplex Doppler with image documentation
EXCLUDES Transplanted kidney ultrasound without duplex doppler (76775)

Do not report with abdominal/pelvic/scrotal contents/retroperitoneal duplex scan (93975, 93976)
 3.78   3.78 Global Days XXX
AMA: 2007, March, 7-8

76800 Ultrasound, spinal canal and contents
 3.54   3.54 Global Days XXX
AMA: 2009, Jan, 11-31; 2008, Jan, 10-25; 2007, January, 13-27

76801-76802 Ultrasound: Pregnancy Less Than 14 Weeks
CMS 100-2,15,80 Physician Supervision Requirements for Diagnostic Tests
CMS 100-3,220.5 Ultrasound Diagnostic Procedures
CMS 100-4,3,10.4 Payment of Nonphysician Services for Inpatients
INCLUDES Determination of the number of gestational sacs and fetuses
Gestational sac/fetal measurement appropriate for gestational (younger than 14 weeks 0 days)
Inspection of the maternal uterus and adnexa
Quality analysis of amniotic fluid volume/gestational sac shape
Visualization of fetal and placental anatomic formation
Written documentation of each component of exam
EXCLUDES Focused ultrasound ablation of uterine leiomyomata (0071T-0072T)
Ultrasound exam that does not include thorough assessment of organ or site, recorded image, and written report

76801 Ultrasound, pregnant uterus, real time with image documentation, fetal and maternal evaluation, first trimester (< 14 weeks 0 days), transabdominal approach; single or first gestation
EXCLUDES Fetal nuchal translucency measurement, first trimester (76813)
 3.23   3.23 Global Days XXX
AMA: 2009, Jan, 11-31; 2008, Jan, 10-25; 2007, January, 13-27; 2005, November, 14-15

+ **76802** each additional gestation (List separately in addition to code for primary procedure)
EXCLUDES Fetal nuchal translucency measurement, first trimester (76814)
Code first single/first gestation (76801)
 1.78   1.78 Global Days ZZZ
AMA: 2009, Jan, 11-31; 2008, Jan, 10-25; 2007, January, 13-27; 2005, November, 14-15

76805-76810 Ultrasound: Pregnancy of 14 Weeks or More
CMS 100-2,15,80 Physician Supervision Requirements for Diagnostic Tests
CMS 100-3,220.5 Ultrasound Diagnostic Procedures
CMS 100-4,3,10.4 Payment of Nonphysician Services for Inpatients
INCLUDES Determination of the number of gestational/chorionic sacs and fetuses
Evaluation of:
Amniotic fluid
Four chambered heart
Intracranial, spinal, abdominal anatomy
Placenta location
Umbilical cord insertion site
Examination of maternal adnexa if visible
Gestational sac/fetal measurement appropriate for gestational (older than or equal to 14 weeks 0 days)
Written documentation of each component of exam
EXCLUDES Focused ultrasound ablation of uterine leiomyomata (0071T-0072T)
Ultrasound exam that does not include thorough assessment of organ or site, recorded image, and written report

76805 Ultrasound, pregnant uterus, real time with image documentation, fetal and maternal evaluation, after first trimester (> or = 14 weeks 0 days), transabdominal approach; single or first gestation
 3.75   3.75 Global Days XXX

+ **76810** each additional gestation (List separately in addition to code for primary procedure)
Code first single/first gestation (76805)
 2.54   2.54 Global Days ZZZ

● New Code   ▲ Revised Code   M Maternity   Age   Unlisted   Not Covered   # Resequenced
CCI   + Add-on   ⊘ Mod 51 Exempt   Mod 63 Exempt   ⊙ Mod Sedation   PQRI
© 2009 Publisher (Blue Ink)   CPT only © 2009 American Medical Association. All Rights Reserved. (Black Ink)   Medicare (Red Ink)   281

76811-76812 Ultrasound: Pregnancy, with Additional Studies of Fetus

CMS 100-3,220.5   Ultrasound Diagnostic Procedures
CMS 100-4,3,10.4   Payment of Nonphysician Services for Inpatients

INCLUDES
Determination of the number of gestational/chorionic sacs and fetuses
Evaluation of:
    Abdominal organ specific anatomy
    Amniotic fluid
    Chest anatomy
    Face
    Fetal brain/ventricles
    Four chambered heart
    Heart/outflow tracts and chest anatomy
    Intracranial, spinal, abdominal anatomy
    Limbs including number, length, and architecture
    Other fetal anatomy as indicated
    Placenta
    Umbilical cord insertion site
Examination of maternal adnexa if visible
Gestational sac/fetal measurement appropriate for gestational (older than or equal to 14 weeks 0 days)
Written documentation of each component of exam

EXCLUDES
Focused ultrasound ablation of uterine leiomyomata (0071T-0072T)
Ultrasound exam that does not include thorough assessment organ or site, recorded image, and written report

76811   Ultrasound, pregnant uterus, real time with image documentation, fetal and maternal evaluation plus detailed fetal anatomic examination, transabdominal approach; single or first gestation
    4.85   4.85   Global Days XXX

+ 76812   each additional gestation (List separately in addition to code for primary procedure)
    Code first single/first gestation (76811)
    5.50   5.50   Global Days ZZZ

76813-76828 Ultrasound: Other Fetal Evaluations

CMS 100-2,15,80   Physician Supervision Requirements for Diagnostic Tests
CMS 100-3,220.5   Ultrasound Diagnostic Procedures
CMS 100-4,3,10.4   Payment of Nonphysician Services for Inpatients

INCLUDES
Required permanent documentation of ultrasound images except when diagnostic purpose is biometric measurement
Written documentation

EXCLUDES
Focused ultrasound ablation of uterine leiomyomata (0071T-0072T)
Ultrasound exam that does not include thorough assessment of organ or site, recorded image, and written report

76813   Ultrasound, pregnant uterus, real time with image documentation, first trimester fetal nuchal translucency measurement, transabdominal or transvaginal approach; single or first gestation
    3.26   3.26   Global Days XXX
    AMA: 2007, March, 7-8

+ 76814   each additional gestation (List separately in addition to code for primary procedure)
    Code first single/first gestation (76813)
    2.16   2.16   Global Days XXX
    AMA: 2007, March, 7-8

76815   Ultrasound, pregnant uterus, real time with image documentation, limited (eg, fetal heart beat, placental location, fetal position and/or qualitative amniotic fluid volume), 1 or more fetuses
    INCLUDES   Focused "quick look" exam of one or more elements
    Reporting only once per exam, instead of per element
    EXCLUDES   Fetal nuchal translucency measurement, first trimester (76813, 76814)
    2.29   2.29   Global Days XXX
    AMA: 2009, Jan, 11-31; 2008, Jan, 10-25; 2007, January, 13-27

76816   Ultrasound, pregnant uterus, real time with image documentation, follow-up (eg, re-evaluation of fetal size by measuring standard growth parameters and amniotic fluid volume, re-evaluation of organ system(s) suspected or confirmed to be abnormal on a previous scan), transabdominal approach, per fetus
    Code also modifier 59 for examination of each additional fetus in a multiple pregnancy
    3.05   3.05   Global Days XXX

76817   Ultrasound, pregnant uterus, real time with image documentation, transvaginal
    EXCLUDES   Transvaginal ultrasound, non-obstetrical (76830)
    Code also transabdominal obstetrical ultrasound, if performed
    2.59   2.59   Global Days XXX

76818   Fetal biophysical profile; with non-stress testing
    Code also modifier 59 for each additional fetus
    3.14   3.14   Global Days XXX
    AMA: 2009, Jan, 11-31; 2008, Jan, 10-25; 2007, January, 13-27

76819   without non-stress testing
    EXCLUDES   Amniotic fluid index without non-stress test (76815)
    Code also modifier 59 for each additional fetus
    2.27   2.27   Global Days XXX
    AMA: 2009, Jan, 11-31; 2008, Jan, 10-25; 2007, January, 13-27

76820   Doppler velocimetry, fetal; umbilical artery
    1.08   1.08   Global Days XXX
    AMA: 2005, December, 3-6

76821   middle cerebral artery
    2.43   2.43   Global Days XXX
    AMA: 2005, December, 3-6

76825   Echocardiography, fetal, cardiovascular system, real time with image documentation (2D), with or without M-mode recording;
    5.66   5.66   Global Days XXX

76826   follow-up or repeat study
    3.34   3.34   Global Days XXX

76827   Doppler echocardiography, fetal, pulsed wave and/or continuous wave with spectral display; complete
    1.60   1.60   Global Days XXX
    AMA: 2005, December, 3-6

76828   follow-up or repeat study
    EXCLUDES   Color mapping (93325)
    1.21   1.21   Global Days XXX
    AMA: 2005, December, 3-6

Current Procedural Coding Expert – Radiology 76936

76830-76886 Ultrasound: Male and Female Genitalia and Extremities

CMS 100-2,15,80 — Physician Supervision Requirements for Diagnostic Tests
CMS 100-3,220.5 — Ultrasound Diagnostic Procedures
CMS 100-4,3,10.4 — Payment of Nonphysician Services for Inpatients

INCLUDES Required permanent documentation of ultrasound images except when diagnostic purpose is biometric measurement
Written documentation

EXCLUDES Focused ultrasound ablation of uterine leiomyomata (0071T-0072T)
Ultrasound exam that does not include thorough assessment of organ or site, recorded image, and written report

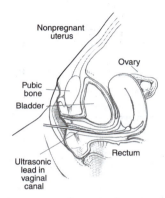

Ultrasound is performed in real time with image documentation by a transvaginal approach

76830 Ultrasound, transvaginal
EXCLUDES Transvaginal ultrasound, obstetric (76817)
Code also transabdominal non-obstetrical ultrasound, if performed
3.16   3.16 Global Days XXX
AMA: 2009, Feb, 22; 2009, Jan, 11-31; 2008, Jan, 10-25; 2007, January, 13-27; 2005, December, 3-6

76831 Saline infusion sonohysterography (SIS), including color flow Doppler, when performed
Code also saline introduction for saline infusion sonohysterography (58340)
3.22   3.22 Global Days XXX
AMA: 2009, Mar, 10-11; 2005, December, 3-6

76856 Ultrasound, pelvic (nonobstetric), real time with image documentation; complete
INCLUDES Total examination of the female pelvic anatomy which includes:
Bladder measurement
Description and measurement of the uterus and adnexa
Description of any pelvic pathology
Measurement of the endometrium
Total examination of the male pelvis which includes:
Bladder measurement
Description of any pelvic pathology
Evaluation of prostate and seminal vesicles
3.13   3.13 Global Days XXX
AMA: 2009, Jan, 11-31; 2009, Feb, 22; 2008, Jan, 10-25; 2007, March, 7-8; 2007, January, 13-27; 2006, March, 15; 2005, December, 3-6

76857 limited or follow-up (eg, for follicles)
INCLUDES Focused evaluation limited to:
Evaluation of one or more elements listed in 76856 and/or
Reevaluation of one or more pelvic abnormalities previously documented on ultrasound
Urinary bladder alone
EXCLUDES Bladder volume or post-voided residual measurement without imaging the bladder (51798)
Urinary bladder and kidneys (76770)
2.40   2.40 Global Days XXX
AMA: 2009, Jan, 11-31; 2009, May, 7&10; 2009, Feb, 22; 2008, Jan, 10-25; 2007, January, 13-27; 2005, December, 3-6

76870 Ultrasound, scrotum and contents
3.10   3.10 Global Days XXX

76872 Ultrasound, transrectal;
3.34   3.34 Global Days XXX
AMA: 2005, May, 3-6

76873 prostate volume study for brachytherapy treatment planning (separate procedure)
4.64   4.64 Global Days XXX

76880 Ultrasound, extremity, nonvascular, real time with image documentation
3.60   3.60 Global Days XXX
AMA: 2009, May, 7&10; 2007, March, 7-8

76885 Ultrasound, infant hips, real time with imaging documentation; dynamic (requiring physician manipulation)
3.68   3.68 Global Days XXX

76886 limited, static (not requiring physician manipulation)
3.18   3.18 Global Days XXX

76930-76970 Imaging Guidance: Ultrasound

CMS 100-3,220.5 — Ultrasound Diagnostic Procedures
CMS 100-4,3,10.4 — Payment of Nonphysician Services for Inpatients

INCLUDES Required permanent documentation of ultrasound images except when diagnostic purpose is biometric measurement
Written documentation

EXCLUDES Focused ultrasound ablation of uterine leiomyomata (0071T-0072T)
Ultrasound exam that does not include thorough assessment of organ or site, recorded image, and written report

76930 Ultrasonic guidance for pericardiocentesis, imaging supervision and interpretation
2.10   2.10 Global Days XXX

76932 Ultrasonic guidance for endomyocardial biopsy, imaging supervision and interpretation
0.00   0.00 Global Days XXX

76936 Ultrasound guided compression repair of arterial pseudoaneurysm or arteriovenous fistulae (includes diagnostic ultrasound evaluation, compression of lesion and imaging)
7.51   7.51 Global Days XXX

Current Procedural Coding Expert – Radiology

76937 Ultrasound guidance for vascular access requiring ultrasound evaluation of potential access sites, documentation of selected vessel patency, concurrent realtime ultrasound visualization of vascular needle entry, with permanent recording and reporting (List separately in addition to code for primary procedure)

EXCLUDES Extremity venous non-invasive vascular diagnostic study performed separately from venous access guidance (93965, 93970, 93971)

Code first primary procedure
Do not report with (37760-37761, 76942)
💲 0.90 💲 0.90 Global Days ZZZ
AMA: 2009, Jan, 7-8

76940 Ultrasound guidance for, and monitoring of, parenchymal tissue ablation

EXCLUDES Ablation (32998, 47370-47382, 50592, 50593)

Do not report with intraoperative ultrasonic guidance (76998)
💲 0.00 💲 0.00 Global Days XXX
AMA: 2007, March, 7-8; 2006, April, 11-18

76941 Ultrasonic guidance for intrauterine fetal transfusion or cordocentesis, imaging supervision and interpretation

Code also surgical procedure (36460, 59012)
💲 0.00 💲 0.00 Global Days XXX

76942 Ultrasonic guidance for needle placement (eg, biopsy, aspiration, injection, localization device), imaging supervision and interpretation

Do not report with (37760-37761, 43232, 43237, 43242, 45341-45342, 76975)
💲 4.88 💲 4.88 Global Days XXX
AMA: 2009, Jan, 11-31; 2009, Mar, 8-9; 2008, Jan, 10-25; 2008, Jun, 8-11; 2007, May, 1-2; 2007, June, 10-11; 2007, January, 13-27; 2006, April, 11-18; 2005, April, 13-14

76945 Ultrasonic guidance for chorionic villus sampling, imaging supervision and interpretation

Code also surgical procedure (59015)
💲 0.00 💲 0.00 Global Days XXX

76946 Ultrasonic guidance for amniocentesis, imaging supervision and interpretation
💲 0.84 💲 0.84 Global Days XXX

76948 Ultrasonic guidance for aspiration of ova, imaging supervision and interpretation
💲 0.93 💲 0.93 Global Days XXX

76950 Ultrasonic guidance for placement of radiation therapy fields

EXCLUDES Placement of interstitial device(s) for radiation therapy guidance (31627, 32553, 49411, 55876)

💲 1.78 💲 1.78 Global Days XXX

76965 Ultrasonic guidance for interstitial radioelement application
💲 2.46 💲 2.46 Global Days XXX

76970 Ultrasound study follow-up (specify)
💲 2.66 💲 2.66 Global Days XXX

76975 Endoscopic Ultrasound

CMS 100-3,220.5   Ultrasound Diagnostic Procedures
CMS 100-4,3,10.4   Payment of Nonphysician Services for Inpatients
CMS 100-4,12,30.1 Upper Gastrointestinal Endoscopy Including Endoscopic Ultrasound (EUS)

INCLUDES Required permanent documentation of ultrasound images except when diagnostic purpose is biometric measurement
Written documentation

EXCLUDES Focused ultrasound ablation of uterine leiomyomata (0071T-0072T)
Ultrasound exam that does not include thorough assessment of organ or site, recorded image, and written report

76975 Gastrointestinal endoscopic ultrasound, supervision and interpretation

Do not report with (43231, 43232, 43237, 43238, 43242, 43259, 45341, 45342, 76942)
💲 0.00 💲 0.00 Global Days XXX
AMA: 2009, Mar, 8-9

76977 Bone Density Measurements: Ultrasound

CMS 100-3,220.5   Ultrasound Diagnostic Procedures
CMS 100-4,13,140   Bone Mass Measurements (BMMs)

INCLUDES Required permanent documentation of ultrasound images except when diagnostic purpose is biometric measurement
Written documentation

EXCLUDES Focused ultrasound ablation of uterine leiomyomata (0071T-0072T)
Ultrasound exam that does not include thorough assessment of organ or site, recorded image, and written report

76977 Ultrasound bone density measurement and interpretation, peripheral site(s), any method
💲 0.19 💲 0.19 Global Days XXX

76998-76999 Imaging Guidance During Surgery: Ultrasound

INCLUDES Required permanent documentation of ultrasound images except when diagnostic purpose is biometric measurement
Written documentation

EXCLUDES Focused ultrasound ablation of uterine leiomyomata (0071T-0072T)
Ultrasound exam that does not include thorough assessment of organ or site, recorded image, and written report

76998 Ultrasonic guidance, intraoperative

EXCLUDES Radiofrequency tissue ablation, open/laparoscopic, ultrasonic guidance (76940)

Do not report with (36475-36479, 37760-37761, 47370-47382)
💲 0.00 💲 0.00 Global Days XXX
AMA: 2007, March, 7-8

76999 Unlisted ultrasound procedure (eg, diagnostic, interventional)
💲 0.00 💲 0.00 Global Days XXX
AMA: 2009, May, 7&10

CPT only © 2009 American Medical Association. All Rights Reserved. (Black Ink)   Medicare (Red Ink)   © 2009 Publisher (Blue Ink)

Current Procedural Coding Expert – Radiology

77001-77022 Imaging Guidance Techniques

+ 77001 Fluoroscopic guidance for central venous access device placement, replacement (catheter only or complete), or removal (includes fluoroscopic guidance for vascular access and catheter manipulation, any necessary contrast injections through access site or catheter with related venography radiologic supervision and interpretation, and radiographic documentation of final catheter position) (List separately in addition to code for primary procedure)

EXCLUDES *Formal extremity venography performed separately from venous access and interpreted separately (36005, 75820, 75822, 75825, 75827)*

Do not report with (77002)
2.96 2.96 Global Days ZZZ
AMA: 2009, Jan, 11-31; 2008, Jul, 9; 2008, Jun, 8-11; 2007, March, 7-8

77002 Fluoroscopic guidance for needle placement (eg, biopsy, aspiration, injection, localization device)

INCLUDES Radiographic arthrography except for supervision and interpretation of CT and MRI arthrography

Code also surgical procedure
Do not report with (49440, 74320, 74355, 74445, 74470, 74475, 75809-75810, 75885, 75887, 75980, 75982, 75989)
1.93 1.93 Global Days XXX
AMA: 2009, Jan, 11-31; 2008, Jan, 10-25; 2008, Jun, 8-11; 2008, Jul, 9; 2007, February, 10-11; 2007, May, 1-2; 2007, June, 10-11; 2007, March, 7-8

▲ 77003 Fluoroscopic guidance and localization of needle or catheter tip for spine or paraspinous diagnostic or therapeutic injection procedures (epidural, transforaminal epidural, subarachnoid, or sacroiliac joint), including neurolytic agent destruction

EXCLUDES *Injection and needle/catheter placement, epidural/subarachnoid (62270-62282, 62310-62319)*
Injection, paravertebral facet joint (64490-64495)
Neurolytic agent destruction (64600-64680)
Sacroiliac joint arthrography (27096, 73542)
Transforaminal epidural needle placement/injection (64479-64484)

1.66 1.66 Global Days XXX
AMA: 2009, Jan, 11-31; 2008, Jul, 9; 2008, Jun, 8-11; 2007, March, 7-8

77011 Computed tomography guidance for stereotactic localization
19.70 19.70 Global Days XXX
AMA: 2007, March, 7-8

77012 Computed tomography guidance for needle placement (eg, biopsy, aspiration, injection, localization device), radiological supervision and interpretation
3.26 3.26 Global Days XXX
AMA: 2007, June, 10-11; 2007, March, 7-8; 2007, May, 1-2

77013 Computed tomography guidance for, and monitoring of, parenchymal tissue ablation

EXCLUDES *Ablation, percutaneous radiofrequency (32998, 47382, 50592)*
Percutaneous radiofrequency ablation (32998, 47382, 50592-50593)

Do not report with (20982)
0.00 0.00 Global Days XXX
AMA: 2007, March, 7-8

77014 Computed tomography guidance for placement of radiation therapy fields

Code also placement of interstitial device(s) for radiation therapy guidance (31627, 32553, 49411, 55876)
4.99 4.99 Global Days XXX
AMA: 2007, March, 7-8

77021 Magnetic resonance guidance for needle placement (eg, for biopsy, needle aspiration, injection, or placement of localization device) radiological supervision and interpretation

EXCLUDES *Surgical procedure*
9.98 9.98 Global Days XXX
AMA: 2008, Jun, 8-11; 2007, May, 1-2; 2007, March, 7-8; 2007, June, 10-11

77022 Magnetic resonance guidance for, and monitoring of, parenchymal tissue ablation

EXCLUDES *Ablation:*
Percutaneous radiofrequency (32998, 47382, 50592-50593)
Uterine leiomyomata by focused ablation (0071T, 0072T)

0.00 0.00 Global Days XXX
AMA: 2007, March, 7-8

77031-77059 Radiography: Breast

CMS 100-3,220.4 Mammograms
CMS 100-4,18,20 Mammography Services
CMS 100-4,18,20.4 FI/A/B MAC Processing Mammography Services

EXCLUDES *Mammographic guidance for needle placement into lesion (77032)*

77031 Stereotactic localization guidance for breast biopsy or needle placement (eg, for wire localization or for injection), each lesion, radiological supervision and interpretation

EXCLUDES *Sentinel node localization injection without lymphoscintigraphy (38792)*

Code also surgical procedure (10022, 19000-19103, 19290-19291)
3.39 3.39 Global Days XXX
AMA: 2007, March, 7-8

77032 Mammographic guidance for needle placement, breast (eg, for wire localization or for injection), each lesion, radiological supervision and interpretation

EXCLUDES *Sentinel node localization injection without lymphoscintigraphy (38792)*

Code also surgical procedure (10022, 19000, 19102-19103, 19290-19291)
1.32 1.32 Global Days XXX
AMA: 2007, March, 7-8

77051 **CURRENT PROCEDURAL CODING EXPERT – Radiology**

+ **77051** Computer-aided detection (computer algorithm analysis of digital image data for lesion detection) with further physician review for interpretation, with or without digitization of film radiographic images; diagnostic mammography (List separately in addition to code for primary procedure)
    Code first mammography (77055, 77056)
    0.25   0.25   Global Days ZZZ
    AMA: 2007, March, 7-8; 2007, April, 1-2; 2006, December, 10-12

+ **77052** screening mammography (List separately in addition to code for primary procedure)
    Code first screening mammography (77057)
    0.25   0.25   Global Days ZZZ
    AMA: 2007, April, 1-2; 2007, March, 7-8; 2006, December, 10-12

77053 Mammary ductogram or galactogram, single duct, radiological supervision and interpretation
    Code also injection procedure (19030)
    1.45   1.45   Global Days XXX
    AMA: 2007, March, 7-8; 2006, December, 10-12

77054 Mammary ductogram or galactogram, multiple ducts, radiological supervision and interpretation
    1.94   1.94   Global Days XXX
    AMA: 2007, March, 7-8

77055 Mammography; unilateral
    Code also computer-aided detection applied to diagnostic mammogram, if performed (77051)
    2.16   2.16   Global Days XXX
    AMA: 2007, March, 7-8

77056 bilateral
    Code also computer-aided detection applied to diagnostic mammogram, if performed (77051)
    2.78   2.78   Global Days XXX
    AMA: 2007, March, 7-8

77057 Screening mammography, bilateral (2-view film study of each breast)
    EXCLUDES Breast electrical impedance scan (76499)
    Code also computer-aided detection applied to screening mammogram, if performed (77052)
    2.00   2.00   Global Days XXX
    AMA: 2007, March, 7-8

77058 Magnetic resonance imaging, breast, without and/or with contrast material(s); unilateral
    13.08   13.08   Global Days XXX
    AMA: 2007, Jul, 6-10; 2007, March, 7-8

77059 bilateral
    12.97   12.97   Global Days XXX
    AMA: 2007, Jul, 6-10; 2007, March, 7-8

77071-77084 Additional Evaluations of Bones and Joints

77071 Manual application of stress performed by physician for joint radiography, including contralateral joint if indicated
    1.31   1.31   Global Days XXX
    AMA: 2007, March, 7-8

77072 Bone age studies
    0.59   0.59   Global Days XXX
    AMA: 2007, March, 7-8

77073 Bone length studies (orthoroentgenogram, scanogram)
    0.99   0.99   Global Days XXX
    AMA: 2007, March, 7-8

77074 Radiologic examination, osseous survey; limited (eg, for metastases)
    1.73   1.73   Global Days XXX
    AMA: 2007, March, 7-8

77075 complete (axial and appendicular skeleton)
    2.56   2.56   Global Days XXX
    AMA: 2007, March, 7-8

77076 Radiologic examination, osseous survey, infant
    2.60   2.60   Global Days XXX
    AMA: 2007, March, 7-8

77077 Joint survey, single view, 2 or more joints (specify)
    1.04   1.04   Global Days XXX
    AMA: 2007, March, 7-8

77078 Computed tomography, bone mineral density study, 1 or more sites; axial skeleton (eg, hips, pelvis, spine)
    4.49   4.49   Global Days XXX
    AMA: 2007, March, 7-8

77079 appendicular skeleton (peripheral) (eg, radius, wrist, heel)
    1.02   1.02   Global Days XXX
    AMA: 2007, March, 7-8

77080 Dual-energy X-ray absorptiometry (DXA), bone density study, 1 or more sites; axial skeleton (eg, hips, pelvis, spine)
    1.24   1.24   Global Days XXX
    AMA: 2007, March, 7-8

77081 appendicular skeleton (peripheral) (eg, radius, wrist, heel)
    0.71   0.71   Global Days XXX
    AMA: 2007, March, 7-8

77082 vertebral fracture assessment
    EXCLUDES Dual-energy x-ray absorptiometry [DXA] body composition study (76499)
    0.70   0.70   Global Days XXX
    AMA: 2007, March, 7-8

77083 Radiographic absorptiometry (eg, photodensitometry, radiogrammetry), 1 or more sites
    0.62   0.62   Global Days XXX
    AMA: 2007, March, 7-8

77084 Magnetic resonance (eg, proton) imaging, bone marrow blood supply
    14.70   14.70   Global Days XXX
    AMA: 2007, March, 7-8

77261-77263 Therapeutic Radiology: Treatment Planning

CMS 100-2,6,10   Medical and Other Services Furnished to Inpatients
CMS 100-4,3,10.4   Payment of Nonphysician Services for Inpatients
INCLUDES Determination of:
    Appropriate treatment devices
    Number and size of treatment ports
    Treatment method
    Treatment time/dosage
    Treatment volume
Interpretation of special testing
Tumor localization

77261 Therapeutic radiology treatment planning; simple
    INCLUDES Planning for single treatment area included in a single port or simple parallel opposed ports with simple or no blocking
    2.08   2.08   Global Days XXX

77262 intermediate
    INCLUDES Planning for three or more converging ports, two separate treatment sites, multiple blocks, or special time dose constraints
    3.13   3.13   Global Days XXX

---

26 PC/TC Comp Only   A2/Z3 ASC Pmt   50 Bilateral   ♂ Male Only   ♀ Female Only   Facility RVU   Non-Facility RVU
AMA: CPT Asst   **MED:** Pub 100   A/Y OPPSI   80 Surg Assist Allowed / w/Doc   Lab Crosswalk   Radiology Crosswalk

Current Procedural Coding Expert – Radiology

77263 complex
INCLUDES Planning for very complex blocking, custom shielding blocks, tangential ports, special wedges or compensators, three or more separate treatment areas, rotational or special beam considerations, combination of treatment modalities
4.66 4.66 Global Days XXX

77280-77299 Radiation Therapy Simulation
CMS 100-2,6,10 Medical and Other Services Furnished to Inpatients
CMS 100-4,3,10.4 Payment of Nonphysician Services for Inpatients
CMS 100-4,4,200.3.2 Additional Billing Instructions for IMRT Planning and Delivery
INCLUDES Simulation provided on a:
Dedicated simulator
Diagnostic x-ray machine
Radiation therapy treatment unit

77280 Therapeutic radiology simulation-aided field setting; simple
INCLUDES Simple or no blocking
Simulation of a single treatment site with either a single port or parallel opposed ports
4.85 4.85 Global Days XXX

77285 intermediate
INCLUDES Multiple blocks
Simulation of converging ports >=3
Two different treatment areas
8.53 8.53 Global Days XXX

77290 complex
INCLUDES Complex blocking
Contrast material
Custom shielding blocks
Hyperthermia probe verification
Rotation or arc therapy
Treatment to >= 3 treatment areas
Simulation of tangential portals
Verification of brachytherapy source
14.03 14.03 Global Days XXX

77295 3-dimensional
INCLUDES Computer-created 3D reconstruction of tumor and surrounding tissue from direct CT scans and/or MRI data
12.09 12.09 Global Days XXX
AMA: 2005, May, 7-12

77299 Unlisted procedure, therapeutic radiology clinical treatment planning
0.00 0.00 Global Days XXX
AMA: 2009, May, 8-9&11

77300-77370 Radiation Physics Services
CMS 100-4,3,10.4 Payment of Nonphysician Services for Inpatients
CMS 100-4,3,10.4 Payment of Nonphysician Services for Inpatients
CMS 100-4,4,61.2 Requirements for Specific Procedures to be Reported With Device Codes
CMS 100-4,4,200.3.1 Billing for IMRT Planning and Delivery
CMS 100-4,4,200.3.2 Additional Billing Instructions for IMRT Planning and Delivery
CMS 100-4,4,220.2 Additional Billing Instructions for IMRT Planning

77300 Basic radiation dosimetry calculation, central axis depth dose calculation, TDF, NSD, gap calculation, off axis factor, tissue inhomogeneity factors, calculation of non-ionizing radiation surface and depth dose, as required during course of treatment, only when prescribed by the treating physician
1.80 1.80 Global Days XXX
AMA: 2009, Jan, 11-31

77301 Intensity modulated radiotherapy plan, including dose-volume histograms for target and critical structure partial tolerance specifications
61.63 61.63 Global Days XXX
AMA: 2005, March, 1-6; 2005, May, 7-12

77305 Teletherapy, isodose plan (whether hand or computer calculated); simple (1 or 2 parallel opposed unmodified ports directed to a single area of interest)
INCLUDES Normal follow-up care during and three months after treatment
1.63 1.63 Global Days XXX

77310 intermediate (3 or more treatment ports directed to a single area of interest)
INCLUDES Normal follow-up care during and three months after treatment
2.36 2.36 Global Days XXX

77315 complex (mantle or inverted Y, tangential ports, the use of wedges, compensators, complex blocking, rotational beam, or special beam considerations)
INCLUDES Normal follow-up care during and three months after treatment
3.71 3.71 Global Days XXX

77321 Special teletherapy port plan, particles, hemibody, total body
2.48 2.48 Global Days XXX

77326 Brachytherapy isodose plan; simple (calculation made from single plane, 1 to 4 sources/ribbon application, remote afterloading brachytherapy, 1 to 8 sources)
3.81 3.81 Global Days XXX

77327 intermediate (multiplane dosage calculations, application involving 5 to 10 sources/ribbons, remote afterloading brachytherapy, 9 to 12 sources)
5.37 5.37 Global Days XXX

77328 complex (multiplane isodose plan, volume implant calculations, over 10 sources/ribbons used, special spatial reconstruction, remote afterloading brachytherapy, over 12 sources)
7.20 7.20 Global Days XXX

77331 Special dosimetry (eg, TLD, microdosimetry) (specify), only when prescribed by the treating physician
1.75 1.75 Global Days XXX

77332 Treatment devices, design and construction; simple (simple block, simple bolus)
2.05 2.05 Global Days XXX

 New Code   Revised Code   Maternity   Age    Unlisted   Not Covered   # Resequenced

CCI   + Add-on   Mod 51 Exempt   Mod 63 Exempt   Mod Sedation   PQRI

© 2009 Publisher (Blue Ink)   CPT only © 2009 American Medical Association. All Rights Reserved. (Black Ink)   Medicare (Red Ink)

77333	intermediate (multiple blocks, stents, bite blocks, special bolus)
	1.46 1.46 Global Days XXX
77334	complex (irregular blocks, special shields, compensators, wedges, molds or casts)
	3.91 3.91 Global Days XXX
77336	Continuing medical physics consultation, including assessment of treatment parameters, quality assurance of dose delivery, and review of patient treatment documentation in support of the radiation oncologist, reported per week of therapy
	1.05 1.05 Global Days XXX
● 77338	Multi-leaf collimator (MLC) device(s) for intensity modulated radiation therapy (IMRT), design and construction per IMRT plan

Do not report with (0073T)
EXCLUDES Immobilization in IMRT treatment (77332-77334)

Do not report more than once per IMRT plan
13.23 13.23 Global Days XXX

77370	Special medical radiation physics consultation
	2.81 2.81 Global Days XXX
	AMA: 2009, May, 8-9;11

77371-77399 Stereotactic Radiosurgery (SRS) Planning and Delivery

CMS 100-4,4,200.3.3   Billing Multi-Source Photon Stereotactic Radiosurgery Planning and Delivery

⊙ 77371	Radiation treatment delivery, stereotactic radiosurgery (SRS), complete course of treatment of cranial lesion(s) consisting of 1 session; multi-source Cobalt 60 based
	0.00 0.00 Global Days XXX
	AMA: 2007, March, 7-8
77372	linear accelerator based
	EXCLUDES Radiation treatment supervision (77432)
	20.89 20.89 Global Days XXX
	AMA: 2007, March, 7-8
77373	Stereotactic body radiation therapy, treatment delivery, per fraction to 1 or more lesions, including image guidance, entire course not to exceed 5 fractions
	EXCLUDES Single fraction cranial lesion(s) (77371-77372)
	Do not report with (77401-77416, 77418)
	38.86 38.86 Global Days XXX
	AMA: 2007, March, 7-8
77399	Unlisted procedure, medical radiation physics, dosimetry and treatment devices, and special services
	0.00 0.00 Global Days XXX

77401-77417 Radiation Treatment

CMS 100-2,6,10   Medical and Other Services Furnished to Inpatients
CMS 100-4,3,10.4   Payment of Nonphysician Services for Inpatients
CMS 100-4,4,220.1   Billing for IMRT Planning and Delivery
CMS 100-4,13,70.3   Radiation Treatment Delivery
EXCLUDES Intra-fraction localization and target tracking (0197T)
INCLUDES Technical component and assorted energy levels

77401	Radiation treatment delivery, superficial and/or ortho voltage
	0.43 0.43 Global Days XXX

77402	Radiation treatment delivery, single treatment area, single port or parallel opposed ports, simple blocks or no blocks; up to 5 MeV
	3.84 3.84 Global Days XXX
77403	6-10 MeV
	3.42 3.42 Global Days XXX
77404	11-19 MeV
	3.84 3.84 Global Days XXX
77406	20 MeV or greater
	3.90 3.90 Global Days XXX
77407	Radiation treatment delivery, 2 separate treatment areas, 3 or more ports on a single treatment area, use of multiple blocks; up to 5 MeV
	6.80 6.80 Global Days XXX
77408	6-10 MeV
	4.71 4.71 Global Days XXX
77409	11-19 MeV
	5.26 5.26 Global Days XXX
77411	20 MeV or greater
	5.26 5.26 Global Days XXX
77412	Radiation treatment delivery, 3 or more separate treatment areas, custom blocking, tangential ports, wedges, rotational beam, compensators, electron beam; up to 5 MeV
	6.21 6.21 Global Days XXX
77413	6-10 MeV
	6.25 6.25 Global Days XXX
77414	11-19 MeV
	7.03 7.03 Global Days XXX
77416	20 MeV or greater
	7.06 7.06 Global Days XXX
77417	Therapeutic radiology port film(s)
	0.34 0.34 Global Days XXX
	AMA: 2009, Jan, 11-31; 2008, Jan, 10-25; 2007, January, 13-27; 2006, February, 16-18

77418 IMRT Delivery

CMS 100-2,6,10   Medical and Other Services Furnished to Inpatients
CMS 100-4,3,10.4   Payment of Nonphysician Services for Inpatients
CMS 100-4,4,220.1   Billing for IMRT Planning and Delivery
EXCLUDES Delivery of compensator-based beam modulation treatment (0073T)
Intra-fraction localization and target tracking (0197T)
Treatment planning (77301)

77418	Intensity modulated treatment delivery, single or multiple fields/arcs, via narrow spatially and temporally modulated beams, binary, dynamic MLC, per treatment session
	12.01 12.01 Global Days XXX
	AMA: 2007, May, 1-2; 2005, March, 1-6; 2005, March, 11-15; 2005, May, 7-12

77421 Stereoscopic Imaging Guidance

CMS 100-2,6,10   Medical and Other Services Furnished to Inpatients
CMS 100-4,3,10.4   Payment of Nonphysician Services for Inpatients
EXCLUDES Placement of interstitial device(s) for radiation therapy guidance (31627, 32553, 49411, 55876)
Do not report with (77432, 77435)

77421	Stereoscopic X-ray guidance for localization of target volume for the delivery of radiation therapy
	2.63 2.63 Global Days XXX

CURRENT PROCEDURAL CODING EXPERT – Radiology

77422-77423 Neutron Therapy

77422 High energy neutron radiation treatment delivery; single treatment area using a single port or parallel-opposed ports with no blocks or simple blocking
  6.18 6.18 Global Days XXX

77423 1 or more isocenter(s) with coplanar or non-coplanar geometry with blocking and/or wedge, and/or compensator(s)
  6.83 6.83 Global Days XXX

77427-77499 Radiation Therapy Management

CMS 100-4,13,70.1 Weekly Radiation Therapy Management

INCLUDES Assessment of patient for medical evaluation and management
Review of:
  Dose delivery
  Dosimetry
  Patient treatment set-up
  Port film
  Treatment parameters
Units of five fractions or treatment sessions regardless of time

77427 Radiation treatment management, 5 treatments
  INCLUDES Fewer than two fractions at the end of a treatment period
  5.64 5.64 Global Days XXX
  AMA: 2005, March, 11-15

77431 Radiation therapy management with complete course of therapy consisting of 1 or 2 fractions only
  2.85 2.85 Global Days XXX

77432 Stereotactic radiation treatment management of cranial lesion(s) (complete course of treatment consisting of 1 session)
  EXCLUDES Stereotactic body radiation therapy treatment (77435)
  Do not report with stereotactic radiosurgery (61796-61800)
  11.76 11.76 Global Days XXX

77435 Stereotactic body radiation therapy, treatment management, per treatment course, to 1 or more lesions, including image guidance, entire course not to exceed 5 fractions
  Do not report with (77427-77432)
  Do not report with stereotactic radiosurgery (63620, 63621)
  19.57 19.57 Global Days XXX
  AMA: 2007, March, 7-8

77470 Special treatment procedure (eg, total body irradiation, hemibody radiation, per oral, endocavitary or intraoperative cone irradiation)
  4.18 4.18 Global Days XXX

77499 Unlisted procedure, therapeutic radiology treatment management
  0.00 0.00 Global Days XXX

77520-77525 Proton Therapy

CMS 100-2,6,10 Medical and Other Services Furnished to Inpatients
CMS 100-4,3,10.4 Payment of Nonphysician Services for Inpatients
EXCLUDES High dose rate electronic brachytherapy, per fraction (0182T)

77520 Proton treatment delivery; simple, without compensation
  INCLUDES Single treatment area using a single nontangential/oblique port
  0.00 0.00 Global Days XXX

77522 simple, with compensation
  INCLUDES Single treatment area using a single nontangential/oblique port
  0.00 0.00 Global Days XXX

77523 intermediate
  INCLUDES Proton therapy delivery to one or more treatment sites using two or more ports or one or more tangential/oblique ports, with custom blocks and compensators
  0.00 0.00 Global Days XXX

77525 complex
  INCLUDES Proton therapy delivery to one or more treatment sites using two or more ports per treatment site with matching or patching fields and/or numerous isocenters, with custom blocks and compensators
  0.00 0.00 Global Days XXX

77600-77620 Hyperthermia Treatment

CMS 100-3,110.1 Hyperthermia for Treatment of Cancer
INCLUDES Interstitial insertion of temperature sensors
  Management during the course of therapy
  Normal follow-up care for three months after completion
  Physics planning
  Use of heat generating devices
EXCLUDES High dose rate electronic brachytherapy, per fraction (0182T)
  Preliminary consultation (99241-99255)
  Radiation therapy treatment (77371-77373, 77401-77416, 77422-77423)

77600 Hyperthermia, externally generated; superficial (ie, heating to a depth of 4 cm or less)
  11.14 11.14 Global Days XXX

77605 deep (ie, heating to depths greater than 4 cm)
  28.30 28.30 Global Days XXX

77610 Hyperthermia generated by interstitial probe(s); 5 or fewer interstitial applicators
  17.13 17.13 Global Days XXX

77615 more than 5 interstitial applicators
  26.17 26.17 Global Days XXX

77620 Hyperthermia generated by intracavitary probe(s)
  13.90 13.90 Global Days XXX

77750

77750-77799 Brachytherapy

CMS 100-4,4,61.4.1 — Brachytherapy Sources - General
CMS 100-4,4,61.4.3 — Brachytherapy Sources Ordered for a Specific Patient
CMS 100-4,4,61.4.4 — Billing for Brachytherapy Source Supervision, Handling, and Loading Costs
CMS 100-4,13,70.4 — Clinical Brachytherapy

INCLUDES Hospital admission and daily visits

EXCLUDES High dose rate electronic brachytherapy, per fraction (0182T)
Placement of:
  Heyman capsules (58346)
  Ovoids and tandems (57155)

Code also brachytherapy sources (C1716-C1719, C2616, C2634-C2643, C2698-C2699)

77750 Infusion or instillation of radioelement solution (includes 3-month follow-up care)
  EXCLUDES Monoclonal antibody infusion (79403)
  Nonantibody radiopharmaceutical therapy infusion with follow-up care (79101)
  9.98 9.98 Global Days 090
  AMA: 2005, September, 1-4

77761 Intracavitary radiation source application; simple
  INCLUDES One to four sources/ribbons
  Do not report with (0182T)
  10.17 10.17 Global Days 090
  AMA: 2009, Jan, 11-31; 2008, Jan, 10-25; 2007, January, 13-27; 2005, September, 1-4

77762 intermediate
  INCLUDES Five to 10 sources/ribbons
  Do not report with (0182T)
  13.68 13.68 Global Days 090
  AMA: 2005, September, 1-4

77763 complex
  INCLUDES More than 10 sources/ribbons
  Do not report with (0182T)
  19.41 19.41 Global Days 090
  AMA: 2005, September, 1-4

77776 Interstitial radiation source application; simple
  INCLUDES One to four sources/ribbons
  11.57 11.57 Global Days 090
  AMA: 2007, May, 1-2; 2005, September, 1-4

77777 intermediate
  INCLUDES Five to 10 sources/ribbons
  15.81 15.81 Global Days 090
  AMA: 2007, May, 1-2; 2005, September, 1-4

77778 complex
  INCLUDES More than 10 sources/ribbons
  23.40 23.40 Global Days 090
  AMA: 2007, May, 1-2; 2005, September, 1-4

77785 Remote afterloading high dose rate radionuclide brachytherapy; 1 channel
  Do not report with (0182T)
  4.89 4.89 Global Days XXX

77786 2-12 channels
  Do not report with (0182T)
  11.35 11.35 Global Days XXX

77787 over 12 channels
  Do not report with (0182T)
  19.07 19.07 Global Days XXX

77789 Surface application of radiation source
  3.16 3.16 Global Days 000
  AMA: 2005, September, 1-4

77790 Supervision, handling, loading of radiation source
  2.55 2.55 Global Days XXX
  AMA: 2005, September, 1-4

77799 Unlisted procedure, clinical brachytherapy
  0.00 0.00 Global Days XXX
  AMA: 2005, September, 1-4

78000-78320 Nuclear Radiology Procedures

CMS 100-3,220.8 — Nuclear Radiology Procedure
CMS 100-3,220.12 — Single Photon Emission Tomography

EXCLUDES Diagnostic services (see appropriate sections)
Follow-up care (see appropriate section)
Radioimmunoassays (82000-84999 [82652])

Code also radiopharmaceuticals (A4641-A4642, A9500-A9605, C1716-C1719, C2616, C2634-C2643, C2698-C2699, C9247, C9898)

78000 Thyroid uptake; single determination
  1.72 1.72 Global Days XXX
  AMA: 2009, Jan, 11-31; 2008, Jan, 10-25; 2007, January, 13-27; 2007, January, 28-31; 2005, December, 7

78001 multiple determinations
  2.21 2.21 Global Days XXX
  AMA: 2007, January, 28-31; 2005, December, 7

78003 stimulation, suppression or discharge (not including initial uptake studies)
  1.98 1.98 Global Days XXX
  AMA: 2007, January, 28-31; 2005, December, 7

78006 Thyroid imaging, with uptake; single determination
  5.86 5.86 Global Days XXX
  AMA: 2007, January, 28-31; 2005, December, 7

78007 multiple determinations
  3.08 3.08 Global Days XXX
  AMA: 2007, January, 28-31; 2005, December, 7

Hypothyroidism is the syndrome caused by a deficiency of thyroid hormone; the condition may be congenital, acquired, or iatrogenic (resulting from medical treatment)

The thyroid gland secretes hormones governing the body's metabolic rate; excess levels result in hyperthyroidism; abnormal enlargement of the gland is called goiter and there are numerous forms

78010 Thyroid imaging; only
  4.01 4.01 Global Days XXX
  AMA: 2007, January, 28-31; 2005, December, 7

78011 with vascular flow
  4.30 4.30 Global Days XXX
  AMA: 2007, January, 28-31; 2005, December, 7

78015 Thyroid carcinoma metastases imaging; limited area (eg, neck and chest only)
  5.21 5.21 Global Days XXX
  AMA: 2007, January, 28-31; 2005, December, 7

Current Procedural Coding Expert – Radiology

78016	with additional studies (eg, urinary recovery)
	6.90 6.90 Global Days XXX
	AMA: 2007, January, 28-31; 2005, December, 7
78018	whole body
	7.57 7.57 Global Days XXX
	AMA: 2007, January, 28-31; 2005, December, 7
+ 78020	Thyroid carcinoma metastases uptake (List separately in addition to code for primary procedure)
	Code first (78018)
	2.03 2.03 Global Days ZZZ
	AMA: 2009, Jan, 11-31; 2008, Jan, 10-25; 2007, January, 28-31; 2007, January, 13-27; 2005, December, 7
78070	Parathyroid imaging
	3.74 3.74 Global Days XXX
	AMA: 2007, January, 28-31; 2005, December, 7
78075	Adrenal imaging, cortex and/or medulla
	10.27 10.27 Global Days XXX
	AMA: 2007, January, 28-31; 2005, December, 7

[Anatomical illustrations of the thyroid gland with labels: Epiglottis, Hyoid bone, Thyroid cartilage, Pyramid lobe, Cricoid cartilage, Thyroid gland, Isthmus, Thyroglossal duct (dotted line), Cricothyroid muscle, Trachea, Esophagus. The thyroid is an important endocrine gland and its size and configuration can vary greatly. A pyramid lobe occurs in about 40 percent of people and is a remnant of the thyroglossal duct.]

78099	**Unlisted endocrine procedure, diagnostic nuclear medicine**
	0.00 0.00 Global Days XXX
	AMA: 2007, January, 28-31; 2005, December, 7
78102	Bone marrow imaging; limited area
	4.03 4.03 Global Days XXX
	AMA: 2007, January, 28-31; 2005, December, 7
78103	multiple areas
	5.30 5.30 Global Days XXX
	AMA: 2007, January, 28-31; 2005, December, 7
78104	whole body
	5.96 5.96 Global Days XXX
	AMA: 2007, January, 28-31; 2005, December, 7
78110	Plasma volume, radiopharmaceutical volume-dilution technique (separate procedure); single sampling
	2.06 2.06 Global Days XXX
	AMA: 2007, January, 28-31; 2005, December, 7
78111	multiple samplings
	1.77 1.77 Global Days XXX
	AMA: 2007, January, 28-31; 2005, December, 7
78120	Red cell volume determination (separate procedure); single sampling
	1.93 1.93 Global Days XXX
	AMA: 2007, January, 28-31; 2005, December, 7
78121	multiple samplings
	1.77 1.77 Global Days XXX
	AMA: 2007, January, 28-31; 2005, December, 7

78122	Whole blood volume determination, including separate measurement of plasma volume and red cell volume (radiopharmaceutical volume-dilution technique)
	2.20 2.20 Global Days XXX
	AMA: 2007, January, 28-31; 2005, December, 7
78130	Red cell survival study;
	3.67 3.67 Global Days XXX
	AMA: 2007, January, 28-31; 2005, December, 7
78135	differential organ/tissue kinetics (eg, splenic and/or hepatic sequestration)
	8.42 8.42 Global Days XXX
	AMA: 2007, January, 28-31; 2005, December, 7
78140	Labeled red cell sequestration, differential organ/tissue (eg, splenic and/or hepatic)
	3.08 3.08 Global Days XXX
	AMA: 2007, January, 28-31; 2005, December, 7
78185	Spleen imaging only, with or without vascular flow
	EXCLUDES Liver imaging (78215-78216)
	4.91 4.91 Global Days XXX
	AMA: 2007, January, 28-31; 2005, December, 7
78190	Kinetics, study of platelet survival, with or without differential organ/tissue localization
	10.18 10.18 Global Days XXX
	AMA: 2007, January, 28-31; 2005, December, 7
78191	Platelet survival study
	3.65 3.65 Global Days XXX
	AMA: 2007, January, 28-31; 2005, December, 7
78195	Lymphatics and lymph nodes imaging
	EXCLUDES Sentinel node identification without scintigraphy (38792)
	Sentinel node removal (38500-38542)
	8.73 8.73 Global Days XXX
	AMA: 2008, Sep, 5-6; 2007, January, 28-31; 2005, December, 7
78199	**Unlisted hematopoietic, reticuloendothelial and lymphatic procedure, diagnostic nuclear medicine**
	0.00 0.00 Global Days XXX
	AMA: 2007, January, 28-31; 2005, December, 7
78201	Liver imaging; static only
	EXCLUDES Spleen imaging only (78185)
	4.70 4.70 Global Days XXX
	AMA: 2007, January, 28-31; 2005, December, 7
78202	with vascular flow
	EXCLUDES Spleen imaging only (78185)
	4.83 4.83 Global Days XXX
	AMA: 2007, January, 28-31; 2005, December, 7
78205	Liver imaging (SPECT);
	5.18 5.18 Global Days XXX
	AMA: 2007, January, 28-31; 2005, December, 7
78206	with vascular flow
	8.49 8.49 Global Days XXX
	AMA: 2007, January, 28-31; 2005, December, 7
78215	Liver and spleen imaging; static only
	4.63 4.63 Global Days XXX
	AMA: 2007, January, 28-31; 2005, December, 7
78216	with vascular flow
	2.95 2.95 Global Days XXX
	AMA: 2007, January, 28-31; 2005, December, 7
78220	Liver function study with hepatobiliary agents, with serial images
	3.07 3.07 Global Days XXX
	AMA: 2007, January, 28-31; 2005, December, 7

● New Code   ▲ Revised Code   M Maternity   A Age   Unlisted   Not Covered   # Resequenced
CCI   + Add-on   Mod 51 Exempt   Mod 63 Exempt   Mod Sedation   PQRI

© 2009 Publisher (*Blue Ink*)   CPT only © 2009 American Medical Association. All Rights Reserved. (Black Ink)   Medicare (Red Ink)

78223   **Current Procedural Coding Expert – Radiology**

78223	Hepatobiliary ductal system imaging, including gallbladder, with or without pharmacologic intervention, with or without quantitative measurement of gallbladder function
	8.23 8.23 Global Days XXX
	AMA: 2007, January, 28-31; 2005, December, 7
78230	Salivary gland imaging;
	4.09 4.09 Global Days XXX
	AMA: 2007, January, 28-31; 2005, December, 7
78231	with serial images
	2.94 2.94 Global Days XXX
	AMA: 2007, January, 28-31; 2005, December, 7
78232	Salivary gland function study
	2.34 2.34 Global Days XXX
	AMA: 2007, January, 28-31; 2005, December, 7
78258	Esophageal motility
	5.90 5.90 Global Days XXX
	AMA: 2007, January, 28-31; 2005, December, 7
78261	Gastric mucosa imaging
	6.03 6.03 Global Days XXX
	AMA: 2007, January, 28-31; 2005, December, 7
78262	Gastroesophageal reflux study
	5.94 5.94 Global Days XXX
	AMA: 2007, January, 28-31; 2005, December, 7
78264	Gastric emptying study
	6.95 6.95 Global Days XXX
	AMA: 2007, January, 28-31; 2005, December, 7
78267	Urea breath test, C-14 (isotopic); acquisition for analysis
	0.00 0.00 Global Days XXX
	AMA: 2007, January, 28-31; 2005, December, 7
78268	analysis
	0.00 0.00 Global Days XXX
	AMA: 2007, January, 28-31; 2005, December, 7
78270	Vitamin B-12 absorption study (eg, Schilling test); without intrinsic factor
	1.93 1.93 Global Days XXX
	AMA: 2007, January, 28-31; 2005, December, 7
78271	with intrinsic factor
	2.23 2.23 Global Days XXX
	AMA: 2007, January, 28-31; 2005, December, 7
78272	Vitamin B-12 absorption studies combined, with and without intrinsic factor
	2.13 2.13 Global Days XXX
	AMA: 2007, January, 28-31; 2005, December, 7
78278	Acute gastrointestinal blood loss imaging
	8.43 8.43 Global Days XXX
	AMA: 2007, January, 28-31; 2005, December, 7
78282	Gastrointestinal protein loss
	0.00 0.00 Global Days XXX
	AMA: 2007, January, 28-31; 2005, December, 7
78290	Intestine imaging (eg, ectopic gastric mucosa, Meckel's localization, volvulus)
	8.03 8.03 Global Days XXX
	AMA: 2007, January, 28-31; 2005, December, 7
78291	Peritoneal-venous shunt patency test (eg, for LeVeen, Denver shunt)
	Code also (49427)
	6.22 6.22 Global Days XXX
	AMA: 2007, January, 28-31; 2005, December, 7
78299	Unlisted gastrointestinal procedure, diagnostic nuclear medicine
	0.00 0.00 Global Days XXX
	AMA: 2007, January, 28-31; 2005, December, 7
78300	Bone and/or joint imaging; limited area
	4.32 4.32 Global Days XXX
	AMA: 2009, Jan, 11-31; 2008, Jan, 10-25; 2007, January, 28-31; 2007, January, 13-27; 2005, December, 7
78305	multiple areas
	5.65 5.65 Global Days XXX
	AMA: 2007, January, 28-31; 2005, December, 7
78306	whole body
	6.07 6.07 Global Days XXX
	AMA: 2009, Jan, 11-31; 2008, Jan, 10-25; 2007, January, 28-31; 2007, January, 13-27; 2005, December, 7
78315	3 phase study
	8.43 8.43 Global Days XXX
	AMA: 2009, Jan, 11-31; 2008, Jan, 10-25; 2007, January, 28-31; 2007, January, 13-27; 2005, December, 7
78320	tomographic (SPECT)
	5.58 5.58 Global Days XXX
	AMA: 2009, Jan, 11-31; 2008, Jan, 8-9; 2007, January, 28-31; 2005, December, 7

78350-78399 Nuclear Radiology: Bone Density Studies

CMS 100-3,150.3   Bone (Mineral) Density Studies
CMS 100-3,220.8   Nuclear Radiology Procedure
EXCLUDES   Radiographic bone density (photodensitometry) (77083)

Code also radiopharmaceuticals (A4641-A4642, A9500-A9605, C1716-C1719, C2616, C2634-C2643, C2698-C2699, C9247, C9898)

78350	Bone density (bone mineral content) study, 1 or more sites; single photon absorptiometry
	0.82 0.82 Global Days XXX
	AMA: 2007, January, 28-31; 2005, December, 7
78351	dual photon absorptiometry, 1 or more sites
	0.43 0.43 Global Days XXX
	AMA: 2007, January, 28-31; 2005, December, 7
78399	Unlisted musculoskeletal procedure, diagnostic nuclear medicine
	0.00 0.00 Global Days XXX
	AMA: 2007, January, 28-31; 2005, December, 7

78414-78499 Nuclear Radiology: Heart and Vascular

CMS 100-3,220.6   Positron Emission Tomography (PET) Scans
CMS 100-3,220.6.1   NCD for PET for Perfusion of the Heart (220.6.1)
CMS 100-3,220.6.8   PET (FDG) for Myocardial Viability
CMS 100-3,220.8   Nuclear Radiology Procedure
CMS 100-3,220.12   Single Photon Emission Tomography
CMS 100-4,13,60   Positron Emission Tomography (PET) Scans - General Information
CMS 100-4,13,60.1   Billing for PET Scans
CMS 100-4,13,60.2   Use of Gamma Cameras, Full and Partial Ring PET Scanners
CMS 100-4,13,60.3   PET Scan Qualifying Conditions
CMS 100-4,13,60.4   PET Scans for Imaging of the Perfusion of the Heart Using Rubidium 82
CMS 100-4,13,60.9   Coverage of PET Scans for Myocardial Viability
CMS 100-4,13,60.11   PET Scans for Perfusion of the Heart Using Ammonia N-13
EXCLUDES   Stress testing (93015-93018)

Code also radiopharmaceuticals (A4641-A4642, A9500-A9605, C1716-C1719, C2616, C2634-C2643, C2698-C2699, C9247, C9898)

78414	Determination of central c-v hemodynamics (non-imaging) (eg, ejection fraction with probe technique) with or without pharmacologic intervention or exercise, single or multiple determinations
	0.00 0.00 Global Days XXX
	AMA: 2007, January, 28-31; 2005, December, 7
78428	Cardiac shunt detection
	4.76 4.76 Global Days XXX
	AMA: 2007, January, 28-31; 2005, December, 7

26/TC PC/TC Comp Only   **A2-Z3** ASC Pmt   **50** Bilateral   ♂ Male Only   ♀ Female Only   Facility RVU   Non-Facility RVU
AMA: CPT Asst   **MED:** Pub 100   **A-Y** OPPSI   **80/80** Surg Assist Allowed / w/Doc   Lab Crosswalk   Radiology Crosswalk

292   CPT only © 2009 American Medical Association. All Rights Reserved. (Black Ink)   Medicare (Red Ink)   © 2009 Publisher (Blue Ink)

Current Procedural Coding Expert – Radiology 78494

78445	Non-cardiac vascular flow imaging (ie, angiography, venography)
	4.16 4.16 Global Days XXX
	AMA: 2007, January, 28-31; 2005, December, 7
● 78451	Myocardial perfusion imaging, tomographic (SPECT) (including attenuation correction, qualitative or quantitative wall motion, ejection fraction by first pass or gated technique, additional quantification, when performed); single study, at rest or stress (exercise or pharmacologic)
	6.16 6.16 Global Days XXX
● 78452	multiple studies, at rest and/or stress (exercise or pharmacologic) and/or redistribution and/or rest reinjection
	10.52 10.52 Global Days XXX
● 78453	Myocardial perfusion imaging, planar (including qualitative or quantitative wall motion, ejection fraction by first pass or gated technique, additional quantification, when performed); single study, at rest or stress (exercise or pharmacologic)
	5.36 5.36 Global Days XXX
● 78454	multiple studies, at rest and/or stress (exercise or pharmacologic) and/or redistribution and/or rest reinjection
	5.16 5.16 Global Days XXX
78456	Acute venous thrombosis imaging, peptide
	8.17 8.17 Global Days XXX
	AMA: 2007, January, 28-31; 2005, December, 7
78457	Venous thrombosis imaging, venogram; unilateral
	4.81 4.81 Global Days XXX
	AMA: 2007, January, 28-31; 2005, December, 7
78458	bilateral
	4.54 4.54 Global Days XXX
	AMA: 2007, January, 28-31; 2005, December, 7
78459	Myocardial imaging, positron emission tomography (PET), metabolic evaluation
	0.00 0.00 Global Days XXX
	AMA: 2007, January, 28-31; 2005, December, 7
~~78460~~	~~Myocardial perfusion imaging; (planar) single study, at rest or stress (exercise and/or pharmacologic), with or without quantification~~
	To report, see code 78453
~~78461~~	~~multiple studies (planar), at rest and/or stress (exercise or pharmacologic), and redistribution and/or rest injection, with or without quantification~~
	To report, see code 78454
~~78464~~	~~tomographic (SPECT), single study (including attenuation correction when performed), at rest or stress (exercise or pharmacologic), with or without quantification~~
	To report, see code 78451
~~78465~~	~~tomographic (SPECT), multiple studies (including attenuation correction when performed), at rest and/or stress (exercise or pharmacologic) and redistribution and/or rest injection, with or without quantification~~
	To report, see code 78452
78466	Myocardial imaging, infarct avid, planar; qualitative or quantitative
	4.27 4.27 Global Days XXX
	AMA: 2007, January, 28-31; 2005, December, 7
78468	with ejection fraction by first pass technique
	5.04 5.04 Global Days XXX
	AMA: 2007, January, 28-31; 2005, December, 7
78469	tomographic SPECT with or without quantification
	5.94 5.94 Global Days XXX
	AMA: 2007, January, 28-31; 2005, December, 7
78472	Cardiac blood pool imaging, gated equilibrium; planar, single study at rest or stress (exercise and/or pharmacologic), wall motion study plus ejection fraction, with or without additional quantitative processing
	Do not report with (78451-78454, 78481, 78483, 78494)
	5.74 5.74 Global Days XXX
	AMA: 2007, January, 28-31; 2005, December, 7
78473	multiple studies, wall motion study plus ejection fraction, at rest and stress (exercise and/or pharmacologic), with or without additional quantification
	Do not report with (78451-78454, 78481, 78483, 78494)
	7.44 7.44 Global Days XXX
	AMA: 2007, January, 28-31; 2005, December, 7
~~78478~~	~~Myocardial perfusion study with wall motion, qualitative or quantitative study (List separately in addition to code for primary procedure)~~
	To report, see code 78451-78454
~~78480~~	~~Myocardial perfusion study with ejection fraction (List separately in addition to code for primary procedure)~~
	To report, see code 78451-78454
78481	Cardiac blood pool imaging (planar), first pass technique; single study, at rest or with stress (exercise and/or pharmacologic), wall motion study plus ejection fraction, with or without quantification
	Do not report with (78451-78454)
	4.63 4.63 Global Days XXX
	AMA: 2007, January, 28-31; 2005, December, 7
78483	multiple studies, at rest and with stress (exercise and/or pharmacologic), wall motion study plus ejection fraction, with or without quantification
	Do not report with (78451-78454)
	EXCLUDES Blood flow studies of the brain (78610)
	6.28 6.28 Global Days XXX
	AMA: 2007, January, 28-31; 2005, December, 7
78491	Myocardial imaging, positron emission tomography (PET), perfusion; single study at rest or stress
	0.00 0.00 Global Days XXX
	AMA: 2007, January, 28-31; 2005, December, 7
78492	multiple studies at rest and/or stress
	0.00 0.00 Global Days XXX
	AMA: 2007, January, 28-31; 2005, December
78494	Cardiac blood pool imaging, gated equilibrium, SPECT, at rest, wall motion study plus ejection fraction, with or without quantitative processing
	5.99 5.99 Global Days XXX
	AMA: 2007, January, 28-31; 2005, December, 7

● New Code ▲ Revised Code Ⓜ Maternity Ⓐ Age Unlisted Not Covered # Resequenced

CCI + Add-on ⊘ Mod 51 Exempt 63 Mod 63 Exempt ⊙ Mod Sedation PQRI

© 2009 Publisher (Blue Ink)   CPT only © 2009 American Medical Association. All Rights Reserved. (Black Ink)   Medicare (Red Ink)

Current Procedural Coding Expert – Radiology

| + | 78496 | Cardiac blood pool imaging, gated equilibrium, single study, at rest, with right ventricular ejection fraction by first pass technique (List separately in addition to code for primary procedure) N1 N 80 |

Code first (78472)
🔧 1.15 🔨 1.15 Global Days ZZZ
AMA: 2009, Jan, 11-31; 2008, Jan, 10-25; 2007, January, 13-27; 2007, January, 28-31; 2005, December, 7

| | 78499 | Unlisted cardiovascular procedure, diagnostic nuclear medicine Z2 S 80 |

🔧 0.00 🔨 0.00 Global Days XXX
AMA: 2007, January, 28-31; 2005, December, 7

78580-78599 Nuclear Radiology: Lungs

CMS 100-2,15,80 Physician Supervision Requirements for Diagnostic Tests
CMS 100-3,220.7 Xenon Scan
CMS 100-3,220.8 Nuclear Radiology Procedure
CMS 100-4,3,10.4 Payment of Nonphysician Services for Inpatients

Code also radiopharmaceuticals (A4641-A4642, A9500-A9605, C1716-C1719, C2616, C2634-C2643, C2698-C2699, C3247, C9898)

| | 78580 | Pulmonary perfusion imaging, particulate Z2 S 80 |

Do not report with (78451-78454)
🔧 5.07 🔨 5.07 Global Days XXX
AMA: 2007, January, 28-31; 2005, December, 7

| | 78584 | Pulmonary perfusion imaging, particulate, with ventilation; single breath Z2 S 80 |

🔧 3.57 🔨 3.57 Global Days XXX
AMA: 2007, January, 28-31; 2005, December, 7

| | 78585 | rebreathing and washout, with or without single breath Z2 S 80 |

🔧 8.51 🔨 8.51 Global Days XXX
AMA: 2007, January, 28-31; 2005, December, 7

| | 78586 | Pulmonary ventilation imaging, aerosol; single projection Z3 S 80 |

🔧 4.03 🔨 4.03 Global Days XXX
AMA: 2007, January, 28-31; 2005, December, 7

| | 78587 | multiple projections (eg, anterior, posterior, lateral views) Z2 S 80 |

🔧 5.04 🔨 5.04 Global Days XXX
AMA: 2007, January, 28-31; 2005, December, 7

| | 78588 | Pulmonary perfusion imaging, particulate, with ventilation imaging, aerosol, 1 or multiple projections Z2 S 80 |

🔧 8.59 🔨 8.59 Global Days XXX
AMA: 2007, January, 28-31; 2005, December, 7

| | 78591 | Pulmonary ventilation imaging, gaseous, single breath, single projection Z3 S 80 |

🔧 4.02 🔨 4.02 Global Days XXX
AMA: 2007, January, 28-31; 2005, December, 7

| | 78593 | Pulmonary ventilation imaging, gaseous, with rebreathing and washout with or without single breath; single projection Z2 S 80 |

🔧 4.65 🔨 4.65 Global Days XXX
AMA: 2007, January, 28-31; 2005, December, 7

| | 78594 | multiple projections (eg, anterior, posterior, lateral views) Z2 S 80 |

🔧 4.94 🔨 4.94 Global Days XXX
AMA: 2007, January, 28-31; 2005, December, 7

| | 78596 | Pulmonary quantitative differential function (ventilation/perfusion) study Z2 S 80 |

🔧 8.90 🔨 8.90 Global Days XXX
AMA: 2007, January, 28-31; 2005, December, 7

| | 78599 | Unlisted respiratory procedure, diagnostic nuclear medicine Z2 S |

🔧 0.00 🔨 0.00 Global Days XXX
AMA: 2007, January, 28-31; 2005, December, 7

78600-78650 Diagnostic Imaging: Brain/Cerebrospinal Fluid

CMS 100-3,220.6.9 FDG PET for Refractory Seizures
CMS 100-3,220.8 Nuclear Radiology Procedure

Code also radiopharmaceuticals (A4641-A4642, A9500-A9605, C1716-C1719, C2616, C2634-C2643, C2698-C2699, C9247, C9898)

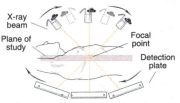
Diagram of tomography principal (left)

Schematic of frontal coronal CT section of skull

Tomogram is a general term for radiographic studies that focus on a single body plane, unimpeded by shadows cast by surrounding tissues and structures. The x-ray tube and the film are rotated around the patient during exposure of the focal point. Computed tomography (CT) offers a "slice" view of the study area and information is typically digitized and viewed on monitors. Magnetic resonance imaging (MRI) places a patient within the field of a powerful magnet while radio waves pass through the body; as with CT studies, views are usually of a "slice" of tissue. Ultrasound and nuclear imaging are other common radiological approaches

| 78600 | Brain imaging, less than 4 static views; Z3 S 80 |

🔧 4.33 🔨 4.33 Global Days XXX
AMA: 2007, January, 28-31; 2005, December, 7

| 78601 | with vascular flow Z3 S 80 |

🔧 5.08 🔨 5.08 Global Days XXX
AMA: 2007, January, 28-31; 2005, December, 7

| 78605 | Brain imaging, minimum 4 static views; Z2 S 80 |

🔧 4.68 🔨 4.68 Global Days XXX
AMA: 2007, January, 28-31; 2005, December, 7

| 78606 | with vascular flow Z3 S 80 |

🔧 8.22 🔨 8.22 Global Days XXX
AMA: 2007, January, 28-31; 2005, December, 7

| 78607 | Brain imaging, tomographic (SPECT) Z3 S 80 |

🔧 8.54 🔨 8.54 Global Days XXX
AMA: 2007, January, 28-31; 2005, December, 7

| 78608 | Brain imaging, positron emission tomography (PET); metabolic evaluation Z2 S 80 |

🔧 0.00 🔨 0.00 Global Days XXX
AMA: 2007, January, 28-31; 2005, December, 7

| 78609 | perfusion evaluation E |

🔧 2.13 🔨 2.13 Global Days XXX
AMA: 2007, January, 28-31; 2005, December, 7

| 78610 | Brain imaging, vascular flow only Z2 S 80 |

🔧 4.10 🔨 4.10 Global Days XXX
AMA: 2007, January, 28-31; 2005, December, 7

| 78630 | Cerebrospinal fluid flow, imaging (not including introduction of material); cisternography Z2 S 80 |

Code also injection procedure (61000-61070, 62270-62319)
🔧 8.17 🔨 8.17 Global Days XXX
AMA: 2007, January, 28-31; 2005, December, 7

| 78635 | ventriculography Z2 S 80 |

Code also injection procedure (61000-61070, 62270-62294)
🔧 8.09 🔨 8.09 Global Days XXX
AMA: 2007, January, 28-31; 2005, December, 7

| 78645 | shunt evaluation Z2 S 80 |

Code also injection procedure (61000-61070, 62270-62294)
🔧 7.77 🔨 7.77 Global Days XXX
AMA: 2007, January, 28-31; 2005, December, 7

| 78647 | tomographic (SPECT) Z3 S 80 |

🔧 6.84 🔨 6.84 Global Days XXX
AMA: 2007, January, 28-31; 2005, December, 7

Current Procedural Coding Expert – Radiology 78804

78650	Cerebrospinal fluid leakage detection and localization

Code also injection procedure (61000-61070, 62270-62294)

7.89   7.89   Global Days XXX

AMA: 2007, January, 28-31; 2005, December, 7

78660-78699 Nuclear Radiology: Lacrimal Duct System

Code also radiopharmaceuticals (A4641-A4642, A9500-A9605, C1716-C1719, C2616, C2634-C2643, C2698-C2699, C9247, C9898)

78660	Radiopharmaceutical dacryocystography

4.34   4.34   Global Days XXX

AMA: 2007, January, 28-31; 2005, December, 7

78699	Unlisted nervous system procedure, diagnostic nuclear medicine

0.00   0.00   Global Days XXX

AMA: 2007, January, 28-31; 2005, December, 7

78700-78725 Nuclear Radiology: Renal Anatomy and Function

CMS 100-2,15,80 Physician Supervision Requirements for Diagnostic Tests
CMS 100-3,220.8 Nuclear Radiology Procedure
CMS 100-3,220.12 Single Photon Emission Tomography
CMS 100-4,3,10.4 Payment of Nonphysician Services for Inpatients

EXCLUDES Renal endoscopy with insertion of radioactive substances (77776-77778)

Code also radiopharmaceuticals (A4641-A4642, A9500-A9605, C1716-C1719, C2616, C2634-C2643, C2698-C2699, C9898)

78700	Kidney imaging morphology;

4.12   4.12   Global Days XXX

AMA: 2007, March, 7-8; 2007, January, 28-31; 2005, December, 7

78701	with vascular flow

5.14   5.14   Global Days XXX

AMA: 2007, January, 28-31; 2007, March, 7-8; 2005, December, 7

78707	with vascular flow and function, single study without pharmacological intervention

5.62   5.62   Global Days XXX

AMA: 2007, March, 7-8; 2007, January, 28-31; 2005, December, 7

78708	with vascular flow and function, single study, with pharmacological intervention (eg, angiotensin converting enzyme inhibitor and/or diuretic)

4.09   4.09   Global Days XXX

AMA: 2007, March, 7-8; 2007, January, 28-31; 2005, December, 7

78709	with vascular flow and function, multiple studies, with and without pharmacological intervention (eg, angiotensin converting enzyme inhibitor and/or diuretic)

9.02   9.02   Global Days XXX

AMA: 2007, March, 7-8; 2007, January, 28-31; 2005, December, 7

78710	tomographic (SPECT)

4.83   4.83   Global Days XXX

AMA: 2007, January, 28-31; 2007, March, 7-8; 2005, December, 7

78725	Kidney function study, non-imaging radioisotopic study

2.54   2.54   Global Days XXX

AMA: 2007, January, 28-31; 2005, December, 7

78730-78799 Nuclear Radiology: Urogenital

CMS 100-2,15,80 Physician Supervision Requirements for Diagnostic Tests
CMS 100-3,220.8 Nuclear Radiology Procedure
CMS 100-4,3,10.4 Payment of Nonphysician Services for Inpatients

Code also radiopharmaceuticals (A4641-A4642, A9500-A9605, C1716-C1719, C2616, C2634-C2643, C2698-C2699, C9247, C9898)

78730	Urinary bladder residual study (List separately in addition to code for primary procedure)

EXCLUDES Measurement of postvoid residual urine and/or bladder capacity using ultrasound (51798)

Ultrasound imaging of the bladder only with measurement of postvoid residual urine (76857)

Code first (78740)

1.66   1.66   Global Days ZZZ

AMA: 2007, March, 7-8; 2007, January, 28-31; 2005, December, 7

78740	Ureteral reflux study (radiopharmaceutical voiding cystogram)

EXCLUDES Catheterization (51701-51703)

Code also urinary bladder residual study (78730)

5.51   5.51   Global Days XXX

AMA: 2007, January, 28-31; 2005, December, 7

78761	Testicular imaging with vascular flow

5.12   5.12   Global Days XXX

AMA: 2007, January, 28-31; 2007, March, 7-8; 2005, December, 7

78799	Unlisted genitourinary procedure, diagnostic nuclear medicine

0.00   0.00   Global Days XXX

AMA: 2007, January, 28-31; 2005, December, 7

78800-78804 Nuclear Radiology: Tumor Localization

CMS 100-2,15,80 Physician Supervision Requirements for Diagnostic Tests
CMS 100-3,220.8 Nuclear Radiology Procedure
CMS 100-3,220.12 Single Photon Emission Tomography
CMS 100-4,3,10.4 Payment of Nonphysician Services for Inpatients

Code also radiopharmaceuticals (A4641-A4642, A9500-A9605, C1716-C1719, C2616, C2634-C2643, C2698-C2699, C9247, C9898)

78800	Radiopharmaceutical localization of tumor or distribution of radiopharmaceutical agent(s); limited area

INCLUDES Ocular radiophosphorus tumor identification

EXCLUDES Specific organ (see appropriate site)

4.61   4.61   Global Days XXX

AMA: 2007, January, 28-31; 2005, December, 7

78801	multiple areas

6.04   6.04   Global Days XXX

AMA: 2007, January, 28-31; 2005, December, 7

78802	whole body, single day imaging

7.75   7.75   Global Days XXX

AMA: 2007, January, 28-31; 2005, December, 7

78803	tomographic (SPECT)

8.23   8.23   Global Days XXX

AMA: 2007, January, 28-31; 2005, December, 7

78804	whole body, requiring 2 or more days imaging

13.74   13.74   Global Days XXX

AMA: 2007, January, 28-31; 2005, December, 7

● New Code   ▲ Revised Code   M Maternity   A Age   Unlisted   Not Covered   # Resequenced
CCI   + Add-on   ⊘ Mod 51 Exempt   Mod 63 Exempt   ⊙ Mod Sedation   PQRI
© 2009 Publisher (Blue Ink)   CPT only © 2009 American Medical Association. All Rights Reserved. (Black Ink)   Medicare (Red Ink)

78805-78807 Nuclear Radiology: Inflammation and Infection

CMS 100-2,15,80   Physician Supervision Requirements for Diagnostic Tests
CMS 100-3,220.8   Nuclear Radiology Procedure
CMS 100-3,220.12   Single Photon Emission Tomography
CMS 100-4,3,10.4   Payment of Nonphysician Services for Inpatients

EXCLUDES
- Brain PET scan (78608-78609)
- Imaging bone infectious or inflammatory disease with bone imaging radiopharmaceutical (78300, 78305-78306)
- PET myocardial imaging (78459, 78491-78492)

Code also radiopharmaceuticals (A4641-A4642, A9500-A9605, C1716-C1719, C2616, C2634-C2643, C2698-C2699, C9247, C9898)

78805   Radiopharmaceutical localization of inflammatory process; limited area
     4.36   4.36   Global Days XXX
     AMA: 2007, January, 28-31; 2005, December, 7

78806   whole body
     7.98   7.98   Global Days XXX
     AMA: 2007, January, 28-31; 2005, December, 7

78807   tomographic (SPECT)
     8.15   8.15   Global Days XXX
     AMA: 2007, January, 28-31; 2005, December, 7

78808 Intravenous Injection for Radiopharmaceutical Localization

Code also radiopharmaceuticals (A4641-A4642, A9500-A9605, C1716-C1719, C2616, C2634-C2643, C2698-C2699, C9247, C9898)

78808   Injection procedure for radiopharmaceutical localization by non-imaging probe study, intravenous (eg, parathyroid adenoma)
     EXCLUDES   Identification of sentinel node (38792)
     1.08   1.08   Global Days XXX

78811-78999 Nuclear Radiology: Diagnosis, Staging, Restaging or Monitoring Cancer

CMS 100-4,3,10.4   Payment of Nonphysician Services for Inpatients
CMS 100-4,13,60.3   PET Scan Qualifying Conditions
CMS 100-4,13,60.3.1   Appropriate Codes for PET Scans

EXCLUDES
- CT scan performed for other than attenuation correction and anatomical localization (report with the appropriate site-specific CT code)
- Ocular radiophosphorus tumor identification (78800)

Code also radiopharmaceuticals (A4641-A4642, A9500-A9605, C1716-C1719, C2616, C2634-C2643, C2698-C2699, C9247, C9898)

Do not report with procedure performed more than once per session

78811   Positron emission tomography (PET) imaging; limited area (eg, chest, head/neck)
     0.00   0.00   Global Days XXX
     AMA: 2007, January, 28-31; 2005, December, 7

78812   skull base to mid-thigh
     0.00   0.00   Global Days XXX
     AMA: 2007, January, 28-31; 2005, December, 7

78813   whole body
     0.00   0.00   Global Days XXX
     AMA: 2007, January, 28-31; 2005, December, 7

78814   Positron emission tomography (PET) with concurrently acquired computed tomography (CT) for attenuation correction and anatomical localization imaging; limited area (eg, chest, head/neck)
     0.00   0.00   Global Days XXX
     AMA: 2009, Jan, 11-31; 2008, Jan, 10-25; 2007, January, 13-27; 2007, January, 28-31; 2005, December, 7; 2005, June, 9-11; 2005, February, 13-16

78815   skull base to mid-thigh
     0.00   0.00   Global Days XXX
     AMA: 2009, Jan, 11-31; 2008, Jan, 10-25; 2007, January, 28-31; 2007, January, 13-27; 2005, December, 7; 2005, June, 9-11; 2005, February, 13-16

78816   whole body
     0.00   0.00   Global Days XXX
     AMA: 2009, Jan, 11-31; 2008, Jan, 10-25; 2007, January, 28-31; 2007, January, 13-27; 2005, June, 9-11; 2005, December, 7; 2005, February, 13-16

78999   Unlisted miscellaneous procedure, diagnostic nuclear medicine
     0.00   0.00   Global Days XXX
     AMA: 2007, January, 28-31; 2005, December, 7

79005-79999 Systemic Radiopharmaceutical Therapy

CMS 100-3,220.8   Nuclear Radiology Procedure

EXCLUDES
- Imaging guidance
- Intra-arterial, intra-cavitory, intra-articular injection (see appropriate injection codes)
- Radiological supervision and interpretation

79005   Radiopharmaceutical therapy, by oral administration
     EXCLUDES   Monoclonal antibody treatment (79403)
     3.47   3.47   Global Days XXX
     AMA: 2005, September, 1-4

79101   Radiopharmaceutical therapy, by intravenous administration
     EXCLUDES
- Administration of nonantibody radioelement solution including follow-up care (77750)
- Radiolabeled monoclonal antibody IV infusion (79403)

Do not report with (36400, 36410, 79403, 96360, 96374-96375, 96409)
     3.89   3.89   Global Days XXX

79200   Radiopharmaceutical therapy, by intracavitary administration
     4.12   4.12   Global Days XXX

79300   Radiopharmaceutical therapy, by interstitial radioactive colloid administration
     0.00   0.00   Global Days XXX

79403   Radiopharmaceutical therapy, radiolabeled monoclonal antibody by intravenous infusion
     EXCLUDES   Pretreatment imaging (78802, 78804)

Do not report with (79101)
     4.83   4.83   Global Days XXX
     AMA: 2005, September, 1-4

79440   Radiopharmaceutical therapy, by intra-articular administration
     3.68   3.68   Global Days XXX

79445   Radiopharmaceutical therapy, by intra-arterial particulate administration
     EXCLUDES   Procedural and radiological supervision and interpretation for angiographic and interventional procedures before intra-arterial radiopharmaceutical therapy

Do not report with (96373, 96420)
     0.00   0.00   Global Days XXX
     AMA: 2006, December, 10-12

79999   Radiopharmaceutical therapy, unlisted procedure
     0.00   0.00   Global Days XXX
     AMA: 2005, March, 11-15

Current Procedural Coding Expert – Pathology and Laboratory

80047-80076 Multi-test Laboratory Panels

CMS 100-2,6,10 — Medical and Other Services Furnished to Inpatients
CMS 100-2,15,80 — Physician Supervision Requirements for Diagnostic Tests
CMS 100-4,3,10.4 — Payment of Nonphysician Services for Inpatients

EXCLUDES Test codes:
 For testing performed at a frequency greater than the number specified by panel definition
 Not specified by panel definition

Do not report two or more panel codes comprising the same tests; report the panel with the highest number of tests to meet the definition of the code, and report the remaining tests individually

80047 Basic metabolic panel (Calcium, ionized)
INCLUDES
Calcium, ionized (82330)
Carbon dioxide (82374)
Chloride (82435)
Creatinine (82565)
Glucose (82947)
Potassium (84132)
Sodium (84295)
Urea nitrogen (BUN) (84520)

0.00 0.00 Global Days XXX
AMA: 2008, Apr, 5-7

80048 Basic metabolic panel (Calcium, total)
INCLUDES
Calcium, total (82310)
Carbon dioxide (82374)
Chloride (82435)
Creatinine (82565)
Glucose (82947)
Potassium (84132)
Sodium (84295)
Urea nitrogen (BUN) (84520)

0.00 0.00 Global Days XXX
AMA: 2008, Apr, 5-7; 2005, August, 9-10; 2005, July, 11-12; 2005, August, 7-8

80050 General health panel
INCLUDES
Complete blood count (CBC) automated and appropriate manual differential WBC count (85007, 85009, 85027)
Complete blood count with differential (CBC) (85004, or 85025, 85027)
Comprehensive metabolic profile OR (80053)
Thyroid stimulating hormones (84443)

0.00 0.00 Global Days XXX
AMA: 2009, Jan, 11-31; 2008, Jan, 10-25; 2007, January, 13-27; 2005, August, 7-8; 2005, August, 9-10; 2005, July, 11-12

80051 Electrolyte panel
INCLUDES
Carbon dioxide (82374)
Chloride (82435)
Potassium (84132)
Sodium (84295)

0.00 0.00 Global Days XXX
AMA: 2009, Jan, 11-31; 2008, Jan, 10-25; 2007, January, 13-27; 2005, August, 7-8; 2005, August, 9-10; 2005, July, 11-12

80053 Comprehensive metabolic panel
INCLUDES
Albumin (82040)
Bilirubin, total (82247)
Calcium, total (82310)
Carbon dioxide (bicarbonate) (82374)
Chloride (82435)
Creatinine (82565)
Glucose (82947)
Phosphatase, alkaline (84075)
Potassium (84132)
Protein, total (84155)
Sodium (84295)
Transferase, alanine amino (ALT) (SGPT) (84460)
Transferase, aspartate amino (AST) (SGOT) (84450)
Urea nitrogen (BUN) (84520)

0.00 0.00 Global Days XXX
AMA: 2009, Jan, 11-31; 2008, Jan, 10-25; 2008, Apr, 5-7; 2007, January, 13-27; 2005, August, 7-8; 2005, January, 46-47; 2005, July, 11-12; 2005, August, 9-10

▲ 80055 Obstetric panel
INCLUDES
Blood typing, ABO and Rh (86900-86901)
CBC (85004, 85007, 85009, 85025, 85027)
Hepatitis B surface antigen (HBsAg) (87340)
RBC antibody screen, each serum technique (86850)
Rubella antibody (86762)
Syphilis test, non-treponemal antibody qualitative (86592)

Do not report panel code 80055 when syphilis screening is provided using a treponemal antibody approach (86780); report individual codes for tests performed in the OB panel instead

0.00 0.00 Global Days XXX
AMA: 2009, Jan, 11-31; 2008, Jan, 10-25; 2007, January, 13-27; 2005, August, 7-8; 2005, August, 9-10; 2005, July, 11-12

80061 Lipid panel
INCLUDES
Cholesterol, serum, total (82465)
Lipoprotein, direct measurement, high density cholesterol (HDL cholesterol) (83718)
Triglycerides (84478)

0.00 0.00 Global Days XXX
AMA: 2009, Jan, 11-31; 2008, Jan, 10-25; 2007, January, 13-27; 2005, August, 9-10; 2005, July, 11-12; 2005, August, 7-8; 2005, February, 7-9

80069 Renal function panel
INCLUDES
Albumin (82040)
Calcium, total (82310)
Carbon dioxide (82374)
Chloride (82435)
Creatinine (82565)
Glucose (82947)
Phosphorus inorganic (84100)
Potassium (84132)
Sodium (84295)
Urea nitrogen (BUN) (84520)

0.00 0.00 Global Days XXX
AMA: 2009, Jan, 11-31; 2008, Jan, 10-25; 2007, January, 13-27; 2005, August, 7-8; 2005, August, 9-10; 2005, July, 11-12

80074 Acute hepatitis panel
INCLUDES
Hepatitis A antibody (HAAb) IgM (86709)
Hepatitis B core antibody (HBcAb), IgM (86705)
Hepatitis B surface antigen (HBsAg) (87340)
Hepatitis C antibody (86803)

0.00   0.00   Global Days XXX
AMA: 2009, Jan, 11-31; 2008, Jan, 10-25; 2007, January, 13-27; 2005, August, 7-8; 2005, July, 11-12; 2005, August, 9-10

80076 Hepatic function panel
INCLUDES
Albumin (82040)
Bilirubin, direct (82248)
Bilirubin, total (82247)
Phosphatase, alkaline (84075)
Protein, total (84155)
Transferase, alanine amino (ALT) (SGPT) (84460)
Transferase, aspartate amino (AST) (SGOT) (84450)

0.00   0.00   Global Days XXX
AMA: 2009, Jan, 11-31; 2008, Jan, 10-25; 2007, January, 13-27; 2005, July, 11-12; 2005, August, 9-10; 2005, August, 7-8

80100-80103 Drug Screening Tests

CMS 100-2,6,10   Medical and Other Services Furnished to Inpatients
CMS 100-2,15,80   Physician Supervision Requirements for Diagnostic Tests
CMS 100-4,3,10.4   Payment of Nonphysician Services for Inpatients

INCLUDES   Qualitative test for drugs or drug classes such as:
Alcohols
Amphetamines
Barbiturates
Benzodiazepines
Cocaine and metabolites
Methadones
Opiates
Phencyclidines
Phenothiazines
Propoxyphenes
Tetrahydrocannabinoids
Tricyclic antidepressants
Stationary and mobile chromatography

EXCLUDES   Drug quantification (80150-80299, 82000-84999 [82652])

80100   Drug screen, qualitative; multiple drug classes chromatographic method, each procedure
0.00   0.00   Global Days XXX
AMA: 2005, July, 11-12; 2005, August, 7-8; 2005, August, 9-10

80101   single drug class method (eg, immunoassay, enzyme assay), each drug class
0.00   0.00   Global Days XXX
AMA: 2009, Jan, 11-31; 2008, Jan, 10-25; 2007, January, 13-27; 2006, December, 10-12; 2005, July, 11-12; 2005, August, 9-10; 2005, August, 7-8

80102   Drug confirmation, each procedure
0.00   0.00   Global Days XXX
AMA: 2005, July, 11-12; 2005, August, 9-10; 2005, August, 7-8

80103   Tissue preparation for drug analysis
0.00   0.00   Global Days XXX
AMA: 2005, August, 7-8; 2005, August, 9-10; 2005, July, 11-12

80150-80299 Therapeutic Drug Levels

CMS 100-2,15,80   Physician Supervision Requirements for Diagnostic Tests
CMS 100-4,3,10.4   Payment of Nonphysician Services for Inpatients
INCLUDES   Tests on specimens from any source
EXCLUDES   Nonquantitative testing (80100-80103)

80150   Amikacin
0.00   0.00   Global Days XXX
AMA: 2005, July, 11-12; 2005, August, 7-8; 2005, August, 9-10

80152   Amitriptyline
0.00   0.00   Global Days XXX
AMA: 2005, July, 11-12; 2005, August, 7-8; 2005, August, 9-10

80154   Benzodiazepines
0.00   0.00   Global Days XXX
AMA: 2005, August, 9-10; 2005, August, 7-8; 2005, July, 11-12

80156   Carbamazepine; total
0.00   0.00   Global Days XXX
AMA: 2005, July, 11-12; 2005, August, 7-8; 2005, August, 9-10

80157   free
0.00   0.00   Global Days XXX
AMA: 2005, July, 11-12; 2005, August, 7-8; 2005, August, 9-10

80158   Cyclosporine
0.00   0.00   Global Days XXX
AMA: 2005, August, 9-10; 2005, July, 11-12; 2005, August, 7-8

80160   Desipramine
0.00   0.00   Global Days XXX
AMA: 2005, August, 7-8; 2005, July, 11-12; 2005, August, 9-10

80162   Digoxin
0.00   0.00   Global Days XXX
AMA: 2005, August, 9-10; 2005, July, 11-12; 2005, August, 7-8

80164   Dipropylacetic acid (valproic acid)
0.00   0.00   Global Days XXX
AMA: 2005, August, 7-8; 2005, July, 11-12; 2005, August, 9-10

80166   Doxepin
0.00   0.00   Global Days XXX
AMA: 2005, August, 7-8; 2005, July, 11-12; 2005, August, 9-10

80168   Ethosuximide
0.00   0.00   Global Days XXX
AMA: 2005, July, 11-12; 2005, August, 9-10; 2005, August, 7-8

80170   Gentamicin
0.00   0.00   Global Days XXX
AMA: 2005, August, 9-10; 2005, August, 7-8; 2005, July, 11-12

80172   Gold
0.00   0.00   Global Days XXX
AMA: 2005, August, 7-8; 2005, August, 9-10; 2005, July, 11-12

80173   Haloperidol
0.00   0.00   Global Days XXX
AMA: 2005, August, 9-10; 2005, July, 11-12; 2005, August, 7-8

80174   Imipramine
0.00   0.00   Global Days XXX
AMA: 2005, August, 9-10; 2005, August, 7-8; 2005, July, 11-12

80176   Lidocaine
0.00   0.00   Global Days XXX
AMA: 2005, August, 7-8; 2005, August, 9-10; 2005, July, 11-12

80178   Lithium
0.00   0.00   Global Days XXX
AMA: 2005, August, 7-8; 2005, July, 11-12; 2005, August, 9-10

80182   Nortriptyline
0.00   0.00   Global Days XXX
AMA: 2005, August, 9-10; 2005, July, 11-12; 2005, August, 7-8

80184   Phenobarbital
0.00   0.00   Global Days XXX
AMA: 2005, August, 9-10; 2005, August, 7-8; 2005, July, 11-12

Current Procedural Coding Expert – Pathology and Laboratory

80185	Phenytoin; total	A
	0.00 0.00 Global Days XXX	
	AMA: 2005, August, 7-8; 2005, July, 11-12; 2005, August, 9-10	

80186 free [A]
 0.00 0.00 Global Days XXX
AMA: 2005, August, 9-10; 2005, August, 7-8; 2005, July, 11-12

80188 Primidone [A]
 0.00 0.00 Global Days XXX
AMA: 2005, August, 9-10; 2005, July, 11-12; 2005, August, 7-8

80190 Procainamide; [A]
 0.00 0.00 Global Days XXX
AMA: 2005, August, 9-10; 2005, August, 7-8; 2005, July, 11-12

80192 with metabolites (eg, n-acetyl procainamide) [A]
 0.00 0.00 Global Days XXX
AMA: 2005, August, 7-8; 2005, July, 11-12; 2005, August, 9-10

80194 Quinidine [A]
 0.00 0.00 Global Days XXX
AMA: 2005, August, 9-10; 2005, July, 11-12; 2005, August, 7-8

80195 Sirolimus [A]
 0.00 0.00 Global Days XXX
AMA: 2006, March, 6-9; 2005, August, 9-10; 2005, August, 7-8

80196 Salicylate [A]
 0.00 0.00 Global Days XXX
AMA: 2005, August, 7-8; 2005, July, 11-12; 2005, August, 9-10

80197 Tacrolimus [A]
 0.00 0.00 Global Days XXX
AMA: 2005, July, 11-12; 2005, August, 9-10; 2005, August, 7-8

80198 Theophylline [A]
 0.00 0.00 Global Days XXX
AMA: 2005, August, 7-8; 2005, August, 9-10; 2005, July, 11-12

80200 Tobramycin [A]
 0.00 0.00 Global Days XXX
AMA: 2005, August, 9-10; 2005, August, 7-8; 2005, July, 11-12

80201 Topiramate [A]
 0.00 0.00 Global Days XXX
AMA: 2005, August, 9-10; 2005, August, 7-8; 2005, July, 11-12

80202 Vancomycin [A]
 0.00 0.00 Global Days XXX
AMA: 2005, August, 7-8; 2005, July, 11-12; 2005, August, 9-10

80299 Quantitation of drug, not elsewhere specified [A]
 0.00 0.00 Global Days XXX
AMA: 2009, Jan, 11-31; 2008, Jan, 10-25; 2007, January, 13-27; 2005, August, 9-10; 2005, August, 7-8; 2005, July, 11-12

80400-80440 Stimulation and Suppression Test Panels

CMS 100-2,15,80 Physician Supervision Requirements for Diagnostic Tests
CMS 100-4,3,10.4 Payment of Nonphysician Services for Inpatients
EXCLUDES *Administration of evocative or suppressive material (96365-96368, 96372-96376, C8957)*
Evocative or suppression test substances (99070, J0120-J7599)
Physician monitoring and attendance during the test (see Evaluation and Management codes)

80400 ACTH stimulation panel; for adrenal insufficiency [A]
 INCLUDES Cortisol x 2 (82533)
 0.00 0.00 Global Days XXX
AMA: 2005, August, 7-8; 2005, August, 9-10; 2005, July, 11-12

80402 for 21 hydroxylase deficiency [A]
 INCLUDES 17 hydroxyprogesterone X 2 (83498)
Cortisol x 2 (82533)
 0.00 0.00 Global Days XXX
AMA: 2005, August, 7-8; 2005, August, 9-10; 2005, July, 11-12

80406 for 3 beta-hydroxydehydrogenase deficiency [A]
 INCLUDES 17 hydroxypregnenolone x 2 (84143)
Cortisol x 2 (82533)
 0.00 0.00 Global Days XXX
AMA: 2005, July, 11-12; 2005, August, 7-8; 2005, August, 9-10

80408 Aldosterone suppression evaluation panel (eg, saline infusion) [A]
 INCLUDES Aldosterone x 2 (82088)
Renin x 2 (84244)
 0.00 0.00 Global Days XXX
AMA: 2005, August, 7-8; 2005, August, 9-10; 2005, July, 11-12

80410 Calcitonin stimulation panel (eg, calcium, pentagastrin) [A]
 INCLUDES Calcitonin x 3 (82308)
 0.00 0.00 Global Days XXX
AMA: 2005, August, 7-8; 2005, August, 9-10; 2005, July, 11-12

80412 Corticotropic releasing hormone (CRH) stimulation panel [A]
 INCLUDES Adrenocorticotropic hormone (ACTH) x 6 (82024)
Cortisol x 6 (82533)
 0.00 0.00 Global Days XXX
AMA: 2005, August, 9-10; 2005, July, 11-12; 2005, August, 7-8

80414 Chorionic gonadotropin stimulation panel; testosterone response ♀ [A]
 INCLUDES Testosterone x 2 on three pooled blood samples (84403)
 0.00 0.00 Global Days XXX
AMA: 2005, August, 7-8; 2005, July, 11-12; 2005, August, 9-10

80415 estradiol response [A]
 INCLUDES Estradiol x 2 on three pooled blood samples (82670)
 0.00 0.00 Global Days XXX
AMA: 2005, August, 7-8; 2005, July, 11-12; 2005, August, 9-10

80416 Renal vein renin stimulation panel (eg, captopril) [A]
 INCLUDES Renin x 6 (84244)
 0.00 0.00 Global Days XXX
AMA: 2005, August, 7-8; 2005, August, 9-10; 2005, July, 11-12

80417 Peripheral vein renin stimulation panel (eg, captopril) [A]
 INCLUDES Renin x 2 (84244)
 0.00 0.00 Global Days XXX
AMA: 2005, August, 7-8; 2005, August, 9-10; 2005, July, 11-12

80418 Combined rapid anterior pituitary evaluation panel [A]
 INCLUDES Adrenocorticotropic hormone (ACTH) x 4 (82024)
Cortisol x 4 (82533)
Follicle stimulating hormone (FSH) x 4 (83001)
Human growth hormone x 4 (83003)
Luteinizing hormone (LH) x 4 (83002)
Prolactin x 4 (84146)
Thyroid stimulating hormone (TSH) x 4 (84443)
 0.00 0.00 Global Days XXX
AMA: 2005, July, 11-12; 2005, August, 7-8; 2005, August, 9-10

80420

80420 Dexamethasone suppression panel, 48 hour
  INCLUDES: Cortisol x 2 (82533)
  Free cortisol, urine x 2 (82530)
  Volume measurement for timed collection x 2 (81050)
  EXCLUDES: Single dose dexamethasone (82533)
  0.00 0.00 Global Days XXX
  AMA: 2005, July, 11-12; 2005, August, 7-8; 2005, August, 9-10

80422 Glucagon tolerance panel; for insulinoma
  INCLUDES: Glucose x 3 (82947)
  Insulin x 3 (83525)
  0.00 0.00 Global Days XXX
  AMA: 2005, August, 7-8; 2005, August, 9-10; 2005, July, 11-12

80424 for pheochromocytoma
  INCLUDES: Catecholamines, fractionated x 2 (82384)
  0.00 0.00 Global Days XXX
  AMA: 2005, July, 11-12; 2005, August, 7-8; 2005, August, 9-10

80426 Gonadotropin releasing hormone stimulation panel
  INCLUDES: Follicle stimulating hormone (FSH) x 4 (83001)
  Luteinizing hormone (LH) x 4 (83002)
  0.00 0.00 Global Days XXX
  AMA: 2005, August, 7-8; 2005, August, 9-10; 2005, July, 11-12

80428 Growth hormone stimulation panel (eg, arginine infusion, l-dopa administration)
  INCLUDES: Human growth hormone (HGH) x 4 (83003)
  0.00 0.00 Global Days XXX
  AMA: 2005, August, 7-8; 2005, August, 9-10; 2005, July, 11-12

80430 Growth hormone suppression panel (glucose administration)
  INCLUDES: Glucose x 3 (82947)
  Human growth hormone (HGH) x 4 (83003)
  0.00 0.00 Global Days XXX
  AMA: 2005, August, 9-10; 2005, July, 11-12; 2005, August, 7-8

80432 Insulin-induced C-peptide suppression panel
  INCLUDES: C-peptide x 5 (84681)
  Glucose x 5 (82947)
  Insulin (83525)
  0.00 0.00 Global Days XXX
  AMA: 2005, August, 7-8; 2005, July, 11-12; 2005, August, 9-10

80434 Insulin tolerance panel; for ACTH insufficiency
  INCLUDES: Cortisol x 5 (82533)
  Glucose x 5 (82947)
  0.00 0.00 Global Days XXX
  AMA: 2005, August, 7-8; 2005, August, 9-10; 2005, July, 11-12

80435 for growth hormone deficiency
  INCLUDES: Glucose x 5 (82947)
  Human growth hormone (HGH) x 5 (83003)
  0.00 0.00 Global Days XXX
  AMA: 2005, August, 9-10; 2005, August, 7-8; 2005, July, 11-12

80436 Metyrapone panel
  INCLUDES: 11 deoxycortisol x 2 (82634)
  Cortisol x 2 (82533)
  0.00 0.00 Global Days XXX
  AMA: 2005, July, 11-12; 2005, August, 9-10; 2005, August, 7-8

80438 Thyrotropin releasing hormone (TRH) stimulation panel; 1 hour
  INCLUDES: Thyroid stimulating hormone (TSH) x 3 (84443)
  0.00 0.00 Global Days XXX
  AMA: 2005, August, 7-8; 2005, July, 11-12; 2005, August, 9-10

80439 2 hour
  INCLUDES: Thyroid stimulating hormone (TSH) x 4 (84443)
  0.00 0.00 Global Days XXX
  AMA: 2005, August, 7-8; 2005, August, 9-10; 2005, July, 11-12

80440 for hyperprolactinemia
  INCLUDES: Prolactin x 3 (84146)
  0.00 0.00 Global Days XXX
  AMA: 2005, August, 7-8; 2005, August, 9-10; 2005, July, 11-12

80500-80502 Consultation By Clinical Pathologist

CMS 100-2,15,80 Physician Supervision Requirements for Diagnostic Tests
CMS 100-4,3,10.4 Payment of Nonphysician Services for Inpatients
CMS 100-4,12,60 Payment for Pathology Services
INCLUDES: Pharmacokinetic consultations
Written report by pathologist for tests requiring additional medical judgement
EXCLUDES: Consultations that include examination of the patient (99241-99255)

80500 Clinical pathology consultation; limited, without review of patient's history and medical records
  0.50 0.56 Global Days XXX
  AMA: 2005, July, 11-12; 2005, August, 7-8; 2005, August, 9-10

80502 comprehensive, for a complex diagnostic problem, with review of patient's history and medical records
  1.74 1.79 Global Days XXX
  AMA: 2005, August, 7-8; 2005, August, 9-10; 2005, July, 11-12

81000-81099 Urine Tests

CMS 100-2,15,80 Physician Supervision Requirements for Diagnostic Tests
CMS 100-4,3,10.4 Payment of Nonphysician Services for Inpatients

81000 Urinalysis, by dip stick or tablet reagent for bilirubin, glucose, hemoglobin, ketones, leukocytes, nitrite, pH, protein, specific gravity, urobilinogen, any number of these constituents; non-automated, with microscopy
  0.00 0.00 Global Days XXX
  AMA: 2005, August, 7-8; 2005, August, 9-10; 2005, July, 11-12

81001 automated, with microscopy
  0.00 0.00 Global Days XXX
  AMA: 2005, August, 9-10; 2005, July, 11-12; 2005, August, 7-8

81002 non-automated, without microscopy
  INCLUDES: Mosenthal test
  0.00 0.00 Global Days XXX
  AMA: 2007, April, 1-2; 2005, August, 7-8; 2005, July, 11-12; 2005, August, 9-10

81003 automated, without microscopy
  0.00 0.00 Global Days XXX
  AMA: 2007, April, 1-2; 2005, August, 7-8; 2005, July, 11-12; 2005, August, 9-10

81005 Urinalysis; qualitative or semiquantitative, except immunoassays
  INCLUDES: Benedict test for dextrose
  EXCLUDES: Immunoassay, qualitative or semiquantitative (83518)
  Microalbumin (82043-82044)
  Nonimmunoassay reagent strip analysis (81000, 81002)
  0.00 0.00 Global Days XXX
  AMA: 2005, August, 7-8; 2005, August, 9-10; 2005, July, 11-12

Current Procedural Coding Expert – Pathology and Laboratory 82105

81007 bacteriuria screen, except by culture or dipstick
  EXCLUDES   Culture (87086-87088)
             Dipstick (81000-81002)
  0.00   0.00   Global Days XXX
  AMA: 2005, August, 9-10; 2005, July, 11-12; 2005, August, 7-8

81015 microscopic only
  EXCLUDES   Sperm evaluation for retrograde ejaculation (89331)
  0.00   0.00   Global Days XXX
  AMA: 2008, Apr, 5-7; 2005, August, 7-8; 2005, July, 11-12; 2005, August, 9-10

81020 2 or 3 glass test
  INCLUDES   Valentine's test
  0.00   0.00   Global Days XXX
  AMA: 2005, August, 9-10; 2005, August, 7-8; 2005, July, 11-12

81025 Urine pregnancy test, by visual color comparison methods
  0.00   0.00   Global Days XXX
  AMA: 2005, August, 7-8; 2005, August, 9-10; 2005, July, 11-12

81050 Volume measurement for timed collection, each
  0.00   0.00   Global Days XXX
  AMA: 2005, August, 9-10; 2005, August, 7-8; 2005, July, 11-12

81099 Unlisted urinalysis procedure
  0.00   0.00   Global Days XXX
  AMA: 2005, August, 7-8; 2005, August, 9-10; 2005, July, 11-12

82000-82030 Chemistry: Acetaldehyde—Adenosine

CMS 100-2,15,80   Physician Supervision Requirements for Diagnostic Tests
CMS 100-4,3,10.4   Payment of Nonphysician Services for Inpatients
INCLUDES   Mathematically calculated results
           Quantitative analysis unless otherwise specified
           Specimens from any source unless otherwise specified
EXCLUDES   Organ or disease panels (80048-80076)
           Therapeutic drug assays (80150-80299)

82000 Acetaldehyde, blood
  0.00   0.00   Global Days XXX
  AMA: 2005, August, 7-8; 2005, July, 11-12; 2005, August, 9-10

82003 Acetaminophen
  0.00   0.00   Global Days XXX
  AMA: 2005, August, 9-10; 2005, August, 7-8; 2005, July, 11-12

82009 Acetone or other ketone bodies, serum; qualitative
  0.00   0.00   Global Days XXX
  AMA: 2005, August, 7-8; 2005, July, 11-12; 2005, August, 9-10

82010 quantitative
  0.00   0.00   Global Days XXX
  AMA: 2005, August, 9-10; 2005, August, 7-8; 2005, July, 11-12

82013 Acetylcholinesterase
  0.00   0.00   Global Days XXX
  AMA: 2005, August, 7-8; 2005, July, 11-12; 2005, August, 9-10

82016 Acylcarnitines; qualitative, each specimen
  0.00   0.00   Global Days XXX
  AMA: 2005, August, 9-10; 2005, July, 11-12; 2005, August, 7-8

82017 quantitative, each specimen
  0.00   0.00   Global Days XXX
  AMA: 2005, August, 9-10; 2005, July, 11-12; 2005, August, 7-8

82024 Adrenocorticotropic hormone (ACTH)
  0.00   0.00   Global Days XXX
  AMA: 2005, August, 7-8; 2005, August, 9-10; 2005, July, 11-12

82030 Adenosine, 5-monophosphate, cyclic (cyclic AMP)
  0.00   0.00   Global Days XXX
  AMA: 2005, August, 9-10; 2005, July, 11-12; 2005, August, 7-8

82040-82045 Chemistry: Albumin

CMS 100-2,15,80   Physician Supervision Requirements for Diagnostic Tests
CMS 100-3,190.10   Laboratory Tests--CRD Patients
CMS 100-4,3,10.4   Payment of Nonphysician Services for Inpatients
INCLUDES   Mathematically calculated results
           Quantitative analysis unless otherwise specified
           Specimens from any other sources unless otherwise specified
EXCLUDES   Organ or disease panels (80048-80076)
           Therapeutic drug assays (80150-80299)

82040 Albumin; serum, plasma or whole blood
  0.00   0.00   Global Days XXX
  AMA: 2005, August, 7-8; 2005, July, 11-12; 2005, August, 9-10

82042 urine or other source, quantitative, each specimen
  0.00   0.00   Global Days XXX
  AMA: 2005, August, 7-8; 2005, August, 9-10; 2005, July, 11-12

82043 urine, microalbumin, quantitative
  0.00   0.00   Global Days XXX
  AMA: 2005, August, 7-8; 2005, August, 9-10; 2005, July, 11-12

82044 urine, microalbumin, semiquantitative (eg, reagent strip assay)
  EXCLUDES   Prealbumin (84134)
  0.00   0.00   Global Days XXX
  AMA: 2009, Jan, 11-31; 2008, Jan, 10-25; 2007, January, 13-27; 2005, August, 9-10; 2005, July, 11-12; 2005, August, 7-8

82045 ischemia modified
  0.00   0.00   Global Days XXX
  AMA: 2005, August, 7-8; 2005, July, 11-12; 2005, August, 9-10

82055-82107 Chemistry: Alcohol—Alpha-fetoprotein (AFP)

CMS 100-2,15,80   Physician Supervision Requirements for Diagnostic Tests
CMS 100-4,3,10.4   Payment of Nonphysician Services for Inpatients
INCLUDES   Mathematically calculated results
           Quantitative analysis unless otherwise specified
           Specimens from any source unless otherwise specified
EXCLUDES   Organ or disease panels (80048-80076)
           Therapeutic drug assays (80150-80299)

82055 Alcohol (ethanol); any specimen except breath
  EXCLUDES   Other types of alcohols, volatiles (84600)
  0.00   0.00   Global Days XXX
  AMA: 2005, August, 7-8; 2005, August, 9-10; 2005, July, 11-12

82075 breath
  0.00   0.00   Global Days XXX
  AMA: 2005, August, 7-8; 2005, August, 9-10; 2005, July, 11-12

82085 Aldolase
  0.00   0.00   Global Days XXX
  AMA: 2005, August, 9-10; 2005, July, 11-12; 2005, August, 7-8

82088 Aldosterone
  0.00   0.00   Global Days XXX
  AMA: 2005, August, 7-8; 2005, July, 11-12; 2005, August, 9-10

82101 Alkaloids, urine, quantitative
  0.00   0.00   Global Days XXX
  AMA: 2005, August, 7-8; 2005, August, 9-10; 2005, July, 11-12

82103 Alpha-1-antitrypsin; total
  0.00   0.00   Global Days XXX
  AMA: 2005, August, 9-10; 2005, July, 11-12; 2005, August, 7-8

82104 phenotype
  0.00   0.00   Global Days XXX
  AMA: 2005, August, 7-8; 2005, July, 11-12; 2005, August, 9-10

82105 Alpha-fetoprotein (AFP); serum
  0.00   0.00   Global Days XXX
  AMA: 2005, August, 7-8; 2005, August, 9-10; 2005, July, 11-12

● New Code   ▲ Revised Code   M Maternity   A Age   Unlisted   Not Covered   # Resequenced
CCI   + Add-on   ⊘ Mod 51 Exempt   Mod 63 Exempt   ⊙ Mod Sedation   PQRI
© 2009 Publisher (Blue Ink)   CPT only © 2009 American Medical Association. All Rights Reserved. (Black Ink)   Medicare (Red Ink)   301

CURRENT PROCEDURAL CODING EXPERT – Pathology and Laboratory

82106	amniotic fluid
	0.00 0.00 Global Days XXX
	AMA: 2005, August, 9-10; 2005, August, 7-8; 2005, July, 11-12
82107	AFP-L3 fraction isoform and total AFP (including ratio)
	0.00 0.00 Global Days XXX

82108 Chemistry: Aluminum

CMS 100-2,15,80 Physician Supervision Requirements for Diagnostic Tests
CMS 100-3,190.10 Laboratory Tests--CRD Patients
CMS 100-4,3,10.4 Payment of Nonphysician Services for Inpatients

INCLUDES
- Mathematically calculated results
- Quantitative analysis unless otherwise specified
- Specimens from any source unless otherwise specified

EXCLUDES
- Organ or disease panels (80048-80076)
- Therapeutic drug assays (80150-80299)

82108	Aluminum
	0.00 0.00 Global Days XXX
	AMA: 2005, August, 9-10; 2005, August, 7-8; July, 11-12

82120-82261 Chemistry: Amines—Biotinidase

CMS 100-2,15,80 Physician Supervision Requirements for Diagnostic Tests
CMS 100-4,3,10.4 Payment of Nonphysician Services for Inpatients

INCLUDES
- Mathematically calculated results
- Quantitative analysis unless otherwise specified
- Specimens from any source unless otherwise specified

EXCLUDES
- Organ or disease panels (80048-80076)
- Therapeutic drug assays (80150-80299)

82120	Amines, vaginal fluid, qualitative
	EXCLUDES Combined pH and amines test for vaginitis (82120, 83986)
	0.00 0.00 Global Days XXX
	AMA: 2005, August, 7-8; 2005, July, 11-12; 2005, August, 9-10
82127	Amino acids; single, qualitative, each specimen
	0.00 0.00 Global Days XXX
	AMA: 2005, August, 7-8; 2005, August, 9-10; 2005, July, 11-12
82128	multiple, qualitative, each specimen
	0.00 0.00 Global Days XXX
	AMA: 2005, August, 9-10; 2005, August, 7-8; 2005, July, 11-12
82131	single, quantitative, each specimen
	INCLUDES Van Slyke method
	0.00 0.00 Global Days XXX
	AMA: 2009, Jan, 11-31; 2008, Jan, 10-25; 2007, January, 13-27; 2005, August, 9-10; 2005, July, 11-12; 2005, August, 7-8
82135	Aminolevulinic acid, delta (ALA)
	0.00 0.00 Global Days XXX
	AMA: 2005, August, 7-8; 2005, July, 11-12; 2005, August, 9-10
82136	Amino acids, 2 to 5 amino acids, quantitative, each specimen
	0.00 0.00 Global Days XXX
	AMA: 2005, August, 9-10; 2005, August, 7-8; 2005, July, 11-12
82139	Amino acids, 6 or more amino acids, quantitative, each specimen
	0.00 0.00 Global Days XXX
	AMA: 2005, August, 9-10; 2005, July, 11-12; 2005, August, 7-8
82140	Ammonia
	0.00 0.00 Global Days XXX
	AMA: 2005, August, 7-8; 2005, July, 11-12; 2005, August, 9-10
82143	Amniotic fluid scan (spectrophotometric)
	EXCLUDES L/S ratio (83661)
	0.00 0.00 Global Days XXX
	AMA: 2005, August, 9-10; 2005, August, 7-8; 2005, July, 11-12

82145	Amphetamine or methamphetamine
	EXCLUDES Qualitative testing (80100-80103)
	0.00 0.00 Global Days XXX
	AMA: 2005, August, 9-10; 2005, July, 11-12; 2005, August, 7-8
82150	Amylase
	0.00 0.00 Global Days XXX
	AMA: 2005, August, 9-10; 2005, August, 7-8; 2005, July, 11-12
82154	Androstanediol glucuronide
	0.00 0.00 Global Days XXX
	AMA: 2005, August, 7-8; 2005, July, 11-12; 2005, August, 9-10
82157	Androstenedione
	0.00 0.00 Global Days XXX
	AMA: 2005, August, 9-10; 2005, August, 7-8; 2005, July, 11-12
82160	Androsterone
	0.00 0.00 Global Days XXX
	AMA: 2005, August, 9-10; 2005, August, 7-8; 2005, July, 11-12
82163	Angiotensin II
	0.00 0.00 Global Days XXX
	AMA: 2005, August, 9-10; 2005, July, 11-12; 2005, August, 7-8
82164	Angiotensin I - converting enzyme (ACE)
	0.00 0.00 Global Days XXX
	AMA: 2005, August, 7-8; 2005, July, 11-12; 2005, August, 9-10
82172	Apolipoprotein, each
	0.00 0.00 Global Days XXX
	AMA: 2005, August, 9-10; 2005, August, 7-8; 2005, July, 11-12
82175	Arsenic
	EXCLUDES Heavy metal screening (83015)
	0.00 0.00 Global Days XXX
	AMA: 2005, August, 9-10; 2005, August, 7-8; 2005, July, 11-12
82180	Ascorbic acid (Vitamin C), blood
	0.00 0.00 Global Days XXX
	AMA: 2005, August, 7-8; 2005, July, 11-12; 2005, August, 9-10
82190	Atomic absorption spectroscopy, each analyte
	0.00 0.00 Global Days XXX
	AMA: 2005, August, 9-10; 2005, July, 11-12; 2005, August, 7-8
82205	Barbiturates, not elsewhere specified
	EXCLUDES Qualitative analysis (80100-80103)
	0.00 0.00 Global Days XXX
	AMA: 2005, August, 9-10; 2005, August, 7-8; 2005, July, 11-12
82232	Beta-2 microglobulin
	0.00 0.00 Global Days XXX
	AMA: 2005, August, 9-10; 2005, August, 7-8; 2005, July, 11-12
82239	Bile acids; total
	0.00 0.00 Global Days XXX
	AMA: 2005, July, 11-12; 2005, August, 7-8; 2005, August, 9-10
82240	cholylglycine
	EXCLUDES Bile pigments, urine (81000-81005)
	0.00 0.00 Global Days XXX
	AMA: 2005, August, 9-10; 2005, July, 11-12; 2005, August, 7-8
82247	Bilirubin; total
	INCLUDES Van Den Bergh test
	0.00 0.00 Global Days XXX
	AMA: 2005, August, 9-10; 2005, August, 7-8; 2005, July, 11-12
82248	direct
	0.00 0.00 Global Days XXX
	AMA: 2005, July, 11-12; 2005, August, 7-8; 2005, August, 9-10
82252	feces, qualitative
	0.00 0.00 Global Days XXX
	AMA: 2005, August, 9-10; 2005, August, 7-8; 2005, July, 11-12
82261	Biotinidase, each specimen
	0.00 0.00 Global Days XXX
	AMA: 2005, August, 9-10; 2005, August, 7-8; 2005, July, 11-12

26/TC PC/TC Comp Only   CLIA Waived   ♂ Male Only   ♀ Female Only
AMA: CPT Asst   **MED:** Pub 100   A-Y OPPSI   Radiology Crosswalk

Current Procedural Coding Expert – Pathology and Laboratory 82373

82270-82274 Chemistry: Occult Blood

CMS 100-2,15,80   Physician Supervision Requirements for Diagnostic Tests
CMS 100-3,190.34   Fecal Occult Blood Test (FOBT)
CMS 100-4,3,10.4   Payment of Nonphysician Services for Inpatients
CMS 100-4,18,60   Colorectal Cancer Screening
CMS 100-4,18,60.1   Payment for Colorectal Screening Services
CMS 100-4,18,60.2   Frequency and Age Requirements for Colorectal Screening
CMS 100-4,18,60.2.1   Common Working File Edits: Colorectal Screening
CMS 100-4,18,60.6   Billing for Colorectal Screening Services

INCLUDES   Mathematically calculated results
Quantitative analysis unless otherwise specified
Specimens from any source unless otherwise specified

EXCLUDES   *Organ or disease panels (80048-80076)*
Therapeutic drug assays (80150-80299)

82270   Blood, occult, by peroxidase activity (eg, guaiac), qualitative; feces, consecutive collected specimens with single determination, for colorectal neoplasm screening (ie, patient was provided 3 cards or single triple card for consecutive collection)
     INCLUDES   Day test
     0.00   0.00   Global Days XXX
     AMA: 2009, Jan, 11-31; 2008, Jan, 10-25; 2008, Apr, 5-7; 2007, January, 13-27; 2006, February, 7-9; 2005, August, 9-10; 2005, July, 11-12; 2005, August, 7-8

82271   other sources
     0.00   0.00   Global Days XXX
     AMA: 2006, February, 7-9; 2005, August, 7-8; 2005, August, 9-10

82272   Blood, occult, by peroxidase activity (eg, guaiac), qualitative, feces, 1-3 simultaneous determinations, performed for other than colorectal neoplasm screening
     0.00   0.00   Global Days XXX
     AMA: 2009, Jun, 10-11; 2008, Apr, 5-7; 2006, February, 7-9; 2005, August, 9-10; 2005, August, 7-8

82274   Blood, occult, by fecal hemoglobin determination by immunoassay, qualitative, feces, 1-3 simultaneous determinations
     0.00   0.00   Global Days XXX
     AMA: 2005, August, 9-10; 2005, August, 7-8; 2005, July, 11-12

82286-82308 [82652] Chemistry: Bradykinin—Calcitonin

CMS 100-2,15,80   Physician Supervision Requirements for Diagnostic Tests
CMS 100-4,3,10.4   Payment of Nonphysician Services for Inpatients

INCLUDES   Mathematically calculated results
Quantitative analysis unless otherwise specified
Specimens from any source unless otherwise specified

EXCLUDES   *Organ or disease panels (80048-80076)*
Therapeutic drug assays (80150-80299)

82286   Bradykinin
     0.00   0.00   Global Days XXX
     AMA: 2005, August, 9-10; 2005, July, 11-12; 2005, August, 7-8

82300   Cadmium
     0.00   0.00   Global Days XXX
     AMA: 2005, July, 11-12; 2005, August, 7-8; 2005, August, 9-10

▲ **82306**   Vitamin D; 25 hydroxy, includes fraction(s), if performed
     0.00   0.00   Global Days XXX
     AMA: 2005, August, 9-10; 2005, August, 7-8; 2005, July, 11-12

#▲ **82652**   1, 25 dihydroxy, includes fraction(s), if performed
     0.00   0.00   Global Days XXX
     AMA: 2005, July, 11-12; 2005, August, 9-10; 2005, August, 7-8

~~82307~~   ~~Calciferol (Vitamin D)~~
To report, see code 82306

82308   Calcitonin
     0.00   0.00   Global Days XXX
     AMA: 2005, July, 11-12; 2005, August, 9-10; 2005, August, 7-8

82310 Chemistry: Total Calcium

CMS 100-2,15,80   Physician Supervision Requirements for Diagnostic Tests
CMS 100-3,190.10   Laboratory Tests--CRD Patients
CMS 100-4,3,10.4   Payment of Nonphysician Services for Inpatients

INCLUDES   Mathematically calculated results
Quantitative analysis unless otherwise specified
Specimens from any source unless otherwise specified

EXCLUDES   *Organ or disease panels (80048-80076)*
Therapeutic drug assays (80150-80299)

82310   Calcium; total
     0.00   0.00   Global Days XXX
     AMA: 2005, August, 9-10; 2005, July, 11-12; 2005, August, 7-8

82330-82373 Chemistry: Calcium, Ionized—Carbohydrate Deficient Transferrin

CMS 100-2,15,80   Physician Supervision Requirements for Diagnostic Tests
CMS 100-4,3,10.4   Payment of Nonphysician Services for Inpatients

INCLUDES   Mathematically calculated results
Quantitative analysis unless otherwise specified
Specimens from any source unless otherwise specified

EXCLUDES   *Organ or disease panels (80048-80076)*
Therapeutic drug assays (80150-80299)

82330   Calcium; ionized
     INCLUDES   Calcium, ionized (82330)
     0.00   0.00   Global Days XXX
     AMA: 2005, July, 11-12; 2005, August, 7-8; 2005, August, 9-10

82331   after calcium infusion test
     0.00   0.00   Global Days XXX
     AMA: 2005, July, 11-12; 2005, August, 9-10; 2005, August, 7-8

82340   urine quantitative, timed specimen
     0.00   0.00   Global Days XXX
     AMA: 2005, July, 11-12; 2005, August, 9-10; 2005, August, 7-8

82355   Calculus; qualitative analysis
     0.00   0.00   Global Days XXX
     AMA: 2005, July, 11-12; 2005, August, 9-10; 2005, August, 7-8

82360   quantitative analysis, chemical
     0.00   0.00   Global Days XXX
     AMA: 2005, July, 11-12; 2005, August, 9-10; 2005, August, 7-8

82365   infrared spectroscopy
     0.00   0.00   Global Days XXX
     AMA: 2005, July, 11-12; 2005, August, 9-10; 2005, August, 7-8

82370   X-ray diffraction
     0.00   0.00   Global Days XXX
     AMA: 2005, July, 11-12; 2005, August, 9-10; 2005, August, 7-8

82373   Carbohydrate deficient transferrin
     0.00   0.00   Global Days XXX
     AMA: 2005, August, 9-10; 2005, July, 11-12; 2005, August, 7-8

● New Code   ▲ Revised Code   M Maternity   A Age   Unlisted   Not Covered   # Resequenced
CCI   + Add-on   Mod 51 Exempt   Mod 63 Exempt   Mod Sedation   PQRI
© 2009 Publisher *(Blue Ink)*   CPT only © 2009 American Medical Association. All Rights Reserved. *(Black Ink)*   Medicare *(Red Ink)*

82374 Chemistry: Carbon Dioxide

CMS 100-2,15,80 — Physician Supervision Requirements for Diagnostic Tests
CMS 100-3,190.10 — Laboratory Tests--CRD Patients
CMS 100-4,3,10.4 — Payment of Nonphysician Services for Inpatients
INCLUDES Mathematically calculated results
Quantitative analysis unless otherwise specified
Specimens from any source unless otherwise specified
EXCLUDES Organ or disease panels (80048-80076)
Therapeutic drug assays (80150-80299)

- **82374** Carbon dioxide (bicarbonate)
  EXCLUDES Blood gases (82803)
  0.00 0.00 Global Days XXX
  AMA: 2005, July, 11-12; 2005, August, 9-10; 2005, August, 7-8

82375-82376 Chemistry: Carboxyhemoglobin (Carbon Monoxide)

CMS 100-2,15,80 — Physician Supervision Requirements for Diagnostic Tests
CMS 100-4,3,10.4 — Payment of Nonphysician Services for Inpatients
INCLUDES Mathematically calculated results
Specimens from any source unless otherwise specified
EXCLUDES Organ or disease panels (80048-80076)
Transcutaneous measurement of carboxyhemoglobin (88740)

- **82375** Carboxyhemoglobin; quantitative
  0.00 0.00 Global Days XXX
  AMA: 2005, August, 9-10; 2005, August, 7-8; 2005, July, 11-12

- **82376** qualitative
  EXCLUDES Transcutaneous measurement of carboxyhemoglobin (88740)
  0.00 0.00 Global Days XXX
  AMA: 2005, July, 11-12; 2005, August, 9-10; 2005, August, 7-8

82378 Chemistry: Carcinoembryonic Antigen (CEA)

CMS 100-2,15,80 — Physician Supervision Requirements for Diagnostic Tests
CMS 100-3,190.26 — Carcinoembryonic Antigen (CEA)
CMS 100-4,3,10.4 — Payment of Nonphysician Services for Inpatients

- **82378** Carcinoembryonic antigen (CEA)
  0.00 0.00 Global Days XXX
  AMA: 2009, Jan, 11-31; 2008, Jan, 10-25; 2007, January, 13-27; 2005, July, 11-12; 2005, August, 7-8; 2005, August, 9-10

82379-82415 Chemistry: Carnitine—Chloramphenicol

CMS 100-2,15,80 — Physician Supervision Requirements for Diagnostic Tests
CMS 100-4,3,10.4 — Payment of Nonphysician Services for Inpatients
INCLUDES Mathematically calculated results
Quantitative analysis unless otherwise specified
Specimens from any source unless otherwise specified
EXCLUDES Organ or disease panels (80048-80076)
Therapeutic drug assays (80150-80299)

- **82379** Carnitine (total and free), quantitative, each specimen
  EXCLUDES Acylcarnitine (82016-82017)
  0.00 0.00 Global Days XXX
  AMA: 2005, August, 7-8; 2005, July, 11-12; 2005, August, 9-10

- **82380** Carotene
  0.00 0.00 Global Days XXX
  AMA: 2005, August, 7-8; 2005, August, 9-10; 2005, July, 11-12

- **82382** Catecholamines; total urine
  0.00 0.00 Global Days XXX
  AMA: 2005, August, 9-10; 2005, August, 7-8; 2005, July, 11-12

- **82383** blood
  0.00 0.00 Global Days XXX
  AMA: 2005, August, 7-8; 2005, July, 11-12; 2005, August, 9-10

- **82384** fractionated
  EXCLUDES Urine metabolites (83835, 84585)
  0.00 0.00 Global Days XXX
  AMA: 2005, August, 9-10; 2005, July, 11-12; 2005, August, 7-8

- **82387** Cathepsin-D
  0.00 0.00 Global Days XXX
  AMA: 2005, July, 11-12; 2005, August, 9-10; 2005, August, 7-8

- **82390** Ceruloplasmin
  0.00 0.00 Global Days XXX
  AMA: 2005, August, 7-8; 2005, July, 11-12; 2005, August, 9-10

- **82397** Chemiluminescent assay
  0.00 0.00 Global Days XXX
  AMA: 2005, July, 11-12; 2005, August, 9-10; 2005, August, 7-8

- **82415** Chloramphenicol
  0.00 0.00 Global Days XXX
  AMA: 2005, July, 11-12; 2005, August, 9-10; 2005, August, 7-8

82435-82438 Chemistry: Chloride

CMS 100-2,15,80 — Physician Supervision Requirements for Diagnostic Tests
CMS 100-3,190.10 — Laboratory Tests--CRD Patients
CMS 100-4,3,10.4 — Payment of Nonphysician Services for Inpatients
INCLUDES Mathematically calculated results
Quantitative analysis unless otherwise specified
Specimens from any source unless otherwise specified
EXCLUDES Organ or disease panels (80048-80076)
Therapeutic drug assays (80150-80299)

- **82435** Chloride; blood
  0.00 0.00 Global Days XXX
  AMA: 2005, July, 11-12; 2005, August, 9-10; 2005, August, 7-8

- **82436** urine
  0.00 0.00 Global Days XXX
  AMA: 2005, August, 9-10; 2005, July, 11-12; 2005, August, 7-8

- **82438** other source
  EXCLUDES Sweat collections by iontophoresis (89230)
  0.00 0.00 Global Days XXX
  AMA: 2005, August, 7-8; 2005, July, 11-12; 2005, August, 9-10

82441 Chemistry: Chlorinated Hydrocarbons

CMS 100-2,15,80 — Physician Supervision Requirements for Diagnostic Tests
CMS 100-4,3,10.4 — Payment of Nonphysician Services for Inpatients
INCLUDES Mathematically calculated results
Quantitative analysis unless otherwise specified
Specimens from any source unless otherwise specified

- **82441** Chlorinated hydrocarbons, screen
  EXCLUDES Chlorpromazine (84022)
  0.00 0.00 Global Days XXX
  AMA: 2005, August, 9-10; 2005, August, 7-8; 2005, July, 11-12

82465 Chemistry: Cholesterol, Total

CMS 100-2,15,80 — Physician Supervision Requirements for Diagnostic Tests
CMS 100-3,190.23 — Lipid Testing
CMS 100-4,3,10.4 — Payment of Nonphysician Services for Inpatients
INCLUDES Mathematically calculated results
Quantitative analysis unless otherwise specified
EXCLUDES Organ or disease panels (80048-80299)

- **82465** Cholesterol, serum or whole blood, total
  EXCLUDES High density lipoprotein (HDL) (83718)
  0.00 0.00 Global Days XXX
  AMA: 2009, Jan, 11-31; 2008, Jan, 10-25; 2007, January, 13-27; 2005, August, 9-10; 2005, August, 7-8; 2005, July, 11-12; 2005, February, 7-9

Current Procedural Coding Expert – Pathology and Laboratory 82553

82480-82492 Chemistry: Cholinesterase—Chromatography

INCLUDES Mathematically calculated results
Quantitative analysis unless otherwise specified
Specimens from any source unless otherwise specified

EXCLUDES *Organ or disease panels (80048-80076)*
Therapeutic drug assays (80048-80299)

82480 Cholinesterase; serum [A]
0.00   0.00 Global Days XXX
AMA: 2005, August, 7-8; 2005, July, 11-12; 2005, August, 9-10

82482 RBC [A]
0.00   0.00 Global Days XXX
AMA: 2005, August, 9-10; 2005, August, 7-8; 2005, July, 11-12

82485 Chondroitin B sulfate, quantitative [A]
0.00   0.00 Global Days XXX
AMA: 2005, August, 9-10; 2005, August, 7-8; 2005, July, 11-12

82486 Chromatography, qualitative; column (eg, gas liquid or HPLC), analyte not elsewhere specified [A]
0.00   0.00 Global Days XXX
AMA: 2005, August, 7-8; 2005, July, 11-12; 2005, August, 9-10

82487 paper, 1-dimensional, analyte not elsewhere specified [A]
0.00   0.00 Global Days XXX
AMA: 2005, August, 9-10; 2005, July, 11-12; 2005, August, 7-8

82488 paper, 2-dimensional, analyte not elsewhere specified [A]
0.00   0.00 Global Days XXX
AMA: 2005, August, 9-10; 2005, July, 11-12; 2005, August, 7-8

82489 thin layer, analyte not elsewhere specified [A]
0.00   0.00 Global Days XXX
AMA: 2005, August, 9-10; 2005, August, 7-8; 2005, July, 11-12

82491 Chromatography, quantitative, column (eg, gas liquid or HPLC); single analyte not elsewhere specified, single stationary and mobile phase [A]
0.00   0.00 Global Days XXX
AMA: 2005, July, 11-12; 2005, August, 9-10; 2005, August, 7-8

82492 multiple analytes, single stationary and mobile phase [A]
0.00   0.00 Global Days XXX
AMA: 2005, July, 11-12; 2005, August, 7-8; 2005, August, 9-10

82495-82520 Chemistry: Chromium—Cocaine

CMS 100-2,15,80 Physician Supervision Requirements for Diagnostic Tests
CMS 100-4,3,10.4 Payment of Nonphysician Services for Inpatients

INCLUDES Mathematically calculated results
Quantitative analysis unless otherwise specified
Specimens from any source unless otherwise specified

EXCLUDES *Organ or disease panels (80048-80076)*
Therapeutic drug assays (80150-80299)

82495 Chromium [A]
0.00   0.00 Global Days XXX
AMA: 2005, July, 11-12; 2005, August, 9-10; 2005, August, 7-8

82507 Citrate [A]
0.00   0.00 Global Days XXX
AMA: 2005, August, 9-10; 2005, July, 11-12; 2005, August, 7-8

82520 Cocaine or metabolite [A]
EXCLUDES *Cocaine, qualitative testing (80100-80103)*
0.00   0.00 Global Days XXX
AMA: 2005, August, 7-8; 2005, July, 11-12; 2005, August, 9-10

82523 Chemistry: Collagen Crosslinks, Any Method

CMS 100-2,15,80 Physician Supervision Requirements for Diagnostic Tests
CMS 100-3,190.19 NCD for Collagen Crosslinks, Any Method
CMS 100-4,3,10.4 Payment of Nonphysician Services for Inpatients

INCLUDES Mathematically calculated results
Quantitative analysis unless otherwise specified
Specimens from any source unless otherwise specified

EXCLUDES *Organ or disease panels (80048-80076)*
Therapeutic drug assays (80150-80299)

82523 Collagen cross links, any method [A][x]
0.00   0.00 Global Days XXX
AMA: 2005, August, 9-10; 2005, August, 7-8; 2005, July, 11-12

82525-82946 Chemistry: Copper—Glucagon Tolerance Test

CMS 100-2,15,80 Physician Supervision Requirements for Diagnostic Tests
CMS 100-4,3,10.4 Payment of Nonphysician Services for Inpatients

INCLUDES Mathematically calculated results
Quantitative analysis unless otherwise specified
Specimens from any source unless otherwise specified

EXCLUDES *Organ or disease panels (80048-80076)*
Therapeutic drug assays (80150-80299)

82525 Copper [A]
0.00   0.00 Global Days XXX
AMA: 2005, August, 7-8; 2005, July, 11-12; 2005, August, 9-10

82528 Corticosterone [A]
INCLUDES Porter-Silber test
0.00   0.00 Global Days XXX
AMA: 2005, July, 11-12; 2005, August, 7-8; 2005, August, 9-10

82530 Cortisol; free [A]
0.00   0.00 Global Days XXX
AMA: 2005, July, 11-12; 2005, August, 9-10; 2005, August, 7-8

82533 total [A]
0.00   0.00 Global Days XXX
AMA: 2005, July, 11-12; 2005, August, 9-10; 2005, August, 7-8

82540 Creatine [A]
0.00   0.00 Global Days XXX
AMA: 2005, July, 11-12; 2005, August, 9-10; 2005, August, 7-8

82541 Column chromatography/mass spectrometry (eg, GC/MS, or HPLC/MS), analyte not elsewhere specified; qualitative, single stationary and mobile phase [A]
0.00   0.00 Global Days XXX
AMA: 2005, July, 11-12; 2005, August, 9-10; 2005, August, 7-8

82542 quantitative, single stationary and mobile phase [A]
0.00   0.00 Global Days XXX
AMA: 2005, August, 7-8; 2005, July, 11-12; 2005, August, 9-10

82543 stable isotope dilution, single analyte, quantitative, single stationary and mobile phase [A]
0.00   0.00 Global Days XXX
AMA: 2005, July, 11-12; 2005, August, 9-10; 2005, August, 7-8

82544 stable isotope dilution, multiple analytes, quantitative, single stationary and mobile phase [A]
0.00   0.00 Global Days XXX
AMA: 2005, July, 11-12; 2005, August, 9-10; 2005, August, 7-8

82550 Creatine kinase (CK), (CPK); total [A][x]
0.00   0.00 Global Days XXX
AMA: 2005, August, 7-8; 2005, July, 11-12; 2005, August, 9-10

82552 isoenzymes [A]
0.00   0.00 Global Days XXX
AMA: 2005, July, 11-12; 2005, August, 9-10; 2005, August, 7-8

82553 MB fraction only [A]
0.00   0.00 Global Days XXX
AMA: 2005, July, 11-12; 2005, August, 9-10; 2005, August, 7-8

● New Code   ▲ Revised Code   M Maternity   A Age   Unlisted   Not Covered   # Resequenced
CCI   + Add-on   ⊘ Mod 51 Exempt   Mod 63 Exempt   ⊙ Mod Sedation   PQRI

82554	isoforms
	AMA: 2005, July, 11-12; 2005, August, 9-10; 2005, August, 7-8
82565	Creatinine; blood
	AMA: 2005, August, 9-10; 2005, August, 7-8; 2005, July, 11-12
82570	other source
	AMA: 2005, August, 9-10; 2005, August, 7-8; 2005, July, 11-12
82575	clearance
	INCLUDES Holten test
	AMA: 2005, August, 9-10; 2005, August, 7-8; 2005, July, 11-12
82585	Cryofibrinogen
	AMA: 2005, July, 11-12; 2005, August, 9-10; 2005, August, 7-8
82595	Cryoglobulin, qualitative or semi-quantitative (eg, cryocrit)
	EXCLUDES Quantitative, cryoglobulin (82784-82785)
	AMA: 2005, August, 7-8; 2005, August, 9-10; 2005, July, 11-12
82600	Cyanide
	AMA: 2005, August, 7-8; 2005, August, 9-10; 2005, July, 11-12
82607	Cyanocobalamin (Vitamin B-12);
	AMA: 2005, August, 9-10; 2005, July, 11-12; 2005, August, 7-8
82608	unsaturated binding capacity
	AMA: 2005, August, 7-8; 2005, July, 11-12; 2005, August, 9-10
82610	Cystatin C
	AMA: 2009, Jan, 11-31; 2008, Apr, 5-7
82615	Cystine and homocystine, urine, qualitative
	AMA: 2005, August, 7-8; 2005, August, 9-10; 2005, July, 11-12
82626	Dehydroepiandrosterone (DHEA)
	AMA: 2005, August, 7-8; 2005, August, 9-10; 2005, July, 11-12
82627	Dehydroepiandrosterone-sulfate (DHEA-S)
	AMA: 2005, July, 11-12; 2005, August, 9-10; 2005, August, 7-8
82633	Desoxycorticosterone, 11-
	AMA: 2005, August, 7-8; 2005, August, 9-10; 2005, July, 11-12
82634	Deoxycortisol, 11-
	AMA: 2005, July, 11-12; 2005, August, 7-8; 2005, August, 9-10
82638	Dibucaine number
	AMA: 2005, August, 7-8; 2005, July, 11-12; 2005, August, 9-10
82646	Dihydrocodeinone
	EXCLUDES Qualitative testing (80100-80103)
	AMA: 2005, July, 11-12; 2005, August, 9-10; 2005, August, 7-8
82649	Dihydromorphinone
	EXCLUDES Qualitative testing (80100-80103)
	AMA: 2005, August, 7-8; 2005, August, 9-10; 2005, July, 11-12
82651	Dihydrotestosterone (DHT)
	AMA: 2005, August, 7-8; 2005, August, 9-10; 2005, July, 11-12
82652	Resequenced code. See code following 82306.
82654	Dimethadione
	EXCLUDES Qualitative testing (80100-80103)
	AMA: 2005, August, 7-8; 2005, August, 9-10; 2005, July, 11-12
82656	Elastase, pancreatic (EL-1), fecal, qualitative or semi-quantitative
	AMA: 2009, Jan, 11-31; 2008, Jan, 10-25; 2007, January, 13-27; 2005, August, 7-8; 2005, September, 9-11; 2005, July, 11-12; 2005, August, 9-10
82657	Enzyme activity in blood cells, cultured cells, or tissue, not elsewhere specified; nonradioactive substrate, each specimen
	AMA: 2005, July, 11-12; 2005, August, 7-8; 2005, August, 9-10
82658	radioactive substrate, each specimen
	AMA: 2005, August, 9-10; 2005, July, 11-12; 2005, August, 7-8
82664	Electrophoretic technique, not elsewhere specified
	AMA: 2005, August, 7-8; 2005, July, 11-12; 2005, August, 9-10
82666	Epiandrosterone
	AMA: 2005, August, 7-8; 2005, August, 9-10
82668	Erythropoietin
	AMA: 2005, August, 9-10; 2005, July, 11-12; 2005, August, 7-8
82670	Estradiol
	AMA: 2005, August, 7-8; 2005, August, 9-10
82671	Estrogens; fractionated
	AMA: 2005, August, 7-8; 2005, August, 9-10; 2005, July, 11-12
82672	total
	AMA: 2005, August, 7-8; 2005, August, 9-10; 2005, July, 11-12
82677	Estriol
	AMA: 2005, July, 11-12; 2005, August, 9-10; 2005, August, 7-8
82679	Estrone
	AMA: 2005, August, 7-8; 2005, August, 9-10; 2005, July, 11-12
82690	Ethchlorvynol
	AMA: 2005, August, 7-8; 2005, August, 9-10; 2005, July, 11-12
82693	Ethylene glycol
	AMA: 2005, August, 7-8; 2005, August, 9-10; 2005, July, 11-12
82696	Etiocholanolone
	EXCLUDES Fractionation of ketosteroids (83593)
	AMA: 2005, August, 9-10; 2005, July, 11-12; 2005, August, 7-8
82705	Fat or lipids, feces; qualitative
	AMA: 2005, August, 7-8; 2005, July, 11-12; 2005, August, 9-10
82710	quantitative
	AMA: 2005, August, 7-8; 2005, August, 9-10; 2005, July, 11-12
82715	Fat differential, feces, quantitative
	AMA: 2005, August, 9-10; 2005, July, 11-12; 2005, August, 7-8
82725	Fatty acids, nonesterified
	AMA: 2005, August, 7-8; 2005, July, 11-12; 2005, August, 9-10

Current Procedural Coding Expert – Pathology and Laboratory   82950

82726	**Very long chain fatty acids** A
	EXCLUDES *Long-chain (C20-22) omega-3 fatty acids in red blood cell (RBC) membranes (0111T)*
	0.00 0.00 **Global Days XXX**
	AMA: 2005, August, 7-8; 2005, August, 9-10; 2005, July, 11-12; 2005, June, 6-8
82728	**Ferritin** A
	0.00 0.00 **Global Days XXX**
	AMA: 2005, August, 7-8; 2005, August, 9-10; 2005, July, 11-12
82731	**Fetal fibronectin, cervicovaginal secretions, semi-quantitative** M ♀ A
	0.00 0.00 **Global Days XXX**
	AMA: 2005, August, 9-10; 2005, August, 7-8; 2005, July, 11-12
82735	**Fluoride** A
	0.00 0.00 **Global Days XXX**
	AMA: 2005, August, 7-8; 2005, July, 11-12; 2005, August, 9-10
82742	**Flurazepam** A
	EXCLUDES *Qualitative testing (80100-80103)*
	0.00 0.00 **Global Days XXX**
	AMA: 2005, August, 9-10; 2005, August, 7-8; 2005, July, 11-12
82746	**Folic acid; serum** A
	0.00 0.00 **Global Days XXX**
	AMA: 2005, August, 7-8; 2005, July, 11-12; 2005, August, 9-10
82747	**RBC** A
	0.00 0.00 **Global Days XXX**
	AMA: 2005, August, 9-10; 2005, July, 11-12; 2005, August, 7-8
82757	**Fructose, semen** ♂ A
	EXCLUDES *Fructosamine (82985)* *Fructose, TLC screen (84375)*
	0.00 0.00 **Global Days XXX**
	AMA: 2005, August, 9-10; 2005, August, 7-8; 2005, July, 11-12
82759	**Galactokinase, RBC** A
	0.00 0.00 **Global Days XXX**
	AMA: 2005, August, 9-10; 2005, August, 7-8; 2005, July, 11-12
82760	**Galactose** A
	0.00 0.00 **Global Days XXX**
	AMA: 2005, August, 7-8; 2005, August, 9-10; 2005, July, 11-12
82775	**Galactose-1-phosphate uridyl transferase; quantitative** A
	0.00 0.00 **Global Days XXX**
	AMA: 2005, August, 9-10; 2005, August, 7-8; 2005, July, 11-12
82776	**screen** A
	0.00 0.00 **Global Days XXX**
	AMA: 2005, August, 9-10; 2005, August, 7-8; 2005, July, 11-12
▲ 82784	**Gammaglobulin (immunoglobulin); IgA, IgD, IgG, IgM, each** A
	INCLUDES Farr test
	0.00 0.00 **Global Days XXX**
	AMA: 2009, Jan, 11-31; 2008, Jan, 10-25; 2007, January, 13-27; 2005, July, 11-12; 2005, August, 9-10; 2005, August, 7-8
▲ 82785	**IgE** A
	INCLUDES Farr test
	EXCLUDES *Allergen specific, IgE (86003, 86005)*
	0.00 0.00 **Global Days XXX**
	AMA: 2005, August, 9-10; 2005, August, 7-8; 2005, July, 11-12
▲ 82787	**immunoglobulin subclasses (eg, IgG1, 2, 3, or 4), each** A
	EXCLUDES *Gamma-glutamyltransferase (GGT) (82977)*
	0.00 0.00 **Global Days XXX**
	AMA: 2005, July, 11-12; 2005, August, 9-10; 2005, August, 7-8
82800	**Gases, blood, pH only** A
	0.00 0.00 **Global Days XXX**
	AMA: 2005, July, 11-12; 2005, August, 9-10; 2005, August, 7-8

82803	**Gases, blood, any combination of pH, pCO2, pO2, CO2, HCO3 (including calculated O2 saturation);** A
	INCLUDES Two or more of the listed analytes
	0.00 0.00 **Global Days XXX**
	AMA: 2005, August, 9-10; 2005, July, 11-12; 2005, August, 7-8
82805	**with O2 saturation, by direct measurement, except pulse oximetry** A
	0.00 0.00 **Global Days XXX**
	AMA: 2005, August, 7-8; 2005, August, 9-10; 2005, July, 11-12
82810	**Gases, blood, O2 saturation only, by direct measurement, except pulse oximetry** A
	EXCLUDES *Pulse oximetry (94760)*
	0.00 0.00 **Global Days XXX**
	AMA: 2005, August, 9-10; 2005, August, 7-8; 2005, July, 11-12
82820	**Hemoglobin-oxygen affinity (pO2 for 50% hemoglobin saturation with oxygen)** A
	0.00 0.00 **Global Days XXX**
	AMA: 2005, August, 9-10; 2005, August, 7-8; 2005, July, 11-12
82926	**Gastric acid, free and total, each specimen** A
	0.00 0.00 **Global Days XXX**
	AMA: 2005, July, 11-12; 2005, August, 7-8; 2005, August, 9-10
82928	**Gastric acid, free or total, each specimen** A
	0.00 0.00 **Global Days XXX**
	AMA: 2005, August, 9-10; 2005, August, 7-8; 2005, July, 11-12
82938	**Gastrin after secretin stimulation** A
	0.00 0.00 **Global Days XXX**
	AMA: 2005, August, 7-8; 2005, July, 11-12; 2005, August, 9-10
82941	**Gastrin** A
	0.00 0.00 **Global Days XXX**
	AMA: 2005, July, 11-12; 2005, August, 7-8; 2005, August, 9-10
82943	**Glucagon** A
	0.00 0.00 **Global Days XXX**
	AMA: 2005, August, 7-8; 2005, August, 9-10; 2005, July, 11-12
82945	**Glucose, body fluid, other than blood** A
	0.00 0.00 **Global Days XXX**
	AMA: 2005, July, 11-12; 2005, August, 7-8; 2005, August, 9-10
82946	**Glucagon tolerance test** A
	0.00 0.00 **Global Days XXX**
	AMA: 2005, August, 7-8; 2005, August, 9-10; 2005, July, 11-12

82947-82962 Chemistry: Glucose Testing

CMS 100-2,15,80 Physician Supervision Requirements for Diagnostic Tests
CMS 100-3,190.20 Blood Glucose Testing
CMS 100-4,3,10.4 Payment of Nonphysician Services for Inpatients
INCLUDES Mathematically calculated results
Quantitative analysis unless otherwise specified
Specimens from any source unless otherwise specified
EXCLUDES *Organ or disease panels (80048-80076)*
Therapeutic drug assays (80150-80299)
Code also glucose administration injection (96374)

82947	**Glucose; quantitative, blood (except reagent strip)** A
	0.00 0.00 **Global Days XXX**
	AMA: 2005, August, 7-8; 2005, August, 9-10; 2005, July, 11-12; 2005, February, 7-9
82948	**blood, reagent strip** A
	0.00 0.00 **Global Days XXX**
	AMA: 2009, Jan, 11-31; 2008, Jan, 10-25; 2007, January, 13-27; 2005, August, 9-10; 2005, August, 7-8; 2005, July, 11-12
82950	**post glucose dose (includes glucose)** A
	0.00 0.00 **Global Days XXX**
	AMA: 2009, Jan, 11-31; 2008, Jan, 10-25; 2007, January, 13-27; 2005, August, 7-8; 2005, July, 11-12; 2005, February, 7-9; 2005, August, 9-10

● New Code ▲ Revised Code M Maternity A Age Unlisted Not Covered # Resequenced
CCI + Add-on ⊘ Mod 51 Exempt @ Mod 63 Exempt ⊙ Mod Sedation PQRI

© 2009 Publisher *(Blue Ink)*   CPT only © 2009 American Medical Association. All Rights Reserved. (Black Ink)   Medicare (Red Ink)   307

82951	tolerance test (GTT), 3 specimens (includes glucose)

AMA: 2009, Jan, 11-31; 2008, Jan, 10-25; 2007, January, 13-27; 2005, August, 9-10; 2005, July, 11-12; 2005, February, 7-9; 2005, August, 7-8

82952	tolerance test, each additional beyond 3 specimens

AMA: 2009, Jan, 11-31; 2008, Jan, 10-25; 2007, January, 13-27; 2005, July, 11-12; 2005, August, 7-8; 2005, August, 9-10

82953	tolbutamide tolerance test

EXCLUDES Semiquantitative urine glucose (81000, 81002, 81005, 81099)

AMA: 2005, August, 7-8; 2005, July, 11-12; 2005, August, 9-10

82955	Glucose-6-phosphate dehydrogenase (G6PD); quantitative

AMA: 2005, July, 11-12; 2005, August, 7-8; 2005, August, 9-10

82960	screen

Code also injection administration (96374)

AMA: 2005, August, 9-10; 2005, July, 11-12; 2005, August, 7-8

82962	Glucose, blood by glucose monitoring device(s) cleared by the FDA specifically for home use

AMA: 2009, Jan, 11-31; 2008, Jan, 10-25; 2007, January, 13-27; 2005, August, 7-8; 2005, July, 11-12; 2005, August, 9-10

82963-83690 Chemistry: Glucosidase—Lipase

CMS 100-2,15,80 Physician Supervision Requirements for Diagnostic Tests
CMS 100-4,3,10.4 Payment of Nonphysician Services for Inpatients

INCLUDES
Mathematically calculated results
Quantitative analysis unless otherwise specified
Specimens from any source unless otherwise specified

EXCLUDES
Organ or disease panels (80048-80076)
Therapeutic drug assays (80150-80299)

82963	Glucosidase, beta

AMA: 2005, August, 7-8; 2005, July, 11-12; 2005, August, 9-10

82965	Glutamate dehydrogenase

AMA: 2005, August, 7-8; 2005, August, 9-10; 2005, July, 11-12

82975	Glutamine (glutamic acid amide)

AMA: 2005, July, 11-12; 2005, August, 7-8; 2005, August, 9-10

82977	Glutamyltransferase, gamma (GGT)

AMA: 2005, August, 9-10; 2005, July, 11-12; 2005, August, 7-8

82978	Glutathione

AMA: 2005, August, 7-8; 2005, July, 11-12; 2005, August, 9-10

82979	Glutathione reductase, RBC

AMA: 2005, August, 7-8; 2005, August, 9-10; 2005, July, 11-12

82980	Glutethimide

AMA: 2005, August, 9-10; 2005, July, 11-12; 2005, August, 7-8

82985	Glycated protein

EXCLUDES Gonadotropin, chorionic (hCG) (84702-84703)

AMA: 2005, August, 9-10; 2005, August, 7-8; 2005, July, 11-12

83001	Gonadotropin; follicle stimulating hormone (FSH)

AMA: 2005, August, 7-8; 2005, July, 11-12; 2005, August, 9-10

83002	luteinizing hormone (LH)

EXCLUDES Luteinizing releasing factor (LRH) (83727)

AMA: 2005, August, 9-10; 2005, July, 11-12; 2005, August, 7-8

83003	Growth hormone, human (HGH) (somatotropin)

EXCLUDES Antibody to human growth hormone (86277)

AMA: 2005, August, 7-8; 2005, August, 9-10; 2005, July, 11-12

83008	Guanosine monophosphate (GMP), cyclic

AMA: 2005, August, 7-8; 2005, July, 11-12; 2005, August, 9-10

83009	Helicobacter pylori, blood test analysis for urease activity, non-radioactive isotope (eg, C-13)

EXCLUDES H. pylori, breath test analysis for urease activity (83013-83014)

AMA: 2005, August, 7-8; 2005, August, 9-10; 2005, July, 11-12

83010	Haptoglobin; quantitative

AMA: 2005, August, 7-8; 2005, August, 9-10; 2005, July, 11-12

83012	phenotypes

AMA: 2005, August, 9-10; 2005, July, 11-12; 2005, August, 7-8

83013	Helicobacter pylori; breath test analysis for urease activity, non-radioactive isotope (eg, C-13)

AMA: 2005, August, 7-8; 2005, July, 11-12; 2005, August, 9-10

83014	drug administration

EXCLUDES H. pylori:
Blood test analysis for urease activity (83009)
Enzyme immunoassay (87339)
Liquid scintillation counter (78267-78268)
Stool (87338)

AMA: 2005, August, 7-8; 2005, August, 9-10; 2005, July, 11-12

83015	Heavy metal (eg, arsenic, barium, beryllium, bismuth, antimony, mercury); screen

INCLUDES Reinsch test

AMA: 2005, August, 9-10; 2005, July, 11-12; 2005, August, 7-8

83018	quantitative, each

AMA: 2005, August, 7-8; 2005, July, 11-12; 2005, August, 9-10

83020	Hemoglobin fractionation and quantitation; electrophoresis (eg, A2, S, C, and/or F)

AMA: 2005, August, 7-8; 2005, August, 9-10; 2005, July, 11-12

83021	chromatography (eg, A2, S, C, and/or F)

EXCLUDES Glycosylated (A1c) hemoglobin analysis by chromatography in the absence of an identified hemoglobin variant (83036)

AMA: 2005, August, 9-10; 2005, July, 11-12; 2005, August, 7-8

83026	Hemoglobin; by copper sulfate method, non-automated

AMA: 2005, August, 7-8; 2005, August, 9-10; 2005, July, 11-12

Current Procedural Coding Expert – Pathology and Laboratory

83030	F (fetal), chemical — 0.00 0.00 Global Days XXX **AMA:** 2005, August, 7-8; 2005, July, 11-12; 2005, August, 9-10
83033	F (fetal), qualitative — 0.00 0.00 Global Days XXX **AMA:** 2005, August, 7-8; 2005, August, 9-10; 2005, July, 11-12
83036	glycosylated (A1C) **EXCLUDES** Glycosylated (A1c) hemoglobin analysis by chromatography in the setting of an identified hemoglobin variant (83021) 0.00 0.00 Global Days XXX **AMA:** 2006, February, 7-9; 2005, August, 9-10; 2005, August, 7-8; 2005, July, 11-12
83037	glycosylated (A1C) by device cleared by FDA for home use **AMA:** 2009, Jan, 11-31; 2008, Jan, 10-25; 2007, January, 13-27; 2006, February, 7-9; 2005, August, 7-8; 2005, August, 9-10
83045	methemoglobin, qualitative — 0.00 0.00 Global Days XXX **AMA:** 2005, August, 7-8; 2005, August, 9-10; 2005, July, 11-12
83050	methemoglobin, quantitative **EXCLUDES** Transcutaneous methemoglobin test (88741) 0.00 0.00 Global Days XXX **AMA:** 2005, August, 7-8; 2005, August, 9-10; 2005, July, 11-12
83051	plasma — 0.00 0.00 Global Days XXX **AMA:** 2005, August, 9-10; 2005, July, 11-12; 2005, August, 7-8
83055	sulfhemoglobin, qualitative — 0.00 0.00 Global Days XXX **AMA:** 2005, August, 7-8; 2005, July, 11-12; 2005, August, 9-10
83060	sulfhemoglobin, quantitative — 0.00 0.00 Global Days XXX **AMA:** 2005, August, 7-8; 2005, August, 9-10; 2005, July, 11-12
83065	thermolabile — 0.00 0.00 Global Days XXX **AMA:** 2005, August, 9-10; 2005, July, 11-12; 2005, August, 7-8
83068	unstable, screen — 0.00 0.00 Global Days XXX **AMA:** 2005, August, 7-8; 2005, August, 9-10; 2005, July, 11-12
83069	urine — 0.00 0.00 Global Days XXX **AMA:** 2005, August, 7-8; 2005, August, 9-10; 2005, July, 11-12
83070	Hemosiderin; qualitative — 0.00 0.00 Global Days XXX **AMA:** 2005, August, 7-8; 2005, August, 9-10; 2005, July, 11-12
83071	quantitative — 0.00 0.00 Global Days XXX **AMA:** 2005, August, 7-8; 2005, August, 9-10; 2005, July, 11-12
83080	b-Hexosaminidase, each assay — 0.00 0.00 Global Days XXX **AMA:** 2005, August, 7-8; 2005, August, 9-10; 2005, July, 11-12
83088	Histamine — 0.00 0.00 Global Days XXX **AMA:** 2005, August, 7-8; 2005, July, 11-12; 2005, August, 9-10
83090	Homocysteine — 0.00 0.00 Global Days XXX **AMA:** 2009, Jan, 11-31; 2008, Jan, 10-25; 2007, January, 13-27; 2005, July, 11-12; 2005, August, 7-8; 2005, August, 9-10
83150	Homovanillic acid (HVA) — 0.00 0.00 Global Days XXX **AMA:** 2005, August, 9-10; 2005, July, 11-12; 2005, August, 7-8
83491	Hydroxycorticosteroids, 17- (17-OHCS) **EXCLUDES** Cortisol (82530, 82533); Deoxycortisol (82634) 0.00 0.00 Global Days XXX **AMA:** 2005, August, 7-8; 2005, July, 11-12; 2005, August, 9-10
83497	Hydroxyindolacetic acid, 5-(HIAA) **EXCLUDES** Urine qualitative test (81005) 0.00 0.00 Global Days XXX **AMA:** 2005, August, 9-10; 2005, August, 7-8; 2005, July, 11-12
83498	Hydroxyprogesterone, 17-d — 0.00 0.00 Global Days XXX **AMA:** 2005, August, 9-10; 2005, July, 11-12; 2005, August, 7-8
83499	Hydroxyprogesterone, 20- — 0.00 0.00 Global Days XXX **AMA:** 2005, July, 11-12; 2005, August, 9-10; 2005, August, 7-8
83500	Hydroxyproline; free — 0.00 0.00 Global Days XXX **AMA:** 2005, July, 11-12; 2005, August, 9-10; 2005, August, 7-8
83505	total — 0.00 0.00 Global Days XXX **AMA:** 2005, July, 11-12; 2005, August, 9-10; 2005, August, 7-8
▲ 83516	Immunoassay for analyte other than infectious agent antibody or infectious agent antigen; qualitative or semiquantitative, multiple step method 0.00 0.00 Global Days XXX **AMA:** 2005, July, 11-12; 2005, August, 9-10; 2005, August, 7-8
▲ 83518	qualitative or semiquantitative, single step method (eg, reagent strip) 0.00 0.00 Global Days XXX **AMA:** 2005, August, 7-8; 2005, August, 9-10; 2005, July, 11-12
▲ 83519	quantitative, by radioimmunoassay (eg, RIA) 0.00 0.00 Global Days XXX **AMA:** 2005, July, 11-12; 2005, August, 7-8; 2005, August, 9-10
▲ 83520	quantitative, not otherwise specified 0.00 0.00 Global Days XXX **AMA:** 2005, July, 11-12; 2005, August, 9-10; 2005, August, 7-8
83525	Insulin; total **EXCLUDES** Proinsulin (84206) 0.00 0.00 Global Days XXX **AMA:** 2005, July, 11-12; 2005, August, 9-10; 2005, August, 7-8
83527	free — 0.00 0.00 Global Days XXX **AMA:** 2005, July, 11-12; 2005, August, 9-10; 2005, August, 7-8
83528	Intrinsic factor **EXCLUDES** Intrinsic factor antibodies (86340) 0.00 0.00 Global Days XXX **AMA:** 2005, July, 11-12; 2005, August, 9-10; 2005, August, 7-8
83540	Iron — 0.00 0.00 Global Days XXX **AMA:** 2005, July, 11-12; 2005, August, 9-10; 2005, August, 7-8
83550	Iron binding capacity — 0.00 0.00 Global Days XXX **AMA:** 2005, July, 11-12; 2005, August, 9-10; 2005, August, 7-8
83570	Isocitric dehydrogenase (IDH) — 0.00 0.00 Global Days XXX **AMA:** 2005, July, 11-12; 2005, August, 9-10; 2005, August, 7-8
83582	Ketogenic steroids, fractionation — 0.00 0.00 Global Days XXX **AMA:** 2005, August, 7-8; 2005, August, 9-10; 2005, July, 11-12
83586	Ketosteroids, 17- (17-KS); total — 0.00 0.00 Global Days XXX **AMA:** 2005, July, 11-12; 2005, August, 9-10; 2005, August, 7-8

● New Code   ▲ Revised Code   Maternity   Age   Unlisted   Not Covered   # Resequenced
CCI   + Add-on   ⊘ Mod 51 Exempt   Mod 63 Exempt   ⊙ Mod Sedation   PQRI

© 2009 Publisher *(Blue Ink)*   CPT only © 2009 American Medical Association. All Rights Reserved. *(Black Ink)*   Medicare *(Red Ink)*

83593	fractionation	[A]
	0.00 0.00 Global Days XXX	
	AMA: 2005, August, 7-8; 2005, July, 11-12; 2005, August, 9-10	
83605	Lactate (lactic acid)	[A][X]
	0.00 0.00 Global Days XXX	
	AMA: 2005, August, 7-8; 2005, August, 9-10; 2005, July, 11-12	
83615	Lactate dehydrogenase (LD), (LDH);	[A]
	0.00 0.00 Global Days XXX	
	AMA: 2005, August, 7-8; 2005, July, 11-12; 2005, August, 9-10	
83625	isoenzymes, separation and quantitation	[A]
	0.00 0.00 Global Days XXX	
	AMA: 2005, July, 11-12; 2005, August, 7-8; 2005, August, 9-10	
83630	Lactoferrin, fecal; qualitative	[A]
	0.00 0.00 Global Days XXX	
	AMA: 2006, February, 7-9; 2005, August, 7-8; 2005, July, 11-12; 2005, August, 9-10	
83631	quantitative	[A]
	0.00 0.00 Global Days XXX	
	AMA: 2009, Jan, 11-31; 2008, Jan, 10-25; 2007, January, 28-31; 2006, February, 7-9; 2005, August, 7-8; 2005, August, 9-10	
83632	Lactogen, human placental (HPL) human chorionic somatomammotropin	[M][♀][A]
	0.00 0.00 Global Days XXX	
	AMA: 2005, August, 7-8; 2005, August, 9-10; 2005, July, 11-12	
83633	Lactose, urine; qualitative	[A]
	0.00 0.00 Global Days XXX	
	AMA: 2005, August, 7-8; 2005, July, 11-12; 2005, August, 9-10	
83634	quantitative	[A]
	EXCLUDES Breath hydrogen test for lactase deficiency (91065)	
	Glucose tolerance test (GTT) (82951-82952)	
	0.00 0.00 Global Days XXX	
	AMA: 2005, August, 7-8; 2005, August, 9-10; 2005, July, 11-12	
83655	Lead	[A][X]
	0.00 0.00 Global Days XXX	
	AMA: 2005, August, 7-8; 2005, July, 11-12; 2005, August, 9-10	
83661	Fetal lung maturity assessment; lecithin sphingomyelin (L/S) ratio	[M][♀][A]
	0.00 0.00 Global Days XXX	
	AMA: 2005, July, 11-12; 2005, August, 7-8; 2005, August, 9-10	
83662	foam stability test	[M][♀][A]
	0.00 0.00 Global Days XXX	
	AMA: 2005, July, 11-12; 2005, August, 7-8; 2005, August, 9-10	
83663	fluorescence polarization	[M][♀][A]
	0.00 0.00 Global Days XXX	
	AMA: 2005, July, 11-12; 2005, August, 7-8; 2005, August, 9-10	
83664	lamellar body density	[M][♀][A]
	EXCLUDES Phosphatidylglycerol (84081)	
	0.00 0.00 Global Days XXX	
	AMA: 2005, July, 11-12; 2005, August, 7-8; 2005, August, 9-10	
83670	Leucine aminopeptidase (LAP)	[A]
	0.00 0.00 Global Days XXX	
	AMA: 2005, July, 11-12; 2005, August, 7-8; 2005, August, 9-10	
83690	Lipase	[A]
	0.00 0.00 Global Days XXX	
	AMA: 2005, August, 7-8; 2005, August, 9-10; 2005, July, 11-12	

83695-83727 Chemistry: Lipoprotein—Luteinizing Releasing Factor

CMS 100-2,15,80 — Physician Supervision Requirements for Diagnostic Tests
CMS 100-3,190.23 — Lipid Testing
CMS 100-4,3,10.4 — Payment of Nonphysician Services for Inpatients

INCLUDES
Mathematically calculated results
Quantitative analysis unless otherwise specified
Specimens from any source unless otherwise specified

EXCLUDES
Organ or disease panels (80048-80076)
Therapeutic drug assays

83695	Lipoprotein (a)	[A]
	0.00 0.00 Global Days XXX	
	AMA: 2006, February, 7-9; 2005, August, 7-8; 2005, August, 9-10	
83698	Lipoprotein-associated phospholipase A2 (Lp-PLA2)	[A]
	0.00 0.00 Global Days XXX	
83700	Lipoprotein, blood; electrophoretic separation and quantitation	[A]
	0.00 0.00 Global Days XXX	
	AMA: 2006, February, 7-9; 2005, August, 7-8; 2005, August, 9-10	
83701	high resolution fractionation and quantitation of lipoproteins including lipoprotein subclasses when performed (eg, electrophoresis, ultracentrifugation)	[A]
	0.00 0.00 Global Days XXX	
	AMA: 2006, February, 7-9; 2005, August, 7-8; 2005, August, 9-10	
83704	quantitation of lipoprotein particle numbers and lipoprotein particle subclasses (eg, by nuclear magnetic resonance spectroscopy)	[A]
	0.00 0.00 Global Days XXX	
	AMA: 2006, February, 7-9; 2005, August, 7-8; 2005, August, 9-10	
83718	Lipoprotein, direct measurement; high density cholesterol (HDL cholesterol)	[A][X]
	0.00 0.00 Global Days XXX	
	AMA: 2009, Jan, 11-31; 2008, Jan, 10-25; 2007, January, 13-27; 2005, February, 7-9; 2005, July, 11-12; 2005, August, 9-10; 2005, August, 7-8	
83719	VLDL cholesterol	[A]
	0.00 0.00 Global Days XXX	
	AMA: 2009, Jan, 11-31; 2008, Jan, 10-25; 2007, January, 13-27; 2005, July, 11-12; 2005, August, 7-8; 2005, August, 9-10	
83721	LDL cholesterol	[A][X]
	EXCLUDES Fractionation by high resolution electrophoresis or ultracentrifugation (83701)	
	Lipoprotein particle numbers and subclasses analysis by nuclear magnetic resonance spectroscopy (83704)	
	0.00 0.00 Global Days XXX	
	AMA: 2009, Jan, 11-31; 2008, Jan, 10-25; 2007, January, 13-27; 2005, August, 7-8; 2005, August, 9-10; 2005, July, 11-12	
83727	Luteinizing releasing factor (LRH)	[A]
	EXCLUDES Qualitative analysis (80100-80103)	
	0.00 0.00 Global Days XXX	
	AMA: 2005, July, 11-12; 2005, August, 7-8; 2005, August, 9-10	

Current Procedural Coding Expert – Pathology and Laboratory

83735-83887 Chemistry: Magnesium—Nicotine

CMS 100-2,15,80   Physician Supervision Requirements for Diagnostic Tests
CMS 100-4,3,10.4   Payment of Nonphysician Services for Inpatients

INCLUDES
Mathematically calculated results
Quantitative analysis unless otherwise specified
Specimens from any source unless otherwise specified

EXCLUDES
Organ or disease panels (80048-80076)
Therapeutic drug assays (80150-80299)

83735 Magnesium [A]
0.00   0.00   Global Days XXX
AMA: 2005, July, 11-12; 2005, August, 7-8; 2005, August, 9-10

83775 Malate dehydrogenase [A]
0.00   0.00   Global Days XXX
AMA: 2005, July, 11-12; 2005, August, 7-8; 2005, August, 9-10

83785 Manganese [A]
0.00   0.00   Global Days XXX
AMA: 2005, July, 11-12; 2005, August, 7-8; 2005, August, 9-10

83788 Mass spectrometry and tandem mass spectrometry (MS, MS/MS), analyte not elsewhere specified; qualitative, each specimen [A]
0.00   0.00   Global Days XXX
AMA: 2005, July, 11-12; 2005, August, 7-8; 2005, August, 9-10

83789 quantitative, each specimen [A]
0.00   0.00   Global Days XXX
AMA: 2005, July, 11-12; 2005, August, 7-8; 2005, August, 9-10

83805 Meprobamate [A]
EXCLUDES Qualitative analysis (80100-80103)
0.00   0.00   Global Days XXX
AMA: 2005, July, 11-12; 2005, August, 7-8; 2005, August, 9-10

83825 Mercury, quantitative [A]
EXCLUDES Mercury screen (83015)
0.00   0.00   Global Days XXX
AMA: 2005, August, 7-8; 2005, July, 11-12; 2005, August, 9-10

83835 Metanephrines [A]
EXCLUDES Catecholamines (82382-82384)
0.00   0.00   Global Days XXX
AMA: 2005, July, 11-12; 2005, August, 7-8; 2005, August, 9-10

83840 Methadone [A]
EXCLUDES Methadone qualitative analysis (80100-80103)
0.00   0.00   Global Days XXX
AMA: 2005, July, 11-12; 2005, August, 7-8; 2005, August, 9-10

83857 Methemalbumin [A]
0.00   0.00   Global Days XXX
AMA: 2005, August, 7-8; 2005, August, 9-10; 2005, July, 11-12

83858 Methsuximide [A]
0.00   0.00   Global Days XXX
AMA: 2005, August, 7-8; 2005, July, 11-12; 2005, August, 9-10

83864 Mucopolysaccharides, acid; quantitative [A]
0.00   0.00   Global Days XXX
AMA: 2005, July, 11-12; 2005, August, 7-8; 2005, August, 9-10

83866 screen [A]
0.00   0.00   Global Days XXX
AMA: 2005, July, 11-12; 2005, August, 7-8; 2005, August, 9-10

83872 Mucin, synovial fluid (Ropes test) [A]
0.00   0.00   Global Days XXX
AMA: 2005, July, 11-12; 2005, August, 7-8; 2005, August, 9-10

83873 Myelin basic protein, cerebrospinal fluid [A]
EXCLUDES Oligoclonal bands (83916)
0.00   0.00   Global Days XXX
AMA: 2005, August, 7-8; 2005, July, 11-12; 2005, August, 9-10

83874 Myoglobin [A]
0.00   0.00   Global Days XXX
AMA: 2005, August, 7-8; 2005, August, 9-10; 2005, July, 11-12

83876 Myeloperoxidase (MPO) [A]
0.00   0.00   Global Days XXX

83880 Natriuretic peptide [A][X]
0.00   0.00   Global Days XXX
AMA: 2005, August, 7-8; 2005, July, 11-12; 2005, August, 9-10

83883 Nephelometry, each analyte not elsewhere specified [A]
0.00   0.00   Global Days XXX
AMA: 2005, August, 7-8; 2005, July, 11-12; 2005, August, 9-10

83885 Nickel [A]
0.00   0.00   Global Days XXX
AMA: 2005, August, 7-8; 2005, July, 11-12; 2005, August, 9-10

83887 Nicotine [A]
0.00   0.00   Global Days XXX
AMA: 2005, August, 7-8; 2005, August, 9-10; 2005, July, 11-12

83890-83914 Chemistry: Nucleic Acid Diagnostics

CMS 100-2,15,80   Physician Supervision Requirements for Diagnostic Tests
CMS 100-4,3,10.4   Payment of Nonphysician Services for Inpatients

INCLUDES
Molecular diagnostic techniques for analysis of nucleic acids
Tests reported by procedure instead of analyte

EXCLUDES
Array technology using more than 10 probes (88384-88386)
Digestate, undigested nucleic acid, or other individually modified nucleic acid sample
Microbial identification (87149-87150, 87152-87153, 87470-87801)

Do not report with or instead of (87140-87158, 87470-87801)

83890 Molecular diagnostics; molecular isolation or extraction, each nucleic acid type (ie, DNA or RNA) [A]
0.00   0.00   Global Days XXX
AMA: 2008, Apr, 5-7; 2006, January, 5-6,48; 2006, February, 7-9; 2005, July, 1-8; 2005, July, 11-12; 2005, August, 9-10; 2005, August, 7-8

83891 isolation or extraction of highly purified nucleic acid, each nucleic acid type (ie, DNA or RNA) [A]
0.00   0.00   Global Days XXX
AMA: 2008, Apr, 5-7; 2006, January, 5-6,48; 2005, August, 7-8; 2005, August, 9-10; 2005, July, 11-12; 2005, July, 1-8

83892 enzymatic digestion, each enzyme treatment [A]
0.00   0.00   Global Days XXX
AMA: 2008, Apr, 5-7; 2006, January, 5-6,48; 2005, August, 7-8; 2005, August, 9-10; 2005, July, 11-12; 2005, July, 1-8

83893 dot/slot blot production, each nucleic acid preparation [A]
0.00   0.00   Global Days XXX
AMA: 2008, Apr, 5-7; 2006, January, 5-6,48; 2005, July, 11-12; 2005, August, 7-8; 2005, August, 9-10; 2005, July, 1-8

83894 separation by gel electrophoresis (eg, agarose, polyacrylamide), each nucleic acid preparation [A]
0.00   0.00   Global Days XXX
AMA: 2008, Apr, 5-7; 2006, January, 5-6,48; 2005, July, 1-8; 2005, August, 7-8; 2005, August, 9-10; 2005, July, 11-12

83896 nucleic acid probe, each [A]
0.00   0.00   Global Days XXX
AMA: 2009, Jan, 11-31; 2008, Jan, 10-25; 2008, Apr, 5-7; 2007, January, 13-27; 2006, January, 5-6,48; 2005, July, 11-12; 2005, August, 9-10; 2005, July, 1-8; 2005, August, 7-8

83897 nucleic acid transfer (eg, Southern, Northern), each nucleic acid preparation [A]
0.00   0.00   Global Days XXX
AMA: 2008, Apr, 5-7; 2006, January, 5-6,48; 2005, July, 11-12; 2005, August, 7-8; 2005, August, 9-10; 2005, July, 1-8

83898 amplification, target, each nucleic acid sequence
EXCLUDES Multiple target amplification (83900-83901)
Signal amplification (83908)
0.00 0.00 Global Days XXX
AMA: 2008, Apr, 5-7; 2006, January, 5-6,48; 2006, February, 7-9; 2005, August, 7-8; 2005, July, 1-8; 2005, July, 11-12; 2005, August, 9-10

83900 amplification, target, multiplex, first 2 nucleic acid sequences
0.00 0.00 Global Days XXX
AMA: 2008, Apr, 5-7; 2006, January, 5-6,48; 2006, February, 7-9; 2005, August, 7-8; 2005, August, 9-10

+ **83901** amplification, target, multiplex, each additional nucleic acid sequence beyond 2 (List separately in addition to code for primary procedure)
Code first (83900)
0.00 0.00 Global Days XXX
AMA: 2008, Apr, 5-7; 2006, January, 5-6,48; 2006, February, 7-9; 2005, July, 1-8; 2005, July, 11-12; 2005, August, 7-8; 2005, August, 9-10

83902 reverse transcription
0.00 0.00 Global Days XXX
AMA: 2008, Apr, 5-7; 2006, January, 5-6,48; 2005, July, 1-8; 2005, August, 7-8; 2005, July, 11-12; 2005, August, 9-10

83903 mutation scanning, by physical properties (eg, single strand conformational polymorphisms [SSCP], heteroduplex, denaturing gradient gel electrophoresis [DGGE], RNA'ase A), single segment, each
0.00 0.00 Global Days XXX
AMA: 2008, Apr, 5-7; 2006, January, 5-6,48; 2005, July, 11-12; 2005, July, 1-8; 2005, August, 7-8; 2005, August, 9-10

83904 mutation identification by sequencing, single segment, each segment
0.00 0.00 Global Days XXX
AMA: 2008, Apr, 5-7; 2006, January, 5-6,48; 2005, July, 1-8; 2005, August, 7-8; 2005, August, 9-10; 2005, July, 11-12

83905 mutation identification by allele specific transcription, single segment, each segment
0.00 0.00 Global Days XXX
AMA: 2008, Apr, 5-7; 2006, January, 5-6,48; 2005, July, 11-12; 2005, August, 7-8; 2005, July, 1-8; 2005, August, 9-10

83906 mutation identification by allele specific translation, single segment, each segment
0.00 0.00 Global Days XXX
AMA: 2008, Apr, 5-7; 2006, January, 5-6,48; 2005, August, 7-8; 2005, July, 1-8; 2005, July, 11-12; 2005, August, 9-10

83907 lysis of cells prior to nucleic acid extraction (eg, stool specimens, paraffin embedded tissue), each specimen
0.00 0.00 Global Days XXX
AMA: 2008, Apr, 5-7; 2006, January, 5-6,48; 2006, February, 7-9; 2005, August, 7-8; 2005, August, 9-10

83908 amplification, signal, each nucleic acid sequence
EXCLUDES Target amplification (83898-83901)
0.00 0.00 Global Days XXX
AMA: 2008, Apr, 5-7; 2006, January, 5-6,48; 2006, February, 7-9; 2005, August, 7-8; 2005, August, 9-10

83909 separation and identification by high resolution technique (eg, capillary electrophoresis), each nucleic acid preparation
0.00 0.00 Global Days XXX
AMA: 2008, Apr, 5-7; 2006, January, 5-6,48; 2006, February, 7-9; 2005, August, 7-8; 2005, August, 9-10

83912 interpretation and report
0.00 0.00 Global Days XXX
AMA: 2008, Apr, 5-7; 2006, January, 5-6,48; 2006, February, 7-9; 2005, August, 7-8; 2005, August, 9-10; 2005, July, 1-8; 2005, July, 11-12

83913 RNA stabilization
0.00 0.00 Global Days XXX
AMA: 2008, Apr, 5-7

83914 Mutation identification by enzymatic ligation or primer extension, single segment, each segment (eg, oligonucleotide ligation assay [OLA], single base chain extension [SBCE], or allele-specific primer extension [ASPE])
0.00 0.00 Global Days XXX
AMA: 2008, Apr, 5-7; 2006, January, 5-6,48; 2006, February, 7-9; 2005, August, 7-8; 2005, August, 9-10

83915-84066 Chemistry: Nucleotidase 5'- —Phosphatase (Acid)

CMS 100-2,15,80 Physician Supervision Requirements for Diagnostic Tests
CMS 100-4,3,10.4 Payment of Nonphysician Services for Inpatients
INCLUDES Mathematically calculated results
Quantitative analysis unless otherwise specified
Specimens from any source unless otherwise specified
EXCLUDES Organ or disease panels (80048-80299)
Therapeutic drug assays (80150-80299)

83915 Nucleotidase 5'-
0.00 0.00 Global Days XXX
AMA: 2005, August, 7-8; 2005, August, 9-10; 2005, July, 11-12

83916 Oligoclonal immune (oligoclonal bands)
0.00 0.00 Global Days XXX
AMA: 2005, August, 7-8; 2005, August, 9-10; 2005, July, 11-12

83918 Organic acids; total, quantitative, each specimen
0.00 0.00 Global Days XXX
AMA: 2009, Jan, 11-31; 2008, Jan, 10-25; 2007, January, 13-27; 2005, August, 7-8; 2005, July, 11-12; 2005, August, 9-10

83919 qualitative, each specimen
0.00 0.00 Global Days XXX
AMA: 2005, August, 7-8; 2005, August, 9-10; 2005, July, 11-12

83921 Organic acid, single, quantitative
0.00 0.00 Global Days XXX
AMA: 2005, August, 7-8; 2005, August, 9-10; 2005, July, 11-12

83925 Opiate(s), drug and metabolites, each procedure
0.00 0.00 Global Days XXX
AMA: 2005, August, 7-8; 2005, July, 11-12; 2005, August, 9-10

83930 Osmolality; blood
0.00 0.00 Global Days XXX
AMA: 2005, August, 7-8; 2005, August, 9-10; 2005, July, 11-12

83935 urine
0.00 0.00 Global Days XXX
AMA: 2005, August, 7-8; 2005, August, 9-10; 2005, July, 11-12

83937 Osteocalcin (bone gla protein)
0.00 0.00 Global Days XXX
AMA: 2005, August, 7-8; 2005, July, 11-12; 2005, August, 9-10

83945 Oxalate
0.00 0.00 Global Days XXX
AMA: 2005, July, 11-12; 2005, August, 7-8; 2005, August, 9-10

83950 Oncoprotein; HER-2/neu
EXCLUDES Tissue (88342, 88365)
0.00 0.00 Global Days XXX
AMA: 2005, August, 7-8; 2005, July, 11-12; 2005, August, 9-10

83951 des-gamma-carboxy-prothrombin (DCP)
0.00 0.00 Global Days XXX

Current Procedural Coding Expert – Pathology and Laboratory 84140

83970	**Parathormone (parathyroid hormone)** [A]
	EXCLUDES — *Chlorinated hydrocarbons (82441)*
	Pesticide, quantitative (see code for specific method)
	0.00 0.00 **Global Days XXX**
	AMA: 2005, August, 7-8; 2005, July, 11-12; 2005, August, 9-10

▲ **83986** pH; body fluid, not otherwise specified [A][X]
EXCLUDES — *Blood pH (82800, 82803)*
0.00 0.00 **Global Days XXX**
AMA: 2005, August, 7-8; 2005, July, 11-12; 2005, August, 9-10

● **83987** exhaled breath condensate [A]
0.00 0.00 **Global Days XXX**

83992 Phencyclidine (PCP) [A]
EXCLUDES — *Qualitative analysis (80100-80103)*
0.00 0.00 **Global Days XXX**
AMA: 2005, July, 11-12; 2005, August, 7-8; 2005, August, 9-10

83993 Calprotectin, fecal [A]
0.00 0.00 **Global Days XXX**
AMA: 2008, Apr, 5-7

84022 Phenothiazine [A]
EXCLUDES — *Qualitative analysis (80100-80101)*
0.00 0.00 **Global Days XXX**
AMA: 2005, August, 7-8; 2005, August, 9-10; 2005, July, 11-12

84030 Phenylalanine (PKU), blood [A]
INCLUDES — Guthrie test
EXCLUDES — *Phenylalanine-tyrosine ratio (84030, 84510)*
0.00 0.00 **Global Days XXX**
AMA: 2005, August, 7-8; 2005, July, 11-12; 2005, August, 9-10

84035 Phenylketones, qualitative [A]
0.00 0.00 **Global Days XXX**
AMA: 2005, August, 7-8; 2005, July, 11-12; 2005, August, 9-10

84060 Phosphatase, acid; total [A]
0.00 0.00 **Global Days XXX**
AMA: 2005, August, 7-8; 2005, August, 9-10; 2005, July, 11-12

84061 forensic examination [A]
0.00 0.00 **Global Days XXX**
AMA: 2005, July, 11-12; 2005, August, 7-8; 2005, August, 9-10

84066 prostatic ♂[A]
0.00 0.00 **Global Days XXX**
AMA: 2005, August, 7-8; 2005, August, 9-10; 2005, July, 11-12

84075-84080 Chemistry: Phosphatase (Alkaline)

CMS 100-2,15,80 Physician Supervision Requirements for Diagnostic Tests
CMS 100-3,190.10 Laboratory Tests--CRD Patients
CMS 100-4,3,10.4 Payment of Nonphysician Services for Inpatients
INCLUDES Mathematically calculated results
Quantitative analysis unless otherwise specified
Specimens from any source unless otherwise specified
EXCLUDES *Organ or disease panels (80048-80076)*

84075 Phosphatase, alkaline; [A][X]
0.00 0.00 **Global Days XXX**
AMA: 2005, July, 11-12; 2005, August, 7-8; 2005, August, 9-10

84078 heat stable (total not included) [A]
0.00 0.00 **Global Days XXX**
AMA: 2005, August, 7-8; 2005, July, 11-12; 2005, August, 9-10

84080 isoenzymes [A]
0.00 0.00 **Global Days XXX**
AMA: 2005, July, 11-12; 2005, August, 7-8; 2005, August, 9-10

84081-84150 Chemistry: Phosphatidylglycerol—Prostaglandin

CMS 100-2,15,80 Physician Supervision Requirements for Diagnostic Tests
CMS 100-4,3,10.4 Payment of Nonphysician Services for Inpatients
INCLUDES Mathematically calculated results
Quantitative analysis unless otherwise specified
Specimens from any source unless otherwise specified
EXCLUDES *Organ or disease panels (80048-80076)*
Therapeutic drug assays (80150-80299)

84081 Phosphatidylglycerol [A]
0.00 0.00 **Global Days XXX**
AMA: 2005, July, 11-12; 2005, August, 7-8; 2005, August, 9-10

84085 Phosphogluconate, 6-, dehydrogenase, RBC [A]
0.00 0.00 **Global Days XXX**
AMA: 2005, August, 7-8; 2005, August, 9-10; 2005, July, 11-12

84087 Phosphohexose isomerase [A]
0.00 0.00 **Global Days XXX**
AMA: 2005, August, 9-10; 2005, August, 7-8; 2005, July, 11-12

84100 Phosphorus inorganic (phosphate); [A]
0.00 0.00 **Global Days XXX**
AMA: 2005, August, 7-8; 2005, July, 11-12; 2005, August, 9-10

84105 urine [A]
0.00 0.00 **Global Days XXX**
AMA: 2005, August, 7-8; 2005, August, 9-10; 2005, July, 11-12

84106 Porphobilinogen, urine; qualitative [A]
0.00 0.00 **Global Days XXX**
AMA: 2005, August, 7-8; 2005, August, 9-10; 2005, July, 11-12

84110 quantitative [A]
0.00 0.00 **Global Days XXX**
AMA: 2005, August, 7-8; 2005, August, 9-10; 2005, July, 11-12

84119 Porphyrins, urine; qualitative [A]
0.00 0.00 **Global Days XXX**
AMA: 2005, July, 11-12; 2005, August, 7-8; 2005, August, 9-10

84120 quantitation and fractionation [A]
0.00 0.00 **Global Days XXX**
AMA: 2005, August, 7-8; 2005, August, 9-10; 2005, July, 11-12

84126 Porphyrins, feces; quantitative [A]
0.00 0.00 **Global Days XXX**
AMA: 2005, July, 11-12; 2005, August, 7-8; 2005, August, 9-10

84127 qualitative [A]
EXCLUDES — *Porphyrin precursors (82135, 84106, 84110)*
0.00 0.00 **Global Days XXX**
AMA: 2005, July, 11-12; 2005, August, 7-8; 2005, August, 9-10

84132 Potassium; serum, plasma or whole blood [A][X]
0.00 0.00 **Global Days XXX**
AMA: 2005, July, 11-12; 2005, August, 7-8; 2005, August, 9-10

84133 urine [A]
0.00 0.00 **Global Days XXX**
AMA: 2005, July, 11-12; 2005, August, 7-8; 2005, August, 9-10

84134 Prealbumin [A]
EXCLUDES — *Microalbumin (82043-82044) (82043-82044)*
0.00 0.00 **Global Days XXX**
AMA: 2005, July, 11-12; 2005, August, 7-8; 2005, August, 9-10

84135 Pregnanediol ♀[A]
0.00 0.00 **Global Days XXX**
AMA: 2005, August, 7-8; 2005, July, 11-12; 2005, August, 9-10

84138 Pregnanetriol ♀[A]
0.00 0.00 **Global Days XXX**
AMA: 2005, August, 7-8; 2005, July, 11-12; 2005, August, 9-10

84140 Pregnenolone [A]
0.00 0.00 **Global Days XXX**
AMA: 2005, July, 11-12; 2005, August, 7-8; 2005, August, 9-10

● New Code   ▲ Revised Code   M Maternity   A Age   Unlisted   Not Covered   # Resequenced
CCI   + Add-on   ⊘ Mod 51 Exempt   ⊘ Mod 63 Exempt   ⊙ Mod Sedation   PQRI

84143	17-hydroxypregnenolone	A
	0.00 0.00 Global Days XXX	
	AMA: 2005, July, 11-12; 2005, August, 7-8; 2005, August, 9-10	
84144	Progesterone	A
	EXCLUDES Progesterone receptor assay (84234)	
	0.00 0.00 Global Days XXX	
	AMA: 2005, August, 7-8; 2005, July, 11-12; 2005, August, 9-10	
● 84145	Procalcitonin (PCT)	A
	0.00 0.00 Global Days XXX	
84146	Prolactin	A
	0.00 0.00 Global Days XXX	
	AMA: 2005, July, 11-12; 2005, August, 7-8; 2005, August, 9-10	
84150	Prostaglandin, each	A
	0.00 0.00 Global Days XXX	
	AMA: 2005, August, 7-8; 2005, August, 9-10; 2005, July, 11-12	

84152-84154 Chemistry: Prostate Specific Antigen

CMS 100-2,15,80 — Physician Supervision Requirements for Diagnostic Tests
CMS 100-3,190.31 — Prostate Specific Antigen (PSA)
CMS 100-3,210.1 — Prostate Cancer Screening Tests
CMS 100-4,3,10.4 — Payment of Nonphysician Services for Inpatients
INCLUDES Mathematically calculated results
Quantitative analysis unless otherwise specified

84152	Prostate specific antigen (PSA); complexed (direct measurement)	♂ A
	0.00 0.00 Global Days XXX	
	AMA: 2005, July, 11-12; 2005, August, 7-8; 2005, August, 9-10	
84153	total	♂ A
	0.00 0.00 Global Days XXX	
	AMA: 2009, Jan, 11-31; 2008, Jan, 10-25; 2007, January, 13-27; 2005, August, 7-8; 2005, August, 9-10; 2005, July, 11-12	
84154	free	♂ A
	0.00 0.00 Global Days XXX	
	AMA: 2009, Jan, 11-31; 2008, Jan, 10-25; 2007, January, 13-27; 2005, August, 7-8; 2005, August, 9-10; 2005, July, 11-12	

84155-84157 Chemistry: Protein, Total (Not by Refractometry)

CMS 100-2,15,80 — Physician Supervision Requirements for Diagnostic Tests
CMS 100-3,190.10 — Laboratory Tests--CRD Patients
CMS 100-4,3,10.4 — Payment of Nonphysician Services for Inpatients
INCLUDES Mathematically calculated results
EXCLUDES Organ or disease panels (80048-80076)

84155	Protein, total, except by refractometry; serum, plasma or whole blood	A
	0.00 0.00 Global Days XXX	
	AMA: 2005, August, 7-8; 2005, July, 11-12; 2005, August, 9-10	
84156	urine	A
	0.00 0.00 Global Days XXX	
	AMA: 2005, August, 7-8; 2005, August, 9-10; 2005, July, 11-12	
84157	other source (eg, synovial fluid, cerebrospinal fluid)	A ✗
	0.00 0.00 Global Days XXX	
	AMA: 2005, August, 7-8; 2005, July, 11-12; 2005, August, 9-10	

84160-84432 Chemistry: Protein, Total (Refractometry)—Thyroglobulin

CMS 100-2,15,80 — Physician Supervision Requirements for Diagnostic Tests
CMS 100-4,3,10.4 — Payment of Nonphysician Services for Inpatients
INCLUDES Mathematically calculated results
Quantitative analysis unless otherwise specified
Specimens from any source unless otherwise specified
EXCLUDES Organ or disease panels (80048-80076)
Therapeutic drug assays (80150-80299)

84160	Protein, total, by refractometry, any source	A
	EXCLUDES Dipstick urine protein (81000-81003)	
	0.00 0.00 Global Days XXX	
	AMA: 2005, August, 7-8; 2005, July, 11-12; 2005, August, 9-10	
84163	Pregnancy-associated plasma protein-A (PAPP-A)	♀ A
	0.00 0.00 Global Days XXX	
	AMA: 2005, August, 7-8; 2005, July, 11-12; 2005, August, 9-10	
84165	Protein; electrophoretic fractionation and quantitation, serum	A
	0.00 0.00 Global Days XXX	
	AMA: 2005, August, 7-8; 2005, July, 11-12; 2005, August, 9-10	
84166	electrophoretic fractionation and quantitation, other fluids with concentration (eg, urine, CSF)	A
	0.00 0.00 Global Days XXX	
	AMA: 2005, August, 7-8; 2005, July, 11-12; 2005, August, 9-10	
84181	Western Blot, with interpretation and report, blood or other body fluid	A
	0.00 0.00 Global Days XXX	
	AMA: 2005, August, 7-8; 2005, July, 11-12; 2005, August, 9-10	
84182	Western Blot, with interpretation and report, blood or other body fluid, immunological probe for band identification, each	A
	EXCLUDES Western Blot tissue testing (88371)	
	0.00 0.00 Global Days XXX	
	AMA: 2005, August, 7-8; 2005, July, 11-12; 2005, August, 9-10	
84202	Protoporphyrin, RBC; quantitative	A
	0.00 0.00 Global Days XXX	
	AMA: 2005, August, 7-8; 2005, July, 11-12; 2005, August, 9-10	
84203	screen	A
	0.00 0.00 Global Days XXX	
	AMA: 2005, August, 7-8; 2005, July, 11-12; 2005, August, 9-10	
84206	Proinsulin	A
	0.00 0.00 Global Days XXX	
	AMA: 2005, July, 11-12; 2005, August, 7-8; 2005, August, 9-10	
84207	Pyridoxal phosphate (Vitamin B-6)	A
	0.00 0.00 Global Days XXX	
	AMA: 2005, July, 11-12; 2005, August, 7-8; 2005, August, 9-10	
84210	Pyruvate	A
	0.00 0.00 Global Days XXX	
	AMA: 2005, July, 11-12; 2005, August, 7-8; 2005, August, 9-10	
84220	Pyruvate kinase	A
	0.00 0.00 Global Days XXX	
	AMA: 2005, August, 7-8; 2005, August, 9-10; 2005, July, 11-12	
84228	Quinine	A
	0.00 0.00 Global Days XXX	
	AMA: 2005, July, 11-12; 2005, August, 7-8; 2005, August, 9-10	
84233	Receptor assay; estrogen	A
	0.00 0.00 Global Days XXX	
	AMA: 2005, August, 7-8; 2005, August, 9-10; 2005, July, 11-12	
84234	progesterone	A
	0.00 0.00 Global Days XXX	
	AMA: 2005, August, 7-8; 2005, August, 9-10; 2005, July, 11-12	

26/TC PC/TC Comp Only   ✗ CLIA Waived   ♂ Male Only   ♀ Female Only
AMA: CPT Asst   **MED:** Pub 100   **A-Y** OPPSI   Radiology Crosswalk

Current Procedural Coding Expert – Pathology and Laboratory 84445

84235	endocrine, other than estrogen or progesterone (specify hormone)	A
	0.00 0.00 Global Days XXX	
	AMA: 2005, August, 7-8; 2005, August, 9-10; 2005, July, 11-12	
84238	non-endocrine (specify receptor)	A
	0.00 0.00 Global Days XXX	
	AMA: 2009, Jan, 11-31; 2008, Jan, 10-25; 2007, January, 13-27; 2006, February, 7-9; 2005, July, 11-12; 2005, August, 9-10; 2005, November, 14-15; 2005, August, 7-8	
84244	Renin	A
	0.00 0.00 Global Days XXX	
	AMA: 2005, August, 7-8; 2005, August, 9-10; 2005, July, 11-12	
84252	Riboflavin (Vitamin B-2)	A
	0.00 0.00 Global Days XXX	
	AMA: 2005, July, 11-12; 2005, August, 7-8; 2005, August, 9-10	
84255	Selenium	A
	0.00 0.00 Global Days XXX	
	AMA: 2005, August, 7-8; 2005, July, 11-12; 2005, August, 9-10	
84260	Serotonin	A
	EXCLUDES Urine metabolites (HIAA) (83497)	
	0.00 0.00 Global Days XXX	
	AMA: 2005, August, 7-8; 2005, August, 9-10; 2005, July, 11-12	
84270	Sex hormone binding globulin (SHBG)	A
	0.00 0.00 Global Days XXX	
	AMA: 2005, August, 7-8; 2005, August, 9-10; 2005, July, 11-12	
84275	Sialic acid	A
	0.00 0.00 Global Days XXX	
	AMA: 2005, August, 7-8; 2005, July, 11-12; 2005, August, 9-10	
84285	Silica	A
	0.00 0.00 Global Days XXX	
	AMA: 2005, August, 7-8; 2005, August, 9-10; 2005, July, 11-12	
84295	Sodium; serum, plasma or whole blood	A
	0.00 0.00 Global Days XXX	
	AMA: 2005, August, 7-8; 2005, August, 9-10; 2005, July, 11-12	
84300	urine	A
	0.00 0.00 Global Days XXX	
	AMA: 2005, July, 11-12; 2005, August, 7-8; 2005, August, 9-10	
84302	other source	A
	0.00 0.00 Global Days XXX	
	AMA: 2005, July, 11-12; 2005, August, 7-8; 2005, August, 9-10	
84305	Somatomedin	A
	0.00 0.00 Global Days XXX	
	AMA: 2005, August, 9-10; 2005, August, 7-8; 2005, July, 11-12	
84307	Somatostatin	A
	0.00 0.00 Global Days XXX	
	AMA: 2005, August, 7-8; 2005, July, 11-12; 2005, August, 9-10	
84311	Spectrophotometry, analyte not elsewhere specified	A
	0.00 0.00 Global Days XXX	
	AMA: 2005, July, 11-12; 2005, August, 7-8; 2005, August, 9-10	
84315	Specific gravity (except urine)	A
	EXCLUDES Urine specific gravity (81000-81003)	
	0.00 0.00 Global Days XXX	
	AMA: 2005, July, 11-12; 2005, August, 7-8; 2005, August, 9-10	
84375	Sugars, chromatographic, TLC or paper chromatography	A
	0.00 0.00 Global Days XXX	
	AMA: 2005, August, 7-8; 2005, July, 11-12; 2005, August, 9-10	
84376	Sugars (mono-, di-, and oligosaccharides); single qualitative, each specimen	A
	0.00 0.00 Global Days XXX	
	AMA: 2005, August, 7-8; 2005, August, 9-10; 2005, July, 11-12	
84377	multiple qualitative, each specimen	A
	0.00 0.00 Global Days XXX	
	AMA: 2005, August, 7-8; 2005, August, 9-10; 2005, July, 11-12

84378	single quantitative, each specimen	A
	0.00 0.00 Global Days XXX	
	AMA: 2005, August, 7-8; 2005, July, 11-12; 2005, August, 9-10	
84379	multiple quantitative, each specimen	A
	0.00 0.00 Global Days XXX	
	AMA: 2005, August, 7-8; 2005, August, 9-10; 2005, July, 11-12	
84392	Sulfate, urine	A
	0.00 0.00 Global Days XXX	
	AMA: 2005, August, 7-8; 2005, August, 9-10; 2005, July, 11-12	
84402	Testosterone; free	A
	0.00 0.00 Global Days XXX	
	AMA: 2005, August, 9-10; 2005, August, 7-8; 2005, July, 11-12	
84403	total	A
	0.00 0.00 Global Days XXX	
	AMA: 2005, August, 7-8; 2005, August, 9-10; 2005, July, 11-12	
84425	Thiamine (Vitamin B-1)	A
	0.00 0.00 Global Days XXX	
	AMA: 2005, August, 7-8; 2005, July, 11-12; 2005, August, 9-10	
84430	Thiocyanate	A
	0.00 0.00 Global Days XXX	
	AMA: 2005, August, 7-8; 2005, August, 9-10; 2005, July, 11-12	
● 84431	Thromboxane metabolite(s), including thromboxane if performed, urine	A
	Code also determination of concurrent urine creatinine (82507)	
	0.00 0.00 Global Days XXX	
84432	Thyroglobulin	A
	EXCLUDES Thyroglobulin antibody (86800)	
	0.00 0.00 Global Days XXX	
	AMA: 2005, August, 7-8; 2005, August, 9-10; 2005, July, 11-12

84436-84445 Chemistry: Thyroid Tests

CMS 100-2,15,80 — Physician Supervision Requirements for Diagnostic Tests
CMS 100-3,190.22 — Thyroid Testing
CMS 100-4,3,10.4 — Payment of Nonphysician Services for Inpatients

INCLUDES
Mathematically calculated results
Quantitative analysis unless otherwise specified
Specimens from any source unless otherwise specified

EXCLUDES
Organ or disease panels (80048-80076)
Therapeutic drug assays (80150-80299)

84436	Thyroxine; total	A
	0.00 0.00 Global Days XXX	
	AMA: 2005, August, 7-8; 2005, July, 11-12; August, 9-10	
84437	requiring elution (eg, neonatal)	A
	0.00 0.00 Global Days XXX	
	AMA: 2005, August, 7-8; 2005, August, 9-10; 2005, July, 11-12	
84439	free	A
	0.00 0.00 Global Days XXX	
	AMA: 2005, July, 11-12; 2005, August, 7-8; 2005, August, 9-10	
84442	Thyroxine binding globulin (TBG)	A
	0.00 0.00 Global Days XXX	
	AMA: 2005, August, 7-8; 2005, August, 9-10; 2005, July, 11-12	
84443	Thyroid stimulating hormone (TSH)	A
	0.00 0.00 Global Days XXX	
	AMA: 2005, July, 11-12; 2005, August, 7-8; 2005, August, 9-10	
84445	Thyroid stimulating immune globulins (TSI)	A
	0.00 0.00 Global Days XXX	
	AMA: 2005, July, 11-12; 2005, August, 7-8; 2005, August, 9-10

● New Code ▲ Revised Code M Maternity A Age Unlisted Not Covered # Resequenced
CCI + Add-on ⊘ Mod 51 Exempt @ Mod 63 Exempt ⊙ Mod Sedation PQRI

© 2009 Publisher *(Blue Ink)*   CPT only © 2009 American Medical Association. All Rights Reserved. (Black Ink)   Medicare (Red Ink)

84446-84449 Chemistry: Tocopherol Alpha—Transcortin

CMS 100-2,15,80 — Physician Supervision Requirements for Diagnostic Tests
CMS 100-4,3,10.4 — Payment of Nonphysician Services for Inpatients
INCLUDES Mathematically calculated results
Quantitative analysis unless otherwise specified
Specimens from any source unless otherwise specified
EXCLUDES Organ or disease panels (80048-80076)
Therapeutic drug assays (80150-80299)

84446 Tocopherol alpha (Vitamin E)
0.00   0.00   Global Days XXX
AMA: 2005, July, 11-12; 2005, August, 7-8; 2005, August, 9-10

84449 Transcortin (cortisol binding globulin)
0.00   0.00   Global Days XXX
AMA: 2005, July, 11-12; 2005, August, 7-8; 2005, August, 9-10

84450-84460 Chemistry: Transferase

CMS 100-2,15,80 — Physician Supervision Requirements for Diagnostic Tests
CMS 100-3,190.10 — Laboratory Tests--CRD Patients
CMS 100-4,3,10.4 — Payment of Nonphysician Services for Inpatients
INCLUDES Mathematically calculated results
Quantitative analysis unless otherwise specified

84450 Transferase; aspartate amino (AST) (SGOT)
0.00   0.00   Global Days XXX
AMA: 2005, August, 7-8; 2005, August, 9-10; 2005, July, 11-12

84460 alanine amino (ALT) (SGPT)
0.00   0.00   Global Days XXX
AMA: 2005, July, 11-12; 2005, August, 7-8; 2005, August, 9-10

84466 Chemistry: Transferrin

CMS 100-2,15,80 — Physician Supervision Requirements for Diagnostic Tests
CMS 100-4,3,10.4 — Payment of Nonphysician Services for Inpatients
INCLUDES Mathematically calculated results
Quantitative analysis unless otherwise specified

84466 Transferrin
EXCLUDES Iron binding capacity (83550)
0.00   0.00   Global Days XXX
AMA: 2005, August, 7-8; 2005, August, 9-10; 2005, July, 11-12

84478 Chemistry: Triglycerides

CMS 100-2,15,80 — Physician Supervision Requirements for Diagnostic Tests
CMS 100-3,190.23 — Lipid Testing
CMS 100-4,3,10.4 — Payment of Nonphysician Services for Inpatients
INCLUDES Mathematically calculated results
EXCLUDES Organ or disease panels (80048-80076)

84478 Triglycerides
0.00   0.00   Global Days XXX
AMA: 2009, Jan, 11-31; 2008, Jan, 10-25; 2007, January, 13-27; 2005, July, 11-12; 2005, August, 9-10; 2005, February, 7-9; 2005, August, 7-8

84479-84482 Chemistry: Thyroid Hormone—Triiodothyronine

CMS 100-2,15,80 — Physician Supervision Requirements for Diagnostic Tests
CMS 100-3,190.22 — Thyroid Testing
CMS 100-4,3,10.4 — Payment of Nonphysician Services for Inpatients
INCLUDES Mathematically calculated results
Quantitative analysis unless otherwise specified
Specimens from any source unless otherwise specified
EXCLUDES Organ or disease panels (80048-80076)

84479 Thyroid hormone (T3 or T4) uptake or thyroid hormone binding ratio (THBR)
0.00   0.00   Global Days XXX
AMA: 2005, August, 7-8; 2005, August, 9-10; 2005, July, 11-12

84480 Triiodothyronine T3; total (TT-3)
0.00   0.00   Global Days XXX
AMA: 2005, July, 11-12; 2005, August, 7-8; 2005, August, 9-10

84481 free
0.00   0.00   Global Days XXX
AMA: 2005, August, 7-8; 2005, August, 9-10; 2005, July, 11-12

84482 reverse
0.00   0.00   Global Days XXX
AMA: 2005, July, 11-12; 2005, August, 7-8; 2005, August, 9-10

84484-84512 Chemistry: Troponin (Quantitative)—Troponin (Qualitative)

CMS 100-2,15,80 — Physician Supervision Requirements for Diagnostic Tests
CMS 100-4,3,10.4 — Payment of Nonphysician Services for Inpatients
INCLUDES Mathematically calculated results
Specimens from any source unless otherwise specified
EXCLUDES Organ or disease panels

84484 Troponin, quantitative
EXCLUDES Qualitative troponin assay (84512)
0.00   0.00   Global Days XXX
AMA: 2005, July, 11-12; 2005, August, 7-8; 2005, August, 9-10

84485 Trypsin; duodenal fluid
0.00   0.00   Global Days XXX
AMA: 2005, August, 7-8; 2005, August, 9-10; 2005, July, 11-12

84488 feces, qualitative
0.00   0.00   Global Days XXX
AMA: 2005, August, 7-8; 2005, August, 9-10; 2005, July, 11-12

84490 feces, quantitative, 24-hour collection
0.00   0.00   Global Days XXX
AMA: 2005, August, 7-8; 2005, August, 9-10; 2005, July, 11-12

84510 Tyrosine
EXCLUDES Urate crystal identification (89060)
0.00   0.00   Global Days XXX
AMA: 2005, July, 11-12; 2005, August, 7-8; 2005, August, 9-10

84512 Troponin, qualitative
EXCLUDES Quantitative tropin assay (84484)
0.00   0.00   Global Days XXX
AMA: 2005, July, 11-12; 2005, August, 7-8; 2005, August, 9-10

84520-84525 Chemistry: Urea Nitrogen (Blood)

CMS 100-2,15,80 — Physician Supervision Requirements for Diagnostic Tests
CMS 100-3,190.10 — Laboratory Tests--CRD Patients
CMS 100-4,3,10.4 — Payment of Nonphysician Services for Inpatients
INCLUDES Mathematically calculated results
EXCLUDES Organ or disease panels (80048-80076)

84520 Urea nitrogen; quantitative
0.00   0.00   Global Days XXX
AMA: 2005, July, 11-12; 2005, August, 7-8; 2005, August, 9-10

Current Procedural Coding Expert – Pathology and Laboratory 85004

84525	semiquantitative (eg, reagent strip test)
	INCLUDES Patterson's test
	0.00 0.00 Global Days XXX
	AMA: 2005, July, 11-12; 2005, August, 7-8; 2005, August, 9-10

84540-84630 Chemistry: Urea Nitrogen (Urine)—Zinc

CMS 100-2,15,80 Physician Supervision Requirements for Diagnostic Tests
CMS 100-4,3,10.4 Payment of Nonphysician Services for Inpatients
INCLUDES Mathematically calculated results
Quantitative analysis unless otherwise specified
Specimens from any source unless otherwise specified
EXCLUDES Organ or disease panels (80048-80076)
Therapeutic drug assays (80150-80299)

84540	Urea nitrogen, urine
	0.00 0.00 Global Days XXX
	AMA: 2005, July, 11-12; 2005, August, 9-10; 2005, August, 7-8
84545	Urea nitrogen, clearance
	0.00 0.00 Global Days XXX
	AMA: 2005, July, 11-12; 2005, August, 7-8; 2005, August, 9-10
84550	Uric acid; blood
	0.00 0.00 Global Days XXX
	AMA: 2005, July, 11-12; 2005, August, 7-8; 2005, August, 9-10
84560	other source
	0.00 0.00 Global Days XXX
	AMA: 2005, August, 7-8; 2005, August, 9-10; 2005, July, 11-12
84577	Urobilinogen, feces, quantitative
	0.00 0.00 Global Days XXX
	AMA: 2005, July, 11-12; 2005, August, 7-8; 2005, August, 9-10
84578	Urobilinogen, urine; qualitative
	0.00 0.00 Global Days XXX
	AMA: 2005, August, 7-8; 2005, August, 9-10; 2005, July, 11-12
84580	quantitative, timed specimen
	0.00 0.00 Global Days XXX
	AMA: 2005, August, 7-8; 2005, August, 9-10; 2005, July, 11-12
84583	semiquantitative
	0.00 0.00 Global Days XXX
	AMA: 2005, August, 7-8; 2005, July, 11-12; 2005, August, 9-10
84585	Vanillylmandelic acid (VMA), urine
	0.00 0.00 Global Days XXX
	AMA: 2005, August, 7-8; 2005, August, 9-10; 2005, July, 11-12
84586	Vasoactive intestinal peptide (VIP)
	0.00 0.00 Global Days XXX
	AMA: 2005, August, 7-8; 2005, July, 11-12; 2005, August, 9-10
84588	Vasopressin (antidiuretic hormone, ADH)
	0.00 0.00 Global Days XXX
	AMA: 2005, August, 7-8; 2005, August, 9-10; 2005, July, 11-12
84590	Vitamin A
	0.00 0.00 Global Days XXX
	AMA: 2005, July, 11-12; 2005, August, 7-8; 2005, August, 9-10
84591	Vitamin, not otherwise specified
	0.00 0.00 Global Days XXX
	AMA: 2005, July, 11-12; 2005, August, 7-8; 2005, August, 9-10
84597	Vitamin K
	0.00 0.00 Global Days XXX
	AMA: 2005, July, 11-12; 2005, August, 7-8; 2005, August, 9-10
84600	Volatiles (eg, acetic anhydride, carbon tetrachloride, dichloroethane, dichloromethane, diethylether, isopropyl alcohol, methanol)
	EXCLUDES Acetaldehyde (82000)
	0.00 0.00 Global Days XXX
	AMA: 2005, July, 11-12; 2005, August, 9-10; 2005, August, 7-8
84620	Xylose absorption test, blood and/or urine
	EXCLUDES Administration (99070)
	0.00 0.00 Global Days XXX
	AMA: 2005, July, 11-12; 2005, August, 7-8; 2005, August, 9-10
84630	Zinc
	0.00 0.00 Global Days XXX
	AMA: 2005, August, 7-8; 2005, August, 9-10; 2005, July, 11-12

84681-84999 Other and Unlisted Chemistry Tests

CMS 100-2,15,80 Physician Supervision Requirements for Diagnostic Tests
CMS 100-4,3,10.4 Payment of Nonphysician Services for Inpatients
INCLUDES Mathematically calculated results
Quantitative analysis unless otherwise specified
Specimens from any source unless otherwise specified
EXCLUDES Organ or disease panels (80048-80076)

84681	C-peptide
	0.00 0.00 Global Days XXX
	AMA: 2005, July, 11-12; 2005, August, 7-8; 2005, August, 9-10
84702	Gonadotropin, chorionic (hCG); quantitative
	0.00 0.00 Global Days XXX
	AMA: 2005, July, 11-12; 2005, August, 7-8; 2005, August, 9-10
84703	qualitative
	EXCLUDES Urine pregnancy test by visual color comparison (81025)
	0.00 0.00 Global Days XXX
	AMA: 2005, July, 11-12; 2005, August, 7-8; 2005, August, 9-10
84704	free beta chain
	0.00 0.00 Global Days XXX
	AMA: 2009, Jan, 11-31; 2008, Apr, 5-7
84830	Ovulation tests, by visual color comparison methods for human luteinizing hormone
	0.00 0.00 Global Days XXX
	AMA: 2005, July, 11-12; 2005, August, 7-8; 2005, August, 9-10
84999	**Unlisted chemistry procedure**
	0.00 0.00 Global Days XXX
	AMA: 2009, Jan, 11-31; 2008, Jan, 10-25; 2007, January, 13-27; 2005, August, 9-10; 2005, July, 11-12; 2005, August, 7-8

85002 Bleeding Time Test

CMS 100-2,15,80 Physician Supervision Requirements for Diagnostic Tests
CMS 100-4,3,10.4 Payment of Nonphysician Services for Inpatients
EXCLUDES Agglutinins (86000, 86156-86157)
Antiplasmin (85410)
Antithrombin III (85300-85301)
Blood banking procedures (86850-86999)

85002	Bleeding time
	0.00 0.00 Global Days XXX
	AMA: 2005, August, 7-8; 2005, August, 9-10; 2005, July, 11-12

85004-85049 Blood Counts

CMS 100-2,15,80 Physician Supervision Requirements for Diagnostic Tests
CMS 100-3,190.15 Blood Counts
CMS 100-4,3,10.4 Payment of Nonphysician Services for Inpatients
EXCLUDES Agglutinins (86000, 86156-86157)
Antiplasmin (85410)
Antithrombin III (85300-85301)
Blood banking procedures (86850-86999)

85004	Blood count; automated differential WBC count
	0.00 0.00 Global Days XXX
	AMA: 2009, Jan, 11-31; 2008, Jan, 10-25; 2007, January, 13-27; 2005, July, 11-12; 2005, August, 9-10; 2005, August, 7-8

85007	**blood smear, microscopic examination with manual differential WBC count** [A]	
	0.00 0.00 Global Days XXX	
	AMA: 2009, Jan, 11-31; 2008, Jan, 10-25; 2007, January, 13-27; 2005, August, 7-8; 2005, August, 9-10; 2005, July, 11-12	
85008	**blood smear, microscopic examination without manual differential WBC count** [A]	
	EXCLUDES Cell count other fluids (eg, CSF) (89050-89051)	
	0.00 0.00 Global Days XXX	
	AMA: 2009, Jan, 11-31; 2008, Jan, 10-25; 2007, January, 13-27; 2005, July, 11-12; 2005, August, 9-10; 2005, August, 7-8	
85009	**manual differential WBC count, buffy coat** [A]	
	0.00 0.00 Global Days XXX	
	AMA: 2009, Jan, 11-31; 2008, Jan, 10-25; 2007, January, 13-27; 2005, July, 11-12; 2005, August, 9-10; 2005, August, 7-8	
85013	**spun microhematocrit** [A] [X]	
	0.00 0.00 Global Days XXX	
	AMA: 2005, July, 11-12; 2005, August, 7-8; 2005, August, 9-10	
85014	**hematocrit (Hct)** [A] [X]	
	0.00 0.00 Global Days XXX	
	AMA: 2005, July, 11-12; 2005, August, 7-8; 2005, August, 9-10	
85018	**hemoglobin (Hgb)** [A] [X]	
	EXCLUDES Immunoassay, hemoglobin, fecal (82274 (82274)	
	Other hemoglobin determination (83020-83069)	
	Transcutaneous hemoglobin measurement (88738)	
	0.00 0.00 Global Days XXX	
	AMA: 2005, July, 11-12; 2005, August, 7-8; 2005, August, 9-10	
85025	**complete (CBC), automated (Hgb, Hct, RBC, WBC and platelet count) and automated differential WBC count** [A]	
	0.00 0.00 Global Days XXX	
	AMA: 2009, Jan, 11-31; 2008, Jan, 10-25; 2007, January, 13-27; 2005, July, 11-12; 2005, August, 9-10; 2005, August, 7-8	
85027	**complete (CBC), automated (Hgb, Hct, RBC, WBC and platelet count)** [A]	
	0.00 0.00 Global Days XXX	
	AMA: 2005, July, 11-12; 2005, August, 7-8; 2005, August, 9-10	
85032	**manual cell count (erythrocyte, leukocyte, or platelet) each** [A]	
	0.00 0.00 Global Days XXX	
	AMA: 2009, Jan, 11-31; 2008, Jan, 10-25; 2007, January, 13-27; 2005, July, 11-12; 2005, August, 7-8; 2005, August, 9-10	
85041	**red blood cell (RBC), automated** [A]	
	Do not report with (85025, 85027)	
	0.00 0.00 Global Days XXX	
	AMA: 2005, August, 7-8; 2005, August, 9-10; 2005, July, 11-12	
85044	**reticulocyte, manual** [A]	
	0.00 0.00 Global Days XXX	
	AMA: 2005, August, 7-8; 2005, July, 11-12; 2005, August, 9-10	
85045	**reticulocyte, automated** [A]	
	0.00 0.00 Global Days XXX	
	AMA: 2005, August, 7-8; 2005, July, 11-12; 2005, August, 9-10	
85046	**reticulocytes, automated, including 1 or more cellular parameters (eg, reticulocyte hemoglobin content [CHr], immature reticulocyte fraction [IRF], reticulocyte volume [MRV], RNA content), direct measurement** [A]	
	0.00 0.00 Global Days XXX	
	AMA: 2005, August, 7-8; 2005, July, 11-12; 2005, August, 9-10	
85048	**leukocyte (WBC), automated** [A]	
	0.00 0.00 Global Days XXX	
	AMA: 2005, August, 7-8; 2005, July, 11-12; 2005, August, 9-10	
85049	**platelet, automated** [A]	
	0.00 0.00 Global Days XXX	
	AMA: 2005, August, 7-8; 2005, July, 11-12; 2005, August, 9-10	

85055-85705 Coagulopathy Testing

CMS 100-2,15,80 Physician Supervision Requirements for Diagnostic Tests
CMS 100-4,3,10.4 Payment of Nonphysician Services for Inpatients
CMS 100-4,3,20.7.3 Payment for Blood Clotting Factor for Hemophilia Inpatients

EXCLUDES Agglutinins (86000, 86156-86157)
Antiplasmin (85410)
Antithrombin III (85300-85301)
Blood banking procedures (86850-86999)

85055	**Reticulated platelet assay** [A]	
	0.00 0.00 Global Days XXX	
	AMA: 2005, August, 7-8; 2005, July, 11-12; 2005, August, 9-10	
85060	**Blood smear, peripheral, interpretation by physician with written report** [B] [80]	
	0.64 0.64 Global Days XXX	
	AMA: 2005, July, 11-12; 2005, August, 7-8; 2005, August, 9-10	
85097	**Bone marrow, smear interpretation** [X] [80]	
	EXCLUDES Bone biopsy (20220, 20225, 20240, 20245, 20250-20251)	
	Special stains (88312-88313)	
	1.30 2.12 Global Days XXX	
	AMA: 2009, Jan, 11-31; 2008, Jan, 10-25; 2007, January, 13-27; 2005, August, 7-8; 2005, August, 9-10; 2005, July, 11-12	
85130	**Chromogenic substrate assay** [A]	
	0.00 0.00 Global Days XXX	
	AMA: 2005, July, 11-12; 2005, August, 7-8; 2005, August, 9-10	
85170	**Clot retraction** [A]	
	0.00 0.00 Global Days XXX	
	AMA: 2005, August, 7-8; 2005, July, 11-12; 2005, August, 9-10	
85175	**Clot lysis time, whole blood dilution** [A]	
	0.00 0.00 Global Days XXX	
	AMA: 2005, August, 7-8; 2005, August, 9-10; 2005, July, 11-12	
85210	**Clotting; factor II, prothrombin, specific** [A]	
	EXCLUDES Prothrombin time (85610-85611)	
	Russel viper venom time (85612-85613 (85612-85613)	
	0.00 0.00 Global Days XXX	
	AMA: 2005, August, 7-8; 2005, July, 11-12; 2005, August, 9-10	
85220	**factor V (AcG or proaccelerin), labile factor** [A]	
	0.00 0.00 Global Days XXX	
	AMA: 2005, August, 7-8; 2005, August, 9-10; 2005, July, 11-12	
85230	**factor VII (proconvertin, stable factor)** [A]	
	0.00 0.00 Global Days XXX	
	AMA: 2005, July, 11-12; 2005, August, 7-8; 2005, August, 9-10	
85240	**factor VIII (AHG), 1-stage** [A]	
	0.00 0.00 Global Days XXX	
	AMA: 2005, August, 7-8; 2005, August, 9-10; 2005, July, 11-12	
85244	**factor VIII related antigen** [A]	
	0.00 0.00 Global Days XXX	
	AMA: 2005, August, 7-8; 2005, July, 11-12; 2005, August, 9-10	
85245	**factor VIII, VW factor, ristocetin cofactor** [A]	
	0.00 0.00 Global Days XXX	
	AMA: 2005, August, 7-8; 2005, August, 9-10; 2005, July, 11-12	
85246	**factor VIII, VW factor antigen** [A]	
	0.00 0.00 Global Days XXX	
	AMA: 2005, August, 7-8; 2005, July, 11-12; 2005, August, 9-10	
85247	**factor VIII, von Willebrand factor, multimetric analysis** [A]	
	0.00 0.00 Global Days XXX	
	AMA: 2005, July, 11-12; 2005, August, 7-8; 2005, August, 9-10	

Current Procedural Coding Expert – Pathology and Laboratory 85441

85250	factor IX (PTC or Christmas)	A
	0.00 0.00 Global Days XXX	
	AMA: 2005, July, 11-12; 2005, August, 7-8; 2005, August, 9-10	
85260	factor X (Stuart-Prower)	A
	0.00 0.00 Global Days XXX	
	AMA: 2005, July, 11-12; 2005, August, 7-8; 2005, August, 9-10	
85270	factor XI (PTA)	A
	0.00 0.00 Global Days XXX	
	AMA: 2005, July, 11-12; 2005, August, 7-8; 2005, August, 9-10	
85280	factor XII (Hageman)	A
	0.00 0.00 Global Days XXX	
	AMA: 2005, July, 11-12; 2005, August, 7-8; 2005, August, 9-10	
85290	factor XIII (fibrin stabilizing)	A
	0.00 0.00 Global Days XXX	
	AMA: 2005, July, 11-12; 2005, August, 7-8; 2005, August, 9-10	
85291	factor XIII (fibrin stabilizing), screen solubility	A
	0.00 0.00 Global Days XXX	
	AMA: 2005, July, 11-12; 2005, August, 7-8; 2005, August, 9-10	
85292	prekallikrein assay (Fletcher factor assay)	A
	0.00 0.00 Global Days XXX	
	AMA: 2005, August, 7-8; 2005, July, 11-12; 2005, August, 9-10	
85293	high molecular weight kininogen assay (Fitzgerald factor assay)	A
	0.00 0.00 Global Days XXX	
	AMA: 2005, July, 11-12; 2005, August, 7-8; 2005, August, 9-10	
85300	Clotting inhibitors or anticoagulants; antithrombin III, activity	A
	0.00 0.00 Global Days XXX	
	AMA: 2005, July, 11-12; 2005, August, 7-8; 2005, August, 9-10	
85301	antithrombin III, antigen assay	A
	0.00 0.00 Global Days XXX	
	AMA: 2005, July, 11-12; 2005, August, 7-8; 2005, August, 9-10	
85302	protein C, antigen	A
	0.00 0.00 Global Days XXX	
	AMA: 2005, July, 11-12; 2005, August, 7-8; 2005, August, 9-10	
85303	protein C, activity	A
	0.00 0.00 Global Days XXX	
	AMA: 2005, July, 11-12; 2005, August, 7-8; 2005, August, 9-10	
85305	protein S, total	A
	0.00 0.00 Global Days XXX	
	AMA: 2005, July, 11-12; 2005, August, 7-8; 2005, August, 9-10	
85306	protein S, free	A
	0.00 0.00 Global Days XXX	
	AMA: 2005, July, 11-12; 2005, August, 7-8; 2005, August, 9-10	
85307	Activated Protein C (APC) resistance assay	A
	0.00 0.00 Global Days XXX	
	AMA: 2005, August, 7-8; 2005, July, 11-12; 2005, August, 9-10	
85335	Factor inhibitor test	A
	0.00 0.00 Global Days XXX	
	AMA: 2005, July, 11-12; 2005, August, 7-8; 2005, August, 9-10	
85337	Thrombomodulin	A
	EXCLUDES Mixing studies for inhibitors (85732)	
	0.00 0.00 Global Days XXX	
	AMA: 2005, July, 11-12; 2005, August, 7-8; 2005, August, 9-10	
85345	Coagulation time; Lee and White	A
	0.00 0.00 Global Days XXX	
	AMA: 2005, July, 11-12; 2005, August, 7-8; 2005, August, 9-10	
85347	activated	A
	0.00 0.00 Global Days XXX	
	AMA: 2005, July, 11-12; 2005, August, 7-8; 2005, August, 9-10	
85348	other methods	A
	0.00 0.00 Global Days XXX	
	AMA: 2005, August, 7-8; 2005, August, 9-10; 2005, July, 11-12	
85360	Euglobulin lysis	A
	0.00 0.00 Global Days XXX	
	AMA: 2005, July, 11-12; 2005, August, 7-8; 2005, August, 9-10	
85362	Fibrin(ogen) degradation (split) products (FDP) (FSP); agglutination slide, semiquantitative	A
	0.00 0.00 Global Days XXX	
	AMA: 2005, July, 11-12; 2005, August, 7-8; 2005, August, 9-10	
85366	paracoagulation	A
	0.00 0.00 Global Days XXX	
	AMA: 2005, August, 7-8; 2005, August, 9-10; 2005, July, 11-12	
85370	quantitative	A
	0.00 0.00 Global Days XXX	
	AMA: 2005, August, 7-8; 2005, August, 9-10; 2005, July, 11-12	
85378	Fibrin degradation products, D-dimer; qualitative or semiquantitative	A
	0.00 0.00 Global Days XXX	
	AMA: 2005, July, 11-12; 2005, August, 7-8; 2005, August, 9-10	
85379	quantitative	
	INCLUDES Ultrasensitive and standard sensitivity quantitative D-dimer	
	0.00 0.00 Global Days XXX	
	AMA: 2005, July, 11-12; 2005, August, 7-8; 2005, August, 9-10	
85380	ultrasensitive (eg, for evaluation for venous thromboembolism), qualitative or semiquantitative	A
	0.00 0.00 Global Days XXX	
	AMA: 2005, July, 11-12; 2005, August, 7-8; 2005, August, 9-10	
85384	Fibrinogen; activity	A
	0.00 0.00 Global Days XXX	
	AMA: 2005, August, 7-8; 2005, August, 9-10; 2005, July, 11-12	
85385	antigen	A
	0.00 0.00 Global Days XXX	
	AMA: 2005, August, 7-8; 2005, August, 9-10; 2005, July, 11-12	
85390	Fibrinolysins or coagulopathy screen, interpretation and report	A
	0.00 0.00 Global Days XXX	
	AMA: 2005, July, 11-12; 2005, August, 7-8; 2005, August, 9-10	
85396	Coagulation/fibrinolysis assay, whole blood (eg, viscoelastic clot assessment), including use of any pharmacologic additive(s), as indicated, including interpretation and written report, per day	N 80
	0.52 0.52 Global Days XXX	
	AMA: 2005, July, 11-12; 2005, August, 7-8; 2005, August, 9-10	
85397	Coagulation and fibrinolysis, functional activity, not otherwise specified (eg, ADAMTS-13), each analyte	A
	0.00 0.00 Global Days XXX	
85400	Fibrinolytic factors and inhibitors; plasmin	A
	0.00 0.00 Global Days XXX	
	AMA: 2005, July, 11-12; 2005, August, 7-8; 2005, August, 9-10	
85410	alpha-2 antiplasmin	A
	0.00 0.00 Global Days XXX	
	AMA: 2005, August, 7-8; 2005, August, 9-10; 2005, July, 11-12	
85415	plasminogen activator	A
	0.00 0.00 Global Days XXX	
	AMA: 2005, July, 11-12; 2005, August, 7-8; 2005, August, 9-10	
85420	plasminogen, except antigenic assay	A
	0.00 0.00 Global Days XXX	
	AMA: 2005, July, 11-12; 2005, August, 7-8; 2005, August, 9-10	
85421	plasminogen, antigenic assay	A
	0.00 0.00 Global Days XXX	
	AMA: 2005, July, 11-12; 2005, August, 7-8; 2005, August, 9-10	
85441	Heinz bodies; direct	A
	0.00 0.00 Global Days XXX	
	AMA: 2005, August, 7-8; 2005, August, 9-10; 2005, July, 11-12

● New Code   ▲ Revised Code   M Maternity   A Age   Unlisted   Not Covered   # Resequenced

CCI   + Add-on   ⊘ Mod 51 Exempt   ⊘ Mod 63 Exempt   ⊙ Mod Sedation   PQRI

© 2009 Publisher *(Blue Ink)* CPT only © 2009 American Medical Association. All Rights Reserved. *(Black Ink)*  Medicare *(Red Ink)*   319

85445

Code	Description
85445	induced, acetyl phenylhydrazine
0.00 0.00 Global Days XXX
AMA: 2005, July, 11-12; 2005, August, 7-8; 2005, August, 9-10
85460	Hemoglobin or RBCs, fetal, for fetomaternal hemorrhage; differential lysis (Kleihauer-Betke)
EXCLUDES Hemoglobin F (83030, 83033)
Hemolysins (86940-86941)
0.00 0.00 Global Days XXX
AMA: 2005, July, 11-12; 2005, August, 7-8; 2005, August, 9-10
85461	rosette
0.00 0.00 Global Days XXX
AMA: 2005, July, 11-12; 2005, August, 7-8; 2005, August, 9-10
85475	Hemolysin, acid
INCLUDES Ham test
EXCLUDES Hemolysins and agglutinins (86940-86941)
0.00 0.00 Global Days XXX
AMA: 2005, July, 11-12; 2005, August, 7-8; 2005, August, 9-10
85520	Heparin assay
0.00 0.00 Global Days XXX
AMA: 2005, August, 7-8; 2005, August, 9-10; 2005, July, 11-12
85525	Heparin neutralization
0.00 0.00 Global Days XXX
AMA: 2005, August, 9-10; 2005, July, 11-12; 2005, August, 7-8
85530	Heparin-protamine tolerance test
0.00 0.00 Global Days XXX
AMA: 2005, August, 7-8; 2005, July, 11-12; 2005, August, 9-10
85536	Iron stain, peripheral blood
EXCLUDES Iron stains on bone marrow or other tissues with physician evaluation (88313)
0.00 0.00 Global Days XXX
AMA: 2005, August, 9-10; 2005, August, 7-8; 2005, July, 11-12
85540	Leukocyte alkaline phosphatase with count
0.00 0.00 Global Days XXX
AMA: 2005, August, 9-10; 2005, July, 11-12; 2005, August, 7-8
85547	Mechanical fragility, RBC
0.00 0.00 Global Days XXX
AMA: 2005, July, 11-12; 2005, August, 7-8; 2005, August, 9-10
85549	Muramidase
0.00 0.00 Global Days XXX
AMA: 2005, August, 9-10; 2005, July, 11-12; 2005, August, 7-8
85555	Osmotic fragility, RBC; unincubated
0.00 0.00 Global Days XXX
AMA: 2005, August, 9-10; 2005, August, 7-8; 2005, July, 11-12
85557	incubated
0.00 0.00 Global Days XXX
AMA: 2005, August, 9-10; 2005, August, 7-8; 2005, July, 11-12
85576	Platelet, aggregation (in vitro), each agent
EXCLUDES Thromboxane metabolite(s), including thromboxane, when performed, in urine (84431)
0.00 0.00 Global Days XXX
AMA: 2009, Jan, 11-31; 2008, Jan, 10-25; 2007, January, 13-27; 2005, August, 7-8; 2005, July, 11-12; 2005, August, 9-10
85597	Platelet neutralization
0.00 0.00 Global Days XXX
AMA: 2005, August, 7-8; 2005, July, 11-12; 2005, August, 9-10
85610	Prothrombin time;
0.00 0.00 Global Days XXX
AMA: 2005, August, 9-10; 2005, August, 7-8; 2005, July, 11-12
85611	substitution, plasma fractions, each
0.00 0.00 Global Days XXX
AMA: 2005, August, 9-10; 2005, July, 11-12
85612	Russell viper venom time (includes venom); undiluted
0.00 0.00 Global Days XXX
AMA: 2005, August, 7-8; 2005, July, 11-12; 2005, August, 9-10
85613	diluted
0.00 0.00 Global Days XXX
AMA: 2005, August, 9-10; 2005, August, 7-8; 2005, July, 11-12
85635	Reptilase test
0.00 0.00 Global Days XXX
AMA: 2005, August, 9-10; 2005, August, 7-8; 2005, July, 11-12
85651	Sedimentation rate, erythrocyte; non-automated
0.00 0.00 Global Days XXX
AMA: 2005, August, 7-8; 2005, July, 11-12; 2005, August, 9-10
85652	automated
INCLUDES Westergren test
0.00 0.00 Global Days XXX
AMA: 2005, August, 9-10; 2005, August, 7-8; 2005, July, 11-12
85660	Sickling of RBC, reduction
EXCLUDES Hemoglobin electrophoresis (83020)
Smears (87207)
0.00 0.00 Global Days XXX
AMA: 2005, August, 9-10; 2005, August, 7-8; 2005, July, 11-12
85670	Thrombin time; plasma
0.00 0.00 Global Days XXX
AMA: 2005, August, 9-10; 2005, August, 7-8; 2005, July, 11-12
85675	titer
0.00 0.00 Global Days XXX
AMA: 2005, August, 7-8; 2005, July, 11-12; 2005, August, 9-10
85705	Thromboplastin inhibition, tissue
EXCLUDES Individual clotting factors (85245-85247)
0.00 0.00 Global Days XXX
AMA: 2005, August, 9-10; 2005, August, 7-8; 2005, July, 11-12

85730-85732 Partial Thromboplastin Time (PTT)

CMS 100-2,15,80 Physician Supervision Requirements for Diagnostic Tests
CMS 100-3,190.16 Partial Thromboplastin Time (PTT)
CMS 100-4,3,10.4 Payment of Nonphysician Services for Inpatients

EXCLUDES Agglutinins (86000, 86156-86157)
  Antiplasmin (85410)
  Antithrombin III (85300-85301)
  Blood banking procedures (86850-86999)

Code	Description
85730	Thromboplastin time, partial (PTT); plasma or whole blood
INCLUDES Hicks-Pitney test
0.00 0.00 Global Days XXX
AMA: 2005, August, 9-10; 2005, August, 7-8; 2005, July, 11-12
85732	substitution, plasma fractions, each
0.00 0.00 Global Days XXX
AMA: 2005, August, 9-10; 2005, August, 7-8; 2005, July, 11-12

85810-85999 Blood Viscosity and Unlisted Hematology Procedures

CMS 100-2,15,80 Physician Supervision Requirements for Diagnostic Tests
CMS 100-4,3,10.4 Payment of Nonphysician Services for Inpatients

Code	Description
85810	Viscosity
0.00 0.00 Global Days XXX
AMA: 2009, Feb, 22; 2005, August, 7-8; 2005, July, 11-12; 2005, August, 9-10
85999	Unlisted hematology and coagulation procedure
0.00 0.00 Global Days XXX
AMA: 2005, August, 9-10; 2005, July, 11-12; 2005, August, 7-8

Current Procedural Coding Expert – Pathology and Laboratory

86000-86063 Antibody Testing

CMS 100-2,15,80 — Physician Supervision Requirements for Diagnostic Tests
CMS 100-4,3,10.4 — Payment of Nonphysician Services for Inpatients

86000 Agglutinins, febrile (eg, Brucella, Francisella, Murine typhus, Q fever, Rocky Mountain spotted fever, scrub typhus), each antigen [A]
0.00   0.00   Global Days XXX
AMA: 2005, August, 9-10; 2005, August, 7-8; 2005, July, 11-12

86001 Allergen specific IgG quantitative or semiquantitative, each allergen [A]
0.00   0.00   Global Days XXX
AMA: 2005, July, 11-12; 2005, August, 7-8; 2005, August, 9-10

86003 Allergen specific IgE; quantitative or semiquantitative, each allergen [A]
EXCLUDES Total quantitative IgE (82785)
0.00   0.00   Global Days XXX
AMA: 2005, August, 9-10; 2005, August, 7-8; 2005, July, 11-12

86005 qualitative, multiallergen screen (dipstick, paddle, or disk) [A]
EXCLUDES Total qualitative IgE (83518)
0.00   0.00   Global Days XXX
AMA: 2005, August, 9-10; 2005, July, 11-12; 2005, August, 7-8

86021 Antibody identification; leukocyte antibodies [A]
0.00   0.00   Global Days XXX
AMA: 2005, August, 9-10; 2005, July, 11-12; 2005, August, 7-8

86022 platelet antibodies [A]
0.00   0.00   Global Days XXX
AMA: 2005, July, 11-12; 2005, August, 7-8; 2005, August, 9-10

86023 platelet associated immunoglobulin assay [A]
0.00   0.00   Global Days XXX
AMA: 2005, August, 9-10; 2005, July, 11-12; 2005, August, 7-8

86038 Antinuclear antibodies (ANA); [A]
0.00   0.00   Global Days XXX
AMA: 2005, August, 9-10; 2005, August, 7-8; 2005, July, 11-12

86039 titer [A]
0.00   0.00   Global Days XXX
AMA: 2005, July, 11-12; 2005, August, 7-8; 2005, August, 9-10

86060 Antistreptolysin O; titer [A]
0.00   0.00   Global Days XXX
AMA: 2005, August, 9-10; 2005, July, 11-12; 2005, August, 7-8

86063 screen [A]
0.00   0.00   Global Days XXX
AMA: 2005, August, 9-10; 2005, August, 7-8; 2005, July, 11-12

86077-86079 Blood Bank Services

CMS 100-2,15,80 — Physician Supervision Requirements for Diagnostic Tests
CMS 100-4,3,10.4 — Payment of Nonphysician Services for Inpatients
CMS 100-4,12,60 — Payment for Pathology Services

86077 Blood bank physician services; difficult cross match and/or evaluation of irregular antibody(s), interpretation and written report [X 80]
1.34   1.42   Global Days XXX
AMA: 2005, August, 7-8; 2005, August, 9-10; 2005, July, 11-12

86078 investigation of transfusion reaction including suspicion of transmissible disease, interpretation and written report [X 80]
1.35   1.43   Global Days XXX
AMA: 2005, July, 11-12; 2005, August, 9-10; 2005, August, 7-8

86079 authorization for deviation from standard blood banking procedures (eg, use of outdated blood, transfusion of Rh incompatible units), with written report [X 80]
1.35   1.43   Global Days XXX
AMA: 2005, August, 7-8; 2005, July, 11-12; 2005, August, 9-10

86140-86344 Diagnostic Immunology Testing

CMS 100-2,15,80 — Physician Supervision Requirements for Diagnostic Tests
CMS 100-4,3,10.4 — Payment of Nonphysician Services for Inpatients

86140 C-reactive protein; [A]
0.00   0.00   Global Days XXX
AMA: 2005, July, 11-12; 2005, August, 7-8; 2005, August, 9-10

86141 high sensitivity (hsCRP) [A]
0.00   0.00   Global Days XXX
AMA: 2005, July, 11-12; 2005, August, 7-8; 2005, August, 9-10

86146 Beta 2 Glycoprotein I antibody, each [A]
0.00   0.00   Global Days XXX
AMA: 2005, July, 11-12; 2005, August, 7-8; 2005, August, 9-10

86147 Cardiolipin (phospholipid) antibody, each Ig class [A]
0.00   0.00   Global Days XXX
AMA: 2005, August, 7-8; 2005, August, 9-10; 2005, July, 11-12

86148 Anti-phosphatidylserine (phospholipid) antibody [A]
EXCLUDES Antiprothrombin (phospholipid cofactor) antibody (0030T)
0.00   0.00   Global Days XXX
AMA: 2005, July, 11-12; 2005, August, 7-8; 2005, August, 9-10

86155 Chemotaxis assay, specify method [A]
0.00   0.00   Global Days XXX
AMA: 2005, July, 11-12; 2005, August, 7-8; 2005, August, 9-10

86156 Cold agglutinin; screen [A]
0.00   0.00   Global Days XXX
AMA: 2005, August, 7-8; 2005, August, 9-10; 2005, July, 11-12

86157 titer [A]
0.00   0.00   Global Days XXX
AMA: 2005, July, 11-12; 2005, August, 7-8; 2005, August, 9-10

86160 Complement; antigen, each component [A]
0.00   0.00   Global Days XXX
AMA: 2005, July, 11-12; 2005, August, 7-8; 2005, August, 9-10

86161 functional activity, each component [A]
0.00   0.00   Global Days XXX
AMA: 2005, July, 11-12; 2005, August, 7-8; 2005, August, 9-10

86162 total hemolytic (CH50) [A]
0.00   0.00   Global Days XXX
AMA: 2005, August, 7-8; 2005, July, 11-12; 2005, August, 9-10

86171 Complement fixation tests, each antigen [A]
0.00   0.00   Global Days XXX
AMA: 2005, August, 7-8; 2005, August, 9-10; 2005, July, 11-12

86185 Counterimmunoelectrophoresis, each antigen [A]
0.00   0.00   Global Days XXX
AMA: 2005, July, 11-12; 2005, August, 7-8; 2005, August, 9-10

86200 Cyclic citrullinated peptide (CCP), antibody [A]
0.00   0.00   Global Days XXX
AMA: 2006, March, 6-9; 2005, August, 7-8; 2005, August, 9-10

86215 Deoxyribonuclease, antibody [A]
0.00   0.00   Global Days XXX
AMA: 2005, July, 11-12; 2005, August, 7-8; 2005, August, 9-10

86225 Deoxyribonucleic acid (DNA) antibody; native or double stranded [A]
EXCLUDES Echinococcus, antibodies (see code for specific method)
0.00   0.00   Global Days XXX
AMA: 2005, July, 11-12; 2005, August, 9-10; 2005, August, 7-8

● New Code   ▲ Revised Code   M Maternity   A Age   Unlisted   Not Covered   # Resequenced
CCI   + Add-on   ⊘ Mod 51 Exempt   Mod 63 Exempt   ⊙ Mod Sedation   PQRI
© 2009 Publisher (Blue Ink)   CPT only © 2009 American Medical Association. All Rights Reserved. (Black Ink)   Medicare (Red Ink)

86226

Code	Description
86226	single stranded
	EXCLUDES Anti D.S, DNA, IFA, eg, using C. lucilae (86255-86256)
	0.00 0.00 **Global Days XXX**
	AMA: 2005, July, 11-12; 2005, August, 7-8; 2005, August, 9-10
86235	Extractable nuclear antigen, antibody to, any method (eg, nRNP, SS-A, SS-B, Sm, RNP, Sc170, J01), each antibody
	0.00 0.00 **Global Days XXX**
	AMA: 2005, July, 11-12; 2005, August, 7-8; 2005, August, 9-10
86243	Fc receptor
	EXCLUDES Filaria antibodies to, (see code for specific method)
	0.00 0.00 **Global Days XXX**
	AMA: 2005, July, 11-12; 2005, August, 9-10; 2005, August, 7-8
86255	Fluorescent noninfectious agent antibody; screen, each antibody
	0.00 0.00 **Global Days XXX**
	AMA: 2005, July, 11-12; 2005, August, 9-10; 2005, August, 7-8
86256	titer, each antibody
	EXCLUDES Fluorescent technique for antigen identification in tissue (88346)
	FTA (86780)
	Gel (agar) diffusion tests (86331)
	Indirect fluorescence (88347)
	0.00 0.00 **Global Days XXX**
	AMA: 2005, July, 11-12; 2005, August, 7-8; 2005, August, 9-10
86277	Growth hormone, human (HGH), antibody
	0.00 0.00 **Global Days XXX**
	AMA: 2005, August, 7-8; 2005, August, 9-10; 2005, July, 11-12
86280	Hemagglutination inhibition test (HAI)
	EXCLUDES Antibodies to infectious agents (86602-86804)
	Rubella (86762)
	0.00 0.00 **Global Days XXX**
	AMA: 2005, July, 11-12; 2005, August, 9-10; 2005, August, 7-8
86294	Immunoassay for tumor antigen, qualitative or semiquantitative (eg, bladder tumor antigen)
	0.00 0.00 **Global Days XXX**
	AMA: 2005, July, 11-12; 2005, August, 7-8; 2005, August, 9-10
86300	Immunoassay for tumor antigen, quantitative; CA 15-3 (27.29)
	0.00 0.00 **Global Days XXX**
	AMA: 2005, August, 7-8; 2005, August, 9-10; 2005, July, 11-12
86301	CA 19-9
	0.00 0.00 **Global Days XXX**
	AMA: 2005, August, 7-8; 2005, July, 11-12; 2005, August, 9-10
86304	CA 125
	EXCLUDES Measurement of serum HER-2/neu oncoprotein (83950)
	0.00 0.00 **Global Days XXX**
	AMA: 2005, July, 11-12; 2005, August, 9-10; 2005, August, 7-8
● 86305	Human epididymis protein 4 (HE4)
	0.00 0.00 **Global Days XXX**
86308	Heterophile antibodies; screening
	EXCLUDES Antibodies to infectious agents (86602-86804)
	0.00 0.00 **Global Days XXX**
	AMA: 2005, August, 7-8; 2005, July, 11-12; 2005, August, 9-10
86309	titer
	EXCLUDES Antibodies to infectious agents (86602-86804)
	0.00 0.00 **Global Days XXX**
	AMA: 2005, August, 7-8; 2005, July, 11-12; 2005, August, 9-10
86310	titers after absorption with beef cells and guinea pig kidney
	EXCLUDES Antibodies to infectious agents (86602-86804)
	0.00 0.00 **Global Days XXX**
	AMA: 2005, July, 11-12; 2005, August, 7-8; 2005, August, 9-10
86316	Immunoassay for tumor antigen, other antigen, quantitative (eg, CA 50, 72-4, 549), each
	0.00 0.00 **Global Days XXX**
	AMA: 2009, Jan, 11-31; 2008, Jan, 10-25; 2007, January, 13-27; 2005, August, 9-10; 2005, July, 11-12; 2005, August, 7-8
86317	Immunoassay for infectious agent antibody, quantitative, not otherwise specified
	0.00 0.00 **Global Days XXX**
	AMA: 2005, August, 7-8; 2005, August, 9-10; 2005, July, 11-12
86318	Immunoassay for infectious agent antibody, qualitative or semiquantitative, single step method (eg, reagent strip)
	0.00 0.00 **Global Days XXX**
	AMA: 2009, Jan, 11-31; 2008, Jan, 10-25; 2007, March, 9-11; 2005, August, 7-8; 2005, August, 9-10; 2005, July, 11-12
86320	Immunoelectrophoresis; serum
	0.00 0.00 **Global Days XXX**
	AMA: 2005, August, 7-8; 2005, July, 11-12; 2005, August, 9-10
86325	other fluids (eg, urine, cerebrospinal fluid) with concentration
	0.00 0.00 **Global Days XXX**
	AMA: 2005, August, 9-10; 2005, August, 7-8; 2005, July, 11-12
86327	crossed (2-dimensional assay)
	0.00 0.00 **Global Days XXX**
	AMA: 2005, July, 11-12; 2005, August, 7-8; 2005, August, 9-10
86329	Immunodiffusion; not elsewhere specified
	0.00 0.00 **Global Days XXX**
	AMA: 2009, Jan, 11-31; 2008, Jan, 10-25; 2007, January, 13-27; 2005, August, 7-8; 2005, August, 9-10; 2005, July, 11-12
86331	gel diffusion, qualitative (Ouchterlony), each antigen or antibody
	0.00 0.00 **Global Days XXX**
	AMA: 2005, July, 11-12; 2005, August, 9-10; 2005, August, 7-8
86332	Immune complex assay
	0.00 0.00 **Global Days XXX**
	AMA: 2005, August, 7-8; 2005, August, 9-10; 2005, July, 11-12
86334	Immunofixation electrophoresis; serum
	0.00 0.00 **Global Days XXX**
	AMA: 2005, July, 11-12; 2005, August, 7-8; 2005, August, 9-10
86335	other fluids with concentration (eg, urine, CSF)
	0.00 0.00 **Global Days XXX**
	AMA: 2005, August, 7-8; 2005, August, 9-10; 2005, July, 11-12
86336	Inhibin A
	0.00 0.00 **Global Days XXX**
	AMA: 2005, August, 7-8; 2005, August, 9-10; 2005, July, 11-12
86337	Insulin antibodies
	0.00 0.00 **Global Days XXX**
	AMA: 2005, July, 11-12; 2005, August, 7-8; 2005, August, 9-10
86340	Intrinsic factor antibodies
	0.00 0.00 **Global Days XXX**
	AMA: 2005, August, 7-8; 2005, August, 9-10; 2005, July, 11-12
86341	Islet cell antibody
	0.00 0.00 **Global Days XXX**
	AMA: 2005, July, 11-12; 2005, August, 7-8; 2005, August, 9-10
86343	Leukocyte histamine release test (LHR)
	0.00 0.00 **Global Days XXX**
	AMA: 2005, August, 9-10; 2005, August, 7-8; 2005, July, 11-12

Current Procedural Coding Expert – Pathology and Laboratory

86344 Leukocyte phagocytosis
0.00   0.00   Global Days XXX
AMA: 2005, August, 7-8; 2005, July, 11-12; 2005, August, 9-10

86352 Assay Cellular Function

● **86352** Cellular function assay involving stimulation (eg, mitogen or antigen) and detection of biomarker (eg, ATP)
0.00   0.00   Global Days XXX

86353 Lymphocyte Mitogen Response Assay

CMS 100-2,15,80   Physician Supervision Requirements for Diagnostic Tests
CMS 100-3,190.8   Lymphocyte Mitogen Response Assays
CMS 100-4,3,10.4   Payment of Nonphysician Services for Inpatients

86353 Lymphocyte transformation, mitogen (phytomitogen) or antigen induced blastogenesis
  EXCLUDES Cellular function assay involving stimulation and detection of biomarker 86352
0.00   0.00   Global Days XXX
AMA: 2005, August, 7-8; 2005, August, 9-10; 2005, July, 11-12

86355-86593 Additional Diagnostic Immunology Testing

CMS 100-2,15,80   Physician Supervision Requirements for Diagnostic Tests
CMS 100-4,3,10.4   Payment of Nonphysician Services for Inpatients

86355 B cells, total count
Do not report with flow cytometry interpretation (88187-88189)
0.00   0.00   Global Days XXX
AMA: 2008, Apr, 5-7; 2006, March, 6-9; 2005, August, 9-10; 2005, August, 7-8

86356 Mononuclear cell antigen, quantitative (eg, flow cytometry), not otherwise specified, each antigen
Do not report with flow cytometry interpretation (88187-88189)
0.00   0.00   Global Days XXX
AMA: 2008, Apr, 5-7

86357 Natural killer (NK) cells, total count
Do not report with flow cytometry interpretation (88187-88189)
0.00   0.00   Global Days XXX
AMA: 2008, Apr, 5-7; 2006, March, 6-9; 2005, August, 7-8; 2005, August, 9-10

86359 T cells; total count
Do not report with flow cytometry interpretation (88187-88189)
0.00   0.00   Global Days XXX
AMA: 2008, Apr, 5-7; 2005, August, 7-8; 2005, July, 11-12; 2005, August, 9-10

86360 absolute CD4 and CD8 count, including ratio
Do not report with flow cytometry interpretation (88187-88189)
0.00   0.00   Global Days XXX
AMA: 2008, Apr, 5-7; 2007, January, 28-31; 2005, July, 11-12; 2005, August, 7-8; 2005, August, 9-10

86361 absolute CD4 count
Do not report with flow cytometry interpretation (88187-88189)
0.00   0.00   Global Days XXX
AMA: 2008, Apr, 5-7; 2005, July, 11-12; 2005, August, 7-8; 2005, August, 9-10

86367 Stem cells (ie, CD34), total count
  EXCLUDES Flow cytometric immunophenotyping for the assessment of potential hematolymphoid neoplasia (88184-88189)
Do not report with flow cytometry interpretation (88187-88189)
0.00   0.00   Global Days XXX
AMA: 2009, Jun, 3-6&11; 2008, Apr, 5-7; 2006, March, 6-9; 2005, August, 9-10; 2005, August, 7-8

86376 Microsomal antibodies (eg, thyroid or liver-kidney), each
0.00   0.00   Global Days XXX
AMA: 2005, August, 7-8; 2005, August, 9-10; 2005, July, 11-12

86378 Migration inhibitory factor test (MIF)
0.00   0.00   Global Days XXX
AMA: 2005, July, 11-12; 2005, August, 7-8; 2005, August, 9-10

86382 Neutralization test, viral
0.00   0.00   Global Days XXX
AMA: 2005, August, 9-10; 2005, August, 7-8; 2005, July, 11-12

86384 Nitroblue tetrazolium dye test (NTD)
0.00   0.00   Global Days XXX
AMA: 2005, July, 11-12; 2005, August, 7-8; 2005, August, 9-10

86403 Particle agglutination; screen, each antibody
0.00   0.00   Global Days XXX
AMA: 2005, July, 11-12; 2005, August, 7-8; 2005, August, 9-10

86406 titer, each antibody
  EXCLUDES Pregnancy test (84702-84703)
            Rapid plasma reagin test (RPR) (86592-86593)
0.00   0.00   Global Days XXX
AMA: 2005, July, 11-12; 2005, August, 7-8; 2005, August, 9-10

86430 Rheumatoid factor; qualitative
0.00   0.00   Global Days XXX
AMA: 2005, August, 9-10; 2005, August, 7-8; 2005, July, 11-12

86431 quantitative
0.00   0.00   Global Days XXX
AMA: 2005, July, 11-12; 2005, August, 7-8; 2005, August, 9-10

86480 Tuberculosis test, cell mediated immunity measurement of gamma interferon antigen response
0.00   0.00   Global Days XXX
AMA: 2006, March, 6-9; 2005, August, 7-8; 2005, August, 9-10

86485 Skin test; candida
0.00   0.00   Global Days XXX
AMA: 2005, August, 7-8; 2005, August, 9-10; 2005, July, 11-12

86486 unlisted antigen, each
0.12   0.12   Global Days XXX
AMA: 2008, Apr, 5-7

86490 coccidioidomycosis
0.12   0.12   Global Days XXX
AMA: 2005, August, 9-10; 2005, August, 7-8; 2005, July, 11-12

86510 histoplasmosis
0.14   0.14   Global Days XXX
AMA: 2005, July, 11-12; 2005, August, 7-8; 2005, August, 9-10

86580 tuberculosis, intradermal
  INCLUDES Heaf test
            Intradermal Mantoux test
  EXCLUDES Skin test for allergy (95010-95199) (95010-95199)
            Tuberculosis test, cell mediated immunity measurement of gamma interferon antigen response (86480 (86480)
0.18   0.18   Global Days XXX
AMA: 2005, August, 7-8; 2005, August, 9-10; 2005, July, 11-12

● New Code   ▲ Revised Code   M Maternity   A Age   Unlisted   Not Covered   # Resequenced
 CCI   + Add-on   Mod 51 Exempt   Mod 63 Exempt   Mod Sedation   PQ PQRI

86590 — Pathology and Laboratory

86590 Streptokinase, antibody [A]
EXCLUDES Antibodies to infectious agents (86602-86804)
Streptolysin O antibody (86060, 86063)
0.00 0.00 Global Days XXX
AMA: 2005, August, 7-8; 2005, August, 9-10; 2005, July, 11-12

▲ **86592** Syphilis test, non-treponemal antibody; qualitative (eg, VDRL, RPR, ART) [A]
INCLUDES Wasserman test
EXCLUDES Antibodies to infectious agents (86602-86804)
0.00 0.00 Global Days XXX
AMA: 2005, July, 11-12; 2005, August, 7-8; 2005, August, 9-10

▲ **86593** quantitative [A]
EXCLUDES Antibodies to infectious agents (86602-86804)
0.00 0.00 Global Days XXX
AMA: 2005, July, 11-12; 2005, August, 7-8; 2005, August, 9-10

86602-86698 Testing for Antibodies to Infectious Agents: Actinomyces—Histoplasma

CMS 100-2,15,80 Physician Supervision Requirements for Diagnostic Tests
CMS 100-4,3,10.4 Payment of Nonphysician Services for Inpatients
INCLUDES Qualitative or semiquantitative immunoassays performed by multiple-step methods for the detection of antibodies to infectious agents
EXCLUDES Detection of:
Antibodies other than those to infectious agents, see specific antibody or method (86021-86023, 86376, 86800, 86850-86870)
Infectious agent/antigen (87260-87899)
Immunoassays by single-step method (86318)

86602 Antibody; actinomyces [A]
0.00 0.00 Global Days XXX
AMA: 2005, July, 11-12; 2005, August, 9-10; 2005, August, 7-8

86603 adenovirus [A]
0.00 0.00 Global Days XXX
AMA: 2005, July, 11-12; 2005, August, 7-8; 2005, August, 9-10

86606 Aspergillus [A]
0.00 0.00 Global Days XXX
AMA: 2005, July, 11-12; 2005, August, 7-8; 2005, August, 9-10

86609 bacterium, not elsewhere specified [A]
0.00 0.00 Global Days XXX
AMA: 2005, July, 11-12; 2005, August, 9-10; 2005, August, 7-8

86611 Bartonella [A]
0.00 0.00 Global Days XXX
AMA: 2005, August, 7-8; 2005, August, 9-10; 2005, July, 11-12

86612 Blastomyces [A]
0.00 0.00 Global Days XXX
AMA: 2005, August, 7-8; 2005, July, 11-12; 2005, August, 9-10

86615 Bordetella [A]
0.00 0.00 Global Days XXX
AMA: 2005, August, 7-8; 2005, July, 11-12; 2005, August, 9-10

86617 Borrelia burgdorferi (Lyme disease) confirmatory test (eg, Western Blot or immunoblot) [A]
0.00 0.00 Global Days XXX
AMA: 2005, August, 9-10; 2005, July, 11-12; 2005, August, 7-8

86618 Borrelia burgdorferi (Lyme disease) [A] [X]
0.00 0.00 Global Days XXX
AMA: 2005, August, 7-8; 2005, August, 9-10; 2005, July, 11-12

86619 Borrelia (relapsing fever) [A]
0.00 0.00 Global Days XXX
AMA: 2005, August, 7-8; 2005, August, 9-10; 2005, July, 11-12

86622 Brucella [A]
0.00 0.00 Global Days XXX
AMA: 2005, August, 7-8; 2005, July, 11-12; 2005, August, 9-10

86625 Campylobacter [A]
0.00 0.00 Global Days XXX
AMA: 2005, July, 11-12; 2005, August, 9-10; 2005, August, 7-8

86628 Candida [A]
EXCLUDES Candida skin test (86485)
0.00 0.00 Global Days XXX
AMA: 2005, August, 7-8; 2005, July, 11-12; 2005, August, 9-10

86631 Chlamydia [A]
0.00 0.00 Global Days XXX
AMA: 2005, July, 11-12; 2005, August, 7-8; 2005, August, 9-10

86632 Chlamydia, IgM [A]
EXCLUDES Chlamydia antigen (87270, 87320)
Fluorescent antibody technique (86255-86256)
0.00 0.00 Global Days XXX
AMA: 2005, July, 11-12; 2005, August, 9-10; 2005, August, 7-8

86635 Coccidioides [A]
0.00 0.00 Global Days XXX
AMA: 2005, August, 7-8; 2005, July, 11-12; 2005, August, 9-10

86638 Coxiella burnetii (Q fever) [A]
0.00 0.00 Global Days XXX
AMA: 2005, August, 7-8; 2005, July, 11-12; 2005, August, 9-10

86641 Cryptococcus [A]
0.00 0.00 Global Days XXX
AMA: 2005, July, 11-12; 2005, August, 9-10; 2005, August, 7-8

86644 cytomegalovirus (CMV) [A]
0.00 0.00 Global Days XXX
AMA: 2005, July, 11-12; 2005, August, 9-10; 2005, August, 7-8

86645 cytomegalovirus (CMV), IgM [A]
0.00 0.00 Global Days XXX
AMA: 2005, August, 7-8; 2005, August, 9-10; 2005, July, 11-12

86648 Diphtheria [A]
0.00 0.00 Global Days XXX
AMA: 2005, July, 11-12; 2005, August, 7-8; 2005, August, 9-10

86651 encephalitis, California (La Crosse) [A]
0.00 0.00 Global Days XXX
AMA: 2005, August, 7-8; 2005, July, 11-12; 2005, August, 9-10

86652 encephalitis, Eastern equine [A]
0.00 0.00 Global Days XXX
AMA: 2005, August, 9-10; 2005, July, 11-12; 2005, August, 7-8

86653 encephalitis, St. Louis [A]
0.00 0.00 Global Days XXX
AMA: 2005, July, 11-12; 2005, August, 7-8; 2005, August, 9-10

86654 encephalitis, Western equine [A]
0.00 0.00 Global Days XXX
AMA: 2005, August, 7-8; 2005, July, 11-12; 2005, August, 9-10

86658 enterovirus (eg, coxsackie, echo, polio) [A]
0.00 0.00 Global Days XXX
AMA: 2005, July, 11-12; 2005, August, 9-10; 2005, August, 7-8

86663 Epstein-Barr (EB) virus, early antigen (EA) [A]
0.00 0.00 Global Days XXX
AMA: 2005, August, 7-8; 2005, August, 9-10; 2005, July, 11-12

86664 Epstein-Barr (EB) virus, nuclear antigen (EBNA) [A]
0.00 0.00 Global Days XXX
AMA: 2005, August, 7-8; 2005, July, 11-12; 2005, August, 9-10

86665 Epstein-Barr (EB) virus, viral capsid (VCA) [A]
0.00 0.00 Global Days XXX
AMA: 2005, July, 11-12; 2005, August, 9-10; 2005, August, 7-8

86666 Ehrlichia [A]
0.00 0.00 Global Days XXX
AMA: 2005, August, 7-8; 2005, August, 9-10; 2005, July, 11-12

86668 Francisella tularensis [A]
0.00 0.00 Global Days XXX
AMA: 2005, July, 11-12; 2005, August, 7-8; 2005, August, 9-10

26/TC PC/TC Comp Only   X CLIA Waived   ♂ Male Only   ♀ Female Only
AMA: CPT Asst   MED: Pub 100   A-Y OPPSI   Radiology Crosswalk

Current Procedural Coding Expert – Pathology and Laboratory   86727

86671	fungus, not elsewhere specified
	0.00 0.00 Global Days XXX
	AMA: 2005, August, 7-8; 2005, July, 11-12; 2005, August, 9-10
86674	Giardia lamblia
	0.00 0.00 Global Days XXX
	AMA: 2005, August, 7-8; 2005, July, 11-12; 2005, August, 9-10
86677	Helicobacter pylori
	0.00 0.00 Global Days XXX
	AMA: 2005, August, 9-10; 2005, August, 7-8; 2005, July, 11-12
86682	helminth, not elsewhere specified
	0.00 0.00 Global Days XXX
	AMA: 2005, August, 7-8; 2005, July, 11-12; 2005, August, 9-10
86684	Haemophilus influenza
	0.00 0.00 Global Days XXX
	AMA: 2005, August, 7-8; 2005, July, 11-12; 2005, August, 9-10
86687	HTLV-I
	0.00 0.00 Global Days XXX
	AMA: 2005, August, 9-10; 2005, August, 7-8; 2005, July, 11-12
86688	HTLV-II
	0.00 0.00 Global Days XXX
	AMA: 2005, August, 7-8; 2005, July, 11-12; 2005, August, 9-10
86689	HTLV or HIV antibody, confirmatory test (eg, Western Blot)
	0.00 0.00 Global Days XXX
	AMA: 2008, Mar, 3&7; 2005, August, 7-8; 2005, July, 11-12; 2005, August, 9-10
86692	hepatitis, delta agent
	EXCLUDES Hepatitis delta agent, antigen (87380)
	0.00 0.00 Global Days XXX
	AMA: 2005, August, 9-10; 2005, July, 11-12; 2005, August, 7-8
86694	herpes simplex, non-specific type test
	0.00 0.00 Global Days XXX
	AMA: 2005, August, 7-8; 2005, July, 11-12; 2005, August, 9-10
86695	herpes simplex, type 1
	0.00 0.00 Global Days XXX
	AMA: 2005, August, 7-8; 2005, July, 11-12; 2005, August, 9-10
86696	herpes simplex, type 2
	0.00 0.00 Global Days XXX
	AMA: 2005, August, 7-8; 2005, July, 11-12; 2005, August, 9-10
86698	histoplasma
	0.00 0.00 Global Days XXX
	AMA: 2005, July, 11-12; 2005, August, 9-10; 2005, August, 7-8

86701-86703 Testing for HIV Antibodies

CMS 100-2,15,80   Physician Supervision Requirements for Diagnostic Tests
CMS 100-3,190.9   Serologic Testing for Acquired Immunodeficiency Syndrome (AIDS)
CMS 100-3,190.14 Human Immunodeficiency Virus Testing (Diagnosis)
CMS 100-4,3,10.4 Payment of Nonphysician Services for Inpatients

INCLUDES Qualitative or semiquantitative immunoassays performed by multiple-step methods for the detection of antibodies to infectious agents

EXCLUDES Confirmatory test for HIV antibody (86689)
Detection of:
Antibodies other than those to infectious agents, see specific antibody or method (86021-86023, 86376, 86800, 86850-86870)
Infectious agent/antigen (87260-87899)
HIV-1 antigen (87390)
HIV-2 antigen (87391)
Immunoassays by single-step method (86318)

86701	Antibody; HIV-1
	0.00 0.00 Global Days XXX
	AMA: 2008, Mar, 3&7; 2008, Apr, 5-7; 2005, August, 7-8; 2005, July, 11-12; 2005, August, 9-10
86702	HIV-2
	0.00 0.00 Global Days XXX
	AMA: 2008, Mar, 3&7; 2008, Apr, 5-7; 2005, August, 7-8; 2005, July, 11-12; 2005, August, 9-10
86703	HIV-1 and HIV-2, single assay
	Code also modifier 92 when HIV antibody testing (86701-86703) is performed using a single use disposable kit or disposable analytic chamber in a transportable instrument.
	0.00 0.00 Global Days XXX
	AMA: 2008, Mar, 3&7; 2008, Apr, 5-7; 2005, August, 7-8; 2005, July, 11-12; 2005, August, 9-10

86704-86804 Testing for Infectious Disease Antibodies: Hepatitis—Yersinia

CMS 100-2,15,80   Physician Supervision Requirements for Diagnostic Tests
CMS 100-4,3,10.4 Payment of Nonphysician Services for Inpatients

INCLUDES Qualitative or semiquantitative immunoassays performed by multiple-step methods for the detection of antibodies to infectious agents

EXCLUDES Detection of:
Antibodies other than those to infectious agents, see specific antibody or method (86021-86023, 86376, 86800, 86850-86870)
Infectious agent/antigen
Immunoassays by single-step method (86318)

86704	Hepatitis B core antibody (HBcAb); total
	0.00 0.00 Global Days XXX
	AMA: 2005, August, 9-10; 2005, August, 7-8; 2005, July, 11-12
86705	IgM antibody
	0.00 0.00 Global Days XXX
	AMA: 2005, August, 7-8; 2005, July, 11-12; 2005, August, 9-10
86706	Hepatitis B surface antibody (HBsAb)
	0.00 0.00 Global Days XXX
	AMA: 2005, August, 7-8; 2005, July, 11-12; 2005, August, 9-10
86707	Hepatitis Be antibody (HBeAb)
	0.00 0.00 Global Days XXX
	AMA: 2005, August, 9-10; 2005, August, 7-8; 2005, July, 11-12
86708	Hepatitis A antibody (HAAb); total
	0.00 0.00 Global Days XXX
	AMA: 2009, Jan, 11-31; 2008, Jan, 10-25; 2007, January, 13-27; 2005, August, 7-8; 2005, July, 11-12; 2005, August, 9-10
86709	IgM antibody
	0.00 0.00 Global Days XXX
	AMA: 2009, Jan, 11-31; 2008, Jan, 10-25; 2007, January, 13-27; 2005, August, 7-8; 2005, July, 11-12; 2005, August, 9-10
86710	Antibody; influenza virus
	0.00 0.00 Global Days XXX
	AMA: 2009, May, 6&10; 2005, July, 11-12; 2005, August, 7-8; 2005, August, 9-10
86713	Legionella
	0.00 0.00 Global Days XXX
	AMA: 2005, July, 11-12; 2005, August, 9-10; 2005, August, 7-8
86717	Leishmania
	0.00 0.00 Global Days XXX
	AMA: 2005, August, 7-8; 2005, July, 11-12; 2005, August, 9-10
86720	Leptospira
	0.00 0.00 Global Days XXX
	AMA: 2005, August, 7-8; 2005, July, 11-12; 2005, August, 9-10
86723	Listeria monocytogenes
	0.00 0.00 Global Days XXX
	AMA: 2005, July, 11-12; 2005, August, 9-10; 2005, August, 7-8
86727	lymphocytic choriomeningitis
	0.00 0.00 Global Days XXX
	AMA: 2005, August, 7-8; 2005, August, 9-10; 2005, July, 11-12

● New Code   ▲ Revised Code   Ⓜ Maternity   Ⓐ Age   Unlisted   Not Covered   # Resequenced
CCI   + Add-on   Ⓢ Mod 51 Exempt   Ⓢ Mod 63 Exempt   Ⓢ Mod Sedation   PQRI

Code	Description
86729	lymphogranuloma venereum [A] 0.00 0.00 Global Days XXX **AMA:** 2005, August, 7-8; 2005, July, 11-12; 2005, August, 9-10
86732	mucormycosis [A] 0.00 0.00 Global Days XXX **AMA:** 2005, August, 7-8; 2005, July, 11-12; 2005, August, 9-10
86735	mumps [A] 0.00 0.00 Global Days XXX **AMA:** 2009, Jan, 11-31; 2008, Jan, 10-25; 2007, January, 13-27; 2006, September, 14-16; 2005, July, 11-12; 2005, August, 9-10; 2005, August, 7-8
86738	mycoplasma [A] 0.00 0.00 Global Days XXX **AMA:** 2005, August, 7-8; 2005, July, 11-12; 2005, August, 9-10
86741	Neisseria meningitidis [A] 0.00 0.00 Global Days XXX **AMA:** 2005, August, 7-8; 2005, August, 9-10; 2005, July, 11-12
86744	Nocardia [A] 0.00 0.00 Global Days XXX **AMA:** 2005, August, 7-8; 2005, July, 11-12; 2005, August, 9-10
86747	parvovirus [A] 0.00 0.00 Global Days XXX **AMA:** 2005, July, 11-12; 2005, August, 9-10; 2005, August, 7-8
86750	Plasmodium (malaria) [A] 0.00 0.00 Global Days XXX **AMA:** 2005, August, 7-8; 2005, August, 9-10; 2005, July, 11-12
86753	protozoa, not elsewhere specified [A] 0.00 0.00 Global Days XXX **AMA:** 2005, August, 7-8; 2005, July, 11-12; 2005, August, 9-10
86756	respiratory syncytial virus [A] 0.00 0.00 Global Days XXX **AMA:** 2005, July, 11-12; 2005, August, 9-10; 2005, August, 7-8
86757	Rickettsia [A] 0.00 0.00 Global Days XXX **AMA:** 2005, August, 7-8; 2005, July, 11-12; 2005, August, 9-10
86759	rotavirus [A] 0.00 0.00 Global Days XXX **AMA:** 2005, July, 11-12; 2005, August, 9-10; 2005, August, 7-8
86762	rubella [A] 0.00 0.00 Global Days XXX **AMA:** 2005, August, 7-8; 2005, July, 11-12; 2005, August, 9-10
86765	rubeola [A] 0.00 0.00 Global Days XXX **AMA:** 2005, August, 7-8; 2005, July, 11-12; 2005, August, 9-10
86768	Salmonella [A] 0.00 0.00 Global Days XXX **AMA:** 2005, July, 11-12; 2005, August, 9-10; 2005, August, 7-8
86771	Shigella [A] 0.00 0.00 Global Days XXX **AMA:** 2005, August, 7-8; 2005, July, 11-12; 2005, August, 9-10
86774	tetanus [A] 0.00 0.00 Global Days XXX **AMA:** 2005, August, 7-8; 2005, August, 9-10; 2005, July, 11-12
86777	Toxoplasma [A] 0.00 0.00 Global Days XXX **AMA:** 2005, August, 9-10; 2005, August, 7-8; 2005, July, 11-12
86778	Toxoplasma, IgM [A] 0.00 0.00 Global Days XXX **AMA:** 2005, August, 7-8; 2005, July, 11-12; 2005, August, 9-10
● 86780	Treponema pallidum [A] **EXCLUDES** Nontreponemal antibody analysis syphilis testing (86592-86593) 0.00 0.00 Global Days XXX
~~86781~~	~~Treponema pallidum, confirmatory test (eg, FTA-abs)~~ To report, see code 86780
86784	Trichinella [A] 0.00 0.00 Global Days XXX **AMA:** 2005, August, 7-8; 2005, July, 11-12; 2005, August, 9-10
86787	varicella-zoster [A] 0.00 0.00 Global Days XXX **AMA:** 2005, July, 11-12; 2005, August, 9-10; 2005, August, 7-8
86788	West Nile virus, IgM [A] 0.00 0.00 Global Days XXX
86789	West Nile virus [A] 0.00 0.00 Global Days XXX
86790	virus, not elsewhere specified [A] 0.00 0.00 Global Days XXX **AMA:** 2005, July, 11-12; 2005, August, 9-10; 2005, August, 7-8
86793	Yersinia [A] 0.00 0.00 Global Days XXX **AMA:** 2005, August, 7-8; 2005, July, 11-12; 2005, August, 9-10
86800	Thyroglobulin antibody [A] 0.00 0.00 Global Days XXX **AMA:** 2005, August, 7-8; 2005, July, 11-12; 2005, August, 9-10
86803	Hepatitis C antibody; [A] 0.00 0.00 Global Days XXX **AMA:** 2005, July, 11-12; 2005, August, 9-10; 2005, August, 7-8
86804	confirmatory test (eg, immunoblot) [A] 0.00 0.00 Global Days XXX **AMA:** 2005, August, 7-8; 2005, July, 11-12; 2005, August, 9-10

86805-86808 Pre-Transplant Antibody Cross Matching

CMS 100-2,15,80 Physician Supervision Requirements for Diagnostic Tests
CMS 100-4,3,10.4 Payment of Nonphysician Services for Inpatients

Code	Description
86805	Lymphocytotoxicity assay, visual crossmatch; with titration [A] 0.00 0.00 Global Days XXX **AMA:** 2005, August, 7-8; 2005, July, 11-12; 2005, August, 9-10
86806	without titration [A] 0.00 0.00 Global Days XXX **AMA:** 2005, August, 9-10; 2005, August, 7-8; 2005, July, 11-12
86807	Serum screening for cytotoxic percent reactive antibody (PRA); standard method [A] 0.00 0.00 Global Days XXX **AMA:** 2009, Jan, 11-31; 2008, Jan, 10-25; 2007, January, 13-27; 2005, August, 7-8; 2005, July, 11-12; 2005, August, 9-10
86808	quick method [A] 0.00 0.00 Global Days XXX **AMA:** 2009, Jan, 11-31; 2008, Jan, 10-25; 2007, January, 13-27; 2005, August, 7-8; 2005, July, 11-12; 2005, August, 9-10

86812-86849 Histocompatibility Testing

CMS 100-2,15,80 Physician Supervision Requirements for Diagnostic Tests
CMS 100-3,190.1 Histocompatibility Testing
CMS 100-3,190.8 Lymphocyte Mitogen Response Assays
CMS 100-4,3,10.4 Payment of Nonphysician Services for Inpatients
EXCLUDES HLA typing by molecular pathology methods (83890-83914)

Code	Description
86812	HLA typing; A, B, or C (eg, A10, B7, B27), single antigen [A] 0.00 0.00 Global Days XXX **AMA:** 2009, Jan, 11-31; 2008, Jan, 10-25; 2007, January, 13-27; 2006, June, 16-17; 2005, August, 7-8; 2005, August, 9-10; 2005, July, 11-12

Current Procedural Coding Expert – Pathology and Laboratory 86922

86813	**A, B, or C, multiple antigens** [A]
	0.00 0.00 Global Days XXX
	AMA: 2009, Jan, 11-31; 2008, Jan, 10-25; 2007, January, 13-27; 2006, June, 16-17; 2005, July, 11-12; 2005, August, 9-10; 2005, August, 7-8
86816	**DR/DQ, single antigen** [A]
	0.00 0.00 Global Days XXX
	AMA: 2009, Jan, 11-31; 2008, Jan, 10-25; 2007, January, 13-27; 2005, July, 11-12; 2005, August, 9-10; 2005, August, 7-8
86817	**DR/DQ, multiple antigens** [A]
	0.00 0.00 Global Days XXX
	AMA: 2009, Jan, 11-31; 2008, Jan, 10-25; 2007, January, 13-27; 2005, August, 7-8; 2005, August, 9-10; 2005, July, 11-12
86821	**lymphocyte culture, mixed (MLC)** [A]
	0.00 0.00 Global Days XXX
	AMA: 2009, Jan, 11-31; 2008, Jan, 10-25; 2007, January, 13-27; 2005, July, 11-12; 2005, August, 9-10; 2005, August, 7-8
86822	**lymphocyte culture, primed (PLC)** [A]
	0.00 0.00 Global Days XXX
	AMA: 2009, Jan, 11-31; 2008, Jan, 10-25; 2007, January, 13-27; 2005, July, 11-12; 2005, August, 9-10; 2005, August, 7-8
● 86825	**Human leukocyte antigen (HLA) crossmatch, non-cytotoxic (eg, using flow cytometry); first serum sample or dilution** [A]
	EXCLUDES *Autologous HLA crossmatch 86825-86826*
	Lymphocytotoxicity visual crossmatch (86805-86806)
	Do not report with (86355, 86359, 88184-88189)
	0.00 0.00 Global Days XXX
+● 86826	**each additional serum sample or sample dilution (List separately in addition to primary procedure)** [A]
	EXCLUDES *Autologous HLA crossmatch (86825-86826)*
	Lymphocytotoxicity visual crossmatch (86805-86806)
	Do not report with (86355, 86359, 88184-88189)
	0.00 0.00 Global Days XXX
86849	**Unlisted immunology procedure** [A]
	0.00 0.00 Global Days XXX
	AMA: 2009, Jan, 11-31; 2008, Jan, 10-25; 2007, January, 13-27; 2005, August, 7-8; 2005, July, 11-12; 2005, August, 9-10

86850-86999 Transfusion Services

CMS 100-2,15,80 Physician Supervision Requirements for Diagnostic Tests
CMS 100-3,110.5 Granulocyte Transfulsions
CMS 100-3,110.7 Blood Transfusions
CMS 100-3,110.8 Blood Platelet Transfusions
CMS 100-4,3,10.4 Payment of Nonphysician Services for Inpatients
EXCLUDES Apheresis (36511-36512)
Therapeutic phlebotomy (99195)

86850	**Antibody screen, RBC, each serum technique** [X]
	0.00 0.00 Global Days XXX
	AMA: 2008, Apr, 5-7; 2005, August, 9-10; 2005, August, 7-8; 2005, July, 11-12
86860	**Antibody elution (RBC), each elution** [X]
	0.00 0.00 Global Days XXX
	AMA: 2005, July, 11-12; 2005, August, 9-10; 2005, August, 7-8
86870	**Antibody identification, RBC antibodies, each panel for each serum technique** [X]
	0.00 0.00 Global Days XXX
	AMA: 2009, Jan, 11-31; 2008, Jan, 10-25; 2008, Apr, 5-7; 2007, January, 13-27; 2005, July, 11-12; 2005, August, 9-10; 2005, August, 7-8

86880	**Antihuman globulin test (Coombs test); direct, each antiserum** [X]
	0.00 0.00 Global Days XXX
	AMA: 2005, August, 7-8; 2005, July, 11-12; 2005, August, 9-10
86885	**indirect, qualitative, each reagent red cell** [X]
	0.00 0.00 Global Days XXX
	AMA: 2008, Apr, 5-7; 2005, August, 7-8; 2005, August, 9-10; 2005, July, 11-12
86886	**indirect, each antibody titer** [X]
	EXCLUDES *Indirect antihuman globulin (Coombs) test for RBC antibody identification using reagent red cell panels (86870)*
	Indirect antihuman globulin (Coombs) test for RBC antibody screening (86850)
	0.00 0.00 Global Days XXX
	AMA: 2008, Apr, 5-7; 2005, August, 9-10; 2005, July, 11-12; 2005, August, 7-8
86890	**Autologous blood or component, collection processing and storage; predeposited** [X]
	0.00 0.00 Global Days XXX
	AMA: 2005, August, 7-8; 2005, July, 11-12; 2005, August, 9-10
86891	**intra- or postoperative salvage** [X]
	EXCLUDES *Physician services to autologous donors (99201-99204)*
	0.00 0.00 Global Days XXX
	AMA: 2005, August, 7-8; 2005, July, 11-12; 2005, August, 9-10
86900	**Blood typing; ABO** [X]
	0.00 0.00 Global Days XXX
	AMA: 2005, August, 9-10; 2005, August, 7-8; 2005, July, 11-12
86901	**Rh (D)** [X]
	0.00 0.00 Global Days XXX
	AMA: 2005, August, 7-8; 2005, August, 9-10; 2005, July, 11-12
86903	**antigen screening for compatible blood unit using reagent serum, per unit screened** [X]
	0.00 0.00 Global Days XXX
	AMA: 2005, August, 7-8; 2005, July, 11-12; 2005, August, 9-10
86904	**antigen screening for compatible unit using patient serum, per unit screened** [X]
	0.00 0.00 Global Days XXX
	AMA: 2005, August, 7-8; 2005, July, 11-12; 2005, August, 9-10
86905	**RBC antigens, other than ABO or Rh (D), each** [X]
	0.00 0.00 Global Days XXX
	AMA: 2005, July, 11-12; 2005, August, 9-10; 2005, August, 7-8
86906	**Rh phenotyping, complete** [X]
	0.00 0.00 Global Days XXX
	AMA: 2005, August, 9-10; 2005, August, 7-8; 2005, July, 11-12
86910	**Blood typing, for paternity testing, per individual; ABO, Rh and MN** [E]
	0.00 0.00 Global Days XXX
	AMA: 2005, August, 7-8; 2005, July, 11-12; 2005, August, 9-10
86911	**each additional antigen system** [E]
	0.00 0.00 Global Days XXX
	AMA: 2005, August, 7-8; 2005, August, 9-10; 2005, July, 11-12
86920	**Compatibility test each unit; immediate spin technique** [X]
	0.00 0.00 Global Days XXX
	AMA: 2006, March, 6-9; 2005, July, 11-12; 2005, August, 9-10; 2005, August, 7-8
86921	**incubation technique** [X]
	0.00 0.00 Global Days XXX
	AMA: 2006, March, 6-9; 2005, August, 7-8; 2005, July, 11-12; 2005, August, 9-10
86922	**antiglobulin technique** [X]
	0.00 0.00 Global Days XXX
	AMA: 2006, March, 6-9; 2005, August, 7-8; 2005, July, 11-12; 2005, August, 9-10

● New Code ▲ Revised Code Ⓜ Maternity Ⓐ Age Unlisted Not Covered # Resequenced
CCI + Add-on ⊘ Mod 51 Exempt ⦸ Mod 63 Exempt ⊙ Mod Sedation PQRI
2009 Publisher *(Blue Ink)* CPT only © 2009 American Medical Association. All Rights Reserved. (Black Ink) Medicare (Red Ink)

86923

Code	Description
86923	electronic [X] Do not report with (86920-86922) 0.00 0.00 Global Days XXX AMA: 2006, March, 6-9; 2005, August, 9-10; 2005, August, 7-8
86927	Fresh frozen plasma, thawing, each unit [X] 0.00 0.00 Global Days XXX AMA: 2005, August, 7-8; 2005, July, 11-12; 2005, August, 9-10
86930	Frozen blood, each unit; freezing (includes preparation) [X] 0.00 0.00 Global Days XXX AMA: 2005, July, 11-12; 2005, August, 7-8; 2005, August, 9-10
86931	thawing [X] 0.00 0.00 Global Days XXX AMA: 2005, July, 11-12; 2005, August, 9-10; 2005, August, 7-8
86932	freezing (includes preparation) and thawing [X] 0.00 0.00 Global Days XXX AMA: 2005, July, 11-12; 2005, August, 7-8; 2005, August, 9-10
86940	Hemolysins and agglutinins; auto, screen, each [A] 0.00 0.00 Global Days XXX AMA: 2005, August, 7-8; 2005, July, 11-12; 2005, August, 9-10
86941	incubated [A] 0.00 0.00 Global Days XXX AMA: 2005, August, 9-10; 2005, July, 11-12; 2005, August, 7-8
86945	Irradiation of blood product, each unit [X] 0.00 0.00 Global Days XXX AMA: 2009, Jan, 11-31; 2007, Dec, 10-179; 2005, August, 9-10; 2005, July, 11-12; 2005, August, 7-8
86950	Leukocyte transfusion [X] EXCLUDES Leukapheresis (36511) 0.00 0.00 Global Days XXX AMA: 2005, July, 11-12; 2005, August, 7-8; 2005, August, 9-10
86960	Volume reduction of blood or blood product (eg, red blood cells or platelets), each unit [X] 0.00 0.00 Global Days XXX AMA: 2006, March, 6-9; 2005, August, 9-10; 2005, August, 7-8
86965	Pooling of platelets or other blood products [X] 0.00 0.00 Global Days XXX AMA: 2005, August, 9-10; 2005, July, 11-12; 2005, August, 7-8
86970	Pretreatment of RBCs for use in RBC antibody detection, identification, and/or compatibility testing; incubation with chemical agents or drugs, each [X] 0.00 0.00 Global Days XXX AMA: 2005, August, 9-10; 2005, July, 11-12; 2005, August, 7-8
86971	incubation with enzymes, each [X] 0.00 0.00 Global Days XXX AMA: 2005, August, 9-10; 2005, August, 7-8; 2005, July, 11-12
86972	by density gradient separation [X] 0.00 0.00 Global Days XXX AMA: 2005, August, 7-8; 2005, August, 9-10; 2005, July, 11-12
86975	Pretreatment of serum for use in RBC antibody identification; incubation with drugs, each [X] 0.00 0.00 Global Days XXX AMA: 2005, August, 9-10; 2005, July, 11-12; 2005, August, 7-8
86976	by dilution [X] 0.00 0.00 Global Days XXX AMA: 2005, August, 9-10; 2005, July, 11-12; 2005, August, 7-8
86977	incubation with inhibitors, each [X] 0.00 0.00 Global Days XXX AMA: 2005, August, 7-8; 2005, August, 9-10; 2005, July, 11-12
86978	by differential red cell absorption using patient RBCs or RBCs of known phenotype, each absorption [X] 0.00 0.00 Global Days XXX AMA: 2005, August, 9-10; 2005, July, 11-12; 2005, August, 7-8
86985	Splitting of blood or blood products, each unit [X] 0.00 0.00 Global Days XXX AMA: 2005, August, 9-10; 2005, July, 11-12; 2005, August, 7-8
86999	Unlisted transfusion medicine procedure [X] 0.00 0.00 Global Days XXX AMA: 2009, Mar, 10-11; 2009, Jan, 11-31; 2008, Jan, 10-25; 2007, January, 13-27; 2005, July, 11-12; 2005, August, 7-8; 2005, November, 14-15; 2005, August, 9-10

87001-87118 Identification of Microorganisms

CMS 100-2,15,80 — Physician Supervision Requirements for Diagnostic Tests
CMS 100-3,190.12 — Urine Culture, Bacterial
CMS 100-4,3,10.4 — Payment of Nonphysician Services for Inpatients

INCLUDES Bacteriology, mycology, parasitology, and virology
EXCLUDES Additional tests using molecular probes, chromatography, nucleic acid resequencing, or immunologic techniques (87140-87158)

Code also modifier 59 for multiple specimens or sites
Code also modifier 91 for repeat procedures performed on the same day

Code	Description
87001	Animal inoculation, small animal; with observation [A] 0.00 0.00 Global Days XXX AMA: 2005, August, 9-10; 2005, July, 11-12; 2005, August, 7-8
87003	with observation and dissection [A] 0.00 0.00 Global Days XXX AMA: 2005, August, 9-10; 2005, July, 11-12; 2005, August, 7-8
87015	Concentration (any type), for infectious agents [A] Do not report with (87177) 0.00 0.00 Global Days XXX AMA: 2005, August, 9-10; 2005, July, 11-12; 2005, August, 7-8
87040	Culture, bacterial; blood, aerobic, with isolation and presumptive identification of isolates (includes anaerobic culture, if appropriate) [A] 0.00 0.00 Global Days XXX AMA: 2009, Jan, 11-31; 2008, Jan, 10-25; 2007, January, 13-27; 2005, July, 11-12; 2005, August, 7-8; 2005, August, 9-10
87045	stool, aerobic, with isolation and preliminary examination (eg, KIA, LIA), Salmonella and Shigella species [A] 0.00 0.00 Global Days XXX AMA: 2005, July, 11-12; 2005, August, 9-10; 2005, August, 7-8
87046	stool, aerobic, additional pathogens, isolation and presumptive identification of isolates, each plate [A] 0.00 0.00 Global Days XXX AMA: 2005, August, 7-8; 2005, July, 11-12; 2005, August, 9-10
87070	any other source except urine, blood or stool, aerobic, with isolation and presumptive identification of isolates [A] EXCLUDES Urine (87088) 0.00 0.00 Global Days XXX AMA: 2009, Jan, 11-31; 2008, Jan, 10-25; 2007, January, 13-27; 2005, July, 11-12; 2005, August, 7-8; 2005, August, 9-10
87071	quantitative, aerobic with isolation and presumptive identification of isolates, any source except urine, blood or stool [A] EXCLUDES Urine (87088) 0.00 0.00 Global Days XXX AMA: 2005, July, 11-12; 2005, August, 7-8; 2005, August, 9-10

Current Procedural Coding Expert – Pathology and Laboratory

87073 — quantitative, anaerobic with isolation and presumptive identification of isolates, any source except urine, blood or stool
> EXCLUDES *Definitive identification of isolates (87076, or 87077)*
> *Typing of isolates (87140-87158)*
> 0.00   0.00   Global Days XXX
> AMA: 2005, July, 11-12; 2005, August, 9-10; 2005, August, 7-8

87075 — any source, except blood, anaerobic with isolation and presumptive identification of isolates
> 0.00   0.00   Global Days XXX
> AMA: 2005, August, 9-10; 2005, August, 7-8; 2005, July, 11-12

87076 — anaerobic isolate, additional methods required for definitive identification, each isolate
> 0.00   0.00   Global Days XXX
> AMA: 2005, July, 11-12; 2005, August, 7-8; 2005, August, 9-10

87077 — aerobic isolate, additional methods required for definitive identification, each isolate
> 0.00   0.00   Global Days XXX
> AMA: 2005, July, 11-12; 2005, August, 9-10; 2005, August, 7-8

87081 — Culture, presumptive, pathogenic organisms, screening only;
> 0.00   0.00   Global Days XXX
> AMA: 2005, July, 11-12; 2005, August, 9-10; 2005, August, 7-8

87084 — with colony estimation from density chart
> 0.00   0.00   Global Days XXX
> AMA: 2005, July, 11-12; 2005, August, 9-10; 2005, August, 7-8

87086 — Culture, bacterial; quantitative colony count, urine
> 0.00   0.00   Global Days XXX
> AMA: 2005, July, 11-12; 2005, August, 7-8; 2005, August, 9-10

87088 — with isolation and presumptive identification of each isolate, urine
> 0.00   0.00   Global Days XXX
> AMA: 2005, August, 9-10; 2005, July, 11-12; 2005, August, 7-8

87101 — Culture, fungi (mold or yeast) isolation, with presumptive identification of isolates; skin, hair, or nail
> 0.00   0.00   Global Days XXX
> AMA: 2009, Jan, 11-31; 2008, Jan, 10-25; 2007, January, 13-27; 2005, August, 9-10; 2005, July, 11-12; 2005, August, 7-8

87102 — other source (except blood)
> 0.00   0.00   Global Days XXX
> AMA: 2005, August, 7-8; 2005, July, 11-12; 2005, August, 9-10

87103 — blood
> 0.00   0.00   Global Days XXX
> AMA: 2005, August, 9-10; 2005, August, 7-8; 2005, July, 11-12

87106 — Culture, fungi, definitive identification, each organism; yeast
> Code also (87101-87103)
> 0.00   0.00   Global Days XXX
> AMA: 2005, August, 9-10; 2005, August, 7-8; 2005, July, 11-12

87107 — mold
> 0.00   0.00   Global Days XXX
> AMA: 2005, July, 11-12; 2005, August, 9-10; 2005, August, 7-8

87109 — Culture, mycoplasma, any source
> 0.00   0.00   Global Days XXX
> AMA: 2005, July, 11-12; 2005, August, 7-8; 2005, August, 9-10

87110 — Culture, chlamydia, any source
> EXCLUDES *Immunofluorescence staining of shell vials (87140)*
> 0.00   0.00   Global Days XXX
> AMA: 2005, August, 9-10; 2005, July, 11-12; 2005, August, 7-8

87116 — Culture, tubercle or other acid-fast bacilli (eg, TB, AFB, mycobacteria) any source, with isolation and presumptive identification of isolates
> EXCLUDES *Concentration (87015)*
> 0.00   0.00   Global Days XXX
> AMA: 2005, August, 9-10; 2005, July, 11-12; 2005, August, 7-8

87118 — Culture, mycobacterial, definitive identification, each isolate
> EXCLUDES *GLC HPLC identification (87143)*
> *Nucleic acid probe identification (87149)*
> 0.00   0.00   Global Days XXX
> AMA: 2005, July, 11-12; 2005, August, 9-10; 2005, August, 7-8

87140-87158 Additional Culture Typing Techniques

CMS 100-2,15,80 Physician Supervision Requirements for Diagnostic Tests
CMS 100-4,3,10.4 Payment of Nonphysician Services for Inpatients
INCLUDES Bacteriology, mycology, parasitology, and virology

Code also definitive identification
Code also modifier 59 for multiple specimens or sites
Code also modifier 91 for repeat procedures performed on the same day
Do not report with or instead of molecular diagnosis codes (83890-83914)

87140 — Culture, typing; immunofluorescent method, each antiserum
> 0.00   0.00   Global Days XXX
> AMA: 2005, July, 11-12; 2005, August, 7-8; 2005, August, 9-10

87143 — gas liquid chromatography (GLC) or high pressure liquid chromatography (HPLC) method
> 0.00   0.00   Global Days XXX
> AMA: 2005, August, 9-10; 2005, July, 11-12; 2005, August, 7-8

87147 — immunologic method, other than immunofluoresence (eg, agglutination grouping), per antiserum
> 0.00   0.00   Global Days XXX
> AMA: 2009, Jan, 11-31; 2008, Jan, 10-25; 2007, January, 13-27; 2005, August, 9-10; 2005, August, 7-8; 2005, July, 11-12

▲ **87149** — identification by nucleic acid (DNA or RNA) probe, direct probe technique, per culture or isolate, each organism probed
> Do not report with (83890-83914)
> 0.00   0.00   Global Days XXX
> AMA: 2005, August, 7-8; 2005, July, 11-12; 2005, August, 9-10

● **87150** — identification by nucleic acid (DNA or RNA) probe, amplified probe technique, per culture or isolate, each organism probed
> Do not report with (83890-83914)
> 0.00   0.00   Global Days XXX

87152 — identification by pulse field gel typing
> Do not report with (83890-83914)
> 0.00   0.00   Global Days XXX
> AMA: 2005, August, 9-10; 2005, July, 11-12; 2005, August, 7-8

● **87153** — identification by nucleic acid sequencing method, each isolate (eg, sequencing of the 16S rRNA gene)
> 0.00   0.00   Global Days XXX

87158 — other methods
> 0.00   0.00   Global Days XXX
> AMA: 2005, August, 7-8; 2005, August, 9-10; 2005, July, 11-12

● New Code   ▲ Revised Code   Maternity   Age   Unlisted   Not Covered   # Resequenced
CCI   + Add-on   Mod 51 Exempt   Mod 63 Exempt   Mod Sedation   PQRI

87164-87255 Identification of Organism from Primary Source and Sensitivity Studies

CMS 100-2,15,80 — Physician Supervision Requirements for Diagnostic Tests
CMS 100-4,3,10.4 — Payment of Nonphysician Services for Inpatients

INCLUDES Bacteriology, mycology, parasitology, and virology

EXCLUDES Additional tests using molecular probes, chromatography, or immunologic techniques (87140-87158)

Code also modifier 59 for multiple specimens or sites
Code also modifier 91 for repeat procedures performed on the same day

87164 Dark field examination, any source (eg, penile, vaginal, oral, skin); includes specimen collection
0.00   0.00   Global Days XXX
AMA: 2005, August, 7-8; 2005, July, 11-12; 2005, August, 9-10

87166 without collection
0.00   0.00   Global Days XXX
AMA: 2005, August, 9-10; 2005, August, 7-8; 2005, July, 11-12

87168 Macroscopic examination; arthropod
0.00   0.00   Global Days XXX
AMA: 2005, August, 9-10; 2005, July, 11-12; 2005, August, 7-8

87169 parasite
0.00   0.00   Global Days XXX
AMA: 2005, August, 9-10; 2005, August, 7-8; 2005, July, 11-12

87172 Pinworm exam (eg, cellophane tape prep)
0.00   0.00   Global Days XXX
AMA: 2005, July, 11-12; 2005, August, 9-10; 2005, August, 7-8

87176 Homogenization, tissue, for culture
0.00   0.00   Global Days XXX
AMA: 2005, August, 7-8; 2005, August, 9-10; 2005, July, 11-12

87177 Ova and parasites, direct smears, concentration and identification
EXCLUDES Coccidia or microsporidia exam (87207)
Complex special stain (trichrome, iron hematoxylin) (87209)
Direct smears from primary source (87207)
Nucleic acid probes in cytologic material (88365)

Do not report with (87015)
0.00   0.00   Global Days XXX
AMA: 2009, Jan, 11-31; 2008, Jan, 10-25; 2007, January, 13-27; 2006, March, 6-9; 2005, August, 9-10; 2005, July, 11-12; 2005, August, 7-8

87181 Susceptibility studies, antimicrobial agent; agar dilution method, per agent (eg, antibiotic gradient strip)
0.00   0.00   Global Days XXX
AMA: 2005, August, 9-10; 2005, August, 7-8; 2005, July, 11-12

87184 disk method, per plate (12 or fewer agents)
0.00   0.00   Global Days XXX
AMA: 2005, August, 7-8; 2005, August, 9-10; 2005, July, 11-12

87185 enzyme detection (eg, beta lactamase), per enzyme
0.00   0.00   Global Days XXX
AMA: 2005, August, 9-10; 2005, July, 11-12; 2005, August, 7-8

87186 microdilution or agar dilution (minimum inhibitory concentration [MIC] or breakpoint), each multi-antimicrobial, per plate
0.00   0.00   Global Days XXX
AMA: 2005, August, 9-10; 2005, August, 7-8; 2005, July, 11-12

+ **87187** microdilution or agar dilution, minimum lethal concentration (MLC), each plate (List separately in addition to code for primary procedure)
Code first (87186, or 87188)
0.00   0.00   Global Days XXX
AMA: 2005, July, 11-12; 2005, August, 9-10; 2005, August, 7-8

87188 macrobroth dilution method, each agent
0.00   0.00   Global Days XXX
AMA: 2005, August, 7-8; 2005, August, 9-10; 2005, July, 11-12

87190 mycobacteria, proportion method, each agent
EXCLUDES Other mycobacterial susceptibility studies (87181, 87184, 87186, or 87188)
0.00   0.00   Global Days XXX
AMA: 2005, August, 9-10; 2005, July, 11-12; 2005, August, 7-8

87197 Serum bactericidal titer (Schlicter test)
0.00   0.00   Global Days XXX
AMA: 2005, August, 7-8; 2005, July, 11-12; 2005, August, 9-10

87205 Smear, primary source with interpretation; Gram or Giemsa stain for bacteria, fungi, or cell types
0.00   0.00   Global Days XXX
AMA: 2005, August, 9-10; 2005, July, 11-12; 2005, August, 7-8

87206 fluorescent and/or acid fast stain for bacteria, fungi, parasites, viruses or cell types
0.00   0.00   Global Days XXX
AMA: 2005, July, 11-12; 2005, August, 7-8; 2005, August, 9-10

87207 special stain for inclusion bodies or parasites (eg, malaria, coccidia, microsporidia, trypanosomes, herpes viruses)
INCLUDES Tzank smear
EXCLUDES Direct smears with concentration and identification (87177)
Fat, meat, fibers, nasal eosinophils, and starch (see miscellaneous section)
Thick smear preparation (87015)

0.00   0.00   Global Days XXX
AMA: 2006, March, 6-9; 2005, August, 9-10; 2005, August, 7-8; 2005, July, 11-12

87209 complex special stain (eg, trichrome, iron hemotoxylin) for ova and parasites
0.00   0.00   Global Days XXX
AMA: 2006, March, 6-9; 2005, August, 9-10; 2005, August, 7-8

87210 wet mount for infectious agents (eg, saline, India ink, KOH preps)
EXCLUDES KOH evaluation of skin, hair, or nails (87220)
0.00   0.00   Global Days XXX
AMA: 2005, August, 7-8; 2005, July, 11-12; 2005, August, 9-10

87220 Tissue examination by KOH slide of samples from skin, hair, or nails for fungi or ectoparasite ova or mites (eg, scabies)
0.00   0.00   Global Days XXX
AMA: 2005, August, 9-10; 2005, July, 11-12; 2005, August, 7-8

87230 Toxin or antitoxin assay, tissue culture (eg, Clostridium difficile toxin)
0.00   0.00   Global Days XXX
AMA: 2005, August, 9-10; 2005, August, 7-8; 2005, July, 11-12

87250 Virus isolation; inoculation of embryonated eggs, or small animal, includes observation and dissection
0.00   0.00   Global Days XXX
AMA: 2005, August, 9-10; 2005, August, 7-8; 2005, July, 11-12

87252 tissue culture inoculation, observation, and presumptive identification by cytopathic effect
0.00   0.00   Global Days XXX
AMA: 2005, July, 11-12; 2005, August, 7-8; 2005, August, 9-10

87253	tissue culture, additional studies or definitive identification (eg, hemabsorption, neutralization, immunofluoresence stain), each isolate		87276	influenza A virus
				0.00 0.00 Global Days XXX
				AMA: 2009, May, 6&10; 2005, August, 9-10; 2005, August, 7-8; 2005, July, 11-12
	EXCLUDES Electron microscopy (88348)		87277	Legionella micdadei
	Inclusion bodies in:			0.00 0.00 Global Days XXX
	Fluids (88106)			AMA: 2005, August, 7-8; 2005, August, 9-10; 2005, July, 11-12
	Smears (87207-87210)		87278	Legionella pneumophila
	Tissue sections (88304-88309)			0.00 0.00 Global Days XXX
	0.00 0.00 Global Days XXX			AMA: 2005, August, 9-10; 2005, July, 11-12; 2005, August, 7-8
	AMA: 2005, August, 9-10; 2005, August, 7-8; 2005, July, 11-12		87279	Parainfluenza virus, each type
87254	centrifuge enhanced (shell vial) technique, includes identification with immunofluorescence stain, each virus			0.00 0.00 Global Days XXX
				AMA: 2005, August, 7-8; 2005, July, 11-12; 2005, August, 9-10
			87280	respiratory syncytial virus
	Code also (87252)			0.00 0.00 Global Days XXX
	0.00 0.00 Global Days XXX			AMA: 2005, August, 9-10; 2005, August, 7-8; 2005, July, 11-12
	AMA: 2005, July, 11-12; 2005, August, 9-10; 2005, August, 7-8		87281	Pneumocystis carinii
87255	including identification by non-immunologic method, other than by cytopathic effect (eg, virus specific enzymatic activity)			0.00 0.00 Global Days XXX
				AMA: 2005, August, 9-10; 2005, July, 11-12; 2005, August, 7-8
			87283	Rubeola
				0.00 0.00 Global Days XXX
	0.00 0.00 Global Days XXX			AMA: 2005, August, 9-10; 2005, August, 7-8; 2005, July, 11-12
	AMA: 2005, August, 7-8; 2005, July, 11-12; 2005, August, 9-10		87285	Treponema pallidum
				0.00 0.00 Global Days XXX
				AMA: 2005, August, 7-8; 2005, July, 11-12; 2005, August, 9-10

87260-87300 Fluorescence Microscopy by Organism

CMS 100-2,15,80   Physician Supervision Requirements for Diagnostic Tests
CMS 100-4,3,10.4   Payment of Nonphysician Services for Inpatients
INCLUDES   Primary source code only
EXCLUDES   Comparable tests on culture material (87140-87158)
Identification of antibodies (86602-86804)

Code also modifier 59 for different species or strains reported by the same code
Do not report with or instead of molecular diagnosis codes (83890-83914)

87260	Infectious agent antigen detection by immunofluorescent technique; adenovirus		87290	Varicella zoster virus
				0.00 0.00 Global Days XXX
	0.00 0.00 Global Days XXX			AMA: 2005, August, 9-10; 2005, August, 7-8; 2005, July, 11-12
	AMA: 2005, August, 9-10; 2005, August, 7-8; 2005, July, 11-12		87299	not otherwise specified, each organism
87265	Bordetella pertussis/parapertussis			0.00 0.00 Global Days XXX
	0.00 0.00 Global Days XXX			AMA: 2005, August, 9-10; 2005, August, 7-8; 2005, July, 11-12
	AMA: 2005, August, 9-10; 2005, July, 11-12; 2005, August, 7-8		87300	Infectious agent antigen detection by immunofluorescent technique, polyvalent for multiple organisms, each polyvalent antiserum
87267	Enterovirus, direct fluorescent antibody (DFA)			
	0.00 0.00 Global Days XXX			
	AMA: 2005, July, 11-12; 2005, August, 7-8; 2005, August, 9-10			EXCLUDES Physician evaluation of infectious disease agents by immunofluorescence (88346)
87269	giardia			0.00 0.00 Global Days XXX
	0.00 0.00 Global Days XXX			AMA: 2005, August, 7-8; 2005, July, 11-12; 2005, August, 9-10
	AMA: 2005, August, 9-10; 2005, August, 7-8; 2005, July, 11-12			

87301-87451 Enzyme Immunoassay Technique by Organism

EXCLUDES   Nonspecific agent detection (87449-87450, 87797-87799, 87899)

Code also modifier 59 for different species or strains reported by the same code.
Do not report with or instead of molecular diagnosis codes (83890-83914)

87270	Chlamydia trachomatis		87301	Infectious agent antigen detection by enzyme immunoassay technique, qualitative or semiquantitative, multiple-step method; adenovirus enteric types 40/41
	0.00 0.00 Global Days XXX			
	AMA: 2005, August, 9-10; 2005, July, 11-12; 2005, August, 7-8			
87271	Cytomegalovirus, direct fluorescent antibody (DFA)			
				0.00 0.00 Global Days XXX
	0.00 0.00 Global Days XXX			AMA: 2005, August, 9-10; 2005, August, 7-8; 2005, July, 11-12
	AMA: 2005, August, 9-10; 2005, July, 11-12; 2005, August, 7-8		87305	Aspergillus
87272	cryptosporidium			0.00 0.00 Global Days XXX
	0.00 0.00 Global Days XXX		87320	Chlamydia trachomatis
	AMA: 2005, August, 7-8; 2005, July, 11-12; 2005, August, 9-10			0.00 0.00 Global Days XXX
87273	Herpes simplex virus type 2			AMA: 2005, August, 9-10; 2005, July, 11-12; 2005, August, 7-8
	0.00 0.00 Global Days XXX		87324	Clostridium difficile toxin(s)
	AMA: 2005, August, 9-10; 2005, July, 11-12; 2005, August, 7-8			0.00 0.00 Global Days XXX
87274	Herpes simplex virus type 1			AMA: 2005, August, 9-10; 2005, August, 7-8; 2005, July, 11-12
	0.00 0.00 Global Days XXX		87327	Cryptococcus neoformans
	AMA: 2005, August, 9-10; 2005, July, 11-12; 2005, August, 7-8			EXCLUDES Cryptococcus latex agglutination (86403)
87275	influenza B virus			0.00 0.00 Global Days XXX
	0.00 0.00 Global Days XXX			AMA: 2005, August, 7-8; 2005, July, 11-12; 2005, August, 9-10
	AMA: 2009, May, 6&10; 2005, August, 7-8; 2005, July, 11-12; 2005, August, 9-10		87328	cryptosporidium
				0.00 0.00 Global Days XXX
				AMA: 2005, July, 11-12; 2005, August, 9-10; 2005, August, 7-8

● New Code   ▲ Revised Code   M Maternity   A Age   Unlisted   Not Covered   # Resequenced
CCI   + Add-on   ⊘ Mod 51 Exempt   ⊚ Mod 63 Exempt   ⊙ Mod Sedation   PQRI
© 2009 Publisher (Blue Ink)   CPT only © 2009 American Medical Association. All Rights Reserved. (Black Ink)   Medicare (Red Ink)

Code	Description
87329	giardia — 0.00 0.00 Global Days XXX AMA: 2005, July, 11-12; 2005, August, 9-10; 2005, August, 7-8
87332	cytomegalovirus — 0.00 0.00 Global Days XXX AMA: 2005, July, 11-12; 2005, August, 9-10; 2005, August, 7-8
87335	Escherichia coli 0157 EXCLUDES Giardia antigen (87329) 0.00 0.00 Global Days XXX AMA: 2005, July, 11-12; 2005, August, 7-8; 2005, August, 9-10
87336	Entamoeba histolytica dispar group — 0.00 0.00 Global Days XXX AMA: 2005, August, 7-8; 2005, August, 9-10; 2005, July, 11-12
87337	Entamoeba histolytica group — 0.00 0.00 Global Days XXX AMA: 2005, August, 9-10; 2005, August, 7-8; 2005, July, 11-12
87338	Helicobacter pylori, stool — 0.00 0.00 Global Days XXX AMA: 2005, August, 7-8; 2005, July, 11-12; 2005, August, 9-10
87339	Helicobacter pylori EXCLUDES H. pylori: Breath and blood by mass spectrometry (83013-83014) Liquid scintillation counter (78267-78268) Stool (87338) 0.00 0.00 Global Days XXX AMA: 2005, July, 11-12; 2005, August, 7-8; 2005, August, 9-10
87340	hepatitis B surface antigen (HBsAg) — 0.00 0.00 Global Days XXX AMA: 2005, July, 11-12; 2005, August, 9-10; 2005, August, 7-8
87341	hepatitis B surface antigen (HBsAg) neutralization — 0.00 0.00 Global Days XXX AMA: 2005, August, 7-8; 2005, July, 11-12; 2005, August, 9-10
87350	hepatitis Be antigen (HBeAg) — 0.00 0.00 Global Days XXX AMA: 2005, August, 7-8; 2005, August, 9-10; 2005, July, 11-12
87380	hepatitis, delta agent — 0.00 0.00 Global Days XXX AMA: 2005, August, 9-10; 2005, July, 11-12; 2005, August, 7-8
87385	Histoplasma capsulatum — 0.00 0.00 Global Days XXX AMA: 2005, July, 11-12; 2005, August, 9-10; 2005, August, 7-8
87390	HIV-1 — 0.00 0.00 Global Days XXX AMA: 2005, August, 7-8; 2005, August, 9-10; 2005, July, 11-12
87391	HIV-2 — 0.00 0.00 Global Days XXX AMA: 2005, August, 7-8; 2005, July, 11-12; 2005, August, 9-10
87400	Influenza, A or B, each — 0.00 0.00 Global Days XXX AMA: 2009, Jan, 11-31; 2009, May, 6&10; 2008, Jan, 10-25; 2007, January, 13-27; 2005, August, 9-10; 2005, July, 11-12; 2005, August, 7-8
87420	respiratory syncytial virus — 0.00 0.00 Global Days XXX AMA: 2005, July, 11-12; 2005, August, 9-10; 2005, August, 7-8
87425	rotavirus — 0.00 0.00 Global Days XXX AMA: 2005, August, 7-8; 2005, July, 11-12; 2005, August, 9-10
87427	Shiga-like toxin — 0.00 0.00 Global Days XXX AMA: 2005, July, 11-12; 2005, August, 9-10; 2005, August, 7-8
87430	Streptococcus, group A — 0.00 0.00 Global Days XXX AMA: 2009, Jan, 11-31; 2008, Jan, 10-25; 2007, January, 13-27; 2005, August, 9-10; 2005, July, 11-12; 2005, August, 7-8
87449	Infectious agent antigen detection by enzyme immunoassay technique qualitative or semiquantitative; multiple step method, not otherwise specified, each organism — 0.00 0.00 Global Days XXX AMA: 2009, Jan, 11-31; 2008, Jan, 10-25; 2007, January, 13-27; 2005, July, 11-12; 2005, August, 7-8; 2005, August, 9-10
87450	single step method, not otherwise specified, each organism — 0.00 0.00 Global Days XXX AMA: 2005, August, 7-8; 2005, August, 9-10; 2005, July, 11-12
87451	multiple step method, polyvalent for multiple organisms, each polyvalent antiserum — 0.00 0.00 Global Days XXX AMA: 2005, July, 11-12; 2005, August, 9-10; 2005, August, 7-8

87470-87801 Detection Infectious Agent by Probe Techniques

87470	Infectious agent detection by nucleic acid (DNA or RNA); Bartonella henselae and Bartonella quintana, direct probe technique — 0.00 0.00 Global Days XXX AMA: 2005, July, 11-12; 2005, August, 9-10; 2005, August, 7-8
87471	Bartonella henselae and Bartonella quintana, amplified probe technique — 0.00 0.00 Global Days XXX AMA: 2005, August, 9-10; 2005, July, 11-12; 2005, August, 7-8
87472	Bartonella henselae and Bartonella quintana, quantification — 0.00 0.00 Global Days XXX AMA: 2005, July, 11-12; 2005, August, 7-8; 2005, August, 9-10
87475	Borrelia burgdorferi, direct probe technique — 0.00 0.00 Global Days XXX AMA: 2005, July, 11-12; 2005, August, 9-10; 2005, August, 7-8
87476	Borrelia burgdorferi, amplified probe technique — 0.00 0.00 Global Days XXX AMA: 2005, August, 9-10; 2005, August, 7-8; 2005, July, 11-12
87477	Borrelia burgdorferi, quantification — 0.00 0.00 Global Days XXX AMA: 2005, August, 7-8; 2005, July, 11-12; 2005, August, 9-10
87480	Candida species, direct probe technique — 0.00 0.00 Global Days XXX AMA: 2005, August, 9-10; 2005, August, 7-8; 2005, July, 11-12
87481	Candida species, amplified probe technique — 0.00 0.00 Global Days XXX AMA: 2005, August, 9-10; 2005, August, 7-8; 2005, July, 11-12
87482	Candida species, quantification — 0.00 0.00 Global Days XXX AMA: 2005, July, 11-12; 2005, August, 7-8; 2005, August, 9-10
87485	Chlamydia pneumoniae, direct probe technique — 0.00 0.00 Global Days XXX AMA: 2005, August, 9-10; 2005, August, 7-8; 2005, July, 11-12
87486	Chlamydia pneumoniae, amplified probe technique — 0.00 0.00 Global Days XXX AMA: 2005, August, 9-10; 2005, August, 7-8; 2005, July, 11-12
87487	Chlamydia pneumoniae, quantification — 0.00 0.00 Global Days XXX AMA: 2005, August, 7-8; 2005, August, 9-10; 2005, July, 11-12

Current Procedural Coding Expert – Pathology and Laboratory

Code	Description
87490	Chlamydia trachomatis, direct probe technique 0.00 0.00 Global Days XXX **AMA:** 2005, August, 7-8; 2005, July, 11-12; 2005, August, 9-10
87491	Chlamydia trachomatis, amplified probe technique 0.00 0.00 Global Days XXX **AMA:** 2005, August, 7-8; 2005, July, 11-12; 2005, August, 9-10
87492	Chlamydia trachomatis, quantification 0.00 0.00 Global Days XXX **AMA:** 2005, August, 7-8; 2005, August, 9-10; 2005, July, 11-12
● 87493	Clostridium difficile, toxin gene(s), amplified probe technique 0.00 0.00 Global Days XXX
87495	cytomegalovirus, direct probe technique 0.00 0.00 Global Days XXX **AMA:** 2005, July, 11-12; 2005, August, 9-10; 2005, August, 7-8
87496	cytomegalovirus, amplified probe technique 0.00 0.00 Global Days XXX **AMA:** 2005, August, 7-8; 2005, July, 11-12; 2005, August, 9-10
87497	cytomegalovirus, quantification 0.00 0.00 Global Days XXX **AMA:** 2005, August, 7-8; 2005, August, 9-10; 2005, July, 11-12
87498	enterovirus, amplified probe technique 0.00 0.00 Global Days XXX
87500	vancomycin resistance (eg, enterococcus species van A, van B), amplified probe technique 0.00 0.00 Global Days XXX **AMA:** 2008, Apr, 5-7
87510	Gardnerella vaginalis, direct probe technique 0.00 0.00 Global Days XXX **AMA:** 2005, August, 7-8; 2005, August, 9-10; 2005, July, 11-12
87511	Gardnerella vaginalis, amplified probe technique 0.00 0.00 Global Days XXX **AMA:** 2005, August, 9-10; 2005, July, 11-12; 2005, August, 7-8
87512	Gardnerella vaginalis, quantification 0.00 0.00 Global Days XXX **AMA:** 2005, August, 7-8; 2005, July, 11-12; 2005, August, 9-10
87515	hepatitis B virus, direct probe technique 0.00 0.00 Global Days XXX **AMA:** 2005, August, 7-8; 2005, July, 11-12; 2005, August, 9-10
87516	hepatitis B virus, amplified probe technique 0.00 0.00 Global Days XXX **AMA:** 2005, July, 11-12; 2005, August, 9-10; 2005, August, 7-8
87517	hepatitis B virus, quantification 0.00 0.00 Global Days XXX **AMA:** 2005, July, 11-12; 2005, August, 9-10; 2005, August, 7-8
87520	hepatitis C, direct probe technique 0.00 0.00 Global Days XXX **AMA:** 2005, August, 7-8; 2005, July, 11-12; 2005, August, 9-10
87521	hepatitis C, amplified probe technique 0.00 0.00 Global Days XXX **AMA:** 2005, August, 7-8; 2005, August, 9-10; 2005, July, 11-12
87522	hepatitis C, quantification 0.00 0.00 Global Days XXX **AMA:** 2005, July, 11-12; 2005, August, 9-10; 2005, August, 7-8
87525	hepatitis G, direct probe technique 0.00 0.00 Global Days XXX **AMA:** 2005, August, 7-8; 2005, August, 9-10; 2005, July, 11-12
87526	hepatitis G, amplified probe technique 0.00 0.00 Global Days XXX **AMA:** 2005, August, 7-8; 2005, July, 11-12; 2005, August, 9-10
87527	hepatitis G, quantification 0.00 0.00 Global Days XXX **AMA:** 2005, July, 11-12; 2005, August, 9-10; 2005, August, 7-8
87528	Herpes simplex virus, direct probe technique 0.00 0.00 Global Days XXX **AMA:** 2005, August, 7-8; 2005, August, 9-10; 2005, July, 11-12
87529	Herpes simplex virus, amplified probe technique 0.00 0.00 Global Days XXX **AMA:** 2005, August, 7-8; 2005, July, 11-12; 2005, August, 9-10
87530	Herpes simplex virus, quantification 0.00 0.00 Global Days XXX **AMA:** 2005, August, 7-8; 2005, August, 9-10; 2005, July, 11-12
87531	Herpes virus-6, direct probe technique 0.00 0.00 Global Days XXX **AMA:** 2005, August, 9-10; 2005, July, 11-12; 2005, August, 7-8
87532	Herpes virus-6, amplified probe technique 0.00 0.00 Global Days XXX **AMA:** 2005, August, 7-8; 2005, August, 9-10; 2005, July, 11-12
87533	Herpes virus-6, quantification 0.00 0.00 Global Days XXX **AMA:** 2005, August, 7-8; 2005, July, 11-12; 2005, August, 9-10
87534	HIV-1, direct probe technique 0.00 0.00 Global Days XXX **AMA:** 2005, August, 7-8; 2005, July, 11-12; 2005, August, 9-10
87535	HIV-1, amplified probe technique 0.00 0.00 Global Days XXX **AMA:** 2008, Mar, 3&7; 2005, August, 9-10; 2005, July, 11-12; 2005, August, 7-8
87536	HIV-1, quantification 0.00 0.00 Global Days XXX **AMA:** 2005, August, 7-8; 2005, August, 9-10; 2005, July, 11-12
87537	HIV-2, direct probe technique 0.00 0.00 Global Days XXX **AMA:** 2005, August, 7-8; 2005, July, 11-12; 2005, August, 9-10
87538	HIV-2, amplified probe technique 0.00 0.00 Global Days XXX **AMA:** 2005, July, 11-12; 2005, August, 9-10; 2005, August, 7-8
87539	HIV-2, quantification 0.00 0.00 Global Days XXX **AMA:** 2005, August, 7-8; 2005, August, 9-10; 2005, July, 11-12
87540	Legionella pneumophila, direct probe technique 0.00 0.00 Global Days XXX **AMA:** 2005, August, 7-8; 2005, July, 11-12; 2005, August, 9-10
87541	Legionella pneumophila, amplified probe technique 0.00 0.00 Global Days XXX **AMA:** 2005, August, 7-8; 2005, July, 11-12; 2005, August, 9-10
87542	Legionella pneumophila, quantification 0.00 0.00 Global Days XXX **AMA:** 2005, July, 11-12; 2005, August, 9-10; 2005, August, 7-8
87550	Mycobacteria species, direct probe technique 0.00 0.00 Global Days XXX **AMA:** 2005, August, 7-8; 2005, July, 11-12; 2005, August, 9-10
87551	Mycobacteria species, amplified probe technique 0.00 0.00 Global Days XXX **AMA:** 2005, August, 7-8; 2005, August, 9-10; 2005, July, 11-12
87552	Mycobacteria species, quantification 0.00 0.00 Global Days XXX **AMA:** 2005, August, 7-8; 2005, July, 11-12; 2005, August, 9-10

● New Code   ▲ Revised Code   M Maternity   A Age   Unlisted   Not Covered   # Resequenced
CCI   + Add-on   ⊘ Mod 51 Exempt   Mod 63 Exempt   Mod Sedation   PQRI

87555

Code	Description
87555	Mycobacteria tuberculosis, direct probe technique [A] 0.00 0.00 Global Days XXX **AMA:** 2005, July, 11-12; 2005, August, 9-10; 2005, August, 7-8
87556	Mycobacteria tuberculosis, amplified probe technique [A] 0.00 0.00 Global Days XXX **AMA:** 2005, July, 11-12; 2005, August, 7-8; 2005, August, 9-10
87557	Mycobacteria tuberculosis, quantification [A] 0.00 0.00 Global Days XXX **AMA:** 2005, August, 7-8; 2005, July, 11-12; 2005, August, 9-10
87560	Mycobacteria avium-intracellulare, direct probe technique [A] 0.00 0.00 Global Days XXX **AMA:** 2005, July, 11-12; 2005, August, 9-10; 2005, August, 7-8
87561	Mycobacteria avium-intracellulare, amplified probe technique [A] 0.00 0.00 Global Days XXX **AMA:** 2005, August, 7-8; 2005, July, 11-12; 2005, August, 9-10
87562	Mycobacteria avium-intracellulare, quantification [A] 0.00 0.00 Global Days XXX **AMA:** 2005, August, 7-8; 2005, July, 11-12; 2005, August, 9-10
87580	Mycoplasma pneumoniae, direct probe technique [A] 0.00 0.00 Global Days XXX **AMA:** 2005, August, 7-8; 2005, August, 9-10; 2005, July, 11-12
87581	Mycoplasma pneumoniae, amplified probe technique [A] 0.00 0.00 Global Days XXX **AMA:** 2005, July, 11-12; 2005, August, 9-10; 2005, August, 7-8
87582	Mycoplasma pneumoniae, quantification [A] 0.00 0.00 Global Days XXX **AMA:** 2005, July, 11-12; 2005, August, 9-10; 2005, August, 7-8
87590	Neisseria gonorrhoeae, direct probe technique [A] 0.00 0.00 Global Days XXX **AMA:** 2005, July, 11-12; 2005, August, 7-8; 2005, August, 9-10
87591	Neisseria gonorrhoeae, amplified probe technique [A] 0.00 0.00 Global Days XXX **AMA:** 2005, August, 9-10; 2005, July, 11-12; 2005, August, 7-8
87592	Neisseria gonorrhoeae, quantification [A] 0.00 0.00 Global Days XXX **AMA:** 2005, July, 11-12; 2005, August, 7-8; 2005, August, 9-10
87620	papillomavirus, human, direct probe technique [A] 0.00 0.00 Global Days XXX **AMA:** 2009, Jan, 11-31; 2008, Jan, 10-25; 2007, January, 13-27; 2005, July, 11-12; 2005, August, 7-8; 2005, August, 9-10
87621	papillomavirus, human, amplified probe technique [A] 0.00 0.00 Global Days XXX **AMA:** 2005, August, 7-8; 2005, July, 11-12; 2005, August, 9-10
87622	papillomavirus, human, quantification [A] 0.00 0.00 Global Days XXX **AMA:** 2005, July, 11-12; 2005, August, 7-8; 2005, August, 9-10
87640	Staphylococcus aureus, amplified probe technique [A] 0.00 0.00 Global Days XXX **AMA:** 2007, Aug, 7-8
87641	Staphylococcus aureus, methicillin resistant, amplified probe technique [A] **EXCLUDES** *Assays that detect methicillin resistance and identify Staphylococcus aureus using a single nucleic acid sequence (87641)* 0.00 0.00 Global Days XXX **AMA:** 2007, Aug, 7-8
87650	Streptococcus, group A, direct probe technique [A] 0.00 0.00 Global Days XXX **AMA:** 2005, August, 7-8; 2005, July, 11-12; 2005, August, 9-10
87651	Streptococcus, group A, amplified probe technique [A] 0.00 0.00 Global Days XXX **AMA:** 2007, Aug, 7-8; 2005, August, 7-8; 2005, August, 9-10; 2005, July, 11-12
87652	Streptococcus, group A, quantification [A] 0.00 0.00 Global Days XXX **AMA:** 2005, August, 7-8; 2005, July, 11-12; 2005, August, 9-10
87653	Streptococcus, group B, amplified probe technique [A] **AMA:** 2007, Aug, 7-8
87660	Trichomonas vaginalis, direct probe technique [A] 0.00 0.00 Global Days XXX **AMA:** 2005, July, 11-12; 2005, August, 9-10; 2005, August, 7-8
87797	Infectious agent detection by nucleic acid (DNA or RNA), not otherwise specified; direct probe technique, each organism [A] 0.00 0.00 Global Days XXX **AMA:** 2005, July, 11-12; 2005, August, 7-8; 2005, August, 9-10
87798	amplified probe technique, each organism [A] 0.00 0.00 Global Days XXX **AMA:** 2007, Aug, 7-8; 2005, August, 7-8; 2005, August, 9-10; 2005, July, 11-12
87799	quantification, each organism [A] 0.00 0.00 Global Days XXX **AMA:** 2005, July, 11-12; 2005, August, 7-8; 2005, August, 9-10
87800	Infectious agent detection by nucleic acid (DNA or RNA), multiple organisms; direct probe(s) technique [A] 0.00 0.00 Global Days XXX **AMA:** 2005, July, 11-12; 2005, August, 7-8; 2005, August, 9-10
87801	amplified probe(s) technique [A] **EXCLUDES** *Detection of specific infectious agents not otherwise specified (87797-87799) Each specific organism nucleic acid detection from a primary source (87470-87660)* 0.00 0.00 Global Days XXX **AMA:** 2005, July, 11-12; 2005, August, 7-8; 2005, August, 9-10

87802-87899 Detection Infectious Agent by Immunoassay with Direct Optical Observation

87802	Infectious agent antigen detection by immunoassay with direct optical observation; Streptococcus, group B [A] 0.00 0.00 Global Days XXX **AMA:** 2005, July, 11-12; 2005, August, 7-8; 2005, August, 9-10
87803	Clostridium difficile toxin A [A] 0.00 0.00 Global Days XXX **AMA:** 2005, July, 11-12; 2005, August, 7-8; 2005, August, 9-10
87804	Influenza [A] 0.00 0.00 Global Days XXX **AMA:** 2009, Jan, 11-31; 2009, May, 6&10; 2007, Dec, 10-179; 2005, August, 7-8; 2005, August, 9-10; 2005, July, 11-12
87807	respiratory syncytial virus [A] 0.00 0.00 Global Days XXX **AMA:** 2005, August, 7-8; 2005, August, 9-10; 2005, July, 11-12
87808	Trichomonas vaginalis [A] 0.00 0.00 Global Days XXX
87809	adenovirus [A] 0.00 0.00 Global Days XXX **AMA:** 2008, Apr, 5-7

Current Procedural Coding Expert – Pathology and Laboratory

Code	Description
87810	**Chlamydia trachomatis**
	0.00 0.00 Global Days XXX
	AMA: 2005, July, 11-12; 2005, August, 7-8; 2005, August, 9-10
87850	**Neisseria gonorrhoeae**
	0.00 0.00 Global Days XXX
	AMA: 2005, July, 11-12; 2005, August, 9-10; 2005, August, 7-8
87880	**Streptococcus, group A**
	0.00 0.00 Global Days XXX
	AMA: 2009, Jan, 11-31; 2008, Jan, 10-25; 2007, January, 13-27; 2005, July, 11-12; 2005, August, 7-8; 2005, August, 9-10
87899	**not otherwise specified**
	0.00 0.00 Global Days XXX
	AMA: 2009, Jan, 11-31; 2008, Jan, 10-25; 2007, January, 13-27; 2005, July, 11-12; 2005, August, 7-8; 2005, August, 9-10

87900-87999 Drug Sensitivity Genotype/Phenotype

87900	**Infectious agent drug susceptibility phenotype prediction using regularly updated genotypic bioinformatics**
	0.00 0.00 Global Days XXX
	AMA: 2006, March, 6-9; 2005, August, 7-8; 2005, August, 9-10
87901	**Infectious agent genotype analysis by nucleic acid (DNA or RNA); HIV-1, reverse transcriptase and protease**
	EXCLUDES Infectious agent drug susceptibility phenotype prediction for HIV-1 (87900)
	0.00 0.00 Global Days XXX
	AMA: 2006, March, 6-9; 2005, July, 11-12; 2005, August, 7-8; 2005, August, 9-10
87902	**Hepatitis C virus**
	0.00 0.00 Global Days XXX
	AMA: 2005, August, 7-8; 2005, August, 9-10; 2005, July, 11-12
87903	**Infectious agent phenotype analysis by nucleic acid (DNA or RNA) with drug resistance tissue culture analysis, HIV 1; first through 10 drugs tested**
	0.00 0.00 Global Days XXX
	AMA: 2006, March, 6-9; 2005, August, 7-8; 2005, July, 11-12; 2005, August, 9-10
+ 87904	**each additional drug tested (List separately in addition to code for primary procedure)**
	Code first (87903)
	0.00 0.00 Global Days XXX
	AMA: 2009, Jan, 11-31; 2008, Jan, 10-25; 2007, January, 13-27; 2006, March, 6-9; 2005, July, 11-12; 2005, August, 7-8; 2005, August, 9-10
87905	**Infectious agent enzymatic activity other than virus (eg, sialidase activity in vaginal fluid)**
	EXCLUDES Isolation of a virus identified by a nonimmunologic method, and by noncytopathic effect (87255)
	0.00 0.00 Global Days XXX
87999	**Unlisted microbiology procedure**
	0.00 0.00 Global Days XXX
	AMA: 2005, July, 11-12; 2005, August, 7-8; 2005, August, 9-10

88000-88099 Autopsy Services

CMS 100-1,5,90.2 Laboratory Defined
CMS 100-2,15,80 Physician Supervision Requirements for Diagnostic Tests
CMS 100-2,15,80.1 Payment for Clinical Laboratory Services
CMS 100-4,16,10 General Coverage: Diagnostic X-ray, Laboratory, and Other Tests
CMS 100-4,16,10.1 Laboratory Definitions
CMS 100-4,16,110.4 Carrier Contacts With Independent Clinical Laboratories
INCLUDES Services for physicians only

88000	**Necropsy (autopsy), gross examination only; without CNS**
	0.00 0.00 Global Days XXX
	AMA: 2005, August, 7-8; 2005, July, 11-12; 2005, August, 9-10
88005	**with brain**
	0.00 0.00 Global Days XXX
	AMA: 2005, August, 7-8; 2005, August, 9-10; 2005, July, 11-12
88007	**with brain and spinal cord**
	0.00 0.00 Global Days XXX
	AMA: 2005, July, 11-12; 2005, August, 7-8; 2005, August, 9-10
88012	**infant with brain**
	0.00 0.00 Global Days XXX
	AMA: 2005, July, 11-12; 2005, August, 9-10; 2005, August, 7-8
88014	**stillborn or newborn with brain**
	0.00 0.00 Global Days XXX
	AMA: 2005, July, 11-12; 2005, August, 7-8; 2005, August, 9-10
88016	**macerated stillborn**
	0.00 0.00 Global Days XXX
	AMA: 2005, August, 7-8; 2005, July, 11-12; 2005, August, 9-10
88020	**Necropsy (autopsy), gross and microscopic; without CNS**
	0.00 0.00 Global Days XXX
	AMA: 2005, July, 11-12; 2005, August, 7-8; 2005, August, 9-10
88025	**with brain**
	0.00 0.00 Global Days XXX
	AMA: 2005, July, 11-12; 2005, August, 9-10; 2005, August, 7-8
88027	**with brain and spinal cord**
	0.00 0.00 Global Days XXX
	AMA: 2005, August, 7-8; 2005, August, 9-10; 2005, July, 11-12
88028	**infant with brain**
	0.00 0.00 Global Days XXX
	AMA: 2005, August, 9-10; 2005, August, 7-8; 2005, July, 11-12
88029	**stillborn or newborn with brain**
	0.00 0.00 Global Days XXX
	AMA: 2005, August, 9-10; 2005, August, 7-8; 2005, July, 11-12
88036	**Necropsy (autopsy), limited, gross and/or microscopic; regional**
	0.00 0.00 Global Days XXX
	AMA: 2005, July, 11-12; 2005, August, 9-10; 2005, August, 7-8
88037	**single organ**
	0.00 0.00 Global Days XXX
	AMA: 2005, August, 7-8; 2005, August, 9-10; 2005, July, 11-12
88040	**Necropsy (autopsy); forensic examination**
	0.00 0.00 Global Days XXX
	AMA: 2005, July, 11-12; 2005, August, 9-10; 2005, August, 7-8
88045	**coroner's call**
	0.00 0.00 Global Days XXX
	AMA: 2005, July, 11-12; 2005, August, 9-10; 2005, August, 7-8
88099	**Unlisted necropsy (autopsy) procedure**
	0.00 0.00 Global Days XXX
	AMA: 2005, July, 11-12; 2005, August, 9-10; 2005, August, 7-8

● New Code   ▲ Revised Code   M Maternity   A Age   Unlisted   Not Covered   # Resequenced
CCI   + Add-on   ⊘ Mod 51 Exempt   Mod 63 Exempt   ⊙ Mod Sedation   PQRI

© 2009 Publisher *(Blue Ink)*   CPT only © 2009 American Medical Association. All Rights Reserved. *(Black Ink)*   Medicare *(Red Ink)*

88104-88140 Cytopathology: Other Than Cervical/Vaginal

CMS 100-2,15,80 — Physician Supervision Requirements for Diagnostic Tests
CMS 100-4,3,10.4 — Payment of Nonphysician Services for Inpatients
CMS 100-4,12,60 — Payment for Pathology Services

88104 Cytopathology, fluids, washings or brushings, except cervical or vaginal; smears with interpretation
1.70   1.70   Global Days XXX
AMA: 2009, Jan, 11-31; 2008, Jun, 14-15; 2005, July, 11-12; 2005, August, 7-8; 2005, August, 9-10

88106 simple filter method with interpretation
2.06   2.06   Global Days XXX
AMA: 2005, July, 11-12; 2005, August, 9-10; 2005, August, 7-8

88107 smears and simple filter preparation with interpretation
EXCLUDES: Nongynecological selective cellular enhancement including filter transfer techniques (88112)
2.64   2.64   Global Days XXX
AMA: 2005, July, 11-12; 2005, August, 9-10; 2005, August, 7-8

88108 Cytopathology, concentration technique, smears and interpretation (eg, Saccomanno technique)
EXCLUDES: Cervical or vaginal smears (88150-88155)
Gastric intubation with lavage (89130-89141, 91055)
74340
1.89   1.89   Global Days XXX
AMA: 2005, July, 11-12; 2005, August, 7-8; 2005, August, 9-10

88112 Cytopathology, selective cellular enhancement technique with interpretation (eg, liquid based slide preparation method), except cervical or vaginal
Do not report with (88108)
2.58   2.58   Global Days XXX
AMA: 2005, July, 11-12; 2005, August, 9-10; 2005, August, 7-8

88125 Cytopathology, forensic (eg, sperm)
0.58   0.58   Global Days XXX
AMA: 2005, July, 11-12; 2005, August, 9-10; 2005, August, 7-8

88130 Sex chromatin identification; Barr bodies
0.00   0.00   Global Days XXX
AMA: 2005, July, 11-12; 2005, August, 9-10; 2005, August, 7-8

88140 peripheral blood smear, polymorphonuclear drumsticks
EXCLUDES: Guard stain (88313)
0.00   0.00   Global Days XXX
AMA: 2006, March, 6-9; 2005, July, 11-12; 2005, August, 7-8; 2005, August, 9-10

88141-88155 Pap Smears

CMS 100-2,15,80 — Physician Supervision Requirements for Diagnostic Tests
CMS 100-3,190.2 — Diagnostic Pap Smears
CMS 100-3,210.2 — Screening Pap Smears/Pelvic Examinations for Early Detection Cervical/Vaginal Cancer
CMS 100-4,3,10.4 — Payment of Nonphysician Services for Inpatients

88141 Cytopathology, cervical or vaginal (any reporting system), requiring interpretation by physician
Code also (88142-88154, 88164-88167, 88174-88175)
0.78   0.78   Global Days XXX
AMA: 2009, Jan, 11-31; 2008, Jan, 10-25; 2007, January, 13-27; 2005, March, 16-17; 2005, August, 7-8; 2005, July, 11-12; 2005, August, 9-10

88142 Cytopathology, cervical or vaginal (any reporting system), collected in preservative fluid, automated thin layer preparation; manual screening under physician supervision
INCLUDES: Bethesda or non-Bethesda method
0.00   0.00   Global Days XXX
AMA: 2005, July, 11-12; 2005, August, 9-10; 2005, August, 7-8

88143 with manual screening and rescreening under physician supervision
INCLUDES: Bethesda or non-Bethesda method
EXCLUDES: Automated screening of automated thin layer preparation (88174-88175)
0.00   0.00   Global Days XXX
AMA: 2009, Jan, 11-31; 2008, Jan, 10-25; 2007, January, 13-27; 2005, March, 16-17; 2005, July, 11-12; 2005, August, 7-8; 2005, August, 9-10

88147 Cytopathology smears, cervical or vaginal; screening by automated system under physician supervision
0.00   0.00   Global Days XXX
AMA: 2009, Jan, 11-31; 2008, Jan, 10-25; 2007, January, 13-27; 2005, July, 11-12; 2005, August, 7-8; 2005, August, 9-10

88148 screening by automated system with manual rescreening under physician supervision
0.00   0.00   Global Days XXX
AMA: 2005, August, 9-10; 2005, August, 7-8; 2005, July, 11-12

88150 Cytopathology, slides, cervical or vaginal; manual screening under physician supervision
EXCLUDES: Bethesda method Pap smears (88164-88167)
0.00   0.00   Global Days XXX
AMA: 2005, August, 9-10; 2005, August, 7-8; 2005, July, 11-12

88152 with manual screening and computer-assisted rescreening under physician supervision
EXCLUDES: Bethesda method Pap smears (88164-88167)
0.00   0.00   Global Days XXX
AMA: 2005, August, 7-8; 2005, August, 9-10; 2005, July, 11-12

88153 with manual screening and rescreening under physician supervision
EXCLUDES: Bethesda method Pap smears (88164-88167)
0.00   0.00   Global Days XXX
AMA: 2009, Jan, 11-31; 2008, Jan, 10-25; 2007, January, 13-27; 2005, July, 11-12; 2005, August, 7-8; 2005, March, 16-17; 2005, August, 9-10

88154 with manual screening and computer-assisted rescreening using cell selection and review under physician supervision
EXCLUDES: Bethesda method Pap smears (88164-88167)
0.00   0.00   Global Days XXX
AMA: 2005, July, 11-12; 2005, August, 9-10; 2005, August, 7-8

+ 88155 Cytopathology, slides, cervical or vaginal, definitive hormonal evaluation (eg, maturation index, karyopyknotic index, estrogenic index) (List separately in addition to code[s] for other technical and interpretation services)
Code first (88142-88154, 88164-88167, 88174-88175)
0.00   0.00   Global Days XXX
AMA: 2005, July, 11-12; 2005, August, 9-10; 2005, August, 7-8

88160-88162 Cytopathology Smears (Other Than Pap)

CMS 100-2,15,80 — Physician Supervision Requirements for Diagnostic Tests
CMS 100-4,12,60 — Payment for Pathology Services

88160 Cytopathology, smears, any other source; screening and interpretation
1.35   1.35   Global Days XXX
AMA: 2006, December, 10-12; 2005, July, 11-12; 2005, August, 7-8; 2005, August, 9-10

Current Procedural Coding Expert – Pathology and Laboratory   88188

88161 preparation, screening and interpretation
1.35 1.35 Global Days XXX
AMA: 2006, December, 10-12; 2005, July, 11-12; 2005, August, 9-10; 2005, August, 7-8

88162 extended study involving over 5 slides and/or multiple stains
EXCLUDES Aerosol collection of sputum (89220)
Special stains (88312-88314)
1.76 1.76 Global Days XXX
AMA: 2005, July, 11-12; 2005, August, 9-10; 2005, August, 7-8

88164-88167 Pap Smears: Bethesda System

CMS 100-2,15,80 Physician Supervision Requirements for Diagnostic Tests
CMS 100-3,190.2 Diagnostic Pap Smears
CMS 100-3,210.2 Screening Pap Smears/Pelvic Examinations for Early Detection Cervical/Vaginal Cancer
CMS 100-4,3,10.4 Payment of Nonphysician Services for Inpatients
EXCLUDES Non-Bethesda method (88150-88154)

88164 Cytopathology, slides, cervical or vaginal (the Bethesda System); manual screening under physician supervision
0.00 0.00 Global Days XXX
AMA: 2005, July, 11-12; 2005, August, 7-8; 2005, August, 9-10

88165 with manual screening and rescreening under physician supervision
0.00 0.00 Global Days XXX
AMA: 2009, Jan, 11-31; 2008, Jan, 10-25; 2007, January, 13-27; 2005, March, 16-17; 2005, July, 11-12; 2005, August, 9-10; 2005, August, 7-8

88166 with manual screening and computer-assisted rescreening under physician supervision
0.00 0.00 Global Days XXX
AMA: 2005, July, 11-12; 2005, August, 9-10; 2005, August, 7-8

88167 with manual screening and computer-assisted rescreening using cell selection and review under physician supervision
EXCLUDES Collection of specimen via fine needle aspiration (10021-10022)
0.00 0.00 Global Days XXX
AMA: 2005, July, 11-12; 2005, August, 7-8; 2005, August, 9-10

88172-88173 Cytopathology of Needle Biopsy

CMS 100-2,15,80 Physician Supervision Requirements for Diagnostic Tests
CMS 100-4,3,10.4 Payment of Nonphysician Services for Inpatients
CMS 100-4,12,60 Payment for Pathology Services

88172 Cytopathology, evaluation of fine needle aspirate; immediate cytohistologic study to determine adequacy of specimen(s)
Do not report with same specimen (88333-88334)
1.46 1.46 Global Days XXX
AMA: 2009, Jan, 11-31; 2008, Jan, 10-25; 2007, Aug, 15; 2007, January, 13-27; 2005, August, 9-10; 2005, August, 7-8; 2005, July, 11-12

88173 interpretation and report
EXCLUDES Fine needle aspiration (10021-10022)
Do not report with same specimen (88333-88334)
3.54 3.54 Global Days XXX
AMA: 2009, Jan, 11-31; 2008, Jan, 10-25; 2007, January, 13-27; 2005, July, 11-12; 2005, August, 7-8; 2005, August, 9-10

88174-88175 Pap Smears: Automated Screening

CMS 100-2,15,80 Physician Supervision Requirements for Diagnostic Tests
CMS 100-3,190.2 Diagnostic Pap Smears
CMS 100-3,210.2 Screening Pap Smears/Pelvic Examinations for Early Detection Cervical/Vaginal Cancer
CMS 100-4,3,10.4 Payment of Nonphysician Services for Inpatients

88174 Cytopathology, cervical or vaginal (any reporting system), collected in preservative fluid, automated thin layer preparation; screening by automated system, under physician supervision
INCLUDES Bethesda or non-Bethesda method
0.00 0.00 Global Days XXX
AMA: 2005, July, 11-12; 2005, August, 9-10; 2005, August, 7-8

88175 with screening by automated system and manual rescreening or review, under physician supervision
INCLUDES Bethesda or non-Bethesda method
EXCLUDES Manual screening (88142-88143)
0.00 0.00 Global Days XXX
AMA: 2006, March, 6-9; 2005, July, 11-12; 2005, August, 9-10; 2005, August, 7-8

88182-88199 Cytopathology Using the Fluorescence-Activated Cell Sorter

CMS 100-2,15,80 Physician Supervision Requirements for Diagnostic Tests
CMS 100-4,3,10.4 Payment of Nonphysician Services for Inpatients
CMS 100-4,12,60 Payment for Pathology Services

88182 Flow cytometry, cell cycle or DNA analysis
EXCLUDES DNA ploidy analysis by morphometric technique (88358)
2.55 2.55 Global Days XXX
AMA: 2009, Jun, 3-6&11; 2005, July, 11-12; 2005, August, 7-8; 2005, August, 9-10

88184 Flow cytometry, cell surface, cytoplasmic, or nuclear marker, technical component only; first marker
1.97 1.97 Global Days XXX
AMA: 2009, Jun, 3-6&11; 2007, Dec, 10-179; 2005, July, 11-12; 2005, August, 9-10; 2005, August, 7-8

+ **88185** each additional marker (List separately in addition to code for first marker)
Code first (88184)
1.20 1.20 Global Days ZZZ
AMA: 2009, Jan, 11-31; 2009, Jun, 3-6&11; 2007, Dec, 10-179; 2005, July, 11-12; 2005, August, 9-10; 2005, August, 7-8

88187 Flow cytometry, interpretation; 2 to 8 markers
EXCLUDES Interpretation (86355-86357, 86359-86361, 86367)
1.89 1.89 Global Days XXX
AMA: 2009, Jun, 3-6&11; 2009, Jan, 11-31; 2008, Jan, 10-25; 2008, Apr, 5-7; 2007, January, 13-27; 2005, July, 11-12; 2005, August, 7-8; 2005, April, 13-14; 2005, August, 9-10

88188 9 to 15 markers
EXCLUDES Interpretation (86355-86357, 86359-86361, 86367)
2.36 2.36 Global Days XXX
AMA: 2009, Jan, 11-31; 2009, Jun, 3-6&11; 2008, Jan, 10-25; 2008, Apr, 5-7; 2007, January, 13-27; 2005, August, 9-10; 2005, August, 7-8; 2005, July, 11-12; 2005, April, 13-14

● New Code   ▲ Revised Code   Maternity   Age   Unlisted    Not Covered   # Resequenced

□ CCI   + Add-on   ⊘ Mod 51 Exempt   Mod 63 Exempt   ⊙ Mod Sedation   PQRI

© 2009 Publisher *(Blue Ink)*   CPT only © 2009 American Medical Association. All Rights Reserved. *(Black Ink)*   Medicare *(Red Ink)*   337

88189	**16 or more markers**
	EXCLUDES Interpretation (86355-86357, 86359-86361, 86367)
	2.89 2.89 **Global Days XXX**
	AMA: 2009, Jan, 11-31; 2009, Jun, 3-6&11; 2008, Jan, 10-25; 2008, Apr, 5-7; 2007, January, 13-27; 2005, April, 13-14; 2005, August, 7-8; 2005, July, 11-12; 2005, August, 9-10
88199	**Unlisted cytopathology procedure**
	0.00 0.00 **Global Days XXX**
	AMA: 2005, August, 9-10; 2005, July, 11-12; 2005, August, 7-8

88230-88299 Cytogenic Studies

CMS 100-1,5,90.2 — Laboratory Defined
CMS 100-2,15,80 — Physician Supervision Requirements for Diagnostic Tests
CMS 100-2,15,80.1 — Payment for Clinical Laboratory Services
CMS 100-3,190.3 — Cytogenic Studies
CMS 100-4,3,10.4 — Payment of Nonphysician Services for Inpatients
CMS 100-4,16,10 — General Coverage: Diagnostic X-ray, Laboratory, and Other Tests
CMS 100-4,16,10.1 — Laboratory Definitions
CMS 100-4,16,110.4 — Carrier Contacts With Independent Clinical Laboratories
Code also genetic testing modifiers for oncologic or inherited disorder

88230	**Tissue culture for non-neoplastic disorders; lymphocyte**
	0.00 0.00 **Global Days XXX**
	AMA: 2008, May, 5-8; 2005, July, 11-12; 2005, August, 9-10; 2005, August, 7-8
88233	**skin or other solid tissue biopsy**
	0.00 0.00 **Global Days XXX**
	AMA: 2008, May, 5-8; 2005, July, 11-12; 2005, August, 7-8; 2005, August, 9-10
88235	**amniotic fluid or chorionic villus cells**
	0.00 0.00 **Global Days XXX**
	AMA: 2008, May, 5-8; 2005, August, 9-10; 2005, July, 11-12; 2005, August, 7-8
88237	**Tissue culture for neoplastic disorders; bone marrow, blood cells**
	0.00 0.00 **Global Days XXX**
	AMA: 2008, May, 5-8; 2005, July, 11-12; 2005, August, 9-10; 2005, August, 7-8
88239	**solid tumor**
	0.00 0.00 **Global Days XXX**
	AMA: 2008, May, 5-8; 2005, August, 9-10; 2005, August, 7-8; 2005, July, 11-12
88240	**Cryopreservation, freezing and storage of cells, each cell line**
	EXCLUDES Therapeutic cryopreservation and storage (38207)
	0.00 0.00 **Global Days XXX**
	AMA: 2009, Jun, 3-6&11; 2005, August, 9-10; 2005, July, 11-12; 2005, August, 7-8
88241	**Thawing and expansion of frozen cells, each aliquot**
	EXCLUDES Therapeutic thawing of previous harvest (38208)
	0.00 0.00 **Global Days XXX**
	AMA: 2009, Jun, 3-6&11; 2005, July, 11-12; 2005, August, 7-8; 2005, August, 9-10
88245	**Chromosome analysis for breakage syndromes; baseline Sister Chromatid Exchange (SCE), 20-25 cells**
	0.00 0.00 **Global Days XXX**
	AMA: 2008, May, 5-8; 2005, July, 1-8; 2005, August, 9-10; 2005, August, 7-8; 2005, July, 11-12
88248	**baseline breakage, score 50-100 cells, count 20 cells, 2 karyotypes (eg, for ataxia telangiectasia, Fanconi anemia, fragile X)**
	0.00 0.00 **Global Days XXX**
	AMA: 2008, May, 5-8; 2005, July, 11-12; 2005, July, 1-8; 2005, August, 9-10; 2005, August, 7-8
88249	**score 100 cells, clastogen stress (eg, diepoxybutane, mitomycin C, ionizing radiation, UV radiation)**
	0.00 0.00 **Global Days XXX**
	AMA: 2008, May, 5-8; 2005, July, 11-12; 2005, July, 1-8; 2005, August, 7-8; 2005, August, 9-10
88261	**Chromosome analysis; count 5 cells, 1 karyotype, with banding**
	0.00 0.00 **Global Days XXX**
	AMA: 2008, May, 5-8; 2007, Dec, 10-179; 2005, July, 11-12; 2005, August, 9-10; 2005, August, 7-8; 2005, July, 1-8
88262	**count 15-20 cells, 2 karyotypes, with banding**
	0.00 0.00 **Global Days XXX**
	AMA: 2008, May, 5-8; 2007, Dec, 10-179; 2005, July, 11-12; 2005, July, 1-8; 2005, August, 9-10; 2005, August, 7-8
88263	**count 45 cells for mosaicism, 2 karyotypes, with banding**
	0.00 0.00 **Global Days XXX**
	AMA: 2008, May, 5-8; 2005, August, 7-8; 2005, July, 11-12; 2005, July, 1-8; 2005, August, 9-10
88264	**analyze 20-25 cells**
	0.00 0.00 **Global Days XXX**
	AMA: 2008, May, 5-8; 2005, July, 1-8; 2005, August, 7-8; 2005, August, 9-10; 2005, July, 11-12
88267	**Chromosome analysis, amniotic fluid or chorionic villus, count 15 cells, 1 karyotype, with banding**
	0.00 0.00 **Global Days XXX**
	AMA: 2008, May, 5-8; 2005, July, 1-8; 2005, August, 9-10; 2005, July, 11-12; 2005, August, 7-8
88269	**Chromosome analysis, in situ for amniotic fluid cells, count cells from 6-12 colonies, 1 karyotype, with banding**
	0.00 0.00 **Global Days XXX**
	AMA: 2008, May, 5-8; 2005, July, 11-12; 2005, July, 1-8; 2005, August, 9-10; 2005, August, 7-8
88271	**Molecular cytogenetics; DNA probe, each (eg, FISH)**
	0.00 0.00 **Global Days XXX**
	AMA: 2009, Jan, 11-31; 2008, May, 5-8; 2008, Jan, 10-25; 2007, January, 13-27; 2005, July, 11-12; 2005, July, 1-8; 2005, August, 7-8; 2005, August, 9-10
88272	**chromosomal in situ hybridization, analyze 3-5 cells (eg, for derivatives and markers)**
	0.00 0.00 **Global Days XXX**
	AMA: 2009, Jan, 11-31; 2008, Jan, 10-25; 2008, May, 5-8; 2007, January, 13-27; 2005, July, 11-12; 2005, July, 1-8; 2005, August, 9-10; 2005, August, 7-8
88273	**chromosomal in situ hybridization, analyze 10-30 cells (eg, for microdeletions)**
	0.00 0.00 **Global Days XXX**
	AMA: 2009, Jan, 11-31; 2008, May, 5-8; 2008, Jan, 10-25; 2007, January, 13-27; 2005, July, 11-12; 2005, July, 1-8; 2005, August, 7-8; 2005, August, 9-10
88274	**interphase in situ hybridization, analyze 25-99 cells**
	0.00 0.00 **Global Days XXX**
	AMA: 2009, Jan, 11-31; 2008, Jan, 10-25; 2008, May, 5-8; 2007, January, 13-27; 2005, July, 1-8; 2005, August, 9-10; 2005, August, 7-8; 2005, July, 11-12

Current Procedural Coding Expert – Pathology and Laboratory   88302

88275   interphase in situ hybridization, analyze 100-300 cells   [A]
    0.00   0.00   **Global Days** XXX
    AMA: 2009, Jan, 11-31; 2008, Jan, 10-25; 2008, May, 5-8; 2007, January, 13-27; 2005, August, 9-10; 2005, August, 7-8; 2005, July, 11-12; 2005, July, 1-8

88280   **Chromosome analysis; additional karyotypes, each study**   [A]
    0.00   0.00   **Global Days** XXX
    AMA: 2008, May, 5-8; 2005, July, 1-8; 2005, August, 7-8; 2005, July, 11-12; 2005, August, 9-10

88283   additional specialized banding technique (eg, NOR, C-banding)   [A]
    0.00   0.00   **Global Days** XXX
    AMA: 2008, May, 5-8; 2005, August, 9-10; 2005, July, 11-12; 2005, August, 7-8; 2005, July, 1-8

88285   additional cells counted, each study   [A]
    0.00   0.00   **Global Days** XXX
    AMA: 2009, Jan, 11-31; 2008, May, 5-8; 2007, Dec, 10-179; 2005, August, 9-10; 2005, July, 1-8; 2005, August, 7-8; 2005, July, 11-12

88289   additional high resolution study   [A]
    0.00   0.00   **Global Days** XXX
    AMA: 2008, May, 5-8; 2005, July, 11-12; 2005, July, 1-8; 2005, August, 7-8; 2005, August, 9-10

88291   **Cytogenetics and molecular cytogenetics, interpretation and report**   [M][26][80]
    0.79   0.79   **Global Days** XXX
    AMA: 2008, May, 5-8; 2005, August, 9-10; 2005, July, 1-8; 2005, August, 7-8; 2005, July, 11-12

88299   **Unlisted cytogenetic study**   [X][80]
    0.00   0.00   **Global Days** XXX
    AMA: 2005, August, 9-10; 2005, August, 7-8; 2005, July, 11-12

88300 Evaluation of Surgical Specimen: Gross Anatomy

CMS 100-1,5,90.2   Laboratory Defined
CMS 100-4,12,60   Payment for Pathology Services
INCLUDES   Attainment, examination, and reporting
    Unit of service is the specimen
EXCLUDES   Additional procedures (88311-88365, 88399)

88300   **Level I - Surgical pathology, gross examination only**   [X][80]
    EXCLUDES   Microscopic exam (88302-88309)
    0.63   0.63   **Global Days** XXX
    AMA: 2009, Jan, 11-31; 2008, Jan, 10-25; 2007, January, 13-27; 2005, July, 11-12; 2005, August, 7-8; 2005, August, 9-10

88302-88309 Evaluation of Surgical Specimens: Gross and Microscopic Anatomy

CMS 100-1,5,90.2   Laboratory Defined
CMS 100-4,12,60   Payment for Pathology Services
INCLUDES   Attainment, examination, and reporting
    Unit of service is the specimen
EXCLUDES   Additional procedures (88311-88365, 88399)
Do not report with Mohs surgery (17311-17315)

88302   **Level II - Surgical pathology, gross and microscopic examination**   [X][80]
    INCLUDES
      Appendix, incidental
      Confirming identification and absence of disease
      Fallopian tube, sterilization
      Fingers or toes traumatic amputation
      Foreskin, newborn
      Hernia sac, any site
      Hydrocele sac
      Nerve
      Skin, plastic repair
      Sympathetic ganglion
      Testis, castration
      Vaginal mucosa, incidental
      Vas deferense, sterilization
    1.30   1.30   **Global Days** XXX
    AMA: 2009, Jan, 11-31; 2008, Jan, 10-25; 2007, January, 28-31; 2007, January, 13-27; 2006, December, 1-3; 2005, August, 9-10; 2005, July, 11-12; 2005, August, 7-8

● New Code   ▲ Revised Code   [M] Maternity   [A] Age   Unlisted   Not Covered   # Resequenced
CCI   + Add-on   ⊘ Mod 51 Exempt   Mod 63 Exempt   Mod Sedation   PQRI
© 2009 Publisher *(Blue Ink)*   CPT only © 2009 American Medical Association. All Rights Reserved. *(Black Ink)*   Medicare *(Red Ink)*

88304 Level III - Surgical pathology, gross and microscopic examination ⊠ 80

INCLUDES
- Abortion, induced
- Abscess
- Anal tag
- Aneurysm-atrial/ventricular
- Appendix, other than incidental
- Artery, atheromatous plaque
- Bartholin's gland cyst
- Bone fragment(s), other than pathologic fracture
- Bursa/ synovial cyst
- Carpal tunnel tissue
- Cartilage, shavings
- Cholesteatoma
- Colon, colostomy stoma
- Conjunctiva-biopsy/pterygium
- Cornea
- Diverticulum-esophagus/small intestine
- Dupuytren's contracture tissue
- Femoral head, other than fracture
- Fissure/fistula
- Foreskin, other than newborn
- Gallbladder
- Ganglion cyst
- Hematoma
- Hemorrhoids
- Hydatid of Morgagni
- Intervertebral disc
- Joint, loose body
- Meniscus
- Mucocele, salivary
- Neuroma-Morton's/traumatic
- Pilonidal cyst/sinus
- Polyps, inflammatory-nasal/sinusoidal
- Skin-cyst/tag/debridement
- Soft tissue, debridement
- Soft tissue, lipoma
- Spermatocele
- Tendon/tendon sheath
- Testicular appendage
- Thrombus or embolus
- Tonsil and/or adenoids
- Varicocele
- Vas deferens, other than sterilization
- Vein, varicosity
- Fallopian tube, biopsy
- Fallopian tube, ectopic pregnancy
- Femoral head, fracture
- Finger/toes, amputation, nontraumatic
- Gingiva/oral mucosa, biopsy
- Heart valve
- Joint resection
- Kidney biopsy
- Larynx biopsy
- Leiomyoma(s), uterine myomectomy-without uterus
- Lip, biopsy/wedge resection
- Lung, transbronchial biopsy
- Lymph node, biopsy
- Muscle, biopsy
- Nasal mucosa, biopsy
- Nasopharynx/oropharynx, biopsy
- Nerve biopsy
- Odontogenic/dental cyst
- Omentum, biopsy
- Ovary, biopsy/wedge resection
- Ovary with or without tube, nonneoplastic
- Parathyroid gland
- Peritoneum, biopsy
- Pituitary tumor
- Placenta, other than third trimester
- Pleura/pericardium-biopsy/tissue
- Polyp:
  - Cervical/endometrial
  - Colorectal
  - Stomach/small intestine
- Prostate:
  - Needle biopsy
  - TUR
- Salivary gland, biopsy
- Sinus, paranasal biopsy
- Skin, other than cyst/tag/debridement/plastic repair
- Small intestine, biopsy
- Soft tissue, other than tumor/mas/lipoma/debridement
- Spleen
- Stomach biopsy
- Synovium
- Testis, other than tumor/biopsy, castration
- Thyroglossal duct/brachial cleft cyst
- Tongue, biopsy
- Tonsil, biopsy
- Trachea biopsy
- Ureter, biopsy
- Urethra, biopsy
- Urinary bladder, biopsy
- Uterus, with or without tubes and ovaries, for prolapse
- Vagina biopsy
- Vulva/labial biopsy

🔾 1.60   🔾 1.60 Global Days XXX
AMA: 2009, Jan, 11-31; 2008, Jan, 10-25; 2007, January, 28-31; 2007, January, 13-27; 2006, December, 1-3; 2005, August, 9-10; 2005, July, 11-12; 2005, August, 7-8

88305 Level IV - Surgical pathology, gross and microscopic examination ⊠ 80

INCLUDES
- Abortion, spontaneous/missed
- Artery, biopsy
- Bone exostosis
- Bone marrow, biopsy
- Brain/meninges, other than for tumor resection
- Breast biopsy without microscopic assessment of surgical margin
- Breast reduction mammoplasty
- Bronchus, biopsy
- Cell block, any source
- Cervix, biopsy
- Colon, biopsy
- Duodenum, biopsy
- Endocervix, curettings/biopsy
- Endometrium, curettings/biopsy
- Esophagus, biopsy
- Extremity, amputation, traumatic

🔾 2.64   🔾 2.64 Global Days XXX
AMA: 2009, Jan, 11-31; 2008, Jan, 10-25; 2007, January, 13-27; 2007, January, 28-31; 2006, December, 1-3; 2005, August, 9-10; 2005, July, 11-12; 2005, March, 11-15; 2005, July, 13-16; 2005, August, 7-8

Current Procedural Coding Expert – Pathology and Laboratory   88313

88307 Level V - Surgical pathology, gross and microscopic examination [X] [80] [CCI] [PQRI]

INCLUDES
- Adrenal resection
- Bone, biopsy/curettings
- Bone fragment(s), pathologic fractures
- Brain, biopsy
- Brain meninges, tumor resection
- Breast, excision of lesion, requiring microscopic evaluation of surgical margins
- Breast, mastectomy-partial/simple
- Cervix, conization
- Colon, segmental resection, other than for tumor
- Extremity, amputation, nontraumatic
- Eye, enucleation
- Kidney, partial/total nephrectomy
- Larynx, partial/total resection
- Liver, biopsy-needle, wedge
- Lung, wedge biopsy
- Lymph nodes, regional resection
- Mediastinum, mass
- Myocardium, biopsy
- Odontogenic tumor
- Ovary with or without tube, neoplastic
- Pancreas, biopsy
- Placenta, third trimester
- Prostate, except radical resection
- Salivary gland
- Sentinel lymph node
- Small intestine, resection, other than for tumor
- Soft tissue mass (except lipoma)-biopsy/simple excision
- Stomach-subtotal/total resection, other than for tumor
- Testis, biopsy
- Thymus, tumor
- Thyroid, total/lobe
- Ureter, resection
- Urinary bladder, TUR
- Uterus, with or without tubes and ovaries, other than neoplastic/prolapse

5.81   5.81   **Global Days XXX**
AMA: 2009, Jan, 11-31; 2008, Jan, 10-25; 2007, January, 13-27; 2007, January, 28-31; 2006, December, 1-3; 2005, July, 11-12; 2005, August, 7-8; 2005, August, 9-10

88309 Level VI - Surgical pathology, gross and microscopic examination [X] [80] [CCI] [PQRI]

INCLUDES
- Bone resection
- Breast, mastectomy-with regional lymph nodes
- Colon:
  - Total resection
  - Segmental resection for tumor
- Esophagus, partial/total resection
- Extremity, disarticulation
- Fetus, with dissection
- Larynx, partial/total resection-with regional lymph nodes
- Lung-total/lobe/segment resection
- Pancreas, total/subtotal resection
- Prostate, radical resection
- Small intestine, resection for tumor
- Soft tissue tumor, extensive resection
- Stomach, subtotal/total resection for tumor
- Testis, tumor
- Tongue/tonsil, resection for tumor
- Urinary bladder, partial/total resection
- Uterus, with or without tubes and ovaries, neoplastic
- Vulva, total/subtotal resection

EXCLUDES
- Evaluation of fine needle aspirate (88172-88173)
- Fine needle aspiration (10021-10022)

8.91   8.91   **Global Days XXX**
AMA: 2009, Jan, 11-31; 2008, Jan, 10-25; 2007, January, 28-31; 2007, January, 13-27; 2006, December, 1-3; 2005, July, 11-12; 2005, August, 9-10; 2005, August, 7-8

88311-88399 Additional Surgical Pathology Services

CMS 100-4,12,60   Payment for Pathology Services

+ 88311 Decalcification procedure (List separately in addition to code for surgical pathology examination) [X] [80]

Code first surgical pathology exam (88302-88309)
0.51   0.51   **Global Days XXX**
AMA: 2009, Jan, 11-31; 2008, Jan, 10-25; 2007, January, 13-27; 2006, December, 1-3; 2005, August, 9-10; 2005, August, 7-8; 2005, July, 11-12

▲ 88312 Special stains; Group I for microorganisms (eg, Gridley, acid fast, methenamine silver), including interpretation and report, each [X] [80]

Code first primary pathology procedure
2.66   2.66   **Global Days XXX**
AMA: 2009, Jan, 11-31; 2008, Jan, 10-25; 2007, January, 13-27; 2006, March, 6-9; 2006, December, 1-3; 2005, July, 11-12; 2005, August, 9-10; 2005, August, 7-8

▲ 88313 Group II, all other (eg, iron, trichrome), except immunocytochemistry and immunoperoxidase stains, including interpretation and report, each [X] [80] [CCI]

EXCLUDES   Immunocytochemistry and immunoperoxidase tissue studies (88342)

Code first primary pathology procedure
1.89   1.89   **Global Days XXX**
AMA: 2009, Jan, 11-31; 2008, Jan, 10-25; 2007, January, 13-27; 2006, December, 1-3; 2006, June, 16-17; 2006, March, 6-9; 2005, July, 11-12; 2005, August, 7-8; 2005, August, 9-10

● New Code   ▲ Revised Code   [M] Maternity   [A] Age   Unlisted   Not Covered   # Resequenced
[CCI] CCI   + Add-on   ⊘ Mod 51 Exempt   @ Mod 63 Exempt   ⊙ Mod Sedation   [PQRI] PQRI
© 2009 Publisher (*Blue Ink*)   CPT only © 2009 American Medical Association. All Rights Reserved. (Black Ink)   Medicare (Red Ink)

+ ▲	**88314**	**histochemical staining with frozen section(s), including interpretation and report** (List separately in addition to code for primary procedure) ☒ 80

Code first primary pathology procedure

Do not report with routine frozen section stain during Mohs surgery (17311-17315)

🔴 2.16 🔵 2.16 **Global Days XXX**

AMA: 2006, December, 1-3; 2005, August, 9-10; 2005, August, 7-8; 2005, July, 11-12

88318 **Determinative histochemistry to identify chemical components (eg, copper, zinc)** ☒ 80

🔴 2.53 🔵 2.53 **Global Days XXX**

AMA: 2005, July, 11-12; 2005, August, 9-10; 2005, August, 7-8

88319 **Determinative histochemistry or cytochemistry to identify enzyme constituents, each** ☒ 80

🔴 3.50 🔵 3.50 **Global Days XXX**

AMA: 2005, July, 11-12; 2005, August, 7-8; 2005, August, 9-10

88321 **Consultation and report on referred slides prepared elsewhere** ☒ 80 ▫

🔴 2.27 🔵 2.49 **Global Days XXX**

AMA: 2009, Jan, 11-31; 2008, Jan, 10-25; 2007, January, 13-27; 2005, July, 11-12; 2005, August, 7-8; 2005, August, 9-10

88323 **Consultation and report on referred material requiring preparation of slides** ☒ 80 ▫

🔴 3.72 🔵 3.72 **Global Days XXX**

AMA: 2009, Jan, 11-31; 2008, Jan, 10-25; 2007, January, 13-27; 2005, August, 7-8; 2005, August, 9-10; 2005, July, 11-12

88325 **Consultation, comprehensive, with review of records and specimens, with report on referred material** ☒ 80 ▫

🔴 3.61 🔵 5.33 **Global Days XXX**

AMA: 2009, Jan, 11-31; 2008, Jan, 10-25; 2007, January, 13-27; 2005, August, 7-8; 2005, July, 11-12; 2005, August, 9-10

88329 **Pathology consultation during surgery;** ☒ 80 ▫

🔴 0.95 🔵 1.38 **Global Days XXX**

AMA: 2009, Jan, 11-31; 2008, Jan, 10-25; 2007, January, 28-31; 2007, January, 13-27; 2005, August, 9-10; 2005, July, 11-12; 2005, August, 7-8

88331 **first tissue block, with frozen section(s), single specimen** ☒ 80 ▫

🔴 2.44 🔵 2.44 **Global Days XXX**

AMA: 2007, January, 28-31; 2006, March, 6-9; 2006, December, 1-3; 2005, August, 7-8; 2005, August, 9-10; 2005, July, 11-12

88332 **each additional tissue block with frozen section(s)** ☒ 80 ▫

🔴 1.09 🔵 1.09 **Global Days XXX**

AMA: 2007, January, 28-31; 2006, December, 1-3; 2006, March, 6-9; 2005, August, 7-8; 2005, July, 11-12; 2005, August, 9-10

88333 **cytologic examination (eg, touch prep, squash prep), initial site** ☒ 80

EXCLUDES *Intraprocedural cytologic evaluation of fine needle aspirate (88172)*
Nonintraoperative cytologic examination (88160-88162)

🔴 2.55 🔵 2.55 **Global Days XXX**

AMA: 2009, Jan, 11-31; 2008, Jun, 14-15; 2007, January, 28-31; 2006, March, 6-9; 2005, August, 9-10; 2005, August, 7-8

88334 **cytologic examination (eg, touch prep, squash prep), each additional site** ☒ 80

EXCLUDES *Intraoperative consultation on a specimen requiring both frozen section and cytologic evaluation (88331, 88334)*
Intraprocedural cytologic evaluation of fine needle aspirate (88172)
Nonintraoperative cytologic examination (88160-88162)
Percutaneous needle biopsy requiring intraprocedural cytologic examination (88333)

🔴 1.57 🔵 1.57 **Global Days XXX**

AMA: 2007, January, 28-31; 2006, March, 6-9; 2005, August, 9-10; 2005, August, 7-8

88342 **Immunohistochemistry (including tissue immunoperoxidase), each antibody** ☒ 80 ▫

EXCLUDES *Quantitative or semiquantitative immunohistochemistry (88360-88361)*

Do not report with testing on the same antibody (88360-88361)

🔴 2.66 🔵 2.66 **Global Days XXX**

AMA: 2009, Jan, 11-31; 2008, Jan, 10-25; 2007, January, 13-27; 2006, December, 1-3; 2005, August, 7-8; 2005, August, 9-10; 2005, July, 11-12

88346 **Immunofluorescent study, each antibody; direct method** ☒ 80

🔴 2.58 🔵 2.58 **Global Days XXX**

AMA: 2005, July, 11-12; 2005, August, 7-8; 2005, August, 9-10

88347 **indirect method** ☒ 80

🔴 1.99 🔵 1.99 **Global Days XXX**

AMA: 2005, July, 11-12; 2005, August, 9-10; 2005, August, 7-8

88348 **Electron microscopy; diagnostic** ☒ 80 ▫

🔴 16.48 🔵 16.48 **Global Days XXX**

AMA: 2005, July, 11-12; 2005, August, 7-8; 2005, August, 9-10

88349 **scanning** ☒ 80

🔴 9.54 🔵 9.54 **Global Days XXX**

AMA: 2005, July, 11-12; 2005, August, 7-8; 2005, August, 9-10

88355 **Morphometric analysis; skeletal muscle** ☒ 80 ▫

🔴 4.51 🔵 4.51 **Global Days XXX**

AMA: 2005, July, 11-12; 2005, August, 7-8; 2005, August, 9-10

88356 **nerve** ☒ 80 ▫

🔴 7.08 🔵 7.08 **Global Days XXX**

AMA: 2005, July, 11-12; 2005, August, 9-10; 2005, August, 7-8

88358 **tumor (eg, DNA ploidy)** ☒ 80 ▫

Do not report with 88313 unless each procedure is for a different special stain (88313)

🔴 1.93 🔵 1.93 **Global Days XXX**

AMA: 2009, Jan, 11-31; 2008, Jan, 10-25; 2007, January, 13-27; 2006, June, 16-17; 2005, July, 11-12; 2005, August, 7-8; 2005, August, 9-10

88360 **Morphometric analysis, tumor immunohistochemistry (eg, Her-2/neu, estrogen receptor/progesterone receptor), quantitative or semiquantitative, each antibody; manual** ☒ 80 ▫

Do not report with 88342 unless each test is for different antibody (88342)

🔴 3.18 🔵 3.18 **Global Days XXX**

AMA: 2005, July, 11-12; 2005, August, 7-8; 2005, August, 9-10

Current Procedural Coding Expert – Pathology and Laboratory

88361 using computer-assisted technology
EXCLUDES *Morphometric analysis using in situ hybridization techniques (88367-88368)*

Do not report with 88342 unless each test is for different antibody (88342)
3.66   3.66   Global Days XXX
AMA: 2005, July, 11-12; 2005, August, 9-10; 2005, August, 7-8

88362 Nerve teasing preparations
7.38   7.38   Global Days XXX
AMA: 2005, July, 11-12; 2005, August, 7-8; 2005, August, 9-10

88365 In situ hybridization (eg, FISH), each probe
Do not report with 88367-88368 for the same probe (88367-88368)
4.23   4.23   Global Days XXX
AMA: 2009, Jan, 11-31; 2008, Jan, 10-25; 2007, January, 13-27; 2005, July, 11-12; 2005, August, 7-8; 2005, March, 16-17; 2005, August, 9-10

88367 Morphometric analysis, in situ hybridization (quantitative or semi-quantitative) each probe; using computer-assisted technology
6.18   6.18   Global Days XXX
AMA: 2009, Jan, 11-31; 2008, Jan, 10-25; 2007, January, 13-27; 2005, March, 16-17; 2005, August, 9-10; 2005, July, 11-12; 2005, August, 7-8

88368 manual
5.43   5.43   Global Days XXX
AMA: 2009, Jan, 11-31; 2008, Jan, 10-25; 2007, January, 13-27; 2005, March, 16-17; 2005, August, 9-10; 2005, August, 7-8; 2005, July, 11-12

88371 Protein analysis of tissue by Western Blot, with interpretation and report;
0.00   0.00   Global Days XXX
AMA: 2005, August, 7-8; 2005, August, 9-10; 2005, July, 11-12

88372 immunological probe for band identification, each
0.00   0.00   Global Days XXX
AMA: 2005, July, 11-12; 2005, August, 7-8; 2005, August, 9-10

88380 Microdissection (ie, sample preparation of microscopically identified target); laser capture
5.10   5.10   Global Days XXX
AMA: 2008, Apr, 5-7; 2005, August, 7-8; 2005, July, 11-12; 2005, August, 9-10

88381 manual
Do not report with 88381
3.59   3.59   Global Days XXX
AMA: 2008, Apr, 5-7

88384 Array-based evaluation of multiple molecular probes; 11 through 50 probes
0.00   0.00   Global Days XXX
AMA: 2006, March, 6-9; 2006, January, 5-6,48; 2005, August, 9-10; 2005, August, 7-8

88385 51 through 250 probes
24.17   24.17   Global Days XXX
AMA: 2008, May, 5-8; 2006, March, 6-9; 2006, January, 5-6,48; 2005, August, 7-8; 2005, August, 9-10

88386 251 through 500 probes
EXCLUDES *Preparation and analysis of fewer than 11 probes (83890-83914)*
Preparation of array-based evaluation (83890-83892, 83898-83901)
15.67   15.67   Global Days XXX
AMA: 2009, Jan, 11-31; 2008, May, 5-8; 2008, May, 9-11; 2006, January, 5-6,48; 2006, March, 6-9; 2005, August, 7-8; 2005, August, 9-10

● **88387** Macroscopic examination, dissection, and preparation of tissue for non-microscopic analytical studies (eg, nucleic acid-based molecular studies); each tissue preparation (eg, a single lymph node)
Do not report for tissues preparation for microbiologic cultures or flow cytometric studies
Do not report with (88329-88384, 88388)
1.09   1.09   Global Days XXX

+ ● **88388** in conjunction with a touch imprint, intraoperative consultation, or frozen section, each tissue preparation (eg, a single lymph node) (List separately in addition to code for primary procedure)
Code first (88329-88334)
Do not report for tissue preparation for microbiologic cultures or flow cytometric studies
0.65   0.65   Global Days XXX

88399 Unlisted surgical pathology procedure
0.00   0.00   Global Days XXX
AMA: 2009, Jan, 11-31; 2008, May, 9-11; 2005, August, 9-10; 2005, July, 11-12; 2005, August, 7-8

88720-88741 Transcutaneous Procedures

88720 Bilirubin, total, transcutaneous
EXCLUDES *Transdermal oxygen saturation testing (94760-94762)*
0.00   0.00   Global Days XXX

● **88738** Hemoglobin (Hgb), quantitative, transcutaneous
EXCLUDES *In vitro hemoglobin measurement (85018)*
0.00   0.00   Global Days XXX

88740 Hemoglobin, quantitative, transcutaneous, per day; carboxyhemoglobin
EXCLUDES *In vitro carboxyhemoglobin measurement (82375)*
0.00   0.00   Global Days XXX

88741 methemoglobin
EXCLUDES *In vitro quantitative methemoglobin measurement (83050)*
0.00   0.00   Global Days XXX

89049-89240 Other Pathology Services

CMS 100-4,3,10.4   Payment of Nonphysician Services for Inpatients

89049 Caffeine halothane contracture test (CHCT) for malignant hyperthermia susceptibility, including interpretation and report
1.85   6.42   Global Days XXX
AMA: 2009, Jan, 11-31; 2008, Jan, 10-25; 2007, January, 13-27; 2006, March, 6-9; 2006, May, 16-20; 2005, August, 7-8; 2005, August, 9-10

89050 Cell count, miscellaneous body fluids (eg, cerebrospinal fluid, joint fluid), except blood;
0.00   0.00   Global Days XXX
AMA: 2005, July, 11-12; 2005, August, 7-8; 2005, August, 9-10

89051 with differential count
0.00   0.00   Global Days XXX
AMA: 2005, July, 11-12; 2005, August, 7-8; 2005, August, 9-10

89055 Leukocyte assessment, fecal, qualitative or semiquantitative
0.00   0.00   Global Days XXX
AMA: 2005, July, 11-12; 2005, August, 7-8; 2005, August, 9-10

CURRENT PROCEDURAL CODING EXPERT — Pathology and Laboratory

89060	Crystal identification by light microscopy with or without polarizing lens analysis, tissue or any body fluid (except urine) [A]
	EXCLUDES Crystal identification on paraffin embedded tissue (89060)
	0.00 0.00 Global Days XXX
	AMA: 2005, July, 11-12; 2005, August, 7-8; 2005, August, 9-10
89100	Duodenal intubation and aspiration; single specimen (eg, simple bile study or afferent loop culture) plus appropriate test procedure [X][80]
	1.16 8.18 Global Days XXX
	AMA: 2005, July, 11-12; 2005, August, 7-8; 2005, August, 9-10
89105	collection of multiple fractional specimens with pancreatic or gallbladder stimulation, single or double lumen tube [X][80]
	EXCLUDES Chemical analyses (see chemistry codes)
	Electrocardiogram (93000-93268)
	Esophagus acid perfusion test (Berstein) (91030)
	74340
	0.95 7.28 Global Days XXX
	AMA: 2005, August, 7-8; 2005, July, 11-12; 2005, August, 9-10
89125	Fat stain, feces, urine, or respiratory secretions [A]
	0.00 0.00 Global Days XXX
	AMA: 2005, July, 11-12; 2005, August, 9-10; 2005, August, 7-8
89130	Gastric intubation and aspiration, diagnostic, each specimen, for chemical analyses or cytopathology; [X][80]
	0.86 6.73 Global Days XXX
	AMA: 2005, July, 11-12; 2005, August, 7-8; 2005, August, 9-10
89132	after stimulation [X][80]
	0.50 6.53 Global Days XXX
	AMA: 2005, July, 11-12; 2005, August, 7-8; 2005, August, 9-10
89135	Gastric intubation, aspiration, and fractional collections (eg, gastric secretory study); 1 hour [X][80]
	1.43 8.36 Global Days XXX
	AMA: 2005, August, 7-8; 2005, August, 9-10; 2005, July, 11-12
89136	2 hours [X][80]
	0.52 6.53 Global Days XXX
	AMA: 2005, July, 11-12; 2005, August, 9-10; 2005, August, 7-8
89140	2 hours including gastric stimulation (eg, histalog, pentagastrin) [X][80]
	1.56 7.69 Global Days XXX
	AMA: 2005, July, 11-12; 2005, August, 7-8; 2005, August, 9-10
89141	3 hours, including gastric stimulation [X][80]
	EXCLUDES Chemical analyses (82926, 82928)
	Joint fluid chemistry (see chemistry codes)
	Therapeutic gastric lavage (91105)
	74340
	1.43 7.55 Global Days XXX
	AMA: 2005, July, 11-12; 2005, August, 7-8; 2005, August, 9-10
89160	Meat fibers, feces [A]
	0.00 0.00 Global Days XXX
	AMA: 2005, July, 11-12; 2005, August, 9-10; 2005, August, 7-8
89190	Nasal smear for eosinophils [A]
	EXCLUDES Occult blood, feces (82270)
	Paternity tests (86910)
	0.00 0.00 Global Days XXX
	AMA: 2005, July, 11-12; 2005, August, 7-8; 2005, August, 9-10
89220	Sputum, obtaining specimen, aerosol induced technique (separate procedure) [X][TC][80]
	0.38 0.38 Global Days XXX
	AMA: 2005, July, 11-12; 2005, August, 7-8; 2005, August, 9-10
89225	Starch granules, feces [A]
	0.00 0.00 Global Days XXX
	AMA: 2005, July, 11-12; 2005, August, 9-10; 2005, August, 7-8
89230	Sweat collection by iontophoresis [X][TC][80]
	0.16 0.16 Global Days XXX
	AMA: 2005, July, 11-12; 2005, August, 9-10; 2005, August, 7-8
89235	Water load test [A]
	0.00 0.00 Global Days XXX
	AMA: 2005, August, 7-8; 2005, July, 11-12; 2005, August, 9-10
89240	Unlisted miscellaneous pathology test [X][80]
	0.00 0.00 Global Days XXX
	AMA: 2009, Jan, 11-31; 2008, Jan, 10-25; 2007, January, 13-27; 2005, November, 14-15; 2005, August, 9-10; 2005, July, 11-12; 2005, August, 7-8

89250-89398 Infertility Treatment Services

CMS 100-2,1,100 Treatment for Infertility
CMS 100-4,3,10.4 Payment of Nonphysician Services for Inpatients

89250	Culture of oocyte(s)/embryo(s), less than 4 days; ♀ [X]
	0.00 0.00 Global Days XXX
	AMA: 2009, Jan, 11-31; 2008, Jan, 10-25; 2007, January, 13-27; 2005, July, 11-12; 2005, August, 7-8; 2005, August, 9-10
89251	with co-culture of oocyte(s)/embryos ♀ [X]
	EXCLUDES Extended culture of oocyte(s)/embryo(s) (89272)
	0.00 0.00 Global Days XXX
	AMA: 2009, Jan, 11-31; 2008, Jan, 10-25; 2007, January, 13-27; 2005, July, 11-12; 2005, August, 9-10; 2005, August, 7-8
89253	Assisted embryo hatching, microtechniques (any method) [X]
	0.00 0.00 Global Days XXX
	AMA: 2009, Jan, 11-31; 2008, Jan, 10-25; 2007, January, 13-27; 2005, July, 11-12; 2005, August, 7-8; 2005, August, 9-10
89254	Oocyte identification from follicular fluid ♀ [X]
	0.00 0.00 Global Days XXX
	AMA: 2009, Jan, 11-31; 2008, Jan, 10-25; 2007, January, 13-27; 2005, August, 7-8; 2005, July, 11-12; 2005, August, 9-10
89255	Preparation of embryo for transfer (any method) [X]
	0.00 0.00 Global Days XXX
	AMA: 2009, Jan, 11-31; 2008, Jan, 10-25; 2007, January, 13-27; 2005, July, 11-12; 2005, August, 9-10; 2005, August, 7-8
89257	Sperm identification from aspiration (other than seminal fluid) [X]
	EXCLUDES Semen analysis (89300-89320)
	Sperm identification from testis tissue (89264)
	0.00 0.00 Global Days XXX
	AMA: 2009, Jan, 11-31; 2008, Jan, 10-25; 2007, January, 13-27; 2005, July, 11-12; 2005, August, 7-8; 2005, August, 9-10
89258	Cryopreservation; embryo(s) [X]
	0.00 0.00 Global Days XXX
	AMA: 2009, Jan, 11-31; 2008, Jan, 10-25; 2007, January, 13-27; 2005, August, 7-8; 2005, August, 9-10; 2005, July, 11-12
89259	sperm [X]
	EXCLUDES Cryopreservation of testicular reproductive tissue (89335)
	0.00 0.00 Global Days XXX
	AMA: 2009, Jan, 11-31; 2008, Jan, 10-25; 2007, January, 13-27; 2005, July, 11-12; 2005, August, 9-10; 2005, August, 7-8
89260	Sperm isolation; simple prep (eg, sperm wash and swim-up) for insemination or diagnosis with semen analysis [X]
	0.00 0.00 Global Days XXX
	AMA: 2009, Jan, 11-31; 2008, Jan, 10-25; 2007, January, 13-27; 2005, July, 11-12; 2005, August, 7-8; 2005, August, 9-10

[26]/[TC] PC/TC Comp Only [X] CLIA Waived ♂ Male Only ♀ Female Only
AMA: CPT Asst MED: Pub 100 [A]-[Y] OPPSI [Radiology Crosswalk]

Current Procedural Coding Expert – Pathology and Laboratory

89261	complex prep (eg, Percoll gradient, albumin gradient) for insemination or diagnosis with semen analysis
	EXCLUDES *Semen analysis without sperm wash or swim-up (89320)*
	0.00 0.00 Global Days XXX
	AMA: 2009, Jan, 11-31; 2008, Jan, 10-25; 2007, January, 13-27; 2005, July, 11-12; 2005, August, 7-8; 2005, August, 9-10
89264	Sperm identification from testis tissue, fresh or cryopreserved
	EXCLUDES *Biopsy of testis (54500, 54505)*
	Semen analysis (89300-89320)
	Sperm identification from aspiration (89257)
	0.00 0.00 Global Days XXX
	AMA: 2009, Jan, 11-31; 2008, Jan, 10-25; 2007, January, 13-27; 2005, July, 11-12; 2005, August, 9-10; 2005, August, 7-8
89268	Insemination of oocytes
	0.00 0.00 Global Days XXX
	AMA: 2009, Jan, 11-31; 2008, Jan, 10-25; 2007, January, 13-27; 2005, August, 7-8; 2005, July, 11-12; 2005, August, 9-10
89272	Extended culture of oocyte(s)/embryo(s), 4-7 days
	0.00 0.00 Global Days XXX
	AMA: 2009, Jan, 11-31; 2008, Jan, 10-25; 2007, January, 13-27; 2005, July, 11-12; 2005, August, 7-8; 2005, August, 9-10
89280	Assisted oocyte fertilization, microtechnique; less than or equal to 10 oocytes
	0.00 0.00 Global Days XXX
	AMA: 2009, Jan, 11-31; 2008, Jan, 10-25; 2007, January, 13-27; 2005, July, 11-12; 2005, August, 7-8; 2005, August, 9-10
89281	greater than 10 oocytes
	0.00 0.00 Global Days XXX
	AMA: 2009, Jan, 11-31; 2008, Jan, 10-25; 2007, January, 13-27; 2005, July, 11-12; 2005, August, 7-8; 2005, August, 9-10
89290	Biopsy, oocyte polar body or embryo blastomere, microtechnique (for pre-implantation genetic diagnosis); less than or equal to 5 embryos
	0.00 0.00 Global Days XXX
	AMA: 2009, Jan, 11-31; 2008, Jan, 10-25; 2007, January, 13-27; 2005, July, 11-12; 2005, August, 9-10; 2005, August, 7-8
89291	greater than 5 embryos
	0.00 0.00 Global Days XXX
	AMA: 2009, Jan, 11-31; 2008, Jan, 10-25; 2007, January, 13-27; 2005, July, 11-12; 2005, August, 7-8; 2005, August, 9-10
89300	Semen analysis; presence and/or motility of sperm including Huhner test (post coital)
	0.00 0.00 Global Days XXX
	AMA: 2009, Jan, 11-31; 2008, Jan, 10-25; 2008, Apr, 5-7; 2007, January, 13-27; 2005, August, 7-8; 2005, August, 9-10; 2005, July, 11-12
89310	motility and count (not including Huhner test)
	0.00 0.00 Global Days XXX
	AMA: 2009, Jan, 11-31; 2008, Jan, 10-25; 2008, Apr, 5-7; 2007, January, 13-27; 2005, August, 9-10; 2005, July, 11-12; 2005, August, 7-8
89320	volume, count, motility, and differential
	0.00 0.00 Global Days XXX
	AMA: 2009, Jan, 11-31; 2008, Jan, 10-25; 2008, Apr, 5-7; 2007, January, 13-27; 2005, August, 7-8; 2005, July, 11-12; 2005, August, 9-10
89321	sperm presence and motility of sperm, if performed
	EXCLUDES *Hyaluronan binding assay (HBA) (89398)*
	0.00 0.00 Global Days XXX
	AMA: 2009, Jan, 11-31; 2008, Jan, 10-25; 2008, Apr, 5-7; 2007, January, 13-27; 2005, July, 11-12; 2005, August, 7-8; 2005, August, 9-10
89322	volume, count, motility, and differential using strict morphologic criteria (eg, Kruger)
	0.00 0.00 Global Days XXX
	AMA: 2009, Jan, 11-31; 2008, Jan, 10-25; 2008, Apr, 5-7
89325	Sperm antibodies
	EXCLUDES *Medicolegal identification of sperm (88125)*
	0.00 0.00 Global Days XXX
	AMA: 2009, Jan, 11-31; 2008, Jan, 10-25; 2007, January, 13-27; 2005, July, 11-12; 2005, August, 7-8; 2005, August, 9-10
89329	Sperm evaluation; hamster penetration test
	0.00 0.00 Global Days XXX
	AMA: 2009, Jan, 11-31; 2008, Jan, 10-25; 2007, January, 13-27; 2005, July, 11-12; 2005, August, 7-8; 2005, August, 9-10
89330	cervical mucus penetration test, with or without spinnbarkeit test
	0.00 0.00 Global Days XXX
	AMA: 2009, Jan, 11-31; 2008, Jan, 10-25; 2007, January, 13-27; 2005, July, 11-12; 2005, August, 7-8; 2005, August, 9-10; 2005, November, 14-15
89331	Sperm evaluation, for retrograde ejaculation, urine (sperm concentration, motility, and morphology, as indicated)
	EXCLUDES *Detection of sperm in urine (81015)*
	Code also semen analysis on concurrent sperm specimen (89300-89322)
	0.00 0.00 Global Days XXX
	AMA: 2009, Jan, 11-31; 2008, Jan, 10-25; 2008, Apr, 5-7
89335	Cryopreservation, reproductive tissue, testicular
	EXCLUDES *Cryopreservation of:*
	Embryo(s) (89258)
	Ovarian reproductive tissue, oocytes (89240)
	Sperm (89259)
	0.00 0.00 Global Days XXX
	AMA: 2009, Jan, 11-31; 2008, Jan, 10-25; 2007, January, 13-27; 2005, August, 7-8; 2005, August, 9-10; 2005, July, 11-12
89342	Storage (per year); embryo(s)
	0.00 0.00 Global Days XXX
	AMA: 2009, Jan, 11-31; 2008, Jan, 10-25; 2007, January, 13-27; 2005, August, 7-8; 2005, August, 9-10; 2005, July, 11-12
89343	sperm/semen
	0.00 0.00 Global Days XXX
	AMA: 2009, Jan, 11-31; 2008, Jan, 10-25; 2007, January, 13-27; 2005, July, 11-12; 2005, August, 7-8; 2005, August, 9-10
89344	reproductive tissue, testicular/ovarian
	0.00 0.00 Global Days XXX
	AMA: 2009, Jan, 11-31; 2008, Jan, 10-25; 2007, January, 13-27; 2005, July, 11-12; 2005, August, 7-8; 2005, August, 9-10
89346	oocyte(s)
	0.00 0.00 Global Days XXX
	AMA: 2009, Jan, 11-31; 2008, Jan, 10-25; 2007, January, 13-27; 2005, August, 7-8; 2005, August, 9-10; 2005, July, 11-12
89352	Thawing of cryopreserved; embryo(s)
	0.00 0.00 Global Days XXX
	AMA: 2009, Jan, 11-31; 2008, Jan, 10-25; 2007, January, 13-27; 2005, July, 11-12; 2005, August, 9-10; 2005, August, 7-8

	89353	sperm/semen, each aliquot	[x]
		🚗 0.00 🔧 0.00 Global Days XXX	
		AMA: 2009, Jan, 11-31; 2008, Jan, 10-25; 2007, January, 13-27; 2005, July, 11-12; 2005, August, 9-10; 2005, August, 7-8	
	89354	reproductive tissue, testicular/ovarian	[x]
		🚗 0.00 🔧 0.00 Global Days XXX	
		AMA: 2009, Jan, 11-31; 2008, Jan, 10-25; 2007, January, 13-27; 2005, July, 11-12; 2005, August, 7-8; 2005, August, 9-10	
	89356	oocytes, each aliquot	[x]
		🚗 0.00 🔧 0.00 Global Days XXX	
		AMA: 2009, Jan, 11-31; 2008, Jan, 10-25; 2007, January, 13-27; 2005, July, 11-12; 2005, August, 7-8; 2005, August, 9-10	
●	89398	Unlisted reproductive medicine laboratory procedure	[x]
		EXCLUDES *Hyaluronan binding assay (HBA) (89398)*	
		🚗 0.00 🔧 0.00 Global Days XXX	

Current Procedural Coding Expert – Medicine

90281-90399 Immunoglobulin Products

CMS 100-2,15,50   Drugs and Biologicals
CMS 100-4,4,20.5   HCPCS Under OPPS

INCLUDES Immune globulin product only
Immune globulins/antioxins/various isoantibodies, and monoclonal antibodies:
    Anti-infective
    Broad-spectrum

Code also (96365-96368, 96372, 96374-96375)

- **90281** Immune globulin (Ig), human, for intramuscular use   [E]
0.00   0.00   Global Days XXX
AMA: 2009, Jan, 11-31; 2008, Jan, 10-25; 2007, January, 13-27

- **90283** Immune globulin (IgIV), human, for intravenous use   [E]
0.00   0.00   Global Days XXX
AMA: 2009, Jan, 11-31; 2008, Jan, 10-25

- **90284** Immune globulin (SCIg), human, for use in subcutaneous infusions, 100 mg, each   [E]
0.00   0.00   Global Days XXX
AMA: 2009, Jan, 11-31; 2008, Jan, 10-25

- **90287** Botulinum antitoxin, equine, any route   [E]
0.00   0.00   Global Days XXX
AMA: 2009, Jan, 11-31; 2008, Jan, 10-25

- **90288** Botulism immune globulin, human, for intravenous use   [E]
0.00   0.00   Global Days XXX
AMA: 2009, Jan, 11-31; 2008, Jan, 10-25

- **90291** Cytomegalovirus immune globulin (CMV-IgIV), human, for intravenous use   [E]
0.00   0.00   Global Days XXX
AMA: 2009, Jan, 11-31; 2008, Jan, 10-25

- **90296** Diphtheria antitoxin, equine, any route   [E]
0.00   0.00   Global Days XXX
AMA: 2009, Jan, 11-31; 2008, Jan, 10-25

- **90371** Hepatitis B immune globulin (HBIg), human, for intramuscular use   [K2][K]
0.00   0.00   Global Days XXX
AMA: 2009, Jan, 11-31; 2008, Jan, 10-25

- **90375** Rabies immune globulin (RIg), human, for intramuscular and/or subcutaneous use   [K2][K]
0.00   0.00   Global Days XXX
AMA: 2009, Jan, 11-31; 2008, Jan, 10-25

- **90376** Rabies immune globulin, heat-treated (RIg-HT), human, for intramuscular and/or subcutaneous use   [K2][K]
0.00   0.00   Global Days XXX
AMA: 2009, Jan, 11-31; 2008, Jan, 10-25

- ▲ **90378** Respiratory syncytial virus, monoclonal antibody, recombinant, for intramuscular use, 50 mg, each   [K2][K]
0.00   0.00   Global Days XXX
AMA: 2009, Jan, 11-31; 2008, Jan, 10-25

- ~~90379~~ ~~Respiratory syncytial virus immune globulin (RSV-IgIV), human, for intravenous use~~
To report, see code 90378

- **90384** Rho(D) immune globulin (RhIg), human, full-dose, for intramuscular use   [E]
0.00   0.00   Global Days XXX
AMA: 2009, Jan, 11-31; 2008, Jan, 10-25

- **90385** Rho(D) immune globulin (RhIg), human, mini-dose, for intramuscular use   [N1][N]
0.00   0.00   Global Days XXX
AMA: 2009, Jan, 11-31; 2008, Jan, 10-25

- **90386** Rho(D) immune globulin (RhIgIV), human, for intravenous use   [E]
0.00   0.00   Global Days XXX
AMA: 2009, Jan, 11-31; 2008, Jan, 10-25

- **90389** Tetanus immune globulin (TIg), human, for intramuscular use   [E]
0.00   0.00   Global Days XXX
AMA: 2009, Jan, 11-31; 2008, Jan, 10-25

- **90393** Vaccinia immune globulin, human, for intramuscular use   [E]
0.00   0.00   Global Days XXX
AMA: 2009, Jan, 11-31; 2008, Jan, 10-25

- **90396** Varicella-zoster immune globulin, human, for intramuscular use   [K2][K]
0.00   0.00   Global Days XXX
AMA: 2009, Jan, 11-31; 2008, Jan, 10-25

- **90399** Unlisted immune globulin   [E]
0.00   0.00   Global Days XXX
AMA: 2009, Jan, 11-31; 2008, Jan, 10-25

90465-90470 Injections Provided with Physician Counseling

CMS 100-2,16,90   Routine Services and Appliances

INCLUDES Patient/family face-to-face counseling

EXCLUDES Administration of influenza and pneumococcal vaccine for Medicare patients (G0008-G0009, G9141)
Allergy testing (95004-95075)
Bacterial/viral/fungal skin tests (86485-86580)

Code also significant, separately identifiable preventive medicine services (99381-99429)
Code also significant separately identifiable evaluation and management service if performed (99201-99215)
Code also therapeutic or diagnostic injections (96372-96379)
Code also toxoid/vaccine (90476-90749)

- **90465** Immunization administration younger than 8 years of age (includes percutaneous, intradermal, subcutaneous, or intramuscular injections) when the physician counsels the patient/family; first injection (single or combination vaccine/toxoid), per day   [A][B][80]
Do not report with intranasal/oral administration (90467)
0.60   0.60   Global Days XXX
AMA: 2009, Jan, 7-8; 2009, Jul, 7; 2009, Jan, 3,4&9; 2005, November, 1-9; 2005, August, 13-15; 2005, April, 1-5

- + **90466** each additional injection (single or combination vaccine/toxoid), per day (List separately in addition to code for primary procedure)   [A][B][80]
Code first initial administration/injection (90465, 90467)
0.22   0.32   Global Days ZZZ
AMA: 2009, Jan, 3,4&9; 2009, Jan, 7-8; 2009, Jul, 7; 2005, August, 13-15; 2005, April, 1-5; 2005, November, 1-9

- **90467** Immunization administration younger than age 8 years (includes intranasal or oral routes of administration) when the physician counsels the patient/family; first administration (single or combination vaccine/toxoid), per day   [A][B][80]
Do not report with percutaneous/intradermal/subcutaneous/intramuscular injection (90465)
0.28   0.44   Global Days XXX
AMA: 2009, Jan, 7-8; 2009, Jan, 3,4&9; 2009, Jul, 7; 2005, April, 1-5; 2005, August, 13-15

● New Code   ▲ Revised Code   [M] Maternity   [A] Age   Unlisted   Not Covered   # Resequenced
CCI   + Add-on   ⊘ Mod 51 Exempt   63 Mod 63 Exempt   ⊙ Mod Sedation   PQRI
© 2009 Publisher (Blue Ink)   CPT only © 2009 American Medical Association. All Rights Reserved. (Black Ink)   Medicare (Red Ink)

90468

+ **90468** each additional administration (single or combination vaccine/toxoid), per day (List separately in addition to code for primary procedure) [A][B][80]
Code first initial administration/injection (90465, 90467)
0.22   0.31   Global Days ZZZ
AMA: 2009, Jan, 3,4&9; 2009, Jul, 7; 2009, Jan, 7-8; 2005, August, 13-15; 2005, April, 1-5

● **90470** H1N1 immunization administration (intramuscular, intranasal), including counseling when performed [E]
0.00   0.00   Global Days XXX

90471-90474 Injections and Other Routes of Administration Without Physician Counseling

CMS 100-2,15,50   Drugs and Biologicals
CMS 100-2,16,90   Routine Services and Appliances
CMS 100-4,18,10.2.1   Vaccines and Administration

EXCLUDES Administration of influenza and pneumococcal vaccine for Medicare patients (G0008-G0009, G9141)
Allergy testing (95004-95075)
Bacterial/viral/fungal skin tests (86485-86580)
Injections, diagnostic/therapeutic (96372-96379)
Patient/family face-to-face counseling

Code also significant, separately identifiable preventive medicine services (99381-99429)
Code also significant separately identifiable evaluation and management service if performed (99201-99215)
Code also toxoid/vaccine (90476-90749)

90471 Immunization administration (includes percutaneous, intradermal, subcutaneous, or intramuscular injections); 1 vaccine (single or combination vaccine/toxoid) [S][80]
Do not report with intranasal/oral administration (90473)
0.60   0.60   Global Days XXX
AMA: 2009, Jan, 11-31; 2009, Jan, 3,4&9; 2009, Jan, 7-8; 2009, Jul, 7; 2008, Jan, 10-25; 2007, Jul, 12-13; 2005, November, 1-9; 2005, April, 1-5

+ **90472** each additional vaccine (single or combination vaccine/toxoid) (List separately in addition to code for primary procedure) [S][80]
EXCLUDES BCG vaccine, intravesical administration (51720, 90586)
Immune globulin administration (96365-96368, 96372-96375)
Immune globulin product (90281-90399)
Code first initial vaccine (90471, 90473)
0.22   0.32   Global Days ZZZ
AMA: 2009, Jan, 11-31; 2009, Jan, 7-8; 2009, Jan, 3,4&9; 2009, Jul, 7; 2008, Jan, 10-25; 2007, Jul, 12-13; 2005, November, 1-9; 2005, April, 1-5

90473 Immunization administration by intranasal or oral route; 1 vaccine (single or combination vaccine/toxoid) [S][80]
Do not report with percutaneous/intradermal/subcutaneous/intramuscular injections (90471)
0.25   0.44   Global Days XXX
AMA: 2009, Jan, 3,4&9; 2009, Jan, 7-8; 2009, Jul, 7; 2005, April, 1-5

+ **90474** each additional vaccine (single or combination vaccine/toxoid) (List separately in addition to code for primary procedure) [S][80]
Code first initial vaccine (90471, 90473)
0.22   0.27   Global Days ZZZ
AMA: 2009, Jan, 7-8; 2009, Jul, 7; 2009, Jan, 3,4&9; 2005, April, 1-5

90476-90749 Vaccination Products

CMS 100-2,15,50   Drugs and Biologicals
CMS 100-2,16,90   Routine Services and Appliances
CMS 100-4,4,20.5   HCPCS Under OPPS

INCLUDES Patient's age for coding purposes, not for product license
Vaccine product only

EXCLUDES Immune globulins and adminstration (90281-90399, 96365, 96372-96375)

Code also administration of vaccine (90465-90474)
Code also office/other outpatient (99201-99215)
Code also preventive medicine (99381-99429)
Code also significant separately identifiable evaluation and management service if performed

90476 Adenovirus vaccine, type 4, live, for oral use [K2][K]
0.00   0.00   Global Days XXX
AMA: 2009, Jul, 7; 2009, Jan, 11-31; 2008, Jan, 10-25; 2007, January, 13-27; 2007, February, 10-11

90477 Adenovirus vaccine, type 7, live, for oral use [E]
0.00   0.00   Global Days XXX
AMA: 2009, Jan, 11-31; 2009, Jul, 7; 2008, Jan, 10-25

90581 Anthrax vaccine, for subcutaneous use [E]
INCLUDES BioThrax
0.00   0.00   Global Days XXX
AMA: 2009, Jul, 7; 2009, Jan, 11-31; 2008, Jan, 10-25

90585 Bacillus Calmette-Guerin vaccine (BCG) for tuberculosis, live, for percutaneous use [K2][K]
INCLUDES Mycobax
0.00   0.00   Global Days XXX
AMA: 2009, Jan, 11-31; 2009, Jul, 7; 2008, Jan, 10-25

90586 Bacillus Calmette-Guerin vaccine (BCG) for bladder cancer, live, for intravesical use [B]
INCLUDES TheraCys
TICE BCG
0.00   0.00   Global Days XXX
AMA: 2009, Jan, 11-31; 2009, Jul, 7; 2008, Jan, 10-25

90632 Hepatitis A vaccine, adult dosage, for intramuscular use [A][N1][N]
INCLUDES HAVRIX 1440EL.U/1mL
VAQTA 50U/1mL
0.00   0.00   Global Days XXX
AMA: 2009, Jan, 11-31; 2009, Jul, 7; 2008, Jan, 10-25

90633 Hepatitis A vaccine, pediatric/adolescent dosage-2 dose schedule, for intramuscular use [A][N1][N]
INCLUDES HAVRIX 720EL.U/0.5mL
VAQTA 25U/0.5mL
0.00   0.00   Global Days XXX
AMA: 2009, Jul, 7; 2009, Jan, 11-31; 2008, Jan, 10-25

90634 Hepatitis A vaccine, pediatric/adolescent dosage-3 dose schedule, for intramuscular use [N1][N]
0.00   0.00   Global Days XXX
AMA: 2009, Jul, 7; 2009, Jan, 11-31; 2008, Jan, 10-25

90636 Hepatitis A and hepatitis B vaccine (HepA-HepB), adult dosage, for intramuscular use [A][N1][N]
INCLUDES TWINRIX
0.00   0.00   Global Days XXX
AMA: 2009, Jan, 11-31; 2009, Jul, 7; 2008, Jan, 10-25

● **90644** Meningococcal conjugate vaccine, serogroups C & Y and Hemophilus influenza b vaccine, tetanus toxoid conjugate (Hib-MenCY-TT), 4-dose schedule, when administered to children 2-15 months of age, for intramuscular use [E]
0.00   0.00   Global Days XXX

Current Procedural Coding Expert – Medicine 90676

90645 Hemophilus influenza b vaccine (Hib), HbOC conjugate (4 dose schedule), for intramuscular use
0.00 0.00 Global Days XXX
AMA: 2009, Jul, 7; 2009, Jan, 11-31; 2008, Jan, 10-25

90646 Hemophilus influenza b vaccine (Hib), PRP-D conjugate, for booster use only, intramuscular use
0.00 0.00 Global Days XXX
AMA: 2009, Jan, 11-31; 2009, Jul, 7; 2008, Jan, 10-25

90647 Hemophilus influenza b vaccine (Hib), PRP-OMP conjugate (3 dose schedule), for intramuscular use
INCLUDES PedvaxHIB
0.00 0.00 Global Days XXX
AMA: 2009, Jul, 7; 2009, Jan, 11-31; 2008, Jan, 10-25

90648 Hemophilus influenza b vaccine (Hib), PRP-T conjugate (4 dose schedule), for intramuscular use
INCLUDES ActHIB
0.00 0.00 Global Days XXX
AMA: 2009, Jan, 11-31; 2009, Jul, 7; 2008, Jan, 10-25

90649 Human Papilloma virus (HPV) vaccine, types 6, 11, 16, 18 (quadrivalent), 3 dose schedule, for intramuscular use
INCLUDES GARDASIL
0.00 0.00 Global Days XXX
AMA: 2009, Jan, 11-31; 2009, Jul, 7; 2008, Jan, 10-25; 2007, Jul, 12-13; 2006, June, 8-10; 2005, December, 9-11

▲ **90650** Human Papilloma virus (HPV) vaccine, types 16, 18, bivalent, 3 dose schedule, for intramuscular use
INCLUDES CERVARIX
0.00 0.00 Global Days XXX
AMA: 2009, Jan, 11-31; 2009, Jul, 7; 2008, Jan, 10-25

90655 Influenza virus vaccine, split virus, preservative free, when administered to children 6-35 months of age, for intramuscular use
INCLUDES Fluzone, no preservative, pediatric dose
0.00 0.00 Global Days XXX
AMA: 2009, Jan, 11-31; 2009, Jul, 7; 2008, Jan, 10-25; 2008, Apr, 8-9; 2007, April, 11-12

90656 Influenza virus vaccine, split virus, preservative free, when administered to individuals 3 years and older, for intramuscular use
INCLUDES AFLURIA (prefilled syringe)
FLUARIX
Fluvirin (prefilled syringe)
Fluzone®, Influenza Virus Vaccine, No Preservative
Fluzone, no preservative
0.00 0.00 Global Days XXX
AMA: 2009, Jan, 11-31; 2009, Jul, 7; 2008, Jan, 10-25; 2008, Apr, 8-9

90657 Influenza virus vaccine, split virus, when administered to children 6-35 months of age, for intramuscular use
INCLUDES Fluzone, 0.25 mL
0.00 0.00 Global Days XXX
AMA: 2009, Jan, 11-31; 2009, Jul, 7; 2008, Jan, 10-25; 2008, Apr, 8-9; 2007, February, 10-11; 2005, April, 1-5

90658 Influenza virus vaccine, split virus, when administered to individuals 3 years of age and older, for intramuscular use
INCLUDES AFLURIA, 0.5mL
FLULAVAL
Fluvirin, 0.5mL
Fluzone, 0.5 mL
Fluzone®, Influenza Virus Vaccine (5mL vial [0.5mL dose])
0.00 0.00 Global Days XXX
AMA: 2009, Jan, 11-31; 2009, Jul, 7; 2008, Jan, 10-25; 2008, Apr, 8-9; 2007, April, 11-12; 2007, February, 10-11

90660 Influenza virus vaccine, live, for intranasal use
INCLUDES FluMist
0.00 0.00 Global Days XXX
AMA: 2009, Jul, 7; 2009, Jan, 11-31; 2008, Jan, 10-25; 2008, Apr, 8-9; 2007, February, 10-11

90661 Influenza virus vaccine, derived from cell cultures, subunit, preservative and antibiotic free, for intramuscular use
0.00 0.00 Global Days XXX
AMA: 2009, Jan, 11-31; 2009, Jul, 7; 2008, Jan, 10-25; 2008, Apr, 8-9

90662 Influenza virus vaccine, split virus, preservative free, enhanced immunogenicity via increased antigen content, for intramuscular use
0.00 0.00 Global Days XXX
AMA: 2009, Jan, 11-31; 2009, Jul, 7; 2008, Jan, 10-25; 2008, Apr, 8-9

▲ **90663** Influenza virus vaccine, pandemic formulation, H1N1
INCLUDES H1N1 vaccine (non-Medicare)
EXCLUDES H1N1 vaccine for Medicare patients (G9142)
0.00 0.00 Global Days XXX
AMA: 2009, Jan, 11-31; 2009, Jul, 7; 2008, Jan, 10-25; 2008, Apr, 8-9

90665 Lyme disease vaccine, adult dosage, for intramuscular use
0.00 0.00 Global Days XXX
AMA: 2009, Jan, 11-31; 2009, Jul, 7; 2008, Jan, 10-25; 2007, February, 10-11

90669 Pneumococcal conjugate vaccine, 7 valent, for intramuscular use
INCLUDES Prevnar
0.00 0.00 Global Days XXX
AMA: 2009, Jan, 11-31; 2009, Jul, 7; 2008, Jan, 10-25; 2007, February, 10-11

● **90670** Pneumococcal conjugate vaccine, 13 valent, for intramuscular use
0.00 0.00 Global Days XXX
AMA: 2009, Jul, 7

90675 Rabies vaccine, for intramuscular use
INCLUDES IMOVAX
RabAvert
0.00 0.00 Global Days XXX
AMA: 2009, Jul, 7; 2009, Jan, 11-31; 2008, Jan, 10-25; 2007, February, 10-11

90676 Rabies vaccine, for intradermal use
0.00 0.00 Global Days XXX
AMA: 2009, Jan, 11-31; 2009, Jul, 7; 2008, Jan, 10-25; 2007, February, 10-11

● New Code ▲ Revised Code M Maternity A Age Unlisted Not Covered # Resequenced
CCI + Add-on Mod 51 Exempt Mod 63 Exempt Mod Sedation PQRI

90680

90680 Rotavirus vaccine, pentavalent, 3 dose schedule, live, for oral use
INCLUDES RotaTeq
0.00 0.00 Global Days XXX
AMA: 2009, Jan, 11-31; 2009, Jul, 7; 2008, Jan, 10-25; 2007, February, 10-11; 2006, June, 8-10; 2005, June, 6-8; 2005, December, 9-11

90681 Rotavirus vaccine, human, attenuated, 2 dose schedule, live, for oral use
INCLUDES Rotarix
0.00 0.00 Global Days XXX
AMA: 2009, Jul, 7; 2009, Jan, 11-31; 2008, Jan, 10-25

90690 Typhoid vaccine, live, oral
INCLUDES Vivotif
0.00 0.00 Global Days XXX
AMA: 2009, Jul, 7; 2009, Jan, 11-31; 2008, Jan, 10-25; 2007, February, 10-11

90691 Typhoid vaccine, Vi capsular polysaccharide (ViCPs), for intramuscular use
INCLUDES Typhim Vi
0.00 0.00 Global Days XXX
AMA: 2009, Jan, 11-31; 2009, Jul, 7; 2008, Jan, 10-25; 2007, February, 10-11

90692 Typhoid vaccine, heat- and phenol-inactivated (H-P), for subcutaneous or intradermal use
0.00 0.00 Global Days XXX
AMA: 2009, Jan, 11-31; 2009, Jul, 7; 2008, Jan, 10-25; 2007, February, 10-11

90693 Typhoid vaccine, acetone-killed, dried (AKD), for subcutaneous use (U.S. military)
0.00 0.00 Global Days XXX
AMA: 2009, Jan, 11-31; 2009, Jul, 7; 2008, Jan, 10-25; 2007, January, 13-27; 2007, February, 10-11

90696 Diphtheria, tetanus toxoids, acellular pertussis vaccine and poliovirus vaccine, inactivated (DTaP-IPV), when administered to children 4 through 6 years of age, for intramuscular use
INCLUDES KINRIX
0.00 0.00 Global Days XXX
AMA: 2009, Jan, 11-31; 2009, Jul, 7; 2008, Jan, 10-25

90698 Diphtheria, tetanus toxoids, acellular pertussis vaccine, haemophilus influenza Type B, and poliovirus vaccine, inactivated (DTaP - Hib - IPV), for intramuscular use
INCLUDES Pentacel
0.00 0.00 Global Days XXX
AMA: 2009, Jan, 11-31; 2009, Jul, 7; 2008, Jan, 10-25; 2007, February, 10-11; 2006, June, 8-10

90700 Diphtheria, tetanus toxoids, and acellular pertussis vaccine (DTaP), when administered to individuals younger than 7 years, for intramuscular use
INCLUDES DAPTACEL
         INFANRIX
         Tripedia
0.00 0.00 Global Days XXX
AMA: 2009, Jul, 7; 2009, Jan, 11-31; 2008, Jan, 10-25; 2007, February, 10-11

90701 Diphtheria, tetanus toxoids, and whole cell pertussis vaccine (DTP), for intramuscular use
0.00 0.00 Global Days XXX
AMA: 2009, Jan, 11-31; 2009, Jul, 7; 2008, Jan, 10-25; 2007, February, 10-11

90702 Diphtheria and tetanus toxoids (DT) adsorbed when administered to individuals younger than 7 years, for intramuscular use
INCLUDES Diphtheria and Tetanus Toxoids Adsorbed USP (For Pediatric Use)
0.00 0.00 Global Days XXX
AMA: 2009, Jan, 11-31; 2009, Jul, 7; 2008, Jan, 10-25; 2007, February, 10-11

90703 Tetanus toxoid adsorbed, for intramuscular use
INCLUDES Tetanus Toxoid Adsorbed
0.00 0.00 Global Days XXX
AMA: 2009, Jan, 11-31; 2009, Jul, 7; 2008, Jan, 10-25; 2007, February, 10-11

90704 Mumps virus vaccine, live, for subcutaneous use
INCLUDES MUMPSVAX
0.00 0.00 Global Days XXX
AMA: 2009, Jan, 11-31; 2009, Jul, 7; 2008, Jan, 10-25; 2007, February, 10-11

90705 Measles virus vaccine, live, for subcutaneous use
INCLUDES ATTENUVAX
0.00 0.00 Global Days XXX
AMA: 2009, Jan, 11-31; 2009, Jul, 7; 2008, Jan, 10-25; 2007, February, 10-11

90706 Rubella virus vaccine, live, for subcutaneous use
INCLUDES MERUVAX II
0.00 0.00 Global Days XXX
AMA: 2009, Jan, 11-31; 2009, Jul, 7; 2008, Jan, 10-25; 2007, February, 10-11

90707 Measles, mumps and rubella virus vaccine (MMR), live, for subcutaneous use
INCLUDES M-M-R II
0.00 0.00 Global Days XXX
AMA: 2009, Jan, 11-31; 2009, Jul, 7; 2008, Jan, 10-25; 2007, February, 10-11; 2005, April, 1-5

90708 Measles and rubella virus vaccine, live, for subcutaneous use
0.00 0.00 Global Days XXX
AMA: 2009, Jan, 11-31; 2009, Jul, 7; 2008, Jan, 10-25; 2007, February, 10-11

90710 Measles, mumps, rubella, and varicella vaccine (MMRV), live, for subcutaneous use
INCLUDES ProQuad
0.00 0.00 Global Days XXX
AMA: 2009, Jan, 11-31; 2009, Jul, 7; 2008, Jan, 10-25; 2007, February, 10-11; 2006, June, 8-10; 2005, December, 9-11

90712 Poliovirus vaccine, (any type[s]) (OPV), live, for oral use
0.00 0.00 Global Days XXX
AMA: 2009, Jul, 7; 2009, Jan, 11-31; 2008, Jan, 10-25; 2007, February, 10-11

90713 Poliovirus vaccine, inactivated (IPV), for subcutaneous or intramuscular use
INCLUDES IPOL
0.00 0.00 Global Days XXX
AMA: 2009, Jul, 7; 2009, Jan, 11-31; 2008, Jan, 10-25; 2007, February, 10-11; 2005, June, 6-8

Current Procedural Coding Expert – Medicine

90714 Tetanus and diphtheria toxoids (Td) adsorbed, preservative free, when administered to individuals 7 years or older, for intramuscular use
INCLUDES DECAVAC
0.00 0.00 Global Days XXX
AMA: 2009, Jan, 11-31; 2009, Jul, 7; 2008, Jan, 10-25; 2007, February, 10-11; 2005, June, 6-8

90715 Tetanus, diphtheria toxoids and acellular pertussis vaccine (Tdap), when administered to individuals 7 years or older, for intramuscular use
INCLUDES Adacel
BOOSTRIX
0.00 0.00 Global Days XXX
AMA: 2009, Jan, 11-31; 2009, Jul, 7; 2008, Jan, 10-25; 2007, February, 10-11; 2006, June, 8-10; 2005, June, 6-8; 2005, December, 9-11

90716 Varicella virus vaccine, live, for subcutaneous use
INCLUDES VARIVAX
0.00 0.00 Global Days XXX
AMA: 2009, Jan, 11-31; 2009, Jul, 7; 2008, Jan, 10-25; 2007, February, 10-11

90717 Yellow fever vaccine, live, for subcutaneous use
INCLUDES YF-VAX
0.00 0.00 Global Days XXX
AMA: 2009, Jan, 11-31; 2009, Jul, 7; 2008, Jan, 10-25; 2007, January, 13-27; 2007, February, 10-11

90718 Tetanus and diphtheria toxoids (Td) adsorbed when administered to individuals 7 years or older, for intramuscular use
INCLUDES Tetanus and Diphtheria Toxoids Adsorbed for Adult Use
0.00 0.00 Global Days XXX
AMA: 2009, Jan, 11-31; 2009, Jul, 7; 2008, Jan, 10-25; 2007, February, 10-11; 2007, January, 13-27

90719 Diphtheria toxoid, for intramuscular use
0.00 0.00 Global Days XXX
AMA: 2009, Jan, 11-31; 2009, Jul, 7; 2008, Jan, 10-25; 2007, February, 10-11; 2007, January, 13-27

90720 Diphtheria, tetanus toxoids, and whole cell pertussis vaccine and Hemophilus influenza B vaccine (DTP-Hib), for intramuscular use
0.00 0.00 Global Days XXX
AMA: 2009, Jul, 7; 2009, Jan, 11-31; 2008, Jan, 10-25; 2007, February, 10-11; 2007, January, 13-27

90721 Diphtheria, tetanus toxoids, and acellular pertussis vaccine and Hemophilus influenza B vaccine (DtaP-Hib), for intramuscular use
INCLUDES TriHIBit
0.00 0.00 Global Days XXX
AMA: 2009, Jan, 11-31; 2009, Jul, 7; 2008, Jan, 10-25; 2007, January, 13-27; 2007, February, 10-11

90723 Diphtheria, tetanus toxoids, acellular pertussis vaccine, Hepatitis B, and poliovirus vaccine, inactivated (DtaP-HepB-IPV), for intramuscular use
INCLUDES PEDIARIX
0.00 0.00 Global Days XXX
AMA: 2009, Jan, 11-31; 2009, Jul, 7; 2008, Jan, 10-25; 2007, January, 13-27; 2007, February, 10-11

90725 Cholera vaccine for injectable use
0.00 0.00 Global Days XXX
AMA: 2009, Jan, 11-31; 2009, Jul, 7; 2008, Jan, 10-25; 2007, February, 10-11; 2007, January, 13-27

90727 Plague vaccine, for intramuscular use
0.00 0.00 Global Days XXX
AMA: 2009, Jul, 7; 2009, Jan, 11-31; 2008, Jan, 10-25; 2007, January, 13-27; 2007, February, 10-11

90732 Pneumococcal polysaccharide vaccine, 23-valent, adult or immunosuppressed patient dosage, when administered to individuals 2 years or older, for subcutaneous or intramuscular use
INCLUDES PNEUMOVAX 23
0.00 0.00 Global Days XXX
AMA: 2009, Jan, 11-31; 2009, Jul, 7; 2008, Jan, 10-25; 2007, January, 13-27; 2007, February, 10-11

90733 Meningococcal polysaccharide vaccine (any group(s)), for subcutaneous use
INCLUDES Menomune-A/C/Y/W-135
0.00 0.00 Global Days XXX
AMA: 2009, Jan, 11-31; 2009, Jul, 7; 2008, Jan, 10-25; 2007, January, 13-27; 2007, February, 10-11

90734 Meningococcal conjugate vaccine, serogroups A, C, Y and W-135 (tetravalent), for intramuscular use
INCLUDES Menactra
0.00 0.00 Global Days XXX
AMA: 2009, Jul, 7; 2009, Jan, 11-31; 2008, Jan, 10-25; 2007, January, 13-27; 2007, February, 10-11

90735 Japanese encephalitis virus vaccine, for subcutaneous use
INCLUDES JE-VAX
0.00 0.00 Global Days XXX
AMA: 2009, Jan, 11-31; 2009, Jul, 7; 2008, Jan, 10-25; 2007, February, 10-11; 2007, January, 13-27

90736 Zoster (shingles) vaccine, live, for subcutaneous injection
INCLUDES ZOSTAVAX
0.00 0.00 Global Days XXX
AMA: 2009, Jan, 11-31; 2009, Jul, 7; 2008, Jan, 10-25; 2007, February, 10-11; 2007, Jul, 12-13; 2007, January, 13-27; 2006, June, 8-10; 2005, December, 9-11

90738 Japanese encephalitis virus vaccine, inactivated, for intramuscular use
0.00 0.00 Global Days XXX
AMA: 2009, Jan, 11-31; 2009, Jul, 7

90740 Hepatitis B vaccine, dialysis or immunosuppressed patient dosage (3 dose schedule), for intramuscular use
INCLUDES RECOMBIVAX HB 40mcg/1mL (dialysis formulation)
0.00 0.00 Global Days XXX
AMA: 2009, Jan, 11-31; 2009, Jul, 7; 2008, Jan, 10-25; 2007, January, 13-27; 2007, February, 10-11

90743 Hepatitis B vaccine, adolescent (2 dose schedule), for intramuscular use
INCLUDES RECOMBIVAX HB 10mcg/1mL
0.00 0.00 Global Days XXX
AMA: 2009, Jan, 11-31; 2009, Jul, 7; 2008, Jan, 10-25; 2007, February, 10-11; 2007, January, 13-27

90744 Hepatitis B vaccine, pediatric/adolescent dosage (3 dose schedule), for intramuscular use
INCLUDES ENGERIX-B 10mcg/0.5mL
RECOMBIVAX HB 5mcg/0.5mL
0.00 0.00 Global Days XXX
AMA: 2009, Jan, 11-31; 2009, Jul, 7; 2008, Jan, 10-25; 2007, February, 10-11; 2007, January, 13-27; 2005, April, 1-5

90746

90746 Hepatitis B vaccine, adult dosage, for intramuscular use [F]
INCLUDES ENGERIX-B 20mcg/1mL
RECOMBIVAX HB 10mcg/1mL
💰 0.00 🔧 0.00 Global Days XXX
AMA: 2009, Jan, 11-31; 2009, Jul, 7; 2008, Jan, 10-25; 2007, January, 13-27; 2007, February, 10-11

90747 Hepatitis B vaccine, dialysis or immunosuppressed patient dosage (4 dose schedule), for intramuscular use [F]
INCLUDES ENGERIX-B 20mcg/1mL x 2 - 40mcg/2mL each dose
💰 0.00 🔧 0.00 Global Days XXX
AMA: 2009, Jan, 11-31; 2009, Jul, 7; 2008, Jan, 10-25; 2007, January, 13-27; 2007, February, 10-11

90748 Hepatitis B and Hemophilus influenza b vaccine (HepB-Hib), for intramuscular use [E]
INCLUDES COMVAX
💰 0.00 🔧 0.00 Global Days XXX
AMA: 2009, Jul, 7; 2009, Jan, 11-31; 2008, Jan, 10-25; 2007, February, 10-11; 2007, January, 13-27

90749 Unlisted vaccine/toxoid [N1][N]
💰 0.00 🔧 0.00 Global Days XXX
AMA: 2009, Jan, 11-31; 2009, Jul, 7; 2008, Jan, 10-25; 2007, February, 10-11

90801-90802 Interactive Psychiatric Evaluation

CMS 100-4,12,110.2 Outpatient Mental Health Limitation
CMS 100-4,12,150 Clinical Social Worker (CSW) Services
CMS 100-4,12,160 Independent Psychologist Services
CMS 100-4,12,160.1 Payment for Independent Psychologists' Services
CMS 100-4,12,170 Clinical Psychologist Services
CMS 100-4,12,170.1 Payment for Clinical Psychologist Services
CMS 100-4,12,210 Outpatient Mental Health Limitation

90801 Psychiatric diagnostic interview examination [03][80][▶][P0]
INCLUDES Communication with family/other sources
Disposition
History
Mental status
Ordering/interpretation of lab studies
Ordering/interpretation of other medical diagnostic studies
💰 3.38 🔧 4.18 Global Days XXX
AMA: 2007, Jul, 6-10; 2006, December, 8-9; 2005, March, 11-15; 2005, May, 1-2

90802 Interactive psychiatric diagnostic interview examination using play equipment, physical devices, language interpreter, or other mechanisms of communication [03][80][▶][P0]
INCLUDES Non-verbal communication
Physical aids
Services furnished to:
  Children
  Other individuals lacking expressive/receptive communication skills
💰 3.70 🔧 4.58 Global Days XXX
AMA: 2005, May, 1-2

90804-90809 Individual Outpatient Psychotherapy

CMS 100-3,130.1 Inpatient Stays for Alcoholism Treatment
CMS 100-3,130.2 Outpatient Hospital Services for Alcoholism
CMS 100-3,130.5 Treatment of Alcoholism/Drug Abuse in a Freestanding Clinic
CMS 100-3,130.6 Treatment of Drug Abuse (Chemical Dependency)
CMS 100-3,130.7 Withdrawal Treatments for Narcotic Addictions
CMS 100-4,12,110.2 Outpatient Mental Health Limitation
CMS 100-4,12,150 Clinical Social Worker (CSW) Services
CMS 100-4,12,160 Independent Psychologist Services
CMS 100-4,12,160.1 Payment for Independent Psychologists' Services
CMS 100-4,12,170 Clinical Psychologist Services
CMS 100-4,12,170.1 Payment for Clinical Psychologist Services
CMS 100-4,12,210 Outpatient Mental Health Limitation

INCLUDES Drug management
Face-to-face time
Insight oriented/behavior modifying/supportive psychotherapy:
  Cognitive discussion of reality
  Development of insight/affective understanding
  Supportive interactions
  Use of behavior modification
Interpretation of lab/other diagnostic studies/observations
Medical diagnostic evaluation:
  Comorbid medical conditions
  Drug interactions
  Physical examination
Physician orders
Psychotherapy only
Psychotherapy with medical evaluation and management services
Services provided in office or other outpatient facility
Treatment for:
  Behavior disturbances
  Mental illness

90804 Individual psychotherapy, insight oriented, behavior modifying and/or supportive, in an office or outpatient facility, approximately 20 to 30 minutes face-to-face with the patient; [03][80][▶][P0]
💰 1.40 🔧 1.72 Global Days XXX
AMA: 2009, Jan, 11-31; 2008, Jan, 10-25; 2007, January, 13-27; 2005, May, 1-2

90805 with medical evaluation and management services [03][80][▶][P0]
💰 1.64 🔧 1.99 Global Days XXX
AMA: 2005, May, 1-2

90806 Individual psychotherapy, insight oriented, behavior modifying and/or supportive, in an office or outpatient facility, approximately 45 to 50 minutes face-to-face with the patient; [03][80][▶][P0]
💰 2.11 🔧 2.29 Global Days XXX
AMA: 2009, Jan, 11-31; 2008, Jan, 10-25; 2007, January, 13-27; 2005, May, 1-2; 2005, March, 11-15; 2005, March, 16-17

90807 with medical evaluation and management services [03][80][▶][P0]
💰 2.43 🔧 2.77 Global Days XXX
AMA: 2005, May, 1-2

90808 Individual psychotherapy, insight oriented, behavior modifying and/or supportive, in an office or outpatient facility, approximately 75 to 80 minutes face-to-face with the patient; [03][80][▶][P0]
💰 3.18 🔧 3.36 Global Days XXX
AMA: 2005, May, 1-2

90809 with medical evaluation and management services [03][80][▶][P0]
💰 3.57 🔧 3.89 Global Days XXX
AMA: 2009, Jul, 8-9; 2005, May, 1-2

Current Procedural Coding Expert – Medicine

90810-90815 Individual Outpatient Interactive Psychotherapy

CMS 100-3,130.2	Outpatient Hospital Services for Alcoholism
CMS 100-3,130.5	Treatment of Alcoholism/Drug Abuse in a Freestanding Clinic
CMS 100-3,130.6	Treatment of Drug Abuse (Chemical Dependency)
CMS 100-3,130.7	Withdrawal Treatments for Narcotic Addictions
CMS 100-4,12,110.2	Outpatient Mental Health Limitation
CMS 100-4,12,150	Clinical Social Worker (CSW) Services
CMS 100-4,12,160	Independent Psychologist Services
CMS 100-4,12,170	Clinical Psychologist Services

INCLUDES
- Drug management
- Face-to-face time
- Interactive psychotherapy:
  - Physical aids/non-verbal communication for individuals lacking expressive/receptive communication skills
  - Usually provided to children
- Interpretation of lab/other diagnostic studies/observations
- Medical diagnostic evaluation:
  - Comorbid medical conditions
  - Drug interactions
  - Physical examination
- Physician orders
- Psychotherapy only
- Psychotherapy with medical evaluation and management services
- Services provided in office or other outpatient facility
- Treatment for:
  - Behavior disturbances
  - Mental illness

90810 Individual psychotherapy, interactive, using play equipment, physical devices, language interpreter, or other mechanisms of non-verbal communication, in an office or outpatient facility, approximately 20 to 30 minutes face-to-face with the patient;
  1.53 1.79 Global Days XXX
  AMA: 2005, May, 1-2

90811 with medical evaluation and management services
  1.79 2.23 Global Days XXX
  AMA: 2005, May, 1-2

90812 Individual psychotherapy, interactive, using play equipment, physical devices, language interpreter, or other mechanisms of non-verbal communication, in an office or outpatient facility, approximately 45 to 50 minutes face-to-face with the patient;
  2.23 2.50 Global Days XXX
  AMA: 2005, May, 1-2

90813 with medical evaluation and management services
  2.55 3.00 Global Days XXX
  AMA: 2005, May, 1-2

90814 Individual psychotherapy, interactive, using play equipment, physical devices, language interpreter, or other mechanisms of non-verbal communication, in an office or outpatient facility, approximately 75 to 80 minutes face-to-face with the patient;
  3.31 3.63 Global Days XXX
  AMA: 2005, May, 1-2

90815 with medical evaluation and management services
  3.70 4.16 Global Days XXX
  AMA: 2009, Jul, 8-9; 2005, May, 1-2

90816-90822 Individual Inpatient Psychotherapy

CMS 100-3,130.1	Inpatient Stays for Alcoholism Treatment
CMS 100-3,130.6	Treatment of Drug Abuse (Chemical Dependency)
CMS 100-3,130.7	Withdrawal Treatments for Narcotic Addictions
CMS 100-4,12,110.2	Outpatient Mental Health Limitation
CMS 100-4,12,150	Clinical Social Worker (CSW) Services
CMS 100-4,12,160	Independent Psychologist Services
CMS 100-4,12,160.1	Payment for Independent Psychologists' Services
CMS 100-4,12,170	Clinical Psychologist Services
CMS 100-4,12,170.1	Payment for Clinical Psychologist Services
CMS 100-4,12,210	Outpatient Mental Health Limitation

INCLUDES
- Drug management
- Face-to-face time
- Insight oriented/behavior modifying/supportive psychotherapy:
  - Cognitive discussion of reality
  - Development of insight/affective understanding
  - Supportive interactions
  - Use of behavior modification
- Interpretation of lab/other diagnostic studies/observations
- Medical diagnostic evaluation:
  - Comorbid medical conditions
  - Drug interactions
  - Physical examination
- Physician orders
- Psychotherapy only
- Psychotherapy with medical evaluation and management services
- Services provided in inpatient hospital/partial hospital/residential care facility
- Treatment for:
  - Behavior disturbances
  - Mental illiness

90816 Individual psychotherapy, insight oriented, behavior modifying and/or supportive, in an inpatient hospital, partial hospital or residential care setting, approximately 20 to 30 minutes face-to-face with the patient;
  1.50 1.50 Global Days XXX
  AMA: 2005, May, 1-2

90817 with medical evaluation and management services
  1.80 1.80 Global Days XXX
  AMA: 2005, May, 1-2

90818 Individual psychotherapy, insight oriented, behavior modifying and/or supportive, in an inpatient hospital, partial hospital or residential care setting, approximately 45 to 50 minutes face-to-face with the patient;
  2.22 2.22 Global Days XXX
  AMA: 2005, May, 1-2

90819 with medical evaluation and management services
  2.57 2.57 Global Days XXX
  AMA: 2005, May, 1-2

90821 Individual psychotherapy, insight oriented, behavior modifying and/or supportive, in an inpatient hospital, partial hospital or residential care setting, approximately 75 to 80 minutes face-to-face with the patient;
  3.31 3.31 Global Days XXX
  AMA: 2005, May, 1-2

90822 with medical evaluation and management services
  3.69 3.69 Global Days XXX
  AMA: 2009, Jul, 8-9; 2005, May, 1-2

● New Code ▲ Revised Code Ⓜ Maternity Ⓐ Age Unlisted Not Covered # Resequenced
CCI + Add-on Ⓢ Mod 51 Exempt ⊚ Mod 63 Exempt ⊙ Mod Sedation PQRI

© 2009 Publisher (Blue Ink)   CPT only © 2009 American Medical Association. All Rights Reserved. (Black Ink)   Medicare (Red Ink)

90823-90829 Inpatient Individual Psychotherapy: Interactive

CMS 100-3,130.1 Inpatient Stays for Alcoholism Treatment
CMS 100-3,130.6 Treatment of Drug Abuse (Chemical Dependency)
CMS 100-3,130.7 Withdrawal Treatments for Narcotic Addictions
CMS 100-4,12,110.2 Outpatient Mental Health Limitation
CMS 100-4,12,150 Clinical Social Worker (CSW) Services
CMS 100-4,12,160 Independent Psychologist Services
CMS 100-4,12,160.1 Payment for Independent Psychologists' Services
CMS 100-4,12,170 Clinical Psychologist Services

INCLUDES
Drug management
Face-to-face time
Interactive psychotherapy:
   Physical aids/non-verbal communication for individuals lacking expressive/receptive communication skills
   Usually provided to children
Interpretation of lab/other diagnostic studies/observations
Medical diagnostic evaluation:
   Comorbid medical conditions
   Drug interactions
   Physical examination
Physician orders
Psychotherapy only
Psychotherapy with medical evaluation and management services
Services provided in inpatient hospital/partial hospital/residential care facility
Treatment for:
   Behavior disturbances
   Mental illness

90823 Individual psychotherapy, interactive, using play equipment, physical devices, language interpreter, or other mechanisms of non-verbal communication, in an inpatient hospital, partial hospital or residential care setting, approximately 20 to 30 minutes face-to-face with the patient;
   1.62   1.62   Global Days XXX
   AMA: 2005, May, 1-2

90824 with medical evaluation and management services
   1.92   1.92   Global Days XXX
   AMA: 2005, May, 1-2

90826 Individual psychotherapy, interactive, using play equipment, physical devices, language interpreter, or other mechanisms of non-verbal communication, in an inpatient hospital, partial hospital or residential care setting, approximately 45 to 50 minutes face-to-face with the patient;
   2.36   2.36   Global Days XXX
   AMA: 2005, May, 1-2

90827 with medical evaluation and management services
   2.69   2.69   Global Days XXX
   AMA: 2005, May, 1-2

90828 Individual psychotherapy, interactive, using play equipment, physical devices, language interpreter, or other mechanisms of non-verbal communication, in an inpatient hospital, partial hospital or residential care setting, approximately 75 to 80 minutes face-to-face with the patient;
   3.40   3.40   Global Days XXX
   AMA: 2005, May, 1-2

90829 with medical evaluation and management services
   3.81   3.81   Global Days XXX
   AMA: 2009, Jul, 8-9; 2005, May, 1-2

90845-90862 Additional Psychotherapy Services

CMS 100-2,15,160 Clinical Psychologist Services
CMS 100-3,130.1 Inpatient Stays for Alcoholism Treatment
CMS 100-3,130.2 Outpatient Hospital Services for Alcoholism
CMS 100-3,130.5 Treatment of Alcoholism/Drug Abuse in a Freestanding Clinic
CMS 100-3,130.6 Treatment of Drug Abuse (Chemical Dependency)
CMS 100-3,130.7 Withdrawal Treatments for Narcotic Addictions
CMS 100-4,12,110.2 Outpatient Mental Health Limitation
CMS 100-4,12,150 Clinical Social Worker (CSW) Services
CMS 100-4,12,160 Independent Psychologist Services
CMS 100-4,12,160.1 Payment for Independent Psychologists' Services
CMS 100-4,12,170 Clinical Psychologist Services
CMS 100-4,12,170.1 Payment for Clinical Psychologist Services

90845 Psychoanalysis
   2.18   2.24   Global Days XXX
   AMA: 2009, Jan, 11-31; 2008, Jan, 10-25; 2007, January, 13-27; 2006, February, 16-18; 2005, May, 1-2

90846 Family psychotherapy (without the patient present)
   2.21   2.29   Global Days XXX
   AMA: 2005, May, 1-2

90847 Family psychotherapy (conjoint psychotherapy) (with patient present)
   2.63   2.85   Global Days XXX
   AMA: 2005, May, 1-2

90849 Multiple-family group psychotherapy
   0.79   0.91   Global Days XXX
   AMA: 2005, May, 1-2

90853 Group psychotherapy (other than of a multiple-family group)
   0.81   0.88   Global Days XXX
   AMA: 2005, May, 1-2

90857 Interactive group psychotherapy
   0.84   0.97   Global Days XXX
   AMA: 2005, May, 1-2

90862 Pharmacologic management, including prescription, use, and review of medication with no more than minimal medical psychotherapy
   EXCLUDES Analysis/programming of neurostimulators for vagus nerve stimulation therapy (95970, 95974, 95975)
   Repetitive transcranial magnetic stimulation for treatment of clinical depression (0160T, 0161T)
   1.25   1.59   Global Days XXX
   AMA: 2006, December, 10-12; 2005, May, 1-2; 2005, March, 11-15

Current Procedural Coding Expert – Medicine

90865-90870 Psychiatric Treatment with Drugs or Electroshock

CMS 100-4,12,110.2 — Outpatient Mental Health Limitation
CMS 100-4,12,150 — Clinical Social Worker (CSW) Services
CMS 100-4,12,160 — Independent Psychologist Services
CMS 100-4,12,160.1 — Payment for Independent Psychologists' Services
CMS 100-4,12,170 — Clinical Psychologist Services
CMS 100-4,12,170.1 — Payment for Clinical Psychologist Services
CMS 100-4,12,210 — Outpatient Mental Health Limitation

EXCLUDES Analysis/programming of neurostimulators for vagus nerve stimulation therapy (95970, 95974, 95975)
Repetitive transcranial magnetic stimulation for treatment of clinical depression (0160T-0161T)

90865 Narcosynthesis for psychiatric diagnostic and therapeutic purposes (eg, sodium amobarbital (Amytal) interview)
3.50   4.39   Global Days XXX
AMA: 2005, May, 1-2

90870 Electroconvulsive therapy (includes necessary monitoring)
2.31   3.79   Global Days 000
AMA: 2005, May, 1-2

90875-90880 Psychiatric Therapy with Biofeedback or Hypnosis

CMS 100-3,30.1 — Biofeedback Therapy
CMS 100-4,12,110.2 — Outpatient Mental Health Limitation
CMS 100-4,12,150 — Clinical Social Worker (CSW) Services
CMS 100-4,12,160 — Independent Psychologist Services
CMS 100-4,12,160.1 — Payment for Independent Psychologists' Services
CMS 100-4,12,170 — Clinical Psychologist Services
CMS 100-4,12,170.1 — Payment for Clinical Psychologist Services
CMS 100-4,12,210 — Outpatient Mental Health Limitation

EXCLUDES Analysis/programming of neurostimulators for vagus nerve stimulation therapy (95970, 95974, 95975)
Repetitive transcranial magnetic stimulation for treatment of clinical depression (0160T, 0161T)

90875 Individual psychophysiological therapy incorporating biofeedback training by any modality (face-to-face with the patient), with psychotherapy (eg, insight oriented, behavior modifying or supportive psychotherapy); approximately 20-30 minutes
1.70   1.96   Global Days XXX
AMA: 2009, Jan, 11-31; 2008, Jan, 10-25; 2007, January, 13-27; 2005, May, 1-2; 2005, March, 16-17

90876 approximately 45-50 minutes
2.69   2.94   Global Days XXX
AMA: 2005, May, 1-2; 2005, March, 16-17

90880 Hypnotherapy
2.53   2.66   Global Days XXX
AMA: 2005, May, 1-2; 2005, March, 16-17

90882-90899 Psychiatric Services without Patient Face-to-Face Contact

CMS 100-1,3,30.3 — Mental Health Diagnostic Services
CMS 100-4,12,110.2 — Outpatient Mental Health Limitation
CMS 100-4,12,150 — Clinical Social Worker (CSW) Services
CMS 100-4,12,160 — Independent Psychologist Services
CMS 100-4,12,160.1 — Payment for Independent Psychologists' Services
CMS 100-4,12,170 — Clinical Psychologist Services
CMS 100-4,12,170.1 — Payment for Clinical Psychologist Services
CMS 100-4,12,210 — Outpatient Mental Health Limitation

EXCLUDES Analysis/programming of neurostimulators for vagus nerve stimulation therapy (95970, 95974, 95975)
Repetitive transcranial magnetic stimulation for treatment of clinical depression (0160T, 0161T)

90882 Environmental intervention for medical management purposes on a psychiatric patient's behalf with agencies, employers, or institutions
0.00   0.00   Global Days XXX
AMA: 2005, May, 1-2; 2005, March, 16-17

90885 Psychiatric evaluation of hospital records, other psychiatric reports, psychometric and/or projective tests, and other accumulated data for medical diagnostic purposes
1.37   1.37   Global Days XXX
AMA: 2009, Jan, 11-31; 2008, Jan, 10-25; 2007, January, 13-27; 2005, March, 16-17; 2005, May, 1-2

90887 Interpretation or explanation of results of psychiatric, other medical examinations and procedures, or other accumulated data to family or other responsible persons, or advising them how to assist patient
2.09   2.38   Global Days XXX
AMA: 2009, Jan, 11-31; 2008, Jan, 10-25; 2007, January, 13-27; 2005, May, 1-2; 2005, March, 16-17

90889 Preparation of report of patient's psychiatric status, history, treatment, or progress (other than for legal or consultative purposes) for other physicians, agencies, or insurance carriers
0.00   0.00   Global Days XXX
AMA: 2005, May, 1-2; 2005, March, 16-17

90899 Unlisted psychiatric service or procedure
0.00   0.00   Global Days XXX
AMA: 2005, May, 1-2; 2005, March, 16-17

90901-90911 Biofeedback Therapy

CMS 100-3,30.1 — Biofeedback Therapy
CMS 100-3,30.1.1 — Biofeedback for Urinary Incontinence

EXCLUDES Psychophysiological therapy utilizing biofeedback training (90875, 90876)

90901 Biofeedback training by any modality
0.56   0.97   Global Days 000
AMA: 2009, Jan, 11-31; 2008, Jan, 10-25; 2007, January, 13-27; 2005, March, 16-17

90911 Biofeedback training, perineal muscles, anorectal or urethral sphincter, including EMG and/or manometry
EXCLUDES Rectal sensation/tone/compliance testing (91120)
Treatment for incontinence, pulsed magnetic neuromodulation (53899)
1.24   2.16   Global Days 000
AMA: 2009, Jan, 11-31; 2008, Jan, 10-25; 2007, January, 13-27; 2005, March, 16-17

90935-90940 Hemodialysis Services: Inpatient ESRD and Outpatient Non-ESRD

CMS 100-2,1,10	Inpatient Hospital Services Covered Under Part A
CMS 100-2,11,20	Coverage of Outpatient Maintenance Dialysis
CMS 100-3,130.8	Hemodialysis for Schizophrenia
CMS 100-3,190.10	Laboratory Tests--CRD Patients
CMS 100-3,230.14	Ultrafiltration Monitor
CMS 100-4,3,100.6	Inpatient Renal Services

EXCLUDES
- Blood specimen collection from partial/complete implantable venous access device (36591)
- Declotting of cannula (36831, 36833, 36860, 36861)
- Hemodialysis home visit by non-physician health care professional (99512)
- Physician attendance for a prolonged period of time (99354-99360)
- Thrombolytic agent declotting of implanted vascular access device/catheter (36593)

Code also significant separately identifiable evaluation and management service not related to dialysis procedure or renal failure, with modifier 25

90935 Hemodialysis procedure with single physician evaluation

INCLUDES All evaluation and management services related to the patient's renal disease rendered on a day dialysis is performed:
- Inpatient ESRD and non-ESRD procedures
- Only one evaluation of the patient related to hemodialysis procedure
- Outpatient non-ESRD dialysis

1.90   1.90   Global Days 000
AMA: 2005, March, 16-17

90937 Hemodialysis procedure requiring repeated evaluation(s) with or without substantial revision of dialysis prescription

INCLUDES All evaluation and management services related to the patient's renal disease rendered on a day dialysis is performed:
- Inpatient ESRD and non-ESRD procedures
- Outpatient non-ESRD dialysis
- Re-evaluation of the patient during hemodialysis procedure

3.13   3.13   Global Days 000
AMA: 2005, March, 16-17

90940 Hemodialysis access flow study to determine blood flow in grafts and arteriovenous fistulae by an indicator method

EXCLUDES Hemodialysis access duplex scan (93990)

0.00   0.00   Global Days XXX
AMA: 2009, Jan, 11-31; 2008, Jan, 10-25; 2007, January, 13-27; 2006, May, 16-20; 2005, March, 16-17

90945-90947 Dialysis Techniques Other Than Hemodialysis

CMS 100-2,1,10	Inpatient Hospital Services Covered Under Part A
CMS 100-3,110.15	Ultrafiltration, Hemoperfusion, and Hemofiltration
CMS 100-3,190.10	Laboratory Tests--CRD Patients
CMS 100-3,240.6	Transvenous (Catheter) Pulmonary Embolectomy
CMS 100-4,3,100.6	Inpatient Renal Services
CMS 100-4,4,20.5	HCPCS Under OPPS

EXCLUDES
- Intraperitoneal cannula/catheter insertion (49420, 49421)
- Physician attendance for a prolonged period of time (99354-99360)

90945 Dialysis procedure other than hemodialysis (eg, peritoneal dialysis, hemofiltration, or other continuous renal replacement therapies), with single physician evaluation

INCLUDES All evaluation and management services related to the patient's renal disease rendered on a day dialysis is performed:
- Continuous renal replacement therapies
- Hemofiltration
- Only one evaluation of the patient related to the procedure
- Peritoneal dialysis

EXCLUDES
- Hemodialysis
- Peritoneal dialysis home infusion (99601, 99602)

Code also significant separately identifiable evaluation and management service not related to dialysis procedure or renal failure, with modifier 25

1.98   1.98   Global Days 000
AMA: 2009, Jan, 11-31; 2008, Jan, 10-25; 2007, January, 13-27; 2005, March, 16-17

90947 Dialysis procedure other than hemodialysis (eg, peritoneal dialysis, hemofiltration, or other continuous renal replacement therapies) requiring repeated physician evaluations, with or without substantial revision of dialysis prescription

INCLUDES All evaluation and management services related to the patient's renal disease rendered on a day dialysis is performed:
- Continuous renal replacement therapies
- Hemofiltration
- Peritoneal dialysis
- Re-evaluation during a procedure

EXCLUDES Hemodialysis

Code also significant separately identifiable evaluation and management service not related to dialysis procedure or renal failure, with modifier 25

3.19   3.19   Global Days 000
AMA: 2009, Jan, 11-31; 2008, Jan, 10-25; 2007, January, 13-27; 2005, March, 16-17

Current Procedural Coding Expert – Medicine

90951-90962 End-stage Renal Disease Monthly Outpatient Services

CMS 100-3,190.10   Laboratory Tests--CRD Patients
CMS 100-3,230.14   Ultrafiltration Monitor

INCLUDES
- Establishing dialyzing cycle
- Management of dialysis visits
- Outpatient evaluation
- Patient management
- Telephone calls

EXCLUDES
Dialysis services provided during an inpatient hospitalization (90935-90937, 90945-90947)
ESRD/non-ESRD dialysis services performed in an inpatient setting (90935-90937, 90945-90947)
Non-ESRD dialysis services performed in an outpatient setting (90935-90937, 90945-90947)
Non-ESRD related evaluation and management services that cannot be performed during the dialysis session

90951 End-stage renal disease (ESRD) related services monthly, for patients younger than 2 years of age to include monitoring for the adequacy of nutrition, assessment of growth and development, and counseling of parents; with 4 or more face-to-face physician visits per month
   27.76   27.76   Global Days XXX
   AMA: 2009, Jan, 3,4&9

90952 with 2-3 face-to-face physician visits per month
   0.00   0.00   Global Days XXX
   AMA: 2009, Jan, 3,4&9

90953 with 1 face-to-face physician visit per month
   0.00   0.00   Global Days XXX
   AMA: 2009, Jan, 3,4&9

90954 End-stage renal disease (ESRD) related services monthly, for patients 2-11 years of age to include monitoring for the adequacy of nutrition, assessment of growth and development, and counseling of parents; with 4 or more face-to-face physician visits per month
   23.32   23.32   Global Days XXX
   AMA: 2009, Jan, 3,4&9

90955 with 2-3 face-to-face physician visits per month
   12.90   12.90   Global Days XXX
   AMA: 2009, Jan, 3,4&9

90956 with 1 face-to-face physician visit per month
   8.53   8.53   Global Days XXX
   AMA: 2009, Jan, 3,4&9

90957 End-stage renal disease (ESRD) related services monthly, for patients 12-19 years of age to include monitoring for the adequacy of nutrition, assessment of growth and development, and counseling of parents; with 4 or more face-to-face physician visits per month
   18.66   18.66   Global Days XXX
   AMA: 2009, Jan, 3,4&9

90958 with 2-3 face-to-face physician visits per month
   12.38   12.38   Global Days XXX
   AMA: 2009, Jan, 3,4&9

90959 with 1 face-to-face physician visit per month
   7.92   7.92   Global Days XXX
   AMA: 2009, Jan, 3,4&9

90960 End-stage renal disease (ESRD) related services monthly, for patients 20 years of age and older; with 4 or more face-to-face physician visits per month
   8.12   8.12   Global Days XXX
   AMA: 2009, Jan, 3,4&9

90961 with 2-3 face-to-face physician visits per month
   6.49   6.49   Global Days XXX
   AMA: 2009, Jan, 3,4&9

90962 with 1 face-to-face physician visit per month
   4.61   4.61   Global Days XXX
   AMA: 2009, Jan, 3,4&9

90963-90966 End-stage Renal Disease Monthly Home Dialysis Services

INCLUDES
- ESRD services for home dialysis patients
- Services provided for a full month services

90963 End-stage renal disease (ESRD) related services for home dialysis per full month, for patients younger than 2 years of age to include monitoring for the adequacy of nutrition, assessment of growth and development, and counseling of parents
   15.15   15.15   Global Days XXX
   AMA: 2009, Jan, 3,4&9

90964 End-stage renal disease (ESRD) related services for home dialysis per full month, for patients 2-11 years of age to include monitoring for the adequacy of nutrition, assessment of growth and development, and counseling of parents
   13.20   13.20   Global Days XXX
   AMA: 2009, Jan, 3,4&9

90965 End-stage renal disease (ESRD) related services for home dialysis per full month, for patients 12-19 years of age to include monitoring for the adequacy of nutrition, assessment of growth and development, and counseling of parents
   12.59   12.59   Global Days XXX
   AMA: 2009, Jan, 3,4&9

90966 End-stage renal disease (ESRD) related services for home dialysis per full month, for patients 20 years of age and older
   6.58   6.58   Global Days XXX
   AMA: 2009, Jan, 3,4&9

90967-90970 End-stage Renal Disease Services: Partial Month

CMS 100-3,190.10   Laboratory Tests--CRD Patients
CMS 100-3,230.14   Ultrafiltration Monitor

INCLUDES ESRD services for less than a full month, such as:
- A patient who is transient, dies, recovers, or undergoes kidney transplant
- Outpatient ESRD-related services initiated prior to completion of assessment
- Patient spending part of the month as a hospital inpatient
- Services reported on a daily basis, less the days of hospitalization

90967 End-stage renal disease (ESRD) related services for dialysis less than a full month of service, per day; for patients younger than 2 years of age
   0.56   0.56   Global Days XXX
   AMA: 2009, Jan, 3,4&9

90968 for patients 2-11 years of age
   0.45   0.45   Global Days XXX
   AMA: 2009, Jan, 3,4&9

90969 for patients 12-19 years of age
   0.43   0.43   Global Days XXX
   AMA: 2009, Jan, 3,4&9

● New Code   ▲ Revised Code   M Maternity   A Age   Unlisted   Not Covered   # Resequenced
CCI   + Add-on   ⊘ Mod 51 Exempt   @ Mod 63 Exempt   ⊙ Mod Sedation   PQRI

© 2009 Publisher *(Blue Ink)*   CPT only © 2009 American Medical Association. All Rights Reserved. *(Black Ink)*   Medicare *(Red Ink)*

90970 for patients 20 years of age and older [A][M][80][P0]
 0.22   0.22 Global Days XXX
AMA: 2009, Jan, 3,4&9

90989-90993 Dialysis Training Services

90989 Dialysis training, patient, including helper where applicable, any mode, completed course [B]
 0.00   0.00 Global Days XXX
AMA: 2009, Jan, 11-31; 2008, Jan, 10-25; 2007, January, 13-27

90993 Dialysis training, patient, including helper where applicable, any mode, course not completed, per training session [B]
 0.00   0.00 Global Days XXX
AMA: 2009, Jan, 11-31; 2008, Jan, 10-25; 2007, January, 13-27

90997-90999 Hemoperfusion and Unlisted Dialysis Procedures

90997 Hemoperfusion (eg, with activated charcoal or resin) [B][80]
 2.52   2.52 Global Days 000

90999 Unlisted dialysis procedure, inpatient or outpatient [B][80]
 0.00   0.00 Global Days XXX

91000 Esophageal Intubation for Cytology Washings

EXCLUDES
Anoscopy (46600-46615)
Colonoscopy (45355-45385)
Duodenal intubation/aspiration (89100-89105)
Esophagoscopy (43200-43228)
Insertion of:
   Esophageal tamponade tube (43460)
   Miller-Abbott tube (44500)
Proctosigmoidoscopy (45300-45321)
Radiologic services, gastrointestinal (74210-74363)
Sigmoidoscopy (45330-45339)
Small intestine/stomal endoscopy (44360-44393)
Upper gastrointestinal endoscopy (43234-43259)

91000 Esophageal intubation and collection of washings for cytology, including preparation of specimens (separate procedure) [X][80]
 2.88   2.88 Global Days 000

91010-91022 Esophageal Manometry

CMS 100-3, 100.4   Esophageal Manometry

EXCLUDES
Anoscopy (46600-46615)
Colonoscopy (45355-45385)
Duodenal intubation/aspiration (89100-89105)
Esophagoscopy (43200-43228)
Insertion of:
   Esophageal tamponade tube (43460)
   Miller-Abbott tube (44500)
Proctosigmoidoscopy (45300-45321)
Radiologic services, gastrointestinal (74210-74363)
Sigmoidoscopy (45330-45339)
Small intestine/stomal endoscopy (44360-44393)
Upper gastrointestinal endoscopy (43234-43259)

91010 Esophageal motility (manometric study of the esophagus and/or gastroesophageal junction) study; [X][80]
 4.52   4.52 Global Days 000
AMA: 2005, May, 3-6

91011 with mecholyl or similar stimulant [X][80]
 6.06   6.06 Global Days 000

91012 with acid perfusion studies [X][80]
 6.12   6.12 Global Days 000

Gastric pertains to the stomach; peptic is a term for ulcers caused by digestive juices in the stomach, duodenum or jejunum; duodenal ulcers are more common in young people, gastric in the elderly

91020 Gastric motility (manometric) studies [X][80]
 5.78   5.78 Global Days 000

91022 Duodenal motility (manometric) study [X][80]
EXCLUDES Fluoroscopy (76000)
Gastric motility study (91020)
 4.32   4.32 Global Days 000

91030-91040 Esophageal Reflux Tests

EXCLUDES
Anoscopy (46600-46615)
Colonoscopy (45355-45385)
Duodenal intubation/aspiration (89100-89105)
Esophagoscopy (43200-43228)
Insertion of:
   Esophageal tamponade tube (43460)
   Miller-Abbott tube (44500)
Proctosigmoidoscopy (45300-45321)
Radiologic services, gastrointestinal (74210-74363)
Sigmoidoscopy (45330-45339)
Small intestine/stomal endoscopy (44360-44393)
Upper gastrointestinal endoscopy (43234-43259)

91030 Esophagus, acid perfusion (Bernstein) test for esophagitis [X][80]
 3.41   3.41 Global Days 000

91034 Esophagus, gastroesophageal reflux test; with nasal catheter pH electrode(s) placement, recording, analysis and interpretation [X][80]
 4.64   4.64 Global Days 000
AMA: 2005, May, 3-6

91035 with mucosal attached telemetry pH electrode placement, recording, analysis and interpretation [X][80]
 11.55   11.55 Global Days 000
AMA: 2005, May, 3-6

91037 Esophageal function test, gastroesophageal reflux test with nasal catheter intraluminal impedance electrode(s) placement, recording, analysis and interpretation; [X][80]
 4.01   4.01 Global Days 000
AMA: 2005, May, 3-6

91038 prolonged (greater than 1 hour, up to 24 hours) [X][80]
 3.54   3.54 Global Days 000
AMA: 2005, May, 3-6

Current Procedural Coding Expert – Medicine

91040 Esophageal balloon distension provocation study
  EXCLUDES: Endoscopic balloon dilation (43220, 43249, 43456, 43458)
  7.10   7.10   Global Days 000
  AMA: 2005, May, 3-6

91052 Gastric Analysis for pH of Stomach Secretions
CMS 100-3,30.6   Intravenous Histamine Therapy
EXCLUDES:
  Anoscopy (46600-46615)
  Colonoscopy (45355-45385)
  Duodenal intubation/aspiration (89100-89105)
  Esophagoscopy (43200-43228)
  Insertion of:
    Esophageal tamponade tube (43460)
    Miller-Abbott tube (44500)
  Proctosigmoidoscopy (45300-45321)
  Radiologic services, gastrointestinal (74210-74363)
  Sigmoidoscopy (45330-45339)
  Small intestine/stomal endoscopy (44360-44393)
  Upper gastrointestinal endoscopy (43234-43259)

91052 Gastric analysis test with injection of stimulant of gastric secretion (eg, histamine, insulin, pentagastrin, calcium and secretin)
  EXCLUDES: Stomach biopsy by capsule/peroral/via tube, one or more specimens (43600)
  89130-89141
  3.31   3.31   Global Days 000

91055 Gastric Intubation for Cytology Washings
EXCLUDES:
  Anoscopy (46600-46615)
  Colonoscopy (45355-45385)
  Duodenal intubation/aspiration (89100-89105)
  Esophagoscopy (43200-43228)
  Insertion of:
    Esophageal tamponade tube (43460)
    Miller-Abbott tube (44500)
  Proctosigmoidoscopy (45300-45321)
  Radiologic services, gastrointestinal (74210-74363)
  Sigmoidoscopy (45330-45339)
  Small intestine/stomal endoscopy (44360-44393)
  Upper gastrointestinal endoscopy (43234-43259)

91055 Gastric intubation, washings, and preparing slides for cytology (separate procedure)
  INCLUDES: Hollander test
    Rehfuss' test
  EXCLUDES: Intestinal biopsy by capsule/mouth/tube, one or more specimens (44100)
    Therapeutic gastric lavage (91105)
  3.84   3.84   Global Days 000

91065 Breath Analysis
CMS 100-3,100.5   Diagnostic Breath Analysis
EXCLUDES:
  Anoscopy (46600-46615)
  Colonoscopy (45355-45385)
  Duodenal intubation/aspiration (89100-89105)
  Esophagoscopy (43200-43228)
  H. pylori breath test analysis, radioactive (C-14) or nonradioactive (C-13) (78268, or 83013)
  Insertion of:
    Esophageal tamponade tube (43460)
    Miller-Abbott tube (44500)
  Proctosigmoidoscopy (45300-45321)
  Radiologic services, gastrointestinal (74210-74363)
  Sigmoidoscopy (45330-45339)
  Small intestine/stomal endoscopy (44360-44393)
  Upper gastrointestinal endoscopy (43234-43259)

91065 Breath hydrogen test (eg, for detection of lactase deficiency, fructose intolerance, bacterial overgrowth, or oro-cecal gastrointestinal transit)
  EXCLUDES: H. pylori breath test analysis
    Nonreactive isotope (C-13) (83013)
    Radioactive isotope (C-14) (78268)
  1.74   1.74   Global Days 000
  AMA: 2005, May, 3-6

91105 Gastric Lavage and Aspiration
CMS 100-4,12,30.6.12   Critical Care Visits
EXCLUDES:
  Anoscopy (46600-46615)
  Colonoscopy (45355-45385)
  Duodenal intubation/aspiration (89100-89105)
  Esophagoscopy (43200-43228)
  Proctosigmoidoscopy (45300-45321)
  Radiologic services, gastrointestinal (74210-74363)
  Sigmoidoscopy (45330-45339)
  Small intestine/stomal endoscopy (44360-44393)
  Upper gastrointestinal endoscopy (43234-43259)

91105 Gastric intubation, and aspiration or lavage for treatment (eg, for ingested poisons)
  EXCLUDES: Cholangiography (47500, 74320)
    Paracentesis, abdominal (49080, 49081)
      With medication instillation (96440, 96445)
    Peritoneoscopy (49320)
      With biopsy (49321)
    Peritoneoscopy with guided transhepatic cholangiography (47560)
      With biopsy (47561)
    Splenoportography (38200, 75810)
  0.48   2.34   Global Days 000
  AMA: 2009, Jan, 11-31; 2008, Jan, 10-25; 2007, Jul, 1-4; 2007, January, 13-27; 2007, February, 10-11

91110-91299 Additional Gastrointestinal Diagnostic/Therapeutic Procedures

EXCLUDES
Anoscopy (46600-46615)
Colonoscopy (45355-45385)
Duodenal intubation, aspiration (89100-89105)
Esophagoscopy (43200-43228)
Proctosigmoidoscopy (45300-45321)
Radiologic services, gastrointestinal (74210-74363)
Sigmoidoscopy (45330-45339)
Small intestine/stomal endoscopy (44360-44393)
Upper gastrointestinal endoscopy (43234-43259)

91110 Gastrointestinal tract imaging, intraluminal (eg, capsule endoscopy), esophagus through ileum, with physician interpretation and report T 80

Code also modifier 52 if ileum is not visualized
Do not report with visualization of the colon separately

21.53 21.53 Global Days XXX
AMA: 2009, Jan, 11-31; 2009, May, 8-9&11; 2008, Jan, 10-25; 2007, January, 13-27; 2005, August, 13-15

91111 Gastrointestinal tract imaging, intraluminal (eg, capsule endoscopy), esophagus with physician interpretation and report T 80

Do not report with imaging, esophagus through ileum (91110)

17.07 17.07 Global Days XXX

91120 Rectal sensation, tone, and compliance test (ie, response to graded balloon distention) T 80

EXCLUDES
Anorectal manometry (91122)
Biofeedback training (90911)

9.69 9.69 Global Days XXX
AMA: 2005, May, 3-6

91122 Anorectal manometry T 80
5.57 5.57 Global Days 000

91123 Pulsed irrigation of fecal impaction N
0.00 0.00 Global Days XXX

91132 Electrogastrography, diagnostic, transcutaneous; X 80
0.00 0.00 Global Days XXX

91133 with provocative testing X 80
0.00 0.00 Global Days XXX

91299 Unlisted diagnostic gastroenterology procedure X 80
0.00 0.00 Global Days XXX
AMA: 2005, August, 13-15

92002-92014 Ophthalmic Medical Services

CMS 100-4,4,20.5 HCPCS Under OPPS
CMS 100-4,4,160 Clinic and Emergency Visits Under OPPS
INCLUDES Routine ophthalmoscopy
EXCLUDES Surgical procedures on the eye/ocular adnexa (65091-68899)

92002 Ophthalmological services: medical examination and evaluation with initiation of diagnostic and treatment program; intermediate, new patient V 80 P0

INCLUDES Evaluation of new/existing condition complicated by new diagnostic or management problem
Integrated services where medical decision making cannot be separated from examination methods
Problems not related to primary diagnosis
Services provided to patients who have received no professional services from this physician or other same-specialty physicians within the same group practice within the past three years
The following for intermediate services:
Biomicroscopy
External ocular/adnexal examination
General medical observation
History
Mydriasis
Ophthalmoscopy
Other diagnostic procedures
Tonometry

1.34 2.09 Global Days XXX
AMA: 2009, Jan, 11-31; 2008, Jan, 1-3; 2008, Jan, 10-25; 2008, Sep, 7-8; 2007, January, 28-31; 2005, June, 9-11; 2005, December, 9-11

92004 comprehensive, new patient, 1 or more visits V 80 P0

INCLUDES General evaluation of complete visual system
Integrated services where medical decision making cannot be separated from examination methods
Services provided to patients who have received no professional services from this physician or other same-specialty physicians within the same group practice within the past three years
Single service that need not be performed at one session
The following for comprehensive services:
Basic sensorimotor examination
Biomicroscopy
Consultations
Dilation (cycloplegia)
External examinations
General medical observation
Gross visual fields
History
Initiation of diagnostic/treatment programs
Laboratory services
Mydriasis
Ophthalmoscopic examinations
Other diagnostic procedures
Prescription of medication
Radiological services
Special diagnostic/treatment services
Tonometry

2.80 3.92 Global Days XXX
AMA: 2008, Jan, 1-3; 2008, Sep, 7-8; 2007, January, 28-31; 2005, March, 11-15; 2005, December, 9-11; 2005, June, 9-11

Current Procedural Coding Expert – Medicine

92012 Ophthalmological services: medical examination and evaluation, with initiation or continuation of diagnostic and treatment program; intermediate, established patient

INCLUDES
- Evaluation of new/existing condition complicated by new diagnostic or management problem
- Integrated services where medical decision making cannot be separated from examination methods
- Problems not related to primary diagnosis
- Services provided to patients who have received professional services from this physician or other same-specialty physicians within the same group practice within the past three years
- The following for intermediate services:
  - External ocular/adnexal examination
  - General medical observation
  - History
  - Other diagnostic procedures
  - Biomicroscopy
  - Mydriasis
  - Ophthalmoscopy
  - Tonometry

1.47   2.22   Global Days XXX
AMA: 2008, Jan, 1-3; 2008, Sep, 7-8; 2007, January, 28-31; 2005, December, 9-11; 2005, March, 11-15; 2005, June, 9-11

92014 comprehensive, established patient, 1 or more visits

INCLUDES
- General evaluation of complete visual system
- Integrated services where medical decision making cannot be separated from examination methods
- Services provided to patients who have received professional services from this physician or other same-specialty physicians within the same group practice within the past three years
- Single service that need not be performed at one session
- The following for comprehensive services:
  - Basic sensorimotor examination
  - Biomicroscopy
  - Consultations
  - Dilation (cycloplegia)
  - External examinations
  - General medical observation
  - Gross visual fields
  - History
  - Initiation of diagnostic/treatment programs
  - Laboratory services
  - Mydriasis
  - Ophthalmoscopic examinations
  - Other diagnostic procedures
  - Prescription of medication
  - Radiological services
  - Special diagnostic/treatment services
  - Tonometry

2.25   3.25   Global Days XXX
AMA: 2009, Jan, 11-31; 2008, Jan, 10-25; 2008, Jan, 1-3; 2008, Sep, 7-8; 2007, January, 28-31; 2007, January, 13-27; 2005, March, 11-15; 2005, December, 9-11; 2005, June, 9-11

92015-92287 Ophthalmic Diagnostic and Other Special Services

CMS 100-2,16,90   Routine Services and Appliances
CMS 100-3,80.1   Hydrophilic Contact lens for Corneal Bandage
CMS 100-3,80.2   Photodynamic Therapy
CMS 100-3,80.4   Hydrophilic Contact Lens
CMS 100-3,80.6   Intraocular Photography
CMS 100-3,80.8   Endothelial Cell Photography
CMS 100-3,80.9   Computer Enhanced Perimetry

INCLUDES   Routine ophthalmoscopy
EXCLUDES   Surgical procedures on the eye/ocular adnexa (65091-68899)

Code also evaluation and management services (99201-99499)
Code also general ophthalmological services (92002-92014)

92015 Determination of refractive state
INCLUDES
- Lens prescription
- Absorptive factor
- Axis
- Impact resistance
- Lens power
- Prism
- Specification of lens type
- Monofocal
- Bifocal

0.54   0.55   Global Days XXX
AMA: 2009, Jan, 11-31; 2008, Jan, 10-25; 2007, January, 13-27; 2006, August, 12-14

92018 Ophthalmological examination and evaluation, under general anesthesia, with or without manipulation of globe for passive range of motion or other manipulation to facilitate diagnostic examination; complete

4.02   4.02   Global Days XXX

92019 limited
1.94   1.94   Global Days XXX

92020 Gonioscopy (separate procedure)
EXCLUDES   Gonioscopy under general anesthesia (92018)
0.59   0.73   Global Days XXX

92025 Computerized corneal topography, unilateral or bilateral, with interpretation and report
EXCLUDES   Manual keratoscopy
Do not report with (65710-65771)
0.97   0.97   Global Days XXX

92060 Sensorimotor examination with multiple measurements of ocular deviation (eg, restrictive or paretic muscle with diplopia) with interpretation and report (separate procedure)
1.69   1.69   Global Days XXX

92065 Orthoptic and/or pleoptic training, with continuing medical direction and evaluation
1.37   1.37   Global Days XXX
AMA: 2009, Jan, 11-31; 2008, Jan, 10-25; 2007, January, 13-27

92070 Fitting of contact lens for treatment of disease, including supply of lens
1.10   1.85   Global Days XXX

92081 Visual field examination, unilateral or bilateral, with interpretation and report; limited examination (eg, tangent screen, Autoplot, arc perimeter, or single stimulus level automated test, such as Octopus 3 or 7 equivalent)
1.50   1.50   Global Days XXX

CURRENT PROCEDURAL CODING EXPERT – Medicine

92082	intermediate examination (eg, at least 2 isopters on Goldmann perimeter, or semiquantitative, automated suprathreshold screening program, Humphrey suprathreshold automatic diagnostic test, Octopus program 33)
	1.99 1.99 Global Days XXX
92083	extended examination (eg, Goldmann visual fields with at least 3 isopters plotted and static determination within the central 30°, or quantitative, automated threshold perimetry, Octopus program G-1, 32 or 42, Humphrey visual field analyzer full threshold programs 30-2, 24-2, or 30/60-2)
	EXCLUDES Gross visual field testing/confrontation testing
	2.29 2.29 Global Days XXX
	AMA: 2005, March, 11-15
92100	Serial tonometry (separate procedure) with multiple measurements of intraocular pressure over an extended time period with interpretation and report, same day (eg, diurnal curve or medical treatment of acute elevation of intraocular pressure)
	1.42 2.50 Global Days XXX
	AMA: 2009, Jan, 11-31; 2008, Jan, 10-25; 2007, January, 13-27
92120	Tonography with interpretation and report, recording indentation tonometer method or perilimbal suction method
	EXCLUDES Ocular blood flow measurement (0198T)
	1.24 2.04 Global Days XXX
92130	Tonography with water provocation
	1.29 2.29 Global Days XXX
92135	Scanning computerized ophthalmic diagnostic imaging, posterior segment, (eg, scanning laser) with interpretation and report, unilateral
	1.30 1.30 Global Days XXX
	AMA: 2009, Jan, 11-31; 2008, Jan, 10-25; 2008, Jan, 1-3; 2007, January, 13-27; 2005, March, 11-15
92136	Ophthalmic biometry by partial coherence interferometry with intraocular lens power calculation
	2.22 2.22 Global Days XXX
	AMA: 2009, Jan, 11-31; 2008, Jan, 10-25; 2007, January, 13-27

Open-angle is the most common type of glaucoma; the disease occurs most frequently in people over age 60

Cornea
Trabecular meshwork
Schlemm's canal
Anterior chamber angle
Iris
Lens
Schematic of anterior chamber
Normal flow of aqueous humor from behind lens to Schlemm's canal

Glaucoma is caused by excessive intraocular pressure and abnormal accumulation of aqueous humor in the anterior chamber of the eye; pressure reduces blood supply to the optic nerve and causes nerve damage

92140	Provocative tests for glaucoma, with interpretation and report, without tonography
	0.75 1.59 Global Days XXX
92225	Ophthalmoscopy, extended, with retinal drawing (eg, for retinal detachment, melanoma), with interpretation and report; initial
	EXCLUDES Ophthalmoscopy under general anesthesia (92018)
	0.60 0.73 Global Days XXX
	AMA: 2009, Jan, 11-31; 2008, Jan, 10-25; 2007, January, 13-27
92226	subsequent
	0.53 0.66 Global Days XXX
92230	Fluorescein angioscopy with interpretation and report
	0.95 1.50 Global Days XXX
92235	Fluorescein angiography (includes multiframe imaging) with interpretation and report
	3.48 3.48 Global Days XXX
	AMA: 2008, Jan, 1-3; 2005, March, 11-15
92240	Indocyanine-green angiography (includes multiframe imaging) with interpretation and report
	6.15 6.15 Global Days XXX
	AMA: 2008, Jan, 1-3
92250	Fundus photography with interpretation and report
	1.95 1.95 Global Days XXX
	AMA: 2008, Jan, 1-3
92260	Ophthalmodynamometry
	EXCLUDES Ophthalmoscopy under general anesthesia (92018)
	0.32 0.49 Global Days XXX
92265	Needle oculoelectromyography, 1 or more extraocular muscles, 1 or both eyes, with interpretation and report
	2.16 2.16 Global Days XXX
92270	Electro-oculography with interpretation and report
	2.31 2.31 Global Days XXX
	AMA: 2009, Jan, 11-31; 2009, May, 8-9&11
92275	Electroretinography with interpretation and report
	EXCLUDES Vestibular function tests/electronystagmography (92541-92548)
	76511-76529
	3.95 3.95 Global Days XXX
92283	Color vision examination, extended, eg, anomaloscope or equivalent
	INCLUDES Farnsworth-Munsell color test Ishihara test
	1.33 1.33 Global Days XXX
92284	Dark adaptation examination with interpretation and report
	1.48 1.48 Global Days XXX
92285	External ocular photography with interpretation and report for documentation of medical progress (eg, close-up photography, slit lamp photography, goniophotography, stereo-photography)
	1.13 1.13 Global Days XXX
	AMA: 2009, Jan, 11-31; 2008, Jan, 10-25; 2008, Jan, 1-3; 2007, January, 13-27
92286	Special anterior segment photography with interpretation and report; with specular endothelial microscopy and cell count
	3.08 3.08 Global Days XXX
	AMA: 2008, Jan, 1-3
92287	with fluorescein angiography
	1.30 3.10 Global Days XXX

26/TC PC/TC Comp Only   A2-Z3 ASC Pmt   50 Bilateral   ♂ Male Only   ♀ Female Only   Facility RVU   Non-Facility RVU
AMA: CPT Asst   MED: Pub 100   A-Y OPPSI   Non-FDA Drug   Lab Crosswalk   Radiology Crosswalk

Current Procedural Coding Expert – Medicine

92310-92326 Services Related to Contact Lenses

CMS 100-2,15,30.4 — Optometrist's Services
CMS 100-2,15,120 — Prosthetic Devices
CMS 100-3,80.1 — Hydrophilic Contact lens for Corneal Bandage
CMS 100-3,80.4 — Hydrophilic Contact Lens
CMS 100-4,4,20.5 — HCPCS Under OPPS

INCLUDES
Incidental revision of lens during training period
Patient training/instruction
Specification of optical/physical characteristics:
  Curvature
  Flexibility
  Gas-permeabililty
  Power
  Size

EXCLUDES
Extended wear lenses follow up (92012-92014)
General ophthalmological services
Therapeutic/surgical use of contact lens (68340, 92070)

92310 Prescription of optical and physical characteristics of and fitting of contact lens, with medical supervision of adaptation; corneal lens, both eyes, except for aphakia [E]
  Code also modifier 52 for one eye
  1.66 2.50 Global Days XXX

92311 corneal lens for aphakia, 1 eye [S][80]
  1.63 2.71 Global Days XXX

92312 corneal lens for aphakia, both eyes [S][80]
  1.85 3.12 Global Days XXX

92313 corneoscleral lens [S][80]
  1.46 2.69 Global Days XXX

92314 Prescription of optical and physical characteristics of contact lens, with medical supervision of adaptation and direction of fitting by independent technician; corneal lens, both eyes except for aphakia [E]
  Code also modifier 52 for one eye
  0.97 2.01 Global Days XXX

92315 corneal lens for aphakia, 1 eye [S][80]
  0.67 1.94 Global Days XXX

92316 corneal lens for aphakia, both eyes [S][80]
  1.11 2.67 Global Days XXX

92317 corneoscleral lens [S][80]
  0.53 2.64 Global Days XXX

92325 Modification of contact lens (separate procedure), with medical supervision of adaptation [S][80]
  0.94 0.94 Global Days XXX

92326 Replacement of contact lens [S][80]
  EXCLUDES Prescription/fitting/medical supervision of ocular prosthetic adaptation by the physician (92002-92014, 99201-99499)
  0.81 0.81 Global Days XXX

92340-92499 Services Related to Eyeglasses

CMS 100-2,15,30.4 — Optometrist's Services
CMS 100-2,15,120 — Prosthetic Devices
CMS 100-2,15,120 — Prosthetic Devices
CMS 100-4,1,30.3.5 — Effect of Assignment on Cataract Glasses from Participating Physician/Supplier
CMS 100-4,4,20.5 — HCPCS Under OPPS
CMS 100-4,4,20.5 — HCPCS Under OPPS

INCLUDES
Anatomical facial characteristics measurement
Final adjustment of spectacles to visual axes/anatomical topography
Written laboratory specifications

EXCLUDES
Supply of materials

92340 Fitting of spectacles, except for aphakia; monofocal [E]
  0.53 0.90 Global Days XXX

92341 bifocal [E]
  0.66 1.04 Global Days XXX

92342 multifocal, other than bifocal [E]
  0.75 1.13 Global Days XXX

92352 Fitting of spectacle prosthesis for aphakia; monofocal [S]
  0.53 1.03 Global Days XXX

92353 multifocal [S]
  0.71 1.22 Global Days XXX

92354 Fitting of spectacle mounted low vision aid; single element system [S]
  0.31 0.31 Global Days XXX

92355 telescopic or other compound lens system [S]
  0.48 0.48 Global Days XXX

92358 Prosthesis service for aphakia, temporary (disposable or loan, including materials) [S]
  0.26 0.26 Global Days XXX

92370 Repair and refitting spectacles; except for aphakia [E]
  0.46 0.79 Global Days XXX

92371 spectacle prosthesis for aphakia [S]
  0.27 0.27 Global Days XXX

92499 Unlisted ophthalmological service or procedure [S][80]
  0.00 0.00 Global Days XXX

92502-92548 Special Procedures of the Ears/Nose/Throat

CMS 100-2,15,80.3 — Audiological Diagnostic Testing
CMS 100-2,15,230.3 — Practice of Speech-Language Pathology

INCLUDES
Diagnostic/treatment services not generally included in a comprehensive otorhinolaryngologic evaluation or office visit (92502-92700)

EXCLUDES
Laryngoscopy with stroboscopy (31579)

Do not report anterior rhinoscopy, tuning fork testing, otoscopy, or removal of cerumen (non-impacted) separately

92502 Otolaryngologic examination under general anesthesia [T][80]
  2.70 2.70 Global Days 000

92504 Binocular microscopy (separate diagnostic procedure) [N][80]
  0.28 0.82 Global Days XXX
  AMA: 2009, Jan, 11-31; 2008, Jan, 10-25; 2007, January, 13-27; 2005, January, 46-47; 2005, July, 13-16

● New Code ▲ Revised Code Maternity Age Unlisted Not Covered # Resequenced
CCI + Add-on Mod 51 Exempt Mod 63 Exempt Mod Sedation PQRI
© 2009 Publisher (Blue Ink)   CPT only © 2009 American Medical Association. All Rights Reserved. (Black Ink)   Medicare (Red Ink)

92506 Evaluation of speech, language, voice, communication, and/or auditory processing
INCLUDES
Evaluation of:
Expressive language abilities
Receptive language
Speech production
Examination of:
Appropriate formulation/utterance of expressive thought
Articulatory movements of oral musculature
Capability of understanding the meaning/intent of written/verbal expressions
Speech sound production

1.30 4.60 Global Days XXX
AMA: 2009, Jan, 11-31; 2009, Mar, 10-11; 2008, Jan, 10-25; 2007, January, 13-27; 2006, January, 7-10,47; 2005, March, 7-10

92507 Treatment of speech, language, voice, communication, and/or auditory processing disorder; individual
EXCLUDES
Auditory rehabilitation:
Postlingual hearing loss (92633)
Prelingual hearing loss (92630)
Programming of cochlear implant (92601-92604)

0.75 1.91 Global Days XXX
AMA: 2006, January, 7-10,47

92508 group, 2 or more individuals
EXCLUDES
Auditory rehabilitation:
Postlingual hearing loss (92633)
Prelingual hearing loss (92630)
Programming of cochlear implant (92601-92604)

0.39 1.02 Global Days XXX

92511 Nasopharyngoscopy with endoscope (separate procedure)
1.66 4.10 Global Days 000

92512 Nasal function studies (eg, rhinomanometry)
0.83 1.61 Global Days XXX

92516 Facial nerve function studies (eg, electroneuronography)
0.65 1.73 Global Days XXX

92520 Laryngeal function studies (ie, aerodynamic testing and acoustic testing)
EXCLUDES
Other laryngeal function testing (92700)
Swallowing/laryngeal sensory testing with flexible fiberoptic endoscope (92611-92617)

Code also modifier 52 for single test
1.14 1.87 Global Days XXX
AMA: 2006, January, 7-10,47

92526 Treatment of swallowing dysfunction and/or oral function for feeding
1.87 2.01 Global Days XXX

92531 Spontaneous nystagmus, including gaze
Do not report with evaluation and management services
0.00 0.00 Global Days XXX

92532 Positional nystagmus test
Do not report with evaluation and management services
0.00 0.00 Global Days XXX

92533 Caloric vestibular test, each irrigation (binaural, bithermal stimulation constitutes 4 tests)
INCLUDES Barany caloric test
0.00 0.00 Global Days XXX

92534 Optokinetic nystagmus test
0.00 0.00 Global Days XXX

● **92540 Basic vestibular evaluation, includes spontaneous nystagmus test with eccentric gaze fixation nystagmus, with recording, positional nystagmus test, minimum of 4 positions, with recording, optokinetic nystagmus test, bidirectional foveal and peripheral stimulation, with recording, and oscillating tracking test, with recording**
Do not report with 92541-92542, 92544-92545, (92541-92542, 92544-92545)
2.63 2.63 Global Days XXX

92541 Spontaneous nystagmus test, including gaze and fixation nystagmus, with recording
Do not report with (92542, 92544-92545)
0.80 0.80 Global Days XXX
AMA: 2009, May, 8-9&11; 2005, February, 13-16

92542 Positional nystagmus test, minimum of 4 positions, with recording
Do not report with (92541, 92544-92545)
0.69 0.69 Global Days XXX
AMA: 2009, May, 8-9&11; 2005, February, 13-16

92543 Caloric vestibular test, each irrigation (binaural, bithermal stimulation constitutes 4 tests), with recording
0.37 0.37 Global Days XXX
AMA: 2009, Jan, 11-31; 2009, May, 8-9&11; 2008, Jan, 10-25; 2007, January, 13-27; 2006, September, 14-16; 2005, February, 13-16

92544 Optokinetic nystagmus test, bidirectional, foveal or peripheral stimulation, with recording
Do not report with (92541-92542, 92545)
0.59 0.59 Global Days XXX
AMA: 2009, May, 8-9&11; 2005, February, 13-16

92545 Oscillating tracking test, with recording
0.55 0.55 Global Days XXX
AMA: 2009, May, 8-9&11; 2005, February, 13-16

92546 Sinusoidal vertical axis rotational testing
2.49 2.49 Global Days XXX
AMA: 2009, Jan, 11-31; 2009, May, 8-9&11; 2008, Jan, 10-25; 2007, January, 13-27; 2005, February, 13-16

+ **92547 Use of vertical electrodes (List separately in addition to code for primary procedure)**
Code first vestibular function tests with recording/medical diagnostic evaluation (92541-92546)
0.13 0.13 Global Days ZZZ
AMA: 2009, Jan, 11-31; 2009, May, 8-9&11; 2008, Jan, 10-25; 2007, January, 13-27; 2005, February, 13-16

92548 Computerized dynamic posturography
2.72 2.72 Global Days XXX

Current Procedural Coding Expert – Medicine

92550-92596 Hearing and Speech Tests

CMS 100-2,15,230.3 — Practice of Speech-Language Pathology
CMS 100-4,5,10.2 — Financial Limitation for Outpatient Rehabilitation Services
CMS 100-4,12,30.3 — Audiological Diagnostic Tests, Speech-Language Evaluations and Treatments

INCLUDES Diagnostic/treatment services not generally included in a comprehensive otorhinolaryngologic evaluation or office visit
Testing of both ears. When one ear is tested, append modifier 52.
Use of calibrated electronic equipment, recording of results, and a report with interpretation

EXCLUDES Evaluation of speech/language/hearing problems using observation/assessment of performance

Do not report tuning fork or whispered voice hearing tests separately

● **92550** Tympanometry and reflex threshold measurements
Do not report with (92567-92568)
0.57 0.57 Global Days XXX

92551 Screening test, pure tone, air only
0.28 0.28 Global Days XXX

92552 Pure tone audiometry (threshold); air only
0.67 0.67 Global Days XXX

92553 air and bone
0.81 0.81 Global Days XXX

92555 Speech audiometry threshold;
0.48 0.48 Global Days XXX

92556 with speech recognition
0.72 0.72 Global Days XXX

92557 Comprehensive audiometry threshold evaluation and speech recognition (92553 and 92556 combined)
EXCLUDES Evaluation/selection of hearing aid (92590-92595)
0.90 1.00 Global Days XXX

92559 Audiometric testing of groups
0.00 0.00 Global Days XXX

92560 Bekesy audiometry; screening
0.00 0.00 Global Days XXX

92561 diagnostic
0.87 0.87 Global Days XXX

92562 Loudness balance test, alternate binaural or monaural
INCLUDES ABLB test
0.97 0.97 Global Days XXX
AMA: 2005, March, 7-10

92563 Tone decay test
0.68 0.68 Global Days XXX

92564 Short increment sensitivity index (SISI)
0.63 0.63 Global Days XXX

92565 Stenger test, pure tone
0.32 0.32 Global Days XXX

92567 Tympanometry (impedance testing)
0.30 0.38 Global Days XXX

▲ **92568** Acoustic reflex testing, threshold
0.43 0.44 Global Days XXX
AMA: 2009, Jan, 11-31; 2009, Jun, 10-11; 2008, Jan, 10-25; 2007, January, 13-27; 2006, January, 7-10,47

~~92569~~ ~~Acoustic reflex testing; decay~~
To report, see code 92570

● **92570** Acoustic immittance testing, includes tympanometry (impedance testing), acoustic reflex threshold testing, and acoustic reflex decay testing
Do not report with (92567-92568)
0.82 0.87 Global Days XXX

92571 Filtered speech test
0.52 0.52 Global Days XXX
AMA: 2005, March, 7-10

92572 Staggered spondaic word test
1.08 1.08 Global Days XXX
AMA: 2005, March, 7-10

92575 Sensorineural acuity level test
1.37 1.37 Global Days XXX

92576 Synthetic sentence identification test
0.75 0.75 Global Days XXX
AMA: 2005, March, 7-10

92577 Stenger test, speech
0.36 0.36 Global Days XXX

92579 Visual reinforcement audiometry (VRA)
1.07 1.23 Global Days XXX

92582 Conditioning play audiometry
1.37 1.37 Global Days XXX

92583 Select picture audiometry
0.99 0.99 Global Days XXX

92584 Electrocochleography
1.52 1.52 Global Days XXX

92585 Auditory evoked potentials for evoked response audiometry and/or testing of the central nervous system; comprehensive
2.99 2.99 Global Days XXX

92586 limited
1.79 1.79 Global Days XXX

92587 Evoked otoacoustic emissions; limited (single stimulus level, either transient or distortion products)
0.88 0.88 Global Days XXX

92588 comprehensive or diagnostic evaluation (comparison of transient and/or distortion product otoacoustic emissions at multiple levels and frequencies)
EXCLUDES Evaluation of central auditory function (92620, 92621)
1.68 1.68 Global Days XXX

92590 Hearing aid examination and selection; monaural
0.00 0.00 Global Days XXX

92591 binaural
0.00 0.00 Global Days XXX

92592 Hearing aid check; monaural
0.00 0.00 Global Days XXX

92593 binaural
0.00 0.00 Global Days XXX

92594 Electroacoustic evaluation for hearing aid; monaural
0.00 0.00 Global Days XXX

92595 binaural
0.00 0.00 Global Days XXX

92596 Ear protector attenuation measurements
1.40 1.40 Global Days XXX

● New Code   ▲ Revised Code   Maternity   Age   Unlisted   Not Covered   # Resequenced
CCI   + Add-on   ⊘ Mod 51 Exempt   Mod 63 Exempt   ⊙ Mod Sedation   PQ PQRI
© 2009 Publisher (Blue Ink)   CPT only © 2009 American Medical Association. All Rights Reserved. (Black Ink)   Medicare (Red Ink)

92597 Services Related to Voice Prosthesis

INCLUDES Diagnostic/treatment services not generally included in a comprehensive otorhinolaryngologic evaluation or office visit
Use of calibrated electronic equipment

92597 Evaluation for use and/or fitting of voice prosthetic device to supplement oral speech

EXCLUDES Communication device services, augmentative/alternative (92605, 92607, 92608)

1.89 1.96 Global Days XXX

92601-92609 Services Related to Hearing and Speech Devices

CMS 100-2,15,80.3 Audiological Diagnostic Testing
CMS 100-3,50.1 Speech Generating Devices
CMS 100-3,50.2 Electronic Speech Aids
CMS 100-3,50.3 Cochlear Implantation
CMS 100-4,32,100 Billing Requirements for Cochlear Implantation

INCLUDES Diagnostic/treatment services not generally included in a comprehensive otorhinolaryngologic evaluation or office visit

92601 Diagnostic analysis of cochlear implant, patient younger than 7 years of age; with programming

INCLUDES Connection to cochlear implant
Postoperative analysis/fitting of previously placed external devices
Stimulator programming

EXCLUDES Cochlear implant placement (69930)

3.41 3.90 Global Days XXX
AMA: 2006, January, 7-10,47

92602 subsequent reprogramming

INCLUDES Internal stimulator re-programming
Subsequent sessions for external transmitter measurements/adjustment

EXCLUDES Aural rehabilitation services after a cochlear implant (92626-92627, 92630-92633)
Cochlear implant placement (69930)

Do not report with 92601

1.90 2.55 Global Days XXX
AMA: 2009, Jan, 11-31; 2008, Jan, 10-25; 2007, January, 13-27; 2006, January, 7-10,47

92603 Diagnostic analysis of cochlear implant, age 7 years or older; with programming

INCLUDES Connection to cochlear implant
Post-operative analysis/fitting of previously placed external devices
Stimulator programming

EXCLUDES Cochlear implant placement (69930)

3.37 3.88 Global Days XXX
AMA: 2006, January, 7-10,47

92604 subsequent reprogramming

INCLUDES Internal stimulator re-programming
Subsequent sessions for external transmitter measurements/adjustment

EXCLUDES Cochlear implant placement (69930)

Do not report with 92603

1.87 2.29 Global Days XXX
AMA: 2009, Jan, 11-31; 2008, Jan, 10-25; 2007, January, 13-27; 2006, January, 7-10,47

92605 Evaluation for prescription of non-speech-generating augmentative and alternative communication device

0.00 0.00 Global Days XXX

92606 Therapeutic service(s) for the use of non-speech-generating device, including programming and modification

0.00 0.00 Global Days XXX

92607 Evaluation for prescription for speech-generating augmentative and alternative communication device, face-to-face with the patient; first hour

EXCLUDES Evaluation for prescription of non-speech generating device (92605)

4.75 4.75 Global Days XXX

+ **92608** each additional 30 minutes (List separately in addition to code for primary procedure)
Code first initial hour (92607)

1.19 1.19 Global Days XXX

92609 Therapeutic services for the use of speech-generating device, including programming and modification

EXCLUDES Therapeutic services for use of non-speech generating device (92606)

2.73 2.73 Global Days XXX

92610-92617 Swallowing Evaluations

CMS 100-2,15,230.3 Practice of Speech-Language Pathology
CMS 100-3,170.3 Speech-language Pathology Services for Dysphagia

92610 Evaluation of oral and pharyngeal swallowing function

EXCLUDES Evaluation with flexible endoscope (92612-92617)
Motion fluoroscopic evaluation of swallowing function (92611)

1.88 2.10 Global Days XXX

92611 Motion fluoroscopic evaluation of swallowing function by cine or video recording

EXCLUDES Diagnostic flexible fiberoptic laryngoscopy (31575)
Evaluation of oral/pharyngeal swallowing function (92610)

74230

2.32 2.32 Global Days XXX
AMA: 2006, January, 7-10,47

92612 Flexible fiberoptic endoscopic evaluation of swallowing by cine or video recording;

EXCLUDES Flexible fiberoptic endoscopic examination/testing without cine or video recording (92700)

Do not report with diagnostic flexible fiberoptic laryngoscopy (31575)

1.92 4.45 Global Days XXX
AMA: 2009, Jan, 11-31; 2008, Jan, 10-25; 2007, January, 13-27; 2006, January, 7-10,47

92613 physician interpretation and report only

EXCLUDES Oral/pharyngeal swallowing function examination (92610)
Swallowing function motion fluoroscopic examination (92611)

Do not report with diagnostic flexible fiberoptic laryngoscopy (31575)

1.07 1.07 Global Days XXX
AMA: 2006, January, 7-10,47

26/TC PC/TC Comp Only	A2-Z3 ASC Pmt	50 Bilateral	♂ Male Only	♀ Female Only	Facility RVU	Non-Facility RVU
AMA: CPT Asst	**MED:** Pub 100	A-Y OPPSI	Non-FDA Drug	Lab Crosswalk	Radiology Crosswalk	

Current Procedural Coding Expert – Medicine 92971

92614	Flexible fiberoptic endoscopic evaluation, laryngeal sensory testing by cine or video recording; [A][80][M]	
	EXCLUDES *Flexible fiberoptic endoscopic examination/testing without cine or video recording (92700)*	
	Do not report with diagnostic flexible fiberoptic laryngoscopy (31575)	
	1.94 4.00 Global Days XXX	
	AMA: 2006, January, 7-10,47	
92615	physician interpretation and report only [E][80][M]	
	Do not report with diagnostic flexible fiberoptic laryngoscopy (31575)	
	0.95 0.95 Global Days XXX	
	AMA: 2006, January, 7-10,47	
92616	Flexible fiberoptic endoscopic evaluation of swallowing and laryngeal sensory testing by cine or video recording; [A][80][M]	
	EXCLUDES *Flexible fiberoptic endoscopic examination/testing without cine or video recording (92700)*	
	Do not report with diagnostic flexible fiberoptic laryngoscopy (31575)	
	2.82 5.32 Global Days XXX	
	AMA: 2006, January, 7-10,47	
92617	physician interpretation and report only [E][80][M]	
	Do not report with diagnostic flexible fiberoptic laryngoscopy (31575)	
	1.18 1.18 Global Days XXX	
	AMA: 2006, January, 7-10,47	

92620-92700 Diagnostic Hearing Evaluations and Rehabilitation

INCLUDES Diagnostic/treatment services not generally included in a comprehensive otorhinolaryngologic evaluation or office visit

92620	Evaluation of central auditory function, with report; initial 60 minutes [X][80][M][PQ]	
	Do not report with (92506)	
	2.30 2.53 Global Days XXX	
	AMA: 2005, March, 7-10	
92621	each additional 15 minutes [N][80][M][PQ]	
	Code first initial hour (92620)	
	Do not report with (92506)	
	0.51 0.59 Global Days ZZZ	
	AMA: 2005, March, 7-10	
92625	Assessment of tinnitus (includes pitch, loudness matching, and masking) [X][80][M][PQ]	
	Code also modifier 52 for unilateral procedure	
	Do not report with (92562)	
	1.71 1.88 Global Days XXX	
	AMA: 2005, March, 7-10	
92626	Evaluation of auditory rehabilitation status; first hour [X][80][PQ]	
	INCLUDES Face-to-face time spent with the patient or family	
	The ability of the patient to use residual hearing in order to identify acoustic characteristics of sounds associated with speech communication	
	2.07 2.36 Global Days XXX	
	AMA: 2006, January, 7-10,47	

+ 92627	each additional 15 minutes (List separately in addition to code for primary procedure) [N][80][PQ]	
	INCLUDES Face-to-face time spent with the patient or family	
	The ability of the patient to use residual hearing in order to identify acoustic characteristics of sounds associated with speech communication	
	Code first initial hour (92626)	
	0.49 0.57 Global Days ZZZ	
	AMA: 2006, January, 7-10,47	
92630	Auditory rehabilitation; prelingual hearing loss [E]	
	0.00 0.00 Global Days XXX	
	AMA: 2006, January, 7-10,47	
92633	postlingual hearing loss [E]	
	0.00 0.00 Global Days XXX	
	AMA: 2006, January, 7-10,47	
92640	Diagnostic analysis with programming of auditory brainstem implant, per hour [X][80][PQ]	
	EXCLUDES *Nonprogramming services (cardiac monitoring)*	
	2.68 3.00 Global Days XXX	
92700	Unlisted otorhinolaryngological service or procedure [X][80]	
	INCLUDES Lombard test	
	0.00 0.00 Global Days XXX	
	AMA: 2009, Jan, 11-31; 2008, Jan, 10-25; 2007, January, 13-27; 2006, September, 14-16; 2006, January, 7-10,47	

92950-92953 Emergency Cardiac Procedures

CMS 100-4,12,30.4   Cardiovascular System

92950	Cardiopulmonary resuscitation (eg, in cardiac arrest) [S][80][M]	
	EXCLUDES *Critical care (99291, 99292)*	
	4.88 7.49 Global Days 000	
	AMA: 2009, Jan, 11-31; 2008, Jan, 10-25; 2007, January, 13-27	
⊙ 92953	Temporary transcutaneous pacing [S][80][M]	
	EXCLUDES *Physician direction of ambulance/rescue personnel outside of the hospital (99288)*	
	0.30 0.30 Global Days 000	
	AMA: 2007, February, 10-11; 2007, Jul, 1-4	

92960-92961 Cardioversion

CMS 100-4,12,30.4   Cardiovascular System

⊙ 92960	Cardioversion, elective, electrical conversion of arrhythmia; external [S][80][M]	
	3.33 5.49 Global Days 000	
	AMA: 2009, Jan, 11-31; 2008, Jan, 10-25; 2007, January, 13-27	
⊙ 92961	internal (separate procedure) [S][M]	
	Do not report with (93282-93284, 93287, 93289, 93295-93296, 93618-93624, 93631, 93640-93642, 93650-93652, 93662)	
	6.67 6.67 Global Days 000	

92970-92971 Circulatory Assist: External/Internal

EXCLUDES *Atrial septostomy, balloon (92992)*
Catheter placement for use in circulatory assist devices (intra-aortic balloon pump) (33970)

92970	Cardioassist-method of circulatory assist; internal [C][80][M]	
	4.79 4.79 Global Days 000	
92971	external [C][80][M]	
	2.56 2.56 Global Days 000	

● New Code   ▲ Revised Code   [M] Maternity   [A] Age   Unlisted   Not Covered   # Resequenced
[CCI] CCI   + Add-on   ⊘ Mod 51 Exempt   ⊗ Mod 63 Exempt   ⊙ Mod Sedation   [PQ] PQRI

© 2009 Publisher *(Blue Ink)*   CPT only © 2009 American Medical Association. All Rights Reserved. (Black Ink)   Medicare (Red Ink)   367

92973-92979 Intravascular Coronary Procedures: Insert Brachytherapy Device; Treatment of Thrombosis; Ultrasound

CMS 100-4,12,30.4   Cardiovascular System

- **92973** Percutaneous transluminal coronary thrombectomy (List separately in addition to code for primary procedure)
  Code first primary procedure (92980, 92982)
  4.53   4.53   Global Days ZZZ
  AMA: 2009, Jan, 11-31; 2008, Jan, 10-25; 2007, January, 13-27

- **92974** Transcatheter placement of radiation delivery device for subsequent coronary intravascular brachytherapy (List separately in addition to code for primary procedure)
  EXCLUDES   Application of intravascular radioelement (77785-77787)
  Code first primary procedure (92980, 92982, 92995, 93508)
  4.17   4.17   Global Days ZZZ

- **92975** Thrombolysis, coronary; by intracoronary infusion, including selective coronary angiography
  EXCLUDES   Thrombolysis, cerebral (37195)
  Thrombolysis other than coronary (37201, 75896)
  10.05   10.05   Global Days 000

- **92977** by intravenous infusion
  EXCLUDES   Thrombolysis, cerebral (37195)
  Thrombolysis other than coronary (37201, 75896)
  1.26   1.26   Global Days XXX

- **92978** Intravascular ultrasound (coronary vessel or graft) during diagnostic evaluation and/or therapeutic intervention including imaging supervision, interpretation and report; initial vessel (List separately in addition to code for primary procedure)
  Code also (C1753)
  Code first primary procedure
  0.00   0.00   Global Days ZZZ
  AMA: 2009, Jan, 11-31; 2008, Jan, 10-25

- **92979** each additional vessel (List separately in addition to code for primary procedure)
  INCLUDES   Transducer manipulations/repositioning in the vessel examined, before and after therapeutic intervention
  EXCLUDES   Intravascular spectroscopy (0205T)
  Code first initial vessel (92978)
  0.00   0.00   Global Days ZZZ

92980-92984 Percutaneous Transluminal Angioplasty and Stent Placement

CMS 100-3,20.7   Percutaneous Transluminal Angioplasty (PTA)
CMS 100-4,12,30.4   Cardiovascular System

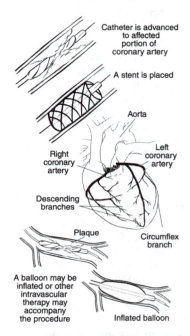

- **92980** Transcatheter placement of an intracoronary stent(s), percutaneous, with or without other therapeutic intervention, any method; single vessel
  INCLUDES   Coronary angioplasty/atherectomy in the same artery
  Coronary artery stenting
  EXCLUDES   Coronary brachytherapy (92974)
  Intravascular ultrasound (92978, 92979)
  Application of intravascular radioelement (77785-77787)
  Percutaneous transluminal coronary thrombectomy (92973)
  Code also (C1874, C1875, C1876, C1877)
  20.65   20.65   Global Days 000
  AMA: 2009, Jan, 11-31; 2008, Jan, 10-25; 2007, January, 13-27; 2005, April, 13-14; 2005, March, 11-15

- **92981** each additional vessel (List separately in addition to code for primary procedure)
  INCLUDES   Coronary angioplasty/atherectomy in the same artery
  Coronary artery stenting
  EXCLUDES   Additional vessels treated by only angioplasty or atherectomy during the same session (92984, 92996)
  Transcatheter placement of radiation delivery device for coronary intravascular brachytherapy (92974)
  Application of intravascular radioelement (77785-77787)
  Code also (C1874, C1875, C1876, C1877)
  Code first single vessel (92980)
  5.75   5.75   Global Days ZZZ
  AMA: 2009, Jan, 11-31; 2008, Jan, 10-25; 2007, January, 13-27

Current Procedural Coding Expert – Medicine

92982 Percutaneous transluminal coronary balloon angioplasty; single vessel
Code also (C1725, C1874, C1876, C1885)
15.31 15.31 Global Days 000
AMA: 2009, Jan, 11-31; 2008, Jan, 10-25; 2007, January, 13-27; 2005, April, 13-14

+ 92984 each additional vessel (List separately in addition to code for primary procedure)
EXCLUDES Application of intravascular radioelement (77785-77787)
Placement of stent after angioplasty/atherectomy completion (92980, 92981)
Transcatheter placement of radiation delivery device for coronary intravascular brachytherapy (92974)
Code also (C1725, C1874, C1876, C1885)
Code first single vessel (92980, 92982, 92995)
4.11 4.11 Global Days ZZZ
AMA: 2009, Jan, 11-31; 2008, Jan, 10-25; 2007, January, 13-27; 2005, April, 13-14

92986-92993 Percutaneous Procedures of Heart Valves and Septum
CMS 100-4,12,30.4 Cardiovascular System

92986 Percutaneous balloon valvuloplasty; aortic valve
34.04 34.04 Global Days 090

92987 mitral valve
35.05 35.05 Global Days 090

92990 pulmonary valve
27.50 27.50 Global Days 090

92992 Atrial septectomy or septostomy; transvenous method, balloon (eg, Rashkind type) (includes cardiac catheterization)
0.00 0.00 Global Days 090
AMA: 2009, Jan, 11-31; 2008, Jan, 10-25

92993 blade method (Park septostomy) (includes cardiac catheterization)
0.00 0.00 Global Days 090

92995-92996 Percutaneous Coronary Atherectomy
CMS 100-4,12,30.4 Cardiovascular System
Code also (C1714, C1724, C1885)

92995 Percutaneous transluminal coronary atherectomy, by mechanical or other method, with or without balloon angioplasty; single vessel
Code also (C1714, C1724, C1885)
16.84 16.84 Global Days 000

+ 92996 each additional vessel (List separately in addition to code for primary procedure)
Code also (C1714, C1724, C1885)
EXCLUDES Additional vessels treated by only angioplasty during the same session (92984)
Placement of stent after angioplasty/atherectomy completion (92980, 92981)
Code first single vessel (92980, 92982, 92995)
4.50 4.50 Global Days ZZZ

92997-92998 Percutaneous Angioplasty: Pulmonary Artery
CMS 100-4,12,30.4 Cardiovascular System

92997 Percutaneous transluminal pulmonary artery balloon angioplasty; single vessel
Code also (C1725, C1874, C1876, C1885, C2625)
16.69 16.69 Global Days 000

+ 92998 each additional vessel (List separately in addition to code for primary procedure)
Code also (C1725, C1874, C1876, C1885, C2625)
Code first single vessel (92997)
8.27 8.27 Global Days ZZZ

93000-93014 Electrocardiographic Services
CMS 100-3,20.15 Electrocardiographic Services
CMS 100-4,12,30.4 Cardiovascular System
INCLUDES Specific order for the service, a separate written and signed report, and documentation of medical necessity
Echocardiography (93303-93350)
EKG with 64 or more leads, graphic presentation, and analysis (0178T-0180T)
Use of these codes for the review of telemetry monitoring strips

93000 Electrocardiogram, routine ECG with at least 12 leads; with interpretation and report
EXCLUDES ECG monitoring (99354-99360)
0.47 0.47 Global Days XXX
AMA: 2008, Jul, 3&14; 2005, March, 1-6; 2005, March, 11-15; 2005, February, 7-9

93005 tracing only, without interpretation and report
EXCLUDES ECG monitoring (99354-99360)
0.23 0.23 Global Days XXX
AMA: 2005, March, 1-6

93010 interpretation and report only
EXCLUDES ECG monitoring (99354-99360)
0.24 0.24 Global Days XXX
AMA: 2007, April, 1-2; 2005, March, 11-15; 2005, March, 1-6

93012 Telephonic transmission of post-symptom electrocardiogram rhythm strip(s), 24-hour attended monitoring, per 30 day period of time; tracing only
3.55 3.55 Global Days XXX
AMA: 2009, Mar, 5-7; 2009, Feb, 3-12; 2005, October, 14-17

93014 physician review with interpretation and report only
Do not report with (93228-93229)
0.72 0.72 Global Days XXX
AMA: 2009, Mar, 5-7; 2009, Feb, 3-12; 2005, October, 14-17

93015-93018 Stress Test
CMS 100-3,20.10 Cardiac Rehabilitation Programs
CMS 100-3,20.15 Electrocardiographic Services
CMS 100-4,12,30.4 Cardiovascular System
EXCLUDES Inert gas rebreathing measurement (0104T, 0105T)

93015 Cardiovascular stress test using maximal or submaximal treadmill or bicycle exercise, continuous electrocardiographic monitoring, and/or pharmacological stress; with physician supervision, with interpretation and report
2.14 2.14 Global Days XXX
AMA: 2009, Jan, 11-31; 2008, Jan, 10-25; 2008, Jul, 3&14; 2007, January, 13-27; 2005, March, 11-15

	93016	physician supervision only, without interpretation and report [B][26][80]
		🔴 0.61 ⚫ 0.61 Global Days XXX
		AMA: 2009, Jan, 11-31; 2008, Jan, 10-25; 2008, Jul, 3&14; 2007, January, 13-27
	93017	tracing only, without interpretation and report [X][TC][80]
		🔴 1.12 ⚫ 1.12 Global Days XXX
		AMA: 2009, Jan, 11-31; 2008, Jan, 10-25; 2008, Jul, 3&14; 2007, January, 13-27
	93018	interpretation and report only [B][26][80]
		🔴 0.41 ⚫ 0.41 Global Days XXX
		AMA: 2009, Jan, 11-31; 2008, Jan, 10-25; 2008, Jul, 3&14; 2007, January, 13-27

93024 Provocation Test for Coronary Vasospasm

CMS 100-3,20.15 — Electrocardiographic Services
CMS 100-4,12,30.4 — Cardiovascular System

	93024	Ergonovine provocation test [X][80]
		🔴 2.89 ⚫ 2.89 Global Days XXX

93025 Microvolt T-Wave Alternans

CMS 100-3,20.30 — Microvolt T-Wave Alternans (MTWA)
CMS 100-4,12,30.4 — Cardiovascular System

INCLUDES Specific order for the service, a separate written and signed report, and documentation of medical necessity

EXCLUDES Echocardiography (93303-93350)
EKG with 64 or more leads, graphic presentation, and analysis (0178T-0180T)
Use of these codes for the review of telemetry monitoring strips

	93025	Microvolt T-wave alternans for assessment of ventricular arrhythmias [X][80]
		🔴 3.94 ⚫ 3.94 Global Days XXX

93040-93042 Rhythm Strips

CMS 100-3,20.15 — Electrocardiographic Services
CMS 100-4,12,30.4 — Cardiovascular System

EXCLUDES Echocardiography (93303-93350)
EKG with 64 or more leads, graphic presentation, and analysis (0178T-0180T)
Specific order for the service, a separate written and signed report, and documentation of medical necessity
Use of these codes for the review of telemetry monitoring strips

	93040	Rhythm ECG, 1-3 leads; with interpretation and report [B][80]
		🔴 0.34 ⚫ 0.34 Global Days XXX
		AMA: 2009, Feb, 3-12
	93041	tracing only without interpretation and report [X][TC][80]
		🔴 0.13 ⚫ 0.13 Global Days XXX
		AMA: 2009, Feb, 3-12
	93042	interpretation and report only [B][26][80]
		🔴 0.21 ⚫ 0.21 Global Days XXX
		AMA: 2009, Feb, 3-12

93224-93272 Ambulatory ECG Monitoring

CMS 100-3,20.15 — Electrocardiographic Services
CMS 100-4,12,30.4 — Cardiovascular System

INCLUDES Wearable mobile cardiovascular monitoring that transmits to a surveillance center for up to 30 days
Wearable mobile cardiovascular monitoring that does transmit to an attended surveillance center

EXCLUDES Echocardiography (93303-93352)
EKG with 64 or more leads, graphic presentation, and analysis (0178T-0180T)
Implantable patient activated cardiac event recorders (33282, 93285, 93291, 93298)

	93224	Wearable electrocardiographic rhythm derived monitoring for 24 hours by continuous original waveform recording and storage, with visual superimposition scanning; includes recording, scanning analysis with report, physician review and interpretation [M][80]
		🔴 2.25 ⚫ 2.25 Global Days XXX
		AMA: 2009, Mar, 5-7; 2009, Feb, 3-12; 2008, Mar, 4-5; 2007, April, 3-6; 2005, October, 14-17
	93225	recording (includes connection, recording, and disconnection) [S][TC][80]
		🔴 0.63 ⚫ 0.63 Global Days XXX
		AMA: 2009, Mar, 5-7; 2009, Feb, 3-12; 2008, Mar, 4-5; 2007, April, 3-6; 2005, October, 14-17
	93226	scanning analysis with report [S][TC][80]
		🔴 0.89 ⚫ 0.89 Global Days XXX
		AMA: 2009, Mar, 5-7; 2009, Feb, 3-12; 2008, Mar, 4-5; 2007, April, 3-6; 2005, October, 14-17
	93227	physician review and interpretation [M][26][80]
		🔴 0.73 ⚫ 0.73 Global Days XXX
		AMA: 2009, Mar, 5-7; 2009, Feb, 3-12; 2008, Mar, 4-5; 2007, April, 3-6; 2005, October, 14-17
	93228	Wearable mobile cardiovascular telemetry with electrocardiographic recording, concurrent computerized real time data analysis and greater than 24 hours of accessible ECG data storage (retrievable with query) with ECG triggered and patient selected events transmitted to a remote attended surveillance center for up to 30 days; physician review and interpretation with report [M][26][80]
		INCLUDES Reporting only once in a 30-day period
		Do not report with (93014)
		🔴 0.74 ⚫ 0.74 Global Days XXX
		AMA: 2009, Mar, 5-7; 2009, Feb, 3-12
	93229	technical support for connection and patient instructions for use, attended surveillance, analysis and physician prescribed transmission of daily and emergent data reports [S][TC][80]
		INCLUDES Reporting only once in a 30-day period
		Do not report with (93014)
		🔴 0.00 ⚫ 0.00 Global Days XXX
		AMA: 2009, Mar, 5-7; 2009, Feb, 3-12
	93230	Wearable electrocardiographic rhythm derived monitoring for 24 hours by continuous original waveform recording and storage without superimposition scanning utilizing a device capable of producing a full miniaturized printout; includes recording, microprocessor-based analysis with report, physician review and interpretation [M][80]
		🔴 2.29 ⚫ 2.29 Global Days XXX
		AMA: 2009, Mar, 5-7; 2009, Feb, 3-12; 2008, Mar, 4-5; 2007, April, 3-6; 2005, October, 14-17

[26/TC] PC/TC Comp Only [12-73] ASC Pmt [50] Bilateral ♂ Male Only ♀ Female Only 🔴 Facility RVU ⚫ Non-Facility RVU
AMA: CPT Asst **MED:** Pub 100 [A-Y] OPPSI ✗ Non-FDA Drug 📘 Lab Crosswalk 📕 Radiology Crosswalk

CPT only © 2009 American Medical Association. All Rights Reserved. (Black Ink) Medicare (Red Ink) © 2009 Publisher (Blue Ink)

Current Procedural Coding Expert – Medicine 93281

93231 recording (includes connection, recording, and disconnection) [S][TC][80]
🔹 0.55 🔹 0.55 **Global Days XXX**
AMA: 2009, Mar, 5-7; 2009, Feb, 3-12; 2008, Mar, 4-5; 2007, April, 3-6; 2005, October, 14-17

93232 microprocessor-based analysis with report [S][TC][80]
🔹 1.03 🔹 1.03 **Global Days XXX**
AMA: 2009, Mar, 5-7; 2009, Feb, 3-12; 2008, Mar, 4-5; 2007, April, 3-6; 2005, October, 14-17

93233 physician review and interpretation [M][26][80]
🔹 0.71 🔹 0.71 **Global Days XXX**
AMA: 2009, Mar, 5-7; 2009, Feb, 3-12; 2008, Mar, 4-5; 2007, April, 3-6; 2005, October, 14-17

93235 Wearable electrocardiographic rhythm derived monitoring for 24 hours by continuous computerized monitoring and non-continuous recording, and real-time data analysis utilizing a device capable of producing intermittent full-sized waveform tracings, possibly patient activated; includes monitoring and real-time data analysis with report, physician review and interpretation [M][80]
INCLUDES Holter monitor procedure
🔹 0.00 🔹 0.00 **Global Days XXX**
AMA: 2009, Mar, 5-7; 2009, Feb, 3-12; 2008, Mar, 4-5; 2007, April, 3-6; 2005, October, 14-17

93236 monitoring and real-time data analysis with report [S][TC][80]
🔹 0.00 🔹 0.00 **Global Days XXX**
AMA: 2009, Mar, 5-7; 2009, Feb, 3-12; 2008, Mar, 4-5; 2007, April, 3-6; 2005, October, 14-17

93237 physician review and interpretation [M][26][80]
🔹 0.62 🔹 0.62 **Global Days XXX**
AMA: 2009, Mar, 5-7; 2009, Feb, 3-12; 2008, Mar, 4-5; 2007, April, 3-6; 2005, October, 14-17

93268 Wearable patient activated electrocardiographic rhythm derived event recording with presymptom memory loop, 24-hour attended monitoring, per 30 day period of time; includes transmission, physician review and interpretation [M][80]
EXCLUDES Implanted patient activated cardiac event recording (33282, 93285, 93291, 93298)
Postsymptom recording (93012, 93014)
🔹 5.44 🔹 5.44 **Global Days XXX**
AMA: 2009, Mar, 5-7; 2009, Feb, 3-12; 2008, Mar, 4-5; 2007, April, 3-6; 2005, October, 14-17

93270 recording (includes connection, recording, and disconnection) [S][TC][80]
🔹 0.22 🔹 0.22 **Global Days XXX**
AMA: 2009, Mar, 5-7; 2009, Feb, 3-12; 2008, Mar, 4-5; 2007, April, 3-6; 2005, October, 14-17

93271 monitoring, receipt of transmissions, and analysis [S][TC][80]
🔹 4.52 🔹 4.52 **Global Days XXX**
AMA: 2009, Mar, 5-7; 2009, Feb, 3-12; 2008, Mar, 4-5; 2007, April, 3-6; 2005, October, 14-17

93272 physician review and interpretation [M][26][80]
🔹 0.70 🔹 0.70 **Global Days XXX**
AMA: 2009, Jan, 11-31; 2009, Mar, 5-7; 2009, Feb, 3-12; 2008, Jan, 10-25; 2008, Mar, 4-5; 2007, April, 3-6; 2007, January, 13-27; 2005, October, 14-17

93278 Signal-averaged Electrocardiography

CMS 100-3,20.15 — Electrocardiographic Services
CMS 100-4,12,30.4 — Cardiovascular System
EXCLUDES Echocardiography (93303-93352)
EKG with 64 or more leads, graphic presentation, and analysis (0178T-0180T)

93278 Signal-averaged electrocardiography (SAECG), with or without ECG [X][80]
🔹 0.78 🔹 0.78 **Global Days XXX**
AMA: 2009, Mar, 5-7; 2008, Mar, 4-5

93279-93299 Monitoring of Cardiovascular Devices

INCLUDES Cardioverter-defibrillator (ICD) interrogation:
Battery
Capture and sensing functions
Leads
Presence or absence of therapy for ventricular tachyarrhythmias
Programmed parameters
Underlying heart rhythm
Implantable cardiovascular monitor (ICM) interrogation:
Analysis of at least one recorded physiologic cardiovascular data element from either internal or external sensors
Programmed parameters
Implantable loop recorder (ILR) interrogation:
Heart rate and rhythm during recorded episodes from both patient-initiated and device detected events
Programmed parameters
Interrogation evaluation of device
Pacemaker interrogation:
Battery
Capture and sensing functions
Heart rhythm
Leads
Programmed parameters
Time period established by the initiation of remote monitoring or the 91st day of ICD or pacemaker monitoring or the 31st day of ILR monitoring and extends for the succeeding 30- or 90-day period
EXCLUDES Wearable device monitoring (93224-93272)

Code also programming device evaluation and remote device interrogation during the remote interrogation device evaluation timeframe.
Do not report in-person and remote interrogation of the same device during the same period
Do not report programming and in-person interrogation on the same day by the same physician

▲ **93279** Programming device evaluation (in person) with iterative adjustment of the implantable device to test the function of the device and select optimal permanent programmed values with physician analysis, review and report; single lead pacemaker system [S][80]
Do not report with (93286, 93288)
🔹 1.29 🔹 1.29 **Global Days XXX**
AMA: 2009, Feb, 3-12

▲ **93280** dual lead pacemaker system [S][80]
Do not report with (93286, 93288)
🔹 1.50 🔹 1.50 **Global Days XXX**
AMA: 2009, Feb, 3-12

▲ **93281** multiple lead pacemaker system [S][80]
Do not report with (93286, 93288)
🔹 1.74 🔹 1.74 **Global Days XXX**
AMA: 2009, Feb, 3-12

● New Code ▲ Revised Code [M] Maternity [A] Age Unlisted Not Covered # Resequenced
[CCI] CCI + Add-on ⊘ Mod 51 Exempt ⊕ Mod 63 Exempt ⊙ Mod Sedation [PQ] PQRI

© 2009 Publisher *(Blue Ink)* CPT only © 2009 American Medical Association. All Rights Reserved. (Black Ink) Medicare (Red Ink) 371

93282 — Current Procedural Coding Expert – Medicine

▲ **93282** single lead implantable cardioverter-defibrillator system [S][80]

Do not report with (93287, 93289, 93745)
🏥 1.62   🏠 1.62   **Global Days** XXX
AMA: 2009, Feb, 3-12

▲ **93283** dual lead implantable cardioverter-defibrillator system [S][80]

Do not report with (93287, 93289)
🏥 2.10   🏠 2.10   **Global Days** XXX
AMA: 2009, Feb, 3-12

▲ **93284** multiple lead implantable cardioverter-defibrillator system [S][80]

Do not report with (93287, 93289)
🏥 2.30   🏠 2.30   **Global Days** XXX
AMA: 2009, Feb, 3-12

▲ **93285** implantable loop recorder system [S][80]

Do not report with (33282, 93279-93284, 93291)
🏥 1.07   🏠 1.07   **Global Days** XXX
AMA: 2009, Mar, 5-7; 2009, Feb, 3-12

▲ **93286** Peri-procedural device evaluation (in person) and programming of device system parameters before or after a surgery, procedure, or test with physician analysis, review and report; single, dual, or multiple lead pacemaker system [N][80]

INCLUDES   One evaluation and programming (if performed once before and once after, report as two units)

Do not report with (93279-93281, 93288)
🏥 0.74   🏠 0.74   **Global Days** XXX
AMA: 2009, Feb, 3-12

▲ **93287** single, dual, or multiple lead implantable cardioverter-defibrillator system [N][80]

INCLUDES   One evaluation and programming (if performed once before and once after, report as two units)

Do not report with (93282-93284, 93289)
🏥 0.97   🏠 0.97   **Global Days** XXX
AMA: 2009, Feb, 3-12

93288 Interrogation device evaluation (in person) with physician analysis, review and report, includes connection, recording and disconnection per patient encounter; single, dual, or multiple lead pacemaker system [S][80]

INCLUDES   Correct operation of:
    Battery
    Capture and sensing
    Heart rhythm
    Lead(s)
    Programmed settings

Do not report with (93012, 93014, 93040-93042, 93279-93281, 93286, 93294, 93296)
🏥 0.94   🏠 0.94   **Global Days** XXX
AMA: 2009, Feb, 3-12

93289 single, dual, or multiple lead implantable cardioverter-defibrillator system, including analysis of heart rhythm derived data elements [S][80]

EXCLUDES   Monitoring physiologic cardiovascular data elements derived from an ICD (93290)

Do not report with (93282-93284, 93287, 93295-93296)
🏥 1.69   🏠 1.69   **Global Days** XXX
AMA: 2009, Feb, 3-12

93290 implantable cardiovascular monitor system, including analysis of 1 or more recorded physiologic cardiovascular data elements from all internal and external sensors [S][80]

EXCLUDES   Heart rhythm derived data (93289)

Do not report with (93297, 93299)
🏥 0.86   🏠 0.86   **Global Days** XXX
AMA: 2009, Feb, 3-12

93291 implantable loop recorder system, including heart rhythm derived data analysis [S][80]

Do not report with (33282, 93288-93290, 93298-93299)
🏥 0.92   🏠 0.92   **Global Days** XXX
AMA: 2009, Mar, 5-7; 2009, Feb, 3-12

93292 wearable defibrillator system [S][80]

Do not report with (93745)
🏥 0.83   🏠 0.83   **Global Days** XXX
AMA: 2009, Feb, 3-12

93293 Transtelephonic rhythm strip pacemaker evaluation(s) single, dual, or multiple lead pacemaker system, includes recording with and without magnet application with physician analysis, review and report(s), up to 90 days [S][80]

EXCLUDES   In-person evaluation (93040-93042)

Do not report more than once in a 90 day period
Do not report when monitoring period is less than 30 days
Do not report with (93294)
🏥 1.33   🏠 1.33   **Global Days** XXX
AMA: 2009, Feb, 3-12

93294 Interrogation device evaluation(s) (remote), up to 90 days; single, dual, or multiple lead pacemaker system with interim physician analysis, review(s) and report(s) [M][26][80]

Do not report more than once in a 90 day period
Do not report when monitoring period is less than 30 days
Do not report with (93288, 93293)
🏥 0.90   🏠 0.90   **Global Days** XXX
AMA: 2009, Feb, 3-12

93295 single, dual, or multiple lead implantable cardioverter-defibrillator system with interim physician analysis, review(s) and reports(s) [M][26][80]

EXCLUDES   Remote monitoring of physiological cardiovascular ICD data (93297)

Do not report more than once in a 90 day period
Do not report when monitoring period is less than 30 days
Do not report with (93289)
🏥 1.78   🏠 1.78   **Global Days** XXX
AMA: 2009, Feb, 3-12

93296 single, dual, or multiple lead pacemaker system or implantable cardioverter-defibrillator system, remote data acquisition(s), receipt of transmissions and technician review, technical support and distribution of results [S][TC][80]

Do not report more than once in a 90 day period
Do not report with (93288-93289, 93299)
🏥 0.72   🏠 0.72   **Global Days** XXX
AMA: 2009, Feb, 3-12

[26/TC] PC/TC Comp Only   [A2-Z3] ASC Pmt   [50] Bilateral   ♂ Male Only   ♀ Female Only   🏥 Facility RVU   🏠 Non-Facility RVU
AMA: CPT Asst   **MED:** Pub 100   [A-Y] OPPSI   ✗ Non-FDA Drug   ▌ Lab Crosswalk   ⊞ Radiology Crosswalk
CPT only © 2009 American Medical Association. All Rights Reserved. (Black Ink)   Medicare (Red Ink)   © 2009 Publisher (Blue Ink)

Current Procedural Coding Expert – Medicine

93297 Interrogation device evaluation(s), (remote) up to 30 days; implantable cardiovascular monitor system, including analysis of 1 or more recorded physiologic cardiovascular data elements from all internal and external sensors, physician analysis, review(s) and report(s) [M][26][80]

    EXCLUDES Heart rhythm derived data (93295)

Do not report more than once in a 30 day period

Do not report when monitoring period is less than 10 days

Do not report with (93290, 93298)

    0.74   0.74 **Global Days XXX**
    AMA: 2009, Feb, 3-12

93298 implantable loop recorder system, including analysis of recorded heart rhythm data, physician analysis, review(s) and report(s) [M][26][80]

Do not report more than once in a 30 day period

Do not report when monitoring period is less than 10 days

Do not report with (33282, 93291, 93297)

    0.73   0.73 **Global Days XXX**
    AMA: 2009, Mar, 5-7; 2009, Feb, 3-12

93299 implantable cardiovascular monitor system or implantable loop recorder system, remote data acquisition(s), receipt of transmissions and technician review, technical support and distribution of results [S][TC][80]

Do not report more than once in a 30 day period

Do not report when monitoring period is less than 10 days

Do not report with (93290-93291, 93296)

    0.00   0.00 **Global Days XXX**
    AMA: 2009, Feb, 3-12

93303-93352 Echocardiography

CMS 100-4,4,200.7.1 Cardiac Echocardiography Without Contrast
CMS 100-4,12,30.4 Cardiovascular System

INCLUDES Interpretation and report
Obtaining ultrasonic signals from heart/great arteries
Report of study which includes:
    Description of recognized abnormalities
    Documentation of all clinically relevent findings which includes obtained quantitative measurements
    Interpretation of all information obtained
Two-dimensional image/doppler ultrasonic signal documentation
Ultrasound exam of:
    Adjacent great vessels
    Cardiac chambers/valves
    Pericardium

EXCLUDES Contrast agents and/or drugs used for pharmacogical stress
Echocardiography, fetal (76825-76828)
Ultrasound without thorough examination of the organ(s) or anatomic region/documentation of the image/final written report

93303 Transthoracic echocardiography for congenital cardiac anomalies; complete [S][80]

    4.90   4.90 **Global Days XXX**
    AMA: 2009, Jan, 11-31; 2008, Mar, 4-5; 2008, Jan, 10-25; 2007, January, 13-27

93304 follow-up or limited study [S][80]

    3.26   3.26 **Global Days XXX**
    AMA: 2008, Mar, 4-5

93306 Echocardiography, transthoracic, real-time with image documentation (2D), includes M-mode recording, when performed, complete, with spectral Doppler echocardiography, and with color flow Doppler echocardiography [S][80]

    INCLUDES 2-dimensional and M-mode
    Doppler and color flow

    EXCLUDES Transthoracic without spectral and color doppler (93307)

    4.81   4.81 **Global Days XXX**

93307 Echocardiography, transthoracic, real-time with image documentation (2D), includes M-mode recording, when performed, complete, without spectral or color Doppler echocardiography [S][80]

    INCLUDES 2-dimensional/selected M-mode exam of:
        Adjacent portions of the aorta
        Aortic/mitral/tricuspid valves
        Left/right atria
        Left/right ventricles
        Pericardium
    Additional structures that may be viewed such as pulmonary vein or artery, pulmonic valve, inferior vena cava
    Obtaining/recording appropriate measurements
    Using multiple views as required to obtain a complete functional/anatomic evaluation

Do not report with (93320-93321, 93325)

    2.82   2.82 **Global Days XXX**
    AMA: 2009, Jan, 11-31; 2008, Mar, 4-5; 2008, Jan, 10-25; 2007, January, 13-27; 2005, March, 11-15; 2005, September, 9-11

93308 Echocardiography, transthoracic, real-time with image documentation (2D), includes M-mode recording, when performed, follow-up or limited study [S][80]

    INCLUDES An exam that does not evaluate/document the attempt to evaluate all the structures that comprise the complete echocardiographic exam

    2.42   2.42 **Global Days XXX**
    AMA: 2009, Jan, 11-31; 2008, Jan, 10-25; 2008, Mar, 4-5; 2007, January, 13-27; 2005, September, 9-11

⊙ **93312** Echocardiography, transesophageal, real-time with image documentation (2D) (with or without M-mode recording); including probe placement, image acquisition, interpretation and report [S][80]

    7.88   7.88 **Global Days XXX**
    AMA: 2009, Jan, 11-31; 2008, Mar, 4-5; 2008, Jan, 10-25; 2007, January, 13-27

⊙ **93313** placement of transesophageal probe only [S][80]

    1.17   1.17 **Global Days XXX**
    AMA: 2008, Mar, 4-5

⊙ **93314** image acquisition, interpretation and report only [N][80]

    7.00   7.00 **Global Days XXX**
    AMA: 2008, Mar, 4-5

⊙ **93315** Transesophageal echocardiography for congenital cardiac anomalies; including probe placement, image acquisition, interpretation and report [S][80]

    0.00   0.00 **Global Days XXX**
    AMA: 2008, Mar, 4-5

⊙ **93316** placement of transesophageal probe only [S][80]

    1.22   1.22 **Global Days XXX**
    AMA: 2008, Mar, 4-5

● New Code   ▲ Revised Code   [M] Maternity   Age   Unlisted   Not Covered   # Resequenced

[CCI]   + Add-on   ⊘ Mod 51 Exempt   Mod 63 Exempt   ⊙ Mod Sedation   [PQ] PQRI

© 2009 Publisher *(Blue Ink)*   CPT only © 2009 American Medical Association. All Rights Reserved. *(Black Ink)*   Medicare *(Red Ink)*

93317 — Current Procedural Coding Expert – Medicine

- **93317** image acquisition, interpretation and report only
  - 0.00 | 0.00 Global Days XXX
  - **AMA:** 2008, Mar, 4-5

- **93318** Echocardiography, transesophageal (TEE) for monitoring purposes, including probe placement, real time 2-dimensional image acquisition and interpretation leading to ongoing (continuous) assessment of (dynamically changing) cardiac pumping function and to therapeutic measures on an immediate time basis
  - 0.00 | 0.00 Global Days XXX
  - **AMA:** 2008, Mar, 4-5

- **+ 93320** Doppler echocardiography, pulsed wave and/or continuous wave with spectral display (List separately in addition to codes for echocardiographic imaging); complete
  - Code first (93303-93304, 93312, 93314-93315, 93317, 93350-93351)
  - 1.16 | 1.16 Global Days ZZZ
  - **AMA:** 2008, Mar, 4-5; 2005, March, 11-15

- **+ 93321** follow-up or limited study (List separately in addition to codes for echocardiographic imaging)
  - Code first (93303-93304, 93308, 93312, 93314-93315, 93317, 93350-93351)
  - 0.61 | 0.61 Global Days ZZZ
  - **AMA:** 2008, Mar, 4-5

- **+ 93325** Doppler echocardiography color flow velocity mapping (List separately in addition to codes for echocardiography)
  - Code first (76825-76828, 93303-93304, 93308, 93312, 93314-93315, 93317, 93350-93351)
  - 0.50 | 0.50 Global Days ZZZ
  - **AMA:** 2008, Mar, 4-5; 2005, March, 11-15

- **93350** Echocardiography, transthoracic, real-time with image documentation (2D), includes M-mode recording, when performed, during rest and cardiovascular stress test using treadmill, bicycle exercise and/or pharmacologically induced stress, with interpretation and report;
  - Code also exercise stress testing (93016-93018)
  - Do not report with (93015)
  - 5.11 | 5.11 Global Days XXX
  - **AMA:** 2009, Jan, 11-31; 2008, Mar, 4-5; 2008, Jan, 10-25; 2007, January, 13-27

- **93351** including performance of continuous electrocardiographic monitoring, with physician supervision
  - Do not report with (93015-93018, 93350)
  - 5.92 | 5.92 Global Days XXX

- **+ 93352** Use of echocardiographic contrast agent during stress echocardiography (List separately in addition to code for primary procedure)
  - Code also (93350, 93351)
  - Do not report more than once for each stress echocardiogram
  - 0.82 | 0.82 Global Days ZZZ

93501-93562 Heart Catheterization and Injection Procedures

CMS 100-4,12,30.4 Cardiovascular System

INCLUDES
Catheter(s):
  Introduction
  Positioning
  Repositioning
Final evaluation
Intracardiac pressure recording
Intravascular pressure recording
Obtaining blood samples
Report

EXCLUDES *Selective injection procedures without cardiac catheterization (36011-36015, 36215-36218)*

- **93501** Right heart catheterization
  - **EXCLUDES** Bundle of His recording (93600)
  - 16.66 | 16.66 Global Days 000
  - **AMA:** 2009, Jan, 11-31; 2008, Jan, 10-25; 2008, Mar, 4-5; 2007, January, 13-27

- **93503** Insertion and placement of flow directed catheter (eg, Swan-Ganz) for monitoring purposes
  - **EXCLUDES** Subsequent monitoring (99356-99357)
  - 3.86 | 3.86 Global Days 000
  - **AMA:** 2008, Mar, 4-5

- **93505** Endomyocardial biopsy
  - 19.65 | 19.65 Global Days 000
  - **AMA:** 2009, Jan, 11-31; 2008, Mar, 4-5; 2008, Jan, 10-25; 2007, January, 13-27

26/TC PC/TC Comp Only | A2-A3 ASC Pmt | 50 Bilateral | ♂ Male Only | ♀ Female Only | Facility RVU | Non-Facility RVU
AMA: CPT Asst | **MED:** Pub 100 | A-Y OPPSI | Non-FDA Drug | Lab Crosswalk | Radiology Crosswalk

Current Procedural Coding Expert – Medicine

93508 Catheter placement in coronary artery(s), arterial coronary conduit(s), and/or venous coronary bypass graft(s) for coronary angiography without concomitant left heart catheterization

> INCLUDES: Reporting only once per procedure
>
> EXCLUDES: Application of intravascular radioelement (77785-77787)
> Left heart catheterization (93510, 93511, 93524, 93526)
> Transcatheter placement of radiation delivery device for coronary intravascular brachytherapy (92974)
>
> Code also imaging supervision, interpretation and report (93556)
> Code also injection procedures (93539, 93540, 93544, 93545)
> 24.93   24.93   Global Days 000
> AMA: 2009, Jan, 11-31; 2008, Jan, 10-25; 2008, Mar, 4-5; 2007, Dec, 10-179; 2007, January, 13-27

93510 Left heart catheterization, retrograde, from the brachial artery, axillary artery or femoral artery; percutaneous
> 24.67   24.67   Global Days 000
> AMA: 2008, Mar, 4-5; 2005, March, 11-15

93511 by cutdown
> 0.00   0.00   Global Days 000
> AMA: 2008, Mar, 4-5

93514 Left heart catheterization by left ventricular puncture
> 0.00   0.00   Global Days 000
> AMA: 2008, Mar, 4-5

93524 Combined transseptal and retrograde left heart catheterization
> 0.00   0.00   Global Days 000
> AMA: 2008, Mar, 4-5

93526 Combined right heart catheterization and retrograde left heart catheterization
> 31.32   31.32   Global Days 000
> AMA: 2008, Mar, 4-5

93527 Combined right heart catheterization and transseptal left heart catheterization through intact septum (with or without retrograde left heart catheterization)
> 0.00   0.00   Global Days 000
> AMA: 2008, Mar, 4-5

93528 Combined right heart catheterization with left ventricular puncture (with or without retrograde left heart catheterization)
> 0.00   0.00   Global Days 000
> AMA: 2008, Mar, 4-5

93529 Combined right heart catheterization and left heart catheterization through existing septal opening (with or without retrograde left heart catheterization)
> 0.00   0.00   Global Days 000
> AMA: 2008, Mar, 4-5

93530 Right heart catheterization, for congenital cardiac anomalies
> 0.00   0.00   Global Days 000
> AMA: 2009, Jan, 11-31; 2008, Jan, 10-25; 2008, Mar, 4-5; 2007, January, 13-27

93531 Combined right heart catheterization and retrograde left heart catheterization, for congenital cardiac anomalies
> 0.00   0.00   Global Days 000
> AMA: 2008, Mar, 4-5

93532 Combined right heart catheterization and transseptal left heart catheterization through intact septum with or without retrograde left heart catheterization, for congenital cardiac anomalies
> 0.00   0.00   Global Days 000
> AMA: 2009, Jan, 11-31; 2008, Jan, 10-25; 2008, Mar, 4-5; 2007, January, 13-27

93533 Combined right heart catheterization and transseptal left heart catheterization through existing septal opening, with or without retrograde left heart catheterization, for congenital cardiac anomalies
> 0.00   0.00   Global Days 000
> AMA: 2008, Mar, 4-5

93539 Injection procedure during cardiac catheterization; for selective opacification of arterial conduits (eg, internal mammary), whether native or used for bypass
> 93556
> 0.55   2.19   Global Days 000
> AMA: 2009, Jan, 11-31; 2008, Jan, 10-25; 2008, Mar, 4-5; 2007, Dec, 10-179; 2007, January, 13-27

93540 for selective opacification of aortocoronary venous bypass grafts, 1 or more coronary arteries
> 93556
> 0.59   6.69   Global Days 000
> AMA: 2008, Mar, 4-5; 2007, Dec, 10-179

93541 for pulmonary angiography
> 93556
> 0.40   0.40   Global Days 000
> AMA: 2008, Mar, 4-5; 2007, Dec, 10-179

93542 for selective right ventricular or right atrial angiography
> 93555
> 0.40   4.10   Global Days 000
> AMA: 2008, Mar, 4-5; 2007, Dec, 10-179

93543 for selective left ventricular or left atrial angiography
> 93555
> 0.40   2.19   Global Days 000
> AMA: 2008, Mar, 4-5; 2007, Dec, 10-179

93544 for aortography
> 93556
> 0.34   1.59   Global Days 000
> AMA: 2008, Mar, 4-5; 2007, Dec, 10-179

93545 for selective coronary angiography (injection of radiopaque material may be by hand)
> 93556
> 0.55   4.67   Global Days 000
> AMA: 2009, Jan, 11-31; 2008, Mar, 4-5; 2008, Jan, 10-25; 2007, Dec, 10-179; 2007, January, 13-27

93555 Imaging supervision, interpretation and report for injection procedure(s) during cardiac catheterization; ventricular and/or atrial angiography
> Code also (93542, 93543)
> 1.22   1.22   Global Days XXX
> AMA: 2009, Jan, 11-31; 2008, Mar, 4-5; 2008, Jan, 10-25; 2007, January, 13-27

93556 pulmonary angiography, aortography, and/or selective coronary angiography including venous bypass grafts and arterial conduits (whether native or used in bypass)
> Code also (93539-93541, 93544-93545)
> 1.43   1.43   Global Days XXX
> AMA: 2009, Jan, 11-31; 2008, Mar, 4-5; 2008, Jan, 10-25; 2007, Dec, 10-179; 2007, January, 13-27

● New Code   ▲ Revised Code   M Maternity   Age   Unlisted   Not Covered   # Resequenced
□ CCI   + Add-on   ⊘ Mod 51 Exempt   Mod 63 Exempt   ⊙ Mod Sedation   PQRI

© 2009 Publisher (Blue Ink)   CPT only © 2009 American Medical Association. All Rights Reserved. (Black Ink)   Medicare (Red Ink)

93561

Current Procedural Coding Expert – Medicine

93561 Indicator dilution studies such as dye or thermal dilution, including arterial and/or venous catheterization; with cardiac output measurement (separate procedure)
EXCLUDES *Cardiac output, radioisotope method (78472, 78473, 78481)*
Do not report with cardiac catheterization codes
0.00   0.00   Global Days 000
AMA: 2009, Jan, 11-31; 2008, Jan, 10-25; 2008, Mar, 4-5; 2007, Jul, 1-4; 2007, February, 10-11

93562 subsequent measurement of cardiac output
EXCLUDES *Cardiac output, radioisotope method (78472, 78473, 78481)*
Do not report with cardiac catheterization codes
0.00   0.00   Global Days 000
AMA: 2008, Mar, 4-5; 2007, February, 10-11; 2007, Jul, 1-4

93571-93572 Coronary Artery Doppler Studies

CMS 100-4,12,30.4   Cardiovascular System
INCLUDES Doppler transducer manipulations/repositioning within the vessel examined, during coronary angiography/therapeutic intervention (angioplasty)

+ 93571 Intravascular Doppler velocity and/or pressure derived coronary flow reserve measurement (coronary vessel or graft) during coronary angiography including pharmacologically induced stress; initial vessel (List separately in addition to code for primary procedure)
Code first primary procedure
0.00   0.00   Global Days ZZZ
AMA: 2008, Mar, 4-5

+ 93572 each additional vessel (List separately in addition to code for primary procedure)
Code first: initial vessel (93571)
0.00   0.00   Global Days ZZZ
AMA: 2008, Mar, 4-5

93580-93581 Percutaneous Repair of Septal Defect

CMS 100-4,12,30.4   Cardiovascular System
INCLUDES Injection of contrast for atrial/ventricular angiograms
Right heart catheterization
EXCLUDES *Closure of ventricular septal defect with transmyocardial implant delivery (0166T, 0167T)*
Echocardiography (93303-93317, 93662)
Do not report with (93501, 93529-93533, 93539, 93543, 93555)

93580 Percutaneous transcatheter closure of congenital interatrial communication (ie, Fontan fenestration, atrial septal defect) with implant
25.16   25.16   Global Days 000
AMA: 2009, Jan, 11-31; 2008, Jan, 10-25; 2008, Mar, 4-5; 2007, January, 13-27

93581 Percutaneous transcatheter closure of a congenital ventricular septal defect with implant
33.97   33.97   Global Days 000
AMA: 2009, Jan, 11-31; 2008, Mar, 4-5; 2008, Jan, 10-25; 2007, January, 13-27

93600-93603 Recording of Intracardiac Electrograms

CMS 100-3,20.13   HIS Bundle Study
CMS 100-4,12,30.4   Cardiovascular System
INCLUDES Unusual situations where there may be recording/pacing/attempt at arrhythmia induction from only one side of the heart

93600 Bundle of His recording
Code also (C1730, C1731, C1732, C1733, C1766, C1892, C1893, C1894, C2629, C2630)
0.00   0.00   Global Days 000
AMA: 2009, Jan, 11-31; 2008, Jan, 10-25; 2008, Mar, 4-5; 2007, Dec, 10-179; 2007, January, 13-27; 2005, August, 13-15

93602 Intra-atrial recording
Code also (C1730, C1731, C1732, C1733, C1766, C1892, C1893, C1894, C2629, C2630)
0.00   0.00   Global Days 000
AMA: 2009, Jan, 11-31; 2008, Jan, 10-25; 2008, Mar, 4-5; 2007, January, 13-27; 2005, August, 13-15

93603 Right ventricular recording
Code also (C1730, C1731, C1732, C1733, C1766, C1892, C1893, C1894, C2629, C2630)
0.00   0.00   Global Days 000
AMA: 2008, Mar, 4-5; 2005, August, 13-15

93609-93613 Intracardiac Mapping and Pacing

CMS 100-3,20.12   Diagnostic Endocardial Electrical Stimulation (Pacing)
CMS 100-4,12,30.4   Cardiovascular System

+ 93609 Intraventricular and/or intra-atrial mapping of tachycardia site(s) with catheter manipulation to record from multiple sites to identify origin of tachycardia (List separately in addition to code for primary procedure)
Code also (C1730, C1731, C1733, C2629, C2630)
Code first comprehensive electrophysiologic evaluation or intracardiac catheter ablation (93620, 93651, 93652)
Do not report with (93613)
0.00   0.00   Global Days ZZZ
AMA: 2008, Mar, 4-5; 2005, August, 13-15

93610 Intra-atrial pacing
INCLUDES Unusual situations where there may be recording/pacing/attempt at arrhythmia induction from only one side of the heart
Code also (C1730, C1731, C1732, C1733, C1766, C1892, C1893, C1894, C2629, C2630)
0.00   0.00   Global Days 000
AMA: 2008, Mar, 4-5; 2005, August, 13-15

93612 Intraventricular pacing
INCLUDES Unusual situations where there may be recording/pacing/attempt at arrhythmia induction from only one side of the heart
Code also (C1730, C1731, C1732, C1733, C1766, C1892, C1893, C1894, C2629, C2630)
Do not report with (93620-93622)
0.00   0.00   Global Days 000
AMA: 2008, Mar, 4-5; 2005, August, 13-15

Current Procedural Coding Expert – Medicine

+ ⊙ **93613** Intracardiac electrophysiologic 3-dimensional mapping (List separately in addition to code for primary procedure)

Code also (C1730, C1731, C1732, C1733, C2630)
Code first comprehensive electrophysiologic evaluation or intracardiac catheter ablation (93620, 93651, 93652)
Do not report with (93609)
🚑 9.67 ✂ 9.67 Global Days ZZZ
AMA: 2008, Mar, 4-5; 2005, August, 13-15

93615-93616 Recording and Pacing via Esophagus

CMS 100-4,12,30.4   Cardiovascular System

⊘ ⊙ **93615** Esophageal recording of atrial electrogram with or without ventricular electrogram(s);

Code also (C1730, C1731, C1732, C1733, C1766, C1892, C1893, C1894, C2629, C2630)
🚑 0.00 ✂ 0.00 Global Days 000
AMA: 2008, Mar, 4-5; 2005, August, 13-15

⊘ ⊙ **93616** with pacing

Code also (C1730, C1731, C1732, C1733, C1756, C1766, C1892, C1893, C1894, C2629, C2630)
🚑 0.00 ✂ 0.00 Global Days 000
AMA: 2008, Mar, 4-5; 2005, August, 13-15

93618 Pacing to Produce an Arrhythmia

CMS 100-4,12,30.4   Cardiovascular System
INCLUDES Unusual situations where there may be recording/pacing/attempt at arrhythmia induction from only one side of the heart
EXCLUDES Intracardiac phonocardiogram (93799)

⊘ ⊙ **93618** Induction of arrhythmia by electrical pacing

INCLUDES Unusual situations where there may be recording/pacing/attempt at arrhythmia induction from only one side of the heart
EXCLUDES Intracardiac phonocardiogram (93799)

Code also (C1730, C1731, C1732, C1733, C1766, C1892, C1893, C1894, C2629, C2630)
🚑 0.00 ✂ 0.00 Global Days 000
AMA: 2009, Jan, 11-31; 2008, Mar, 4-5; 2008, Jan, 10-25; 2007, Dec, 10-179; 2007, January, 13-27; 2005, August, 13-15

93619-93623 Comprehensive Electrophysiological Studies

CMS 100-3,20.12   Diagnostic Endocardial Electrical Stimulation (Pacing)
CMS 100-4,12,30.4   Cardiovascular System

⊙ **93619** Comprehensive electrophysiologic evaluation with right atrial pacing and recording, right ventricular pacing and recording, His bundle recording, including insertion and repositioning of multiple electrode catheters, without induction or attempted induction of arrhythmia

INCLUDES Evaluation of sinus node/atrioventricular node/His-Purkinje conduction system without arrhythmia induction

Code also (C1730, C1731, C1732, C1733, C1766, C1892, C1893, C1894, C2629, C2630)
Do not report with (93600, 93602, 93610, 93612, 93618, 93620-93622)
🚑 0.00 ✂ 0.00 Global Days 000
AMA: 2009, Jan, 11-31; 2008, Mar, 4-5; 2008, Jan, 10-25; 2007, Dec, 10-179; 2007, January, 13-27; 2005, August, 13-15

⊙ **93620** Comprehensive electrophysiologic evaluation including insertion and repositioning of multiple electrode catheters with induction or attempted induction of arrhythmia; with right atrial pacing and recording, right ventricular pacing and recording, His bundle recording

INCLUDES Recording/pacing/attempted arrhythmia induction from one or more site(s) in the heart

Code also (C1730, C1731, C1732, C1733, C1766, C1892, C1893, C1894, C2629, C2630)
Do not report with (93600, 93602, 93610, 93612, 93618, 93619)
🚑 0.00 ✂ 0.00 Global Days 000
AMA: 2009, Jan, 11-31; 2008, Jan, 10-25; 2008, Mar, 4-5; 2008, Oct, 10-11; 2007, Dec, 10-179; 2007, January, 13-27; 2005, August, 13-15

+ ⊙ **93621** with left atrial pacing and recording from coronary sinus or left atrium (List separately in addition to code for primary procedure)

INCLUDES Recording/pacing/attempted arrhythmia induction from one or more site(s) in the heart

Code also (C1730, C1731, C1732, C1733, C1766, C1892, C1893, C1894, C2629, C2630)
Code first right atrial/ventricular pacing/recording (93620)
🚑 0.00 ✂ 0.00 Global Days ZZZ
AMA: 2009, Jan, 11-31; 2008, Mar, 4-5; 2008, Jan, 10-25; 2008, Oct, 10-11; 2007, Dec, 10-179; 2007, January, 13-27; 2005, August, 13-15

+ ⊙ **93622** with left ventricular pacing and recording (List separately in addition to code for primary procedure)

Code also (C1730, C1731, C1732, C1733, C1766, C1892, C1893, C1894, C2629, C2630)
Code first right atrial/ventricular pacing/recording (93620)
🚑 0.00 ✂ 0.00 Global Days ZZZ
AMA: 2009, Jan, 11-31; 2008, Jan, 10-25; 2008, Mar, 4-5; 2007, Dec, 10-179; 2007, January, 13-27; 2005, August, 13-15

+ **93623** Programmed stimulation and pacing after intravenous drug infusion (List separately in addition to code for primary procedure)

INCLUDES Recording/pacing/attempted arrhythmia induction from one or more site(s) in the heart

Code also (C1730, C1731, C1732, C1733, C1766, C1892, C1893, C1894, C2629, C2630)
Code first comprehensive eletrophysiologic evaluation (93619, 93620)
🚑 0.00 ✂ 0.00 Global Days ZZZ
AMA: 2009, Jan, 11-31; 2008, Mar, 4-5; 2008, Oct, 10-11; 2007, Dec, 10-179; 2005, August, 13-15

● New Code   ▲ Revised Code   M Maternity   A Age   Unlisted   Not Covered   # Resequenced
CCI   + Add-on   ⊘ Mod 51 Exempt   ⊚ Mod 63 Exempt   ⊙ Mod Sedation   PQRI

93624-93631 Followup and Intraoperative Electrophysiologic Studies

CMS 100-3,20.11 — Intraoperative Ventricular Mapping
CMS 100-3,20.12 — Diagnostic Endocardial Electrical Stimulation (Pacing)
CMS 100-4,12,30.4 — Cardiovascular System

- **93624** Electrophysiologic follow-up study with pacing and recording to test effectiveness of therapy, including induction or attempted induction of arrhythmia
  - **INCLUDES** Recording/pacing/attempted arrhythmia induction from one or more site(s) in the heart
  - Code also (C1730, C1731, C1732, C1733, C1766, C1892, C1893, C1894)
  - 0.00 0.00 Global Days 000
  - **AMA:** 2008, Mar, 4-5; 2007, Dec, 10-179; 2005, August, 13-15

- **93631** Intra-operative epicardial and endocardial pacing and mapping to localize the site of tachycardia or zone of slow conduction for surgical correction
  - **EXCLUDES** Operative ablation of an arrhythmogenic focus or pathway by a separate provider (33250-33261)
  - Code also (C1730, C1731, C1732, C1733, C1766, C1892, C1893, C1894, C2629, C2630)
  - 0.00 0.00 Global Days 000
  - **AMA:** 2008, Mar, 4-5; 2007, Dec, 10-179; 2005, August, 13-15

93640-93642 Electrophysiologic Studies of Pacing Cardioverter-Defibrillators

CMS 100-3,20.8.2 — Self-contained Pacemaker Monitors
CMS 100-3,20.12 — Diagnostic Encocardial Electrical Stimulation (Pacing)
CMS 100-4,12,30.4 — Cardiovascular System

INCLUDES Recording/pacing/attempted arrhythmia induction from one or more site(s) in the heart

- **93640** Electrophysiologic evaluation of single or dual chamber pacing cardioverter-defibrillator leads including defibrillation threshold evaluation (induction of arrhythmia, evaluation of sensing and pacing for arrhythmia termination) at time of initial implantation or replacement;
  - 0.00 0.00 Global Days 000
  - **AMA:** 2008, Mar, 4-5; 2005, August, 13-15

- **93641** with testing of single or dual chamber pacing cardioverter-defibrillator pulse generator
  - **EXCLUDES** Single/dual chamber pacing cardioverter-defibrillators reprogramming/electronic analysis, subsequent/periodic (93282-93283, 93289, 93292, 93295, 93642)
  - 0.00 0.00 Global Days 000
  - **AMA:** 2008, Mar, 4-5; 2005, August, 13-15

- **93642** Electrophysiologic evaluation of single or dual chamber pacing cardioverter-defibrillator (includes defibrillation threshold evaluation, induction of arrhythmia, evaluation of sensing and pacing for arrhythmia termination, and programming or reprogramming of sensing or therapeutic parameters)
  - 9.93 9.93 Global Days 000
  - **AMA:** 2008, Mar, 4-5; 2005, August, 13-15

93650-93652 Intracardiac Ablation

CMS 100-4,12,30.4 — Cardiovascular System

- **93650** Intracardiac catheter ablation of atrioventricular node function, atrioventricular conduction for creation of complete heart block, with or without temporary pacemaker placement
  - Code also (C1732, C1733, C1766, C1892, C1893, C1894, C2629, C2630)
  - 14.75 14.75 Global Days 000
  - **AMA:** 2008, Mar, 4-5; 2005, August, 13-15

- **93651** Intracardiac catheter ablation of arrhythmogenic focus; for treatment of supraventricular tachycardia by ablation of fast or slow atrioventricular pathways, accessory atrioventricular connections or other atrial foci, singly or in combination
  - **INCLUDES** Delivery of radiofrequency energy to the area to selectively destroy cardiac tissue
    Services that may be performed independently on a date subsequent to or at the same time as a diagnostic electrophysiologic study/tachycardia(s) induction/mapping
  - Code also (C1732, C1733, C1766, C1892, C1893, C1894, C2629, C2630)
  - 22.46 22.46 Global Days 000
  - **AMA:** 2008, Mar, 4-5; 2007, Dec, 10-179; 2005, August, 13-15

- **93652** for treatment of ventricular tachycardia
  - **INCLUDES** Delivery of radiofrequency energy to the area to selectively destroy cardiac tissue
    Services that may be performed independently on a date subsequent to or at the same time as a diagnostic electrophysiologic study/tachycardia(s) induction/mapping
  - Code also (C1732, C1733, C1766, C1892, C1893, C1894, C2629, C2630)
  - 24.45 24.45 Global Days 000
  - **AMA:** 2009, Jan, 11-31; 2008, Jan, 10-25; 2008, Mar, 4-5; 2007, January, 13-27; 2005, August, 13-15

93660-93662 Other Tests for Cardiac Function

CMS 100-4,12,30.4 — Cardiovascular System

- **93660** Evaluation of cardiovascular function with tilt table evaluation, with continuous ECG monitoring and intermittent blood pressure monitoring, with or without pharmacological intervention
  - **EXCLUDES** Autonomic nervous system function testing (95921-95923)
  - 3.99 3.99 Global Days 000
  - **AMA:** 2008, Mar, 4-5

+ **93662** Intracardiac echocardiography during therapeutic/diagnostic intervention, including imaging supervision and interpretation (List separately in addition to code for primary procedure)
  - Code also (C1759)
  - Code first 92987, 93527, 93532, 93580, 93581, 93621, 93622, 93651, 93652
  - Do not report with internal cardioversion (92961)
  - 0.00 0.00 Global Days ZZZ
  - **AMA:** 2009, Jan, 11-31; 2008, Jan, 10-25; 2008, Mar, 4-5; 2007, January, 13-27

Current Procedural Coding Expert – Medicine

93668 Rehabilitation Services: Peripheral Arterial Disease
INCLUDES 45-60 minutes per session
Monitoring:
  Other cardiovascular limitations for adjustment of workload
  Patient's claudication threshold
Motorized treadmill or track
Supervision by exercise physiologist/nurse
Code also evaluation and management service, if appropriate

93668 Peripheral arterial disease (PAD) rehabilitation, per session [E]
  0.45   0.45   Global Days XXX
  AMA: 2008, Mar, 4-5

93701 Thoracic Electrical Bioimpedance
CMS 100-3,20.16   Cardiac Output Monitoring by Thoracic Electrical Bioimpedance (TEB)
CMS 100-4,12,30.4   Cardiovascular System

▲ **93701** Bioimpedance-derived physiologic cardiovascular analysis [S][TC][80]
  EXCLUDES Indirect measurement of left vetricular filling pressure by computerized calibration of the arterial waveform response to Valsalva (93799)
  0.57   0.57   Global Days XXX
  AMA: 2008, Mar, 4-5

93720-93722 Total Body Plethysmography
CMS 100-3,20.14   Plethysmography
EXCLUDES Penile plethysmography (54240)
Regional plethysmography (93875-93931)

93720 Plethysmography, total body; with interpretation and report [B][80]
  1.19   1.19   Global Days XXX
  AMA: 2009, Jan, 11-31; 2008, Mar, 4-5; 2008, Jan, 10-25; 2007, January, 13-27

93721 tracing only, without interpretation and report [X][TC][80]
  0.96   0.96   Global Days XXX
  AMA: 2008, Mar, 4-5

93722 interpretation and report only [B][26][80]
  0.23   0.23   Global Days XXX
  AMA: 2008, Mar, 4-5

93724 Electronic Analysis of Pacemaker Function
CMS 100-3,20.8   Cardiac Pacemakers
CMS 100-3,20.8.1   Cardiac Pacemaker Evaluation Services
CMS 100-3,20.14   Plethysmography
CMS 100-4,12,30.4   Cardiovascular System
EXCLUDES Arterial cannulization/recording of direct arterial pressure (36620)
Chemotherapy (96409-96549)
Hemodialysis vascular cannulization (36800-36821)
Radiographic injection services (36000-36299)

93724 Electronic analysis of antitachycardia pacemaker system (includes electrocardiographic recording, programming of device, induction and termination of tachycardia via implanted pacemaker, and interpretation of recordings) [S][80]
  7.28   7.28   Global Days 000
  AMA: 2008, Mar, 4-5

93740 Temperature Gradient Assessment
CMS 100-4,12,30.4   Cardiovascular System

93740 Temperature gradient studies [X]
  0.24   0.24   Global Days XXX

93745 Wearable Cardioverter-Defibrillator System Services
CMS 100-4,12,30.4   Cardiovascular System
EXCLUDES Arterial cannulization/recording of direct arterial pressure (36620)
Chemotherapy (96409-96549)
Hemodialysis vascular cannulization (36800-36821)
Radiographic injection services (36000-36299)

93745 Initial set-up and programming by a physician of wearable cardioverter-defibrillator includes initial programming of system, establishing baseline electronic ECG, transmission of data to data repository, patient instruction in wearing system and patient reporting of problems or events [S][80]
  Do not report with (93282, 93292)
  0.00   0.00   Global Days XXX
  AMA: 2009, Mar, 5-7; 2009, Feb, 3-12

93750 Ventricular Assist Device (VAD) Interrogation

● **93750** Interrogation of ventricular assist device (VAD), in person, with physician analysis of device parameters (eg, drivelines, alarms, power surges), review of device function (eg, flow and volume status, septum status, recovery), with programming, if performed, and report [S][80]
  Do not report with (33975-33976, 33979, 33981-33983)
  1.27   1.45   Global Days XXX

93770 Peripheral Venous Blood Pressure Assessment
CMS 100-4,12,30.4   Cardiovascular System

93770 Determination of venous pressure [N]
  EXCLUDES Cannulization, central venous (36500, 36555-36556)
  0.24   0.24   Global Days XXX

93784-93790 Ambulatory Blood Pressure Monitoring
CMS 100-3,20.19   Ambulatory Blood Pressure Monitoring
CMS 100-4,12,30.4   Cardiovascular System
CMS 100-4,32,10.1   Ambulatory Blood Pressure Monitoring Billing Requirements
EXCLUDES Arterial cannulization/recording of direct arterial pressure (36620)
Chemotherapy (96409-96549)
Hemodialysis vascular cannulization (36800-36821)
Radiographic injection services (36000-36299)

93784 Ambulatory blood pressure monitoring, utilizing a system such as magnetic tape and/or computer disk, for 24 hours or longer; including recording, scanning analysis, interpretation and report [E][80]
  1.66   1.66   Global Days XXX

93786 recording only [S][TC][80]
  0.72   0.72   Global Days XXX

93788 scanning analysis with report [S][TC][80]
  0.41   0.41   Global Days XXX

93790 physician review with interpretation and report [M][26][80]
  0.53   0.53   Global Days XXX

● New Code   ▲ Revised Code   [M] Maternity   [A] Age   Unlisted   Not Covered   # Resequenced
[CCI] CCI   + Add-on   Mod 51 Exempt   Mod 63 Exempt   Mod Sedation   [PQ] PQRI

© 2009 Publisher *(Blue Ink)*   CPT only © 2009 American Medical Association. All Rights Reserved. *(Black Ink)*   Medicare *(Red Ink)*

93797-93799 Cardiac Rehabilitation

CMS 100-3,20.10   Cardiac Rehabilitation Programs
CMS 100-4,4,200.5   Cardiac Rehabilitation Services
CMS 100-4,12,30.4   Cardiovascular System

EXCLUDES   Arterial cannulization/recording of direct arterial pressure (36620)
Chemotherapy (96409)
Hemodialysis vascular cannulization (36800-36821)
Radiographic injection services (36000-36299)

93797 Physician services for outpatient cardiac rehabilitation; without continuous ECG monitoring (per session)
    0.26   0.45   Global Days 000

93798 with continuous ECG monitoring (per session)
    0.39   0.63   Global Days 000
    AMA: 2005, November, 1-9

93799 Unlisted cardiovascular service or procedure
    0.00   0.00   Global Days XXX
    AMA: 2009, Jan, 11-31; 2009, Mar, 5-7; 2008, Jan, 10-25; 2007, January, 13-27; 2005, November, 14-15

93875-93893 Noninvasive Tests Extracranial/Intracranial Arteries

CMS 100-3,20.17   Noninvasive Tests of Carotid Function

93875 Noninvasive physiologic studies of extracranial arteries, complete bilateral study (eg, periorbital flow direction with arterial compression, ocular pneumoplethysmography, Doppler ultrasound spectral analysis)
    INCLUDES Evaluation of
      Doppler analysis of bi-directional blood flow
      Non-imaging physiologic recordings of pressures
      Oxygen tension measurements
      Plethysmography
    2.61   2.61   Global Days XXX
    AMA: 2009, Jan, 11-31; 2008, Jan, 10-25; 2007, January, 13-27; 2005, December, 3-6

93880 Duplex scan of extracranial arteries; complete bilateral study
    6.03   6.03   Global Days XXX
    AMA: 2005, March, 11-15; 2005, December, 3-6

93882 unilateral or limited study
    EXCLUDES   Common carotid intima-media thickness study for coronary heart disease risk factor assessment or evaluation of atherosclerotic burden (0126T)
    4.42   4.42   Global Days XXX
    AMA: 2005, December, 3-6

93886 Transcranial Doppler study of the intracranial arteries; complete study
    INCLUDES Complete transcranial doppler (TCD) study
      Ultrasound evaluation of right/left anterior circulation territories and posterior circulation territory
    8.84   8.84   Global Days XXX
    AMA: 2005, December, 3-6

93888 limited study
    INCLUDES Limited TCD study
      Ultrasound examination of two or fewer of these territories (right/left anterior circulation, posterior circulation)
    5.53   5.53   Global Days XXX
    AMA: 2005, December, 3-6

93890 vasoreactivity study
Do not report with limited TCD study (93888)
    7.79   7.79   Global Days XXX
    AMA: 2005, December, 3-6

93892 emboli detection without intravenous microbubble injection
Do not report with limited TCD study (93888)
    9.94   9.94   Global Days XXX
    AMA: 2005, December, 3-6

93893 emboli detection with intravenous microbubble injection
Do not report with limited TCD study (93888)
    9.27   9.27   Global Days XXX
    AMA: 2005, December, 3-6

93922-93990 Noninvasive Vascular Studies: Abdomen/Extremities/Thorax

CMS 100-3,20.14   Plethysmography

INCLUDES Patient care required to perform/supervise studies and interpret results
Use of simple hand-held devices

93922 Noninvasive physiologic studies of upper or lower extremity arteries, single level, bilateral (eg, ankle/brachial indices, Doppler waveform analysis, volume plethysmography, transcutaneous oxygen tension measurement)
    INCLUDES Evaluation of:
      Doppler analysis of bi-directional blood flow
      Nonimaging physiologic recordings of pressures
      Oxygen tension measurements
      Plethysmography
    3.12   3.12   Global Days XXX
    AMA: 2005, December, 3-6

93923 Noninvasive physiologic studies of upper or lower extremity arteries, multiple levels or with provocative functional maneuvers, complete bilateral study (eg, segmental blood pressure measurements, segmental Doppler waveform analysis, segmental volume plethysmography, segmental transcutaneous oxygen tension measurements, measurements with postural provocative tests, measurements with reactive hyperemia)
    INCLUDES Evaluation of
      Doppler analysis of bi-directional blood flow
      Non-imaging physiologic recordings of pressures
      Oxygen tension measurements
      Plethysmography
    4.76   4.76   Global Days XXX
    AMA: 2009, Jan, 11-31; 2008, Jan, 10-25; 2007, January, 13-27; 2005, December, 3-6

Current Procedural Coding Expert – Medicine

93924 Noninvasive physiologic studies of lower extremity arteries, at rest and following treadmill stress testing, complete bilateral study [S] [80]
  INCLUDES Evaluation of
    Doppler analysis of bi-directional blood flow
    Non-imaging physiologic recordings of pressures
    Oxygen tension measurements
    Plethysmography
  5.79 5.79 Global Days XXX
  AMA: 2005, December, 3-6

93925 Duplex scan of lower extremity arteries or arterial bypass grafts; complete bilateral study [S] [80]
  7.66 7.66 Global Days XXX
  AMA: 2005, December, 3-6

93926 unilateral or limited study [S] [80]
  5.10 5.10 Global Days XXX
  AMA: 2005, December, 3-6

93930 Duplex scan of upper extremity arteries or arterial bypass grafts; complete bilateral study [S] [80]
  6.14 6.14 Global Days XXX
  AMA: 2005, December, 3-6

93931 unilateral or limited study [S] [80]
  4.06 4.06 Global Days XXX
  AMA: 2005, December, 3-6

93965 Noninvasive physiologic studies of extremity veins, complete bilateral study (eg, Doppler waveform analysis with responses to compression and other maneuvers, phleborheography, impedance plethysmography) [S] [80]
  INCLUDES Evaluation of:
    Doppler analysis of bi-directional blood flow
    Nonimaging physiologic recordings of pressures
    Oxygen tension measurements
    Plethysmography
  3.05 3.05 Global Days XXX
  AMA: 2005, December, 3-6

93970 Duplex scan of extremity veins including responses to compression and other maneuvers; complete bilateral study [S] [80]
  6.32 6.32 Global Days XXX
  AMA: 2005, December, 3-6

93971 unilateral or limited study [S] [80]
  4.11 4.11 Global Days XXX
  AMA: 2009, Jan, 11-31; 2008, Jan, 10-25; 2007, January, 13-27; 2005, December, 3-6

93975 Duplex scan of arterial inflow and venous outflow of abdominal, pelvic, scrotal contents and/or retroperitoneal organs; complete study [S] [80]
  9.26 9.26 Global Days XXX
  AMA: 2009, Jan, 11-31; 2008, Jan, 10-25; 2007, January, 13-27; 2005, December, 3-6

93976 limited study [S] [80]
  5.28 5.28 Global Days XXX
  AMA: 2009, Jan, 11-31; 2008, Jan, 10-25; 2007, January, 13-27; 2005, December, 3-6

93978 Duplex scan of aorta, inferior vena cava, iliac vasculature, or bypass grafts; complete study [S] [80]
  5.99 5.99 Global Days XXX
  AMA: 2005, December, 3-6

93979 unilateral or limited study [S] [80]
  4.10 4.10 Global Days XXX
  AMA: 2005, December, 3-6

93980 Duplex scan of arterial inflow and venous outflow of penile vessels; complete study ♂ [S] [80]
  4.32 4.32 Global Days XXX
  AMA: 2005, December, 3-6

93981 follow-up or limited study ♂ [S] [80]
  2.79 2.79 Global Days XXX
  AMA: 2005, December, 3-6

93982 Noninvasive physiologic study of implanted wireless pressure sensor in aneurysmal sac following endovascular repair, complete study including recording, analysis of pressure and waveform tracings, interpretation and report [S] [80]
  Do not report with (34806)
  1.10 1.10 Global Days XXX

93990 Duplex scan of hemodialysis access (including arterial inflow, body of access and venous outflow) [S] [80]
  EXCLUDES Hemodialysis access flow measurement by indicator method (90940)
  5.43 5.43 Global Days XXX
  AMA: 2005, December, 3-6

94002-94005 Ventilator Management Services

94002 Ventilation assist and management, initiation of pressure or volume preset ventilators for assisted or controlled breathing; hospital inpatient/observation, initial day [S] [80]
  Do not report with (99201-99499)
  2.57 2.57 Global Days XXX
  AMA: 2009, Jan, 11-31; 2008, Jan, 10-25; 2007, February, 10-11; 2007, April, 3-6; 2007, March, 9-11; 2007, Jul, 1-4

94003 hospital inpatient/observation, each subsequent day [S] [80]
  Do not report with (99201-99499)
  1.85 1.85 Global Days XXX
  AMA: 2007, February, 10-11; 2007, Jul, 1-4; 2007, April, 3-6

94004 nursing facility, per day [B] [80]
  Do not report with (99201-99499)
  1.33 1.33 Global Days XXX
  AMA: 2007, February, 10-11; 2007, April, 3-6; 2007, Jul, 1-4

94005 Home ventilator management care plan oversight of a patient (patient not present) in home, domiciliary or rest home (eg, assisted living) requiring review of status, review of laboratories and other studies and revision of orders and respiratory care plan (as appropriate), within a calendar month, 30 minutes or more [M]
  Do not report with (99339-99340, 99374-99378)
  2.50 2.50 Global Days XXX
  AMA: 2009, Jan, 11-31; 2008, Jan, 10-25; 2007, April, 3-6; 2007, March, 9-11; 2007, Jul, 1-4

94010-94799 Respiratory Services: Diagnostic and Therapeutic

INCLUDES Laboratory procedure(s)
  Test results interpretation
EXCLUDES Separate identifiable evaluation and management service (99201-99499)

94010 Spirometry, including graphic record, total and timed vital capacity, expiratory flow rate measurement(s), with or without maximal voluntary ventilation [X] [80]
  0.90 0.90 Global Days XXX
  AMA: 2009, Jan, 11-31; 2008, Jan, 10-25; 2008, Nov, 5-6; 2007, January, 13-27; 2005, July, 11-12

● New Code   ▲ Revised Code   [M] Maternity   [△] Age   Unlisted   Not Covered   # Resequenced
[CCI]   + Add-on   ⊘ Mod 51 Exempt   ⊚ Mod 63 Exempt   ⊙ Mod Sedation   [PQ] PQRI
© 2009 Publisher *(Blue Ink)*   CPT only © 2009 American Medical Association. All Rights Reserved. *(Black Ink)*   Medicare *(Red Ink)*   381

Current Procedural Coding Expert – Medicine

94011 Measurement of spirometric forced expiratory flows in an infant or child through 2 years of age
    2.67   2.67 Global Days XXX

94012 Measurement of spirometric forced expiratory flows, before and after bronchodilator, in an infant or child through 2 years of age
    4.12   4.12 Global Days XXX

94013 Measurement of lung volumes (ie, functional residual capacity [FRC], forced vital capacity [FVC], and expiratory reserve volume [ERV]) in an infant or child through 2 years of age
    0.87   0.87 Global Days XXX

94014 Patient-initiated spirometric recording per 30-day period of time; includes reinforced education, transmission of spirometric tracing, data capture, analysis of transmitted data, periodic recalibration and physician review and interpretation
    1.27   1.27 Global Days XXX
AMA: 2008, Nov, 5-6; 2005, July, 11-12

94015 recording (includes hook-up, reinforced education, data transmission, data capture, trend analysis, and periodic recalibration)
    0.58   0.58 Global Days XXX
AMA: 2008, Nov, 5-6; 2005, July, 11-12

94016 physician review and interpretation only
    0.69   0.69 Global Days XXX
AMA: 2008, Nov, 5-6; 2005, July, 11-12

94060 Bronchodilation responsiveness, spirometry as in 94010, pre- and post-bronchodilator administration
    EXCLUDES Bronchospasm prolonged exercise test with pre- and post-spirometry (94620)
    Code also bronchodilator supply with appropriate supply code or 99070
    1.53   1.53 Global Days XXX
AMA: 2009, Jan, 11-31; 2008, Jan, 10-25; 2008, Nov, 5-6; 2007, January, 13-27; 2005, July, 11-12

94070 Bronchospasm provocation evaluation, multiple spirometric determinations as in 94010, with administered agents (eg, antigen[s], cold air, methacholine)
    Code also antigen(s) administration with appropriate supply code or 99070
    1.56   1.56 Global Days XXX
AMA: 2008, Nov, 5-6; 2005, July, 11-12

94150 Vital capacity, total (separate procedure)
    0.61   0.61 Global Days XXX
AMA: 2008, Nov, 5-6; 2005, July, 11-12

94200 Maximum breathing capacity, maximal voluntary ventilation
    0.60   0.60 Global Days XXX
AMA: 2009, Jan, 11-31; 2008, Jan, 10-25; 2008, Nov, 5-6; 2007, January, 13-27; 2005, July, 11-12

94240 Functional residual capacity or residual volume: helium method, nitrogen open circuit method, or other method
    1.00   1.00 Global Days XXX
AMA: 2008, Nov, 5-6; 2005, July, 11-12

94250 Expired gas collection, quantitative, single procedure (separate procedure)
    0.60   0.60 Global Days XXX
AMA: 2008, Nov, 5-6; 2005, July, 11-12

94260 Thoracic gas volume
    EXCLUDES Plethysmography (93720-93722)
    0.80   0.80 Global Days XXX
AMA: 2008, Nov, 5-6; 2005, July, 11-12

94350 Determination of maldistribution of inspired gas: multiple breath nitrogen washout curve including alveolar nitrogen or helium equilibration time
    0.86   0.86 Global Days XXX
AMA: 2008, Nov, 5-6; 2005, July, 11-12

94360 Determination of resistance to airflow, oscillatory or plethysmographic methods
    1.12   1.12 Global Days XXX
AMA: 2008, Nov, 5-6; 2005, July, 11-12

94370 Determination of airway closing volume, single breath tests
    0.85   0.85 Global Days XXX
AMA: 2008, Nov, 5-6; 2005, July, 11-12

94375 Respiratory flow volume loop
    0.98   0.98 Global Days XXX
AMA: 2008, Nov, 5-6; 2007, Jul, 1-4; 2006, May, 1-9; 2005, July, 11-12

94400 Breathing response to CO2 (CO2 response curve)
    1.36   1.36 Global Days XXX
AMA: 2008, Nov, 5-6; 2005, July, 11-12

94450 Breathing response to hypoxia (hypoxia response curve)
    EXCLUDES HAST - high altitude simulation test (94452, 94453)
    1.76   1.76 Global Days XXX
AMA: 2008, Nov, 5-6; 2005, July, 11-12

94452 High altitude simulation test (HAST), with physician interpretation and report;
    EXCLUDES Obtaining arterial blood gases (36600)
    Do not report with (94453, 94760-94761)
    1.40   1.40 Global Days XXX
AMA: 2008, Nov, 5-6; 2005, July, 11-12

94453 with supplemental oxygen titration
    EXCLUDES Obtaining arterial blood gases (36600)
    Do not report with (94452, 94760-94761)
    1.90   1.90 Global Days XXX
AMA: 2008, Nov, 5-6; 2005, July, 11-12

94610 Intrapulmonary surfactant administration by a physician through endotracheal tube
    INCLUDES Reporting once per dosing episode
    EXCLUDES Intubation, endotracheal (31500)
    Do not report with (99468-99472)
    1.67   1.67 Global Days XXX
AMA: 2008, Jul, 7-8&15; 2008, Nov, 5-6; 2007, April, 3-6; 2007, Jul, 1-4

94620 Pulmonary stress testing; simple (eg, 6-minute walk test, prolonged exercise test for bronchospasm with pre- and post-spirometry and oximetry)
    1.42   1.42 Global Days XXX
AMA: 2009, Jan, 11-31; 2008, Jan, 10-25; 2008, Nov, 5-6; 2007, June, 10-11; 2007, January, 13-27; 2007, April, 3-6; 2005, July, 13-16; 2005, July, 11-12

94621 complex (including measurements of CO2 production, O2 uptake, and electrocardiographic recordings)
    4.11   4.11 Global Days XXX
AMA: 2009, Jan, 11-31; 2008, Jan, 10-25; 2008, Nov, 5-6; 2007, January, 13-27; 2005, July, 11-12

| 26/TC PC/TC Comp Only | 52 ASC Pmt | 50 Bilateral | ♂ Male Only | ♀ Female Only | Facility RVU | Non-Facility RVU |

AMA: CPT Asst   **MED:** Pub 100   A/Y OPPSI   Non-FDA Drug   Lab Crosswalk   Radiology Crosswalk

Current Procedural Coding Expert – Medicine

94640 Pressurized or nonpressurized inhalation treatment for acute airway obstruction or for sputum induction for diagnostic purposes (eg, with an aerosol generator, nebulizer, metered dose inhaler or intermittent positive pressure breathing [IPPB] device)
- EXCLUDES: 1 hour or more of continuous inhalation treatment (94644, 94645)
- Code also modifier 76 when more than 1 inhalation treatment is performed on the same date
- 0.42 0.42 Global Days XXX
- AMA: 2009, Jan, 11-31; 2008, Jan, 10-25; 2008, Nov, 5-6; 2007, April, 3-6; 2007, January, 13-27; 2005, July, 11-12

94642 Aerosol inhalation of pentamidine for pneumocystis carinii pneumonia treatment or prophylaxis
- 0.00 0.00 Global Days XXX
- AMA: 2008, Nov, 5-6; 2005, July, 11-12

94644 Continuous inhalation treatment with aerosol medication for acute airway obstruction; first hour
- EXCLUDES: Services that are less than 1 hour (94640)
- 1.02 1.02 Global Days XXX
- AMA: 2008, Nov, 5-6; 2007, April, 3-6

+ 94645 each additional hour (List separately in addition to code for primary procedure)
- Code first initial hour (94644)
- 0.33 0.33 Global Days XXX
- AMA: 2008, Nov, 5-6; 2007, April, 3-6

94660 Continuous positive airway pressure ventilation (CPAP), initiation and management
- 1.04 1.60 Global Days XXX
- AMA: 2009, Jan, 11-31; 2008, Jan, 10-25; 2008, Nov, 5-6; 2007, Jul, 1-4; 2007, January, 13-27; 2007, February, 10-11; 2006, May, 1-9; 2005, July, 11-12

94662 Continuous negative pressure ventilation (CNP), initiation and management
- 1.00 1.00 Global Days XXX
- AMA: 2009, Jan, 11-31; 2008, Jan, 10-25; 2008, Nov, 5-6; 2007, February, 10-11; 2007, Jul, 1-4; 2007, January, 13-27; 2005, July, 11-12

94664 Demonstration and/or evaluation of patient utilization of an aerosol generator, nebulizer, metered dose inhaler or IPPB device
- INCLUDES: Reporting only one time per day of service
- 0.41 0.41 Global Days XXX
- AMA: 2009, Jan, 11-31; 2008, Jan, 10-25; 2008, Nov, 5-6; 2007, January, 13-27; 2005, July, 11-12

94667 Manipulation chest wall, such as cupping, percussing, and vibration to facilitate lung function; initial demonstration and/or evaluation
- 0.55 0.55 Global Days XXX
- AMA: 2008, Nov, 5-6; 2005, July, 11-12

94668 subsequent
- 0.54 0.54 Global Days XXX
- AMA: 2008, Nov, 5-6; 2005, July, 11-12

94680 Oxygen uptake, expired gas analysis; rest and exercise, direct, simple
- 1.38 1.38 Global Days XXX
- AMA: 2008, Nov, 5-6; 2005, July, 11-12

94681 including CO2 output, percentage oxygen extracted
- 1.27 1.27 Global Days XXX
- AMA: 2008, Nov, 5-6; 2005, July, 11-12

94690 rest, indirect (separate procedure)
- EXCLUDES: Arterial puncture (36600)
- 1.19 1.19 Global Days XXX
- AMA: 2008, Nov, 5-6; 2005, July, 11-12

94720 Carbon monoxide diffusing capacity (eg, single breath, steady state)
- 1.28 1.28 Global Days XXX
- AMA: 2009, Jan, 11-31; 2009, Mar, 10-11; 2008, Nov, 5-6; 2005, July, 11-12

94725 Membrane diffusion capacity
- 1.22 1.22 Global Days XXX
- AMA: 2009, Mar, 10-11; 2008, Nov, 5-6; 2005, July, 11-12

94750 Pulmonary compliance study (eg, plethysmography, volume and pressure measurements)
- 1.97 1.97 Global Days XXX
- AMA: 2008, Nov, 5-6; 2005, July, 11-12

94760 Noninvasive ear or pulse oximetry for oxygen saturation; single determination
- EXCLUDES: Blood gases (82803-82810)
- 0.07 0.07 Global Days XXX
- AMA: 2009, Jan, 11-31; 2008, Jan, 10-25; 2008, Nov, 5-6; 2007, February, 10-11; 2007, Jul, 1-4; 2007, January, 13-27; 2007, April, 1-2; 2006, May, 1-9; 2006, February, 10-15; 2005, July, 11-12

94761 multiple determinations (eg, during exercise)
- 0.11 0.11 Global Days XXX
- AMA: 2009, Jan, 11-31; 2008, Jan, 10-25; 2008, Nov, 5-6; 2007, February, 10-11; 2007, June, 10-11; 2007, April, 1-2; 2007, Jul, 1-4; 2007, January, 13-27; 2006, February, 10-15; 2006, May, 1-9; 2005, July, 11-12

94762 by continuous overnight monitoring (separate procedure)
- 0.27 0.27 Global Days XXX
- AMA: 2008, Nov, 5-6; 2007, April, 1-2; 2007, Jul, 1-4; 2007, February, 10-11; 2006, May, 1-9; 2006, February, 10-15; 2005, July, 11-12

94770 Carbon dioxide, expired gas determination by infrared analyzer
- EXCLUDES:
  - Arterial catheterization/cannulation (36620)
  - Arterial puncture (36600)
  - Bronchoscopy (31622-31656)
  - Flow directed catheter placement (93503)
  - Needle biopsy of the lung (32405)
  - Orotracheal/nasotracheal intubation (31500)
  - Placement of central venous catheter (36555-36556)
  - Therapeutic phlebotomy (99195)
  - Thoracentesis (32421)
  - Venipuncture (36410)
- 0.99 0.99 Global Days XXX
- AMA: 2008, Nov, 5-6; 2005, July, 11-12

94772 Circadian respiratory pattern recording (pediatric pneumogram), 12-24 hour continuous recording, infant
- EXCLUDES: Separate procedure codes for electromyograms/EEG/ECG/respiration recordings
- 0.00 0.00 Global Days XXX
- AMA: 2008, Nov, 5-6; 2005, July, 11-12

94774 Pediatric home apnea monitoring event recording including respiratory rate, pattern and heart rate per 30-day period of time; includes monitor attachment, download of data, physician review, interpretation, and preparation of a report
- INCLUDES: Oxygen saturation monitoring
- EXCLUDES: Sleep testing (95805-95811)
- Do not report with (93224-93272, 94775-94777)
- 0.00 0.00 Global Days YYY
- AMA: 2008, Mar, 4-5; 2008, Nov, 5-6; 2007, April, 3-6

● New Code ▲ Revised Code M Maternity A Age Unlisted Not Covered # Resequenced
CCI + Add-on ⊘ Mod 51 Exempt ⊚ Mod 63 Exempt ⊙ Mod Sedation PQRI

© 2009 Publisher (Blue Ink)   CPT only © 2009 American Medical Association. All Rights Reserved. (Black Ink)   Medicare (Red Ink)   383

94775

94775 monitor attachment only (includes hook-up, initiation of recording and disconnection) [S] [TC] [80]
  INCLUDES Oxygen saturation monitoring
  EXCLUDES Sleep testing (95805-95811)
  Do not report with 93224-93272
  ⊕ 0.00 ⌇ 0.00 Global Days YYY
  AMA: 2008, Mar, 4-5; 2008, Nov, 5-6; 2007, April, 3-6

94776 monitoring, download of information, receipt of transmission(s) and analyses by computer only [S] [TC] [80]
  INCLUDES Oxygen saturation monitoring
  EXCLUDES Sleep testing (95805-95811)
  Do not report with 93224-93272
  ⊕ 0.00 ⌇ 0.00 Global Days YYY
  AMA: 2008, Mar, 4-5; 2008, Nov, 5-6; 2007, April, 3-6

94777 physician review, interpretation and preparation of report only [B] [26] [80]
  INCLUDES Oxygen saturation monitoring
  EXCLUDES Sleep testing (95805-95811)
  Do not report with (93224-93272)
  ⊕ 0.00 ⌇ 0.00 Global Days YYY
  AMA: 2008, Mar, 4-5; 2008, Nov, 5-6; 2007, April, 3-6

94799 Unlisted pulmonary service or procedure [X] [80]
  ⊕ 0.00 ⌇ 0.00 Global Days XXX
  AMA: 2009, Jan, 11-31; 2008, Jan, 10-25; 2008, Nov, 5-6; 2007, January, 13-27; 2005, July, 11-12

95004-95075 Allergy Tests

CMS 100-2,15,20.2 Physician Expense for Allergy Treatment
CMS 100-3,110.12 Challenge Ingestion Food Testing
CMS 100-3,110.13 Cytotoxic Food Tests
CMS 100-4,12,200 Allergy Testing and Immunotherapy
EXCLUDES Intractable/severe allergic disease therapy (96365-96368, 96372, 96374-96375)

Code also significant, separately identifiable E/M services using modifier 25
Do not report with codes for evaluation and management services when reporting test interpretation/report

95004 Percutaneous tests (scratch, puncture, prick) with allergenic extracts, immediate type reaction, including test interpretation and report by a physician, specify number of tests [X] [80] ▪
  ◼ 86000-86999
  ⊕ 0.16 ⌇ 0.16 Global Days XXX
  AMA: 2007, Dec, 9

95010 Percutaneous tests (scratch, puncture, prick) sequential and incremental, with drugs, biologicals or venoms, immediate type reaction, including test interpretation and report by a physician, specify number of tests [X] [80] ▪
  ◼ 86000-86999
  ⊕ 0.47 ⌇ 0.47 Global Days XXX

95012 Nitric oxide expired gas determination [X] [80]
  ◼ 86000-86999
  ⊕ 0.48 ⌇ 0.48 Global Days XXX
  AMA: 2009, Jan, 11-31; 2008, Jan, 10-25; 2007, April, 3-6; 2007, March, 9-11

95015 Intracutaneous (intradermal) tests, sequential and incremental, with drugs, biologicals, or venoms, immediate type reaction, including test interpretation and report by a physician, specify number of tests [X] [80] ▪
  ◼ 86000-86999
  ⊕ 0.36 ⌇ 0.36 Global Days XXX

95024 Intracutaneous (intradermal) tests with allergenic extracts, immediate type reaction, including test interpretation and report by a physician, specify number of tests [X] [80] ▪
  ◼ 86000-86999
  ⊕ 0.18 ⌇ 0.18 Global Days XXX
  AMA: 2007, Dec, 9

95027 Intracutaneous (intradermal) tests, sequential and incremental, with allergenic extracts for airborne allergens, immediate type reaction, including test interpretation and report by a physician, specify number of tests [X] [80] ▪
  ◼ 86000-86999
  ⊕ 0.12 ⌇ 0.12 Global Days XXX
  AMA: 2009, Jan, 11-31; 2008, Jan, 10-25; 2007, Dec, 9; 2007, January, 13-27

95028 Intracutaneous (intradermal) tests with allergenic extracts, delayed type reaction, including reading, specify number of tests [X] [TC] [80] ▪
  ◼ 86000-86999
  ⊕ 0.33 ⌇ 0.33 Global Days XXX

95044 Patch or application test(s) (specify number of tests) [X] [80] ▪
  ◼ 86000-86999
  ⊕ 0.14 ⌇ 0.14 Global Days XXX

95052 Photo patch test(s) (specify number of tests) [X] [80] ▪
  ◼ 86000-86999
  ⊕ 0.15 ⌇ 0.15 Global Days XXX

95056 Photo tests [X] [80] ▪
  ◼ 86000-86999
  ⊕ 1.04 ⌇ 1.04 Global Days XXX

95060 Ophthalmic mucous membrane tests [X] [TC] [80]
  ◼ 86000-86999
  ⊕ 0.79 ⌇ 0.79 Global Days XXX

95065 Direct nasal mucous membrane test [X] [TC] [80] ▪
  ◼ 86000-86999
  ⊕ 0.61 ⌇ 0.61 Global Days XXX

95070 Inhalation bronchial challenge testing (not including necessary pulmonary function tests); with histamine, methacholine, or similar compounds [X] [TC] [80] ▪
  EXCLUDES Pulmonary function tests (94060, 94070)
  ◼ 86000-86999
  ⊕ 0.69 ⌇ 0.69 Global Days XXX

95071 with antigens or gases, specify [X] [TC] [80] ▪
  EXCLUDES Pulmonary function tests (94060, 94070)
  ◼ 86000-86999
  ⊕ 0.84 ⌇ 0.84 Global Days XXX

95075 Ingestion challenge test (sequential and incremental ingestion of test items, eg, food, drug or other substance such as metabisulfite) [X] [80]
  ◼ 86000-86999
  ⊕ 1.33 ⌇ 1.73 Global Days XXX
  AMA: 2009, Jan, 11-31; 2008, Jan, 10-25; 2007, January, 13-27

Current Procedural Coding Expert – Medicine 95251

95115-95199 Allergy Immunotherapy

CMS 100-2,15,20.2 — Physician Expense for Allergy Treatment
CMS 100-3,110.9 — Antigens Prepared for Sublingual Administration
CMS 100-4,12,200 — Allergy Testing and Immunotherapy

INCLUDES Allergen immunotherapy professional services

EXCLUDES Bacterial/viral/fungal extracts skin testing (86485-86486, 95028)
Special reports for allergy patients (99080)
The following procedures for testing (see Pathology/Immunology section or 95199)
  Leukocyte histamine release (LHR)
  Lymphocytic transformation test (LTT)
  Mast cell degranulation test (MCDT)
  Migration inhibitory factor test (MIF)
  Nitroblue tetrazolium dye test (NTD)
  Radioallergosorbent testing (RAST)
  Rat mast cell technique (RMCT)
  Transfer factor test (TFT)

Code also significantly separate identifiable evaluation and management services, if provided

95115 Professional services for allergen immunotherapy not including provision of allergenic extracts; single injection
 0.23 0.23 Global Days XXX
 AMA: 2007, Dec, 9; 2006, December, 10-12; 2005, November, 1-9; 2005, February, 10-12

95117 2 or more injections
 0.27 0.27 Global Days XXX
 AMA: 2009, Jan, 11-31; 2008, Jan, 10-25; 2007, Dec, 9; 2007, January, 13-27; 2006, December, 10-12; 2005, February, 10-12; 2005, November, 1-9

95120 Professional services for allergen immunotherapy in prescribing physicians office or institution, including provision of allergenic extract; single injection
 0.00 0.00 Global Days XXX
 AMA: 2005, February, 10-12

95125 2 or more injections
 0.00 0.00 Global Days XXX
 AMA: 2009, Jan, 11-31; 2008, Jan, 10-25; 2007, January, 13-27; 2005, February, 10-12

95130 single stinging insect venom
 0.00 0.00 Global Days XXX
 AMA: 2009, Jan, 11-31; 2008, Jan, 10-25; 2007, January, 13-27; 2005, February, 10-12

95131 2 stinging insect venoms
 0.00 0.00 Global Days XXX
 AMA: 2009, Jan, 11-31; 2008, Jan, 10-25; 2007, January, 13-27; 2005, February, 10-12

95132 3 stinging insect venoms
 0.00 0.00 Global Days XXX
 AMA: 2009, Jan, 11-31; 2008, Jan, 10-25; 2007, January, 13-27; 2005, February, 10-12

95133 4 stinging insect venoms
 0.00 0.00 Global Days XXX
 AMA: 2009, Jan, 11-31; 2008, Jan, 10-25; 2007, January, 13-27; 2005, February, 10-12

95134 5 stinging insect venoms
 0.00 0.00 Global Days XXX
 AMA: 2009, Jan, 11-31; 2008, Jan, 10-25; 2007, January, 13-27; 2005, February, 10-12

95144 Professional services for the supervision of preparation and provision of antigens for allergen immunotherapy, single dose vial(s) (specify number of vials)
 INCLUDES Single dose vial/single dose of antigen administered in one injection
 0.09 0.32 Global Days XXX
 AMA: 2009, Jan, 11-31; 2008, Jan, 10-25; 2007, January, 13-27; 2005, February, 10-12

95145 Professional services for the supervision of preparation and provision of antigens for allergen immunotherapy (specify number of doses); single stinging insect venom
 0.09 0.39 Global Days XXX
 AMA: 2009, Jan, 11-31; 2008, Jan, 10-25; 2007, January, 13-27; 2005, February, 10-12

95146 2 single stinging insect venoms
 0.09 0.66 Global Days XXX
 AMA: 2005, February, 10-12

95147 3 single stinging insect venoms
 0.09 0.65 Global Days XXX
 AMA: 2005, February, 10-12

95148 4 single stinging insect venoms
 0.09 0.93 Global Days XXX
 AMA: 2005, February, 10-12

95149 5 single stinging insect venoms
 0.09 1.21 Global Days XXX
 AMA: 2005, February, 10-12

95165 Professional services for the supervision of preparation and provision of antigens for allergen immunotherapy; single or multiple antigens (specify number of doses)
 0.09 0.32 Global Days XXX
 AMA: 2009, Jan, 11-31; 2008, Jan, 10-25; 2007, January, 13-27; 2005, June, 9-11; 2005, February, 10-12

95170 whole body extract of biting insect or other arthropod (specify number of doses)
 INCLUDES A dose which is the amount of antigen(s) administered in a single injection from a multiple dose vial
 0.09 0.25 Global Days XXX
 AMA: 2009, Jan, 11-31; 2008, Jan, 10-25; 2007, January, 13-27; 2005, June, 9-11; 2005, February, 10-12

95180 Rapid desensitization procedure, each hour (eg, insulin, penicillin, equine serum)
 2.89 3.68 Global Days XXX

95199 Unlisted allergy/clinical immunologic service or procedure
 0.00 0.00 Global Days XXX

95250-95251 Glucose Monitoring By Subcutaneous Device

Do not report with physiologic data collection/interpretation (99091)

95250 Ambulatory continuous glucose monitoring of interstitial tissue fluid via a subcutaneous sensor for a minimum of 72 hours; sensor placement, hook-up, calibration of monitor, patient training, removal of sensor, and printout of recording
 Do not report more than once per month
 Do not report with (99091)
 3.57 3.57 Global Days XXX

95251 interpretation and report
 Do not report more than once per month
 Do not report with (99091)
 1.23 1.23 Global Days XXX

95803-95811 Sleep Studies

CMS 100-2,6,50   Sleep Disorder Clinics

INCLUDES
Diagnosis of sleep disorders
Evaluation of patient's response to therapies
Physician:
   Interpretation
   Recording
   Report
   Review
Simultaneous/continuous monitoring/recording of physiological/pathophysiological sleep parameters of 6 hours or more

EXCLUDES
Clinical depression treatment by repetitive transcranial magnetic stimulation (0160T-0161T)
Consultation services (99241-99255)
Evaluation and management services (99201-99499)
Unattended sleep studies (95806)

Code also modifier 52 for fewer than 6 hours of recording or other reduced services

95803   Actigraphy testing, recording, analysis, interpretation, and report (minimum of 72 hours to 14 consecutive days of recording)
  Do not report more than once in any 14 day period
  Do not report with (95806-95811)
  0.00   0.00   **Global Days XXX**

95805   Multiple sleep latency or maintenance of wakefulness testing, recording, analysis and interpretation of physiological measurements of sleep during multiple trials to assess sleepiness
  EXCLUDES   Polysomnography (95808-95811)
    Sleep study, not attended (95806)
  8.30   8.30   **Global Days XXX**
  AMA: 2008, Mar, 4-5

▲ **95806**   Sleep study, unattended, simultaneous recording of, heart rate, oxygen saturation, respiratory airflow, and respiratory effort (eg, thoracoabdominal movement)
  Do not report with (0203T-0204T, 93012, 93014, 93041-93272)
    Other unattended sleep studies (0203T-0204T)
    Attended sleep study (95807)
  EXCLUDES   Attended polysomnograhy (95808-95811)
  5.46   5.46   **Global Days XXX**
  AMA: 2009, Jan, 11-31; 2008, Jan, 10-25; 2008, Mar, 4-5; 2007, January, 13-27

95807   Sleep study, simultaneous recording of ventilation, respiratory effort, ECG or heart rate, and oxygen saturation, attended by a technologist
  EXCLUDES   Polysomnography (95808-95811)
    Sleep study, not attended (95806)
  11.33   11.33   **Global Days XXX**
  AMA: 2008, Mar, 4-5

95808   Polysomnography; sleep staging with 1-3 additional parameters of sleep, attended by a technologist
  EXCLUDES   Sleep study, not attended (95806)
  19.08   19.08   **Global Days XXX**
  AMA: 2009, Jan, 11-31; 2008, Jan, 10-25; 2008, Mar, 4-5; 2007, January, 13-27

95810   sleep staging with 4 or more additional parameters of sleep, attended by a technologist
  EXCLUDES   Sleep study, not attended (95806)
  19.64   19.64   **Global Days XXX**
  AMA: 2008, Mar, 4-5

95811   sleep staging with 4 or more additional parameters of sleep, with initiation of continuous positive airway pressure therapy or bilevel ventilation, attended by a technologist
  EXCLUDES   Sleep study, not attended (95806)
  21.63   21.63   **Global Days XXX**
  AMA: 2008, Mar, 4-5

95812-95830 Evaluation of Brain Activity by Electroencephalogram

EXCLUDES
Clinical depression treatment by repetitive transcranial magnetic stimulation (0160T-0161T)
Consultation services (99241-99255)
Evaluation and management services (99201-99499)

95812   Electroencephalogram (EEG) extended monitoring; 41-60 minutes
  INCLUDES
    Hyperventilation
    Photic stimulation
    Physician interpretation
    Recording of 41-60 minutes
    Report
  EXCLUDES
    EEG digital analysis (95957)
    EEG during nonintracranial surgery (95955)
    EEG monitoring, 24-hour (95950-95953, 95956)
    Wada test (95958)
  Code also modifier 26 for physician interpretation only
  9.43   9.43   **Global Days XXX**

95813   greater than 1 hour
  INCLUDES
    Hyperventilation
    Photic stimulation
    Physician interpretation
    Recording of 61 minutes or more
    Report
  EXCLUDES
    EEG digital analysis (95957)
    EEG during nonintracranial surgery (95955)
    EEG monitoring, 24-hour (95950-95953, 95956)
    Wada test (95958)
  Code also modifier 26 for physician interpretation only
  10.71   10.71   **Global Days XXX**

95816   Electroencephalogram (EEG); including recording awake and drowsy
  INCLUDES
    Photic stimulation
    Physician interpretation
    Recording of 20-40 minutes
    Report
  EXCLUDES
    EEG digital analysis (95957)
    EEG during nonintracranial surgery (95955)
    EEG monitoring, 24-hour (95950-95953, 95956)
    Wada test (95958)
  Code also modifier 26 for physician interpretation only
  8.65   8.65   **Global Days XXX**
  AMA: 2009, Jan, 11-31; 2008, Jan, 10-25; 2007, January, 13-27

Current Procedural Coding Expert – Medicine

95819 including recording awake and asleep [S][80]
- **INCLUDES**
  - Hyperventilation
  - Photic stimulation
  - Physician interpretation
  - Recording of 20-40 minutes
  - Report
- **EXCLUDES**
  - EEG digital analysis (95957)
  - EEG during nonintracranial surgery (95955)
  - EEG monitoring, 24-hour (95950-95953, 95956)
  - Wada test (95958)

Code also modifier 26 for interpretation only
9.84   9.84   Global Days XXX

95822 recording in coma or sleep only [S][80]
- **INCLUDES**
  - Hyperventilation
  - Photic stimulation
  - Physician interpretation
  - Recording of 20-40 minutes
  - Report
- **EXCLUDES**
  - EEG digital analysis (95957)
  - EEG during nonintracranial surgery (95955)
  - EEG monitoring, 24-hour (95950-95953, 95956)
  - Wada test (95958)

Code also modifier 26 for interpretation only
8.93   8.93   Global Days XXX

95824 cerebral death evaluation only [S][80]
- **INCLUDES**
  - Physician interpretation
  - Recording
  - Report
- **EXCLUDES**
  - EEG digital analysis (95957)
  - EEG during nonintracranial surgery (95955)
  - EEG monitoring, 24-hour (95950-95953, 95956)
  - Wada test (95958)

Code also modifier 26 for physician interpretation only
0.00   0.00   Global Days XXX

95827 all night recording [S][80]
- **INCLUDES**
  - Physician interpretation
  - Recording
  - Report
- **EXCLUDES**
  - EEG digital analysis (95957)
  - EEG during nonintracranial surgery (95955)
  - EEG monitoring, 24-hour (95950-95953, 95956)
  - Wada test (95958)

Code also modifier 26 for interpretation only
18.16   18.16   Global Days XXX

95829 Electrocorticogram at surgery (separate procedure) [N][80]
- **INCLUDES**
  - Physician interpretation
  - Recording
  - Report

Code also modifier 26 for interpretation only
42.02   42.02   Global Days XXX

95830 Insertion by physician of sphenoidal electrodes for electroencephalographic (EEG) recording [B][80]
2.43   5.56   Global Days XXX

95831-95857 Evaluation of Muscles and Range of Motion

- **EXCLUDES**
  - Clinical depression treatment by repetitive transcranial magnetic stimulation (0160T-0161T)
  - Consultation services (99241-99255)
  - Evaluation and management services (99201-99499)

95831 Muscle testing, manual (separate procedure) with report; extremity (excluding hand) or trunk [A][80]
0.41   0.79   Global Days XXX
AMA: 2009, Jan, 11-31; 2008, Jan, 10-25; 2008, May, 9-11; 2007, January, 13-27

95832 hand, with or without comparison with normal side [A][80]
0.45   0.79   Global Days XXX
AMA: 2009, Jan, 11-31; 2008, May, 9-11; 2008, Jan, 10-25; 2007, January, 13-27

95833 total evaluation of body, excluding hands [A][80]
0.61   0.98   Global Days XXX
AMA: 2008, May, 9-11

95834 total evaluation of body, including hands [A][80]
0.82   1.28   Global Days XXX
AMA: 2008, May, 9-11

95851 Range of motion measurements and report (separate procedure); each extremity (excluding hand) or each trunk section (spine) [A][80]
0.22   0.47   Global Days XXX
AMA: 2009, Jan, 11-31; 2008, Jan, 10-25; 2008, May, 9-11; 2007, Dec, 10-179; 2007, January, 13-27

95852 hand, with or without comparison with normal side [A][80]
0.16   0.41   Global Days XXX
AMA: 2008, May, 9-11

95857 Tensilon test for myasthenia gravis [S][80]
0.80   1.34   Global Days XXX

95860-95920 Evaluation of Nerve and Muscle Function: Electromyography/Nerve Conduction Studies

CMS 100-2,15,80 Physician Supervision Requirements for Diagnostic Tests
CMS 100-3,160.10 Evoked Response Tests
- **INCLUDES**
  - Physician interpretation
  - Recording
  - Report
- **EXCLUDES**
  - Clinical depression treatment by repetitive transcranial magnetic stimulation (0160T-0161T)
  - Consultation services (99241-99255)
  - Evaluation and management services (99201-99499)

95860 Needle electromyography; 1 extremity with or without related paraspinal areas [S][80]
- **EXCLUDES**
  - Dynamic electromyography during motion analysis studies (96002-96003)

Do not report with (95873, 95874, 96000-96004)
2.53   2.53   Global Days XXX
AMA: 2009, Jan, 11-31; 2009, Jan, 7-8; 2008, Jan, 10-25; 2007, January, 13-27; 2006, September, 5-8; 2006, June, 8-10

95861 2 extremities with or without related paraspinal areas [S][80]
- **EXCLUDES**
  - Dynamic electromyography during motion analysis studies (96002-96003)

Do not report with (95873, 95874, 96000-96004)
3.76   3.76   Global Days XXX
AMA: 2009, Jan, 7-8; 2009, Jan, 11-31; 2008, Jan, 10-25; 2007, January, 13-27; 2006, September, 5-8; 2006, June, 8-10; 2005, June, 9-11

● New Code   ▲ Revised Code   M Maternity   A Age   Unlisted   Not Covered   # Resequenced
CCI   + Add-on   ⊘ Mod 51 Exempt   Mod 63 Exempt   ⊙ Mod Sedation   PQRI

© 2009 Publisher (*Blue Ink*)   CPT only © 2009 American Medical Association. All Rights Reserved. (Black Ink)   Medicare (Red Ink)

95863

	95863	**3 extremities with or without related paraspinal areas** [S][80][□]
		Do not report with (95873-95874, 96000-96004)
		🚗 4.55 🚶 4.55 **Global Days XXX**
		AMA: 2009, Jan, 11-31; 2009, Jan, 7-8; 2008, Jan, 10-25; 2007, January, 13-27; 2006, June, 8-10; 2006, September, 5-8
	95864	**4 extremities with or without related paraspinal areas** [S][80][□]
		Do not report with (95873-95874, 96000-96004)
		🚗 4.87 🚶 4.87 **Global Days XXX**
		AMA: 2009, Jan, 11-31; 2009, Jan, 7-8; 2008, Jan, 10-25; 2007, January, 13-27; 2006, September, 5-8; 2006, June, 8-10
	95865	**larynx** [S][80]
		Code also modifier 52 for unilateral procedure.
		Do not report with (95873-95874, 96000-96004)
		🚗 3.31 🚶 3.31 **Global Days XXX**
		AMA: 2009, Jan, 11-31; 2009, Jan, 7-8; 2008, Jan, 10-25; 2007, Dec, 10-179; 2007, January, 13-27; 2006, September, 5-8
	95866	**hemidiaphragm** [S][80][50]
		Do not report with (95873-95874, 96000-96004)
		🚗 3.00 🚶 3.00 **Global Days XXX**
		AMA: 2009, Jan, 7-8; 2009, Jan, 11-31; 2008, Jan, 10-25; 2007, January, 13-27; 2006, September, 5-8
	95867	**cranial nerve supplied muscle(s), unilateral** [S][80][□]
		Do not report with (95873-95874, 96000-96004)
		🚗 2.29 🚶 2.29 **Global Days XXX**
		AMA: 2009, Jan, 11-31; 2009, Jan, 7-8; 2008, Jan, 10-25; 2007, Dec, 10-179; 2007, January, 13-27; 2006, September, 5-8; 2006, June, 8-10
	95868	**cranial nerve supplied muscles, bilateral** [S][80][□]
		Do not report with (95873-95874, 96000-96004)
		🚗 3.09 🚶 3.09 **Global Days XXX**
		AMA: 2009, Jan, 11-31; 2009, Jan, 7-8; 2008, Jan, 10-25; 2007, Dec, 10-179; 2007, January, 13-27; 2006, September, 5-8; 2006, June, 8-10
	95869	**thoracic paraspinal muscles (excluding T1 or T12)** [S][80][□]
		Do not report with (95873-95874, 96000-96004)
		🚗 1.79 🚶 1.79 **Global Days XXX**
		AMA: 2009, Jan, 11-31; 2009, Jan, 7-8; 2008, Jan, 10-25; 2007, January, 13-27; 2006, September, 5-8; 2006, June, 8-10
	95870	**limited study of muscles in 1 extremity or non-limb (axial) muscles (unilateral or bilateral), other than thoracic paraspinal, cranial nerve supplied muscles, or sphincters** [S][80]
		INCLUDES Adson test
		EXCLUDES *Anal/urethral sphincter/detrusor/urethra/perineum musculature (51785-51792)*
		Complete study of extremities (95860-95864)
		Eye muscles (92265)
		Do not report with (95873-95874, 96000-96004)
		🚗 1.73 🚶 1.73 **Global Days XXX**
		AMA: 2009, Jan, 11-31; 2009, Jan, 7-8; 2008, Jan, 10-25; 2007, January, 13-27; 2006, June, 8-10; 2006, September, 5-8; 2005, June, 9-11
	95872	**Needle electromyography using single fiber electrode, with quantitative measurement of jitter, blocking and/or fiber density, any/all sites of each muscle studied** [S][80]
		Do not report with motion analysis (96000-96004)
		🚗 5.13 🚶 5.13 **Global Days XXX**
		AMA: 2009, Jan, 11-31; 2009, Jan, 7-8; 2008, Jan, 10-25; 2007, January, 13-27; 2006, September, 5-8

+	95873	**Electrical stimulation for guidance in conjunction with chemodenervation (List separately in addition to code for primary procedure)** [N][80]
		Code first chemodenervation (64612-64614)
		Do not report with (95860-95870, 95874, 96000-96004)
		🚗 1.74 🚶 1.74 **Global Days ZZZ**
		AMA: 2009, Jan, 11-31; 2009, Jan, 7-8; 2008, Jan, 10-25; 2007, January, 13-27; 2006, September, 5-8
+	95874	**Needle electromyography for guidance in conjunction with chemodenervation (List separately in addition to code for primary procedure)** [N][80]
		Code first chemodenervation (64612-64614)
		Do not report with (95860-95870, 95873, 96000-96004)
		🚗 1.67 🚶 1.67 **Global Days ZZZ**
		AMA: 2009, Jan, 11-31; 2009, Jan, 7-8; 2009, Jun, 10-11; 2008, Jan, 10-25; 2007, January, 13-27; 2006, September, 5-8
	95875	**Ischemic limb exercise test with serial specimen(s) acquisition for muscle(s) metabolite(s)** [S][80][□]
		Do not report with (96000-96004)
		🚗 2.99 🚶 2.99 **Global Days XXX**
		AMA: 2009, Jan, 11-31; 2008, Jan, 10-25; 2007, January, 13-27
⊘	95900	**Nerve conduction, amplitude and latency/velocity study, each nerve; motor, without F-wave study** [S][80]
		INCLUDES Reporting this service only once when multiple sites on the same nerve are stimulated/recorded
		🚗 1.65 🚶 1.65 **Global Days XXX**
		AMA: 2009, Jan, 11-31; 2008, Jan, 10-25; 2008, Feb, 2; 2008, Feb, 1; 2007, January, 13-27; 2006, September, 5-8; 2006, June, 8-10; 2005, March, 16-17; 2005, December, 9-11
⊘	95903	**motor, with F-wave study** [S][80][□]
		INCLUDES Reporting this service only once when multiple sites on the same nerve are stimulated/recorded
		🚗 1.92 🚶 1.92 **Global Days XXX**
		AMA: 2009, Jan, 11-31; 2008, Jan, 10-25; 2008, Feb, 2; 2008, Feb, 1; 2007, January, 13-27; 2006, June, 8-10; 2006, September, 5-8; 2005, December, 9-11; 2005, March, 16-17
⊘	95904	**sensory** [S][80]
		INCLUDES Reporting this service only once when multiple sites on the same nerve are stimulated/recorded
		🚗 1.45 🚶 1.45 **Global Days XXX**
		AMA: 2009, Jan, 11-31; 2008, Jan, 10-25; 2008, Feb, 2; 2008, Feb, 1; 2007, January, 13-27; 2007, Jul, 12-13; 2006, September, 5-8; 2006, June, 8-10; 2005, March, 16-17; 2005, December, 9-11
⊘ ●	95905	**Motor and/or sensory nerve conduction, using preconfigured electrode array(s), amplitude and latency/velocity study, each limb, includes F-wave study when performed, with interpretation and report** [S][80]
		INCLUDES Reporting this code only once for each limb studied
		Study with preconfigured electrodes that are customized to a specific body location
		Do not report with (95900-95904, 95934-95936)
		🚗 2.11 🚶 2.11 **Global Days XXX**

| [26]/[10] **PC/TC Comp Only** | [A2]-[Z3] **ASC Pmt** | [50] **Bilateral** | ♂ **Male Only** | ♀ **Female Only** | 🚗 **Facility RVU** | 🚶 **Non-Facility RVU** |
| **AMA:** CPT Asst | **MED:** Pub 100 | [A]-[Y] **OPPSI** | ✗ **Non-FDA Drug** | 🔲 **Lab Crosswalk** | 🔲 **Radiology Crosswalk** |

CPT only © 2009 American Medical Association. All Rights Reserved. (Black Ink)   Medicare (Red Ink)   © 2009 Publisher (Blue Ink)

Current Procedural Coding Expert – Medicine

+ 95920 Intraoperative neurophysiology testing, per hour (List separately in addition to code for primary procedure) [N][80][P0]

INCLUDES:
- Electrophysiologic testing/monitoring that is ongoing while surgical procedures are performed
- Ongoing electrophysiologic monitoring time that is distinct from:
  - Interpretation of specific type(s) of baseline electrophysiologic study(s) (92585, 95822, 95870, 95925-95928, 95929, 95930)
  - Performance of specific type(s) of baseline electrophysiologic study(s) (95860, 95861, 95867, 95868, 95870, 95900, 95904, 95928, 95929, 95933-95937)
- Use of baseline electrophysiologic study(s) only once per operative session
- Use of code only once per hour, even if multiple electrophysiologic studies are performed

EXCLUDES:
- Electrocorticography (95829)
- Intraoperative:
  - EEG during nonintracranial surgery (95955)
  - Functional cortical/subcortical mapping (95961-95962)
  - Neurostimulator programming/analysis (95970-95975)
  - Time spent performing/interpreting baseline electrophysiologic study(s)

Code first primary procedure (92585, 95822, 95860, 95861, 95867, 95868, 95870, 95900, 95904, 95925-95937)

4.41   4.41   Global Days ZZZ

AMA: 2009, Jan, 11-31; 2008, Jan, 10-25; 2007, January, 13-27; 2005, June, 9-11

95921-95923 Evaluation of Autonomic Nervous System

INCLUDES:
- Physician interpretation
- Recording
- Report

EXCLUDES:
- Clinical depression treatment by repetitive transcranial magnetic stimulation (0160T-0161T)

95921 Testing of autonomic nervous system function; cardiovagal innervation (parasympathetic function), including 2 or more of the following: heart rate response to deep breathing with recorded R-R interval, Valsalva ratio, and 30:15 ratio [S][80][CCI]

2.20   2.20   Global Days XXX

AMA: 2009, Jan, 11-31; 2008, Jan, 10-25; 2007, January, 13-27; 2006, February, 16-18

95922 vasomotor adrenergic innervation (sympathetic adrenergic function), including beat-to-beat blood pressure and R-R interval changes during Valsalva maneuver and at least 5 minutes of passive tilt [S][80][CCI]

2.75   2.75   Global Days XXX

AMA: 2009, Jan, 11-31; 2008, Jan, 10-25; 2007, January, 13-27; 2006, December, 10-12; 2006, February, 16-18

95923 sudomotor, including 1 or more of the following: quantitative sudomotor axon reflex test (QSART), silastic sweat imprint, thermoregulatory sweat test, and changes in sympathetic skin potential [S][80][CCI]

4.14   4.14   Global Days XXX

AMA: 2009, Jan, 11-31; 2008, Jan, 10-25; 2007, January, 13-27; 2006, February, 16-18

95925-95937 Neurotransmission Studies

95925 Short-latency somatosensory evoked potential study, stimulation of any/all peripheral nerves or skin sites, recording from the central nervous system; in upper limbs [S][80]

EXCLUDES: Auditory evoked potentials (92585)

4.63   4.63   Global Days XXX

95926 in lower limbs [S][80]

EXCLUDES: Auditory evoked potentials (92585)

4.49   4.49   Global Days XXX

AMA: 2009, Jan, 11-31; 2008, Jan, 10-25; 2007, January, 13-27

95927 in the trunk or head [S][80]

EXCLUDES: Auditory evoked potentials (92585)

Code also modifier 52 for unilateral test

3.94   3.94   Global Days XXX

95928 Central motor evoked potential study (transcranial motor stimulation); upper limbs [S][80]

6.85   6.85   Global Days XXX

95929 lower limbs [S][80]

7.27   7.27   Global Days XXX

95930 Visual evoked potential (VEP) testing central nervous system, checkerboard or flash [S][80]

3.78   3.78   Global Days XXX

95933 Orbicularis oculi (blink) reflex, by electrodiagnostic testing [S][80]

2.17   2.17   Global Days XXX

95934 H-reflex, amplitude and latency study; record gastrocnemius/soleus muscle [S][80][50]

1.65   1.65   Global Days XXX

AMA: 2009, Jan, 11-31; 2008, Jan, 10-25; 2007, January, 13-27; 2006, June, 8-10

95936 record muscle other than gastrocnemius/soleus muscle [S][80][50]

1.32   1.32   Global Days XXX

AMA: 2006, June, 8-10

95937 Neuromuscular junction testing (repetitive stimulation, paired stimuli), each nerve, any 1 method [S][80][CCI]

1.84   1.84   Global Days XXX

AMA: 2006, June, 8-10

95950-95962 Electroencephalography For Seizure Monitoring/Intraoperative Use

EXCLUDES:
- Clinical depression treatment by repetitive transcranial magnetic stimulation (0160T-0161T)
- Consultation services (99241-99255)
- Evaluation and management services (99201-99499)

95950 Monitoring for identification and lateralization of cerebral seizure focus, electroencephalographic (eg, 8 channel EEG) recording and interpretation, each 24 hours [S][80][CCI]

8.44   8.44   Global Days XXX

95951 Monitoring for localization of cerebral seizure focus by cable or radio, 16 or more channel telemetry, combined electroencephalographic (EEG) and video recording and interpretation (eg, for presurgical localization), each 24 hours [S][80][CCI]

0.00   0.00   Global Days XXX

AMA: 2009, Jan, 11-31; 2008, Jan, 10-25; 2007, January, 13-27

● New Code   ▲ Revised Code   M Maternity   A Age   Unlisted   Not Covered   # Resequenced
CCI   + Add-on   ⊘ Mod 51 Exempt   Mod 63 Exempt   ⊙ Mod Sedation   PQRI

© 2009 Publisher *(Blue Ink)*   CPT only © 2009 American Medical Association. All Rights Reserved. *(Black Ink)*   Medicare *(Red Ink)*   389

95953	Monitoring for localization of cerebral seizure focus by computerized portable 16 or more channel EEG, electroencephalographic (EEG) recording and interpretation, each 24 hours 13.77 13.77 Global Days XXX
95954	Pharmacological or physical activation requiring physician attendance during EEG recording of activation phase (eg, thiopental activation test) 8.70 8.70 Global Days XXX
95955	Electroencephalogram (EEG) during nonintracranial surgery (eg, carotid surgery) 4.80 4.80 Global Days XXX
95956	Monitoring for localization of cerebral seizure focus by cable or radio, 16 or more channel telemetry, electroencephalographic (EEG) recording and interpretation, each 24 hours 21.57 21.57 Global Days XXX
95957	Digital analysis of electroencephalogram (EEG) (eg, for epileptic spike analysis) 10.17 10.17 Global Days XXX
95958	Wada activation test for hemispheric function, including electroencephalographic (EEG) monitoring 13.22 13.22 Global Days XXX
95961	Functional cortical and subcortical mapping by stimulation and/or recording of electrodes on brain surface, or of depth electrodes, to provoke seizures or identify vital brain structures; initial hour of physician attendance 7.22 7.22 Global Days XXX
+ 95962	each additional hour of physician attendance (List separately in addition to code for primary procedure) Code first initial hour (95961) 6.41 6.41 Global Days ZZZ

95965-95967 Magnetoencephalography

INCLUDES Physician interpretation
Recording
Report

EXCLUDES Clinical depression treatment by repetitive transcranial magnetic stimulation (0160T-0161T)
Consultation services (99241-99255)
CT provided along with magnetoencephalography (70450-70470, 70496)
Electroencephalography provided along with magnetoencephalography (95812-95827)
Evaluation and management services (99201-99499)
MRI provided along with magnetoencephalography (70551-70553)
Somatosensory evoked potentials/auditory evoked potentials/visual evoked potentials provided along with magnetic evoked field responses (92585, 95925, 95926, 95930)

95965	Magnetoencephalography (MEG), recording and analysis; for spontaneous brain magnetic activity (eg, epileptic cerebral cortex localization) 0.00 0.00 Global Days XXX
95966	for evoked magnetic fields, single modality (eg, sensory, motor, language, or visual cortex localization) 0.00 0.00 Global Days XXX
+ 95967	for evoked magnetic fields, each additional modality (eg, sensory, motor, language, or visual cortex localization) (List separately in addition to code for primary procedure) Code first single modality (95966) 0.00 0.00 Global Days ZZZ

95970-95982 Evaluation of Implanted Neurostimulator

CMS 100-3,160.12 Neuromuscular Electrical Stimulation (NMES)
CMS 100-3,160.13 Supplies Used for Transcutaneous Electrical Nerve Stimulation and Neuromuscular Electrical Stimulation (NMES)
CMS 100-4,32,50 Deep Brain Stimulation for Essential Tremor and Parkinson's Disease

INCLUDES Simple neurostimulator (three or less of the following); or complex neurostimulator (three or more of the following):
8 or more electrode contacts
Alternating electrode polarities
Cycling
Dose time
More than 1 clinical feature
Number of channels
Number of programs
Pulse amplitude
Pulse duration
Pulse frequency
Stimulation train duration
Train spacing

EXCLUDES Clinical depression treatment by repetitive transcranial magnetic stimulation (0160T-0161T)
Consultation services (99241-99255)
Evaluation and management services (99201-99499)
Neurostimulator electrodes:
   Implantation (0155T-0157T, 43647, 43881, 61850-61875, 63650-63655, 64553-64580)
   Revision/removal (0156T, 0158T, 43648, 43882, 61880, 63661-63664, 64585)
Neurostimulator pulse generator/receiver
   Insertion (61885, 63685, 64590)
   Revision/removal (61888, 63688, 64595)

95970	Electronic analysis of implanted neurostimulator pulse generator system (eg, rate, pulse amplitude and duration, configuration of wave form, battery status, electrode selectability, output modulation, cycling, impedance and patient compliance measurements); simple or complex brain, spinal cord, or peripheral (ie, cranial nerve, peripheral nerve, autonomic nerve, neuromuscular) neurostimulator pulse generator/transmitter, without reprogramming 0.66 1.67 Global Days XXX **AMA:** 2009, Jan, 11-31; 2008, Jan, 10-25; 2007, January, 13-27; 2006, December, 10-12; 2005, August, 7-8; 2005, September, 9-11
95971	simple spinal cord, or peripheral (ie, peripheral nerve, autonomic nerve, neuromuscular) neurostimulator pulse generator/transmitter, with intraoperative or subsequent programming 1.10 1.51 Global Days XXX **AMA:** 2005, August, 7-8
95972	complex spinal cord, or peripheral (except cranial nerve) neurostimulator pulse generator/transmitter, with intraoperative or subsequent programming, first hour 2.18 2.91 Global Days XXX **AMA:** 2006, May, 12-15; 2005, August, 7-8
+ 95973	complex spinal cord, or peripheral (except cranial nerve) neurostimulator pulse generator/transmitter, with intraoperative or subsequent programming, each additional 30 minutes after first hour (List separately in addition to code for primary procedure) Code first initial hour (95972) 1.35 1.69 Global Days ZZZ **AMA:** 2006, May, 12-15; 2005, August, 7-8

Current Procedural Coding Expert – Medicine

95974	complex cranial nerve neurostimulator pulse generator/transmitter, with intraoperative or subsequent programming, with or without nerve interface testing, first hour [S][80]

4.31 5.21 Global Days XXX
AMA: 2009, Jan, 11-31; 2008, Jan, 10-25; 2007, January, 13-27; 2006, December, 10-12; 2005, September, 9-11

+ **95975** complex cranial nerve neurostimulator pulse generator/transmitter, with intraoperative or subsequent programming, each additional 30 minutes after first hour (List separately in addition to code for primary procedure) [S][80]
Code first initial hour (95974)
2.46 2.79 Global Days ZZZ
AMA: 2009, Jan, 11-31; 2008, Jan, 10-25; 2007, January, 13-27; 2006, December, 10-12; 2005, September, 9-11

95978 Electronic analysis of implanted neurostimulator pulse generator system (eg, rate, pulse amplitude and duration, battery status, electrode selectability and polarity, impedance and patient compliance measurements), complex deep brain neurostimulator pulse generator/transmitter, with initial or subsequent programming; first hour [S][80]
5.20 6.36 Global Days XXX
AMA: 2005, August, 7-8

+ **95979** each additional 30 minutes after first hour (List separately in addition to code for primary procedure) [S][80]
Code first initial hour (95978)
2.42 2.79 Global Days ZZZ
AMA: 2005, August, 7-8

95980 Electronic analysis of implanted neurostimulator pulse generator system (eg, rate, pulse amplitude and duration, configuration of wave form, battery status, electrode selectability, output modulation, cycling, impedance and patient measurements) gastric neurostimulator pulse generator/transmitter; intraoperative, with programming [N][80]
INCLUDES Gastric neurostimulator of lesser curvature (95980-95982)
1.26 1.26 Global Days XXX
AMA: 2008, Jan, 8-9

95981 subsequent, without reprogramming [S][80]
0.49 0.82 Global Days XXX
AMA: 2008, Jan, 8-9

95982 subsequent, with reprogramming [S][80]
1.01 1.39 Global Days XXX
AMA: 2008, Jan, 8-9

95990-95991 Refill/Upkeep of Implanted Drug Delivery Pump to Central Nervous System

CMS 100-3,280.14 Infusion Pumps
EXCLUDES Clinical depression treatment by repetitive transcranial magnetic stimulation (0160T-0161T)
Consultation services (99241-99255)
Evaluation and management services (99201-99499)

95990 Refilling and maintenance of implantable pump or reservoir for drug delivery, spinal (intrathecal, epidural) or brain (intraventricular); [S][80]
EXCLUDES Analysis/reprogramming of implanted pump for infusion (62367-62368)
Refilling/maintenance implantable drug delivery pump (96522)
2.14 2.14 Global Days XXX
AMA: 2009, Jan, 11-31; 2008, Jan, 10-25; 2007, January, 13-27; 2006, April, 19-20; 2005, January, 46-47; 2005, November, 1-9

95991 administered by physician [S][80]
1.11 3.02 Global Days XXX
AMA: 2006, April, 19-20; 2005, November, 1-9

95992-95999 Other and Unlisted Neurological Procedures

⊘ **95992** Canalith repositioning procedure(s) (eg, Epley maneuver, Semont maneuver), per day [E]
Do not report with (92531-92532)
1.06 1.17 Global Days XXX
AMA: 2009, Jan, 3,4&9

95999 Unlisted neurological or neuromuscular diagnostic procedure [S][80]
0.00 0.00 Global Days XXX
AMA: 2009, Jan, 11-31; 2008, Jan, 10-25; 2007, March, 4-5; 2007, April, 7-10; 2007, January, 13-27

96000-96004 Motion Analysis Studies

CMS 100-2,15,80 Physician Supervision Requirements for Diagnostic Tests
CMS 100-2,15,230.4 Services By a Physical/Occupational Therapist in Private Practice
INCLUDES Services provided as part of major therapeutic/diagnostic decision making
Services provided in a dedicated motion analysis department capable of
3-D kinetics/dynamic electromyography
Computerized 3-D kinematics
Videotaping from the front/back/both sides
EXCLUDES Clinical depression treatment by repetitive transcranial magnetic stimulation (0160T-0161T)
Consultation services (99241-99255)
Evaluation and management services (99201-99499)
Gait training (97116)
Needle electromyography (95860-95875)

96000 Comprehensive computer-based motion analysis by video-taping and 3D kinematics; [S][80]
2.59 2.59 Global Days XXX
AMA: 2007, May, 3-4

96001 with dynamic plantar pressure measurements during walking [S][80]
3.01 3.01 Global Days XXX

96002 Dynamic surface electromyography, during walking or other functional activities, 1-12 muscles [S][80]
Do not report with (95860-95864, 95869-95872)
0.58 0.58 Global Days XXX

96003 Dynamic fine wire electromyography, during walking or other functional activities, 1 muscle [S][80]
Do not report with (95860-95864, 95869-95872)
0.54 0.54 Global Days XXX

96004 Physician review and interpretation of comprehensive computer-based motion analysis, dynamic plantar pressure measurements, dynamic surface electromyography during walking or other functional activities, and dynamic fine wire electromyography, with written report [B][26][80]
3.12 3.12 Global Days XXX

● New Code ▲ Revised Code [M] Maternity [A] Age Unlisted Not Covered # Resequenced
[CCI] + Add-on ⊘ Mod 51 Exempt Mod 63 Exempt ⊙ Mod Sedation [PQ] PQRI

96020 Neurofunctional Brain Testing

96020 Neurofunctional testing selection and administration during noninvasive imaging functional brain mapping, with test administered entirely by a physician or psychologist, with review of test results and report

INCLUDES Selection/administration of testing of:
- Cognition
- Determination of validity of neurofunctional testing relative to separately interpreted functional magnetic resonance images
- Functional neuroimaging
- Language
- Memory
- Monitoring performance of testing
- Movement
- Other neurological functions
- Sensation

EXCLUDES Clinical depression treatment by repetitive transcranial magnetic stimulation (0160T-0161T)
Consultation services (99241-99255)
Evaluation and management services (99201-99499)

Do not report with (70554, 96101-96103, 96116-96120, 99201-99499)

↔ 70555

💰 0.00 💰 0.00 Global Days XXX
AMA: 2007, February, 6-7

96040 Genetic Counseling Services

INCLUDES
- Analysis for genetic risk assessment
- Counseling of patient/family
- Counseling services
- Face-to-face interviews
- Obtaining structured family genetic history
- Pedigree construction
- Review of medical data/family information
- Services provided by trained genetic counselor
- Services provided during one or more sessions

EXCLUDES
Education/genetic counseling by a physician to a group (99078)
Education/genetic counseling by a physician to an individual (99201-99499)
Education regarding genetic risks by a nonphysician to a group (98961, 98962)
Genetic counseling and/or risk factor reduction intervention from a physician, provided to patients without symptoms/diagnosis (99401-99412)

96040 Medical genetics and genetic counseling services, each 30 minutes face-to-face with patient/family

INCLUDES
- Analysis for genetic risk assessment
- Counseling of patient/family
- Counseling services
- Face-to-face interviews
- Obtaining structured family genetic history
- Pedigree construction
- Review of medical data/family information
- Services provided by trained genetic counselor
- Services provided during one or more sessions

💰 1.06 💰 1.06 Global Days XXX
AMA: 2007, Aug, 9-12

96101-96125 Cognitive Capability Assessments

CMS 100-1,3,30 Outpatient Mental Health Treatment Limitation
CMS 100-1,3,30.1 Application of Mental Health Limitation - Status of Patient
CMS 100-1,3,30.2 Disorders Subject to Mental Health Limitation
CMS 100-2,15,80.2 Psychological and Neuropsychological Tests
CMS 100-2,15,160 Clinical Psychologist Services
CMS 100-4,12,150 Clinical Social Worker (CSW) Services
CMS 100-4,12,160 Independent Psychologist Services
CMS 100-4,12,170 Clinical Psychologist Services
CMS 100-4,12,170.1 Payment for Clinical Psychologist Services
CMS 100-4,12,210 Outpatient Mental Health Limitation

INCLUDES Cognitive function testing of the central nervous system

EXCLUDES Cognitive skills development (97532, 97533)
Physician conducted mini-mental status examination (99201-99499)

96101 Psychological testing (includes psychodiagnostic assessment of emotionality, intellectual abilities, personality and psychopathology, eg, MMPI, Rorschach, WAIS), per hour of the psychologist's or physician's time, both face-to-face time administering tests to the patient and time interpreting these test results and preparing the report

INCLUDES Situations when more time is needed to assimilate other clinical data sources including tests administered by a technician or computer and previously reported

EXCLUDES Interpretation and report of (96102-96103)

💰 2.14 💰 2.15 Global Days XXX
AMA: 2006, December, 8-9

96102 Psychological testing (includes psychodiagnostic assessment of emotionality, intellectual abilities, personality and psychopathology, eg, MMPI and WAIS), with qualified health care professional interpretation and report, administered by technician, per hour of technician time, face-to-face

💰 0.63 💰 1.51 Global Days XXX
AMA: 2006, December, 8-9

96103 Psychological testing (includes psychodiagnostic assessment of emotionality, intellectual abilities, personality and psychopathology, eg, MMPI), administered by a computer, with qualified health care professional interpretation and report

💰 0.68 💰 1.63 Global Days XXX
AMA: 2006, December, 8-9

96105 Assessment of aphasia (includes assessment of expressive and receptive speech and language function, language comprehension, speech production ability, reading, spelling, writing, eg, by Boston Diagnostic Aphasia Examination) with interpretation and report, per hour

💰 2.49 💰 2.49 Global Days XXX
AMA: 2005, May, 1-2

96110 Developmental testing; limited (eg, Developmental Screening Test II, Early Language Milestone Screen), with interpretation and report

💰 0.21 💰 0.21 Global Days XXX
AMA: 2005, May, 1-2

96111 extended (includes assessment of motor, language, social, adaptive and/or cognitive functioning by standardized developmental instruments) with interpretation and report

💰 3.59 💰 3.72 Global Days XXX
AMA: 2005, May, 1-2

Current Procedural Coding Expert – Medicine

96116 Neurobehavioral status exam (clinical assessment of thinking, reasoning and judgment, eg, acquired knowledge, attention, language, memory, planning and problem solving, and visual spatial abilities), per hour of the psychologist's or physician's time, both face-to-face time with the patient and time interpreting test results and preparing the report [03] [80] [PQ]
  2.38   2.51   Global Days XXX
  AMA: 2009, Jan, 11-31; 2008, Jan, 10-25; 2007, January, 13-27; 2006, September, 14-16; 2006, December, 8-9

96118 Neuropsychological testing (eg, Halstead-Reitan Neuropsychological Battery, Wechsler Memory Scales and Wisconsin Card Sorting Test), per hour of the psychologist's or physician's time, both face-to-face time administering tests to the patient and time interpreting these test results and preparing the report [03] [80]
  EXCLUDES Interpretation and report of (96119-96120)
  INCLUDES Situations when more time is needed to assimilate other clinical data sources including tests administered by a technician or computer and previously reported
  2.12   2.48   Global Days XXX
  AMA: 2006, December, 8-9; 2006, September, 14-16

96119 Neuropsychological testing (eg, Halstead-Reitan Neuropsychological Battery, Wechsler Memory Scales and Wisconsin Card Sorting Test), with qualified health care professional interpretation and report, administered by technician, per hour of technician time, face-to-face [03] [80]
  0.64   1.74   Global Days XXX
  AMA: 2006, September, 14-16; 2006, December, 8-9

96120 Neuropsychological testing (eg, Wisconsin Card Sorting Test), administered by a computer, with qualified health care professional interpretation and report [03] [80]
  0.67   2.30   Global Days XXX
  AMA: 2009, Jan, 11-31; 2008, Jan, 10-25; 2007, January, 13-27; 2006, September, 14-16; 2006, December, 8-9

96125 Standardized cognitive performance testing (eg, Ross Information Processing Assessment) per hour of a qualified health care professional's time, both face-to-face time administering tests to the patient and time interpreting these test results and preparing the report [A] [80]
  EXCLUDES Neuropsychological testing by a physician or psychologist (96118-96120)
  Psychological testing by a physician or psychologist (96101-96103)
  2.36   2.78   Global Days XXX

96150-96155 Biopsychosocial Assessment/Intervention

INCLUDES Services for patients that have primary physical illnesses/diagnoses/symptoms who may benefit from assessments/interventions that focus on the biopsychosocial factors related to the patient's health status
Services used to identify the following factors which are important to the prevention/treatment/management of physical health problems:
  Behavioral
  Cognitive
  Emotional
  Psychological
  Social

EXCLUDES Health and behavior assessment/intervention done by a physician (99201-99499)
Preventive medicine counseling/risk factor reduction/behavioral change (99401-99412)

Do not report evaluation and management service codes, including 99401-99412, on the same day
Do not report with (90801-90899, 99401-99404, 99411-99412)

96150 Health and behavior assessment (eg, health-focused clinical interview, behavioral observations, psychophysiological monitoring, health-oriented questionnaires), each 15 minutes face-to-face with the patient; initial assessment [03] [80] [PQ]
  0.56   0.57   Global Days XXX
  AMA: 2009, Jan, 11-31; 2008, Jan, 10-25; 2007, January, 13-27; 2005, June, 9-11; 2005, May, 1-2

96151 re-assessment [03] [80] [PQ]
  0.54   0.55   Global Days XXX
  AMA: 2009, Jan, 11-31; 2008, Jan, 10-25; 2007, January, 13-27; 2005, May, 1-2; 2005, June, 9-11

96152 Health and behavior intervention, each 15 minutes, face-to-face; individual [03] [80] [PQ]
  0.52   0.53   Global Days XXX
  AMA: 2009, Jan, 11-31; 2008, Jan, 10-25; 2007, January, 13-27; 2005, May, 1-2; 2005, June, 9-11

96153 group (2 or more patients) [03] [80]
  0.12   0.13   Global Days XXX
  AMA: 2009, Jan, 11-31; 2008, Jan, 10-25; 2007, January, 13-27; 2005, May, 1-2; 2005, June, 9-11

96154 family (with the patient present) [03] [80]
  0.51   0.51   Global Days XXX
  AMA: 2009, Jan, 11-31; 2008, Jan, 10-25; 2007, January, 13-27; 2005, June, 9-11; 2005, May, 1-2

96155 family (without the patient present) [E]
  0.62   0.62   Global Days XXX
  AMA: 2009, Jan, 11-31; 2008, Jan, 10-25; 2007, January, 13-27; 2005, May, 1-2; 2005, June, 9-11

● New Code ▲ Revised Code M Maternity A Age Unlisted Not Covered # Resequenced
CCI + Add-on ⊘ Mod 51 Exempt ⊘ Mod 63 Exempt ⊙ Mod Sedation PQRI
© 2009 Publisher *(Blue Ink)* CPT only © 2009 American Medical Association. All Rights Reserved. *(Black Ink)* Medicare *(Red Ink)*

96360-96361 Intravenous Fluid Infusion for Hydration (Nonchemotherapy)

CMS 100-4,12,30.5   Payment for Injections and Infusions: Chemotherapy and Nonchemotherapy

INCLUDES Coding hierarchy rules for facility reporting only:
- Diagnostic, prophylactic, and therapeutic services are primary to hydration services
- Chemotherapy services are primary to diagnostic, prophylactic, and therapeutic services
- Infusions are primary to pushes
- Pushes are primary to injections

Direct physician supervision:
- Direction of personnel

Minimal supervision for:
- Consent
- Safety oversight
- Supervision of personnel

Physicians report the initial code for the primary reason for the visit regardless of the order in which the infusions or injections are given

Pre-packaged fluid/electrolytes

The following if done to facilitate the injection/infusion:
- Flush at the end of infusion
- Indwelling IV, subcutaneous catheter/port access
- Local anesthesia
- Start of IV
- Supplies/tubing/syringes
- Treatment plan verification

EXCLUDES Catheter/port declotting (36593)
Drugs/other substances
Significant separately identifiable evaluation and management service if performed

Do not report with infusion for hydration that is 30 minutes or less

96360   **Intravenous infusion, hydration; initial, 31 minutes to 1 hour** [S] [80]
- Do not report hydration infusions of 30 minutes or less
- Do not report if performed as a concurrent infusion
- 1.32   1.32   Global Days XXX
- AMA: 2009, Feb, 17-21

+ 96361   **each additional hour (List separately in addition to code for primary procedure)** [S] [80]
- **INCLUDES** Hydration infusion of more than 30 minutes beyond 1 hour
- Hydration provided as a secondary or subsequent service after a different initial service via the same IV access site
- Code first (96360)
- 0.36   0.36   Global Days ZZZ
- AMA: 2009, May, 8-9&11; 2009, Feb, 17-21

96365-96371 Infusions: Diagnostic/Preventive/Therapeutic

CMS 100-4,12,30.5   Payment for Injections and Infusions: Chemotherapy and Nonchemotherapy
CMS 100-4,20,160.1   Billing for Total Parenteral Nutrition Furnished to Part B Inpatients

INCLUDES Administration of fluid
Administration of substances/drugs
An infusion of 15 minutes or less
Coding heirarchy rules for facility reporting:
- Chemotherapy services are primary to diagnostic, prophylactic, and therapeutic services
- Diagnostic, prophylactic, and therapeutic services are primary to hydration services
- Infusions are primary to pushes
- Pushes are primary to injections

Constant presence of health care professional administering the substance/drug

Direct physician supervision:
- Consent
- Direction of personnel
- Patient assessment
- Safety oversight
- Supervision of personnel

The following if done to facilitate the injection/infusion:
- Flush at the end of infusion
- Indwelling IV, subcutaneous catheter/port access
- Local anesthesia
- Start of IV
- Supplies/tubing/syringes

Training to assess patient and monitor vital signs
Training to prepare/dose/dispose
Treatment plan verification

EXCLUDES Catheter/port declotting (36593)
Significant separately identifiable evaluation and management service if performed

Code also drugs/materials

Do not report with codes for which IV push or infusion is an integral part of the procedure

96365   **Intravenous infusion, for therapy, prophylaxis, or diagnosis (specify substance or drug); initial, up to 1 hour** [S] [80]
- 1.67   1.67   Global Days XXX
- AMA: 2009, Feb, 17-21

+ 96366   **each additional hour (List separately in addition to code for primary procedure)** [S] [80]
- **INCLUDES** Additional hours of sequential infusion
- Infusion intervals of more than 30 minutes beyond one hour
- Code first (96365, 96367)
- 0.53   0.53   Global Days ZZZ
- AMA: 2009, Feb, 17-21

+ 96367   **additional sequential infusion, up to 1 hour (List separately in addition to code for primary procedure)** [S] [80]
- **INCLUDES** A secondary or subsequent service after a different initial service via the same IV access
- Code also (96365, 96374, 96409, 96413)
- Do not report more than once per sequential infusion of the same mix
- 0.75   0.75   Global Days ZZZ
- AMA: 2009, Feb, 17-21

Current Procedural Coding Expert – Medicine

+ 96368 concurrent infusion (List separately in addition to code for primary procedure)
Code also (96365, 96366, 96413, 96415, 96416)
Do not report more than once per encounter
0.47 0.47 Global Days ZZZ
AMA: 2009, Feb, 17-21

96369 Subcutaneous infusion for therapy or prophylaxis (specify substance or drug); initial, up to 1 hour, including pump set-up and establishment of subcutaneous infusion site(s)
EXCLUDES Infusions of 15 minutes or less (96372)
3.58 3.58 Global Days XXX
AMA: 2009, Feb, 17-21

+ 96370 each additional hour (List separately in addition to code for primary procedure)
INCLUDES Infusions of more than 30 minutes beyond one hour
Code first (96369)
Do not report more than once per encounter
0.41 0.41 Global Days ZZZ
AMA: 2009, Feb, 17-21

+ 96371 additional pump set-up with establishment of new subcutaneous infusion site(s) (List separately in addition to code for primary procedure)
Code also (96369)
Do not report more than once per encounter
2.19 2.19 Global Days ZZZ
AMA: 2009, Feb, 17-21

96372-96379 Injections: Diagnostic/Preventive/Therapeutic

CMS 100-4,12,30.5   Payment for Injections and Infusions: Chemotherapy and Nonchemotherapy

INCLUDES
Administration of fluid
Administration of substances/drugs
Coding heirarchy rules for facility reporting:
    Chemotherapy services are primary to diagnostic, prophylactic, and therapeutic services
    Infusions are primary to pushes
    Pushes are primary to injections
Constant presence of health care professional administering the substance/drug
Direct physician supervision:
    Consent
    Direction of personnel
    Patient assessment
    Safety oversight
    Supervision of personnel
Infusion of 15 minutes or less
The following if done to facilitate the injection/infusion:
    Flush at the end of infusion
    Indwelling IV, subcutaneous catheter/port access
    Local anesthesia
    Start of IV
    Supplies/tubing/syringes
Training to assess patient and monitor vital signs
Training to prepare/dose/dispose
Treatment plan verification

EXCLUDES
Catheter/port declotting (36593)
Significant separately identifiable evaluation and management service if performed

Code also drugs/materials
Do not report with codes for which IV push or infusion is an integral part of the procedure

96372 Therapeutic, prophylactic, or diagnostic injection (specify substance or drug); subcutaneous or intramuscular
INCLUDES Direct physician supervision when reported by the physician. When reported by a hospital, physician need not be present.
EXCLUDES Administration of vaccines/toxiods (90465, 90466, 90471, 90472)
Allergen immunotherapy injections (95115-95117)
Antineoplastic hormonal injections (96402)
Antineoplastic nonhormonal injections (96401)
Hormonal therapy injections (non-antineoplastic) (96372)
0.60 0.60 Global Days XXX
AMA: 2009, Feb, 17-21

96373 intra-arterial
0.50 0.50 Global Days XXX
AMA: 2009, Feb, 17-21

96374 intravenous push, single or initial substance/drug
1.29 1.29 Global Days XXX
AMA: 2009, May, 8-9&11; 2009, Feb, 17-21

96375 — 96411

+ 96375 each additional sequential intravenous push of a new substance/drug (List separately in addition to code for primary procedure) [S] [80]
  INCLUDES IV push of a new substance/drug provided as a secondary or subsequent service after a different initial service via same IV access site
  Code also (96365, 96374, 96409, 96413)
  0.52 0.52 Global Days ZZZ
  AMA: 2009, Feb, 17-21

+ 96376 each additional sequential intravenous push of the same substance/drug provided in a facility (List separately in addition to code for primary procedure) [N]
  INCLUDES Facilities only
  EXCLUDES Services performed by any provider that is not a facility
  Do not report a push performed within 30 minutes of a reported push of the same substance or drug
  0.00 0.00 Global Days ZZZ
  AMA: 2009, May, 8-9&11; 2009, Feb, 17-21

96379 Unlisted therapeutic, prophylactic, or diagnostic intravenous or intra-arterial injection or infusion [S] [80]
  0.00 0.00 Global Days XXX
  AMA: 2009, Feb, 17-21

96401-96411 Chemotherapy and Other Complex Drugs, Biologicals: Injection

CMS 100-3,110.2 Certain Drugs Distributed by the National Cancer Institute
CMS 100-3,110.6 Scalp Hypothermia During Chemotherapy, to Prevent Hair Loss
CMS 100-4,4,230.2.2 Chemotherapy Drug Administration
CMS 100-4,12,30.5 Payment for Injections and Infusions: Chemotherapy and Nonchemotherapy

INCLUDES An infusion of 15 minutes or less
Constant presence of the health care professional administering the drug or substance
Highly complex services that require direct supervision for:
  Consent
  Patient assessment
  Safety oversight
  Supervision
Intravenous/intra-arterial push
More intense physician work and monitoring of clinical staff due to greater risk of severe patient reactions.
Parenteral administration of:
  Anti-neoplastic agents for noncancer diagnoses
  Monoclonal antibody agents
  Nonradionuclide antineoplastic drugs
  Other biologic response modifiers
Do not report with physician services provided in the facility setting with these codes.

96401 Chemotherapy administration, subcutaneous or intramuscular; non-hormonal anti-neoplastic [S] [80] [PQ]
  1.70 1.70 Global Days XXX
  AMA: 2009, Feb, 17-21; 2009, Jan, 11-31; 2008, Jan, 10-25; 2007, May, 3-4; 2007, June, 4-6; 2007, January, 13-27; 2007, January, 28-31; 2005, November, 1-9

96402 hormonal anti-neoplastic [S] [80] [PQ]
  0.77 0.77 Global Days XXX
  AMA: 2009, Jan, 11-31; 2009, Feb, 17-21; 2008, Jan, 10-25; 2007, January, 13-27; 2007, June, 4-6; 2007, January, 28-31; 2007, May, 3-4; 2005, November, 1-9

96405 Chemotherapy administration; intralesional, up to and including 7 lesions [S] [▫] [PQ]
  0.82 2.00 Global Days 000
  AMA: 2009, Jan, 11-31; 2009, Feb, 17-21; 2008, Jan, 10-25; 2007, May, 3-4; 2007, January, 13-27; 2007, June, 4-6; 2007, January, 28-31; 2005, November, 1-9

96406 intralesional, more than 7 lesions [S] [▫] [PQ]
  1.22 2.82 Global Days 000
  AMA: 2009, Jan, 11-31; 2009, Feb, 17-21; 2008, Jan, 10-25; 2007, January, 28-31; 2007, May, 3-4; 2007, June, 4-6; 2007, January, 13-27; 2005, November, 1-9

96409 intravenous, push technique, single or initial substance/drug [S] [80] [PQ]
  Do not report with 36823
  2.49 2.49 Global Days XXX
  AMA: 2009, Jan, 11-31; 2009, Feb, 17-21; 2008, Jan, 10-25; 2007, May, 3-4; 2007, June, 4-6; 2007, January, 28-31; 2007, January, 13-27; 2005, November, 1-9

+ 96411 intravenous, push technique, each additional substance/drug (List separately in addition to code for primary procedure) [S] [80] [PQ]
  Code first initial substance/drug (96409, 96413)
  Do not report with 36823
  1.41 1.41 Global Days ZZZ
  AMA: 2009, Jan, 11-31; 2009, Feb, 17-21; 2008, Jan, 10-25; 2007, June, 4-6; 2007, January, 28-31; 2007, January, 13-27; 2007, May, 3-4; 2005, November, 1-9

Current Procedural Coding Expert – Medicine

96413-96417 Chemotherapy and Complex Drugs, Biologicals: Intravenous Infusion

CMS 100-3,110.2 — Certain Drugs Distributed by the National Cancer Institute
CMS 100-3,110.6 — Scalp Hypothermia During Chemotherapy, to Prevent Hair Loss
CMS 100-4,4,230.2 — Coding and Payment for Drug Administration
CMS 100-4,4,230.2.2 — Chemotherapy Drug Administration
CMS 100-4,12,30.5 — Payment for Injections and Infusions: Chemotherapy and Nonchemotherapy

INCLUDES
- An infusion of 15 minutes or less
- Constant presence of the health care professional administering the drug or substance
- Highly complex services that require direct supervision for:
  - Consent
  - Patient assessment
  - Safety oversight
  - Supervision
- Intravenous/intra-arterial push
- More intense physician work and monitoring of clinical staff due to greater risk of severe patient reactions
- Parenteral administration of:
  - Anti-neoplastic agents for noncancer diagnoses
  - Monoclonal antibody agents
  - Nonradionuclide antineoplastic drugs
  - Other biologic response modifiers
- The following in the administration:
  - Access to IV/catheter/port
  - Drug preparation
  - Flushing at the completion of the infusion
  - Hydration fluid
  - Routine tubing/syringe/supplies
  - Starting the IV
  - Use of local anesthesia

EXCLUDES
- Administration of nonchemotherapy agents such as antibiotics/steriods/analgesics
- Declotting of catheter/port (36593)
- Home infusion (99601-99602)

Code also drug or substance
Code also significant separately identifiable evaluation and management service, if performed
Do not report with 36823
Do not report with physician services provided in the facility setting with these codes.

96413 Chemotherapy administration, intravenous infusion technique; up to 1 hour, single or initial substance/drug

EXCLUDES
- Hydration administered as secondary or subsequent service via same IV access site (96361)
- Therapeutic/prophylactic/diagnostic drug infusion/injection through the same intravenous access (96366, 96367, 96375)

3.20   3.20 Global Days XXX
AMA: 2009, Jan, 11-31; 2009, Feb, 17-21; 2008, Jan, 10-25; 2007, May, 3-4; 2007, Dec, 10-179; 2007, June, 4-6; 2007, January, 13-27; 2007, January, 28-31; 2005, November, 1-9

+ 96415 each additional hour (List separately in addition to code for primary procedure)

INCLUDES Infusion intervals of more than 30 minutes past 1-hour increments

Code first initial hour (96413)
0.72   0.72 Global Days ZZZ
AMA: 2009, Jan, 11-31; 2009, Feb, 17-21; 2008, Jan, 10-25; 2007, May, 3-4; 2007, Dec, 10-179; 2007, June, 4-6; 2007, January, 28-31; 2007, January, 13-27; 2005, November, 1-9

96416 initiation of prolonged chemotherapy infusion (more than 8 hours), requiring use of a portable or implantable pump

EXCLUDES Portable or implantable infusion pump/reservoir refilling/maintenance for drug delivery (96521-96523)

3.49   3.49 Global Days XXX
AMA: 2009, Jan, 11-31; 2009, Feb, 17-21; 2008, Jan, 10-25; 2007, Dec, 10-179; 2007, June, 4-6; 2007, January, 13-27; 2007, May, 3-4; 2007, January, 28-31; 2005, November, 1-9

+ 96417 each additional sequential infusion (different substance/drug), up to 1 hour (List separately in addition to code for primary procedure)

INCLUDES Reporting only once per sequential infusion
EXCLUDES Additional hour(s) of sequential infusion (96415)

Code first initial substance/drug (96413)
1.60   1.60 Global Days ZZZ
AMA: 2009, Jan, 11-31; 2009, Feb, 17-21; 2008, Jan, 10-25; 2007, May, 3-4; 2007, January, 13-27; 2007, June, 4-6; 2007, January, 28-31; 2005, November, 1-9

96420-96425 Chemotherapy and Complex Drugs, Biologicals: Intra-arterial

CMS 100-3,110.2	Certain Drugs Distributed by the National Cancer Institute
CMS 100-3,110.6	Scalp Hypothermia During Chemotherapy, to Prevent Hair Loss
CMS 100-4,4,230.2	Coding and Payment for Drug Administration
CMS 100-4,4,230.2.2	Chemotherapy Drug Administration
CMS 100-4,12,30.5	Payment for Injections and Infusions: Chemotherapy and Nonchemotherapy

INCLUDES Highly complex services that require direct supervision for:
- Consent
- Patient assessment
- Safety oversight
- Supervision

More intense physician work and monitoring of clinical staff due to greater risk of severe patient reactions

Parenteral administration of:
- Anti-neoplastic agents for noncancer diagnoses
- Monoclonal antibody agents
- Non-radionuclide antineoplastic drugs
- Other biologic response modifiers

The following in the administration:
- Access to IV/catheter/port
- Drug preparation
- Flushing at the completion of the infusion
- Hydration fluid
- Routine tubing/syringe/supplies
- Starting the IV
- Use of local anesthesia

EXCLUDES Administration of non-chemotherapy agents such as antibiotics/steriods/analgesics
Declotting of catheter/port (36593)
Home infusion (99601-99602)

Code also drug or substance
Code also significant separately identifiable evaluation and management service, if performed
Do not report with physician services provided in the facility setting with these codes.

96420 Chemotherapy administration, intra-arterial; push technique [S] [80] [◻] [P0]
  INCLUDES Regional chemotherapy perfusion
  EXCLUDES Placement of intra-arterial catheter
  Do not report with 36823
  🩺 2.42 ✂ 2.42 Global Days XXX
  AMA: 2009, Jan, 11-31; 2009, Feb, 17-21; 2008, Jan, 10-25; 2007, May, 3-4; 2007, January, 13-27; 2007, June, 4-6; 2007, January, 28-31; 2006, December, 10-12; 2005, November, 1-9

96422 infusion technique, up to 1 hour [S] [80] [◻] [P0]
  INCLUDES Regional chemotherapy perfusion
  EXCLUDES Placement of intra-arterial catheter
  Do not report with 36823
  🩺 3.80 ✂ 3.80 Global Days XXX
  AMA: 2009, Jan, 11-31; 2009, Feb, 17-21; 2008, Jan, 10-25; 2007, May, 3-4; 2007, Dec, 10-179; 2007, January, 13-27; 2007, January, 28-31; 2007, June, 4-6; 2005, November, 1-9

+ **96423** infusion technique, each additional hour (List separately in addition to code for primary procedure) [S] [80] [◻] [P0]
  INCLUDES Infusion intervals of more than 30 minutes past 1-hour increments
  Regional chemotherapy perfusion
  EXCLUDES Arterial/venous cannula insertion with regional chemotherapy perfusion to an extremity (36823)
  Placement of intra-arterial catheter
  Code first initial hour (96422)
  Do not report with 36823
  🩺 1.78 ✂ 1.78 Global Days ZZZ
  AMA: 2009, Feb, 17-21; 2009, Jan, 11-31; 2008, Jan, 10-25; 2007, Dec, 10-179; 2007, June, 4-6; 2007, January, 13-27; 2007, May, 3-4; 2007, January, 28-31; 2005, November, 1-9

96425 infusion technique, initiation of prolonged infusion (more than 8 hours), requiring the use of a portable or implantable pump [S] [80] [◻] [P0]
  INCLUDES Regional chemotherapy perfusion
  EXCLUDES Placement of intra-arterial catheter
  Portable or implantable infusion pump/reservoir refilling/maintenance for drug delivery (96521-96523)
  Do not report with 36823
  🩺 4.07 ✂ 4.07 Global Days XXX
  AMA: 2009, Jan, 11-31; 2009, Feb, 17-21; 2008, Jan, 10-25; 2007, May, 3-4; 2007, January, 28-31; 2007, January, 13-27; 2007, June, 4-6; 2005, November, 1-9

96440-96450 Chemotherapy Administration: Intrathecal/Peritoneal Cavity/Pleural Cavity

96440 Chemotherapy administration into pleural cavity, requiring and including thoracentesis [S] [80] [◻] [P0]
  EXCLUDES Blood specimen collection from completely implantable venous access device (36591)
  🩺 3.82 ✂ 21.09 Global Days 000
  AMA: 2009, Jan, 11-31; 2009, Feb, 17-21; 2008, Jan, 10-25; 2007, May, 3-4; 2007, January, 28-31; 2007, January, 13-27; 2007, June, 4-6; 2005, November, 1-9

96445 Chemotherapy administration into peritoneal cavity, requiring and including peritoneocentesis [S] [80] [◻] [P0]
  EXCLUDES Blood specimen collection from completely implantable venous access device (36591)
  🩺 3.28 ✂ 6.68 Global Days 000
  AMA: 2009, Jan, 11-31; 2009, Feb, 17-21; 2008, Jan, 10-25; 2007, May, 3-4; 2007, June, 4-6; 2007, January, 13-27; 2007, January, 28-31; 2007, May, 9-11; 2005, November, 1-9

96450 Chemotherapy administration, into CNS (eg, intrathecal), requiring and including spinal puncture [S] [80] [◻] [P0]
  EXCLUDES Blood specimen collection from completely implantable venous access device (36591)
  Chemotherapy administration, intravesical/bladder (51720)
  Insertion of catheter/reservoir:
    Intraventricular (61210, 61215)
    Subarachnoid (62350, 62351, 62360-62362)
  🩺 2.24 ✂ 4.49 Global Days 000
  AMA: 2009, Jan, 11-31; 2009, Feb, 17-21; 2008, Jan, 10-25; 2007, January, 28-31; 2007, June, 4-6; 2007, May, 3-4; 2007, January, 13-27; 2005, November, 1-9

CURRENT PROCEDURAL CODING EXPERT – Medicine   96570

96521-96523 Refill/Upkeep of Drug Delivery Device

CMS 100-4,4,230.2 — Coding and Payment for Drug Administration

INCLUDES Highly complex services that require direct supervision for:
  Consent
  Patient assessment
  Safety oversight
  Supervision
Parenteral administration of:
  Anti-neoplastic agents for noncancer diagnoses
  Monoclonal antibody agents
  Non-radionuclide antineoplastic drugs
  Other biologic response modifiers
The following in the administration:
  Access to IV/catheter/port
  Drug preparation
  Flushing at the completion of the infusion
  Hydration fluid
  Routine tubing/syringe/supplies
  Starting the IV
  Use of local anesthesia
Therapeutic drugs other than chemotherapy

EXCLUDES *Administratoin of non-chemotherapy agents such as antibiotics/steriods/analgesics*
Blood specimen collection from completely implantable venous access device (36591)
Declotting of catheter/port (36593)
Home infusion (99601-99602)

Code also drug or substance
Code also significant separately identifiable evaluation and management service, if performed

96521 Refilling and maintenance of portable pump
  3.02 3.02 Global Days XXX
  AMA: 2009, Feb, 17-21; 2007, June, 4-6; 2007, May, 3-4; 2007, January, 28-31; 2005, November, 1-9

96522 Refilling and maintenance of implantable pump or reservoir for drug delivery, systemic (eg, intravenous, intra-arterial)
  EXCLUDES *Implantable infusion pump refilling/maintenance for spinal/brain drug delivery (95990-95991)*
  2.55 2.55 Global Days XXX
  AMA: 2009, Feb, 17-21; 2007, January, 28-31; 2007, May, 3-4; 2007, June, 4-6; 2006, April, 19-20; 2005, November, 1-9

96523 Irrigation of implanted venous access device for drug delivery systems
  EXCLUDES *Direct physician supervision*
  Do not report with any other services on the same date of service.
  0.56 0.56 Global Days XXX
  AMA: 2009, Feb, 17-21; 2007, June, 4-6; 2007, January, 28-31; 2007, May, 3-4; 2005, November, 1-9

96542-96549 Chemotherapy Injection Into Brain

CMS 100-3,110.2 — Certain Drugs Distributed by the National Cancer Institute
CMS 100-4,4,230.2.2 — Chemotherapy Drug Administration
CMS 100-4,12,30.5 — Payment for Injections and Infusions: Chemotherapy and Nonchemotherapy

INCLUDES Highly complex services that require direct supervision for:
  Consent
  Patient assessment
  Safety oversight
  Supervision
Parenteral administration of:
  Anti-neoplastic agents for noncancer diagnoses
  Monoclonal antibody agents
  Non-radionuclide antineoplastic drugs
  Other biologic response modifiers
The following in the administration:
  Access to IV/catheter/port
  Drug preparation
  Flushing at the completion of the infusion
  Hydration fluid
  Routine tubing/syringe/supplies
  Starting the IV
  Use of local anesthesia

EXCLUDES *Administration of non-chemotherapy agents such as antibiotics/steriods/analgesics*
Blood specimen collection from completely implantable venous access device (36591)
Declotting of catheter/port (36593)
Home infusion (99601-99602)

Code also drug or substance
Code also significant separately identifiable evaluation and management service, if performed

96542 Chemotherapy injection, subarachnoid or intraventricular via subcutaneous reservoir, single or multiple agents
  79005
  1.15 2.78 Global Days XXX
  AMA: 2009, Feb, 17-21; 2007, May, 3-4; 2007, June, 4-6; 2007, January, 28-31; 2005, November, 1-9

96549 Unlisted chemotherapy procedure
  0.00 0.00 Global Days XXX
  AMA: 2009, Jan, 11-31; 2009, Feb, 17-21; 2008, Jan, 10-25; 2007, May, 3-4; 2007, June, 4-6; 2007, January, 28-31; 2005, November, 1-9

96567-96571 Destruction of Lesions: Photodynamic Therapy

EXCLUDES *Ocular photodynamic therapy (67221)*

96567 Photodynamic therapy by external application of light to destroy premalignant and/or malignant lesions of the skin and adjacent mucosa (eg, lip) by activation of photosensitive drug(s), each phototherapy exposure session
  3.18 3.18 Global Days XXX

+ ▲ **96570** Photodynamic therapy by endoscopic application of light to ablate abnormal tissue via activation of photosensitive drug(s); first 30 minutes (List separately in addition to code for endoscopy or bronchoscopy procedures of lung and gastrointestinal tract)
  Code first (31641, 43228)
  1.60 1.60 Global Days ZZZ
  AMA: 2008, Oct, 6-7

● New Code ▲ Revised Code Maternity Age Unlisted Not Covered # Resequenced
CCI + Add-on ⊘ Mod 51 Exempt Ⓔ Mod 63 Exempt ⊙ Mod Sedation PQRI

© 2009 Publisher *(Blue Ink)* CPT only © 2009 American Medical Association. All Rights Reserved. *(Black Ink)* Medicare *(Red Ink)* 399

96571   Current Procedural Coding Expert – Medicine

+ ▲ **96571** each additional 15 minutes (List separately in addition to code for endoscopy or bronchoscopy procedures of lung and gastrointestinal tract) [T]
Code first (31641, 43228)
0.73 0.73 **Global Days ZZZ**
AMA: 2008, Oct, 6-7

96900-96999 Diagnostic/Therapeutic Skin Procedures

CMS 100-3,190.6 Hair Analysis
CMS 100-3,250.1 Treatment of Psoriasis
CMS 100-3,250.4 Treatment of Actinic Keratosis
EXCLUDES Consultation services (99241-99255)
Evaluation and management services (99201-99499)
Injection, intralesional (11900-11901)

96900 Actinotherapy (ultraviolet light) [S][80]
88160-88161
0.49 0.49 **Global Days XXX**
AMA: 2009, Jan, 11-31; 2008, Jan, 10-25; 2007, January, 13-27; 2006, December, 10-12; 2006, August, 12-14

96902 Microscopic examination of hairs plucked or clipped by the examiner (excluding hair collected by the patient) to determine telogen and anagen counts, or structural hair shaft abnormality [N]
88160-88161
0.58 0.60 **Global Days XXX**

96904 Whole body integumentary photography, for monitoring of high risk patients with dysplastic nevus syndrome or a history of dysplastic nevi, or patients with a personal or familial history of melanoma [N][80]
88160-88161
1.51 1.51 **Global Days XXX**
AMA: 2006, December, 10-12

96910 Photochemotherapy; tar and ultraviolet B (Goeckerman treatment) or petrolatum and ultraviolet B [S][80]
88160-88161
1.67 1.67 **Global Days XXX**

96912 psoralens and ultraviolet A (PUVA) [S][80]
88160-88161
2.14 2.14 **Global Days XXX**

96913 Photochemotherapy (Goeckerman and/or PUVA) for severe photoresponsive dermatoses requiring at least 4-8 hours of care under direct supervision of the physician (includes application of medication and dressings) [S][80]
88160-88161
3.01 3.01 **Global Days XXX**

96920 Laser treatment for inflammatory skin disease (psoriasis); total area less than 250 sq cm [T]
EXCLUDES Destruction by laser of:
Benign lesions (17110-17111)
Cutaneous vascular proliferative lesions (17106-17108)
Malignant lesions (17260-17286)
Premalignant lesions (17000-17004)
88160-88161
1.87 4.36 **Global Days 000**

96921 250 sq cm to 500 sq cm [T]
EXCLUDES Destruction by laser of:
Benign lesions (17110-17111)
Cutaneous vascular proliferative lesions (17106-17108)
Malignant lesions (17260-17286)
Premalignant lesions (17000-17004)
88160-88161
1.89 4.49 **Global Days 000**

96922 over 500 sq cm [T]
EXCLUDES Destruction by laser of:
Benign lesions (17110-17111)
Cutaneous vascular proliferative lesions (17106-17108)
Malignant lesions (17260-17286)
Premalignant lesions (17000-17004)
88160-88161
3.42 6.38 **Global Days 000**

96999 Unlisted special dermatological service or procedure [T][80]
0.00 0.00 **Global Days XXX**

97001-97006 Physical Medicine Assessments

CMS 100-2,15,230.4 Services By a Physical/Occupational Therapist in Private Practice
CMS 100-3,20.10 Cardiac Rehabilitation Programs
CMS 100-4,5,10 Part B Outpatient Rehabilitation/Comprehensive Outpatient Rehabilitation Facility Services
CMS 100-4,5,10.2 Financial Limitation for Outpatient Rehabilitation Services
CMS 100-4,5,20 HCPCS Coding Requirement
EXCLUDES EMG biofeedback training (90901)
Muscle/range of motion testing and electromyography (95831-95904)
TNS - transcutaneous nerve stimulation (64550)

⊘ **97001** Physical therapy evaluation [A][80][P0]
2.01 2.01 **Global Days XXX**
AMA: 2009, Jan, 11-31; 2008, Jan, 10-25; 2008, May, 9-11; 2007, January, 13-27; 2006, August, 12-14

⊘ **97002** Physical therapy re-evaluation [A][80][P0]
1.10 1.10 **Global Days XXX**
AMA: 2009, Jan, 11-31; 2008, May, 9-11; 2008, Jan, 10-25; 2007, January, 13-27

⊘ **97003** Occupational therapy evaluation [A][80][P0]
2.25 2.25 **Global Days XXX**
AMA: 2009, Jan, 11-31; 2008, May, 9-11; 2008, Jan, 10-25; 2007, January, 13-27; 2006, August, 12-14

⊘ **97004** Occupational therapy re-evaluation [A][80][P0]
1.35 1.35 **Global Days XXX**
AMA: 2009, Jan, 11-31; 2008, May, 9-11; 2008, Jan, 10-25; 2007, January, 13-27

⊘ **97005** Athletic training evaluation [E]
0.00 0.00 **Global Days XXX**

⊘ **97006** Athletic training re-evaluation [E]
0.00 0.00 **Global Days XXX**

Current Procedural Coding Expert – Medicine

97010-97028 Physical Therapy Treatment Modalities: Supervised

CMS 100-2,15,230 — Practice of Physical Therapy, Occupational Therapy, and Speech-Language Pathology
CMS 100-2,15,230.1 — Practice of Physical Therapy
CMS 100-2,15,230.4 — Services By a Physical/Occupational Therapist in Private Practice
CMS 100-3,20.10 — Cardiac Rehabilitation Programs
CMS 100-4,5,10 — Part B Outpatient Rehabilitation/Comprehensive Outpatient Rehabilitation Facility Services
CMS 100-4,5,10.2 — Financial Limitation for Outpatient Rehabilitation Services
CMS 100-4,5,20 — HCPCS Coding Requirement

EXCLUDES Direct patient contact by the provider
EMG biofeedback training (90901)
Muscle/range of motion testing and electromyography (95831-95904)
TNS - transcutaneous nerve stimulation (64550)

97010 Application of a modality to 1 or more areas; hot or cold packs
0.15   0.15 Global Days XXX
AMA: 2009, Jan, 11-31; 2008, Jan, 10-25; 2007, January, 13-27; 2006, August, 12-14

97012 traction, mechanical
0.43   0.43 Global Days XXX
AMA: 2009, Jan, 11-31; 2008, Jan, 10-25; 2007, January, 13-27

97014 electrical stimulation (unattended)
EXCLUDES Acupuncture with electrical stimulation (97813, 97814)
0.40   0.40 Global Days XXX
AMA: 2009, Jan, 11-31; 2008, Jan, 10-25; 2007, January, 13-27

97016 vasopneumatic devices
0.48   0.48 Global Days XXX
AMA: 2005, May, 13-14

97018 paraffin bath
0.26   0.26 Global Days XXX

97022 whirlpool
0.58   0.58 Global Days XXX

97024 diathermy (eg, microwave)
0.17   0.17 Global Days XXX

97026 infrared
0.15   0.15 Global Days XXX

97028 ultraviolet
0.19   0.19 Global Days XXX

97032-97039 Physical Therapy Treatment Modalities: Constant Attendance

CMS 100-2,15,230 — Practice of Physical Therapy, Occupational Therapy, and Speech-Language Pathology
CMS 100-2,15,230.1 — Practice of Physical Therapy
CMS 100-2,15,230.2 — Practice of Occupational Therapy
CMS 100-2,15,230.4 — Services By a Physical/Occupational Therapist in Private Practice
CMS 100-3,20.10 — Cardiac Rehabilitation Programs
CMS 100-4,5,10 — Part B Outpatient Rehabilitation/Comprehensive Outpatient Rehabilitation Facility Services
CMS 100-4,5,10.2 — Financial Limitation for Outpatient Rehabilitation Services
CMS 100-4,5,20 — HCPCS Coding Requirement

INCLUDES Direct patient contact by the provider
EXCLUDES EMG biofeedback training (90901)
Muscle/range of motion testing and electromyography (95831-95904)
TNS - transcutaneous nerve stimulation (64550)

97032 Application of a modality to 1 or more areas; electrical stimulation (manual), each 15 minutes
0.50   0.50 Global Days XXX
AMA: 2009, Jan, 11-31; 2008, Jan, 10-25; 2007, January, 13-27

97033 iontophoresis, each 15 minutes
0.80   0.80 Global Days XXX

97034 contrast baths, each 15 minutes
0.46   0.46 Global Days XXX

97035 ultrasound, each 15 minutes
0.34   0.34 Global Days XXX
AMA: 2009, Jan, 11-31; 2008, Jan, 10-25; 2007, January, 13-27

97036 Hubbard tank, each 15 minutes
0.83   0.83 Global Days XXX

97039 Unlisted modality (specify type and time if constant attendance)
0.00   0.00 Global Days XXX
AMA: 2009, Jan, 11-31; 2008, Jan, 10-25; 2007, January, 13-27; 2005, May, 13-14

97110-97546 Other Therapeutic Techniques With Direct Patient Contact

CMS 100-2,15,230 — Practice of Physical Therapy, Occupational Therapy, and Speech-Language Pathology
CMS 100-2,15,230.1 — Practice of Physical Therapy
CMS 100-2,15,230.2 — Practice of Occupational Therapy
CMS 100-2,15,230.4 — Services By a Physical/Occupational Therapist in Private Practice
CMS 100-3,20.10 — Cardiac Rehabilitation Programs
CMS 100-4,5,10 — Part B Outpatient Rehabilitation/Comprehensive Outpatient Rehabilitation Facility Services
CMS 100-4,5,10.2 — Financial Limitation for Outpatient Rehabilitation Services
CMS 100-4,5,20 — HCPCS Coding Requirement

INCLUDES Application of clinical skills/services to improve function
Direct patient contact by the provider

EXCLUDES EMG biofeedback training (90901)
Muscle/range of motion testing and electromyography (95831-95904)
TNS - transcutaneous nerve stimulation (64550)

97110 Therapeutic procedure, 1 or more areas, each 15 minutes; therapeutic exercises to develop strength and endurance, range of motion and flexibility
0.84   0.84 Global Days XXX
AMA: 2009, Jan, 11-31; 2008, Jan, 10-25; 2008, May, 9-11; 2007, January, 13-27; 2006, August, 12-14; 2006, March, 15; 2005, April, 13-14; 2005, December, 8; 2005, March, 11-15; 2005, August, 11-12

97112 neuromuscular reeducation of movement, balance, coordination, kinesthetic sense, posture, and/or proprioception for sitting and/or standing activities
0.88   0.88 Global Days XXX
AMA: 2009, Jan, 11-31; 2008, Jan, 10-25; 2008, May, 9-11; 2007, January, 13-27; 2006, March, 15; 2006, August, 12-14; 2005, August, 11-12; 2005, April, 13-14

97113 aquatic therapy with therapeutic exercises
1.09   1.09 Global Days XXX
AMA: 2009, Jan, 11-31; 2008, Jan, 10-25; 2008, May, 9-11; 2007, January, 13-27; 2006, March, 15; 2006, August, 12-14; 2005, April, 13-14

97116 gait training (includes stair climbing)
EXCLUDES Comprehensive gait/motion analysis (96000-96003)
0.74   0.74 Global Days XXX
AMA: 2009, Jan, 11-31; 2008, May, 9-11; 2008, Jan, 10-25; 2007, January, 13-27; 2007, February, 8-9; 2006, March, 15; 2006, August, 12-14; 2005, April, 13-14

● New Code   ▲ Revised Code   Ⓜ Maternity   Ⓐ Age   Unlisted   Not Covered   # Resequenced
CCI   + Add-on   ⊘ Mod 51 Exempt   Mod 63 Exempt   ⊙ Mod Sedation   PQRI

© 2009 Publisher (Blue Ink)   CPT only © 2009 American Medical Association. All Rights Reserved. (Black Ink)   Medicare (Red Ink)

	97124	massage, including effleurage, petrissage and/or tapotement (stroking, compression, percussion) [A][80]
		EXCLUDES Myofascial release (97140)
		0.63 0.68 Global Days XXX
		AMA: 2009, Jan, 11-31; 2008, Jan, 10-25; 2008, May, 9-11; 2007, January, 13-27; 2006, March, 15; 2006, August, 12-14; 2005, April, 13-14; 2005, May, 13-14
	97139	Unlisted therapeutic procedure (specify) [A][80]
		0.00 0.00 Global Days XXX
		AMA: 2009, Jan, 11-31; 2008, May, 9-11; 2008, Jan, 10-25; 2007, January, 13-27; 2006, August, 12-14; 2005, April, 13-14
	97140	Manual therapy techniques (eg, mobilization/manipulation, manual lymphatic drainage, manual traction), 1 or more regions, each 15 minutes [A][80]
		0.78 0.78 Global Days XXX
		AMA: 2009, Jan, 11-31; 2009, May, 8-9&11; 2008, May, 9-11; 2008, Jan, 10-25; 2007, January, 13-27; 2005, March, 11-15; 2005, January, 46-47
	97150	Therapeutic procedure(s), group (2 or more individuals) [A][80]
		INCLUDES Constant attendance by the physician/therapist
		Reporting this procedure for each member of group
		EXCLUDES Osteopathic manipulative treatment (98925-98929)
		0.54 0.54 Global Days XXX
		AMA: 2009, Jan, 11-31; 2008, May, 9-11; 2008, Jan, 10-25; 2007, January, 13-27; 2006, August, 12-14; 2005, April, 13-14
	97530	Therapeutic activities, direct (one-on-one) patient contact by the provider (use of dynamic activities to improve functional performance), each 15 minutes [A][80]
		0.90 0.90 Global Days XXX
		AMA: 2009, Jan, 11-31; 2008, May, 9-11; 2008, Jan, 10-25; 2007, January, 13-27; 2005, August, 11-12
	97532	Development of cognitive skills to improve attention, memory, problem solving (includes compensatory training), direct (one-on-one) patient contact by the provider, each 15 minutes [A][80]
		0.71 0.71 Global Days XXX
		AMA: 2008, May, 9-11
	97533	Sensory integrative techniques to enhance sensory processing and promote adaptive responses to environmental demands, direct (one-on-one) patient contact by the provider, each 15 minutes [A][80]
		0.77 0.77 Global Days XXX
		AMA: 2008, May, 9-11
	97535	Self-care/home management training (eg, activities of daily living (ADL) and compensatory training, meal preparation, safety procedures, and instructions in use of assistive technology devices/adaptive equipment) direct one-on-one contact by provider, each 15 minutes [A][80]
		0.90 0.90 Global Days XXX
		AMA: 2009, Jan, 11-31; 2008, Jan, 10-25; 2008, May, 9-11; 2007, January, 13-27
	97537	Community/work reintegration training (eg, shopping, transportation, money management, avocational activities and/or work environment/modification analysis, work task analysis, use of assistive technology device/adaptive equipment), direct one-on-one contact by provider, each 15 minutes [A][80]
		EXCLUDES Wheelchair management/propulsion training (97542)
		0.79 0.79 Global Days XXX
		AMA: 2008, May, 9-11

	97542	Wheelchair management (eg, assessment, fitting, training), each 15 minutes [A][80]
		0.80 0.80 Global Days XXX
		AMA: 2008, May, 9-11
	97545	Work hardening/conditioning; initial 2 hours [A][80]
		0.00 0.00 Global Days XXX
		AMA: 2009, Jan, 11-31; 2008, May, 9-11; 2008, Jan, 10-25; 2007, January, 13-27
+	97546	each additional hour (List separately in addition to code for primary procedure) [A][80]
		Code first initial 2 hours (97545)
		0.00 0.00 Global Days ZZZ
		AMA: 2009, Jan, 11-31; 2008, May, 9-11

97597-97606 Treatment of Wounds

CMS 100-2,15,230.4 Services By a Physical/Occupational Therapist in Private Practice
CMS 100-3,270.1 Electrical Stimulation and Electromagnetic Therapy for the Treatment of Wounds
CMS 100-3,270.2 Noncontact Normothermic Wound Therapy
CMS 100-3,270.3 Blood-derived Products for Chronic Nonhealing Wounds
CMS 100-3,270.4 Treatment of Decubitus
CMS 100-4,5,10 Part B Outpatient Rehabilitation/Comprehensive Outpatient Rehabilitation Facility Services
CMS 100-4,5,20 HCPCS Coding Requirement

	97597	Removal of devitalized tissue from wound(s), selective debridement, without anesthesia (eg, high pressure waterjet with/without suction, sharp selective debridement with scissors, scalpel and forceps), with or without topical application(s), wound assessment, and instruction(s) for ongoing care, may include use of a whirlpool, per session; total wound(s) surface area less than or equal to 20 square centimeters [T][80]
		INCLUDES Direct patient contact
		Removing devitalized/necrotic tissue and promoting healing
		Do not report with debridement (11040-11044)
		0.76 1.95 Global Days XXX
		AMA: 2009, Jan, 11-31; 2008, Jan, 10-25; 2007, January, 13-27; 2005, June, 1-4; 2005, June, 9-11
	97598	total wound(s) surface area greater than 20 square centimeters [T][80]
		INCLUDES Direct patient contact
		Removing devitalized/necrotic tissue and promoting healing
		Do not report with debridement (11040-11044)
		1.04 2.39 Global Days XXX
		AMA: 2005, June, 1-4; 2005, June, 9-11
	97602	Removal of devitalized tissue from wound(s), non-selective debridement, without anesthesia (eg, wet-to-moist dressings, enzymatic, abrasion), including topical application(s), wound assessment, and instruction(s) for ongoing care, per session [T]
		INCLUDES Direct patient contact
		Removing devitalized/necrotic tissue and promoting healing
		Do not report with debridement (11040-11044)
		0.00 0.00 Global Days XXX
		AMA: 2009, Jan, 11-31; 2008, Sep, 10-11; 2005, June, 1-4; 2005, June, 9-11

Current Procedural Coding Expert – Medicine

⊘ **97605** Negative pressure wound therapy (eg, vacuum assisted drainage collection), including topical application(s), wound assessment, and instruction(s) for ongoing care, per session; total wound(s) surface area less than or equal to 50 square centimeters [T][80]
- INCLUDES: Direct patient contact
- Removing devitalized/necrotic tissue and promoting healing
- 0.74 1.09 Global Days XXX
- **AMA:** 2009, Jan, 11-31; 2008, Jan, 10-25; 2007, January, 13-27; 2005, June, 1-4; 2005, April, 13-14; 2005, June, 9-11

⊘ **97606** total wound(s) surface area greater than 50 square centimeters [T][80]
- INCLUDES: Direct patient contact
- Removing devitalized/necrotic tissue and promoting healing
- 0.82 1.18 Global Days XXX
- **AMA:** 2009, Jan, 11-31; 2008, Jan, 10-25; 2007, January, 13-27; 2005, April, 13-14; 2005, June, 1-4; 2005, June, 9-11

97750-97799 Assessments and Training

- **CMS** 100-2,15,230 — Practice of Physical Therapy, Occupational Therapy, and Speech-Language Pathology
- **CMS** 100-2,15,230.1 — Practice of Physical Therapy
- **CMS** 100-2,15,230.2 — Practice of Occupational Therapy
- **CMS** 100-2,15,230.4 — Services By a Physical/Occupational Therapist in Private Practice
- **CMS** 100-3,20.10 — Cardiac Rehabilitation Programs
- **CMS** 100-4,5,10 — Part B Outpatient Rehabilitation/Comprehensive Outpatient Rehabilitation Facility Services
- **CMS** 100-4,5,20 — HCPCS Coding Requirement

⊘ **97750** Physical performance test or measurement (eg, musculoskeletal, functional capacity), with written report, each 15 minutes [A][80]
- INCLUDES: Direct patient contact
- EXCLUDES: Muscle/range of motion testing and electromyography/nerve velocity determination (95831-95904)
- 0.86 0.86 Global Days XXX
- **AMA:** 2009, Jan, 11-31; 2008, May, 9-11; 2008, Jan, 10-25; 2007, February, 10-11; 2007, January, 13-27

⊘ **97755** Assistive technology assessment (eg, to restore, augment or compensate for existing function, optimize functional tasks and/or maximize environmental accessibility), direct one-on-one contact by provider, with written report, each 15 minutes [A][80]
- INCLUDES: Direct patient contact
- EXCLUDES: Augmentative/alternative communication device (92605, 92607)
- Muscle/range of motion testing and electromyography/nerve velocity determination (95831-95904)
- 0.96 0.96 Global Days XXX

97760 Orthotic(s) management and training (including assessment and fitting when not otherwise reported), upper extremity(s), lower extremity(s) and/or trunk, each 15 minutes [A][80]
- Do not report with gait training, if performed on the same extremity (97116)
- 0.98 0.98 Global Days XXX
- **AMA:** 2007, February, 8-9; 2005, December, 8

97761 Prosthetic training, upper and/or lower extremity(s), each 15 minutes [A][80]
- 0.86 0.86 Global Days XXX
- **AMA:** 2009, Jan, 11-31; 2008, Jan, 10-25; 2007, February, 8-9; 2007, January, 13-27; 2005, December, 8

97762 Checkout for orthotic/prosthetic use, established patient, each 15 minutes [A][80]
- 1.15 1.15 Global Days XXX
- **AMA:** 2007, February, 8-9; 2005, December, 8

97799 Unlisted physical medicine/rehabilitation service or procedure [A][80]
- 0.00 0.00 Global Days XXX

97802-97804 Medical Nutrition Therapy Services

- **CMS** 100-3,40.1 — Diabetes Outpatient Self-management Training
- **CMS** 100-3,40.5 — Treatment of Obesity
- **CMS** 100-3,180.1 — Medical Nutrition Therapy
- **CMS** 100-4,4,300 — Medical Nutrition Therapy Services
- EXCLUDES: Physician provided medical nutrition therapy assessment/intervention (99201-99499)

97802 Medical nutrition therapy; initial assessment and intervention, individual, face-to-face with the patient, each 15 minutes [A][80][PQ]
- 0.74 0.78 Global Days XXX
- **AMA:** 2009, Feb, 13-16

97803 re-assessment and intervention, individual, face-to-face with the patient, each 15 minutes [A][80][PQ]
- 0.63 0.67 Global Days XXX
- **AMA:** 2009, Feb, 13-16

97804 group (2 or more individual(s)), each 30 minutes [A][80][PQ]
- 0.35 0.36 Global Days XXX
- **AMA:** 2009, Feb, 13-16

97810-97814 Acupuncture

- **CMS** 100-3,30.3 — Acupuncture
- **CMS** 100-3,30.3.1 — Acupuncture for Fibromyalgia
- **CMS** 100-3,30.3.2 — Acupuncture for Osteoarthritis
- INCLUDES: 15 minute increments of face-to-face contact with the patient
- Reporting only one code for each 15 minute increment

Code also evaluation and mangement time, if performed
Code also significant separately identifiable evaluation and management code (99201-99499)

97810 Acupuncture, 1 or more needles; without electrical stimulation, initial 15 minutes of personal one-on-one contact with the patient [E]
- EXCLUDES: Electrical stimulation (97813-97814)
- Do not report with (97813)
- 0.85 0.98 Global Days XXX
- **AMA:** 2009, Jan, 11-31; 2008, Jan, 10-25; 2007, January, 13-27; 2006, August, 3-5; 2006, June, 16-17; 2005, June, 5; 2005, January, 16-18

+ **97811** without electrical stimulation, each additional 15 minutes of personal one-on-one contact with the patient, with re-insertion of needle(s) (List separately in addition to code for primary procedure) [E]
- EXCLUDES: Electrical stimulation (97813-97814)
- Code first initial 15 minutes (97810, 97813)
- 0.71 0.75 Global Days ZZZ
- **AMA:** 2006, August, 3-5; 2005, January, 16-18; 2005, June, 5

97813 with electrical stimulation, initial 15 minutes of personal one-on-one contact with the patient [E]
- INCLUDES: Electrical stimulation
- Do not report with (97810)
- 0.92 1.05 Global Days XXX
- **AMA:** 2006, August, 3-5; 2006, June, 16-17; 2005, June, 5; 2005, January, 16-18

● New Code ▲ Revised Code Ⓜ Maternity △ Age Unlisted Not Covered # Resequenced
CCI + Add-on ⊘ Mod 51 Exempt Mod 63 Exempt ⊙ Mod Sedation PQRI

© 2009 Publisher (Blue Ink)   CPT only © 2009 American Medical Association. All Rights Reserved. (Black Ink)   Medicare (Red Ink)

+ 97814 with electrical stimulation, each additional 15 minutes of personal one-on-one contact with the patient, with re-insertion of needle(s) (List separately in addition to code for primary procedure) [E]
  INCLUDES Electrical stimulation
  Code first initial 15 minutes (97810, 97813)
  🚑 0.78 ✂ 0.85 Global Days ZZZ
  AMA: 2006, August, 3-5; 2005, June, 5; 2005, January, 16-18

98925-98929 Osteopathic Manipulation

CMS 100-3,150.1 Manipulation
INCLUDES Physician applied manual treatment done to eliminate/alleviate somatic dysfunction and related disorders using a variety of techniques
  The following body regions:
    Abdomen/viscera region
    Cervical region
    Head region
    Lower extremities
    Lumbar region
    Pelvic region
    Rib cage region
    Sacral region
    Thoracic region
    Upper extremities
Code also significant separately identifiable evaluation and management service (99201-99499)

98925 Osteopathic manipulative treatment (OMT); 1-2 body regions involved [S][80][□]
  🚑 0.64 ✂ 0.84 Global Days 000
  AMA: 2009, Jan, 11-31; 2008, Jan, 10-25; 2007, January, 13-27

98926 3-4 body regions involved [S][80][□]
  🚑 0.91 ✂ 1.15 Global Days 000
  AMA: 2009, Jan, 11-31; 2008, Jan, 10-25; 2007, January, 13-27

98927 5-6 body regions involved [S][80][□]
  🚑 1.20 ✂ 1.49 Global Days 000
  AMA: 2009, Jan, 11-31; 2008, Jan, 10-25; 2007, January, 13-27

98928 7-8 body regions involved [S][80][□]
  🚑 1.41 ✂ 1.72 Global Days 000
  AMA: 2009, Jan, 11-31; 2008, Jan, 10-25; 2007, January, 13-27

98929 9-10 body regions involved [S][80][□]
  🚑 1.64 ✂ 2.00 Global Days 000
  AMA: 2009, Jan, 11-31; 2008, Jan, 10-25; 2007, January, 13-27

98940-98943 Chiropractic Manipulation

CMS 100-1,5,70.6 Chiropractors
CMS 100-2,15,240 Chiropractic Services - General
CMS 100-3,150.1 Manipulation
INCLUDES Form of manual treatment performed to influence joint/neurophysical function
  The following five extraspinal regions:
    Abdomen
    Head, including temporomandibular joint, excluding atlanto-occipital region
    Lower extremities
    Rib cage, not including costotransverse/costovertebral joints
    Upper extremities
  The following five spinal regions:
    Cervical region (atlanto-occipital joint)
    Lumbar region
    Pelvic region (sacro-iliac joint)
    Sacral region
    Thoracic region (costovertebral/costotransverse joints)
Code also signficant separately identifiable evaluation and management service (99201-99499)

98940 Chiropractic manipulative treatment (CMT); spinal, 1-2 regions [S][80][□][P0]
  🚑 0.59 ✂ 0.71 Global Days 000
  AMA: 2009, Jan, 11-31; 2008, Jan, 10-25; 2007, Dec, 10-179; 2007, January, 13-27; 2006, March, 15; 2005, March, 11-15; 2005, January, 46-47

98941 spinal, 3-4 regions [S][80][□][P0]
  🚑 0.86 ✂ 0.98 Global Days 000
  AMA: 2009, Jan, 11-31; 2008, Jan, 10-25; 2007, Dec, 10-179; 2007, January, 13-27; 2006, March, 15; 2005, March, 11-15; 2005, January, 46-47

98942 spinal, 5 regions [S][80][□][P0]
  🚑 1.14 ✂ 1.27 Global Days 000
  AMA: 2009, Jan, 11-31; 2008, Jan, 10-25; 2007, Dec, 10-179; 2007, January, 13-27; 2006, March, 15; 2005, January, 46-47

98943 extraspinal, 1 or more regions [E]
  🚑 0.57 ✂ 0.65 Global Days XXX
  AMA: 2009, Jan, 11-31; 2008, Jan, 10-25; 2007, Dec, 10-179; 2007, January, 13-27; 2006, March, 15; 2005, January, 46-47

Current Procedural Coding Expert – Medicine

98960-98962 Self-Management Training

INCLUDES
- Education/training services:
  - Prescribed by a physician
  - Provided by a qualified nonphysician health care provider
- Standardized curriculum that may be modified as necessary for:
  - Clinical needs
  - Cultural norms
  - Health literacy
- Teaching the patient how to manage the illness/delay the comorbidity(s)

EXCLUDES
- Genetic counseling education services (96040)
- Health/behavior assessment (96150-96155)
- Medical nutrition therapy (97802-97804)
- The following services provided by physicians:
  - Counseling/education to a group (99078)
  - Counseling/education to individuals (99201-99499)
  - Counseling/risk factor reduction without symptoms/established disease (99401-99412)

98960 Education and training for patient self-management by a qualified, nonphysician health care professional using a standardized curriculum, face-to-face with the patient (could include caregiver/family) each 30 minutes; individual patient [E] [PQ]
0.63   0.63   Global Days XXX
AMA: 2009, Feb, 13-16

98961 2-4 patients [E] [PQ]
INCLUDES Group education regarding genetic risks
0.31   0.31   Global Days XXX
AMA: 2009, Feb, 13-16; 2007, Aug, 9-12

98962 5-8 patients [E] [PQ]
INCLUDES Group education regarding genetic risks
0.23   0.23   Global Days XXX
AMA: 2009, Feb, 13-16; 2007, Aug, 9-12

98966-98968 Nonphysician Telephone Services

CMS 100-1,5,70   Definition of Physician

INCLUDES
- Assessment and management services provided by telephone by a qualified health care professional
- Episode of care initiated by an established patient or his/her guardian

EXCLUDES
- Call initiated by the qualified health care professional
- Calls during the postoperative period of a procedure
- Decision to see the patient at the next available urgent care appointment
- Decision to see the patient within 24 hours of the call
- Telephone services provided by a physician (99441-99443)
- Telephone services that are considered a part of a previous or subsequent service

Do not report with 98966-98968, 98969 if performed in the seven preceding days

98966 Telephone assessment and management service provided by a qualified nonphysician health care professional to an established patient, parent, or guardian not originating from a related assessment and management service provided within the previous 7 days nor leading to an assessment and management service or procedure within the next 24 hours or soonest available appointment; 5-10 minutes of medical discussion [E]
0.35   0.38   Global Days XXX
AMA: 2008, Mar, 6-7

98967 11-20 minutes of medical discussion [E]
0.71   0.74   Global Days XXX
AMA: 2008, Mar, 6-7

98968 21-30 minutes of medical discussion [E]
1.06   1.09   Global Days XXX
AMA: 2008, Mar, 6-7

98969 Nonphysician Online Service

INCLUDES
- On-line assessment and management service provided by a qualified health care professional
- Timely reply to the patient as well as:
  - Ordering laboratory services
  - Permanent record of the service; either hard copy or electronic
  - Providing a prescription
  - Related telephone calls

EXCLUDES
- On-line evaluation service:
  - Provided during the postoperative period of a procedure
  - Provided more than once in a seven day period
  - Related to a service provided in the previous seven days

Do not report with (99339-99340, 99363-99364, 99374-99380)
Do not report with (99363-99364)

98969 Online assessment and management service provided by a qualified nonphysician health care professional to an established patient, guardian, or health care provider not originating from a related assessment and management service provided within the previous 7 days, using the Internet or similar electronic communications network [E]
0.00   0.00   Global Days XXX
AMA: 2009, Jul, 5-6

99000-99091 Supplemental Services and Supplies

INCLUDES Supplemental reporting for services adjunct to the basic service provided

99000 Handling and/or conveyance of specimen for transfer from the physician's office to a laboratory [E]
0.00   0.00   Global Days XXX
AMA: 2009, Jan, 11-31; 2008, Jan, 10-25; 2007, January, 28-31; 2007, January, 13-27; 2006, September, 14-16; 2006, August, 6-8

99001 Handling and/or conveyance of specimen for transfer from the patient in other than a physician's office to a laboratory (distance may be indicated) [E]
0.00   0.00   Global Days XXX
AMA: 2009, Jan, 11-31; 2008, Jan, 10-25; 2007, January, 28-31; 2007, January, 13-27; 2006, September, 14-16; 2006, August, 6-8

99002 Handling, conveyance, and/or any other service in connection with the implementation of an order involving devices (eg, designing, fitting, packaging, handling, delivery or mailing) when devices such as orthotics, protectives, prosthetics are fabricated by an outside laboratory or shop but which items have been designed, and are to be fitted and adjusted by the attending physician [B]
EXCLUDES Venous blood routine collection (36415)
0.00   0.00   Global Days XXX
AMA: 2009, Jan, 11-31; 2008, Jan, 10-25; 2007, January, 13-27; 2007, January, 28-31; 2006, September, 14-16; 2006, August, 6-8

99024 Postoperative follow-up visit, normally included in the surgical package, to indicate that an evaluation and management service was performed during a postoperative period for a reason(s) related to the original procedure [B]
0.00   0.00   Global Days XXX
AMA: 2009, Jan, 11-31; 2008, Jan, 10-25; 2007, January, 13-27; 2007, January, 28-31; 2006, September, 14-16; 2006, August, 6-8

● New Code   ▲ Revised Code   Ⓜ Maternity   Ⓐ Age   Unlisted   Not Covered   # Resequenced
CCI   + Add-on   ⊘ Mod 51 Exempt   @ Mod 63 Exempt   ⊙ Mod Sedation   PQRI

© 2009 Publisher (Blue Ink)   CPT only © 2009 American Medical Association. All Rights Reserved. (Black Ink)   Medicare (Red Ink)   405

99026 Hospital mandated on call service; in-hospital, each hour [E]
    EXCLUDES   *Physician stand-by services with prolonged physician attendance (99360)*
    0.00   0.00   Global Days XXX
    AMA: 2009, Jan, 11-31; 2008, Jan, 10-25; 2007, January, 28-31; 2007, January, 13-27; 2006, August, 6-8; 2006, September, 14-16

99027 out-of-hospital, each hour [E]
    EXCLUDES   *Physician stand-by services with prolonged physician attendance (99360)*
    0.00   0.00   Global Days XXX
    AMA: 2009, Jan, 11-31; 2008, Jan, 10-25; 2007, January, 28-31; 2007, January, 13-27; 2006, September, 14-16; 2006, August, 6-8

99050 Services provided in the office at times other than regularly scheduled office hours, or days when the office is normally closed (eg, holidays, Saturday or Sunday), in addition to basic service [B]
    0.00   0.00   Global Days XXX
    AMA: 2009, Jan, 11-31; 2008, Jan, 10-25; 2007, January, 13-27; 2007, January, 28-31; 2006, September, 14-16; 2006, August, 6-8; 2006, May, 16-20

99051 Service(s) provided in the office during regularly scheduled evening, weekend, or holiday office hours, in addition to basic service [B]
    0.00   0.00   Global Days XXX
    AMA: 2009, Jan, 11-31; 2008, Jan, 10-25; 2007, January, 13-27; 2007, January, 28-31; 2006, September, 14-16; 2006, May, 16-20; 2006, August, 6-8

99053 Service(s) provided between 10:00 PM and 8:00 AM at 24-hour facility, in addition to basic service [B]
    0.00   0.00   Global Days XXX
    AMA: 2009, Jan, 11-31; 2008, Jan, 10-25; 2007, January, 28-31; 2007, January, 13-27; 2006, May, 16-20; 2006, August, 6-8; 2006, September, 14-16

99056 Service(s) typically provided in the office, provided out of the office at request of patient, in addition to basic service [B]
    0.00   0.00   Global Days XXX
    AMA: 2009, Jan, 11-31; 2008, Jan, 10-25; 2007, January, 13-27; 2007, January, 28-31; 2006, September, 14-16; 2006, August, 6-8; 2006, May, 16-20

99058 Service(s) provided on an emergency basis in the office, which disrupts other scheduled office services, in addition to basic service [B]
    0.00   0.00   Global Days XXX
    AMA: 2009, Jan, 11-31; 2008, Jan, 10-25; 2007, January, 13-27; 2007, January, 28-31; 2006, August, 6-8; 2006, September, 14-16; 2006, May, 16-20

99060 Service(s) provided on an emergency basis, out of the office, which disrupts other scheduled office services, in addition to basic service [B]
    0.00   0.00   Global Days XXX
    AMA: 2009, Jan, 11-31; 2008, Jan, 10-25; 2007, January, 28-31; 2007, January, 13-27; 2006, September, 14-16; 2006, May, 16-20; 2006, August, 6-8

99070 Supplies and materials (except spectacles), provided by the physician over and above those usually included with the office visit or other services rendered (list drugs, trays, supplies, or materials provided) [B]
    EXCLUDES   *Spectacles supply*
    0.00   0.00   Global Days XXX
    AMA: 2009, Jan, 11-31; 2009, May, 8-9&11; 2008, Jan, 10-25; 2008, Sep, 10-11; 2007, January, 28-31; 2007, January, 13-27; 2007, February, 8-9; 2006, September, 14-16; 2006, August, 6-8; 2006, April, 19-20; 2005, June, 1-4; 2005, July, 11-12

99071 Educational supplies, such as books, tapes, and pamphlets, provided by the physician for the patient's education at cost to physician [B]
    0.00   0.00   Global Days XXX
    AMA: 2009, Jan, 11-31; 2008, Jan, 10-25; 2007, January, 13-27; 2007, January, 28-31; 2006, August, 6-8; 2006, September, 14-16

99075 Medical testimony [E]
    0.00   0.00   Global Days XXX
    AMA: 2009, Jan, 11-31; 2008, Jan, 10-25; 2007, January, 28-31; 2007, January, 13-27; 2006, September, 14-16; 2006, August, 6-8

99078 Physician educational services rendered to patients in a group setting (eg, prenatal, obesity, or diabetic instructions) [N] [P0]
    0.00   0.00   Global Days XXX
    AMA: 2009, Jan, 11-31; 2008, Jan, 10-25; 2007, Aug, 9-12; 2007, January, 28-31; 2007, January, 13-27; 2006, September, 14-16; 2006, August, 6-8

99080 Special reports such as insurance forms, more than the information conveyed in the usual medical communications or standard reporting form [B]
    Do not report with 99455, 99456 for completion of workmen's compensation forms
    0.00   0.00   Global Days XXX
    AMA: 2009, Jan, 11-31; 2008, Jan, 10-25; 2007, January, 13-27; 2007, January, 28-31; 2006, August, 6-8; 2006, September, 14-16

99082 Unusual travel (eg, transportation and escort of patient) [B] [80]
    0.00   0.00   Global Days XXX
    AMA: 2009, Jan, 11-31; 2008, Jan, 10-25; 2007, January, 28-31; 2007, January, 13-27; 2006, September, 14-16; 2006, August, 6-8

99090 Analysis of clinical data stored in computers (eg, ECGs, blood pressures, hematologic data) [B]
    EXCLUDES   *Collection/interpretation by health care professional/physician of physiologic data stored/transmitted by patient or caregiver (99091)*
    This service if there exists a more specific CPT code for cardiographic services, glucose monitoring or musculoskeletal function testing (93014, 93227, 93233, 93272, 95250, 97750)
    0.00   0.00   Global Days XXX
    AMA: 2009, Jan, 11-31; 2008, Jan, 10-25; 2008, Jan, 6-7; 2007, February, 10-11; 2007, Jul, 1-4; 2007, January, 13-27; 2007, January, 28-31; 2006, September, 14-16; 2006, August, 6-8

99091 Collection and interpretation of physiologic data (eg, ECG, blood pressure, glucose monitoring) digitally stored and/or transmitted by the patient and/or caregiver to the physician or other qualified health care professional, requiring a minimum of 30 minutes of time [N]
    INCLUDES   Reporting only once in a 30-day period
    EXCLUDES   *This service if there exists a more specific CPT code for cardiographic services or glucose monitoring (93014, 93227, 93233, 93272, 95250)*
    Transfer/interpretation of data from hospital/clinical laboratory computers
    Do not report with care plan oversight services if within 30 days (99374-99380)
    1.56   1.56   Global Days XXX
    AMA: 2009, Jan, 11-31; 2008, Jan, 10-25; 2007, January, 13-27; 2007, January, 28-31; 2006, September, 14-16; 2006, August, 6-8

Current Procedural Coding Expert – Medicine

99100-99140 Modifying Factors for Anesthesia Services

CMS 100-4,12,50 — Anesthesia Services
CMS 100-4,12,140 — Certified Registered Nurse Anesthetist Services
CMS 100-4,12,140.2 — Payment for CRNA Services
CMS 100-4,12,140.3.2 — Calculation of Anesthesia Time

+ 99100 Anesthesia for patient of extreme age, younger than 1 year and older than 70 (List separately in addition to code for primary anesthesia procedure) [A][B]

EXCLUDES: Services performed on infants that are less that 1 year old at the time of surgery (00326, 00561, 00834, 00836)

Code first primary anesthesia procedure
0.00   0.00   Global Days ZZZ
AMA: 2008, Apr, 3-4

+ 99116 Anesthesia complicated by utilization of total body hypothermia (List separately in addition to code for primary anesthesia procedure) [B]

Code first primary anesthesia procedure
0.00   0.00   Global Days ZZZ
AMA: 2008, Apr, 3-4

+ 99135 Anesthesia complicated by utilization of controlled hypotension (List separately in addition to code for primary anesthesia procedure) [B]

Code first primary anesthesia procedure
0.00   0.00   Global Days ZZZ
AMA: 2008, Apr, 3-4

+ 99140 Anesthesia complicated by emergency conditions (specify) (List separately in addition to code for primary anesthesia procedure) [B]

INCLUDES: Circumstances where a delay in treatment would lead to a significant increase in the threat to life or body part

Code first primary anesthesia procedure
0.00   0.00   Global Days ZZZ
AMA: 2009, Jan, 11-31; 2008, Jan, 10-25; 2008, Apr, 3-4; 2007, January, 13-27

99143-99150 Moderate Sedation Services

INCLUDES:
- Administration of medication
- IV access
- Maintenance of sedation
- Monitoring of oxygen saturation/heart rate/blood pressure
- Patient assessment
- Recovery (not included in intraservice time)

EXCLUDES: Minimal sedation/anxiolysis/deep sedation/monitored anesthesia care (00100-01999)

Do not report with pulse oximetry (94760-94762)

⊘ **99143** Moderate sedation services (other than those services described by codes 00100-01999) provided by the same physician performing the diagnostic or therapeutic service that the sedation supports, requiring the presence of an independent trained observer to assist in the monitoring of the patient's level of consciousness and physiological status; younger than 5 years of age, first 30 minutes intra-service time [N][80]

0.00   0.00   Global Days XXX
AMA: 2009, Jan, 11-31; 2008, Jan, 10-25; 2008, Feb, 5-6; 2007, January, 13-27; 2006, February, 10-15; 2006, September, 1-4; 2006, May, 16-20

⊘ **99144** age 5 years or older, first 30 minutes intra-service time [A][N][80]

0.00   0.00   Global Days XXX
AMA: 2008, Feb, 5-6; 2006, September, 1-4; 2006, May, 16-20; 2006, February, 10-15

+ 99145 Moderate sedation services (other than those services described by codes 00100-01999) provided by the same physician performing the diagnostic or therapeutic service that the sedation supports, requiring the presence of an independent trained observer to assist in the monitoring of the patient's level of consciousness and physiological status; each additional 15 minutes intra-service time (List separately in addition to code for primary service) [N][80]

Code first initial 30 minutes (99143, 99144)
0.00   0.00   Global Days ZZZ
AMA: 2008, Feb, 5-6; 2006, September, 1-4; 2006, May, 16-20; 2006, February, 10-15

99148 Moderate sedation services (other than those services described by codes 00100-01999), provided by a physician other than the health care professional performing the diagnostic or therapeutic service that the sedation supports; younger than 5 years of age, first 30 minutes intra-service time [N][80]

0.00   0.00   Global Days XXX
AMA: 2009, Jan, 11-31; 2008, Jan, 10-25; 2007, January, 13-27; 2006, May, 16-20; 2006, February, 10-15

99149 age 5 years or older, first 30 minutes intra-service time [A][N][80]

0.00   0.00   Global Days XXX
AMA: 2006, February, 10-15; 2006, May, 16-20

+ 99150 each additional 15 minutes intra-service time (List separately in addition to code for primary service) [N][80]

Code first initial 30 minutes (99148, 99149)
0.00   0.00   Global Days ZZZ
AMA: 2006, May, 16-20; 2006, February, 10-15

99170 Specialized Examination of Child

99170 Anogenital examination with colposcopic magnification in childhood for suspected trauma [A][T]

EXCLUDES: Conscious sedation (99143-99150)

2.54   3.65   Global Days 000
AMA: 2006, April, 1-7

99172-99173 Visual Acuity Screening Tests

CMS 100-2,16,90 — Routine Services and Appliances

99172 Visual function screening, automated or semi-automated bilateral quantitative determination of visual acuity, ocular alignment, color vision by pseudoisochromatic plates, and field of vision (may include all or some screening of the determination[s] for contrast sensitivity, vision under glare) [E]

INCLUDES:
- Graduated visual acuity stimuli that allow a quantitative determination of visual acuity
- Ocular photoscreening

Do not report with (99173)

Do not report with evaluation and management service or general ophthalmological service (92002-92014, 99201-99499)

0.00   0.00   Global Days XXX
AMA: 2009, Jan, 11-31; 2008, Jan, 10-25; 2007, January, 13-27; 2005, March, 1-6

99173 Screening test of visual acuity, quantitative, bilateral   E
  INCLUDES   Graduated visual acuity stimuli that allow a quantitative estimate of visual acuity
   Ocular photoscreening
  Do not report with (99172)
  0.07   0.07   Global Days XXX
  AMA: 2005, March, 1-6

99174 Screening For Amblyogenic Factors

Do not report with (92002-92014, 99172-99173)

99174 Ocular photoscreening with interpretation and report, bilateral   E
  0.68   0.68   Global Days XXX

99175 Drug Administration to Induce Vomiting

99175 Ipecac or similar administration for individual emesis and continued observation until stomach adequately emptied of poison   N 80
  EXCLUDES   Diagnostic gastric lavage (91055)
   Diagnostic intubation (82926-82928, 89130-89141)
  0.56   0.56   Global Days XXX

99183 Hyperbaric Oxygen Therapy

CMS 100-3,20.29   Hyperbaric Oxygen Therapy

99183 Physician attendance and supervision of hyperbaric oxygen therapy, per session   B 80
  EXCLUDES   Evaluation and management services if performed
   Other procedures such as wound debridement, if performed
  3.32   5.60   Global Days XXX
  AMA: 2009, Jan, 11-31; 2008, Jan, 10-25; 2007, January, 13-27

99190-99192 Assemble and Manage Pump with Oxygenator/Heat Exchange

99190 Assembly and operation of pump with oxygenator or heat exchanger (with or without ECG and/or pressure monitoring); each hour   C
  0.00   0.00   Global Days XXX

99191 45 minutes   C
  0.00   0.00   Global Days XXX

99192 30 minutes   C
  0.00   0.00   Global Days XXX

99195-99199 Therapeutic Phlebotomy and Unlisted Procedures

99195 Phlebotomy, therapeutic (separate procedure)   X 80
  2.12   2.12   Global Days XXX
  AMA: 2009, Jan, 11-31; 2008, Jan, 10-25; 2007, January, 13-27

99199 Unlisted special service, procedure or report   B 80
  0.00   0.00   Global Days XXX

99500-99602 Home Visit By Non-Physician Professionals

INCLUDES   Services performed by non-physician providers
  Services provided in patient's:
   Assisted living apartment
   Custodial care facility
   Group home
   Non-traditional private home
   Residence
   School

EXCLUDES   Home visits performed by physicians (99341-99350)
   Other services/procedures provided by physicians to patients at home

Code also home visit evaluation and management codes if health care provider is authorized to use (99341-99350)

Code also significant separately identifiable evaluation and management service

99500 Home visit for prenatal monitoring and assessment to include fetal heart rate, non-stress test, uterine monitoring, and gestational diabetes monitoring   M ♀ E
  0.00   0.00   Global Days XXX
  AMA: 2009, Jan, 11-31; 2008, Jan, 10-25; 2007, January, 28-31

99501 Home visit for postnatal assessment and follow-up care   ♀ E
  0.00   0.00   Global Days XXX
  AMA: 2007, January, 28-31

99502 Home visit for newborn care and assessment   A E
  0.00   0.00   Global Days XXX
  AMA: 2007, January, 28-31

99503 Home visit for respiratory therapy care (eg, bronchodilator, oxygen therapy, respiratory assessment, apnea evaluation)   E
  0.00   0.00   Global Days XXX
  AMA: 2007, January, 28-31

99504 Home visit for mechanical ventilation care   E
  0.00   0.00   Global Days XXX
  AMA: 2007, January, 28-31

99505 Home visit for stoma care and maintenance including colostomy and cystostomy   E
  0.00   0.00   Global Days XXX
  AMA: 2007, January, 28-31

99506 Home visit for intramuscular injections   E
  0.00   0.00   Global Days XXX
  AMA: 2007, January, 28-31

99507 Home visit for care and maintenance of catheter(s) (eg, urinary, drainage, and enteral)   E
  0.00   0.00   Global Days XXX
  AMA: 2007, January, 28-31

99509 Home visit for assistance with activities of daily living and personal care   E
  EXCLUDES   Medical nutrition therapy/assessment home services (97802-97804)
   Self-care/home management training (97535)
   Speech therapy home services (92507-92508)
  0.00   0.00   Global Days XXX
  AMA: 2007, January, 28-31

99510 Home visit for individual, family, or marriage counseling   E P0
  0.00   0.00   Global Days XXX
  AMA: 2007, January, 28-31

99511 Home visit for fecal impaction management and enema administration   E
  0.00   0.00   Global Days XXX
  AMA: 2007, January, 28-31

Current Procedural Coding Expert – Medicine

99512 Home visit for hemodialysis [E]
  EXCLUDES: *Peritoneal dialysis home infusion (99601, 99602)*
  0.00 0.00 Global Days XXX
  AMA: 2007, January, 28-31

99600 **Unlisted home visit service or procedure** [E]
  0.00 0.00 Global Days XXX
  AMA: 2009, Jan, 11-31; 2008, Jan, 10-25; 2007, January, 28-31

99601 Home infusion/specialty drug administration, per visit (up to 2 hours); [E]
  0.00 0.00 Global Days XXX
  AMA: 2005, November, 1-9

+ **99602** each additional hour (List separately in addition to code for primary procedure) [E]
  Code first initial 2 hours (99601)
  0.00 0.00 Global Days XXX
  AMA: 2005, November, 1-9

99605-99607 Medication Management By Pharmacist

INCLUDES Direct (face-to-face) assessment and intervention by a pharmacist for the purpose of:
  Managing medication complications and/or interactions
  Maximizing the patient's response to drug therapy
  Documenting the following required elements:
    Advice given regarding improvement of treatment compliance and outcomes
    Profile of medications (prescription and nonprescription)
    Review of applicable patient history

EXCLUDES *Routine tasks associated with dispensing and related activities (e.g., providing product information)*

99605 Medication therapy management service(s) provided by a pharmacist, individual, face-to-face with patient, with assessment and intervention if provided; initial 15 minutes, new patient [E]
  0.00 0.00 Global Days XXX

99606 initial 15 minutes, established patient [E]
  0.00 0.00 Global Days XXX

+ **99607** each additional 15 minutes (List separately in addition to code for primary service) [E]
  Code first (99605, 99606)
  0.00 0.00 Global Days XXX
  AMA: 2009, Jan, 11-31

Evaluation and Management (E/M) Services Guidelines

In addition to the information presented in the Introduction, several other items unique to this section are defined or identified here.

CLASSIFICATION OF EVALUATION AND MANAGEMENT (E/M) SERVICES

The E/M section is divided into broad categories such as office visits, hospital visits, and consultations. Most of the categories are further divided into two or more subcategories of E/M services. For example, there are two subcategories of office visits (new patient and established patient) and there are two subcategories of hospital visits (initial and subsequent). The subcategories of E/M services are further classified into levels of E/M services that are identified by specific codes. This classification is important because the nature of physician work varies by type of service, place of service, and the patient's status.

The basic format of the levels of E/M services is the same for most categories. First, a unique code number is listed. Second, the place and/or type of service is specified, eg, office consultation. Third, the content of the service is defined, eg, comprehensive history and comprehensive examination. Fourth, the nature of the presenting problem(s) usually associated with a given level is described. Fifth, the time typically required to provide the service is specified.

DEFINITIONS OF COMMONLY USED TERMS

Certain key words and phrases are used throughout the E/M section. The following definitions are intended to reduce the potential for differing interpretations and to increase the consistency of reporting by physicians in differing specialties. E/M services may also be reported by other qualified health care professionals who are authorized to perform such services within the scope of their practice.

New and Established Patient

Solely for the purposes of distinguishing between new and established patients, professional services are those face-to-face services rendered by a physician and reported by a specific CPT code(s). A new patient is one who has not received any professional services from the physician or another physician of the same specialty who belongs to the same group practice, within the past three years.

An established patient is one who has received professional services from the physician or another physician of the same specialty who belongs to the same group practice, within the past three years.

In the instance where a physician is on call for or covering for another physician, the patient's encounter will be classified as it would have been by the physician who is not available.

No distinction is made between new and established patients in the emergency department. E/M services in the emergency department category may be reported for any new or established patient who presents for treatment in the emergency department.

The decision tree is provided to aid in determining whether to report the E/M service provided as a new or an established patient encounter.

Chief Complaint

A chief complaint is a concise statement describing the symptom, problem, condition, diagnosis, or other factor that is the reason for the encounter, usually stated in the patient's words.

Concurrent Care

Concurrent care is the provision of similar services (e.g., hospital visits) to the same patient by more than one physician on the same day. When concurrent care is provided, no special reporting is required. Transfer of care is the process whereby a physician who is managing some or all of a patient's problems relinquishes this responsibility to another physician who explicitly agrees to accept this responsibility and who, from the initial encounter, is not providing consultative services. The physician transferring care is then no longer providing care for these problems though he or she may continue providing care for other conditions when appropriate. Consultation codes should not be reported by the physician who has agreed to accept transfer of care before an initial evaluation but are appropriate to report if the decision to accept transfer of care cannot be made until after the initial consultation evaluation, regardless of the site of service.

Counseling

Counseling is a discussion with a patient and/or family concerning one or more of the following areas:

- Diagnostic results, impressions, and/or recommended diagnostic studies
- Prognosis
- Risks and benefits of management (treatment) options
- Instructions for management (treatment) and/or follow-up
- Importance of compliance with chosen management (treatment) options
- Risk factor reduction
- Patient and family education

(For psychotherapy, see 90804-90857)

Family History

A review of medical events in the patient's family that includes significant information about:

- The health status or cause of death of parents, siblings, and children
- Specific diseases related to problems identified in the Chief Complaint or History of the Present Illness, and/or System Review
- Diseases of family members that may be hereditary or place the patient at risk

History of Present Illness

A chronological description of the development of the patient's present illness from the first sign and/or symptom to the present. This includes a description of location, quality, severity, timing, context, modifying factors, and associated signs and symptoms significantly related to the presenting problem(s).

Levels of E/M Services

Within each category or subcategory of E/M service, there are three to five levels of E/M services available for reporting purposes. Levels of E/M services are not interchangeable among the different categories or subcategories of service. For example, the first level of E/M services in the subcategory of office visit, new patient, does not have the same definition as the first level of E/M services in the subcategory of office visit, established patient.

The levels of E/M services include examinations, evaluations, treatments, conferences with or concerning patients, preventive pediatric and adult health supervision, and similar medical services, such as the determination of the need and/or location for appropriate care. Medical screening includes the history, examination, and medical decision-making required to determine the need and/or location for appropriate care and treatment of the patient (eg, office and other outpatient setting, emergency department, nursing facility). The levels of E/M services encompass the wide variations in skill, effort, time, responsibility, and medical knowledge required for the prevention or diagnosis and treatment of illness or injury and the promotion of optimal health. Each level of E/M services may be used by all physicians.

The descriptors for the levels of E/M services recognize seven components, six of which are used in defining the levels of E/M services. These components are:

- History
- Examination
- Medical decision making
- Counseling
- Coordination of care

Evaluation and Management (E/M) Services Guidelines

- Nature of presenting problem
- Time

The first three of these components (history, examination, and medical decision making) are considered the key components in selecting a level of E/M services.

The next three components (counseling, coordination of care, and the nature of the presenting problem) are considered contributory factors in the majority of encounters. Although the first two of these contributory factors are important E/M services, it is not required that these services be provided at every patient encounter.

Coordination of care with other providers or agencies without a patient encounter on that day is reported using the case management codes.

Decision Tree for New vs. Established patients

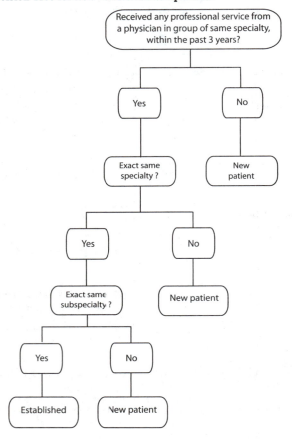

The final component, time, is discussed in detail.

Any specifically identifiable procedure (ie, identified with a specific CPT code) performed on or subsequent to the date of initial or subsequent E/M services should be reported separately.

The actual performance and/or interpretation of diagnostic tests/studies ordered during a patient encounter are not included in the levels of E/M services. Physician performance of diagnostic tests/studies for which specific CPT codes are available may be reported separately, in addition to the appropriate E/M code. The physician's interpretation of the results of diagnostic tests/studies (ie, professional component) with preparation of a separate distinctly identifiable signed written report may also be reported separately, using the appropriate CPT code with modifier 26 appended.

The physician may need to indicate that on the day a procedure or service identified by a CPT code was performed, the patient's condition required a significant separately identifiable E/M service above and beyond other services provided or beyond the usual preservice and postservice care associated with the procedure that was performed. The E/M service may be caused or prompted by the symptoms or condition for which the procedure and/or service was provided. This circumstance may be reported by adding modifier 25 to the appropriate level of E/M service. As such, different diagnoses are not required for reporting of the procedure and the E/M services on the same date.

Nature of Presenting Problem

A presenting problem is a disease, condition, illness, injury, symptom, sign, finding, complaint, or other reason for encounter, with or without a diagnosis being established at the time of the encounter. The E/M codes recognize five types of presenting problems that are defined as follows:

Minimal: A problem that may not require the presence of the physician, but service is provided under the physician's supervision.

Self-limited or minor: A problem that runs a definite and prescribed course, is transient in nature, and is not likely to permanently alter health status OR has a good prognosis with management/compliance.

Low severity: A problem where the risk of morbidity without treatment is low; there is little to no risk of mortality without treatment; full recovery without functional impairment is expected.

Moderate severity: A problem where the risk of morbidity without treatment is moderate; there is moderate risk of mortality without treatment; uncertain prognosis OR increased probability of prolonged functional impairment.

High severity: A problem where the risk of morbidity without treatment is high to extreme; there is a moderate to high risk of mortality without treatment OR high probability of severe, prolonged functional impairment.

Past History

A review of the patient's past experiences with illnesses, injuries, and treatments that includes significant information about:

- Prior major illnesses and injuries
- Prior operations
- Prior hospitalizations
- Current medications
- Allergies (eg, drug, food)
- Age appropriate immunization status
- Age appropriate feeding/dietary status

Social History

An age appropriate review of past and current activities that includes significant information about:

- Marital status and/or living arrangements
- Current employment
- Occupational history
- Use of drugs, alcohol, and tobacco
- Level of education
- Sexual history
- Other relevant social factors

System Review (Review of Systems)

An inventory of body systems obtained through a series of questions seeking to identify signs and/or symptoms that the patient may be experiencing or has experienced. For the purposes of the CPT codebook the following elements of a system review have been identified:

- Constitutional symptoms (fever, weight loss, etc)
- Eyes
- Ears, nose, mouth, throat
- Cardiovascular
- Respiratory
- Gastrointestinal
- Genitourinary
- Musculoskeletal
- Integumentary (skin and/or breast)
- Neurological
- Psychiatric

- Endocrine
- Hematologic/lymphatic
- Allergic/immunologic

The review of systems helps define the problem, clarify the differential diagnosis, identify needed testing, or serves as baseline data on other systems that might be affected by any possible management options.

Time

The inclusion of time in the definitions of levels of E/M services has been implicit in prior editions of the CPT codebook. The inclusion of time as an explicit factor beginning in CPT 1992 is done to assist physicians in selecting the most appropriate level of E/M services. It should be recognized that the specific times expressed in the visit code descriptors are averages and, therefore, represent a range of times that may be higher or lower depending on actual clinical circumstances.

Time is not a descriptive component for the emergency department levels of E/M services because emergency department services are typically provided on a variable intensity basis, often involving multiple encounters with several patients over an extended period of time. Therefore, it is often difficult for physicians to provide accurate estimates of the time spent face-to-face with the patient.

Studies to establish levels of E/M services employed surveys of practicing physicians to obtain data on the amount of time and work associated with typical E/M services. Since "work" is not easily quantifiable, the codes must rely on other objective, verifiable measures that correlate with physicians' estimates of their "work." It has been demonstrated that physicians' estimations of intraservice time (as explained on the next page), both within and across specialties, is a variable that is predictive of the "work" of E/M services. This same research has shown there is a strong relationship between intraservice time and total time for E/M services. Intraservice time, rather than total time, was chosen for inclusion with the codes because of its relative ease of measurement and because of its direct correlation with measurements of the total amount of time and work associated with typical E/M services.

Intraservice times are defined as face-to-face time for office and other outpatient visits and as unit/floor time for hospital and other inpatient visits. This distinction is necessary because most of the work of typical office visits takes place during the face-to-face time with the patient, while most of the work of typical hospital visits takes place during the time spent on the patient's floor or unit.

Face-to-face time (office and other outpatient visits and office consultations): For coding purposes, face-to-face time for these services is defined as only that time that the physician spends face-to-face with the patient and/or family. This includes the time in which the physician performs such tasks as obtaining a history, performing an examination, and counseling the patient.

Physicians also spend time doing work before or after the face-to-face time with the patient, performing such tasks as reviewing records and tests, arranging for further services, and communicating further with other professionals and the patient through written reports and telephone contact.

This non-face-to-face time for office services—also called pre- and postencounter time—is not included in the time component described in the E/M codes. However, the pre- and post-face-to-face work associated with an encounter was included in calculating the total work of typical services in physician surveys.

Thus, the face-to-face time associated with the services described by any E/M code is a valid proxy for the total work done before, during, and after the visit.

Unit/floor time (hospital observation services, inpatient hospital care, initial hospital consultations, nursing facility): For reporting purposes, intraservice time for these services is defined as unit/floor time, which includes the time that the physician is present on the patient's hospital unit and at the bedside rendering services for that patient. This includes the time in which the physician establishes and/or reviews the patient's chart, examines the patient, writes notes, and communicates with other professionals and the patient's family.

In the hospital, pre- and post-time includes time spent off the patient's floor performing such tasks as reviewing pathology and radiology findings in another part of the hospital.

This pre- and postvisit time is not included in the time component described in these codes. However, the pre- and postwork performed during the time spent off the floor or unit was included in calculating the total work of typical services in physician surveys.

Thus, the unit/floor time associated with the services described by any code is a valid proxy for the total work done before, during, and after the visit.

UNLISTED SERVICE

An E/M service may be provided that is not listed in this section of the CPT codebook. When reporting such a service, the appropriate "Unlisted" code may be used to indicate the service, identifying it by "Special Report," as discussed in the following paragraph. The "Unlisted Services" and accompanying codes for the E/M section are as follows:

99429	Unlisted preventive medicine service
99499	Unlisted evaluation and management service

SPECIAL REPORT

An unlisted service or one that is unusual, variable, or new may require a special report demonstrating the medical appropriateness of the service. Pertinent information should include an adequate definition or description of the nature, extent, and need for the procedure and the time, effort, and equipment necessary to provide the service. Additional items that may be included are complexity of symptoms, final diagnosis, pertinent physical findings, diagnostic and therapeutic procedures, concurrent problems, and follow-up care.

INSTRUCTIONS FOR SELECTING A LEVEL OF E/M SERVICE

Identify the Category and Subcategory of Service

Identify the category and subcategory of service codes available for reporting E/M services.

The categories and subcategories of codes available for reporting E/M services are shown in Table 1.

Review the Reporting Instructions for the Selected Category or Subcategory

Most of the categories and many of the subcategories of service have special guidelines or instructions unique to that category or subcategory. Where these are indicated, eg, "Inpatient Hospital Care," special instructions will be presented preceding the levels of E/M services.

Review the Level of E/M Service Descriptors and Examples in the Selected Category or Subcategory

The descriptors for the levels of E/M services recognize seven components, six of which are used in defining the levels of E/M services. These components are:

- History
- Examination
- Medical decision making
- Counseling
- Coordination of care
- Nature of presenting problem
- Time

The first three of these components (ie, history, examination, and medical decision making) should be considered the key components in selecting the level of E/M services. An exception to this rule is in the case of visits that consist predominantly of counseling or coordination of care.

The nature of the presenting problem and time are provided in some levels to assist the physician in determining the appropriate level of E/M service.

Determine the Extent of History Obtained

The extent of the history is dependent upon clinical judgment and on the nature of the presenting problems(s). The levels of E/M services recognize four types of history that are defined as follows:

Problem focused: Chief complaint; brief history of present illness or problem.

Evaluation and Management (E/M) Services Guidelines

Expanded problem focused: Chief complaint; brief history of present illness; problem pertinent system review.

Detailed: Chief complaint; extended history of present illness; problem pertinent system review extended to include a review of a limited number of additional systems; pertinent past, family, and/or social history directly related to the patient's problems.

Comprehensive: Chief complaint; extended history of present illness; review of systems that is directly related to the problem(s) identified in the history of the present illness plus a review of all additional body systems; complete past, family, and social history.

The comprehensive history obtained as part of the preventive medicine E/M service is not problem-oriented and does not involve a chief complaint or present illness. It does, however, include a comprehensive system review and comprehensive or interval past, family, and social history as well as a comprehensive assessment/history of pertinent risk factors.

Determine the Extent of Examination Performed

The extent of the examination performed is dependent on clinical judgment and on the nature of the presenting problem(s). The levels of E/M services recognize four types of examination that are defined as follows:

Problem focused: A limited examination of the affected body area or organ system.

Expanded problem focused: A limited examination of the affected body area or organ system and other symptomatic or related organ system(s).

Detailed: An extended examination of the affected body area(s) and other symptomatic or related organ system(s).

Comprehensive: A general multisystem examination or a complete examination of a single organ system. Note: The comprehensive examination performed as part of the preventive medicine E/M service is multisystem, but its extent is based on age and risk factors identified.

For the purposes of these CPT definitions, the following body areas are recognized:

- Head, including the face
- Neck
- Chest, including breasts and axilla
- Abdomen
- Genitalia, groin, buttocks
- Back
- Each extremity

For the purposes of these CPT definitions, the following organ systems are recognized:

- Eyes
- Ears, nose, mouth, and throat
- Cardiovascular
- Respiratory
- Gastrointestinal
- Genitourinary
- Musculoskeletal
- Skin
- Neurologic
- Psychiatric
- Hematologic/lymphatic/immunologic

Determine the Complexity of Medical Decision Making

Medical decision making refers to the complexity of establishing a diagnosis and/or selecting a management option as measured by:

- The number of possible diagnoses and/or the number of management options that must be considered
- The amount and/or complexity of medical records, diagnostic tests, and/or other information that must be obtained, reviewed, and analyzed
- The risk of significant complications, morbidity, and/or mortality, as well as comorbidities, associated with the patient's presenting problems(s), the diagnostic procedure(s), and/or the possible management options

Four types of medical decision making are recognized: straightforward, low complexity, moderate complexity, and high complexity. To qualify for a given type of decision making, two of the three elements in Table 2 must be met or exceeded.

Comorbidities/underlying diseases, in and of themselves, are not considered in selecting a level of E/M services unless their presence significantly increases the complexity of the medical decision making.

Select the Appropriate Level of E/M Services Based on the Following

1. For the following categories/subcategories, all of the key components, ie, history, examination, and medical decision making, must meet or exceed the stated requirements to qualify for a particular level of E/M service: office, new patient; hospital observation services; initial hospital care; office consultations; initial inpatient consultations; emergency department services; initial nursing facility care; domiciliary care, new patient; and home, new patient.

2. For the following categories/subcategories, two of the three key components (ie, history, examination, and medical decision making) must meet or exceed the stated requirements to qualify for a particular level of E/M services: office, established patient; subsequent hospital care; subsequent nursing facility care; domiciliary care, established patient; and home, established patient.

3. When counseling and/or coordination of care dominates (more than 50%) the physician/patient and/or family encounter (face-to-face time in the office or other outpatient setting or floor/unit time in the hospital or nursing facility), then time may be considered the key or controlling factor to qualify for a particular level of E/M services. This includes time spent with parties who have assumed responsibility for the care of the patient or decision making whether or not they are family members (eg, foster parents, person acting in loco parentis, legal guardian). The extent of counseling and/or coordination of care must be documented in the medical record.

TABLE 1

Complexity of Medical Decision Making

Number of Diagnoses or Management Options	Amount and/or Complexity of Data to be Reviewed	Risk of Complications and/or Morbidity or Mortality	Type of Decision Making
minimal	minimal or none	minimal	straightforward
limited	limited	low	low complexity
multiple	moderate	moderate	moderate complexity
extensive	extensive	high	high complexity

CONSULTATION CODES FOR MEDICARE REIMBURSEMENT

The Centers for Medicare and Medicaid Services (CMS) have proceeded with their proposal from July to no longer pay for the consultation CPT codes. CMS has redistributed the value of the consultation codes across the other E/M codes for Medicare services. CMS retained values for codes 99241-99255 in the Medicare Physician Fee Schedule for those private payers who utilize this data for reimbursement. Note that private payers may choose to follow CMS or CPT guidelines, and the use of consultation codes should be verified with individual payers.

In the 2010 Physician Services Final Rule, CMS stated that despite refinements to coding and documentation guidelines, consultations continue to be reported inappropriately. As a result of the confusion regarding consultations, CMS has adopted new policies regarding the use of consultation codes. Under these guidelines, the inpatient and office/outpatient consultation codes contained in the CPT manual will not be covered services for CMS. However, Medicare will cover telehealth consultations when reported with the appropriate HCPCS Level II G code.

In past years, the guidelines regarding consultations have been revised, and attempts at clarification have been made by both the American Medical Association (AMA) and Centers for Medicare and Medicaid Services (CMS). Despite these efforts confusion regarding consultations, including the required documentation and appropriate use of the consultation codes, continues.

For 2010, the AMA included additional guidance in the CPT manual regarding consultations. A consultation is now defined as a service that must be requested by a physician or other appropriate source "to either recommend care for a specific condition or problem or to determine whether to accept responsibility for ongoing management of the patient's entire care or for the care of a specific condition or problem." CPT guidelines state that the request may be verbal but must be documented in the patient record "by either the consulting or requesting physician or appropriate source." New guidelines also emphasize that a consultation initiated by the patient is not reported using the consultation codes.

Additional changes regarding inpatient services will also be initiated in 2010 by CMS. All outpatient services will be reported using the appropriate new or established evaluation and management (E/M) codes. Inpatient services will be reported with the first inpatient encounter by any physician reported with initial hospital care codes 99221-99223 and subsequent inpatient encounters using codes 99231-99233. As only one physician may be the admitting physician, CMS has added HCPCS Level II modifier AI, Principal physician of record, to be appended to the initial hospital care code by the attending physician.

Current Procedural Coding Expert – Evaluation and Management

99201-99215 Outpatient and Other Visits

CMS 100-3,70.3   Physician's Offices Within an Institution--"Incident-to" Provision
CMS 100-4,12,30.6.7   Payment for Office or Other Outpatient Evaluation and Management (E/M) Visits

INCLUDES
Established patients: received prior care from the physician or another physician in the practice of the same specialty in the previous three years (99211-99215)
New patients: have not received care from the physician or any other physician in the same practice within the same specialty in the previous three years (99201-99205)
Office visits
Outpatient services prior to formal admission to a facility

EXCLUDES
Office/outpatient services that require more than the customary E/M service (99354-99355, 99358-99359)

99201 Office or other outpatient visit for the evaluation and management of a new patient, which requires these 3 key components: A problem focused history; A problem focused examination; Straightforward medical decision making. Counseling and/or coordination of care with other providers or agencies are provided consistent with the nature of the problem(s) and the patient's and/or family's needs. Usually, the presenting problem(s) are self limited or minor. Physicians typically spend 10 minutes face-to-face with the patient and/or family.
0.72   1.12   **Global Days XXX**
AMA: 2009, Mar, 3,4&7; 2009, Jan, 11-31; 2009, Jul, 7; 2009, Jul, 8-9; 2008, Jan, 10-25; 2007, April, 11-12; 2007, Jul, 1-4; 2007, March, 9-11; 2007, January, 13-27; 2006, June, 1-7; 2006, May, 1-9; 2005, May, 1-2; 2005, March, 11-15; 2005, April, 1-5; 2005, June, 9-11; 2005, December, 9-11; 2005, February, 1-6

99202 Office or other outpatient visit for the evaluation and management of a new patient, which requires these 3 key components: An expanded problem focused history; An expanded problem focused examination; Straightforward medical decision making. Counseling and/or coordination of care with other providers or agencies are provided consistent with the nature of the problem(s) and the patient's and/or family's needs. Usually, the presenting problem(s) are of low to moderate severity. Physicians typically spend 20 minutes face-to-face with the patient and/or family.
1.39   1.96   **Global Days XXX**
AMA: 2009, Jan, 11-31; 2009, Mar, 3,4&7; 2009, Jul, 8-9; 2009, Jul, 7; 2008, Jan, 10-25; 2007, January, 13-27; 2007, Jul, 1-4; 2007, March, 9-11; 2007, April, 11-12; 2006, May, 1-9; 2006, June, 1-7; 2005, February, 1-6; 2005, April, 1-5; 2005, December, 9-11; 2005, May, 1-2; 2005, March, 11-15; 2005, June, 9-11

99203 Office or other outpatient visit for the evaluation and management of a new patient, which requires these 3 key components: A detailed history; A detailed examination; Medical decision making of low complexity. Counseling and/or coordination of care with other providers or agencies are provided consistent with the nature of the problem(s) and the patient's and/or family's needs. Usually, the presenting problem(s) are of moderate severity. Physicians typically spend 30 minutes face-to-face with the patient and/or family.
2.11   2.83   **Global Days XXX**
AMA: 2009, Jan, 11-31; 2009, Mar, 3,4&7; 2009, Jul, 7; 2009, Jul, 8-9; 2008, Jan, 10-25; 2007, January, 13-27; 2007, April, 11-12; 2007, Jul, 1-4; 2007, March, 9-11; 2006, May, 1-9; 2006, June, 1-7; 2005, June, 9-11; 2005, December, 9-11; 2005, April, 1-5; 2005, May, 1-2; 2005, February, 7-9; 2005, February, 1-6; 2005, March, 11-15

99204 Office or other outpatient visit for the evaluation and management of a new patient, which requires these 3 key components: A comprehensive history; A comprehensive examination; Medical decision making of moderate complexity. Counseling and/or coordination of care with other providers or agencies are provided consistent with the nature of the problem(s) and the patient's and/or family's needs. Usually, the presenting problem(s) are of moderate to high severity. Physicians typically spend 45 minutes face-to-face with the patient and/or family.
3.59   4.39   **Global Days XXX**
AMA: 2009, Mar, 3,4&7; 2009, Jul, 8-9; 2009, Jul, 7; 2009, Jan, 11-31; 2008, Jan, 10-25; 2007, January, 13-27; 2007, April, 11-12; 2007, Jul, 1-4; 2007, March, 9-11; 2006, June, 1-7; 2006, May, 1-9; 2005, March, 11-15; 2005, June, 9-11; 2005, December, 9-11; 2005, April, 1-5; 2005, May, 1-2; 2005, February, 1-6

99205 A comprehensive examination; Medical decision making of high complexity. Counseling and/or coordination of care with other providers or agencies are provided consistent with the nature of the problem(s) and the patient's and/or family's needs. Usually, the presenting problem(s) are of moderate to high severity. Physicians typically spend 60 minutes face-to-face with the patient and/or family.
4.61   5.47   **Global Days XXX**
AMA: 2009, Jan, 11-31; 2009, Mar, 3,4&7; 2009, Jul, 7; 2009, Jul, 8-9; 2008, Jan, 10-25; 2007, April, 11-12; 2007, Jul, 1-4; 2007, March, 9-11; 2007, January, 13-27; 2006, June, 1-7; 2006, May, 1-9; 2005, May, 1-2; 2005, June, 9-11; 2005, April, 1-5; 2005, February, 1-6; 2005, December, 9-11; 2005, March, 11-15

99211 Office or other outpatient visit for the evaluation and management of an established patient, that may not require the presence of a physician. Usually, the presenting problem(s) are minimal. Typically, 5 minutes are spent performing or supervising these services.
0.26   0.50   **Global Days XXX**
AMA: 2009, Jan, 11-31; 2009, Mar, 3,4&7; 2009, Jul, 8-9; 2009, Jul, 7; 2008, Jan, 10-25; 2008, Mar, 3&7; 2007, Dec, 9; 2007, Jul, 1-4; 2007, January, 13-27; 2007, March, 9-11; 2007, April, 11-12; 2006, June, 1-7; 2006, May, 1-9; 2006, May, 16-20; 2005, November, 1-9; 2005, March, 11-15; 2005, June, 9-11; 2005, May, 1-2; 2005, April, 1-5; 2005, February, 1-6; 2005, February, 13-16; 2005, December, 9-11

99212 Office or other outpatient visit for the evaluation and management of an established patient, which requires at least 2 of these 3 key components: A problem focused history; A problem focused examination; Straightforward medical decision making. Counseling and/or coordination of care with other providers or agencies are provided consistent with the nature of the problem(s) and the patient's and/or family's needs. Usually, the presenting problem(s) are self limited or minor. Physicians typically spend 10 minutes face-to-face with the patient and/or family.
0.71   1.12   **Global Days XXX**
AMA: 2009, Jan, 11-31; 2009, Mar, 3,4&7; 2009, Jul, 7; 2009, Jul, 8-9; 2008, Jan, 10-25; 2008, Mar, 3&7; 2007, January, 13-27; 2007, April, 11-12; 2007, March, 9-11; 2007, Jul, 1-4; 2006, May, 1-9; 2006, June, 11-15; 2006, June, 1-7; 2006, September, 9-13; 2005, May, 1-2; 2005, June, 9-11; 2005, February, 1-6; 2005, December, 9-11; 2005, March, 11-15; 2005, April, 1-5

99213 Office or other outpatient visit for the evaluation and management of an established patient, which requires at least 2 of these 3 key components: An expanded problem focused history; An expanded problem focused examination; Medical decision making of low complexity. Counseling and coordination of care with other providers or agencies are provided consistent with the nature of the problem(s) and the patient's and/or family's needs. Usually, the presenting problem(s) are of low to moderate severity. Physicians typically spend 15 minutes face-to-face with the patient and/or family.

🔹 1.41   🔹 1.90   **Global Days XXX**

AMA: 2009, Jan, 11-31; 2009, Mar, 3,4&7; 2009, Jul, 8-9; 2009, Jul, 7; 2008, Jan, 10-25; 2008, Mar, 3&7; 2007, April, 11-12; 2007, Jul, 1-4; 2007, January, 13-27; 2007, March, 9-11; 2006, June, 11-15; 2006, September, 9-13; 2006, June, 1-7; 2006, May, 1-9; 2005, May, 1-2; 2005, March, 11-15; 2005, June, 9-11; 2005, April, 1-5; 2005, February, 1-6; 2005, December, 9-11

99214 Office or other outpatient visit for the evaluation and management of an established patient, which requires at least 2 of these 3 key components: A detailed history; A detailed examination; Medical decision making of moderate complexity. Counseling and/or coordination of care with other providers or agencies are provided consistent with the nature of the problem(s) and the patient's and/or family's needs. Usually, the presenting problem(s) are of moderate to high severity. Physicians typically spend 25 minutes face-to-face with the patient and/or family.

🔹 2.16   🔹 2.82   **Global Days XXX**

AMA: 2009, Jan, 11-31; 2009, Mar, 3,4&7; 2009, Jul, 7; 2009, Jul, 8-9; 2008, Jan, 10-25; 2008, Mar, 3&7; 2008, Jun, 12&15; 2007, January, 13-27; 2007, April, 11-12; 2007, Jul, 1-4; 2007, March, 9-11; 2006, September, 9-13; 2006, June, 1-7; 2006, June, 11-15; 2006, September, 14-16; 2006, May, 1-9; 2005, April, 1-5; 2005, June, 9-11; 2005, February, 1-6; 2005, December, 9-11; 2005, May, 1-2; 2005, March, 11-15

99215 Office or other outpatient visit for the evaluation and management of an established patient, which requires at least 2 of these 3 key components: A comprehensive history; A comprehensive examination; Medical decision making of high complexity. Counseling and/or coordination of care with other providers or agencies are provided consistent with the nature of the problem(s) and the patient's and/or family's needs. Usually, the presenting problem(s) are of moderate to high severity. Physicians typically spend 40 minutes face-to-face with the patient and/or family.

🔹 3.04   🔹 3.81   **Global Days XXX**

AMA: 2009, Mar, 3,4&7; 2009, Jul, 7; 2009, Jul, 8-9; 2009, Jan, 11-31; 2008, Jan, 10-25; 2008, Mar, 3&7; 2007, January, 13-27; 2007, March, 9-11; 2007, April, 11-12; 2007, Jul, 1-4; 2006, September, 9-13; 2006, June, 11-15; 2006, May, 1-9; 2006, June, 1-7; 2005, February, 1-6; 2005, May, 1-2; 2005, June, 9-11; 2005, April, 1-5; 2005, December, 9-11; 2005, March, 11-15; 2005, November, 10-13

99217-99220 Facility Observation Visits: Initial and Discharge

CMS 100-1,5,70   Definition of Physician
CMS 100-2,15,30   Physician Services
CMS 100-3,70.1   Consultations with a Beneficiary's Family and Associates
CMS 100-4,12,30.6.8   Payment for Hospital Observation Services

INCLUDES
Services provided on the same date in other settings (e.g. emergency department, physician's office) associated with the observation status admission

Services provided to new and established patients admitted to a hospital specifically for observation (not required to be a designated area of the hospital)

EXCLUDES *Post-surgical care services*

Services provided by physicians other than the admitting physician (99241-99245)

Services provided to patients who are admitted and discharged from observation status on the same date (99234-99236)

99217 Observation care discharge day management (This code is to be utilized by the physician to report all services provided to a patient on discharge from "observation status" if the discharge is on other than the initial date of "observation status." To report services to a patient designated as "observation status" or "inpatient status" and discharged on the same date, use the codes for Observation or Inpatient Care Services [including Admission and Discharge Services, 99234-99236 as appropriate.])

INCLUDES
Discussing the observation admission with the patient
Final patient evaluation
Discharge instructions
Sign off on discharge medical records

Do not report with hospital discharge day management services (99238-99239)

Do not report with observation/inpatient admission/discharge on the same date (99234-99236)

🔹 1.94   🔹 1.94   **Global Days XXX**

AMA: 2009, Jul, 7; 2007, March, 9-11; 2007, Jul, 1-4; 2006, December, 14-15; 2006, May, 1-9; 2006, September, 9-13; 2005, May, 1-2; 2005, February, 1-6; 2005, November, 10-13

99218 Initial observation care, per day, for the evaluation and management of a patient which requires these 3 key components: A detailed or comprehensive history; A detailed or comprehensive examination; and Medical decision making that is straightforward or of low complexity. Counseling and/or coordination of care with other providers or agencies are provided consistent with the nature of the problem(s) and the patient's and/or family's needs. Usually, the problem(s) requiring admission to "observation status" are of low severity.

🔹 1.82   🔹 1.82   **Global Days XXX**

AMA: 2009, Jan, 11-31; 2009, Jul, 7; 2008, Jan, 10-25; 2007, January, 13-27; 2007, March, 9-11; 2007, Jul, 1-4; 2006, September, 9-13; 2006, December, 14-15; 2006, May, 1-9; 2005, May, 1-2; 2005, November, 10-13; 2005, February, 1-6

99219 Initial observation care, per day, for the evaluation and management of a patient, which requires these 3 key components: A comprehensive history; A comprehensive examination; and Medical decision making of moderate complexity. Counseling and/or coordination of care with other providers or agencies are provided consistent with the nature of the problem(s) and the patient's and/or family's needs. Usually, the problem(s) requiring admission to "observation status" are of moderate severity. [B][80][=][PQ]
🚑 3.04   3.04 **Global Days XXX**
AMA: 2009, Jul, 7; 2009, Jan, 11-31; 2008, Jan, 10-25; 2007, January, 13-27; 2007, March, 9-11; 2007, Jul, 1-4; 2006, December, 14-15; 2006, September, 9-13; 2006, May, 1-9; 2005, February, 1-6; 2005, May, 1-2; 2005, November, 10-13

99220 A comprehensive examination; and Medical decision making of high complexity. Counseling and/or coordination of care with other providers or agencies are provided consistent with the nature of the problem(s) and the patient's and/or family's needs. Usually, the problem(s) requiring admission to "observation status" are of high severity. [B][80][=][PQ]
🚑 4.21   4.21 **Global Days XXX**
AMA: 2009, Jan, 11-31; 2009, Jul, 7; 2008, Jan, 10-25; 2007, Jul, 1-4; 2007, March, 9-11; 2007, January, 13-27; 2006, September, 9-13; 2006, December, 14-15; 2006, May, 1-9; 2005, February, 1-6; 2005, May, 1-2; 2005, November, 10-13

99221-99233 Inpatient Hospital Visits: Initial and Subsequent

CMS 100-1,5,70   Definition of Physician
CMS 100-2,15,30   Physician Services
CMS 100-3,70.1   Consultations with a Beneficiary's Family and Associates
CMS 100-4,12,30.6.8   Payment for Hospital Observation Services
CMS 100-4,12,30.6.9   Hospital Visit and Critical Care on Same Day
CMS 100-4,12,30.6.9.1   Initial Hospital Care and Observation or Inpatient Care Services

INCLUDES   All services provided on the date of admission in other sites of service (e.g., emergency department, physician's office, nursing facility)
Initial physician services provided to the patient in the hospital or "partial" hospital settings (99221-99223)
Services provided to a new or established patient

EXCLUDES   *Consultation services provided by other than the admitting physician (99251)*
Inpatient E/M services provided by other than the admitting physician (99231-99233)
Observation/inpatient care when the patient is admitted/discharged on the same date (99234-99236)
Physician services provided to the patient in the hospital or "partial" hospital settings after the initial care (99231-99233)

99221 Initial hospital care, per day, for the evaluation and management of a patient, which requires these 3 key components: A detailed or comprehensive history; A detailed or comprehensive examination; and Medical decision making that is straightforward or of low complexity. Counseling and/or coordination of care with other providers or agencies are provided consistent with the nature of the problem(s) and the patient's and/or family's needs. Usually, the problem(s) requiring admission are of low severity. Physicians typically spend 30 minutes at the bedside and on the patient's hospital floor or unit. [B][80][=][PQ]
🚑 2.72   2.72 **Global Days XXX**
AMA: 2009, Jul, 7; 2009, Jul, 8-9; 2009, Jan, 11-31; 2008, Jan, 10-25; 2007, January, 13-27; 2007, March, 9-11; 2007, Jul, 1-4; 2007, Jul, 12-13; 2006, September, 9-13; 2005, May, 1-2; 2005, February, 1-6

99222 Initial hospital care, per day, for the evaluation and management of a patient, which requires these 3 key components: A comprehensive history; A comprehensive examination; and Medical decision making of moderate complexity. Counseling and/or coordination of care with other providers or agencies are provided consistent with the nature of the problem(s) and the patient's and/or family's needs. Usually, the problem(s) requiring admission are of moderate severity. Physicians typically spend 50 minutes at the bedside and on the patient's hospital floor or unit. [B][80][=][PQ]
🚑 3.70   3.70 **Global Days XXX**
AMA: 2009, Jul, 7; 2009, Jul, 8-9; 2009, Jan, 11-31; 2008, Jan, 10-25; 2007, March, 9-11; 2007, Jul, 1-4; 2007, January, 13-27; 2007, Jul, 12-13; 2006, September, 9-13; 2005, March, 11-15; 2005, May, 1-2; 2005, February, 1-6

99223 A comprehensive examination; and Medical decision making of high complexity. Counseling and/or coordination of care with other providers or agencies are provided consistent with the nature of the problem(s) and the patient's and/or family's needs. Usually, the problem(s) requiring admission are of high severity. Physicians typically spend 70 minutes at the bedside and on the patient's hospital floor or unit. [B][80][=][PQ]
🚑 5.42   5.42 **Global Days XXX**
AMA: 2009, Jul, 8-9; 2009, Jul, 7; 2009, Jan, 11-31; 2008, Jan, 10-25; 2007, March, 9-11; 2007, January, 13-27; 2007, Jul, 1-4; 2007, Jul, 12-13; 2006, September, 9-13; 2005, March, 11-15; 2005, February, 1-6; 2005, May, 1-2

99231 Subsequent hospital care, per day, for the evaluation and management of a patient, which requires at least 2 of these 3 key components: A problem focused interval history; A problem focused examination; Medical decision making that is straightforward or of low complexity. Counseling and/or coordination of care with other providers or agencies are provided consistent with the nature of the problem(s) and the patient's and/or family's needs. Usually, the patient is stable, recovering or improving. Physicians typically spend 15 minutes at the bedside and on the patient's hospital floor or unit. [B][80][=][PQ]
🚑 1.08   1.08 **Global Days XXX**
AMA: 2009, Jan, 11-31; 2009, Mar, 3,4&7; 2009, Jul, 8-9; 2009, Jul, 7; 2008, Jan, 10-25; 2007, January, 13-27; 2007, March, 9-11; 2007, Jul, 1-4; 2006, May, 16-20; 2006, May, 1-9; 2006, June, 1-7; 2005, March, 11-15; 2005, February, 1-6; 2005, May, 1-2

99232 Subsequent hospital care, per day, for the evaluation and management of a patient, which requires at least 2 of these 3 key components: An expanded problem focused interval history; An expanded problem focused examination; Medical decision making of moderate complexity. Counseling and/or coordination of care with other providers or agencies are provided consistent with the nature of the problem(s) and the patient's and/or family's needs. Usually, the patient is responding inadequately to therapy or has developed a minor complication. Physicians typically spend 25 minutes at the bedside and on the patient's hospital floor or unit. [B][80][=][PQ]
🚑 1.98   1.98 **Global Days XXX**
AMA: 2009, Jan, 11-31; 2009, Mar, 3,4&7; 2009, Jul, 8-9; 2009, Jul, 7; 2008, Jan, 10-25; 2008, Jun, 12&15; 2007, January, 13-27; 2007, March, 9-11; 2007, Jul, 1-4; 2006, June, 1-7; 2006, May, 16-20; 2006, May, 1-9; 2005, May, 1-2; 2005, February, 1-6; 2005, March, 11-15

99233 — Current Procedural Coding Expert – Evaluation and Management

99233 Subsequent hospital care, per day, for the evaluation and management of a patient, which requires at least 2 of these 3 key components: A detailed interval history; A detailed examination; Medical decision making of high complexity. Counseling and/or coordination of care with other providers or agencies are provided consistent with the nature of the problem(s) and the patient's and/or family's needs. Usually, the patient is unstable or has developed a significant complication or a significant new problem. Physicians typically spend 35 minutes at the bedside and on the patient's hospital floor or unit.
 2.83 2.83 Global Days XXX
AMA: 2009, Jan, 11-31; 2009, Mar, 3,4&7; 2009, Jul, 7; 2009, Jul, 8-9; 2008, Jan, 10-25; 2007, March, 9-11; 2007, Jul, 1-4; 2006, June, 1-7; 2006, May, 16-20; 2006, May, 1-9; 2005, May, 1-2; 2005, March, 11-15; 2005, February, 1-6

99234-99236 Observation/Inpatient Visits: Admitted/Discharged on Same Date

CMS 100-1,5,70 — Definition of Physician
CMS 100-2,15,30 — Physician Services
CMS 100-3,70.1 — Consultations with a Beneficiary's Family and Associates
CMS 100-4,12,30.6.8 — Payment for Hospital Observation Services
CMS 100-4,12,30.6.9 — Hospital Visit and Critical Care on Same Day
CMS 100-4,12,30.6.9.1 — Initial Hospital Care and Observation or Inpatient Care Services
CMS 100-4,12,40.2 — Global Surgery Billing Requirements

INCLUDES
Admission to observation and discharge services on the same date
All services provided by admitting physician on same date of service, even when initiated in another setting (e.g., emergency department, nursing facility, physician's office)

EXCLUDES
Inpatient discharge services (99238-99239)
Inpatient subsequent care services (99231-99233)
Services provided to patients admitted to observation and discharged on a different date (99217-99220)

99234 Observation or inpatient hospital care, for the evaluation and management of a patient including admission and discharge on the same date, which requires these 3 key components: A detailed or comprehensive history; A detailed or comprehensive examination; and Medical decision making that is straightforward or of low complexity. Counseling and/or coordination of care with other providers or agencies are provided consistent with the nature of the problem(s) and the patient's and/or family's needs. Usually the presenting problem(s) requiring admission are of low severity.
 3.66 3.66 Global Days XXX
AMA: 2009, Jan, 11-31; 2009, Jul, 7; 2008, Jan, 10-25; 2007, January, 13-27; 2007, Jul, 1-4; 2007, March, 9-11; 2006, September, 9-13; 2006, December, 14-15; 2006, May, 1-9; 2005, February, 1-6; 2005, November, 10-13; 2005, May, 1-2

99235 Observation or inpatient hospital care, for the evaluation and management of a patient including admission and discharge on the same date, which requires these 3 key components: A comprehensive history; A comprehensive examination; and Medical decision making of moderate complexity. Counseling and/or coordination of care with other providers or agencies are provided consistent with the nature of the problem(s) and the patient's and/or family's needs. Usually the presenting problem(s) requiring admission are of moderate severity.
 4.85 4.85 Global Days XXX
AMA: 2009, Jan, 11-31; 2009, Jul, 7; 2008, Jan, 10-25; 2007, January, 13-27; 2007, March, 9-11; 2007, Jul, 1-4; 2006, May, 1-9; 2006, December, 14-15; 2006, September, 9-13; 2005, May, 1-2; 2005, November, 10-13; 2005, February, 1-6

99236 A comprehensive examination; and Medical decision making of high complexity. Counseling and/or coordination of care with other providers or agencies are provided consistent with the nature of the problem(s) and the patient's and/or family's needs. Usually the presenting problem(s) requiring admission are of high severity.
 6.02 6.02 Global Days XXX
AMA: 2009, Jan, 11-31; 2009, Jul, 7; 2008, Jan, 10-25; 2007, January, 13-27; 2007, March, 9-11; 2007, Jul, 1-4; 2006, September, 9-13; 2006, December, 14-15; 2006, May, 1-9; 2005, May, 1-2; 2005, February, 1-6; 2005, November, 10-13

99238-99239 Inpatient Hospital Discharge Services

CMS 100-4,12,30.6.9.2 — Hospital Discharge Management

INCLUDES
Discharge instructions
Final preparation of the pateint's medical records
Provision of prescriptions/referrals, as needed
Review of the inpatient admission

EXCLUDES
Discharge from observation (99217)
Admission/discharge on same date (99234-99236)
Discharge from nursing facility (99315, 99316)
Discharge services for newborns admitted and discharged the same day (99463)
Final patient evaluation
Healthy newborn evaluated and discharged on same date (99463)
Services provided by other than attending physician on date of discharge (99231-99233)

99238 Hospital discharge day management; 30 minutes or less
 1.95 1.95 Global Days XXX
AMA: 2009, Jul, 7; 2009, Jan, 11-31; 2008, Jan, 10-25; 2007, January, 13-27; 2007, March, 9-11; 2007, Jul, 1-4; 2006, September, 9-13; 2005, May, 1-2; 2005, March, 11-15; 2005, February, 1-6

99239 more than 30 minutes
 2.87 2.87 Global Days XXX
AMA: 2009, Jan, 11-31; 2009, Jul, 7; 2008, Jan, 10-25; 2007, January, 13-27; 2007, March, 9-11; 2007, Jul, 1-4; 2006, September, 9-13; 2005, May, 1-2; 2005, March, 11-15; 2005, February, 1-6

Current Procedural Coding Expert – Evaluation and Management

99241-99245 Consultations: Office and Outpatient

CMS 100-1,5,70 — Definition of Physician
CMS 100-2,15,30 — Physician Services
CMS 100-3,70.1 — Consultations with a Beneficiary's Family and Associates
CMS 100-4,12,30.6.10 — Consultation Services

INCLUDES
- A third-party mandated consultation
- All outpatient consultations provided in the physician's office, outpatient or other ambulatory facility, domiciliary/rest home, emergency department, patient's home, and hospital observation
- Documentation of a request for a consultation from an appropriate source
- Documentation of the need for consultation in the patient's medical record
- One consultation per consultant
- Provision by a physician or qualified nonphysician practitioner whose advice, opinion, recommendation, suggestion, direction, or counsel, etc., is requested for evaluating/treating a patient since that individual's expertise in a specific medical area is beyond the scope of knowledge of the requesting physician
- Provision of a written report of findings/recommendations from the consultant to the referring physician

EXCLUDES
- Another appropriately requested and documented consultation pertaining to the same/new problem; repeat use of consultation codes
- Any distinctly recognizable procedure/service provided on or following the consultation
- Assumption of care (all or partial); report subsequent codes as appropriate for the place of service (99211-99215, 99334-99337, 99347-99350)
- Consultation prompted by the patient/family; report codes for office, domiciliary/rest home, or home visits instead (99201-99215, 99324-99337, 99341-99350)

99241 Office consultation for a new or established patient, which requires these 3 key components: A problem focused history; A problem focused examination; and Straightforward medical decision making. Counseling and/or coordination of care with other providers or agencies are provided consistent with the nature of the problem(s) and the patient's and/or family's needs. Usually, the presenting problem(s) are self limited or minor. Physicians typically spend 15 minutes face-to-face with the patient and/or family. E ▭ PQ
0.93 1.35 **Global Days XXX**
AMA: 2009, Jan, 11-31; 2009, Jul, 7; 2009, Jul, 8-9; 2008, Jan, 10-25; 2007, March, 9-11; 2007, April, 11-12; 2007, January, 13-27; 2007, Jul, 1-4; 2006, September, 9-13; 2006, May, 16-20; 2006, May, 1-9; 2006, June, 1-7; 2005, May, 1-2; 2005, February, 1-6; 2005, December, 9-11

99242 Office consultation for a new or established patient, which requires these 3 key components: An expanded problem focused history; An expanded problem focused examination; and Straightforward medical decision making. Counseling and/or coordination of care with other providers or agencies are provided consistent with the nature of the problem(s) and the patient's and/or family's needs. Usually, the presenting problem(s) are of low severity. Physicians typically spend 30 minutes face-to-face with the patient and/or family. E ▭ PQ
1.95 2.54 **Global Days XXX**
AMA: 2009, Jul, 8-9; 2009, Jul, 7; 2009, Jan, 11-31; 2008, Jan, 10-25; 2007, January, 13-27; 2007, March, 9-11; 2007, April, 11-12; 2007, Jul, 1-4; 2006, May, 1-9; 2006, June, 1-7; 2006, September, 9-13; 2006, May, 16-20; 2005, May, 1-2; 2005, February, 1-6; 2005, December, 9-11; 2005, March, 11-15

99243 Office consultation for a new or established patient, which requires these 3 key components: A detailed history; A detailed examination; and Medical decision making of low complexity. Counseling and/or coordination of care with other providers or agencies are provided consistent with the nature of the problem(s) and the patient's and/or family's needs. Usually, the presenting problem(s) are of moderate severity. Physicians typically spend 40 minutes face-to-face with the patient and/or family. E ▭ PQ
2.72 3.47 **Global Days XXX**
AMA: 2009, Jul, 8-9; 2009, Jul, 7; 2009, Jan, 11-31; 2008, Jan, 10-25; 2007, March, 9-11; 2007, January, 13-27; 2007, Jul, 1-4; 2007, April, 11-12; 2006, September, 9-13; 2006, May, 16-20; 2006, June, 1-7; 2006, May, 1-9; 2005, May, 1-2; 2005, February, 1-6; 2005, December, 9-11; 2005, March, 11-15

99244 Office consultation for a new or established patient, which requires these 3 key components: A comprehensive history; A comprehensive examination; and Medical decision making of moderate complexity. Counseling and/or coordination of care with other providers or agencies are provided consistent with the nature of the problem(s) and the patient's and/or family's needs. Usually, the presenting problem(s) are of moderate to high severity. Physicians typically spend 60 minutes face-to-face with the patient and/or family. E ▭ PQ
4.32 5.14 **Global Days XXX**
AMA: 2009, Jan, 11-31; 2009, Jul, 7; 2009, Jul, 8-9; 2008, Jan, 10-25; 2007, April, 11-12; 2007, Jul, 1-4; 2007, March, 9-11; 2007, January, 13-27; 2006, June, 1-7; 2006, May, 1-9; 2006, September, 9-13; 2006, May, 16-20; 2005, May, 1-2; 2005, February, 1-6; 2005, December, 9-11; 2005, March, 11-15

99245 A comprehensive examination; and Medical decision making of high complexity. Counseling and/or coordination of care with other providers or agencies are provided consistent with the nature of the problem(s) and the patient's and/or family's needs. Usually, the presenting problem(s) are of moderate to high severity. Physicians typically spend 80 minutes face-to-face with the patient and/or family. E ▭ PQ
5.36 6.28 **Global Days XXX**
AMA: 2009, Jul, 8-9; 2009, Jul, 7; 2009, Jan, 11-31; 2008, Jan, 10-25; 2007, January, 13-27; 2007, March, 9-11; 2007, April, 11-12; 2007, Jul, 1-4; 2006, September, 9-13; 2006, May, 16-20; 2006, May, 1-9; 2006, June, 1-7; 2005, March, 11-15; 2005, February, 1-6; 2005, December, 9-11; 2005, May, 1-2

99251-99255 Consultations: Inpatient

CMS 100-1,5,70 — Definition of Physician
CMS 100-2,15,30 — Physician Services
CMS 100-3,70.1 — Consultations with a Beneficiary's Family and Associates
CMS 100-4,12,30.6.10 — Consultation Services

INCLUDES
A third-party mandated consultation
All inpatient consultations include services provided in the hospital inpatient or partial hospital settings and nursing facilities
Documentation of a request for a consultation from an appropriate source
Documentation of the need for consultation in the patient's medical record
One consultation by consultant per admission
Provision by a physician or qualified nonphysician practitioner whose advice, opinion, recommendation, suggestion, direction, or counsel, etc. is requested for evaluating/treating a patient since that individual's expertise in a specific medical area is beyond the scope of knowledge of the requesting physician
Provision of a written report of findings/recommendations from the consultant to the referring physician

EXCLUDES
Another appropriately requested and documented consultation pertaining to the same/new problem: repeat use of consultation codes
Any distinctly recognizable procedure/service provided on or following the consultation
Assumption of care (all or partial): report subsequent codes as appropriate for the place of service (99231-99233, 99307-99310)
Consultation prompted by the patient/family: report codes for office, domiciliary/rest home, or home visits instead (99201-99215, 99324-99337, 99341-99350)

Do not report an outpatient consultation and an inpatient consutation for the same addmission

99251 Inpatient consultation for a new or established patient, which requires these 3 key components: A problem focused history; A problem focused examination; and Straightforward medical decision making. Counseling and/or coordination of care with other providers or agencies are provided consistent with the nature of the problem(s) and the patient's and/or family's needs. Usually, the presenting problem(s) are self limited or minor. Physicians typically spend 20 minutes at the bedside and on the patient's hospital floor or unit. E P0
  🚗 1.37   ✎ 1.37   **Global Days XXX**
  AMA: 2009, Jan, 11-31; 2009, Jul, 7; 2009, Jul, 8-9; 2008, Jan, 10-25; 2007, January, 13-27; 2007, March, 9-11; 2007, Jul, 1-4; 2006, May, 16-20; 2006, June, 1-7; 2006, May, 1-9; 2005, May, 1-2; 2005, December, 9-11; 2005, February, 1-6

99252 Inpatient consultation for a new or established patient, which requires these 3 key components: An expanded problem focused history; An expanded problem focused examination; and Straightforward medical decision making. Counseling and/or coordination of care with other providers or agencies are provided consistent with the nature of the problem(s) and the patient's and/or family's needs. Usually, the presenting problem(s) are of low severity. Physicians typically spend 40 minutes at the bedside and on the patient's hospital floor or unit. E P0
  🚗 2.11   ✎ 2.11   **Global Days XXX**
  AMA: 2009, Jan, 11-31; 2009, Jul, 8-9; 2009, Jul, 7; 2008, Jan, 10-25; 2007, January, 13-27; 2007, March, 9-11; 2007, Jul, 1-4; 2006, June, 1-7; 2006, May, 1-9; 2006, May, 16-20; 2005, March, 11-15; 2005, December, 9-11; 2005, May, 1-2; 2005, February, 1-6

99253 Inpatient consultation for a new or established patient, which requires these 3 key components: A detailed history; A detailed examination; and Medical decision making of low complexity. Counseling and/or coordination of care with other providers or agencies are provided consistent with the nature of the problem(s) and the patient's and/or family's needs. Usually, the presenting problem(s) are of moderate severity. Physicians typically spend 55 minutes at the bedside and on the patient's hospital floor or unit. E P0
  🚗 3.22   ✎ 3.22   **Global Days XXX**
  AMA: 2009, Jul, 7; 2009, Jul, 8-9; 2009, Jan, 11-31; 2008, Jan, 10-25; 2007, January, 13-27; 2007, March, 9-11; 2007, Jul, 1-4; 2006, June, 1-7; 2006, May, 1-9; 2006, May, 16-20; 2005, May, 1-2; 2005, December, 9-11; 2005, March, 11-15; 2005, February, 1-6

99254 Inpatient consultation for a new or established patient, which requires these 3 key components: A comprehensive history; A comprehensive examination; and Medical decision making of moderate complexity. Counseling and/or coordination of care with other providers or agencies are provided consistent with the nature of the problem(s) and the patient's and/or family's needs. Usually, the presenting problem(s) are of moderate to high severity. Physicians typically spend 80 minutes at the bedside and on the patient's hospital floor or unit. E P0
  🚗 4.65   ✎ 4.65   **Global Days XXX**
  AMA: 2009, Jan, 11-31; 2009, Jul, 8-9; 2009, Jul, 7; 2008, Jan, 10-25; 2007, January, 13-27; 2007, Jul, 1-4; 2007, March, 9-11; 2006, May, 16-20; 2006, May, 1-9; 2006, June, 1-7; 2005, March, 11-15; 2005, February, 1-6; 2005, May, 1-2; 2005, December, 9-11

99255 A comprehensive examination; and Medical decision making of high complexity. Counseling and/or coordination of care with other providers or agencies are provided consistent with the nature of the problem(s) and the patient's and/or family's needs. Usually, the presenting problem(s) are of moderate to high severity. Physicians typically spend 110 minutes at the bedside and on the patient's hospital floor or unit. E P0
  🚗 5.62   ✎ 5.62   **Global Days XXX**
  AMA: 2009, Jul, 7; 2009, Jul, 8-9; 2009, Jan, 11-31; 2008, Jan, 10-25; 2007, March, 9-11; 2007, Jul, 1-4; 2007, January, 13-27; 2006, June, 1-7; 2006, May, 16-20; 2006, May, 1-9; 2005, March, 11-15; 2005, February, 1-6; 2005, December, 9-11; 2005, May, 1-2

Current Procedural Coding Expert – Evaluation and Management

99281-99288 Emergency Department Visits

CMS 100-1,5,70   Definition of Physician
CMS 100-2,15,30   Physician Services
CMS 100-3,70.1   Consultations with a Beneficiary's Family and Associates
CMS 100-4,12,30.6.11   Emergency Department Visits

INCLUDES Any amount of time spent with the patient, which usually involves a series of encounters while the patient is in the emergency department
Care provided to new and established patients

EXCLUDES Critical care services (99291-99292)
Observation services (99217-99220, 99234-99236)

99281 Emergency department visit for the evaluation and management of a patient, which requires these 3 key components: A problem focused history; A problem focused examination; and Straightforward medical decision making. Counseling and/or coordination of care with other providers or agencies are provided consistent with the nature of the problem(s) and the patient's and/or family's needs. Usually, the presenting problem(s) are self limited or minor.
0.60   0.60   **Global Days XXX**
AMA: 2009, Jan, 11-31; 2009, Jul, 7; 2008, Jan, 10-25; 2007, Dec, 10-179; 2007, March, 9-11; 2007, January, 13-27; 2007, Jul, 1-4; 2006, December, 14-15; 2006, February, 16-18; 2005, February, 1-6; 2005, May, 1-2; 2005, November, 10-13

99282 Emergency department visit for the evaluation and management of a patient, which requires these 3 key components: An expanded problem focused history; An expanded problem focused examination; and Medical decision making of low complexity. Counseling and/or coordination of care with other providers or agencies are provided consistent with the nature of the problem(s) and the patient's and/or family's needs. Usually, the presenting problem(s) are of low to moderate severity.
1.16   1.16   **Global Days XXX**
AMA: 2009, Jan, 11-31; 2009, Jul, 7; 2008, Jan, 10-25; 2007, Dec, 10-179; 2007, January, 13-27; 2007, March, 9-11; 2007, Jul, 1-4; 2006, December, 14-15; 2006, February, 16-18; 2005, February, 1-6; 2005, November, 10-13; 2005, May, 1-2

99283 An expanded problem focused examination; and Medical decision making of moderate complexity. Counseling and/or coordination of care with other providers or agencies are provided consistent with the nature of the problem(s) and the patient's and/or family's needs. Usually, the presenting problem(s) are of moderate severity.
1.75   1.75   **Global Days XXX**
AMA: 2009, Jul, 7; 2009, Jan, 11-31; 2008, Jan, 10-25; 2007, January, 13-27; 2007, Dec, 10-179; 2007, March, 9-11; 2007, Jul, 1-4; 2006, February, 16-18; 2006, December, 14-15; 2005, March, 11-15; 2005, February, 1-6; 2005, May, 1-2; 2005, November, 10-13

99284 Emergency department visit for the evaluation and management of a patient, which requires these 3 key components: A detailed history; A detailed examination; and Medical decision making of moderate complexity. Counseling and/or coordination of care with other providers or agencies are provided consistent with the nature of the problem(s) and the patient's and/or family's needs. Usually, the presenting problem(s) are of high severity, and require urgent evaluation by the physician but do not pose an immediate significant threat to life or physiologic function.
3.27   3.27   **Global Days XXX**
AMA: 2009, Jan, 11-31; 2009, Jul, 7; 2008, Jan, 10-25; 2007, Dec, 10-179; 2007, March, 9-11; 2007, January, 13-27; 2007, Jul, 1-4; 2006, December, 14-15; 2006, February, 16-18; 2005, May, 1-2; 2005, February, 1-6; 2005, March, 11-15; 2005, November, 10-13

99285 Emergency department visit for the evaluation and management of a patient, which requires these 3 key components within the constraints imposed by the urgency of the patient's clinical condition and/or mental status: A comprehensive history; A comprehensive examination; and Medical decision making of high complexity. Counseling and/or coordination of care with other providers or agencies are provided consistent with the nature of the problem(s) and the patient's and/or family's needs. Usually, the presenting problem(s) are of high severity and pose an immediate significant threat to life or physiologic function.
4.78   4.78   **Global Days XXX**
AMA: 2009, Jan, 11-31; 2009, Jul, 7; 2008, Jan, 10-25; 2007, Dec, 10-179; 2007, Jul, 1-4; 2007, March, 9-11; 2007, January, 13-27; 2006, December, 14-15; 2006, February, 16-18; 2005, May, 1-2; 2005, March, 11-15; 2005, February, 1-6; 2005, November, 10-13

99288 Physician direction of emergency medical systems (EMS) emergency care, advanced life support
INCLUDES Management provided by an emergency/intensive care based physician via voice contact to ambulance/rescue staff for services such as heart monitoring and drug administration
0.00   0.00   **Global Days XXX**
AMA: 2009, Jul, 7; 2007, Jul, 1-4; 2007, March, 9-11; 2005, May, 1-2; 2005, February, 1-6

99291-99292 Critical Care Visits: Patients 25 Months of Age and Older

CMS 100-1,5,70 — Definition of Physician
CMS 100-2,15,30 — Physician Services
CMS 100-3,70.1 — Consultations with a Beneficiary's Family and Associates
CMS 100-4,12,30.6.9 — Hospital Visit and Critical Care on Same Day
CMS 100-4,12,30.6.12 — Critical Care Visits

INCLUDES
- 30 minutes or more of direct care provided by the physician to a critically ill or injured patient, regardless of the location
- All time spent exclusively with patient/family/caregivers on the nursing unit or elsewhere
- Blood gases (82800-82810)
- Chest films (71010-71020)
- Customary monitoring, blood gases
- Gastric intubation (43752, 91105)
- Includes physician presence during interfacility transfer for critically ill/injured patients over 24 months of age
- Measurement of cardiac output (93561-93562)
- Other computer stored information (99090)
- Outpatient critical care provided to neonates and pediatric patients up through 71 months of age
- Pulse oximetry (94760-94762)
- Transcutaneous pacing, temporary (92953)
- Venous access, arterial puncture (36000, 36410, 36415, 36591, 36600)
- Ventilation assistance and management, includes CPAP, CNP (94002-94004, 94660, 94662)

EXCLUDES
- All services that are less than 30 minutes; report appropriate E/M code
- Critical care services provided via remote real-time interactive videoconferencing (0188T, 0189T)
- Inpatient critical care services provided to neonates that are age 28 days or less (99468-99469)
- Other procedures not listed as included performed by the physician rendering critical care
- Physician presence during interfacility transfer for critically ill/injured patients under 24 months of age (99466, 99467)

Do not report activities performed outside of the unit or off the floor

▲ **99291** Critical care, evaluation and management of the critically ill or critically injured patient; first 30-74 minutes

6.12　7.26　Global Days XXX
AMA: 2009, Jan, 5&10; 2009, Jan, 11-31; 2009, Jul, 7; 2009, Mar, 3,4&7; 2008, Jan, 10-25; 2008, Jul, 7-8&15; 2007, March, 9-11; 2007, Jul, 1-4; 2007, January, 13-27; 2006, May, 1-9; 2006, December, 13; 2005, May, 1-2; 2005, February, 1-6; 2005, March, 11-15; 2005, November, 10-13; 2005, July, 13-16

+ **99292** each additional 30 minutes (List separately in addition to code for primary service)

Code first (99291)
3.06　3.30　Global Days ZZZ
AMA: 2009, Jan, 11-31; 2009, Mar, 3,4&7; 2009, Jan, 5&10; 2009, Jul, 7; 2008, Jan, 10-25; 2008, Jul, 7-8&15; 2007, January, 13-27; 2007, March, 9-11; 2007, Jul, 1-4; 2006, December, 13; 2006, May, 1-9; 2005, May, 1-2; 2005, February, 1-6; 2005, November, 10-13; 2005, July, 13-16

99304-99318 Nursing Facility Visits

CMS 100-1,5,70 — Definition of Physician
CMS 100-2,15,30 — Physician Services
CMS 100-3,70.1 — Consultations with a Beneficiary's Family and Associates
CMS 100-3,70.2 — Consultation by a Podiatrist in a Skilled Nursing Facility
CMS 100-3,70.3 — Physician's Offices Within an Institution--"Incident-to" Provision
CMS 100-4,12,30.6.9 — Swing Bed Visits
CMS 100-4,12,30.6.13 — Nursing Facility Visits

INCLUDES
- All E/M services provided by the admitting physican on the date of nursing facility admission in other locations (e.g. office, emergency department)
- Discharge services include all time spent by the physician for:
- Initial care, subsequent care, discharge, and yearly assessments
- Initial services include patient assessment and physician participation in developing a plan of care (99304-99306)
- Services provided to new and established patients in a nursing facility (skilled, intermediate, and long-term care facilities)
- Subsequent services include physician review of medical records, reassessment, review of test results (99307-99310)

EXCLUDES Care plan oversight services (99379-99380)

▲ **99304** Initial nursing facility care, per day, for the evaluation and management of a patient, which requires these 3 key components: a detailed or comprehensive history; A detailed or comprehensive examination; and medical decision making that is straightforward or of low complexity. Counseling and/or coordination of care with other providers or agencies are provided consistent with the nature of the problem(s) and the patient's and/or family's needs. Usually, the problem(s) requiring admission are of low severity. Physicians typically spend 25 minutes at the bedside and on the patient's facility floor or unit.

2.47　2.47　Global Days XXX
AMA: 2009, Jul, 7; 2009, Jul, 8-9; 2009, Jul, 3-4; 2007, Jul, 1-4; 2007, March, 9-11; 2006, June, 1-7

▲ **99305** Initial nursing facility care, per day, for the evaluation and management of a patient, which requires these 3 key components: a comprehensive history; a comprehensive examination; and medical decision making of moderate complexity. Counseling and/or coordination of care with other providers or agencies are provided consistent with the nature of the problem(s) and the patient's and/or family's needs. Usually, the problem(s) requiring admission are of moderate severity. Physicians typically spend 35 minutes at the bedside and on the patient's facility floor or unit.

3.49　3.49　Global Days XXX
AMA: 2009, Jul, 7; 2009, Jul, 8-9; 2009, Jul, 3-4; 2007, March, 9-11; 2007, Jul, 1-4; 2006, June, 1-7

▲ **99306** a comprehensive examination; and medical decision making of high complexity. Counseling and/or coordination of care with other providers or agencies are provided consistent with the nature of the problem(s) and the patient's and/or family's needs. Usually, the problem(s) requiring admission are of high severity. Physicians typically spend 45 minutes at the bedside and on the patient's facility floor or unit.

4.45　4.45　Global Days XXX
AMA: 2009, Jul, 7; 2009, Jul, 8-9; 2009, Jul, 3-4; 2007, March, 9-11; 2007, Jul, 1-4; 2006, June, 1-7

Current Procedural Coding Expert – Evaluation and Management

▲ **99307** Subsequent nursing facility care, per day, for the evaluation and management of a patient, which requires at least 2 of these 3 key components: a problem-focused interval history; a problem-focused examination; straightforward medical decision making. Counseling and/or coordination of care with other providers or agencies are provided consistent with the nature of the problem(s) and the patient's and/or family's needs. Usually, the patient is stable, recovering, or improving. Physicians typically spend 10 minutes at the bedside and on the patient's facility floor or unit.
   1.20   1.20 Global Days XXX
   AMA: 2009, Jul, 8-9; 2009, Jul, 3-4; 2009, Jul, 7; 2009, Jan, 11-31; 2008, Jan, 10-25; 2007, March, 9-11; 2007, Jul, 1-4; 2006, June, 1-7; 2006, May, 1-9; 2006, May, 16-20

▲ **99308** Subsequent nursing facility care, per day, for the evaluation and management of a patient, which requires at least 2 of these 3 key components: an expanded problem-focused interval history; an expanded problem-focused examination; medical decision making of low complexity. Counseling and/or coordination of care with other providers or agencies are provided consistent with the nature of the problem(s) and the patient's and/or family's needs. Usually, the patient is responding inadequately to therapy or has developed a minor complication. Physicians typically spend 15 minutes at the bedside and on the patient's facility floor or unit.
   1.85   1.85 Global Days XXX
   AMA: 2009, Jul, 8-9; 2009, Jul, 7; 2009, Jul, 3-4; 2007, Jul, 1-4; 2007, March, 9-11; 2006, June, 1-7; 2006, May, 16-20; 2006, May, 1-9

▲ **99309** Subsequent nursing facility care, per day, for the evaluation and management of a patient, which requires at least 2 of these 3 key components: a detailed interval history; a detailed examination; medical decision making of moderate complexity. Counseling and/or coordination of care with other providers or agencies are provided consistent with the nature of the problem(s) and the patient's and/or family's needs. Usually, the patient has developed a significant complication or a significant new problem. Physicians typically spend 25 minutes at the bedside and on the patient's facility floor or unit.
   2.45   2.45 Global Days XXX
   AMA: 2009, Jul, 3-4; 2009, Jul, 8-9; 2009, Jul, 7; 2007, Jul, 1-4; 2007, March, 9-11; 2006, May, 1-9; 2006, June, 1-7; 2006, May, 16-20

▲ **99310** Subsequent nursing facility care, per day, for the evaluation and management of a patient, which requires at least 2 of these 3 key components: a comprehensive interval history; a comprehensive examination; medical decision making of high complexity. Counseling and/or coordination of care with other providers or agencies are provided consistent with the nature of the problem(s) and the patient's and/or family's needs. The patient may be unstable or may have developed a significant new problem requiring immediate physician attention. Physicians typically spend 35 minutes at the bedside and on the patient's facility floor or unit.
   3.62   3.62 Global Days XXX
   AMA: 2009, Jan, 11-31; 2009, Jul, 7; 2009, Jul, 8-9; 2009, Jul, 3-4; 2008, Jan, 10-25; 2007, March, 9-11; 2007, Jul, 1-4; 2006, May, 1-9; 2006, June, 1-7; 2006, May, 16-20

99315 Nursing facility discharge day management; 30 minutes or less
   1.75   1.75 Global Days XXX
   AMA: 2009, Jul, 3-4; 2009, Jul, 7; 2009, Jan, 11-31; 2008, Jan, 10-25; 2007, January, 13-27; 2007, March, 9-11; 2007, Jul, 1-4; 2005, May, 1-2; 2005, February, 1-6

99316 more than 30 minutes
   2.29   2.29 Global Days XXX
   AMA: 2009, Jan, 11-31; 2009, Jul, 7; 2009, Jul, 3-4; 2008, Jan, 10-25; 2007, March, 9-11; 2007, Jul, 1-4; 2007, January, 13-27; 2005, May, 1-2; 2005, February, 1-6

▲ **99318** Evaluation and management of a patient involving an annual nursing facility assessment, which requires these 3 key components: a detailed interval history; a comprehensive examination; and medical decision making that is of low to moderate complexity. Counseling and/or coordination of care with other providers or agencies are provided consistent with the nature of the problem(s) and the patient's and/or family's needs. Usually, the patient is stable, recovering, or improving. Physicians typically spend 30 minutes at the bedside and on the patient's facility floor or unit.
   Do not report with the same date of service as (99304-99316)
   2.61   2.61 Global Days XXX
   AMA: 2009, Jul, 7; 2009, Jul, 3-4; 2007, March, 9-11; 2007, Jul, 1-4; 2006, June, 1-7

99324-99337 Domiciliary Care, Rest Home, Assisted Living Visits

CMS 100-3,70.1   Consultations with a Beneficiary's Family and Associates
CMS 100-4,12,30.6.14   Domiciliary Care, Rest Home, Assisted Living Visits
INCLUDES   E/M services for patients residing in assisted living, domiciliary care, and rest homes where medical care is not included
   Services provided to new patients or established patients (99324-99328, or 99334-99337)
EXCLUDES   Rest home/home care plan oversight services (99339-99340)

99324 Domiciliary or rest home visit for the evaluation and management of a new patient, which requires these 3 key components: A problem focused history; A problem focused examination; and Straightforward medical decision making. Counseling and/or coordination of care with other providers or agencies are provided consistent with the nature of the problem(s) and the patient's and/or family's needs. Usually, the presenting problem(s) are of low severity. Physicians typically spend 20 minutes with the patient and/or family or caregiver.
   1.50   1.50 Global Days XXX
   AMA: 2009, Jul, 7; 2009, Jul, 8-9; 2007, Jul, 1-4; 2007, March, 9-11; 2006, June, 1-7

99325 Domiciliary or rest home visit for the evaluation and management of a new patient, which requires these 3 key components: An expanded problem focused history; An expanded problem focused examination; and Medical decision making of low complexity. Counseling and/or coordination of care with other providers or agencies are provided consistent with the nature of the problem(s) and the patient's and/or family's needs. Usually, the presenting problem(s) are of moderate severity. Physicians typically spend 30 minutes with the patient and/or family or caregiver.
   2.20   2.20 Global Days XXX
   AMA: 2009, Jul, 7; 2009, Jul, 8-9; 2007, March, 9-11; 2007, Jul, 1-4; 2006, June, 1-7

99326 Domiciliary or rest home visit for the evaluation and management of a new patient, which requires these 3 key components: A detailed history; A detailed examination; and Medical decision making of moderate complexity. Counseling and/or coordination of care with other providers or agencies are provided consistent with the nature of the problem(s) and the patient's and/or family's needs. Usually, the presenting problem(s) are of moderate to high severity. Physicians typically spend 45 minutes with the patient and/or family or caregiver. B 80 PQ
  3.85   3.85   Global Days XXX
  AMA: 2009, Jul, 8-9; 2009, Jul, 7; 2007, March, 9-11; 2007, Jul, 1-4; 2006, June, 1-7

99327 Domiciliary or rest home visit for the evaluation and management of a new patient, which requires these 3 key components: A comprehensive history; A comprehensive examination; and Medical decision making of moderate complexity. Counseling and/or coordination of care with other providers or agencies are provided consistent with the nature of the problem(s) and the patient's and/or family's needs. Usually, the presenting problem(s) are of high severity. Physicians typically spend 60 minutes with the patient and/or family or caregiver. B 80 PQ
  5.07   5.07   Global Days XXX
  AMA: 2009, Jul, 7; 2009, Jul, 8-9; 2007, Jul, 1-4; 2007, March, 9-11; 2006, June, 1-7

99328 A comprehensive examination; and Medical decision making of high complexity. Counseling and/or coordination of care with other providers or agencies are provided consistent with the nature of the problem(s) and the patient's and/or family's needs. Usually, the patient is unstable or has developed a significant new problem requiring immediate physician attention. Physicians typically spend 75 minutes with the patient and/or family or caregiver. B 80 PQ
  5.89   5.89   Global Days XXX
  AMA: 2009, Jul, 7; 2009, Jul, 8-9; 2007, March, 9-11; 2007, Jul, 1-4; 2006, June, 1-7

99334 Domiciliary or rest home visit for the evaluation and management of an established patient, which requires at least 2 of these 3 key components: A problem focused interval history; A problem focused examination; Straightforward medical decision making. Counseling and/or coordination of care with other providers or agencies are provided consistent with the nature of the problem(s) and the patient's and/or family's needs. Usually, the presenting problem(s) are self-limited or minor. Physicians typically spend 15 minutes with the patient and/or family or caregiver. B 80 PQ
  1.64   1.64   Global Days XXX
  AMA: 2009, Jul, 7; 2009, Jul, 8-9; 2007, March, 9-11; 2007, Jul, 1-4; 2006, June, 1-7

99335 Domiciliary or rest home visit for the evaluation and management of an established patient, which requires at least 2 of these 3 key components: An expanded problem focused interval history; An expanded problem focused examination; Medical decision making of low complexity. Counseling and/or coordination of care with other providers or agencies are provided consistent with the nature of the problem(s) and the patient's and/or family's needs. Usually, the presenting problem(s) are of low to moderate severity. Physicians typically spend 25 minutes with the patient and/or family or caregiver. B 80 PQ
  2.58   2.58   Global Days XXX
  AMA: 2009, Jul, 7; 2009, Jul, 8-9; 2007, March, 9-11; 2007, Jul, 1-4; 2006, June, 1-7

99336 Domiciliary or rest home visit for the evaluation and management of an established patient, which requires at least 2 of these 3 key components: A detailed interval history; A detailed examination; Medical decision making of moderate complexity. Counseling and/or coordination of care with other providers or agencies are provided consistent with the nature of the problem(s) and the patient's and/or family's needs. Usually, the presenting problem(s) are of moderate to high severity. Physicians typically spend 40 minutes with the patient and/or family or caregiver. B 80 PQ
  3.67   3.67   Global Days XXX
  AMA: 2009, Jul, 7; 2009, Jul, 8-9; 2007, March, 9-11; 2007, Jul, 1-4; 2006, June, 1-7

99337 Domiciliary or rest home visit for the evaluation and management of an established patient, which requires at least 2 of these 3 key components: A comprehensive interval history; A comprehensive examination; Medical decision making of moderate to high complexity. Counseling and/or coordination of care with other providers or agencies are provided consistent with the nature of the problem(s) and the patient's and/or family's needs. Usually, the presenting problem(s) are of moderate to high severity. The patient may be unstable or may have developed a significant new problem requiring immediate physician attention. Physicians typically spend 60 minutes with the patient and/or family or caregiver. B 80 PQ
  5.28   5.28   Global Days XXX
  AMA: 2009, Jul, 8-9; 2009, Jul, 7; 2007, March, 9-11; 2007, Jul, 1-4; 2006, June, 1-7

99339-99340 Care Plan Oversight: Rest Home, Domiciliary Care, Assisted Living, and Home

CMS 100-4,12,30.6.14   Domiciliary Care, Rest Home, Assisted Living Visits

INCLUDES   Care plan oversight for patients residing in assisted living, domiciliary care, private residences, and rest homes

EXCLUDES   Care plan oversight services furnished under a home health agency, nursing facility, or hospice (99374-99380)

Do not report with (98966-98969, 99441-99444)

99339 Individual physician supervision of a patient (patient not present) in home, domiciliary or rest home (eg, assisted living facility) requiring complex and multidisciplinary care modalities involving regular physician development and/or revision of care plans, review of subsequent reports of patient status, review of related laboratory and other studies, communication (including telephone calls) for purposes of assessment or care decisions with health care professional(s), family member(s), surrogate decision maker(s) (eg, legal guardian) and/or key caregiver(s) involved in patient's care, integration of new information into the medical treatment plan and/or adjustment of medical therapy, within a calendar month; 15-29 minutes B

  Do not report with time peroid reported for (98966-98969, 99441-99444)
  2.08   2.08   Global Days XXX
  AMA: 2009, Jul, 5-6; 2009, Jul, 7; 2009, Jul, 10; 2008, Mar, 6-7; 2008, Sep, 3-4; 2007, Jul, 1-4; 2007, April, 3-6; 2007, March, 9-11; 2006, December, 4-7

99340 30 minutes or more B

  Do not report with time peroid reported for (98966-98969, 99441-99444)
  2.92   2.92   Global Days XXX
  AMA: 2009, Jul, 5-6; 2009, Jul, 10; 2009, Jul, 7; 2008, Mar, 6-7; 2008, Sep, 3-4; 2007, April, 3-6; 2007, Jul, 1-4; 2007, March, 9-11; 2006, December, 4-7

Current Procedural Coding Expert – Evaluation and Management

99341-99350 Home Visits

CMS 100-4,12,30.6.14.1 Home Visits

INCLUDES
Services for a new patient or an established patient (99341-99345, or 99347-99350)
Services provided to a patient in a private home

EXCLUDES
Services provided to patients under home health agency or hospice care (99374-99378)

99341 Home visit for the evaluation and management of a new patient, which requires these 3 key components: A problem focused history; A problem focused examination; and Straightforward medical decision making. Counseling and/or coordination of care with other providers or agencies are provided consistent with the nature of the problem(s) and the patient's and/or family's needs. Usually, the presenting problem(s) are of low severity. Physicians typically spend 20 minutes face-to-face with the patient and/or family. [B][80][][PQ]
  🚑 1.50   ⚕ 1.50   **Global Days XXX**
  AMA: 2009, Jul, 7; 2009, Jul, 8-9; 2007, March, 9-11; 2007, Jul, 1-4; 2007, January, 28-31; 2006, January, 2-4,48; 2005, May, 1-2; 2005, February, 1-6

99342 Home visit for the evaluation and management of a new patient, which requires these 3 key components: An expanded problem focused history; An expanded problem focused examination; and Medical decision making of low complexity. Counseling and/or coordination of care with other providers or agencies are provided consistent with the nature of the problem(s) and the patient's and/or family's needs. Usually, the presenting problem(s) are of moderate severity. Physicians typically spend 30 minutes face-to-face with the patient and/or family. [B][80][][PQ]
  🚑 2.17   ⚕ 2.17   **Global Days XXX**
  AMA: 2009, Jul, 8-9; 2009, Jul, 7; 2007, January, 28-31; 2007, March, 9-11; 2007, Jul, 1-4; 2006, January, 2-4,48; 2005, May, 1-2; 2005, February, 1-6

99343 Home visit for the evaluation and management of a new patient, which requires these 3 key components: A detailed history; A detailed examination; and Medical decision making of moderate complexity. Counseling and/or coordination of care with other providers or agencies are provided consistent with the nature of the problem(s) and the patient's and/or family's needs. Usually, the presenting problem(s) are of moderate to high severity. Physicians typically spend 45 minutes face-to-face with the patient and/or family. [B][80][][PQ]
  🚑 3.62   ⚕ 3.62   **Global Days XXX**
  AMA: 2009, Jul, 7; 2009, Jul, 8-9; 2007, March, 9-11; 2007, Jul, 1-4; 2007, January, 28-31; 2006, January, 2-4,48; 2005, February, 1-6; 2005, May, 1-2

99344 Home visit for the evaluation and management of a new patient, which requires these 3 key components: A comprehensive history; A comprehensive examination; and Medical decision making of moderate complexity. Counseling and/or coordination of care with other providers or agencies are provided consistent with the nature of the problem(s) and the patient's and/or family's needs. Usually, the presenting problem(s) are of high severity. Physicians typically spend 60 minutes face-to-face with the patient and/or family. [B][80][][PQ]
  🚑 4.96   ⚕ 4.96   **Global Days XXX**
  AMA: 2009, Jul, 8-9; 2009, Jul, 7; 2007, Jul, 1-4; 2007, January, 28-31; 2007, March, 9-11; 2006, January, 2-4,48; 2005, May, 1-2; 2005, February, 1-6

99345 A comprehensive examination; and Medical decision making of high complexity. Counseling and/or coordination of care with other providers or agencies are provided consistent with the nature of the problem(s) and the patient's and/or family's needs. Usually, the patient is unstable or has developed a significant new problem requiring immediate physician attention. Physicians typically spend 75 minutes face-to-face with the patient and/or family. [B][80][][PQ]
  🚑 5.99   ⚕ 5.99   **Global Days XXX**
  AMA: 2009, Jul, 7; 2009, Jul, 8-9; 2007, March, 9-11; 2007, Jul, 1-4; 2007, January, 28-31; 2006, January, 2-4,48; 2005, February, 1-6; 2005, May, 1-2

99347 Home visit for the evaluation and management of an established patient, which requires at least 2 of these 3 key components: A problem focused interval history; A problem focused examination; Straightforward medical decision making. Counseling and/or coordination of care with other providers or agencies are provided consistent with the nature of the problem(s) and the patient's and/or family's needs. Usually, the presenting problem(s) are self limited or minor. Physicians typically spend 15 minutes face-to-face with the patient and/or family. [B][80][][PQ]
  🚑 1.51   ⚕ 1.51   **Global Days XXX**
  AMA: 2009, Jul, 7; 2009, Jul, 8-9; 2007, March, 9-11; 2007, Jul, 1-4; 2007, January, 28-31; 2006, January, 2-4,48; 2005, May, 1-2; 2005, February, 1-6

99348 Home visit for the evaluation and management of an established patient, which requires at least 2 of these 3 key components: An expanded problem focused interval history; An expanded problem focused examination; Medical decision making of low complexity. Counseling and/or coordination of care with other providers or agencies are provided consistent with the nature of the problem(s) and the patient's and/or family's needs. Usually, the presenting problem(s) are of low to moderate severity. Physicians typically spend 25 minutes face-to-face with the patient and/or family. [B][80][][PQ]
  🚑 2.31   ⚕ 2.31   **Global Days XXX**
  AMA: 2009, Jul, 8-9; 2009, Jul, 7; 2007, March, 9-11; 2007, Jul, 1-4; 2007, January, 28-31; 2006, January, 2-4,48; 2005, February, 1-6; 2005, May, 1-2

99349 Home visit for the evaluation and management of an established patient, which requires at least 2 of these 3 key components: A detailed interval history; A detailed examination; Medical decision making of moderate complexity. Counseling and/or coordination of care with other providers or agencies are provided consistent with the nature of the problem(s) and the patient's and/or family's needs. Usually, the presenting problem(s) are moderate to high severity. Physicians typically spend 40 minutes face-to-face with the patient and/or family. [B][80][][PQ]
  🚑 3.49   ⚕ 3.49   **Global Days XXX**
  AMA: 2009, Jul, 8-9; 2009, Jul, 7; 2007, Jul, 1-4; 2007, January, 28-31; 2007, March, 9-11; 2006, January, 2-4,48; 2005, May, 1-2; 2005, February, 1-6

99350

99350 Home visit for the evaluation and management of an established patient, which requires at least 2 of these 3 key components: A comprehensive interval history; A comprehensive examination; Medical decision making of moderate to high complexity. Counseling and/or coordination of care with other providers or agencies are provided consistent with the nature of the problem(s) and the patient's and/or family's needs. Usually, the presenting problem(s) are of moderate to high severity. The patient may be unstable or may have developed a significant new problem requiring immediate physician attention. Physicians typically spend 60 minutes face-to-face with the patient and/or family.

4.86   4.86 Global Days XXX
AMA: 2009, Jul, 7; 2009, Jul, 8-9; 2007, January, 28-31; 2007, Jul, 1-4; 2007, March, 9-11; 2006, January, 2-4,48; 2005, May, 1-2; 2005, February, 1-6

99354-99357 Prolonged Services Direct Contact

CMS 100-1,5,70 — Definition of Physician
CMS 100-2,15,30 — Physician Services
CMS 100-4,12,30.6.15 — Extended Services Outside Customary Services
CMS 100-4,12,30.6.15.1 — Prolonged Services With Direct Face-to-Face Patient Contact

INCLUDES Personal contact with the patient (99354-99357)
Services provided prior to and after personal contact with the patient (99358, 99359)
Services that extend beyond the customary service provided in the inpatient or outpatient setting
Time spent providing prolonged services on a date of service, even when the time is not continuous

Do not report any service less than 30 minutes
Do not report any service that fails to extend into the next time period by 15 minutes or more

+ **99354** Prolonged physician service in the office or other outpatient setting requiring direct (face-to-face) patient contact beyond the usual service; first hour (List separately in addition to code for office or other outpatient Evaluation and Management service)
Code first (90809, 90815, 99201-99215, 99241-99245, 99324-99337, 99341-99350)
2.53   2.69 Global Days ZZZ
AMA: 2009, Jul, 8-9; 2008, Sep, 3-4; 2008, Jun, 12&15; 2007, March, 9-11; 2007, Jul, 1-4; 2005, May, 1-2; 2005, November, 10-13; 2005, February, 1-6

+ **99355** each additional 30 minutes (List separately in addition to code for prolonged physician service)
Code first (99354)
2.49   2.65 Global Days ZZZ
AMA: 2009, Jul, 8-9; 2008, Jun, 12&15; 2008, Sep, 3-4; 2007, March, 9-11; 2007, Jul, 1-4; 2005, May, 1-2; 2005, November, 10-13; 2005, February, 1-6

+ **99356** Prolonged physician service in the inpatient setting, requiring unit/floor time beyond the usual service; first hour (List separately in addition to code for inpatient Evaluation and Management service)
Code first (90822, 90829, 99221-99233, 99251-99255, 99304-99310)
2.48   2.48 Global Days ZZZ
AMA: 2009, Jul, 8-9; 2008, Sep, 3-4; 2008, Jun, 12&15; 2007, Jul, 1-4; 2007, March, 9-11; 2005, February, 1-6; 2005, November, 10-13; 2005, May, 1-2

+ **99357** each additional 30 minutes (List separately in addition to code for prolonged physician service)
Code first (99356)
2.48   2.48 Global Days ZZZ
AMA: 2009, Jul, 8-9; 2008, Sep, 3-4; 2008, Jun, 12&15; 2007, March, 9-11; 2007, Jul, 1-4; 2005, May, 1-2; 2005, November, 10-13; 2005, February, 1-6

99358-99359 Prolonged Services Indirect Contact

CMS 100-1,5,70 — Definition of Physician
CMS 100-2,15,30 — Physician Services
CMS 100-4,12,30.6.15 — Extended Services Outside Customary Services
CMS 100-4,12,30.6.15.2 — Prolonged Services Without Face to Face Service

INCLUDES Prolonged services performed in a day that are not continuous
Time spent after direct face-to-face contact beyond the usual not necessarily on the same date of service.

EXCLUDES Anticoagulation services
Care plan oversight
On-line medical services
Other indirect services that have a more specific code and no upper time limit in the code
Time spent in medical team conference

Code also evaluation and management or other services provided
Code also non-face-to-face service codes that have an upper time limit
Code also the code for each additional service for the last 15-30 minutes.
Do not report services less than 15 minutes beyond the first hour
Do not report services less than 30 minutes

▲ **99358** Prolonged evaluation and management service before and/or after direct (face-to-face) patient care; first hour
3.01   3.01 Global Days XXX
AMA: 2008, Jun, 12&15; 2008, Sep, 3-4; 2007, March, 9-11; 2007, Jul, 1-4; 2005, May, 1-2; 2005, November, 10-13; 2005, February, 1-6

+ ▲ **99359** each additional 30 minutes (List separately in addition to code for prolonged physician service)
Code first (99358)
1.45   1.45 Global Days ZZZ
AMA: 2008, Jun, 12&15; 2008, Sep, 3-4; 2007, Jul, 1-4; 2007, March, 9-11; 2005, February, 1-6; 2005, November, 10-13; 2005, May, 1-2

99360 Standby Services

CMS 100-4,12,30.6.15.3 — Standby Services

INCLUDES Services requested by another physician that involve no direct pateint contact

EXCLUDES History/examination of normal newborn (99460-99461, 99463)
Less than 30 minutes of standby time
On-call services ordered by the hospital (99026, 99027)
Resuscitation of newborn (99465)

Do not report with (99464)

99360 Physician standby service, requiring prolonged physician attendance, each 30 minutes (eg, operative standby, standby for frozen section, for cesarean/high risk delivery, for monitoring EEG)
EXCLUDES Hospital mandated on call services (99026-99027)
Code also as appropriate (99460, 99465)
Do not report with (99464)
1.70   1.70 Global Days XXX
AMA: 2009, Jan, 11-31; 2008, Jan, 10-25; 2008, Mar, 14-15; 2007, January, 13-27; 2007, March, 9-11; 2007, Jul, 1-4; 2006, December, 10-12; 2005, May, 1-2; 2005, November, 10-13; 2005, February, 1-6

Current Procedural Coding Expert – Evaluation and Management

99363-99364 Supervision of Warfarin Therapy

INCLUDES Services provided on an outpatient basis only
Supervision of therapy with warfarin: ordering, dosage adjustments, analysis of International Normalized Ration (INR) tests, patient discussion

EXCLUDES Initial services provided/continued in the hospital or in observation: new period of subsequent therapy starts with discharge (99364)
Services provided for less than 60 uninterrupted days
Services that fail to meet the required criteria (e.g., at least 8 INR tests/initial 90 days; 3 INR tests/each following 90 days)
Warfarin therapy supervision accomplished online or via telephone contact (98969, 99444)

Do not report with (99217-99239, 99291-99292, 99304-99318, 99471-99480)

99363 Anticoagulant management for an outpatient taking warfarin, physician review and interpretation of International Normalized Ratio (INR) testing, patient instructions, dosage adjustment (as needed), and ordering of additional tests; initial 90 days of therapy (must include a minimum of 8 INR measurements) [B]
2.33 ⚕ 3.31 **Global Days XXX**
AMA: 2009, Jul, 5-6; 2008, Mar, 6-7; 2007, March, 9-11; 2007, Jul, 1-4

99364 each subsequent 90 days of therapy (must include a minimum of 3 INR measurements) [B]
0.89 ⚕ 1.14 **Global Days XXX**
AMA: 2009, Jul, 5-6; 2008, Mar, 6-7; 2007, March, 9-11; 2007, Jul, 1-4

99366-99368 Interdisciplinary Conferences

CMS 100-1,5,70 Definition of Physician
CMS 100-2,15,30 Physician Services
CMS 100-4,11,40.1.3 Attending Physician Services Under Hospice

INCLUDES Documentation of participation, contribution, and recommendations of the conference
Face-to-face participation by minimum of three qualified people from different specialties or disciplines
Only participants who have performed face-to-face evaluations or direct treatment to the patient within the previous 60 days
Start of the review of an individual patient and ends at conclusion of review

EXCLUDES Conferences of less than 30 minutes (not reportable)
More than one individual from the same specialty at the same encounter
Time spent record keeping or writing a report.

99366 Medical team conference with interdisciplinary team of health care professionals, face-to-face with patient and/or family, 30 minutes or more, participation by nonphysician qualified health care professional [N]
INCLUDES Team conferences of 30 minutes or more
EXCLUDES Team conferences by a physician with patient or family present (99201-99499)
1.16 ⚕ 1.18 **Global Days XXX**
AMA: 2009, Jan, 11-31; 2008, Jun, 14-15; 2008, Sep, 3-4

99367 Medical team conference with interdisciplinary team of health care professionals, patient and/or family not present, 30 minutes or more; participation by physician [N]
INCLUDES Team conferences of 30 minutes or more
1.56 ⚕ 1.56 **Global Days XXX**
AMA: 2008, Sep, 3-4

99368 participation by nonphysician qualified health care professional [N]
INCLUDES Team conferences of 30 minutes or more
1.02 ⚕ 1.02 **Global Days XXX**
AMA: 2009, Jan, 11-31; 2008, Sep, 3-4; 2008, Jun, 14-15

99374-99380 Care Plan Oversight: Patient Under Care of HHA, Hospice, or Nursing Facility

CMS 100-4,11,40.1.3.1 CPO Services with Hospice Care
CMS 100-4,12,180 Payment of Care Plan Oversight (CPO)
CMS 100-4,12,180.1 Billing for Care Plan Oversight (CPO)

INCLUDES Analysis of reports, diagnostic tests, treatment plans
Discussions with other health care providers, outside of the practice, involved in the patient's care
Establishment of and revisions to care plans within a 30-day period
Payment to one physician per month for covered care plan oversight services (must be the same one who signed the plan of care)

EXCLUDES Care plan oversight services provided in assisted living, domiciliary care, or private residence, not under care of a home health agency or hospice (99339, 99340)
Routine postoperative care provided during a global surgery period
Time discussing treatment with patient and/or caregivers

Code also office/outpatient visits, hospital, home, nursing facility, domiciliary, or non-face-to-face services
Do not report with (98966-98969, 99441-99444)

99374 Physician supervision of a patient under care of home health agency (patient not present) in home, domiciliary or equivalent environment (eg, Alzheimer's facility) requiring complex and multidisciplinary care modalities involving regular physician development and/or revision of care plans, review of subsequent reports of patient status, review of related laboratory and other studies, communication (including telephone calls) for purposes of assessment or care decisions with health care professional(s), family member(s), surrogate decision maker(s) (eg, legal guardian) and/or key caregiver(s) involved in patient's care, integration of new information into the medical treatment plan and/or adjustment of medical therapy, within a calendar month; 15-29 minutes [B]
1.56 ⚕ 1.87 **Global Days XXX**
AMA: 2009, Jul, 10; 2009, Jul, 5-6; 2008, Mar, 6-7; 2008, Sep, 3-4; 2007, April, 3-6; 2007, Jul, 1-4; 2007, March, 9-11; 2006, December, 4-7; 2005, May, 1-2; 2005, February, 1-6

99375 30 minutes or more [E]
2.45 ⚕ 2.82 **Global Days XXX**
AMA: 2009, Jul, 10; 2009, Jul, 5-6; 2008, Mar, 6-7; 2008, Sep, 3-4; 2007, April, 3-6; 2007, March, 9-11; 2007, Jul, 1-4; 2006, December, 4-7; 2005, February, 1-6; 2005, May, 1-2

99377 Physician supervision of a hospice patient (patient not present) requiring complex and multidisciplinary care modalities involving regular physician development and/or revision of care plans, review of subsequent reports of patient status, review of related laboratory and other studies, communication (including telephone calls) for purposes of assessment or care decisions with health care professional(s), family member(s), surrogate decision maker(s) (eg, legal guardian) and/or key caregiver(s) involved in patient's care, integration of new information into the medical treatment plan and/or adjustment of medical therapy, within a calendar month; 15-29 minutes [B]
1.56 ⚕ 1.87 **Global Days XXX**
AMA: 2009, Jul, 10; 2009, Jul, 5-6; 2008, Mar, 6-7; 2008, Sep, 3-4; 2007, April, 3-6; 2007, March, 9-11; 2007, Jul, 1-4; 2006, December, 4-7; 2005, February, 1-6; 2005, May, 1-2

● New Code ▲ Revised Code Ⓜ Maternity Ⓐ Age Unlisted Not Covered # Resequenced
▢ CCI + Add-on ⊘ Mod 51 Exempt Ⓢ Mod 63 Exempt ⊙ Mod Sedation ▣ PQRI

© 2009 Publisher *(Blue Ink)* CPT only © 2009 American Medical Association. All Rights Reserved. *(Black Ink)* Medicare *(Red Ink)*

99378 30 minutes or more E
 💰 2.45 ✋ 2.82 Global Days XXX
 AMA: 2009, Jul, 5-6; 2009, Jul, 10; 2008, Mar, 6-7; 2008, Sep, 3-4; 2007, March, 9-11; 2007, Jul, 1-4; 2007, April, 3-6; 2006, December, 4-7; 2005, February, 1-6; 2005, May, 1-2

99379 Physician supervision of a nursing facility patient (patient not present) requiring complex and multidisciplinary care modalities involving regular physician development and/or revision of care plans, review of subsequent reports of patient status, review of related laboratory and other studies, communication (including telephone calls) for purposes of assessment or care decisions with health care professional(s), family member(s), surrogate decision maker(s) (eg, legal guardian) and/or key caregiver(s) involved in patient's care, integration of new information into the medical treatment plan and/or adjustment of medical therapy, within a calendar month; 15-29 minutes B
 💰 1.56 ✋ 1.87 Global Days XXX
 AMA: 2009, Jul, 5-6; 2008, Mar, 6-7; 2008, Sep, 3-4; 2007, Jul, 1-4; 2007, March, 9-11; 2006, December, 4-7; 2005, February, 1-6; 2005, May, 1-2

99380 30 minutes or more B
 💰 2.45 ✋ 2.82 Global Days XXX
 AMA: 2009, Jul, 5-6; 2008, Mar, 6-7; 2008, Sep, 3-4; 2007, March, 9-11; 2007, Jul, 1-4; 2006, December, 4-7; 2005, May, 1-2; 2005, February, 1-6

99381-99397 Preventive Medicine Visits

CMS 100-1,5,70 Definition of Physician
CMS 100-2,15,30 Physician Services
CMS 100-4,12,30.6.2 Medically Necessary and Preventive Medicine Service on Same Date

INCLUDES
Care of a small problem or preexisting condition that requires no extra work
New patients or established patients (99381-99387, or 99391-99397)
Regular preventive care (e.g., well-child exams) for all age groups

EXCLUDES
Counseling/risk factor reduction interventions not provided with a preventive medical examination (99401-99412)
Diagnostic tests and other procedures
Immunizations (90465-90474, 90476-90749)
Substantial problems that require additional work

99381 Initial comprehensive preventive medicine evaluation and management of an individual including an age and gender appropriate history, examination, counseling/anticipatory guidance/risk factor reduction interventions, and the ordering of laboratory/diagnostic procedures, new patient; infant (age younger than 1 year) A E
 💰 1.68 ✋ 2.45 Global Days XXX
 AMA: 2009, Mar, 3,4&7; 2009, Jul, 7; 2009, Jan, 11-31; 2008, Jan, 10-25; 2007, March, 9-11; 2007, January, 13-27; 2007, Jul, 1-4; 2005, February, 1-6; 2005, May, 1-2; 2005, August, 13-15

99382 early childhood (age 1 through 4 years) A E
 💰 1.93 ✋ 2.69 Global Days XXX
 AMA: 2009, Jul, 7; 2007, March, 9-11; 2007, Jul, 1-4; 2005, May, 1-2; 2005, February, 1-6; 2005, August, 13-15

99383 late childhood (age 5 through 11 years) A E
 💰 1.93 ✋ 2.69 Global Days XXX
 AMA: 2009, Jul, 7; 2007, March, 9-11; 2007, Jul, 1-4; 2005, February, 1-6; 2005, August, 13-15; 2005, May, 1-2

99384 adolescent (age 12 through 17 years) A E
 💰 2.17 ✋ 2.93 Global Days XXX
 AMA: 2009, Jul, 7; 2007, March, 9-11; 2007, Jul, 1-4; 2005, May, 1-2; 2005, August, 13-15; 2005, February, 1-6

99385 18-39 years A E
 💰 2.17 ✋ 2.93 Global Days XXX
 AMA: 2009, Jul, 7; 2007, Jul, 1-4; 2007, March, 9-11; 2005, May, 1-2; 2005, February, 1-6; 2005, August, 13-15

99386 40-64 years A E
 💰 2.66 ✋ 3.42 Global Days XXX
 AMA: 2009, Jul, 7; 2007, March, 9-11; 2007, Jul, 1-4; 2005, February, 1-6; 2005, May, 1-2; 2005, August, 13-15

99387 65 years and older A E
 💰 2.91 ✋ 3.77 Global Days XXX
 AMA: 2009, Jul, 7; 2007, March, 9-11; 2007, Jul, 1-4; 2005, February, 1-6; 2005, August, 13-15; 2005, May, 1-2

99391 Periodic comprehensive preventive medicine reevaluation and management of an individual including an age and gender appropriate history, examination, counseling/anticipatory guidance/risk factor reduction interventions, and the ordering of laboratory/diagnostic procedures, established patient; infant (age younger than 1 year) A E
 💰 1.44 ✋ 2.11 Global Days XXX
 AMA: 2009, Mar, 3,4&7; 2009, Jul, 7; 2007, Jul, 1-4; 2007, March, 9-11; 2005, May, 1-2; 2005, August, 13-15; 2005, February, 1-6

99392 early childhood (age 1 through 4 years) A E
 💰 1.68 ✋ 2.35 Global Days XXX
 AMA: 2009, Jul, 7; 2007, March, 9-11; 2007, Jul, 1-4; 2005, February, 1-6; 2005, May, 1-2; 2005, August, 13-15

99393 late childhood (age 5 through 11 years) A E
 💰 1.68 ✋ 2.34 Global Days XXX
 AMA: 2009, Jul, 7; 2007, March, 9-11; 2007, Jul, 1-4; 2005, August, 13-15; 2005, May, 1-2; 2005, February, 1-6

99394 adolescent (age 12 through 17 years) A E
 💰 1.93 ✋ 2.58 Global Days XXX
 AMA: 2009, Jul, 7; 2007, March, 9-11; 2007, Jul, 1-4; 2005, May, 1-2; 2005, February, 1-6; 2005, August, 13-15

99395 18-39 years A E
 💰 1.93 ✋ 2.59 Global Days XXX
 AMA: 2009, Jul, 7; 2008, Mar, 3&7; 2007, Jul, 1-4; 2007, March, 9-11; 2005, February, 1-6; 2005, May, 1-2; 2005, August, 13-15

99396 40-64 years A E
 💰 2.17 ✋ 2.83 Global Days XXX
 AMA: 2009, Jul, 7; 2007, March, 9-11; 2007, Jul, 1-4; 2005, February, 1-6; 2005, May, 1-2; 2005, August, 13-15

99397 65 years and older A E
 💰 2.42 ✋ 3.19 Global Days XXX
 AMA: 2009, Jan, 11-31; 2009, Jul, 7; 2008, Jan, 10-25; 2007, January, 13-27; 2007, March, 9-11; 2007, Jul, 1-4; 2005, May, 1-2; 2005, August, 13-15; 2005, February, 1-6

Current Procedural Coding Expert – Evaluation and Management 99443

99401-99429 Counseling Services: Risk Factor and Behavioral Change Modification

CMS 100-1,5,70	Definition of Physician
CMS 100-2,15,30	Physician Services
CMS 100-2,16,90	Routine Services and Appliances
CMS 100-3,210.4	Smoking and Tobacco-Use Cessation Counseling
CMS 100-4,4,200.6	Alcohol and/or Substance Abuse Assessment and Intervention Services
CMS 100-4,12,10	General Processing Instructions
CMS 100-4,32,12	Smoking and Tobacco-Use Cessation Counseling Services
CMS 100-4,32,12.1	Smoking And Tobacco- Use Cessation Counseling
CMS 100-4,32,12.2	Carrier Billing: Smoking and Tobacco Use Cessation Counseling
CMS 100-4,32,12.3	FI Billing: Smoking and Tobacco Use Cessation Counseling

INCLUDES Administration and analysis of a health risk assessment (99420)
Face-to-face services for new and established patients based on time increments of 15 to 60 minutes
Issues such as a healthy diet, exercise, alcohol and drug abuse
Services provided by a physician or other qualified healthcare professional for the purpose of promoting health and reducing illness and injury

EXCLUDES Counseling and risk factor reduction interventions included in preventive medicine services (99381-99397)
Counseling services provided to patient groups with existing symptoms or illness (99078)

Code also distinct evaluation and management services when performed in addition
Do not report with heath and behavioral services (96150-96155)

99401 Preventive medicine counseling and/or risk factor reduction intervention(s) provided to an individual (separate procedure); approximately 15 minutes   E
   0.68   0.94   Global Days XXX
AMA: 2007, Aug, 9-12; 2007, Jul, 1-4; 2007, March, 9-11; 2005, May, 1-2; 2005, February, 1-6

99402 approximately 30 minutes   E
   1.39   1.65   Global Days XXX
AMA: 2007, Aug, 9-12; 2007, March, 9-11; 2007, Jul, 1-4; 2005, February, 1-6; 2005, May, 1-2

99403 approximately 45 minutes   E
   2.06   2.33   Global Days XXX
AMA: 2007, Aug, 9-12; 2007, March, 9-11; 2007, Jul, 1-4; 2005, May, 1-2; 2005, February, 1-6

99404 approximately 60 minutes   E
   2.76   3.03   Global Days XXX
AMA: 2007, Aug, 9-12; 2007, March, 9-11; 2007, Jul, 1-4; 2005, February, 1-6; 2005, May, 1-2

99406 Smoking and tobacco use cessation counseling visit; intermediate, greater than 3 minutes up to 10 minutes   X 80
   0.34   0.38   Global Days XXX
AMA: 2008, Jan, 1-3

99407 intensive, greater than 10 minutes   X 80
Do not report with (99406)
   0.70   0.75   Global Days XXX
AMA: 2008, Jan, 1-3

99408 Alcohol and/or substance (other than tobacco) abuse structured screening (eg, AUDIT, DAST), and brief intervention (SBI) services; 15 to 30 minutes   E
INCLUDES Only initial screening and brief intervention Services of 15 minutes or more.

Do not report with (99420)
   0.92   0.96   Global Days XXX
AMA: 2008, May, 3-4; 2008, Jul, 11-13

99409 greater than 30 minutes   E
INCLUDES Only initial screening and brief intervention
Do not report with (99408, 99420)
   1.84   1.89   Global Days XXX
AMA: 2008, Jul, 11-13; 2008, May, 3-4

99411 Preventive medicine counseling and/or risk factor reduction intervention(s) provided to individuals in a group setting (separate procedure); approximately 30 minutes   E
   0.21   0.41   Global Days XXX
AMA: 2007, Aug, 9-12; 2007, March, 9-11; 2007, Jul, 1-4; 2005, May, 1-2; 2005, February, 1-6

99412 approximately 60 minutes   E
   0.35   0.55   Global Days XXX
AMA: 2007, Aug, 9-12; 2007, March, 9-11; 2007, Jul, 1-4; 2005, May, 1-2; 2005, February, 1-6

99420 Administration and interpretation of health risk assessment instrument (eg, health hazard appraisal)   E
   0.25   0.25   Global Days XXX
AMA: 2007, Jul, 1-4; 2007, March, 9-11; 2005, May, 1-2; 2005, February, 1-6

99429 Unlisted preventive medicine service   E
   0.00   0.00   Global Days XXX
AMA: 2007, March, 9-11; 2007, Jul, 1-4; 2005, May, 1-2; 2005, February, 1-6

99441-99443 Telephone Calls for Patient Management

CMS 100-1,5,70	Definition of Physician
CMS 100-2,15,30	Physician Services
CMS 100-4,11,40.1.3	Attending Physician Services Under Hospice
CMS 100-4,12,10	General Processing Instructions

INCLUDES Episodes of care initiated by an established patient or the patient or guardian of an established patient
Non-face-to-face evaluation and management services provided by a physician

EXCLUDES Services provided by a qualified nonphysician healthcare professional (98966-98968)

Do not report with anticoagulation management reported with codes: (99363-99364)
Do not report with a related evaluation and management visit within the next 24 hours or as the next available urgent visit
Do not report with a related evaluation and management service performed and reported within the previous seven days or within the postoperative period of a completed procedure
Do not report with a related evaluation and management service perfomed in the previous seven days (99441-99444)
Do not report with the same call reported with codes: (99339-99340, 99374-99380)

99441 Telephone evaluation and management service provided by a physician to an established patient, parent, or guardian not originating from a related E/M service provided within the previous 7 days nor leading to an E/M service or procedure within the next 24 hours or soonest available appointment; 5-10 minutes of medical discussion   E
   0.35   0.38   Global Days XXX
AMA: 2008, Mar, 6-7

99442 11-20 minutes of medical discussion   E
   0.71   0.74   Global Days XXX
AMA: 2008, Mar, 6-7

99443 21-30 minutes of medical discussion   E
   1.06   1.09   Global Days XXX
AMA: 2008, Mar, 6-7

● New Code   ▲ Revised Code   M Maternity   A Age   Unlisted   Not Covered   # Resequenced
CCI   + Add-on   ⊘ Mod 51 Exempt   63 Mod 63 Exempt   ⊙ Mod Sedation   PQRI

© 2009 Publisher (Blue Ink)   CPT only © 2009 American Medical Association. All Rights Reserved. (Black Ink)   Medicare (Red Ink)   431

99444 Online Patient Management Services

INCLUDES
- All related communications such as related phone calls, prescription and lab orders
- Permanent electronic or hardcopy storage
- Physician evaluation and management services provided via the internet in response to a patient's on-line inquiry
- The physician's personal timely response

Do not report with more than once per seven day period for the same episode of care

Do not report with when related to an evaluation service performed and reported within the previous seven days

Do not report with when within the postoperative period of a previously completed procedure

99444 Online evaluation and management service provided by a physician to an established patient, guardian, or health care provider not originating from a related E/M service provided within the previous 7 days, using the Internet or similar electronic communications network

EXCLUDES On-line medical evaluation by a qualified nonphysician healthcare professional (98969)

Do not report with (99339-99340, 99363-99364, 99374-99380)

0.00 0.00 Global Days XXX

AMA: 2009, Jul, 5-6

99450-99456 Life/Disability Insurance Eligibility Visits

CMS 100-1,5,70 Definition of Physician
CMS 100-2,15,30 Physician Services

INCLUDES
- Assessment services for insurance eligibility and work-related disability without medical management of the patient's illness/injury
- Services provided to new/established patients at any site of service

EXCLUDES Any additional E/M services or procedures performed on the same date of service: report with appropriate code

99450 Basic life and/or disability examination that includes: Measurement of height, weight, and blood pressure; Completion of a medical history following a life insurance pro forma; Collection of blood sample and/or urinalysis complying with "chain of custody" protocols; and Completion of necessary documentation/certificates.

0.00 0.00 Global Days XXX

AMA: 2007, March, 9-11; 2007, Jul, 1-4; 2005, May, 1-2; 2005, February, 1-6

99455 Work related or medical disability examination by the treating physician that includes: Completion of a medical history commensurate with the patient's condition; Performance of an examination commensurate with the patient's condition; Formulation of a diagnosis, assessment of capabilities and stability, and calculation of impairment; Development of future medical treatment plan; and Completion of necessary documentation/certificates and report.

Do not report with (99080)

0.00 0.00 Global Days XXX

AMA: 2007, March, 9-11; 2007, Jul, 1-4; 2005, May, 1-2; 2005, February, 1-6

99456 Work related or medical disability examination by other than the treating physician that includes: Completion of a medical history commensurate with the patient's condition; Performance of an examination commensurate with the patient's condition; Formulation of a diagnosis, assessment of capabilities and stability, and calculation of impairment; Development of future medical treatment plan; and Completion of necessary documentation/certificates and report.

Do not report with (99080)

0.00 0.00 Global Days XXX

AMA: 2007, March, 9-11; 2007, Jul, 1-4; 2005, May, 1-2; 2005, February, 1-6

99460-99463 Evaluation and Management Services for Age 28 Days or Less

INCLUDES
- Family consultation
- Healthy newborn history and physical
- Medical record documentation
- Ordering of diagnostic test and treatments
- Services provied to healthy newborns age 28 days or less

EXCLUDES
- Attendance at delivery (99464)
- Circumcision (54150)
- Emergency resuscitation services (99465)
- Neonatal intensive and critical care services (99466-99469, 99477-99480)

99460 Initial hospital or birthing center care, per day, for evaluation and management of normal newborn infant

1.67 1.67 Global Days XXX

AMA: 2009, Mar, 3,4&7

99461 Initial care, per day, for evaluation and management of normal newborn infant seen in other than hospital or birthing center

1.78 2.54 Global Days XXX

99462 Subsequent hospital care, per day, for evaluation and management of normal newborn

0.88 0.88 Global Days XXX

99463 Initial hospital or birthing center care, per day, for evaluation and management of normal newborn infant admitted and discharged on the same date

EXCLUDES Services to newborns admitted and discharged on a date other than the admission date (99238-99239)

2.28 2.28 Global Days XXX

AMA: 2009, Mar, 3,4&7

99464-99465 Newborn Delivery Attendance/Resuscitation

99464 Attendance at delivery (when requested by the delivering physician) and initial stabilization of newborn

Code also (99460, 99468, 99477)

Do not report with (99465)

2.08 2.08 Global Days XXX

AMA: 2009, Mar, 3,4&7

99465 Delivery/birthing room resuscitation, provision of positive pressure ventilation and/or chest compressions in the presence of acute inadequate ventilation and/or cardiac output

Code also any necessary procedures performed as part of the resuscitation

Code also as appropriate (99460, 99468, 99477)

Do not report with (99464)

4.15 4.15 Global Days XXX

AMA: 2009, Mar, 3,4&7

Current Procedural Coding Expert – Evaluation and Management 99480

99466-99467 Critical Care Transport Age 24 Months or Younger

INCLUDES All services included for neonatal and pediatric critical care
Physician presence during interfacility transfer of critically ill/injured patient 24 months of age or less

EXCLUDES Patient critical care transport services with personal contact with patient of less than 30 minutes
Physician directed emergency care via two-way voice communication with transporting staff (99288)

Do not report for services less than 30 minutes duration (see evaluation and management codes)

99466 Critical care services delivered by a physician, face-to-face, during an interfacility transport of critically ill or critically injured pediatric patient, 24 months of age or younger; first 30-74 minutes of hands-on care during transport A N 80
  6.80 6.80 Global Days XXX
  AMA: 2009, Mar, 3,4&7

+ **99467** each additional 30 minutes (List separately in addition to code for primary service) A N 80
  Code first (99466)
  3.47 3.47 Global Days ZZZ
  AMA: 2009, Mar, 3,4&7

99468-99476 Critical Care Age 5 Years or Younger

INCLUDES All services included in codes 99291-99292 as well as:
Administration of blood/blood components (36430, 36440)
Administration of intravenous fluids (96360-96361)
Administration of surfactant (94610)
Bladder aspiration, suprapubic (51100)
Bladder catheterization (51701, 51702)
Catheterization umbilical artery (36660)
Catheterization umbilical vein (36510)
Central venous catheter, centrally inserted (36555)
Endotracheal intubation (31500)
Lumbar puncture (62270)
Oral or nasogastric tube placement (43752)
Pulmonary function testing, performed at the bedside (94375)
Pulse or ear oximetry (94760-94762)
Vascular access, arteries (36140, 36620)
Vascular access, venous (36420, 36400-36406, 36600)
Ventilatory management (94002-94004, 94660)
Initial and subsequent care provided to a critically ill infant or child

EXCLUDES Critical care services for patients 6 years of age or older (99291-99292)
Critical care services provided by a second physician or physician of a different specialty (99291-99292)
Critical care services to an outpatient (99291-99292)

Do not report with remote critical care (0188T-0189T)

99468 Initial inpatient neonatal critical care, per day, for the evaluation and management of a critically ill neonate, 28 days of age or younger A C 80
  26.37 26.37 Global Days XXX
  AMA: 2009, Jan, 5&10; 2009, Mar, 3,4&7

99469 Subsequent inpatient neonatal critical care, per day, for the evaluation and management of a critically ill neonate, 28 days of age or younger A C 80
  11.04 11.04 Global Days XXX
  AMA: 2009, Jan, 5&10; 2009, Mar, 3,4&7

99471 Initial inpatient pediatric critical care, per day, for the evaluation and management of a critically ill infant or young child, 29 days through 24 months of age A C 80
  22.08 22.08 Global Days XXX
  AMA: 2009, Jan, 5&10; 2009, Mar, 3,4&7

99472 Subsequent inpatient pediatric critical care, per day, for the evaluation and management of a critically ill infant or young child, 29 days through 24 months of age A C 80
  11.14 11.14 Global Days XXX
  AMA: 2009, Jan, 5&10; 2009, Mar, 3,4&7

99475 Initial inpatient pediatric critical care, per day, for the evaluation and management of a critically ill infant or young child, 2 through 5 years of age A C 80
  15.24 15.24 Global Days XXX
  AMA: 2009, Jan, 5&10; 2009, Jan, 3,4&9; 2009, Mar, 3,4&7

99476 Subsequent inpatient pediatric critical care, per day, for the evaluation and management of a critically ill infant or young child, 2 through 5 years of age A C 80
  9.15 9.15 Global Days XXX
  AMA: 2009, Jan, 3,4&9; 2009, Mar, 3,4&7; 2009, Jan, 5&10

99477-99499 Initial Inpatient Neonatal Intensive Care and Other Services

INCLUDES Initial and subsequent services for non-critically ill infants and neonates that continue to require any of the following:
Adjustments to enteral and/or parenteral nutrition
Constant and/or frequent monitoring of vitals signs
Continuous observation by the healthcare team
Heat maintenance
Intensive cardiac or respiratory monitoring
Monitoring of laboratory and oxygen values

EXCLUDES Subsequent care of a sick neonate, under 28 days of age, more than 5000 grams, not requiring critical or intensive care services (99231-99233)

99477 Initial hospital care, per day, for the evaluation and management of the neonate, 28 days of age or younger, who requires intensive observation, frequent interventions, and other intensive care services A C 80
  EXCLUDES Initiation of care of a critically ill neonate (99468)
  Initiation of inpatient care of a normal newborn (99460)
  Initiation of inpatient hospital care of a neonate not requiring:
    Frequent interventions
    Intensive observation
    Other intensive services
  9.60 9.60 Global Days XXX
  AMA: 2009, Mar, 3,4&7; 2008, Jan, 1-3; 2008, Jan, 8-9; 2008, Jul, 10&13

99478 Subsequent intensive care, per day, for the evaluation and management of the recovering very low birth weight infant (present body weight less than 1500 grams) A C 80
  3.98 3.98 Global Days XXX
  AMA: 2009, Mar, 3,4&7

99479 Subsequent intensive care, per day, for the evaluation and management of the recovering low birth weight infant (present body weight of 1500-2500 grams) A C 80
  3.62 3.62 Global Days XXX
  AMA: 2009, Mar, 3,4&7

99480 Subsequent intensive care, per day, for the evaluation and management of the recovering infant (present body weight of 2501-5000 grams) A C 80
  3.43 3.43 Global Days XXX
  AMA: 2009, Mar, 3,4&7

99499 Unlisted evaluation and management service
0.00 0.00 Global Days XXX
AMA: 2009, Jan, 11-31; 2008, Jan, 10-25; 2007, Jul, 1-4; 2007, January, 13-27; 2007, March, 9-11; 2006, January, 46-47; 2006, September, 9-13; 2005, May, 1-2; 2005, March, 11-15; 2005, February, 1-6

Current Procedural Coding Expert – Category II Codes

0001F-0015F Quality Measures with Multiple Components

INCLUDES Several measures grouped within a single code descriptor to make possible reporting for clinical conditions when all of the components have been met

0001F Heart failure assessed (includes assessment of all the following components) (CAD, HF): Blood pressure measured (2000F) Level of activity assessed (1003F) Clinical symptoms of volume overload (excess) assessed (1004F) Weight, recorded (2001F) Clinical signs of volume overload (excess) assessed (2002F) [M]

> **INCLUDES**
> Blood pressure measured (2000F)
> Clinical signs of volume overload (excess) assessed (2002F)
> Clinical symptoms of volume overload (excess) assessed (1004F)
> Level of activity assessed (1003F)
> Weight recorded (2001F)

💰 0.00 ✂ 0.00 **Global Days XXX**
AMA: 2006, December, 10-12; 2005, October, 1-5

0005F Osteoarthritis assessed (OA) Includes assessment of all the following components: Osteoarthritis symptoms and functional status assessed (1006F) Use of anti-inflammatory or over-the-counter (OTC) analgesic medications assessed (1007F) Initial examination of the involved joint(s) (includes visual inspection, palpation, range of motion) (2004F) [M]

> **INCLUDES**
> Initial examination of the involved joint(s) (includes visual inspection/palpation/range of motion) (2004F)
> Osteoarthritis symptoms and functional status assessed (1006F)
> Use of anti-inflammatory or over-the-counter (OTC) analgesic medications assessed (1007F)
>
> **EXCLUDES** Tobacco use cessation intervention (4001F)

💰 0.00 ✂ 0.00 **Global Days XXX**
AMA: 2005, October, 1-5

0012F Community-acquired bacterial pneumonia assessment (includes all of the following components) (CAP): Co-morbid conditions assessed (1026F) Vital signs recorded (2010F) Mental status assessed (2014F) Hydration status assessed (2018F) [M]

> **INCLUDES**
> Co-morbid conditions assessed (1026F)
> Hydration status assessed (2018F)
> Mental status assessed (2014F)
> Vital signs recorded (2010F)

💰 0.00 ✂ 0.00 **Global Days XXX**

0014F Comprehensive preoperative assessment performed for cataract surgery with intraocular lens (IOL) placement (includes assessment of all of the following components) (EC): Dilated fundus evaluation performed within 12 months prior to cataract surgery (2020F) Pre-surgical (cataract) axial length, corneal power measurement and method of intraocular lens power calculation documented (must be performed within 12 months prior to surgery) (3073F) Preoperative assessment of functional or medical indication(s) for surgery prior to the cataract surgery with intraocular lens placement (must be performed within 12 months prior to cataract surgery) (3325F) [M] [PQ]

> **INCLUDES**
> Evaluation of dilated fundus done within 12 months prior to surgery (2020F)
> Preoperative assessment of functional or medical indications done within 12 months prior to sugery (3325F)
> Presurgical measurement of axial length and corneal power and IOL power calculation performed within 12 months prior to sugery (3325F)

💰 0.00 ✂ 0.00 **Global Days XXX**
AMA: 2008, Mar, 8-12

0015F Melanoma follow-up completed (includes assessment of all of the following components) (ML): History obtained regarding new or changing moles (1050F) Complete physical skin exam performed (2029F) Patient counseled to perform a monthly self skin examination (5005F) [M] [PQ]

> **INCLUDES**
> Complete physical skin exam (2029F)
> Counseling to perform monthly skin self-examination (5005F)
> History obtained of new or changing moles (1050F)

💰 0.00 ✂ 0.00 **Global Days XXX**
AMA: 2008, Mar, 8-12

0500F-0575F Care Provided According to Prevailing Guidelines

INCLUDES Measures of utilization or patient care provided for certain clinical purposes

▲ **0500F** Initial prenatal care visit (report at first prenatal encounter with health care professional providing obstetrical care. Report also date of visit and, in a separate field, the date of the last menstrual period [LMP]) (Prenatal) [M] ♀ [M]

💰 0.00 ✂ 0.00 **Global Days XXX**
AMA: 2005, October, 1-5

0501F Prenatal flow sheet documented in medical record by first prenatal visit (documentation includes at minimum blood pressure, weight, urine protein, uterine size, fetal heart tones, and estimated date of delivery). Report also: date of visit and, in a separate field, the date of the last menstrual period [LMP] (Note: If reporting 0501F Prenatal flow sheet, it is not necessary to report 0500F Initial prenatal care visit) (Prenatal) [M] ♀ [M]

💰 0.00 ✂ 0.00 **Global Days XXX**

Category II Codes

0502F

0502F Subsequent prenatal care visit (Prenatal) [Excludes: patients who are seen for a condition unrelated to pregnancy or prenatal care (eg, an upper respiratory infection; patients seen for consultation only, not for continuing care)]

> **EXCLUDES** Patients seen for an unrelated pregnancy/prenatal care condition (e.g., upper respiratory infection; patients seen for consultation only, not for continuing care)

0.00   0.00   Global Days XXX

0503F Postpartum care visit (Prenatal)
0.00   0.00   Global Days XXX

0505F Hemodialysis plan of care documented (ESRD, P-ESRD)
0.00   0.00   Global Days XXX
AMA: 2008, Mar, 8-12

0507F Peritoneal dialysis plan of care documented (ESRD)
0.00   0.00   Global Days XXX
AMA: 2008, Mar, 8-12

0509F Urinary incontinence plan of care documented (GER)
0.00   0.00   Global Days XXX

0513F Elevated blood pressure plan of care documented (CKD)
0.00   0.00   Global Days XXX
AMA: 2008, Mar, 8-12

▲ **0514F** Plan of care for elevated hemoglobin level documented for patient receiving erythropoiesis-stimulating agent therapy (ESA) (CKD)
0.00   0.00   Global Days XXX
AMA: 2008, Mar, 8-12

0516F Anemia plan of care documented (ESRD)
0.00   0.00   Global Days XXX
AMA: 2008, Mar, 8-12

0517F Glaucoma plan of care documented (EC)
0.00   0.00   Global Days XXX
AMA: 2008, Mar, 8-12

0518F Falls plan of care documented (GER)
0.00   0.00   Global Days XXX
AMA: 2008, Mar, 8-12

0519F Planned chemotherapy regimen, including at a minimum: drug(s) prescribed, dose, and duration, documented prior to initiation of a new treatment regimen (ONC)
0.00   0.00   Global Days XXX
AMA: 2008, Mar, 8-12

0520F Radiation dose limits to normal tissues established prior to the initiation of a course of 3D conformal radiation for a minimum of 2 tissues/organs (ONC)
0.00   0.00   Global Days XXX
AMA: 2008, Mar, 8-12

0521F Plan of care to address pain documented (COA) (ONC)
0.00   0.00   Global Days XXX
AMA: 2008, Mar, 8-12

0525F Initial visit for episode (BkP)
0.00   0.00   Global Days XXX
AMA: 2008, Mar, 8-12

0526F Subsequent visit for episode (BkP)
0.00   0.00   Global Days XXX
AMA: 2008, Mar, 8-12

● **0528F** Recommended follow-up interval for repeat colonoscopy of at least 10 years documented in colonoscopy report (End/Polyp)
0.00   0.00   Global Days XXX

● **0529F** Interval of 3 or more years since patient's last colonoscopy, documented (End/Polyp)
0.00   0.00   Global Days XXX

● **0535F** Dyspnea management plan of care, documented (Pall Cr)
0.00   0.00   Global Days XXX

● **0540F** Glucorticoid Management Plan Documented (RA)
0.00   0.00   Global Days XXX

● **0545F** Plan for follow-up care for major depressive disorder, documented (MDD ADOL)
0.00   0.00   Global Days XXX

0575F HIV RNA control plan of care, documented (HIV)
0.00   0.00   Global Days XXX

1000F-1220F Elements of History/Review of Systems

> **INCLUDES** Measures for specific aspects of patient history or review of systems

1000F Tobacco use assessed (CAD, CAP, COPD, PV) (DM)
0.00   0.00   Global Days XXX
AMA: 2005, October, 1-5

1002F Anginal symptoms and level of activity assessed (CAD)
0.00   0.00   Global Days XXX

1003F Level of activity assessed (HF)
0.00   0.00   Global Days XXX
AMA: 2006, December, 10-12

1004F Clinical symptoms of volume overload (excess) assessed (HF)
0.00   0.00   Global Days XXX
AMA: 2006, December, 10-12

1005F Asthma symptoms evaluated (includes physician documentation of numeric frequency of symptoms or patient completion of an asthma assessment tool/survey/questionnaire) (Asthma)

1006F Osteoarthritis symptoms and functional status assessed (may include the use of a standardized scale or the completion of an assessment questionnaire, such as the SF-36, AAOS Hip & Knee Questionnaire) (OA) [Instructions: Report when osteoarthritis is addressed during the patient encounter]

> **INCLUDES** Osteoarthritis when it is addressed during the patient encounter

0.00   0.00   Global Days XXX

1007F Use of anti-inflammatory or analgesic over-the-counter (OTC) medications for symptom relief assessed (OA)
0.00   0.00   Global Days XXX

1008F Gastrointestinal and renal risk factors assessed for patients on prescribed or OTC non-steroidal anti-inflammatory drug (NSAID) (OA)
0.00   0.00   Global Days XXX

1015F Chronic obstructive pulmonary disease (COPD) symptoms assessed (Includes assessment of at least 1 of the following: dyspnea, cough/sputum, wheezing), or respiratory symptom assessment tool completed (COPD)
0.00   0.00   Global Days XXX

1018F Dyspnea assessed, not present (COPD)
0.00   0.00   Global Days XXX

1019F Dyspnea assessed, present (COPD)
0.00   0.00   Global Days XXX

1022F Pneumococcus immunization status assessed (CAP, COPD)
0.00   0.00   Global Days XXX
AMA: 2008, Mar, 8-12

Current Procedural Coding Expert – Category II Codes

1026F	Co-morbid conditions assessed (eg, includes assessment for presence or absence of: malignancy, liver disease, congestive heart failure, cerebrovascular disease, renal disease, chronic obstructive pulmonary disease, asthma, diabetes, other co-morbid conditions) (CAP) [M] 0.00　0.00　Global Days XXX
1030F	Influenza immunization status assessed (CAP) [M] 0.00　0.00　Global Days XXX AMA: 2008, Mar, 8-12
1034F	Current tobacco smoker (CAD, CAP, COPD, PV) (DM) [M][PQ] 0.00　0.00　Global Days XXX AMA: 2008, Mar, 8-12
1035F	Current smokeless tobacco user (eg, chew, snuff) (PV) [M][PQ] 0.00　0.00　Global Days XXX AMA: 2008, Mar, 8-12
1036F	Current tobacco non-user (CAD, CAP, COPD, PV) (DM) [M][PQ] 0.00　0.00　Global Days XXX AMA: 2008, Mar, 8-12
1038F	Persistent asthma (mild, moderate or severe) (Asthma) [M][PQ] 0.00　0.00　Global Days XXX
1039F	Intermittent asthma (Asthma) [M][PQ] 0.00　0.00　Global Days XXX
▲ 1040F	DSM-IV (TM) criteria for major depressive disorder documented at the initial evaluation (MDD, MDD ADOL) [M][PQ] 0.00　0.00　Global Days XXX AMA: 2008, Mar, 8-12
1050F	History obtained regarding new or changing moles (ML) [M] 0.00　0.00　Global Days XXX AMA: 2008, Mar, 8-12
1055F	Visual functional status assessed (EC) [M] 0.00　0.00　Global Days XXX
1060F	Documentation of permanent OR persistent OR paroxysmal atrial fibrillation (STR) [M] 0.00　0.00　Global Days XXX
1061F	Documentation of absence of permanent AND persistent AND paroxysmal atrial fibrillation (STR) [M] 0.00　0.00　Global Days XXX
1065F	Ischemic stroke symptom onset of less than 3 hours prior to arrival (STR) [M][PQ] 0.00　0.00　Global Days XXX
1066F	Ischemic stroke symptom onset greater than or equal to 3 hours prior to arrival (STR) [M][PQ] 0.00　0.00　Global Days XXX
1070F	Alarm symptoms (involuntary weight loss, dysphagia, or gastrointestinal bleeding) assessed; none present (GERD) [M] 0.00　0.00　Global Days XXX
1071F	1 or more present (GERD) [M] 0.00　0.00　Global Days XXX
1090F	Presence or absence of urinary incontinence assessed (GER) [M][PQ] 0.00　0.00　Global Days XXX
▲ 1091F	Urinary incontinence characterized (eg, frequency, volume, timing, type of symptoms, how bothersome) (GER) [M][PQ] 0.00　0.00　Global Days XXX
▲ 1100F	Patient screened for future fall risk; documentation of 2 or more falls in the past year or any fall with injury in the past year (GER) [M][PQ] 0.00　0.00　Global Days XXX AMA: 2008, Mar, 8-12
1101F	documentation of no falls in the past year or only 1 fall without injury in the past year (GER) [M][PQ] 0.00　0.00　Global Days XXX AMA: 2008, Mar, 8-12
1110F	Patient discharged from an inpatient facility (eg, hospital, skilled nursing facility, or rehabilitation facility) within the last 60 days (GER) [M] 0.00　0.00　Global Days XXX
1111F	Discharge medications reconciled with the current medication list in outpatient medical record (COA) (GER) [M] 0.00　0.00　Global Days XXX
1116F	Auricular or periauricular pain assessed (AOE) [M][PQ] 0.00　0.00　Global Days XXX AMA: 2008, Mar, 8-12
1118F	GERD symptoms assessed after 12 months of therapy (GERD) [M] 0.00　0.00　Global Days XXX AMA: 2008, Mar, 8-12
▲ 1119F	Initial evaluation for condition (HEP C)(EPI) [M][PQ] 0.00　0.00　Global Days XXX AMA: 2008, Mar, 8-12
▲ 1121F	Subsequent evaluation for condition (HEP C)(EPI) [M][PQ] 0.00　0.00　Global Days XXX AMA: 2008, Mar, 8-12
1123F	Advance Care Planning discussed and documented; advance care plan or surrogate decision maker documented in the medical record (GER, Pall Cr) [M][PQ] 0.00　0.00　Global Days XXX AMA: 2008, Mar, 8-12
1124F	Advance Care Planning discussed and documented in the medical record; patient did not wish or was not able to name a surrogate decision maker or provide an advance care plan (GER, Pall Cr) [M][PQ] 0.00　0.00　Global Days XXX AMA: 2008, Mar, 8-12
1125F	Pain severity quantified; pain present (COA) (ONC) [M][PQ] 0.00　0.00　Global Days XXX AMA: 2008, Mar, 8-12
1126F	no pain present (COA) (ONC) [M][PQ] 0.00　0.00　Global Days XXX AMA: 2008, Mar, 8-12
~~1127F~~	~~New episode for condition (ML)~~
~~1128F~~	~~Subsequent episode for condition (ML)~~
1130F	Back pain and function assessed, including all of the following: Pain assessment AND functional status AND patient history, including notation of presence or absence of "red flags" (warning signs) AND assessment of prior treatment and response, AND employment status (BkP) [M][PQ] 0.00　0.00　Global Days XXX AMA: 2008, Mar, 8-12
1134F	Episode of back pain lasting 6 weeks or less (BkP) [M] 0.00　0.00　Global Days XXX AMA: 2008, Mar, 8-12
1135F	Episode of back pain lasting longer than 6 weeks (BkP) [M] 0.00　0.00　Global Days XXX AMA: 2008, Mar, 8-12

● New Code　▲ Revised Code　[M] Maternity　[A] Age　Unlisted　Not Covered　# Resequenced
CCI　+ Add-on　⊘ Mod 51 Exempt　⊚ Mod 63 Exempt　⊙ Mod Sedation　[PQ] PQRI

© 2009 Publisher *(Blue Ink)*　CPT only © 2009 American Medical Association. All Rights Reserved. *(Black Ink)*　Medicare *(Red Ink)*

Current Procedural Coding Expert – Category II Codes

1136F	Episode of back pain lasting 12 weeks or less (BkP) [M] 0.00 0.00 Global Days XXX **AMA:** 2008, Mar, 8-12
1137F	Episode of back pain lasting longer than 12 weeks (BkP) [M] 0.00 0.00 Global Days XXX **AMA:** 2008, Mar, 8-12
● 1150F	Documentation that a patient has a substantial risk of death within one year (Pall Cr) [E] 0.00 0.00 Global Days XXX
● 1151F	Documentation that a patient does not have a substantial risk of death within 1 year (Pall Cr) [E] 0.00 0.00 Global Days XXX
● 1152F	Documentation of advanced disease diagnosis, goals of care prioritize comfort (Pall Cr) [E] 0.00 0.00 Global Days XXX
● 1153F	Documentation of advanced disease diagnosis, goals of care do not prioritize comfort (Pall Cr) [E] 0.00 0.00 Global Days XXX
● 1157F	Advance care plan or similar legal document present in the medical record (COA) [E] 0.00 0.00 Global Days XXX
● 1158F	Advance care planning discussion documented in the medical record (COA) [M] 0.00 0.00 Global Days XXX
● 1159F	Medication list documented in medical record (COA) [E] 0.00 0.00 Global Days XXX
● 1160F	Review of all medications by a prescribing practitioner or clinical pharmacist (such as, prescriptions, OTCs, herbal therapies and supplements) documented in the medical record (COA) [E] 0.00 0.00 Global Days XXX
● 1170F	Functional status assessed (COA) (RA) [M][PQ] 0.00 0.00 Global Days XXX
1180F	All specified thromboembolic risk factors assessed (AFIB) [E] 0.00 0.00 Global Days XXX
● 1200F	Seizure type(s) and current seizure frequency(ies) documented (EPI) [E] 0.00 0.00 Global Days XXX
● 1205F	Etiology of epilepsy or epilepsy syndrome(s) reviewed and documented (EPI) [E] 0.00 0.00 Global Days XXX
1220F	Patient screened for depression (SUD) [M] 0.00 0.00 Global Days XXX

2000F-2060F Elements of Examination

INCLUDES Components of clinical assessment or physical exam

2000F	Blood pressure measured (CAD, CKD, HF, HTN)(DM) [M][PQ] 0.00 0.00 Global Days XXX **AMA:** 2008, Mar, 8-12; 2006, December, 10-12; 2005, October, 1-5
2001F	Weight recorded (HF, PAG) [M] 0.00 0.00 Global Days XXX **AMA:** 2006, December, 10-12
2002F	Clinical signs of volume overload (excess) assessed (HF) [M] 0.00 0.00 Global Days XXX **AMA:** 2006, December, 10-12
2004F	Initial examination of the involved joint(s) (includes visual inspection, palpation, range of motion) (OA) [Instructions: Report only for initial osteoarthritis visit or for visits for new joint involvement] [M] **INCLUDES** Visits for initial osteoarthritis examination or new joint involvement 0.00 0.00 Global Days XXX
2010F	Vital signs (temperature, pulse, respiratory rate, and blood pressure) documented and reviewed (CAP) (EM) [M][PQ] 0.00 0.00 Global Days XXX
2014F	Mental status assessed (CAP) (EM) [M][PQ] 0.00 0.00 Global Days XXX
2018F	Hydration status assessed (normal/mildly dehydrated/severely dehydrated) (CAP) [M] 0.00 0.00 Global Days XXX
2019F	Dilated macular exam performed, including documentation of the presence or absence of macular thickening or hemorrhage AND the level of macular degeneration severity (EC) [M][PQ] 0.00 0.00 Global Days XXX
2020F	Dilated fundus evaluation performed within 12 months prior to cataract surgery (EC) [M] 0.00 0.00 Global Days XXX **AMA:** 2008, Mar, 8-12
2021F	Dilated macular or fundus exam performed, including documentation of the presence or absence of macular edema AND level of severity of retinopathy (EC) [M][PQ] 0.00 0.00 Global Days XXX
2022F	Dilated retinal eye exam with interpretation by an ophthalmologist or optometrist documented and reviewed (DM) [M][PQ] 0.00 0.00 Global Days XXX **AMA:** 2008, Mar, 8-12
2024F	7 standard field stereoscopic photos with interpretation by an ophthalmologist or optometrist documented and reviewed (DM) [M][PQ] 0.00 0.00 Global Days XXX **AMA:** 2008, Mar, 8-12
▲ 2026F	Eye imaging validated to match diagnosis from 7 standard field stereoscopic photos results documented and reviewed (DM) [M][PQ] 0.00 0.00 Global Days XXX **AMA:** 2008, Mar, 8-12
2027F	Optic nerve head evaluation performed (EC) [M][PQ] 0.00 0.00 Global Days XXX
2028F	Foot examination performed (includes examination through visual inspection, sensory exam with monofilament, and pulse exam - report when any of the 3 components are completed) (DM) [M][PQ] 0.00 0.00 Global Days XXX
2029F	Complete physical skin exam performed (ML) [M] 0.00 0.00 Global Days XXX **AMA:** 2008, Mar, 8-12
2030F	Hydration status documented, normally hydrated (PAG) [M] 0.00 0.00 Global Days XXX
2031F	Hydration status documented, dehydrated (PAG) [M] 0.00 0.00 Global Days XXX
2035F	Tympanic membrane mobility assessed with pneumatic otoscopy or tympanometry (OME) [M][PQ] 0.00 0.00 Global Days XXX **AMA:** 2008, Mar, 8-12

Current Procedural Coding Expert – Category II Codes

2040F Physical examination on the date of the initial visit for low back pain performed, in accordance with specifications (BkP)
0.00 0.00 Global Days XXX
AMA: 2008, Mar, 8-12

2044F Documentation of mental health assessment prior to intervention (back surgery or epidural steroid injection) or for back pain episode lasting longer than 6 weeks (BkP)
0.00 0.00 Global Days XXX
AMA: 2008, Mar, 8-12

● **2050F** Wound characteristics including size AND nature of wound base tissue AND amount of drainage prior to debridement documented (CWC)
0.00 0.00 Global Days XXX

● **2060F** Patient interviewed directly by evaluating clinician on or before date of diagnosis of major depressive disorder (MDD ADOL)
0.00 0.00 Global Days XXX

3006F-3650F Findings from Diagnostic Tests

INCLUDES Ordered test results and medical decision making:of:
Clinical laboratory tests
Other procedural examinations
Radiological examinations

3006F Chest X-ray results documented and reviewed (CAP)
0.00 0.00 Global Days XXX

● **3008F** Body Mass Index (BMI), documented (PV)
0.00 0.00 Global Days XXX

3011F Lipid panel results documented and reviewed (must include total cholesterol, HDL-C, triglycerides and calculated LDL-C) (CAD)
0.00 0.00 Global Days XXX

3014F Screening mammography results documented and reviewed (PV)
0.00 0.00 Global Days XXX
AMA: 2008, Mar, 8-12

● **3015F** Cervical cancer screening results documented and reviewed (PV)
0.00 0.00 Global Days XXX

3016F Patient screened for unhealthy alcohol use using a systematic screening method (PV)
0.00 0.00 Global Days XXX

3017F Colorectal cancer screening results documented and reviewed (PV)
0.00 0.00 Global Days XXX
AMA: 2008, Mar, 8-12

3018F Pre-procedure risk assessment AND depth of insertion AND quality of the bowel prep AND complete description of polyp(s) found, including location of each polyp, size, number and gross morphology AND recommendations for follow-up in final colonoscopy report, documented (End/Polyp)
0.00 0.00 Global Days XXX

3020F Left ventricular function (LVF) assessment (eg, echocardiography, nuclear test, or ventriculography) documented in the medical record (Includes quantitative or qualitative assessment results) (HF)
0.00 0.00 Global Days XXX
AMA: 2006, December, 10-12

▲ **3021F** Left ventricular ejection fraction (LVEF) less than 40% or documentation of moderately or severely depressed left ventricular systolic function (CAD, HF)
0.00 0.00 Global Days XXX

3022F Left ventricular ejection fraction (LVEF) greater than or equal to 40% or documentation as normal or mildly depressed left ventricular systolic function (CAD, HF)
0.00 0.00 Global Days XXX

3023F Spirometry results documented and reviewed (COPD)
0.00 0.00 Global Days XXX

3025F Spirometry test results demonstrate FEV1/FVC less than 70% with COPD symptoms (eg, dyspnea, cough/sputum, wheezing) (CAP, COPD)
0.00 0.00 Global Days XXX

3027F Spirometry test results demonstrate FEV1/FVC greater than or equal to 70% or patient does not have COPD symptoms (COPD)
0.00 0.00 Global Days XXX

3028F Oxygen saturation results documented and reviewed (includes assessment through pulse oximetry or arterial blood gas measurement) (CAP, COPD) (EM)
0.00 0.00 Global Days XXX

▲ **3035F** Oxygen saturation less than or equal to 88% or a PaO2 less than or equal to 55 mm Hg (COPD).
0.00 0.00 Global Days XXX

▲ **3037F** Oxygen saturation greater than 88% or PaO2 greater than 55 mmHg (COPD)
0.00 0.00 Global Days XXX

● **3038F** Pulmonary function test performed within 12 months prior to surgery (Lung/Esop Cx)
0.00 0.00 Global Days XXX

3040F Functional expiratory volume (FEV1) less than 40% of predicted value (COPD)
0.00 0.00 Global Days XXX

3042F Functional expiratory volume (FEV1) greater than or equal to 40% of predicted value (COPD)
0.00 0.00 Global Days XXX

3044F Most recent hemoglobin A1c (HbA1c) level less than 7.0% (DM)
0.00 0.00 Global Days XXX

▲ **3045F** Most recent hemoglobin A1c (HbA1c) level 7.0–9.0% (DM)
0.00 0.00 Global Days XXX

3046F Most recent hemoglobin A1c level greater than 9.0% (DM)
0.00 0.00 Global Days XXX

3048F Most recent LDL-C less than 100 mg/dL (DM)
0.00 0.00 Global Days XXX

3049F Most recent LDL-C 100-129 mg/dL (DM)
0.00 0.00 Global Days XXX

3050F Most recent LDL-C greater than or equal to 130 mg/dL (DM)
0.00 0.00 Global Days XXX

3060F Positive microalbuminuria test result documented and reviewed (DM)
0.00 0.00 Global Days XXX

3061F Negative microalbuminuria test result documented and reviewed (DM)
0.00 0.00 Global Days XXX

3062F Positive macroalbuminuria test result documented and reviewed (DM)
0.00 0.00 Global Days XXX

● New Code ▲ Revised Code Maternity Age Unlisted Not Covered # Resequenced
CCI + Add-on ⊘ Mod 51 Exempt Mod 63 Exempt ⊙ Mod Sedation PQRI

3066F	Documentation of treatment for nephropathy (eg, patient receiving dialysis, patient being treated for ESRD, CRF, ARF, or renal insufficiency, any visit to a nephrologist) (DM) — 0.00 / 0.00 Global Days XXX
3072F	Low risk for retinopathy (no evidence of retinopathy in the prior year) (DM) — 0.00 / 0.00 Global Days XXX — AMA: 2008, Mar, 8-12
▲ 3073F	Pre-surgical (cataract) axial length, corneal power measurement and method of intraocular lens power calculation documented within 12 months prior to surgery (EC) — 0.00 / 0.00 Global Days XXX — AMA: 2008, Mar, 8-12
3074F	Most recent systolic blood pressure less than 130 mm Hg (DM) (HTN, CKD) — 0.00 / 0.00 Global Days XXX — AMA: 2008, Mar, 8-12
▲ 3075F	Most recent systolic blood pressure 130-139 mm Hg (DM) (HTN, CKD) — 0.00 / 0.00 Global Days XXX — AMA: 2008, Mar, 8-12
▲ 3077F	Most recent systolic blood pressure greater than or equal to 140 mm Hg (HTN, CKD) (DM) — 0.00 / 0.00 Global Days XXX — AMA: 2008, Mar, 8-12
3078F	Most recent diastolic blood pressure less than 80 mm Hg (HTN, CKD) (DM) — 0.00 / 0.00 Global Days XXX — AMA: 2008, Mar, 8-12
3079F	Most recent diastolic blood pressure 80-89 mm Hg (HTN, CKD) (DM) — 0.00 / 0.00 Global Days XXX — AMA: 2008, Mar, 8-12
▲ 3080F	Most recent diastolic blood pressure greater than or equal to 90 mm Hg (HTN, CKD) (DM) — 0.00 / 0.00 Global Days XXX — AMA: 2008, Mar, 8-12
3082F	Kt/V less than 1.2 (Clearance of urea [Kt]/volume [V]) (ESRD, P-ESRD) — 0.00 / 0.00 Global Days XXX — AMA: 2008, Mar, 8-12
3083F	Kt/V equal to or greater than 1.2 and less than 1.7 (Clearance of urea [Kt]/volume [V]) (ESRD, P-ESRD) — 0.00 / 0.00 Global Days XXX — AMA: 2008, Mar, 8-12
3084F	Kt/V greater than or equal to 1.7 (Clearance of urea [Kt]/volume [V]) (ESRD, P-ESRD) — 0.00 / 0.00 Global Days XXX — AMA: 2008, Mar, 8-12
▲ 3085F	Suicide risk assessed (MDD, MDD ADOL) — 0.00 / 0.00 Global Days XXX
3088F	Major depressive disorder, mild (MDD) — 0.00 / 0.00 Global Days XXX
3089F	Major depressive disorder, moderate (MDD) — 0.00 / 0.00 Global Days XXX
3090F	Major depressive disorder, severe without psychotic features (MDD) — 0.00 / 0.00 Global Days XXX
3091F	Major depressive disorder, severe with psychotic features (MDD) — 0.00 / 0.00 Global Days XXX
3092F	Major depressive disorder, in remission (MDD) — 0.00 / 0.00 Global Days XXX
3093F	Documentation of new diagnosis of initial or recurrent episode of major depressive disorder (MDD) — 0.00 / 0.00 Global Days XXX — AMA: 2008, Mar, 8-12
▲ 3095F	Central dual-energy X-ray absorptiometry (DXA) results documented (OP) — 0.00 / 0.00 Global Days XXX
3096F	Central dual-energy X-ray absorptiometry (DXA) ordered (OP)
3100F	Carotid imaging study report (includes direct or indirect reference to measurements of distal internal carotid diameter as the denominator for stenosis measurement) (STR, RAD) — 0.00 / 0.00 Global Days XXX — AMA: 2008, Mar, 8-12
▲ 3110F	Documentation in final CT or MRI report of presence or absence of hemorrhage and mass lesion and acute infarction (STR) — 0.00 / 0.00 Global Days XXX
▲ 3111F	CT or MRI of the brain performed in the hospital within 24 hours of arrival OR performed in an outpatient imaging center, to confirm initial diagnosis of stroke, TIA or hemorrhage (STR) — 0.00 / 0.00 Global Days XXX
▲ 3112F	CT or MRI of the brain performed greater than 24 hours after arrival to the hospital OR performed in an outpatient imaging center for purpose other than confirmation of initial diagnosis of stroke, TIA, or hemorrhage (STR) — 0.00 / 0.00 Global Days XXX
3120F	12-Lead ECG Performed (EM) — 0.00 / 0.00 Global Days XXX
3130F	Upper gastrointestinal endoscopy performed (GERD) — 0.00 / 0.00 Global Days XXX
3132F	Documentation of referral for upper gastrointestinal endoscopy (GERD) — 0.00 / 0.00 Global Days XXX
3140F	Upper gastrointestinal endoscopy report indicates suspicion of Barrett's esophagus (GERD) — 0.00 / 0.00 Global Days XXX
3141F	Upper gastrointestinal endoscopy report indicates no suspicion of Barrett's esophagus (GERD) — 0.00 / 0.00 Global Days XXX
3142F	Barium swallow test ordered (GERD) — 0.00 / 0.00 Global Days XXX
3150F	Forceps esophageal biopsy performed (GERD) — 0.00 / 0.00 Global Days XXX
3155F	Cytogenetic testing performed on bone marrow at time of diagnosis or prior to initiating treatment (HEM) — 0.00 / 0.00 Global Days XXX — AMA: 2008, Mar, 8-12
3160F	Documentation of iron stores prior to initiating erythropoietin therapy (HEM) — 0.00 / 0.00 Global Days XXX — AMA: 2008, Mar, 8-12
3170F	Flow cytometry studies performed at time of diagnosis or prior to initiating treatment (HEM) — 0.00 / 0.00 Global Days XXX — AMA: 2008, Mar, 8-12
3200F	Barium swallow test not ordered (GERD) — 0.00 / 0.00 Global Days XXX

CPT only © 2009 American Medical Association. All Rights Reserved. (Black Ink) Medicare (Red Ink) © 2009 Publisher (Blue Ink)

Current Procedural Coding Expert – Category II Codes

3210F Group A Strep Test Performed (PHAR) [M][PQ]
 0.00 0.00 Global Days XXX
 AMA: 2008, Mar, 8-12

3215F Patient has documented immunity to Hepatitis A (HEP-C) [M][PQ]
 0.00 0.00 Global Days XXX
 AMA: 2008, Mar, 8-12

3216F Patient has documented immunity to Hepatitis B (HEP-C) [M][PQ]
 0.00 0.00 Global Days XXX
 AMA: 2008, Mar, 8-12

3218F RNA testing for Hepatitis C documented as performed within 6 months prior to initiation of antiviral treatment for Hepatitis C (HEP-C) [M][PQ]
 0.00 0.00 Global Days XXX
 AMA: 2008, Mar, 8-12

3220F Hepatitis C quantitative RNA testing documented as performed at 12 weeks from initiation of antiviral treatment (HEP-C) [M][PQ]
 0.00 0.00 Global Days XXX
 AMA: 2008, Mar, 8-12

3230F Documentation that hearing test was performed within 6 months prior to tympanostomy tube insertion (OME) [M][PQ]
 0.00 0.00 Global Days XXX
 AMA: 2008, Mar, 8-12

▲ **3250F** Specimen site other than anatomic location of primary tumor (PATH) [M][PQ]
 0.00 0.00 Global Days XXX
 AMA: 2008, Mar, 8-12

3260F pT category (primary tumor), pN category (regional lymph nodes), and histologic grade documented in pathology report (PATH) [M][PQ]
 0.00 0.00 Global Days XXX
 AMA: 2008, Mar, 8-12

3265F Ribonucleic acid (RNA) testing for Hepatitis C viremia ordered or results documented (HEP C) [M][PQ]
 0.00 0.00 Global Days XXX
 AMA: 2008, Mar, 8-12

3266F Hepatitis C genotype testing documented as performed prior to initiation of antiviral treatment for Hepatitis C (HEP C) [M][PQ]
 0.00 0.00 Global Days XXX
 AMA: 2008, Mar, 8-12

3268F Prostate-specific antigen (PSA), AND primary tumor (T) stage, AND Gleason score documented prior to initiation of treatment (PRCA) [M]
 0.00 0.00 Global Days XXX
 AMA: 2008, Mar, 8-12

3269F Bone scan performed prior to initiation of treatment or at any time since diagnosis of prostate cancer (PRCA) [M][PQ]
 0.00 0.00 Global Days XXX
 AMA: 2008, Mar, 8-12

3270F Bone scan not performed prior to initiation of treatment nor at any time since diagnosis of prostate cancer (PRCA) [M][PQ]
 0.00 0.00 Global Days XXX
 AMA: 2008, Mar, 8-12

3271F Low risk of recurrence, prostate cancer (PRCA) [M][PQ]
 0.00 0.00 Global Days XXX
 AMA: 2008, Mar, 8-12

3272F Intermediate risk of recurrence, prostate cancer (PRCA) [M][PQ]
 0.00 0.00 Global Days XXX
 AMA: 2008, Mar, 8-12

3273F High risk of recurrence, prostate cancer (PRCA) [M][PQ]
 0.00 0.00 Global Days XXX
 AMA: 2008, Mar, 8-12

3274F Prostate cancer risk of recurrence not determined or neither low, intermediate nor high (PRCA) ♂ [M][PQ]
 0.00 0.00 Global Days XXX
 AMA: 2008, Mar, 8-12

3278F Serum levels of calcium, phosphorus, intact Parathyroid Hormone (PTH) and lipid profile ordered (CKD) [M][PQ]
 0.00 0.00 Global Days XXX
 AMA: 2008, Mar, 8-12

3279F Hemoglobin level greater than or equal to 13 g/dL (CKD, ESRD) [M][PQ]
 0.00 0.00 Global Days XXX
 AMA: 2008, Mar, 8-12

3280F Hemoglobin level 11 g/dL to 12.9 g/dL (CKD, ESRD) [M][PQ]
 0.00 0.00 Global Days XXX
 AMA: 2008, Mar, 8-12

3281F Hemoglobin level less than 11 g/dL (CKD, ESRD) [M][PQ]
 0.00 0.00 Global Days XXX
 AMA: 2008, Mar, 8-12

3284F Intraocular pressure (IOP) reduced by a value of greater than or equal to 15% from the pre-intervention level (EC) [M][PQ]
 0.00 0.00 Global Days XXX
 AMA: 2008, Mar, 8-12

3285F Intraocular pressure (IOP) reduced by a value less than 15% from the pre-intervention level (EC) [M][PQ]
 0.00 0.00 Global Days XXX
 AMA: 2008, Mar, 8-12

3288F Falls risk assessment documented (GER) [M][PQ]
 0.00 0.00 Global Days XXX
 AMA: 2008, Mar, 8-12

3290F Patient is D (Rh) negative and unsensitized (Pre-Cr) [M]
 0.00 0.00 Global Days XXX
 AMA: 2008, Mar, 8-12

3291F Patient is D (Rh) positive or sensitized (Pre-Cr) [M]
 0.00 0.00 Global Days XXX
 AMA: 2008, Mar, 8-12

3292F HIV testing ordered or documented and reviewed during the first or second prenatal visit (Pre-Cr) [M]
 0.00 0.00 Global Days XXX

● **3293F** ABO and Rh blood typing documented as performed (Pre-Cr) [E]
 0.00 0.00 Global Days XXX

● **3294F** Group B Streptococcus (GBS) screening documented as performed during week 35-37 gestation (Pre-Cr) [E]
 0.00 0.00 Global Days XXX

3300F American Joint Committee on Cancer (AJCC) stage documented and reviewed (ONC) [M]
 0.00 0.00 Global Days XXX
 AMA: 2008, Mar, 8-12

3301F Cancer stage documented in medical record as metastatic and reviewed (ONC) [M]
 0.00 0.00 Global Days XXX
 AMA: 2008, Mar, 8-12

3315F Estrogen receptor (ER) or progesterone receptor (PR) positive breast cancer (ONC) [M][PQ]
 0.00 0.00 Global Days XXX
 AMA: 2008, Mar, 8-12

3316F Estrogen receptor (ER) and progesterone receptor (PR) negative breast cancer (ONC) [M][PQ]
 0.00 0.00 Global Days XXX
 AMA: 2008, Mar, 8-12

● New Code ▲ Revised Code [M] Maternity [A] Age Unlisted Not Covered # Resequenced
 CCI + Add-on ⊘ Mod 51 Exempt ⊛ Mod 63 Exempt ⊙ Mod Sedation [PQ] PQRI
© 2009 Publisher *(Blue Ink)*   CPT only © 2009 American Medical Association. All Rights Reserved. *(Black Ink)*   Medicare *(Red Ink)*

3317F	Pathology report confirming malignancy documented in the medical record and reviewed prior to the initiation of chemotherapy (ONC) [M] 0.00 0.00 Global Days XXX AMA: 2008, Mar, 8-12
3318F	Pathology report confirming malignancy documented in the medical record and reviewed prior to the initiation of radiation therapy (ONC) [M] 0.00 0.00 Global Days XXX AMA: 2008, Mar, 8-12
▲ 3319F	1 of the following diagnostic imaging studies ordered: chest x-ray, CT, ultrasound, MRI, PET, or nuclear medicine scans (ML) [M] 0.00 0.00 Global Days XXX AMA: 2008, Mar, 8-12
3320F	None of the following diagnostic imaging studies ordered: chest X-ray, CT, Ultrasound, MRI, PET, or nuclear medicine scans (ML) [M] 0.00 0.00 Global Days XXX AMA: 2008, Mar, 8-12
▲ 3321F	AJCC cancer Stage 0 or IA melanoma, documented (ML) [E] 0.00 0.00 Global Days XXX
3322F	Melanoma greater than AJCC Stage 0 or IA (ML) [E] 0.00 0.00 Global Days XXX
● 3323F	Clinical tumor, node and metastases (TNM) staging documented and reviewed prior to surgery (Lung/Esop Cx) [M] 0.00 0.00 Global Days XXX
● 3324F	MRI or CT scan ordered, reviewed or requested (EPI) [E] 0.00 0.00 Global Days XXX
3325F	Preoperative assessment of functional or medical indication(s) for surgery prior to the cataract surgery with intraocular lens placement (must be performed within 12 months prior to cataract surgery) (EC) [M] 0.00 0.00 Global Days XXX AMA: 2008, Mar, 8-12
● 3328F	Performance status documented and reviewed within 2 weeks prior to surgery (Lung/Esop Cx) [E] 0.00 0.00 Global Days XXX
3330F	Imaging study ordered (BkP) [M] 0.00 0.00 Global Days XXX AMA: 2008, Mar, 8-12
3331F	Imaging study not ordered (BkP) [M] 0.00 0.00 Global Days XXX AMA: 2008, Mar, 8-12
3340F	Mammogram assessment category of "incomplete: need additional imaging evaluation", documented (RAD) ♀ [M] [P0] 0.00 0.00 Global Days XXX AMA: 2008, Mar, 8-12
3341F	Mammogram assessment category of "negative", documented (RAD) ♀ [M] [P0] 0.00 0.00 Global Days XXX AMA: 2008, Mar, 8-12
3342F	Mammogram assessment category of "benign", documented (RAD) ♀ [M] [P0] 0.00 0.00 Global Days XXX AMA: 2008, Mar, 8-12
3343F	Mammogram assessment category of "probably benign", documented (RAD) ♀ [M] [P0] 0.00 0.00 Global Days XXX AMA: 2008, Mar, 8-12
3344F	Mammogram assessment category of "suspicious", documented (RAD) ♀ [M] [P0] 0.00 0.00 Global Days XXX AMA: 2008, Mar, 8-12
3345F	Mammogram assessment category of "highly suggestive of malignancy", documented (RAD) ♀ [M] [P0] 0.00 0.00 Global Days XXX AMA: 2008, Mar, 8-12
3350F	Mammogram assessment category of "known biopsy proven malignancy", documented (RAD) ♀ [M] [P0] 0.00 0.00 Global Days XXX AMA: 2008, Mar, 8-12
3351F	Negative screen for depressive symptoms as categorized by using a standardized depression screening/assessment tool (MDD) [E] 0.00 0.00 Global Days XXX
3352F	No significant depressive symptoms as categorized by using a standardized depression assessment tool (MDD) [E] 0.00 0.00 Global Days XXX
3353F	Mild to moderate depressive symptoms as categorized by using a standardized depression screening/assessment tool (MDD) [E] 0.00 0.00 Global Days XXX
3354F	Clinically significant depressive symptoms as categorized by using a standardized depression screening/assessment tool (MDD) [E] 0.00 0.00 Global Days XXX
3370F	AJCC Breast Cancer Stage 0, documented (ONC) [M] [P0] 0.00 0.00 Global Days XXX
3372F	AJCC Breast Cancer Stage I: T1mic, T1a or T1b (tumor size <= 1 cm), documented (ONC) [M] [P0] 0.00 0.00 Global Days XXX
3374F	AJCC Breast Cancer Stage I: T1c (tumor size > 1 cm to 2 cm), documented (ONC) [M] [P0] 0.00 0.00 Global Days XXX
3376F	AJCC Breast Cancer Stage II, documented (ONC) [M] [P0] 0.00 0.00 Global Days XXX
3378F	AJCC Breast Cancer Stage III, documented (ONC) [M] [P0] 0.00 0.00 Global Days XXX
3380F	AJCC Breast Cancer Stage IV, documented (ONC) [M] [P0] 0.00 0.00 Global Days XXX
3382F	AJCC colon cancer, Stage 0, documented (ONC) [M] [P0] 0.00 0.00 Global Days XXX
3384F	AJCC colon cancer, Stage I, documented (ONC) [M] [P0] 0.00 0.00 Global Days XXX
3386F	AJCC colon cancer, Stage II, documented (ONC) [M] [P0] 0.00 0.00 Global Days XXX
3388F	AJCC colon cancer, Stage III, documented (ONC) [M] [P0] 0.00 0.00 Global Days XXX
3390F	AJCC colon cancer, Stage IV, documented (ONC) [M] [P0] 0.00 0.00 Global Days XXX
● 3450F	Dyspnea screened, no dyspnea or mild dyspnea (Pall Cr) [E] 0.00 0.00 Global Days XXX
● 3451F	Dyspnea screened, moderate or severe dyspnea (Pall Cr) [E] 0.00 0.00 Global Days XXX
● 3452F	Dyspnea not screened (Pall Cr) [E] 0.00 0.00 Global Days XXX

Current Procedural Coding Expert – Category II Codes

- **3455F** TB screening performed and results interpreted within six months prior to initiation of first-time biologic disease modifying anti-rheumatic drug therapy for RA (RA) [M][PQ]
  0.00 0.00 Global Days XXX

- **3470F** Rheumatoid arthritis (RA) disease activity, low (RA) [M][PQ]
  0.00 0.00 Global Days XXX

- **3471F** Rheumatoid arthritis (RA) disease activity, moderate (RA) [M][PQ]
  0.00 0.00 Global Days XXX

- **3472F** Rheumatoid arthritis (RA) disease activity, high (RA) [M][PQ]
  0.00 0.00 Global Days XXX

- **3475F** Disease prognosis for rheumatoid arthritis assessed, poor prognosis documented (RA) [M][PQ]
  0.00 0.00 Global Days XXX

- **3476F** Disease prognosis for rheumatoid arthritis assessed, good prognosis documented (RA) [M][PQ]
  0.00 0.00 Global Days XXX

- **3490F** History of AIDS-defining condition (HIV) [M]
  0.00 0.00 Global Days XXX

- **3491F** HIV indeterminate (infants of undetermined HIV status born of HIV-infected mothers) (HIV) [E]
  0.00 0.00 Global Days XXX

- **3492F** History of nadir CD4+ cell count <350 cells/mm3 (HIV) [M]
  0.00 0.00 Global Days XXX

- **3493F** No history of nadir CD4+ cell count <350 cells/mm3 AND no history of AIDS-defining condition (HIV) [M]
  0.00 0.00 Global Days XXX

- **3494F** CD4+ cell count <200 cells/mm3 (HIV) [M]
  0.00 0.00 Global Days XXX

- **3495F** CD4+ cell count 200 - 499 cells/mm3 (HIV) [M]
  0.00 0.00 Global Days XXX

- **3496F** CD4+ cell count >=500 cells/mm3 (HIV) [M]
  0.00 0.00 Global Days XXX

- **3497F** CD4+ cell percentage <15% (HIV) [E]
  0.00 0.00 Global Days XXX

- **3498F** CD4+ cell percentage >=15% (HIV) [E]
  0.00 0.00 Global Days XXX

3500F CD4+ cell count or CD4+ cell percentage documented as performed (HIV) [M]
0.00 0.00 Global Days XXX

3502F HIV RNA viral load below limits of quantification (HIV) [M]
0.00 0.00 Global Days XXX

3503F HIV RNA viral load not below limits of quantification (HIV) [M]
0.00 0.00 Global Days XXX

3510F Documentation that tuberculosis (TB) screening test performed and results interpreted (HIV) [E]
0.00 0.00 Global Days XXX

3511F Chlamydia and gonorrhea screenings documented as performed (HIV) [M]
0.00 0.00 Global Days XXX

3512F Syphilis screening documented as performed (HIV) [M]
0.00 0.00 Global Days XXX

3513F Hepatitis B screening documented as performed (HIV) [E]
0.00 0.00 Global Days XXX

3514F Hepatitis C screening documented as performed (HIV) [E]
0.00 0.00 Global Days XXX

3515F Patient has documented immunity to Hepatitis C (HIV) [E]
0.00 0.00 Global Days XXX

3550F Low risk for thromboembolism (AFIB) [E]
0.00 0.00 Global Days XXX

3551F Intermediate risk for thromboembolism (AFIB) [E]
0.00 0.00 Global Days XXX

3552F High risk for thromboembolism (AFIB) [E]
0.00 0.00 Global Days XXX

3555F Patient had International Normalized Ratio (INR) measurement performed (AFIB) [E]
0.00 0.00 Global Days XXX

3570F Final report for bone scintigraphy study includes correlation with existing relevant imaging studies (eg, x-ray, MRI, CT) corresponding to the same anatomical region in question (NUC_MED) [M][PQ]
0.00 0.00 Global Days XXX

3572F Patient considered to be potentially at risk for fracture in a weight-bearing site (NUC_MED) [E]
0.00 0.00 Global Days XXX

3573F Patient not considered to be potentially at risk for fracture in a weight-bearing site (NUC_MED) [E]
0.00 0.00 Global Days XXX

- **3650F** Electroencephalogram (EEG) ordered, reviewed or requested (EPI) [E]
  0.00 0.00 Global Days XXX

4000F-4340F Therapies Provided (Includes Preventive Services)

INCLUDES Behavioral/pharmacologic/procedural therapies
Preventive services including patient education/counseling

4000F Tobacco use cessation intervention, counseling (COPD, CAP, CAD) (DM) (PV) [M][PQ]
0.00 0.00 Global Days XXX
AMA: 2008, Mar, 8-12; 2005, October, 1-5

4001F Tobacco use cessation intervention, pharmacologic therapy (COPD, CAD, CAP, PV) (DM)(PV) [M][PQ]
0.00 0.00 Global Days XXX
AMA: 2008, Mar, 8-12

4002F Statin therapy, prescribed (CAD) [M]
0.00 0.00 Global Days XXX

4003F Patient education, written/oral, appropriate for patients with heart failure, performed (HF) [M]
0.00 0.00 Global Days XXX

- **4004F** Patient screened for tobacco use AND received tobacco cessation counseling, if identified as a tobacco user (PV) [E]
  0.00 0.00 Global Days XXX

4005F Pharmacologic therapy (other than minerals/vitamins) for osteoporosis prescribed (OP) [M][PQ]
0.00 0.00 Global Days XXX

▲ **4006F** Beta-blocker therapy prescribed (CAD, HF) [M]
0.00 0.00 Global Days XXX

4009F Angiotensin converting enzyme (ACE) inhibitor or angiotensin receptor blocker (ARB) therapy prescribed (HF, CAD, CKD), (DM) [M][PQ]
0.00 0.00 Global Days XXX
AMA: 2008, Mar, 8-12

4011F Oral antiplatelet therapy prescribed (CAD) [M][PQ]
0.00 0.00 Global Days XXX

4012F Warfarin therapy prescribed (HF) [M]
0.00 0.00 Global Days XXX

● New Code ▲ Revised Code [M] Maternity [A] Age Unlisted Not Covered # Resequenced
[CCI] CCI + Add-on ⊘ Mod 51 Exempt Mod 63 Exempt ⊙ Mod Sedation [PQ] PQRI

© 2009 Publisher *(Blue Ink)* CPT only © 2009 American Medical Association. All Rights Reserved. *(Black Ink)* Medicare *(Red Ink)*

Category II Codes

4014F Written discharge instructions provided to heart failure patients discharged home (Instructions include all of the following components: activity level, diet, discharge medications, follow-up appointment, weight monitoring, what to do if symptoms worsen) (HF) (Excludes patients less than 18 years of age)
EXCLUDES   Patients younger than 18 years of age
0.00   0.00   Global Days XXX

4015F Persistent asthma, preferred long term control medication or an acceptable alternative treatment, prescribed (Asthma) (Note: There are no medical exclusion criteria)
Code also modifier 2P for patient reasons for not prescribing
Do not report with with modifier 1P
0.00   0.00   Global Days XXX

4016F Anti-inflammatory/analgesic agent prescribed (OA) (Use for prescribed or continued medication[s], including over-the-counter medication[s])
INCLUDES   Over-the-counter medication(s)
Prescribed/continued medication(s)
0.00   0.00   Global Days XXX

4017F Gastrointestinal prophylaxis for NSAID use prescribed (OA)
0.00   0.00   Global Days XXX

4018F Therapeutic exercise for the involved joint(s) instructed or physical or occupational therapy prescribed (OA)
0.00   0.00   Global Days XXX

4019F Documentation of receipt of counseling on exercise AND either both calcium and vitamin D use or counseling regarding both calcium and vitamin D use (OP)
0.00   0.00   Global Days XXX

4025F Inhaled bronchodilator prescribed (COPD)
0.00   0.00   Global Days XXX

4030F Long-term oxygen therapy prescribed (more than 15 hours per day) (COPD)
0.00   0.00   Global Days XXX

4033F Pulmonary rehabilitation exercise training recommended (COPD)
Code also dyspnea assessed, present (1019F)
0.00   0.00   Global Days XXX

4035F Influenza immunization recommended (COPD)
0.00   0.00   Global Days XXX
AMA: 2008, Mar, 8-12

4037F Influenza immunization ordered or administered (COPD, PV, CKD, ESRD)
0.00   0.00   Global Days XXX
AMA: 2008, Mar, 8-12

4040F Pneumococcal vaccine administered or previously received (COPD), (PV)
0.00   0.00   Global Days XXX
AMA: 2008, Mar, 8-12

4041F Documentation of order for cefazolin OR cefuroxime for antimicrobial prophylaxis (PERI 2)
0.00   0.00   Global Days XXX

4042F Documentation that prophylactic antibiotics were neither given within 4 hours prior to surgical incision nor given intraoperatively (PERI 2)
0.00   0.00   Global Days XXX

4043F Documentation that an order was given to discontinue prophylactic antibiotics within 48 hours of surgical end time, cardiac procedures (PERI 2)
0.00   0.00   Global Days XXX

4044F Documentation that an order was given for venous thromboembolism (VTE) prophylaxis to be given within 24 hrs prior to incision time or 24 hours after surgery end time (PERI 2)
0.00   0.00   Global Days XXX

4045F Appropriate empiric antibiotic prescribed (CAP), (EM)

4046F Documentation that prophylactic antibiotics were given within 4 hours prior to surgical incision or given intraoperatively (PERI 2)
0.00   0.00   Global Days XXX

▲ **4047F** Documentation of order for prophylactic parenteral antibiotics to be given within 1 hour (if fluoroquinolone or vancomycin, 2 hours) prior to surgical incision (or start of procedure when no incision is required) (PERI 2)
0.00   0.00   Global Days XXX

▲ **4048F** Documentation that administration of prophylactic parenteral antibiotic was initiated within 1 hour (if fluoroquinolone or vancomycin, 2 hours) prior to surgical incision (or start of procedure when no incision is required), as ordered (PERI 2)
0.00   0.00   Global Days XXX

4049F Documentation that order was given to discontinue prophylactic antibiotics within 24 hours of surgical end time, non-cardiac procedure (PERI 2)
0.00   0.00   Global Days XXX

4050F Hypertension plan of care documented as appropriate (HTN)
0.00   0.00   Global Days XXX

4051F Referred for an arteriovenous (AV) fistula (ESRD, CKD)
0.00   0.00   Global Days XXX
AMA: 2008, Mar, 8-12

4052F Hemodialysis via functioning arteriovenous (AV) fistula (ESRD)
0.00   0.00   Global Days XXX
AMA: 2008, Mar, 8-12

4053F Hemodialysis via functioning arteriovenous (AV) graft (ESRD)
0.00   0.00   Global Days XXX
AMA: 2008, Mar, 8-12

4054F Hemodialysis via catheter (ESRD)
0.00   0.00   Global Days XXX
AMA: 2008, Mar, 8-12

4055F Patient receiving peritoneal dialysis (ESRD)
0.00   0.00   Global Days XXX
AMA: 2008, Mar, 8-12

4056F Appropriate oral rehydration solution recommended (PAG)
0.00   0.00   Global Days XXX

4058F Pediatric gastroenteritis education provided to caregiver (PAG)
0.00   0.00   Global Days XXX

▲ **4060F** Psychotherapy services provided (MDD, MDD ADOL)
0.00   0.00   Global Days XXX

4062F Patient referral for psychotherapy documented (MDD)
0.00   0.00   Global Days XXX

● **4063F** Antidepressant pharmacotherapy considered and not prescribed (MDD ADOL)
0.00   0.00   Global Days XXX

Current Procedural Coding Expert – Category II Codes

▲ **4064F** Antidepressant pharmacotherapy prescribed (MDD, MDD ADOL) [M]
0.00 0.00 Global Days XXX

4065F Antipsychotic pharmacotherapy prescribed (MDD) [M]
0.00 0.00 Global Days XXX

4066F Electroconvulsive therapy (ECT) provided (MDD) [M]
0.00 0.00 Global Days XXX

4067F Patient referral for electroconvulsive therapy (ECT) documented (MDD) [M]
0.00 0.00 Global Days XXX

4070F Deep vein thrombosis (DVT) prophylaxis received by end of hospital day 2 (STR) [M][PQ]
0.00 0.00 Global Days XXX

4073F Oral antiplatelet therapy prescribed at discharge (STR) [M][PQ]
0.00 0.00 Global Days XXX

4075F Anticoagulant therapy prescribed at discharge (STR) [M]
0.00 0.00 Global Days XXX

4077F Documentation that tissue plasminogen activator (t-PA) administration was considered (STR) [M][PQ]
0.00 0.00 Global Days XXX

4079F Documentation that rehabilitation services were considered (STR) [M][PQ]
0.00 0.00 Global Days XXX

4084F Aspirin received within 24 hours before emergency department arrival or during emergency department stay (EM) [M][PQ]
0.00 0.00 Global Days XXX

4090F Patient receiving erythropoietin therapy (HEM) [M][PQ]
0.00 0.00 Global Days XXX
AMA: 2008, Mar, 8-12

4095F Patient not receiving erythropoietin therapy (HEM) [M][PQ]
0.00 0.00 Global Days XXX
AMA: 2008, Mar, 8-12

4100F Bisphosphonate therapy, intravenous, ordered or received (HEM) [M][PQ]
0.00 0.00 Global Days XXX
AMA: 2008, Mar, 8-12

4110F Internal mammary artery graft performed for primary, isolated coronary artery bypass graft procedure (CABG) [M][PQ]
0.00 0.00 Global Days XXX

4115F Beta blocker administered within 24 hours prior to surgical incision (CABG) [M][PQ]
0.00 0.00 Global Days XXX

4120F Antibiotic prescribed or dispensed (URI, PHAR), (A-BRONCH) [M][PQ]
0.00 0.00 Global Days XXX
AMA: 2008, Mar, 8-12

▲ **4124F** Antibiotic neither prescribed nor dispensed (URI, PHAR), (A-BRONCH) [M][PQ]
0.00 0.00 Global Days XXX
AMA: 2008, Mar, 8-12

4130F Topical preparations (including OTC) prescribed for acute otitis externa (AOE) [M][PQ]
0.00 0.00 Global Days XXX
AMA: 2008, Mar, 8-12

4131F Systemic antimicrobial therapy prescribed (AOE) [M][PQ]
0.00 0.00 Global Days XXX
AMA: 2008, Mar, 8-12

4132F Systemic antimicrobial therapy not prescribed (AOE) [M][PQ]
0.00 0.00 Global Days XXX
AMA: 2008, Mar, 8-12

4133F Antihistamines or decongestants prescribed or recommended (OME) [M]
0.00 0.00 Global Days XXX
AMA: 2008, Mar, 8-12

4134F Antihistamines or decongestants neither prescribed nor recommended (OME) [M]
0.00 0.00 Global Days XXX
AMA: 2008, Mar, 8-12

4135F Systemic corticosteroids prescribed (OME) [M]
0.00 0.00 Global Days XXX
AMA: 2008, Mar, 8-12

4136F Systemic corticosteroids not prescribed (OME) [M]
0.00 0.00 Global Days XXX
AMA: 2008, Mar, 8-12

4148F Hepatitis A vaccine injection administered or previously received (HEP-C) [M][PQ]
0.00 0.00 Global Days XXX

4149F Hepatitis B vaccine injection administered or previously received (HEP-C) [M][PQ]
0.00 0.00 Global Days XXX

4150F Patient receiving antiviral treatment for Hepatitis C (HEP-C) [M][PQ]
0.00 0.00 Global Days XXX

4151F Patient not receiving antiviral treatment for Hepatitis C (HEP-C) [M][PQ]
0.00 0.00 Global Days XXX
AMA: 2008, Mar, 8-12

4153F Combination peginterferon and ribavirin therapy prescribed (HEP-C) [M][PQ]
0.00 0.00 Global Days XXX
AMA: 2008, Mar, 8-12

4155F Hepatitis A vaccine series previously received (HEP-C) [M]
0.00 0.00 Global Days XXX
AMA: 2008, Mar, 8-12

4157F Hepatitis B vaccine series previously received (HEP-C) [M]
0.00 0.00 Global Days XXX
AMA: 2008, Mar, 8-12

4158F Patient counseled about risks of alcohol use (HEP-C) [M][PQ]
0.00 0.00 Global Days XXX
AMA: 2008, Mar, 8-12

4159F Counseling regarding contraception received prior to initiation of antiviral treatment (HEP-C) [M][PQ]
0.00 0.00 Global Days XXX
AMA: 2008, Mar, 8-12

4163F Patient counseling at a minimum on all of the following treatment options for clinically localized prostate cancer: active surveillance, AND interstitial prostate brachytherapy, AND external beam radiotherapy, AND radical prostatectomy, provided prior to initiation of treatment (PRCA) [M]
0.00 0.00 Global Days XXX
AMA: 2008, Mar, 8-12

4164F Adjuvant (ie, in combination with external beam radiotherapy to the prostate for prostate cancer) hormonal therapy (gonadotropin-releasing hormone [GnRH] agonist or antagonist) prescribed/administered (PRCA) [M][PQ]
0.00 0.00 Global Days XXX
AMA: 2008, Mar, 8-12

● New Code   ▲ Revised Code   [M] Maternity   Age   Unlisted   Not Covered   # Resequenced
CCI   + Add-on   ⊘ Mod 51 Exempt   Mod 63 Exempt   ⊙ Mod Sedation   [PQ] PQRI

© 2009 Publisher *(Blue Ink)*   CPT only © 2009 American Medical Association. All Rights Reserved. *(Black Ink)*   Medicare *(Red Ink)*

4165F	3-dimensional conformal radiotherapy (3D-CRT) or intensity modulated radiation therapy (IMRT) received (PRCA) 0.00 0.00 Global Days XXX AMA: 2008, Mar, 8-12
4167F	Head of bed elevation (30-45 degrees) on first ventilator day ordered (CRIT) 0.00 0.00 Global Days XXX AMA: 2008, Mar, 8-12
4168F	Patient receiving care in the intensive care unit (ICU) and receiving mechanical ventilation, 24 hours or less (CRIT) 0.00 0.00 Global Days XXX AMA: 2008, Mar, 8-12
4169F	Patient either not receiving care in the intensive care unit (ICU) OR not receiving mechanical ventilation OR receiving mechanical ventilation greater than 24 hours (CRIT) 0.00 0.00 Global Days XXX AMA: 2008, Mar, 8-12
4171F	Patient receiving erythropoiesis-stimulating agents (ESA) therapy (CKD) 0.00 0.00 Global Days XXX AMA: 2008, Mar, 8-12
4172F	Patient not receiving erythropoiesis-stimulating agents (ESA) therapy (CKD) 0.00 0.00 Global Days XXX AMA: 2008, Mar, 8-12
4174F	Counseling about the potential impact of glaucoma on visual functioning and quality of life, and importance of treatment adherence provided to patient and/or caregiver(s) (EC) 0.00 0.00 Global Days XXX AMA: 2008, Mar, 8-12
4175F	Best-corrected visual acuity of 20/40 or better (distance or near) achieved within the 90 days following cataract surgery (EC) 0.00 0.00 Global Days XXX AMA: 2008, Mar, 8-12
▲ 4176F	Counseling about value of protection from UV light and lack of proven efficacy of nutritional supplements in prevention or progression of cataract development provided to patient and/or caregiver(s) (NMA-No Measure Assoc.) 0.00 0.00 Global Days XXX
4177F	Counseling about the benefits and/or risks of the Age-Related Eye Disease Study (AREDS) formulation for preventing progression of age-related macular degeneration (AMD) provided to patient and/or caregiver(s) (EC) 0.00 0.00 Global Days XXX AMA: 2008, Mar, 8-12
4178F	Anti-D immune globulin received between 26 and 30 weeks gestation (Pre-Cr) 0.00 0.00 Global Days XXX AMA: 2008, Mar, 8-12
4179F	Tamoxifen or aromatase inhibitor (AI) prescribed (ONC) 0.00 0.00 Global Days XXX AMA: 2008, Mar, 8-12
4180F	Adjuvant chemotherapy referred, prescribed, or previously received for Stage III colon cancer (ONC) 0.00 0.00 Global Days XXX AMA: 2008, Mar, 8-12
4181F	Conformal radiation therapy received (NMA-No Measure Assoc.) 0.00 0.00 Global Days XXX
4182F	Conformal radiation therapy not received (NMA-No Measure Assoc.) 0.00 0.00 Global Days XXX
4185F	Continuous (12-months) therapy with proton pump inhibitor (PPI) or histamine H2 receptor antagonist (H2RA) received (GERD) 0.00 0.00 Global Days XXX AMA: 2008, Mar, 8-12
4186F	No continuous (12-months) therapy with either proton pump inhibitor (PPI) or histamine H2 receptor antagonist (H2RA) received (GERD) 0.00 0.00 Global Days XXX AMA: 2008, Mar, 8-12
4187F	Disease modifying anti-rheumatic drug therapy prescribed or dispensed (RA) 0.00 0.00 Global Days XXX AMA: 2008, Mar, 8-12
4188F	Appropriate angiotensin converting enzyme (ACE)/angiotensin receptor blockers (ARB) therapeutic monitoring test ordered or performed (AM) 0.00 0.00 Global Days XXX AMA: 2008, Mar, 8-12
4189F	Appropriate digoxin therapeutic monitoring test ordered or performed (AM) 0.00 0.00 Global Days XXX AMA: 2008, Mar, 8-12
4190F	Appropriate diuretic therapeutic monitoring test ordered or performed (AM) 0.00 0.00 Global Days XXX AMA: 2008, Mar, 8-12
4191F	Appropriate anticonvulsant therapeutic monitoring test ordered or performed (AM) 0.00 0.00 Global Days XXX AMA: 2008, Mar, 8-12
● 4192F	Patient not receiving glucocorticoid therapy (RA) 0.00 0.00 Global Days XXX
● 4193F	Patient receiving <10 mg daily prednisone (or equivalent), or RA activity is worsening, or glucocorticoid use is for less than 6 months (RA) 0.00 0.00 Global Days XXX
● 4194F	Patient receiving >= 10 mg daily prednisone (or equivalent) for longer than 6 months, and improvement or no change in disease activity (RA) 0.00 0.00 Global Days XXX
● 4195F	Patient receiving first-time biologic disease modifying anti-rheumatic drug therapy for rheumatoid arthritis (RA) 0.00 0.00 Global Days XXX
● 4196F	Patient not receiving first-time biologic disease modifying anti-rheumatic drug therapy for rheumatoid arthritis (RA) 0.00 0.00 Global Days XXX
4200F	External beam radiotherapy as primary therapy to the prostate with or without nodal irradiation (PRCA) 0.00 0.00 Global Days XXX AMA: 2008, Mar, 8-12
4201F	External beam radiotherapy with or without nodal irradiation as adjuvant or salvage therapy for prostate cancer patient (PRCA) 0.00 0.00 Global Days XXX AMA: 2008, Mar, 8-12

Current Procedural Coding Expert – Category II Codes

4210F Angiotensin converting enzyme (ACE) or angiotensin receptor blockers (ARB) medication therapy for 6 months or more (MM) [M]
 0.00 0.00 Global Days XXX
 AMA: 2008, Mar, 8-12

4220F Digoxin medication therapy for 6 months or more (MM) [M]
 0.00 0.00 Global Days XXX
 AMA: 2008, Mar, 8-12

4221F Diuretic medication therapy for 6 months or more (MM) [M]
 0.00 0.00 Global Days XXX
 AMA: 2008, Mar, 8-12

4230F Anticonvulsant medication therapy for 6 months or more (MM) [M]
 0.00 0.00 Global Days XXX
 AMA: 2008, Mar, 8-12

4240F Instruction in therapeutic exercise with follow-up by the physician provided to patients during episode of back pain lasting longer than 12 weeks (BkP) [M]
 0.00 0.00 Global Days XXX
 AMA: 2008, Mar, 8-12

4242F Counseling for supervised exercise program provided to patients during episode of back pain lasting longer than 12 weeks (BkP) [M]
 0.00 0.00 Global Days XXX
 AMA: 2008, Mar, 8-12

4245F Patient counseled during the initial visit to maintain or resume normal activities (BkP) [M][PQ]
 0.00 0.00 Global Days XXX
 AMA: 2008, Mar, 8-12

4248F Patient counseled during the initial visit for an episode of back pain against bed rest lasting 4 days or longer (BkP) [M][PQ]
 0.00 0.00 Global Days XXX
 AMA: 2008, Mar, 8-12

4250F Active warming used intraoperatively for the purpose of maintaining normothermia, OR at least 1 body temperature equal to or greater than 36 degrees Centigrade (or 96.8 degrees Fahrenheit) recorded within the 30 minutes immediately before or the 15 minutes immediately after anesthesia end time (CRIT) [M]
 0.00 0.00 Global Days XXX
 AMA: 2008, Mar, 8-12

● **4255F** Duration of general or neuraxial anesthesia 60 minutes or longer, as documented in the anesthesia record [M]
 0.00 0.00 Global Days XXX

● **4256F** Duration of general or neuraxial anesthesia less than 60 minutes, as documented in the anesthesia record [M]
 0.00 0.00 Global Days XXX

● **4260F** Wound surface culture technique used (CWC) [E]
 0.00 0.00 Global Days XXX

● **4261F** Technique other than surface culture of the wound exudate used (eg, Levine/deep swab technique, semi-quantitative or quantitative swab technique) OR wound surface culture technique not used (CWC) [E]
 0.00 0.00 Global Days XXX

● **4265F** Use of wet to dry dressings prescribed or recommended (CWC) [E]
 0.00 0.00 Global Days XXX

● **4266F** Use of wet to dry dressings neither prescribed nor recommended (CWC) [E]
 0.00 0.00 Global Days XXX

● **4267F** Compression therapy prescribed (CWC) [M][PQ]
 0.00 0.00 Global Days XXX

● **4268F** Patient education regarding the need for long term compression therapy including interval replacement of compression stockings, received (CWC) [E]
 0.00 0.00 Global Days XXX

● **4269F** Appropriate method of offloading (pressure relief) prescribed (CWC) [E]
 0.00 0.00 Global Days XXX

4270F Patient receiving potent antiretroviral therapy for 6 months or longer (HIV) [E]
 0.00 0.00 Global Days XXX

4271F Patient receiving potent antiretroviral therapy for less than 6 months or not receiving potent antiretroviral therapy (HIV) [M]
 0.00 0.00 Global Days XXX

4274F Influenza immunization administered or previously received (HIV) (P-ESRD) [M][PQ]
 0.00 0.00 Global Days XXX

4275F Hepatitis B vaccine injection administered or previously received (HIV) [E]
 0.00 0.00 Global Days XXX

● **4276F** Potent antiretroviral therapy prescribed (HIV) [M]
 0.00 0.00 Global Days XXX

● **4279F** Pneumocystis jiroveci pneumonia prophylaxis prescribed (HIV) [E]
 0.00 0.00 Global Days XXX

● **4280F** Pneumocystis jiroveci pneumonia prophylaxis prescribed within 3 months of low CD4+ cell count or percentage (HIV) [E]
 0.00 0.00 Global Days XXX

4290F Patient screened for injection drug use (HIV) [M]
 0.00 0.00 Global Days XXX

4293F Patient screened for high-risk sexual behavior (HIV) [M]
 0.00 0.00 Global Days XXX

4300F Patient receiving warfarin therapy for nonvalvular atrial fibrillation or atrial flutter (AFIB) [E]
 0.00 0.00 Global Days XXX

4301F Patient not receiving warfarin therapy for nonvalvular atrial fibrillation or atrial flutter (AFIB) [E]
 0.00 0.00 Global Days XXX

● **4305F** Patient education regarding appropriate foot care AND daily inspection of the feet received (CWC) [E]
 0.00 0.00 Global Days XXX

● **4306F** Patient counseled regarding psychosocial AND pharmacologic treatment options for opioid addiction (SUD) [E]
 0.00 0.00 Global Days XXX

4320F Patient counseled regarding psychosocial AND pharmacologic treatment options for alcohol dependence (SUD) [E]
 0.00 0.00 Global Days XXX

● **4330F** Counseling about epilepsy specific safety issues provided to patient (or caregiver(s)) (EPI) [E]
 0.00 0.00 Global Days XXX

● **4340F** Counseling for women of childbearing potential with epilepsy (EPI) [E]
 0.00 0.00 Global Days XXX

5005F-5200F Results Conveyed and Documented

INCLUDES Patient's:
- Functional status
- Morbidity/mortality
- Satisfaction/experience with care
- Review/communication of test results to patients

5005F Patient counseled on self-examination for new or changing moles (ML) [M]
0.00 0.00 Global Days XXX
AMA: 2008, Mar, 8-12

5010F Findings of dilated macular or fundus exam communicated to the physician managing the diabetes care (EC) [M] [P0]
0.00 0.00 Global Days XXX

5015F Documentation of communication that a fracture occurred and that the patient was or should be tested or treated for osteoporosis (OP) [M] [P0]
0.00 0.00 Global Days XXX

5020F Treatment summary report communicated to physician(s) managing continuing care and to the patient within 1 month of completing treatment (ONC) [E]
0.00 0.00 Global Days XXX
AMA: 2008, Mar, 8-12

5050F Treatment plan communicated to provider(s) managing continuing care within 1 month of diagnosis (ML) [M] [P0]
0.00 0.00 Global Days XXX
AMA: 2008, Mar, 8-12

5060F Findings from diagnostic mammogram communicated to practice managing patient's on-going care within 3 business days of exam interpretation (RAD) ♀ [M]
0.00 0.00 Global Days XXX
AMA: 2008, Mar, 8-12

5062F Findings from diagnostic mammogram communicated to the patient within 5 days of exam interpretation (RAD) ♀ [M]
0.00 0.00 Global Days XXX
AMA: 2008, Mar, 8-12

● **5100F** Potential risk for fracture communicated to the referring physician within 24 hours of completion of the imaging study (NUC_MED) [E]
0.00 0.00 Global Days XXX

● **5200F** Consideration of referral for a neurological evaluation of appropriateness for surgical therapy for intractable epilepsy within the past 3 years (EPI) [E]
0.00 0.00 Global Days XXX

6005F-6070F Elements Related to Patient Safety Processes

INCLUDES Patient safety practices

6005F Rationale (eg, severity of illness and safety) for level of care (eg, home, hospital) documented (CAP) [M]
0.00 0.00 Global Days XXX

6010F Dysphagia screening conducted prior to order for or receipt of any foods, fluids or medication by mouth (STR) [M] [P0]
0.00 0.00 Global Days XXX

6015F Patient receiving or eligible to receive foods, fluids or medication by mouth (STR) [M] [P0]
0.00 0.00 Global Days XXX

6020F NPO (nothing by mouth) ordered (STR) [M] [P0]
0.00 0.00 Global Days XXX

▲ **6030F** All elements of maximal sterile barrier technique followed including: cap AND mask AND sterile gown AND sterile gloves AND a large sterile sheet AND hand hygiene AND 2% chlorhexidine for cutaneous antisepsis (or acceptable alternative antiseptics, per current guideline) (CRIT) [M] [P0]
0.00 0.00 Global Days XXX
AMA: 2008, Mar, 8-12

6040F Use of appropriate radiation dose reduction devices OR manual techniques for appropriate moderation of exposure, documented (RAD) [M]
0.00 0.00 Global Days XXX

6045F Radiation exposure or exposure time in final report for procedure using fluoroscopy, documented (RAD) [M] [P0]
0.00 0.00 Global Days XXX
AMA: 2008, Mar, 8-12

● **6070F** Patient queried and counseled about anti-epileptic drug (AED) side-effects (EPI) [E]
0.00 0.00 Global Days XXX

7010F-7025F Recall/Reminder System in Place

INCLUDES
- Capabilities of the provider
- Measures that address the setting or system of care provided

▲ **7010F** Patient information entered into a recall system that includes: target date for the next exam specified AND a process to follow up with patients regarding missed or unscheduled appointments (ML) [M] [P0]
0.00 0.00 Global Days XXX
AMA: 2008, Mar, 8-12

▲ **7020F** Mammogram assessment category (eg, Mammography Quality Standards Act [MQSA], Breast Imaging Reporting and Data System [BI-RADS®], or FDA-approved equivalent categories) entered into an internal database to allow for analysis of abnormal interpretation (recall) rate (RAD) ♀ [M]
0.00 0.00 Global Days XXX
AMA: 2008, Mar, 8-12

7025F Patient information entered into a reminder system with a target due date for the next mammogram (RAD) ♀ [M]
0.00 0.00 Global Days XXX
AMA: 2008, Mar, 8-12

Current Procedural Coding Expert – Category III Codes

0016T-0017T

0016T Destruction of localized lesion of choroid (eg, choroidal neovascularization), transpupillary thermotherapy
0.00   0.00   Global Days XXX

0017T Destruction of macular drusen, photocoagulation
0.00   0.00   Global Days XXX

0019T-0042T

0019T Extracorporeal shock wave involving musculoskeletal system, not otherwise specified, low energy
EXCLUDES High energy:
 Extracorporeal shock wave (0101T)
 Lateral humeral epicondyle extracorporeal shock wave (0102T)
0.00   0.00   Global Days XXX
AMA: 2006, March, 1-5; 2005, June, 6-8

0030T Antiprothrombin (phospholipid cofactor) antibody, each Ig class
0.00   0.00   Global Days XXX

0042T Cerebral perfusion analysis using computed tomography with contrast administration, including post-processing of parametric maps with determination of cerebral blood flow, cerebral blood volume, and mean transit time
0.00   0.00   Global Days XXX

0048T-0053T

CMS 100-4,3,90.2.1   Artificial Hearts and Related Devices

0048T Implantation of a ventricular assist device, extracorporeal, percutaneous transseptal access, single or dual cannulation
0.00   0.00   Global Days XXX

0050T Removal of a ventricular assist device, extracorporeal, percutaneous transseptal access, single or dual cannulation
EXCLUDES Replacement of ventricular assist device, extracorporeal, via percutaneous transseptal access (33999)
0.00   0.00   Global Days XXX

0051T Implantation of a total replacement heart system (artificial heart) with recipient cardiectomy
EXCLUDES Ventricular assist device implant (33975-33976)
0.00   0.00   Global Days XXX

0052T Replacement or repair of thoracic unit of a total replacement heart system (artificial heart)
EXCLUDES Exchange or repair of other artificial heart components (0053T)
0.00   0.00   Global Days XXX

0053T Replacement or repair of implantable component or components of total replacement heart system (artificial heart), excluding thoracic unit
EXCLUDES Exchange or repair of thoracic unit of artificial heart (0052T)
0.00   0.00   Global Days XXX

0054T-0055T

+ **0054T** Computer-assisted musculoskeletal surgical navigational orthopedic procedure, with image-guidance based on fluoroscopic images (List separately in addition to code for primary procedure)
Code first primary procedure
0.00   0.00   Global Days XXX
AMA: 2009, Jan, 11-31; 2007, January, 13-27

+ **0055T** Computer-assisted musculoskeletal surgical navigational orthopedic procedure, with image-guidance based on CT/MRI images (List separately in addition to code for primary procedure)
INCLUDES Performance of both CT and MRI in same session (1 unit)
Code first primary procedure
0.00   0.00   Global Days XXX
AMA: 2009, Jan, 11-31; 2007, January, 13-27

0062T-0063T

~~**0062T** Percutaneous intradiscal annuloplasty, any method except electrothermal, unilateral or bilateral including fluoroscopic guidance; single level~~
To report, see code 22526-22527, 22899

~~**0063T** 1 or more additional levels (List separately in addition to 0062T for primary procedure)~~
To report, see code 22526-22527, 22899

0064T

~~**0064T** Spectroscopy, expired gas analysis (eg, nitric oxide/carbon dioxide test)~~
To report, see code 94799

0066T-0067T

~~**0066T** Computed tomographic (CT) colonography (ie, virtual colonoscopy); screening~~
To report, see code 74263

~~**0067T** diagnostic~~
To report, see code 74261-74262

0068T-0070T

~~**0068T** Acoustic heart sound recording and computer analysis; with interpretation and report~~
To report, see code 93799

~~**0069T** acoustic heart sound recording and computer analysis only~~
To report, see code 93799

~~**0070T** interpretation and report only~~
To report, see code 93799

0071T-0072T

Do not report with (51702, 77022)

0071T Focused ultrasound ablation of uterine leiomyomata, including MR guidance; total leiomyomata volume less than 200 cc of tissue
0.00   0.00   Global Days XXX
AMA: 2005, December, 3-6; 2005, March, 1-6

● New Code   ▲ Revised Code   M Maternity   Age   Unlisted   Not Covered   # Resequenced
CCI   + Add-on   ⊘ Mod 51 Exempt   Mod 63 Exempt   ⊙ Mod Sedation   PQRI
© 2009 Publisher (Blue Ink)   CPT only © 2009 American Medical Association. All Rights Reserved. (Black Ink)   Medicare (Red Ink)

0072T — 0095T Category III Codes

0072T   total leiomyomata volume greater or equal to 200 cc of tissue ♀ S 80
     0.00   0.00   Global Days XXX
     AMA: 2005, March, 1-6; 2005, December, 3-6

0073T
CMS 100-4,4,220.1   Billing for IMRT Planning and Delivery

0073T   Compensator-based beam modulation treatment delivery of inverse planned treatment using 3 or more high resolution (milled or cast) compensator convergent beam modulated fields, per treatment session   72 S TC 80
     EXCLUDES   Radiotherapy treatment planning (77301)
     Do not report with other treatment delivery (77401-77416, 77418)
     12.01   12.01   Global Days XXX
     AMA: 2005, March, 1-6; 2005, May, 7-12

0075T-0077T

0075T   Transcatheter placement of extracranial vertebral or intrathoracic carotid artery stent(s), including radiologic supervision and interpretation, percutaneous; initial vessel   C 80 P0
     INCLUDES   All diagnostic services for stenting Ipsilateral extracranial vertebral or intrathoracic selective carotid when confirming the need for stenting
     EXCLUDES   Selective catheterization and imaging when stenting is not required (report only slective catheterition codes)
     0.00   0.00   Global Days XXX
     AMA: 2005, May, 7-12

+ **0076T**   each additional vessel (List separately in addition to code for primary procedure)   C 80
     Code first 0075T
     0.00   0.00   Global Days XXX
     AMA: 2005, May, 7-12

~~**0077T**~~   ~~Implanting and securing cerebral thermal perfusion probe, including twist drill or burr hole, to measure absolute cerebral tissue perfusion~~
     To report, see code 61107, 61210

0078T-0081T
Code also when performed outside the endoprosthesis target zone (35454, 37205-37208)
Do not report with (34800-34805, 35081, 35102, 35452, 35454, 35472, 37205-37208)

0078T   Endovascular repair using prosthesis of abdominal aortic aneurysm, pseudoaneurysm or dissection, abdominal aorta involving visceral branches (superior mesenteric, celiac and/or renal artery[s])   C 80
     Code also when performed outside the target area of the endoprosthesis (35454, 37205)
     0.00   0.00   Global Days XXX
     AMA: 2005, May, 7-12; 2005, June, 6-8

+ **0079T**   Placement of visceral extension prosthesis for endovascular repair of abdominal aortic aneurysm involving visceral vessels, each visceral branch (List separately in addition to code for primary procedure)   C 80
     Code first (0078T)
     0.00   0.00   Global Days XXX
     AMA: 2005, June, 6-8; 2005, May, 7-12

0080T   Endovascular repair of abdominal aortic aneurysm, pseudoaneurysm or dissection, abdominal aorta involving visceral vessels (superior mesenteric, celiac or renal), using fenestrated modular bifurcated prosthesis (2 docking limbs), radiological supervision and interpretation   C 80 P0
     0.00   0.00   Global Days XXX
     AMA: 2005, May, 7-12; 2005, June, 6-8

+ **0081T**   Placement of visceral extension prosthesis for endovascular repair of abdominal aortic aneurysm involving visceral vessels, each visceral branch, radiological supervision and interpretation (List separately in addition to code for primary procedure)   C 80
     Code first 0080T
     0.00   0.00   Global Days XXX
     AMA: 2005, June, 6-8; 2005, May, 7-12

0084T-0087T

~~**0084T**~~   ~~Insertion of a temporary prostatic urethral stent~~
     To report, see code 53855

0085T   Breath test for heart transplant rejection   E
     0.00   0.00   Global Days XXX
     AMA: 2005, May, 7-12

~~**0086T**~~   ~~Left ventricular filling pressure indirect measurement by computerized calibration of the arterial waveform response to Valsalva maneuver~~
     To report, see code 93799

~~**0087T**~~   ~~Sperm evaluation, Hyaluronan sperm binding test~~
     To report, see code 89398

0092T-0098T
INCLUDES   Fluoroscopy
Do not report with these procedures when performed at the same level (22851, 49010)

+ **0092T**   Total disc arthroplasty (artificial disc), anterior approach, including discectomy with end plate preparation (includes osteophytectomy for nerve root or spinal cord decompression and microdissection), each additional interspace, cervical (List separately in addition to code for primary procedure)   C 80
     EXCLUDES   Lumbar arthroplasty (0163T)
     Code first 0090T (22856)
     Do not report with total disc arthroplasty (22851)
     0.00   0.00   Global Days XXX
     AMA: 2006, February, 1-6; 2005, June, 6-8

+ **0095T**   Removal of total disc arthroplasty (artificial disc), anterior approach, each additional interspace, cervical (List separately in addition to code for primary procedure)   C 80
     EXCLUDES   Lumbar disc (0164T)
          Total disc arthroplasty removal (22865)
     Code first (22864)
     0.00   0.00   Global Days XXX
     AMA: 2006, February, 1-6; 2005, June, 6-8

Current Procedural Coding Expert – Category III Codes

+ **0098T** Revision including replacement of total disc arthroplasty (artificial disc), anterior approach, each additional interspace, cervical (List separately in addition to code for primary procedure) [C][80]
　EXCLUDES *Spinal cord decompression (63001-63048)*

　Code first (22861)
　Do not report with (0095T, 22861)
　Do not report with instrumentation at the same level (22851)
　　0.00　0.00　Global Days XXX
　AMA: 2006, February, 1-6; 2005, June, 6-8

0099T-0140T

0099T Implantation of intrastromal corneal ring segments [R2][T][80]
　　0.00　0.00　Global Days XXX
　AMA: 2006, February, 1-6; 2005, June, 6-8

0100T Placement of a subconjunctival retinal prosthesis receiver and pulse generator, and implantation of intra-ocular retinal electrode array, with vitrectomy [G2][T][80]
　　0.00　0.00　Global Days XXX
　AMA: 2006, February, 1-6; 2005, June, 6-8

0101T Extracorporeal shock wave involving musculoskeletal system, not otherwise specified, high energy [G2][T][80]
　EXCLUDES *Low energy extracorporeal shock wave (0019T)*
　　0.00　0.00　Global Days XXX
　AMA: 2006, March, 1-5; 2005, June, 6-8

0102T Extracorporeal shock wave, high energy, performed by a physician, requiring anesthesia other than local, involving lateral humeral epicondyle [G2][T][80]
　EXCLUDES *Low energy extracorporeal shock wave (0019T)*
　　0.00　0.00　Global Days XXX
　AMA: 2006, March, 1-5; 2005, June, 6-8

0103T Holotranscobalamin, quantitative [A][80]
　　0.00　0.00　Global Days XXX
　AMA: 2006, March, 1-5; 2005, June, 6-8

0104T Inert gas rebreathing for cardiac output measurement; during rest [A][80]
　　0.00　0.00　Global Days XXX
　AMA: 2006, March, 1-5; 2005, June, 6-8

0105T 　during exercise [A][80]
　　0.00　0.00　Global Days XXX
　AMA: 2006, March, 1-5; 2005, June, 6-8

0106T Quantitative sensory testing (QST), testing and interpretation per extremity; using touch pressure stimuli to assess large diameter sensation [X][80]
　　0.00　0.00　Global Days XXX
　AMA: 2006, March, 1-5; 2005, June, 6-8

0107T 　using vibration stimuli to assess large diameter fiber sensation [X][80]
　　0.00　0.00　Global Days XXX
　AMA: 2006, March, 1-5; 2005, June, 6-8

0108T 　using cooling stimuli to assess small nerve fiber sensation and hyperalgesia [X][80]
　　0.00　0.00　Global Days XXX
　AMA: 2006, March, 1-5; 2005, June, 6-8

0109T 　using heat-pain stimuli to assess small nerve fiber sensation and hyperalgesia [X][80]
　　0.00　0.00　Global Days XXX
　AMA: 2006, March, 1-5; 2005, June, 6-8

0110T 　using other stimuli to assess sensation [X][80]
　　0.00　0.00　Global Days XXX
　AMA: 2006, March, 1-5; 2005, June, 6-8

0111T Long-chain (C20-22) omega-3 fatty acids in red blood cell (RBC) membranes [A][80]
　EXCLUDES *Very long chain fatty acids (82726)*
　　0.00　0.00　Global Days XXX
　AMA: 2006, March, 1-5; 2005, June, 6-8

0123T Fistulization of sclera for glaucoma, through ciliary body [G2][T][80]
　　0.00　0.00　Global Days XXX
　AMA: 2006, April, 11-18

0124T Conjunctival incision with posterior extrascleral placement of pharmacological agent (does not include supply of medication) [R2][T][80]
　EXCLUDES *Suprachoroidal delivery of medication (0186T)*
　Code also medication
　　0.00　0.00　Global Days XXX
　AMA: 2008, Jan, 6-7; 2006, April, 11-18

0126T Common carotid intima-media thickness (IMT) study for evaluation of atherosclerotic burden or coronary heart disease risk factor assessment [N1][01][80]
　　0.00　0.00　Global Days XXX
　AMA: 2006, April, 11-18

0130T Validated, statistically reliable, randomized, controlled, single-patient clinical investigation of FDA approved chronic care drugs, provided by a pharmacist, interpretation and report to the prescribing health care professional [B][80]
　　0.00　0.00　Global Days XXX
　AMA: 2006, April, 11-18

~~**0140T** Exhaled breath condensate pH~~
See 83987

0141T-0143T

INCLUDES Administration and management of:
　Antibiotics
　Immunotherapy
　Islet cells
　Pain medication
　Sedation
Recovery services
　All other therapeutic, infusions, and injections during islet cell infusion
　Blood glucose and insulin therapy
　Portal and hemodynamics

0141T Pancreatic islet cell transplantation through portal vein, percutaneous [E]
　EXCLUDES *Catheterization of portal vein (36481)*
　　　Laparoscopic procedure (0143T)
　　　Open procedure (0142T)
　　75887
　　0.00　0.00　Global Days XXX
　AMA: 2007, June, 7-9; 2006, April, 11-18

0142T Pancreatic islet cell transplantation through portal vein, open [E]
　EXCLUDES *Laparoscopic procedure (0143T)*
　　　Percutaneous procedure (0141T)
　Do not report with (49000, 49002)
　　0.00　0.00　Global Days XXX
　AMA: 2007, June, 7-9; 2006, April, 11-18

0143T Laparoscopy, surgical, pancreatic islet cell transplantation through portal vein [E]
　EXCLUDES *Open procedure (0142T)*
　　　Percutaneous procedure (0141T)
　Do not report with diagnostic laparoscopy (49320)
　　0.00　0.00　Global Days XXX
　AMA: 2007, June, 7-9; 2006, April, 11-18

0144T-0151T

~~0144T~~ ~~Computed tomography, heart, without contrast material, including image postprocessing and quantitative evaluation of coronary calcium~~
To report, see code 75571

~~0145T~~ ~~Computed tomography, heart, with contrast material(s), including noncontrast images, if performed, cardiac gating and 3D image postprocessing; cardiac structure and morphology~~
To report, see code 75572-75574

~~0146T~~ ~~computed tomographic angiography of coronary arteries (including native and anomalous coronary arteries, coronary bypass grafts), without quantitative evaluation of coronary calcium~~
To report, see code 75572-75574

~~0147T~~ ~~computed tomographic angiography of coronary arteries (including native and anomalous coronary arteries, coronary bypass grafts), with quantitative evaluation of coronary calcium~~
To report, see code 75572-75574

~~0148T~~ ~~cardiac structure and morphology and computed tomographic angiography of coronary arteries (including native and anomalous coronary arteries, coronary bypass grafts), without quantitative evaluation of coronary calcium~~
To report, see code 75572-75574

~~0149T~~ ~~cardiac structure and morphology and computed tomographic angiography of coronary arteries (including native and anomalous coronary arteries, coronary bypass grafts), with quantitative evaluation of coronary calcium~~
To report, see code 75572-75574

~~0150T~~ ~~cardiac structure and morphology in congenital heart disease~~
To report, see code 75572-75574

~~0151T~~ ~~Computed tomography, heart, with contrast material(s), including noncontrast images, if performed, cardiac gating and 3D image postprocessing, function evaluation (left and right ventricular function, ejection-fraction and segmental wall motion) (List separately in addition to code for primary procedure)~~
To report, see code 75572-75574

0155T-0156T

EXCLUDES Electronic study and programming of gastric neurostimulator pulse generator (95999)
Open procedure (0157T-0158T)

0155T Laparoscopy, surgical; implantation or replacement of gastric stimulation electrodes, lesser curvature (ie, morbid obesity) [T][80]
0.00   0.00   Global Days XXX
AMA: 2007, April, 7-10; 2007, March, 4-5; 2006, May, 12-15

0156T revision or removal of gastric stimulation electrodes, lesser curvature (ie, morbid obesity) [T][80]
EXCLUDES Electronic analysis and programming of:
Antral gastric neurostimulator pulse generator (95980-95982)
Insertion, revision or removal of gastric neurostimulator pulse generator (64590, 64595)
Laproscopic or open insertion, revision, or removal of antral gastric neurostimulator (43647-43648, 43881-43882)
Open approach (0157T-0158T)
0.00   0.00   Global Days XXX
AMA: 2007, April, 7-10; 2007, March, 4-5; 2006, May, 12-15

0157T-0158T

EXCLUDES Electronic analysis and programming of antral gastric neurostimulator pulse generator (95980-95982)
Laparoscopic procedure (0155T-0156T)
Placement of gastric neurostimulator pulse generator (64590)
Revision or removal of gastric neurostimulator pulse generator (64595)

0157T Laparotomy, implantation or replacement of gastric stimulation electrodes, lesser curvature (ie, morbid obesity) [C][80]
0.00   0.00   Global Days XXX
AMA: 2007, April, 7-10; 2006, May, 12-15

0158T Laparotomy, revision or removal of gastric stimulation electrodes, lesser curvature (ie, morbid obesity) [C][80]
0.00   0.00   Global Days XXX
AMA: 2007, April, 7-10; 2006, May, 12-15

0159T

+ 0159T Computer-aided detection, including computer algorithm analysis of MRI image data for lesion detection/characterization, pharmacokinetic analysis, with further physician review for interpretation, breast MRI (List separately in addition to code for primary procedure) [M][N][80]
Do not report with (76376-76377)
76376-76377, 77058-77059
0.00   0.00   Global Days ZZZ
AMA: 2007, Jul, 6-10; 2007, March, 7-8; 2006, May, 12-15; 2006, April, 11-18

0160T-0161T

0160T Therapeutic repetitive transcranial magnetic stimulation treatment planning [S][80]
INCLUDES Pretreatment:
Determination of magnetic field strength
Stimulation limits
Treatment site
0.00   0.00   Global Days XXX
AMA: 2007, Jul, 6-10; 2006, May, 12-15; 2006, December, 10-12

0161T Therapeutic repetitive transcranial magnetic stimulation treatment delivery and management, per session [S][80]
INCLUDES Monitoring
Treatment limit review
0.00   0.00   Global Days XXX
AMA: 2007, Jul, 6-10; 2006, December, 10-12; 2006, May, 12-15

Current Procedural Coding Expert – Category III Codes

0163T-0165T

INCLUDES Fluoroscopy
EXCLUDES Cervical disc procedures (22856)
Decompression (63001-63048)

Do not report with these procedures when performed at the same level (22851, 49010)

+ **0163T** Total disc arthroplasty (artificial disc), anterior approach, including discectomy to prepare interspace (other than for decompression), each additional interspace, lumbar (List separately in addition to code for primary procedure) [C] [80]
   Code first 22857
   0.00 0.00 Global Days YYY
   AMA: 2007, June, 1-3

+ **0164T** Removal of total disc arthroplasty, (artificial disc), anterior approach, each additional interspace, lumbar (List separately in addition to code for primary procedure) [C] [80]
   Code first 22865
   0.00 0.00 Global Days YYY
   AMA: 2007, June, 1-3

+ **0165T** Revision including replacement of total disc arthroplasty (artificial disc), anterior approach, each additional interspace, lumbar (List separately in addition to code for primary procedure) [C] [80]
   Code first 22862
   0.00 0.00 Global Days YYY
   AMA: 2007, June, 1-3

0166T-0167T

EXCLUDES Percutaneous ventricular septal defect repair (93581)

Do not report with (32551, 33210-33211)

0166T Transmyocardial transcatheter closure of ventricular septal defect, with implant; without cardiopulmonary bypass [C] [80]
   EXCLUDES Ventricular septal defect closure via percutaneous transcatheter implant delivery (93581)
   0.00 0.00 Global Days XXX
   AMA: 2007, Jul, 6-10; 2006, December, 8-9

0167T with cardiopulmonary bypass [C] [80]
   EXCLUDES Ventricular septal defect closure via percutaneous transcatheter implant delivery (93581)
   0.00 0.00 Global Days XXX
   AMA: 2007, Jul, 6-10; 2006, December, 8-9

0168T-0177T

0168T Rhinophototherapy, intranasal application of ultraviolet and visible light, bilateral [T] [80]
   0.00 0.00 Global Days XXX
   AMA: 2007, Jul, 6-10; 2006, December, 8-9

0169T Stereotactic placement of infusion catheter(s) in the brain for delivery of therapeutic agent(s), including computerized stereotactic planning and burr hole(s) [C] [80]
   Do not report with (20660, 61107, 61795)
   0.00 0.00 Global Days XXX
   AMA: 2009, Jan, 11-31; 2008, Jul, 4; 2008, May, 9-11; 2007, Jul, 6-10; 2006, December, 8-9

~~0170T~~ ~~Repair of anorectal fistula with plug (eg, porcine small intestine submucosa [SIS])~~
   To report, see code 46707

0171T Insertion of posterior spinous process distraction device (including necessary removal of bone or ligament for insertion and imaging guidance), lumbar; single level [T] [80]
   0.00 0.00 Global Days XXX
   AMA: 2007, Jul, 6-10; 2006, December, 8-9

+ **0172T** each additional level (List separately in addition to code for primary procedure) [T] [80]
   Code first 0171T
   0.00 0.00 Global Days XXX
   AMA: 2007, Jul, 6-10; 2006, December, 8-9

+ **0173T** Monitoring of intraocular pressure during vitrectomy surgery (List separately in addition to code for primary procedure) [N] [80]
   Code first (67036, 67039-67043, 67108, 67112, 67112, 67112-67113)
   0.00 0.00 Global Days XXX
   AMA: 2008, Oct, 1-5; 2007, Jul, 6-10; 2006, December, 8-9

+ **0174T** Computer-aided detection (CAD) (computer algorithm analysis of digital image data for lesion detection) with further physician review for interpretation and report, with or without digitization of film radiographic images, chest radiograph(s), performed concurrent with primary interpretation (List separately in addition to code for primary procedure) [N1] [N] [80]
   Code first primary procedure
   71010, 71020-71022, 71030
   0.00 0.00 Global Days XXX
   AMA: 2007, March, 7-8; 2007, Jul, 6-10; 2006, December, 8-9

0175T Computer-aided detection (CAD) (computer algorithm analysis of digital image data for lesion detection) with further physician review for interpretation and report, with or without digitization of film radiographic images, chest radiograph(s), performed remote from primary interpretation [N1] [N] [80]
   Do not report with (71010, 71020-71022, 71030)
   0.00 0.00 Global Days XXX
   AMA: 2007, March, 7-8; 2007, Jul, 6-10; 2006, December, 8-9

0176T Transluminal dilation of aqueous outflow canal; without retention of device or stent [A2] [T] [80]
   0.00 0.00 Global Days XXX
   AMA: 2007, Jul, 6-10; 2006, December, 8-9

0177T with retention of device or stent [A2] [T] [80]
   0.00 0.00 Global Days XXX
   AMA: 2007, Jul, 6-10; 2006, December, 8-9

0178T-0180T

EXCLUDES Separately performed 12-lead electrocardiogram (93000-93010)

0178T Electrocardiogram, 64 leads or greater, with graphic presentation and analysis; with interpretation and report [B] [80]
   0.00 0.00 Global Days XXX

0179T tracing and graphics only, without interpretation and report [X] [TC] [80]
   0.00 0.00 Global Days XXX

0180T interpretation and report only [B] [26] [80]
   0.00 0.00 Global Days XXX

0181T-0187T

0181T Corneal hysteresis determination, by air impulse stimulation, bilateral, with interpretation and report [S] [80]
   0.00 0.00 Global Days XXX

● New Code   ▲ Revised Code   M Maternity   A Age   Unlisted   Not Covered   # Resequenced
CCI   + Add-on   ⊘ Mod 51 Exempt   Mod 63 Exempt   ⊙ Mod Sedation   PQRI

© 2009 Publisher *(Blue Ink)*   CPT only © 2009 American Medical Association. All Rights Reserved. *(Black Ink)*   Medicare *(Red Ink)*

Current Procedural Coding Expert – Category III Codes

0182T High dose rate electronic brachytherapy, per fraction
  EXCLUDES Placement or removal of an applicator into breast for radiation therapy (C9726)
  Do not report with (77761-77763, 77776-77778, 77785-77787, 77789)
  0.00 0.00 Global Days XXX

0183T Low frequency, non-contact, non-thermal ultrasound, including topical application(s), when performed, wound assessment, and instruction(s) for ongoing care, per day
  0.00 0.00 Global Days XXX

0184T Excision of rectal tumor, transanal endoscopic microsurgical approach (ie, TEMS)
  INCLUDES Operating microscope (66990)
  EXCLUDES Nonendoscopic excision of rectal tumor (45160, 45171-45172)
  Do not report with (45300-45327)
  0.00 0.00 Global Days XXX
  AMA: 2008, Jan, 6-7

▲ **0185T** Multivariate analysis of patient-specific findings with quantifiable computer probability assessment, including report
  Do not report with (99090)
  0.00 0.00 Global Days XXX
  AMA: 2008, Jan, 6-7

0186T Suprachoroidal delivery of pharmacologic agent (does not include supply of medication)
  0.00 0.00 Global Days XXX
  AMA: 2008, Jan, 6-7

0187T Scanning computerized ophthalmic diagnostic imaging, anterior segment, with interpretation and report, unilateral
  0.00 0.00 Global Days XXX
  AMA: 2008, Jan, 6-7

0188T-0189T

INCLUDES
  30 minutes or more of direct medical care by a physician(s) to a critically ill or critically injured patient from an off-site location.
  Additional on-site critical care services when a critically ill or injured patient requires critical care resources not available on-site
Real time ability to:
  Document the remote care services in the medical record
  Enter orders electronically
  Evaluate patients with high fidelity audio/video capabilities
  Talk to patients and family members
  Videoconference with the health care team on-site in the patient's room
Real-time access to the patient's:
  Clinical laboratory test results
  Diagnostic test results
  Medical records
  Radiographic images
Review and/or interpretation of all diagnostic information
Time spent with the patient, family, or surrogate decision makers to obtain a medical history, review the patient's condition/prognosis, or discuss treatment options from the remote site

Do not report for time spent away from the remote site without real-time capabilities
Do not report time spent for services that do not directly contribute to patient treatment

0188T Remote real-time interactive video-conferenced critical care, evaluation and management of the critically ill or critically injured patient; first 30-74 minutes
  INCLUDES First 30 to 74 minutes of remote critical care each day
  Do not report remote critical care less than 30 minutes total duration
  0.00 0.00 Global Days XXX
  AMA: 2009, Jan, 5&10; 2008, Jan, 6-7

+ **0189T** each additional 30 minutes (List separately in addition to code for primary service)
  INCLUDES Up to 30 minutes each beyond the first 74 minutes
  Code first (0188T)
  0.00 0.00 Global Days XXX
  AMA: 2009, Jan, 5&10; 2008, Jan, 6-7

0190T-0194T

+ **0190T** Placement of intraocular radiation source applicator (List separately in addition to primary procedure)
  EXCLUDES Insertion of brachytherapy source by radiation oncologist (see Clinical Brachytherapy Section)
  Code first (67036)
  Code also brachytherapy source
  0.00 0.00 Global Days XXX
  AMA: 2008, Jan, 6-7

0191T Insertion of anterior segment aqueous drainage device, without extraocular reservoir; internal approach
  0.00 0.00 Global Days XXX
  AMA: 2008, Jan, 6-7

0192T external approach
  0.00 0.00 Global Days XXX
  AMA: 2008, Jan, 6-7

26/TC PC/TC Comp Only   A2-73 ASC Pmt   50 Bilateral   ♂ Male Only   ♀ Female Only   Facility RVU   Non-Facility RVU
AMA: CPT Asst   MED: Pub 100   A-Y OPPSI   80/80 Surg Assist Allowed / w/Doc   Lab Crosswalk   Radiology Crosswalk
CPT only © 2009 American Medical Association. All Rights Reserved. (Black Ink)   Medicare (Red Ink)   © 2009 Publisher (Blue Ink)

Current Procedural Coding Expert – Category III Codes

0193T Transurethral, radiofrequency micro-remodeling of the female bladder neck and proximal urethra for stress urinary incontinence
Do not report with (51701)
0.00 0.00 Global Days XXX

~~0194T~~ ~~Procalcitonin (PCT)~~
To report, see code 84145

0195T-0196T
Do not report with (22558, 22845, 22851, 76000, 76380, 76496, 76497)

0195T Arthrodesis, pre-sacral interbody technique, including instrumentation, imaging (when performed), and discectomy to prepare interspace, lumbar; single interspace
0.00 0.00 Global Days XXX

+ 0196T each additional interspace (List separately in addition to code for primary procedure)
Code first (0195T)
0.00 0.00 Global Days XXX

0197T-0199T

0197T Intra-fraction localization and tracking of target or patient motion during delivery of radiation therapy (eg, 3D positional tracking, gating, 3D surface tracking), each fraction of treatment
0.00 0.00 Global Days XXX

0198T Measurement of ocular blood flow by repetitive intraocular pressure sampling, with interpretation and report
0.00 0.00 Global Days XXX

▲ 0199T Physiologic recording of tremor using accelerometer(s) and/or gyroscope(s) (including frequency and amplitude) including interpretation and report
0.00 0.00 Global Days XXX

0200T-0201T
EXCLUDES Bone biopsy (20220, 20225)

⊙ ● 0200T Percutaneous sacral augmentation (sacroplasty), unilateral injection(s), including the use of a balloon or mechanical device (if utilized), 1 or more needles
72291-72292
0.00 0.00 Global Days XXX

⊙ ● 0201T Percutaneous sacral augmentation (sacroplasty), bilateral injections, including the use of a balloon or mechanical device (if utilized), 2 or more needles
72291-72292
0.00 0.00 Global Days XXX

0202T

● 0202T Posterior vertebral joint(s) arthroplasty (e.g., facet joint(s) replacement) including facetectomy, laminectomy, foraminotomy and vertebral column fixation, with or without injection of bone cement, including fluoroscopy, single level, lumbar spine
Do not report the following codes when performed at the same level: (22521, 22524, 22840, 22851, 22857, 63005, 63012, 63017, 63030, 63042, 63047, 63056)
0.00 0.00 Global Days XXX

0203T-0204T
EXCLUDES Measurement of a minimum of heart rate, oxygen saturation, respiratory airflow, and respiratory effort unattended sleep study (95806)

● 0203T Sleep study, unattended, simultaneous recording; heart rate, oxygen saturation, respiratory analysis (eg, by airflow or peripheral arterial tone) and sleep time
EXCLUDES Measurement of a minimum of heart rate, oxygen saturation, and respiratory analysis unattended sleep study. (0204T)
Do not report with (93014, 93012, 95803, 95806, 93041-93272, 0204T)
0.00 0.00 Global Days XXX

● 0204T minimum of heart rate, oxygen saturation, and respiratory analysis (eg, by airflow or peripheral arterial tone)
EXCLUDES Unattended sleep study that measures heart rate, oxygen saturation, respiratory analysis and sleep time (0203T)
Do not report with (0203T, 93012, 93014, 93041-93272, 95806)
0.00 0.00 Global Days XXX

0205T-0207T

+ ● 0205T Intravascular catheter-based coronary vessel or graft spectroscopy (eg, infrared) during diagnostic evaluation and/or therapeutic intervention including imaging supervision, interpretation, and report, each vessel (List separately in addition to code for primary procedure)
Code first (92980, 92982, 92995, 93508, 93510-93533)
0.00 0.00 Global Days ZZZ

● 0206T Algorithmic analysis, remote, of electrocardiographic-derived data with computer probability assessment, including report
Code also 12-lead ECG when performed (93000-93010)

● 0207T Evacuation of meibomian glands, automated, using heat and intermittent pressure, unilateral
0.00 0.00 Global Days XXX

0208T-0212T
EXCLUDES Manual audiometric testing by a qualified health care professional, using audiometers (92551-92557)

● 0208T Pure tone audiometry (threshold), automated (includes use of computer-assisted device); air only
0.00 0.00 Global Days XXX

● 0209T air and bone
0.00 0.00 Global Days XXX

● 0210T Speech audiometry threshold, automated (includes use of computer-assisted device);
0.00 0.00 Global Days XXX

● 0211T with speech recognition
0.00 0.00 Global Days XXX

● 0212T Comprehensive audiometry threshold evaluation and speech recognition (0209T, 0211T combined), automated (includes use of computer-assisted device)
0.00 0.00 Global Days XXX

● New Code ▲ Revised Code M Maternity Age Unlisted Not Covered # Resequenced
CCI + Add-on ⊘ Mod 51 Exempt Mod 63 Exempt ⊙ Mod Sedation PQRI
© 2009 Publisher (Blue Ink) CPT only © 2009 American Medical Association. All Rights Reserved. (Black Ink) Medicare (Red Ink)

0213T-0215T

- ● **0213T** Injection(s), diagnostic or therapeutic agent, paravertebral facet (zygapophyseal) joint (or nerves innervating that joint) with ultrasound guidance, cervical or thoracic; single level [62] [T] [80] [50]
  0.00 0.00 Global Days XXX

+ ● **0214T** second level (List separately in addition to code for primary procedure) [62] [T] [80] [50]
  Code first (0213T)
  0.00 0.00 Global Days ZZZ

+ ● **0215T** third and any additional level(s) (List separately in addition to code for primary procedure) [62] [T] [80] [50]
  Code first (0213T)
  Do not report more than once per day.
  0.00 0.00 Global Days ZZZ

0216T-0218T

- ● **0216T** Injection(s), diagnostic or therapeutic agent, paravertebral facet (zygapophyseal) joint (or nerves innervating that joint) with ultrasound guidance, lumbar or sacral; single level [62] [T] [80] [50]
  0.00 0.00 Global Days XXX

+ ● **0217T** second level (List separately in addition to code for primary procedure) [62] [T] [80] [50]
  Code first (0216T)
  0.00 0.00 Global Days ZZZ

+ ● **0218T** third and any additional level(s) (List separately in addition to code for primary procedure) [62] [T] [80] [50]
  Do not report more than once a day
  Code first (0216T)
  0.00 0.00 Global Days ZZZ

0219T-0221T

Do not report with any x-ray procedure
Do not report when performed at the same level (20930-20931, 22600-22614, 22840, 22851)

- ● **0219T** Placement of posterior intrafacet implant(s), unilateral or bilateral, including imaging and placement of bone graft(s) or synthetic device(s), single level; cervical [C] [80]
  0.00 0.00 Global Days XXX

- ● **0220T** thoracic [C] [80]
  0.00 0.00 Global Days XXX

- ● **0221T** lumbar [T] [80]
  0.00 0.00 Global Days XXX

0222T

+ ● **0222T** Placement of posterior intrafacet implant(s), unilateral or bilateral, including imaging and placement of bone graft(s) or synthetic device(s), single level; each additional vertebral segment (List separately in addition to code for primary procedure) [T] [80]
  EXCLUDES Posterior or posterolateral arthrodesis procedure (22600-22614)
  Code first (0219T-0221T)
  0.00 0.00 Global Days ZZZ

APPENDIX A — MODIFIERS

CPT Modifiers

A modifier is a two-position alpha or numeric code that is appended to a CPT code to clarify the services being billed. Modifiers provide a means by which a service can be altered without changing the procedure code. They add more information, such as the anatomical site, to the code. In addition, they help to eliminate the appearance of duplicate billing and unbundling. Modifiers are used to increase accuracy in reimbursement, coding consistency, editing, and to capture payment data.

22 **Increased Procedural Services:** When the work required to provide a service is substantially greater than typically required, it may be identified by adding modifier 22 to the usual procedure code. Documentation must support the substantial additional work and the reason for the additional work (ie, increased intensity, time, technical difficulty of procedure, severity of patient's condition, physical and mental effort required).

Note: This modifier should not be appended to an E/M service.

23 **Unusual Anesthesia:** Occasionally, a procedure, which usually requires either no anesthesia or local anesthesia, because of unusual circumstances must be done under general anesthesia. This circumstance may be reported by adding modifier 23 to the procedure code of the basic service.

24 **Unrelated Evaluation and Management Service by the Same Physician During a Postoperative Period:** The physician may need to indicate that an evaluation and management service was performed during a postoperative period for a reason(s) unrelated to the original procedure. This circumstance may be reported by adding modifier 24 to the appropriate level of E/M service.

25 **Significant, Separately Identifiable Evaluation and Management Service by the Same Physician on the Same Day of the Procedure or Other Service:** It may be necessary to indicate that on the day a procedure or service identified by a CPT code was performed, the patient's condition required a significant, separately identifiable E/M service above and beyond the other service provided or beyond the usual preoperative and postoperative care associated with the procedure that was performed. A significant, separately identifiable E/M service is defined or substantiated by documentation that satisfies the relevant criteria for the respective E/M service to be reported (see Evaluation and Management Services Guidelines for instructions on determining level of E/M service). The E/M service may be prompted by the symptom or condition for which the procedure and/or service was provided. As such, different diagnoses are not required for reporting of the E/M services on the same date. This circumstance may be reported by adding modifier 25 to the appropriate level of E/M service. Note: This modifier is not used to report an E/M service that resulted in a decision to perform surgery. See modifier 57. For significant, separately identifiable non-E/M services, see modifier 59.

26 **Professional Component:** Certain procedures are a combination of a physician component and a technical component. When the physician component is reported separately, the service may be identified by adding modifier 26 to the usual procedure number.

32 **Mandated Services:** Services related to mandated consultation and/or related services (eg, third-party payer, governmental, legislative or regulatory requirement) may be identified by adding modifier 32 to the basic procedure.

47 **Anesthesia by Surgeon:** Regional or general anesthesia provided by the surgeon may be reported by adding modifier 47 to the basic service. (This does not include local anesthesia.) Note: Modifier 47 would not be used as a modifier for the anesthesia procedures 00100-01999.

50 **Bilateral Procedure:** Unless otherwise identified in the listings, bilateral procedures that are performed at the same operative session should be identified by adding modifier 50 to the appropriate 5-digit code.

51 **Multiple Procedures:** When multiple procedures, other than Evaluation and Management Services, are performed at the same session by the same provider, the primary procedure or service may be reported as listed. The additional procedure(s) or service(s) may be identified by appending modifier 51 to the additional procedure or service code(s). Note: This modifier should not be appended to designated "add-on" codes.

52 **Reduced Services:** Under certain circumstances a service or procedure is partially reduced or eliminated at the physician's discretion. Under these circumstances the service provided can be identified by its usual procedure number and the addition of modifier 52, signifying that the service is reduced. This provides a means of reporting reduced services without disturbing the identification of the basic service. Note: For hospital outpatient reporting of a previously scheduled procedure/service that is partially reduced or cancelled as a result of extenuating circumstances or those that threaten the well-being of the patient prior to or after administration of anesthesia, see modifiers 73 and 74 (see modifiers approved for ASC hospital outpatient use).

53 **Discontinued Procedure:** Under certain circumstances, the physician may elect to terminate a surgical or diagnostic procedure. Due to extenuating circumstances or those that threaten the well being of the patient, it may be necessary to indicate that a surgical or diagnostic procedure was started but discontinued. This circumstance may be reported by adding modifier 53 to the code reported by the physician for the discontinued procedure. Note: This modifier is not used to report the elective cancellation of a procedure prior to the patient's anesthesia induction and/or surgical preparation in the operating suite. For outpatient hospital/ambulatory surgery center (ASC) reporting of a previously scheduled procedure/service that is partially reduced or cancelled as a result of extenuating circumstances or those that threaten the well being of the patient prior to or after administration of anesthesia, see modifiers 73 and 74 (see modifiers approved for ASC hospital outpatient use).

54 **Surgical Care Only:** When 1 physician performs a surgical procedure and another provides preoperative and/or postoperative management, surgical services may be identified by adding modifier 54 to the usual procedure number.

55 **Postoperative Management Only:** When 1 physician performs the postoperative management and another physician has performed the surgical procedure, the postoperative component may be identified by adding modifier 55 to the usual procedure number.

56 **Preoperative Management Only:** When 1 physician performs the preoperative care and evaluation and another physician performs the surgical procedure, the preoperative component may be identified by adding modifier 56 to the usual procedure number.

57 **Decision for Surgery:** An evaluation and management service that resulted in the initial decision to perform the surgery may be identified by adding modifier 57 to the appropriate level of E/M service.

58 **Staged or Related Procedure or Service By the Same Physician During the Postoperative Period:** It may be necessary to indicate that the performance of a procedure or service during the postoperative period was (a) planned or anticipated (staged); (b) more extensive than the original procedure; or (c) for therapy following a surgical procedure. This circumstance may be reported by adding modifier 58 to the staged or related procedure. Note: For treatment of a problem that requires a return to the operating or procedure room (eg, unanticipated clinical condition), see modifier 78.

59 **Distinct Procedural Service:** Under certain circumstances, it may be necessary to indicate that a procedure or service was distinct or independent from other non-E/M services performed on the same day. Modifier 59 is used to identify procedures or services, other than E/M services, that are not normally reported together but are appropriate under the circumstances. Documentation must support a different session, different procedure or surgery, different site or organ system, separate incision or excision, separate lesion, or separate injury (or area of injury in extensive injuries) not ordinarily encountered or performed on the same day by the same individual. However, when another already established modifier is appropriate it should be used rather than modifier 59. Only if no more descriptive modifier is available and the use of modifier 59 best explains the circumstances should modifier 59 be used.

Appendix A — Modifiers

Note: Modifier 59 should not be appended to an E/M service. To report a separate and distinct E/M service with a non-E/M service performed on the same date, see modifier 25.

62 Two Surgeons: When 2 surgeons work together as primary surgeons performing distinct part(s) of a procedure, each surgeon should report his/her distinct operative work by adding modifier 62 to the procedure code and any associated add-on code(s) for that procedure as long as both surgeons continue to work together as primary surgeons. Each surgeon should report the co-surgery once using the same procedure code. If an additional procedure(s) (including an add-on procedure(s)) is performed during the same surgical session, a separate code(s) may be reported with the modifier 62 added.

Note: If a co-surgeon acts as an assistant in the performance of an additional procedure(s) during the same surgical session, the service(s) may be reported using a separate procedure code(s) with modifier 80 or modifier 82 added, as appropriate.

63 Procedure Performed on Infants less than 4 kg: Procedures performed on neonates and infants up to a present body weight of 4 kg may involve significantly increased complexity and physician work commonly associated with these patients. This circumstance may be reported by adding the modifier 63 to the procedure number.

Note: Unless otherwise designated, this modifier may only be appended to procedures/services listed in the 20000-69999 code series. Modifier 63 should not be appended to any CPT codes in the **Evaluation and Management Services, Anesthesia, Radiology, Pathology/Laboratory or Medicine** sections.

66 Surgical Team: Under some circumstances, highly complex procedures (requiring the concomitant services of several physicians, often of different specialties, plus other highly skilled, specially trained personnel, various types of complex equipment) are carried out under the "surgical team" concept. Such circumstances may be identified by each participating physician with the addition of modifier 66 to the basic procedure number used for reporting services.

76 Repeat Procedure or Service by Same Physician It may be necessary to indicate that a procedure or service was repeated subsequent to the original procedure or service. This circumstance may be reported by adding modifier 76 to the repeated procedure or service.

77 Repeat Procedure by Another Physician: The physician may need to indicate that a basic procedure or service performed by another physician had to be repeated. This situation may be reported by adding modifier 77 to the repeated procedure/service.

78 Unplanned Return to the Operating/Procedure Room by the Same Physician Following Initial Procedure for a Related Procedure During the Postoperative Period: It may be necessary to indicate that another procedure was performed during the postoperative period of the initial procedure (unplanned procedure following initial procedure). When this procedure is related to the first and requires the use of an operating or procedure room, it may be reported by adding modifier 78 to the related procedure. (For repeat procedures, see modifier 76.)

79 Unrelated Procedure or Service by the Same Physician During the Postoperative Period: The physician may need to indicate that the performance of a procedure or service during the postoperative period was unrelated to the original procedure. This circumstance may be reported by using modifier 79. (For repeat procedures on the same day, see modifier 76.)

80 Assistant Surgeon: Surgical assistant services may be identified by adding modifier 80 to the usual procedure number(s).

81 Minimum Assistant Surgeon: Minimum surgical assistant services are identified by adding modifier 81 to the usual procedure number.

82 Assistant Surgeon (when qualified resident surgeon not available): The unavailability of a qualified resident surgeon is a prerequisite for use of modifier 82 appended to the usual procedure code number(s).

90 Reference (Outside) Laboratory: When laboratory procedures are performed by a party other than the treating or reporting physician, the procedure may be identified by adding modifier 90 to the usual procedure number.

91 Repeat Clinical Diagnostic Laboratory Test: In the course of treatment of the patient, it may be necessary to repeat the same laboratory test on the same day to obtain subsequent (multiple) test results. Under these circumstances, the laboratory test performed can be identified by its usual procedure number and the addition of modifier 91.

Note: This modifier may not be used when tests are rerun to confirm initial results; due to testing problems with specimens or equipment; or for any other reason when a normal, one-time, reportable result is all that is required. This modifier may not be used when another code(s) describes a series of test results (eg, glucose tolerance tests, evocative/suppression testing). This modifier may only be used for a laboratory test(s) performed more than once on the same day on the same patient.

92 Alternative Laboratory Platform Testing When laboratory testing is being performed using a kit or transportable instrument that wholly or in part consists of a single use, disposable analytical chamber, the service may be identified by adding modifier 92 to the usual laboratory procedure code (HIV testing 86701-86703). The test does not require permanent dedicated space; hence by its design it may be hand carried or transported to the vicinity of the patient for immediate testing at that site, although location of the testing is not in itself determinative of the use of this modifier.

99 Multiple Modifiers: Under certain circumstances 2 or more modifiers may be necessary to completely delineate a service. In such situations, modifier 99 should be added to the basic procedure and other applicable modifiers may be listed as part of the description of the service.

Anesthesia Physical Status Modifiers

All anesthesia services are reported by use of the five-digit anesthesia procedure code with the appropriate physical status modifier appended.

Under certain circumstances, when other modifier(s) are appropriate, they should be reported in addition to the physical status modifier.

- **P1** A normal healthy patient
- **P2** A patient with mild systemic disease
- **P3** A patient with severe systemic disease
- **P4** A patient with severe systemic disease that is a constant threat to life
- **P5** A moribund patient who is not expected to survive without the operation
- **P6** A declared brain-dead patient whose organs are being removed for donor purposes

Modifiers Approved for Ambulatory Surgery Center (ASC) Hospital Outpatient Use

CPT Level I Modifiers

25 Significant, Separately Identifiable Evaluation and Management Service by the Same Physician on the Same Day of the Procedure or Other Service: It may be necessary to indicate that on the day a procedure or service identified by a CPT code was performed, the patient's condition required a significant, separately identifiable E/M service above and beyond the other service provided or beyond the usual preoperative and postoperative care associated with the procedure that was performed. A significant, separately identifiable E/M service is defined or substantiated by documentation that satisfies the relevant criteria for the respective E/M service to be reported (see **Evaluation and Management Services Guidelines** for instructions on determining level of E/M service). The E/M service may be prompted by the symptom or condition for which the procedure and/or service was provided. As such, different diagnoses are not required for reporting of the E/M services on the same date. This circumstance may be reported by adding modifier 25 to the appropriate level of E/M service.

Note: This modifier is not used to report an E/M service that resulted in a decision to perform surgery. See modifier 57. For significant, separately identifiable non-E/M services, see modifier 59.

27 Multiple Outpatient Hospital E/M Encounters on the Same Date: For hospital outpatient reporting purposes, utilization of hospital resources related to separate and distinct E/M encounters performed in multiple outpatient hospital settings on the same date may be reported by adding modifier 27 to each appropriate level outpatient and/or emergency department E/M code(s). This modifier provides a means of reporting circumstances involving evaluation and management services provided by a physician(s) in more than one (multiple) outpatient hospital setting(s) (eg, hospital emergency department, clinic). Note: This modifier is not to be used for physician reporting of multiple E/M services performed by the same physician on the same date. For physician reporting of all outpatient evaluation and management services provided by the same physician on the same date and performed in multiple outpatient settings (eg, hospital emergency department, clinic), see **Evaluation and Management, Emergency Department, or Preventive Medicine Services** codes.

50 **Bilateral Procedure:** Unless otherwise identified in the listings, bilateral procedures that are performed at the same operative session should be identified by adding modifier 50 to the appropriate five digit code.

52 **Reduced Services:** Under certain circumstances a service or procedure is partially reduced or eliminated at the physician's discretion. Under these circumstances the service provided can be identified by its usual procedure number and the addition of modifier 52, signifying that the service is reduced. This provides a means of reporting reduced services without disturbing the identification of the basic service. Note: For hospital outpatient reporting of a previously scheduled procedure/service that is partially reduced or cancelled as a result of extenuating circumstances or those that threaten the well-being of the patient prior to or after administration of anesthesia, see modifiers 73 and 74 (see modifiers approved for ASC hospital outpatient use).

58 **Staged or Related Procedure or Service by the Same Physician During the Postoperative Period:** It may be necessary to indicate that the performance of a procedure or service during the postoperative period was (a) planned or anticipated (staged); (b) more extensive than the original procedure; or (c) for therapy following a surgical procedure. This circumstance may be reported by adding modifier 58 to the staged or related procedure.

Note: For treatment of a problem that requires a return to the operating or procedure room (eg, unanticipated clinical condition), see modifier 78.

59 **Distinct Procedural Service:** Under certain circumstances, it may be necessary to indicate that a procedure or service was distinct or independent from other non-E/M services performed on the same day. Modifier 59 is used to identify procedures or services, other than E/M services, that are not normally reported together but are appropriate under the circumstances. Documentation must support a different session, different procedure or surgery, different site or organ system, separate incision or excision, separate lesion, or separate injury (or area of injury in extensive injuries) not ordinarily encountered or performed on the same day by the same individual. However, when another already established modifier is appropriate it should be used rather than modifier 59. Only if no more descriptive modifier is available and the use of modifier 59 best explains the circumstances should modifier 59 be used. Note: Modifier 59 should not be appended to an E/M service. To report a separate and distinct E/M service with a non-E/M service performed on the same date, see modifier 25.

73 **Discontinued Out-Patient Hospital/Ambulatory Surgery Center (ASC) Procedure Prior to the Administration of Anesthesia:** Due to extenuating circumstances or those that threaten the well being of the patient, the physician may cancel a surgical or diagnostic procedure subsequent to the patient's surgical preparation (including sedation when provided, and being taken to the room where the procedure is to be performed), but prior to the administration of anesthesia (local, regional block(s), or general). Under these circumstances, the intended service that is prepared for but cancelled can be reported by its usual procedure number and the addition of modifier 73. Note: The elective cancellation of a service prior to the administration of anesthesia and/or surgical preparation of the patient should not be reported. For physician reporting of a discontinued procedure, see modifier 53.

74 **Discontinued Out-Patient Hospital/Ambulatory Surgery Center (ASC) Procedure After Administration of Anesthesia:** Due to extenuating circumstances or those that threaten the well being of the patient, the physician may terminate a surgical or diagnostic procedure after the administration of anesthesia (local, regional block(s), general) or after the procedure was started (incision made, intubation started, scope inserted, etc.). Under these circumstances, the procedure started but terminated can be reported by its usual procedure number and the addition of modifier 74. Note: The elective cancellation of a service prior to the administration of anesthesia and/or surgical preparation of the patient should not be reported. For physician reporting of a discontinued procedure, see modifier 53.

76 **Repeat Procedure or Service by Same Physician:** It may be necessary to indicate that a procedure or service was repeated subsequent to the original procedure or service. This circumstance may be reported by adding modifier 76 to the repeated procedure or service.

77 **Repeat Procedure by Another Physician:** The physician may need to indicate that a basic procedure or service performed by another physician had to be repeated. This situation may be reported by adding modifier 77 to the repeated procedure/service.

78 **Unplanned Return to the Operating/Procedure Room by the Same Physician Following Initial Procedure for a Related Procedure During the Postoperative Period:** It may be necessary to indicate that another procedure was performed during the postoperative period of the initial procedure (unplanned procedure following initial procedure). When this procedure is related to the first and requires the use of an operating or procedure room, it may be reported by adding modifier 78 to the related procedure. (For repeat procedures, see modifier 76.)

79 **Unrelated Procedure or Service by the Same Physician During the Postoperative Period:** The physician may need to indicate that the performance of a procedure or service during the postoperative period was unrelated to the original procedure. This circumstance may be reported by using modifier 79. (For repeat procedures on the same day, see modifier 76.)

91 **Repeat Clinical Diagnostic Laboratory Test:** In the course of treatment of the patient, it may be necessary to repeat the same laboratory test on the same day to obtain subsequent (multiple) test results. Under these circumstances, the laboratory test performed can be identified by its usual procedure number and the addition of modifier 91. Note: This modifier may not be used when tests are rerun to confirm initial results; due to testing problems with specimens or equipment; or for any other reason when a normal, one-time, reportable result is all that is required. This modifier may not be used when another code(s) describe a series of test results (eg, glucose tolerance tests, evocative/suppression testing). This modifier may only be used for a laboratory test(s) performed more than once on the same day on the same patient.

Level II (HCPCS/National) Modifiers
Anatomical Modifiers

E1	Upper left, eyelid
E2	Lower left, eyelid
E3	Upper right, eyelid
E4	Lower right, eyelid
F1	Left hand, second digit
F2	Left hand, third digit
F3	Left hand, fourth digit
F4	Left hand, fifth digit
F5	Right hand, thumb
F6	Right hand, second digit
F7	Right hand, third digit
F8	Right hand, fourth digit
F9	Right hand, fifth digit
FA	Left hand, thumb
LT	Left side (used to identify procedures performed on the left side of the body)
RT	Right side (used to identify procedures performed on the right side of the body)
T1	Left foot, second digit

Appendix A — Modifiers

T2	Left foot, third digit
T3	Left foot, fourth digit
T4	Left foot, fifth digit
T5	Right foot, great toe
T6	Right foot, second digit
T7	Right foot, third digit
T8	Right foot, fourth digit
T9	Right foot, fifth digit
TA	Left foot, great toe

Anesthesia Modifiers

AA	Anesthesia services performed personally by anesthesiologist
AD	Medical supervision by a physician: more than four concurrent anesthesia procedures
G8	Monitored anesthesia care (MAC) for deep complex, complicated, or markedly invasive surgical procedure
G9	Monitored anesthesia care for patient who has history of severe cardio-pulmonary condition
QK	Medical direction of two, three, or four concurrent anesthesia procedures involving qualified individuals
QS	Monitored anesthesia care service
QX	CRNA service: with medical direction by a physician
QY	Medical direction of one certified registered nurse anesthetist (CRNA) by an anesthesiologist
QZ	CRNA service: without medical direction by a physician
P1	A normal healthy patient
P2	A patient with mild systemic disease
P3	A patient with severe systemic disease
P4	A patient with severe systemic disease that is a constant threat to life
P5	A moribund patient who is not expected to survive without the operation
P6	A declared brain-dead patient whose organs are being removed for donor purposes

Coronary Artery Modifiers

LC	Left circumflex coronary artery (Hospitals use with codes 92980-92984, 92995, 92996)
LD	Left anterior descending coronary artery (Hospitals use with codes 92980-92984, 92995, 92996)
RC	Right coronary artery (Hospitals use with codes 92980-92984, 92995, 92996)

Ophthalmology Modifiers

AP	Determination of refractive state was not performed in the course of diagnostic ophthalmological examination
LS	FDA-monitored intraocular lens implant
PL	Progressive addition lenses
VP	Aphakic patient

Other Modifiers

AE	Registered dietician
AF	Specialty physician
AG	Primary physician
AH	Clinical psychologist
AI	Principal physician of record
AJ	Clinical social worker
AK	Nonparticipating physician
AM	Physician, team member service
AQ	Physician providing a service in an unlisted health professional shortage area (HPSA)
AR	Physician provider services in a physician scarcity area
AS	Physician assistant, nurse practitioner, or clinical nurse specialist services for assistant at surgery
AT	Acute treatment (this modifier should be used when reporting service 98940, 98941, 98942)
CA	Procedure payable only in the inpatient setting when performed emergently on an outpatient who expires prior to admission
CB	Service ordered by a renal dialysis facility (RDF) physician as part of the ESRD beneficiary's dialysis benefit, is not part of the composite rate, and is separately reimbursable
CC	Procedure code change (use 'CC' when the procedure code submitted was changed either for administrative reasons or because an incorrect code was filed)
CG	Policy criteria applied
CR	Catastrophe/disaster related
EP	Service provided as part of Medicaid early periodic screening diagnosis and treatment (EPSDT) program
ET	Emergency services
EY	No physician or other licensed health care provider order for this item or service
FB	Item provided without cost to provider, supplier or practitioner, or full credit received for replaced device (examples, but not limited to covered under warranty, replaced due to defect, free samples)
FC	Partial credit received for replacement device
FP	Service provided as part of family planning program
G7	Pregnancy resulted from rape or incest or pregnancy certified by physician as life threatening
GA	Waiver of liability statement on file
GB	Claim being resubmitted for payment because it is no longer covered under a global payment demonstration
GC	This service has been performed in part by a resident under the direction of a teaching physician
GD	Units of service exceeds medically unlikely edit value and represents reasonable and necessary services
GE	This service has been performed by a resident without the presence of a teaching physician under the primary care exception
GF	Non-physician (e.g. nurse practitioner (NP), certified registered nurse anesthetist (CRNA), certified registered nurse (CRN), clinical nurse specialist (CNS), physician assistant (PA)) services in a critical access hospital
GG	Performance and payment of a screening mammogram and diagnostic mammogram on the same patient, same day
GH	Diagnostic mammogram converted from screening mammogram on same day
GJ	Opt out physician or practitioner emergency or urgent service
GK	Reasonable and necessary item/service associated with GA or GZ modifier
GN	Service delivered under an outpatient speech-language pathology plan of care
GO	Service delivered an outpatient occupational therapy plan of care
GP	Service delivered under an outpatient physical therapy plan of care
GQ	Via asynchronous telecommunications system
GR	This service was performed in whole or in part by a resident in a department of veterans affairs medical center or clinic, supervised in accordance with VA policy
GT	Via interactive audio and video telecommunication systems
GV	Attending physician not employed or paid under arrangement by the patient's hospice provider
GW	Service not related to the hospice patient's terminal condition
GX	Notice of liability issued, voluntary under payer policy *(Effective April 5, 2010)*
GY	Item or service statutorily excluded, does not meet the definition of any Medicare benefit or for non-Medicare insurers, is not a contract benefit
GZ	Item or service expected to be denied as not reasonable and necessary
H9	Court-ordered
HA	Child/adolescent program
HB	Adult program, nongeriatric
HC	Adult program, geriatric

HD	Pregnant/parenting women's program
HE	Mental health program
HF	Substance abuse program
HG	Opioid addiction treatment program
HH	Integrated mental health/substance abuse program
HI	Integrated mental health and mental retardation/developmental disabilities program
HJ	Employee assistance program
HK	Specialized mental health programs for high-risk populations
HL	Intern
HM	Less than bachelor degree level
HN	Bachelors degree level
HO	Masters degree level
HP	Doctoral level
HQ	Group setting
HR	Family/couple with client present
HS	Family/couple without client present
HT	Multi-disciplinary team
HU	Funded by child welfare agency
HV	Funded state addictions agency
HW	Funded by state mental health agency
HX	Funded by county/local agency
HY	Funded by juvenile justice agency
HZ	Funded by criminal justice agency
KB	Beneficiary requested upgrade for ABN, more than four modifiers identified on claim
KX	Requirements specified in the medical policy have been met
KZ	New coverage not implemented by managed care
LR	Laboratory round trip
M2	Medicare secondary payer (MSP)
PA	Surgical or other invasive procedure on wrong body part
PB	Surgical or other invasive procedure on wrong patient
PC	Wrong surgery or other invasive procedure on patient
PI	Positron emission tomography (PET) or PET/computed tomography (CT) to inform the initial treatment strategy of tumors that are biopsy proven or strongly suspected of being cancerous based on other diagnostic testing, once per cancer diagnosis
PS	Positron emission tomography (PET) or PET/computed tomography (CT) to inform the subsequent treatment strategy of cancerous tumor when the beneficiary's treating physician determines that the PET study is needed to inform subsequent anti-tumor strategy
Q0	Investigational clinical service provided in a clinical research study that is in an approved clinical research study
Q1	Routine clinical service provided in a clinical research study that is in an approved clinical research study
Q2	HCFA/ORD demonstration project procedure/service
Q3	Live kidney donor surgery and related services
Q4	Service for ordering/referring physician qualifies as a service exemption
Q5	Service furnished by a substitute physician under a reciprocal billing arrangement
Q6	Service furnished by a locum tenens physician
Q7	One Class A finding
Q8	Two Class B findings
Q9	One Class B and two Class C findings
QC	Single channel monitoring
QD	Recording and storage in solid state memory by a digital recorder
QJ	Services/items provided to a prisoner or patient in state or local custody, however the state or local government, as applicable, meets the requirements in 42 CRF 411.4 (B)
QP	Documentation is on file showing that the laboratory test(s) was ordered individually or ordered as a CPT-recognized panel other than automated profile codes 80002-80019, G0058, G0059, and G0060
QT	Recording and storage on tape by an analog tape recorder
QW	CLIA waived test
RE	Furnished in full compliance with FDA-mandated risk evaluation and mitigation strategy (REMS)
SA	Nurse practitioner rendering service in collaboration with a physician
SB	Nurse Midwife
SC	Medically necessary service or supply
SD	Services provided by registered nurse with specialized, highly technical home infusion training
SE	State and/or federally funded programs/services
SF	Second opinion ordered by a professional review organization (PRO) per section 9401, P.L.99-272 (100% reimbursement - no Medicare deductible or coinsurance)
SG	Ambulatory surgical center (ASC) facility service
SH	Second concurrently administered infusion therapy
SJ	Third or more concurrently administered infusion therapy
SK	Member of high risk population (use only with codes for immunization)
SL	State supplied vaccine
SM	Second surgical opinion
SN	Third surgical opinion
SQ	Item ordered by home health
SS	Home infusion services provided in the infusion suite of the IV therapy provider
ST	Related to trauma or injury
SU	Procedure performed in physician's office (to denote use of facility and equipment)
SW	Services provided by a certified diabetic educator
SY	Persons who are in close contact with member of high-risk population (use only with codes for immunization)
TC	Technical component. Under certain circumstances, a charge may be made for the technical component alone. Under those circumstances the technical component charge is identified by adding modifier 'TC' to the usual procedure number. Technical component charges are institutional charges and not billed separately by physicians. However, portable x-ray suppliers only bill for technical component and should utilize modifier TC. The charge data from portable x-ray suppliers will then be used to build customary and prevailing profiles.
TD	RN
TE	LPN/LVN
TF	Intermediate level of care
TG	Complex/high level of care
TH	Obstetrical treatment/services, prenatal or postpartum
TJ	Program group, child and/or adolescent
TK	Extra patient or passenger, nonambulance
TL	Early intervention/individualized family service plan (IFSP)
TM	Individualized education program (IEP)
TN	Rural/outside providers' customary service area
TR	School-based individualized education program (IEP) services provided outside the public school district responsible for the student
TS	Follow-up service
TT	Individualized service provided to more than one patient in same setting
TU	Special payment rate, overtime
TV	Special payment rates, holidays/weekends
U1	Medicaid level of care 1, as defined by each state

Appendix A — Modifiers

U2	Medicaid level of care 2, as defined by each state
U3	Medicaid level of care 3, as defined by each state
U4	Medicaid level of care 4, as defined by each state
U5	Medicaid level of care 5, as defined by each state
U6	Medicaid level of care 6, as defined by each state
U7	Medicaid level of care 7, as defined by each state
U8	Medicaid level of care 8, as defined by each state
U9	Medicaid level of care 9, as defined by each state
UA	Medicaid level of care 10, as defined by each state
UB	Medicaid level of care 11, as defined by each state
UC	Medicaid level of care 12, as defined by each state
UD	Medicaid level of care 13, as defined by each state
UF	Services provided in the morning
UG	Services provided in the afternoon
UH	Services provided in the evening
UJ	Services provided at night
UK	Services provided on behalf of the client to someone other than the client (collateral relationship)
UN	Two patients served
UP	Three patients served
UQ	Four patients served
UR	Five patients served
US	Six or more patients served
V5	Vascular catheter
V6	Arteriovenous graft
V7	Arteriovenous fistula
V8	Infection present
V9	No infection present

Category II Modifiers

- **1P** Performance measure exclusion modifier due to medical reasons

  Includes:
  - Not indicated (absence of organ/limb, already received/performed, other)
  - Contraindicated (patient allergic history, potential adverse drug interaction, other)
  - Other medical reasons

- **2P** Performance measure exclusion modifier due to patient reasons

  Includes:
  - Patient declined
  - Economic, social, or religious reasons
  - Other patient reasons

- **3P** Performance measure exclusion modifier due to system reasons

  Includes:
  - Resources to perform the services not available (eg, equipment, supplies)
  - Insurance coverage or payer-related limitations
  - Other reasons attributable to health care delivery system

- **8P** Performance measure reporting modifier - action not performed, reason not otherwise specified

  Includes:
  - Reporting of circumstances that describe a service in the measure's numerator is not performed and the reason is not otherwise specified

Dental Modifiers

- **ET** Emergency services (dental procedures performed in emergency situations should show the modifier ET)

ESRD Modifiers

- **CD** AMCC test has been ordered by an ESRD facility or MCP physician that is a part of the composite rate and is not separately billable
- **CE** AMCC test has been ordered by an ESRD facility or MCP physician that is a composite rate test but is beyond the normal frequency covered under the rate and is separately reimbursable based on medically necessary
- **CF** AMCC test has been ordered by an ESRD facility or MCP physician that is not part of the composite rate and is separately billable
- **G6** ESRD patient for whom less than six dialysis sessions have been provided in a month
- **GS** Dosage of EPO or darbepoietin alfa has been reduced and maintained in response to hematocrit or hemoglobin level
- **Q3** Live kidney donor: services associated with postoperative medical complications directly related to the donation

Genetic Testing Modifiers

Neoplasia (Solid Tumor, Excluding Sarcoma and Lymphoma)

0A	BRCA1 (Hereditary breast/ovarian cancer)
0B	BRCA2 (Hereditary breast cancer)
0C	Neurofibromin (Neurofibromatosis, type 1)
0D	Merlin (Neurofibromatosis, type 2)
0E	c-RET (Multiple endocrine neoplasia, types 2A/B, familial medullary thyroid carcinoma)
0F	VHL (Von Hippel Lindau disease, renal carcinoma)
0G	SDHD (Hereditary paraganglioma)
0H	SDHB (Hereditary paraganglioma)
0I	ERRB2, commonly called Her-2/neu
0J	MLH1 (HNPCC mismatch repair genes)
0K	MSH2, MSH6, or PMS2 (HNPCC, mismatch repair genes)
0L	APC (Hereditary polyposis coli)
0M	Rb (Retinoblastoma)
0N	TP53, commonly called p53
0O	PTEN (Cowden's syndrome)
0P	KIT, also called CD117 (gastrointestinal stromal tumor)
0Z	Solid tumor gene, not otherwise specified

Neoplasia (Sarcoma)

1A	WT1 or WT2 (Wilm's tumor)
1B	PAX3, PAX7, or FOX01A (Alveolar rhabdomyosarcoma)
1C	FLI1, ERG, ETV1, or EWSR1 (Ewing's sarcoma, desmoplastic round cell)
1D	DDIT3 or FUS (Myxoid liposarcoma)
1E	NR4A3, RBF56, or TCF12 (Myxoid chondrosarcoma)
1F	SSX1, SSX2, or SYT (Synovial sarcoma)
1G	MYCN (Neuroblastoma)
1H	COL1A1 or PDGFB (Dermatofibrosarcoma protuberans)
1I	TFE3 or ASPSCR1 (Alveolar soft parts sarcoma)
1J	JAZF1 or JJAZ1 (Endometrial stromal sarcoma)
1Z	Sarcoma gene, not otherwise specified

Neoplasia (Lymphoid/Hemtopoietic)

2A	RUNX1 or CBFA2T1, commonly called AML1 or ETO, (genes associated with t(8;21) AML1–also ETO (Acute myeloid leukemia)
2B	BCR or ABL, genes associated with t(9;22) (Chronic myelogenous or acute leukemia) BCR—also ABL (Chronic myeloid, acute lymphoid leukemia)
2C	PBX1 or TCF3, genes associated with t(1;19) (Acute lymphoblastic leukemia) CGF1
2D	CBFB or MYH11, genes associated with inv 16 (Acute myelogenous leukemia) CBF betas (leukemia)
2E	MML (Acute leukemia)
2F	PML or RARA, genes associated with t (15;17) (Acute promyelocytic leukemia) PML/RAR alpha (Promyelocytic leukemia)
2G	ETV6, commonly called TEL, gene associated with t (12;21 (acute leukemia) TEL (Leukemia)
2H	BCL2 (B cell lymphoma, follicle center cell origin) BCL-2 (Lymphoma)

Current Procedural Coding Expert

Appendix A — Modifiers

- **2I** CCND1, commonly called BCL1, cyclin D1 (Mantle cell lymphoma, myeloma) BCL-1 (Lymphoma)
- **2J** Myc (Burkitt lymphoma) c-Myc (Lymphoma)
- **2K** IgH (Lymphoma/leukemia)
- **2L** IGK (Lymphoma/leukemia)
- **2M** TRB, T cell receptor beta (Lymphoma/leukemia)
- **2N** TRG, T cell receptor gamma (Lymphoma/leukemia)
- **2O** SIL or TAL1 (T cell leukemia)
- **2T** BCL6 (B cell lymphoma)
- **2Q** API1 or MALT1 (MALT lymphoma)
- **2R** NPM or ALK, genes associated with t (2;5) (anaplastic large cell lymphoma)
- **2S** FLT3 (Acute myelogenous leukemia)
- **2Z** Lymphoid/hematopoetic neoplasia, not otherwise specified)

Non-Neoplastic Hematology/Coagulation
- **3A** F5, commonly called Factor V (Leiden, others) (Hypercoagulable state)
- **3B** FACC (Fanconi anemia)
- **3C** FACD (Fanconi anemia)
- **3D** HBB, Beta globin (Thalassemia, sickle cell anemia, other hemoglobinopathies)
- **3E** HBA, commonly called alpha globin (thalassemia)
- **3F** MTHFR (Elevated homocystinemia)
- **3G** F2, commonly called prothrombin (20210, others) (Hypercoagulable state) prothrombin (Factor II, 20210A) (Hypercoagulable state)
- **3H** F8, commonly called Factor VII (Hemophilia A/VWF)
- **3I** F9, commonly called Factor IX (Hemophilia B)
- **3K** F13, commonly called factor XIII (bleeding or hypercoagulable state) beta globin
- **3Z** Non-neoplastic hematology/coagulation, not otherwise specified

Histocompatibility/Blood Typing/Identity/Microsatellite
- **4A** HLA-A
- **4B** HLA-B
- **4C** HLA-C
- **4D** HLA-D
- **4E** HLA-DR
- **4F** HLA-DQ
- **4G** HLA-DP
- **4H** Kell
- **4I** Fingerprint for engraftment (postallogenic progenitor cell transplant)
- **4J** Fingerprint for donor allelotype (allogeneic transplant)
- **4K** Fingerprint for recipient allelotype (allogeneic transplant)
- **4L** Fingerprint for leukocyte chimerism (allogeneic solid organ transplant)
- **4M** Fingerprint for maternal versus fetal origin
- **4N** Microsatellite instability
- **4O** Microsatelite loss (loss of heterozygosity)
- **4Z** Histocompatibility/blood typing, not otherwise specified

Neurologic, NonNeoplastic
- **5A** ASPA, commonly called Aspartoacylase A (Canavan disease)
- **5B** FMR-1 (Fragile X, FRAXA, syndrome)
- **5C** FRDA, commonly called Frataxin (Freidreich's ataxia)
- **5D** HD, commonly called Huntington (Huntington's disease)
- **5E** GABRA5, NIPA1, UBE3A, or ANCR GABRA (Prader Willi-Angelman syndrome)
- **5F** GJB2, commonly called Connexin-26 (Hereditary hearing loss) Connexin-26 (GJB2) (Hereditary deafness)
- **5G** GJB1, commonly called Connexin-32 (X-linked Charcot-Marie-Tooth disease)
- **5H** SNRPN (Prader Willi-Angelman syndrome)
- **5I** SCA1, commonly called Ataxin-1 (Spinocerebellar ataxia, type 1)
- **5J** SCA2, commonly called Ataxin-2 (Spinocerebellar ataxia, type 2)
- **5K** MJD, commonly called Ataxin-3 (Spinocerebellar ataxia, type 3, Machado-Joseph disease)
- **5L** CACNA1A (Spinocerebellar ataxia, type 6)
- **5M** ATXN7 Ataxin-7 (Spinocerebellar ataxia, type 7)
- **5N** PMP-22 (Charcot-Marie-Tooth disease, type 1A)
- **5O** MECP2 (Rett syndrome)
- **5Z** Neurologic, nonneoplastic, not otherwise specified

Muscular, NonNeoplastic
- **6A** DMD, commonly called Dystrophin (Duchenne/Becker muscular dystrophy)
- **6B** DMPK (Myotonic dystrophy, type 1)
- **6C** ZNF-9 (Myotonic dystrophy, type 2)
- **6D** SMN1/SMN2 (Autosomal recessive spinal muscular atrophy)
- **6E** MTTK, commonly called tRNAlys (mytonic epilepsy, MERRF)
- **6F** MTTL1, commonly called tRNAleu (mitochondrial encephalomyopathy, MELAS)
- **6Z** Muscular, not otherwise specified

Metabolic, Other
- **7A** APOE, commonly called Apolipoprotein E (Cardiovascular disease or Alzheimer's disease)
- **7B** NPC1 or NPC2, commonly called sphingomyelin phosphodiesterase (Nieman-Pick disease)
- **7C** GBA, commonly called Acid Beta Glucosidase (Gaucher disease)
- **7D** HFE (Hemochromatosis)
- **7E** HEXA, commonly called Hexosaminidase A (Tay-Sachs disease)
- **7F** ACADM (medium chain acyl CoA dehydrogenase deficiency)
- **7Z** Metabolic, other, not otherwise specified

Metabolic, Transport
- **8A** CFTR (Cystic fibrosis)
- **8B** PRSS1 (Hereditary pancreatitis)
- **8C** Long QT syndrome, KCN (Jervell and Lange-Nielsen syndromes, types 1, 2, 5, and 6) and SCN (Brugada syndrome, SIDS and type 3)
- **8Z** Metabolic, transport, not otherwise specified)

Metabolic-Pharmacogenetics
- **9A** TPMT, commonly called (thiopurine methyltransferase) (patients on antimetabolite therapy)
- **9B** CYP2 genes, commonly called cytochrome p450 (drug metabolism)
- **9C** ABCB1, commonly called MDR1 or p-glycoprotein (drug transport)
- **9D** NAT2 (drug metabolism)
- **9L** Metabolic-pharmacogenetics, not otherwise specified

Dysmorphology
- **9M** FGFR1 (Pfeiffer and Kallmann syndromes)
- **9N** FGFR2 (Crouzon, Jackson-Weiss, Apert, Saethre-Chotzen syndromes)
- **9O** FGFR3 (Achondroplasia, Hypochondroplasia, Thanatophoric dysplasia, types I and II, Crouzon syndrome with acanthosis nigricans, Muencke syndromes)
- **9P** TWIST (Saethre-Chotzen syndrome)
- **9Q** DCGR, commonly called CATCH-22 (DiGeorge and 22q11 deletion syndromes)
- **9Z** Dysmorphology, not otherwise specified

Appendix B — New, Changed, Deleted, and Modified Codes

The following lists include codes ear-marked as new, changed, and deleted.

New Codes

- **14301** Adjacent tissue transfer or rearrangement, any area; defect 30.1 sq cm to 60.0 sq cm
- **14302** Adjacent tissue transfer or rearrangement, any area; each additional 30.0 sq cm, or part thereof (List separately in addition to code for primary procedure)
- **21011** Excision, tumor, soft tissue of face or scalp, subcutaneous; less than 2 cm
- **21012** Excision, tumor, soft tissue of face or scalp, subcutaneous; 2 cm or greater
- **21013** Excision, tumor, soft tissue of face and scalp, subfascial (eg, subgaleal, intramuscular); less than 2 cm
- **21014** Excision, tumor, soft tissue of face and scalp, subfascial (eg, subgaleal, intramuscular); 2 cm or greater
- **21016** Radical resection of tumor (eg, malignant neoplasm), soft tissue of face or scalp; 2 cm or greater
- **21552** Excision, tumor, soft tissue of neck or anterior thorax, subcutaneous; 3 cm or greater
- **21554** Excision, tumor, soft tissue of neck or anterior thorax, subfascial (eg, intramuscular); 5 cm or greater
- **21558** Radical resection of tumor (eg, malignant neoplasm), soft tissue of neck or anterior thorax; 5 cm or greater
- **21931** Excision, tumor, soft tissue of back or flank, subcutaneous; 3 cm or greater
- **21932** Excision, tumor, soft tissue of back or flank, subfascial (eg, intramuscular); less than 5 cm
- **21933** Excision, tumor, soft tissue of back or flank, subfascial (eg, intramuscular); 5 cm or greater
- **21936** Radical resection of tumor (eg, malignant neoplasm), soft tissue of back or flank; 5 cm or greater
- **22901** Excision, tumor, soft tissue of abdominal wall, subfascial (eg, intramuscular); 5 cm or greater
- **22902** Excision, tumor, soft tissue of abdominal wall, subcutaneous; less than 3 cm
- **22903** Excision, tumor, soft tissue of abdominal wall, subcutaneous; 3 cm or greater
- **22904** Radical resection of tumor (eg, malignant neoplasm), soft tissue of abdominal wall; less than 5 cm
- **22905** Radical resection of tumor (eg, malignant neoplasm), soft tissue of abdominal wall; 5 cm or greater
- **23071** Excision, tumor, soft tissue of shoulder area, subcutaneous; 3 cm or greater
- **23073** Excision, tumor, soft tissue of shoulder area, subfascial (eg, intramuscular); 5 cm or greater
- **23078** Radical resection of tumor (eg, malignant neoplasm), soft tissue of shoulder area; 5 cm or greater
- **24071** Excision, tumor, soft tissue of upper arm or elbow area, subcutaneous; 3 cm or greater
- **24073** Excision, tumor, soft tissue of upper arm or elbow area, subfascial (eg, intramuscular); 5 cm or greater
- **24079** Radical resection of tumor (eg, malignant neoplasm), soft tissue of upper arm or elbow area; 5 cm or greater
- **25071** Excision, tumor, soft tissue of forearm and/or wrist area, subcutaneous; 3 cm or greater
- **25073** Excision, tumor, soft tissue of forearm and/or wrist area, subfascial (eg, intramuscular); 3 cm or greater
- **25078** Radical resection of tumor (eg, malignant neoplasm), soft tissue of forearm and/or wrist area; 3 cm or greater
- **26111** Excision, tumor or vascular malformation, soft tissue of hand or finger, subcutaneous; 1.5 cm or greater
- **26113** Excision, tumor, soft tissue, or vascular malformation, of hand or finger, subfascial (eg, intramuscular); 1.5 cm or greater
- **26118** Radical resection of tumor (eg, malignant neoplasm), soft tissue of hand or finger; 3 cm or greater
- **27043** Excision, tumor, soft tissue of pelvis and hip area, subcutaneous; 3 cm or greater
- **27045** Excision, tumor, soft tissue of pelvis and hip area, subfascial (eg, intramuscular); 5 cm or greater
- **27059** Radical resection of tumor (eg, malignant neoplasm), soft tissue of pelvis and hip area; 5 cm or greater
- **27337** Excision, tumor, soft tissue of thigh or knee area, subcutaneous; 3 cm or greater
- **27339** Excision, tumor, soft tissue of thigh or knee area, subfascial (eg, intramuscular); 5 cm or greater
- **27364** Radical resection of tumor (eg, malignant neoplasm), soft tissue of thigh or knee area; 5 cm or greater
- **27616** Radical resection of tumor (eg, malignant neoplasm), soft tissue of leg or ankle area; 5 cm or greater
- **27632** Excision, tumor, soft tissue of leg or ankle area, subcutaneous; 3 cm or greater
- **27634** Excision, tumor, soft tissue of leg or ankle area, subfascial (eg, intramuscular); 5 cm or greater
- **28039** Excision, tumor, soft tissue of foot or toe, subcutaneous; 1.5 cm or greater
- **28041** Excision, tumor, soft tissue of foot or toe, subfascial (eg, intramuscular); 1.5 cm or greater
- **28047** Radical resection of tumor (eg, malignant neoplasm), soft tissue of foot or toe; 3 cm or greater
- **29581** Application of multi-layer venous wound compression system, below knee
- **31626** Bronchoscopy, rigid or flexible, including fluoroscopic guidance, when performed; with placement of fiducial markers, single or multiple
- **31627** Bronchoscopy, rigid or flexible, including fluoroscopic guidance, when performed; with computer-assisted, image-guided navigation (List separately in addition to code for primary procedure[s])
- **32552** Removal of indwelling tunneled pleural catheter with cuff
- **32553** Placement of interstitial device(s) for radiation therapy guidance (eg, fiducial markers, dosimeter), percutaneous, intra-thoracic, single or multiple
- **32561** Instillation(s), via chest tube/catheter, agent for fibrinolysis (eg, fibrinolytic agent for break-up of multiloculated effusion); initial day
- **32562** Instillation(s), via chest tube/catheter, agent for fibrinolysis (eg, fibrinolytic agent for break-up of multiloculated effusion); subsequent day
- **33782** Aortic root translocation with ventricular septal defect and pulmonary stenosis repair (ie, Nikaidoh procedure); without coronary ostium reimplantation
- **33783** Aortic root translocation with ventricular septal defect and pulmonary stenosis repair (ie, Nikaidoh procedure); with reimplantation of 1 or both coronary ostia
- **33981** Replacement of extracorporeal ventricular assist device, single or biventricular, pump(s), single or each pump
- **33982** Replacement of ventricular assist device pump(s); implantable intracorporeal, single ventricle, without cardiopulmonary bypass
- **33983** Replacement of ventricular assist device pump(s); implantable intracorporeal, single ventricle, with cardiopulmonary bypass
- **36147** Introduction of needle and/or catheter, arteriovenous shunt created for dialysis (graft/fistula); initial access with complete radiological evaluation of dialysis access, including fluoroscopy, image documentation and report (includes access of shunt, injection[s] of contrast, and all necessary imaging from the arterial anastomosis and adjacent artery through entire venous outflow, including the inferior or superior vena cava)
- **36148** Introduction of needle and/or catheter, arteriovenous shunt created for dialysis (graft/fistula); additional access for therapeutic intervention (List separately in addition to code for primary procedure)

Current Procedural Coding Expert
Appendix B — New, Changed, Deleted, and Modified Codes

New Codes (continued)

- 37761 Ligation of perforator vein(s), subfascial, open, including ultrasound guidance, when performed, 1 leg
- 43281 Laparoscopy, surgical, repair of paraesophageal hernia, includes fundoplasty, when performed; without implantation of mesh
- 43282 Laparoscopy, surgical, repair of paraesophageal hernia, includes fundoplasty, when performed; with implantation of mesh
- 43775 Laparoscopy, surgical, gastric restrictive procedure; longitudinal gastrectomy (ie, sleeve gastrectomy)
- 45171 Excision of rectal tumor, transanal approach; not including muscularis propria (ie, partial thickness)
- 45172 Excision of rectal tumor, transanal approach; including muscularis propria (ie, full thickness)
- 46707 Repair of anorectal fistula with plug (eg, porcine small intestine submucosa [SIS])
- 49411 Placement of interstitial device(s) for radiation therapy guidance (eg, fiducial markers, dosimeter), percutaneous, intra-abdominal, intra-pelvic (except prostate), and/or retroperitoneum, single or multiple
- 51727 Complex cystometrogram (ie, calibrated electronic equipment); with urethral pressure profile studies (ie, urethral closure pressure profile), any technique
- 51728 Complex cystometrogram (ie, calibrated electronic equipment); with voiding pressure studies (ie, bladder voiding pressure), any technique
- 51729 Complex cystometrogram (ie, calibrated electronic equipment); with voiding pressure studies (ie, bladder voiding pressure) and urethral pressure profile studies (ie, urethral closure pressure profile), any technique
- 53855 Insertion of a temporary prostatic urethral stent, including urethral measurement
- 57426 Revision (including removal) of prosthetic vaginal graft, laparoscopic approach
- 63661 Removal of spinal neurostimulator electrode percutaneous array(s), including fluoroscopy, when performed
- 63662 Removal of spinal neurostimulator electrode plate/paddle(s) placed via laminotomy or laminectomy, including fluoroscopy, when performed
- 63663 Revision including replacement, when performed, of spinal neurostimulator electrode percutaneous array(s), including fluoroscopy, when performed
- 63664 Revision including replacement, when performed, of spinal neurostimulator electrode plate/paddle(s) placed via laminotomy or laminectomy, including fluoroscopy, when performed
- 64490 Injection(s), diagnostic or therapeutic agent, paravertebral facet (zygapophyseal) joint (or nerves innervating that joint) with image guidance (fluoroscopy or CT), cervical or thoracic; single level
- 64491 Injection(s), diagnostic or therapeutic agent, paravertebral facet (zygapophyseal) joint (or nerves innervating that joint) with image guidance (fluoroscopy or CT), cervical or thoracic; second level (List separately in addition to code for primary procedure)
- 64492 Injection(s), diagnostic or therapeutic agent, paravertebral facet (zygapophyseal) joint (or nerves innervating that joint) with image guidance (fluoroscopy or CT), cervical or thoracic; third and any additional level(s) (List separately in addition to code for primary procedure)
- 64493 Injection(s), diagnostic or therapeutic agent, paravertebral facet (zygapophyseal) joint (or nerves innervating that joint) with image guidance (fluoroscopy or CT), lumbar or sacral; single level
- 64494 Injection(s), diagnostic or therapeutic agent, paravertebral facet (zygapophyseal) joint (or nerves innervating that joint) with image guidance (fluoroscopy or CT), lumbar or sacral; second level (List separately in addition to code for primary procedure)
- 64495 Injection(s), diagnostic or therapeutic agent, paravertebral facet (zygapophyseal) joint (or nerves innervating that joint) with image guidance (fluoroscopy or CT), lumbar or sacral; third and any additional level(s) (List separately in addition to code for primary procedure)
- 74261 Computed tomographic (CT) colonography, diagnostic, including image postprocessing; without contrast material
- 74262 Computed tomographic (CT) colonography, diagnostic, including image postprocessing; with contrast material(s) including non-contrast images, if performed
- 74263 Computed tomographic (CT) colonography, screening, including image postprocessing
- 75565 Cardiac magnetic resonance imaging for velocity flow mapping (List separately in addition to code for primary procedure)
- 75571 Computed tomography, heart, without contrast material, with quantitative evaluation of coronary calcium
- 75572 Computed tomography, heart, with contrast material, for evaluation of cardiac structure and morphology (including 3D image postprocessing, assessment of cardiac function, and evaluation of venous structures, if performed)
- 75573 Computed tomography, heart, with contrast material, for evaluation of cardiac structure and morphology in the setting of congenital heart disease (including 3D image postprocessing, assessment of LV cardiac function, RV structure and function and evaluation of venous structures, if performed)
- 75574 Computed tomographic angiography, heart, coronary arteries and bypass grafts (when present), with contrast material, including 3D image postprocessing (including evaluation of cardiac structure and morphology, assessment of cardiac function, and evaluation of venous structures, if performed)
- 75791 Angiography, arteriovenous shunt (eg, dialysis patient fistula/graft), complete evaluation of dialysis access, including fluoroscopy, image documentation and report (includes injections of contrast and all necessary imaging from the arterial anastomosis and adjacent artery through entire venous outflow, including the inferior or superior vena cava), radiological supervision and interpretation
- 77338 Multi-leaf collimator (MLC) device(s) for intensity modulated radiation therapy (IMRT), design and construction per IMRT plan
- 78451 Myocardial perfusion imaging, tomographic (SPECT) (including attenuation correction, qualitative or quantitative wall motion, ejection fraction by first pass or gated technique, additional quantification, when performed); single study, at rest or stress (exercise or pharmacologic)
- 78452 Myocardial perfusion imaging, tomographic (SPECT) (including attenuation correction, qualitative or quantitative wall motion, ejection fraction by first pass or gated technique, additional quantification, when performed); multiple studies, at rest and/or stress (exercise or pharmacologic) and/or redistribution and/or rest reinjection
- 78453 Myocardial perfusion imaging, planar (including qualitative or quantitative wall motion, ejection fraction by first pass or gated technique, additional quantification, when performed); single study, at rest or stress (exercise or pharmacologic)
- 78454 Myocardial perfusion imaging, planar (including qualitative or quantitative wall motion, ejection fraction by first pass or gated technique, additional quantification, when performed); multiple studies, at rest and/or stress (exercise or pharmacologic) and/or redistribution and/or rest reinjection
- 83987 pH; exhaled breath condensate
- 84145 Procalcitonin (PCT)
- 84431 Thromboxane metabolite(s), including thromboxane if performed, urine
- 86305 Human epididymis protein 4 (HE4)
- 86352 Cellular function assay involving stimulation (eg, mitogen or antigen) and detection of biomarker (eg, ATP)
- 86780 Antibody; Treponema pallidum
- 86825 Human leukocyte antigen (HLA) crossmatch, non-cytotoxic (eg, using flow cytometry); first serum sample or dilution
- 86826 Human leukocyte antigen (HLA) crossmatch, non-cytotoxic (eg, using flow cytometry); each additional serum sample or sample dilution (List separately in addition to primary procedure)
- 87150 Culture, typing; identification by nucleic acid (DNA or RNA) probe, amplified probe technique, per culture or isolate, each organism probed
- 87153 Culture, typing; identification by nucleic acid sequencing method, each isolate (eg, sequencing of the 16S rRNA gene)

Appendix B — New, Changed, Deleted, and Modified Codes

New Codes (continued)

- 87493 Infectious agent detection by nucleic acid (DNA or RNA); Clostridium difficile, toxin gene(s), amplified probe technique
- 88387 Macroscopic examination, dissection, and preparation of tissue for non-microscopic analytical studies (eg, nucleic acid-based molecular studies); each tissue preparation (eg, a single lymph node)
- 88388 Macroscopic examination, dissection, and preparation of tissue for non-microscopic analytical studies (eg, nucleic acid-based molecular studies); in conjunction with a touch imprint, intraoperative consultation, or frozen section, each tissue preparation (eg, a single lymph node) (List separately in addition to code for primary procedure)
- 88738 Hemoglobin (Hgb), quantitative, transcutaneous
- 89398 Unlisted reproductive medicine laboratory procedure
- 90470 H1N1 immunization administration (intramuscular, intranasal), including counseling when performed
- 90644 Meningococcal conjugate vaccine, serogroups C & Y and Hemophilus influenza b vaccine, tetanus toxoid conjugate (Hib-MenCY-TT), 4-dose schedule, when administered to children 2-15 months of age, for intramuscular use
- 92540 Basic vestibular evaluation, includes spontaneous nystagmus test with eccentric gaze fixation nystagmus, with recording, positional nystagmus test, minimum of 4 positions, with recording, optokinetic nystagmus test, bidirectional foveal and peripheral stimulation, with recording, and oscillating tracking test, with recording
- 92550 Tympanometry and reflex threshold measurements
- 92570 Acoustic immittance testing, includes tympanometry (impedance testing), acoustic reflex threshold testing, and acoustic reflex decay testing
- 93750 Interrogation of ventricular assist device (VAD), in person, with physician analysis of device parameters (eg, drivelines, alarms, power surges), review of device function (eg, flow and volume status, septum status, recovery), with programming, if performed, and report
- 94011 Measurement of spirometric forced expiratory flows in an infant or child through 2 years of age
- 94012 Measurement of spirometric forced expiratory flows, before and after bronchodilator, in an infant or child through 2 years of age
- 94013 Measurement of lung volumes (ie, functional residual capacity [FRC], forced vital capacity [FVC], and expiratory reserve volume [ERV]) in an infant or child through 2 years of age
- 95905 Motor and/or sensory nerve conduction, using preconfigured electrode array(s), amplitude and latency/velocity study, each limb, includes F-wave study when performed, with interpretation and report
- 0199T Physiologic recording of tremor using accelerometer(s) and/or gyroscope(s) (including frequency and amplitude) including interpretation and report
- 0203T Sleep study, unattended, simultaneous recording; heart rate, oxygen saturation, respiratory analysis (eg, by airflow or peripheral arterial tone) and sleep time
- 0204T Sleep study, unattended, simultaneous recording; minimum of heart rate, oxygen saturation, and respiratory analysis (eg, by airflow or peripheral arterial tone)
- 0205T Intravascular catheter-based coronary vessel or graft spectroscopy (eg, infrared) during diagnostic evaluation and/or therapeutic intervention including imaging supervision, interpretation, and report, each vessel (List separately in addition to code for primary procedure)
- 0206T Algorithmic analysis, remote, of electrocardiographic-derived data with computer probability assessment, including report
- 0207T Evacuation of meibomian glands, automated, using heat and intermittent pressure, unilateral
- 0208T Pure tone audiometry (threshold), automated (includes use of computer-assisted device); air only
- 0209T Pure tone audiometry (threshold), automated (includes use of computer-assisted device); air and bone
- 0210T Speech audiometry threshold, automated (includes use of computer-assisted device);
- 0211T Speech audiometry threshold, automated (includes use of computer-assisted device); with speech recognition
- 0212T Comprehensive audiometry threshold evaluation and speech recognition (0209T, 0211T combined), automated (includes use of computer-assisted device)
- 0213T Injection(s), diagnostic or therapeutic agent, paravertebral facet (zygapophyseal) joint (or nerves innervating that joint) with ultrasound guidance, cervical or thoracic; single level
- 0214T Injection(s), diagnostic or therapeutic agent, paravertebral facet (zygapophyseal) joint (or nerves innervating that joint) with ultrasound guidance, cervical or thoracic; second level (List separately in addition to code for primary procedure)
- 0215T Injection(s), diagnostic or therapeutic agent, paravertebral facet (zygapophyseal) joint (or nerves innervating that joint) with ultrasound guidance, cervical or thoracic; third and any additional level(s) (List separately in addition to code for primary procedure)
- 0216T Injection(s), diagnostic or therapeutic agent, paravertebral facet (zygapophyseal) joint (or nerves innervating that joint) with ultrasound guidance, lumbar or sacral; single level
- 0217T Injection(s), diagnostic or therapeutic agent, paravertebral facet (zygapophyseal) joint (or nerves innervating that joint) with ultrasound guidance, lumbar or sacral; second level (List separately in addition to code for primary procedure)
- 0218T Injection(s), diagnostic or therapeutic agent, paravertebral facet (zygapophyseal) joint (or nerves innervating that joint) with ultrasound guidance, lumbar or sacral; third and any additional level(s) (List separately in addition to code for primary procedure)
- 0219T Placement of posterior intrafacet implant(s), unilateral or bilateral, including imaging and placement of bone graft(s) or synthetic device(s), single level; cervical
- 0220T Placement of posterior intrafacet implant(s), unilateral or bilateral, including imaging and placement of bone graft(s) or synthetic device(s), single level; thoracic
- 0221T Placement of posterior intrafacet implant(s), unilateral or bilateral, including imaging and placement of bone graft(s) or synthetic device(s), single level; lumbar
- 0222T Placement of posterior intrafacet implant(s), unilateral or bilateral, including imaging and placement of bone graft(s) or synthetic device(s), single level; each additional vertebral segment (List separately in addition to code for primary procedure)
- 0529F Interval of 3 or more years since patient's last colonoscopy, documented (End/Polyp)
- 0535F Dyspnea management plan of care, documented (Pall Cr)
- 0540F Glucorticoid Management Plan Documented (RA)
- 0545F Plan for follow-up care for major depressive disorder, documented (MDD ADOL)
- 1150F Documentation that a patient has a substantial risk of death within one year (Pall Cr)
- 1151F Documentation that a patient does not have a substantial risk of death within 1 year (Pall Cr)
- 1152F Documentation of advanced disease diagnosis, goals of care prioritize comfort (Pall Cr)
- 1153F Documentation of advanced disease diagnosis, goals of care do not prioritize comfort (Pall Cr)
- 1157F Advance care plan or similar legal document present in the medical record (COA)
- 1158F Advance care planning discussion documented in the medical record (COA)
- 1159F Medication list documented in medical record (COA)
- 1160F Review of all medications by a prescribing practitioner or clinical pharmacist (such as, prescriptions, OTCs, herbal therapies and supplements) documented in the medical record (COA)
- 1170F Functional status assessed (COA) (RA)
- 1200F Seizure type(s) and current seizure frequency(ies) documented (EPI)
- 1205F Etiology of epilepsy or epilepsy syndrome(s) reviewed and documented (EPI)

Current Procedural Coding Expert — Appendix B — New, Changed, Deleted, and Modified Codes

New Codes (continued)

- **2050F** Wound characteristics including size AND nature of wound base tissue AND amount of drainage prior to debridement documented (CWC)
- **2060F** Patient interviewed directly by evaluating clinician on or before date of diagnosis of major depressive disorder (MDD ADOL)
- **3008F** Body Mass Index (BMI), documented (PV)
- **3015F** Cervical cancer screening results documented and reviewed (PV)
- **3016F** Patient screened for unhealthy alcohol use using a systematic screening method (PV)
- **3018F** Pre-procedure risk assessment AND depth of insertion AND quality of the bowel prep AND complete description of polyp(s) found, including location of each polyp, size, number and gross morphology AND recommendations for follow-up in final colonoscopy report, documented (End/Polyp)
- **3038F** Pulmonary function test performed within 12 months prior to surgery (Lung/Esop Cx)
- **3293F** ABO and Rh blood typing documented as performed (Pre-Cr)
- **3294F** Group B Streptococcus (GBS) screening documented as performed during week 35-37 gestation (Pre-Cr)
- **3323F** Clinical tumor, node and metastases (TNM) staging documented and reviewed prior to surgery (Lung/Esop Cx)
- **3324F** MRI or CT scan ordered, reviewed or requested (EPI)
- **3328F** Performance status documented and reviewed within 2 weeks prior to surgery(Lung/Esop Cx)
- **3450F** Dyspnea screened, no dyspnea or mild dyspnea (Pall Cr)
- **3451F** Dyspnea screened, moderate or severe dyspnea (Pall Cr)
- **3452F** Dyspnea not screened (Pall Cr)
- **3455F** TB screening performed and results interpreted within six months prior to initiation of first-time biologic disease modifying anti-rheumatic drug therapy for RA (RA)
- **3470F** Rheumatoid arthritis (RA) disease activity, low (RA)
- **3471F** Rheumatoid arthritis (RA) disease activity, moderate (RA)
- **3472F** Rheumatoid arthritis (RA) disease activity, high (RA)
- **3475F** Disease prognosis for rheumatoid arthritis assessed, poor prognosis documented (RA)
- **3476F** Disease prognosis for rheumatoid arthritis assessed, good prognosis documented (RA)
- **3490F** History of AIDS-defining condition (HIV)
- **3491F** HIV indeterminate (infants of undetermined HIV status born of HIV-infected mothers) (HIV)
- **3492F** History of nadir CD4+ cell count <350 cells/mm3 (HIV)
- **3493F** No history of nadir CD4+ cell count <350 cells/mm3 AND no history of AIDS-defining condition (HIV)
- **3494F** CD4+ cell count <200 cells/mm3 (HIV)
- **3495F** CD4+ cell count 200 - 499 cells/mm3 (HIV)
- **3496F** CD4+ cell count >=500 cells/mm3 (HIV)
- **3497F** CD4+ cell percentage <15% (HIV)
- **3498F** CD4+ cell percentage >=15% (HIV)
- **3650F** Electroencephalogram (EEG) ordered, reviewed or requested (EPI)
- **4004F** Patient screened for tobacco use AND received tobacco cessation counseling, if identified as a tobacco user (PV)
- **4063F** Antidepressant pharmacotherapy considered and not prescribed (MDD ADOL)
- **4192F** Patient not receiving glucocorticoid therapy (RA)
- **4193F** Patient receiving <10 mg daily prednisone (or equivalent), or RA activity is worsening, or glucocorticoid use is for less than 6 months (RA)
- **4194F** Patient receiving >= 10 mg daily prednisone (or equivalent) for longer than 6 months, and improvement or no change in disease activity (RA)
- **4195F** Patient receiving first-time biologic disease modifying anti-rheumatic drug therapy for rheumatoid arthritis (RA)
- **4196F** Patient not receiving first-time biologic disease modifying anti-rheumatic drug therapy for rheumatoid arthritis (RA)
- **4255F** Duration of general or neuraxial anesthesia 60 minutes or longer, as documented in the anesthesia record
- **4256F** Duration of general or neuraxial anesthesia less than 60 minutes, as documented in the anesthesia record
- **4260F** Wound surface culture technique used (CWC)
- **4261F** Technique other than surface culture of the wound exudate used (eg, Levine/deep swab technique, semi-quantitative or quantitative swab technique) OR wound surface culture technique not used (CWC)
- **4265F** Use of wet to dry dressings prescribed or recommended (CWC)
- **4266F** Use of wet to dry dressings neither prescribed nor recommended (CWC)
- **4267F** Compression therapy prescribed (CWC)
- **4268F** Patient education regarding the need for long term compression therapy including interval replacement of compression stockings, received (CWC)
- **4269F** Appropriate method of offloading (pressure relief) prescribed (CWC)
- **4276F** Potent antiretroviral therapy prescribed (HIV)
- **4279F** Pneumocystis jiroveci pneumonia prophylaxis prescribed (HIV)
- **4280F** Pneumocystis jiroveci pneumonia prophylaxis prescribed within 3 months of low CD4+ cell count or percentage (HIV)
- **4305F** Patient education regarding appropriate foot care AND daily inspection of the feet received (CWC)
- **4306F** Patient counseled regarding psychosocial AND pharmacologic treatment options for opioid addiction (SUD)
- **4330F** Counseling about epilepsy specific safety issues provided to patient (or caregiver (s)) (EPI)
- **4340F** Counseling for women of childbearing potential with epilepsy (EPI)
- **5100F** Potential risk for fracture communicated to the referring physician within 24 hours of completion of the imaging study (NUC_MED)
- **5200F** Consideration of referral for a neurological evaluation of appropriateness for surgical therapy for intractable epilepsy within the past 3 years (EPI)
- **6070F** Patient queried and counseled about anti-epileptic drug (AED) side-effects (EPI)

Changed Codes

- **19295** Image guided placement, metallic localization clip, percutaneous, during breast biopsy/aspiration (List separately in addition to code for primary procedure)
- **21015** Radical resection of tumor (eg, malignant neoplasm), soft tissue of face or scalp; less than 2 cm
- **21555** Excision, tumor, soft tissue of neck or anterior thorax, subcutaneous; less than 3 cm
- **21556** Excision, tumor, soft tissue of neck or anterior thorax, subfascial (eg, intramuscular); less than 5 cm
- **21557** Radical resection of tumor (eg, malignant neoplasm), soft tissue of neck or anterior thorax; less than 5 cm
- **21930** Excision, tumor, soft tissue of back or flank, subcutaneous; less than 3 cm
- **21935** Radical resection of tumor (eg, malignant neoplasm), soft tissue of back or flank; less than 5 cm
- **22520** Percutaneous vertebroplasty, 1 vertebral body, unilateral or bilateral injection; thoracic
- **22521** Percutaneous vertebroplasty, 1 vertebral body, unilateral or bilateral injection; lumbar
- **22527** Percutaneous intradiscal electrothermal annuloplasty, unilateral or bilateral, including fluoroscopic guidance; 1 or more additional levels (List separately in addition to code for primary procedure)
- **22900** Excision, tumor, soft tissue of abdominal wall, subfascial (eg, intramuscular); less than 5 cm
- **23075** Excision, tumor, soft tissue of shoulder area, subcutaneous; less than 3 cm
- **23076** Excision, tumor, soft tissue of shoulder area, subfascial (eg, intramuscular); less than 5 cm

Appendix B — New, Changed, Deleted, and Modified Codes

Changed Codes (continued)

- 23077 Radical resection of tumor (eg, malignant neoplasm), soft tissue of shoulder area; less than 5 cm
- 23200 Radical resection of tumor; clavicle
- 23210 Radical resection of tumor; scapula
- 23220 Radical resection of tumor, proximal humerus
- 24075 Excision, tumor, soft tissue of upper arm or elbow area, subcutaneous; less than 3 cm
- 24076 Excision, tumor, soft tissue of upper arm or elbow area, subfascial (eg, intramuscular); less than 5 cm
- 24077 Radical resection of tumor (eg, malignant neoplasm), soft tissue of upper arm or elbow area; less than 5 cm
- 24150 Radical resection of tumor, shaft, or distal humerus
- 24152 Radical resection of tumor, radial head or neck
- 25075 Excision, tumor, soft tissue of forearm and/or wrist area, subcutaneous; less than 3 cm
- 25076 Excision, tumor, soft tissue of forearm and/or wrist area, subfascial (eg, intramuscular); less than 3 cm
- 25077 Radical resection of tumor (eg, malignant neoplasm), soft tissue of forearm and/or wrist area; less than 3 cm
- 25170 Radical resection of tumor, radius or ulna
- 26115 Excision, tumor or vascular malformation, soft tissue of hand or finger, subcutaneous; less than 1.5 cm
- 26116 Excision, tumor, soft tissue, or vascular malformation, of hand or finger, subfascial (eg, intramuscular); less than 1.5 cm
- 26117 Radical resection of tumor (eg, malignant neoplasm), soft tissue of hand or finger; less than 3 cm
- 26250 Radical resection of tumor, metacarpal
- 26260 Radical resection of tumor, proximal or middle phalanx of finger
- 26262 Radical resection of tumor, distal phalanx of finger
- 27047 Excision, tumor, soft tissue of pelvis and hip area, subcutaneous; less than 3 cm
- 27048 Excision, tumor, soft tissue of pelvis and hip area, subfascial (eg, intramuscular); less than 5 cm
- 27049 Radical resection of tumor (eg, malignant neoplasm), soft tissue of pelvis and hip area; less than 5 cm
- 27075 Radical resection of tumor; wing of ilium, 1 pubic or ischial ramus or symphysis pubis
- 27076 Radical resection of tumor; ilium, including acetabulum, both pubic rami, or ischium and acetabulum
- 27077 Radical resection of tumor; innominate bone, total
- 27078 Radical resection of tumor; ischial tuberosity and greater trochanter of femur
- 27327 Excision, tumor, soft tissue of thigh or knee area, subcutaneous; less than 3 cm
- 27328 Excision, tumor, soft tissue of thigh or knee area, subfascial (eg, intramuscular); less than 5 cm
- 27329 Radical resection of tumor (eg, malignant neoplasm), soft tissue of thigh or knee area; less than 5 cm
- 27365 Radical resection of tumor, femur or knee
- 27615 Radical resection of tumor (eg, malignant neoplasm), soft tissue of leg or ankle area; less than 5 cm
- 27618 Excision, tumor, soft tissue of leg or ankle area, subcutaneous; less than 3 cm
- 27619 Excision, tumor, soft tissue of leg or ankle area, subfascial (eg, intramuscular); less than 5 cm
- 27640 Partial excision (craterization, saucerization, or diaphysectomy), bone (eg, osteomyelitis); tibia
- 27641 Partial excision (craterization, saucerization, or diaphysectomy), bone (eg, osteomyelitis); fibula
- 27645 Radical resection of tumor; tibia
- 27646 Radical resection of tumor; fibula
- 27647 Radical resection of tumor; talus or calcaneus
- 28043 Excision, tumor, soft tissue of foot or toe, subcutaneous; less than 1.5 cm
- 28045 Excision, tumor, soft tissue of foot or toe, subfascial (eg, intramuscular); less than 1.5 cm
- 28046 Radical resection of tumor (eg, malignant neoplasm), soft tissue of foot or toe; less than 3 cm
- 28171 Radical resection of tumor; tarsal (except talus or calcaneus)
- 28173 Radical resection of tumor; metatarsal
- 28175 Radical resection of tumor; phalanx of toe
- 30801 Ablation, soft tissue of inferior turbinates, unilateral or bilateral, any method (eg, electrocautery, radiofrequency ablation, or tissue volume reduction); superficial
- 30802 Ablation, soft tissue of inferior turbinates, unilateral or bilateral, any method (eg, electrocautery, radiofrequency ablation, or tissue volume reduction); intramural (ie, submucosal)
- 31622 Bronchoscopy, rigid or flexible, including fluoroscopic guidance, when performed; diagnostic, with cell washing, when performed (separate procedure)
- 31623 Bronchoscopy, rigid or flexible, including fluoroscopic guidance, when performed; with brushing or protected brushings
- 31624 Bronchoscopy, rigid or flexible, including fluoroscopic guidance, when performed; with bronchial alveolar lavage
- 31625 Bronchoscopy, rigid or flexible, including fluoroscopic guidance, when performed; with bronchial or endobronchial biopsy(s), single or multiple sites
- 31628 Bronchoscopy, rigid or flexible, including fluoroscopic guidance, when performed; with transbronchial lung biopsy(s), single lobe
- 31629 Bronchoscopy, rigid or flexible, including fluoroscopic guidance, when performed; with transbronchial needle aspiration biopsy(s), trachea, main stem and/or lobar bronchus(i)
- 31630 Bronchoscopy, rigid or flexible, including fluoroscopic guidance, when performed; with tracheal/bronchial dilation or closed reduction of fracture
- 31631 Bronchoscopy, rigid or flexible, including fluoroscopic guidance, when performed; with placement of tracheal stent(s) (includes tracheal/bronchial dilation as required)
- 31632 Bronchoscopy, rigid or flexible, including fluoroscopic guidance, when performed; with transbronchial lung biopsy(s), each additional lobe (List separately in addition to code for primary procedure)
- 31633 Bronchoscopy, rigid or flexible, including fluoroscopic guidance, when performed; with transbronchial needle aspiration biopsy(s), each additional lobe (List separately in addition to code for primary procedure)
- 31635 Bronchoscopy, rigid or flexible, including fluoroscopic guidance, when performed; with removal of foreign body
- 31636 Bronchoscopy, rigid or flexible, including fluoroscopic guidance, when performed; with placement of bronchial stent(s) (includes tracheal/bronchial dilation as required), initial bronchus
- 31637 Bronchoscopy, rigid or flexible, including fluoroscopic guidance, when performed; each additional major bronchus stented (List separately in addition to code for primary procedure)
- 31638 Bronchoscopy, rigid or flexible, including fluoroscopic guidance, when performed; with revision of tracheal or bronchial stent inserted at previous session (includes tracheal/bronchial dilation as required)
- 31640 Bronchoscopy, rigid or flexible, including fluoroscopic guidance, when performed; with excision of tumor
- 31641 Bronchoscopy, rigid or flexible, including fluoroscopic guidance, when performed; with destruction of tumor or relief of stenosis by any method other than excision (eg, laser therapy, cryotherapy)
- 31643 Bronchoscopy, rigid or flexible, including fluoroscopic guidance, when performed; with placement of catheter(s) for intracavitary radioelement application
- 31645 Bronchoscopy, rigid or flexible, including fluoroscopic guidance, when performed; with therapeutic aspiration of tracheobronchial tree, initial (eg, drainage of lung abscess)
- 31646 Bronchoscopy, rigid or flexible, including fluoroscopic guidance, when performed; with therapeutic aspiration of tracheobronchial tree, subsequent

Changed Codes (continued)

- 31656 Bronchoscopy, rigid or flexible, including fluoroscopic guidance, when performed; with injection of contrast material for segmental bronchography (fiberscope only)
- 32560 Instillation, via chest tube/catheter, agent for pleurodesis (eg, talc for recurrent or persistent pneumothorax)
- 33216 Insertion of a single transvenous electrode, permanent pacemaker or cardioverter-defibrillator
- 33217 Insertion of 2 transvenous electrodes, permanent pacemaker or cardioverter-defibrillator
- 33223 Revision of skin pocket for cardioverter-defibrillator
- 33522 Coronary artery bypass, using venous graft(s) and arterial graft(s); 5 venous grafts (List separately in addition to code for primary procedure)
- 36481 Percutaneous portal vein catheterization by any method
- 37760 Ligation of perforator veins, subfascial, radical (Linton type), including skin graft, when performed, open,1 leg
- 42894 Resection of pharyngeal wall requiring closure with myocutaneous or fasciocutaneous flap or free muscle, skin, or fascial flap with microvascular anastomosis
- 43761 Repositioning of a naso- or oro-gastric feeding tube, through the duodenum for enteric nutrition
- 46200 Fissurectomy, including sphincterotomy, when performed
- 46220 Excision of single external papilla or tag, anus
- 46221 Hemorrhoidectomy, internal, by rubber band ligation(s)
- 46230 Excision of multiple external papillae or tags, anus
- 46250 Hemorrhoidectomy, external, 2 or more columns/groups
- 46255 Hemorrhoidectomy, internal and external, single column/group;
- 46257 Hemorrhoidectomy, internal and external, single column/group; with fissurectomy
- 46258 Hemorrhoidectomy, internal and external, single column/group; with fistulectomy, including fissurectomy, when performed
- 46260 Hemorrhoidectomy, internal and external, 2 or more columns/groups;
- 46261 Hemorrhoidectomy, internal and external, 2 or more columns/groups; with fissurectomy
- 46262 Hemorrhoidectomy, internal and external, 2 or more columns/groups; with fistulectomy, including fissurectomy, when performed
- 46275 Surgical treatment of anal fistula (fistulectomy/fistulotomy); intersphincteric
- 46280 Surgical treatment of anal fistula (fistulectomy/fistulotomy); transsphincteric, suprasphincteric, extrasphincteric or multiple, including placement of seton, when performed
- 46320 Excision of thrombosed hemorrhoid, external
- 46945 Hemorrhoidectomy, internal, by ligation other than rubber band; single hemorrhoid column/group
- 46946 Hemorrhoidectomy, internal, by ligation other than rubber band; 2 or more hemorrhoid columns/groups
- 47382 Ablation, 1 or more liver tumor(s), percutaneous, radiofrequency
- 47425 Choledochotomy or choledochostomy with exploration, drainage, or removal of calculus, with or without cholecystotomy; with transduodenal sphincterotomy or sphincteroplasty
- 51726 Complex cystometrogram (ie, calibrated electronic equipment);
- 51797 Voiding pressure studies, intra-abdominal (ie, rectal, gastric, intraperitoneal) (List separately in addition to code for primary procedure)
- 52282 Cystourethroscopy, with insertion of permanent urethral stent
- 55873 Cryosurgical ablation of the prostate (includes ultrasonic guidance and monitoring)
- 55876 Placement of interstitial device(s) for radiation therapy guidance (eg, fiducial markers, dosimeter), percutaneous, prostate, single or multiple
- 59897 Unlisted fetal invasive procedure, including ultrasound guidance, when performed
- 63043 Laminotomy (hemilaminectomy), with decompression of nerve root(s), including partial facetectomy, foraminotomy and/or excision of herniated intervertebral disc, re-exploration, single interspace; each additional cervical interspace (List separately in addition to code for primary procedure)
- 63044 Laminotomy (hemilaminectomy), with decompression of nerve root(s), including partial facetectomy, foraminotomy and/or excision of herniated intervertebral disc, re-exploration, single interspace; each additional lumbar interspace (List separately in addition to code for primary procedure)
- 64834 Suture of 1 nerve; hand or foot, common sensory nerve
- 64835 Suture of 1 nerve; median motor thenar
- 64836 Suture of 1 nerve; ulnar motor
- 72291 Radiological supervision and interpretation, percutaneous vertebroplasty, vertebral augmentation, or sacral augmentation (sacroplasty), including cavity creation, per vertebral body or sacrum; under fluoroscopic guidance
- 72292 Radiological supervision and interpretation, percutaneous vertebroplasty, vertebral augmentation, or sacral augmentation (sacroplasty), including cavity creation, per vertebral body or sacrum; under CT guidance
- 77003 Fluoroscopic guidance and localization of needle or catheter tip for spine or paraspinous diagnostic or therapeutic injection procedures (epidural, transforaminal epidural, subarachnoid, or sacroiliac joint), including neurolytic agent destruction
- 77371 Radiation treatment delivery, stereotactic radiosurgery (SRS), complete course of treatment of cranial lesion(s) consisting of 1 session; multi-source Cobalt 60 based
- 78600 Brain imaging, less than 4 static views;
- 80055 Obstetric panel
- 82306 Vitamin D; 25 hydroxy, includes fraction(s), if performed
- 82652 Vitamin D; 1, 25 dihydroxy, includes fraction(s), if performed
- 82784 Gammaglobulin (immunoglobulin); IgA, IgD, IgG, IgM, each
- 82785 Gammaglobulin (immunoglobulin); IgE
- 82787 Gammaglobulin (immunoglobulin); immunoglobulin subclasses (eg, IgG1, 2, 3, or 4), each
- 83516 Immunoassay for analyte other than infectious agent antibody or infectious agent antigen; qualitative or semiquantitative, multiple step method
- 83518 Immunoassay for analyte other than infectious agent antibody or infectious agent antigen; qualitative or semiquantitative, single step method (eg, reagent strip)
- 83519 Immunoassay for analyte other than infectious agent antibody or infectious agent antigen; quantitative, by radioimmunoassay (eg, RIA)
- 83520 Immunoassay for analyte other than infectious agent antibody or infectious agent antigen; quantitative, not otherwise specified
- 83986 pH; body fluid, not otherwise specified
- 86592 Syphilis test, non-treponemal antibody; qualitative (eg, VDRL, RPR, ART)
- 86593 Syphilis test, non-treponemal antibody; quantitative
- 87149 Culture, typing; identification by nucleic acid (DNA or RNA) probe, direct probe technique, per culture or isolate, each organism probed
- 88312 Special stains; Group I for microorganisms (eg, Gridley, acid fast, methenamine silver), including interpretation and report, each
- 88313 Special stains; Group II, all other (eg, iron, trichrome), except immunocytochemistry and immunoperoxidase stains, including interpretation and report, each
- 88314 Special stains; histochemical staining with frozen section(s), including interpretation and report (List separately in addition to code for primary procedure)
- 90378 Respiratory syncytial virus, monoclonal antibody, recombinant, for intramuscular use, 50 mg, each
- 90650 Human Papilloma virus (HPV) vaccine, types 16, 18, bivalent, 3 dose schedule, for intramuscular use
- 90663 Influenza virus vaccine, pandemic formulation, H1N1
- 90669 Pneumococcal conjugate vaccine, 7 valent, for intramuscular use

Appendix B — New, Changed, Deleted, and Modified Codes

Changed Codes (continued)

- 90738 Japanese encephalitis virus vaccine, inactivated, for intramuscular use
- 92568 Acoustic reflex testing, threshold
- 93279 Programming device evaluation (in person) with iterative adjustment of the implantable device to test the function of the device and select optimal permanent programmed values with physician analysis, review and report; single lead pacemaker system
- 93280 Programming device evaluation (in person) with iterative adjustment of the implantable device to test the function of the device and select optimal permanent programmed values with physician analysis, review and report; dual lead pacemaker system
- 93281 Programming device evaluation (in person) with iterative adjustment of the implantable device to test the function of the device and select optimal permanent programmed values with physician analysis, review and report; multiple lead pacemaker system
- 93282 Programming device evaluation (in person) with iterative adjustment of the implantable device to test the function of the device and select optimal permanent programmed values with physician analysis, review and report; single lead implantable cardioverter-defibrillator system
- 93283 Programming device evaluation (in person) with iterative adjustment of the implantable device to test the function of the device and select optimal permanent programmed values with physician analysis, review and report; dual lead implantable cardioverter-defibrillator system
- 93284 Programming device evaluation (in person) with iterative adjustment of the implantable device to test the function of the device and select optimal permanent programmed values with physician analysis, review and report; multiple lead implantable cardioverter-defibrillator system
- 93285 Programming device evaluation (in person) with iterative adjustment of the implantable device to test the function of the device and select optimal permanent programmed values with physician analysis, review and report; implantable loop recorder system
- 93286 Peri-procedural device evaluation (in person) and programming of device system parameters before or after a surgery, procedure, or test with physician analysis, review and report; single, dual, or multiple lead pacemaker system
- 93287 Peri-procedural device evaluation (in person) and programming of device system parameters before or after a surgery, procedure, or test with physician analysis, review and report; single, dual, or multiple lead implantable cardioverter-defibrillator system
- 93308 Echocardiography, transthoracic, real-time with image documentation (2D), includes M-mode recording, when performed, follow-up or limited study
- 93701 Bioimpedance-derived physiologic cardiovascular analysis
- 95806 Sleep study, unattended, simultaneous recording of, heart rate, oxygen saturation, respiratory airflow, and respiratory effort (eg, thoracoabdominal movement)
- 96570 Photodynamic therapy by endoscopic application of light to ablate abnormal tissue via activation of photosensitive drug(s); first 30 minutes (List separately in addition to code for endoscopy or bronchoscopy procedures of lung and gastrointestinal tract)
- 96571 Photodynamic therapy by endoscopic application of light to ablate abnormal tissue via activation of photosensitive drug(s); each additional 15 minutes (List separately in addition to code for endoscopy or bronchoscopy procedures of lung and gastrointestinal tract)
- 99304 Initial nursing facility care, per day, for the evaluation and management of a patient, which requires these 3 key components: a detailed or comprehensive history; A detailed or comprehensive examination; and medical decision making that is straightforward or of low complexity. Counseling and/or coordination of care with other providers or agencies are provided consistent with the nature of the problem(s) and the patient's and/or family's needs. Usually, the problem(s) requiring admission are of low severity. Physicians typically spend 25 minutes at the bedside and on the patient's facility floor or unit.
- 99305 Initial nursing facility care, per day, for the evaluation and management of a patient, which requires these 3 key components: a comprehensive history; a comprehensive examination; and medical decision making of moderate complexity. Counseling and/or coordination of care with other providers or agencies are provided consistent with the nature of the problem(s) and the patient's and/or family's needs. Usually, the problem(s) requiring admission are of moderate severity. Physicians typically spend 35 minutes at the bedside and on the patient's facility floor or unit.
- 99306 Initial nursing facility care, per day, for the evaluation and management of a patient, which requires these 3 key components: a comprehensive history; a comprehensive examination; and medical decision making of high complexity. Counseling and/or coordination of care with other providers or agencies are provided consistent with the nature of the problem(s) and the patient's and/or family's needs. Usually, the problem(s) requiring admission are of high severity. Physicians typically spend 45 minutes at the bedside and on the patient's facility floor or unit.
- 99307 Subsequent nursing facility care, per day, for the evaluation and management of a patient, which requires at least 2 of these 3 key components: a problem-focused interval history; a problem-focused examination; straightforward medical decision making. Counseling and/or coordination of care with other providers or agencies are provided consistent with the nature of the problem(s) and the patient's and/or family's needs. Usually, the patient is stable, recovering, or improving. Physicians typically spend 10 minutes at the bedside and on the patient's facility floor or unit.
- 99308 Subsequent nursing facility care, per day, for the evaluation and management of a patient, which requires at least 2 of these 3 key components: an expanded problem-focused interval history; an expanded problem-focused examination; medical decision making of low complexity. Counseling and/or coordination of care with other providers or agencies are provided consistent with the nature of the problem(s) and the patient's and/or family's needs. Usually, the patient is responding inadequately to therapy or has developed a minor complication. Physicians typically spend 15 minutes at the bedside and on the patient's facility floor or unit.
- 99309 Subsequent nursing facility care, per day, for the evaluation and management of a patient, which requires at least 2 of these 3 key components: a detailed interval history; a detailed examination; medical decision making of moderate complexity. Counseling and/or coordination of care with other providers or agencies are provided consistent with the nature of the problem(s) and the patient's and/or family's needs. Usually, the patient has developed a significant complication or a significant new problem. Physicians typically spend 25 minutes at the bedside and on the patient's facility floor or unit.
- 99310 Subsequent nursing facility care, per day, for the evaluation and management of a patient, which requires at least 2 of these 3 key components: a comprehensive interval history; a comprehensive examination; medical decision making of high complexity. Counseling and/or coordination of care with other providers or agencies are provided consistent with the nature of the problem(s) and the patient's and/or family's needs. The patient may be unstable or may have developed a significant new problem requiring immediate physician attention. Physicians typically spend 35 minutes at the bedside and on the patient's facility floor or unit.
- 99318 Evaluation and management of a patient involving an annual nursing facility assessment, which requires these 3 key components: a detailed interval history; a comprehensive examination; and medical decision making that is of low to moderate complexity. Counseling and/or coordination of care with other providers or agencies are provided consistent with the nature of the problem(s) and the patient's and/or family's needs. Usually, the patient is stable, recovering, or improving. Physicians typically spend 30 minutes at the bedside and on the patient's facility floor or unit.
- 99358 Prolonged evaluation and management service before and/or after direct (face-to-face) patient care; first hour
- 99359 Prolonged evaluation and management service before and/or after direct (face-to-face) patient care; each additional 30 minutes (List separately in addition to code for prolonged physician service)
- 0185T Multivariate analysis of patient-specific findings with quantifiable computer probability assessment, including report

Changed Codes (continued)

0500F Initial prenatal care visit (report at first prenatal encounter with health care professional providing obstetrical care. Report also date of visit and, in a separate field, the date of the last menstrual period [LMP]) (Prenatal)

0502F Subsequent prenatal care visit (Prenatal) [Excludes: patients who are seen for a condition unrelated to pregnancy or prenatal care (eg, an upper respiratory infection; patients seen for consultation only, not for continuing care)]

0505F Hemodialysis plan of care documented (ESRD, P-ESRD)

0514F Plan of care for elevated hemoglobin level documented for patient receiving erythropoiesis-stimulating agent therapy (ESA) (CKD)

1040F DSM-IV (TM) criteria for major depressive disorder documented at the initial evaluation (MDD, MDD ADOL)

1091F Urinary incontinence characterized (eg, frequency, volume, timing, type of symptoms, how bothersome) (GER)

1100F Patient screened for future fall risk; documentation of 2 or more falls in the past year or any fall with injury in the past year (GER)

1101F Patient screened for future fall risk; documentation of no falls in the past year or only 1 fall without injury in the past year (GER)

1111F Discharge medications reconciled with the current medication list in outpatient medical record (COA) (GER)

1119F Initial evaluation for condition (HEP C)(EPI)

1121F Subsequent evaluation for condition (HEP C)(EPI)

2026F Eye imaging validated to match diagnosis from 7 standard field stereoscopic photos results documented and reviewed (DM)

3020F Left ventricular function (LVF) assessment (eg, echocardiography, nuclear test, or ventriculography) documented in the medical record (Includes quantitative or qualitative assessment results) (HF)

3025F Spirometry test results demonstrate FEV1/FVC less than 70% with COPD symptoms (eg, dyspnea, cough/sputum, wheezing) (CAP, COPD)

3028F Oxygen saturation results documented and reviewed (includes assessment through pulse oximetry or arterial blood gas measurement) (CAP, COPD) (EM)

3035F Oxygen saturation less than or equal to 88% or a PaO2 less than or equal to 55 mm Hg (COPD).

3037F Oxygen saturation greater than 88% or PaO2 greater than 55 mmHg (COPD)

3045F Most recent hemoglobin A1c (HbA1c) level 7.0–9.0% (DM)

3073F Pre-surgical (cataract) axial length, corneal power measurement and method of intraocular lens power calculation documented within 12 months prior to surgery (EC)

3075F Most recent systolic blood pressure 130-139 mm Hg (DM) (HTN, CKD)

3077F Most recent systolic blood pressure greater than or equal to 140 mm Hg (HTN, CKD) (DM)

3078F Most recent diastolic blood pressure less than 80 mm Hg (HTN, CKD) (DM)

3079F Most recent diastolic blood pressure 80-89 mm Hg (HTN, CKD) (DM)

3080F Most recent diastolic blood pressure greater than or equal to 90 mm Hg (HTN, CKD) (DM)

3085F Suicide risk assessed (MDD, MDD ADOL)

3095F Central dual-energy X-ray absorptiometry (DXA) results documented (OP)

3110F Documentation in final CT or MRI report of presence or absence of hemorrhage and mass lesion and acute infarction (STR)

3111F CT or MRI of the brain performed in the hospital within 24 hours of arrival OR performed in an outpatient imaging center, to confirm initial diagnosis of stroke, TIA or hemorrhage (STR)

3112F CT or MRI of the brain performed greater than 24 hours after arrival to the hospital OR performed in an outpatient imaging center for purpose other than confirmation of initial diagnosis of stroke, TIA, or hemorrhage(STR)

3140F Upper gastrointestinal endoscopy report indicates suspicion of Barrett's esophagus (GERD)

3141F Upper gastrointestinal endoscopy report indicates no suspicion of Barrett's esophagus (GERD)

3250F Specimen site other than anatomic location of primary tumor (PATH)

3292F HIV testing ordered or documented and reviewed during the first or second prenatal visit (Pre-Cr)

3319F 1 of the following diagnostic imaging studies ordered: chest x-ray, CT, ultrasound, MRI, PET, or nuclear medicine scans (ML)

3321F AJCC cancer Stage 0 or IA melanoma, documented (ML)

4001F Tobacco use cessation intervention, pharmacologic therapy (COPD, CAD, CAP, PV) (DM)(PV)

4006F Beta-blocker therapy prescribed (CAD, HF)

4040F Pneumococcal vaccine administered or previously received (COPD), (PV)

4047F Documentation of order for prophylactic parenteral antibiotics to be given within 1 hour (if fluoroquinolone or vancomycin, 2 hours) prior to surgical incision (or start of procedure when no incision is required) (PERI 2)

4048F Documentation that administration of prophylactic parenteral antibiotic was initiated within 1 hour (if fluoroquinolone or vancomycin, 2 hours) prior to surgical incision (or start of procedure when no incision was required), as ordered (PERI 2)

4060F Psychotherapy services provided (MDD, MDD ADOL)

4064F Antidepressant pharmacotherapy prescribed (MDD, MDD ADOL)

4120F Antibiotic prescribed or dispensed (URI, PHAR), (A-BRONCH)

4124F Antibiotic neither prescribed nor dispensed (URI, PHAR), (A-BRONCH)

4165F 3-dimensional conformal radiotherapy (3D-CRT) or intensity modulated radiation therapy (IMRT) received (PRCA)

4171F Patient receiving erythropoiesis-stimulating agents (ESA) therapy (CKD)

4172F Patient not receiving erythropoiesis-stimulating agents (ESA) therapy (CKD)

4176F Counseling about value of protection from UV light and lack of proven efficacy of nutritional supplements in prevention or progression of cataract development provided to patient and/or caregiver(s) (NMA-No Measure Assoc.)

4201F External beam radiotherapy with or without nodal irradiation as adjuvant or salvage therapy for prostate cancer patient (PRCA)

6030F All elements of maximal sterile barrier technique followed including: cap AND mask AND sterile gown AND sterile gloves AND a large sterile sheet AND hand hygiene AND 2% chlorhexidine for cutaneous antisepsis (or acceptable alternative antiseptics, per current guideline) (CRIT)

7010F Patient information entered into a recall system that includes: target date for the next exam specified AND a process to follow up with patients regarding missed or unscheduled appointments (ML)

7020F Mammogram assessment category (eg, Mammography Quality Standards Act [MQSA], Breast Imaging Reporting and Data System [BI-RADS®], or FDA-approved equivalent categories) entered into an internal database to allow for analysis of abnormal interpretation (recall) rate (RAD)

Deleted Codes

01632	14300	23221	23222	24151	24153	26255
26261	27079	29220	36145	36834	45170	46210
46211	46937	46938	51772	51795	63660	64470
64472	64475	64476	75558	75560	75562	75564
75790	78460	78461	78464	78465	78478	78480
82307	86781	90379	92569	99185	99186	0062T
0063T	0064T	0066T	0067T	0068T	0069T	0070T
0077T	0084T	0086T	0087T	0140T	0144T	0145T
0146T	0147T	0148T	0149T	0150T	0151T	0170T
0194T	1127F	1128F				

APPENDIX C — CROSSWALK OF DELETED CODES

Deleted CPT 2009 Codes	CPT 2010 Code	Deleted CPT 2009 Codes	CPT 2010 Code	Deleted CPT 2009 Codes	CPT 2010 Code
01632	01630, 01638	64475	64493	0068T	93799
14300	14301-14302	64476	64494-64495	0069T	93799
23221	23220	75558	75565	0070T	93799
23222	23220	75560	75565	0077T	61107, 61210
24151	24150	75562	75565	0084T	53855
24153	24152	75564	75565	0086T	93799
26255	26250	75790	75791	0087T	89398
26261	26260	78460	78453	0140T	83987
27079	27078	78461	78454	0144T	75571
29220	29799	78464	78451	0145T	75572-75574
36145	36147-36148	78465	78452	0146T	75572-75574
36834	36832	78478	78451-78454	0147T	75572-75574
45170	45171-45172	78480	78451-78454	0148T	75572-75574
46210	46999	82307	82306	0149T	75572-75574
46211	46999	86781	86780	0150T	75572-75574
46937	45190	90379	90378	0151T	75572-75574
46938	45190	92569	92570	0170T	46707
51772	51727, 51729	0062T	22526-22527, 22899	0194T	84145
51795	51728-51729	0063T	22526-22527, 22899		
63660	63661	0064T	94799		
64470	64490	0066T	74263		
64472	64491-64492	0067T	74261-74262		

APPENDIX D: RESEQUENCED CODES

Code	Description	Numeric see ref note
21552	Excision, tumor, soft tissue of neck or anterior thorax, subcutaneous; 3 cm or greater	Resequenced code. See code following 21555.
21554	Excision, tumor, soft tissue of neck or anterior thorax, subfascial (eg, intramuscular); 5 cm or greater	Resequenced code. See code following 21556.
23071	Excision, tumor, soft tissue of shoulder area, subcutaneous; 3 cm or greater	Resequenced code. See code following 23075.
23073	Excision, tumor, soft tissue of shoulder area, subfascial (eg, intramuscular); 5 cm or greater	Resequenced code. See code following 23076.
24071	Excision, tumor, soft tissue of upper arm or elbow area, subcutaneous; 3 cm or greater	Resequenced code. See code following 24075.
24073	Excision, tumor, soft tissue of upper arm or elbow area, subfascial (eg, intramuscular); 5 cm or greater	Resequenced code. See code following 24076.
25071	Excision, tumor, soft tissue of forearm and/or wrist area, subcutaneous; 3 cm or greater	Resequenced code. See code following 25075.
25073	Excision, tumor, soft tissue of forearm and/or wrist area, subfascial (eg, intramuscular); 3 cm or greater	Resequenced code. See code following 25076.
26111	Excision, tumor or vascular malformation, soft tissue of hand or finger, subcutaneous; 1.5 cm or greater	Resequenced code. See code following 26115.
26113	Excision, tumor, soft tissue, or vascular malformation, of hand or finger, subfascial (eg, intramuscular); 1.5 cm or greater	Resequenced code. See code following 26116.
27043	Excision, tumor, soft tissue of pelvis and hip area, subcutaneous; 3 cm or greater	Resequenced code. See code following 27047.
27045	Excision, tumor, soft tissue of pelvis and hip area, subfascial (eg, intramuscular); 5 cm or greater	Resequenced code. See code following 27048.
27059	Radical resection of tumor (eg, malignant neoplasm), soft tissue of pelvis and hip area; 5 cm or greater	Resequenced code. See code following 27049.
27329	Radical resection of tumor (eg, malignant neoplasm), soft tissue of thigh or knee area; less than 5 cm	Resequenced code. See code following 27360.
27337	Excision, tumor, soft tissue of thigh or knee area, subcutaneous; 3 cm or greater	Resequenced code. See code following 27327.
27339	Excision, tumor, soft tissue of thigh or knee area, subfascial (eg, intramuscular); 5 cm or greater	Resequenced code. See code following 27328.
27632	Excision, tumor, soft tissue of leg or ankle area, subcutaneous; 3 cm or greater	Resequenced code. See code following 27618.
27634	Excision, tumor, soft tissue of leg or ankle area, subfascial (eg, intramuscular); 5 cm or greater	Resequenced code. See code following 27619.
28039	Excision, tumor, soft tissue of foot or toe, subcutaneous; 1.5 cm or greater	Resequenced code. See code following 28043.
28041	Excision, tumor, soft tissue of foot or toe, subfascial (eg, intramuscular); 1.5 cm or greater	Resequenced code. See code following 28045.
46220	Excision of single external papilla or tag, anus	Resequenced code. See code above 46230.
46320	Excision of thrombosed hemorrhoid, external	Resequenced code. See code following 46230.
46945	Hemorrhoidectomy, internal, by ligation other than rubber band; single hemorrhoid column/group	Resequenced code. See code range 46221-46230.
46946	Hemorrhoidectomy, internal, by ligation other than rubber band; 2 or more hemorrhoid columns/groups	Resequenced code. See code range 46221-46230.
46947	Hemorrhoidopexy (eg, for prolapsing internal hemorrhoids) by stapling	Resequenced code. See code following 46762.
51797	Voiding pressure studies, intra-abdominal (ie, rectal, gastric, intraperitoneal) (List separately in addition to code for primary procedure)	Resequenced code. See code following 51729.
82652	Vitamin D; 1, 25 dihydroxy, includes fraction(s), if performed	Resequenced code. See code following 82306.

APPENDIX E: ADD-ON CODES, MODIFIER 51, 63, AND MODERATE SEDATION CODES

Codes specified as add-on, exempt from modifier 51 and 63, and include conscious sedation are listed. The lists are designed to be read left to right rather than vertically.

Add-on Codes

0054T	0055T	0063T	0076T	0079T	0081T	0092T
0095T	0098T	0151T	0159T	0163T	0164T	0165T
0172T	0173T	0174T	0189T	0190T	1953	1968
1969	0196T	0205T	0214T	0215T	0217T	0218T
0222T	11001	11008	11101	11201	11732	11922
13102	13122	13133	13153	14302	15003	15005
15101	15111	15116	15121	15131	15136	15151
15152	15156	15157	15171	15176	15201	15221
15241	15261	15301	15321	15331	15336	15341
15361	15366	15401	15421	15431	15787	15847
16036	17003	17312	17314	17315	19001	19126
19291	19295	19297	20930	20931	20936	20937
20938	20985	22103	22116	22208	22216	22226
22328	22522	22525	22527	22534	22585	22614
22632	22840	22841	22842	22843	22844	22845
22846	22847	22848	22851	26125	26861	26863
27358	27692	31620	31627	31632	31633	31637
32501	33141	33225	33257	33258	33259	33508
33517	33518	33519	33521	33522	33523	33530
33572	33768	33884	33924	33961	34806	34808
34813	34826	35306	35390	35400	35500	35572
35600	35681	35682	35683	35685	35686	35697
35700	36148	36218	36248	36476	36479	37185
37186	37206	37208	37250	37251	38102	38746
38747	43273	43635	44015	44121	44128	44139
44203	44213	44701	44955	47001	47550	48400
49326	49435	49568	49905	51797	56606	57267
58110	58611	59525	60512	61316	61517	61609
61610	61611	61612	61641	61642	61795	61797
61799	61800	61864	61868	62148	62160	63035
63043	63044	63048	63057	63066	63076	63078
63082	63086	63088	63091	63103	63295	63308
63621	64472	64476	64480	64484	64491	64492
64494	64495	64623	64627	64727	64778	64783
64787	64832	64837	64859	64872	64874	64876
64901	64902	65757	66990	67225	67320	67331
67332	67334	67335	67340	69990	74301	75565
75774	75946	75964	75968	75993	75996	76125
76802	76810	76812	76814	76937	77001	77051
77052	78020	78478	78480	78496	78730	83901
86826	87187	87904	88155	88185	88311	88314
88388	90466	90468	90472	90474	92547	92608
92627	92973	92974	92978	92979	92981	92984
92996	92998	93320	93321	93325	93352	93571
93572	93609	93613	93621	93622	93623	93662
94645	95873	95874	95920	95962	95967	95973
95975	95979	96361	96366	96367	96368	96370
96371	96375	96376	96411	96415	96417	96423
96570	96571	97546	97811	97814	99100	99116
99135	99140	99145	99150	99292	99354	99355
99356	99357	99359	99467	99602	99607	

Modifier 51 Exempt Codes

17004	20697	20974	20975	31500	36620	44500
61107	90281	90283	90284	90287	90288	90291
90296	90371	90375	90376	90378	90379	90384
90385	90386	90389	90393	90396	90399	93503
93539	93540	93544	93545	93555	93556	93600
93602	93603	93610	93612	93615	93616	93618
93631	94610	95900	95903	95904	95905	95992
97001	97002	97003	97004	97005	97006	97010
97012	97014	97016	97018	97022	97024	97026
97028	97032	97033	97034	97035	97036	97110
97112	97113	97116	97124	97140	97150	97530
97532	97533	97535	97537	97542	97545	97546
97597	97598	97602	97605	97606	97750	97755
99143	99144					

Modifier 63 Exempt Codes

30540	30545	31520	33401	33403	33470	33472
33502	33503	33505	33506	33610	33611	33619
33647	33670	33690	33694	33730	33732	33735
33736	33750	33755	33762	33778	33786	33922
33960	33961	36415	36420	36450	36460	36510
36660	39503	43313	43314	43520	43831	44055
44126	44127	44128	46070	46705	46715	46716
46730	46735	46740	46742	46744	47700	47701
49215	49491	49492	49495	49496	49600	49605
49606	49610	49611	53025	54000	54150	54160
63700	63702	63704	63706	65820		

Moderate Sedation Codes

19298	20982	22520	22521	22526	22527	31615
31620	31622	31623	31624	31625	31626	31627
31628	31629	31635	31645	31646	31656	31725
32201	32550	32551	32553	33010	33011	33206
33207	33208	33210	33211	33212	33213	33214
33216	33217	33218	33220	33222	33223	33233
33234	33235	33240	33241	33244	33249	33570
35471	35472	35473	35474	35475	35476	36147
36148	36481	36555	36557	36558	36560	36561
36563	36565	36566	36568	36570	36571	36576
36578	36581	36582	36583	36585	36590	36870
37183	37184	37185	37186	37187	37188	37203
37210	37215	37216	43200	43201	43202	43204
43205	43215	43216	43217	43219	43220	43226
43227	43228	43231	43232	43234	43235	43236
43237	43238	43239	43240	43241	43242	43243
43244	43245	43246	43247	43248	43249	43250
43251	43255	43256	43257	43258	43259	43260
43261	43262	43263	43264	43265	43267	43268
43269	43271	43272	43273	43453	43456	43458
44360	44361	44363	44364	44365	44366	44369
44370	44372	44373	44376	44377	44378	44379
44380	44382	44383	44385	44386	44388	44389
44390	44391	44392	44393	44394	44397	44500
44901	45303	45305	45307	45308	45309	45315
45317	45320	45321	45327	45332	45333	45334
45335	45337	45338	45339	45340	45341	45342
45345	45355	45378	45379	45380	45381	45382
45383	45384	45385	45386	45387	45391	45392
47011	47382	47525	48511	49021	49041	49061
49411	49440	49441	49442	49446	50021	50200
50382	50384	50385	50386	50387	50592	50593
58823	66720	69300	77371	77600	77605	77610
77615	92953	92960	92961	92973	92974	92975
92978	92979	92980	92981	92982	92984	92986
92987	92995	92996	93312	93313	93314	93315
93316	93317	93318	93501	93505	93508	93510
93511	93514	93524	93526	93527	93528	93529
93530	93539	93540	93541	93542	93543	93544
93545	93555	93556	93561	93562	93571	93572
93609	93613	93615	93616	93618	93619	93620
93621	93622	93624	93640	93641	93642	93650
93651	93652	94011	94012	94013	0200T	0201T

APPENDIX F — PLACE OF SERVICE AND TYPE OF SERVICE

Place-of-Service Codes for Professional Claims

Listed below are place of service codes and descriptions. These codes should be used on professional claims to specify the entity where service(s) were rendered. Check with individual payers (e.g., Medicare, Medicaid, other private insurance) for reimbursement policies regarding these codes. To comment on a code(s) or description(s), please send your request to posinfo@cms.hhs.gov.

Code	Name	Description
01	Pharmacy	A facility or location where drugs and other medically related items and services are sold, dispensed, or otherwise provided directly to patients.
02	Unassigned	N/A
03	School	A facility whose primary purpose is education.
04	Homeless shelter	A facility or location whose primary purpose is to provide temporary housing to homeless individuals (e.g., emergency shelters, individual or family shelters).
05	Indian Health Service freestanding facility	A facility or location, owned and operated by the Indian Health Service, which provides diagnostic, therapeutic (surgical and non-surgical), and rehabilitation services to American Indians and Alaska natives who do not require hospitalization.
06	Indian Health Service provider-based facility	A facility or location, owned and operated by the Indian Health Service, which provides diagnostic, therapeutic (surgical and nonsurgical), and rehabilitation services rendered by, or under the supervision of, physicians to American Indians and Alaska natives admitted as inpatients or outpatients.
07	Tribal 638 freestanding facility	A facility or location owned and operated by a federally recognized American Indian or Alaska native tribe or tribal organization under a 638 agreement, which provides diagnostic, therapeutic (surgical and nonsurgical), and rehabilitation services to tribal members who do not require hospitalization.
08	Tribal 638 Provider-based Facility	A facility or location owned and operated by a federally recognized American Indian or Alaska native tribe or tribal organization under a 638 agreement, which provides diagnostic, therapeutic (surgical and nonsurgical), and rehabilitation services to tribal members admitted as inpatients or outpatients.
09	Prison/correctional facility	A prison, jail, reformatory, work farm, detention center, or any other similar facility maintained by either federal, state or local authorities for the purpose of confinement or rehabilitation of adult or juvenile criminal offenders.
10	Unassigned	N/A
11	Office	Location, other than a hospital, skilled nursing facility (SNF), military treatment facility, community health center, State or local public health clinic, or intermediate care facility (ICF), where the health professional routinely provides health examinations, diagnosis, and treatment of illness or injury on an ambulatory basis.
12	Home	Location, other than a hospital or other facility, where the patient receives care in a private residence.
13	Assisted living facility	Congregate residential facility with self-contained living units providing assessment of each resident's needs and on-site support 24 hours a day, 7 days a week, with the capacity to deliver or arrange for services including some health care and other services.
14	Group home	A residence, with shared living areas, where clients receive supervision and other services such as social and/or behavioral services, custodial service, and minimal services (e.g., medication administration).
15	Mobile unit	A facility/unit that moves from place-to-place equipped to provide preventive, screening, diagnostic, and/or treatment services.
16	Temporary lodging	A short-term accommodation such as a hotel, campground, hostel, cruise ship or resort where the patient receives care, and which is not identified by any other POS code.
17-19	Unassigned	N/A
20	Urgent care facility	Location, distinct from a hospital emergency room, an office, or a clinic, whose purpose is to diagnose and treat illness or injury for unscheduled, ambulatory patients seeking immediate medical attention.
21	Inpatient hospital	A facility, other than psychiatric, which primarily provides diagnostic, therapeutic (both surgical and nonsurgical), and rehabilitation services by, or under, the supervision of physicians to patients admitted for a variety of medical conditions.
22	Outpatient hospital	A portion of a hospital which provides diagnostic, therapeutic (both surgical and nonsurgical), and rehabilitation services to sick or injured persons who do not require hospitalization or institutionalization.
23	Emergency room—hospital	A portion of a hospital where emergency diagnosis and treatment of illness or injury is provided.
24	Ambulatory surgical center	A freestanding facility, other than a physician's office, where surgical and diagnostic services are provided on an ambulatory basis.
25	Birthing center	A facility, other than a hospital's maternity facilities or a physician's office, which provides a setting for labor, delivery, and immediate post-partum care as well as immediate care of new born infants.
26	Military treatment facility	A medical facility operated by one or more of the uniformed services. Military treatment facility (MTF) also refers to certain former U.S. Public Health Service (USPHS) facilities now designated as uniformed service treatment facilities (USTF).
27-30	Unassigned	N/A
31	Skilled nursing facility	A facility which primarily provides inpatient skilled nursing care and related services to patients who require medical, nursing, or rehabilitative services but does not provide the level of care or treatment available in a hospital.

Appendix F — Place of Service and Type of Service

Code	Place	Description
32	Nursing facility	A facility which primarily provides to residents skilled nursing care and related services for the rehabilitation of injured, disabled, or sick persons, or, on a regular basis, health-related care services above the level of custodial care to other than mentally retarded individuals.
33	Custodial care facility	A facility which provides room, board, and other personal assistance services, generally on a long-term basis, and which does not include a medical component.
34	Hospice	A facility, other than a patient's home, in which palliative and supportive care for terminally ill patients and their families are provided.
35-40	Unassigned	N/A
41	Ambulance—land	A land vehicle specifically designed, equipped and staffed for lifesaving and transporting the sick or injured.
42	Ambulance—air or water	An air or water vehicle specifically designed, equipped and staffed for lifesaving and transporting the sick or injured.
43-48	Unassigned	N/A
49	Independent clinic	A location, not part of a hospital and not described by any other place-of-service code, that is organized and operated to provide preventive, diagnostic, therapeutic, rehabilitative, or palliative services to outpatients only.
50	Federally qualified health center	A facility located in a medically underserved area that provides Medicare beneficiaries preventive primary medical care under the general direction of a physician.
51	Inpatient psychiatric facility	A facility that provides inpatient psychiatric services for the diagnosis and treatment of mental illness on a 24-hour basis, by or under the supervision of a physician.
52	Psychiatric facility-partial hospitalization	A facility for the diagnosis and treatment of mental illness that provides a planned therapeutic program for patients who do not require full time hospitalization, but who need broader programs than are possible from outpatient visits to a hospital-based or hospital-affiliated facility.
53	Community mental health center	A facility that provides the following services: outpatient services, including specialized outpatient services for children, the elderly, individuals who are chronically ill, and residents of the CMHC's mental health services area who have been discharged from inpatient treatment at a mental health facility; 24 hour a day emergency care services; day treatment, other partial hospitalization services, or psychosocial rehabilitation services; screening for patients being considered for admission to state mental health facilities to determine the appropriateness of such admission; and consultation and education services.
54	Intermediate care facility/mentally retarded	A facility which primarily provides health-related care and services above the level of custodial care to mentally retarded individuals but does not provide the level of care or treatment available in a hospital or SNF.
55	Residential substance abuse treatment facility	A facility which provides treatment for substance (alcohol and drug) abuse to live-in residents who do not require acute medical care. Services include individual and group therapy and counseling, family counseling, laboratory tests, drugs and supplies, psychological testing, and room and board.
56	Psychiatric residential treatment center	A facility or distinct part of a facility for psychiatric care which provides a total 24-hour therapeutically planned and professionally staffed group living and learning environment.
57	Non-residential substance abuse treatment facility	A location which provides treatment for substance (alcohol and drug) abuse on an ambulatory basis. Services include individual and group therapy and counseling, family counseling, laboratory tests, drugs and supplies, and psychological testing.
58-59	Unassigned	N/A
60	Mass immunization center	A location where providers administer pneumococcal pneumonia and influenza virus vaccinations and submit these services as electronic media claims, paper claims, or using the roster billing method. This generally takes place in a mass immunization setting, such as, a public health center, pharmacy, or mall but may include a physician office setting.
61	Comprehensive inpatient rehabilitation facility	A facility that provides comprehensive rehabilitation services under the supervision of a physician to inpatients with physical disabilities. Services include physical therapy, occupational therapy, speech pathology, social or psychological services, and orthotics and prosthetics services.
62	Comprehensive outpatient rehabilitation facility	A facility that provides comprehensive rehabilitation services under the supervision of a physician to outpatients with physical disabilities. Services include physical therapy, occupational therapy, and speech pathology services.
63-64	Unassigned	N/A
65	End-stage renal disease treatment facility	A facility other than a hospital, which provides dialysis treatment, maintenance, and/or training to patients or caregivers on an ambulatory or home-care basis.
66-70	Unassigned	N/A
71	State or local public health clinic	A facility maintained by either state or local health departments that provides ambulatory primary medical care under the general direction of a physician.
72	Rural health clinic	A certified facility which is located in a rural medically underserved area that provides ambulatory primary medical care under the general direction of a physician.
73-80	Unassigned	N/A
81	Independent laboratory	A laboratory certified to perform diagnostic and/or clinical tests independent of an institution or a physician's office.
82-98	Unassigned	N/A
99	Other place of service	Other place of service not identified above.

Appendix F — Place of Service and Type of Service

Type of Service

Common Working File Type of Service (TOS) Indicators

For submitting a claim to the Common Working File (CWF), use the following table to assign the proper TOS. Some procedures may have more than one applicable TOS. CWF will reject alerts on codes with incorrect TOS designations. CWF is rejecting codes with incorrect TOS designations.

The only exceptions to this table are:

- Surgical services billed for dates of service through December 31, 2007, containing the ASC facility service modifier SG must be reported as TOS F. Effective for services on or after January 1, 2008, the SG modifier is no longer applicable for Medicare services. ASC providers should discontinue applying the SG modifier on ASC facility claims. The indicator F does not appear in the TOS table because its use depends upon claims submitted with POS 24 (ASC facility) from an ASC (specialty 49). This became effective for dates of service January 1, 2008, or after.

- Surgical services billed with an assistant-at-surgery modifier (80-82, AS,) must be reported with TOS 8. The 8 indicator does not appear on the TOS table because its use is dependent upon the use of the appropriate modifier. (See Pub. 100-4 *Medicare Claims Processing Manual*, chapter 12, "Physician/Practitioner Billing," for instructions on when assistant-at-surgery is allowable.)

- Psychiatric treatment services that are subject to the outpatient mental health treatment limitation should be reported with TOS T.

- TOS H appears in the list of descriptors. However, it does not appear in the table. In CWF, "H" is used only as an indicator for hospice. The carrier should not submit TOS H to CWF at this time.

- For outpatient services, when a transfusion medicine code appears on a claim that also contains a blood product, the service is paid under reasonable charge at 80 percent; coinsurance and deductible apply. When transfusion medicine codes are paid under the clinical laboratory fee schedule they are paid at 100 percent; coinsurance and deductible do not apply.

Note: For injection codes with more than one possible TOS designation, use the following guidelines when assigning the TOS:

When the choice is L or 1:

- Use TOS L when the drug is used related to ESRD; or
- Use TOS 1 when the drug is not related to ESRD and is administered in the office.

When the choice is G or 1:

- Use TOS G when the drug is an immunosuppressive drug; or
- Use TOS 1 when the drug is used for other than immunosuppression.

When the choice is P or 1:

- Use TOS P if the drug is administered through durable medical equipment (DME); or
- Use TOS 1 if the drug is administered in the office.

The place of service or diagnosis may be considered when determining the appropriate TOS. The descriptors for each of the TOS codes listed in the following table are:

0	Whole blood
1	Medical care
2	Surgery
3	Consultation
4	Diagnostic radiology
5	Diagnostic laboratory
6	Therapeutic radiology
7	Anesthesia
8	Assistant at surgery
9	Other medical items or services
A	Used DME
B	High risk screening mammography
C	Low risk screening mammography
D	Ambulance
E	Enteral/parenteral nutrients/supplies
F	Ambulatory surgical center (facility usage for surgical services)
G	Immunosuppressive drugs
H	Hospice
J	Diabetic shoes
K	Hearing items and services
L	ESRD supplies
M	Monthly capitation payment for dialysis
N	Kidney donor
P	Lump sum purchase of DME, prosthetics, orthotics
Q	Vision items or services
R	Rental of DME
S	Surgical dressings or other medical supplies
T	Outpatient mental health treatment limitation
U	Occupational therapy
V	Pneumococcal/flu vaccine
W	Physical therapy

Berenson-Eggers Type of Service (BETOS) Codes

The BETOS coding system was developed primarily for analyzing the growth in Medicare expenditures. The coding system covers all HCPCS codes; assigns a HCPCS code to only one BETOS code; consists of readily understood clinical categories (as opposed to statistical or financial categories); consists of categories that permit objective assignment; is stable over time; and is relatively immune to minor changes in technology or practice patterns.

BETOS Codes and Descriptions:

1. **Evaluation and Management**
   1. M1A Office visits—new
   2. M1B Office visits—established
   3. M2A Hospital visit—initial
   4. M2B Hospital visit—subsequent
   5. M2C Hospital visit—critical care
   6. M3   Emergency room visit
   7. M4A Home visit
   8. M4B Nursing home visit
   9. M5A Specialist—pathology
   10. M5B Specialist—psychiatry
   11. M5C Specialist—ophthalmology
   12. M5D Specialist—other
   13. M6 Consultations

2. **Procedures**
   1. P0   Anesthesia
   2. P1A Major procedure—breast
   3. P1B Major procedure—colectomy
   4. P1C Major procedure—cholecystectomy
   5. P1D Major procedure—TURP
   6. P1E Major procedure—hysterectomy
   7. P1F Major procedure—explor/decompr/excis disc
   8. P1G Major procedure—other
   9. P2A Major procedure, cardiovascular—CABG
   10. P2B Major procedure, cardiovascular—aneurysm repair
   11. P2C Major procedure, cardiovascular—thromboendarterectomy
   12. P2D Major procedure, cardiovascular—coronary angioplasty (PTCA)
   13. P2E Major procedure, cardiovascular—pacemaker insertion
   14. P2F Major procedure, cardiovascular—other

Appendix F — Place of Service and Type of Service

15.	P3A	Major procedure, orthopedic—hip fracture repair
16.	P3B	Major procedure, orthopedic—hip replacement
17.	P3C	Major procedure, orthopedic—knee replacement
18.	P3D	Major procedure, orthopedic—other
19.	P4A	Eye procedure—corneal transplant
20.	P4B	Eye procedure—cataract removal/lens insertion
21.	P4C	Eye procedure—retinal detachment
22.	P4D	Eye procedure—treatment of retinal lesions
23.	P4E	Eye procedure—other
24.	P5A	Ambulatory procedures—skin
25.	P5B	Ambulatory procedures—musculoskeletal
26.	P5C	Ambulatory procedures—groin hernia repair
27.	P5D	Ambulatory procedures—lithotripsy
28.	P5E	Ambulatory procedures—other
29.	P6A	Minor procedures—skin
30.	P6B	Minor procedures—musculoskeletal
31.	P6C	Minor procedures—other (Medicare fee schedule)
32.	P6D	Minor procedures—other (non-Medicare fee schedule)
33.	P7A	Oncology—radiation therapy
34.	P7B	Oncology—other
35.	P8A	Endoscopy—arthroscopy
36.	P8B	Endoscopy—upper gastrointestinal
37.	P8C	Endoscopy—sigmoidoscopy
38.	P8D	Endoscopy—colonoscopy
39.	P8E	Endoscopy—cystoscopy
40.	P8F	Endoscopy—bronchoscopy
41.	P8G	Endoscopy—laparoscopic cholecystectomy
42.	P8H	Endoscopy—laryngoscopy
43.	P8I	Endoscopy—other
44.	P9A	Dialysis services (Medicare fee schedule)
45.	P9B	Dialysis services (non-Medicare fee schedule)

3. **Imaging**
   1. I1A Standard imaging—chest
   2. I1B Standard imaging—musculoskeletal
   3. I1C Standard imaging—breast
   4. I1D Standard imaging—contrast gastrointestinal
   5. I1E Standard imaging—nuclear medicine
   6. I1F Standard imaging—other
   7. I2A Advanced imaging—CAT/CT/CTA; brain/head/neck
   8. I2B Advanced imaging—CAT/CT/CTA; other
   9. I2C Advanced imaging—MRI/MRA; brain/head/neck
   10. I2D Advanced imaging—MRI/MRA; other
   11. I3A Echography—eye
   12. I3B Echography—abdomen/pelvis
   13. I3C Echography—heart
   14. I3D Echography—carotid arteries
   15. I3E Echography—prostate, transrectal
   16. I3F Echography—other
   17. I4A Imaging/procedure—heart, including cardiac catheterization
   18. I4B Imaging/procedure—other

4. **Tests**
   1. T1A Lab tests—routine venipuncture (non-Medicare fee schedule)
   2. T1B Lab tests—automated general profiles
   3. T1C Lab tests—urinalysis
   4. T1D Lab tests—blood counts
   5. T1E Lab tests—glucose
   6. T1F Lab tests—bacterial cultures
   7. T1G Lab tests—other (Medicare fee schedule)
   8. T1H Lab tests—other (non-Medicare fee schedule)
   9. T2A Other tests—electrocardiograms
   10. T2B Other tests—cardiovascular stress tests
   11. T2C Other tests—EKG monitoring
   12. T2D Other tests—other

5. **Durable Medical Equipment**
   1. D1A Medical/surgical supplies
   2. D1B Hospital beds
   3. D1C Oxygen and supplies
   4. D1D Wheelchairs
   5. D1E Other DME
   6. D1F Prosthetic/orthotic devices
   7. D1G Drugs administered through DME

6. **Other**
   1. O1A Ambulance
   2. O1B Chiropractic
   3. O1C Enteral and parenteral
   4. O1D Chemotherapy
   5. O1E Other drugs
   6. O1F Hearing and speech services
   7. O1G Immunizations/vaccinations

7. **Exceptions/Unclassified**
   1. Y1 Other—Medicare fee schedule
   2. Y2 Other—Non-Medicare fee schedule
   3. Z1 Local codes
   4. Z2 Undefined codes

APPENDIX G — PUB 100 REFERENCES

The Centers for Medicare and Medicaid Services restructured its paper-based manual system as a web-based system on October 1, 2003. Called the online CMS manual system, it combines all of the various program instructions into internet-only manuals (IOMs), which are used by all CMS programs and contractors. In many instances, the references from the online manuals in appendix E contain a mention of the old paper manuals from which the current information was obtained when the manuals were converted. This information is shown in the header of the text, in the following format, when applicable, as A3-3101, HO-210, and B3-2049. Complete versions of all of the manuals can be found at http://www.cms.hhs.gov/manuals.

Effective with implementation of the IOMs, the former method of publishing program memoranda (PMs) to communicate program instructions was replaced by the following four templates:

- One-time notification
- Manual revisions
- Business requirements
- Confidential requirements

The web-based system has been organized by functional area (e.g., eligibility, entitlement, claims processing, benefit policy, program integrity) in an effort to eliminate redundancy within the manuals, simplify updating, and make CMS program instructions available more quickly. The web-based system contains the functional areas included below:

Pub. 100	Introduction
Pub. 100-1	Medicare General Information, Eligibility, and Entitlement Manual
Pub. 100-2	Medicare Benefit Policy Manual
Pub. 100-3	Medicare National Coverage Determinations Manual
Pub. 100-4	Medicare Claims Processing Manual
Pub. 100-5	Medicare Secondary Payer Manual
Pub. 100-6	Medicare Financial Management Manual
Pub. 100-7	State Operations Manual
Pub. 100-8	Medicare Program Integrity Manual
Pub. 100-9	Medicare Contractor Beneficiary and Provider Communications Manual
Pub. 100-10	Quality Improvement Organization Manual
Pub. 100-11	Reserved
Pub. 100-12	State Medicaid Manual (under development)
Pub. 100-13	Medicaid State Children's Health Insurance Program (under development)
Pub. 100-14	Medicare ESRD Network Organizations Manual
Pub. 100-15	State Buy-In Manual
Pub. 100-16	Medicare Managed Care Manual
Pub. 100-17	CMS/Business Partners Systems Security Manual
Pub. 100-18	Medicare Prescription Drug Benefit Manual
Pub. 100-19	Demonstrations
Pub. 100-20	One-Time Notification
Pub. 100-21	Recurring Update Notification

A brief description of the Medicare manuals primarily used for *CPC Expert* follows:

The **National Coverage Determinations Manual** (NCD), is organized according to categories such as diagnostic services, supplies, and medical procedures. The table of contents lists each category and subject within that category. Revision transmittals identify any new or background material, recap the changes, and provide an effective date for the change.

When complete, the manual will contain two chapters. Chapter 1 currently includes a description of CMS's national coverage determinations. When available, chapter 2 will contain a list of HCPCS codes related to each coverage determination. The manual is organized in accordance with CPT category sequences.

The **Medicare Benefit Policy Manual** contains Medicare general coverage instructions that are not national coverage determinations. As a general rule, in the past these instructions have been found in chapter II of the **Medicare Carriers Manual**, the **Medicare Intermediary Manual**, other provider manuals, and program memoranda.

The **Medicare Claims Processing Manual** contains instructions for processing claims for contractors and providers.

The **Medicare Program Integrity Manual** communicates the priorities and standards for the Medicare integrity programs.

Medicare IOM references

100-1, 3, 20.5
Blood Deductibles (Part A and Part B)
Program payment may not be made for the first 3 pints of whole blood or equivalent units of packed red cells received under Part A and Part B combined in a calendar year. However, blood processing (e.g., administration, storage) is not subject to the deductible.

The blood deductibles are in addition to any other applicable deductible and coinsurance amounts for which the patient is responsible.

The deductible applies only to the first 3 pints of blood furnished in a calendar year, even if more than one provider furnished blood.

100-1, 3, 20.5.2
Part B Blood Deductible
Blood is furnished on an outpatient basis or is subject to the Part B blood deductible and is counted toward the combined limit. It should be noted that payment for blood may be made to the hospital under Part B only for blood furnished in an outpatient setting. Blood is not covered for inpatient Part B services.

100-1, 3, 20.5.3
Items Subject to Blood Deductibles
The blood deductibles apply only to whole blood and packed red cells. The term whole blood means human blood from which none of the liquid or cellular components have been removed. Where packed red cells are furnished, a unit of packed red cells is considered equivalent to a pint of whole blood. Other components of blood such as platelets, fibrinogen, plasma, gamma globulin, and serum albumin are not subject to the blood deductible. However, these components of blood are covered as biologicals.

Refer to Pub. 100-04, Medicare Claims Processing Manual, chapter 4, Sec.231 regarding billing for blood and blood products under the Hospital Outpatient Prospective Payment System (OPPS).

100-1, 3, 30
Outpatient Mental Health Treatment Limitation
Regardless of the actual expenses a beneficiary incurs for treatment of mental, psychoneurotic, and personality disorders while the beneficiary is not an inpatient of a hospital at the time such expenses are incurred, the amount of those expenses that may be recognized for Part B deductible and payment purposes is limited to 62.5 percent of the Medicare allowed amount for these services. The limitation is called the outpatient mental health treatment limitation. Since Part B deductible also applies the program pays for about half of the allowed amount recognized for mental health therapy services.

Expenses for diagnostic services (e.g., psychiatric testing and evaluation to diagnose the patient's illness) are not subject to this limitation. This limitation applies only to therapeutic services and to services performed to evaluate the progress of a course of treatment for a diagnosed condition.

100-1, 3, 30.1
Application of Mental Health Limitation - Status of Patient
The limitation is applicable to expenses incurred in connection with the treatment of an individual who is not an inpatient of a hospital. Thus, the limitation applies to mental health services furnished to a person in a physician's office, in the patient's home, in a skilled nursing facility, as an outpatient, and so forth. The term "hospital" in this context means an institution which is primarily engaged in providing to inpatients, by or under the supervision of a physician(s):

- Diagnostic and therapeutic services for medical diagnosis, and treatment, and care of injured, disabled, or sick persons;
- Rehabilitation services for injured, disabled, or sick persons; or
- Psychiatric services for the diagnosis and treatment of mentally ill patients.

100-1, 3, 30.2
Disorders Subject to Mental Health Limitation
The term "mental, psychoneurotic, and personality disorders" is defined as the specific psychiatric conditions described in the American Psychiatric Association's Diagnostic and Statistical Manual of Mental Disorders, Third Edition - Revised (DSM-III-R).

If the treatment services rendered are for both a psychiatric condition and one or more nonpsychiatric conditions, the charges are separated to apply the limitation only to the mental health charge. Normally HCPCS code and diagnoses are used. Where HCPCS code is not available on the claim, revenue code is used.

Appendix G — Pub 100 References

If the service is primarily on the basis of a diagnosis of Alzheimer's Disease (coded 331.0 in the International Classification of Diseases, 9th Revision) or Alzheimer's or other disorders (coded 290.XX in DSM-III-R), treatment typically represents medical management of the patient's condition (rather than psychiatric treatment) and is not subject to the limitation.

100-1, 3, 30.3
Diagnostic Services

The mental health limitation does not apply to tests and evaluations performed to establish or confirm the patient's diagnosis. Diagnostic services include psychiatric or psychological tests and interpretations, diagnostic consultations, and initial evaluations. However, testing services performed to evaluate a patient's progress during treatment are considered part of treatment and are subject to the limitation.

100-1, 5, 70
Physician Defined

Physician means doctor of medicine, doctor of osteopathy (including osteopathic practitioner), doctor of dental surgery or dental medicine (within the limitations in subsection Sec.70.2), doctor of podiatric medicine (within the limitations in subsection Sec.70.3), or doctor of optometry (within the limitations of subsection Sec.70.5), and, with respect to certain specified treatment, a doctor of chiropractic legally authorized to practice by a State in which he/she performs this function. The services performed by a physician within these definitions are subject to any limitations imposed by the State on the scope of practice. The issuance by a State of a license to practice medicine constitutes legal authorization. Temporary State licenses also constitute legal authorization to practice medicine. If State law authorizes local political subdivisions to establish higher standards for medical practitioners than those set by the State licensing board, the local standards determine whether a particular physician has legal authorization. If State licensing law limits the scope of practice of a particular type of medical practitioner, only the services within the limitations are covered. The issuance by a State of a license to practice medicine constitutes legal authorization. Temporary State licenses also constitute legal authorization to practice medicine. If State law authorizes local political subdivisions to establish higher standards for medical practitioners than those set by the State licensing board, the local standards determine whether a particular physician has legal authorization. If State licensing law limits the scope of practice of a particular type of medical practitioner, only the services within the limitations are covered. NOTE: The term physician does not include such practitioners as a Christian Science practitioner or naturopath.

100-1, 5, 70.6
Chiropractors

A. General

A licensed chiropractor who meets uniform minimum standards (see subsection C) is a physician for specified services. Coverage extends only to treatment by means of manual manipulation of the spine to correct a subluxation demonstrated by X-ray, provided such treatment is legal in the State where performed. All other services furnished or ordered by chiropractors are not covered. An X-ray obtained by a chiropractor for his or her own diagnostic purposes before commencing treatment may suffice for claims documentation purposes. This means that if a chiropractor orders, takes, or interprets an X-ray to demonstrate a subluxation of the spine, the X-ray can be used for claims processing purposes. However, there is no coverage or payment for these services or for any other diagnostic or therapeutic service ordered or furnished by the chiropractor. In addition, in performing manual manipulation of the spine, some chiropractors use manual devices that are hand-held with the thrust of the force of the device being controlled manually. While such manual manipulation may be covered, there is no separate payment permitted for use of this device.

B. Licensure and Authorization to Practice

A chiropractor must be licensed or legally authorized to furnish chiropractic services by the State or jurisdiction in which the services are furnished.

C. Uniform Minimum Standards

1. Prior to July 1, 1974, Chiropractors licensed or authorized to practice prior to July 1, 1974, and those individuals who commenced their studies in a chiropractic college before that date must meet all of the following minimum standards to render payable services under the program:

    a. Preliminary education equal to the requirements for graduation from an accredited high school or other secondary school;

    b. Graduation from a college of chiropractic approved by the State's chiropractic examiners that included the completion of a course of study covering a period of not less than 3 school years of 6 months each year in actual continuous attendance covering adequate course of study in the subjects of anatomy, physiology, symptomatology and diagnosis, hygiene and sanitation, chemistry, histology, pathology, and principles and practice of chiropractic, including clinical instruction in vertebral palpation, nerve tracing and adjusting; and

    c. Passage of an examination prescribed by the State's chiropractic examiners covering the subjects listed in subsection b.

2. After June 30, 1974 - Individuals commencing their studies in a chiropractic college after June 30, 1974, must meet all of the following additional requirements:

    a. Satisfactory completion of 2 years of pre-chiropractic study at the college level;

    b. Satisfactory completion of a 4-year course of 8 months each year (instead of a 3-year course of 6 months each year) at a college or school of chiropractic that includes not less than 4,000 hours in the scientific and chiropractic courses specified in subsection 1.b, plus courses in the use and effect of X-ray and chiropractic analysis; and

    c. The practitioner must be over 21 years of age.

100-1, 5, 90.2
Laboratory Defined

Laboratory means a facility for the biological, microbiological, serological, chemical, immuno-hematological, immunohematological, biophysical, cytological, pathological, or other examination of materials derived from the human body for the purpose of providing information for the diagnosis, prevention, or treatment of any disease or impairment of, or the assessment of the health of, human beings. These examinations also include procedures to determine, measure, or otherwise describe the presence or absence of various substances or organisms in the body. Facilities only collecting or preparing specimens (or both) or only serving as a mailing service and not performing testing are not considered laboratories.

100-2, 1, 10
Covered Inpatient Hospital Services Covered Under Part A

A3-3101, HO-210

Patients covered under hospital insurance are entitled to have payment made on their behalf for inpatient hospital services. (Inpatient hospital services do not include extended care services provided by hospitals pursuant to swing bed approvals. See Pub. 100-1, Chapter 8, Sec.10.1, "Hospital Providers of Extended Care Services."). However, both inpatient hospital and inpatient SNF benefits are provided under Part A - Hospital Insurance Benefits for the Aged and Disabled, of Title XVIII).

Additional information concerning the following topics can be found in the following manual chapters:

- Benefit periods is found in Chapter 3, "Duration of Covered Inpatient Services";
- Copayment days is found in Chapter 2, "Duration of Covered Inpatient Services";
- Lifetime reserve days is found in Chapter 5, "Lifetime Reserve Days";
- Related payment information is housed in the Provider Reimbursement Manual.

Blood must be furnished on a day which counts as a day of inpatient hospital services to be covered as a Part A service and to count toward the blood deductible. Thus, blood is not covered under Part A and does not count toward the Part A blood deductible when furnished to an inpatient after the inpatient has exhausted all benefit days in a benefit period, or where the individual has elected not to use lifetime reserve days. However, where the patient is discharged on their first day of entitlement or on the hospital's first day of participation, the hospital is permitted to submit a billing form with no accommodation charge, but with ancillary charges including blood.

The records for all Medicare hospital inpatient discharges are maintained in CMS for statistical analysis and use in determining future PPS DRG classifications and rates.

Non-PPS hospitals do not pay for noncovered services generally excluded from coverage in the Medicare Program. This may result in denial of a part of the billed charges or in denial of the entire admission, depending upon circumstance. In PPS hospitals, the following are also possible:

1. In appropriately admitted cases where a noncovered procedure was performed, denied services may result in payment of a different DRG (i.e., one which excludes payment for the noncovered procedure); or

2. In appropriately admitted cases that become cost outlier cases, denied services may lead to denial of some or all of an outlier payment.

The following examples illustrate this principle. If care is noncovered because a patient does not need to be hospitalized, the intermediary denies the admission and makes no Part A (i.e., PPS) payment unless paid under limitation on liability. Under limitation on liability, Medicare payment may be made when the provider and the beneficiary were not aware the services were not necessary and could not reasonably be expected to know that the services were not necessary. For detailed instructions, see the Medicare Claims Processing Manual, Chapter 30, "Limitation on Liability." If a patient is appropriately hospitalized but receives (beyond routine services) only noncovered care, the admission is denied.

NOTE: The intermediary does not deny an admission that includes covered care, even if noncovered care was also rendered. Under PPS, Medicare assumes that it is paying for only the covered care rendered whenever covered services needed to treat and/or diagnose the illness were in fact provided.

If a noncovered procedure is provided along with covered nonroutine care, a DRG change rather than an admission denial might occur. If noncovered procedures are elevating costs into the cost outlier category, outlier payment is denied in whole or in part.

When the hospital is included in PPS, most of the subsequent discussion regarding coverage of inpatient hospital services is relevant only in the context of determining the appropriateness of admissions, which DRG, if any, to pay, and the appropriateness of payment for any outlier cases.

If a patient receives items or services in excess of, or more expensive than, those for which payment can be made, payment is made only for the covered items or services or for only the appropriate prospective payment amount. This provision applies not only to inpatient services, but also to all hospital services under Parts A and B of the program. If the items or services were requested by the patient, the hospital may charge him the difference between the amount customarily charged for the services requested and the amount customarily charged for covered services.

An inpatient is a person who has been admitted to a hospital for bed occupancy for purposes of receiving inpatient hospital services. Generally, a patient is considered an inpatient if formally admitted as inpatient with the expectation that he or she will remain at least overnight and occupy a bed even though it later develops that the patient can be discharged or transferred to another hospital and not actually use a hospital bed overnight.

The physician or other practitioner responsible for a patient's care at the hospital is also responsible for deciding whether the patient should be admitted as an inpatient. Physicians should use a 24-hour period as a benchmark, i.e., they should order admission for patients who are expected to need hospital care for 24 hours or more, and treat other patients on an outpatient basis. However, the decision to admit a patient is a complex medical judgment which can be made only after the physician has considered a number of factors, including the patient's medical history and current medical needs, the types of facilities available to inpatients and to outpatients, the hospital's by-laws and admissions policies, and the relative appropriateness of treatment in each setting. Factors to be considered when making the decision to admit include such things as:

- The severity of the signs and symptoms exhibited by the patient;
- The medical predictability of something adverse happening to the patient;
- The need for diagnostic studies that appropriately are outpatient services (i.e., their performance does not ordinarily require the patient to remain at the hospital for 24 hours or more) to assist in assessing whether the patient should be admitted; and
- The availability of diagnostic procedures at the time when and at the location where the patient presents.

Admissions of particular patients are not covered or noncovered solely on the basis of the length of time the patient actually spends in the hospital. In certain specific situations coverage of services on an inpatient or outpatient basis is determined by the following rules:

Minor Surgery or Other Treatment - When patients with known diagnoses enter a hospital for a specific minor surgical procedure or other treatment that is expected to keep them in the hospital for only a few hours (less than 24), they are considered outpatients for coverage purposes regardless of: the hour they came to the hospital, whether they used a bed, and whether they remained in the hospital past midnight.

Renal Dialysis - Renal dialysis treatments are usually covered only as outpatient services but may under certain circumstances be covered as inpatient services depending on the patient's condition. Patients staying at home, who are ambulatory, whose conditions are stable and who come to the hospital for routine chronic dialysis treatments, and not for a diagnostic workup or a change in therapy, are considered outpatients. On the other hand, patients undergoing short-term dialysis until their kidneys recover from an acute illness (acute dialysis), or persons with borderline renal failure who develop acute renal failure every time they have an illness and require dialysis (episodic dialysis) are usually inpatients. A patient may begin dialysis as an inpatient and then progress to an outpatient status.

Under original Medicare, the Quality Improvement Organization (QIO), for each hospital is responsible for deciding, during review of inpatient admissions on a case-by-case basis, whether the admission was medically necessary. Medicare law authorizes the QIO to make these judgments, and the judgments are binding for purposes of Medicare coverage. In making these judgments, however, QIOs consider only the medical evidence which was available to the physician at the time an admission decision had to be made. They do not take into account other information (e.g., test results) which became available only after admission, except in cases where considering the post-admission information would support a finding that an admission was medically necessary.

Refer to Parts 4 and 7 of the QIO Manual with regard to initial determinations for these services. The QIO will review the swing bed services in these PPS hospitals as well.

NOTE: When patients requiring extended care services are admitted to beds in a hospital, they are considered inpatients of the hospital. In such cases, the services furnished in the hospital will not be considered extended care services, and payment may not be made under the program for such services unless the services are extended care services furnished pursuant to a swing bed agreement granted to the hospital by the Secretary of Health and Human Services.

100-2, 1, 90
Termination of Pregnancy
B3-4276.1,.2

Effective for services furnished on or after October 1, 1998, Medicare will cover abortions procedures in the following situations:

1. If the pregnancy is the result of an act or rape or incest; or
2. In the case where a woman suffers from a physical disorder, physical injury, or physical illness, including a life-endangering physical condition caused by the pregnancy itself that would, as certified by a physician, place the woman in danger of death unless an abortion is performed.

NOTE: The "G7" modifier must be used with the following CPT codes in order for these services to be covered when the pregnancy resulted from rape or incest, or the pregnancy is certified by a physician as life threatening to the mother:

59840, 59841, 59850, 59851, 59852, 59855, 59856, 59857, 59866

100-2, 1, 100
Treatment for Infertility
A3-3101.13

Effective for services rendered on or after January 15, 1980, reasonable and necessary services associated with treatment for infertility are covered under Medicare. Like pregnancy (see Sec. 80 above), infertility is a condition sufficiently at variance with the usual state of health to make it appropriate for a person who normally would be expected to be fertile to seek medical consultation and treatment. Contractors should coordinate with QIOs to see that utilization guidelines are established for this treatment if inappropriate utilization or abuse is suspected.

100-2, 6, 10
Medical and Other Health Services Furnished to Inpatients of Participating Hospitals

Payment may be made under Part B for physician services and for the nonphysician medical and other health services listed below when furnished by a participating hospital (either directly or under arrangements) to an inpatient of the hospital, but only if payment for these services cannot be made under Part A.

In PPS hospitals, this means that Part B payment could be made for these services if:

- No Part A prospective payment is made at all for the hospital stay because of patient exhaustion of benefit days before admission;
- The admission was disapproved as not reasonable and necessary (and waiver of liability payment was not made);
- The day or days of the otherwise covered stay during which the services were provided were not reasonable and necessary (and no payment was made under waiver of liability);
- The patient was not otherwise eligible for or entitled to coverage under Part A (See the Medicare Benefit Policy Manual, Chapter 1, Sec.150, for services received as a result of noncovered services); or
- No Part A day outlier payment is made (for discharges before October 1997) for one or more outlier days due to patient exhaustion of benefit days after admission but before the case's arrival at outlier status, or because outlier days are otherwise not covered and waiver of liability payment is not made.

However, if only day outlier payment is denied under Part A (discharges before October 1997), Part B payment may be made for only the services covered under Part B and furnished on the denied outlier days.

In non-PPS hospitals, Part B payment may be made for services on any day for which Part A payment is denied (i.e., benefit days are exhausted; services are not at the hospital level of care; or patient is not otherwise eligible or entitled to payment under Part A).

Services payable are:

- Diagnostic x-ray tests, diagnostic laboratory tests, and other diagnostic tests;
- X-ray, radium, and radioactive isotope therapy, including materials and services of technicians;
- Surgical dressings, and splints, casts, and other devices used for reduction of fractures and dislocations;
- Prosthetic devices (other than dental) which replace all or part of an internal body organ (including contiguous tissue), or all or part of the function of a permanently inoperative or malfunctioning internal body organ, including replacement or repairs of such devices;
- Leg, arm, back, and neck braces, trusses, and artificial legs, arms, and eyes including adjustments, repairs, and replacements required because of breakage, wear, loss, or a change in the patient's physical condition;
- Outpatient physical therapy, outpatient speech-language pathology services, and outpatient occupational therapy (see the Medicare Benefit Policy Manual, Chapter 15, "Covered Medical and Other Health Services," Sec.Sec.220 and 230);
- Screening mammography services;
- Screening pap smears;
- Influenza, pneumococcal pneumonia, and hepatitis B vaccines;
- Colorectal screening;
- Bone mass measurements;
- Diabetes self-management;
- Prostate screening;
- Ambulance services;
- Hemophilia clotting factors for hemophilia patients competent to use these factors without supervision);
- Immunosuppressive drugs;
- Oral anti-cancer drugs;
- Oral drug prescribed for use as an acute anti-emetic used as part of an anti-cancer chemotherapeutic regimen; and Epoetin Alfa (EPO).

Coverage rules for these services are described in the Medicare Benefit Policy Manual, Chapters: 11, "End Stage Renal Disease (ESRD);" 14, "Medical Devices;" or 15, "Medical and Other Health Services."

For services to be covered under Part A or Part B, a hospital must furnish nonphysician services to its inpatients directly or under arrangements. A nonphysician service is one which does not meet the criteria defining physicians' services specifically provided for in regulation at 42 CFR 415.102. Services "incident to" physicians' services (except for the services of nurse anesthetists employed by anesthesiologists) are nonphysician services for purposes of this provision. This provision is applicable to all hospitals participating in Medicare, including those paid under alternative arrangements such as State cost control systems, and to emergency hospital services furnished by nonparticipating hospitals.

In all hospitals, every service provided to a hospital inpatient other than those listed in the next paragraph must be treated as an inpatient hospital service to be paid for under Part A, if Part A coverage is available and the beneficiary is entitled to Part A. This is because every hospital must provide directly or arrange for any nonphysician service rendered to its inpatients, and a hospital can be paid under Part B for a service provided in this manner only if Part A coverage does not exist.

Appendix G — Pub 100 References

These services, when provided to a hospital inpatient, may be covered under Part B, even though the patient has Part A coverage for the hospital stay. This is because these services are covered under Part B and not covered under Part A. They are:

- Physicians' services (including the services of residents and interns in unapproved teaching programs);
- Influenza vaccine;
- Pneumoccocal vaccine and its administration;
- Hepatitis B vaccine and its administration;
- Screening mammography services;
- Screening pap smears and pelvic exams;
- Colorectal screening;
- Bone mass measurements;
- Diabetes self management training services; and
- Prostate screening.

However, note that in order to have any Medicare coverage at all (Part A or Part B), any nonphysician service rendered to a hospital inpatient must be provided directly or arranged for by the hospital.

100-2, 6, 50
Sleep Disorder Clinics
A3-3112.5

Sleep disorder clinics are facilities in which certain conditions are diagnosed through the study of sleep. Such clinics are for diagnosis, therapy, and research. Sleep disorder clinics may provide some diagnostic or therapeutic services that are covered under Medicare. These clinics may be affiliated either with a hospital or a freestanding facility. Whether a clinic is hospital-affiliated or freestanding, coverage for diagnostic services under some circumstances is covered under provisions of the law different from those for coverage of therapeutic services.

100-2, 11, 20
Coverage of Outpatient Maintenance Dialysis
A3-3167, B3-2230.2, RDF-202, SOM-2272, RDF-317.1, PM AB-03-001

Medicare covers maintenance dialysis treatments when they are provided to ESRD patients by an approved hospital-based dialysis facility, an independent dialysis facility, or a special purpose dialysis facility. Outpatient dialysis treatments are covered in various settings: hospital outpatient facility, independent dialysis facility, or the patient's home. Dialysis treatments at dialysis facilities differ according to the types of patients being treated, the types of equipment and supplies used, the preferences of the treating physician, and the capability and makeup of the staff. Although not all facilities provide an identical range of services, the most common elements of a dialysis treatment are:

a. Personnel services;
b. Equipment and supplies - dialysis machine and its maintenance;
c. Administrative services;
d. Overhead costs;
e. Monitoring access and related declotting the access or referring the patient;
f. ESRD related laboratory tests; and
g. Biologicals.

Direct nursing services include registered nurses, licensed practical nurses, technicians, social workers, and dietitians. Facilities with self-dialysis units must meet specific health and safety requirements. Certain standards applicable to staff assisted dialysis have been adjusted for self-dialysis units in consideration of the differences in the two modalities. Before participating in self-dialysis, patients must have completed an appropriate training program in emergency procedures and have a safe storage area for their supplies. Access to the self-dialysis unit is limited to patients for whom the facility maintains patient care plans in order to exclude transient patients who might not be familiar with the facility's equipment or emergency procedures. The self-dialysis unit need not be physically separate from the rest of the facility nor operate on a separate shift.

100-2, 13, 30
Rural Health Clinic and Federally Qualified Health Center Service Defined

Payments for covered RHC/FQHC services furnished to Medicare beneficiaries are made on the basis of an all-inclusive rate per covered visit (except for pneumococcal and influenza vaccines and their administration, which is paid at 100 percent of reasonable cost). The term "visit" is defined as a face-to-face encounter between the patient and a physician, physician assistant, nurse practitioner, certified nurse midwife, visiting nurse, clinical psychologist, or clinical social worker during which an RHC/FQHC service is rendered. As a result of section 5114 of the Deficit Reduction Act of 2005 (DRA), the FQHC definition of a face-to-face encounter is expanded to include encounters with qualified practitioners of Outpatient Diabetes Self-Management Training Services (DSMT) and medical nutrition therapy (MNT) services when the FQHC meets all relevant program requirements for the provision of such services.

Encounters with (1) more than one health professional; and (2) multiple encounters with the same health professional which take place on the same day and at a single location, constitute a single visit. An exception occurs in cases in which the patient, subsequent to the first encounter, suffers an illness or injury requiring additional diagnosis or treatment.

100-2, 15, 20.1
Physician Expense for Surgery, Childbirth, and Treatment for Infertility
B3-2005.I

A. Surgery and Childbirth
Skilled medical management is covered throughout the events of pregnancy, beginning with diagnosis, continuing through delivery and ending after the necessary postnatal care. Similarly, in the event of termination of pregnancy, regardless of whether terminated spontaneously or for therapeutic reasons (i.e., where the life of the mother would be endangered if the fetus were brought to term), the need for skilled medical management and/or medical services is equally important as in those cases carried to full term. After the infant is delivered and is a separate individual, items and services furnished to the infant are not covered on the basis of the mother's eligibility.

Most surgeons and obstetricians bill patients an all-inclusive package charge intended to cover all services associated with the surgical procedure or delivery of the child. All expenses for surgical and obstetrical care, including preoperative/prenatal examinations and tests and post-operative/postnatal services, are considered incurred on the date of surgery or delivery, as appropriate. This policy applies whether the physician bills on a package charge basis, or itemizes the bill separately for these items.

Occasionally, a physician's bill may include charges for additional services not directly related to the surgical procedure or the delivery. Such charges are considered incurred on the date the additional services are furnished.

The above policy applies only where the charges are imposed by one physician or by a clinic on behalf of a group of physicians. Where more than one physician imposes charges for surgical or obstetrical services, all preoperative/prenatal and post-operative/postnatal services performed by the physician who performed the surgery or delivery are considered incurred on the date of the surgery or delivery. Expenses for services rendered by other physicians are considered incurred on the date they were performed.

B. Treatment for Infertility
Reasonable and necessary services associated with treatment for infertility are covered under Medicare. Infertility is a condition sufficiently at variance with the usual state of health to make it appropriate for a person who normally is expected to be fertile to seek medical consultation and treatment.

100-2, 15, 20.2
Physician Expense for Allergy Treatment

B3-2005.2, B3-4145 Allergists commonly bill separately for the initial diagnostic workup and for the treatment (See Sec.60.2). Where it is necessary to provide treatment over an extended period, the allergist may submit a single bill for all of the treatments, or may bill periodically. In either case the Form CMS-1500 claim shows the Healthcare Common Procedure Coding System (HCPCS) codes and from and through dates of service, or the Form CMS-1450 outpatient claim shows the HCPCS code and date of service (except for critical access hospital (CAH) claims).

100-2, 15, 20.3
Artificial Limbs, Braces, and Other Custom Made Items Ordered But Not Furnished
B3-2005.3

A. Date of Incurred Expense
If a custom-made item was ordered but not furnished to a beneficiary because the individual died or because the order was canceled by the beneficiary or because the beneficiary's condition changed and the item was no longer reasonable and necessary or appropriate, payment can be made based on the supplier's expenses. (See subsection B for determination of the allowed amount.) In such cases, the expense is considered incurred on the date the beneficiary died or the date the supplier learned of the cancellation or that the item was no longer reasonable and necessary or appropriate for the beneficiary's condition. If the beneficiary died or the beneficiary's condition changed and the item was no longer reasonable and necessary or appropriate, payment can be made on either an assigned or unassigned claim. If the beneficiary, for any other reason, canceled the order, payment can be made to the supplier only.

B. Determination of Allowed Amount
The allowed amount is based on the services furnished and materials used, up to the date the supplier learned of the beneficiary's death or of the cancellation of the order or that the item was no longer reasonable and necessary or appropriate. The Durable Medical Equipment Regional Carrier (DMERC), carrier or intermediary, as appropriate, determines the services performed and the allowable amount appropriate in the particular situation. It takes into account any salvage value of the device to the supplier. Where a supplier breaches an agreement to make a prosthesis, brace, or other custom-made device for a Medicare beneficiary, e.g., an unexcused failure to provide the article within the time specified in the contract, payment may not be made for any work or material expended on the item. Whether a particular supplier has lived up to its agreement, of course, depends on the facts in the individual case.

100-2, 15, 30
Physician Services
B3-2020, B3-4142

A. General
Physician services are the professional services performed by a physician or physicians for a patient including diagnosis, therapy, surgery, consultation, and care plan oversight. The physician must render the service for the service to be covered. (See Publication 100-1, the Medicare General Information, Eligibility, and Entitlement Manual, Chapter 5, Sec.70, for definition of physician.) A service may be considered to be a physician's service where the physician either examines the patient in person or is able to visualize some aspect of the patient's condition without the interposition of a third person's judgment. Direct visualization would be possible by means of x-rays, electrocardiogram and electroencephalogram tapes, tissue samples, etc. For example, the interpretation by a physician of an actual

electrocardiogram or electroencephalogram reading that has been transmitted via telephone (i.e., electronically rather than by means of a verbal description) is a covered service. Professional services of the physician are covered if provided within the United States, and may be performed in a home, office, institution, or at the scene of an accident. A patient's home, for this purpose, is anywhere the patient makes his or her residence, e.g., home for the aged, a nursing home, a relative's home.

B. Telephone Services
Services by means of a telephone call between a physician and a beneficiary, or between a physician and a member of a beneficiary's family, are covered under Medicare, but carriers may not make separate payment for these services under the program. The physician work resulting from telephone calls is considered to be an integral part of the prework and postwork of other physician services, and the fee schedule amount for the latter services already includes payment for the telephone calls. See the Medicare Benefit Policy Manual, Chapter 15, "Covered Medical and Other Health Services," Sec.270, for coverage of telehealth services.

C. Consultations
A consultation may be paid when the consulting physician initiates treatment on the same day as the consultation. It is only after a transfer of care has occurred that evaluation and management (E&M) services may not be billed as consultations; they must be billed as subsequent office/outpatient visits. Therefore, if covered, a consultation is reimbursable when it is a professional service furnished a patient by a second physician at the request of the attending physician. Such a consultation includes the history and examination of the patient as well as the written report, which is furnished to the attending physician for inclusion in the patient's permanent medical record. These reports must be prepared and submitted to the provider for retention when they involve patients of institutions responsible for maintaining such records, and submitted to the attending physician's office for other patients. To reimburse laboratory consultations, the services must: Be requested by the patient's attending physician; Relate to a test result that lies outside of the clinically significant normal or expected/established range relative to the condition of the patient; Result in a written narrative report included in the patient's medical record; andRequire medical judgment by the consultant physician. A consultation must involve a medical judgment that ordinarily requires a physician. Where a nonphysician laboratory specialist could furnish the information, the service of the physician is not a consultation payable under Part B. The following indicators can ordinarily distinguish attending physician's claims:Therapeutic services are included on the bill in addition to an examination;The patient's history is before the examiner while the claim is reviewed and the billing physician has previously rendered other services to the patient; orInformation in the file indicates that the patient was not referred. The attending physician may remove himself from the care of the patient and turn the patient over to the person who performed a consultation service. In this situation, the initial examination would be a consultation if the above requirements were met at that time.

D. Patient-Initiated Second Opinions
Patient-initiated second opinions that relate to the medical need for surgery or for major nonsurgical diagnostic and therapeutic procedures (e.g., invasive diagnostic techniques such as cardiac catheterization and gastroscopy) are covered under Medicare. In the event that the recommendation of the first and second physician differs regarding the need for surgery (or other major procedure), a third opinion is also covered. Second and third opinions are covered even though the surgery or other procedure, if performed, is determined not covered. Payment may be made for the history and examination of the patient, and for other covered diagnostic services required to properly evaluate the patient's need for a procedure and to render a professional opinion. In some cases, the results of tests done by the first physician may be available to the second physician.

E. Concurrent Care
Concurrent care exists where more than one physician renders services more extensive than consultative services during a period of time. The reasonable and necessary services of each physician rendering concurrent care could be covered where each is required to play an active role in the patient's treatment, for example, because of the existence of more than one medical condition requiring diverse specialized medical services. In order to determine whether concurrent physicians' services are reasonable and necessary, the carrier must decide the following:

1. Whether the patient's condition warrants the services of more than one physician on an attending (rather than consultative) basis, and
2. Whether the individual services provided by each physician are reasonable and necessary.

In resolving the first question, the carrier should consider the specialties of the physicians as well as the patient's diagnosis, as concurrent care is usually (although not always) initiated because of the existence of more than one medical condition requiring diverse specialized medical or surgical services. The specialties of the physicians are an indication of the necessity for concurrent services, but the patient's condition and the inherent reasonableness and necessity of the services, as determined by the carrier's medical staff in accordance with locality norms, must also be considered. For example, although cardiology is a sub-specialty of internal medicine, the treatment of both diabetes and of a serious heart condition might require the concurrent services of two physicians, each practicing in internal medicine but specializing in different sub-specialties.

While it would not be highly unusual for concurrent care performed by physicians in different specialties (e.g., a surgeon and an internist) or by physicians in different sub-specialties of the same specialty (e.g., an allergist and a cardiologist) to be found medically necessary, the need for such care by physicians in the same specialty or sub-specialty (e.g., two internists or two cardiologists) would occur infrequently since in most cases both physicians would possess the skills and knowledge necessary to treat the patient. However, circumstances could arise which would necessitate such care. For example, a patient may require the services of two physicians in the same specialty or sub-specialty when one physician has further limited his or her practice to some unusual aspect of that specialty, e.g., tropical medicine. Similarly, concurrent services provided by a family physician and an internist may or may not be found to be reasonable and necessary, depending on the circumstances of the specific case. If it is determined that the services of one of the physicians are not warranted by the patient's condition, payment may be made only for the other physician's (or physicians') services.

Once it is determined that the patient requires the active services of more than one physician, the individual services must be examined for medical necessity, just as where a single physician provides the care. For example, even if it is determined that the patient requires the concurrent services of both a cardiologist and a surgeon, payment may not be made for any services rendered by either physician which, for that condition, exceed normal frequency or duration unless there are special circumstances requiring the additional care.

The carrier must also assure that the services of one physician do not duplicate those provided by another, e.g., where the family physician visits during the post-operative period primarily as a courtesy to the patient.

Hospital admission services performed by two physicians for the same beneficiary on the same day could represent reasonable and necessary services, provided, as stated above, that the patient's condition necessitates treatment by both physicians. The level of difficulty of the service provided may vary between the physicians, depending on the severity of the complaint each one is treating and that physician's prior contact with the patient. For example, the admission services performed by a physician who has been treating a patient over a period of time for a chronic condition would not be as involved as the services performed by a physician who has had no prior contact with the patient and who has been called in to diagnose and treat a major acute condition.

Carriers should have sufficient means for identifying concurrent care situations. A correct coverage determination can be made on a concurrent care case only where the claim is sufficiently documented for the carrier to determine the role each physician played in the patient's care (i.e., the condition or conditions for which the physician treated the patient). If, in any case, the role of each physician involved is not clear, the carrier should request clarification.

F. Completion of Claims Forms
Separate charges for the services of a physician in completing a Form CMS-1500, a statement in lieu of a Form CMS-1500, or an itemized bill are not covered. Payment for completion of the Form CMS-1500 claim form is considered included in the fee schedule amount.

G. Care Plan Oversight Services
Care plan oversight is supervision of patients under care of home health agencies or hospices that require complex and multidisciplinary care modalities involving regular physician development and/or revision of care plans, review of subsequent reports of patient status, review of laboratory and other studies, communication with other health professionals not employed in the same practice who are involved in the patient's care, integration of new information into the care plan, and/or adjustment of medical therapy.

Such services are covered for home health and hospice patients, but are not covered for patients of skilled nursing facilities (SNFs), nursing home facilities, or hospitals. These services are covered only if all the following requirements are met:

1. The beneficiary must require complex or multi-disciplinary care modalities requiring ongoing physician involvement in the patient's plan of care;
2. The care plan oversight (CPO) services should be furnished during the period in which the beneficiary was receiving Medicare covered HHA or hospice services;
3. The physician who bills CPO must be the same physician who signed the home health or hospice plan of care;
4. The physician furnished at least 30 minutes of care plan oversight within the calendar month for which payment is claimed. Time spent by a physician's nurse or the time spent consulting with one's nurse is not countable toward the 30-minute threshold. Low-intensity services included as part of other evaluation and management services are not included as part of the 30 minutes required for coverage;
5. The work included in hospital discharge day management (codes 99238-99239) and discharge from observation (code 99217) is not countable toward the 30 minutes per month required for work on the same day as discharge but only for those services separately documented as occurring after the patient is actually physically discharged from the hospital;
6. The physician provided a covered physician service that required a face-to-face encounter with the beneficiary within the six months immediately preceding the first care plan oversight service. Only evaluation and management services are acceptable prerequisite face-to-face encounters for CPO. EKG, lab, and surgical services are not sufficient face-to-face services for CPO;
7. The care plan oversight billed by the physician was not routine post-operative care provided in the global surgical period of a surgical procedure billed by the physician;
8. If the beneficiary is receiving home health agency services, the physician did not have a significant financial or contractual interest in the home health agency. A physician who is an employee of a hospice, including a volunteer medical director, should not bill CPO services. Payment for the services of a physician employed by the hospice is included in the payment to the hospice;
9. The physician who bills the care plan oversight services is the physician who furnished them;
10. Services provided incident to a physician's service do not qualify as CPO and do not count toward the 30-minute requirement;
11. The physician is not billing for the Medicare end stage renal disease (ESRD) capitation payment for the same beneficiary during the same month; and
12. The physician billing for CPO must document in the patient's record the services furnished and the date and length of time associated with those services.

100-2, 15, 30.4
Optometrist's Services
B3-2020.25

Effective April 1, 1987, a doctor of optometry is considered a physician with respect to all services the optometrist is authorized to perform under State law or regulation. To be covered under Medicare, the services must be medically reasonable and necessary for the diagnosis or treatment of illness or injury, and must meet all applicable coverage requirements. See the Medicare Benefit Policy Manual, Chapter 16, "General Exclusions from Coverage," for exclusions from coverage that apply to vision care services, and the Medicare Claims Processing Manual, Chapter 12, "Physician/Practitioner Billing," for information dealing with payment for items and services furnished by optometrists.

A. FDA Monitored Studies of Intraocular Lenses
Special coverage rules apply to situations in which an ophthalmologist is involved in a Food and Drug Administration (FDA) monitored study of the safety and efficacy of an investigational Intraocular Lens (IOL). The investigation process for IOLs is unique in that there is a core period and an adjunct period. The core study is a traditional, well-controlled clinical investigation with full record keeping and reporting requirements. The adjunct study is essentially an extended distribution phase for lenses in which only limited safety data are compiled. Depending on the lens being evaluated, the adjunct study may be an extension of the core study or may be the only type of investigation to which the lens may be subject.

All eye care services related to the investigation of the IOL must be provided by the investigator (i.e., the implanting ophthalmologist) or another practitioner (including a doctor of optometry) who provides services at the direction or under the supervision of the investigator and who has an agreement with the investigator that information on the patient is given to the investigator so that he or she may report on the patient to the IOL manufacturer. Eye care services furnished by anyone other than the investigator (or a practitioner who assists the investigator, as described in the preceding paragraph) are not covered during the period the IOL is being investigated, unless the services are not related to the investigation.

B. Concurrent Care
Where more than one practitioner furnishes concurrent care, services furnished to a beneficiary by both an ophthalmologist and another physician (including an optometrist) may be recognized for payment if it is determined that each practitioner's services were reasonable and necessary. (See Sec.30.E

100-2, 15, 30.5
Chiropractor's Services
B3-2020.26

A chiropractor must be licensed or legally authorized to furnish chiropractic services by the State or jurisdiction in which the services are furnished. In addition, a licensed chiropractor must meet the following uniform minimum standards to be considered a physician for Medicare coverage. Coverage extends only to treatment by means of manual manipulation of the spine to correct a subluxation provided such treatment is legal in the State where performed. All other services furnished or ordered by chiropractors are not covered. If a chiropractor orders, takes, or interprets an x-ray or other diagnostic procedure to demonstrate a subluxation of the spine, the x-ray can be used for documentation. However, there is no coverage or payment for these services or for any other diagnostic or therapeutic service ordered or furnished by the chiropractor. For detailed information on using x-rays to determine subluxation, see Sec.240.1.2. In addition, in performing manual manipulation of the spine, some chiropractors use manual devices that are hand-held with the thrust of the force of the device being controlled manually. While such manual manipulation may be covered, there is no separate payment permitted for use of this device.

A. Uniform Minimum Standards
Prior to July 1, 1974 Chiropractors licensed or authorized to practice prior to July 1, 1974, and those individuals who commenced their studies in a chiropractic college before that date must meet all of the following three minimum standards to render payable services under the program:

Preliminary education equal to the requirements for graduation from an accredited high school or other secondary school;Graduation from a college of chiropractic approved by the State's chiropractic examiners that included the completion of a course of study covering a period of not less than 3 school years of 6 months each year in actual continuous attendance covering adequate course of study in the subjects of anatomy, physiology, symptomatology and diagnosis, hygiene and sanitation, chemistry, histology, pathology, and principles and practice of chiropractic, including clinical instruction in vertebral palpation, nerve tracing, and adjusting; andPassage of an examination prescribed by the State's chiropractic examiners covering the subjects listed above.

After June 30, 1974Individuals commencing their studies in a chiropractic college after June 30, 1974, must meet all of the above three standards and all of the following additional requirements:Satisfactory completion of 2 years of pre-chiropractic study at the college level;Satisfactory completion of a 4-year course of 8 months each year (instead of a 3-year course of 6 months each year) at a college or school of chiropractic that includes not less than 4,000 hours in the scientific and chiropractic courses specified in the second bullet under "Prior to July 1, 1974" above, plus courses in the use and effect of x-ray and chiropractic analysis; andThe practitioner must be over 21 years of age.

B. Maintenance Therapy
Under the Medicare program, Chiropractic maintenance therapy is not considered to be medically reasonable or necessary, and is therefore not payable. Maintenance therapy is defined as a treatment plan that seeks to prevent disease, promote health, and prolong and enhance the quality of life; or therapy that is performed to maintain or prevent deterioration of a chronic condition. When further clinical improvement cannot reasonably be expected from continuous ongoing care, and the chiropractic treatment becomes supportive rather than corrective in nature, the treatment is then considered maintenance therapy. For information on how to indicate on a claim a treatment is or is not maintenance, see Sec.240.1.

100-2, 15, 50
Drugs and Biologicals
B3-2049, A3-3112.4.B, HO-230.4.B

The Medicare program provides limited benefits for outpatient drugs. The program covers drugs that are furnished "incident to" a physician's service provided that the drugs are not usually self-administered by the patients who take them. Generally, drugs and biologicals are covered only if all of the following requirements are met:

- They meet the definition of drugs or biologicals (see Sec.50.1);
- They are of the type that are not usually self-administered. (see Sec.50.2);
- They meet all the general requirements for coverage of items as incident to a physician's services (see Sec.Sec.50.1 and 50.3);
- They are reasonable and necessary for the diagnosis or treatment of the illness or injury for which they are administered according to accepted standards of medical practice (see Sec.50.4);
- They are not excluded as noncovered immunizations (see Sec.50.4.4.2); and
- They have not been determined by the FDA to be less than effective. (See Sec.Sec.50.4.4).

Medicare Part B does generally not cover drugs that can be self-administered, such as those in pill form, or are used for self-injection. However, the statute provides for the coverage of some self-administered drugs. Examples of self-administered drugs that are covered include blood-clotting factors, drugs used in immunosuppressive therapy, erythropoietin for dialysis patients, osteoporosis drugs for certain homebound patients, and certain oral cancer drugs. (See Sec.110.3 for coverage of drugs, which are necessary to the effective use of Durable Medical Equipment (DME) or prosthetic devices.)

100-2, 15, 50.4.4.2
Immunizations
A3-3157.A, B3-2049.4, HO-230.4.C

Vaccinations or inoculations are excluded as immunizations unless they are directly related to the treatment of an injury or direct exposure to a disease or condition, such as anti-rabies treatment, tetanus antitoxin or booster vaccine, botulin antitoxin, antivenin sera, or immune globulin. In the absence of injury or direct exposure, preventive immunization (vaccination or inoculation) against such diseases as smallpox, polio, diphtheria, etc., is not covered. However, pneumococcal, hepatitis B, and influenza virus vaccines are exceptions to this rule. (See items A, B, and C below.) In cases where a vaccination or inoculation is excluded from coverage, related charges are also not covered.

A. Pneumococcal Pneumonia Vaccinations
Effective for services furnished on or after May 1, 1981, the Medicare Part B program covers pneumococcal pneumonia vaccine and its administration when furnished in compliance with any applicable State law by any provider of services or any entity or individual with a supplier number. This includes revaccination of patients at highest risk of pneumococcal infection. Typically, these vaccines are administered once in a lifetime except for persons at highest risk. Effective July 1, 2000, Medicare does not require for coverage purposes that a doctor of medicine or osteopathy order the vaccine. Therefore, the beneficiary may receive the vaccine upon request without a physician's order and without physician supervision.

An initial vaccine may be administered only to persons at high risk (see below) of pneumococcal disease. Revaccination may be administered only to persons at highest risk of serious pneumococcal infection and those likely to have a rapid decline in pneumococcal antibody levels, provided that at least five years have [passed since the previous doe of pneumococcal vaccine. Persons at high risk for whom an initial vaccine may be administered include all people age 65 and older; immunocompetent adults who are at increased risk of pneumococcal disease or its complications because of chronic illness (e.g., cardiovascular disease, pulmonary disease, diabetes mellitus, alcoholism, cirrhosis, or cerebrospinal fluid leaks); and individuals with compromised immune systems (e.g., splenic dysfunction or anatomic asplenia, Hodgkin's disease, lymphoma, multiple myeloma, chronic renal failure, HIV infection, nephrotic syndrome, sickle cell disease, or organ transplantation). Persons at highest risk and those most likely to have rapid declines in antibody levels are those for whom revaccination may be appropriate. This group includes persons with functional or anatomic asplenia (e.g., sickle cell disease, splenectomy), HIV infection, leukemia, lymphoma, Hodgkin's disease, multiple myeloma, generalized malignancy, chronic renal failure, nephrotic syndrome, or other conditions associated with immunosuppression such as organ or bone marrow transplantation, and those receiving immunosuppressive chemotherapy. It is not appropriate for routine revaccination of people age 65 or older that are not at highest risk. Those administering the vaccine should not require the patient to present an immunization record prior to administering the pneumococcal vaccine, nor should they feel compelled to review the patient's complete medical record if it is not available. Instead, provided that the patient is competent, it is acceptable to rely on the patient's verbal history to determine prior vaccination status. If the patient is uncertain about his or her vaccination history in the past five years, the vaccine should be given. However, if the patient is certain he/she was were vaccinated in the last five years, the vaccine should not be given. If the patient is certain that the vaccine was given more than five years ago, revaccination is covered only if the patient is at high risk.

B. Hepatitis B Vaccine
Effective for services furnished on or after September 1, 1984, P.L. 98-369 provides coverage under Part B for hepatitis B vaccine and its administration, furnished to a Medicare beneficiary who is at high or intermediate risk of contracting hepatitis B. This coverage is effective for services furnished on or after September 1, 1984. High-risk groups currently identified include (see exception below):ESRD patients;Hemophiliacs who receive Factor VIII or IX concentrates;Clients of institutions for the mentally retarded;Persons who live in the same household as an Hepatitis B Virus (HBV) carrier;Homosexual men; andIllicit injectable drug abusers.

Intermediate risk groups currently identified include: Staff in institutions for the mentally retarded; and Workers in health care professions who have frequent contact with blood or blood-derived body fluids during routine work. EXCEPTION: Persons in both of the above-listed groups in paragraph B, would not be considered at high or intermediate risk of contracting hepatitis B, however, if there were laboratory evidence positive for antibodies to hepatitis B. (ESRD patients are routinely tested for hepatitis B antibodies as part of their continuing monitoring and therapy.) For Medicare program purposes, the vaccine may be administered upon the order of a doctor of medicine or osteopathy, by a doctor of medicine or osteopathy, or by home health agencies, skilled nursing facilities, ESRD facilities, hospital outpatient departments, and persons recognized under the incident to physicians' services provision of law. A charge separate from the ESRD composite rate will be recognized and paid for administration of the vaccine to ESRD patients.

C. Influenza Virus Vaccine

Effective for services furnished on or after May 1, 1993, the Medicare Part B program covers influenza virus vaccine and its administration when furnished in compliance with any applicable State law by any provider of services or any entity or individual with a supplier number. Typically, these vaccines are administered once a year in the fall or winter. Medicare does not require, for coverage purposes, that a doctor of medicine or osteopathy order the vaccine. Therefore, the beneficiary may receive the vaccine upon request without a physician's order and without physician supervision.

100-2, 15, 50.5
Self-Administered Drugs and Biologicals

B3-2049.5 Medicare Part B does not cover drugs that are usually self-administered by the patient unless the statute provides for such coverage. The statute explicitly provides coverage, for blood clotting factors, drugs used in immunosuppressive therapy, erythropoietin for dialysis patients, certain oral anti-cancer drugs and anti-emetics used in certain situations.

100-2, 15, 60.3
Incident to Physician's Service in Clinic

B3-2050.3

Services and supplies incident to a physician's service in a physician directed clinic or group association are generally the same as those described above.

A physician directed clinic is one where:

1. A physician (or a number of physicians) is present to perform medical (rather than administrative) services at all times the clinic is open;
2. Each patient is under the care of a clinic physician; and
3. The nonphysician services are under medical supervision.

In highly organized clinics, particularly those that are departmentalized, direct physician supervision may be the responsibility of several physicians as opposed to an individual attending physician. In this situation, medical management of all services provided in the clinic is assured. The physician ordering a particular service need not be the physician who is supervising the service. Therefore, services performed by auxiliary personnel and other aides are covered even though they are performed in another department of the clinic. Supplies provided by the clinic during the course of treatment are also covered. When the auxiliary personnel perform services outside the clinic premises, the services are covered only if performed under the direct supervision of a clinic physician. If the clinic refers a patient for auxiliary services performed by personnel who are not supervised by clinic physicians, such services are not incident to a physician's servic

100-2, 15, 80
Requirements for Diagnostic X-Ray, Diagnostic Laboratory, and Other Diagnostic Tests

This section describes the levels of physician supervision required for furnishing the technical component of diagnostic tests for a Medicare beneficiary who is not a hospital inpatient or outpatient. Section 410.32(b) of the Code of Federal Regulations (CFR) requires that diagnostic tests covered under Sec.1861(s)(3) of the Act and payable under the physician fee schedule, with certain exceptions listed in the regulation, have to be performed under the supervision of an individual meeting the definition of a physician (Sec.1861(r) of the Act) to be considered reasonable and necessary and, therefore, covered under Medicare. The regulation defines these levels of physician supervision for diagnostic tests as follows:

General Supervision - means the procedure is furnished under the physician's overall direction and control, but the physician's presence is not required during the performance of the procedure. Under general supervision, the training of the nonphysician personnel who actually performs the diagnostic procedure and the maintenance of the necessary equipment and supplies are the continuing responsibility of the physician.

Direct Supervision - in the office setting means the physician must be present in the office suite and immediately available to furnish assistance and direction throughout the performance of the procedure. It does not mean that the physician must be present in the room when the procedure is performed.

Personal Supervision - means a physician must be in attendance in the room during the performance of the procedure.

One of the following numerical levels is assigned to each CPT or HCPCS code in the Medicare Physician Fee Schedule Database:

0 Procedure is not a diagnostic test or procedure is a diagnostic test which is not subject to the physician supervision policy.

1 Procedure must be performed under the general supervision of a physician.

2 Procedure must be performed under the direct supervision of a physician.

3 Procedure must be performed under the personal supervision of a physician.

4 Physician supervision policy does not apply when procedure is furnished by a qualified, independent psychologist or a clinical psychologist or furnished under the general supervision of a clinical psychologist; otherwise must be performed under the general supervision of a physician.

5 Physician supervision policy does not apply when procedure is furnished by a qualified audiologist; otherwise must be performed under the general supervision of a physician.

6 Procedure must be performed by a physician or by a physical therapist (PT) who is certified by the American Board of Physical Therapy Specialties (ABPTS) as a qualified electrophysiologic clinical specialist and is permitted to provide the procedure under State law.

6a Supervision standards for level 66 apply; in addition, the PT with ABPTS certification may supervise another PT but only the PT with ABPTS certification may bill.

7a Supervision standards for level 77 apply; in addition, the PT with ABPTS certification may supervise another PT but only the PT with ABPTS certification may bill.

9 Concept does not apply.

21 Procedure must be performed by a technician with certification under general supervision of a physician; otherwise must be performed under direct supervision of a physician.

22 Procedure may be performed by a technician with on-line real-time contact with physician.

66 Procedure must be performed by a physician or by a PT with ABPTS certification and certification in this specific procedure.

77 Procedure must be performed by a PT with ABPTS certification or by a PT without certification under direct supervision of a physician, or by a technician with certification under general supervision of a physician.

Nurse practitioners, clinical nurse specialists, and physician assistants are not defined as physicians under Sec.1861(r) of the Act. Therefore, they may not function as supervisory physicians under the diagnostic tests benefit (Sec.1861(s)(3) of the Act). However, when these practitioners personally perform diagnostic tests as provided under Sec.1861(s)(2)(K) of the Act, Sec.1861(s)(3) does not apply and they may perform diagnostic tests pursuant to State scope of practice laws and under the applicable State requirements for physician supervision or collaboration. Because the diagnostic tests benefit set forth in Sec.1861(s)(3) of the Act is separate and distinct from the incident to benefit set forth in Sec.1861(s)(2) of the Act, diagnostic tests need not meet the incident to requirements. Diagnostic tests may be furnished under situations that meet the incident to requirements but this is not required. However, carriers must not scrutinize claims for diagnostic tests utilizing the incident to requirements.

100-2, 15, 80.1
Clinical Laboratory Services

Section 1833 and 1861 of the Act provides for payment of clinical laboratory services under Medicare Part B. Clinical laboratory services involve the biological, microbiological, serological, chemical, immunohematological, hematological, biophysical, cytological, pathological, or other examination of materials derived from the human body for the diagnosis, prevention, or treatment of a disease or assessment of a medical condition. Laboratory services must meet all applicable requirements of the Clinical Laboratory Improvement Amendments of 1988 (CLIA), as set forth at 42 CFR part 493. Section 1862(a)(1)(A) of the Act provides that Medicare payment may not be made for services that are not reasonable and necessary. Clinical laboratory services must be ordered and used promptly by the physician who is treating the beneficiary as described in 42 CFR 410.32(a), or by a qualified nonphysician practitioner, as described in 42 CFR 410.32(a)(3).

See section 80.6 of this manual for related physician ordering instructions.

See the Medicare Claims Processing Manual Chapter 16 for related claims processing instructions.

100-2, 15, 80.2
Psychological Tests and Neuropsychological Tests

Medicare Part B coverage of psychological tests and neuropsychological tests is authorized under section 1861(s)(3) of the Social Security Act. Payment for psychological and neuropsychological tests is authorized under section 1842(b)(2)(A) of the Social Security Act. The payment amounts for the new psychological and neuropsychological tests (CPT codes 96102, 96103, 96119 and 96120) that are effective January 1, 2006, and are billed for tests administered by a technician or a computer reflect a site of service payment differential for the facility and non-facility settings.

Additionally, there is no authorization for payment for diagnostic tests when performed on an "incident to" basis.

Under the diagnostic tests provision, all diagnostic tests are assigned a certain level of supervision. Generally, regulations governing the diagnostic tests provision require that only physicians can provide the assigned level of supervision for diagnostic tests.

However, there is a regulatory exception to the supervision requirement for diagnostic psychological and neuropsychological tests in terms of who can provide the supervision.

That is, regulations allow a clinical psychologist (CP) or a physician to perform the general supervision assigned to diagnostic psychological and neuropsychological tests.

In addition, nonphysician practitioners such as nurse practitioners (NPs), clinical nurse specialists (CNSs) and physician assistants (PAs) who personally perform diagnostic psychological and neuropsychological tests are excluded from having to perform these tests under the general supervision of a physician or a CP. Rather, NPs and CNSs must perform such tests under the requirements of their respective benefit instead of the requirements for diagnostic psychological and neuropsychological tests. Accordingly, NPs and CNSs must perform tests in collaboration (as defined under Medicare law at section 1861(aa)(6) of the Act) with a physician. PAs perform tests under the general supervision of a physician as required for services furnished under the PA benefit.

Furthermore, physical therapists (PTs), occupational therapists (OTs) and speech language pathologists (SLPs) are authorized to bill three test codes as "sometimes therapy" codes. Specifically, CPT codes 96105, 96110 and 96111 may be performed by these therapists. However, when PTs, OTs and SLPs perform these three tests, they must be performed under the general supervision of a physician or a CP.

Who May Bill for Diagnostic Psychological and Neuropsychological Tests

- CPs - see qualifications under chapter 15, section 160 of the Benefits Policy Manual, Pub. 100-02.
- NPs -to the extent authorized under State scope of practice. See qualifications under chapter 15, section 200 of the Benefits Policy Manual, Pub. 100-02.
- CNSs -to the extent authorized under State scope of practice. See qualifications under chapter 15, section 210 of the Benefits Policy Manual, Pub. 100-02.
- PAs - to the extent authorized under State scope of practice. See qualifications under chapter 15, section 190 of the Benefits Policy Manual, Pub. 100-02.
- Independently Practicing Psychologists (IPPs)
- PTs, OTs and SLPs - see qualifications under chapter 15, sections 220-230.6 of the Benefits Policy Manual, Pub. 100-02.

Psychological and neuropsychological tests performed by a psychologist (who is not a CP) practicing independently of an institution, agency, or physician's office are covered when a physician orders such tests. An IPP is any psychologist who is licensed or certified to practice psychology in the State or jurisdiction where furnishing services or, if the jurisdiction does not issue licenses, if provided by any practicing psychologist. (It is CMS' understanding that all States, the District of Columbia, and Puerto Rico license psychologists, but that some trust territories do not. Examples of psychologists, other than CPs, whose psychological and neuropsychological tests are covered under the diagnostic tests provision include, but are not limited to, educational psychologists and counseling psychologists.)

The carrier must secure from the appropriate State agency a current listing of psychologists holding the required credentials to determine whether the tests of a particular IPP are covered under Part B in States that have statutory licensure or certification. In States or territories that lack statutory licensing or certification, the carrier checks individual qualifications before provider numbers are issued. Possible reference sources are the national directory of membership of the American Psychological Association, which provides data about the educational background of individuals and indicates which members are board-certified, the records and directories of the State or territorial psychological association, and the National Register of Health Service Providers. If qualification is dependent on a doctoral degree from a currently accredited program, the carrier verifies the date of accreditation of the school involved, since such accreditation is not retroactive. If the listed reference sources do not provide enough information (e.g., the psychologist is not a member of one of these sources), the carrier contacts the psychologist personally for the required information. Generally, carriers maintain a continuing list of psychologists whose qualifications have been verified.

NOTE: When diagnostic psychological tests are performed by a psychologist who is not practicing independently, but is on the staff of an institution, agency, or clinic, that entity bills for the psychological tests.

The carrier considers psychologists as practicing independently when:

- They render services on their own responsibility, free of the administrative and professional control of an employer such as a physician, institution or agency;
- The persons they treat are their own patients; and
- They have the right to bill directly, collect and retain the fee for their services.

A psychologist practicing in an office located in an institution may be considered an independently practicing psychologist when both of the following conditions exist:

- The office is confined to a separately-identified part of the facility which is used solely as the psychologist's office and cannot be construed as extending throughout the entire institution; and
- The psychologist conducts a private practice, i.e., services are rendered to patients from outside the institution as well as to institutional patients.

Payment for Diagnostic Psychological and Neuropsychological Tests Expenses for diagnostic psychological and neuropsychological tests are not subject to the outpatient mental health treatment limitation, that is, the payment limitation on treatment services for mental, psychoneurotic and personality disorders as authorized under Section 1833(c) of the Act. The payment amount for the new psychological and neuropsychological tests (CPT codes 96102, 96103, 96119 and 96120) that are billed for tests performed by a technician or a computer reflect a site of service payment differential for the facility and non-facility settings. CPs, NPs, CNSs and PAs are required by law to accept assigned payment for psychological and neuropsychological tests. However, while IPPs are not required by law to accept assigned payment for these tests, they must report the name and address of the physician who ordered the test on the claim form when billing for tests.

CPT Codes for Diagnostic Psychological and Neuropsychological Tests The range of CPT codes used to report psychological and neuropsychological tests is 96101-96120. CPT codes 96101, 96102, 96103, 96105, 96110, and 96111 are appropriate for use when billing for psychological tests. CPT codes 96116, 96118, 96119 and 96120 are appropriate for use when billing for neuropsychological tests.

All of the tests under this CPT code range 96101-96120 are indicated as active codes under the physician fee schedule database and are covered if medically necessary.

Payment and Billing Guidelines for Psychological and Neuropsychological Tests The technician and computer CPT codes for psychological and neuropsychological tests include practice expense, malpractice expense and professional work relative value units.

Accordingly, CPT psychological test code 96101 should not be paid when billed for the same tests or services performed under psychological test codes 96102 or 96103. CPT neuropsychological test code 96118 should not be paid when billed for the same tests or services performed under neuropsychological test codes 96119 or 96120. However, CPT codes 96101 and 96118 can be paid separately on the rare occasion when billed on the same date of service for different and separate tests from 96102, 96103, 96119 and 96120.

Under the physician fee schedule, there is no payment for services performed by students or trainees. Accordingly, Medicare does not pay for services represented by CPT codes 96102 and 96119 when performed by a student or a trainee. However, the presence of a student or a trainee while the test is being administered does not prevent a physician, CP, IPP, NP, CNS or PA from performing and being paid for the psychological test under 96102 or the neuropsychological test under 96119.

100-2, 15, 80.3

Audiological Diagnostic Testing

References.

1861(ll)(3)(B) of the Social Security Act for qualifications of audiologists.

Pub. 100-04, chapter 12, section 30.3 for coding and billing information related to audiological services and aural rehabilitation.

Pub. 100-02, chapter 15, sections 220 and 230 for the physical therapy and speech-language pathology policies relative to aural rehabilitation and balance, section 60 for services incident to a physician, and section 80.5 for policies relevant to ordering for diagnostic tests.

Pub. 100-02, chapter 16, section 100 for hearing aid policies.

Benefit.

Audiological diagnostic testing refers to tests of the audiological and vestibular systems, e.g., hearing, balance, auditory processing, tinnitus and diagnostic programming of certain prosthetic devices, performed by qualified audiologists. Audiological testing is covered as "other diagnostic tests" under Sec.1861(s)(3) of the Act when a physician orders such testing for the purpose of obtaining information necessary for the physician's diagnostic medical evaluation or to determine the appropriate medical or surgical treatment of a hearing deficit or related medical problem. For the purposes of ordering audiological diagnostic tests, a nonphysician practitioner may perform the same service as a physician when the nonphysician practitioner orders diagnostic tests within their scope of practice, State and local laws and any policies applicable to the setting. See subsections of section 80 of this chapter for policies relative to ordering diagnostic tests.

Audiological diagnostic tests are not covered under the benefit for incident to a physician (described in Pub. 100-02, chapter 15, section 60), because they have their own benefit as "other diagnostic tests". See Pub. 100-04, chapter 13 for diagnostic test policies.

Orders

If a beneficiary undergoes diagnostic testing performed by an audiologist without a physician order, the tests are not covered even if the audiologist discovers a pathologic condition. See the policies on ordering diagnostic tests in section 80.6 of this chapter.

When a qualified physician or qualified nonphysician practitioner orders a specific audiological test using the CPT descriptor for the test, only that test may be provided on that order. Further orders are necessary if the ordered test indicates that other tests are necessary to evaluate, for example, the type or cause of the condition. Orders for specific tests are required for technicians. When the qualified physician or qualified nonphysician practitioner orders diagnostic audiological tests by an audiologist without naming specific tests, the audiologist may select the appropriate battery of tests.

Coverage and Payment for Audiological Services.

Diagnostic services performed by a qualified audiologist and meeting the requirements at Sec.1861(ll)(3)(B) are payable as "other diagnostic tests." Audiological diagnostic tests are not covered as services incident to physician's services or as services incident to audiologist's services.

The payment for audiological diagnostic tests is determined by the reason the tests were performed, rather than by the diagnosis or the patient's condition.

Payment for audiological diagnostic tests is not allowed by virtue of Sec.1862(a)(7) when:

- The type and severity of the current hearing, tinnitus or balance status needed to determine the appropriate medical or surgical treatment is known to the physician before the test; or
- The test was ordered for the specific purpose of fitting or modifying a hearing aid.

Payment of audiological diagnostic tests is allowed for other reasons (see Documentation subsection below) and is not limited, for example, by:

- Any information resulting from the test including, for example:
  - Confirmation of a prior diagnosis;
  - Post-evaluation diagnoses; or
  - Treatment provided after diagnosis, including hearing aids, or
- The type of evaluation or treatment the physician anticipates before the diagnostic test; or
- Timing of re-evaluation. Re-evaluation is appropriate at a schedule dictated by the ordering physician when the information provided by the diagnostic test is required, for example, to determine changes in hearing, to evaluate the appropriate medical or surgical treatment or evaluate the results of treatment. For example, re-evaluation may be appropriate, even when the evaluation was recent, in cases where the hearing loss, balance or tinnitus may be progressive or fluctuating, the patient or caregiver complains of new symptoms, or treatment (such as medication or surgery) may have changed the patient's audiological condition with or without awareness by the patient.

Payment for these services is based on the physician fee schedule amount except for audiology services furnished in a hospital outpatient department, which are paid under the Outpatient Prospective Payment System.

Computer-administered hearing tests are screening tests, do not require the skilled services of an audiologist and are not covered or payable using codes for diagnostic audiological testing. Examples include, but are not limited to "otograms" and pure tone or imittance screening devices that do not require the skills of an audiologist.

Diagnostic analysis of cochlear or brainstem implant and programming are audiology diagnostic services covered under the "other diagnostic test" benefit. Audiological diagnostic tests before and periodically after implantation of auditory prosthetic devices are covered services.

For descriptions of hearing aids and auditory prosthetic devices including osseointegrated devices, see Pub. 100-02, chapter16, section 100.

If a physician refers a beneficiary to an audiologist for testing related to signs or symptoms associated with hearing loss, balance disorder, tinnitus, ear disease, or ear injury, the audiologist's diagnostic testing services should be covered even if the only outcome is the prescription of a hearing aid.

Individuals Who Provide Audiological Tests.

Some diagnostic audiological tests require, for both the technical and professional components, the skills of an audiologist to perform the test and interpret not only the data output, but also the manner of the patient's response to the test. These tests must be personally furnished by an audiologist or a physician. The skills of an audiologist required when furnishing the ordered diagnostic tests involve skilled judgment or assessment including but not limited to:

- Interpretation, comparison or consideration of the anatomical or physiological implications of test results or patient responsiveness to stimuli during the test;
- Modification of the stimulus based on responses obtained during the test;
- Choices for subsequent presentations of stimuli, or tests in a battery of tests;
- Tests related to implantation of auditory prosthetic devices, central auditory processing, contralateral masking; and/or
- Tests designed to identify central auditory processing disorders, tinnitus, or nonorganic hearing loss.

The technical components of certain audiological diagnostic tests i.e., tympanometry (92567) and vestibular function tests (e.g., 92541) that do not require the skills of an audiologist may be performed by a qualified technician or by an audiologist, physician or nonphysician practitioner acting within their scope of practice. If performed by a technician, the service must be provided under the direct supervision [42 CFR Sec.410.32(3)] of a physician or qualified nonphysician practitioner who is responsible for all clinical judgment and for the appropriate provision of the service. The physician or qualified nonphysician practitioner bills the directly supervised service as a diagnostic test.

Documenting for Audiological Tests.

The "other diagnostic tests" benefit requires an order from a physician, or, where allowed by State and local law, by a non-physician practitioner. See section 80.6 of this chapter for policies concerning orders for diagnostic tests.

The reason for the test should be documented either on the order, on the audiological evaluation report, or in the patient's medical record. (See subsection of this section titled "Benefit".) Examples of appropriate reasons include but are not limited to:

- Evaluation of suspected change in hearing, tinnitus, or balance;
- Evaluation of the cause of disorders of hearing, tinnitus, or balance.
- Determination of the effect of medication, surgery or other treatment;

Reevaluation to follow-up changes in hearing, tinnitus or balance that may be caused for example, but not limited to otosclerosis, atelectatic tympanic membrane, tymposclerosis, cholesteatoma, resolving middle ear infection, Meniere's disease, sudden idiopathic sensorineural hearing loss, autoimmune inner ear disease, acoustic neuroma, demyelinating diseases, ototoxicity secondary to medications, genetic, vascular and viral conditions. Screening tests are not payable, but failure of a screening test may be an appropriate reason for diagnostic audiological tests.

The medical record shall identify the name and professional identity of the person who ordered and the person who actually performed the service. When the medical record is subject to medical review, it is necessary that the contractor determine that the service qualifies as an audiological diagnostic test that requires the skills of an audiologist. A technician must meet qualifications determined by the Medicare contractor to whom the claim is billed. At a minimum, the qualifications must include the requirements of any applicable State or local laws, and successful completion of a curriculum including both classroom training and supervised clinical experience in administration of the audiological service.

If a technician performs the technical component of a service that does not require the skills of an audiologist, the physician supervisor shall provide and document the physician's professional component of the service including, e.g., clinical decision making, and other active participation in the delivery of the service. This participation may not also be billed as evaluation and management or as part of other billed services.

Audiological Treatment.

There is no provision in the law for Medicare to pay audiologists for therapeutic services. For example, vestibular treatment, auditory rehabilitation and auditory processing treatment, while they are within the scope of practice of audiologists, are not diagnostic tests, and therefore, shall not be billed by audiologists to Medicare. Services related to hearing aid evaluation and fitting are not covered regardless of how they are billed. Services identified as "always" therapy in Pub. 100-04 chapter 5, section 20 may not be billed when provided by audiologists. (See also Pub 100-04, chapter 12, section 30.3.)

Services that are not diagnostic tests and are also not "always" therapy (according to the list and the policy in Pub.100-04, chapter 5, section 20) and are provided by qualified personnel (who may be audiologists), may be billed "incident to" when all other appropriate requirements are met. (See policies in Pub. 100-02, chapter 15, sections 60, 200, and 230.)

Treatment related to hearing may be covered under the speech-language pathology benefit when the services are provided by speech-language pathologists. Treatment related to balance (e.g., using "always therapy" codes 97001-97004, 97110, 97112, 97116, and 97750) may be covered under the physical therapy or occupational therapy benefit when the services are provided by physical or occupational therapists or their assistants, where appropriate. Covered therapy services incident to a physician's service must conform to policies in chapter 15, sections 60, 220 and 230. Audiological treatment provided under the benefit for physical therapy and speech-language pathology services may be personally provided and billed by physicians and nonphysician practitioners when the services are within their scope of practice and consistent with State and local laws.

For example, aural rehabilitation and signed communication training may be payable according to the benefit for speech-language pathology services or as speech-language pathology services incident to a physician's or nonphysician practitioner's service. Treatment for balance disorders may be payable according to the benefit for physical therapy services or as a physical therapy service incident to the services of a physician or nonphysician practitioner. See the policies in Pub 100-02, chapter 15, section 220 and 230 for details.

Assignment.

Nonhospital entities billing for the audiologist's services may accept assignment under the usual procedure or, if not accepting assignment, may charge the patient and submit a nonassigned claim on their beha

100-2, 15, 80.5.4
Conditions for Coverage

Medicare covers BMM under the following conditions:

1. Is ordered by the physician or qualified nonphysician practitioner who is treating the beneficiary following an evaluation of the need for a BMM and determination of the appropriate BMM to be used. A physician or qualified nonphysician practitioner treating the beneficiary for purposes of this provision is one who furnishes a consultation or treats a beneficiary for a specific medical problem, and who uses the results in the management of the patient. For the purposes of the BMM benefit, qualified nonphysician practitioners include physician assistants, nurse practitioners, clinical nurse specialists, and certified nurse midwives.

2. Is performed under the appropriate level of physician supervision as defined in 42 CFR 410.32(b).

3. Is reasonable and necessary for diagnosing and treating the condition of a beneficiary who meets the conditions described in Sec.80.5.6.

4. In the case of an individual being monitored to assess the response to or efficacy of an FDA-approved osteoporosis drug therapy, is performed with a dual-energy x-ray absorptiometry system (axial skeleton).

5. In the case of any individual who meets the conditions of 80.5.6 and who has a confirmatory BMM, is performed by a dual-energy x-ray absorptiometry system (axial skeleton) if the initial BMM was not performed by a dual-energy x-ray absorptiometry system (axial skeleton). A confirmatory baseline BMM is not covered if the initial BMM was performed by a dual-energy x-ray absorptiometry system (axial skeleton).

100-2, 15, 80.5.5
Frequency Standards

Medicare pays for a screening BMM once every 2 years (at least 23 months have passed since the month the last covered BMM was performed).

When medically necessary, Medicare may pay for more frequent BMMs. Examples include, but are not limited to, the following medical circumstances: Monitoring beneficiaries on long-term glucocorticoid (steroid) therapy of more than 3 months.

Confirming baseline BMMs to permit monitoring of beneficiaries in the future.

100-2, 15, 80.5.6
Beneficiaries Who May be Covered

To be covered, a beneficiary must meet at least one of the five conditions listed below:

1. A woman who has been determined by the physician or qualified nonphysician practitioner treating her to be estrogen-deficient and at clinical risk for osteoporosis, based on her medical history and other findings.

    NOTE: Since not every woman who has been prescribed estrogen replacement therapy (ERT) may be receiving an "adequate" dose of the therapy, the fact that a woman is receiving ERT should not preclude her treating physician or other qualified treating nonphysician practitioner from ordering a bone mass measurement for her. If a BMM is ordered for a woman following a careful evaluation of her medical need, however, it is expected that the ordering treating physician (or other qualified treating nonphysician practitioner) will document in her medical record why he or she believes that the woman is estrogen-deficient and at clinical risk for osteoporosis.

2. An individual with vertebral abnormalities as demonstrated by an x-ray to be indicative of osteoporosis, osteopenia, or vertebral fracture.

3. An individual receiving (or expecting to receive) glucocorticoid (steroid) therapy equivalent to an average of 5.0 mg of prednisone, or greater, per day, for more than 3 months.

4. An individual with primary hyperparathyroidism.

5. An individual being monitored to assess the response to or efficacy of an FDAapproved osteoporosis drug therapy.

100-2, 15, 100
Surgical Dressings, Splints, Casts, and Other Devices Used for Reductions of Fractures and Dislocations
B3-2079, A3-3110.3, HO-228.3

Surgical dressings are limited to primary and secondary dressings required for the treatment of a wound caused by, or treated by, a surgical procedure that has been performed by a physician or other health care professional to the extent permissible under State law. In addition, surgical dressings required after debridement of a wound are also covered, irrespective of the type of debridement, as long as the debridement was reasonable and necessary and was performed by a health care professional acting within the scope of his/her legal authority when performing this function. Surgical dressings are covered for as long as they are medically necessary.

Primary dressings are therapeutic or protective coverings applied directly to wounds or lesions either on the skin or caused by an opening to the skin. Secondary dressing materials that serve a therapeutic or protective function and that are needed to secure a primary dressing are also covered. Items such as adhesive tape, roll gauze, bandages, and disposable compression material are examples of secondary dressings. Elastic stockings, support hose, foot coverings, leotards, knee supports, surgical leggings, gauntlets, and pressure garments for the arms and hands are examples of items that are not ordinarily covered as surgical dressings. Some items, such as transparent film, may be used as a primary or secondary dressing.

If a physician, certified nurse midwife, physician assistant, nurse practitioner, or clinical nurse specialist applies surgical dressings as part of a professional service that is billed to Medicare, the surgical dressings are considered incident to the professional services of the health care practitioner. (See Sec. 60.1, 180, 190, 200, and 210.) When surgical dressings are not covered incident to the services of a health care practitioner and are obtained by the patient from a supplier (e.g., a drugstore, physician, or other health care practitioner that qualifies as a supplier) on an order from a physician or other health care professional authorized under State law or regulation to make such an order, the surgical dressings are covered separately under Part B.

Splints and casts, and other devices used for reductions of fractures and dislocations are covered under Part B of Medicare. This includes dental splints.

100-2, 15, 120
Prosthetic Devices
B3-2130, A3-3110.4, HO-228.4, A3-3111, HO-229

A. General
Prosthetic devices (other than dental) which replace all or part of an internal body organ (including contiguous tissue), or replace all or part of the function of a permanently inoperative or malfunctioning internal body organ are covered when furnished on a physician's order. This does not require a determination that there is no possibility that the patient's condition may improve sometime in the future. If the medical record, including the judgment of the attending physician, indicates the condition is of long and indefinite duration, the test of permanence is considered met. (Such a device may also be covered under Sec.60.l as a supply when furnished incident to a physician's service.)

Examples of prosthetic devices include artificial limbs, parenteral and enteral (PEN) nutrition, cardiac pacemakers, prosthetic lenses (see subsection B), breast prostheses (including a surgical brassiere) for postmastectomy patients, maxillofacial devices, and devices which replace all or part of the ear or nose. A urinary collection and retention system with or without a tube is a prosthetic device replacing bladder function in case of permanent urinary incontinence. The foley catheter is also considered a prosthetic device when ordered for a patient with permanent urinary incontinence. However, chucks, diapers, rubber sheets, etc., are supplies that are not covered under this provision. Although hemodialysis equipment is a prosthetic device, payment for the rental or purchase of such equipment in the home is made only for use under the provisions for payment applicable to durable medical equipment.

An exception is that if payment cannot be made on an inpatient's behalf under Part A, hemodialysis equipment, supplies, and services required by such patient could be covered under Part B as a prosthetic device, which replaces the function of a kidney. See the Medicare Benefit Policy Manual, Chapter 11, "End Stage Renal Disease," for payment for hemodialysis equipment used in the home. See the Medicare Benefit Policy Manual, Chapter 1, "Inpatient Hospital Services," Sec.10, for additional instructions on hospitalization for renal dialysis.

NOTE: Medicare does not cover a prosthetic device dispensed to a patient prior to the time at which the patient undergoes the procedure that makes necessary the use of the device. For example, the carrier does not make a separate Part B payment for an intraocular lens (IOL) or pacemaker that a physician, during an office visit prior to the actual surgery, dispenses to the patient for his or her use. Dispensing a prosthetic device in this manner raises health and safety issues. Moreover, the need for the device cannot be clearly established until the procedure that makes its use possible is successfully performed. Therefore, dispensing a prosthetic device in this manner is not considered reasonable and necessary for the treatment of the patient's condition.

Colostomy (and other ostomy) bags and necessary accouterments required for attachment are covered as prosthetic devices. This coverage also includes irrigation and flushing equipment and other items and supplies directly related to ostomy care, whether the attachment of a bag is required. Accessories and/or supplies which are used directly with an enteral or parenteral device to achieve the therapeutic benefit of the prosthesis or to assure the proper functioning of the device may also be covered under the prosthetic device benefit subject to the additional guidelines in the Medicare National Coverage Determinations Manual.

Covered items include catheters, filters, extension tubing, infusion bottles, pumps (either food or infusion), intravenous (I.V.) pole, needles, syringes, dressings, tape, Heparin Sodium (parenteral only), volumetric monitors (parenteral only), and parenteral and enteral nutrient solutions. Baby food and other regular grocery products that can be blenderized and used with the enteral system are not covered. Note that some of these items, e.g., a food pump and an I.V. pole, qualify as DME. Although coverage of the enteral and parenteral nutritional therapy systems is provided on the basis of the prosthetic device benefit, the payment rules relating to lump sum or monthly payment for DME apply to such items.

The coverage of prosthetic devices includes replacement of and repairs to such devices as explained in subsection D.

Finally, the Benefits Improvement and Protection Act of 2000 amended Sec.1834(h)(1) of the Act by adding a provision (1834 (h)(1)(G)(i)) that requires Medicare payment to be made for the replacement of prosthetic devices which are artificial limbs, or for the replacement of any part of such devices, without regard to continuous use or useful lifetime restrictions if an ordering physician determines that the replacement device, or replacement part of such a device, is necessary.

Payment may be made for the replacement of a prosthetic device that is an artificial limb, or replacement part of a device if the ordering physician determines that the replacement device or part is necessary because of any of the following:

1. A change in the physiological condition of the patient;
2. An irreparable change in the condition of the device, or in a part of the device; or
3. The condition of the device, or the part of the device, requires repairs and the cost of such repairs would be more than 60 percent of the cost of a replacement device, or, as the case may be, of the part being replaced.

This provision is effective for items replaced on or after April 1, 2001. It supersedes any rule that that provided a 5-year or other replacement rule with regard to prosthetic devices.

B. Prosthetic Lenses
The term "internal body organ" includes the lens of an eye. Prostheses replacing the lens of an eye include post-surgical lenses customarily used during convalescence from eye surgery in which the lens of the eye was removed. In addition, permanent lenses are also covered when required by an individual lacking the organic lens of the eye because of surgical removal or congenital absence. Prosthetic lenses obtained on or after the beneficiary's date of entitlement to supplementary medical insurance benefits may be covered even though the surgical removal of the crystalline lens occurred before entitlement.

1. Prosthetic Cataract Lenses
   One of the following prosthetic lenses or combinations of prosthetic lenses furnished by a physician (see Sec.30.4 for coverage of prosthetic lenses prescribed by a doctor of optometry) may be covered when determined to be reasonable and necessary to restore essentially the vision provided by the crystalline lens of the eye:

   - Prosthetic bifocal lenses in frames;
   - Prosthetic lenses in frames for far vision, and prosthetic lenses in frames for near vision; or
   - When a prosthetic contact lens(es) for far vision is prescribed (including cases of binocular and monocular aphakia), make payment for the contact lens(es) and prosthetic lenses in frames for near vision to be worn at the same time as the contact lens(es), and prosthetic lenses in frames to be worn when the contacts have been removed.

   Lenses which have ultraviolet absorbing or reflecting properties may be covered, in lieu of payment for regular (untinted) lenses, if it has been determined that such lenses are medically reasonable and necessary for the individual patient.

   Medicare does not cover cataract sunglasses obtained in addition to the regular (untinted) prosthetic lenses since the sunglasses duplicate the restoration of vision function performed by the regular prosthetic lenses.

2. Payment for Intraocular Lenses (IOLs) Furnished in Ambulatory Surgical Centers (ASCs)
   Effective for services furnished on or after March 12, 1990, payment for intraocular lenses (IOLs) inserted during or subsequent to cataract surgery in a Medicare certified ASC is included with the payment for facility services that are furnished in connection with the covered surgery.

   Refer to the Medicare Claims Processing Manual, Chapter 14, "Ambulatory Surgical Centers," for more information.

3. Limitation on Coverage of Conventional Lenses One pair of conventional eyeglasses or conventional contact lenses furnished after each cataract surgery with insertion of an IOL is covered.

C. Dentures
Dentures are excluded from coverage. However, when a denture or a portion of the denture is an integral part (built-in) of a covered prosthesis (e.g., an obturator to fill an opening in the palate), it is covered as part of that prosthesis.

D. Supplies, Repairs, Adjustments, and Replacement
Supplies are covered that are necessary for the effective use of a prosthetic device (e.g., the batteries needed to operate an artificial larynx). Adjustment of prosthetic devices required by wear or by a change in the patient's condition is covered when ordered by a physician. General provisions relating to the repair and replacement of durable medical equipment in Sec.110.2 for the repair and replacement of prosthetic devices are applicable. (See the Medicare Benefit Policy Manual, Chapter 16, "General Exclusions from Coverage," Sec.40.4, for payment for devices replaced under a warranty.) Replacement of conventional eyeglasses or contact lenses furnished in accordance with Sec.120.B.3 is not covered. Necessary supplies, adjustments, repairs, and replacements are covered even when the device had been in use before the user enrolled in Part B of the program, so long as the device continues to be medically required.

100-2, 15, 150
Dental Services
B3-2136

As indicated under the general exclusions from coverage, items and services in connection with the care, treatment, filling, removal, or replacement of teeth or structures directly supporting the teeth are not covered. "Structures directly supporting the teeth" means the periodontium, which includes the gingivae, dentogingival junction, periodontal membrane, cementum of the teeth, and alveolar process.

In addition to the following, see Pub 100-01, the Medicare General Information, Eligibility, and Entitlement Manual, Chapter 5, Definitions and Pub 3, the Medicare National Coverage Determinations Manual for specific services which may be covered when furnished by a dentist. If an otherwise noncovered procedure or service is performed by a dentist as incident to and as an integral part of a covered procedure or service performed by the dentist, the total service performed by the dentist on such an occasion is covered.

EXAMPLE 1: The reconstruction of a ridge performed primarily to prepare the mouth for dentures is a noncovered procedure. However, when the reconstruction of a ridge is performed as a result of and at the same time as the surgical removal of a tumor (for other than dental purposes), the totality of surgical procedures is a covered service.

EXAMPLE 2: Medicare makes payment for the wiring of teeth when this is done in connection with the reduction of a jaw fracture.

The extraction of teeth to prepare the jaw for radiation treatment of neoplastic disease is also covered. This is an exception to the requirement that to be covered, a noncovered procedure or service performed by a dentist must be an incident to and an integral part of a covered procedure or service performed by the dentist. Ordinarily, the dentist extracts the patient's teeth, but another physician, e.g., a radiologist, administers the radiation treatments.

When an excluded service is the primary procedure involved, it is not covered, regardless of its complexity or difficulty. For example, the extraction of an impacted tooth is not covered. Similarly, an alveoplasty (the surgical improvement of the shape and condition of the alveolar process) and a frenectomy are excluded from coverage when either of these procedures is performed in connection with an excluded service, e.g., the preparation of the mouth for dentures. In a like manner, the removal of a torus palatinus (a bony protuberance of the hard palate) may be a covered service. However, with rare exception, this surgery is performed in connection with an excluded service, i.e., the preparation of the mouth for dentures. Under such circumstances, Medicare does not pay for this procedure.

Dental splints used to treat a dental condition are excluded from coverage under 1862(a)(12) of the Act. On the other hand, if the treatment is determined to be a covered medical condition (i.e., dislocated upper/lower jaw joints), then the splint can be covered.

Whether such services as the administration of anesthesia, diagnostic x-rays, and other related procedures are covered depends upon whether the primary procedure being performed by the dentist is itself covered. Thus, an x-ray taken in connection with the reduction of a fracture of the jaw or facial bone is covered. However, a single x-ray or x-ray survey taken in connection with the care or treatment of teeth or the periodontium is not covered.

Medicare makes payment for a covered dental procedure no matter where the service is performed. The hospitalization or nonhospitalization of a patient has no direct bearing on the coverage or exclusion of a given dental procedure.

Payment may also be made for services and supplies furnished incident to covered dental services. For example, the services of a dental technician or nurse who is under the direct supervision of the dentist or physician are covered if the services are included in the dentist's or physician's bill.

100-2, 15, 160
Clinical Psychologist Services
A. Clinical Psychologist (CP) Defined
To qualify as a clinical psychologist (CP), a practitioner must meet the following requirements:

- Hold a doctoral degree in psychology;
- Be licensed or certified, on the basis of the doctoral degree in psychology, by the State in which he or she practices, at the independent practice level of psychology to furnish diagnostic, assessment, preventive, and therapeutic services directly to individuals.

B. Qualified Clinical Psychologist Services Defined
Effective July 1, 1990, the diagnostic and therapeutic services of CPs and services and supplies furnished incident to such services are covered as the services furnished by a physician or as incident to physician's services are covered. However, the CP must be legally authorized to perform the services under applicable licensure laws of the State in which they are furnished.

C. Types of Clinical Psychologist Services That May Be Covered
Diagnostic and therapeutic services that the CP is legally authorized to perform in accordance with State law and/or regulation. Carriers pay all qualified CPs based on the physician fee schedule for the diagnostic and therapeutic services. (Psychological tests by practitioners who do not meet the requirements for a CP may be covered under the provisions for diagnostic tests as described in Sec.80.2.

Services and supplies furnished incident to a CP's services are covered if the requirements that apply to services incident to a physician's services, as described in Sec.60 are met. These services must be:

- Mental health services that are commonly furnished in CPs' offices;
- An integral, although incidental, part of professional services performed by the CP;
- Performed under the direct personal supervision of the CP; i.e., the CP must be physically present and immediately available;
- Furnished without charge or included in the CP's bill; and
- Performed by an employee of the CP (or an employee of the legal entity that employs the supervising CP) under the common law control test of the Act, as set forth in 20 CFR 404.1007 and Sec.RS 2101.020 of the Retirement and Survivors Insurance part of the Social Security Program Operations Manual System.
- Diagnostic psychological testing services when furnished under the general supervision of a CP.

Carriers are required to familiarize themselves with appropriate State laws and/or regulations governing a CP's scope of practice.

D. Noncovered Services
The services of CPs are not covered if the service is otherwise excluded from Medicare coverage even though a clinical psychologist is authorized by State law to perform them.

For example, Sec.1862(a)(1)(A) of the Act excludes from coverage services that are not "reasonable and necessary for the diagnosis or treatment of an illness or injury or to improve the functioning of a malformed body member." Therefore, even though the services are authorized by State law, the services of a CP that are determined to be not reasonable and necessary are not covered. Additionally, any therapeutic services that are billed by CPs under CPT psychotherapy codes that include medical evaluation and management services are not covered.

E. Requirement for Consultation
When applying for a Medicare provider number, a CP must submit to the carrier a signed Medicare provider/supplier enrollment form that indicates an agreement to the effect that, contingent upon the patient's consent, the CP will attempt to consult with the patient's attending or primary care physician in accordance with accepted professional ethical norms, taking into consideration patient confidentiality.

If the patient assents to the consultation, the CP must attempt to consult with the patient's physician within a reasonable time after receiving the consent. If the CP's attempts to consult directly with the physician are not successful, the CP must notify the physician within a reasonable time that he or she is furnishing services to the patient. Additionally, the CP must document, in the patient's medical record, the date the patient consented or declined consent to consultations, the date of consultation, or, if attempts to consult did not succeed, that date and manner of notification to the physician.

The only exception to the consultation requirement for CPs is in cases where the patient's primary care or attending physician refers the patient to the CP. Also, neither a CP nor a primary care nor attending physician may bill Medicare or the patient for this required consultation.

F. Outpatient Mental Health Services Limitation
All covered therapeutic services furnished by qualified CPs are subject to the outpatient mental health services limitation in Pub 100-01, Medicare General Information, Eligibility, and Entitlement Manual, Chapter 3, "Deductibles, Coinsurance Amounts, and Payment Limitations," Sec.30, (i.e., only 62 1/2 percent of expenses for these services are considered incurred expenses for Medicare purposes). The limitation does not apply to diagnostic services.

G. Assignment Requirement
Assignment Sec. required.

100-2, 15, 170
Clinical Social Worker (CSW) Services
B3-2152

See the Medicare Claims Processing Manual Chapter 12, Physician/Nonphysician Practitioners, Sec.150, "Clinical Social Worker Services," for payment requirements.

A. Clinical Social Worker Defined
Section 1861(hh) of the Act defines a "clinical social worker" as an individual who:

- Possesses a master's or doctor's degree in social work;
- Has performed at least two years of supervised clinical social work; and
- Is licensed or certified as a clinical social worker by the State in which the services are performed; or
- In the case of an individual in a State that does not provide for licensure or certification, has completed at least 2 years or 3,000 hours of post master's degree supervised clinical social work practice under the supervision of a master's level social worker in an appropriate setting such as a hospital, SNF, or clinic.

B. Clinical Social Worker Services Defined
Section 1861(hh)(2) of the Act defines "clinical social worker services" as those services that the CSW is legally authorized to perform under State law (or the State regulatory mechanism provided by State law) of the State in which such services are performed for the diagnosis and treatment of mental illnesses. Services furnished to an inpatient of a hospital or an inpatient of a SNF that the SNF is required to provide as a requirement for participation are not included. The services that are covered are those that are otherwise covered if furnished by a physician or as incident to a physician's professional service.

C. Covered Services
Coverage is limited to the services a CSW is legally authorized to perform in accordance with State law (or State regulatory mechanism established by State law). The services of a CSW may be covered under Part B if they are: The type of services that are otherwise covered if furnished by a physician, or as incident to a physician's service. (See Sec.30 for a description of physicians' services and Sec.70 of Pub 100-1, the Medicare General Information, Eligibility and Entitlement Manual, Chapter 5, for the definition of a physician.); Performed by a person who meets the definition of a CSW (See subsection A.); and Not otherwise excluded from coverage. Carriers should become familiar with the State law or regulatory mechanism governing a CSW's scope of practice in their service area.

Appendix G — Pub 100 References

D. Noncovered Services
Services of a CSW are not covered when furnished to inpatients of a hospital or to inpatients of a SNF if the services furnished in the SNF are those that the SNF is required to furnish as a condition of participation in Medicare. In addition, CSW services are not covered if they are otherwise excluded from Medicare coverage even though a CSW is authorized by State law to perform them. For example, the Medicare law excludes from coverage services that are not "reasonable and necessary for the diagnosis or treatment of an illness or injury or to improve the functioning of a malformed body member."

E. Outpatient Mental Health Services
Limitation All covered therapeutic services furnished by qualified CSWs are subject to the outpatient psychiatric services limitation in Pub 100-01, Medicare General Information, Eligibility, and Entitlement Manual, Chapter 3, "Deductibles, Coinsurance Amounts, and Payment Limitations," Sec.30, (i.e., only 62 1/2 percent of expenses for these services are considered incurred expenses for Medicare purposes). The limitation does not apply to diagnostic services.

F. Assignment Requirement
Assignment is required.

100-2, 15, 180
Nurse-Midwife (CNM) Services
B3-2154

A. General
Effective on or after July 1, 1988, the services provided by a certified nurse-midwife or incident to the certified nurse-midwife's services are covered. Payment is made under assignment only. See the Medicare Claims Processing Manual, Chapter 12, "Physician and Nonphysician Practitioners," Sec.130, for payment methodology for nurse midwife services.

B. Certified Nurse-Midwife Defined
A certified nurse-midwife is a registered nurse who has successfully completed a program of study and clinical experience in nurse-midwifery, meeting guidelines prescribed by the Secretary, or who has been certified by an organization recognized by the Secretary. The Secretary has recognized certification by the American College of Nurse-Midwives and State qualifying requirements in those States that specify a program of education and clinical experience for nurse-midwives for these purposes. A nurse-midwife must:

- Be currently licensed to practice in the State as a registered professional nurse; and
- Meet one of the following requirements:
    1. Be legally authorized under State law or regulations to practice as a nurse-midwife and have completed a program of study and clinical experience for nurse-midwives, as specified by the State; or
    2. If the State does not specify a program of study and clinical experience that nurse-midwives must complete to practice in that State, the nurse-midwife must:
        a. Be currently certified as a nurse-midwife by the American College of Nurse-Midwives;
        b. Have satisfactorily completed a formal education program (of at least one academic year) that, upon completion, qualifies the nurse to take the certification examination offered by the American College of Nurse-Midwives; or
        c. Have successfully completed a formal education program for preparing registered nurses to furnish gynecological and obstetrical care to women during pregnancy, delivery, the postpartum period, and care to normal newborns, and have practiced as a nurse-midwife for a total of 12 months during any 18-month period from August 8, 1976, to July 16, 1982.

C. Covered Services
1. General - Effective January 1, 1988, through December 31, 1993, the coverage of nurse-midwife services was restricted to the maternity cycle. The maternity cycle is a period that includes pregnancy, labor, and the immediate postpartum period.

   Beginning with services furnished on or after January 1, 1994, coverage is no longer limited to the maternity cycle. Coverage is available for services furnished by a nurse-midwife that he or she is legally authorized to perform in the State in which the services are furnished and that would otherwise be covered if furnished by a physician, including obstetrical and gynecological services.

2. Incident To- Services and supplies furnished incident to a nurse midwife's service are covered if they would have been covered when furnished incident to the services of a doctor of medicine or osteopathy, as described in Sec.60.

D. Noncovered Services
The services of nurse-midwives are not covered if they are otherwise excluded from Medicare coverage even though a nurse-midwife is authorized by State law to perform them. For example, the Medicare program excludes from coverage routine physical checkups and services that are not reasonable and necessary for the diagnosis or treatment of an illness or injury or to improve the functioning of a malformed body member. Coverage of service to the newborn continues only to the point that the newborn is or would normally be treated medically as a separate individual. Items and services furnished the newborn from that point are not covered on the basis of the mother's eligibility.

E. Relationship With Physician
Most States have licensure and other requirements applicable to nurse-midwives. For example, some require that the nurse-midwife have an arrangement with a physician for the referral of the patient in the event a problem develops that requires medical attention. Others may require that the nurse-midwife function under the general supervision of a physician. Although these and similar State requirements must be met in order for the nurse-midwife to provide Medicare covered care, they have no effect on the nurse-midwife's right to personally bill for and receive direct Medicare payment. That is, billing does not have to flow through a physician or facility. See Sec.60.2 for coverage of services performed by nurse-midwives incident to the service of physicians.

F. Place of Service
There is no restriction on place of service. Therefore, nurse-midwife services are covered if provided in the nurse-midwife's office, in the patient's home, or in a hospital or other facility, such as a clinic or birthing center owned or operated by a nurse-midwife.

G. Assignment Requirement
Assignment is required.

100-2, 15, 230
Practice of Physical Therapy, Occupational Therapy, and Speech-Language Pathology

A. Group Therapy Services.
Contractors pay for outpatient physical therapy services (which includes outpatient speech-language pathology services) and outpatient occupational therapy services provided simultaneously to two or more individuals by a practitioner as group therapy services (97150). The individuals can be, but need not be performing the same activity. The physician or therapist involved in group therapy services must be in constant attendance, but one-on-one patient contact is not required.

B. Therapy Students
1. General

   Only the services of the therapist can be billed and paid under Medicare Part B. The services performed by a student are not reimbursed even if provided under "line of sight" supervision of the therapist; however, the presence of the student "in the room" does not make the service unbillable. Pay for the direct (one-to-one) patient contact services of the physician or therapist provided to Medicare Part B patients. Group therapy services performed by a therapist or physician may be billed when a student is also present "in the room".

   EXAMPLES:

   Therapists may bill and be paid for the provision of services in the following scenarios:

   - The qualified practitioner is present and in the room for the entire session. The student participates in the delivery of services when the qualified practitioner is directing the service, making the skilled judgment, and is responsible for the assessment and treatment.
   - The qualified practitioner is present in the room guiding the student in service delivery when the therapy student and the therapy assistant student are participating in the provision of services, and the practitioner is not engaged in treating another patient or doing other tasks at the same time
   - The qualified practitioner is responsible for the services and as such, signs all documentation. (A student may, of course, also sign but it is not necessary since the Part B payment is for the clinician's service, not for the student's services).

2. Therapy Assistants as Clinical Instructors

   Physical therapist assistants and occupational therapy assistants are not precluded from serving as clinical instructors for therapy students, while providing services within their scope of work and performed under the direction and supervision of a licensed physical or occupational therapist to a Medicare beneficiary.

3. Services Provided Under Part A and Part B

   The payment methodologies for Part A and B therapy services rendered by a student are different. Under the MPFS (Medicare Part B), Medicare pays for services provided by physicians and practitioners that are specifically authorized by statute. Students do not meet the definition of practitioners under Medicare Part B. Under SNF PPS, payments are based upon the case mix or Resource Utilization Group (RUG) category that describes the patient. In the rehabilitation groups, the number of therapy minutes delivered to the patient determines the RUG category. Payment levels for each category are based upon the costs of caring for patients in each group rather than providing pecific payment for each therapy service as is done in Medicare Part B.

100-2, 15, 230.1
Practice of Physical Therapy
A. General
Physical therapy services are those services provided within the scope of practice of physical therapists and necessary for the diagnosis and treatment of impairments, functional limitations, disabilities or changes in physical function and health status. (See Pub. 100-03, the Medicare National Coverage Determinations Manual, for specific conditions or services.) For descriptions of aquatic therapy in a community center pool see section 220C of this chapter.

B. Qualified Physical Therapist Defined
Reference: 42CFR484.4

The new personnel qualifications for physical therapists were discussed in the 2008 Physician Fee Schedule. See the Federal Register of November 27, 2007, for the full text. See also the correction notice for this rule, published in the Federal Register on January 15, 2008.

The regulation provides that a qualified physical therapist (PT) is a person who is licensed, if applicable, as a PT by the state in which he or she is practicing unless licensure does not apply, has graduated from an accredited PT education program and passed a national examination approved by the state in which PT services are provided. The phrase, "by the state in which practicing" includes any authorization to practice provided by the same state in which the service is provided, including temporary licensure, regardless of the location of the entity billing the services. The curriculum accreditation is provided by the Commission on Accreditation in

Physical Therapy Education (CAPTE) or, for those who graduated before CAPTE, curriculum approval was provided by the American Physical Therapy Association (APTA). For internationally educated PTs, curricula are approved by a credentials evaluation organization either approved by the APTA or identified in 8 CFR 212.15(e) as it relates to PTs. For example, in 2007, 8 CFR 212.15(e) approved the credentials evaluation provided by the Federation of State Boards of Physical Therapy (FSBPT) and the Foreign Credentialing Commission on Physical Therapy (FCCPT). The requirements above apply to all PTs effective January 1, 2010, if they have not met any of the following requirements prior to January 1, 2010.

Physical therapists whose current license was obtained on or prior to December 31, 2009, qualify to provide PT services to Medicare beneficiaries if they:

- graduated from a CAPTE approved program in PT on or before December 31, 2009 (examination is not required); or,
- graduated on or before December 31, 2009, from a PT program outside the U.S. that is determined to be substantially equivalent to a U.S. program by a credentials evaluating organization approved by either the APTA or identified in 8 CFR 212.15(e) and also passed an examination for PTs approved by the state in which practicing.

Or, PTs whose current license was obtained before January 1, 2008, may meet the requirements in place on that date (i.e., graduation from a curriculum approved by either the APTA, the Committee on Allied Health Education and Accreditation of the American Medical Association, or both).

Or, PTs meet the requirements who are currently licensed and were licensed or qualified as a PT on or before December 31, 1977, and had 2 years appropriate experience as a PT, and passed a proficiency examination conducted, approved, or sponsored by the U.S. Public Health Service.

Or, PTs meet the requirements if they are currently licensed and before January 1, 1966, they were:

- admitted to membership by the APTA; or
- admitted to registration by the American Registry of Physical Therapists; or
- graduated from a 4-year PT curriculum approved by a State Department of Education; or
- licensed or registered and prior to January 1, 1970, they had 15 years of fulltime experience in PT under the order and direction of attending and referring doctors of medicine or osteopathy.

Or, PTs meet requirements if they are currently licensed and they were trained outside the U.S. before January 1, 2008, and after 1928 graduated from a PT curriculum approved in the country in which the curriculum was located, if that country had an organization that was a member of the World Confederation for Physical Therapy, and that PT qualified as a member of the organization.

For outpatient PT services that are provided incident to the services of physicians/NPPs, the requirement for PT licensure does not apply; all other personnel qualifications do apply. The qualified personnel providing PT services incident to the services of a physician/NPP must be trained in an accredited PT curriculum. For example, a person who, on or before December 31, 2009, graduated from a PT curriculum accredited by CAPTE, but who has not passed the national examination or obtained a license, could provide Medicare outpatient PT therapy services incident to the services of a physician/NPP if the physician assumes responsibility for the services according to the incident to policies. On or after January 1, 2010, although licensure does not apply, both education and examination requirements that are effective January 1, 2010, apply to qualified personnel who provide PT services incident to the services of a physician/NPP.

C. Services of Physical Therapy Support Personnel

Reference: 42CFR 484.4

Personnel Qualifications. The new personnel qualifications for physical therapist assistants (PTA) were discussed in the 2008 Physician Fee Schedule. See the Federal Register of November 27, 2007, for the full text. See also the correction notice for this rule, published in the Federal Register on January 15, 2008.

The regulation provides that a qualified PTA is a person who is licensed as a PTA unless licensure does not apply, is registered or certified, if applicable, as a PTA by the state in which practicing, and graduated from an approved curriculum for PTAs, and passed a national examination for PTAs. The phrase, "by the state in which practicing" includes any authorization to practice provided by the same state in which the service is provided, including temporary licensure, regardless of the location or the entity billing for the services. Approval for the curriculum is provided by CAPTE or, if internationally or military trained PTAs apply, approval will be through a credentialing body for the curriculum for PTAs identified by either the American Physical Therapy Association or identified in 8 CFR 212.15(e). A national examination for PTAs is, for example the one furnished by the Federation of State Boards of Physical Therapy. These requirements above apply to all PTAs effective January 1, 2010, if they have not met any of the following requirements prior to January 1, 2010.

Those PTAs also qualify who, on or before December 31, 2009, are licensed, registered or certified as a PTA and met one of the two following requirements:

1. Is licensed or otherwise regulated in the state in which practicing; or
2. In states that have no licensure or other regulations, or where licensure does not apply, PTAs have:

- graduated on or before December 31, 2009, from a 2-year college-level program approved by the APTA or CAPTE; and
- effective January 1, 2010, those PTAs must have both graduated from a CAPTE approved curriculum and passed a national examination for PTAs; or

PTAs may also qualify if they are licensed, registered or certified as a PTA, if applicable and meet requirements in effect before January 1, 2008, that is,

- they have graduated before January 1, 2008, from a 2 year college level program approved by the APTA; or
- on or before December 31, 1977, they were licensed or qualified as a PTA and passed a proficiency examination conducted, approved, or sponsored by the U.S. Public Health Service.

Services. The services of PTAs used when providing covered therapy benefits are included as part of the covered service. These services are billed by the supervising physical therapist. PTAs may not provide evaluation services, make clinical judgments or decisions or take responsibility for the service. They act at the direction and under the supervision of the treating physical therapist and in accordance with state laws.

A physical therapist must supervise PTAs. The level and frequency of supervision differs by setting (and by state or local law). General supervision is required for PTAs in all settings except private practice (which requires direct supervision) unless state practice requirements are more stringent, in which case state or local requirements must be followed. See specific settings for details. For example, in clinics, rehabilitation services, either on or off the organization's premises, those services are supervised by a qualified physical therapist who makes an onsite supervisory visit at least once every 30 days or more frequently if required by state or local laws or regulation.

The services of a PTA shall not be billed as services incident to a physician/NPP's service, because they do not meet the qualifications of a therapist.

The cost of supplies (e.g., theraband, hand putty, electrodes) used in furnishing covered therapy care is included in the payment for the HCPCS codes billed by the physical therapist, and are, therefore, not separately billable. Separate coverage and billing provisions apply to items that meet the definition of brace in Sec.130.

Services provided by aides, even if under the supervision of a therapist, are not therapy services and are not covered by Medicare. Although an aide may help the therapist by providing unskilled services, those services that are unskilled are not covered by Medicare and shall be denied as not reasonable and necessary if they are billed as therapy services.

D. Application of Medicare Guidelines to PT Services

This subsection will be used in the future to illustrate the application of the above guidelines to some of the physical therapy modalities and procedures utilized in the treatment of patient

100-2, 15, 230.2
Practice of Occupational Therapy

(Rev. 88, Issued: 05-07-08, Effective: 01-01-08, Implementation: 06-09-08)

A. General

Occupational therapy services are those services provided within the scope of practice of occupational therapists and necessary for the diagnosis and treatment of impairments, functional disabilities or changes in physical function and health status. (See Pub. 100- 03, the Medicare National Coverage Determinations Manual, for specific conditions or services.)

Occupational therapy is medically prescribed treatment concerned with improving or restoring functions which have been impaired by illness or injury or, where function has been permanently lost or reduced by illness or injury, to improve the individual's ability to perform those tasks required for independent functioning. Such therapy may involve:

The evaluation, and reevaluation as required, of a patient's level of function by administering diagnostic and prognostic tests;

The selection and teaching of task-oriented therapeutic activities designed to restore physical function; e.g., use of woodworking activities on an inclined table to restore shoulder, elbow, and wrist range of motion lost as a result of burns;

The planning, implementing, and supervising of individualized therapeutic activity programs as part of an overall "active treatment" program for a patient with a diagnosed psychiatric illness; e.g., the use of sewing activities which require following a pattern to reduce confusion and restore reality orientation in a schizophrenic patient;

The planning and implementing of therapeutic tasks and activities to restore sensoryintegrative function; e.g., providing motor and tactile activities to increase sensory input and improve response for a stroke patient with functional loss resulting in a distorted body image;

The teaching of compensatory technique to improve the level of independence in the activities of daily living, for example:

- Teaching a patient who has lost the use of an arm how to pare potatoes and chop vegetables with one hand;
- Teaching an upper extremity amputee how to functionally utilize a prosthesis;
- Teaching a stroke patient new techniques to enable the patient to perform feeding, dressing, and other activities as independently as possible; or
- Teaching a patient with a hip fracture/hip replacement techniques of standing tolerance and balance to enable the patient to perform such functional activities as dressing and homemaking tasks.

The designing, fabricating, and fitting of orthotics and self-help devices; e.g., making a hand splint for a patient with rheumatoid arthritis to maintain the hand in a functional position or constructing a device which would enable an individual to hold a utensil and feed independently; or Vocational and prevocational assessment and training, subject to the limitations specified in item B below.

Only a qualified occupational therapist has the knowledge, training, and experience required to evaluate and, as necessary, reevaluate a patient's level of function, determine whether an occupational therapy program could reasonably be expected to improve, restore, or compensate for lost function and, where appropriate, recommend to the physician/NPP a plan of treatment.

B. Qualified Occupational Therapist Defined
Reference: 42CFR484.4 The new personnel qualifications for occupational therapists (OT) were discussed in the 2008 Physician Fee Schedule. See the Federal Register of November 27, 2007, for the full text. See also the correction notice for this rule, published in the Federal Register on January 15, 2008.

The regulation provides that a qualified OT is an individual who is licensed, if licensure applies, or otherwise regulated, if applicable, as an OT by the state in which practicing, and graduated from an accredited education program for OTs, and is eligible to take or has passed the examination for OTs administered by the National Board for Certification in Occupational Therapy, Inc. (NBCOT). The phrase, "by the state in which practicing" includes any authorization to practice provided by the same state in which the service is provided, including temporary licensure, regardless of the location of the entity billing the services. The education program for U.S. trained OTs is accredited by the Accreditation Council for Occupational Therapy Education (ACOTE). The requirements above apply to all OTs effective January 1, 2010, if they have not met any of the following requirements prior to January 1, 2010.

The OTs may also qualify if on or before December 31, 2009:

- they are licensed or otherwise regulated as an OT in the state in which practicing (regardless of the qualifications they met to obtain that licensure or regulation); or
- when licensure or other regulation does not apply, OTs have graduated from an OT education program accredited by ACOTE and are eligible to take, or have successfully completed the NBCOT examination for OTs.

Also, those OTs who met the Medicare requirements for OTs that were in 42CFR484.4 prior to January 1, 2008, qualify to provide OT services for Medicare beneficiaries if:

- on or before January 1, 2008, they graduated an OT program approved jointly by the American Medical Association and the AOTA, or
- they are eligible for the National Registration Examination of AOTA or the National Board for Certification in OT.

Also, they qualify who on or before December 31, 1977, had 2 years of appropriate experience as an occupational therapist, and had achieved a satisfactory grade on a proficiency examination conducted, approved, or sponsored by the U.S. Public Health Service.

Those educated outside the U.S. may meet the same qualifications for domestic trained OTs. For example, they qualify if they were licensed or otherwise regulated by the state in which practicing on or before December 31, 2009. Or they are qualified if they:

- graduated from an OT education program accredited as substantially equivalent to a U.S. OT education program by ACOTE, the World Federation of Occupational Therapists, or a credentialing body approved by AOTA; and
- passed the NBCOT examination for OT; and
- Effective January 1, 2010, are licensed or otherwise regulated, if applicable as an OT by the state in which practicing.

For outpatient OT services that are provided incident to the services of physicians/NPPs, the requirement for OT licensure does not apply; all other personnel qualifications do apply. The qualified personnel providing OT services incident to the services of a physician/NPP must be trained in an accredited OT curriculum. For example, a person who, on or before December 31, 2009, graduated from an OT curriculum accredited by ACOTE and is eligible to take or has successfully completed the entry-level certification examination for OTs developed and administered by NBCOT, could provide Medicare outpatient OT services incident to the services of a physician/NPP if the physician assumes responsibility for the services according to the incident to policies. On or after January 1, 2010, although licensure does not apply, both education and examination requirements that are effective January 1, 2010, apply to qualified personnel who provide OT services incident to the services of a physician/NPP.

C. Services of Occupational Therapy Support Personnel
Reference: 42CFR 484.4

The new personnel qualifications for occupational therapy assistants were discussed in the 2008 Physician Fee Schedule. See the Federal Register of November 27, 2007, for the full text. See also the correction notice for this rule, published in the Federal Register on January 15, 2008.

The regulation provides that an occupational therapy assistant is a person who is licensed, unless licensure does not apply, or otherwise regulated, if applicable, as an OTA by the state in which practicing, and graduated from an OTA education program accredited by ACOTE and is eligible to take or has successfully completed the NBCOT examination for OTAs. The phrase, "by the state in which practicing" includes any authorization to practice provided by the same state in which the service is provided, including temporary licensure, regardless of the location of the entity billing the services.

If the requirements above are not met, an OTA may qualify if, on or before December 31, 2009, the OTA is licensed or otherwise regulated as an OTA, if applicable, by the state in which practicing, or meets any qualifications defined by the state in which practicing.

Or, where licensure or other state regulation does not apply, OTAs may qualify if they have, on or before December 31, 2009:

- completed certification requirements to practice as an OTA established by a credentialing organization approved by AOTA; and
- after January 1, 2010, they have also completed an education program accredited by ACOTE and passed the NBCOT examination for OTAs.

OTAs who qualified under the policies in effect prior to January 1, 2008, continue to qualify to provide OT directed and supervised OTA services to Medicare beneficiaries.

Therefore, OTAs qualify who after December 31, 1977, and on or before December 31, 2007:

- completed certification requirements to practice as an OTA established by a credentialing organization approved by AOTA; or
- completed the requirements to practice as an OTA applicable in the state in which practicing.

Those OTAs who were educated outside the U.S. may meet the same requirements as domestically trained OTAs. Or, if educated outside the U.S. on or after January 1, 2008, they must have graduated from an OTA program accredited as substantially equivalent to OTA entry level education in the U.S. by ACOTE, its successor organization, or the World Federation of Occupational Therapists or a credentialing body approved by AOTA. In addition, they must have passed an exam for OTAs administered by NBCOT.

Services. The services of OTAs used when providing covered therapy benefits are included as part of the covered service. These services are billed by the supervising occupational therapist. OTAs may not provide evaluation services, make clinical judgments or decisions or take responsibility for the service. They act at the direction and under the supervision of the treating occupational therapist and in accordance with state laws.

An occupational therapist must supervise OTAs. The level and frequency of supervision differs by setting (and by state or local law). General supervision is required for OTAs in all settings except private practice (which requires direct supervision) unless state practice requirements are more stringent, in which case state or local requirements must be followed. See specific settings for details. For example, in clinics, rehabilitation agencies, and public health agencies, 42CFR485.713 indicates that when an OTA provides services, either on or off the organization's premises, those services are supervised by a qualified occupational therapist who makes an onsite supervisory visit at least once every 30 days or more frequently if required by state or local laws or regulation.

The services of an OTA shall not be billed as services incident to a physician/NPP's service, because they do not meet the qualifications of a therapist.

The cost of supplies (e.g., looms, ceramic tiles, or leather) used in furnishing covered therapy care is included in the payment for the HCPCS codes billed by the occupational therapist and are, therefore, not separately billable. Separate coverage and billing provisions apply to items that meet the definition of brace in Sec.130 of this manual.

Services provided by aides, even if under the supervision of a therapist, are not therapy services in the outpatient setting and are not covered by Medicare. Although an aide may help the therapist by providing unskilled services, those services that are unskilled are not covered by Medicare and shall be denied as not reasonable and necessary if they are billed as therapy services.

D. Application of Medicare Guidelines to Occupational Therapy Services
Occupational therapy may be required for a patient with a specific diagnosed psychiatric illness. If such services are required, they are covered assuming the coverage criteria are met. However, where an individual's motivational needs are not related to a specific diagnosed psychiatric illness, the meeting of such needs does not usually require an individualized therapeutic program. Such needs can be met through general activity programs or the efforts of other professional personnel involved in the care of the patient. Patient motivation is an appropriate and inherent function of all health disciplines, which is interwoven with other functions performed by such personnel for the patient. Accordingly, since the special skills of an occupational therapist are not required, an occupational therapy program for individuals who do not have a specific diagnosed psychiatric illness is not to be considered reasonable and necessary for the treatment of an illness or injury. Services furnished under such a program are not covered.

Occupational therapy may include vocational and prevocational assessment and training. When services provided by an occupational therapist are related solely to specific employment opportunities, work skills, or work settings, they are not reasonable or necessary for the diagnosis or treatment of an illness or injury and are not covered. However, carriers and intermediaries exercise care in applying this exclusion, because the assessment of level of function and the teaching of compensatory techniques to improve the level of function, especially in activities of daily living, are services which occupational therapists provide for both vocational and nonvocational purposes. For example, an assessment of sitting and standing tolerance might be nonvocational for a mother of young children or a retired individual living alone, but could also be a vocational test for a sales clerk. Training an amputee in the use of prosthesis for telephoning is necessary for everyday activities as well as for employment purposes. Major changes in life style may be mandatory for an individual with a substantial disability. The techniques of adjustment cannot be considered exclusively vocational or nonvocational.

100-2, 15, 230.3

Practice of Speech-Language Pathology

A. General
Speech-language pathology services are those services provided within the scope of practice of speech-language pathologists and necessary for the diagnosis and treatment of speech and language disorders, which result in communication disabilities and for the diagnosis and treatment of swallowing disorders (dysphagia), regardless of the presence of a communication disability. (See Pub. 100-03, chapter 1, Sec.170.3)

B. Qualified Speech-Language Pathologist Defined
A qualified speech-language pathologist for program coverage purposes meets one of the following requirements:

- The education and experience requirements for a Certificate of Clinical Competence in (speech-language pathology) granted by the American Speech- Language Hearing Association; or
- Meets the educational requirements for certification and is in the process of accumulating the supervised experience required for certification.

For outpatient speech-language pathology services that are provided incident to the services of physicians/NPPs, the requirement for speech-language pathology licensure does not apply; all other personnel qualifications do apply. Therefore, qualified personnel providing speech-language pathology services incident to the services of a physician/NPP must meet the above qualifications.

C. Services of Speech-Language Pathology Support Personnel
Services of speech-language pathology assistants are not recognized for Medicare coverage. Services provided by speech-language pathology assistants, even if they are licensed to provide services in their states, will be considered unskilled services and denied as not reasonable and necessary if they are billed as therapy services.

Services provided by aides, even if under the supervision of a therapist, are not therapy services and are not covered by Medicare. Although an aide may help the therapist by providing unskilled services, those services are not covered by Medicare and shall be denied as not reasonable and necessary if they are billed as therapy services.

D. Application of Medicare Guidelines to Speech-Language Pathology Services

1. Evaluation Services
Speech-language pathology evaluation services are covered if they are reasonable and necessary and not excluded as routine screening by Sec.1862(a)(7) of the Act. The speechlanguage pathologist employs a variety of formal and informal speech, language, and dysphagia assessment tests to ascertain the type, causal factor(s), and severity of the speech and language or swallowing disorders. Reevaluation of patients for whom speech, language and swallowing were previously contraindicated is covered only if the patient exhibits a change in medical condition. However, monthly reevaluations; e.g., a Western Aphasia Battery, for a patient undergoing a rehabilitative speech-language pathology program, are considered a part of the treatment session and shall not be covered as a separate evaluation for billing purposes. Although hearing screening by the speechlanguage pathologist may be part of an evaluation, it is not billable as a separate service.

2. Therapeutic Services
The following are examples of common medical disorders and resulting communication deficits, which may necessitate active rehabilitative therapy. This list is not all-inclusive:
- Cerebrovascular disease such as cerebral vascular accidents presenting with dysphagia, aphasia/dysphasia, apraxia, and dysarthria;
- Neurological disease such as Parkinsonism or
- Multiple Sclerosis with dysarthria, dysphagia, inadequate respiratory volume/control, or voice disorder; or
- Laryngeal carcinoma requiring laryngectomy resulting in aphonia.

3. Impairments of the Auditory System
The terms, aural rehabilitation, auditory rehabilitation, auditory processing, lipreading and speech reading are among the terms used to describe covered services related to perception and comprehension of sound through the auditory system. See Pub. 100-04, chapter 12, section 30.3 for billing instructions. For example:
- Auditory processing evaluation and treatment may be covered and medically necessary. Examples include but are not limited to services for certain neurological impairments or the absence of natural auditory stimulation that results in impaired ability to process sound. Certain auditory processing disorders require diagnostic audiological tests in addition to speech-language pathology evaluation and treatment.
- Evaluation and treatment for disorders of the auditory system may be covered and medically necessary, for example, when it has been determined by a speechlanguage pathologist in collaboration with an audiologist that the hearing impaired beneficiary's current amplification options (hearing aid, other amplification device or cochlear implant) will not sufficiently meet the patient's functional communication needs. Audiologists and speech-language pathologists both evaluate beneficiaries for disorders of the auditory system using different skills and techniques, but only speech-language pathologists may provide treatment.

Assessment for the need for rehabilitation of the auditory system (but not the vestibular system) may be done by a speech language pathologist. Examples include but are not limited to: evaluation of comprehension and production of language in oral, signed or written modalities; speech and voice production, listening skills, speech reading, communications strategies, and the impact of the hearing loss on the patient/client and family.

Examples of rehabilitation include but are not limited to treatment that focuses on comprehension, and production of language in oral, signed or written modalities; speech and voice production, auditory training, speech reading, multimodal (e.g., visual, auditory-visual, and tactile) training, communication strategies, education and counseling. In determining the necessity for treatment, the beneficiary's performance in both clinical and natural environment should be considered.

4. Dysphagia
Dysphagia, or difficulty in swallowing, can cause food to enter the airway, resulting in coughing, choking, pulmonary problems, aspiration or inadequate nutrition and hydration with resultant weight loss, failure to thrive, pneumonia and death. It is most often due to complex neurological and/or structural impairments including head and neck trauma, cerebrovascular accident, neuromuscular degenerative diseases, head and neck cancer, dementias, and encephalopathies. For these reasons, it is important that only qualified professionals with specific training and experience in this disorder provide evaluation and treatment.

The speech-language pathologist performs clinical and instrumental assessments and analyzes and integrates the diagnostic information to determine candidacy for intervention as well as appropriate compensations and rehabilitative therapy techniques.

The equipment that is used in the examination may be fixed, mobile or portable.

Professional guidelines recommend that the service be provided in a team setting with a physician/NPP who provides supervision of the radiological examination and interpretation of medical conditions revealed in it.

Swallowing assessment and rehabilitation are highly specialized services. The professional rendering care must have education, experience and demonstrated competencies. Competencies include but are not limited to: identifying abnormal upper aerodigestive tract structure and function; conducting an oral, pharyngeal, laryngeal and respiratory function examination as it relates to the functional assessment of swallowing; recommending methods of oral intake and risk precautions; and developing a treatment plan employing appropriate compensations and therapy techniques.

100-2, 15, 230.4
Services Furnished by a Physical or Occupational Therapist in Private Practice
A. General
In order to qualify to bill Medicare directly as a therapist, each individual must be enrolled as a private practitioner and employed in one of the following practice types: an unincorporated solo practice, unincorporated partnership, unincorporated group practice, physician/NPP group or groups that are not professional corporations, if allowed by state and local law. Physician/NPP group practices may employ physical therapists in private practice (PTPP) and/or occupational therapists in private practice (OTPP) if state and local law permits this employee relationship.

For purposes of this provision, a physician/NPP group practice is defined as one or more physicians/NPPs enrolled with Medicare who may bill as one entity. For further details on issues concerning enrollment, see the provider enrollment Web site at www.cms.hhs.gov/providers/enrollment.

Private practice also includes therapists who are practicing therapy as employees of another supplier, of a professional corporation or other incorporated therapy practice. Private practice does not include individuals when they are working as employees of an institutional provider.

Services should be furnished in the therapist's or group's office or in the patient's home. The office is defined as the location(s) where the practice is operated, in the state(s) where the therapist (and practice, if applicable) is legally authorized to furnish services, during the hours that the therapist engages in the practice at that location. If services are furnished in a private practice office space, that space shall be owned, leased, or rented by the practice and used for the exclusive purpose of operating the practice. For descriptions of aquatic therapy in a community center pool see section 220C of this chapter.

Therapists in private practice must be approved as meeting certain requirements, but do not execute a formal provider agreement with the Secretary.

If therapists who have their own Medicare Personal Identification number (PIN) or National Provider Identifier (NPI) are employed by therapist groups, physician/NPP groups, or groups that are not professional organizations, the requirement that therapy space be owned, leased, or rented may be satisfied by the group that employs the therapist. Each physical or occupational therapist employed by a group should enroll as a PT or OT in private practice.

When therapists with a Medicare PIN/NPI provide services in the physician's/NPP's office in which they are employed, and bill using their PIN/NPI for each therapy service, then the direct supervision requirement for PTAs and OTAs apply.

When the PT or OT who has a Medicare PIN/ NPI is employed in a physician's/NPP's office the services are ordinarily billed as services of the PT or OT, with the PT or OT identified on the claim as the supplier of services. However, services of the PT or OT who has a Medicare PIN/NPI may also be billed by the physician/NPP as services incident to the physician's/NPP's service. (See Sec.230.5 for rules related to PTA and OTA services incident to a physician.) In that case, the physician/NPP is the supplier of service, the Unique Provider Identification Number (UPIN) or NPI of the physician/NPP (ordering or supervising, as indicated) is reported on the claim with the service and all the rules for incident to services (Sec.230.5) must be followed.

B. Private Practice Defined
Reference: Federal Register November, 1998, pages 58863-58869; 42CFR 410.38(b)

The carrier considers a therapist to be in private practice if the therapist maintains office space at his or her own expense and furnishes services only in that space or the patient's home. Or, a therapist is employed by another supplier and furnishes services in facilities provided at the expense of that supplier.

The therapist need not be in full-time private practice but must be engaged in private practice on a regular basis; i.e., the therapist is recognized as a private practitioner and for that purpose has access to the necessary equipment to provide an adequate program of therapy.

The physical or occupational therapy services must be provided either by or under the direct supervision of the therapist in private practice. Each physical or occupational therapist in a practice should be enrolled as a Medicare provider. If a physical or occupational therapist is not enrolled, the services of that therapist must be directly supervised by an enrolled physical or occupational therapist. Direct supervision requires that the supervising private practice therapist be present in the office suite at the time the service is performed. These direct supervision requirements apply only in the private practice setting and only for physical therapists and occupational therapists and their assistants. In other outpatient settings, supervision rules differ. The services of support personnel must be included in the therapist's bill. The supporting personnel, including other therapists, must be W-2 or 1099 employees of the therapist in private practice or other qualified employer.

Coverage of outpatient physical therapy and occupational therapy under Part B includes the services of a qualified therapist in private practice when furnished in the therapist's office or the beneficiary's home. For this purpose, "home" includes an institution that is used as a home, but not a hospital, CAH or SNF, (Federal Register Nov. 2, 1998, pg 58869). Place of Service (POS) includes:
- 03/School, only if residential,
- 04/Homeless Shelter,

Appendix G — Pub 100 References

- 12/Home, other than a facility that is a private residence,
- 14/Group Home, 33/Custodial Care Facility.

C. Assignment
Reference: Nov. 2, 1998 Federal Register, pg. 58863

See also Pub. 100-04 chapter 1, Sec.30.2.

When physicians, NPPs, PTPPs or OTPPs obtain provider numbers, they have the option of accepting assignment (participating) or not accepting assignment (nonparticipating). In contrast, providers, such as outpatient hospitals, SNFs, rehabilitation agencies, and CORFs, do not have the option. For these providers, assignment is mandatory.

If physicians/NPPs, PTPPs or OTPPs accept assignment (are participating), they must accept the Medicare Physician Fee Schedule amount as payment. Medicare pays 80% and the patient is responsible for 20%. In contrast, if they do not accept assignment, Medicare will only pay 95% of the fee schedule amount. However, when these services are not furnished on an assignment-related basis, the limiting charge applies. (See Sec.1848(g)(2)(c) of the Act.)

NOTE: Services furnished by a therapist in the therapist's office under arrangements with hospitals in rural communities and public health agencies (or services provided in the beneficiary's home under arrangements with a provider of outpatient physical or occupational therapy services) are not covered under this provision. See section 230.6.

100-2, 15, 240
Chiropractic Services - General
B3-2250, B3-4118

The term "physician" under Part B includes a chiropractor who meets the specified qualifying requirements set forth in Sec.30.5 but only for treatment by means of manual manipulation of the spine to correct a subluxation.

Effective for claims with dates of services on or after January 1, 2000, an x-ray is not required to demonstrate the subluxation.

Implementation of the chiropractic benefit requires an appreciation of the differences between chiropractic theory and experience and traditional medicine due to fundamental differences regarding etiology and theories of the pathogenesis of disease. Judgments about the reasonableness of chiropractic treatment must be based on the application of chiropractic principles. So that Medicare beneficiaries receive equitable adjudication of claims based on such principles and are not deprived of the benefits intended by the law, carriers may use chiropractic consultation in carrier review of Medicare chiropractic claims.

Payment is based on the physician fee schedule and made to the beneficiary or, on assignment, to the chiropractor.

A. Verification of Chiropractor's Qualifications
Carriers must establish a reference file of chiropractors eligible for payment as physicians under the criteria in Sec.30.1. They pay only chiropractors on file. Information needed to establish such files is furnished by the CMS RO.

The RO is notified by the appropriate State agency which chiropractors are licensed and whether each meets the national uniform standards.

100-2, 15, 260
Ambulatory Surgical Center Services
Facility services furnished by ambulatory surgical centers (ASCs) in connection with certain surgical procedures are covered under Part B. To receive coverage of and payment for its services under this provision, a facility must be certified as meeting the requirements for an ASC and enter into a written agreement with CMS. Medicare periodically updates the list of covered procedures and related payment amounts through release of regulations and Program Memoranda. The ASC must accept Medicare's payment for such procedures as payment in full with respect to those services defined as ASC facility services.

Where services are performed in an ASC, the physician and others who perform covered services may also be paid for his/her professional services; however, the "professional" rate is then adjusted since the ASC incurs the facility costs.

100-2, 15, 290
Foot Care
A. Treatment of Subluxation of Foot
Subluxations of the foot are defined as partial dislocations or displacements of joint surfaces, tendons ligaments, or muscles of the foot. Surgical or nonsurgical treatments undertaken for the sole purpose of correcting a subluxated structure in the foot as an isolated entity are not covered.

However, medical or surgical treatment of subluxation of the ankle joint (talo-crural joint) is covered. In addition, reasonable and necessary medical or surgical services, diagnosis, or treatment for medical conditions that have resulted from or are associated with partial displacement of structures is covered. For example, if a patient has osteoarthritis that has resulted in a partial displacement of joints in the foot, and the primary treatment is for the osteoarthritis, coverage is provided.

B. Exclusions from Coverage
The following foot care services are generally excluded from coverage under both Part A and Part B. (See Sec.290.F and Sec.290.G for instructions on applying foot care exclusions.)

1. Treatment of Flat Foot

    The term "flat foot" is defined as a condition in which one or more arches of the foot have flattened out. Services or devices directed toward the care or correction of such conditions, including the prescription of supportive devices, are not covered.

2. Routine Foot Care

    Except as provided above, routine foot care is excluded from coverage. Services that normally are considered routine and not covered by Medicare include the following:
    - The cutting or removal of corns and calluses;
    - The trimming, cutting, clipping, or debriding of nails; and
    - Other hygienic and preventive maintenance care, such as cleaning and soaking the feet, the use of skin creams to maintain skin tone of either ambulatory or bedfast patients, and any other service performed in the absence of localized illness, injury, or symptoms involving the foot.

3. Supportive Devices for Feet

    Orthopedic shoes and other supportive devices for the feet generally are not covered. However, this exclusion does not apply to such a shoe if it is an integral part of a leg brace, and its expense is included as part of the cost of the brace. Also, this exclusion does not apply to therapeutic shoes furnished to diabetics.

C. Exceptions to Routine Foot Care Exclusion

1. Necessary and Integral Part of Otherwise Covered Services

    In certain circumstances, services ordinarily considered to be routine may be covered if they are performed as a necessary and integral part of otherwise covered services, such as diagnosis and treatment of ulcers, wounds, or infections.

2. Treatment of Warts on Foot

    The treatment of warts (including plantar warts) on the foot is covered to the same extent as services provided for the treatment of warts located elsewhere on the body.

3. Presence of Systemic Condition

    The presence of a systemic condition such as metabolic, neurologic, or peripheral vascular disease may require scrupulous foot care by a professional that in the absence of such condition(s) would be considered routine (and, therefore, excluded from coverage). Accordingly, foot care that would otherwise be considered routine may be covered when systemic condition(s) result in severe circulatory embarrassment or areas of diminished sensation in the individual's legs or feet. (See subsection A.)

    In these instances, certain foot care procedures that otherwise are considered routine (e.g., cutting or removing corns and calluses, or trimming, cutting, clipping, or debriding nails) may pose a hazard when performed by a nonprofessional person on patients with such systemic conditions. (See Sec.290.G for procedural instructions.)

4. Mycotic Nails

    In the absence of a systemic condition, treatment of mycotic nails may be covered.

    The treatment of mycotic nails for an ambulatory patient is covered only when the physician attending the patient's mycotic condition documents that (1) there is clinical evidence of mycosis of the toenail, and (2) the patient has marked limitation of ambulation, pain, or secondary infection resulting from the thickening and dystrophy of the infected toenail plate.

    The treatment of mycotic nails for a nonambulatory patient is covered only when the physician attending the patient's mycotic condition documents that (1) there is clinical evidence of mycosis of the toenail, and (2) the patient suffers from pain or secondary infection resulting from the thickening and dystrophy of the infected toenail plate.

    For the purpose of these requirements, documentation means any written information that is required by the carrier in order for services to be covered. Thus, the information submitted with claims must be substantiated by information found in the patient's medical record. Any information, including that contained in a form letter, used for documentation purposes is subject to carrier verification in order to ensure that the information adequately justifies coverage of the treatment of mycotic nails.

D. Systemic Conditions That Might Justify Coverage
Although not intended as a comprehensive list, the following metabolic, neurologic, and peripheral vascular diseases (with synonyms in parentheses) most commonly represent the underlying conditions that might justify coverage for routine foot care.

- Diabetes mellitus *
- Arteriosclerosis obliterans (A.S.O., arteriosclerosis of the extremities, occlusive peripheral arteriosclerosis)
- Buerger's disease (thromboangiitis obliterans)
- Chronic thrombophlebitis *
- Peripheral neuropathies involving the feet -

    Associated with malnutrition and vitamin deficiency *
    - Malnutrition (general, pellagra)
    - Alcoholism
    - Malabsorption (celiac disease, tropical sprue)
    - Pernicious anemia

        Associated with carcinoma *

        Associated with diabetes mellitus *

        Associated with drugs and toxins *

        Associated with multiple sclerosis *

        Associated with uremia (chronic renal disease) *

        Associated with traumatic injury

        Associated with leprosy or neurosyphilis

        Associated with hereditary disorders

- Hereditary sensory radicular neuropathy
- Angiokeratoma corporis diffusum (Fabry's)
- Amyloid neuropathy

When the patient's condition is one of those designated by an asterisk (*), routine procedures are covered only if the patient is under the active care of a doctor of medicine or osteopathy who documents the condition.

E. Supportive Devices for Feet
Orthopedic shoes and other supportive devices for the feet generally are not covered. However, this exclusion does not apply to such a shoe if it is an integral part of a leg brace, and its expense is included as part of the cost of the brace. Also, this exclusion does not apply to therapeutic shoes furnished to diabetics.

F. Presumption of Coverage
In evaluating whether the routine services can be reimbursed, a presumption of coverage may be made where the evidence available discloses certain physical and/or clinical findings consistent with the diagnosis and indicative of severe peripheral involvement. For purposes of applying this presumption the following findings are pertinent:

Class A Findings
- Nontraumatic amputation of foot or integral skeletal portion thereof.

Class B Findings
- Absent posterior tibial pulse;
- Advanced trophic changes as: hair growth (decrease or absence) nail changes (thickening) pigmentary changes (discoloration) skin texture (thin, shiny) skin color (rubor or redness) (Three required); and
- Absent dorsalis pedis pulse.

Class C Findings
- Claudication;
- Temperature changes (e.g., cold feet);
- Edema;
- Paresthesias (abnormal spontaneous sensations in the feet); and
- Burning.

The presumption of coverage may be applied when the physician rendering the routine foot care has identified:

1. A Class A finding;
2. Two of the Class B findings; or
3. One Class B and two Class C findings.

Cases evidencing findings falling short of these alternatives may involve podiatric treatment that may constitute covered care and should be reviewed by the intermediary's medical staff and developed as necessary.

For purposes of applying the coverage presumption where the routine services have been rendered by a podiatrist, the contractor may deem the active care requirement met if the claim or other evidence available discloses that the patient has seen an M.D. or D.O. for treatment and/or evaluation of the complicating disease process during the 6-month period prior to the rendition of the routine-type services. The intermediary may also accept the podiatrist's statement that the diagnosing and treating M.D. or D.O. also concurs with the podiatrist's findings as to the severity of the peripheral involvement indicated.

Services ordinarily considered routine might also be covered if they are performed as a necessary and integral part of otherwise covered services, such as diagnosis and treatment of diabetic ulcers, wounds, and infections.

G. Application of Foot Care Exclusions to Physician's Services
The exclusion of foot care is determined by the nature of the service. Thus, payment for an excluded service should be denied whether performed by a podiatrist, osteopath, or a doctor of medicine, and without regard to the difficulty or complexity of the procedure.

When an itemized bill shows both covered services and noncovered services not integrally related to the covered service, the portion of charges attributable to the noncovered services should be denied. (For example, if an itemized bill shows surgery for an ingrown toenail and also removal of calluses not necessary for the performance of toe surgery, any additional charge attributable to removal of the calluses should be denied.)

In reviewing claims involving foot care, the carrier should be alert to the following exceptional situations:

1. Payment may be made for incidental noncovered services performed as a necessary and integral part of, and secondary to, a covered procedure. For example, if trimming of toenails is required for application of a cast to a fractured foot, the carrier need not allocate and deny a portion of the charge for the trimming of the nails. However, a separately itemized charge for such excluded service should be disallowed. When the primary procedure is covered the administration of anesthesia necessary for the performance of such procedure is also covered.

2. Payment may be made for initial diagnostic services performed in connection with a specific symptom or complaint if it seems likely that its treatment would be covered even though the resulting diagnosis may be one requiring only noncovered care.

The name of the M.D. or D.O. who diagnosed the complicating condition must be submitted with the claim. In those cases, where active care is required, the approximate date the beneficiary was last seen by such physician must also be indicated.

NOTE: Section 939 of P.L. 96-499 removed "warts" from the routine foot care exclusion effective July 1, 1981.

Relatively few claims for routine-type care are anticipated considering the severity of conditions contemplated as the basis for this exception. Claims for this type of foot care should not be paid in the absence of convincing evidence that nonprofessional performance of the service would have been hazardous for the beneficiary because of an underlying systemic disease. The mere statement of a diagnosis such as those mentioned in Sec.D above does not of itself indicate the severity of the condition. Where development is indicated to verify diagnosis and/or severity the carrier should follow existing claims processing practices which may include review of carrier's history and medical consultation as well as physician contacts.

The rules in Sec.290.F concerning presumption of coverage also apply.

Codes and policies for routine foot care and supportive devices for the feet are not exclusively for the use of podiatrists. These codes must be used to report foot care services regardless of the specialty of the physician who furnishes the services. Carriers must instruct physicians to use the most appropriate code available when billing for routine foot care.

100-2, 16, 10
General Exclusions From Coverage
A3-3150, HO-260, HHA-232, B3-2300

No payment can be made under either the hospital insurance or supplementary medical insurance program for certain items and services, when the following conditions exist:

- Not reasonable and necessary (Sec.20);
- No legal obligation to pay for or provide (Sec.40);
- Paid for by a governmental entity (Sec.50);
- Not provided within United States (Sec.60);
- Resulting from war (Sec.70);
- Personal comfort (Sec.80);
- Routine services and appliances (Sec.90);
- Custodial care (Sec.110);
- Cosmetic surgery (Sec.120);
- Charges by immediate relatives or members of household (Sec.130);
- Dental services (Sec.140);
- Paid or expected to be paid under workers' compensation (Sec.150);
- Nonphysician services provided to a hospital inpatient that were not provided directly or arranged for by the hospital (Sec.170);
- Services Related to and Required as a Result of Services Which are not Covered Under Medicare (Sec.180);
- Excluded foot care services and supportive devices for feet (Sec.30); or
- Excluded investigational devices (See Chapter 14, Sec.30).

100-2, 16, 20
Services Not Reasonable and Necessary
A3-3151, HO-260.1, B3-2303, AB-00-52 - 6/00

Items and services which are not reasonable and necessary for the diagnosis or treatment of illness or injury or to improve the functioning of a malformed body member are not covered, e.g., payment cannot be made for the rental of a special hospital bed to be used by the patient in their home unless it was a reasonable and necessary part of the patient's treatment. See also Sec.80.

A health care item or service for the purpose of causing, or assisting to cause, the death of any individual (assisted suicide) is not covered. This prohibition does not apply to the provision of an item or service for the purpose of alleviating pain or discomfort, even if such use may increase the risk of death, so long as the item or service is not furnished for the specific purpose of causing death.

100-2, 16, 90
Routine Services and Appliances
A3-3157, HO-260.7, B3-2320, R-1797A3 - 5/00

Routine physical checkups; eyeglasses, contact lenses, and eye examinations for the purpose of prescribing, fitting, or changing eyeglasses; eye refractions by whatever practitioner and for whatever purpose performed; hearing aids and examinations for hearing aids; and immunizations are not covered.

The routine physical checkup exclusion applies to (a) examinations performed without relationship to treatment or diagnosis for a specific illness, symptom, complaint, or injury; and (b) examinations required by third parties such as insurance companies business establishments, or Government agencies.

If the claim is for a diagnostic test or examination performed solely for the purpose of establishing a claim under title IV of Public Law 91-173, "Black Lung Benefits," the service is not covered under Medicare and the claimant should be advised to contact their Social Security office regarding the filing of a claim for reimbursement under the "Black Lung" program.

The exclusions apply to eyeglasses or contact lenses, and eye examinations for the purpose of prescribing, fitting, or changing eyeglasses or contact lenses for refractive errors. The exclusions do not apply to physicians' services (and services incident to a physicians' service) performed in conjunction with an eye disease, as for example, glaucoma or cataracts, or to post-surgical prosthetic lenses which are customarily used during convalescence from eye surgery in which the lens of the eye was removed, or to permanent prosthetic lenses required by an individual lacking the organic lens of the eye whether by surgical removal or congenital disease. Such prosthetic lens is a replacement for an internal body organ - the lens of the eye. (See the Medicare Benefit Policy Manual, Chapter 15, "Covered Medical and Other Health Services," Sec.120). Expenses for all refractive procedures, whether performed by an ophthalmologist (or any other physician) or an optometrist and without regard to the reason for performance of the refraction, are excluded from coverage.

A. Immunizations
Vaccinations or inoculations are excluded as immunizations unless they are either

- Directly related to the treatment of an injury or direct exposure to a disease or condition, such as antirabies treatment, tetanus antitoxin or booster vaccine, botulin antitoxin, antivenin sera, or immune globulin. (In the absence of injury or direct exposure, preventive immunization (vaccination or inoculation) against such diseases as smallpox, polio, diphtheria, etc., is not covered.); or
- Specifically covered by statute, as described in the Medicare Benefit Policy Manual, Chapter 15, "Covered Medical and Other Health Services," Sec.50.

B. Antigens
Prior to the Omnibus Reconciliation Act of 1980, a physician who prepared an antigen for a patient could not be reimbursed for that service unless the physician also administered the antigen to the patient. Effective January 1, 1981, payment may be made for a reasonable supply of antigens that have been prepared for a particular patient even though they have not been administered to the patient by the same physician who prepared them if:

- The antigens are prepared by a physician who is a doctor of medicine or osteopathy, and
- The physician who prepared the antigens has examined the patient and has determined a plan of treatment and a dosage regimen.

A reasonable supply of antigens is considered to be not more than a 12-week supply of antigens that has been prepared for a particular patient at any one time. The purpose of the reasonable supply limitation is to assure that the antigens retain their potency and effectiveness over the period in which they are to be administered to the patient. (See the Medicare Benefit Policy Manual, Chapter 15, "Covered Medical and Other Health Services," Sec.50.4.4.2)

100-2, 16, 100
Hearing Aids and Auditory Implants
Section 1862(a)(7) of the Social Security Act states that no payment may be made under part A or part B for any expenses incurred for items or services "where such expenses are for . . . hearing aids or examinations therefore. . . ." This policy is further reiterated at 42 CFR 411.15(d) which specifically states that "hearing aids or examination for the purpose of prescribing, fitting, or changing hearing aids" are excluded from coverage.

Hearing aids are amplifying devices that compensate for impaired hearing. Hearing aids include air conduction devices that provide acoustic energy to the cochlea via stimulation of the tympanic membrane with amplified sound. They also include bone conduction devices that provide mechanical energy to the cochlea via stimulation of the scalp with amplified mechanical vibration or by direct contact with the tympanic membrane or middle ear ossicles.

Certain devices that produce perception of sound by replacing the function of the middle ear, cochlea or auditory nerve are payable by Medicare as prosthetic devices. These devices are indicated only when hearing aids are medically inappropriate or cannot be utilized due to congenital malformations, chronic disease, severe sensorineural hearing loss or surgery. The following are prosthetic devices:

- Cochlear implants and auditory brainstem implants, i.e., devices that replace the function of cochlear structures or auditory nerve and provide electrical energy to auditory nerve fibers and other neural tissue via implanted electrode arrays.
- Osseointegrated implants, i.e., devices implanted in the skull that replace the function of the middle ear and provide mechanical energy to the cochlea via a mechanical transducer.

Medicare contractors deny payment for an item or service that is associated with any hearing aid as defined above. See Sec.180 for policy for the medically necessary treatment of complications of implantable hearing aids, such as medically necessary removals of implantable hearing aids due to infection.

100-2, 16, 120
Cosmetic Surgery
A3-3160, HO-260.11, B3-2329

Cosmetic surgery or expenses incurred in connection with such surgery is not covered. Cosmetic surgery includes any surgical procedure directed at improving appearance, except when required for the prompt (i.e., as soon as medically feasible) repair of accidental injury or for the improvement of the functioning of a malformed body member. For example, this exclusion does not apply to surgery in connection with treatment of severe burns or repair of the face following a serious automobile accident, or to surgery for therapeutic purposes which coincidentally also serves some cosmetic purpose.

100-2, 16, 180
Services Related to and Required as a Result of Services Which Are Not Covered Under Medicare
B3-2300.1, A3-3101.14, HO-210.12

Medical and hospital services are sometimes required to treat a condition that arises as a result of services that are not covered because they are determined to be not reasonable and necessary or because they are excluded from coverage for other reasons. Services "related to" noncovered services (e.g., cosmetic surgery, noncovered organ transplants, noncovered artificial organ implants, etc.), including services related to follow-up care and complications of noncovered services which require treatment during a hospital stay in which the noncovered service was performed, are not covered services under Medicare. Services "not related to" noncovered services are covered under Medicare.

Following are examples of services "related to" and "not related to" noncovered services while the beneficiary is an inpatient:

- A beneficiary was hospitalized for a noncovered service and broke a leg while in the hospital. Services related to care of the broken leg during this stay is a clear example of "not related to" services and are covered under Medicare.
- A beneficiary was admitted to the hospital for covered services, but during the course of hospitalization became a candidate for a noncovered transplant or implant and actually received the transplant or implant during that hospital stay. When the original admission was entirely unrelated to the diagnosis that led to a recommendation for a noncovered transplant or implant, the services related to the admitting condition would be covered.
- A beneficiary was admitted to the hospital for covered services related to a condition which ultimately led to identification of a need for transplant and receipt of a transplant during the same hospital stay. If, on the basis of the nature of the services and a comparison of the date they are received with the date on which the beneficiary is identified as a transplant candidate, the services could reasonably be attributed to preparation for the noncovered transplant, the services would be "related to" noncovered services and would also be noncovered.

Following is an example of services received subsequent to a noncovered inpatient stay:

- After a beneficiary has been discharged from the hospital stay in which the beneficiary received noncovered services, medical and hospital services required to treat a condition or complication that arises as a result of the prior noncovered services may be covered when they are reasonable and necessary in all other respects. Thus, coverage could be provided for subsequent inpatient stays or outpatient treatment ordinarily covered by Medicare, even if the need for treatment arose because of a previous noncovered procedure. Some examples of services that may be found to be covered under this policy are the reversal of intestinal bypass surgery for obesity, repair of complications from transsexual surgery or from cosmetic surgery, removal of a noncovered bladder stimulator, or treatment of any infection at the surgical site of a noncovered transplant that occurred following discharge from the hospital.

However, any subsequent services that could be expected to have been incorporated into a global fee are considered to have been paid in the global fee, and may not be paid again. Thus, where a patient undergoes cosmetic surgery and the treatment regimen calls for a series of postoperative visits to the surgeon for evaluating the patient's progress, these visits are not paid.

100-3, 10.1
NCD for Use of Visual Tests Prior to and General Anesthesia During Cataract Surgery (10.1)
A - Pre-Surgery Evaluations
Cataract surgery with an intraocular lens (IOL) implant is a high volume Medicare procedure. Along with the surgery, a substantial number of preoperative tests are available to the surgeon. In most cases, a comprehensive eye examination (ocular history and ocular examination) and a single scan to determine the appropriate pseudophakic power of the IOL are sufficient. In most cases involving a simple cataract, a diagnostic ultrasound A-scan is used. For patients with a dense cataract, an ultrasound B-scan may be used.

Accordingly, where the only diagnosis is cataract(s), Medicare does not routinely cover testing other than one comprehensive eye examination (or a combination of a brief/intermediate examination not to exceed the charge of a comprehensive examination) and an A-scan or, if medically justified, a B-scan. Claims for additional tests are denied as not reasonable and necessary unless there is an additional diagnosis and the medical need for the additional tests is fully documented.

Because cataract surgery is an elective procedure, the patient may decide not to have the surgery until later, or to have the surgery performed by a physician other than the diagnosing physician. In these situations, it may be medically appropriate for the operating physician to conduct another examination. To the extent the additional tests are considered reasonable and necessary by the carrier's medical staff, they are covered.

B - General Anesthesia
The use of general anesthesia in cataract surgery may be considered reasonable and necessary if, for particular medical indications, it is the accepted procedure among ophthalmologists in the local community to use general anesthesia.

100-3, 10.2
NCD for Transcutaneous Electrical Nerve Stimulation (TENS) for Acute Post-Operative Pain (10.2)
The use of TENS for the relief of acute post-operative pain is covered under Medicare. TENS may be covered whether used as an adjunct to the use of drugs, or as an alternative to drugs, in the treatment of acute pain resulting from surgery.

TENS devices, whether durable or disposable, may be used in furnishing this service. When used for the purpose of treating acute post-operative pain, TENS devices are considered supplies. As such they may be hospital supplies furnished inpatients covered under Part A, or supplies incident to a physician's service when furnished in connection with surgery done on an outpatient basis, and covered under Part B.

It is expected that TENS, when used for acute post-operative pain, will be necessary for relatively short periods of time, usually 30 days or less. In cases when TENS is used for longer periods, contractors should attempt to ascertain whether TENS is no longer being used for acute pain but rather for chronic pain, in which case the TENS device may be covered as durable medical equipment as described in 280.13.

Current Procedural Coding Expert

Appendix G — Pub 100 References

100-3,10.3
NCD for Inpatient Hospital Pain Rehabilitation Programs (10.3)

Since pain rehabilitation programs of a lesser scope than that described above would raise a question as to whether the program could be provided in a less intensive setting than on an inpatient hospital basis, carefully evaluate such programs to determine whether the program does, in fact, necessitate a hospital level of care. Some pain rehabilitation programs may utilize services and devices which are excluded from coverage, e.g., acupuncture (see 35-8), biofeedback (see 35-27), dorsal column stimulator (see 65-8), and family counseling services (see 35-14). In determining whether the scope of a pain program does necessitate inpatient hospital care, evaluate only those services and devices which are covered. Although diagnostic tests may be an appropriate part of pain rehabilitation programs, such tests would be covered in an individual case only where they can be reasonably related to a patient's illness, complaint, symptom, or injury and where they do not represent an unnecessary duplication of tests previously performed.

An inpatient program of 4 weeks' duration is generally required to modify pain behavior. After this period it would be expected that any additional rehabilitation services which might be required could be effectively provided on an outpatient basis under an outpatient pain rehabilitation program (see 10.4 of the NCD Manual) or other outpatient program. The first 7-10 days of such an inpatient program constitute, in effect, an evaluation period. If a patient is unable to adjust to the program within this period, it is generally concluded that it is unlikely that the program will be effective and the patient is discharged from the program. On occasions a program longer than 4 weeks may be required in a particular case. In such a case there should be documentation to substantiate that inpatient care beyond a 4-week period was reasonable and necessary. Similarly, where it appears that a patient participating in a program is being granted frequent outside passes, a question would exist as to whether an inpatient program is reasonable and necessary for the treatment of the patient's condition.

An inpatient hospital stay for the purpose of participating in a pain rehabilitation program would be covered as reasonable and necessary to the treatment of a patient's condition where the pain is attributable to a physical cause, the usual methods of treatment have not been successful in alleviating it, and a significant loss of ability to function independently has resulted from the pain. Chronic pain patients often have psychological problems which accompany or stem from the physical pain and it is appropriate to include psychological treatment in the multidisciplinary approach. However, patients whose pain symptoms result from a mental condition, rather than from any physical cause, generally cannot be succesfully treated in a pain rehabilitation program.

100-3,10.4
NCD for Outpatient Hospital Pain Rehabilitation Programs (10.4)

Coverage of services furnished under outpatient hospital pain rehabilitation programs, including services furnished in group settings under individualized plans of treatment, is available if the patient's pain is attributable to a physical cause, the usual methods of treatment have not been successful in alleviating it, and a significant loss of ability by the patient to function independently has resulted from the pain. If a patient meets these conditions and the program provides services of the types discussed in 10.3 of the NCD Manual, the services provided under the program may be covered. Noncovered services (e.g., vocational counseling, meals for outpatients, or acupuncture) continue to be excluded from coverage, and intermediaries would not be precluded from finding, in the case of particular patients, that the pain rehabilitation program is not reasonable and necessary under 1862(a)(1) of the Act for the treatment of their conditions.

100-3,10.5
NCD for Autogenous Epidural Blood Graft (10.5)

Autogenous epidural blood grafts are considered a safe and effective remedy for severe headaches that may occur after performance of spinal anesthesia, spinal taps or myelograms, and are covered.

100-3, 10.6

The use of general or monitored anesthesia during transvenous cardiac pacemaker surgery may be reasonable and necessary and therefore covered under Medicare only if adequate documentation of medical necessity is provided on a case-by-case basis. The contractor obtains advice from its medical consultants or from appropriate specialty physicians or groups in its locality regarding the adequacy of documentation before deciding whether a particular claim should be covered.

A second type of pacemaker surgery that is sometimes performed involves the use of the thoracic method of implantation which requires open surgery. Where the thoracic method is employed, general anesthesia is always used and should not require special medical documentation.

100-3, 20.1
NCD for Vertebral Artery Surgery (20.1)

- These procedures can be medically reasonable and necessary, but only if each of the following conditions is met:
- Symptoms of vertebral artery obstruction exist;
- Other causes have been considered and ruled out;
- There is radiographic evidence of a valid vertebral artery obstruction; and
- Contraindications to the procedure do not exist, such as coexistent obstructions of multiple cerebral vessels.

Angiograms documenting a valid obstruction should show not only the aortic arch with the vessels off the arch, but also show the vessels in the neck and head (providing biplane views of the carotid and vertebral vascular system). In addition, serial views are needed to diagnose "subclavian steal," the condition in which subclavian artery obstruction causes the symptoms of vertebral artery obstruction. Because the symptoms are not specific for vertebral artery obstruction, other causes must be considered. In addition to vertebral artery obstruction, the differential diagnosis should include various degenerative disorders of the brain, orthostatic hypotension, acoustic neuroma, labyrinthitis, diabetes mellitus and hypoglycemia related disorders.

Obstructions which can cause symptoms of blocked vertebral artery blood flow and which can be documented by an angiogram include:

- Intravascular obstructions - arteriosclerotic lesions within the vertebral artery or in other arteries.
- Extravascular obstructions.
- Bony tissue or osteophytes, located laterally in the C6(C7)-C2 cervical vertebral area course of the vertebral artery, most commonly at C5 -C6.
- Anatomical variations - Anomalous location of the origin of the vertebral artery, a congenital aberration, and tortuosity and kinks of the vertebral artery.
- Fibrous tissue - Tissue changed as a result of manipulation of the neck for neck pain or injury associated with hematoma; external bands, tendinous slings, and fibrous bands.

The most controversial obstructions include vertebral artery tortuosity and kinks and connective tissue along the course of the vertebral artery, and variously called external bands, tendinous slings and fibrous bands. In the absence of symptoms of vertebral artery obstruction, vascular surgeons feel such abnormalities are insignificant. Vascular surgery experts, however, agree that these abnormalities in very rare cases do cause symptoms of vertebral artery obstruction and do necessitate surgical correction.

Vertebral artery construction and vertebral artery surgery are phrases which most physicians interpret to include only surgical cleaning (endarterectomy) and bypass (resection) procedures. However, some physicians who use these terms mean all operative manipulations which remove vertebral artery blood flow obstructions. Also, some physicians use general terms of vascular surgery, such as endarterectomy when vertebral artery related surgery is performed. Use of the above terminology specifies neither the surgical procedure performed nor its relationship to the vertebral artery. Therefore, in developing claims for this type of procedure, require specific identification of the obstruction in question and the surgical procedure performed. Also, in view of the specific coverage criteria given, develop all claims for vertebral artery surgery on a case-by-case basis.

Make payment for a surgical procedure listed above if: (1) it is reasonable and necessary for the individual patient to have the surgery performed to remove or relieve an obstruction to vertebral artery flow, and (2) the four conditions noted are met.

In all other cases, these procedures cannot be considered reasonable and necessary within the meaning of Sec.1862(a)(1) of the Act and are not reimbursable under the program.

100-3, 20.3
NCD for Thoracic Duct Drainage (TDD) in Renal Transplants (20.3)

TDD is performed on an inpatient basis, and the inpatient stay is covered for patients admitted for treatment in advance of a kidney transplant as well as for those receiving it post-transplant. TDD is a covered technique when furnished to a kidney transplant recipient or an individual approved to receive kidney transplantation in a hospital approved to perform kidney transplantation.

100-3, 20.4
NCD for Implantable Automatic Defibrillators (20.4)

A. General

The implantable automatic defibrillator is an electronic device designed to detect and treat life-threatening tachyarrhythmias. The device consists of a pulse generator and electrodes for sensing and defibrillating.

B. Covered Indications

1. Documented episode of cardiac arrest due to ventricular fibrillation (VF), not due to a transient or reversible cause (effective July 1, 1991).

2. Documented sustained ventricular tachyarrhythmia (VT), either spontaneous or induced by an electrophysiology (EP) study, not associated with an acute myocardial infarction (MI) and not due to a transient or reversible cause (effective July 1, 1999).

3. Documented familial or inherited conditions with a high risk of life-threatening VT, such as long QT syndrome or hypertrophic cardiomyopathy (effective July 1, 1999).

    Additional indications effective for services performed on or after October 1, 2003:

4. Coronary artery disease with a documented prior MI, a measured left ventricular ejection fraction (LVEF) <0.35, and inducible, sustained VT or VF at EP study. (The MI must have occurred more than 40 days prior to defibrillator insertion. The EP test must be performed more than 4 weeks after the qualifying MI.)

5. Documented prior MI and a measured LVEF <0.30 and a QRS duration of >120 milliseconds (the QRS restriction does not apply to services performed on or after January 27, 2005). Patients must not have:

    a. New York Heart Association (NYHC) classification IV;

    b. Cardiogenic shock or symptomatic hypotension while in a stable baseline rhythm;

    c. Had a coronary artery bypass graft (CABG) or percutaneous transluminal coronary angioplasty (PTCA) within past 3 months;

    d. Had an enzyme positive MI within past month (Effective for services on or after January 27, 2005, patients must not have an acute MI in the past 40 days);

    e. Clinical symptoms or findings that would make them a candidate for coronary revascularization; or

Appendix G — Pub 100 References

f. Any disease, other than cardiac disease (e.g., cancer, uremia, liver failure), associated with a likelihood of survival less than 1 year.

Additional indications effective for services performed on or after January 27, 2005:

6. Patients with ischemic dilated cardiomyopathy (IDCM), documented prior MI, NYHA Class II and III heart failure, and measured LVEF <35%;

7. Patients with non-ischemic dilated cardiomyopathy (NIDCM) >9 months, NYHA Class II and III heart failure, and measured LVEF <35%;

8. Patients who meet all current Centers for Medicare & Medicaid Services (CMS) coverage requirements for a cardiac resynchronization therapy (CRT) device and have NYHA Class IV heart failure;

All indications must meet the following criteria:

a. Patients must not have irreversible brain damage from preexisting cerebral disease;

b. MIs must be documented and defined according to the consensus document of the Joint European Society of Cardiology/American College of Cardiology Committee for the Redefinition of Myocardial Infarction[1];

Either one of the following criteria satisfies the diagnosis for an acute, evolving or recent MI:

1. Typical rise and gradual fall (troponin) or more rapid rise and fall (CK-MB) of biochemical markers of myocardial necrosis with at least one of the following:

    a. ischemic symptoms;

    b. development of pathologic Q waves on the ECG;

    c. ECG changes indicative of ischemia (ST segment elevation or depression); or

    d. coronary artery intervention (e.g., coronary angioplasty).

2. Pathologic findings of an acute MI.

Criteria for established MI.

Any one of the following criteria satisfies the diagnosis of established MI:

Indications 3-8 (primary prevention of sudden cardiac death) must also meet the following critera:

a. Patients must be able to give informed consent;

b. Patients must have:

   • Cardiogenic shock or symptomatic hypotension while in a stable baseline rhythm;

   • Had a CABG or PTCA within the past 3 months;

   • Had an acute MI within the past 40 days;

   • Clinical symptoms or findings that would make them a candidate for coronary revascularization;

   • Any disease, other than cardiac disease (e.g., cancer, uremia, liver failure), associated with a likelihood of survival less than 1 year;

c. Ejection fractions must be measured by angiography, radionuclide scanning, or echocardiography;

d. The beneficiary receiving the defibrillator implantation for primary prevention is enrolled in either a Food and Drug Administration (FDA)-approved category B investigational device exemption (IDE) clinical trial (42 CFR Sec.405.201), a trial under the CMS Clinical Trial Policy (National Coverage Determination (NCD) Manual Sec.310.1) or a qualifying data collection system including approved clinical trials and registries. Initially, an implantable cardiac defibrillator (ICD) database will be maintained using a data submission mechanism that is already in use by Medicare participating hospitals to submit data to the Iowa Foundation for Medical Care (IFMC)--a Quality Improvement Organization (QIO) contractor--for determination of reasonable and necessary and quality improvement. Initial hypothesis and data elements are specified in this decision (Appendix VI) and are the minimum necessary to ensure that the device is reasonable and necessary. Data collection will be completed using the ICDA (ICD Abstraction Tool) and transmitted via QNet (Quality Network Exchange) to the IFMC who will collect and maintain the database. Additional stakeholder-developed data collection systems to augment or replace the initial QNet system, addressing at a minimum the hypotheses specified in this decision, must meet the following basic criteria:

   • Written protocol on file;

      1) Development of new pathologic Q waves on serial ECGs. The patient may or may not remember previous symptoms. Biochemical markers of myocardial necrosis may have normalized, depending on the length of time that has passed since the infarct developed.

      2) Pathologic findings of a healed or healing MI.

         • Institutional review board review and approval;

         • Scientific review and approval by two or more qualified individuals who are not part of the research team;

         • Certification that investigators have not been disqualified.

e. For purposes of this coverage decision, CMS will determine whether specific registries or clinical trials meet these criteria.

f. Providers must be able to justify the medical necessity of devices other than single lead devices. This justification should be available in the patient's medical record.

9. Patients with NIDCM >3 months, NYHA Class II or III heart failure, and measured LVEF = 35%, only if the following additional criteria are also met:

a. Patients must be able to give informed consent;

b. Patients must not have:

   • Cardiogenic shock or symptomatic hypotension while in a stable baseline rhythm;

   • Had a CABG or PTCA within the past 3 months;

   • Had an acute MI within the past 40 days;

   • Clinical symptoms or findings that would make them a candidate for coronary revascularization;

   • Irreversible brain damage from preexisting cerebral disease;

   • Any disease, other than cardiac disease (e.g. cancer, uremia, liver failure), associated with a likelihood of survival less than 1 year;

c. Ejection fractions must be measured by angiography, radionuclide scanning, or echocardiography;

d. MIs must be documented and defined according to the consensus document of the Joint European Society of Cardiology/American College of Cardiology Committee for the Redefinition of Myocardial Infarction;[2]

e. The beneficiary receiving the defibrillator implantation for this indication is enrolled in either an FDA-approved category B IDE clinical trial (42 CFR §405.201), a trial under the CMS Clinical Trial Policy (NCD Manual §310.1), or a prospective data collection system meeting the following basic criteria:

   • Written protocol on file;

   • Institutional Review Board review and approval;

   • Scientific review and approval by two or more qualified individuals who are not part of the research team;

   • Certification that investigators have not been disqualified.

For purposes of this coverage decision, CMS will determine whether specific registries or clinical trials meet these criteria.

d. Providers must be able to justify the medical necessity of devices other than single lead devices. This justification should be available in the patient's medical record.

C. Other Indications

All other indications for implantable automatic defibrillators not currently covered in accordance with this decision will continue to be covered under Category B IDE trials (42 CFR §405.201) and the CMS routine clinical trials policy (NCD §310.1).

(This NCD last reviewed February 2005.)

100-3, 20.5

NCD for Extracorporeal Immunoadsorption (ECI) Using Protein A Columns (20.5)

For claims with dates of service on or after January 1, 2001, Medicare covers the use of Protein A columns for the treatment of ITP. In addition, Medicare will cover Protein A columns for the treatment of rheumatoid arthritis (RA) under the following conditions:

• Patient has severe RA. Patient disease is active, having >5 swollen joints, >20 tender joints, and morning stiffness >60 minutes.

• Patient has failed an adequate course of a minimum of 3 Disease Modifying Anti-Rheumatic Drugs (DMARDs). Failure does not include intolerance.

Other uses of these columns are currently considered to be investigational and, therefore, not reasonable and necessary under the Medicare law. (See Sec.1862(a)(1)(A) of the Act.)

100-3, 20.6

NCD for Transmyocardial Revascularization (TMR) (20.6)

CMS therefore covers TMR as a late or last resort for patients with severe (Canadian Cardiovascular Society classification Classes III or IV) angina (stable or unstable), which has been found refractory to standard medical therapy, including drug therapy at the maximum tolerated or maximum safe dosages. In addition, the angina symptoms must be caused by areas of the heart not amenable to surgical therapies such as percutaneous transluminal coronary angioplasty, stenting, coronary atherectomy or coronary bypass. Coverage is further limited to those uses of the laser used in performing the procedure which have been approved by the Food and Drug Administration for the purpose for which they are being used.

Patients would have to meet the following additional selection guidelines:

• An ejection fraction of 25% or greater;

• Have areas of viable ischemic myocardium (as demonstrated by diagnostic study) which are not capable of being revascularized by direct coronary intervention; and

• Have been stabilized, or have had maximal efforts to stabilize acute conditions such as severe ventricular arrhythmias, decompensated congestive heart failure or acute myocardial infarction.

---

1. Alpert and Thygesen et al., 2000. Criteria for acute, evolving or recent MI.

2. Ibid.

Coverage is limited to physicians who have been properly trained in the procedure. Providers of this service is performed must also document that all ancillary personnel, including physicians, nurses, operating room personnel and technicians, are trained in the procedure and the proper use of the equipment involved. Coverage is further limited to providers which have dedicated cardiac care units, including the diagnostic and support services necessary for care of patients undergoing this therapy. In addition, these providers must conform to the standards for laser safety set by the American National Standards Institute, ANSIZ1363.

100-3, 20.7

NCD for Percutaneous Transluminal Angioplasty (PTA) (20.7)

A. General

This procedure involves inserting a balloon catheter into a narrow or occluded blood vessel to recanalize and dilate the vessel by inflating the balloon. The objective of the procedure is to improve the blood flow through the diseased segment of a vessel so that vessel patency is increased and embolization is decreased. With the development and use of balloon angioplasty for treatment of atherosclerotic and other vascular stenoses, PTA (with and without the placement of a stent) is a widely used technique for dilating lesions of peripheral, renal, and coronary arteries.

Indications and Limitations of Coverage

B. Nationally Covered Indications

The PTA is covered when used under the following conditions:

1. Treatment of Atherosclerotic Obstructive Lesions

   In the lower extremities, i.e., the iliac, femoral, and popliteal arteries, or in the upper extremities, i.e., the innominate, subclavian, axillary, and brachial arteries. The upper extremities do not include head or neck vessels.

   Of a single coronary artery for patients for whom the likely alternative treatment is coronary bypass surgery and who exhibit the following characteristics:

   - Angina refractory to optimal medical management;
   - Objective evidence of myocardial ischemia; and
   - Lesions amenable to angioplasty.

   Of the renal arteries for patients in whom there is an inadequate response to a thorough medical management of symptoms and for whom surgery is the likely alternative. The PTA for this group of patients is an alternative to surgery, not simply an addition to medical management.

   Of arteriovenous dialysis fistulas and grafts when performed through either a venous or arterial approach.

2. Concurrent with Carotid Stent Placement Food and Drug Administration(FDA)-Approved Category B Investigational Device Exemption(IDE) Clinical Trials

   Effective July 1, 2001, Medicare covers PTA of the carotid artery concurrent with carotid stent placement when furnished in accordance with the Food and Drug Administration (FDA)-approved protocols governing Category B Investigational Device Exemption (IDE) clinical trials. The PTA of the carotid artery, when provided solely for the purpose of carotid artery dilation concurrent with carotid stent placement, is considered to be a reasonable and necessary service only when provided in the context of such a clinical trial.

3. Concurrent With Carotid Stent Placement in FDA-Approved Post Approval Studies

   Effective October 12, 2004, Medicare covers PTA of the carotid artery concurrent with the placement of an FDA-approved carotid stent for an FDA-approved indication when furnished in accordance with FDA-approved protocols governing post-approval studies. CMS determines that coverage of PTA of the carotid artery is reasonable and necessary under these circumstances.

4. Concurrent With Carotid Stent Placement in Patients at High Risk for Carotid Endarterectomy (CEA)

   Effective March 17, 2005, Medicare covers PTA of the carotid artery concurrent with the placement of an FDA-approved carotid stent with embolic protection for the following:

   - Patients who are at high risk for CEA and who also have symptomatic carotid artery stenosis >70 percent. Coverage is limited to procedures performed using FDA-approved carotid artery stenting systems and embolic protection devices;
   - Patients who are at high risk for CEA and have symptomatic carotid artery stenosis between 50 percent and 70 percent, in accordance with the Category B IDE clinical trials regulation (42 CFR 405.201), as a routine cost under the clinical trials policy (Medicare NCD Manual 310.1), or in accordance with the NCD on carotid artery stenting (CAS) post-approval studies (Medicare NCD Manual 20.7);
   - Patients who are at high risk for CEA and have asymptomatic carotid artery stenosis >80 percent, in accordance with the Category B IDE clinical trials regulation (42 CFR 405.201), as a routine cost under the clinical trials policy (Medicare NCD Manual 310.1), or in accordance with the NCD on CAS post-approval studies (Medicare NCD Manual 20.7).

Coverage is limited to procedures performed using FDA approved carotid artery stents and embolic protection devices.

The use of a distal embolic protection device is required. If deployment of the distal embolic protection device is not technically possible, then the procedure should be aborted given the risks of CAS without distal embolic protection.

Patients at high risk for CEA are defined as having significant comorbidities and/or anatomic risk factors (i.e., recurrent stenosis and/or previous radical neck dissection), and would be poor candidates for CEA. Significant comorbid conditions include but are not limited to:

- Congestive heart failure (CHF) class III/IV;
- Left ventricular ejection fraction (LVEF) < 30 percent;
- Unstable angina;
- Contralateral carotid occlusion;
- Recent myocardial infarction (MI);
- Previous CEA with recurrent stenosis;
- Prior radiation treatment to the neck; and
- Other conditions that were used to determine patients at high risk for CEA in the prior carotid artery stenting trials and studies, such as ARCHER, CABERNET, SAPPHIRE, BEACH, and MAVERIC II.

Symptoms of carotid artery stenosis include carotid transient ischemic attack (distinct focal neurological dysfunction persisting less than 24 hours), focal cerebral ischemia producing a non-disabling stroke (modified Rankin scale >3) shall be excluded from coverage.

The determination that a patient is at high risk for CEA and the patient's symptoms of carotid artery stenosis shall be available in the patient medical records prior to performing any procedure.

The degree of carotid artery stenosis shall be measured by duplex Doppler ultrasound or carotid artery angiography and recorded in the patient's medical records. If the stenosis is measured by ultrasound prior to the procedure, then the degree of stenosis must be

confirmed by angiography at the start of the procedure. If the stenosis is determined to be less than 70 percent by angiography, then CAS should not proceed.

In addition, CMS has determined that CAS with embolic protection is reasonable and necessary only if performed in facilities that have been determined to be competent in performing the evaluation, procedure and follow-up necessary to ensure optimal patient outcomes. Standards to determine competency include specific physician training standards, facility support requirements and data collection to evaluate outcomes during a required reevaluation.

The CMS has created a list of minimum standards modeled in part on professional society statements on competency. All facilities must at least meet CMS's standards in order to receive coverage for carotid artery stenting for high-risk patients.

- Facilities must have necessary imaging equipment, device inventory, staffing, and infrastructure to support a dedicated carotid stent program. Specifically, high-quality x-ray imaging equipment is a critical component of any carotid interventional suite, such as high-resolution digital imaging systems with the capability of subtraction, magnification, road mapping, and orthogonal angulation.
- Advanced physiologic monitoring must be available in the interventional suite. This includes real time and archived physiologic, hemodynamic, and cardiac rhythm monitoring equipment, as well as support staff who are capable of interpreting the findings and responding appropriately.
- Emergency management equipment and systems must be readily available in the interventional suite such as resuscitation equipment, a defibrillator, vasoactive and antiarrhythmic drugs, endotracheal intubation capability, and anesthesia support.
- Each institution shall have a clearly delineated program for granting carotid stent privileges and for monitoring the quality of the individual interventionalists and the program as a whole. The oversight committee for this program shall be empowered to identify the minimum case volume for an operator to maintain privileges, as well as the (risk-adjusted) threshold for complications that the institution will allow before suspending privileges or instituting measures for remediation. Committees are encouraged to apply published standards from national specialty societies recognized by the American Board of Medical Specialties to determine appropriate physician qualifications. Examples of standards and clinical competence guidelines include those published in the December 2004 edition of the American Journal of Neuroradiology, and those published in the August 18, 2004, Journal of the American College of Cardiology.
- To continue to receive Medicare payment for CAS under this decision, the facility or a contractor to the facility must collect data on all carotid artery stenting procedures done at that particular facility. This data must be analyzed routinely to ensure patient safety. This data must be made available to CMS upon request. The interval for data analysis will be determined by the facility but shall not be less frequent than every 6 months.

Since there currently is no recognized entity that evaluates CAS facilities, CMS has established a mechanism for evaluating facilities. Facilities must provide written documentation to CMS that the facility meets one of the following:

1. The facility was an FDA approved site that enrolled patients in prior CAS IDE trials, such as SAPPHIRE, and ARCHER;
2. The facility is an FDA approved site that is participating and enrolling patients in ongoing CAS IDE trials, such as CREST;
3. The facility is an FDA approved site for one or more FDA post approval studies; or
4. The facility has provided a written affidavit to CMS attesting that the facility has met the minimum facility standards. This should be sent to:

   Director, Coverage and Analysis Group
   7500 Security Boulevard, Mailstop C1-09-06
   Baltimore, MD 21244

The letter must include the following information:

- Facility's name and complete address;
- Facility's national provider identifier (formerly referred to as the Medicare provider number);
- Point-of-contact for questions with telephone number;
- Discussion of how each standard has been met by the hospital;

Appendix G — Pub 100 References

- Mechanism of data collection of CAS procedures; and
- Signature of a senior facility administrative official.

A list of certified facilities will be made available and viewable at: http://www.cms.hhs.gov/coverage/carotid-stent-facilities.asp. In addition, CMS will publish a list of approved facilities in the Federal Register.

Facilities must recertify every two (2) years in order to maintain Medicare coverage of CAS procedures. Recertification will occur when the facility documents that and describes how it continues to meet the CMS standards.

The process for recertification is as follows:

1. At 23 months after initial certification:
   - Submission of a letter to CMS stating how the facility continues to meet the minimum facility standards as listed above.
2. At 27 months after initial certification:
   - Submission of required data elements for all CAS procedures performed on patients during the previous two (2) years of certification.
   - Data elements:
     a. Patients' Medicare identification number if a Medicare beneficiary;
     b. Patients' date of birth;
     c. Date of procedure;
     d. Does the patient meet high surgical risk criteria (defined below)?
        - Age >80;
        - Recent (< 30 days) Myocardial Infarction (MI);
        - Left Ventricle Ejection Fraction (LVEF) < 30 percent;
        - Contralateral carotid occlusion;
        - New York Heart Association (NYHA) Class III or IV congestive heart failure;
        - Unstable angina: Canadian Cardiovascular Society (CCS) Class III/IV;
        - Renal failure: end stage renal disease on dialysis;
        - Common Carotid Artery (CCA) lesion(s) below clavicle;
        - Severe chronic lung disease;
        - Previous neck radiation;
        - High cervical Internal Carotid Artery (ICA) lesion(s);
        - Restenosis of prior carotid endarterectomy (CEA);
        - Tracheostomy;
        - Contralateral laryngeal nerve palsy.
     e. Is the patient symptomatic (defined below)?
        - Carotid Transient Ischemic Attack (TIA) persisting less than 24 hours;
        - Non-disabling stroke: Modified Rankin Scale
        - Transient monocular blindness: amaurosis fugax.
     f. Modified Rankin Scale score if the patient experienced a stroke.
     g. Percent stenosis of stented lesion(s) by angiography.
     h. Was embolic protection used?
     i. Were there any complications during hospitalization (defined below)?
        - All stroke: an ischemic neurologic deficit that persisted more than 24 hours;
        - MI;
        - All death.

Recertification is effective for two (2) additional years during which facilities will be required to submit the requested data every April 1 and October 1.

The CMS will consider the approval of national carotid artery stenting registries that provide CMS with a comprehensive overview of the registry and its capabilities, and the manner in which the registry meets CMS data collection and evaluation requirements. Specific standards for CMS approval are listed below. Facilities enrolled in a CMS approved national carotid artery stenting registry will automatically meet the data collection standards required for initial and continued facility certification. Hospitals' contracts with an approved registry may include authority for the registry to submit required data to CMS for the hospital. A list of approved registries will be available on the CMS Coverage Web Site.

National Registries

As noted above, CMS will approve national registries developed by professional societies and other organizations and allow these entities to collect and submit data to CMS on behalf of participating facilities to meet facility certification and recertification requirements. To be eligible to perform these functions and become a CMS approved registry, the national registry, at a minimum, must be able to:

1. Enroll facilities in every U.S. state and territory;
2. Assure data confidentiality and compliance with HIPPA;
3. Collect the required CMS data elements as listed in the above section;
4. Assure data quality and data completeness;
5. Address deficiencies in the facility data collection, quality, and submission;
6. Validate the data submitted by facilities as needed;
7. Track long term outcomes such as stroke and death;
8. Conduct data analyses and produce facility specific data reports and summaries;
9. Submit data to CMS on behalf of the individual facilities; and
10. Provide quarterly reports to CMS on facilities that do not meet or no longer meet the CMS facility certification and recertification requirements pertaining to data collection and analysis.

Registries wishing to receive this designation from CMS must submit evidence that they meet or exceed our standards. Though the registry requirements pertain to CAS, CMS strongly encourages all national registries to establish a similar mechanism to collect

comparable data on CEA. Having both CAS and CEA data will help answer questions about carotid revascularization, in general, in the Medicare population.

The CAS for patients who are not at high risk for CEA remains covered only in FDA-approved Category B IDE clinical trials under 42 CFR 405.201.

The CMS has determined that PTA of the carotid artery concurrent with the placement of an FDA-approved carotid stent is not reasonable and necessary for all other patients.

Concurrent with Intracranial Stent Placement in FDA-Approved Category B IDE Clinical Trials

Effective November 6, 2006, Medicare covers PTA and stenting of intracranial arteries for the treatment of cerebral artery stenosis >50 percent in patients with intracranial atherosclerotic disease when furnished in accordance with the FDA-approved protocols governing Category B IDE clinical trials. CMS determines that coverage of intracranial PTA and stenting is reasonable and necessary under these circumstances.

C. Nationally Non-covered Indications
All other indications for PTA with or without stenting to treat obstructive lesions of the vertebral and cerebral arteries remain non-covered. The safety and efficacy of these procedures are not established.

All other indications for PTA without stenting for which CMS has not specifically indicated coverage remain non-covered.

D. Other
Coverage of PTA with stenting not specifically addressed or discussed in this NCD is at local Medicare contractor discretion.

(This NCD last reviewed May 2008.)

100-3, 20.8

NCD for Cardiac Pacemakers (20.8)

Cardiac pacemakers are self-contained, battery-operated units that send electrical stimulation to the heart. They are generally implanted to alleviate symptoms of decreased cardiac output related to abnormal heart rate and/or rhythm. Pacemakers are generally used for persistent, symptomatic second- or third-degree atrioventricular (AV) block and symptomatic sinus bradycardia.

Cardiac pacemakers are covered as prosthetic devices under the Medicare program, subject to the following conditions and limitations. While cardiac pacemakers have been covered under Medicare for many years, there were no specific guidelines for their use other than the general Medicare requirement that covered services be reasonable and necessary for the treatment of the condition. Services rendered for cardiac pacing on or after the effective dates of this instruction are subject to these guidelines, which are based on certain assumptions regarding the clinical goals of cardiac pacing. While some uses of pacemakers are relatively certain or unambiguous, many other uses require considerable expertise and judgment.

Consequently, the medical necessity for permanent cardiac pacing must be viewed in the context of overall patient management. The appropriateness of such pacing may be conditional on other diagnostic or therapeutic modalities having been undertaken. Although significant complications and adverse side effects of pacemaker use are relatively rare, they cannot be ignored when considering the use of pacemakers for dubious medical conditions, or marginal clinical benefit.

These guidelines represent current concepts regarding medical circumstances in which permanent cardiac pacing may be appropriate or necessary. As with other areas of medicine, advances in knowledge and techniques in cardiology are expected. Consequently, judgments about the medical necessity and acceptability of new uses for cardiac pacing in new classes of patients may change as more more conclusive evidence becomes available. This instruction applies only to permanent cardiac pacemakers, and does not address the use of temporary, non-implanted pacemakers.

The two groups of conditions outlined below deal with the necessity for cardiac pacing for patients in general. These are intended as guidelines in assessing the medical necessity for pacing therapies, taking into account the particular circumstances in each case. However, as a general rule, the two groups of current medical concepts may be viewed as representing:

Group I: Single-Chamber Cardiac Pacemakers — a) conditions under which single chamber pacemaker claims may be considered covered without further claims development; and b) conditions under which single-chamber pacemaker claims would be denied unless further claims development shows that they fall into the covered category, or special medical circumstances exist of the sufficiency to convince the contractor that the claim should be paid.

Group II: Dual-Chamber Cardiac Pacemakers - a) conditions under which dual-chamber pacemaker claims may be considered covered without further claims development, and b) conditions under which dual-chamber pacemaker claims would be denied unless further claims development shows that they fall into the covered categories for single- and dual-chamber pacemakers, or special medical circumstances exist sufficient to convince the contractor that the claim should be paid.

The CMS opened the NCD on Cardiac Pacemakers to afford the public an opportunity to comment on the proposal to revise the language contained in the instruction. The revisions transfer the focus of the NCD from the actual pacemaker implantation procedure itself to the reasonable and necessary medical indications that justify cardiac

pacing. This is consistent with our findings that pacemaker implantation is no longer considered routinely harmful or an experimental procedure.

Group I: Single-Chamber Cardiac Pacemakers (Effective March 16, 1983)

A. Nationally Covered Indications
Conditions under which cardiac pacing is generally considered acceptable or necessary, provided that the conditions are chronic or recurrent and not due to transient causes such as acute myocardial infarction, drug toxicity, or electrolyte imbalance. (In cases where there is a rhythm disturbance, if the rhythm disturbance is chronic or recurrent, a single episode of a symptom such as syncope or seizure is adequate to establish medical necessity.)

1. Acquired complete (also referred to as third-degree) AV heart block.
2. Congenital complete heart block with severe bradycardia (in relation to age), or significant physiological deficits or significant symptoms due to the bradycardia.
3. Second-degree AV heart block of Type II (i.e., no progressive prolongation of P-R interval prior to each blocked beat. P-R interval indicates the time taken for an impulse to travel from the atria to the ventricles on an electrocardiogram).
4. Second-degree AV heart block of Type I (i.e., progressive prolongation of P-R interval prior to each blocked beat) with significant symptoms due to hemodynamic instability associated with the heart block.
5. Sinus bradycardia associated with major symptoms (e.g., syncope, seizures, congestive heart failure); or substantial sinus bradycardia (heart rate less than 50) associated with dizziness or confusion. The correlation between symptoms and bradycardia must be documented, or the symptoms must be clearly attributable to the bradycardia rather than to some other cause.
6. In selected and few patients, sinus bradycardia of lesser severity (heart rate 50-59) with dizziness or confusion. The correlation between symptoms and bradycardia must be documented, or the symptoms must be clearly attributable to the bradycardia rather than to some other cause.
7. Sinus bradycardia is the consequence of long-term necessary drug treatment for which there is no acceptable alternative when accompanied by significant symptoms (e.g., syncope, seizures, congestive heart failure, dizziness or confusion). The correlation between symptoms and bradycardia must be documented, or the symptoms must be clearly attributable to the bradycardia rather than to some other cause.
8. Sinus node dysfunction with or without tachyarrhythmias or AV conduction block (i.e., the bradycardia-tachycardia syndrome, sino-atrial block, sinus arrest) when accompanied by significant symptoms (e.g., syncope, seizures, congestive heart failure, dizziness or confusion).
9. Sinus node dysfunction with or without symptoms when there are potentially life-threatening ventricular arrhythmias or tachycardia secondary to the bradycardia (e.g., numerous premature ventricular contractions, couplets, runs of premature ventricular contractions, or ventricular tachycardia).
10. Bradycardia associated with supraventricular tachycardia (e.g., atrial fibrillation, atrial flutter, or paroxysmal atrial tachycardia) with high-degree AV block which is unresponsive to appropriate pharmacological management and when the bradycardia is associated with significant symptoms (e.g., syncope, seizures, congestive heart failure, dizziness or confusion).
11. The occasional patient with hypersensitive carotid sinus syndrome with syncope due to bradycardia and unresponsive to prophylactic medical measures.
12. Bifascicular or trifascicular block accompanied by syncope which is attributed to transient complete heart block after other plausible causes of syncope have been reasonably excluded.
13. Prophylactic pacemaker use following recovery from acute myocardial infarction during which there was temporary complete (third-degree) and/or Mobitz Type II second-degree AV block in association with bundle branch block.
14. In patients with recurrent and refractory ventricular tachycardia, "overdrive pacing" (pacing above the basal rate) to prevent ventricular tachycardia.

(Effective May 9, 1985)

15. Second-degree AV heart block of Type I with the QRS complexes prolonged.

B. Nationally Noncovered Indications
Conditions which, although used by some physicians as a basis for permanent cardiac pacing, are considered unsupported by adequate evidence of benefit and therefore should not generally be considered appropriate uses for single-chamber pacemakers in the absence of the above indications. Contractors should review claims for pacemakers with these indications to determine the need for further claims development prior to denying the claim, since additional claims development may be required. The object of such further development is to establish whether the particular claim actually meets the conditions in a) above. In claims where this is not the case or where such an event appears unlikely, the contractor may deny the claim

1 Syncope of undetermined cause.

2. Sinus bradycardia without significant symptoms.
3. Sino-atrial block or sinus arrest without significant symptoms.
4. Prolonged P-R intervals with atrial fibrillation (without third-degree AV block) or with other causes of transient ventricular pause.
5. Bradycardia during sleep.
6. Right bundle branch block with left axis deviation (and other forms of fascicular or bundle branch block) without syncope or other symptoms of intermittent AV block.
7. Asymptomatic second-degree AV block of Type I unless the QRS complexes are prolonged or electrophysiological studies have demonstrated that the block is at or beyond the level of the His bundle (a component of the electrical conduction system of the heart).

Effective October 1, 2001

8. Asymptomatic bradycardia in post-mycardial infarction patients about to initiate long-term beta-blocker drug therapy.

C. Other
All other indications for single-chamber cardiac pacing for which CMS has not specifically indicated coverage remain nationally noncovered, except for Category B Investigational Device Exemption (IDE) clinical trials, or as routine costs of single-chamber cardiac pacing associated with clinical trials, in accordance with section 310.1 of the NCD Manual.

Group II: Dual-Chamber Cardiac Pacemakers – (Effective May 9, 1985)

A. Nationally Covered Indications
Conditions under dual-chamber cardiac pacing are considered acceptable or necessary in the general medical community unless conditions 1 and 2 under Group II. B., are present:

1. Patients in who single-chamber (ventricular pacing) at the time of pacemaker insertion elicits a definite drop in blood pressure, retrograde conduction, or discomfort.
2. Patients in whom the pacemaker syndrome (atrial ventricular asynchrony), with significant symptoms, has already been experienced with a pacemaker that is being replaced.
3. Patients in whom even a relatively small increase in cardiac efficiency will importantly improve the quality of life, e.g., patients with congestive heart failure despite adequate other medical measures.
4. Patients in whom the pacemaker syndrome can be anticipated, e.g., in young and active people, etc.

Dual-chamber pacemakers may also be covered for the conditions, as listed in Group I. A., if the medical necessity is sufficiently justified through adequate claims development. Expert physicians differ in their judgments about what constitutes appropriate criteria for dual-chamber pacemaker use. The judgment that such a pacemaker is warranted in the patient meeting accepted criteria must be based upon the individual needs and characteristics of that patient, weighing the magnitude and likelihood of anticipated benefits against the magnitude and likelihood of disadvantages to the patient.

B. Nationally Noncovered Indications
Whenever the following conditions (which represent overriding contraindications) are present, dual-chamber pacemakers are not covered:

1. Ineffective atrial contractions (e.g., chronic atrial fibrillation or flutter, or giant left atrium).
2. Frequent or persistent supraventricular tachycardias, except where the pacemaker is specifically for the control of the tachycardia.
3. A clinical condition in which pacing takes place only intermittently and briefly, and which is not associated with a reasonable likelihood that pacing needs will become prolonged, e.g., the occasional patient with hypersensitive carotid sinus syndrome with syncope due to bradycardia and unresponsive to prophylactic medical measures.
4. Prophylactic pacemaker use following recovery from acute myocardial infarction during which there was temporary complete (third-degree) and/or Type II second-degree AV block in association with bundle branch block.

C. Other
All other indications for dual-chamber cardiac pacing for which CMS has not specifically indicated coverage remain nationally noncovered, except for Category B IDE clinical trials, or as routine costs of dual-chamber cardiac pacing associated with clinical trials, in accordance with section 310.1 of the NCD Manual.

(This NCD last reviewed June 2004.)

100-3, 20.8.1

NCD for Cardiac Pacemaker Evaluation Services (20.8.1)

Medicare covers a variety of services for the post-implant follow-up and evaluation of implanted cardiac pacemakers. The following guidelines are designed to assist contractors in identifying and processing claims for such services.

NOTE: These new guidelines are limited to lithium battery-powered pacemakers, because mercury-zinc battery-powered pacemakers are no longer being manufactured and virtually all have been replaced by lithium units. Contractors still receiving claims for monitoring such units should continue to apply the guidelines published in 1980 to those units until they are replaced.

One fact of which contractors should be aware is that many dual-chamber units may be programmed to pace only the ventricles; this may be done either at the time the pacemaker is implanted or at some time afterward. In such cases, a dual-chamber unit, when programmed or reprogrammed for ventricular pacing, should be treated as a single-chamber pacemaker in applying screening guidelines.

The decision as to how often any patient's pacemaker should be monitored is the responsibility of the patient's physician who is best able to take into account the condition and circumstances of the individual patient. These may vary over time, requiring modifications of the frequency with which the patient should be monitored. In cases where monitoring is done by some entity other than the patient's physician, such as a commercial monitoring service or hospital outpatient department, the physician's prescription for monitoring is required and should be periodically renewed (at least annually) to assure that the frequency of monitoring is proper for the patient. When a patient is monitered both during clinica visits and transtelephonically, the contractor should be sure to include frequency data on both ypes of monitoring in evaluating the reasonableness of the frequency of monitoring services received by the patient.

Since there are over 200 pacemaker models in service at any given point, and a variety of patient conditions that give rise to the need for pacemakers, the question of the appropriate frequency of monitorings is a complex one. Nevertheless, it is possible to develop guidelines within which the vast majority of pacemaker monitorings will fall and contractors should do this, using their own data and experience, as well as the frequency guidelines which follow, in order to limit extensive claims development to those cases requiring special attention.

100-3, 20.8.2
NCD for Self-Contained Pacemaker Monitors (20.8.2)
Self-contained pacemaker monitors are accepted devices for monitoring cardiac pacemakers. Accordingly, program payment may be made for the rental or purchase of either of the following pacemaker monitors when it is prescribed by a physician for a patient with a cardiac pacemaker:

A. Digital Electronic Pacemaker Monitor.
This device provides the patient with an instantaneous digital readout of his pacemaker pulse rate. Use of this device does not involve professional services until there has been a change of five pulses (or more) per minute above or below the initial rate of the pacemaker; when such change occurs, the patient contacts his physician.

B. Audible/Visible Signal Pacemaker Monitor.
This device produces an audible and visible signal which indicates the pacemaker rate. Use of this device does not involve professional services until a change occurs in these signals; at such time, the patient contacts his physician.

NOTE: The design of the self-contained pacemaker monitor makes it possible for the patient to monitor his pacemaker periodically and minimizes the need for regular visits to the outpatient department of the provider.

Therefore, documentation of the medical necessity for pacemaker evaluation in the outpatient department of the provider should be obtained where such evaluation is employed in addition to the self-contained pacemaker monitor used by the patient in his home.

100-3, 20.10
NCD for Cardiac Rehabilitation Programs (20.10)
A. General
Phase II cardiac rehabilitation, as described by the U.S. Public Health Service, is a comprehensive, long-term program including medical evaluation, prescribed exercise, cardiac risk factor modification, education, and counseling. Phase II refers to outpatient, medically supervised programs that are typically initiated 1-3 weeks after hospital discharge and provide appropriate electrocardiographic monitoring.

B. Nationally Covered Indications
Effective for services performed on or after March 22, 2006, Medicare coverage of cardiac rehabilitation programs is considered reasonable and necessary only for patients who: (1) have a documented diagnosis of acute myocardial infarction within the preceding 12 months; or (2) have had coronary bypass surgery; or (3) have stable angina pectoris; or (4) have had heart valve repair/replacement; or (5) have had percutaneous transluminal coronary angioplasty (PTCA) or coronary stenting; or (6) have had a heart or heart-lung transplant.

1. Program Requirements
   a. Duration

      Services provided in connection with a cardiac rehabilitation exercise program may be considered reasonable and necessary for up to 36 sessions. Patients generally receive 2 to 3 sessions per week for 12 to 18 weeks. Coverage of additional sessions is discussed in section D below.

   b. Components

      Cardiac rehabilitation programs must be comprehensive and to be comprehensive they must include a medical evaluation, a program to modify cardiac risk factors (e.g., nutritional counseling), prescribed exercise, education, and counseling.

   c. Facility

      The facility must have available for immediate use the necessary cardio-pulmonary, emergency, diagnostic, and therapeutic life-saving equipment accepted by the medical community as medically necessary, e.g., oxygen, cardiopulmonary resuscitation equipment, or defibrillator.

   d. Staff

      The program must be staffed by personnel necessary to conduct the program safely and effectively, who are trained in both basic and advanced life support techniques and in exercise therapy for coronary disease. The program must be under the direct supervision of a physician, as defined in 42 CFR Sec.410.26(a)(2) (defined through cross reference to 42 CFR Sec.410.32(b)(3)(ii), or 42 CFR Sec.410.27(f)).

C. Nationally Non-Covered Indications
Except as provided in section D., all other indications are not covered.

D. Other
The contractor has the discretion to cover cardiac rehabilitation services beyond 18 weeks. Coverage must not exceed a total of 72 sessions for 36 weeks.

(This NCD last reviewed March 2006.)

100-3, 20.11
NCD for Intraoperative Ventricular Mapping (20.11)
Intraoperative ventricular mapping is the technique of recording cardiac electrical activity directly from the heart. The recording sites are usually identified from an anatomical grid and may consist of epicardial, intramural, and endocardial sites. A probe with electrodes is used to explore these surfaces and generate a map that displays the sequence of electrical activation. This information is used by the surgeon to locate precisely the site of an operative intervention.

The intraoperative ventricular mapping procedure is covered under Medicare only for the uses and medical conditions described below:

- Localize accessory pathways associated with the Wolff-Parkinson-White (WPW) and other preexcitation syndromes;
- Map the sequence of atrial and ventricular activation for drug-resistant supraventricular tachycardias;
- Delineate the anatomical course of His bundle and/or bundle branches during corrective cardiac surgery for congenital heart diseases; and
- Direct the surgical treatment of patients with refractory ventricular tachyarrhythmias.

100-3, 20.12
NCD for Diagnostic Endocardial Electrical Stimulation (Pacing) (20.12)
Diagnostic endocardial electrical stimulation (EES), also called programmed electrical stimulation of the heart, is covered under Medicare when used for patients with severe cardiac arrhythmias.

100-3, 20.13
NCD for HIS Bundle Study (20.13)
Medicare coverage of the procedure would be limited to selected patients: those with complex ongoing acute arrhythmias, those with intermittent or permanent heart block in whom pacemaker implantation is being considered, and those patients who have recently developed heart block secondary to a myocardial infarction. When heart catheterization and the HIS Bundle Study are performed at the same time, the program will cover only one catheterization and a small additional charge for the study.

When a HIS bundle cardiogram is obtained as part of a diagnostic endocardial electrical stimulation, no separate charge will be recognized for the His bundle study.

100-3, 20.14
NCD for Plethysmography (20.14)
Medicare coverage is extended to those procedures listed in Category I below when used for the accepted medical indications mentioned above. The procedures in Category II are still considered experimental and are not covered at this time. Denial of claims because a noncovered procedure was used or because there was no medical indication for plethysmographic evaluation of any type should be based on Sec.1862(a)(1) of the Act.

Category I - Covered
Segmental Plethysmography - Included under this procedure are services performed with a regional plethysmograph, differential plethysmograph, recording oscillometer, and a pulse volume recorder.

Electrical Impedance Plethysmography

Ultrasonic Measurement of Blood Flow (Doppler) - While not strictly a plethysmographic method, this is also a useful tool in the evaluation of suspected peripheral vascular disease or preoperative screening of podiatric patients with suspected peripheral vascular compromise. (See Sec.50-7 for the applicable coverage policy on this procedure.)

Oculoplethysmography - See NCD on Noninvasive Tests of Carotid Function, Sec.20.17.

Strain Gauge Plethysmography - This test is based on recording the non-pulsatile aspects of inflowing blood at various points on an extremity by a mercury-in-silastic strain gauge sensor. The instrument consists of a chart recorder, an automatic cuff inflation and deflation system, and a recording manometer.

Category II - Experimental
The following methods have not yet reached a level of development such as to allow their routine use in the evaluation of suspected peripheral vascular disease.

Inductance Plethysmography - This method is considered experimental and does not provide reproducible results.

Capacitance Plethysmography - This method is considered experimental and does not provide reproducible results.

Mechanical Oscillometry - This is a non-standardized method which offers poor sensitivity and is not considered superior to the simple measurement of peripheral blood pressure.

Photoelectric Plethysmography - This method is considered useful only in determining whether or not a pulse is present and does not provide reproducible measurements of blood flow.

Differential plethysmography, on the other hand, is a system which uses an impedance technique to compare pulse pressures at various points along a limb, with a reference pressure at the mid-brachial or wrist level. It is not clear whether this technique, as usually performed in the physician's office, meets the definition of plethysmography because quantitative measurements of blood flow are usually not made. It has been concluded, in any event, that the differential plethysmography system is a blood pulse recorder of undetermined value, which has the potential for significant overutilization. Therefore, reimbursement for studies done by techniques other than venous occlusive pneumoplethysmography should be denied, at least until additional data on these devices, including controlled clinical studies, become available.

100-3, 20.15
NCD for Electrocardiographic (EKG) Services (20.15)
Nationally Covered Indications

The following indications are covered nationally unless otherwise indicated:

1. Computer analysis of EKGs when furnished in a setting and under the circumstances required for coverage of other EKG services.
2. EKG services rendered by an independent diagnostic testing facility (IDTF), including physician review and interpretation. Separate physician services are not covered unless he/she is the patient's attending or consulting physician.
3. Emergency EKGs (i.e., when the patient is or may be experiencing a lifethreatening event) performed as a laboratory or diagnostic service by a portable x-ray supplier only when a physician is in attendance at the time the service is performed or immediately thereafter.
4. Home EKG services with documentation of medical necessity.
5. Trans-telephonic EKG transmissions (effective March 1, 1980) as a diagnostic service for the indications described below, when performed with equipment meeting the standards described below, subject to the limitations and conditions specified below. Coverage is further limited to the amounts payable with respect to the physician's service in interpreting the results of such transmissions, including charges for rental of the equipment. The device used by the beneficiary is part of a total diagnostic system and is not considered DME separately. Covered uses are to:
   a. Detect, characterize, and document symptomatic transient arrhythmias;
   b. Initiate, revise, or discontinue arrhythmic drug therapy; or,
   c. Carry out early post-hospital monitoring of patients discharged after myocardial infarction (MI); (only if 24-hour coverage is provided, see C.5. below).

   Certain uses other than those specified above may be covered if, in the judgment of the local contractor, such use is medically necessary.

   Additionally, the transmitting devices must meet at least the following criteria:
   a. They must be capable of transmitting EKG Leads, I, II, or III; and,
   b. The tracing must be sufficiently comparable to a conventional EKG.

24-hour attended coverage used as early post-hospital monitoring of patients discharged after MI is only covered if provision is made for such 24-hour attended coverage in the manner described below:

24-hour attended coverage means there must be, at a monitoring site or central data center, an EKG technician or other non-physician, receiving calls and/or EKG data; tape recording devices do not meet this requirement. Further, such technicians should have immediate, 24-hour access to a physician to review transmitted data and make clinical decisions regarding the patient. The technician should also be instructed as to when and how to contact available facilities to assist the patient in case of emergencies.

C. Nationally Non-covered Indications
The following indications are non-covered nationally unless otherwise specified below:

1. The time-sampling mode of operation of ambulatory EKG cardiac event monitoring/recording.
2. Separate physician services other than those rendered by an IDTF unless rendered by the patient's attending or consulting physician.
3. Home EKG services without documentation of medical necessity.
4. Emergency EKG services by a portable x-ray supplier without a physician in attendance at the time of service or immediately thereafter.
5. 24-hour attended coverage used as early post-hospital monitoring of patients discharged after MI unless provision is made for such 24-hour attended coverage in the manner described in section B.5. above.
6. Any marketed Food and Drug Administration (FDA)-approved ambulatory cardiac monitoring device or service that cannot be categorized according to the framework below.

D. Other
Ambulatory cardiac monitoring performed with a marketed, FDA-approved device, is eligible for coverage if it can be categorized according to the framework below. Unless there is a specific NCD for that device or service, determination as to whether a device or service that fits into the framework is reasonable and necessary is according to local contractor discretion.

Electrocardiographic Services Framework

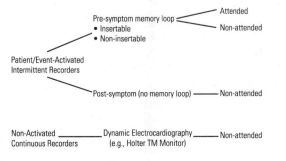

(This NCD last reviewed December 2004.)

100-3, 20.16
NCD for Cardiac Output Monitoring by Thoracic Electrical Bioimpedance (TEB) (20.16)

Indications and Limitations of Coverage

B. Nationally Covered Indications
Effective for services performed on and after January 23, 2004, TEB is covered for the following uses:

1. Differentiation of cardiogenic from pulmonary causes of acute dyspnea when medical history, physical examination, and standard assessment tools provide insufficient information, and the treating physician has determined that TEB hemodynamic data are necessary for appropriate management of the patient.
2. Optimization of atrioventricular (A/V) interval for patients with A/V sequential cardiac pacemakers when medical history, physical examination, and standard assessment tools provide insufficient information, and the treating physician has determined that TEB hemodynamic data are necessary for appropriate management of the patient.
3. Monitoring of continuous inotropic therapy for patients with terminal congestive heart failure, when those patients have chosen to die with comfort at home, or for patients waiting at home for a heart transplant.
4. Evaluation for rejection in patients with a heart transplant as a predetermined alternative to a myocardial biopsy. Medical necessity must be documented should a biopsy be performed after TEB.
5. Optimization of fluid management in patients with congestive heart failure when medical history, physical examination, and standard assessment tools provide insufficient information, and the treating physician has determined that TEB hemodynamic data are necessary for appropriate management of the patient.

C. Nationally Non-Covered Indications
1. TEB is non-covered when used for patients:
   - With proven or suspected disease involving severe regurgitation of the aorta;
   - With minute ventilation (MV) sensor function pacemakers, since the device may adversely affect the functioning of that type of pacemaker;
   - During cardiac bypass surgery; or,
   - In the management of all forms of hypertension (with the exception of drug-resistant hypertension as outlined below).
2. All other uses of TEB not otherwise specified remain non-covered.

D. Other
Contractors have discretion to determine whether the use of TEB for the management of drug-resistant hypertension is reasonable and necessary. Drug resistant hypertension is defined as failure to achieve goal blood pressure in patients who are adhering to full doses of an appropriate 3-drug regimen that includes a diuretic. Effective November 24, 2006, after reconsideration of Medicare policy, CMS will continue current Medicare policy for TEB.

(This NCD last reviewed November 2006.)

100-3, 20.17
NCD for Noninvasive Tests of Carotid Function (20.17)

It is important to note that the names of these tests are not standardized. Following are some of the acceptable tests, recognizing that this list is not inclusive and that local medical consultants should make determinations:

Direct Tests
- Carotid Phonoangiography
- Direct Bruit Analysis
- Spectral Bruit Analysis
- Doppler Flow Velocity
- Ultrasound Imaging including Real Time
- B-Scan and Doppler Devices

Indirect Tests
- Periorbital Directional Doppler Ultrasonography
- Oculoplethysmography
- Ophthalmodynamometry

100-3, 20.18
NCD for Carotid Body Resection/Carotid Body Denervation (20.18)

Carotid body resection is occasionally used to relieve pulmonary symptoms, including asthma, but has been shown to lack general acceptance of the professional medical community. In addition, controlled clinical studies establishing the safety and effectiveness of this procedure are needed. Therefore, all carotid body resections to relieve pulmonary symptoms must be considered investigational and cannot be considered reasonable and necessary within the meaning of section 1862(a)(l) of the law. No program reimbursement may be made in such cases.

There is, however, one instance where carotid body resection has been accepted by the medical community as effective. That instance is when evidence of a mass in the carotid body, with or without symptoms, indicates the need for surgery to remove the carotid body tumor.

Denervation of a carotid sinus to treat hypersensitive carotid sinus reflex is another procedure performed in the area of the carotid body. In the case of hypersensitive carotid sinus, light pressure on the upper part of the neck (such as might be experienced when turning or raising one's head) results in symptoms such as dizziness or syncope due to hypotension and slowed heart rate. Failure of medical therapy and continued deterioration in the condition of the patient in such cases may indicate need for surgery. Denervation of the carotid sinus is rarely performed, but when elected as the therapy of choice with the above indications, this procedure may be considered reasonable and necessary.

100-3, 20.19
NCD for Ambulatory Blood Pressure Monitoring (20.19)

ABPM must be performed for at least 24 hours to meet coverage criteria.

ABPM is only covered for those patients with suspected white coat hypertension. Suspected white coat hypertension is defined as

1) office blood pressure >140/90 mm Hg on at least three separate clinic/office visits with two separate measurements made at each visit;
2) at least two documented blood pressure measurements taken outside the office which are <140/90 mm Hg; and
3) no evidence of end-organ damage.

The information obtained by ABPM is necessary in order to determine the appropriate management of the patient. ABPM is not covered for any other uses. In the rare circumstance that ABPM needs to be performed more than once in a patient, the qualifying criteria described above must be met for each subsequent ABPM test.

For those patients that undergo ABPM and have an ambulatory blood pressure of <135/85 with no evidence of end-organ damage, it is likely that their cardiovascular risk is similar to that of normotensives. They should be followed over time. Patients for which ABPM demonstrates a blood pressure of >135/85 may be at increased cardiovascular risk, and a physician may wish to consider antihypertensive therapy.

100-3, 20.23
NCD for Fabric Wrapping of Abdominal Aneurysms (20.23)

Fabric wrapping of abdominal aneurysms is not a covered Medicare procedure. This is a treatment for abdominal aneurysms which involves wrapping aneurysms with cellophane or fascia lata. This procedure has not been shown to prevent eventual rupture. In extremely rare instances, external wall reinforcement may be indicated when the current accepted treatment (excision of the aneurysm and reconstruction with synthetic materials) is not a viable alternative, but external wall reinforcement is not fabric wrapping. Accordingly, fabric wrapping of abdominal aneurysms is not considered reasonable and necessary within the meaning of Sec.1862(a)(1) of the Act.

100-3, 20.25
NCD for Cardiac Catheterization Performed in Other than a Hospital Setting (20.25)
(Effective January 12, 2006 - Repealed)

100-3, 20.26
NCD for Partial Ventriculectomy (20.26)

Since the mortality rate is high and there are no published scientific articles or clinical studies regarding partial ventriculectomy, this procedure cannot be considered reasonable and necessary within the meaning of Sec.1862(a)(1) of the Act. Therefore, partial ventriculectomy is not covered by Medicare.

100-3, 20.28
NCD for Therapeutic Embolization (20.28)

Therapeutic embolization is covered when done for hemorrhage, and for other conditions amenable to treatment by the procedure, when reasonable and necessary for the individual patient. Renal embolization for the treatment of renal adenocarcinoma continues to be covered, effective December 15, 1978, as one type of therapeutic embolization, to:

- Reduce tumor vascularity preoperatively;
- Reduce tumor bulk in inoperable cases; or
- Palliate specific symptoms.

100-3, 20.29
NCD for Hyperbaric Oxygen Therapy (20.29)
A. Covered Conditions

Program reimbursement for HBO therapy will be limited to that which is administered in a chamber (including the one man unit) and is limited to the following conditions:

1. Acute carbon monoxide intoxication,
2. Decompression illness,
3. Gas embolism,
4. Gas gangrene,
5. Acute traumatic peripheral ischemia. HBO therapy is a valuable adjunctive treatment to be used in combination with accepted standard therapeutic measures when loss of function, limb, or life is threatened.
6. Crush injuries and suturing of severed limbs. As in the previous conditions, HBO therapy would be an adjunctive treatment when loss of function, limb, or life is threatened.
7. Progressive necrotizing infections (necrotizing fasciitis),
8. Acute peripheral arterial insufficiency,
9. Preparation and preservation of compromised skin grafts (not for primary management of wounds),
10. Chronic refractory osteomyelitis, unresponsive to conventional medical and surgical management,
11. Osteoradionecrosis as an adjunct to conventional treatment,
12. Soft tissue radionecrosis as an adjunct to conventional treatment,
13. Cyanide poisoning,
14. Actinomycosis, only as an adjunct to conventional therapy when the disease process is refractory to antibiotics and surgical treatment,
15. Diabetic wounds of the lower extremities in patients who meet the following three criteria:
    a. Patient has type I or type II diabetes and has a lower extremity wound that is due to diabetes;
    b. Patient has a wound classified as Wagner grade III or higher; and
    c. Patient has failed an adequate course of standard wound therapy.

The use of HBO therapy is covered as adjunctive therapy only after there are no measurable signs of healing for at least 30-days of treatment with standard wound therapy and must be used in addition to standard wound care. Standard wound care in patients with diabetic wounds includes: assessment of a patient's vascular status and correction of any vascular problems in the affected limb if possible, optimization of nutritional status, optimization of glucose control, debridement by any means to remove devitalized tissue, maintenance of a clean, moist bed of granulation tissue with appropriate moist dressings, appropriate off-loading, and necessary treatment to resolve any infection that might be present. Failure to respond to standard wound care occurs when there are no measurable signs of healing for at least 30 consecutive days. Wounds must be evaluated at least every 30 days during administration of HBO therapy. Continued treatment with HBO therapy is not covered if measurable signs of healing have not been demonstrated within any 30-day period of treatment.

B. Noncovered Conditions

All other indications not specified under Sec.270.4(A) are not covered under the Medicare program. No program payment may be made for any conditions other than those listed in Sec.270.4(A).

No program payment may be made for HBO in the treatment of the following conditions:

1. Cutaneous, decubitus, and stasis ulcers.
2. Chronic peripheral vascular insufficiency.
3. Anaerobic septicemia and infection other than clostridial.
4. Skin burns (thermal).
5. Senility.
6. Myocardial infarction.
7. Cardiogenic shock.
8. Sickle cell anemia.
9. Acute thermal and chemical pulmonary damage, i.e., smoke inhalation with pulmonary insufficiency.
10. Acute or chronic cerebral vascular insufficiency.
11. Hepatic necrosis.
12. Aerobic septicemia.
13. Nonvascular causes of chronic brain syndrome (Pick's disease, Alzheimer's disease, Korsakoff's disease).
14. Tetanus.
15. Systemic aerobic infection.
16. Organ transplantation.
17. Organ storage.
18. Pulmonary emphysema.
19. Exceptional blood loss anemia.
20. Multiple Sclerosis.
21. Arthritic Diseases.
22. Acute cerebral edema.

C. Topical Application of Oxygen

This method of administering oxygen does not meet the definition of HBO therapy as stated above. Also, its clinical efficacy has not been established. Therefore, no Medicare reimbursement may be made for the topical application of oxygen.

100-3, 20.30
NCD for Microvolt T-Wave Alternans (MTWA) (20.30)

B. Nationally Covered Indications
Microvolt T-wave Alternans diagnostic testing is covered for the evaluation of patients at risk for SCD, only when the spectral analysis method is used.

C. Nationally Non-Covered Indications
Microvolt T-wave Alternans diagnostic test is non-covered for the evaluation of patients at risk for SCD if measurement is not performed employing the spectral analysis.

D. Other
N/A

100-3, 30.1
NCD for Biofeedback Therapy (30.1)
Biofeedback therapy is covered under Medicare only when it is reasonable and necessary for the individual patient for muscle re-education of specific muscle groups or for treating pathological muscle abnormalities of spasticity, incapacitating muscle spasm, or weakness, and more conventional treatments (heat, cold, massage, exercise, support) have not been successful. This therapy is not covered for treatment of ordinary muscle tension states or for psychosomatic conditions. (See the Medicare Benefit Policy Manual, Chapter 15, for general coverage requirements about physical therapy requirements.)

100-3, 30.1.1
NCD for Biofeedback Therapy for the Treatment of Urinary Incontinence (30.1.1)
This policy applies to biofeedback therapy rendered by a practitioner in an office or other facility setting.

Biofeedback is covered for the treatment of stress and/or urge incontinence in cognitively intact patients who have failed a documented trial of pelvic muscle exercise (PME)training. Biofeedback is not a treatment, per se, but a tool to help patients learn how to perform PME. Biofeedback-assisted PME incorporates the use of an electronic or mechanical device to relay visual and/or auditory evidence of pelvic floor muscle tone, in order to improve awareness of pelvic floor musculature and to assist patients in the performance of PME.

A failed trial of PME training is defined as no clinically significant improvement in urinary incontinence after completing 4 weeks of an ordered plan of pelvic muscle exercises to increase periurethral muscle strength.

Contractors may decide whether or not to cover biofeedback as an initial treatment modality.

Home use of biofeedback therapy is not covered.

100-3, 30.5
NCD for Transcendental Meditation (TM) (30.5)
After review of this issue, CMS has concluded that the evidence concerning the medical efficacy of TM is incomplete at best and does not demonstrate effectiveness and that a professional level of skill is not required for the training of patients to engage in TM.

Although many articles have been written about application of TM for patients with certain forms of hypertension and anxiety, there are no rigorous scientific studies that demonstrate the effectiveness of TM for use as an adjunct medical therapy for such conditions. Accordingly, neither TM nor the training of patients for its use are covered under the Medicare program.

100-3, 30.6
NCD for Intravenous Histamine Therapy (30.6)
However, there is no scientifically valid clinical evidence that histamine therapy is effective for any condition regardless of the method of administration, nor is it accepted or widely used by the medical profession. Therefore, histamine therapy cannot be considered reasonable and necessary, and program payment for such therapy is not made.

100-3, 40.1
NCD for Diabetes Outpatient Self-Management Training (40.1)
Please refer to 42 CFR 410.140 - 410.146 for conditions that must be met for Medicare coverage.

100-3, 40.5
NCD for Treatment of Obesity (40.5)
B. Nationally Covered Indications

Certain designated surgical services for the treatment of obesity are covered for Medicare beneficiaries who have a BMI >=35, have at least one co-morbidity related to obesity and have been previously unsuccessful with the medical treatment of obesity. See Sec.100.1.

C. Nationally Noncovered Indications

1. Treatments for obesity alone remain non-covered.
2. Supplemented fasting is not covered under the Medicare program as a general treatment for obesity (see section D. below for discretionary local coverage).

D. Other

Where weight loss is necessary before surgery in order to ameliorate the complications posed by obesity when it coexists with pathological conditions such as cardiac and respiratory diseases, diabetes, or hypertension (and other more conservative techniques to achieve this end are not regarded as appropriate), supplemented fasting with adequate monitoring of the patient is eligible for coverage on a case-by-case basis or pursuant to a local coverage determination. The risks associated with the achievement of rapid weight loss must be carefully balanced against the risk posed by the condition requiring surgical treatment.

(This NCD last reviewed February 2006.)

100-3, 50.1
NCD for Speech Generating Devices (50.1)
Effective January 1, 2001, augmentative and alternative communication devices or communicators, which are hereafter referred to as "speech generating devices" are now considered to fall within the DME benefit category established by Sec.1861(n) of the Act. They may be covered if the contractor's medical staff determines that the patient suffers from a severe speech impairment and that the medical condition warrants the use of a device based on the definitions above.

100-3, 50.2
NCD for Electronic Speech Aids (50.2)
Electronic speech aids are covered under Part B as prosthetic devices when the patient has had a laryngectomy or his larynx is permanently inoperative.

100-3, 50.3
NCD for Cochlear Implantation (50.3)
B. Nationally Covered Indications

1. Effective for services performed on or after April 4, 2005, cochlear implantation may be covered for treatment of bilateral pre- or post-linguistic, sensorineural, moderate-to-profound hearing loss in individuals who demonstrate limited benefit from amplification. Limited benefit from amplification is defined by test scores of less than or equal to 40% correct in the best-aided listening condition on tape-recorded tests of open-set sentence cognition. Medicare coverage is provided only for those patients who meet all of the following selection guidelines.

   - Diagnosis of bilateral moderate-to-profound sensorineural hearing impairment with limited benefit from appropriate hearing (or vibrotactile) aids;
   - Cognitive ability to use auditory clues and a willingness to undergo an extended program of rehabilitation;
   - Freedom from middle ear infection, an accessible cochlear lumen that is structurally suited to implantation, and freedom from lesions in the auditory nerve and acoustic areas of the central nervous system;
   - No contraindications to surgery; and
   - The device must be used in accordance with Food and Drug Administration (FDA)-approved labeling.

2. Effective for services performed on or after April 4, 2005, cochlear implantation may be covered for individuals meeting the selection guidelines above and with hearing test scores of greater than 40% and less than or equal to 60% only when the provider is participating in, and patients are enrolled in, either an FDA-approved category B investigational device exemption clinical trial as defined at 42 CFR 405.201, a trial under the Centers for Medicare & Medicaid (CMS) Clinical Trial Policy as defined at section 310.1 of the National Coverage Determinations Manual, or a prospective, controlled comparative trial approved by CMS as consistent with the evidentiary requirements for National Coverage Analyses and meeting specific quality standards.

C. Nationally Noncovered Indications

Medicare beneficiaries not meeting all of the coverage criteria for cochlear implantation listed are deemed not eligible for Medicare coverage under section 1862(a)(1)(A) of the Social Security Act.

D. Other

All other indications for cochlear implantation not otherwise indicated as nationally covered or non-covered above remain at local contractor discretion.

(This NCD last reviewed May 2005.)

100-3, 70.1
NCD for Consultations with a Beneficiary's Family and Associates (70.1)
In certain types of medical conditions, including when a patient is withdrawn and uncommunicative due to a mental disorder or comatose, the physician may contact relatives and close associates to secure background information to assist in diagnosis and treatment planning. When a physician contacts his patient's relatives or associates for this purpose, expenses of such interviews are properly chargeable as physician's services to the patient on whose behalf the information was secured. If the beneficiary is not an inpatient of a hospital, Part B reimbursement for such an interview is subject to the special limitation on payments for physicians' services in connection with mental, psychoneurotic, and personality disorders.

A physician may also have contacts with a patient's family and associates for purposes other than securing background information. In some cases, the physician will provide counseling to members of the household. Family counseling services are covered only where the primary purpose of such counseling is the treatment of the patient's condition. For example, two situations where family counseling services would be appropriate are as follows: (1) where there is a need to observe the patient's interaction with family members; and/or (2) where there is a need to assess the capability of and assist the family members in aiding in the management of the patient. Counseling principally concerned with the effects of the patient's condition on the individual being interviewed would not be reimbursable as part of the physician's personal services to the patient. While to a limited degree, the counseling described in the second situation may be used to modify the behavior of the family members, such services nevertheless are covered because they relate primarily to the management of the patient's problems and not to the treatment of the family member's problems.

100-3, 70.2
NCD for Consultation Services Rendered by a Podiatrist in a Skilled Nursing Facility (70.2)
Consultation services rendered by a podiatrist in a skilled nursing facility are covered if the services are reasonable and necessary and do not come within any of the specific statutory exclusions. Section 1862(a)(13) of the Act excludes payment for the treatment of flat foot conditions, the treatment of subluxations of the foot, and routine foot care. To determine whether the consultation comes within the foot care exclusions, apply the same rule as for initial diagnostic examinations, i.e., where services are performed in connection with specific symptoms or complaints which suggest the need for covered services, the services are covered regardless of the resulting diagnosis. The exclusion of routine physician examinations is also

Appendix G — Pub 100 References

pertinent and would generally exclude podiatric consultation performed on all patients in a skilled nursing facility on a routine basis for screening purposes, except in those cases where a specific foot ailment is involved. Section 1862(a)(7) of the Act excludes payment for routine physical checkups.

100-3, 70.2.1
NCD for Services Provided for the Diagnosis and Treatment of Diabetic Sensory Neuropathy with Loss of Protective Sensation (AKA Diabetic Peripheral Neuropathy) (70.2.1)

Diabetic sensory neuropathy with LOPS is a localized illness of the feet and falls within the regulation's exception to the general exclusionary rule (see 42 CFR Sec.411.15(I)(1)(i)). Foot exams for people with diabetic sensory neuropathy with LOPS are reasonable and necessary to allow for early intervention in serious complications that typically afflict diabetics with the disease.

Effective for services furnished on or after July 1, 2002, Medicare covers, as a physician service, an evaluation (examination and treatment) of the feet no more often than every six months for individuals with a documented diagnosis of diabetic sensory neuropathy and LOPS, as long as the beneficiary has not seen a foot care specialist for some other reason in the interim. LOPS shall be diagnosed through sensory testing with the 5.07 monofilament using established guidelines, such as those developed by the National Institute of Diabetes and Digestive and Kidney Diseases guidelines. Five sites should be tested on the plantar surface of each foot, according to the National Institute of Diabetes and Digestive and Kidney Diseases guidelines. The areas must be tested randomly since the loss of protective sensation may be patchy in distribution, and the patient may get clues if the test is done rhythmically. Heavily callused areas should be avoided. As suggested by the American Podiatric Medicine Association, an absence of sensation at two or more sites out of 5 tested on either foot when tested with the 5.07 Semmes-Weinstein monofilament must be present and documented to diagnose peripheral neuropathy with loss of protective sensation.

The examination includes:

1. A patient history.
2. A physical examination that must consist of at least the following elements:
   - Visual inspection of forefoot and hindfoot (including toe web spaces).
   - Evaluation of protective sensation.
   - Evaluation of foot structure and biomechanics.
   - Evaluation of vascular status and skin integrity.
   - Evaluation of the need for special footwear.
3. Patient education.

A. Treatment includes, but is not limited to:

- Local care of superficial wounds.
- Debridement of corns and calluses.
- Trimming and debridement of nails.

The diagnosis of diabetic sensory neuropathy with LOPS should be established and documented prior to coverage of foot care. Other causes of peripheral neuropathy should be considered and investigated by the primary care physician prior to initiating or referring for foot care for persons with LOPS.

100-3, 80.1
NCD for Hydrophilic Contact Lens For Corneal Bandage (80.1)

Payment may be made under Sec.1861(s)(2) of the Act for a hydrophilic contact les approved by the Food and Drug Administration (FDA) and used as a supply incident to a pphysician's service. Payment for the lens is included in the payment for the physician's service to which the lens is incident. Contractors are authorized to accept an FDA letter of approval or other FDA published material as evidence of FDA approval. (See Sec.80.4 of the NCD Manual for coverage of a hydrophilic contact lens as prosthetic device.)

100-3, 80.2
Photodynamic Therapy
(Rev. 1, 10-03-03)

CIM 35-100

Photodynamic therapy is a medical procedure which involves the infusion of a photosensitive (light-activated) drug with a very specific absorption peak. This drug is chemically designed to have a unique affinity for the diseased tissue intended for treatment. Once introduced to the body, the drug accumulates and is retained in diseased tissue to a greater degree than in normal tissue. Infusion is followed by the targeted irradiation of this tissue with a non-thermal laser, calibrated to emit light at a wavelength that corresponds to the drug's absorption peak. The drug then becomes active and locally treats the diseased tissue.

Ocular photodynamic therapy (OPT)

The OPT is used in the treatment of ophthalmologic diseases. OPT is only covered when used in conjunction with verteporfin (see §80.3, "Photosensitive Drugs").

- Classic Subfoveal Choroidal Neovascular (CNV) Lesions - OPT is covered with a diagnosis of neovascular age-related macular degeneration (AMD) with predominately classic subfoveal choroidal neovascular (CNV) lesions (where the area of classic CNV occupies ≥ 50 percent of the area of the entire lesion) at the initial visit as determined by a fluorescein angiogram. Subsequent follow-up visits will require a fluorescein angiogram prior to treatment. There are no requirements regarding visual acuity, lesion size, and number of re-treatments.

- Occult Subfoveal Choroidal Neovascular (CNV) Lesions - OPT is noncovered for patients with a diagnosis of age-related macular degeneration (AMD) with occult and no classic CNV lesions.

- Other Conditions - Use of OPT with verteporfin for other types of AMD (e.g., patients with minimally classic CNV lesions, atrophic, or dry AMD) is noncovered. OPT with verteporfin for other ocular indications such as pathologic myopia or presumed ocular histoplasmosis syndrome, is eligible for coverage through individual contractor discretion.

100-3, 80.4
NCD for Hydrophilic Contact Lenses (80.4)

Hydrophilic contact lenses are eyeglasses within the meaning of the exclusion in Sec.1862(a)(7) of the Act and are not covered when used in the treatment of nondiseased eyes with spherical ametrophia, refractive astigmatism, and/or corneal astigmatism. Payment may be made under the prosthetic device benefit, however, for hydrophilic contact lenses when prescribed for an aphakic patient.

Contractors are authorized to accept an FDA letter of approval or other FDA published material as evidence of FDA approval. (See Sec.80.1 of the NCD Manual for coverage of a hydrophilic lens as a corneal bandage.)

100-3, 80.6
NCD for Intraocular Photography (80.6)

Intraocular photography is covered when used for the diagnosis of such conditions as macular degeneration, retinal neoplasms, choroid disturbances and diabetic retinopathy, or to identify glaucoma, multiple sclerosis and other central nervous system abnormalities. Make Medicare payment for the use of this procedure by an opthalmologist in these situations when it is reasonable and necessary for the individual patient to receive these services.

100-3, 80.7
NCD for Refractive Keratoplasty (80.7)

The correction of common refractive errors by eyeglasses, contact lenses or other prosthetic devices is specifically excluded from coverage. The use of radial keratotomy and/or keratoplasty for the purpose of refractive error compensation is considered a substitute or alternative to eye glasses or contact lenses, which are specifically excluded by Sec.1862(a)(7) of the Act (except in certain cases in connection with cataract surgery). In addition, many in the medical community consider such procedures cosmetic surgery, which is excluded by section Sec.1862(a)(10) of the Act. Therefore, radial keratotomy and keratoplasty to treat refractive defects are not covered.

Keratoplasty that treats specific lesions of the cornea, such as phototherapeutic keratectomy that removes scar tissue from the visual field, deals with an abnormality of the eye and is not cosmetic surgery. Such cases may be covered under Sec.1862(a)(1)(A) of the Act.

The use of lasers to treat ophthalmic disease constitutes opthalmologic surgery. Coverage is restricted to practitioners who have completed an approved training program in ophthalmologic surgery.

100-3, 80.8
NCD for Endothelial Cell Photography (80.8)

Endothelial cell photography is a covered procedure under Medicare when reasonable and necessary for patients who meet one or more of the following criteria:

- Have slit lamp evidence of endothelial dystrophy (cornea guttata),
- Have slit lamp evidence of corneal edema (unilateral or bilateral),
- Are about to undergo a secondary intraocular lens implantation,
- Have had previous intraocular surgery and require cataract surgery,
- Are about to undergo a surgical procedure associated with a higher risk to corneal endothelium; i.e., phacoemulsification, or refractive surgery (see Sec.80.7 for excluded refractive procedures),
- With evidence of posterior polymorphous dystrophy of the cornea or irido-corneal-endothelium syndrome, or
- Are about to be fitted with extended wear contact lenses after intraocular surgery.

When a pre-surgical examination for cataract surgery is performed and the conditions of this section are met, if the only visual problem is cataracts, endothelial cell photography is covered as part of the presurgical comprehensive eye examination or combination brief/intermediate examination provided prior to cataract surgery, and not in addition to it. (See Sec.10.1.)

100-3, 80.9
NCD for Computer Enhanced Perimetry (80.9)

It is a covered service when used in assessing visual fields in patients with glaucoma or other neuropathologic defects.

100-3, 80.10
NCD for Phaco-Emulsification procedure - cataract extraction (80.10)

In view of recommendations of authoritative sources in the field of ophthalmology, the subject technique is viewed as an accepted procedure for removal of cataracts. Accordingly, program reimbursement may be made for necessary services furnished in connection with cataract extraction utilizing the phaco-emulsification procedure.

100-3, 80.11
NCD for Vitrectomy (80.11)

Vitrectomy may be considered reasonable and necessary for the following conditions: vitreous loss incident to cataract surgery, vitreous opacities due to vitreous hemorrhage or other causes, retinal detachments secondary to vitreous strands, proliferative retinopathy, and vitreous retraction. See Chapter 23 of the Medicare Claims Manual for how to determine payment for physician vitrectomy services and Chapter 14 Sec.40 for how to determine payment for ASC facility vitrectomy services. Also, see Chapter 23 Sec.20.9 to identify when, for Medicare payment purposes, certain vitrectomy codes are included in other codes or when codes for other services include vitrectomy codes.

100-3, 80.12
NCD for Intraocular Lenses (IOLs) (80.12)
Intraocular lens implantation services, as well as the lens itself, may be covered if reasonable and necessary for the individual. Implantation services may include hospital, surgical, and other medical services, including pre-implantation ultrasound (A-scan) eye measurement of one or both eyes.

100-3, 100.1
NCD for Bariatric Surgery for Treatment of Morbid Obesity (100.1)
NCD for Bariatric Surgery for Treatment of Morbid Obesity (100.1)

A. General
Bariatric surgery procedures are performed to treat comorbid conditions associated with morbid obesity. Two types of surgical procedures are employed. Malabsorptive procedures divert food from the stomach to a lower part of the digestive tract where the normal mixing of digestive fluids and absorption of nutrients cannot occur. Restrictive procedures restrict the size of the stomach and decrease intake. Surgery can combine both types of procedures.

The following are descriptions of bariatric surgery procedures:

1. Roux-en-Y Gastric Bypass (RYGBP)
   The RYGBP achieves weight loss by gastric restriction and malabsorption. Reduction of the stomach to a small gastric pouch (30 cc) results in feelings of satiety following even small meals. This small pouch is connected to a segment of the jejunum, bypassing the duodenum and very proximal small intestine, thereby reducing absorption. RYGBP procedures can be open or laparoscopic.

2. Biliopancreatic Diversion with Duodenal Switch (BPD/DS)
   The BPD achieves weight loss by gastric restriction and malabsorption. The stomach is partially resected, but the remaining capacity is generous compared to that achieved with RYGBP. As such, patients eat relatively normal-sized meals and do not need to restrict intake radically, since the most proximal areas of the small intestine (i.e., the duodenum and jejunum) are bypassed, and substantial malabsorption occurs. The partial BPD/DS is a variant of the BPD procedure. It involves resection of the greater curvature of the stomach, preservation of the pyloric sphincter, and transection of the duodenum above the ampulla of Vater with a duodeno-ileal anastomosis and a lower ileo-ileal anastomosis. BPD/DS procedures can be open or laparoscopic.

3. Adjustable Gastric Banding (AGB)
   The AGB achieves weight loss by gastric restriction only. A band creating a gastric pouch with a capacity of approximately 15 to 30 cc's encircles the uppermost portion of the stomach. The band is an inflatable doughnut-shaped balloon, the diameter of which can be adjusted in the clinic by adding or removing saline via a port that is positioned beneath the skin. The bands are adjustable, allowing the size of the gastric outlet to be modified as needed, depending on the rate of a patient's weight loss. AGB procedures are laparoscopic only.

4. Sleeve Gastrectomy
   Sleeve gastrectomy is a 70%-80% greater curvature gastrectomy (sleeve resection of the stomach) with continuity of the gastric lesser curve being maintained while simultaneously reducing stomach volume. It may be the first step in a two-stage procedure when performing RYGBP. Sleeve gastrectomy procedures can be open or laparoscopic.

5. Vertical Gastric Banding (VGB)
   The VGB achieves weight loss by gastric restriction only. The upper part of the stomach is stapled, creating a narrow gastric inlet or pouch that remains connected with the remainder of the stomach. In addition, a non-adjustable band is placed around this new inlet in an attempt to prevent future enlargement of the stoma (opening). As a result, patients experience a sense of fullness after eating small meals. Weight loss from this procedure results entirely from eating less. VGB procedures are essentially no longer performed.

B. Nationally Covered Indications
Effective for services performed on and after February 21, 2006, Open and laparoscopic Roux-en-Y gastric bypass (RYGBP), open and laparoscopic Biliopancreatic Diversion with Duodenal Switch (BPD/DS), and laparoscopic adjustable gastric banding (LAGB) are covered for Medicare beneficiaries who have a body-mass index > 35, have at least one co-morbidity related to obesity, and have been previously unsuccessful with medical treatment for obesity. These procedures are only covered when performed at facilities that are: (1) certified by the American College of Surgeons as a Level 1 Bariatric Surgery Center (program standards and requirements in effect on February 15, 2006); or (2) certified by the American Society for Bariatric Surgery as a Bariatric Surgery Center of Excellence (program standards and requirements in effect on February 15, 2006).

Effective for services performed on and after February 12, 2009, the Centers for Medicare & Medicaid Services (CMS) determines that Type 2 diabetes mellitus is a co-morbidity for purposes of this NCD.

A list of approved facilities and their approval dates are listed and maintained on the CMS Coverage Web site at http://www.cms.hhs.gov/center/coverage.asp, and published in the Federal Register.

C. Nationally Non-Covered Indications
The following bariatric surgery procedures are non-covered for all Medicare beneficiaries:

- Open adjustable gastric banding;
- Open and laparoscopic sleeve gastrectomy; and,
- Open and laparoscopic vertical banded gastroplasty.

The two previous non-coverage determinations remain unchanged - Gastric Balloon (Section 100.11) and Intestinal Bypass (Section 100.8).

D. Other
N/A

100-3, 100.2
NCD for Endoscopy (100.2)
Endoscopic procedures are covered when reasonable and necessary for the individual patient.

100-3, 100.4
NCD for Esophageal Manometry (100.4)
Esophageal manometry is covered under Medicare where it is determined to be reasonable and necessary for the individual patient.

100-3, 100.5
NCD for Diagnostic Breath Analyses (100.5)
The Following Breath Test is Covered:

- Lactose breath hydrogen to detect lactose malabsorption.

The Following Breath Tests are Excluded from Coverage;

- Lactulose breath hydrogen for diagnosing small bowel bacterial overgrowth and measuring small bowel transit time.
- CO2 for diagnosing bile acid malabsorption.
- CO2 for diagnosing fat malabsorption.

100-3, 100.8
NCD for Intestinal By-Pass Surgery (100.8)
The safety of intestinal bypass surgery for treatment of obesity has not been demonstrated. Severe adverse reactions such as steatorrhea, electrolyte depletion, liver failure, arthralgia, hypoplasia of bone marrow, and avitaminosis have sometimes occurred as a result of this procedure. It does not meet the reasonable and necessary provisions of Sec.1862(a)(1) of the Act and is not a covered Medicare procedure.

100-3, 100.9
NCD for Implantation of Anti-Gastroesophageal Reflux Device (100.9)
The implantation of this device may be considered reasonable and necessary in specific clinical situations where a conventional valvuloplasty procedure is contraindicated. The implantation of an anti-gastroesophageal reflux device is covered only for patients with documented severe or life threatening gastroesophageal reflux disease whose conditions have been resistant to medical treatment and who also:

- have esophageal involvement with progressive systemic sclerosis; or
- have foreshortening of the esophagus such that insufficient tissue exists to permit a valve reconstruction; or
- are poor surgical risks for a valvuloplasty procedure; or
- have failed previous attempts at surgical treatment with valvuloplasty procedures.

100-3, 100.10
NCD for Injection Sclerotherapy for Esophageal Variceal Bleeding (100.10)
This procedure is covered under Medicare.

100-3, 100.12
NCD for Gastrophotography (100.12)
Gastrophotography is an accepted procedure for diagnosis and treatment of gastrointestinal disorders. The photographic record provided by this procedure is often necessary for consultation and/or followup purposes and when required for such purposes, is more valuable than a conventional gastroscopic examination. Such a record facilitates the documentation and evaluation (healing or worsening) of lesions such as the gastric ulcer, facilitates consultation between physicians concerning difficult-to-interpret lesions, provides preoperative characterization for the surgeon, and permits better diagnosis of postoperative gastric bleeding to help determine whether there is a need for reoperation. Therefore, program reimbursement may be made for this procedure.

100-3, 100.13
NCD for Laparoscopic Cholecystectomy (100.13)
Laparoscopic cholecystectomy is a covered surgical procedure in which a diseased gall bladder is removed through the use of instruments introduced via cannulae, with vision of the operative field maintained by use of a high-resolution television camera-monitor system (video laparoscope). For inpatient claims, use ICD-9-CM code 51.23, Laparoscopic cholecystectomy. For all other claims, use CPT codes 49310 for laparoscopy, surgical; cholecystectomy (any method), and 49311 for laparoscopy, surgical: cholecystectomy with cholangiography.

100-3, 110.1
NCD for Hyperthermia for Treatment of Cancer (110.1)
Local hyperthermia is covered under Medicare when used in connection with radiation therapy for the treatment of primary or metastatic cutaneous or subcutaneous superficial malignancies. It is not covered when used alone or in connection with chemotherapy.

100-3, 110.2
NCD for Certain Drugs Distributed by the National Cancer Institute (110.2)
A physician is eligible to receive Group C drugs from the Division of Cancer Treatment only if the following requirements are met:

Appendix G — Pub 100 References

- A physician must be registered with the NCI as an investigator by having completed an FD-Form 1573;
- A written request for the drug, indicating the disease to be treated, must be submitted to the NCI;
- The use of the drug must be limited to indications outlined in the NCI's guidelines; and
- All adverse reactions must be reported to the Investigational Drug Branch of the Division of Cancer Treatment.

In view of these NCI controls on distribution and use of Group C drugs, intermediaries may assume, in the absence of evidence to the contrary, that a Group C drug and the related hospital stay are covered if all other applicable coverage requirements are satisfied.

If there is reason to question coverage in a particular case, the matter should be resolved with the assistance of the Quality improvemetn organization (QIO), or if there is none, the assistance of your medical consultants.

Information regarding those drugs which are classified as Group C drugs may be obtained from:

Office of the Chief, Investigational Drug Branch
Division of Cancer Treatment, CTEP, Landow Building
Room 4C09, National Cancer Institute
Bethesda, Maryland 20205

100-3, 110.3
NCD for Anti-Inhibitor Coagulant Complex (AICC) (110.3)
Anti-inhibitor coagulant complex, AICC, is a drug used to treat hemophilia in patients with factor VIII inhibitor antibodies. AICC has been shown to be safe and effective and has Medicare coverage when furnished to patients with hemophilia A and inhibitor antibodies to factor VIII who have major bleeding episodes and who fail to respond to other, less expensive therapies.

100-3, 110.4
NCD for Extracorporeal Photopheresis (110.4)
B. Nationally Covered Indications
The CMS has determined that extracorporeal photopheresis is reasonable and necessary under Sec.1862(a)(1)(A) of the Social Security Act under the following circumstances:

1. Effective April 8, 1988, Medicare provides coverage for:

    Palliative treatment of skin manifestations of CTCL that has not responded to other therapy.

2. Effective December 19, 2006, Medicare also provides coverage for:

    Patients with acute cardiac allograft rejection whose disease is refractory to standard immunosuppressive drug treatment; and

    Patients with chronic graft versus host disease whose disease is refractory to standard immunosuppressive drug treatment.

C. Nationally Noncovered Indications
All other indications for extracorporeal photopheresis remain noncovered.

D. Other
Claims processing instructions can be found in chapter 32, section 190 of the Medicare Claims Processing Manual.

(This NCD last reviewed December 2006.)

100-3, 110.5
NCD for Granulocyte Transfusions (110.5)
Granulocyte transfusions to patients suffering from severe infection and granulocytopenia are a covered service under Medicare. Granulocytopenia is usually identified as fewer than 500 granulocytes/mm 3 whole blood. Accepted indications for granulocyte transfusions include:

Granulocytopenia with evidence of gram negative sepsis; and

Granulocytopenia in febrile patients with local progressive infections unresponsive to appropriate antibiotic therapy, thought to be due to gram negative organisms.

100-3, 110.6
NCD for Scalp Hypothermia During Chemotherapy, to Prevent Hair Loss (110.6)
While ice-filled bags or bandages or other devices used for scalp hypothermia during chemotherapy may be covered as supplies of the kind commonly furnished without a separate charge, no separate charge for them would be recognized.

100-3, 110.7
NCD for Blood Transfusions (110.7)
B. Policy Governing Transfusions
For Medicare coverage purposes, it is important to distinguish between a transfusion itself and preoperative blood services; e.g., collection, processing, storage. Medically necessary transfusion of blood, regardless of the type, may generally be a covered service under both Part A and Part B of Medicare. Coverage does not make a distinction between the transfusion of homologous, autologous, or donor-directed blood. With respect to the coverage of the services associated with the preoperative collection, processing, and storage of autologous and donor-directed blood, the following policies apply.

1. Hospital Part A and B Coverage and Payment

    Under Sec.1862(a)(14) of the Act, non-physician services furnished to hospital patients are covered and paid for as hospital services. As provided in Sec.1886 of the Act, under the prospective [payment system (PPS), the diganosis related group (DRG) payment to the hospital includes all covered blood and blood processing expenses, whether or not the blood is eventually used.

    Under its provider agreement, a hospital is required to furnish or arrange for all covered services furnished to hospital patients. medicare payment is made to the hospital, under PPS or cost reimbursement, for covered inpatient services, and it is intended to reflect payment for all costs of furnishing those services.

2. Nonhospital Part B Coverage

    Under Part B, to be eligible for separate coverage, a service must fit the definition of one of the services authorized by Sec.1832 of the Act. These services are defined in 42 CFR 410.10 and do not include a separate category for a supplier's services associated with blood donation services, either autologous or donor-directed. That is, the collection, processing, and storage of blood for later transfusion into the beneficiary is not recognized as a separate service under Part B. Therefore, there is no avenue through which a blood supplier can receive direct payment under Part B for blood donation services.

C. Perioperative Blood Salvage
When the perioperative blood salvage process is used in surgery on a hospital patient, payment made to the hospital (under PPS or through cost reimbursement) for the procedure in which that process is used is intended to encompass payment for all costs relating to that process.

100-3, 110.8
NCD for Blood Platelet Transfusions (110.8)
Blood platelet transplants are safe and effective for the correction of thrombocytopenia and other blood defects. It is covered under Medicare when treatment is reasonable and necessary for the individual patient.

100-3, 110.8.1
NCD for Stem Cell Transplantation (110.8.1)
1. Allogeneic Stem Cell Transplantation

    Allogeneic stem cell transplantation is a procedure in which a portion of a healthy donor's stem cell or bone marrow is obtained and prepared for intravenous infusion.

    a. Covered Indications

        The following uses of allogeneic bone marrow transplantation are covered under Medicare:

        - Effective for services performed on or after August 1, 1978, for the treatment of leukemia, leukemia in remission, or aplastic anemia when it is reasonable and necessary; and
        - Effective for services performed on or after June 3, 1985, for the treatment of severe combined immunodeficiency disease (SCID), and for the treatment of Wiskott-Aldrich syndrome.

    b. Noncovered Indications

        Effective for services performed on or after May 24, 1996, allogeneic stem cell transplantation is not covered as treatment for multiple myeloma.

2. Autologous Stem Cell Transplantation (AuSCT)

    Autologous stem cell transplantation (AuSCT) is a technique for restoring stem cells using the patient's own previously stored cells.

    a. Covered Indications

        Effective for services performed on or after April 28, 1989, AuSCT is considered reasonable and necessary under Sec.l862(a)(1)(A) of the Social Security Act (the Act) for the following conditions and is covered under Medicare for patients with:

        - Acute leukemia in remission who have a high probability of relapse and who have no human leucocyte antigens (HLA)-matched;
        - Resistant non-Hodgkin's lymphomas or those presenting with poor prognostic features following an initial response;
        - Recurrent or refractory neuroblastoma; or
        - Advanced Hodgkin's disease who have failed conventional therapy and have no HLA-matched donor.

        Effective October 1, 2000, single AuSCT is only covered for Durie-Salmon Stage II or III patients that fit the following requirements:

        - Newly diagnosed or responsive multiple myeloma. This includes those patients with previously untreated disease, those with at least a partial response to prior chemotherapy (defined as a 50% decrease either in measurable paraprotein [serum and/or urine] or in bone marrow infiltration, sustained for at least 1 month), and those in responsive relapse; and
        - Adequate cardiac, renal, pulmonary, and hepatic function.

        Effective for services performed on or after March 15, 2005, when recognized clinical risk factors are employed to select patients for transplantation, high dose melphalan (HDM) together with AuSCT is reasonable and necessary for Medicare beneficiaries of any age group with primary amyloid light chain (AL) amyloidosis who meet the following criteria:

        - Amyloid deposition in 2 or fewer organs; and,
        - Cardiac left ventricular ejection fraction (EF) greater than 45%.

    b. Noncovered Indications

        Insufficient data exist to establish definite conclusions regarding the efficacy of AuSCT for the following conditions:

        - Acute leukemia not in remission;
        - Chronic granulocytic leukemia;

- Solid tumors (other than neuroblastoma);
- Up to October 1, 2000, multiple myeloma;
- Tandem transplantation (multiple rounds of AuSCT) for patients with multiple myeloma;
- Effective October 1, 2000, non primary AL amyloidosis; and,
- Effective October 1, 2000, thru March 14, 2005, primary AL amyloidosis for Medicare beneficiaries age 64 or older.

In these cases, AuSCT is not considered reasonable and necessary within the meaning of Sec.I862(a)(1)(A) of the Act and is not covered under Medicare.

B. Other
All other indications for stem cell transplantation not otherwise noted above as covered or noncovered nationally remain at local contractor discretion.

(This NCD last reviewed November 2005.)

100-3, 110.9
NCD for Antigens Prepared for Sublingual Administration (110.9)
For antigens provided to patients on or after November 17, 1996, Medicare does not cover such antigens if they are to be administered sublingually, i.e., by placing drops under the patient's tongue. This kind of allergy therapy has not been proven to be safe and effective. Antigens are covered only if they are administered by injection.

100-3, 110.10
NCD for Intravenous Iron Therapy (110.10)
Effective December 1, 2000, Medicare covers sodium ferric gluconate complex in sucrose injection as a first line treatment of iron deficiency anemia when furnished intravenously to patients undergoing chronic hemodialysis who are receiving supplemental erythropoeitin therapy.

Effective October 1, 2001, Medicare also covers iron sucrose injection as a first line treatment of iron deficiency anemia when furnished intravenously to patients undergoing chronic hemodialysis who are receiving supplemental erythropoietin therapy.

100-3, 110.12
NCD for Challenge Ingestion Food Testing (110.12)
This procedure is covered when it is used on an outpatient basis if it is reasonable and necessary for the individual patient.

Challenge ingestion food testing has not been proven to be effective in the diagnosis of rheumatoid arthritis, depression, or respiratory disorders. Accordingly, its use in the diagnosis of these conditions is not reasonable and necessary within the meaning of section 1862(a)(1) of the Medicare law, and no program payment is made for this procedure when it is so used.

100-3, 110.14
NCD for Apheresis (Therapeutic Pheresis) (110.14)
B. Indications
Apheresis is covered for the following indications:

- Plasma exchange for acquired myasthenia gravis;
- Leukapheresis in the treatment of leukemekia
- Plasmapheresis in the treatment of primary macroglobulinemia (Waldenstrom);
- Treatment of hyperglobulinemias, including (but not limited to) multiple myelomas, cryoglobulinemia and hyperviscosity syndromes;
- Plasmapheresis or plasma exchange as a last resort treatment of thrombotic thrombocytopenic purpura (TTP);
- Plasmapheresis or plasma exchange in the last resort treatment of life threatening rheumatoid vasculitis;
- Plasma perfusion of charcoal filters for treatment of pruritis of cholestatic liver disease;
- Plasma exchange in the treatment of Goodpasture's Syndrome;
- Plasma exchange in the treatment of glomerulonephritis associated with antiglomerular basement membrane antibodies and advancing renal failure or pulmonary hemorrhage;
- Treatment of chronic relapsing polyneuropathy for patients with severe or life threatening symptoms who have failed to respond to conventional therapy;
- Treatment of life threatening scleroderma and polymyositis when the patient is unresponsive to conventional therapy;
- Treatment of Guillain-Barre Syndrome; and
- Treatment of last resort for life threatening systemic lupus erythematosus (SLE) when conventional therapy has failed to prevent clinical deterioration.

C. Settings
Apheresis is covered only when performed in a hospital setting (either inpatient or outpatient). or in a nonhospital setting. e.g. physician directed clinic when the following conditions are met:

- A physician (or a number of physicians) is present to perform medical services and to respond to medical emergencies at all times during patient care hours;
- Each patient is under the care of a physician; and
- All nonphysician services are furnished under the direct, personal supervision of a physician.

100-3, 110.15
NCD for Ultrafiltration, Hemoperfusion and Hemofiltration (110.15)
A. Ultrafiltration.
This is a process for removing excess fluid from the blood through the dialysis membrane by means of pressure. It is not a substitute for dialysis. Ultrafiltration is utilized in cases where excess fluid cannot be removed easily during the regular course of hemodialysis. When it is performed, it is commonly done during the first hour or two of each hemodialysis on patients who, e.g., have refractory edema. Ultrafiltration is a covered procedure under the Medicare program (effective for services performed on and after 9/1/79).

Predialysis Ultrafiltration.--While this procedure requires additional staff care, the facility dialysis rate is intended to cover the full range of complicated and uncomplicated nonacute dialysis treatments. Therefore, no additional facility charge is recognized for predialysis ultrafiltration. The physician's role in ultrafiltration varies with the stability of the patient's condition. In unstable patients, the physician may need to be present at the initiation of dialysis, and available either in- house or in close proximity to monitor the patient carefully. In patients who are relatively stable, but who seem to accumulate excessive weight gain, the procedure requires only a modest increase in physician involvement over routine outpatient hemodialysis.

Occasionally, medical complications may occur which require that ultrafiltration be performed separate from the dialysis treatment, and in these cases an additional charge can be recognized. However, the claim must be documented as to why the ultrafiltration could not have been performed at the same time as the dialysis.

B. Hemoperfusion.
This is a process which removes substances from the blood using a charcoal or resin artificial kidney. When used in the treatment of life threatening drug overdose, hemoperfusion is a covered service for patients with or without renal failure (effective for services performed on and after 9/1/79). Hemoperfusion generally requires a physician to be present to initiate treatment and to be present in the hospital or an adjacent medical office during the entire procedure, as changes may be sudden. Special staff training and equipment are required.

Develop charges for hemoperfusion in the same manner as for any new or unusual service. One or two treatments are usually all that is necessary to remove the toxic compound; document additional treatments. Hemoperfusion may be performed concurrently with dialysis, and in those cases payment for the hemoperfusion reflects only the additional care rendered over and above the care given with dialysis.

The effects of using hemoperfusion to improve the results of chronic hemodialysis are not known. Therefore, hemoperfusion is not a covered service when used to improve the results of hemodialysis. In addition, it has not been demonstrated that the use of hemoperfusion in conjunction with deferoxamine (DFO), in treating symptomatic patients with iron overload, is efficacious. There is also a paucity of data regarding its efficacy in treating asymptomatic patients with iron overload. Therefore, hemoperfusion used in conjunction with DFO in treating patients with iron overload is not a covered service; i.e., it is not considered reasonable and necessary within the meaning of Sec.1862(a)(1) of the Act.

However, the use of hemoperfusion in conjunction with DFO for the treatment of patients with aluminum toxicity has been demonstrated to be clinically efficacious and is therefore regarded as a covered service.

C. Hemofiltration.
This is a process which removes fluid, electrolytes and other low molecular weight toxic substances from the blood by filtration through hollow artificial membranes and may be routinely performed in 3 weekly sessions. Hemofiltration (which is also known as diafiltration) is a covered procedure under Medicare and is a safe and effective technique for the treatment of ESRD patients and an alternative to peritoneal dialysis and hemodialysis (effective for services performed on and after August 20, 1987). In contrast to both hemodialysis and peritoneal dialysis treatments, which eliminate dissolved substances via diffusion across semipermeable membranes, hemofiltration mimics the filtration process of the normal kidney. The technique requires an arteriovenous access. Hemofiltration may be performed either in facility or at home.

The procedure is most advantageous when applied to high-risk unstable patients, such as older patients with cardiovascular diseases or diabetes, because there are fewer side effects such as hypotension, hypertension or volume overload.

100-3, 110.16
NCD for Nonselective (Random) Transfusions and Living Related Donor Specific Transfusions (DST) in Kidney Transplantation (110.16)
These pretransplant transfusions are covered under Medicare without a specific limitation on the number of transfusions, subject to the normal Medicare blood deductible provisions. Where blood is given directly to the transplant patient; e.g., in the case of donor specific transfusions, the blood is considered replaced for purposes of the blood deductible provisions.

100-3, 130.1
NCD for Inpatient Hospital Stays for the Treatment of Alcoholism (130.1)
A. Inpatient Hospital Stay for Alcohol Detoxification
Many hospitals provide detoxification services during the more acute stages of alcoholism or alcohol withdrawal. When the high probability or occurrence of medical complications (e.g., delirium, confusion, trauma, or unconsciousness) during detoxification for acute alcoholism or alcohol withdrawal necessitates the constant availability of physicians and/or complex medical equipment found only in the hospital setting, inpatient hospital care during this period is considered reasonable and necessary and is therefore covered under the program. Generally, detoxification can be accomplished within 2-3 days with an occasional need for up to 5 days where the patient's condition dictates. This limit (5 days) may be extended in an individual case where there is a need for a longer period for detoxification for a particular patient. In such cases, however, there should be documentation by a physician which substantiates that a longer period of detoxification was reasonable and necessary. When the detoxification needs of an individual

no longer require an inpatient hospital setting, coverage should be denied on the basis that inpatient hospital care is not reasonable and necessary as required by section l862(a)(l) of the Act. Following detoxification a patient may be transferred to an inpatient rehabilitation unit or discharged to a residential treatment program or outpatient treatment setting.

B. Inpatient Hospital Stay for Alcohol Rehabilitation
Hospitals may also provide structured inpatient alcohol rehabilitation programs to the chronic alcoholic. These programs are composed primarily of coordinated educational and psychotherapeutic services provided on a group basis. Depending on the subject matter, a series of lectures, discussions, films, and group therapy sessions are led by either physicians, psychologists, or alcoholism counselors from the hospital or various outside organizations. In addition, individual psychotherapy and family counseling (see Sec.70.1 of the NCD Manual) may be provided in selected cases. These programs are conducted under the supervision and direction of a physician. Patients may directly enter an inpatient hospital rehabilitation program after having undergone detoxification in the same hospital or in another hospital or may enter an inpatient hospital rehabilitation program without prior hospitalization for detoxification.

Alcohol rehabilitation can be provided in a variety of settings other than the hospital setting. In order for an inpatient hospital stay for alcohol rehabilitation to be covered under Medicare it must be medically necessary for the care to be provided in the inpatient hospital setting rather than in a less costly facility or on an outpatient basis. Inpatient hospital care for receipt of an alcohol rehabilitation program would generally be medically necessary where either (l) there is documentation by the physician that recent alcohol rehabilitation services in a less intensive setting or on an outpatient basis have proven unsuccessful and, as a consequence, the patient requires the supervision and intensity of services which can only be found in the controlled environment of the hospital, or (2) only the hospital environment can assure the medical management or control of the patient's concomitant conditions during the course of alcohol rehabilitation. (However, a patient's concomitant condition may make the use of certain alcohol treatment modalities medically inappropriate.) In addition, the "active treatment" criteria (see the Medicare Benefit Policy Manual, Chapter 2, "Inpatient Psychiatric Hospital Services," Sec.20) should be applied to psychiatric care in the general hospital as well as to psychiatric care in a psychiatric hospital. Since alcoholism is classifiable as a psychiatric condition the "active treatment" criteria must also be met in order for alcohol rehabilitation services to be covered under Medicare. (Thus, it is the combined need for "active treatment" and for covered care which can only be provided in the inpatient hospital setting, rather than the fact that rehabilitation immediately follows a period of detoxification, which provides the basis for coverage of inpatient hospital alcohol rehabilitation programs.)

Generally 16-19 days of rehabilitation services are sufficient to bring a patient to a point where care could be continued in other than an inpatient hospital setting. An inpatient hospital stay for alcohol rehabilitation may be extended beyond this limit in an individual case where a longer period of alcohol rehabilitation is medically necessary. In such cases, however, there should be documentation by a physician which substantiates the need for such care. Where the rehabilitation needs of an individual no longer require an inpatient hospital setting, coverage should be denied on the basis that inpatient hospital care is not reasonable and necessary as required by section l862(a)(l) of the Act..

Subsequent admissions to the inpatient hospital setting for alcohol rehabilitation followup, reinforcement, or "recap" treatments are considered to be readmissions (rather than an extension of the original stay) and must meet the requirements of this section for coverage under Medicare. Prior admissions to the inpatient hospital setting--either in the same hospital or in a different hospital--may be an indication that the "active treatment" requirements are not met (i.e., there is no reasonable expectation of improvement) and the stay should not be covered. Accordingly, there should be documentation to establish that "readmission" to the hospital setting for alcohol rehabilitation services can reasonably be expected to result in improvement of the patient's condition. For example, the documentation should indicate what changes in the patient's medical condition, social or emotional status, or treatment plan make improvement likely, or why the patient's initial hospital treatment was not sufficient.

C. Combined Alcohol Detoxification/Rehabilitation Programs.
Fiscal intermediaries should apply the guidelines in A. and B. above to both phases of a combined inpatient hospital alcohol detoxification/rehabilitation program. Not all patients who require the inpatient hospital setting for detoxification also need the inpatient hospital setting for rehabilitation. (See Sec.130.1 of the NCD Manual for coverage of outpatient hospital alcohol rehabilitation services.) Where the inpatient hospital setting is medically necessary for both alcohol detoxification and rehabilitation, generally a 3-week period is reasonable and necessary to bring the patient to the point where care can be continued in other than an inpatient hospital setting.

Decisions regarding reasonableness and necessity of treatment, the need for an inpatient hospital level of care, and length of treatment should be made by intermediaries based on accepted medical practice with the advice of their medical consultant. (In hospitals under PSRO review, PSRO determinations of medical necessity of services and appropriateness of the level of care at which services are provided are binding on the title XVIII fiscal intermediaries for purposes of adjudicating claims for payment.)

100-3, 130.2

NCD for Outpatient Hospital Services for Treatment of Alcoholism (130.2)

Coverage is available for both diagnostic and therapeutic services furnished for the treatment of alcoholism by the hospital to outpatients subject to the same rules applicable to outpatient hospital services in general. While there is no coverage for day hospitalization programs, per se, individual services which meet the requirements in the Medicare Benefit Policy Manual, Chapter 6, Sec.20 may be covered. (Meals, transportation and recreational and social activities do not fall within the scope of covered outpatient hospital services under Medicare.)

All services must be reasonable and necessary for diagnosis or treatment of the patient's condition (see the Medicare Benefit Policy Manual, chapter 16 Sec.20). Thus, educational services and family counseling would only be covered where they are directly related to treatment of the patient's condition. The frequency of treatment and period of time over which it occurs must also be reasonable and necessary.

100-3, 130.3

NCD for Chemical Aversion Therapy for Treatment of Alcoholism (130.3)

Available evidence indicates that chemical aversion therapy may be an effective component of certain alcoholism treatment programs, particularly as part of multimodality treatment programs which include other behavioral techniques and therapies, such as psychotherapy. Based on this evidence, CMS's medical consultants have recommended that chemical aversion therapy be covered under Medicare. However, since chemical aversion therapy is a demanding therapy which may not be appropriate for all Medicare beneficiaries needing treatment for alcoholism, a physician should certify to the appropriateness of chemical aversion therapy in the individual case. Therefore, if chemical aversion therapy for treatment of alcoholism is determined to be reasonable and necessary for an individual patient, it is covered under Medicare.

When it is medically necessary for a patient to receive chemical aversion therapy as a hospital inpatient, coverage for care in that setting is available. (See Sec.130.1 regarding coverage of multimodality treatment programs.) Followup treatments for chemical aversion therapy can generally be provided on an outpatient basis. Thus, where a patient is admitted as an inpatient for receipt of chemical aversion therapy, there must be documentation by the physician of the need in the individual case for the inpatient hospital admission.

Decisions regarding reasonableness and necessity of treatment and the need for an inpatient hospital level of care should be made by intermediaries based on accepted medical practice with the advice of their medical consultant. (In hospitals under QIO review, QIO determinations of medical necessity of services and appropriateness of the level of care at which services are provided are binding on the title XVIII fiscal intermediaries for purposes of adjudicating claims for payment.)

100-3, 130.4

NCD for Electrical Aversion Therapy for Treatment of Alcoholism (130.4)

Electrical aversion therapy has not been shown to be safe and effective and therefore is excluded from coverage.

100-3, 130.5

NCD for Treatment of Alcoholism and Drug Abuse in a Freestanding Clinic (130.5)

Coverage is available for alcoholism or drug abuse treatment services (such as drug therapy, psychotherapy, and patient education) that are provided incident to a physician's professional service in a freestanding clinic to patients who, for example, have been discharged from an inpatient hospital stay for the treatment of alcoholism or drug abuse or to individuals who are not in the acute stages of alcoholism or drug abuse but require treatment. The coverage available for these services is subject to the same rules generally applicable to the coverage of clinic services. Of course, the services also must be reasonable and necessary for the diagnosis or treatment of the individual's alcoholism or drug abuse. The Part B psychiatric limitation would apply to alcoholism or drug abuse treatment services furnished by physicians to individuals who are not hospital inpatients.

100-3, 130.6

NCD for Treatment of Drug Abuse (Chemical Dependency) (130.6)

Accordingly, when it is medically necessary for a patient to receive detoxification and/or rehabilitation for drug substance abuse as a hospital inpatient, coverage for care in that setting is available. Coverage is also available for treatment services that are provided in the outpatient department of a hospital to patients who, for example, have been discharged from an inpatient stay for the treatment of drug substance abuse or who require treatment but do not require the availability and intensity of services found only in the inpatient hospital setting. The coverage available for these services is subject to the same rules generally applicable to the coverage of outpatient hospital services. The services must also be reasonable and necessary for treatment of the individual's condition. Decisions regarding reasonableness and necessity of treatment, the need for an inpatient hospital level of care, and length of treatment should be made by intermediaries based on accepted medical practice with the advice of their medical consultant. (In hospitals under QIO review, QIO determinations of medical necessity of services and appropriateness of the level of care at which services are provided are binding on the title XVIII fiscal intermediaries for purposes of adjudicating claims for payment.)

100-3, 130.7

NCD for Withdrawal Treatments for Narcotic Addictions (130.7)

Withdrawal is an accepted treatment for narcotic addiction, and Part B payment can be made for these services if they are provided by the physician directly or under his personal supervision and if they are reasonable and necessary. In reviewing claims, reasonableness and necessity are determined with the aid of the contractor's medical staff.

Drugs that the physician provides in connection with this treatment are also covered if they cannot be self-administered and meet all other statutory requirements.

100-3, 130.8

NCD for Hemodialysis for Treatment of Schizophrenia (130.8)

Scientific evidence supporting use of hemodialysis as a safe and effective means of treatment for schizophrenia is inconclusive at this time. Accordingly, Medicare does not cover hemodialysis for treatment of schizophrenia.

100-3, 140.1

NCD for Abortion (140.1)

Abortions are not covered Medicare procedures except:

1. If the pregnancy is the result of an act of rape or incest; or
2. In the case where a woman suffers from a physical disorder, physical injury, or physical illness, including a life-endangering physical condition caused by or arising from the pregnancy itself, that would, as certified by a physician, place the woman in danger of death unless an abortion is performed.

100-3, 140.2
NCD for Breast Reconstruction Following Mastectomy (140.2)
Reconstruction of the affected and the contralateral unaffected breast following a medically necessary mastectomy is considered a relatively safe and effective noncosmetic procedure. Accordingly, program payment may be made for breast reconstruction surgery following removal of a breast for any medical reason.

Program payment may not be made for breast reconstruction for cosmetic reasons. (Cosmetic surgery is excluded from coverage under Sec.1862(a)(10) of the Social Security Act.)

100-3, 140.3
NCD for Transsexual Surgery (140.3)
Transsexual surgery for sex reassignment of transsexuals is controversial. Because of the lack of well controlled, long term studies of the safety and effectiveness of the surgical procedures and attendant therapies for transsexualism, the treatment is considered experimental. Moreover, there is a high rate of serious complications for these surgical procedures. For these reasons, transsexual surgery is not covered.

100-3, 140.4
NCD for Plastic Surgery to Correct "Moon Face" (140.4)
The cosmetic surgery exclusion precludes payment for any surgical procedure directed at improving appearance. The condition giving rise to the patient's preoperative appearance is generally not a consideration. The only exception to the exclusion is surgery for the prompt repair of an accidental injury or for the improvement of a malformed body member which coincidentally serves some cosmetic purpose. Since surgery to correct a condition of "moon face" which developed as a side effect of cortisone therapy does not meet the exception to the exclusion, it is not covered under Medicare (Sec.1862(a)(10) of the Act).

100-3, 140.5
NCD for Laser Procedures (140.5)
Medicare recognizes the use of lasers for many medical indications. Procedures performed with lasers are sometimes used in place of more conventional techniques. In the absence of a specific noncoverage instruction, and where a laser has been approved for marketing by the Food and Drug Administration, contractor discretion may be used to determine whether a procedure performed with a laser is reasonable and necessary and, therefore, covered.

The determination of coverage for a procedure performed using a laser is made on the basis that the use of lasers to alter, revise, or destroy tissue is a surgical procedure. Therefore, coverage of laser procedures is restricted to practitioners with training in the surgical management of the disease or condition being treated.

100-3, 150.1
NCD for Manipulation (150.1)
A. Manipulation of the Rib Cage.
Manual manipulation of the rib cage contributes to the treatment of respiratory conditions such as bronchitis, emphysema, and asthma as part of a regimen which includes other elements of therapy, and is covered only under such circumstances.

B. Manipulation of the Head.
Manipulation of the occipitocervical or temporomandibular regions of the head when indicated for conditions affecting those portions of the head and neck is a covered service.

100-3, 150.2
NCD for Osteogenic Stimulators (150.2)
Electrical Osteogenic Stimulators

B. Nationally Covered Indications

1. Noninvasive Stimulator.

    The noninvasive stimulator device is covered only for the following indications:
    - Nonunion of long bone fractures;
    - Failed fusion, where a minimum of nine months has elapsed since the last surgery;
    - Congenital pseudarthroses; and
    - Effective July 1, 1996, as an adjunct to spinal fusion surgery for patients at high risk of pseudarthrosis due to previously failed spinal fusion at the same site or for those undergoing multiple level fusion. A multiple level fusion involves 3 or more vertebrae (e.g., L3-L5, L4-S1, etc).
    - Effective September 15, 1980, nonunion of long bone fractures is considered to exist only after 6 or more months have elapsed without healing of the fracture.
    - Effective April 1, 2000, nonunion of long bone fractures is considered to exist only when serial radiographs have confirmed that fracture healing has ceased for 3 or more months prior to starting treatment with the electrical osteogenic stimulator. Serial radiographs must include a minimum of 2 sets of radiographs, each including multiple views of the fracture site, separated by a minimum of 90 days.

2. Invasive (Implantable) Stimulator.

    The invasive stimulator device is covered only for the following indications:
    - Nonunion of long bone fractures
    - Effective July 1, 1996, as an adjunct to spinal fusion surgery for patients at high risk of pseudarthrosis due to previously failsed spinal fusion at the same site or for those undergoing multiple level fusion. A multiple level fusion involves 3 or more vertebrae (e.g., L3-5, L4-S1, etc.)
    - Effective September 15, 1980, nonunion of long bone fractures is considered to exist only after 6 or more months have elapsed without healing of the fracture.
    - Effective April 1, 2000, non union of long bone fractures is considered to exist only when serial radiographs have confirmed that fracture healing has ceased for 3 or more months prior to starting treatment with the electrical osteogenic stimulator. Serial radiographs must include a minimum of 2 sets of radiographs, each including multiple views of the fracture site, separated by a minimum of 90 days.
    - Effective for services performed on or after January 1, 2001, ultrasonic osteogenic stimulators are covered as medically reasonable and necessary for the treatment of non-union fractures. In demonstrating nonunion of fractures, we would expect:
    - A minimum of two sets of radiographs obtained prior to starting treatment with the osteogenic stimulator, separated by a minimum of 90 days. Each radiograph must include multiple views of the fracture site accompanied with a written interpretation by a physician stating that there has been no clinically significant evidence of fracture healing between the two sets of radiographs.
    - Indications that the patient failed at least one surgical intervention for the treatment of the fracture.
    - Effective April 27, 2005, upon the recommendation of the ultrasound stimulation for nonunion fracture healing, CMS determins that the evidence is adequate to condlude that noninvasive ultrasound stimulation for the treatment of nonunion bone fractures prior to surfical intervention is reasonable and necessary. In demonstrating non-union fracturs, CMS expects:
    - A minimum of 2 sets of radiographs, obtained prior to starting treating with the osteogenic stimulator, separated by a minimum of 90 days. Each radiograph set must include multiple views of the fracture site accompanied with a written interpretation by a physician stating that there has been no clinically significant evidence of fracture healing between the 2 sets of radiographs.

C. Nationally Non-Covered Indications
Nonunion fractures of the skull, vertebrae and those that are tumor-related are excluded from coverage.

Ultrasonic osteogenic stimulators may not be used concurrently with other non-invasive osteogenic devices.

Ultrasonic osteogenic stimulators for fresh fracturs and delayed unions remain non-covered.

(This NCD last reviewed June 2005)

100-3, 150.3
NCD for Bone (Mineral) Density Studies (150.3)
Conditions for coverage of bone mass measurements are now contained in chapter 15, section 80.5 of Pub. 100-02, Medicare Benefit Policy Manual . Claims processing instructions can be found in chapter 13, section 140 of Pub. 100-04, Medicare Claims Processing Manual .

100-3, 150.5
NCD for Diathermy Treatment (150.5)
High energy pulsed wave diathermy machines have been found to produce some degree of therapeutic benefit for essentially the same conditions and to the same extent as standard diathermy. Accordingly, where the contractor's medical staff has determined that the pulsed wave diathermy apparatus used is one which is considered therapeutically effective, the treatments are considered a covered service, but only for those conditions for which standard diathermy is medically indicated and only when rendered by a physician or incident to a physician's professional services.

100-3, 150.6
NCD for Vitamin B12 Injections to Strengthen Tendons, Ligaments, etc., of the Foot (150.6)
Vitamin B12 injections to strengthen tendons, ligaments, etc., of the foot are not covered under Medicare because (1) there is no evidence that vitamin B12 injections are effective for the purpose of strengthening weakened tendons and ligaments, and (2) this is nonsurgical treatment under the subluxation exclusion. Accordingly, vitamin B12 injections are not considered reasonable and necessary within the meaning of Sec.1862(a)(1) of the Act.

100-3, 150.7
NCD for Prolotherapy, Joint Sclerotherapy, and Ligamentous Injections with Sclerosing Agents (150.7)
The medical effectiveness of the above therapies has not been verified by scientifically controlled studies. Accordingly, reimbursement for these modalities should be denied on the ground that they are not reasonable and necessary as required by Sec.1862(a)(1) of the Act.

100-3, 150.10
NCD for Lumbar Artificial Disc Replacement (LADR) (150.10)
B. Nationally Covered IndicationsN/AC. Nationally Non-Covered Indications
Effective for services performed from May 16, 2006 through August 13, 2007, the Centers for Medicare and Medicaid Services (CMS) has found that LADR with the Charite TM lumbar artificial disc is not reasonable and necessary for the Medicare population over 60 years of age; therefore, LADR with the Charite TM lumbar artificial disc is non-covered for Medicare beneficiaries over 60 years of age.

Effective for services performed on or after August 14, 2007, CMS has found that LADR is not reasonable and necessary for the Medicare population over 60 years of age; therefore, LADR is non-covered for Medicare beneficiaries over 60 years of age.

Appendix G — Pub 100 References

D. Other
For Medicare beneficiaries 60 years of age and younger, there is no national coverage determination for LADR, leaving such determinations to continue to be made by the local contractors.

For dates of service May 16, 2006 through August 13, 2007, Medicare coverage under the investigational device exemption (IDE) for LADR with a disc other than the Charite TM lumbar disc in eligible clinical trials is not impacted.

(This NCD last reviewed August 2007.)

100-3, 150.11
Thermal Intradiscal Procedures (TIPs)

A. General
Percutaneous thermal intradiscal procedures (TIPs) involve the insertion of a catheter(s)/probe(s) in the spinal disc under fluoroscopic guidance for the purpose of producing or applying heat and/or disruption within the disc to relieve low back pain.

The scope of this national coverage determination on TIPs includes percutaneous intradiscal techniques that employ the use of a radiofrequency energy source or electrothermal energy to apply or create heat and/or disruption within the disc for coagulation and/or decompression of disc material to treat symptomatic patients with annular disruption of a contained herniated disc, to seal annular tears or fissures, or destroy nociceptors for the purpose of relieving pain. This includes techniques that use single or multiple probe(s)/catheter(s), which utilize a resistance coil or other delivery system technology, are flexible or rigid, and are placed within the nucleus, the nuclear-annular junction, or the annulus. Although not intended to be an all inclusive list, TIPs are commonly identified as intradiscal electrothermal therapy (IDET), intradiscal thermal annuloplasty (IDTA), percutaneous intradiscal radiofrequency thermocoagulation (PIRFT), radiofrequency annuloplasty (RA), intradiscal biacuplasty (IDB), percutaneous (or plasma) disc decompression (PDD) or coblation, or targeted disc decompression (TDD). At times, TIPs are identified or labeled based on the name of the catheter/probe that is used (e.g., SpineCath, discTRODE, SpineWand, Accutherm, or TransDiscal electrodes). Each technique or device has it own protocol for application of the therapy. Percutaneous disc decompression or nucleoplasty procedures that do not utilize a radiofrequency energy source or electrothermal energy (such as the disc decompressor procedure or laser procedure) are not within the scope of this NCD.

B. Nationally Covered Indications
N/A

C. Nationally Non-Covered Indications
Effective for services performed on or after September 29, 2008, the Centers for Medicare and Medicaid Services has determined that TIPs are not reasonable and necessary for the treatment of low back pain. Therefore, TIPs, which include procedures that employ the use of a radiofrequency energy source or electrothermal energy to apply or create heat and/or disruption within the disc for the treatment of low back pain, are noncovered.

D. Other
N/A

(This NCD last reviewed September 2008.)

100-3, 160.1
NCD for Induced Lesions of Nerve Tracts (160.1)
Accordingly, program payment may be made for these denervation procedures when used in selected cases (concurred in by contractor's medical staff) to treat chronic pain.

100-3, 160.2
NCD for Treatment of Motor Function Disorders with Electric Nerve Stimulation (160.2)
Where electric nerve stimulation is employed to treat motor function disorders, no reimbursement may be made for the stimulator or for the services related to its implantation since this treatment cannot be considered reasonable and necessary.

Note: For Medicare coverage of deep brain stimulation for essential tremor and Parkinson's disease, see Sec.160.24 of the NCD Manual.

100-3, 160.4
NCD for Stereotactic Cingulotomy as a Means of Psychosurgery (160.4)
Stereotactic cingulotomy is not covered under Medicare because the procedure is considered to be investigational.

100-3, 160.5
NCD for Stereotaxic Depth Electrode Implantation (160.5)
Stereotaxic depth electrode implantation prior to surgical treatment of focal epilepsy for patients who are unresponsive to anticonvulsant medications has been found both safe and effective for diagnosing resectable seizure foci that may go undetected by conventional scalp electroencephalographs (EEGs).

100-3, 160.6
NCD for Carotid Sinus Nerve Stimulator (160.6)
Implantation of the carotid sinus nerve stimulator is indicated for relief of angina pectoris in carefully selected patients who are refractory to medical therapy and who after undergoing coronary angiography study either are poor candidates for or refuse to have coronary bypass surgery. In such cases, Medicare reimbursement may be made for this device and for the related services required for its implantation.

However, the use of the carotid sinus nerve stimulator in the treatment of paroxysmal supraventricular tachycardia is considered investigational and is not in common use by the medical community. The device and related services in such cases cannot be considered as reasonable and necessary for the treatment of an illness or injury or to improve the functioning of a malformed body member as required by Sec.1862(a)(1) of the Act.

100-3, 160.7
NCD for Electrical Nerve Stimulators (160.7)
Two general classifications of electrical nerve stimulators are employed to treat chronic intractable pain: peripheral nerve stimulators and central nervous system stimulators.

A. Implanted Peripheral Nerve Stimulators
Payment may be made under the prosthetic device benefit for implanted peripheral nerve stimulators. Use of this stimulator involves implantation of electrodes around a selected peripheral nerve. The stimulating electrode is connected by an insulated lead to a receiver unit which is implanted under the skin at a depth not greater than 1/2 inch. Stimulation is induced by a generator connected to an antenna unit which is attached to the skin surface over the receiver unit. Implantation of electrodes requires surgery and usually necessitates an operating room.

Note: Peripheral nerve stimulators may also be employed to assess a patient's suitability for continued treatment with an electric nerve stimulator. As explained in Sec.160.7.1, such use of the stimulator is covered as part of the total diagnostic service furnished to the beneficiary rather than as a prosthesis.

B. Central Nervous System Stimulators (Dorsal Column and Depth Brain Stimulators)
The implantation of central nervous system stimulators may be covered as therapies for the relief of chronic intractable pain, subject to the following conditions:

1. Types of Implantations

    There are two types of implantations covered by this instruction:

    Dorsal Column (Spinal Cord) Neurostimulation - The surgical implantation of neurostimulator electrodes within the dura mater (endodural) or the percutaneous insertion of electrodes in the epidural space is covered.

    Depth Brain Neurostimulation - The stereotactic implantation of electrodes in the deep brain (e.g., thalamus and periaqueductal gray matter) is covered.

2. Conditions for Coverage

    No payment may be made for the implantation of dorsal column or depth brain stimulators or services and supplies related to such implantation, unless all of the conditions listed below have been met:

    The implantation of the stimulator is used only as a late resort (if not a last resort) for patients with chronic intractable pain;

    With respect to item a, other treatment modalities (pharmacological, surgical, physical, or psychological therapies) have been tried and did not prove satisfactory, or are judged to be unsuitable or contraindicated for the given patient;

    Patients have undergone careful screening, evaluation and diagnosis by a multidisciplinary team prior to implantation. (Such screening must include psychological, as well as physical evaluation);

    All the facilities, equipment, and professional and support personnel required for the proper diagnosis, treatment training, and followup of the patient (including that required to satisfy item c) must be available; and

    Demonstration of pain relief with a temporarily implanted electrode precedes permanent implantation.

    Contractors may find it helpful to work with QIOs to obtain the information needed to apply these conditions to claims.

100-3, 160.7.1
NCD for Assessing Patient's Suitability for Electrical Nerve Stimulation Therapy (160.7.1)
Indications and Limitations of Coverage
CIM 35-46

Electrical nerve stimulation is an accepted modality for assessing a patient's suitability for ongoing treatment with a transcutaneous or an implanted nerve stimulator.

Accordingly, program payment may be made for the following techniques when used to determine the potential therapeutic usefulness of an electrical nerve stimulator:

A. Transcutaneous Electrical Nerve Stimulation(TENS)
This technique involves attachment of a transcutaneous nerve stimulator to the surface of the skin over the peripheral nerve to be stimulated. It is used by the patient on a trial basis and its effectiveness in modulating pain is monitored by the physician, or physical therapist. Generally, the physician or physical therapist is able to determine whether the patient is likely to derive a significant therapeutic benefit from continuous use of a transcutaneous stimulator within a trial period of 1 month; in a few cases this determination may take longer to make. Document the medical necessity for such services which are furnished beyond the first month. (See Sec.160.13 for an explanation of coverage of medically necessary supplies for the effective use of TENS.)

If TENS significantly alleviates pain, it may be considered as primary treatment; if it produces no relief or greater discomfort than the original pain electrical nerve stimulation therapy is ruled out. However, where TENS produces incomplete relief, further evaluation with percutaneous electrical nerve stimulation may be considered to determine whether an implanted peripheral nerve stimulator would provide significant relief from pain.

Usually, the physician or physical therapist providing the services will furnish the equipment necessary for assessment. Where the physician or physical therapist advises the patient to rent the TENS from a supplier during the trial period rather than supplying it himself/herself, program payment may be made for rental of the TENS as well as for the services of the physician or physical therapist who is evaluating its use. However, the combined program payment which is made for the physician's or physical therapist's services and the rental of the stimulator from a supplier should not exceed the amount which would be payable for the total service, including the stimulator, furnished by the physician or physical therapist alone.

B. Percutaneous Electrical Nerve Stimulation (PENS)
This diagnostic procedure which involves stimulation of peripheral nerves by a needle electrode inserted through the skin is performed only in a physician's office, clinic, or hospital outpatient department. Therefore, it is covered only when performed by a physician or incident to physician's service. If pain is effectively controlled by percutaneous stimulation, implantation of electrodes is warranted.

As in the case of TENS (described in subsection A), generally the physician should be able to determine whether the patient is likely to derive a significant therapeutic benefit from continuing use of an implanted nerve stimulator within a trial period of 1 month. In a few cases, this determination may take longer to make. The medical necessity for such diagnostic services which are furnished beyond the first month must be documented.

NOTE: Electrical nerve stimulators do not prevent pain but only alleviate pain as it occurs. A patient can be taught how to employ the stimulator, and once this is done, can use it safely and effectively without direct physician supervision. Consequently, it is inappropriate for a patient to visit his/her physician, physical therapist, or an outpatient clinic on a continuing basis for treatment of pain with electrical nerve stimulation. Once it is determined that electrical nerve stimulation should be continued as therapy and the patient has been trained to use the stimulator, it is expected that a stimulator will be implanted or the patient will employ the TENS on a continual basis in his/her home. Electrical nerve stimulation treatments furnished by a physician in his/her office, by a physical therapist or outpatient clinic are excluded from coverage by Sec.1862(a)(1) of the Act. (See Sec.160.7 for an explanation of coverage of the therapeutic use of implanted peripheral nerve stimulators under the prosthetic devices benefit. See Sec.280.13 for an explanation of coverage of the therapeutic use of TENS under the durable medical equipment benefit.)

100-3, 160.8
NCD for Electroencephalographic (EEG) Monitoring During Surgical Procedures Involving the Cerebral Vasculature (160.8)
CIM 35-57

Electroencephalographic (EEG) monitoring is a safe and reliable technique for the assessment of gross cerebral blood flow during general anesthesia and is covered under Medicare. Very characteristic changes in the EEG occur when cerebral perfusion is inadequate for ce rebral function. EEG monitoring as an indirect measure of cerebral perfusion requires the expertise of an electroencephalographer, a neurologist trained in EEG, or an advanced EEG technician for its proper interpretation.

The EEG monitoring may be covered routinely in carotid endarterectomies and in other neurological procedures where cerebral perfusion could be reduced. Such other procedures might include aneurysm surgery where hypotensive anesthesia is used or other cerebral vascular procedures where cerebral blood flow may be interrupted.

100-3, 160.9
NCD for Electroencephalographic (EEG) Monitoring during Open-Heart Surgery (160.9)
The value of EEG monitoring during open heart surgery and in the immediate post-operative period is debatable because there are little published data based on well designed studies regarding its clinical effectiveness. The procedure is not frequently used and does not enjoy widespread acceptance of benefit.

Accordingly, Medicare does not cover EEG monitoring during open heart surgery and during the immediate post-operative period.

100-3, 160.10
NCD for Evoked Response Tests (160.10)
Evoked response tests, including brain stem evoked response and visual evoked response tests, are generally accepted as safe and effective diagnostic tools. Program payment may be made for these procedures.

100-3, 160.12
NCD for Neuromuscular Electrical Stimulaton (NMES) (160.12)
Indications and Limitations of Coverage

Treatment of Muscle Atrophy
Coverage of NMES to treat muscle atrophy is limited to the treatment of disuse atrophy where nerve supply to the muscle is intact, including brain, spinal cord and peripheral nerves, and other non-neurological reasons for disuse atrophy. Some examples would be casting or splinting of a limb, contracture due to scarring of soft tissue as in burn lesions, and hip replacement surgery (until orthotic training begins). (See Sec.160.13 of the NCD Manual for an explanation of coverage of medically necessary supplies for the effective use of NMES.)

Use for Walking in Patients with Spinal Cord Injury (SCI)
The type of NMES that is use to enhance the ability to walk of SCI patients is commonly referred to as functional electrical stimulation (FES). These devices are surface units that use electrical impulses to activate paralyzed or weak muscles in precise sequence. Coverage for the use of NMES/FES is limited to SCI patients for walking, who have completed a training program which consists of at least 32 physical therapy sessions with the device over a period of three months. The trial period of physical therapy will enable the physician treating the patient for his or her spinal cord injury to properly evaluate the person's ability to use these devices frequently and for the long term. Physical therapy necessary to perform this training must be directly performed by the physical therapist as part of a one-on-one training program.

The goal of physical therapy must be to train SCI patients on the use of NMES/FES devices to achieve walking, not to reverse or retard muscle atrophy.

Coverage for NMES/FES for walking will be covered in SCI patients with all of the following characteristics:

- Persons with intact lower motor unite (L1 and below) (both muscle and peripheral nerve);
- Persons with muscle and joint stability for weight bearing at upper and lower extremities that can demonstrate balance and control to maintain an upright support posture independently;
- Persons that demonstrate brisk muscle contraction to NMES and have sensory perception electrical stimulation sufficient for muscle contraction;
- Persons that possess high motivation, commitment and cognitive ability to use such devices for walking;
- Persons that can transfer independently and can demonstrate independent standing tolerance for at least 3 minutes;
- Persons that can demonstrate hand and finger function to manipulate controls;
- Persons with at least 6-month post recovery spinal cord injury and restorative surgery;
- Persons with hip and knee degenerative disease and no history of long bone fracture secondary to osteoporosis; and
- Persons who have demonstrated a willingness to use the device long-term.

NMES/FES for walking will not be covered in SCI patient with any of the following:

- Persons with cardiac pacemakers;
- Severe scoliosis or severe osteoporosis;
- Skin disease or cancer at area of stimulation;
- Irreversible contracture; or
- Autonomic dysflexia.

The only settings where therapists with the sufficient skills to provide these services are employed, are inpatient hospitals; outpatient hospitals; comprehensive outpatient rehabilitation facilities; and outpatient rehabilitation facilities. The physical therapy necessary to perform this training must be part of a one-on-one training program.

Additional therapy after the purchase of the DME would be limited by our general policies in converge of skilled physical therapy.

100-3, 160.13
NCD for Supplies Used in the Delivery of Transcutaneous Electrical Nerve Stimulation (TENS) and Neuromuscular Electrical Stimulation (NMES) (160.13)
A form-fitting conductive garment (and medically necessary related supplies) may be covered under the program only when:

1. It has received permission or approval for marketing by the Food and Drug Administration;
2. It has been prescribed by a physician for use in delivering covered TENS or NMES treatment; and
3. One of the medical indications outlined below is met:
    - The patient cannot manage without the conductive garment because there is such a large area or so many sites to be stimulated and the stimulation would have to be delivered so frequently that it is not feasible to use conventional electrodes, adhesive tapes and lead wires;
    - The patient cannot manage without the conductive garment for the treatment of chronic intractable pain because the areas or sites to be stimulated are inaccessible with the use of conventional electrodes, adhesive tapes and lead wires;
    - The patient has a documented medical condition such as skin problems that preclude the application of conventional electrodes, adhesive tapes and lead wires;
    - The patient requires electrical stimulation beneath a cast either to treat disuse atrophy, where the nerve supply to the muscle is intact, or to treat chronic intractable pain; or
    - The patient has a medical need for rehabilitation strengthening (pursuant to a written plan of rehabilitation) following an injury where the nerve supply to the muscle is intact.

A conductive garment is not covered for use with a TENS device during the trial period specified in Sec.160.3 unless:

- The patient has a documented skin problem prior to the start of the trial period; and
- The carrier's medical consultants are satisfied that use of such an item is medically necessary for the patient.

100-3, 160.15
NCD for Electrotherapy for Treatment of Facial Nerve Paralysis (Bell's Palsy) (160.15)
Electrotherapy for the treatment of facial nerve paralysis, commonly known as Bell's Palsy, is not covered under Medicare because its clinical effectiveness has not been established.

100-3, 160.17
NCD for L-DOPA (160.17)

A - Part A Payment for L-Dopa and Associated Inpatient Hospital Services

A hospital stay and related ancillary services for the administration of L-Dopa are covered if medically required for this purpose. Whether a drug represents an allowable inpatient hospital cost during such stay depends on whether it meets the definition of a drug in Sec.1861(t) of the Act; i.e., on its inclusion in the compendia named in the Act or approval by the hospital's pharmacy and drug therapeutics (P&DT) or equivalent committee. (Levodopa (L-Dopa) has been favorably evaluated for the treatment of Parkinsonism by A.M.A. Drug Evaluations, First Edition 1971, the replacement compendia for "New Drugs.")

Inpatient hospital services are frequently not required in many cases when L-Dopa therapy is initiated. Therefore, determine the medical need for inpatient hospital services on the basis of medical facts in the individual case. It is not necessary to hospitalize the typical, well-functioning, ambulatory Parkinsonian patient who has no concurrent disease at the start of L-Dopa treatment. It is reasonable to provide inpatient hospital services for Parkinsonian patients with concurrent diseases, particularly of the cardiovascular, gastrointestinal, and neuropsychiatric systems. Although many patients require hospitalization for a period of under 2 weeks, a 4-week period of inpatient care is not unreasonable.

Laboratory tests in connection with the administration of L-Dopa - The tests medically warranted in connection with the achievement of optimal dosage and the control of the side effects of L-Dopa include a complete blood count, liver function tests such as SGOT, SGPT, and/or alkaline phosphatase, BUN or creatinine and urinalysis, blood sugar, and electrocardiogram.

Whether or not the patient is hospitalized, laboratory tests in certain cases are reasonable at weekly intervals although some physicians prefer to perform the tests much less frequently.

Physical therapy furnished in connection with administration of L-Dopa - Where, following administration of the drug, the patient experiences a reduction of rigidity which permits the reestablishment of a restorative goal for him/her, physical therapy services required to enable him/her to achieve this goal are payable provided they require the skills of a qualified physical therapist and are furnished by or under the supervision of such a therapist. However, once the individual's restoration potential has been achieved, the services required to maintain him/her at this level do not generally require the skills of a qualified physical therapist. In such situations, the role of the therapist is to evaluate the patient's needs in consultation with his/her physician and design a program of exercise appropriate to the capacity and tolerance of the patient and treatment objectives of the physician, leaving to others the actual carrying out of the program. While the evaluative services rendered by a qualified physical therapist are payable as physical therapy, services furnished by others in connection with the carrying out of the maintenance program established by the therapist are not.

B - Part A Reimbursement for L-Dopa Therapy in SNFs

Initiation of L-Dopa therapy can be appropriately carried out in the SNF setting, applying the same guidelines used for initiation of L-Dopa therapy in the hospital, including the types of patients who should be covered for inpatient services, the role of physical therapy, and the use of laboratory tests. (See subsection A.)

Where inpatient care is required and L-Dopa therapy is initiated in the SNF, limit the stay to a maximum of 4 weeks; but in many cases the need may be no longer than 1 or 2 weeks, depending upon the patient's condition. However, where L-Dopa therapy is begun in the hospital and the patient is transferred to an SNF for continuation of the therapy, a combined length of stay in hospital and SNF of no longer than 4 weeks is reasonable (i.e., 1 week hospital stay followed by 3 weeks SNF stay; or 2 weeks hospital stay followed by 2 weeks SNF stay; etc.). Medical need must be demonstrated in cases where the combined length of stay in hospital and SNF is longer than 4 weeks. The choice of hospital or SNF, and the decision regarding the relative length of time spent in each, should be left to the medical judgment of the treating physician.

C - L-Dopa Coverage Under Part B

Part B reimbursement may not be made for the drug L-Dopa since it is a self-administrable drug. However, physician services rendered in connection with its administration and control of its side effects are covered if determined to be reasonable and necessary. Initiation of L-Dopa therapy on an outpatient basis is possible in most cases. Visit frequency ranging from every week to every 2 or 3 months is acceptable. However, after half a year of therapy, visits more frequent than every month would usually not be reasonable.

100-3, 160.18
NCD for Vagus Nerve Stimulation for Treatment of Seizures (160.18)

B. Nationally Covered Indications

Effective for services performed on or after July 1, 1999, VNS is reasonable and necessary for patients with medically refractory partial onset seizures for whom surgery is not recommended or for whom surgery has failed.

C. Nationally Non-Covered Indications

Effective for services performed on or after July 1, 1999, VNS is not reasonable and necessary for all other types of seizure disorders which are medically refractory and for whom surgery is not recommended or for whom surgery has failed.

Effective for services performed on or after May 4, 2007, VNS is not reasonable and necessary for resistant depression. (Information on the national coverage analysis leading to this determination can be found at: http://www.cms.hhs.gov/mcd/viewnca.asp?where=index&nca_id= 195.)

D. Other

Also see Sec.160, "Electrical Nerve Stimulators."

(This NCD last reviewed May 2007.)

100-3, 160.20
NCD for Transfer Factor for Treatment of Multiple Sclerosis (160.20)

Transfer factor is the dialysate of an extract from sensitized leukocytes which increases cellular immune activity in the recipient. It is not covered as a treatment for multiple sclerosis because its use for the purpose is still experimental.

100-3, 160.21
NCD for Telephone Transmission of Electroencephalograms (EEGs) (160.21)

Telephone transmission of electroencephalograms (EEGs) is covered as a physician's service or as incident to a physician's service when reasonable and necessary for the individual patient, under appropriate circumstances. The service is safe, and may save time and cost in sending EEGs from remote areas without special competence in neurology, neurosurgery, and electroencephalography, by avoiding the need to transport patients to large medical centers for standard EEG testing.

100-3, 160.22
NCD for Ambulatory EEG Monitoring (160.22)

Ambulatory EEG monitoring is a diagnostic procedure for patients in whom a seizure diathesis is suspected but not defined by history, physical or resting EEG. Ambulatory EEG can be utilized in the differential diagnosis of syncope and transient ischemic attacks if not elucidated by conventional studies. Ambulatory EEG should always be preceded by a resting EEG.

Ambulatory EEG monitoring is considered an established technique and covered under Medicare for the above purposes.

100-3, 170.3
NCD for Speech Pathology Services for the Treatment of Dysphagia (170.3)

Speech-language pathology services are covered under Medicare for the treatment of dysphagia, regardless of the presence of a communication disability.

100-3, 180.1
NCD for Medical Nutrition Therapy (180.1)

Effective October 1, 2002, basic coverage of MNT for the first year a beneficiary receives MNT with either a diagnosis of renal disease or diabetes as defined at 42 CFR Sec.410.130 is 3 hours. Also effective October 1, 2002, basic coverage in subsequent years for renal disease or diabetes is 2 hours. The dietitian/nutritionist may choose how many units are performed per day as long as all of the other requirements in this NCD and 42 CFR Secs.410.130-410.134 are met. Pursuant to the exception at 42 CFR Sec.410.132(b)(5), additional hours are considered to be medically necessary and covered if the treating physician determines that there is a change in medical condition, diagnosis, or treatment regimen that requires a change in MNT and orders additional hours during that episode of care.

Effective October 1, 2002, if the treating physician determines that receipt of both MNT and DSMT is medically necessary in the same episode of care, Medicare will cover both DSMT and MNT initial and subsequent years without decreasing either benefit as long as DSMT and MNT are not provided on the same date of service. The dietitian/nutritionist may choose how many units are performed per day as long as all of the other requirements in the NCD and 42 CFR Secs.410.130-410.134 are met. Pursuant to the exception at 42 CFR 410.132(b)(5), additional hours are considered to be medically necessary and covered if the treating physician determines that there is a change in medical condition, diagnosis, or treatment regimen that requires a change in MNT and orders additional hours during that episode of care.

100-3, 190.1
NCD for Histocompatibility Testing (190.1)

This testing is safe and effective when it is performed on patients:

- In preparation for a kidney transplant;
- In preparation for bone marrow transplantation;
- In preparation for blood platelet transfusions (particularly where multiple infusions are involved); or
- Who are suspected of having ankylosing spondylitis.

This testing is covered under Medicare when used for any of the indications listed in A, B, and C and if it is reasonable and necessary for the patient.

It is covered for ankylosing spondylitis in cases where other methods of diagnosis would not be appropriate or have yielded inconclusive results. Request documentation supporting the medical necessity of the test from the physician in all cases where ankylosing spondylitis is indicated as the reason for the test.

100-3, 190.2
NCD for Diagnostic Pap Smears (190.2)

CIM 50-20, CIM 50-20.1

A diagnostic pap smear and related medically necessary services are covered under Medicare Part B when ordered by a physician under one of the following conditions:

- Previous cancer of the cervix, uterus, or vagina that has been or is presently being treated;
- Previous abnormal pap smear;
- Any abnormal findings of the vagina, cervix, uterus, ovaries, or adnexa;
- Any significant complaint by the patient referable to the female reproductive system; or
- Any signs or symptoms that might in the physician's judgment reasonably be related to a gynecologic disorder.

Screening Pap Smears and Pelvic Examinations for Early Detection of Cervical or Vaginal Cancer. (See section 210.2.)

100-3, 190.3
NCD for Cytogenetic Studies (190.3)
Medicare covers these tests when they are reasonable and necessary for the diagnosis or treatment of the following conditions:

Genetic disorders (e.g., mongolism) in a fetus (See Medicare Benefit Policy Manual, Chapter 15, "Covered medical and Other health Services," Sec.20.1)

Failure of sexual development;

Chronic myelogenous leukemia;

Acute leukemias lymphoid (FAB L1-L3), myeloid (FAB M0-M7), and unclassified; or

Mylodysplasia

100-3, 190.4
NCD for Electron Microscope (190.4)
The electron microscope has been used in the examination of biopsies for years; its efficacy, and therefore its Medicare coverage, is not being questioned. However, there are less expensive methods for examining biopsies which are normally adequate. The additional expense for the electron microscope is normally warranted only when distinguishing different types of nephritis from renal needle biopsies or when there is an uncertain diagnosis from the pathologist. When an uncertain diagnosis from the pathologists results from a less expensive method of examination and an electron microscope examination is therefore necessary, both biopsy examinations are covered. Where the additional expense for an electron microscope examination is not warranted, payment is based upon the less costly methods of examining biopsies.

100-3, 190.5
NCD for Sweat Test (190.5)
Indications and Limitations of Coverage

The sweat test is an important diagnostic tool in cystic fibrosis and may be covered when used for that purpose. Usage of the sweat test as a predictor of efficacy of sympathectomy in peripheral vascular disease is unproven and, therefore, is not covered.

100-3, 190.6
NCD for Hair Analysis (190.6)
Indications and Limitations of Coverage

Hair analysis to detect mineral traces as an aid in diagnosing human disease is not a covered service under Medicare.

The correlation of hair analysis to the chemical state of the whole body is not possible at this time, and therefore this diagnostic procedure cannot be considered to be reasonable and necessary under Sec.1862(a)(1) of the Act.

100-3, 190.8
NCD for Lymphocyte Mitogen Response Assays (190.8)
It is a covered test under Medicare when it is medically necessary to assess lymphocytic function in diagnosed immunodeficiency diseases and to monitor immunotherapy.

It is not covered when it is used to monitor the treatment of cancer, because its use for that purpose is experimental.

100-3, 190.9
NCD for Serologic Testing for Acquired Immunodeficiency Syndrome (AIDS) (190.9)
These tests may be covered when performed to help determine a diagnosis for symptomaticpatients. They are not covered when furnished as part of a screening program for asymptomatic persons.

Note: Two enzyme-linked immunosorbent assay (ELISA) tests that were conducted on the same specimen must both be positive before Medicare will cover the Western blot test.

100-3, 190.10
NCD for Laboratory Tests - CRD Patients (190.10)
Laboratory tests are essential to monitor the progress of CRD patients. The following list and frequencies of tests constitute the level and types of routine laboratory tests that are covered. Bills for other types of tests are considered nonroutine. Routine tests at greater frequencies must include medical justification. Nonroutine tests generally are justified by the diagnosis.

The routinely covered regimen includes the following tests:

Per Dialysis

- All hematocrit or hemoglobin and clotting time tests furnished incident to dialysis treatments.

Per Week

- Prothrombin time for patients on anticoagulant therapy
- Serum Creatinine

Per Week or Thirteen Per Quarter

- BUN

Monthly

- CBC
- Serum Calcium
- Serum Potassium
- Serum Chloride
- Serum Bicarbonate
- Serum Phosphorous
- Total Protein
- Serum Albumin
- Alkaline Phospatase
- AST, SGOT
- LDH

Guidelines for tests other than those routinely performed include:

- Serum Aluminum - one every 3 months
- Serum Ferritin - one every 3 months

The following tests for hepatitis B are covered when patients first enter a dialysis facility:

- Hepatitis B surface antigen (HBsAg)
- Anti-HBs

Coverage of future testing in these patients depends on their serologic status and on whether they have been successfully immunized against hepatitis B virus. The following table summarizes the frequency of serologic surveillance for hepatitis B. Tests furnished according to this table do not require additional documentation and are paid separately because payment for maintenance dialysis treatments does not take them into account.

Frequency of Screening

	Vaccination and Serologic Status	HbsAg Patients	Anti-HBs Patients
Unvaccinated	Susceptible	Monthly	Semiannually
Unvaccinated	HBsAg Carrier	Annually	None
Unvaccinated	Anti-HBs-Positive (1)	None	Annually
Vaccinated	Anti-HBs-Positive (1)	None	Annually
Vaccinated	Low Level or No Anti-HBs	Monthly	Semiannually

(1) At least 10 sample ration units by radioimmunoassay or positive by enzyme immunoassay.

Patients who are in the process of receiving hepatitis B vaccines, but have not received the complete series, should continue to be routinely screened as susceptible. Between one and six months after the third dose, all vaccines should be tested for anti-HBs to confirm their response to the vaccine. Patients who have a level of anti-HBs of at least 10 sample ratio units (SRUs) by radioimmunoassay (RIA) or who are positive by enzyme immunoassay (EIA) are considered adequate responders to vaccine and need only be tested for anti-HBs annually to verify their immune status. If anti-HBs drops below 10 SRUs by RIA or is negative by EIA, a booster dose of hepatitis B vaccine should be given.

Laboratory tests are subject to the normal coverage requirements. If the laboratory services are performed by a free-standing facility, be sure it meets the conditions of coverage for independent laboratories.

100-3, 190.11
NCD for Home Prothrombin Time International Normalized Ratio (INR) Monitoring for Anticoagulation Management (190.11)

A. General

Use of the International Normalized Ratio (INR) or prothrombin time (PT) - standard measurement for reporting the blood's clotting time) - allows physicians to determine the level of anticoagulation in a patient independent of the laboratory reagents used. The INR is the ratio of the patient's PT (extrinsic or tissue-factor dependent coagulation pathway) compared to the mean PT for a group of normal individuals. Maintaining patients within his/her prescribed therapeutic range minimizes adverse events associated with inadequate or excessive anticoagulation such as serious bleeding or thromboembolic events. Patient self-testing and self-management through the use of a home INR monitor may be used to improve the time in therapeutic rate (TTR) for select groups of patients. Increased TTR leads to improved clinical outcomes and reductions in thromboembolic and hemorrhagic events.

Warfarin (also prescribed under other trade names, e.g., Coumadin(R)) is a self-administered, oral anticoagulant (blood thinner) medication that affects the vitamin K- dependent clotting factors II, VII, IX and X. It is widely used for various medical conditions, and has a narrow therapeutic index, meaning it is a drug with less than a 2-fold difference between median lethal dose and median effective dose. For this reason, since October 4, 2006, it falls under the category of a Food and Drug dministration (FDA) "black-box" drug whose dosage must be closely monitored to avoid serious complications. A PT/INR monitoring system is a portable testing device that includes a finger-stick and an FDA-cleared meter that measures the time it takes for a person's blood plasma to clot.

B. Nationally Covered Indications

For services furnished on or after March 19, 2008, Medicare will cover the use of home PT/INR monitoring for chronic, oral anticoagulation management for patients with mechanical heart valves, chronic atrial fibrillation, or venous thromboembolism (inclusive of deep venous thrombosis and pulmonary embolism) on warfarin. The monitor and the home testing must be prescribed by a treating physician as provided at 42 CFR 410.32(a), and all of the following requirements must be met:

1. The patient must have been anticoagulated for at least 3 months prior to use of the home INR device; and,

Appendix G — Pub 100 References

2. The patient must undergo a face-to-face educational program on anticoagulation anagement and must have demonstrated the correct use of the device prior to its use in the home; and,
3. The patient continues to correctly use the device in the context of the management of the anticoagulation therapy following the initiation of home monitoring; and,
4. Self-testing with the device should not occur more frequently than once a week.

C. Nationally Non-Covered Indications
N/A

D. Other
1. All other indications for home PT/INR monitoring not indicated as nationally covered above remain at local Medicare contractor discretion.
2. This national coverage determination (NCD) is distinct from, and makes no changes to, the PT clinical laboratory NCD at section 190.17 of Publication 100-03 of the NCD Manual.

100-3, 190.12
NCD for Urine Culture, Bacterial (190.12)
Indications

1. A patient's urinalysis is abnormal suggesting urinary tract infection, for example, abnormal microscopic (hematuria, pyuria, bacteriuria); abnormal biochemical urinalysis (positive leukocyte esterase, nitrite, protein, blood); a Gram's stain positive for microorganisms; positive bacteriuria screen by a non?culture technique; or other significant abnormality of a urinalysis. While it is not essential to evaluate a urine specimen by one of these methods before a urine culture is performed, certain clinical presentations with highly suggestive signs and symptoms may lend themselves to an antecedent urinalysis procedure where follow-up culture depends upon an initial positive or abnormal test result.
2. A patient has clinical signs and symptoms indicative of a possible urinary tract infection (UTI). Acute lower UTI may present with urgency, frequency, nocturia, dysuria, discharge or incontinence. These findings may also be noted in upper UTI with additional systemic symptoms (for example, fever, chills, lethargy); or pain in the costovertebral, abdominal, or pelvic areas. Signs and symptoms may overlap considerably with other inflammatory conditions of the genitourinary tract (for example, prostatitis, urethritis, vaginitis, or cerviciitis). Elderly or immunocompromised patients, or patients with neurologic disorders may present atypically (for example, general debility, acute mental status changes, declining functional status).
3. The patient is being evaluated for suspected urosepsis, fever of unknown origin, or other systemic manifestations of infection but without a known source. Signs and symptoms used to define sepsis have been well established.
4. A test-of cure is generally not indicated in an uncomplicated infection. However, it may be indicated if the patient is being evaluated for response to therapy and there is a complicating co-existing urinary abnormality including structural or functional abnormalities, calculi, foreign bodies, or ureteral/renal stents or there is clinical or laboratory evidence of failure to respond as described in Indications 1 and 2.
5. In surgical procedures involving major manipulations of the genitourinary tract, preoperative examination to detect occult infection may be indicated in selected cases (for example, prior to renal transplantation, manipulation or removal of kidney stones, or transurethral surgery of the bladder or prostate).
6. Urine culture may be indicated to detect occult infection in renal transplant recipients on immunosuppressive therapy.

Limitations

1. CPT 87086 may be used one time per encounter.
2. Colony count restrictions on coverage of CPT 87088 do not apply as they may be highly variable according to syndrome or other clinical circumstances (for example, antecedent therapy, collection time, degree of hydration).
3. CPT 87088, 87184, and 87186 may be used multiple times in association with or independent of 87086, as urinary tract infections may be polymicrobial.
4. Testing for asymptomatic bacteriuria as part of a prenatal evaluation may be medically appropriate but is considered screening and, therefore, not covered by Medicare. The US Preventive Services Task Force has concluded that screening for asymptomatic bacteriuria outside of the narrow indication for pregnant women is generally not indicated. There are insufficient data to recommend screening in ambulatory elderly patients including those with diabetes. Testing may be clinically indicated on other grounds including likelihood of recurrence or potential adverse effects of antibiotics, but is considered screening in the absence of clinical or laboratory evidence of infection.

100-3, 190.13
NCD for Human Immunodeficiency Virus (HIV) Testing (Prognosis Including Monitoring) (190.13)
Indications

1. A plasma HIV RNA baseline level may be medically necessary in any patient with confirmed HIV infection.
2. Regular periodic measurement of plasma HIV RNA levels may be medically necessary to determine risk for disease progression in an HIV-infected individual and to determine when to initiate or modify antiretroviral treatment regimens.
3. In clinical situations where the risk of HIV infection is significant and initiation of therapy is anticipated, a baseline HIV quantification may be performed. These situations include:
   a. Persistence of borderline or equivocal serologic reactivity in an at-risk individual.
   b. Signs and symptoms of acute retroviral syndrome characterized by fever, malaise, lymphadenopathy and rash in an at-risk individual.

Limitations

1. Viral quantification may be appropriate for prognostic use including baseline determination, periodic monitoring, and monitoring of response to therapy. Use as a diagnostic test method is not indicated.
2. Measurement of plasma HIV RNA levels should be performed at the time of establishment of an HIV infection diagnosis. For an accurate baseline, 2 specimens in a 2-week period are appropriate.
3. For prognosis including anti-retroviral therapy monitoring, regular, periodic measurements are appropriate. The frequency of viral load testing should be consistent with the most current Centers for Disease Control and Prevention guidelines for use of anti-retroviral agents in adults and adolescents or pediatrics.
4. Because differences in absolute HIV copy number are known to occur using different assays, plasma HIV RNA levels should be measured by the same analytical method. A change in assay method may necessitate re-establishment of a baseline.
5. Nucleic acid quantification techniques are representative of rapidly emerging and evolving new technologies. As such, users are advised to remain current on FDA-approval status.

100-3, 190.14
NCD for Human Immunodeficiency Virus (HIV) Testing (Diagnosis) (190.14)
Indications and Limitations of Coverage

Indications

Diagnostic testing to establish HIV infection may be indicated when there is a strong clinical suspicion supported by one or more of the following clinical findings:

1. The patient has a documented, otherwise unexplained, AIDS-defining or AIDS-associated opportunistic infection.
2. The patient has another documented sexually transmitted disease which identifies significant risk of exposure to HIV and the potential for an early or subclinical infection.
4. The patient has documented acute or chronic hepatitis B or C infection that identifies a significant risk of exposure to HIV and the potential for an early or subclinical infection.
5. The patient has a documented AIDS-defining or AIDS-associated neoplasm.
6. The patient has a documented AIDS-associated neurologic disorder or otherwise unexplained dementia.
7. The patient has another documented AIDS-defining clinical condition, or a history of other severe, recurrent, or persistent conditions which suggest an underlying immune deficiency (for example, cutaneous or mucosal disorders).
8. The patient has otherwise unexplained generalized signs and symptoms suggestive of a chronic process with an underlying immune deficiency (for example, fever, weight loss, malaise, fatigue, chronic diarrhea, failure to thrive, chronic cough, hemoptysis, shortness of breath, or lymphadenopathy).
9. The patient has otherwise unexplained laboratory evidence of a chronic disease process with an underlying immune deficiency (for example, anemia, leukopenia, pancytopenia, lymphopenia, or low CD4+ lymphocyte count).
10. The patient has signs and symptoms of acute retroviral syndrome with fever, malaise, lymphadenopathy, and skin rash.
11. The patient has documented exposure to blood or body fluids known to be capable of transmitting HIV (for example, needlesticks and other significant blood exposures) and antiviral therapy is initiated or anticipated to be initiated.
12. The patient is undergoing treatment for rape. (HIV testing is a part of the rape treatment protocol.)

Limitations

1. HIV antibody testing in the United States is usually performed using HIV-1 or HIV-¾ combination tests. HIV-2 testing is indicated if clinical circumstances suggest HIV-2 is likely (that is, compatible clinical findings and HIV-1 test negative). HIV-2 testing may also be indicated in areas of the country where there is greater prevalence of HIV-2 infections.
2. The Western Blot test should be performed only after documentation that the initial EIA tests are repeatedly positive or equivocal on a single sample.
3. The HIV antigen tests currently have no defined diagnostic usage.
4. Direct viral RNA detection may be performed in those situations where serologic testing does not establish a diagnosis but strong clinical suspicion persists (for example, acute retroviral syndrome, nonspecific serologic evidence of HIV, or perinatal HIV infection).
5. If initial serologic tests confirm an HIV infection, repeat testing is not indicated.
6. If initial serologic tests are HIV EIA negative and there is no indication for confirmation of infection by viral RNA detection, the interval prior to retesting is 3-6 months.
7. Testing for evidence of HIV infection using serologic methods may be medically appropriate in situations where there is a risk of exposure to HIV. However, in the absence of a documented AIDS defining or HIV- associated disease, an HIV associated sign or symptom, or documented exposure to a known HIV-infected source, the testing is considered by Medicare to be screening and thus is not covered by Medicare (for example, history of multiple blood component transfusions, exposure to blood or body fluids not resulting in consideration of therapy, history of transplant, history of illicit drug use, multiple sexual partners, same-sex encounters, prostitution, or contact with prostitutes).
8. The CPT Editorial Panel has issued a number of codes for infectious agent detection by direct antigen or nucleic acid probe techniques that have not yet been developed or are only being used on an investigational basis. Laboratory providers are advised to remain current on FDA-approval status for these tests

Current Procedural Coding Expert

Appendix G — Pub 100 References

100-3, 190.15

NCD for Blood Counts (190.15)

Indications

Indications for a CBC or hemogram include red cell, platelet, and white cell disorders. Examples of these indications are enumerated individually below.

1. Indications for a CBC generally include the evaluation of bone marrow dysfunction as a result of neoplasms, therapeutic agents, exposure to toxic substances, or pregnancy. The CBC is also useful in assessing peripheral destruction of blood cells, suspected bone marrow failure or bone marrow infiltrate, suspected myeloproliferative, myelodysplastic, or lymphoproliferative processes, and immune disorders.
2. Indications for hemogram or CBC related to red cell (RBC) parameters of the hemogram include signs, symptoms, test results, illness, or disease that can be associated with anemia or other red blood cell disorder (e.g., pallor, weakness, fatigue, weight loss, bleeding, acute injury associated with blood loss or suspected blood loss, abnormal menstrual bleeding, hematuria, hematemesis, hematochezia, positive fecal occult blood test, malnutrition, vitamin deficiency, malabsorption, neuropathy, known malignancy, presence of acute or chronic disease that may have associated anemia, coagulation or hemostatic disorders, postural dizziness, syncope, abdominal pain, change in bowel habits, chronic marrow hypoplasia or decreased RBC production, tachycardia, systolic heart murmur, congestive heart failure, dyspnea, angina, nailbed deformities, growth retardation, jaundice, hepatomegaly, splenomegaly, lymphadenopathy, ulcers on the lower extremities).
3. Indications for hemogram or CBC related to red cell (RBC) parameters of the hemogram include signs, symptoms, test results, illness, or disease that can be associated with polycythemia (for example, fever, chills, ruddy skin, conjunctival redness, cough, wheezing, cyanosis, clubbing of the fingers, orthopnea, heart murmur, headache, vague cognitive changes including memory changes, sleep apnea, weakness, pruritus, dizziness, excessive sweating, visual symptoms, weight loss, massive obesity, gastrointestinal bleeding, paresthesias, dyspnea, joint symptoms, epigastric distress, pain and erythema of the fingers or toes, venous or arterial thrombosis, thromboembolism, myocardial infarction, stroke, transient ischemic attacks, congenital heart disease, chronic obstructive pulmonary disease, increased erythropoietin production associated with neoplastic, renal or hepatic disorders, androgen or diuretic use, splenomegaly, hepatomegaly, diastolic hypertension.)
4. Specific indications for CBC with differential count related to the WBC include signs, symptoms, test results, illness, or disease associated with leukemia, infections or inflammatory processes, suspected bone marrow failure or bone marrow infiltrate, suspected myeloproliferative, myelodysplastic or lymphoproliferative disorder, use of drugs that may cause leukopenia, and immune disorders (e.g., fever, chills, sweats, shock, fatigue, malaise, tachycardia, tachypnea, heart murmur, seizures, alterations of consciousness, meningismus, pain such as headache, abdominal pain, arthralgia, odynophagia, or dysuria, redness or swelling of skin, soft tissue bone, or joint, ulcers of the skin or mucous membranes, gangrene, mucous membrane discharge, bleeding, thrombosis, respiratory failure, pulmonary infiltrate, jaundice, diarrhea, vomiting, hepatomegaly, splenomegaly, lymphadenopathy, opportunistic infection such as oral candidiasis.)
5. Specific indications for CBC related to the platelet count include signs, symptoms, test results, illness, or disease associated with increased or decreased platelet production and destruction, or platelet dysfunction (e.g., gastrointestinal bleeding, genitourinary tract bleeding, bilateral epistaxis, thrombosis, ecchymosis, purpura, jaundice, petechiae, fever, heparin therapy, suspected DIC, shock, pre-eclampsia, neonate with maternal ITP, massive transfusion, recent platelet transfusion, cardiopulmonary bypass, hemolytic uremic syndrome, renal diseases, lymphadenopathy, hepatomegaly, splenomegaly, hypersplenism, neurologic abnormalities, viral or other infection, myeloproliferative, myelodysplastic, or lymphoproliferative disorder, thrombosis, exposure to toxic agents, excessive alcohol ingestion, autoimmune disorders (SLE, RA and other).
6. Indications for hemogram or CBC related to red cell (RBC) parameters of the hemogram include, in addition to those already listed, thalassemia, suspected hemoglobinopathy, lead poisoning, arsenic poisoning, and spherocytosis.
7. Specific indications for CBC with differential count related to the WBC include, in addition to those already listed, storage diseases; mucopolysaccharidoses, and use of drugs that cause leukocytosis such as G-CSF or GM-CSF
8. Specific indications for CBC related to platelet count include, in addition to those already listed, May-Hegglin syndrome and Wiskott-Aldrich syndrome.

Limitations

1. Testing of patients who are asymptomatic, or who do not have a condition that could be expected to result in a hematological abnormality, is screening and is not a covered service.
2. In some circumstances it may be appropriate to perform only a hemoglobin or hematocrit to assess the oxygen carrying capacity of the blood. When the ordering provider requests only a hemoglobin or hematocrit, the remaining components of the CBC are not covered.
3. When a blood count is performed for an end-stage renal disease (ESRD) patient, and is billed outside the ESRD rate, documentation of the medical necessity for the blood count must be submitted with the claim.
4. In some patients presenting with certain signs, symptoms or diseases, a single CBC may be appropriate. Repeat testing may not be indicated unless abnormal results are found, or unless there is a change in clinical condition. If repeat testing is performed, a more descriptive diagnosis code (e.g., anemia) should be reported to support medical necessity. However, repeat testing may be indicated where results are normal in patients with conditions where there is a continued risk for the development of hematologic abnormality.

100-3, 190.16

NCD for Partial Thromboplastin Time (PTT) (190.16)

Indications and Limitations of Coverage

Indications

1. The PTT is most commonly used to quantitate the effect of therapeutic unfractionated heparin and to regulate its dosing. Except during transitions between heparin and warfarin therapy, in general both the PTT and PT are not necessary together to assess the effect of anticoagulation therapy. PT and PTT must be justified separately.
2. A PTT may be used to assess patients with signs or symptoms of hemorrhage or thrombosis. For example: abnormal bleeding, hemorrhage or hematoma petechiae or other signs of thrombocytopenia that could be due to disseminated intravascular coagulation; swollen extremity with or without prior trauma.
3. A PTT may be useful in evaluating patients who have a history of a condition known to be associated with the risk of hemorrhage or thrombosis that is related to the intrinsic coagulation pathway. Such abnormalities may be genetic or acquired. For example: dysfibrinogenemia; afibrinogenemia (complete); acute or chronic liver dysfunction or failure, including Wilson's disease; hemophilia; liver disease and failure; infectious processes; bleeding disorders; disseminated intravascular coagulation; lupus erythematosus or other conditions associated with circulating inhibitors, e.g., Factor VIII Inhibitor, lupus-like anticoagulant, etc.; sepsis; von Willebrand's disease; arterial and venous thrombosis, including the evaluation of hypercoagulable states; clinical conditions associated with nephrosis or renal failure; other acquired and congenital coagulopathies as well as thrombotic states.
4. A PTT may be used to assess the risk of thrombosis or hemorrhage in patients who are going to have a medical intervention known to be associated with increased risk of bleeding or thrombosis. An example is as follows: evaluation prior to invasive procedures or operations of patients with personal or family history of bleeding or who are on heparin therapy.

Limitations

1. The PTT is not useful in monitoring the effects of warfarin on a patient's coagulation routinely. However, a PTT may be ordered on a patient being treated with warfarin as heparin therapy is being discontinued. A PTT may also be indicated when the PT is markedly prolonged due to warfarin toxicity.
2. The need to repeat this test is determined by changes in the underlying medical condition and/or the dosing of heparin.
3. Testing prior to any medical intervention associated with a risk of bleeding and thrombosis (other than thrombolytic therapy) will generally be considered medically necessary only where there are signs or symptoms of a bleeding or thrombotic abnormality or a personal history of bleeding, thrombosis or a condition associated with a coagulopathy. Hospital/clinic-specific policies, protocols, etc., in and of themselves, cannot alone justify coverage.

100-3, 190.17

NCD for Prothrombin Time (PT) (190.17)

Indications

1. A PT may be used to assess patients taking warfarin. The prothrombin time is generally not useful in monitoring patients receiving heparin who are not taking warfarin.
2. A PT may be used to assess patients with signs or symptoms of abnormal bleeding or thrombosis. For example: swollen extremity with or without prior trauma; unexplained bruising; abnormal bleeding, hemorrhage or hematoma; petechiae or other signs of thrombocytopenia that could be due to disseminated intravascular coagulation.
3. A PT may be useful in evaluating patients who have a history of a condition known to be associated with the risk of bleeding or thrombosis that is related to the extrinsic coagulation pathway. Such abnormalities may be genetic or acquired. For example: dysfibrinogenemia; afibrinogenemia (complete); acute or chronic liver dysfunction or failure, including Wilson's disease and Hemochromatosis; disseminated intravascular coagulation (DIC); congenital and acquired deficiencies of factors II, V, VII, X; vitamin K deficiency; lupus erythematosus; hypercoagulable state; paraproteinemia; lymphoma; amyloidosis; acute and chronic leukemias; plasma cell dyscrasia; HIV infection; malignant neoplasms; hemorrhagic fever; salicylate poisoning; obstructive jaundice; intestinal fistula; malabsorption syndrome; colitis; chronic diarrhea; presence of peripheral venous or arterial thrombosis or pulmonary emboli or myocardial infarction; patients with bleeding or clotting tendencies; organ transplantation; presence of circulating coagulation inhibitors.
4. A PT may be used to assess the risk of hemorrhage or thrombosis in patients who are going to have a medical intervention known to be associated with increased risk of bleeding or thrombosis. For example: evaluation prior to invasive procedures or operations of patients with personal history of bleeding or a condition associated with coagulopathy prior to the use of thrombolytic medication.

Limitations

1. When an ESRD patient is tested for PT, testing more frequently than weekly requires documentation of medical necessity, e.g., other than chronic renal failure or renal failure, unspecified.
2. The need to repeat this test is determined by changes in the underlying medical condition and/or the dosing of warfarin. In a patient on stable warfarin therapy, it is ordinarily not necessary to repeat testing more than every two to three weeks. When testing is performed to evaluate a patient with signs or symptoms of abnormal bleeding or thrombosis and the initial test result is normal, it is ordinarily not necessary to repeat testing unless there is a change in the patient's medical status.
3. Since the INR is a calculation, it will not be paid in addition to the PT when expressed in seconds, and is considered part of the conventional prothrombin time.

Appendix G — Pub 100 References

Appendix G — Pub 100 References

4. Testing prior to any medical intervention associated with a risk of bleeding and thrombosis (other than thrombolytic therapy) will generally be considered medically necessary only where there are signs or symptoms of a bleeding or thrombotic abnormality or a personal history of bleeding, thrombosis or a condition associated with a coagulopathy. Hospital/clinic-specific policies, protocols, etc., in and of themselves, cannot alone justify coverage.

100-3, 190.18
100-3, 190.18
Indications

1. Ferritin (82728), iron (83540) and either iron binding capacity (83550) or transferrin (84466) are useful in the differential diagnosis of iron deficiency, anemia, and for iron overload conditions.

    a. The following presentations are examples that may support the use of these studies for evaluating iron deficiency:

    - Certain abnormal blood count values (i.e., decreased mean corpuscular volume (MCV), decreased hemoglobin/hematocrit when the MCV is low or normal, or increased red cell distribution width (RDW) and low or normal MCV);
    - Abnormal appetite (pica);
    - Acute or chronic gastrointestinal blood loss;
    - Hematuria;
    - Menorrhagia;
    - Malabsorption;
    - Status post-gastrectomy;
    - Status post-gastrojejunostomy;
    - Malnutrition;
    - Preoperative autologous blood collection(s);
    - Malignant, chronic inflammatory and infectious conditions associated with anemia which may present in a similar manner to iron deficiency anemia;
    - Following a significant surgical procedure where blood loss had occurred and had not been repaired with adequate iron replacement.

    b. The following presentations are examples that may support the use of these studies for evaluating iron overload:

    - Chronic Hepatitis;
    - Diabetes;
    - Hyperpigmentation of skin;
    - Arthropathy;
    - Cirrhosis;
    - Hypogonadism;
    - Hypopituitarism;
    - Impaired porphyrin metabolism;
    - Heart failure;
    - Multiple transfusions;
    - Sideroblastic anemia;
    - Thalassemia major;
    - Cardiomyopathy, cardiac dysrhythmias and conduction disturbances.

2. Follow-up testing may be appropriate to monitor response to therapy, e.g., oral or parenteral iron, ascorbic acid, and erythropoietin.

3. Iron studies may be appropriate in patients after treatment for other nutritional deficiency anemias, such as folate and vitamin B12, because iron deficiency may not be revealed until such a nutritional deficiency is treated.

4. Serum ferritin may be appropriate for monitoring iron status in patients with chronic renal disease with or without dialysis.

5. Serum iron may also be indicated for evaluation of toxic effects of iron and other metals (e.g., nickel, cadmium, aluminum, lead) whether due to accidental, intentional exposure or metabolic causes.

Limitations

1. Iron studies should be used to diagnose and manage iron deficiency or iron overload states. These tests are not to be used solely to assess acute phase reactants where disease management will be unchanged. For example, infections and malignancies are associated with elevations in acute phase reactants such as ferritin, and decreases in serum iron concentration, but iron studies would only be medically necessary if results of iron studies might alter the management of the primary diagnosis or might warrant direct treatment of an iron disorder or condition.

2. If a normal serum ferritin level is documented, repeat testing would not ordinarily be medically necessary unless there is a change in the patient's condition, and ferritin assessment is needed for the ongoing management of the patient. For example, a patient presents with new onset insulin-dependent diabetes mellitus and has a serum ferritin level performed for the suspicion of hemochromatosis. If the ferritin level is normal, the repeat ferritin for diabetes mellitus would not be medically necessary.

3. When an End Stage Renal Disease (ESRD) patient is tested for ferritin, testing more frequently than every three months (the frequency authorized by 3167.3, Fiscal Intermediary manual) requires documentation of medical necessity [e.g., other than "Chronic Renal Failure" (ICD-9-CM 585) or "Renal Failure, Unspecified" (ICD-9-CM 586)].

4. It is ordinarily not necessary to measure both transferrin and TIBC at the same time because TIBC is an indirect measure of transferrin. When transferrin is ordered as part of the nutritional assessment for evaluating malnutrition, it is not necessary to order other iron studies unless iron deficiency or iron overload is suspected as well.

5. It is not ordinarily necessary to measure both iron/TIBC (or transferrin) and ferritin in initial patient testing. If clinically indicated after evaluation of the initial iron studies, it may be appropriate to perform additional iron studies either on the initial specimen or on a subsequently obtained specimen. After a diagnosis of iron deficiency or iron overload is established, either iron/TIBC (or transferrin) or ferritin may be medically necessary for monitoring, but not both.

6. It would not ordinarily be considered medically necessary to do a ferritin as a preoperative test except in the presence of anemia or recent autologous blood collections prior to the surgery.

100-3, 190.19
Collagen Crosslinks, Any Method
Indications

Generally speaking, collagen crosslink testing is useful mostly in "fast losers" of bone. The age when these bone markers can help direct therapy is often pre-Medicare. By the time a fast loser of bone reaches age 65, she will most likely have been stabilized by appropriate therapy or have lost so much bone mass that further testing is useless. Coverage for bone marker assays may be established, however, for younger Medicare beneficiaries and for those men and women who might become fast losers because of some other therapy such as glucocorticoids. Safeguards should be incorporated to prevent excessive use of tests in patients for whom they have no clinical relevance.

Collagen crosslinks testing is used to:

1. Identify individuals with elevated bone resorption, who have osteoporosis in whom response to treatment is being monitored;
2. Predict response (as assessed by bone mass measurements) to FDA approved antiresorptive therapy in postmenopausal women; and
3. Assess response to treatment of patients with osteoporosis, Paget's disease of the bone, or risk for osteoporosis where treatment may include FDA approved antiresorptive agents, anti-estrogens or selective estrogen receptor moderators.

Limitations

Because of significant specimen to specimen collagen crosslink physiologic variability (15-20%), current recommendations for appropriate utilization include: one or two base-line assays from specified urine collections on separate days; followed by a repeat assay about three months after starting anti-resorptive therapy; followed by a repeat assay in 12 months after the three-month assay; and thereafter not more than annually, unless there is a change in therapy in which circumstance an additional test may be indicated three months after the initiation of new therapy.

Some collagen crosslink assays may not be appropriate for use in some disorders, according to FDA labeling restrictions.

100-3, 190.20
NCD for Blood Glucose Testing (190.20)
Indications

Blood glucose values are often necessary for the management of patients with diabetes mellitus, where hyperglycemia and hypoglycemia are often present. They are also critical in the determination of control of blood glucose levels in the patient with impaired fasting glucose (FPG 110-125 mg/dL), the patient with insulin resistance syndrome and/or carbohydrate intolerance (excessive rise in glucose following ingestion of glucose or glucose sources of food), in the patient with a hypoglycemia disorder such as nesidioblastosis or insulinoma, and in patients with a catabolic or malnutrition state. In addition to those conditions already listed, glucose testing may be medically necessary in patients with tuberculosis, unexplained chronic or recurrent infections, alcoholism, coronary artery disease (especially in women), or unexplained skin conditions (including pruritis, local skin infections, ulceration and gangrene without an established cause).

Many medical conditions may be a consequence of a sustained elevated or depressed glucose level. These include comas, seizures or epilepsy, confusion, abnormal hunger, abnormal weight loss or gain, and loss of sensation. Evaluation of glucose may also be indicated in patients on medications known to affect carbohydrate metabolism.

Effective January 1, 2005, the Medicare law expanded coverage to diabetic screening services. Some forms of blood glucode testing covered under this national coverage determination may be covered for screening purposes subject to specified frequencies. See 42 CFR 410.18 and section 90, chapter 18 of the Claims Processing Manual, for a full description of this screening benefit.

Limitations

Frequent home blood glucose testing by diabetic patients should be encouraged. In stable, non-hospitalized patients who are unable or unwilling to do home monitoring, it may be reasonable and necessary to measure quantitative blood glucose up to four times annually.

Depending upon the age of the patient, type of diabetes, degree of control, complications of diabetes, and other co-morbid conditions, more frequent testing than four times annually may be reasonable and necessary.

In some patients presenting with nonspecific signs, symptoms, or diseases not normally associated with disturbances in glucose metabolism, a single blood glucose test may be medically necessary. Repeat testing may not be indicated unless abnormal results are found or unless there is a change in clinical condition. If repeat testing is performed, a specific diagnosis code (e.g., diabetes) should be reported to support medical necessity. However, repeat testing may be indicated where results are normal in patients with conditions where there is a confirmed continuing risk of glucose metabolism abnormality (e.g., monitoring glucocorticoid therapy).

100-3, 190.21
NCD for Glycated Hemoglobin/Glycated Protein (190.21)
Indications

Glycated hemoglobin/protein testing is widely accepted as medically necessary for the management and control of diabetes. It is also valuable to assess hyperglycemia, a history of hyperglycemia or dangerous hypoglycemia. Glycated protein testing may be used in place of glycated hemoglobin in the management of diabetic patients, and is particularly useful in patients who have abnormalities of erythrocytes such as hemolytic anemia or hemoglobinopathies.

Limitations

It is not considered reasonable and necessary to perform glycated hemoglobin tests more often than every three months on a controlled diabetic patient to determine whether the patient's metabolic control has been on average within the target range. It is not considered reasonable and necessary for these tests to be performed more frequently than once a month for diabetic pregnant women. Testing for uncontrolled type one or two diabetes mellitus may require testing more than four times a year. The above Description Section provides the clinical basis for those situations in which testing more frequently than four times per annum is indicated, and medical necessity documentation must support such testing in excess of the above guidelines.

Many methods for the analysis of glycated hemoglobin show significant interference from elevated levels of fetal hemoglobin or by variant hemoglobin molecules. When the glycated hemoglobin assay is initially performed in these patients, the laboratory may inform the ordering physician of a possible analytical interference. Alternative testing, including glycated protein, for example, fructosamine, may be indicated for the monitoring of the degree of glycemic control in this situation. It is therefore conceivable that a patient will have both a glycated hemoglobin and glycated protein ordered on the same day. This should be limited to the initial assay of glycated hemoglobin, with subsequent exclusive use of glycated protein. These tests are not considered to be medically necessary for the diagnosis of diabetes.

100-3, 190.22
NCD for Thyroid Testing (190.22)
Indications

Thyroid function tests are used to define hyper function, euthyroidism, or hypofunction of thyroid disease. Thyroid testing may be reasonable and necessary to:

- Distinguish between primary and secondary hypothyroidism;
- Confirm or rule out primary hypothyroidism;
- Monitor thyroid hormone levels (for example, patients with goiter, thyroid nodules, or thyroid cancer);
- Monitor drug therapy in patients with primary hypothyroidism;
- Confirm or rule out primary hyperthyroidism; and
- Monitor therapy in patients with hyperthyroidism.

Thyroid function testing may be medically necessary in patients with disease or neoplasm of the thyroid and other endocrine glands. Thyroid function testing may also be medically necessary in patients with metabolic disorders; malnutrition; hyperlipidemia; certain types of anemia; psychosis and non-psychotic personality disorders; unexplained depression; ophthalmologic disorders; various cardiac arrhythmias; disorders of menstruation; skin conditions; myalgias; and a wide array of signs and symptoms, including alterations in consciousness; malaise; hypothermia; symptoms of the nervous and musculoskeletal system; skin and integumentary system; nutrition and metabolism; cardiovascular; and gastrointestinal system.

It may be medically necessary to do follow-up thyroid testing in patients with a personal history of malignant neoplasm of the endocrine system and in patients on long-term thyroid drug therapy.

Limitations

Testing may be covered up to two times a year in clinically stable patients; more frequent testing may be reasonable and necessary for patients whose thyroid therapy has been altered or in whom symptoms or signs of hyperthyroidism or hypothyroidism are noted.

100-3, 190.23
NCD for Lipid Testing (190.23)
Indications and Limitations of Coverage

Indications

The medical community recognizes lipid testing as appropriate for evaluating atherosclerotic cardiovascular disease. Conditions in which lipid testing may be indicated include:

- Assessment of patients with atherosclerotic cardiovascular disease.
- Evaluation of primary dyslipidemia.
- Any form of atherosclerotic disease, or any disease leading to the formation of atherosclerotic disease.
- Diagnostic evaluation of diseases associated with altered lipid metabolism, such as: nephrotic syndrome, pancreatitis, hepatic disease, and hypo and hyperthyroidism.
- Secondary dyslipidemia, including diabetes mellitus, disorders of gastrointestinal absorption, chronic renal failure.
- Signs or symptoms of dyslipidemias, such as skin lesions.
- As follow-up to the initial screen for coronary heart disease (total cholesterol + HDL cholesterol) when total cholesterol is determined to be high (>240 mg/dL), or borderline-high (200-240 mg/dL) plus two or more coronary heart disease risk factors, or an HDL cholesterol, <35 mg/dl.

To monitor the progress of patients on anti-lipid dietary management and pharmacologic therapy for the treatment of elevated blood lipid disorders, total cholesterol, HDL cholesterol and LDL cholesterol may be used. Triglycerides may be obtained if this lipid fraction is also elevated or if the patient is put on drugs (for example, thiazide diuretics, beta blockers, estrogens, glucocorticoids, and tamoxifen) which may raise the triglyceride level.

When monitoring long term anti-lipid dietary or pharmacologic therapy and when following patients with borderline high total or LDL cholesterol levels, it may be reasonable to perform the lipid panel annually. A lipid panel at a yearly interval will usually be adequate while measurement of the serum total cholesterol or a measured LDL should suffice for interim visits if the patient does not have hypertriglyceridemia.

Any one component of the panel or a measured LDL may be reasonable and necessary up to six times the first year for monitoring dietary or pharmacologic therapy. More frequent total cholesterol HDL cholesterol, LDL cholesterol and triglyceride testing may be indicated for marked elevations or for changes to anti-lipid therapy due to inadequate initial patient response to dietary or pharmacologic therapy. The LDL cholesterol or total cholesterol may be measured three times yearly after treatment goals have been achieved.

Electrophoretic or other quantitation of lipoproteins may be indicated if the patient has a primary disorder of lipoid metabolism.

Effective January 1, 2005, the Medicare law expanded coverage to cardiovascular screening services. Several of the procedures included in this NCD may be covered for screening purposes subject to specified frequencies. See 42 CFR 410.17 and section 100, chapter 18, of the Claims Processing Manual, for a full description of this benefit.Limitations

Limitations

Lipid panel and hepatic panel testing may be used for patients with severe psoriasis which has not responded to conventional therapy and for which the retinoid etretinate has been prescribed and who have developed hyperlipidemia or hepatic toxicity. Specific examples include erythrodermia and generalized pustular type and psoriasis associated with arthritis.

Routine screening and prophylactic testing for lipid disorder are not covered by Medicare. While lipid screening may be medically appropriate, Medicare by statute does not pay for it. Lipid testing in asymptomatic individuals is considered to be screening regardless of the presence of other risk factors such as family history, tobacco use, etc.

Once a diagnosis is established, one or several specific tests are usually adequate for monitoring the course of the disease. Less specific diagnoses (for example, other chest pain) alone do not support medical necessity of these tests.

When monitoring long term anti-lipid dietary or pharmacologic therapy and when following patients with borderline high total or LDL cholesterol levels, it is reasonable to perform the lipid panel annually. A lipid panel at a yearly interval will usually be adequate while measurement of the serum total cholesterol or a measured LDL should suffice for interim visits if the patient does not have hypertriglyceridemia.

Any one component of the panel or a measured LDL may be medically necessary up to six times the first year for monitoring dietary or pharmacologic therapy. More frequent total cholesterol HDL cholesterol, LDL cholesterol and triglyceride testing may be indicated for marked elevations or for changes to anti-lipid therapy due to inadequate initial patient response to dietary or pharmacologic therapy. The LDL cholesterol or total cholesterol may be measured three times yearly after treatment goals have been achieved.

If no dietary or pharmacological therapy is advised, monitoring is not necessary.

When evaluating non-specific chronic abnormalities of the liver (for example, elevations of transaminase, alkaline phosphatase, abnormal imaging studies, etc.), a lipid panel would generally not be indicated more than twice per year

100-3, 190.24
NCD for Digoxin Therapeutic Drug Assay (190.24)
Indications and Limitations of Coverage

Indications

Digoxin levels may be performed to monitor drug levels of individuals receiving digoxin therapy because the margin of safety between side effects and toxicity is narrow or because the blood level may not be high enough to achieve the desired clinical effect.

Clinical indications may include individuals on digoxin:

- With symptoms, signs or electrocardiogram (ECG) suggestive of digoxin toxicity.
- Taking medications that influence absorption, bioavailability, distribution, and/or elimination of digoxin.
- With impaired renal, hepatic, gastrointestinal, or thyroid function.
- With pH and/or electrolyte abnormalities.
- With unstable cardiovascular status, including myocarditis.
- Requiring monitoring of patient compliance.

Clinical indications may include individuals:

- Suspected of accidental or intended overdose.

Appendix G — Pub 100 References

- Who have an acceptable cardiac diagnosis (as listed) and for whom an accurate history of use of digoxin is unobtainable.

The value of obtaining regular serum digoxin levels is uncertain, but it may be reasonable to check levels once yearly after a steady state is achieved. In addition, it may be reasonable to check the level if:

- Heart failure status worsens.
- Renal function deteriorates.
- Additional medications are added that could affect the digoxin level.
- Signs or symptoms of toxicity develop.

Steady state will be reached in approximately 1 week in patients with normal renal function, although 2?3 weeks may be needed in patients with renal impairment. After changes in dosages or the addition of a medication that could affect the digoxin level, it is reasonable to check the digoxin level one week after the change or addition. Based on the clinical situation, in cases of digoxin toxicity, testing may need to be done more than once a week.

Digoxin is indicated for the treatment of patients with heart failure due to systolic dysfunction and for reduction of the ventricular response in patients with atrial fibrillation or flutter. Digoxin may also be indicated for the treatment of other supraventricular arrhythmias, particularly in the presence of heart failure.

Limitations
This test is not appropriate for patients on digitoxin or treated with digoxin FAB (fragment antigen binding) antibody.

100-3, 190.25
NCD for Alpha-fetoprotein (AFP) (190.25)
Indications and Limitations of Coverage
AFP is useful for the diagnosis of hepatocellular carcinoma in high-risk patients (such as alcoholic cirrhosis, cirrhosis of viral etiology, hemochromatosis, and alpha 1-antitrypsin deficiency) and in separating patients with benign hepatocellular neoplasms or metastases from those with hepatocellular carcinoma and, as a non-specific tumor associated antigen, serves in marking germ cell neoplasms of the testis, ovary, retro peritoneum, and mediastinum.

100-3, 190.26
NCD for Carcinoembryonic Antigen (CEA) (190.26)
Indications
CEA may be medically necessary for follow-up of patients with colorectal carcinoma. It would however only be medically necessary at treatment decision?making points. In some clinical situations (e.g. adenocarcinoma of the lung, small cell carcinoma of the lung, and some gastrointestinal carcinomas) when a more specific marker is not expressed by the tumor, CEA may be a medically necessary alternative marker for monitoring. Preoperative CEA may also be helpful in determining the post?operative adequacy of surgical resection and subsequent medical management. In general, a single tumor marker will suffice in following patients with colorectal carcinoma or other malignancies that express such tumor markers.

In following patients who have had treatment for colorectal carcinoma, ASCO guideline suggests that if resection of liver metastasis would be indicated, it is recommended that post-operative CEA testing be performed every two to three months in patients with initial stage II or stage III disease for at least two years after diagnosis.

For patients with metastatic solid tumors which express CEA, CEA may be measured at the start of the treatment and with subsequent treatment cycles to assess the tumor's response to therapy.

Limitations
Serum CEA determinations are generally not indicated more frequently than once per chemotherapy treatment cycle for patients with metastatic solid tumors which express CEA or every two months post-surgical treatment for patients who have had colorectal carcinoma. However, it may be proper to order the test more frequently in certain situations, for example, when there has been a significant change from prior CEA level or a significant change in patient status which could reflect disease progression or recurrence.

Testing with a diagnosis of an in situ carcinoma is not reasonably done more frequently than once, unless the result is abnormal, in which case the test may be repeated once.

100-3, 190.27
NCD for Human Chorionic Gonadotropin (hCG) (190.27)
Indications and Limitations of Coverage

Indications
hCG is useful for monitoring and diagnosis of germ cell neoplasms of the ovary, testis, mediastinum, retroperitoneum, and central nervous system. In addition, hCG is useful for monitoring pregnant patients with vaginal bleeding, hypertension and/or suspected fetal loss.

Limitations
It is not reasonable and necessary to perform hCG testing more than once per month for diagnostic purposes. It may be performed as needed for monitoring of patient progress and treatment. Qualitative hCG assays are not appropriate for medically managing patients with known or suspected germ cell neoplasms.

100-3, 190.28
NCD for Tumor Antigen by Immunoassay - CA125 (190.28)
Indications
CA 125 is a high molecular weight serum tumor marker elevated in 80% of patients who present with epithelial ovarian carcinoma. It is also elevated in carcinomas of the fallopian tube, endometrium, and endocervix. An elevated level may also be associated with the presence of a malignant mesothelioma or primary peritoneal carcinoma.

A CA125 level may be obtained as part of the initial pre-operative work-up for women presenting with a suspicious pelvic mass to be used as a baseline for purposes of post-operative monitoring. Initial declines in CA 125 after initial surgery and/or chemotherapy for ovarian carcinoma are also measured by obtaining three serum levels during the first month post treatment to determine the patient's CA 125 half-life, which has significant prognostic implications.

The CA 125 levels are again obtained at the completion of chemotherapy as an index of residual disease. Surveillance CA125 measurements are generally obtained every 3 months for 2 years, every 6 months for the next 3 years, and yearly thereafter. CA 125 levels are also an important indicator of a patient's response to therapy in the presence of advanced or recurrent disease. In this setting, CA 125 levels may be obtained prior to each treatment cycle.

Limitations
These services are not covered for the evaluation of patients with signs or symptoms suggestive of malignancy. The service may be ordered at times necessary to assess either the presence of recurrent disease or the patient's response to treatment with subsequent treatment cycles.

The CA 125 is specifically not covered for aiding in the differential diagnosis of patients with a pelvic mass as the sensitivity and specificity of the test is not sufficient. In general, a single "tumor marker" will suffice in following a patient with one of these malignancies.

100-3, 190.29
NCD for Tumor Antigen by Immunoassay CA 15-3/CA 27.29 (190.29)
Indications
Multiple tumor markers are available for monitoring the response of certain malignancies to therapy and assessing whether residual tumor exists post-surgical therapy.

CA 15-3 is often medically necessary to aid in the management of patients with breast cancer. Serial testing must be used in conjunction with other clinical methods for monitoring breast cancer. For monitoring, if medically necessary, use consistently either CA 15-3 or CA 27.29, not both.

CA 27.29 is equivalent to CA 15-3 in its usage in management of patients with breast cancer.

Limitations
These services are not covered for the evaluation of patients with signs or symptoms suggestive of malignancy. The service may be ordered at times necessary to assess either the presence of recurrent disease or the patient's response to treatment with subsequent treatment cycles.

100-3, 190.30
NCD for Tumor Antigen by Immunoassay CA 19-9 (190.30)
Indications
Multiple tumor markers are available for monitoring the response of certain malignancies to therapy and assessing whether residual tumor exists post-surgical therapy.

Levels are useful in following the course of patients with established diagnosis of pancreatic and biliary ductal carcinoma. The test is not indicated for diagnosing these two diseases.

Limitations
These services are not covered for the evaluation of patients with signs or symptoms suggestive of malignancy. The service may be ordered at times necessary to assess either the presence of recurrent disease or the patient's response to treatment with subsequent treatment cycles.

100-3, 190.31
NCD for Prostate Specific Antigen (PSA) (190.31)
Indications
PSA is of proven value in differentiating benign from malignant disease in men with lower urinary tract signs and symptoms (e.g., hematuria, slow urine stream, hesitancy, urgency, frequency, nocturia and incontinence) as well as with patients with palpably abnormal prostate glands on physician exam, and in patients with other laboratory or imaging studies that suggest the possibility of a malignant prostate disorder. PSA is also a marker used to follow the progress of prostate cancer once a diagnosis has been established, such as in detecting metastatic or persistent disease in patients who may require additional treatment. PSA testing may also be useful in the differential diagnosis of men presenting with as yet undiagnosed disseminated metastatic disease.

Limitations
Generally, for patients with lower urinary tract signs or symptoms, the test is performed only once per year unless there is a change in the patient's medical condition.

Testing with a diagnosis of in situ carcinoma is not reasonably done more frequently than once, unless the result is abnormal, in which case the test may be repeated once.

100-3, 190.32
NCD for Gamma Glutamyl Transferase (GGT) (190.32)
Indications

1. To provide information about known or suspected hepatobiliary disease, for example:
   a. Following chronic alcohol or drug ingestion.
   b. Following exposure to hepatotoxins.
   c. When using medication known to have a potential for causing liver toxicity (e.g., following the drug manufacturer's recommendations).
   d. Following infection (e.g., viral hepatitis and other specific infections such as amoebiasis, tuberculosis, psittacosis, and similar infections).

2. To assess liver injury/function following diagnosis of primary or secondary malignant neoplasms.

3. To assess liver injury/function in a wide variety of disorders and diseases known to cause liver involvement (e.g., diabetes mellitus, malnutrition, disorders of iron and mineral metabolism, sarcoidosis, amyloidosis, lupus, and hypertension).
4. To assess liver function related to gastrointestinal disease.
5. To assess liver function related to pancreatic disease.
6. To assess liver function in patients subsequent to liver transplantation.
7. To differentiate between the different sources of elevated alkaline phosphatase activity.

Limitations

When used to assess liver dysfunction secondary to existing non-hepatobiliary disease with no change in signs, symptoms, or treatment, it is generally not necessary to repeat a GGT determination after a normal result has been obtained unless new indications are present.

If the GGT is the only "liver" enzyme abnormally high, it is generally not necessary to pursue further evaluation for liver disease for this specific indication.

When used to determine if other abnormal enzyme tests reflect liver abnormality rather than other tissue, it generally is not necessary to repeat a GGT more than one time per week.

Because of the extreme sensitivity of GGT as a marker for cytochrome oxidase induction or cell membrane permeability, it is generally not useful in monitoring patients with known liver disease.

100-3, 190.33
NCD for Hepatitis Panel/Acute Hepatitis Panel (190.33)
Indications

1. To detect viral hepatitis infection when there are abnormal liver function test results, with or without signs or symptoms of hepatitis.
2. Prior to and subsequent to liver transplantation.

Limitations

After a hepatitis diagnosis has been established, only individual tests, rather than the entire panel, are needed.

100-3, 190.34
NCD for Fecal Occult Blood Test (FOBT) (190.34)
NCD for Fecal Occult Blood Test (FOBT) (190.34)

Indications

1. To evaluate known or suspected alimentary tract conditions that might cause bleeding into the intestinal tract.
2. To evaluate unexpected anemia.
3. To evaluate abnormal signs, symptoms, or complaints that might be associated with loss of blood.
4. To evaluate patient complaints of black or red-tinged stools.

Limitations

1. The FOBT is reported once for the testing of up to three separate specimens (comprising either one or two tests per specimen).
2. In patients who are taking non-steroidal anti-inflammatory drugs and have a history of gastrointestinal bleeding but no other signs, symptoms, or complaints associated with gastrointestinal blood loss, testing for occult blood may generally be appropriate no more than once every three months.

When testing is done for the purpose of screening for colorectal cancer in the absence of signs, symptoms, conditions, or complaints associated with gastrointestinal blood loss, report the HCPCS code for colorectal cancer screening; fecal-occult blood test, 1-3 simultaneous determinations should be used.

100-3, 210.1
NCD for Prostate Cancer Screening Tests (210.1)
Indications and Limitations of Coverage

CIM 50-55

Covered

A. General

Section 4103 of the Balanced Budget Act of 1997 provides for coverage of certain prostate cancer screening tests subject to certain coverage, frequency, and payment limitations. Medicare will cover prostate cancer screening tests/procedures for the early detection of prostate cancer. Coverage of prostate cancer screening tests includes the following procedures furnished to an individual for the early detection of prostate cancer:

- Screening digital rectal examination; and
- Screening prostate specific antigen blood test

B. Screening Digital Rectal Examinations

Screening digital rectal examinations are covered at a frequency of once every 12 months for men who have attained age 50 (at least 11 months have passed following the month in which the last Medicare-covered screening digital rectal examination was performed). Screening digital rectal examination means a clinical examination of an individual's prostate for nodules or other abnormalities of the prostate. This screening must be performed by a doctor of medicine or osteopathy (as defined in §1861(r)(1) of the Act), or by a physician assistant, nurse practitioner, clinical nurse specialist, or certified nurse midwife (as defined in §1861(aa) and §1861(gg) of the Act) who is authorized under State law to perform the examination, fully knowledgeable about the beneficiary's medical condition, and would be responsible for using the results of any examination performed in the overall management of the beneficiary's specific medical problem.

C. Screening Prostate Specific Antigen Tests

Screening prostate specific antigen tests are covered at a frequency of once every 12 months for men who have attained age 50 (at least 11 months have passed following the month in which the last Medicare-covered screening prostate specific antigen test was performed). Screening prostate specific antigen tests (PSA) means a test to detect the marker for adenocarcinoma of prostate. PSA is a reliable immunocytochemical marker for primary and metastatic adenocarcinoma of prostate. This screening must be ordered by the beneficiary's physician or by the beneficiary's physician assistant, nurse practitioner, clinical nurse specialist, or certified nurse midwife (the term "attending physician" is defined in §1861(r)(1) of the Act to mean a doctor of medicine or osteopathy and the terms "physician assistant, nurse practitioner, clinical nurse specialist, or certified nurse midwife" are defined in §1861(aa) and §1861(gg) of the Act) who is fully knowledgeable about the beneficiary's medical condition, and who would be responsible for using the results of any examination (test) performed in the overall management of the beneficiary's specific medica

100-3, 210.2
NCD for Screening Pap Smears and Pelvic Examinations for Early Detection of Cervical or Vaginal Cancer (210.2)
Indications and Limitations of Coverage

CIM 50-20.1

Screening Pap Smear

A screening pap smear and related medically necessary services provided to a woman for the early detection of cervical cancer (including collection of the sample of cells and a physician's interpretation of the test results) and pelvic examination (including clinical breast examination) are covered under Medicare Part B when ordered by a physician (or authorized practitioner) under one of the following conditions:

- She has not had such a test during the preceding two years or is a woman of childbearing age (§1861(nn) of the Act).
- There is evidence (on the basis of her medical history or other findings) that she is at high risk of developing cervical cancer and her physician (or authorized practitioner) recommends that she have the test performed more frequently than every two years.

High risk factors for cervical and vaginal cancer are:

- Early onset of sexual activity (under 16 years of age).
- Multiple sexual partners (five or more in a lifetime).
- History of sexually transmitted disease (including HIV infection).
- Fewer than three negative or any pap smears within the previous 7 years.; and
- DES (diethylstilbestrol) - exposed daughters of women who took DES during pregnancy.

NOTE: Claims for pap smears must indicate the beneficiary's low or high risk status by including the appropriate ICD-9-CM on the line item (Item 24E of the Form CMS-1500).

Definitions

- A woman as described in §1861(nn) of the Act is a woman who is of childbearing age and has had a pap smear test during any of the preceding three years that indicated the presence of cervical or vaginal cancer or other abnormality, or is at high risk of developing cervical or vaginal cancer.
- A woman of childbearing age is one who is premenopausal and has been determined by a physician or other qualified practitioner to be of childbearing age, based upon the medical history or other findings.
- Other qualified practitioner, as defined in 42 CFR 410.56(a) includes a certified nurse midwife (as defined in §1861(gg) of the Act), or a physician assistant, nurse practitioner, or clinical nurse specialist (as defined in §1861(aa) of the Act) who is authorized under State law to perform the examination.

Screening Pelvic Examination

Section 4102 of the Balanced Budget Act of 1997 provides for coverage of screening pelvic examinations (including a clinical breast examination) for all female beneficiaries, subject to certain frequency and other limitations. A screening pelvic examination (including a clinical breast examination) should include at least seven of the following eleven elements:

- Inspection and palpation of breasts for masses or lumps, tenderness, symmetry, or nipple discharge.
- Digital rectal examination including sphincter tone, presence of hemorrhoids, and rectal masses. Pelvic examination (with or without specimen collection for smears and cultures) including:
- External genitalia (for example, general appearance, hair distribution, or lesions).
- Urethral maetus (for example, size, location, lesions, or prolapse).
- Urethra (for example, masses, tenderness, or scarring).
- Bladder (for example, fullness, masses, or tenderness).
- Vagina (for example, general appearance, estrogen effect, discharge lesions, pelvic support, cystocele, or rectocele).
- Cervix (for example, general appearance, lesions, or discharge).
- Uterus (for example, size, contour, position, mobility, tenderness, consistency, descent, or support).
- Adnexa/parametria (for example, masses, tenderness, organomegaly, or nodularity).

Appendix G — Pub 100 References

- Anus and perineum.

This description is from Documentation Guidelines for Evaluation and Management Services, published in May 1997 and was developed by the Centers for Medicare and Medicaid

100-3, 210.3
Colorectal Cancer Screening Tests

A. General

Section 4104 of the Balanced Budget Act of 1997 provides for coverage of screening colorectal cancer procedures under Medicare Part B. Medicare currently covers: (1) annual fecal occult blood tests (FOBTs); (2) flexible sigmoidoscopy over 4 years; (3) screening colonoscopy for persons at average risk for colorectal cancer every 10 years, or for persons at high risk for colorectal cancer every 2 years; (4) barium enema every 4 years as an alternative to flexible sigmoidoscopy, or every 2 years as an alternative to colonoscopy for persons at high risk for colorectal cancer; and, (5) other procedures the Secretary finds appropriate based on consultation with appropriate experts and organizations.

Coverage of the above screening examinations was implemented in regulations through a final rule that was published on October 31, 1997 (62 FR 59079), and was effective January 1, 1998. At that time, based on consultation with appropriate experts and organizations, the definition of the term "FOBT" was defined in 42 CFR Sec.410.37(a)(2) of the regulation to mean a "guaiac-based test for peroxidase activity, testing two samples from each of three consecutive stools."

In the 2003 Physician Fee Schedule Final Rule (67 FR 79966) effective March 1, 2003, the Centers for Medicare & Medicaid Services (CMS) amended the FOBT screening test regulation definition to provide that it could include either: (1) a guaiac-based FOBT, or, (2) other tests determined by the Secretary through a national coverage determination.

B. Nationally Covered Indications

Fecal Occult Blood Tests (FOBT) (effective for services performed on or after January 1, 2004)

1. History
The FOBTs are generally divided into two types: immunoassay and guaiac types. Immunoassay (or immunochemical) fecal occult blood tests (iFOBT) use "antibodies directed against human globin epitopes. While most iFOBTs use spatulas to collect stool samples, some use a brush to collect toilet water surrounding the stool. Most iFOBTs require laboratory processing.

    Guaiac fecal occult blood tests (gFOBT) use a peroxidase reaction to indicate presence of the heme portion of hemoglobin. Guaiac turns blue after oxidation by oxidants or peroxidases in the presence of an oxygen donor such as hydrogen peroxide. Most FOBTs use sticks to collect stool samples and may be developed in a physician's office or a laboratory. In 1998, Medicare began reimbursement for guaiac FOBTs, but not immunoassay type tests for colorectal cancer screening. Since the fundamental process is similar for other iFOBTs, CMS evaluated colorectal cancer screening using immunoassay FOBTs in general.

2. Expanded Coverage
Medicare covers one screening FOBT per annum for the early detection of colorectal cancer. This means that Medicare will cover one guaiac-based (gFOBT) or one immunoassay-based (iFOBT) at a frequency of every 12 months; i.e., at least 11 months have passed following the month in which the last covered screening FOBT was performed, for beneficiaries aged 50 years and older. The beneficiary completes the existing gFOBT by taking samples from two different sites of three consecutive stools; the beneficiary completes the iFOBT by taking the appropriate number of stool samples according to the specific manufacturer's instructions. This screening requires a written order from the beneficiary's attending physician. ("Attending physician means a doctor of medicine or osteopathy (as defined in Sec.1861(r)(1) of the Social Security Act) who is fully knowledgeable about the beneficiary's medical condition, and who would be responsible for using the results of any examination performed in the overall management of the beneficiary's specific medical problem.)

C. Nationally Non-Covered Indications

All other indications for colorectal cancer screening not otherwise specified above remain non-covered. Non-coverage specifically includes:

1. Screening DNA (Deoxyribonucleic acid) stool tests, effective April 28, 2008, and,
2. Screening computed tomographic colonography (CTC), effective May 12, 2009.

D. Other

N/A

(This NCD last reviewed May 2009.)

100-3, 220.1
NCD for Computerized Tomography (220.1)

A. General

Diagnostic examinations of the head (head scans) and of other parts of the body (body scans) performed by computerized tomography (CT) scanners are covered if you find that the medical and scientific literature and opinion support the effective use of a scan for the condition, and the scan is: (1) reasonable and necessary for the individual patient; and (2) performed on a model of CT equipment that meets the criteria in C below.

CT scans have become the primary diagnostic tool for many conditions and symptoms. CT scanning used as the primary diagnostic tool can be cost effective because it can eliminate the need for a series of other tests, is non-invasive and thus virtually eliminates complications, and does not require hospitalization.

B. Determining Whether a CT Scan Is Reasonable and Necessary

Sufficient information must be provided with claims to differentiate CT scans from other radiology services and to make coverage determinations. Carefully review claims to insure that a scan is reasonable and necessary for the individual patient; i.e., the use must be found to be medically appropriate considering the patient's symptoms and preliminary diagnosis.

There is no general rule that requires other diagnostic tests to be tried before CT scanning is used. However, in an individual case the contractor's medical staff may determine that use of a CT scan as the initial diagnostic test was not reasonable and necessary because it was not supported by the patient's symptoms or complaints stated on the claim form; e.g., "periodic headaches."

Claims for CT scans are reviewed for evidence of abuse which might include the absence of reasonable indications for the scans, an excessive number of scans or unnecessarily expensive types of scans considering the facts in the particular cases.

C-Approved Models of CT Equipment

1. Criteria for Approval

    In the absence of evidence to the contrary, you may assume that a CT scan for which payment is requested has been performed on equipment that meets the following criteria:

    a. The model must be known to the Food and Drug Administration, and

    b. Must be in the full market release phase of development.

    Should it be necessary to confirm that those criteria are met, ask the manufacturer to submit the information in subsection C.2. If manufacturers inquire about obtaining Medicare approval for their equipment, inform them of the foregoing criteria.

2. Evidence of Approval

    a. The letter sent by the Bureau of Radiological Health, Food and Drug Administration (FDA), to the manufacturer acknowledging the FDA's receipt of information on the specific CT scanner system model submitted as required under Public Law 90-602, "The Radiation Control for Health and Safety Act of 1968."

    b. A letter signed by the chief executive officer or other officer acting in a similar capacity for the manufacturer which:

        1) Furnishes the CT scanner system model number, all names that hospitals and physicians' offices may use to refer to the CT scanner system on claims, and the accession number assigned by FDA to the specific model; \

        2) Specifies whether the scanner performs head scans only, body scans only (i.e., scans of parts of the body other than the head), or head and body scans;

        3) States that the company or corporation is satisfied with the results of the developmental stages that preceded the full market release phase of the equipment, that the equipment is in the full market release phase, and the date on which it was decided to put the product into the full market release phase.

D-Mobile Ct Equipment

CT scans performed on mobile units are subject to the same Medicare coverage requirements applicable to scans performed on stationary units, as well as certain health and safety requirements recommended by PHS. As with scans performed on stationary units, the scans must be determined medically necessary for the individual patient. The scans must be performed on types of CT scanning equipment that have been approved for use as stationary units (see C above), and must be in compliance with applicable State laws and regulations for control of radiation.

1. Hospital Setting

    The hospital must assume responsibility for the quality of the scan furnished to inpatients and outpatients and must assure that a radiologist or other qualified physician is in charge of the procedure. The radiologist or other physician (i.e., one who is with the mobile unit) who is responsible for the procedure must be approved by the hospital for similar privileges.

2. Ambulatory Setting

    If mobile CT scan services are furnished at an ambulatory health care facility other than a hospital-based facility, e.g., a freestanding physician-directed clinic, the diagnostic procedure must be performed by or under the direct personal supervision of a radiologist or other qualified physician. In addition, the facility must maintain a record of the attending physician's order for a scan performed on a mobile unit.

3. Billing for Mobile CT Scans

    Hospitals, hospital-associated radiologists, ambulatory health care facilities, and physician owner/operators of mobile units may bill for mobile scans as they would for scans performed on stationary equipment.

4. Claims Review

    Evidence of compliance with applicable State laws and regulations for control of radiation should be requested from owners of mobile CT scan units upon receipt of the first claims. All mobile scan claims should be reviewed very carefully in accordance with instructions applicable to scans performed on fixed units, with particular emphasis on the medical necessity for scans performed in an ambulatory setting.

E-Multi-Planar Diagnostic Imaging (MPDI)

In usual computerized tomography (CT) scanning procedures, a series of transverse or axial images are reproduced. These transverse images are routinely translated into coronal and/or sagittal views. Multiplanar diagnostic imaging (MPDI) is a process which further translates the data produced by CT scanning by providing reconstructed oblique images which can contribute to diagnostic information. MPDI, also known as planar image reconstruction or reformatted imaging, is covered under Medicare when provided as a service to an entity performing a covered CT scan.

100-3, 220.2
NCD for Magnetic Resonance Imaging (MRI) (220.2)
B - Nationally Covered Indications (Effective November 22, 1985)

Although several uses of MRI are still considered investigational and some uses are clearly contraindicated (see subsection D), MRI is considered medically efficacious for a number of uses. Use the following descriptions as general guidelines or examples of what may be considered covered rather than as a restrictive list of specific covered indications. Coverage is limited to MRI units that have received FDA premarket approval, and such units must be operated within the parameters specified by the approval. In addition, the services must be reasonable and necessary for the diagnosis or treatment of the specific patient involved.

The MRI is useful in examining the head, central nervous system, and spine. Multiple sclerosis can be diagnosed with MRI and the contents of the posterior fossa are visible. The inherent tissue contrast resolution of MRI makes it an appropriate standard diagnostic modality for general neuroradiology.

The MRI can assist in the differential diagnosis of mediastinal and retroperitoneal masses, including abnormalities of the large vessels such as aneurysms and dissection. When a clinical need exists to visualize the parenchyma of solid organs to detect anatomic disruption or neoplasia, this can be accomplished in the liver, urogenital system, adrenals, and pelvic organs without the use of radiological contrast materials. When MRI is considered reasonable and necessary, the use of paramagnetic contrast materials may be covered as part of the study. MRI may also be used to detect and stage pelvic and retroperitoneal neoplasms and to evaluate disorders of cancellous bone and soft tissues. It may also be used in the detection of pericardial thickening. Primary and secondary bone neoplasm and aseptic necrosis can be detected at an early stage and monitored with MRI. Patients with metallic prostheses, especially of the hip, can be imaged in order to detect the early stages of infection of the bone to which the prothesis is attached.

Disc Disease Diagnosis (Effective March 22, 1994)

The MRI may also be covered to diagnose disc disease without regard to whether radiological imaging has been tried first to diagnose the problem.

Gating Devices and Surface Coils (Effective March 4, 1991)

Gating devices that eliminate distorted images caused by cardiac and respiratory movement cycles are now considered state of the art techniques and may be covered. Surface and other specialty coils may also be covered, as they are used routinely for high resolution imaging where small limited regions of the body are studied. They produce high signal-to-noise ratios resulting in images of enhanced anatomic detail.

C - Contraindications and Nationally Noncovered Indications

1. Contraindications
   The MRI is not covered when the following patient-specific contraindications are present. It is not covered for patients with cardiac pacemakers or with metallic clips on vascular aneurysms. MRI during a viable pregnancy is also contraindicated at this time. The danger inherent in bringing ferromagnetic materials within range of MRI units generally constrains the use of MRI on acutely ill patients requiring life support systems and monitoring devices that employ ferromagnetic materials. In addition, the long imaging time and the enclosed position of the patient may result in claustrophobia, making patients who have a history of claustrophobia unsuitable candidates for MRI procedures.

2. Nationally Noncovered Indications
   The CMS has determined that blood flow measurement, imaging of cortical bone and calcifications, and procedures involving spatial resolution of bone and calcifications, are not considered reasonable and necessary indications within the meaning of section 1862(a)(1)(A) of the Social Security Act, and are therefore noncovered.

D. Other
All other uses of MRI for which CMS has not specifically indicated coverage or noncoverage continue to be eligible for coverage through individual local contractor discretion.

(This NCD last reviewed September 2004.)

100-3, 220.3
NCD for Magnetic Resonance Angiography (MRA) (220.3)
B. Nationally Covered Indications

1. Head and Neck
   Studies have proven that MRA is effective for evaluating flow in internal carotid vessels of the head and neck. However, not all potential applications of MRA have been shown to be reasonable and necessary. All of the following criteria must apply in order for Medicare to provide coverage for MRA of the head and neck:
   a. MRA is used to evaluate the carotid arteries, the circle of Willis, the anterior, middle or posterior cerebral arteries, the vertebral or basilar arteries or the venous sinuses;
   b. MRA is performed on patients with conditions of the head and neck for which surgery is anticipated and may be found to be appropriate based on the MRA. These conditions include, but are not limited to, tumor, aneurysms, vascular malformations, vascular occlusion or thrombosis. Within this broad category of disorders, medical necessity is the underlying determinant of the need for an MRA in specific diseases. The medical records should clearly justify and demonstrate the existence of medical necessity; and
   c. MRA and contrast angiography (CA) are not expected to be performed on the same patient for diagnostic purposes prior to the application of anticipated therapy. Only one of these tests will be covered routinely unless the physician can demonstrate the medical need to perform both tests.

2. Peripheral Arteries of Lower Extremities
   Studies have proven that MRA of peripheral arteries is useful in determining the presence and extent of peripheral vascular disease in lower extremities. This procedure is non-invasive and has been shown to find occult vessels in some patients for which those vessels were not apparent when CA was performed. Medicare will cover either MRA or CA to evaluate peripheral arteries of the lower extremities. However, both MRA and CA may be useful is some cases, such as:
   a. A patient has had CA and this test was unable to identify a viable run-off vessel for bypass. When exploratory surgery is not believed to be a reasonable medical course of action for this patient, MRA may be performed to identify the viable runoff vessel; or
   b. A patient has had MRA, but the results are inconclusive.

3. Abdomen and Pelvis
   a. Pre-operative Evaluation of Patients Undergoing Elective Abdominal Aortic Aneurysm (AAA) Repair (Effective July 1, 1999)

      The MRA is covered for pre-operative evaluation of patients undergoing elective AAA repair if the scientific evidence reveals MRA is considered comparable to CA in determining the extent of AAA, as well as in evaluating aortoiliac occlusion disease and renal artery pathology that may be necessary in the surgical planning of AAA repair. These studies also reveal that MRA could provide a net benefit to the patient. If preoperative CA is avoided, then patients are not exposed to the risks associated with invasive procedures, contrast media, end-organ damage, or arterial injury.

   b. Imaging the Renal Arteries and the Aortoiliac Arteries in the Absence of AAA or Aortic Dissection (Effective July 1, 2003)

      The MRA coverage is expanded to include imaging the renal arteries and the aortoiliac arteries in the absence of AAA or aortic dissection. MRA should be obtained in those circumstances in which using MRA is expected to avoid obtaining CA, when physician history, physical examination, and standard assessment tools provide insufficient information for patient management, and obtaining an MRA has a high probability of positively affecting patient management. However, CA may be ordered after obtaining the results of an MRA in those rare instances where medical necessity is demonstrated.

4. Chest
   a. Diagnosis of Pulmonary Embolism

      Current scientific data has shown that diagnostic pulmonary MRAs are improving due to recent developments such as faster imaging capabilities and gadolinium-enhancement. However, these advances in MRA are not significant enough to warrant replacement of pulmonary angiography in the diagnosis of pulmonary embolism for patients who have no contraindication to receiving intravenous iodinated contrast material. Patients who are allergic to iodinated contrast material face a high risk of developing complications if they undergo pulmonary angiography or computed tomography angiography. Therefore, Medicare will cover MRA of the chest for diagnosing a suspected pulmonary embolism when it is contraindicated for the patient to receive intravascular iodinated contrast material.

   b. Evaluation of Thoracic Aortic Dissection and Aneurysm

      Studies have shown that MRA of the chest has a high level of diagnostic accuracy for pre-operative and post-operative evaluation of aortic dissection of aneurysm. Depending on the clinical presentation, MRA may be used as an alternative to other non-invasive imaging technologies, such as transesophageal echocardiography and CT. Generally, Medicare will provide coverage only for MRA or for CA when used as a diagnostic test. However, if both MRA and CA of the chest are used, the physician must demonstrate the medical need for performing these tests.

      While the intent of this policy is to provide reimbursement for either MRA or CA, CMS is also allowing flexibility for physicians to make appropriate decisions concerning the use of these tests based on the needs of individual patients. CMS anticipates, however, low utilization of the combined use of MRA and CA. As a result, CMS encourages contractors to monitor the use of these tests and, where indicated, requires evidence of the need to perform both MRA and CA.

C. Nationally Noncovered Indications
All other uses of MRA for which CMS has not specifically indicated coverage continue to be noncovered.

D. Other
Not applicable.

(This NCD last reviewe

100-3, 220.5
NCD for Ultrasound Diagnostic Procedures (220.5)
A. General
Ultrasound diagnostic procedures utilizing low energy sound waves are being widely employed to determine the composition and contours of nearly all body tissues except bone and air-filled spaces. This technique permits noninvasive visualization of even the deepest structures in the body. The use of the ultrasound technique is sufficiently developed that it can be considered essential to good patient care in diagnosing a wide variety of conditions.

Ultrasound diagnostic procedures are listed below and are divided into two categories. Medicare coverage is extended to the procedures listed in Category I. Periodic claims review by the intermediary's medical consultants should be conducted to ensure that the techniques are medically appropriate and the general indications specified in these categories are met. Techniques in Category II are considered experimental and should not be covered at this time.

Indications and Limitations of Coverage

B. Nationally Covered Indications
Category I - (Clinically effective, usually part of initial patient evaluation, may be an adjunct to radiologic and nuclear medicine diagnostic technique)

Appendix G — Pub 100 References

- Echoencephalography, (Diencephalic Midline) (A-Mode).
- Echoencephalography, Complete (Diencephalic Midline and Ventricular Size).
- Ocular and Orbital Echography (A-Mode).
- Covered procedures include efforts to determine the suitability of aphakic patients for implantation of an artificial lens (pseudophakoi) following cataract surgery.
- Ocular and Orbital Sonography (B-Mode).
- Echocardiography, Pericardial Effusion (M-Mode).
- Pericardiocentesis, by Ultrasonic Guidance.
- Echocardiography, Cardiac Valve(s) (M-Mode).
- Echocardiography, Complete (M-Mode).
- Echocardiography, limited (e.g., follow-up or limited study) (M-Mode).
- Pleural Effusion Echography.
- Thoracentesis, by Ultrasonic Guidance.
- Abdominal Sonography, complete survey study (B-Scan).
- Abdominal Sonography, limited (e.g., follow-up or limited study) (B-Scan).
- Abdominal Sonography is not synonymous with ultrasound examination of individual organs.
- Renal Cyst Aspiration, by Ultrasonic Guidance.
- Renal Biopsy, by Ultrasonic Guidance.
- Pancreas Sonography (B-Scan).
- Pancreatic Sonography has proven effective in diagnosing pseudocysts.
- Spleen Sonography (B-Scan).
- Abdominal Aorta Echography (A-Mode).
- Abdominal Aorta Sonography (B-Scan).
- Retroperitoneal Sonography (B-Scan).
- Retroperitoneal Sonography does not include planning of fields for radiation therapy.
- Urinary Bladder Sonography (B-Scan).
- Urinary bladder Sonography does not include staging of bladder tumors.
- Pregnancy Diagnosis Sonography (B-Scan).
- Fetal Age Determination (Biparietal Diameter) Sonography (B-Scan).
- Fetal Growth Rate Sonography (B-Scan).
- Placenta Localization Sonography (B-Scan).
- Pregnancy Sonography, Complete (B-Scan).
- Molar Pregnancy Diagnosis Sonography (B-Scan).
- Ectopic Pregnancy Diagnosis Sonography (B-Scan).
- Passive Testing (Antepartum Monitoring of Fetal Heart Rate In the Resting Fetus).
- Intrauterine Contraceptive Device Sonography (B-Scan).
- Pelvic Mass Diagnosis Sonography (B-Scan).
- Amniocentesis, by Ultrasonic Guidance.
- Arterial Flow Study, Peripheral (Doppler).
- Venous Flow Study, Peripheral (Doppler).
- Arterial Aneurysm, Peripheral (B-Scan).
- Radiation Therapy Planning Sonography (B-Scan).
- Thyroid Echography (A-Mode).
- Thyroid Sonography (B-Scan).
- Breast Echography (A-Mode).
- Breast Sonography (B-Scan).
- Hepatic Sonography (B-Scan).
- Gallbladder Sonography.
- Renal Sonography.
- Two-Dimensional Echocardiography (B-Mode).
- Monitoring of cardiac output(Esophageal Doppler) for ventilated patients in the ICU and operative patients with a need for intra-operative fluid optimization

C. Nationally Non-Covered Indications
Category II - (Clinical reliability and efficacy not proven):

- B-Scan for atherosclerotic narrowing of peripheral arteries.

D. Other
Uses for ultrasound diagnostic procedures not listed in Category I or II above are left to local contractor discretion. In view of the rapid changes in the field of ultrasound diagnosis, uses for ultrasound diagnostic procedures other than those listed under Categories I and II should be carefully reviewed before payment. Medical justification may be required.

(This NCD last reviewed June 2007.)

100-3, 220.6
NCD for PET Scans (220.6) (Effective April 6, 2009)
Positron Emission Tomography (PET) is a minimally invasive diagnostic imaging procedure used to evaluate metabolism in normal tissue as well as in diseased tissues in conditions such as cancer, ischemic heart disease, and some neurologic disorders. A radiopharmaceutical is injected into the patient that gives off sub-atomic particles, known as positrons, as it decays. PET uses a positron camera (tomograph) to measure the decay of the radiopharmaceutical. The rate of decay provides biochemical information on the metabolism of the tissue being studied.

(This NCD last reviewed March 2009.)

100-3, 220.6.2
NCD for PET (FDG) for Lung Cancer (220.6.2)
(See section 220.6.17)

100-3, 220.6.3
NCD for PET (FDG) for Esophageal Cancer (220.6.3)
(See section 220.6.17)

100-3, 220.6.4
NCD for PET (FDG) for Colorectal Cancer (220.6.4)
(See section 220.6.17)

100-3, 220.6.5
NCD for PET (FDG) for Lymphoma (220.6.5)
(See section 220.6.17)

100-3, 220.6.6
NCD for PET (FDG) for Melanoma (220.6.6)
(See section 220.6.17)

100-3, 220.6.7
NCD for PET (FDG) for Head and Neck Cancers (220.6.7)
(See section 220.6.17)

100-3, 220.6.8
NCD for PET (FDG) for Myocardial Viability (220.6.8)

1. FDG PET is covered for the determination of myocardial viability following an inconclusive single photon emission computed tomography (SPECT) test from July 1, 2001, through September 30, 2002. Only full ring PET scanners are covered from July 1, 2001, through December 31, 2001. However, as of January 1, 2002, full and partial ring scanners are covered.
2. Beginning October 1, 2002, Medicare covers FDG PET for the determination of myocardial viability as a primary or initial diagnostic study prior to revascularization, or following an inconclusive SPECT. Studies performed by full and partial ring scanners are covered.

Limitations
In the event a patient receives a SPECT test with inconclusive results, a PET scan may be covered. However, if a patient receives a FDG PET study with inconclusive results, a follow up SPECT test is not covered.

Documentation that these conditions are met should be maintained by the referring physician in the beneficiary's medical record, as is normal business practice.

(This NCD last reviewed September 2002.)

100-3, 220.6.9
NCD for PET (FDG) for Refractory Seizures (220.6.9)
Beginning July 1, 2001, Medicare covers FDG PET for pre-surgical evaluation for the purpose of localization of a focus of refractory seizure activity.

Limitations: Covered only for pre-surgical evaluation.

Documentation that these conditions are met should be maintained by the referring physician in the beneficiary's medical record, as is normal business practice.

(This NCD last reviewed June 2001.)

100-3, 220.6.10
NCD for PET (FDG) for Breast Cancer (220.6.10)
(See section 220.6.17)

100-3, 220.6.11
NCD for PET (FDG) for Thyroid Cancer (220.6.11)
(See section 220.6.17)

100-3, 220.6.12
FDG PET for Soft Tissue Sarcoma
(See section 220.6.17)

100-3, 220.6.14
NCD for PET (FDG) for Brain, Cervical, Ovarian, Pancreatic, Small Cell Lung, and Testicular Cancers (220.6.14)
See section 220.6.17

100-3, 220.6.17
Positron Emission Tomography (FDG) for Oncologic Conditions

General
The Centers for Medicare and Medicaid Services (CMS) was asked to reconsider section 220.6 of the National Coverage Determinations (NCD) Manual to end the prospective data collection

requirements across all oncologic indications of FDG PET except for monitoring response to treatment. Section 220.6, of this chapter, establishes the requirement for prospective data collection for FDG PET used in the diagnosis, staging, restaging, and monitoring response to treatment for brain, cervical, ovarian, pancreatic, small cell lung and testicular cancers, as well as for cancer indications not previously specified in section 220.6 in its entirety.

The CMS received public input indicating that the current coverage framework, which required cancer-by-cancer consideration of diagnosis, staging, restaging, and monitoring response to treatment should be replaced by a more omnibus consideration. Thus, CMS broadened the scope of this review through an announcement on the CMS Web site and solicited additional public comment on the use of FDG PET imaging for solid tumors so that it could transparently consider this possibility.

1. Framework

    The CMS is adopting a coverage framework that replaces the four-part diagnosis, staging, restaging and monitoring response to treatment categories with a two-part framework that differentiates FDG PET imaging used to inform the initial antitumor treatment strategy from other uses related to guiding subsequent antitumor treatment strategies after the completion of initial treatment. CMS is making this change for all NCDs that address coverage of FDG PET for the specific oncologic conditions addressed in this decision.

2. Initial Anti-tumor Treatment Strategy

    The CMS has determined that the evidence is adequate to determine that the results of FDG PET imaging are useful in determining the appropriate initial treatment strategy for beneficiaries with suspected solid tumors and myeloma and improve health outcomes and thus are reasonable and necessary under Sec.1862(a)(1)(A) of the Social Security Act (the Act).

    Therefore, CMS will cover only one FDG PET study for beneficiaries who have solid tumors that are biopsy proven or strongly suspected based on other diagnostic testing when the beneficiary's treating physician determines that the FDG PET study is needed to determine the location and/or extent of the tumor for the following therapeutic purposes related to the initial treatment strategy:

    - To determine whether or not the beneficiary is an appropriate candidate for an invasive diagnostic or therapeutic procedure; or
    - To determine the optimal anatomic location for an invasive procedure; or
    - To determine the anatomic extent of tumor when the recommended anti-tumor treatment reasonably depends on the extent of the tumor.

    As exceptions to the initial treatment strategy section above:

    a. CMS has reviewed evidence on the use of FDG PET imaging to determine initial anti-tumor treatment in patients with adenocarcinoma of the prostate. CMS has determined that the available evidence does not demonstrate that FDG PET imaging improves physician decision making in the determination of initial anti-tumor treatment strategy in Medicare beneficiaries who have adenocarcinoma of the prostate, does not improve health outcomes and is thus not reasonable and necessary under Sec.1862(a)(1)(A) of the Act. Therefore, FDG PET is nationally non-covered for this indication of this tumor type.

    b. CMS received no new evidence demonstrating a change was warranted with respect to the use of FDG PET imaging to determine initial anti-tumor treatment in breast cancer; thus CMS is not making any change to the current coverage policy for FDG PET in breast cancer. CMS continues to cover FDG PET imaging for the initial treatment strategy for male and female breast cancer only when used in staging distant metastasis. FDG PET imaging for diagnosis and initial staging of axillary nodes will remain non-covered.

    c. CMS received no new evidence demonstrating a change was warranted with respect to use of FDG PET imaging of regional lymph nodes in melanoma; thus CMS is not changing the current NCD for FDG PET in melanoma. CMS will continue non-coverage of FDG PET for the evaluation of regional lymph nodes in melanoma. Other uses to determine initial treatment strategy remain covered.

    d. CMS received no new evidence demonstrating a change was warranted with respect to use of FDG PET imaging in the initial treatment strategy for cervical cancer. CMS continues to cover FDG PET imaging as an adjunct test for the detection of pre-treatment metastasis (i.e., staging) in newly diagnosed cervical cancers following conventional imaging that is negative for extra-pelvic metastasis. All other uses of FDG PET for the initial treatment strategy for beneficiaries diagnosed with cervical cancer will continue to only be covered as research under Sec.1862(a)(1)(E) of the Act through Coverage with Evidence Development (CED) as outlined immediately below and in section 3.

    Therefore, we will cover one initial FDG PET study for newly diagnosed cervical cancer when not used as an adjunct test for the detection of pre-treatment metastases following conventional imaging that is negative for extra-pelvic metastasis only when the beneficiary's treating physician determines that the FDG PET study is needed to inform the initial anti-tumor treatment strategy and the beneficiary is enrolled in, and the FDG PET provider is participating in, the following type of prospective clinical study:

    An FDG PET clinical study that is designed to collect additional information at the time of the scan to assist in patient management. Qualifying clinical studies must ensure that specific hypotheses are addressed; appropriate data elements are collected; hospitals and providers are qualified to provide the PET scan and interpret the results; participating hospitals and providers accurately report data on all enrolled patients not included in other qualifying trials through adequate auditing mechanisms; and all patient confidentiality, privacy, and other Federal laws must be followed.

    The clinical studies for which we will provide coverage must answer one or more of the following three questions:

    Prospectively, in Medicare beneficiaries with newly diagnosed cervical cancer who have not been found following conventional imaging to be negative for extra-pelvic metastases and whose treating physician determines that the FDG PET study is needed to inform the initial anti-tumor treatment strategy, does the addition of FDG PET imaging lead to:

    - A change in the likelihood of appropriate referrals for palliative care;
    - Improved quality of life; or,
    - Improved survival?

    The study must adhere to the standards of scientific integrity and relevance to the Medicare population as described in section 3 below.

3. Subsequent Anti-tumor Treatment Strategy

    The CMS reviewed evidence on the use of FDG PET in the subsequent treatment strategy for patients with tumor types other than breast, colorectal, esophagus, head and neck (non-CNS/thyroid), lymphoma, melanoma, non-small cell lung, and thyroid.

    For tumor types other than breast, colorectal, esophagus, head and neck (non-CNS/thyroid), lymphoma, melanoma, non-small cell lung, and thyroid, CMS has determined that the available evidence is not adequate to determine that FDG PET imaging improves physician decision making in the determination of subsequent anti-tumor treatment strategy or improves health outcomes in Medicare beneficiaries and thus is not reasonable and necessary under Sec.1862(a)(1)(A) of the Act.

    However, CMS has determined that the available evidence is sufficient to determine that FDG PET imaging for subsequent anti-tumor treatment strategy for tumor types other than breast, colorectal, esophagus, head and neck (non-CNS/thyroid), lymphoma, melanoma, non-small cell lung, and thyroid may be covered as research under Sec.1862(a)(1)(E) of the Act through CED.

    Therefore, CMS will cover a subsequent FDG PET study for tumor types other than breast, colorectal, esophagus, head and neck (non-CNS/thyroid), lymphoma, melanoma, non-small cell lung, and thyroid when the beneficiary's treating physician determines that the FDG PET study is needed to inform the subsequent anti-tumor treatment strategy and the beneficiary is enrolled in, and the FDG PET provider is participating in, the following type of prospective clinical study:

    An FDG PET clinical study that is designed to collect additional information at the time of the scan to assist in patient management. Qualifying clinical studies must ensure that specific hypotheses are addressed; appropriate data elements are collected; hospitals and providers are qualified to provide the FDG PET scan and interpret the results; participating hospitals and providers accurately report data on all enrolled patients not included in other qualifying trials through adequate auditing mechanisms; and all patient confidentiality, privacy, and other Federal laws must be followed.

    The clinical studies for which CMS will provide coverage, must answer one or more of the following three questions:

    Prospectively, in Medicare beneficiaries whose treating physician determines that the FDG PET study is needed to inform the subsequent anti-tumor treatment strategy, does the addition of FDG PET imaging lead to:

    - A change in the likelihood of appropriate referrals for palliative care;
    - Improved quality of life; or,
    - Improved survival?

    The study must adhere to the following standards of scientific integrity and relevance to the Medicare population:

    a. The principal purpose of the research study is to test whether a particular intervention potentially improves the participants' health outcomes.

    b. The research study is well-supported by available scientific and medical information or it is intended to clarify or establish the health outcomes of interventions already in common clinical use.

    c. The research study does not unjustifiably duplicate existing studies.

    d. The research study design is appropriate to answer the research question being asked in the study.

    e. The research study is sponsored by an organization or individual capable of executing the proposed study successfully.

    f. The research study is in compliance with all applicable Federal regulations concerning the protection of human subjects found in the Code of Federal Regulations (CFR) at 45 CFR Part 46. If a study is regulated by the Food and Drug Administration (FDA), it also must be in compliance with 21 CFR Parts 50 and 56.

    g. All aspects of the research study are conducted according to the appropriate standards of scientific integrity.

    h. The research study has a written protocol that clearly addresses, or incorporates by reference, the Medicare standards.

    i. The clinical research study is not designed to exclusively test toxicity or disease pathophysiology in healthy individuals. Trials of all medical technologies measuring therapeutic outcomes as one of the objectives meet this standard only if the disease or condition being studied is life-threatening as defined in 21 CFR Sec.312.81(a) and the patient has no other viable treatment options.

    j. The clinical research study is registered on the www.ClinicalTrials.gov Web site by the principal sponsor/investigator prior to the enrollment of the first study subject.

Appendix G — Pub 100 References

k. The research study protocol specifies the method and timing of public release of all pre-specified outcomes to be measured including release of outcomes if outcomes are negative or study is terminated early. The results must be made public within 24 months of the end of data collection. If a report is planned to be published in a peer-reviewed journal, then that initial release may be an abstract that meets the requirements of the International Committee of Medical Journal Editors. However, a full report of the outcomes must be made public no later than 3 years after the end of data collection.

l. The research study protocol must explicitly discuss subpopulations affected by the treatment under investigation, particularly traditionally underrepresented groups in clinical studies, how the inclusion and exclusion criteria affect enrollment of these populations, and a plan for the retention and reporting of said populations on the trial. If the inclusion and exclusion criteria are expected to have a negative effect on the recruitment or retention of underrepresented populations, the protocol must discuss why these criteria are necessary.

m. The research study protocol explicitly discusses how the results are or are not expected to be generalizable to the Medicare population to infer whether Medicare patients may benefit from the intervention. Separate discussions in the protocol may be necessary for populations eligible for Medicare due to age, disability or Medicaid eligibility.

Consistent with section 1142 of the Act, the Agency for Healthcare Research and Quality (AHRQ), supports clinical research studies that CMS determines meet the above-listed standards and address the above-listed research questions.

As exceptions to the subsequent treatment strategy section above:

a. CMS has reviewed evidence on the use of FDG PET imaging to determine subsequent treatment strategy in patients with ovarian cancer. CMS has determined that the available evidence is adequate to determine that FDG PET imaging improves physician decision making in the determination of subsequent treatment strategy in Medicare beneficiaries who have ovarian cancer, improves health outcomes, and is thus reasonable and necessary under Sec.1862(a)(1)(A) of the Act. Therefore, CMS has determined that FDG PET imaging is nationally covered for this indication for this tumor type.

b. CMS has reviewed evidence on the use of FDG PET imaging to determine subsequent treatment strategy in patients with cervical cancer. CMS has determined that the available evidence is adequate to determine that FDG PET imaging improves physician decision making in the determination of subsequent treatment strategy in Medicare beneficiaries who have cervical cancer, improves health outcomes, and is thus reasonable and necessary under Sec.1862(a)(1)(A) of the Act. Therefore, CMS has determined that FDG PET imaging is nationally covered for this indication for this tumor type.

4. Myeloma
The CMS reviewed evidence on the use of FDG PET in the initial and subsequent treatment strategy for myeloma. CMS has determined that the available evidence is sufficient to determine that FDG PET imaging improves physician decision making for these uses in Medicare beneficiaries who have myeloma, improves health outcomes, and is thus reasonable and necessary under Sec.1862(a)(1)(A) of the Act. Therefore, CMS has determined that FDG PET imaging is nationally covered for this indication for this tumor type.

5. Further Exceptions
The CMS specifically requested public comments with respect to treatment strategy of nine cancers that were covered in prior NCDs under Sec.1862(a)(1)(A). For the nine tumor types listed below, we will continue to cover FDG PET for those specific indications currently covered under Sec.1862(a)(1)(A) of the Act. CMS has not received public input suggesting coverage for these uses should be restricted. These include specific indications pertinent to:

- Breast
- Cervix
- Colorectal
- Esophagus
- Head and Neck (non-CNS/thyroid)
- Lymphoma
- Melanoma
- Non-small cell lung
- Thyroid

The CMS has transitioned the prior framework-diagnosis, staging, restaging, and monitoring response to treatment-into the initial treatment strategy and subsequent treatment strategy framework while maintaining current coverage.

The chart below summarizes section 220.6.1:

Tumor Type	Initial Treatment Strategy *	Subsequent Treatment Strategy **
Colorectal	Cover	Cover
Esophagus	Cover	Cover
Head & Neck (not thyroid or CNS)	Cover	Cover
Lymphoma	Cover	Cover
Non-small cell lung	Cover	Cover

Tumor Type	Initial Treatment Strategy *	Subsequent Treatment Strategy **
Ovary	Cover	Cover
Brain	Cover	CED
Cervix	1 or CED	Cover
Small cell lung	Cover	CED
Soft Tissue Sarcoma	Cover	CED
Pancreas	Cover	CED
Testes	Cover	CED
Breast (female and male)	2	Cover
Melanoma	3	Cover
Prostate	N/C	Cover
Thyroid	Cover	4 or CED
All other solid tumors	Cover	CED
Myeloma	Cover	Cover
All other cancers not listed herein	CED	CED

* Formerly "diagnosis" and "staging"

** Formerly "restaging" and "monitoring response to treatment"

N/C = noncover

(1) Cervix: Covered for the detection of pre-treatment metastases (i.e., staging) in newly diagnosed cervical cancer subsequent to conventional imaging that is negative for extra-pelvic metastasis. All other uses are CED.

(2) Breast: Non-covered for initial diagnosis and/or staging of axillary lymph nodes. Covered for initial staging of metastatic disease.

(3) Melanoma: Non-covered for initial staging of regional lymph nodes. All other uses for initial staging are covered.

(4) Thyroid: Covered for subsequent treatment strategy of recurrent or residual thyroid cancer of follicular cell origin previously treated by thyroidectomy and radioiodine ablation and have a serum thyroglobulin >10ng/ml and have a negative I-131 whole body scan. All other uses for subsequent treatment strategy are CED.

(This NCD last reviewed April 2009.)

100-3, 220.7

NCD for Xenon Scan (220.7)

Program payment may be made for this diagnostic procedure which involves perfusion lung imaging with 133 xenon. However, review for evidence of abuse which might include absence of reasonable indications, inappropriate sequence, or excessive number or kinds of procedures used in the care of individual patients.

100-3, 220.8

NCD for Nuclear Radiology Procedure (220.8)

Nuclear radiology procedures, including nuclear examinations performed with mobile radiological equipment, are covered if reasonable and necessary for the individual patient. Although these procedures may not be widely used, they are generally accepted. Review claims for these procedures for evidence of abuse which might absence of reasonable indications, inappropriate sequence, or excessive number or kinds of procedures used in the care of individual patients.

100-3, 220.12

NCD for Single Photon Emission Computed Tomography (SPECT) (220.12)

Frequency limitations: Contractor discretion.

In the case of myocardial viability, FDG PET may be used following a SPECT that was found to be inconclusive. However, SPECT may not be used following an inconclusive FDG PET performed to evaluate myocardial viability.

100-3, 220.13

NCD for Percutaneous Image-Guided Breast Biopsy (220.13)

The Breast Imaging Reporting and Data System (or BIRADS system) employed by the American College of Radiology provides a standardized lexicon with which radiologists may report their interpretation of a mammogram. The BIRADS grading of mammograms is as follows: Grade I-Negative, Grade II-Benign finding, Grade III-Probably benign, Grade IV-Suspicious abnormality, and Grade V-Highly suggestive of malignant neoplasm.

A. Nonpalpable Breast Lesions.
Effective January 1, 2003, Medicare covers percutaneous image-guided breast biopsy using stereotactic or ultrasound imaging for a radiographic abnormality that is nonpalpable and is graded as a BIRADS III, IV, or V.

B. Palpable Breast Lesions.

Effective January 1, 2003, Medicare covers percutaneous image guided breast biopsy using stereotactic or ultrasound imaging for palpable lesions that are difficult to biopsy using palpation alone. Contractors have the discretion to decide what types of palpable lesions are difficult to biopsy using palpation.

100-3, 230.1
NCD for Treatment of Kidney Stones (230.1)

In addition to the traditional surgical/endoscopic techniques for the treatment of kidney stones, the following lithotripsy techniques are also covered for services rendered on or after March 15, 1985.

A. Extracorporeal Shock Wave Lithotripsy.

Extracorporeal Shock Wave Lithotripsy (ESWL) is a non-invasive method of treating kidney stones using a device called a lithotriptor. The lithotriptor uses shock waves generated outside of the body to break up upper urinary tract stones. It focuses the shock waves specifically on stones under X-ray visualization, pulverizing them by repeated shocks. ESWL is covered under Medicare for use in the treatment of upper urinary tract kidney stones.

B. Percutaneous Lithotripsy.

Percutaneous lithotripsy (or nephrolithotomy) is an invasive method of treating kidney stones by using ultrasound, electrohydraulic or mechanical lithotripsy. A probe is inserted through an incision in the skin directly over the kidney and applied to the stone. A form of lithotripsy is then used to fragment the stone. Mechanical or electrohydraulic lithotripsy may be used as an alternative or adjunct to ultrasonic lithotripsy. Percutaneous lithotripsy of kidney stones by ultrasound or by the related techniques of electrohydraulic or mechanical lithotripsy is covered under Medicare.

The following is covered for services rendered on or after January 16, 1988.

C. Transurethral Ureteroscopic Lithotripsy.

Transurethral ureteroscopic lithotripsy is a method of fragmenting and removing ureteral and renal stones through a cystoscope. The cystoscope is inserted through the urethra into the bladder. Catheters are passed through the scope into the opening where the ureters enter the bladder. Instruments passed through this opening into the ureters are used to manipulate and ultimately disintegrate stones, using either mechanical crushing, transcystoscopic electrohydraulic shock waves, ultrasound or laser. Transurethral ureteroscopic lithotripsy for the treatment of urinary tract stones of the kidney or ureter is covered under Medicare.

100-3, 230.2
NCD for Uroflowmetric Evaluations (230.2)

Uroflowmetric evaluations (also referred to as urodynamic voiding or urodynamic flow studies) are covered under Medicare for diagnosing various urological dysfunctions, including bladder outlet obstructions.

100-3, 230.3
NCD for Sterilization (230.3)

- Payment may be made only where sterilization is a necessary part of the treatment of an illness or injury, e.g., removal of a uterus because of a tumor, removal of diseased ovaries (bilateral oophorectomy), or bilateral orchidectomy in a case of cancer of the prostate. Deny claims when the pathological evidence of the necessity to perform any such procedures to treat an illness or injury is absent; and
- Sterilization of a mentally retarded beneficiary is covered if it is a necessary part of the treatment of an illness or injury.
- Monitor such surgeries closely and obtain the information needed to determine whether in fact the surgery was performed as a means of treating an illness or injury or only to achieve sterilization.
- **B - Noncovered Conditions**
  Elective hysterectomy, tubal ligation, and vasectomy, if the stated reason for these procedures is sterilization;
- A sterilization that is performed because a physician believes another pregnancy would endanger the overall general health of the woman is not considered to be reasonable and necessary for the diagnosis or treatment of illness or injury within the meaning of Sec.1862(a)(1) of the Act. The same conclusion would apply where the sterilization is performed only as a measure to prevent the possible development of, or effect on, a mental condition should the individual become pregnant; and Sterilization of a mentally retarded person where the purpose is to prevent conception, rather than the treatment of an illness or injury.

100-3, 230.4
NCD for Diagnosis and Treatment of Impotence (230.4)

Program payment may be made for diagnosis and treatment of sexual impotence.¬

100-3, 230.6
NCD for Vabra Aspirator (230.6)

Program payment cannot be made for the aspirator or the related diagnostic services when furnished in connection with the examination of an asymptomatic patient. Payment for routine physical checkups is precluded under the statute (Sec.1862(a)(7) of the Act).

100-3, 230.9
NCD for Cryosurgery of Prostate (230.9)

Cryosurgery of the prostate as a salvage therapy is not covered for any services performed prior to June 30, 2001.

Salvage Cryosurgery of Prostate After Radiation Failure. Salvage cryosurgery of the prostate for recurrent cancer is medically necessary and appropriate only for those patients with localized disease who:

1. Have failed a trial of radiation therapy as their primary treatment; and
2. Meet one of the following conditions: Stage T2B or below, Gleason score <9, PSA <8 ng/mL.

Cryosurgery as salvage therapy is therefore not covered under Medicare after failure of other therapies as the primary treatment. Cryosurgery as salvage is only covered after the failure of a trial of radiation therapy, under the conditions noted above.

100-3, 230.10
NCD for Incontinence Control Devices (230.10)

A - Mechanical/Hydraulic Incontinence Control Devices

Mechanical/hydraulic incontinence control devices are accepted as safe and effective in the management of urinary incontinence in patients with permanent anatomic and neurologic dysfunctions of the bladder. This class of devices achieves control of urination by compression of the urethra. The materials used and the success rate may vary somewhat from device to device. Such a device is covered when its use is reasonable and necessary for the individual patient.

B - Collagen Implant

A collagen implant, which is injected into the submucosal tissues of the urethra and/or the bladder neck and into tissues adjacent to the urethra, is a prosthetic device used in the treatment of stress urinary incontinence resulting from intrinsic sphincter deficiency (ISD). ISD is a cause of stress urinary incontinence in which the urethral sphincter is unable to contract and generate sufficient resistance in the bladder, especially during stress maneuvers.

Prior to collagen implant therapy, a skin test for collagen sensitivity must be administered and evaluated over a 4 week period.

In male patients, the evaluation must include a complete history and physical examination and a simple cystometrogram to determine that the bladder fills and stores properly. The patient then is asked to stand upright with a full bladder and to cough or otherwise exert abdominal pressure on his bladder. If the patient leaks, the diagnosis of ISD is established.

In female patients, the evaluation must include a complete history and physical examination (including a pelvic exam) and a simple cystometrogram to rule out abnormalities of bladder compliance and abnormalities of urethral support. Following that determination, an abdominal leak point pressure (ALLP) test is performed. Leak point pressure, stated in cm H2O, is defined as the intra-abdominal pressure at which leakage occurs from the bladder (around a catheter) when the bladder has been filled with a minimum of 150 cc fluid. If the patient has an ALLP of less than 100 cm H2O, the diagnosis of ISD is established.

To use a collagen implant, physicians must have urology training in the use of a cystoscope and must complete a collagen implant training program.

Coverage of a collagen implant, and the procedure to inject it, is limited to the following types of patients with stress urinary incontinence due to ISD:

- Male or female patients with congenital sphincter weakness secondary to conditions such as myelomeningocele or epispadias;
- Male or female patients with acquired sphincter weakness secondary to spinal cord lesions;
- Male patients following trauma, including prostatectomy and/or radiation; and
- Female patients without urethral hypermobility and with abdominal leak point pressures of 100 cm H2O or less.

Patients whose incontinence does not improve with 5 injection procedures (5 separate treatment sessions) are considered treatment failures, and no further treatment of urinary incontinence by collagen implant is covered. Patients who have a reoccurrence of incontinence following successful treatment with collagen implants in the past (e.g., 6-12 months previously) may benefit from additional treatment sessions. Coverage of additional sessions may be allowed but must be supported by medical justification.

100-3, 230.12
NCD for Dimethyl Sulfoxide (DMSO) (230.12)

The Food and Drug Administration has determined that the only purpose for which DMSO is safe and effective for humans is in the treatment of the bladder condition, interstitial cystitis. Therefore, the use of DMSO for all other indications is not considered to be reasonable and necessary. Payment may be made for its use only when reasonable and necessary for a patient in the treatment of interstitial cystitis.

100-3, 230.14
NCD for Ultrafiltration Monitor (230.14)

Covered:

Ultrafiltration and ultrafiltration monitoring as a component of hemodialysis has an established and critical role in maintaining the well-being of ESRD patients and is a covered service. The Ultrafiltration Monitor is covered under the Medicare program when it is used to calculate fluid rates for those recipients who present difficult fluid management problems. Determine the medical necessity of this device on a case-by-case basis.

Not Covered:

Ultrafiltration, independent of conventional dialysis, is considered experimental, and technology exclusively designed for this purpose is not covered under Medicare.

100-3, 240.3
NCD for Heat Treatment, including the Use of Diathermy and Ultrasound for Pulmonary Conditions (240.3)

There is no physiological rationale or valid scientific documentation of effectiveness of diathermy or ultrasound heat treatments for asthma, bronchitis, or any other pulmonary condition and for such purpose this treatment cannot be considered reasonable and necessary within the meaning of section 1862(a)(1) of the Act.

100-3, 240.4.1
Sleep Testing for Obstructive Sleep Apnea (OSA) (Effective March 3, 2009)

A. General

Obstructive sleep apnea (OSA) is the collapse of the oropharyngeal walls and the obstruction of airflow occurring during sleep. Diagnostic tests for OSA have historically been classified into four types. The most comprehensive is designated Type I attended facility based polysomnography (PSG), which is considered the reference standard for diagnosing OSA. Attended facility based polysomnogram is a comprehensive diagnostic sleep test including at least electroencephalography (EEG), electro-oculography (EOG), electromyography (EMG), heart rate or electrocardiography (ECG), airflow, breathing/respiratory effort, and arterial oxygen saturation (SaO2) furnished in a sleep laboratory facility in which a technologist supervises the recording during sleep time and has the ability to intervene if needed. Overnight PSG is the conventional diagnostic test for OSA. The American Thoracic Society and the American Academy of Sleep Medicine have recommended supervised PSG in the sleep laboratory over 2 nights for the diagnosis of OSA and the initiation of continuous positive airway pressure (CPAP).

Three categories of portable monitors (used both in attended and unattended settings) have been developed for the diagnosis of OSA. Type II monitors have a minimum of 7 channels (e.g., EEG, EOG, EMG, ECG-heart rate, airflow, breathing/respiratory effort, SaO2)-this type of device monitors sleep staging, so AHI can be calculated. Type III monitors have a minimum of 4 monitored channels including ventilation or airflow (at least two channels of respiratory movement or respiratory movement and airflow), heart rate or ECG, and oxygen saturation. Type IV devices may measure one, two, three or more parameters but do not meet all the criteria of a higher category device. Some monitors use an actigraphy algorithm to identify periods of sleep and wakefulness.

B. Nationally Covered Indications

Effective for claims with dates of service on and after March 3, 2009, the Centers for Medicare & Medicaid Services finds that the evidence is sufficient to determine that the results of the sleep tests identified below can be used by a beneficiary's treating physician to diagnose OSA, that the use of such sleep testing technologies demonstrates improved health outcomes in Medicare beneficiaries who have OSA and receive the appropriate treatment, and that these tests are thus reasonable and necessary under section 1862(a)(1)(A) of the Social Security Act.

1. Type I PSG is covered when used to aid the diagnosis of OSA in beneficiaries who have clinical signs and symptoms indicative of OSA if performed attended in a sleep lab facility.
2. Type II or Type III sleep testing devices are covered when used to aid the diagnosis of OSA in beneficiaries who have clinical signs and symptoms indicative of OSA if performed unattended in or out of a sleep lab facility or attended in a sleep lab facility.
3. Type IV sleep testing devices measuring three or more channels, one of which is airflow, are covered when used to aid the diagnosis of OSA in beneficiaries who have signs and symptoms indicative of OSA if performed unattended in or out of a sleep lab facility or attended in a sleep lab facility.
4. Sleep testing devices measuring three or more channels that include actigraphy, oximetry, and peripheral arterial tone, are covered when used to aid the diagnosis of OSA in beneficiaries who have signs and symptoms indicative of OSA if performed unattended in or out of a sleep lab facility or attended in a sleep lab facility.

C. Nationally Non-Covered Indications

Effective for claims with dates of services on and after March 3, 2009, other diagnostic sleep tests for the diagnosis of OSA, other than those noted above for prescribing CPAP, are not sufficient for the coverage of CPAP and are not covered.

D. Other

N/A

(This NCD last reviewed March 2009.)

100-3, 240.6
NCD for Transvenous (Catheter) Pulmonary Embolectomy (240.6)

It is not covered under Medicare because it is still experimental.

100-3, 240.7
NCD for Postural Drainage Procedures and Pulmonary Exercises (240.7)

In most cases, postural drainage procedures and pulmonary exercises can be carried out safely and effectively by nursing personnel. However, in some cases patients may have acute or severe pulmonary conditions involving complex situations in which these procedures or exercises require the knowledge and skills of a physical therapist or a respiratory therapist. Therefore, if the attending physician determines as part of his/her plan of treatment that for the safe and effective administration of such services the procedures or exercises in question need to be performed by a physical therapist, the services of such a therapist constitute covered physical therapy when provided as an inpatient hospital service, extended care service, home health service, or outpatient physical therapy service.

NOTE: Physical therapy furnished in the outpatient department of a hospital is covered under the outpatient physical therapy benefit.

If the attending physician determines that the services should be performed by a respiratory therapist, the services of such a therapist constitute covered respiratory therapy when provided as an inpatient hospital service, outpatient hospital service, or extended care service, assuming that such services are furnished to the skilled nursing facility by a hospital with which the facility has a transfer agreement. Since the services of a respiratory therapist are not covered under the home health benefit, payment may not be made under the home health benefit for visits by a respiratory therapist to a patient's home to provide such services. Postural drainage procedures and pulmonary exercises are also covered when furnished by a physical therapist or a respiratory therapist as incident to a physician's professional service.

100-3, 250.1
NCD for Treatment of Psoriasis (250.1)

Psoriasis is a chronic skin disease, for which several conventional methods of treatment have been recognized as covered. These include topical application of steroids or other drugs; ultraviolet light (actinotherapy); and coal tar alone or in combination with ultraviolet B light (Goeckerman treatment).

A newer treatment for psoriasis uses a psoralen derivative drug in combination with ultraviolet A light, known as PUVA. PUVA therapy is covered for treatment of intractable, disabling psoriasis, but only after the psoriasis has not responded to more conventional treatment. The contractor should document this before paying for PUVA therapy.

In addition, reimbursement for PUVA therapy should be limited to amounts paid for other types of photochemotherapy; ordinarily, payment should not be allowed for more than 30 days of treatment, unless improvement is documented.

100-3, 250.3
NCD for Intravenous Immune Globulin for the Treatment of Autoimmune Mucocutaneous Blistering Diseases (250.3)

Effective October 1, 2002, IVIg is covered for the treatment of biopsy-proven (1) Pemphigus Vulgaris, (2) Pemphigus Foliaceus, (3) Bullous Pemphigoid, (4) Mucous Membrane Pemphigoid (a.k.a., Cicatricial Pemphigoid), and (5) Epidermolysis Bullosa Acquisita for the following patient subpopulations:

- Patients who have failed conventional therapy. Contractors have the discretion to define what constitutes failure of conventional therapy;
- Patients in whom conventional therapy is otherwise contraindicated. Contractors have the discretion to define what constitutes contraindications to conventional therapy; or
- Patients with rapidly progressive disease in whom a clinical response could not be affected quickly enough using conventional agents. In such situations IVIg therapy would be given along with conventional treatment(s) and the IVIg would be used only until the conventional therapy could take effect.

In addition, IVIg for the treatment of autoimmune mucocutaneous blistering diseases must be used only for short-term therapy and not as a maintenance therapy. Contractors have the discretion to decide what constitutes short-term therapy.

100-3, 250.4
NCD for Treatment of Actinic Keratosis (AKs) (250.4)

Actinic keratoses (AKs), also known as solar keratoses, are common, sun-induced skin lesions that are confined to the epidermis and have the potential to become a skin cancer.

Various options exist for treating AKs. Clinicians should select an appropriate treatment based on the patient's medical history, the lesion's characteristics, and on the patient's preference for a specific treatment. Commonly performed treatments for AKs include cryosurgery with liquid nitrogen, topical drug therapy, and curettage. Less commonly performed treatments for AK include dermabrasion, excision, chemical peels, laser therapy, and photodynamic therapy (PDT). An alternative approach to treating AKs is to observe the lesions over time and remove them only if they exhibit specific clinical features suggesting possible transformation to invasive squamous cell carcinoma (SCC).

Effective for services performed on and after November 26, 2001, Medicare covers the destruction of actinic keratoses without restrictions based on lesion or patient characteristics.

100-3, 260.1
NCD for Adult Liver Transplantation (260.1)

A - General

Effective July 15, 1996, adult liver transplantation when performed on beneficiaries with end stage liver disease other than hepatitis B or malignancies is covered under Medicare when performed in a facility which is approved by CMS as meeting institutional coverage criteria.

Effective December 10, 1999, adult liver transplantation when performed on beneficiaries with end stage liver disease other than malignancies is covered under Medicare when performed in a facility which is approved by CMS as meeting institutional coverage criteria.

Effective September 1, 2001, Medicare covers adult liver transplantation for hepatocellular carcinoma when the following conditions are met:

- The patient is not a candidate for subtotal liver resection;
- The patient's tumor(s) is less than or equal to 5 cm in diameter;
- There is no macrovascular involvement;
- There is no identifiable extrahepatic spread of tumor to surrounding lymph nodes, lungs, abdominal organs or bone; and
- The transplant is furnished in a facility which is approved by CMS as meeting institutional coverage criteria for liver transplants (See 65 FR 15006).

Adult liver transplantation for other malignancies remains excluded from coverage.

Coverage of adult liver transplantation is effective as of the date of the facility's approval, but for applications received before July 13, 1991, can be effective as early as March 8, 1990. (See "Federal Register" 56 FR 15006 dated April 12, 1991.)

B - Follow-up Care
Follow-up care or retransplantation (ICD-9-M 996.82, Complications of Transplanted Organ, Liver required as a result of a covered liver transplant is covered, provided such services are otherwise reasonable and necessary. Follow-up care is also covered for patients who have been discharged from a hospital after receiving noncoverd liver transplant. Coverage for follow-up care is for items and services that are reasonable and necessary as determined by Medicare guidelines.

C - Immunosuppressive Drugs
See the Medicare Benefit Policy Manual, Chapter 15, "Covered Medical and Other Health Services," Sec.50.5.1 and the Medicare Claims Processing Manual, Chapter 17, "Drugs and Biologicals," Sec.80.3.

100-3, 260.2
NCD for Pediatric Liver Transplantation (260.2)
Liver transplantation is covered for children (under age 18) with extrahepatic biliary atresia or any other form of end stage liver disease, except that coverage is not provided for children with a malignancy extending beyond the margins of the liver or those with persistent viremia.

Liver transplantation is covered for Medicare beneficiaries when performed in a pediatric hospital that performs pediatric liver transplants if the hospital submits an application which CMS approves documenting that:

The hospital's pediatric liver transplant program is operated jointly by the hospital and another facility that has been found by CMS to meet the institutional coverage criteria in the "Federal Register" notice of April 12, 1991;

- The unified program shares the same transplant surgeons and quality assurance program (including oversight committee, patient protocol, and patient selection criteria); and
- The hospital is able to provide the specialized facilities, services, and personnel that are required by pediatric liver transplant patients.

100-3, 260.3
NCD for Pancreas Transplants (260.3)
B. Nationally Covered Indications
Effective for services performed on or after July 1, 1999, whole organ pancreas transplantation is nationally covered by Medicare when performed simultaneous with or after a kidney transplant. If the pancreas transplant occurs after the kidney transplant, immunosuppressive therapy begins with the date of discharge from the inpatient stay for the pancreas transplant.

Effective for services performed on or after April 26, 2006, pancreas transplants alone (PA) are reasonable and necessary for Medicare beneficiaries in the following limited circumstances:

1. PA will be limited to those facilities that are Medicare-approved for kidney transplantation. (Approved centers can be found at http://www.cms.hhs.gov/ESRDGeneralInformation/02_Data.asp#TopOfPage
2. Patients must have a diagnosis of type I diabetes: ul.mylist2 li{list-style-type : circle}
    - Patient with diabetes must be beta cell autoantibody positive; or
    - Patient must demonstrate insulinopenia defined as a fasting C-peptide level that is less than or equal to 110% of the lower limit of normal of the laboratory's measurement method. Fasting C-peptide levels will only be considered valid with a concurrently obtained fasting glucose <225 mg/dL;
3. Patients must have a history of medically-uncontrollable labile (brittle) insulin-dependent diabetes mellitus with documented recurrent, severe, acutely life-threatening metabolic complications that require hospitalization. Aforementioned complications include frequent hypoglycemia unawareness or recurring severe ketoacidosis, or recurring severe hypoglycemic attacks;
4. Patients must have been optimally and intensively managed by an endocrinologist for at least 12 months with the most medically-recognized advanced insulin formulations and delivery systems;
5. Patients must have the emotional and mental capacity to understand the significant risks associated with surgery and to effectively manage the lifelong need for immunosuppression; and,
6. Patients must otherwise be a suitable candidate for transplantation.

C. Nationally Non-Covered Indications
The following procedure is not considered reasonable and necessary within the meaning of section 1862(a)(1)(A) of the Social Security Act:

1. Transplantation of partial pancreatic tissue or islet cells (except in the context of a clinical trial (see section 260.3.1 of the National Coverage Determinations Manual).

D. Other
Not applicable.

(This NCD last reviewed April 2006.)

100-3, 260.7
NCD for Lymphocyte Immune Globulin, Anti-Thymocyte Globulin (Equine) (260.7)
The FDA has approved one lymphocyte immune globulin preparation for marketing, lymphocyte immune globulin, anti-thymocyte globulin (equine). This drug is indicated for the management of allograft rejection episodes in renal transplantation. It is covered under Medicare when used for this purpose. Other forms of lymphocyte globulin preparation which the FDA approves for this indication in the future may be covered under Medicare.

100-3, 260.9
NCD for Heart Transplants (260.9)
A - General
Cardiac transplantation is covered under Medicare when performed in a facility which is approved by Medicare as meeting institutional coverage criteria. (See CMS Ruling 87-1.)

B - Exceptions
In certain limited cases, exceptions to the criteria may be warranted if there is justification and if the facility ensures our objectives of safety and efficacy. Under no circumstances will exceptions be made for facilities whose transplant programs have been in existence for less than two years, and applications from consortia will not be approved.

Although consortium arrangements will not be approved for payment of Medicare heart transplants, consideration will be given to applications from heart transplant facilities that consist of more than one hospital where all of the following conditions exist:

The hospitals are under the common control or have a formal affiliation arrangement with each other under the auspices of an organization such as a university or a legally-constituted medical research institute; and

The hospitals share resources by routinely using the same personnel or services in their transplant programs. The sharing of resources must be supported by the submission of operative notes or other information that documents the routine use of the same personnel and services in all of the individual hospitals. At a minimum, shared resources means:

- The individual members of the transplant team, consisting of the cardiac transplant surgeons, cardiologists and pathologists, must practice in all the hospitals and it can be documented that they otherwise function as members of the transplant team;
- The same organ procurement organization, immunology, and tissue-typing services must be used by all the hospitals;
- The hospitals submit, in the manner required (Kaplan-Meier method) their individual and pooled experience and survival data; and
- The hospitals otherwise meet the remaining Medicare criteria for heart transplant facilities; that is, the criteria regarding patient selection, patient management, program commitment, etc.

C - Pediatric Hospitals
Cardiac transplantation is covered for Medicare beneficiaries when performed in a pediatric hospital that performs pediatric heart transplants if the hospital submits an application which CMS approves as documenting that:

- The hospital's pediatric heart transplant program is operated jointly by the hospital and another facility that has been found by CMS to meet the institutional coverage criteria in CMS Ruling 87-1;
- The unified program shares the same transplant surgeons and quality assurance program (including oversight committee, patient protocol, and patient selection criteria); and
- The hospital is able to provide the specialized facilities, services, and personnel that are required by pediatric heart transplant patients.

D - Follow-Up Care
Follow-up care required as a result of a covered heart transplant is covered, provided such services are otherwise reasonable and necessary. Follow-up care is also covered for patients who have been discharged from a hospital after receiving a noncovered heart transplant. Coverage for follow-up care would be for items and services that are reasonable and necessary, as determined by Medicare guidelines. (See the Medicare Benefit Policy Manual, Chapter 16, "General Exclusions from Coverage," Sec.180.)

E - Immunosuppressive Drugs
See the Medicare Claims Processing Manual, Chapter 17, "Drugs and Biologicals," Sec.80.3.1, and Chapter 8, "Outpatient ESRD Hospital, Independent Facility, and Physician/Supplier Claims," Sec.120.1.

F - Artificial Hearts
Medicare does not cover the use of artificial hearts as a permanent replacement for a human heart or as a temporary life-support system until a human heart becomes available for transplant (often referred to as a "bridge to transplant"). Medicare does cover a ventricular assist device (VAD) when used in conjunction with specific criteria listed in Sec.20.9 of the NCD Manual.

100-3, 270.1
NCD for Electrical Stimulation (ES) and Electromagnetic Therapy for the Treatment of Wounds (270.1)
A. Nationally Covered Indications
The use of ES and electromagnetic therapy for the treatment of wounds are considered adjunctive therapies, and will only be covered for chronic Stage III or Stage IV pressure ulcers, arterial ulcers, diabetic ulcers, and venous stasis ulcers. Chronic ulcers are defined as ulcers that have not healed within 30 days of occurrence. ES or electromagnetic therapy will be covered only after appropriate standard wound therapy has been tried for at least 30 days and there are no measurable signs of improved healing. This 30-day period may begin while the wound is acute.

Standard wound care includes: optimization of nutritional status, debridement by any means to remove devitalized tissue, maintenance of a clean, moist bed of granulation tissue with appropriate moist dressings, and necessary treatment to resolve any infection that may be present. Standard wound care based on the specific type of wound includes: frequent repositioning of a patient with pressure ulcers (usually every 2 hours), offloading of pressure and good glucose control for diabetic ulcers, establishment of adequate circulation for arterial ulcers, and the use of a compression system for patients with venous ulcers.

Measurable signs of improved healing include: a decrease in wound size (either surface area or volume), decrease in amount of exudates, and decrease in amount of necrotic tissue. ES or electromagnetic therapy must be discontinued when the wound demonstrates 100% epithelilized wound bed.

ES and electromagnetic therapy services can only be covered when performed by a physician, physical therapist, or incident to a physician service. Evaluation of the wound is an integral part of wound therapy. When a physician, physical therapist, or a clinician incident to a physician, performs ES or electromagnetic therapy, the practitioner must evaluate the wound and contact the treating physician if the wound worsens. If ES or electromagnetic therapy is being used, wounds must be evaluated at least monthly by the treating physician.

B. Nationally Noncovered Indications

1. ES and electromagnetic therapy will not be covered as an initial treatment modality.
2. Continued treatment with ES or electromagnetic therapy is not covered if measurable signs of healing have not been demonstrated within any 30-day period of treatment.
3. Unsupervised use of ES or electromagnetic therapy for wound therapy will not be covered, as this use has not been found to be medically reasonable and necessary.

C. Other

All other uses of ES and electromagnetic therapy not otherwise specified for the treatment of wounds remain at local contractor discretion.

(This NCD last reviewed March 2004.)

100-3, 270.2
NCD for Noncontact Normothermic Wound Therapy (NNWT) (270.2)

There is insufficient scientific or clinical evidence to consider this device as reasonable and necessary for the treatment of wounds within the meaning of Sec.1862(a)(1)(A) of the Social Security Act and will not be covered by Medicare.

100-3, 270.4
NCD for Treatment of Decubitus Ulcers (270.4)

An accepted procedure for healing decubitus ulcers is to remove dead tissue from the lesions and to keep them clean to promote the growth of new tissue. This may be accomplished by hydrotherapy (whirlpool) treatments. Hydrotherapy (whirlpool) treatment for decubitus ulcers is a covered service under Medicare for patients when treatment is reasonable and necessary. Some other methods of treating decubitus ulcers, the safety and effectiveness of which have not been established, are not covered under the Medicare program. Some examples of these types of treatments are: ultraviolet light, low intensity direct current, topical application of oxygen, and topical dressings with Balsam of Peru in castor oil.

100-3, 270.5
NCD for Porcine Skin and Gradient Pressure Dressings (270.5)

Porcine (pig) skin dressings are covered, if reasonable and necessary for the individual patient as an occlusive dressing for burns, donor sites of a homograft, and decubiti and other ulcers.

100-3, 280.13
NCD for Transcutaneous Electrical Nerve Stimulators (TENS) (280.13)

(Rev. 1, 10-03-03)

CIM 60-20

The TENS is a type of electrical nerve stimulator that is employed to treat chronic intractable pain. This stimulator is attached to the surface of the patient's skin over the peripheral nerve to be stimulated. It may be applied in a variety of settings (in the patient's home, a physician's office, or in an outpatient clinic). Payment for TENS may be made under the durable medical equipment benefit. (See §160.13 for an explanation of coverage of medically necessary supplies for the effective use of TENS and §10.2 for an explanation of coverage of TENS for acute post-operative pain.)

100-3, 280.14
NCD for Infusion Pumps (280.14)

B. Nationally Covered Indications

The following indications for treatment using infusion pumps are covered under Medicare:

1. External Infusion Pumps

   a. Iron Poisoning (Effective for Services Performed On or After September 26, 1984)

   When used in the administration of deferoxamine for the treatment of acute iron poisoning and iron overload, only external infusion pumps are covered.

   b. Thromboembolic Disease (Effective for Services Performed On or After September 26, 1984)

   When used in the administration of heparin for the treatment of thromboembolic disease and/or pulmonary embolism, only external infusion pumps used in an institutional setting are covered.

   c. Chemotherapy for Liver Cancer (Effective for Services Performed On or After January 29, 1985)

   The external chemotherapy infusion pump is covered when used in the treatment of primary hepatocellular carcinoma or colorectal cancer where this disease is unresectable; OR, where the patient refuses surgical excision of the tumor.

   d. Morphine for Intractable Cancer Pain (Effective for Services Performed On or After April 22, 1985)

   Morphine infusion via an external infusion pump is covered when used in the treatment of intractable pain caused by cancer (in either an inpatient or outpatient setting, including a hospice).

   e. Continuous Subcutaneous Insulin Infusion (CSII) Pumps (Effective for Services Performed On or after December 17, 2004)

   Continuous subcutaneous insulin infusion (CSII) and related drugs/supplies are covered as medically reasonable and necessary in the home setting for the treatment of diabetic patients who: (1) either meet the updated fasting C-Peptide testing requirement, or, are beta cell autoantibody positive; and, (2) satisfy the remaining criteria for insulin pump therapy as described below. Patients must meet either Criterion A or B as follows:

   Criterion A: The patient has completed a comprehensive diabetes education program, and has been on a program of multiple daily injections of insulin (i.e., at least 3 injections per day), with frequent self-adjustments of insulin doses for at least 6 months prior to initiation of the insulin pump, and has documented frequency of glucose self-testing an average of at least 4 times per day during the 2 months prior to initiation of the insulin pump, and meets one or more of the following criteria while on the multiple daily injection regimen:

   - Glycosylated hemoglobin level (HbAlc) > 7.0 percent;
   - History of recurring hypoglycemia;
   - Wide fluctuations in blood glucose before mealtime;
   - Dawn phenomenon with fasting blood sugars frequently exceeding 200 mg/dl; or,
   - History of severe glycemic excursions.

   Criterion B: The patient with diabetes has been on a pump prior to enrollment in Medicare and has documented frequency of glucose self-testing an average of at least 4 times per day during the month prior to Medicare enrollment.

   General CSII Criteria

   In addition to meeting Criterion A or B above, the following general requirements must be met:

   The patient with diabetes must be insulinopenic per the updated fasting C-peptide testing requirement, or, as an alternative, must be beta cell autoantibody positive.

   Updated fasting C-peptide testing requirement:

   - Insulinopenia is defined as a fasting C-peptide level that is less than or equal to 110% of the lower limit of normal of the laboratory's measurement method.
   - For patients with renal insufficiency and creatinine clearance (actual or calculated from age, gender, weight, and serum creatinine) <50 ml/minute, insulinopenia is defined as a fasting C-peptide level that is less than or equal to 200% of the lower limit of normal of the laboratory's measurement method.
   - Fasting C-peptide levels will only be considered valid with a concurrently obtained fasting glucose <225 mg/dL.
   - Levels only need to be documented once in the medical records.

   Continued coverage of the insulin pump would require that the patient be seen and evaluated by the treating physician at least every 3 months.

   The pump must be ordered by and follow-up care of the patient must be managed by a physician who manages multiple patients with CSII and who works closely with a team including nurses, diabetes educators, and dietitians who are knowledgeable in the use of CSII.

   Other Uses of CSII

   The CMS will continue to allow coverage of all other uses of CSII in accordance with the Category B investigational device exemption (IDE) clinical trials regulation (42 CFR 405.201) or as a routine cost under the clinical trials policy (Medicare National Coverage Determinations (NCD) Manual 310.1).

   f. Other Uses

   Other uses of external infusion pumps are covered if the contractor's medical staff verifies the appropriateness of the therapy and the prescribed pump for the individual patient.

   NOTE: Payment may also be made for drugs necessary for the effective use of a covered external infusion pump as long as the drug being used with the pump is itself reasonable and necessary for the patient's treatment.

2. Implantable Infusion Pumps

   a. Chemotherapy for Liver Cancer (Effective for Services Performed On or After September 26, 1984)

   The implantable infusion pump is covered for intra-arterial infusion of 5-FUdR for the treatment of liver cancer for patients with primary hepatocellular carcinoma or Duke's Class D colorectal cancer, in whom the metastases are limited to the liver, and where: (1) the disease is unresectable, or (2) the patient refuses surgical excision of the tumor.

   b. Anti-Spasmodic Drugs for Severe Spasticity

   An implantable infusion pump is covered when used to administer anti-spasmodic drugs intrathecally (e.g., baclofen) to treat chronic intractable spasticity in patients who have proven unresponsive to less invasive medical therapy as determined by the following criteria:

   As indicated by at least a 6-week trial, the patient cannot be maintained on noninvasive methods of spasm control, such as oral anti-spasmodic drugs, either because these methods fail to control adequately the spasticity or produce intolerable side effects, and prior to pump implantation, the patient must have responded favorably to a trial intrathecal dose of the anti-spasmodic drug.

c. Opioid Drugs for Treatment of Chronic Intractable Pain

An implantable infusion pump is covered when used to administer opioid drugs (e.g., morphine) intrathecally or epidurally for treatment of severe chronic intractable pain of malignant or nonmalignant origin in patients who have a life expectancy of at least 3 months, and who have proven unresponsive to less invasive medical therapy as determined by the following criteria:

The patient's history must indicate that he/she would not respond adequately to noninvasive methods of pain control, such as systemic opioids (including attempts to eliminate physical and behavioral abnormalities which may cause an exaggerated reaction to pain); and a preliminary trial of intraspinal opioid drug administration must be undertaken with a temporary intrathecal/epidural catheter to substantiate adequately acceptable pain relief and degree of side effects (including effects on the activities of daily living) and patient acceptance.

d. Coverage of Other Uses of Implanted Infusion Pumps

Determinations may be made on coverage of other uses of implanted infusion pumps if the contractor's medical staff verifies that:

- The drug is reasonable and necessary for the treatment of the individual patient;
- It is medically necessary that the drug be administered by an implanted infusion pump; and,
- The Food and Drug Administration (FDA)-approved labeling for the pump must specify that the drug being administered and the purpose for which it is administered is an indicated use for the pump.

e. Implantation of Infusion Pump Is Contraindicated

The implantation of an infusion pump is contraindicated in the following patients:

- With a known allergy or hypersensitivity to the drug being used (e.g., oral baclofen, morphine, etc.);
- Who have an infection;
- Whose body size is insufficient to support the weight and bulk of the device; and,
- With other implanted programmable devices since crosstalk between devices may inadvertently change the prescription.

NOTE: Payment may also be made for drugs necessary for the effective use of an implantable infusion pump as long as the drug being used with the pump is itself reasonable and necessary for the patient's treatment.

C. Nationally Noncovered Indications
The following indications for treatment using infusion pumps are not covered under Medicare:

1. External Infusion Pumps

    a. Vancomycin (Effective for Services Beginning On or After September 1, 1996)

    Medicare coverage of vancomycin as a durable medical equipment infusion pump benefit is not covered. There is insufficient evidence to support the necessity of using an external infusion pump, instead of a disposable elastomeric pump or the gravity drip method, to administer vancomycin in a safe and appropriate manner.

2. Implantable Infusion Pump

    a. Thromboembolic Disease (Effective for Services Performed On or After September 26, 1984)

    According to the Public Health Service, there is insufficient published clinical data to support the safety and effectiveness of the heparin implantable pump. Therefore, the use of an implantable infusion pump for infusion of heparin in the treatment of recurrent thromboembolic disease is not covered.

    b. Diabetes

    An implanted infusion pump for the infusion of insulin to treat diabetes is not covered. The data does not demonstrate that the pump provides effective administration of insulin.

D. Other
Not applicable.

(This NCD last reviewed January 2005.)

100-3, 300.1
NCD for Obsolete or Unreliable Diagnostic Tests (300.1)
CIM 50-34

A. Diagnostic Tests
Do not routinely pay for the following diagnostic tests because they are obsolete and have been replaced by more advanced procedures. The listed tests may be paid for only if the medical need for the procedure is satisfactorily justified by the physician who performs it. When the services are subject to the Quality Improvement Organization (QIO) Review, the QIO is responsible for determining that satisfactory medical justification exists. When the services are not subject to QIO review, the intermediary or carrier is responsible for determining that satisfactory medical justification exists. This includes:

- Amylase, blood isoenzymes, electrophoretic,
- Chromium, blood,
- Guanase, blood,
- Zinc sulphate turbidity, blood,
- Skin test, cat scratch fever,
- Skin test, lymphopathia venereum,
- Circulation time, one test,
- Cephalin flocculation,
- Congo red, blood,
- Hormones, adrenocorticotropin quantitative animal tests,
- Hormones, adrenocorticotropin quantitative bioassay,
- Thymol turbidity, blood,
- Skin test, actinomycosis,
- Skin test, brucellosis,
- Skin test, psittacosis,
- Skin test, trichinosis,
- Calcium, feces, 24-hour quantitative,
- Starch, feces, screening,
- Chymotrypsin, duodenal contents,
- Gastric analysis, pepsin,
- Gastric analysis, tubeless,
- Calcium saturation clotting time,
- Capillary fragility test (Rumpel-Leede),
- Colloidal gold,
- Bendien's test for cancer and tuberculosis,
- Bolen's test for cancer,
- Rehfuss test for gastric acidity, and
- Serum seromucoid assay for cancer and other diseases.

B. Cardiovascular Tests
Do not pay for the following phonocardiography and vectorcardiography diagnostic tests because they have been determined to be outmoded and of little clinical value. They include:

- Phonocardiogram with or without ECG lead; with supervision during recording with interpretation and report (when equipment is supplied by the physician),
- Phonocardiogram; tracing only, without interpretation and report (e.g., when equipment is supplied by the hospital, clinic),
- Phonocardiogram; interpretation and report,
- Phonocardiogram with ECG lead, with indirect carotid artery and/or jugular vein tracing, and/or apex cardiogram; with interpretation and report,
- Phonocardiogram; without interpretation and report,
- Phonocardiogram; interpretation and report only,
- Intracardiac,
- Vectorcardiogram (VCG), with or without ECG; with interpretation and report,
- Vectorcardiogram; tracing only, without interpretation and report, and
- Vectorcardiogram; interpretation and report only.

100-4, 1, 30.3.5
Effect of Assignment Upon Purchase of Cataract Glasses FromParticipating Physician or Supplier on Claims Submitted to Carriers
B3-3045.4

A pair of cataract glasses is comprised of two distinct products: a professional product (the prescribed lenses) and a retail commercial product (the frames). The frames serve not only as a holder of lenses but also as an article of personal apparel. As such, they are usually selected on the basis of personal taste and style. Although Medicare will pay only for standard frames, most patients want deluxe frames. Participating physicians and suppliers cannot profitably furnish such deluxe frames unless they can make an extra (noncovered) charge for the frames even though they accept assignment.

Therefore, a participating physician or supplier (whether an ophthalmologist, optometrist, or optician) who accepts assignment on cataract glasses with deluxe frames may charge the Medicare patient the difference between his/her usual charge to private pay patients for glasses with standard frames and his/her usual charge to such patients for glasses with deluxe frames, in addition to the applicable deductible and coinsurance on glasses with standard frames, if all of the following requirements are met:

A. The participating physician or supplier has standard frames available, offers them for sale to the patient, and issues and ABN to the patient that explains the price and other differences between standard and deluxe frames. Refer to Chapter 30.

B. The participating physician or supplier obtains from the patient (or his/her representative) and keeps on file the following signed and dated statement:

_____
Name of Patient   Medicare Claim Number

Having been informed that an extra charge is being made by the physician or supplier for deluxe frames, that this extra charge is not covered by Medicare, and that standard frames

Appendix G — Pub 100 References

are available for purchase from the physician or supplier at no extra charge, I have chosen to purchase deluxe frames.

Signature					Date

C. The participating physician or supplier itemizes on his/her claim his/her actual charge for the lenses, his/her actual charge for the standard frames, and his/her actual extra charge for the deluxe frames (charge differential). Once the assigned claim for deluxe frames has been processed, the carrier will follow the ABN instructions as described in Sec.60.

100-4, 3, 10.4
Payment of Nonphysician Services for Inpatients

All items and nonphysician services furnished to inpatients must be furnished directly by the hospital or billed through the hospital under arrangements. This provision applies to all hospitals, regardless of whether they are subject to PPS.

Other Medical Items, Supplies, and Services the following medical items, supplies, and services furnished to inpatients are covered under Part A. Consequently, they are covered by the prospective payment rate or reimbursed as reasonable costs under Part A to hospitals excluded from PPS.

- Laboratory services (excluding anatomic pathology services and certain clinical pathology services);
- Pacemakers and other prosthetic devices including lenses, and artificial limbs, knees, and hips;
- Radiology services including computed tomography (CT) scans furnished to inpatients by a physician's office, other hospital, or radiology clinic;
- Total parenteral nutrition (TPN) services; and
- Transportation, including transportation by ambulance, to and from another hospital or freestanding facility to receive specialized diagnostic or therapeutic services not available at the facility where the patient is an inpatient.

The hospital must include the cost of these services in the appropriate ancillary service cost center, i.e., in the cost of the diagnostic or therapeutic service. It must not show them separately under revenue code 0540.

EXCEPTIONS

- Pneumococcal Vaccine -is payable under Part B only and is billed by the hospital on the Form CMS-1450.
- Ambulance Service For purposes of this section "hospital inpatient" means beneficiary who has been formally admitted it does not include a beneficiary who is in the process of being transferred from one hospital to another. Where the patient is transferred from one hospital to another, and is admitted as an inpatient to the second, the ambulance service is payable under only Part B. If transportation is by a hospital owned and operated ambulance, the hospital bills separately on Form CMS-1450 as appropriate. Similarly, if the hospital arranges for the ambulance transportation with an ambulance operator, including paying the ambulance operator, it bills separately. However, if the hospital does not assume any financial responsibility, the billing is to the carrier by the ambulance operator or beneficiary, as appropriate, if an ambulance is used for the transportation of a hospital inpatient to another facility for diagnostic tests or special treatment the ambulance trip is considered part of the DRG, and not separately billable, if the resident hospital is under PPS.
- Part B Inpatient Services Where Part A benefits are not payable, payment maybe made to the hospital under Part B for certain medical and other health services. See Chapter 4 for a description of Part B inpatient services.
- Anesthetist Services "Incident to" Physician Services-If a physician's practice was to employ anesthetists and to bill on a reasonable charge basis for these services and that practice was in effect as of the last day of the hospital's most recent 12-month cost reporting period ending before September 30, 1983, the physician may continue that practice through cost reporting periods beginning October 1, 1984. However, if the physician chooses to continue this practice, the hospital may not add costs of the anesthetist's service to its base period costs for purposes of its transition payment rates. If it is the existing or new practice of the physician to employ certified registered nurse anesthetists (CRNAs) and other qualified anesthetists and include charges for their services in the physician bills for anesthesiology services for the hospital's cost report periods beginning on or after October 1, 1984, and before October 1, 1987, the physician may continue to do so.

B. Exceptions/Waivers

These provisions were waived before cost reporting periods beginning on or after October1, 1986, under certain circumstances. The basic criteria for waiver was that services furnished by outside suppliers are so extensive that a sudden change in billing practices would threaten the stability of patient care. Specific criteria for waiver and processing procedures are in Sec.2804 of the Provider Reimbursement Manual (CMS Pub. 15-1).

100-4, 3, 20.1.2.8
Special Outlier Payments for Burn Cases

For discharges occurring on or after April 1, 1988, the additional payment amount for the DRGs related to burn cases, which are identified in the most recent annual notice of prospective payment rates is computed using the same methodology (as stated above in section 20.1.2.3) except that the payment is made using a marginal cost factor of 90 percent instead of 80 percent.

100-4, 3, 20.2.1
Medicare Code Editor (MCE)

A. General

The MCE edits claims to detect incorrect billing data. In determining the appropriate DRG for a Medicare patient, the age, sex, discharge status, principal diagnosis, secondary diagnosis, and procedures performed must be reported accurately to the Grouper program. The logic of the Grouper software assumes that this information is accurate and the Grouper does not make any attempt to edit the data for accuracy. Only where extreme inconsistencies occur in the patient information will a patient not be assigned to a DRG. Therefore, the MCE is used to improve the quality of information given to Grouper.

The MCE addresses three basic types of edits which will support the DRG assignment:

- Code Edits - Examines a record for the correct use of ICD-9-CM codes that describe a patient's diagnoses and procedures. They include basic consistency checks on the interrelationship among a patient's age, sex, and diagnoses and procedures.
- Coverage Edits - Examines the type of patient and procedures performed to determine if the services where covered.
- Clinical Edits - Examines the clinical consistency of the diagnostic and procedural information on the medical claim to determine if they are clinically reasonable and, therefore, should be paid.

B. Implementation Requirements

The FI processes all inpatient Part A discharge/transfer bills for both PPS and non-PPS facilities (including waiver States, long-term care hospitals, and excluded units) through the MCE. It processes claims that have been reviewed by the QIO prior to billing through the MCE only for edit types 1, 2, 3, 4, 7, and 12. It does not process the following kinds of bills through the MCE:

- Where no Medicare payment is due (amounts reported by value codes 12, 13, 14, 15, or 16 equal or exceed charges).
- Where no Medicare payment is being made. Where partial payment is made, editing is required.
- Where QIO reviewed prior to billing (code C1 or C3 in FL 24-30). It may process these exceptions through the program and ignore development codes or bypass the program.

The MCE software contains multiple versions. The version of the MCE accessed by the program depends upon the patient discharge date entered on the claim.

C. Bill System/MCE Interface

The FI installs the MCE online, if possible, so that prepayment edit requirements identified in subsection C can be directed to hospitals without clerical handling.

The MCE needs the following data elements to analyze the bill:

- Age;
- Sex;
- Discharge status;
- Diagnosis (9 maximum - principal diagnosis and up to 8 additional diagnoses);
- Procedures (6 maximum); and
- Discharge date.

The MCE provides the FI an analysis of "errors" on the bill as described in subsection D. The FI develops its own interface program to provide data to MCE and receive data from it.

The MCE Installation Manual describes the installation and operation of the program, including data base formats and locations.

D. Processing Requirements

The hospital must follow the procedure described below for each error code. For bills returned to the provider, the FI considers the bill improperly completed for control and processing time purposes. (See chapter 1.)

1. Invalid Diagnosis or Procedure Code
   The MCE checks each diagnosis code, including the admitting diagnosis, and each procedure code against a table of valid ICD-9-CM codes. An admitting diagnosis, a principle diagnosis, and up to eight additional diagnoses may be reported. Up to six total procedure codes may be reported on an inpatient claim. If the recorded code is not in this table, the code is invalid, and the FI returns the bill to the provider.

   For a list of all valid ICD-9-CM codes see "International Classification of Diseases, 9th Revision, Clinical Modification (ICD-9-CM), January 1979, Volume I (Diseases)" and "Volume 3 (Procedures)," and the "Addendum/Errata" and new codes furnished by the FI. The hospital must review the medical record and/or face sheet and enter the correct diagnosis/procedure codes before returning the bill.

2. Invalid Fourth or Fifth Digit
   The MCE identifies any diagnosis code, including the admitting diagnosis or any procedure that requires a fourth or fifth digit, which is either missing or not valid for the code in question.

   For a list of all valid fourth and fifth digit ICD-9-CM codes see "International Classification of Diseases, 9th Revision, Clinical Modification (ICD-9-CM), January 1979, Volume 1 (Diseases)" and "Volume 3 (Procedures)," and the "Addendum/Errata" and new codes furnished by the FI. The FI returns claims edited for this reason to the hospital. The hospital must review the medical record and/or face sheet and enter the correct diagnosis/procedure before returning the bill.

3. E-Code as Principal Diagnosis
   E-codes describe the circumstances that caused an injury, not the nature of the injury, and therefore are not recognized by the Grouper program as acceptable principal diagnoses. E-codes are all ICD-9-CM diagnosis codes that begin with the letter E. For a list of all E-codes,

see "International Classification of Diseases, 9th Revision, Clinical Modification (ICD-9-CM), January 1979, Volume I (Diseases)." The hospital must review the medical record and/or face sheet and enter the correct diagnosis before returning the bill.

4. Duplicate of PDX
Any secondary diagnosis that is the same code as the principal diagnosis is identified as a duplicate of the principal diagnoses. This is unacceptable because the secondary diagnosis may cause an erroneous assignment to a higher severity MS-DRG. Hospitals may not repeat a diagnosis code. The FI will delete the duplicate secondary diagnosis and process the bill.

5. Age Conflict
The MCE detects inconsistencies between a patient's age and any diagnosis on the patient's record. Examples are:
- A 5-year-old patient with benign prostatic hypertrophy.
- A 78-year-old delivery.

In the above cases, the diagnosis is clinically impossible in a patient of the stated age. Therefore, either the diagnosis or age is presumed to be incorrect. Four age code categories are described below.
- A subset of diagnoses is intended only for newborns and neonates. These are "Newborn" diagnoses. For "Newborn" diagnoses, the patient's age must be 0 years.
- Certain diagnoses are considered reasonable only for children between the ages of 0 and 17. These are "Pediatric" diagnoses.
- Diagnoses identified as "Maternity" are coded only for patients between the ages of 12 and 55 years.
- A subset of diagnoses is considered valid only for patients over the age of 14. These are "Adult" diagnoses. For "Adult" diagnoses the age range is 15 through 124.

The diagnoses described in the Medicare Code Editor, posted on the CMS Webpage at: http://www.cms.hhs.gov/AcuteInpatientPPS/FFD/itemdetail.asp?filterType=none&filterByDID=-99&sortByDID=2&sortOrder=ascending&itemID=CMS1206058&intNumPerPage=10 are acceptable only for the age categories shown. If the FI edits online, it will return such bills for a proper diagnosis or correction of age as applicable. If the FI edits in batch operations after receipt of the admission query response, it uses the age based on CMS records and returns bills that fail this edit. The hospital must review the medical record and/or face sheet and enter the proper diagnosis or patient's age before returning the bill.

6. Sex Conflict
The MCE detects inconsistencies between a patient's sex and a diagnosis or procedure on the patient's record. Examples are:
- Male patient with cervical cancer (diagnosis).
- Male patient with a hysterectomy (procedure).

In both instances, the indicated diagnosis or the procedure conflicts with the stated sex of the patient. Therefore, either the patient's diagnosis, procedure or sex is incorrect.

The Medicare Code Editor contains listings of male and female related ICD-9-CM diagnosis and procedure codes and the corresponding English descriptions. The hospital should review the medical record and/or face sheet and enter the proper sex, diagnosis, and procedure before returning the bill.

7. Manifestation Code As Principal Diagnosis
A manifestation code describes the manifestation of an underlying disease, not the disease itself, and therefore, cannot be a principal diagnosis. The Medicare Code Editor contains listings of ICD-9-CM diagnoses identified as manifestation codes. The hospital should review the medical record and/or face sheet and enter the proper diagnosis before returning the bill.

8. Nonspecific Principal Diagnosis
Effective October 1, 2007 (FY 2008), the non-specific principal diagnosis edit was discontinued and will appear for claims processed using MCE version 2.0-23.0 only.

9. Questionable Admission
There are some diagnoses which are not usually sufficient justification for admission to an acute care hospital. For example, if a patient is given a principal diagnosis of:

4011 - Benign Hypertension

then this patient would have a questionable admission, since benign hypertension is not normally sufficient justification for admission.

The Medicare Code Editor contains a listing of ICD-9-CM diagnosis codes identified as "Questionable Admission" when used as principal diagnosis.

The A/B MACs or the FIs may review on a post-payment basis all questionable admission cases. Where the A/B MACs or the FIs determines the denial rate is sufficiently high to warrant, it may review the claim before payment.

10. Unacceptable Principal Diagnosis
There are selected codes that describe a circumstance which influences an individual's health status but is not a current illness or injury; therefore, they are unacceptable as a principal diagnosis. For example, VI73 (Family History of Ischemic Heart Disease) is an unacceptable principal diagnosis.

In a few cases, there are codes that are acceptable if a secondary diagnosis is coded. If no secondary diagnosis is present for them, MCE returns the message "requires secondary dx." The A/B MAC or the FI may review claims with diagnosis V571, V5721, V5722, V573, V5789, and V579 and a secondary diagnosis. A/B MACs or FIs may choose to review as a principal diagnosis if data analysis deems it a priority.

If these codes are identified without a secondary diagnosis, the FI returns the bill to the hospital and requests a secondary diagnosis that describes the origin of the impairment. Also, bills containing other "unacceptable principal diagnosis" codes are returned.

The hospital reviews the medical record and/or face sheet and enters the principal diagnosis that describes the illness or injury before returning the bill.

11. Nonspecific O.R. Procedures
Effective October 1, 2007 (FY 2008), the non-specific O.R. procedure edit was discontinued and will appear for claims processed using MCE version 2.0-23.0 only.

12. Noncovered O.R. Procedures
There are some O.R. procedures for which Medicare does not provide payment. The FI will return the bill requesting either:
- A no pay bill, or
- A correction in the procedure code.
- A bill indicating the covered and noncovered procedures.

If the hospital indicates that there are covered and noncovered procedures, the FI refers the bill to the QIO for prepayment review. Upon receipt of the QIOs response, it either deletes the noncovered procedures and charges or requires the hospital to delete them. It does not process the noncovered procedures through Grouper or the noncovered charges through Pricer.

13. Open Biopsy Check
Biopsies can be performed as open (i.e., a body cavity is entered surgically), percutaneously, or endoscopically. The DRG Grouper logic assign a patient to different DRGs depending upon whether or not the biopsy was open. In general, for most organ systems, open biopsies are performed infrequently.

Effective October 1, 1987, there are revised biopsy codes that distinguish between open and closed biopsies. To make sure that hospitals are using ICD-9-CM codes correctly, the FI requests O.R. reports on a sample of 10 percent of claims with open biopsy procedures for review on a post payment basis.

If the O.R. report reveals that the biopsy was closed (performed percutaneously, endoscopically, etc.) the FI changes the procedure code on the bill to the closed biopsy code and processes an adjustment bill. Some biopsy codes (3328 and 5634) have two related closed biopsy codes, one for closed endoscopic and for closed percutaneous biopsies. The FI assigns the appropriate closed biopsy code after reviewing the medical information.

14. Medicare as Secondary Payer - MSP Alert
The MCE identifies situations that may involve automobile medical, no-fault or liability insurance. The hospital must develop other insurance coverage as provided in the Medicare Secondary Payer Manuals, before billing Medicare.

15. Bilateral Procedure
There are codes that do not accurately reflect performed procedures in one admission on two or more different bilateral joints of the lower extremities. A combination of these codes show a bilateral procedure when, in fact, they could be single joint procedures (i.e., duplicate procedures).

If two more of these procedures are coded, and the principal diagnosis is in MDC 8, the claim is flagged for post-pay development. The FI processes the bill as coded but requests an O.R. report. If the report substantiates bilateral surgery, no further action is necessary. If the O.R. report does not substantiate bilateral surgery, an adjustment bill is processed.

If the error rate for any provider is sufficiently high, the FI may develop claims prior to payment on a provider-specific basis.

16. Invalid Age
If the hospital reports an age over 124, the FI requests the hospital to determine if it made a bill preparation error. If the beneficiary's age is established at over 124, the hospital enters 123.

17. Invalid Sex
A patient's sex is sometimes necessary for appropriate DRG determination. Usually the FI can resolve the issue without hospital assistance. The sex code reported must be either 1 (male) or 2 (female).

18. Invalid Discharge Status
A patient's discharge status is sometimes necessary for appropriate DRG determination. Discharge status must be coded according to the Form CMS-1450 conventions. See Chapter 25.

19. Invalid Discharge Date
An invalid discharge date is a discharge date that does not fall into the acceptable range of numbers to represent, either the month, day or year (e.g., 13/03/01, 12/32/01). If no discharge date is entered, it is also invalid. MCE reports when an invalid discharge date is entered.

20. Limited Coverage
Effective October 1, 2003, for certain procedures whose medical complexity and serious nature incur extraordinary associated costs, Medicare limits coverage. The edit message indicates the type of limited coverage (e.g., LVRS, heart transplant, etc). The procedures receiving limited coverage edits previously were listed as non-covered procedures, but were covered under Medicare in certain circumstances. The FIs will handle these procedures as they had previously.

100-4, 3, 20.7.3
Payment for Blood Clotting Factor Administered to Hemophilia Patients
Section 6011 of Public Law (P.L.) 101-239 amended Sec.1886(a)(4) of the Social Security Act (the Act) to provide that prospective payment system (PPS) hospitals receive anadditional payment for the costs of administering blood clotting factor to Medicare hemophiliacs who are hospital inpatients. Section 6011(b) of P.L. 101.239 specified that the payment be based on a predetermined price per unit of clotting factor multiplied by the number of units provided. This add-on payment originally was effective for blood clotting factors furnished on or after June 19, 1990, and before December 19, 1991. Section 13505 of P. L. 103-66 amended Sec.6011 (d) of P.L.

Appendix G — Pub 100 References

101-239 to extend the period covered by the add-on payment for blood clotting factors administered to Medicare inpatients with hemophilia through September 30, 1994. Section 4452 of P.L. 105-33 amended Sec.6011(d) of P.L. 101-239 to reinstate the add-on payment for the costs of administering blood clotting factor to Medicare beneficiaries who have hemophilia and who are hospital inpatients for discharges occurring on or after October 1, 1998.

Local carriers shall process non-institutional blood clotting factor claims.

The FIs shall process institutional blood clotting factor claims payable under either Part A or Part B.

A. Inpatient Bills

Under the Inpatient Prospective Payment System (PPS), hospitals receive a special add-on payment for the costs of furnishing blood clotting factors to Medicare beneficiaries with hemophilia, admitted as inpatients of PPS hospitals. The clotting factor add-on payment is calculated using the number of units (as defined in the HCPCS code long descriptor) billed by the provider under special instructions for units of service.

The PPS Pricer software does not calculate the payment amount. The Fiscal Intermediary Standard System (FISS) calculates the payment amount and subtracts the charges from those submitted to Pricer so that the clotting factor charges are not included in cost outlier computations.

Blood clotting factors not paid on a cost or PPS basis are priced as a drug/biological under the Medicare Part B Drug Pricing File effective for the specific date of service. As of January 1, 2005, the average sales price (ASP) plus 6 percent shall be used.

If a beneficiary is in a covered Part A stay in a PPS hospital, the clotting factors are paid in addition to the DRG/HIPPS payment (For FY 2004, this payment is based on 95 percent of average wholesale price.) For a SNF subject to SNF/PPS, the payment is bundled into the SNF/PPS rate.

For SNF inpatient Part A, there is no add-on payment for blood clotting factors.

The codes for blood-clotting factors are found on the Medicare Part B Drug Pricing File. This file is distributed on a quarterly basis.

For discharges occurring on or after October 1, 2000, and before December 31, 2005, report HCPCS Q0187 based on 1 billing unit per 1.2 mg. Effective January 1, 2006, HCPCS code J7189 replaces Q0187 and is defined as 1 billing unit per 1 microgram (mcg).

The examples below include the HCPCS code and indicate the dosage amount specified in the descriptor of that code. Facilities use the units field as a multiplier to arrive at the dosage amount.

EXAMPLE 1

HCPCS	Drug	Dosage
J7189	Factor VIIa	1 mcg

Actual dosage: 13,365 mcg

On the bill, the facility shows J7189 and 13,365 in the units field (13,365 mcg divided by 1 mcg = 13,365 units).

NOTE: The process for dealing with one international unit (IU) is the same as the process of dealing with one microgram.

EXAMPLE 2

HCPCS	Drug	Dosage
J9355	Trastuzumab	10 mg

Actual dosage: 140 mg

On the bill, the facility shows J9355 and 14 in the units field (140 mg divided by 10mg = 14 units).

When the dosage amount is greater than the amount indicated for the HCPCS code, the facility rounds up to determine units. When the dosage amount is less than the amount indicated for the HCPCS code, use 1 as the unit of measure.

EXAMPLE 3

HCPCS	Drug	Dosage
J3100	Tenecteplase	50 mg

Actual Dosage: 40 mg

The provider would bill for 1 unit, even though less than 1 full unit was furnished.

At times, the facility provides less than the amount provided in a single use vial and there is waste, i.e.; some drugs may be available only in packaged amounts that exceed the needs of an individual patient. Once the drug is reconstituted in the hospital's pharmacy, it may have a limited shelf life. Since an individual patient may receive less than the fully reconstituted amount, we encourage hospitals to schedule patients in such a way that the hospital can use the drug most efficiently. However, if the hospital must discard the remainder of a vial after administering part of it to a Medicare patient, the provider may bill for the amount of drug discarded plus the amount administered.

Example 1:

Drug X is available only in a 100-unit size. A hospital schedules three Medicare patients to receive drug X on the same day within the designated shelf life of the product. An appropriate hospital staff member administers 30 units to each patient. The remaining 10 units are billed to Medicare on the account of the last patient. Therefore, 30 units are billed on behalf of the first patient seen and 30 units are billed on behalf of the second patient seen. Forty units are billed on behalf of the last patient seen because the hospital had to discard 10 units at that point.

Example 2:

An appropriate hospital staff member must administer 30 units of drug X to a Medicare patient, and it is not practical to schedule another patient who requires the same drug. For example, the hospital has only one patient who requires drug X, or the hospital sees the patient for the first time and did not know the patient's condition. The hospital bills for 100 units on behalf of the patient, and Medicare pays for 100 units.

When the number of units of blood clotting factor administered to hemophiliac inpatients exceeds 99,999, the hospital reports the excess as a second line for revenue code 0636 and repeats the HCPCS code. One hundred thousand fifty (100,050) units are reported on one line as 99,999, and another line shows 1,051.

Revenue Code 0636 is used. It requires HCPCS. Some other inpatient drugs continue to be billed without HCPCS codes under pharmacy.

No changes in beneficiary notices are required. Coverage is applicable to hospital Part A claims only. Coverage is also applicable to inpatient Part B services in SNFs and all types of hospitals, including CAHs. Separate payment is not made to SNFs for beneficiaries in an inpatient Part A stay.

B. FI Action

The FI is responsible for the following:

- It accepts HCPCS codes for inpatient services;
- It edits to require HCPCS codes with Revenue Code 0636. Multiple iterations of the revenue code are possible with the same or different HCPCS codes. It does not edit units except to ensure a numeric value;
- It reduces charges forwarded to Pricer by the charges for hemophilia clotting factors in revenue code 0636. It retains the charges and revenue and HCPCS codes for CWF; and
- It modifies data entry screens to accept HCPCS codes for hospital (including CAH) swing bed, and SNF inpatient claims (bill types 11X, 12X, 18x, 21x and, 22x).

The September 1, 1993, IPPS final rule (58 FR 46304) states that payment will be made for the blood clotting factor only if an ICD-9-CM diagnosis code for hemophilia is included on the bill.

Since inpatient blood-clotting factors are covered only for beneficiaries with hemophilia, the FI must ensure that one of the following hemophilia diagnosis codes is listed on the bill before payment is made:

286.0 Congenital factor VIII disorder

286.1 Congenital factor IX disorder

286.2 Congenital factor IX disorder

286.3 Congenital deficiency of other clotting factor

286.4 von Willebrands' disease

Effective for discharges on or after August 1, 2001, payment may also be made if one of the following diagnosis codes is reported:

286.5 Hemorrhagic disorder due to circulating anticoagulants

286.7 Acquired coagulation factor deficiency

C. Part A Remittance Advice

1. X12.835 Ver. 003030M

   For remittance reporting PIP and/or non-PIP payments, the Hemophilia Add on will be reported in a claims level 2-090-CAS segment (CAS is the element identifier) exhibiting an "OA" Group Code and adjustment reason code "97" (payment is included in the allowance for the basic service/ procedure) followed by the associated dollar amount (POSITIVE) and units of service. For this version of the 835, "OA" group coded line level CAS segments are informational and are not included in the balancing routine. The Hemophilia Add On amount will always be included in the 2-010-CLP04 Claim Payment Amount.

   For remittance reporting PIP payments, the Hemophilia Add On will also be reported in the provider level adjustment (element identifier PLB) segment with the provider level adjustment reason code "CA" (Manual claims adjustment) followed by the associated dollar amount (NEGATIVE).

   NOTE: A data maintenance request will be submitted to ANSI ASC X12 for a new PLB adjustment reason code specifically for PIP payment Hemophilia Add On situations for future use. However, continue to use adjustment reason code "CA" until further notice.

   The FIs enter MA103 (Hemophilia Add On) in an open MIA (element identifier) remark code data element. This will alert the provider that the reason code 97 and PLB code "CA" adjustments are related to the Hemophilia Add On.

2. X12.835 Ver. 003051

   For remittances reporting PIP and/or non-PIP payments, Hemophilia Add On information will be reported in the claim level 2-062-AMT and 2-064-QTY segments. The 2-062-AMT01 element will carry a "ZK" (Federal Medicare claim MANDATE - Category 1) qualifier code followed by the total claim level Hemophilia Add On amount (POSITIVE). The 2-064QTY01 element will carry a "FL" (Units) qualifier code followed by the number of units approved for the Hemophilia Add On for the claim. The Hemophilia Add On amount will always be included in the 2-010-CLP04 Claim Payment Amount.

NOTE: A data maintenance request will be submitted to ANSI ASC X12 for a new AMT qualifier code specifically for the Hemophilia Add On for future use. However, continue to use adjustment reason code "ZK" until further notice.

For remittances reporting PIP payments, the Hemophilia Add On will be reported in the provider level adjustment PLB segment with the provider level adjustment reason "ZZ" followed by the associated dollar amount (NEGATIVE).

NOTE: A data maintenance request will be submitted to ANSI ASC X12 for a new PLB, adjustment reason code specifically for the Hemophilia Add On for future use. However, continue to use PLB adjustment reason code "ZZ" until further notice. The FIs enter MA103 (Hemophilia Add On) in an open MIA remark code data element. This will alert the provider that the ZK, FL and ZZ entries are related to the Hemophilia Add On. (Effective with version 4010 of the 835, report ZK in lieu of FL in the QTY segment.)

3. Standard Hard Copy Remittance Advice
For paper remittances reporting non-PIP payments involving Hemophilia Add On, add a "Hemophilia Add On" category to the end of the "Pass Thru Amounts" listings in the "Summary" section of the paper remittance. Enter the total of the Hemophilia Add On amounts due for the claims covered by this remittance next to the Hemophilia Add On heading.

The FIs add the Remark Code "MA103" (Hemophilia Add On) to the remittance advice under the REM column for those claims that qualify for Hemophilia Add On payments.

This will be the full extent of Hemophilia Add On reporting on paper remittance notices; providers wishing more detailed information must subscribe to the Medicare Part A specifications for the ANSI ASC X12N 835, where additional information is available.

See chapter 22, for detailed instructions and definitions.

100-4, 3, 40.2.2
Charges to Beneficiaries for Part A Services

The hospital submits a bill even where the patient is responsible for a deductible which covers the entire amount of the charges for non-PPS hospitals, or in PPS hospitals, where the DRG payment amount will be less than the deductible.

A hospital receiving payment for a covered hospital stay (or PPS hospital that includes at least one covered day, or one treated as covered under guarantee of payment or limitation on liability) may charge the beneficiary, or other person, for items and services furnished during the stay only as described in subsections A through H. If limitation of liability applies, a beneficiary's liability for payment is governed by the limitation on liability notification rules in Chapter 30 of this manual. For related notices for inpatient hospitals, see CMS Transmittal 594, Change Request3903, dated June 24, 2005.

A. Deductible and Coinsurance
The hospital may charge the beneficiary or other person for applicable deductible and coinsurance amounts. The deductible is satisfied only by charges for covered services. The FI deducts the deductible and coinsurance first from the PPS payment. Where the deductible exceeds the PPS amount, the excess will be applied to a subsequent payment to the hospital. (See Chapter 3 of the Medicare General Information, Eligibility, and Entitlement Manual for specific policies.)

B. Blood Deductible
The Part A blood deductible provision applies to whole blood and red blood cells, and reporting of the number of pints is applicable to both PPS and non-PPS hospitals. (See Chapter 3 of the Medicare General Information, Eligibility, and Entitlement Manual for specific policies.) Hospitals shall report charges for red blood cells using revenue code 381, and charges for whole blood using revenue code 382.

C. Inpatient Care No Longer Required
The hospital may charge for services that are not reasonable and necessary or that constitute custodial care. Notification may be required under limitation of liability. See CMS Transmittal 594, Change Request3903, dated June 24, 2005, section V. of the attachment, for specific notification requirements. Note this transmittal will be placed in Chapter 30 of this manual at a future point. Chapter 1, section 150 of this manual also contains related billing information in addition to that provided below.

In general, after proper notification has occurred, and assuming an expedited decision is received from a Quality Improvement Organization (QIO), the following entries are required on the bill the hospital prepares:

- Occurrence code 31 (and date) to indicate the date the hospital notified the patient in accordance with the first bullet above;
- Occurrence span code 76 (and dates) to indicate the period of noncovered care for which it is charging the beneficiary;
- Occurrence span code 77 (and dates) to indicate the period of noncovered care for which the provider is liable, when it is aware of this prior to billing; and
- Value code 31 (and amount) to indicate the amount of charges it may bill the beneficiary for days for which inpatient care was no longer required. They are included as noncovered charges on the bill.

D. Change in the Beneficiary's Condition
If the beneficiary remains in the hospital after receiving notice as described in subsection C, and the hospital, the physician who concurred in the hospital's determination, or the QIO, subsequently determines that the beneficiary again requires inpatient hospital care, the hospital may not charge the beneficiary or other person for services furnished after the beneficiary again required inpatient hospital care until proper notification occurs (see subsection C).

If a patient who needs only a SNF level of care remains in the hospital after the SNF bed becomes available, and the bed ceases to be available, the hospital may continue to charge the beneficiary. It need not provide the beneficiary with another notice when the patient chose not to be discharged to the SNF bed.

E. Admission Denied
If the entire hospital admission is determined to be not reasonable or necessary, limitation of liability may apply. See 2005 CMS transmittal 594, section V. of the attachment, for specific notification requirements.

NOTE: This transmittal will be placed in Chapter 30 of this manual at a future point.

In such cases the following entries are required on the bill:

- Occurrence code 31 (and date) to indicate the date the hospital notified the beneficiary.
- Occurrence span code 76 (and dates) to indicate the period of noncovered care for which the hospital is charging the beneficiary.
- Occurrence span code 77 (and dates) to indicate any period of noncovered care for which the provider is liable (e.g., the period between issuing the notice and the time it may charge the beneficiary) when the provider is aware of this prior to billing.
- Value code 31 (and amount) to indicate the amount of charges the hospital may bill the beneficiary for hospitalization that was not necessary or reasonable. They are included as noncovered charges on the bill.

F. Procedures, Studies and Courses of Treatment That Are Not Reasonable or Necessary
If diagnostic procedures, studies, therapeutic studies and courses of treatment are excluded from coverage as not reasonable and necessary (even though the beneficiary requires inpatient hospital care) the hospital may charge the beneficiary or other person for the services or care according the procedures given in CMS Transmittal 594, Change Request3903, dated June 24, 2005.

The following bill entries apply to these circumstances:

- Occurrence code 32 (and date) to indicate the date the hospital provided the notice to the beneficiary.
- Value code 31 (and amount) to indicate the amount of such charges to be billed to the beneficiary. They are included as noncovered charges on the bill.

G. Nonentitlement Days and Days after Benefits Exhausted
If a hospital stay exceeds the day outlier threshold, the hospital may charge for some, or all, of the days on which the patient is not entitled to Medicare Part A, or after the Part A benefits are exhausted (i.e., the hospital may charge its customary charges for services furnished on those days). It may charge the beneficiary for the lesser of:

- The number of days on which the patient was not entitled to benefits or after the benefits were exhausted; or
- The number of outlier days. (Day outliers were discontinued at the end of FY 1997.)

If the number of outlier days exceeds the number of days on which the patient was not entitled to benefits, or after benefits were exhausted, the hospital may charge for all days on which the patient was not entitled to benefits or after benefits were exhausted. If the number of days on which the beneficiary was not entitled to benefits, or after benefits were exhausted, exceeds the number of outlier days, the hospital determines the days for which it may charge by starting with the last day of the stay (i.e., the day before the day of discharge) and identifying and counting off in reverse order, days on which the patient was not entitled to benefits or after the benefits were exhausted, until the number of days counted off equals the number of outlier days. The days counted off are the days for which the hospital may charge.

H. Contractual Exclusions
In addition to receiving the basic prospective payment, the hospital may charge the beneficiary for any services that are excluded from coverage for reasons other than, or in addition to, absence of medical necessity, provision of custodial care, non-entitlement to Part A, or exhaustion of benefits. For example, it may charge for most cosmetic and dental surgery.

I. Private Room Care
Payment for medically necessary private room care is included in the prospective payment. Where the beneficiary requests private room accommodations, the hospital must inform the beneficiary of the additional charge. (See the Medicare Benefit Policy Manual, Chapter 1.) When the beneficiary accepts the liability, the hospital will supply the service, and bill the beneficiary directly. If the beneficiary believes the private room was medically necessary, the beneficiary has a right to a determination and may initiate a Part A appeal.

J. Deluxe Item or Service
Where a beneficiary requests a deluxe item or service, i.e., an item or service which is more expensive than is medically required for the beneficiary's condition, the hospital may collect the additional charge if it informs the beneficiary of the additional charge. That charge is the difference between the customary charge for the item or service most commonly furnished by the hospital to private pay patients with the beneficiary's condition, and the charge for the more expensive item or service requested. If the beneficiary believes that the more expensive item or service was medically necessary, the beneficiary has a right to a determination and may initiate a Part A appeal.

K. Inpatient Acute Care Hospital Admission Followed By a Death or Discharge Prior To Room Assignment
A patient of an acute care hospital is considered an inpatient upon issuance of written doctor's orders to that effect. If a patient either dies or is discharged prior to being assigned and/or occupying a room, a hospital may enter an appropriate room and board charge on the claim. If a patient leaves of their own volition prior to being assigned and/or occupying a room, a hospital may enter an appropriate room and board charge on the claim as well as a patient status code 07 which indicates they left against medical advice. A hospital is not required to enter a room and board charge, but failure to do so may have a minimal impact on future DRG weight calculations.

Appendix G — Pub 100 References

100-4, 3, 40.3
Outpatient Services Treated as Inpatient Services
A3-3610.3, HO-415.6, HO-400D, A-03-008, A-03-013, A-03-054

A Outpatient Services Followed by Admission Before Midnight of the Following Day
(Effective For Services Furnished Before October 1, 1991)

When a beneficiary receives outpatient hospital services during the day immediately preceding the hospital admission, the outpatient hospital services are treated as inpatient services if the beneficiary has Part A coverage. Hospitals and FIs apply this provision only when the beneficiary is admitted to the hospital before midnight of the day following receipt of outpatient services. The day on which the patient is formally admitted as an inpatient is counted as the first inpatient day.

When this provision applies, services are included in the applicable PPS payment and not billed separately. When this provision applies to hospitals and units excluded from the hospital PPS, services are shown on the bill and included in the Part A payment. See Chapter 1 for FI requirements for detecting duplicate claims in such cases.

B Preadmission Diagnostic Services
(Effective for Services Furnished On or After January 1, 1991)

Diagnostic services (including clinical diagnostic laboratory tests) provided to a beneficiary by the admitting hospital, or by an entity wholly owned or wholly operated by the admitting hospital (or by another entity under arrangements with the admitting hospital), within 3 days prior to and including the date of the beneficiary's admission are deemed to be inpatient services and included in the inpatient payment, unless there is no Part A coverage. For example, if a patient is admitted on a Wednesday, outpatient services provided by the hospital on Sunday, Monday, Tuesday, or Wednesday are included in the inpatient Part A payment.

This provision does not apply to ambulance services and maintenance renal dialysis services (see the Medicare Benefit Policy Manual, Chapters 10 and 11, respectively). Additionally, Part A services furnished by skilled nursing facilities, home health agencies, and hospices are excluded from the payment window provisions.

For services provided before October 31, 1994, this provision applies to both hospitals subject to the hospital inpatient prospective payment system (IPPS) as well as those hospitals and units excluded from IPPS.

For services provided on or after October 31, 1994, for hospitals and units excluded from IPPS, this provision applies only to services furnished within one day prior to and including the date of the beneficiary's admission. The hospitals and units that are excluded from IPPS are: psychiatric hospitals and units; inpatient rehabilitation facilities (IRF) and units; long-term care hospitals (LTCH); children's hospitals; and cancer hospitals.

Critical access hospitals (CAHs) are not subject to the 3-day (nor 1-day) DRG payment window.

An entity is considered to be "wholly owned or operated" by the hospital if the hospital is the sole owner or operator. A hospital need not exercise administrative control over a facility in order to operate it. A hospital is considered the sole operator of the facility if the hospital has exclusive responsibility for implementing facility policies (i.e., conducting or overseeing the facility's routine operations), regardless of whether it also has the authority to make the policies.

For this provision, diagnostic services are defined by the presence on the bill of the following revenue and/or CPT codes:

0254 -	Drugs incident to other diagnostic services
0255 -	Drugs incident to radiology
030X -	Laboratory
031X -	Laboratory pathological
032X -	Radiology diagnostic
0341, 0343 -	Nuclear medicine, diagnostic/Diagnostic Radiopharmaceuticals
035X -	CT scan
0371 -	Anesthesia incident to Radiology
0372 -	Anesthesia incident to other diagnostic services
040X -	Other imaging services
046X -	Pulmonary function
0471 -	Audiology diagnostic
0481, 0489-	Cardiology, Cardiac Catheter Lab/Other Cardiology with CPT codes 93501, 93503, 93505, 93508, 93510, 93526, 93541, 93542, 93543, 93544, 93556, 93561, or 93562 diagnostic
0482-	Cardiology, Stress Test
0483-	Cardiology, Echocardiology
053X -	Osteopathic services
061X -	MRT
062X -	Medical/surgical supplies, incident to radiology or other diagnostic services
073X -	EKG/ECG
074X -	EEG
0918-	Testing- Behavioral Health
092X -	Other diagnostic services

The CWF rejects services furnished January 1, 1991, or later when outpatient bills for diagnostic services with through dates or last date of service (occurrence span code 72) fall on the day of admission or any of the 3 days immediately prior to admission to an IPPS or IPPS-excluded hospital. This reject applies to the bill in process, regardless of whether the outpatient or inpatient bill is processed first. Hospitals must analyze the two bills and report appropriate corrections. For services on or after October 31, 1994, for hospitals and units excluded from IPPS, CWF will reject outpatient diagnostic bills that occur on the day of or one day before admission. For IPPS hospitals, CWF will continue to reject outpatient diagnostic bills for services that occur on the day of or any of the 3 days prior to admission. Effective for dates of service on or after July 1, 2008, CWF will reject diagnostic services when the line item date of service (LIDOS) falls on the day of admission or any of the 3 days immediately prior to an admission to an IPPS hospital or on the day of admission or one day prior to admission for hospitals excluded from IPPS.

Hospitals in Maryland that are under the jurisdiction of the Health Services Cost Review Commission are subject to the 3-day payment window.

C Other Preadmission Services
(Effective for Services Furnished On or After October 1, 1991)

Nondiagnostic outpatient services that are related to a patient's hospital admission and that are provided by the hospital, or by an entity wholly owned or wholly operated by the admitting hospital (or by another entity under arrangements with the admitting hospital), to the patient during the 3 days immediately preceding and including the date of the patient's admission are deemed to be inpatient services and are included in the inpatient payment. Effective March 13, 1998, we defined nondiagnostic preadmission services as being related to the admission only when there is an exact match (for all digits) between the ICD-9-CM principal diagnosis code assigned for both the preadmission services and the inpatient stay. Thus, whenever Part A covers an admission, the hospital may bill nondiagnostic preadmission services to Part B as outpatient services only if they are not related to the admission. The FI shall assume, in the absence of evidence to the contrary, that such bills are not admission related and, therefore, are not deemed to be inpatient (Part A) services. If there are both diagnostic and nondiagnostic preadmission services and the nondiagnostic services are unrelated to the admission, the hospital may separately bill the nondiagnostic preadmission services to Part B. This provision applies only when the patient has Part A coverage. This provision does not apply to ambulance services and maintenance renal dialysis. Additionally, Part A services furnished by skilled nursing facilities, home health agencies, and hospices are excluded from the payment window provisions.

For services provided before October 31, 1994, this provision applies to both hospitals subject to IPPS as well as those hospitals and units excluded from IPPS (see section B above).

For services provided on or after October 31, 1994, for hospitals and units excluded from IPPS, this provision applies only to services furnished within one day prior to and including the date of the beneficiary's admission.

Critical access hospitals (CAHs) are not subject to the 3-day (nor 1-day) DRG payment window.

Hospitals in Maryland that are under the jurisdiction of the Health Services Cost Review Commission are subject to the 3-day payment window.

Effective for dates of service on or after July 1, 2008, CWF will reject therapeutic services when the line item date of service (LIDOS) falls on the day of admission or any of the 3 days immediately prior to an admission to an IPPS hospital or on the day of admission or one day prior to admission for hospitals excluded from IPPS.

100-4, 3, 90.1
Kidney Transplant - General
A3-3612, HO-E414

A major treatment for patients with ESRD is kidney transplantation. This involves removing a kidney, usually from a living relative of the patient or from an unrelated person who has died, and surgically placing the kidney into the patient. After the beneficiary receives a kidney transplant, Medicare pays the transplant hospital for the transplant and appropriate standard acquisition charges. Special provisions apply to payment. For the list of approved Medicare certified transplant facilities, refer to the following Web site:
http://www.cms.hhs.gov/CertificationandComplianc/20_Transplant.asp#TopOfPage

A transplant hospital may acquire cadaver kidneys by:

- Excising kidneys from cadavers in its own hospital; and
- Arrangements with a freestanding organ procurement organization (OPO) that provides cadaver kidneys to any transplant hospital or by a hospital based OPO.

A transplant hospital that is also a certified organ procurement organization may acquire cadaver kidneys by:

- Having its organ procurement team excise kidneys from cadavers in other hospitals;
- Arrangements with participating community hospitals, whether they excise kidneys on a regular or irregular basis; and
- Arrangements with an organ procurement organization that services the transplant hospital as a member of a network.

When the transplant hospital also excises the cadaver kidney, the cost of the procedure is included in its kidney acquisition costs and is considered in arriving at its standard cadaver kidney acquisition charge. When the transplant hospital excises a kidney to provide another hospital, it may use its standard cadaver kidney acquisition charge or its standard detailed departmental charges to bill that hospital.

When the excising hospital is not a transplant hospital, it bills its customary charges for services used in excising the cadaver kidney to the transplant hospital or organ procurement agency.

If the transplanting hospital's organ procurement team excises the cadaver kidney at another hospital, the cost of operating such a team is included in the transplanting hospital's kidney acquisition costs, along with the reasonable charges billed by the other hospital of its services.

100-4, 3, 90.1.1
The Standard Kidney Acquisition Charge
A3-3612.1, A3-3612.3, HO-E417, HO-406, HO-E408, HO-E410, HO-E412, HO-E416,HO-E418, HO-E420

There are two basic standard charges that must be developed by transplant hospitals fromcosts expected to be incurred in the acquisition of kidneys:

- The standard charge for acquiring a live donor kidney; and
- The standard charge for acquiring a cadaver kidney.

The standard charge is not a charge representing the acquisition cost of a specific kidney;rather, it is a charge that reflects the average cost associated with each type of kidney acquisition.When the transplant hospital bills the program for the transplant, it shows its standard kidney acquisition charge on a separate line on the billing form.Acquisition services are billed from the excising hospital to the transplant hospital. A billing form is not submitted from the excising hospital to the FI. The transplant hospital keeps an itemized statement that identifies the services furnished, the charges, the person receiving the service (donor/recipient), and whether this is a potential transplant donor orrecipient. These charges are reflected in the transplant hospital's kidney acquisition costcenter and are used in determining the hospital's standard charge for acquiring a live donor's kidney or a cadaver's kidney. The standard charge is not a charge representing theacquisition cost of a specific kidney. Rather, it is a charge that reflects the average costassociated with each type of kidney acquisition. Also, it is an all-inclusive charge for allservices required in acquisition of a kidney, i.e., tissue typing, post-operative evaluation.

A. Billing For Blood And Tissue Typing of the Transplant Recipient Whether or NotMedicare Entitlement Is Established
Tissue typing and pre-transplant evaluation can be reflected only through the kidney acquisition charge of the hospital where the transplant will take place. The transplant hospital includes in its kidney acquisition cost center the reasonable charges it pays to the independent laboratory or other hospital which typed the potential transplant recipient,either before or after his entitlement. It also includes reasonable charges paid for physician tissue typing services, applicable to live donors and recipients (during the preentitlement period and after entitlement, but prior to hospital admission for transplantation).

B. Billing for Blood and Tissue Typing and Other Pre-Transplant Evaluation of LiveDonors
The entitlement date of the beneficiary who will receive the transplant is not aconsideration in reimbursing for the services to donors, since no bill is submitted directly to Medicare. All charges for services to donors prior to admission into the hospital fo rexcision are "billed" indirectly to Medicare through the live donor acquisition charge oftransplanting hospitals.

C. Billing Donor And Recipient Pre-Transplant Services (Performed by Transplant Hospitals or Other Providers) to the Kidney Acquisition Cost Center
The transplant hospital prepares an itemized statement of the services rendered for submittal to its cost accounting department. Regular Medicare billing forms are not necessary for this purpose, since no bills are submitted to the FI at this point.The itemized statement should contain information that identifies the person receiving theservice (donor/recipient), the health care insurance number, the service rendered and the charge for the service, as well as a statement as to whether this is a potential transplantdonor or recipient. If it is a potential donor, the provider must identify the prospective recipient.

EXAMPLE:

Mary Jones
Health care insurance number
200 Adams St.
Anywhere, MS

Transplant donor evaluation services for recipient:

John Jones
Health care insurance number
200 Adams St.
Anywhere, MS

Services performed in a hospital other than the potential transplant hospital or by an independent laboratory are billed by that facility to the potential transplant hospital. This holds true regardless of where in the United States the service is performed. For example, if the donor services are performed in a Florida hospital and the transplant is to take place in a California hospital, the Florida hospital bills the California hospital (as described inabove). The Florida hospital is paid by the California hospital, which recoups the monies through the kidney acquisition cost center.

D. Billing for Cadaveric Donor Services
Normally, various tests are performed to determine the type and suitability of a cadaver kidney. Such tests may be performed by the excising hospital (which may also be a transplant hospital) or an independent laboratory. When the excising-only hospital performs the tests, it includes the related charges on its bill to the transplant hospital or tothe organ procurement agency.When the tests are performed by the transplant hospital, it uses the related costs in establishing the standard charge for acquiring the cadaver kidney. The transplant hospitalincludes the costs and charges in the appropriate departments for final cost settlementpurposes.When the tests are performed by an independent laboratory for the excising-only hospital or the transplant hospital, the laboratory bills the hospital that engages its services or the organ procurement agency. The excising-only hospital includes such charges in itscharges to the transplant hospital, which then includes the charges in developing its standard charge for acquiring the cadaver kidney. It is the transplant hospitals'responsibility to assure that the independent laboratory does not bill both hospitals.The cost of these services cannot be billed directly to the program, since such tests andother procedures performed on a cadaver are not identifiable to a specific patient.

E. Billing For Physicians' Services Prior to Transplantation
Physicians' services applicable to kidney excisions involving live donors and recipients (during the pre-entitlement period and after entitlement, but prior to entrance into the hospital for transplantation) as well as all physicians' services applicable to cadavers are considered Part A hospital services (kidney acquisition costs).

F. Billing for Physicians' Services After Transplantation
All physicians' services rendered to the living donor and all physicians' services renderedto the transplant recipient are billed to the Medicare program in the same manner as all Medicare Part B services are billed. All donor physicians' services must be billed to the account of the recipient (i.e., the recipient's Medicare number).

G. Billing For Physicians' Renal Transplantation Services
To ensure proper payment when submitting a Part B bill for the renal surgeon's services to the recipient, the appropriate HCPCS codes must be submitted, including HCPCS codes for concurrent surgery, as applicable.The bill must include all living donor physicians' services, e.g., Revenue Center code 081X.

100-4, 3, 90.1.2
Billing for Kidney Transplant and Acquisition Services
Applicable standard kidney acquisition charges are identified separately in FL 42 by revenue code 0811 (Living Donor Kidney Acquisition) or 0812 (Cadaver Donor Kidney Acquisition). Where interim bills are submitted, the standard acquisition charge appears on the billing form for the period during which the transplant took place. This charge is in addition to the hospital's charges for services rendered directly to the Medicare recipient.

The contractor deducts kidney acquisition charges for PPS hospitals for processing through Pricer. These costs, incurred by approved kidney transplant hospitals, are not included in the prospective payment DRG 302 (kidney transplant). They are paid on a reasonable cost basis. Interim payment is paid as a "pass through" item. (See the Provider Reimbursement Manual, Part 1, Sec.2802 B.8.) The contractor includes kidney acquisition charges under the appropriate revenue code in CWF.

Bill Review Procedures
The Medicare Code Editor (MCE) creates a Limited Coverage edit for procedure code 55.69 (kidney transplant). Where this procedure code is identified by MCE, the contractor checks the provider number to determine if the provider is an approved transplant center, and checks the effective approval date. The contractor shall also determine if the facility is certified for adults and/or pediatric transplants dependent upon the patient's age. If payment is appropriate (i.e., the center is approved and the service is on or after the approval date) it overrides the limited coverage edit.

100-4, 3, 90.2
Heart Transplants
A3-3613, HO-416

Cardiac transplantation is covered under Medicare when performed in a facility which is approved by Medicare as meeting institutional coverage criteria. On April 6, 1987, CMS Ruling 87-1, "Criteria for Medicare Coverage of Heart Transplants" was published in the "Federal Register." For Medicare coverage purposes, heart transplants are medically reasonable and necessary when performed in facilities that meet these criteria. If a hospital wishes to bill Medicare for heart transplants, it must submit an application and documentation, showing its ongoing compliance with each criterion.

If a contractor has any questions concerning the effective or approval dates of its hospitals, it should contact its RO.

For a complete list of approved transplant centers, visit:
http://www.cms.hhs.gov/CertificationandComplianc/20_Transplant.asp#TopOfPage

A. Effective Dates
The effective date of coverage for heart transplants performed at facilities applying after July 6, 1987, is the date the facility receives approval as a heart transplant facility. Coverage is effective for discharges October 17, 1986 for facilities that would have qualified and that applied by July 6, 1987. All transplant hospitals will be recertified under the final rule, Federal Register / Vol. 72, No. 61 / Friday, March 30, 2007, / Rules and Regulations.

The CMS informs each hospital of its effective date in an approval letter.

B. Drugs
Medicare Part B covers immunosuppressive drugs following a covered transplant in an approved facility.

C. Noncovered Transplants
Medicare will not cover transplants or re-transplants in facilities that have not been approved as meeting the facility criteria. If a beneficiary is admitted for and receives a heart transplant from a hospital that is not approved, physicians' services, and inpatient services associated with the transplantation procedure are not covered.

If a beneficiary received a heart transplant from a hospital while it was not an approved facility and later requires services as a result of the noncovered transplant, the services are covered when they are reasonable and necessary in all other respects.

D. Charges for Heart Acquisition Services
The excising hospital bills the OPO, who in turn bills the transplant (implant) hospital for applicable services. It should not submit a bill to its contractor. The transplant hospital must keep an itemized statement that identifies the services rendered, the charges, the person receiving the service (donor/recipient), and whether this person is a potential transplant donor or recipient.

Appendix G — Pub 100 References

These charges are reflected in the transplant hospital's heart acquisition cost center and are used in determining its standard charge for acquiring a donor's heart. The standard charge is not a charge representing the acquisition cost of a specific heart; rather, it reflects the average cost associated with each type of heart acquisition. Also, it is an all inclusive charge for all services required in acquisition of a heart, i.e., tissue typing, post-operative evaluation, etc.

E. Bill Review Procedures

The contractor takes the following actions to process heart transplant bills. It may accomplish them manually or modify its MCE and Grouper interface programs to handle the processing.

1. Change in MCE Interface
   The MCE creates a Limited Coverage edit for procedure code 37.51 (heart transplant). Where this procedure code is identified by MCE, the contractor checks the provider number to determine if the provider is an approved transplant center, and checks the effective approval date. The contractor shall also determine if the facility is certified for adults and/or pediatric transplants dependent upon the patient's age. If payment is appropriate (i.e., the center is approved and the service is on or after the approval date) it overrides the limited coverage edit.

2. Handling Heart Transplant Billings From Nonapproved Hospitals
   Where a heart transplant and covered services are provided by a nonapproved hospital, the bill data processed through Grouper and Pricer must exclude transplant procedure codes and related charges.

100-4, 3, 90.2.1
Artificial Hearts and Related Devices

Effective for discharges before May 1, 2008, Medicare does not cover the use of artificial hearts, either as a permanent replacement for a human heart or as a temporary life-support system until a human heart becomes available for transplant (often referred to as "bridge to transplant").

Medicare does cover a Ventricular Assist Device (VAD). A VAD is used to assist a damaged or weakened heart in pumping blood. VADs are used as a bridge to a heart transplant, for support of blood circulation postcardiotomy or destination therapy. Refer to the NCD Manual, section 20.9 for coverage criteria.

The MCE creates a Limited Coverage edit for procedure code 37.66. This procedure code has limited coverage due to the stringent conditions that must be met by hospitals. Where this procedure code is identified by MCE, the FI shall determine if coverage criteria is met and override the MCE if appropriate.

Effective for discharges on or after May 1, 2008, the use of artificial hearts will be covered by Medicare under Coverage with Evidence Development when beneficiaries are enrolled in a clinical study that meets all of the criteria listed in Pub. 100-03, Medicare NCD Manual, section 20.9.

100-4, 3, 90.3
Stem Cell Transplantation

Stem cell transplantation is a process in which stem cells are harvested from either a patient's or donor's bone marrow or peripheral blood for intravenous infusion. Autologous stem cell transplants (AuSCT) must be used to effect hematopoietic reconstitution following severely myelotoxic doses of chemotherapy (HDCT) and/or radiotherapy used to treat various malignancies. Allogeneic stem cell transplant may also be used to restore function in recipients having an inherited or acquired deficiency or defect.

Bone marrow and peripheral blood stem cell transplantation is a process which includes mobilization, harvesting, and transplant of bone marrow or peripheral blood stem cells and the administration of high dose chemotherapy or radiotherapy prior to the actual transplant. When bone marrow or peripheral blood stem cell transplantation is covered, all necessary steps are included in coverage. When bone marrow or peripheral blood stem cell transplantation is non-covered, none of the steps are covered.

Allogeneic and autologous stem cell transplants are covered under Medicare for specific diagnoses. Effective October 1, 1990, these cases were assigned to MS-DRG 009, Bone Marrow Transplant.

The FI's Medicare Code Editor (MCE) will edit stem cell transplant procedure codes 4101, 4102, 4103, 4104, 4105, 4107, 4108, and 4109 against diagnosis codes to determine which cases meet specified coverage criteria. Cases with a diagnosis code for a covered condition will pass (as covered) the MCE noncovered procedure edit. When a stem cell transplant case is selected for review based on the random selection of beneficiaries, the QIO will review the case on a post-payment basis to assure proper coverage decisions.

Procedure code 41.00 (bone marrow transplant, not otherwise specified) will be classified as noncovered and the claim will be returned to the hospital for a more specific procedure code.

The A/B MACs or the FI may choose to review if data analysis deems it a priority.

100-4, 3, 90.3.1
Allogeneic Stem Cell Transplantation
A3-3614.1, HO-416.2, A3-3614.2, HO-416.3

A. General

Allogeneic stem cell transplantation (ICD-9-CM Procedure Codes 41.02, 41.03, 41.05, and 41.08, CPT-4 Code 38240) is a procedure in which a portion of a healthy donor's stem cells are obtained and prepared for intravenous infusion to restore normal hematopoietic function in recipients having an inherited or acquired hematopoietic deficiency or defect.

See the National Coverage Determinations Manual for more information.

Expenses incurred by a donor are a covered benefit to the recipient/beneficiary but, except for physician services, are not paid separately. Services to the donor include physician services, hospital care in connection with screening the stem cell, and ordinary follow-up care.

B. Covered Conditions

1. Effective for services performed on or after August 1, 1978:
   - For the treatment of leukemia, leukemia in remission (ICD-9-CM codes 204.00 through 208.91), or aplastic anemia (ICD-9-CM codes 284.0 through 284.9) when it is reasonable and necessary; and

2. Effective for services performed on or after June 3, 1985:
   - For the treatment of severe combined immunodeficiency disease (SCID) (ICD-9-CM code 279.2), and for the treatment of Wiskott - Aldrich syndrome (ICD-9-CM 279.12).

C. Noncovered Conditions

3. Effective for services performed on or after May 24, 1996:
   - Allogeneic stem cell transplantation is not covered as treatment for multiple myeloma (ICD-9-CM codes 203.00 and 203.01).

NOTE: Coverage for conditions other than these specifically designated as covered or noncovered in this section or National Coverage Determination Manual are left to individual FI's discretion.

100-4, 3, 90.3.2
Autologous Stem Cell Transplantation (AuSCT)

A. General

Autologous stem cell transplantation (AuSCT) (ICD-9-CM procedure code 41.01, 41.04, 41.07, and 41.09 and CPT-4 code 38241) is a technique for restoring stem cells using the patient's own previously stored cells. AuSCT must be used to effect hematopoietic reconstitution following severely myelotoxic doses of chemotherapy (high dose chemotherapy (HDCT)) and/or radiotherapy used to treat various malignancies.

B. Covered Conditions

1. Effective for services performed on or after April 28, 1989:
   - Acute leukemia in remission (ICD-9-CM codes 204.01, lymphoid; 205.01, myeloid; 206.01, monocytic; 207.01, acute erythremia and erythroleukemia; and 208.01 unspecified cell type) patients who have a high probability of relapse and who have no human leucocyte antigens (HLA)-matched;
   - Resistant non-Hodgkin's lymphomas (ICD-9-CM codes 200.00-200.08, 200.10-200.18, 200.20-200.28, 200.80-200.88, 202.00-202.08, 202.80-202.88, and 202.90-202.98) or those presenting with poor prognostic features following an initial response;
   - Recurrent or refractory neuroblastoma (see ICD-9-CM Neoplasm by site, malignant); or
   - Advanced Hodgkin's disease (ICD-9-CM codes 201.00-201.98) patients who have failed conventional therapy and have no HLA-matched donor.

2. Effective for services performed on or after October 1, 2000:
   - Durie-Salmon Stage II or III that fit the following requirement: Newly diagnosed or responsive multiple myeloma (ICD-9-CM codes 203.00 and 238.6). This includes those patients with previously untreated disease, those with at least a partial response to prior chemotherapy (defined as a 50% decrease either in measurable paraprotein [serum and/or urine] or in bone marrow infiltration, sustained for at least 1 month), and those in responsive relapse, and adequate cardiac, renal, pulmonary, and hepatic function.

3. Effective for services performed on or after March 15, 2005, when recognized clinical risk factors are employed to select patients for transplantation, high-dose melphalan (HDM), together with AuSCT, in treating Medicare beneficiaries of any age group with primary amyloid light-chain (AL) amyloidosis who meet the following criteria:
   1. Amyloid deposition in 2 or fewer organs; and,
   2. Cardiac left ventricular ejection fraction (EF) of 45% or greater.

C. Noncovered Conditions

Insufficient data exist to establish definite conclusions regarding the efficacy of autologous stem cell transplantation for the following conditions:

- Acute leukemia not in remission (ICD-9-CM codes 204.00, 205.00, 206.00, 207.00 and 208.00);
- Chronic granulocytic leukemia (ICD-9-CM codes 205.10 and 205.11);
- Solid tumors (other than neuroblastoma) (ICD-9-CM codes 140.0-199.1);
- Multiple myeloma (ICD-9-CM code 203.00 and 238.6), through September 30, 2000.
- Tandem transplantation (multiple rounds of autologous stem cell transplantation) for patients with multiple myeloma (ICD-9-CM code 203.00 and 238.6)
- Non-primary (AL) amyloidosis (ICD-9-CM code 277.3), effective October 1, 2000; or
- Primary (AL) amyloidosis (ICD-9-CM code 277.3) for Medicare beneficiaries age 64 or older, effective October 1, 2000, through March 14, 2005.

NOTE: Coverage for conditions other than these specifically designated as covered or non-covered is left to the FI's discretion.

100-4, 3, 90.3.3
Billing for Stem Cell Transplantation

A. Billing for Allogeneic Stem Cell Transplants

1. Definition of Acquisition Charges for Allogeneic Stem Cell Transplants
   Acquisition charges for allogeneic stem cell transplants include, but are not limited to, charges for the costs of the following services:

Current Procedural Coding Expert

Appendix G — Pub 100 References

- National Marrow Donor Program fees, if applicable, for stem cells from an unrelated donor;
- Tissue typing of donor and recipient;
- Donor evaluation;
- Physician pre-admission/pre-procedure donor evaluation services;
- Costs associated with harvesting procedure (e.g., general routine and special care services, procedure/operating room and other ancillary services, apheresis services, etc.);
- Post-operative/post-procedure evaluation of donor; and
- Preparation and processing of stem cells.

Payment for these acquisition services is included in the MS-DRG payment for the allogeneic stem cell transplant. The Medicare contractor does not make separate payment for these acquisition services, because hospitals may bill and receive payment only for services provided to the Medicare beneficiary who is the recipient of the stem cell transplant and whose illness is being treated with the stem cell transplant. Unlike the acquisition costs of solid organs for transplant (e.g., hearts and kidneys), which are paid on a reasonable cost basis, acquisition costs for allogeneic stem cells are included in prospective payment.

Acquisition charges for stem cell transplants apply only to allogeneic transplants, for which stem cells are obtained from a donor (other than the recipient himself or herself). Acquisition charges do not apply to autologous transplants (transplanted stems cells are obtained from the recipient himself or herself), because autologous transplants involve services provided to the beneficiary only (and not to a donor), for which the hospital may bill and receive payment (see paragraph B of this section). 2. Billing for Acquisition Services

The hospital identifies stem cell acquisition charges for allogeneic bone marrow/stem cell transplants separately in FL 42 of Form CMS-1450 (or electronic equivalent) by using revenue code 0819 (Other Organ Acquisition). Revenue code 0819 charges should include all services required to acquire stem cells from a donor, as defined above.

On the recipient's transplant bill, the hospital reports the acquisition charges, cost report days, and utilization days for the donor's hospital stay (if applicable) and/or charges for other encounters in which the stem cells were obtained from the donor. The donor is covered for medically necessary inpatient hospital days of care or outpatient care provided in connection with the allogeneic stem cell transplant under Part A. Expenses incurred for complications are paid only if they are directly and immediately attributable to the stem cell donation procedure. The hospital reports the acquisition charges on the billing form for the recipient, as described in the first paragraph of this section. It does not charge the donor's days of care against the recipient's utilization record. For cost reporting purposes, it includes the covered donor days and charges as Medicare days and charges.

The transplant hospital keeps an itemized statement that identifies the services furnished, the charges, the person receiving the service (donor/recipient), and whether this is a potential transplant donor or recipient. These charges will be reflected in the transplant hospital's stem cell/bone marrow acquisition cost center. For allogeneic stem cell acquisition services in cases that do not result in transplant, due to death of the intended recipient or other causes, hospitals include the costs associated with the acquisition services on the Medicare cost report.

The hospital shows charges for the transplant itself in revenue center code 0362 or another appropriate cost center. Selection of the cost center is up to the hospital.

B. Billing for Autologous Stem Cell Transplants
The hospital bills and shows all charges for autologous stem cell harvesting, processing, and transplant procedures based on the status of the patient (i.e., inpatient or outpatient) when the services are furnished. It shows charges for the actual transplant, described by the appropriate ICD-9-CM procedure or CPT codes, in revenue center code 0362 or another appropriate cost center.

The CPT codes describing autologous stem cell harvesting procedures may be billed and are separately payable under the Outpatient Prospective Payment System (OPPS) when provided in the hospital outpatient setting of care. Autologous harvesting procedures are distinct from the acquisition services described in section A. above for allogeneic stem cell transplants, which include services provided when stem cells are obtained from a donor and not from the patient undergoing the stem cell transplant. The CPT codes describing autologous stem cell processing procedures also may be billed and are separately payable under the OPPS when provided to hospital outpatients. Payment for stem cell harvesting procedures performed in the hospital inpatient setting of care, with transplant also occurring in the inpatient setting of care, is included in the MS-DRG payment for the autologous stem cell transplant.

100-4, 3, 90.4
Liver Transplants
A. Background
For Medicare coverage purposes, liver transplants are considered medically reasonable and necessary for specified conditions when performed in facilities that meet specific criteria.

To review the current list of approved Liver Transplant Centers, see
http://www.cms.hhs.gov/CertificationandComplianc/20_Transplant.asp#TopOfPage

100-4, 3, 90.4.1
Standard Liver Acquisition Charge
A3-3615.1, A3-3615.3

Each transplant facility must develop a standard charge for acquiring a cadaver liver from costs it expects to incur in the acquisition of livers.

This standard charge is not a charge that represents the acquisition cost of a specific liver. Rather, it is a charge that reflects the average cost associated with a liver acquisition.

Services associated with liver acquisition are billed from the organ procurement organization or, in some cases, the excising hospital to the transplant hospital. The excising hospital does not submit a billing form to the FI. The transplant hospital keeps an itemized statement that identifies the services furnished, the charges, the person receiving the service (donor/recipient), and the potential transplant donor. These charges are reflected in the transplant hospital's liver acquisition cost center and are used in determining the hospital's standard charge for acquiring a cadaver's liver. The standard charge is not a charge representing the acquisition cost of a specific liver. Rather, it is a charge that reflects the average cost associated with liver acquisition. Also, it is an all inclusive charge for all services required in acquisition of a liver, e.g., tissue typing, transportation of organ, and surgeons' retrieval fees.

100-4, 3, 90.4.2
Billing for Liver Transplant and Acquisition Services
Form CMS-1450 or its electronic equivalent is completed in accordance with instructions in chapter 25 for the beneficiary who receives a covered liver transplant. Applicable standard liver acquisition charges are identified separately in FL 42 by revenue code 0817 (Donor-Liver). Where interim bills are submitted, the standard acquisition charge appears on the billing form for the period during which the transplant took place. This charge is in addition to the hospital's charge for services furnished directly to the Medicare recipient.

The contractor deducts liver acquisition charges for IPPS hospitals prior to processing through Pricer. Costs of liver acquisition incurred by approved liver transplant facilities are not included in prospective payment DRG 480 (Liver Transplant). They are paid on a reasonable cost basis. This item is a "pass-through" cost for which interim payments are made. (See the Provider Reimbursement Manual, Part 1, Sec.2802 B.8.) The contractor includes liver acquisition charges under revenue code 0817 in the HUIP record that it sends to CWF and the QIO.

A. Bill Review Procedures
The contractor takes the following actions to process liver transplant bills.

1. Operative Report
   The contractor requires the operative report with all claims for liver transplants, or sends a development request to the hospital for each liver transplant with a diagnosis code for a covered condition.

2. MCE Interface
   Code 50.51 (Auxiliary liver transplant) is always a non-covered procedure. However, the MCE contains a limited coverage edit for procedure code 50.59 (liver transplant). Where procedure code 50.59 is identified by the MCE, the contractor shall check the provider number and effective date to determine if the provider is an approved liver transplant facility at the time of the transplant, and the contractor shall also determine if the facility is certified for adults and/or pediatric transplants dependent upon the patient's age. If yes, the claim is suspended for review of the operative report to determine whether the beneficiary has at least one of the covered conditions when the diagnosis code is for a covered condition. If payment is appropriate (i.e., the facility is approved, the service is furnished on or after the approval date, and the beneficiary has a covered condition), the contractor sends the claim to Grouper and Pricer.

   If none of the diagnoses codes are for a covered condition, or if the provider is not an approved liver transplant facility, the contractor denies the claim.

   NOTE: Some non-covered conditions are included in the covered diagnostic codes. (The diagnostic codes are broader than the covered conditions. For example, primary biliary cirrhosis is a covered condition, secondary biliary cirrhosis is not a covered condition. Both primary and secondary biliary cirrhosis have the same diagnosis code ICD 9 571.6) Do not pay for noncovered conditions.

3. Grouper
   If the bill shows a discharge date before March 8, 1990, the liver transplant procedure is not covered. If the discharge date is March 8, 1990 or later, the contractor processes the bill through Grouper and Pricer. If the discharge date is after March 7, 1990, and before October 1, 1990, Grouper assigned CMS DRG 191 or 192. The contractor sent the bill to Pricer with review code 08. Pricer would then overlay CMS DRG 191 or 192 with CMS DRG 480 and the weights and thresholds for CMS DRG 480 to price the bill. If the discharge date is after September 30, 1990, Grouper assigns CMS DRG 480 and Pricer is able to price without using review code 08. If the discharge date is after September 30, 2007, Grouper assigns MS-DRG 005 or 006 (Liver transplant with MCC or Intestinal Transplant or Liver transplant without MCC, respectively) and Pricer is able to price without using review code 08.

4. Liver Transplant Billing From Non-approved Hospitals
   Where a liver transplant and covered services are provided by a non-approved hospital, the bill data processed through Grouper and Pricer must exclude transplant procedure codes and related charges.

   When CMS approves a hospital to furnish liver transplant services, it informs the hospital of the effective date in the approval letter. The contractor will receive a copy of the letter.

100-4, 3, 90.5
Pancreas Transplants Kidney Transplants
A. Background
Effective July 1, 1999, Medicare covered pancreas transplantation when performed simultaneously with or following a kidney transplant (ICD-9-CM procedure code 55.69). Pancreas transplantation is performed to induce an insulin independent, euglycemic state in diabetic patients. The procedure is generally limited to those patients with severe secondary complications of diabetes including kidney failure. However, pancreas transplantation is sometimes performed on patients with labile diabetes and hypoglycemic unawareness.

Appendix G — Pub 100 References

Medicare has had a policy of not covering pancreas transplantation. The Office of Health Technology Assessment performed an assessment on pancreas-kidney transplantation in 1994. They found reasonable graft survival outcomes for patients receiving either simultaneous pancreas-kidney (SPK) transplantation or pancreas after kidney (PAK) transplantation. For a list of facilities approved to perform SPK or PAK, refer to the following Web site: http://www.cms.hhs.gov/CertificationandComplianc/20_Transplant.asp#TopOfPage

B. Billing for Pancreas Transplants

There are no special provisions related to managed care participants. Managed care plans are required to provide all Medicare covered services. Medicare does not restrict which hospitals or physicians may perform pancreas transplantation.

The transplant procedure and revenue code 0360 for the operating room are paid under these codes. Procedures must be reported using the current ICD-9-CM procedure codes for pancreas and kidney transplants. Providers must place at least one of the following transplant procedure codes on the claim:

- 52.80 Transplant of pancreas
- 52.82 Homotransplant of pancreas

The Medicare Code Editor (MCE) has been updated to include 52.80 and 52.82 as limited coverage procedures. The contractor must determine if the facility is approved for the transplant and certified for either pediatric or adult transplants dependent upon the age of the patient.

Effective October 1, 2000, ICD-9-CM code 52.83 was moved in the MCE to non-covered. The contractor must override any deny edit on claims that came in with 52.82 prior to October 1, 2000 and adjust, as 52.82 is the correct code.

If the discharge date is July 1, 1999, or later: the contractor processes the bill through Grouper and Pricer.

Pancreas transplantation is reasonable and necessary for the following diagnosis codes. However, since this is not an all-inclusive list, the contractor is permitted to determine if any additional diagnosis codes will be covered for this procedure.

Diabetes Diagnosis Codes

- 250.00 Diabetes mellitus without mention of complication, type II (non-insulin dependent) (NIDDM) (adult onset) or unspecified type, not stated as uncontrolled.
- 250.01 Diabetes mellitus without mention of complication, type I (insulin dependent) (IDDM) (juvenile), not stated as uncontrolled.
- 250.02 Diabetes mellitus without mention of complication, type II (non-insulin dependent) (NIDDM) (adult onset) or unspecified type, uncontrolled.
- 250.03 Diabetes mellitus without mention of complication, type I (insulin dependent) (IDDM) (juvenile), uncontrolled.
- 250.1X Diabetes with ketoacidosis
- 250.2X Diabetes with hyperosmolarity
- 250.3X Diabetes with coma
- 250.4X Diabetes with renal manifestations
- 250.5X Diabetes with ophthalmic manifestations
- 250.6X Diabetes with neurological manifestations
- 250.7X Diabetes with peripheral circulatory disorders
- 250.8X Diabetes with other specified manifestations
- 250.9X Diabetes with unspecified complication

NOTE: X=0-3

Hypertensive Renal Diagnosis Codes:

- 403.01 Malignant hypertensive renal disease, with renal failure
- 403.11 Benign hypertensive renal disease, with renal failure
- 403.91 Unspecified hypertensive renal disease, with renal failure
- 404.02 Malignant hypertensive heart and renal disease, with renal failure
- 404.03 Malignant hypertensive heart and renal disease, with congestive heart failure or renal failure
- 404.12 Benign hypertensive heart and renal disease, with renal failure
- 404.13 Benign hypertensive heart and renal disease, with congestive heart failure or renal failure
- 404.92 Unspecified hypertensive heart and renal disease, with renal failure
- 404.93 Unspecified hypertensive heart and renal disease, with congestive heart failure or renal failure
- 585.1-585.6, 585.9 Chronic Renal Failure Code

NOTE: If a patient had a kidney transplant that was successful, the patient no longer has chronic kidney failure, therefore it would be inappropriate for the provider to bill 585.1 - 585.6, 585.9 on such a patient. In these cases one of the following V-codes should be present on the claim or in the beneficiary's history.

The provider uses the following V-codes only when a kidney transplant was performed before the pancreas transplant:

- V42.0 Organ or tissue replaced by transplant kidney
- V43.89 Organ tissue replaced by other means, kidney or pancreas

NOTE: If a kidney and pancreas transplants are performed simultaneously, the claim should contain a diabetes diagnosis code and a renal failure code or one of the hypertensive renal failure diagnosis codes. The claim should also contain two transplant procedure codes. If the claim is for a pancreas transplant only, the claim should contain a diabetes diagnosis code and a V-code to indicate a previous kidney transplant. If the V-code is not on the claim for the pancreas transplant, the contractor will search the beneficiary's claim history for a V-code.

C. Drugs

If the pancreas transplant occurs after the kidney transplant, immunosuppressive therapy will begin with the date of discharge from the inpatient stay for the pancreas transplant.

D. Charges for Pancreas Acquisition Services

A separate organ acquisition cost center has been established for pancreas transplantation. The Medicare cost report will include a separate line to account for pancreas transplantation costs. The 42 CFR 412.2(e)(4) was changed to include pancreas in the list of organ acquisition costs that are paid on a reasonable cost basis.

Acquisition costs for pancreas transplantation as well as kidney transplants will occur in Revenue Center 081X. The contractor overrides any claims that suspend due to repetition of revenue code 081X on the same claim if the patient had a simultaneous kidney/pancreas transplant. It pays for acquisition costs for both kidney and pancreas organs if transplants are performed simultaneously. It will not pay for more than two organ acquisitions on the same claim.

E. Medicare Summary Notices (MSN) and Remittance Advice Messages

If the provider submits a claim for simultaneous pancreas kidney transplantation or pancreas transplantation following a kidney transplant, and omits one of the appropriate diagnosis/procedure codes, the contractor rejects the claim, using the following MSN:

- MSN 16.32, "Medicare does not pay separately for this service."
- Use the following Remittance Advice Message:
- Claim adjustment reason code B15, "Claim/service denied/reduced because this procedure or service is not paid separately."
- If a claim is denied because no evidence of a prior kidney transplant is presented, use the following MSN message:
- MSN 15.4, "The information provided does not support the need for this service or item."

The contractor uses the following Remittance Advice Message:

- Claim adjustment reason code 50, "These are non-covered services because this is not deemed a 'medical necessity' by the payer."

To further clarify the situation, the contractor should also use new claim level remark code MA 126, "Pancreas transplant not covered unless kidney transplant performed."

100-4, 3, 90.6
Intestinal and Multi-Visceral Transplants
A. Background

Effective for services on or after April 1, 2001, Medicare covers intestinal and multi-visceral transplantation for the purpose of restoring intestinal function in patients with irreversible intestinal failure. Intestinal failure is defined as the loss of absorptive capacity of the small bowel secondary to severe primary gastrointestinal disease or surgically induced short bowel syndrome. Intestinal failure prevents oral nutrition and may be associated with both mortality and profound morbidity. Multi-Visceral transplantation includes organs in the digestive system (stomach, duodenum, liver, and intestine). See Sec.260.5 of the National Coverage Determinations Manual for further information.

B. Approved Transplant Facilities

Medicare will cover intestinal transplantation if performed in an approved facility. The approved facilities are located at:
http://www.cms.hhs.gov/CertificationandComplianc/20_Transplant.asp#TopOfPage

C. Billing

ICD-9-CM procedure code 46.97 is effective for discharges on or after April 1, 2001. The Medicare Code Editor (MCE) lists this code as a limited coverage procedure. The contractor shall override the MCE when this procedure code is listed and the coverage criteria are met in an approved transplant facility, and also determine if the facility is certified for adults and/or pediatric transplants dependent upon the patient's age.

For this procedure where the provider is approved as transplant facility and certified for the adult and/or pediatric population, and the service is performed on or after the transplant approval date, the contractor must suspend the claim for clerical review of the operative report to determine whether the beneficiary has at least one of the covered conditions listed when the diagnosis code is for a covered condition.

This review is not part of the contractor's medical review workload. Instead, the contractor should complete this review as part of its claims processing workload.

Charges for ICD-9-CM procedure code 46.97 should be billed under revenue code 0360, Operating Room Services.

For discharge dates on or after October 1, 2001, acquisition charges are billed under revenue code 081X, Organ Acquisition. For discharge dates between April 1, 2001, and September 30, 2001, hospitals were to report the acquisition charges on the claim, but there was no interim pass-through payment made for these costs.

Bill the procedure used to obtain the donor's organ on the same claim, using appropriate ICD-9-CM procedure codes.

The 11X bill type should be used when billing for intestinal transplants.

Immunosuppressive therapy for intestinal transplantation is covered and should be billed consistent with other organ transplants under the current rules.

There is no specific ICD-9-CM diagnosis code for intestinal failure. Diagnosis codes exist to capture the causes of intestinal failure. Some examples of intestinal failure include, but are not limited to:

- Volvulus 560.2,
- Volvulus gastroschisis 756.79, other [congenital] anomalies of abdominal wall,
- Volvulus gastroschisis 569.89, other specified disorders of intestine,
- Necrotizing enterocolitis 777.5, necrotizing enterocolitis in fetus or newborn,
- Necrotizing enterocolitis 014.8, other tuberculosis of intestines, peritoneum, and mesenteric,
- Necrotizing enterocolitis and splanchnic vascular thrombosis 557.0, acute vascular insufficiency of intestine,
- Inflammatory bowel disease 569.9, unspecified disorder of intestine,
- Radiation enteritis 777.5, necrotizing enterocolitis in fetus or newborn, and
- Radiation enteritis 558.1.

D. Acquisition Costs
A separate organ acquisition cost center was established for acquisition costs incurred on or after October 1, 2001. The Medicare Cost Report will include a separate line to account for these transplantation costs. For intestinal and multi-visceral transplants performed between April 1, 2001, and October 1, 2001, the DRG payment was payment in full for all hospital services related to this procedure.

E. Medicare Summary Notices (MSN), Remittance Advice Messages, and Notice of Utilization Notices (NOU)
If an intestinal transplant is billed by an unapproved facility after April 1, 2001, the contractor shall deny the claim and use MSN message 21.6, "This item or service is not covered when performed, referred, or ordered by this provider;" 21.18, "This item or service is not covered when performed or ordered by this provider;" or, 16.2, "This service cannot be paid when provided in this location/facility;" and Remittance Advice Message, Claim Adjustment Reason Code 52, "The referring/prescribing/rendering provider is not eligible to refer/prescribe/order/perform the service billed."

100-4, 3, 100.1
Billing for Abortion Services
A3-3652

Effective October 1, 1998, abortions are not covered under the Medicare program except for instances where the pregnancy is a result of an act of rape or incest; or the woman suffers from a physical disorder, physical injury, or physical illness, including a life endangering physical condition caused by the pregnancy itself that would, as certified by a physician, place the woman in danger of death unless an abortion is performed.

A. "G" Modifier
The "G7" modifier is defined as "the pregnancy resulted from rape or incest, or pregnancy certified by physician as life threatening."

Beginning July 1, 1999, providers should bill for abortion services using the new Modifier G7. This modifier can be used on claims with dates of services October 1, 1998, and after. CWF will be able to recognize the modifier beginning July 1, 1999.

B. FI Billing Instructions
1. Hospital Inpatient Billing
    Hospitals will bill the FI on Form CMS-1450 using bill type 11X. Medicare will pay only when condition code A7 or A8 is used in FLs 24-30 of UB92 along with an appropriate ICD-9-CM principal diagnosis code that will group to DRG 380 or with an appropriate ICD-9-CM principal diagnosis code and one of the four appropriate ICD-9-CM operating room procedure codes listed below that will group to DRG 381.

    69.01 69.02 69.51 74.91

    Providers must use ICD-9-CM codes 69.01 and 69.02 to describe exactly the procedure or service performed.

    The FI must manually review claims with the above ICD-9-CM procedure codes to verify that all of the above conditions are met.

2. Outpatient Billing
    Hospitals will bill the FI on Form CMS-1450 using bill type 13X, 83X and 85X.

    Medicare will pay only if one of the following CPT codes is used with the "G7" modifier.

    59840 59851 59856
    59841 59852 59857
    59850 59855 59866

C. Common Working File (CWF) Edits
For hospital outpatient claims, CWF will bypass its edits for a managed care beneficiary who is having an abortion outside their plan and the claim is submitted with the "G7" modifier and one of the above CPT codes.

For hospital inpatient claims, CWF will bypass its edits for a managed care beneficiary who is having an abortion outside their plan and the claim is submitted with one of the above ICD-9-CM procedure codes.

D. Medicare Summary Notices (MSN)/Explanation of Your Medicare Benefits
Remittance Advice Message

If a claim is submitted with one of the above CPT procedure codes but no "G7" modifier, the claim is denied. The FI states on the MSN the following message:

This service was denied because Medicare covers this service only under certain circumstances." (MSN Message 21.21).

For the remittance advice the FI uses existing American National Standard Institute (ANSI) X12-835 claim adjustment reason code B5, "Claim/service denied/reduced because coverage guidelines were not met or were exceeded."

100-4, 3, 100.2
Payment for CRNA or AA Services
A3-3660.9

Anesthesia services furnished on or after January 1, 1990, at a qualified rural hospital by a hospital employed or contracted CRNA or AA can be paid on a reasonable cost basis. The FI determines the hospital's qualification using the following criteria.

The hospital must be located in a rural area (as defined for PPS purposes) to be considered. A rural hospital that qualified and was paid on a reasonable cost basis for CRNA or AA services during calendar year 1989 could continue to be paid on a reasonable cost basis for these services furnished during calendar year 1990 if it could establish before January 1, 1990, that it did not provide more than 500 surgical procedures, both inpatient and outpatient, requiring anesthesia services during 1989.

A rural hospital that was not paid on a reasonable cost basis for CRNA or AA services during calendar year 1989 could be paid on a reasonable cost basis for these services furnished during calendar year 1990 if it established before January 1, 1990, that:

- As of January 1, 1988, it employed or contracted with a CRNA or AA (but not more than one full-time equivalent CRNA or AA); and
- In both 1987 and 1989, it had a volume of 500 or fewer surgical procedures, including inpatient and outpatient procedures, requiring anesthesia services.

Each CRNA or AA employed by, or under contract with the hospital, must agree in writing not to bill on a fee schedule basis for services furnished at the hospital. A rural hospital can qualify and continue to be paid on a reasonable cost basis for qualified CRNA or AA services for a calendar year beyond 1990 if it could establish before January 1 of that year that it did not provide more than 500 surgical procedures, both inpatient and outpatient, requiring anesthesia services during the preceding year. For a calendar year beyond 1990, it must make its election after September 30, but before January 1. The FI determines the number of anesthetics by annualizing the number of surgical procedures for the 9-month period ending September 30.

A rural hospital that first elects reasonable cost payment for CRNA services for a calendar year after 1990 must demonstrate that:

- It had a volume of 500 or fewer surgical procedures, including inpatient and outpatient, requiring anesthesia services in the preceding year; and
- It meets the criteria that would have been met by a rural hospital first electing reasonable cost in calendar year 1990.

To prevent duplicate payments, the FI informs carriers of the names of CRNAs or AAs, the hospitals with which they have agreements, and the effective dates of the agreements. If the CRNA or AA bills Part B for anesthesia services furnished prior to the hospital's election of reasonable cost payments, the carrier must recover the overpayment from the CRNA or AA.

100-4, 3, 100.6
Inpatient Renal Services
HO-E400

Section 405.103I of Subpart J of Regulation 5 stipulates that only approved hospitals may bill for ESRD services. Hence, to allow hospitals to bill and be reimbursed for inpatient dialysis services furnished under arrangements, both facilities participating in the arrangement must meet the conditions of 405.2120 and 405.2160 of Subpart U of Regulation 5. In order for renal dialysis facilities to have a written arrangement with each other to provide inpatient dialysis care both facilities must meet the minimum utilization rate requirement, i.e., two dialysis stations with a performance capacity of at least four dialysis treatments per week.

Dialysis may be billed by an SNF as a service if: (a) it is provided by a hospital with which the facility has a transfer agreement in effect, and that hospital is approved to provide staff-assisted dialysis for the Medicare program; or (b) it is furnished directly by an SNF meeting all nonhospital maintenance dialysis facility requirements, including minimum utilization requirements. (See 1861(h)(6), 1861(h)(7), title XVIII.)

100-4, 3, 100.7
Lung Volume Reduction Surgery (LVRS) (also known as reduction pneumoplasty, lung shaving, or lung contouring) is an invasive surgical procedure to reduce the volume of a hyperinflated lung in order to allow the underlying compressed lung to expand, and thus, establish improved respiratory function.

Effective for discharges on or after January 1, 2004, Medicare will cover LVRS under certain conditions as described in 240 of Pub. 100-03, "National Coverage Determinations".

The Medicare Code Editor (MCE) creates a Limited Coverage edit for procedure code 32.22. This procedure code has limited coverage due to the stringent conditions that must be met by hospitals. Where this procedure code is identified by MCE, the FI shall determine if coverage criteria is met and override the MCE if appropriate.

The LVRS can only be performed in the facilities listed on the following Web site: www.cms.hhs.gov/coverage/lvrsfacility.pdf

Appendix G — Pub 100 References

Medicare previously only covered LVRS as part of the National Emphysema Treatment Trial (NETT). The study was limited to 18 hospitals, and patients were randomized into two arms, either medical management and LVRS or medical management. The study was conducted by The National Heart, Lung, and Blood Institute of the National Institutes of Health and coordinated by Johns Hopkins University (JHU). Hospital claims for patients in the NETT were identified by the presence of Condition Code EY. The JHU instructed hospitals of the correct billing procedures for billing claims under the NETT.

100-4, 4, 10.4
Packaging

Under the OPPS, packaged services are items and services that are considered to be an integral part of another service that is paid under the OPPS. No separate payment is made for packaged services, because the cost of these items and services is included in the APC payment for the service of which they are an integral part. For example, routine supplies, anesthesia, recovery room use, and most drugs are considered to be an integral part of a surgical procedure so payment for these items is packaged into the APC payment for the surgical procedure.

A. Packaging for Claims Resulting in APC Payments
If a claim contains services that result in an APC payment but also contains packaged services, separate payment for the packaged services is not made since payment is included in the APC. However, charges related to the packaged services are used for outlier and Transitional Corridor Payments (TOPs) as well as for future rate setting.

Therefore, it is extremely important that hospitals report all HCPCS codes and all charges for all services they furnish, whether payment for the services is made separately paid or is packaged.

B. Packaging for Claims Resulting in No APC Payments
If the claim contains only services payable under cost reimbursement, such as corneal tissue, and services that would be packaged services if an APC were payable, then the packaged services are not separately payable. In addition, these charges for the packaged services are not used to calculate TOPs.

If the claim contains only services payable under a fee schedule, such as clinical diagnostic laboratory tests, and also contains services that would be packaged services if an APC were payable, the packaged services are not separately payable. In addition, the charges are not used to calculate TOPs.

If a claim contains services payable under cost reimbursement, services payable under a fee schedule, and services that would be packaged services if an APC were payable, the packaged services are not separately payable. In addition, the charges are not used to calculate TOPs payments.

C. Packaging Types Under the OPPS
1. Unconditionally packaged services are services for which separate payment is never made because the payment for the service is always packaged into the payment for other services. Unconditionally packaged services are identified in the OPPS Addendum B with status indictor of N. See the OPPS Web site at http://www.cms.hhs.gov/HospitalOutpatientPPS/ for the most recent Addendum B (HCPCS codes with status indicators). In general, the charges for unconditionally packaged services are used to calculate outlier and TOPS payments when they appear on a claim with a service that is separately paid under the OPPS because the packaged service is considered to be part of the package of services for which payment is being made through the APC payment for the separately paid service.

2. STVX-packaged services are services for which separate payment is made only if there is no service with status indicator S, T, V or X reported with the same date of service on the same claim. If a claim includes a service that is assigned status indicator S, T, V, or X reported on the same date of service as the STVXpackaged service, the payment for the STVX-packaged service is packaged into the payment for the service(s) with status indicator S, T, V or X and no separate payment is made for the STVX-packaged service. STVX-packaged services are assigned status indicator Q. See the OPPS Webpage at http://www.cms.hhs.gov/HospitalOutpatientPPS/ for identification of STVXpackaged codes.

3. T-packaged services are services for which separate payment is made only if there is no service with status indicator T reported with the same date of service on the same claim. When there is a claim that includes a service that is assigned status indicator T reported on the same date of service as the T-packaged service, the payment for the T-packaged service is packaged into the payment for the service(s) with status indicator T and no separate payment is made for the T-packaged service. T-packaged services are assigned status indicator Q. See the OPPS Web site at http://www.cms.hhs.gov/HospitalOutpatientPPS/ for identification of T-packaged codes.

4. A service that is assigned to a composite APC is a major component of a single episode of care. The hospital receives one payment through a composite APC for multiple major separately identifiable services. Services mapped to composite APCs are assigned status indicator Q. See the discussion of composite APCs in section 10.2.1.

100-4, 4, 10.5
Discounting

- Fifty percent of the full OPPS amount is paid if a procedure for which anesthesia is planned is discontinued after the patient is prepared and taken to the room where the procedure is to be performed but before anesthesia is provided.

- Fifty percent of the full OPPS amount is paid if a procedure for which anesthesia is not planned is discontinued after the patient is prepared and taken to the room where the procedure is to be performed.

- Multiple surgical procedures furnished during the same operative session are discounted.
  - The full amount is paid for the surgical procedure with the highest weight;
  - Fifty percent is paid for any other surgical procedure(s) performed at the same time;
  - Similar discounting occurs now under the physician fee schedule and the payment system for ASCs;
- When multiple surgical procedures are performed during the same operative session, beneficiary coinsurance is discounted in proportion to the APC payment.

100-4, 4, 10.10
Biweekly Interim Payments for Certain Hospital OutpatientItems and Services That Are Paid on a Cost Basis, and Direct Medical Education Payments, Not Included in the Hospital Outpatient Prospective Payment System
A-01-32

For hospitals subject to the OPPS, payment for certain items that are not paid under the OPPS, but which are reimbursable in addition to OPPS, are made through biweekly interim payments subject to retrospective adjustment based on a settled cost report.

These payments include:

- Direct medical education payments;
- Costs of nursing and allied health programs;
- Costs associated with interns and residents not in an approved teaching program as described in 42 CFR 415.202;
- Teaching physicians costs attributable to Part B services for hospitals that elect cost-based reimbursement for teaching physicians under 42 CFR 415.160;
- CRNA services;
- For hospitals that meet the requirements under 42 CFR 412.113(c), the reasonable costs of anesthesia services furnished to hospital outpatients by qualified nonphysician anesthetists (i.e., certified registered nurse anesthetists and anesthesiologists' assistants) employed by the hospital or obtained under arrangements;
- Bad debts for uncollectible deductibles and coinsurance;
- Organ acquisition costs paid under Part B.

For hospitals that are paid under the OPPS, interim payments for these items attributable to both hospital outpatients, as well as inpatients whose services are paid under Part B of the Medicare program are made on a biweekly basis. The FI determines the amount of the biweekly payment by estimating a hospital's reimbursement amount for these items for the cost reporting period by using:

- Medicare principles of cost reimbursement for cost-based items; and
- Medicare rules for determining payment for graduate medical education for direct medical education, and dividing the total annual estimated amount for these items into 26 equal biweekly payments.

The estimated annual amount is based on the most current data available. Biweekly interim payments are reviewed and, if necessary, adjusted at least twice during the reporting period, with final settlement based on a submitted cost report. Because hospitals subject to the OPPS have not received payment for these items attributable to services furnished on or after August 1, 2000, the date the OPPS was implemented, the first payment to each hospital included all the payments due to the hospital retroactive to August 1, 2000. Thereafter, FIs continue to make payment on a biweekly basis. Each payment is made two weeks after the end of a biweekly period of services. The FI was required to make retroactive payments and begin making biweekly interim payments to all hospitals that are due these payments no later than 60 days after March 8, 2001.

These biweekly payments may be combined with the inpatient biweekly payments that the FI makes under 2405.2 of the Medicare Provider Reimbursement Manual (CMS Pub.15-I). However, if a single payment is made, for purposes of final cost report settlement, they must maintain records to separately identify the amount of the hospital's combined payment that is paid out of the Part A or Part B trust fund.

100-4, 4, 61.4.1
Billing for Brachytherapy Sources - General

Brachytherapy sources (e.g., brachytherapy devices or seeds, solutions) are paid separately from the services to administer and deliver brachytherapy in the OPPS, per section 1833(t)(2)(H) of the Act, reflecting the number, isotope, and radioactive intensity of devices furnished, as well as stranded versus non-stranded configurations of sources. Therefore, providers must bill for brachytherapy sources in addition to the brachytherapy services with which the sources are applied, in order to receive payment for the sources. The list of separately payable sources is found in Addendum B of the most recent OPPS annual update published in the Federal Register, as well as in the recurring update notifications of the current year for billing purposes. New sources meeting the OPPS definition of a brachytherapy source may be added for payment beginning any quarter, and the new source codes and descriptors are announced in the recurring update notifications. Each unit of a billable source is identified by the unit measurement in the respective source's long descriptor. Seed-like sources are generally billed and paid "per source" based on the number of units of the source HCPCS code reported, including the billing of the number of sources within a stranded configuration of sources. Providers therefore must bill the number of units of a source used with the brachytherapy service rendered.

100-4, 4, 61.4.2
Definition of Brachytherapy Source for Separate Payment

Brachytherapy sources eligible for separate billing and payment must be radioactive sources, meaning that the source contains a radioactive isotope. Separate brachytherapy source payments reflect the number, isotope, and radioactive intensity of sources furnished to patients, as well as stranded and non-stranded configurations.

100-4, 4, 61.4.3
Billing of Brachytherapy Sources Ordered for a Specific Patient

A hospital may report and charge Medicare and the Medicare beneficiary for all brachytherapy sources that are ordered by the physician for a specific patient, acquired by the hospital, and used in the care of the patient. Specifically, brachytherapy sources prescribed by the physician in accordance with high quality clinical care, acquired by the hospital, and actually implanted in the patient may be reported and charged. In the case where most, but not all, prescribed sources are implanted in the patient, CMS will consider the relatively few brachytherapy sources that were ordered but not implanted due to specific clinical considerations to be used in the care of the patient and billable to Medicare under the following circumstances. The hospital may charge for all sources if they were specifically acquired by the hospital for the particular patient according to a physician's prescription for the sources that was consistent with standard clinical practice and high quality brachytherapy treatment, in order to ensure that the clinically appropriate number of sources was available for the implantation procedure, and they were not implanted in any other patient. Those sources that were not implanted must have been disposed of in accordance with all appropriate requirements for their handling.

In general, the number of sources used in the care of the patient but not implanted would not be expected to constitute more than a small fraction of the sources actually implanted in the patient. Under these circumstances, the beneficiary is liable for the copayment for all the sources billed to Medicare.

100-4, 4, 61.4.4
Billing for Brachytherapy Source Supervision, Handling and Loading Costs

Providers should report charges related to supervision, handling, and loading of radiation sources, including brachytherapy sources, in one of two ways:

1. Report the charge separately using CPT code 77790 (Supervision, handling, loading of radiation source), in addition to reporting the associated HCPCS procedure code(s) for application of the radiation source;
2. Include the supervision, handling, and/or loading charges as part of the charge reported with the HCPCS procedure code(s) for application of the radiation source.

Do not bill a separate charge for brachytherapy source storage costs. These costs are treated as part of the department's overhead costs.

100-4, 4, 160
Clinic and Emergency Visits

CMS has acknowledged from the beginning of the OPPS that CMS believes that CPT Evaluation and Management (E/M) codes were designed to reflect the activities of physicians and do not describe well the range and mix of services provided by hospitals during visits of clinic and emergency department patients. While awaiting the development of a national set of facility-specific codes and guidelines, providers should continue to apply their current internal guidelines to the existing CPT codes. Each hospital's internal guidelines should follow the intent of the CPT code descriptors, in that the guidelines should be designed to reasonably relate the intensity of hospital resources to the different levels of effort represented by the codes. Hospitals should ensure that their guidelines accurately reflect resource distinctions between the five levels of codes.

Effective January 1, 2007, CMS is distinguishing between two types of emergency departments: Type A emergency departments and Type B emergency departments.

A Type A emergency department is defined as an emergency department that is available 24 hours a day, 7 days a week and is either licensed by the State in which it is located under applicable State law as an emergency room or emergency department or it is held out to the public (by name, posted signs, advertising, or other means) as a place that provides care for emergency medical conditions on an urgent basis without requiring a previously scheduled appointment.

A Type B emergency department is defined as an emergency department that meets the definition of a "dedicated emergency department" as defined in 42 CFR 489.24 under the EMTALA regulations. It must meet at least one of the following requirements:

(1) It is licensed by the State in which it is located under applicable State law as an emergency room or emergency department;
(2) It is held out to the public (by name, posted signs, advertising, or other means) as a place that provides care for emergency medical conditions on an urgent basis without requiring a previously scheduled appointment; or
(3) During the calendar year immediately preceding the calendar year in which a determination under 42 CFR 489.24 is being made, based on a representative sample of patient visits that occurred during that calendar year, it provides at least one-third of all of its outpatient visits for the treatment of emergency medical conditions on an urgent basis without requiring a previously scheduled appointment.

Hospitals must bill for visits provided in Type A emergency departments using CPT emergency department E/M codes. Hospitals must bill for visits provided in Type B emergency departments using the G-codes that describe visits provided in Type B emergency departments.

Hospitals that will be billing the new Type B ED visit codes may need to update their internal guidelines to report these codes.

Emergency department and clinic visits are paid in some cases separately and in other cases as part of a composite APC payment. See section 10.2.1 of this chapter for further details.

100-4, 4, 160.1
Critical Care Services

Beginning January 1, 2007, critical care services will be paid at two levels, depending on the presence or absence of trauma activation. Providers will receive one payment rate for critical care without trauma activation and will receive additional payment when critical care is associated with trauma activation.

To determine whether trauma activation occurs, follow the National Uniform Billing Committee (NUBC) guidelines in the Claims Processing Manual, Pub 100-04, Chapter 25, Sec.75.4 related to the reporting of the trauma revenue codes in the 68x series. The revenue code series 68x can be used only by trauma centers/hospitals as licensed or designated by the state or local government authority authorized to do so, or as verified by the American College of Surgeons. Different subcategory revenue codes are reported by designated Level 1-4 hospital trauma centers. Only patients for whom there has been prehospital notification based on triage information from prehospital caregivers, who meet either local, state or American College of Surgeons field triage criteria, or are delivered by inter-hospital transfers, and are given the appropriate team response can be billed a trauma activation charge.

When critical care services are provided without trauma activation, the hospital may bill CPT code 99291, Critical care, evaluation and management of the critically ill or critically injured patient; first 30-74 minutes (and 99292, if appropriate). If trauma activation occurs under the circumstances described by the NUBC guidelines that would permit reporting a charge under 68x, the hospital may also bill one unit of code G0390, which describes trauma activation associated with hospital critical care services. Revenue code 68x must be reported on the same date of service. The OCE will edit to ensure that G0390 appears with revenue code 68x on the same date of service and that only one unit of G0390 is billed. CMS believes that trauma activation is a one-time occurrence in association with critical care services, and therefore, CMS will only pay for one unit of G0390 per day.

The CPT code 99291 is defined by CPT as the first 30-74 minutes of critical care. This 30 minute minimum has always applied under the OPPS. The CPT code 99292, Critical care, evaluation and management of the critically ill or critically injured patient; each additional 30 minutes, remains a packaged service under the OPPS, so that hospitals do not have the ongoing administrative burden of reporting precisely the time for each critical service provided. As the CPT guidelines indicate, hospitals that provide less than 30 minutes of critical care should bill for a visit, typically an emergency department visit, at a level consistent with their own internal guidelines.

Under the OPPS, the time that can be reported as critical care is the time spent by a physician and/or hospital staff engaged in active face-to-face critical care of a critically ill or critically injured patient. If the physician and hospital staff or multiple hospital staff members are simultaneously engaged in this active face-to-face care, the time involved can only be counted once.

- In CY 2007 hospitals may continue to report a charge with RC 68x without any HCPCS code when trauma team activation occurs. In order to receive additional payment when critical care services are associated with trauma activation, the hospital must report G0390 on the same date of service as RC 68x, in addition to CPT code 99291 (or 99292, if appropriate.)

In CY 2007 hospitals should continue to report 99291 (and 99292 as appropriate) for critical care services furnished without trauma team activation. CPT 99291 maps to APC 0617 (Critical Care). (CPT 99292 is packaged and not paid separately, but should be reported if provided.)

Critical care services are paid in some cases separately and in other cases as part of a composite APC payment. See Section 10.2.1 of this chapter for further details.

100-4, 4, 180.3
Unlisted Service or Procedure

This section does not apply to OPPS hospitals.

There may be services or procedures performed that are not found in HCPCS. These are typically services that are rarely performed, unusual, variable, or new. A number of specific code numbers have been designated for reporting unlisted procedures. When an unlisted procedure code is used, a report describing the service is submitted with the claim. Pertinent information includes a definition or description of the nature, extent, and need for the procedure and the time, effort, and equipment necessary to provide the service.

When an FI receives a claim with an unlisted procedure code, it reviews it to verify that there is no existing code that adequately describes the procedure. If it determines that an adequately descriptive code is contained in HCPCS, it advises the hospital of the proper code and processes the claim. If it determines that no existing code is sufficiently descriptive, it pays the claim using the unlisted procedure code. If the frequency of the procedure warrants assignment of a local code, the FI forwards a copy and the operative report to the RO HCPCS coordinator for a code determination. When it receives a determination, the FI informs the hospital of the correct code for future reporting. Local codes are not accepted under OPPS and line items for local codes are no longer paid on cost.

NOTE: If the claim is submitted via EMC or identified after the bill has been processed, an operative report, the provider number, revenue codes, and charges are sufficient.

The "Unlisted Procedures" and codes for surgery are:

HCPCS code	Unlisted Procedure
15999	Unlisted procedure, excision pressure ulcer
17999	Unlisted procedure, skin, mucous membrane and subcutaneous tissue
19499	Unlisted procedure, breast
20999	Unlisted procedure, musculoskeletal system, general
21299	Unlisted craniofacial and maxillofacial procedures
21499	Unlisted orthopedic procedure, head
21899	Unlisted procedure, neck or thorax

Appendix G — Pub 100 References

HCPCS code	Unlisted Procedure
22899	Unlisted procedure, spine
22999	Unlisted procedure, abdomen, musculoskeletal system
23929	Unlisted procedure, shoulder
24999	Unlisted procedure, humerus or elbow
25999	Unlisted procedure, forearm or wrist
26989	Unlisted procedure, hands or fingers
27299	Unlisted procedure, pelvis or hip joint
27599	Unlisted procedure, femur or knee
27899	Unlisted procedure, leg or ankle
28899	Unlisted procedure, foot or toes
29799	Unlisted procedure, casting or strapping
29909	Unlisted procedure, arthroscopy
30999	Unlisted procedure, nose
31299	Unlisted procedure, accessory sinuses
31599	Unlisted procedure, larynx
31899	Unlisted procedure, trachea, bronchi
32999	Unlisted procedure, lungs, and pleura
33999	Unlisted procedure, cardiac surgery
36299	Unlisted procedure, vascular injection
37799	Unlisted procedure, vascular surgery
38999	Unlisted procedure, hemic or lymphatic system
39499	Unlisted procedure, mediastinum
39599	Unlisted procedure, diaphragm
40799	Unlisted procedure, lips
40899	Unlisted procedure, vestibule of mouth
41599	Unlisted procedure, tongue, floor of mouth
41899	Unlisted procedure, dentoalveolar structures
42299	Unlisted procedure, palate, uvula
42699	Unlisted procedure, salivary glands or ducts
42999	Unlisted procedure, pharynx, adenoids, or tonsils
43499	Unlisted procedure, esophag
43999	Unlisted procedure, stomach
44799	Unlisted procedure, intestine
44899	Unlisted procedure, Meckel's diverticulum and the mesentery
45999	Unlisted procedure, rectum
46999	Unlisted procedure, anus
47399	Unlisted procedure, liver
47999	Unlisted procedure, biliary tract
48999	Unlisted procedure, pancreas
49999	Unlisted procedure, abdomen, peritoneum, and omentum
53899	Unlisted procedure, urinary system
55899	Unlisted procedure, male genital system
56399	Unlisted procedure, laparoscopy, hysteroscopy
58999	Unlisted procedure, female genital system non-obstetrical
59899	Unlisted procedure, maternity care and delivery
60699	Unlisted procedure, endocrine system
64999	Unlisted procedure, nervous system
66999	Unlisted procedure, anterior segment of eye
67299	Unlisted procedure, posterior segment
67399	Unlisted procedure, ocular muscle
67599	Unlisted procedure, orbit
67999	Unlisted procedure, eyelids
68399	Unlisted procedure, conjunctiva
68899	Unlisted procedure, lacrimal system
69399	Unlisted procedure, external ear
69799	Unlisted procedure, middle ear
69949	Unlisted procedure, inner ear
69979	Unlisted procedure, temporal bone, middle fossa approach

100-4, 4, 200, 3.1
Billing for IMRT Planning and Delivery

Effective for services furnished on or after April 1, 2002, HCPCS codes G0174 (IMRT delivery) and G0178 (IMRT planning) are no longer valid codes. HCPCS code G0174 has been replaced with CPT codes 77418 and 0073T for IMRT delivery and HCPCS code G0178 with CPT code 77301. Therefore, hospitals must use CPT codes 77418 or 0073T for IMRT delivery and CPT code 77301 for IMRT planning. Any of the CPT codes 77401 through 77416 or 77418 may be reported on the same day as long as the services are furnished at separate treatment sessions. In these cases, modifier -59 must be appended to the appropriate codes. Additionally, in the context of billing 77301, regardless of the same or different dates of service, CPT codes 77014, 77280-77295, 77305-77321, 77331, 77336, and 77370 may only be billed in addition to 77301 if they are not provided as part of developing the IMRT treatment plan.

- 7730   Intensity modulated radiotherapy plan, including dose-volume histograms for target and critical structure partial tolerance specifications
- 77418   Intensity modulated treatment delivery, single or multiple fields/arcs, via narrow spatially and temporally modulated beams, binary, dynamic MLC, per treatment session
- 0073T   Compensator-based beam modulation treatment delivery of inverse planned treatment using three or more high resolution (milled or cast) compensator convergent beam modulated fields, per treatment session

100-4, 4, 200.3.2
Additional Billing Instructions for IMRT Planning

Payment for the services identified by CPT codes 77014, 77280-77295, 77305-77321, 77331, 77336, and 77370 is included in the APC payment for IMRT planning when these services are performed as part of developing an IMRT plan that is reported using CPT code 77301. Under those circumstances, these codes should not be billed in addition to CPT code 77301 for IMRT planning.

100-4, 4, 200.3.3
Billing for Multi-Source Photon (Cobalt 60-Based) Stereotactic

Radiosurgery (SRS) Planning and Delivery

Effective for services furnished on or after January 1, 2006, hospitals must bill for multisource photon (cobalt 60-based) SRS planning using existing CPT codes that most accurately describe the service furnished, and HCPCS code G0243 for the delivery. For CY 2007, HCPCS code G0243 is no longer be reportable under the hospital OPPS because the code has been deleted and replaced with CPT code 77371, effective January 1, 2007.

- 77371   Radiation treatment delivery, stereotactic radiosurgery (SRS) (complete course of treatment of cerebral lesion[s] consisting of 1 session); multisource Cobalt 60 based.

Payment for CPT code 20660 is included in CPT code 77371; therefore, hospitals should not report 20660 separately.

100-4, 4, 200.4
Billing for Amniotic Membrane

Hospitals should report HCPCS code V2790 (Amniotic membrane for surgical reconstruction, per procedure) to report amniotic membrane tissue when the tissue is used. A specific procedure code associated with use of amniotic membrane tissue is CPT code 65780 (Ocular surface reconstruction; amniotic membrane transplantation).

Payment for the amniotic membrane tissue is packaged into payment for CPT code 65780 or other procedures with which the amniotic membrane is used.

100-4, 4, 200.5
Billing and Payment for Cardiac Rehabilitation Services

The National Coverage Determination for cardiac rehabilitation programs requires that programs must be comprehensive and to be comprehensive they must include a medical evaluation, a program to modify cardiac risk factors (e.g., nutritional counseling), prescribed exercise, education, and counseling. See the National Coverage Determination (NCD) Manual, Pub. 100-03, section 20.10, for more information. A cardiac rehabilitation session may include more than one aspect of the comprehensive program. For CY 2008, hospitals will continue to use CPT code 93797 (Physician services for outpatient cardiac rehabilitation, without continuous ECG monitoring (per session)) and CPT code 93798 (Physician services for outpatient cardiac rehabilitation, with continuous ECG monitoring (per session)) to report cardiac rehabilitation services.

However, effective for dates of service on or after January 1, 2008, hospitals may report more than one unit of HCPCS code 93797 or 97398 for a date of service if more than one cardiac rehabilitation session lasting at least 1 hour each is provided on the same day.

In order to report more than one session for a given date of service, each session must last a minimum of 60 minutes. For example, if the cardiac rehabilitation services provided on a given day total 1 hour and 50 minutes, then only one session should be billed to report the cardiac rehabilitation services provided on that day.

100-4, 4, 200.6
Billing and Payment for Alcohol and/or Substance Abuse Assessment and Intervention Services

For CY 2008, the CPT Editorial Panel has created two new Category I CPT codes for reporting alcohol and/or substance abuse screening and intervention services. They are CPT code 99408 (Alcohol and/or substance (other than tobacco) abuse structured screening (e.g., AUDIT, DAST), and brief intervention (SBI) services; 15 to 30 minutes); and CPT code 99409 (Alcohol and/or substance (other than tobacco) abuse structured screening (e.g., AUDIT, DAST), and brief intervention (SBI) services; greater than 30 minutes). However, screening services are not covered by Medicare without specific statutory authority, such as has been provided for mammography, diabetes, and colorectal cancer screening. Therefore, beginning January 1, 2008, the OPPS recognizes two parallel G-codes (HCPCS codes G0396 and G0397) to allow for appropriate reporting and payment of alcohol and substance abuse structured assessment and intervention services that are not provided as screening services, but that are performed in the context of the diagnosis or treatment of illness or injury.

Contractors shall make payment under the OPPS for HCPCS code G0396 (Alcohol and/or substance (other than tobacco) abuse structured assessment (e.g., AUDIT, DAST) and brief intervention, 15 to 30 minutes) and HCPCS code G0397, (Alcohol and/or substance(other than tobacco) abuse structured assessment (e.g., AUDIT, DAST) and intervention greater than 30 minutes), only when reasonable and necessary (i.e., when the service is provided to evaluate patients with signs/symptoms of illness or injury) as per section 1862(a)(1)(A) of the Act.

HCPCS codes G0396 and G0397 are to be used for structured alcohol and/or substance (other than tobacco) abuse assessment and intervention services that are distinct from other clinic and emergency department visit services performed during the same encounter. Hospital resources expended performing services described by HCPCS codes G0396 and G0397 may not be counted as resources for determining the level of a visit service and vice versa (i.e., hospitals may not double count the same facility resources in order to reach a higher level clinic or emergency department visit). However, alcohol and/or substance structured assessment or intervention services lasting less than 15 minutes should not be reported using these HCPCS codes, but the hospital resources expended should be included in determining the level of the visit service reported.

100-4, 4, 200.7.1
Cardiac Echocardiography Without Contrast
Hospitals are instructed to bill for echocardiograms without contrast in accordance with the CPT code descriptors and guidelines associated with the applicable Level I CPT code(s) (93303-93350).

100-4, 4, 230.2
Coding and Payment for Drug Administration
A. Overview
Drug administration services furnished under the Hospital Outpatient Prospective Payment System (OPPS) during CY 2005 were reported using CPT codes 90780, 90781, and 96400-96459.

Effective January 1, 2006, some of these CPT codes were replaced with more detailed CPT codes incorporating specific procedural concepts, as defined and described by the CPT manual, such as initial, concurrent, and sequential.

Hospitals are instructed to use the full set of CPT codes, including those codes referencing concepts of initial, concurrent, and sequential, to bill for drug administration services furnished in the hospital outpatient department beginning January 1, 2007. In addition, hospitals are instructed to continue billing the HCPCS codes that most accurately describe the service(s) provided.

Hospitals are reminded to bill a separate Evaluation and Management code (with modifier 25) only if a significant, separately identifiable E/M service is performed in the same encounter with OPPS drug administration services.

B. Billing for Infusions and Injections
In CY 2007, hospitals are instructed to use the full set of drug administration CPT codes (90760-90779; 96401-96549) when billing for drug administration services provided in the hospital outpatient department. In addition, hospitals are to continue to bill HCPCS code C8957 (Intravenous infusion for therapy/diagnosis; initiation of prolonged infusion (more than 8 hours), requiring use of portable or implantable pump) when appropriate.

Hospitals are expected to report all drug administration CPT codes in a manner consistent with their descriptors, CPT instructions, and correct coding principles. Hospitals should note the conceptual changes between CY 2006 drug administration codes effective under the OPPS and the CY 2007 CPT codes in order to ensure accurate billing under the OPPS.

Medicare's general policy regarding physician supervision within hospital outpatient departments meets the physician supervision requirements for use of CPT codes 90760- 90779, 96401-96549. (Reference: Medicare Benefit Policy Manual, Pub.100-02, Chapter 6, Sec.20.4.1.)

C. Payments For Drug Administration Services
For CY 2007, OPPS drug administration APCs have been restructured resulting in a sixlevel hierarchy where active HCPCS codes have been assigned according to their clinical coherence and resource use. Contrary to the CY 2006 payment structure that bundled payment for several instances of a type of service (non-chemotherapy, chemotherapy by infusion, non-infusion chemotherapy) into a per-encounter APC payment, the CY 2007 structure provides a separate APC payment for each reported unit of a separately payable HCPCS code.

Hospitals should note that the transition to the full set of CPT drug administration codes provides for conceptual differences when reporting, such as those noted below.

- In CY 2006, hospitals were instructed to bill for the first hour (and any additional hours) by each type of infusion service (non-chemotherapy, chemotherapy by infusion, non-infusion chemotherapy). In CY 2007, the first hour concept no longer exists. CY 2007 CPT codes allow for only one initial service per encounter, for each vascular access site, no matter how many types of infusion services are provided; however, hospitals will receive an APC payment for the initial service and separate APC payment(s) for additional hours of infusion or other drug administration services provided that are separately payable .

- In CY 2006, hospitals providing infusion services of different types (nonchemotherapy, chemotherapy by infusion, non-infusion chemotherapy) received payment for the associated per-encounter infusion APC even if these infusions occurred during the same time period. In CY 2007, CPT instructions allow reporting of only one initial drug administration service, including infusion services, per encounter for each distinct vascular access site, with other services through the same vascular access site being reported via the sequential, concurrent or additional hour codes.

(NOTE: This list provides a brief overview of a limited number of the conceptual changes between CY 2006 OPPS drug administration codes and CY 2007 OPPS drug administration codes - this list is not comprehensive and does not include all items hospitals will need to consider during this transition) For CY 2007 APC payment rates, refer to Addendum B on the CMS Web site at http://www.cms.hhs.gov/HospitalOutpatientPPS/.

D. Infusions Started Outside the Hospital
Hospitals may receive Medicare beneficiaries for outpatient services who are in the process of receiving an infusion at their time of arrival at the hospital (e.g. a patient who arrives via ambulance with an ongoing intravenous infusion initiated by paramedics during transport). Hospitals are reminded to bill for all services provided using the HCPCS code(s) that most accurately describe the service(s) they provided. This includes hospitals reporting an initial hour of infusion, even if the hospital did not initiate the infusion, and additional HCPCS codes for additional or sequential infusion services if needed.

100-4, 4, 231.4
Billing for Split Unit of Blood
HCPCS code P9011 was created to identify situations where one unit of blood or a blood product is split and some portion of the unit is transfused to one patient and the other portions are transfused to other patients or to the same patient at other times. When a patient receives a transfusion of a split unit of blood or blood product, OPPS providers should bill P9011 for the blood product transfused, as well as CPT 86985 (Splitting, blood products) for each splitting procedure performed to prepare the blood product for a specific patient.

Providers should bill split units of packed red cells and whole blood using Revenue Code 389 (Other blood), and should not use Revenue Codes 381 (Packed red cells) or 382 (Whole blood). Providers should bill split units of other blood products using the applicable revenue codes for the blood product type, such as 383 (Plasma) or 384 (Platelets), rather than 389. Reporting revenue codes according to these specifications will ensure the Medicare beneficiary's blood deductible is applied correctly.

EXAMPLE: OPPS provider splits off a 100cc aliquot from a 250 cc unit of leukocytereduced red blood cells for a transfusion to Patient X. The hospital then splits off an 80cc aliquot of the remaining unit for a transfusion to Patient Y. At a later time, the remaining 70cc from the unit is transfused to Patient Z.

In billing for the services for Patient X and Patient Y, the OPPS provider should report the charges by billing P9011 and 86985 in addition to the CPT code for the transfusion service, because a specific splitting service was required to prepare a split unit for transfusion to each of those patients. However, the OPPS provider should report only P9011 and the CPT code for the transfusion service for Patient Z because no additional splitting was necessary to prepare the split unit for transfusion to Patient Z. The OPPS provider should bill Revenue Code 0389 for each split unit of the leukocyte-reduced red blood cells that was transfused.

100-4, 4, 231.9
Billing for Pheresis and Apheresis Services
Apheresis/pheresis services are billed on a per visit basis and not on a per unit basis. OPPS providers should report the charge for an Evaluation and Management (E&M) visit only if there is a separately identifiable E&M service performed which extends beyond the evaluation and management portion of a typical apheresis/pheresis service. If the OPPS provider is billing an E&M visit code in addition to the apheresis/pheresis service, it may be appropriate to use the HCPCS modifier -25.

100-4, 4, 240
Inpatient Part B Hospital Services
Inpatient Part B services which are paid under OPPS include:

- Diagnostic x-ray tests, and other diagnostic tests (excluding clinical diagnostic laboratory tests);
- X-ray, radium, and radioactive isotope therapy, including materials and services of technicians;
- Surgical dressings applied during an encounter at the hospital and splints, casts, and other devices used for reduction of fractures and dislocations (splints and casts, etc., include dental splints);
- Implantable prosthetic devices;
- Hepatitis B vaccine and its administration, and certain preventive screening services (pelvic exams, screening sigmoidoscopies, screening colonoscopies, bone mass measurements, and prostate screening.)
- Bone Mass measurements;
- Prostate screening;
- Immunosuppressive drugs;
- Oral anti-cancer drugs;
- Oral drug prescribed for use as an acute anti-emetic used as part of an anti-cancer chemotherapeutic regimen; and
- Epoetin Alfa (EPO)

When a hospital that is not paid under the OPPS furnishes an implantable prosthetic device that meets the criteria for coverage in Medicare Benefits Policy Manual, Pub.100-02, Chapter 6, Sec.10 to an inpatient who has coverage under Part B, payment for the implantable prosthetic device is made under the payment mechanism that applies to other hospital outpatient services (e.g. reasonable cost, all inclusive rate, waiver).

When a hospital that is paid under the OPPS furnishes an implantable prosthetic device to an inpatient who has coverage under Part B, but who does not have coverage of inpatient services on the date that the implanted prosthetic device is furnished, the hospital should report new HCPCS code, C9899, Implanted Prosthetic Device, Payable Only for Inpatients who do not Have Inpatient Coverage, that will be effective for services furnished on or after January 1, 2009. This code may be reported only on claims with TOB 12X when the prosthetic device is implanted on a day on which the beneficiary does not have coverage of the hospital inpatient services he or she is receiving. The line containing this new code will be rejected if it is reported on a claim that is not a TOB 12X or if it is reported with a line item date of service on which the beneficiary has coverage of inpatient hospital services. By reporting C9899, the hospital is reporting that all of the criteria for payment under Part B are met as specified in the Medicare Benefits Policy Manual, Pub.100-02, Chapter 6, Sec.10, and that the item meets all Medicare criteria for coverage as an implantable prosthetic device as defined in that section.

Medicare contractors shall first determine that the item furnished meets the Medicare criteria for coverage as an implantable prosthetic device as specified in the Medicare Benefits Policy Manual, Pub. 100-02, Chapter 6, Sec.10. If the item does not meet the criteria for coverage as an implantable prosthetic device, the contractor shall deny payment on the basis that the item is outside the scope of the benefits for which there is coverage for Part B inpatients. The beneficiary is liable for the charges for the noncovered item when the item does not meet the criteria for coverage as an implanted prosthetic device as specified in the Medicare Benefits Policy Manual, Pub.100-02, Chapter 6, Sec.10.

If the contractor determines that the device is covered, the contractor shall determine if the device has pass through status under the OPPS. If so, the contractor shall establish the payment amount for the device at the product of the charge for the device and the hospital specific cost to charge ratio. Where the device does not have pass through status under the OPPS, the contractor shall establish the payment amount for the device at the amount for a comparable device in the DMEPOS fee schedule where there is such an amount. Payment under the DMEPOS fee schedule is made at the lesser of charges or the fee schedule amount and therefore if there is a fee for the specific item on the DMEPOS fee schedule, the payment amount for the item will be set at the lesser of the actual charges or the DMEPOS fee schedule amount. Where the item does not have pass through payment status and where there is no amount for a comparable device in the DMEPOS fee schedule, the contractor shall establish a payment amount that is specific to the particular implanted prosthetic device for the applicable calendar year. This amount (less applicable unpaid deductible and coinsurance) will be paid for that specific device for services furnished in the applicable calendar year unless the actual charge for the item is less than the established amount). Where the actual charge is less than the established amount, the contractor will pay the actual charge for the item (less applicable unpaid deductible and coinsurance).

In setting a contractor established payment rate for the specific device, the contractor takes into account the cost information available at the time the payment rate is established. This information may include, but is not limited to, the amount of device cost that would be removed from an applicable APC payment for implantation of the device if the provider received a device without cost or a full credit for the cost of the device.

If the contractor chooses to use this amount, see www.cms.hhs.gov/HospitalOutpatientPPS/ for the amount of reduction to the APC payment that would apply in these cases. From the OPPS webpage, select "Device, Radiolabeled Product, and Procedure Edits" from the list on the left side of the page. Open the file "Procedure to Device edits" to determine the HCPCS code that best describes the procedure in which the device would be used. Then identify the APC to which that procedure code maps from the most recent Addenda B on the OPPS webpage and open the file "FB/FC Modifier Procedures and Devices". Select the applicable year's file of APCs subject to full and partial credit reductions (for example: CY 2008 APCs Subject to Full and Partial Credit Reduction Policy"). Select the "Full offset reduction amount" that pertains to the APC that is most applicable to the device described by C9899. It would be reasonable to set this amount as a payment for a device furnished to a Part B inpatient.

For example, if C9899 is reporting insertion of a single chamber pacemaker (C1786 or equivalent narrative description on the claim in "remarks") the file of procedure to device edits shows that a single chamber pacemaker is the dominant device for APC 0089 (APC 0089 is for insertion of both pacemaker and electrodes and therefore would not apply if electrodes are not also billed). The table of offset reduction amounts for CY 2008 shows that the estimated cost of a single chamber pacemaker for APC 0090 is $4881.77. It would therefore be reasonable for the contractor/MAC to set the payment rate for a single chamber pacemaker furnished to a Part B inpatient to $4881.77. In this case the coinsurance would be $936.75 (20 percent of $4881.77, which is less than the inpatient deductible).

The beneficiary coinsurance is 20 percent of the payment amount for the device (i.e. the pass through payment amount, the DMEPOS fee schedule amount, the contractor established amount, or the actual charge if less than the DMEPOS fee schedule amount or the contractor established amount for the specific device), not to exceed the Medicare inpatient deductible that is applicable to the year in which the implanted prosthetic device is furnished.

Inpatient Part B services paid under other payment methods include:

- Clinical diagnostic laboratory tests, prosthetic devices other than implantable ones and other than dental which replace all or part of an internal body organ (including contiguous tissue), or all or part of the function of a permanently inoperative or malfunctioning internal body organ, including replacement or repairs of such devices;
- Leg, arm, back and neck braces; trusses and artificial legs; arms and eyes including adjustments, repairs, and replacements required because of breakage, wear, loss, or a change in the patient's physical condition; take home surgical dressings; outpatient physical therapy; outpatient occupational therapy; and outpatient speech-language pathology services;
- Ambulance services;
- Screening pap smears, screening colorectal tests, and screening mammography;
- Influenza virus vaccine and its administration, pneumococcal vaccine and its administration;
- Diabetes self-management training;
- Hemophilia clotting factors for hemophilia patients competent to use these factors without supervision.

See Chapter 6 of the Medicare Benefit Policy Manual for a discussion of the circumstances under which the above services may be covered as Part B Inpatient services.

100-4, 4, 250.3.2

Physician Rendering Anesthesia in a Hospital Outpatient Setting

When a medically necessary anesthesia service is furnished within a HPSA area by a physician, a HPSA bonus is payable. In addition to using the PC/TC indicator on the CORF extract of the MPFS Summary File to identify HPSA services, pay physicians the HPSA bonus when CPT codes 00100 through 01999 are billed with the following modifiers: QY, QK, AA, or GC and "QB" or "QU" in revenue code 963. Modifier QB or QU must be submitted to receive payment of the HPSA bonus for claims with dates of service prior to January 01, 2006. Effective for claims with dates of service on or after January 01, 2006, the modifier AQ, physician providing a service in a health professional shortage area, may be required to receive the HPSA bonus. Refer to 250.2.2 of this chapter for more information on when modifier AQ is required.

The modifiers signify that a physician performed an anesthesia service. Using the Anesthesia File (See Section above) the physician service will be 115 percent times the payment amount to be paid to a CAH on Method II payment plus 10 percent HPSA bonus payment.

Anesthesiology modifiers:

AA	anesthesia services performed personally by anesthesiologist.
GC	service performed, in part, by a resident under the direction of a teaching physician.
QK	medical direction of two, three, or four concurrent anesthesia procedures involving qualified individuals.
QY	medical direction of one CRNA by an anesthesiologist.

Modifiers AA and GC result in physician payment at 80% of the allowed amount. Modifiers QK and QY result in physician payment at 50% of the allowed amount.

Data elements needed to calculate payment:

- HCPCS plus Modifier,
- Base Units,
- Time units, based on standard 15 minute intervals,
- locality specific anesthesia Conversion factor, and
- Allowed amount minus applicable deductions and coinsurance amount.

Formula 1: Calculate payment for a physician performing anesthesia alone

HCPCS = xxxxx

Modifier = AA

Base Units = 4

Anesthesia Time is 60 minutes. Anesthesia time units = 4 (60/15)

Sum of Base Units plus Time Units = 4 + 4 = 8

Locality specific Anesthesia conversion factor = $17.00 (varies by localities)

Coinsurance = 20%

Example 1: Physician personally performs the anesthesia case

Base Units plus time units - 4+4=8

Total units multiplied by the anesthesia conversion factor times .80

8 x $17= ($136.00 - (deductible*) x .80 = $108.80

Payment amount times 115 percent for the CAH method II payment.

$108.80 x 1.15 = $125.12 (Payment amount)

$125.12 x .10 = $12.51 (HPSA bonus payment)

*Assume the Part B deductible has already been met for the calendar year

Formula 2: Calculate the payment for the physician's medical direction service when the physician directs two concurrent cases involving CRNAs. The medical direction allowance is 50% of the allowance for the anesthesia service personally performed by the physician.

HCPCS = xxxxx

Modifier = QK

Base Units = 4

Time Units 60/15=4

Sum of base units plus time units = 8

Locality specific anesthesia conversion factor = $17(varies by localities)

Coinsurance = 20 %

(Allowed amount adjusted for applicable deductions and coinsurance and to reflect payment percentage for medical direction).

Example 2: Physician medically directs two concurrent cases involving CRNAs

Base units plus time - 4+4=8

Total units multiplied by the anesthesia conversion factor times. 50 equal allowed amount minus any remaining deductible

Current Procedural Coding Expert

Appendix G — Pub 100 References

8 x $17 = $136 x .50 = $68.00 -(deductible*) = $68.00

Allowed amount Times 80 percent times 1.15

$68.00 x .80 = $54.40 x 1.15 = 62.56 (Payment amount)

$62.56 x .10 = $6.26 (HPSA bonus payment)

*Assume the deductible has already been met for the calendar year.

100-4, 4, 290.5.1
Billing and Payment for Observation Services Beginning January 1, 2008

Observation services are reported using HCPCS code G0378 (Hospital observation service, per hour). Beginning January 1, 2008, HCPCS code G0378 for hourly observation services is assigned status indicator N, signifying that its payment is always packaged. No separate payment is made for observation services reported with HCPCS code G0378, and APC 0339 is deleted as of January 1, 2008. In most circumstances, observation services are supportive and ancillary to the other services provided to a patient. In certain circumstances when observation care is billed in conjunction with a high level clinic visit (Level 5), high level Type A emergency department visit (Level 4 or 5), high level Type B emergency department visit (Level 5), critical care services, or a direct referral as an integral part of a patient's extended encounter of care, payment may be made for the entire extended care encounter through one of two composite APCs when certain criteria are met. For information about payment for extended assessment and management composite APCs, see Sec.10.2.1 (Composite APCs) of this chapter.

APC 8002 (Level I Extended Assessment and Management Composite) describes an encounter for care provided to a patient that includes a high level (Level 5) clinic visit or direct referral for observation in conjunction with observation services of substantial duration (8 or more hours). APC 8003 (Level II Extended Assessment and Management Composite) describes an encounter for care provided to a patient that includes a high level (Level 4 or 5) emergency department visit or critical care services in conjunction with observation services of substantial duration. Beginning January 1, 2009, APC 8003 also includes high level (Level 5) Type B emergency department visits. There is no limitation on diagnosis for payment of these composite APCs; however, composite APC payment will not be made when observation services are reported in association with a surgical procedure (T status procedure) or the hours of observation care reported are less than 8. The I/OCE evaluates every claim received to determine if payment through a composite APC is appropriate. If payment through a composite APC is inappropriate, the I/OCE, in conjunction with the Pricer, determines the appropriate status indicator, APC, and payment for every code on a claim.

All of the following requirements must be met in order for a hospital to receive an APC payment for an extended assessment and management composite APC:

1. Observation Time
    a. Observation time must be documented in the medical record.
    b. Hospital billing for observation services begins at the clock time documented in the patient's medical record, which coincides with the time that observation services are initiated in accordance with a physician's order for observation services.
    c. A beneficiary's time receiving observation services (and hospital billing) ends when all clinical or medical interventions have been completed, including follow-up care furnished by hospital staff and physicians that may take place after a physician has ordered the patient be released or admitted as an inpatient.
    d. The number of units reported with HCPCS code G0378 must equal or exceed 8 hours.
2. Additional Hospital Services
    a. The claim for observation services must include one of the following services in addition to the reported observation services. The additional services listed below must have a line item date of service on the same day or the day before the date reported for observation:
        - A Type A or B emergency department visit (CPT codes 99284 or 99285 or HCPCS code G0384); or
        - A clinic visit (CPT code 99205 or 99215); or
        - Critical care (CPT code 99291); or
        - Direct referral for observation care reported with HCPCS code G0379 (APC 0604) must be reported on the same date of service as the date reported for observation services.
    b. No procedure with a T status indicator can be reported on the same day or day before observation care is provided.
3. Physician Evaluation
    a. The beneficiary must be in the care of a physician during the period of observation, as documented in the medical record by outpatient registration, discharge, and other appropriate progress notes that are timed, written, and signed by the physician.
    b. he medical record must include documentation that the physician explicitly assessed patient risk to determine that the beneficiary would benefit from observation care.

Criteria 1 and 3 related to observation care beginning and ending time and physician evaluation apply regardless of whether the hospital believes that the criteria will be met for payment of the extended encounter through extended assessment and management composite payment.

Only visits, critical care and observation services that are billed on a 13X bill type may be considered for a composite APC payment.

Non-repetitive services provided on the same day as either direct referral for observation care or observation services must be reported on the same claim because the OCE claim-by-claim logic cannot function properly unless all services related to the episode of observation care, including hospital clinic visits, emergency department visits, critical care services, and T status procedures, are reported on the same claim. Additional guidance can be found in chapter 1, section 50.2.2 of this manual.

If a claim for services provided during an extended assessment and management encounter including observation care does not meet all of the requirements listed above, then the usual APC logic will apply to separately payable items and services on the claim; the special logic for direct admission will apply, and payment for the observation care will be packaged into payments for other separately payable services provided to the beneficiary in the same encounter.

100-4, 4, 300
Medical Nutrition Therapy (MNT) Services

Section 105 of the Medicare, Medicaid, and SCHIP Benefits Improvement and Protection Act of 2000 (BIPA) permits Medicare coverage of Medical Nutrition Therapy (MNT) services when furnished by a registered dietitian or nutrition professional meeting certain requirements. The benefit is available for beneficiaries with diabetes or renal disease, when referral is made by a physician as defined in Sec.1861(r)(l) of the Act. It also allows registered dietitians and nutrition professionals to receive direct Medicare reimbursement for the first time. The effective date of this provision is January 1, 2002.

The benefit consists of an initial visit for an assessment; follow-up visits for interventions; and reassessments as necessary during the 12-month period beginning with the initial assessment ("episode of care") to assure compliance with the dietary plan. Effective October 1, 2002, basic coverage of MNT for the first year a beneficiary receives MNT with either a diagnosis of renal disease or diabetes as defined at 42 CFR, 410.130 is 3 hours. Also effective October 1, 2002, basic coverage in subsequent years for renal disease is 2 hours.

For the purposes of this benefit, renal disease means chronic renal insufficiency or the medical condition of a beneficiary who has been discharged from the hospital after a successful renal transplant within the last 6 months. Chronic renal insufficiency means a reduction in renal function not severe enough to require dialysis or transplantation (glomerular filtration rate (GFR) 13-50 ml/min/1.73m−ð). Effective January 1, 2004, CMS updated the definition of diabetes to be as follows: Diabetes is defined as diabetes mellitus, a condition of abnormal glucose metabolism diagnosed using the following criteria: a fasting blood sugar greater than or equal to 126 mg/dL on two different occasions; a 2 hour post-glucose challenge greater than or equal to 200 mg/dL on 2 different occasions; or a random glucose test over 200 mg/dL for a person with symptoms of uncontrolled diabetes.

The MNT benefit is a completely separate benefit from the diabetes self-management training (DSMT) benefit. CMS had originally planned to limit how much of both benefits a beneficiary might receive in the same time period. However, the national coverage decision, published May 1, 2002, allows a beneficiary to receive the full amount of both benefits in the same period. Therefore, a beneficiary can receive the full 10 hours of initial DSMT and the full 3 hours of MNT. However, providers are not allowed to bill for both DSMT and MNT on the same date of service for the same beneficiary

100-4, 5, 10
Part B Outpatient Rehabilitation and Comprehensive Outpatient Rehabilitation Facility (CORF) Services - General

Language in this section is defined or described in Pub. 100-02, chapter 15, sections 220 and 230.

Section 4541(a)(2) of the Balanced Budget Act (BBA) (P.L. 105-33), which added Sec.1834(k)(5) to the Social Security Act (the Act), required that all claims for outpatient rehabilitation, certain audiology services and comprehensive outpatient rehabilitation facility (CORF) services, be reported using a uniform coding system. The CMS chose HCPCS (Healthcare Common Procedure Coding System) as the coding system to be used for the reporting of these services. This coding requirement is effective for all claims for outpatient rehabilitation services including certain audiology services and CORF services submitted on or after April 1, 1998.

The BBA also required payment under a prospective payment system for outpatient rehabilitation services including audiology and CORF services. Effective for claims with dates of service on or after January 1, 1999, the Medicare Physician Fee Schedule (MPFS) became the method of payment for outpatient therapy services furnished by:

- Comprehensive outpatient rehabilitation facilities (CORFs);
- Outpatient physical therapy providers (OPTs);
- Other rehabilitation facilities (ORFs);
- Hospitals (to outpatients and inpatients who are not in a covered Part A stay);
- Skilled nursing facilities (SNFs) (to residents not in a covered Part A stay and to nonresidents who receive outpatient rehabilitation services from the SNF); and
- Home health agencies (HHAs) (to individuals who are not homebound or otherwise are not receiving services under a home health plan of care (POC)).

NOTE: No provider or supplier other than the SNF will be paid for therapy services during the time the beneficiary is in a covered SNF Part A stay. For information regarding SNF consolidated billing see chapter 6, section 10 of this manual.

Similarly, under the HH prospective payment system, HHAs are responsible to provide, either directly or under arrangements, all outpatient rehabilitation therapy services to beneficiaries receiving services under a home health POC. No other provider or supplier will be paid for these services during the time the beneficiary is in a covered Part A stay. For information regarding HH consolidated billing see chapter10, section 20 of this manual. Section 143 of the Medicare Improvements for Patients and Provider's Act of 2008 (MIPPA) authorizes the Centers for Medicare & Medicaid Services (CMS) to enroll speech-language pathologists (SLP) as suppliers of Medicare services and for SLPs to begin billing Medicare for outpatient speech-language pathology services furnished in private practice beginning July 1, 2009. Enrollment will allow SLPs in private practice to bill Medicare and receive direct payment for their services. Previously,

Appendix G — Pub 100 References

the Medicare program could only pay SLP services if an institution, physician or nonphysician practitioner billed them.

In Chapter 23, as part of the CY 2009 Medicare Physician Fee Schedule Database, the descriptor for PC/TC indicator "7", as applied to certain HCPCS/CPT codes, is described as specific to the services of privately practicing therapists. Payment may not be made if the service is provided to either a hospital outpatient or a hospital inpatient by a physical therapist, occupational therapist, or speech-language pathologist in private practice.

The MPFS is used as a method of payment for outpatient rehabilitation services furnished under arrangement with any of these providers.

In addition, the MPFS is used as the payment system for audiology and CORF services identified by the HCPCS codes in Sec.20. Assignment is mandatory.

The Medicare allowed charge for the services is the lower of the actual charge or the MPFS amount. The Medicare payment for the services is 80 percent of the allowed charge after the Part B deductible is met. Coinsurance is made at 20 percent of the lower of the actual charge or the MPFS amount. The general coinsurance rule (20 percent of the actual charges) does not apply when making payment under the MPFS. This is a final payment.

The MPFS does not apply to outpatient rehabilitation services furnished by critical access hospitals (CAHs). CAHs are to be paid on a reasonable cost basis.

Contractors process outpatient rehabilitation claims from hospitals, including CAHs, SNFs, HHAs, CORFs, outpatient rehabilitation agencies, and outpatient physical therapy providers for which they have received a tie in notice from the RO. These provider types submit their claims to the contractors using the 837 Institutional electronic claim format or the UB-04 paper form when permissible. Contractors also process claims from physicians, certain nonphysician practitioners (NPPs), therapists in private practices (TPPs), (which are limited to physical and occupational therapists, and speech-language pathologists in private practices), and physician-directed clinics that bill for services furnished incident to a physician's service (see chapter 15 in Pub. 100-02, Medicare Benefit Policy Manual for a definition of "incident to"). These provider types submit their claims to the contractor using the 837 Professional electronic claim format or the CMS-1500 paper form when permissible.

There are different fee rates for nonfacility and facility services. Chapter 23 describes the differences in these two rates. (See fields 28 and 29 of the record therein described).

Facility rates apply to professional services performed in a facility other than the professional's office. Nonfacility rates apply when the service is performed in the professional's office. The nonfacility rate (that is paid when the provider performs the services in its own facility) accommodates overhead and indirect expenses the provider incurs by operating its own facility. Thus it is somewhat higher than the facility rate.

Contractors pay the nonfacility rate on institutional claims for services performed in the provider's facility. Contractors may pay professional claims using the facility or nonfacility rate depending upon where the service is performed (place of service on the claim), and the provider specialty.

Contractors pay the codes in Sec.20 under the MPFS on professional claims regardless of whether they may be considered rehabilitation services. However, contractors must use this list for institutional claims to determine whether to pay under outpatient rehabilitation rules or whether payment rules for other types of service may apply, e.g., OPPS for hospitals, reasonable costs for CAHs.

Note that because a service is considered an outpatient rehabilitation service does not automatically imply payment for that service. Additional criteria, including coverage, plan of care and physician certification must also be met. These criteria are described in Pub. 100-02, Medicare Benefit Policy Manual, chapters 1 and 15.

Payment for rehabilitation services provided to Part A inpatients of hospitals or SNFs is included in the respective PPS rate. Also, for SNFs (but not hospitals), if the beneficiary has Part B, but not Part A coverage (e.g., Part A benefits are exhausted), the SNF must bill for any rehabilitation service (but not audiologic function services).

Audiologists in private practice using a professional claim may bill directly for services rendered to Part B Medicare entitled beneficiaries residing in a SNF, but not in a SNF Part A covered stay. Payment is made based on the MPFS, whether on an institutional or professional claim. For beneficiaries not in a covered Part A SNF stay, who are sometimes referred to as beneficiaries in a Part B SNF stay, audiologic function tests are payable under Part B when billed by the SNF on an institutional claim as type of bill 22X, or when billed directly by the provider or supplier of the service on a professional claim. For tests that include both a professional component and technical component, the SNF may elect to bill the technical component on an institutional claim, but is not required to bill the service. (The professional component of a service is the direct patient care provided by the physician or audiologist, e.g., the interpretation of a test when the test is valued by the American Medical Association to include interpretation in the professional component.)

Payment for rehabilitation therapy services provided by home health agencies under a home health plan of care is included in the home health PPS rate. HHAs may submit bill type 34X and be paid under the MPFS if there are no home health services billed under a home health plan of care at the same time, and there is a valid rehabilitation POC (e.g., the patient is not homebound).

An institutional employer (other than a SNF) of the TPPs, or physician performing outpatient services, (e.g., hospital, CORF, etc.), or a clinic billing on behalf of the physician or therapist may bill the contractor on a professional claim.

The MPFS is the basis of payment for outpatient rehabilitation services furnished by TPPs, physicians, and certain nonphysician practitioners or for diagnostic tests provided incident to the services of such physicians or nonphysician practitioners. (See Pub. 100-02, Medicare Benefit Policy Manual, chapter 15, for a definition of "incident to, therapist, therapy and related instructions.") Such services are billed to the contractor on the professional claim format. Assignment is mandatory.

The following table identifies the provider and supplier types, and identifies which claim format they may use to submit bills to the contractor.

"Provider/Supplier Service" Type	Format	Bill Type	Comment
Inpatient hospital Part A	Institutional	11X	Included in PPS
Inpatient SNF Part A	Institutional	21X	Included in PPS
Inpatient hospital Part B	Institutional	12X	Hospital may obtain services under arrangements and bill, or rendering provider may bill.
Inpatient SNF Part B except for audiology function tests.	Institutional	22X	SNF must provide and bill, or obtain under arrangements and bill.
Inpatient SNF Part B audiology function tests only.	Institutional	22X	SNF may bill the contractor using the institutional claim format or the supplier of services may bill the contractor using the professional claim form.
Outpatient hospital	Institutional	13X	Hospital may provide and bill or obtain under arrangements and bill, or rendering provider may bill.
Outpatient SNF	Institutional	23X	SNF must provide and bill or obtain under arrangements and bill.
HHA billing for services rendered under a Part A or Part B home health plan of care.	Institutional	32X	Service is included in PPS rate. CMS determines whether payment is from Part A or Part B trust fund.
HHA billing for services not rendered under a Part A or Part B home health plan of care, but rendered under a therapy plan of care.	Institutional	34X	Service not under home health plan of care.
Other Rehabilitation Facility (ORF)	Institutional	74X	Paid MPFS for outpatient rehabilitation services effective January 1, 1999, and all other services except drugs effective July 1, 2000. Starting April 1, 2002, drugs are paid 95% of the AWP. For claims with dates of service on or after July 1, 2003, drugs and biologicals do not apply in an OPT setting. Therefore, FIs are to advise their OPTs not to bill for them.
Comprehensive Outpatient Rehabilitation Facility (CORF)	Institutional	75X	Paid MPFS for outpatient rehabilitation services effective January 1, 1999, and all other services except drugs effective July 1, 2000. Starting April 1, 2002, drugs are paid 95% of the AWP.
Physician, NPPs, TPPs, and, for diagnostic tests only, audiologists (service in hospital or SNF)	Professional	See Chapter 26 for place of service, and type of service coding.	Payment may not be made for therapy services to Part A inpatients of hospitals or SNFs, or for Part B SNF residents. Otherwise, suppliers bill to the contractor using the professional claim format. Note that services of a physician/ NPP/TPP employee of a facility may be billed by the facility to a contractor.
Physician/NPP/TPPs office, independent clinic or patient's home	Professional	See Chapter 26 for place of service, and type of service coding.	Paid via Physician fee schedule.

"Provider/Supplier Service" Type	Format	Bill Type	Comment
Practicing audiologist for services defined as diagnostic tests only	Professional	See Chapter 26 for place of service, and type of service coding.	Some audiologists tests provided in hospitals are considered other diagnostic tests and are subject to OPPS instead of MPFS for outpatient therapy fee schedule.
Critical Access Hospital - inpatient Part A	Institutional	11X	Rehabilitation services are paid cost.
Critical Access Hospital - inpatient Part B	Institutional	85X	Rehabilitation services are paid cost.
Critical Access Hospital – outpatient Part B	Institutional	85X	Rehabilitation services are paid cost.

Complete Claim form completion requirements are contained in chapters 25 and 26.

For a list of the outpatient rehabilitation HCPCS codes see Sec.20.

If a contractor receives an institutional claim for one of these HCPCS codes with dates of service on or after July 1, 2003, that does not appear on the supplemental file it currently uses to pay the therapy claims, it contacts its professional claims area to obtain the non-facility price in order to pay the claim.

NOTE: The list of codes in Sec.20 contains commonly utilized codes for outpatient rehabilitation services. Contractors may consider other codes on institutional claims for payment under the MPFS as outpatient rehabilitation services to the extent that such codes are determined to be medically reasonable and necessary and could be performed within the scope of practice of the therapist providing the service.

100-4, 5, 10.2

A. Financial Limitation Prior to the Balanced Budget Refinement Act (BBRA)

Section 4541(a)(2) of the Balanced Budget Act (BBA) (P.L. 105-33) of 1997, which added §1834(k)(5) to the Act, required payment under a prospective payment system for outpatient rehabilitation services (except those furnished by or under arrangements with a hospital). Outpatient rehabilitation services include the following services:

- Physical therapy (which includes outpatient speech-language pathology); and
- Occupational therapy.

Section 4541(c) of the BBA required application of a financial limitation to all outpatient rehabilitation services (except those furnished by or under arrangements with a hospital). In 1999, an annual per beneficiary limit of $1,500 applied to all outpatient physical therapy services (including speech-language pathology services). A separate limit applied to all occupational therapy services. The limit is based on incurred expenses and includes applicable deductible and coinsurance. The BBA provided that the limits be indexed by the Medicare Economic Index (MEI) each year beginning in 2002.

The limitation is based on therapy services the Medicare beneficiary receives, not the type of practitioner who provides the service. Physical therapists, speech-language pathologists, occupational therapists as well as physicians and certain nonphysician practitioners could render a therapy service.

As a transitional measure, effective in 1999, providers/suppliers were instructed to keep track of the allowed incurred expenses. This process was put in place to assure providers/suppliers did not bill Medicare for patients who exceeded the annual limitations for physical therapy, and for occupational therapy services rendered by individual providers/suppliers. In 2003 and later, the limitation was applied through CMS systems.

B. Moratoria and Exceptions for Therapy Claims

Section 221 of the BBRA of 1999 placed a 2-year moratorium on the application of the financial limitation for claims for therapy services with dates of service January 1, 2000, through December 31, 2001.

Section 421 of the Medicare, Medicaid, and SCHIP Benefits Improvement and Protection Act (BIPA) of 2000, extended the moratorium on application of the financial limitation to claims for outpatient rehabilitation services with dates of service January 1, 2002, through December 31, 2002. Therefore, the moratorium was for a 3-year period and applied to outpatient rehabilitation claims with dates of service January 1, 2000, through December 31, 2002.

In 2003, there was not a moratorium on therapy caps. Implementation was delayed until September 1, 2003. Therapy caps were in effect for services rendered on September 1, 2003 through December 7, 2003.

Congress re-enacted a moratorium on financial limitations on outpatient therapy services on December 8, 2003 that extended through December 31, 2005. Caps were implemented again on January 1, 2006 and policies were modified to allow exceptions as directed by the Deficit Reduction Act of 2005 only for calendar year 2006. The Tax Relief and Health Care Act of 2006 extended the cap exceptions process through calendar year 2007. The Medicare, Medicaid, and SCHIP Extension Act of 2007 extended the cap exceptions process for services furnished through June 30, 2008. The Medicare Improvements for Patients and Providers Act of 2008 extended the exceptions process from July 1, 2008 through December 31, 2009.

Future exceptions. The cap exception for therapy services billed by outpatient hospitals was part of the original legislation and applies as long as caps are in effect. Exceptions to caps based on the medical necessity of the service are in effect only when Congress legislates the exceptions, as noted above. References to the exceptions process in subsection C of this section apply only when the exceptions are in effect.

C. Application of Financial Limitations

Financial limitations on outpatient therapy services, as described above, began for therapy services rendered on or after on January 1, 2006. See C 1 to C 7 of this section when exceptions to therapy caps apply. The limits were $1740 in 2006 and $1780 in 2007, $1810 for 2008. For 2009, the annual limit on the allowed amount for outpatient physical therapy and speech-language pathology combined is $1840; the limit for occupational therapy is $1840. Limits apply to outpatient Part B therapy services from all settings except outpatient hospital and hospital emergency room. These excluded hospital services are reported on types of bill 12x or 13x, or 85x.

Contractors apply the financial limitations to the Medicare Physician Fee Schedule (MPFS) amount (or the amount charged if it is smaller) for therapy services for each beneficiary.

As with any Medicare payment, beneficiaries pay the coinsurance (20 percent) and any deductible that may apply. Medicare will pay the remaining 80 percent of the limit after the deductible is met. These amounts will change each calendar year. Medicare Contractors shall publish the financial limitation amount in educational articles. It is also available at 1-800-Medicare.

Medicare shall apply these financial limitations in order, according to the dates when the claims were received. When limitations apply, the Common Working File (CWF) tracks the limits. Shared system maintainers are not responsible for tracking the dollar amounts of incurred expenses of rehabilitation services for each therapy limit.

In processing claims where Medicare is the secondary payer, the shared system takes the lowest secondary payment amount from MSPPAY and sends this amount on to CWF as the amount applied to therapy limits.

1. Exceptions to Therapy Caps - General
   The Deficit Reduction Act of 2005 directed CMS to develop exceptions to therapy caps for calendar year 2006 and those exceptions have been extended several times by subsequent legislation. The following policies concerning exceptions to caps due to medical necessity apply only when the exceptions process is in effect. With the exception of the use of the KX modifier, the guidance in this section concerning medical necessity applies as well to services provided before caps are reached.

   Instructions for contractors to manage automatic process for exceptions will be found in the Program Integrity Manual, chapter 3, section 3.4.1.2. Provider and supplier information concerning exceptions is in this manual and in IOM Pub. 100-02, chapter 15, section 220.3. Exceptions shall be identified by a modifier on the claim and supported by documentation.

   Since the providers and suppliers will take an active role in obtaining an exception for a beneficiary, this manual section is written to address them as well as Medicare contractors.

   The beneficiary may qualify for use of the cap exceptions at any time during the episode when documented medically necessary services exceed caps. All covered and medically necessary services qualify for exceptions to caps.

   In 2006, the Exception Processes fell into two categories, Automatic Process Exceptions, and Manual Process Exceptions. Beginning January 1, 2007, there is no manual process for exceptions. All services that require exceptions to caps shall be processed using the automatic process. All requests for exception are in the form of a KX modifier added to claim lines. (See subsection C6 for use of the KX modifier.)

   Use of the automatic process for exceptions increases the responsibility of the provider/supplier for determining and documenting that services are appropriate.

   Also, use of the automatic process for exception does not exempt services from manual or other medical review processes as described in 100-08, Chapter 3, Section 3.4.1.1.1. Rather, atypical use of the automatic exception process may invite contractor scrutiny. Particular care should be taken to document improvement and avoid billing for services that do not meet the requirements for skilled services, or for services which are maintenance rather than rehabilitative treatment (See Pub. 100-02, chapter 15, sections 220.2, 220.3, and 230).

   The KX modifier, described in subsection C6, is added to claim lines to indicate that the clinician attests that services are medically necessary and justification is documented in the medical record.

2. Automatic Process Exceptions
   The term "automatic process exceptions" indicates that the claims processing for the exception is automatic, and not that the exception is automatic. An exception may be made when the patient's condition is justified by documentation indicating that the beneficiary requires continued skilled therapy, i.e., therapy beyond the amount payable under the therapy cap, to achieve their prior functional status or maximum expected functional status within a reasonable amount of time.

   No special documentation is submitted to the contractor for automatic process exceptions. The clinician is responsible for consulting guidance in the Medicare manuals and in the professional literature to determine if the beneficiary may qualify for the automatic process exception because documentation justifies medically necessary services above the caps. The clinician's opinion is not binding on the Medicare contractor who makes the final determination concerning whether the claim is payable.

   Documentation justifying the services shall be submitted in response to any Additional Documentation Request (ADR) for claims that are selected for medical review. Follow the documentation requirements in Pub. 100-02, chapter 15, section 220.3. If medical records are requested for review, clinicians may include, at their discretion, a summary that specifically addresses the justification for therapy cap exception.

   In making a decision about whether to utilize the automatic process exception, clinicians shall consider, for example, whether services are appropriate to--

   - The patient's condition including the diagnosis, complexities and severity (A list of the excepted evaluation codes are in C.2.a. A list of the ICD-9 codes for conditions and complexities that might qualify a beneficiary for exception to caps is in 10.2 C3. The list

Appendix G — Pub 100 References

is a guideline and neither assures that services on the list will be excepted nor limits provision of covered and medically necessary services for conditions not on the list);

- The services provided including their type, frequency and duration;
- The interaction of current active conditions and complexities that directly and significantly influence the treatment such that it causes services to exceed caps.

In addition, the following should be considered before using the automatic exception process:

a. Exceptions for Services
Evaluation. The CMS will except therapy evaluations from caps after the therapy caps are reached when evaluation is necessary, e.g., to determine if the current status of the beneficiary requires therapy services. For example, the following evaluation procedures may be appropriate:

92506, 92597, 92607, 92608, 92610, 92611, 92612, 92614, 92616, 96105, 97001, 97002, 97003, 97004.

These codes will continue to be reported as outpatient therapy procedures as described in the Claims Processing Manual, Chapter 5, Section 20(B) "Applicable Outpatient Rehabilitation HCPCS Codes." They are not diagnostic tests. Definition of evaluations and documentation is found in Pub. 100-02, sections 220 and 230.

Other Services. There are a number of sources that suggest the amount of certain services that may be typical, either per service, per episode, per condition, or per discipline. For example, see the CSC - Therapy Cap Report, 3/21/2008, and CSC – Therapy Edits Tables 4/14/2008 at www.cms.hhs.gov/TherapyServices (Studies and Reports). Professional literature and guidelines from professional associations also provide a basis on which to estimate whether the type, frequency and intensity of services are appropriate to an individual. Clinicians and contractors should utilize available evidence related to the patient's condition to justify provision of medically necessary services to individual beneficiaries, especially when they exceed caps. Contractors shall not limit medically necessary services that are justified by scientific research applicable to the beneficiary. Neither contractors nor clinicians shall utilize professional literature and scientific reports to justify payment for continued services after an individual's goals have been met earlier than is typical. Conversely, professional literature and scientific reports shall not be used as justification to deny payment to patients whose needs are greater than is typical or when the patient's condition is not represented by the literature.

b. Exceptions for Conditions or Complexities Identified by ICD-9 codes.
Clinicians may utilize the automatic process for exception for any diagnosis for which they can justify services exceeding the cap. Based upon analysis of claims data, research and evidence based practice guidelines, CMS has identified conditions and complexities represented by ICD-9 codes that may be more likely than others to require therapy services that exceed therapy caps. This list appears in 10.2 C3. Clinicians may use the automatic process of exception for beneficiaries who do not have a condition or complexity on this list when they justify the provision of therapy services that exceed caps for that patient's condition.

Not all patients who have a condition or complexity on the list are "automatically" excepted from therapy caps. See Pub. 100-02, chapter 15, section 230.3 for documenting the patient's condition and complexities. Contractors may scrutinize claims from providers whose services exceed caps more frequently than is typical.

Regardless of the condition, the patient must also meet other requirements for coverage. For example, the patient must require skilled treatment for a covered, medically necessary service; the services must be appropriate in type, frequency and duration for the patient's condition and service must be documented appropriately. Guidelines for utilization of therapy services may be found in Medicare manuals, local coverage determinations of Medicare contractors, and professional guidelines issued by associations and states.

Bill the most relevant diagnosis. As always, when billing for therapy services, the ICD-9 code that best relates to the reason for the treatment shall be on the claim, unless there is a compelling reason. For example, when a patient with diabetes is being treated for gait training due to amputation, the preferred diagnosis is abnormality of gait (which characterizes the treatment). Where it is possible in accordance with State and local laws and the contractors local coverage determinations, avoid using vague or general diagnoses. When a claim includes several types of services, or where the physician/NPP must supply the diagnosis, it may not be possible to use the most relevant therapy code in the primary position. In that case, the relevant code should, if possible, be on the claim in another position.

Codes representing the medical condition that caused the treatment are used when there is no code representing the treatment. Complicating conditions are preferably used in non-primary positions on the claim and are billed in the primary position only in the rare circumstance that there is no more relevant code.

The condition or complexity that caused treatment to exceed caps must be related to the therapy goals and must either be the condition that is being treated or a complexity that directly and significantly impacts the rate of recovery of the condition being treated such that it is appropriate to exceed the caps. Codes marked as complexities represented by ICD-9 codes on the list below are unlikely to require therapy services that would exceed the caps unless they occur in a patient who also has another condition (either listed or not listed). Therefore, documentation for an exception should indicate how the complexity (or combination of complexities) directly and significantly affects treatment for a therapy condition. For example, if the condition underlying the reason for therapy is V43.64, hip replacement, the treatment may have a goal to ambulate 60' with stand-by assistance and a KX modifier may be appropriate for gait training (assuming the severity of the patient is such that the services exceed the cap). Alternatively, it would not be appropriate to use the KX modifier for a patient who recovered from hip replacement last year and is being treated this year for a sprain of a severity which does not justify extensive therapy exceeding caps.

3. ICD-9 Codes That are More Likely to Qualify for the Automatic Process Therapy Cap Exception Based Upon Clinical Condition or Complexity
When using this table, refer to the ICD-9 code book for coding instructions. Some contractors' local coverage determinations do not allow the use of some of the codes on this list in the primary diagnosis position on a claim. If the contractor has determined that these codes do not characterize patients who require medically necessary services, providers/suppliers may not use these codes, but must utilize a billable diagnosis code allowed by their contractor to describe the patient's condition. Contractors shall not apply therapy caps to services based on the patient's condition, but only on the medical necessity of the service for the condition. If a service would be payable before the cap is reached and is still medically necessary after the cap is reached, that service is excepted. This list is illustrative and not exclusive. Providers/suppliers may use the automatic process for exception for medically necessary services when the patient has a billable condition that is not on the list below. The diagnosis on the list below may be put in a secondary position on the claim and/or in the medical records, as the contractor directs.

When two codes are listed in the left cell in a row, all the codes between them are also eligible for exception. If one code is in the cell, only that one code is likely to qualify for exception. The descriptions in the table are not always identical to those in the ICD-9 code book, but may be summaries. Contact your contractor for interpretation if you are not sure that a condition or complexity is applicable for automatic process exception.

It is very important to recognize that most of the conditions on this list would not ordinarily result in services exceeding the cap. Use the KX modifier only in cases where the condition of the individual patient is such that services are APPROPRIATELY provided in an episode that exceeds the cap. In most cases, the severity of the condition, comorbidities, or complexities will contribute to the necessity of services exceeding the cap, and these should be documented. Routine use of the KX modifier for all patients with these conditions will likely show up on data analysis as aberrant and invite inquiry. Be sure that documentation is sufficiently detailed to support the use of the modifier.

The following ICD-9 codes describe the conditions (etiology or underlying medical conditions) that may result in excepted conditions (marked X) and complexities (marked *) that MIGHT cause medically necessary therapy services to qualify for the automatic process exception for each discipline separately. When the field corresponding to the therapy discipline treating and the diagnosis code is marked with a dash (–) services by that discipline are not appropriate for that diagnosis and, therefore, services do not qualify for exception to caps.

These codes are grouped only to facilitate reference to them. The codes may be used only when the code is applicable to the condition being actively treated. For example, an exception should not be claimed for a diagnosis of hip replacement when the service provided is for an unrelated dysphagia.

ICD-9 Cluster	ICD-9 (Cluster) Description	PT	OT	SLP
V43.61-V43.69	Joint Replacement	X	X	--
V45.4	Arthrodesis Status	*	*	--
V45.81-V45.82 and V45.89	Other Postprocedural Status	*	*	--
V49.61-V49.67	Upper Limb Amputation Status	X	X	--
V49.71-V49.77	Lower Limb Amputation Status	X	X	--
V54.10-V54.29	Aftercare for Healing Traumatic or Pathologic Fracture	X	X	--
V58.71-V58.78	Aftercare Following Surgery to Specified Body Systems, Not Elsewhere Classified	*	*	*
244.0-244.9	Acquired Hypothyroidism	*	*	*
250.00-251.9	Diabetes Mellitus and Other Disorders of Pancreatic Internal Secretion	*	*	*
276.0-276.9	Disorders of Fluid, Electrolyte, and Acid-Base Balance	*	*	*
278.00-278.01	Obesity and Morbid Obesity	*	*	*
280.0-289.9	Diseases of the blood and blood-forming organs	*	*	*
290.0-290.43	Dementias	*	*	*
294.0-294.9	Persistent Mental Disorders due to Conditions Classified Elsewhere	*	*	*
295.00-299.91	Other Psychoses	*	*	*
300.00-300.9	Anxiety, Disassociative and Somatoform Disorders	*	*	*
310.0-310.9	Specific Nonpsychotic Mental Disorders due to Brain Damage	*	*	*

X   Automatic (only ICD-9 needed on claim)
*   Complexity (requires another ICD-9 on claim)
--   Does not serve as qualifying ICD-9 on claim

Current Procedural Coding Expert

Appendix G — Pub 100 References

ICD-9 Cluster	ICD-9 (Cluster) Description	PT	OT	SLP
311	Depressive Disorder, Not Elsewhere Classified	*	*	*
315.00-315.9	Specific delays in Development	*	*	*
317	Mild Mental Retardation	*	*	*
320.0-326	Inflammatory Diseases of the Central Nervous System	*	*	*
330.0-337.9	Hereditary and Degenerative Diseases of the Central Nervous System	X	X	X
340-345.91 and 348.0-349.9	Other Disorders of the Central Nervous System	X	X	X
353.0-359.9	Disorders of the Peripheral Nervous system	X	X	--
365.00-365.9	Glaucoma	*	*	*
369.00-369.9	Blindness and Low Vision	*	*	*
386.00-386.9	Vertiginous Syndromes and Other Disorders of Vestibular System	*	*	*
389.00-389.9	Hearing Loss	*	*	*
401.0-405.99	Hypertensive Disease	*	*	*
410.00-414.9	Ischemic Heart Disease	*	*	*
415.0-417.9	Diseases of Pulmonary Circulation	*	*	*
420.0-429.9	Other Forms of Heart Disease	*	*	*
430-438.9	Cerebrovascular Disease	X	X	X
451.0-453.9 and 456.0-459.9	Diseases of Veins and Lymphatics, and Other Diseases of Circulatory System	*	*	*
465.0-466.19	Acute Respiratory Infections	*	*	*
478.30-478.5	Paralysis, Polyps, or Other Diseases of Vocal Cords	*	*	*
480.0-486	Pneumonia	*	*	*
490-496	Chronic Obstructive Pulmonary Disease and Allied Conditions	*	*	*
507.0-507.8	Pneumonitis due to solids and liquids	*	*	*
510.0-519.9	Other Diseases of Respiratory System	*	*	*
560.0-560.9	Intestinal Obstruction Without Mention of Hernia	*	*	*
578.0-578.9	Gastrointestinal Hemorrhage	*	*	*
584.5-586	Renal Failure and Chronic Kidney Disease	*	*	*
590.00-599.9	Other Diseases of Urinary System	*	*	*
682.0-682.8	Other Cellulitis and Abscess	*	*	--
707.00-707.9	Chronic Ulcer of Skin	*	*	--
710.0-710.9	Diffuse Diseases of Connective Tissue	*	*	*
711.00-711.99	Arthropathy Associated with Infections	*	*	--
712.10-713.8	Crystal Arthropathies and Arthropathy Associated with Other Disorders Classified Elsewhere	*	*	--
714.0-714.9	Rheumatoid Arthritis and Other Inflammatory Polyarthropathies	*	*	*
715.00-715.98	Osteoarthrosis and Allied Disorders (Complexity except as listed below)	*	*	--
715.09	Osteoarthritis and allied disorders, multiple sites	X	X	--
715.11	Osteoarthritis, localized, primary, shoulder region	X	X	--
715.15	Osteoarthritis, localized, primary, pelvic region and thigh	X	X	--
715.16	Osteoarthritis, localized, primary, lower leg	X	X	--
715.91	Osteoarthritis, unspecified id gen. or local, shoulder	X	X	--
715.96	Osteoarthritis, unspecified if gen. or local, lower leg	X	X	--
716.00-716.99	Other and Unspecified Arthropathies	*	*	--
717.0-717.9	Internal Derangement of Knee	*	*	--

X   Automatic (only ICD-9 needed on claim)
*   Complexity (requires another ICD-9 on claim)
--   Does not serve as qualifying ICD-9 on claim

ICD-9 Cluster	ICD-9 (Cluster) Description	PT	OT	SLP
718.00-718.99	Other Derangement of Joint (Complexity except as listed below)	*	*	--
718.49	Contracture of Joint, Multiple Sites	X	X	--
719.00-719.99	Other and Unspecified Disorders of Joint (Complexity except as listed below)	*	*	--
719.7	Difficulty Walking	X	X	--
720.0-724.9	Dorsopathies	*	*	--
725-729.9	Rheumatism, Excluding Back (Complexity except as listed below)	*	*	--
726.10-726.19	Rotator Cuff Disorder and Allied Syndromes	X	X	--
727.61-727.62	Rupture of Tendon, Nontraumatic	X	X	--
730.00-739.9	Osteopathies, Chondropathies, and Acquired Musculoskeletal Deformities (Complexity except as listed below)	*	*	--
733.00	Osteoporosis	X	X	--
741.00-742.9 and 745.0-748.9 and 754.0-756.9	Congenital Anomalies	*	*	*
780.31-780.39	Convulsions	*	*	*
780.71-780.79	Malaise and Fatigue	*	*	*
780.93	Memory Loss	*	*	*
781.0-781.99	Symptoms Involving Nervous and Musculoskeletal System (Complexity except as listed below)	*	*	*
781.2	Abnormality of Gait	X	X	--
781.3	Lack of Coordination	X	X	--
783.0-783.9	Symptoms Concerning Nutrition, Metabolism, and Development	*	*	*
784.3-784.69	Aphasia, Voice and Other Speech Disturbance, Other Symbolic Dysfunction	*	*	X
785.4	Gangrene	*	*	--
786.00-786.9	Symptoms involving Respiratory System and Other Chest Symptoms	*	*	*
787.2	Dysphagia	*	*	X
800.00-828.1	Fractures (Complexity except as listed below)	*	*	--
806.00-806.9	Fracture of Vertebral Column With Spinal Cord Injury	X	X	--
810.11-810.13	Fracture of Clavicle	X	X	--
811.00-811.19	Fracture of Scapula	X	X	--
812.00-812.59	Fracture of Humerus	X	X	--
813.00-813.93	Fracture of Radius and Ulna	X	X	--
820.00-820.9	Fracture of Neck of Femur	X	X	--
821.00-821.39	Fracture of Other and Unspecified Parts of Femur	X	X	--
828.0-828.1	Multiple Fractures Involving Both Lower Limbs, Lower with Upper Limb, and Lower Limb(s) with Rib(s) and Sternum	X	X	--
830.0-839.9	Dislocations	X	X	--
840.0-848.8	Sprains and Strains of Joints and Adjacent Muscles	*	*	--
851.00-854.19	Intracranial Injury, excluding those With Skull Fracture	X	X	X
880.0-884.2	Open Wound of Upper Limb	*	*	--
885.0-887.7	Traumatic Amputation, Thumb(s), Finger(s), Arm and Hand (complete)(partial)	X	X	--
890.0-894.2	Open Wound Lower Limb	*	*	--
895.0-897.7	Traumatic Amputation, Toe(s), Foot/Feet, Leg(s) (complete)(partial)	X	X	--
905.0-905.9	Late Effects of Musculoskeletal and Connective Tissue Injuries	*	*	*

X   Automatic (only ICD-9 needed on claim)
*   Complexity (requires another ICD-9 on claim)
--   Does not serve as qualifying ICD-9 on claim

Appendix G — Pub 100 References

ICD-9 Cluster	ICD-9 (Cluster) Description	PT	OT	SLP
907.0-907.9	Late Effects of Injuries to the Nervous System	*	*	*
941.00-949.5	Burns	*	*	*
952.00-952.9	Spinal Cord Injury Without Evidence of Spinal Bone Injury	X	X	X
953.0-953.8	Injury to Nerve Roots and Spinal Plexus	X	X	*
959.01	Head Injury, Unspecified	X	X	X

X Automatic (only ICD-9 needed on claim)
* Complexity (requires another ICD-9 on claim)
-- Does not serve as qualifying ICD-9 on claim

100-4, 5, 20
HCPCS Coding Requirement

A. Uniform Coding

Section 1834(k)(5) of the Act requires that all claims for outpatient rehabilitation therapy services and all comprehensive outpatient rehabilitation facility (CORF) services be reported using a uniform coding system. The current Healthcare Common Procedure Coding System/Current Procedural Terminology is used for the reporting of these services. The uniform coding requirement in the Act is specific to payment for all CORF services and outpatient rehabilitation therapy services - including physical therapy, occupational therapy, and speech-language pathology - that is provided and billed to carriers and fiscal intermediaries (FIs). The Medicare physician fee schedule (MPFS) is used to make payment for these therapy services at the nonfacility rate.

Effective for claims submitted on or after April 1, 1998, providers that had not previously reported HCPCS/CPT for outpatient rehabilitation and CORF services began using HCPCS to report these services. This requirement does not apply to outpatient rehabilitation services provided by:

- Critical access hospitals, which are paid on a cost basis, not MPFS;
- RHCs, and FQHCs for which therapy is included in the all-inclusive rate; or
- Providers that do not furnish therapy services.

The following "providers of services" must bill the FI for outpatient rehabilitation services using HCPCS codes:

- Hospitals (to outpatients and inpatients who are not in a covered Part A1 stay);
- Skilled nursing facilities (SNFs) (to residents not in a covered Part A1 stay and to nonresidents who receive outpatient rehabilitation services from the SNF);
- Home health agencies (HHAs) (to individuals who are not homebound or otherwise are not receiving services under a home health plan of care2 (POC);
- Comprehensive outpatient rehabilitation facilities (CORFs); and
- Providers of outpatient physical therapy and speech-language pathology services (OPTs), also known as rehabilitation agencies (previously termed outpatient physical therapy facilities in this instruction).

Note 1. The requirements for hospitals and SNFs apply to inpatient Part B and outpatient services only. Inpatient Part A services are bundled into the respective prospective payment system payment; no separate payment is made.

Note 2. For HHAs, HCPCS/CPT coding for outpatient rehabilitation services is required only when the HHA provides such service to individuals that are not homebound and, therefore, not under a home health plan of care.

The following practitioners must bill the carriers for outpatient rehabilitation therapy services using HCPCS/CPT codes:

- Physical therapists in private practice (PTPPs),
- Occupational therapists in private practice (OTPPs),
- Physicians, including MDs, DOs, podiatrists and optometrists, and
- Certain nonphysician practitioners (NPPs), acting within their State scope of practice, e.g., nurse practitioners and clinical nurse specialists.

Providers billing to intermediaries shall report:

- The date the therapy plan of care was either established or last reviewed (see Sec.220.1.3B) in Occurrence Code 17, 29, or 30.
- The first day of treatment in Occurrence Code 35, 44, or 45.

B. Applicable Outpatient Rehabilitation HCPCS Codes

The CMS identifies the following codes as therapy services, regardless of the presence of a financial limitation. Therapy services include only physical therapy, occupational therapy and speech-language pathology services. Therapist means only a physical therapist, occupational therapist or speech-language pathologist. Therapy modifiers are GP for physical therapy, GO for occupational therapy, and GN for speech-language pathology. Check the notes below the chart for details about each code.

When in effect, any financial limitation will also apply to services represented by the following codes, except as noted below.

NOTE: Listing of the following codes does not imply that services are covered or applicable to all provider settings.

64550+	90901+	92506¿	92507¿	92508	92526
92597	92605****	92606****	92607	92608	92609
92610+	92611+	92612+	92614+	92616+	95831+
95832+	95833+	95834+	95851+	95852+	95992****
96105+	96110+				

100-4, 5, 100.10
Group Therapy Services (Code 97150)

Policies for group therapy services for CORF are the same as group therapy services for other Part B outpatient services. See Pub 100-02, chapter 15, section 230.

100-4, 8, 140
Monthly Capitation Payment Method for Physicians' Services Furnished to Patients on Maintenance Dialysis

Physicians and practitioners managing patients on dialysis (center based) are paid a monthly capitation payment (MCP) for most outpatient dialysis-related physician services furnished to a Medicare end stage renal disease (ESRD) beneficiary. The payment amount varies based on the number of visits provided within each month and the age of the ESRD beneficiary. Physicians and practitioners managing ESRD patients who dialyze at home are paid a single monthly rate based on the age of the ESRD beneficiary, regardless of the number of face-to-face physician or practitioner visits. The MCP is reported once per month for services performed in an outpatient setting that are related to the patients' ESRD.

Physicians and practitioners may receive payment for managing patients on dialysis for less than a full month of care in specific circumstances as discussed in section 140.2. Payment for ESRD related services, less than a full month, is made on a per diem bases.

Payment for ESRD-related services is made at 80 percent of the Medicare approved amount (lesser of the actual charge or applicable Medicare fee schedule amount) after the beneficiary's Part B deductible is met. The beneficiary is responsible for the Part B deductible and the 20 percent coinsurance for physician and practitioner ESRD-related services.

A. Services Included in Monthly Capitation Payment

The following physician services are included in the MCP:

- Assessment of the need for a specified diet and the need for nutritional supplementation for the control of chronic renal failure. Specification of the quantity of total protein, high biologic protein, sodium, potassium, and amount of fluids to be allowed during a given time period. For diabetic patients with chronic renal failure, the prescription usually specifies the number of calories in the diet.

- Assessment of which mode(s) of chronic dialysis (types of hemodialysis or peritoneal dialysis) are suitable for a given patient and recommendation of the type(s) of therapy for a given patient.

- Assessment and determination of which type of dialysis access is best suited for a given patient and arrangement for creation of dialysis access.

- Assessment of whether the patient meets preliminary criteria as a renal transplant candidate and presentation of this assessment to the patient and family.

- Prescription of the parameters of intradialytic management. For chronic hemodialysis therapies, this includes the type of dialysis access, the type and amount of anticoagulant to be employed, blood flow rates, dialysate flow rate, ultrafiltration rate, dialysate temperature, type of dialysate (acetate versus bicarbonate) and composition of the electrolytes in the dialysate, size of hemodialyzer (surface area) and composition of the dialyzer membrane (conventional versus high flux), duration and frequency of treatments, the type and frequency of measuring indices of clearance, and intradialytic medications to be administered. For chronic peritoneal dialysis therapies, this includes the type of peritoneal dialysis, the volume of dialysate, concentration of dextrose in the dialysate, electrolyte composition of the dialysate, duration of each exchange, and addition of medication to the dialysate, such as heparin, and the type and frequency of measuring indices of clearance. For diabetics, the quantity of insulin to be added to each exchange is prescribed.

- Assessment of whether the patient has significant renal failure-related anemia, determination of the etiology(ies) for the anemia based on diagnostic tests, and prescription of therapy for correction of the anemia, such as vitamins, oral or parenteral iron, and hormonal therapy such as erythropoietin.

- Assessment of whether the patient has hyperparathyroidism and/or renal osteodystrophy secondary to chronic renal failure and prescription of appropriate therapy, such as calcium and phosphate binders for control of hyperphosphatemia. Based upon assessment of parahormone levels, serum calcium levels, and evaluation for the presence of metabolic bone disease, the physician determines whether oral or parenteral therapy with vitamin D or its analogs is indicated and prescribes the appropriate therapy. Based upon assessment and diagnosis of bone disease, the physician may prescribe specific chelation therapy with deferoxamine and the use of hemoperfusion for removal of aluminum and the chelation.

- Assessment of whether the patient has dialysis-related arthropathy or neuropathy and adjustment of the patient's prescription accordingly. Referral of the patient for any additional needed specialist evaluation and management of these endorgan problems.

- Assessment of whether the patient has fluid overload resulting from renal failure and establishment of an estimated "ideal (dry) weight." The physician determines the need for fluid removal independent of the dialysis prescription and implements these measures when indicated.

- Determination of the need for and prescription of antihypertensive medications and their timing relative to dialysis when the patient is hypertensive in spite of correction of fluid overload.
- Periodic review of the dialysis records to ascertain whether the patient is receiving the prescribed amount of dialysis and ordering of indices of clearance, such as urea kinetics, in order to ascertain whether the dialysis prescription is producing adequate dialysis. If the indices of clearance suggest that the prescription requires alteration, the physician orders changes in the hemodialysis prescription, such as blood flow rate, dialyzer surface area, dialysis frequency, and/or dialysis duration (length of treatment). For peritoneal dialysis patients, the physician may order changes in the volume of dialysate, dextrose concentration of the dialysate, and duration of the exchanges.
- Periodic visits (at least one per month) to the patient during dialysis to ascertain whether the dialysis is working well and whether the patient is tolerating the procedure well (physiologically and psychologically). During these visits, the physician determines whether alteration in any aspect of a given patient's prescription is indicated, such as changes in the estimate of the patient's dry weight. Review of the treatment with the nurse or technician performing the therapy is also included. The frequency of these visits will vary depending upon the patient's medical status, complicating conditions, and other determinants.
- Performance of periodic physical assessments, based upon the patient's clinical stability, in order to determine the necessity for alterations in various aspects of the patient's prescription. Similarly, the physician reviews the results of periodic laboratory testing in order to determine the need for alterations in the patient's prescription, such as changes in the amount and timing of phosphate binders or dose of erythropoietin.
- Periodic assessment of the adequacy and function of the patient's dialysis access appropriate tests and antibiotic therapy.
- Interpretations of the following tests:
  - Bone mineral density studies (CPT codes 76070, 76075, 78350, and 78351);
  - Noninvasive vascular diagnostic studies of hemodialysis access (CPT codes 93925, 93926, 93930, 93931, and 93990);
  - Nerve conduction studies (CPT codes 95900, 95903, 95904, 95925, 95926, 95927, 95934, 95935, and 95936);
  - Electromyography studies (CPT codes 95860, 95861, 95863, 95864, 95867, 95867, 95869, and 95872).
- Periodic review and update of the patient's short-term and long-term care plans with staff.
- Coordination and direction of the care of patients by other professional staff, such as dieticians and social workers.
- Certification of the need for items and services such as durable medical equipment and home health care services. Care plan oversight services described by CPT code 99375 are included in the MCP and may not be separately reported.

B. Services Excluded from Monthly Capitation Payment
The following physician services furnished to the physician's ESRD patients are excluded from the MCP and should be paid in accordance with the physician fee schedule:

1. Administration of hepatitis B vaccine.
2. Surgical services such as:
   - Temporary or permanent hemodialysis catheter placement;
   - Temporary or permanent peritoneal dialysis catheter placement;
   - Repair of existing dialysis accesses;
   - Placement of catheter(s) for thrombolytic therapy;
   - Thrombolytic therapy (systemic, regional, or access catheter only; hemodialysis or peritoneal dialysis);
   - Thrombectomy of clotted cannula;
   - Arthrocentesis;
   - Bone marrow aspiration; and
   - Bone marrow biopsy.
3. Interpretation of tests that have a professional component such as:
   - Electrocardiograms (12 lead, Holter monitor, stress tests, etc.);
   - Echocardiograms;
   - 24-hour blood pressure monitor;
   - Biopsies; and
   - Spirometry and complete pulmonary function tests.
4. Complete evaluation for renal transplantation. While the physician assessment of whether the patient meets preliminary criteria as a renal transplant candidate is included under the MCP, the complete evaluation for renal transplantation is excluded from the MCP.
5. Evaluation of potential living transplant donors.
6. The training of patients to perform home hemodialysis, self hemodialysis, and the various forms of self peritoneal dialysis.
7. Non-renal related physician's services. These services may be furnished by the physician providing renal care or by another physician. They may not be incidental to services furnished during a dialysis session or office visit necessitated by the renal condition. The physician must provide documentation that the illness is not related to the renal condition and that the added visits are required. The contractor's medical staff determines whether additional reimbursement is warranted for treatment of the unrelated illness. For example, the medical management of diabetes mellitus that is not related to the dialysis or furnished during a dialysis session is excluded.
8. Covered physician services furnished to hospital inpatients.
9. All physician services that antedate the initiation of outpatient dialysis.
10. Covered physician services furnished by another physician when the patient is not available to receive the outpatient services as usual; for example, when the patient is traveling out of tow

100-4, 9, 182
Medical Nutrition Therapy (MNT) Services

A - FQHCs
Previously, MNT type services were considered incident to services under the FQHC benefit, if all relevant program requirements were met. Therefore, separate all-inclusive encounter rate payment could not be made for the provision of MNT services. With passage of DRA, effective January 1, 2006, FQHCs are eligible for a separate payment under Part B for these services provided they meet all program requirements. Payment is made at the all-inclusive encounter rate to the FQHC. This payment can be in addition to payment for any other qualifying visit on the same date of service as the beneficiary received qualifying MNT services.

For FQHCs to qualify for a separate visit payment for MNT services, the services must be a one-on-one face-to-face encounter. Group sessions don't constitute a billable visit for any FQHC services. Rather, the cost of group sessions is included in the calculation of the all-inclusive FQHC visit rate. To receive payment for MNT services, the MNT services must be billed on TOB 73X with the appropriate individual MNT HCPCS code (codes 97802, 97803, or G0270) and with the appropriate site of service revenue code in the 052X revenue code series. This payment can be in addition to payment for any other qualifying visit on the same date of service as the beneficiary received qualifying MNT services as long as the claim for MNT services contain the appropriate coding specified above.

NOTE: MNT is not a qualifying visit on the same day that DSMT is provided.

Additional information on MNT can be found in Chapter 4, section 300 of this manual.

Group services (HCPCS 97804 or G0271) do not meet the criteria for a separate qualifying encounter. All line items billed on TOB 73x with HCPCS code 97804 or G0271 will be denied.

B - RHCs
Separate payment to RHCs for these practitioners/services continues to be precluded as these services are not within the scope of Medicare-covered RHC benefits. All line items billed on TOB 71x with HCPCS codes for MNT services will be denied.

100-4, 11, 10
Overview
Medicare beneficiaries entitled to hospital insurance (Part A) who have terminal illnesses and a life expectancy of six months or less have the option of electing hospice benefits in lieu of standard Medicare coverage for treatment and management of their terminal condition. Only care provided by a Medicare certified hospice is covered under the hospice benefit provisions.

Hospice care is available for two 90-day periods and an unlimited number of 60-day periods during the remainder of the hospice patient's lifetime. However, a beneficiary may voluntarily terminate his hospice election period. Election/termination dates are retained on CWF.

When hospice coverage is elected, the beneficiary waives all rights to Medicare Part B payments for services that are related to the treatment and management of his/her terminal illness during any period his/her hospice benefit election is in force, except for professional services of an attending physician, which may include a nurse practitioner. If the attending physician, who may be a nurse practitioner, is an employee of the designated hospice, he or she may not receive compensation from the hospice for those services under Part B. These physician professional services are billed to Medicare Part A by the hospice.

To be covered, hospice services must be reasonable and necessary for the palliation or management of the terminal illness and related conditions. The individual must elect hospice care and a certification that the individual is terminally ill must be completed by the patient's attending physician (if there is one), and the Medical Director (or the physician member of the Interdisciplinary Group (IDG)). Nurse practitioners serving as the attending physician may not certify or re-certify the terminal illness. A plan of care must be established before services are provided. To be covered, services must be consistent with the plan of care. Certification of terminal illness is based on the physician's or medical director's clinical judgment regarding the normal course of an individual's illness. It should be noted that predicting life expectancy is not always exact.

See the Medicare Benefit Policy Manual, Chapter 9, for additional general information about the Hospice benefit.

See Chapter 29 of this manual for information on the appeals process that should be followed when an entity is dissatisfied with the determination made on a claim.

See Chapter 9 of the Medicare Benefit Policy Manual for hospice eligibility requirements and election of hospice care.

100-4, 11, 40.1.3
Attending Physician Services
When hospice coverage is elected, the beneficiary waives all rights to Medicare Part B payments for professional services that are related to the treatment and management of his/her terminal illness during any period his/her hospice benefit election is in force, except for professional services of an "attending physician," who is not an employee of the designated hospice nor receives compensation from the hospice for those services. For purposes of administering the hospice benefit provisions, an "attending physician" means an individual who:

Appendix G — Pub 100 References

- Is a doctor of medicine or osteopathy or
- A nurse practitioner (for professional services related to the terminal illness that are furnished on or after December 8, 2003); and
- Is identified by the individual, at the time he/she elects hospice coverage, as having the most significant role in the determination and delivery of their medical care.

Even though a beneficiary elects hospice coverage, he/she may designate and use an attending physician, who is not employed by nor receives compensation from the hospice for professional services furnished, in addition to the services of hospice-employed physicians. The professional services of an attending physician, who may be a nurse practitioner as defined in Chapter 9, that are reasonable and necessary for the treatment and management of a hospice patient's terminal illness are not considered hospice services.

Where the service is considered a hospice service (i.e., a service related to the hospice patient's terminal illness that was furnished by someone other than the designated "attending physician" [or a physician substituting for the attending physician]) the physician or other provider must look to the hospice for payment.

Professional services related to the hospice patient's terminal condition that were furnished by the "attending physician", who may be a nurse practitioner, are billed to carriers. When the attending physician furnishes a terminal illness related service that includes both a professional and technical component (e.g., x-rays), he/she bills the professional component of such services to the carrier and looks to the hospice for payment for the technical component. Likewise, the attending physician, who may be a nurse practitioner, would look to the hospice for payment for terminal illness related services furnished that have no professional component (e.g., clinical lab tests). The remainder of this section explains this in greater detail.

When a Medicare beneficiary elects hospice coverage he/she may designate an attending physician, who may be a nurse practitioner, not employed by the hospice, in addition to receiving care from hospice-employed physicians. The professional services of a non-hospice affiliated attending physician for the treatment and management of a hospice patient's terminal illness are not considered "hospice services." These attending physician services are billed to the carrier, provided they were not furnished under a payment arrangement with the hospice. The attending physician codes services with the GV modifier "Attending physician not employed or paid under agreement by the patient's hospice provider" when billing his/her professional services furnished for the treatment and management of a hospice patient's terminal condition. Carriers make payment to the attending physician or beneficiary, as appropriate, based on the payment and deductible rules applicable to each covered service.

Payments for the services of attending physician are not counted in determining whether the hospice cap amount has been exceeded because services provided by an independent attending physician are not part of the hospice's care.

Services provided by an independent attending physician who may be a nurse practitioner must be coordinated with any direct care services provided by hospice physicians.

Only the direct professional services of an independent attending physician, who may be a nurse practitioner, to a patient may be billed; the costs for services such as lab or x-rays are not to be included in the bill.

If another physician covers for a hospice patient's designated attending physician, the services of the substituting physician are billed by the designated attending physician under the reciprocal or locum tenens billing instructions. In such instances, the attending physician bills using the GV modifier in conjunction with either the Q5 or Q6 modifier.

When services related to a hospice patient's terminal condition are furnished under a payment arrangement with the hospice by the designated attending physician who may be a nurse practitioner, the physician must look to the hospice for payment. In this situation the physicians' services are hospice services and are billed by the hospice to its FI.

Carriers must process and pay for covered, medically necessary Part B services that physicians furnish to patients after their hospice benefits are revoked even if the patient remains under the care of the hospice. Such services are billed without the GV or GW modifiers. Make payment based on applicable Medicare payment and deductible rules for each covered service even if the beneficiary continues to be treated by the hospice after hospice benefits are revoked.

The CWF response contains the period of hospice entitlement. This information is a permanent part of the notice and is furnished on all CWF replies and automatic notices. Carriers use the CWF reply for validating dates of hospice coverage and to research, examine and adjudicate services coded with the GV or GW modifiers.

100-4, 11, 40.1.3.1
Care Plan Oversight

Care plan oversight (CPO) exists where there is physician supervision of patients under care of hospices that require complex and multidisciplinary care modalities involving regular physician development and/or revision of care plans. Implicit in the concept of CPO is the expectation that the physician has coordinated an aspect of the patient's care with the hospice during the month for which CPO services were billed.

For a physician or NP employed by or under arrangement with a hospice agency, CPO functions are incorporated and are part of the hospice per diem payment and as such may not be separately billed.

For information on separately billable CPO services by the attending physician or nurse practitioner see Chapter 12, 180 of this manual.

100-4, 12, 30
Correct Coding Policy
B3-15068

The Correct Coding Initiative was developed to promote national correct coding methodologies and to control improper coding leading to inappropriate payment in Part B claims. Refer to Chapter 23 for additional information on the initiative.

The principles for the correct coding policy are:

- The service represents the standard of care in accomplishing the overall procedure;
- The service is necessary to successfully accomplish the comprehensive procedure.
- Failure to perform the service may compromise the success of the procedure; and
- The service does not represent a separately identifiable procedure unrelated to the comprehensive procedure planned.

For a detailed description of the correct coding policy, refer to http://www.cms.hhs.gov/medlearn/ncci.asp.

The CMS as well as many third party payers have adopted the HCPCS/CPT coding system for use by physicians and others to describe services rendered. The system contains three levels of codes. Level I contains the American Medical Association's Current Procedural Terminology (CPT) numeric codes. Level II contains alpha-numeric codes primarily for items and services not included in CPT. Level III contains carrier specific codes that are not included in either Level I or Level II. For a list of CPT and HCPCS codes refer to the CMS Web site.

The following general coding policies encompass coding principles that are to be applied in the review of Medicare claims. They are the basis for the correct coding edits that are installed in the claims processing systems effective January 1, 1996.

A. Coding Based on Standards of Medical/Surgical Practice
All services integral to accomplishing a procedure are considered bundled into that procedure and, therefore, are considered a component part of the comprehensive code. Many of these generic activities are common to virtually all procedures and, on other occasions, some are integral to only a certain group of procedures, but are still essential to accomplish these particular procedures. Accordingly, it is inappropriate to separately report these services based on standard medical and surgical principles.

Because many services are unique to individual CPT coding sections, the rationale for rebundling is described in that particular section of the detailed coding narratives that are transmitted to carriers periodically.

B. CPT Procedure Code Definition
The format of the CPT manual includes descriptions of procedures, which are, in order to conserve space, not listed in their entirety for all procedures. The partial description is indented under the main entry. The main entry then encompasses the portion of the description preceding the semicolon. The main entry applies to and is a part of all indented entries, which follow with their codes.

In the course of other procedure descriptions, the code definition specifies other procedures that are included in this comprehensive code. In addition, a code description may define a rebundling relationship where one code is a part of another based on the language used in the descriptor.

C. CPT Coding Manual Instruction/Guideline
Each of the six major subsections include guidelines that are unique to that section.

These directions are not all inclusive of nor limited to, definitions of terms, modifiers, unlisted procedures or services, special or written reports, details about reporting separate, and multiple or starred procedures and qualifying circumstances.

D. Coding Services Supplemental to Principal Procedure (Add-On Codes) Code
Generally, these are identified with the statement "list separately in addition to code for primary procedure" in parentheses, and other times the supplemental code is used only with certain primary codes, which are parenthetically identified. The reason for these CPT codes is to enable physicians and others to separately identify a service that is performed in certain situations as an additional service. Incidental services that are necessary to accomplish the primary procedure (e.g., lysis of adhesions in the course of an open cholecystectomy) are not separately billed.

E. Separate Procedures
The narrative for many CPT codes includes a parenthetical statement that the procedure represents a "separate procedure."

The inclusion of this statement indicates that the procedure, while possible to perform separately, is generally included in a more comprehensive procedure, and the service is not to be billed when a related, more comprehensive, service is performed. The "separate procedure" designation is used with codes in the surgery (CPT codes 10000-69999), radiology (CPT codes 70000-79999), and medicine (CPT codes 90000-99199) sections.

When a related procedure from the same section, subsection, category, or subcategory is performed, a code with the designation of "separate procedure" is not to be billed with the primary procedure.

F. Designation of Sex
Many procedure codes have a sex designation within their narrative. These codes are not billed with codes having an opposite sex designation because this would reflect a conflict in sex classification either by the definition of the code descriptions themselves, or by the fact that the performance of these procedures on the same beneficiary would be anatomically impossible.

G. Family of Codes
In a family of codes, there are two or more component codes that are not billed separately because they are included in a more comprehensive code as members of the code family.

Comprehensive codes include certain services that are separately identifiable by other component codes. The component codes as members of the comprehensive code family represent parts of the procedure that should not be listed separately when the complete procedure is done. However, the component codes are considered individually if performed independently of the complete procedure and if not all the services listed in the comprehensive codes were rendered to make up the total service.

H. Most Extensive Procedures
When procedures are performed together that are basically the same or performed on the same site but are qualified by an increased level of complexity, the less extensive procedure is bundled into the more extensive procedure.

I. Sequential Procedures
An initial approach to a procedure may be followed at the same encounter by a second, usually more invasive approach. There may be separate CPT codes describing each service. The second procedure is usually performed because the initial approach was unsuccessful in accomplishing the medically necessary service. These procedures are considered "sequential procedures." Only the CPT code for one of the services, generally the more invasive service, should be billed.

J. With/Without Procedures
In the CPT manual, there are various procedures that have been separated into two codes with the definitional difference being "with" versus "without" (e.g., with and without contrast). Both procedure codes cannot be billed. When done together, the "without" procedure is bundled into the "with" procedure.

K. Laboratory Panels
When components of a specific organ or disease oriented laboratory panel (e.g., codes 80061 and 80059) or automated multi-channel tests (e.g., codes 80002 - 80019) are billed separately, they must be bundled into the comprehensive panel or automated multichannel test code as appropriate that includes the multiple component tests. The individual tests that make up a panel or can be performed on an automated multi-channel test analyzer are not to be separately billed.

L Mutually Exclusive Procedures
There are numerous procedure codes that are not billed together because they are mutually exclusive of each other. Mutually exclusive codes are those codes that cannot reasonably be done in the same session.

An example of a mutually exclusive situation is when the repair of the organ can be performed by two different methods. One repair method must be chosen to repair the organ and must be billed. Another example is the billing of an "initial" service and a subsequent" service. It is contradictory for a service to be classified as an initial and a subsequent service at the same time.

CPT codes which are mutually exclusive of one another based either on the CPT definition or the medical impossibility/improbability that the procedures could be performed at the same session can be identified as code pairs. These codes are not necessarily linked to one another with one code narrative describing a more comprehensive procedure compared to the component code, but can be identified as code pairs which should not be billed together.

M. Use of Modifiers
When certain component codes or mutually exclusive codes are appropriately furnished, such as later on the same day or on a different digit or limb, it is appropriate that these services be reported using a HCPCS code modifier. Such modifiers are modifiers E1 -E4, FA, F1 - F9, TA, T1 - T9, LT, RT, LC, LD, RC, -58, -78, -79, and -94.

Modifier -59 is not appropriate to use with weekly radiation therapy management codes (77427) or with evaluation and management services codes (99201 - 99499).

Application of these modifiers prevent erroneous denials of claims for several procedures performed on different anatomical sites, on different sides of the body, or at different sessions on the same date of service. The medical record must reflect that the modifier is being used appropriately to describe separate services.

100-4, 12, 30.1
Digestive System (Codes 40000 - 49999)
B3-15100

A. Upper Gastrointestinal Endoscopy Including Endoscopic Ultrasound (EUS) (Code 43259)
If the person performing the original diagnostic endoscopy has access to the EUS and the clinical situation requires an EUS, the EUS may be done at the same time. The procedure, diagnostic and EUS, is reported under the same code, CPT 43259. This code conforms to CPT guidelines for the indented codes. The service represented by the indented code, in this case code 43259 for EUS, includes the service represented by the unintended code preceding the list of indented codes. Therefore, when a diagnostic examination of the upper gastrointestinal tract "including esophagus, stomach, and either the duodenum or jejunum as appropriate," includes the use of endoscopic ultrasonography, the service is reported by a single code, namely 43259.

Interpretation, whether by a radiologist or endoscopist, is reported under CPT code 76975-26. These codes may both be reported on the same day.

B. Incomplete Colonoscopies (Codes 45330 and 45378)
An incomplete colonoscopy, e.g., the inability to extend beyond the splenic flexure, is billed and paid using colonoscopy code 45378 with modifier "-53." The Medicare physician fee schedule database has specific values for code 45378-53. These values are the same as for code 45330, sigmoidoscopy, as failure to extend beyond the splenic flexure means that a sigmoidoscopy rather than a colonoscopy has been performed.

However, code 45378-53 should be used when an incomplete colonoscopy has been done because other MPFSDB indicators are different for codes 45378 and 45330.

100-4, 12, 30.2
Urinary and Male Genital Systems (Codes 50010 - 55899)
B3-15200

A. Cystourethroscopy With Ureteral Catheterization (Code 52005)
Code 52005 has a zero in the bilateral field (payment adjustment for bilateral procedure does not apply) because the basic procedure is an examination of the bladder and urethra (cystourethroscopy), which are not paired organs. The work RVUs assigned take into account that it may be necessary to examine and catheterize one or both ureters. No additional payment is made when the procedure is billed with bilateral modifier "-50." Neither is any additional payment made when both ureters are examined and code 52005 is billed with multiple surgery modifier "-51." It is inappropriate to bill code 52005 twice, once by itself and once with modifier "-51," when both ureters are examined.

B. Cystourethroscopy With Fulgration and/or Resection of Tumors (Codes 52234, 52235, and 52240)
The descriptors for codes 52234 through 52240 include the language "tumor(s)." This means that regardless of the number of tumors removed, only one unit of a single code can be billed on a given date of service. It is inconsistent to allow payment for removal of a small (code 52234) and a large (code 52240) tumor using two codes when only one code is allowed for the removal of more than one large tumor. For these three codes only one unit may be billed for any of these codes, only one of the codes may be billed, and the billed code reflects the size of the largest tumor removed.

100-4, 12, 30.3
Audiological Diagnostic Tests, Speech-Language Evaluations and Treatments
A. Correct Coding
Contact the Medicare contractor for guidance if the CPT codebook changes the description of codes mentioned in this section.

Speech-Language Pathology Services. Speech-language pathology (SLP) services are included in the list of therapy services in Pub. 100-04, Chapter 5, Sec.20. Policies for outpatient therapy services are in Pub. 100-02, Chapter 15, Secs.220 and 230. Most of the CPT codes that apply to SLP services are untimed codes that may only be billed once for each encounter. A common error is the billing of untimed codes for multiple units of time. For example, the evaluation code 92506 is billed once a day regardless of the number of types of evaluation included or the length of time that is involved. Bill the code that most appropriately describes the service that is being provided.

Audiology Services. Policies concerning audiology services are found in Pub. 100-02, Chapter 15, Sec.80.3.

Audiologists shall bill for the global service if they perform both technical and professional components of the diagnostic tests that have both components.

Audiologists are to be encouraged to enroll as soon as possible after they obtain their National Provider Identifier (NPI). For audiologists who are enrolled and bill independently for services they render, the audiologist's NPI is required on all claims.

Audiologists must be enrolled and use their NPI on all claims for services they render on or after October 1, 2008, (for additional information about enrollment, please refer to Chapter 10 of the Program Integrity Manual, Pub.100-08). Before October 1, 2008, audiologists who are not yet enrolled may continue to have their services billed by a physician or group who employs the audiologist. Audiologists shall use the billing instructions in the Medicare manuals; for example, see this manual, Chapter 1, Sec.30.

See the most recent Physician Fee Schedule for pricing and supervision levels for audiology services: http://www.cms.hhs.gov/PFSlookup/01_Overview.asp#TopOfPage.

B. Implant Processing
Payment for diagnostic testing of implants, such as cochlear, osseointegrated or brainstem implants, including programming or reprogramming following implantation surgery is not included in the global fee for the surgery.

The diagnostic analysis of a cochlear implant shall be billed using CPT codes 92601 through 92604.

Osseointegrated prosthetic devices should be billed and paid for under provisions of the applicable payment system. For example, payment may differ depending upon whether the device is furnished on an inpatient or outpatient basis, and by a hospital subject to the OPPS, or by a Critical Access Hospital, physician's clinic, or a Federally Qualified Health Center.

C. Aural Rehabilitation Services
General Policy for Evaluation and Treatment of Conditions Related to the Auditory System.

For evaluation of auditory processing disorders and speech-reading or lip-reading, by a speech-language pathologists use the untimed code 92506 with "1" as the unit of service, regardless of the duration of the service on a given day. This "always therapy" evaluation code must be provided by speech-language pathologists according to the policies in Pub. 100-02, Chapter 15, Secs.220 and 230. The codes 92620 and 92621 are diagnostic audiological tests and may not be used for SLP services.

For treatment of auditory processing disorders or auditory rehabilitation/auditory training (including speech-reading or lip-reading), 92507, and 92508 are used to report a single encounter with "1" as the unit of service, regardless of the duration of the service on a given day. These codes always represent SLP services. See Pub. 100-02, Chapter 15, Sec.220 and 230 for SLP policies. These SLP evaluation and treatment services are not covered when performed or billed by audiologists, even if they are supervised by physicians or nonphysician practitioners.

For evaluation of auditory rehabilitation to instruct the use of residual hearing provided by an implant or hearing aid related to hearing loss, the timed codes 92626 and 92627 are used. These are not "always therapy" codes. Evaluation of auditory rehabilitation shall be appropriately provided by an audiologist or speech-language pathologist. Evaluation services may be billed by an audiologist. Also, these services may be provided incident to a physician or nonphysician practitioner's service by a speech-language pathologist, or personally by a physician or nonphysician practitioner within their scope of practice. Evaluation of auditory rehabilitation is a covered diagnostic test when performed and billed by an audiologist and is a SLP evaluation service covered under the SLP benefit when performed by a speech-language pathologist.

Appendix G — Pub 100 References

General Policies for Post implant Services.
The services of a speech-language pathologist may be covered for SLP services provided after implantation of auditory devices. For example, a speech-language pathologist may provide evaluation and treatment of speech, language, cognition, voice, and auditory processing using code 92506 and 92507. Use 92626 and 92627 for auditory (aural) rehabilitation evaluation following cochlear implantation or for other hearing impairments.

For diagnostic testing of cochlear implants, audiologists use codes 92601, 92602, 92603 and 92604. These services may not be provided by speech-language pathologists or others, with the exception of physicians and non-physician practitioners who may personally provide the services that are within their scope of practice.

D. Computer Administered Hearing Testing
Services using devices that do not require the skills of an audiologist are not covered audiological diagnostic tests. See Pub. 100-02, Chapter 15 concerning descriptions of services that require the skills of an audiologist.

There are some computerized testing devices (e.g., certain audiometers, Bekesy audiometry - 92561) that may be used to produce diagnostic tests when personally performed by an audiologist or physician. Codes for audiological diagnostic tests may be used when an audiologist or physician utilizes an audiometer to furnish a diagnostic test, even if the audiometer has some computerized functions, if the skills of an audiologist are applied to complete the test. (See Pub 100-02, Chapter 15, Sec.80.3.)

Otograms. This is one example of the use of computer-administered hearing tests. Otograms may be coded as unlisted otorhinolaryngological services or procedures (92700). However, these computer-administered hearing tests do not require the skills of an audiologist and are not payable.

Comprehensive audiometry threshold evaluation and speech recognition. Comprehensive audiometry threshold evaluation and speech recognition (92557) are not payable when a computer administers the test e.g., tracks or evaluates responses, automatically adjusts the stimulus or suggests a diagnosis.

100-4, 12, 30.4
Cardiovascular System (Codes 92950-93799)
A. Echocardiography Contrast Agents
Effective October 1, 2000, physicians may separately bill for contrast agents used in echocardiography. Physicians should use HCPCS Code A9700 (Supply of Injectable Contrast Material for Use in Echocardiography, per study). The type of service code is 9. This code will be carrier-priced.

B. Electronic Analyses of Implantable Cardioverter-defibrillators and Pacemakers
The CPT codes 93731, 93734, 93741 and 93743 are used to report electronic analyses of single or dual chamber pacemakers and single or dual chamber implantable cardioverterdefibrillators. In the office, a physician uses a device called a programmer to obtain information about the status and performance of the device and to evaluate the patient's cardiac rhythm and response to the implanted device. Advances in information technology now enable physicians to evaluate patients with implanted cardiac devices without requiring the patient to be present in the physician's office. Using a manufacturer's specific monitor/transmitter, a patient can send complete device data and specific cardiac data to a distant receiving station or secure Internet server. The electronic analysis of cardiac device data that is remotely obtained provides immediate and long-term data on the device and clinical data on the patient's cardiac functioning equivalent to that obtained during an in-office evaluation. Physicians should report the electronic analysis of an implanted cardiac device using remotely obtained data as described above with CPT code 93731, 93734, 93741 or 93743, depending on the type of cardiac device implanted in the patient.

100-4, 12, 30.5
Payment for Codes for Chemotherapy Administration and Nonchemotherapy Injections and Infusions
A. General
Codes for Chemotherapy administration and nonchemotherapy injections and infusions include the following three categories of codes in the American Medical Association's Current Procedural Terminology (CPT):

1. Hydration;
2. Therapeutic, prophylactic, and diagnostic injections and infusions (excluding chemotherapy); and
3. Chemotherapy administration.

Physician work related to hydration, injection, and infusion services involves the affirmation of the treatment plan and the supervision (pursuant to incident to requirements) of nonphysician clinical staff.

B. Hydration
The hydration codes are used to report a hydration IV infusion which consists of a prepackaged fluid and /or electrolytes (e.g. normal saline, D5-1/2 normal saline +30 mg EqKC1/liter) but are not used to report infusion of drugs or other substances.

C. Therapeutic, prophylactic, and diagnostic injections and infusions (excluding chemotherapy)
A therapeutic, prophylactic, or diagnostic IV infusion or injection, other than hydration, is for the administration of substances/drugs. The fluid used to administer the drug (s) is incidental hydration and is not separately payable.

If performed to facilitate the infusion or injection or hydration, the following services and items are included and are not separately billable:

1. Use of local anesthesia;
2. IV start;
3. Access to indwelling IV, subcutaneous catheter or port;
4. Flush at conclusion of infusion; and
5. Standard tubing, syringes and supplies.

Payment for the above is included in the payment for the chemotherapy administration or nonchemotherapy injection and infusion service.

If a significant separately identifiable evaluation and management service is performed, the appropriate E & M code should be reported utilizing modifier 25 in addition to the chemotherapy administration or nonchemotherapy injection and infusion service. For an evaluation and management service provided on the same day, a different diagnosis is not required.

The CPT 2006 includes a parenthetical remark immediately following CPT code 90772 (Therapeutic, prophylactic or diagnostic injection; (specify substance or drug); subcutaneous or intramuscular.) It states, "Do not report 90772 for injections given without direct supervision. To report, use 99211." This coding guideline does not apply to Medicare patients. If the RN, LPN or other auxiliary personnel furnishes the injection in the office and the physician is not present in the office to meet the supervision requirement, which is one of the requirements for coverage of an incident to service, then the injection is not covered. The physician would also not report 99211 as this would not be covered as an incident to service.

D. Chemotherapy Administration
Chemotherapy administration codes apply to parenteral administration of nonradionuclide anti-neoplastic drugs; and also to anti-neoplastic agents provided for treatment of noncancer diagnoses (e.g., cyclophosphamide for auto-immune conditions) or to substances such as monoclonal antibody agents, and other biologic response modifiers. The following drugs are commonly considered to fall under the category of monoclonal antibodies: infliximab, rituximab, alemtuzumb, gemtuzumab, and trastuzumab. Drugs commonly considered to fall under the category of hormonal antineoplastics include leuprolide acetate and goserelin acetate. The drugs cited are not intended to be a complete list of drugs that may be administered using the chemotherapy administration codes. Local carriers may provide additional guidance as to which drugs may be considered to be chemotherapy drugs under Medicare.

The administration of anti-anemia drugs and anti-emetic drugs by injection or infusion for cancer patients is not considered chemotherapy administration.

If performed to facilitate the chemotherapy infusion or injection, the following services and items are included and are not separately billable:

1. Use of local anesthesia;
2. IV access;
3. Access to indwelling IV, subcutaneous catheter or port;
4. Flush at conclusion of infusion;
5. Standard tubing, syringes and supplies; and
6. Preparation of chemotherapy agent(s).

Payment for the above is included in the payment for the chemotherapy administration service.

If a significant separately identifiable evaluation and management service is performed, the appropriate E & M code should be reported utilizing modifier 25 in addition to the chemotherapy code. For an evaluation and management service provided on the same day, a different diagnosis is not required.

E. Coding Rules for Chemotherapy Administration and Nonchemotherapy Injections and Infusion Services
Instruct physicians to follow the CPT coding instructions to report chemotherapy administration and nonchemotherapy injections and infusions services with the exception listed in subsection C for CPT code 90772. The physician should be aware of the following specific rules.

When administering multiple infusions, injections or combinations, the physician should report only one "initial" service code unless protocol requires that two separate IV sites must be used. The initial code is the code that best describes the key or primary reason for the encounter and should always be reported irrespective of the order in which the infusions or injections occur. If an injection or infusion is of a subsequent or concurrent nature, even if it is the first such service within that group of services, then a subsequent or concurrent code should be reported. For example, the first IV push given subsequent to an initial one-hour infusion is reported using a subsequent IV push code.

If more than one "initial" service code is billed per day, the carrier shall deny the second initial service code unless the patient has to come back for a separately identifiable service on the same day or has two IV lines per protocol. For these separately identifiable services, instruct physician to report with modifier 59.

The CPT includes a code for a concurrent infusion in addition to an intravenous infusion for therapy, prophylaxis or diagnosis. Allow only one concurrent infusion per patient per encounter. Do not allow payment for the concurrent infusion billed with modifier 59 unless it is provided during a second encounter on the same day with the patient and is documented in the medical record.

For chemotherapy administration and therapeutic, prophylactic and diagnostic injections and infusions, an intravenous or intra-arterial push is defined as: 1.) an injection in which the healthcare professional is continuously present to administer the substance/drug and observe the patient; or 2.) an infusion of 15 minutes or less.

The physician may report the infusion code for "each additional hour" only if the infusion interval is greater than 30 minutes beyond the 1 hour increment. For example if the patient receives an infusion of a single drug that lasts 1 hour and 45 minutes, the physician would report the "initial" code up to 1 hour and the add-on code for the additional 45 minutes.

Several chemotherapy administration and nonchemotherapy injection and infusion service codes have the following parenthetical descriptor included as a part of the CPT code, "List separately in addition to code for primary procedure." Each of these codes has a physician fee schedule indicator of "ZZZ" meaning this service is allowed if billed with another chemotherapy administration or nonchemotherapy injection and infusion service code.

Do not interpret this parenthetical descriptor to mean that the add-on code can be billed only if it is listed with another drug administration primary code. For example, code 90761 will be ordinarily billed with code 90760. However, there may be instances when only the add-on code, 90761, is billed because an "initial" code from another section in the drug administration codes, instead of 90760, is billed as the primary code.

Pay for code 96523, "Irrigation of implanted venous access device for drug delivery systems," if it is the only service provided that day. If there is a visit or other chemotherapy administration or nonchemotherapy injection or infusion service provided on the same day, payment for 96523 is included in the payment for the other service.

F. Chemotherapy Administration (or Nonchemotherapy Injection and Infusion) and Evaluation and Management Services Furnished on the Same Day

For services furnished on or after January 1, 2004, do not allow payment for CPT code 99211, with or without modifier 25, if it is billed with a nonchemotherapy drug infusion code or a chemotherapy administration code. Apply this policy to code 99211 when it is billed with a diagnostic or therapeutic injection code on or after January 1, 2005.

Physicians providing a chemotherapy administration service or a nonchemotherapy drug infusion service and evaluation and management services, other than CPT code 99211, on the same day must bill in accordance with 30.6.6 using modifier 25. The carriers pay for evaluation and management services provided on the same day as the chemotherapy administration services or a nonchemotherapy injection or infusion service if the evaluation and management service meets the requirements of section 30.6.6 even though the underlying codes do not have global periods. If a chemotherapy service and a significant separately identifiable evaluation and management service are provided on the same day, a different diagnosis is not required.

In 2005, the Medicare physician fee schedule status database indicators for therapeutic and diagnostic injections were changed from T to A. Thus, beginning in 2005, the policy on evaluation and management services, other than 99211, that is applicable to a chemotherapy or a nonchemotherapy injection or infusion service applies equally to these codes.

100-4, 12, 30.6.1
Selection of Level of Evaluation and Management Service
A. Use of CPT Codes

Advise physicians to use CPT codes (level 1 of HCPCS) to code physician services, including evaluation and management services. Medicare will pay for E/M services for specific non-physician practitioners (i.e., nurse practitioner (NP), clinical nurse specialist (CNS) and certified nurse midwife (CNM)) whose Medicare benefit permits them to bill these services. A physician assistant (PA) may also provide a physician service, however, the physician collaboration and general supervision rules as well as all billing rules apply to all the above non-physician practitioners. The service provided must be medically necessary and the service must be within the scope of practice for a nonphysician practitioner in the State in which he/she practices. Do not pay for CPT evaluation and management codes billed by physical therapists in independent practice or by occupational therapists in independent practice.

Medical necessity of a service is the overarching criterion for payment in addition to the individual requirements of a CPT code. It would not be medically necessary or appropriate to bill a higher level of evaluation and management service when a lower level of service is warranted. The volume of documentation should not be the primary influence upon which a specific level of service is billed. Documentation should support the level of service reported. The service should be documented during, or as soon as practicable after it is provided in order to maintain an accurate medical record.

B. Selection of Level Of Evaluation and Management Service

Instruct physicians to select the code for the service based upon the content of the service. The duration of the visit is an ancillary factor and does not control the level of the service to be billed unless more than 50 percent of the face-to-face time (for non-inpatient services) or more than 50 percent of the floor time (for inpatient services) is spent providing counseling or coordination of care as described in subsection C.

Any physician or non-physician practitioner (NPP) authorized to bill Medicare services will be paid by the carrier at the appropriate physician fee schedule amount based on the rendering UPIN/PIN.

"Incident to" Medicare Part B payment policy is applicable for office visits when the requirements for "incident to" are met (refer to sections 60.1, 60.2, and 60.3, chapter 15 in IOM 100-02).

SPLIT/SHARED E/M SERVICE
Office/Clinic Setting

In the office/clinic setting when the physician performs the E/M service the service must be reported using the physician's UPIN/PIN. When an E/M service is a shared/split encounter between a physician and a non-physician practitioner (NP, PA, CNS or CNM), the service is considered to have been performed "incident to" if the requirements for "incident to" are met and the patient is an established patient. If "incident to" requirements are not met for the shared/split E/M service, the service must be billed under the NPP's UPIN/PIN, and payment will be made at the appropriate physician fee schedule payment.

Hospital Inpatient/Outpatient/Emergency Department Setting When a hospital inpatient/hospital outpatient or emergency department E/M is shared between a physician and an NPP from the same group practice and the physician provides any face-to-face portion of the E/M encounter with the patient, the service may be billed under either the physician's or the NPP's UPIN/PIN number. However, if there was no face-to-face encounter between the patient and the physician (e.g., even if the physician participated in the service by only reviewing the patient's medical record) then the service may only be billed under the NPP's UPIN/PIN. Payment will be made at the appropriate physician fee schedule rate based on the UPIN/PIN entered on the claim.

EXAMPLES OF SHARED VISITS

1. If the NPP sees a hospital inpatient in the morning and the physician follows with a later face-to-face visit with the patient on the same day, the physician or the NPP may report the service.
2. In an office setting the NPP performs a portion of an E/M encounter and the physician completes the E/M service. If the "incident to" requirements are met, the physician reports the service. If the "incident to" requirements are not met, the service must be reported using the NPP's UPIN/PIN.

In the rare circumstance when a physician (or NPP) provides a service that does not reflect a CPT code description, the service must be reported as an unlisted service with CPT code 99499. A description of the service provided must accompany the claim. The carrier has the discretion to value the service when the service does not meet the full terms of a CPT code description (e.g., only a history is performed). The carrier also determines the payment based on the applicable percentage of the physician fee schedule depending on whether the claim is paid at the physician rate or the non-physician practitioner rate. CPT modifier -52 (reduced services) must not be used with an evaluation and management service. Medicare does not recognize modifier -52 for this purpose.

C. Selection Of Level Of Evaluation and Management Service Based On Duration Of Coordination Of Care and/or Counseling

Advise physicians that when counseling and/or coordination of care dominates (more than 50 percent) the face-to-face physician/patient encounter or the floor time (in the case of inpatient services), time is the key or controlling factor in selecting the level of service.

In general, to bill an E/M code, the physician must complete at least 2 out of 3 criteria applicable to the type/level of service provided. However, the physician may document time spent with the patient in conjunction with the medical decision-making involved and a description of the coordination of care or counseling provided. Documentation must be in sufficient detail to support the claim.

EXAMPLE: A cancer patient has had all preliminary studies completed and a medical decision to implement chemotherapy. At an office visit the physician discusses the treatment options and subsequent lifestyle effects of treatment the patient may encounter or is experiencing. The physician need not complete a history and physical examination in order to select the level of service. The time spent in counseling/coordination of care and medical decision-making will determine the level of service billed.

The code selection is based on the total time of the face-to-face encounter or floor time, not just the counseling time. The medical record must be documented in sufficient detail to justify the selection of the specific code if time is the basis for selection of the code.

In the office and other outpatient setting, counseling and/or coordination of care must be provided in the presence of the patient if the time spent providing those services is used to determine the level of service reported. Face-to-face time refers to the time with the physician only. Counseling by other staff is not considered to be part of the face-to-face physician/patient encounter time. Therefore, the time spent by the other staff is not considered in selecting the appropriate level of service. The code used depends upon the physician service provided.

In an inpatient setting, the counseling and/or coordination of care must be provided at the bedside or on the patient's hospital floor or unit that is associated with an individual patient. Time spent counseling the patient or coordinating the patient's care after the patient has left the office or the physician has left the patient's floor or begun to care for another patient on the floor is not considered when selecting the level of service to be reported.

The duration of counseling or coordination of care that is provided face-to-face or on the floor may be estimated but that estimate, along with the total duration of the visit, must be recorded when time is used for the selection of the level of a service that involves predominantly coordination of care or counseling.

D. Use of Highest Levels of Evaluation and Management Codes

Carriers must advise physicians that to bill the highest levels of visit and consultation codes, the services furnished must meet the definition of the code (e.g., to bill a Level 5 new patient visit, the history must meet CPT's definition of a comprehensive history).

The comprehensive history must include a review of all the systems and a complete past (medical and surgical) family and social history obtained at that visit. In the case of an established patient, it is acceptable for a physician to review the existing record and update it to reflect only changes in the patient's medical, family, and social history from the last encounter, but the physician must review the entire history for it to be considered a comprehensive history.

The comprehensive examination may be a complete single system exam such as cardiac, respiratory, psychiatric, or a complete multi-system examination.

100-4, 12, 30.6.2
Billing for Medically Necessary Visit on Same Occasion as Preventive Medicine Service

See Chapter 18 for payment for covered preventive services.

When a physician furnishes a Medicare beneficiary a covered visit at the same place and on the same occasion as a noncovered preventive medicine service (CPT codes 99381- 99397), consider the covered visit to be provided in lieu of a part of the preventive medicine service of equal value to the visit. A preventive medicine service (CPT codes 99381-99397) is a noncovered service. The physician may charge the beneficiary, as a charge for the noncovered remainder of the service, the amount by which the physician's current established charge for the preventive medicine service exceeds his/her current established charge for the covered visit. Pay for the covered visit based on the lesser of the fee schedule amount or the physician's actual charge for the visit. The physician is not required to give the beneficiary written advance notice of noncoverage of the part of the visit that constitutes a routine preventive visit. However, the physician is responsible for notifying the patient in advance of his/her liability for the charges for services that are not medically necessary to treat the illness or injury.

There could be covered and noncovered procedures performed during this encounter (e.g., screening x-ray, EKG, lab tests.). These are considered individually. Those procedures which are for screening for asymptomatic conditions are considered noncovered and, therefore, no payment is made. Those procedures ordered to diagnose or monitor a symptom, medical condition, or treatment are evaluated for medical necessity and, if covered, are paid.

100-4, 12, 30.6.4
Evaluation and Management (E/M) Services Furnished Incident to Physician's Service by Nonphysician Practitioners

When evaluation and management services are furnished incident to a physician's service by a nonphysician practitioner, the physician may bill the CPT code that describes the evaluation and management service furnished.

When evaluation and management services are furnished incident to a physician's service by a nonphysician employee of the physician, not as part of a physician service, the physician bills code 99211 for the service.

A physician is not precluded from billing under the "incident to" provision for services provided by employees whose services cannot be paid for directly under the Medicare program. Employees of the physician may provide services incident to the physician's service, but the physician alone is permitted to bill Medicare.

Services provided by employees as "incident to" are covered when they meet all the requirements for incident to and are medically necessary for the individual needs of the patien

100-4, 12, 30.6.7
Payment for Office or Other Outpatient Evaluation and Management (E/M) Visits (Codes 99201 - 99215)

A. Definition of New Patient for Selection of E/M Visit Code
Interpret the phrase "new patient" to mean a patient who has not received any professional services, i.e., E/M service or other face-to-face service (e.g., surgical procedure) from the physician or physician group practice (same physician specialty) within the previous 3 years. For example, if a professional component of a previous procedure is billed in a 3 year time period, e.g., a lab interpretation is billed and no E/M service or other face-to-face service with the patient is performed, then this patient remains a new patient for the initial visit. An interpretation of a diagnostic test, reading an x-ray or EKG etc., in the absence of an E/M service or other face-to-face service with the patient does not affect the designation of a new patient.

B. Office/Outpatient E/M Visits Provided on Same Day for Unrelated Problems
As for all other E/M services except where specifically noted, carriers may not pay two E/M office visits billed by a physician (or physician of the same specialty from the same group practice) for the same beneficiary on the same day unless the physician documents that the visits were for unrelated problems in the office or outpatient setting which could not be provided during the same encounter (e.g., office visit for blood pressure medication evaluation, followed five hours later by a visit for evaluation of leg pain following an accident).

C. Office/Outpatient or Emergency Department E/M Visit on Day of Admission to Nursing Facility
Carriers may not pay a physician for an emergency department visit or an office visit and a comprehensive nursing facility assessment on the same day. Bundle E/M visits on the same date provided in sites other than the nursing facility into the initial nursing facility care code when performed on the same date as the nursing facility admission by the same physician.

D. Drug Administration Services and E/M Visits Billed on Same Day of Service
Carriers must advise physicians that CPT code 99211 cannot be paid if it is billed with a drug administration service such as a chemotherapy or nonchemotherapy drug infusion code (effective January 1, 2004). This drug administration policy was expanded in the Physician Fee Schedule Final Rule, November 15, 2004, to also include a therapeutic or diagnostic injection code (effective January 1, 2005). Therefore, when a medically necessary, significant and separately identifiable E/M service (which meets a higher complexity level than CPT code 99211) is performed, in addition to one of these drug administration services, the appropriate E/M CPT code should be reported with modifier -25. Documentation should support the level of E/M service billed. For an E/M service provided on the same day, a different diagnosis is not required.

100-4, 12, 30.6.8
Payment for Hospital Observation Services (Codes 99217‚Äì 99220) and Observation or Inpatient Care Services (Including Admission and Discharge Services–(Codes 99234–99236))

A. Who May Bill Initial Observation Care
Contractors pay for initial observation care billed by only the physician who admitted the patient to hospital observation and was responsible for the patient during his/her stay in observation. A physician who does not have inpatient admitting privileges but who is authorized to admit a patient to observation status may bill these codes.

For a physician to bill the initial observation care codes, there must be a medical observation record for the patient which contains dated and timed physician's admitting orders regarding the care the patient is to receive while in observation, nursing notes, and progress notes prepared by the physician while the patient was in observation status.

This record must be in addition to any record prepared as a result of an emergency department or outpatient clinic encounter.

Payment for an initial observation care code is for all the care rendered by the admitting physician on the date the patient was admitted to observation. All other physicians who see the patient while he or she is in observation must bill the office and other outpatient service codes or outpatient consultation codes as appropriate when they provide services to the patient.

For example, if an internist admits a patient to observation and asks an allergist for a consultation on the patient's condition, only the internist may bill the initial observation care code. The allergist must bill using the outpatient consultation code that best represents the services he or she provided. The allergist cannot bill an inpatient consultation since the patient was not a hospital inpatient.

B. Physician Billing for Observation Care Following Admission to Observation
When a patient is admitted for observation care for less than 8 hours on the same calendar date, the Initial Observation Care, from CPT code range 99218 - 99220, shall be reported by the physician. The Observation Care Discharge Service, CPT code 99217, shall not be reported for this scenario.

When a patient is admitted for observation care and then discharged on a different calendar date, the physician shall report Initial Observation Care, from CPT code range 99218 - 99220 and CPT observation care discharge CPT code 99217.

When a patient has been admitted for observation care for a minimum of 8 hours, but less than 24 hours and discharged on the same calendar date, Observation or Inpatient Care Services (Including Admission and Discharge Services) from CPT code range 99234 - 99236, shall be reported. The observation discharge, CPT code 99217, cannot also be reported for this scenario.

C. Documentation Requirements for Billing Observation or Inpatient Care Services (Including Admission and Discharge Services (Codes 99234 - 99236))
The physician shall satisfy the E/M documentation guidelines for admission to and discharge from observation care or inpatient hospital care. In addition to meeting the documentation requirements for history, examination, and medical decision making documentation in the medical record shall include:

- Documentation stating the stay for observation care or inpatient hospital care involves 8 hours, but less than 24 hours;
- Documentation identifying the billing physician was present and personally performed the services; and
- Documentation identifying the admission and discharge notes were written by the billing physician.

In the rare circumstance when a patient is held in observation status for more than 2 calendar dates, the physician shall bill a visit furnished before the discharge date using the outpatient/office visit codes. The physician may not use the subsequent hospital care codes since the patient is not an inpatient of the hospital.

D. Admission to Inpatient Status from Observation
If the same physician who admitted a patient to observation status also admits the patient to inpatient status from observation before the end of the date on which the patient was admitted to observation, pay only an initial hospital visit for the evaluation and management services provided on that date. Medicare payment for the initial hospital visit includes all services provided to the patient on the date of admission by that physician, regardless of the site of service. The physician may not bill an initial observation care code for services on the date that he or she admits the patient to inpatient status. If the patient is admitted to inpatient status from observation subsequent to the date of admission to observation, the physician must bill an initial hospital visit for the services provided on that date. The physician may not bill the hospital observation discharge management code (code 99217) or an outpatient/office visit for the care provided in observation on the date of admission to inpatient status.

E. Hospital Observation During Global Surgical Period
The global surgical fee includes payment for hospital observation (codes 99217, 99218, 99219, and 99220, 99234, 99235, 99236) services unless the criteria for use of CPT modifiers "-24," "-25," or "-57" are met. Contractors must pay for these services in addition to the global surgical fee only if both of the following requirements are met:

- The hospital observation service meets the criteria needed to justify billing it with CPT modifiers "-24," "-25," or "-57" (decision for major surgery); and
- The hospital observation service furnished by the surgeon meets all of the criteria for the hospital observation code billed.

Examples of the decision for surgery during a hospital observation period are:

- A patient is admitted by an emergency department physician to an observation unit for observation of a head injury. A neurosurgeon is called in to do a consultation on the need for surgery while the patient is in the observation unit and decides that the patient requires surgery. The surgeon would bill an outpatient consultation with the "-57" modifier to indicate that the decision for surgery was made during the consultation. The surgeon must bill an outpatient consultation because the patient in an observation unit is not an inpatient of the hospital. Only the physician who admitted the patient to hospital observation may bill for initial observation care.

- A patient is admitted by a neurosurgeon to a hospital observation unit for observation of a head injury. During the observation period, the surgeon makes the decision for surgery. The surgeon would bill the appropriate level of hospital observation code with the "-57" modifier to indicate that the decision for surgery was made while the surgeon was providing hospital observation care.

Examples of hospital observation services during the postoperative period of a surgery are:

- A patient at the 80th day following a TURP is admitted to observation with abdominal pain from a kidney stone by the surgeon who performed the procedure. The surgeon decides that the patient does not require surgery. The surgeon would bill the observation code with CPT modifier "-24" and documentation to support that the observation services are unrelated to the surgery.

- A patient at the 80th day following a TURP is admitted to observation with abdominal pain by the surgeon who performed the procedure. While the patient is in hospital observation, the surgeon decides that the patient requires kidney surgery. The surgeon would bill the observation code with HCPCS modifier "-57" to indicate that the decision for surgery was made while the patient was in hospital observation. The subsequent surgical procedure would be reported with modifier "-79."

- A patient at the 20th day following a resection of the colon is admitted to observation for abdominal pain by the surgeon who performed the surgery. The surgeon determines that the patient requires no further colon surgery and discharges the patient. The surgeon may not bill for the observation services furnished during the global period because they were related to the previous surgery.

An example of a billable hospital observation service on the same day as a procedure is a patient is admitted to the hospital observation unit for observation of a head injury by a physician who repaired a laceration of the scalp in the emergency department. The physician would bill the observation code with a CPT modifier 25 and the procedure

100-4, 12, 30.6.9
Payment for Inpatient Hospital Visits - General (Codes 99221 - 99239)
A. Hospital Visit and Critical Care on Same Day
When a hospital inpatient or office/outpatient evaluation and management service (E/M) are furnished on a calendar date at which time the patient does not require critical care and the patient subsequently requires critical care both the critical Care Services (CPT codes 99291 and 99292) and the previous E/M service may be paid on the same date of service. Hospital emergency department services are not paid for the same date as critical care services when provided by the same physician to the same patient.

During critical care management of a patient those services that do not meet the level of critical care shall be reported using an inpatient hospital care service with CPT Subsequent Hospital Care using a code from CPT code range 99231 - 99233.

Both Initial Hospital Care (CPT codes 99221 - 99223) and Subsequent Hospital Care codes are "per diem" services and may be reported only once per day by the same physician or physicians of the same specialty from the same group practice.

Physicians and qualified nonphysician practitioners (NPPs) are advised to retain documentation for discretionary contractor review should claims be questioned for both hospital care and critical care claims. The retained documentation shall support claims for critical care when the same physician or physicians of the same specialty in a group practice report critical care services for the same patient on the same calendar date as other E/M services.

B. Two Hospital Visits Same Day
Contractors pay a physician for only one hospital visit per day for the same patient, whether the problems seen during the encounters are related or not. The inpatient hospital visit descriptors contain the phrase "per day" which means that the code and the payment established for the code represent all services provided on that date. The physician should select a code that reflects all services provided during the date of the service.

C. Hospital Visits Same Day But by Different Physicians
In a hospital inpatient situation involving one physician covering for another, if physician A sees the patient in the morning and physician B, who is covering for A, sees the same patient in the evening, carriers do not pay physician B for the second visit. The hospital visit descriptors include the phrase "per day" meaning care for the day.

If the physicians are each responsible for a different aspect of the patient's care, pay both visits if the physicians are in different specialties and the visits are billed with different diagnoses. There are circumstances where concurrent care may be billed by physicians of the same specialty.

D. Visits to Patients in Swing Beds
If the inpatient care is being billed by the hospital as inpatient hospital care, the hospital care codes apply. If the inpatient care is being billed by the hospital as nursing facility care, then the nursing facility codes apply.

100-4, 12, 30.6.9.1
Payment for Initial Hospital Care Services (Codes 99221–99223 and Observation or Inpatient Care Services (Including Admission and Discharge Services) (Codes 99234–99236)
A. Initial Hospital Care From Emergency Room
Contractors pay for an initial hospital care service or an initial inpatient consultation if a physician sees his/her patient in the emergency room and decides to admit the person to the hospital. They do not pay for both E/M services. Also, they do not pay for an emergency department visit by the same physician on the same date of service. When the patient is admitted to the hospital via another site of service (e.g., hospital emergency department, physician's office, nursing facility), all services provided by the physician in conjunction with that admission are considered part of the initial hospital care when performed on the same date as the admission.

B. Initial Hospital Care on Day Following Visit
Contractors pay both visits if a patient is seen in the office on one date and admitted to the hospital on the next date, even if fewer than 24 hours has elapsed between the visit and the admission.

C. Initial Hospital Care and Discharge on Same Day
When the patient is admitted to inpatient hospital care for less than 8 hours on the same date, then Initial Hospital Care, from CPT code range 99221 - 99223, shall be reported by the physician. The Hospital Discharge Day Management service, CPT codes 99238 or 99239, shall not be reported for this scenario.

When a patient is admitted to inpatient initial hospital care and then discharged on a different calendar date, the physician shall report an Initial Hospital Care from CPT code range 99221 - 99223 and a Hospital Discharge Day Management service, CPT code 99238 or 99239.

When a patient has been admitted to inpatient hospital care for a minimum of 8 hours but less than 24 hours and discharged on the same calendar date, Observation or Inpatient Hospital Care Services (Including Admission and Discharge Services), from CPT code range 99234 - 99236, shall be reported.

D. Documentation Requirements for Billing Observation or Inpatient Care Services (Including Admission and Discharge Services), CPT codes 99234 - 99236
The physician shall satisfy the E/M documentation guidelines for admission to and discharge from inpatient observation or hospital care. In addition to meeting the documentation requirements for history, examination and medical decision making documentation in the medical record shall include:

- Documentation stating the stay for hospital treatment or observation care status involves 8 hours but less than 24 hours;
- Documentation identifying the billing physician was present and personally performed the services; and
- Documentation identifying the admission and discharge notes were written by the billing physician.

E. Physician Services Involving Transfer From One Hospital to Another; Transfer Within Facility to Prospective Payment System (PPS) Exempt Unit of Hospital; Transfer From One Facility to Another Separate Entity Under Same Ownership and/or Part of Same Complex; or Transfer From One Department to Another Within Single Facility
Physicians may bill both the hospital discharge management code and an initial hospital care code when the discharge and admission do not occur on the same day if the transfer is between:

- Different hospitals;
- Different facilities under common ownership which do not have merged records; or
- Between the acute care hospital and a PPS exempt unit within the same hospital when there are no merged records.

In all other transfer circumstances, the physician should bill only the appropriate level of subsequent hospital care for the date of transfer.

F. Initial Hospital Care Service History and Physical That Is Less Than Comprehensive
When a physician performs a visit or consultation that meets the definition of a Level 5 office visit or consultation several days prior to an admission and on the day of admission performs less than a comprehensive history and physical, he or she should report the office visit or consultation that reflects the services furnished and also report the lowest level initial hospital care code (i.e., code 99221) for the initial hospital admission. Contractors pay the office visit as billed and the Level 1 initial hospital care code.

G. Initial Hospital Care Visits by Two Different M.D.s or D.O.s When They Are Involved in Same Admission
Physicians use the initial hospital care codes (codes 99221-99223) to report the first hospital inpatient encounter with the patient when he or she is the admitting physician.

Contractors consider only one M.D. or D.O. to be the admitting physician and permit only the admitting physician to use the initial hospital care codes. Physicians that participate in the care of a patient but are not the admitting physician of record should bill the inpatient evaluation and management services codes that describe their participation in the patient's care (i.e., subsequent hospital visit or inpatient consultation).

H. Initial Hospital Care and Nursing Facility Visit on Same Day
Pay only the initial hospital care code if the patient is admitted to a hospital following a nursing facility visit on the same date by the same physician. Instruct physicians that they may not report a nursing facility service and an initial hospital care service on the same day. Payment for the initial hospital care service includes all work performed by in all sites of service on that dat

100-4, 12, 30.6.9.2
Subsequent Hospital Visit and Hospital Discharge Day Management (Codes 99231 - 99239)
A. Subsequent Hospital Visits During the Global Surgery Period
(Refer to Secs.40-40.4 on global surgery)

The Medicare physician fee schedule payment amount for surgical procedures includes all services (e.g., evaluation and management visits) that are part of the global surgery payment; therefore, contractors shall not pay more than that amount when a bill is fragmented for staged procedures.

B. Hospital Discharge Day Management Service
Hospital Discharge Day Management Services, CPT code 99238 or 99239 is a face-to-face evaluation and management (E/M) service between the attending physician and the patient. The E/M discharge day management visit shall be reported for the date of the actual visit by the physician or qualified nonphysician practitioner even if the patient is discharged from the facility on a different calendar date. Only one hospital discharge day management service is payable per patient per hospital stay.

Only the attending physician of record reports the discharge day management service. Physicians or qualified nonphysician practitioners, other than the attending physician, who have been managing concurrent health care problems not primarily managed by the attending physician, and who are not acting on behalf of the attending physician, shall use Subsequent Hospital Care (CPT code range 99231 - 99233) for a final visit.

Medicare pays for the paperwork of patient discharge day management through the pre- and post- service work of an E/M service.

Appendix G — Pub 100 References

Current Procedural Coding Expert

Appendix G — Pub 100 References

C. Subsequent Hospital Visit and Discharge Management on Same Day
Pay only the hospital discharge management code on the day of discharge (unless it is also the day of admission, in which case, refer to Sec.30.6.9.1 C for the policy on Observation or Inpatient Care Services (Including Admission and Discharge Services CPT Codes 99234 - 99236). Contractors do not pay both a subsequent hospital visit in addition to hospital discharge day management service on the same day by the same physician. Instruct physicians that they may not bill for both a hospital visit and hospital discharge management for the same date of service.

D. Hospital Discharge Management (CPT Codes 99238 and 99239) and Nursing Facility Admission Code When Patient Is Discharged From Hospital and Admitted to Nursing Facility on Same Day
Contractors pay the hospital discharge code (codes 99238 or 99239) in addition to a nursing facility admission code when they are billed by the same physician with the same date of service.

If a surgeon is admitting the patient to the nursing facility due to a condition that is not as a result of the surgery during the postoperative period of a service with the global surgical period, he/she bills for the nursing facility admission and care with a modifier "-24" and provides documentation that the service is unrelated to the surgery (e.g., return of an elderly patient to the nursing facility in which he/she has resided for five years following discharge from the hospital for cholecystectomy).

Contractors do not pay for a nursing facility admission by a surgeon in the postoperative period of a procedure with a global surgical period if the patient's admission to the nursing facility is to receive post operative care related to the surgery (e.g., admission to a nursing facility to receive physical therapy following a hip replacement). Payment for the nursing facility admission and subsequent nursing facility services are included in the global fee and cannot be paid separately.

E. Hospital Discharge Management and Death Pronouncement
Only the physician who personally performs the pronouncement of death shall bill for the face-to-face Hospital Discharge Day Management Service, CPT code 99238 or 99239. The date of the pronouncement shall reflect the calendar date of service on the day it was performed even if the paperwork is delayed to a subsequent date.

100-4, 12, 30.6.10

Consultation Services (Codes 99241 - 99255)

A. Consultation Services versus Other Evaluation and Management (E/M) Visits
Carriers pay for a reasonable and medically necessary consultation service when all of the following criteria for the use of a consultation code are met:

- Specifically, a consultation service is distinguished from other evaluation and management (E/M) visits because it is provided by a physician or qualified nonphysician practitioner (NPP) whose opinion or advice regarding evaluation and/or management of a specific problem is requested by another physician or other appropriate source. The qualified NPP may perform consultation services within the scope of practice and licensure requirements for NPPs in the State in which he/she practices. Applicable collaboration and general supervision rules apply as well as billing rules;
- A request for a consultation from an appropriate source and the need for consultation (i.e., the reason for a consultation service) shall be documented by the consultant in the patient's medical record and included in the requesting physician or qualified NPP's plan of care in the patient's medical record; and
- After the consultation is provided, the consultant shall prepare a written report of his/her findings and recommendations, which shall be provided to the referring physician.

The intent of a consultation service is that a physician or qualified NPP or other appropriate source is asking another physician or qualified NPP for advice, opinion, a recommendation, suggestion, direction, or counsel, etc. in evaluating or treating a patient because that individual has expertise in a specific medical area beyond the requesting professional's knowledge. Consultations may be billed based on time if the counseling/coordination of care constitutes more than 50 percent of the face-to-face encounter between the physician or qualified NPP and the patient. The preceding requirements (request, evaluation (or counseling/coordination) and written report) shall also be met when the consultation is based on time for counseling/coordination.

A consultation shall not be performed as a split/shared E/M visit.

B. Consultation Followed by Treatment
A physician or qualified NPP consultant may initiate diagnostic services and treatment at the initial consultation service or subsequent visit. Ongoing management, following the initial consultation service by the consultant physician, shall not be reported with consultation service codes. These services shall be reported as subsequent visits for the appropriate place of service and level of service. Payment for a consultation service shall be made regardless of treatment initiation unless a transfer of care occurs.

Transfer of Care A transfer of care occurs when a physician or qualified NPP requests that another physician or qualified NPP take over the responsibility for managing the patients' complete care for the condition and does not expect to continue treating or caring for the patient for that condition.

When this transfer is arranged, the requesting physician or qualified NPP is not asking for an opinion or advice to personally treat this patient and is not expecting to continue treating the patient for the condition. The receiving physician or qualified NPP shall document this transfer of the patient's care, to his/her service, in the patient's medical record or plan of care.

In a transfer of care the receiving physician or qualified NPP would report the appropriate new or established patient visit code according to the place of service and level of service performed and shall not report a consultation service.

C. Initial and Follow-Up Consultation Services
Initial Consultation Service
In the hospital setting, the consulting physician or qualified NPP shall use the appropriate Initial Inpatient Consultation codes (99251 - 99255) for the initial consultation service.

In the nursing facility setting, the consulting physician or qualified NPP shall use the appropriate Initial Inpatient Consultation codes (99251 - 99255) for the initial consultation service.

The Initial Inpatient Consultation may be reported only once per consultant per patient per facility admission.

In the office or other outpatient setting, the consulting physician or qualified NPP shall use the appropriate Office or Other Outpatient Consultation (new or established patient) codes (99241 - 99245) for the initial consultation service.

If an additional request for an opinion or advice, regarding the same or a new problem with the same patient, is received from the same or another physician or qualified NPP and documented in the medical record, the Office or Other Outpatient Consultation (new or established patient) codes (99241 - 99245) may be used again. However, if the consultant continues to care for the patient for the original condition following his/her initial consultation, repeat consultation services shall not be reported by this physician or qualified NPP during his/her ongoing management of this condition.

Follow-Up Consultation Service
Effective January 1, 2006, the follow-up inpatient consultation codes (99261 - 99263) are deleted.

In the hospital setting, following the initial consultation service, the Subsequent Hospital Care codes (99231 - 99233) shall be reported for additional follow-up visits.

In the nursing facility setting, following the initial consultation service, the Subsequent Nursing Facility (NF) Care codes (new CPT codes 99307 - 99310) shall be reported for additional follow-up visits. Effective January 1, 2006, CPT codes 99311 - 99313 are deleted and not valid for Subsequent NF visits.

In the office or other outpatient setting, following the initial consultation service, the Office or Other Outpatient Established Patient codes (99212 - 99215) shall be reported for additional follow-up visits. The CPT code 99211 shall not be reported as a consultation service. The CPT code 99211 is not included by Medicare for a consultation service since this service typically does not require the presence of a physician or qualified NPP and would not meet the consultation service criteria.

D. Second Opinion E/M Service Requests
Effective January 1, 2006, the Confirmatory Consultation codes (99271 - 99275) are deleted.

A second opinion E/M service is a request by the patient and/or family or mandated (e.g., by a third-party payer) and is not requested by a physician or qualified NPP. A consultation service requested by a physician, qualified NPP or other appropriate source that meets the requirements stated in Section A shall be reported using the initial consultation service codes as discussed in Section C. A written report is not required by Medicare to be sent to a physician when an evaluation for a second opinion has been requested by the patient and/or family.

A second opinion, for Medicare purposes, is generally performed as a request for a second or third opinion of a previously recommended medical treatment or surgical procedure. A second opinion E/M service initiated by a patient and/or family is not reported using the consultation codes.

In both the inpatient hospital setting and the NF setting, a request for a second opinion would be made through the attending physician or physician of record. If an initial consultation is requested of another physician or qualified NPP by the attending physician and meets the requirements for a consultation service (as identified in Section A) then the appropriate Initial Inpatient Consultation code shall be reported by the consultant. If the service does not meet the consultation requirements, then the E/M service shall be reported using the Subsequent Hospital Care codes (99231 - 99233) in the inpatient hospital setting and the Subsequent NF Care codes (99307 - 99310) in the NF setting.

A second opinion E/M service performed in the office or other outpatient setting shall be reported using the Office or Other Outpatient new patient codes (99201 - 99205) for a new patient and established patient codes (99212 - 99215) for an established patient, as appropriate. The 3 year rule regarding "new patient" status applies. Any medically necessary follow-up visits shall be reported using the appropriate subsequent visit/established patient E/M visit codes.

The CPT modifier -32 (Mandated Services) is not recognized as a payment modifier in Medicare. A second opinion evaluation service to satisfy a requirement for a third party payer is not a covered service in Medicare.

E. Consultations Requested by Members of Same Group
Carriers pay for a consultation if one physician or qualified NPP in a group practice requests a consultation from another physician in the same group practice when the consulting physician or qualified NPP has expertise in a specific medical area beyond the requesting professional's knowledge. A consultation service shall not be reported on every patient as a routine practice between physicians and qualified NPPs within a group practice setting.

F. Documentation for Consultation Services
Consultation Request
A written request for a consultation from an appropriate source and the need for a consultation must be documented in the patient's medical record. The initial request may be a verbal interaction between the requesting physician and the consulting physician; however, the verbal conversation shall be documented in the patient's medical record, indicating a request for a consultation service was made by the requesting physician or qualified NPP.

The reason for the consultation service shall be documented by the consultant (physician or qualified NPP) in the patient's medical record and included in the requesting physician or qualified NPP's plan of care. The consultation service request may be written on a physician order form by the requestor in a shared medical record.

Consultation Report
A written report shall be furnished to the requesting physician or qualified NPP.

In an emergency department or an inpatient or outpatient setting in which the medical record is shared between the referring physician or qualified NPP and the consultant, the request may be documented as part of a plan written in the requesting physician or qualified NPP's progress note, an order in the medical record, or a specific written request for the consultation. In these settings, the report may consist of an appropriate entry in the common medical record.

In an office setting, the documentation requirement may be met by a specific written request for the consultation from the requesting physician or qualified NPP or if the consultant's records show a specific reference to the request. In this setting, the consultation report is a separate document communicated to the requesting physician or qualified NPP.

In a large group practice, e.g., an academic department or a large multi-specialty group, in which there is often a shared medical record, it is acceptable to include the consultant's report in the medical record documentation and not require a separate letter from the consulting physician or qualified NPP to the requesting physician or qualified NPP. The written request and the consultation evaluation, findings and recommendations shall be available in the consultation report.

G. Consultation for Preoperative Clearance
Preoperative consultations are payable for new or established patients performed by any physician or qualified NPP at the request of a surgeon, as long as all of the requirements for performing and reporting the consultation codes are met and the service is medically necessary and not routine screening.

H. Postoperative Care by Physician Who Did Preoperative Clearance Consultation
If subsequent to the completion of a preoperative consultation in the office or hospital, the consultant assumes responsibility for the management of a portion or all of the patient's condition(s) during the postoperative period, the consultation codes should not be used postoperatively. In the hospital setting, the physician or qualified NPP who has performed a preoperative consultation and assumes responsibility for the management of a portion or all of the patient's condition(s) during the postoperative period should use the appropriate subsequent hospital care codes to bill for the concurrent care he or she is providing. In the office setting, the appropriate established patient visit codes should be used during the postoperative period.

A physician (primary care or specialist) or qualified NPP who performs a postoperative evaluation of a new or established patient at the request of the surgeon may bill the appropriate consultation code for evaluation and management services furnished during the postoperative period following surgery when all of the criteria for the use of the consultation codes are met and that same physician has not already performed a preoperative consultation.

I. Surgeon's Request That Another Physician Participate In Postoperative Care
If the surgeon asks a physician or qualified NPP who had been treating the patient preoperatively or who had not seen the patient for a preoperative consultation to take responsibility for the management of an aspect of the patient's condition during the postoperative period, the physician or qualified NPP may not bill a consultation because the surgeon is not asking the physician or qualified NPP's opinion or advice for the surgeon's use in treating the patient. The physician or qualified NPP's services would constitute concurrent care and should be billed using the appropriate subsequent hospital care codes in the hospital inpatient setting, subsequent NF care codes in the SNF/NF setting or the appropriate office or other outpatient visit codes in the office or outpatient settings.

J. Examples That Meet the Criteria for Consultation Services
For brevity, the consultation request and the consultation written report is not repeated in each of these examples. Criteria for consultation services shall always include a request and a written report in the medical record as described above.

EXAMPLE 1: An internist sees a patient that he has followed for 20 years for mild hypertension and diabetes mellitus. He identifies a questionable skin lesion and asks a dermatologist to evaluate the lesion. The dermatologist examines the patient and decides the lesion is probably malignant and needs to be removed. He removes the lesion which is determined to be an early melanoma. The dermatologist dictates and forwards a report to the internist regarding his evaluation and treatment of the patient. Modifier -25 shall be used with the consultation service code in addition to the procedure code. Modifier -25 is required to identify the consultation service as a significant, separately identifiable E/M service in addition to the procedure code reported for the incision/removal of lesion. The internist resumes care of the patient and continues surveillance of the skin on the advice of the dermatologist.

EXAMPLE 2: A rural family practice physician examines a patient who has been under his care for 20 years and diagnoses a new onset of atrial fibrillation. The family practitioner sends the patient to a cardiologist at an urban cardiology center for advice on his care and management. The cardiologist examines the patient, suggests a cardiac catheterization and other diagnostic tests which he schedules and then sends a written report to the requesting physician. The cardiologist subsequently periodically sees the patient once a year as follow-up. Subsequent visits provided by the cardiologist should be billed as an established patient visit in the office or other outpatient setting, as appropriate.

Following the advice and intervention by the cardiologist the family practice physician resumes the general medical care of the patient.

EXAMPLE 3: A family practice physician examines a female patient who has been under his care for some time and diagnoses a breast mass. The family practitioner sends the patient to a general surgeon for advice and management of the mass and related patient care. The general surgeon examines the patient and recommends a breast biopsy, which he schedules, and then sends a written report to the requesting physician. The general surgeon subsequently performs a biopsy and then periodically sees the patient once a year as follow-up. Subsequent visits provided by the surgeon should be billed as an established patient visit in the office or other outpatient setting, as appropriate.

Following the advice and intervention by the surgeon the family practice physician resumes the general medical care of the patient.

I. Examples That Do Not Meet the Criteria for Consultation Services
EXAMPLE 1: Standing orders in the medical record for consultations.

EXAMPLE 2: No order for a consultation.

EXAMPLE 3: No written report of a consultation.

EXAMPLE 4: The emergency room physician treats the patient for a sprained ankle.

The patient is discharged and instructed to visit the orthopedic clinic for follow-up. The physician in the orthopedic clinic shall not report a consultation service because advice or opinion is not required by the emergency room physician. The orthopedic physician shall report the appropriate office or other outpatient visit code.

100-4, 12, 30.6.11
Emergency Department Visits (Codes 99281 - 99288)
B3-15507

A. Use of Emergency Department Codes by Physicians Not Assigned to Emergency Department
Any physician seeing a patient registered in the emergency department may use emergency department visit codes (for services matching the code description). It is not required that the physician be assigned to the emergency department.

B. Use of Emergency Department Codes In Office
Emergency department coding is not appropriate if the site of service is an office or outpatient setting or any sight of service other than an emergency department. The emergency department codes should only be used if the patient is seen in the emergency department and the services described by the HCPCS code definition are provided. The emergency department is defined as an organized hospital-based facility for the provision of unscheduled or episodic services to patients who present for immediate medical attention.

C. Use of Emergency Department Codes to Bill Nonemergency Services
Services in the emergency department may not be emergencies. However the codes (99281 - 99288) are payable if the described services are provided.

However, if the physician asks the patient to meet him or her in the emergency department as an alternative to the physician's office and the patient is not registered as a patient in the emergency department, the physician should bill the appropriate office/outpatient visit codes. Normally a lower level emergency department code would be reported for a nonemergency condition.

D. Emergency Department or Office/Outpatient Visits on Same Day As Nursing Facility Admission
Emergency department visit provided on the same day as a comprehensive nursing facility assessment are not paid. Payment for evaluation and management services on the same date provided in sites other than the nursing facility are included in the payment for initial nursing facility care when performed on the same date as the nursing facility admission.

E. Physician Billing for Emergency Department Services Provided to Patient by Both Patient's Personal Physician and Emergency Department Physician
If a physician advises his/her own patient to go to an emergency department (ED) of a hospital for care and the physician subsequently is asked by the ED physician to come to the hospital to evaluate the patient and to advise the ED physician as to whether the patient should be admitted to the hospital or be sent home, the physicians should bill as follows:

- If the patient is admitted to the hospital by the patient's personal physician, then the patient's regular physician should bill only the appropriate level of the initial hospital care (codes 99221 - 99223) because all evaluation and management services provided by that physician in conjunction with that admission are considered part of the initial hospital care when performed on the same date as the admission. The ED physician who saw the patient in the emergency department should bill the appropriate level of the ED codes.

- If the ED physician, based on the advice of the patient's personal physician who came to the emergency department to see the patient, sends the patient home, then the ED physician should bill the appropriate level of emergency department service. The patient's personal physician should also bill the level of emergency department code that describes the service he or she provided in the emergency department. The patient's personal physician would not bill a consultation because he or she is not providing information to the emergency department physician for his or her use in treating the patient. If the patient's personal physician does not come to the hospital to see the patient, but only advises the emergency department physician by telephone, then the patient's personal physician may not bill.

F. Emergency Department Physician Requests Another Physician to See the Patient in Emergency Department or Office/Outpatient Setting
If the emergency department physician requests that another physician evaluate a given patient, the other physician should bill a consultation if the criteria for consultation are met. If the criteria for a consultation are not met and the patient is discharged from the Emergency Department or admitted to the hospital by another physician, the physician contacted by the Emergency Department physician should bill an emergency department visit. If the consulted physician admits the patient to the hospital and the criteria for a consultation are not met, he/she should bill an initial hospital care code.

100-4, 12, 30.6.12
Critical Care Visits and Neonatal Intensive Care (Codes 99291 - 99292)
CRITICAL CARE SERVICES (CODES 99291-99292)

A. Use of Critical Care Codes
Pay for services reported with CPT codes 99291 and 99292 when all the criteria for critical care and critical care services are met. Critical care is defined as the direct delivery by a physician(s) medical care for a critically ill or critically injured patient. A critical illness or injury acutely impairs one or more vital organ systems such that there is a high probability of imminent or life threatening deterioration in the patient's condition.

Critical care involves high complexity decision making to assess, manipulate, and support vital system functions(s) to treat single or multiple vital organ system failure and/or to prevent further life threatening deterioration of the patient's condition.

Examples of vital organ system failure include, but are not limited to: central nervous system failure, circulatory failure, shock, renal, hepatic, metabolic, and/or respiratory failure. Although critical care typically requires interpretation of multiple physiologic parameters and/or application of advanced technology(s), critical care may be provided in life threatening situations when these elements are not present.

Providing medical care to a critically ill, injured, or post-operative patient qualifies as a critical care service only if both the illness or injury and the treatment being provided meet the above requirements.

Critical care is usually, but not always, given in a critical care area such as a coronary care unit, intensive care unit, respiratory care unit, or the emergency department. However, payment may be made for critical care services provided in any location as long as the care provided meets the definition of critical care.

Consult the American Medical Association (AMA) CPT Manual for the applicable codes and guidance for critical care services provided to neonates, infants and children.

B. Critical Care Services and Medical Necessity
Critical care services must be medically necessary and reasonable. Services provided that do not meet critical care services or services provided for a patient who is not critically ill or injured in accordance with the above definitions and criteria but who happens to be in a critical care, intensive care, or other specialized care unit should be reported using another appropriate E/M code (e.g., subsequent hospital care, CPT codes 99231 - 99233).

As described in Section A, critical care services encompass both treatment of "vital organ failure" and "prevention of further life threatening deterioration of the patient's condition." Therefore, although critical care may be delivered in a moment of crisis or upon being called to the patient's bedside emergently, this is not a requirement for providing critical care service. The treatment and management of the patient's condition, while not necessarily emergent, shall be required, based on the threat of imminent deterioration (i.e., the patient shall be critically ill or injured at the time of the physician's visit).

Chronic Illness and Critical Care:

Examples of patients whose medical condition may not warrant critical care services:

1. Daily management of a patient on chronic ventilator therapy does not meet the criteria for critical care unless the critical care is separately identifiable from the chronic long term management of the ventilator dependence.
2. Management of dialysis or care related to dialysis for a patient receiving ESRD hemodialysis does not meet the criteria for critical care unless the critical care is separately identifiable from the chronic long term management of the dialysis dependence (refer to Chapter 8, Sec.160.4). When a separately identifiable condition (e.g., management of seizures or pericardial tamponade related to renal failure) is being managed, it may be billed as critical care if critical care requirements are met. Modifier -25 should be appended to the critical care code when applicable in this situation.

Examples of patients whose medical condition may warrant critical care services:

1. An 81 year old male patient is admitted to the intensive care unit following abdominal aortic aneurysm resection. Two days after surgery he requires fluids and pressors to maintain adequate perfusion and arterial pressures. He remains ventilator dependent.
2. A 67 year old female patient is 3 days status post mitral valve repair. She develops petechiae, hypotension and hypoxia requiring respiratory and circulatory support.
3. A 70 year old admitted for right lower lobe pneumococcal pneumonia with a history of COPD becomes hypoxic and hypotensive 2 days after admission.
4. A 68 year old admitted for an acute anterior wall myocardial infarction continues to have symptomatic ventricular tachycardia that is marginally responsive to antiarrhythmic therapy.

Examples of patients who may not satisfy Medicare medical necessity criteria, or do not meet critical care criteria or who do not have a critical care illness or injury and therefore not eligible for critical care payment:

1. Patients admitted to a critical care unit because no other hospital beds were available;
2. Patients admitted to a critical care unit for close nursing observation and/or frequent monitoring of vital signs (e.g., drug toxicity or overdose); and
3. Patients admitted to a critical care unit because hospital rules require certain treatments (e.g., insulin infusions) to be administered in the critical care unit.

Providing medical care to a critically ill patient should not be automatically deemed to be a critical care service for the sole reason that the patient is critically ill or injured. While more than one physician may provide critical care services to a patient during the critical care episode of an illness or injury each physician must be managing one or more critical illness(es) or injury(ies) in whole or in part.

EXAMPLE: A dermatologist evaluates and treats a rash on an ICU patient who is maintained on a ventilator and nitroglycerine infusion that are being managed by an intensivist. The dermatologist should not report a service for critical care.

C. Critical Care Services and Full Attention of the Physician
The duration of critical care services to be reported is the time the physician spent evaluating, providing care and managing the critically ill or injured patient's care. That time must be spent at the immediate bedside or elsewhere on the floor or unit so long as the physician is immediately available to the patient.

For example, time spent reviewing laboratory test results or discussing the critically ill patient's care with other medical staff in the unit or at the nursing station on the floor may be reported as critical care, even when it does not occur at the bedside, if this time represents the physician's full attention to the management of the critically ill/injured patient.

For any given period of time spent providing critical care services, the physician must devote his or her full attention to the patient and, therefore, cannot provide services to any other patient during the same period of time. D. Critical Care Services and Qualified Non-Physician Practitioners (NPP) Critical care services may be provided by qualified NPPs and reported for payment under the NPP's National Provider Identifier (NPI) when the services meet the definition and requirements of critical care services in Sections A and B. The provision of critical care services must be within the scope of practice and licensure requirements for the State in which the qualified NPP practices and provides the service(s). Collaboration, physician supervision and billing requirements must also be met. A physician assistant shall meet the general physician supervision requirements.

E. Critical Care Services and Physician Time
Critical care is a time- based service, and for each date and encounter entry, the physician's progress note(s) shall document the total time that critical care services were provided. More than one physician can provide critical care at another time and be paid if the service meets critical care, is medically necessary and is not duplicative care. Concurrent care by more than one physician (generally representing different physician specialties) is payable if these requirements are met (refer to the Medicare Benefit Policy Manual, Pub. 100-02, Chapter 15, Sec.30 for concurrent care policy discussion).

The CPT critical care codes 99291 and 99292 are used to report the total duration of time spent by a physician providing critical care services to a critically ill or critically injured patient, even if the time spent by the physician on that date is not continuous. Non-continuous time for medically necessary critical care services may be aggregated. Reporting CPT code 99291 is a prerequisite to reporting CPT code 99292. Physicians of the same specialty within the same group practice bill and are paid as though they were a single physician (Sec.30.6.5).

1. Off the Unit/Floor
   Time spent in activities (excluding those identified previously in Section C) that occur outside of the unit or off the floor (i.e., telephone calls, whether taken at home, in the office, or elsewhere in the hospital) may not be reported as critical care because the physician is not immediately available to the patient. This time is regarded as pre- and post service work bundled in evaluation and management services.
2. Split/Shared Service
   A split/shared E/M service performed by a physician and a qualified NPP of the same group practice (or employed by the same employer) cannot be reported as a critical care service. Critical care services are reflective of the care and management of a critically ill or critically injured patient by an individual physician or qualified non-physician practitioner for the specified reportable period of time.

   Unlike other E/M services where a split/shared service is allowed the critical care service reported shall reflect the evaluation, treatment and management of a patient by an individual physician or qualified non-physician practitioner and shall not be representative of a combined service between a physician and a qualified NPP.

   When CPT code time requirements for both 99291 and 99292 and critical care criteria are met for a medically necessary visit by a qualified NPP the service shall be billed using the appropriate individual NPI number. Medically necessary visit(s) that do not meet these requirements shall be reported as subsequent hospital care services.
3. Unbundled Procedures
   Time involved performing procedures that are not bundled into critical care (i.e., billed and paid separately) may not be included and counted toward critical care time. The physician's progress note(s) in the medical record should document that time involved in the performance of separately billable procedures was not counted toward critical care time.
4. Family Counseling/Discussions
   Critical care CPT codes 99291 and 99292 include pre and post service work. Routine daily updates or reports to family members and or surrogates are considered part of this service. However, time involved with family members or other surrogate decision makers, whether to obtain a history or to discuss treatment options (as described in CPT), may be counted toward critical care time when these specific criteria are met:

   a) The patient is unable or incompetent to participate in giving a history and/or making treatment decisions, and

   b) The discussion is necessary for determining treatment decisions.

   For family discussions, the physician should document:

   a. The patient is unable or incompetent to participate in giving history and/or making treatment decisions

   b. The necessity to have the discussion (e.g., "no other source was available to obtain a history" or "because the patient was deteriorating so rapidly I needed to immediately discuss treatment options with the family",

   c. Medically necessary treatment decisions for which the discussion was needed, and

   d. A summary in the medical record that supports the medical necessity of the discussion All other family discussions, no matter how lengthy, may not be additionally counted towards critical care. Telephone calls to family members and or surrogate decision-makers may be counted towards critical care time, but only if they meet the same criteria as described in the aforementioned paragraph.
5. Inappropriate Use of Time for Payment of Critical Care Services.
   Time involved in activities that do not directly contribute to the treatment of the critically ill or injured patient may not be counted towards the critical care time, even when they are performed in the critical care unit at a patient's bedside (e.g., review of literature, and

teaching sessions with physician residents whether conducted on hospital rounds or in other venues).

F. Hours and Days of Critical Care that May Be Billed

Critical care service is a time-based service provided on an hourly or fraction of an hour basis. Payment should not be restricted to a fixed number of hours, a fixed number of physicians, or a fixed number of days, on a per patient basis, for medically necessary critical care services. Time counted towards critical care services may be continuous or intermittent and aggregated in time increments (e.g., 50 minutes of continuous clock time or (5) 10 minute blocks of time spread over a given calendar date). Only one physician may bill for critical care services during any one single period of time even if more than one physician is providing care to a critically ill patient.

For Medicare Part B physician services paid under the physician fee schedule, critical care is not a service that is paid on a "shift" basis or a "per day" basis. Documentation may be requested for any claim to determine medical necessity. Examples of critical care billing that may require further review could include: claims from several physicians submitting multiple units of critical care for a single patient, and submitting claims for more than 12 hours of critical care time by a physician for one or more patients on the same given calendar date. Physicians assigned to a critical care unit (e.g., hospitalist, intensivist, etc.) may not report critical care for patients based on a "per shift" basis.

The CPT code 99291 is used to report the first 30 - 74 minutes of critical care on a given calendar date of service. It should only be used once per calendar date per patient by the same physician or physician group of the same specialty. CPT code 99292 is used to report additional block(s) of time, of up to 30 minutes each beyond the first 74 minutes of critical care (See table below). Critical care of less than 30 minutes total duration on a given calendar date is not reported separately using the critical care codes. This service should be reported using another appropriate E/M code such as subsequent hospital care.

Clinical Example of Correct Billing of Time:
A patient arrives in the emergency department in cardiac arrest. The emergency department physician provides 40 minutes of critical care services. A cardiologist is called to the ED and assumes responsibility for the patient, providing 35 minutes of critical care services. The patient stabilizes and is transferred to the CCU. In this instance, the ED physician provided 40 minutes of critical care services and reports only the critical care code (CPT code 99291) and not also emergency department services. The cardiologist may report the 35 minutes of critical care services (also CPT code 99291) provided in the ED. Additional critical care services by the cardiologist in the CCU may be reported on the same calendar date using 99292 or another appropriate E/M code depending on the clock time involved.

G. Counting of Units of Critical Care Services

The CPT code 99291 (critical care, first hour) is used to report the services of a physician providing full attention to a critically ill or critically injured patient from 30-74 minutes on a given date. Only one unit of CPT code 99291 may be billed by a physician for a patient on a given date. Physicians of the same specialty within the same group practice bill and are paid as though they were a single physician and would not each report CPT 99291on the same date of service.

The following illustrates the correct reporting of critical care services:

Total Duration of Critical Care	Code(s)
Less than 30 minutes	99232 or 99233 or other appropriate E/M code
30-74 minutes	99291 x 1
75-104 minutes	99291 x 1 and 99292 x 1
105-134 minutes	99291 x 1 and 99292 x 2
135-164 minutes	99291 x 1 and 99292 x 3
165-194 minutes	99291 x 1 and 99292 x 4
194 minutes or longer	99291 - 99292 as appropriate (per the above illustrations)

H. Critical Care Services and Other Evaluation and Management Services Provided on Same Day

When critical care services are required upon the patient's presentation to the hospital emergency department, only critical care codes 99291 - 99292 may be reported. An emergency department visit code may not also be reported.

When critical care services are provided on a date where an inpatient hospital or office/outpatient evaluation and management service was furnished earlier on the same date at which time the patient did not require critical care, both the critical care and the previous evaluation and management service may be paid. Hospital emergency department services are not payable for the same calendar date as critical care services when provided by the same physician to the same patient.

Physicians are advised to submit documentation to support a claim when critical care is additionally reported on the same calendar date as when other evaluation and management services are provided to a patient by the same physician or physicians of the same specialty in a group practice.

I. Critical Care Services Provided by Physicians in Group Practice(s)

Medically necessary critical care services provided on the same calendar date to the same patient by physicians representing different medical specialties that are not duplicative services are payable. The medical specialists may be from the same group practice or from different group practices.

Critically ill or critically injured patients may require the care of more than one physician medical specialty. Concurrent critical care services provided by each physician must be medically necessary and not provided during the same instance of time. Medical record documentation must support the medical necessity of critical care services provided by each physician (or qualified NPP). Each physician must accurately report the service(s) he/she provided to the patient in accordance with any applicable global surgery rules or concurrent care rules. (Refer to Medicare Claims Processing Manual, Pub. 100-04, Chapter 12, Sec.40, and the Medicare Benefit Policy Manual, Pub. 100-02, Chapter 15, Sec.30.)

CPT Code 99291
The initial critical care time, billed as CPT code 99291, must be met by a single physician or qualified NPP. This may be performed in a single period of time or be cumulative by the same physician on the same calendar date. A history or physical exam performed by one group partner for another group partner in order for the second group partner to make a medical decision would not represent critical care services.

CPT Code 99292
Subsequent critical care visits performed on the same calendar date are reported using CPT code 99292. The service may represent aggregate time met by a single physician or physicians in the same group practice with the same medical specialty in order to meet the duration of minutes required for CPT code 99292. The aggregated critical care visits must be medically necessary and each aggregated visit must meet the definition of critical care in order to combine the times.

Physicians in the same group practice who have the same specialty may not each report CPT initial critical care code 99291 for critical care services to the same patient on the same calendar date. Medicare payment policy states that physicians in the same group practice who are in the same specialty must bill and be paid as though each were the single physician. (Refer to the Medicare Claims Processing Manual, Pub. 100-04, Chapter 12, Sec.30.6.) Physician specialty means the self-designated primary specialty by which the physician bills Medicare and is known to the contractor that adjudicates the claims. Physicians in the same group practice who have different medical specialties may bill and be paid without regard to their membership in the same group. For example, if a cardiologist and an endocrinologist are group partners and the critical care services of each are medically necessary and not duplicative, the critical care services may be reported by each regardless of their group practice relationship.

Two or more physicians in the same group practice who have different specialties and who provide critical care to a critically ill or critically injured patient may not in all cases each report the initial critical care code (CPT 99291) on the same date. When the group physicians are providing care that is unique to his/her individual medical specialty and managing at least one of the patient's critical illness(es) or critical injury(ies) then the initial critical care service may be payable to each.

However, if a physician or qualified NPP within a group provides "staff coverage" or "follow-up" for each other after the first hour of critical care services was provided on the same calendar date by the previous group clinician (physician or qualified NPP), the subsequent visits by the "covering" physician or qualified NPP in the group shall be billed using CPT critical care add-on code 99292. The appropriate individual NPI number shall be reported on the claim. The services will be paid at the specific physician fee schedule rate for the individual clinician (physician or qualified NPP) billing the service.

Clinical Examples of Critical Care Services

1. Drs. Smith and Jones, pulmonary specialists, share a group practice. On Tuesday Dr. Smith provides critical care services to Mrs. Benson who is comatose and has been in the intensive care unit for 4 days following a motor vehicle accident. She has multiple organ dysfunction including cerebral hematoma, flail chest and pulmonary contusion. Later on the same calendar date Dr. Jones covers for Dr. Smith and provides critical care services. Medically necessary critical care services provided at the different time periods may be reported by both Drs. Smith and Jones. Dr. Smith would report CPT code 99291 for the initial visit and Dr. Jones, as part of the same group practice would report CPT code 99292 on the same calendar date if the appropriate time requirements are met.

2. Mr. Marks, a 79 year old comes to the emergency room with vague joint pains and lethargy. The ED physician evaluates Mr. Marks and phones his primary care physician to discuss his medical evaluation. His primary care physician visits the ER and admits Mr. Marks to the observation unit for monitoring, and diagnostic and laboratory tests. In observation Mr. Marks has a cardiac arrest. His primary care physician provides 50 minutes of critical care services. Mr. Marks' is admitted to the intensive care unit. On the same calendar day Mr. Marks' condition deteriorates and he requires intermittent critical care services. In this scenario the ED physician should report an emergency department visit and the primary care physician should report both an initial hospital visit and critical care services.

J. Critical Care Services and Other Procedures Provided on the Same Day by the Same Physician as Critical Care Codes 99291 - 99292

The following services when performed on the day a physician bills for critical care are included in the critical care service and should not be reported separately:

- The interpretation of cardiac output measurements (CPT 93561, 93562);
- Chest x-rays, professional component (CPT 71010, 71015, 71020);
- Blood draw for specimen (CPT 36415);
- Blood gases, and information data stored in computers (e.g., ECGs, blood pressures, hematologic data-CPT 99090);
- Gastric intubation (CPT 43752, 91105);
- Pulse oximetry (CPT 94760, 94761, 94762);
- Temporary transcutaneous pacing (CPT 92953);
- Ventilator management (CPT 94002 - 94004, 94660, 94662); and
- Vascular access procedures (CPT 36000, 36410, 36415, 36591, 36600).

No other procedure codes are bundled into the critical care services. Therefore, other medically necessary procedure codes may be billed separately.

K. Global Surgery
Critical care services shall not be paid on the same calendar date the physician also reports a procedure code with a global surgical period unless the critical care is billed with CPT modifier -25 to indicate that the critical care is a significant, separately identifiable evaluation and management service that is above and beyond the usual pre and post operative care associated with the procedure that is performed.

Services such as endotracheal intubation (CPT code 31500) and the insertion and placement of a flow directed catheter e.g., Swan-Ganz (CPT code 93503) are not bundled into the critical care codes. Therefore, separate payment may be made for critical care in addition to these services if the critical care was a significant, separately identifiable service and it was reported with modifier -25. The time spent performing the pre, intra, and post procedure work of these unbundled services, e.g., endotracheal intubation, shall be excluded from the determination of the time spent providing critical care.

This policy applies to any procedure with a 0, 10 or 90 day global period including cardiopulmonary resuscitation (CPT code 92950). CPR has a global period of 0 days and is not bundled into critical care codes. Therefore, critical care may be billed in addition to CPR if critical care was a significant, separately identifiable service and it was reported with modifier -25. The time spent performing CPR shall be excluded from the determination of the time spent providing critical care. In this instance it must be the physician who performs the resuscitation who bills for this service. Members of a code team must not each bill Medicare Part B for this service.

When postoperative critical care services (for procedures with a global surgical period) are provided by a physician other than the surgeon, no modifier is required unless all surgical postoperative care has been officially transferred from the surgeon to the physician performing the critical care services. In this situation, CPT modifiers "-54" (surgical care only) and "-55"(postoperative management only) must be used by the surgeon and intensivist who are submitting claims. Medical record documentation by the surgeon and the physician who assumes a transfer (e.g., intensivist) is required to support claims for services when CPT modifiers -54 and -55 are used indicating the transfer of care from the surgeon to the intensivist. Critical care services must meet all the conditions previously described in this manual section.

L. Critical Care Services Provided During Preoperative Portion and Postoperative Portion of Global Period of Procedure with 90 Day Global Period in Trauma and Burn Cases

Preoperative

Preoperative critical care may be paid in addition to a global fee if the patient is critically ill and requires the full attention of the physician, and the critical care is unrelated to the specific anatomic injury or general surgical procedure performed. Such patients may meet the definition of being critically ill and criteria for conditions where there is a high probability of imminent or life threatening deterioration in the patient's condition.

Preoperatively, in order for these services to be paid, two reporting requirements must be met. Codes 99291 - 99292 and modifier -25 (significant, separately identifiable evaluation and management services by the same physician on the day of the procedure) must be used, and documentation identifying that the critical care was unrelated to the specific anatomic injury or general surgical procedure performed shall be submitted. An ICD-9-CM code in the range 800.0 through 959.9 (except 930.0 - 939.9), which clearly indicates that the critical care was unrelated to the surgery, is acceptable documentation.

Postoperative

Postoperatively, in order for critical care services to be paid, two reporting requirements must be met. Codes 99291 - 99292 and modifier -24 (unrelated evaluation and management service by the same physician during a postoperative period) must be used, and documentation that the critical care was unrelated to the specific anatomic injury or general surgical procedure performed must be submitted. An ICD-9-CM code in the range 800.0 through 959.9 (except 930.0 - 939.9), which clearly indicates that the critical care was unrelated to the surgery, is acceptable documentation.

Medicare policy allows separate payment to the surgeon for postoperative critical care services during the surgical global period when the patient has suffered trauma or burns. When the surgeon provides critical care services during the global period, for reasons unrelated to the surgery, these are separately payable as well.

M. Teaching Physician Criteria
In order for the teaching physician to bill for critical care services the teaching physician must meet the requirements for critical care described in the preceding sections. For CPT codes determined on the basis of time, such as critical care, the teaching physician must be present for the entire period of time for which the claim is submitted. For example, payment will be made for 35 minutes of critical care services only if the teaching physician is present for the full 35 minutes. (See IOM, Pub 100-04, Chapter12, Sec. 100.1.4)

1. Teaching
   Time spent teaching may not be counted towards critical care time. Time spent by the resident, in the absence of the teaching physician, cannot be billed by the teaching physician as critical care or other time-based services. Only time spent by the resident and teaching physician together with the patient or the teaching physician alone with the patient can be counted toward critical care time.
2. Documentation
   A combination of the teaching physician's documentation and the resident's documentation may support critical care services. Provided that all requirements for critical care services are met, the teaching physician documentation may tie into the resident's documentation. The teaching physician may refer to the resident's documentation for specific patient history, physical findings and medical assessment. However, the teaching physician medical record documentation must provide substantive information including: (1) the time the teaching physician spent providing critical care, (2) that the patient was critically ill during the time the teaching physician saw the patient, (3) what made the patient critically ill, and (4) the nature of the treatment and management provided by the teaching physician. The medical review criteria are the same for the teaching physician as for all physicians. (See the Medicare Claims Processing, Pub. 100-04, Chapter 12, Sec.100.1.1 for teaching physician documentation guidance.)

Unacceptable Example of Documentation:

"I came and saw (the patient) and agree with (the resident)".

Acceptable Example of Documentation:

"Patient developed hypotension and hypoxia; I spent 45 minutes while the patient was in this condition, providing fluids, pressor drugs, and oxygen. I reviewed the resident's documentation and I agree with the resident's assessment and plan of care."

N. Ventilator Management
Medicare recognizes the ventilator codes (CPT codes 94002 - 94004, 94660 and 94662) as physician services payable under the physician fee schedule. Medicare Part B under the physician fee schedule does not pay for ventilator management services in addition to an evaluation and management service (e.g., critical care services, CPT codes 99291 - 99292) on the same day for the patient even when the evaluation and management service is billed with CPT modifier -2

100-4, 12, 30.6.13

Nursing Facility Services (Codes 99304 - 99318)

A. Visits to Perform the Initial Comprehensive Assessment and Annual Assessments
The distinction made between the delegation of physician visits and tasks in a skilled nursing facility (SNF) and in a nursing facility (NF) is based on the Medicare Statute. Section 1819 (b) (6) (A) of the Social Security Act (the Act) governs SNFs while section 1919 (b) (6) (A) of the Act governs NFs. For further information refer to Medlearn Matters article number SE0418 at www.cms.hhs.gov/medlearn/matters The initial visit in a SNF and NF must be performed by the physician except as otherwise permitted (42 CFR 483.40 (c) (4)). The initial visit is defined in S&C-04-08 (see www.cms.hhs.gov/medlearn/matters) as the initial comprehensive assessment visit during which the physician completes a thorough assessment, develops a plan of care and writes or verifies admitting orders for the nursing facility resident. For Survey and Certification requirements, a visit must occur no later than 30 days after admission.

Further, per the Long Term Care regulations at 42 CFR 483.40 (c)(4) and (e) (2), the physician may not delegate a task that the physician must personally perform. Therefore, as stated in S&C-04-08 the physician may not delegate the initial visit in a SNF. This also applies to the NF with one exception.

The only exception, as to who performs the initial visit, relates to the NF setting. In the NF setting, a qualified NPP (i.e., a nurse practitioner (NP), physician assistant (PA), or a clinical nurse specialist (CNS), who is not employed by the facility, may perform the initial visit when the State law permits this. The evaluation and management (E/M) visit shall be within the State scope of practice and licensure requirements where the E/M visit is performed and the requirements for physician collaboration and physician supervision shall be met.

Under Medicare Part B payment policy, other medically necessary E/M visits may be performed and reported prior to and after the initial visit, if the medical needs of the patient require an E/M visit. A qualified NPP may perform medically necessary E/M visits prior to and after the initial visit if all the requirements for collaboration, general physician supervision, licensure and billing are met.

The CPT Nursing Facility Services codes shall be used with place of service (POS) 31 (SNF) if the patient is in a Part A SNF stay. They shall be used with POS 32 (nursing facility) if the patient does not have Part A SNF benefits or if the patient is in a NF or in a non-covered SNF stay (e.g., there was no preceding 3-day hospital stay). The CPT Nursing Facility code definition also includes POS 54 (Intermediate Care Facility/Mentally Retarded) and POS 56 (Psychiatric Residential Treatment Center). For further guidance on POS codes and associated CPT codes refer to Sec.30.6.14.

Effective January 1, 2006, the Initial Nursing Facility Care codes 99301- 99303 are deleted.

Beginning January 1, 2006, the new CPT codes, Initial Nursing Facility Care, per day, (99304 - 99306) shall be used to report the initial visit. Only a physician may report

these codes for an initial visit performed in a SNF or NF (with the exception of the qualified NPP in the NF setting who is not employed by the facility and when State law permits, as explained above).

A readmission to a SNF or NF shall have the same payment policy requirements as an initial admission in both the SNF and NF settings.

A physician who is employed by the SNF/NF may perform the E/M visits and bill independently to Medicare Part B for payment. An NPP who is employed by the SNF or NF may perform and bill Medicare Part B directly for those services where it is permitted as discussed above. The employer of the PA shall always report the visits performed by the PA. A physician, NP or CNS has the option to bill Medicare directly or to reassign payment for his/her professional service to the facility.

As with all E/M visits for Medicare Part B payment policy, the E/M documentation guidelines apply.

B. Visits to Comply With Federal Regulations (42 CFR 483.40 (c) (1)) in the SNF and NF
Payment is made under the physician fee schedule by Medicare Part B for federally mandated visits. Following the initial visit by the physician, payment shall be made for federally mandated visits that monitor and evaluate residents at least once every 30 days for the first 90 days after admission and at least once every 60 days thereafter.

Effective January 1, 2006, the Subsequent Nursing Facility Care, per day, codes 99311- 99313 are deleted.

Beginning January 1, 2006, the new CPT codes, Subsequent Nursing Facility Care, per day, (99307 - 99310) shall be used to report federally mandated physician E/M visits and medically necessary E/M visits.

Carriers shall not pay for more than one E/M visit performed by the physician or qualified NPP for the same patient on the same date of service. The Nursing Facility Services codes represent a "per day" service.

The federally mandated E/M visit may serve also as a medically necessary E/M visit if the situation arises (i.e., the patient has health problems that need attention on the day the scheduled mandated physician E/M visit occurs). The physician/qualified NPP shall bill only one E/M visit.

Beginning January 1, 2006, the new CPT code, Other Nursing Facility Service (99318), may be used to report an annual nursing facility assessment visit on the required schedule of visits on an annual basis. For Medicare Part B payment policy, an annual nursing facility assessment visit code may substitute as meeting one of the federally mandated physician visits if the code requirements for CPT code 99318 are fully met and in lieu of reporting a Subsequent Nursing Facility Care, per day, service (codes 99307 - 99310). It shall not be performed in addition to the required number of federally mandated physician visits. The new CPT annual assessment code does not represent a new benefit service for Medicare Part B physician services.

Qualified NPPs, whether employed or not by the SNF, may perform alternating federally mandated physician visits, at the option of the physician, after the initial visit by the physician in a SNF.

Qualified NPPs in the NF setting, who are not employed by the NF, may perform federally mandated physician visits, at the option of the State, after the initial visit by the physician.

Medicare Part B payment policy does not pay for additional E/M visits that may be required by State law for a facility admission or for other additional visits to satisfy facility or other administrative purposes. E/M visits, prior to and after the initial physician visit, that are reasonable and medically necessary to meet the medical needs of the individual patient (unrelated to any State requirement or administrative purpose) are payable under Medicare Part B.

C. Visits by Qualified Nonphysician Practitioners
All E/M visits shall be within the State scope of practice and licensure requirements where the visit is performed and all the requirements for physician collaboration and physician supervision shall be met when performed and reported by qualified NPPs. General physician supervision and employer billing requirements shall be met for PA services in addition to the PA meeting the State scope of practice and licensure requirements where the E/M visit is performed.

Medically Necessary Visits Qualified NPPs may perform medically necessary E/M visits prior to and after the physician's initial visit in both the SNF and NF. Medically necessary E/M visits for the diagnosis or treatment of an illness or injury or to improve the functioning of a malformed body member are payable under the physician fee schedule under Medicare Part B. CPT codes, Subsequent Nursing Facility Care, per day (99307 - 99310), shall be reported for these E/M visits even if the visits are provided prior to the initial visit by the physician.

SNF Setting--Place of Service Code 31

Following the initial visit by the physician, the physician may delegate alternate federally mandated physician visits to a qualified NPP who meets collaboration and physician supervision requirements and is licensed as such by the State and performing within the scope of practice in that State.

NF Setting--Place of Service Code 32

Per the regulations at 42 CFR 483.40 (f), a qualified NPP, who meets the collaboration and physician supervision requirements, the State scope of practice and licensure requirements, and who is not employed by the NF, may at the option of the State, perform the initial visit in a NF, and may perform any other federally mandated physician visit in a NF in addition to performing other medically necessary E/M visits.

Questions pertaining to writing orders or certification and recertification issues in the SNF and NF settings shall be addressed to the appropriate State Survey and Certification Agency departments for clarification.

D. Medically Complex Care
Payment is made for E/M visits to patients in a SNF who are receiving services for medically complex care upon discharge from an acute care facility when the visits are reasonable and medically necessary and documented in the medical record. Physicians and qualified NPPs shall report E/M visits using the Subsequent Nursing Facility Care, per day (codes 99307 - 99310) for these E/M visits even if the visits are provided prior to the initial visit by the physician.

E. Incident to Services
Where a physician establishes an office in a SNF/NF, the "incident to" services and requirements are confined to this discrete part of the facility designated as his/her office. "Incident to" E/M visits, provided in a facility setting, are not payable under the Physician Fee Schedule for Medicare Part B. Thus, visits performed outside the designated "office" area in the SNF/NF would be subject to the coverage and payment rules applicable to SNF/NF setting and shall not be reported using the CPT codes for office or other outpatient visits or use place of service code 11.

F. Use of the Prolonged Services Codes and Other Time-Related Services
Beginning January 1, 2008, typical/average time units for E/M visits in the SNF/NF settings are reestablished. Medically necessary prolonged services for E/M visits (codes 99356 and 99357) in a SNF or NF may be billed with the Nursing Facility Services in the code ranges (99304 - 99306, 99307 - 99310 and 99318).

Counseling and Coordination of Care Visits With the reestablishment of typical/average time units, medically necessary E/M visits for counseling and coordination of care, for Nursing Facility Services in the code ranges (99304 - 99306, 99307 - 99310 and 99318) that are time-based services, may be billed with the appropriate prolonged services codes (99356 and 99357).

G. Gang Visits
The complexity level of an E/M visit and the CPT code billed must be a covered and medically necessary visit for each patient (refer to Secs.1862 (a)(1)(A) of the Act). Claims for an unreasonable number of daily E/M visits by the same physician to multiple patients at a facility within a 24-hour period may result in medical review to determine medical necessity for the visits. The E/M visit (Nursing Facility Services) represents a "per day" service per patient as defined by the CPT code. The medical record must be personally documented by the physician or qualified NPP who performed the E/M visit and the documentation shall support the specific level of E/M visit to each individual patient.

H. Split/Shared E/M Visit
A split/shared E/M visit cannot be reported in the SNF/NF setting. A split/shared E/M visit is defined by Medicare Part B payment policy as a medically necessary encounter with a patient where the physician and a qualified NPP each personally perform a substantive portion of an E/M visit face-to-face with the same patient on the same date of service. A substantive portion of an E/M visit involves all or some portion of the history, exam or medical decision making key components of an E/M service. The physician and the qualified NPP must be in the same group practice or be employed by the same employer. The split/shared E/M visit applies only to selected E/M visits and settings (i.e., hospital inpatient, hospital outpatient, hospital observation, emergency department, hospital discharge, office and non facility clinic visits, and prolonged visits associated with these E/M visit codes). The split/shared E/M policy does not apply to consultation services, critical care services or procedures.

I. SNF/NF Discharge Day Management Service
Medicare Part B payment policy requires a face-to-face visit with the patient provided by the physician or the qualified NPP to meet the SNF/NF discharge day management service as defined by the CPT code. The E/M discharge day management visit shall be reported for the date of the actual visit by the physician or qualified NPP even if the patient is discharged from the facility on a different calendar date. The CPT codes 99315 - 99316 shall be reported for this visit. The Discharge Day Management Service may be reported using CPT code 99315 or 99316, depending on the code requirement, for a patient who has expired, but only if the physician or qualified NPP personally performed the death pronouncement.

100-4, 12, 30.6.14
Home Care and Domiciliary Care Visits (Codes 99324- 99350)
Physician Visits to Patients Residing in Various Places of Service
The American Medical Association's Current Procedural Terminology (CPT) 2006 new patient codes 99324 - 99328 and established patient codes 99334 - 99337(new codes beginning January 2006), for Domiciliary, Rest Home (e.g., Boarding Home), or Custodial Care Services, are used to report evaluation and management (E/M) services to residents residing in a facility which provides room, board, and other personal assistance services, generally on a long-term basis. These CPT codes are used to report E/M services in facilities assigned places of service (POS) codes 13 (Assisted Living Facility), 14 (Group Home), 33 (Custodial Care Facility) and 55 (Residential Substance Abuse Facility). Assisted living facilities may also be known as adult living facilities.

Physicians and qualified nonphysician practitioners (NPPs) furnishing E/M services to residents in a living arrangement described by one of the POS listed above must use the level of service code in the CPT code range 99324 - 99337 to report the service they provide. The CPT codes 99321 - 99333 for Domiciliary, Rest Home (e.g., Boarding Home), or Custodial Care Services are deleted beginning January, 2006.

Beginning in 2006, reasonable and medically necessary, face-to-face, prolonged services, represented by CPT codes 99354 - 99355, may be reported with the appropriate companion E/M codes when a physician or qualified NPP, provides a prolonged service involving direct (face-to-face) patient contact that is beyond the usual E/M visit service for a Domiciliary, Rest Home (e.g., Boarding Home) or Custodial Care Service. All the requirements for prolonged services at Sec.30.6.15.1 must be met.

The CPT codes 99341 through 99350, Home Services codes, are used to report E/M services furnished to a patient residing in his or her own private residence (e.g., private home, apartment, town home) and not residing in any type of congregate/shared facility living arrangement including assisted living facilities and group homes. The Home Services codes apply only to the specific 2-digit POS 12 (Home). Home Services codes may not be used for billing E/M services provided in settings other than in the private residence of an individual as described above.

Beginning in 2006, E/M services provided to patients residing in a Skilled Nursing Facility (SNF) or a Nursing Facility (NF) must be reported using the appropriate CPT level of service code within the range identified for Initial Nursing Facility Care (new CPT codes 99304 - 99306) and Subsequent Nursing Facility Care (new CPT codes 99307 - 99310). Use the CPT code, Other Nursing Facility Services (new CPT code 99318), for an annual nursing facility assessment. Use CPT codes 99315 - 99316 for SNF/NF discharge services. The CPT codes 99301 - 99303 and 99311 - 99313 are deleted beginning January, 2006. The Home Services codes should not be used for these places of service.

The CPT SNF/NF code definition includes intermediate care facilities (ICFs) and long term care facilities (LTCFs). These codes are limited to the specific 2-digit POS 31 (SNF), 32 (Nursing Facility), 54 (Intermediate Care Facility/Mentally Retarded) and 56 (Psychiatric Residential Treatment Center).

The CPT nursing facility codes should be used with POS 31 (SNF) if the patient is in a Part A SNF stay and POS 32 (nursing facility) if the patient does not have Part A SNF benefits. There is no longer a different payment amount for a Part A or Part B benefit period in these POS settings.

100-4, 12, 30.6.14.1
Home Services (Codes 99341 - 99350)
B3-15515, B3-15066

Appendix G — Pub 100 References

A. Requirement for Physician Presence
Home services codes 99341-99350 are paid when they are billed to report evaluation and management services provided in a private residence. A home visit cannot be billed by a physician unless the physician was actually present in the beneficiary's home.

B. Homebound Status
Under the home health benefit the beneficiary must be confined to the home for services to be covered. For home services provided by a physician using these codes, the beneficiary does not need to be confined to the home. The medical record must document the medical necessity of the home visit made in lieu of an office or outpatient visit.

C. Fee Schedule Payment for Services to Homebound Patients under General Supervision
Payment may be made in some medically underserved areas where there is a lack of medical personnel and home health services for injections, EKGs, and venipunctures that are performed for homebound patients under general physician supervision by nurses and paramedical employees of physicians or physician-directed clinics. Section 10 provides additional information on the provision of services to homebound Medicare patients.

100-4, 12, 30.6.15.1
Prolonged Services With Direct Face-to-Face Patient Contact Service (Codes 99354 - 99357) (ZZZ codes)

A. Definition
Prolonged physician services (CPT code 99354) in the office or other outpatient setting with direct face-to-face patient contact which require one hour beyond the usual service are payable when billed on the same day by the same physician or qualified nonphysician practitioner (NPP) as the companion evaluation and management codes. The time for usual service refers to the typical/average time units associated with the companion evaluation and management service as noted in the CPT code. Each additional 30 minutes of direct face-to-face patient contact following the first hour of prolonged services may be reported by CPT code 99355.

Prolonged physician services (code 99356) in the inpatient setting, with direct face-to-face patient contact which require one hour beyond the usual service are payable when they are billed on the same day by the same physician or qualified NPP as the companion evaluation and management codes. Each additional 30 minutes of direct face-to-face patient contact following the first hour of prolonged services may be reported by CPT code 99357.

Prolonged service of less than 30 minutes total duration on a given date is not separately reported because the work involved is included in the total work of the evaluation and management codes.

Code 99355 or 99357 may be used to report each additional 30 minutes beyond the first hour of prolonged services, based on the place of service. These codes may be used to report the final 15 - 30 minutes of prolonged service on a given date, if not otherwise billed. Prolonged service of less than 15 minutes beyond the first hour or less than 15 minutes beyond the final 30 minutes is not reported separately.

B. Required Companion Codes
- The companion evaluation and management codes for 99354 are the Office or Other Outpatient visit codes (99201 - 99205, 99212 - 99215), the Office or Other Outpatient Consultation codes (99241 - 99245), the Domiciliary, Rest Home, or Custodial Care Services codes (99324 - 99328, 99334 - 99337), the Home Services codes (99341 - 99345, 99347 - 99350);
- The companion codes for 99355 are 99354 and one of the evaluation and management codes required for 99354 to be used;
- The companion evaluation and management codes for 99356 are the Initial Hospital Care codes and Subsequent Hospital Care codes (99221 - 99223, 99231 - 99233), the Inpatient Consultation codes (99251 - 99255); Nursing Facility Services codes (99304 -99318) or
- The companion codes for 99357 are 99356 and one of the evaluation and management codes required for 99356 to be used.

Prolonged services codes 99354 - 99357 are not paid unless they are accompanied by the companion codes as indicated.

C. Requirement for Physician Presence
Physicians may count only the duration of direct face-to-face contact between the physician and the patient (whether the service was continuous or not) beyond the typical/average time of the visit code billed to determine whether prolonged services can be billed and to determine the prolonged services codes that are allowable. In the case of prolonged office services, time spent by office staff with the patient, or time the patient remains unaccompanied in the office cannot be billed. In the case of prolonged hospital services, time spent reviewing charts or discussion of a patient with house medical staff and not with direct face-to-face contact with the patient, or waiting for test results, for changes in the patient's condition, for end of a therapy, or for use of facilities cannot be billed as prolonged services.

D. Documentation
Documentation is not required to accompany the bill for prolonged services unless the physician has been selected for medical review. Documentation is required in the medical record about the duration and content of the medically necessary evaluation and management service and prolonged services billed. The medical record must be appropriately and sufficiently documented by the physician or qualified NPP to show that the physician or qualified NPP personally furnished the direct face-to-face time with the patient specified in the CPT code definitions. The start and end times of the visit shall be documented in the medical record along with the date of service.

E. Use of the Codes
Prolonged services codes can be billed only if the total duration of all physician or qualified NPP direct face-to-face service (including the visit) equals or exceeds the threshold time for the evaluation and management service the physician or qualified NPP provided (typical/average time associated with the CPT E/M code plus 30 minutes). If the total duration of direct face-to-face time does not equal or exceed the threshold time for the level of evaluation and management service the physician or qualified NPP provided, the physician or qualified NPP may not bill for prolonged services.

F. Threshold Times for Codes 99354 and 99355 (Office or Other Outpatient Setting)
If the total direct face-to-face time equals or exceeds the threshold time for code 99354, but is less than the threshold time for code 99355, the physician should bill the evaluation and management visit code and code 99354. No more than one unit of 99354 is acceptable. If the total direct face-to-face time equals or exceeds the threshold time for code 99355 by no more than 29 minutes, the physician should bill the visit code 99354 and one unit of code 99355. One additional unit of code 99355 is billed for each additional increment of 30 minutes extended duration. Contractors use the following threshold times to determine if the prolonged services codes 99354 and/or 99355 can be billed with the office or other outpatient settings including outpatient consultation services and domiciliary, rest home, or custodial care services and home services codes.

Threshold Time for Prolonged Visit Codes 99354 and/or 99355 Billed with Office/Outpatient and Consultation Codes

Code	Typical Time for Code	Threshold Time to Bill Code 99354	Threshold Time to Bill Codes 99354 and 99355
99201	10	40	85
99202	20	50	95
99203	30	60	105
99204	45	75	120
99205	60	90	135
99212	10	40	85
99213	15	45	90
99214	25	55	100
99215	40	70	115
99241	15	45	90
99242	30	60	105
99243	40	70	115
99244	60	90	135
99245	80	110	155
99324	20	50	95
99325	30	60	105
99326	45	75	120
99327	60	90	135
99328	75	105	150
99334	15	45	90
99335	25	55	100
99336	40	70	115
99337	60	90	135
99341	20	50	95
99342	30	60	105
99343	45	75	120
99344	60	90	135
99345	75	105	150
99347	15	45	90
99348	25	55	100
99349	40	70	115
99350	60	90	135

Add 30 minutes to the threshold time for billing codes 99354 and 99355 to get the threshold time for billing code 99354 and two units of code 99355. For example, to bill code 99354 and two units of code 99355 when billing a code 99205, the threshold time is 150 minutes.

G. Threshold Times for Codes 99356 and 99357 (Inpatient Setting)
If the total direct face-to-face time equals or exceeds the threshold time for code 99356, but is less than the threshold time for code 99357, the physician should bill the visit and code 99356. Contractors do not accept more than one unit of code 99356. If the total direct face-to-face time equals or exceeds the threshold time for code 99356 by no more than 29 minutes, the physician bills the visit code 99356 and one unit of code 99357. One additional unit of code 99357 is billed for each additional increment of 30 minutes extended duration. Contractors use the following threshold times to determine if the prolonged services codes 99356 and/or 99357 can be billed with the inpatient setting codes.

Current Procedural Coding Expert

Appendix G — Pub 100 References

Threshold Time for Prolonged Visit Codes 99356 and/or 99357 Billed with Inpatient Setting Codes

Code	Typical Time for Code	Threshold Time to Bill Code 99356	Threshold Time to Bill Codes 99356 and 99357
99221	30	60	105
99222	50	80	125
99223	70	100	145
99231	15	45	90
99232	25	55	100
99233	35	65	110
99251	20	50	95
99252	40	70	115
99253	55	85	130
99254	80	110	155
99255	110	140	185
99304	25	55	100
99305	35	65	110
99306	45	75	120
99307	10	40	85
99308	15	45	90
99309	25	55	100
99310	35	65	110
99318	30	60	105

Add 30 minutes to the threshold time for billing codes 99356 and 99357 to get the threshold time for billing code 99356 and two units of 99357.

H. Prolonged Services Associated With Evaluation and Management Services Based on Counseling and/or Coordination of Care (Time-Based)

When an evaluation and management service is dominated by counseling and/or coordination of care (the counseling and/or coordination of care represents more than 50% of the total time with the patient) in a face-to-face encounter between the physician or qualified NPP and the patient in the office/clinic or the floor time (in the scenario of an inpatient service), then the evaluation and management code is selected based on the typical/average time associated with the code levels. The time approximation must meet or exceed the specific CPT code billed (determined by the typical/average time associated with the evaluation and management code) and should not be "rounded" to the next higher level.

In those evaluation and management services in which the code level is selected based on time, prolonged services may only be reported with the highest code level in that family of codes as the companion code.

I. Examples of Billable Prolonged Services

EXAMPLE 1. A physician performed a visit that met the definition of an office visit code 99213 and the total duration of the direct face-to-face services (including the visit) was 65 minutes. The physician bills code 99213 and one unit of code 99354.

EXAMPLE 2. A physician performed a visit that met the definition of a domiciliary, rest home care visit code 99327 and the total duration of the direct face-to-face contact (including the visit) was 140 minutes. The physician bills codes 99327, 99354, and one unit of code 99355.

EXAMPLE 3. A physician performed an office visit to an established patient that was predominantly counseling, spending 75 minutes (direct face-to-face) with the patient. The physician should report CPT code 99215 and one unit of code 99354.

J. Examples of Nonbillable Prolonged Services

EXAMPLE 1. A physician performed a visit that met the definition of visit code 99212 and the total duration of the direct face-to-face contact (including the visit) was 35 minutes. The physician cannot bill prolonged services because the total duration of direct face-to-face service did not meet the threshold time for billing prolonged services.

EXAMPLE 2. A physician performed a visit that met the definition of code 99213 and, while the patient was in the office receiving treatment for 4 hours, the total duration of the direct face-to-face service of the physician was 40 minutes. The physician cannot bill prolonged services because the total duration of direct face-to-face service did not meet the threshold time for billing prolonged services.

EXAMPLE 3. A physician provided a subsequent office visit that was predominantly counseling, spending 60 minutes (face-to-face) with the patient. The physician cannot code 99214, which has a typical time of 25 minutes, and one unit of code 99354. The physician must bill the highest level code in the code family (99215 which has 40 minutes typical/average time units associated with it). The additional time spent beyond this code is 20 minutes and does not meet the threshold time for billing prolonged services.

100-4, 12, 30.6.15.2
Prolonged Services Without Direct Face-to-Face Patient Contact Service (Codes 99358–99359)

Contractors may not pay prolonged services codes 99358 and 99359, which do not require any direct patient face-to-face contact (e.g., telephone calls). Payment for these services is included in the payment for direct face-to-face services that physicians bill. The physician cannot bill the patient for these services since they are Medicare covered services and payment is included in the payment for other billable services.

100-4, 12, 30.6.15.3
Physician Standby Service (Code 99360)

Standby services are not payable to physicians. Physicians may not bill Medicare or beneficiaries for standby services. Payment for standby services is included in the Part A payment to the facility. Such services are a part of hospital costs to provide quality care.

If hospitals pay physicians for standby services, such services are part of hospital costs to provide quality care.

100-4, 12, 30.6.16
Case Management Services (Codes 99362 and 99371 - 99373)

A. Team Conferences
Team conferences (codes 99361-99362) may not be paid separately. Payment for these services is included in the payment for the services to which they relate.

B. Telephone Calls
Telephone calls (codes 99371-99373) may not be paid separately. Payment for telephone calls is included in payment for billable services (e.g., visit, surgery, diagnostic procedure results).

100-4, 12, 40.2
Billing Requirements for Global Surgeries

To ensure the proper identification of services that are, or are not, included in the global package, the following procedures apply.

A. Procedure Codes and Modifiers
Use of the modifiers in this section apply to both major procedures with a 90-day postoperative period and minor procedures with a 10-day postoperative period (and/or a zero day postoperative period in the case of modifiers "-22" and "-25").

1. Physicians Who Furnish the Entire Global Surgical Package
   Physicians who perform the surgery and furnish all of the usual pre-and postoperative work bill for the global package by entering the appropriate CPT code for the surgical procedure only. Billing is not allowed for visits or other services that are included in the global package.

2. Physicians in Group Practice
   When different physicians in a group practice participate in the care of the patient, the group bills for the entire global package if the physicians reassign benefits to the group. The physician who performs the surgery is shown as the performing physician. (For dates of service prior to January 1, 1994, however, where a new physician furnishes the entire postoperative care, the group billed for the surgical care and the postoperative care as separate line items with the appropriate modifiers.)

3. Physicians Who Furnish Part of a Global Surgical Package
   Where physicians agree on the transfer of care during the global period, the following modifiers are used:

   - "-54" for surgical care only; or
   - "-55" for postoperative management only.

   Both the bill for the surgical care only and the bill for the postoperative care only, will contain the same date of service and the same surgical procedure code, with the services distinguished by the use of the appropriate modifier.

   Providers need not specify on the claim that care has been transferred. However, the date on which care was relinquished or assumed, as applicable, must be shown on the claim. This should be indicated in the remarks field/free text segment on the claim form/format. Both the surgeon and the physician providing the postoperative care must keep a copy of the written transfer agreement in the beneficiary's medical record.

   Where a transfer of postoperative care occurs, the receiving physician cannot bill for any part of the global services until he/she has provided at least one service. Once the physician has seen the patient, that physician may bill for the period beginning with the date on which he/she assumes care of the patient.

   EXCEPTIONS:

   - Where a transfer of care does not occur, occasional post-discharge services of a physician other than the surgeon are reported by the appropriate evaluation and management code. No modifiers are necessary on the claim.

   - If the transfer of care occurs immediately after surgery, the physician other than the surgeon who provides the in-hospital postoperative care bills using subsequent hospital care codes for the inpatient hospital care and the surgical code with the "-55" modifier for the post-discharge care. The surgeon bills the surgery code with the "-54" modifier.

   - Physicians who provide follow-up services for minor procedures performed in emergency departments bill the appropriate level of office visit code. The physician who performs the emergency room service bills for the surgical procedure without a modifier.

   - If the services of a physician other than the surgeon are required during a postoperative period for an underlying condition or medical complication, the other physician reports the appropriate evaluation and management code. No modifiers are necessary on the claim. An example is a cardiologist who manages underlying cardiovascular conditions of a patient.

Appendix G — Pub 100 References

4. **Evaluation and Management Service Resulting in the Initial Decision to Perform Surgery**
   Evaluation and management services on the day before major surgery or on the day of major surgery that result in the initial decision to perform the surgery are not included in the global surgery payment for the major surgery and, therefore, may be billed and paid separately.

   In addition to the CPT evaluation and management code, modifier "-57" (decision for surgery) is used to identify a visit which results in the initial decision to perform surgery. (Modifier "-QI" was used for dates of service prior to January 1, 1994.)

   If evaluation and management services occur on the day of surgery, the physician bills using modifier "-57," not "-25." The "-57" modifier is not used with minor surgeries because the global period for minor surgeries does not include the day prior to the surgery. Moreover, where the decision to perform the minor procedure is typically done immediately before the service, it is considered a routine preoperative service and a visit or consultation is not billed in addition to the procedure.

5. **Return Trips to the Operating Room During the Postoperative Period**
   When treatment for complications requires a return trip to the operating room, physicians must bill the CPT code that describes the procedure(s) performed during the return trip. If no such code exists, use the unspecified procedure code in the correct series, i.e., 47999 or 64999. The procedure code for the original surgery is not used except when the identical procedure is repeated.

   In addition to the CPT code, physicians use CPT modifier "-78" for these return trips (return to the operating room for a related procedure during a postoperative period.)

   The physician may also need to indicate that another procedure was performed during the postoperative period of the initial procedure. When this subsequent procedure is related to the first procedure and requires the use of the operating room, this circumstance may be reported by adding the modifier "-78" to the related procedure.

   NOTE: The CPT definition for this modifier does not limit its use to treatment for complications.

6. **Staged or Related Procedures**
   Modifier "-58" was established to facilitate billing of staged or related surgical procedures done during the postoperative period of the first procedure. This modifier is not used to report the treatment of a problem that requires a return to the operating room.

   The physician may need to indicate that the performance of a procedure or service during the postoperative period was:

   a. Planned prospectively or at the time of the original procedure;
   b. More extensive than the original procedure; or
   c. For therapy following a diagnostic surgical procedure.

   These circumstances may be reported by adding modifier "-58" to the staged procedure. A new postoperative period begins when the next procedure in the series is billed.

7. **Unrelated Procedures or Visits During the Postoperative Period**
   Two CPT modifiers were established to simplify billing for visits and other procedures which are furnished during the postoperative period of a surgical procedure, but which are not included in the payment for the surgical procedure.

   Modifier "-79": Reports an unrelated procedure by the same physician during a postoperative period. The physician may need to indicate that the performance of a procedure or service during a postoperative period was unrelated to the original procedure.

   A new postoperative period begins when the unrelated procedure is billed.

   Modifier "-24": Reports an unrelated evaluation and management service by same physician during a postoperative period. The physician may need to indicate that an evaluation and management service was performed during the postoperative period of an unrelated procedure. This circumstance is reported by adding the modifier "-24" to the appropriate level of evaluation and management service.

   Services submitted with the "-24" modifier must be sufficiently documented to establish that the visit was unrelated to the surgery. An ICD-9-CM code that clearly indicates that the reason for the encounter was unrelated to the surgery is acceptable documentation.

   A physician who is responsible for postoperative care and has reported and been paid using modifier "-55" also uses modifier "-24" to report any unrelated visits.

8. **Significant Evaluation and Management on the Day of a Procedure**
   Modifier "-25" is used to facilitate billing of evaluation and management services on the day of a procedure for which separate payment may be made.

   It is used to report a significant, separately identifiable evaluation and management service by same physician on the day of a procedure. The physician may need to indicate that on the day a procedure or service that is identified with a CPT code was performed, the patient's condition required a significant, separately identifiable evaluation and management service above and beyond the usual preoperative and postoperative care associated with the procedure or service that was performed. This circumstance may be reported by adding the modifier "-25" to the appropriate level of evaluation and management service.

   Claims containing evaluation and management codes with modifier "-25" are not subject to prepayment review except in the following situations:

   - Effective January 1, 1995, all evaluation and management services provided on the same day as inpatient dialysis are denied without review with the exception of CPT Codes 99221-9223, 99251-99255, and 99238. These codes may be billed with modifier "-25" and reviewed for possible allowance if the evaluation and management service is unrelated to the treatment of ESRD and was not, and could not, have been provided during the dialysis treatment;

   - When preoperative critical care codes are being billed for within a global surgical period; and

   - When carriers have conducted a specific medical review process and determined, after reviewing the data, that an individual or group have high statistics in terms of the use of modifier "-25," have done a case-by-case review of the records to verify that the use of modifier "-25" was inappropriate, and have educated the individual or group as to the proper use of this modifier.

9. **Critical Care**
   Critical care services provided during a global surgical period for a seriously injured or burned patient are not considered related to a surgical procedure and may be paid separately under the following circumstances.

   Preoperative and postoperative critical care may be paid in addition to a global fee if:

   - The patient is critically ill and requires the constant attendance of the physician; and
   - The critical care is above and beyond, and, in most instances, unrelated to the specific anatomic injury or general surgical procedure performed.

   Such patients are potentially unstable or have conditions that could pose a significant threat to life or risk of prolonged impairment.

   In order for these services to be paid, two reporting requirements must be met:

   - Codes 99291/99292 and modifier "-25" (for preoperative care) or "-24" (for postoperative care) must be used; and
   - Documentation that the critical care was unrelated to the specific anatomic injury or general surgical procedure performed must be submitted. An ICD-9-CM code in the range 800.0 through 959.9 (except 930-939), which clearly indicates that the critical care was unrelated to the surgery, is acceptable documentation.

10. **Unusual Circumstances**
    Surgeries for which services performed are significantly greater than usually required may be billed with the "-22" modifier added to the CPT code for the procedure. Surgeries for which services performed are significantly less than usually required may be billed with the "-52" modifier. The biller must provide:

    - A concise statement about how the service differs from the usual; and
    - An operative report with the claim.

    Modifier "-22" should only be reported with procedure codes that have a global period of 0, 10, or 90 days. There is no such restriction on the use of modifier "-52."

B. Date(s) of Service

Physicians, who bill for the entire global surgical package or for only a portion of the care, must enter the date on which the surgical procedure was performed in the "From/To" date of service field. This will enable carriers to relate all appropriate billings to the correct surgery. Physicians who share postoperative management with another physician must submit additional information showing when they assumed and relinquished responsibility for the postoperative care. If the physician who performed the surgery relinquishes care at the time of discharge, he or she need only show the date of surgery when billing with modifier "-54."

However, if the surgeon also cares for the patient for some period following discharge, the surgeon must show the date of surgery and the date on which postoperative care was relinquished to another physician. The physician providing the remaining postoperative care must show the date care was assumed. This information should be shown in Item 19 on the paper Form CMS-1500, in the narrative portion of the HAO record on the National Standard Format, and in the NTE segment for ANSI X12N electronic claims.

C. Care Provided in Different Payment Localities

If portions of the global period are provided in different payment localities, the services should be billed to the carriers servicing each applicable payment locality. For example, if the surgery is performed in one state and the postoperative care is provided in another state, the surgery is billed with modifier "-54" to the carrier servicing the payment locality where the surgery was performed and the postoperative care is billed with modifier "-55" to the carrier servicing the payment locality where the postoperative care was performed. This is true whether the services were performed by the same physician/group or different physicians/groups.

D. Health Professional Shortage Area (HPSA) Payments for Services Which are Subject to the Global Surgery Rules

HPSA bonus payments may be made for global surgeries when the services are provided in HPSAs. The following are guidelines for the appropriate billing procedures:

- If the entire global package is provided in a HPSA, physicians should bill for the appropriate global surgical code with the applicable HPSA modifier.
- If only a portion of the global package is provided in a HPSA, the physician should bill using a HPSA modifier for the portion which is provided in the HPSA.

EXAMPLE

The surgical portion of the global service is provided in a non-HPSA and the postoperative portion is provided in a HPSA. The surgical portion should be billed with the "-54" modifier and no HPSA modifier. The postoperative portion should be billed with the "-55" modifier and the appropriate HPSA modifier. The 10 percent bonus will be paid on the appropriate postoperative portion only. If a claim is submitted with a global surgical code and a HPSA modifier, the carrier assumes that the entire global service was provided in a HPSA in the absence of evidence otherwise.

NOTE: The sum of the payments made for the surgical and postoperative services provided in different localities will not equal the global amount in either of the localities because of geographic adjustments made through the Geographic Practice Cost Indices.

100-4, 12, 40.6
Claims for Multiple Surgeries
B3-4826, B3-15038, B3-15056

A. General

Multiple surgeries are separate procedures performed by a single physician or physicians in the same group practice on the same patient at the same operative session or on the same day for which separate payment may be allowed. Co-surgeons, surgical teams, or assistants-at-surgery may participate in performing multiple surgeries on the same patient on the same day.

Multiple surgeries are distinguished from procedures that are components of or incidental to a primary procedure. These intra-operative services, incidental surgeries, or components of more major surgeries are not separately billable. See Chapter 23 for a description of mandatory edits to prevent separate payment for those procedures. Major surgical procedures are determined based on the MFSDB approved amount and not on the submitted amount from the providers. The major surgery, as based on the MFSDB, may or may not be the one with the larger submitted amount.

Also, see subsection D below for a description of the standard payment policy on multiple surgeries. However, these standard payment rules are not appropriate for certain procedures. Field 21 of the MFSDB indicates whether the standard payment policy rules apply to a multiple surgery, or whether special payment rules apply. Site of service payment adjustments (codes with an indicator of "1" in Field 27 of the MFSDB) should be applied before multiple surgery payment adjustments.

B. Billing Instructions

The following procedures apply when billing for multiple surgeries by the same physician on the same day.

- Report the more major surgical procedure without the multiple procedures modifier "-51."
- Report additional surgical procedures performed by the surgeon on the same day with modifier "-51."

There may be instances in which two or more physicians each perform distinctly different, unrelated surgeries on the same patient on the same day (e.g., in some multiple trauma cases). When this occurs, the payment adjustment rules for multiple surgeries may not be appropriate. In such cases, the physician does not use modifier "-51" unless one of the surgeons individually performs multiple surgeries.

C. Carrier Claims Processing System Requirements

Carriers must be able to:

1. Identify multiple surgeries by both of the following methods:
    - The presence on the claim form or electronic submission of the "-51" modifier; and
    - The billing of more than one separately payable surgical procedure by the same physician performed on the same patient on the same day, whether on different lines or with a number greater than 1 in the units column on the claim form or inappropriately billed with modifier "-78" (i.e., after the global period has expired);

2. Access Field 34 of the MFSDB to determine the Medicare fee schedule payment amount for each surgery;

3. Access Field 21 for each procedure of the MFSDB to determine if the payment rules for multiple surgeries apply to any of the multiple surgeries billed on the same day;

4. If Field 21 for any of the multiple procedures contains an indicator of "0," the multiple surgery rules do not apply to that procedure. Base payment on the lower of the billed amount or the fee schedule amount (Field 34 or 35) for each code unless other payment adjustment rules apply;

5. For dates of service prior to January 1, 1995, if Field 21 contains an indicator of "1," the standard rules for pricing multiple surgeries apply (see items 6-8 below);

6. Rank the surgeries subject to the standard multiple surgery rules (indicator "1") in descending order by the Medicare fee schedule amount;

7. Base payment for each ranked procedure on the lower of the billed amount, or:
    - 100 percent of the fee schedule amount (Field 34 or 35) for the highest valued procedure;
    - 50 percent of the fee schedule amount for the second highest valued procedure; and
    - 25 percent of the fee schedule amount for the third through the fifth highest valued procedures;

8. If more than five procedures are billed, pay for the first five according to the rules listed in 5, 6, and 7 above and suspend the sixth and subsequent procedures for manual review and payment, if appropriate, "by report." Payment determined on a "by report" basis for these codes should never be lower than 25 percent of the full payment amount;

9. For dates of service on or after January 1, 1995, new standard rules for pricing multiple surgeries apply. If Field 21 contains an indicator of "2," these new standard rules apply (see items 10-12 below);

10. Rank the surgeries subject to the multiple surgery rules (indicator "2") in descending order by the Medicare fee schedule amount;

11. Base payment for each ranked procedure (indicator "2") on the lower of the billed amount:
    - 100 percent of the fee schedule amount (Field 34 or 35) for the highest valued procedure; and
    - 50 percent of the fee schedule amount for the second through the fifth highest valued procedures; or

12. If more than five procedures with an indicator of "2" are billed, pay for the first five according to the rules listed in 9, 10, and 11 above and suspend the sixth and subsequent procedures for manual review and payment, if appropriate, "by report." Payment determined on a "by report" basis for these codes should never be lower than 50 percent of the full payment amount. Pay by the unit for services that are already reduced (e.g., 17003). Pay for 17340 only once per session, regardless of how many lesions were destroyed;

    NOTE: For dates of service prior to January 1, 1995, the multiple surgery indicator of "2" indicated that special dermatology rules applied. The payment rules for these codes have not changed. The rules were expanded, however, to all codes that previously had a multiple surgery indicator of "1." For dates of service prior to January 1, 1995, if a dermatological procedure with an indicator of "2" was billed with the "-51" modifier with other procedures that are not dermatological procedures (procedures with an indicator of "1" in Field 21), the standard multiple surgery rules applied. Pay no less than 50 percent for the dermatological procedures with an indicator of "2." See 40.6.C.6-8 for required actions.

13. If Field 21 contains an indicator of "3," and multiple endoscopies are billed, the special rules for multiple endoscopic procedures apply. Pay the full value of the highest valued endoscopy, plus the difference between the next highest and the base endoscopy. Access Field 31A of the MFSDB to determine the base endoscopy.

    EXAMPLE

    In the course of performing a fiber optic colonoscopy (CPT code 45378), a physician performs a biopsy on a lesion (code 45380) and removes a polyp (code 45385) from a different part of the colon. The physician bills for codes 45380 and 45385. The value of codes 45380 and 45385 have the value of the diagnostic colonoscopy (45378) built in.

    Rather than paying 100 percent for the highest valued procedure (45385) and 50 percent for the next (45380), pay the full value of the higher valued endoscopy (45385), plus the difference between the next highest endoscopy (45380) and the base endoscopy (45378).

    Carriers assume the following fee schedule amounts for these codes:

    45378 - $255.40

    45380 - $285.98

    45385 - $374.56

    Pay the full value of 45385 ($374.56), plus the difference between 45380 and 45378 ($30.58), for a total of $405.14.

    NOTE: If an endoscopic procedure with an indicator of "3" is billed with the "-51" modifier with other procedures that are not endoscopies (procedures with an indicator of "1" in Field 21), the standard multiple surgery rules apply. See 40.6.C.6-8 for required actions.

14. Apply the following rules where endoscopies are performed on the same day as unrelated endoscopies or other surgical procedures:
    - Two unrelated endoscopies (e.g., 46606 and 43217): Apply the usual multiple surgery rules;
    - Two sets of unrelated endoscopies (e.g., 43202 and 43217; 46606 and 46608): Apply the special endoscopy rules to each series and then apply the multiple surgery rules. Consider the total payment for each set of endoscopies as one service;
    - Two related endoscopies and a third, unrelated procedure: Apply the special endoscopic rules to the related endoscopies, and, then apply the multiple surgery rules. Consider the total payment for the related endoscopies as one service and the unrelated endoscopy as another service.

15. If two or more multiple surgeries are of equal value, rank them in descending dollar order billed and base payment on the percentages listed above (i.e., 100 percent for the first billed procedure, 50 percent for the second, etc.);

16. If any of the multiple surgeries are bilateral surgeries, consider the bilateral procedure at 150 percent as one payment amount, rank this with the remaining procedures, and apply the appropriate multiple surgery reductions. See 40.7 for bilateral surgery payment instructions.);

17. Round all adjusted payment amounts to the nearest cent;

18. If some of the surgeries are subject to special rules while others are subject to the standard rules, automate pricing to the extent possible. If necessary, price manually;

19. In cases of multiple interventional radiological procedures, both the radiology code and the primary surgical code are paid at 100 percent of the fee schedule amount. The subsequent surgical procedures are paid at the standard multiple surgical percentages (50 percent, 50 percent, 50 percent and 50 percent);

20. Apply the requirements in 40 on global surgeries to multiple surgeries;

21. Retain the "-51" modifier in history for any multiple surgeries paid at less than the full global amount; and

22. Follow the instructions on adjudicating surgery claims submitted with the "-22" modifier. Review documentation to determine if full payment should be made for those distinctly different, unrelated surgeries performed by different physicians on the same day.

D. Ranking of Same Day Multiple Surgeries When One Surgery Has a "-22" Modifier and Additional Payment is Allowed

B3-4826

If the patient returns to the operating room after the initial operative session on the same day as a result of complications from the original surgery, the complications rules apply to each procedure required to treat the complications from the original surgery. The multiple surgery rules would not apply.

However, if the patient is returned to the operating room during the postoperative period of the original surgery, not on the same day of the original surgery, for multiple procedures that are required as a result of complications from the original surgery, the complications rules would apply. The multiple surgery rules would also not apply.

Multiple surgeries are defined as separate procedures performed by a single physician or physicians in the same group practice on the same patient at the same operative session or on the same day for which separate payment may be allowed. Co-surgeons, surgical teams, or assistants-at-surgery may participate in performing multiple surgeries on the same patient on the same day.

Multiple surgeries are distinguished from procedures that are components of or incidental to a primary procedure. These intra-operative services, incidental surgeries, or components of more major surgeries are not separately billable. See Chapter 23 for a description of mandatory edits to prevent separate payment for those procedures.

100-4, 12, 40.7
Claims for Bilateral Surgeries
B3-4827, B3-15040

A. General
Bilateral surgeries are procedures performed on both sides of the body during the same operative session or on the same day.

The terminology for some procedure codes includes the terms "bilateral" (e.g., code 27395; Lengthening of the hamstring tendon; multiple, bilateral.) or "unilateral or bilateral" (e.g., code 52290; cystourethroscopy; with ureteral meatotomy, unilateral or bilateral). The payment adjustment rules for bilateral surgeries do not apply to procedures identified by CPT as "bilateral" or "unilateral or bilateral" since the fee schedule reflects any additional work required for bilateral surgeries.

Field 22 of the MFSDB indicates whether the payment adjustment rules apply to a surgical procedure.

B. Billing Instructions for Bilateral Surgeries
If a procedure is not identified by its terminology as a bilateral procedure (or unilateral or bilateral), physicians must report the procedure with modifier "-50." They report such procedures as a single line item. (NOTE: This differs from the CPT coding guidelines which indicate that bilateral procedures should be billed as two line items.)

If a procedure is identified by the terminology as bilateral (or unilateral or bilateral), as in codes 27395 and 52290, physicians do not report the procedure with modifier "-50."

C. Claims Processing System Requirements
Carriers must be able to:

1. Identify bilateral surgeries by the presence on the claim form or electronic submission of the "-50" modifier or of the same code on separate lines reported once with modifier "-LT" and once with modifier "-RT";

2. Access Field 34 or 35 of the MFSDB to determine the Medicare payment amount;

3. Access Field 22 of the MFSDB.
   - If Field 22 contains an indicator of "0," "2," or "3," the payment adjustment rules for bilateral surgeries do not apply. Base payment on the lower of the billed amount or 100 percent of the fee schedule amount (Field 34 or 35) unless other payment adjustment rules apply.

   NOTE: Some codes which have a bilateral indicator of "0" in the MFSDB may be performed more than once on a given day. These are services that would never be considered bilateral and thus should not be billed with modifier "-50." Where such a code is billed on multiple line items or with more than 1 in the units field and carriers have determined that the code may be reported more than once, bypass the "0" bilateral indicator and refer to the multiple surgery field for pricing;

   - If Field 22 contains an indicator of "1," the standard adjustment rules apply. Base payment on the lower of the billed amount or 150 percent of the fee schedule amount (Field 34 or 35). (Multiply the payment amount in Field 34 or 35 for the surgery by 150 percent and round to the nearest cent.)

4. Apply the requirements 40 - 40.4 on global surgeries to bilateral surgeries; and

5. Retain the "-50" modifier in history for any bilateral surgeries paid at the adjusted amount.
   (NOTE: The "-50" modifier is not retained for surgeries which are bilateral by definition such as code 27395.)

100-4, 12, 40.8
Claims for Co-Surgeons and Team Surgeons
B3-4828, B3-15046

A. General
Under some circumstances, the individual skills of two or more surgeons are required to perform surgery on the same patient during the same operative session. This may be required because of the complex nature of the procedure(s) and/or the patient's condition.

In these cases, the additional physicians are not acting as assistants-at-surgery.

B. Billing Instructions
The following billing procedures apply when billing for a surgical procedure or procedures that required the use of two surgeons or a team of surgeons:

- If two surgeons (each in a different specialty) are required to perform a specific procedure, each surgeon bills for the procedure with a modifier "-62." Co-surgery also refers to surgical procedures involving two surgeons performing the parts of the procedure simultaneously, i.e., heart transplant or bilateral knee replacements. Documentation of the medical necessity for two surgeons is required for certain services identified in the MFSDB. (See 40.8.C.5.);

- If a team of surgeons (more than 2 surgeons of different specialties) is required to perform a specific procedure, each surgeon bills for the procedure with a modifier "-66." Field 25 of the MFSDB identifies certain services submitted with a "-66" modifier which must be sufficiently documented to establish that a team was medically necessary. All claims for team surgeons must contain sufficient information to allow pricing "by report."

- If surgeons of different specialties are each performing a different procedure (with specific CPT codes), neither co-surgery nor multiple surgery rules apply (even if the procedures are performed through the same incision). If one of the surgeons performs multiple procedures, the multiple procedure rules apply to that surgeon's services. (See 40.6 for multiple surgery payment rules.)

For co-surgeons (modifier 62), the fee schedule amount applicable to the payment for each co-surgeon is 62.5 percent of the global surgery fee schedule amount. Team surgery (modifier 66) is paid for on a "By Report" basis.

C. Claims Processing System Requirements
Carriers must be able to:

1. Identify a surgical procedure performed by two surgeons or a team of surgeons by the presence on the claim form or electronic submission of the "-62" or "-66" modifier;

2. Access Field 34 or 35 of the MFSDB to determine the fee schedule payment amount for the surgery;

3. Access Field 24 or 25, as appropriate, of the MFSDB. These fields provide guidance on whether two or team surgeons are generally required for the surgical procedure;

4. If the surgery is billed with a "-62" or "-66" modifier and Field 24 or 25 contains an indicator of "0," payment adjustment rules for two or team surgeons do not apply:
   - Carriers pay the first bill submitted, and base payment on the lower of the billed amount or 100 percent of the fee schedule amount (Field 34 or 35) unless other payment adjustment rules apply;
   - Carriers deny bills received subsequently from other physicians and use the appropriate MSN message in 40.8.D. As these are medical necessity denials, the instructions in the Program Integrity Manual regarding denial of unassigned claims for medical necessity are applied;

5. If the surgery is billed with a "-62" modifier and Field 24 contains an indicator of "1," suspend the claim for manual review of any documentation submitted with the claim. If the documentation supports the need for co-surgeons, base payment for each physician on the lower of the billed amount or 62.5 percent of the fee schedule amount (Field 34 or 35);

6. If the surgery is billed with a "-62" modifier and Field 24 contains an indicator of "2," payment rules for two surgeons apply. Carriers base payment for each physician on the lower of the billed amount or 62.5 percent of the fee schedule amount (Field 34 or 35);

7. If the surgery is billed with a "-66" modifier and Field 25 contains an indicator of "1," carriers suspend the claim for manual review. If carriers determine that team surgeons were medically necessary, each physician is paid on a "by report" basis;

8. If the surgery is billed with a "-66" modifier and Field 25 contains an indicator of "2," carriers pay "by report";

   NOTE: A Medicare fee may have been established for some surgical procedures that are billed with the "-66" modifier. In these cases, all physicians on the team must agree on the percentage of the Medicare payment amount each is to receive. If carriers receive a bill with a "-66" modifier after carriers have paid one surgeon the full Medicare payment amount (on a bill without the modifier), deny the subsequent claim.

9. Apply the rules global surgical packages to each of the physicians participating in a co- or team surgery; and

10. Retain the "-62" and "-66" modifiers in history for any co- or team surgeries.

D. Beneficiary Liability on Denied Claims for Assistant, Co- surgeon and Team Surgeons
MSN message 23.10 which states "Medicare does not pay for a surgical assistant for this kind of surgery," was established for denial of claims for assistant surgeons. Where such payment is denied because the procedure is subject to the statutory restriction against payment for assistants-at-surgery. Carriers include the following statement in the MSN:

"You cannot be charged for this service." (Unnumbered add-on message.)

Carriers use Group Code CO on the remittance advice to the physician to signify that the beneficiary may not be billed for the denied service and that the physician could be subject to penalties if a bill is issued to the beneficiary.

If Field 23 of the MFSDB contains an indicator of "0" or "1" (assistant-at-surgery may not be paid) for procedures CMS has determined that an assistant surgeon is not generally medically necessary.

For those procedures with an indicator of "0," the limitation on liability provisions described in Chapter 30 apply to assigned claims. Therefore, carriers include the appropriate limitation of liability language from Chapter 21. For unassigned claims, apply the rules in the Program Integrity Manual concerning denial for medical necessity.

Where payment may not be made for a co- or team surgeon, use the following MSN message (MSN message number 15.13):

Medicare does not pay for team surgeons for this procedure.

Where payment may not be made for a two surgeons, use the following MSN message (MSN message number 15.12):

Medicare does not pay for two surgeons for this procedure.

Also see limitation of liability remittance notice REF remark codes M25, M26, and M27.

Use the following message on the remittance notice:

Multiple physicians/assistants are not covered in this case. (Reason code 54.)

100-4, 12, 50
Payment for Anesthesiology Services

A. General Payment Rule
The fee schedule amount for physician anesthesia services furnished on or after January 1, 1992 is, with the exceptions noted, based on allowable base and time units multiplied by an anesthesia conversion factor specific to that locality. The base unit for each anesthesia procedure is communicated to the carriers by means of the HCPCS file released annually. The public can access the base units on the CMS homepage through the anesthesiologists center. The way in which time units are calculated is described in 50.G. CMS releases the conversion factor annually.

B. Payment at Personally Performed Rate
Carriers must determine the fee schedule payment, recognizing the base unit for the anesthesia code and one time unit per 15 minutes of anesthesia time if:

- The physician personally performed the entire anesthesia service alone;
- The physician is involved with one anesthesia case with a resident, the physician is a teaching physician as defined in 100, and the service is furnished on or after January 1, 1996;
- The physician is continuously involved in a single case involving a student nurse anesthetist;
- The physician is continuously involved in one anesthesia case involving a CRNA (or AA) and the service was furnished prior to January 1, 1998. If the physician is involved with a single case with a CRNA (or AA) and the service was furnished on or after January 1, 1998, carriers may pay the physician service and the CRNA (or AA) service in accordance with the medical direction payment policy; or
- The physician and the CRNA (or AA) are involved in one anesthesia case and the services of each are found to be medically necessary. Documentation must be submitted by both the CRNA and the physician to support payment of the full fee for each of the two providers. The physician reports the "AA" modifier and the CRNA reports the "QZ" modifier for a nonmedically directed case.

C. Payment at the Medically Directed Rate
Carriers determine payment for the physician's medical direction service furnished on or after January 1, 1998, on the basis of 50 percent of the allowance for the service performed by the physician alone. Medical direction occurs if the physician medically directs qualified individuals in two, three, or four concurrent cases and the physician performs the following activities.

- Performs a pre-anesthetic examination and evaluation;
- Prescribes the anesthesia plan;
- Personally participates in the most demanding procedures in the anesthesia plan, including induction and emergence;
- Ensures that any procedures in the anesthesia plan that he or she does not perform are performed by a qualified anesthetist;
- Monitors the course of anesthesia administration at frequent intervals;
- Remains physically present and available for immediate diagnosis and treatment of emergencies; and
- Provides indicated-post-anesthesia care.

Prior to January 1, 1999, the physician was required to participate in the most demanding procedures of the anesthesia plan, including induction and emergence.

For medical direction services furnished on or after January 1, 1999, the physician must participate only in the most demanding procedures of the anesthesia plan, including, if applicable, induction and emergence. Also for medical direction services furnished on or after January 1, 1999, the physician must document in the medical record that he or she performed the pre-anesthetic examination and evaluation. Physicians must also document that they provided indicated post-anesthesia care, were present during some portion of the anesthesia monitoring, and were present during the most demanding procedures, including induction and emergence, where indicated.

For services furnished on or after January 1, 1994, the physician can medically direct two, three, or four concurrent procedures involving qualified individuals, all of whom could be CRNAs, AAs, interns, residents or combinations of these individuals. The medical direction rules apply to cases involving student nurse anesthetists if the physician directs two concurrent cases, each of which involves a student nurse anesthetist, or the physician directs one case involving a student nurse anesthetist and another involving a CRNA, AA, intern or resident.

If anesthesiologists are in a group practice, one physician member may provide the pre-anesthesia examination and evaluation while another fulfills the other criteria. Similarly, one physician member of the group may provide post-anesthesia care while another member of the group furnishes the other component parts of the anesthesia service. However, the medical record must indicate that the services were furnished by physicians and identify the physicians who furnished them.

A physician who is concurrently directing the administration of anesthesia to not more than four surgical patients cannot ordinarily be involved in furnishing additional services to other patients. However, addressing an emergency of short duration in the immediate area, administering an epidural or caudal anesthetic to ease labor pain, or periodic, rather than continuous, monitoring of an obstetrical patient does not substantially diminish the scope of control exercised by the physician in directing the administration of anesthesia to surgical patients. It does not constitute a separate service for the purpose of determining whether the medical direction criteria are met. Further, while directing concurrent anesthesia procedures, a physician may receive patients entering the operating suite for the next surgery, check or discharge patients in the recovery room, or handle scheduling matters without affecting fee schedule payment.

However, if the physician leaves the immediate area of the operating suite for other than short durations or devotes extensive time to an emergency case or is otherwise not available to respond to the immediate needs of the surgical patients, the physician's services to the surgical patients are supervisory in nature. Carriers may not make payment under the fee schedule.

See 50.J for a definition of concurrent anesthesia procedures.

D. Payment at Medically Supervised Rate
Carriers may allow only three base units per procedure when the anesthesiologist is involved in furnishing more than four procedures concurrently or is performing other services while directing the concurrent procedures. An additional time unit may be recognized if the physician can document he or she was present at induction.

E. Billing and Payment for Multiple Anesthesia Procedures
Physicians bill for the anesthesia services associated with multiple bilateral surgeries by reporting the anesthesia procedure with the highest base unit value with the multiple procedure modifier "-51." They report the total time for all procedures in the line item with the highest base unit value.

If the same anesthesia CPT code applies to two or more of the surgical procedures, billers enter the anesthesia code with the "-51" modifier and the number of surgeries to which the modified CPT code applies.

Payment can be made under the fee schedule for anesthesia services associated with multiple surgical procedures or multiple bilateral procedures. Payment is determined based on the base unit of the anesthesia procedure with the highest base unit value and time units based on the actual anesthesia time of the multiple procedures. See 40.6-40.7 for a definition and appropriate billing and claims processing instructions for multiple and bilateral surgeries.

F. Payment for Medical and Surgical Services Furnished in Addition to Anesthesia Procedure
Payment may be made under the fee schedule for specific medical and surgical services furnished by the anesthesiologist as long as these services are reasonable and medically necessary or provided that other rebundling provisions (see 30 and Chapter 23) do not preclude separate payment. These services may be furnished in conjunction with the anesthesia procedure to the patient or may be furnished as single services, e.g., during the day of or the day before the anesthesia service. These services include the insertion of a Swan Ganz catheter, the insertion of central venous pressure lines, emergency intubation, and critical care visits.

G. Anesthesia Time and Calculation of Anesthesia Time Units
Anesthesia time is defined as the period during which an anesthesia practitioner is present with the patient. It starts when the anesthesia practitioner begins to prepare the patient for anesthesia services in the operating room or an equivalent area and ends when the anesthesia practitioner is no longer furnishing anesthesia services to the patient, that is, when the patient may be placed safely under postoperative care. Anesthesia time is a continuous time period from the start of anesthesia to the end of an anesthesia service. In counting anesthesia time for services furnished on or after January 1, 2000, the anesthesia practitioner can add blocks of time around an interruption in anesthesia time as long as the anesthesia practitioner is furnishing continuous anesthesia care within the time periods around the interruption.

Actual anesthesia time in minutes is reported on the claim. For anesthesia services furnished on or after January 1, 1994, carriers compute time units by dividing reported anesthesia time by 15 minutes. Round the time unit to one decimal place. Carriers do not recognize time units for CPT codes 01995 or 01996.

For purposes of this section, anesthesia practitioner means a physician who performs the anesthesia service alone, a CRNA who is not medically directed, or a CRNA or AA, who is medically directed. The physician who medically directs the CRNA or AA would ordinarily report the same time as the CRNA or AA reports for the CRNA service.

H. Base Unit Reduction for Concurrent Medically Directed Procedures
If the physician medically directs concurrent medically directed procedures prior to January 1, 1994, reduce the number of base units for each concurrent procedure as follows.

- For two concurrent procedures, the base unit on each procedure is reduced 10 percent.
- For three concurrent procedures, the base unit on each procedure is reduced 25 percent.
- For four concurrent procedures, the base on each concurrent procedure is reduced 40 percent.
- If the physician medically directs concurrent procedures prior to January 1, 1994, and any of the concurrent procedures are cataract or iridectomy anesthesia, reduce the base units for each cataract or iridectomy procedure by 10 percent.

I. Monitored Anesthesia Care
Carriers pay for reasonable and medically necessary monitored anesthesia care services on the same basis as other anesthesia services. Anesthesiologists use modifier QS to report monitored anesthesia care cases. Monitored anesthesia care involves the intra-operative monitoring by a physician or qualified individual under the medical direction of a physician or of the patient's vital physiological signs in anticipation of the need for administration of general anesthesia or of the development of adverse physiological patient reaction to the surgical procedure. It also includes the performance of a pre-anesthetic examination and evaluation, prescription of the anesthesia care required, administration of any necessary oral or parenteral medications (e.g., atropine, demerol, valium) and provision of indicated postoperative anesthesia care.

Payment is made under the fee schedule using the payment rules in subsection B if the physician personally performs the monitored anesthesia care case or under the rules in subsection C if the physician medically directs four or fewer concurrent cases and monitored anesthesia care represents one or more of these concurrent cases.

J. Definition of Concurrent Medically Directed Anesthesia Procedures
Concurrency is defined with regard to the maximum number of procedures that the physician is medically directing within the context of a single procedure and whether these other procedures overlap each other. Concurrency is not dependent on each of the cases involving a Medicare

Appendix G — Pub 100 References

patient. For example, if an anesthesiologist directs three concurrent procedures, two of which involve non-Medicare patients and the remaining a Medicare patient, this represents three concurrent cases. The following example illustrates this concept and guides physicians in determining how many procedures they are directing.

EXAMPLE:

Procedures A through E are medically directed procedures involving CRNAs and furnished between January 1, 1992 and December 31, 1997 (1998 concurrent instructions can be found in subsection C.) The starting and ending times for each procedure represent the periods during which anesthesia time is counted. Assume that none of the procedures were cataract or iridectomy anesthesia.

Procedure A begins at 8:00 a.m. and lasts until 8:20 a.m.

Procedure B begins at 8:10 a.m. and lasts until 8:45 a.m.

Procedure C begins at 8:30 a.m. and lasts until 9:15 a.m.

Procedure D begins at 9:00 a.m. and lasts until 12:00 noon.

Procedure E begins at 9:10 a.m. and lasts until 9:55 a.m.

Procedure	Number of Concurrent Medically Directed Procedures	Base Unit Reduction Percentage
A	2	10%
B	2	10%
C	3	25%
D	3	25%
E	3	25%

From 8:00 a.m. to 8:20 a.m., the length of procedure A, the anesthesiologist medically directed two concurrent procedures, A and B. From 8:10 a.m. to 8:45 a.m., the length of procedure B, the anesthesiologist medically directed two concurrent procedures.

From 8:10 to 8:20 a.m., the anesthesiologist medically directed procedures A and B. From 8:20 to 8:30 a.m., the anesthesiologist medically directed only procedure B. From 8:30 to 8:45 a.m., the anesthesiologist medically directed procedures B and C. Thus, during procedure B, the anesthesiologist medically directed, at most, two concurrent procedures.

From 8:30 a.m. to 9:15 a.m., the length of procedure C, the anesthesiologist medically directed three concurrent procedures.

From 8:30 to 8:45 a.m., the anesthesiologist medically directed procedures B and C. From 8:45 to 9:00 a.m., the anesthesiologist medically directed procedure C. From 9:00 to 9:10 a.m., the anesthesiologist medically directed procedures C and D. From 9:10 to 9:15 a.m., the anesthesiologist medically directed procedures C, D and E. Thus, during procedure C, the anesthesiologist medically directed, at most, three concurrent procedures.

The same analysis shows that during procedure D or E, the anesthesiologist medically directed, at most, three concurrent procedures.

K. Anesthesia Claims Modifiers

Physicians report the appropriate anesthesia modifier to denote whether the service was personally performed, medically directed, or medically supervised.

Specific anesthesia modifiers include:

AA Anesthesia Services performed personally by the anesthesiologist

AD Medical Supervision by a physician; more than 4 concurrent anesthesia procedures;

G8 Monitored anesthesia care (MAC) for deep complex complicated, or markedly invasive surgical procedures;

G9 Monitored anesthesia care for patient who has a history of severe cardio-pulmonary condition

QK Medical direction of two, three or four concurrent anesthesia procedures involving qualified individuals

QS Monitored anesthesia care service

QX CRNA service; with medical direction by a physician

QY Medical direction of one certified registered nurse anesthetist by an anesthesiologist

QZ CRNA service: Without medical direction by a physician.

The QS modifier is for informational purposes. Providers must report actual anesthesia time on the claim.

Carriers must determine payment for anesthesia in accordance with these instructions. They must be able to determine the uniform base unit that is assigned to the anesthesia code and apply the appropriate reduction where the anesthesia procedure is medically directed. They must also be able to determine the number of anesthesia time units from actual anesthesia time reported on the claim. Carriers must multiply allowable units by the anesthesia-specific conversion factor used to determine fee schedule payment for the payment area.

L. Anesthesia and Medical/Surgical Service Provided by the Same Physician

Anesthesia services range in complexity. The continuum of anesthesia services, from least intense to most intense in complexity is as follows: local or topical anesthesia, moderate (conscious) sedation, regional anesthesia and general anesthesia. Prior to 2006, Medicare did not recognize separate payment if the same physician provided the medical or surgical procedure and the anesthesia needed for the procedure.

Moderate sedation is a drug induced depression of consciousness during which the patient responds purposefully to verbal commands, either alone or accompanied by light tactile stimulation. Moderate sedation does not include minimal sedation, deep sedation or monitored anesthesia care. In 2006, the CPT added new codes 99143 to 99150 for moderate or conscious sedation. The moderate (conscious) sedation codes are carrier priced under the Medicare physician fee schedule.

CPT codes 99143 to 99145 describe moderate sedation provided by the same physician performing the diagnostic or therapeutic service that the sedation supports, requiring the presence of an independent trained observer to assist in the monitoring of the patient's level of consciousness and physiological status. The physician can bill the conscious sedation codes 99143 to 99145 as long as the procedure with it is billed is not listed in Appendix G of CPT. CPT codes 99148 to 99150 describe moderate sedation provided by a physician other than the health care professional performing the diagnostic or therapeutic service that the sedation supports.

The CPT includes Appendix G, Summary of CPT Codes That Include Moderate (Conscious) Sedation. This appendix lists those procedures for which moderate (conscious) sedation is an inherent part of the procedure itself. CPT coding guidelines instruct practices not to report CPT codes 99143 to 99145 in conjunction with codes listed in Appendix G. The National Correct Coding Initiative has established edits that bundle CPT codes 99143 and 99144 into the procedures listed in Appendix G.

In the unusual event when a second physician other than the health care professional performing the diagnostic or therapeutic services provides moderate sedation in the facility setting for the procedures listed in Appendix G, the second physician can bill 99148 to 99150. The term, facility, includes those places of service listed in Chapter 23 Addendum -- field 29. However, when these services are performed by the second physician in the nonfacility setting, CPT codes 99148 to 99150 are not to be reported.

If the anesthesiologist or CRNA provides anesthesia for diagnostic or therapeutic nerve blocks or injections and a different provider performs the block or injection, then the anesthesiologist or CRNA may report the anesthesia service using CPT code 01991. The service must meet the criteria for monitored anesthesia care. If the anesthesiologist or CRNA provides both the anesthesia service and the block or injection, then the anesthesiologist or CRNA may report the anesthesia service using the conscious sedation code and the injection or block. However, the anesthesia service must meet the requirements for conscious sedation and if a lower level complexity anesthesia service is provided, then the conscious sedation code should not be reported.

If the physician performing the medical or surgical procedure also provides a level of anesthesia lower in intensity than moderate or conscious sedation, such as a local or topical anesthesia, then the conscious sedation code should not be reported and no payment shall be allowed by the carrier. There is no CPT code for the performance of local anesthesia and as payment for this service is considered in the payment for the underlying medical or surgical service.

100-4, 12, 60
Payment for Pathology Services
B3-15020, AB-01-47 (CR1499)

A. General Payment Rule

Payment may be made under the fee schedule for the professional component of physician laboratory or physician pathology services furnished to hospital inpatients or outpatients by hospital physicians or by independent laboratories, if they qualify as the reassignee for the physician service.. Payment may be made under the fee schedule, as noted below, for the technical component (TC) of pathology services furnished by an independent laboratory to hospital inpatients or outpatients. Payment may be made under the fee schedule for the technical component of physician pathology services furnished by an independent laboratory, or a hospital if it is acting as an independent laboratory, to non-hospital patients. The Medicare physician fee schedule identifies those physician laboratory or physician pathology services that have a technical component service.

CMS published a final regulation in 1999 that would no longer allow independent laboratories to bill under the physician fee schedule for the TC of physician pathology services. The implementation of this regulation was delayed by Section 542 of the Benefits and Improvement and Protection Act of 2000 (BIPA). Section 542 allows the Medicare carrier to continue to pay for the TC of physician pathology services when an independent laboratory furnishes this service to an inpatient or outpatient of a covered hospital. This provision is applicable to TC services furnished in 2001, 2002, 2003, 2004, 2005 or 2006.

For this provision, a covered hospital is a hospital that had an arrangement with an independent laboratory that was in effect as of July 22, 1999, under which a laboratory furnished the TC of physician pathology services to fee-for-service Medicare beneficiaries who were hospital inpatients or outpatients, and submitted claims for payment for the TC to a carrier. The TC could have been submitted separately or combined with the professional component and reported as a combined service.

The term, fee-for-service Medicare beneficiary, means an individual who:

Is entitled to benefits under Part A or enrolled under Part B of title XVIII or both; and

Is not enrolled in any of the following: A Medicare + Choice plan under Part C of such title; a plan offered by an eligible organization under 1876 of the Social Security Act; a program of all-inclusive care for the elderly under 1894; or a social health maintenance organization demonstration project established under Section 4108 of the Omnibus Budget Reconciliation Act of 1987.

In implementing Section 542, the carriers should consider as independent laboratories those entities that it has previously recognized as independent laboratories. An independent laboratory that has acquired another independent laboratory that had an arrangement of July 22, 1999, with a covered hospital, can bill the TC of physician pathology services for that hospital's inpatients and outpatients under the physician fee schedule.

An independent laboratory that furnishes the TC of physician pathology services to inpatients or outpatients of a hospital that is not a covered hospital may not bill the carrier for the TC of physician pathology services during the time 542 is in effect.

If the arrangement between the independent laboratory and the covered hospital limited the provision of TC physician pathology services to certain situations or at particular times, then the independent laboratory can bill the carrier only for these limited services.

The carrier shall require independent laboratories that had an arrangement, on or prior to July 22, 1999 with a covered hospital, to bill for the technical component of physician pathology services to provide a copy of this agreement, or other documentation substantiating that an arrangement was in effect between the hospital and the independent laboratory as of this date. The independent laboratory must submit this documentation for each covered hospital that the independent laboratory services.

See Chapter 16 for additional instruction on laboratory services including clinical diagnostic laboratory services.

Physician laboratory and pathology services are limited to:

- Surgical pathology services;
- Specific cytopathology, hematology and blood banking services that have been identified to require performance by a physician and are listed below;
- Clinical consultation services that meet the requirements in subsection D below;
- and
- Clinical laboratory interpretation services that meet the requirements and which are specifically listed in subsection E below.

B. Surgical Pathology Services
Surgical pathology services include the gross and microscopic examination of organ tissue performed by a physician, except for autopsies, which are not covered by Medicare. Surgical pathology services paid under the physician fee schedule are reported under the following CPT codes:

88300, 88302, 88304, 88305, 88307, 88309, 88311, 88312, 88313, 88314, 88318, 88319, 88321, 88323, 88325, 88329, 88331, 88332, 88342, 88346, 88347, 88348, 88349, 88355, 88356, 88358, 88361, 88362, 88365, 88380.

Depending upon circumstances and the billing entity, the carriers may pay professional component, technical component or both.

C. Specific Hematology, Cytopathology and Blood Banking Services
Cytopathology services include the examination of cells from fluids, washings, brushings or smears, but generally excluding hematology. Examining cervical and vaginal smears are the most common service in cytopathology. Cervical and vaginal smears do not require interpretation by a physician unless the results are or appear to be abnormal. In such cases, a physician personally conducts a separate microscopic evaluation to determine the nature of an abnormality. This microscopic evaluation ordinarily does require performance by a physician. When medically necessary and when furnished by a physician, it is paid under the fee schedule.

These codes include 88104, 88106, 88107, 88108, 88112, 88125, 88141, 88160, 88161, 88162, 88172, 88173, 88180, 88182.

For services furnished prior to January 1, 1999, carriers pay separately under the physician fee schedule for the interpretation of an abnormal pap smear furnished to a hospital inpatient by a physician. They must pay under the clinical laboratory fee schedule for pap smears furnished in all other situations. This policy also applies to screening pap smears requiring a physician interpretation. For services furnished on or after January 1, 1999, carriers allow separate payment for a physician's interpretation of a pap smear to any patient (i.e., hospital or non-hospital) as long as: (1) the laboratory's screening personnel suspect an abnormality; and (2) the physician reviews and interprets the pap smear.

This policy also applies to screening pap smears requiring a physician interpretation and described in the National Coverage Determination Manual and Chapter 18. These services are reported under codes P3000 or P3001.

Physician hematology services include microscopic evaluation of bone marrow aspirations and biopsies. It also includes those limited number of peripheral blood smears which need to be referred to a physician to evaluate the nature of an apparent abnormality identified by the technologist. These codes include 85060, 38220, 85097, and 38221.

Carriers pay the professional component for the interpretation of an abnormal blood smear (code 85060) furnished to a hospital inpatient by a hospital physician or an independent laboratory.

For the other listed hematology codes, payment may be made for the professional component if the service is furnished to a patient by a hospital physician or independent laboratory. In addition, payment may be made for these services furnished to patients by an independent laboratory.

Codes 38220 and 85097 represent professional-only component services and have no technical component values.

Blood banking services of hematologists and pathologists are paid under the physician fee schedule when analyses are performed on donor and/or patient blood to determine compatible donor units for transfusion where cross matching is difficult or where contamination with transmissible disease of donor is suspected.

The blood banking codes are 86077, 86078, and 86079 and represent professional component only services. These codes do not have a technical component.

D. Clinical Consultation Services
Clinical consultations are paid under the physician fee schedule only if they:

- Are requested by the patient's attending physician;
- Relate to a test result that lies outside the clinically significant normal or expected range in view of the condition of the patient;
- Result in a written narrative report included in the patient's medical record; and
- Require the exercise of medical judgment by the consultant physician.

Clinical consultations are professional component services only. There is no technical component. The clinical consultation codes are 80500 and 80502.

Routine conversations held between a laboratory director and an attending physician about test orders or results do not qualify as consultations unless all four requirements are met. Laboratory personnel, including the director, may from time to time contact attending physicians to report test results or to suggest additional testing or be contacted by attending physicians on similar matters. These contacts do not constitute clinical consultations. However, if in the course of such a contact, the attending physician requests a consultation from the pathologist, and if that consultation meets the other criteria and is properly documented, it is paid under the fee schedule.

EXAMPLE: A pathologist telephones a surgeon about a patient's suitability for surgery based on the results of clinical laboratory test results. During the course of their conversation, the surgeon ask the pathologist whether, based on test results, patient history and medical records, the patient is a candidate for surgery. The surgeon's request requires the pathologist to render a medical judgment and provide a consultation. The athologist follows up his/her oral advice with a written report and the surgeon notes in the patient's medical record that he/she requested a consultation. This consultation is paid under the fee schedule.

In any case, if the information could ordinarily be furnished by a nonphysician laboratory specialist, the service of the physician is not a consultation payable under the fee schedule.

See the Program Integrity Manual for guidelines for related data analysis to identify inappropriate patterns of billing for consultations.

E. Clinical Laboratory Interpretation Services
Only clinical laboratory interpretation services listed below and which meet the criteria in subsections D.1, D.3, and D.4 for clinical consultations and, as a result, are billable under the fee schedule. These services are reported under the clinical laboratory code with modifier 26. These services can be paid under the physician fee schedule if they are furnished to a patient by a hospital pathologist or an independent laboratory. Note that a hospital's standing order policy can be used as a substitute for the individual request by the patient's attending physician. Carriers are not allowed to revise CMS's list to accommodate local medical practice. The CMS periodically reviews this list and adds or deletes clinical laboratory codes as warranted.

Clinical Laboratory Interpretation Services

Code	Definition
83020	Hemoglobin; electrophoresis
83912	Nucleic acid probe, with electrophoresis, with examination and report
84165	Protein, total, serum; electrophoretic fractionation and quantitation
84181	Protein; Western Blot with interpretation and report, blood or other body fluid
84182	Protein; Western Blot, with interpretation and report, blood or other body fluid, immunological probe for band identification; each
85390	Fibrinolysin; screening
85576	Platelet; aggregation (in vitro), any agent
86255	Fluorescent antibody; screen
86256	Fluorescent antibody; titer
86320	Immunoelectrophoresis; serum, each specimen
86325	Immunoelectrophoresis; other fluids (e.g.urine) with concentration, each specimen
86327	Immunoelectrophoresis; crossed (2 dimensional assay)
86334	Immunofixation electrophoresis
87164	Dark field examination, any source (e.g. penile, vaginal, oral, skin); includes specimen collection
87207	Smear, primary source, with interpretation; special stain for inclusion bodies or intracellular parasites (e.g. malaria, kala azar, herpes)
88371	Protein analysis of tissue by Western Blot, with interpretation and report.
88372	Protein analysis of tissue by Western Blot, immunological probe for band identification, each
89060	Crystal identification by light microscopy with or without polarizing lens analysis, any body fluid (except urine)

100-4, 12, 80.3
Unusual Travel (CPT Code 99082)
B3-15026 In general, travel has been incorporated in the MPFSDB individual fees and is thus not separately payable. Carriers must pay separately for unusual travel (CPT code 99082) only when the physician submits documentation to demonstrate that the travel was very unusual.

100-4, 12, 90.3
Physicians' Services Performed in Ambulatory Surgical Centers (ASC)
B3-2265, B3-2265.4

See Chapter 14, for a description of services that may be billed by an ASC and services separately billed by physicians.

Appendix G — Pub 100 References

The ASC payment does not include the professional services of the physician. These are billed separately by the physician. Physicians' services include the services of anesthesiologists administering or supervising the administration of anesthesia to ASC patients and the patients' recovery from the anesthesia. The term physicians' services also includes any routine pre- or postoperative services, such as office visits, consultations, diagnostic tests, removal of stitches, changing of dressings, and other services which the individual physician usually performs.

The physician must enter the place of service code (POS) 24 on the claim to show that the procedure was performed in an ASC.

The carrier pays the "facility" fee from the MPFSDB to the physician. The facility fee is for services done in a facility other than the physician's office and is less then the nonfacility fee for services performed in the physician's office.

100-4, 12, 100
Teaching Physician Services
Definitions

For purposes of this section, the following definitions apply.

Resident -An individual who participates in an approved graduate medical education (GME) program or a physician who is not in an approved GME program but who is authorized to practice only in a hospital setting. The term includes interns and fellows in GME programs recognized as approved for purposes of direct GME payments made by the FI. Receiving a staff or faculty appointment or participating in a fellowship does not by itself alter the status of "resident". Additionally, this status remains unaffected regardless of whether a hospital includes the physician in its full time equivalency count of residents.

Student- An individual who participates in an accredited educational program (e.g., a medical school) that is not an approved GME program. A student is never considered to be an intern or a resident. Medicare does not pay for any service furnished by a student. See 100.1.1B for a discussion concerning E/M service documentation performed by students.

Teaching Physician -A physician (other than another resident) who involves residents in the care of his or her patients.

Direct Medical and Surgical Services -Services to individual beneficiaries that are either personally furnished by a physician or furnished by a resident under the supervision of a physician in a teaching hospital making the reasonable cost election for physician services furnished in teaching hospitals. All payments for such services are made by the FI for the hospital.

Teaching Hospital -A hospital engaged in an approved GME residency program in medicine, osteopathy, dentistry, or podiatry.

Teaching Setting -Any provider, hospital-based provider, or nonprovider setting in which Medicare payment for the services of residents is made by the FI under the direct graduate medical education payment methodology or freestanding SNF or HHA in which such payments are made on a reasonable cost basis.

Critical or Key Portion- That part (or parts) of a service that the teaching physician determines is (are) a critical or key portion(s). For purposes of this section, these terms are interchangeable.

Documentation- Notes recorded in the patient's medical records by a resident, and/or teaching physician or others as outlined in the specific situations below regarding the service furnished. Documentation may be dictated and typed or hand-written, or computer-generated and typed or handwritten. Documentation must be dated and include a legible signature or identity. Pursuant to 42 CFR 415.172 (b), documentation must identify, at a minimum, the service furnished, the participation of the teaching physician in providing the service, and whether the teaching physician was physically present. In the context of an electronic medical record, the term 'macro' means a command in a computer or dictation application that automatically generates predetermined text that is not edited by the user.

When using an electronic medical record, it is acceptable for the teaching physician to use a macro as the required personal documentation if the teaching physician adds it personally in a secured (password protected) system. In addition to the teaching physician's macro, either the resident or the teaching physician must provide customized information that is sufficient to support a medical necessity determination. The note in the electronic medical record must sufficiently describe the specific services furnished to the specific patient on the specific date. It is insufficient documentation if both the resident and the teaching physician use macros only.

Physically Present- The teaching physician is located in the same room (or partitioned or curtained area, if the room is subdivided to accommodate multiple patients) as the patient and/or performs a face-to-face service.

100-4, 12, 110.2
Outpatient Mental Health Limitation
B3-4112, B3-2472.4 The carrier must apply the outpatient mental health limitation to all covered mental health therapeutic services furnished by PAs. The reduction is 62.5 percent applied after the 85 percent.

Refer to 210 below for a complete discussion of the outpatient mental health limitation.

100-4, 12, 140
Certified Registered Nurse Anesthetist (CRNA) Services
B3-16003, B3-16003 A, B3-3040.4, B3-4172 Section 9320 of OBRA 1986 provides for payment under a fee schedule to certified registered nurse anesthetists (CRNAs) and anesthesia assistants (AAs). CRNAs and AAs may bill Medicare directly for their services or have payment made to an employer or an entity under which they have a contract. This could be a hospital, physician or ASC. This provision is effective for services rendered on or after January 1, 1989.

Anesthesia services are subject to the usual Part B coinsurance and deductible and when furnished on or after January 1, 1992 by a qualified nurse anesthetist and are paid at the lesser of the actual charge, the physician fee schedule, or the CRNA fee schedule. Payment for CRNA services is made only on an assignment basis.

100-4, 12, 140.2
Entity or Individual to Whom CRNA Fee Schedule is Payable
B3-16003.C, B3-4830.A

Payment for the services of a CRNA may be made to the CRNA who furnished the anesthesia services or to a hospital, physician, group practice, or ASC with which the CRNA has an employment or contractual relationship.

100-4, 12, 140.3.2
Anesthesia Time and Calculation of Anesthesia Time Units
B3-15018.G Anesthesia time means the time during which a CRNA is present with the patient. It starts when the CRNA begins to prepare the patient for anesthesia services in the operating room or an equivalent area and ends when the CRNA is no longer furnishing anesthesia services to the patient, that is, when the patient may be placed safely under postoperative care. Anesthesia time is a continuous time period from the start of anesthesia to the end of an anesthesia service. In counting anesthesia time for services furnished on or after January 1, 2000, the CRNA can add blocks of time around an interruption in anesthesia time as long as the CRNA is furnishing continuous anesthesia care within the time periods around the interruption.

100-4, 12, 150
Clinical Social Worker (CSW) Services
B3-2152, B3-17000 See Medicare Benefit Policy Manual, Chapter 15, for coverage requirements.

Assignment of benefits is required.

Payment is at 75 percent of the physician fee schedule.

CSWs are identified on the provider file by specialty code 80 and provider type 56.

Medicare applies the outpatient mental health limitation to all covered therapeutic services furnished by qualified CSWs. Refer to 210, below, for a discussion of the outpatient mental health limitation. The modifier "AJ" must be applied on CSN services.

100-4, 12, 160
Independent Psychologist Services
B3-2150, B3-2070.2 See the Medicare Benefit Policy Manual, Chapter 15, for coverage requirements.

There are a number of types of psychologists. Educational psychologists engage in identifying and treating education-related issues. In contrast, counseling psychologists provide services that include a broader realm including phobias, familial issues, etc.

Psychometrists are psychologists who have been trained to administer and interpret tests.

However, clinical psychologists are defined as a provider of diagnostic and therapeutic services. Because of the differences in services provided, services provided by psychologists who do not provide clinical services are subject to different billing guidelines. One service often provided by nonclinical psychologist is diagnostic testing.

NOTE:Diagnostic psychological testing services performed by persons who meet these requirements are covered as other diagnostic tests. When, however, the psychologist is not practicing independently, but is on the staff of an institution, agency, or clinic, that entity bills for the diagnostic services.

Expenses for such testing are not subject to the payment limitation on treatment for mental, psychoneurotic, and personality disorders. Independent psychologists are not required by law to accept assignment when performing psychological tests. However, regardless of whether the psychologist accepts assignment, he or she must report on the claim form the name and address of the physician who ordered the test.

100-4, 12, 160.1
Payment
Diagnostic testing services are not subject to the outpatient mental health limitation. Refer to §210, below, for a discussion of the outpatient mental health limitation.

The diagnostic testing services performed by a psychologist (who is not a clinical psychologist) practicing independently of an institution, agency, or physician's office are covered as other diagnostic tests if a physician orders such testing. Medicare covers this type of testing as an outpatient service if furnished by any psychologist who is licensed or certified to practice psychology in the State or jurisdiction where he or she is furnishing services or, if the jurisdiction does not issue licenses, if provided by any practicing psychologist. (It is CMS' understanding that all States, the District of Columbia, and Puerto Ricolicense psychologists, but that some trust territories do not. Examples of psychologists, other than clinical psychologists, whose services are covered under this provision include, but are not limited to, educational psychologists and counseling psychologists.)

To determine whether the diagnostic psychological testing services of a particular independent psychologist are covered under Part B in States which have statutory licensure or certification, carriers must secure from the appropriate State agency a current listing of psychologists holding the required credentials. In States or territories which lack statutory licensing and certification, carriers must check individual qualifications as claims are submitted. Possible reference sources are the national directory of membership of the American Psychological Association, which provides data about the educational background of individuals and indicates which members are board-certified, and records and directories of the State or territorial psychological association. If qualification is dependent on a doctoral degree from a currently accredited program, carriers must verify the date of accreditation of the school involved, since such accreditation is not retroactive. If the reference sources listed above do not provide enough information (e.g., the psychologist is not a member of the association), carriers must contact the psychologist personally for the required information. Carriers may wish to maintain a continuing list of psychologists whose qualifications have been verified.

Medicare excludes expenses for diagnostic testing from the payment limitation on treatment for mental/psychoneurotic/personality disorders.

Carriers must identify the independent psychologist's choice whether or not to accept assignment when performing psychological tests.

Carriers must accept an independent psychologist claim only if the psychologist reports the name/UPIN of the physician who ordered a test.

Carriers pay nonparticipating independent psychologists at 95 percent of the physician fee schedule allowed amount. Carriers pay participating independent psychologists at 100 percent of the physician fee schedule allowed amount.

Independent psychologists are identified on the provider file by specialty code 62 and provider type 35.

100-4, 12, 170
Clinical Psychologist Services
B3-2150 See Medicare Benefit Policy Manual, Chapter 15, for general coverage requirements.

Direct payment may be made under Part B for professional services. However, services furnished incident to the professional services of CPs to hospital patients remain bundled.

Therefore, payment must continue to be made to the hospital (by the FI) for such "incident to" services.

100-4, 12, 170.1
Payment
B3-2150, B3-17001.1 All covered therapeutic services furnished by qualified CPs are subject to the outpatient mental health services limitation (i.e., only 62 1/2 percent of expenses for these services are considered incurred expenses for Medicare purposes). The limitation does not apply to diagnostic services. Refer to 210 below for a discussion of the outpatient mental health limitation.

Payment for the services of CPs is made on the basis of a fee schedule or the actual charge, whichever is less, and only on the basis of assignment.

CPs are identified by specialty code 68 and provider type 27. Modifier "AH" is required on CP services.

100-4, 12, 180
Care Plan Oversight Services
The Medicare Benefit Policy Manual, Chapter 15, contains requirements for coverage for medical and other health services including those of physicians and non-physician practitioners.

Care plan oversight (CPO) is the physician supervision of a patient receiving complex and/or multidisciplinary care as part of Medicare-covered services provided by a participating home health agency or Medicare approved hospice.

CPO services require complex or multidisciplinary care modalities involving:

- Regular physician development and/or revision of care plans;
- Review of subsequent reports of patient status;
- Review of related laboratory and other studies;
- Communication with other health professionals not employed in the same practice who are involved in the patient's care;
- Integration of new information into the medical treatment plan; and/or
- Adjustment of medical therapy.

The CPO services require recurrent physician supervision of a patient involving 30 or more minutes of the physician's time per month. Services not countable toward the 30 minutes threshold that must be provided in order to bill for CPO include, but are not limited to:

- Time associated with discussions with the patient, his or her family or friends to adjust medication or treatment;
- Time spent by staff getting or filing charts;
- Travel time; and/or
- Physician's time spent telephoning prescriptions into the pharmacist unless the telephone conversation involves discussions of pharmaceutical therapies.

Implicit in the concept of CPO is the expectation that the physician has coordinated an aspect of the patient's care with the home health agency or hospice during the month for which CPO services were billed. The physician who bills for CPO must be the same physician who signs the plan of care.

Nurse practitioners, physician assistants, and clinical nurse specialists, practicing within the scope of State law, may bill for care plan oversight. These non-physician practitioners must have been providing ongoing care for the beneficiary through evaluation and management services. These non-physician practitioners may not bill for CPO if they have been involved only with the delivery of the Medicare-covered home health or hospice service.

A. Home Health CPO
Non-physician practitioners can perform CPO only if the physician signing the plan of care provides regular ongoing care under the same plan of care as does the NPP billing for CPO and either:

- The physician and NPP are part of the same group practice; or

- If the NPP is a nurse practitioner or clinical nurse specialist, the physician signing the plan of care also has a collaborative agreement with the NPP; or
- If the NPP is a physician assistant, the physician signing the plan of care is also the physician who provides general supervision of physician assistant services for the practice.

Billing may be made for care plan oversight services furnished by an NPP when:

- The NPP providing the care plan oversight has seen and examined the patient;
- The NPP providing care plan oversight is not functioning as a consultant whose participation is limited to a single medical condition rather than multidisciplinary coordination of care; and
- The NPP providing care plan oversight integrates his or her care with that of the physician who signed the plan of care.

NPPs may not certify the beneficiary for home health care.

B. Hospice CPO
The attending physician or nurse practitioner (who has been designated as the attending physician) may bill for hospice CPO when they are acting as an "attending physician".

An "attending physician" is one who has been identified by the individual, at the time he/she elects hospice coverage, as having the most significant role in the determination and delivery of their medical care. They are not employed nor paid by the hospice. The care plan oversight services are billed using Form CMS-1500 or electronic equivalent.

For additional information on hospice CPO, see Chapter 11, 40.1.3.1 of this manual.

100-4, 12, 180.1
Care Plan Oversight Billing Requirements
A. Codes for Which Separate Payment May Be Made
Effective January 1, 1995, separate payment may be made for CPO oversight services for 30 minutes or more if the requirements specified in the Medicare Benefits Policy Manual, Chapter 15 are met.

Providers billing for CPO must submit the claim with no other services billed on that claim and may bill only after the end of the month in which the CPO services were rendered. CPO services may not be billed across calendar months and should be submitted (and paid) only for one unit of service.

Physicians may bill and be paid separately for CPO services only if all the criteria in the Medicare Benefit Policy Manual, Chapter 15 are met.

B. Physician Certification and Recertification of Home Health Plans of Care
Effective 2001, two new HCPCS codes for the certification and recertification and development of plans of care for Medicare-covered home health services were created.

See the Medicare General Information, Eligibility, and Entitlement Manual, Pub. 100-01, Chapter 4, "Physician Certification and Recertification of Services," 10-60, and the Medicare Benefit Policy Manual, Pub. 100-02, Chapter 7, "Home Health Services", 30.

The home health agency certification code can be billed only when the patient has not received Medicare-covered home health services for at least 60 days. The home health agency recertification code is used after a patient has received services for at least 60 days (or one certification period) when the physician signs the certification after the initial certification period. The home health agency recertification code will be reported only once every 60 days, except in the rare situation when the patient starts a new episode before 60 days elapses and requires a new plan of care to start a new episode.

C. Provider Number of Home Health Agency (HHA) or Hospice
For claims for CPO submitted on or after January 1, 1997, physicians must enter on the Medicare claim form the 6-character Medicare provider number of the HHA or hospice providing Medicare-covered services to the beneficiary for the period during which CPO services was furnished and for which the physician signed the plan of care. Physicians are responsible for obtaining the HHA or hospice Medicare provider numbers.

Additionally, physicians should provide their UPIN to the HHA or hospice furnishing services to their patient.

NOTE: There is currently no place on the HIPAA standard ASC X12N 837 professional format to specifically include the HHA or hospice provider number required for a care plan oversight claim. For this reason, the requirement to include the HHA or hospice provider number on a care plan oversight claim is temporarily waived until a new version of this electronic standard format is adopted under HIPAA and includes a place to provide the HHA and hospice provider numbers for care plan oversight claims.

100-4, 12, 190.3
List of Medicare Telehealth Services
The use of a telecommunications system may substitute for a face-to-face, "hands on" encounter for consultation, office visits, individual psychotherapy, pharmacologic management, psychiatric diagnostic interview examination, end stage renal disease related services, and individual medical nutrition therapy. These services and corresponding current procedure terminology (CPT) or Healthcare Common Procedure Coding System (HCPCS) codes are listed below.

- Consultations (CPT codes 99241 - 99275) - Effective October 1, 2001 - December 31, 2005;
- Consultations (CPT codes 99241 - 99255) - Effective January 1, 2006;
- Office or other outpatient visits (CPT codes 99201 - 99215);
- Individual psychotherapy (CPT codes 90804 - 90809);
- Pharmacologic management (CPT code 90862);
- Psychiatric diagnostic interview examination (CPT code 90801) - Effective March 1, 2003;

Appendix G — Pub 100 References
Current Procedural Coding Expert
Appendix G — Pub 100 References

- End Stage Renal Disease (ESRD) related services (HCPCS codes G0308, G0309, G0311, G0312, G0314, G0315, G0317, and G0318) - Effective January 1, 2005 - December 31, 2008;
- End Stage Renal Disease (ESRD) related services (CPT codes 90951, 90952, 90954, 90955, 90957, 90958, 90960, and 90961) - Effective January 1, 2009;
- Individual Medical Nutrition Therapy (HCPCS codes G0270, 97802, and 97803) - Effective January 1, 2006;
- Neurobehavioral status exam (CPT code 96116) - Effective January 1, 2008; and
- Follow-up inpatient telehealth consultations (HCPCS codes G0406, G0407, and G0408) - Effective January 1, 2009.

100-4, 12, 190.7

Contractor Editing of Telehealth Claims

Medicare telehealth services (as listed in section 190.3) are billed with either the "GT" or "GQ" modifier. The contractor shall approve covered telehealth services if the physician or practitioner is licensed under State law to provide the service. Contractors must familiarize themselves with licensure provisions of States for which they process claims and disallow telehealth services furnished by physicians or practitioners who are not authorized to furnish the applicable telehealth service under State law. For example, if a nurse practitioner is not licensed to provide individual psychotherapy under State law, he or she would not be permitted to receive payment for individual psychotherapy under Medicare. The contractor shall install edits to ensure that only properly licensed physicians and practitioners are paid for covered telehealth services.

If a contractor receives claims for professional telehealth services coded with the "GQ" modifier (representing "via asynchronous telecommunications system"), it shall approve/pay for these services only if the physician or practitioner is affiliated with a Federal telemedicine demonstration conducted in Alaska or Hawaii. The contractor may require the physician or practitioner at the distant site to document his or her participation in a Federal telemedicine demonstration program conducted in Alaska or Hawaii prior to paying for telehealth services provided via asynchronous, store and forward technologies.

If a contractor denies telehealth services because the physician or practitioner may not bill for them, the contractor uses MSN message 21.18: "This item or service is not covered when performed or ordered by this practitioner." The contractor uses remittance advice message 52 when denying the claim based upon MSN message 21.18.

If a service is billed with one of the telehealth modifiers and the procedure code is not designated as a covered telehealth service, the contractor denies the service using MSN message 9.4: "This item or service was denied because information required to make payment was incorrect." The remittance advice message depends on what is incorrect, e.g., B18 if procedure code or modifier is incorrect, 125 for submission billing errors, 4-12 for difference inconsistencies. The contractor uses B18 as the explanation for the denial of the claim.

The only claims from institutional facilities that FIs shall pay for telehealth services at the distant site, except for MNT services, are for physician or practitioner services when the distant site is located in a CAH that has elected Method II, and the physician or practitioner has reassigned his/her benefits to the CAH. The CAH bills its regular FI for the professional services provided at the distant site via a telecommunications system, in any of the revenue codes 096x, 097x or 098x. All requirements for billing distant site telehealth services apply.

Claims from hospitals or CAHs for MNT services are submitted to the hospital's or CAH's regular FI. Payment is based on the non-facility amount on the Medicare Physician Fee Schedule for the particular HCPCS codes.

100-4, 12, 200

Allergy Testing and Immunotherapy

B3-15050

A. Allergy Testing

The MPFSDB fee amounts for allergy testing services billed under codes 95004-95078 are established for single tests. Therefore, the number of tests must be shown on the claim.

EXAMPLE: If a physician performs 25 percutaneous tests (scratch, puncture, or prick) with allergenic extract, the physician must bill code 95004 and specify 25 in the units field of Form CMS-1500 (paper claims or electronic format). To compute payment, the Medicare carrier multiplies the payment for one test (i.e., the payment listed in the fee schedule) by the quantity listed in the units field.

B. Allergy Immunotherapy

For services rendered on or after January 1, 1995, all antigen/allergy immunotherapy services are paid for under the Medicare physician fee schedule. Prior to that date, only the antigen injection services, i.e., only codes 95115 and 95117, were paid for under the fee schedule. Codes representing antigens and their preparation and single codes representing both the antigens and their injection were paid for under the Medicare reasonable charge system. A legislative change brought all of these services under the fee schedule at the beginning of 1995 and the following policies are effective as of January 1, 1995:

1. CPT codes 95120 through 95134 are not valid for Medicare. Codes 95120 through 95134 represent complete services, i.e., services that include both the injection service as well as the antigen and its preparation.
2. Separate coding for injection only codes (i.e., codes 95115 and 95117) and/or the codes representing antigens and their preparation (i.e., codes 95144 through 95170) must be used.

   If both services are provided both codes are billed.

   This includes allergists who provide both services through the use of treatment boards.
3. If a physician bills both an injection code plus either codes 95165 or 95144, carriers pay the appropriate injection code (i.e., code 95115 or code 95117) plus the code 95165 rate. When a provider bills for codes 95115 or 95117 plus code 95144, carriers change 95144 to 95165 and pay accordingly. Code 95144 (single dose vials of antigen) should be billed only if the physician providing the antigen is providing it to be injected by some other entity. Single dose vials, which should be used only as a means of insuring proper dosage amounts for injections, are more costly than multiple dose vials (i.e., code 95165) and therefore their payment rate is higher. Allergists who prepare antigens are assumed to be able to administer proper doses from the less costly multiple dose vials. Thus, regardless of whether they use or bill for single or multiple dose vials at the same time that they are billing for an injection service, they are paid at the multiple dose vial rate.
4. The fee schedule amounts for the antigen codes (95144 through 95170) are for a single dose. When billing those codes, physicians are to specify the number of doses provided. When making payment, carriers multiply the fee schedule amount by the number of doses specified in the units field.
5. If a patient's doses are adjusted, e.g., because of patient reaction, and the antigen provided is actually more or fewer doses than originally anticipated, the physician is to make no change in the number of doses for which he or she bills. The number of doses anticipated at the time of the antigen preparation is the number of doses to be billed. This is consistent with the notes on page 30 of the Spring 1994 issue of the American Medical Association's CPT Assistant. Those notes indicate that the antigen codes mean that the physician is to identify the number of doses "prospectively planned to be provided." The physician is to "identify the number of doses scheduled when the vial is provided." This means that in cases where the patient actually gets more doses than originally anticipated (because dose amounts were decreased during treatment) and in cases where the patient gets fewer doses (because dose amounts were increased), no change is to be made in the billing. In the first case, carriers are not to pay more because the number of doses provided in the original vial(s) increased. In the second case, carriers are not to seek recoupment (if carriers have already made payment) because the number of doses is less than originally planned. This is the case for both venom and nonvenom antigen codes.
6. Venom Doses and Catch-Up Billing - Venom doses are prepared in separate vials and not mixed together - except in the case of the three vespid mix (white and yellow hornets and yellow jackets). A dose of code 95146 (the two-venom code) means getting some of two venoms. Similarly, a dose of code 95147 means getting some of three venoms; a dose of code 95148 means getting some of four venoms; and a dose of 95149 means getting some of five venoms. Some amount of each of the venoms must be provided. Questions arise when the administration of these venoms does not remain synchronized because of dosage adjustments due to patient reaction. For example, a physician prepares ten doses of code 95148 (the four venom code) in two vials - one containing 10 doses of three vespid mix and another containing 10 doses of wasp venom. Because of dose adjustment, the three vespid mix doses last longer, i.e., they last for 15 doses. Consequently, questions arise regarding the amount of "replacement" wasp venom antigen that should be prepared and how it should be billed. Medicare pricing amounts have savings built into the use of the higher venom codes. Therefore, if a patient is in two venom, three venom, four venom or five venom therapy, the carrier objective is to pay at the highest venom level possible. This means that, to the greatest extent possible, code 95146 is to be billed for a patient in two venom therapy, code 95147 is to be billed for a patient in three venom therapy, code 95148 is to be billed for a patient in four venom therapy, and code 95149 is to be billed for a patient in five venom therapy. Thus, physicians are to be instructed that the venom antigen preparation, after dose adjustment, must be done in a manner that, as soon as possible, synchronizes the preparation back to the highest venom code possible. In the above example, the physician should prepare and bill for only 5 doses of "replacement" wasp venom - billing five doses of code 95145 (the one venom code). This will permit the physician to get back to preparing the four venoms at one time and therefore billing the doses of the "cheaper" four venom code. Use of a code below the venom treatment number for the particular patient should occur only for the purpose of "catching up."
7. Code 95165 Doses. - Code 95165 represents preparation of vials of non-venom antigens. As in the case of venoms, some non-venom antigens cannot be mixed together, i.e., they must be prepared in separate vials. An example of this is mold and pollen. Therefore, some patients will be injected at one time from one vial - containing in one mixture all of the appropriate antigens - while other patients will be injected at one time from more than one vial. In establishing the practice expense component for mixing a multidose vial of antigens, we observed that the most common practice was to prepare a 10 cc vial; we also observed that the most common use was to remove aliquots with a volume of 1 cc. Our PE computations were based on those facts. Therefore, a physician's removing 10 1cc aliquot doses captures the entire PE component for the service.

   This does not mean that the physician must remove 1 cc aliquot doses from a multidose vial. It means that the practice expenses payable for the preparation of a 10cc vial remain the same irrespective of the size or number of aliquots removed from the vial. Therefore, a physician may not bill this vial preparation code for more than 10 doses per vial; paying more than 10 doses per multidose vial would significantly overpay the practice expense component attributable to this service. (Note that this code does not include the injection of antigen(s); injection of antigen(s) is separately billable.) When a multidose vial contains less than 10cc, physicians should bill Medicare for the number of 1 cc aliquots that may be removed from the vial. That is, a physician may bill Medicare up to a maximum of 10 doses per multidose vial, but should bill Medicare for fewer than 10 doses per vial when there is less than 10cc in the vial.

   If it is medically necessary, physicians may bill Medicare for preparation of more than one multidose vial.

   EXAMPLES:

   (1) If a 10cc multidose vial is filled to 6cc with antigen, the physician may bill Medicare for 6 doses since six 1cc aliquots may be removed from the vial.

   (2) If a 5cc multidose vial is filled completely, the physician may bill Medicare for 5 doses for this vial.

(3) If a physician removes ¬¾ cc aliquots from a 10cc multidose vial for a total of 20 doses from one vial, he/she may only bill Medicare for 10 doses. Billing for more than 10 doses would mean that Medicare is overpaying for the practice expense of making the vial.

(4) If a physician prepares two 10cc multidose vials, he/she may bill Medicare for 20 doses. However, he/she may remove aliquots of any amount from those vials. For example, the physician may remove ¬¾ aliquots from one vial, and 1cc aliquots from the other vial, but may bill no more than a total of 20 doses.

(5) If a physician prepares a 20cc multidose vial, he/she may bill Medicare for 20 doses, since the practice expense is calculated based on the physician's removing 1cc aliquots from a vial. If a physician removes 2cc aliquots from this vial, thus getting only 10 doses, he/she may nonetheless bill Medicare for 20 doses because the PE for 20 doses reflects the actual practice expense of preparing the vial.

(6) If a physician prepares a 5cc multidose vial, he may bill Medicare for 5 doses, based on the way that the practice expense component is calculated. However, if the physician removes ten ¬¾ cc aliquots from the vial, he/she may still bill only 5 doses because the practice expense of preparing the vial is the same, without regard to the number of additional doses that are removed from the vial.

C. Allergy Shots and Visit Services on the Same Day

At the outset of the physician fee schedule, the question was posed as to whether visits should be billed on the same day as an allergy injection (CPT codes 95115-95117), since these codes have status indicators of A rather than T. Visits should not be billed with allergy injection services 95115 or 95117 unless the visit represents another separately identifiable service. This language parallels CPT editorial language that accompanies the allergen immunotherapy codes, which include codes 9515 and 95117. Prior to January 1, 1995, you appeared to be enforcing this policy through three (3) different means:

- Advising physician to use modifier 25 with the visit service;
- Denying payment for the visit unless documentation has been provided; and
- Paying for both the visit and the allergy shot if both are billed for.

For services rendered on or after January 1, 1995, you are to enforce the requirement that visits not be billed and paid for on the same day as an allergy injection through the following means. Effective for services rendered on or after that date, the global surgery policies will apply to all codes in the allergen immunotherapy series, including the allergy shot codes 95115 and 95117. To accomplish this, CMS changed the global surgery indicator for allergen immunotherapy codes from XXX, which meant that the global surgery concept did not apply to those codes, to 000, which means that the global surgery concept applies, but that there are no days in the postoperative global period.

Now that the global surgery policies apply to these services, you are to rely on the use of modifier 25 as the only means through which you can make payment for visit services provided on the same day as allergen immunotherapy services. In order for a physician to receive payment for a visit service provided on the same day that the physician also provides a service in the allergen immunotherapy series (i.e., any service in the series from 95115 through 95199), the physician is to bill a modifier 25 with the visit code, indicating that the patient's condition required a significant, separately identifiable visit service above and beyond the allergen immunotherapy service provided.

D. Reasonable Supply of Antigens

See CMS Manual System, Internet Only Manual, Medicare Benefits Policy Manual, CMS Pub. 100-02 Chapter 15, section 50.4.4, regarding the coverage of antigens, including what constitutes a reasonable supply of antige

100-4, 12, 210
Outpatient Mental Health Limitation
B3-2470

Regardless of the actual expenses a beneficiary incurs for treatment of mental, psychoneurotic, and personality disorders while the beneficiary is not an inpatient of a hospital at the time such expenses are incurred, the amount of those expenses that may be recognized for Part B deductible and payment purposes is limited to 62.5 percent of the Medicare allowed amount for those services. This limitation is called the outpatient mental health treatment limitation. Expenses for diagnostic services (e.g., psychiatric testing and evaluation to diagnose the patient's illness) are not subject to this limitation.

This limitation applies only to therapeutic services and to services performed to evaluate the progress of a course of treatment for a diagnosed condition.

100-4, 13, 10
ICD-9-CM Coding for Diagnostic Tests

The ICD-9-CM Coding Guidelines for Outpatient Services (hospital-based and physician office) have instructed physicians to report diagnoses based on test results. Instructions and examples for coding specialists, contractors, physicians, hospitals, and other health care providers to use in determining the use of ICD-9-CM codes for coding diagnostic test results is found in Chapter 23.

100-4, 13, 30
Computerized Axial Tomography (CT) Procedures

Carriers do not reduce or deny payment for medically necessary multiple CT scans of different areas of the body that are performed on the same day.

The TC RVUs for CT procedures that specify "with contrast" include payment for high osmolar contrast media. When separate payment is made for low osmolar contrast media under the conditions set forth in 30.1.1, reduce payment for the contrast media as set forth in 30.1.2.

100-4, 13, 40
Magnetic Resonance Imaging (MRI) Procedures
Prior to January 1, 2007

Carriers do not make additional payments for three or more MRI sequences. The RVUs reflect payment levels for two sequences.

The TC RVUs for MRI procedures that specify "with contrast" include payment for paramagnetic contrast media. Carriers do not make separate payment under code A4647.

A diagnostic technique has been developed under which an MRI of the brain or spine is first performed without contrast material, then another MRI is performed with a standard (0.1mmol/kg) dose of contrast material and, based on the need to achieve a better image, a third MRI is performed with an additional double dosage (0.2mmol/kg) of contrast material. When the high-dose contrast technique is utilized, carriers:

- Do not pay separately for the contrast material used in the second MRI procedure;
- Pay for the contrast material given for the third MRI procedure through supply code Q9952, the replacement code for A4643, when billed with CPT codes 70553, 72156, 72157, and 72158;
- Do not pay for the third MRI procedure. For example, in the case of an MRI of the brain, if CPT code 70553 (without contrast material, followed by with contrast material(s) and further sequences) is billed, make no payment for CPT code 70551 (without contrast material(s)), the additional procedure given for the purpose of administering the double dosage, furnished during the same session. Medicare does not pay for the third procedure (as distinguished from the contrast material) because the CPT definition of code 70553 includes all further sequences; and
- Do not apply the payment criteria for low osmolar contrast media in 30.1.2 to billings for code Q9952, the replacement code for A4643.

Effective January 1, 2007

With the implementation for calendar year 2007 of a bottom-up methodology, which utilizes the direct inputs to determine the practice expense (PE) relative value units (RVUs), the cost of the contrast media is not included in the PE RVUs. Therefore, a separate payment for the contrast media used in various imaging procedures is paid. In addition to the CPT code representing the imaging procedure, separately bill the appropriate HCPCS "Q" code (Q9945 - Q9954; Q9958-Q9964) for the contrast medium utilized in performing the service.

100-4, 13, 40.1.1
Magnetic Resonance Angiography Coverage Summary

Section 1861(s)(2)(C) of the Act provides for coverage of diagnostic testing. Coverage of magnetic resonance angiography (MRA) of the head and neck, and MRA of the peripheral vessels of the lower extremities is limited as described in the Medicare National Coverage Determinations Manual. This instruction has been revised as of July 1, 2003, based on a determination that coverage is reasonable and necessary in additional circumstances. Under that instruction, MRA is generally covered only to the extent that it is used as a substitute for contrast angiography, except to the extent that there are documented circumstances consistent with that instruction that demonstrate the medical necessity of both tests. There is no coverage of MRA outside of the indications and circumstances described in that instruction.

Because the status codes for HCPCS 71555, 71555-TC, 71555-26, 74185, 74185- TC, and 74185-26 were changed in the MPFSDB from N to R on April 1, 1998, any MRA claims with those HCPCS codes with dates of service between April 1, 1998, and June 30, 1999, are to be processed according to the contractor's discretionary authority to determine payment in the absence of national policy.

100-4, 13, 60
Positron Emission Tomography (PET) Scans - General Information

Positron emission tomography (PET) is a noninvasive imaging procedure that assesses perfusion and the level of metabolic activity in various organ systems of the human body. A positron camera (tomograph) is used to produce cross-sectional tomographic images which are obtained by detecting radioactivity from a radioactive tracer substance radiopharmaceutical) that emits a radioactive tracer substance (radiopharmaceutical FDG) such as 2 -[F-18] flouro-D-glucose FDG, that is administered intravenously to the patient.

The Medicare National Coverage Determinations (NCD) Manual, Chapter 1, Sec.220.6, contains additional coverage instructions to indicate the conditions under which a PET scan is performed.

A. Definitions

For all uses of PET, excluding Rubidium 82 for perfusion of the heart, myocardial viability and refractory seizures, the following definitions apply:

Diagnosis: PET is covered only in clinical situations in which the PET results may assist in avoiding an invasive diagnostic procedure, or in which the PET results may assist in determining the optimal anatomical location to perform an invasive diagnostic procedure. In general, for most solid tumors, a tissue diagnosis is made prior to the performance of PET scanning. PET scans following a tissue diagnosis are generally performed for the purpose of staging, rather than diagnosis. Therefore, the use of PET in the diagnosis of lymphoma, esophageal and colorectal cancers, as well as in melanoma, should be rare. PET is not covered for other diagnostic uses, and is not covered for screening (testing of patients without specific signs and symptoms of disease).

Staging: PET is covered in clinical situations in which (1) (a) the stage of the cancer remains in doubt after completion of a standard diagnostic workup, including conventional imaging (computed tomography, magnetic resonance imaging, or ultrasound) or, (b) the use of PET would also be considered reasonable and necessary if it could potentially replace one or more conventional imaging studies when it is expected that conventional study information is insufficient for the clinical management of the patient and, (2) clinical management of the patient would differ depending on the stage of the cancer identified.

Appendix G — Pub 100 References

Restaging: PET will be covered for restaging: (1) after the completion of treatment for the purpose of detecting residual disease, (2) for detecting suspected recurrence, or metastasis, (3) to determine the extent of a known recurrence, or (4) if it could potentially replace one or more conventional imaging studies when it is expected that conventional study information is to determine the extent of a known recurrence, or if study information is insufficient for the clinical management of the patient. Restaging applies to testing after a course of treatment is completed and is covered subject to the conditions above.

Monitoring: Use of PET to monitor tumor response to treatment during the planned course of therapy (i.e., when a change in therapy is anticipated).

NOTE: Effective for services on or after April 6, 2009, the terms "restaging" and "monitoring" will be replaced with "Subsequent Treatment Strategy." For further information on this new term, refer to Pub. 100-03, section 220.6.17.

B. Limitations

For staging and restaging: PET is covered in either/or both of the following circumstances:

The stage of the cancer remains in doubt after completion of a standard diagnostic workup, including conventional imaging (computed tomography, magnetic resonance imaging, or ultrasound); and/or

The clinical management of the patient would differ depending on the stage of the cancer identified. PET will be covered for restaging after the completion of treatment for the purpose of detecting residual disease, for detecting suspected recurrence, or to determine the extent of a known recurrence. Use of PET would also be considered reasonable and necessary if it could potentially replace one or more conventional imaging studies when it is expected that conventional study information is insufficient for the clinical management of the patient.

The PET is not covered for other diagnostic uses, and is not covered for screening (testing of patients without specific symptoms). Use of PET to monitor tumor response during the planned course of therapy (i.e. when no change in therapy is being contemplated) is not covered.

100-4, 13, 60.1
Billing Instructions

A. Billing and Payment Instructions or Responsibilities for Carriers

Claims for PET scan services must be billed on Form-CMS 1500 or the electronic equivalent with the appropriate HCPCS or CPT code and diagnosis codes to the local carrier. Effective for claims received on or after July 1, 2001, PET modifiers were discontinued and are no longer a claims processing requirement for PET scan claims.

Therefore, July 1, 2001, and after the MSN messages regarding the use of PET modifiers can be discontinued. The type of service (TOS) for the new PET scan procedure codes is TOS 4, Diagnostic Radiology. Payment is based on the Medicare Physician Fee Schedule.

B. Billing and Payment Instructions or Responsibilities for FIs

Claims for PET scan procedures must be billed to the FI on Form CMS-1450 (UB-92) or the electronic equivalent with the appropriate diagnosis and HCPCS "G" code or CPT code to indicate the conditions under which a PET scan was done. These codes represent the technical component costs associated with these procedures when furnished to hospital and SNF outpatients. They are paid as follows:

- under OPPS for hospitals subject to OPPS
- under current payment methodologies for hospitals not subject to OPPS
- on a reasonable cost basis for critical access hospitals.
- on a reasonable cost basis for skilled nursing facilities.

Institutional providers bill these codes under Revenue Code 0404 (PET Scan).

Medicare contractors shall pay claims submitted for services provided by a critical access hospital (CAH) as follows: Method I technical services are paid at 101% of reasonable cost; Method II technical services are paid at 101% of reasonable cost, and professional services are paid at 115% of the Medicare Physician Fee Schedule Data Base.

C. Frequency

In the absence of national frequency limitations, for all indications covered on and after July 1, 2001, contractors can, if necessary, develop frequency limitations on any or all covered PET scan services.

D. Post-Payment Review for PET Scans

As with any claim, but particularly in view of the limitations on this coverage, Medicare may decide to conduct post-payment reviews to determine that the use of PET scans is consistent with coverage instructions. Pet scanning facilities must keep patient record information on file for each Medicare patient for whom a PET scan claim is made. These medical records can be used in any post-payment reviews and must include the information necessary to substantiate the need for the PET scan. These records must include standard information (e.g., age, sex, and height) along with sufficient patient histories to allow determination that the steps required in the coverage instructions were followed. Such information must include, but is not limited to, the date, place and results of previous diagnostic tests (e.g., cytopathology and surgical pathology reports, CT), as well as the results and reports of the PET scan(s) performed at the center. If available, such records should include the prognosis derived from the PET scan, together with information regarding the physician or institution to which the patient proceeded following the scan for treatment or evaluation. The ordering physician is responsible for forwarding appropriate clinical data to the PET scan facility.

Effective for claims received on or after July 1, 2001, CMS no longer requires paper documentation to be submitted up front with PET scan claims. Contractors shall be aware and advise providers of the specific documentation requirements for PET scans for dementia and neurodegenerative diseases. This information is outlined in section 60.12.

Documentation requirements such as physician referral and medical necessity determination are to be maintained by the provider as part of the beneficiary's medical record. This information must be made available to the carrier or FI upon request of additional documentation to determine appropriate payment of an individual claim.

100-4, 13, 60.2
Use of Gamma Cameras and Full Ring and Partial Ring PET Scanners for PET Scans

See the Medicare NCD Manual, Section 220.6, concerning 2-[F-18] Fluoro-D-Glucose (FDG) PET scanners and details about coverage.

On July 1, 2001, HCPCS codes G0210 - G0230 were added to allow billing for all currently covered indications for FDG PET. Although the codes do not indicate the type of PET scanner, these codes were used until January 1, 2002, by providers to bill for services in a manner consistent with the coverage policy.

Effective January 1, 2002, HCPCS codes G0210 - G0230 were updated with new descriptors to properly reflect the type of PET scanner used. In addition, four new HCPCS codes became effective for dates of service on and after January 1, 2002, (G0231, G0232, G0233, G0234) for covered conditions that may be billed if a gamma camera is used for the PET scan. For services performed from January 1, 2002, through January 27, 2005, providers should bill using the revised HCPCS codes G0210 - G0234.

Beginning January 28, 2005 providers should bill using the appropriate CPT code.

100-4, 13, 60.3
PET Scan Qualifying Conditions and HCPCS Code Chart

Below is a summary of all covered PET scan conditions, with effective dates.

NOTE: The G codes below except those a # can be used to bill for PET Scan services through January 27, 2005. Effective for dates of service on or after January 28, 2005, providers must bill for PET Scan services using the appropriate CPT codes. See section 60.3.1. The G codes with a # can continue to be used for billing after January 28, 2005 and these remain non-covered by Medicare. (NOTE: PET Scanners must be FDA-approved.)

Conditions	Coverage Effective Date	****HCPCS/CPT
*Myocardial perfusion imaging (following previous PET G0030-G0047) single study, rest or stress (exercise and/or pharmacologic)	3/14/95	G0030
*Myocardial perfusion imaging (following previous PET G0030-G0047) multiple studies, rest or stress (exercise and/or pharmacologic)	3/14/95	G0031
*Myocardial perfusion imaging (following rest SPECT, 78464); single study, rest or stress (exercise and/or pharmacologic)	'3/14/95	G0032
*Myocardial perfusion imaging (following rest SPECT 78464); multiple studies, rest or stress (exercise and/or pharmacologic)	3/14/95	G0033
*Myocardial perfusion (following stress SPECT 78465); single study, rest or stress (exercise and/or pharmacologic)	3/14/95	G0034
*Myocardial Perfusion Imaging (following stress SPECT 78465); multiple studies, rest or stress (exercise and/or pharmacologic)	3/14/95	G0035
*Myocardial Perfusion Imaging (following coronary angiography 93510-93529); single study, rest or stress (exercise and/or pharmacologic)	3/14/95	G0036
*Myocardial Perfusion Imaging, (following coronary angiography), 93510-93529; multiple studies, rest or stress (exercise and/or pharmacologic)	3/14/95	G0037
*Myocardial Perfusion Imaging (following stress planar myocardial perfusion, 78460); single study, rest or stress (exercise and/or pharmacologic)	3/14/95	G0038
*Myocardial Perfusion Imaging (following stress planar myocardial perfusion, 78460); multiple studies, rest or stress (exercise and/or pharmacologic)	3/14/95	G0039
*Myocardial Perfusion Imaging (following stress echocardiogram 93350); single study, rest or stress (exercise and/or pharmacologic)	3/14/95	G0040
*Myocardial Perfusion Imaging (following stress echocardiogram, 93350); multiple studies, rest or stress (exercise and/or pharmacologic)	3/14/95	G0041
*Myocardial Perfusion Imaging (following stress nuclear ventriculogram 78481 or 78483); single study, rest or stress (exercise and/or pharmacologic)	3/14/95	G0042
*Myocardial Perfusion Imaging (following stress nuclear ventriculogram 78481 or 78483); multiple studies, rest or stress (exercise and/or pharmacologic)	3/14/95	G0043

*   Carriers must report A4641 for the tracer Rubidium 82 when used with PET scan codes G0030 through G0047 for services performed on or before January 27, 2005
** Not FDG PET
*** For dates of service October 1, 2003, through December 31, 2003, use temporary code Q4078 for billing this radiopharmaceutical.

Current Procedural Coding Expert

Appendix G — Pub 100 References

Conditions	Coverage Effective Date	****HCPCS/CPT
*Myocardial Perfusion Imaging (following stress ECG, 93000); single study, rest or stress (exercise and/or pharmacologic)	3/14/95	G0044
*Myocardial perfusion (following stress ECG, 93000), multiple studies; rest or stress (exercise and/or pharmacologic)	3/14/95	G0045
*Myocardial perfusion (following stress ECG, 93015), single study; rest or stress (exercise and/or pharmacologic)	3/14/95	G0046
*Myocardial perfusion (following stress ECG, 93015); multiple studies; rest or stress (exercise and/or pharmacologic)	3/14/95	G0047
PET imaging regional or whole body; single pulmonary nodule	1/1/98	G0125
Lung cancer, non-small cell (PET imaging whole body) Diagnosis, Initial Staging, Restaging	7/1/01	G0210 G0211 G0212
Colorectal cancer (PET imaging whole body) Diagnosis, Initial Staging, Restaging	7/1/01	G0213 G0214 G0215
Melanoma (PET imaging whole body) Diagnosis, Initial Staging, Restaging	7/1/01	G0216 G0217 G0218
Melanoma for non-covered indications	7/1/01	G0219
Lymphoma (PET imaging whole body) Diagnosis, Initial Staging, Restaging	7/1/01	G0220 G0221 G0222
Head and neck cancer; excluding thyroid and CNS cancers (PET imaging whole body or regional) Diagnosis, Initial Staging, Restaging	7/1/01	G0223 G0224 G0225
Esophageal cancer (PET imaging whole body) Diagnosis, Initial Staging, Restaging	7/1/01	G0226 G0227 G0228
Metabolic brain imaging for pre-surgical evaluation of refractory seizures	7/1/01	G0229
Metabolic assessment for myocardial viability following inconclusive SPECT study	7/1/01	G0230
Recurrence of colorectal or colorectal metastatic cancer (PET whole body, gamma cameras only)	1/1/02	G0231
Staging and characterization of lymphoma (PET whole body, gamma cameras only)	1/1/02	G0232
Recurrence of melanoma or melanoma metastatic cancer (PET whole body, gamma cameras only)	1/1/02	G0233
Regional or whole body, for solitary pulmonary nodule following CT, or for initial staging of nonsmall cell lung cancer (gamma cameras only)	1/1/02	G0234
Non-Covered Service PET imaging, any site not otherwise specified	1/28/05	G0235
Non-Covered Service Initial diagnosis of breast cancer and/or surgical planning for breast cancer (e.g., initial staging of axillary lymph nodes), not covered (full- and partialring PET scanners only)	10/1/02	G0252
Breast cancer, staging/restaging of local regional recurrence or distant metastases, i.e., staging/restaging after or prior to course of treatment (full- and partial-ring PET scanners only)	10/1/02	G0253
Breast cancer, evaluation of responses to treatment, performed during course of treatment (full- and partial-ring PET scanners only)	10/1/02	G0254
Myocardial imaging, positron emission tomography (PET), metabolic evaluation	10/1/02	78459
Restaging or previously treated thyroid cancer of follicular cell origin following negative I-131 whole body scan (full- and partial-ring PET scanner only)	10/1/03	G0296
Tracer Rubidium**82 (Supply of Radiopharmaceutical Diagnostic Imaging Agent) (This is only billed through Outpatient Perspective Payment System, OPPS.) (Carriers must use HCPCS Code A4641).	10/1/03	Q3000
Supply of Radiopharmaceutical Diagnostic Imaging Agent, Ammonia N-13	01/1/04	A9526

*   Carriers must report A4641 for the tracer Rubidium 82 when used with PET scan codes G0030 through G0047 for services performed on or before January 27, 2005
**   Not FDG PET
***   For dates of service October 1, 2003, through December 31, 2003, use temporary code Q4078 for billing this radiopharmaceutical.

Conditions	Coverage Effective Date	****HCPCS/CPT
PET imaging, brain imaging for the differential diagnosis of Alzheimer's disease with aberrant features vs. fronto-temporal dementia	09/15/04	Appropriate CPT Code from section 60.3.1
PET Cervical Cancer Staging as adjunct to conventional imaging, other staging, diagnosis, restaging, monitoring	1/28/05	Appropriate CPT Code from section 60.3.1

*   Carriers must report A4641 for the tracer Rubidium 82 when used with PET scan codes G0030 through G0047 for services performed on or before January 27, 2005
**   Not FDG PET
***   For dates of service October 1, 2003, through December 31, 2003, use temporary code Q4078 for billing this radiopharmaceutical.

100-4, 13, 60.3.1
Appropriate CPT Codes Effective for PET Scans for Services Performed on or After January 28, 2005
NOTE: All PET scan services require the use of a radiopharmaceutical diagnostic imaging agent (tracer). The applicable tracer code should be billed when billing for a PET scan service. See section 60.3.2 below for applicable tracer codes.

CPT Code	Description
78459	Myocardial imaging, positron emission tomography (PET), metabolic evaluation
78491	Myocardial imaging, positron emission tomography (PET), perfusion, single study at rest or stress
78492	Myocardial imaging, positron emission tomography (PET), perfusion, multiple studies at rest and/or stress
78608	Brain imaging, positron emission tomography (PET); metabolic evaluation
78811	Tumor imaging, positron emission tomography (PET); limited area (eg, chest, head/neck)
78812	Tumor imaging, positron emission tomography (PET); skull base to mid-thigh
78813	Tumor imaging, positron emission tomography (PET); whole body
78814	Tumor imaging, positron emission tomography (PET) with concurrently acquired computed tomography (CT) for attenuation correction and anatomical localization; limited area (eg, chest, head/neck)
78815	Tumor imaging, positron emission tomography (PET) with concurrently acquired computed tomography (CT) for attenuation correction and anatomical localization; skull base to mid-thigh
78816	Tumor imaging, positron emission tomography (PET) with concurrently acquired computed tomography (CT) for attenuation correction and anatomical localization; whole body

100-4, 13, 60.3.2
Tracer Codes Required for PET Scans
The following tracer codes are applicable only to CPT 78491 and 78492. They can not be reported with any other code.

Institutional providers billing the fiscal intermediary.

HCPCS	Description
*A9555	Rubidium Rb-82, Diagnostic, Per study dose, Up To 60 Millicuries
* Q3000 (Deleted effective 12/31/05)	Supply of Radiopharmaceutical Diagnostic Imaging Agent, Rubidium Rb-82, per dose
A9526	Nitrogen N-13 Ammonia, Diagnostic, Per study dose, Up To 40 Millicuries

NOTE: For claims with dates of service prior to 1/01/06, providers report Q3000 for supply of radiopharmaceutical diagnostic imaging agent, Rubidium Rb-82. For claims with dates of service 1/01/06 and later, providers report A9555 for radiopharmaceutical diagnostic imaging agent, Rubidium Rb-82 in place of Q3000.

Physicians / practitioners billing the carrier:

*A4641	Supply of Radiopharmaceutical Diagnostic Imaging Agent, Not Otherwise Classified
A9526	Nitrogen N-13 Ammonia, Diagnostic, Per study dose, Up To 40 Millicuries
A9555	Rubidium Rb-82, Diagnostic, Per study dose, Up To 60 Millicuries

*   NOTE: Effective January 1, 2008, tracer code A4641 is not applicable for PET Scans.
The following tracer codes are applicable only to CPT 78459, 78608, 78811-78816. They can not be reported with any other code:

Appendix G — Pub 100 References

Institutional providers billing the fiscal intermediary:

* A9552	Fluorodeoxyglucose F18, FDG, Diagnostic, Per study dose, Up to 45 Millicuries
* C1775 (Deleted effective 12/31/05)	Supply of Radiopharmaceutical Diagnostic Imaging Agent, Fluorodeoxyglucose F18, (2-Deoxy-2-18F Fluoro-D-Glucose), Per dose (4-40 Mci/MI)
**A4641	Supply of Radiopharmaceutical Diagnostic Imaging Agent, Not Otherwise Classified

* NOTE: For claims with dates of service prior to 1/01/06, OPPS hospitals report C1775 for supply of radiopharmaceutical diagnostic imaging agent, Fluorodeoxyglucose F18. For claims with dates of service 1/01/06 and later, providers report A9552 for radiopharmaceutical diagnostic imaging agent, Fluorodeoxyglucose F18 in place of C1775.
** NOTE: Effective January 1, 2008, tracer code A4641 is not applicable for PET Scans.

Physicians / practitioners billing the carrier:

A9552	Fluorodeoxyglucose F18, FDG, Diagnostic, Per study dose, Up to 45 Millicuries
*A4641	Supply of Radiopharmaceutical Diagnostic Imaging Agent, Not Otherwise Classified

* NOTE: Effective January 1, 2008, tracer code A4641 is not applicable for PET Scans.

100-4, 13, 60.4
PET Scans for Imaging of the Perfusion of the Heart Using Rubidium 82 (Rb 82)(Rev. 223, Issued: 07-02-04) (Effective/Implementation: Not Applicable)

For dates of service on or after March 14, 1995, Medicare covers one PET scan for imaging of the perfusion of the heart using Rubidium 82 (Rb 82), provided that the following conditions are met:

- The PET is done at a PET imaging center with a PET scanner that has been approved by the FDA;
- The PET scan is a rest alone or rest with pharmacologic stress PET scan, used for noninvasive imaging of the perfusion of the heart for the diagnosis and management of patients with known or suspected coronary artery disease, using Rb 82; and
- Either the PET scan is used in place of, but not in addition to, a single photon emission computed tomography (SPECT) or the PET scan is used following a SPECT that was found inconclusive.

100-4, 13, 60.15
Billing Requirements for CMS - Approved Clinical Trial and Coverage With Evidence Development Claims for PET Scans for Neurodegenerative Diseases, Previously Specified Cancer Indications, and All Other Cancer Indications Not Previously Specified

Effective for services on or after January 28, 2005, contractors shall accept and pay for claims for PET scans for lung cancer, esophageal cancer, colorectal cancer, lymphoma, melanoma, head & neck cancer, breast cancer, thyroid cancer, soft tissue sarcoma, brain cancer, cervical cancer, ovarian cancer, pancreatic cancer, small cell lung cancer, and testicular cancer, as well as for neurodegenerative diseases and all other cancer indications not previously mentioned in this chapter, if these scans were performed as part of a CMS-approved clinical trial. (See Pub. 100-03, sections 220.6.2-220.6.7 and 220.6.10-220.6.15.)

Contractors shall also be aware that PET scans for all cancers not previously specified at Pub. 100-03, section 220.6.15, remain nationally non-covered unless performed in conjunction with a CMS-approved clinical trial.

- Carriers Only
Carriers shall pay claims for PET scans for beneficiaries participating in a CMS-approved clinical trial submitted with an appropriate CPT code from 60.3.1 and the QR (Item or Service Provided in a Medicare Specified Study) modifier.

- FIs Only
In order to pay claims for PET scans on behalf of beneficiaries participating in a CMSapproved clinical trial, FIs require providers to submit claims with ICD-9 code V70.7 in the second diagnosis position on the CMS-1450 (UB-92), or the electronic equivalent, with the appropriate principal diagnosis code and an appropriate CPT code from section 60.3.1. Effective for PET scan claims for dates of service on or after January 28, 2005, FIs shall accept claims with the QR modifier on other than inpatient claims.

NOTE: Effective for services on or after January 1, 2008, -Q0 (Investigational clinical service provided in a clinical research study that is in an approved clinical research study) replaces the -QR modifier.

100-4, 13, 60.16
Billing and Coverage Changes for PET Scans Effective for Services on or After April 6, 2009

A. Summary of Changes
Effective for services on or after April 6, 2009, CMS will nationally non-cover the use of FDG PET imaging to determine initial treatment strategy in patients with adenocarcinoma of the prostate. CMS will also non-cover FDG PET imaging for subsequent anti-tumor treatment strategy for tumor types other than breast, colorectal, esophagus, head and neck (non-CNS/thyroid), lymphoma, melanoma, non-small cell lung, and thyroid, unless the FDG PET is provided under the coverage with evidence modifier -Q0, see section 60.15).

Effective for services on or after April 6, 2009, CMS will cover one FDG PET study for beneficiaries who have solid tumors that are biopsy-proven or strongly suspected based on other diagnostic testing when the beneficiary's treating physician determines that the FDG PET study is needed to determine the location and/or extent of the tumor for the following specific therapeutic purposes outlined in Pub. 100-03, section 220.6.17.

Additionally, effective for services on or after April 6, 2009, CMS will cover the use of FDG PET imaging to determine subsequent treatment strategy in patients with ovarian and cervical cancers. For further information regarding the changes in coverage, refer to Pub.100-03, section 220.6.17.

B. New ICD-9 Diagnosis Codes for FDG PET Imaging for Oncologic Indications for Services on or after April 6, 2009
Contractors shall accept claims for these PET scans within the ICD-9 code range 140.xx through 239.xx as these are considered appropriate cancer diagnosis codes for FDG PET scans.

C. New Modifiers for PET Scans
Effective for claims with dates of service on or after April 6, 2009, the following modifiers have been created for usage to inform for the initial treatment strategy of tumors or subsequent treatment strategy of cancerous tumors:

PI -Positron Emission Tomography (PET) or PET/Computed Tomography (CT) to inform the initial treatment strategy of tumors that are biopsy proven or strongly suspected of being cancerous based on other diagnostic testing.

Short descriptor: PET tumor init tx strat

PS - Positron Emission Tomography (PET) or PET/Computed Tomography (CT) to inform the subsequent treatment strategy of cancerous tumors when the beneficiary's treatment physician determines that the PET study is needed to inform subsequent anti-tumor strategy.

Short descriptor: PS - PET tumor subsq tx strategy

KX - requirements specified in the medical policy have been met.

NOTE: Contractors shall use this modifier for PET FDG oncologic claims where an alternate ICD-9 diagnosis code determined by the local contractor is the only payable diagnosis submitted on the claim (i.e. outside the 140.xx through 239.xx range). This modifier is required in addition to either the -PI or -PS modifier.

D. Billing Changes for A/B MACs, FIs and Carriers
Effective for claims with dates of service on or after April 6, 2009, contractors shall accept PET (FDG) claims billed to inform initial treatment strategy with the following CPT codes and modifier -PI used to identify PET (FDG) performed (1) one time per cancer type only: CPT 78811, 78812, 78813, 78814, 78815, 78816

Contractors have been instructed to accept PET (FDG) claims with modifier -PS and an appropriate cancer diagnosis code from the range in 60.16C for the subsequent treatment strategy for solid tumors.

Contractors shall also accept FDG PET claims billed to inform initial treatment strategy or subsequent treatment strategy when performed under CED with one of the PET or PET/CT CPT codes above AND CPT modifier -PI or -PS along with an ICD-9 diagnosis code from the range in 60.16C AND modifier -Q0: Investigational clinical service provided in a clinical research study that is in an approved clinical research study.

NOTE: For institutional claims diagnosis code V70.7 and condition code 30 must also be on the claim.

E. Medicare Summary Notices, Remittance Advice Remark Codes, and Claim Adjustment Reason Codes
Effective for dates of service on or after April 6, 2009, that are received after July 5, 2009, contractors have been instructed to return as unprocessable/return to provider claims that do not include the -PI modifier with one of the following PET/PET/CT CPT codes listed below AND an ICD-9 diagnosis code from the range in 60.16C when billing for the initial treatment strategy for solid tumors in accordance with Pub.100-03, section 220.6.17.

In addition, contractors have been instructed to return as unprocessable/return to provider claims that do not include the -PS modifier with one of the CPT codes listed in section B above, AND an ICD-9 diagnosis code from the range in 60.16C when billing for the subsequent treatment strategy for solid tumors.

The following messages apply:

- Claim Adjustment Reason Code 4 - the procedure code is inconsistent with the modifier used or a required modifier is missing.
- Remittance Advice Remark Code MA-130 - Your claim contains incomplete and/or invalid information, and no appeal rights are afforded because the claim is unprocessable. Submit a new claim with the complete/correct information.
- Remittance Advice Remark Code M16 - Alert: See our Web site, mailings, or bulletins for more details concerning this policy/procedure/decision.

Contractors shall deny FDG PET claims billed without an ICD-9 cancer diagnosis code listed in 60.16C or an appropriate locally determined diagnosis code and modifier -KX using the following messages

MSN 15.4 - The information provided does not support the need for this service or item.

Claim Adjustment Reason Code 167 - This (these) diagnosis(es) is (are) not covered.

If an ABN is provided with a GA modifier indicating there is a signed ABN on file, contractors shall use Group Code PR (Patient Responsibility) and the liability falls to the beneficiary.

If an ABN is provided with a GA modifier indicating no ABN was provided, contractors shall use Group Code CO (Contractual Obligation) and the liability falls to the provider.

Contractors shall also use the following messages when denying claims for the initial treatment strategy for solid tumors, billed more than one (1) time per cancer type:

- MSN 15.22 - The information provided does not support the need for this many services or items in this period of time so Medicare will not pay for this item or service
- Claim Adjustment Reason Code 119 - Benefit maximum for this time period or occurrence has been reached
- Remittance Advice Remark Code M86 - Service denied because payment already made for same/similar procedure within set time frame.
- Remittance Advice Remark Code M16 - Alert: See our Web site, mailings, or bulletins for more details concerning this policy/procedure/decision
- Contractors shall use group code CO (Contractual Obligation).

Effective April 6, 2009, contractors are instructed to deny claims with ICD-9 diagnosis code 185 for FDG PET imaging for the initial treatment strategy of patients with adenocarcinoma of the prostate, and with ICD-9 diagnosis codes for FDG PET imaging for subsequent anti-tumor treatment strategy for tumor types other than breast, colorectal, esophagus, head and neck (non-CNS/thyroid), lymphoma, melanoma, non-small cell lung and thyroid unless the FDG PET is provided under CED/CSP (Submitted with the -Q0 modifier) and use the following messages:

- Medicare Summary Notice 15.4 - Medicare does not support the need for this service or item
- Claim Adjustment Reason Code 50 - These are non-covered services because this is not deemed a 'medical necessity' by the payer.
- Contractors shall use Group Code CO (Contractual Obligation)

100-4, 13, 60.9
Coverage of PET Scans for Myocardial Viability

FDG PET is covered for the determination of myocardial viability following an inconclusive single photon computed tomography test (SPECT) from July 1, 2001, through September 30, 2002. Only full ring scanners are covered as the scanning medium for this service from July 1, 2001, through December 31, 2001. However, as of January 1, 2002, full and partial ring scanners are covered for myocardial viability following an inconclusive SPECT.

Beginning October 1, 2002, Medicare will cover FDG PET for the determination of myocardial viability as a primary or initial diagnostic study prior to revascularization, and will continue to cover FDG PET when used as a follow-up to an inconclusive SPECT.

However, if a patient received a FDG PET study with inconclusive results, a follow-up SPECT is not covered. FDA full and partial ring PET scanners are covered. In the event that a patient receives a SPECT with inconclusive results, a PET scan may be performed and covered by Medicare. However, a SPECT is not covered following a FDG PET with inconclusive results. See the Medicare National Coverage Determinations Manual, Section 220.6 for specific frequency limitations for Myocardial Viability following an inconclusive SPECT.

Documentation that these conditions are met should be maintained by the referring provider as part of the beneficiary's medical record.

HCPCS Code for PET Scan for Myocardial Viability

78459 Myocardial imaging, positron emission tomography (PET), metabolic evaluation

100-4, 13, 60.11
Coverage of PET Scans for Perfusion of the Heart Using Ammonia N-13

Effective for service performed on or after October 1, 2003, PET scans performed at rest or with pharmacological stress used for noninvasive imaging of the perfusion of the heart for the diagnosis and management of patients with known or suspected coronary artery disease using the FDA-approved radiopharmaceutical ammonia N-13 are covered, provided the following requirements are met.

100-4, 13, 60.12
Coverage for PET Scans for Dementia and Neurodegenerative Diseases

Effective for dates of service on or after September 15, 2004, Medicare will cover FDG PET scans for a differential diagnosis of fronto-temporal dementia (FTD) and Alzheimer's disease OR; its use in a CMS-approved practical clinical trial focused on the utility of FDG-PET in the diagnosis or treatment of dementing neurodegenerative diseases. Refer to Pub. 100-03, NCD Manual, section 220.6.13, for complete coverage conditions and clinical trial requirements and section 60.15 of this manual for claims processing information.

A. Carrier and FI Billing Requirements for PET Scan Claims for FDG-PET for the Differential Diagnosis of Fronto-temporal Dementia and Alzheimer's Disease:

- CPT Code for PET Scans for Dementia and Neurodegenerative Diseases

    Contractors shall advise providers to use the appropriate CPT code from section 60.3.1 for dementia and neurodegenerative diseases for services performed on or after January 28, 2005.

- Diagnosis Codes for PET Scans for Dementia and Neurodegenerative Diseases

    The contractor shall ensure one of the following appropriate diagnosis codes is present on claims for PET Scans for AD:

    - 290.0, 290.10 - 290.13, 290.20 - 290, 21, 290.3, 331.0, 331.11, 331.19, 331.2, 331.9, 780.93

    Medicare contractors shall use an appropriate Medicare Summary Notice (MSN) message such as 16.48, "Medicare does not pay for this item or service for this condition" to deny claims when submitted with an appropriate CPT code from section 60.3.1 and with a diagnosis code other than the range of codes listed above. Also, contractors shall use an appropriate Remittance Advice (RA) such as 11, "The diagnosis is inconsistent with the procedure."

    Medicare contractors shall instruct providers to issue an Advanced Beneficiary Notice to beneficiaries advising them of potential financial liability prior to delivering the service if one of the appropriate diagnosis codes will not be present on the claim.

- Provider Documentation Required with the PET Scan Claim

    Medicare contractors shall inform providers to ensure the conditions mentioned in the NCD Manual, section 220.6.13, have been met. The information must also be maintained in the beneficiary's medical record:

    - Date of onset of symptoms;
    - Diagnosis of clinical syndrome (normal aging, mild cognitive impairment or MCI: mild, moderate, or severe dementia);
    - Mini mental status exam (MMSE) or similar test score;
    - Presumptive cause (possible, probably, uncertain AD);
    - Any neuropsychological testing performed;
    - Results of any structural imaging (MRI, CT) performed;
    - Relevant laboratory tests (B12, thyroid hormone); and,
    - Number and name of prescribed medications.

100-4, 13, 70.1
Weekly Radiation Therapy Management (CPT 77419 - 77430)

Carriers must pay for a physician's weekly treatment management services under code 77427. Billing entities must indicate on each claim the number of fractions for which payment is sought.

A weekly unit of treatment management is equal to five fractions or treatment sessions.

A week for the purpose of making payments under these codes is comprised of five fractions regardless of the actual time period in which the services are furnished. It is not necessary that the radiation therapist personally examine the patient during each fraction for the weekly treatment management code to be payable. Multiple fractions representing two or more treatment sessions furnished on the same day may be counted as long as there has been a distinct break in therapy sessions, and the fractions are of the character usually furnished on different days. If, at the final billing of the treatment course, there are three or four fractions beyond a multiple of five, those three or four fractions are paid for as a week. If there are one or two fractions beyond a multiple of five, payment for these services is considered as having been made through prior payments.

EXAMPLE:

18 fractions = 4 weekly services

62 fractions = 12 weekly services

8 fractions = 2 weekly services

6 fractions = 1 weekly service

If billings have occurred which indicate that the treatment course has ended (and, therefore, the number of residual fractions has been determined), but treatments resume, adjust carrier payments for the additional services consistent with the above policy.

EXAMPLE:

8 fractions = payment for 2 weeks

2 additional fractions are furnished by the same physician. No additional Medicare payment is made for the 2 additional fractions.

A. SNF Treatment Management Delivery Services

A SNF may not bill weekly treatment management services for its outpatients (codes 77419, 77420, 77425, 77430, and 77431). Instead, the SNF should bill for radiation treatment delivery (codes 77401 - 77404, 77406 - 77409, 77411 - 77414, and 77416).

Also, SNFs bill for therapeutic radiology port film (code 77417), which was previously a part of the weekly services. They enter the number of services in the units field.

100-4, 13, 70.3
Radiation Treatment Delivery (CPT 77401 - 77417)

Carriers pay for these TC services on a daily basis under CPT codes 77401-77416 for radiation treatment delivery. They do not use local codes and RVUs in paying for the TC of radiation oncology services. Multiple treatment sessions on the same day are payable as long as there has been a distinct break in therapy services, and the individual sessions are of the character usually furnished on different days. Carriers pay for CPT code 77417 (Therapeutic radiology port film(s)) on a weekly (five fractions) basis.

100-4, 13, 70.4
Clinical Brachytherapy (CPT Codes 77750 - 77799)

Carriers must apply the bundled services policy to procedures in this family of codes other than CPT code 77776. For procedures furnished in settings in which TC payments are made, carriers must pay separately for the expendable source associated with these procedures under CPT code 79900 except in the case of remote after-loading high intensity brachytherapy procedures (CPT codes 77781-77784). In the four codes cited, the expendable source is included in the RVUs for the TC of the procedures.

100-4, 13, 70.5
Radiation Physics Services (CPT Codes 77300 - 77399)
Carriers pay for the PC and TC of CPT codes 77300-77334 and 77399 on the same basis as they pay for radiologic services generally. For professional component billings in all settings, carriers presume that the radiologist participated in the provision of the service, e.g., reviewed/validated the physicist's calculation. CPT codes 77336 and 77370 are technical services only codes that are payable by carriers in settings in which only technical component is are payable.

100-4, 13, 80.1
Physician Presence
Radiologic supervision and interpretation (S&I) codes are used to describe the personal supervision of the performance of the radiologic portion of a procedure by one or more physicians and the interpretation of the findings. In order to bill for the supervision aspect of the procedure, the physician must be present during its performance. This kind of personal supervision of the performance of the procedure is a service to an individual beneficiary and differs from the type of general supervision of the radiologic procedures performed in a hospital for which FIs pay the costs as physician services to the hospital. The interpretation of the procedure may be performed later by another physician. In situations in which a cardiologist, for example, bills for the supervision (the "S") of the S&I code, and a radiologist bills for the interpretation (the "I") of the code, both physicians should use a "-52" modifier indicating a reduced service, e.g., only one of supervision and/or interpretation. Payment for the fragmented S&I code is no more than if a single physician furnished both aspects of the procedure.

100-4, 13, 80.2
Multiple Procedure Reduction
Carriers make no multiple procedure reductions in the S&I or primary non-radiologic codes in these types of procedures, or in any procedure codes for which the descriptor and RVUs reflect a multiple service reduction. For additional procedure codes that do not reflect such a reduction, carriers apply the multiple procedure reductions.

100-4, 13, 100
Interpretation of Diagnostic Tests
B3-15023

100-4, 13, 140
Bone Mass Measurements (BMMs)
Sections H1861(s)(15)H and H(rr)(1)H of the Social Security Act (the Act) (as added by 4106 of the Balanced Budget Act (BBA) of 1997) standardize Medicare coverage of medically necessary bone mass measurements by providing for uniform coverage under Medicare Part B. This coverage is effective for claims with dates of service furnished on or after July 1, 1998.

Effective for dates of service on and after January 1, 2007, the CY 2007 Physician Fee Schedule final rule expanded the number of beneficiaries qualifying for BMM by reducing the dosage requirement for glucocorticoid (steroid) therapy from 7.5 mg of prednisone per day to 5.0 mg. It also changed the definition of BMM by removing coverage for a single-photon absorptiometry as it is not considered reasonable and necessary under section 1862 (a)(1)(A) of the Act. Finally, it required that in the case of monitoring and confirmatory baseline BMMs, they be performed with a dual-energy xray absorptiometry (axial) test.

Conditions of Coverage for BMMs are located in Pub.100-02, Medicare Benefit Policy Manual, chapter 15.

100-4, 13, 140.1
Payment Methodology and HCPCS Coding
Carriers pay for BMM procedures based on the Medicare physician fee schedule. Claims from physicians, other practitioners, or suppliers where assignment was not taken are subject to the Medicare limiting charge.

The FIs pay for BMM procedures under the current payment methodologies for radiology services according to the type of provider.

Do not pay BMM procedure claims for dual photon absorptiometry, CPT procedure code 78351.

Deductible and coinsurance apply.

Any of the following CPT procedure codes may be used when billing for BMMs through December 31, 2006. All of these codes are bone densitometry measurements except code 76977, which is bone sonometry measurements. CPT procedure codes are applicable to billing FIs and carriers.

76070 76071 76075 76076 76078 76977 78350 G0130

Effective for dates of services on and after January 1, 2007, the following changes apply to BMM:

- New 2007 CPT bone mass procedure codes have been assigned for BMM. The following codes will replace current codes, however the CPT descriptors for the services remain the same:

    77078 replaces 76070

    77079 replaces 76071

    77080 replaces 76075

    77081 replaces 76076

    77083 replaces 76078

- Certain BMM tests are covered when used to screen patients for osteoporosis subject to the frequency standards described in chapter 15, section 80.5.5 of the Medicare Benefit Policy Manual.

- Contractors will pay claims for screening tests when coded as follows:
    - Contains CPT procedure code 77078, 77079, 77080, 77081, 77083, 76977 or G0130, and
    - Contains a valid ICD-9-CM diagnosis code indicating the reason for the test is postmenopausal female, vertebral fracture, hyperparathyroidism, or steroid therapy. Contractors are to maintain local lists of valid codes for the benefit's screening categories.

- Contractors will deny claims for screening tests when coded as follows:
    - Contains CPT procedure code 77078, 77079, 77081, 77083, 76977 or G0130, but
    - Does not contain a valid ICD-9-CM diagnosis code from the local lists of valid ICD-9-CM diagnosis codes maintained by the contractor for the benefit's screening categories indicating the reason for the test is postmenopausal female, vertebral fracture, hyperparathyroidism, or steroid therapy.

- Dual-energy x-ray absorptiometry (axial) tests are covered when used to monitor FDA-approved osteoporosis drug therapy subject to the 2-year frequency standards described in chapter 15, section 80.5.5 of the Medicare Benefit Policy Manual.

- Contractors will pay claims for monitoring tests when coded as follows:
    - Contains CPT procedure code 77080, and
    - Contains 733.00, 733.01, 733.02, 733.03, 733.09, 733.90, or 255.0 as the ICD-9-CM diagnosis code.

- Contractors will deny claims for monitoring tests when coded as follows:
    - Contains CPT procedure code 77078, 77079, 77081, 77083, 76977 or G0130, and
    - Contains 733.00, 733.01, 733.02, 733.03, 733.09, 733.90, or 255.0 as the ICD-9-CM diagnosis code, but
    - Does not contain a valid ICD-9-CM diagnosis code from the local lists of valid ICD-9-CM diagnosis codes maintained by the contractor for the benefit's screening categories indicating the reason for the test is postmenopausal female, vertebral fracture, hyperparathyroidism, or steroid therapy.

- Single photon absorptiometry tests are not covered. Contractors will deny CPT procedure code 78350.

The FIs are billed using the ANSI X12N 837 I or hardcopy Form CMS-1450. The appropriate bill types are: 12X, 13X, 22X, 23X, 34X, 71X (Provider-based and independent), 72X, 73X (Provider-based and freestanding), 83X, and 85X. Effective April 1, 2006, type of bill 14X is for non-patient laboratory specimens and is no longer applicable for bone mass measurements. Information regarding the claim form locators that correspond to the HCPCS/CPT code or Type of Bill and a table to crosswalk its CMS-1450 form locators to the 837 transaction are found in Chapter 25.

Providers must report HCPCS codes for bone mass measurements under revenue code 320 with number of units and line item dates of service per revenue code line for each bone mass measurement reported.

Carriers are billed for bone mass measurement procedures using the ANSI X12N 837 P or hardcopy Form CMS-1500.

100-4, 14, 10
General
Payment is made under Part B for certain surgical procedures that are furnished in ASCs and are approved for being furnished in an ASC. These procedures are those that generally do not exceed 90 minutes in length and do not require more than four hours recovery or convalescent time.

To be paid under this provision, a facility must be certified as meeting the requirements for an ASC and must enter into a written agreement with the Centers for Medicare & Medicaid Services (CMS). The certification process is described in the State Operations Manual.

Medicare will not pay an ASC for those procedures that require more than an ASC level of care, or for minor procedures that are normally performed in a physician's office.

The CMS publishes updates to the list of procedures for which an ASC may be paid each year. The complete list of procedures is available through the Public Use files (PUF) at http://www.cms.hhs.gov/researchers/. This includes applicable codes, payment groups, and payment amounts for each ASC group before adjustments for regional wage variations. Applicable wage indices are also published via program memorandum.

ASCs must accept Medicare's payment for such procedures as payment in full for the facility service with respect to those services defined as ASC facility services. The physician and anesthesiologist may bill and be paid for the professional component of the service also.

Certain other services may be performed in an ASC facility, billed by the appropriate certified provider/supplier, or in certain cases by the ASC facility itself, and paid outside of the facility rate.

100-4, 14, 40.3
Payment for Intraocular Lens (IOL)
Prior to January 1, 2008, payment for facility services furnished by an ASC for IOL insertion during or subsequent to cataract surgery includes an allowance for the lens. The procedures that include insertion of an IOL are: Payment Group 6: CPT-4 Codes 66985 and 66986 Payment Group 8: CPT-4 Codes 66982, 66983 and 66984 Physicians or suppliers are not paid for an IOL furnished to a beneficiary in an ASC after July 1, 1988. Separate claims for IOLs furnished to ASC patients beginning March 12, 1990 are denied. Also, effective March 12, 1990, procedures 66983 and 66984 are treated as single procedures for payment purposes.

Beginning January 1, 2008, the Medicare payment for the IOL is included in the Medicare ASC payment for the associated surgical procedure. Consequently, no separate payment for the IOL is made, except for a payment adjustment for NTIOLs established according to the process outlined in 42 CFR 416.185. ASCs should not report separate charges for conventional IOLs because their payment is included in the Medicare payment for the associated surgical procedure. The ASC payment system logic that excluded $150 for IOLs for purposes of the multiple surgery reduction in cases of cataract surgery prior to January 1, 2008 no longer applies, effective for dates of service on or after January 1, 2008.

Effective for dates of service on and after February 27, 2006, through February 26, 2011, Medicare pays an additional $50 for specified Category 3 NTIOLs that are provided in association with a covered ASC surgical procedure. The list of Category 3 NTIOLS is available at: http://www.cms.hhs.gov/ASCPayment/08_NTIOLs.asp#TopOfPage.

ASCs should use HCPCS code Q1003 to bill for a Category 3 NTIOL. HCPCS code Q1003, along with one of the approved surgical procedure codes (CPT codes 66982, 66983, 66984, 66985, 66986) are to be used on all NTIOL Category 3 claims associated with reduced spherical aberration from February 27, 2006, through February 26, 2011. The payment adjustment for the NTIOL is subject to beneficiary coinsurance but is not wage-adjusted.

Any subsequent IOL recognized by CMS as having the same characteristics as the first NTIOL recognized by CMS for a payment adjustment as a Category III NTIOL (those of reduced spherical aberration) will receive the same adjustment for the remainder of the 5-year period established by the first recognized IOL.

100-4, 14, 40.6
Payment for Extracorporeal Shock Wave Lithotripsy (ESWL)
A ninth ASC payment group was established in a "Federal Register" notice (56 FR 67666) published December 31, 1991. The ninth payment group amount ($1,150) was assigned to only one procedure, CPT code 50590, extracorporeal shock wave lithotripsy (ESWL). However, a court order issued March 12, 1992, has stayed the Group 9 payment rate until the Secretary publishes all information relevant to the setting of the ESWL rate, receives comments, and publishes a subsequent final notice. This has not yet been completed.

In a previous instruction (Medicare Carrier's Manual Transmittal 1435), CMS advised carriers to make payment to ASCs for ESWL services furnished after January 29, 1992, and through the date when the ASC received notice from the carrier of the court order staying the Group 9 payment rate. This was a temporary measure to avoid penalizing ASCs that furnished ESWL services in accordance with the December 31, 1991, "Federal Register" notice and that could not have been expected to know that the March 12, 1992, court order set aside the ESWL provisions of that notice. Carriers did not make Medicare payment for ESWL as an ASC procedure when such services were furnished after the date that the carrier advised an ASC of the court order.

However carriers were instructed to retain all ASC claims for ESWL with a service date after January 29, 1992, and before the date when they were notified about the court order. It may be necessary to retrieve these clams for further action at some later date.

Beginning January 1, 2008 with the revised ASC payment system, contractors may pay for any of the ESWL services that are included on the ASC list of covered surgical procedures.

100-4, 14, 40.8
40.8 - Payment When a Device is Furnished With No Cost or With Full or Partial Credit Beginning January 1, 2008
Contractors pay ASCs a reduced amount for certain specified procedures when a specified device is furnished without cost or for which either a partial or full credit is received (e.g., device recall). For specified procedure codes that include payment for a device, ASCs are required to include modifier -FB on the procedure code when a specified device is furnished without cost or for which full credit is received. If the ASC receives a partial credit of 50 percent or more of the cost of a specified device, the ASC is required to include modifier -FC on the procedure code if the procedure is on the list of specified procedures to which the -FC reduction applies. A single procedure code should not be submitted with both modifiers -FB and -FC. The pricing determination related to modifiers -FB and -FC is made prior to the application of multiple procedure payment reductions. Contractors adjust beneficiary coinsurance to reflect the reduced payment amount. Tables listing the procedures and devices to which the payment adjustments apply, and the full and partial adjustment amounts, are available on the CMS Web site.

In order to report that the receipt of a partial credit of 50 percent or more of the cost of a device, ASCs have the option of either: 1) Submitting the claim for the procedure to their Medicare contractor after the procedure's performance but prior to manufacturer acknowledgement of credit for a specified device, and subsequently contacting the contractor regarding a claims adjustment once the credit determination is made; or 2) holding the claim for the procedure until a determination is made by the manufacturer on the partial credit and submitting the claim with modifier -FC appended to the implantation procedure HCPCS code if the partial credit is 50 percent or more of the cost of the device. If choosing the first billing option, to request a claims adjustment once the credit determination is made, ASCs should keep in mind that the initial Medicare payment for the procedure involving the device is conditional and subject to adjustment.

100-4, 16, 10
Background
B3-2070, B3-2070.1, B3-4110.3, B3-5114

Diagnostic X-ray, laboratory, and other diagnostic tests, including materials and the services of technicians, are covered under the Medicare program. Some clinical laboratory procedures or tests require Food and Drug Administration (FDA) approval before coverage is provided.

A diagnostic laboratory test is considered a laboratory service for billing purposes, regardless of whether it is performed in:

A physician's office, by an independent laboratory;

By a hospital laboratory for its outpatients or nonpatients;

In a rural health clinic; or

In an HMO or Health Care Prepayment Plan (HCPP) for a patient who is not a member.

When a hospital laboratory performs laboratory tests for nonhospital patients, the laboratory is functioning as an independent laboratory, and still bills the fiscal intermediary (FI). Also, when physicians and laboratories perform the same test, whether manually or with automated equipment, the services are deemed similar. Laboratory services furnished by an independent laboratory are covered under SMI if the laboratory is an approved Independent Clinical Laboratory. However, as is the case of all diagnostic services, in order to be covered these services must be related to a patient's illness or injury (or symptom or complaint) and ordered by a physician. A small number of laboratory tests can be covered as a preventive screening service.

See the Medicare Benefit Policy Manual, Chapter 15, for detailed coverage requirements.

See the Medicare Program Integrity Manual, Chapter 10, for laboratory/supplier enrollment guidelines.

See the Medicare State Operations Manual for laboratory/supplier certification requirements.

100-4, 16, 70.8
Certificate of Waiver
Effective September 1, 1992, all laboratory testing sites (except as provided in 42 CFR 493.3(b)) must have either a CLIA certificate of waiver, certificate for provider-performed microscopy procedures, certificate of registration, certificate of compliance, or certificate of accreditation to legally perform clinical laboratory testing on specimens from individuals in the United States.

The Food and Drug Administration approves CLIA waived tests on a flow basis. The CMS identifies CLIA waived tests by providing an updated list of waived tests to the Medicare contractors on a quarterly basis via a Recurring Update Notification. To be recognized as a waived test, some CLIA waived tests have unique HCPCS procedure codes and some must have a QW modifier included with the HCPCS code.

For a list of specific HCPCS codes subject to CLIA see http://www.cms.hhs.gov/CLIA/downloads/waivetbl.pdf

100-4, 17, 20.5.7
Injection Services
Where the sole purpose of an office visit was for the patient to receive an injection, payment may be made only for the injection service (if it is covered). Conversely, injection services (codes 90782, 90783, 90784, 90788, and 90799) included in the Medicare Physician Fee Schedule (MPFS) are not paid for separately, if the physician is paid for any other physician fee schedule service furnished at the same time. Pay separately for those injection services only if no other physician fee schedule service is being paid. However, pay separately for cancer chemotherapy injections (CPT codes 96400-96549) in addition to the visit furnished on the same day. In either case, the drug is separately payable. All injection claims must include the specific name of the drug and dosage. Identification of the drug enables you to pay for the services.

100-4, 18, 10.2.1
Healthcare Common Procedure Coding System (HCPCS) Codes
Vaccines and their administration are reported using separate codes. The following codes are for reporting the vaccines only.

HCPCS	Definition
90655	Influenza virus vaccine, split virus, preservative free, for children 6-35 months of age, for intramuscular use;
90656	Influenza virus vaccine, split virus, preservative free, for use in individuals 3 years and above, for intramuscular use;
90657	Influenza virus vaccine, split virus, for children 6-35 months of age, for intramuscular use;
90658	Influenza virus vaccine, split virus, for use in individuals 3 years of age and above, for intramuscular use;
90659	Influenza virus vaccine, whole virus, for intramuscular or jet injection use (Discontinued December 31, 2003);
90660	Influenza virus vaccine, live, for intranasal use;
90669	Pneumococcal conjugate vaccine, polyvalent, for children under 5 years, for intramuscular use
90732	Pneumococcal polysaccharide vaccine, 23-valent, adult or immunosuppressed patient dosage, for use in individuals 2 years or older, for subcutaneous or intramuscular use;
90740	Hepatitis B vaccine, dialysis or immunosuppressed patient dosage (3 dose schedule), for intramuscular use;
90743	Hepatitis B vaccine, adolescent (2 dose schedule), for intramuscular use;
90744	Hepatitis B vaccine, pediatric/adolescent dosage (3 dose schedule), for intramuscular use;
90746	Hepatitis B vaccine, adult dosage, for intramuscular use; and
90747	Hepatitis B vaccine, dialysis or immunosuppressed patient dosage (4 dose schedule), for intramuscular use.

Appendix G — Pub 100 References

The following codes are for reporting administration of the vaccines only. The administration of the vaccines is billed using:

HCPCS	Definition
G0008	Administration of influenza virus vaccine;
G0009	Administration of pneumococcal vaccine; and
*G0010	Administration of hepatitis B vaccine.
*90471	Immunization administration. (For OPPS hospitals billing for the hepatitis B vaccine administration)
*90472	Each additional vaccine. (For OPPS hospitals billing for the hepatitis B vaccine administration)

* NOTE: For claims with dates of service prior to January 1, 2006, OPPS and non-OPPS hospitals report G0010 for Hepatitis B vaccine administration. For claims with dates of service January 1, 2006 and later, OPPS hospitals report 90471 or 90472 for hepatitis B vaccine administration as appropriate in place of G0010.

One of the following diagnosis codes must be reported as appropriate. If the sole purpose for the visit is to receive a vaccine or if a vaccine is the only service billed on a claim the applicable following diagnosis code may be used.

Diagnosis Code	Description
V03.82	Pneumococcus
V04.81**	Influenza
V06.6***	Pneumococcus and Influenza
V05.3	Hepatitis B

** Effective for influenza virus claims with dates of service October 1, 2003 and later.
*** Effective October 1, 2006, providers may report diagnosis code V06.6 on claims for pneumococcus and/or influenza virus vaccines when the purpose of the visit was to receive both vaccines.

If a diagnosis code for pneumococcus, hepatitis B, or influenza virus vaccination is not reported on a claim, contractors may not enter the diagnosis on the claim. Contractors must follow current resolution processes for claims with missing diagnosis codes.

If the diagnosis code and the narrative description are correct, but the HCPCS code is incorrect, the carrier or intermediary may correct the HCPCS code and pay the claim. For example, if the reported diagnosis code is V04.81 and the narrative description (if annotated on the claim) says "flu shot" but the HCPCS code is incorrect, contractors may change the HCPCS code and pay for the flu vaccine. Effective October 1, 2006, carriers/AB MACs should follow the instructions in Pub. 100-04, Chapter 1, Section 80.3.2.1.1 (Carrier Data Element Requirements) for claims submitted without a HCPCS code.

Claims for Hepatitis B vaccinations must report the I.D. Number of referring physician. In addition, if a doctor of medicine or osteopathy does not order the influenza virus vaccine, the intermediary claims require:

- UPIN code SLF000 to be reported on claims submitted prior to the date when Medicare will no longer accept identifiers other than NPIs, or
- The provider's own NPI to be reported in the NPI field for the attending physician on claims submitted when NPI requirements are implemented.

100-4, 18, 10.2.2.1
FI /AB MAC Payment for Pneumococcal Pneumonia Virus, and Hepatitis B Virus Vaccines and Their Administration
Payment for Vaccines
Payment for all of these vaccines is on a reasonable cost basis for hospitals, home health agencies (HHAs), skilled nursing facilities (SNFs), critical access hospitals (CAHs), and hospital-based renal dialysis facilities (RDFs). Payment for comprehensive outpatient rehabilitation facilities (CORFs), Indian Health Service hospitals (IHS), IHS CAHs and independent RDFs is based on 95 percent of the average wholesale price (AWP). Section 10.2.4 of this chapter contains information on payment of these vaccines when provided by RDFs or hospices. See Sec.10.2.2.2 for payment to independent and provider- based Rural Health Centers and Federally Qualified Health Clinics.

Payment for these vaccines is as follows:

Facility	Type of Bill	Payment
Hospitals, other than Indian Health Service (IHS) Hospitals and Critical Access Hospitals (CAHs)	12x, 13x	Reasonable cost
IHS Hospitals	12x, 13x, 83x	95% of AWP
IHS CAHs	85x	95% of AWP
CAHs Method I and Method II	85x	Reasonable cost
Skilled Nursing Facilities	22x, 23x	Reasonable cost
Home Health Agencies	34x	Reasonable cost
Comprehensive Outpatient Rehabilitation Facilities	75x	95% of the AWP
Independent Renal Dialysis Facilities	72x	95% of the AWP
Hospital-based Renal Dialysis Facilities	72x	Reasonable cost

Payment for Vaccine Administration
Payment for the administration of Influenza Virus and PPV vaccines is as follows:

Facility	Type of Bill	Payment
Hospitals, other than IHS Hospitals and CAHs	12x, 13x	Outpatient Prospective Payment System (OPPS) for hospitals subject to OPPS Reasonable cost for hospitals not subject to OPPS
IHS Hospitals	12x, 13x, 83x	MPFS as indicated in guidelines below.
IHS CAHs	85x	MPFS as indicated in guidelines below.
CAHs Method I and II	85x	Reasonable cost
Skilled Nursing Facilities	22x, 23x	MPFS as indicated in the guidelines below
Home Health Agencies	34x	OPPS
Comprehensive Outpatient Rehabilitation Facilities	75x	MPFS as indicated in the guidelines below
Independent RDFs	72x	MPFS as indicated in the guidelines below
Hospital-based RDFs	72x	Reasonable cost

Guidelines for pricing PPV and Influenza vaccine administration under the MPFS.

Make reimbursement based on the rate in the MPFS associated with the CPT code 90782 or 90471 as follows:

HCPCS code	Effective prior to March 1, 2003	Effective on and after March 1, 2003
G0008	90782	90471
G0009	90782	90471

See Sec.10.2.2.2 for payment to independent and provider based Rural Health Centers and Federally Qualified Health Clinics.

Payment for the administration of Hepatitis B vaccine is as follows:

Facility	Type of Bill	Payment
Hospitals other than IHS hospitals and CAHs	12x, 13x	Outpatient Prospective Payment System (OPPS) for hospitals subject to OPPS Reasonable cost for hospitals not subject to OPPS
IHS Hospitals	12x, 13x, 83x	MPFS as indicated in the guidelines below
CAHs Method I and II	85x	Reasonable cost
IHS CAHs	85x	MPFS as indicated in guidelines below.
Skilled Nursing Facilities	22x, 23x	MPFS as indicated in the chart below
Home Health Agencies	34x	OPPS
Comprehensive Outpatient Rehabilitation Facilities	75x	MPFS as indicated in the guidelines below
Independent RDFs	72x	MPFS as indicated in the chart below
Hospital-based RDFs	72x	Reasonable cost

Guidelines for pricing Hepatitis B vaccine administration under the MPFS.

Make reimbursement based on the rate in the MPFS associated with the CPT code 90782 or 90471 as follows:

HCPCS code	Effective prior to March 1, 2003	Effective on and after March 1, 2003
G0010	90782	90471

See Sec.10.2.2.2 for payment to independent and provider based Rural Health Centers and Federally Qualified Health Clinics.

100-4, 18, 10.4
CWF Edits
In order to prevent duplicate payments for influenza virus and pneumococcal vaccination claims by the local contractor/AB MAC and the centralized billing contractor, effective for claims received on or after July 1, 2002, CWF has implemented a number of edits.

NOTE: 90659 was discontinued December 31, 2003.

CWF returns information in Trailer 13 information from the history claim. The following fields are returned to the contractor:

- Trailer Code;
- Contractor Number;

Current Procedural Coding Expert
Appendix G — Pub 100 References

- Document Control Number;
- First Service Date;
- Last Service Date;
- Provider, Physician, Supplier Number;
- Claim Type; Procedure code;
- Alert Code (where applicable); and,
- More history (where applicable.)

100-4, 18, 10.4.1
CWF Edits on FI/AB MAC Claims
(Rev. 1586, Issued: 09-05-08, Effective: 10-06-08, Implementation: 10-06-08)

In order to prevent duplicate payment by the same FI/AB MAC, CWF edits by line item on the FI/AB MAC number, the beneficiary Health Insurance Claim (HIC) number, and the date of service, the influenza virus procedure codes 90657, 90658, or 90659, the pneumonia procedure code 90732, and the administration codes G0008 or G0009.

If CWF receives a claim with either HCPCS codes 90657, 90658 or 90659, and it already has on record a claim with the same HIC number, same FI/AB MAC number, same date of service, and any one of those HCPCS codes, the second claim submitted to CWF rejects.

If CWF receives a claim with HCPCS code 90732 and it already has on record a claim with the same HIC number, same FI/AB MAC number, same date of service, and the same HCPCS code, the second claim submitted to CWF rejects when all four items match.

If CWF receives a claim with HCPCS administration codes G0008 or G0009 and it already has on record a claim with the same HIC number, same FI/AB MAC number, same date of service, and same procedure code, CWF rejects the second claim submitted when all four items match.

CWF returns to the FI/AB MAC a reject code "7262" for this edit. FIs/AB MACs must deny the second claim and use the same messages they currently use for the denial of duplicate claims.

100-4, 18, 20
Mammography Services (Screening and Diagnostic)
A. Screening Mammography
Beginning January 1, 1991, Medicare provides Part B coverage of screening mammographies for women. Screening mammographies are radiologic procedures for early detection of breast cancer and include a physician's interpretation of the results. A doctor's prescription or referral is not necessary for the procedure to be covered.

Whether payment can be made is determined by a woman's age and statutory frequency parameter. See Pub. 100-02, Medicare Benefit Policy Manual, chapter 15, section 280.3 for additional coverage information for a screening mammography.

Section 4101 of the Balanced Budget Act (BBA) of 1997 provides for annual screening mammographies for women over age 39 and waives the Part B deductible. Coverage applies as follows:

Age Groups	Screening Period
Under age 35	No payment allowed for screening mammography.
35-39	Baseline (pay for only one screening mammography performed on a woman between her 35thand 40thbirthday)
Over age 39	Annual (11 full months have elapsed following the month of last screening

NOTE:Count months between screening mammographies beginning the month after the date of the examination. For example, if Mrs. Smith received a screening mammography examination in January 2005, begin counting the next month (February 2005) until 11 months have elapsed. Payment can be made for another screening mammography in January 2006.

B. Diagnostic Mammography
A diagnostic mammography is a radiological mammogram and is a covered diagnostic test under the following conditions:

- A patient has distinct signs and symptoms for which a mammogram is indicated;
- A patient has a history of breast cancer; or
- A patient is asymptomatic, but based on the patient's history and other factors the physician considers significant, the physician's judgment is that a mammogram is appropriate.

Beginning January 1, 2005, Medicare Prescription Drug, Improvement, and Modernization Act (MMA) of 2003, Sec. 644, Public Law 108-173 has changed the way Medicare pays for diagnostic mammography. Medicare will pay based on the MPFS in lieu of OPPS or the lower of the actual change.

100-4, 18, 20.4
Billing Requirements - FI/A/B MAC Claims
Contractors use the weekly-updated MQSA file to verify that the billing facility is certified by the FDA to perform mammography services, and has the appropriate certification to perform the type of mammogram billed (film and/or digital). (See Sec.20.1.) FIs/A/B MACs use the provider number submitted on the claim to identify the facility and use the MQSA data file to verify the facility's certification(s). FIs/A/B MACs complete the following activities in processing mammography claims:

- If the provider number on the claim does not correspond with a certified mammography facility on the MQSA file, then intermediaries/A/B MACs deny the claim.

- When a film mammography HCPCS code is on a claim, the claim is checked for a "1" film indicator.
- If a film mammography HCPCS code comes in on a claim and the facility is certified for film mammography, the claim is paid if all other relevant Medicare criteria are met.
- If a film mammography HCPCS code is on a claim and the facility is certified for digital mammography only, the claim is denied.
- When a digital mammography HCPCS code is on a claim, the claim is checked for "2" digital indicator.
- If a digital mammography HCPCS code is on a claim and the facility is certified for digital mammography, the claim is paid if all other relevant Medicare criteria are met.
- If a digital mammography HCPCS code is on a claim and the facility is certified for film mammography only, the claim is denied.

NOTE: The Common Working File (CWF) no longer receives the mammography file for editing purposes.

Except as provided in the following sections for RHCs and FQHCs, the following procedures apply to billing for screening mammographies: The technical component portion of the screening mammography is billed on Form CMS-1450 under bill type 12X, 13X, 14X**, 22X, 23X or 85X using revenue code 0403 and HCPCS code 77057* (76092*).

The technical component portion of the diagnostic mammography is billed on Form CMS-1450 under bill type 12X, 13X, 14X**, 22X, 23X or 85X using revenue code 0401 and HCPCS code 77055* (76090*), 77056* (76091*), G0204 and G0206.

Separate bills are required for claims for screening mammographies with dates of service prior to January 1, 2002. Providers include on the bill only charges for the screening mammography. Separate bills are not required for claims for screening mammographies with dates of service on or after January 1, 2002.

See separate instructions below for rural health clinics (RHCs) and federally qualified health centers (FQHCs).

* For claims with dates of service prior to January 1, 2007, providers report CPT codes 76090, 76091, and 76092. For claims with dates of service January 1, 2007 and later, providers report CPT codes 77055, 77056, and 77057 respectively.

** For claims with dates of service April 1, 2005 and later, hospitals bill for all mammography services under the 13X type of bill or for dates of service April 1, 2007 and later, 12X or 13X as appropriate. The 14X type of bill is no longer applicable. Appropriate bill types for providers other than hospitals are 22X, 23X, and 85X.

In cases where screening mammography services are self-referred and as a result an attending physician NPI is not available, the provider shall duplicate their facility NPI in the attending physician identifier field on the claim.

100-4, 18, 20.5
Carrier Processing Requirements
Contractors use the weekly-updated file to verify that the billing facility is certified by the FDA to perform mammography services, and has the appropriate certification to perform the type of mammogram billed (film and/or digital). Carriers/B MACs match the FDA assigned, 6-digit mammography certification number on the claim to the FDA mammography certification number appearing on the file for the billing facility. Carriers/B MACs complete the following activities in processing mammography claims: If the claim does not contain the facility's 6-digit certification number, or if a 6-digit certification number is not reported in item 32 of the Form CMS-1500 for paper claims, or in the 2400 loop (REF 02 segment, where 01=EW segment) of the ASC X12N 837 professional claim format, version 4010A1, for electronic claims, then carriers/B MACs return the claim as unprocessable.

- If the claim contains a 6-digit certification number that is reported in the proper field or segment (as specified in the previous bullet) but such number does not correspond to the number specified in the MQSA file for the facility, then Carriers/B MACs deny the claim.
- When a film mammography HCPCS code is on a claim, the claim is checked for a "1" film indicator.
- If a film mammography HCPCS code comes in on a claim and the facility is certified for film mammography, the claim is paid if all other relevant Medicare criteria are met.
- If a film mammography HCPCS code is on a claim and the facility is certified for digital mammography only, the claim is denied.
- When a digital mammography HCPCS code is on a claim, the claim is checked for "2" digital indicator.
- If a digital mammography HCPCS code is on a claim and the facility is certified for digital mammography, the claim is paid if all other relevant Medicare criteria are met.
- If a digital mammography HCPCS code is on a claim and the facility is certified for film mammography only, the claim is denied.
- Process the claim to the point of payment based on the information provided on the claim and in carrier claims history.
- Identify the claim as a screening mammography claim by the CPT-4 code listed in field 24D and the diagnosis code(s) listed in field 21 of Form CMS-1500.
- Assign physician specialty code 45 to facilities that are certified to perform only screening mammography.
- Ensure that entities that bill globally for screening mammography contain a blank in modifier position #1.
- Ensure that entities that bill for the technical component use only HCPCS modifier "-TC." Ensure that physicians who bill the professional component separately use HCPCS modifier "-26." Send the mammography modifier to CWF in the first modifier position on the claim. If

Appendix G — Pub 100 References

more than one modifier is necessary, e.g., if the service was performed in a rural Health Manpower Shortage Area (HMSA) facility, instruct providers to bill the mammography modifier in modifier position 1 and the rural (or other) modifier in modifier position 2.

- Ensure all those who are qualified include the 6-digit FDA-assigned certification number of the screening center in field 32 of Form CMS-1500 and in the REF02
- segment (where 01 = EW segment) of the 2400 loop for the ASC X12N 837 professional claim format, version 4010A1. Carriers/B MACs retain this number in their provider files.
- Waive Part B deductible and apply coinsurance for a screening mammography.
- Add diagnosis code V76.12 if a claim comes in for screening mammography without a diagnosis and the carrier file data shows this is appropriate. If there are other diagnoses on the claim, but not code V76.12, add it. (Do not change or overlay code V76.12 but ADD it). At a minimum, edit for age, frequency, and place of service (POS).
- After May 23, 2008, accept the screening mammography facility's NPI number in place of the attending/referring physician NPI number for self-referred mammography claims.

NOTE: Beginning October 1, 2003, carriers/B MACs are no longer permitted to add the ICD-9 code for a screening mammography when the screening mammography claim has no diagnosis code. Screening mammography claims with no diagnosis code must be returned as unprocessable for assigned claims. For unassigned claims, deny the claim.

Carrier Provider Education

- Educate providers that when a screening mammography turns to a diagnostic mammography on the same day for the same beneficiary, add the "-GG" modifier to the diagnostic code and bill both codes on the same claim. Both services are reimbursable by Medicare.
- Educate providers that they cannot bill an add-on code without also billing for the appropriate mammography code. If just the add-on code is billed, the service will be denied. Both the add-on code and the appropriate mammography code should be on the same claim.
- Educate providers to submit their own NPI in place of an attending/referring physician NPI in cases where screening mammography services are self-referred.

100-4, 18, 60.1
Payment

Payment (contractor) is under the MPFS except as follows:

- Fecal occult blood tests (82270* (G0107*) and G0328) are paid under the clinical diagnostic lab fee schedule except reasonable cost is paid to all non-OPPS hospitals, including CAHs, but not IHS hospitals billing on TOB 83x. IHS hospitals billing on TOB 83x are paid the ASC payment amount. Other IHS hospitals (billing on TOB 13x) are paid the OMB approved AIR, or the facility specific per visit amount as applicable. Deductible and coinsurance do not apply for these tests. See section A below for payment to Maryland waiver on TOB 13X. Payment from all hospitals for non-patient laboratory specimens on TOB 14X will be based on the clinical diagnostic fee schedule, including CAHs and Maryland waiver hospitals.
- Flexible sigmoidoscopy (code G0104) is paid under OPPS for hospital outpatient departments and on a reasonable cost basis for CAHs; or current payment methodologies for hospitals not subject to OPPS.
- Colonoscopies (G0105 and G0121) and barium enemas (G0106 and G0120) are paid under OPPS for hospital outpatient departments and on a reasonable cost basis for CAHs or current payment methodologies for hospitals not subject to OPPS. Also colonoscopies may be done in an Ambulatory Surgical Center (ASC) and when done in an ASC the ASC rate applies. The ASC rate is the same for diagnostic and screening colonoscopies. The ASC rate is paid to IHS hospitals when the service is billed on TOB 83x.

Prior to January 1, 2007, deductible and coinsurance apply to HCPCS codes G0104, G0105, G0106, G0120, and G0121. Beginning with services provided on or after January 1, 2007, Section 5113 of the Deficit Reduction Act of 2005 waives the requirement of the annual Part B deductible for these screening services. Coinsurance still applies. Coinsurance and deductible applies to the diagnostic colorectal service codes listed below.

The following screening codes must be paid at rates consistent with the diagnostic codes indicated.

Screening Code	Diagnostic Code
G0104	45330
G0105 and G0121	45378
G0106 and G0120	74280

A. Special Payment Instructions for TOB 13X Maryland Waiver Hospitals
For hospitals in Maryland under the jurisdiction of the Health Services Cost Review Commission, screening colorectal services HCPCS codes G0104, G0105, G0106, 82270* (G0107*), G0120, G0121 and G0328 are paid according to the terms of the waiver, that is 94% of submitted charges minus any unmet existing deductible, co-insurance and non-covered charges. Maryland Hospitals bill TOB 13X for outpatient colorectal cancer screenings.

B. Special Payment Instructions for Non-Patient Laboratory Specimen (TOB 14X) for all hospitals
Payment for colorectal cancer screenings (82270* (G0107*) and G0328) to a hospital for a non-patient laboratory specimen (TOB 14X), is the lesser of the actual charge, the fee schedule amount, or the National Limitation Amount (NLA), (including CAHs and Maryland Waiver hospitals). Part B deductible and coinsurance do not apply.

*NOTE: For claims with dates of service prior to January 1, 2007, physicians, suppliers, and providers report HCPCS code G0107. Effective January 1, 2007, code G0107 is discontinued and replaced with CPT code 82270.

100-4, 18, 60.2
HCPCS Codes, Frequency Requirements, and Age Requirements (If Applicable)

Effective for services furnished on or after January 1, 1998, the following codes are used for colorectal cancer screening services:

- 82270* (G0107*) - Colorectal cancer screening; fecal-occult blood tests, 1-3 simultaneous determinations;
- G0104 - Colorectal cancer screening; flexible sigmoidoscopy;
- G0105 - Colorectal cancer screening; colonoscopy on individual at high risk;
- G0106 - Colorectal cancer screening; barium enema; as an alternative to G0104, screening sigmoidoscopy;
- G0120 - Colorectal cancer screening; barium enema; as an alternative to G0105, screening colonoscopy.

Effective for services furnished on or after July 1, 2001, the following codes are used for colorectal cancer screening services:

- G0121 - Colorectal cancer screening; colonoscopy on individual not meeting criteria for high risk. Note that the description for this code has been revised to remove the term "noncovered."
- G0122 - Colorectal cancer screening; barium enema (noncovered).

Effective for services furnished on or after January 1, 2004, the following code is used for colorectal cancer screening services as an alternative to 82270* (G0107*):

- G0328 - Colorectal cancer screening; immunoassay, fecal-occult blood test, 1-3 simultaneous determinations

*NOTE: For claims with dates of service prior to January 1, 2007, physicians, suppliers, and providers report HCPCS code G0107. Effective January 1, 2007, code G0107 is discontinued and replaced with CPT code 82270.

G0104 - Colorectal Cancer Screening; Flexible Sigmoidoscopy

Screening flexible sigmoidoscopies (code G0104) may be paid for beneficiaries who have attained age 50, when performed by a doctor of medicine or osteopathy at the frequencies noted below.

For claims with dates of service on or after January 1, 2002, contractors pay for screening flexible sigmoidoscopies (code G0104) for beneficiaries who have attained age 50 when these services were performed by a doctor of medicine or osteopathy, or by a physician assistant, nurse practitioner, or clinical nurse specialist (as defined in Sec.1861(aa)(5) of the Act and in the Code of Federal Regulations at 42 CFR 410.74, 410.75, and 410.76) at the frequencies noted above. For claims with dates of service prior to January 1, 2002, contractors pay for these services under the conditions noted only when a doctor of medicine or osteopathy performs them.

For services furnished from January 1, 1998, through June 30, 2001, inclusive:

- Once every 48 months (i.e., at least 47 months have passed following the month in which the last covered screening flexible sigmoidoscopy was done).

For services furnished on or after July 1, 2001:

- Once every 48 months as calculated above unless the beneficiary does not meet the criteria for high risk of developing colorectal cancer (refer to Sec.60.3 of this chapter) and he/she has had a screening colonoscopy (code G0121) within the preceding 10 years. If such a beneficiary has had a screening colonoscopy within the preceding 10 years, then he or she can have covered a screening flexible sigmoidoscopy only after at least 119 months have passed following the month that he/she received the screening colonoscopy (code G0121).

NOTE: If during the course of a screening flexible sigmoidoscopy a lesion or growth is detected which results in a biopsy or removal of the growth; the appropriate diagnostic procedure classified as a flexible sigmoidoscopy with biopsy or removal should be billed and paid rather than code G0104.

G0105 - Colorectal Cancer Screening; Colonoscopy on Individual at High Risk

Screening colonoscopies (code G0105) may be paid when performed by a doctor of medicine or osteopathy at a frequency of once every 24 months for beneficiaries at high risk for developing colorectal cancer (i.e., at least 23 months have passed following the month in which the last covered G0105 screening colonoscopy was performed). Refer to Sec.60.3 of this chapter for the criteria to use in determining whether or not an individual is at high risk for developing colorectal cancer.

NOTE: If during the course of the screening colonoscopy, a lesion or growth is detected which results in a biopsy or removal of the growth, the appropriate diagnostic procedure classified as a colonoscopy with biopsy or removal should be billed and paid rather than code G0105.

A. Colonoscopy Cannot be Completed Because of Extenuating Circumstances

1. FIs
   When a covered colonoscopy is attempted but cannot be completed because of extenuating circumstances, Medicare will pay for the interrupted colonoscopy as long as the coverage conditions are met for the incomplete procedure. However, the frequency standards associated with screening colonoscopies will not be applied by CWF. When a covered colonoscopy is next attempted and completed, Medicare will pay for that colonoscopy according to its payment methodology for this procedure as long as coverage conditions are met, and the frequency standards will be applied by CWF. This policy is applied to both screening and diagnostic colonoscopies.

   When submitting a facility claim for the interrupted colonoscopy, providers are to suffix the colonoscopy HCPCS codes with a modifier of "-73" or "-74" as appropriate to indicate that the procedure was interrupted. Payment for covered incomplete screening colonoscopies shall be consistent with payment methodologies currently in place for complete screening colonoscopies, including those contained in 42 CFR 419.44(b). In situations where a critical

Current Procedural Coding Expert
Appendix G — Pub 100 References

access hospital (CAH) has elected payment Method II for CAH patients, payment shall be consistent with payment methodologies currently in place as outlined in Chapter 3. As such, instruct CAHs that elect Method II payment to use modifier "-53" to identify an incomplete screening colonoscopy (physician professional service(s) billed in revenue code 096X, 097X, and/or 098X). Such CAHs will also bill the technical or facility component of the interrupted colonoscopy in revenue code 075X (or other appropriate revenue code) using the "-73" or "-74" modifier as appropriate.

Note that Medicare would expect the provider to maintain adequate information in the patient's medical record in case it is needed by the contractor to document the incomplete procedure.

2. Carriers

When a covered colonoscopy is attempted but cannot be completed because of extenuating circumstances (see Chapter 12), Medicare will pay for the interrupted colonoscopy at a rate consistent with that of a flexible sigmoidoscopy as long as coverage conditions are met for the incomplete procedure. When a covered colonoscopy is next attempted and completed, Medicare will pay for that colonoscopy according to its payment methodology for this procedure as long as coverage conditions are met. This policy is applied to both screening and diagnostic colonoscopies.

When submitting a claim for the interrupted colonoscopy, professional providers are to suffix the colonoscopy code with a modifier of "-53" to indicate that the procedure was interrupted. When submitting a claim for the facility fee associated with this procedure, Ambulatory Surgical Centers (ASCs) are to suffix the colonoscopy code with "-73" or "-74" as appropriate. Payment for covered screening colonoscopies, including that for the associated ASC facility fee when applicable, shall be consistent with payment for diagnostic colonoscopies, whether the procedure is complete or incomplete.

Note that Medicare would expect the provider to maintain adequate information in the patient's medical record in case it is needed by the contractor to document the incomplete procedure.

G0106 - Colorectal Cancer Screening; Barium Enema; as an Alternative to G0104, Screening Sigmoidoscopy

Screening barium enema examinations may be paid as an alternative to a screening sigmoidoscopy (code G0104). The same frequency parameters for screening sigmoidoscopies (see those codes above) apply. In the case of an individual aged 50 or over, payment may be made for a screening barium enema examination (code G0106) performed after at least 47 months have passed following the month in which the last screening barium enema or screening flexible sigmoidoscopy was performed. For example, the beneficiary received a screening barium enema examination as an alternative to a screening flexible sigmoidoscopy in January 1999. Start counts beginning February 1999. The beneficiary is eligible for another screening barium enema in January 2003. The screening barium enema must be ordered in writing after a determination that the test is the appropriate screening test. Generally, it is expected that this will be a screening double contrast enema unless the individual is unable to withstand such an exam. This means that in the case of a particular individual, the attending physician must determine that the estimated screening potential for the barium enema is equal to or greater than the screening potential that has been estimated for a screening flexible sigmoidoscopy for the same individual. The screening single contrast barium enema also requires a written order from the beneficiary's attending physician in the same manner as described above for the screening double contrast barium enema examination.

82270* (G0107*) - Colorectal Cancer Screening; Fecal-Occult Blood Test, 1-3 Simultaneous Determinations

Effective for services furnished on or after January 1, 1998, screening FOBT (code 82270* (G0107*) may be paid for beneficiaries who have attained age 50, and at a frequency of once every 12 months (i.e., at least 11 months have passed following the month in which the last covered screening FOBT was performed). This screening FOBT means a guaiac-based test for peroxidase activity, in which the beneficiary completes it by taking samples from two different sites of three consecutive stools. This screening requires a written order from the beneficiary's attending physician. (The term "attending physician" is defined to mean a doctor of medicine or osteopathy (as defined in Sec.1861(r)(1)of the Act) who is fully knowledgeable about the beneficiary's medical condition, and who would be responsible for using the results of any examination performed in the overall management of the beneficiary's specific medical problem.)

Effective for services furnished on or after January 1, 2004, payment may be made for a immunoassay-based FOBT (G0328, described below) as an alternative to the guaiacbased FOBT, 82270* (G0107*). Medicare will pay for only one covered FOBT per year, either 82270* (G0107*) or G0328, but not both.

*NOTE: For claims with dates of service prior to January 1, 2007, physicians, suppliers, and providers report HCPCS code G0107. Effective January 1, 2007, code G0107 is discontinued and replaced with CPT code 82270.

G0328 - Colorectal Cancer Screening; Immunoassay, Fecal-Occult Blood Test, 1-3 Simultaneous Determinations

Effective for services furnished on or after January 1, 2004, screening FOBT, (code G0328) may be paid as an alternative to 82270* (G0107*) for beneficiaries who have attained age 50. Medicare will pay for a covered FOBT (either 82270* (G0107*) or G0328, but not both) at a frequency of once every 12 months (i.e., at least 11 months have passed following the month in which the last covered screening FOBT was performed). Screening FOBT, immunoassay, includes the use of a spatula to collect the appropriate number of samples or the use of a special brush for the collection of samples, as determined by the individual manufacturer's instructions. This screening requires a written order from the beneficiary's attending physician. (The term "attending physician" is defined to mean a doctor of medicine or osteopathy (as defined in Sec.1861(r)(1) of the Act) who is fully knowledgeable about the beneficiary's medical condition, and who would be responsible for using the results of any examination performed in the overall management of the beneficiary's specific medical problem.)

G0120 - Colorectal Cancer Screening; Barium Enema; as an Alternative to or G0105, Screening Colonoscopy

Screening barium enema examinations may be paid as an alternative to a screening colonoscopy (code G0105) examination. The same frequency parameters for screening colonoscopies (see those codes above) apply. In the case of an individual who is at high risk for colorectal cancer, payment may be made for a screening barium enema examination (code G0120) performed after at least 23 months have passed following the month in which the last screening barium enema or the last screening colonoscopy was performed. For example, a beneficiary at high risk for developing colorectal cancer received a screening barium enema examination (code G0120) as an alternative to a screening colonoscopy (code G0105) in January 2000. Start counts beginning February 2000. The beneficiary is eligible for another screening barium enema examination (code G0120) in January 2002. The screening barium enema must be ordered in writing after a determination that the test is the appropriate screening test. Generally, it is expected that this will be a screening double contrast enema unless the individual is unable to withstand such an exam. This means that in the case of a particular individual, the attending physician must determine that the estimated screening potential for the barium enema is equal to or greater than the screening potential that has been estimated for a screening colonoscopy, for the same individual. The screening single contrast barium enema also requires a written order from the beneficiary's attending physician in the same manner as described above for the screening double contrast barium enema examination.

G0121 - Colorectal Screening; Colonoscopy on Individual Not Meeting Criteria for High Risk - Applicable On and After July 1, 2001

Effective for services furnished on or after July 1, 2001, screening colonoscopies (code G0121) performed on individuals not meeting the criteria for being at high risk for developing colorectal cancer (refer to Sec.60.3 of this chapter) may be paid under the following conditions:

- At a frequency of once every 10 years (i.e., at least 119 months have passed following the month in which the last covered G0121 screening colonoscopy was performed.)
- If the individual would otherwise qualify to have covered a G0121 screening colonoscopy based on the above but has had a covered screening flexible sigmoidoscopy (code G0104), then he or she may have covered a G0121 screening colonoscopy only after at least 47 months have passed following the month in which the last covered G0104 flexible sigmoidoscopy was performed.

NOTE: If during the course of the screening colonoscopy, a lesion or growth is detected which results in a biopsy or removal of the growth, the appropriate diagnostic procedure classified as a colonoscopy with biopsy or removal should be billed and paid rather than code G0121.

G0122 - Colorectal Cancer Screening; Barium Enema
The code is not covered by Medicare.

100-4, 18, 60.6
Billing Requirements for Claims Submitted to FIs

Follow the general bill review instructions in Chapter 25. Hospitals use the ANSI X12N 837I to bill the FI or on the hardcopy Form CMS-1450. Hospitals bill revenue codes and HCPCS codes as follows:

Screening Test/Procedure	Revenue Code	HCPCS Code	TOB
Fecal Occult blood test	030X	82270*** (G0107***), G0328	13X, 14X**, 22X, 23X, 83X, 85X
Barium enema	032X	G0106, G0120, G0122	13X, 22X, 23X, 85X****
Flexible Sigmoidoscopy	*	G0104	13X, 22X, 23X, 83X, 85X****
Colonoscopy-high risk	*	G0105, G0121	13X, 22X, 23X, 83X, 85X**** *

*   The appropriate revenue code when reporting any other surgical procedure.
**   14X is only applicable for non-patient laboratory specimens.
*** For claims with dates of service prior to January 1, 2007, physicians, suppliers, and providers report HCPCS code G0107. Effective January 1, 2007, code G0107, is discontinued and replaced with CPT code 82270.
**** CAHs that elect Method II bill revenue code 096X, 097X, and/or 098X for professional services and 075X (or other appropriate revenue code) for the technical or facility component.

A Special Billing Instructions for Hospital Inpatients
When these tests/procedures are provided to inpatients of a hospital, they are covered under this benefit. However, the provider bills on bill type 13X using the discharge date of the hospital stay to avoid editing in the Common Working File (CWF) as a result of the hospital bundling rules.

100-4, 20, 100.2.2
Evidence of Medical Necessity for Parenteral and Enteral Nutrition (PEN) Therapy

The PEN coverage is determined by information provided by the treating physician and the PEN supplier. A completed certification of medical necessity (CMN) must accompany and support initial claims for PEN to establish whether coverage criteria are met and to ensure that the PEN therapy provided is consistent with the attending or ordering physician's prescription.

Contractors ensure that the CMN contains pertinent information from the treating physician. Uniform specific medical data facilitate the review and promote consistency in coverage determinations and timelier claims processing.The medical and prescription information on a PEN CMN can be most appropriatelycompleted by the treating physician or from information in the patient's records by an employee of the physician for the physician's review and signature.

Although PEN suppliers sometimes may assist in providing the PEN services, they cannot complete the CMN since they do not have the same access to patient information needed to properly enter medical or prescription information. Contractors use appropriate professional relations issuances, training sessions, and meetings to ensure that all persons and PEN suppliers are aware of this limitation of their role. When properly completed, the PEN CMN includes the elements of a prescription as well as other data needed to determine whether Medicare coverage is possible. This practice will facilitate prompt delivery of PEN services and timely submittal of the related claim.

100-4, 32, 10.1
Ambulatory Blood Pressure Monitoring (ABPM) Billing Requirements
A. Coding Applicable to Local Carriers & Fiscal Intermediaries (FIs)

Effective April 1, 2002, a National Coverage Decision was made to allow for Medicare coverage of ABPM for those beneficiaries with suspected "white coat hypertension" (WCH). ABPM involves the use of a non-invasive device, which is used to measure blood pressure in 24-hour cycles. These 24-hour measurements are stored in the device and are later interpreted by a physician. Suspected "WCH" is defined as: (1) Clinic/office blood pressure >140/90 mm Hg on at least three separate clinic/office visits with two separate measurements made at each visit; (2) At least two documented separate blood pressure measurements taken outside the clinic/office which are < 140/90 mm Hg; and (3) No evidence of end-organ damage. ABPM is not covered for any other uses. Coverage policy can be found in Medicare National Coverage Determinations Manual, Chapter 1, Section 20.19. (www.cms.hhs.gov/masnuals/103 cov determ/ncd103index.asp).

The ABPM must be performed for at least 24 hours to meet coverage criteria. Payment is not allowed for institutionalized beneficiaries, such as those receiving Medicare covered skilled nursing in a facility. In the rare circumstance that ABPM needs to be performed more than once for a beneficiary, the qualifying criteria described above must be met for each subsequent ABPM test.

Effective dates for applicable Common Procedure Coding System (HCPCS) codes for ABPM for suspected WCH and their covered effective dates are as follows:

HCPCS	Definition	Effective Date
93784	ABPM, utilizing a system such as magnetic tape and/or computer disk, for 24 hours or longer; including recording, scanning analysis, interpretation and report.	04/01/2002
93786	ABPM, utilizing a system such as magnetic tape and/or computer disk, for 24 hours or longer; recording only.	04/01/2002
93788	ABPM, utilizing a system such as magnetic tape and/or computer disk, for 24 hours or longer; scanning analysis with report.	01/01/2004

HCPCS Definition Effective Date

93790	ABPM, utilizing a system such as magnetic tape and/or computer disk, for 24 hours or longer; physician review with interpretation and report.	04/01/2002

In addition, the following diagnosis code must be present:

Diagnosis Code	Description
796.2	Elevated blood pressure reading without diagnosis of hypertension.

B. FI Billing Instructions
The applicable types of bills acceptable when billing for ABPM services are 13X, 23X, 71X, 73X, 75X, and 85X. Chapter 25 of this manual provides general billing instructions that must be followed for bills submitted to FIs. The FIs pay for hospital outpatient ABPM services billed on a 13X type of bill with HCPCS 93786 and/or 93788 as follows: (1) Outpatient Prospective Payment System (OPPS) hospitals pay based on the Ambulatory Payment Classification (APC); (2) non-OPPS hospitals (Indian Health Services Hospitals, Hospitals that provide Part B services only, and hospitals located in American Samoa, Guam, Saipan and the Virgin Islands) pay based on reasonable cost, except for Maryland Hospitals which are paid based on a percentage of cost. Effective 4/1/06, type of bill 14X is for non-patient laboratory specimens and is no longer applicable for ABPM.

The FIs pay for comprehensive outpatient rehabilitation facility (CORF) ABPM services billed on a 75x type of bill with HCPCS code 93786 and/or 93788 based on the Medicare Physician Fee Schedule (MPFS) amount for that HCPCS code.

The FIs pay for ABPM services for critical access hospitals (CAHs) billed on a 85x type of bill as follows: (1) for CAHs that elected the Standard Method and billed HCPCS code 93786 and/or 93788, pay based on reasonable cost for that HCPCS code; and (2) for CAHs that elected the Optional Method and billed any combination of HCPCS codes 93786, 93788 and 93790 pay based on reasonable cost for HCPCS 93786 and 93788 and pay 115% of the MPFS amount for HCPCS 93790.

The FIs pay for ABPM services for skilled nursing facility (SNF) outpatients billed on a 23x type of bill with HCPCS code 93786 and/or 93788, based on the MPFS.

The FIs accept independent and provider-based rural health clinic (RHC) bills for visits under the all-inclusive rate when the RHC bills on a 71x type of bill with revenue code 052x for providing the professional component of ABPM services. The FIs should not make a separate payment to a RHC for the professional component of ABPM services in

addition to the all-inclusive rate. RHCs are not required to use ABPM HCPCS codes for professional services covered under the all-inclusive rate.

The FIs accept free-standing and provider-based federally qualified health center (FQHC) bills for visits under the all-inclusive rate when the FQHC bills on a 73x type of bill with revenue code 052x for providing the professional component of ABPM services.

The FIs should not make a separate payment to a FQHC for the professional component of ABPM services in addition to the all-inclusive rate. FQHCs are not required to use ABPM HCPCS codes for professional services covered under the all-inclusive rate.

The FIs pay provider-based RHCs/FQHCs for the technical component of ABPM services when billed under the base provider's number using the above requirements for that particular base provider type, i.e., a OPPS hospital based RHC would be paid for the ABPM technical component services under the OPPS using the APC for code 93786 and/or 93788 when billed on a 13x type of bill.

Independent and free-standing RHC/FQHC practitioners are only paid for providing the technical component of ABPM services when billed to the carrier following the carrier instructions.

C. Carrier Claims
Local carriers pay for ABPM services billed with diagnosis code 796.2 and HCPCS codes 93784 or for any combination of 93786, 93788 and 93790, based on the MPFS for the specific HCPCS code billed.

D. Coinsurance and Deductible
The FIs and local carriers shall apply coinsurance and deductible to payments for ABPM services except for services billed to the FI by FQHCs. For FQHCs only co-insurance applies.

100-4, 32, 12
Smoking and Tobacco-Use Cessation Counseling Services
Background: Effective for services furnished on or after March 22, 2005, a National Coverage Determination (NCD) provides for coverage of smoking and tobacco-use cessation counseling services. Conditions of Medicare Part A and Medicare Part B coverage for smoking and tobacco-use cessation counseling services are located in the Medicare National Coverage Determinations Manual, Publication 100-3, section 210.4.

100-4, 32, 12.1
HCPCS and Diagnosis Coding
The following HCPCS codes should be reported when billing for smoking and tobacco-use cessation counseling services:

- 99406 Smoking and tobacco-use cessation counseling visit; intermediate, greater than 3 minutes up to 10 minutes
- 99407 Smoking and tobacco-use cessation counseling visit; intensive, greater than 10 minutes

Note the above codes are payable for dates of service on or after January 1, 2008. Codes G0375 and G0376, below, are not valid or payable for dates of service on or after January 1, 2008.

- G0375 Smoking and tobacco-use cessation counseling visit; intermediate, greater than 3 minutes up to 10 minutes

    Short Descriptor: Smoke/Tobacco counseling 3-10

- G0376 Smoking and tobacco-use cessation counseling visit; intensive, greater than 10 minutes

    Short Descriptor: Smoke/Tobacco counseling greater than 10

NOTE: The above G codes will NOT be active in contractors' systems until July 5, 2005. Therefore, contractors shall advise providers to use unlisted code 99199 to bill for smoking and tobacco-use cessation counseling services during the interim period of March 22, 2005, through July 4, 2005, and received prior to July 5, 2005.

On July 5, 2005, contractors' systems will accept the new G codes for services performed on and after March 22, 2005.

Contractors shall allow payment for a medically necessary E/M service on the same day as the smoking and tobacco-use cessation counseling service when it is clinically appropriate. Physicians and qualified non-physician practitioners shall use an appropriate HCPCS code, such as HCPCS 99201- 99215, to report an E/M service with modifier 25 to indicate that the E/M service is a separately identifiable service from G0375 or G0376.

Contractors shall only pay for 8 Smoking and Tobacco-Use Cessation Counseling sessions in a 12-month period. The beneficiary may receive another 8 sessions during a second or subsequent year after 11 full months have passed since the first Medicare covered cessation session was performed. To start the count for the second or subsequent 12-month period, begin with the month after the month in which the first Medicare covered cessation session was performed and count until 11 full months have elapsed.

Claims for smoking and tobacco use cessation counseling services shall be submitted with an appropriate diagnosis code. Diagnosis codes should reflect: the condition the patient has that is adversely affected by tobacco use or the condition the patient is being treated for with a therapeutic agent whose metabolism or dosing is affected by tobacco use.

NOTE: This decision does not modify existing coverage for minimal cessation counseling (defined as 3 minutes or less in duration) which is already considered to be covered as part of each Evaluation and Management (E/M) visit and is not separately billable.

Current Procedural Coding Expert
Appendix G — Pub 100 References

100-4, 32, 12.2
Carrier Billing:
Carriers shall pay for counseling services billed with codes 99406 and 99407 for dates of service on or after January 1, 2008. Carriers shall pay for counseling services billed with codes G0375 and G0376 for dates of service performed on and after March 22, 2005 through Dec. 31, 2007. The type of service (TOS) for each of the new codes is 1.

Carriers pay for counseling services billed based on the Medicare Physician Fee Schedule (MPFS). Deductible and coinsurance apply. Claims from physicians or other providers where assignment was not taken are subject to the Medicare limiting charge, which means that charges to the beneficiary may be no more than 115 percent of the allowed amount.

Physicians or qualified non-physician practitioners shall bill the carrier for smoking and tobacco-use cessation counseling services on the Form CMS-1500 or an approved electronic format.

100-4, 32, 12.3
FI Billing Requirements
The FIs shall pay for Smoking and Tobacco-Use Cessation Counseling services with codes 99406 and 99407 for dates of service on or after January 1, 2008. FIs shall pay for counseling services billed with codes G0375 and G0376 for dates of service performed on or after March 22, 2005 through December 31, 2007.

A. Claims for Smoking and Tobacco-Use Cessation Counseling Services should be submitted on Form CMS-1450 or its electronic equivalent.

The applicable bill types are 12X, 13X, 22X, 23X, 34X, 71X, 73X, 83X, and 85X. Effective 4/1/06, type of bill 14X is for non-patient laboratory specimens and is no longer applicable for Smoking and Tobacco-Use Cessation Counseling services.

Applicable revenue codes are as follows:

Provider Type	Revenue Code
Rural Health Centers (RHCs)/Federally Qualified Health Centers (FQHCs)	052X
Indian Health Services (IHS)	0510
Critical Access Hospitals (CAHs) Method II	096X, 097X, 098X
All Other Providers	0942

NOTE: When these services are provided by a clinical nurse specialist in the RHC/FQHC setting, they are considered "incident to" and do not constitute a billable visit.

Payment for outpatient services is as follows:

Type of Facility	Method of Payment
Rural Health Centers (RHCs)/Federally Qualified Health Centers (FQHCs)	All-inclusive rate (AIR) for the encounter
Indian Health Service (IHS)/Tribally owned or operated hospitals and hospital-based facilities	All-inclusive rate (AIR)
IHS/Tribally owned or operated non-hospital-based facilities	Medicare Physician Fee Schedule (MPFS)
IHS/Tribally owned or operated Critical Access Hospitals (CAHs)	Facility Specific Visit Rate
Hospitals subject to the Outpatient Prospective Payment System (OPPS)	Ambulatory Payment Classification (APC)
Hospitals not subject to OPPS	Payment is made under current methodologies
Skilled Nursing Facilities (SNFs) NOTE: Included in Part A PPS for skilled patients.	Medicare Physician Fee Schedule (MPFS)
Home Health Agencies (HHAs)	Medicare Physician Fee Schedule (MPFS)
Critical Access Hospitals (CAHs)	Method I: Technical services are paid at 101% of reasonable cost. Method II: technical services are paid at 101% of reasonable cost, and Professional services are paid at 115% of the MMPFS Data Base
Maryland Hospitals	Payment is based according to the Health Services Cost Review Commission (HSCRC). That is 94% of submitted charges subject to any unmet deductible, coinsurance, and non-covered charges policies.

NOTE: Inpatient claims submitted with Smoking and Tobacco-Use Cessation Counseling Services are processed under the current payment methodologies.

100-4, 32, 30.1
Billing Requirements for HBO Therapy for the Treatment of Diabetic Wounds of the Lower Extremities
Hyperbaric Oxygen Therapy is a modality in which the entire body is exposed to oxygen under increased atmospheric pressure. Effective April 1, 2003, a National Coverage Decision expanded the use of HBO therapy to include coverage for the treatment of diabetic wounds of the lower extremities. For specific coverage criteria for HBO Therapy, refer to the National Coverage Determinations Manual, chapter 1, section 20.29.

NOTE: Topical application of oxygen does not meet the definition of HBO therapy as stated above. Also, its clinical efficacy has not been established. Therefore, no Medicare reimbursement may be made for the topical application of oxygen.

I. Billing Requirements for Intermediaries
Claims for HBO therapy should be submitted on Form CMS-1450 or its electronic equivalent.

   a. Applicable Bill Types
      The applicable hospital bill types are 11X, 13X and 85X.

   b. Procedural Coding

      99183 Physician attendance and supervision of hyperbaric oxygen therapy, per session.

      C1300 Hyperbaric oxygen under pressure, full body chamber, per 30-minute interval.

NOTE: Code C1300 is not available for use other than in a hospital outpatient department. In skilled nursing facilities (SNFs), HBO therapy is part of the SNF PPS payment for beneficiaries in covered Part A stays.

For hospital inpatients and critical access hospitals (CAHs) not electing Method I, HBO therapy is reported under revenue code 940 without any HCPCS code. For inpatient services, show ICD-9-CM procedure code 93.59.

For CAHs electing Method I, HBO therapy is reported under revenue code 940 along with HCPCS code 99183.

   c. Payment Requirements for Intermediaries
      Payment is as follows:

      Intermediary payment is allowed for HBO therapy for diabetic wounds of the lower extremities when performed as a physician service in a hospital outpatient setting and for inpatients. Payment is allowed for claims with valid diagnostic ICD-9 codes as shown above with dates of service on or after April 1, 2003. Those claims with invalid codes should be denied as not medically necessary.

      For hospitals, payment will be based upon the Ambulatory Payment Classification (APC) or the inpatient Diagnosis Related Group (DRG). Deductible and coinsurance apply.

      Payment to Critical Access Hospitals (electing Method I) is made under cost reimbursement. For Critical Access Hospitals electing Method II, the technical component is paid under cost reimbursement and the professional component is paid under the Physician Fee Schedule.

NOTE: Information regarding the form locator numbers that correspond to these data element names and a table to crosswalk UB-04 form locators to the 837 transaction is found in Chapter 25.

II. Carrier Billing Requirements
Claims for this service should be submitted on Form CMS-1500 or its electronic equivalent.

The following HCPCS code applies:

- 99183 - Physician attendance and supervision of hyperbaric oxygen therapy, per session.

   a. Payment Requirements for Carriers
      Payment and pricing information will occur through updates to the Medicare Physician Fee Schedule Database (MPFSDB). Pay for this service on the basis of the MPFSDB. Deductible and coinsurance apply. Claims from physicians or other practitioners where assignment was not taken, are subject to the Medicare limiting charge.

III. Medicare Summary Notices (MSNs)
Use the following MSN Messages where appropriate:

In situations where the claim is being denied on the basis that the condition does not meet our coverage requirements, use one of the following MSN Messages:

      "Medicare does not pay for this item or service for this condition." (MSN Message 16.48)

The Spanish version of the MSN message should read:

      "Medicare no paga por este articulo o servicio para esta afeccion."

In situations where, based on the above utilization policy, medical review of the claim results in a determination that the service is not medically necessary, use the following MSN message:

      "The information provided does not support the need for this service or item." (MSN Message 15.4)

The Spanish version of the MSN message should read:

      "La informacion proporcionada no confirma la necesidad para este servicio o articulo."

IV. Remittance Advice Notices
Use appropriate existing remittance advice and reason codes at the line level to express the specific reason if you deny payment for HBO therapy for the treatment of diabetic wounds of lower extremities.

100-4, 32, 40
Sacral Nerve Stimulation
A sacral nerve stimulator is a pulse generator that transmits electrical impulses to the sacral nerves through an implanted wire. These impulses cause the bladder muscles to contract, which gives the patient ability to void more properly.

Appendix G — Pub 100 References

100-4, 32, 40.1
Coverage Requirements

Effective January 1, 2002, sacral nerve stimulation is covered for the treatment of urinary urge incontinence, urgency-frequency syndrome and urinary retention. Sacral nerve stimulation involves both a temporary test stimulation to determine if an implantable stimulator would be effective and a permanent implantation in appropriate candidates. Both the test and the permanent implantation are covered.

The following limitations for coverage apply to all indications:

- Patient must be refractory to conventional therapy (documented behavioral, pharmacologic and/or surgical corrective therapy) and be an appropriate surgical candidate such that implantation with anesthesia can occur.
- Patients with stress incontinence, urinary obstruction, and specific neurologic diseases (e.g., diabetes with peripheral nerve involvement) that are associated with secondary manifestations of the above three indications are excluded.
- Patient must have had a successful test stimulation in order to support subsequent implantation. Before a patient is eligible for permanent implantation, he/she must demonstrate a 50% or greater improvement through test stimulation. Improvement is measured through voiding diaries.
- Patient must be able to demonstrate adequate ability to record voiding diary data such that clinical results of the implant procedure can be properly evaluated.

100-4, 32, 50
Deep Brain Stimulation for Essential Tremor and Parkinson's Disease

Deep brain stimulation (DBS) refers to high-frequency electrical stimulation of anatomic regions deep within the brain utilizing neurosurgically implanted electrodes. These DBS electrodes are stereotactically placed within targeted nuclei on one (unilateral) or both (bilateral) sides of the brain. There are currently three targets for DBS -- the thalamic ventralis intermedius nucleus (VIM), subthalamic nucleus (STN) and globus pallidus interna (GPi).

Essential tremor (ET) is a progressive, disabling tremor most often affecting the hands. ET may also affect the head, voice and legs. The precise pathogenesis of ET is unknown. While it may start at any age, ET usually peaks within the second and sixth decades. Beta-adrenergic blockers and anticonvulsant medications are usually the first line treatments for reducing the severity of tremor. Many patients, however, do not adequately respond or cannot tolerate these medications. In these medically refractory ET patients, thalamic VIM DBS may be helpful for symptomatic relief of tremor.

Parkinson's disease (PD) is an age-related progressive neurodegenerative disorder involving the loss of dopaminergic cells in the substantia nigra of the midbrain. The disease is characterized by tremor, rigidity, bradykinesia and progressive postural instability. Dopaminergic medication is typically used as a first line treatment for reducing the primary symptoms of PD. However, after prolonged use, medication can become less effective and can produce significant adverse events such as dyskinesias and other motor function complications. For patients who become unresponsive to medical treatments and/or have intolerable side effects from medications, DBS for symptom relief may be considere

100-4, 32, 60.4.1
Allowable Covered Diagnosis Codes

For services furnished on or after July 1, 2002, the applicable ICD-9-CM diagnosis code for this benefit is V43.3, organ or tissue replaced by other means; heart valve.

For services furnished on or after March 19, 2008, the applicable ICD-9-CM diagnosis codes for this benefit are:

- V43.3 (organ or tissue replaced by other means; heart valve),
- 289.81 (primary hypercoagulable state),
- 451.0-451.9 (includes 451.11, 451.19, 451.2, 451.80-451.84, 451.89) (phlebitis & thrombophlebitis),
- 453.0-453.3 (other venous embolism & thrombosis),
- 453.40-453.49 (includes 453.40-453.42, 453.8-453.9) (venous embolism and thrombosis of the deep vessels of the lower extremity, and other specified veins/unspecified sites)
- 415.11-415.12, 415.19 (pulmonary embolism & infarction) or,
- 427.31 (atrial fibrillation (established) (paroxysmal)).

100-4, 32, 60.5.2
Applicable Diagnosis Codes for Carriers

For services furnished on or after July 1, 2002, the applicable ICD-9-CM diagnosis code for this benefit is V43.3, organ or tissue replaced by other means; heart valve.

For services furnished on or after March 19, 2008, the applicable ICD-9-CM diagnosis codes for this benefit are:

- V43.3 (organ or tissue replaced by other means; heart valve),
- 289.81 (primary hypercoagulable state),
- 451.0-451.9 (includes 451.11, 451.19, 451.2, 451.80-451.84, 451.89) (phlebitis & thrombophlebitis),
- 453.0-453.3 (other venous embolism & thrombosis),
- 453.40-453.49 (includes 453.40-453.42, 453.8-453.9) (venous embolism and thrombosis of the deep vessels of the lower extremity, and other specified veins/unspecified sites)
- 415.11-415.12, 415.19 (pulmonary embolism & infarction) or,
- 427.31 (atrial fibrillation (established) (paroxysmal)).

100-4, 32, 80.8
CWF Utilization Edits

Edit 1 - Should CWF receive a claim from an FI for G0245 or G0246 and a second claim from a contractor for either G0245 or G0246 (or vice versa) and they are different dates of service and less than 6 months apart, the second claim will reject. CWF will edit to allow G0245 or G0246 to be paid no more than every 6 months for a particular beneficiary, regardless of who furnished the service. If G0245 has been paid, regardless of whether it was posted as a facility or professional claim, it must be 6 months before G0245 can be paid again or G0246 can be paid. If G0246 has been paid, regardless of whether it was posted as a facility or professional claim, it must be 6 months before G0246 can be paid again or G0245 can be paid. CWF will not impose limits on how many times each code can be paid for a beneficiary as long as there has been 6 months between each service.

The CWF will return a specific reject code for this edit to the contractors and FIs that will be identified in the CWF documentation. Based on the CWF reject code, the contractors and FIs must deny the claims and return the following messages:

> MSN 18.4 -- This service is being denied because it has not been __ months since your last examination of this kind (NOTE: Insert 6 as the appropriate number of months.)

RA claim adjustment reason code 96 - Non-covered charges, along with remark code M86 - Service denied because payment already made for same/similar procedure within set time frame.

Edit 2 - The CWF will edit to allow G0247 to pay only if either G0245 or G0246 has been submitted and accepted as payable on the same date of service. CWF will return a specific reject code for this edit to the contractors and FIs that will be identified in the CWF documentation. Based on this reject code, contractors and FIs will deny the claims and return the following messages:

> MSN 21.21 - This service was denied because Medicare only covers this service under certain circumstances.

RA claim adjustment reason code 107 - The related or qualifying claim/service was not identified on this claim.

Edit 3 - Once a beneficiary's condition has progressed to the point where routine foot care becomes a covered service, payment will no longer be made for LOPS evaluation and management services. Those services would be considered to be included in the regular exams and treatments afforded to the beneficiary on a routine basis. The physician or provider must then just bill the routine foot care codes, per Pub 100-02, Chapter 15, Sec.290.

The CWF will edit to reject LOPS codes G0245, G0246, and/or G0247 when on the beneficiary's record it shows that one of the following routine foot care codes were billed and paid within the prior 6 months: 11055, 11056, 11057, 11719, 11720, and/or 11721.

The CWF will return a specific reject code for this edit to the contractors and FIs that will be identified in the CWF documentation. Based on the CWF reject code, the contractors and FIs must deny the claims and return the following messages:

> MSN 21.21 - This service was denied because Medicare only covers this service under certain circumstances.

The RA claim adjustment reason code 96 - Non-covered charges, along with remark code M86 - Service denied because payment already made for same/similar procedure within set time frame.

100-4, 32, 90
Stem Cell Transplantation

Stem cell transplantation is a process in which stem cells are harvested from either a patient's or donor's bone marrow or peripheral blood for intravenous infusion. Autologous stem cell transplantation (AuSCT) must be used to effect hematopoietic reconstitution following severely myelotoxic doses of chemotherapy (HDCT) and/or radiotherapy used to treat various malignancies. Allogeneic stem cell transplant may also be used to restore function in recipients having an inherited or acquired deficiency or defect.

Bone marrow and peripheral blood stem cell transplantation is a process which includes mobilization, harvesting, and transplant of bone marrow or peripheral blood stem cells and the administration of high dose chemotherapy or radiotherapy prior to the actual transplant. When bone marrow or peripheral blood stem cell transplantation is covered, all necessary steps are included in coverage. When bone marrow or peripheral blood stem cell transplantation is non-covered, none of the steps are covered.

Allogeneic and autologous stem cell transplants are covered under Medicare for specific diagnoses. See Pub. 100-03, National Coverage Determinations Manual, section 110.8.1, for a complete description of covered and noncovered conditions. The following sections contain claims processing instructions for carrier claims. For institutional claims processing instructions, please refer to Pub. 100-04, chapter 3, section 90.3.

100-4, 32, 100
Billing Requirements for Expanded Coverage of Cochlear Implantation

Effective for dates of services on and after April 4, 2005, the Centers for Medicare & Medicaid Services (CMS) has expanded the coverage for cochlear implantation to cover moderate-to-profound hearing loss in individuals with hearing test scores equal to or less than 40% correct in the best aided listening condition on tape-recorded tests of open-set sentence recognition and who demonstrate limited benefit from amplification. (See Publication 100-03, chapter 1, section 50.3, for specific coverage criteria).

In addition CMS is covering cochlear implantation for individuals with open-set sentence recognition test scores of greater than 40% to less than or equal to 60% correct but only when the provider is participating in, and patients are enrolled in, either:

A Food and Drug Administration (FDA)-approved category B investigational device exemption (IDE) clinical trial; or

A trial under the CMS clinical trial policy (see Pub. 100-03, section 310.1); or

A prospective, controlled comparative trial approved by CMS as consistent with the evidentiary requirements for national coverage analyses and meeting specific quality standards.

100-4, 32, 120.2
Coding and General Billing Requirements
Physicians and hospitals must report one of the following Current Procedural Terminology (CPT) codes on the claim:

- 66982 Extracapsular cataract removal with insertion of intraocular lens prosthesis (one stage procedure), manual or mechanical technique (e.g., irrigation and aspiration or phacoemulsification), complex requiring devices or techniques not generally used in routine cataract surgery (e.g., iris expansion device, suture support for intraocular lens, or primary posterior capsulorrhexis) or performed on patients in the amblyogenic development stage.
- 66983 Intracapsular cataract with insertion of intraocular lens prosthesis (one stage procedure)
- 66984 Extracapsular cataract removal with insertion of intraocular lens prosthesis (one stage procedure), manual or mechanical technique (e.g., irrigation and aspiration or phacoemulsification)
- 66985 Insertion of intraocular lens prosthesis (secondary implant), not associated with concurrent cataract extraction
- 66986 Exchange of intraocular lens

In addition, physicians inserting a P-C IOL or A-C IOL in an office setting may bill code V2632 (posterior chamber intraocular lens) for the IOL. Medicare will make payment for the lens based on reasonable cost for a conventional IOL. Place of Service (POS) = 11.

Effective for dates of service on and after January 1, 2006, physician, hospitals and ASCs may also bill the non-covered charges related to the P-C function of the IOL using HCPCS code V2788. Effective for dates of service on and after January 22, 2007 through January 1, 2008, non-covered charges related to A-C function of the IOL can be billed using HCPCS code V2788. The type of service indicator for the non-covered billed charges is Q. (The type of service is applied by the Medicare carrier and not the provider). Effective for A-C IOL insertion services on or after January 1, 2008, physicians, hospitals and ASCs should use V2787 rather than V2788 to report any additional charges that accrue.

When denying the non-payable charges submitted with V2787 or V2788, contractors shall use an appropriate Medical Summary Notice (MSN) such as 16.10 (Medicare does not pay for this item or service) and an appropriate claim adjustment reason code such as 96 (non-covered charges) for claims submitted with the non-payable charges.

Hospitals and physicians may use the proper CPT code(s) to bill Medicare for evaluation and management services usually associated with services following cataract extraction surgery, if appropriate.

A - Applicable Bill Types
The hospital applicable bill types are 12X, 13X, 83X and 85X.

B - Other Special Requirements for Hospitals
Hospitals shall continue to pay CAHs method 2 claims under current payment methodologies for conditional IOLs.

100-4, 32, 130
External Counterpulsation (ECP) Therapy
Commonly referred to as enhanced external counterpulsation, is a non-invasive outpatient treatment for coronary artery disease refractory medical and/or surgical therapy. Effective for dates of service July 1, 1999, and after, Medicare will cover ECP when its use is in patients with stable angina (Class III or Class IV, Canadian Cardiovascular Society Classification or equivalent classification) who, in the opinion of a cardiologist or cardiothoracic surgeon, are not readily amenable to surgical intervention, such as PTCA or cardiac bypass, because:

- Their condition is inoperable, or at high risk of operative complications or post-operative failure;
- Their coronary anatomy is not readily amenable to such procedures; or
- They have co-morbid states that create excessive risk.

(Refer to Publication 100-03, section 20.20 for further coverage criteria.)

100-4, 32, 130.1
Billing and Payment Requirements
Effective for dates of service on or after January 1, 2000, use HCPCS code G0166 (External counterpulsation, per session) to report ECP services. The codes for external cardiac assist (92971), ECG rhythm strip and report (93040 or 93041), pulse oximetry (94760 or 94761) and plethysmography (93922 or 93923) or other monitoring tests for examining the effects of this treatment are not clinically necessary with this service and should not be paid on the same day, unless they occur in a clinical setting not connected with the delivery of the ECP. Daily evaluation and management service, e.g., 99201-99205, 99211-99215, 99217-99220, 99241-99245, cannot be billed with the ECP treatments. Any evaluation and management service must be justified with adequate documentation of the medical necessity of the visit. Deductible and coinsurance apply.

100-4, 32, 140
Cardiac Rehabilitation Programs
Medicare covers cardiac rehabilitation exercise programs for patients who meet the following criteria:

- Have a documented diagnosis of acute myocardial infarction within the preceding 12 months; or
- Have had coronary bypass surgery; or
- Have stable angina pectoris; or
- Have had heart valve repair/replacement; or
- Have had percutaneous transluminal coronary angioplasty (PTCA) or coronary stenting; or
- Have had a heart or heart-lung transplant.

Effective for dates of services on or after March 22, 2006, services provided in connection with a cardiac rehabilitation exercise program may be considered reasonable and necessary for up to 36 sessions. Patients generally receive 2 to 3 sessions per week for 12 to 18 weeks. The contractor has discretion to cover cardiac rehabilitation services beyond 18 weeks. Coverage must not exceed a total of 72 sessions for 36 weeks.

Cardiac rehabilitation programs shall be performed incident to physician's services in outpatient hospitals, or outpatient settings such as clinics or offices. Follow the policies for services incident to the services of a physician as they apply in each setting. For example, see Pub. 100-02, chapter 6, section 2.4.1, and Pub. 100-02, chapter 15, section 60.1.

(Refer to Publication 100-03, section 20.10 for further coverage guidelines.)

100-4, 32, 150.1
General

A. Covered Bariatric Surgery Procedures
Effective for services on or after February 21, 2006, Medicare has determined that the following bariatric surgery procedures are reasonable and necessary under certain conditions for the treatment of morbid obesity. The patient must have a body-mass index (BMI) >=35, have at least one co-morbidity related to obesity, and have been previously unsuccessful with medical treatment for obesity. This medical information must be documented in the patient's medical record. In addition, the procedure must be performed at an approved facility. A list of approved facilities may be found at
http://www.cms.hhs.gov/MedicareApprovedFacilitie/BSF/list.asp#TopOfPage.

Open Roux-en-Y gastric bypass (RYGBP).

Laparoscopic Roux-en-Y gastric bypass (RYGBP).

Laparoscopic adjustable gastric banding (LAGB).

Open biliopancreatic diversion with duodenal switch (BPD/DS).

Laparoscopic biliopancreatic diversion with duodenal switch (BPD/DS).

B. Non-Covered Bariatric Surgery Procedures
Effective for services on or after February 21, 2006, Medicare has determined that the following bariatric surgery procedures are not reasonable and necessary for the treatment of morbid obesity.

Open vertical banded gastroplasty.

Laparoscopic vertical banded gastroplasty.

Open sleeve gastrectomy.

Laparoscopic sleeve gastrectomy.

Open adjustable gastric banding.

Effective for services performed on and after February 12, 2009, CMS determines that open and laparoscopic Roux-en-Y gastric bypass (RYGBP), laparoscopic adjustable gastric banding (LAGB), and open and laparoscopic biliopancreatic diversion with duodenal switch (BPD/DS) in Medicare beneficiaries who have type 2 diabetes mellitus (T2DM) and a BMI <35 are not reasonable and necessary under section 1862(a)(1)(A) of the Social Security Act, and therefore are not covered.

Complete coverage guidelines can be found in the National Coverage Determination Manual (Pub. 100-03), sections 40.5 and 100.1.

100-4, 32, 150.2
HCPCS Procedure Codes for Bariatric Surgery

A. Covered HCPCS Procedure Codes
For services on or after February 21, 2006, the following HCPCS procedure codes are covered for bariatric surgery:

- 43770 Laparoscopy, surgical, gastric restrictive procedure; placement of adjustable gastric band (gastric band and subcutaneous port components).
- 43644 Laparoscopy, surgical, gastric restrictive procedure; with gastric bypass and Roux-en-Y gastroenterostomy (roux limb 150 cm or less).
- 43645 Laparoscopy with gastric bypass and small intestine reconstruction to limit absorption. (Do not report 43645 in conjunction with 49320, 43847.)
- 43845 Gastric restrictive procedure with partial gastrectomy, pylorus-preserving duodenoileostomy and ileoieostomy (50 to 100 cm common channel) to limit absorption (biliopancreatic diversion with duodenal switch).
- 43846 Gastric restrictive procedure, with gastric bypass for morbid obesity; with short limb (150 cm or less Roux-en-Y gastroenterostomy. (For greater than 150 cm, use 43847.) (For laparoscopic procedure, use 43644.)

Appendix G — Pub 100 References

43847 With small intestine reconstruction to limit absorption.

B. Noncovered HCPCS Procedure Codes
For services on or after February 21, 2006, the following HCPCS procedure codes are non-covered for bariatric surgery:

43842 Gastric restrictive procedure, without gastric bypass, for morbid obesity; vertical banded gastroplasty.

NOC code 43999 used to bill for:

- Laparoscopic vertical banded gastroplasty.
- Open sleeve gastrectomy.
- Laparoscopic sleeve gastrectomy.
- Open adjustable gastric banding.

100-4, 32, 150.6
ICD-9 Procedure Codes for Bariatric Procedures

150.6 - Claims Guidance for Payment

A. Covered Bariatric Surgery Procedures
Contractors shall process covered bariatric surgery claims as follows:

1. Identify bariatric surgery claims.
   - Contractors identify inpatient bariatric surgery claims by the presence of ICD-9-CM diagnosis code 278.01 as the primary diagnosis (for morbid obesity) and one of the covered ICD-9-CM procedure codes listed in Sec.150.3.
   - Contractors identify practitioner bariatric surgery claims by the presence of ICD-9-CM diagnosis code 278.01 as the primary diagnosis (for morbid obesity) and one of the covered HCPCS procedure codes listed in Sec.150.2.
2. Perform facility certification validation for all bariatric surgery claims on a pre-pay basis.
   - A list of approved facilities may be found at: http://www.cms.hhs.gov/MedicareApprovedFacilitie/BSF/list.asp#TopOfPage.
3. Review bariatric surgery claims data and determine whether a pre- or post-pay sample of bariatric surgery claims need further review to assure that the beneficiary has a BMI >=35 (V85.35 - V85.4), and at least one co-morbidity related to obesity.
   - The carrier/FI/A/B MAC medical director may define the appropriate method for addressing the obesity-related co-morbid requirement.

NOTE: If ICD-9-CM diagnosis code 278.01 is present, but a covered procedure code (listed in Sec.150.2 or Sec.150.3) is/are not present, the claim is not for bariatric surgery and should be processed under normal procedures.

B. Non-Covered Bariatric Surgery Procedures
Carriers, FIs and A/B MACs are to process non-covered practitioner bariatric surgery claims according to the conditions outlined below:

1. Deny claims billed with HCPCS procedure code 43842 when used for:
   - Open vertical banded gastroplasty.
2. Deny claims billed with HCPCS NOC code 43999 when used for:
   - Laparoscopic vertical banded gastroplasty.
   - Open sleeve gastrectomy.
   - Laparoscopic sleeve gastrectomy.
   - Open adjustable gastric banding.

The FIs and A/B MACs are to process non-covered inpatient bariatric surgery claims according to the conditions outlined below:

1. Reject claims billed with principal ICD-9 CM diagnosis code 278.01 and ICD-9 procedure code 44.68 when used for:
   - Open adjustable gastric banding.
   - Laparoscopic vertical banded gastroplasty.
2. Reject claims billed with principal ICD-9 CM diagnosis code 278.01 and ICD-9 procedure code 44.69 when used for:
   - Open vertical banded gastroplasty.
3. Reject claims billed with principal ICD-9 CM diagnosis code 278.01 and ICD-9 procedure code 43.89 when used for:
   - Open sleeve gastrectomy.
   - Laparoscopic sleeve gastrectomy.

NOTE: If ICD-9 procedure code 43.89 appears on the claim along with 45.51 and 45.91 to describe open or laparoscopic BPD/DS, process as a covered procedure according to Sec.150.6.A.

100-4, 32, 170.1
General
Effective for services performed from May 16, 2006 through August 13, 2007, the Centers for Medicare & Medicaid Services (CMS) made the decision that lumbar artificial disc replacement (LADR) with the ChariteTM lumbar artificial disc is non-covered for Medicare beneficiaries over 60 years of age. See Pub. 100-03, Medicare National Coverage Determinations Manual, section 150.10, for more information about the non-covered determination.

Effective for services performed on or after August 14, 2007, CMS made the decision that LADR with any lumbar artificial disc is non-covered for Medicare beneficiaries over 60 years of age, (i.e. on or after a beneficiary's 61st birthday).

For Medicare beneficiaries 60 years of age and younger, there is no national coverage determination for LADR, leaving such determinations to continue to be made by the local contractors.

100-4, 32, 170.2
Carrier Billing Requirements
Effective for services performed on or after May 16, 2006 through December 31, 2006, carriers shall deny claims, for Medicare beneficiaries over 60 years of age, submitted with the following Category III Codes:

0091T Single interspace, lumbar; and

0092T Each additional interspace (List separately in addition to code for primary procedure.)

Effective for services performed on or after January 1, 2007 through August 13, 2007, for Medicare beneficiaries over 60 years of age, LADR with the ChariteTM lumbar artificial disc, carriers shall deny claims submitted with the following codes:

22857 Total disc arthroplasty (artificial disc), anterior approach, including discectomy to prepare interspace (other than for decompression), lumbar, single interspace; and

0163T Total disc arthroplasty (artificial disc), anterior approach, including discectomy to prepare interspace (other than for decompression), lumbar, each additional interspace.

Carriers shall continue to follow their normal claims processing criteria for IDEs for LADR performed with an implant eligible under the IDE criteria.

For dates of service May 16, 2006 through August 13, 2007, Medicare coverage under the investigational device exemption (IDE) for LADR with a disc other than the ChariteTM lumbar disc in eligible clinical trials is not impacted.

Effective for services performed on or after August 14, 2007, carriers shall deny claims for LADR surgery, for Medicare beneficiaries over 60 years of age, (i.e. on or after a beneficiary's 61st birthday) submitted with the following codes:

22857 Total disc arthroplasty (artificial disc), anterior approach, including discectomy to prepare interspace (other than for decompression), lumbar, single interspace; and

0163T Total disc arthroplasty (artificial disc), anterior approach, including discectomy to prepare interspace (other than for decompression), lumbar, each additional interspace.

100-4, 32, 180.1
Coverage Requirements
Medicare covers cryosurgery of the prostate gland effective for claims with dates of service on or after July 1, 1999. The coverage is for:

1. Primary treatment of patients with clinically localized prostate cancer, Stages T1 - T3 (diagnosis code is 185 - malignant neoplasm of prostate).
2. Salvage therapy (effective for claims with dates of service on or after July 1, 2001 for patients:
   a. Having recurrent, localized prostate cancer;
   b. Failing a trial of radiation therapy as their primary treatment; and
   c. Meeting one of these conditions: State T2B or below; Gleason score less than 9 or; PSA less than 8 ng/ml.

100-4, 32, 180.2
Billing Requirements
Claims for cryosurgery for the prostate gland are to be submitted on the ANSI X12 ASC 837, or, in exceptional circumstances, on a hard copy Form CMS - 1450. This procedure can be rendered in an inpatient or outpatient hospital setting (types of bill (TOBs) 11x 13x, 83x, and 85x).

The FI will look for the following when processing claims with cryosurgery services:

- Diagnosis Code 185 (must be on all cryosurgical claims);
- For outpatient claims HCPCS 55873 and revenue codes 0360, 0361, or 0369 Cryosurgery ablation of localized prostate cancer, stages T1- T3 (includes ultrasonic guidance for interstitial cryosurgery probe placement, postoperative irrigations and aspiration of sloughing tissue included) must be on all outpatient claims; and
- For inpatient claims procedure code 60.62 (perineal prostatectomy- the definition includes cryoablation of prostate, cryostatectomy of prostate, and radical cryosurgical ablation of prostate) must be on the claim.

100-4, 32, 190
Billing Requirements for Extracorporeal Photopheresis
Effective for dates of services on and after December 19, 2006, Medicare has expanded coverage for extracorporeal photopheresis for patients with acute cardiac allograft rejection whose disease is refractory to standard immunosuppresive drug treatment and patients with chronic graft versus host disease whose disease is refractory to standard immunosuppresive drug treatment. (See Pub. 100-03, chapter 1, section 110.4, for complete coverage guidelines).

100-4,32,190.2
Healthcare Common Procedural Coding System (HCPCS), Applicable Diagnosis Codes and Procedure Code

The following HCPCS procedure code is used for billing extracorporeal photopheresis

36522   Photopheresis, extracorporeal

The following are the applicable ICD-9-CM diagnosis codes for the new expanded coverage:

996.83   Complications of transplanted heart, or

996.85   Complications of transplanted bone marrow.

The following is the applicable ICD-9-CM procedure code for the new expanded coverage:

99.88   Therapeutic photopheresis.

NOTE:Contractors shall edit for an appropriate oncological and autoimmune disorder diagnosis for payment of extracorporeal photopheresis according to the National Coverage Determination

100-4, 32, 220.1
220.1 - General

Effective for services on or after September 29, 2008, the Center for Medicare & Medicaid Services (CMS) made the decision that Thermal Intradiscal Procedures (TIPS) are not reasonable and necessary for the treatment of low back pain. Therefore, TIPs are non-covered. Refer to Pub.100-03, Medicare National Coverage Determination (NCD) Manual Chapter 1, Part 2, Section 150.11, for further information on the NCD.

100-4, 32, 220.2
220.2 - Contractors, A/B Medicare Administrative Contractors (MACs)

The following Healthcare Common Procedure Coding System (HCPCS) codes will be nationally non-covered by Medicare effective for dates of service on and after September 29, 2008: 22526: Percutaneous intradiscal electrothermal annuloplasty, unilateral or bilateral including fluoroscopic guidance; single level 22527: Percutaneous intradiscal electrothermal annuloplasty, unilateral or bilateral including fluoroscopic guidance; one or more additional levels 0062T: Percutaneous intradiscal annuloplasty, any method except electrothermal, unilateral or bilateral including fluoroscopic guidance; single level 0063T: Percutaneous intradiscal annuloplasty, any method except electrothermal, unilateral or bilateral including fluoroscopic guidance; one or more additional levels NOTE: The change to add the non-covered indicator for the above HCPCS codes will be part of the January 2009 Medicare Physician Fee Schedule Update. The change to the status indicator to non-cover the above HCPCS will be part of the January Integrated Outpatient Code Editor (IOCE) update.

Claims submitted with the non-covered HCPCS codes on or after September 29, 2008, will be denied by Medicare contractors

APPENDIX H — GLOSSARY

-centesis. Puncture, as with a needle, trocar, or aspirator; often done for withdrawing fluid from a cavity.

-ectomy. Excision, removal.

-orrhaphy. Suturing.

-ostomy. Indicates a surgically created artificial opening.

-otomy. Making an incision or opening.

-plasty. Indicates surgically formed or molded.

abdominal lymphadenectomy. Surgical removal of the abdominal lymph nodes grouping, with or without para-aortic and vena cava nodes.

ablation. Removal or destruction of a body part or tissue or its function. Ablation may be performed by surgical means, hormones, drugs, radiofrequency, heat, chemical application, or other methods.

absorbable sutures. Strands prepared from collagen or a synthetic polymer and capable of being absorbed by tissue over time. Examples include surgical gut and collagen sutures; or synthetics like polydioxanone (PDS), polyglactin 910 (Vicryl), poliglecaprone 25 (Monocryl), polyglyconate (Maxon), and polyglycolic acid (Dexon). For wound repair, see CPT codes 12001-13160. Correct code assignment is dependent upon the type of closure performed (i.e., simple, intermediate, or complex), the anatomical site, and the wound size.

acetabuloplasty. Surgical repair or reconstruction of the large cup-shaped socket in the hipbone (acetabulum) with which the head of the femur articulates.

Achilles tendon. Tendon attached to the back of the heel bone (calcaneus) that flexes the foot downward.

acromioclavicular joint. Junction between the clavicle and the scapula. The acromion is the projection from the back of the scapula that forms the highest point of the shoulder and connects with the clavicle. Trauma or injury to the acromioclavicular joint is often referred to as a dislocation of the shoulder. This is not correct, however, as a dislocation of the shoulder is a disruption of the glenohumeral joint. Synonym: AC joint.

acromionectomy. Surgical treatment for acromioclavicular arthritis in which the distal portion of the acromion process is removed.

acromioplasty. Repair of the part of the shoulder blade that connects to the deltoid muscles and clavicle.

actigraphy. Science of monitoring activity levels, particularly during sleep. In most cases, the patient wears a wristband that records motion while sleeping. The data are recorded, analyzed, and interpreted to study sleep/wake patterns and circadian rhythms.

air conduction. Transportation of sound from the air, through the external auditory canal, to the tympanic membrane and ossicular chain. Air conduction hearing is tested by presenting an acoustic stimulus through earphones or a loudspeaker to the ear.

air puff device. Instrument that measures intraocular pressure by evaluating the force of a reflected amount of air blown against the cornea.

allograft. Graft from one individual to another of the same species.

amniocentesis. Surgical puncture through the abdominal wall, with a specialized needle and under ultrasonic guidance, into the interior of the pregnant uterus and directly into the amniotic sac to collect fluid for diagnostic analysis or therapeutic reduction of fluid levels.

anastomosis. Surgically created connection between ducts, blood vessels, or bowel segments to allow flow from one to the other.

anesthesia time. Time period factored into anesthesia procedures beginning with the anesthesiologist preparing the patient for surgery and ending when the patient is turned over to the recovery department.

angioplasty. Reconstruction or repair of a diseased or damaged blood vessel.

annuloplasty. Surgical plicaton of weakened tissue of the heart, to improve its muscular function. Annuli are thick, fibrous rings and one is found surrounding each of the cardiac chambers. The atrial and ventricular muscle fibers attach to the annuli. In annuloplasty, weakened annuli may be surgically plicated, or tucked, to improve muscular functions.

anorectal anometry. Measurement of pressure generated by anal sphincter to diagnose incontinence.

anterior chamber lenses. Lenses inserted into the anterior chamber following intracapsular cataract extraction.

applanation tonometer. Instrument that measures intraocular pressure by recording the force required to flatten an area of the cornea.

arthrotomy. Surgical incision into a joint that may include exploration, drainage, or removal of a foreign body.

aspirate. To withdraw fluid or air from a body cavity by suction.

atrial septal defect. Cardiac anomaly consisting of a patent opening in the atrial septum due to a fusion failure, classified as ostium secundum type, ostium primum defect, or endocardial cushion defect.

attended surveillance. Ability of a technician at a remote surveillance center or location to respond immediately to patient transmissions regarding rhythm or device alerts as they are produced and received at the remote location. These transmissions may originate from wearable or implanted therapy or monitoring devices.

auricle. External ear, which is a single elastic cartilage covered in skin and normal adnexal features (hair follicles, sweat glands, and sebaceous glands), shaped to channel sound waves into the acoustic meatus.

autogenous transplant. Tissue, such as bone, that is harvested from the patient and used for transplantation back into the same patient.

autograft. Any tissue harvested from one anatomical site of a person and grafted to another anatomical site of the same person. Most commonly, blood vessels, skin, tendons, fascia, and bone are used as autografts.

backbench preparation. Procedures performed on a donor organ following procurement to prepare the organ for transplant into the recipient. Excess fat and other tissue may be removed, the organ may be perfused, and vital arteries may be sized, repaired, or modified to fit the patient. These procedures are done on a back table in the operating room before transplantation can begin.

Bartholin's gland. Mucous-producing gland found in the vestibular bulbs on either side of the vaginal orifice and connected to the mucosal membrane at the opening by a duct.

Bartholin's gland abscess. Pocket of pus and surrounding cellulitis caused by infection of the Bartholin's gland and causing localized swelling and pain in the posterior labia majora that may extend into the lower vagina.

Berman locator. Small, sensitive tool used to detect the location of a metallic foreign body in the eye.

bifurcated. Having two branches or divisions, such as the left pulmonary veins that split off from the left atrium to carry oxygenated blood away from the heart.

biopsy. Tissue or fluid removed for diagnostic purposes through analysis of the cells in the biopsy material.

Blalock-Hanlon procedure. Excision of a segment of the right atrium, creating an atrial septal defect.

Blalock-Taussig procedure. Anastomosis of the left subclavian artery to the left pulmonary artery or the right subclavian artery to the right pulmonary artery in order to shunt some of the blood flow from the systemic to the pulmonary circulation.

blepharochalasis. Loss of elasticity and relaxation of skin of the eyelid, thickened or indurated skin on the eyelid associated with recurrent episodes of edema, and intracellular atrophy.

blepharoplasty. Plastic surgery of the eyelids to remove excess fat and redundant skin weighting down the lid. The eyelid is pulled tight and sutured to support sagging muscles.

blepharoptosis. Droop or displacement of the upper eyelid, caused by paralysis, muscle problems, or outside mechanical forces.

blepharorrhaphy. Suture of a portion or all of the opposing eyelids to shorten the palpebral fissure or close it entirely.

blue baby. Infant born with bluish discoloration due to cyanosis.

Current Procedural Coding Expert — Appendix H — Glossary

bone conduction. Transportation of sound through the bones of the skull to the inner ear.

bone mass measurement. Radiologic or radioisotopic procedure or other procedure approved by the FDA for identifying bone mass, detecting bone loss, or determining bone quality. The procedure includes a physician's interpretation of the results. Qualifying individuals must be an estrogen-deficient woman at clinical risk for osteoporosis with vertebral abnormalities.

brachytherapy. Form of radiation therapy in which radioactive pellets or seeds are implanted directly into the tissue being treated to deliver their dose of radiation in a more directed fashion. Brachytherapy provides radiation to the prescribed body area while minimizing exposure to normal tissue.

Bristow procedure. Anterior capsulorrhaphy prevents chronic separation of the shoulder. In this procedure, the bone block is affixed to the anterior glenoid rim with a screw.

buccal mucosa. Tissue from the mucous membrane on the inside of the cheek.

Caldwell-Luc operation. Intraoral antrostomy approach into the maxillary sinus for the removal of tooth roots or tissue, or for packing the sinus to reduce zygomatic fractures by creating a window above the teeth in the canine fossa area.

canthorrhaphy. Suturing of the palpebral fissure, the juncture between the eyelids, at either end of the eye.

canthotomy. Horizontal incision at the canthus (junction of upper and lower eyelids) to divide the outer canthus and enlarge lid margin separation.

cardio-. Relating to the heart.

cardiopulmonary bypass. Venous blood is diverted to a heart-lung machine, which mechanically pumps and oxygenates the blood temporarily so the heart can be bypassed while an open procedure on the heart or coronary arteries is performed. During bypass, the lungs are deflated and immobile.

cardioverter-defibrillator. Device that uses both low energy cardioversion or defibrillating shocks and antitachycardia pacing to treat ventricular tachycardia or ventricular fibrillation.

care plan oversight services. Physician's ongoing review and revision of a patient's care plan involving complex or multidisciplinary care modalities.

case management services. Physician case management is a process of involving direct patient care as well as coordinating and controlling access to the patient or initiating and/or supervising other necessary health care services.

cataract extraction. Anterior chamber lenses are inserted in conjunction with intracapsular cataract extraction and posterior chamber lenses are inserted in conjunction with extracapsular cataract extraction.

catheter. Flexible tube inserted into an area of the body for introducing or withdrawing fluid.

certified nurse midwife. Registered nurse who has successfully completed a program of study and clinical experience or has been certified by a recognized organization for the care of pregnant or delivering patients.

cervical cap. Contraceptive device similar in form and function to the diaphragm but that can be left in place for 48 hours.

Chiari osteotomy. Top of the femur is altered to correct a dislocated hip caused by congenital conditions or cerebral palsy. Plate and screws are often used.

choanal atresia. Congenital, membranous, or bony closure of one or both posterior nostrils due to failure of the embryonic bucconasal membrane to rupture and open up the nasal passageway.

chondromalacia. Condition in which the articular cartilage softens, seen in various body sites but most often in the patella, and may be congenital or acquired.

chondroplasty. Surgical repair of cartilage.

chorionic villus sampling. Aspiration of a placental sample through a catheter, under ultrasonic guidance. The specialized needle is placed transvaginally through the cervix or transabdominally into the uterine cavity.

chronic pain management services. Distinct services frequently performed by anesthesiologists who have additional training in pain management procedures. Pain management services include initial and subsequent evaluation and management (E/M) services, trigger point injections, spine and spinal cord injections, and nerve blocks.

cineplastic amputation. Amputation in which muscles and tendons of the remaining portion of the extremity are arranged so that they may be utilized for motor functions. Following this type of amputation, a specially constructed prosthetic device allows the individual to execute more complex movements because the muscles and tendons are able to communicate independent movements to the device.

circadian. Relating to a cyclic, 24-hour period.

clinical social worker. Individual who possesses a master's or doctor's degree in social work and, after obtaining the degree, has performed at least two years of supervised clinical social work. A clinical social worker must be licensed by the state or, in the case of states without licensure, must completed at least two years or 3,000 hours of post-master's degree supervised clinical social work practice under the supervision of a master's level social worker.

CMS. Centers for Medicare and Medicaid Services. Federal agency that administers the public health programs.

CO2 laser. Carbon dioxide laser that emits an invisible beam and vaporizes water-rich tissue. The vapor is suctioned from the site.

colostomy. Artificial surgical opening anywhere along the length of the colon to the skin surface for the diversion of feces.

commissurotomy. Surgical division or disruption of any two parts that are joined to form a commissure in order to increase the opening. The procedure most often refers to opening the adherent leaflet bands of fibrous tissue in a stenosed mitral valve.

community mental health center. Facility providing outpatient mental health day treatment, assessments, and education as appropriate to community members.

computerized corneal topography. Digital imaging and analysis by computer of the shape of the corneal.

conjunctiva. Mucous membrane lining of the eyelids and covering of the exposed, anterior sclera.

conjunctivodacryocystostomy. Surgical connection of the lacrimal sac directly to the conjunctival sac.

conjunctivorhinostomy. Correction of an obstruction of the lacrimal canal achieved by suturing the posterior flaps and removing any lacrimal obstruction, preserving the conjunctiva.

consultation. Advice or an opinion regarding diagnosis and treatment of a patient rendered by a medical professional at the request of the primary care provider.

core needle biopsy. Large-bore biopsy needle inserted into a mass and a core of tissue is removed for diagnostic study.

corpectomy. Removal of the body of a bone, such as a vertebra.

costochondral. Pertaining to the ribs and the scapula.

CPT. Current Procedural Terminology. Definitive procedural coding system developed by the American Medical Association that lists descriptive terms and identifying codes to provide a uniform language that describes medical, surgical, and diagnostic services for nationwide communication among physicians, patients, and third parties, used in outpatient reporting of services.

craniosynostosis. Congenital condition in which one or more of the cranial sutures fuse prematurely, creating a deformed or aberrant head shape.

craterization. Excision of a portion of bone creating a crater-like depression to facilitate drainage from infected areas of bone.

cricoid. Circular cartilage around the trachea.

CRNA. Certified registered nurse anesthetist. Nurse trained and specializing in the administration of anesthesia.

cryolathe. Tool used for reshaping a button of corneal tissue.

Appendix H — Glossary

cryosurgery. Application of intense cold, usually produced using liquid nitrogen, to locally freeze diseased or unwanted tissue and induce tissue necrosis without causing harm to adjacent tissue.

CT. Computed tomography.

cutdown. Small, incised opening in the skin to expose a blood vessel, especially over a vein (venous cutdown) to allow venipuncture and permit a needle or cannula to be inserted for the withdrawal of blood or administration of fluids.

cytogenetic studies. Procedures in CPT that are related to the branch of genetics that studies cellular (cyto) structure and function as it relates to heredity (genetics). White blood cells, specifically T-lymphocytes, are the most commonly used specimen for chromosome analysis.

dacryocystotome. Instrument used for incising the lacrimal duct strictures.

debride. To remove all foreign objects and devitalized or infected tissue from a burn or wound to prevent infection and promote healing.

definitive identification. Identification of microorganisms using additional tests to specify the genus or species (e.g. slide cultures or biochemical panels).

dermis. Skin layer found under the epidermis that contains a papillary upper layer and the deep reticular layer of collagen, vascular bed, and nerves.

dermis graft. Skin graft that has been separated from the epidermal tissue and the underlying subcutaneous fat, used primarily as a substitute for fascia grafts in plastic surgery.

desensitization. 1) Administration of extracts of allergens periodically to build immunity in the patient. 2) Application of medication to decrease the symptoms, usually pain, associated with a dental condition or disease.

destruction. Ablation or eradication of a structure or tissue.

diabetes outpatient self-management training services. Educational and training services furnished by a certified provider in an outpatient setting. The physician managing the individual's diabetic condition must certify that the services are needed under a comprehensive plan of care and provide the patient with the skills and knowledge necessary for therapeutic program compliance (including skills related to the self-administration of injectable drugs). The provider must meet applicable standards established by the National Diabetes Advisory or be recognized by an organization that represents individuals with diabetes as meeting standards for furnishing the services.

diagnostic procedures. Procedure performed on a patient to obtain information to assess the medical condition of the patient or to identify a disease and to determine the nature and severity of an illness or injury.

diaphragm. 1) Muscular wall separating the thorax and its structures from the abdomen. 2) Flexible disk inserted into the vagina and against the cervix as a method of birth control.

diaphysectomy. Surgical removal of a portion of the shaft of a long bone, often done to facilitate drainage from infected bone.

diathermy. Applying heat to body tissues by various methods for therapeutic treatment or surgical purposes to coagulate and seal tissue.

dilation. Artificial increase in the diameter of an opening or lumen made by medication or by instrumentation.

dissect. Cut apart or separate tissue for surgical purposes or for visual or microscopic study.

dorsal. Pertaining to the back or posterior aspect.

drugs and biologicals. Drugs and biologicals included - or approved for inclusion - in the United States Pharmacopoeia, the National Formulary, the United States Homeopathic Pharmacopoeia, in New Drugs or Accepted Dental Remedies, or approved by the pharmacy and drug therapeutics committee of the medical staff of the hospital. Also included are medically accepted and FDA approved drugs used in an anticancer chemotherapeutic regimen. The carrier determines medical acceptance based on supportive clinical evidence.

dual-lead device. Implantable cardiac device (pacemaker or implantable cardioverter-defibrillator [ICD]) in which pacing and sensing components are placed in only two chambers of the heart.

DuToit staple capsulorrhaphy. Reattachment of the capsule of the shoulder and glenoid labrum to the glenoid lip using staples to anchor the avulsed capsule and glenoid labrum.

Dx. Diagnosis.

DXA. Dual energy x-ray absorptiometry. Radiological technique for bone density measurement using a two-dimensional projection system in which two x-ray beams with different levels of energy are pulsed alternately and the results are given in two scores, reported as standard deviations from peak bone mass density.

ECMO. Extracorporeal membrane oxygenation.

ectropion. Drooping of the lower eyelid away from the eye or outward turning or eversion of the edge of the eyelid, exposing the palpebral conjunctiva and causing irritation.

Eden-Hybinette procedure. Anterior shoulder repair using an anterior bone block to augment the bony anterior glenoid lip.

EDTA. Drug used to inhibit damage to the cornea by collagenase. EDTA is especially effective in alkali burns as it neutralizes soluable alkali, including lye.

effusion. Escape of fluid from within a body cavity.

electrocardiographic rhythm derived. Analysis of data obtained from readings of the heart's electrical activation, including heart rate and rhythm, variability of heart rate, ST analysis, and T-wave alternans. Other data may also be assessed when warranted.

electrocautery. Division or cutting of tissue using high-frequency electrical current to produce heat, which destroys cells.

emergency. Serious medical condition or symptom (including severe pain) resulting from injury, sickness, or mental illness that arises suddenly and requires immediate care and treatment, generally received within 24 hours of onset, to avoid jeopardy to the life, limb, or health of a covered person.

empyema. Accumulation of pus within the respiratory, or pleural, cavity.

endarterectomy. Removal of the thickened, endothelial lining of a diseased or damaged artery.

entropion. Inversion of the eyelid, turning the edge in toward the eyeball and causing irritation from contact of the lashes with the surface of the eye.

enucleation. Removal of a growth or organ cleanly so as to extract it in one piece.

epidermis. Outermost, nonvascular layer of skin that contains four to five differentiated layers depending on its body location: stratum corneum, lucidum, granulosum, spinosum, and basale.

epiphysiodesis. Surgical fusion of an epiphysis performed to prematurely stop further bone growth.

escharotomy. Surgical incision into the scab or crust resulting from a severe burn in order to relieve constriction and allow blood flow to the distal unburned tissue.

established patient. 1) Patient who has received professional services in a face-to-face setting within the last three years from the same physician or another physician of the same specialty who belongs to the same group practice. 2) For OPPS hosptials, patient who has been registered as an inpatient or outpatient in a hospital's provider-based clinic or emergency department within the past three years.

evacuation. Removal or purging of waste material.

evaluation and management codes. Assessment and management of a patient's health care using CPT codes 99201-99499.

evaluation and management service components. Key components of history, examination, and medical decision making that are key to selecting the correct E/M codes. Other non-key components include counseling, coordination of care, nature of presenting problem, and time.

event recorder. Portable, ambulatory heart monitor worn by the patient that makes electrocardiographic recordings of the length and frequency of aberrant cardiac rhythm to help diagnose heart conditions and to assess pacemaker functioning or programming.

exenteration. Surgical removal of the entire contents of a body cavity, such as the pelvis or orbit.

extended care services. Items and services provided to an inpatient of a skilled nursing facility, including nursing care, physical or occupational therapy, speech pathology, drugs and supplies, and medical social services.

external electrical capacitor device. External electrical stimulation device designed to promote bone healing. This device may also promote neural regeneration, revascularization, epiphyseal growth, and ligament maturation.

external pulsating electromagnetic field. External stimulation device designed to promote bone healing. This device may also promote neural regeneration, revascularization, epiphyseal growth, and ligament maturation.

extracorporeal. Located or taking place outside the body.

Eyre-Brook capsulorrhaphy. Reattachment of the capsule of the shoulder and glenoid labrum to the glenoid lip.

fascia. Fibrous sheet or band of tissue that envelops organs, muscles, and groupings of muscles.

fasciectomy. Excision of fascia or strips of fascial tissue.

fasciotomy. Incision or transection of fascial tissue.

fat graft. Graft composed of fatty tissue completely freed from surrounding tissue that is used primarily to fill in depressions.

FDA. Food and Drug Administration. Federal agency responsible for protecting public health by substantiating the safety, efficacy, and security of human and veterinary drugs, biological products, medical devices, national food supply, cosmetics, and items that give off radiation.

filtered speech test. Test most commonly used to identify central auditory dysfunction in which the patient is presented monosyllabic words that are low pass filtered, allowing only the parts of each word below a certain pitch to be presented. A score is given on the number of correct responses. This may be a subset of a standard battery of tests provided during a single encounter.

fissure. Deep furrow, groove, or cleft in tissue structures.

fistulization. Creation of a communication between two structures that were not previously connected.

flexor digitorum profundus tendon. Tendon originating in the proximal forearm and extending to the index finger and wrist. A thickened FDP sheath, usually caused by age, illness, or injury, can fill the carpal canal and lead to impingement of the median nerve.

fluoroscopy. Radiology technique that allows visual examination of part of the body or a function of an organ using a device that projects an x-ray image on a fluorescent screen.

focal length. Distance between the object in focus and the lens.

free flap. Tissue that is completely detached from the donor site and transplanted to the recipient site, receiving its blood supply from capillary ingrowth at the recipient site.

free microvascular flap. Tissue that is completely detached from the donor site following careful dissection and preservation of the blood vessels, then attached to the recipient site with the transferred blood vessels anastomosed to the vessels in the recipient bed.

fulguration. Destruction of living tissue by using sparks from a high-frequency electric current.

gas tamponade. Absorbable gas may be injected to force the retina against the choroid. Common gases include room air, short-acting sulfahexafluoride, intermediate-acting perfluoroethane, or long-acting perfluorooctane.

HCPCS. Healthcare Common Procedure Coding System. HCPCS Level I Healthcare Common Procedure Coding System Level I. Numeric coding system used by physicians, facility outpatient departments, and ambulatory surgery centers (ASC) to code ambulatory, laboratory, radiology, and other diagnostic services for Medicare billing. This coding system contains only the American Medical Association's Physicians' Current Procedural Terminology (CPT) codes. The AMA updates codes annually. HCPCS Level II Healthcare Common Procedure Coding System Level II. National coding system, developed by CMS, that contains alphanumeric codes for physician and nonphysician services not included in the CPT coding system. HCPCS Level II covers such things as ambulance services, durable medical equipment, and orthotic and prosthetic devices. HCPCS modifiers Two-character code (AA-ZZ) that identifies circumstances that alter or enhance the description of a service or supply. They are recognized by carriers nationally and are updated annually by CMS.

Hct. Hematocrit.

hemilaminectomy. Excision of a portion of the vertebral lamina.

hemodialysis. Cleansing of wastes and contaminating elements from the blood by virtue of different diffusion rates through a semipermeable membrane, which separates blood from a filtration solution that diffuses other elements out of the blood.

hemoperitoneum. Effusion of blood into the peritoneal cavity, the space between the continuous membrane lining the abdominopelvic walls and encasing the visceral organs.

heterograft. Surgical graft of tissue from one animal species to a different animal species. A common type of heterograft is porcine (pig) tissue, used for temporary wound closure.

heterotopic transplant. Tissue transplanted from a different anatomical site for usage as is natural for that tissue, for example, buccal mucosa to a conjunctival site.

Hickman catheter. Central venous catheter used for long-term delivery of medications, such as antibiotics, nutritional substances, or chemotherapeutic agents.

HLA. Human leukocyte antigen.

home health services. Services furnished to patients in their homes under the care of physicians. These services include part-time or intermittent skilled nursing care, physical therapy, medical social services, medical supplies and some rehabilitation equipment. Home health supplies and services must be prescribed by a physician, and the beneficiary must be confined at home in order for Medicare to pay the benefits in full.

homograft. Graft from one individual to another of the same species. Synonym(s): allogeneic graft, allograft.

hospice care. Items and services provided to a terminally ill individual by a hospice program under a written plan established and periodically reviewed by the individual's attending physician and by the medical director: Nursing care provided by or under the supervision of a registered professional nurse; Physical or occupational therapy or speech-language pathology services; Medical social services under the direction of a physician; Services of a home health aide who has successfully completed a training program; Medical supplies (including drugs and biologicals) and the use of medical appliances; Physicians' services; Short-term inpatient care (including both respite care and procedures necessary for pain control and acute and chronic symptom management) in an inpatient facility on an intermittent basis and not consecutively over longer than five days; Counseling (including dietary counseling) with respect to care of the terminally ill individual and adjustment to his death; Any item or service which is specified in the plan and for which payment may be made.

hospital. Institution that provides, under the supervision of physicians, diagnostic, therapeutic, and rehabilitation services for medical diagnosis, treatment, and care of patients. Hospitals receiving federal funds must maintain clinical records on all patients, provide 24-hour nursing services, and have a discharge planning process in place. The term "hospital" also includes religious nonmedical health care institutions and facilities of 50 beds or less located in rural areas.

IA. Intra-arterial.

ICD. Implantable cardioverter defibrillator.

ICM. Implantable cardiovascular monitor.

ileostomy. Artificial surgical opening that brings the end of the ileum out through the abdominal wall to the skin surface for the diversion of feces through a stoma.

iliopsoas tendon. Fibrous tissue that connects muscle to bone in the pelvic region, common to the iliacus and psoas major.

ILR. Implantable loop recorder.

IM. 1) Infectious mononucleosis. 2) Internal medicine. 3) Intramuscular.

Appendix H — Glossary

implant. Material or device inserted or placed within the body for therapeutic, reconstructive, or diagnostic purposes.

implantable cardiovascular monitor. Implantable electronic device that stores cardiovascular physiologic data such as intracardiac pressure waveforms collected from internal sensors or data such as weight and blood pressure collected from external sensors. The information stored in these devices is used as an aid in managing patients with heart failure and other cardiac conditions that are non-rhythm related. The data may be transmitted via local telemetry or remotely to a surveillance technician or an internet-based file server. Synonym: ICM.

implantable cardioverter-defibrillator. Implantable electronic cardiac device used to control rhythm abnormalities such as tachycardia, fibrillation, or bradycardia by producing high- or low-energy stimulation and pacemaker functions. It may also have the capability to provide the functions of an implantable loop recorder or implantable cardiovascular monitor. Synonym: ICD.

implantable loop recorder. Implantable electronic cardiac device that constantly monitors and records electrocardiographic rhythm. It may be triggered by the patient when a symptomatic episode occurs or activated automatically by rapid or slow heart rates. This may be the sole purpose of the device or it may be a component of another cardiac device such as a pacemaker or implantable cardioverter-defibrillator. The data can be transmitted via local telemetry or remotely to a surveillance technician or an internet-based file server. Synonym: ILR.

implantable loop recorder. Implantable electronic cardiac device that constantly monitors and records electrocardiographic rhythm. It may be triggered by the patient when a symptomatic episode occurs or activated automatically by rapid or slow heart rates. This may be the sole purpose of the device or it may be a component of another cardiac device such as a pacemaker or implantable cardioverter-defibrillator. The data can be transmitted via local telemetry or remotely to a surveillance technician or an internet-based file server. Synonym: ILR.

implantable venous access device. Catheter implanted for continuous access to the venous system for long-term parenteral feeding or for the administration of fluids or medications.

in situ. Located in the natural position or contained within the origin site, not spread into neighboring tissue.

incontinence. Inability to control urination or defecation.

infundibulectomy. Excision of the anterosuperior portion of the right ventricle of the heart.

internal direct current stimulator. Electrostimulation device placed directly into the surgical site designed to promote bone regeneration by encouraging cellular healing response in bone and ligaments.

interrogation device evaluation. Assessment of an implantable cardiac device (pacemaker, cardioverter-defibrillator, cardiovascular monitor, or loop recorder) in which collected data about the patient's heart rate and rhythm, battery and pulse generator function, and any leads or sensors present, are retrieved and evaluated. Determinations regarding device programming and appropriate treatment settings are made based on the findings. CPT provides required components for evaluation of the various types of devices.

intramedullary implants. Nail, rod, or pin placed into the intramedullary canal at the fracture site. Intramedullary implants not only provide a method of aligning the fracture, they also act as a splint and may reduce fracture pain. Implants may be rigid or flexible. Rigid implants are preferred for prophylactic treatment of diseased bone, while flexible implants are preferred for traumatic injuries.

intraocular lens. Artificial lens implanted into the eye to replace a damaged natural lens or cataract.

intravenous. Within a vein or veins.

introducer. Instrument, such as a catheter, needle, or tube, through which another instrument or device is introduced into the body.

IP. 1) Interphalangeal. 2) Intraperitoneal.

irrigation. To wash out or cleanse a body cavity, wound, or tissue with water or other fluid.

keratoprosthesis. Surgical procedure in which the physician creates a new anterior chamber with a plastic optical implant to replace a severely damaged cornea that cannot be repaired.

krypton laser. Laser light energy that uses ionized krypton by electric current as the active source, has a radiation beam between the visible yellow-red spectrum, and is effective in photocoagulation of retinal bleeding, macular lesions, and vessel aberrations of the choroid.

lacrimal. Tear-producing gland or ducts that provides lubrication and flushing of the eyes and nasal cavities.

lacrimal punctum. Opening of the lacrimal papilla of the eyelid through which tears flow to the canaliculi to the lacrimal sac.

lacrimotome. Knife for cutting the lacrimal sac or duct.

lacrimotomy. Incision of the lacrimal sac or duct.

laparotomy. Incision through the flank or abdomen for therapeutic or diagnostic purposes.

larynx. Musculocartilaginous structure between the trachea and the pharynx that functions as the valve preventing food and other particles from entering the respiratory tract, as well as the voice mechanism. Also called the voicebox, the larynx is composed of three single cartilages: cricoid, epiglottis, and thyroid; and three paired cartilages: arytenoid, corniculate, and cuneiform.

laser surgery. Use of concentrated, sharply defined light beams to cut, cauterize, coagulate, seal, or vaporize tissue.

LEEP. Loop electrode excision procedure. Biopsy specimen or cone shaped wedge of cervical tissue is removed using a hot cautery wire loop with an electrical current running through it.

levonorgestrel. Drug inhibiting ovulation and preventing sperm from penetrating cervical mucus. It is delivered subcutaneously in polysiloxone capsules. The capsules can be effective for up to five years, and provide a cumulative pregnancy rate of less than 2 percent. The capsules are not biodegradable, and therefore must be removed. Removal is more difficult than insertion of levonorgestrel capsules because fibrosis develops around the capsules. Normal hormonal activity and a return to fertility begins immediately upon removal.

ligament. Band or sheet of fibrous tissue that connects the articular surfaces of bones or supports visceral organs.

ligation. Tying off a blood vessel or duct with a suture or a soft, thin wire.

lymphadenectomy. Dissection of lymph nodes free from the vessels and removal for examination by frozen section in a separate procedure to detect early-stage metastases.

lysis. Destruction, breakdown, dissolution, or decomposition of cells or substances by a specific catalyzing agent.

Magnuson-Stack procedure. Treatment for recurrent anterior dislocation of the shoulder that involves tightening and realigning the subscapularis tendon.

Manchester colporrhaphy. Preservation of the uterus following prolapse by amputating the vaginal portion of the cervix, shortening the cardinal ligaments, and performing a colpoperineorrhaphy posteriorly.

marsupialization. Creation of a pouch in surgical treatment of a cyst in which one wall is resected and the remaining cut edges are sutured to adjacent tissue creating an open pouch of the previously enclosed cyst.

mastectomy. Surgical removal of one or both breasts.

McDonald procedure. Polyester tape is placed around the cervix with a running stitch to assist in the prevention of pre-term delivery. Tape is removed at term for vaginal delivery.

MCP. Metacarpophalangeal.

medial. Middle or midline.

Medicare contractor. Medicare Part A fiscal intermediary, Medicare Part B carrier, Medicare administrative contractor (MAC), or a Medicare durable medical equipment regional carrier (DMERC).

mitral valve. Valve with two cusps that is between the left atrium and left ventricle of the heart.

moderate sedation. Medically controlled state of depressed consciousness, with or without analgesia, while maintaining the patient's airway, protective reflexes, and ability to respond to stimulation or verbal commands.

Mohs micrographic surgery. Special technique used to treat complex or ill-defined skin cancer and requires a single physician to provide two distinct services. The first service is surgical and involves the destruction of the lesion by a combination of chemosurgery and excision. The second service is that of a pathologist and includes mapping, color coding of specimens, microscopic examination of specimens, and complete histopathologic preparation.

monitored anesthesia care. Sedation, with or without analgesia, used to achieve a medically controlled state of depressed consciousness while maintaining the patient's airway, protective reflexes, and ability to respond to stimulation or verbal commands. In dental conscious sedation, the patient is rendered free of fear, apprehension, and anxiety through the use of pharmacological agents.

multiple-lead device. Implantable cardiac device (pacemaker or implantable cardioverter-defibrillator [ICD]) in which pacing and sensing components are placed in at least three chambers of the heart.

Mustard procedure. Corrective measure for transposition of great vessels involves an intra-atrial baffle made of pericardial tissue or synthetic material. The baffle is secured between pulmonary veins and mitral valve and between mitral and tricuspid valves. The baffle directs systemic venous flow into the left ventricle and lungs and pulmonary venous flow into the right ventricle and aorta.

myasthenia gravis. Autoimmune neuromuscular disorder caused by antibodies to the acetylcholine receptors at the neuromuscular junction, interfering with proper binding of the neurotransmitter from the neuron to the target muscle, causing muscle weakness, fatigue, and exhaustion, without pain or atrophy.

myotomy. Surgical cutting of a muscle to gain access to underlying tissues or for therapeutic reasons.

myringotomy. Incision in the eardrum done to prevent spontaneous rupture precipitated by fluid pressure build-up behind the tympanic membrane and to prevent stagnant infection and erosion of the ossicles.

nasal polyp. Fleshy outgrowth projecting from the mucous membrane of the nose or nasal sinus cavity that may obstruct ventilation or affect the sense of smell.

nasal sinus. Air-filled cavities in the cranial bones lined with mucous membrane and continuous with the nasal cavity, draining fluids through the nose.

nasogastric tube. Long, hollow, cylindrical catheter made of soft rubber or plastic that is inserted through the nose down into the stomach, and is used for feeding, instilling medication, or withdrawing gastric contents.

nasolacrimal punctum. Opening of the lacrimal duct near the nose.

nasopharynx. Membranous passage above the level of the soft palate.

Nd:YAG laser. Laser light energy that uses an yttrium, aluminum, and garnet crystal doped with neodymium ions as the active source, has a radiation beam nearing the infrared spectrum, and is effective in photocoagulation, photoablation, cataract extraction, and lysis of vitreous strands.

nebulizer. Latin for mist, a device that converts liquid into a fine spray and is commonly used to deliver medicine to the upper respiratory, bronchial, and lung areas.

neurectomy. Excision of all or a portion of a nerve.

new patient. Patient who is receiving face-to-face care from a provider or another physician of the same specialty who belongs to the same group practice for the first time in three years. For OPPS hospitals, a patient who has not been registered as an inpatient or outpatient, including off-campus provider based clinic or emergency department, of the hospital within the past three years.

Nissen fundoplasty. Surgical repair technique that involves the fundus of the stomach being wrapped around the lower end of the esophagus to treat reflux esophagitis.

Nissen fundoplasty. Surgical repair technique that involves the fundus of the stomach being wrapped around the lower end of the esophagus to treat reflux esophagitis.

nonabsorbable sutures. Strands of natural or synthetic material that resist absorption into living tissue and are removed once healing is under way. Nonabsorbable sutures are commonly used to close skin wounds and repair tendons or collagenous tissue.

obturator. Prosthesis used to close an acquired or congenital opening in the palate that aids in speech and chewing.

obturator nerve. Lumbar plexus nerve with anterior and posterior divisions that innervate the adductor muscles (e.g., adductor longus, adductor brevis) of the leg and the skin over the medial area of the thigh or a sacral plexus nerve with anterior and posterior divisions that innervate the superior gemellus muscles.

occult blood test. Chemical or microscopic test to determine the presence of blood in a specimen.

ocular implant. Implant inside muscular cone.

oophorectomy. Surgical removal of all or part of one or both ovaries, either as open procedure or laparoscopically. Menstruation and childbearing ability continues when one ovary is removed.

orthosis. Derived from a Greek word meaning "to make straight," it is an artificial appliance that supports, aligns, or corrects an anatomical deformity or improves the use of a moveable body part. Unlike a prosthesis, an orthotic device is always functional in nature.

osteo-. Having to do with bone.

osteogenesis stimulator. Device used to stimulate the growth of bone by electrical impulses or ultrasound.

osteotomy. Surgical cutting of a bone.

ostomy. Artificial (surgical) opening in the body used for drainage or for delivery of medications or nutrients.

pacemaker. Implantable cardiac device that controls the heart's rhythm and maintains regular beats by artificial electric discharges. This device consists of the pulse generator with a battery and the electrodes, or leads, which are placed in single or dual chambers of the heart, usually transvenously.

palmaris longus tendon. Tendon located in the hand that flexes the wrist joint.

paratenon graft. Graft composed of the fatty tissue found between a tendon and its sheath.

passive mobilization. Pressure, movement, or pulling of a limb or body part utilizing an apparatus or device.

pedicle flap. Full-thickness skin and subcutaneous tissue for grafting that remains partially attached to the donor site by a pedicle or stem in which the blood vessels supplying the flap remain intact.

Pemberton osteotomy. Osteotomy is performed to position triradiate cartilage as a hinge for rotating the acetabular roof in cases of dysplasia of the hip in children.

percutaneous intradiscal electrothermal annuloplasty. Procedure corrects tears in the vertebral annulus by applying heat to the collagen disc walls percutaneously through a catheter. The heat contracts and thickens the wall, which may contract and close any annular tears.

percutaneous skeletal fixation. Treatment that is neither open nor closed. In this procedure, the injury site is not directly visualized. Instead, fixation devices (pins, screws) are placed to stabilize the dislocation using x-ray guidance.

pericardium. Thin and slippery case in which the heart lies that is lined with fluid so that the heart is free to pulse and move as it beats.

peritoneal. Space between the lining of the abdominal wall, or parietal peritoneum, and the surface layer of the abdominal organs, or visceral peritoneum. It contains a thin, watery fluid that keeps the peritoneal surfaces moist. p. dialysis Dialysis that filters waste from blood inside the body using the peritoneum, the natural lining of the abdomen, as the semipermeable membrane across which ultrafiltration is accomplished. A special catheter is inserted into the abdomen and a dialysis solution is drained into the

Appendix H — Glossary

abdomen. This solution extracts fluids and wastes, which are then discarded when the fluid is drained. Various forms of peritoneal dialysis include CAPD, CCPD, and NIDP. p. effusion Persistent escape of fluid within the peritoneal cavity.

pessary. Device placed in the vagina to support and reposition a prolapsing or retropositioned uterus, rectum, or vagina.

photocoagulation. Application of an intense laser beam of light to disrupt tissue and condense protein material to a residual mass, used especially for treating ocular conditions.

physical status modifiers. Alphanumeric modifier used to identify the patient's health status as it affects the work related to providing the anesthesia service.

physical therapy modality. Therapeutic agent or regimen applied or used to provide appropriate treatment of the musculoskeletal system.

PICC. Peripherally inserted central catheter. PICC is inserted into one of the large veins of the arm and threaded through the vein until the tip sits in a large vein just above the heart.

PKR. Photorefractive therapy. Procedure involving the removal of the surface layer of the cornea (epithelium) by gentle scraping and use of a computer-controlled excimer laser to reshape the stroma.

pleurodesis. Injection of a sclerosing agent into the pleural space for creating adhesions between the parietal and the visceral pleura to treat a collapsed lung caused by air trapped in the pleural cavity, or severe cases of pleural effusion.

plication. Surgical technique involving folding, tucking, or pleating to reduce the size of a hollow structure or organ.

Potts-Smith-Gibson procedure. Side-to-side anastomosis of the aorta and left pulmonary artery creating a shunt that enlarges as the child grows.

presumptive identification. Identification of microorganisms using media growth, colony morphology, gram stains, or up to three specific tests (e.g., catalase, indole, oxidase, urease).

profunda. Denotes a part of a structure that is deeper from the surface of the body than the rest of the structure.

prolonged physician services. Extended pre- or post-service care provided to a patient whose condition requires services beyond the usual.

prostate. Male gland surrounding the bladder neck and urethra that secretes a substance into the seminal fluid.

prosthetic. Device that replaces all or part of an internal body organ or body part, or that replaces part of the function of a permanently inoperable or malfunctioning internal body organ or body part.

provider of services. Institution, individual, or organization that provides health care.

proximal. Located closest to a specified reference point, usually the midline.

psychiatric hospital. Specialized institution that provides, under the supervision of physicians, services for the diagnosis and treatment of mentally ill persons.

pterygium. Benign, wedge-shaped, conjunctival thickening that advances from the inner corner of the eye toward the cornea.

pterygomaxillary fossa. Wide depression on the external surface of the maxilla above and to the side of the canine tooth socket.

pulmonary artery banding. Surgical constriction of the pulmonary artery to prevent irreversible pulmonary vascular obstructive changes and overflow into the left ventricle.

Putti-Platt procedure. Realignment of the subscapularis tendon to treat recurrent anterior dislocation, thereby partially eliminating external rotation. The anterior capsule is also tightened and reinforced.

pyloroplasty. Enlargement and reconstruction of the lower portion of the stomach opening into the duodenum performed after vagotomy to speed gastric emptying and treat duodenal ulcers.

radioactive substances. Materials used in the diagnosis and treatment of disease that emit high-speed particles and energy-containing rays.

radiology services. Services that include diagnostic and therapeutic radiology, nuclear medicine, CT scan procedures, magnetic resonance imaging services, ultrasound, and other imaging procedures.

radiotherapy afterloading. Part of the radiation therapy process in which the chemotherapy agent is actually instilled into the tumor area subsequent to surgery and placement of an expandable catheter into the void remaining after tumor excision. The specialized catheter remains in place and the patient may come in for multiple treatments with radioisotope placed to treat the margin of tissue surrounding the excision. After the radiotherapy is completed, the patient returns to have the catheter emptied and removed. This is a new therapy in breast cancer treatment.

Rashkind procedure. Transvenous balloon atrial septectomy or septostomy performed by cardiac catheterization. A balloon catheter is inserted into the heart either to create or enlarge an opening in the interatrial septal wall.

repair. Surgical closure of a wound. The wound may be a result of injury/trauma or it may be a surgically created defect. Repairs are divided into three categories: simple, intermediate, and complex. Simple repair is performed when the wound is superficial and only requires simple, one layer, primary suturing. Intermediate repair is performed for wounds and lacerations in which one or more of the deeper layers of subcutaneous tissue and non-muscle fascia are repaired in addition to the skin and subcutaneous tissue. Complex repair includes repair of wounds requiring more than layered closure.

ribbons. In oncology, small plastic tubes containing radioactive sources for interstitial placement that may be cut into specific lengths tailored to the size of the area receiving ionizing radiation treatment.

Ridell sinusotomy. Frontal sinus tissue is destroyed to eliminate tumors.

rural health clinic. Clinic in an area where there is a shortage of health services staffed by a nurse practitioner, physician assistant, or certified nurse midwife under physician direction that provides routine diagnostic services, including clinical laboratory services, drugs, and biologicals and that has prompt access to additional diagnostic services from facilities meeting federal requirements.

Salter osteotomy. Innominate bone of the hip is cut, removed, and repositioned to repair a congenital dislocation, subluxation, or deformity.

saucerization. Creation of a shallow, saucer-like depression in the bone to facilitate drainage of infected areas.

Schiotz tonometer. Instrument that measures intraocular pressure by recording the depth of an indentation on the cornea by a plunger of known weight.

screening mammography. Radiologic images taken of the female breast for the early detection of breast cancer.

screening mammography services. Radiological procedures provided to women for early detection of breast cancer. A physician must interpret the results of the procedure. No symptoms need to be present for a screening mammography to be covered. Coverage for this service was added to the Medicare program effective January 1, 1991.

screening pap smear. Diagnostic laboratory test consisting of a routine exfoliative cytology test (Papanicolaou test) provided to a woman for the early detection of cervical or vaginal cancer. The exam includes a clinical breast examination and a physician's interpretation of the results.

seeds. Small (1 mm or less) sources of radioactive material that are permanently placed directly into tumors.

senning procedure. Flaps of intra-atrial septum and right atrial wall are used to create two interatrial channels to divert the systemic and pulmonary venous circulation.

sensitivity tests. Number of methods of applying selective suspected allergens to the skin or mucous.

sensorineural conduction. Transportation of sound from the cochlea to the acoustic nerve and central auditory pathway to the brain.

sentinel lymph node. First node to which lymph drainage and metastasis from a cancer can occur.

separate procedures. Services commonly carried out as a fundamental part of a total service, and as such usually do not warrant a separate identification. They are noted in the CPT book with the parenthetical phrase (separate procedure) at the end of the description, and are payable only when they are performed alone.

separate procedures. Services commonly carried out as a fundamental part of a total service, and as such usually do not warrant a separate identification. They are noted in the CPT book with the parenthetical phrase (separate procedure) at the end of the description, and are payable only when they are performed alone.

septectomy. 1) Surgical removal of all or part of the nasal septum. 2) Submucosal resection of the nasal septum.

Shirodkar procedure. Treatment of an incompetent cervical os by placing nonabsorbent suture material in purse-string sutures as a cerclage to support the cervix.

sialodochoplasty. Surgical repair of a salivary gland duct.

single-lead device. Implantable cardiac device (pacemaker or implantable cardioverter-defibrillator [ICD]) in which pacing and sensing components are placed in only one chamber of the heart.

sinus of Valsalva. Any of three sinuses corresponding to the individual cusps of the aortic valve, located in the most proximal part of the aorta just above the cusps. These structures are contained within the pericardium and appear as distinct but subtle outpouchings or dilations of the aortic wall between each of the semilunar cusps of the valve.

speculoscopy. Viewing the cervix utilizing a magnifier and a special wavelength of light, allowing detection of abnormalities that may not be discovered on a routine Pap smear.

speech-language pathology services. Speech, language, and related function assessment and rehabilitation service furnished by a qualified speech-language pathologist. Audiology services include hearing and balance assessment services furnished by a qualified audiologist. A qualified speech pathologist and audiologist must have a master's or doctoral degree in their respective fields and be licensed to serve in the state. Speech pathologists and audiologists practicing in states without licensure must complete 350 hours of supervised clinical work and perform at least nine months of supervised full-time service after earning their degrees.

sphincteroplasty. Surgical repair done to correct, augment, or improve the muscular function of a sphincter, such as the anus or intestines.

spirometry. Measurement of the lungs' breathing capacity.

splint. Brace or support. A dynamic splint permits movement of an anatomical structure such as a hand, wrist, foot, or other part of the body after surgery or injury. A static splint prevents movement and maintains support and position for an anatomical structure after surgery or injury.

stent. Tube to provide support in a body cavity or lumen.

stereotactic radiosurgery. Delivery of externally-generated ionizing radiation to specific targets for destruction or inactivation. Most often utilized in the treatment of brain or spinal tumors, high-resolution stereotactic imaging is used to identify the target and then deliver the treatment. Computer-assisted planning may also be employed. Simple and complex cranial lesions and spinal lesions are typically treated in a single planning and treatment session, although a maximum of five sessions may be required. No incision is made for stereotactic radiosurgery procedures.

stereotaxis. Three-dimensional method for precisely locating structures.

Stoffel rhizotomy. Nerve roots are sectioned to relieve pain or spastic paralysis.

strabismus. Misalignment of the eyes due to an imbalance in extraocular muscles.

surgical package. Normal, uncomplicated performance of specific surgical services, with the assumption that, on average, all surgical procedures of a given type are similar with respect to skill level, duration, and length of normal follow-up care.

symblepharopterygium. Adhesion in which the eyelid is adhered to the eyeball by a band that resembles a pterygium.

sympathectomy. Surgical interruption or transection of a sympathetic nervous system pathway.

tarso-. 1) Relating to the foot. 2) Relating to the margin of the eyelid.

tarsocheiloplasty. Plastic operation upon the edge of the eyelid for the treatment of trichiasis.

tarsorrhaphy. Suture of a portion or all of the opposing eyelids together for the purpose of shortening the palpebral fissure or closing it entirely.

technical component. Portion of a health care service that identifies the provision of the equipment, supplies, technical personnel, and costs attendant to the performance of the procedure other than the professional services.

tendon. Fibrous tissue that connects muscle to bone, consisting primarily of collagen and containing little vasculature.

tendon allograft. Allografts are tissues obtained from another individual of the same species. Tendon allografts are usually obtained from cadavers and frozen or freeze dried for later use in soft tissue repairs where the physician elects not to obtain an autogenous graft (a graft obtained from the individual on whom the surgery is being performed).

tendon suture material. Tendons are composed of fibrous tissue consisting primarily of collagen and containing few cells or blood vessels. This tissue heals more slowly than tissues with more vascularization. Because of this, tendons are usually repaired with nonabsorbable suture material. Examples include surgical silk, surgical cotton, linen, stainless steel, surgical nylon, polyester fiber, polybutester (Novafil), polyethylene (Dermalene), and polypropylene (Prolene, Surilene).

tendon transplant. Replacement of a tendon with another tendon.

tenon's capsule. Connective tissue that forms the capsule enclosing the posterior eyeball, extending from the conjunctival fornix and continuous with the muscular fascia of the eye.

tenonectomy. Excision of a portion of a tendon to make it shorter.

tenotomy. Cutting into a tendon.

TENS. Transcutaneous electrical nerve stimulator. Applied by placing electrode pads over the area to be stimulated and connecting the electrodes to a transmitter box, which sends a current through the skin to sensory nerve fibers to help decrease pain in that nerve distribution.

tensilon. Edrophonium chloride. Agent used for evaluation and treatment of myasthenia gravis.

terminally ill. Individual whose medical prognosis for life expectancy is six months or less.

tetralogy of Fallot. Specific combination of congenital cardiac defects: obstruction of the right ventricular outflow tract with pulmonary stenosis, interventricular septal defect, malposition of the aorta, overriding the interventricular septum and receiving blood from both the venous and arterial systems, and enlargement of the right ventricle.

therapeutic services. Services performed for treatment of a specific diagnosis. These services include performance of the procedure, various incidental elements, and normal, related follow-up care.

thoracentesis. Surgical puncture of the chest cavity with a specialized needle or hollow tubing to aspirate fluid from within the pleural space for diagnostic or therapeutic reasons.

thoracic lymphadenectomy. Procedure to cut out the lymph nodes near the lungs, around the heart, and behind the trachea.

thoracostomy. Creation of an opening in the chest wall for drainage.

thyroglossal duct. Embryonic duct at the front of the neck, which becomes the pyramidal lobe of the thyroid gland with obliteration of the remaining duct, but may form a cyst or sinus in adulthood if it persists.

total disc arthroplasty with artificial disc. Removal of an intravertebral disc and its replacement with an implant. The implant is an artificial disc consisting of two metal plates with a weight-bearing surface of polyethylene between the plates. The plates are anchored to the vertebral immediately above and below the affected disc.

total shoulder replacement. Prosthetic replacement of the entire shoulder joint, including the humeral head and the glenoid fossa.

trabeculae carneae cordis. Bands of muscular tissue that line the walls of the ventricles in the heart.

Appendix H — Glossary

tracheostomy. Formation of a tracheal opening on the neck surface with tube insertion to allow for respiration in cases of obstruction or decreased patency. A tracheostomy may be planned or performed on an emergency basis for temporary or long-term use.

tracheotomy. Formation of a tracheal opening on the neck surface with tube insertion to allow for respiration in cases of obstruction or decreased patency. A tracheotomy may be planned or performed on an emergency basis for temporary or long-term use.

traction. Drawing out or holding tension on an area by applying a direct therapeutic pulling force.

transcranial magnetic stimulation. Application of electromagnetic energy to the brain through a coil placed on the scalp. The procedure stimulates cortical neurons and is intended to activate and normalize their processes.

trephine. 1) Specialized round saw for cutting circular holes in bone, especially the skull. 2) Instrument that removes small disc-shaped buttons of corneal tissue for transplanting.

tricuspid atresia. Congenital absence of the valve that may occur with other defects, such as atrial septal defect, pulmonary atresia, and transposition of great vessels.

turbinates. Scroll or shell-shaped elevations from the wall of the nasal cavity, the inferior turbinate being a separate bone, while the superior and middle turbinates are of the ethmoid bone.

tympanic membrane. Thin, sensitive membrane across the entrance to the middle ear that vibrates in response to sound waves, allowing the waves to be transmitted via the ossicular chain to the internal ear.

tympanoplasty. Surgical repair of the structures of the middle ear, including the eardrum and the three small bones, or ossicles.

unlisted procedure. Procedural descriptions used when the overall procedure and outcome of the procedure are not adequately described by an existing procedure code. Such codes are used as a last resort and only when there is not a more appropriate procedure code.

ureterorrhaphy. Surgical repair using sutures to close an open wound or injury of the ureter.

vagotomy. Division of the vagus nerves, interrupting impulses resulting in lower gastric acid production and hastening gastric emptying. Used in the treatment of chronic gastric, pyloric, and duodenal ulcers that can cause severe pain and difficulties in eating and sleeping.

vasectomy. Surgical procedure involving the removal of all or part of the vas deferens, usually performed for sterilization or in conjunction with a prostatectomy.

ventricular septal defect. Congenital cardiac anomaly resulting in a continual opening in the septum between the ventricles that, in severe cases, causes oxygenated blood to flow back into the lungs, resulting in pulmonary hypertension.

vertebral interspace. Non-bony space between two adjacent vertebral bodies that contains the cushioning intervertebral disk.

volar. Palm of the hand (palmar) or sole of the foot (plantar).

Waterston procedure. Type of aortopulmonary shunting done to increase pulmonary blood flow where the ascending aorta is anastomosed to the right pulmonary artery.

Wharton's ducts. Salivary ducts below the mandible.

wick catheter. Device used to monitor interstitial fluid pressure, and sometimes used intraoperatively during fasciotomy procedures to evaluate the effectiveness of the decompression.

xenograft. Tissue that is nonhuman and harvested from one species and grafted to another. Pigskin is the most common xenograft for human skin and is applied to a wound as a temporary closure until a permanent option is performed.

z-plasty. Plastic surgery technique used primarily to release tension or elongate contractured scar tissue in which a Z-shaped incision is made with the middle line of the Z crossing the area of greatest tension. The triangular flaps are then rotated so that they cross the incision line in the opposite direction, creating a reversed Z.

ZPIC. Zone Program Integrity Contractor. CMS newly created entities currently being transitioned to eventually replace the existing Program Safeguard Contractors (PSC). These new contractors will be responsible for ensuring the integrity of all Medicare-related claims under Parts A and B (hospital, skilled nursing, home health, provider and durable medical equipment claims), Part C (Medicare Advantage health plans), Part D (prescription drug plans) and coordination of Medicare-Medicaid data matches (Medi-Medi).

APPENDIX I — LISTING OF SENSORY, MOTOR, AND MIXED NERVES

This summary assigns each sensory, motor, and mixed nerve with its appropriate nerve conduction study code in order to enhance accurate reporting of codes 95900, 95903, and 95904. Each nerve constitutes one unit of service.

Motor Nerves Assigned to Codes 95900 and 95903.

I. Upper extremity, cervical plexus, and brachial plexus motor nerves
   A. Axillary motor nerve to the deltoid
   B. Long thoracic motor nerve to the serratus anterior
   C. Median nerve
      1. Median motor nerve to the abductor pollicis brevis
      2. Median motor nerve, anterior interosseous branch, to the flexor pollicis longus
      3. Median motor nerve, anterior interosseous branch, to the pronator quadratus
      4. Median motor nerve to the first lumbrical
      5. Median motor nerve to the second lumbrical
   D. Musculocutaneous motor nerve to the biceps brachii
   E. Radial nerve
      1. Radial motor nerve to the extensor carpi ulnaris
      2. Radial motor nerve to the extensor digitorum communis
      3. Radial motor nerve to the extensor indicis proprius
      4. Radial motor nerve to the brachioradialis
   F. Suprascapular nerve
      1. Suprascapular motor nerve to the supraspinatus
      2. Suprascapular motor nerve to the infraspinatus
   G. Thoracodorsal motor nerve to the latissimus dorsi
   H. Ulnar nerve
      1. Ulnar motor nerve to the abductor digiti minimi
      2. Ulnar motor nerve to the palmar interosseous
      3. Ulnar motor nerve to the first dorsal interosseous
      4. Ulnar motor nerve to the flexor carpi ulnaris
   I. Other

II. Lower extremity motor nerves
   A. Femoral motor nerve to the quadriceps
      1. Femoral motor nerve to the vastus medialis
      2. Femoral motor nerve to vastus lateralis
      3. Femoral motor nerve to vastus intermedialis
      4. Femoral motor nerve to rectus femoris
   B. Ilioinguinal motor nerve
   C. Peroneal (fibular) nerve
      1. Peroneal motor nerve to the extensor digitorum brevis
      2. Peroneal motor nerve to the peroneus brevis
      3. Peroneal motor nerve to the peroneus longus
      4. Peroneal motor nerve to the tibialis anterior
   D. Plantar motor nerve
   E. Sciatic nerve
   F. Tibial nerve
      1. Tibial motor nerve, inferior calcaneal branch, to the abductor digiti minimi
      2. Tibial motor nerve, medial plantar branch, to the abductor hallucis
      3. Tibial motor nerve, lateral plantar branch, to the flexor digiti minimi brevis
   G. Other

III. Cranial nerves and trunk
   A. Cranial nerve VII (facial motor nerve)
      1. Facial nerve to the frontalis
      2. Facial nerve to the nasalis
      3. Facial nerve to the orbicularis oculi
      4. Facial nerve to the orbicularis oris
   B. Cranial nerve XI (spinal accessory motor nerve)
   C. Cranial nerve XII (hypoglossal motor nerve)
   D. Intercostal motor nerve
   E. Phrenic motor nerve to the diaphragm
   F. Recurrent laryngeal nerve
   G. Other

IV. Nerve Roots
   A. Cervical nerve root stimulation
      1. Cervical level 5 (C5)
      2. Cervical level 6 (C6)
      3. Cervical level 7 (C7)
      4. Cervical level 8 (C8)
   B. Thoracic nerve root stimulation
      1. Thoracic level 1 (T1)
      2. Thoracic level 2 (T2)
      3. Thoracic level 3 (T3)
      4. Thoracic level 4 (T4)
      5. Thoracic level 5 (T5)
      6. Thoracic level 6 (T6)
      7. Thoracic level 7 (T7)
      8. Thoracic level 8 (T8)
      9. Thoracic level 9 (T9)
      10. Thoracic level 10 (T10)
      11. Thoracic level 11 (T11)
      12. Thoracic level 12 (T12)
   C. Lumbar nerve root stimulation
      1. Lumbar level 1 (L1)
      2. Lumbar level 2 (L2)
      3. Lumbar level 3 (L3)
      4. Lumbar level 4 (L4)
      5. Lumbar level 5 (L5)
   D. Sacral nerve root stimulation
      1. Sacral level 1 (S1)
      2. Sacral level 2 (S2)
      3. Sacral level 3 (S3)
      4. Sacral level 4 (S4)

Sensory and Mixed Nerves Assigned to Code 95904

I. Upper extremity sensory and mixed nerves
   A. Lateral antebrachial cutaneous sensory nerve
   B. Medial antebrachial cutaneous sensory nerve
   C. Medial brachial cutaneous sensory nerve
   D. Median nerve
      1. Median sensory nerve to the first digit
      2. Median sensory nerve to the second digit
      3. Median sensory nerve to the third digit
      4. Median sensory nerve to the fourth digit

Appendix I — Listing of Sensory, Motor, and Mixed Nerves

      5. Median palmar cutaneous sensory nerve
      6. Median palmar mixed nerve
   E. Posterior antebrachial cutaneous sensory nerve
   F. Radial sensory nerve
      1. Radial sensory nerve to the base of the thumb
      2. Radial sensory nerve to digit 1
   G. Ulnar nerve
      1. Ulnar dorsal cutaneous sensory nerve
      2. Ulnar sensory nerve to the fourth digit
      3. Ulnar sensory nerve to the fifth digit
      4. Ulnar palmar mixed nerve
   H. Intercostal sensory nerve
   I. Other
II. Lower extremity sensory and mixed nerves
   A. Lateral femoral cutaneous sensory nerve
   B. Medical calcaneal sensory nerve
   C. Medial femoral cutaneous sensory nerve
   D. Peroneal nerve
      1. Deep peroneal sensory nerve
      2. Superficial peroneal sensory nerve, medial dorsal cutaneous branch
      3. Superficial peroneal sensory nerve, intermediate dorsal cutaneous branch
   E. Posterior femoral cutaneous sensory nerve
   F. Saphenous nerve
      1. Saphenous sensory nerve (distal technique)
      2. Saphenous sensory nerve (proximal technique)
   G. Sural nerve
      1. Sural sensory nerve, lateral dorsal cutaneous branch
      2. Sural sensory nerve
   H. Tibial sensory nerve (digital nerve to toe 1)
   I. Tibial sensory nerve (medial plantar nerve)
   J. Tibial sensory nerve (lateral plantar nerve)
   K. Other
III. Head and trunk sensory nerves
   A. Dorsal nerve of the penis
   B. Greater auricular nerve
   C. Ophthalmic branch of the trigeminal nerve
   D. Pudendal sensory nerve
   E. Suprascapular sensory nerves
   F. Other

The following table provides a reasonable maximum number of studies performed per diagnostic category necessary for a physician to arrive at a diagnosis in 90% of patients with that final diagnosis. The numbers in each column represent the number of studies recommended. The appropriate number of studies to be performed is based upon the physician's discretion.

Indication	Needle EMG (95860-95864, 95867-95870)	Motor NCS With and/or Without F wave	Sensory NCS	H-Reflex	Neuromuscular Junction Testing (Repetitive Stimulation)
Carpal Tunnel (Unilateral)	1	3	4	—	—
Carpal Tunnel (Bilateral)	2	4	6	—	—
Radiculopathy	2	3	2	2	—
Mononeuropathy	1	3	3	2	—
Polyneuropathy/Mononeuropathy Multiplex	3	4	4	2	—
Myopathy	2	2	2	—	2
Motor Neuronopathy (e.g., ALS)	4	4	2	—	2
Plexopathy	2	4	6	2	-
Neuromuscular Junction	2	2	2	—	3
Tarsal Tunnel Syndrome (Unilateral)	1	4	4	—	—
Tarsal Tunnel Syndrome (Bilateral)	2	5	6	—	—
Weakness, Fatigue, Cramps, or Twitching (Focal)	2	3	4	—	2
Weakness, Fatigue, Cramps, or Twitching (General)	4	4	4	—	2
Pain, Numbness, or Tingling (Unilateral)	1	3	4	2	—
Pain, Numbness, or Tingling (Bilateral)	2	4	6	2	—

Type of Study/Maximum Number of Studies — Nerve Conduction Studies (95900, 95903, 95904) — Other EMG Studies (95934, 95936, 95937)

APPENDIX J — VASCULAR FAMILIES

This table assumes that the starting point is catheterization of the aorta. This categorization would not be accurate, for instance, if a femoral or carotid artery were catheterized with the blood's flow. The names of the arteries that appear in bold face type in the following table indicate those arteries that are most often the subject of arteriographic procedures.

First Order	Second Order Branch	Third Order Branch	Beyond Third Order Branches
Innominate	Right Common Carotid	**Right Internal Carotid**	Right Ophthalmic Right Posterior Communicating Right Middle Cerebral Right Anterior Cerebral
		Right External Carotid	Right Superior Thyroid Right Ascending Pharyngeal Right Facial Right Lingual Right Occipital Right Posterior Auricular Right Superficial Temporal Right Internal Maxillary Right Middle Meningeal
	Right Subclavian and	**Right Vertebral** ———— Basilar	
		Right Internal Thoracic (Internal Mammary)	
		Right Thyrocervical Trunk	Right Inferior Thyroid Right Surascapular Right Transverse Cervical
		Right Costocervical Trunk	Right Highest Intercostal Right Deep Cervical
		Right Lateral Thoracic Right Thoracromial Right Humeral Circumflex (A/P)	
		Right Subcapular ———— Right Circumflex Scapular	
		Right Brachial	
		Right Deep Brachial	Right Ulnar Right Radial Right Interosseous Right Deep Palmar Arch Right Superficial Palmar Arch Right Metacarpals and Digitals
Left Common Carotid		**Left Internal Carotid**	Left Ophthalmic Left Posterior Communicating Left Middle Cerebral Left Anterior Cerebral
		Left External Carotid	Left Superior Thyroid Left Ascending Pharyngeal Left Facial Left Lingual Left Occipital Left Posterior Auricular Left Superficial Temporal
		Left Internal Maxillary ———— Left Middle Meningeal	

Appendix J — Vascular Families

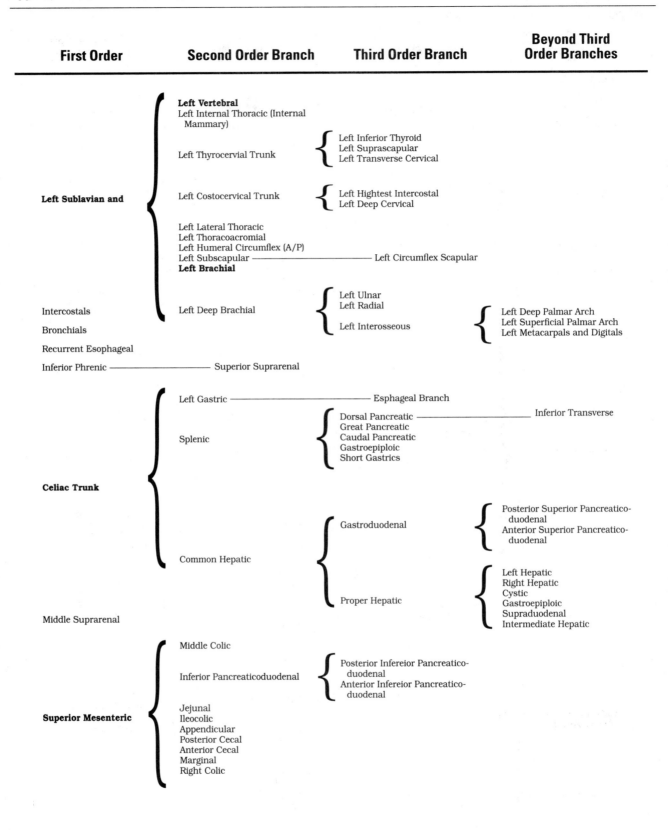

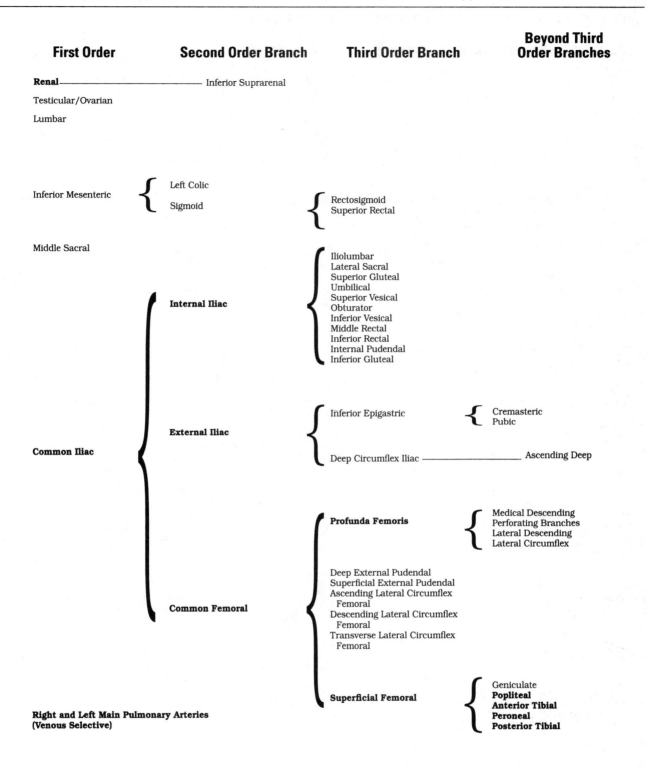

Reference: Kadir S. *Atlas of Normal and Variant Angiographic Anatomy*. Philadelphia, Pa: WB Saunders Co; 1991

APPENDIX K — PHYSICIAN QUALITY REPORTING INITIATIVE (PQRI)

Numerator	Associated Diagnostic Denominator	Associated Procedure Denominator	Associated Modifiers
3471F, 3472F, 3476F, 4192F, 4193F, 4195F, 4196F	714.0-714.2, 714.81	99201-99205, 99212-99215, 99241-99245, 99341-99350, 99455-99456	N/A
3570F	N/A	78300-78320	3P, 8P
4000F	N/A	99201-99205, 99212-99220, 99241-99245	8P
4001F, G8455, G8456, G8457	N/A	99201-99205, 99212-99220, 99241-99245	N/A
4005F	733.00-733.09, 733.12-733.14, 805.00-805.08, 805.2, 805.4, 805.6, 805.8, 813.40-813.42, 813.44-813.45, 813.50-813.52, 813.54, 820.00-820.09, 820.20-820.22, 820.8	99201-99205, 99212-99215, 99241-99245, 22305-22327, 22520-22521, 22523-22524, 25600-25609, 27230-27248	1P, 2P, 3P, 8P
4009F	402.01, 402.11, 402.91, 404.01, 404.03, 404.11, 404.13, 404.91, 404.93, 428.0-428.1, 428.20-428.23, 428.30-428.33, 428.9	99201-99205, 99212-99215, 99238-99245, 99304-99310, 99324-99337, 99341-99350	1P, 2P, 3P, 8P
4011F	410.00-410.02, 410.10-410.12, 410.20-410.22, 410.30-410.32, 410.40-410.42, 410.50-410.52, 410.60-410.62, 410.70-410.72, 410.80-410.82, 410.90-410.92, 411.0-411.1, 411.81-412, 413.0-413.9, 414.00-414.07, 414.8-414.9, V45.82	99201-99205, 99212-99215, 99238-99245, 99304-99310, 99324-99337, 99341-99350	1P, 2P, 3P, 8P
4015F	493.00-493.02, 493.10-493.12, 493.20-493.22, 493.81-493.82, 493.92	99201-99205, 99212-99215, 99241-99245	2P, 8P
4037F	585.6	99201-99205, 99212-99215, 99241-99245, 90935-90937, 90945-90947, 90957-90962, 90965-90966, 90969-90970	1P, 2P, 3P, 8P
4040F	N/A	99201-99205, 99212-99215, 99218-99220, 99241-99245, 99324-99337, 99341-99350, 99356-99357	1P, 8P
4041F	N/A	15734, 15738, 19260-19272, 19301-19307, 19361-19369, 21627, 21632, 21740, 21750, 21805, 21825, 22325, 22524, 22554, 22558, 22600, 22612, 22630, 22800-22804, 27125-27138, 27235-27236, 27244-27245, 27269, 27440-27447, 27702-27704, 27758-27759, 27766, 27769, 27792, 27814, 27870, 28192-28193, 28293, 28296, 28299-28300, 28306-28310, 28320-28322, 28415-28420, 28445, 28465, 28485, 28505, 28525, 28531, 28555, 28585, 28615, 28645, 28675-28760, 31760-31775, 31786, 31805, 32095-32150, 32215-32320, 32402, 32440-32501, 32800-32815, 32900-32940, 33020-33202, 33250-33251, 33256, 33261, 33300-33322, 33332-33411, 33413, 33416, 33422-33465, 33475, 33496, 33510-33572, 33877-33883, 33886, 33891, 34051, 34800-34805, 34825, 34830-34832, 34900, 35021, 35081, 35091, 35102, 35131, 35141, 35151, 35211-35216, 35241-35246, 35271-35276, 35301, 35311, 35481, 35526, 35601-35671, 36830, 37616, 38115, 38381, 38746, 39000-39220, 39545, 39561, 43045-43135, 43300-43313, 43320-43425, 43496, 43500-43520, 43605-43634, 43640-43641, 43653, 43800-43840, 43843-43870, 44005-44010, 44020-44021, 44050-44100, 44120, 44125-44127, 44130-44136, 47420-47480, 47560-47561, 47570, 47600-47620, 47700-47800, 47802-47900, 48020-48100, 48120-48155, 48500-48550, 48554-48556, 49215, 49568, 50300-50320, 50340-50380, 60521-60522, 61154, 61312-61313, 61315, 61510-61512, 61518, 61548, 61697, 61700, 61750-61751, 61867, 62223, 62230, 63015, 63020-63030, 63042, 63045, 63047, 63056, 63075, 63081, 63267, 63276, 64746	1P, 8P

Numerator	Associated Diagnostic Denominator	Associated Procedure Denominator	Associated Modifiers
4042F, 4046F	N/A	15734, 15738, 19260-19272, 19301-19307, 19361-19369, 21346-21348, 21422-21423, 21432-21436, 21454-21470, 21627, 21632, 21740, 21750, 21805, 21825, 22325, 22524, 22554, 22558, 22600, 22612, 22630, 22800-22804, 27125-27138, 27235-27236, 27244-27245, 27269, 27440-27447, 27702-27704, 27758-27759, 27766, 27769, 27792, 27814, 27870, 28192-28193, 28293, 28296, 28299-28300, 28306-28310, 28320-28322, 28415-28420, 28445, 28465, 28485, 28505, 28525, 28531, 28555, 28585, 28615, 28645, 28675-28760, 31360-31395, 31760-31775, 31786, 31805, 32095-32150, 32215-32320, 32402, 32440-32501, 32800-32815, 32900-32940, 33020-33208, 33212-33256, 33261, 33300-33322, 33332-33411, 33413, 33416, 33422-33465, 33475, 33496, 33510-33572, 33877-33883, 33886, 33891, 34051, 34800-34805, 34825, 34830-34832, 34900, 35021, 35081, 35091, 35102, 35131, 35141, 35151, 35211-35216, 35241-35246, 35271-35276, 35301, 35311, 35481, 35526, 35601-35671, 36830, 37616, 38381, 38746, 39000-39220, 39545, 39561, 41130-41155, 43045-43135, 43300-43313, 43320-43425, 43496, 43500-43520, 43605-43634, 43640-43641, 43653, 43800-43840, 43843-43880, 44005-44010, 44020-44120, 44125-44127, 44130-44136, 44140-44160, 44202, 44204-44212, 44300-44346, 44615-44661, 44700, 44950, 45108-45190, 45500-45825, 47420-47480, 47560-47561, 47570, 47600-47620, 47700-47800, 47802-47900, 48020-48100, 48120-48155, 48500-48550, 48554-48556, 49215, 49568, 50300-50320, 50340-50380, 51597, 58150-58210, 58260-58294, 60521-60522, 61154, 61312-61313, 61315, 61510-61512, 61518, 61520, 61526-61530, 61548, 61591, 61595-61596, 61598, 61606, 61616-61619, 61697, 61700, 61750-61751, 61867, 62223, 62230, 63015, 63020-63030, 63042, 63045, 63047, 63056, 63075, 63081, 63267, 63276, 64746, 69720, 69930, 69955-69970	N/A
4043F	N/A	33120-33141, 33250-33251, 33256, 33261, 33305, 33315, 33332-33411, 33413, 33416, 33422-33465, 33475, 33496, 33510-33572	1P, 8P
4044F	N/A	19260-19272, 19301-19330, 19342-19380, 22558, 22600, 22612, 22630, 27125-27138, 27235-27236, 27244-27245, 27269, 27440-27447, 38100-38101, 38115-38120, 38571-38572, 38700-38745, 38747-38780, 39501-39561, 43020-43135, 43279-43280, 43300-43425, 43496, 43500-43520, 43605-43634, 43640-43645, 43651-43653, 43770-43830, 43832-43840, 43843-43880, 43886-43888, 44005-44010, 44020-44055, 44110-44120, 44125-44127, 44130, 44140-44202, 44204-44212, 44227, 44300-44346, 44602-44700, 44800-44850, 44900, 44950, 44960-44970, 45000, 45020-45190, 45395-45402, 45500-45505, 45550-45825, 46715-46762, 47010, 47100-47130, 47135-47142, 47300-47371, 47380-47382, 47400-47480, 47500-47505, 47560-47570, 47600-47900, 48000-48100, 48105-48155, 48500-48510, 48520-48548, 48554-48556, 49000-49020, 49040, 49060, 49203-49323, 49560-49566, 49570, 50020, 50220-50240, 50320, 50340-50380, 50543, 50545-50548, 50715-50728, 50760-50820, 50947-50948, 51550-51597, 51800-51820, 51900-51925, 51960, 55810-55845, 55866, 56630-56640, 58200-58240, 58285, 58951, 58953-58956, 60200-60281, 60500-60505, 60520-60650, 61313, 61510-61512, 61518, 61548, 61697, 61700, 62230, 63015, 63020, 63047, 63056, 63081, 63267, 63276	1P, 8P

Appendix K — Physician Quality Reporting Initiative (PQRI)

Numerator	Associated Diagnostic Denominator	Associated Procedure Denominator	Associated Modifiers
4047F, 4048F	N/A	00100-00103, 00120, 00140, 00145-00147, 00160-00322, 00350-00406, 00450-00500, 00528-00634, 00670-00700, 00730, 00750-00802, 00820-00832, 00840, 00844-00870, 00880-00944, 01120, 01140-01150, 01170-01190, 01202-01215, 01230-01320, 01360, 01382, 01392-01404, 01430-01444, 01464-01486, 01500-01610, 01622-01670, 01710-01716, 01732-01810, 01829-01852, 01924-01926, 01951-01953, 01961-01966, 01968-01969, 15734, 15738, 19260-19272, 19301-19307, 19361-19369, 21346-21348, 21422-21423, 21432-21436, 21454-21470, 21627, 21632, 21740, 21750, 21805, 21825, 22325, 22524, 22554, 22558, 22600, 22612, 22630, 22800-22804, 27125-27138, 27235-27236, 27244-27245, 27269, 27440-27447, 27702-27704, 27758-27759, 27766, 27769, 27792, 27814, 27870, 28192-28193, 28293, 28296, 28299-28300, 28306-28310, 28320-28322, 28415-28420, 28445, 28465, 28485, 28505, 28525, 28531, 28555, 28585, 28615, 28645, 28675-28760, 31360-31395, 31760-31775, 31786, 31805, 32095-32150, 32215-32320, 32402, 32440-32501, 32800-32815, 32900-32940, 33020-33208, 33212-33256, 33261, 33300-33322, 33332-33411, 33413, 33416, 33422-33465, 33475, 33496, 33510-33572, 33877-33883, 33886, 33891, 34051, 34800-34805, 34825, 34830-34832, 34900, 35021, 35081, 35091, 35102, 35131, 35141, 35151, 35211-35216, 35241-35246, 35271-35276, 35301, 35311, 35481, 35526, 35601-35671, 36830, 37616, 38115, 38381, 38746, 39000-39220, 39545, 39561, 41130-41155, 43045-43135, 43300-43313, 43320-43425, 43496, 43500-43520, 43605-43634, 43640-43641, 43653, 43800-43840, 43843-43880, 44005-44010, 44020-44120, 44125-44127, 44130-44136, 44140-44160, 44202, 44204-44212, 44300-44346, 44602-44661, 44700, 44950, 45108-45190, 45500-45825, 47133-47142, 47420-47480, 47560-47561, 47570, 47600-47620, 47700-47800, 47802-47900, 48020-48100, 48120-48155, 48500-48550, 48554-48556, 49215, 49568, 50300-50320, 50340-50380, 51550-51597, 51920-51925, 52450, 52601, 52630, 52647-52649, 54401-54410, 54415-54416, 55801-55845, 58150-58210, 58260-58294, 60521-60522, 61154, 61312-61313, 61315, 61510-61512, 61518, 61520, 61526-61530, 61548, 61591, 61595-61596, 61598, 61606, 61616-61619, 61697, 61700, 61750-61751, 61867, 62223, 62230, 63015, 63020-63030, 63042, 63045, 63047, 63056, 63075, 63081, 63267, 63276, 64746, 69720, 69930, 69955-69970	1P, 8P
4049F	N/A	15734, 15738, 19260-19272, 19301-19307, 19361-19369, 21346-21348, 21422-21423, 21432-21436, 21454-21470, 21627, 21632, 21740, 21750, 21805, 21825, 22325, 22524, 22554, 22558, 22600, 22612, 22630, 22800-22804, 27125-27138, 27235-27236, 27244-27245, 27269, 27440-27447, 27702-27704, 27758-27759, 27766, 27769, 27792, 27814, 27870, 28192-28193, 28293, 28296, 28299-28300, 28306-28310, 28320-28322, 28415-28420, 28445, 28465, 28485, 28505, 28525, 28531, 28555, 28585, 28615, 28645, 28675-28760, 31360-31395, 31760-31775, 31786, 31805, 32095-32150, 32215-32320, 32402, 32440-32501, 32800-32815, 32900-32940, 33020-33050, 33202-33208, 33212-33249, 33254-33255, 33300, 33310, 33320-33322, 33877-33883, 33886, 33891, 34051, 34800-34805, 34825, 34830-34832, 34900, 35021, 35081, 35091, 35102, 35131, 35141, 35151, 35211-35216, 35241-35246, 35271-35276, 35301, 35311, 35481, 35526, 35601-35671, 36830, 37616, 38381, 38746, 39000-39220, 39545, 39561, 41130-41155, 43045-43135, 43300-43313, 43320-43425, 43496, 43500-43520, 43605-43634, 43640-43641, 43653, 43800-43840, 43843-43880, 44005-44010, 44020-44120, 44125-44127, 44130-44136, 44140-44160, 44202, 44204-44212, 44300-44346, 44615-44661, 44700, 44950, 45108-45190, 45500-45825, 47420-47480, 47560-47561, 47570, 47600-47620, 47700-47800, 47802-47900, 48020-48100, 48120-48155, 48500-48550, 48554-48556, 49215, 49568, 50300-50320, 50340-50380, 51597, 58150-58210, 58260-58294, 60521-60522, 61154, 61312-61313, 61315, 61510-61512, 61518, 61520, 61526-61530, 61548, 61591, 61595-61596, 61598, 61606, 61616-61619, 61697, 61700, 61750-61751, 61867, 62223, 62230, 63015, 63020-63030, 63042, 63045, 63047, 63056, 63075, 63081, 63267, 63276, 64746, 69720, 69930, 69955-69970	1P, 8P
4070F	431, 433.01, 433.11, 433.21, 433.31, 433.81, 433.91, 434.01, 434.11, 434.91	99221-99223, 99251-99255, 99291	1P, 2P, 8P
4073F	433.01, 433.11, 433.21, 433.31, 433.81, 433.91, 434.01, 434.11, 434.91, 435.9	99238-99239, 99251-99255	1P, 2P, 8P
4077F	433.01, 433.11, 433.21, 433.31, 433.81, 433.91, 434.01, 434.11, 434.91	99221-99223, 99251-99255, 99291	8P

Numerator	Associated Diagnostic Denominator	Associated Procedure Denominator	Associated Modifiers
4079F	431, 433.01, 433.11, 433.21, 433.31, 433.81, 433.91, 434.01, 434.11, 434.91	99238-99239, 99251-99255	8P
4084F	410.01, 410.11, 410.21, 410.31, 410.41, 410.51, 410.61, 410.71, 410.81, 410.91	99281-99285, 99291	1P, 2P, 8P
4090F, 4095F	238.75	99201-99205, 99212-99215, 99241-99245	N/A
4100F	203.00, 203.02	99201-99205, 99212-99215, 99241-99245	1P, 2P, 8P
4110F, 4115F	N/A	33510-33523, 33533-33536	1P, 8P
4120F	034.0, 460, 462-463, 465.0-465.9, 466.0	99201-99205, 99212-99220, 99241-99245	1P
4124F	034.0, 460, 462-463, 465.0-465.9, 466.0	99201-99205, 99212-99220, 99241-99245	N/A
4130F	380.10-380.13, 380.22	99201-99205, 99212-99215, 99241-99245	1P, 2P, 8P
4131F	380.10-380.13, 380.22	99201-99205, 99212-99215, 99241-99245	1P
4132F	380.10-380.13, 380.22	99201-99205, 99212-99215, 99241-99245	N/A
4148F, 4149F	070.51, 070.54, 070.70	99201-99205, 99212-99215	1P, 2P, 8P
4150F, 4151F, G8458, G8459, G8460, G8461, G8462, G8463	070.54	99201-99205, 99212-99215, 99241-99245	N/A
4153F	070.54	99201-99205, 99212-99215, 99241-99245	1P, 2P, 3P, 8P
4158F	070.51, 070.54, 070.70	99201-99205, 99212-99215, 99241-99245	8P
4164F	185	77407-77416, 77418, 77427	1P, 2P, 8P
4165F	185	77401-77416, 77418, 77427	8P
4177F	362.52	99201-99205, 99212-99215, 99241-99245, 99307-99310, 99324-99337, 92002-92014	3P, 8P
4179F	174.9	99201-99205, 99212-99215	1P, 2P, 3P, 8P
4180F	153.9	99201-99205, 99212-99215	1P, 2P, 3P, 8P
4200F, 4201F	185	77401-77416, 77418, 77427	N/A
4267F	459.31, 459.33, 459.81, 707.19	99201-99205, 99212-99215, 99241-99245	1P, 2P, 3P, 8P
4274F	585.6	90951-90959, 90963-90965	1P, 2P, 3P, 8P
5010F	362.06	99201-99205, 99212-99215, 99241-99245, 99304-99310, 99324-99337, 92002-92014	2P, 3P, 8P
5015F	733.12-733.14, 805.00-805.08, 805.2, 805.4, 805.6, 805.8, 813.40-813.42, 813.44-813.45, 813.50-813.52, 813.54, 820.00-820.09, 820.20-820.22, 820.8	99201-99205, 99212-99215, 99241-99245, 22305-22327, 22520-22521, 22523-22524, 25600-25609, 27230-27248	1P, 2P, 8P
5050F	172.9	99201-99205, 99212-99215, 99241-99245	2P, 3P, 8P
6010F	431, 433.01, 433.11, 433.21, 433.31, 433.81, 433.91, 434.01, 434.11, 434.91	99221-99223, 99251-99255	1P, 8P
6015F, 6020F	431, 433.01, 433.11, 433.21, 433.31, 433.81, 433.91, 434.01, 434.11, 434.91	99221-99223, 99251-99255	N/A
6030F	N/A	36555-36571, 36578-36585, 93503	1P, 8P
6045F	N/A	0062T, 0075T, 0080T, 24516, 25606, 25651, 26608, 26650, 26676, 26706, 26727, 27235, 27244-27245, 27506, 27509, 27756, 27759, 28406, 28436, 28456, 28476, 36597-36598, 37182-37184, 37187-37188, 37210, 43260-43272, 43752, 44500, 49440-49465, 50382-50389, 50590, 61623, 62263-62264, 62280-62282, 62318-62319, 63610, 64510, 64520-64530, 64561, 64605-64610, 64620-64622, 64626, 64680-64681, 70010-70015, 70170, 70332, 70370-70373, 70390, 71023, 71034, 71040-71090, 72240-72291, 72295, 73040, 73085, 73115, 73525, 73542, 73580, 73615, 74190-74300, 74305-74485, 74740-74742, 75600-75630, 75650-75756, 75790-75940, 75952-75962, 75966, 75970-75984, 75992, 75994-75995, 76000-76001, 76080, 76100-76120, 76150, 76496, 77001-77003, 77031, 77053-77054, 77071, 92611, 93555-93556, G0106, G0120, G0259-G0260, G0275-G0278, G0365	8P

Appendix K — Physician Quality Reporting Initiative (PQRI)

Numerator	Associated Diagnostic Denominator	Associated Procedure Denominator	Associated Modifiers
99201, 99202, 99203, 99204, 99205, 99212, 99213, 99214, 99215	034.0, 042, 070.51, 070.54, 070.70, 079.53, 140.0-140.9, 141.0-141.9, 142.0-142.9, 143.0-143.9, 144.0-144.9, 145.0-145.9, 146.0-146.9, 147.0-147.9, 148.0-148.9, 149.0-149.9, 150.0-150.9, 151.0-151.9, 152.0-152.9, 153.0-153.9, 154.0-154.8, 155.0-155.2, 156.0-156.9, 157.0-157.9, 158.0-158.9, 159.0-159.9, 160.0-160.9, 161.0-161.9, 162.0-162.9, 163.0-163.9, 164.0-164.9, 165.0-165.9, 170.0-170.9, 171.0-171.9, 172.0-172.9, 173.0-173.9, 174.0-174.9, 175.0-175.9, 176.0-179, 180.0-181, 182.0-182.8, 183.0-183.9, 184.0-185, 186.0-186.9, 187.1-187.9, 188.0-188.9, 189.0-189.9, 190.0-190.9, 191.0-191.9, 192.0-193, 194.0-194.9, 195.0-195.8, 196.0-196.9, 197.0-197.8, 198.0-198.7, 198.81-198.89, 199.0-199.2, 200.00-200.08, 200.10-200.18, 200.20-200.28, 200.30-200.38, 200.40-200.48, 200.50-200.58, 200.60-200.68, 200.70-200.78, 200.80-200.88, 201.00-201.08, 201.10-201.18, 201.20-201.28, 201.40-201.48, 201.50-201.58, 201.60-201.68, 201.70-201.78, 201.90-201.98, 202.00-202.08, 202.10-202.18, 202.20-202.28, 202.30-202.38, 202.40-202.48, 202.50-202.58, 202.60-202.68, 202.70-202.78, 202.80-202.88, 202.90-202.98, 203.00-203.02, 203.10-203.12, 203.80-203.82, 204.00-204.02, 204.10-204.12, 204.20-204.22, 204.80-204.82, 204.90-204.92, 205.00-205.02, 205.10-205.12, 205.20-205.22, 205.30-205.32, 205.80-205.82, 205.90-205.92, 206.00-206.02, 206.10-206.12, 206.20-206.22, 206.80-206.82, 206.90-206.92, 207.00-207.02, 207.10-207.12, 207.20-207.22, 207.80-207.82, 208.00-208.02, 208.10-208.12, 208.20-208.22, 208.80-208.82, 208.90-208.92, 209.00-209.03, 209.10-209.17, 209.20-209.29, 209.30, 235.0-235.9, 236.0-236.7, 236.90-236.99, 237.0-237.6, 237.70-237.9, 238.0-238.6, 238.71-238.77, 238.8-238.9, 239.0-239.8, 239.9, 250.00-250.03, 250.10-250.13, 250.20-250.23, 250.30-250.33, 250.40-250.43, 250.50-250.53, 250.60-250.63, 250.70-250.73, 250.80-250.83, 250.90-250.93, 296.20-296.25, 296.30-296.35, 298.0, 300.4, 307.6, 309.0-309.1, 311, 357.2, 362.01-362.07, 362.50-362.52, 365.01, 365.10-365.12, 365.15, 366.41, 380.10-380.13, 380.22, 381.10-381.19, 381.20-381.4, 402.01, 402.11, 402.91, 404.01, 404.03, 404.11, 404.13, 404.91, 404.93, 410.00-410.02, 410.10-410.12, 410.20-410.22, 410.30-410.32, 410.40-410.42, 410.50-410.52, 410.60-410.62, 410.70-410.72, 410.80-410.82, 410.90-410.92, 411.0-411.1, 411.81-412, 413.0-413.9, 414.00-414.07, 414.8-414.9, 428.0-428.1, 428.20-428.23, 428.30-428.33, 428.40-428.9, 459.31, 459.33, 459.81, 460, 462-463, 465.0-465.9, 466.0, 481, 482.0-482.2, 482.30-482.39, 482.40-482.49, 482.81-482.9, 483.0-483.8, 485-486, 487.0, 491.0-491.1, 491.20-491.9, 492.0-492.8, 493.00-493.02, 493.10-493.12, 493.20-493.22, 493.81-493.82, 493.90-493.92, 496, 585.4-585.5, 625.6, 648.00-648.04, 707.12-707.19, 714.0-714.2, 714.81, 715.00-715.09, 715.10-715.18, 715.20-715.28, 715.30-715.38, 715.80-715.89, 715.90-715.98, 721.3, 721.41-721.42, 721.90, 722.0, 722.10-722.2, 722.30-722.4, 722.51-722.6, 722.70-722.73, 722.80-722.83, 722.90-722.93, 723.0, 724.00-724.09, 724.2-724.6, 724.70-724.79, 733.00-733.09, 733.12-733.14, 738.4-738.5, 739.3-739.4, 756.12, 788.30-788.31, 788.33-788.39, 805.00-805.08, 805.2, 805.4, 805.6, 805.8, 813.40-813.42, 813.44-813.45, 813.50-813.52, 813.54, 820.00-820.09, 820.20-820.22, 820.8, 846.0-846.9, 847.2, V08, V10.82, V22.0-V22.2, V23.0-V23.3, V23.41-V23.7, V23.81-V23.84, V23.89-V23.9, V45.82	99201-99285, 99291, 99304-99316, 99324-99337, 99341-99350, 99356-99357, 99455-99456, 00100-01999, 11040-11057, 11719-11730, 11740, 22210, 22214, 22220-22327, 22520-22521, 22523-22524, 22532-22600, 22612-22632, 22818-22849, 25600-25609, 27230-27248, 51720, 63001-63048, 63055-63200, 77427-77470, 90801-90815, 90821-90824, 90829-90845, 90849-90862, 92002-92014, 92541-92545, 92547-92548, 92552-92555, 92557, 92561-92582, 92584-92588, 92601-92604, 92620-92627, 92640, 95920, 96116, 96150-96152, 96401-96549, 97001-97004, 97750, 97802-97804, 98940-98942, 98960-98962, 99078, 99510, D7140-D7210, G0101, G0108-G0109, G0271	N/A

Appendix K — Physician Quality Reporting Initiative (PQRI)

Numerator	Associated Diagnostic Denominator	Associated Procedure Denominator	Associated Modifiers
99324, 99325, 99326, 99327, 99328, 99334, 99335, 99336, 99337	250.00-250.03, 250.10-250.13, 250.20-250.23, 250.30-250.33, 250.40-250.43, 250.50-250.53, 250.60-250.63, 250.70-250.73, 250.80-250.83, 250.90-250.93, 307.6, 357.2, 362.01-362.07, 362.50-362.52, 365.01, 365.10-365.12, 365.15, 366.41, 402.01, 402.11, 402.91, 404.01, 404.03, 404.11, 404.13, 404.91, 404.93, 410.00-410.02, 410.10-410.12, 410.20-410.22, 410.30-410.32, 410.40-410.42, 410.50-410.52, 410.60-410.62, 410.70-410.72, 410.80-410.82, 410.90-410.92, 411.0-411.1, 411.81-412, 413.0-413.9, 414.00-414.07, 414.8-414.9, 428.0-428.1, 428.20-428.23, 428.30-428.33, 428.40-428.9, 481, 482.0-482.2, 482.30-482.39, 482.40-482.49, 482.81-482.9, 483.0-483.8, 485-486, 487.0, 625.6, 648.00-648.04, 788.30-788.31, 788.33-788.39, V45.82	99201-99215, 99218-99285, 99291, 99304-99316, 99324-99337, 99341-99350, 99356-99357, 00100-01999, 11040-11057, 11719-11730, 11740, 90801-90809, 92002-92014, 97001-97004, 97802-97804, 98960, D7140-D7210, G0101, G0108, G0271	N/A
99341, 99342, 99343, 99344, 99345, 99347, 99348, 99349, 99350	250.00-250.03, 250.10-250.13, 250.20-250.23, 250.30-250.33, 250.40-250.43, 250.50-250.53, 250.60-250.63, 250.70-250.73, 250.80-250.83, 250.90-250.93, 296.20-296.25, 296.30-296.35, 298.0, 300.4, 307.6, 309.0-309.1, 311, 357.2, 362.01-362.07, 366.41, 402.01, 402.11, 402.91, 404.01, 404.03, 404.11, 404.13, 404.91, 404.93, 410.00-410.02, 410.10-410.12, 410.20-410.22, 410.30-410.32, 410.40-410.42, 410.50-410.52, 410.60-410.62, 410.70-410.72, 410.80-410.82, 410.90-410.92, 411.0-411.1, 411.81-412, 413.0-413.9, 414.00-414.07, 414.8-414.9, 428.0-428.1, 428.20-428.23, 428.30-428.33, 428.40-428.9, 481, 482.0-482.2, 482.30-482.39, 482.40-482.49, 482.81-482.9, 483.0-483.8, 485-486, 487.0, 625.6, 648.00-648.04, 714.0-714.2, 714.81, 788.30-788.31, 788.33-788.39, V45.82	99201-99215, 99218-99285, 99291, 99304-99316, 99324-99337, 99341-99350, 99356-99357, 99455-99456, 00100-01999, 11040-11057, 11719-11730, 11740, 90801-90815, 90821-90824, 90829-90845, 90849-90862, 92002-92014, 97001-97004, 97802-97804, 98960, 99078, 99510, D7140-D7210, G0101, G0108, G0271	N/A
G8126, G8127, G8128	296.20-296.25, 296.30-296.35, 298.0, 300.4, 309.0-309.1, 311	99201-99205, 99212-99215, 99241-99245, 99341-99350, 90801-90815, 90821-90824, 90829-90845, 90849-90862, 99078, 99510	N/A
G8395, G8396, G8450, G8451, G8452	402.01, 402.11, 402.91, 404.01, 404.03, 404.11, 404.13, 404.91, 404.93, 428.0-428.1, 428.20-428.23, 428.30-428.33, 428.9	99201-99205, 99212-99215, 99241-99245, 99304-99310, 99324-99337, 99341-99350	N/A
G8397, G8398	362.06	99201-99205, 99212-99215, 99241-99245, 99304-99310, 99324-99337, 92002-92014	N/A
G8399, G8400, G8401	N/A	99201-99205, 99212-99215	N/A
G8404, G8405, G8406, G8410, G8415, G8416	250.00-250.03, 250.10-250.13, 250.20-250.23, 250.30-250.33, 250.40-250.43, 250.50-250.53, 250.60-250.63, 250.70-250.73, 250.80-250.83, 250.93	99201-99205, 99212-99215, 99241-99255, 99304-99310, 99324-99337, 99341-99350, 11040-11057, 11719-11730, 11740, 97001-97002, 97802-97803	N/A
G8417, G8418, G8419, G8420, G8421, G8422	N/A	99201-99215, 99241-99245, 99324-99337, 99341-99350, 00100-01999, 90801-90809, 97001, 97003, 97802-97803, 98960, D7140-D7210, G0101, G0108, G0270	N/A
G8427, G8428, G8429, G8430, G8507	N/A	99201-99215, 99241-99245, 00100-01999, 90801-90802, 92002-92014, 92541-92545, 92547-92548, 92557, 92567-92569, 92585, 92588, 92626, 96116, 96150, 96152, 97001-97004, 97802-97803, 98960, G0101, G0108, G0270	N/A
G8431, G8432, G8433, G8510, G8511	N/A	90801-90809, 92557, 92567-92568, 92625, 97003	N/A
G8440, G8441, G8442, G8508, G8509	N/A	90801-90802, 96116, 96150, 97001, 97003, 98940-98942	N/A
G8447, G8448	N/A	99201-99215, 99241-99245, 90801-90809, 92002-92014, 92541-92544, 92548, 92552-92555, 92557, 92561-92582, 92584-92588, 92601-92604, 92620-92627, 92640, 95920, 96150-96152, 97001-97004, 97750, 97802-97804, 98940-98942, D7140-D7210, G0101, G0108-G0109, G0271	N/A
G8464, G8465	185	77407-77416, 77418, 77427	N/A

Appendix K — Physician Quality Reporting Initiative (PQRI)

Numerator	Associated Diagnostic Denominator	Associated Procedure Denominator	Associated Modifiers
G8468, G8469, G8470, G8471, G8472, G8473, G8474, G8475	250.00-250.03, 250.10-250.13, 250.20-250.23, 250.30-250.33, 250.40-250.43, 250.50-250.53, 250.60-250.63, 250.70-250.73, 250.80-250.83, 250.90-250.93, 410.00-410.02, 410.10-410.12, 410.20-410.22, 410.30-410.32, 410.40-410.42, 410.50-410.52, 410.60-410.62, 410.70-410.72, 410.80-410.82, 410.90-410.92, 411.0-411.1, 411.81-412, 413.0-413.9, 414.00-414.07, 414.8-414.9, 648.00-648.04, V45.82	99201-99205, 99212-99215, 99241-99245, 99304-99310, 99324-99337, 99341-99350	N/A
G8482, G8483, G8484	N/A	99201-99205, 99212-99215, 99304-99316, 99324-99337, 99341-99350	N/A
G8518, G8519, G8520	150.3-150.5, 162.5	32440-32488, 32500, 32503-32504, 32657, 32663, 43107-43113, 43117-43123	N/A
G8524, G8525, G8526	N/A	35301	N/A
G8530, G8531, G8532	585.4-585.6, 996.73	36818-36821, 36825-36830	N/A
G8534, G8535, G8536, G8537, G8538	N/A	90801-90802, 96116, 96150, 97003, 97802-97803, G0270	N/A
G8539, G8540, G8541, G8542, G8543	N/A	98940-98942	N/A

APPENDIX L — MEDICALLY UNLIKELY EDITS (MUES)

The Centers for Medicare & Medicaid Services (CMS) began to publish many of the edits used in the medically unlikely edits (MUE) program for the first time effective October 2008. What follows below is a list of the published CPT codes that have MUEs assigned to them and the number of units allowed with each code. CMS publishes the updates on a quarterly basis. Not all MUEs will be published, however. MUEs intended to detect and discourage any questionable payments will not be published as the agency feels the efficacy of these edits would be compromised.

The quarterly updates will be published on the CMS website at http://www.cms.hhs.gov/NationalCorrectCodInitEd/08_MUE.asp#TopOfPage.

Professional

CPT	MUE	CPT	MUE	CPT	MUE	CPT	MUE	CPT	MUE	CPT	MUE	CPT	MUE	CPT	MUE
0016T	2	0151T	1	11720	1	13121	1	15783	2	16035	1	20150	2	21044	1
0017T	2	0159T	2	11721	1	13131	1	15786	1	17000	1	20200	3	21045	1
0019T	1	0160T	1	11730	1	13132	1	15787	3	17003	13	20205	4	21046	2
0030T	2	0161T	1	11770	1	13150	1	15788	1	17004	1	20206	3	21047	2
0042T	1	0163T	2	11771	1	13151	1	15789	1	17106	1	20250	3	21048	2
0048T	1	0164T	4	11772	1	13152	1	15792	1	17107	1	20251	3	21049	2
0050T	1	0165T	4	11900	1	13160	3	15793	1	17108	1	20526	2	21050	1
0051T	1	0169T	1	11901	1	14300	3	15819	1	17110	1	20552	1	21060	1
0052T	1	0170T	1	11920	1	15002	1	15820	1	17111	1	20553	1	21070	1
0053T	1	0171T	1	11921	1	15004	1	15821	1	17264	3	20555	1	21073	1
0054T	2	0172T	3	11922	1	15040	1	15822	1	17266	2	20660	1	21076	1
0055T	2	0173T	1	11950	1	15050	1	15823	1	17276	3	20661	1	21077	2
0064T	1	0174T	1	11951	1	15100	1	15824	1	17286	3	20662	1	21079	1
0067T	1	0175T	1	11952	1	15110	1	15825	1	17340	1	20663	2	21080	1
0068T	1	0176T	1	11954	1	15115	1	15826	1	17360	1	20664	1	21081	1
0069T	1	0177T	1	11960	3	15120	1	15828	1	17380	1	20665	1	21082	1
0070T	1	0179T	1	11970	2	15130	1	15829	1	19000	2	20670	2	21083	1
0071T	1	0180T	1	11971	2	15135	1	15830	1	19001	5	20680	2	21084	1
0072T	1	0181T	1	11976	1	15150	1	15832	2	19020	2	20692	3	21085	1
0073T	2	0182T	3	11980	1	15151	1	15833	2	19030	2	20693	2	21086	2
0075T	1	0183T	1	11981	1	15155	1	15834	2	19101	3	20696	3	21087	1
0076T	2	0184T	1	11982	1	15156	1	15835	1	19110	2	20697	3	21088	1
0077T	2	0187T	2	11983	1	15170	1	15836	2	19112	2	20802	2	21100	1
0078T	1	0190T	2	12001	1	15175	1	15838	1	19120	2	20805	2	21110	2
0079T	4	0191T	2	12002	1	15200	1	15839	2	19125	2	20808	2	21116	2
0080T	1	0192T	2	12004	1	15220	1	15840	1	19126	3	20824	2	21120	1
0081T	4	0193T	1	12005	1	15240	1	15841	2	19260	2	20827	2	21121	1
0084T	1	0194T	1	12006	1	15260	1	15842	2	19271	2	20838	2	21122	1
0085T	1	0195T	1	12007	1	15300	1	15845	2	19272	2	20900	2	21123	1
0086T	1	0197T	2	12011	1	15320	1	15847	1	19290	3	20910	2	21125	2
0087T	1	0198T	2	12013	1	15330	1	15851	1	19296	2	20912	1	21127	2
0092T	1	01996	1	12014	1	15335	1	15852	2	19297	2	20920	2	21137	1
0095T	1	10040	1	12015	1	15340	1	15860	1	19298	2	20922	2	21138	1
0098T	1	10060	1	12016	1	15360	1	15876	1	19300	2	20924	4	21139	1
0099T	2	10061	1	12017	1	15365	1	15877	1	19301	2	20926	2	21141	1
0100T	2	10080	1	12018	1	15400	1	15878	2	19302	2	20937	3	21142	1
0101T	1	10081	1	12020	3	15420	1	15879	2	19303	2	20938	3	21143	1
0102T	2	10180	3	12021	3	15430	1	15920	1	19304	2	20955	1	21145	1
0103T	1	11000	1	12031	1	15570	3	15922	1	19305	2	20956	1	21146	1
0104T	1	11004	1	12032	1	15572	2	15931	1	19306	2	20957	1	21147	1
0105T	1	11005	1	12034	1	15574	2	15933	1	19307	2	20962	1	21150	1
0106T	4	11006	1	12035	1	15576	2	15934	1	19316	1	20969	2	21151	1
0107T	4	11008	1	12036	1	15600	2	15935	1	19318	1	20970	2	21154	1
0108T	4	11010	1	12037	1	15610	2	15936	1	19324	1	20972	2	21155	1
0109T	1	11011	1	12041	1	15620	2	15937	1	19325	2	20973	2	21159	1
0110T	4	11012	1	12042	1	15630	2	15940	2	19328	1	20974	1	21160	1
0111T	1	11055	1	12044	1	15650	1	15941	2	19330	1	20975	1	21172	1
0123T	2	11056	1	12045	1	15731	1	15944	2	19340	1	20979	1	21175	1
0124T	2	11057	1	12046	1	15740	3	15945	2	19342	1	20982	1	21179	1
0126T	1	11100	1	12047	1	15750	1	15946	2	19350	1	20985	1	21180	1
0130T	1	11200	1	12051	1	15756	1	15950	2	19355	1	21010	1	21181	1
0140T	1	11201	1	12052	1	15757	3	15951	2	19357	1	21015	1	21182	2
0144T	1	11446	3	12053	1	15758	3	15952	2	19366	1	21025	2	21183	2
0145T	1	11450	2	12054	1	15760	2	15953	2	19370	1	21026	2	21184	2
0146T	1	11451	2	12055	1	15770	2	15956	2	19371	1	21029	1	21188	1
0147T	1	11462	2	12056	1	15775	1	15958	2	19380	1	21030	2	21193	1
0148T	1	11463	2	12057	1	15776	1	16000	1	19396	1	21031	2	21194	1
0149T	1	11471	2	13100	1	15780	1	16020	1	20100	2	21032	1	21195	1
0150T	1	11646	3	13101	1	15781	2	16025	1	20102	4	21034	1	21196	1
		11719	1	13120	1	15782	2	16030	1	20103	4	21040	2	21198	1

Appendix L — Medically Unlikely Edits (MUEs) — Professional

CPT	MUE	CPT	MUE	CPT	MUE	CPT	MUE	CPT	MUE	CPT	MUE	CPT	MUE	CPT	MUE
21199	1	21445	2	22326	1	23106	2	23625	2	24362	2	25105	2	25500	2
21206	1	21450	1	22327	1	23107	2	23630	2	24363	2	25107	2	25505	2
21208	2	21451	1	22328	8	23120	2	23650	2	24365	2	25110	3	25515	2
21209	2	21452	1	22505	1	23125	2	23655	2	24366	2	25111	2	25520	2
21210	2	21453	1	22520	1	23130	2	23660	2	24400	2	25112	2	25525	2
21215	2	21454	1	22521	1	23145	1	23665	2	24410	2	25115	2	25526	2
21230	2	21461	1	22522	5	23146	1	23670	2	24420	2	25116	2	25530	2
21235	2	21462	1	22523	1	23150	1	23675	2	24430	2	25119	2	25535	2
21240	2	21465	2	22524	1	23155	1	23680	2	24435	2	25120	2	25545	2
21242	2	21470	1	22525	5	23156	1	23700	2	24470	2	25125	1	25560	2
21243	2	21480	2	22526	1	23170	1	23800	2	24495	2	25126	1	25565	2
21244	1	21485	2	22527	1	23172	1	23802	2	24498	2	25130	2	25574	2
21245	2	21490	2	22532	1	23174	1	23900	1	24500	2	25135	2	25575	2
21246	2	21495	1	22533	1	23180	1	23920	2	24505	2	25136	2	25600	2
21247	2	21497	1	22534	3	23182	1	23921	2	24515	2	25145	1	25605	2
21255	2	21501	3	22548	1	23184	1	23930	2	24516	2	25150	1	25606	2
21256	2	21502	1	22554	1	23190	1	23931	2	24530	2	25151	1	25607	2
21260	1	21510	1	22556	1	23195	1	23935	2	24535	2	25170	1	25608	2
21261	1	21550	3	22558	1	23200	1	24000	2	24538	2	25210	2	25609	2
21263	1	21556	3	22585	7	23210	1	24006	2	24545	2	25215	2	25622	2
21267	2	21557	1	22590	1	23220	1	24065	2	24546	2	25230	2	25624	2
21268	2	21610	2	22595	1	23221	1	24066	2	24560	2	25240	2	25628	2
21270	2	21615	2	22600	1	23222	1	24077	2	24565	2	25246	2	25630	2
21275	1	21616	2	22610	1	23330	2	24100	2	24566	2	25248	3	25635	2
21280	2	21620	1	22612	1	23331	2	24101	2	24575	2	25250	2	25650	2
21282	2	21627	1	22614	15	23332	2	24102	2	24576	2	25251	2	25651	2
21295	2	21630	1	22630	1	23350	2	24105	2	24577	2	25259	2	25652	2
21296	2	21632	1	22632	4	23395	1	24110	1	24579	2	25275	2	25660	2
21310	1	21685	1	22800	1	23397	1	24115	2	24582	2	25295	9	25670	2
21315	1	21700	2	22802	1	23400	1	24116	1	24586	2	25300	2	25671	2
21320	1	21705	2	22804	1	23405	2	24120	2	24587	2	25301	2	25675	2
21325	1	21720	1	22808	1	23406	2	24125	1	24600	2	25315	2	25676	2
21330	1	21725	1	22810	1	23410	2	24126	1	24605	2	25316	2	25680	2
21335	1	21740	1	22812	1	23412	2	24130	2	24615	2	25320	2	25685	2
21336	1	21742	1	22818	1	23415	2	24134	1	24620	2	25332	2	25690	2
21337	1	21743	1	22819	1	23420	2	24136	1	24635	2	25335	2	25695	2
21338	1	21750	1	22830	1	23430	2	24138	2	24640	2	25337	2	25800	2
21339	1	21805	3	22840	1	23440	2	24140	2	24650	2	25350	2	25805	2
21340	1	21810	1	22842	1	23450	2	24145	2	24655	2	25355	2	25810	2
21343	1	21820	1	22843	1	23455	2	24147	2	24665	2	25360	2	25820	2
21344	1	21825	1	22844	1	23460	2	24149	2	24666	2	25365	2	25825	2
21345	1	21920	3	22845	1	23462	2	24150	1	24670	2	25370	2	25830	2
21346	1	21925	3	22846	1	23465	2	24151	1	24675	2	25375	2	25900	2
21347	1	21935	1	22847	1	23466	2	24152	1	24685	2	25390	2	25905	2
21348	1	22010	2	22848	1	23470	2	24153	1	24800	2	25391	2	25907	2
21355	2	22015	2	22849	1	23472	2	24155	2	24802	2	25392	2	25909	2
21356	2	22100	1	22850	1	23480	2	24160	2	24900	2	25393	2	25915	2
21360	2	22101	1	22851	9	23485	2	24164	2	24920	2	25394	2	25920	2
21365	2	22102	1	22852	1	23490	2	24200	3	24925	2	25400	2	25922	2
21366	2	22103	3	22855	1	23491	2	24201	3	24930	2	25405	2	25924	2
21385	2	22110	1	22857	1	23500	2	24220	2	24931	2	25415	2	25927	2
21386	2	22112	1	22862	1	23505	2	24300	2	24935	2	25420	2	25929	2
21387	2	22114	1	22865	1	23515	2	24301	2	24940	2	25425	2	25931	2
21390	2	22116	3	22900	3	23520	2	24305	4	25000	2	25426	2	26010	3
21395	2	22206	1	23000	2	23525	2	24320	2	25001	2	25430	2	26011	3
21400	2	22207	1	23020	2	23530	2	24330	2	25020	2	25431	2	26025	2
21401	2	22210	1	23030	2	23532	2	24331	2	25023	2	25440	2	26030	2
21406	2	22212	1	23031	2	23540	2	24332	2	25024	2	25441	2	26034	2
21407	2	22214	1	23035	2	23545	2	24340	2	25025	2	25442	2	26035	3
21408	2	22216	6	23040	2	23550	2	24342	2	25031	2	25443	2	26037	2
21421	1	22220	1	23044	2	23552	2	24343	2	25035	2	25444	2	26040	2
21422	1	22222	1	23065	2	23570	2	24344	2	25040	2	25445	2	26045	2
21423	1	22224	1	23066	2	23575	2	24345	2	25065	5	25446	2	26070	3
21431	1	22305	1	23075	4	23585	2	24346	2	25066	3	25449	2	26100	2
21432	1	22310	1	23076	2	23600	2	24357	2	25076	5	25450	2	26105	2
21433	1	22315	1	23077	1	23605	2	24358	2	25077	2	25455	2	26110	3
21435	1	22318	1	23100	2	23615	2	24359	2	25085	2	25490	2	26117	2
21436	1	22319	1	23101	2	23616	2	24360	2	25100	2	25491	2	26121	2
21440	2	22325	1	23105	2	23620	2	24361	2	25101	2	25492	2	26123	2

CPT	MUE	CPT	MUE	CPT	MUE	CPT	MUE	CPT	MUE	CPT	MUE	CPT	MUE	CPT	MUE
26185	1	27054	2	27246	2	27425	2	27594	2	27756	2	28113	2	28545	2
26205	2	27057	1	27248	2	27427	2	27596	2	27758	2	28114	2	28546	2
26215	2	27060	2	27250	2	27428	2	27598	2	27759	2	28116	2	28555	2
26230	3	27062	2	27252	2	27429	2	27600	2	27760	2	28118	2	28570	2
26236	3	27065	2	27253	2	27430	2	27601	2	27762	2	28119	2	28575	2
26250	2	27066	2	27254	2	27435	2	27602	2	27766	2	28120	2	28576	2
26255	2	27067	2	27256	2	27437	2	27604	2	27767	2	28130	2	28585	2
26260	2	27070	2	27257	2	27438	2	27605	2	27768	2	28171	2	28600	3
26261	2	27071	2	27258	2	27440	2	27606	2	27769	2	28173	2	28605	3
26262	2	27075	1	27259	2	27441	2	27607	2	27780	2	28175	2	28630	3
26357	3	27076	2	27265	2	27442	2	27610	2	27781	2	28192	2	28705	2
26358	3	27077	2	27266	2	27443	2	27612	2	27784	2	28193	2	28715	2
26390	3	27078	2	27267	2	27445	2	27615	2	27786	2	28202	2	28725	2
26392	3	27079	2	27268	2	27446	2	27620	2	27788	2	28210	2	28730	2
26416	2	27080	1	27269	2	27447	2	27625	2	27792	2	28220	2	28735	2
26428	2	27086	2	27275	2	27454	2	27626	2	27808	2	28222	2	28737	2
26432	2	27087	2	27282	1	27465	2	27630	2	27810	2	28225	2	28750	2
26433	2	27090	2	27284	2	27466	2	27635	2	27814	2	28226	2	28755	2
26434	3	27091	2	27286	2	27468	2	27637	2	27816	2	28230	2	28760	2
26494	2	27093	2	27290	1	27470	2	27638	2	27818	2	28238	2	28800	2
26496	2	27095	2	27295	2	27472	2	27640	2	27822	2	28240	2	28805	2
26497	2	27097	2	27303	2	27475	2	27641	2	27823	2	28250	2	28890	2
26498	2	27098	2	27305	2	27477	2	27645	1	27824	2	28260	2	29000	1
26508	2	27100	2	27306	2	27479	2	27646	1	27825	2	28261	2	29010	1
26516	2	27105	2	27307	2	27485	2	27647	2	27826	2	28262	2	29015	1
26517	2	27110	2	27310	2	27486	2	27648	2	27827	2	28264	2	29020	1
26518	2	27111	2	27325	1	27487	2	27650	2	27828	2	28280	2	29025	1
26548	3	27120	2	27326	1	27488	2	27652	2	27829	2	28286	2	29035	1
26550	2	27122	2	27329	2	27495	2	27654	2	27830	2	28289	2	29040	1
26551	2	27125	2	27330	2	27496	2	27656	2	27831	2	28290	2	29044	1
26553	2	27130	2	27331	2	27497	2	27658	2	27832	2	28292	2	29046	1
26554	2	27132	2	27332	2	27498	2	27659	2	27840	2	28293	2	29049	1
26555	2	27134	2	27333	2	27499	2	27664	2	27842	2	28294	2	29055	1
26556	2	27137	2	27334	2	27500	2	27665	2	27846	2	28296	2	29058	1
26560	2	27138	2	27335	2	27501	2	27675	2	27848	2	28297	2	29065	2
26561	2	27140	2	27340	2	27502	2	27676	2	27860	2	28298	2	29075	2
26562	2	27146	2	27345	2	27503	2	27680	3	27870	2	28299	2	29085	2
26580	2	27147	2	27347	2	27506	2	27681	2	27871	2	28300	2	29086	2
26641	2	27151	2	27350	2	27507	2	27685	2	27880	2	28302	2	29105	2
26645	2	27156	2	27355	2	27508	2	27686	2	27881	2	28304	2	29125	2
26650	2	27158	1	27356	2	27509	2	27687	2	27882	2	28305	2	29126	2
26665	2	27161	2	27357	2	27510	2	27690	2	27884	2	28306	2	29200	1
26740	3	27165	2	27358	2	27511	2	27691	2	27886	2	28307	2	29220	1
26742	3	27170	2	27365	2	27513	2	27695	2	27888	2	28309	2	29240	2
26746	3	27175	2	27370	2	27514	2	27696	2	27889	2	28310	2	29260	2
26820	2	27176	2	27380	2	27516	2	27698	2	27892	2	28315	2	29280	2
26841	2	27177	2	27381	2	27517	2	27700	2	27893	2	28320	2	29305	1
26842	2	27178	2	27385	2	27519	2	27702	2	27894	2	28322	2	29325	1
26860	1	27179	2	27386	2	27520	2	27703	2	28001	2	28340	2	29345	2
26862	1	27181	2	27390	2	27524	2	27704	2	28002	3	28341	2	29355	2
26990	2	27185	2	27391	1	27530	2	27705	2	28003	2	28344	2	29358	2
26991	2	27187	2	27392	1	27532	2	27707	2	28005	3	28360	2	29365	2
26992	2	27193	1	27393	2	27535	2	27709	2	28035	2	28400	2	29405	2
27000	2	27194	1	27394	1	27536	2	27712	2	28052	2	28405	2	29425	2
27001	1	27200	1	27395	1	27538	2	27715	2	28054	2	28406	2	29435	2
27003	1	27202	1	27396	2	27540	2	27720	2	28060	2	28415	2	29440	2
27005	2	27220	2	27397	2	27550	2	27722	2	28062	2	28420	2	29445	2
27006	2	27222	2	27400	2	27552	2	27724	2	28086	2	28430	2	29450	1
27027	1	27226	2	27403	2	27556	2	27725	2	28088	2	28435	2	29505	2
27030	2	27227	2	27405	2	27557	2	27726	2	28090	2	28436	2	29515	2
27033	2	27228	2	27407	2	27558	2	27727	2	28092	2	28445	2	29520	2
27035	2	27230	2	27409	2	27560	2	27730	2	28100	2	28446	2	29530	2
27036	2	27232	2	27412	2	27562	2	27732	2	28102	2	28490	2	29540	2
27040	2	27235	2	27415	2	27566	2	27734	2	28103	2	28495	2	29550	2
27041	3	27236	2	27416	2	27570	2	27740	2	28106	2	28496	2	29580	2
27048	2	27238	2	27418	2	27580	2	27742	2	28107	2	28505	2	29590	2
27049	2	27240	2	27420	2	27590	2	27745	2	28108	2	28530	2	29700	2
27050	2	27244	2	27422	2	27591	2	27750	2	28110	2	28531	2	29705	2
27052	2	27245	2	27424	2	27592	2	27752	2	28111	2	28540	2	29710	2

Appendix L — Medically Unlikely Edits (MUEs) — Professional

CPT	MUE	CPT	MUE	CPT	MUE	CPT	MUE	CPT	MUE	CPT	MUE	CPT	MUE	CPT	MUE
29715	1	29899	2	31087	2	31578	1	32150	1	33015	1	33406	1	33660	1
29720	1	29900	2	31090	2	31579	1	32151	1	33020	1	33410	1	33675	1
29730	2	29901	2	31200	2	31580	1	32160	1	33025	1	33411	1	33681	1
29740	2	29902	2	31201	2	31582	1	32200	2	33030	1	33412	1	33684	1
29750	1	29904	2	31205	2	31584	1	32201	2	33031	1	33413	1	33688	1
29800	2	29905	2	31225	2	31587	1	32215	2	33050	1	33414	1	33690	1
29804	2	29906	2	31230	1	31588	1	32220	2	33120	1	33415	1	33692	1
29805	2	29907	2	31231	1	31590	1	32225	2	33130	1	33416	1	33694	1
29806	2	30000	1	31233	2	31595	2	32400	2	33140	1	33417	1	33697	1
29807	2	30020	1	31235	2	31600	1	32402	2	33141	1	33420	1	33702	1
29819	2	30100	3	31237	2	31601	1	32405	2	33202	1	33422	1	33710	1
29820	2	30110	1	31238	2	31603	1	32420	2	33203	1	33425	1	33720	1
29821	2	30115	1	31239	2	31605	1	32421	3	33206	1	33426	1	33722	1
29822	2	30117	2	31240	2	31610	1	32422	3	33207	1	33427	1	33724	1
29823	2	30118	2	31254	2	31611	1	32440	1	33208	1	33430	1	33730	1
29824	2	30120	1	31255	2	31612	1	32442	1	33210	1	33460	1	33732	1
29825	2	30124	2	31256	2	31613	1	32445	1	33211	1	33463	1	33735	1
29826	2	30125	1	31267	2	31614	1	32480	2	33212	1	33464	1	33736	1
29827	2	30130	2	31276	2	31615	1	32482	1	33213	1	33465	1	33737	1
29828	2	30140	2	31287	2	31620	1	32484	2	33214	1	33468	1	33750	1
29830	2	30150	1	31288	2	31622	1	32486	1	33215	2	33470	1	33755	1
29834	2	30160	1	31290	2	31623	1	32488	1	33216	1	33471	1	33762	1
29835	2	30200	1	31291	2	31624	1	32500	2	33217	1	33472	1	33764	1
29836	2	30210	1	31292	2	31625	1	32501	1	33218	1	33474	1	33766	1
29837	2	30220	1	31293	2	31628	1	32540	1	33220	1	33475	1	33767	1
29838	2	30300	1	31294	2	31629	1	32550	2	33222	1	33476	1	33768	1
29840	2	30310	1	31300	1	31630	2	32560	1	33223	1	33478	1	33770	1
29843	2	30320	1	31320	1	31631	1	32601	1	33224	1	33496	1	33771	1
29844	2	30400	1	31360	1	31632	4	32602	1	33225	1	33500	1	33774	1
29845	2	30410	1	31365	1	31633	4	32603	1	33226	1	33501	1	33775	1
29846	2	30420	1	31367	1	31635	1	32604	1	33233	1	33502	1	33776	1
29847	2	30430	1	31368	1	31636	1	32605	1	33234	1	33503	1	33777	1
29848	2	30435	1	31370	1	31637	2	32606	1	33235	1	33504	1	33778	1
29850	2	30450	1	31375	1	31638	2	32650	2	33236	1	33505	1	33779	1
29851	2	30460	1	31380	1	31640	1	32651	2	33237	1	33506	1	33780	1
29855	2	30462	1	31382	1	31641	1	32652	2	33238	1	33507	1	33781	1
29856	2	30465	1	31390	1	31643	1	32653	1	33240	1	33508	1	33786	1
29860	2	30520	1	31395	1	31645	1	32654	2	33241	1	33510	1	33788	1
29861	2	30540	1	31400	1	31646	2	32655	2	33243	1	33511	1	33800	1
29862	2	30545	1	31420	1	31656	1	32656	2	33244	1	33512	1	33802	1
29863	2	30560	1	31500	2	31715	1	32657	2	33249	1	33513	1	33803	1
29866	2	30580	2	31502	1	31717	1	32658	1	33250	1	33514	1	33813	1
29867	2	30600	1	31505	1	31720	1	32659	1	33251	1	33516	1	33814	1
29868	2	30620	1	31510	1	31725	1	32660	1	33254	1	33517	1	33820	1
29870	2	30630	1	31511	1	31730	1	32661	1	33255	1	33518	1	33822	1
29871	2	30801	1	31512	1	31750	1	32662	1	33256	1	33519	1	33824	1
29873	2	30802	1	31513	1	31755	1	32663	2	33257	1	33521	1	33840	1
29874	2	30901	1	31515	1	31760	1	32664	2	33258	1	33522	1	33845	1
29875	2	30903	1	31520	1	31766	1	32665	1	33259	1	33523	1	33851	1
29876	2	30905	1	31525	1	31770	2	32800	1	33261	1	33530	1	33852	1
29877	2	30906	1	31526	1	31775	1	32810	1	33265	1	33533	1	33853	1
29879	2	30915	1	31527	1	31780	1	32815	1	33266	1	33534	1	33860	1
29880	2	30920	1	31528	1	31781	1	32820	1	33282	1	33535	1	33861	1
29881	2	30930	1	31529	1	31785	1	32850	1	33284	1	33536	1	33863	1
29882	2	31000	1	31530	1	31786	1	32851	1	33300	1	33542	1	33864	1
29883	2	31002	2	31531	1	31800	1	32852	1	33305	1	33545	1	33870	1
29884	2	31020	1	31535	1	31805	1	32853	1	33310	1	33548	1	33875	1
29885	2	31030	1	31536	1	31820	1	32854	1	33315	1	33572	3	33877	1
29886	2	31032	1	31540	1	31825	1	32855	1	33320	1	33606	1	33880	1
29887	2	31040	2	31541	1	31830	1	32856	1	33321	1	33608	1	33881	1
29888	2	31050	2	31545	2	32035	2	32900	1	33322	1	33610	1	33883	1
29889	2	31051	2	31546	2	32036	2	32905	1	33330	1	33611	1	33884	3
29891	2	31070	2	31560	1	32095	2	32906	1	33332	1	33612	1	33886	1
29892	2	31075	2	31561	1	32100	1	32940	1	33335	1	33615	1	33889	1
29893	2	31080	2	31570	1	32110	2	32960	1	33400	1	33617	1	33891	1
29894	2	31081	2	31571	1	32120	1	32997	2	33401	1	33619	1	33910	1
29895	2	31084	2	31575	1	32124	2	32998	2	33403	1	33641	1	33915	1
33897	2	31085	2	31576	1	32140	1	33010	1	33404	1	33645	1	33916	1
29898	2	31086	2	31577	1	32141	1	33011	1	33405	1	33647	1	33917	1

Appendix L — Medically Unlikely Edits (MUEs) — Professional

CPT	MUE	CPT	MUE	CPT	MUE	CPT	MUE	CPT	MUE	CPT	MUE	CPT	MUE	CPT	MUE
33920	1	35122	1	35506	1	35691	2	36561	2	37210	1	38760	1	41114	2
33922	1	35131	2	35508	1	35693	2	36563	2	37215	2	38765	1	41115	1
33924	1	35132	2	35509	1	35694	2	36565	2	37250	1	38770	1	41116	3
33925	1	35141	2	35510	1	35695	2	36566	2	37500	2	38780	1	41120	1
33926	1	35142	2	35511	1	35697	2	36568	2	37565	2	38790	1	41130	1
33930	1	35151	2	35512	1	35700	2	36569	2	37600	1	38792	2	41135	1
33933	1	35152	2	35515	1	35701	2	36570	2	37605	2	38794	1	41140	1
33935	1	35180	2	35516	1	35721	2	36571	2	37606	2	39000	1	41145	1
33940	1	35182	2	35518	1	35741	2	36575	2	37607	1	39010	1	41150	1
33944	1	35184	2	35521	2	35761	2	36576	2	37609	2	39200	1	41153	1
33945	1	35188	2	35522	1	35800	2	36578	2	37615	2	39220	1	41155	1
33960	1	35189	1	35523	2	35820	2	36580	2	37616	1	39400	1	41250	2
33961	1	35190	2	35525	1	35840	2	36581	2	37617	3	39501	1	41251	2
33967	1	35201	2	35526	3	35860	2	36582	2	37618	1	39502	1	41252	2
33968	1	35206	2	35531	2	35870	1	36583	2	37620	1	39503	1	41500	1
33970	1	35207	3	35533	1	35875	2	36584	2	37650	1	39520	1	41510	1
33971	1	35211	3	35535	2	35876	2	36585	2	37660	2	39530	1	41512	1
33973	1	35216	3	35536	1	35879	2	36589	2	37700	1	39531	1	41520	1
33974	1	35221	3	35537	1	35881	2	36590	2	37718	1	39540	1	41800	2
33975	1	35226	3	35538	1	35883	1	36592	1	37722	1	39541	1	41820	4
33976	1	35231	2	35539	1	35884	1	36593	2	37735	1	39545	1	41822	1
33977	1	35236	2	35540	1	35901	1	36595	2	37760	1	39560	1	41823	1
33978	1	35241	2	35548	1	35903	2	36596	2	37765	2	39561	1	41825	2
34001	1	35246	2	35549	1	35905	1	36597	2	37766	2	40500	2	41826	2
34051	1	35251	2	35551	1	35907	1	36598	2	37780	1	40510	2	41827	2
34101	2	35256	2	35556	2	36002	2	36620	3	37785	2	40520	2	41828	4
34111	2	35261	1	35558	2	36005	2	36625	2	37788	1	40525	2	41850	2
34151	2	35266	2	35560	2	36010	2	36640	1	37790	1	40527	2	41872	4
34201	2	35271	2	35563	2	36013	2	36660	1	38100	1	40530	2	41874	4
34203	2	35276	2	35565	2	36014	2	36680	1	38101	1	40650	2	42000	1
34401	1	35281	2	35566	2	36100	2	36800	1	38102	1	40652	2	42100	3
34421	2	35286	2	35570	2	36120	2	36810	1	38115	1	40654	2	42104	3
34451	1	35302	2	35571	2	36145	2	36815	1	38120	1	40700	1	42106	2
34471	1	35303	2	35572	2	36160	1	36818	1	38200	1	40701	1	42107	2
34490	2	35304	2	35583	2	36200	2	36819	1	38205	1	40702	1	42120	1
34501	2	35305	2	35585	2	36260	1	36820	2	38206	1	40720	1	42140	1
34510	2	35306	2	35587	2	36261	1	36821	2	38220	2	40761	1	42145	1
34520	1	35311	2	35600	2	36262	1	36822	1	38221	2	40800	1	42160	1
34530	2	35321	2	35601	2	36400	1	36823	1	38230	1	40801	1	42180	1
34800	1	35331	1	35606	1	36405	1	36825	1	38240	1	40806	2	42182	1
34802	1	35351	2	35612	1	36406	1	36830	2	38241	1	40816	2	42200	1
34803	1	35355	2	35616	1	36410	3	36831	1	38242	1	40818	2	42205	1
34804	1	35361	1	35621	2	36420	2	36832	2	38300	2	40819	2	42210	1
34805	1	35363	1	35623	2	36425	1	36833	1	38305	2	40820	2	42215	1
34806	1	35371	2	35626	3	36430	1	36834	1	38308	1	40830	2	42220	1
34808	1	35372	2	35632	2	36440	1	36835	1	38380	1	40831	2	42225	1
34813	1	35390	2	35633	2	36450	1	36838	2	38381	1	40840	1	42226	1
34825	2	35400	1	35634	2	36455	1	36860	2	38382	1	40842	1	42227	1
34826	4	35450	2	35636	1	36468	1	36861	1	38500	2	40843	1	42235	1
34830	1	35452	1	35637	1	36469	1	36870	2	38505	3	40844	2	42260	1
34831	1	35456	2	35638	1	36470	2	37140	1	38510	2	40845	1	42280	1
34832	1	35458	3	35642	1	36471	2	37145	1	38520	2	41000	1	42281	1
35001	2	35459	2	35645	1	36475	2	37160	1	38525	2	41005	1	42300	2
35002	2	35471	3	35646	1	36478	2	37180	1	38530	2	41006	2	42305	2
35005	2	35472	1	35647	1	36479	2	37181	1	38542	2	41007	2	42310	2
35011	2	35474	2	35650	1	36481	1	37182	1	38550	1	41008	2	42320	1
35013	2	35480	2	35651	2	36510	1	37183	1	38555	1	41009	2	42330	3
35021	2	35481	1	35654	1	36511	1	37184	2	38562	1	41010	1	42335	2
35022	2	35483	2	35656	2	36512	1	37185	1	38564	1	41015	2	42340	2
35045	2	35484	2	35661	1	36513	1	37186	1	38570	1	41016	1	42400	2
35081	1	35485	2	35663	2	36514	1	37187	1	38571	1	41017	2	42405	2
35082	1	35490	2	35665	2	36515	1	37188	2	38572	1	41018	2	42408	1
35091	1	35491	1	35666	2	36516	1	37195	1	38700	1	41019	1	42409	1
35092	1	35492	2	35671	2	36522	1	37200	2	38720	1	41100	3	42410	2
35102	1	35493	2	35681	2	36555	2	37201	1	38724	2	41105	3	42415	2
35103	1	35494	3	35682	1	36556	2	37203	2	38740	2	41108	2	42420	2
35111	1	35495	2	35683	1	36557	2	37205	2	38745	2	41110	2	42425	2
35112	1	35500	2	35685	2	36558	2	37207	2	38746	1	41112	2	42426	2
35121	2	35501	2	35686	1	36560	2	37209	2	38747	1	41113	2	42440	2

Appendix L — Medically Unlikely Edits (MUEs) — Professional

CPT	MUE	CPT	MUE	CPT	MUE	CPT	MUE	CPT	MUE	CPT	MUE	CPT	MUE	CPT	MUE
42450	1	43204	1	43401	1	43888	1	44369	1	45170	1	46083	2	47011	3
42500	2	43205	1	43405	1	44005	1	44370	1	45190	1	46200	1	47015	1
42505	1	43215	1	43410	1	44010	1	44372	1	45300	1	46210	1	47100	3
42507	1	43216	1	43415	1	44015	1	44373	1	45303	1	46211	1	47120	1
42508	1	43217	1	43420	1	44020	2	44376	1	45305	1	46220	2	47122	1
42509	1	43219	1	43425	1	44021	1	44377	1	45307	1	46221	1	47125	1
42510	1	43220	1	43450	1	44025	1	44378	1	45308	1	46230	1	47130	1
42550	2	43226	1	43453	1	44050	1	44379	1	45309	1	46250	1	47133	1
42600	1	43227	2	43456	1	44055	1	44380	1	45315	1	46255	1	47135	1
42650	2	43228	1	43458	1	44100	1	44382	1	45317	1	46257	1	47136	1
42660	2	43231	1	43460	1	44110	1	44383	1	45320	1	46258	1	47140	1
42665	2	43232	1	43496	1	44111	1	44385	1	45321	1	46260	1	47141	1
42700	2	43234	1	43500	1	44120	1	44386	1	45327	1	46261	1	47142	1
42720	1	43235	1	43501	1	44125	1	44388	1	45330	1	46262	1	47143	1
42725	2	43236	1	43502	1	44126	1	44389	1	45331	1	46270	1	47144	1
42800	3	43237	1	43510	1	44127	1	44390	1	45332	1	46275	1	47145	1
42802	2	43238	1	43520	1	44128	2	44391	1	45333	1	46280	1	47147	3
42806	1	43239	1	43600	1	44132	1	44392	1	45334	1	46285	1	47300	2
42808	2	43240	1	43605	1	44133	1	44393	1	45335	1	46288	1	47350	1
42809	1	43241	1	43610	1	44135	1	44394	1	45337	1	46320	2	47360	1
42810	2	43242	1	43611	1	44136	1	44397	1	45338	1	46500	1	47361	1
42815	2	43243	1	43620	1	44137	1	44500	1	45339	1	46505	1	47362	1
42820	1	43244	1	43621	1	44139	1	44602	1	45340	1	46600	1	47370	1
42821	1	43245	1	43622	1	44140	2	44603	1	45341	1	46604	1	47371	1
42825	1	43246	1	43631	1	44141	1	44604	1	45342	1	46606	1	47380	1
42826	1	43247	1	43632	1	44143	1	44605	1	45345	1	46608	1	47381	1
42830	1	43248	1	43633	1	44144	1	44620	2	45355	1	46610	1	47382	1
42831	1	43249	1	43634	1	44145	1	44625	1	45378	1	46611	1	47400	1
42835	1	43250	1	43635	1	44146	1	44626	1	45379	1	46612	1	47420	1
42836	1	43251	1	43640	1	44147	1	44640	2	45380	1	46614	1	47425	1
42842	1	43255	2	43641	1	44150	1	44650	2	45381	1	46615	1	47460	1
42844	1	43256	1	43644	1	44151	1	44660	1	45382	2	46700	1	47480	1
42845	1	43257	1	43645	1	44155	1	44661	1	45383	1	46705	1	47490	1
42860	1	43258	1	43647	1	44156	1	44680	1	45384	1	46706	2	47500	2
42870	1	43259	1	43648	1	44157	1	44700	1	45385	1	46710	1	47505	2
42890	1	43260	1	43651	1	44158	1	44701	1	45386	1	46712	1	47510	2
42892	1	43261	1	43652	1	44160	1	44715	1	45387	1	46715	1	47511	2
42894	1	43262	2	43653	1	44180	1	44720	2	45391	1	46716	1	47525	3
42900	1	43263	2	43752	2	44186	1	44721	2	45392	1	46730	1	47530	3
42950	1	43264	1	43760	2	44187	1	44800	1	45395	1	46735	1	47550	1
42953	1	43265	1	43761	2	44188	1	44820	2	45397	1	46740	1	47552	1
42955	1	43267	1	43770	1	44202	1	44850	1	45400	1	46742	1	47553	1
42960	1	43268	2	43771	1	44203	2	44900	1	45402	1	46744	1	47554	1
42961	1	43269	2	43772	1	44204	2	44901	1	45500	1	46746	1	47555	1
42962	1	43271	1	43773	1	44205	1	44950	1	45505	1	46748	1	47556	1
42970	1	43272	1	43774	1	44206	1	44955	1	45520	1	46750	1	47560	1
42971	1	43273	1	43800	1	44207	1	44960	1	45540	1	46751	1	47561	1
42972	1	43279	1	43810	1	44208	1	44970	1	45541	1	46753	1	47562	1
43020	1	43280	1	43820	1	44210	1	45000	1	45550	1	46754	1	47563	1
43030	1	43300	1	43825	1	44211	1	45005	1	45560	1	46760	1	47564	1
43045	1	43305	1	43830	1	44212	1	45020	1	45562	1	46761	1	47570	1
43100	1	43310	1	43831	1	44213	1	45100	1	45563	1	46762	1	47600	1
43101	1	43312	1	43832	1	44227	1	45108	1	45800	1	46900	1	47605	1
43107	1	43313	1	43840	2	44300	1	45110	1	45805	1	46910	1	47610	1
43108	1	43314	1	43843	1	44310	2	45111	1	45820	1	46916	1	47612	1
43112	1	43320	1	43845	1	44312	1	45112	1	45825	1	46917	1	47620	1
43113	1	43324	1	43846	1	44314	1	45113	1	45900	1	46922	1	47630	1
43116	1	43325	1	43847	1	44316	1	45114	1	45905	1	46924	1	47700	1
43117	1	43326	1	43848	1	44320	1	45116	1	45910	1	46930	1	47701	1
43118	1	43330	1	43850	1	44322	1	45119	1	45915	1	46937	1	47711	1
43121	1	43331	1	43855	1	44340	1	45120	1	45990	1	46938	1	47712	1
43122	1	43340	1	43860	1	44345	1	45121	1	46020	1	46940	1	47715	1
43123	1	43341	1	43865	1	44346	1	45123	1	46030	1	46942	1	47720	1
43124	1	43350	1	43870	1	44360	1	45126	1	46040	2	46945	1	47721	1
43130	1	43351	1	43880	1	44361	1	45130	1	46045	2	46946	1	47740	1
43135	1	43352	1	43881	1	44363	1	45135	1	46050	2	46947	1	47741	1
43200	1	43360	1	43882	1	44364	1	45136	1	46060	2	47000	3	47760	1
43201	1	43361	1	43886	1	44365	1	45150	1	46070	1	47001	3	47765	1
43202	1	43400	1	43887	1	44366	1	45160	1	46080	1	47010	3	47780	1

Appendix L — Medically Unlikely Edits (MUEs) — Professional

CPT	MUE	CPT	MUE	CPT	MUE	CPT	MUE	CPT	MUE	CPT	MUE	CPT	MUE	CPT	MUE
47785	1	49427	1	50125	2	50600	2	51600	1	52325	1	53515	1	54408	1
47800	1	49428	1	50130	2	50605	2	51605	2	52327	2	53520	1	54410	1
47801	1	49429	1	50135	2	50610	2	51610	1	52330	2	53600	1	54411	1
47802	1	49435	1	50200	2	50620	2	51700	1	52332	1	53601	1	54415	1
47900	1	49436	1	50205	2	50630	2	51701	2	52334	2	53605	1	54416	1
48000	1	49440	1	50220	2	50650	2	51702	2	52341	2	53620	1	54417	1
48001	1	49441	1	50225	2	50660	2	51703	2	52342	2	53621	1	54420	1
48020	1	49442	1	50230	2	50684	2	51705	1	52343	2	53660	1	54430	1
48100	1	49446	1	50234	2	50686	2	51710	1	52344	2	53661	1	54435	1
48102	2	49450	1	50236	2	50688	2	51715	1	52345	2	53665	1	54440	1
48120	1	49451	1	50240	2	50690	2	51720	1	52346	2	53850	1	54450	1
48140	1	49452	1	50250	1	50700	2	51725	1	52351	1	53852	1	54500	2
48145	1	49460	1	50280	2	50722	2	51726	1	52352	2	54000	1	54505	1
48146	1	49465	1	50290	1	50725	1	51736	1	52353	2	54001	1	54512	2
48148	1	49491	1	50300	1	50727	1	51741	1	52354	2	54015	1	54520	1
48150	1	49492	1	50320	1	50728	1	51772	1	52355	2	54050	1	54522	2
48152	1	49495	1	50323	1	50740	2	51784	1	52400	1	54055	1	54530	2
48153	1	49496	1	50325	1	50750	2	51785	1	52402	1	54056	1	54535	1
48154	1	49500	1	50327	3	50760	2	51792	1	52450	1	54057	1	54550	1
48155	1	49501	1	50328	3	50770	1	51795	1	52500	1	54060	1	54560	1
48400	1	49505	1	50329	2	50782	2	51797	1	52601	1	54065	1	54600	2
48500	1	49507	1	50360	1	50783	2	51798	1	52630	1	54100	3	54620	1
48510	1	49520	1	50365	1	50810	1	51800	1	52640	1	54105	2	54640	1
48511	1	49521	1	50370	1	50825	1	51820	1	52647	1	54110	1	54650	2
48520	1	49525	1	50380	1	50830	1	51840	1	52648	1	54111	1	54660	1
48540	1	49540	1	50382	1	50845	1	51841	1	52649	1	54112	1	54670	1
48545	1	49550	1	50384	1	50900	2	51845	1	52700	1	54115	1	54680	1
48547	1	49553	1	50385	2	50920	2	51860	1	53000	1	54120	1	54690	2
48550	1	49555	1	50386	2	50930	2	51865	1	53010	1	54125	1	54692	2
48551	1	49557	1	50387	1	50940	2	51880	1	53020	1	54130	1	54700	2
48552	2	49565	2	50389	2	50945	2	51900	1	53025	1	54135	1	54800	2
48554	1	49566	2	50390	2	50947	2	51920	1	53040	1	54150	1	54830	2
48556	1	49570	1	50391	2	50948	2	51925	1	53060	1	54160	1	54840	2
49000	1	49572	1	50392	2	50951	2	51940	1	53080	1	54161	1	54860	1
49002	1	49580	1	50393	2	50953	2	51960	1	53085	1	54162	1	54861	1
49010	1	49582	1	50394	2	50955	2	51980	1	53200	1	54163	1	54865	1
49020	2	49585	1	50395	2	50957	2	51990	1	53210	1	54164	1	54900	1
49021	3	49587	1	50396	2	50961	2	51992	1	53215	1	54200	1	54901	1
49040	2	49590	1	50398	2	50970	2	52000	1	53220	1	54205	1	55000	2
49041	3	49600	1	50400	2	50972	2	52001	1	53230	1	54220	1	55040	1
49060	2	49605	1	50405	2	50974	2	52005	2	53235	1	54230	1	55041	1
49061	3	49606	1	50500	1	50976	2	52007	2	53240	1	54231	1	55060	2
49062	1	49610	1	50520	1	50980	2	52010	1	53250	1	54235	1	55100	2
49080	1	49611	1	50525	1	51020	1	52204	1	53260	1	54240	1	55110	1
49081	2	49650	1	50526	1	51030	1	52214	1	53265	1	54250	1	55120	1
49180	3	49651	1	50540	1	51040	1	52224	1	53270	1	54300	1	55150	1
49203	1	49652	1	50541	2	51045	1	52234	1	53275	1	54304	1	55175	1
49204	1	49653	1	50542	2	51050	1	52235	1	53400	1	54308	1	55180	1
49205	1	49654	2	50543	2	51060	2	52240	1	53405	1	54312	1	55200	1
49215	1	49655	2	50544	2	51065	1	52250	1	53410	1	54316	1	55250	1
49220	1	49656	2	50545	2	51080	2	52260	1	53415	1	54318	1	55300	1
49250	1	49657	2	50546	2	51100	1	52265	1	53420	1	54322	1	55400	1
49255	1	49900	1	50547	1	51101	1	52270	1	53425	1	54324	1	55450	1
49320	1	49904	1	50548	2	51102	1	52275	1	53430	1	54326	1	55500	2
49321	1	49905	1	50551	2	51500	1	52276	1	53431	1	54328	1	55520	2
49322	1	49906	1	50553	2	51520	1	52277	1	53440	1	54332	1	55530	2
49323	1	50010	2	50555	1	51525	1	52281	1	53442	1	54336	1	55535	2
49324	1	50020	1	50557	2	51530	1	52282	1	53444	1	54340	1	55540	2
49325	1	50021	2	50561	2	51550	1	52283	1	53445	1	54344	1	55550	2
49326	1	50040	2	50562	1	51555	1	52285	1	53446	1	54348	1	55600	1
49400	1	50045	2	50570	2	51565	1	52290	1	53447	1	54352	1	55605	2
49402	1	50060	2	50572	2	51570	1	52300	1	53448	1	54360	1	55680	2
49419	1	50065	2	50574	1	51575	1	52301	1	53449	1	54380	1	55700	1
49421	1	50070	2	50575	2	51580	1	52305	1	53450	1	54385	1	55705	1
49422	1	50075	2	50576	2	51585	1	52310	1	53460	1	54390	1	55706	1
49423	3	50080	2	50580	1	51590	1	52315	2	53500	1	54400	1	55720	1
49424	3	50081	2	50590	1	51595	1	52317	1	53502	1	54401	1	55725	1
49425	1	50100	2	50592	1	51596	1	52318	1	53505	1	54405	1	55801	1
49426	1	50120	2	50593	2	51597	1	52320	2	53510	1	54406	1	55810	1

Appendix L — Medically Unlikely Edits (MUEs) — Professional

CPT	MUE	CPT	MUE	CPT	MUE	CPT	MUE	CPT	MUE	CPT	MUE	CPT	MUE	CPT	MUE
55812	1	57260	1	58260	1	58805	1	59866	1	61470	1	61613	1	62165	1
55815	1	57265	1	58262	1	58820	2	59870	1	61480	1	61615	1	62180	1
55821	1	57267	3	58263	1	58822	2	59871	1	61500	3	61616	1	62190	1
55831	1	57268	1	58267	1	58823	2	60000	1	61501	1	61618	2	62192	1
55840	1	57270	1	58270	1	58825	1	60200	2	61512	3	61619	1	62194	2
55842	1	57280	1	58275	1	58900	1	60210	1	61514	2	61623	2	62200	1
55845	1	57282	1	58280	1	58920	1	60212	1	61516	2	61624	2	62201	1
55860	1	57283	1	58285	1	58925	1	60220	1	61517	1	61626	2	62220	1
55862	1	57284	1	58290	1	58940	1	60225	1	61518	2	61680	1	62223	1
55865	1	57285	1	58291	1	58943	1	60240	1	61519	2	61682	1	62225	2
55866	1	57287	1	58292	1	58950	1	60252	1	61520	1	61684	1	62230	2
55870	1	57288	1	58293	1	58951	1	60254	1	61521	1	61686	1	62252	2
55873	1	57289	1	58294	1	58952	1	60260	1	61522	2	61690	1	62256	1
55875	1	57291	1	58301	1	58953	1	60270	1	61524	1	61692	1	62258	1
55876	1	57292	1	58321	1	58954	1	60271	1	61526	1	61697	3	62263	1
55920	1	57295	1	58322	1	58956	1	60280	1	61530	1	61698	2	62264	1
56405	2	57296	1	58323	1	58957	1	60281	1	61533	2	61700	3	62268	1
56420	1	57300	1	58340	1	58958	1	60500	1	61534	1	61702	2	62269	2
56440	1	57305	1	58345	2	58960	1	60502	1	61535	2	61703	1	62270	2
56441	1	57307	1	58346	1	58970	1	60505	1	61536	1	61705	1	62272	1
56442	1	57308	1	58350	2	58974	1	60512	1	61537	1	61708	2	62273	2
56501	1	57310	1	58353	1	58976	2	60520	1	61538	1	61710	2	62280	1
56515	1	57311	1	58356	1	59020	1	60521	1	61539	1	61711	1	62281	1
56605	1	57320	1	58400	1	59025	1	60522	1	61540	1	61720	2	62282	1
56620	1	57330	1	58410	1	59050	1	60545	2	61541	1	61735	2	62284	1
56625	1	57335	1	58520	1	59051	1	60600	1	61542	1	61750	2	62287	1
56630	1	57400	1	58540	1	59100	1	60605	1	61543	1	61751	3	62290	5
56631	1	57410	1	58541	1	59120	1	60650	2	61544	2	61760	1	62292	1
56632	1	57415	1	58542	1	59121	1	61000	1	61545	1	61770	1	62294	1
56633	1	57420	1	58543	1	59130	1	61001	1	61546	1	61790	2	62310	2
56634	1	57421	1	58544	1	59135	1	61020	2	61548	1	61791	2	62311	2
56637	1	57423	1	58545	1	59136	1	61026	2	61550	1	61795	2	62318	1
56640	1	57425	1	58546	1	59140	1	61050	1	61552	1	61796	1	62319	1
56700	1	57452	1	58548	1	59150	1	61055	1	61556	1	61798	1	62350	1
56740	2	57454	1	58550	1	59151	1	61070	2	61557	1	61800	1	62351	1
56800	1	57455	1	58552	1	59160	1	61105	2	61558	1	61850	1	62355	1
56805	1	57456	1	58553	1	59200	1	61107	2	61559	1	61860	1	62360	1
56810	1	57460	1	58554	1	59300	1	61108	2	61563	2	61863	2	62361	1
56820	1	57461	1	58555	1	59320	1	61120	1	61564	2	61864	1	62362	1
56821	1	57500	1	58558	1	59325	1	61140	2	61566	1	61867	2	62365	1
57000	1	57505	1	58559	1	59350	1	61150	2	61567	1	61868	2	62367	1
57010	1	57510	1	58560	1	59400	1	61151	2	61570	2	61870	1	62368	1
57020	1	57511	1	58561	1	59410	1	61154	2	61571	2	61875	1	63001	1
57022	2	57513	1	58562	1	59412	2	61156	2	61575	1	61880	1	63003	1
57023	2	57520	1	58563	1	59414	1	61210	1	61576	1	61885	2	63005	1
57061	1	57522	1	58565	1	59425	1	61215	1	61580	1	61886	1	63011	1
57065	1	57530	1	58570	1	59426	1	61250	1	61581	1	61888	2	63012	1
57100	3	57531	1	58571	1	59430	1	61253	1	61582	1	62000	1	63015	1
57105	2	57540	1	58572	1	59510	1	61304	1	61583	1	62005	1	63016	1
57106	1	57545	1	58573	1	59514	1	61305	1	61584	1	62010	1	63017	1
57107	1	57550	1	58600	1	59515	1	61312	2	61585	1	62100	1	63020	1
57109	1	57555	1	58605	1	59525	1	61313	2	61586	1	62115	1	63030	1
57110	1	57556	1	58611	1	59610	1	61314	2	61590	1	62116	1	63035	6
57111	1	57558	1	58615	1	59614	1	61315	1	61591	1	62117	1	63040	1
57112	1	57700	1	58660	1	59618	1	61316	1	61592	1	62120	1	63042	1
57120	1	57720	1	58661	1	59620	1	61320	2	61595	1	62121	1	63043	6
57130	1	57800	1	58662	1	59622	1	61321	2	61596	1	62140	1	63044	4
57135	2	58100	1	58670	1	59812	1	61322	1	61597	1	62141	1	63045	1
57150	1	58110	1	58671	1	59820	1	61323	1	61598	1	62142	2	63046	1
57155	1	58120	1	58672	1	59821	1	61330	1	61600	1	62143	2	63047	1
57160	1	58140	1	58673	1	59830	1	61332	2	61601	1	62145	2	63048	9
57170	1	58145	1	58700	1	59840	1	61333	2	61605	1	62146	1	63050	1
57180	1	58146	1	58720	1	59841	1	61334	2	61606	1	62147	2	63051	1
57200	1	58150	1	58740	1	59850	1	61343	1	61607	1	62148	2	63055	1
57210	1	58152	1	58750	2	59851	1	61345	1	61608	1	62160	1	63056	1
57220	1	58180	1	58752	2	59852	1	61440	1	61609	1	62161	1	63057	8
57230	1	58200	1	58760	2	59855	1	61450	1	61610	1	62162	1	63064	1
57240	1	58210	1	58770	2	59856	1	61458	1	61611	1	62163	1	63066	3
57250	1	58240	1	58800	1	59857	1	61460	1	61612	1	62164	1	63075	1

Appendix L — Medically Unlikely Edits (MUEs) — Professional

CPT	MUE	CPT	MUE	CPT	MUE	CPT	MUE	CPT	MUE	CPT	MUE	CPT	MUE	CPT	MUE
63076	6	63700	1	64713	2	64907	1	66020	2	67120	2	67911	4	69110	2
63077	1	63702	1	64714	2	64910	3	66030	2	67121	2	67912	2	69120	1
63078	5	63704	1	64718	2	64911	2	66130	2	67141	2	67914	4	69140	2
63081	1	63706	1	64719	2	65091	2	66150	2	67145	2	67915	4	69145	2
63082	6	63707	1	64721	2	65093	2	66155	2	67208	2	67916	4	69150	1
63085	1	63709	1	64726	2	65101	2	66160	2	67210	2	67917	4	69155	1
63086	6	63710	1	64727	3	65103	2	66165	2	67218	2	67921	4	69200	2
63087	1	63740	1	64732	2	65105	2	66170	2	67220	2	67922	4	69205	2
63088	5	63741	1	64734	2	65110	2	66172	2	67221	1	67923	4	69210	1
63090	1	63744	1	64736	2	65112	2	66180	2	67225	1	67924	4	69220	1
63101	1	63746	1	64738	2	65114	2	66185	2	67227	2	67930	2	69222	1
63102	1	64402	2	64740	2	65125	2	66220	2	67228	2	67935	2	69300	1
63170	1	64405	1	64742	2	65130	2	66225	2	67229	1	67938	2	69310	2
63172	1	64408	2	64744	2	65135	2	66250	2	67250	2	67950	2	69320	2
63173	1	64410	2	64746	2	65140	2	66500	2	67255	2	67961	4	69400	2
63180	1	64412	2	64752	1	65150	2	66505	2	67311	2	67966	4	69401	2
63182	1	64413	2	64755	1	65155	2	66600	2	67312	2	67971	2	69405	2
63185	1	64415	2	64760	1	65175	2	66605	2	67314	2	67973	2	69420	2
63190	1	64416	2	64761	1	65205	2	66625	2	67316	2	67974	2	69421	2
63194	1	64417	2	64763	1	65210	2	66630	2	67318	2	67975	2	69424	1
63195	1	64418	2	64766	1	65220	2	66635	2	67320	2	68020	2	69433	1
63196	1	64420	3	64771	2	65222	2	66680	2	67331	2	68040	2	69436	1
63197	1	64421	3	64772	2	65235	2	66682	2	67332	2	68100	2	69440	2
63198	1	64425	2	64774	3	65260	2	66700	2	67334	2	68110	2	69450	2
63199	1	64430	2	64776	1	65265	2	66710	2	67335	2	68115	2	69501	1
63200	1	64435	2	64778	3	65270	2	66711	2	67340	2	68130	2	69502	1
63250	1	64445	1	64782	2	65272	2	66720	2	67343	2	68135	2	69505	1
63251	1	64446	1	64783	2	65273	2	66740	2	67345	2	68200	2	69511	1
63252	1	64447	2	64786	2	65275	2	66761	2	67346	1	68320	2	69530	1
63265	1	64448	2	64790	1	65280	2	66762	2	67400	2	68325	2	69535	1
63266	1	64449	2	64792	2	65285	2	66770	2	67405	2	68326	2	69540	2
63267	1	64455	2	64795	2	65286	2	66820	2	67412	2	68328	2	69550	1
63268	1	64479	1	64802	1	65290	2	66821	2	67413	2	68330	2	69552	1
63270	1	64483	1	64804	1	65400	2	66825	2	67414	2	68335	2	69554	1
63271	1	64505	2	64821	2	65410	2	66830	2	67415	2	68340	2	69601	1
63272	1	64508	2	64822	2	65420	2	66840	2	67420	2	68360	2	69602	1
63273	1	64510	2	64823	2	65426	2	66850	2	67430	2	68362	2	69603	1
63275	1	64517	1	64831	2	65430	2	66852	2	67440	2	68371	1	69604	1
63276	1	64520	2	64834	2	65435	2	66920	2	67445	2	68400	2	69605	1
63277	1	64530	2	64835	2	65436	2	66930	2	67450	2	68420	2	69610	2
63278	1	64553	1	64836	2	65450	2	66940	2	67500	2	68440	2	69620	2
63280	1	64555	2	64837	3	65600	2	66982	2	67505	2	68500	2	69631	2
63281	1	64560	1	64840	2	65710	2	66983	2	67515	2	68505	2	69632	1
63282	1	64561	2	64856	2	65730	2	66984	2	67550	2	68510	2	69633	1
63283	1	64565	2	64857	3	65750	2	66985	2	67560	2	68520	2	69635	1
63285	1	64573	1	64858	2	65755	2	66986	2	67570	2	68525	2	69636	1
63286	1	64575	2	64859	2	65756	2	66990	2	67700	4	68530	2	69637	1
63287	1	64577	1	64861	2	65757	2	67005	2	67710	2	68540	1	69641	1
63290	1	64580	2	64862	2	65770	2	67010	2	67715	2	68550	1	69642	1
63295	1	64581	2	64864	2	65772	2	67015	2	67800	1	68700	2	69643	1
63300	1	64585	2	64865	1	65775	2	67025	2	67801	1	68705	2	69644	1
63301	1	64590	1	64866	1	65780	2	67027	2	67805	1	68720	2	69645	1
63302	1	64595	1	64868	1	65781	2	67028	2	67808	1	68745	2	69646	1
63303	1	64600	2	64870	1	65782	2	67030	2	67820	2	68750	2	69650	1
63304	1	64605	2	64872	3	65800	2	67031	2	67825	2	68760	4	69660	1
63305	1	64610	2	64874	1	65805	2	67036	2	67830	3	68761	4	69661	1
63306	1	64612	2	64876	1	65810	2	67039	2	67835	2	68770	2	69662	2
63307	1	64613	1	64885	1	65815	2	67040	2	67850	4	68801	4	69666	2
63308	4	64614	1	64886	1	65820	2	67041	2	67875	2	68810	1	69667	2
63600	2	64622	1	64890	3	65850	2	67042	2	67880	2	68811	1	69670	1
63610	1	64626	1	64891	2	65855	2	67043	2	67882	2	68815	1	69676	1
63615	1	64630	1	64892	2	65860	2	67101	2	67900	2	68816	1	69700	2
63620	1	64632	2	64893	2	65865	2	67105	2	67901	2	68840	2	69711	2
63621	2	64650	1	64895	2	65870	2	67107	2	67902	2	68850	2	69714	2
63650	2	64653	1	64896	2	65875	2	67108	2	67903	2	69000	2	69715	1
63655	1	64680	1	64897	2	65880	2	67110	2	67904	2	69005	2	69717	1
63660	1	64681	1	64898	2	65900	2	67112	2	67906	2	69020	2	69718	1
63685	2	64702	2	64901	2	65920	2	67113	2	67908	2	69100	3	69720	2
63688	2	64712	2	64905	1	65930	2	67115	2	67909	2	69105	2	69725	2

Appendix L — Medically Unlikely Edits (MUEs) — Professional

CPT	MUE	CPT	MUE	CPT	MUE	CPT	MUE	CPT	MUE	CPT	MUE	CPT	MUE	CPT	MUE
69740	2	70545	1	72158	1	73660	2	74710	1	75961	2	76940	1	77522	1
69745	2	70546	1	72170	1	73700	2	74740	1	75962	1	76942	1	77523	1
69801	1	70547	1	72190	1	73701	2	74742	2	75964	3	76945	1	77525	1
69802	1	70548	1	72191	1	73702	2	74775	1	75966	1	76946	1	77600	1
69805	1	70549	1	72192	1	73706	2	75557	1	75968	2	76948	1	77605	1
69806	1	70551	1	72193	1	73718	2	75559	1	75970	2	76950	2	77610	1
69820	1	70552	1	72194	1	73719	2	75561	1	75980	1	76965	2	77615	1
69840	1	70553	1	72195	1	73720	2	75563	1	75982	2	76970	1	77620	1
69905	1	70554	1	72196	1	73721	4	75600	1	75984	2	76975	1	77750	1
69910	1	70555	1	72197	1	73722	2	75605	1	75989	2	76977	1	77761	1
69915	1	70557	1	72198	1	73723	4	75625	1	75992	1	76998	1	77762	1
69930	2	70558	1	72200	1	73725	2	75630	1	75994	2	77001	1	77763	1
69950	2	70559	1	72202	1	74000	3	75635	1	75995	1	77002	1	77776	1
69955	2	71015	2	72220	1	74010	2	75650	2	75996	2	77003	1	77777	1
69960	2	71021	1	72240	1	74020	2	75658	2	76000	3	77011	1	77778	1
69970	1	71022	1	72255	1	74022	2	75660	1	76001	2	77012	1	77785	3
69990	1	71023	2	72265	1	74150	1	75662	1	76010	2	77013	1	77786	3
70010	1	71030	2	72270	1	74160	1	75665	1	76080	2	77014	2	77787	3
70015	1	71034	1	72275	3	74170	1	75671	1	76100	2	77021	1	77789	2
70030	2	71035	2	72292	3	74175	1	75676	1	76101	1	77022	1	77790	2
70100	1	71040	1	73000	2	74181	1	75680	1	76102	1	77053	2	78000	1
70110	1	71060	1	73010	2	74182	1	75685	2	76120	1	77054	2	78001	1
70120	2	71090	1	73020	2	74183	1	75710	1	76125	1	77071	1	78003	1
70130	2	71100	1	73030	2	74185	1	75716	1	76350	1	77261	1	78006	1
70134	1	71101	1	73040	2	74190	1	75722	1	76376	2	77262	1	78007	1
70140	1	71110	1	73050	1	74210	1	75724	1	76377	2	77263	1	78010	1
70150	1	71111	1	73060	2	74220	1	75726	2	76380	1	77280	1	78011	1
70160	1	71120	1	73070	2	74230	1	75731	1	76506	1	77285	1	78015	1
70170	2	71130	1	73080	2	74235	1	75733	1	76510	2	77290	1	78016	1
70190	1	71250	1	73085	2	74240	1	75736	1	76511	2	77295	1	78018	1
70200	1	71260	1	73090	2	74241	1	75741	1	76512	2	77301	1	78020	1
70210	1	71270	1	73092	2	74245	1	75743	1	76513	2	77305	2	78070	1
70220	1	71275	1	73100	2	74246	1	75746	1	76514	1	77310	2	78075	1
70240	1	71550	1	73110	2	74247	1	75756	2	76516	1	77315	2	78102	1
70250	1	71551	1	73115	2	74249	1	75790	2	76519	2	77321	1	78103	1
70260	1	71552	1	73120	2	74250	1	75801	1	76529	2	77326	1	78104	1
70300	1	71555	1	73130	2	74251	1	75803	1	76536	1	77327	1	78110	1
70310	1	72010	1	73140	2	74260	1	75805	1	76604	1	77328	1	78111	1
70320	1	72020	4	73200	2	74270	1	75807	1	76645	1	77332	4	78120	1
70328	1	72040	3	73201	2	74280	1	75809	1	76700	1	77333	4	78121	1
70330	1	72050	1	73202	2	74283	1	75810	1	76705	2	77336	1	78122	1
70332	2	72052	1	73206	2	74290	1	75820	1	76770	1	77370	1	78130	1
70336	1	72069	1	73218	2	74291	1	75822	1	76775	2	77371	1	78135	1
70350	1	72070	1	73219	2	74300	1	75825	1	76776	1	77372	1	78140	1
70355	1	72072	1	73220	2	74301	2	75827	1	76800	1	77373	1	78185	1
70360	1	72074	1	73221	2	74305	1	75831	1	76801	1	77401	2	78190	1
70370	1	72080	1	73222	2	74320	1	75833	1	76802	3	77402	2	78191	1
70371	1	72090	1	73223	2	74327	1	75840	1	76805	1	77403	2	78195	1
70373	1	72100	1	73500	2	74328	1	75842	1	76810	3	77404	2	78201	1
70380	2	72110	2	73510	2	74329	1	75860	2	76811	1	77406	2	78202	1
70390	2	72114	1	73520	2	74330	1	75870	1	76812	3	77407	2	78205	1
70450	3	72120	1	73525	2	74340	1	75872	1	76813	1	77408	2	78206	1
70460	1	72125	1	73530	2	74355	1	75880	2	76814	3	77409	2	78215	1
70470	2	72126	1	73540	1	74360	1	75885	1	76815	1	77411	2	78216	1
70480	1	72127	1	73542	2	74363	2	75887	1	76817	1	77412	2	78220	1
70481	1	72128	1	73550	2	74400	1	75889	1	76830	1	77413	2	78223	1
70482	1	72129	1	73560	2	74410	1	75891	1	76831	1	77414	2	78230	1
70486	1	72130	1	73562	2	74415	1	75900	3	76856	1	77416	2	78231	1
70487	1	72131	1	73564	2	74420	2	75901	1	76857	1	77417	1	78232	1
70488	1	72132	1	73565	1	74425	1	75902	2	76870	1	77418	2	78258	1
70490	1	72133	1	73580	2	74430	1	75940	1	76872	1	77421	1	78261	1
70491	1	72141	1	73590	2	74440	2	75945	1	76873	1	77422	1	78262	1
70492	1	72142	1	73592	2	74445	1	75952	1	76880	2	77423	1	78264	1
70496	1	72146	1	73600	2	74450	1	75953	4	76885	1	77427	1	78267	1
70498	1	72147	1	73610	2	74455	1	75954	2	76886	1	77431	1	78268	1
70540	1	72148	1	73615	2	74470	2	75956	1	76930	1	77432	1	78270	1
70542	1	72149	1	73620	2	74475	2	75957	1	76932	1	77435	1	78271	1
70543	1	72156	1	73630	2	74480	2	75958	2	76936	2	77470	1	78272	1
70544	1	72157	1	73650	2	74485	2	75959	1	76937	2	77520	1	78278	2

Appendix L — Medically Unlikely Edits (MUEs) — Professional

CPT	MUE	CPT	MUE	CPT	MUE	CPT	MUE	CPT	MUE	CPT	MUE	CPT	MUE	CPT	MUE
78282	1	78804	1	80418	1	82205	1	82600	1	83012	1	83789	2	84163	1
78290	1	78805	1	80420	1	82232	2	82607	1	83013	1	83805	1	84165	1
78291	1	78806	1	80422	1	82239	1	82608	1	83014	1	83825	2	84166	2
78300	1	78807	1	80424	1	82240	1	82610	1	83015	1	83835	2	84202	1
78305	1	78808	1	80426	1	82247	2	82615	1	83018	7	83840	2	84203	1
78306	1	78811	1	80428	1	82248	2	82626	1	83020	2	83857	1	84206	1
78315	1	78812	1	80430	1	82252	1	82627	1	83021	2	83858	1	84207	1
78320	1	78813	1	80432	1	82261	1	82633	1	83026	1	83864	1	84210	2
78414	1	78814	1	80434	1	82270	1	82634	2	83030	1	83866	1	84220	1
78428	1	78815	1	80435	1	82271	1	82638	1	83033	1	83872	2	84228	1
78445	1	78816	1	80436	1	82272	1	82646	1	83036	1	83873	1	84233	2
78456	1	79005	1	80438	1	82274	1	82649	1	83037	1	83874	2	84234	2
78457	1	79101	1	80439	1	82286	1	82651	1	83045	1	83880	1	84235	1
78458	1	79200	1	80440	1	82300	1	82652	1	83050	1	83885	2	84238	3
78459	1	79300	1	80500	1	82306	1	82654	1	83051	1	83887	2	84252	1
78460	1	79403	1	80502	1	82307	1	82656	1	83055	1	83912	1	84255	2
78461	1	79440	1	81000	2	82308	3	82657	3	83060	1	83915	1	84260	1
78464	1	79445	1	81001	2	82310	2	82658	2	83065	1	83916	2	84270	1
78465	1	80047	2	81002	2	82330	2	82666	1	83068	1	83918	2	84275	1
78466	1	80048	2	81003	2	82331	1	82668	1	83069	1	83919	1	84285	1
78468	1	80051	2	81005	2	82340	1	82670	2	83070	1	83921	2	84295	3
78469	1	80053	1	81007	1	82355	3	82671	1	83071	1	83925	4	84300	2
78472	1	80061	1	81015	1	82360	3	82672	1	83080	2	83930	2	84302	1
78473	1	80069	1	81020	1	82365	3	82677	1	83088	1	83935	1	84305	1
78478	1	80074	1	81025	1	82370	3	82679	1	83090	2	83937	1	84307	1
78480	1	80076	1	81050	2	82373	1	82690	1	83150	1	83945	2	84311	2
78481	1	80103	2	82000	1	82374	1	82693	2	83491	1	83950	1	84315	2
78483	1	80150	2	82003	2	82375	1	82696	1	83497	1	83951	1	84375	1
78491	1	80152	2	82009	1	82378	2	82705	1	83498	2	83970	2	84376	1
78492	1	80154	2	82010	4	82379	1	82710	1	83499	1	83986	2	84377	1
78494	1	80156	2	82013	1	82380	1	82715	1	83500	1	83992	2	84378	2
78496	1	80157	2	82016	1	82382	1	82725	1	83505	1	83993	1	84379	1
78580	1	80158	2	82017	1	82383	1	82726	1	83518	2	84022	2	84392	1
78584	2	80160	2	82030	1	82384	2	82728	1	83527	1	84030	1	84402	1
78585	2	80162	2	82040	1	82387	1	82731	1	83528	1	84035	1	84403	2
78586	1	80164	2	82042	2	82390	1	82735	1	83540	2	84060	1	84425	1
78587	1	80166	2	82043	1	82415	1	82742	1	83550	1	84061	1	84430	1
78588	1	80168	2	82044	1	82435	2	82746	1	83570	1	84066	1	84432	1
78591	1	80170	2	82045	1	82436	1	82747	1	83582	1	84075	2	84436	1
78593	1	80172	2	82055	2	82438	1	82757	1	83586	1	84078	1	84437	1
78594	1	80173	2	82075	2	82441	1	82759	1	83593	1	84080	1	84439	1
78596	1	80174	2	82085	1	82465	1	82760	1	83605	3	84081	1	84442	1
78600	1	80176	1	82101	1	82480	2	82775	1	83615	2	84085	1	84445	1
78601	1	80178	2	82103	1	82482	1	82776	1	83625	1	84087	1	84446	1
78605	1	80182	2	82104	1	82485	1	82784	6	83630	1	84100	3	84449	1
78606	2	80184	2	82105	1	82486	2	82785	1	83631	1	84105	1	84450	1
78607	1	80185	2	82106	4	82487	2	82787	4	83632	1	84106	1	84460	1
78608	1	80186	2	82107	1	82488	1	82820	1	83633	1	84110	1	84466	1
78610	1	80188	2	82108	1	82489	2	82928	1	83634	1	84119	1	84478	1
78630	2	80190	2	82120	1	82492	2	82941	1	83655	2	84120	1	84479	1
78635	1	80192	2	82127	2	82495	1	82943	1	83661	4	84126	1	84480	1
78645	1	80194	2	82128	2	82507	1	82946	1	83662	4	84127	1	84481	1
78647	1	80195	2	82131	3	82520	2	82950	3	83663	4	84132	3	84482	1
78650	1	80197	2	82135	1	82523	1	82951	1	83664	4	84133	2	84484	2
78660	1	80198	2	82136	3	82525	2	82952	3	83670	1	84134	1	84485	1
78700	1	80200	2	82139	3	82528	1	82953	1	83690	2	84135	1	84488	1
78701	2	80201	2	82140	2	82530	2	82955	1	83695	1	84138	1	84490	1
78707	1	80202	2	82143	2	82540	1	82960	1	83698	1	84140	1	84510	1
78708	1	80299	3	82145	1	82543	2	82963	1	83700	1	84143	2	84512	1
78709	1	80400	1	82150	4	82544	2	82965	1	83701	1	84144	1	84520	4
78710	1	80402	1	82154	1	82550	3	82975	1	83704	1	84146	3	84525	1
78725	1	80406	1	82157	1	82552	3	82977	1	83718	1	84150	2	84540	2
78730	1	80408	1	82160	1	82553	3	82978	1	83719	1	84152	1	84545	1
78740	1	80410	1	82163	1	82554	1	82979	1	83721	1	84153	1	84550	1
78761	1	80412	1	82164	1	82565	2	82980	1	83727	1	84154	1	84560	2
78800	1	80414	1	82172	3	82570	3	82985	1	83735	4	84155	1	84577	1
78801	1	80415	1	82175	2	82575	1	83008	1	83775	1	84156	1	84578	1
78802	1	80416	1	82180	1	82585	1	83009	1	83785	1	84157	3	84580	1
78803	1	80417	1	82190	4	82595	1	83010	1	83788	3	84160	2	84583	1

Appendix L — Medically Unlikely Edits (MUEs) — Professional

CPT	MUE	CPT	MUE	CPT	MUE	CPT	MUE	CPT	MUE	CPT	MUE	CPT	MUE	CPT	MUE
84585	1	85384	2	86309	1	86703	2	87169	2	87495	2	88104	4	88380	1
84586	1	85385	1	86310	1	86704	1	87172	2	87496	2	88106	3	88381	1
84588	2	85390	3	86316	3	86705	1	87177	3	87497	2	88125	1	88384	1
84590	1	85396	1	86320	1	86706	2	87197	1	87498	2	88130	1	88385	1
84591	1	85400	2	86325	2	86707	2	87207	3	87500	1	88140	1	88386	1
84597	1	85410	2	86327	1	86708	1	87220	3	87510	2	88141	1	88720	1
84600	2	85415	2	86332	1	86709	1	87230	3	87511	2	88142	1	88740	1
84620	1	85420	2	86334	1	86713	3	87250	3	87512	2	88143	1	88741	1
84630	2	85421	2	86335	2	86720	2	87255	2	87515	2	88147	1	89049	1
84702	2	85441	1	86336	1	86723	2	87260	2	87516	2	88148	1	89050	2
84703	1	85445	1	86337	1	86727	2	87265	2	87517	2	88150	1	89051	2
84704	1	85460	1	86340	1	86732	2	87267	2	87520	2	88152	1	89055	2
84830	1	85461	1	86341	1	86738	2	87269	3	87521	2	88153	1	89060	2
85002	1	85475	1	86343	1	86741	2	87270	2	87522	2	88154	1	89100	1
85004	2	85525	2	86344	1	86744	2	87271	2	87525	2	88155	1	89105	1
85007	1	85530	1	86355	1	86747	2	87272	3	87526	2	88160	4	89125	2
85008	1	85536	1	86357	1	86750	4	87273	2	87527	2	88161	4	89130	1
85009	1	85540	1	86359	1	86756	2	87274	2	87528	2	88162	3	89132	1
85013	2	85547	1	86360	1	86759	2	87275	2	87529	2	88164	1	89135	1
85014	2	85549	1	86361	1	86762	2	87276	2	87530	2	88165	1	89136	1
85018	2	85555	1	86367	1	86768	5	87277	2	87531	2	88166	1	89140	1
85025	2	85557	1	86376	2	86771	2	87278	3	87532	2	88167	1	89141	1
85032	3	85597	2	86378	1	86774	2	87280	2	87533	2	88172	3	89160	1
85041	1	85611	2	86382	3	86777	2	87283	2	87534	2	88173	3	89190	1
85044	1	85612	1	86384	1	86778	2	87285	2	87535	2	88174	1	89220	1
85045	1	85613	1	86406	2	86781	2	87290	2	87536	2	88175	1	89225	1
85046	1	85635	1	86430	2	86784	2	87299	2	87537	2	88182	2	89230	1
85048	2	85651	1	86431	2	86787	2	87301	2	87538	2	88184	1	89235	1
85049	2	85652	1	86480	1	86788	2	87305	2	87539	2	88187	1	89250	1
85055	1	85660	1	86485	1	86789	2	87320	2	87540	2	88188	1	89251	1
85060	1	85670	2	86490	1	86793	2	87324	3	87541	2	88189	1	89253	1
85097	2	85675	1	86510	1	86800	1	87327	2	87542	2	88230	2	89254	1
85130	2	85705	1	86580	1	86803	2	87328	3	87550	2	88233	3	89255	1
85170	1	85732	4	86590	1	86804	1	87329	3	87551	2	88239	3	89257	1
85175	1	85810	2	86592	2	86807	1	87332	2	87552	2	88240	3	89258	1
85210	2	86021	1	86593	2	86808	1	87335	2	87557	2	88241	3	89259	1
85220	2	86022	1	86602	3	86812	1	87336	3	87560	2	88245	1	89260	1
85230	2	86023	2	86603	2	86813	1	87337	3	87561	2	88248	1	89261	1
85240	2	86038	1	86612	2	86816	1	87338	1	87562	2	88249	1	89264	1
85244	2	86039	1	86617	2	86817	1	87339	1	87580	2	88261	2	89268	1
85245	2	86060	1	86618	2	86821	3	87340	1	87581	2	88262	2	89272	1
85246	2	86063	1	86619	2	86822	3	87341	1	87582	2	88263	1	89280	1
85247	2	86077	1	86625	2	86850	3	87350	1	87590	3	88264	2	89281	1
85250	2	86078	1	86628	3	86860	2	87380	2	87591	3	88267	2	89290	1
85260	2	86079	1	86632	3	86885	3	87385	2	87592	2	88269	2	89291	1
85270	2	86140	1	86641	2	86906	1	87390	2	87620	2	88273	3	89300	1
85280	2	86141	1	86645	1	86930	2	87391	2	87621	3	88283	2	89310	1
85290	2	86146	3	86648	2	86940	1	87400	2	87622	2	88289	1	89320	1
85291	2	86147	4	86651	2	86941	1	87420	2	87640	2	88291	1	89321	1
85292	2	86148	1	86652	2	86945	3	87425	2	87650	1	88300	2	89322	1
85293	2	86155	1	86653	2	86950	1	87427	3	87651	1	88302	2	89325	1
85300	2	86156	1	86654	2	86960	3	87430	2	87652	1	88309	3	89329	1
85301	2	86157	1	86663	2	86975	2	87449	3	87653	1	88311	4	89330	1
85302	2	86160	4	86664	2	86976	2	87450	2	87660	1	88318	3	89331	1
85303	2	86161	3	86665	2	86977	2	87451	2	87797	3	88321	1	89335	1
85305	2	86162	1	86668	2	87001	1	87470	2	87799	3	88323	1	89342	1
85306	2	86171	2	86674	3	87003	1	87471	2	87800	2	88325	1	89343	1
85307	2	86200	1	86677	3	87045	3	87472	2	87802	2	88329	4	89344	1
85335	2	86215	1	86684	2	87073	3	87475	2	87803	3	88331	11	89346	1
85337	1	86225	1	86687	2	87084	2	87476	2	87804	2	88333	4	89352	1
85345	2	86226	1	86688	2	87086	3	87477	2	87807	2	88347	4	89353	1
85348	1	86243	1	86689	2	87103	3	87480	2	87808	1	88348	1	89354	1
85360	1	86277	1	86692	2	87109	3	87482	2	87810	2	88349	1	89356	2
85362	2	86280	1	86694	2	87110	2	87485	2	87850	1	88355	1	90284	1
85366	2	86294	1	86695	2	87118	3	87486	2	87880	2	88356	1	90296	1
85370	2	86300	2	86696	2	87143	2	87487	2	87900	1	88358	2	90371	1
85378	2	86301	1	86698	3	87164	2	87490	2	87901	1	88362	1	90375	1
85379	2	86304	1	86701	1	87166	2	87491	2	87902	1	88371	1	90376	1
85380	2	86308	1	86702	2	87168	2	87492	2	87903	1	88372	1	90378	1

CPT	MUE	CPT	MUE	CPT	MUE	CPT	MUE	CPT	MUE	CPT	MUE	CPT	MUE	CPT	MUE
90385	1	90735	1	90969	1	92502	1	92982	1	93313	2	93720	2	94681	1
90465	1	90736	1	90970	1	92504	1	92984	2	93314	2	93721	2	94690	1
90466	4	90738	1	90989	1	92507	1	92986	1	93315	2	93722	1	94720	1
90467	1	90740	1	90993	1	92508	1	92987	1	93316	2	93724	2	94725	1
90468	3	90743	1	90997	1	92511	1	92990	1	93317	2	93745	1	94750	1
90471	1	90744	1	91000	1	92512	1	92992	1	93318	2	93784	1	94760	1
90472	4	90746	1	91010	1	92516	1	92993	1	93320	1	93786	1	94761	1
90473	1	90747	1	91011	1	92520	1	92995	1	93321	1	93788	1	94762	1
90474	1	90801	1	91012	1	92526	1	92996	2	93325	1	93790	1	94770	1
90476	1	90802	1	91020	1	92541	1	92997	1	93350	1	93797	3	94772	1
90477	1	90804	1	91022	1	92542	1	92998	2	93351	1	93798	3	94775	1
90581	1	90805	1	91030	1	92543	4	93000	3	93352	1	93875	1	94776	1
90585	1	90806	1	91034	1	92544	1	93005	3	93501	2	93880	1	94777	1
90586	1	90807	1	91035	1	92545	1	93012	1	93503	2	93882	1	95012	2
90632	1	90808	1	91037	1	92546	1	93014	1	93505	1	93886	1	95056	1
90633	1	90809	1	91038	1	92548	1	93015	2	93508	2	93888	1	95060	1
90634	1	90810	1	91040	1	92552	1	93016	2	93510	2	93890	1	95065	1
90636	1	90811	1	91052	1	92553	1	93017	2	93511	1	93892	1	95070	1
90645	1	90812	1	91055	1	92555	1	93018	2	93514	1	93893	1	95071	1
90646	1	90813	1	91065	1	92556	1	93024	1	93524	1	93922	2	95075	1
90647	1	90814	1	91105	2	92557	1	93025	1	93526	2	93923	1	95115	1
90648	1	90815	1	91110	1	92561	1	93040	3	93527	1	93924	1	95117	1
90649	1	90816	1	91111	1	92562	1	93041	2	93528	1	93925	1	95250	1
90650	1	90817	1	91120	1	92563	1	93042	3	93529	1	93926	1	95251	1
90655	1	90818	1	91122	1	92564	1	93224	1	93530	1	93930	1	95805	1
90656	1	90819	1	91132	1	92565	1	93225	1	93531	1	93931	1	95806	1
90657	1	90821	1	91133	1	92567	1	93226	1	93532	1	93965	1	95807	1
90658	1	90822	1	92002	1	92568	1	93227	1	93533	1	93970	1	95808	1
90660	1	90823	1	92004	1	92569	1	93228	1	93539	2	93971	1	95810	1
90661	1	90824	1	92012	1	92571	1	93229	1	93540	2	93975	1	95811	1
90662	1	90826	1	92014	1	92572	1	93230	1	93541	1	93976	1	95812	1
90663	1	90827	1	92018	1	92575	1	93231	1	93542	1	93978	1	95813	1
90665	1	90828	1	92019	1	92576	1	93232	1	93543	1	93979	1	95816	1
90669	1	90829	1	92020	1	92577	1	93233	1	93544	1	93980	1	95819	1
90675	1	90845	1	92025	1	92579	1	93235	1	93545	2	93981	1	95822	1
90676	1	90846	1	92060	1	92582	1	93236	1	93555	2	93982	1	95824	1
90680	1	90847	1	92065	1	92583	1	93237	1	93556	2	93990	2	95827	1
90681	1	90849	1	92070	2	92584	1	93268	1	93561	1	94002	1	95829	1
90690	1	90853	1	92081	1	92585	1	93270	1	93562	3	94003	1	95830	1
90691	1	90857	1	92082	1	92586	1	93271	1	93571	1	94004	1	95832	1
90692	1	90862	1	92083	1	92587	1	93272	1	93572	2	94010	1	95852	1
90693	1	90865	1	92100	1	92588	1	93278	1	93580	1	94014	1	95857	1
90696	1	90870	1	92120	1	92596	1	93279	1	93581	1	94015	1	95860	1
90698	1	90880	1	92130	1	92601	1	93280	1	93600	1	94016	1	95861	1
90700	1	90901	1	92135	2	92602	1	93281	1	93602	1	94060	1	95863	1
90701	1	90911	1	92140	1	92603	1	93282	1	93603	1	94070	1	95864	1
90702	1	90935	1	92225	2	92604	1	93283	1	93609	1	94200	1	95865	1
90703	1	90937	1	92226	2	92609	1	93284	1	93610	1	94240	1	95866	2
90704	1	90940	2	92230	2	92610	1	93285	1	93612	1	94250	1	95867	1
90705	1	90945	1	92235	2	92613	1	93286	2	93613	1	94260	1	95868	1
90706	1	90947	1	92240	2	92615	1	93287	2	93615	1	94350	1	95869	1
90707	1	90951	1	92250	1	92617	1	93288	1	93616	1	94360	1	95873	1
90708	1	90952	1	92260	1	92620	1	93289	1	93618	1	94370	1	95874	1
90710	1	90953	1	92265	1	92625	1	93290	1	93619	1	94375	1	95875	2
90712	1	90954	1	92270	1	92626	1	93291	1	93620	1	94400	1	95921	1
90713	1	90955	1	92275	1	92950	3	93292	1	93621	1	94450	1	95922	1
90714	1	90956	1	92283	1	92953	2	93293	1	93622	1	94452	1	95923	1
90715	1	90957	1	92284	1	92960	2	93294	1	93623	1	94453	1	95925	1
90716	1	90958	1	92285	1	92961	1	93295	1	93624	1	94610	2	95926	1
90717	1	90959	1	92286	1	92970	1	93296	1	93631	1	94620	1	95927	1
90718	1	90960	1	92287	1	92971	1	93297	1	93640	1	94621	1	95928	1
90719	1	90961	1	92311	1	92973	2	93298	1	93641	1	94642	1	95929	1
90720	1	90962	1	92312	1	92974	1	93299	1	93642	1	94644	1	95930	1
90721	1	90963	1	92313	1	92975	1	93303	1	93650	1	94645	2	95933	1
90725	1	90964	1	92315	1	92977	1	93304	1	93651	1	94660	1	95934	1
90727	1	90965	1	92316	1	92978	1	93306	1	93652	1	94662	1	95936	2
90732	1	90966	1	92317	1	92979	2	93307	1	93660	1	94664	2	95950	1
90733	1	90967	1	92325	1	92980	1	93308	2	93662	1	94667	1	95951	1
90734	1	90968	1	92326	2	92981	2	93312	2	93701	1	94680	1	95953	1

Appendix L — Medically Unlikely Edits (MUEs) — Professional

CPT	MUE	CPT	MUE	CPT	MUE	CPT	MUE	CPT	MUE	CPT	MUE	CPT	MUE	CPT	MUE
95954	1	97150	1	99308	1	A6501	2	E0114	1	E0291	1	E0617	1	E0890	1
95955	1	97545	1	99309	1	A6502	2	E0116	2	E0292	1	E0618	1	E0900	1
95956	1	97546	2	99310	1	A6503	2	E0117	2	E0293	1	E0619	1	E0910	1
95957	1	97597	1	99315	1	A6509	2	E0118	2	E0294	1	E0620	1	E0911	1
95958	1	97598	1	99316	1	A6510	2	E0130	1	E0295	1	E0621	1	E0912	1
95961	1	97605	1	99318	1	A6511	2	E0135	1	E0296	1	E0627	1	E0920	1
95965	1	97606	1	99324	1	A6513	2	E0140	1	E0297	1	E0628	1	E0930	1
95966	1	98925	1	99325	1	A7027	1	E0141	1	E0300	1	E0629	1	E0940	1
95967	3	98926	1	99326	1	A7039	1	E0143	1	E0301	1	E0630	1	E0941	1
95970	1	98927	1	99327	1	A7040	2	E0144	1	E0302	1	E0635	1	E0942	1
95971	1	98928	1	99328	1	A7041	2	E0147	1	E0303	1	E0636	1	E0944	1
95972	1	98929	1	99334	1	A7042	2	E0148	1	E0304	1	E0637	1	E0945	2
95974	1	98940	1	99335	1	A7043	2	E0149	1	E0310	2	E0638	1	E0946	1
95975	2	98941	1	99336	1	A9500	3	E0153	2	E0316	1	E0639	1	E0947	1
95978	1	98942	1	99337	1	A9501	3	E0154	2	E0325	1	E0640	1	E0948	1
95980	1	99082	1	99341	1	A9502	3	E0155	1	E0326	1	E0641	1	E0950	1
95981	1	99143	1	99342	1	A9503	1	E0156	1	E0350	1	E0642	1	E0951	2
95982	1	99144	1	99343	1	A9504	1	E0157	2	E0371	1	E0650	1	E0952	1
95990	2	99148	1	99344	1	A9507	1	E0158	1	E0372	1	E0651	1	E0955	1
95991	2	99149	1	99345	1	A9510	1	E0163	1	E0373	1	E0652	1	E0957	2
95992	1	99170	1	99347	1	A9521	2	E0165	1	E0424	1	E0655	2	E0958	2
96000	1	99175	1	99348	1	A9526	2	E0167	1	E0431	1	E0660	2	E0959	2
96001	1	99183	1	99349	1	A9536	1	E0168	1	E0434	1	E0665	2	E0960	2
96002	1	99185	1	99350	1	A9537	1	E0170	1	E0439	1	E0666	2	E0961	2
96003	1	99186	1	99354	1	A9538	1	E0171	1	E0441	1	E0667	2	E0966	1
96004	1	99191	1	99356	1	A9539	2	E0175	2	E0442	1	E0668	2	E0967	2
96020	1	99192	1	99406	1	A9540	2	E0181	1	E0443	1	E0669	2	E0968	1
96103	1	99195	2	99407	1	A9541	1	E0182	1	E0444	1	E0671	2	E0970	2
96120	1	99201	1	99455	1	A9542	1	E0184	1	E0450	2	E0672	2	E0971	2
96360	2	99202	1	99456	1	A9543	1	E0185	1	E0455	1	E0673	2	E0973	2
96368	2	99203	1	99460	1	A9544	1	E0186	1	E0457	1	E0675	1	E0974	2
96369	1	99204	1	99461	1	A9545	1	E0187	1	E0459	1	E0691	1	E0978	1
96371	1	99205	1	99462	1	A9546	1	E0188	1	E0460	1	E0692	1	E0981	1
96373	2	99211	1	99463	1	A9550	1	E0189	1	E0461	1	E0693	1	E0982	1
96374	2	99217	1	99464	1	A9551	1	E0193	1	E0462	1	E0694	1	E0983	1
96402	2	99218	1	99465	1	A9552	1	E0194	1	E0463	1	E0705	1	E0984	1
96405	1	99219	1	99466	1	A9553	1	E0196	1	E0464	1	E0720	1	E0985	1
96406	1	99220	1	99468	1	A9554	1	E0197	1	E0470	1	E0730	1	E0986	1
96409	2	99221	1	99469	1	A9555	3	E0198	1	E0471	1	E0731	1	E0990	2
96413	2	99222	1	99471	1	A9557	2	E0199	1	E0472	1	E0740	1	E0992	1
96416	1	99223	1	99472	1	A9559	1	E0200	1	E0480	1	E0744	1	E0994	2
96420	2	99231	1	99475	1	A9560	2	E0202	1	E0481	1	E0745	1	E0995	2
96422	2	99232	1	99476	1	A9561	1	E0205	1	E0482	1	E0746	1	E1002	1
96425	1	99233	1	99477	1	A9562	2	E0210	1	E0483	1	E0747	1	E1003	1
96440	1	99234	1	99478	1	A9566	1	E0215	1	E0484	1	E0748	1	E1004	1
96445	1	99235	1	99479	1	A9567	2	E0217	1	E0485	1	E0749	1	E1005	1
96450	1	99236	1	99480	1	A9569	1	E0218	1	E0486	1	E0755	1	E1006	1
96521	2	99238	1	99605	1	A9570	1	E0225	1	E0500	1	E0760	1	E1007	1
96522	1	99239	1	99606	1	A9571	1	E0235	1	E0550	1	E0762	1	E1008	1
96523	1	99241	1	99607	1	A9700	2	E0236	1	E0555	1	E0764	1	E1009	2
96542	1	99242	1	A4221	1	B4034	1	E0238	1	E0560	1	E0765	1	E1010	1
96567	1	99243	1	A4253	1	B4035	1	E0239	1	E0561	1	E0776	1	E1011	1
96570	1	99244	1	A4255	1	B4036	1	E0249	1	E0562	1	E0779	1	E1014	1
96571	3	99245	1	A4259	1	B4087	1	E0250	1	E0565	1	E0780	1	E1015	2
96900	1	99251	1	A4470	1	B4088	1	E0251	1	E0570	1	E0781	1	E1016	2
96904	1	99252	1	A4480	1	B4216	1	E0255	1	E0571	1	E0782	1	E1017	2
96910	1	99253	1	A4561	2	B4220	1	E0256	1	E0572	1	E0783	1	E1018	2
96912	1	99254	1	A4562	2	B4222	1	E0260	1	E0574	1	E0784	1	E1020	2
96913	1	99255	1	A4642	1	B4224	1	E0261	1	E0575	1	E0785	1	E1028	4
96920	1	99281	1	A4660	1	B9000	1	E0265	1	E0580	1	E0786	1	E1029	1
96921	1	99282	1	A4663	1	B9002	1	E0266	1	E0585	1	E0791	1	E1030	1
96922	1	99283	1	A5500	2	B9004	1	E0270	1	E0600	1	E0840	1	E1031	1
97012	1	99284	1	A5501	2	B9006	1	E0271	1	E0601	1	E0849	1	E1035	1
97016	1	99285	1	A5503	2	E0100	1	E0272	1	E0605	1	E0850	1	E1037	1
97018	1	99291	1	A5504	2	E0105	1	E0275	1	E0606	1	E0855	1	E1038	1
97022	1	99304	1	A5505	2	E0110	1	E0276	1	E0607	1	E0856	1	E1039	1
97024	1	99305	1	A5506	2	E0111	2	E0277	1	E0610	1	E0860	1	E1050	1
97026	1	99306	1	A5508	2	E0112	1	E0280	1	E0615	1	E0870	1	E1060	1
97028	1	99307	1	A5510	2	E0113	2	E0290	1	E0616	1	E0880	1	E1070	1

Appendix L — Medically Unlikely Edits (MUEs) — Professional

CPT	MUE	CPT	MUE	CPT	MUE	CPT	MUE	CPT	MUE	CPT	MUE	CPT	MUE	CPT	MUE
E1083	1	E1594	1	E2325	1	G0103	1	G0393	1	K0815	1	L0470	1	L1300	1
E1084	1	E1600	1	E2326	1	G0104	1	G0396	1	K0816	1	L0472	1	L1310	1
E1085	1	E1610	1	E2327	1	G0105	1	G0397	1	K0820	1	L0480	1	L1500	1
E1086	1	E1615	1	E2328	1	G0106	1	G0398	1	K0821	1	L0482	1	L1510	1
E1087	1	E1620	1	E2329	1	G0117	1	G0399	1	K0822	1	L0484	1	L1520	1
E1088	1	E1625	1	E2330	1	G0118	1	G0400	1	K0823	1	L0486	1	L1600	1
E1089	1	E1630	1	E2331	1	G0120	1	G0416	1	K0824	1	L0488	1	L1610	1
E1090	1	E1635	1	E2340	1	G0121	1	G0417	1	K0825	1	L0490	1	L1620	1
E1092	1	E1639	1	E2341	1	G0123	1	G0418	1	K0826	1	L0491	1	L1630	1
E1093	1	E1700	1	E2342	1	G0124	1	G0419	1	K0827	1	L0492	1	L1640	1
E1100	1	E1800	2	E2343	1	G0127	1	K0001	1	K0828	1	L0621	1	L1650	1
E1110	1	E1801	2	E2351	1	G0130	1	K0002	1	K0829	1	L0622	1	L1652	1
E1130	1	E1802	2	E2361	2	G0141	1	K0003	1	K0830	1	L0623	1	L1660	1
E1140	1	E1805	2	E2363	2	G0143	1	K0004	1	K0831	1	L0624	1	L1680	1
E1150	1	E1806	2	E2365	2	G0144	1	K0005	1	K0835	1	L0625	1	L1685	1
E1160	1	E1810	2	E2366	1	G0145	1	K0006	1	K0836	1	L0626	1	L1686	1
E1161	1	E1811	2	E2367	1	G0147	1	K0007	1	K0837	1	L0627	1	L1690	1
E1170	1	E1812	2	E2368	2	G0148	1	K0009	1	K0838	1	L0628	1	L1700	1
E1171	1	E1815	2	E2369	2	G0166	2	K0015	2	K0839	1	L0629	1	L1710	1
E1172	1	E1816	2	E2370	2	G0173	1	K0017	2	K0840	1	L0630	1	L1720	2
E1180	1	E1818	2	E2371	2	G0175	1	K0018	2	K0841	1	L0631	1	L1730	1
E1190	1	E1820	2	E2375	1	G0179	1	K0019	2	K0842	1	L0632	1	L1755	2
E1195	1	E1821	1	E2381	2	G0180	1	K0020	1	K0843	1	L0633	1	L1800	2
E1200	1	E1825	2	E2382	2	G0181	1	K0037	2	K0848	1	L0634	1	L1810	2
E1220	1	E1830	2	E2383	2	G0182	1	K0038	2	K0849	1	L0635	1	L1815	2
E1221	1	E1840	2	E2384	4	G0186	1	K0039	2	K0850	1	L0636	1	L1820	2
E1222	1	E1841	2	E2385	4	G0202	1	K0040	2	K0851	1	L0637	1	L1825	2
E1223	1	E1902	1	E2387	4	G0204	1	K0041	2	K0852	1	L0638	1	L1830	2
E1224	1	E2000	1	E2389	4	G0206	1	K0042	2	K0854	1	L0639	1	L1831	2
E1225	1	E2100	1	E2391	4	G0239	1	K0043	2	K0855	1	L0640	1	L1832	2
E1226	1	E2101	1	E2392	4	G0245	1	K0044	2	K0856	1	L0700	1	L1834	2
E1228	1	E2120	1	E2393	4	G0246	1	K0045	2	K0857	1	L0710	1	L1836	2
E1230	1	E2201	1	E2395	4	G0247	1	K0046	2	K0858	1	L0810	1	L1840	2
E1231	1	E2202	1	E2396	4	G0248	1	K0047	2	K0859	1	L0820	1	L1843	2
E1232	1	E2203	1	E2397	1	G0249	1	K0050	2	K0860	1	L0830	1	L1844	2
E1233	1	E2204	1	E2402	1	G0250	1	K0051	2	K0861	1	L0859	1	L1845	2
E1234	1	E2205	2	E2500	1	G0251	1	K0052	2	K0862	1	L0861	1	L1846	2
E1235	1	E2206	2	E2502	1	G0259	2	K0053	2	K0863	1	L0970	1	L1847	2
E1236	1	E2207	2	E2504	1	G0260	2	K0056	1	K0864	1	L0972	1	L1850	2
E1237	1	E2208	1	E2506	1	G0268	1	K0065	2	K0868	1	L0974	1	L1860	2
E1238	1	E2209	2	E2508	1	G0275	1	K0069	2	K0869	1	L0976	1	L1900	2
E1240	1	E2211	2	E2510	1	G0278	1	K0070	2	K0877	1	L0978	2	L1901	2
E1250	1	E2212	2	E2511	1	G0281	1	K0071	2	K0880	1	L0980	1	L1902	2
E1260	1	E2213	2	E2512	1	G0283	1	K0072	2	K0884	1	L1000	1	L1904	2
E1270	1	E2214	2	E2601	1	G0288	1	K0073	2	L0112	1	L1005	1	L1906	2
E1280	1	E2215	2	E2602	1	G0289	2	K0077	2	L0120	1	L1010	2	L1907	2
E1285	1	E2216	2	E2603	1	G0290	1	K0105	1	L0130	1	L1020	2	L1910	2
E1290	1	E2217	2	E2604	1	G0291	2	K0195	2	L0140	1	L1025	1	L1920	2
E1295	1	E2218	2	E2605	1	G0293	1	K0455	1	L0150	1	L1030	1	L1930	2
E1310	1	E2219	2	E2606	1	G0294	1	K0462	1	L0160	1	L1040	1	L1932	2
E1353	1	E2220	2	E2607	1	G0302	1	K0606	1	L0170	1	L1050	1	L1940	2
E1355	1	E2221	2	E2608	1	G0303	1	K0607	1	L0172	1	L1060	1	L1945	2
E1372	1	E2222	2	E2609	1	G0304	1	K0608	1	L0174	1	L1070	2	L1950	2
E1390	1	E2223	2	E2611	1	G0305	1	K0609	1	L0180	1	L1080	2	L1951	2
E1391	1	E2224	2	E2612	1	G0306	2	K0730	1	L0190	1	L1085	1	L1960	2
E1392	1	E2225	2	E2613	1	G0307	2	K0733	2	L0200	1	L1090	1	L1970	2
E1405	1	E2226	2	E2614	1	G0328	1	K0734	1	L0210	1	L1100	2	L1971	2
E1406	1	E2227	2	E2615	1	G0329	1	K0735	1	L0220	1	L1110	2	L1980	2
E1500	1	E2228	2	E2616	1	G0337	1	K0736	1	L0430	1	L1120	3	L1990	2
E1510	1	E2300	1	E2617	1	G0339	1	K0737	1	L0450	1	L1200	1	L2000	2
E1520	1	E2301	1	E2619	2	G0340	1	K0738	1	L0452	1	L1210	2	L2005	2
E1530	1	E2310	1	E2620	1	G0341	1	K0800	1	L0454	1	L1220	1	L2010	2
E1540	1	E2311	1	E2621	1	G0342	1	K0801	1	L0456	1	L1230	1	L2020	2
E1550	1	E2312	1	G0008	1	G0343	1	K0802	1	L0458	1	L1240	1	L2030	2
E1560	1	E2313	1	G0009	1	G0364	2	K0806	1	L0460	1	L1250	2	L2034	2
E1570	1	E2321	1	G0010	1	G0365	2	K0807	1	L0462	1	L1260	1	L2035	2
E1580	1	E2322	1	G0027	1	G0372	1	K0808	1	L0464	1	L1270	3	L2036	2
E1590	1	E2323	1	G0101	1	G0389	1	K0813	1	L0466	1	L1280	2	L2037	2
E1592	1	E2324	1	G0102	1	G0392	1	K0814	1	L0468	1	L1290	2	L2038	2

Appendix L — Medically Unlikely Edits (MUEs) — Professional

CPT	MUE	CPT	MUE	CPT	MUE	CPT	MUE	CPT	MUE	CPT	MUE	CPT	MUE	CPT	MUE
L2040	1	L3002	2	L3660	1	L4055	2	L5637	2	L5810	2	L6386	2	L6940	2
L2050	1	L3003	2	L3670	1	L4060	2	L5638	2	L5811	2	L6388	2	L6945	2
L2060	1	L3010	2	L3671	1	L4070	2	L5639	2	L5812	2	L6400	2	L6950	2
L2070	1	L3020	2	L3672	1	L4080	2	L5640	2	L5814	2	L6450	2	L6955	2
L2080	1	L3030	2	L3673	1	L4100	2	L5642	2	L5816	2	L6500	2	L6960	2
L2090	1	L3031	2	L3675	1	L4130	2	L5643	2	L5818	2	L6550	2	L6965	2
L2106	2	L3040	2	L3677	1	L4350	2	L5644	2	L5822	2	L6570	2	L6970	2
L2108	2	L3050	2	L3700	2	L4360	2	L5645	2	L5824	2	L6580	2	L6975	2
L2112	2	L3060	2	L3701	2	L4370	2	L5646	2	L5826	2	L6582	2	L7040	2
L2114	2	L3070	2	L3702	2	L4380	2	L5647	2	L5828	2	L6584	2	L7045	2
L2116	2	L3080	2	L3710	2	L4386	2	L5648	2	L5830	2	L6586	2	L7170	2
L2126	2	L3090	2	L3720	2	L4392	2	L5649	2	L5840	2	L6588	2	L7180	2
L2128	2	L3100	2	L3730	2	L4394	2	L5650	2	L5845	2	L6590	2	L7181	2
L2132	2	L3140	1	L3740	2	L4396	2	L5651	2	L5848	2	L6600	2	L7185	2
L2134	2	L3150	1	L3760	2	L4398	2	L5652	2	L5850	2	L6605	2	L7186	2
L2136	2	L3160	2	L3762	2	L5000	2	L5653	2	L5855	2	L6610	2	L7190	2
L2180	2	L3170	2	L3763	2	L5010	2	L5654	2	L5856	2	L6615	2	L7191	2
L2188	2	L3215	2	L3764	2	L5020	2	L5655	2	L5857	2	L6616	2	L7260	2
L2190	2	L3216	2	L3765	2	L5050	2	L5656	2	L5858	2	L6620	2	L7261	2
L2192	2	L3217	2	L3766	2	L5060	2	L5658	2	L5910	2	L6621	2	L7266	2
L2230	2	L3219	2	L3806	2	L5100	2	L5661	2	L5920	2	L6623	2	L7272	2
L2232	2	L3221	2	L3807	2	L5105	2	L5665	2	L5925	2	L6625	2	L7274	2
L2240	2	L3222	2	L3808	2	L5150	2	L5666	2	L5930	2	L6628	2	L7362	1
L2250	2	L3224	2	L3900	2	L5160	2	L5668	2	L5940	2	L6629	2	L7366	1
L2260	2	L3225	2	L3901	2	L5200	2	L5670	2	L5950	2	L6630	2	L7368	1
L2265	2	L3230	2	L3904	2	L5210	2	L5671	2	L5960	2	L6635	2	L7400	2
L2270	2	L3250	2	L3905	2	L5220	2	L5672	2	L5962	2	L6637	2	L7401	2
L2275	2	L3251	2	L3906	2	L5230	2	L5676	2	L5964	2	L6638	2	L7402	2
L2280	2	L3252	2	L3908	2	L5250	2	L5677	2	L5966	2	L6640	2	L7403	2
L2300	1	L3253	2	L3909	2	L5270	2	L5678	2	L5968	2	L6641	2	L7404	2
L2310	1	L3330	2	L3911	2	L5280	2	L5680	2	L5970	2	L6642	2	L7405	2
L2320	2	L3332	2	L3912	2	L5301	2	L5681	2	L5971	2	L6645	2	L7900	1
L2330	2	L3340	2	L3913	2	L5311	2	L5682	2	L5972	2	L6646	2	L8030	2
L2335	2	L3350	2	L3917	2	L5321	2	L5683	2	L5974	2	L6647	2	L8035	2
L2340	2	L3360	2	L3919	2	L5331	2	L5684	2	L5975	2	L6648	2	L8039	2
L2350	2	L3370	2	L3921	2	L5341	2	L5686	2	L5976	2	L6650	2	L8040	1
L2360	2	L3380	2	L3923	2	L5400	2	L5688	2	L5978	2	L6670	2	L8041	1
L2370	2	L3390	2	L3929	2	L5410	2	L5690	2	L5979	2	L6672	2	L8042	2
L2375	2	L3400	2	L3931	2	L5420	2	L5692	2	L5980	2	L6675	2	L8043	1
L2380	2	L3410	2	L3933	3	L5430	2	L5694	2	L5981	2	L6676	2	L8044	1
L2500	2	L3420	2	L3935	3	L5450	2	L5695	2	L5982	2	L6677	2	L8045	2
L2510	2	L3430	2	L3960	1	L5460	2	L5696	2	L5984	2	L6686	2	L8046	1
L2520	2	L3440	2	L3961	1	L5500	2	L5697	2	L5985	2	L6687	2	L8047	1
L2525	2	L3450	2	L3962	1	L5505	2	L5698	2	L5986	2	L6688	2	L8300	1
L2526	2	L3455	2	L3964	2	L5510	2	L5699	2	L5987	2	L6689	2	L8310	1
L2530	2	L3460	2	L3965	2	L5520	2	L5700	2	L5988	2	L6690	2	L8320	2
L2540	2	L3465	2	L3966	2	L5530	2	L5701	2	L5990	2	L6693	2	L8330	2
L2550	2	L3470	2	L3967	1	L5535	2	L5702	2	L6000	2	L6694	2	L8500	1
L2570	2	L3480	2	L3968	2	L5540	2	L5703	2	L6010	2	L6695	2	L8501	2
L2580	2	L3485	2	L3969	2	L5560	2	L5704	2	L6020	2	L6696	2	L8507	3
L2600	2	L3500	2	L3970	2	L5570	2	L5705	2	L6025	2	L6697	2	L8509	1
L2610	2	L3510	2	L3971	1	L5580	2	L5706	2	L6050	2	L6698	2	L8510	1
L2620	2	L3520	2	L3972	2	L5585	2	L5707	2	L6055	2	L6805	2	L8511	1
L2622	2	L3530	2	L3973	1	L5590	2	L5710	2	L6100	2	L6810	2	L8514	1
L2624	2	L3540	2	L3974	2	L5595	2	L5711	2	L6110	2	L6881	2	L8515	1
L2627	1	L3550	2	L3975	1	L5600	2	L5712	2	L6120	2	L6882	2	L8600	2
L2628	1	L3560	2	L3976	2	L5610	2	L5714	2	L6130	2	L6883	2	L8610	2
L2630	1	L3570	2	L3977	1	L5611	2	L5716	2	L6200	2	L6884	2	L8612	2
L2640	1	L3580	2	L3978	1	L5613	2	L5718	2	L6205	2	L6885	2	L8613	2
L2650	2	L3590	2	L3980	2	L5614	2	L5722	2	L6250	2	L6890	2	L8614	2
L2660	1	L3595	2	L3982	2	L5616	2	L5724	2	L6300	2	L6895	2	L8615	2
L2670	2	L3600	2	L3984	2	L5617	2	L5726	2	L6310	2	L6900	2	L8616	2
L2680	2	L3610	2	L4000	1	L5628	2	L5728	2	L6320	2	L6905	2	L8617	2
L2795	2	L3620	2	L4010	2	L5629	2	L5780	2	L6350	2	L6910	2	L8618	2
L2800	2	L3630	2	L4020	2	L5630	2	L5781	2	L6360	2	L6915	2	L8619	2
L2820	2	L3640	1	L4030	2	L5631	2	L5782	2	L6370	2	L6920	2	L8622	2
L2830	2	L3650	1	L4040	2	L5632	2	L5785	2	L6380	2	L6925	2	L8630	4
L3000	2	L3651	1	L4045	2	L5634	2	L5790	2	L6382	2	L6930	2	L8631	4
L3001	2	L3652	1	L4050	2	L5636	2	L5795	2	L6384	2	L6935	2	L8641	4

Appendix L — Medically Unlikely Edits (MUEs) — Professional

CPT	MUE	CPT	MUE	CPT	MUE	CPT	MUE	CPT	MUE	CPT	MUE	CPT	MUE	CPT	MUE
L8642	2	P3001	1	Q0492	1	R0070	2	V2203	2	V2304	2	V2503	2	V2631	2
L8658	4	P9612	1	Q0493	1	R0075	2	V2204	2	V2305	2	V2510	2	V2632	2
L8659	4	P9615	1	Q0494	1	V2020	1	V2205	2	V2306	2	V2511	2	V2700	2
L8670	4	Q0035	1	Q0495	1	V2101	2	V2206	2	V2307	2	V2512	2	V2710	2
L8681	1	Q0091	1	Q0497	2	V2102	2	V2207	2	V2308	2	V2513	2	V2718	2
L8682	2	Q0111	2	Q0498	1	V2104	2	V2208	2	V2309	2	V2520	2	V2730	2
L8683	1	Q0112	3	Q0499	1	V2105	2	V2209	2	V2310	2	V2521	2	V2761	2
L8684	1	Q0113	2	Q0501	1	V2106	2	V2210	2	V2311	2	V2522	2	V2770	2
L8685	1	Q0114	1	Q0502	1	V2107	2	V2211	2	V2312	2	V2523	2	V2780	2
L8686	2	Q0115	1	Q0503	3	V2108	2	V2212	2	V2313	2	V2530	2	V2781	2
L8687	2	Q0480	1	Q0504	1	V2109	2	V2213	2	V2314	2	V2531	2	V2782	2
L8688	2	Q0481	1	Q1003	2	V2110	2	V2214	2	V2315	2	V2600	1	V2783	2
L8689	1	Q0482	1	Q1004	2	V2111	2	V2215	2	V2318	2	V2610	1	V2785	2
L8690	1	Q0483	1	Q1005	2	V2112	2	V2218	2	V2319	2	V2615	2	V2790	1
L8691	1	Q0484	1	Q4001	1	V2113	2	V2219	2	V2320	2	V2623	2	V2797	1
L8695	1	Q0485	1	Q4002	1	V2114	2	V2220	2	V2321	2	V2624	2	V5008	1
M0064	1	Q0486	1	Q4003	2	V2115	2	V2221	2	V2399	2	V2625	2	V5010	1
P2028	1	Q0487	1	Q4004	2	V2118	2	V2299	2	V2410	2	V2626	2	V5011	1
P2029	1	Q0488	1	Q4025	1	V2121	2	V2300	2	V2430	2	V2627	2		
P2033	1	Q0489	1	Q4026	1	V2200	2	V2301	2	V2500	2	V2628	2		
P2038	1	Q0490	1	Q4027	1	V2201	2	V2302	2	V2501	2	V2629	2		
P3000	1	Q0491	1	Q4028	1	V2202	2	V2303	2	V2502	2	V2630	2		

Appendix L — Medically Unlikely Edits (MUEs) — OPPS

OPPS

CPT	MUE	CPT	MUE	CPT	MUE	CPT	MUE	CPT	MUE	CPT	MUE	CPT	MUE	CPT	MUE
0016T	2	11055	1	12054	1	15788	1	17266	2	20922	2	21244	1	22100	1
0017T	2	11056	1	12055	1	15789	1	17276	3	20924	4	21245	2	22101	1
0019T	1	11057	1	12056	1	15792	1	17286	3	20926	2	21246	2	22102	1
0030T	2	11100	1	12057	1	15793	1	17340	1	20972	2	21260	1	22103	3
0054T	2	11200	1	13100	1	15819	1	17360	1	20973	2	21261	1	22222	1
0055T	2	11201	1	13101	1	15820	1	17380	1	20974	1	21263	1	22305	1
0064T	1	11446	3	13120	1	15821	1	19000	2	20975	1	21267	2	22310	1
0067T	1	11450	2	13121	1	15822	1	19001	5	20979	1	21270	2	22315	1
0071T	1	11451	2	13131	1	15823	1	19020	2	20982	1	21275	1	22505	1
0072T	1	11462	2	13132	1	15824	1	19101	3	21010	1	21280	2	22520	1
0073T	2	11463	2	13150	1	15825	1	19110	2	21015	1	21282	2	22521	1
0084T	1	11471	2	13151	1	15826	1	19112	2	21025	2	21295	2	22522	5
0085T	1	11646	3	13152	1	15828	1	19120	2	21026	2	21296	2	22523	1
0087T	1	11719	1	13160	3	15829	1	19125	2	21029	1	21310	1	22524	1
0099T	2	11720	1	14300	3	15830	1	19126	3	21030	2	21315	1	22525	5
0100T	2	11721	1	15002	1	15832	2	19260	2	21031	2	21320	1	22612	1
0101T	1	11730	1	15004	1	15833	2	19296	2	21032	1	21325	1	22614	15
0102T	2	11770	1	15040	1	15834	2	19297	2	21034	1	21330	1	22851	9
0103T	1	11771	1	15050	1	15835	1	19298	2	21040	2	21335	1	22900	3
0104T	1	11772	1	15100	1	15836	2	19300	2	21044	1	21336	1	23000	2
0105T	1	11900	1	15110	1	15838	1	19301	2	21046	2	21337	1	23020	2
0106T	4	11901	1	15115	1	15839	2	19302	2	21047	2	21338	1	23030	2
0107T	4	11920	1	15120	1	15840	1	19303	2	21048	2	21339	1	23031	2
0108T	4	11921	1	15130	1	15841	2	19304	2	21049	2	21340	1	23035	2
0109T	4	11922	1	15135	1	15842	2	19307	2	21050	1	21345	1	23040	2
0110T	4	11950	1	15150	1	15845	2	19316	1	21060	1	21355	2	23044	2
0111T	1	11951	1	15151	1	15847	1	19318	1	21070	1	21356	2	23065	2
0123T	2	11952	1	15155	1	15850	1	19324	1	21073	1	21390	2	23066	2
0124T	2	11954	1	15156	1	15851	1	19325	1	21076	1	21400	2	23075	4
0140T	1	11960	3	15170	1	15852	2	19328	1	21077	2	21401	2	23076	2
0144T	1	11970	2	15175	1	15860	1	19330	1	21079	1	21406	2	23077	1
0145T	1	11971	2	15200	1	15876	1	19340	1	21080	1	21407	2	23100	2
0146T	1	11976	1	15220	1	15877	1	19342	1	21081	1	21408	2	23101	2
0147T	1	11980	1	15240	1	15878	2	19350	1	21082	1	21421	1	23105	2
0148T	1	11981	1	15260	1	15879	2	19355	1	21083	1	21440	2	23106	2
0149T	1	11982	1	15300	1	15920	1	19357	1	21084	1	21445	2	23107	2
0150T	1	11983	1	15320	1	15922	1	19366	1	21085	1	21450	1	23120	2
0151T	1	12001	1	15330	1	15931	1	19370	1	21086	2	21451	1	23125	2
0160T	1	12002	1	15335	1	15933	1	19371	1	21087	1	21452	1	23130	2
0161T	1	12004	1	15340	1	15934	1	19380	1	21088	1	21453	1	23145	1
0170T	1	12005	1	15360	1	15935	1	19396	1	21100	1	21454	1	23146	1
0171T	1	12006	1	15365	1	15936	1	20100	2	21110	2	21461	1	23150	1
0172T	3	12007	1	15400	1	15937	1	20102	4	21120	1	21462	1	23155	1
0176T	1	12011	1	15420	1	15940	2	20103	4	21121	1	21465	2	23156	1
0177T	1	12013	1	15430	1	15941	2	20150	2	21122	1	21470	1	23170	1
0179T	1	12014	1	15570	3	15944	2	20200	3	21123	1	21480	2	23172	1
0181T	1	12015	1	15572	2	15945	2	20205	4	21125	2	21485	2	23174	1
0182T	3	12016	1	15574	2	15946	2	20206	3	21127	2	21490	2	23180	1
0183T	1	12017	1	15576	2	15950	2	20250	3	21137	1	21495	1	23182	1
0190T	2	12018	1	15600	2	15951	2	20251	3	21138	1	21497	1	23184	1
0191T	2	12020	3	15610	2	15952	2	20526	2	21139	1	21501	3	23190	1
0192T	2	12021	3	15620	2	15953	2	20552	1	21150	1	21502	1	23195	1
0193T	1	12031	1	15630	2	15956	2	20553	1	21175	1	21550	3	23330	2
0194T	1	12032	1	15650	1	15958	2	20555	1	21181	1	21556	3	23331	2
0197T	2	12034	1	15731	1	16000	1	20662	1	21195	1	21557	1	23395	1
0198T	2	12035	1	15740	3	16020	1	20663	2	21198	1	21610	2	23397	1
10040	1	12036	1	15750	2	16025	1	20665	1	21199	1	21685	1	23400	1
10060	1	12037	1	15760	2	16030	1	20670	2	21206	1	21700	2	23405	2
10061	1	12041	1	15770	2	17000	1	20680	2	21208	2	21720	1	23406	2
10080	1	12042	1	15775	1	17003	13	20692	3	21209	2	21725	1	23410	2
10081	1	12044	1	15776	1	17004	1	20693	2	21210	2	21742	1	23412	2
10180	3	12045	1	15780	1	17106	1	20696	3	21215	2	21743	1	23415	2
11000	1	12046	1	15781	2	17107	1	20697	2	21230	2	21805	3	23420	2
11010	1	12047	1	15782	2	17108	1	20900	2	21235	2	21820	1	23430	2
11011	1	12051	1	15783	2	17110	1	20910	2	21240	2	21920	3	23440	2
11012	1	12052	1	15786	1	17111	1	20912	1	21242	2	21925	3	23450	2
		12053	1	15787	3	17264	3	20920	2	21243	2	21935	1	23455	2

Appendix L — Medically Unlikely Edits (MUEs) — OPPS

CPT	MUE	CPT	MUE	CPT	MUE	CPT	MUE	CPT	MUE	CPT	MUE	CPT	MUE	CPT	MUE
23460	2	24152	1	24800	2	25415	2	26034	2	27048	2	27397	2	27640	2
23462	2	24153	1	24802	2	25420	2	26035	3	27049	2	27400	2	27641	2
23465	2	24155	2	24925	2	25425	2	26037	2	27050	2	27403	2	27647	2
23466	2	24160	2	24935	2	25426	2	26040	2	27052	2	27405	2	27650	2
23470	2	24164	2	25000	2	25430	2	26045	2	27057	1	27407	2	27652	2
23480	2	24200	3	25001	2	25431	2	26070	3	27060	2	27409	2	27654	2
23485	2	24201	3	25020	2	25440	2	26100	2	27062	2	27412	2	27656	2
23490	2	24300	2	25023	2	25441	2	26105	2	27065	2	27415	2	27658	2
23491	2	24301	2	25024	2	25442	2	26110	3	27066	2	27416	2	27659	2
23500	2	24305	4	25025	2	25443	2	26117	2	27067	2	27418	2	27664	2
23505	2	24320	2	25031	2	25444	2	26121	2	27080	1	27420	2	27665	2
23515	2	24330	2	25035	2	25445	2	26123	2	27086	2	27422	2	27675	2
23520	2	24331	2	25040	2	25446	2	26185	1	27087	2	27424	2	27676	2
23525	2	24332	2	25065	5	25449	2	26205	2	27096	1	27425	2	27680	3
23530	2	24340	2	25066	3	25450	2	26215	2	27097	2	27427	2	27681	2
23532	2	24342	2	25076	5	25455	2	26230	3	27098	2	27428	2	27685	2
23540	2	24343	2	25077	2	25490	2	26236	3	27100	2	27429	2	27686	2
23545	2	24344	2	25085	2	25491	2	26250	2	27105	2	27430	2	27687	2
23550	2	24345	2	25100	2	25492	2	26255	2	27110	2	27435	2	27690	2
23552	2	24346	2	25101	2	25500	2	26260	2	27111	2	27437	2	27691	2
23570	2	24357	2	25105	2	25505	2	26261	2	27193	1	27438	2	27695	2
23575	2	24358	2	25107	2	25515	2	26262	2	27194	1	27440	2	27696	2
23585	2	24359	2	25110	3	25520	2	26357	3	27200	1	27441	2	27698	2
23600	2	24360	2	25111	2	25525	2	26358	3	27202	1	27442	2	27700	2
23605	2	24361	2	25112	2	25526	2	26390	3	27220	2	27443	2	27704	2
23615	2	24362	2	25115	2	25530	2	26392	3	27230	2	27446	2	27705	2
23616	2	24363	2	25116	2	25535	2	26416	2	27235	2	27475	2	27707	2
23620	2	24365	2	25119	2	25545	2	26428	2	27238	2	27496	2	27709	2
23625	2	24366	2	25120	2	25560	2	26432	2	27246	2	27497	2	27720	2
23630	2	24400	2	25125	1	25565	2	26433	2	27250	2	27498	2	27722	2
23650	2	24410	2	25126	1	25574	2	26434	3	27252	2	27499	2	27726	2
23655	2	24420	2	25130	2	25575	2	26494	2	27256	2	27500	2	27730	2
23660	2	24430	2	25135	2	25600	2	26496	2	27257	2	27501	2	27732	2
23665	2	24435	2	25136	2	25605	2	26497	2	27265	2	27502	2	27734	2
23670	2	24470	2	25145	1	25606	2	26498	2	27266	2	27503	2	27740	2
23675	2	24495	2	25150	1	25607	2	26508	2	27267	2	27508	2	27742	2
23680	2	24498	2	25151	1	25608	2	26516	2	27275	2	27509	2	27745	2
23700	2	24500	2	25170	1	25609	2	26517	2	27305	2	27510	2	27750	2
23800	2	24505	2	25210	2	25622	2	26518	2	27306	2	27516	2	27752	2
23802	2	24515	2	25215	2	25624	2	26548	3	27307	2	27517	2	27756	2
23921	2	24516	2	25230	2	25628	2	26550	2	27310	2	27520	2	27758	2
23930	2	24530	2	25240	2	25630	2	26555	2	27325	1	27524	2	27759	2
23931	2	24535	2	25248	3	25635	2	26560	2	27326	1	27530	2	27760	2
23935	2	24538	2	25250	2	25650	2	26561	2	27329	2	27532	2	27762	2
24000	2	24545	2	25251	2	25651	2	26562	2	27330	2	27538	2	27766	2
24006	2	24546	2	25259	2	25652	2	26580	2	27331	2	27550	2	27767	2
24065	2	24560	2	25275	2	25660	2	26641	2	27332	2	27552	2	27768	2
24066	2	24565	2	25295	9	25670	2	26645	2	27333	2	27560	2	27769	2
24077	2	24566	2	25300	2	25671	2	26650	2	27334	2	27562	2	27780	2
24100	2	24575	2	25301	2	25675	2	26665	2	27335	2	27566	2	27781	2
24101	2	24576	2	25315	2	25676	2	26740	3	27340	2	27570	2	27784	2
24102	2	24577	2	25316	2	25680	2	26742	3	27345	2	27594	2	27786	2
24105	2	24579	2	25320	2	25685	2	26746	3	27347	2	27600	2	27788	2
24110	1	24582	2	25332	2	25690	2	26820	2	27350	2	27601	2	27792	2
24115	2	24586	2	25335	2	25695	2	26841	2	27355	2	27602	2	27808	2
24116	1	24587	2	25337	2	25800	2	26842	2	27356	2	27604	2	27810	2
24120	2	24600	2	25350	2	25805	2	26860	1	27357	2	27605	2	27814	2
24125	1	24605	2	25355	2	25810	2	26862	1	27358	2	27606	2	27816	2
24126	1	24615	2	25360	2	25820	2	26990	2	27380	2	27607	2	27818	2
24130	2	24620	2	25365	2	25825	2	26991	2	27381	2	27610	2	27822	2
24134	1	24635	2	25370	2	25830	2	27000	2	27385	2	27612	2	27823	2
24136	1	24640	2	25375	2	25907	2	27001	1	27386	2	27615	2	27824	2
24138	2	24650	2	25390	2	25922	2	27003	1	27390	2	27620	2	27825	2
24140	2	24655	2	25391	2	25929	2	27006	2	27391	2	27625	2	27826	2
24145	2	24665	2	25392	2	25931	2	27027	1	27392	1	27626	2	27827	2
24147	2	24666	2	25393	2	26010	3	27033	2	27393	2	27630	2	27828	2
24149	2	24670	2	25394	2	26011	3	27035	2	27394	1	27635	2	27829	2
24150	1	24675	2	25400	2	26025	2	27040	2	27395	1	27637	2	27830	2
24151	1	24685	2	25405	2	26030	2	27041	3	27396	2	27638	2	27831	2

Appendix L — Medically Unlikely Edits (MUEs) — OPPS

CPT	MUE	CPT	MUE	CPT	MUE	CPT	MUE	CPT	MUE	CPT	MUE	CPT	MUE	CPT	MUE
27832	2	28298	2	29086	2	29860	2	30520	1	31527	1	32421	3	35459	2
27840	2	28299	2	29105	2	29861	2	30540	1	31528	1	32422	3	35471	3
27842	2	28300	2	29125	2	29862	2	30545	1	31529	1	32550	2	35472	1
27846	2	28302	2	29126	2	29863	2	30560	1	31530	1	32560	2	35474	2
27848	2	28304	2	29200	1	29866	2	30580	2	31531	1	32601	1	35484	2
27860	2	28305	2	29220	1	29867	2	30600	1	31535	1	32602	1	35485	2
27870	2	28306	2	29240	2	29868	2	30620	1	31536	1	32603	1	35490	2
27871	2	28307	2	29260	2	29870	2	30630	1	31540	1	32604	1	35491	1
27884	2	28309	2	29280	2	29871	2	30801	1	31541	1	32605	1	35492	2
27889	2	28310	2	29305	1	29873	2	30802	1	31545	2	32606	1	35493	2
27892	2	28315	2	29325	1	29874	2	30901	1	31546	2	32960	1	35494	3
27893	2	28320	2	29345	2	29875	2	30903	1	31560	1	32998	2	35495	2
27894	2	28322	2	29355	2	29876	2	30905	1	31561	1	33010	1	35500	2
28001	2	28340	2	29358	2	29877	2	30906	1	31570	1	33011	1	35685	2
28002	3	28341	2	29365	2	29879	2	30915	1	31571	1	33206	1	35686	1
28003	2	28344	2	29405	2	29880	2	30920	1	31575	1	33207	1	35761	2
28005	3	28360	2	29425	2	29881	2	30930	1	31576	1	33208	1	35860	2
28035	2	28400	2	29435	2	29882	2	31000	1	31577	1	33210	1	35875	2
28052	2	28405	2	29440	2	29883	2	31002	2	31578	1	33211	1	35876	2
28054	2	28406	2	29445	2	29884	2	31020	1	31579	1	33212	1	35879	2
28060	2	28415	2	29450	1	29885	2	31030	1	31580	1	33213	1	35881	2
28062	2	28420	2	29505	2	29886	2	31032	1	31582	1	33214	1	35883	1
28086	2	28430	2	29515	2	29887	2	31040	2	31588	1	33215	2	35884	1
28088	2	28435	2	29520	2	29888	2	31050	2	31590	1	33216	1	35903	2
28090	2	28436	2	29530	2	29889	2	31051	2	31595	2	33217	1	36002	2
28092	2	28445	2	29540	2	29891	2	31070	2	31600	1	33218	1	36260	1
28100	2	28446	2	29550	2	29892	2	31075	2	31601	1	33220	1	36261	1
28102	2	28490	2	29580	2	29893	2	31080	2	31603	1	33222	1	36262	1
28103	2	28495	2	29590	2	29894	2	31081	2	31605	1	33223	1	36420	2
28106	2	28496	2	29700	2	29895	2	31084	2	31610	1	33224	1	36425	3
28107	2	28505	2	29705	2	29897	2	31085	2	31611	1	33225	1	36430	1
28108	2	28530	2	29710	2	29898	2	31086	2	31612	1	33226	1	36440	1
28110	2	28531	2	29715	1	29899	2	31087	2	31613	1	33233	1	36450	1
28111	2	28540	2	29720	1	29900	2	31090	2	31614	1	33234	1	36455	1
28113	2	28545	2	29730	2	29901	2	31200	2	31615	1	33235	1	36468	1
28114	2	28546	2	29740	1	29902	2	31201	2	31620	1	33240	1	36469	1
28116	2	28555	2	29750	1	29904	2	31205	2	31622	1	33241	1	36470	2
28118	2	28570	2	29800	2	29905	2	31231	1	31623	1	33244	1	36471	2
28119	2	28575	2	29804	2	29906	2	31233	2	31624	1	33249	1	36475	2
28120	2	28576	2	29805	2	29907	2	31235	2	31625	1	33282	1	36478	2
28130	2	28585	2	29806	2	30000	1	31237	2	31628	1	33284	1	36479	2
28171	2	28600	3	29807	2	30020	1	31238	2	31629	1	34101	2	36511	1
28173	2	28605	3	29819	2	30100	3	31239	2	31630	2	34111	2	36512	1
28175	2	28630	3	29820	2	30110	1	31240	2	31631	1	34201	2	36513	1
28192	2	28705	2	29821	2	30115	1	31254	2	31632	4	34203	2	36514	1
28193	2	28715	2	29822	2	30117	2	31255	2	31633	4	34421	2	36515	2
28202	2	28725	2	29823	2	30118	2	31256	2	31635	1	34471	1	36516	1
28210	2	28730	2	29824	2	30120	1	31267	2	31636	1	34490	2	36522	1
28220	2	28735	2	29825	2	30124	2	31276	2	31637	2	34501	2	36555	2
28222	2	28737	2	29826	2	30125	1	31287	2	31638	2	34510	2	36556	2
28225	2	28750	2	29827	2	30130	2	31288	2	31640	1	34520	1	36557	2
28226	2	28755	2	29828	2	30140	2	31292	2	31641	1	34530	2	36558	2
28230	2	28760	2	29830	2	30150	1	31293	2	31643	1	35011	2	36560	2
28238	2	28890	2	29834	2	30160	1	31294	2	31645	1	35180	2	36561	2
28240	2	29000	1	29835	2	30200	1	31300	1	31646	2	35184	2	36563	2
28250	2	29010	1	29836	2	30210	1	31320	1	31656	1	35188	2	36565	2
28260	2	29015	1	29837	2	30220	1	31400	1	31717	1	35190	2	36566	2
28261	2	29020	1	29838	2	30300	1	31420	1	31720	2	35201	2	36568	2
28262	2	29025	1	29840	2	30310	1	31500	2	31730	1	35206	2	36569	3
28264	2	29035	1	29843	2	30320	1	31502	1	31750	1	35207	3	36570	2
28280	2	29040	1	29844	2	30400	1	31505	1	31755	1	35226	3	36571	2
28286	2	29044	1	29845	2	30410	1	31510	1	31785	1	35231	2	36575	2
28289	2	29046	1	29846	2	30420	1	31511	1	31820	1	35236	2	36576	2
28290	2	29049	1	29847	2	30430	1	31512	1	31825	1	35256	2	36578	2
28292	2	29055	1	29848	2	30435	1	31513	1	31830	1	35261	1	36580	2
28293	2	29058	1	29850	2	30450	1	31515	1	32201	2	35266	2	36581	2
28294	2	29065	2	29851	2	30460	1	31520	1	32400	2	35286	2	36582	2
28296	2	29075	2	29855	2	30462	2	31525	1	32405	2	35321	2	36583	2
28297	2	29085	2	29856	2	30465	1	31526	1	32420	2	35458	3	36584	2

Appendix L — Medically Unlikely Edits (MUEs) — OPPS

CPT	MUE	CPT	MUE	CPT	MUE	CPT	MUE	CPT	MUE	CPT	MUE	CPT	MUE	CPT	MUE
36585	2	38230	1	41110	2	42509	1	43248	1	44386	1	46030	1	47530	3
36589	2	38240	1	41112	2	42510	1	43249	1	44388	1	46040	2	47552	1
36590	2	38241	1	41113	2	42600	1	43250	1	44389	1	46045	2	47553	1
36592	1	38242	1	41114	2	42650	2	43251	1	44390	1	46050	2	47554	1
36593	2	38300	2	41115	1	42660	2	43255	2	44391	1	46060	2	47555	1
36595	2	38305	2	41116	3	42665	2	43256	1	44392	1	46070	1	47556	1
36596	2	38308	1	41120	1	42700	2	43257	1	44393	1	46080	1	47560	1
36597	2	38500	2	41250	2	42720	1	43258	1	44394	1	46083	2	47561	1
36598	2	38505	3	41251	2	42725	2	43259	1	44397	1	46200	1	47562	1
36640	1	38510	2	41252	2	42800	3	43260	1	44500	1	46210	1	47563	1
36680	1	38520	2	41500	1	42802	2	43261	1	44901	1	46211	1	47564	1
36800	1	38525	2	41510	1	42806	1	43262	2	44970	1	46220	2	47630	1
36810	1	38530	2	41512	1	42808	2	43263	2	45000	1	46221	1	48102	2
36815	1	38542	2	41520	1	42809	1	43264	1	45005	1	46230	1	48511	1
36818	1	38550	1	41800	2	42810	2	43265	1	45020	1	46250	1	49021	3
36819	1	38555	1	41820	4	42815	2	43267	1	45100	1	46255	1	49041	3
36820	2	38570	1	41822	1	42820	1	43268	2	45108	1	46257	1	49061	3
36821	2	38571	1	41823	1	42821	1	43269	2	45150	1	46258	1	49080	1
36825	1	38572	1	41825	2	42825	1	43271	1	45160	1	46260	1	49081	2
36830	2	38700	1	41826	2	42826	1	43272	1	45170	1	46261	1	49180	3
36831	1	38720	1	41827	2	42830	1	43273	1	45190	1	46262	1	49250	1
36832	2	38740	2	41828	4	42831	1	43280	1	45300	1	46270	1	49320	1
36833	1	38745	2	41850	2	42835	1	43450	1	45303	1	46275	1	49321	1
36834	1	38760	1	41872	4	42836	1	43453	1	45305	1	46280	1	49322	1
36835	1	38792	2	41874	4	42842	1	43456	1	45307	1	46285	1	49323	1
36838	2	39400	1	42000	1	42844	1	43458	1	45308	1	46288	1	49324	1
36860	2	40500	2	42100	3	42860	1	43510	1	45309	1	46320	2	49325	1
36861	2	40510	2	42104	3	42870	1	43600	1	45315	1	46500	1	49326	1
36870	2	40520	2	42106	2	42890	1	43647	1	45317	1	46505	1	49402	1
37183	1	40525	2	42107	2	42892	1	43648	1	45320	1	46600	1	49419	1
37184	2	40527	2	42120	1	42900	1	43651	1	45321	1	46604	1	49421	1
37185	2	40530	2	42140	1	42950	1	43652	1	45327	1	46606	1	49422	1
37186	2	40650	2	42145	1	42955	1	43653	1	45330	1	46608	1	49423	3
37187	2	40652	2	42160	1	42960	1	43752	2	45331	1	46610	1	49426	1
37188	2	40654	2	42180	1	42962	1	43760	2	45332	1	46611	1	49429	1
37195	1	40700	1	42182	1	42970	1	43761	2	45333	1	46612	1	49435	1
37200	2	40701	1	42200	1	42972	1	43830	1	45334	1	46614	1	49436	1
37201	1	40702	1	42205	1	43020	1	43831	1	45335	1	46615	1	49440	1
37203	2	40720	1	42210	1	43030	1	43870	1	45337	1	46700	1	49441	1
37205	1	40761	1	42215	1	43130	1	43886	1	45338	1	46706	2	49442	1
37207	1	40800	1	42220	1	43200	1	43887	1	45339	1	46750	1	49446	1
37209	2	40801	1	42225	1	43201	1	43888	1	45340	1	46753	1	49450	1
37210	1	40806	2	42226	1	43202	1	44100	1	45341	1	46754	1	49451	1
37250	1	40816	2	42227	1	43204	1	44180	1	45342	1	46760	1	49452	1
37500	2	40818	2	42235	1	43205	1	44186	1	45345	1	46761	1	49460	1
37565	2	40819	2	42260	1	43215	1	44206	1	45355	1	46762	1	49465	1
37600	1	40820	2	42280	1	43216	1	44207	1	45378	1	46900	1	49491	1
37605	2	40830	2	42281	1	43217	1	44208	1	45379	1	46910	1	49492	1
37606	2	40831	2	42300	2	43219	1	44213	1	45380	1	46916	1	49495	1
37607	1	40840	1	42305	2	43220	1	44312	1	45381	1	46917	1	49496	1
37609	2	40842	1	42310	2	43226	1	44340	1	45382	2	46922	1	49500	1
37615	2	40843	1	42320	2	43227	2	44360	1	45383	1	46924	1	49501	1
37620	1	40844	2	42330	3	43228	1	44361	1	45384	1	46930	1	49505	1
37650	1	40845	1	42335	2	43231	1	44363	1	45385	1	46937	1	49507	1
37700	1	41000	1	42340	2	43232	1	44364	1	45386	1	46938	1	49520	1
37718	1	41005	1	42400	2	43234	1	44365	1	45387	1	46940	1	49521	1
37722	1	41006	2	42405	2	43235	1	44366	1	45391	1	46942	1	49525	1
37735	1	41007	2	42408	1	43236	1	44369	1	45392	1	46945	1	49540	1
37760	1	41008	2	42409	1	43237	1	44370	1	45500	1	46946	1	49550	1
37765	2	41009	2	42410	2	43238	1	44372	1	45505	1	46947	1	49553	1
37766	2	41010	1	42415	2	43239	1	44373	1	45520	1	47000	3	49555	1
37780	1	41015	2	42420	2	43240	1	44376	1	45541	1	47011	3	49557	1
37785	1	41016	1	42425	2	43241	1	44377	1	45560	1	47370	1	49565	2
37790	1	41017	2	42440	2	43242	1	44378	1	45900	1	47371	1	49566	2
38120	1	41018	2	42450	1	43243	1	44379	1	45905	1	47382	1	49570	1
38205	1	41019	1	42500	2	43244	1	44380	1	45910	1	47490	1	49572	1
38206	1	41100	3	42505	1	43245	1	44382	1	45915	1	47510	2	49580	1
38220	2	41105	3	42507	1	43246	1	44383	1	45990	1	47511	2	49582	1
38221	2	41108	2	42508	1	43247	1	44385	1	46020	1	47525	3	49585	1

Appendix L — Medically Unlikely Edits (MUEs) — OPPS

CPT	MUE	CPT	MUE	CPT	MUE	CPT	MUE	CPT	MUE	CPT	MUE	CPT	MUE	CPT	MUE
49587	1	51080	2	52345	2	53852	1	54640	1	57023	2	58100	1	59160	1
49590	1	51100	1	52346	2	54000	1	54660	1	57061	1	58110	1	59200	1
49600	1	51101	1	52351	1	54001	1	54670	2	57065	1	58120	1	59300	1
49650	1	51102	1	52352	2	54015	1	54680	1	57100	3	58145	1	59320	1
49651	1	51500	1	52353	2	54050	1	54690	2	57105	2	58260	1	59412	2
49652	1	51520	1	52354	2	54055	1	54692	1	57106	1	58262	1	59414	1
49653	1	51535	1	52355	2	54056	1	54700	2	57107	1	58263	1	59812	1
49654	2	51700	1	52400	1	54057	1	54800	2	57109	1	58270	1	59820	1
49655	2	51701	2	52402	1	54060	1	54830	2	57120	1	58290	1	59821	1
49656	2	51702	2	52450	1	54065	1	54840	2	57130	1	58291	1	59840	1
49657	2	51703	2	52500	1	54100	3	54860	1	57135	2	58292	1	59841	1
50020	1	51705	2	52601	1	54105	2	54861	1	57150	1	58294	1	59866	1
50021	2	51710	1	52630	1	54110	1	54865	1	57155	1	58301	1	59870	1
50080	2	51715	1	52640	1	54111	1	54900	1	57160	1	58321	1	59871	1
50081	2	51720	1	52647	1	54112	1	54901	1	57170	1	58322	1	60000	1
50200	2	51725	1	52648	1	54115	1	55000	2	57180	1	58323	1	60200	2
50382	1	51726	1	52649	1	54120	1	55040	1	57200	1	58345	2	60210	1
50384	1	51736	1	52700	1	54150	1	55041	1	57210	1	58346	1	60212	1
50385	2	51741	1	53000	1	54160	1	55060	2	57220	1	58350	2	60220	1
50386	2	51772	1	53010	1	54161	1	55100	2	57230	1	58353	1	60225	1
50387	1	51784	1	53020	1	54162	1	55110	1	57240	1	58356	1	60240	1
50389	2	51785	1	53025	1	54163	1	55120	1	57250	1	58541	1	60252	1
50390	2	51792	1	53040	1	54164	1	55150	1	57260	1	58542	1	60260	1
50391	2	51795	1	53060	1	54200	1	55175	1	57265	1	58543	1	60271	1
50392	2	51797	1	53080	1	54205	1	55180	1	57267	3	58544	1	60280	1
50393	2	51798	1	53085	1	54220	1	55200	1	57268	1	58545	1	60281	1
50395	2	51880	1	53200	1	54231	1	55250	1	57282	1	58546	1	60500	1
50396	2	51990	1	53210	1	54235	1	55400	1	57283	1	58550	1	60502	1
50398	2	51992	1	53215	1	54240	1	55450	1	57284	1	58552	1	60512	1
50541	2	52000	1	53220	1	54250	1	55500	2	57285	1	58553	1	60520	1
50542	2	52001	1	53230	1	54300	1	55520	2	57287	1	58554	1	61000	1
50543	2	52005	2	53235	1	54304	1	55530	2	57288	1	58555	1	61001	1
50544	2	52007	2	53240	1	54308	1	55535	2	57289	1	58558	1	61020	2
50551	2	52010	1	53250	1	54312	1	55540	2	57291	1	58559	1	61026	2
50553	2	52204	1	53260	1	54316	1	55550	2	57292	1	58560	1	61050	1
50555	1	52214	1	53265	1	54318	1	55600	1	57295	1	58561	1	61055	1
50557	2	52224	1	53270	1	54322	1	55680	2	57300	1	58562	1	61070	2
50561	2	52234	1	53275	1	54324	1	55700	1	57310	1	58563	1	61215	1
50562	1	52235	1	53400	1	54326	1	55705	1	57320	1	58565	1	61330	1
50570	2	52240	1	53405	1	54328	1	55706	1	57330	1	58570	1	61334	2
50572	2	52250	1	53410	1	54340	1	55720	1	57335	1	58571	1	61623	2
50574	1	52260	1	53420	1	54344	1	55725	1	57400	1	58572	1	61626	2
50575	2	52265	1	53425	1	54348	1	55860	1	57410	1	58573	1	61720	2
50576	2	52270	1	53430	1	54352	1	55870	1	57415	1	58600	1	61770	1
50580	1	52275	1	53431	1	54360	1	55873	1	57420	1	58615	1	61790	2
50590	1	52276	1	53440	1	54380	1	55875	1	57421	1	58660	1	61791	2
50592	1	52277	1	53442	1	54385	1	55876	1	57423	1	58661	1	61795	2
50593	2	52281	1	53444	1	54400	1	55920	1	57425	1	58662	1	61796	2
50686	2	52282	1	53445	1	54401	1	56405	2	57452	1	58670	1	61798	2
50688	2	52283	1	53446	1	54405	1	56420	1	57454	1	58671	1	61800	1
50945	2	52285	1	53447	1	54406	1	56440	1	57455	1	58672	1	61880	1
50947	2	52290	1	53449	1	54408	1	56441	1	57456	1	58673	1	61885	2
50948	2	52300	1	53450	1	54410	1	56442	1	57460	1	58770	2	61886	1
50951	2	52301	1	53460	1	54415	1	56501	1	57461	1	58800	1	61888	2
50953	2	52305	1	53500	1	54416	1	56515	1	57500	1	58805	1	62000	1
50955	2	52310	1	53502	1	54420	1	56605	1	57505	1	58820	2	62160	1
50957	2	52315	2	53505	1	54435	1	56620	1	57510	1	58823	2	62194	2
50961	2	52317	1	53510	1	54440	1	56625	1	57511	1	58900	1	62225	2
50970	2	52318	1	53515	1	54450	1	56700	1	57513	1	58920	1	62230	2
50972	2	52320	2	53520	1	54500	2	56740	2	57520	1	58925	1	62252	2
50974	2	52325	1	53600	1	54505	1	56800	1	57522	1	58970	1	62263	1
50976	2	52327	2	53601	1	54512	2	56805	1	57530	1	58974	1	62264	1
50980	2	52330	2	53605	1	54520	1	56810	1	57550	1	58976	2	62268	1
51020	1	52332	1	53620	1	54522	2	56820	1	57555	1	59020	4	62269	2
51030	1	52334	2	53621	1	54530	2	56821	1	57556	1	59025	1	62270	2
51040	1	52341	2	53660	1	54550	1	57000	1	57558	1	59051	1	62272	2
51045	2	52342	2	53661	1	54560	1	57010	1	57700	1	59100	1	62273	2
51050	1	52343	2	53665	1	54600	2	57020	1	57720	1	59150	1	62280	1
51065	1	52344	2	53850	1	54620	1	57022	2	57800	1	59151	1	62281	1

Appendix L — Medically Unlikely Edits (MUEs) — OPPS

CPT	MUE	CPT	MUE	CPT	MUE	CPT	MUE	CPT	MUE	CPT	MUE	CPT	MUE	CPT	MUE
62282	1	64446	2	64792	2	65400	2	66825	2	67415	2	68340	2	69605	1
62287	1	64447	2	64795	2	65410	2	66830	2	67420	2	68360	2	69610	2
62292	1	64448	2	64802	1	65420	2	66840	2	67430	2	68362	2	69620	2
62294	2	64449	2	64804	1	65426	2	66850	2	67440	2	68371	1	69631	2
62310	2	64455	2	64821	2	65430	2	66852	2	67445	2	68400	2	69632	1
62311	2	64479	1	64822	2	65435	2	66920	2	67450	2	68420	2	69633	1
62318	1	64483	1	64823	2	65436	2	66930	2	67500	2	68440	2	69635	1
62319	1	64505	2	64831	2	65450	2	66940	2	67505	2	68500	2	69636	1
62350	1	64508	2	64834	2	65600	2	66982	2	67515	2	68505	2	69637	1
62351	1	64510	2	64835	2	65710	2	66983	2	67550	2	68510	2	69641	1
62355	1	64517	1	64836	2	65730	2	66984	2	67560	2	68520	2	69642	1
62360	1	64520	2	64837	3	65750	2	66985	2	67570	2	68525	2	69643	1
62361	1	64530	2	64840	2	65755	2	66986	2	67700	4	68530	2	69644	1
62362	1	64553	1	64856	2	65756	2	67005	2	67710	2	68540	1	69645	1
62365	1	64555	2	64857	3	65757	2	67010	2	67715	2	68550	1	69646	1
62367	1	64560	1	64858	2	65770	2	67015	2	67800	1	68700	2	69650	1
62368	1	64561	2	64859	2	65772	2	67025	2	67801	1	68705	2	69660	1
63001	1	64565	2	64861	2	65775	2	67027	2	67805	1	68720	2	69661	1
63003	1	64573	1	64862	2	65780	2	67028	2	67808	1	68745	2	69662	2
63005	1	64575	2	64864	2	65781	2	67030	2	67820	2	68750	2	69666	2
63011	1	64577	1	64865	1	65782	2	67031	2	67825	2	68760	4	69667	2
63012	1	64580	2	64870	1	65800	2	67036	2	67830	3	68761	4	69670	1
63015	1	64581	2	64872	3	65805	2	67039	2	67835	2	68770	2	69676	1
63016	1	64585	2	64874	1	65810	2	67040	2	67850	4	68801	4	69700	2
63017	1	64590	1	64876	1	65815	2	67041	2	67875	2	68810	1	69711	2
63020	1	64595	1	64885	1	65820	2	67042	2	67880	2	68811	1	69714	2
63030	1	64600	2	64886	1	65850	2	67043	2	67882	2	68815	1	69715	1
63035	6	64605	2	64890	3	65855	2	67101	2	67900	2	68816	1	69717	1
63040	1	64610	2	64891	2	65860	2	67105	2	67901	2	68840	2	69718	1
63042	1	64612	2	64892	2	65865	2	67107	2	67902	2	69000	2	69720	2
63045	1	64613	1	64893	2	65870	2	67108	2	67903	2	69005	2	69725	2
63046	1	64614	2	64895	2	65875	2	67110	2	67904	2	69020	2	69740	2
63047	1	64622	1	64896	2	65880	2	67112	2	67906	2	69100	3	69745	2
63048	9	64626	1	64897	2	65900	2	67113	2	67908	2	69105	2	69801	1
63055	1	64630	1	64898	2	65920	2	67115	2	67909	2	69110	2	69802	1
63056	1	64632	2	64901	2	65930	2	67120	2	67911	4	69120	1	69805	2
63057	8	64650	1	64905	1	66020	2	67121	2	67912	2	69140	2	69806	1
63064	1	64653	1	64907	1	66030	2	67141	2	67914	4	69145	2	69820	1
63066	3	64680	1	64910	3	66130	2	67145	2	67915	4	69150	1	69840	1
63075	1	64681	1	64911	2	66150	2	67208	2	67916	4	69200	2	69905	1
63600	2	64702	2	65091	2	66155	2	67210	2	67917	4	69205	2	69910	1
63610	1	64712	2	65093	2	66160	2	67218	2	67921	4	69210	1	69915	1
63615	1	64713	2	65101	2	66165	2	67220	2	67922	4	69220	1	69930	2
63620	1	64714	2	65103	2	66170	2	67221	1	67923	4	69222	1	69955	2
63621	2	64718	2	65105	2	66172	2	67225	1	67924	4	69300	1	69960	2
63650	2	64719	2	65110	2	66180	2	67227	2	67930	2	69310	2	70010	1
63655	1	64721	2	65112	2	66185	2	67228	2	67935	2	69320	2	70015	1
63660	1	64726	2	65114	2	66220	2	67229	1	67938	2	69400	2	70030	2
63685	2	64727	3	65125	2	66225	2	67250	2	67950	2	69401	2	70100	1
63688	2	64732	2	65130	2	66250	2	67255	2	67961	4	69405	2	70110	1
63741	1	64734	2	65135	2	66500	2	67311	2	67966	4	69420	2	70120	2
63744	1	64736	2	65140	2	66505	2	67312	2	67971	2	69421	2	70130	2
63746	1	64738	2	65150	2	66600	2	67314	2	67973	2	69424	1	70134	1
64402	2	64740	2	65155	2	66605	2	67316	2	67974	2	69433	1	70140	1
64405	1	64742	2	65175	2	66625	2	67318	2	67975	2	69436	1	70150	1
64408	2	64744	2	65205	2	66630	2	67320	2	68020	2	69440	2	70160	1
64410	2	64746	2	65210	2	66635	2	67331	2	68040	2	69450	2	70170	2
64412	2	64761	1	65220	2	66680	2	67332	2	68100	2	69501	1	70190	1
64413	2	64763	1	65222	2	66682	2	67334	2	68110	2	69502	1	70200	1
64415	2	64766	1	65235	2	66700	2	67335	2	68115	2	69505	1	70210	1
64416	2	64771	2	65260	2	66710	2	67340	2	68130	2	69511	1	70220	1
64417	2	64772	2	65265	2	66711	2	67343	2	68135	2	69530	1	70240	1
64418	2	64774	3	65270	2	66720	2	67345	2	68200	2	69540	2	70250	1
64420	3	64776	1	65272	2	66740	2	67346	1	68320	2	69550	1	70260	1
64421	3	64778	3	65275	2	66761	2	67400	2	68325	2	69552	1	70300	1
64425	2	64782	2	65280	2	66762	2	67405	2	68326	2	69601	1	70310	1
64430	2	64783	2	65285	2	66770	2	67412	2	68328	2	69602	1	70320	1
64435	2	64786	2	65286	2	66820	2	67413	2	68330	2	69603	1	70328	1
64445	1	64790	1	65290	2	66821	2	67414	2	68335	2	69604	1	70330	1

Appendix L — Medically Unlikely Edits (MUEs) — OPPS

CPT	MUE	CPT	MUE	CPT	MUE	CPT	MUE	CPT	MUE	CPT	MUE	CPT	MUE	CPT	MUE
70332	2	72069	1	73220	2	74320	1	75860	2	76873	1	77750	1	78428	1
70336	1	72070	1	73221	2	74327	1	75870	1	76880	2	77761	1	78445	1
70350	1	72072	1	73222	2	74340	1	75872	1	76885	1	77762	1	78456	1
70355	1	72074	1	73223	2	74355	1	75880	2	76886	1	77763	1	78457	1
70360	1	72080	2	73500	2	74360	1	75885	1	76930	1	77776	1	78458	1
70370	1	72090	1	73510	2	74363	2	75887	1	76932	1	77777	1	78459	1
70371	1	72100	1	73520	2	74400	1	75889	1	76936	2	77778	1	78460	1
70373	1	72110	1	73525	2	74410	1	75891	1	76940	1	77785	3	78461	1
70380	2	72114	1	73530	2	74415	1	75901	1	76942	1	77786	3	78464	1
70390	2	72120	1	73540	1	74420	2	75902	2	76945	1	77787	3	78465	1
70450	3	72125	1	73542	2	74425	1	75940	1	76946	1	77789	2	78466	1
70460	1	72126	1	73550	2	74430	1	75945	1	76948	1	78000	1	78468	1
70470	2	72127	1	73560	2	74440	2	75961	2	76950	2	78001	1	78469	1
70480	1	72128	1	73562	2	74445	1	75962	1	76965	2	78003	1	78472	1
70481	1	72129	1	73564	2	74450	1	75966	1	76970	1	78006	1	78473	1
70482	1	72130	1	73565	1	74455	1	75968	2	76975	1	78007	1	78478	1
70486	1	72131	1	73580	2	74470	2	75970	2	76977	1	78010	1	78480	1
70487	1	72132	1	73590	2	74475	2	75980	1	76998	1	78011	1	78481	1
70488	1	72133	1	73592	2	74480	2	75982	2	77011	1	78015	1	78483	1
70490	1	72141	1	73600	2	74485	2	75984	2	77014	2	78016	1	78491	1
70491	1	72142	1	73610	2	74710	1	75992	1	77022	1	78018	1	78492	1
70492	1	72146	1	73615	2	74740	1	75994	2	77053	2	78020	1	78494	1
70496	1	72147	1	73620	2	74742	2	75995	1	77054	2	78070	1	78496	1
70498	1	72148	1	73630	2	74775	1	75996	2	77071	1	78075	1	78580	1
70540	1	72149	1	73650	2	75557	1	76000	3	77280	2	78102	1	78584	2
70542	1	72156	1	73660	2	75559	1	76010	2	77285	1	78103	1	78585	2
70543	1	72157	1	73700	2	75561	1	76080	2	77290	1	78104	1	78586	1
70544	1	72158	1	73701	2	75563	1	76100	2	77295	1	78110	1	78587	1
70545	1	72170	1	73702	2	75600	1	76101	1	77301	1	78111	1	78588	1
70546	1	72190	1	73706	2	75605	1	76102	1	77305	2	78120	1	78591	1
70547	1	72191	1	73718	2	75625	1	76120	1	77310	2	78121	1	78593	1
70548	1	72192	1	73719	2	75630	1	76125	1	77315	2	78122	1	78594	1
70549	1	72193	1	73720	2	75635	1	76376	2	77321	1	78130	1	78596	1
70551	1	72194	1	73721	4	75650	2	76377	2	77326	1	78135	1	78600	1
70552	1	72195	1	73722	2	75658	2	76380	2	77327	1	78140	1	78601	1
70553	1	72196	1	73723	4	75660	1	76506	1	77328	1	78185	1	78605	1
70554	1	72197	1	74000	3	75662	1	76510	2	77332	4	78190	1	78606	2
70555	1	72200	1	74010	2	75665	1	76511	2	77333	4	78191	1	78607	1
70557	1	72202	1	74020	2	75671	1	76512	2	77336	1	78195	1	78608	1
70558	1	72220	1	74022	2	75676	1	76513	2	77370	1	78201	1	78610	1
70559	1	72240	1	74150	1	75680	1	76514	1	77371	1	78202	1	78630	2
71015	2	72255	1	74160	1	75685	2	76516	1	77401	2	78205	1	78635	1
71021	1	72265	1	74170	1	75710	1	76519	2	77402	2	78206	1	78645	1
71022	1	72270	1	74175	1	75716	1	76529	2	77403	2	78215	1	78647	1
71023	2	72292	3	74181	1	75722	1	76536	1	77404	2	78216	1	78650	1
71030	2	73000	2	74182	1	75724	1	76604	1	77406	2	78220	1	78660	1
71034	1	73010	2	74183	1	75726	2	76645	1	77407	2	78223	1	78700	1
71035	2	73020	2	74190	1	75731	1	76700	1	77408	2	78230	1	78701	2
71040	1	73030	2	74210	1	75733	1	76705	2	77409	2	78231	1	78707	1
71060	1	73040	2	74220	1	75736	1	76770	1	77411	1	78232	1	78708	1
71090	1	73050	1	74230	1	75741	1	76775	2	77412	2	78258	1	78709	1
71100	1	73060	2	74235	1	75743	1	76776	1	77413	2	78261	1	78710	1
71101	1	73070	2	74240	1	75746	1	76800	1	77414	2	78262	1	78725	1
71110	1	73080	2	74241	1	75756	2	76801	1	77416	2	78264	1	78730	1
71111	1	73085	2	74245	1	75790	2	76802	3	77417	1	78267	1	78740	1
71120	1	73090	2	74246	1	75801	1	76805	1	77418	2	78268	1	78761	1
71130	1	73092	2	74247	1	75803	1	76810	3	77421	2	78270	1	78800	1
71250	1	73100	2	74249	1	75805	1	76811	1	77422	1	78271	1	78801	1
71260	1	73110	2	74250	1	75807	1	76812	3	77423	1	78272	1	78802	1
71270	1	73115	2	74251	1	75809	1	76813	1	77470	1	78278	2	78803	1
71275	1	73120	2	74260	1	75810	1	76814	3	77520	1	78282	1	78804	1
71550	1	73130	2	74270	1	75820	1	76815	1	77522	1	78290	1	78805	1
71551	1	73140	2	74280	1	75822	1	76817	1	77523	1	78291	1	78806	1
71552	1	73200	2	74283	1	75825	1	76830	1	77525	1	78300	1	78807	1
72010	1	73201	2	74290	1	75827	1	76831	1	77600	1	78305	1	78808	1
72020	4	73202	2	74291	1	75831	1	76856	1	77605	1	78306	1	78811	1
72040	3	73206	2	74300	1	75833	1	76857	1	77610	1	78315	1	78812	1
72050	1	73218	2	74301	2	75840	1	76870	1	77615	1	78320	1	78813	1
72052	1	73219	2	74305	1	75842	1	76872	1	77620	1	78414	1	78814	1

Appendix L — Medically Unlikely Edits (MUEs) — OPPS

CPT	MUE	CPT	MUE	CPT	MUE	CPT	MUE	CPT	MUE	CPT	MUE	CPT	MUE	CPT	MUE
78815	1	80436	1	82272	1	82646	1	83036	1	83873	1	84233	2	84703	1
78816	1	80438	1	82274	1	82649	1	83037	1	83874	4	84234	2	84704	1
79005	1	80439	1	82286	1	82651	1	83045	1	83880	1	84235	1	84830	1
79101	1	80440	1	82300	1	82652	1	83050	4	83885	2	84238	3	85002	2
79200	1	80500	1	82306	1	82654	1	83051	1	83887	2	84252	1	85004	2
79300	1	80502	1	82307	1	82656	1	83055	1	83912	1	84255	2	85007	1
79403	1	81000	2	82308	3	82657	3	83060	1	83915	1	84260	1	85008	2
79440	1	81001	2	82310	4	82658	2	83065	1	83916	2	84270	1	85009	1
79445	1	81002	2	82330	4	82666	1	83068	1	83918	2	84275	1	85013	2
80047	2	81003	2	82331	1	82668	1	83069	1	83919	1	84285	1	85014	4
80048	2	81005	2	82340	1	82670	2	83070	1	83921	2	84295	4	85018	4
80051	4	81007	1	82355	3	82671	1	83071	1	83925	4	84300	2	85025	2
80053	1	81015	1	82360	3	82672	1	83080	2	83930	2	84302	3	85032	3
80061	1	81020	1	82365	3	82677	1	83088	1	83935	2	84305	1	85041	2
80069	1	81025	1	82370	3	82679	1	83090	2	83937	1	84307	1	85044	1
80074	1	81050	2	82373	1	82690	1	83150	1	83945	2	84311	1	85045	1
80076	1	82000	1	82374	3	82693	2	83491	1	83950	1	84315	2	85046	1
80150	2	82003	3	82375	4	82696	1	83497	1	83951	1	84375	1	85048	2
80152	2	82009	3	82378	2	82705	1	83498	2	83970	4	84376	1	85049	2
80154	2	82010	4	82379	1	82710	1	83499	1	83986	2	84377	1	85055	1
80156	2	82013	1	82380	1	82715	1	83500	1	83992	2	84378	2	85097	2
80157	2	82016	1	82382	1	82725	1	83505	1	83993	1	84379	1	85130	2
80158	3	82017	1	82383	1	82726	1	83518	2	84022	2	84392	1	85170	1
80160	2	82030	1	82384	2	82728	1	83527	1	84030	1	84402	1	85175	1
80162	2	82040	1	82387	1	82731	1	83528	1	84035	1	84403	1	85210	2
80164	2	82042	2	82390	1	82735	1	83540	2	84060	1	84425	1	85220	2
80166	1	82043	1	82415	1	82742	1	83550	1	84061	1	84430	1	85230	2
80168	2	82044	1	82435	3	82746	1	83570	1	84066	1	84432	1	85240	3
80170	2	82045	2	82436	1	82747	1	83582	1	84075	2	84436	1	85244	2
80172	2	82055	3	82438	1	82757	1	83586	1	84078	1	84437	1	85245	2
80173	2	82075	2	82441	1	82759	1	83593	1	84080	1	84439	1	85246	2
80174	2	82085	1	82465	1	82760	1	83605	3	84081	1	84442	1	85247	2
80176	1	82101	1	82480	2	82775	1	83615	3	84085	1	84445	1	85250	2
80178	2	82103	1	82482	1	82776	1	83625	1	84087	1	84446	1	85260	2
80182	2	82104	1	82485	1	82784	6	83630	1	84100	3	84449	1	85270	2
80184	2	82105	1	82486	2	82785	1	83631	1	84105	1	84450	1	85280	2
80185	2	82106	4	82487	2	82787	4	83632	1	84106	1	84460	1	85290	2
80186	2	82107	1	82488	1	82820	1	83633	1	84110	1	84466	1	85291	2
80188	2	82108	1	82489	2	82928	1	83634	1	84119	1	84478	1	85292	2
80190	2	82120	1	82492	2	82941	1	83655	2	84120	1	84479	1	85293	2
80192	2	82127	2	82495	1	82943	1	83661	4	84126	1	84480	1	85300	2
80194	2	82128	2	82507	1	82946	1	83662	4	84127	1	84481	1	85301	2
80195	2	82131	3	82520	2	82950	3	83663	4	84132	4	84482	1	85302	2
80197	2	82135	1	82523	1	82951	1	83664	4	84133	2	84484	3	85303	2
80198	2	82136	3	82525	2	82952	3	83670	1	84134	1	84485	1	85305	2
80200	2	82139	3	82528	1	82953	1	83690	2	84135	1	84488	1	85306	2
80201	2	82140	2	82530	2	82955	1	83695	1	84138	1	84490	1	85307	2
80202	2	82143	2	82540	1	82960	1	83698	1	84140	1	84510	1	85335	2
80299	3	82145	1	82543	2	82963	1	83700	1	84143	2	84512	3	85337	1
80400	1	82150	4	82544	2	82965	1	83701	1	84144	1	84520	4	85345	2
80402	1	82154	1	82550	3	82975	1	83704	1	84146	3	84525	1	85348	2
80406	1	82157	1	82552	3	82977	1	83718	1	84150	2	84540	2	85360	1
80408	1	82160	1	82553	3	82978	1	83719	1	84152	1	84545	1	85362	2
80410	1	82163	1	82554	2	82979	1	83721	1	84153	1	84550	1	85366	2
80412	1	82164	1	82565	3	82980	1	83727	1	84154	1	84560	2	85370	2
80414	1	82172	3	82570	3	82985	1	83735	4	84155	1	84577	1	85378	2
80415	1	82175	2	82575	1	83008	1	83775	1	84156	1	84578	1	85379	2
80416	1	82180	1	82585	1	83009	1	83785	1	84157	3	84580	1	85380	2
80417	1	82190	4	82595	1	83010	1	83788	3	84160	2	84583	1	85384	2
80418	1	82205	1	82600	1	83012	1	83789	2	84163	1	84585	1	85385	1
80420	1	82232	1	82607	1	83013	1	83805	1	84165	1	84586	1	85390	3
80422	1	82239	1	82608	1	83014	1	83825	2	84166	2	84588	2	85400	2
80424	1	82240	1	82610	1	83015	1	83835	2	84202	1	84590	1	85410	2
80426	1	82247	2	82615	1	83018	7	83840	2	84203	1	84591	1	85415	2
80428	1	82248	2	82626	1	83020	2	83857	1	84206	1	84597	1	85420	2
80430	1	82252	1	82627	1	83021	2	83858	1	84207	1	84600	2	85421	2
80432	1	82261	1	82633	1	83026	1	83864	1	84210	2	84620	1	85441	1
80434	1	82270	1	82634	2	83030	1	83866	1	84220	1	84630	2	85445	1
80435	1	82271	3	82638	1	83033	1	83872	2	84228	1	84702	2	85460	1

Appendix L — Medically Unlikely Edits (MUEs) — OPPS

CPT	MUE	CPT	MUE	CPT	MUE	CPT	MUE	CPT	MUE	CPT	MUE	CPT	MUE	CPT	MUE
85461	1	86341	1	86738	2	87269	3	87521	2	88154	1	89130	1	90818	2
85475	1	86343	1	86741	2	87270	2	87522	2	88155	1	89132	1	90819	2
85525	2	86344	1	86744	2	87271	2	87525	2	88160	4	89135	1	90821	2
85530	1	86355	1	86747	2	87272	3	87526	2	88161	4	89136	1	90822	2
85536	1	86357	1	86750	4	87273	2	87527	2	88162	3	89140	1	90823	2
85540	1	86359	1	86756	2	87274	2	87528	2	88164	1	89141	1	90824	2
85547	1	86360	1	86759	2	87275	2	87529	2	88165	1	89160	1	90826	2
85549	1	86361	1	86762	2	87276	2	87530	2	88166	1	89190	1	90827	2
85555	1	86367	2	86768	5	87277	2	87531	2	88167	1	89220	2	90828	2
85557	1	86376	2	86771	2	87278	3	87532	2	88172	3	89225	1	90829	2
85597	2	86378	1	86774	2	87280	2	87533	2	88173	3	89230	1	90845	1
85611	2	86382	3	86777	2	87283	2	87534	2	88174	1	89235	1	90846	1
85612	1	86384	1	86778	2	87285	2	87535	2	88175	1	89250	1	90847	1
85613	1	86406	2	86781	2	87290	2	87536	2	88182	2	89251	1	90849	1
85635	1	86430	2	86784	2	87299	2	87537	2	88184	1	89253	1	90853	3
85651	1	86431	2	86787	2	87301	2	87538	2	88187	1	89254	1	90857	5
85652	1	86480	1	86788	2	87305	2	87539	2	88188	1	89255	1	90862	1
85660	1	86485	1	86789	2	87320	2	87540	2	88189	1	89257	1	90865	1
85670	2	86490	1	86793	2	87324	3	87541	2	88230	2	89258	1	90870	1
85675	1	86510	1	86800	1	87327	2	87542	2	88233	2	89259	1	90880	1
85705	1	86580	1	86803	2	87328	3	87550	2	88239	3	89260	1	90901	1
85732	4	86590	1	86804	1	87329	3	87551	2	88240	3	89261	1	90911	1
85810	2	86592	2	86807	1	87332	2	87552	2	88241	3	89264	1	90935	1
86021	1	86593	2	86808	1	87335	2	87557	2	88245	1	89268	1	90945	1
86022	1	86602	3	86812	1	87336	3	87560	2	88248	1	89272	1	91000	1
86023	2	86603	2	86813	1	87337	3	87561	2	88249	1	89280	1	91010	1
86038	1	86612	2	86816	1	87338	2	87562	2	88261	2	89281	1	91011	1
86039	1	86617	2	86817	1	87339	1	87580	2	88262	2	89290	1	91012	1
86060	1	86618	2	86821	3	87340	1	87581	2	88263	1	89291	1	91020	1
86063	1	86619	2	86822	3	87341	1	87582	2	88264	2	89300	1	91022	1
86077	1	86625	2	86850	3	87350	1	87590	3	88267	2	89310	1	91030	1
86078	1	86628	3	86860	2	87380	1	87591	3	88269	2	89320	1	91034	1
86079	1	86632	3	86885	3	87385	2	87592	2	88273	3	89321	1	91035	1
86140	1	86641	2	86906	1	87390	2	87620	2	88283	2	89322	1	91037	1
86141	1	86645	1	86930	3	87391	2	87621	3	88289	1	89325	1	91038	1
86146	3	86648	2	86940	3	87400	2	87622	2	88300	2	89329	1	91040	1
86147	4	86651	2	86941	3	87420	2	87640	2	88302	2	89330	1	91052	1
86148	1	86652	2	86945	3	87425	2	87650	1	88309	3	89331	1	91055	1
86155	1	86653	2	86950	1	87427	3	87651	1	88311	4	89335	1	91065	1
86156	1	86654	2	86960	3	87430	2	87652	1	88318	3	89342	1	91105	2
86157	1	86663	2	86975	2	87449	3	87653	1	88321	1	89343	1	91110	1
86160	4	86664	2	86976	2	87450	2	87660	1	88323	1	89344	1	91111	1
86161	3	86665	2	86977	2	87451	2	87797	3	88325	1	89346	1	91120	1
86162	1	86668	2	87001	1	87470	2	87799	3	88329	4	89352	1	91122	1
86171	3	86674	3	87003	1	87471	2	87800	2	88331	11	89353	1	91132	1
86200	1	86677	3	87045	3	87472	2	87802	2	88333	4	89354	1	91133	1
86215	1	86684	2	87073	3	87475	2	87803	3	88347	4	89356	2	92002	1
86225	1	86687	2	87084	2	87476	2	87804	2	88348	1	90471	1	92004	1
86226	1	86688	2	87086	3	87477	2	87807	2	88349	1	90472	4	92012	1
86243	1	86689	2	87103	3	87480	2	87808	1	88355	1	90473	1	92014	1
86277	1	86692	2	87109	3	87482	2	87810	2	88356	1	90474	1	92018	1
86280	1	86694	2	87110	2	87485	2	87850	1	88358	2	90681	1	92019	1
86294	1	86695	2	87118	3	87486	2	87880	2	88362	1	90696	1	92020	1
86300	2	86696	2	87143	2	87487	2	87900	1	88371	1	90801	2	92025	1
86301	1	86698	3	87164	2	87490	2	87901	1	88372	1	90802	2	92060	1
86304	1	86701	2	87166	2	87491	2	87902	1	88384	1	90804	2	92065	1
86308	1	86702	2	87168	2	87492	2	87903	1	88385	1	90805	2	92081	1
86309	1	86703	2	87169	2	87495	2	88104	4	88386	1	90806	2	92082	1
86310	1	86704	1	87172	2	87496	2	88106	3	88720	1	90807	2	92083	1
86316	3	86705	1	87177	3	87497	2	88125	1	88740	1	90808	2	92120	1
86320	1	86706	2	87197	1	87498	2	88130	1	88741	1	90809	2	92130	1
86325	2	86707	2	87207	3	87500	1	88140	1	89049	1	90810	2	92135	2
86327	1	86708	1	87220	3	87510	2	88142	1	89050	2	90811	2	92140	1
86332	1	86709	1	87230	3	87511	2	88143	1	89051	2	90812	2	92225	2
86334	1	86713	3	87250	3	87512	2	88147	1	89055	2	90813	2	92226	2
86335	2	86720	2	87255	2	87515	2	88148	1	89060	2	90814	2	92230	2
86336	1	86723	2	87260	2	87516	2	88150	1	89100	1	90815	2	92235	2
86337	1	86727	2	87265	2	87517	2	88152	1	89105	1	90816	2	92240	2
86340	1	86732	2	87267	2	87520	2	88153	1	89125	2	90817	2	92250	1

Appendix L — Medically Unlikely Edits (MUEs) — OPPS

CPT	MUE	CPT	MUE	CPT	MUE	CPT	MUE	CPT	MUE	CPT	MUE	CPT	MUE	CPT	MUE
92260	1	92950	4	93508	2	93978	1	95824	1	96413	2	A6501	2	E1100	1
92265	1	92953	2	93510	1	93979	1	95827	1	96416	1	A6502	2	E1110	1
92270	1	92960	2	93511	1	93980	1	95829	1	96420	2	A6503	2	E1130	1
92275	1	92961	1	93514	1	93981	1	95832	1	96422	2	A6509	2	E1140	1
92283	1	92973	2	93524	1	93982	1	95852	1	96425	1	A6510	2	E1160	1
92284	1	92974	1	93526	2	93990	2	95857	1	96440	1	A6511	2	E1161	1
92285	1	92977	1	93527	1	94002	1	95860	1	96445	1	A7027	1	E1170	1
92286	1	92978	1	93528	1	94003	1	95861	1	96450	1	A7040	2	E1171	1
92287	1	92979	2	93529	1	94010	1	95863	1	96521	2	A7041	2	E1172	1
92311	1	92980	1	93530	1	94014	1	95864	1	96522	1	A7042	2	E1180	1
92312	1	92981	2	93531	1	94015	1	95865	1	96523	1	A7043	2	E1190	1
92313	1	92982	1	93532	1	94016	1	95866	2	96542	1	B4087	1	E1195	1
92315	1	92984	2	93533	1	94060	1	95867	1	96567	1	B4088	1	E1200	1
92316	1	92986	1	93571	1	94070	1	95868	1	96570	1	C8900	1	E1220	1
92317	1	92987	1	93572	2	94150	2	95869	1	96571	3	C8901	1	E1221	1
92325	1	92990	1	93580	1	94200	1	95873	1	96900	1	C8902	1	E1222	1
92326	2	92995	1	93581	1	94240	1	95874	1	96910	1	C8903	1	E1223	1
92502	1	92996	2	93600	1	94250	1	95875	2	96912	1	C8904	1	E1224	1
92507	1	92997	1	93602	1	94260	1	95921	1	96913	1	C8905	1	E1240	1
92508	1	92998	2	93603	1	94350	1	95922	1	96920	1	C8906	1	E1250	1
92511	1	93005	3	93609	1	94360	1	95923	1	96921	1	C8907	1	E1260	1
92512	1	93017	2	93610	1	94370	1	95925	1	96922	1	C8908	1	E1270	1
92516	1	93024	1	93612	1	94375	1	95926	1	97010	1	C8909	1	E1280	1
92520	1	93025	1	93613	1	94400	1	95927	1	97012	1	C8910	1	E1285	1
92526	1	93041	3	93615	1	94450	1	95928	1	97016	1	C8911	1	E1290	1
92541	1	93225	1	93616	1	94452	1	95929	1	97018	1	C8912	2	E1295	1
92542	1	93226	1	93618	1	94453	1	95930	1	97022	1	C8913	2	E1500	1
92543	4	93229	1	93619	1	94610	2	95933	1	97024	1	C8914	2	E1510	1
92544	1	93231	1	93620	1	94620	1	95934	1	97026	1	C8918	1	E1520	1
92545	1	93232	1	93621	1	94621	1	95936	2	97028	1	C8919	1	E1530	1
92546	1	93236	1	93622	1	94642	1	95950	1	97150	1	C8920	1	E1540	1
92548	1	93270	1	93623	1	94644	1	95951	1	97545	1	C8921	1	E1550	1
92552	1	93271	1	93624	1	94645	2	95953	1	97546	2	C8922	1	E1560	1
92553	1	93278	1	93631	1	94660	1	95954	1	97597	1	C8923	1	E1570	1
92555	1	93279	1	93642	1	94662	1	95955	1	97598	1	C8924	1	E1580	1
92556	1	93280	1	93650	1	94664	2	95956	1	97602	1	C8925	1	E1590	1
92557	1	93281	1	93651	1	94667	1	95957	1	97605	1	C8926	1	E1592	1
92561	1	93282	1	93652	1	94680	1	95958	1	97606	1	C8927	1	E1594	1
92562	1	93283	1	93660	1	94681	1	95961	1	98925	1	C8928	1	E1600	1
92563	1	93284	1	93662	1	94690	1	95965	1	98926	1	C8929	1	E1610	1
92564	1	93285	1	93701	1	94720	1	95966	1	98927	1	C8930	1	E1615	1
92565	1	93286	2	93721	2	94725	1	95967	3	98928	1	C8957	1	E1620	1
92567	1	93287	2	93724	2	94750	1	95970	1	98929	1	C9716	1	E1625	1
92568	1	93288	1	93740	1	94762	1	95971	1	98940	1	C9724	1	E1630	1
92569	1	93289	1	93745	1	94770	1	95972	1	98941	1	C9725	1	E1635	1
92571	1	93290	1	93786	1	94772	1	95974	1	98942	1	C9726	2	E1639	1
92572	1	93291	1	93788	1	94775	1	95975	2	99170	1	C9727	1	E1902	1
92575	1	93292	1	93797	3	94776	1	95978	1	99195	2	C9728	1	E2313	1
92576	1	93293	1	93798	3	95012	2	95981	1	99201	1	E0618	1	E2397	1
92577	1	93296	1	93875	1	95056	1	95982	1	99202	1	E0619	1	E2609	1
92579	1	93299	1	93880	1	95060	1	95990	2	99203	1	E0746	1	E2617	1
92582	1	93303	1	93882	1	95065	1	95991	2	99204	1	E0856	1	G0008	1
92583	1	93304	1	93886	1	95070	1	95992	1	99205	1	E0950	1	G0009	1
92584	1	93306	1	93888	1	95071	1	96000	1	99211	3	E0951	2	G0027	1
92585	1	93307	1	93890	1	95075	1	96001	1	99281	2	E0952	2	G0101	1
92586	1	93308	2	93892	1	95115	1	96002	1	99282	2	E0958	2	G0103	1
92587	1	93312	2	93893	1	95117	1	96003	1	99283	2	E1050	1	G0104	1
92588	1	93313	2	93922	2	95250	1	96020	1	99284	2	E1060	1	G0105	1
92596	1	93315	2	93923	1	95805	1	96103	1	99285	2	E1070	1	G0106	1
92601	1	93316	2	93924	1	95806	1	96120	1	99291	1	E1083	1	G0117	1
92602	1	93318	2	93925	1	95807	1	96360	2	99406	1	E1084	1	G0118	1
92603	1	93320	1	93926	1	95808	1	96369	1	99407	1	E1085	1	G0120	1
92604	1	93321	1	93930	1	95810	1	96371	1	99460	1	E1086	1	G0121	1
92609	1	93325	1	93931	1	95811	1	96373	3	99463	1	E1087	1	G0123	1
92610	1	93350	1	93965	1	95812	1	96374	2	99465	1	E1088	1	G0127	1
92613	1	93351	1	93970	1	95813	1	96402	2	A4470	1	E1089	1	G0129	3
92620	1	93501	2	93971	1	95816	1	96405	1	A4480	1	E1090	1	G0130	1
92625	1	93503	2	93975	1	95819	1	96406	1	A4660	1	E1092	1	G0143	1
92626	1	93505	1	93976	1	95822	1	96409	2	A4663	1	E1093	1	G0144	1

Appendix L — Medically Unlikely Edits (MUEs) — OPPS

CPT	MUE	CPT	MUE	CPT	MUE	CPT	MUE	CPT	MUE	CPT	MUE	CPT	MUE	CPT	MUE
G0145	1	L0190	1	L1085	1	L1960	2	L2624	2	L3540	2	L4010	2	L5629	2
G0147	1	L0200	1	L1090	1	L1970	2	L2627	1	L3550	2	L4020	2	L5630	2
G0148	1	L0210	1	L1100	2	L1971	2	L2628	1	L3560	2	L4030	2	L5631	2
G0166	2	L0220	1	L1110	2	L1980	2	L2630	1	L3570	2	L4040	2	L5632	2
G0173	1	L0430	1	L1120	3	L1990	2	L2640	1	L3580	2	L4045	2	L5634	2
G0175	1	L0450	1	L1200	1	L2000	2	L2650	2	L3590	2	L4050	2	L5636	2
G0176	5	L0452	1	L1210	2	L2005	2	L2660	1	L3595	2	L4055	2	L5637	2
G0186	1	L0454	1	L1220	1	L2010	2	L2670	2	L3600	2	L4060	2	L5638	2
G0202	1	L0456	1	L1230	1	L2020	2	L2680	2	L3610	2	L4070	2	L5639	2
G0204	1	L0458	1	L1240	1	L2030	2	L2795	2	L3620	2	L4080	2	L5640	2
G0206	1	L0460	1	L1250	2	L2034	2	L2800	2	L3630	2	L4100	2	L5642	2
G0239	2	L0462	1	L1260	1	L2035	2	L2820	2	L3640	1	L4130	2	L5643	2
G0245	1	L0464	1	L1270	3	L2036	2	L2830	2	L3650	1	L4350	2	L5644	2
G0246	1	L0466	1	L1280	2	L2037	2	L3000	2	L3651	1	L4360	2	L5645	2
G0247	1	L0468	1	L1290	2	L2038	2	L3001	2	L3652	1	L4370	2	L5646	2
G0248	1	L0470	1	L1300	1	L2040	1	L3002	2	L3660	1	L4380	2	L5647	2
G0249	3	L0472	1	L1310	1	L2050	1	L3003	2	L3670	1	L4386	2	L5648	2
G0251	1	L0480	1	L1500	1	L2060	1	L3010	2	L3671	1	L4392	2	L5649	2
G0257	2	L0482	1	L1510	1	L2070	1	L3020	2	L3672	1	L4394	2	L5650	2
G0260	2	L0484	1	L1520	1	L2080	1	L3030	2	L3673	1	L4396	2	L5651	2
G0268	1	L0486	1	L1600	1	L2090	1	L3031	2	L3675	1	L4398	2	L5652	2
G0281	1	L0488	1	L1610	1	L2106	2	L3040	2	L3700	2	L5000	2	L5653	2
G0283	1	L0490	1	L1620	1	L2108	2	L3050	2	L3701	2	L5010	2	L5654	2
G0288	1	L0491	1	L1630	1	L2112	2	L3060	2	L3702	2	L5020	2	L5655	2
G0290	1	L0492	1	L1640	1	L2114	2	L3070	2	L3710	2	L5050	2	L5656	2
G0291	2	L0621	1	L1650	1	L2116	2	L3080	2	L3720	2	L5060	2	L5658	2
G0293	1	L0622	1	L1652	1	L2126	2	L3090	2	L3730	2	L5100	2	L5661	2
G0294	1	L0623	1	L1660	1	L2128	2	L3100	2	L3740	2	L5105	2	L5665	2
G0302	1	L0624	1	L1680	1	L2132	2	L3140	1	L3760	2	L5150	2	L5666	2
G0303	1	L0625	1	L1685	1	L2134	2	L3150	1	L3762	2	L5160	2	L5668	2
G0304	1	L0626	1	L1686	1	L2136	2	L3160	2	L3763	2	L5200	2	L5670	2
G0305	1	L0627	1	L1690	1	L2180	2	L3170	2	L3764	2	L5210	2	L5671	2
G0306	2	L0628	1	L1700	1	L2188	2	L3215	2	L3765	2	L5220	2	L5672	2
G0307	2	L0629	1	L1710	1	L2190	2	L3216	2	L3766	2	L5230	2	L5676	2
G0328	1	L0630	1	L1720	2	L2192	2	L3217	2	L3806	2	L5250	2	L5677	2
G0329	1	L0631	1	L1730	1	L2230	2	L3219	2	L3807	2	L5270	2	L5678	2
G0339	1	L0632	1	L1755	2	L2232	2	L3221	2	L3808	2	L5280	2	L5680	2
G0340	1	L0633	1	L1800	2	L2240	2	L3222	2	L3900	2	L5301	2	L5681	2
G0364	2	L0634	1	L1810	2	L2250	2	L3224	2	L3901	2	L5311	2	L5682	2
G0365	2	L0635	1	L1815	2	L2260	2	L3225	2	L3904	2	L5321	2	L5683	2
G0379	1	L0636	1	L1820	2	L2265	2	L3230	2	L3905	2	L5331	2	L5684	2
G0380	2	L0637	1	L1825	2	L2270	2	L3250	2	L3906	2	L5341	2	L5686	2
G0381	2	L0638	1	L1830	2	L2275	2	L3251	2	L3908	2	L5400	2	L5688	2
G0382	2	L0639	1	L1831	2	L2280	2	L3252	2	L3909	2	L5410	2	L5690	2
G0383	2	L0640	1	L1832	2	L2300	1	L3253	2	L3911	2	L5420	2	L5692	2
G0384	2	L0700	1	L1834	2	L2310	1	L3330	2	L3912	2	L5430	2	L5694	2
G0389	1	L0710	1	L1836	2	L2320	2	L3332	2	L3913	2	L5450	2	L5695	2
G0390	1	L0810	1	L1840	2	L2330	2	L3340	2	L3917	2	L5460	2	L5696	2
G0392	1	L0820	1	L1843	2	L2335	2	L3350	2	L3919	2	L5500	2	L5697	2
G0393	1	L0830	1	L1844	2	L2340	2	L3360	2	L3921	2	L5505	2	L5698	2
G0396	1	L0859	1	L1845	2	L2350	2	L3370	2	L3923	2	L5510	2	L5699	2
G0397	1	L0861	1	L1846	2	L2360	2	L3380	2	L3929	2	L5520	2	L5700	2
G0398	1	L0970	1	L1847	2	L2370	2	L3390	2	L3931	2	L5530	2	L5701	2
G0399	1	L0972	1	L1850	2	L2375	2	L3400	2	L3933	3	L5535	2	L5702	2
G0400	1	L0974	1	L1860	2	L2380	2	L3410	2	L3935	3	L5540	2	L5703	2
G0416	1	L0976	1	L1900	2	L2500	2	L3420	2	L3960	1	L5560	2	L5704	2
G0417	1	L0978	2	L1901	2	L2510	2	L3430	2	L3961	1	L5570	2	L5705	2
G0418	1	L0980	1	L1902	2	L2520	2	L3440	2	L3962	1	L5580	2	L5706	2
G0419	1	L1000	1	L1904	2	L2525	2	L3450	2	L3967	1	L5585	2	L5707	2
L0112	1	L1005	1	L1906	2	L2526	2	L3455	2	L3971	1	L5590	2	L5710	2
L0120	1	L1010	2	L1907	2	L2530	2	L3460	2	L3973	1	L5595	2	L5711	2
L0130	1	L1020	2	L1910	2	L2540	2	L3465	2	L3975	1	L5600	2	L5712	2
L0140	1	L1025	1	L1920	2	L2550	2	L3470	2	L3976	1	L5610	2	L5714	2
L0150	1	L1030	1	L1930	2	L2570	2	L3480	2	L3977	1	L5611	2	L5716	2
L0160	1	L1040	1	L1932	2	L2580	2	L3485	2	L3978	1	L5613	2	L5718	2
L0170	1	L1050	1	L1940	2	L2600	2	L3500	2	L3980	2	L5614	2	L5722	2
L0172	1	L1060	1	L1945	2	L2610	2	L3510	2	L3982	2	L5616	2	L5724	2
L0174	1	L1070	2	L1950	2	L2620	2	L3520	2	L3984	2	L5617	2	L5726	2
L0180	1	L1080	2	L1951	2	L2622	2	L3530	2	L4000	1	L5628	2	L5728	2

Appendix L — Medically Unlikely Edits (MUEs) — OPPS

CPT	MUE	CPT	MUE	CPT	MUE	CPT	MUE	CPT	MUE	CPT	MUE	CPT	MUE	CPT	MUE
L5780	2	L5980	2	L6600	2	L6884	2	L8030	2	Q0091	1	V2108	2	V2313	2
L5781	2	L5981	2	L6605	2	L6885	2	L8035	2	Q0111	2	V2109	2	V2314	2
L5782	2	L5982	2	L6610	2	L6890	2	L8039	2	Q0112	3	V2110	2	V2315	2
L5785	2	L5984	2	L6615	2	L6895	2	L8040	1	Q0113	2	V2111	2	V2318	2
L5790	2	L5985	2	L6616	2	L6900	2	L8041	1	Q0114	1	V2112	2	V2319	2
L5795	2	L5986	2	L6620	2	L6905	2	L8042	2	Q0115	1	V2113	2	V2320	2
L5810	2	L5987	2	L6621	2	L6910	2	L8043	1	Q0480	1	V2114	2	V2321	2
L5811	2	L5988	2	L6623	2	L6915	2	L8044	1	Q0481	1	V2115	2	V2399	2
L5812	2	L5990	2	L6625	2	L6920	2	L8045	2	Q0482	1	V2118	2	V2410	2
L5814	2	L6000	2	L6628	2	L6925	2	L8046	1	Q0483	1	V2121	2	V2430	2
L5816	2	L6010	2	L6629	2	L6930	2	L8047	1	Q0484	1	V2200	2	V2500	2
L5818	2	L6020	2	L6630	2	L6935	2	L8300	1	Q0485	1	V2201	2	V2501	2
L5822	2	L6025	2	L6635	2	L6940	2	L8310	1	Q0486	1	V2202	2	V2502	2
L5824	2	L6050	2	L6637	2	L6945	2	L8320	2	Q0487	1	V2203	2	V2503	2
L5826	2	L6055	2	L6638	2	L6950	2	L8330	1	Q0488	1	V2204	2	V2510	2
L5828	2	L6100	2	L6640	2	L6955	2	L8500	1	Q0489	1	V2205	2	V2511	2
L5830	2	L6110	2	L6641	2	L6960	2	L8501	2	Q0490	1	V2206	2	V2512	2
L5840	2	L6120	2	L6642	2	L6965	2	L8507	3	Q0491	1	V2207	2	V2513	2
L5845	2	L6130	2	L6645	2	L6970	2	L8509	1	Q0492	1	V2208	2	V2520	2
L5848	2	L6200	2	L6646	2	L6975	2	L8510	1	Q0493	1	V2209	2	V2521	2
L5850	2	L6205	2	L6647	2	L7040	2	L8511	1	Q0494	1	V2210	2	V2522	2
L5855	2	L6250	2	L6648	2	L7045	2	L8514	1	Q0495	1	V2211	2	V2523	2
L5856	2	L6300	2	L6650	2	L7170	2	L8515	1	Q0497	2	V2212	2	V2530	2
L5857	2	L6310	2	L6670	2	L7180	2	L8615	2	Q0498	1	V2213	2	V2531	2
L5858	2	L6320	2	L6672	2	L7181	2	L8616	2	Q0499	1	V2214	2	V2600	1
L5910	2	L6350	2	L6675	2	L7185	2	L8617	2	Q0501	1	V2215	2	V2610	1
L5920	2	L6360	2	L6676	2	L7186	2	L8618	2	Q0502	1	V2218	2	V2615	2
L5925	2	L6370	2	L6677	2	L7190	2	L8619	2	Q0503	3	V2219	2	V2623	2
L5930	2	L6380	2	L6686	2	L7191	2	L8622	2	Q0504	1	V2220	2	V2624	2
L5940	2	L6382	2	L6687	2	L7260	2	L8681	1	Q4001	1	V2221	2	V2625	2
L5950	2	L6384	2	L6688	2	L7261	2	L8683	1	Q4002	1	V2299	2	V2626	2
L5960	2	L6386	2	L6689	2	L7266	2	L8684	1	Q4003	2	V2300	2	V2627	2
L5962	2	L6388	2	L6690	2	L7272	2	L8689	1	Q4004	2	V2301	2	V2628	2
L5964	2	L6400	2	L6693	2	L7274	2	L8691	1	Q4025	1	V2302	2	V2629	2
L5966	2	L6450	2	L6694	2	L7362	1	L8695	1	Q4026	1	V2303	2	V2700	2
L5968	2	L6500	2	L6695	2	L7366	1	M0064	1	Q4027	1	V2304	2	V2710	2
L5970	2	L6550	2	L6696	2	L7368	1	P2028	1	Q4028	1	V2305	2	V2718	2
L5971	2	L6570	2	L6697	2	L7400	2	P2029	1	V2020	1	V2306	2	V2730	2
L5972	2	L6580	2	L6698	2	L7401	2	P2033	1	V2101	2	V2307	2	V2770	2
L5974	2	L6582	2	L6805	2	L7402	2	P2038	1	V2102	2	V2308	2	V2780	2
L5975	2	L6584	2	L6810	2	L7403	2	P3000	1	V2104	2	V2309	2	V2782	2
L5976	2	L6586	2	L6881	2	L7404	2	P9612	1	V2105	2	V2310	2	V2783	2
L5978	2	L6588	2	L6882	2	L7405	2	P9615	1	V2106	2	V2311	2	V2797	1
L5979	2	L6590	2	L6883	2	L7900	1	Q0035	1	V2107	2	V2312	2		

NOTES

NOTES

NOTES